October 19-23, 2015
Melbourne, Australia

Association for
Computing Machinery

Advancing Computing as a Science & Profession

CIKM'15

Proceedings of the 24th ACM International Conference on Information and Knowledge Management

Sponsored by:

ACM SIGIR and ACM SIGWEB

Supported by:

Microsoft Research, Sportsbet, Google, City of Melbourne, Professor Ram Kumar Memorial Foundation, Yahoo! Labs, Deakin University, RMIT University, and The University of Melbourne

Association for
Computing Machinery

Advancing Computing as a Science & Profession

The Association for Computing Machinery
2 Penn Plaza, Suite 701
New York, New York 10121-0701

Notice to Past Authors of ACM-Published Articles
ACM intends to create a complete electronic archive of all articles and/or other material previously published by ACM. If you have written a work that has been previously published by ACM in any journal or conference proceedings prior to 1978, or any SIG Newsletter at any time, and you do NOT want this work to appear in the ACM Digital Library, please inform permissions@acm.org, stating the title of the work, the author(s), and where and when published.

ISBN: 978-1-4503-3794-6 (Digital)

ISBN: 978-1-4503-4115-8 (Print)

Additional copies may be ordered prepaid from:

ACM Order Department
PO Box 30777
New York, NY 10087-0777, USA

Phone: 1-800-342-6626 (USA and Canada)
+1-212-626-0500 (Global)
Fax: +1-212-944-1318
E-mail: acmhelp@acm.org
Hours of Operation: 8:30 am – 4:30 pm ET

Printed in the USA

General Chairs' Preface

It is our great pleasure to welcome you to the 24th ACM International Conference on Information and Knowledge Management (CIKM 2015). CIKM is a top-tier ACM conference in the areas of databases, information retrieval, and knowledge management. It has successfully brought together leading researchers and developers from these three communities since 1992, with the purpose of identifying challenging problems facing the development of advanced knowledge and information systems, and shaping future research directions through the publication of high-quality applied and theoretical research findings. The 24th edition of CIKM continues this tradition, placing particular emphasis on the utility of data science across structured and semi-structured data.

We are delighted to present three outstanding keynote speakers: Jaime Teevan, from Microsoft; Andrew Tomkins, from Google; and Xiaofang Zhou, from the University of Queensland. We are also honored to host six distinguished invited speakers for the conference's Industry Track: Hang Li (Huawei Noah's Ark), Wei-Ying Ma (Microsoft Research Asia), Sofus A. Macskassy (Facebook), Igor Perisic (LinkedIn), Amy Shi-Nash (SingTel DataSpark), and Andrew Tomkins (Google).

We are indebted to the many authors who submitted their work to the CIKM technical program, and to the team of people who evaluated them. The Program Committee was expertly led by six PC Chairs: Timos Sellis and Jeffrey Xu Yu (Database Track); Maarten de Rijke and Vanessa Murdock (Information Retrieval Track); and Charu Aggarwal and Ravi Kumar (Knowledge Management Track). The review process was supported by the Microsoft CMT system. A report on the paper selection process appears in the PC Chairs' Preface.

We also thank the other chairs in the organization team: Shonali Krishnaswamy and Marc Najork (Industry Track); Wei Wang and Grace Hui Yang (Tutorials); Shane Culpepper and Chee Yong Chan (Workshops); and Yun Sing Koh (Publicity). CIKM 2015 includes a machine learning competition, sponsored by Sportsbet, with participants tackling the challenge of predicting the outcomes of the Australian Rules Football Finals. A substantial prize will be awarded to the best-performing system on the third day of the conference.

Running a conference the scale of CIKM is a serious undertaking and we are grateful to our local organization team for their effective and efficient handling of logistics. In particular, the Local Arrangements Chairs Tony Wirth and Rui Zhang provided extensive support, as did the team of student volunteers that Tony and Rui helped recruit and manage.

We gratefully acknowledge the support of our sponsors for the conference: Microsoft as Gold Sponsor; Sportsbet as Silver Sponsor; Google, The City of Melbourne, The Professor Ram Kumar Memorial Foundation, and Yahoo Labs, as Bronze sponsors; and The University of Melbourne, RMIT University, and Deakin University, as Academic Sponsors. We also received support from the CIKM Steering Committee, and from the Association for Computing Machinery and their special interest groups SIGIR and SIGWEB.

ICMS Australasia provided expert assistance with the logistics of the event, and we thank them for their professional advice and guidance. We also benefited greatly from the support provided by the Melbourne Convention Bureau during the early stages of our planning; and from the knowledge and skills of the many expert staff at the Melbourne Convention and Exhibition Center, the venue for CIKM 2015.

We trust that you enjoy the conference, and also the other activities you are able to fit in during your visit to Melbourne. Indeed, there are many things to see and enjoy in Victoria and in the whole Australasian region at this time of year, and we hope that you will be able to combine business and pleasure in to a memorable experience while you are here. Finally, CIKM 2016 will be in Indianapolis, in the USA, and we hope to see you again there.

James Bailey and Alistair Moffat
The University of Melbourne

August 2015.

CIKM2015
19–23 October 2015 Melbourne Australia

PC Chairs' Preface

We are delighted to welcome you to the 24th ACM International Conference on Information and Knowledge Management (CIKM 2015), held in Melbourne from October 19–23, 2015. CIKM is now well-established as a leading venue for bringing together researchers from across the Database, Information Retrieval, and Knowledge Management communities.

Continuing the pattern of previous years, we received a large number of high-quality submissions in all three tracks, in both full- and short-paper categories. As a result, we are confident that CIKM 2015 has succeeded in creating an outstanding technical program including research paper presentations; short-paper presentations during the poster session; plenary talks; and an engaging Industry Track arranged by the Industry Track Chairs. In total, we received 646 full-paper (10-page) submissions and 276 short-paper (4-page) submissions, which were reviewed and discussed by 88 area chairs, 471 program committee members, and a further 145 expert external reviewers.

We accepted 165 full papers (26%) and 69 short papers (25%). The acceptance statistics per track were as follows: Databases, 35/129 full papers and 6/37 short papers; Information Retrieval, 43/171 full papers and 27/101 short papers; and Knowledge Management, 87/346 papers and 36/138 short papers. Two of the Knowledge Management short papers were withdrawn by their authors prior to the proceedings being finalized. Our work was greatly eased by the support provided by the Microsoft CMT service, and we thank the CMT team for their assistance.

We are grateful to the many people who helped with the process of bringing this program together. We would in particular like to recognize the immense efforts of the area chairs, program committee members, and external reviewers, who each volunteered many hours of time, and contributed their deep expertise in order to allow the selection of the work that you can see in this volume. Most importantly of all, we thank the authors who submitted contributions for consideration. Without the drive and energy of the several thousand researchers and students who prepared manuscripts and carried out evaluations, the conference would be doomed to failure; but with that drive and energy, we have been able to achieve the success that you see here. We hope that participants in the conference in Melbourne, as well as subsequent readers of the proceedings, will find the technical program of CIKM 2015 to be both inspiring and rewarding.

Charu C. Aggarwal, IBM
Maarten de Rijke, University of Amsterdam
Ravi Kumar, Google
Vanessa Murdock, Microsoft
Timos Sellis, RMIT University
Jeffrey Xu Yu, Chinese University of Hong Kong

August 2015.

CIKM2015
19–23 October 2015 Melbourne Australia

Table of Contents

Session 1D: Text Processing

Session 1E: Applications

Session 1F: Social Media 1

Session 2A: Graphs

Session Chair: Sourav S. Bhowmick *(Nanyang Technological University)*

Session 2B: Retrieval Algorithms

Session Chair: Guido Zuccon *(Queensland University of Technology)*

Session 2C: Text Analysis

Session Chair: Krisztian Balog *(University Of Stavanger)*

Session 2D: Clustering

Session Chair: Ravi Kumar *(Google)*

Session 2E: Users and Predictions

Session Chair: James Caverlee *(Texas A&M University)*

Session 2F: Heterogeneous Networks

Session Chair: Michael Quan Z. Sheng *(The University of Adelaide)*

Session 3A: Veracity

Session Chair: Laure Berti-Équille *(Qatar Computing Research Institute)*

Session 3B: Social Networks 1

Session Chair: Niloy Ganguly *(Indian Institute of Technology Kharagpur)*

Session 3C: Query Completion

Session Chair: Maarten de Rijke *(University of Amsterdam)*

Session 3D: Microblogs

Session Chair: Antoine Doucet *(Université de La Rochelle)*

Session 3E: Graph-Based Analysis

Session Chair: Lina Yao *(The University of Adelaide)*

Session 3F: Classification 1

Session Chair: Alexandra Uitdenbogerd *(RMIT University)*

Keynote Address II

Session Chair: James Bailey *(The University of Melbourne)*

Session 4A: Location-Based Services

Session Chair: Timos Sellis *(RMIT University)*

Session 4B: Query Explanation

Session Chair: Sebastian Link *(The University of Auckland)*

Session 4C: Crowds

Session Chair: Falk Scholer *(RMIT University)*

Session 4D: Optimization

Session Chair: Xuan Vinh Nguyen *(The University of Melbourne)*

Session 4E: Social Networks 2

Session Chair: Hongzhi Yin *(The University of Queensland)*

Session 4F: Matrix Factorization

Session Chair: Jeffrey Chan *(RMIT University)*

Session 5A: Trips and Trajectories

Session Chair: Iadh Ounis *(University of Glasgow)*

Session 5E: Classification 2

Session Chair: Ping Luo *(Chinese Academy of Sciences)*

Session 5F: Sentiment and Content Analysis

Session Chair: Ke Deng *(RMIT University)*

Session 6A: Time Series and Streams

Session Chair: Jenny Xuizhen Zhang *(RMIT University)*

Session 6B: Adaptive Learning

Session Chair: Damiano Spina *(RMIT University)*

Session 6C: Points-of-Interest

Session Chair: Egemen Tanin *(The University of Melbourne)*

Session 6D: Matrices

Session Chair: Weidong Cai *(The University of Sydney)*

Session 6E: Citation Networks

Session Chair: Zhifeng Bao *(RMIT University)*

Session 6F: Knowledge Bases

Session Chair: Vanessa Murdock *(Microsoft)*

Keynote Address III
Session Chair: Shonali Krishnaswamy *(Institute for Infocomm Research)*

Session 7A: Database Optimization
Session Chair: Sven Helmer *(Free University of Bozen-Bolzano)*

Session 7B: Retrieval Enhancements 2
Session Chair: Mark Sanderson *(RMIT University)*

Session 7C: Search Mechanisms
Session Chair: Justin Zobel *(The University of Melbourne)*

Session 7D: Social Networks 3
Session Chair: Carsten Eickhoff *(ETH Zurich)*

Session 8A: Query Evaluation

Session Chair: Yiqun Liu *(Tsinghua University)*

Session 8B: Web Search

Session Chair: David Hawking *(Microsoft)*

Session 8C: Social Media 2

Session Chair: Karin Verspoor *(The University of Melbourne)*

Session 8D: Recommendation

Session Chair: Gangshan Wu *(Nanjing University)*

Short Papers: Databases

Short Papers: Information Retrieval

Short Papers: Knowledge Management

Workshop Reports

Conference Organization

General Chairs

James Bailey (*The University of Melbourne*)
Alistair Moffat (*The University of Melbourne*)

Program Committee Chairs

Charu C. Aggarwal (*IBM*)
Maarten de Rijke (*University of Amsterdam*)
Ravi Kumar (*Google*)
Vanessa Murdock (*Microsoft*)
Timos Sellis (*RMIT University*)
Jeffrey Xu Yu (*Chinese University of Hong Kong*)

Industry Track Chairs

Shonali Krishnaswamy (*Institute for Infocomm Research*)
Marc Najork (*Google*)

Tutorial Chairs

Wei Wang (*University of New South Wales*)
Grace Hui Yang (*Georgetown University*)

Workshop Chairs

Chee Yong Chan (*National University of Singapore*)
Shane Culpepper (*RMIT University*)

Local Arrangements Chairs

Tony Wirth (*The University of Melbourne*)
Rui Zhang (*The University of Melbourne*)

Publicity Chair

Yin Sing Koh (*The University of Auckland*)

Best Papers Chair

Ramamohanarao Kotagiri (*The University of Melbourne*)

Principal Conference Organizers

ICMS Australasia (`http://icmsaust.com.au`)

Program Committee and Referees

Database Track Senior Program Committee Members

Klaus Berberich (*Max Planck Institut*)
Selcuk Candan (*Arizona State U.*)
Lei Chen (*Hong Kong U. Sc. Tech.*)
Minos Garofalakis (*Tech. U. Crete*)
Wook-Shin Han (*PosTech*)
Nick Koudas (*U. Toronto*)
Laks Lakshmanan (*U. British Columbia*)
Huan Liu (*Arizona State U.*)
Vivek Narasayya (*Microsoft Research*)
Tamer Ozsu (*U. Waterloo*)
Kian-Lee Tan (*National U. Singapore*)
Yufei Tao (*Chinese U. Hong Kong*)
X. Sean Wang (*Fudan U.*)
Jun Yang (*Duke U.*)
Haruo Yokota (*Tokyo Institute Tech.*)
Wenjie Zhang (*U. New South Wales*)
Xiaofang Zhou (*U. Queensland*)

Information Retrieval Track Senior Program Committee Members

Eugene Agichtein (*Emory U.*)
James Allan (*U. Massachusetts Amherst*)
Omar Alonso (*Microsoft*)
Jaime Arguello (*U. North Carolina*)
Javed Aslam (*Northeastern U.*)
Leif Azzopardi (*U. Glasgow*)
Peter Bailey (*Microsoft*)
Krisztian Balog (*U. Stavanger*)
Michael Bendersky (*Google*)
Klaus Berberich (*Max Planck Institut*)
Roi Blanco (*Yahoo Labs*)
Jamie Callan (*Carnegie Mellon U.*)
David Carmel (*Yahoo Labs*)
Ben Carterette (*U. Delaware*)
Carlos Castillo (*QCRI*)
James Caverlee (*Texas A&M U.*)
Charles L.A. Clarke (*U. Waterloo*)
Nick Craswell (*Microsoft*)
Fabio Crestani (*U. Lugano*)
Bruce Croft (*U. Massachusetts Amherst*)
Shane Culpepper (*RMIT U.*)
Brian Davison (*Lehigh U.*)
Franciska de Jong (*U. Twente*)
Gianluca Demartini (*U. Sheffield*)
Fernando Diaz (*Microsoft*)
Debora Donato (*StumbleUpon*)
Shlomo Geva (*Queensland U. Tech.*)
Aristides Gionis (*Aalto U.*)
Claudia Hauff (*TU Delft*)
Ben He (*Chinese Academy Sc.*)
Qi He (*LinkedIn*)
Hideo Joho (*U. Tsukuba*)
Gareth Jones (*Dublin City U.*)
Jaap Kamps (*U. Amsterdam*)
Evangelos Kanoulas (*U. Amsterdam*)
Jussi Karlgren (*Gavagai & KTH*)
Gabriella Kazai (*Lumi*)
Diane Kelly (*U. North Carolina Chapel Hill*)
Oren Kurland (*Technion*)
Mounia Lalmas (*Yahoo Labs*)
Matthew Lease (*U. Texas Austin*)
Yoelle Maarek (*Yahoo Labs*)
Craig Macdonald (*U. Glasgow*)
Donald Metzler (*Google*)
Gonzalo Navarro (*U. Chile*)
Filip Radlinski (*Microsoft*)
Tetsuya Sakai (*Waseda U.*)
Mark Sanderson (*RMIT U.*)
Pavel Serdyukov (*Yandex*)
Ian Soboroff (*NIST*)
Ryen W. White (*Microsoft*)
Emine Yilmaz (*U. College London*)

Knowledge Management Track Senior Program Committee Members

Deepak Agarwal (*LinkedIn*)
Diego Calvanese (*Free U. Bozen-Bolzano*)
Anirban Dasgupta (*IIT Gandhinagar*)
Evgeniy Gabrilovich (*Google*)
Sreenivas Gollapudi (*Google*)
Murat Kantarcioglu (*U. Texas Dallas*)
Yan Liu (*USC*)
Nikos Mamoulis (*U. Hong Kong*)
Qiaozhu Mei (*U. Michigan*)
Wen-Chih Peng (*NTU*)
B. Aditya Prakash (*Virginia Tech.*)
Kunal Punera (*Bento Labs*)
Guojun Qi (*U. Central Florida*)
Sujith Ravi (*Google*)
Chandan Reddy (*Wayne State U.*)
Joerg Sander (*U. Alberta*)
Jimeng Sun (*Georgia Tech*)
Evimaria Terzi (*Boston U.*)
Hanghang Tong (*City U. New York*)
Wei Wang (*UCLA*)

Database Track Program Committee Members

Ashraf Aboulnaga (*QCRI*)
Periklis Andritsos (*U. Toronto*)
Walid Aref (*Purdue U.*)
Spiros Bakiras (*City U. New York*)
Zhifeng Bao (*RMIT U.*)
Spyros Blanas (*Ohio State U.*)
Panagiotis Bouros (*HU-Berlin*)
Bogdan Cautis (*U. Paris-Sud*)
Lijun Chang (*U. New South Wales*)
Muhammad Cheema (*Monash U.*)
Hong Cheng (*Chinese U. Hong Kong*)
Reynold Cheng (*U. Hong Kong*)
Gao Cong (*Nanyang Tech. U.*)
Alfredo Cuzzocrea (*ICAR-CNR & U. Calabria*)
Ke Deng (*RMIT U.*)
Prasad Deshpande (*IBM India*)
Gill Dobbie (*U. Auckland*)
Josep Domingo-Ferrer (*U. Rovira i Virgili*)
Markus Endres (*U. Augsburg*)
Csilla Farkas (*U. South Carolina*)
Ada Fu (*Chinese U. Hong Kong*)
Ariel Fuxman (*Google*)
Floris Geerts (*U. Antwerp*)
Dimitrios Gunopulos (*U. Athens*)
Yeye He (*Microsoft Research*)
Seung-won Hwang (*PosTech*)
Stratos Idreos (*Harvard U.*)
Yoshiharu Ishikawa (*Nagoya U.*)
Mizuho Iwaihara (*Waseda U.*)
Lili Jiang (*Max Planck Institut*)
Anastasios Kementsietsidis (*Google*)
Yannis Kotidis (*AUEB Greece*)
Julien Leblay (*AIST*)
Justin Levandoski (*Microsoft Research*)
Chengkai Li (*U. Texas Arlington*)
Guoliang Li (*Tsinghua U.*)
Chengfei Liu (*Swinburne U. Tech.*)
Mengchi Liu (*Carleton U.*)
Lei Liu (*HP Labs*)
Hua Lu (*Aalborg U.*)
Jiebo Luo (*U. Rochester*)
Balaji Palanisamy (*U. Pittsburgh*)
Ippokratis Pandis (*Cloudera*)
Stavros Papadopoulos (*Intel and MIT*)
Milan Petkovic (*Eindhoven U. Tech.*)
Weining Qian (*East China Normal U.*)
Lu Qin (*UTS*)
Matthias Renz (*U. Munich*)
Senjuti Roy (*U. Washington Tacoma*)
Pierangela Samarati (*U. Milan*)
Rusty Sears (*Pure Storage*)
Mohamed Sharaf (*U. Queensland*)
Fabian Suchanek (*Télécom ParisTech U.*)
Dimitri Theodoratos (*New Jersey Inst. Tech.*)
Yannis Theodoridis (*U. Piraeus*)
Aibo Tian (*LinkedIn*)
Pinar Tozun (*IBM Almaden*)
Goce Trajcevski (*Northwestern U.*)
Stratis Viglas (*U. Edinburgh*)
Chi Wang (*Microsoft*)
Jianyong Wang (*Tsinghua U.*)
Wei Wang (*U. New South Wales*)
Raymond Chi-Wing Wong (*Hong Kong U. Sc. Tech.*)
Yinghui Wu (*UCSB*)
Xiaokui Xiao (*Nanyang Tech. U.*)
Yanghua Xiao (*Fudan U.*)
De-Nian Yang (*Academia Sinica*)

Xiaochun Yang (*Northeastern U.*)
Mi-Yen Yeh (*Academia Sinica*)
Man Lung Yiu (*Hong Kong Polytechnic U.*)
Hwanjo Yu (*Pohang U. Sc. Tech.*)
Ji Zhang (*U. Southern Queensland*)
Ying Zhang (*UTS*)
Kevin Zheng (*U. Queensland*)
Yongluan Zhou (*U. Southern Denmark*)
Lei Zou (*Peking U.*)

Information Retrieval Track Program Committee Members

Pal Aditya (*IBM*)
Dirk Ahlers (*NTNU*)
M-Dyaa Albakour (*U. Glasgow*)
Ismail Altingovde (*Middle East Tech. U.*)
Gianni Amati (*Fondazione Ugo Bordoni*)
Linda Andersson (*Vienna U. Tech.*)
Akash Anil (*IIT Guwahati*)
Avi Arampatzis (*Democritus U. Thrace*)
Ioannis Arapakis (*Yahoo Labs*)
Olga Arkhipova (*Yandex*)
Diego Arroyuelo (*U. Técn. Federico Santa María*)
Paul Baecke (*Microsoft Research Cambridge*)
Niranjan Balasubramanian (*U. Washington*)
Andras Benczur (*Hungarian Acad. Sc.*)
Bodo Billerbeck (*Microsoft*)
Ilaria Bordino (*Yahoo Labs*)
Gloria Bordogna (*CNR Italy*)
Pavel Braslavski (*Ural Federal U.*)
Marc Bron (*Yahoo Labs*)
Eric Brown (*IBM Research*)
Fei Cai (*U. Amsterdam*)
Rui Cai (*Microsoft Research*)
B. Barla Cambazoglu (*Yahoo Labs*)
Bin Cao (*Microsoft Research Asia*)
Mark Carman (*Monash U.*)
Marc-Allen Cartright (*Google*)
Pablo Castells (*U. Autónoma Madrid*)
Suleyman Cetintas (*Yahoo Labs*)
Sunandan Chakraborty (*New York U.*)
Praveen Chandar (*U. Delaware*)
Yi Chang (*Yahoo Labs*)
Francine Chen (*FX Palo Alto Laboratory*)
Lin Chen (*U. Illinois Chicago*)
Wei Chen (*Microsoft Research*)
Aleksandr Chuklin (*U. Amsterdam*)
Francisco Claude (*U. Diego Portales*)
Paul Clough (*U. Sheffield*)
Michael Cole (*Rutgers U.*)
Gordon V. Cormack (*U. Waterloo*)
Peng Cui (*Tsinghua U.*)
Ronan Cummins (*U. Greenwich*)
Sally Jo Cunningham (*U. Waikato*)
Mahashweta Das (*HP Labs*)
Gianmarco De Francisci Morales (*Yahoo Labs*)
Alexey Drutsa (*Yandex*)
Sergio Duarte (*U. Twente*)
Thanh Tran Duc (*San Jose State U.*)
Sourav Dutta (*Max Planck Institut*)
Carsten Eickhoff (*ETH Zurich*)
Andrea Esuli (*ISTI-CNR*)
Henry Feild (*Endicott College*)
Dan Feldman (*MIT*)
Nicola Ferro (*U. Padova*)
Luanne Freund (*U. British Columbia*)
Ingo Frommholz (*U. Bedfordshire*)
Bin Gao (*Microsoft Research Asia*)
Judith Gelernter (*Carnegie Mellon U.*)
Lorraine Goeuriot ()
Simon Gog (*Karlsruhe Inst. Tech.*)
Marcos Goncalves (*UFMG*)
Julio Gonzalo (*UNED*)
David Graus (*U. Amsterdam*)
Artem Grotov (*U. Amsterdam*)
Fan Guo (*Carnegie Mellon U.*)
Qi Guo (*Microsoft*)
Manish Gupta (*Microsoft*)
Gleb Gusev (*Yandex*)
Ido Guy (*Yahoo Labs*)
Martin Halvey (*U. Strathclyde*)
Donna Harman (*NIST*)
Jiyin He (*CWI*)
Bruce Hedin (*H5*)
Tomi Heimonen (*U. Tampere*)
Katja Hofmann (*Microsoft*)
Frank Hopfgartner (*U. Glasgow*)
Winston Hsu (*National Taiwan U.*)
Samuel Huston (*U. Massachusetts Amherst*)
Ichiro Ide (*Nagoya U.*)
Adam Jatowt (*Kyoto U.*)
Jiepu Jiang (*U. Massachussetts*)
Noriko Kando (*National Institute of Informatics*)
Nattiya Kanhabua (*L3S Research Center*)

Sarvnaz Karimi (*CSIRO*)
Mostafa Keikha (*U. Massachusetts Amherst*)
Liadh Kelly (*Trinity College Dublin*)
Tom Kenter (*U. Amsterdam*)
Sadegh Kharazmi (*RMIT U.*)
Eugene Kharitonov (*Yandex*)
Yubin Kim (*Carnegie Mellon U.*)
Akisato Kimura (*NTT Japan*)
Irwin King (*Chinese U. Hong Kong*)
Julia Kiseleva (*Eindhoven U. Tech.*)
Pranam Kolari (*Walmart Labs*)
Bevan Koopman (*CSIRO*)
Yehuda Koren (*Google*)
Udo Kruschwitz (*U. Essex*)
Séamus Lawless (*Trinity College Dublin*)
Chia-Jung Lee (*U. Massachusetts Amherst*)
Kyumin Lee (*Utah State U.*)
Teerapong Leelanupab (*KMITL Thailand*)
Jochen Leidner (*Thomson Reuters*)
Johannes Leveling (*Dublin City U.*)
David D. Lewis (*David D. Lewis Consulting*)
Lei Li (*Florida International U.*)
Shangsong Liang (*U. Amsterdam*)
Daniel Liebling (*Microsoft Research*)
Ee-Peng Lim (*Singapore Management U.*)
Nut Limsopatham (*U. Glasgow*)
Christina Lioma (*U. Copenhagen*)
Suzanne Little (*Dublin City U.*)
Claudio Lucchese (*ISTI-CNR*)
Roger Jie Luo (*Yahoo Labs*)
Yuan Luo (*IBM & MIT*)
Mihai Lupu (*Vienna U. Tech.*)
Yuanhua Lv (*Microsoft*)
Dimitrios Lymberopoulos (*Microsoft Research*)
Andrew MacFarlane (*City U. London*)
Walid Magdy (*QCRI*)
Stephane Marchand-Maillet (*U. Geneva*)
Miguel Martinez Alvarez (*Signal*)
Flavio Martins (*U. Nova de Lisboa*)
Maarten Marx (*U. Amsterdam*)
Yosi Mass (*IBM*)
Richard McCreadie (*U. Glasgow*)
Paul McNamee (*JHU*)
Edgar Meij (*Yahoo Labs*)
Yelena Mejova (*QCRI*)
Marcelo Mendoza (*Yahoo Labs*)
Thomas Mensink (*U. Amsterdam*)
Peter Mika (*Yahoo Labs*)
Natasa Milic-Frayling (*Microsoft Research*)
Bhaskar Mitra (*Microsoft*)
Prasenjit Mitra (*Pennsylvania State U.*)
Marie-Francine Moens (*Katholieke U. Leuven*)
Samaneh Moghaddam (*eBay*)
Yashar Moshfeghi (*U. Glasgow*)
Josiane Mothe (*IRIT U. Toulouse*)
Isabelle Moulinier (*Thomson Reuters*)
Hidetsugu Nanba (*Hiroshima U.*)
Franco Maria Nardini (*ISTI-CNR*)
Wolfgang Nejdl (*L3S Research Center*)
Vincent Ng (*U. Texas Dallas*)
Dong Nguyen (*Twente U.*)
Quoc Viet Hung Nguyen (*EPFL*)
Tu Nguyen (*L3S Research Center*)
Feiping Nie (*UT Arlington*)
Jian-Yun Nie (*U. Montreal*)
Alexandros Ntoulas (*Microsoft Research*)
Neil O'Hare (*Yahoo Labs*)
Daan Odijk (*U. Amsterdam*)
Denis Parra (*PUC Chile*)
Gabriella Pasi (*U. Milano-Bicocca*)
Virgil Pavlu (*Northeastern U.*)
Raffaele Perego (*ISTI-CNR*)
Alvaro Pereira Jr (*Federal U. Ouro Preto*)
Barbara Poblete (*U. Chile*)
John Prager (*IBM Research*)
Mu Qiao (*IBM Research*)
Tao Qin (*Microsoft*)
Edie Rasmussen (*U. British Columbia*)
Mohammad Raza (*Microsoft Cambridge*)
Yongli Ren (*RMIT U.*)
Zhaochun Ren (*U. Amsterdam*)
Haggai Roitman (*IBM Research Haifa*)
Stevan Rudinac (*U. Amsterdam*)
Stefan Rüger (*The Open U.*)
Egor Samosvat (*Yandex*)
Jose San Pedro (*Telefonica Research*)
Rodrygo Santos (*U. Federal de Minas Gerais*)
Shin'ichi Satoh (*NII Japan*)
Klaus Schoeffmann (*Klagenfurt U.*)
Anne Schuth (*U. Amsterdam*)
Satoshi Sekine (*New York U.*)
Jangwon Seo (*Google*)
Jialie Shen (*Singapore Management U.*)
Xiaolin Shi (*Microsoft*)
Milad Shokouhi (*Microsoft*)
Edleno Silva de Moura (*Federal U. Amazonas*)
Fabrizio Silvestri (*Yahoo Labs*)
Marc Sloan (*U. College London*)

Yang Song (*Microsoft Research*)
Hanna Suominen (*NICTA & ANU*)
Idan Szpektor (*Yahoo Labs*)
James Thom (*RMIT U.*)
Paul Thomas (*CSIRO*)
Xinmei Tian (*U. Sc. Tech. China*)
Gabriele Tolomei (*Yahoo Labs*)
Elaine Toms (*U. Sheffield*)
Nicola Tonellotto (*ISTI-CNR*)
Dolf Trieschnigg (*U. Twente*)
Andrew Trotman (*eBay*)
Manos Tsagkias (*904Labs*)
Theodora Tsikrika (*CERTH*)
Julián Urbano (*U. Pompeu Fabra*)
Christophe Van Gysel (*U. Amsterdam*)
Suzan Verberne (*Radboud U. Nijmegen*)
Changhu Wang (*Microsoft Research China*)
Hongning Wang (*U. Virginia*)
Lidan Wang (*U. Maryland College Park*)
Meng Wang (*Hefei U. Tech.*)
Shuaiqiang Wang (*U. Jyväskylä*)
William Webber (*Willaim Webber Consulting*)
Wouter Weerkamp (*904Labs*)
Xing Wei (*Inmobi*)
Jerome White (*New York U.*)
Xiaobing Xue (*Twitter*)
Grace Hui Yang (*Georgetown U.*)
Kuiyuan Yang (*Microsoft Research*)
Liu Yang (*U. Massachusetts Amherst*)
Xuchen Yao (*Johns Hopkins U.*)
Jie Yin (*CSIRO*)
Muhammad Bilal Zafar (*Max Planck Institut*)
Duo Zhang (*Twitter*)
Jianwen Zhang (*Microsoft Research Asia*)
Lanbo Zhang (*Twitter*)
Yongfeng Zhang (*Tsinghua U.*)
Zhiwei Zhang (*Purdue U.*)
Ke Zhou (*Yahoo Labs*)
Imed Zitouni (*Microsoft*)
Guido Zuccon (*Queensland U. Tech.*)

Knowledge Management Track Program Committee Members

Gail-Joon Ahn (*Arizona State U.*)
Mohammad AlHassan (*IUPUI*)
David Anastasiu (*U. Minnesota*)
Azin Ashkan (*Technicolor*)
Bahman Bahmani (*Stanford U.*)
Gustavo Batista (*U. Sao Paulo*)
Srikanta Bedathur (*IBM Research India*)
Kanishka Bhaduri (*Netflix*)
Arnab Bhattacharya (*IIT Kanpur*)
Albert Bifet (*U. Waikato*)
Petko Bogdanov (*SUNY Albany*)
Klemens Böhm (*Karlsruhe Institut Tech.*)
Mohamed Bouguessa (*U. Quebec*)
Christos Boutsidis (*Yahoo Labs*)
Andrea Cali (*Birkbeck College London*)
Ricardo Campello (*U. São Paulo*)
Huiping Cao (*New Mexico State U.*)
Jeffrey Chan (*U. Melbourne*)
Varun Chandola (*U. Buffalo*)
Michael Chau (*U. Hong Kong*)
Nitesh Chawla (*Notre Dame*)
Ye Chen (*Microsoft*)
Zhiyuan Chen (*U. Illinois Chicago*)
Jaegul Choo (*Korea U.*)
Vassilis Christophides (*U. Crete*)
Kun-Ta Chuang (*National Cheng Kung U.*)
James Cook (*Google*)
Bernardo Cuenca-Grau (*U. Oxford*)
Alfredo Cuzzocrea (*U. Calabria*)
Na Dai (*Google*)
Theodore Dalamagas (*Athena Research Greeve*)
Abhimanyu Das (*Google*)
Antonios Deligiannakis (*Tech. U. Crete*)
Christos Doulkeridis (*U. Piraeus*)
Dora Erdos (*Boston U.*)
Alex Fabrikant (*Google*)
Elena Ferrari (*U. Insubria*)
Avrilia Floratou (*IBM Almaden*)
Esther Galbrun (*Boston U.*)
Jing Gao (*SUNY Buffalo*)
Dinesh Garg (*IBM India Research Lab*)
Chiara Ghidini (*FBK Trento*)
Nikos Giatrakos (*Tech. U. Crete*)
Kasneci Gjergji (*Hasso Plattner Institut*)
Aris Gkoulalas-Divanis (*IBM*)
Bart Goethals (*U. Antwerp*)
Manuel Gomez Rodriguez (*MPI*)
Amit Goyal (*Yahoo Labs*)
Francesco Gullo (*Yahoo Labs*)
Stephan Günnemann (*Carnegie Mellon U.*)
Sunil Gupta (*Deakin*)
Maxim Gurevich (*Bento Labs*)

Akrivi Vlachou (*AUEB Greece*)
Anil Vullikanti (*Virginia Tech*)
Dong Wang (*U. Notre Dame*)
Jason Wang (*New Jersey Inst. Tech.*)
Shengrui Wang (*U. Sherbrooke*)
William Yang Wang (*Carnegie Mellon U.*)
Yue Wang (*U. Michigan*)
Tim Weninger (*Notre Dame*)
Anthony Wirth (*U. Melbourne*)
Dingming Wu (*U. Hong Kong*)
Donghui Wu (*Lexis Nexis*)
Zhaoming Wu (*Georgia Tech*)
Rongjing Xiang (*Google*)
Li Xiong (*Emory U.*)
Shengqi Yang (*Facebook*)
Yuan Yao (*Nanjing U.*)
Ke Yiping (*Nanyang Tech. U.*)
Philip S. Yu (*U. Illinois Chicago*)
Wenchao Yu (*UCLA*)
Reza Zafarani (*Arizona State U.*)
Hessam Zakerzadeh (*U. Calgary*)
Ce Zhang (*U. Wisconsin Madison*)
Jiawei Zhang (*UIC*)
Qin Zhang (*Indiana*)
Ruofei Zhang (*Microsoft*)
Yuchen Zhao (*AppDynamics*)
Zhe Zhao (*U. Michigan*)
Dmitriy Zheleznyakov (*U. Oxford*)
Arthur Zimek (*LMU Munich*)
Andreas Zuefle (*LMU Munich*)

Additional Referees

Karam Abdulahhad (*CNRS Grenoble*)
Tenindra Abeywickrama (*Monash U.*)
Cem Aksoy (*New Jersey Inst. Tech.*)
Daniel Alejandro Garcia Ulloa (*Emory U.*)
Akhil Arora (*Xerox Research Bangalore*)
Besim Avci (*Northwestern U.*)
Alexander Beloborodov (*Ural Federal U.*)
Rafael Berlanga Llavori (*U. Jaume I Castellon*)
Nikos Bikakis (*Athena Research Greece*)
Fei Bi (*U. New South Wales*)
Dritan Bleco (*AUEB Greece*)
Luca Bonomi (*Emory U.*)
Matteo Catena (*ISTI-CNR*)
Kai Ho Chan (*Hong Kong U. Sc. Tech.*)
Anveshi Charuvaka (*George Mason U.*)
Abon Chaudhuri (*Walmart Labs*)
Jiecao Chen (*Indiana U. Bloomington*)
Lisi Chen (*Nanyang Tech. U.*)
Liu Chen (*Wuhan U.*)
Xu Chu (*U. Waterloo*)
David Corney (*Signal*)
Ananya Dass (*New Jersey Inst. Tech.*)
Sabrina De Capitani di Vimercati (*U. degli Studi di Milano*)
Alberto De Francesco (*ISTI-CNR*)
Amra Delic (*Tech. U. Wien*)
Aggeliki Dimitriou (*National Tech. U. Athens*)
Daniel Ditursi (*SUNY Albany*)
Vasilis Efthymiou (*FORTH-ICS Greece*)
Pavlos Fafalios (*FORTH-ICS Greece*)
Xing Feng (*U. New South Wales*)
Ioanna Filippidou (*AUEB Greece*)
Christian Frey (*Ludwig Maximilians U.*)
Debasis Ganguly (*Dublin City U.*)
Cheng Gao (*U. Kansas*)
Konstantinos Georgoulas (*AUEB Greece*)
Giorgos Giannopoulos (*Athena Research Greece*)
Benoit Groz (*U. Paris Sud*)
Kshiteesh Hegde (*Rensselaer Polytechnic Inst.*)
Zhenying He (*Fudan U.*)
Chuan Hu (*New Mexico State U.*)
Mas-ud Hussain (*Northwestern U.*)
Go Irie (*NTT Japan*)
Saiful Islam (*Swinburne U. Tech.*)
Alankar Jain (*IBM Research India*)
Nandish Jayaram (*U. Texas Austin*)
Meng Jiang (*Tsinghua U.*)
Minhao Jiang (*Hong Kong U. Sc. Tech.*)
Salil Joshi (*IBM Research India*)
Gregor Josse (*Ludwig Maximilians U.*)
Ilias Kanellos (*Athena Research Greece*)
Maria Karanasou (*U. Piraeus*)
Enkelejda Kasneci (*U. Tuebingen*)
Akshar Kaul (*IBM Research India*)
Evgeny Kharlamov (*U. Oxford*)
Roberto Konow (*U. Chile*)
Egor Kostylev (*U. Oxford*)
Jitin Krishnan (*George Mason U.*)
Anastasia Krithara (*IIT Demokritos Greece*)
Alexander Krumpholz (*CSIRO*)
Durgesh Kumar (*IIT Guwahati*)
Christina Lantzaki (*FORTH-ICS Greece*)

Chao Lan (*U. Kansas*)
Léa Laporte (*INSA Lyon*)
Haoran Li (*Emory U.*)
Jianxin Li (*RMIT U.*)
Lei Li (*Hefei U. Tech.*)
Wei Li (*Google*)
Xiaoli Li (*U. Kansas*)
Yuchen Li (*National U. Singapore*)
Zechao Li (*Nanjing U. Sc. Tech.*)
Kewen Liao (*U. Melbourne*)
Aldo Lipani (*Tech. U. Vienna*)
Ruifeng Liu (*Chinese U. Hong Kong*)
Yubao Liu (*Sun Yat Sen U.*)
Cheng Long (*Hong Kong U. Sc. Tech.*)
Xin Lu (*Pennsylvania State U.*)
Nantia Makrynioti (*AUEB Greece*)
Sebastian Mattheis (*BMW Car IT*)
Nianzu Ma (*U. Illinois Chicago*)
Meenakshi Mishra (*U. Kansas*)
Cristina Muntean (*ISTI-CNR*)
Nikhil Muralidhar (*George Mason U.*)
Masaya Murata (*NTT Japan*)
Bin Mu (*City U. New York*)
Azad Naik (*George Mason U.*)
Julia Neidhardt (*Tech. U. Wien*)
Konstantinos Nikolopoulos (*City U. New York*)
Koninika Pal (*Tech. U. Kaiserslautern*)
Panayiotis Papadakos (*FORTH-ICS Greece*)
Theodore Patkos (*FORTH-ICS Greece*)
Kostas Patroumpas (*National Tech. U. Athens*)
Nikos Pelekis (*U. Piraeus*)
Gerardo Pelosi (*Politecnico di Milano*)
Wei Pengfei (*Nanyang Tech. U.*)
Matthias Petri (*U. Melbourne*)
Trang T.M. Pham (*Deakin U.*)
Tuan Anh Nguyen Pham (*Nanyang Tech. U.*)
Layla Pournajaf (*Emory U.*)
Bo Qin (*Hong Kong U. Sc. Tech.*)
Jianbin Qin (*U. New South Wales*)
Ridho Reinanda (*U. Amsterdam*)
Navid Rekabsaz (*Tech. U. Vienna*)
Zhiyun Ren (*George Mason U.*)
Bryan Reynaert (*Akori S.A.*)
Klaus Schmid (*Ludwig Maximilians U.*)
Baoxu Shi (*U. Notre Dame*)
Vasilis Spyropoulos (*AUEB Greece*)
Joseph St.Amand (*U. Kansas*)
Li Su (*U. Southern Denmark*)
Dan Suciu (*U. Washington*)
Yifang Sun (*U. New South Wales*)
Mack Sweeney (*George Mason U.*)
Natasha Tagasovska (*U. Lausanne*)
Aditya Telang (*IBM Research India*)
Camilo Thorne (*U. Mannheim*)
Salvatore Trani (*ISTI-CNR*)
Erald Troja (*City U. New York*)
Yannis Tzitzikas (*FORTH-ICS Greece*)
Utkarsh Upadhyay (*Max Planck Institut*)
Tassos Venetis (*AUEB Greece*)
Thanasis Vergoulis (*Athena Research Greece*)
Hongjian Wang (*Pennsylvania State U.*)
Shuai Wang (*U. Illinois Chicago*)
Xiang Wang (*U. New South Wales*)
Xiaoyang Wang (*U. New South Wales*)
Victor Junqiu Wei (*Hong Kong U. Sc. Tech.*)
Udi Weinsberg (*Facebook*)
Buwen Wu (*U. Southern Denmark*)
Fei Wu (*Pennsylvania State U.*)
Xiaoying Wu (*Wuhan U.*)
Yingjun Wu (*National U. Singapore*)
Xike Xie (*Aalborg U.*)
Xiaofeng Xu (*Emory U.*)
Bin Yang (*Aalborg U.*)
Shiyu Yang (*U. New South Wales*)
Yang Yang (*U. Electronic Sc. Tech. China*)
Zhengwei Yang (*Chinese U. Hong Kong*)
Peifeng Yin (*IBM*)
Quan Yuan (*U. Illinois Urbana-Champaign*)
Ting Yu (*Wuhan U.*)
Shuangfei Zhai (*SUNY Binghamton*)
Bing Zhang (*Northwestern U.*)
Jingyuan Zhang (*U. Illinois Chicago*)
Xu Zhiqiang (*Institute Infocomm Research*)
Rui Zhou (*Victoria U.*)

Sponsors and Supporters

Sponsors

SIGIR
Special Interest Group
on Information Retrieval

sig web

Gold Supporter

Microsoft®
Research

Silver Supporter

sportsbet
.com.au

Bronze Supporters

Academic Supporters

Slow Search: Improving Information Retrieval Using Human Assistance

Jaime Teevan
Microsoft Research, Redmond, WA USA
teevan@microsoft.com

ABSTRACT

We live in a world where the pace of everything from communication to transportation is getting faster. In recent years a number of "slow movements" have emerged that advocate for reducing speed in exchange for increasing quality, including the slow food movement, slow parenting, slow travel, and even slow science. We propose the concept of "slow search," where search engines use additional time to provide a higher quality search experience than is possible given conventional time constraints. While additional time can be used to identify relevant results within the existing search engine framework, it can also be used to create new search artifacts and enable previously unimaginable user experiences. This talk will focus on how search engines can make use of additional time to employ a resource that is inherently slow: other people. Using crowdsourcing and friendsourcing, it will highlight opportunities for search systems to support new search experiences with high quality result content that takes time to identify.

Categories and Subject Descriptors

H.3.3 [**Information Storage and Retrieval**]: Information Search and Retrieval – *search process.*

Keywords

Slow search, crowdsourcing, speed, information retrieval.

1. INTRODUCTION TO SLOW SEARCH

Substantial research and engineering effort has been devoted to achieving low latency in large, complex computing systems like search engines. Search engines target speed for good reason. Research suggests that people perceive results that are delivered quickly as higher quality and more engaging than those delivered more slowly [10]. To achieve near-instantaneous speed, search engines make a number of compromises and limit the complexity of the features and models used to identify relevant documents. The resulting fast, word-oriented matching used by search engines ignores the rich semantics of text but is an efficient way to capture some aspects of the similarity between queries and documents.

Although searchers have grown accustomed to rapid responses to their queries, recent advances in our understanding of how people search suggest there are scenarios where a search engine could take significantly longer than a fraction of a second to return relevant content [9]. People often invest minutes, hours, or even days in more complex or exploratory search tasks. A person planning a vacation or researching a medical diagnosis, for example, may be willing to wait for better results or insights. By building slow search user experiences [2], search engines can make use of additional time to identify the most relevant content [4, 6], load balance responses over time, and incorporate slow resources [1, 3].

One slow resource that is particularly interesting to explore is people. Although computers can consider billions of documents much faster than a person can, a person can better understand each document. Crowdsourcing research suggests paid crowd workers can be incorporated into the search process in a way that is personalized [8] and accounts for privacy considerations [5]. This enables underperforming search engine components, such as those for query understanding and result processing, to be done by crowd workers [4]. Initial explorations show that while incorporating crowd workers into existing search pipelines increases robustness, the increase in performance is not significant enough to warrant the extra time and cost involved. Instead, approaches that use crowd workers to drastically change the search experience [1, 3] or that incorporate feedback from highly relevant people (e.g., friends) [3, 7] appear most likely to be successful.

Our hope is that slow search will inspire new and creative research into how search experiences can be enriched with a more nuanced notion of relevant search resources and time constraints.

CIKM '15, October 19–23, 2015, Melbourne, VIC, Australia.
ACM 978-1-4503-3794-6/15/10.
http://dx.doi.org/10.1145/2806416.2806417

2. REFERENCES

[1] Bernstein, M., Teevan, J., Dumais, S.T., Libeling, D. and Horvitz, E. Direct answers for search queries in the long tail. CHI 2012.

[2] Eickhoff, C., Teevan, J., White, R. and Dumais, S.T. Lessons from the journey: A query log analysis of within-session learning. WSDM 2014.

[3] Jeong, J., Morris, M., Teevan, J. and Liebling, D. A crowd-powered socially embedded search engine. ICWSM 2013.

[4] Kim, Y., Collins-Thompson, K. and Teevan, J. Crowdsourcing for robustness in web search. TREC 2013.

[5] Lasecki, W., Teevan, J., and Kamar, E. Information extraction and manipulation threats in crowd-powered systems. CSCW 2014.

[6] Livne, A., Gokuladas, V., Teevan, J., Dumais, S.T. and Adar, E. CiteSight: Supporting contextual citation recommendation using differential search. SIGIR 2014.

[7] Morris, M.R., Teevan, J. and Panovich, K. A comparison of information seeking using search engines and social networks. ICWSM 2010.

[8] Organisciak, P., Teevan, J., Dumais, S.T., Miller, R.C. and Kalai, A.T. A crowd of your own: Crowdsourcing for on-demand personalization. HCOMP 2014.

[9] Teevan, J., Collins-Thompson, K., White, R.W. and Dumais, S.T. Viewpoint: Slow search. CACM, 57(8), 2014.

[10] Teevan, J., Collins-Thompson, K., White, R.W., Dumais, S.T. and Kim, Y. Slow search: Information retrieval without time constraints. HCIR 2013.

External Data Access and Indexing in AsterixDB

Abdullah Alamoudi, Raman Grover, Michael J. Carey, Vinayak Borkar

Dept. of Computer Science,
University of California Irvine, CA, USA - 92697
{alamouda, ramang, mjcarey, vborkar}@uci.edu

ABSTRACT

Traditional database systems offer rich query interfaces (SQL) and efficient query execution for data that they store. Recent years have seen the rise of Big Data analytics platforms offering query-based access to "raw" external data, e.g., file-resident data (often in HDFS). In this paper, we describe techniques to achieve the qualities offered by DBMSs when accessing external data. This work has been built into Apache AsterixDB, an open source Big Data Management System. We describe how we build distributed indexes over external data, partition external indexes, provide query consistency across access paths, and manage external indexes amidst concurrent activities. We compare the performance of this new AsterixDB capability to an external-only solution (Hive) and to its internally managed data and indexes.

Categories and Subject Descriptors: H.2 [DATABASE MANAGEMENT]: Systems - Query Processing

Keywords: AsterixDB, External data, HDFS, Access, Indexing.

1. INTRODUCTION

Database management systems employ many techniques to achieve good performance. These include storage structures, access methods, caching, and efficient query execution. As a prerequisite, a DBMS requires data to be stored into its storage layer and modified through its interface. Having to pre-load data can be a major obstacle, particularly when data is being produced in huge quantities by multiple sources and being persisted in different storage systems and formats. Providing full-scan access to external data from a DBMS is a first step that enables the use of queries rather than error-prone ad hoc analysis scripts. However, the lack of indexes is bound to give unacceptable query response times. A natural next step is to support indexing for external data.

CIKM'15, October 19–23, 2015, Melbourne, Australia.

DOI: http://dx.doi.org/10.1145/2806416.2806428.

1.1 External Access and Indexing Challenges

Efficient and flexible external data access in a parallel data manager involves challenges stemming from lack of control over the representation of records, their storage locations, and the data modification path(s). These include:
C1) *Disparate Data Sources and Formats*: An external access facility must be generic and extensible to allow access to data in different data sources and formats.
C2) *Seamless Integration*: The distinction between external and internal data should not be visible to the end-user when framing queries in the language offered by the system.
C3) *Parallel/Efficient Access*: A parallel data manager must exploit parallelism in accessing external data and utilize distributed index structures to achieve load balancing.
C4) *Maintenance of Indexes*: External data may change, causing indexes to become stale. The system must enable users to refresh the indexes with *transactional* behavior.
C5) *Consistency of Query Results*: The system should offer consistent query results for external data regardless of the access path used and concurrent changes to external data.

1.2 Contributions

We describe how we have recently enhanced AsterixDB to enable users to efficiently query externally stored data. Our solution supports a set of popular external data source types and formats but is extensible to cater to new data sources and formats. It allows users to build multiple distributed indexes (e.g., B+ Trees and/or R-Trees) over external data. The query compiler then utilizes these indexes to accelerate queries. We offer the following contributions:
(1) *External Data Access and Indexing*: We provide a complete conceptual and technical design for providing access to and building distributed indexes over external data.
(2) *Access Semantics*: We introduce *external data snapshot* semantics for queries accessing indexed external data. We describe mechanisms to keep indexes in known synchrony with the data and provide consistent query results.
(3) *Incremental Updates*: We detail the design for refreshing a dataset's indexes incrementally in AsterixDB in an efficient and robust manner.
(4) *Contribution to Open-Source*: AsterixDB is open-source. Its support for adapters, parsers, and indexing is extensible to allow other project contributors to add new adapters and parsers for other external data sources and formats.
(5) *Experimental Evaluation*: We measure the external data access performance for different HDFS formats, comparing AsterixDB's performance when data resides externally in Hive tables [2] to that of Hive itself. We also compare per-

formance for internal versus external data to see what can be attained without moving data into AsterixDB.

The rest of the paper is organized as follows. Section 2 covers related work. We review AsterixDB and the Hadoop Distributed File System (HDFS) in Section 3. Section 4 introduces the language-level support and concepts related to external data access. We detail the corresponding design and implementation in Section 5. Section 6 presents experimental results, and Section 7 concludes the paper.

2. RELATED WORK

The need to access external data has been long recognized in the database community [16] and was added to the SQL standard. Leading DBMSs provide raw data scanning capabilities via features such as External Tables in Oracle and MySQL and External Link and Open Row Set in MS SQL. For extensibility, Oracle and DB2 offer Table Functions and MS SQL provides Table-Valued User Defined Functions. Use of these features involve full scans over external data, which perform worse than queries over internally stored data. In contrast to using a DBMS to access and query external data, [15] described the use of Unix tools (awk, grep) as an alternative, introducing FlatSQL as a language to operate over text files. The trade-offs involved in using Unix tools when accessing external data were further explored in [14] and influenced the "NoDB" system [4].

It is common today to have large data files that span multiple machines in a distributed file system such as HDFS. Loading such data into a DBMS imposes significant costs. Several efforts (e.g. [18]) have focused on integrating Hadoop (Map-Reduce) with a DBMS to avoid the costs involved in movement of data. HadoopDB [3] allowed running queries on raw HDFS files using MapReduce and provided support for incrementally loading data into the DBMS's storage layer. Other efforts to improve query execution over data in HDFS include the use of Split-oriented indexes [12] to prune unwanted input splits to reduce I/O costs and building Trojan indexes [11] into the physical file splits when loading data into HDFS storage using user-defined functions. In the High Performance Computing field, SciHadoop field[9] provide different mechanism to prune HDFS data partitions and avoid the full scan cost. More recent related work can be found in [7] and [10].

Our approach to external data access is unique in several ways. It allows users to build distributed record-level indexes over external data. It doesn't cache or re-write data, the query results are access path independent, and data is not loaded into the AsterixDB storage layer at any time. The presence of indexes doesn't affect the external data, and we support indexing of multiple HDFS input formats. This is accomplished largely by making externally stored data "look" like internally stored data from the perspective of most of the system's query processing components.

Our work has key differences from the concurrent effort to index HDFS data in Polybase [13]. The differences, detailed later in the paper, include a location-aware index partitioning strategy, a Record Id (RID) optimization, the exploitation of AsterixDB's Log-Structured Merge (LSM) trees when updating indexes atomically, support for indexing RC-Files, snapshot-based consistency of query results, and the roles of MapReduce (in Polybase) and HDFS in query processing.

3. BACKGROUND

We begin by briefly reviewing AsterixDB and HDFS, the systems for which this work was designed, implemented, and evaluated.

AsterixDB: AsterixDB is an Apache incubator open source Big Data management system. It has its own flexible data model – ADM (inspired by JSON) – and comes with a full query language – AQL – for querying and analyzing semi-structured data. Its shared-nothing architecture involves a central Cluster Controller (CC) and a set of *worker* nodes referred to as Node Controllers (NCs). Data resides as records in datasets that are hash-partitioned on their primary keys and stored in primary B+ tree indexes. Secondary indexes (when created) are co-located with the corresponding partitions of the primary index [5]. To execute queries, AsterixDB uses Hyracks [8] as its execution engine. A Hyracks job is a DAG built using data *operators* and *connectors*.

HDFS: HDFS is the distributed file system of Hadoop [1]. HDFS files are partitioned into replicated binary blocks to enable parallel reads and hardware failure tolerance. HDFS consists of a *NameNode* that stores files' metadata information and a set of *DataNode(s)* that store the binary blocks of data. HDFS files are append-only, meaning that records contained in a file cannot be modified.

4. EXTERNAL DATASETS

External datasets in AsterixDB enable users to query data stored in external sources. Unlike internal datasets, external datasets do not support AQL *load*, *insert*, or *delete* statements. External sources may store data in a variety of formats and have specific protocols for fetching data. To cater to the diversity of data sources and formats, a data manager must also be extensible.

4.1 Dataset Adapters

Connecting to an external data source and receiving, parsing, and translating its data into binary ADM records (for AsterixDB processing) is done by a *dataset adapter*. The use of an adapter includes providing a set of parameters that it uses when interfacing with the source. AsterixDB offers a set of initial adapters for common data sources; its design also offers a plug-and-play model to allow new adapters to be added. Common external data sources and their handling by their respective AsterixDB adapters include:

(1) **Data Files in Local File Systems**: Files residing in the local file systems of the AsterixDB nodes are accessible using the Local File System adapter. This adapter is configured with a set of file identifiers, where an identifier combines the host name (AsterixDB node) and absolute path of a local file on the host. The format associated with the file is additionally specified. AsterixDB's built-in text parsers support parsing of data that is in delimited, JSON, or ADM format. AsterixDB also allows using a custom implementation of a parser for additional formats. Multiple files on a given node or on different nodes are read and parsed in parallel to exploit node-level and cluster-level parallelism.

(2) **Data Files in HDFS**: The HDFS adapter performs the same function for data files residing in HDFS. This adaptor takes an additional argument that describes the InputFileFormat of the dataset's files.

(3) **Data in Web Resources**: AsterixDB's web adapters read data from resources identified by URIs. The level of parallelism when using this adapter is dictated by the num-

```
create external dataset ExLineitem(lineitemType)
using hdfs (
("hdfs"="hdfs://namenode:54311"),
("path"="/data/tpch/lineitem"),
("input-format"="text-input-format"),
("format"="delimited-text"),("delimiter"="|"));
for $l in dataset ExLineitem
where $l.lshipdate <= date("1998-09-02")
order by $l.lextendedprice
return $l;
```

Listing 1: Creating and querying an External Dataset

```
create index OrdIdx on Lineitem(lorderkey);
create index OrdIdx on ExLineitem(lorderkey);
```

Listing 2: Creating a B+ Tree Index over Internal and External datasets

```
refresh external dataset ExLineitem;
```

Listing 3: Refreshing an External Dataset

ber of URIs, and the task of reading and parsing records is assigned to different nodes during query compilation.

An adapter is referred to in AQL by its *alias* and specified as part of the *create external dataset* statement. The example statement in Listing 1 uses the HDFS adapter and provides parameters to describe the HDFS instance and contained data. There is no subsequent distinction between internal and external datasets when using them in AQL queries.

4.2 Indexing of External Datasets

The current version of AsterixDB supports full-scan access to external data. The extensions detailed here add support for indexing a variety of HDFS-resident data formats and allow users to build distributed B+ tree and/or R-tree indexes to quickly access records without having to load them into AsterixDB's storage. They were designed to fit in with the typical data lifecycle for a large enterprise Hadoop system, which involves rolling-in and rolling-out data batches in HDFS files. The AQL syntax for defining an index over a set of attributes for any dataset is illustrated in Listing 2. The create index statement syntax is common to both kinds of datasets, internal or external. However, unlike an internal dataset (Lineitem), the data referenced by an external dataset (ExLineitem) can change outside the purview of AsterixDB, causing indexes to become stale. We now explain the consistency model we provide for indexed external data.

4.3 User Experience and Semantics

Manipulation of data in an external source impacts the referencing queries within AsterixDB in two ways. First, external data could change during query execution. Second, creating secondary indexes at different points in time could yield inconsistencies across indexes. To obtain consistent access semantics for external data, we introduce the concept of an *external dataset metadata snapshot*. An external dataset metadata snapshot denotes the state of an external dataset's files at a given point in time. The information contained in a snapshot is used in preserving consistency across an external dataset's indexes and in enforcing a consistent shared view over data between different access paths (full scans or alternative index-based access paths).

The first use of a *create index* statement (Listing 2) with an external dataset implicitly creates a *metadata snapshot* for the external dataset. A metadata snapshot contains only a list of files' absolute paths, sizes, and modification times, and is thus lightweight. It is used to guide subsequent dataset access or index creation. Records added to the external source after a snapshot will remain hidden from AsterixDB until the snapshot and indexes are re-synchronized with the external data via an explicit *refresh external dataset* statement (Listing 3). The refresh operation is executed in a distributed way over an AsterixDB cluster with transactional semantics; in the event of a failure during a refresh operation, the metadata snapshot and all indexes associated with the external dataset are restored to their previous state. We ensure that a refresh statement does not impact concurrent queries and that an executing query always uses the same metadata snapshot associated with an external dataset.

Our user-guided snapshot consistency model differs from the consistency model of Polybase [13]. Polybase computes a metadata delta for HDFS files before answering queries and it aims to deliver results based on the current state of indexed HDFS files. To do so, it resorts to using a more costly Hybrid access path when an index is found to be stale. We avoid this overhead and provide older consistent results.

5. IMPLEMENTATION DETAILS

We now turn to the physical aspects of creating and maintaining snapshots and indexes and using them for queries.

5.1 Unindexed External Data

Consider the example query from Listing 1. In the absence of indexes, the query involves a full scan of the external dataset ExLineitem. The compiler first refers to the Metadata to find the associated dataset adapter and its parameter values. Access to an external dataset is done by an *ExternalDataScan* operator. Multiple instances of this operator may run in parallel, each fetching and parsing records from the external source. A dataset adapter has an associated *factory* class used by AsterixDB to create instance(s) of the adapter. The factory class uses configuration parameters to determine the degree of parallelism (*count constraint*) and any specific set of AsterixDB nodes (*location constraint*) where instances of the adapter should run. As an example, the factory for the HDFS adapter connects with the HDFS NameNode to determine the count and location of input partitions. In determining the location constraint, it gives preference to co-located AsterixDB nodes to facilitate local reads.

5.2 Index Design and Implementation

A parallel external indexing facility needs a way to identify records, to distribute index components in a cluster, and to maintain any/all information in a way that minimizes internode communication when an index is used at runtime.

5.2.1 Identifying Records

Indexing requires each data record to have a unique id, hereafter referred to as its RID. (For internal data, the primary key serves as the RID.) RIDs must enable fast

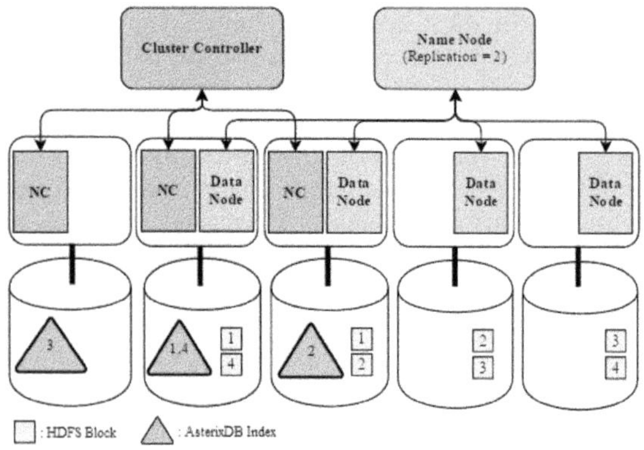

Figure 1: External Data and Index Distribution

record retrieval and must be small in size. As a single external dataset can map to multiple external files, an external record's RID is a combination of a *file id* and a *record locator*. The file id consists of the file's path and modification time. Discovering a file with the same path but a different modification time implies a deletion of the file followed by a creation of a new file. Since storing the file path and modification time in each RID in an index would be very expensive, we replace the long file id with an assigned 4 byte (*integer*) value and store the file id mappings for external datasets' files in a separate B+ Tree index referred to as the *snapshot index*.

The other component of an RID, the record locator, depends on the format of the HDFS file. For the TextInput and SequenceInput formats, the record locator is just the 8 byte (*long*) offset of the record within the file[1]. The RCFile format stores records in columnar order and groups them into row groups of configurable size. Its record locator is then a combination of the 8 byte (*long*) row group offset and 4 byte (*integer*) row number within the containing group.

Support for an additional HDFS file format can be achieved by providing three components. The first is the structure of the RID for the file format; this is used by AsterixDB's query compiler when utilizing operators for index-building or index-accessing jobs. The second component is a runtime indexing adapter that produces RIDs for records being read from HDFS. The third is a runtime lookup adapter that uses the stored RIDs to read the selected records.

5.2.2 Index Distribution

Distribution of data is critical to load-balancing and scalability in a parallel data manager. Records contained in an internal dataset in AsterixDB are hash-partitioned by primary key and stored in primary B+tree indexes across the nodes in a cluster. This achieves near-uniform distribution of records and allows optimizations of joins involving primary keys. Secondary index partitions of internal AsterixDB datasets are co-located with their primary index partitions, which ensures zero extra communication between nodes when accessing data through a secondary index.

External files in HDFS are partitioned into blocks that are replicated and distributed across a set of Data Nodes. Given this, our external indexes use a block-based distribution strategy aimed at achieving locality and load balancing. Co-locating indexes with data reduces communication and allows accessing of HDFS records directly in a short-circuited manner without going through HDFS Data Nodes. The HDFS replication factor and the overlap between AsterixDB NCs and HDFS Data Nodes affect the choices made when selecting an index partition for records in HDFS blocks.

An AsterixDB cluster and an HDFS cluster with data to be externally accessed can have different degrees of node overlap. They may overlap completely, not at all, or partially (the general case, shown in Figure 1). Copies of an HDFS data block may thus be stored on an HDFS node that also hosts an AsterixDB NC (blocks 1, 2, and 4 in Figure 1) or is outside the AsterixDB cluster (block 3 in Figure 1). This yields an index responsibility assignment optimization problem whose objective is to maximize the number of local assignments while minimizing the variance in the number of blocks assigned to each NC. To solve this, we give priority to locality and use a greedy 2-pass algorithm to pick the location of each block's index partition. We first identify the locations of the targeted HDFS blocks and keep track of the number of assignments per NC. In the first pass, we loop over the blocks, assigning overlapping blocks to a co-located NC with the lowest number of assignments (skipping remote blocks). In the second pass, we loop over any unassigned blocks and assign them to the NC with the lowest number of assignments. Ties are broken using node ids.

5.2.3 Snapshot Management

AsterixDB stores metadata about the HDFS files of indexed external datasets; it is used to maintain consistency when interacting with an external dataset. For each external file, the path, modification time, and size in bytes are used to remember its external state at a given point in time and are collectively referred to as the metadata snapshot. (Including the file size is critical because an HDFS file can, in some cases, grow without changing its modification time.) When creating an external index or accessing an external dataset using the *ExternalDataScan* operator, any records lying beyond the stored size of an external file are ignored (treated as not yet visible) to ensure a consistent view of the dataset.

The metadata snapshot of an external dataset is captured from HDFS when the first index on the dataset is created. This snapshot is subsequently updated in a transactional manner when performing external dataset refresh operations. The information contained in the snapshot is stored in AsterixDB's Metadata in a special dataset, the *ExternalFile* dataset. External files are assigned integer ids before capturing their information in a snapshot; these ids are used in the RIDs of external records in place of file paths and modification times. To perform external index accesses, AsterixDB nodes need to lookup metadata snapshots using these assigned ids. This could cause an additional communication overhead and become a bottleneck when accessing AsterixDB Metadata. To avoid this, a *snapshot index* is created for each external dataset in an AsterixDB node. This snapshot index contains the metadata records of external files that belong to the index's associated dataset and it is used to lookup files for indexed access.

5.2.4 Constructing an Index

We now describe the runtime for the *create external index* statement (Listing 2) and the operators involved in the gen-

[1] This is reminiscent of NoDB's positional map[4].

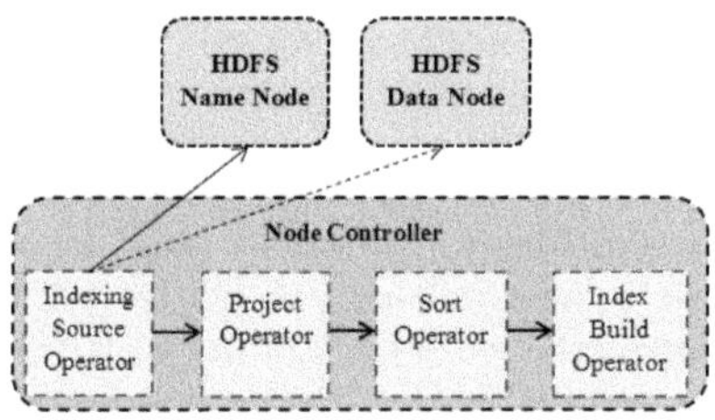

Figure 2: Dataflow for Index Construction

erated Hyracks job. When a user creates a secondary index over an external dataset, the Cluster Controller (CC) first checks whether a metadata snapshot for the dataset exists in the ExternalFile dataset. If one is not found, the CC queries the HDFS NameNode to get the status of the dataset's files and stores it in the ExternalFile dataset. The captured snapshot is then broadcast to all participating nodes in the AsterixDB cluster and stored in B+ tree indexes. The CC then uses the intersection of the stored metadata and the existing files in HDFS to create a list of HDFS block-sized logical file splits to be indexed. Indexing of records in different blocks is assigned to different nodes in AsterixDB as per the distribution strategy described earlier in Section 5.2.2.

A Hyracks load pipeline consisting of four operators is constructed on each participating NC (Figure 2). The *IndexingSource* operator at the head of the pipeline uses an indexing adapter that fetches records and their RIDs. This indexing operator queries the HDFS NameNode to locate the assigned blocks. For blocks local to an NC (e.g., blocks 1, 2 and 4 in Figure 1), the operator can read records directly from the node's disk without communicating with the DataNode as illustrated by the optional dotted connection in Figure 2. For remote blocks (e.g., block 3 in Figure 1), the operator reads records from one of the DataNodes holding the block.

Output from the *IndexingSource* operator is fed into a *Project* operator that extracts the secondary keys from the parsed records and passes them with their RIDs to the *Sort* operator. Tuples sorted on the secondary keys are consumed by the *IndexBuild* operator, which builds the index tree in a bottom up fashion. When the job completes execution on all nodes the index can be used to access the dataset.

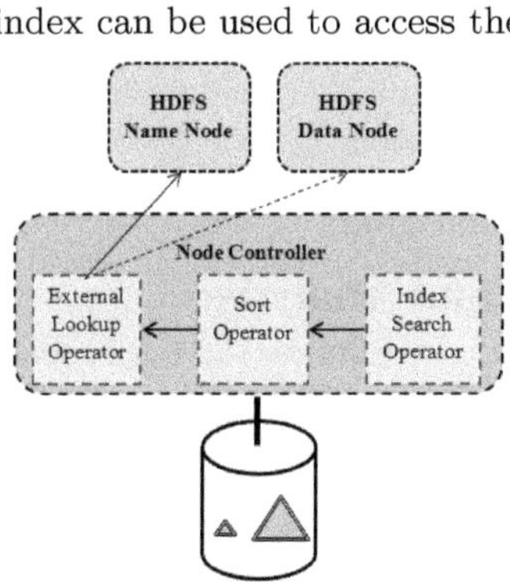

Figure 3: Dataflow for Index Use in Queries

5.2.5 *Using an Index*

When querying an indexed external dataset, AsterixDB's compiler can choose to access the dataset using a secondary index. To access an external dataset through an index, the compiler produces a Hyracks job that contains the pipeline shown in Figure 3. The *IndexSearch* operator uses search predicates to search the secondary index, producing RIDs that point to external records. These RIDs are then sorted by the *Sort* operator and fed to an *ExternalLookup* operator. Sorting RIDs prior to accessing records reduces the associated I/O cost due to sequential access when the number of records are large and incurs a negligible cost when accessing few records since the sort operation would take place in memory. In HDFS case, this also reduces the number of connections made to DataNodes.

The *ExternalLookup* operator uses a lookup adapter to selectively fetch external records by RID. This operator uses the NC's local snapshot index to retrieve files' metadata. Before opening an external file, the operator contacts the HDFS Name Node to validate the existence of the file. If the file was not found, subsequent RIDs with the same file id are dropped. If the block containing accessed records is found to be local, the operator can skip the connection to the DataNode and read directly from its local disk; otherwise the operator reads the records from one of the HDFS DataNodes that holds the block. The operator parses and sends the fetched records in binary ADM format to the consuming operator in the query execution pipeline.

5.3 Updating an External Dataset

Data can change over time, causing external indexes to become stale. To advance the metadata snapshot associated with an external dataset to the current point in time and update all of its secondary indexes, the *refresh external dataset* AQL statement is used. The refresh operation follows the presumed-abort 2-Phase Commit (2PC) protocol [17] to atomically update an external dataset. We exploit AsterixDB's usage of LSM indexes [6] to perform shadow-based transactional batch updates. An LSM index consists of multiple disk-resident immutable components plus a mutable in-memory component. When beginning an external dataset refresh transaction, a new shadow index component is created. All operations under the refresh transaction will be applied to the shadow component. Such components can handle the addition of new records as well as the deletion of existing records. When a refresh transaction commits, its shadow components are revealed and added to the LSM indexes to be used in answering subsequent queries [17, 6]. Aborting a refresh transaction results simply in the deletion of its shadow components.[2] Our failure handling before the decision to commit is fail-backward and we don't support resume operations.

Each external dataset refresh operation starts by computing a snapshot delta that consists of a set of deleted files, a set of record-appended files, and a set of new files. If all three sets are empty, the operation is complete, and otherwise the delta is recorded on disk and the transaction enters the "presumed abort" state. AsterixDB updates both the snapshot index and the secondary indexes of the dataset undergoing the refresh transaction in each NC. In the shadowed component of the snapshot index, new tuples are added for new files and anti-matter tuples (delete flags) for deleted files. Subsequently, and for each secondary index, a Hyracks job similar to the index building job is constructed to update the index.

[2]Shadow components are only used for external data refresh transactions and are not used with internal datasets.

Deletion of index entries for records in deleted files is important to enhance index performance and to reclaim space, but adding an anti-matter tuple for each deleted record would require expensive scans of deleted index components and yield large shadow components. To avoid this, a special "buddy B+ Tree" is paired with each external LSM index component; it is used to store the file numbers of newly deleted files that potentially had entries in older index components. During an index search, the buddy B+ Trees enable deleted records to be filtered out early. Each buddy B+ Tree is accompanied by a Bloom filter to further reduce the number of I/O operations during searches. When merging LSM index components, the buddy B+ Trees of the index are used to filter out the deleted record entries and reclaim disk space.

A refresh transaction moves into the "ready-to-commit" state when all of the dataset's indexes have their shadow components ready. The CC then records the transaction state on disk and instructs all nodes to commit the transaction locally. After it has committed on all NCs, the delta is added to the ExternalFile dataset and the transaction is marked complete. This use of 2PC enables external indexes to recover from crashes and maintain a consistent state. When bootstrapping, the CC loops over all incomplete transactions to perform global recovery. Transactions in the presumed abort state are rolled back, and transactions in the ready-to-commit state are rolled forward. Since refresh operations always bulk load their changes into shadow components, no record-level logging is required.

5.4 Consistency and Concurrency

The semantics of our logical design forbid external data refresh transactions from affecting external data access in queries that began before the transaction is committed. The semantics are maintained while allowing datasets to be accessed (using indexes or using a scan) and refreshed simultaneously. In this section, we explain how different external datasets' operations correctly interleave.

AsterixDB's CC maintains up to two versions (transiently) of the state of each external dataset plus a pointer to the more recent version. It also tracks the number of queries accessing each version. NCs similarly manage two versions for each external index. Each of these corresponds to one of the versions at the CC and is just a list of pointers to a subset of the index's LSM components. (Index components can be shared between the two versions of the index.)

Before a query accesses an external dataset, the compiler marks it with the id of the most recent version of the dataset and increments the number of queries accessing that version. During query execution, external index search operators use the assigned id to only search the LSM index components that belong to the matching version of the index. When a query finishes execution, the access count for each of its accessed datasets' versions is decremented. When the number of queries accessing the older version of a dataset reaches 0, it becomes *inactive* and can be deleted.

A dataset refresh can start only when the older version of the dataset is inactive. When committing a refresh transaction locally, new versions of the dataset's indexes are created that contain existing index components in addition to newly uncovered shadow components. On a global commit, the pointer to the most recent view of the index is updated and it is then ready to accept queries. This allows queries to run and use external indexes for a dataset that is concurrently being refreshed without affecting their results.

Most operations on external datasets can be executed in parallel. Multiple indexes can be created concurrently. However, refresh operations for a dataset must be serialized. A dataset refresh is also mutually exclusive with index creation, as indexes are created according to a captured snapshot (which is updated through refresh operations).

6. EXPERIMENTAL EVALUATION

We now compare the performance of AsterixDB external datasets, on Hive-created data, against that of Hive itself on the same data files. We also compare external and internal dataset performance for the same data content; this shows the trade-offs involved in moving data into the system versus indexing it externally.

6.1 Experimental Setup

We used a 10 node cluster; each node had a dual core processor, 8GB RAM and 2x 1TB 7200rpm hard drives. AsterixDB (0.8.6) and Hadoop (2.2.0) were set up to utilize all nodes in the cluster. Hadoop was configured with an I/O buffer size of 64 KB, a block size of 64 MB, and a replication factor of 3. We used TPC-H data at scale=250. The data (delimited-text) was put uniformly into HDFS with an equal number of blocks on each of the 20 disks on the cluster. Hive (0.13.0) tables were created (using *insert into select* style queries) with data in three different formats – Text file, Sequence file, and RCFile. Data in the RCFile format used 4 MB as the row group size. Table 1 shows the sizes for the Hive tables in each format. Datatypes were defined in AsterixDB to model TPC-H data. The time and space involved in loading the Lineitem, Order, and Customer data into internal AsterixDB datasets are shown in Table 2. The time includes the cost to fetch and parse data from HDFS, hash-partitioning and sort received records by primary key, and bulk-load them into B-Tree indexes partitioned across the cluster.

The queries in the following section were run in sequence. Each was run multiple times ranging from 5 times for full scan queries to 50 for expensive range lookups and 500 for low cost queries, and results were averaged. Predicate ranges were controlled for each point in the x-axis and their position was selected using a uniform random number generator. In contrast, simply creating an external dataset amounts to an insert of a row in AsterixDB's Metadata and requires negligible space and time.

6.2 Results and Analysis

In this section, we compare the performance of full scan operations using Hive, AsterixDB external datasets, and AsterixDB internal datasets. We also show the time and space implications of indexing different external and internal datasets. Subsequently, we evaluate the performance of indexed access to external versus internal datasets for several different query scenarios.

6.2.1 *Aggregation and Lookup Queries (Full Scan)*

We first ran queries to aggregate a single attribute and to look up a single record. Aggregates highlight performance when computation is performed on a single attribute, which affects the minimum deserialization requirements (taken advantage of by Hive with its RCFile formatted records). List-

Dataset	Format	Size (GB)	Number of files
Lineitem	Text	187.2	749
	Sequence	207.6	
	RCFile	173.9	
Orders	Text	41.9	167
	Sequence	46.1	
	RCFile	39.35	
Customer	Text	5.75	23
	Sequence	6.22	
	RCFile	5.6	

Table 1: HDFS raw data files

Dataset	Loading time (mins)	Primary Index Size
Lineitem	43	334GB
Orders	9	60GB
Customer	1.25	7.7GB

Table 2: Cost of loading data

```
--Aggregate Query
SELECT MAX(l.L_PARTKEY) FROM lineitem l;
--Lookup Query
SELECT * FROM lineitem li
  WHERE li.L_SUPPKEY = a
  AND li.L_LINENUMBER = b
  AND li.L_QUANTITY = c
  AND li.L_EXTENDEDPRICE = d;
--Aggregate Query
SELECT MIN(o.O_TOTALPRICE) FROM orders o;
--Lookup Query
SELECT * FROM orders o
  WHERE o.O_CUSTKEY = a
  AND o.O_TOTALPRICE = b
  AND o.O_OSHIPPRIORITY = c;
--Aggregate Query
SELECT MAX(c.C_BALANCE) FROM customer c;
--Lookup Query
SELECT * FROM customer c
  WHERE c.C_CNAME = a AND c.C_ADDRESS =
    b;
```

Listing 4: Aggregation and Lookup queries in HiveQL

ings 4 and 5 show the queries in HiveQL and AQL. The parameters *a*, *b*, *c*, and *d* were picked from specific records in different files. In the absence of an index, each query involved a full scan of the data. Figures 4(a), 4(b) and 4(c) show the results for the Lineitem, Customer and Order datasets, respectively, for data in different platforms and formats. The following are the key observations.

1) ***Querying Internal Data***: Queries against AsterixDB's internal datasets are faster than querying HDFS data, in any format, using either Hive or AsterixDB's external datasets. This is due to internal data being stored in AsterixDB's binary data format (ADM), requiring no translation. Further, the I/O done by AsterixDB is sequential, with a single thread reading from each I/O device with no concurrent I/O activities. For HDFS data, multiple threads may access different splits of data simultaneously and interfere.

2) ***Querying External Data***

(a) *Text and Sequence File Format*: AQL queries on external data in Text and Sequence File formats in HDFS run faster than the corresponding Hive queries. This is due to the different execution engines of AsterixDB and Hive. An

```
let $litems := for $li in dataset Lineitem
               return $li.partkey
return max($litems);
for $li in dataset Lineitem
  where $li.lsuppkey = a
  and $li.llinenumber = b
  and $li.lquantity = c
  and $li.lextendedprice = d
return $li;
let $price := for $ord in dataset Orders
              return $ord.ototalprice
return min($price);
for $ord in dataset Orders
  where $ord.ocustkey = a
  and $ord.ototalprice = b
  and $ord.oshippriority = c
return $ord;
let $balance := for $cust in dataset Customer
                return $cust.cbalance
return max($balance);
for $cust in dataset Customer
  where $cust.cname = a and $cust.caddress = b
return $cust;
```

Listing 5: Aggregation and Lookup queries in AQL

AQL query is compiled into one Hyracks job, while a Hive query is compiled into a Map-Reduce job (or jobs) to run on Hadoop. Hyracks exploits partitioned and pipelined parallelism to offer a more efficient execution model than Hadoop. Additional details on Hyracks can be found in [8].

(b) *RCFile Format*: Queries against the largest dataset, Lineitem, for the RCFile format, run faster in Hive than in AsterixDB as an external dataset being queried with AQL. Also, Hive performs relatively worse for simple selects as compared to aggregates. This is due to its need for additional field deserialization. However, this is mitigated by the use of a lazy deserializer that only deserializes fields when needed. AsterixDB, however, parses all the external fields. This difference lessens for datasets with smaller numbers of fields, e.g., Orders and Customers. In addition, AsterixDB does two-step parsing in its current Hive parser, deserializing records into Hive objects before converting them to ADM.

6.2.2 Joins (Full Scan)

Next, we evaluate a join between Customer and Order data on customer key. The result sizes were limited to around 1000 records via a range predicate on CustKey of Orders. The ranges, *a* and *b*, were picked randomly from the range of CustKeys where *b* is greater than *a* by 100. Listings 6 and 7 show the join query in HiveQL and AQL respectively. Figure 5 compares the query execution times for different storage platform and data format combinations. AsterixDB employs a completely hash-based join algorithm that is more efficent than the sort-and-shuffle-based join algorithm used by Hive. In addition, Hyracks jobs have lower cost than Map-Reduce jobs. Therefore, joins in AsterixDB run faster than joins in Hive. The internal dataset join achieves the best performance, as only the (selected) Orders records are shuffled to the nodes containing the matching Customer records (since the join key is a primary key) and internal datasets avoid parsing overhead.

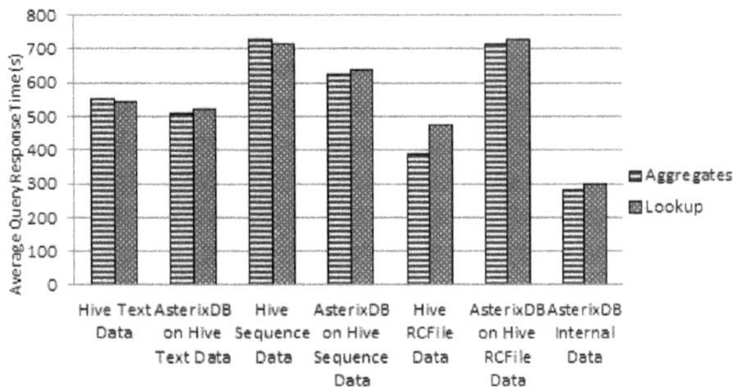

(a) Lineitem Dataset

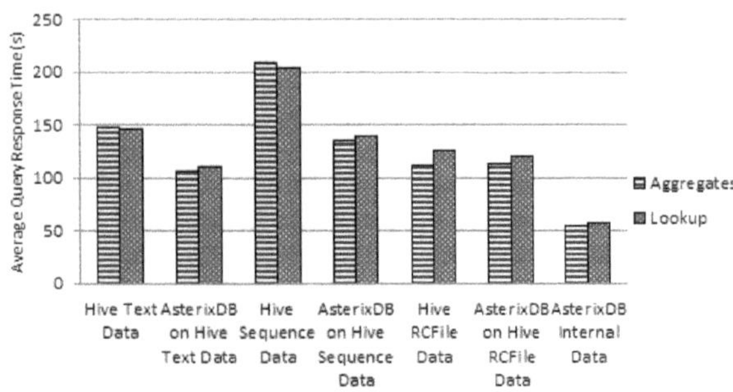

(b) Orders Dataset

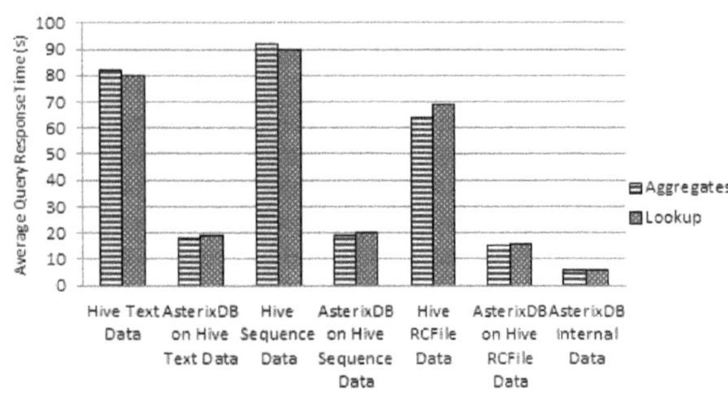

(c) Customer Dataset

Figure 4: Performance comparison: Aggregate and Lookup queries (Full Scan)

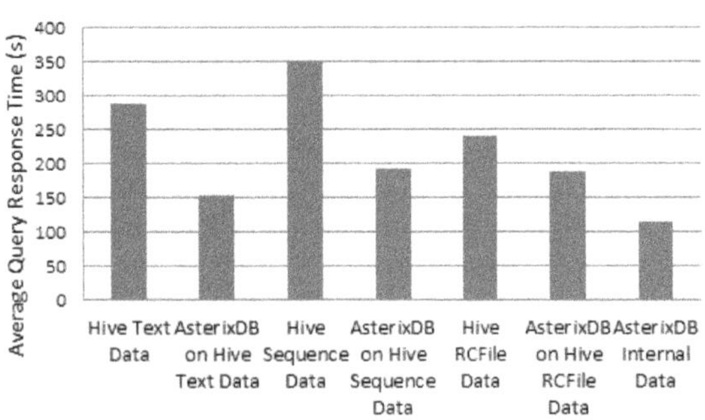

Figure 5: Performance comparison: Join of Customers and Orders (Full Scan)

6.2.3 *Constructing Indexes: Internal vs. External*

Next, we explore the costs of building secondary indexes on internal AsterixDB data versus external HDFS data. As shown in Table 3, indexing external data is slower than internal data. To see why, recall the index-construction pipeline from Figure 2. Indexing an external dataset requires parsing the data into ADM format. In addition, larger composite Record IDs slow down the sort operation. Further, an HDFS record reader may scan multiple files from partitions on the same I/O device, causing interference and non-deterministic delays. (The Hadoop 2.2.0 API doesn't provide a way to determine the I/O device hosting each block and to schedule accordingly.) Note that the index size for the RCFile format is larger due to the additional row number field in each RID.

TPC-H Data	Key	Format	Time (secs)	Size (GB)
Lineitem	order key	Text	1458	48.8
		Sequence	1678	48.8
		RCFile	1796	58.6
	part key	Internal	1313	40
		Text	1632	48.8
		Sequence	1802	48.8
		RCFile	2156	58.6
Orders	customer key	Internal	297	7.7
		Text	356	12
		Sequence	422	12
		RCFile	473	14.5
	order key	Text	300	48.8
		Sequence	362	48.8
		RCFile	341	58.6
Customer	customer key	Text	38	1
		Sequence	39	1
		RCFile	49	1.47

Table 3: Indexing of external and internal datasets

```
SELECT cust.ccustkey, cust.cname, ord.oorderkey
    FROM orders ord JOIN
customer cust ON(ord.ocustkey = cust.ccustkey)
WHERE ord.ocustkey > a and ord.ocustkey < b;
```

Listing 6: Join query example in HiveQL

```
for $ord in dataset Orders
for $cus in dataset Customer
where $ord.ocustkey = $cus.ccustkey
and $ord.ocustkey > a and $ord.ocustkey < b
return { "key":$cus.ccustkey,
   "name":$cus.ccname,
   "orderkey":$ord.oorderkey };
```

Listing 7: Join query example in AQL

```
count(for $ord in dataset Orders
      where $ord.oorderkey > a and $ord.oorderkey < b
      return $ord);
```

Listing 8: Range query on Orders using order index

6.2.4 *Index Access: Internal vs. External*

Having built indexes on both internal and external datasets, we then ran queries to use them. Each query was run for multiple data ranges to show its performance for different result sizes. The parameters a and b in Listings 8, 9, 10, and 11 were substituted with values picked from their respective data ranges using a uniformly distributed random value generator. The difference between a and b was used to control the result sizes. Throughout our experiments, the measured queries just count the results rather than return-

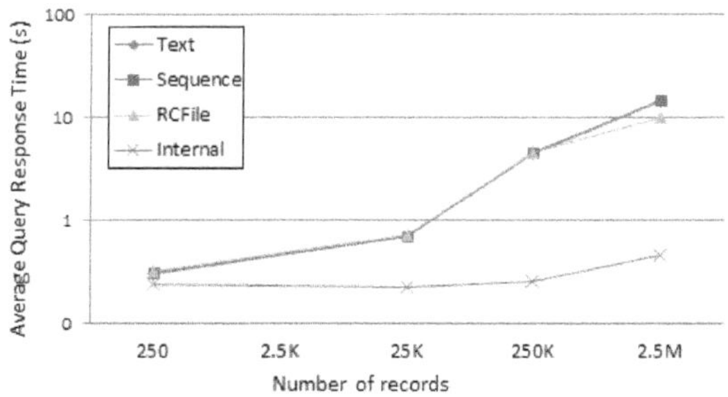

Figure 6: AsterixDB range queries on Orders dataset using order index

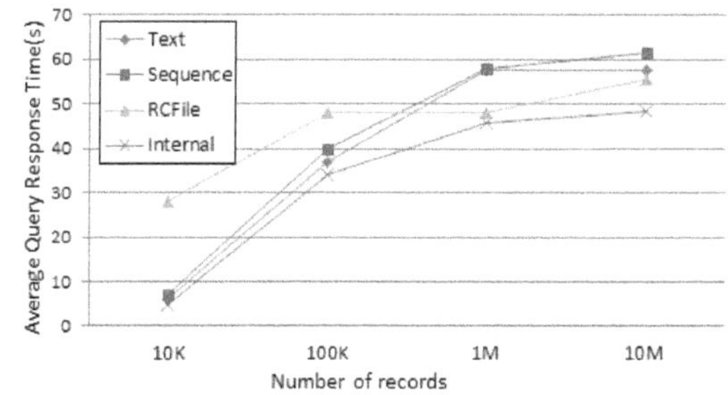

Figure 7: AsterixDB range queries on Orders dataset using customer index

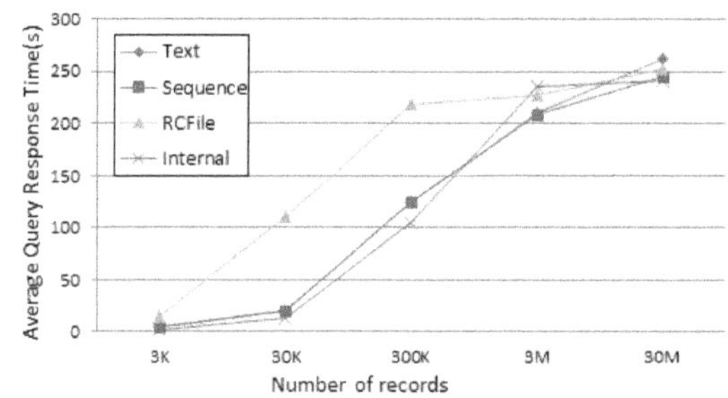

Figure 8: AsterixDB range queries on Lineitem dataset using part index

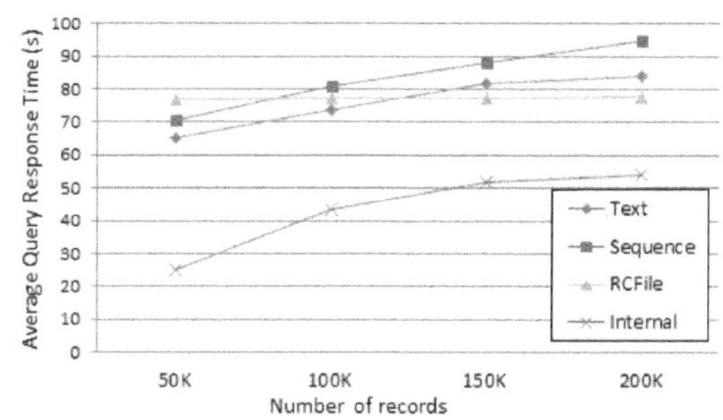

Figure 9: AsterixDB index-based join of Orders and Customers datasets on customer key

ing their data; we did so to isolate computation costs from the cost of result delivery. We now examine the results.

(1)*External Secondary Index vs. Internal Primary Index:* Queries on primary keys benefit when data storage is internal using a primary index. To gain similar efficiency, such queries on external data need secondary indexes (as external datasets lack primary keys). We ran an example query (Listing 8) on an internal dataset as well as on external datasets with different HDFS formats. Figure 6 shows the results. At a result size of 250 records, internal and external data perform similarly; times are dominated by query compilation and running a small Hyracks job. As we increase the result size to 2.5 million records by altering the order key predicate, the time for the internal dataset remains well below 1 second. In contrast, the time for external datasets increases by factors of 10 and 14 for the RCFile and Sequence/Text formats. Querying an internal dataset benefits from evenly distributed processing due to hash-partitioning of records on search key. Moreover, the primary index access requires a sequential scan just of the index leaves, as opposed to random accesses of leaves and internal nodes of primary indexes when accessing data via secondary indexes. Querying external datasets involves additional steps (and overheads) including a secondary index search, sorting RIDs to ensure more clustered access, using RIDs to read external records, and parsing records into ADM binary format.

The generated raw data for the Orders dataset was initially sorted on the order key. Hence, external index access in the query involved sequential I/O. In the case of the RCFile format, groups of records (4 MB in size) were read together, whereas records in the Text/Sequence file formats were read one at a time (causing additional context switching overhead). For this reason, querying external data in the RCFile format was observed to be faster than querying the same data in the Sequence and Text formats (by a factor of 1.4) when reading 2.5 million records.

(2)*Secondary Index Access - Internal vs. External:* To compare secondary index access on external and internal datasets, we ran the range queries shown in Listings 9 and 10. Such a range query does not benefit from hash-partitioned distribution of data records. Furthermore, secondary access paths for internal datasets incur additional CPU and I/O costs to search the primary index to fetch the records. External datasets, on the other hand, can directly use the records' physical locations (embedded in their RIDs) to fetch them from HDFS. Figures 7 and 8 show the results with different range predicates. Both figures show fairly comparable performance for internal data and external data with Text and Sequence formats. In contrast, secondary index access for the RCFile format starts out being about 3 times slower than the other formats (at 10K in Figure 7 and at 30K in Figure 8). This is because accessing RCFile records requires reading their containing row groups (4 MB in size). Starting at the 100K range for the Orders dataset and 300K for the Lineitem dataset, the rate of increase of the RCFile access time decreases, and the cost eventually becomes lower than the other formats. This is due to the increase in the ratio of records to row groups, as the benefits of performing sequential reads and less context switching eventually outweighs the cost of reading extra records. The I/O and parsing costs associated with reading Text and Sequence records are similar. A single read etches a minimum of 64 KB for both formats. However, the actual location of their HDFS blocks and indexes on disks are different, creating small differences in their performance for individual queries.

(3)*Index Nested Loop Joins - Internal vs. External:* Finally, we evaluate an AQL index nested loop (INL) join (Listing 11). This query counts the output of a select on the

```
count(for $ord in dataset Orders
      where $ord.ocustkey > a and $ord.ocustkey < b
      return $ord);
```

Listing 9: Range query on Orders using customer index

```
count(for $li in dataset Lineitem
      where $li.lpartkey > a and $li.lpartkey < b
      return $li);
```

Listing 10: Range query on Lineitem using part index

```
count(for $ord in dataset Orders
for $cus in dataset Customer
where $ord.ocustkey = /*+indexnl*/ $cus.ccustkey
and $ord.ocustkey > a and $ord.ocustkey < b
return $cus);
```

Listing 11: Index nested loop join query

Orders dataset using a predicate on the customer key followed by an INL join on this key with the Customer dataset. As shown in Figure 9, the join runs faster against internal datasets by a factor ranging between 1.4 and 3. For the internal dataset, only Orders records are re-partitioned since the nodes with matching Customer records are known (Customer is hash-partitioned on the customer key). This is not so for external datasets, where partitioning knowledge is unavailable and each produced record must be *broadcast* to all participating nodes. To get the matching record, the internal dataset need only search the primary index, while external datasets first search their secondary indexes and then perform seek, read and parse operations before joining the records. Note that join performance is fairly similar across the three external file formats. As seen previously, RCFile access is slower than the other formats at smaller ranges due to the additional I/O cost. RCFile access cost remained fairly flat even when the join size increased from 50K records to 200K records. This shows that reading more records when accessing RCFile data doesn't necessarily increase the I/O cost, which dominates for this query. The text and Sequence formats showed linear increases in access time while maintaining their difference (around 35 seconds) from internal joins.

7. CONCLUSION

We have described how AsterixDB provides efficient query access to data living outside the system (e.g., in HDFS). Pluggable adapters and parsers provide an extensible framework to support a variety of non-native data sources and formats. To support queries with small to medium selectivity, we added incrementally refreshable distributed indexes that provide carefully enforced access semantics to ensure answer consistency across access paths. We also explained how consistency is ensured when building, using, and refreshing external indexes as well as how failures are handled. We showed that AsterixDB's support for external HDFS data provides both good full scan performance (compared to Hive) as well as significant improvements from indexing. We also compared external and internal data access costs for different queries to gauge the relative performance of external data access. AsterixDB will release these features in its first official Apache incubation release in 2015. Applying these techniques on new data formats (e.g., Parquet or ORC) and/or measuring performance against new "SQL on Hadoop" platforms (such as Impala, Stinger, or SparkSQL) are possible future work. We may also explore HDFS's new inotify feature to automate external index refresh and investigate support for resuming index refresh on failures.
Acknowledgements This work was supported by NSF IIS award 0910989 and CNS awards 1305430 and 1059436.

8. REFERENCES

[1] Apache Hadoop. http://www.hadoop.org/.
[2] Apache Hive. http://oozie.apache.org.
[3] A. Abouzied et al. Invisible Loading: Access-driven Data Transfer from Raw Files into Database Systems. *Proc. EDBT Conf.*, 2013.
[4] I. Alagiannis et al. NoDB: Efficient Query Execution on Raw Data Files. *Proc. SIGMOD Conf.*, 2012.
[5] S. Alsubaiee et al. AsterixDB: A Scalable, Open Source BDMS. *Proc. VLDB Endow.*, 7(14), 2014.
[6] S. Alsubaiee et al. Storage Management in AsterixDB. *Proc. VLDB Endow.*, 7(10), 2014.
[7] S. Blanas et al. Parallel Data Analysis Directly on Scientific File Formats. *Proc. SIGMOD Conf.*, 2014.
[8] V. Borkar, M. Carey, et al. Hyracks: A Flexible and Extensible Foundation for Data-intensive Computing. *Proc. ICDE Conf.*, 2011.
[9] J. B. Buck et al. SciHadoop: Array-based Query Processing in Hadoop. *Proc. ACM Int'l. Conf. on High Perf. Comp., Netw., Storage and Analysis*, 2011.
[10] Y. Cheng and F. Rusu. Parallel In-situ Data Processing with Speculative Loading. *Proc. SIGMOD Conf.*, 2014.
[11] J. Dittrich et al. Hadoop++: Making a Yellow Elephant Run Like a Cheetah (Without It Even Noticing). *Proc. VLDB Endow.*, 3(1-2), 2010.
[12] M. Y. Eltabakh, F. Özcan, Y. Sismanis, et al. Eagle-eyed Elephant: Split-oriented Indexing in Hadoop. *Proc. EDBT Conf.*, 2013.
[13] V. R. Gankidi et al. Indexing HDFS Data in PDW: Splitting the Data from the Index. *Proc. VLDB Endow.*, 7(13), 2014.
[14] S. Idreos et al. Here Are My Data Files. Here Are My Queries. Where Are My Results? *Proc. CIDR Conf.*, 2011.
[15] K. Lorincz, K. Redwine, and J. Tov. Grep versus FlatSQL versus MySQL: Queries using UNIX tools vs. a DBMS, 2003.
[16] J. Melton et al. SQL and Management of External Data. *ACM SIGMOD Rec.*, 30(1), 2001.
[17] C. Mohan et al. Transaction Management in the R* Distributed Database Management System. *ACM TODS*, 11(4), 1986.
[18] Y. Xu, P. Kostamaa, and L. Gao. Integrating Hadoop and Parallel DBMS. *Proc. SIGMOD Conf.*, 2010.

Dynamic Resource Management In a Massively Parallel Stream Processing Engine

Kasper Grud Skat Madsen, Yongluan Zhou
University of Southern Denmark
{kaspergsm, zhou}@imada.sdu.dk

ABSTRACT

The emerging interest in Massively Parallel Stream Processing Engines (MPSPEs), which are able to process long-standing computations over data streams with ever-growing velocity at a large-scale cluster, calls for efficient dynamic resource management techniques to avoid any waste of resources and/or excessive processing latency. In this paper, we propose an approach to integrate dynamic resource management with passive fault-tolerance mechanisms in a MPSPE so that we can harvest the checkpoints prepared for failure recovery to enhance the efficiency of dynamic load migrations. To maximize the opportunity of reusing checkpoints for fast load migration, we formally define a checkpoint allocation problem and provide a pragmatic algorithm to solve it. We implement all the proposed techniques on top of Apache Storm, an open-source MPSPE, and conduct extensive experiments using a real dataset to examine various aspects of our techniques. The results show that our techniques can greatly improve the efficiency of dynamic resource reconfiguration without imposing significant overhead or latency to the normal job execution.

Categories and Subject Descriptors

H.2.4 [**Database Management**]: Systems

Keywords

Fault-Tolerance; Elasticity; Resource Management

1. INTRODUCTION

Recently, a new generation of Massively Parallel Stream Processing Engines have emerged, such as Apache Storm [19], Apache S4 [13] and Muppet [11]. These systems are tuned towards low-latency processing and massive scale-out to achieve high throughput. With such systems comes a plethora of issues to be handled, such as hardware and software failures, load skewness, overload and underload.

CIKM'15, October 19-23, 2015, Melbourne, VIC, Australia
© 2015 ACM. ISBN 978-1-4503-3794-6/15/10...$15.00.
DOI: http://dx.doi.org/10.1145/2806416.2806449.

As the main task of stream processing systems is to execute continuous and long-standing queries, it is easy to encounter failures especially when running on large-scale clusters. Therefore, it is widely recognized that fault-tolerance is an essential requirement for a large-scale MPSPE. A typical approach to achieve fault-tolerance is to make periodic checkpoints of the computation state of each task and store them on other processing nodes. A failed task can be recovered by loading the latest checkpoint and replaying the data that arrived after the checkpoint was made. To achieve low recovery latency, i.e. the time it takes to completely recover a failed task, the frequency of checkpointing should be reasonably high. Frequent checkpointing incurs significant overhead, especially when the state is large and subject to frequent updates. However, this price has to be paid for fault-tolerance and fast recovery.

Another important requirement of an MPSPE is the ability to perform dynamic resource reconfiguration to adapt to runtime changes of system workload incurred by, for example, the fluctuation of data input rates, the change of data distributions, etc. Resource reconfigurations include rebalancing load distribution among the processing nodes, adaptively increasing and decreasing the number of processing nodes. An essential operation in dynamic reconfiguration is to migrate tasks among the processing nodes, which often incurs significant latency and overhead and hence hinder the system from performing frequent reconfigurations.

In this paper, we propose an approach to integrate checkpoint-based fault-tolerance and dynamic resource reconfiguration. Such an integration can achieve low-cost and fast state migration by exploiting the checkpoints made for fault-tolerance. This is because checkpoints contain the computation states of the tasks and migrating a task is essentially equivalent to recovering the task at another location. Since the price of maintaining checkpoints have to be paid anyway, this benefit comes almost for free. In summary, the main contributions of this paper are as follows:

- An integrated approach that combines passive fault-tolerance with dynamic resource reconfiguration in a general MPSPE and supports using the checkpointing mechanism of a general checkpoint-based fault tolerance framework to achieve efficient state migrations.
- New state migration techniques to minimize the processing latency and overhead caused by state migrations. Given a recent checkpoint, our techniques can achieve very fast state migrations that cause negligible latency to the normal processing.

- We formulate the problem of checkpoint allocation to maximize the probability that a checkpoint is available for fast state-migration and propose a pragmatic algorithm, which achieves significant improvements in comparing to a simpler approach.

- All the proposed techniques are implemented on top of Apache Storm and verified by extensive experiments.

2. RELATED WORK AND BACKGROUND

In this section, we present related work and relevant background on some of the problems faced by MPSPEs, such as fault-tolerance and dynamic resource management.

2.1 Fault-Tolerance

The basic fault-tolerance techniques in distributed stream processing systems can be categorized into *upstream backup*, *passive backup* and *active backup* [9, 6, 17, 3].

Upstream backup requires that every tuple included in the processing state of an operator instance (o_i) is kept in an output buffer on an upstream operator instance, until the processing state of o_i no longer depends on it. In case of a fault, the buffered tuples are replayed to restore the failed state. Upstream backup has a significant problem when used alone, as the size of the upstream buffers are not bounded.

Passive backup relies on checkpoints, which are basically copies of the current processing state. When a checkpoint has been stored on a separate node, the buffers can safely be trimmed. In case of a fault, a checkpoint can be used to install an "old" state, which can then be made up-to-date, by replaying the buffered tuples, from the output buffers on the upstream operator instances.

The recovery latency of upstream and passive backup can be in the order of tens of seconds. For some applications such a recovery latency can be unacceptable, in which case *active backup* is often used. Active backup works by executing a duplicate computation on a separate location, such that if either the primary or a duplicate fails, the other can take over. The recovery latency, in this case, is to synchronize the computation. However, active backup is very expensive and basically needs double resources.

There is much work on trying to improve the performance of these basic techniques, such as [10, 16, 6]. Some of these defines the benefits of making checkpoints more fine-grained, some discusses proper checkpoint schedules and some even investigates the tradeoff between all of these techniques.

A recent article [22] presented a tweaked passive backup strategy. The idea is to treat the streaming computation as a series of small deterministic batch computations, and store the history (lineage) of computations. One of the benefits this provides is that parallel recovery can be easily supported, such that if one node fails, multiple nodes can work together to calculate the failed state.

2.2 Dynamic Resource Management

Supporting intra-operator data partitioning at runtime has been investigated in [18]. As their work focuses strictly on load-balancing and not on scaling, it can be considered as part of the solution towards dynamic resource management.

Multiple papers [20, 23, 24] have studied how to allocate operators to achieve load-balancing. In their models, a query is composed of an operator network and each operator does not need to be partitioned. In other words, their models cannot handle dynamic scaling of individual operators.

The authors in [15] studied how to provide an abstraction to decouple the number of threads and the number of processing units to achieve dynamic intra-operator scaling, i.e. changing the number of threads used for processing on runtime. While their work mainly focused on multi-core systems, our system also provide such an abstraction in the context of a large-scale cluster.

To support scaling, one of the key operations is to change the parallelization degree of state-partitioned operators at runtime. This unfortunately poses problems, one of which is that the partitioning often depends on the number of instances. Changing the number of instances thus requires repartitioning some state. The authors in [2], discusses how to avoid this, by adding another operator to perform aggregation of the partial results of the scaled reduce operators.

There is a recent research work [5], which focuses on how to design an adaptation algorithm to achieve elasticity in a distributed stream processing system. They rely on two simple metrics (congestion and throughput), to determine how/when to scale. Their algorithms can be adopted in our system to make scaling decisions.

There are some efforts on developing systems to support both load-balancing and elastic scaling. ESC [14] is a distributed stream processing platform, which supports elasticity and load-balancing by using an Autonomic Manager, which has access to information about the workload of each node, and the queue lengths of the worker processes, to make global decisions. StreamCloud [7] is another recent distributed stream processing engine that supports both elasticity and load-balancing. Load-balancing is supported by defining a point in time p, such that all tuples of a bucket (group) earlier than p, are processed by the old "owner", and tuples later than p are processed by the new one. This simple technique has a problem for stateful operators, as one tuple might contribute to multiple windows, which means there will be tuples that needs to be processed by both the old and new owners (and thus duplicated).

While the above work mostly focuses on how to make better adaptation decisions, our work differs by focusing on how to make adaptations, more specifically state migrations, more efficient and less intrusive to the system's normal execution.

A recent article [4] studied how to integrate the operations of fault-tolerance and scaling out. Our work can be considered as another step in this direction. In their model, the checkpoints of an operator are stored on its upstream operators and hence there are limited opportunities to exploit the fast state migration strategies introduced in this paper. To solve the problem, we design a system that allows checkpoints be placed at any node, and we provide an algorithm to derive a good checkpoint allocation plan.

3. PRELIMINARIES

3.1 Data Model

Data is modelled as a number of continuous streams of tuples in the form of $\langle id, key, value, ts\rangle$. The *id* is a unique identifier of the tuple, composed by the unique id of the stream that the tuple comes from and the per-stream unique sequence number of the tuple. The *key* is the key of the tuple, as a blob in arbitrary form, that is opaque to the

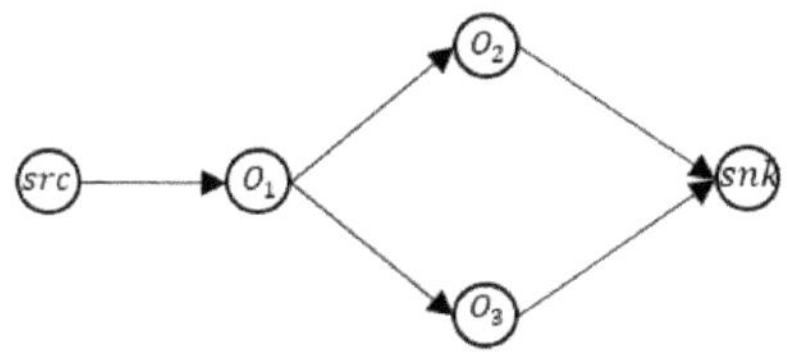

Figure 1: Operator network

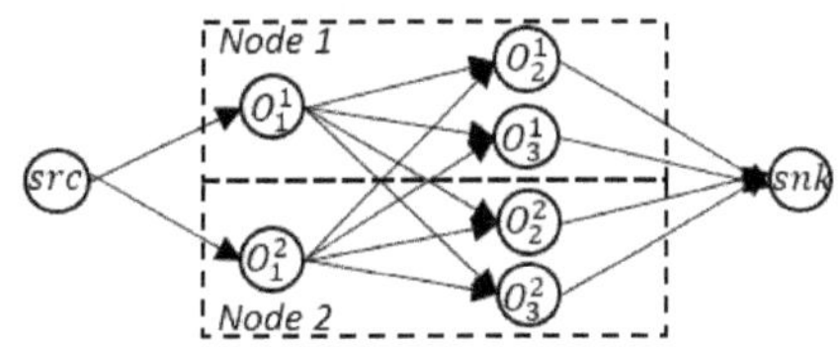

Figure 2: System perspective

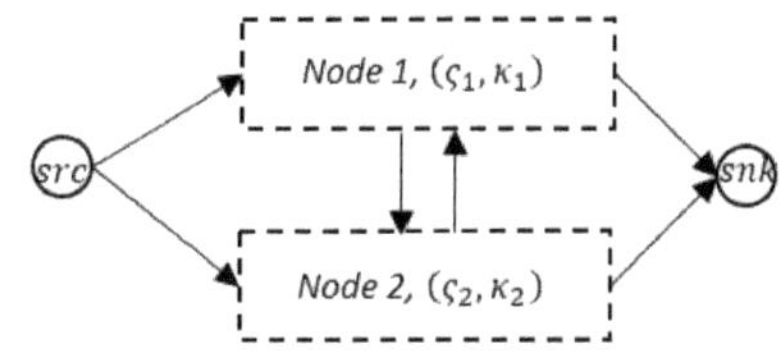

Figure 3: User perspective

system. It is the value of the key that decides how the tuple is routed, which is similar to other systems, e.g. Hadoop. The *value* is the value of the tuple, also as a blob in an arbitrary form that is opaque to the system. The *ts* is a timestamp associated with the tuple, which can be used to indicate the time that the tuple is generated and to define time-based window computations.

3.2 Programming Model

The programming model consists of one function:

$$compute(key, tuple) \rightarrow list(key, tuple)$$

which takes a key-tuple pair and returns a list of key-tuples pairs. The function is associated with a local storage to keep track of the current state of the computation. This programming model can be considered similar to other typical programming models used in MPSPEs. For example, both the *Update* and the *Map* function in the MapUpdate framework [11] are equivalent to our *compute* function with and without using the local storage to store computation state respectively.

3.3 Query Model

A job can be considered as a set of continuous queries represented as an operator network. An operator network is a directed acyclic graph $\langle O, E \rangle$, where each vertex is an operator O_i, and each edge E_i is a stream where the direction represents the direction of data flow. Figure 1 shows an example with five operators.

3.4 Operator Model

An operator has a set of input streams In_i, and a set of output streams Out_i. On each incoming tuple, a function F_i is invoked, which updates processing-state σ_i and a map $m_{key \rightarrow seq}$, which, for each key processed by the operator, contains the *id* of the latest tuple contributing to σ_i. The operator adds tuples to a set of output streams Out_i as specified by the function. An operator O_i is defined by function $F_i : (\eta(In_i), \sigma_i, m_{key \rightarrow seq}) \rightarrow (\psi(Out_i), \sigma'_i, m'_{key \rightarrow seq})$, where $\eta(In_i)$ returns the next incoming tuple, and $\psi(Out_i)$ returns the set of resulting tuples.

3.5 Execution Model

An operator O_i in the operator network can be parallelized to several instances o^i_j, where i is the id of the operator and j is the id of the operator instance. Formally, an operator O_i, is modelled as

$$O_i = \{o^i_1, o^i_2, ..., o^i_n\}, \text{ where } n \in N^+$$

where n describes the degree of parallelization of O_i.

Each input tuple of O_i is associated with a key from a set of independent keys K_i. The keys K_i are partitioned into a set of key groups, such that each group contains a non-overlapping subset of K_i. The set of key groups of K_i is modelled as

$$G_i = \{g^i_1, g^i_2, ..., g^i_p\}, \text{ where } p \geq n$$

Every operator instance o^i_j will handle a non-overlapping subset of G_i. There is a trade-off between avoiding excessive overhead and maintaining sufficient fine-grained control when partitioning state, e.g. if using $|G_i| = 1$, the system would need to maintain one output queue per key, which would incur excessive overhead, while using $|G_i| = |K_i|$ would hinder useful state-migration.

Based on the model above, the main assumption is that the processing of key groups are independent of one another. Each key group $g^i_j \in G_i$ has an independent processing state σ^i_j and a corresponding set of checkpoints

$$CP^i_j = \{cp^i_{j,1}, cp^i_{j,2}, ..., cp^i_{j,m}\}, \text{ where } m < n$$

A cluster has a set of nodes $N = \{n_1, \ldots, n_n\}$. Each node executes exactly one instance of every operator, which means each node has the capability to process any logic. Figure 2 shows how the operator network shown in figure 1 is executed in a cluster with two nodes.

Every node n processes a non-overlapping subset of key groups ς_n from all key groups, defined in the operator network. Furthermore each node n stores a set of checkpoints κ_n. Any node n can thus process any subset of key groups and store a subset of checkpoints. From the users' perspective, the execution graph becomes similar to Figure 3.

Proceessing Order. Given that an operator has several input sources, obtaining a reproducible ordering of input tuples is costly [3]. We assume out-of-order processing, which means that operators eventually produce the same result, given the same data as long as the unorderedness is within some bound [12]. If the computation relies on a strict ordering of the input, then one has to order the data using an additional function before feeding the data to the actual computation, e.g. the SUnion function proposed in [3]. Therefore, the assumption of out-of-order processing does not exclude applications that require a strict input order.

Symbol	Explanation
O_i	Operator i
o^i_j	Instance j of operator i
G_i	Set of key groups of operator i
g^i_j	Key group j of operator i
σ^i_j	Processing state of key group j of operator i
CP^i_j	Set of checkpoints of key group j of operator i
$cp^i_{j,m}$	Checkpoint m of key group j of operator i
ς_n	Set of key groups processed at node n
κ_n	Set of checkpoints stored at node n

Table 1: Symbol overview

4. SYSTEM ARCHITECTURE

Our system is built on top of Apache Storm [19], an open-source MPSPE. In Storm, a job is specified as an instance of a topology, which defines how the job is executed, such as how the operators are parallelized, how the data are transferred between the operators, etc. Storm comes with a basic topology which implements some essential functionalities of parallel stream processing, and allows a user to build a stream processing job by simply creating a topology object, and adding operators to it. Most of our functionalities are implemented as an advanced topology on top of the basic one, and is thus very loosely coupled with Storm. Figure 4 gives an overview of how our system is built on top of Storm.

The *Controller* is a system level operator, used to make global decisions. The controller executes the Fault-Tolerance Manager and the Adaptation Manager. In addition, it is responsible for periodically requesting statistics from all operator instances in the job and preparing it such that the information is easily accessible. Each operator keeps statistics on the utilizations of CPU, memory and network bandwidths and the input rate of each key group.

The *Adaptation Manager* is responsible for making global decisions on scale-in/out, and load-balancing. It executes the adaptation algorithm, which bases its decisions on the statistics collected by the controller.

The *Elastic Scheduler* is the key component used to facilitate dynamic horizontal scaling. Storm provides a basic scheduler that is responsible for managing the assignment of operator instances to the cluster nodes. Each time the basic scheduler is invoked, it will look for any operator instances that have not been allocated to any node. This happens when the job is initially submitted or some faults occur. The scheduler will then distribute the non-allocated operator instances to the nodes as evenly as possible. This basic scheduler is insufficient for our framework as it always attempts to allocate all the operator instances. Note that in Storm, a topology is static in the sense that the number of instances of each operator is fixed, and cannot be increased and decreased dynamically at runtime. To dynamically increase or decrease the instances, one has to pause the whole job, rebuild, and redeploy the complete topology. This will incur prohibitive latency to runtime adaptation.

In order to achieve low-cost runtime reconfiguration while keeping the simple implementation of static topology, we implement a customized elastic scheduler in Storm by employing the following technique. Given the operators of a submitted job, a pre-defined set of instances for each operator is prepared. Initially, only a subset of instances of each operator is scheduled over the initial cluster. The scheduler will maintain that each node has one instance of each operator in the topology. This allows us to flexibly allocate the key groups of each operator to any node. If an instance is not assigned any key group, then it will not be run, and hence will consume negligible resources on its host node.

The *Fault-Tolerance Manager* runs in a separate thread as part of the controller. It detects failures by reading Storm heartbeats directly from Zookeeper [8]. If a failure is detected, it stops the processing of all the failed operator instances, and waits until the scheduler has reallocated the failed instances. Then it invokes the recovery process to restore the computing state and recreate checkpoints.

The system uses a combination of upstream backup and passive backup, as this combination requires fewer computation resources compared to active backup, and has the potential of using checkpoints to achieve faster state-migration. The technique was proposed in previous papers as a general technique which can provide at-least-once or exactly-once processing [10].

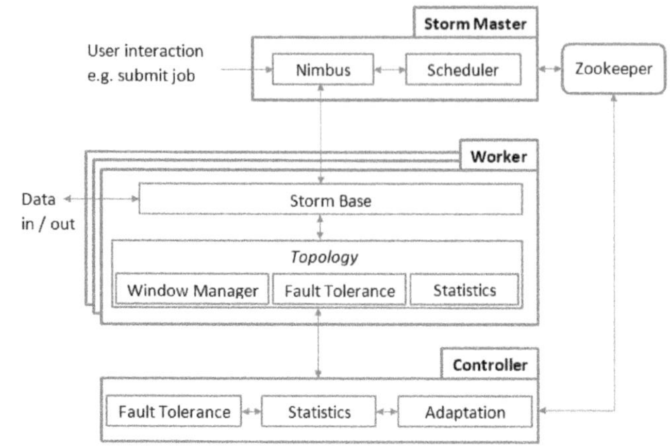

Figure 4: System architecture

To speed up the recovery, a checkpoint will be periodically created for each key group and upon failure of a key group, its latest checkpoint will be loaded and the input data which arrived after its latest checkpoint, will be replayed.

Dynamic partitioning of data is necessary to support migrating key groups from one node to another. To support this kind of operation, the system uses dynamic partitioners between all operators. It works by first calculating which key group a tuple belongs to by a simple hash function. Then it looks up in a routing table to see, which operator instance is currently responsible for processing the key group, and then sends the tuple there. The routing table is updated directly by the controller as part of the state-migration policies.

Messages. There is one FIFO message stream between each operator instance, such that all messages (data and control messages) are sent on the same stream. When receiving a message, the corresponding key group g_x is calculated from the key of the message. A message can be *fast*, in which case it is processed immediately without going through the FIFO queue. Alternatively, a message can also be *normal*, in which case it is put into the input queue for the calculated key group, and will be processed in a FIFO manner. Furthermore, a message can be *stateful*, if it contains data. Supporting two different priorities of messages is especially useful for control messages, as these can often skip dataqueues, leading to a system which can be controlled more efficiently.

5. DYNAMIC RESOURCE MANAGEMENT

In this section, we explore different techniques to obtain dynamic resource management in a general stream processing system. The crucial operation is to move a subset of key groups from ς_n to ς_m. In this section, we present our state-migration protocols, which support this operation for partitioned stateful operators.

In order to analyse the different protocols' completion time, and the data processing latency incurred by them, we first need to model the time that it takes for a message to be

Actions	Cost
Fast Message	1
Normal Message	$1 + C$
Fast Stateful Message	$msgSize$
Normal Stateful Message	$msgSize + C$
Processing one message at o_b^i	$\beta_{o_b^i}$
Size of output buffer from o_a^i to g_x^j	$\chi_{o_a^i \rightarrow g_x^j}$

Table 2: Cost-model overview

transferred over the network. The time from sending a *fast* message to being seen at the receiver is defined as 1, while the time from sending a *normal* message, until being seen at the receiver depends on the input queue at the receiver. For the sake of our analysis we assume the size of input queues is bounded by a constant and we define the time of sending a *normal* message as $1 + C$, where C is to account for the queuing time of the message. Lastly in case a fast message is *stateful*, we define the time as $msgSize$, and in case a normal message is *stateful*, we define the time as $msgSize + C$. To explain the protocols, we make heavy use of the shorthand $\mathcal{O}_{i-1}$, which is the set of upstream operator instances of O_i.

5.1 CP-Assisted Migration

Moving g_x^i from o_a^i to o_b^i using direct state-migration, could potentially incur a large overhead, if the processing state $\sigma_{g_x^i}$ is large. The reason is that the cost of serializing and deserializing $\sigma_{g_x^i}$, heavily dominates the completion time and the latency of the operation, as will be shown later and verified by our experiments. It is possible to avoid this cost, if migrating to an operator instance, which already has the newest checkpoint of g_x^i, by converting the checkpoint to state and replaying the upstream buffers. The technique is described by Algorithm 1.

Algorithm 1: CP-Assisted Migration (abbreviated: CPA)

```
1  Controller informs O_{i-1}: g_x^i moves from o_a^i to o_b^i
2  when o in O_{i-1} receives information do
3      Send toState to o_b^i              ▷ contains output buffer
4      Redirect data for g_x^i to o_b^i
5      Send toCheckpoint to o_a^i
6  when o_a^i gets toCheckpoint from all o in O_{i-1} do
7      Convert state σ_{g_x} to checkpoint
8  when o_b^i gets toState from any o in O_{i-1} do
9      if σ_{g_x} is null: convert checkpoint to state σ_{g_x}
10     Process replayed data
```

Since this state-migration protocol (CPA) relies on the system's fault-tolerance, it naturally inherits the processing guarantee of the fault-tolerance. For example if the system is currently providing a processing guarantee of exactly-once, then when using this technique, the duplicate tuples can automatically be discarded. In case the system provides at-most-once or at-least-once, it is assumed, as this guarantee is sufficient for fault-tolerance, it is also sufficient for state-migration.

Description. First each operator instance o, from the set of upstream operator instances of O_i, sends a toState message to o_b^i. The toState message contains the output buffer, and is sent as a fast message, as o_b^i must process the output buffers before processing other data. After having sent the toState message, new data for g_x^i is redirected from o_a^i to o_b^i. Lastly a toCheckpoint message is sent as a normal message to o_a^i. The algorithm now proceeds in parallel at o_a^i and o_b^i, where o_a^i handles the toCheckpoint messages, and o_b^i handles the toState messages.

When receiving all normal toCheckpoint messages at o_a^i, it is known that no more data will ever be received. For this reason it is safe to convert the state to a checkpoint.

When receiving a toState message at o_b^i, it is known there is already a checkpoint at o_b^i, which can be converted to state, after which the output buffer contained within the toState message is processed. Notice that the checkpoint is only converted to state, when receiving the first toState message.

Analysis. The cost-model captures the cost of moving g_x^i, from o_a^i to o_b^i, when o_b^i has a checkpoint from the set of newest checkpoints of $\sigma_{g_x^i}$. The cost of step $2 + 3$ is not considered, as this step exists in all the state-migration algorithms.

The *completion time* is defined, as the time from the migration was ordered at the controller until effectuated.

$$max_{o_k^j \in \mathcal{O}_{i-1}}(\chi_{o_k^j \rightarrow g_x^i}) + sum_{o_k^j \in \mathcal{O}_{i-1}}(\chi_{o_k^j \rightarrow g_x^i} \cdot \beta_{o_b^i})$$

The *latency* is defined, as the amount of time the processing of g_x^i is paused. For this protocol it equals the maximum time it takes to send, and the sum of time to process all output buffers (done sequentially). The completion time and latency is thus equal.

5.2 CP-Assisted Low-Latency Migration

When moving key group g_x^i from o_a^i to o_b^i, using the cp-assisted state-migration protocol (CPA), the latency and completion time heavily depends on $\chi_{o_k^j \rightarrow g_x^i}$. Using the protocol, as described in algorithm 2, we show how to achieve a significantly lower latency, which is independent on $\chi_{o_k^j \rightarrow g_x^i}$.

Algorithm 2: CP-Assisted Low-Latency Migration (abbreviated: CPAL)

```
1  Controller informs O_{i-1}: g_x^i moves from o_a^i to o_b^i
2  when o in O_{i-1} receives information do
3      Send toState to o_b^i              ▷ contains output buffer
4      Duplicate data for g_x^i to o_a^i and o_b^i
5  when o_b^i gets toState from any o in O_{i-1} do
6      if σ_{g_x} is null: convert checkpoint to state σ_{g_x}
7      Process replayed data
8      if o_b^i has toState from all o in O_{i-1}:
9          Send processedAllReplay to all o in O_{i-1}
10 when o in O_{i-1} gets processedAllReplay do
11     Send syncGroup to o_b^i
12     Stop sending data for g_x^i to o_a^i
13     Send toCheckpoint to o_a^i
14 when o_a^i gets toCheckpoint from all o in O_{i-1} do
15     Convert state σ_{g_x^i} to checkpoint
16 when o_b^i gets syncGroup from any o in O_{i-1} do
17     Begin buffering incoming data to g_x^i from o
18 when o_b^i has syncGroup from all o in O_{i-1} do
19     Process all buffered data for g_x^i and stop buffer
```

Technique	Completion Time	Latency
Direct Migration	$\sigma_{g_x^i} + 4$	equals time
CP-Assisted Migration (CPA)	$max_{o_k^j \in \mathcal{O}_{i-1}}(\chi_{o_k^j \to g_x^i}) + sum_{o_k^j \in \mathcal{O}_{i-1}}(\chi_{o_k^j \to g_x^i} \cdot \beta_{o_b^i})$	equals time
CP-Assisted Low-Latency Migration (CPAL)	$max_{o_k^j \in \mathcal{O}_{i-1}}(\chi_{o_k^j \to g_x^i}) + sum_{o_k^j \in \mathcal{O}_{i-1}}(\chi_{o_k^j \to g_x^i} \cdot \beta_{o_b^i}) + 2 + C$	$1 + C$

Table 3: State-Migration techniques and associated cost in terms of completion time and latency

Description. First each operator instance o in $\mathcal{O}_{i-1}$ sends a normal message called toState, which contains the output buffer for g_x^i, to o_b^i, and o begins duplicating new data for g_x^i to both o_a^i and o_b^i.

When o_b^i gets the toState message, it converts any checkpoint to state for the key group g_x^i, and processes all data contained within the toState message. This idea is similar to the previously described technique, with the exception that data is currently being duplicated to both o_a^i and o_b^i, which means the processing at o_a^i is not paused. When o_b^i has received and processed all toState messages, the state of o_a^i and o_b^i must be synchronized, such that o_b^i can continue the computation exactly where o_a^i stops. This is done by sending a fast message from o_b^i to all o in $\mathcal{O}_{i-1}$, called processedAllReplay.

When a operator instance o in $\mathcal{O}_{i-1}$, gets a processedAllReplay message, it knows o_b^i has processed all replayed data, and that synchronization between o_a^i and o_b^i should be done. First a normal message called syncGroup is sent from o to o_b^i, and then o stops duplicating data for g_x^i to o_a^i. Lastly a normal message called toCheckpoint is sent to o_a^i. The algorithm now proceeds in parallel at o_a^i and o_b^i, where o_a^i handles the toCheckpoint messages and o_b^i handles the syncGroup messages.

When receiving a toCheckpoint at o_a^i from all o in $\mathcal{O}_{i-1}$, it is known that no more data will be received. It is thus safe to convert the state to a checkpoint.

When receving a syncGroup from o in $\mathcal{O}_{i-1}$ at o_b^i, the operator instance must buffer all new incoming data from o to g_x^i. The synchronization is complete, when having received a syncGroup from all o in $\mathcal{O}_{i-1}$, and all buffered data can be processed.

Analysis. The cost-model captures the cost of moving g_x^i, from o_a^i to o_b^i, when o_b^i has a checkpoint from the set of newest checkpoints of $\sigma_{g_x^i}$. The cost of step $2+3$ is not considered, as this step exists in all the state-migration algorithms.

The completion time is defined, as the time from the migration was ordered at the controller until effectuated.

$$max_{o_k^j \in \mathcal{O}_{i-1}}(\chi_{o_k^j \to g_x^i}) + sum_{o_k^j \in \mathcal{O}_{i-1}}(\chi_{o_k^j \to g_x^i} \cdot \beta_{o_b^i}) + 2 + C$$

The latency is defined as the time from buffering begins, until all buffered data is processed:

$$1 + C$$

5.3 Direct Migration

Using direct state-migration to move g_x^i from o_a^i to o_b^i, is done by requesting o_a^i to create a new checkpoint of g_x^i and send it to o_b^i. After o_b^i acknowledges the checkpoint, o_a^i requests all operator instances o in $\mathcal{O}_{i-1}$ to trim output buffers. When the trimming is done, algorithm 1 is executed.

For analyzing the cost of direct state-migration, we simplify our analysis by assuming the amount of data, which needs to be replayed from the upstream operator instances are negligible, due to the recent trim operation. By considering the completion time and latency costs from table 3, it can be seen that if $\chi_{o_k^j \to g_x^i}$ is assumed to be negligible, then the completion time and latency of CPA is also negligible. The completion time and latency of direct state-migration becomes $\sigma_{g_x^i} + 4$, where sigma is the processing-state.

6. CHECKPOINT ALLOCATION

In this section, we show how to allocate checkpoints, such that the probability they can be used with the cp-assisted state-migration protocols (CPA or CPAL), is maximized. This is important, because the latency and in many cases the completion time of state-migration is significantly less for the cp-assisted state-migration protocols (verified in the evaluation section). Checkpoint allocation can therefore be considered as proactive load-balancing.

In this work we consider *partial checkpoints* [16], where each new checkpoint only contains the difference between the current computation state and the last checkpoint. Compared to other checkpointing techniques, partial checkpointing has low overhead and is widely used. Partial checkpointing has been been implemented in well-known systems such as Google MillWheel [1] and Storm Trident [19]. For partial checkpoints, the checkpoint allocation is only updated periodically, as it is costly, and the migration of key groups can only use cp-assisted strategies opportunistically. Therefore, a good checkpoint allocation algorithm is needed to maximize the opportunity.

Algorithm - Baseline. The simplest algorithm for allocating checkpoints to nodes, which works by ensuring a checkpoint, cannot be on the same node, as an identical checkpoint, or the key group it is checkpointing.

Algorithm - Even Distribution. Even Distribution is an extension of the baseline algorithm and we believe it represents most existing systems' behavior. The algorithm imposes two constraints the allocation. Constraint 1 states that a checkpoint cannot be on the same node as an identical checkpoint, or the key group it is checkpointing. Constraint 2 states that checkpoints must be divided fairly on all nodes, such that no node has more checkpoints than $\lceil \frac{\#cps}{\#nodes} \rceil$.

Intuition - Correlated Distribution. A set of nodes can become overloaded, if the load of the key groups allocated to them increases. The change in workload of the key groups could affect the workload of other key groups, which can be measured by correlations. Assume a set of key groups A gets an increased workload, and introduces overload on the set of nodes, where it is allocated. Now the adaptation algorithm would try to migrate a subset of the key groups to a set of nodes, which are not overloaded. In order to do so efficiently, it is beneficial, if as many checkpoints as possible for key groups in A are available on the nodes that are not overloaded. To increase the probability of this, we allocate the checkpoints of the key groups in A to the nodes having key groups that are as negatively as possible correlated with the key groups of A.

6.1 Problem Formulation

In this section we define the optimal solution to the problem of allocating partial checkpoints, as a minimization problem. The solution consists of a mapping from each checkpoint to a node. In the formulation below each checkpoint is allocated to node i.

$$min \sum_{g_1 \in G} \sum_{cp \in g_1} \min_{i=0,\ldots,|N|} \left(\sum_{g_2 \in G_i} corr(g_1, g_2) \cdot load(g_1) \right)$$

where G is the set of all key groups, N is the set of nodes in the cluster, G_i is the set of key groups at node i, such that

1. A node can contain one cp_j^i, if it doesn't contain g_j^i
2. $\sum_{cp_j^i \in N} \left(load(g_j^i)\right) < \alpha * \frac{\sum_{cp_j^i \in N} load(g_j^i)}{|N|}$

Constraint 1 ensures no node can contain both a key group and a corresponding checkpoint. This is needed to ensure fault-tolerance. Also in case multiple checkpoints are defined for one key group, these cannot be allocated at the same node either.

Constraint 2 guarantees the load of the key groups being checkpointed, are distributed fairly even among all the nodes. It can be important to spread out checkpoints, as it increases the amount of unused processing capacity, which can be "reached" by the cp-assisted state-migration policies from any node.

The minimization can be proved to be NP-hard by a polynomial reduction from the NP-hard problem called *The Multi-Resource Generalized Assignment Problem* [21]. Due to space issues, we omit the proof.

6.2 Algorithm

As the problem formulation is NP-hard, we simplify the problem in order to obtain a solution with polynomial complexity. We simplify the problem by assuming that once a checkpoint is allocated to a node, its allocation does not need to be changed again to achieve a satisfactory solution. This reduces the problem to finding a good order of allocating checkpoints. Our proposed algorithm 3, is polynomial with a complexity of $O(|N| \cdot \#checkpoints)$.

Heuristic. We aim to design an algorithm which allocates the checkpoints in a order, such that the largest benefit in terms of the minimization problem can be obtained. For each checkpoint we calculate the potential impact on the minimization problem, of allocating it to any possible node. Then we allocate checkpoints in turn, such that the checkpoint with the largest decrease in benefit if not placed at the current best node, is to be allocated next. The reasoning behind this heuristic is to prioritize allocating the checkpoints, which harms the value of the minimization problem most, if they cannot be assigned to their current best nodes. In this way the algorithm allocates the most "sensitive" checkpoints first.

Explanation. If the checkpoint to allocate next, satisfies constraints 1 and 2 at the best node, then it is simply allocated. Otherwise, the calculation is updated to consider the difference in benefit between the 2nd and the 3rd best node assignment for the checkpoint, and the next checkpoint to allocate is recalculated. Sometimes multiple nodes M achieve the same correlation value for a given checkpoint, and satisfy both constraints 1 and 2. This happens often, when there is no correlation, i.e. the value is 0. When this happens, we allocate the checkpoint to the node in M, which has the lowest checkpoint load, i.e. the minimum sum of loads for each key group corresponding to the checkpoints on the node. The reasoning is to divide the checkpoints evenly over all the nodes in the set, because each node is equally good.

Algorithm 3: Partial Checkpoint Allocation

```
Input: The set of checkpoints and nodes
Output: Map with checkpoint to node allocation
Procedure calcOptimizedAllocation
    cps ← new List
    for each cp in checkpoints do
        for each node in nodes do
            cp.vals(node, corr(cp, node) · load(cp))
        cps.add(cp)
    sort cps in desc order of best - 2'th best vals
    while cps.size > 0 do
        cp ← cps.peek
        bNodes ← getBestNodes(cp)
        if hasAllNodesBeenConsidered(cp) then
            assign cp to node with min correlation
            value, secondly to node with min cp load
            continue
        else if bNodes is null then
            // no node currently satisfies constraint 1
            updateSortValue(cp)
            sort cps in desc order by sortValue
            continue
        cpPlaced ← false
        for each node in bNodes do
            if satisfies2(cp, node, assign) then
                assign.put(cps.poll, node)
                cpPlaced ← true
                break
        if !cpPlaced then
            updateSortValue(cp)
            sort cps in desc order by Sortvalue
    return assign
Procedure getBestNodes (cp)
    safeNodes ← nodes satisfying constraint 1 for cp
    IthBest ← i'th best nodes for placing cp,
      i=sortIndex
    return safeNodes ∩ IthBest
Procedure updateSortValue (cp)
    cp.sortIndex++
    cp.sortVal ← cp.atIthBestNode(cp.sortIndex)
```

Temporal changes. The "quality" of a checkpoint allocation may deteriorate over time, as each checkpoint-assisted state-migration operation changes the location of at least one checkpoint, and thus introduces noise. The quality of a given checkpoint allocation is measured by the value of the minimization problem. The lower the score, the better the allocation.

Each time the checkpoint algorithm is executed, the system calculates the score of the current checkpoint allocation and also an approximate solution to the minimization problem using algorithm 3. If the difference is greater than a user-definable threshold γ, the checkpoint allocation is updated, by moving the checkpoints with improves the score maximally, until the difference is lower or equal to the user-defined threshold γ. In this way, the checkpoint allocation is updated to ensure it remains useable for maximizing the number of checkpoint assisted state-migrations.

By setting γ to a low value, the deterioration of the checkpoint allocation can be prevented by frequent migration of key groups. On the other hand, setting γ to a high value, can result in significant deterioration of the checkpoint allocation over time, which will decrease the possibility of using the checkpoint-assisted state-migration policies. The lower the value of γ, the higher the overhead, due to the need for more state-migrations.

7. EVALUATION

All experiments are carried out on Amazon EC2. Spouts are executed on instance type *m3.xlarge*. All other nodes are of type *m1.medium*. Spouts are executed on faster instances to ensure they can output enough tuples to stress the system if needed. The controller, master and zookeeper are co-located on a dedicated node of type *m1.medium*, called the *control node*. There is always exactly one checkpoint per key group.

The **Airline On-Time** dataset is provided by the Research and Innovative Technology Administration, United States Department of Transportation[1].

We use data for the period from January 2004 to December 2013, which contains information about airplanes, such as departure, arrival, expected time of arrival and so on. The data contains 67,328,899 tuples, and is approximately 28gb uncompressed. The dataset is rich with more than 100 attributes per tuple. We split the data into multiple slices, and stream it in parallel from each of the inputs.

7.1 State-Migration Protocols

The proposed state-migration protocols are evaluated on *latency*, i.e. the additional processing latency of the input tuples incurred by the migration protocol and *completion time*, i.e. the time to complete the whole migration.

The job processes air-flight data and extracts delays, which are then stored per plane over a window of a year. To achieve this functionality, the job consists of one input and two ordinary operators. The input operator parses the data, and sends to operator 1. Operator 1 extracts delays, and sends events (delays) along to operator 2. Operator 2 sums delays by airplane per year, and stores all events with delay in a key-value store.

The job is parallelized over 25 nodes, with 1 control node and 4 inputnodes. The remaining 20 nodes are used to processing operator 1 and 2. Each operator is divided into 20 key groups (evenly allocated the 20 nodes used to process the operators). The input rate is 8000 tuples per second, which guarantees no node is overloaded. The job was left running for 500 seconds, before a key group of operator 2 was migrated from node 2 to node 4.

Figure 5 and 6 shows the latency and completion time of the state-migration operations with varying number of tuples to replay (achieved by adjusting the trimming). The results show that the latency of CPA depends on the amount of data to replay. CPAL does not depend on the replay size, but instead on the time to synchronize, which is shown to be very short for this experiment. Both CPA and CPAL have similar completion time, which depends on the size of data to replay, as expected.

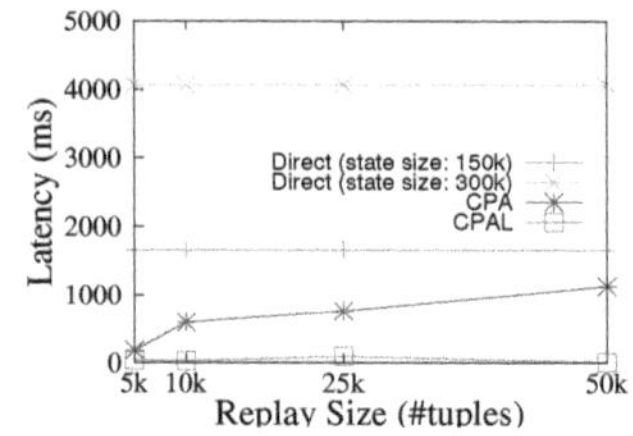

Figure 5: Latency

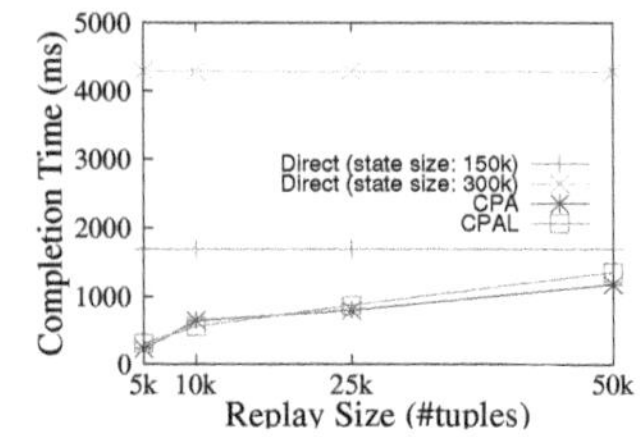

Figure 6: Completion T.

In summary we conclude that both CPA and CPAL outperform direct state-migration in terms of latency and completion time for this experimental setting, especially, when state size is large, and replay size is small. Furthermore, we have shown that by using the CPAL technique, the system incurs negligible latency to tuple processing.

Obtaining negligible latency is good from the users point of view, but the system also gets an easily overlooked benefit. Consider that latency during state-migration, comes from the periods where the processing is paused. When the processing resumes, all the buffered data must be processed. If the system is processing high-volume input, then the amount of buffered data might be very significant. This means it can take a long time to process, leading to bad performance and even to severe problems such as timeout of a node, due to extreme load for an extended period. The low-latency state-migration technique, thus represents a very significant improvement over existing methods.

7.2 Checkpoint Allocation

The following set of experiments requires an adaptation algorithm. As this paper mainly focuses on how to increase the efficiency of adaptations, we adopt a simple adaptation algorithm that supports load-balancing, scale-in and scale-out. Scale-in is done by migrating key groups away from the resources to be freed, and scale-out is done by acquiring new resources followed by allocating key groups there. Load-balancing is done through active repartitioning of key groups, which is similar to the method in [18].

We use $\alpha = \infty$ (see constraint 2 in problem formulation) for the optimized checkpoint allocation, because we want to explore the limits of what can be obtained from considering only the correlations.

7.2.1 *Exhaustive search*

The optimum checkpoint allocation is defined by our problem formulation, and can be calculated for small problem sizes, using exhaustive search. Unfortunately the problem is so expensive to calculate using this technique, that we are unable to do so for any reasonably sized job. Solving this problem for 20 nodes, with only 7 checkpoints, took more than 1.5 hour (we stopped it), on a desktop with an Intel Core i7 processor (3,4 GHz) and 8GB RAM.

7.2.2 *Simple Job*

The job consists of one input and two operators each with 10 key groups. The input is synthetic, and the calculation is a simple count. Initially the input emits all data to operator 1, but each second it begins redirecting one percent of data more to operator 2, such that all data is being sent to opera-

[1] `http://www.rita.dot.gov/bts/`

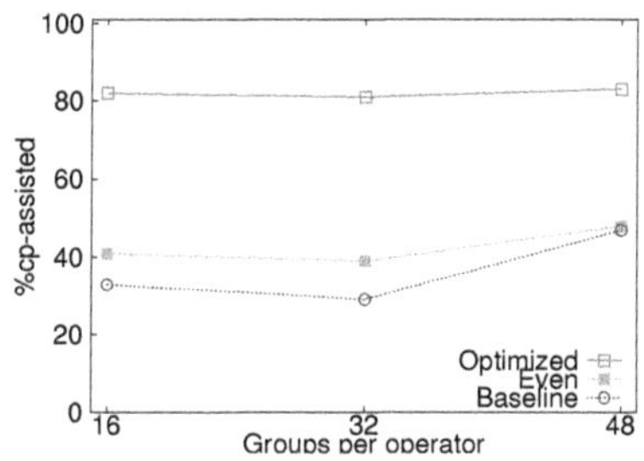

Figure 7: %cp-assisted moves

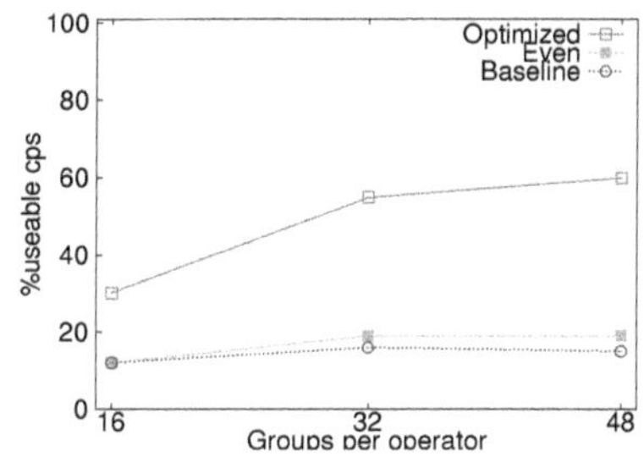

Figure 8: %useable checkpoints

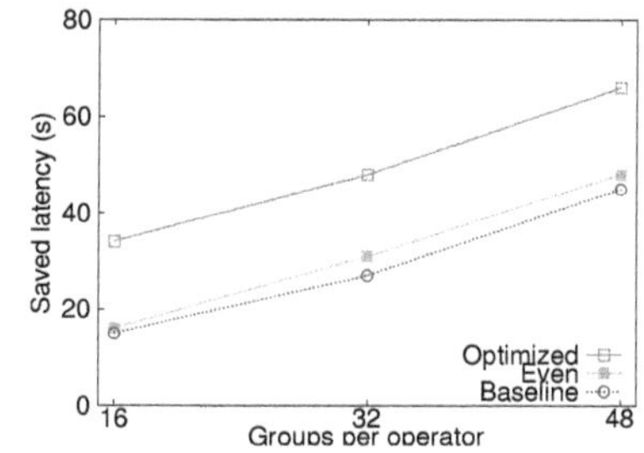

Figure 9: Saved latency

tor 2 after 100 seconds. Operator 1 and operator 2 are thus negatively correlated with a value of -1.

The job is parallelized over 4 nodes. Node 0 is dedicated to process inputs and nodes 1 and 2 are worker nodes, dedicated to processing the two operators. All the key groups of operator 1 are assigned to node 1, and all the key groups of operator 2 are assigned to node 2. Furthermore, both node 0 and node 2 are under an external load that consumes 70% of their CPU. Finally, node 3 is the control node, and is not considered by the adaptation algorithm.

For this job, the worst, average and best checkpoint allocation can be deduced. The optimal checkpoint allocation is to place all checkpoints of operator 2 on node 1, and all checkpoints of operator 1 on node 2. To see why, consider that operator 2 is assigned to node 2, and node 2 is already loaded to the overload threshold. As more and more data is sent to operator 2 from the input, this workload must be transferred to a node, which is not overloaded (node 1).

Placing the checkpoints of operator 2 on node 1 enables CPA or CPAL to perform fast migration. On the contrary, if all checkpoints of operator 2 are placed on node 0, only direct state-migration can be done, which is the worst-case assignment. The even distribution approach, will result in 50% of the checkpoints being available for cp-assisted state-migration, because it randomly spreads out the checkpoints evenly over all the available nodes. *Our checkpoint allocation algorithm, achieves the best possible checkpoint allocation for this experiment. It provides twice the amount of available checkpoints, compared to the even distribution approach.*

7.2.3 Sophisticated Job

Having considered a simple job, we now want to evaluate the checkpoint allocation algorithm for a more realistic job.

We extend the aforementioned sophisticated job (in Section 7.1) with two operators (3 and 4). Operator 3 subscribes to tuples from operator 1 and calculates the percentage of time each airplane has been in the air. Operator 4 receives a random data tuple from each instance of operator 1 for every 200 milliseconds, and calculates the percentage of delayed flights on randomly sampled data to reduce the computation cost.

Calculating a result on randomly sampled data to reduce computation cost, is typical for real-life jobs. Operator 4 is independent on the input and hence theoretically completely uncorrelated with the rest of the operators in the job. The correlation between operator 1 and operator 2 should be close to one, because the percentage of delays is stable in the input data. The correlation between operator 1 and operator 3 should also be close to one. When increasing the load of the system, the load of operator 1, 2 and 3 will increase almost linearly, whereas the load of Operator 4 will remain fixed.

The job is parallelized over 25 nodes. 1 node is used as control node, and 4 are dedicated to parse input. We use 16 nodes to process operator 1, 2 and 3 and 4 nodes to process Operator 4. In addition, we vary the number of key groups from 16 per operator to 48 per operator.

Each experiment is run for 48 minutes, to investigate if the checkpoint allocation impacts the system for more than a short period. The first 15 minutes is used to collect statistics about the system, after which, the checkpoints are allocated with either our checkpoint allocation algorithm, the even distribution or the baseline approach.

Figure 7 compares the percentage of checkpoint assisted state-migrations which were effectuated when using different techniques to allocate checkpoints. The lazy-move technique is intended for full checkpoints, and works as described in previous sections, by lazily updating the checkpoint allocation, then doing CPA afterwards.

The figure shows that both even and baseline follow a similar trend and give similar results. This is because the expected number of checkpoints at any node is equal in the average case. When increasing the number of groups, the percentage of checkpoint assisted state-migrations are shown to increase, which is simply explained by the fact that there are more key groups in total.

Our proposed checkpoint allocation technique outperforms the even and baseline approaches with a factor of approximately two. In order to understand why our optimized approach is only improving slightly with an increasing number of key groups, consider that when the number of key groups are doubled, then the load of each key group is halved in average. Remember that one checkpoint per key group is used, which means that when doubling the number of key groups, the potential load of each checkpoint is halved in average. This means the number of key groups have no impact on the α threshold, which in turn tells us that the optimized technique will not spread out the extra checkpoints. The reason for the improvement, is that more key groups leads to more potential to use the correlations in order to guide the placement of checkpoints.

Figure 8 compares the percentage of checkpoints which were "useable" over the period. The calculation is done as follows: for each key group on an overloaded node, consider if the corresponding checkpoint could be used for state-migration, without introducing overload at the node hosting the checkpoint. The percentage of "useable" checkpoints are important, because it allows the adaptation to make better decisions, i.e. there are more potential places where checkpoint-assisted state-migration can be done.

The figure shows that the percentage of useable checkpoints for baseline and even are fairly independent on the number of key groups, which is reasonable, as a random allocation like baseline and even, should not benefit from an increased number of key groups in percent. The optimized technique on the contrary benefits from an increased number of key groups, because this increases the possibility of using correlations to guide placing of checkpoints. Our proposed checkpoint allocation technique outperforms the even and baseline approaches with a factor of $2-3$.

Figure 9 compares the accumulated processing latencies incurred by all state-migration operations. For the considered job, the latency of doing direct and checkpoint assisted state-migrations were fairly similar. The reason, is that the state-size of the sophisticated job is fairly small. Still, even in this case, our approach is beneficial.

The reason the saved latency increases with the number of key groups, is because using more key groups, leads to a larger number of state-migrations. This happens as the adaptation algorithm will be able to handle overload more finegrained.

8. CONCLUSION

In this paper, we have presented an approach to integrate passive fault-tolerance and dynamic resource management in a general MPSPE. The integration allows us to employ more efficient runtime state-migration strategies to achieve dynamic load-balancing and scaling. The techniques are implemented as a significant extension over Apache Storm's static execution framework. The experiments shows, that our CPAL strategy would only incur negligible latency to the normal computation, while its completion time only depends on the size of the data that needs to be replayed. This is a very significant improvement over the traditional techniques, which usually exhibits much longer latencies.

Finally, we have proposed a new checkpoint allocation technique, and the experimental results show that it can significantly increase the opportunities to make use of our fast and more efficient state migration strategies, and hence minimize the latency incurred to the normal computations.

9. REFERENCES

[1] T. Akidau, A. Balikov, Bekiroğlu, et al. Millwheel: fault-tolerant stream processing at internet scale. *VLDB*, 2013.

[2] D. Alves, P. Bizarro, and P. Marques. Flood: elastic streaming mapreduce. In *DEBS '10*, 2010.

[3] M. Balazinska, H. Balakrishnan, S. R. Madden, and M. Stonebraker. Fault-tolerance in the borealis distributed stream processing system. *ACM Trans. Database Syst.*, 33(1), Mar. 2008.

[4] R. Castro Fernandez, M. Migliavacca, E. Kalyvianaki, and P. Pietzuch. Integrating scale out and fault tolerance in stream processing using operator state management. In *SIGMOD*, 2013.

[5] B. Gedik, S. Schneider, M. Hirzel, and K.-L. Wu. Elastic scaling for data stream processing. *TPDS*, 2013.

[6] Y. Gu et al. An empirical study of high availability in stream processing systems. In *Middleware*, 2009.

[7] V. Gulisano, R. Jimenez-Peris, M. Patino-Martinez, C. Soriente, and P. Valduriez. Streamcloud: An elastic and scalable data streaming system. *IEEE Trans. Parallel Distrib. Syst.*, 2012.

[8] P. Hunt, M. Konar, F. P. Junqueira, and B. Reed. Zookeeper: wait-free coordination for internet-scale systems. In *USENIXATC'10*, 2010.

[9] J.-H. Hwang, M. Balazinska, A. Rasin, U. Cetintemel, M. Stonebraker, and S. Zdonik. High-availability algorithms for distributed stream processing. In *ICDE '05*, 2005.

[10] J. hyon Hwang, Y. Xing, and S. Zdonik. A cooperative, self-configuring high-availability solution for stream processing. In *In ICDE*, 2007.

[11] W. Lam, L. Liu, S. Prasad, A. Rajaraman, Z. Vacheri, and A. Doan. Muppet: Mapreduce-style processing of fast data. *PVLDB*, 5(12), 2012.

[12] J. Li, K. Tufte, V. Shkapenyuk, V. Papadimos, T. Johnson, and D. Maier. Out-of-order processing: A new architecture for high-performance stream systems. *Proc. VLDB Endow.*, 1(1), Aug. 2008.

[13] L. Neumeyer, B. Robbins, A. Nair, and A. Kesari. S4: Distributed stream computing platform. In *ICDMW '10*, 2010.

[14] B. Satzger, W. Hummer, P. Leitner, and S. Dustdar. Esc: Towards an Elastic Stream Computing Platform for the Cloud. In *CLOUD'11*, 2011.

[15] S. Schneider, H. Andrade, B. Gedik, A. Biem, and K.-L. Wu. Elastic scaling of data parallel operators in stream processing. In *IPDPS '09*, 2009.

[16] Z. Sebepou and K. Magoutis. Cec: Continuous eventual checkpointing for data stream processing operators. In *DSN*, 2011.

[17] M. A. Shah, J. M. Hellerstein, and E. Brewer. Highly available, fault-tolerant, parallel dataflows. In *SIGMOD*, 2004.

[18] M. A. Shah, J. M. Hellerstein, S. Chandrasekaran, and M. J. Franklin. Flux: An adaptive partitioning operator for continuous query systems. In *ICDE*, 2003.

[19] A. Toshniwal, S. Taneja, A. Shukla, K. Ramasamy, J. M. Patel, S. Kulkarni, J. Jackson, K. Gade, M. Fu, J. Donham, N. Bhagat, S. Mittal, and D. Ryaboy. Storm@twitter. In *SIGMOD '14*, 2014.

[20] Y. Xing, S. Zdonik, and J.-H. Hwang. Dynamic load distribution in the borealis stream processor. In *ICDE*, 2005.

[21] M. Yagiura, S. Iwasaki, T. Ibaraki, and F. Glover. A very large-scale neighborhood search algorithm for the multi-resource generalized assignment problem. *Discrete Optimization*, 1(1), 2004.

[22] M. Zaharia, T. Das, H. Li, S. Shenker, and I. Stoica. Discretized streams: An efficient and fault-tolerant model for stream processing on large clusters. In *HotCloud*, 2012.

[23] Y. Zhou, K. Aberer, and K.-L. Tan. Toward massive query optimization in large-scale distributed stream systems. In *Middleware*, 2008.

[24] Y. Zhou, B. C. Ooi, K. Tan, and J. Wu. Efficient dynamic operator placement in a locally distributed continuous query system. In *OTM*, 2006.

A Parallel GPU-Based Approach to Clustering Very Fast Data Streams

Pengtao Huang, Xiu Li and Bo Yuan*
Intelligent Computing Lab, Division of Informatics
Graduate School at Shenzhen, Tsinghua University
Shenzhen 518055, P.R. China
hpt13@mails.tsinghua.edu.cn, li.xiu@sz.tsinghua.edu.cn, yuanb@sz.tsinghua.edu.cn

ABSTRACT

Clustering data streams has become a hot topic in the era of big data. Driven by the ever increasing volume, velocity and variety of data, more efficient algorithms for clustering large-scale complex data streams are needed. In this paper, we present a parallel algorithm called PaStream, which is based on advanced Graphics Processing Unit (GPU) and follows the online-offline framework of CluStream. Our approach can achieve hundreds of times speedup on high-speed and high-dimensional data streams compared with CluStream. It can also discover clusters with arbitrary shapes and handle outliers properly. The efficiency and scalability of PaStream are demonstrated through comprehensive experiments on synthetic and standard benchmark datasets with various problem factors.

Categories and Subject Descriptors

H.3.3 [**Information Search and Retrieval**]: Clustering; I.5.3 [**Clustering**]: Algorithms

General Terms

Algorithms, Experimentation

Keywords

PaStream, data stream, clustering, GPU

1. INTRODUCTION

Data stream is a special form of data,which is very common in the real world. Unlike traditional static data stored in databases or data warehouses, data stream is a dynamic, continuous, massive, unbounded and rapid sequence of data. Examples of data stream include multimedia data, trajectory data, web click data and financial data[4, 23].

*Corresponding author.

CIKM'15, October 19–23, 2015, Melbourne, VIC, Australia
© 2015 ACM. ISBN 978-1-4503-3794-6/15/10 ...$15.00
DOI: http://dx.doi.org/10.1145/2806416.2806545.

Due to the characteristics of data stream, it is infeasible to control the order in which elements arrive, nor is it possible to store all elements of a data stream. Consequently, each new element in the data stream should be processed instantly when it arrives and there is no enough time to examine it more than once. Furthermore, the memory requirement should be confined finitely, although new data elements arrive continuously [16, 17].

Clustering is a popular technique of data mining, which aims at discovering groups of similar data elements measured by a given set of criteria [21]. Most traditional clustering algorithms do not apply to data streams because of the one pass constraint and storage limitation. Barbará [6] summarized three basic requirements for clustering data streams: compactness of representation, fast and incremental processing of new data points, clear and fast identification of outliers. Aggarwal et al. [2] further claimed that the quality of clusters should be assured when the data evolves considerably over time and the capability of discovering clusters over different portions of stream should also be maintained. A number of stream clustering algorithms have been proposed, which more or less meet the above requirements. However, in recent years, people are faced with some new challenges in data stream mining.

With the rise of big data, the volume and speed of data streams are far beyond the capacity of most algorithms running on traditional computing architecture and infrastructure. For example, the vast amount of security monitoring data in a city needs to be analyzed in real time so that we can timely handle emergencies. So it is increasingly urgent to explore new efficient data stream mining algorithms based on more powerful hardware. The emerging heterogeneous platforms such as GPU, Hadoop, FPGA and DSP bring us powerful tools to cope with massive and complex big data. Among them, GPU is a lightweight, efficient and promising platform for both personal supercomputing and large scale supercomputing.

In this paper, we present PaStream, a parallel algorithm framework for clustering very high speed and high dimensional data streams with arbitrary cluster shapes based on NVIDIA GPUs. PaStream follows the basic online-offline framework of the well-known CluStream [2]. For the online part, we propose a parallel mechanism to fully exploit the computing power of GPUs, making PaStream hundreds of times faster than CluStream on maintaining micro-clusters. For the offline part, we extend one of the latest clustering algorithms [25] so that it can be used to cluster micro-clusters and find macro-clusters of arbitrary shapes and handle outliers properly. Furthermore, it is accelerated using GPUs and can achieve dozens of times speedup. In summary, the key contributions in PaStream include a new parallel approach to online micro-cluster maintenance and a more powerful method for offline macro-cluster creation.

The remainder of this paper is organized as follows. In Section 2, we review existing work on data stream clustering, and analyse their strengths and weaknesses. We also give an introduction of the CUDA programming model based on NVIDIA GPUs. An overall description of PaStream is given in Section 3. We present the details of the GPU-based algorithm for online micro-clustering in Section 4 and a powerful new approach to offline macro-clustering in Section 5. Section 6 reports the performance of our algorithm and compares it with CluStream. The conclusion and future work of this paper are presented in Section 7.

2. RELATED WORK

2.1 Data Stream Clustering

Zhang et al. [30, 31] proposed BIRCH to efficiently cluster data in very large databases. The algorithm builds a CF Tree to incrementally and dynamically cluster incoming multi-dimensional metric data points. It can typically find a good clustering pattern with a single scan of the data and refine the quality further with a few additional scans.

Guha et al. [19, 18] investigated data stream clustering using K-median and proposed constant-factor approximation algorithms for the K-median problem in the data stream model with a single pass. Charikar et al. [11] gave an improved streaming algorithm for the K-median problem with an arbitrary distance function.

O'Callaghan et al. [24] proposed LOCALSEARCH and STREAM algorithms for high-quality clustering. They are also single-pass algorithms, but they evaluate the performance by a combination of SSQ (Sum of Squared Distance) and the number of centers used. In many applications, they exhibit superior performance compared with algorithms such as BIRCH.

Barbara and Chen [7] presented the Fractal Clustering (FC) algorithm. The algorithm clusters points incrementally and places them in certain clusters. After adding the point, the change in the fractal dimension of the cluster should be the least. It can effectively handle large data sets with high-dimensionality and noise and is capable of recognizing clusters of arbitrary shapes.

Babcock et al. [5] extended the STREAM algorithm with sliding window and solved two important and related problems in the sliding window model: maintaining variance and maintaining the K-median clustering.

Most algorithms above are one-pass algorithms and can address the scalability issue of data stream clustering, but they can hardly cope with fast evolving data streams. Aggarwal et al. [2] proposed the CluStream algorithm, a novel framework for clustering fast evolving data streams. It divides the clustering process into an online phase, which periodically stores detailed summary statistics, and an offline phase, which only relies on these summary statistics. CluStream provides desired functionality in discovering and exploring clusters over different portions of the stream, but it can not discover clusters with arbitrary shapes. Afterwards they proposed HPStream [3], which is a framework for projected clustering of high dimensional data streams.

In order to find clusters of arbitrary shapes in data streams, a number of new algorithms were proposed, such as CDS-Tree [27] based on an improved space partition, DenStream [9] and D-Stream [12] based on density, ACluStream [34] and MGDDS [33] based on grid and FCluStream [20] based on fractal. Most of them followed the online-offline framework of CluStream and incorporated new methods to find clusters of arbitrary shapes.

Dedicated software tools and libraries have also been developed for data stream analysis. For example, Bifet et al. [8] developed a software environment called MOA (Massive Online Analysis)[22] for online learning from evolving data streams. Zhang and Mueller [32] provided a C++ template library for parallel data streaming applications based on the streaming abstraction and GPUs.

2.2 GPU High Performance Computing

In recent years, GPUs have evolved into highly parallel, multi-threaded, many-core processors and are widely used for general purpose computing [14]. Compared with CPU based distributed systems such as Hadoop, GPU based parallel computing systems are more lightweight, portable and energy-efficient.

CUDA (Compute Unified Device Architecture) is a general purpose parallel computing platform and programming model, which was first introduced by NVIDIA in November 2006. CUDA makes it convenient to exploit the parallel capabilities of NVIDIA GPUs to solve computationally intensive problems much more efficiently. CUDA is designed to support various programming languages and interfaces such as CUDA C, OpneCL, Python [1] and FORTRAN.

Threads and kernels are the most important concepts in CUDA. Threads are lightweight processes executed on independent processors in GPU, and they are easy to be created and synchronized. Kernels are functions that are executed on the GPU in parallel by massive threads organized into blocks and grids [13].

There are different types of memory in GPUs, which can significantly affect the performance of programs. Each thread has its private local memory called register, which is the fastest type of memory. Each thread block features shared memory accessible by all threads within a block, which can be as fast as registers if accessed properly. All threads have access to the same global memory, which is the largest and slowest storage and the only memory visible to the CPU. Constant memory and texture memory are two read-only memory spaces accessible by all threads [29]. The global, constant, and texture memory spaces are persistent across kernel launches by the same application.

For devices of compute capability 3.5 or higher, a new functionality of CUDA called dynamic parallelism is available, which enables a CUDA kernel to create new work directly from the GPU without the intervention of CPU, reducing the need to transfer instructions and data between host and device. This feature is very helpful for the parallelization of algorithms and programming patterns that contain recursion, irregular loop structure, or other constructs that do not fit a flat, single-level of parallelism [14].

Cao and Zhou [10] made some attempts to accelerate data stream clustering algorithms using GPUs. However, they only focused on calculating and comparing distances in parallel without making necessary changes to the algorithm flow. Due to the limitations of the algorithm architecture and early GPU architectures, the GPU-based algorithms were only about 7 times faster than the CPU-based algorithms. Meanwhile, Roger et al. [26] presented an efficient algorithm to remove unwanted elements from a stream of outputs on the GPU and Verner et al. [28] proposed an efficient and practical algorithm for processing streams with hard real-time constraints on heterogeneous systems.

3. PRELIMINARIES

Similar to CluStream [2], PaStream consists of an online phase and an offline phase. The online phase groups data points into micro-clusters and the offline phase aggregates micro-clusters into macro-clusters. The schematic diagram of our algorithm is illustrated in Fig. 1.

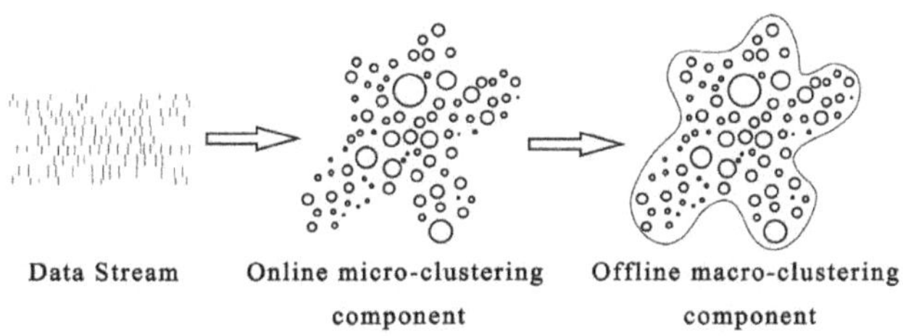

Figure 1: Schematic diagram of PaStream

In our model, each micro-cluster can be regarded as a hyper-sphere containing a set of d-dimensional data points. Using the concept of *clustering feature* (CF) [30], we can represent the i-th micro-cluster containing data points $X_{i_1}, X_{i_2}, \cdots, X_{i_{n_i}}$ with time stamps $T_{i_1}, T_{i_2}, \cdots, T_{i_{n_i}}$ by $(\overline{CF2_i^x}, \overline{CF1_i^x}, CF2_i^t, CF1_i^t, n_i)$, where $\overline{CF2_i^x}$ and $\overline{CF1_i^x}$ are d-dimensional vectors and the other three are scalar values.

$\overline{CF2_i^x}$ maintains the sum of squares of the data points, whose j-th entry can be expressed as:

$$CF2_{i_j}^x = \sum_{k=1}^{n_i} (X_{i_{kj}})^2 \tag{1}$$

$\overline{CF1_i^x}$ maintains the sum of the data points, whose j-th entry can be expressed as:

$$CF1_{i_j}^x = \sum_{k=1}^{n_i} X_{i_{kj}} \tag{2}$$

$CF2t_i$ maintains the sum of squares of the time stamps, which can be expressed as:

$$CF2_i^t = \sum_{k=1}^{n_i} T_{i_k}^2 \tag{3}$$

$CF1t_i$ maintains the sum of the time stamps, which can be expressed as:

$$CF1_i^t = \sum_{k=1}^{n_i} T_{i_k} \tag{4}$$

n_i is the number of data points contained in the i-th micro-cluster. In this way, a micro-cluster is represented by a $(2 * d + 3)$ tuple instead of a $(n_i * d)$ tuple, reducing the memory requirements significantly for a typical $n_i \gg 2$.

From the five attributes above, we can get the *centroid*, *radius* and *relevance stamp* of a micro-cluster. The j-th entry of the centroid of the i-th micro-cluster is:

$$Centroid_{i_j} = \frac{CF1_{i_j}^x}{n_i} \tag{5}$$

Radius reflects the dispersion of the data points in a micro-cluster, which can be measured by the RMS (Root Mean Square) deviation of the data points from the centroid:

$$Radius_i = \frac{1}{d} \sum_{j=1}^{d} \sqrt{\frac{CF2_{i_j}^x}{n_i} - \left(\frac{CF1_{i_j}^x}{n_i}\right)^2} \tag{6}$$

In the micro-clustering phase, whether a data point can be absorbed by a micro-cluster is determined by its *maximal boundary*. For a fast evolving data stream, it is difficult to judge whether to absorb a data point since the radii of micro-clusters may be unstable. If the criterion of absorbing a data point relies on the radius of the nearest micro-cluster, there may be many new micro-clusters created and many existing micro-clusters merged, which is much slower than the absorbing process. To improve efficiency, we introduce an expanding factor so that micro-clusters can expand gradually in each time.

Relevance stamp reflects the recency of the last m data points of a micro-cluster, which is defined as the time of arrival of the $\frac{m}{2 \cdot n_i}$-th percentile of the points. The time-stamps of the data points are assumed to obey normal distribution, the j-th entry of whose mean and standard deviation are:

$$\mu_{i_j} = \frac{CF1_{i_j}^t}{n_i} \tag{7}$$

$$\sigma_{i_j} = \sqrt{\frac{CF2_{i_j}^t}{n_i} - \left(\frac{CF1_{i_j}^t}{n_i}\right)^2} \tag{8}$$

Actually, each micro-cluster can be regarded as a hyper-sphere containing a set of d-dimensional data points. At the very beginning of the algorithm, we need to establish q micro-clusters by buffering *InitNum* data points on disk and clustering them using a standard k-means algorithm. Then, whenever a new data point arrives, the online phase determines whether it is absorbed by a micro-cluster, or a new micro-cluster is created after an old micro-cluster being deleted or two closest micro-clusters being merged. We define the proportion of absorbed points as *absorption rate*. At the same time, the micro-clusters are stored as snapshots following a pyramidal time pattern [2], so that for a given time horizon, the offline phase can determine the micro-clusters by using two related snapshots.

The efficiency of the online phase determines the speed of processing and should be as simple as possible and easy to be parallelized. It is obvious that online micro-clustering methods based on spherical clusters are much simpler than those based on density grids [9, 12] or space partition [27, 34]. So, there is a need to investigate whether spherical micro-clusters can meet the requirements of discovering macro-clusters of arbitrary shapes in the offline phase. To show its feasibility, we consider the following proposition.

PROPOSITION 1. *A confined space of any shape can be approximated infinitely well by an arrangement of non-overlapping spheres of the same dimension.*

A typical circle packing problem[1] is to find an arrangement in which the circles can fill as large a proportion of the space as possible. Note that Proposition 1 describes a similar problem where both the number of circles and the radii of circles are flexible. So, it is feasible to approximate macro-clusters of any shapes by many micro-clusters.

4. ONLINE MICRO-CLUSTERING

In this section, we focus on the key challenges in designing the parallel framework for online micro-clustering in order to handle fast and complex data streams efficiently.

Challenge 1. Transferring data points from host (CPU) to device (GPU) on a one by one basis can be very time consuming.

In a data stream, only a single data point arrives at any given moment. Consequently, data points should be processed one after another according to the order of arrival. However, in order to conduct computing on the GPU, there is a need to transfer data from CPU to GPU, which is a time consuming operation compared with the computing power of the GPU. If each data point is transferred to the GPU upon its arrival, significant amount of time will be wasted on the transferring operation. To reduce the average communication cost of each data point, we create a buffer where *BufferSize* data points can be stored in the CPU memory for a short time and then transferred to device together. Furthermore, as shown in Fig. 2, if the CPU is not able to finish processing a data point before another point arrives, the time lag will get larger over time. By contrast, all the points in the buffer may be timely processed on the GPU. The practicability and accuracy of our method will be verified by experiments in Section 6.

Challenge 2. The shapes of macro-clusters may be irregular or complex, and the number of them may vary tremendously.

For macro-clusters of regular shapes, a small number of micro-clusters can approximate them well enough and excessive number of micro-clusters may waste memory and time. However, for macro-clusters of complex shapes, many more micro-clusters will be needed to approximate them. So, the number of micro-clusters should be self-adaptive within the limits of memory. We propose a scheme according to which adjacent micro-clusters are merged based on their merging factor instead of the number of unabsorbed points. The merging factor is defined as Definition 1, which means any micro-clusters closer than their merging factor will merge.

Definition 1. (Merging Factor) The merging factor Mg_{ij} of the i-th and the j-th micro-clusters is defined as a factor of the sum of the radii of the two adjacent micro-clusters, which can be expressed as:

$$MG_{ij} = t(Radius_i + Radius_j) \tag{9}$$

where t is a relaxation factor, typically between 0.5 and 2.

[1]In three dimensions, it is called sphere packing problem. In higher dimensions, it is called hyper-sphere packing problem.

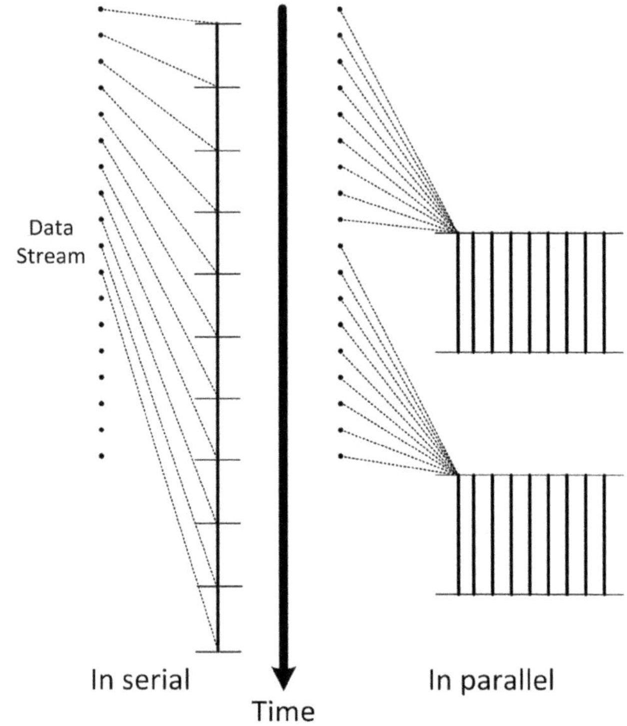

Figure 2: Micro-clustering in serial and in parallel

Based on the discussion above, the parallel micro-clustering framework based on GPU is shown as Algorithm 1 using pseudo-code.

There are several computation-intensive parts in the algorithm, which are very suitable for running on the GPU:

- ☐ Obtaining the cluster label of each point in the initialization part. For each iteration in the loop, there are *PointNum*ClusterNum* Euclidean distances to compute.
- ☐ Finding the closest micro-clusters. For each pass, there are *BufferSize*q* Euclidean distances to compute. The minimum distance and its index are also needed.
- ☐ Finding very old micro-clusters. For each pass, there are q relevance stamps to compute. The minimum distance and its index are also needed.
- ☐ Finding very adjacent micro-clusters. For each pass, there are $\frac{q(q-1)}{2}$ Euclidean distances to compute.

When finding the closest micro-clusters, each point can be processed in a single *block*, and a specific number of Euclidean distances are computed by a single *thread*. For very high dimensionality, we can take advantage of *dynamic parallelism* to launch some child kernels to deal with each dimension within the limits of hardware resource. Furthermore, the data needed by all the threads in the same block can be placed in *shared memory* for faster access, such as the centers of micro-clusters.

According to Amdahl's Law, the maximum speedup that can be achieved depends on the proportion of a program

Algorithm 1 GPU Based Online Micro-clustering

Input: Micro-clusters, *imic*; Buffered data points, *data*; Time stamps, *t*
Output: New micro-clusters, *omic*

```
function MICROCLUSTERING(imic, data, t)
    Get centers, CF2t, CF1t and point numbers of imic
    for i = 0 → BufferSize − 1 in parallel do
        for j = 0 → MicroClusterNum − 1 do
            Calculate DistMat[i, j]
        end for
    end for
    for i = 0 → BufferSize − 1 do
        MinDist ← min(DistMat(i, :))
        MinIdx ← argmin(DistMat(i, :))
        Calculate MaxBoundary of the MinIdx-th micro-cluster
        if MinDist <= MaxBoundary then AbsorbPoint(data(i), t(i))
        end if
    end for
    for i = 0 → BufferSize − 1 in parallel do
        Calculate RelevStmpVec
        if RelevStmpVec[i] < threshold then DeleteCluster(i)
        end if
    end for
    for i = 0 → BufferSize − 2 in parallel do
        for j = i → BufferSize − 1 do
            Calculate ClusterDistMat[i, j]
            if ClusterDistMat[i, j] <= MG_ij then MergeClusters(i,j)
            end if
        end for
    end for
    for each remain point do
        CreateNewClusters()
    end for
    return omic
end function
```

that can be made parallel and the number of processors [15]. Let us denote the number of processors using n and the proportion using P, the theoretical speedup of the parallel code over the serial code can be expressed as:

$$S(n) = \frac{1}{(1-P)+P/n} \tag{10}$$

With the increase of the number of micro-clusters and dimensionality, P gets larger, and more processors can be used. As a result, *(1-P)* gets smaller while P/n almost remains the same, resulting in higher $S(n)$ value. In this way, the algorithm is expected to feature good scalability with regard to the number of micro-clusters and dimensionality. However, the number of processors in a GPU may be up to thousands but still limited, and the memory space in a GPU is also limited. If the number of micro-clusters or dimensionality is out of range, processors or memory space will be short supply and the maximum speedup will increase at a much lower speed and can not go beyond n. In this case, more powerful computing devices are needed to break through the limitation.

In addition to the above factors, there are also some parts that consume significant time but are very difficult to run in parallel, such as the deletion of old clusters and the creation of new clusters. This is because these parts involve object creation and destruction, resulting in memory allocation and release, a slow operation on the GPU. Consequently, for fast evolving data streams, the speedup rate will drop with the decrease of *absorption rate.* In this case, we propose a *Distance Matrix,* which maintains the Euclidean distance between each pair of micro-clusters. Each time a micro-cluster is modified, created or deleted, the *Distance Matrix* updates the corresponding value in it, making it easier to find adjacent objects frequently.

5. OFFLINE MACRO-CLUSTERING

In this section, we describe how to cluster micro-clusters into macro-clusters of arbitrary shapes and detect outliers and present GPU accelerated version of the algorithm.

Rodriguez and Laio [25] proposed a powerful and concise clustering algorithm in 2014, which is able to recognize a large number of clusters with random noise regardless of their shapes and dimensionality. The core idea is that clusters are characterized by a higher density than their neighbours and by a relatively large distance from points with high densities. However, for the offline macro-clustering phase in PaStream, the objects to be clustered are not common data points, but micro-clusters containing different numbers of data points, or weighted points. So, we need to make some improvement to meet the new requirements.

There are two quantities to evaluate the i-th micro-cluster, which are defined as follows:

Definition 2. (Local Density) The local density ρ_i with a Gaussian kernel is defined as the total Gaussian weight of all the data points, which can be expressed as:

$$\rho_i = \sum_{j=1}^{n} \frac{d_{ij}}{d_c} \exp(-\frac{d_{ij}}{d_c}) \tag{11}$$

where n is the number of data points, and d_{ij} is the Euclidean distance between the i-th and the j-th micro-cluster, and d_c is a cutoff distance.

Definition 3. (Local Distance) The local distance ψ_i is defined as the minimum distance between the i-th micro-cluster and any other micro-cluster with higher local density, which can be expressed as:

$$\psi_i = min_{j,\rho_j > \rho_i}(d_{ij}) \tag{12}$$

First of all, for all the cluster centers, we need to calculate the Euclidean distances between each other, which is stored in *CenterDistMat.* Afterwards, for each micro-cluster, we calculate its *local density* and *local distance*, and then we can plot the *decision graph.* The *spiral* dataset is plotted in Fig. 3, and its *decision graph* is shown in Fig. 4.

Typically, the *local distance* of the local density maxima is much larger than others, which makes it very easy to distinguish the number and centers of the clusters.

The parallel macro-clustering framework based on GPU is shown as Algorithm 2 using pseudo-code.

The tasks listed below are computation-intensive but very convenient to parallelize:

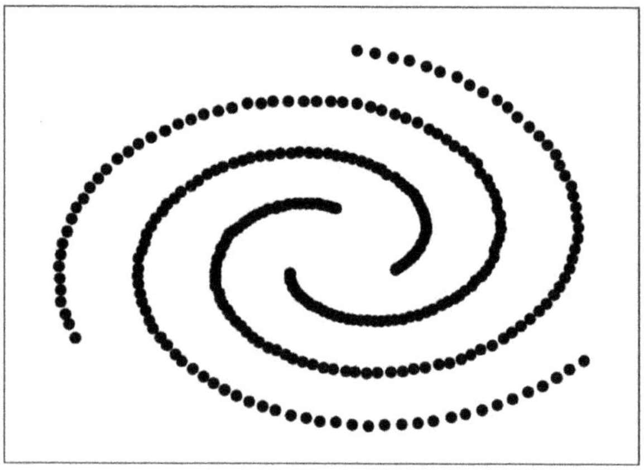

Figure 3: Spiral

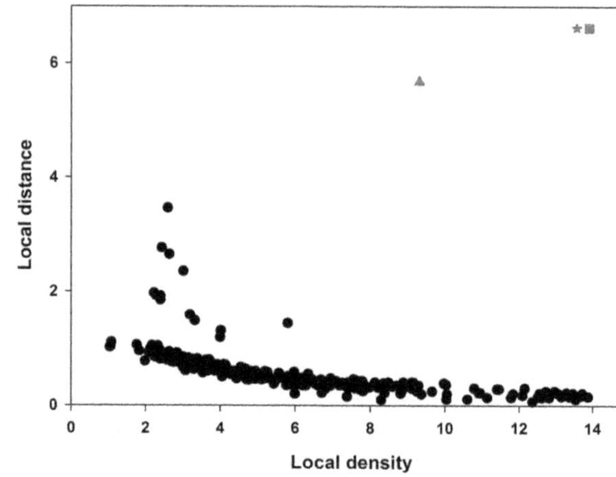

Figure 4: Decision graph of spiral

Algorithm 2 GPU Based Offline Macro-clustering

Input: Micro-clusters, *mic*
Output: Macro-clusters, *mac*:

function MACROCLUSTERING(mic)
  for $i = 0 \to MicNum - 2$ **in parallel do**
    for $j = i \to MicNum - 1$ **do**
      Calculate $CenterDistMat[i, j]$
    end for
  end for
  Get d_c by sorting the $CenterDistMat$
  for $i = 0 \to MicNum - 1$ **in parallel do**
    Calculate $\rho[i]$
  end for
  for $i = 0 \to MicNum - 1$ **in parallel do**
    Calculate $\psi[i]$
  end for
  Plot *Decision Graph* and choose macro-cluster centers
  for $i = 0 \to MicNum - 1$ **in parallel do**
    Assign *cluster labels*
  end for
  return *mac*
end function

- ☐ Calculating *CenterDistMat*. There are $\frac{n(n-1)}{2}$ Euclidean distances to compute.
- ☐ Calculating local densities. There are $\frac{n(n-1)}{2}$ Gaussian wights to compute.
- ☐ Calculating local distances. There are $\frac{n(n-1)}{2}$ comparisons needed.
- ☐ Assigning cluster labels. There are n comparisons needed to assign cluster labels for all the normal points. Besides, in order to distinguish outliers, $\frac{n(n-1)}{2}$ comparisons are needed.

Similarly, each task can be divided into many independent parts to be executed by different blocks and threads. Within the limits of processors and memories, we should try to use more threads to simplify the task of a single thread. For sorting operations, *Thrust* offers several functions such as *thrust::sort* and *thrust::stable_sort* to sort data or rearrange data according to a given criterion very efficiently.

6. EXPERIMENTAL RESULTS

We conducted the experiments on a PC with Intel-i7 CPU (3.40GHz, 4 cores / 8 threads) and NVIDIA GeForce GTX 750 GPU. The programming environment was Visual Studio 2012 with CUDA 6.5 running on Windows 8.1 (64bit).

Both synthetic datasets and real datasets were used in our experiments. The synthetic datasets have a varying number of clusters ranging from 1 to 1000, and dimensionality ranging from 2 to 100. The widely used real dataset in data stream clustering KDD-CUP'99, which contains a set of Network Intrusion Detection stream data, was also included in experiments. This dataset contains 4898431 records, 5 clusters and 42 attributes of which 34 are continuous and the other 8 are discrete. In our experiments, all the 34 continuous attributes were used and normalized to [0, 1].

6.1 Micro-Clustering Performance

We evaluated the online micro-clustering phase of PaStream by its efficiency and quality compared with CluStream [2], including the (single-threaded) CPU version and the OpenMP version.

Fig. 5 shows the running time of PaStream compared with the CPU version and OpenMP version CluStream with varying numbers of micro-clusters, as well as the speedup rates relative to the CPU version CluStream. We can see that the speedup rate of the OpenMP version CluStream varied between 2 and 3.5 while the speedup rate of PaStream kept growing with the increase of the number of micro-clusters,which shows excellent scalability with regard to the micro-cluster number. However, too many micro-clusters will increase the running time significantly, so the number of micro-clusters should be controlled within a certain scope.

Fig. 6 shows the running time of PaStream compared with the CPU version and OpenMP version CluStream with varying dimensionality, as well as their speedup rates relative to the CPU version CluStream. We can see that the speedup rate of PaStream kept growing when the dimensionality increased from 2 to 70 and the running time remained below 10 seconds, which shows excellent scalability with regard

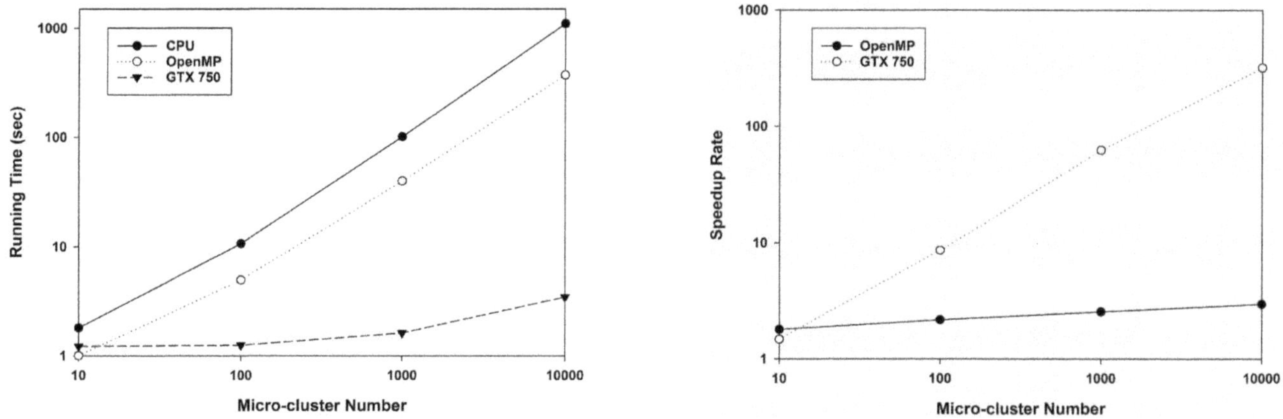

Figure 5: Running time and speedup rate comparison with varying numbers of micro-clusters (Dimensionality = 2, Buffer Size = 1000, Absorption Rate = 95%)

to dimensionality. However, when the dimensionality exceeded 70, the speedup dropped a bit and stopped increasing, which is caused by the limits of processor number and memory space in the GPU. If the dimensionality is too high, too much data will remain in the global memory of GPU, reducing the computing speed.

Fig. 7 shows the running time of PaStream with varying buffer sizes, as well as their speedup rates relative to the CPU version CluStream. We can see that the running time of PaStream dropped significantly when the buffer size increased from 1 to 10 and the speedup rate kept growing with the increase of buffer size, which is consistent with the analysis above. Obviously, the buffer size should be selected rationally to keep the balance between speedup rate and clustering quality. If the buffer size is too large (relative to data stream speed), speedup rate will increase much slower while clustering quality will drop significantly.

Fig. 8 shows the speedup rate of PaStream with varying absorption rates. We can see that the speedup rate decreased for fast evolving data streams because of the frequent deletion of old clusters and creation of new clusters, but the algorithm still shows very high efficiency.

6.2 Macro-Clustering Performance

We evaluated the offline phase of PaStream by its efficiency and quality compared with its CPU version.

Fig. 9 shows the 7 macro-clusters by clustering 1000 micro-clusters. We can see that the macro-clusters were of high quality and most outliers (marked as black dots) were correctly detected.

Fig. 10 shows the SSQ and clustering quality of macro-clustering algorithm with varying buffer sizes based on the KDD-CUP'99 dataset. We can see that the SSQ increased very slowly with the increase of buffer size and the clustering quality was only affected slightly. In practice, the buffer size can be chosen properly according to the speed and complexity of data stream.

Fig. 11 shows the running time and speedup of the GPU version macro-clustering algorithm compared with its CPU version with varying numbers of micro-clusters. We can see that the GPU version can reach up to more than one hundred times faster for complex data streams.

Fig. 12 shows the running time and speedup of the GPU version macro-clustering algorithm compared with its CPU version with varying dimensionality. We can see that the running time of the GPU version algorithm showed excellent scalability with regard to dimensionality and the speedup kept increasing within the permitted scope of hardware resources.

7. CONCLUSION AND FUTURE WORK

In this paper, we present PaStream, a highly efficient parallel algorithm for clustering very fast and complex data streams based on NVIDIA GPUs. With the help of a new parallel framework and a series of innovative techniques, the online micro-clustering phase of PaStream can achieve hundreds of times speedup using inexpensive commodity GPUs and features excellent scalability with regard to cluster number and dimensionality. By incorporating a local density based algorithm into the macro-clustering phase, PaStream can discover clusters with arbitrary shapes and handle outliers effectively. Meanwhile, the macro-clustering algorithm can be accelerated by dozens of times using GPUs, without compromising the clustering quality.

As to future work, it will be a tremendous advantage if we can reduce the I/O overhead significantly and run the algorithm totally on the GPU. Other advanced high-performance computing platforms such as Mars, Spark etc. can also be exploited to handle very fast and complex data streams. It is equally important to consider some special data types (e.g., spatio-temporal data) and more realistic scenarios (e.g., uncertainties and spatial constraints).

8. ACKNOWLEDGMENTS

This work was supported by the NVIDIA CUDA Teaching Center awarded to Tsinghua University.

9. REFERENCES

[1] Accelerate Continuum Documentation. http://docs.continuum.io/accelerate.

[2] C. Aggarwal, J. Han, J. Wang, and P. Yu. A framework for clustering evolving data streams. In *Proceedings of the 29th International Conference on Very Large Data Bases*, pages 81–92, 2003.

[3] C. Aggarwal, J. Han, J. Wang, and P. Yu. A framework for projected clustering of high dimensional

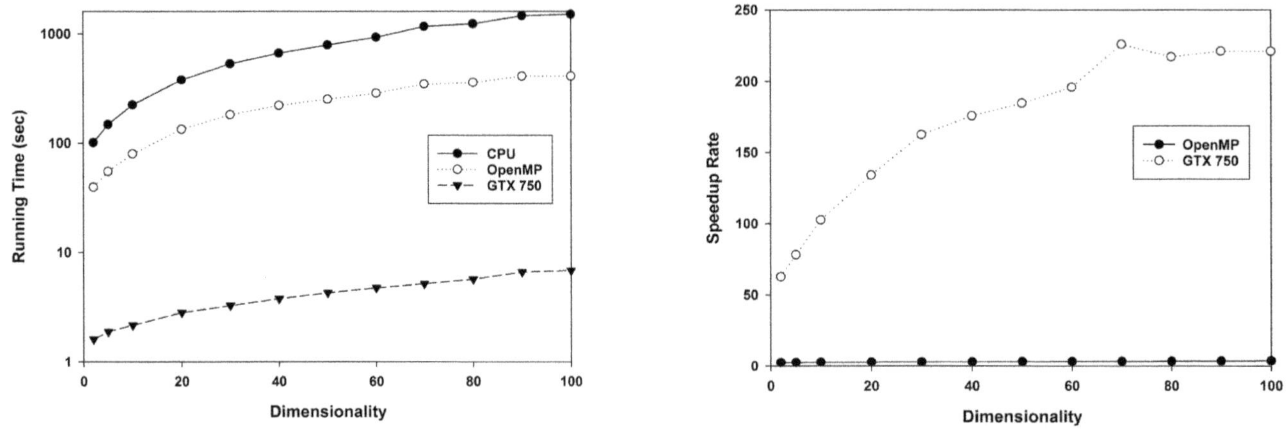

Figure 6: Running time and speedup rate comparison with varying dimensionality (Micro-cluster Number = 1000, Buffer Size = 1000, Absorption Rate = 95%)

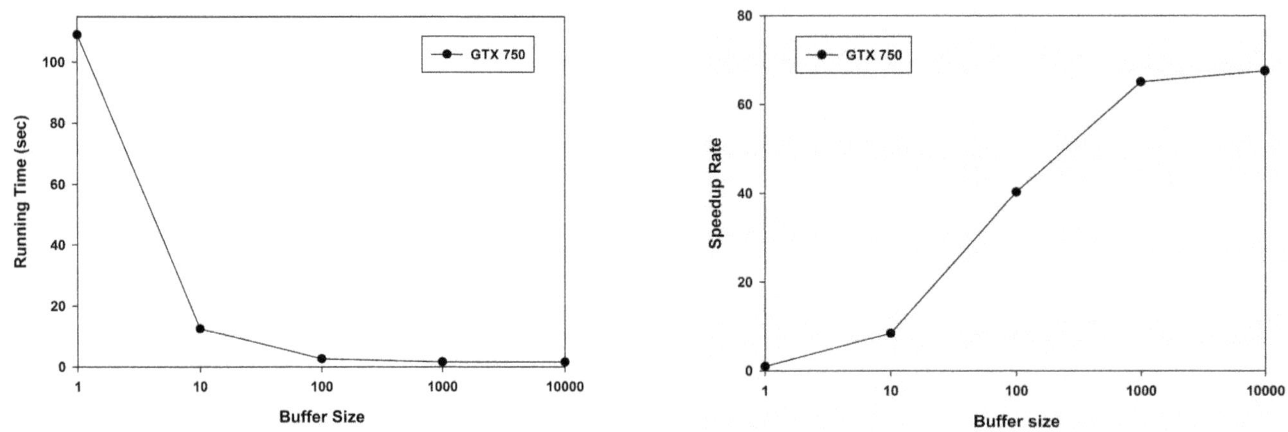

Figure 7: Running time and speedup rate with varying buffer sizes (Micro-cluster Number = 1000, Dimensionality = 2, Absorption Rate = 95%)

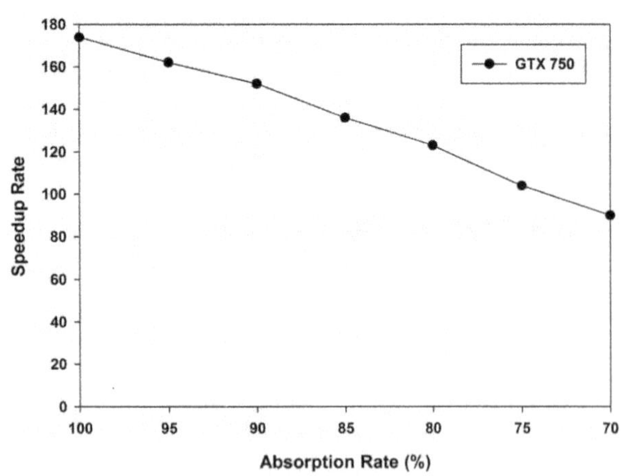

Figure 8: Speedup comparison with varying absorption rates (Micro-cluster Number = 1000, Dimensionality = 30, Buffer Size = 1000)

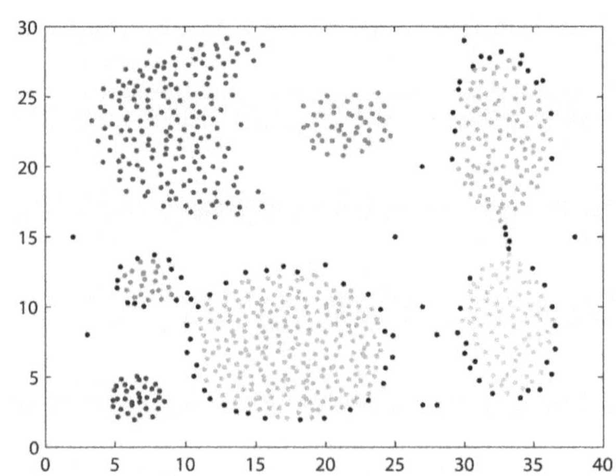

Figure 9: Macro-clusters with outliers

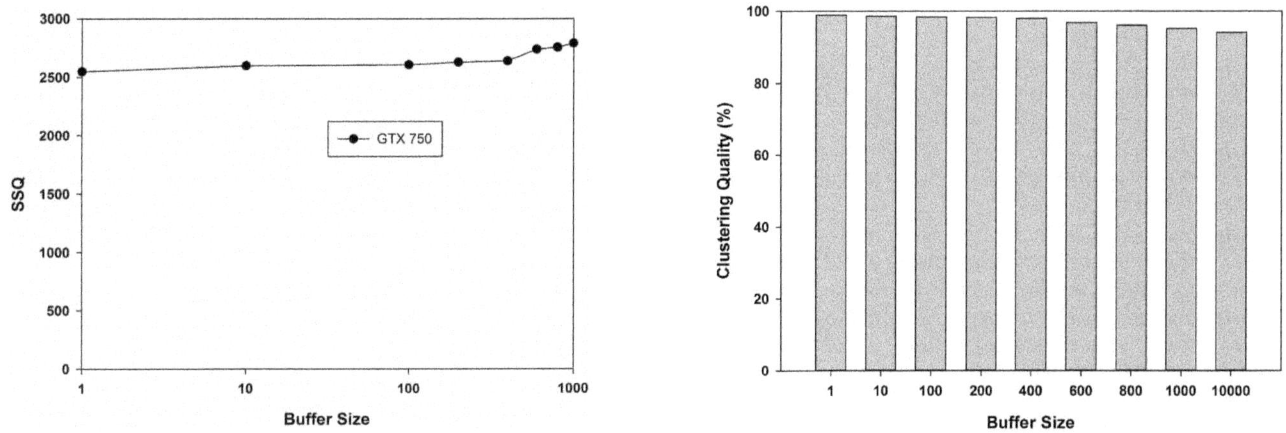

Figure 10: SSQ and clustering quality with varying buffer sizes (Micro-cluster Number = 1000, Dimensionality = 2, Absorption Rate = 95%)

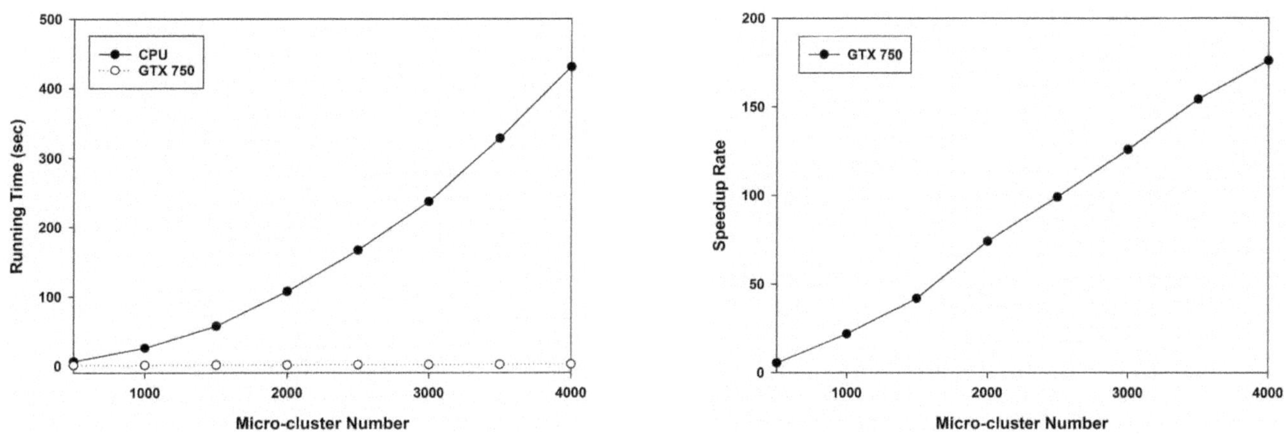

Figure 11: Running time and speedup with varying numbers of micro-clusters (Dimensionality = 60)

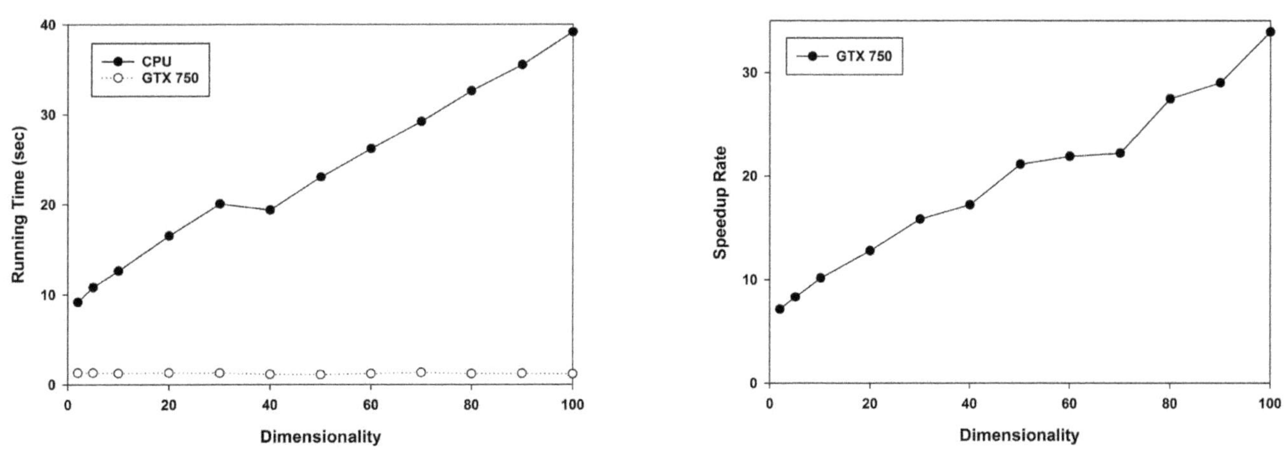

Figure 12: Running time and speedup with varying dimensionality (Micro-cluster Number = 1000)

data streams. In *Proceedings of the Thirtieth International Conference on Very Large Data Bases*, pages 852–863, 2004.

[4] B. Babcock, S. Babu, M. Datar, R. Motwani, and J. Widom. Models and issues in data stream systems. In *Proceedings of the Twenty-first ACM SIGMOD-SIGACT-SIGART Symposium on Principles of Database Systems*, pages 1–16, New York, USA, 2002. ACM Press.

[5] B. Babcock, M. Datar, R. Motwani, and L. O'Callaghan. Maintaining variance and k-medians over data stream windows. In *Proceedings of the twenty-second ACM SIGMOD-SIGACT-SIGART symposium on Principles of database systems - PODS '03*, pages 234–243, New York, USA, June 2003. ACM Press.

[6] D. Barbará. Requirements for clustering data streams. *ACM SIGKDD Explorations Newsletter*, 3(2):23–27, 2002.

[7] D. Barbara and P. Chen. Using the Fractal Dimension to Cluster Datasets. In *Proceedings of the sixth ACM SIGKDD international conference on Knowledge discovery and data mining*, pages 260–264, New York, USA, 2000.

[8] A. Bifet, G. Holmes, R. Kirkby, and B. Pfahringer. MOA : Massive Online Analysis. *The Journal of Machine Learning Research*, 11:1601–1604, 2010.

[9] F. Cao, M. Ester, W. Qian, and A. Zhou. Density-Based Clustering over an Evolving Data Stream with Noise. In *Proceedings of the 2006 SIAM International Conference on Data Mining*, pages 328–339, 2006.

[10] F. Cao and A. Zhou. Fast Clustering of Data Streams Using Graphics Processors. *Journal of Software*, 18(2):291–302, 2007.

[11] M. Charikar, L. O'Callaghan, and R. Panigrahy. Better streaming algorithms for clustering problems. In *Proceedings of the Thirty-fifth ACM Symposium on Theory of Computing - STOC '03*, pages 30–39, New York, USA, 2003. ACM Press.

[12] Y. Chen and L. Tu. Density-based clustering for real-time stream data. In *Proceedings of the 13th ACM SIGKDD International Conference on Knowledge Discovery and Data Mining*, pages 133–142, New York, USA, 2007. ACM Press.

[13] S. Cook. *CUDA Programming: A Developer's Guide to Parallel Computing with GPUs*. Newnes, 2012.

[14] CUDA Toolkit Documentation. http://docs.nvidia.com/cuda/index.html.

[15] R. Farber. *CUDA Application Design and Development*. Elsevier, 2011.

[16] M. Gaber, A. Zaslavsky, and S. Krishnaswamy. Mining data streams: a review. *ACM Sigmod Record*, 34(2):18–26, 2005.

[17] L. Golab and M. T. Özsu. Issues in data stream management. *ACM SIGMOD Record*, 32(2):5–14, June 2003.

[18] S. Guha, A. Meyerson, N. Mishra, R. Motwani, and L. O'Callaghan. Clustering Data Streams: Theory and Practice. *IEEE Transactions on Knowledge and Data Engineering*, 15(3):515–528, May 2003.

[19] S. Guha, N. Mishra, R. Motwani, and L. O'Callaghan. Clustering data streams. In *Proceedings of the 41st Annual Symposium on Foundations of Computer Science*, pages 359–366. IEEE Comput. Soc, 2000.

[20] Y. Luo, Z. Ni, and Z. Yangge. New fractal clustering algorithm on data stream. *Computer Engineering and Applications*, 46(6):136–138, 2010.

[21] A. Mahdiraji. Clustering data stream: A survey of algorithms. *International Journal of Knowledge-based and Intelligent Engineering Systems*, 13:39–44, 2009.

[22] MOA. http://moa.cms.waikato.ac.nz/.

[23] H. Nasereddin. Stream Data Mining. *International Journal of Web Applications (IJWA)*, 1(4):183–190, 2009.

[24] L. O'Callaghan, N. Mishra, and A. Meyerson. Streaming-data algorithms for high-quality clustering. In *Proceedings of the 18th International Conference on Data Engineering*, pages 685–694, Washington, DC, 2002.

[25] A. Rodriguez and A. Laio. Clustering by fast search and find of density peaks. *Science*, 344(6191):1492–1496, June 2014.

[26] D. Roger, U. Assarsson, and N. Holzschuch. Efficient stream reduction on the GPU. In *Workshop on General Purpose Processing on Graphics Processing Units*, Boston, United States, 2007.

[27] H. Sun, G. Yu, Y. Bao, F. Zhao, and D. Wang. CDS-Tree : An Effective Index for Clustering Arbitrary Shapes in Data Streams. In *Proceedings of the 15th International Workshop on Research Issues in Data Engineering: Stream Data Mining and Applications (RIDE-SDMA'05)*, pages 81–88. IEEE, 2005.

[28] U. Verner, A. Schuster, and M. Silberstein. Processing data streams with hard real-time constraints on heterogeneous systems. In *Proceedings of the 25th International Conference on Supercomputing*, Tucson, Arizona, 2011.

[29] N. Wilt. *The CUDA Handbook: A Comprehensive Guide to GPU Programming*. Addison-Wesley, 2013.

[30] T. Zhang, R. Ramakrishnan, and M. Livny. BIRCH: an efficient data clustering method for very large databases. In *Proceedings of the 1996 ACM SIGMOD International Conference on Management of Data*, volume 1, pages 103–114, 1996.

[31] T. Zhang, R. Ramakrishnan, and M. Livny. BIRCH: A new data clustering algorithm and its applications. *Data Mining and Knowledge Discovery*, 1(2):141–182, 1997.

[32] Y. Zhang and F. Mueller. GStream: A general-purpose data streaming framework on GPU clusters. In *International Conference on Parallel Processing (ICPP)*, number 1, pages 245 – 254, Taipei City, 2011. IEEE.

[33] Y. Zheng, Z. Ni, S. Wu, and L. Wang. Data stream cluster algorithm based on mobile grid and density. *Computer Engineering and Applications*, 45(8):129–131, 2009.

[34] W. Zhu, J. Yin, and Y. Xie. Arbitrary Shape Cluster Algorithm for Clustering Data Stream. *Journal of Software*, 17(3):379–387, 2006.

Scalable Clustering Algorithm via a Triangle Folding Processing for Complex Networks

Ying Kang[1,2], Xiaoyan Gu[1]*, Weiping Wang[1], Dan Meng[1]
[1]Institute of Information Engineering, Chinese Academy of Sciences, Beijing, China
[2]University of Chinese Academy of Sciences, Beijing, China
{kangying, guxiaoyan}@iie.ac.cn

ABSTRACT

Facing up to the incessant growth of complex networks, more and more researchers start turning to a multilevel computing paradigm with high scalability for clustering. By virtue of iterative coarsening level by level, the clustering results which are obtained from the coarsest network and then projected to the original network, is superior to the ones from mining the original complex network explicitly. Empirical works reflect that the local-aggregation characteristic is a key point for multilevel clustering algorithms, thus techniques like modularity, label propagation etc. are used to discover the micro-clusters for coarsening. In this paper, we propose a scalable clustering algorithm via a triangle folding processing for complex networks(SCAFT). Based on the strong cluster property of triangle, we fold each traversed triangle of the network into a superverex to realize coarsening. And each generated coarsened network by iteration is capable of reserving the cluster structures of last level network, or even the intrinsic cluster structures of original complex network, improving the computational accuracy. What's more, a streaming algorithm is embedded in our novel approach to generate a serial input sequence of vertices, reducing the heavy burdens of memory usage of system. Experimental results on real-world complex networks show that, SCAFT outperforms the state-of-the-art multilevel clustering algorithms in terms of clustering accuracy, running time, especially in memory usage.

Categories and Subject Descriptors

I.5 [**Pattern Recognition**]: Clustering

General Terms

Algorithms

Keywords

multilevel clustering, triangle folding, streaming algorithm

CIKM'15, October 19-23, 2015, Melbourne, VIC, Australia.
Copyright 2015 ACM 978-1-4503-3794-6/15/10 ... $15.00.
http://dx.doi.org/10.1145/2806416.2806563.

1. INTRODUCTION

Clustering is an efficient and foundational technique for analyzing complex networks, which are derived from a wide range of application domains like biological networks, social networks, the World-Wide-Web etc. By means of identifying the dominant structures and grouping the similar instances together [37], clustering converts the perspective of analyzing complex networks to a mesoscale (cluster) to simplify the difficulty of studying. In addition, the potential information is easier to discover, and the deep insight on complex networks becomes possible. However, the unprecedent expansion of complex networks has posed lots of new challenges, inducing the traditional clustering algorithms like spectral clustering [2], divisive clustering [21] etc. hard to analyze the networks with millions of vertices or more. Therefore, how to extend the capability of clustering algorithms to large-scale complex networks is paramount.

Except for the improved existing clustering algorithms by heuristic skills, lots of researchers focus on data preprocessing, i.e. collecting available meta-data [28], sampling for sparsification [36], reducing the dimensions of feature space [6] etc. As is known to us, it is impractical to have some valuable information about data in hand for the unsupervised learning scenarios. Lack of valid sampling probability, the accuracy of clustering results from data sparsification is often out of expectation. Although dimensional reduction stresses the predominant sub-space, the quantity of data in primitive space has not been cut down, which inevitably leads to a high computational task. The deficiencies of the discussed methods above limit their further researches and applications.

To analyze the large-scale complex networks, plenty of approximate methods emerge successively, of which a multilevel clustering paradigm is proved more fast and scalable. This paradigm is stemmed from the typical algorithm Metis [14], subsequently is used for all kinds of learning scenarios. With respect to the clustering applications, there are many multilevel algorithms such as the modularity-based method [25], the density-based method [12] and the label-propagation-based method [31] etc. By coarsening the input large-scale complex network level by level into a sequence of coarsened networks, the cluster structures of the initial complex network can be approximately projected by the initial clustering results from the coarsest network. Many empirical works demonstrate that the implicit clustering results from the deduction of initial mined clusters after multilevel coarsening are better than the results from analyzing the original complex network explicitly [1]. In-depth studying in multilevel clustering paradigm shows that the local-aggregation characteristic is a key factor. Therefore, based on the local strong cluster property of triangle [29], we propose a scalable clustering algorithm via a triangle folding processing for complex networks(SCAFT). By virtue of folding the traversed triangles which stand for micro-clusters, the multilevel coarsening process is realized and the intrinsic cluster structures of original complex network have been kept, improving the clustering accuracy. In addition, a streaming algorithm is employed to reduce the memory usage. Experimental results on real-world complex networks demonstrate the prominent performances of our proposed approach SCAFT.

2. RELATED WORK

Clustering analysis in complex networks has been proceeded and developed for decades in manifold fields. To meet the versatile application demands, apart from the traditional clustering algorithms like k-means [23], agglomerative hierarchical clustering [11], modularity-based clustering [26] etc., many mixture models equipped with other discipline theories have appeared, such as maximum margin clustering [34] which comes from the supervised learning scenario of support vector machine, probability generation modeling which originates from statistics [18], random walking based clustering [30], genetic algorithm based clustering [5], Potts-model based clustering [24], resistance analog modeling [33] etc. The advantages of these clustering algorithms have been exhibited in many applications, but their ability of mining large-scale complex networks is restricted by the high computational complexity.

Within a certain error tolerance, approximating computation is a better choice to settle the clustering problems with large-scale complex networks. According to some probability, a proportion of sub-network can be sampled to represent the original complex network, lowing the actual size of network to be analyzed. Of these approximate methods, the Nyström method based spectral clustering [10] or kernel k-means [32] are more efficient. To expand the scalability of spectral clustering with high accuracy and global optimal solution, or reduce the computational complexity of kernel k-means caused by dimensional increment, many researches adopt the Nyström method to generate low-rank approximate matrices to speed up the entire clustering procedure. However, the saved time and space are obtained at the cost of the accuracy of clustering results.

Multilevel clustering is a rising popular technique with superior scalability. It is initially proposed for graph partitioning (Metis [14]) by Karypis, and then developed for clustering such as Graclus [9] by Dhillon, and MMLSC [25] by Rotta etc. These algorithms have the common 'maximal matching based edge selection' coarsening policy. A matching of network is to select a set of edges so that in the set there are no two edges incident on a same vertex, and a maximal matching means that the number of matched edges ready for coarsening is as large as possible. This sort of coarsening policy has several drawbacks as follows: (1) the maximal matching is a hard problem [13]; (2) despite the collapsed two vertices are joined by a same edge, it is uncertain that both of them belong to a same cluster; (3) it is unsuitable for a category of special networks whose degree of nodes follows a power-law distribution [1].

To break the limitation of existing multilevel clustering algorithms listed above, recently lots of researches on multilevel clustering have been promoted. Shiokawa et al. coarsened the input network by the modularity-based incremental aggregation and pruning process [27]. Although there is no need to traverse all vertices, the computation of modularity and additional optimization of vertex-selecting order is costly, and the cluster information for pruning is often insufficient. Huang et al. shrunk the micro-clusters detected by DBSCAN into supervertices [12]. Similar to DBSCAN, even though the discovery of micro-clusters based on local density is relative easier than the global searching, the computational complexity of mining parameter-free micro-clusters is higher. Wang et al. utilized the label propagation algorithm to search for the micro-clusters of network for coarsening [31], which was implemented fast. However, the over shrinkage of vertices is liable to induce confusion between adjacent micro-clusters. Thus the refinement step which adds extra operations into the entire system is indispensable.

3. OVERVIEW OF MULTILEVEL CLUSTERING

In general, a complex network is depicted as a graph $G = (V, E, W)$, where vertex $v \in V$ represents one data instance (or entity) of complex network, edge $e \in E$ represents some kind of relationships between vertices, edge weight $w \in W$ represents the degree of connection and the value of w could be unit or numerical. The computing process of multilevel clustering consists of three phases which is displayed in Figure 1. And the definition of multilevel clustering is depicted as follows [14]:

Definition 1 (Multilevel Clustering)
Input: *Large-scale graph G, iterator $i=0$ and initialize a transitional graph $G_i = G$, threshold T.*
Output: *k clusters of G.*
Process:
1. ***Coarsening phase:*** *search for vertex subsets of G_i based on some coarsening policy and fold each vertex subset into a supervertex; generate the coarsened graph G_{i+1} and save it; if $(|V_{G_{i+1}}| \leq T?)$ continue next step, else $i = i + 1$ and return to 1;*
2. ***Initial clustering phase:*** *mine k initial clusters of the coarsest graph G_m by some high-performance clustering algorithm;*
3. ***Uncoarsening and refinement phase:*** *unfold each coarsened graph from the coarsest G_m level by level in an inverse order, project the initial clusters to graph G and refine the cluster affiliation of unfolded vertices from supervertices to obtain the eventually clustering results.*

There are three key points which concern the computational complexity of multilevel clustering algorithms in Definition 1. One is to select a high-quality clustering algorithm for initial clustering, meanwhile focus on the accumulated edge weights. Another is to refine the cluster affiliation of random free vertices which are generated by unfolding supervertices during uncoarsening, improving the eventual accuracy of clustering results. The last one is how to detect an appropriate subset of vertices to be folded into a supervertex, which is the most important. If all vertices folded into a supervertex actually belong to the same cluster, the uncertainty of whether the vertices unfolded from a super-

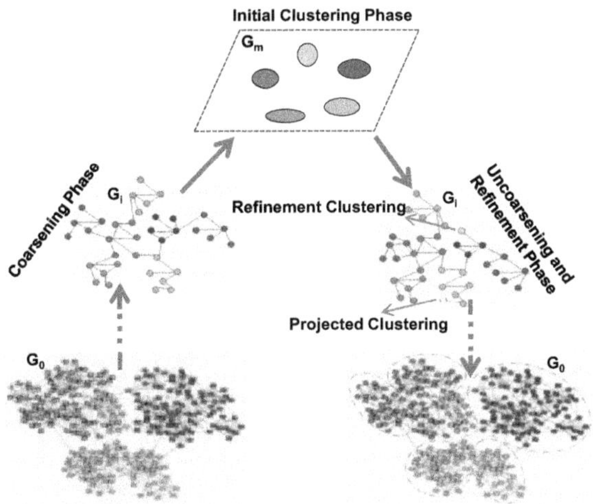

Figure 1: The composed three phases of multilevel clustering

vertex pertaining to a same cluster or not will be eliminated. Moreover, it's obvious that the cluster structures of original graph (or network) would not be destroyed by the iterative coarsening, so the initial clustering results from the coarsest graph G_m can project the basic clusters of original graph almost identically, and the refining operations can be omitted nearly or simplified enormously during the uncoarsening procedure. Shrinking two vertices incident on one edge tends to lose this promise, and the maximal matching is hard to match completely, especially when the distribution of node degree is out of balance. Micro-cluster computed by means of modularity or density has the better local-aggregation property which can keep up this promise, but in essence, the computation of these methods is a kind of local cluster mining process which is time-consuming.

Differing from all the multilevel clustering algorithms discussed above, in this paper we select triangles as the vertex subsets, and fold each traversed triangle of network for coarsening to realize the multilevel clustering. In theory, because of the complete connection among all the inner vertices, clique is a local definition of cluster [22], thus clique with any order (n-clique) ought to be considered as a micro-cluster. However, the computational difficulty of higher-order clique (n-clique, $n \geq 4$) will rise exponentially with the increasing of value of order and size of network, even for 4-clique. To the contrary, triangle (3-clique) owns the most simple structure, while its traversing procedure is the easiest. And relative to other local-aggregation micro-cluster detected by some clustering algorithm, the complexity of multilevel clustering based on searching for triangles of networks will be reduced greatly. Meanwhile, triangle is able to comply with the promise of the vertices which one supervertex contains affiliating to the same cluster, thus the initial clustering and eventual clustering results are much better. In addition, to lower the space complexity of multilevel clustering, we input the vertices of network serially by a streaming algorithm. And with respect to all the triangles incident on each streaming-input vertex, we only traverse the triangle with the largest modularity gain [8], reducing the randomness of triangle selection for folding and coarsening results.

4. PROPOSED APPROACH: SCAFT

4.1 Foundation

Triangle is the ubiquitous topological structures in vast majority of complex networks [7], thus lots of research works adopt triangle as an entry point for deep learning on complex networks. According to Latapy's analysis [17], counting all triangles of a network graph needs $\Theta(m^{3/2})$ time and $\Theta(3m + 3n)$ memory, where m is the number of edges and n is the number of vertices. But fortunately, there is no need to search for all triangles in the coarsening procedure for our proposed multilevel clustering algorithm SCAFT. Let's consider an example in Figure 2. Obviously, there are three clusters of the simple network graph in Figure 2(a), while Figure 2(b) shows the coarsened graph by triangle folding (TF), and edges $\langle b, e\rangle$, $\langle f, i\rangle$ and $\langle m, o\rangle$ are newly generated. Obviously, the coarsened graph in Figure 2(b) keeps the basic cluster structures. Moreover, Figure 2(a) contains 9 triangles, but only 4 triangles are used to be folded, the remaining triangles disappear with the adjacent folded triangles, which can reduce the entire computational complexity of multilevel clustering enormously.

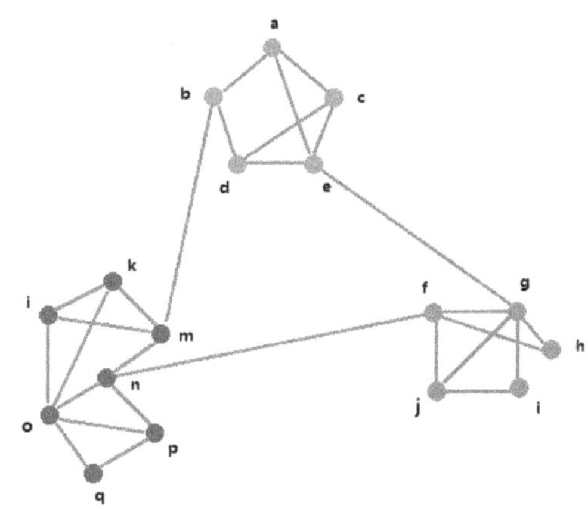

(a) a simple network graph

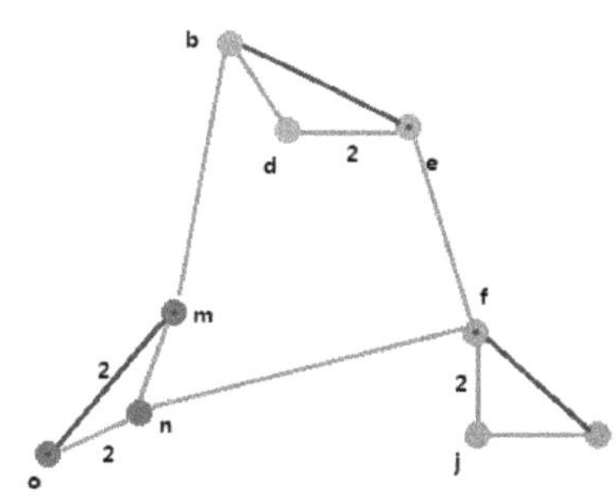

(b) coarsened graph by triangle folding

Figure 2: Coarsening based on triangle folding.

The structures of real-world networks are much more complicated so that the iterative coarsening is going on level by level. When the coarsening levels are built up, the high-order polygons of network graph will become lower-order polygons or even triangles of next level coarsened graph. This transformation is produced by the adjacent relation between polygons and folded triangles as well. It is significant for SCAFT that, when the original network graph is coarsened deeper and deeper, the process of high-order polygons gradually evolving into triangles can make the sustainability of iterative coarsening.

4.2 Streaming-based Triangle Folding Process

Due to the $\Theta(3m + 3n)$ memory usage for counting triangles, the space complexity of multilevel clustering by folding the traversed triangles for large-scale complex networks is higher. Therefore, in order to reduce the memory usage in each level coarsening, we adopt a streaming algorithm to input each vertex of graph serially, and search for one of its adjacent triangles to be folded into a supervertex. The streaming detection is not executed in the beginning, owing to lack of sufficient vertices which are affiliated to the same triangle with the input vertex. Here two policies are proposed to tackle this problem. One is to input the subsequent vertex as close to the last vertex as possible. The other is to save the header sequence of streaming input vertices into memory, and start searching for a triangle incident on the next input vertex when 30 percent of memory is occupied. these two policies are the premise of streaming-based triangle folding process. In essence, the initial overlook of triangles incident on a certain number of vertices input firstly will not affect the eventual clustering results, because they can be saved for next level coarsening. The whole process is described as follows:

Definition 2 (Streaming-based Triangle Folding Process (STF))
Input: *Streaming input vertex* v^t *of* G_i *at time t.*
Output: *Generated supervertex* v_s*.*
Process: *Detect all triangles incident on* v^t*; if existing, then select an optimal triangle to be folded into a supervertex* v_s*, else place* v^t *in memory explicitly;* $t = t + 1$*.*

Until now, someone may doubt what does 'an optimal triangle' mean? As is known to us, vertices with high degree often have more adjacent triangles than vertices with low degree. This imbalance will lead to the randomness of coarsening results, similarly signifies that different choice of triangles incident on the input vertex will generate different coarsened graphs. One efficient settlement to this problem is to order the vertex selection, but it is not applicable to the streaming algorithm. Therefore, we make use of the modularity gain as a metric to measure the quality of micro-clusters (adjacent triangles), and select the triangle with an optimal modularity gain to be folded. Based on a weighted network graph, the modularity Q is defined in Equation 1 [20]:

$$Q = \frac{1}{\sum_{ij} w_{ij}} \sum_{ij} [w_{ij} - \frac{\sum_j w_{ij} \sum_i w_{ij}}{\sum_{ij} w_{ij}}] \delta(c_i, c_j) \quad (1)$$

where w_{ij} denotes the weight of edges between cluster i and j, function $\delta(c_i, c_j)$ equals 1 if $c_i = c_j$, otherwise equals 0. And the definition of modularity gain ΔQ is depicted in Equation 2.

$$\Delta Q = [\frac{W_T + W_{v^t,in}}{2m} - (\frac{W_{all} + W_{v^t}}{2m})^2] - [\frac{W_T}{2m} - (\frac{W_{tot}}{2m})^2 - (\frac{W_{v^t}}{2m})^2] \quad (2)$$

where W_T is the sum of edge weights in triangle T, $W_{v^t,in}$ is the sum of weights of edges incident on v^t in T, W_{tot} is the sum of weights of edges incident on T, W_{v^t} is the sum of weights of edges incident on v^t, m is the sum of edge weights in graph.

Let's view back the streaming-based triangle folding process briefly. Initially, each streaming input vertex of graph is assigned to an independent cluster. Starting at some time t, detect all triangles incident on a streaming input vertex v^t, compute the modularity gain ΔQ by Equation 2 for each triangle which is assumed as a micro-cluster, and select the triangle with maximum gain to be folded. By virtue of the modularity gain ΔQ, two kinds of randomness are eliminated with furthest but not completely. One is the selection of triangles incident on the streaming input vertex v^t, the other is the orders of the streaming input vertices. Because of the optimal triangle selected by ΔQ to be folded, no matter what the streaming input order of vertices is, the overall coarsening process is proceeded by the continuous optimized modularity gain ΔQ, which can make the final results in line with the optimal value of modularity Q.

4.3 Algorithm SCAFT

The implementation of the proposed scalable clustering algorithm via a triangle folding processing for complex networks (SCAFT) is depicted in Algorithm 1. And the concrete description of *Detectalltriangle()* in Algorithm 1 is shown in Algorithm 2, where $D(v)$ denotes the degree of vertex v, $F(v)$ denotes a flag bit, and $N(v)$ denotes the set of vertices adjacent to v.

The core of SCAFT is the streaming-based triangle folding process (STF) for coarsening. During the iterative coarsening procedure, a sequence of coarsened graphs G_1, G_2,..., G_m are generated, satisfying $|V_G| \geq |V_{G_1}| \geq |V_{G_2}| \geq ... \geq |V_{G_m}|$. Each level coarsening based on the traversed triangles folding of graph G_i is an independent procedure, by loop iteration of which the whole coarsening procedure of SCAFT is built up. Note that the information of each level intermediate coarsened graph has to be stored, in support of the subsequent uncoarsening operations.

SCAFT appreciates the initial clustering phase much more than the uncoarsening phase, which is different from most of current multilevel clustering algorithms. As is discussed before, due to the same cluster affiliation of the vertices of one triangle, the triangle folding based coarsening process can maintain the intrinsic consistency of cluster structures between the coarsened graph G_i and the original graph G, thus the initial clustering results determine the entire computational accuracy of SCAFT immensely. Therefore, we select a high-quality spectral clustering algorithm [2] for the initial analysis of cluster structures, which is superior to other traditional clustering algorithms and the computing results are globally optimal.

Under the premise of the first two phases of SCAFT, one of which is guaranteeing the basic cluster structures, and the other is making use of the high-quality clustering algorithm, the cluster structures of the input large-scale network have been mined and restored mostly by initial clustering. In consequence to some extent, there is no need to refine the

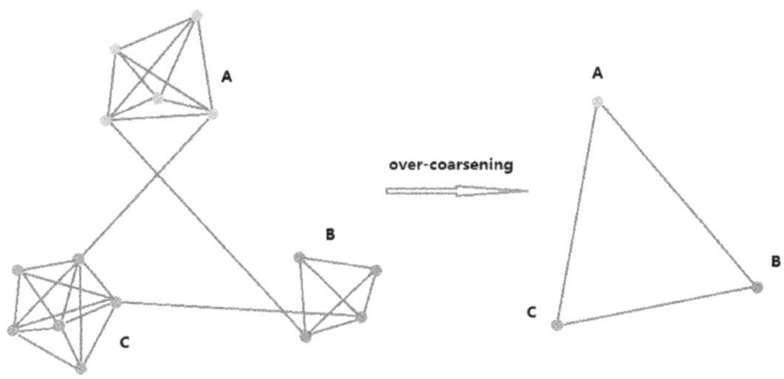

Figure 3: The phenomenon of over coarsening.

cluster affiliation results from the intermediate uncoarsened graphs, because the random free vertices which are generated by unfolding supervertices do not exist.

In another way, by means of the streaming algorithm producing a vertex input sequence, lots of memory usage during coarsening is saved, lowing the space complexity of SCAFT. And the randomness of adjacent-triangle searching can be eliminated maximally but not completely by acquired optimal modularity gain value (ΔQ). After all, all of the multilevel clustering algorithms are approximate computing methods.

Here we need to pay attention to a special phenomenon 'over coarsening', which is shown in Figure 3. The over coarsening phenomenon is a random event with low probability, but happens when the folded triangles locate in the same high-order maximal complete subgraph. If without any constraints, the number of edges within clusters will decrease dramatically, so that it is almost equivalent to the ones between clusters, obscuring the boundary and losing the meaningful cluster structures with local-aggregation property. As is exhibited in Figure 3, clusters A, B and C eventually degenerated into three vertices. Whereas in *Detectalltriangle()*, we make use of the flag bit $F(v)$ set to prevent over coarsening efficiently, and experiences reflect that the best situation is that the number of coarsened triangles incident on a same vertex is no more than 2.

In summary, compared with the state-of-the-art multilevel clustering algorithms like Metis, Mmc and Shrink etc., the proposed algorithm SCAFT skips the heavy computation of maximal matching, and leaves out searching for the local micro-clusters and the refining operations, accelerating the entire analyzing process of multilevel clustering. And the initial clustering adopts a high-quality spectral clustering algorithm to enhance the accuracy. Furthermore, the computing procedure of SCAFT based on a streaming algorithm saves much memory usage of system.

4.4 Complexity Analysis

In the sequel, let's analyze the computational complexity of SCAFT.

Lemma 1 (Complexity) *The time complexity of SCAFT is $\Theta(Lm^{3/2})$ and the space complexity is smaller than or identical to the main memory, where m is the number of edges of graph G, L is the number of coarsening iteration.*

Algorithm 1 SCAFT

Input: Large-scale network graph $G = (V, E, W)$, iterator $i = 0$, threshold T
Output: k clusters of G
1: Initialize a transitional graph $G_i = G$
2: **Coarsening:**
3: **repeat:**
4: Scan vertex v^t of G_i at time t
5: **while** occupation of memory $\leq 30\%$ **do**
6: Save v^t in memory, $t = t + 1$ and return step 2
7: **endwhile**
8: *Detectalltriangles*(v^t)
9: **if** there is no triangle
10: Save v^t in G_{i+1} explicitly
11: **else**
12: Compute ΔQ for each triangle
13: Select the triangle with the optimal value of ΔQ to be folded into supervertex v_s
14: Save v_s in G_{i+1}
15: **until** No available vertex remained in G_i
16: **if** $|G_{i+1}| \leq T$
17: i=i+1 and go on
18: **else**
19: i=i+1 and return step 2
20: **Initial Clustering:**
21: Clustering the coarsest graph G_i by a high-quality spectral clustering algorithm
22: **Uncoarsening without Refinement:**
23: Project the initial clustering results to G by unfolding supervertices of each coarsened graph level by level inversely, eventually obtaining k clusters of G

Proof. Relative to the original large-scale network graph, the size of the generated coarsest graph could be nearly ignored, and owing to the refinement omitted, the time consumption of initial clustering and uncoarsening is far little. Thus the time complexity of SCAFT mainly depends on coarsening. Review Algorithm 1, there are two nested loops during the coarsening procedure, the aim of which is to traverse all the edges of graph in $\Theta(m)$ time; while the innermost loop concealed by *Detectalltriangle()* is the intersecting computation, which can be completed in $\Theta(\sqrt{m})$ time; thus the whole procedure of counting all triangles of graph takes $\Theta(m^{3/2})$ time in the worst case. But SCAFT has not to traverse all the triangles on account of the adjacent relation with the folded triangles(refer to aforementioned section). The other hand is the coarsening iteration, and the number of iteration levels L differs far from m in several orders of magnitude. Therefore to sum up, the The time complexity of SCAFT is little than $\Theta(Lm^{3/2})$. In addition, due to the efficient streaming algorithm which is high-spatial-compression, the memory usage of SCAFT for clustering large-scale graph has been saved enormously.

5. EXPERIMENTS

In this section, we will evaluate the performances of our proposed algorithm SCAFT on several real-world complex networks. Two sub-experiments will be executed respectively. Firstly in comparison with the 'maximal matching based edge selection coarsening policy' which is embedded in Metis [14], we demonstrate that SCAFT which assumes the

Algorithm 2 Detectalltriangle()

```
Input: one vertex v of network graph G
Output: one set of detected triangles which are all incident on vertex v
Begin
    Initialize a triangle set Δ_v = NULL;
    If (F(v) ⩽ 1) Then
       Break;
    Else
       For (each vertex u in N(v)) Do
          If (D(u) ⩾ D(v)&&F(u) ⩽ 1) Then
              Continue;
          End If
          For (each vertex w in N(v) ∩ N(u)) Do
                If (D(w) ⩾ D(v)&&D(w) ⩾ D(u)&&F(w) ⩽ 1) Then
                  Continue;
               Else
                  Put triangle(u,v,w) in Δ_v;
                  F(v) = F(v)+1; F(u) = F(u)+1; F(w) = F(w) + 1;
                  Break;
               End If
          End For
       End For
   Output Δ_v;
   End If
End
```

triangle folding based coarsening policy is fit for the power-law complex networks. Secondly by contrast to SCAFT, we choose four multilevel clustering algorithms such as Metis, Mmc [27], Shrink [12] and Mlp [31] as baseline for experiments. Both Metis and Mlp are the graph partitioning algorithms, which need to be varied a little for clustering before experimental operations. All of the experiments are executed on a Linux machine with a 2.6GHz 4Core CPU and 8G main memory, and all algorithms are implemented in Java.

5.1 Datasets and Experimental Setup

Our experimental datasets are listed in two tables respectively for two different sub-experiments. The datasets in Table 1 come from the Stanford University's SNAP networks [35], and the two networks Actor and Google are the typical instances whose degree of nodes follows the power-law distribution. With regard to the first sub-experiment, we only focus on the coarsening phase of both algorithms (Metis and SCAFT) on Actor and Google. And along with the coarsening process goes on level by level, the ratio of the size (number of nodes or number of edges) of each level coarsened graph to the one of the original network graph varies, which are plotted as the charts in Figure 4.

The datasets in Table 2 are collected from a wide range of repository. Wiki-Talk, Parents, LiveJournal and Twitter are online networks from the Stanford University's SNAP Database [35]. R-MAT is a random-generated scale 24 network [4]. Wiki-Links is an article-link-represented network [15]. Sk-2005 is a crawl of Slovakian domain using UbiCrawler [3]. Structured RDF network DBpedia is generated from Wikipedian data [19].

All the real-world complex networks in Table 2 own their

Table 1: Complex networks with power-law distribution.

Network	Vertex Number	Edge Number	$N_v = \alpha d^{\beta}$(power-law function, N_v is the number of nodes, d is the degree of nodes, α, β are parameters)	
			α	β
Actor	625,058	2,011,703	2.61	-1.89
Google	875,713	5,105,039	1.41	-2.23

Table 2: Description of real-world complex networks.

Network	Vertex Number	Edge Number	Diameter
Wiki-Talk	2.1M	4.6M	9
Parents	3.8M	16.5M	22
LiveJournal	4M	34.7M	16
R-MAT	7.2M	129M	8
Twitter	12.3M	91.8M	21
Wiki-Links	25.5M	498M	170
sk-2005	51M	1.8B	308
DBpedia	62M	190M	8

real clusters, which can be referred as the ground-truth clustering results. Thus we can compare the analyzing accuracy of each algorithm by the following two criteria, and no matter which one is selected, the greater calculated value means the better clustering results.

1. ***Normalized Mutual Information (NMI).*** **NMI** [16] is such a metric that it is able to maintain the balance between clustering quality and number of clusters, the definition of which is:

$$NMI = \frac{-2\sum_{ij} N_{ij}\log(\frac{N_{ij}N}{N_{i.}N_{.j}})}{\sum_i N_{i.}\log(\frac{N_{i.}}{N}) + \sum_j N_{.j}\log(\frac{N_{.j}}{N})} \quad (3)$$

where N denotes the confusion matrix, N_{ij} is the number of vertices in $C_i \bigcap C_j$ (C denotes cluster), $N_{i.}$ and $N_{.j}$ denote the sum on row i and column j of N respectively.

2. ***Rand Index (RI).*** **RI** [16] is a measure of similarity, and its definition is:

$$RI = \frac{TP + TN}{TP + FP + FN + TN} \quad (4)$$

where TP, FP, FN, TN respectively denote true positives, true negatives, false positives, false negatives. Their concrete meanings are omitted here.

We partition the second sub-experiment into two parts to evaluate SCAFT. The first part is used to test the elimination of random searching for the objective folded triangles by the modularity gain. Based on **NMI**, we compute the clustering results of eight real-world networks by SCAFT on two different conditions. One is selecting the folded triangle randomly, the other is selecting an optimal triangle base on the maximal modularity gain ΔQ. The comparative results are drawn in Figure 4. The second part is to compare the performances of SCAFT with other multilevel clustering algorithms in terms of accuracy, time complexity and space occupation. The results of **RI**, running time and memory usage on eight networks are collected in Table 3, Table 4, Table 5 respectively.

5.2 Analysis of Experimental Results

The trend of folding lines in Figure 4 (no matter Figure 4(a) or Figure 4(b)) exhibits that, the capability of SCAFT to coarsen networks complied with the power-law distribution is superior to Metis. Obviously, the folding line of Metis has an asymptotic ratio value more than zero, which implies that the coarsening process of Metis is terminated much earlier. The main reason of this phenomenon is that the imbalance of node-degree distribution limits the maximal matching extremely. To the contrary, the coarsening process of SCAFT goes on. Therefore, SCAFT is suitable to analyze the power-law networks. In addition, under the same horizontal axis, the coarsening reduction ratio of Metis is lower than SCAFT after the identical number of coarsening levels; under the same vertical axis, Metis needs more coarsening levels than SCAFT to obtain the equivalent coarsening reduction ratio. Therefore, we can also conclude from Figure 4 that, SCAFT is able and suitable to analyze the power-law complex networks, which can also be an explanation for further measuring results of SCAFT in running time and memory usage.

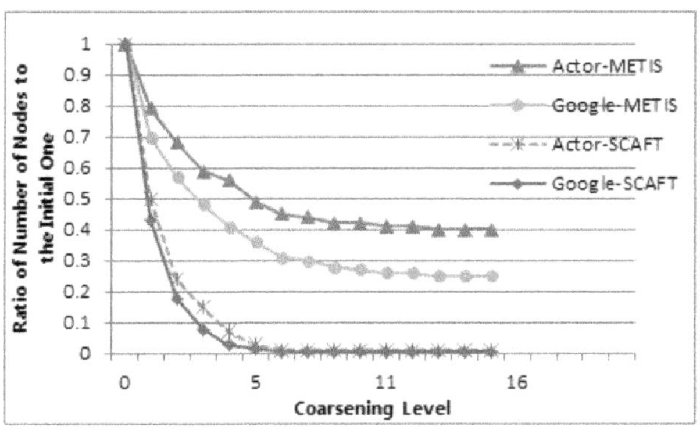

(a) the reduction of nodes

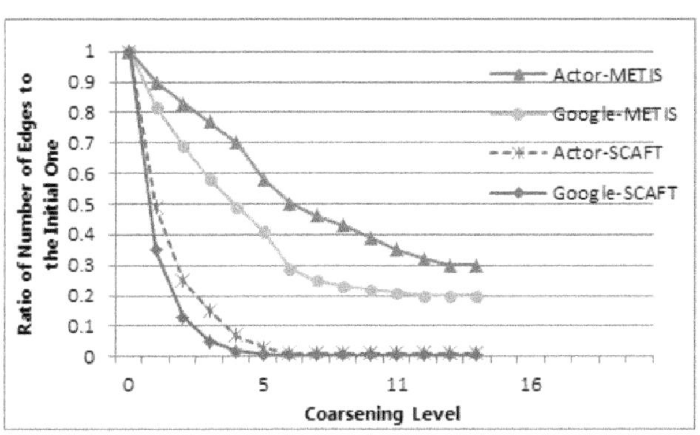

(b) the reduction of edges

Figure 4: The comparison of coarsening capability on power-law complex networks.

Table 3: RI comparison of different algorithms on datasets.

Network	Metis	Mmc	Shrink	Mlp	SCAFT
Wiki-Talk	0.835	0.879	0.901	0.812	0.905
Parents	0.669	0.707	0.715	0.684	0.717
LiveJournal	0.772	0.811	0.836	0.817	0.829
R-MAT	0.646	0.682	0.703	0.673	0.701
Twitter	0.751	0.795	0.806	0.789	0.810
Wiki-Links	0.713	0.725	0.724	0.716	0.728
sk-2005	0.808	0.827	0.839	0.821	0.843
DBpedia	0.747	0.768	0.798	0.782	0.803

Subsequently, let's analyze the clustering results in Figure 5. With regard to the graph of each network, there are two broken lines expressing the different clustering accuracy of **NMI** on two conditions. One is the clustering results from searching for one folded triangle incident on the streaming-input vertex randomly, the other is the results from selecting the triangle with the largest value of modularity gain ΔQ as a micro-cluster. Each broken line of each graph is composed of eight independent executing results under the same experimental condition (by random or ΔQ). Obviously, the value of **NMI** with random searching is volatile, that is because, if there are many triangles incident on one streaming-input vertex, different selections of adjacent triangle to be folded result in different coarsened graphs. Moreover, the generated coarsened graphs and clustering results are different from each other. By contrast, the value of **NMI** based on the modularity gain is plain, demonstrating that the clustering results from SCAFT by folding triangles with the optimal modularity gains ΔQ for coarsening are much more stable.

The scalability of multilevel graph clustering can be concluded from all the experimental results in Table 3, Table 4 and Table 5. Any one of the five algorithms in comparison can analyze the large-scale network graphs efficiently. In the sequel, let's compare the different performance indices of five algorithms in detail separately.

The **RI** comparison of different algorithms is shown in Table 3, which is used to measure and compare the clustering accuracy. From Table 3, we can observe that the **RI** of Metis is the lowest, that is because the coarsened graphs generated by shrinking two vertices incident on one edge, is not capable of guaranteeing the consistence of cluster structures of the coarsened graphs with the ones of the original graph. To the contrary, the other algorithms promise this point. But due to the over shrinkage of vertices which is prone to induce boundary confusion among adjacent micro-clusters, the **RI** of Mlp is relative lower than Mmc, Shrink and SCAFT. The reason of the **RI** of Shrink being higher than Mmc is that, Shrink is realized by two metrics of modularity and density. By contrast with Shrink, the **RI** of SCAFT is higher except for LiveJournal and R-MAT which are caused by random errors in accident, displaying the better performances of SCAFT in computational accuracy.

The different running time results of five algorithms on eight network graphs are listed in Table 4. There is on doubt that the time consuming of Metis is the largest, which is mainly caused by the computational procedure of maximal matching and the low coarsening reduction ratio. The

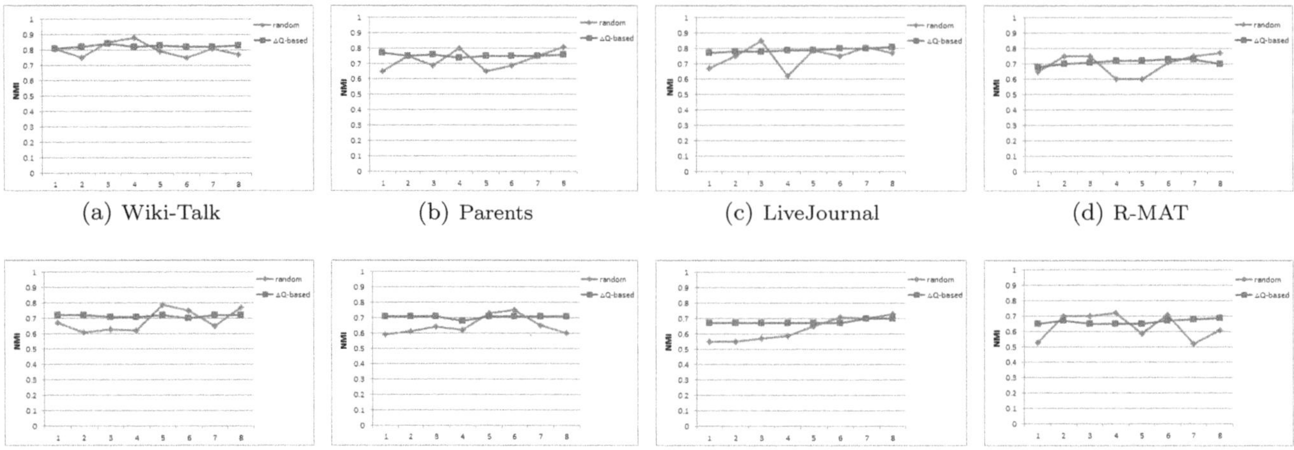

(a) Wiki-Talk (b) Parents (c) LiveJournal (d) R-MAT

(e) Twitter (f) Wiki-Links (g) sk-2005 (h) DBpedia

Figure 5: The different clustering accuracy NMI of SCAFT on two conditions. One is selecting one folded triangle incident on the streaming input vertex randomly, the other is selecting the triangle with the highest value of modularity gain ΔQ to be folded.

Table 4: Running time(s) comparison of different algorithms on datasets.

Network	Metis	Mmc	Shrink	Mlp	SCAFT
Wiki-Talk	376	139	158	102	91
Parents	485	187	209	156	113
LiveJournal	591	192	216	179	122
R-MAT	887	376	403	345	217
Twitter	1670	730	791	679	395
Wiki-Links	3110	1400	1490	1260	746
sk-2005	4940	2270	2310	2010	1210
DBpedia	8140	3660	3700	3280	1490

Table 5: Memory usage(GB) comparison of different algorithms on datasets.

Network	Metis	Mmc	Shrink	Mlp	SCAFT
Wiki-Talk	4.87	0.97	1.12	0.53	0.03
Parents	8.93	1.61	1.83	0.87	0.05
LiveJournal	9.79	1.80	2.05	1.01	0.06
R-MAT	19.2	2.92	3.31	1.55	0.13
Twitter	28.4	4.05	4.97	2.46	0.18
Wiki-Links	67.1	11.6	13.0	6.4	0.49
sk-2005	142.5	25.3	27.8	13.1	1.16
DBpedia	150.8	28.9	31.4	15.2	1.28

detection of local micro-clusters, which is based on the modularity or density clustering algorithms, needs to take much time to complete, thus the running time of Mmc and Shrink is more than Mlp and SCAFT. Because of the boundary confusion resulted from the over shrinkage, there demands plenty of extra time to refine the initial clustering results, thus the time complexity of Mlp is higher than SCAFT. Moreover, the omitted computational processes of the micro-cluster searching and refining operations have saved lots of CPU time for SCAFT.

By virtue of embedding a streaming algorithm into our proposed multilevel clustering approach, the space complexity of SCAFT can be reduced vastly, which is proved by the comparison results of memory usage on eight complex networks, with the smallest space occupation of SCAFT in Table 5. Corresponding to the highest time complexity of Metis, its memory usage is the largest of five algorithms. Different from the analytical accuracy on **RI** and running time, the size of coarsened graphs which are generated from the over shrinkage of vertices is much smaller, thus the space occupation of Mlp is smaller than Metis, Mmc and Shrink. The larger memory usage of Shrink than Mmc is caused by the much more computation on double micro-cluster discovery metrics.

6. CONCLUSION

Inspired by the performance preponderance of multilevel clustering paradigm and the local-aggregation characteristic, we propose a scalable clustering algorithm via a triangle folding processing for complex networks (SCAFT). Different from the existing multilevel algorithms, SCAFT assumes a novel traversed-triangle folding based coarsening policy to put the performance of multilevel clustering forward. On account of the strong cluster effect of triangle, the cluster structures of coarsened graphs generated by SCAFT are in line with the basic ones of the original network. Thus the initial clustering results from the coarsest network after iterative coarsening level by level, suffice for the entire projection of the clusters in the initial large-scale complex network nearly, promoting the analytical accuracy of multilevel clustering paradigm. Moreover, by means of an embedded streaming algorithm, the memory usage of SCAFT is reduced greatly, and the randomness of searching for the folded triangle incident on each serially streaming-input vertex is eliminated mostly by the optimal modularity gain. Lots of experimental results on large-scale real-world complex networks demonstrate that, the computational complexity of SCAFT is far lower than the state-of-the-art multilevel clustering algorithms, especially in memory usage, and the RI comparison of five algorithms on eight datasets displays the prominent performance of SCAFT in clustering accuracy. Besides, there is only one limitation of that SCAFT is applicable to the learning scenarios where the objective complex networks are rich in triangles.

Acknowledgments

This work is supported by the National Science Foundation of China under grant number 61402473, KeJiZhiCheng Project under grant number 2012BAH46B03, National HeGaoJi Key Project under grant number 2013ZX01039-002-001-001, and "Strategic Priority Research Program" of the Chinese Academy of Sciences under grant number XDA06030200.

7. REFERENCES

[1] A. Abou-Rjeili and G. Karypis. Multilevel algorithms for partitioning power-law graphs. In *The 20th International Parallel and Distributed Processing Symposium (IPDPS 2006)*, April 2006.

[2] M. Belkin and P. Niyogi. Laplacian eigenmaps and spectral techniques for embedding and clustering. In *Advances in Neural Information Processing Systems 14*, pages 585–591, 2001.

[3] P. Boldi, B. Codenotti, M. Santini, and S. Vigna. Ubicrawler: a scalable fully distributed web crawler. *Software: Practice & Experience*, 34, 2003.

[4] D. Chakrabarti, Y. Zhan, and C. Faloutsos. R-mat: A recursive model for graph mining. In *SIAM International Conference on Data Mining*, 2004.

[5] C. Chira, A. Gog, and D. Iclanzan. Evolutionary detection of community structures in complex networks: A new fitness function. In *Evolutionary Computation (CEC), 2012 IEEE Congress on*, pages 1–8, June 2012.

[6] R. Chitta, R. Jin, and A. K. Jain. Efficient kernel clustering using random fourier features. In *IEEE 12th International Conference on Data Mining (ICDM 2012)*, pages 161–170, Dec 2012.

[7] S. Chu and J. Cheng. Triangle listing in massive networks and its applications. In *Proceedings of the 17th ACM SIGKDD International Conference on Knowledge Discovery and Data Mining*, (KDD 2011), pages 672–680, 2011.

[8] L. Danon, A. Díaz-Guilera, and A. Arenas. The effect of size heterogeneity on community identification in complex networks. *Journal of Statistical Mechanics*, 2006(11):P11010, 2006.

[9] I. S. Dhillon, G. Y, and B. Kulis. Weighted graph cuts without eigenvectors: A multilevel approach. *IEEE Transactions on Pattern Analysis and Machine Intelligence*, 29(11):1944–1957, 2007.

[10] C. Fowlkes, S. Belongie, F. Chung, and J. Malik. Spectral grouping using the nystrom method. *IEEE Transactions on Pattern Analysis and Machine Intelligence*, 26(2):214–225, Feb 2004.

[11] R. Gil-Garcia, J. M. Badia-Contelles, and A. Pons-Porrata. A general framework for agglomerative hierarchical clustering algorithms. In *The 18th International Conference on Pattern Recognition (ICPR 2006)*, volume 2, pages 569–572, 2006.

[12] J. Huang, H. Sun, J. Han, H. Deng, Y. Sun, and Y. Liu. Shrink: A structural clustering algorithm for detecting hierarchical communities in networks. In *Proceedings of the 19th ACM International Conference on Information and Knowledge Management*, (CIKM 2010), pages 219–228, 2010.

[13] G. Karypis, R. Aggarwal, V. Kumar, and S. Shekhar. Multilevel hypergraph partitioning: applications in vlsi domain. *Very Large Scale Integration (VLSI) Systems, IEEE Transactions on*, 7(1):69–79, March 1999.

[14] G. Karypis and V. Kumar. A fast and high quality multilevel scheme for partitioning irregular graphs. *SIAM J. Sci. Comput.*, 20(1):359–392, 1998.

[15] J. Kunrgis. Konect–the koblenz network collection. 2014.

[16] V. Labatut. Generalized measures for the evaluation of community detection methods. *CoRR*, abs/1303.5441, 2013.

[17] M. Latapy. Main-memory triangle computations for very large (sparse (power-law)) graphs. *Theor. Comput. Sci.*, 407:458–473, 2008.

[18] C. Li and G. Biswas. Improving clustering with hidden markov models using bayesian model selection. In *2000 IEEE International Conference on Systems, Man, and Cybernetics*, volume 1, pages 194–199, 2000.

[19] M. Morsey, J. Lehmann, S. Auer, and A. N. Ngomo. Dbpedia sparql benchmark: Performance assessment with real queries on real data. In *Proceedings of the 10th International Conference on The Semantic Web*, (ISWC 2011), pages 454–469, 2011.

[20] M. Newman. Fast algorithm for detecting community structure in networks. *Physical Review E*, 69, September 2003.

[21] M. E. J. Newman and M. Girvan. Finding and evaluating community structure in networks. *Phys. Rev. E*, 69(2):026113, feb 2004.

[22] G. Palla, I. Derl̨enyi, I. Farkas, and T. Vicsek. Uncovering the overlapping community structure of complex networks in nature and society. *Nature*, 435(7043):814–818, June 2005.

[23] W. L. Ping and A. T. L. Phuan. Centroid stability with k-means fast learning artificial neural networks. In *Proceedings of the International Joint Conference on Neural Networks*, volume 2, pages 1517–1522, July 2003.

[24] J. Reichardt and S. Bornholdt. Detecting fuzzy community structures in complex networks with a potts model. *Physical Review Letters*, 93(21):218701, 2004.

[25] R. Rotta and A. Noack. Multilevel local search algorithms for modularity clustering. *J. Exp. Algorithmics*, 16:257–268, 2011.

[26] P. Schuetz and A. Caflisch. Efficient modularity optimization by multistep greedy algorithm and vertex mover refinement. *Physical Review E*, 77(4):046112, 2008.

[27] H. Shiokawa, Y. Fujiwara, and M. Onizuka. Fast algorithm for modularity-based graph clustering. In *AAAI*. AAAI Press, 2013.

[28] G. M. Slota, K. Madduri, and S. Rajamanickam. Pulp: Scalable multi-objective multi-constraint partitioning

for small-world networks. In *IEEE International Conference on Big Data (ICBD 2014)*, pages 481–490, Oct 2014.

[29] P. Sun and L. Gao. Fast algorithms for detecting overlapping functional modules in protein-protein interaction networks. In *IEEE Symposium on Computational Intelligence in Bioinformatics and Computational Biology (CIBCB 2009)*, pages 247–254, March 2009.

[30] S. A. Tabrizi, A. Shakery, and M. A. et al. Personalized pagerank clustering: A graph clustering algorithm based on random walks. *Physica A: Statistical Mechanics and its Applications*, 392(22):5772–5785, 2013.

[31] L. Wang, H. W. Y. Xiao, and B. Shao. How to partition a billion-node graph. In *IEEE 30th International Conference on Data Engineering (ICDE 2014)*, pages 568–579, March 2014.

[32] C. K. I. Williams and M. Seeger. Using the nyström method to speed up kernel machines. In *Advances in Neural Information Processing Systems*, pages 682–688, 2001.

[33] F. Wu and B. A. Huberman. Finding communities in linear time: a physics approach. In *The European Physical Journal B - Condensed Matter and Complex Systems*, volume 38, pages 331–338, 2004.

[34] L. Xu, J. Neufeld, B. Larson, and D. Schuurmans. Maximum margin clustering. In *Advances in Neural Information Processing Systems*, pages 1537–1544, 2005.

[35] J. Yang and J. Leskovec. Defining and evaluating network communities based on ground-truth. In *IEEE 12th International Conference on Data Mining (ICDM 2012)*, pages 745–754, Dec 2012.

[36] L. Yue, A. Joshi, P. Aashish, L. John, and J. Ghosh. Analyzing and improving clustering based sampling for microprocessor simulation. In *The 17th International Symposium on Computer Architecture and High Performance Computin (SBAC-PAD 2005)*, pages 193–200, Oct 2005.

[37] K. Zhang, I. W. Tsang, and J. T. Kwok. Maximum margin clustering made practical. *IEEE Transactions on Neural Networks*, 20(4):583–596, April 2009.

Understanding the Impact of the Role Factor in Collaborative Information Retrieval

Lynda Tamine
Université de Toulouse UPS IRIT
118 Route de Narbonne
F-31062 Toulouse, France
tamine@irit.fr

Laure Soulier
Université de Toulouse UPS IRIT
118 Route de Narbonne
F-31062 Toulouse, France
soulier@irit.fr

ABSTRACT

Collaborative information retrieval systems often rely on division of labor policies. Such policies allow work to be divided among collaborators with the aim of preventing redundancy and optimizing the synergic effects of collaboration. Most of the underlying methods achieve these goals by the means of explicit vs. implicit role-based mediation. In this paper, we investigate whether and how different factors, such as users' behavior, search strategies, and effectiveness, are related to role assignment within a collaborative exploratory search. Our main findings suggest that: (1) spontaneous and cohesive implicit roles might emerge during the collaborative search session implying users with no prior roles, and that these implicit roles favor the search precision, (2) role drift might occur alongside the search session performed by users with prior-assigned roles.

Categories and Subject Descriptors

H.3.3 [**INFORMATION STORAGE AND RETRIEVAL**]: Information Search and Retrieval - *Search process*

General Terms

Collaborative Information Retrieval

Keywords

Collaborative information retrieval; user behavior analysis; user study

1. INTRODUCTION

In [11], the authors define collaborative information seeking (CIS) as *"the study of the systems and practices that enable individuals to collaborate during the seeking, searching, and retrieval of information"*. Broadly speaking, collaboration allows people to create and share collective knowledge within a work team to identify and resolve a shared complex problem [24].

CIKM'15, October 19–23, 2015, Melbourne, Australia.

ACM 978-1-4503-3794-6/15/10 ...$15.00.
DOI: http://dx.doi.org/10.1145/2806416.2806481.

Collaboration outlines three main paradigms (division of labor, awareness and sharing of knowledge) that avoid redundancy between collaborators and favor the synergic effects of collaboration [10, 25]. Division of labor has been highlighted as the most important paradigm for allowing a work team to cover different facets of a search while minimizing the redundancy between the actions of the involved members [25, 26]. To address these concerns, CIS tools are based on three main approaches to division of labor: user-driven approaches [20, 7], system-mediated approaches [10, 23, 29], and user-driven system-mediated approaches [31]. Focusing on the commonalities that exist between them, we can observe that all of them rely on the user's role as the means of work coordination toward the achievement of the overall task goal. The primary difference among these approaches is the underlying users' role specifications and uses during the collaborative task. In user-driven approaches to the division of labor, users' roles can be either (1) fixed (e.g., searcher/writer) and then assigned to users before the search or (2) freely negotiated and created by the collaborators during the search according to their preferences and search and knowledge skills. In both cases, communicative and interactive interfaces are used to ensure search awareness and coordination. In contrast, in the case of system-mediated approaches, users' roles are automatically leveraged via algorithmic mediation to optimize the search session effectiveness. However, this mediation adapts the search toward the same fixed roles regardless of the user's involvement in the search activity. To maintain the advantages of the two former approaches and address their limitations, a hybrid approach, which is referred to as the user-driven system-mediated approach [31], has been proposed. In this approach, based on users' activities, the roles (from within a set of fixed roles) in which they fit best are dynamically learned, and then the search is algorithmically mediated accordingly.

Based on these approaches and the related studies, we conjecture that regardless of the underlying mediation policy, proper specification of users' roles, whether performed in advance or dynamically during the search, is critical because it might alter the synergic effects of the collaborative task. How the synergic effects are altered depends on the gap between (1) how the users are expected to behave under (system or human) role assignment and (2) how they really behave during the collaborative search activity. This potential alteration is problematic for CIS designers because it leads to the creation of processes and technologies that do not fit with natural, collaborative information behavior. Relatively few fundamental studies have addressed this issue

[19, 25], and to the best of our knowledge, this work is the first empirical comparison of an assigned, role-based collaborative information search and a non-assigned-role-based one in terms of users' search behavior and effectiveness. Through close examination of users' interaction processes and search strategies, we thoroughly study the importance of role factor within a collaborative search process, with the goal of achieving useful and effective collaboration. The results can inform the design of future CIS/collaborative information retrieval (CIR) systems.

The remainder of this paper is organized as follows. Section 2 presents the background for our study, including previous work regarding CIS and the research questions addressed in the paper. Section 3 describes the study design. Section 4 details the study results and presents related discussions. Section 5 highlights the study implications, and Section 6 concludes the paper.

2. BACKGROUND

2.1 Related Work

A collaborative search task can be defined as a complex process that involves several users who interact with each other with the goal of addressing a shared information need. Previous studies [28, 29] have demonstrated the benefits of such a setting for gathering the complementary skills of individual users to solve complex tasks, such as fact-finding tasks (e.g., travel planning) [19] or exploratory search tasks [29]. Within the latter, insufficient knowledge or skills of individual users is the main reason that motivates them to collaborate, which allows collaborators to attain a synergic effect in which *"the whole (is) greater than the sum of all"* [28]. CIS results in collaborative information behavior processes, such as information sharing, evaluation, synthesis, sense-making and utilization of the retrieved information [14]. Whereas search behavior model in an individual search context is well-studied [32, 17], few research works have focused on the collaborative setting [15, 18, 8]. Evans and Chi [8] examined the collaboration process in social searches and defined three main phases in which collaborators interact with each other to optimize the task outcome. Before a search, collaborators' interactions mainly focus on refining the information need and structuring the task guidelines. During the search, users interact within a sense-making process via querying or information foraging, with the aim of increasing the search effectiveness. After the search, they collaboratively interact to assess the collective relevance of the results. Other works investigated a deeper level in the search behavior understanding by focusing either on the collaboration search pratices [19] or the impact of communication channels on collaborative search [13]. Using qualitative and quantitative analysis, the authors highlighted the important need to propose adapted collaborative systems (e.g., relying on audio tools) which would avoid redundant search actions or limit the cognitive effort of collaborators.

To optimize search behaviors among collaborators, three main principles guide the collaboration process: (1) avoiding redundancy between users' actions (division of labor), either at the document level [9] or role level [23, 29], (2) favoring information flow among users (sharing of knowledge), either implicitly by search inference [10] or explicitly by collaborative-based interfaces [22, 26], and (3) informing users of other collaborators' actions (awareness) [26]. In this paper, we focus specifically on the division of labor principle, which can be traced through three levels of mediation that result in specific user behaviors [25]. First, coordination between collaborators can be naturally induced through explicit discussions or exchanges. For this reason, interfaces that allow the users to be freed from specific actions by providing communication and organization-based support have been proposed [28]. The authors examined the communication process in collaborative search settings and found that even if it does not impact the search effectiveness, communication helps collaborators to address many aspects of the information needs. Second, designing adaptive interfaces for collaboration is a key challenge, as noted by Joho et al. [16]. Some of the proposed interfaces [20, 22] facilitate division of labor by allowing users to split and manually distribute the search results among collaborators. Third, algorithmic mediation [9, 23, 29] focuses on the interface background; this process consists of automatically ranking documents in response to queries formulated by the users. Collaborators are no longer the owners of the search session progress because their search results are the outcomes of a ranking algorithm that takes their context into consideration. Recently, a hybrid mediation-based approach was proposed [31]. The core of the underlying method is to assign roles to users based on the differences in their search actions, with the aim of optimizing information retrieval performance.

For all of these approaches, division of labor can be exercised based on collaborators' roles, thus enabling structuring of the search process [25] among collaborators and minimizing redundant actions. Golovchinsky et al. [12] define a role taxonomy that involves several pairs of roles, such as domain A expert/domain B expert, search expert/search novice and prospector/miner (PM). Within the last pair of roles, the *prospector* favors diversity in the search results by opening new exploration fields in the information space, whereas the *miner* ensures the quality and richness of the explored documents. Practically, the role of the prospector is to identify several facets of the information need by skimming documents, whereas the miner is responsible for in-depth reading of the documents to select the most relevant ones. In [29], the authors define the pair of gatherer/surveyor (GS). Whereas the *gatherer* aims at quickly selecting relevant documents, the *surveyor* has the objective of covering a wide range of results to better understand the nature of the information needed to explore the potential exploratory fields and to determine why queries are suboptimal. These roles are complementary because the gatherer can search relevant information alone, whereas the surveyor needs the collective intelligence to ensure topical diversity, which enables a better understanding of the information need landscape.

2.2 Research Questions

The two main conclusions that one can draw from the literature review are the following: (1) the synergic effects of collaboration may be achieved through coordination approaches regardless of whether roles are explicitly assigned to collaborators, (2) a collaborative search task results in a large range of specific user behavioral facets (e.g., communicating with peers, formulating queries, skimming or reading in-depth documents, selecting/splitting results, and sense-making). To design efficient support processes for CIS and CIR, we need to (1) fully understand how users' search behavior changes in a collaborative search session with respect to the division of labor policy and (2) measure how these changes impact the synergic effects of collaboration. However, there is a lack of studies that address role specification as a critical factor that can either facilitate or inhibit the collaboration effectiveness. Unlike previous work that focused on the synergic effects of collaboration compared with individual searches [28], we want to extend our understanding of the differences in users' behaviors in role-oriented and non-role-oriented CIR scenarios. In particular, we wish to focus on an exploratory web search task for which we believe that role-based coordination is challenging. Indeed, several studies have previously demonstrated that role-based coordination particularly benefits from synergic collaboration among searchers to address different aspects of the search results [6, 23, 26]. We address this issue by performing a user study that allows comparing and contrasting both search scenarios. In the study, the role-based scenario relies on well-known, state-of-the-art roles, namely the PM [23] (defined in the role taxonomy of [12]) and GS [29] pairs. Our study provides insight into the real manifestations of division of labor policies in each collaborative search scenario and enables us to emphasize the strengths of each, which could be combined to achieve synergic collaboration. We address the following research questions:

- RQ1: How do user search behaviors that result from collaborating with assigned roles differ from those of users that collaborate without pre-defined roles?
- RQ2: To what extent, if any, does the coordination of a collaborative group with assigned roles differ from the coordination of a collaborative group without roles?
- RQ3: Do users with assigned roles respect the role guidelines? If not, what are the main underlying reasons that they do not?
- RQ4: What is the effect of role assignment on the search results effectiveness?

To answer these research questions, we postulate the following hypotheses:

- H1: The behaviors of collaborators are complementary with respect to division of labor policies [30].
- H2: Differences in the behaviors of members that belong to the same working group represent complementarity signals [31].

3. METHODOLOGY

Our user study involved 75 pairs of users that performed a collaborative exploratory search task. With respect to the study objective, users were assigned to different collaborative search scenarios: (1) search with no-prior roles and (2) search with a prior fixed role, either the prospector and miner [12, 23] or the gatherer and surveyor [29] pair of roles. The log data from the user study are available under the conditions specified[1]. Below, we describe the experimental protocol, including participants, system, search tasks, and processed data.

3.1 Participants

In this study, we recruited participants by dyads, under the constraint that they already knew each other and had already worked on collaborative projects together, to facilitate collaboration during the experiments. The collaborators, who were mainly undergrad and Ph.D. students, were between 18 and 30 years old. All of them had experience in browsing the web and using search engines. For their involvement in the user study, participants received material compensation (worth $20), and the three most effective groups received an additional gift (worth $50). Participants were randomly assigned to one of the search settings that we considered: 25 dyads for the scenario in which there was no prior explicit role assignment, which we refer to as W/oRole, and 50 dyads for the scenario in which there was fixed role assignment prior to the search, which we refer to as W/Role. The dyads were split into PM and GS pairs.

[1]contact authors: tamine,soulier@irit.fr

Table 1: **Collaborative task example**

The mayor of your countryside village must choose between building a huge industrial complex or developing a nature reserve for animal conservation. As forest preservationists, you must raise awareness about the possibility of wildlife extinction surrounding such an industrial complex. ***Yet, before warning all citizens, including the mayor, you must do extensive research and collect all the facts about the matter. Your objective is to create a claim report together, outlining all the possible outcomes for wildlife should the industrial complex be built.*** *Your focus is on wildlife extinction. You must investigate the animal species involved, the efforts done by other countries and the association worldwide to protect them and the reasons we, as humans, must protect our environment in order to survive.* ***You must identify all relevant documents, facts, and pieces of information by using bookmarks, annotations, or saving snippets. If one document discusses several pieces of useful information, you must save each piece separately using snippets. Please assume that this research task is preliminary to your writing, enabling you to provide all relevant information to support your claims in your report.***

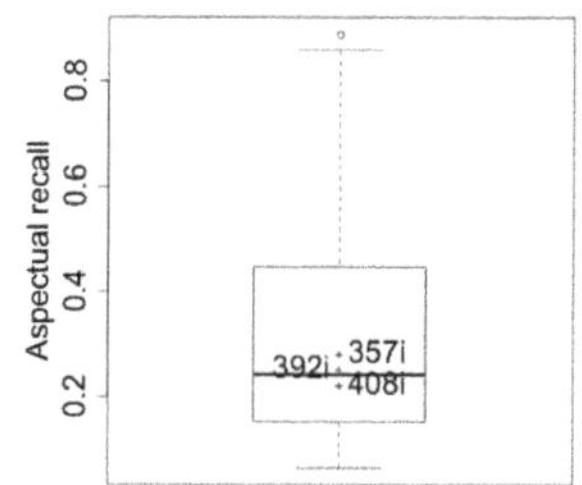

Figure 1: **Aspectual recall analysis over TREC Interactive topics**

3.2 System

To support collaborative search actions, we used an extension of the lab-study open-source Coagmento collaborative search system[2] [27], which we downloaded in December 2013. This version consists of a Firefox plugin that enables tracking of collaborators' actions throughout a web search session and consists of a toolbar that allows participants to rate, annotate and snip web pages. We extended the open-source version by replacing the bookmark option with a page rating tool and including a sidebar with a chat system and an action viewer that enable participants to see the results of the actions (namely, bookmarked, annotated and snipped pages) of their collaborators. To capture all of the participants' actions, we asked them to exchange information only through the chat system.

[2]https://github.com/kevinAlbs/CoagmentoCollaboratory

Table 2: **Pre-task and post-task questionnaires**

	Questions	Possible responses
Pre-Task Questions	1. How old are you?	a) 15-20 years old b) 21-25 years old c) 26-30 years old d)+30 years old
	2. What is your gender?	a) Female b) Male
	3. How often do you use search engines?	a) More 10 times/day b) 2-3 times/day c) Less than 1 time/day d) Less than 1 time/week
	4. How much experienced in web browsing are you?	From 1 (very experienced) to 4 (not experienced at all)
	5. What kind of tools do you use for web search?	a) Search engines b) Social networks c) Direct browsing d) Other
	6. Which web searcher do you use the most?	a) Bing b) Google c) Yahoo d) Other
	7. Are you used to collaboratively work on project or web search?	a) Daily b) Weekly c) Monthly d) Yearly e) Never
	8. What do you think about collaborative work?	a) Enriching b) Useful c) Useless d) Conflictual
Post-Task Questions	1. Have you already participated in such user study? If yes, please describe it.	Free-answer
	2. What do you think about this collaborative manner of seeking information?	Free-answer
	3. What was the level of difficulty of the task?	a) Easy (Not difficult) b) Moderately difficult c) Difficult
	4. What was task difficulty related to?	Free-answer
	5. Could you say that the collaborative system supports your search?	a) Yes b) Not totally c) Not at all
	6. How could we improve this system?	Free-answer

3.3 Tasks

All of the groups within each search setting aimed to solve the same synchronous, collocated, exploratory information search task for which information needs were extracted from the Text Retrieval Conference (TREC) 6-7-8 Interactive track. Because the TREC Interactive topics are designed for exploratory search tasks and lead TREC participants to cover all the aspects (i.e., facets) of the information needs [21], they have already been used in previous CIR research [9, 23]. According to the study objective, we modified the formulation of the TREC topics into collaborative search tasks. An example task description is presented in Table 1. The collaborative facets of the task are highlighted in bold. To limit the effects of knowledge on the search behaviors and effectiveness [32], we allowed the groups that belonged to different search settings to select the topics to be explored. However, to control the effect of the search topic across the different search settings, we first identified homogeneous topics. To achieve this goal, we used the TREC Interactive search logs to select topics that had similar aspectual recall scores [21] that were near the median, as illustrated in Figure 1 (topics 329*i*, 347*i* and 408*i*). Finally, we assigned the topics to the participants with their agreement.

Role guidelines were also supplied to guide the division of labor policy within the search task. We used the PM and GS role pairs, which were designed in previous work for solving exploratory search tasks. The pairs of roles are complementary in the sense that each pair corresponds to one of the two dimensions of the division of labor (search activity [12, 23] and content exploration [29]), and they enable collaboration between dyads or within a small group of collaborators. To allow for fair comparisons between the W/oRole and each of the W/Role pairs, namely PM and GS, we considered collaborative settings based on dyads. Below, we describe the peculiarities of each search setting:

- *W/oRole* (topic 408i): This setting did not include any role guidelines and thus allowed participants to freely organize collaboration throughout the search session.
- *PM* (topic 392i): We used the role guidelines described in [23]: (1) the prospector "opens new fields for exploration into a data collection" and (2) the miner "ensures that rich veins of information are explored".
- *GS* (topic 347i): The role guidelines were extracted from [29]: (1) the gatherer "scan[s] results of the joint search activity of team members to discover the most immediately relevant information", (2) the surveyor "browse[s] a wider diversity of information to obtain a better understanding of the nature of the collection being searched, to understand where the current queries might be failing, and to identify potential avenues of exploration".

The role guidelines were first presented to participants in a written format and then orally explained during a separate face-to-face meeting to highlight the main differences: (1) both the gatherer and miner aim to identify the most relevant documents for the core of the information need, but the former briefly analyses documents, whereas the latter looks deeper into the document content. (2) The surveyor and prospector both focus on diversity, but the role of the surveyor is more than a simple "new content tracker"; rather, the surveyor aims to explore a large area of the information need landscape.

3.4 Data

The user study consisted of a 4-step task:

1. *A sign-up and pre-task questionnaire*, which is described in Table 2, in which the pairs of participants registered their team and provided some demographic information, such as their age, gender and browsing behavior. To assign the roles for the most suited member in the team, the questionnaire included 2 additional questions extracted from [23, 29]. For the GS role allocation, we asked "Who is the most likely to fit with these behaviors: (1) quickly scan pages displayed by a web searcher? and (2) browse documents not necessarily related to the main topic?" For the PM, the question was, "Who is the most likely to fit with these behaviors: (1) identifying the most highly relevant documents? and (2) browse documents not necessarily related to the main topic?"

2. *A training step* during which participants completed a system tutorial that introduced the collaborative system and let them test its functionalities for a few minutes.

3. *The 30-minute search task.* The automatically collected data included participants' search log data, which were issued from physical actions such as visiting pages or expressing feedback (annotations, snippets, and bookmarks)

Table 3: **Behavior-based features**

Feature	Description
npq	Average number of visited pages by query
dt	Average time spent between two visited pages
nf	Average number of relevance feedback information (snippets, annotations & bookmarks)
qn	Average number of submitted queries
ql	Average number of query tokens
qo	Average ratio of shared tokens among successive queries
nbm	Average number of exchanged messages within the search groups

Table 4: **Chat message categories [13]**

	Description	Examples issued from our studies
(TC)	Task coordination: All types of statements which involve decision making about how the task should be performed	Let's divide the work. Look at the definition, I look on the issues.
(TN)	Task content: All types of statements which include information assessment, layout, structure, and revision of report	I found something interesting *www.nhc.noaa.gov/*
(TS)	Task social: All types of statements that concern group functioning, effort, or latitude, as well as opinions regarding to information obtained or information sources	What do you think about this definition? We are doing well
(NT)	Non-task related: All statements that are not related to the assignment or regarding technical issues of system being used	I can't see my snippets How to remove snippets?
(NC)	Non-codable: All types of statements that do not belong to any category specificities	Ok Thanks

according to the features presented in Table 3. These features, which were defined based on the literature [1], model users' behaviors and search experience. All of the behavioral features analyzed in our study were tested for homogeneity in the different collaborative settings by performing outlier detection based on the Chebyshev inequality [2]. To exploit the chat messages exchanged between the collaborative group members, we manually annotated the entire pool of messages following the categorization proposed in [13] and presented in Table 4. Each message was qualitatively examined for content by two graduate students and then categorized. For categorization, strong evidence regarding the participants' feelings had to be expressed in the message, according to the category description. The agreement level between the two assessors was estimated using Cohen's kappa coefficient. We obtained a value equal to 0.71, which indicated substantial agreement. To check the coding consistency, the students met to make consensual decisions about the final categorization.

4. A *post-task questionnaire* (Table 2) that collected participants' feedback after the search task. In this study, we focused on questions 3 and 4 of the post-task questionnaire, which concerned the level and type of difficulty, respectively, that participants encountered during the search. We note that question 4 was a free-answer question for which a coding scheme was constructed with the six main categories presented in Table 5. Because one answer could be labeled in multiple categories, the agreement level between the two assessors was estimated using the Jaccard index; the value was 0.77, which indicates substantial agreement. The assessors

Table 5: **Categorization of participants' responses about the nature of task difficulty**

Categ.	Description	Examples
Page	All statements about web page relevance	Identify relevant information within noisy pages
Comm.	All statements including communication concerns	Exchange through the chat system instead of by voice
Org.	All statements focusing on task organisation	Split search tasks
Topic	All statements concerning the task topic	Focus on the task and do not disgress
Technic.	All statements related to system technical issues	The chat system window is too small
Role	All statements connected to role assignment	It is difficult to keep my role

discussed the cases of disagreement to assign a consensual category.

4. RESULTS AND DISCUSSION

In this section, we present and discuss the results. Then, we enumerate the primary findings that emerged from them. We used both quantitative and qualitative methods for the analysis, as detailed below.

4.1 Analyzing users' behavioral differences

Our aim here was to examine the effects of the role factor on the users' behavior. The search groups' behavioral activities were inferred from physical actions such as visiting pages or expressing feedback (annotations, snippets, and bookmarks). For this purpose, we collected search log data and modeled the users' behavior according to the features presented in Table 3. Following [31], we employed a temporal, feature-based representation of each user's u search session using a matrix $S_u^{(t)} \in \mathcal{R}^{t \times n}$, where n is the number of features. Each element $S_u^{(t)}(t_l, f_k)$ corresponds to the cumulative value of feature f_k for user u aggregated from the beginning of the search session until timestamp t_l. Consequently, we performed Kolmogorov-Smirnov tests to assess the significance of the differences between the *W/oRole* scenario and each of the *W/Role* search scenarios. Table 6 provides a summary of groups' search behavior feature values and the associated standard statistical indicators at the end of the search session ($t_l = 30$). To check wether the *W/Role* intra-group users behaved differently as they were assigned different explicit roles, we computed the differences in their intrinsic search behavioral features ($IGDiff^p$ where p represents the significance value of users' difference estimated through a Student test). To further determine whether the observed differences between the search scenarios varied because of the general underlying division of labor policy, either *W/oRole* or *W/Role*, regardless of the role specifications, we lumped the PM and GS pairs of roles together and performed a one-way analysis of variance (ANOVA). Specifically, because the settings *W/oRole* and *W/Role* had unequal sample sizes, which can lead to inhomogeneous variances, we used a one-way Welch ANOVA [5]. The significance of each role factor as determined by the obtained p-value is reported in the last row of Table 6.

We confirm from Table 6 that intra-group users performing a *W/Role* search had significantly different behavioral facets ($IGDiff^p$). We can also see from Table 6 that the search behaviors collected from *W/oRole* collaborative

Table 6: **Search behavior analysis. Mean(s.d.): Mean value of the feature over the groups (standard deviation).** $IGDiff^p$: **Mean value and significance value of the feature difference between collaborators. p-value/role-base setting (PM,GS): significance of the average differences between the no-role-based setting and the role-based setting; ANOVA p-val.: significance of the role factor** ($W/Role$ **vs.** $W/oRole$). ($0.01 < p < 0.05$): **moderately significant *,** ($0.001 < p < 0.01$): **significant ** ,** ($p < 0.001$): **highly significant *****

			Mean(s.d.)						
			npq	*dt*	*nf*	*qn*	*ql*	*qo*	*nbm*
W/Role	GS	Group	1.719(1.06)	9.993(3.37)	58.522(27.13)	65.913(31.54)	4.640(1.11)	0.438(0.18)	20(14.50)
		$IGDiff^p$	-0.524	-3.469***	1.304***	2.087***	1.160***	0.139***	2.230***
	PM	Group	1.884(1.53)	10.469(3.11)	56.308(27.95)	56.308(27.95)	2.791(0.70)	0.391(0.08)	15(12.88)
		$IGDiff^p$	0.242***	1.453***	-2.423***	-1.692***	0.058***	0-0.232***	0.045***
W/oRole		Group	2.085(1.01)	13.159(3.92)	24.125(12.81)	43.583(16.28)	3.673(0.67)	0.446(0.10)	19(11.34)
		p-value/GS	***	***	***	***	***	***	
		p-value/PM	***	***	***	***	***	***	*
W/Role vs. *W/oRole*	ANOVA p-val.			**	***	**		*	

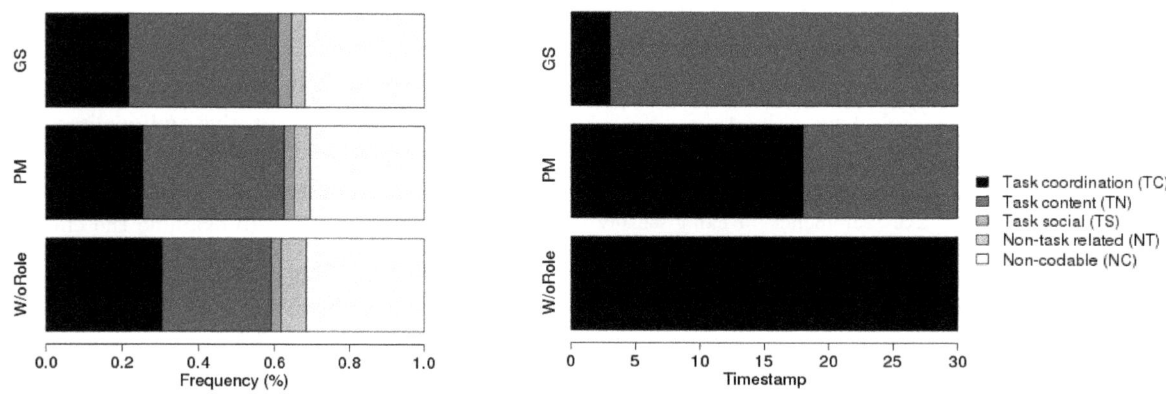

(a) Proportion of message categories for each search setting

(b) Distribution of the most important message categories over the search session timeline

Figure 2: **Communication analysis.**

search sessions differed significantly from those obtained from the *W/Role* search scenarios for almost all features and that the differences in the search policies for the two scenarios explained most of the observed differences. In particular, we observed that groups without prior roles spent a longer time on results pages ($Mean(dt) = 13.159$) than did groups with assigned roles ($Mean(dt) \leq 10.159$), although the former annotated, bookmarked, and snipped less pages ($Mean(nf) = 24.125$) vs. $Mean(nf) \geq 56.308$). This result suggests that given that the users that performed a *W/oRole* search scenario had no search policy, they spent more time scanning pages before selecting a result or refining the query. Therefore, in the same limited search time (30 minutes) as groups with prior roles, groups without prior roles provide less feedback on pages. This result is also confirmed by the analysis of the average number of pages visited per query (*npq*). This slow and exhaustive evaluation style has been demonstrated to be more common among less-experienced users [3]. Thus, we may conclude that the users in the *W/oRole* scenario relied on their limited knowledge about the topic to select web pages according to the relevance of their content, whereas the others used role guidelines to quickly select or discard web pages. Through examination of the query length feature (*ql*), we can note that in the *W/oRole* scenario, the query lengths are significantly different from those of the *W/Role* scenario. The GS (PM) dyads had longer (shorter) query lengths than those in the *W/oRole* scenario. To gain a better understanding of the cause of this result, we analyzed the average difference in the intra-query length features within each collaborative group involved in each scenario. We found relatively important and significant differences for GS search scenarios ($Mean = 1.116, p < 0.001$) but very low differences for both PM ($Mean = 0.058, p < 0.001$) and *W/oRole* ($Mean = 0.549, p < 0.001$) search scenarios. As evident from the role specification, the GS pair of roles is more inclined toward verbose queries because they favor searching diversity [4]. Combining these observations, we can conclude that the differences in query length can be explained by the differences in the role policies involved in the *W/Role* search scenarios, not by the prior assignment of explicit roles. A similar conclusion can be obtained from analysis of the query overlap feature (*qo*). Regarding communication through chat message exchanges (*nbm*), there were few, mostly non-significant differences between the different search scenarios.

To understand why participants communicate, we analyzed the chat messages, categorized as detailed above. Figure 2a reports the proportion of each message category within the communication stream of the collaborative groups in the different search settings. The general outcome of this analysis highlights that collaboration, either

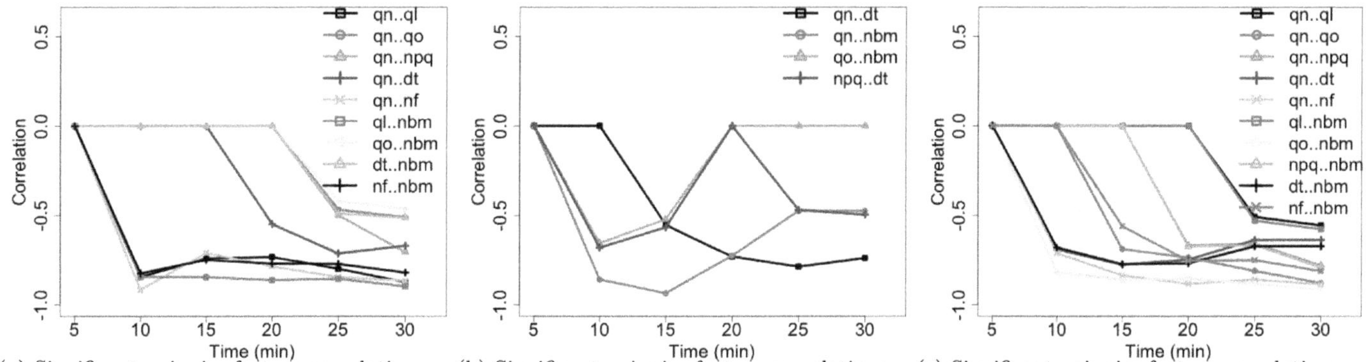

(a) Significant pairwise feature correlations for GS

(b) Significant pairwise feature correlations for PM

(c) Significant pairwise feature correlations for W/oRole

Figure 3: **Collaborators' behavior-based correlation analysis.**

with or without assigned roles, mainly triggered coordinative and content messages. More particularly, we can observe that the most important communication category in the *W/oRole* search scenarios was task coordination (*30.43%*); the fraction of messages in this category was significantly greater than in both the *PM* (*25.42%*) and GS (*21.66%*) search scenarios. This difference reflects the specific need of the users involved in *W/oRole* to bridge the gap, through communication messages, between individual and collaborative perception of the search task as no explicit policy guided their involvement. In contrast, communicating about results was less common in the *W/oRole* searches (*28.64%*) than in the *W/Role* searches (*PM: 37.28%*; *GS: 39.33%*). This could be obviously explained by the increase of coordinative messages in the case of *W/oRole* scenario as shown above. Another assumption is that the role assignment is more functional oriented than content oriented; thus users within role condition are more likely to look for additional knowledge from their peers in order to achieve their involvement in the task. In contrast, users within no role condition are more willing to negotiate their roles according to their skills, which presumably indicates that they are more likely to have a more adequate level of knowledge (than users without prior roles) to perform the task. No apparent differences were observed for the remaining categories. To check whether this tendency was evident over the entire search session, Figure 2b shows the highest proportion of categories for each timestamp ($1-30$). We can confirm that coordination was the main goal underlying communication for collaborators involved in the *W/oRole* scenario and that it dominated all the other categories within the entire timeline of the search. Interestingly, Figure 2b reveals that although the *PM* and *GS* scenarios were quantitatively not significantly different in terms of task coordination and content, they were qualitatively different. The users involved in the *PM* setting needed to coordinate much more than those involved in the *GS* setting. This result suggests that some roles can lead to role ambiguity, which induces overlap in the functional assignments. This may lead users to clarify, through coordination messages, their responsibilities and involvement in the search.

4.2 Analyzing users' division of labor strategies

Here, we analyze how the intra-group members' search strategies differed alongside the search session among the studied search scenarios. Following [31] and according to our research hypotheses ($H1$ and $H2$), our particular objective was to investigate and contrast the complementarities of the user's behaviors toward the achievement of the collaborative task within the different settings by computing the significance of the differences between their behavioral features. To achieve this, we computed the correlation between the participants' cumulative behavior pairs of features alongside the search session for each one-minute timestamp as follows [31]:

$$C^{(t_l)}_{1,2}(f_k, f_{k'}) = \begin{cases} \rho(\Delta^{(t_l)}_{1,2}(f_k), \Delta^{(t_l)}_{1,2}(f_{k'})) & if\ p(\Delta^{(t_l)}_{1,2}(f_k)) < \theta \\ & and\ p(\Delta^{(t_l)}_{1,2}(f_{k'})) < \theta \\ 0 & otherwise \end{cases} \qquad (1)$$

where $\Delta^{(t_l)}_{1,2}(f_k) = S^{(t_l)}_{u_1}(f_k) - S^{(t_l)}_{u_2}(f_k)$ represents the cumulative difference in the feature values of user u_1 and user u_2 and θ is a significance threshold. Negative correlations between the difference values, rather than the feature values themselves, at the session level signify complementarities, i.e., search skills for which collaborators exhibit differences and are effective [31]. Figures 3a, 3b and 3c represent the significant negative correlations of pairwise feature differences for the GS, PM and *W/oRole* search scenarios, respectively, for each five-minute timestamp (5-30). The sets of the negative correlations over the pairwise features evolved across the session, thus highlighting the participants' involvement. We conjecture that the stability of the correlation curve trend across time indicates behavior convergence, thus suggesting that participants achieved complementary skills at the corresponding search stage. We can observe that a higher number of significant correlated features resulted from the *W/oRole* setting (10) than in both of the *W/Role* scenarios (4). This observation indicates that self-organization provided users without roles, with a higher flexibility in their behavior leading to the emergence of a wider range of complementarity skills. We emphasize that according to Figure 3b, 2 of the 4 features implied in the PM correlations varied between negative and null correlations over the search session. For instance, the correlations between the number of pages per query (*npq*) and the page dwell time feature (*dt*) differences were not significant at the beginning of the session, became negative between the 10th and 20th minutes, were non-significant from minutes 20 to 25, and finally became negative again at the end of the session. Furthermore, from Figure 3a, we can observe that in the

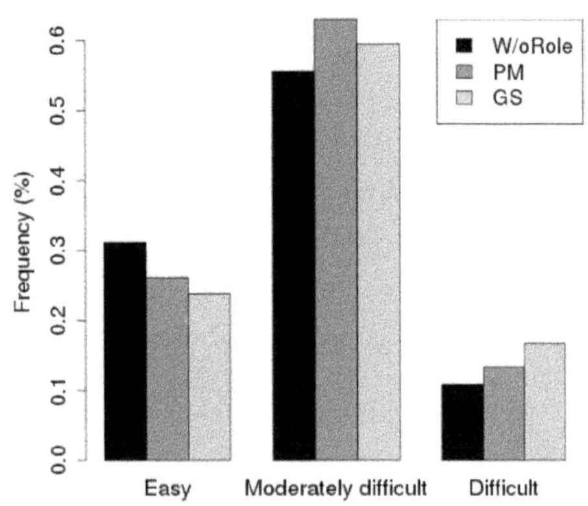

(a) Proportion of users assessing task difficulty for each search setting

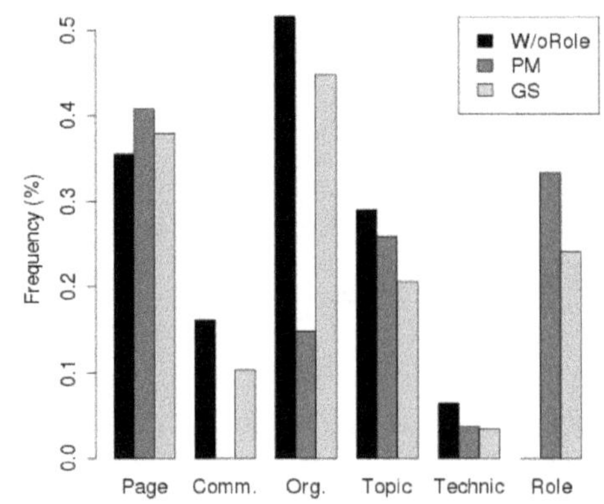

(b) Proportion of answers belonging to each category of difficulty across answers assessing that task is either difficult or moderately difficult

Figure 4: **Qualitative analysis of task difficulty**

GS scenario, 55% (5/9) of the pairwise features exhibited significant negative correlations at 20 minutes, and all of the implied features converged to significant correlations after 25 minutes. In contrast, Figure 3c indicates that collaborators in the *W/oRole* scenario, 80% (8/10) of the feature pairs reached correlation convergence earlier in the session, after 15 minutes. This indicates that roles have weakened the interdependence between the users and it appears that this fact had a negative effect on intra-group coordination stability, especially in the PM setting, in which collaborators seemed to exhibit role drift. To extend our investigation of the features that characterized collaborators' complementarities across time, we examined the pairwise features that were significantly correlated in the *W/oRole* setting but not in the GS or PM settings. These features are listed in the legends of Figures 3a, 3b and 3c. Although there was no significant difference between the GS and *W/oRole* scenarios, we can observe that the most frequent pairwise features, as indicated by the set of non-significantly correlated features within the PM setting, were those that could be connected to the role characteristics: the miner should identify the most relevant documents (a behavior that can be characterized by the number of feedbacks (nf)), and the prospector should favor diversity by submitting a higher number of queries (qn) with low overlap (qo). All of the above observations suggest the following: (1) the no role condition offers to the users a wider range (than the role condition) of opportunities allowing them to give rise to complementarities in which they are the most effective toward the achievement of the shared goal; and (2) roles do not guarantee a cohesive intra-group search.

To gain a deeper qualitative understanding of these observations, we analyzed the post-task questionnaires. Using the provided codes (Table 2, post-task question 3), we assessed the number of participants involved in each scenario that assessed the task as *easy*, *moderately difficult* or *difficult*; the results are shown in Figure 4a. As we can see, most of the users, regardless of the search scenario, found that the task was moderately *difficult*. However it seems that it was more likely that the task is assessed as *easy* when performed in a no role condition. In contrast, it was more likely that the task is assessed as *difficult* when performed in a role condition. However, a χ^2 test between the role and the difficulty level factors ($\chi^2(2, N = 150) = 0.58, p > 0.05$) found that the reported differences are not significant. Figure 4b shows the qualitative differences in terms of what made the task particularly *difficult* or *moderately difficult* within each setting as determined from the participants' answers (Table 2, post-task questions and related codes (Table 5)). We observed that the most important underlying reasons were related to communication (*Comm*), organization (*Org*) and roles (*Role*). It is clear that the latter are linked to the overall task coordination. We can conclude the following: (1) setting up useful communication and organization was particularly and relatively easy within the PM setting; this fact could be explained by the high proportion of chat messages exchanged between users with PM roles, as revealed by the communication analysis, (2) establishing roles was easy in the *W/oRole* setting, whereas fitting pre-assigned roles was difficult in the *W/Role* setting, especially in the PM scenario. Four participants involved in the PM scenarios explicitly mentioned that they had difficulty following the role guidelines (e.g., "*It is difficult to keep my role*" and "*restrict myself to my role*"). These observations confirm our previous expectations that were based on quantitative analysis of the feature-based behavior correlations. We can also observe from Figure 4b that the other types of difficulty, namely *Page*, *Topic* and *Technical*, were mentioned with similar frequencies by the participants in the different settings.

4.3 Search Effectiveness

To evaluate the effectiveness of the various collaborative search settings, we calculated some common metrics and then averaged the values over all of the groups that were in a given search setting. The common metrics used were the following [28]:

- The search precision of collaborative group g:

$$Precision(g) = \frac{RelevantCoverage(g)}{Coverage(g)} \quad (2)$$

where $Coverage(g)$ is the set of unique pages annotated, bookmarked and snipped by group g. $RelevantCoverage(g)$ denotes the set of unique annotated, bookmarked and snipped pages among those of $Coverage(g)$ with a minimal agreement level of 2 participants belonging to distinct groups.

• The search recall of collaborative group g:

$$Recall(g) = \frac{RelevantCoverage(g)}{GT} \quad (3)$$

where $GT = \bigcup_g RelevantCoverage(g)$ is the ground truth computed as the total number of unique annotated, bookmarked and snipped pages over all the search groups with a minimal agreement level of 2 participants belonging to distinct groups.

• The F-measure of a group g combining precision and recall:

$$F(g) = \frac{2 \times Precision(g) \times Recall(g)}{Precision(g) + Recall(g)} \quad (4)$$

The goal of the recall-precision analysis was to determine the impact of role assignment on the search effectiveness. Table 7 presents statistics regarding the obtained precision, recall and F-measure scores. Because the test queries differed from one search setting to another, we centered and reduced the effectiveness measures to make the comparisons of the studied settings fair. The statistical measure transformation was performed over each group within each search setting. The last row reports the significance values of the role factor within each search setting obtained by performing an ANOVA on the transformed scores. We can observe that the precision was significantly higher when searches were performed without prior role assignment ($Mean = 0.557$ vs. $GS : Mean = 0.435/PM : Mean = 0.422$); however, no significant differences were found for the recall and F-measure scores. According to the behavior analysis, we observed that users without prior roles (1) were more likely to spend a longer time on the results pages, (2) were more involved in making assessments (annotations, bookmarks, and snippets) on the results pages, which were considered as relevance signals, and (3) were less communicative about the document content suggesting that spontaneous roles are expected to emerge according to their knowledge skills. Combining all these facts about the search effectiveness and the users' behavior, we can conclude that although users in both settings were able to make fair judgments about relevance, which led to similar levels of recall, users that defined their roles themselves were more successful at discarding irrelevant page results because of their more in-depth page visits and understanding of the search topic. Thus, we hypothesize that performing searches without prior roles may lead to more precision-oriented searches.

5. DESIGN IMPLICATIONS

In this section, we discuss the potential future directions for designing CIS/CIR systems that are revealed by our results.

5.1 Mining latent evolving roles

Our findings indicate that users in prior-role-based settings found it difficult to coordinate among themselves according to the role guidelines. In contrast, user-driven roles enabled users to achieve a reasonable level of coordination,

Table 7: **Search effectiveness analysis. Mean(s.d.): Mean value of the effectiveness metric over the search session (standard deviation). ANOVA p-value: significance of the role factor** ($W/Role$ **vs.** $W/oRole$)**.** ($0.01 < p < 0.05$)**: moderately significant *,** ($0.001 < p < 0.01$)**: significant **,** ($p < 0.001$)**: highly significant *****

		Mean(s.d.)		
		Precision	*Recall*	*F-measure*
W/Role	GS	0.435(0.14)	0.042(0.02)	0.075(0.03)
	PM	0.422(0.16)	0.038(0.02)	0.069(0.03)
W/oRole		0.557(0.17)	0.042(0.01)	0.074(0.03)
	ANOVA/GS	***		
	ANOVA/PM	***		

even though this coordination relied on intensive communication. The implication of these observations is that it would be helpful to design processes that are able to determine the most effective roles for users in a "just-in-time" fashion based on their evolving behavior and then automatically re-inject the determined roles in the ranking model to mediate the subsequent searches. Recently, a method for determining roles based on users' behavior has been proposed [31]. However, this method relies on fixed taxonomic roles that may not be ideal or relevant to users' search skills. Considering our findings, there is room for combining system-based and user-based mediation approaches to design algorithms building unlabeled and latent roles based on collaborators' differences to appropriately personalize collaborative searches. Such approaches may reduce both collaborative search drift and communication costs.

5.2 Providing task-based role templates

The qualitative analysis of communication reported in section 4.1 demonstrated that in both role-based and no-role-based search settings, the chat messages exchanged between users mostly concerned task coordination. The division of labor costs required to build the search task background over the collaborators would be small if the system offered content-based role templates (in addition to functional explicit roles if any) that are appropriate for different types of collaborative search tasks. For instance, in exploratory search tasks in which guidance in exploring unfamiliar topics is helpful, the system could play a virtual role in facilitating query refinement and mediation among collaborators by suggesting the most relevant information nuggets according to the differences in users' knowledge regarding the information landscape of the topic. Accordingly, there is an opportunity for designing systems that are able to detect the collaborative search intent and the individual collaborator's level of knowledge, and then to use this information accordingly in methods that engage the user to better drive the search.

5.3 Enhancing role-based awareness

The analysis of the division of labor strategies and post-task questionnaires highlighted the difficulty that collaborators faced in strictly following their role guidelines. Although roles seem to constrain the users too much, they can structure collaboration and reduce communication costs, and they might be required for some tasks. One underlying challenge concerns the interface design for enhancing collaborators' awareness of their ability to follow role guidelines. Studying users' search behavior across a number of taxonomic collaborative tasks may lead to a set of indicator(s) associated with each pair of task-role (for instance, query overlap for prospectors) that could help CIS/CIR systems automatically detect role drift and monitor support for users in order to let them better suit with role specifications.

6. CONCLUSION

In this paper, we have presented a user study of collaborative, exploratory web-search behavior, and effectiveness. This study is the first empirical investigation of how well roles, either implicit or explicit, explain users' behavior and their methods of using division of labor to achieve a shared exploratory task. Our overall conclusion was that role, either implicitly build by the users or explicitly assigned to the users, appears to have a significant effect on users' behavior, collaborative search strategy, and search results effectiveness. The results of both the quantitative and qualitative analyses reported here particularly that: (1) users without prior roles had a more slow and exhaustive search behavior and worked less independently than users with prior roles, (2) users with no prior roles were more likely to broaden their complementarities and structure their roles relatively early in the search session while users with prior roles had difficulties to fit with their roles, (3) roles limited the precision of the search results. Finally, we discussed several methods that hold promise perspectives for improving the synergic effect of collaborative mediation and coordination. In this work, we only studied the effect of role in collaborative exploraty search within dyads, which might be different than other search settings. However, we hope that this study will improve our understanding of collaborative information behavior from the user role perspective and enable the emergence of a new generation of CIS/CIR systems that bridge the gap between system-centered and user-centered approaches to collaboration.

7. ACKNOWLEDGMENTS

We thank the undergrad and PhD students from Paul Sabatier University who participated to the user study.

8. REFERENCES

[1] E. Agichtein, E. Brill, S. Dumais, and R. Ragno. Learning user interaction models for predicting web search result preferences. In *ACM SIGIR*, pages 3–10, 2006.

[2] B. Amidan, T. Ferryman, and S. Cooley. Data outlier detection using the chebyshev theorem. In *Aerospace Conference, 2005 IEEE*, pages 3814–3819, 2005.

[3] A. Aula, P. Majaranta, and K.-J. Räihä. Eye-tracking reveals the personal styles for search result evaluation. In *INTERACT*, pages 1058–1061, 2005.

[4] M. Benderski and B. Croft. Do longer queries retrieve more diverse results? Research report 764, Center for Intelligent Information Retrieval, University of Massachusetts, 2010.

[5] R. Day and G. Quinn. *Ecol. Monogr.*, 59:433–463, 1989.

[6] P. J. Denning and P. Yaholkovsky. Getting to "we". *Commun. ACM*, 51(4):19–24, 2008.

[7] T. Erickson. A social proxy for collective search. In *CIS Workshop at ACM CSCW*, 2010.

[8] B. M. Evans and E. H. Chi. An elaborated model of social search. *Inf. Process. Manage.*, 46(6):656–678, 2010.

[9] C. Foley and A. F. Smeaton. Synchronous collaborative information retrieval: Techniques and evaluation. In *Springer ECIR*, pages 42–53, 2009.

[10] C. Foley and A. F. Smeaton. Division of labour and sharing of knowledge for synchronous collaborative information retrieval. *Inf. Process. Manage.*, 46(6):762–772, 2010.

[11] J. Foster. Collaborative information seeking and retrieval. *Annual Review of Information Science and Technology*, 40(1), 2006.

[12] G. Golovchinsky, O. Qvarfordt, and J. Pickens. Collaborative information seeking. *IEEE Computer*, 42(3):47–51, 2009.

[13] R. González-Ibáñez, H. Muge, and S. Chirag. Let's search together, but not too close! an analysis of communication and performance in collaborative information seeking. *Inf. Process. Manage.*, 49(5):1165–1179, 2013.

[14] P. Hansen and K. Järvelin. Collaborative information retrieval in an information-intensive domain. *Inf. Process. Manage.*, 41(5):1101–1119, 2005.

[15] J. Hyldegard. Collaborative information behaviour-exploring kuhlthau's information search process model in a group-based educational setting. *Inf. Process. Manage.*, 42(1):276 – 298, 2006.

[16] H. Joho, D. Hannah, and J. M. Jose. Revisiting ir techniques for collaborative search strategies. In *Springer ECIR*, pages 66–77, 2009.

[17] C. C. Kuhlthau. Inside the search process: Information seeking from the user's perspective. *Journal of the American Society for Information Science*, 42(5):361–371, 1991.

[18] T. Kussmann, S. Elbeshausen, T. Mandl, and C. Womser-Hacker. Discovering ellis' phases of information seeking behavior in collaborative search processes. In *CIS Workshop at ACM CSCW*, 2013.

[19] M. R. Morris. A survey of collaborative web search practices. In *ACM SIGCHI*, pages 1657–1660, 2008.

[20] M. R. Morris and E. Horvitz. Searchtogether: an interface for collaborative web search. In *UIST*, pages 3–12, 2007.

[21] P. Over. The trec interactive track: an annotated bibliography. *Inf. Process. Manage.*, 37(3):369–381, 2001.

[22] S. A. Paul and M. R. Morris. Cosense: Enhancing sensemaking for collaborative web search. In *ACM SIGCHI*, pages 1771–1780, 2009.

[23] J. Pickens, G. Golovchinsky, C. Shah, P. Qvarfordt, and M. Back. Algorithmic mediation for collaborative exploratory search. In *ACM SIGIR*, pages 315–322, 2008.

[24] S. Poltrock, R. Fidel, and H. Bruce. Information seeking and sharing in design teams. In *GROUP*, pages 239–247, 2003.

[25] K. Ryan and P. Stephen J. Division of labour in collaborative information seeking: current approaches and future directions. In *CIS Workshop at ACM CSCW*, pages 4–8, 2013.

[26] C. Shah. *Collaborative Information Seeking: The Art and Science of Making The Whole Greater Than The Sum of All.* Springer, 2012.

[27] C. Shah and R. González-Ibáñez. Coagmento - a system for supporting collaborative information seeking. In *ASIST*, pages 9–12, 2011.

[28] C. Shah and R. González-Ibáñez. Evaluating the synergic effect of collaboration in information seeking. In *ACM SIGIR*, pages 913–922, 2011.

[29] C. Shah, J. Pickens, and G. Golovchinsky. Role-based results redistribution for collaborative information retrieval. *Inf. Process. Manage.*, 46(6):773–781, 2010.

[30] D. H. Sonnenwald. Communication roles that support collaboration during the design process. *Design Studies*, 17(3):277–301, 1996.

[31] L. Soulier, C. Shah, and L. Tamine. User-driven system-mediated collaborative information retrieval. In *SIGIR*, pages 485–494, 2014.

[32] I. Xie and S. Joo. Factors affecting the selection of search tactics: Tasks, knowledge, process, and systems. *Inf. Process. Manage.*, 48(2):254 – 270, 2012.

Experiments with a Venue-Centric Model for Personalised and Time-Aware Venue Suggestion

Romain Deveaud, M-Dyaa Albakour, Craig Macdonald and Iadh Ounis
University of Glasgow, UK
firstname.lastname@glasgow.ac.uk

ABSTRACT

Location-based social networks (LBSNs), such as Foursquare, fostered the emergence of new tasks such as recommending venues a user might wish to visit. In the literature, recommending venues has typically been addressed using user-centric recommendation approaches relying on collaborative filtering techniques. Such approaches not only require many users with detailed profiles to be effective, but they also cannot recommend venues to users who are not actually members of the LBSN. In contrast, in this paper, we introduce a venue-centric yet personalised probabilistic approach that suggests personalised and popular venues for users to visit in the near future. In our approach, we probabilistically incorporate two components, a popularity component for predicting the popularity of a venue at a given point in time, as estimated from the attendance of the venue in the LBSN (i.e. number of check-ins), and a personalisation component for identifying its interestingness with respect to the estimated preferences of the user. The popularity of each venue is predicted using time series forecasting models that are trained on the recent attendance trends of the venue, while the users' interests are modelled from the entity pages that they like on Facebook. Using three major cities, we conduct a user study to evaluate the effectiveness of the two components of our approach in suggesting venues for different types of users at different times of the day. Our experimental results show that an approach that combines the popularity and personalisation components is able to consistently outperform the recommendation service of the leading Foursquare LBSN. We also find that combining popularity and personalisation is effective for both new visitors and residents, while former visitors prefer popular venues.

1. INTRODUCTION

With the prevalence of smartphones and ever improving mobile access to the Internet, new behaviours have emerged. People stay connected and rapidly share their opinions, interests, locations and many other aspects of their lives on social networks. The users of these social networks therefore act as Internet-connected sensors of the real world and provide a wealth of information about what is currently happening around them. At the heart of these user-generated information lie Location-based Social Networks (LBSNs) [40], such as Foursquare, Flickr or to some extent Twitter. All such services allow their users to share their location, whether by tweeting a message, posting a photo on Flickr, or entering a review about a venue on Foursquare.

New applications have emerged [40] with these rising technologies, such as the suggestion of venues that might be of interest to a user. This task of venue suggestion has been mainly tackled in the literature using *user-centric* recommendation approaches that rely on collaborative filtering [3, 12, 38, 39], where suggestions are based on venues that were highly rated by users that have the same preferences as the current user (i.e. similar users). The main drawback of such approaches is that they require many users with detailed profiles to learn individual preferences. Moreover, they are not able to recommend venues to those users that are not members of the same social network. To overcome these limitations, instead of relying on similar users, some recent approaches directly model the likelihood of suggesting venues with *venue-centric* methods [16, 21], which focus on the features that make a venue relevant rather than on venues that similar users like. However, all the applications derived from these user- and venue-centric methods have been restricted to specific sub-problems of venue suggestion. These include the recommendation of only new venues [3] (venues in a city that the user has not visited before), the prediction of the next location of the user [16, 21], or the suggestion of only a certain type of venues [21] (e.g. restaurants). In addition, none of the aforementioned studies explored how the quality of their suggestions vary for different types of users (e.g. residents or visitors), or at different times of the day. More importantly, no study so far has reported results derived from the judgments of users.

In this paper, we address all of these issues by proposing a general venue-centric model, which suggests personalised venues at different times of the day. Along with the modelling of the user's preferences, the proposed model additionally predicts the popularity of a venue at a given time to provide the user with timely and high quality suggestions.

Our model is composed of two components. The first one estimates the popularity of a venue (an indicator of high quality) by measuring its level of attendance: the most popular venues are the most attended ones. Following recent work on estimating venues' attendance at different times of the day [25, 32], we use the data generated by the Foursquare users when they "check-in"[1] at venues to regularly measure

[1] A term used by Foursquare to denote users sharing their current location with the LBSN.

CIKM'15, October 19–23, 2015, Melbourne, Australia.
© 2015 ACM. ISBN 978-1-4503-3794-6/15/10 ...$15.00.
DOI: http://dx.doi.org/10.1145/2806416.2806484.

the venues' level of attendance throughout the day. We then predict the future level of attendance of a given venue by applying state-of-the-art time series forecasting models, such as those in [18]. By doing so, we predict the future popularity of venues at a given point in time, thereby adapting the suggestions as a function of the date and the time of the day. Indeed, while harnessing the Foursquare venues' popularity has already been studied [22], no past work attempted to estimate this popularity at future points in time.

The second component of our model takes advantage of the Facebook profile of the users to suggest personalised venues by inferring their interests. People indeed openly share pieces of their interests on Facebook by "liking" various pages, which can be viewed as records of their personality [20]. Our model uses the pages users like to estimate the likelihood of a venue being of interest to them. With nearly 1.5 billion users in 2014[2], Facebook is a central and widely used repository of user interests. Leveraging this centrality allows us to avoid the usual cold-start and sparsity problems that plague recommender systems [13].

While we use specific information sources in this study (i.e. Foursquare and Facebook), our model is general enough to be adapted to other sensors of attendance (e.g. CCTV cameras) or sources of user interests (e.g. Google+). Unlike in previous work, we evaluate the effectiveness of our venue suggestions by asking judgments from users. In particular, we conduct a user study, where we examine the quality of venue suggestions over various dimensions such as the time of the day or the profile of the user (i.e. visitor or resident). Hence, this paper presents a three-fold contribution:

- We propose a principled probabilistic model that suggests personalised venues based on their estimated interestingness and popularity over time;
- We separately evaluate the two components of our model by conducting experiments on: (1) the inference of the user's interests; and (2) the prediction of the venues' level of attendance by applying time series forecasting models;
- We integrate our observations and analysis from the above experiments to build an effective instantiation of our venue suggestion model, which we validate through a user study that involves 100 participants over three major cities. The experimental results from the user study show that: (1) Taken separately or in combination, both components of our model significantly outperform the Foursquare recommendation service, thus validating our approaches for estimating the popularity of a venue and the user's interests; (2) New visitors and residents tend to prefer personalised venues, while former visitors prefer popular venues.

The remainder of this paper is organised as follows. Section 2 reviews approaches related to the task of venue suggestion. In Section 3, we describe our proposed model. We experiment in Section 4 with the two components of our model taken separately, before combining them and carrying a user study in Section 5. We conclude and discuss future work in Section 6.

2. RELATED WORK

Suggesting venues or activities to users is an emerging application that is currently receiving attention due to the growing interest in smart cities [6] and location-based social networks (LBSNs) [40]. These applications are often classified in the literature as Point-of-Interest (POI) [28] (or also sometimes Location [38]) Recommendation. Approaches studied for POI recommendation range from traditional user-centric collaborative filtering [3, 12, 38, 39] to venue-centric topic modelling [16, 21]. User-centric approaches focus on the user and perform recommendation based on the venues that similar users have liked or visited in the past. One weakness of collaborative filtering is that it requires detailed profiles from many users to be able to accurately infer their interests. For example, Bao et al. [3] tackled the sparsity of the user profiles and the cold start problem in collaborative filtering by identifying experts in high-level categories of venues, which are estimated to be of interest to the user from previous interactions on the LBSN (previous visits). Unlike these approaches, we do not rely on previous interactions on LBSNs to model the users' interests.

In contrast, venue-centric approaches to venue suggestion can abstract from the need of detailed profiles, and also offer the advantage of being able to accommodate a wide range of users by not being restricted to users of a single LBSN. Thus far, the venue-centric approaches have relied on probabilistic topic models [16, 21]. Kurashima et al. [21] showed that a topic model can effectively mine logs of GPS trajectories to infer the next visit of a user. Hu et al. [16] proposed a very similar model that uses text and locations extracted from social media (e.g. Twitter). However, the venue-centric approaches [16, 21] only predict the next location of the user, which may not be a venue, thus leading to a low suggestion precision. Moreover, while all of the aforementioned user- and venue-centric approaches relate to our work in that they can all recommend venues, they only consider two parameters: the users and (sometimes) their current location, but they do not consider time. Our approach is different in the sense that it models the quality of venues with respect to both their popularity and the user's interests, and also tracks their popularity over time.

A few studies are closely related to ours. Yuan et al. [39] and Gao et al. [12] proposed time-aware recommendation models that incorporate the temporal check-in behaviour of each user in the LBSN. Both use collaborative filtering, and incorporate the similarity between users that exhibit similar temporal patterns (i.e. users that visit the same locations at the same time of the day). Although these two approaches take time into account for POI recommendation, they are both user-centric and thus suffer from the drawbacks mentioned earlier. Our approach distinguishes itself from those studies by being venue-centric, and by modelling the temporal behaviours of the venues instead of those of the users. Brilhante et al. [8] proposed an approach for mining Flickr and Wikipedia to build sequences of visits for users before they start their trip. However, this last approach only generates a static path of venues given a target city. In contrast, our proposed model adapts to the city, the time, the user, and her/his current location.

The TREC Contextual Suggestion track [10] is investigating research questions related to the personalised suggestion of places. The most effective approaches [11, 31, 37] heavily rely on the high quality search results of the recommendation APIs in various LBSNs such as Google Places, Yelp, or Foursquare. Achieving a personalised ranking is then mostly a matter of re-ranking those results to better fit the user's interests. In the context of the Contextual Suggestion track, these interests are expressed through a list of previously visited places associated with ratings, as for user-

[2] http://www.statisticbrain.com/facebook-statistics

centric approaches. One issue when considering such profiles is that suggestions will always be biased towards categories of venues that the user rated highly, thereby harming the exploration or discovery of new kinds of venues. Again, our approach does not require the user to have a detailed profile of previously visited venues.

The approach we present in this paper differs from all of the above in the sense that it tracks the popularity of venues over time, and proposes a novel method for inferring the interests of the user by using an independent source of preferences (i.e. Facebook). Our proposed model is principled and flexible enough that it could be instantiated using different approaches to represent the popularity and the interestingness of a venue. It is specifically designed to tackle the *zero-query retrieval* task, where suggestions are presented to the user without requiring her/him to issue a query [23].

We present this model and detail the specific instantiations we explore in this paper in the following section.

3. MODEL FORMULATION

For a given user u at a location l and at a certain time t, we aim to model the likelihood of a venue v to be of interest to the user. This model can be formally written as:

$$P(v|u,l,t) \propto P(v|u) \cdot P(v|l,t') \qquad (1)$$

and is composed of two components: an *interestingness* component, which estimates the likelihood $P(v|u)$ that a venue v would correspond to the interests of user u; and a *popularity* component, which estimates the likelihood $P(v|l,t')$ that v would be accessible to the user currently at location l, and that it would be popular at some point in the near future t', where $t' = t + \epsilon$. In other words, our model can suggest venues that may be of interest in the near future by anticipating the needs of the user. The parameter ϵ controls the length of this "near future"; we will discuss its setup in Section 5. Note that the model in Equation (1) assumes independence between the user u and the location and time (l,t). This assumption simplifies the model allowing us to study the interestingness and the popularity components, independently or in combination, by making use of judgments from users. It is also consistent with a venue-centric approach that does not require data detailing the locations of the users at different times. Our model is a venue-centric approach in the sense that it models the likelihood of a venue to be of interest given three parameters, namely the user, its location, and the current time. Venues are modelled both in a conceptual space (finding venues that match the interests of a user) and in a physical space (finding nearby venues that are usually popular at certain points in time). The core of our approach lies in the estimation of the two probabilities of Equation (1), which we describe in the following sections: first, we detail in Section 3.1 our approach for predicting the popularity of a venue at a certain point in the future; then, in Section 3.2 we describe how we can leverage elements of the Facebook profile of a user to infer her/his interests.

3.1 Predicting venue popularity

We now address the issue of estimating the popularity of a venue as expressed by $P(v|l,t')$. In our model, this popularity acts as a surrogate for the quality of the venue suggestion for the user, and depends both on the time and on the user's current location. The quality of a venue would for example decrease if it is far from the current location of the user. We safely assume that a venue will not become popular just because the user is nearby. We thus consider the current location l of the user to be independent of the time t'. The right-hand term of Equation (1) can then be written as:

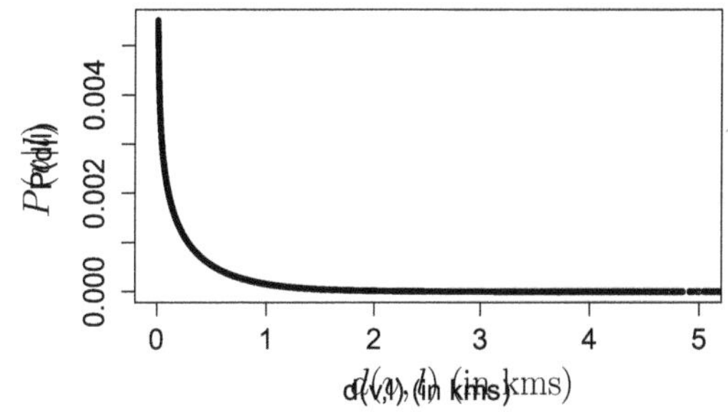

Figure 1: Probability that users check-in at a venue given its distance to their own location. The x-axis represents the distance (in km) between the venue v and the user's location l.

$$P(v|l,t') \propto P(v|l) \cdot P(v|t') \qquad (2)$$

We detail in the two following sections how we model both the venue proximity $P(v|l)$ and the likelihood $P(v|t')$ that the venue will be highly attended in the near future.

3.1.1 Venue proximity

It has been shown in previous studies [30, 38] that users tend to visit venues that are near their current location. Ideally, the probability $P(v|l)$ would thus be high when the distance $d(v,l)$ between the venue v and the user's location l is short. To do so, we look at pairs of Foursquare venues at which the user has checked in over short periods of time (i.e. less than three hours), and fit a Gamma distribution on this distance distribution. The resulting probabilities, expressed as a function of the distance $d(v,l)$ between the venue v and the user's location l, are displayed on Figure 1. Finally, the probability that a venue v would be of interest given the current location l of the user is expressed as: $P(v|l) = P(d(v,l))$. Note that evidence other than distance can be used for estimating $P(v|l)$, for example search logs [4], but we leave the use of this additional evidence for future work.

3.1.2 Attendance forecasting

In our model, the popularity of a venue is mainly related to its predicted level of attendance . We follow the ongoing initiatives in the development of smart cities and use social sensors [1, 33] to construct a time series of attendance for each individual venue. Time series are numerical information that are observed sequentially over time. In this work, we use the Foursquare API[3] as a social sensor. When asking for information about a venue, the API permits to obtain the number of people currently visiting the venue. We query the API every hour for each venue to build a comprehensive time series of venue attendance. It is important to note that we do not depend on using Foursquare as a particular type of sensors. Indeed, any other kind of sensors (or combination of sensors) that can measure crowd density could be used here, such as CCTV cameras for example [34]. Since we focus on predicting popularity, we build a time series of attendance for each venue and rely on three state-of-the-art time series forecasting algorithms [24]. Time series forecasting encompasses a family of methods that can predict not only the value of the next point of the time series, but the values of the next N points. State-of-the-art forecasting algorithms

[3] http://developer.foursquare.com/docs/venues/herenow

such as ARIMA (Auto-Regressive Integrated Moving Average), Neural Networks, and Exponential Smoothing use past observations to learn trends, seasonal variations, and recurring patterns in the data [18, 24].

We use these forecasting models to estimate the probability $P(v|t')$ in Equation (2). We apply Bayesian smoothing with a Dirichlet prior to avoid zero probabilities:

$$P(v|t') = \frac{\hat{y}(v,t') + \mu \cdot P(v|\mathcal{T})}{\sum_{v' \in \mathcal{V}} \hat{y}(v',t') + \mu} \quad (3)$$

where $\hat{y}(v,t')$ is a forecast of the number of people attending the venue v at time t', using either ARIMA, Neural Networks, or Exponential Smoothing as forecasting models. $\mathcal{V}$ is the complete set of venues for a given city. $P(v|\mathcal{T})$ models the popularity of the venue v over an entire timespan $\mathcal{T}$ of past observations, where $\mathcal{T}$ also represents the training period of the forecasting models. This background probability is expressed as $P(v|\mathcal{T}) = \frac{y(v,\mathcal{T})}{\sum_{v' \in \mathcal{V}} y(v',\mathcal{T})}$, where $y(v,\mathcal{T})$ is the total number of people that attended the venue v during $\mathcal{T}$.

The Dirichlet prior μ is the mean of the counts for all venues in the same city, over the entire timespan $\mathcal{T}$. The rationale behind applying such a smoothing is analogous to traditional information retrieval: we avoid eliminating the candidate venues with 0 attendances. Without any smoothing, the probability $P(v|t')$ is null when $\hat{y}(v,t')$ is predicted to be 0. However, even if a venue has a low level of attendance, it may still be interesting to some users. For example, we observed in our data that a board game shop is a very unlikely venue to check-in; however, a person who likes such games would be highly interested by this kind of suggestions. Hence, smoothing this probability helps us to tackle the inevitable sparsity of our observations.

3.2 Modelling venue interestingness

The second component of our approach models the interests of the user in order to personalise the suggestions. Users supply a wealth of information about their personality on social networking websites. With its ever growing number of users, Facebook is one of the most popular publicly available personality repository [20]. On Facebook, people can explicitly share their interests by "liking" pages that refer to entities such as public figures, bands, venues, events, or even fictional characters. The personality of users can then be represented as sets of entities covering their various interests [20]. We leverage this entity representation in a probabilistic model, which extracts the interests of a user with the aim of suggesting personalised venues. More specifically, we compute the probability $P(v|u)$ that a venue fits the interests of user u by marginalising over the space of all known entities of the entire Facebook Graph[4] (with the fair assumption of independence between the user and an entity):

$$P(v|u) = \sum_{e} P(v|e)P(e|u) \quad (4)$$

We reasonably hypothesise that a "like" is an indicator of relevance, hence a page e will always be relevant for a user u if that user has liked it in the past. Therefore, we define in this work $P(e|u) = \frac{\text{like}(e,u)}{\sum_{e'} \text{like}(e',u)}$, where $like(e,u) = 1$ if the user u likes the entity e, and 0 otherwise.

Estimating $P(v|e)$ is thus the core part of this component. Since venues and entities do not share the same space, we map them into a common space of categories and apply machine learning. We detail in the remainder of this section the categorisation and classification approaches we employ.

3.2.1 *From interests to categories*

Our approach for estimating the probability that a venue is relevant given an entity relies on the categories of the DMOZ[5] Open Directory Project, a curated directory of web pages that have been manually categorised. This allows us to represent both venues and Facebook entities as sets of categories, thus enabling their comparison to measure how well a venue corresponds to the interests expressed by an entity. Bi et al. [5] recently proposed a method that relies on DMOZ to map Facebook profiles with search profiles in the Bing search engine, using proprietary search logs. However this previous work is limited in that only the number of similar categories are counted, which we overcome by directly computing probabilities. Moreover, Bi et al. only predicted specific personality traits such as the age, the gender, or the political views of the users. Here, we propose a method that can match two types of entities of very different natures, e.g. a Facebook page and a venue, by categorising each in a space of DMOZ categories. Formally, given $\mathcal{C}$, the set of DMOZ categories, we rewrite the expression of $P(v|e)$ used in Equation (4) as (with the fair assumption of independence between the entity and a category):

$$P(v|e) = \sum_{c \in \mathcal{C}} P(v|c)P(c|e) \quad (5)$$

Using Bayes' rule, $P(v|c)$ can be expressed as:

$$P(v|c) = \frac{P(c|v)P(v)}{P(c)} \propto \frac{P(c|v)}{P(c)} \quad (6)$$

As we do not consider any prior information about venues in this component of the model, $P(v)$ is constant and does not affect ranking and can be removed from Equation (6).

We can then rewrite Equation (5) as:

$$P(v|e) \propto \sum_{c \in \mathcal{C}} \frac{1}{P(c)} P(c|v)P(c|e) \quad (7)$$

Estimating $P(v|e)$ comes down to estimating the category distribution $P(c|\bullet)$, where $\bullet \in \{v, e\}$. We cover this estimation in the following section.

3.2.2 *Learning to categorise*

Our approach to entity and venue classification builds upon recent work in query classification. In particular, predicting the categories of queries has been studied in the past, and successful approaches agreed on the fact that context is needed [5, 36] to tackle the sparsity problem. This context is usually obtained by retrieving documents that are topically relevant to the query, and classifying the top results into a predefined set of categories. We take the same approach to predict the category distribution of venues and Facebook entities. We train three state-of-the-art classifiers using web pages previously labelled with the top-level DMOZ[6] category information. Venues and Facebook Likes can be entities of very different types, we thus intentionally consider the highest level of the DMOZ hierarchy to represent these entities in a general and diverse category space. We show

[4] `http://facebook.com/about/graphsearch`

[5] `http://dmoz.org` [6] The DMOZ hierarchy has 16 top-level categories. Our training data has a total of 13 categories as it does not contain "Kids and Teens", "World" and "Regional".

in Section 4.2 that using the highest-level categories of the DMOZ hierarchy is valid for this task. Future work could however address more refined taxonomies.

Like Bi et al. [5], we transform each Facebook entity e into a query by using its title. Similarly, for each venue v, we concatenate its name and its city to provide some disambiguation, and use this as a query. Let $\mathcal{R}(\bullet)$ be the set of top search results using $\bullet$ as a query. The retrieval model can be of any kind, as long as the retrieved documents are topically relevant to $\bullet$. Each retrieved document of this set is then classified, yielding a probability distribution over the DMOZ categories. More formally, the probability $P(c|\bullet)$ that $\bullet$ would be of category c is expressed as:

$$P(c|\bullet) = \frac{1}{|\mathcal{R}(\bullet)|} \sum_{D \in \mathcal{R}(\bullet)} P(c|D) \tag{8}$$

where $|\mathcal{R}(\bullet)|$ is the number of retrieved documents. These documents are retrieved from a general repository of web pages that we detail in Section 4.2. The probabilities $P(c|D)$ are directly derived from the predictions of the classifier, which models the category distribution of unseen documents. Different retrieval models and classifiers can be deployed to estimate $P(c|\bullet)$, as we detail in Section 4.2.

We rewrite Equation (7) using Equation (8) as:

$$P(v|e) \propto \sum_{c \in \mathcal{C}} \frac{1}{P(c)} \left(\frac{1}{|\mathcal{R}(v)|} \sum_{D_v \in \mathcal{R}(v)} P(c|D_v) \times \frac{1}{|\mathcal{R}(e)|} \sum_{D_e \in \mathcal{R}(e)} P(c|D_e) \right) \tag{9}$$

It is important to note that our approach could be instantiated using other sources of user preferences in lieu of Facebook (e.g. Google+) to infer the user's interests. We could also imagine a combination of social networks to improve the coverage of the user personality. We leave these improvements for future work.

4. EXPERIMENTS

As detailed in the previous section, our model is built upon two principal components that model the popularity and the interestingness of a venue. In this section, we evaluate the two components separately before carrying a user study of the entire model in Section 5. More specifically, we seek to answer the following research questions:

RQ1: What is the best time series forecasting algorithm for predicting venue attendance levels? (Section 4.1)

RQ2: Which choice of retrieval model and classifier enables to effectively model the categories of users' interests? (Section 4.2)

4.1 Forecast accuracy evaluation

We describe in this section the dataset, the measures, the baselines, and the results of our experiments in order to answer our first research question.

4.1.1 Cities dataset

We chose three major cities to evaluate our model and answer our first research question: London, Amsterdam, and San Francisco. London is a major capital with a large population (more than 8 million). Amsterdam has a higher density and counts more than 800,000 inhabitants. We completed our test bed with San Francisco in order to see if the observations made on two European capitals generalise to a major American city.

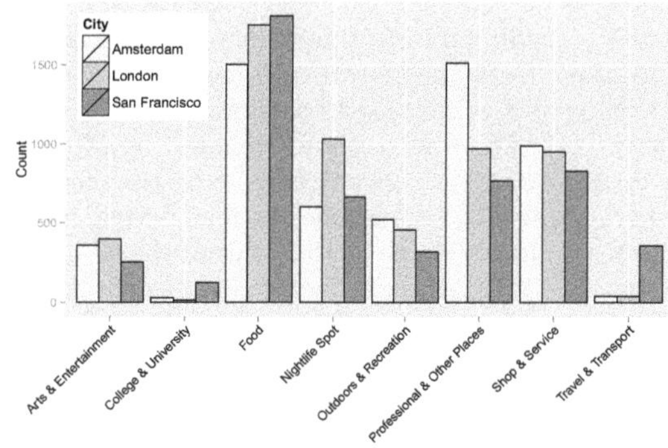

Figure 2: Distribution of venues over their Foursquare categories for the three cities we consider in this study.

We used 3 different Foursquare API accounts belonging to the researchers involved in this study to measure the levels of attendance of venues. The Foursquare API limits the number of calls per account to 5,000 per hour, thus adding up to 15,000 possible API calls per hour. We reasonably limited the frequency of obtaining the levels of attendance to one measurement per hour for each venue. This rate allowed us to both accurately keep track of each venue's attendance while considering a large amount of venues. We equally divided the API calls across the three cities, and monitored 4,950 venues for each city[7] from 5th November 2013 to 17th January 2014. However, tens of thousands of Foursquare venues are available for these cities. Initial experiments showed that the 3,000 venues with the highest total number of check-ins contained the majority of the most popular venues for the three cities. We then performed a selection of venues by choosing the 3,000 ones with the highest number of check-ins, and randomly selected the remaining 1,950 venues from those that had at least 25 check-ins at the time we began our experiments. This threshold of 25 check-ins was used to ensure that we did not include fictitious venues. While performing this selection, we omitted venues falling under the Foursquare categories "College & University" and "Travels & Transport". While airports and train stations for example are very popular among Foursquare users (who like to check-in at these locations to show that they are travelling), they may not be useful suggestions. Some Foursquare venues can belong to multiple Foursquare categories, hence we kept venues that belong to the two blacklisted categories above if they also belong to other (whitelisted) categories. Overall, this selection policy allowed us to build a diverse dataset that includes the most popular venues, which might be of interest to visitors, while also containing less well attended venues. Statistics on this dataset are available in Figure 2, which shows the number of venues for each category in each city.

4.1.2 Forecast accuracy measures and baselines

We detail here the baselines and evaluation measures we use to answer RQ1. Forecast accuracy is determined by computing the errors of the forecasts with respect to the real observations. We report the results in terms of *root mean squared error* (RMSE), which is a commonly used er-

[7] The last 50 API calls were used as a safety buffer in case of an intermittent unavailability of the Foursquare service.

ror measure[8]. As already mentioned in Sections 2 and 3.1.2, we explore the effectiveness of three forecasting models. We compare them to 3 widely used baselines that proved to be competitive [24]. The first baseline, denoted by Mean, forecasts all future values for a given venue to be the mean of the past observations. The second one is called Naïve, for which all forecasts are simply set to be the value of the last observation. It was shown to be very effective in the context of economic and financial time series forecasting [24]. The last one is the Seasonal Naïve method, with the forecast being equal to the previous day. All the time series forecasting models were built using the well-known `forecast` package of `R` [17].

4.1.3 Results

Research question RQ1 aims to explore the accuracy of time series forecasting algorithms for predicting the venue attendance levels. To this end, we evaluate daily forecasts by predicting the attendance of each of the venues for the following 24 hours. In this case, all the days prior to the prediction can be considered as training data. We forecast the attendance of each venue for 10 randomly chosen days (while allowing at least 21 days for training), then average their accuracy. The results are reported in Table 1, where we evaluate the three widely used forecasting models: Neural Networks (Neural), ARIMA, and Exponential Smoothing (Smooth.) with respect to three baselines commonly used in forecasting studies [17]: Mean, Naïve, and Seasonal Naïve (S. Naïve). We vary the number of training days between 7 and 21, and we report the averaged RMSE for all venues in each city. Since RMSE measures a forecast error, the best results are the lowest numbers.

On analysis of Table 1, we see that the Mean method is the most effective method when trained using a small number of observations (7 days). However, with more historical data, ARIMA achieves the best accuracy. The good results of the very basic Mean baseline can be explained by the sparsity of the observations. When building time series of attendance, we consider that a venue is empty if no Foursquare user has checked-in for the current hour. This can result in time series that are mostly composed of zeros for venues that have low levels of attendance, or that attract few Foursquare users. This explains the high results of the Mean baseline, which predicts very low levels of attendance for unattended venues. However, state-of-the-art forecasting models improve their accuracy when we use more historical data, as they are able to model daily and weekly trends even for venues with very few check-ins. ARIMA achieves almost the best results for all cities when using more training days, and Exponential Smoothing models are on par with the three baselines. In contrast, we see that Neural Networks tend to over-fit and hence cannot cope with large daily variations. Nevertheless, we conclude that state-of-the-art time series forecasting models are in general able to outperform these competitive baselines, unless they have a limited amount of training data.

To summarise, in order to address RQ1, we conducted the first systematic series of experiments on the evaluation of forecasting models for predicting the levels of attendance of the venues. Moreover, the forecasting accuracies are very similar across three different cities, which is promising for other potential applications in other cities. It should be

Table 1: Accuracy of the three used forecasting models compared to the three standard baselines. We report the average RMSE for all the venues of each city, varying the number of training days. Numbers in bold are the best results per city and per number of training days.

	7 days			21 days		
	Lon.	Amst.	S. Fran.	Lon.	Amst.	S. Fran.
Mean	**0.633**	**0.563**	**0.868**	0.533	0.357	0.794
Naïve	0.785	0.686	1.131	0.670	0.440	1.015
S. Naïve	0.784	0.696	1.020	0.651	0.446	0.879
Neural	0.822	0.739	1.107	0.796	0.543	1.093
ARIMA	0.677	0.590	0.908	**0.514**	**0.353**	**0.737**
Smooth.	0.787	0.701	1.108	0.640	0.444	1.031

noted that despite the computational requirements of the state-of-the-art forecasting models, they are still suitable for practical deployments, since the forecasting process is done offline on a regular basis and not in real-time..

In the user study we conduct in Section 5, we use the ARIMA models built from the past 21 days as the instantiation of the *popularity* component of our model.

4.2 Evaluation of models of user interests

We now answer RQ2 by evaluating the component that models the user's interests. As described in Section 3.2, this component is a two-step approach, where it first retrieves documents related to a Facebook entity, before classifying them into DMOZ categories. We detail in this section the retrieval models and the classifiers that we use, our evaluation methodology, and the results of this experiment.

4.2.1 Classifiers and retrieval models

As already presented in Section 3.2, our method for estimating the interests of a user has two sequential steps: the retrieval of documents related to a Facebook entity, and their classification into 13 DMOZ categories. We detail here the different retrieval models and classifiers we experimented with in order to answer our second research question RQ2.

The retrieved documents come from the category B of ClueWeb09, a corpus of 50M web pages. We use the Terrier IR platform [26] for indexing and retrieval. We experimented with three different well-known retrieval models using their default settings in Terrier: Language Modelling (LM) [15], BM25 [29] and the DPH model [2] (an effective parameter-free model from the Divergence From Randomness framework). It is well-known that ClueWeb09 contains many spam documents, which we overcome by using the Waterloo spam list [9] that provides spam percentiles for all documents. We follow [9] and only retain documents with a percentile score higher than 70.

We use the Weka machine learning software [14] for training and classifying web pages, and test three different classifiers. We take a traditional text classification approach and consider word frequencies as features. Our baseline classifier is the well-known Naïve Bayes [19]. We also experiment with two other state-of-the-art classifiers: Random forests [7] and Decision trees (J48) [27]. Each classifier is trained using 5,000[9] randomly selected examples from 197,125 documents that were previously labelled in the DMOZ categories.

[8] We noticed in our preliminary experiments that RMSE was highly correlated with other common error measures (such as MAE or MASE).

[9] Increasing the number of training examples only resulted in reducing efficiency and had no significant effect on classification accuracy.

Table 2: **Results for modelling user interests, expressed by the Jensen-Shannon (JS) divergence between the estimated and the reference DMOZ category distributions. We use a two-sided pairwise t-test (with $p < 0.05$) to determine statistically significant differences over: (1) a random baseline that generates random category distributions, and that has a JS divergence of 16.038 ($^{\triangle}$ and $^{\triangledown}$), and (2) the Naïve Bayes baseline ($^{\blacktriangle}$ and $^{\blacktriangledown}$).**

		Number of retrieved documents					
Classifier	**Retrieval Model**	5	10	20	30	40	50
Naïve Bayes [19]	DPH [2]	12.846	5.465$^{\triangle}$	3.113$^{\triangle}$	2.591$^{\triangle}$	2.419$^{\triangle}$	2.002$^{\triangle}$
	BM25 [29]	9.189$^{\triangle}$	3.922$^{\triangle}$	2.693$^{\triangle}$	2.041$^{\triangle}$	1.284$^{\triangle}$	1.262$^{\triangle}$
	LM [15]	51.530$^{\triangledown}$	32.083$^{\triangledown}$	16.451	10.658	8.776$^{\triangle}$	6.457$^{\triangle}$
Random Forests [7]	DPH	13.061$^{\triangle}$	11.424$^{\triangle\blacktriangledown}$	8.237$^{\triangle\blacktriangledown}$	5.052$^{\triangle}$	2.804$^{\triangle}$	2.316$^{\triangle}$
	BM25	13.405$^{\triangle\blacktriangledown}$	11.386$^{\triangle\blacktriangledown}$	10.351$^{\triangle\blacktriangledown}$	8.698$^{\triangle\blacktriangledown}$	7.437$^{\triangle\blacktriangledown}$	1.803$^{\triangle}$
	LM	23.659$^{\triangledown\blacktriangle}$	17.588$^{\blacktriangle}$	15.082	15.073	14.390	13.469$^{\triangle\blacktriangledown}$
Decision trees (J48) [27]	DPH	3.532$^{\triangle\blacktriangle}$	1.316$^{\triangle\blacktriangle}$	1.293$^{\triangle}$	0.577$^{\triangle\blacktriangle}$	0.542$^{\triangle\blacktriangle}$	0.540$^{\triangle\blacktriangle}$
	BM25	1.367$^{\triangle\blacktriangle}$	0.534$^{\triangle\blacktriangle}$	0.498$^{\triangle\blacktriangle}$	0.499$^{\triangle\blacktriangle}$	0.480$^{\triangle\blacktriangle}$	0.489$^{\triangle\blacktriangle}$
	LM	**0.441**$^{\triangle\blacktriangle}$	**0.435**$^{\triangle\blacktriangle}$	**0.431**$^{\triangle\blacktriangle}$	**0.408**$^{\triangle\blacktriangle}$	**0.398**$^{\triangle\blacktriangle}$	**0.406**$^{\triangle\blacktriangle}$

4.2.2 Gold standard and evaluation measure

The nine combinations of classifiers and retrieval models that we described above all output a probability distribution over the DMOZ categories that estimate the interests of the user. In order to quantify the ability of this approach to approximate interests as per RQ2, we first need users to explicitly state their "true" interests in terms of the DMOZ categories. We obtained this gold standard by using the Amazon Mechanical Turk[10] crowdsourcing service. We presented workers with the list of the 13 DMOZ categories and asked them the following question: "*What are your general interests?*". They had to rate each of these categories in order to answer this question. Ratings ranged from 0 (not interested at all) to 10 (extremely interested). We paid users $0.05 for this task, which was completed in 32 seconds on average. We asked users to connect with their Facebook account, using Facebook's software development kit[11], in order to obtain the titles of the pages they like while they were performing the task. The users were explicitly asked to authorise access to the titles of pages they like on Facebook and nothing else. This login step also allowed us to entirely prevent our task from being completed by robots or malicious workers. We obtained a total of 25 manually entered user profiles, which constitute our gold standard.

We then converted the ratings of this gold standard into a reference probability distribution over categories, in order to be able to compare this reference to our automatically generated distributions using statistical distances. Categories from which users attributed a high rating received a high probability, and *vice versa*. In order to measure the statistical distance between our estimated category distribution and the reference distribution, we used the Jensen-Shannon (JS) divergence, which is the symmetric version of the well-known Kullback-Leibler divergence. We use this measure as it is a natural and principled choice for dealing with and comparing probability distributions, and quantifying their differences. We also experimented with the Kendall's τ rank correlation coefficient, from which we made similar observations.

4.2.3 Results

We experiment with the three classifiers and the three retrieval models presented earlier, and vary the number of retrieved documents for each Facebook entity used as a query. For each of these settings, we compute the average JS divergence across the estimated profiles and the crowdsourced references profiles. We report the results of these experiments in Table 2. As the numbers represent divergences, lower are better. As a simple baseline, we randomly generate the category distributions, which achieves a JS divergence of 16.038 (not shown in Table 2).

On analysis of Table 2, we see that increasing the amount of retrieved documents always improves the quality of the estimation, which stabilises around 40-50 documents for a majority of settings. The DPH and BM25 retrieval models have similar behaviours with all classifiers: using BM25 allows to achieve marginally better results than DPH, with one exception for random forest. Language models are ineffective when used in conjunction with Naïve Bayes and Random Forest, but achieve the best results when the retrieved documents are classified with decision trees. Using decision trees for this task significantly outperforms both the random and Naïve Bayes baselines for all settings (according to a pairwise t-test at $p < 0.05$), except for DPH when using 20 retrieved documents.

To summarise, in this section we conducted a comprehensive experiment, which revealed that our approach can automatically quantify the interests of a Facebook user from the pages she/he likes. In answer to our research question RQ2, we conclude that our approach performs best using language models (LM) to retrieve 40 retrieved documents that are classified by decision trees (J48); we adopt this setting to instantiate our model for the following user study. While the evaluation in this section focused on estimating the interests of the users without considering the venues, in the next section, we evaluate the effectiveness of the personalised venue suggestions through our user study.

5. USER STUDY

We now conduct our user study, where we obtain judgments from users (recruited volunteers), to measure the effectiveness of our model for *time-aware* and *personalised* venue suggestion. Specifically, we seek to answer three further research questions:

RQ3: Is our model effective with respect to a state-of-the-art venue suggestion baseline?

RQ4: Is our model effective for different times of the day?

RQ5: Is our model able to accommodate different types of users (such as visitors or residents)?

To answer these questions, we developed a web interface for assessing venue suggestions and asked 100 volunteers (using word-of-mouth and social networks) from across the

[10] `http://mturk.com/mturk` [11] `http://developers.facebook.com/docs/facebook-login`

world to judge these suggestions. Participants had to judge the relevance of a set of venues with respect to three conditions: their own interests, their location in the city and the time of the day. They first had to connect with their Facebook account, so that our model could infer their preferences. As in the experiment in Section 4.2, the participants were explicitly asked to authorise access to the titles of pages they like on Facebook. Then, they had to choose a city: (London, Amsterdam, or San Francisco). The presumed location of the participant during these assessments was randomly chosen within the city they selected. We used the local time of the participants as the time of the day, and set the ϵ parameter (see Section 3) to 1 hour. We specifically chose this value for two reasons. First, the terms of use of the Foursquare API prevented us from choosing a smaller ϵ without reducing the total number of venues in our dataset. Second, we assume that 1 hour is a reasonable duration for a user to walk in a busy area of a major city, while still having the time to visit a few venues. We further clustered the assessments from different times of the day by "time periods" that represent the main parts of the day. The "morning/lunch" part includes assessments performed between 7am and 1pm, the "afternoon" one focuses on the time period between 2pm and 6pm, and the "evening/night" closes the day by covering assessments between 7pm and 2am. Before displaying the suggestions to be judged, we asked participants for their previous knowledge of the city.[12] We divided this knowledge into three levels, allowing us to explore the effectiveness of our model for different types of users: people who have never been, people who have already visited, or people who live/have lived in the city. We display in Table 3 a summary of the 100 total participants broken down by city, time period, and knowledge. As said earlier, we left the choice of the city to the participants, who showed a high preference towards London. We thus take London as our main test city, and consider Amsterdam and San Francisco as additional cities in order to show generalisation. We also observe that a majority of the participants had already visited the city they chose, while a lower number of residents participated in our study. However, as we will see in the results below, the improvements over the baselines were consistent enough so that we could still identify statistical differences.

After the user had selected a city, the ranking lists of venue suggestions were computed using five different algorithms: Nearby (N), Foursquare (F), Popularity (P), Interestingness (I), and our Full model (Full). Nearby is a simple baseline that selects venues that are located near the user within a 500 meters radius (this value has been set according to the probability density function depicted in Figure 1), and ranks them randomly. Foursquare is a competitive, but a blackbox baseline that uses the API of the Foursquare LBSN, i.e. it uses the same data. It uses its own data to recommend venues near a given location[13]. Since it is currently an industrial application, we do not know the implementation details of the Foursquare recommendation algorithm. However, considering the current leadership role of Foursquare among LBSNs, we reasonably use its recommendation service as a state-of-the-art venue suggestion system. Since less than 5 of the participants had a

[12] Due to the limited space, we have not provided screenshots of the interface used by the recruited volunteers. To preserve anonymity, we will provide a URL to the interface when the paper is published.

[13] `http://developer.foursquare.com/docs/venues/explore`

Table 3: Number of participants for the three cities, as a function of their level of knowledge of the city and of the time of the day.

		London	Amst.	San Fran.	Total
Participant knowledge	never been	20	10	7	37
	visited	33	10	9	52
	live/lived in	10	1	0	11
Total		63	21	16	100
Time period	morning/lunch	16	3	1	20
	afternoon	28	12	9	49
	evening/night	19	6	6	31

Foursquare account (which would be required to obtain personalised suggestions from Foursquare), these suggestions were not personalised. The (Full) system is the instantiation of the model we propose in this paper as expressed in Equation (1). The (P) and (I) variants aim at exploring the influence of the two components of our model on suggestion effectiveness. For (P), venues are ranked based on their level of forecasted attendance only and according to the following equation: $P(v|u,l,t) \propto P(v|l,t)$. The (I) model is the opposite of (P) and only considers venues that match the user's interests. In other words, venues are ranked according to $P(v|u,l,t) \propto P(v|u)$ for this model. Details on these probabilities are available in Section 3.

We retained the 10 venues with the highest scores for each of these algorithms. The union of these rankings constitutes the pool of venues to be judged. The average size of the pool for all users is 38.31 venues. We randomised the order of the venues in the pool so that participants could perceive changes of quality in the suggestions. The web interface sequentially presented participants with a single venue, asking them to judge it with respect to the time, the location, and their own interests. Each venue was located on a map, which also shows the participant's location. Before assessing, the participants were presented with a paragraph that detailed the situation (city, exact location, time of the day), and were provided with instructions for judging the relevance of the venue. We also displayed a description of the venue, which included a photo, a list of categories, and a link to the Foursquare homepage of the venue. Participants were then asked to judge on a 3-point scale how likely they would visit the venue (not likely, likely, highly likely). Once an assessment is submitted, the next venue in the randomised pool is displayed. At the end of the study, participants had the opportunity to enter free comments in a dedicated text box[14]. We believe that obtaining user judgments on venues by asking the users to imagine that they are in a certain location of the city is realistic and indeed it has been used for evaluating venue suggestions in the TREC Contextual Suggestion track [10]. We follow the evaluation methodology of previous work in venue suggestion [38, 39] and report performances in terms of precision and nDCG after ranking 10 suggestions.

The first results, reported in Table 4, are averages over the 100 participants. We see that each of the three instantiations of our model outperforms the two baselines (N) and (F) in terms of P@10 and nDCG@10 by a statistically significant margin ($p < 0.05$, according to a pairwise t-test). While (I) gave the best suggestions according to the participants, (P) and (Full) achieve comparable results. The

[14] We received a lot of positive feedback from the participants of our study, who noted the promising applications and thanked us for making them want to travel.

Table 4: Average effectiveness results over all the participants of our study. $^{\alpha}$ and $^{\beta}$ represent statistically significant improvements (using a two-sided paired wise t-test) over the Nearby and Foursquare baselines (with $p < 0.05$), respectively.

		P@10	nDCG@10
Baselines	**Nearby** (N)	0.359	0.327
	Foursquare (F)	0.393	0.345
Our approaches	**Popularity** (P)	$0.466^{\alpha,\beta}$	$0.393^{\alpha,\beta}$
	Interestingness (I)	$\mathbf{0.480}^{\alpha,\beta}$	$\mathbf{0.408}^{\alpha,\beta}$
	Full model (Full)	$0.459^{\alpha,\beta}$	$0.389^{\alpha,\beta}$

Table 5: Effectiveness results for the 3 different cities. Notations are identical to those in Table 4.

	London		Amsterdam		San Francisco	
	P@10	nDCG@10	P@10	nDCG@10	P@10	nDCG@10
(N)	0.386	0.355	0.310	0.265	0.313	0.284
(F)	0.398	0.346	0.467^{α}	0.387^{α}	0.267	0.273
(P)	$0.475^{\alpha,\beta}$	0.394^{α}	$\mathbf{0.486}^{\alpha}$	$\mathbf{0.427}^{\alpha}$	$0.400^{\alpha,\beta}$	0.337
(I)	$\mathbf{0.514}^{\alpha,\beta}$	$\mathbf{0.453}^{\alpha,\beta}$	0.410^{α}	0.295	$\mathbf{0.433}^{\alpha,\beta}$	$\mathbf{0.376}^{\beta}$
(Full)	$0.492^{\alpha,\beta}$	$0.401^{\alpha,\beta}$	0.405^{α}	0.375^{α}	$0.393^{\alpha,\beta}$	0.354^{β}

Foursquare recommendation service (F) achieves a low performance, even when compared to (N). The full model (Full) achieves a 17% improvement in terms of P@10 over the baseline (F), while (I) achieves a 22% improvement (respectively +13% and +18% in terms of nDCG@10).

We report in Table 5 the suggestion effectiveness results when looking at each city separately. We note that the results are similar to those in Table 4. However, Foursquare achieved similar results to (P) for Amsterdam, and slightly outperformed (I) and (Full). For this particular city, (F) was able to provide participants with diversified suggestions of either "Food", "Nightlife Spot", "Arts & Entertainment", or "Outdoors & Recreation" venues. (F) failed to do the same for London and San Francisco, where 64.8% of its suggestions were "Food" venues. From the observations we make in Tables 4 and 5, and in answer to RQ3, we find that (P), (I), and (Full) are effective and consistently outperform Foursquare in terms of P@10 and nDCG@10.

We explore in Table 6 the quality of the suggestions for different time periods. When looking at the "morning" row, we see that all methods achieve similar results. Often, people's activities are very personal during this period of the day and highly depend on their activities and the time at which they start their day. While one user may want to have a breakfast, another user may already have visited a museum or might be at her/his office. By suggesting personalised venues, (I) hence achieves slightly better results than the other methods. Moreover, it is interesting to see that (P) achieves the best results on the evening. When looking at the judgments, we see that 32% of the "evening/night" relevant suggestions belong to the "Nightlife Spot" category, 44% belong to "Food", and 10% belong to "Arts & Entertainment". The fact that 86% of the relevant suggestions are evening-related activities (even if the food venues are popular for the entire day), along with the high performance of (P) for this time period, demonstrates the validity of our forecasting approach for timely promoting high quality venues. As a summary and in answer to RQ4, we find that venue suggestion is a time-dependent problem and that our model is able to cope with time variations by providing a good balance between mornings and evenings.

Table 6: Effectiveness results for 3 different time periods. Notations are identical to those in Table 4.

	morning/lunch		afternoon		evening/night	
	P@10	nDCG@10	P@10	nDCG@10	P@10	nDCG@10
(N)	0.430	0.319	0.331	0.339	0.355	0.314
(F)	0.480	0.423	0.344	0.303	0.413	0.361
(P)	0.500	$\mathbf{0.474}^{\alpha}$	$0.427^{\alpha,\beta}$	0.359^{β}	$\mathbf{0.503}^{\alpha,\beta}$	0.392^{α}
(I)	$\mathbf{0.555}^{\alpha}$	0.393	$0.446^{\alpha,\beta}$	$\mathbf{0.400}^{\alpha,\beta}$	$0.484^{\alpha,\beta}$	$\mathbf{0.430}^{\alpha,\beta}$
(Full)	0.455	0.379	$\mathbf{0.450}^{\alpha,\beta}$	$\mathbf{0.400}^{\alpha,\beta}$	$0.474^{\alpha,\beta}$	0.378^{α}

Finally, Table 7 explores the effectiveness of the venue suggestions for users with various prior knowledge of the city. The results show that while Foursquare is rather effective for people that never visited the city, it is clearly ineffective for residents or former visitors. On the other hand, our model is effective for all types of users. The results achieved by (I) when suggesting venues to residents (i.e. "live/lived in") are interesting. We observe that this class of users are not interested in popular venues and rather want to go to venues that suit their interests. The venues that residents labelled as relevant have a total number of check-ins of 2707 on average, while visitors are attracted by more popular venues (3419 and 3587 check-ins on average for new and former visitors, respectively). In answer to RQ5, we find that our model is able to accommodate different types of users with suggestions of both personalised and popular venues.

6. CONCLUSIONS

In this paper, we proposed a venue-centric and time-aware model that suggests venues based on their estimated popularity and interestingness to the user. We presented an application of time series forecasting algorithms, and an approach for categorising the interests of a user by using the Facebook pages she/he likes. We evaluated these two different components separately using a dataset of 15000 Foursquare venues spread across three cities. The experimental results showed that state-of-the-art time series forecasting models, especially ARIMA, proved to be effective at predicting the levels of venue attendance, although highly dependent on the amount of training data. By crowdsourcing the categorised Facebook user profiles, we demonstrated that users' interests can be inferred using the title of the Facebook pages they like as queries and classifying the top retrieved web documents using decision trees. Despite evaluating on Facebook, we argue that our model can generalise to other sources of user interests. For example, "liked entities" can be replaced with URLs or entities from searching/browsing logs.

Through a user study involving 100 users, we evaluated our complete probabilistic model . We also saw through our user study that our model was effective in different cities, at different times of the day, and for different types of users. Moreover, we showed that the level of attendance of a venue is a good indicator of its popularity. Residents were found to prefer personalised suggestions, while participants preferred highly popular venues during the evening. Hence, as future work, we plan to address the problem of balancing the influence of the two components in function of different parameters, such as the knowledge of the user or the category of the venue (e.g. Food, Shop). We also aim to reuse the judgments of our user study to learn this trade-off, for example by applying Learning to Rank techniques.

Overall, the user study showed that our proposed model is versatile by generalising over different types of users, and times of the day. It also demonstrated that we can model venues using social sensors (user check-ins), paving the way

Table 7: Effectiveness results for different levels of knowledge of the participants in our study. Notations are identical to those mentioned in Table 4.

	never been		visited		live/lived in	
	P@10	nDCG@10	P@10	nDCG@10	P@10	nDCG@10
(N)	0.383	0.376	0.369	0.306	0.227	0.272
(F)	0.439	0.316	0.381	0.380^{α}	0.300	0.274
(P)	0.494^{α}	0.364^{β}	$\mathbf{0.471}^{\alpha,\beta}$	$\mathbf{0.434}^{\alpha,\beta}$	0.345^{α}	0.289
(I)	$\mathbf{0.531}^{\alpha,\beta}$	$0.411^{\alpha,\beta}$	$0.452^{\alpha,\beta}$	0.397^{α}	$\mathbf{0.445}^{\alpha,\beta}$	$\mathbf{0.449}^{\alpha,\beta}$
(Full)	0.508^{α}	$\mathbf{0.423}^{\alpha,\beta}$	0.433^{α}	0.367^{α}	$0.418^{\alpha,\beta}$	$0.378^{\alpha,\beta}$

to a wider use of such data. Note that in our evaluation, we chose large cities with a relatively large number of Foursquare venues and Foursquare adoptions. We aim to consider in future work how our model performs in small cities, rural environments or in developing countries with lesser adoption of LBSNs. Finally, our approach could be extended to combine data coming from other sources, such as the physical sensors of mobile phones [35].

Acknowledgments

This work has been carried out in the scope of the EC co-funded project SMART (FP7-287583).

7. REFERENCES

[1] M.-D. Albakour, C. Macdonald, and I. Ounis. Identifying Local Events by Using Microblogs as Social Sensors. In *Proc. of OAIR*, 2013.

[2] G. Amati, E. Ambrosi, M. Bianchi, C. Gaibisso, and G. Gambosi. FUB, IASI-CNR and Univ. of Tor Vergata at TREC 2007 Blog Track. In *Proc. of TREC*, 2007.

[3] J. Bao, Y. Zheng, and M. F. Mokbel. Location-based and Preference-aware Recommendation Using Sparse Geo-social Networking Data. In *Proc. of SIGSPATIAL*, 2012.

[4] K. Berberich, A. C. König, D. Lymberopoulos, and P. Zhao. Improving Local Search Ranking through External Logs. In *Proc. of SIGIR*, 2011.

[5] B. Bi, M. Shokouhi, M. Kosinski, and T. Graepel. Inferring the Demographics of Search Users: Social Data Meets Search Queries. In *Proc. of WWW*, 2013.

[6] V. Bicer and V. Lopez. Searching in the City of Knowledge: Challenges and Recent Developments. In *Proc. of SIGIR*, 2013.

[7] L. Breiman. Random forests. *Machine Learning*, 45(1), 2001.

[8] I. Brilhante, J. A. Macedo, F. M. Nardini, R. Perego, and C. Renso. Where Shall We Go Today?: Planning Touristic Tours with Tripbuilder. In *Proc. of CIKM*, 2013.

[9] G. V. Cormack, M. D. Smucker, and C. L. Clarke. Efficient and Effective Spam Filtering and Re-ranking for Large Web Datasets. *Information Retrieval*, 14(5), 2011.

[10] A. Dean-Hall, C. L. Clarke, J. Kamps, P. Thomas, N. Simone, and E. M. Voorhees. Overview of the TREC 2013 Contextual Suggestion track. In *Proc. of TREC*, 2013.

[11] R. Deveaud, M.-D. Albakour, C. Macdonald, and I. Ounis. On the Importance of Venue-Dependent Features for Learning to Rank Contextual Suggestions. In *Proc. of CIKM*, 2014.

[12] H. Gao, J. Tang, X. Hu, and H. Liu. Exploring temporal effects for location recommendation on location-based social networks. In *Proceedings of RecSys*, pages 93–100. ACM, 2013.

[13] G. Guo. Resolving Data Sparsity and Cold Start in Recommender Systems. In *Proc. of UMAP*, 2012.

[14] M. Hall, E. Frank, G. Holmes, B. Pfahringer, P. Reutemann, and I. H. Witten. The WEKA Data Mining Software: An Update. *SIGKDD Explor. Newsl.*, 11(1), 2009.

[15] D. Hiemstra. *Using Language Models for Information Retrieval.* PhD thesis, University of Twente, 2001.

[16] B. Hu and M. Ester. Spatial Topic Modeling in Online Social Media for Location Recommendation. In *Proc. of RecSys*, 2013.

[17] R. J. Hyndman and Y. Khandakar. Automatic Time Series Forecasting: The forecast Package for R. *Journal of Statistical Software*, 27(3), 2008.

[18] R. J. Hyndman, A. B. Koehler, R. D. Snyder, and S. Grose. A State Space Framework for Automatic Forecasting using Exponential Smoothing Methods. *Inter. Journal of Forecasting*, 18(3), 2002.

[19] G. H. John and P. Langley. Estimating Continuous Distributions in Bayesian Classifiers. In *Eleventh Conference on Uncertainty in Artificial Intelligence*, San Mateo, 1995. Morgan Kaufmann.

[20] M. Kosinski, D. Stillwell, and T. Graepel. Private Traits and Attributes are Predictable from Digital Records of Human Behavior. *Proceedings of the National Academy of Sciences*, 2013.

[21] T. Kurashima, T. Iwata, T. Hoshide, N. Takaya, and K. Fujimura. Geo Topic Model: Joint Modeling of User's Activity Area and Interests for Location Recommendation. In *Proc. of WSDM*, 2013.

[22] Y. Li, M. Steiner, L. Wang, Z.-L. Zhang, and J. Bao. Exploring Venue Popularity in Foursquare. In *Proc. of INFOCOM*, 2013.

[23] Y. Lv, D. Lymberopoulos, and Q. Wu. An Exploration of Ranking Heuristics in Mobile Local Search. In *Proc. of SIGIR*, 2012.

[24] S. G. Makridakis, S. Wheelwright, and R. Hyndman. *Forecasting: Methods and Applications.* Wiley, 1998.

[25] D. Milne, P. Thomas, and C. Paris. Finding, Weighting and Describing Venues: CSIRO at The 2012 TREC Contextual Suggestion Track. In *Proc. of TREC*, 2012.

[26] I. Ounis, G. Amati, V. Plachouras, B. He, C. Macdonald, and C. Lioma. Terrier: A High Performance and Scalable Information Retrieval Platform. In *Proc. of OSIR at SIGIR*, 2006.

[27] R. Quinlan. *C4.5: Programs for Machine Learning.* Morgan Kaufmann Publishers, 1993.

[28] A. Rae, V. Murdock, A. Popescu, and H. Bouchard. Mining the Web for Points of Interest. In *Proc. of SIGIR*, 2012.

[29] S. E. Robertson, S. Walker, S. Jones, M. Hancock-Beaulieu, and M. Gatford. Okapi at TREC-3. In *Proc. of TREC*, 1994.

[30] D. Saez-Trumper, D. Quercia, and J. Crowcroft. Ads and the City: Considering Geographic Distance Goes a Long Way. In *Proc. of RecSys*, 2012.

[31] M. Sappelli, S. Verberne, and W. Kraaij. Recommending Personalized Touristic Sights Using Google Places. In *Proc. of SIGIR*, 2013.

[32] B. Shaw, J. Shea, S. Sinha, and A. Hogue. Learning to rank for spatiotemporal search. In *Proc. of WSDM*, pages 717–726, 2013.

[33] J. Soldatos, M. Draief, C. Macdonald, and I. Ounis. Multimedia Search over Integrated Social and Sensor Networks. In *Proc. of WWW*, 2012.

[34] T. Teixeira and A. Savvides. Lightweight People Counting and Localizing in Indoor Spaces Using Camera Sensor Nodes. In *Proc. of ICDSC*, 2007.

[35] H. Wang, D. Lymberopoulos, and J. Liu. Local Business Ambience Characterization Through Mobile Audio Sensing. In *Proc. of WWW*, 2014.

[36] R. W. White, P. Bailey, and L. Chen. Predicting User Interests from Contextual Information. In *Proc. of SIGIR*, 2009.

[37] P. Yang and H. Fang. An Opinion-aware Approach to Contextual Suggestion. In *Proc. of TREC*, 2013.

[38] M. Ye, P. Yin, and W.-C. Lee. Location Recommendation for Location-based Social Networks. In *Proc. of SIGSPATIAL GIS*, 2010.

[39] Q. Yuan, G. Cong, Z. Ma, A. Sun, and N. Magnenat-Thalmann. Time-aware Point-of-interest Recommendation. In *Proc. of SIGIR*, 2013.

[40] Y. Zheng. Location-Based Social Networks: Users. In *Computing with Spatial Trajectories.* Springer, 2011.

Search Result Diversification Based on Hierarchical Intents

Sha Hu[1,3], Zhicheng Dou[2,3,*], Xiaojie Wang[2,3], Tetsuya Sakai[4], and Ji-Rong Wen[1,3]
[1]Beijing Key Laboratory of Big Data Management and Analysis Methods, China
[2]Key Laboratory of Data Engineering and Knowledge Engineering, MOE, China
[3]School of Information, Renmin University of China
[4]Waseda University
[1]{sallyshahu,jirong.wen}@gmail.com, [2]{dou,wangxiaojie}@ruc.edu.cn,
[4]tetsuyasakai@acm.org

ABSTRACT

A large percentage of queries issued to search engines are broad or ambiguous. Search result diversification aims to solve this problem, by returning diverse results that can fulfill as many different information needs as possible. Most existing intent-aware search result diversification algorithms formulate user intents for a query as a flat list of subtopics. In this paper, we introduce a new hierarchical structure to represent user intents and propose two general hierarchical diversification models to leverage hierarchical intents. Experimental results show that our hierarchical diversification models outperform state-of-the-art diversification methods that use traditional flat subtopics.

Keywords

Search result diversification; hierarchical diversification; hierarchical intents

1. INTRODUCTION

In web search, the majority of short queries are ambiguous or broad when it comes to specifying a user's information need [16, 18, 25, 33, 34]. For example, by issuing an ambiguous query `[apple]`, one user might be searching for information about the IT company Apple, whereas another user might be looking for information about the fruit. By issuing a broad query `[harry potter]`, a user may want to seek contents covering various aspects, such as `[harry potter movie]`, `[harry potter book]`, or `[harry potter characters]` within this broad topic. Traditional search may fail to cover these different intents in the top ranks.

As an effective way to solve this problem, search result diversification, which aims to return diverse search results that cover as many user intents as possible, has received a lot of attention in recent years. Many search result diversification algorithms [1, 2, 5, 14, 23, 25, 26, 31, 32, 36, 37, 42] and evaluation metrics [1, 4, 8, 9, 28, 39] have been developed to improve and evaluate search result diversity. Some public search result diversification evaluation tasks, including the TREC Web Track Diversity task [11] and the NTCIR Intent/IMine task [22, 27], have been organized to evaluate diversification approaches via public test collections.

In diversification, most existing algorithms generalize user intents in a flat list of independent subtopics, such as topical categories [1, 35], query reformulations by search engine [12, 13, 30], words or phrases extracted from top retrieved documents [3, 13], or combined subtopics from multiple external resources [14, 17]. For instance, Santos *et al.* [30] represented different query intents as a set of Google suggestions or related queries. Dang and Croft [13] extracted words or phrases from top retrieved documents. Dou *et al.* [14] mined subtopics from different types of resources.

In typical search result diversification tasks (such as TREC and NTCIR), the intents of a query are predefined by human labellers. To achieve good performance, it is critical to automatically mine subtopics for a query and the mined subtopics should properly match the predefined intents. However, as the intents and subtopics are independently obtained, it is not easy to match them, especially when a flat intent list is used.

Let us take the query "defender" (topic number 20) in TREC 2009 [6] as an example. Table 1 shows six manually defined intents for it, including "Windows Defender Homepage", "Land Rover Defender", "Defender Marine Supply", "Defender Arcade Game Online", "Windows Defender Reports," and "Chicago Defender Newspaper". To mine subtopics for the query, we use the approach proposed in [12, 13, 30]. We send the query "defender" to a commercial search engine and get back query suggestions "defender windows", "defender arcade game," and "defender land rover" (The first-level subtopics in Figure 1). When we take them as subtopics for the query "defender", we find that they are too coarse to distinguish the user intents. For instance, the subtopic "defender windows" (t_1) covers both the user intents "Windows Defender homepage" (s_1) and "Windows Defender Reports" (s_5). So the diversity algorithm has the risk to only select documents from subtopic t_1 with respect to the intent s_1 without covering subtopic s_5, or vice versa.

An easy remedy to the above problem is to use fine-grained intents in diversification. By further sending the three subtopics as queries to the search engine, we can get their query suggestions as fine-grained subtopics (the second-level subtopics in Figure 1). With the fine-grained subtopics, we can do a better job to distinguish user intents. For example, "defender windows home" ($t_{1,1}$) and "defender windows prob-

* Corresponding Author

CIKM'15, October 19–23, 2015, Melbourne, VIC, Australia.
© 2015 ACM. ISBN 978-1-4503-3794-6/15/10 ...$15.00.
DOI: http://dx.doi.org/10.1145/2806416.2806455.

Table 1: **Subtopics of query "defender" in TREC 2009 Web Track.**

no.	subtopic description
s_1	I'm looking for the homepage of Windows Defender, an anti-spyware program. **(Windows Defender Homepage)**
s_2	Find information on the Land Rover Defender sport-utility vehicle. **(Land Rover Defender)**
s_3	I want to go to the homepage for Defender Marine Supplies. **(Defender Marine Supply)**
s_4	I'm looking for information on Defender, an arcade game by Williams. Is it possible to play it online? **(Defender Arcade Game Online)**
s_5	I'd like to find user reports about Windows Defender, particularly problems with the software. **(Windows Defender Reports)**
s_6	Take me to the homepage for the Chicago Defender newspaper. **(Chicago Defender Newspaper)**

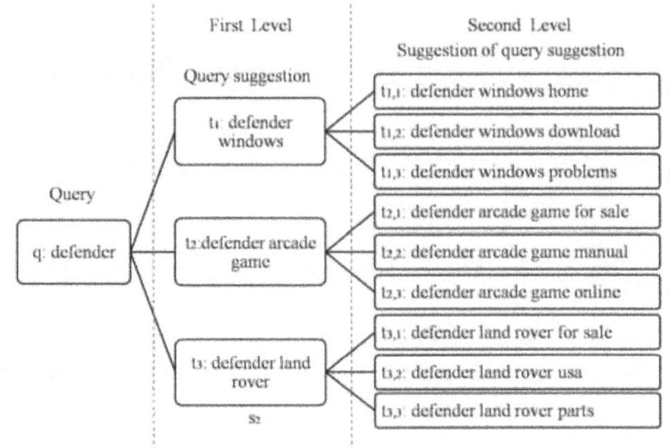

Figure 1: Two-level hierarchical subtopics of query "defender" from query suggestions of a commercial search engine.

lems" ($t_{1,3}$) can be easily matched to user intents "Windows Defender homepage" (s_1) and "Windows Defender Reports" (s_5). However, the fine-grained subtopics bring in a new problem that multiple subtopics are matched to the same user intent. For example, "defender land rover for sale" ($t_{3,1}$), "defender land rover usa" ($t_{3,2}$), and "defender land rover parts" ($t_{3,3}$) are all related to the user intent "Land Rover Defender" (s_2). When simply combining the fine-grained subtopics in a flat list, the diversity algorithm may first select one document from subtopic $t_{3,1}$ ("defender land rover for sale"), and then select another document from subtopic $t_{3,2}$ ("defender land rover usa"), unaware of the fact that the selected documents match the same user intent s_2 ("Land Rover Defender").

To solve the above problems, we explore a new way of organizing subtopics in a hierarchical structure. Figure 1 shows the two-level hierarchical subtopic structure for the query "defender". We can see that the six user intents in Table 1 are mapped to the subtopics in both two levels. This hierarchical structure maintains user intents with different granularity levels and the relationships between different levels. It provides the flexibility of applying and balancing different levels of intent granularity in diversification, which ultimately increases the probability of correctly matching more diverse intents.

In this paper, we propose a diversification framework to explicitly leverage the hierarchical intents. In particular, we extend the state-of-the-art diversification algorithms xQuAD and PM2, and propose a Hierarchical xQuAD model (HxQuAD) and a Hierarchical PM2 model (HPM2). These hierarchical models select documents that maximize diversity in the hierarchical structure. For the example in Figure 1, if the previously selected documents have already cover the subtopic "defender windows home", the next selected document for the intent "defender windows" should better come from the subtopic "defender windows download" or "defender windows problems". Without the hierarchical structure, it is difficult for traditional diversification methods to distinguish and balance these second-level subtopics. Moreover, after selecting documents for the second-level subtopics "defender windows home" and "defender windows problems", which belong to the same first-level subtopic "defender windows," the next document is better to be related to another first-level subtopic such as "defender arcade game" or "defender land rover". This situation is not considered in traditional diversification methods when only the flat intent list is used.

We argue that real user intents are in a hierarchical structure sometimes. Recent work [15, 19] understands queries by query facets and represents query facets by multiple groups of facet items, where these query facets and their facet items can be viewed as a two-level hierarchical explanation of the query. In Table 1, real user intents of the query also lie in a two-level hierarchy. It contains five first-level subtopics "Windows Defender", "Land Rover Defender" (s_2), "Defender Marine" (s_3), "Defender Arcade Game" (s_4), and "Chicago Defender Newspaper" (s_6). The subtopic "Windows Defender" contains two second-level subtopics "Windows Defender Homepage" (s_1) and "Windows Defender Reports". To measure the real user satisfaction on the query, it would be ideal to evaluate diversity based on hierarchical intents. Unfortunately we do not have such diversity judgment data and evaluation metrics. In this paper, we still use existing metrics to evaluate our algorithms.

Our experiments are conducted on two-level hierarchical subtopics which are automatically extracted from a commercial search engine. The algorithms are evaluated on the public TREC [7] dataset and the NTCIR [22] dataset. Experimental results show that by using hierarchical subtopics, our hierarchical algorithms (HxQuAD and HPM2) outperform most state-of-the-art models including xQuAD [30], PM2 [12], TxQuAD, and TPM2 [13], in terms of ERR-IA [4], α-NDCG [8], NRBP [9], and D$\sharp$-nDCG [28]. Even when only using single-level subtopics in the hierarchical structure, our hierarchical algorithms still outperform their corresponding algorithms which represent the same subtopics in a flat list, in terms of ERR-IA, α-NDCG, and NRBP. The results show that exploiting the hierarchical intent structure can benefit search result diversification.

2. RELATED WORK

In early diversification algorithms, query intents were *implicitly* considered to promote diversity by selecting documents with little content similarity. Maximal Marginal Relevance (MMR) [2] measured documents with cosine similarities in vocabulary, and attempted to reduce redundancy while maintaining query relevance in re-ranking. Some work estimated document similarity in different ways, such as using Kullback-Leibler divergence [38], ranking sentences by random walks in an absorbing Markov chain [42], and modeling directed graphs based on the document link structure [40]. These approaches assume that similar documents will cover similar query intents, without considering exactly which query intents are being covered.

Many researchers noticed the above problem and *explicitly* considered query intents for diversification. IA-Select [1] developed an intent-aware diversifying method by classified topical categories for queries and documents based on ODP taxonomy. xQuAD [30] used a greedy algorithm to maximize the coverage of query aspects. RxQuAD [35] explicitly provided a relevance formulation for query aspects. PM2 [12] divided diversification into two processes: finding the best unsatisfied topic-by-topic proportionality, and then choosing the best document based on the selected subtopic. Intrinsic diversity [26] predicted the successor queries for initiator query to seek which content to cover. Yu and Ren [36] formulated diversification as a 0-1 multiple subtopic knapsack problem. Fusion diversification [21] inferred latent subtopics based on topic modeling. Some work promoted diversity by leveraging subtopics from multiple external resources, such as involving user clicks to help query aspects [24], combining subtopics from different data types [14, 17]. Although these approaches generate query intents from various sources, combinations or models, they commonly represent intents in a flat list. In contrast, our work utilizes hierarchical intents and provides hierarchical frameworks to promote diversity of search results.

Some researchers use machine learning techniques to diversify search results, such as Structural SVMs [37] and R-LTR [43]. In this paper, we focus on the unsupervised intent-aware diversification. More specifically, we extend xQuAD to hierarchical novelty-based model, and adapt PM2 for hierarchical proportionality-based model.

There are a few prior art that are somewhat similar to ours. Term level diversification [13] represented a subtopic by a set of key terms, which is similar to our idea of denoting a subtopic with a group of child subtopics in hierarchical subtopic structure. Unlike considering hierarchical information as we do, term level diversification integrated all terms to build subtopics. We implement their basic models as our baselines in our experiments. Concept hierarchy based diversification [41] considered subtopic relations in result diversification. Instead of providing hierarchical frameworks to handle hierarchical subtopics, it exploited concept hierarchies to extract query subtopics in a flat list, utilized hierarchical relations of subtopics to propose a structural similarity function for subtopics, and incorporated this function into the traditional xQuAD framework. This function iteratively selected documents covering important subtopics that are less structurally similar to the subtopics covered by the selected documents. This work was done in enterprise search domain, as it is hard to build high-quality concept hierarchies in web search. We implement this method by adopting our hierarchical subtopics used in our hierarchical models as their input concept hierarchy.

There have been some approaches [15, 19, 20, 29] that mine hierarchical information for a query. In the present study, we use Google suggestions as the source of hierarchical subtopics, following previous work [12, 13, 30]. We will explore our own subtopic mining methods in future work.

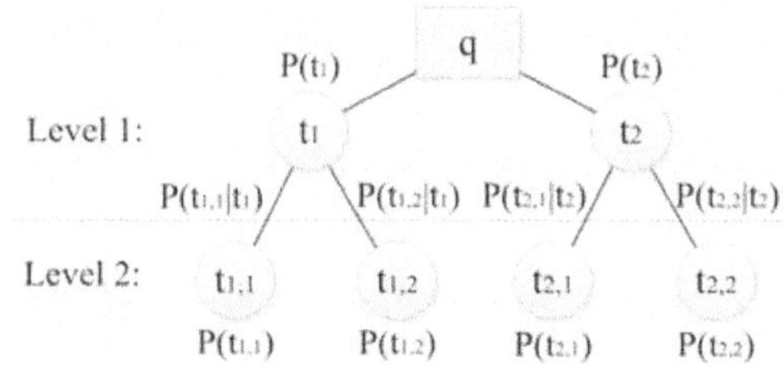

Figure 2: An example of hierarchical subtopic tree.

3. HIERARCHICAL DIVERSIFICATION

3.1 Hierarchical Intents

As mentioned earlier, most intent-aware diversification algorithms model user intents as a group of subtopics and boost diversity based on them. In this paper, we propose to present subtopics in a hierarchical structure.

Formally, we use $T_q = \{t_1, t_2, ...\}$ to indicate a set of first-level subtopics $\{t_{i_1}\}$ for query q where $i_1 = 1, 2...$ is the position of subtopic t_{i_1} in T_q. For subtopic t_{i_1}, we use $T_{i_1} = \{t_{i_1,1}, t_{i_1,2}, ...\}$ to denote a set of its child subtopics $\{t_{i_1,i_2}\}$. For each subtopic $t_{i_1,i_2} \in T_{i_1}$, i_2 is the relative index of subtopic t_{i_1,i_2} within all child subtopics of t_{i_1}. To generalize, we use $t_{i_1,.,i_j}$ to denote a subtopic at level j and use $T_{i_1,.,i_j}$ to denote a set of its child subtopics. $t_{i_1,.,i_{j+1}} \in T_{i_1,.,i_j}$ and $t_{i_1,.,i_{j+1}}$ is a specific child subtopic of $t_{i_1,.,i_j}$ at level $j+1$.

Figure 2 shows an example of the hierarchical subtopics in two levels. The first level contains two subtopics t_1, t_2 and the second level has four subtopics $t_{1,1}, t_{1,2}, t_{2,1}, t_{2,2}$. $t_{1,1}$ and $t_{1,2}$ are child subtopics of t_1, and $t_{2,1}$ and $t_{2,2}$ are child subtopics of t_2. Here exists $T_1 = \{t_{1,1}, t_{1,2}\}$ and $T_2 = \{t_{2,1}, t_{2,2}\}$.

Let us reuse the example topic "defender" in Figure 1 to illustrate the process. The subtopic "defender windows" contains three child subtopics: "defender windows home" shows users want the homepage of the software, "defender windows download" indicates the download requirement of the software, and "defender windows problems" denotes users are interested in the problems of the software. Similarly, the first-level subtopics "defender arcade game" and "defender land rover" have their own second-level child subtopics.

It is worth noting that term level diversification [13] also indicates a subtopic by a set of terms $t_i = \{t_i^1, t_i^2, ., t_i^j, ...\}$. They treat each t_i^j as an independent subtopic, and integrate them together to build a larger flat term level subtopics $\{t_1^1, t_1^2, ..., t_1^{|t_1|}, ..., t_n^1, t_n^2, ..., t_n^{|t_n|}\}$. Its diversification algorithm is not aware of the relationship between t_i^j and t_i, and the relationship between two terms. In contrast, we maintain the subtopics in hierarchy structure and diversify search results based on these hierarchical subtopics.

For a given query q, we use $R = \{d_1, d_2, ..., d_m\}$ to denote its initial ranked documents set. For traditional diversification algorithms that use a flat list of subtopics, we use $T = \{t_1, t_2, ..., t_n\}$ to denote subtopics of the query. Let $P(d|q)$ be the probability that document d is relevant to query q, $P(d|t)$ indicate the probability that d satisfies subtopic t, and $P(t|q)$ denote the importance of subtopic t for query q. Existing diversification algorithms use T, $P(d|q)$, $P(d|t)$, and $P(t|q)$ to select a list of diversified documents D out of R. Similarly, for hierarchical diversification, we define the following probabilities:

$\mathbf{P(t_{i_1,..,i_{j+1}}|t_{i_1,..,i_j})}$. $P(t_{i_1,..,i_{j+1}}|t_{i_1,..,i_j})$ is the importance of a subtopic $t_{i_1,..,i_{j+1}}$ with respect to its parent subtopic $t_{i_1,..,i_j}$. We assume that $t_{i_1,..,i_j}$ is fully covered by its child subtopic set $T_{i_1,..,i_j}$ and each of the child subtopic is independent to each other. Hence we have:

$$\sum_{t_{i_1,..,i_{j+1}} \in T_{i_1,..,i_j}} P(t_{i_1,..,i_{j+1}}|t_{i_1,..,i_j}) = 1$$

In Figure 2, we have $P(t_{1,1}|t_1)+P(t_{1,2}|t_1)=1$ and $P(t_{2,1}|t_2)+P(t_{2,2}|t_2)=1$.

$\mathbf{P(t_{i_1,..,i_j}|q)}$. $P(t_{i_1,..,i_n}|q)$ is the importance of subtopic $t_{i_1,..,i_j}$ with respect to the query q. The way of calculating $P(t_{i_1,..,i_j}|q)$ may vary in different applications. If the importance of leaf subtopics is known (for example, when parent subtopics are generated by clustering child subtopics), we can update the importance of their ancestors by iteratively summing up the importance of child subtopics, i.e., we have:

$$P(t_{i_1,..,i_j}|q) = \sum_{t_{i_1,..,i_{j+1}} \in T_{i_1,..,i_j}} P(t_{i_1,..,i_{j+1}}|q) \qquad (1)$$

In some other cases, we may just know the importance of the first-level subtopics. For example, when building the hierarchy subtopics based on Google suggestion, we need to first retrieve first-level subtopics, and then retrieve second-level subtopics by issuing the first-level subtopics as queries. In this case, we may calculate the weight of each child subtopic by using Bayes's formula:

$$P(t_{i_1,..,i_{j+1}}|q) = P(t_{i_1,..,i_j}|q) \cdot P(t_{i_1,..,i_{j+1}}|t_{i_1,..,i_j})$$

In Figure 2, if $P(t_1|q)$ is given, $P(t_{1,1}|q)=P(t_1|q)\cdot P(t_{1,1}|t_1)$, $P(t_{1,2}|q)=P(t_1|q) \cdot P(t_{1,2}|t_1)$. If $P(t_{1,1}|q)$ and $P(t_{1,2}|q)$ are known, $P(t_1|q)=P(t_{1,1}|q) + P(t_{1,2}|q)$.

$\mathbf{P(d|t_{i_1,..,i_j})}$. $P(d|t_{i_1,..,i_j})$ is the probability that document d satisfies $t_{i_1,..,i_j}$. $P(d|t_{i_1,..,i_j}) = P(d|t_{i_1,..,i_j}, q)$ because we assume $P(q|t_{i_1,..,i_j}) = 1$. We assume that leaf subtopics $t_{i_1,..,i_n}$ are usually represented as words or phrases, and we can directly calculate $P(d|t_{i_1,..,i_n})$ on leaf subtopics using language model or other retrieval model. For non-leaf subtopics, instead of words or phrases, they may be organized as groups of their child subtopics (e.g., when second-level subtopics are Google suggestions, and the first-level subtopics are clusters of these suggestions). In this case, we use a bottom-up method to recursively calculate $P(d|t_{i_1,..,i_j})$ for a subtopic $t_{i_1,..,i_j}$ based on its child subtopics $T_{i_1,..,i_j}$ as follows:

$$P(d|t_{i_1,..,i_j}) = 1 - \prod_{t_{i_1,..,i_{j+1}} \in T_{i_1,..,i_j}} (1 - P(d|t_{i_1,..,i_{j+1}})) \qquad (2)$$

where $(1 - P(d|t_{i_1,..,i_{j+1}}))$ is the probability that d dose not satisfy $t_{i_1,..,i_{j+1}}$. The product denotes the probability that d fails to satisfy every child subtopic for $t_{i_1,..,i_j}$. One minus that product equals the probability that d will satisfy at least one child subtopic $t_{i_1,..,i_{j+1}}$ within $T_{i_1,..,i_j}$.

3.2 Hierarchical Diversification Algorithms

3.2.1 Topic novelty model

The topic novelty model, inspired by MMR [2], is a widely used framework in diversification. It considers both the relevance between the document and the query, and the topic diversity of the document among the selected documents. It iteratively selects a next best document d that is relevant to query q and can maximize the diversity of selected documents D. The formulation of the model is as below.

$$d^* = \arg \max_{d \in R \setminus D} (1 - \lambda) \cdot P(d|q) + \lambda \cdot \Phi(d, D) \qquad (3)$$

Different probabilistic models are proposed to measure the diversity $\Phi(d, D)$ in previous work [1, 3, 30]. We select xQuAD, one of the state-of-the-art diversification methods, to adapt a diversity model to use hierarchical structured subtopics. xQuAD explicitly estimates the diversity of a document by calculating the coverage of matched subtopics.

$$\Phi(d, D) = \sum_{t \in T_q} [P(d|t) \cdot P(t|q) \cdot \prod_{d' \in D} (1 - P(d'|t))] \qquad (4)$$

In the above equation, $(1-P(d'|t))$ indicates the probability that an existing document d' does not satisfy t. The product shows the probability that all the selected documents D fail to satisfies t. Summing up over all subtopics, weighted by $P(t|q)$, the diversity is the probability that d covers the subtopics while the existing document list D fail to satisfy.

However, Equation (4) is designed for the subtopics formed as a flat list, which may fail when real user intents are hierarchical. We take the query intents shown in Figure 2 as an example. Assume there are four documents: d_1 and d_2 relevant to $t_{1,1}$, d_3 relevant to $t_{1,2}$, and d_4 relevant to $t_{2,1}$. One of the ideal rank lists is $(d_1 \to d_4 \to d_3 \to d_2)$ and the diversity is maximized within the top three results. If we just use the first-level subtopics in xQuAD, the returned diversified rank list might be $(d_1 \to d_4 \to d_2 \to d_3)$. In the third iteration, it fails to distinguish the difference between d_2 and d_3 because both are relevant to t_1. If we just use the second-level subtopics in xQuAD, the resulting list might be $(d_1 \to d_3 \to d_4 \to d_2)$. In this case, it assumes that d_3 and d_4 are equally important because both can offer a new subtopic, but in fact, d_4 is better because both d_3 and d_1 belong to subtopic t_1.

To solve the above problem, we adapt xQuAD so that it can handle hierarchical subtopics. We propose **HxQuAD**, a hierarchical xQuAD model, to explicitly model result diversity based on the hierarchical subtopics. Specifically, at each level j of the hierarchical subtopic tree, HxQuAD estimates result diversity by:

$$\Phi(d, D, j) = \sum_{|i_1,..,i_j|=j} [P(d|t_{i_1,..,i_j}) \cdot P(t_{i_1,..,i_j}|q) \cdot \prod_{d' \in D} (1 - P(d'|t_{i_1,..,i_j}))] \qquad (5)$$

Here $|i_1, .., i_j| = j$ means $t_{i_1,..,i_j}$ is a subtopic at level j. $P(d|t_{i_1,..,i_j})$ and $P(t_{i_1,..,i_j}|q)$ estimate the probabilities that d satisfies $t_{i_1,..,i_j}$ and $t_{i_1,..,i_j}$ satisfies q, and we have

$$P(d|t_{i_1,..,i_j}) = 1 - \prod_{t_{i_1,..,i_{j+1}} \in T_{i_1,..,i_j}} (1 - P(d|t_{i_1,..,i_{j+1}}))$$

which is the same as Equation (2). This model evaluates the importance of document d based on whether it can improve overall diversity in terms of the subtopics at level j.

We then combine these components, and evaluate the overall importance of a document in terms of all levels within the hierarchy. A parameter α is introduced to control the granularity of subtopics that the diversification tends to optimize for. We have:

$$\Phi(d, D) = \alpha \cdot \Phi(d, D, 1) + (1-\alpha) \cdot \Phi(d, D, 2) + \frac{(1-\alpha)^2}{\alpha} \cdot \Phi(d, D, 3) + ... + \frac{(1-\alpha)^{n-1}}{\alpha^{n-2}} \cdot \Phi(d, D, n) \quad (6)$$

Here $\alpha \in (0, 1]$ and $\alpha = 0.5$ indicates that all the subtopic levels are equally weighted. A value larger than 0.5 means that the algorithm tends to diversify result based on coarse subtopics; whereas a value lower than 0.5 indicates that it provides fine-grained diversify. Specially, if $\alpha = 1$, then it only uses the first-level subtopics; whereas, if α is close to 0, the model tends to take the leaf subtopics. Note that α could be 0 if there are only two levels in hierarchy.

In summary, HxQuAD extends xQuAD to hierarchical subtopics by redefining a multi-level diversity function. Besides balancing the relevance and diversity by parameter λ, we use a parameter α to control the impact of subtopics at different depth.

3.2.2 *Topic proportionality model*

Instead of considering diversity of subtopics and documents at the same time, the topic proportionality based diversification model selects subtopics and documents separately. At each iteration, the algorithm first selects the best subtopic based on the proportionality strategy, and then finds the most relevant document optimized for the selected subtopic.

PM2 [12] is one of the state-of-the-art topic proportionality based diversification algorithms. It considers the diversification problem as assigning seats to members of competing political parties and follows a highest quotient (Sainte-Lague) method to select subtopics as allocating seats. In the beginning, PM2 computes the quotient qt_i for each subtopic t_i by the Sainte-Lague formula[1].

$$qt_i = \frac{w_i}{2s_i + 1} \quad (7)$$

To maintain the proportionality of the subtopic distribution, PM2 assigns the subtopic with the largest quotient as the selected subtopic t_{i^*}. Then, it calculates the diversity function $\Phi(d, D, t^*)$ to find the document d^* that is most relevant to t_{i^*} and relatively relevant to other subtopics.

$$d^* = \arg \max_{d \in R \setminus D} \Phi(d, D, t^*)$$

where

$$\Phi(d, D, t^*) = \lambda \cdot qt_{i^*} \cdot P(d|t_{i^*}) + (1-\lambda) \cdot \sum_{i \neq i^*} qt_i \cdot P(d|t_i) \quad (8)$$

After document d^* is selected, to punish its highly relevant subtopics, PM2 increases the "portion" of occupied seats s_i for each subtopic t_i by its normalized relevance to d^*.

$$s_i = s_i + \frac{P(d^*|t_i)}{\sum_{t_j \in T_q} P(d^*|t_j)} \quad (9)$$

[1]Sainte-Lague: `http://www.elections.org.nz/voting/mmp/sainte-lague.html`

The algorithm repeats the above process to iteratively select next best documents from R to D.

In this paper, we modify the framework of PM2 to adapt hierarchical subtopics and propose the hierarchical PM2 model (**HPM2**). HPM2 maintains the basic idea of finding the best document based on the preselected subtopic by proportionality. Moreover, since each level of hierarchical subtopics may contain different diversity information, HPM2 selects one best subtopic for each level of the subtopic tree, and combine them together to find the best document. Considering Figure 2 as an example, we may select t_1 with max quotient from the first-level and $t_{1,1}$ with max quotient for the second-level, and find the best document based on them. Note that we may choose t_1 and $t_{2,1}$ sometimes, as the best subtopics are selected independently.

First of all, HPM2 computes the quotient values for the subtopics in each level, respectively. For the subtopic $t_{i_1,..,i_j}$ at level j, the quotient is similarly formulated as Equation (7). Note that $P(t_{i_1,..,i_j}|q)$ is the probability that $t_{i_1,..,i_j}$ satisfies q.

$$qt_{i_1,..,i_j} = \frac{P(t_{i_1,..,i_j}|q)}{2s_{i_1,..,i_j} + 1} \quad (10)$$

Comparing all the quotients of the subtopics at level j, HPM2 selects the best subtopic $t^*_{i_1,..,i_j}$ with max quotient value $qt^*_{i_1,..,i_j}$. The best subtopics $t^*_{i_1}$, $t^*_{i_1,i_2}$, ..., $t^*_{i_1,..,i_n}$ are respectively chosen from level $1, 2, ..., n$ in hierarchy. HPM2 calculates the document diversity for each level of hierarchical subtopics and combines all to select the best document.

For level j in the hierarchical subtopics, since $t^*_{i_1,..,i_j}$ is the preselected subtopic at level j, according to the diversity definition in PM2, a document is more diverse if it is relevant to $t^*_{i_1,..,i_j}$ and fairly related to other subtopics of this level. Therefore, we define $\Phi(d, D, t^*_{i_1,..,i_j})$ as:

$$\Phi(d, D, t^*_{i_1,..,i_j}) = \lambda \cdot qt^*_{i_1,..,i_j} \cdot P(d|t^*_{i_1,..,i_j}) + (1-\lambda) \cdot \sum_{t_k \neq t^*_{i_1,..,i_j}, |k|=j} qt_k \cdot P(d|t_k) \cdot P(t_k|t^*_{i_1,..,i_j}) \quad (11)$$

Here $P(t_k|t^*_{i_1,..,i_j})$ is used to model the dependency between t_k and the selected subtopic $t^*_{i_1,..,i_j}$. We use it because treating all the unselected subtopics equally is not fair in the hierarchy. A close subtopic t, which may share common parent, grandparent, or ancestor with t^*, is more related to t^* than other subtopics. For instance, if $t_{1,1}$ is the selected subtopic, $t_{1,2}$ is usually more semantically related to $t_{1,1}$ than $t_{2,1}$ and $t_{2,2}$. So we should assign a higher weight to $t_{1,2}$ than $t_{2,1}$ and $t_{2,2}$ in Equation (11). We use the following function to evaluate the weight of a subtopic based on its distance to the selected subtopic.

$$P(t_{i_1,..,i_j}|t^*_{i_1,..,i_j}) = \frac{2j - dis(t_{i_1,..,i_j}, t^*_{i_1,..,i_j}) + 1}{2j} \quad (12)$$

where $dis(t, t^*)$ is the length of the path for moving from t to t^*. Since both subtopics are at level j, the maximal distance between t and t^* is $2j$. It is used to normalize the distance. Considering the example in Figure 2, we have $P(t_2|t_1) = (2 \cdot 1 - 2 + 1)/(2 \cdot 1) = 0.5$, $P(t_{1,1}|t_{1,2}) = (2 \cdot 2 - 2 + 1)/(2 \cdot 2) = 0.75$ and $P(t_{2,1}|t_{1,2}) = (2 \cdot 2 - 4 + 1)/(2 \cdot 2) = 0.25$.

Based on Equation (11), we further combine all levels, and find the best document d^* by the following formula.

$$d^* = \arg\max_{d \in R \setminus D} \alpha \cdot \Phi(d, D, t^*_{i_1}) + (1-\alpha) \cdot \Phi(d, D, t^*_{i_1,i_2}) + \frac{(1-\alpha)^2}{\alpha} \cdot \Phi(d, D, t^*_{i_1,i_2,i_3}) + ... + \frac{(1-\alpha)^{n-1}}{\alpha^{n-2}} \cdot \Phi(d, D, t^*_{i_1,..,i_n}) \quad (13)$$

Similar to Equation (6), parameter $\alpha \in (0, 1]$ is used to control the impact of subtopic granularity.

At last, HPM2 updates the occupied seat $s_{i_1,..,i_j}$ for the subtopic $t_{i_1,..,i_j}$ based on the selected document d^* as follows. Note that the update is respectively done for each level in hierarchy, as the best subtopic is selected at each level.

$$s_{i_1,..,i_j} = s_{i_1,..,i_j} + \frac{P(d^*|t_{i_1,..,i_j})}{\sum_{|k|=j} P(d^*|t_k)} \quad (14)$$

In short, HPM2 selects each best subtopic by proportionality, finds the document based on selected subtopics and updates the occupied seats by the chosen document, following the steps of PM2. In addition, HPM2 performs subtopic selecting and seats updating at each level of the hierarchical subtopics and finds the best document by considering n selected subtopics at the same time. It uses a distance function to control the influence of the unselected subtopics by considering their distances to selected subtopics.

4. EXPERIMENTAL SETUP

4.1 Datasets

We experiment with the proposed algorithms on four topic sets provided by TREC Web Tracks from 2009 [6] to 2012 [7]. Every topic set contains 50 topics, each of which includes three to eight subtopics. Topics 95 and 100 in the TREC 2010 topic set were removed as they lack diversity relevance judgments. Following the official task definitions, we use the ClueWeb09 [10] document collection for the four topic sets. We merge the four datasets into one and name it as TREC in this paper.

For each topic, we retrieve top 1,000 documents using the batch search service provided by Lemur project[2]. Similar to existing approaches [12, 13], we remove the documents with spam score larger than 70 using the Waterloo Spam Filter[3] for ClueWeb09. We take these filtered documents as our initial non-diversified ranking results, and conduct our experimental results on top 50 documents as existing work has found that both xQuAD and PM2 achieve their best performance when using 50 documents [12]. We estimate the relevance between documents and topics by the language model used in Lemur[2]. And we use the same model to calculate the relevance between documents and subtopics.

In addition, we use the dataset provided by the IMine (Intent Mining) task in NTCIR-11 [22]. We use the Chinese topic set which is comprised of 18 clear queries and 32 ambiguous or broad queries, and name this dataset as NTCIR in this paper. We evaluate the algorithms using the 32 ambiguous or broad queries, as diversity relevance judgments are not provided for the clear queries. We use the official non-diversified baseline retrieval results from the SogouT2008[4] corpus provided by the organizers. Note that, in contrast to the TREC data, IMine task provides two-level human annotated subtopics and we can evaluate diversity using both coarse-grained and fine-grained search intents.

[2]Batch Service Clueweb09: `http://boston.lti.cs.cmu.edu/Services/clueweb09_batch/`

[3]Waterloo Spam Filter: `http://plg.uwaterloo.ca/~gvcormac/clueweb09spam/`

4.2 Evaluation Metrics

We use ERR-IA [4], α-NDCG [8], and NRBP [9], which are official evaluation metrics at TREC Web Track, to evaluate result diversity. They measure the diversity of a result list by explicitly rewarding novelty and penalizing redundancy observed at every rank. We use the same parameters as those used in official TREC tasks, and hence per-subtopic graded relevance assessments are treated as binary. In addition, we use D♯-measures [28], the primary metric that used in NTCIR IMine task, which actually utilizes graded diversity relevance judgments. All metrics are computed based on the top 20 ranking results, consistent with the official tasks in TREC 2010-2012. Moreover, we use the two-tailed paired t-test for statistically significance testing and report a significant difference if the p-value is lower than 0.05.

4.3 Generation of hierarchical subtopics

Similar to previous work [12, 30], we use query suggestions extracted from Google search engine as subtopics (as shown in Figure 1). To avoid Google's personalized suggestions, we clean the cookies and set the location to United States before query suggestion crawling.

For each topic, we collect its query suggestions from Google as the first-level subtopics. To generate subtopic hierarchy, we further issue the first-level subtopics as queries to Google and retrieve their query suggestions as the second-level subtopics. Sometimes Google fails to provide suggestions for some queries. When a topic has no suggestion, we view this topic as invalid and omit it. If a first-level subtopic from a valid topic has no suggestion, we add itself as its second-level subtopic to ensure the two-level structure. Finally, we collect 1,696 first-level subtopics and 10,527 second-level subtopics for 194 queries. We only consider two-level hierarchical subtopics in this paper, and leave the investigation of using third and deeper levels to future work.

Consistent with existing research [30, 12], we assume a uniform probability distribution for all the first-level subtopics, i.e., $P(t_i|q) = \frac{1}{|T_q|}$ where T_q is the set of the first-level subtopics. We also assume a uniform probability distribution for the second-level subtopics with respect to their parent subtopics. We use Equation (1) to calculate the importance of a second-level subtopic with respect to the query. For example, for the jth second-level subtopic $t_{i,j}$ of the ith first-level subtopic t_i, its importance $P(t_{i,j}|q)$ is $\frac{1}{|T_q|*|T_i|}$ where $|T_i|$ is the count of second-level subtopics of t_i.

4.4 Baseline Models

We compare our proposed models with the following baseline approaches: the non-diversified baseline ranking (Baseline), xQuAD, PM2, TxQuAD, TPM2, and ConceptH. We already introduced **xQuAD** and **PM2** in Section 3.2 and we recall that our hierarchical diversification models are extended from them. Term level diversification models, viz., **TxQuAD** and **TPM2** [13], split the original subtopics (used by xQuAD and PM2) into terms and use these terms as

[4]SogouT2008: `http://www.sogou.com/labs/dl/t-e.html`

Table 2: **Performance comparison on TREC 2009-2012. The best result is in bold. Statistically significant differences between the hierarchical methods (HxQuAD and HPM2) and the baseline methods (xQuAD, TxQuAD, PM2, TPM2, and ConceptH) are marked with $*$, $\star$, $\diamond$, $\circ$, $\dagger$, respectively.**

	ERR-IA	α-nDCG	NRBP	D$\sharp$-nDCG
Baseline	.2630	.3610	.2238	.4124
xQuAD*	.2842	.3822	.2465	.4109
TxQuAD*	.2792	.3835	.2396	.4189
PM2$^\diamond$	.2952	.3990	.2548	.4289
TPM2°	.2805	.3895	.2385	.4256
ConceptH†	.3002	.4064	.2607	.4366
HxQuAD	$.3206^{*\star\dagger}_{\diamond\circ}$	$.4229^{*\star}_{\diamond\circ}$	$.2845^{*\star\dagger}_{\diamond\circ}$	$.4378^{*\star}_{\diamond\circ}$
HPM2	$\mathbf{.3235}^{*\star\dagger}_{\diamond\circ}$	$\mathbf{.4234}^{*\star}_{\diamond\circ}$	$\mathbf{.2880}^{*\star\dagger}_{\diamond\circ}$	$\mathbf{.4381}^{*\star}_{\diamond\circ}$

their subtopics. In order to maintain the consistency of the subtopics, we did not use the DSPApprox method introduced in [13] that extracts terms from search results. **ConceptH** [41] exploits concept hierarchies to find flat query subtopics and infers subtopic relations in traditional diversification by hierarchical similarities of subtopics. We directly take our subtopic hierarchy (See Subsection 4.3) as the concept hierarchy in ConceptH, which means that ConceptH shares the same subtopic hierarchy with HxQuAD and HPM2. All the baseline methods have a parameter λ that requires tuning. Our hierarchical models have two parameters to tune: the traditional parameter λ and the hierarchical weight parameter α. We use a **5-fold cross validation** to tune these parameters in terms of ERR-IA@20 on TREC data and NTCIR data, respectively.

The hierarchical subtopics and all runs can be found on the website: `http://www.playbigdata.com/dou/hdiv` .

5. EXPERIMENTAL RESULTS

5.1 Overall results

We compare our models with the baseline approaches. For the baseline models, we use the first-level subtopics which is a common approach in existing work [12, 13, 30]. The results are shown in Table 2 and Table 3. We find that:

(1) The hierarchical diversification models, i.e., HxQuAD and HPM2, outperform all baseline methods on the TREC 2009-2012 dataset. Table 2 shows that HxQuAD and HPM2 have statistically significant improvements in terms of ERR-IA, α-nDCG, NRBP, and D$\sharp$-nDCG ($p<0.05$ with two-tailed paired t-tests). Specifically, HPM2 outperforms xQuAD, TxQuAD, and TPM2 by more than three hundredths; outperforms PM2 by more than two hundredths; outperforms ConceptH by more than one hundredth, in terms of ERR-IA, α-nDCG, and NRBP.

(2) As mentioned before, the diversity on the NTCIR IMine dataset can be evaluated either on the coarse-grained intents or on the fine-grained intents. Table 3 shows that HxQuAD and HPM2 outperform all baseline algorithms in terms of ERR-IA, α-nDCG, and NRBP at either the coarse-grained level or the fine-grained level, though their improvements are not statistically significant. Please note that there are only 32 topics on NTCIR data. The results indicate that the hierarchical models provide more diverse results than the

Table 3: **Performance comparison on NTCIR data.**

	ERR-IA	α-nDCG	NRBP	D$\sharp$-nDCG
(a) Evaluated by using coarse-grained intents				
Baseline	.3044	.4508	.2644	.3952
xQuAD*	.3146	.4666	.2682	.4079
TxQuAD*	.3282	.4915	.2852	.4266
PM2$^\diamond$	.3200	.4865	.2702	.3596
TPM2°	.3239	.5115	.2699	.4493
ConceptH†	.3203	.4807	.2731	.4185
HxQuAD	.3436	.4901	**.3064**	.4094
HPM2	**.3449**	**.5150**	.2975	**.4507**
(b) Evaluated by using fine-grained intents				
Baseline	.1596	.3497	.1338	.2782
xQuAD*	.1669	.3616	.1396	.2853
TxQuAD*	.1717	.3836	.1458	.2929
PM2$^\diamond$	.1641	.3695	.1348	.2825
TPM2°	.1609	.3929	.1222	**.3135**
ConceptH†	.1684	.3652	.1403	.2837
HxQuAD	**.1831**	.3823	**.1598**	.2881
HPM2	**.1831**	**.3994**	.1543	.3081

baseline models when users are interested in either coarse-grained subtopics or fine-grained subtopics.

(3) Both HxQuAD and HPM2 significantly outperform their corresponding models xQuAD, TxQuAD, PM2, and TPM2 on TREC data, and outperform their corresponding models by more than one to three hundredths on both levels of NTCIR data, in terms of ERR-IA, α-nDCG, and NRBP. This indicates that utilizing hierarchical subtopics, even just containing two levels, could help promote result diversity than traditional subtopics formed as a flat list.

(4) Recall that ConceptH leveraged subtopic hierarchies to calculate subtopic dependencies for traditional flat subtopics. The results show that ConceptH outperforms all the other baseline models on TREC data. However, both HxQuAD and HPM2 outperform ConceptH in terms of all metrics. They significantly outperform ConceptH in terms of ERR-IA and NRBP on TREC data, and outperform ConceptH by more than one to three hundredths on both levels of NTCIR data, in terms of ERR-IA, α-nDCG, and NRBP. Therefore, when using subtopic hierarchies in diversification, proposing hierarchical frameworks for hierarchical subtopics works better than improving traditional frameworks on subtopic relations for flat subtopics.

(5) Consistent with the recent work [12], PM2 performs slightly better than xQuAD in terms of all metrics on the TREC dataset in Table 2. And they perform similarly in the coarse-grained intent of the NTCIR data in Table 3. Term level models TxQuAD and TPM2 perform differently on different datasets. On the TREC data, they underperform their corresponding models xQuAD and PM2 in terms of most metrics. But on NTCIR IMine data, they outperform their corresponding models in terms of most metrics, and are the top performers in some cases. Based on the study made by Dang *et al.* [13], they work very closely to their corresponding models. After analyzing the results, we found that term level models do not work well on topics containing phrases. For instance, considering topic number 165 "blue throated hummingbird" in TREC 2012, it has a subtopic "blue throated hummingbird picture" meaning to find the pictures of the specific bird. Term level models

in our experiments use the split terms "blue", "throated", "hummingbird," and "picture" as the subtopics, which may select some noisy irrelevant documents relevant to "blue" or "picture". Dang et al. [13] claimed that they could identify phrases within the subtopics (for example, split the above example subtopic to "blue throated hummingbird" and "picture"), which may help improve the performance of term-level diversification algorithms. However, we used the Stanford Tokenizor[5] and it failed to detect such kinds of phrases. This might be one of reasons why TxQuAD and TPM2 do not work well in our experiments. For the NTCIR data, we use the ICTCLAS Chinese tokenizer[6]. The tokenizer can recognize named entities and phrases, and may generate better term-level subtopics than on TREC data.

5.2 Impact of using different levels of subtopics

The analysis so far has shown that the proposed hierarchical models using hierarchical subtopics outperform the baseline models with flat-formed subtopics (xQuAD, TxQuAD, PM2, and TPM2). There are at least two possible explanations for it. The first is that our two-level hierarchical approach for diversification is indeed effective. The second is that our approach outperformed the baseline models simply because we used extra subtopics (i.e., second-level subtopics) while the baseline models only used first-level subtopics.

To clarify this problem, we experiment with baseline models using different levels of subtopics. We want to investigate whether our models still outperform baseline models with the same subtopics in a flat list. For fair comparison, we provide baseline models exactly the same subtopics as hierarchical models, by organizing hierarchical subtopics into a flat list, and set a uniform weight for them. We use xQuAD$_{1st}$, xQuAD$_{2nd}$, and xQuAD$_{all}$ to denote using first-level subtopics, second-level subtopics, and all subtopics (merged by the obtained suggestions in two levels) for xQuAD model. Similar symbols are used for other models.

Recall that, in hierarchical models, the impact of first-level subtopics and second-level subtopics are controlled by a parameter α according to Equation (6) and Equation (11). When $\alpha = 1$, only the first-level subtopics are used in hierarchical models. When $\alpha = 0$, hierarchical models only use the second-level subtopics. Due to space limitation of the paper, we only report the results on the TREC dataset. The results are shown in Table 4 and Table 5. The best results are in bold, statistically significant differences between hierarchical methods and their corresponding methods are respectively marked in the upper right corner, and all related parameters are tuned by 5-fold cross validations.

5.2.1 *Using first-level subtopics only*

Table 4 and Table 5 show that, by utilizing first-level subtopics, hierarchical models outperform all their corresponding models in terms of ERR-IA, α-nDCG, and NRBP. Specifically, HxQuAD$_{1st}$ significantly outperforms xQuAD$_{1st}$ in terms of all metrics.

The difference between hierarchical models and their counterparts is **the relevance estimation $P(d|t_i)$ between the document d and the first-level subtopic t_i**. In traditional diversification models, i.e., xQuAD$_{1st}$ and PM2$_{1st}$, the probability that document d satisfies subtopic t_i, i.e., $P(d|t_i)$, is calculated by language model [30]. For hierarchical models, only the relevances between documents and second-level (leaf) subtopics are directly computed as traditional methods. The relevances between documents and first-level (non-leaf) subtopics are estimated by $P(d|t_i) = 1 - \prod_{t_{i,j} \in T_i}(1 - P(d|t_{i,j}))$ as Equation (2) in Subsection 3.1. This design makes our hierarchical models more flexible to handle different subtopic mining algorithms, which may contain virtual subtopics at the non-leaf levels in hierarchy.

[5]Stanford Tokenizor: `http://nlp.stanford.edu/software/tokenizer.shtml`
[6]ICTCLAS: `http://www.ictclas.org/`

Table 4: Performance comparison of HxQuAD and its corresponding methods using different subtopics.

	ERR-IA	α-nDCG	NRBP	D♯-nDCG
(a) Using first-level subtopics only				
xQuAD$^{*}_{1st}$	.2842	.3822	.2465	.4109
TxQuAD$^{\diamond}_{1st}$	.2792	.3835	.2396	.4189
HxQuAD$^{\dagger}_{1st}$	**.3054**$^{*\diamond}$	**.4041***	**.2683***	**.4259***
(b) Using second-level subtopics only				
xQuAD$^{\star}_{2nd}$	.2956	.3940	.2609	.4207
TxQuAD$^{\circ}_{2nd}$	.2850	.3903	.2452	.4171
HxQuAD$^{\ddagger}_{2nd}$	**.3145**$^{*\star\circledast}_{\diamond\circ}$	**.4160**$^{*\star\circledast}_{\diamond\circ\bullet}$	**.2782**$^{*\circledast}_{\diamond\circ}$	**.4334**$^{*\circledast}_{\diamond\circ\bullet}$
(c) Using all subtopics (both two levels)				
xQuAD$^{\circledast}_{all}$	.2948	.3930	.2572	.4193
TxQuAD$^{\bullet}_{all}$	.2898	.3930	.2508	.4185
HxQuAD$_{all}$	**.3206**$^{*\star\circledast\dagger}_{\diamond\circ\bullet\ddagger}$	**.4229**$^{*\star\circledast\dagger}_{\diamond\circ\bullet\ddagger}$	**.2845**$^{*\star\circledast\dagger}_{\diamond\circ\bullet\ddagger}$	**.4378**$^{*\star\circledast\dagger}_{\diamond\circ\bullet\ddagger}$

The results indicate that using the relevance estimation between documents and subtopics in hierarchical models, makes the results more diverse than the traditional way. One of the possible reasons is that, by involving the child subtopics into estimation, finding a relevant document for the subtopic becomes finding a relevant document for its child subtopics. The document related to more child second-level subtopics will be viewed as more relevant to the parent first-level subtopic. For example, a first-level subtopic t_1 has two relevant documents d_1, d_2. Traditional models find that the documents' relevances are $P(d_1|t_1) = 0.8$ and $P(d_2|t_1) = 0.7$, and think d_1 is more relevant to t_1. Hierarchical models check the child second-level subtopics of t_1 and find that d_1 is related to one child subtopic $P(d_1|t_{1,1}) = 0.7$ and d_2 is related to two child subtopics $P(d_2|t_{1,1}) = 0.6$, $P(d_2|t_{1,2}) = 0.4$. Then hierarchical models treat d_2 as more relevant to t_1 as $P(d_2|t_1)=1-(1-0.6)*(1-0.4)=0.76$ and $P(d_1|t_1)=1-(1-0.7)=0.7$. In fact, since d_2 covers more child subtopics, it contains more diversity information than d_1 and should be valued more in diversification. By utilizing the child subtopics to find relevant documents for the first-level subtopics, hierarchical models increase the relevances for the documents covering more child subtopics, and provide better result diversity than traditional models.

5.2.2 *Using second-level subtopics only*

When adopting second-level subtopics, hierarchical models still outperform all their corresponding models in terms of ERR-IA, α-nDCG, and NRBP, as shown in Table 4 and Table 5. In particular, HxQuAD$_{2nd}$ significantly outperforms xQuAD$_{2nd}$ in terms of ERR-IA and α-nDCG, and HPM2$_{2nd}$ outperforms PM2$_{2nd}$ by more than one hundredth in terms of ERR-IA, α-nDCG, and NRBP.

The difference between hierarchical models and their counterparts is **the relevance probability $P(t_{i,j}|q)$ between**

Table 5: **Performance comparison of HPM2 and its corresponding methods using different subtopics.**

	ERR-IA	α-nDCG	NRBP	D♯-nDCG
(a) Using first-level subtopics only				
PM2^{*}_{1st}	.2952	.3990	.2548	**.4289**
$\text{TPM2}^{\diamond}_{1st}$	.2805	.3895	.2385	.4256
$\text{HPM2}^{\dagger}_{1st}$	**.3070**$^{\diamond}$	**.4055**	**.2693**$^{\diamond}$	.4280
(b) Using second-level subtopics only				
$\text{PM2}^{\star}_{2nd}$	.3054	.4104	.2670	**.4380**
$\text{TPM2}^{\circ}_{2nd}$	.2847	.3925	.2435	.4206
$\text{HPM2}^{\ddagger}_{2nd}$	**.3172**$^{*\circledast}_{\diamond\circ\bullet}$	**.4189**$^{*\circledast\dagger}_{\diamond\circ\bullet}$	**.2806**$^{*\circledast}_{\diamond\circ\bullet}$	.4373$^{*\dagger}_{\diamond\circ\bullet}$
(c) Using all subtopics (both two levels)				
$\text{PM2}^{\circledast}_{all}$	.3022	.4072	.2620	.4353
$\text{TPM2}^{\bullet}_{all}$	.2879	.3948	.2485	.4211
HPM2_{all}	**.3225**$^{*\star\circledast\dagger}_{\diamond\circ\bullet\ddagger}$	**.4234**$^{*\star\circledast\dagger}_{\diamond\circ\bullet\ddagger}$	**.2880**$^{*\star\circledast\dagger}_{\diamond\circ\bullet\ddagger}$	**.4381**$^{*\dagger}_{\diamond\circ\bullet}$

the query q and the second-level subtopic $t_{i,j}$. Recall that, in subtopic hierarchy, we set a uniform probability distribution for the first-level subtopics of the query, i.e., $P(t_i|q) = \frac{1}{|T_q|}$ where $|T_q|$ is the count of the first-level subtopics (See Subsection 4.3). And we set a uniform weight for each second-level subtopic with respect to its parent first-level subtopic, i.e., $P(t_{i,j}|t_i) = \frac{1}{|T_i|}$, where $|T_i|$ is the count of the child subtopics in the first-level subtopic t_i. Then we calculate the relevance probabilities between queries and second-level subtopics by Equation (1) in Subsection 3.1, i.e., $P(t_{i,j}|q) = P(t_{i,j}|t_i) * P(t_i|q) = \frac{1}{|T_q|*|T_i|}$. On the other side, in traditional models, since their subtopics are in a flat list, they set a uniform relevance probability distribution for the second-level subtopics of the query, i.e., $P(t_{i,j}|q) = \frac{1}{\sum|T_i|}$, where $\sum|T_i|$ indicates the total number of all the second-level subtopics. For example, consider topic number 3 "getting organized" in TREC 2009, which has 9 first-level subtopics and 52 second-level subtopics in total. In traditional models, all second-level subtopics share the same relevance to the query $P(t_{i,j}|q) = \frac{1}{52} = 0.019$. In hierarchical models, for a first-level subtopic t_1, "getting organized at work", it has 9 child second-level subtopics and their relevance probabilities to the query are $P(t_{1,j}|q) = \frac{1}{9} * \frac{1}{9} = 0.012$; for another first-level subtopic t_2, "getting organized for college", it has 3 child second-level subtopics whose relevance probabilities to the query are $P(t_{2,j}|q) = \frac{1}{9} * \frac{1}{3} = 0.037$.

The results indicate that hierarchical models assign better relevance probabilities for second-level subtopics with respect to queries than traditional models with flat subtopics. One possible reason is that, many second-level subtopics may come from some coarse first-level subtopics, so the documents related to these coarse subtopics may be overvalued in traditional models who treat all second-level subtopics as equally important. On the contrary, by passing the relevance of queries uniformly from first-level subtopics to second-level subtopics, hierarchical models control the total contribution of second-level subtopics from coarse first-level subtopics in diversification. Continue the upper example, assume that document d_1 is highly related to all second-level subtopics from t_1, $P(d_1|t_{1,i})$=1 (i=1,2,.,9), and document d_2 is highly related to all second-level subtopics from t_2, $P(d_2|t_{2,j})$=1 (j=1,2,3). Traditional models think d_1 is more diverse as d_1 is related to more subtopics. $\sum P(d|t_{1,i}) * P(t_{1,i}|q)$=$9 * 1 * 0.019$=0.171 $> \sum P(d|t_{2,j}) * P(t_{2,j}|q)$ =$3 * 1 * 0.019$=0.057. Hierarchical models find that d_2 is also important because d_2 is related to more relevant subtopics. $\sum P(d|t_{1,i}) * P(t_{1,i}|q)$ =$9 * 1 * 0.012$=0.11 = $\sum P(d|t_{2,j}) * P(t_{2,j}|q)$=$3*1*0.037$=0.11. Accurately, d_1 and d_2 should be equally important in diversity since either d_1 or d_2 is only related to one first-level subtopic (t_1 or t_2). Therefore, involving first-level subtopics in assigning relevances for second-level subtopics is a fair choice in hierarchical models. The experimental results show that considering first-level subtopics in estimating the relevances between subtopics and queries is very helpful in result diversification.

5.2.3 *Using all subtopics*

Table 4 and Table 5 show that, by using all the subtopics, our hierarchical models significantly outperform their corresponding models in terms of ERR-IA, α-nDCG, and NRBP. This indicate that, when considering two level subtopics in diversification, our hierarchical models with two-level hierarchy are better than traditional diversification models which merge two-level subtopics in a flat list.

Moreover, for HxQuAD and HPM2, using subtopic hierarchy is always better than using single-level subtopics, and the improvements are significant in terms of ERR-IA, α-nDCG, and NRBP. This means that incorporating the entire hierarchy is better than the sole use of a single-level of subtopics in hierarchical models. Each level plays its own role on diversifying search results.

The results also show that all traditional models with the second-level subtopics outperform their counterparts with the first-level subtopics in terms of most metrics. The improvements are mostly not significant, but they indicate that the traditional models perform better by using the second-level (fine-grained) subtopics than by using the first-level (coarse) subtopics. In a preliminary study in TREC data, we found that there are more fine-grained or specific subtopics than coarse or general subtopics. For example, for the "defender" example shown in Section 1, many predefined subtopics (including s_1, s_4, and s_5) correspond to second-level subtopics we extracted from the commercial search engine. This means that exploiting more fine-grained subtopics could help improve result diversity. xQuAD and PM2 perform worse when using all subtopics than using second-level subtopics. One possible reason is that the merged subtopics include many overlapped subtopics, which may involve redundant documents in search results. So the second-level subtopics is good enough for the flat-subtopic based models, and involving the all subtopics is unnecessary and risky.

In short, our hierarchical models with subtopic hierarchy significantly outperform all their corresponding models with different levels of subtopics in terms of ERR-IA, α-nDCG, and NRBP. This indicates that our two-level hierarchical models are indeed effective in diversification.

6. CONCLUSIONS

In this paper, we argued that the user intents covered by a query can be hierarchical. We leveraged hierarchical intents and proposed hierarchical diversification models to promote search result diversification. Specifically, hierarchical diversification calculated the document diversity on each level of hierarchical subtopics and combined these diversity scores together to help select the best document. We conducted our experiments with two-level hierarchical subtopics generated automatically from Google suggestions. The experimental results showed that our approaches based on hierarchical subtopics outperformed their counterparts with the traditional subtopics in a flat list. Even when using single-level subtopics, hierarchical diversification also provided reasonable benefits, as these single-level subtopics from hierarchical tree implicitly utilize hierarchical information to help diversify search results, while the traditional diversification algorithms use pure subtopics in a flat list without additional information.

7. ACKNOWLEDGMENT

This work was partially supported by the National Key Basic Research 973 Program of China under grant No. 2014CB340403 and the Fundamental Research Funds for the Central Universities, the Research Funds of Renmin University of China No. 14XNLF05 and No. 15XNLF03.

8. REFERENCES

[1] R. Agrawal, S. Gollapudi, A. Halverson, and S. Ieong. Diversifying search results. In *WSDM*, 2009.

[2] J. Carbonell and J. Goldstein. The use of MMR, diversity-based reranking for reordering documents and producing summaries. In *SIGIR*, 1998.

[3] B. Carterette and P. Chandar. Probabilistic models of ranking novel documents for faceted topic retrieval. In *CIKM*, pages 1287–1296, Hong Kong, China, 2009.

[4] O. Chapelle, D. Metlzer, Y. Zhang, and P. Grinspan. Expected reciprocal rank for graded relevance. In *CIKM*, pages 621–630, Hong Kong, China, 2009.

[5] H. Chen and D. R. Karger. Less is more: Probabilistic models for retrieving fewer relevant documents. In *SIGIR*, pages 429–436, Seattle, Washington, 2006.

[6] C. L. Clarke, N. Craswell, and I. Soboroff. Overview of the TREC 2009 web track. In *Proc. the 18th TREC*, 2009.

[7] C. L. Clarke, N. Craswell, and E. M. Voorhees. Overview of the TREC 2012 web track. In *Proc. the 21st TREC*, 2012.

[8] C. L. Clarke, M. Kolla, G. V. Cormack, O. Vechtomova, A. Ashkan, S. Büttcher, and I. MacKinnon. Novelty and diversity in information retrieval evaluation. In *SIGIR*, pages 659–666, 2008.

[9] C. L. Clarke, M. Kolla, and O. Vechtomova. An effectiveness measure for ambiguous and underspecified queries. In *ICTIR*, 2009.

[10] The ClueWeb09 dataset. `http://boston.lti.cs.cmu.edu/Data/clueweb09/`.

[11] K. Collins-Thompson, P. Bennett, F. Diaz, C. L. A. Clarke, and E. M. Voorhees. TREC 2013 Web track overview. In *TREC*, 2013.

[12] V. Dang and W. B. Croft. Diversity by proportionality: An election-based approach to search result diversification. In *SIGIR*, pages 65–74, 2012.

[13] V. Dang and W. B. Croft. Term level search result diversification. In *SIGIR*, pages 603–612, 2013.

[14] Z. Dou, S. Hu, K. Chen, R. Song, and J.-R. Wen. Multi-dimensional search result diversification. In *WSDM*, pages 475–484, Hong Kong, China, 2011.

[15] Z. Dou, S. Hu, Y. Luo, R. Song, and J.-R. Wen. Finding dimensions for queries. In *CIKM*, 2011.

[16] Z. Dou, R. Song, and J.-R. Wen. A large-scale evaluation and analysis of personalized search strategies. In *WWW*, pages 581–590, 2007.

[17] J. He, V. Hollink, and A. de Vries. Combining implicit and explicit topic representations for result diversification. In *SIGIR*, pages 851–860, 2012.

[18] B. J. Jansen, A. Spink, and T. Saracevic. Real life, real users, and real needs: a study and analysis of user queries on the web. *Inf. Process. Manage.*, 36(2):207–227, 2000.

[19] W. Kong and J. Allan. Extracting query facets from search results. In *SIGIR*, pages 93–102, 2013.

[20] D. Lawrie, W. B. Croft, and A. Rosenberg. Finding topic words for hierarchical summarization. In *SIGIR*, pages 349–357, New Orleans, Louisiana, USA, 2001.

[21] S. Liang, Z. Ren, and M. de Rijke. Fusion helps diversification. In *SIGIR*, pages 303–312, 2014.

[22] Y. Liu, R. Song, M. Zhang, Z. Dou, T. Yamamoto, M. Kato, H. Ohshima, and K. Zhou. Overview of the NTCIR-11 IMine task. In *NTCIR-11*, 2014.

[23] F. Radlinski and S. Dumais. Improving personalized web search using result diversification. In *SIGIR*, 2006.

[24] F. Radlinski, R. Kleinberg, and T. Joachims. Learning diverse rankings with multi-armed bandits. In *ICML*, 2008.

[25] D. Rafiei, K. Bharat, and A. Shukla. Diversifying web search results. In *WWW '10*, pages 781–790, 2010.

[26] K. Raman, P. N. Bennett, and K. Collins-Thompson. Toward whole-session relevance: Exploring intrinsic diversity in web search. In *SIGIR*, 2013.

[27] T. Sakai, Z. Dou, T. Yamamoto, Y. Liu, M. Zhang, and R. Song. Overview of the NTCIR-10 INTENT-2 task. In *NTCIR-10*, 2013.

[28] T. Sakai and R. Song. Evaluating diversified search results using per-intent graded relevance. In *SIGIR*, pages 1043–1052, Beijing, China, 2011.

[29] M. Sanderson and B. Croft. Deriving concept hierarchies from text. In *Research and Development in Information Retrieval*, 1999.

[30] R. L. Santos, C. Macdonald, and I. Ounis. Exploiting query reformulations for web search result diversification. In *WWW*, pages 881–890, 2010.

[31] R. L. Santos, C. Macdonald, and I. Ounis. Selectively diversifying web search results. In *CIKM*, 2010.

[32] R. L. Santos, C. Macdonald, and I. Ounis. Intent-aware search result diversification. In *SIGIR*, pages 595–604, 2011.

[33] C. Silverstein, H. Marais, M. Henzinger, and M. Moricz. Analysis of a very large web search engine query log. *SIGIR Forum*, 33(1):6–12, 1999.

[34] R. Song, Z. Luo, J.-Y. Nie, Y. Yu, and H.-W. Hon. Identification of ambiguous queries in web search. *IPM*, 45(2), 2009.

[35] S. Vargas, P. Castells, and D. Vallet. Explicit relevance models in intent-oriented information retrieval diversification. In *SIGIR*, pages 75–84, 2012.

[36] H.-T. Yu and F. Ren. Search result diversification via filling up multiple knapsacks. In *CIKM*, pages 609–618, 2014.

[37] Y. Yue and T. Joachims. Predicting diverse subsets using structural svms. In *ICML*, 2008.

[38] C. Zhai and J. Lafferty. A risk minimization framework for information retrieval. *IPM*, 42(1):31–55, 2006.

[39] C. X. Zhai, W. W. Cohen, and J. Lafferty. Beyond independent relevance: methods and evaluation metrics for subtopic retrieval. In *SIGIR*, 2003.

[40] B. Zhang, H. Li, Y. Liu, L. Ji, W. Xi, W. Fan, Z. Chen, and W.-Y. Ma. Improving web search results using affinity graph. In *SIGIR*, pages 504–511, 2005.

[41] W. Zheng, H. Fang, and C. Yao. Exploiting concept hierarchy for result diversification. In *CIKM*, 2012.

[42] X. Zhu, A. Goldberg, J. Van Gael, and D. Andrzejewski. Improving diversity in ranking using absorbing random walks. *HLT-NAACL*, 2007.

[43] Y. Zhu, Y. Lan, J. Guo, X. Cheng, and S. Niu. Learning for search result diversification. In *SIGIR*, pages 293–302, 2014.

Category-Driven Approach for Local Related Business Recommendations

Yonathan Perez *
Stanford University
yperez@cs.stanford.edu

Michael Schueppert
Google New York
mschueppert@google.com

Matthew Lawlor
Google New York
mflawlor@google.com

Shaunak Kishore
Google New York
skishore@google.com

ABSTRACT

When users search online for a business, the search engine may present them with a list of related business recommendations. We address the problem of constructing a useful and diverse list of such recommendations that would include an optimal combination of substitutes and complements. Substitutes are similar potential alternatives to the searched business, whereas complements are local businesses that can offer a more comprehensive and better rounded experience for a user visiting the searched locality. In our problem setting, each business belongs to a category in an *ontology of business categories*. Two businesses are defined as substitutes of one another if they belong to the same category, and as complements if they are otherwise relevant to each other.

We empirically demonstrate that the related business recommendation lists generated by Google's search engine are too homogeneous, and overemphasize substitutes. We then use various data sources such as crowdsourcing, mobile maps directions queries, and the existing Google's related business graph to mine association rules to determine to which extent do categories complement each other, and establish relevance between businesses, using both category-level and individual business-level information. We provide an algorithmic approach that incorporates these signals to produce a list of recommended businesses that balances pairwise business relevance with overall diversity of the list. Finally, we use human raters to evaluate our system, and show that it significantly improves on the current Google system in usefulness of the generated recommendation lists.

1. INTRODUCTION

Related business recommendations help users discover businesses or establishments that would be useful when searching for a specific source business. Search engines today answer this need by providing recommendations similar to the searched business, relying mostly on search-based association rules of the form "users who search for business x also search for business y". Such recommendations are often *substitutes* to the searched business - establishments that the user could visit instead of the searched business.

Yet, such substitutes may not be the only relevant recommendations for a source business. In some cases a user could benefit more from recommended *complements* – local businesses that one could visit in conjunction to the source business and that could provide the user with a better rounded experience at the searched locality. For example, a user searching for a *specific* hotel might benefit more from recommendations for good restaurants and attractions near that hotel than from only recommendations for other hotels. Some major commercial recommender systems use both substitute and complement notions of relevance in making product recommendations [7, 10]. We aim to leverage both notions of relevance in generating a list of recommended local businesses given a source business.

The usefulness of recommended complements for a source business x can depend on many factors. Later in the paper we show that the type, or category, of x affects heavily on the usefulness of complementary recommendations for it, as well as on the categories of other businesses that could serve as useful complements.

Another important factor is the user's intent - whether she is considering x among other alternatives, or she is planning a visit to x or even already at the locality of x. User intent was not modeled in this paper, and is a topic for future work. However, our approach of combining complements in the related business recommendations, rather than only similar substitutes, is geared towards users who plan a visit to the source business. Thus, lessons from the approach taken in this paper could be more relevant in settings where such user intent is more likely (e.g. mobile searches where the user is near the searched locality, or on the way there).

Our problem setting is that of a non-personalized recommender system, and is demonstrated in Figure 1. When an anonymous user searches for a specific business name, in addition to search results for that business, the system provides a list of k related business recommendations. We aim to improve user satisfaction from the generated recommendation list by constructing a relevant and diverse list of substitute and complement recommendations using both category and business-specific information.

*This work was mostly done while at Google New York

CIKM'15, October 19–23, 2015, Melbourne, Australia.
ACM 978-1-4503-3794-6/15/10.
DOI: http://dx.doi.org/10.1145/2806416.2806495 .

In our problem setting, there exists an ontology of business categories. Each business is a member of some subset of categories in this ontology. In our approach, the relevance of a potential related business recommendation y to the source business x can be established by looking at: (i) the relevance of the set of categories to which y belongs to the set of categories to which x belongs, and (ii) the relevance of y to x given a recommendation category. If the recommendation category is common to both x and y, then y is a substitute recommendation for x. Otherwise, it is a complement recommendation.

One simple approach is to recommend the k businesses that are most relevant to the searched business. Yet, such an approach would typically yield a very homogeneous recommended business list, with the majority of businesses belonging to the category c most relevant to the searched business - i.e. a list of only complements, or more commonly - only substitutes as the source business itself often belongs to c. While each recommended business is highly relevant in these cases, the list as a whole can be redundant. Thus, it is desirable to recommend relevant businesses of varying types and include both substitutes and various types of complements. We use the ontology defined over the business categories to define and promote intra-list diversity, by penalizing recommendations of multiple businesses of the same category. We explore and compare several methods for such penalization.

Unfortunately, as described later in section 4, such penalization in settings where every business can belong to multiple categories makes the problem of finding an optimal recommendation list NP-hard. To make the problem solvable in polynomial time, we associate every business with a single category of interest.

We use crowdsourcing and association rules mined from category-aggregated mobile maps directions queries to establish category-to-category relevance scores. To determine relevance between businesses given category information, we use current Google's business recommendation scores as a baseline. We then adjust these scores using the directions queries data. Using these signals, we establish business-to-business relevance scores, and we produce top-k recommendation lists that optimize for these scores along with category redundancy penalties.

The main contributions of our paper are:

(1) An empirical demonstration that users find complementary related business recommendations useful, whereas the current Google system is strongly focused on making recommendations similar to the searched business. This evidence is shown clearly in Figure 2 and discussed in section 3.

(2) An algorithmic approach for constructing a useful, and often diverse, related business recommendation list in a setting where a business categorization exists. The constructed list consists of a useful mixture of substitute and complement recommendations. This approach is presented in section 4.

(3) Establishment of relevance scores between businesses that take into account the business category ontology. We used multiple data sources to mine and construct the relevance scores: crowdsourcing, mobile maps directions queries, and the current Google related business graph. The construction of relevance scores is explained in section 5.

(4) Large-scale human-based empirical evaluation of several variations of our system. We demonstrate that our system achieves a significant improvement over the current Google system in recommendation list usefulness. The evaluation process and the results and insights that arise from it are discussed in section 6.

Figure 1: The related business recommendations (circled in red) for the source business "Hotel 373 Fifth Avenue" - a boutique hotel in Midtown East, Manhattan. All of the recommendations by the existing system are similar hotels, that serve as substitutes for the source business.

2. RELATED WORK

Item-to-item relevance notions of substitutes and complements have been used by some recommender systems [7, 10, 21]. In these personalized product recommender systems, substitute and complement relations were mined from user browsing and purchasing data. In such e-commerce product recommender systems, different notions of relevance can be used for different stages of the user experience - i.e. recommending substitutes before the user makes a purchase and complements after the purchase. Related business recommendations differ in the sense that its harder for the system to acquire information about different stages in the user behavior and clear signals of when to recommend substitutes and when to recommend complements. Thus, we took the approach of constructing a recommendation list that mixes the two.

Business categorization in our system serves a double purpose – on one hand, we use category information as a factor in determining business-to-business relevance by measuring relevance of category sets to each other, and on the other hand, we use categories to limit redundancy in the produced recommendation list. Thus, in our use of category information to construct a mix of substitutes and complements to the source business, we use *implicit diversification* of the recommendation list as a mean to reduce redundancy and increase user satisfaction. The settings of our problem are those of a non-personalized recommender system, and share traits of both traditional recommender system settings and web search settings. On one hand, the system discovers new useful recommendations that were not searched by the user, and on the other hand, the system is non-personalized and provides its suggestions in response to a web search query for a specific business.

Significant work has been done on result diversification in both recommender systems [18, 14, 20, 22, 13] as well as web search [6, 8, 11, 12, 19, 5]. There are two main notions of such diversification in literature [4] – one is resolving ambiguity and reaching high or sufficient coverage of several topics [2, 12, 14, 19, 5], and the other is avoiding redundancy [22, 3, 20]. A recent work, [13], is also aiming to address both notions.

Multiple approaches have been suggested in coping with ambiguous queries or covering multiple meanings or subtopics. One such approach is the IA-Select [2], where the settings include a taxonomy of the results and a distribution of user intents over this taxonomy given an ambiguous query. IA-Select then aims to maximize the probability that at least one returned result is relevant to the user. Another well-known approach is xQuAD [12], where ranking results for an ambiguous query is done by estimating how well does a result cover an uncovered aspect of the answer. In our problem settings however, coverage is not an objective. We do not aim to cover any number of categories, and we do not try to guarantee at least one useful result, but to maximize user satisfaction from the entire recommendation list, hoping that the user would find as many as possible of the provided recommendations useful. In [5], the goal is to return a result list with per-topic coverage that is proportional to that topic's popularity. While the number of recommendations from a specific category is often higher for categories that are highly relevant to the source business, this is not an objective of our system. Categories assist in determining relevance of businesses to the source business, but are not used for impose any constraints on the composition or coverage of the generated recommendation list.

Our system does aim to reduce redundancy of multiple businesses from the same category and implicitly increase intra-list diversity. In [22], intra-list diversification was pursued as a mean for user satisfaction from book recommendations in a personalized collaborative-filtering system. Similarity and diversity were measured using a taxonomy of books, and the intra-list similarity between items was minimized using a greedy algorithm. The output of the system was combined with a non-diversified list using a diversification factor. Our approach differs significantly in the sense that we do not scale a "diversified list" with an "accurate list", but introduce diversification natively into our optimization objective by enforcing a diminishing returns effect of multiple recommendations from the same category. Explicitly penalizing redundancy was done in [3]. Instead of ranking results by similarity to the query, the MMR (Maximal Marginal Relevance) method uses a linear combination of that similarity with a penalty for similarity to previous results. However, MMR does not take into account a diminishing returns effect and does not increase penalty severity with increased redundancy.

Another aspect touched by our system is that of locality aware recommendations. This is done implicitly as scores of local businesses tend to be higher in the signals we use to establish business-to-business relevance scores. While location is only used implicitly in our system, location-awareness plays a more explicit part in several locality-aware recommender systems [9, 17]. Location is actively used in ranking results for hyper-local web queries [15], and indeed used in determining the relevance between businesses in Google related business graph (see next section).

3. BACKGROUND AND MOTIVATION

Google's current source of related business recommendations is the *Related Business Graph (RBG)*. The RBG is a directed graph where a business x is linked to several (typically hundreds) related businesses and the weight of an edge (x, y) expresses the relevance of y to x. There are multiple signals that contribute to such relevance scores, and we cannot disclose them in this paper. However, search-based association rules (i.e. "users who search x also search for y") are a major component in the RBG's edge weights. Additional important signals include the geographical proximity of y to x (closer businesses are preferred), as well as various measures of *similarity* between x and y. The current RBG-based system produces related business recommendations for a searched business x by returning the top k neighbors of x in the RBG by weight. The RBG-based system is the main system used by Google in production, and for most source business queries [1], the related business recommendation list displayed to the user is produced by that system. Such recommendations tend to be similar to the searched business and to one another, and mostly constitute of substitutes to the source business.

Yet, similar businesses are not always what users want to see as recommendations when they search for a business. To demonstrate this we turned to crowdsourcing and conducted a survey, asking users what information they would find useful when searching for a business from a specific category of interest. The survey was conducted using Google Consumer Surveys[2], and includes 372 participants (web users accessing premium content online).

In the survey, and throughout this paper, we limited ourselves to the geographical scope of New York City (NYC). This controls for geographic settings and cultures, as user preferences and business relevance can vary significantly between different regions, between urban and rural environments, and so on. Thus, all of our businesses of interest are in NYC, and our survey takers are either NYC residents or frequent visitors to NYC (this was used as a filtering question to be allowed to participate in the survey). We also limited the scope of our problem in terms of categories of interest. As we aim to construct a well rounded experience for a user visiting a source business, we limited ourselves to categories of businesses that people visit in person and that answer some recreational need. The list of categories we consider is shown in Table 1.

We asked the survey participants to tell us what information they find useful when they search for a specific business of some category c (in addition to information about the searched business). The answer options included:

1. Information about other nearby businesses from the same category

2. Information about nearby businesses from category c', for three candidate categories c' related to c

3. "None of the above"

The survey results are depicted in Figure 2a. The survey clearly showed that for any source category c, additional information about nearby businesses of some category $c' \neq c$ was found useful by a significant fraction of the survey takers. Furthermore, $c' \neq c$ was often the most useful category for additional information.

[1]For a small number of high-profile establishments (e.g. major tourist attractions like the Empire State Building), Google uses higher-precision data from its Knowledge graph to provide recommendations in its production system. Nethertheless, such establishments also appear like any other establishment in the RBG.

[2]http://www.google.com/insights/consumersurveys/home.

Indoor Lodging	Bars
Movie Theaters	Liquor Stores
Performing Arts Venues	Nightclubs
Sporting Goods Stores	Gyms
Beauty Salons	Restaurants and Cafes
Sports Complexes (e.g. Stadiums)	Tourist Attractions
Grocery Stores	Gift Shops

Table 1: **Categories of interest**. We only look at businesses in NYC that belong to one of the above categories as potential related business recommendations or as source businesses. Grocery Stores and Gift Shops are viewed only as potential recommendations, and we are not interested in them as source businesses.

We then examine how these user preferences match the current recommendations generated using Google's RBG. For every source category c, we examine the businesses x that belong to that category. We compare the fraction of x's top 20 RBG neighbors of category c to the fraction of neighbors in the top complementary category $c' \neq c$ of c according to the survey, and we aggregate these statistics over all businesses in category c. As portrayed by Figure 2b, in the vast majority of cases, the top RBG neighbors are businesses of the same category as the source business x, which does not match user preferences from the survey. There are only two cases where the complementary category c' is significantly popular among RBG neighbors of businesses of category c : $(c, c') = (Bar, Restaurant)$ and $(c, c') = (Nightclub, Bar)$. In both of these cases, the categories themselves are close to each other, and many businesses can be classified as both.

The above experiment demonstrates that Google's current related business recommendation system produces recommendations which are similar substitutes to the source business. However, users often prefer seeing nearby businesses of other, complementary, categories. This motivates our approach to provide more heterogeneous related business recommendation lists which include businesses complementary recommendations, in addition to substitutes.

4. ALGORITHMIC APPROACH

In this section we describe an algorithmic approach for generating a useful and diverse list of related businesses for a source business x. We assume that we are given the relevance scores between every pair of categories, and how relevant a business y is to x given a desired recommendation category. In the next section, we explain how we mine such signals from data, and for the purpose of the discussion in this section, we treat these two signals as given.

We first construct an optimization problem for generating a useful and diverse list of related business recommendations in the more general setting where each business can belong to any number of categories, and we explain the reasoning behind that construction. Since the problem under this setting is NP-hard, we relax the problem by associating each business to a single category, which results in an optimization problem that can be solved in polynomial time using a simple greedy algorithm.

Relevance Scores: We begin by explaining how the relevance between businesses is determined, and introducing notation that we will use in this section and throughout the rest of the paper.

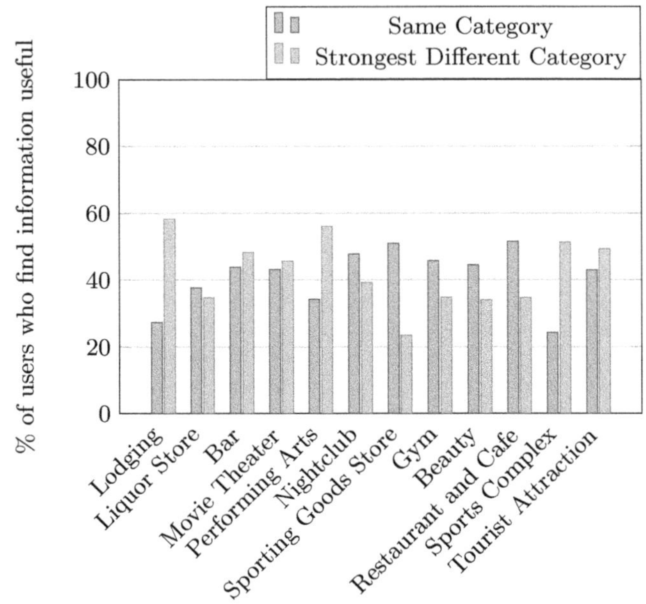

(a) **Survey Results:** When searching for a business of source category c: Percentage of users who find information about other nearby businesses of category c useful vs. percentage of users who find information about businesses of the top complementary category $c' \neq c$ useful. These numbers were normalized to exclude users who indicated that they don't find any information useful.

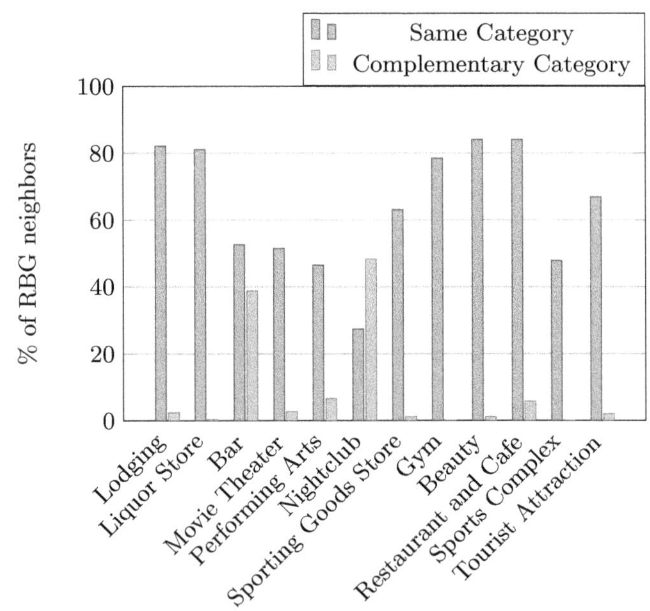

(b) **Top RGB neighbors:** For the top 20 neighbors of businesses of category c (aggregated): The fraction of neighbors of category c vs. the fraction of businesses of category $c' \neq c$ which was indicated most popular compilementary category for c by survey data.

Figure 2: **Same category vs. complementary category recommendations:** User preference compared to current Related Business Graph.

Let $r(y|x,c) \in [0,1]$ denote the relevance score of related business y to the source business x given that we are making a recommendation of category c. The relevance can be either relevance as a substitute if both x and y belong to category c, or as a complement otherwise.

Let Γ denote the set of all categories of interest, and let $R_{CC}: \Gamma \times \Gamma \rightarrow [0,1]$ be a function that gives the relevance between categories - that is, $R_{CC}(c_1, c_2) \in [0,1]$ denotes the relevance of category c_2 to category c_1 (the more relevant c_2 is to c_1, the higher the score is). Note that R_{CC} is not a symmetric function. Furthermore, R_{CC} is a function of categories only, and is agnostic of the source business. The semantics of R_{CC} are further discussed in the next section. As explained earlier, we treat r and R_{CC} as given in this section.

We define the relevance of a category c to a business x as the average relevance of c to the categories of x:

$$R_{BC}(x,c) = \frac{1}{\mid C(x) \mid} \cdot \sum_{c' \in C(x)} R_{CC}\left(c', c\right) \tag{1a}$$

where $C(x) \subseteq \Gamma$ is the set of categories to which x belongs. The relevance of a business y to x is then defined as:

$$R_{BB}(x,y) = \max_{c \in C(y)} \left\{ R_{BC}(x,c) \cdot r(y|x,c) \right\} \tag{2a}$$

The relevance of y to x is determined through a single category in $C(y)$ - the one that maximizes the relevance to the source business - so a business's relevance is not penalized for belonging to multiple categories.

Optimization Problem - Multi-Category Setting: The output of our optimization problem is a list $S = (y_1, y_2, \ldots y_k)$ of k distinct businesses related to the source business x. One simple approach would be to display the k businesses that are most relevant to x under the above definition of business-to-business relevance. This approach would yield a list of related business recommendations where each recommendation y is highly relevant to x, but the list is a whole would be redundant. We would like to introduce diversity to the recommendation list by penalizing multiple recommendations from the same category.

The penalty for recommending multiple businesses from the same category should depend on the category, as redundancy may be worse for some categories than others. Also, to model diminishing returns in contributions made by recommendations of the same category, we would like the penalties for businesses in a category to be increasingly severe as we recommend more businesses from that category.

To satisfy these requirements, when constructing the list of related business recommendations $S = (y_1, y_2, \ldots y_k)$, we penalize multiple recommendations of the same category c by multiplying the business-to-business relevance terms with penalty terms of the form $d_c(rank_{c,S}(y))$. Here, y is a potential recommendation for category c, $d_c(n)$ is a category-c-specific *decay function* which is monotonically non-increasing, and $rank_{c,S}(y)$ is the number of businesses that occur before the index of y in S and belong to category c:

$$rank_{c,S}(y) = \mid \{ j \in \{1, 2, \ldots k\} \mid j < ind_S(y) \wedge c \in C(y_j) \} \mid \tag{3a}$$

$$ind_S(y) = \min(\{ i \in \{1, 2, \ldots k\} | y_i = y \} \cup \{k+1\})$$

(Note that the index of y in S is well-defined even if $y \notin S$, and that for such y, $rank_{c,S}(y)$ is just the number of businesses in S that belong to category c.) Adding the penalty terms gives us the final formulation of the optimization problem that yields a list of k related business recommendations that balances pairwise relevance to the source business x with overall list diversity:

$$Rec(x) = \operatorname*{argmax}_{S=(y_1, y_2, \ldots y_k)} \sum_{i=1}^{k} \left[R_{BB}(x, y_i) \cdot \max_{c \in C(y_i)} \left\{ d_c\left(rank_{c,S}(y_i)\right) \right\} \right] \tag{4a}$$

Note that the max operator over the possible penalty factors means that the penalty for adding a related business y to the list S is the least severe penalty out of all categories to which y belongs. The reasoning for this choice is that a potential related business should not be overly penalized because it belongs to multiple categories - for example, when recommending a bar as a related place for x, a bar-grill y that is classified as both a bar and restaurant should not be penalized just because other restaurants have already been recommended for x.

Optimization Problem - Single-Category Setting: Unfortunately, the optimization problem described in equation 4a, where every potential related business y can belong to a set of categories $C(y) \subseteq \Gamma$ of an arbitrary size, is NP-hard. We show NP-hardness of the problem using a reduction from the maximum k-subset intersection problem [16], and the proof is posted as supplementary material [1].

To enable a polynomial-time solution to the problem, we have decided to solve a relaxed version of the problem in which each business y is associated to a single category $c(y) \in \Gamma$. Belonging to multiple categories in Γ means that business y's (unique) immediate category is a subset of multiple categories in Γ under the given category ontology. For each such immediate category, we determined the most relevant superset category in Γ (see section 5 for further details).

After associating each business y to a single category $c(y)$, equations 1a to 4a takes the following form:

$$R_{BC}(x,c) = R_{CC}\left(c(x), c(y)\right) \tag{1b}$$

$$R_{BB}(x,y) = R_{BC}\left(x, c(y)\right) \cdot r\left(y|x, c(y)\right) \tag{2b}$$

$$rank_{c,S}(y) = \mid \{ j \in \{1, 2, \ldots k\} \mid j < ind_S(y) \wedge c = c(y) \} \mid \tag{3b}$$

$$Rec(x) = \operatorname*{argmax}_{S=(y_1, y_2, \ldots y_k)} \sum_{i=1}^{k} \left[R_{BB}(x, y_i) \cdot d_{c(y_i)}\left(rank_{c(y_i),S}(y_i)\right) \right] \tag{4b}$$

A simple greedy algorithm, as described in Algorithm 1, finds an optimal solution to the relaxed optimization problem 4b in $O(\mid \Gamma \mid \cdot k)$ given a candidate pool of businesses sorted by their relevance score r (see online supplementary materials for proof of optimality and runtime).

Decay Functions To conclude this section, we discuss the decay functions d_c used for penalizing multiple recommendations of the same category. As mentioned before, these are monotonically non-increasing functions that model the diminishing returns of the contributions of same-category recommendations. The decay functions are category-specific,

Algorithm 1 Greedy algorithm for generating related business recommendation list under single category per. business relaxation

function $\text{REC}(x)$
  $S \leftarrow$ empty list
  while $|S| < k$ **do**
    $y^* \leftarrow \text{argmax}_{y \notin S} R_{BB}(x, y) \cdot d_{c(y)}(rank_{c(y),S}(y))$
    Append y^* to S
  return S

$d_c^1(n) = \exp(-\alpha_c n)$
$d_c^2(n) = \exp(-\alpha_c n/2)$
$d_c^3(n) = \alpha_c^{-n}$
$d_c^4(n) \equiv 1$ (no decay)

Table 2: **Four decay functions**, from strongest to weakest, used in our experiments

and should provide a stronger decay, or steeper decrease, for categories in which multiple recommendations would cause highly diminished contributions. For this purpose, we introduce category-specific *decay factors:* $\alpha_c = R_{CC}(c, c)^{-1}$. The decay factor α_c is higher the less relevant a category c is to itself, which can be interpreted as how disadvantageous redundancy is among businesses recommendations of category c. The decay factors can then be used as a parameter for controlling the strength of the decay.

Table 2 lists the four families of decay functions we experimented with, from strongest to weakest. A strong decay function means that the algorithm would be fast to transition between categories, which can lead to a very diverse recommendation list. However, a strong decay function can also lead to transitions to categories with irrelevant businesses in them due to premature exhaustion of the most relevant categories. On the other hand, a weak decay function would make the algorithm stay within highly relevant categories, but may lead to an overly homogenous recommendation list. We will extensively compare the algorithm's empirical performance when using the different decay functions in section 6.

5. GENERATING RELEVANCE SCORES

In this section we explain how we constructed the signals R_{CC} and r which are used as inputs to the algorithmic framework presented in section 4. As mentioned before, $R_{CC}(c, c')$ measures relevance between of category c' to category c, and $r(y|x, c)$ measures the relevance of y to x as a recommendation of category c. These two signals were mined and composed from several data sources, including crowdsourcing, mobile maps queries, and the RBG edge weights. We begin this section with a description of the business category ontology used by the system, and then describe the construction of R_{CC} and r.

5.1 The Business Category Ontology

Google's business category ontology is based on a directed acyclic graph, G^{ONT} where vertices are categories and edges represent *"is-a"* relationships. An edge $(c_1 \rightarrow c_2)$ will be present if c_2 is a subset of c_1. For example, the edge (restaurant $\rightarrow$ chinese restaurant) is present in the graph. Every business is associated with a single immediate category which can be any vertex in G^{ONT}. However, for most businesses, the immediate category is quite specific.

We selected a set of categories Γ which is listed in Table 1. The categories in Γ are categories of recreational businesses, and are fairly general, so each $c \in \Gamma$ has many descendants in G^{ONT}. We would like to associate each immediate category c with all of its ancestors in Γ. However, the multi-category recommendation problem from section 4 is NP-hard, so for each immediate category c, we instead hand-pick the best ancestor of that category in Γ. As a result, each business is associated with a single category in Γ.

We were able to do this task manually because Γ is small, and because the number of immediate categories with multiple ancestors in Γ is also small (a few dozen). However, one could choose ancestors in Γ for each category using more scalable heuristics based on the topology of G^{ONT}, such as by choosing the closest ancestor in the graph.

5.2 Category-To-Category Relevance Scores

R_{CC} is a signal that measures the relevance between categories in Γ, such that $R_{CC}(c, c') \in [0, 1]$ is a score of how relevant category c' is to category c. $R_{CC}(c, c')$ measures how likely is a user visiting a source business of category c to visit another business of category c' (including the case of $c' = c$). Therefore, $R_{CC}(c, c')$ measures the extent to which c' *complements* c. We do not make any special additions to $R_{CC}(c, c)$ to account for increased relevance as a substitute, as the business-to-business scores $r(x|y, c)$, which are mostly based on the existing RBG, are already biased towards relevance as substitute.

R_{CC} is derived from three signals that give such category-to-category relevance scores:
(1) R^S is based on a crowdsourcing survey
(2) R^E is based on explicit mobile maps directions queries
(3) R^I is based on mobile maps search queries which can be treated as implicit directions queries

The signal R^S was computed using a crowdsourcing survey. The survey was conducted through the Google Consumer Surveys platform and included 500 participants who are residents or frequent visitors to NYC (similarly to the survey in section 3). The survey participants were asked to indicate which types of businesses they often *visit* in conjunction to a visit in a business of a specific category. For example, the survey participants were asked to answer the following: "When you visit a bar, which of the following types of establishments do you often visit in conjunction to that bar?". The answer options included:

1. Nearby businesses of the same category (e.g. nearby bars)
2. Nearby businesses of three candidate related categories (e.g. nearby restaurants or nightclubs)
3. I don't visit businesses of that category
4. None of the above - i.e. I visit businesses of that category, but I don't typically visit other businesses in conjunction

$R^S(c, c')$ is then the fraction of survey takers who indicated that they visit a business of category c' when visiting a business of category c. R^S was normalized to exclude survey takers who chose answer 3, but to include survey takers who chose answer 4. We take answer 4 to indicate that showing complementary recommendations for source category c is less beneficial, so we diminish the magnitude of $R^S(c, c')$ for all potential related categories c' (including $c' = c$).

The signals R^E and R^I are generated using data from Google's mobile maps of both explicit (R^E) and implicit

(R^I) directions queries. An explicit directions query is a query where a user asks for directions from business x to business y on the mobile maps application. Unlike a directions query, in a mobile maps search query, a user searches only the location of the business on the mobile maps application. An implicit directions query from x to y is a pair of such maps search queries for x and then for y issued by the same user within a short time window. Both for data reliability and robustness, and to avoid any potential privacy concerns, when computing these signals, we only look at aggregated counts for pairs of businesses (x, y) that occur sufficiently often in the dataset. Before aggregating by source and destination categories, our dataset included 1 million explicit directions queries and 10 million implicit directions queries. Direction queries are a strong indicator of complement relations between businesses - i.e. if there are many directions queries between x and y, then this is an indicator that y complements x.

Directions queries are highly biased towards queries by tourists and other visitors, so hotels, restaurants, and tourist attractions are by far the most common categories associated with almost any category. Therefore, simply mining association rules using commonly occurring pairs of source and destination categories would not work, so we must consider another metric. We use a notion similar to tf-idf for extracting relevance from the directions query dataset. If E is the multi-set of category-annotated explicit queries $q = (c_{src}, c_{dst})$, then we define R^E as follows:

$$R^E(c, c') = \frac{|\{q \in E | q.c_{src} = c \wedge q.c_{dst} = c'\}|}{|\{q \in E | q.c_{src} = c\}| + 1} \times \log\left(\frac{|E|}{|\{q \in E | q.c_{dst} = c'\}| + 1}\right)$$

We define R^I in a similar way using the multi-set of implicit queries.

We combine R^S, R^E, and R^I into a single signal R_{CC} by taking a weighted average. R^S is sparse, as only 48 out of the 168 possible directed pairs of categories were included in the survey. Thus, R^S is only counted towards R_{CC} for pairs of categories included in the survey $(c, c') \in Srv$. R^S is based on answers by people who live in NYC, or visit there frequently, whereas the directions queries are biased towards tourists and other non-locals. To account for both crowds, we take the average of R^S and a signal composed of R^E, and R^I. Since explicit directions queries are higher precision and a clearer signal of user intent, we weight each explicit query twice as much as an implicit query, and since we have 10 times as many implicit as explicit queries, we average R^E and R^I in a ratio of 1:5. This gives us the final formula for R_{CC}:

$$R_{CC}(c, c') = \begin{cases} \frac{1}{2} \cdot R^S(c, c') + \frac{5}{12} \cdot R^I(c, c') + \frac{1}{12} \cdot R^E(c, c') & (c, c') \in Srv \\ \frac{5}{6} \cdot R^I(c, c') + \frac{1}{6} \cdot R^E(c, c') & (c, c') \notin Srv \end{cases} \tag{5}$$

In the approach described in section 4, the signal R_{CC} is used for both establishing business-to-business relevance through category adjustment, as well as to control for the strength of the decay functions. Typically, our approach produces a more diverse related business recommendation list than the current Google RBG-based system does. However, in cases $R_{CC}(c, \tilde{c})$ is very high, and $R_{CC}(c, c')$ is low for all $c' \neq \tilde{c}$, our system might in fact un-diversify the recommendation list by making recommendations only, or mostly, from category $\tilde{c}$. As we will explain in section 6, this case did come up in our evaluations.

5.3 Business-To-Business Relevance Scores

$r(y|x, c)$ is a signal that measures the relevance of a potential related business y to the source business x given that we want to make a recommendation of category c. To compute $r(y|x, c)$, we combine three signals that give business-to-business relevance scores:

1. $r^{RBG}(y|x)$ is the normalized weight of the edge (x, y) in Google RBG: $r^{RBG}(y|x) = \frac{w(x,y)}{\sum_{y'} w(x,y')}$
2. $r^E(y|x)$ is the fraction of queries with destination y among explicit mobile maps directions queries from x
3. $r^I(y|x)$ is the fraction of queries with destination y among implicit directions mobile maps queries from x

For each of the above three $r(y|x)$ signals, we define $r(y|x, c)$ to be $r(y|x)$ if y is of category c, and zero otherwise.

r^{RBG} has far greater coverage of possible business pairs than r^I does. On the other hand, directions queries give more obvious and direct evidence of business-to-business relevance and complementarity. So r^{RBG} is a higher recall and lower precision signal than r^I, which is in turn a higher recall and lower precision signal than r^E. We combine a higher recall and lower precision f_1 with a lower recall and higher precision signal f_2 by using f_2 as an amplifier for the f_1 scores: $combine(f_1, f_2) = f_1 \times (1 + f_2)$. r^{RBG} is used as the basis for r, and we successively combine each signal with the next high recall signal, so we get the final formulation for $r(y|x, c)$:

$$\begin{aligned} r(y|x, c) &= combine(r^{RBG}, combine(r^I, r^E)) \\ &= r^{RBG}(y|x, c) + r^{RBG}(y|x, c) \times r^I(y|x, c) \\ &+ r^{RBG}(y|x, c) \times r^I(y|x, c) \times r^E(y|x, c) \end{aligned} \tag{6}$$

Locality is implicitly a factor in $r(y|x, c)$. The RBG takes into account locality, so high geographic proximity between x and y will increase the weight of the edge (x, y), and thus increase $r(y|x, c)$.

6. EVALUATION

We evaluate several variants of our system using human raters, and compare them against Google current RBG-based system.

The Evaluation Procedure: The raters are professionals who undergo training by Google for ranking results, and are experienced in side-by-side comparison of alternative business result sets. If a rater is not familiar enough with any displayed business, she is instructed to research that business. We gave the raters items that showed a source business x and two lists of 5 related businesses each - one produced by selecting the top neighbors of x in the RBG, and the other produced by our system. The instructions for the item asked the raters to assume that a user had searched and was considering visiting x. The side that our list appeared on was randomized.

For each item, we gave the raters two tasks. The first was to rate how useful each related business recommendation y was for the user. For each recommendation y, the raters had to choose one of three options:
(1) 'Useful as a Complement' - y is a useful suggestion for a complementary business that the user could visit in conjunction to x
(2) 'Useful as a Substitute' - y is a useful suggestion for a substitute that the user could visit instead of x
(3) 'Not Useful'
The second task was to compare the two lists for overall usefulness for the user. The raters had to choose whether the list generated by our system was Much Better / Better / Slightly Better / About the Same / Slightly Worse / Worse / Much Worse than the list generated by the current RBG-based system. Furthermore, they had to give a one sentence explanation for their rating.

We selected 500 items by choosing the 500 businesses with the largest number of explicit directions queries with that business as an origin. Since the explicit directions queries is our sparsest data source, this approach allowed us to utilize as many of our available data sources as possible. We had each of these items rated by three independent raters, for a total of 1500 comparison ratings per evaluation procedure.

We repeated this evaluation procedure for a variant of our system using each of the decay functions listed in Table 3. The choice of decay function had a significant impact on the recommendation lists, and we found that the stronger the decay was, the further our system's recommendation lists were from the RBG-based lists. Table 3 shows the average set overlap between our system's recommendation list and the RBG-based list for the same source business for each decay function.

Overall List Ratings: We start by analyzing the results of the raters' second task, as this task's ratings are the indicator of our system's relative performance compared to that of the current Google system. We explore the ratings for the lists generated by our system for each of the decay options. These ratings compare the lists against the equivalent lists generated by the current Google RBG-based system and give the gain or loss of our system compared to the current system. The distribution of the results is described in Figure 3. We assign a numeric score to each rating option — from (-3) for 'Much Worse' to (+3) for 'Much Better', and display the statistics of the improvement compared to the current RBG-based system in Table 4.

For all of the decay options, the lists generated by our system received a positive average rating (with a confidence level of at least 95%). This means that our system achieves a statistically significant improvement in recommendation list ratings, and that on average, our system produced a more useful recommendation list than the original RBG-based system.

The choice of decay function has a significant impact on the rating distribution. A strong decay function may lead to premature exhaustion of relevant categories and switching to irrelevant categories. Such a scenario usually leads to strong losses, which are more common when using strong exponential decay. On the other hand, using no decay would commonly lead to an homogenous recommendations list, missing some of the opportunities for high gain that arise from diversifying the list. An intermediate decay function,

Decay Function	Average Overlap with RBG list
$d_c^1(n) = \exp(-\alpha_c n)$	37%
$d_c^2(n) = \exp(-\alpha_c n/2)$	46.5%
$d_c^3(n) = \alpha_c^{-n}$	51.1%
$d_c^4(n) \equiv 1$ (no decay)	69%

Table 3: **Decay functions and average overlap:** The four decay functions we explored, from strongest to weakest, and the average set overlap between a recommendation list generated by our system using that decay function and the original recommendation list for that same source business as generated from the RBG.

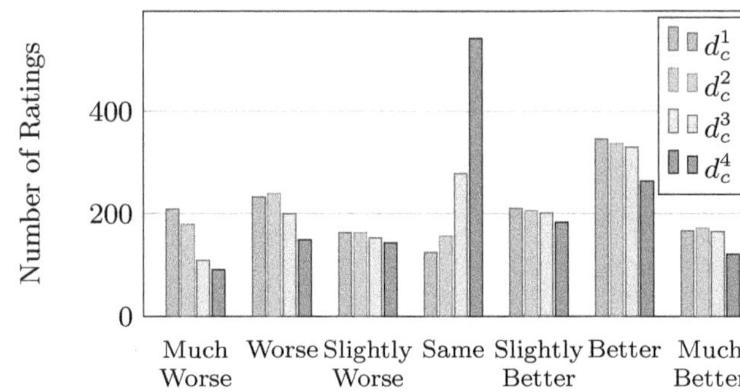

Figure 3: **Comparison to RBG - overall rating distribution:** For each decay function, the distribution of the comparison scores between lists generated by our system using that decay function and lists generated from the RBG.

$d_c^3(n) = \alpha_c^{-n}$, achieved the best improvement in the generated lists.

Individual Business Ratings: Next, we analyze the results of the raters' first task, where they had to classify each recommendation as a useful complement, useful substitute, or neither with respect to the source business. The results are listed in Table 5. As expected, the recommendations generated by the original RBG-based system have a strong majority of useful substitutes and a small fraction of useful complements, but also a small fraction of not useful outliers. The stronger the decay is, the farther the rating distribution is from that of the RBG-based system, and the stronger the decay is the lower is the fraction of useful substitutes among the recommended businesses, and the higher are the fractions of useful complements on one hand and the fraction of not useful suggestions on the other. Note that even when no decay is used and there is no incentive to switch between categories, the fraction of useful complements is higher in our system compared to the RBG-based system, and the fraction of the substitutes is lower. This is mostly due to cases where the most relevant category according to R_{CC} is a category different than the category of the source business, as the RBG-based system tends to make recommendations similar to the searched business.

Per Category List Ratings: The items that we have analyzed are for the 500 most popular source businesses in the explicit directions queries dataset. This dataset has a strong bias towards tourists and other non-locals, so the set of 500 businesses includes many lodging options (258), restaurants and cafes (94), and tourist attractions (72). We now analyze the performance of our system by *source category* (i.e. the

Decay	Average Rating	95% Confidence Interval	positive ratings	negative ratings
d_c^1	0.10	0.0-0.21	49.8%	41.6%
d_c^2	0.15	0.04-0.25	49.2%	40.0%
d_c^3	0.33	0.23-0.42	48.4%	32.2%
d_c^4	0.24	0.16-0.32	38.0%	25.7%

Table 4: **Comparison to RBG - rating statistics:** Comparison of the lists generated by our system to the original RBG-based lists. The ratings are in the scale of (-3) to (+3) with a positive rating indicating improvement compared to the original system, and a negative rating indicating a loss. For all decay options, the average rating is positive with a confidence level of 95%

Decay	Complement	Substitute	Not Useful
d_c^1	43.6%	32.3%	24.1%
d_c^2	36.6%	42.1%	21.3%
d_c^3	35.8%	45.4%	18.8%
d_c^4	21.5%	64.4%	14.1%
RBG	14.4%	71.6%	14%

Table 5: **Distribution of individual recommendation ratings:** For each variant of our system, and for the original RBG-based system. Every recommendation was classified by the raters as either 'Useful Complement', 'Useful Substitute', or 'Not Useful'.

category of the searched source business) to see when is our approach the most applicable.

Since indoor lodging, restaurants and cafes, and tourist attractions are the only categories represented in significant numbers in the previously evaluated business set, we ran separate evaluations for the rest of the source categories listed in Table 1. For each of the remaining source categories, we selected the most popular 50 source businesses of that category in the explicit directions dataset. The results of comparing the list generated by our system using d_c^3 as a decay function against the equivalent lists generated by the current RBG-based system appear in Table 6.

Our system achieved a significant improvement in recommendation list usefulness for the beauty, indoor lodging, liquor store, and sporting goods store. Our system achieved an improvement, but failed to do so with a 95% confidence level, for the bar, nightclub, performing arts venue, movie theater, gym, and sports complex categories, and suffered small losses on average for the restaurant and tourist attraction categories. To reason about the cases in which our system achieved improvement, we also address the ratings of individual recommended businesses (i.e 'useful complementary' / 'useful substitute' / 'not useful') which are not listed here for the by-category evaluations for space considerations.

In the case of the beauty category, our system actually recommends more useful substitutes than the RBG-based system does. The high fraction of useful substitutes in the suggestions is due to the high relevance of beauty to itself, i.e. high $R_{CC}\,(beauty, beauty)$, and the low relevance of other categories to beauty. The category adjustment encourages the system to start with other beauty recommendations, and not to quickly switch to other categories due to a low decay factor. Furthermore, as businesses in the beauty category are often geographically sparse, the RBG-based system, which considers distance more directly than our system does, would often recommend similar but not

Category	Average Rating	95% C.I.	positive ratings	negative ratings
Beauty	0.71	0.41-0.99	53.7%	23.1%
Indoor Lodging	0.52	0.38-0.66	59.4%	34.4%
Liquor Stores	0.37	0.15-0.58	29.9%	13.6%
Sport Stores	0.33	0.1-0.54	33.3%	19.7%
Sports Complexes	0.26	(-0.04)-0.54	45.1%	34.7%
Bars	0.18	(-0.07)-0.42	39.4%	28.6%
Nightclubs	0.15	(-0.09)-0.37	30.6%	23.1%
Performing Arts	0.10	(-0.13)-0.34	33.3%	29.9%
Movie Theaters	0.07	(-0.16)-0.29	29.9%	25.9%
Gyms	0.06	(-0.12)-0.24	18.8%	20.1%
Restaurants	0.00	(-0.16)-0.15	29.9%	27.0%
Tourist Attractions	-0.01	(-0.25)-0.21	38.3%	37.8%

Table 6: **Overall list ratings organized by source category** - comparing the lists generated by our system, when using d_c^3, to the original RBG-based lists. The categories are sorted from highest to lowest improvement, as indicated by the average rating.

directly related businesses such as clothing stores that are close geographically. Raters often do not find such loosely related recommendations useful, and harshly penalize the RBG-based list. A similar scenario explains the gain our system achieved for the liquor store, sporting goods store, and to a lesser extent, the bar and nightclub categories. All of these five categories have very high self-relevance scores $R_{CC}\,(c, c) > 0.75$.

In the case of the indoor lodging category, our system suggested significantly more useful complementary businesses (45.1%) than the the RBG-based system did (6.8%). For example, the related businesses recommendations the RBG-based system provides for the source business "Hotel 373 Fifth Avenue" - a boutique in Midtown East, Manhattan are as follows: $(y_1, y_2, y_3, y_4, y_5) =$ (Hotel Giraffe, Courtyard NY Manhattan-Fifth Avenue, New York Marriott Marquis, Courtyard Times Square South, 70 Park Avenue: A Kimpton Hotel) - all are Midtown hotels similar to the source business. On the other hand, our system makes the following recommendation list: (Hotel Giraffe, American Girl Place Cafe, Courtyard NY Manhattan-Fifth Avenue, Bryant Park, Tenpenny) - i.e. the list is a mix of two similar hotels, two restaurants, and a famous park - all in Midtown East. The raters favored the diversity, even at the expense of a higher fraction of not useful recommendations. A similar scenario explains the improvements that our system achieved in the cases of the sports complex and performing arts venue categories. For all three categories, survey takers in the survey described in section 3 indeed indicated a strong preference for information about complementary businesses when searching for a source business belonging to one of these categories.

In the cases of movie Theater and gym in which our system achieved a very small improvement, the distributions of individual recommendation ratings is very similar for both our system and the RBG-based system. In the cases of restaurant and cafe and tourist attraction categories, our system recommended less useful substitutes, more useful complements, and slightly more not useful recommendations, and suffered a small loss compared to the RBG-based system. Some of the losses are due to locality being less explicitly taken into account in establishing business-to-business relevance compared to the RBG, and some recommendations lose relevance drastically if not immediately close to the source business (e.g. recommending a gift shop not immediately close to the searched tourist attraction). A future improvement to our system could be including distance-based regularization that could more directly account for locality.

7. CONCLUSION AND FUTURE WORK

We studied the problem of improving the usefulness of the list of related business recommendations a search engine provides in response to a specific business search. Our approach was to build a relevant and diverse mixture of substitute and complement recommendations. In our problem settings, an ontology of business categories exists. We mined multiple data sources to establish business-to-business relevance scores that take that ontology into account. We introduced an algorithm that constructs a list of related business recommendations for a given source business. The algorithm balances pairwise business-to-business relevance scores with diversification through penalizing multiple recommendations from the same category. We explored several penalization options through different families of decay functions.

Compared to the current Google system, our system typically generates recommendation lists with more complementary business recommendations and fewer substitutes similar to the source business. The evaluation results show a significant improvement in recommendation list usefulness for the lists generated by our system compared to the current Google system, which demonstrates the added value in including local complementary businesses recommendations. However, the extent to which a source business would benefit from complementary vs. substitute recommendations varies greatly on the source business and its category. In some cases, our system actually gained user satisfaction through offering more substitutes similar to the source business.

Furthermore, in this work we treat two businesses as substitutes if they belong to the same category, and as complements if they are otherwise relevant to one another. However, this is just one interpretation for substitute vs. complementary. Another interpretation could be clustering categories and determining substitute relation iff two businesses are in categories belonging to the same cluster. Other possible interpretations of business to business substitute vs. complement relations can be completely unrelated to the ontology and rely on entirely different features or data sources (e.g. online reviews or social network based connections).

Lastly, our work did not take into account user-specific features, and addressed providing recommendations to an anonymous random search engine user. However, user settings could and should be taken into account, even for providing non-personalized recommendations. In particular, the system could use the user's location and whether they are using a mobile or non-mobile device to provide the best recommendations for a well-rounded and satisfying experience wherever they may go.

The factors that make two business substitute or complement each other, the different interpretations for such relations, and the circumstances in which substitutes vs. complements should be recommended, are all possible lines for future work on the topic.

Acknowledgments. We thank the local search quality team at Google New York, and to Mayur Thakur in particular, for their support and feedback. We also thank Jure Leskovec and the SNAP group at Stanford, and to Austin Benson and Julian McAuley in particular, for their useful feedback. Additionally, we thank Tilman Achberger for his help with the evaluation process. Yonathan Perez is supported by P. Michael Farmwald Stanford Graduate Fellowship.

8. REFERENCES

[1] Supplementary Materials. `https://www.dropbox.com/sh/wau25zqwusnv8mc/AADJta6Ybc6RzyJiJRRCCk_ea?dl=0`.
[2] R. Agrawal, S. Gollapudi, A. Halverson, and S. Ieong. Diversifying search results. In *WSDM*, 2009.
[3] J. Carbonell and J. Goldstein. The use of mmr, diversity-based reranking for reordering documents and producing summaries. In *SIGIR*, 1998.
[4] C. Clarke, M. Kolla, G. Cormack, O. Vechtomova, A. Ashkan, S. Buttcher, and I. MacKinnon. Novelty and diversity in information retrieval evaluation. In *SIGIR*, 2008.
[5] V. Dang and B. Croft. Diversity by proportionality: An election-based approach to search result diversification. In *SIGIR*, 2012.
[6] M. Drosou and E. Pitoura. Search result diversification. *SIGMOD Record*, 39(1):41–47, 2010.
[7] G.Linden, B.Smith, and J.York. Amazon.com recommendations: Item-to-item collaborative filtering. In *IEEE Internet Computing*, 2003.
[8] S. Gollapudi and A. Sharma. An axiomatic approach for result diversification. In *WWW*, 2009.
[9] J. Levandoski, M. Sarwat, A. Eldawy, and M. Mokbel. Lars: A location-aware recommender system. In *ICDE*, 2012.
[10] J. McAuley, R. Pandey, and J. Leskovec. Inferring Networks of Substitutable and Complementary Products. In *KDD*, 2015.
[11] D. Rafiei, K. Bharat, and A. Shukla. Diversifying web search results. In *WWW*, 2010.
[12] R. Santos, C. Macdonald, and I. Ounis. Exploiting query reformulations for web search result diversification. In *WWW*, 2010.
[13] S. Vargas, L. Baltrunas, A. Karatzoglou, and P. Castells. Coverage, redundancy and size-awareness in genre diversity for recommender systems. In *RecSys*, 2014.
[14] E. Vee, U. Srivastava, J. Shanmugasundaram, P. Bhat, and S. Amer-Yahia. Efficient computation of diverse query results. In *ICDE*, 2008.
[15] P. Venetis, H. Gonzalez, C. Jensen, and A. Halevy. Hyper-local, directions-based ranking of places. In *VLDB*, 2011.
[16] E. Xavier. A note on a maximum k-subset intersection problem. *Information Processing Letters*, 112(48):358–373, September 2011.
[17] M. Ye, P. Yin, and W. Lee. Location recommendation for location-based social networks. In *GIS*, 2010.
[18] C. Yu, L. Lakshmanan, and S. Amer-Yahia. It takes variety to make a world: Diversification in recommender systems. In *EDBT*, 2009.
[19] C. Zhai, W. Cohen, and J. Lafferty. Beyond independent relevance: Methods and evaluation metrics for subtopic retrieval. In *SIGIR*, 2003.
[20] M. Zhang and N. Hurley. Avoiding monotony: Improving the diversity of recommendation lists. In *RecSys*, 2008.
[21] J. Zheng, X. Wu, J. Niu, and A. Bolivar. Substitutes and complements: Another step forward in recommendations. In *EC*, 2009.
[22] C. Ziegler, S. McNee, J. Konstan, and G. Lausen. Improving recommendation lists through topic diversification. In *WWW*, 2005.

A Soft Computing Approach for Learning to Aggregate Rankings

Javier A. Vargas
University of Campinas
Campinas, Brazil
jalvarm.acm@gmail.com

Ricardo da S. Torres
University of Campinas
Campinas, Brazil
rtorres@ic.unicamp.br

Marcos André Gonçalves
Universidade Federal de Minas Gerais
Belo Horizonte, Brazil
mgoncalv@dcc.ufmg.br

ABSTRACT

This paper presents an approach to combine rank aggregation techniques using a soft computing technique – Genetic Programming – in order to improve the results in Information Retrieval tasks. Previous work shows that by combining rank aggregation techniques in an agglomerative way, it is possible to get better results than with individual methods. However, these works either combine only a small set of lists or are performed in a completely ad-hoc way. Therefore, given a set of ranked lists and a set of rank aggregation techniques, we propose to use a supervised genetic programming approach to search combinations of them that maximize effectiveness in large search spaces. Experimental results conducted using four datasets with different properties show that our proposed approach reaches top performance in most datasets. Moreover, this cross-dataset performance is not matched by any other baseline among the many we experiment with, some being the state-of-the-art in learning-to-rank and in the supervised rank aggregation tasks. We also show that our proposed framework is very efficient, flexible, and scalable.

Categories and Subject Descriptors

H.3 [**Information Storage and Retrieval**]: Information Search and Retrieval

General Terms

Algorithms, Experimentation

Keywords

Rank Aggregation, Soft Computing, Genetic Programming

1. INTRODUCTION

Rank aggregation is a research line broadly studied in the literature, focused on exploring the complementarity among ranked lists produced by different rankers. The problem of rank aggregation refers to how to combine a set of ranked lists so that the final combination is better (more effective) than any individual lists. Rank aggregation has been applied in the last years in several tasks such as document filtering [13], genome database construction [24], informative gene selection [16], metasearch [7, 15, 23], spam webpage detection [7], word association finding [7], and similarity search [9].

Rank aggregation techniques may be divided into two main categories: score-based and order-based. In the first group, the aggregation function takes the score information associated with each lists' object as input. Examples of methods in this category are the Comb* family of rank aggregation methods (e.g., CombMAX, CombMIN, CombSUM, CombANZ, CombMNZ, and CombMED) [25] and the RL-Sim Rank Aggregation [18]. In the second category, only the relative order among the documents is required to aggregate the lists. Examples of methods of that category are Borda Count [2], Median Rank Aggregation [9], Markov Chain based rank aggregation [7], Footrule Optimal Aggregation [7], and Reciprocal Rank Fusion [3].

Given the large amount of existing techniques, each with different properties, recent work (e.g., [19]) has started to explore the idea of combining the outputs of these methods. For instance, in [19] the authors describe a model to combine in an agglomerative way results of different rank aggregation techniques and show that this model can obtain better results than the individual methods. However, in that and other works, the selection of the rank aggregation techniques was done arbitrarily, in an ad-hoc, not principled way and without exploring the large search space for combinations of rank aggregation techniques. Moreover, usually only a few techniques are exploited in this combination.

In fact, finding the optimal (Kemeny) combination of ranked lists is an NP-hard problem, even for a small set of lists [8].[1] Soft computing techniques are well suited for this type of scenario. Soft Computing refers to the use of inexact solutions to computationally hard tasks. In this work, we explore a supervised soft computing technique – genetic programming – to combine a large set of methods. We model a problem as an optimization one, i.e., we try to optimize some metric of ranking quality while aggregating the lists produced by the individual methods. Our motivations to use genetic programming are threefold: (1) its solid theoretical background [14]; (2) its powerful global exploration capability in large search spaces, with the capability of finding close-to-optimum solutions in many situations; and (3) a history of

[1]To be more precise, four or more lists.

CIKM'15, October 19–23, 2015, Melbourne, Australia.
© 2015 ACM. ISBN 978-1-4503-3794-6/15/10 ...$15.00.
DOI: http://dx.doi.org/10.1145/2806416.2806478.

success of applications of this technique in many information retrieval tasks (e.g., [4,12,27]) and related areas, getting in some cases comparable or better results than state-of-the-art machine learning techniques.

Our experimental results show that when compared to a large set of baselines (32 in total), including state-of-the-art unsupervised and supervised rank aggregation methods as well as Learning-To-Rank (L2R) baselines, our GP Aggregation framework is the only one to achieve top performance (top 1 or top 2) in all tested datasets. Moreover, we show that our method is very efficient and more scalable than several supervised alternatives. Finally, our solution is a general one which is very flexible; any new rank aggregation method to be developed in the future can be easily incorporated into our framework.

The rest of this paper is organized as follows. Section 2 introduces the problem of rank aggregation and describes briefly some methods of the state of the art. Section 3 covers related work. Section 4 presents principal concepts about genetic programming. Section 5 describes the proposed model for rank aggregation. Section 6 presents the experimental protocol, setup and the results, respectively. In section 7, we conclude the paper, presenting future research directions.

2. BACKGROUND ON RANK AGGREGATION

The problem of rank aggregation refers to combining a set of preference lists to produce a unique combined list. In the context of information retrieval, the scheme of rank aggregation is illustrated in Figure 1. Each ranker produces a ranked list, ordering the database's elements with respect to the relevance for the query. Then, using a rank aggregation function, the lists are combined to produce a final list. More formally, let $\mathcal{D} = \{D_1, D_2, \ldots, D_m\}$ be a set of rankers based on which we can compute m ranked lists, $R_{D_1}, R_{D_2}, \ldots, R_{D_m}$, given a query q. Let $\mathcal{R}_q$ be the set formed by these ranked lists, i.e., $\mathcal{R}_q = \{R_{D_1}, R_{D_2}, \ldots, R_{D_m}\}$. A rank aggregation function f is used to define a ranked list $R_{q,f}$ for q, such that $R_{q,f} = f(\mathcal{R}_q)$.

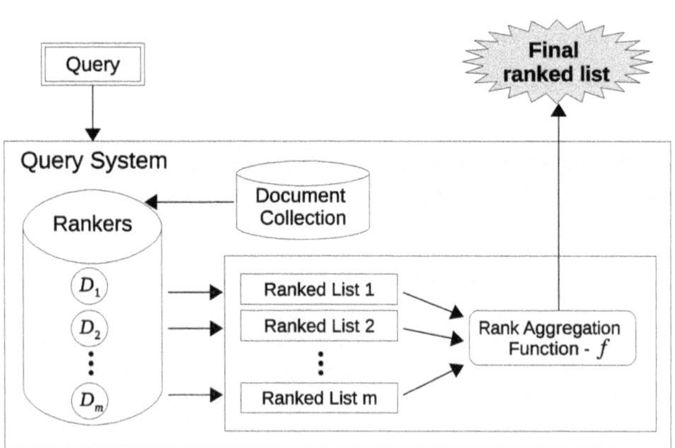

Figure 1: Scheme of rank aggregation in information retrieval.

One of the most cited applications of rank aggregation is meta-search, this is, the problem of creating a search engine that uses the results of a set of search engines to produce better results [7].

Table 1: Formulas to get the final score of an object, by Fox and Shaw [25], where $r(x)$ is the score of x in the ranked list r and R is the set of ranked lists

$CombMAX(x)$	$\max_{r \in R} r(x)$
$CombMIN(x)$	$\min_{r \in R} r(x)$
$CombSUM(x)$	$\sum_{r \in R} r(x)$
$CombMED(x)$	$CombSUM(x) \div \lvert R \rvert$
$CombANZ(x)$	$CombSUM(x) \div \lvert \{r \mid r \in R \text{ and } x \in r\} \rvert$
$CombMNZ(x)$	$CombSUM(x) \times \lvert \{r \mid r \in R \text{ and } x \in r\} \rvert$

There are many unsupervised methods proposed in the literature. The principal advantage of these methods is their low computational complexity. However, they assume that all ranked lists have the same level of importance, which in practice is not a good idea, because the ranked lists were produced by systems with different levels of precision. Some of these methods are described in the following.

Borda [2] proposed the Borda Count algorithm in the context of the social-choice theory. It is an order-based method, where to an element x is assigned a score, in the ranked list r_i, equal to $|r_i| - r_i(x)$, where $r_i(x)$ is the position of the element x in r_i. The final score of an element is the sum of the scores obtained in each ranked list.

Fox and Shaw [25] proposed six score-based techniques: CombMAX, CombMIN, CombSUM, CombMED, CombANZ, and CombMNZ. These methods assign to each object a score using the formulas showed in Table 1. The score of the objects in the ranked list needs to be normalized before using these methods.

The method *RL-Sim Rank Aggregation* was proposed by Pedronette and Torres [18]. It is score-based technique, where the final score of an object is given by the product of their scores in each ranked list. This method is inspired by the Naïve Bayes classifiers, in the sense that it considers that the lists are independent and the score multiplication can be seen like the probability computation of the objects.

Cormack et al. [3] proposed the *Reciprocal Rank Fusion* algorithm, which is an order-based method that simply assigns the final score to an object using the formula showed in Equation 1, where C is the set objects, R the set of ranked lists, $r(x)$ the position of the object x in the list r, and k is a constant (authors report better results with $k = 60$):

$$RRFscore(x \in C) = \sum_{r \in R} \frac{1}{k + r(x)} \qquad (1)$$

Fagin et al. [9] proposed the *Median Rank Aggregation* algorithm, which works as follows. It goes through the ranked lists simultaneously and counts the number of occurrences of the objects. The first object that appears in more than half of the lists is taken as the first object of the combined list. Then, the second object that appears in more than half of the lists is taken as the second, and so on, until the k-top objects are found.

3. RELATED WORK

As we are exploiting a supervised GP framework, the closest methods to ours are learning-to-rank (L2R) approaches and supervised rank aggregation techniques.

L2R methods are usually classified into three categories:

pointwise, pairwise, and listwise. Pointwise strategies can be viewed as regression approaches that predict relevance by minimizing a loss function. Differently, pairwise approaches learn, for any given two documents, if one is more relevant than the other. Finally, listwise approaches iteratively optimize a specialized ranking performance measure, such as Mean Average Precision (MAP). Our approach is more related to listwise approaches as we directly optimize a ranking measure. However, we use an extensive list of L2R methods covering all three categories as baselines in our experiments.

The supervised rank aggregation problem has received considerable attention in recent years and a number of supervised approaches have been proposed [17, 20, 26, 28–30]. Notably, Volkovs and Zemel [28] have recently shown that by applying SVD factorization to pairwise preference matrices effective item features can be extracted. The features transform the problem into a standard L2R one, allowing to apply any of the existing L2R methods to optimize the aggregating function for the target metric. While the authors of that work have shown superior empirical effectiveness of this approach to many existing aggregation methods, it also has a major drawback as it requires computing SVD factors at training or test time. For large problems with many documents per query, applying SVD at training or even test time can be prohibitively expensive, limiting the application of this method. A number of other popular supervised aggregation methods share the same disadvantage and also require applying complex optimization procedures such as semi-definite programming [17].

In [29], on the other hand, the authors address the complexity at testing time by developing a flexible Conditional Random Field (CRF) framework for supervised rank aggregation. This framework uses preference matrices directly in order to avoid costly optimizations. The authors demonstrate that CRF has superior effectiveness when compared to some supervised alternatives. We use this method as one of our baselines. Although efficient at testing time, this method is very costly at training time, mainly when aggregating large ranked lists. Indeed, it took more than a week to run in the biggest dataset we experimented with.

Genetic programming has been previously exploited in [31] for the task of L2R. In that work the authors use genetic programming to discover a ranking function composed of a non-linear combination of the feature values of the document-query pairs, using simple arithmetic operations ($\times$, $+$ and $-$) and a set of fixed constants. We include this method as baseline (RankGP).

In [1] the authors proposed an unsupervised rank aggregation method using genetic algorithms to search a permutation that minimizes the normalized aggregated footrule distance between this permutation and the ranked lists generated by the rankers. An advantage of this method is that it does not require labeled data. An important disadvantage is that if there is a majority of "bad" rankers, the final ranked list will be very correlated to those. Another significant drawback is that the process of optimization is performed at query time, which, generally, can be very expensive and not really suitable for online (web) search. In contrast, our supervised solution, which is run offline, is used only to discover a close to optimal combination of lists, which is very fast to be applied at query time, as we shall see in our experiments.

Several of these methods have explored weighted aggregation rules [20, 26] to learn the importance of individual ranked lists before combining them, using a well-explored social choice aggregation rule, such as Borda or Kemeny. The weights are tuned on the training data to reflect each expert "agreement" with the ground truth preferences. We use the two approaches proposed in [26] (SupBordaCount and SupKemeny) as baselines.

Finally, a recent proposal [30] has used linear discriminant analysis (LDA) to train the weights along with the Condorcet ranking aggregation algorithm. This method, which learns the weights automatically, can be efficient at both, training and testing time. We also use it as a baseline (SupCondorcet).

4. GENETIC PROGRAMMING

Genetic Programming (GP) is an evolutionary methodology introduced by [14]. It is a problem-solving technique based on the principles of biological inheritance and evolution of individuals in a population. The search space of a problem, i.e., the space of all possible solutions to the problem, is searched by applying a set of operations that follow the theory of evolution, combining natural selection and genetic operations, to create more diverse and better performing individuals in subsequent generations with the aim of providing a way to find near-optimal solutions for a given task.

GP evolves a number of candidate solutions, called *individuals*, represented in memory as binary tree structures. Every internal node of the tree is a function and every leaf node, known as terminal, represents either a variable or a constant. The maximum number of available nodes of an individual is determined by the depth of the tree, which is defined before the evolution process begins.

A common GP individual representation is given by a tree, as shown in Figure 2, where the individual represents the function $f(a, b) = a \times b + \sqrt{b} \div a$. The leaf nodes of the tree (a and b) are called *terminals* and the internal nodes ($+$, $\sqrt{}$, $\times$, and $\div$) are called *functions*. The functions (usually mathematical operators) are used to combine terminals.

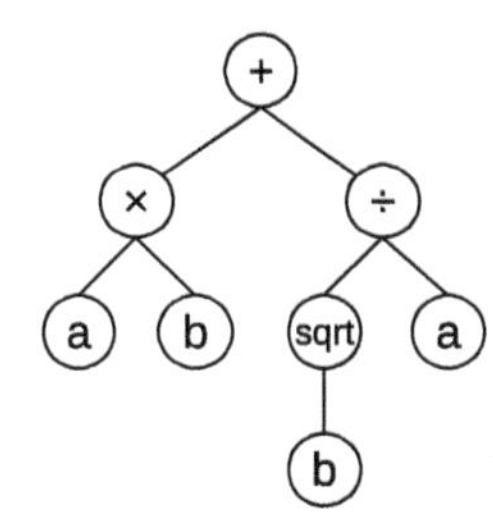

Figure 2: Example of a tree representation of an individual.

The evolution process starts with an *initial population* composed of a set of individuals (the initial population) randomly generated. Each individual is evaluated by a fitness function and associated with a fitness value. This fitness function is commonly modeled by a user-defined measure to score the ability of an individual to adapt to the environment (which in most cases correspond to the best solution for a given problem) and it is used to eliminate from the population all *unfit* individuals, selecting only those closer to the desired goal or those that achieve higher scores. In the case of search systems, this fitness function is the ranking quality measure we want to optimize. Individuals evolve generation by generation through genetic operations such as *reproduction*, *crossover*, and *mutation*.

Reproduction is the process that copies the "best" individuals from one generation to the next one, without modifying them. The individuals selected participate in the crossover and selection operations. The crossover operator allows genetic content exchange between two other individuals, the parents. In a GP process, two parent trees are selected according to a matching selection policy. Next, a random subtree is selected from each parent. The children trees result from the swap of the selected sub-trees between the parents.

Finally, the mutation operator has the role of keeping a minimum level of individuals diversity in a population. In the mutation operation, a random node in a tree is selected and then replaced by a new randomly created sub-tree.

Thus, at the end of the evolutionary process, a new population is created to replace the current one. The fitness value is measured for each new individual, and the process is repeated over many generations until the termination criterion has been satisfied. This criterion can be a pre-established maximum number of generations or some additional problem-specific success measure to be reached (e.g., an intended value of fitness for a specific individual).

We adopt the GP process suggested in [5]. Its main steps are described in Algorithm 1. Basically, the learning process is an iterative process with two main phases: *training* (Lines 1–10) and *validation* (Lines 11–14). For each phase, a distinct set of queries is selected, which we call the *training set* and the *validation set*, respectively. It is important to stress that in this approach the whole GP process is performed offline, only once, when processing a training collection. After the process derives a ranking function, this (mathematical) function is applied to combine features at query processing time. For this reason, GP is an extremely low-cost method when considering run-time query processing computational costs.

Data: Let $\mathcal{T}$ be a training set of queries.
Data: Let $\mathcal{V}$ be a validation set of queries.
Data: Let N_g be the number of generations.
Data: N_b be the number of best individuals.

1 $\mathcal{P} \leftarrow$ Initial random population of individuals;
2 $\mathcal{B}_t \leftarrow \varnothing$;
3 **foreach** *generation g of N_g generations* **do**
4 $\quad \mathcal{F}_t \leftarrow \varnothing$;
5 $\quad$ **foreach** *individual* $i \in \mathcal{P}$ **do**
6 $\quad\quad \mathcal{F}_t \leftarrow \mathcal{F}_t \cup \{g, i, \mathit{fitness}(i, \mathcal{T})$
7 $\quad$ **end**
8 $\quad \mathcal{B}_t \leftarrow \mathcal{B}_t \cup \mathit{getBestIndividuals}(N_b, \mathcal{F}_t)$;
9 $\quad \mathcal{P} \leftarrow \mathit{applyGeneticOperations}(\mathcal{P}, \mathcal{F}_t, \mathcal{B}_t, g)$;
10 **end**
11 $\mathcal{B}_v \leftarrow \varnothing$;
12 **foreach** *individual* $i \in \mathcal{B}_t$ **do**
13 $\quad \mathcal{B}_v \leftarrow \mathcal{B}_v \cup \{i, \mathit{fitness}(i, \mathcal{V})\}$;
14 **end**
15 BestIndividual $\leftarrow \mathit{applySelectionMethod}(\mathcal{B}_t, \mathcal{B}_v)$;

Algorithm 1: GP-based learning process [5].

The process starts with the creation of an initial random population of individuals (Line 1) that evolves generation by generation using genetic operations (reproduction, crossover, and mutation) – Line 9. The process continues until a stopping criterion is met. In the case of Algorithm 1, the criterion is the maximum number of generations of the evolutionary process.

In the training phase, a fitness function is applied to evaluate all individuals of each generation (Lines 5–7), so that only the fittest individuals are selected to continue evolving (Line 8). The fitness of an individual corresponds to the quality of the ranking generated by the individual for each training query.

After the last generation is created, to avoid selecting individuals that work well in the training set but do not generalize for different queries (a problem known as *over-fitting*), a validation phase is applied. In this phase, the fitness function is also used, but at this time over the validation set of queries and documents (Lines 12–14). Individuals that perform the best in this phase are selected as the final solutions (Line 15).

5. RANK AGGREGATION BASED ON GENETIC PROGRAMMING

Our proposed model (hereafter called **GP-Agg** for *GP-Based Rank Aggregation*) uses genetic programming to search the best combinations of different rank aggregation techniques in an agglomerative way, that is, using the result of one as input of another. The principal reasons to use genetic programming for this task are: (i) the inherent complementarity between the results of different rank aggregation techniques studied in [19]; (ii) the large size of the search space for combination functions; and (iii) previous success of using GP in information retrieval.

We use the representation of trees for the GP-Agg individuals, where the terminals are composed of a set of ranked lists $\mathcal{R} = \{R_1, R_2, .., R_m\}$ generated by a set of base rankers. The functions (internal nodes) are composed of a set of unsupervised rank aggregation techniques $\mathcal{F} = \{f_1, f_2, ..., f_k\}$ proposed in the literature. We create randomly the initial population and evolve it through a number of generations. Also, we use the classic genetic operators of reproduction, mutation, and crossover.

Figure 3 illustrates the whole process of learning to aggregate rankings. In part A of the figure, we have the set of rankers that are used to create ranked lists, given query documents available in the document collection (data repository indicated by C). The defined ranked lists are then combined by rank aggregation functions f_i (see B). The GP-based approach described in Section 4 (see D) is then used to define the best combination function represented as a binary tree (see E). Note that the GP-based aggregation function process uses not only the available rank aggregation functions, but also the training and the validation sets (see Algorithm 1). Finally, the best individual is used to rank documents in the test set (module indicated as F).

A clear example of an individual is shown in Figure 4, where the individual represents the composed function: $\hat{f} = f_3(f_2(f_1(R_1, R_2), R_1), f_1(R_3, R_4))$. In this case, the ranked lists R_1 and R_2 are combined using the function f_1; then the result is combined with R_1 using f_2, and finally this result is aggregated using the function f_3 with the result of combining the ranked lists R_3 and R_4 through f_1.

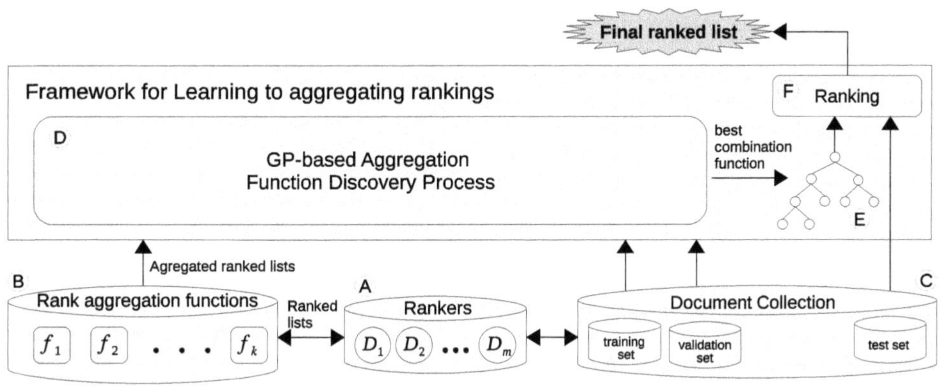

Figure 3: Illustration of the proposed approach for learning to aggregate rankings.

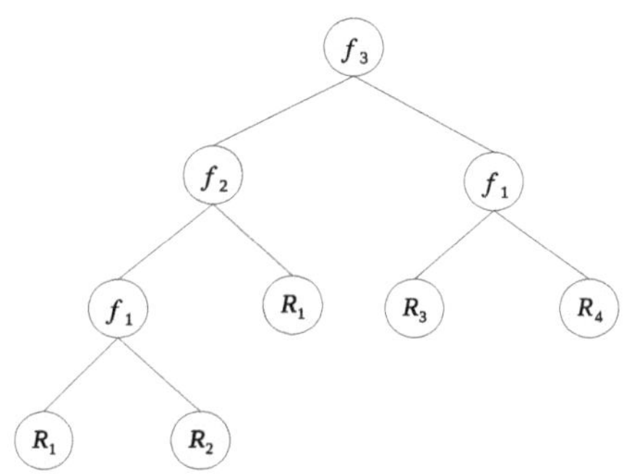

Figure 4: Example of an individual in our proposed model for rank aggregation.

6. EXPERIMENTS

6.1 GP-Agg Experimental Configuration

6.1.1 Rank Aggregation techniques

We used score and order based methods to combine the ranked lists generated by the base rankers. The list of the methods used in our model are shown in Table 2. We selected classical and recent unsupervised methods proposed in the literature.

Table 2: Set of rank aggregation methods used in the proposed GP-Agg framework.

Method	Initials	Type
CombMAX	CombMAX	score-based
CombMIN	CombMIN	score-based
CombSUM	CombSUM	score-based
CombMED	CombMED	score-based
CombANZ	CombANZ	score-based
CombMNZ	CombMNZ	score-based
RL-Sim. Rank Aggregation	RLSIM	score-based
Borda Count	BC	order-based
Reciprocal Rank Fusion	RRF	order-based
Median Rank Aggregation	MRA	order-based

6.1.2 GP-Agg Setup

The following items describe details of the implementation of the proposed model along with the parameter choices selected for GP-Agg. In the parameterization process, we start with values used in previously tested successful GP configurations in related tasks [5, 27], but perform an very comprehensive parameter search, always using a cross-validation procedure in the training set.[2]

- **List of terminals:** As explained in Section 5, the list of terminals is composed of ranked lists generated by the base rankers (as previously described).

- **Functions:** The proposed model uses the rank aggregation methods as functions to combine the terminals. The list of functions used are described in Section 6.1.1.

- **Initial population:** The set of initial trees, constrained to have a maximum depth of four levels, was created using the *ramped half-and-half method* [14]. We considered a population of 50, 100, 500, and 1000 individuals in our experiments. Faster convergence was achieved with 500.

- **Fitness functions:** To evaluate the performance of the individual, we experiment with several functions, including NDCG, MAP, and the FFP* functions proposed in [10]. Overall best results were obtained with the FFP1 function defined as

$$F_{FFP1} = \sum_{i=1}^{|N|} r(\hat{l}_i) \times k_1 \times \ln^{-1}(i + k_2) \qquad (2)$$

where i is the document position after retrieval and $\hat{l}_i$ is the document at position i. $r(\hat{l}_i) \in \{0, 1\}$ is the relevance score assigned to a document, being 1 if the document is relevant and 0 otherwise. $|N|$ is the total number of retrieved documents. k_1, k_2 are scaling factors. Based on [27], we choose $k_1 = 6$ and $k_2 = 1.2$ in our experiments. Although it may seem a counter-intuitive results that directly optimizing the evaluation function did not produce the best results (although they were among the best) this is consistent with the results of [10]. In any case, we believe that a further investigation on this matter should be performed in future work. But such investigation can only make our results even better.

[2]The use of a more systematic methodology [11] for defining the values of GP parameters is left as future work.

- **Genetic operators:** We use the classical GP operators of reproduction, crossover, and mutation, as described in Section 4. Reproduction operator clones the top 10% of the population to the next generation. Crossover rate is 35% and mutation is random and applied at to 1 out of 12 individuals in the whole population. These were the best values found in experiments using cross-validation in the training set and a large pool of alternatives values for the parameters.

- **Stopping criterion:** We stop the evolution after 70 generations. We have empirically observed in our experiments that between the 70th and the 150th generations the individuals' performance does not change significantly. In other words, the evolutionary process converged around the 70th generation.

6.2 Datasets

We use four datasets in our experiments: the informational datasets of Letor 3.0 (TD2003 and TD2004), and the Rank Aggregation datasets of Letor 4.0 (MQ2007-agg and MQ2008-agg). We describe each of these datasets in more details next. These sets of datasets have different properties which help to demonstrate the properties of our proposed framework in different scenarios.

6.2.1 Letor 3.0 Datasets

These datasets[3] were chosen because they are publicly available, include several baseline results, and provide evaluation tools to ensure accurate comparison between methods. In these and the other datasets, information is represented as (query, document) pairs by means of 'meta-level' features that try to capture important relationships between these two central components of an information retrieval system (a.k.a. query-dependent features (QD)). These features vary from simple strategies such as computing Term Frequency (TF), Inverse Document Frequency (IDF), or the combined TF-IDF metric of the query terms in different parts of the document (e.g., whole document, body, anchor text, title, URL) or by the application of traditional (e.g., BM25) or more recent state-of-the-art rankers such as those based on Language Models [32] or Relevance Propagation Methods (e.g., Hyperlink and Score based Propagation models [22].

Other features that are largely exploited in these datasets are the so-called query-independent features (QI), which do not depend on query terms, but are usually related to hyperlinked information available in many collections, most notably the Web. Among these features, we may cite Inlink number, PageRank, HITs hub, and authority. Accordingly, each query-document pair (q,d) is represented by a set of QD and QI features, usually in the form of a feature vector, and labeled with a numerical score indicating how relevant document d is to query q.

Among the datasets in this benchmark, The TD2003 and TD2004 datasets comprise informational queries, while the other datasets (NP and HP ones) comprise navigational queries, for which there is usually only one 'good answer.' Rank aggregation techniques are more suitable for informational queries as there are usually several 'good documents' to fulfill an information need.

[3] `http://research.microsoft.com/en-us/um/beijing/projects/letor/` (As of May 2015).

These datasets are composed of feature vectors for (query, document) pairs, along with a corresponding binary relevance judgements (1 = relevant and 0 = irrelevant) indicating whether the document is relevant or not for the query. Particularly in the case of the TD2003 and TD2004 datasets, there are 64 features per pair: 47 query-dependent features and 17 query-independent ones. Each feature can be considered as an independent ranker, whose ranked list will be aggregated by the base methods. These two datasets together comprise around 100 queries and 100.000 labeled documents. Each dataset comes with five precomputed folds with 60/20/20 splits for training/validation/testing. The results shown for each model are the averages of the test set results for the five folds.

Also available on the benchmark's web page, we find 12 different L2R baselines, namely: AdaRank-MAP, AdaRank-NDCG, FRank, ListNet, RankBoost, RankSVM, RankSVM-Struct, RankSVM-Primal, Regression, Regression+L2reg, SVMMAP, and SmoothRank. Aside from FRank and RankBoost, all of the algorithms use linear ranking functions.

6.2.2 The Letor 4.0 Rank Aggregation Datasets

IN LETOR4.0, there are two datasets especially designed for rank aggregation tasks: MQ2007-agg and MQ2008-agg. MQ2007-agg contains 1692 queries with a total of 69623 documents, while MQ2008-agg contains 784 queries and a total of 15211 documents. Each query contains rankings of the documents under that query. There are 21 features (rankers) in MQ2007-agg and 25 in MQ2008-agg. In addition, in both datasets, to each document is assigned one of three relevance levels (2 = highly relevant, 1 = relevant and 0 = irrelevant). Finally, as before the training, validation, and test sets are pre-computed and results correspond to the average of the five test folds.

6.3 Experimental Setup and Evaluation Metrics

The experimental results presented in this section were carried out using a *5-fold leave-one-out cross-validation* protocol as discussed before, with best parameters being found in the validation sets and results reported only in the test sets. We used the Normalized Discounted Cumulative Gain *NDCG*, *Precison* (at cut-off point 10, for both metrics) as well as Mean Average Precision (*MAP*) metrics to evaluate the results, based on the tools provided by the Letor benchmark.

NDCG for the top k results is defined as:

$$NDCG(Q,k) = \frac{1}{|Q|}\sum_{j=1}^{|Q|} Z_k \sum_{m=1}^{k} \frac{2^{R(j,m)}-1}{log(1+m)} \quad (3)$$

where $R(j,d)$ is the score given by assessors to document d for query j (NB: non-binary notion of relevance) and Z_k is a normalization factor (perfect ranking at k).

Unlike NDCG, MAP only allows binary (relevant/not relevant) document relevance, and is defined in terms of average precision (AP). The average precision (AP) of a query is computed based on the average of precision scores considering each relevant document retrieved. More formally, let q be a query, N_r be the number of relevant items in a collection for a given query q, and let $\langle r_i | i = 1,2,\ldots,d\rangle$ be a ranked relevance vector to depth d, where r_i indicates the relevance of the i-th ranked document scored as either 0 (not relevant) or 1 (relevant), the AP is defined as $AP = \frac{1}{N_r}\sum_{i=1}^{d}\left(P@i \times r_i\right)$, where $P@i = \sum_{j=1}^{i}\frac{r_i}{i}$. MAP is then computed by averaging AP over all queries. To compute P@k and MAP on the MQ datasets the relevance levels are binarised with 2 and 1 converted to 1 and 0 remains unchanged.

As we do have a large number of combinations among base methods, baselines and datasets, a global analysis of the performance of all these combinations is not an easy task. For this, we resort to a performance measure proposed in [21], called *winning number*. This measure tries to assess the most competitive methods among a series of candidates, given a large series of pre-defined tasks they have to perform. That is, the *winning number* of a method i in the context of a performance measure $\mathcal{M}$, is given as $S_i(\mathcal{M}) = \sum_{j=1}^{N}\sum_{k=1}^{M}\mathbf{1}_{\mathcal{M}_i(j)>\mathcal{M}_k(j)}$, where j is the dataset index (N datasets considered), i and k are the methods' index (M methods considered), $\mathcal{M}_i(j)$ is the performance of the $i-th$ method on $j-th$ dataset in terms of measure $\mathcal{M}$, and $\mathbf{1}_{\mathcal{M}_i(j)>\mathcal{M}_k(j)}$ is the indicator function:

$$\mathbf{1}_{\mathcal{M}_i(j)>\mathcal{M}_k(j)} = \begin{cases} 1 & \text{if } \mathcal{M}_i(j) > \mathcal{M}_k(j), \\ 0 & \text{otherwise.} \end{cases}$$

Thus, the larger $S_i(\mathcal{M})$ is, the better the $i-th$ method performs compared to the others.

For all methods we have run ourselves (base aggregation methods, supervised rank aggregation baselines) and for the TD and MQ benchmark baselines for which per-query results were made available, we assess the statistical significance of the GP-Agg results by means of a per-query paired t-test with 95% confidence. A ▲ symbol indicates that GP-Agg was statistically superior to the alternative, ▼ means the opposite, and • means that both methods are statistically tied.

As we have no per-query results in the L2R baseline results in TD2003 and TD2004 for some baselines, as well as for the rank aggregation baselines of the Letor 4.0, and given: 1) the high variability among folds due to both, the small number of queries and highly disparate performances among queries, and 2) the small number of points (only five folds), statistical tests comparing GP-Agg with these baselines cannot be computed reliably. This issue is better discussed in [6]. In this case, for ordering purposes only, we rely on the absolute values of the metrics. In these situations, the absence of statistical results is marked with a –, because of the absence of per-query results of a particular baseline in the official benchmarks.

6.4 Baselines

We consider as baselines:

1. In *Letor 3.0* datasets: all previously mentioned "official" L2R supervised baselines available in the datasets, corresponding to 12 baselines. We also included our own implementation of the RankGP method [31].

2. In *Letor 4.0* datasets: all "official baselines" available for the rank aggregation task, namely CPS-Spearman RankCorrelation, CPS-SpearmanFootrule, and CPS-KendallTau. In the case of BordaCount, we use our own implementation, as it produced better results than those reported in this benchmark;

3. In *all* datasets:
   (a) *Unsupervised Rank Aggregation Methods* – we included all base rank aggregation methods used as terminals in the GP-Agg process (10 methods). Since we had to implement the unsupervised versions of Kemeny and Condorcet in order implement their supervised version, we also include these two baselines in our comparisons.
   (b) *Supervised Rank Aggregation Methods* – we included the following supervised rank aggregation baselines described in Section 3: SupervisedCondorcet [30], Supervised Kemeny [26], Supervised-BordaCount [26], and CRF [29].

Overall we have an impressive set of 32 different baselines across four different datasets with very different properties.

6.5 Experimental Results

6.5.1 Letor 3.0 Datasets

Results for the GP-Agg framework and all considered baselines in the TD2003 and TD2004 are shown in Tables 3 and 4, respectively. Results are ordered by NDCG(@10), which we think is the most representative metric for this type of experiments, besides being the most used metric in recent rank aggregation studies (e.g., [29]).

We start by noticing that the performance of the base (unsupervised) methods used by GP-Agg are very far from the performance of GP-Agg itself. In TD2003 the best unsupervised methods are the Comb* family of methods while in TD2004 is RRF. These methods are statistically worse than GP-Agg, with gains for of around 35% and 27% in the respective datasets for GP-Agg. This indicates that indeed the supervised learning process of GP-Agg can find a proper combination of these methods which maximizes effectiveness.

We can also see in these datasets that, amongst all supervised alternatives, GP-Agg stands out with the highest results for NDCG in TD2003 and the second highest in TD2004.[4] This impressive performance is better captured by its winning numbers in these datasets, shown in Figure 5,[5] comparing GP-Agg with the L2R and supervised rank aggregation methods. In the figure, we can see that amongst all methods, GP-Agg has the best winning numbers outperforming all other baselines. CRF and ListNet are the most competitive L2R methods under this evaluation metric, but they are still far from GP-Agg, mainly when considering P@10.

Moreover, the supervised rank aggregation methods are indeed better than their unsupervised counterparts, but still far from GP-Agg, and still much worse than the L2R approaches, with the exception of CRF, which demonstrated to be competitive in TD2004. In particular, the SupCondorcet's effectiveness in these datasets (it does not figure among the top performers) may be explained by the large number of lists to be aggregated. In [30], the authors indeed demonstrate that there is a decline in performance as the numbers of lists grow.

[4]The large number of statistical ties in theses datasets is due to the small number of points (only 50 queries) and large variety in performance among queries.

[5]In the figure, we did not consider statistical ties and considered only the absolute values of the metrics.

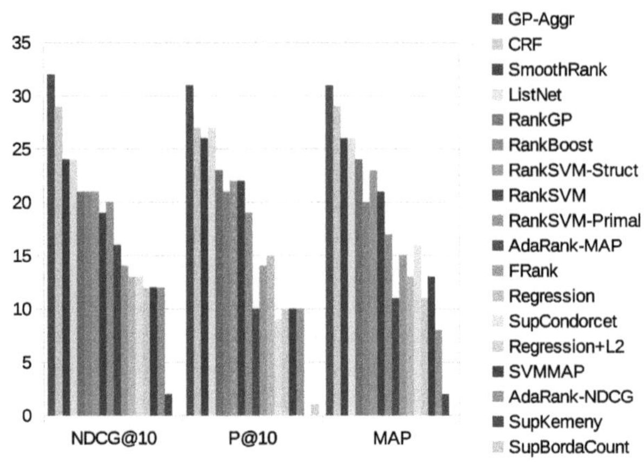

Figure 5: Winning Numbers for the TD2003 and TD2004 datasets.

Finally, in the TD2003 and TD2004 datasets, the CRF method showed be one of the most competitive baselines. However, this method requires the pre-computation of unary and pairwise potentials (to make the learning process more efficient), which has a complexity of $O(|q| \times |d|^2 \times |\mathcal{R}|)$, in which $|q|$ is the number of queries in the training set, $|d|$ is the number of documents per query in each ranked list to be aggregated, and $|\mathcal{R}|$ is the number of ranked lists. This pre-computation, in cases when there are larger ranked lists in the training set, becomes more expensive than the training process itself (depending of the training parameters, e.g. the number of iterations). As in these datasets, the number of documents per query in each ranked list to be aggregated $|d|$ is around 1,000, and there is a total of 64 ranked lists, this enormously increase the time complexity.

Table 3: Results on TD2003

Method	NDCG@10	P@10	MAP
GP-Agg	35.86	19.00	27.36
RankSVM-Primal	– 35.71	– 19.40	– 26.53
ListNet	• 34.84	• 20.00	• 27.53
RankSVM-Struct	– 34.67	– 18.60	– 27.13
RankSVM	• 34.61	• 18.80	• 26.28
CRF	▲ 33.74	• 18.40	▲ 26.55
SmoothRank	– 33.67	– 18.80	– 26.95
Regression+L2	– 32.97	– 17.60	– 24.34
SVMMAP	– 32.82	– 17.00	– 24.45
Regression	▲ 32.63	▲ 17.80	▲ 24.09
RankGP	▲ 32.40	▲ 17.80	▲ 25.19
RankBoost	▲ 31.22	▲ 17.00	▲ 22.74
AdaRank-MAP	▲ 30.69	▲ 15.80	▲ 22.83
AdaRank-NDCG	▲ 30.36	▲ 16.40	▲ 23.68
SupCondorcet	▲ 29.39	▲ 15.40	▲ 22.98
FRank	▲ 26.90	▲ 15.20	▲ 20.31
SupKemeny	▲ 22.30	▲ 11.40	▲ 17.28
SupBordaCount	▲ 19.55	▲ 12.80	▲ 14.97
CombSUM	▲ 26.62	▲ 13.20	▲ 19.03
CombMED	▲ 26.62	▲ 13.20	▲ 19.03
CombANZ	▲ 26.62	▲ 13.20	▲ 19.03
CombMNZ	▲ 26.62	▲ 13.20	▲ 19.03
RLSim	▲ 25.13	▲ 12.60	▲ 18.12
RRF	▲ 24.94	▲ 13.00	▲ 19.85
Condorcet	▲ 23.74	▲ 12.40	▲ 17.84
MRA	▲ 22.99	▲ 12.20	▲ 17.49
Kemeny	▲ 22.90	▲ 11.80	▲ 17.48
CombMIN	▲ 18.88	▲ 10.40	▲ 13.04
CombMAX	▲ 18.58	▲ 10.20	▲ 13.37
BordaCount	▲ 14.18	▲ 9.80	▲ 11.85

Table 4: Results on TD2004

Method	NDCG@10	P@10	MAP
CRF	• 35.68	• 27.60	• 25.80
GP-Agg	• 35.04	• 27.60	• 25.47
RankBoost	• 35.04	• 27.47	• 26.14
RankGP	• 35.00	• 27.33	▲ 24.25
SmoothRank	– 33.43	– 26.53	– 23.26
FRank	• 33.31	• 26.27	▲ 23.88
AdaRank-MAP	▲ 32.85	▲ 24.93	▲ 21.89
SupCondorcet	▲ 32.79	▲ 24.93	▲ 22.71
ListNet	▲ 31.75	▲ 25.60	▲ 22.31
AdaRank-NDCG	▲ 31.63	▲ 24.80	▲ 19.36
RankSVM-Struct	– 30.90	– 25.60	– 21.96
RankSVM	▲ 30.78	▲ 25.20	▲ 22.37
Regression	▲ 30.31	▲ 24.93	▲ 20.78
RankSVM-Primal	– 29.13	– 24.27	– 20.61
SVMMAP	– 29.07	– 24.67	– 20.49
Regression+L2	– 28.32	– 23.47	– 19.92
SupKemeny	▲ 23.28	▲ 18.53	▲ 16.37
SupBordaCount	▲ 22.85	▲ 18.53	▲ 16.11
RRF	▲ 25.60	▲ 20.67	▲ 18.54
MRA	▲ 24.79	▲ 19.87	▲ 16.89
CombSUM	▲ 24.27	▲ 19.20	▲ 17.28
CombMED	▲ 24.27	▲ 19.20	▲ 17.28
CombANZ	▲ 24.27	▲ 19.20	▲ 17.28
CombMNZ	▲ 24.27	▲ 19.20	▲ 17.28
RLSim	▲ 23.71	▲ 19.07	▲ 17.01
Condorcet	▲ 23.26	▲ 18.80	▲ 16.68
Kemeny	▲ 23.24	▲ 18.67	▲ 16.38
CombMIN	▲ 20.57	▲ 16.13	▲ 15.67
BordaCount	▲ 19.94	▲ 16.27	▲ 14.67
CombMAX	▲ 19.76	▲ 15.87	▲ 15.02

6.5.2 Letor 4.0 Datasets

Similarly to the previous results, in Letor 4.0, the GP-Agg performance is outstanding, statistically tied with CRF in first place in all datasets and under all metrics but MAP in MQ2007-agg in which it lost, but by no more than 2% of difference. Against all other baselines, including the supervised baselines and the Letor 4.0 benchmark methods, GP-Agg is statistically superior by large margins of difference. These results, for both datasets, are better summarized in the winning numbers shown in Figure 6.[6]

Experiments with the CRF baseline showed us scalability issues related to the combination of large lists. This aspect along with the effectiveness results discussed in this and in the previous section, demonstrate that our solution is a very competitive one for several possible rank aggregation scenarios.

6.5.3 Efficiency Issues

Since our model combines methods of the literature in an agglomerative way, the time of application of an individual, to a given lists set is equal to the sum of the times required to perform each one of the methods combined. Since it takes only a few milliseconds to run these baselines at test time, this time is very negligible. Moreover, it is possible to run the baselines in parallel to obtain the ranked lists and, by doing so, the time would only correspond to the time to run the slowest base method individually. Similarly, asymptotically, the complexity of an individual would be proportional to the highest complexity among the combined methods.

[6]To keep consistency with the figure for the previous datasets, we again did not consider the statistical ties and use the absolute values of the metrics to calculate the winning numbers. However, we should point out that statistical results are much more reliable in these datasets given the large amount of considered points (hundreds) and the smaller variability among queries.

Table 5: Results on MQ2007-agg

Method	NDCG@10	P@10	MAP
CRF	• 49.34	• 41.63	▼ 50.35
GP-Agg	48.66	41.44	49.92
SupBordaCount	▲ 45.00	▲ 38.42	▲ 46.50
SupCondorcet	▲ 44.20	▲ 37.84	▲ 45.40
CPS-S.RankCorrel.	– 37.18	– 34.51	– 40.69
SupKemeny	▲ 35.44	▲ 32.10	▲ 39.47
CPS-S.Footrule	– 34.85	– 33.54	– 38.98
CPS-KendallTau	– 34.83	– 33.53	– 38.91
RRF	▲ 44.82	▲ 38.29	▲ 46.44
MRA	▲ 44.81	▲ 38.20	▲ 46.63
CombSUM	▲ 44.75	▲ 37.79	▲ 46.58
CombMED	▲ 44.75	▲ 37.79	▲ 46.58
CombMNZ	▲ 44.59	▲ 37.75	▲ 46.60
BordaCount	▲ 44.57	▲ 38.07	▲ 46.12
RLSim	▲ 42.84	▲ 35.53	▲ 44.42
Condorcet	▲ 41.88	▲ 35.70	▲ 44.01
CombMAX	▲ 35.43	▲ 31.30	▲ 37.90
CombANZ	▲ 35.18	▲ 30.51	▲ 38.47
Kemeny	▲ 34.93	▲ 31.63	▲ 38.98
CombMIN	▲ 28.44	▲ 28.30	▲ 34.22

Table 6: Results on MQ2008-agg

Method	NDCG@10	P@10	MAP
GP-Agg	25.18	25.11	49.91
CRF	• 24.98	• 25.31	• 50.51
SupBordaCount	▲ 22.85	• 24.94	▲ 48.05
SupCondorcet	▲ 22.22	▲ 24.52	▲ 45.85
CPS-KendallTau	– 18.92	– 23.24	– 42.19
CPS-S.RankCorrel.	– 18.64	– 22.54	– 41.02
CPS-S.Footrule	– 17.71	– 22.97	– 40.27
SupKemeny	▲ 11.36	▲ 18.84	▲ 31.60
RRF	▲ 22.76	▲ 24.55	▲ 47.73
MRA	▲ 22.74	▲ 24.74	▲ 47.86
BordaCount	▲ 22.70	▲ 24.81	▲ 47.97
CombMNZ	▲ 22.68	▲ 24.52	▲ 47.48
CombSUM	▲ 22.40	▲ 24.45	▲ 47.29
CombMED	▲ 22.40	▲ 24.45	▲ 47.29
Condorcet	▲ 21.27	▲ 23.92	▲ 44.67
RLSim	▲ 20.34	▲ 22.22	▲ 43.59
CombMAX	▲ 14.26	▲ 19.60	▲ 32.09
Kemeny	▲ 10.95	▲ 18.57	▲ 31.08
CombANZ	▲ 10.73	▲ 18.38	▲ 28.28
CombMIN	▲ 08.14	▲ 17.16	▲ 25.32

We measure the overall time for training of our model (average of five training processes in the 5-fold cross-validation process) and the average time required to apply the best individual (best discovered function) on the test-set queries (average of 5 test folds), in each one of the datasets. These results are shown in Figures 7 and 8 respectively. For the average query time, we assume that the lists were generated by the rankers and are ready to be combined. Empirical results show a reasonable time for training and a very fast time of application of the best discovered function. In other words, applying the best GP-Agg individual at test time in real situations requires basically no additional costs.

6.5.4 *Analysis of the Individuals*

The best individuals found by the GP-Agg process in each dataset are listed below. In this case, we chose the individual from the fold whose effectiveness was the closest to the average of the 5 test folds. This may be considered as the most representative individuals.

- **MQ2007-agg**: CombMNZ(BC(L8, L5), RRF(L18, CombMNZ(RLSIM(L19, CombMIN(L21, L18)), RLSIM(L19, CombMIN(CombMIN(L21, L18), L19))))
- **MQ2008-agg**: CombANZ(RRF(L18, L15), BC(CombMED(CombANZ(CombMED(L18, L15), L21), L15), BC(CombANZ(L18, L21), L9)))
- **TD2003**: CombMED(CombSUM(L41, RRF(L32, L52)), RRF(L50, CombMNZ(CombMED(CombMED(RRF(L42, L52), L22), L22), L53)))
- **TD2004**: CombSUM(RRF(L52, BC(L23, L60)), RLSIM(CombMED(RRF(L50, L12), RRF(L41, BC(L23, L60))), RRF(L50, L12)))

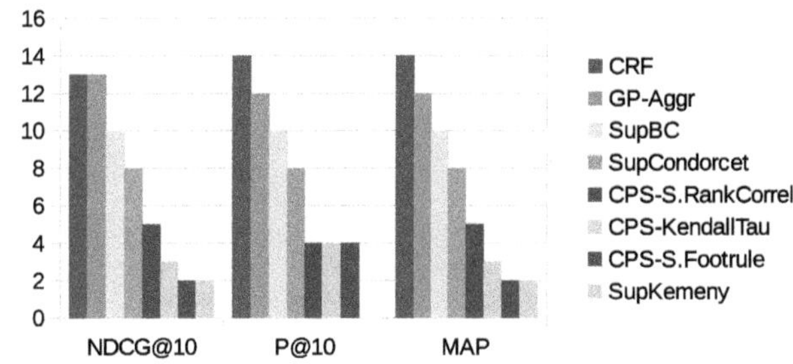

Figure 6: Winning Points for the MQ2007-agg and MQ2008-agg datasets.

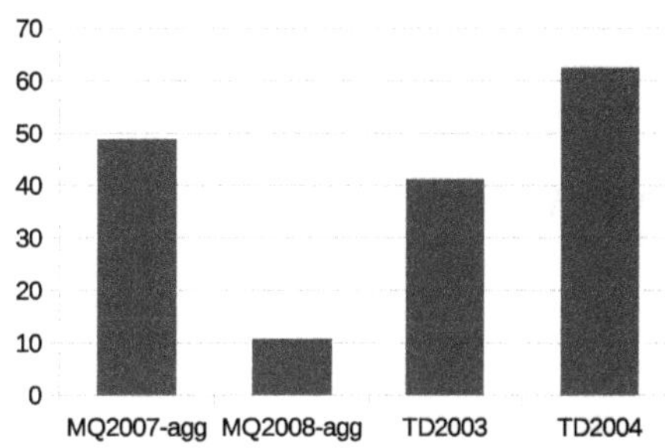

Figure 7: Time for training in minutes.

For these individuals and others of the last generation of GP-Agg process, we observed that ranked lists with better performances are included in most of the individuals. We also observed that methods proposed by Fox and Shaw [25] are used more frequently by individuals with higher fitness of the last generation.

7. CONCLUSIONS

We proposed a soft computing method which, using GP, search for combinations of different rank aggregation techniques, aiming at producing a combination which is more effective than any method used in isolation. The main idea of our work consists in exploiting the complementarity of the results produced by different rank aggregation techniques. Experimental results show significant gains over: (i) classic and recent state-of-the-art unsupervised techniques; (ii) state-of-the-art supervised ranking aggregation techniques; (iii) learning-to-ranking strategies present in the Letor benchmarks. Our method also demonstrated to scale better than some state-of-the-art supervised ranking aggregation methods at learning time, while the impact of its application at running (testing) time is negligible. The method is also very flexible and extensible; any new rank aggregation method can be easily incorporated to it. As future work, we intend to exploit the proposed method in other applications such as

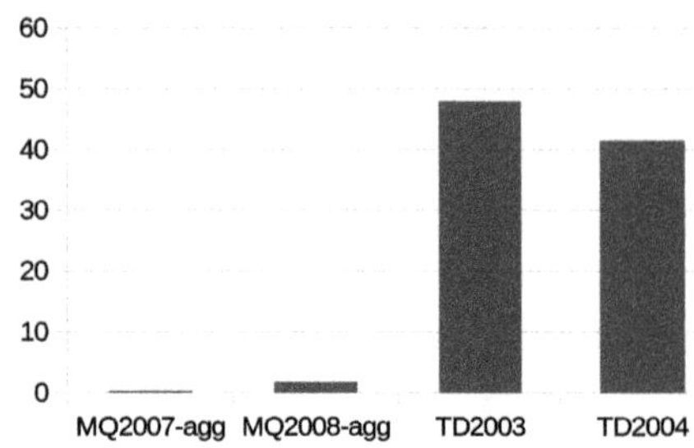

Figure 8: Average time for a query in test set, in milliseconds.

image retrieval and include some of the supervised baselines in our combination to improve results even further. We also want to better investigate issues related to the choice of the fitness function in the overall process.

8. ACKNOWLEDGMENTS

This work was supported by FAPESP, FAPESP-Microsoft Virtual Institute (Proc. 2013/50169-1), FAPEMIG, CNPq, and CAPES.

9. REFERENCES

[1] M. S. Beg and N. Ahmad. Soft computing techniques for rank aggregation on the world wide web. *World Wide Web*, 6(1):5–22, 2003.

[2] J. C. Borda. *Mémoire sur les élections au scrutin*. Histoire de l'Académie Royale des Sciences, 1781.

[3] G. V. Cormack, C. L. Clarke, and S. Buettcher. Reciprocal rank fusion outperforms condorcet and individual rank learning methods. In *Proceedings of the 32nd international ACM SIGIR conference on Research and development in information retrieval*, pages 758–759. ACM, 2009.

[4] R. Cummins, M. Lalmas, and C. O'Riordan. Learning aggregation functions for expert search. In *ECAI*, pages 535–540, 2010.

[5] M. G. de Carvalho, A. H. F. Laender, M. A. Gonçalves, and A. S. da Silva. A genetic programming approach to record deduplication. *IEEE Trans. Knowl. Data Eng.*, 24(3):399–412, 2012.

[6] G. de Castro Mendes Gomes, V. C. de Oliveira, J. M. Almeida, and M. A. Gonçalves. Is learning to rank worth it? A statistical analysis of learning to rank methods in the LETOR benchmarks. *JIDM*, 4(1):57–66, 2013.

[7] C. Dwork, R. Kumar, M. Naor, and D. Sivakumar. Rank aggregation methods for the web. In *Proceedings of the 10th international conference on World Wide Web*, pages 613–622. ACM, 2001.

[8] C. Dwork, R. Kumar, M. Naor, and D. Sivakumar. Rank aggregation methods for the web. In *Proceedings of the 10th International Conference on World Wide Web*, WWW '01, pages 613–622, 2001.

[9] R. Fagin, R. Kumar, and D. Sivakumar. Efficient similarity search and classification via rank aggregation. In *Proceedings of the 2003 ACM SIGMOD international conference on Management of data*, pages 301–312. ACM, 2003.

[10] W. Fan, E. A. Fox, P. Pathak, and H. Wu. The effects of fitness functions on genetic programming-based ranking discovery for web search. *Journal of the American Society for Information Science and Technology*, 55(7):628–636, 2004.

[11] R. Feldt and P. Nordin. Using factorial experiments to evaluate the effect of genetic programming parameters. In *Genetic programming*, pages 271–282. Springer, 2000.

[12] C. D. Ferreira, J. Santos, R. da S Torres, M. A. Gonçalves, R. C. Rezende, and W. Fan. Relevance feedback based on genetic programming for image retrieval. *Pattern Recognition Letters*, 32(1):27–37, 2011.

[13] D. A. Hull, J. O. Pedersen, and H. Schütze. Method combination for document filtering. In *Proceedings of the 19th annual international ACM SIGIR conference on Research and development in information retrieval*, pages 279–287. ACM, 1996.

[14] J. R. Koza. *Genetic programming: on the programming of computers by means of natural selection*, volume 1. MIT press, 1992.

[15] K. W. Lam and C. H. Leung. Rank aggregation for meta-search engines. In *Proceedings of the 13th international World Wide Web conference on Alternate track papers & posters*, pages 384–385. ACM, 2004.

[16] K. Li, N. Du, and A. Zhang. A link prediction based unsupervised rank aggregation algorithm for informative gene selection. In *Bioinformatics and Biomedicine (BIBM), 2012 IEEE International Conference on*, pages 1–6. IEEE, 2012.

[17] Y.-T. Liu, T.-Y. Liu, T. Qin, Z.-M. Ma, and H. Li. Supervised rank aggregation. In *Proceedings of the 16th International Conference on World Wide Web*, WWW '07, pages 481–490, 2007.

[18] D. C. G. Pedronette and R. d. S. Torres. Image re-ranking and rank aggregation based on similarity of ranked lists. In *Computer analysis of images and patterns*, pages 369–376. Springer, 2011.

[19] D. C. G. Pedronette and R. d. S. Torres. Combining re-ranking and rank aggregation methods. In *Progress in Pattern Recognition, Image Analysis, Computer Vision, and Applications*, pages 170–178. Springer, 2012.

[20] M. Pujari and R. Kanawati. Supervised rank aggregation approach for link prediction in complex networks. In *Proceedings of the 21st World Wide Web Conference, WWW 2012, Lyon, France, April 16-20, 2012 (Companion Volume)*, pages 1189–1196, 2012.

[21] T. Qin, T.-Y. Liu, J. Xu, and H. Li. Letor: A benchmark collection for research on learning to rank for information retrieval. *Inf. Retr.*, 13(4), Aug. 2010.

[22] T. Qin, T.-Y. Liu, X.-D. Zhang, Z. Chen, and W.-Y. Ma. A study of relevance propagation for web search. In *Proceedings of the 28th Annual International ACM SIGIR Conference on Research and Development in Information Retrieval*, SIGIR '05, pages 408–415, 2005.

[23] M. E. Renda and U. Straccia. Web metasearch: rank vs. score based rank aggregation methods. In *Proceedings of the 2003 ACM symposium on Applied computing*, pages 841–846. ACM, 2003.

[24] J. Sese and S. Morishita. Rank aggregation method for biological databases. *GENOME INFORMATICS SERIES*, pages 506–507, 2001.

[25] J. A. Shaw, E. A. Fox, J. A. Shaw, and E. A. Fox. Combination of multiple searches. In *The Second Text REtrieval Conference (TREC-2*, pages 243–252, 1994.

[26] K. Subbian and P. Melville. Supervised rank aggregation for predicting influencers in twitter. In *PASSAT/SocialCom 2011, Privacy, Security, Risk and Trust (PASSAT), 2011 IEEE Third International Conference on and 2011 IEEE Third International Conference on Social Computing (SocialCom), Boston, MA, USA, 9-11 Oct., 2011*, pages 661–665, 2011.

[27] R. d. S. Torres, A. X. Falcão, M. A. Gonçalves, J. P. Papa, B. Zhang, W. Fan, and E. A. Fox. A genetic programming framework for content-based image retrieval. *Pattern Recognition*, 42(2):283–292, 2009.

[28] M. N. Volkovs, H. Larochelle, and R. S. Zemel. Learning to rank by aggregating expert preferences. In *Proceedings of the 21st ACM International Conference on Information and Knowledge Management*, CIKM '12, pages 843–851, 2012.

[29] M. N. Volkovs and R. S. Zemel. Crf framework for supervised preference aggregation. In *Proceedings of the 22Nd ACM International Conference on Conference on Information and Knowledge Management*, CIKM '13, pages 89–98, 2013.

[30] S. Wu. The weighted condorcet fusion in information retrieval. *Inf. Process. Manage.*, 49(1):108–122, 2013.

[31] J.-Y. Yeh, J.-Y. Lin, H.-R. Ke, and W.-P. Yang. Learning to rank for information retrieval using genetic programming. In *Proceedings of SIGIR 2007 Workshop on Learning to Rank for Information Retrieval (LR4IR 2007)*, 2007.

[32] C. Zhai and J. Lafferty. A study of smoothing methods for language models applied to ad hoc information retrieval. In *Proceedings of the 24th Annual International ACM SIGIR Conference on Research and Development in Information Retrieval*, SIGIR '01, pages 334–342, 2001.

Approximate String Matching by End-Users using Active Learning

Lutz Büch
Institute of Computer Science
Heidelberg University, Germany
lutz.buech@informatik.uni-heidelberg.de

Artur Andrzejak
Institute of Computer Science
Heidelberg University, Germany
artur.andrzejak@informatik.uni-heidelberg.de

ABSTRACT

Identifying approximately identical strings is key for many data cleaning and data integration processes, including similarity join and record matching. The accuracy of such tasks crucially depends on appropriate choices of string similarity measures and thresholds for the particular dataset. Manual selection of similarity measures and thresholds is infeasible. Other approaches rely on the existence of adequate historic ground-truth or massive manual effort.

To address this problem, we propose an Active Learning algorithm which selects a best performing similarity measure in a given set while optimizing a decision threshold. Active Learning minimizes the number of user queries needed to arrive at an appropriate classifier. Queries require only the label *match/no match*, which end users can easily provide in their domain. Evaluation on well-known string matching benchmark data sets shows that our approach achieves highly accurate results with a small amount of manual labeling required.

Categories and Subject Descriptors

H.2.m [**Database Management**]: Miscellaneous—*Data cleaning*

Keywords

Active Learning; string similarity; similarity measures; similarity join; string matching; record matching; deduplication

1. INTRODUCTION

Data integration and -cleaning are fields with longstanding importance, that still have space for improvement [19]. Many of the tasks in those fields rely on string similarity measures, sometimes also a threshold that allows string matching. These include record matching [11], similarity join [21] and schema matching [17].

CIKM'15, October 19–23, 2015, Melbourne, Australia.

ACM 978-1-4503-3794-6/15/10 ...$15.00.
DOI: http://dx.doi.org/10.1145/2806416.2806453.

One immediate application of approximate string matching is similarity join. It is the simple form of record matching, where the matching depends only on one key attribute. Differently from a simple join operation, equivalent entities from both databases may only have similar values in this key attribute. Specification of a similarity measure and threshold define a solution to the similarity join problem. It can then be reduced to an algorithmic problem, that can be efficiently solved, depending on the similarity measure [21].

Record matching relies on similarity measures to compute similarity values on attribute level [11]. In the Fellegi-Sunter model, binary comparison vectors are based on similarity measures and thresholds for the involved attributes, that need to be specified. In many other popular approaches similarity measures need to be specified, while thresholds for these functions themselves are not relevant. E.g., in SVM-based approaches, similarity values of several attributes are combined to a similarity vector. Then, a decision hyperplane is learned from training data. In decision tree based approaches, several thresholds are learned to constitute predicates in logical rules. These thresholds may be inconsistent for the same attribute and similarity measure across different predicates used in a tree.

Bleiholder et al. point out that the effectiveness of the record matching step in data integration is mostly affected by the quality of the similarity measure and the choice of a similarity threshold [5]. Figure 1 illustrates that the choice of a similarity measure can make a huge difference. Here, the measure TagLink equipped with a suitable threshold can match pairs of strings perfectly, while MongeElkan will produce many errors with any threshold.

In [11], a large scale comparison of frameworks for record matching is done. The authors find that supervised matching approaches require less configuration effort and knowledge than others, but aspects like the choice of similarity measures still have to be determined manually.

In this paper we study how to find a suitable similarity measure from a given pool and optimize a corresponding threshold semi-automatically. We propose an Active Learning approach to this problem, in order to minimize human input. The user is iteratively queried for the ground-truth, i.e., whether a pair of strings is equivalent or not. A stopping criterion suggests that a sufficiently accurate choice can be done and will terminate this loop. It will return the chosen similarity measure along with an appropriately tuned threshold as the final output.

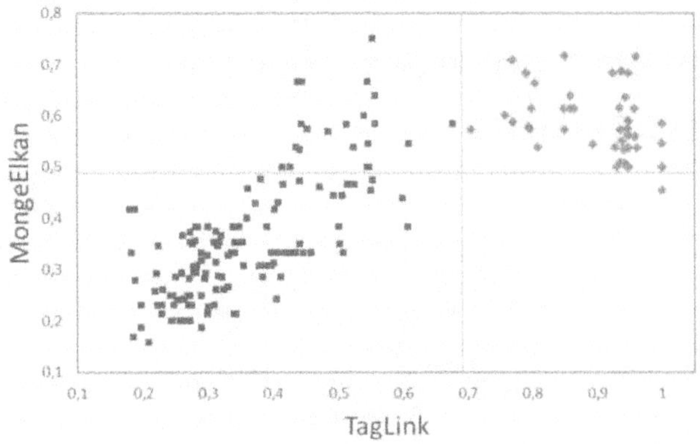

Figure 1: Similarity values and F1-optimal thresholds in data set *ucdFolks* for similarity measures MongeElkan and TagLink; blue squares represent matching pairs, red diamonds non-matching pairs w.r.t the ground-truth

Contribution. The contribution of this paper can be summarized as:

1. We propose an Active Learning algorithm to solve the string matching problem by finding the most appropriate similarity measure from a given pool, while tuning its threshold at the same time.
2. We devise a heuristic stopping criterion that measures a notion of progress of the algorithm. It is designed to stop the querying process early to prevent unnecessary labeling effort for the user.
3. We evaluate our approach on 17 benchmark string matching problems using 24 similarity measures. The results show that the stopping criterion holds after reasonably many queries and the results are close to optimal w.r.t. the hypothesis space.
4. We introduce four new string matching benchmark data sets. We propose corrections to the ground-truth of three widely used benchmark data sets.

2. BACKGROUND

Before proceeding to the introduction of Active String Matching, we provide some important notions and observations.

2.1 String similarity measures

Different fields such as databases, statistics, artificial intelligence and information retrieval have yielded a variety of similarity measures. They account for different variations in strings, like typos, swapping of words, misspellings, format inconsistencies or mishearings (i.e., phonetic variation). There are similarity measures combining others or using them on a lower level of tokens, such as MongeElkan. Others take into account information about the frequency of tokens over the whole data set. For an introduction to string similarity measures, see [7, 15]. A comprehensive account of similarity measures with special focus on name matching can be found in [6]. We regard the different similarity measures simply as black boxes that map pairs of strings on a range of real values, where higher values mean higher similarity. This is usually the interval $[0, 1]$, but this is not required.

2.2 Label distribution

String matching can be cast as a classification problem, where the instances are pairs of strings and the label reads *match* or *non-match.* However, differently from many other classification tasks, it has an inherent skewed label distribution. In a matching problem, the number of pairs will grow quadratically with the size of the involved data sets. At the same time, the number of matches can only grow linearly. In a deduplication task, this is different in theory, as the clusters of duplicates may be of any size. Yet, in practical scenarios, the clusters are limited to small sizes.

Dealing with skewed label distributions is known as the *class imbalance problem* [18, 4]. In [18], there is one short subchapter on it and [4] gives pointers for further reading.

There are two ramifications for this skewed label distribution. First, it influences the choice of quality measure and second, it requires procedures known as *indexing* and *blocking* in the record matching community.

Quality Metric

We measure the quality of a string matching process by *F-measure* (or F_1*-score*). It combines both precision and recall by calculating the harmonic mean of both values. It is widely used in record matching and in information retrieval.

See [13] for a discussion of different quality measures for record matching and especially deduplication. The arguments translate directly to string matching, since it can be seen as a special case, where records have exactly one data field. Most importantly, neither optimizing for precision nor for recall alone will yield useful results in the context of record matching.

Indexing

A skewed label distribution makes learning hard. One idea to mitigate this is to undersample the larger class (i.e., non-matches). The process of undersampling non-matches is called *indexing* (see, e.g. [6, 7]). Indexing can be viewed as a classification of matches aiming for high precision under the constraint of perfect recall. That is, it should eliminate many non-matches without dismissing any matches.

The indexing technique *blocking* eliminates non-matches by requiring the agreement of a *blocking key* that captures a broad measure of similarity. A blocking key can be, e.g., the phonetic code of a name attribute.

We use the *n-gram* blocking implemented in SecondString [2] (with parameter $n = 4$). N-gram blocking is a type of blocking that uses many blocking keys. It generates all n-grams of both strings of a pair and when they agree on at least one n-gram, the pair will be considered for matching. E.g., with $n = 4$, the pair "Franklin Delano Roosevelt", "Grover Cleveland" will be considered, as they share the 4-gram "evel".

2.3 Active Learning

Active Learning is defined as the problem of learning a hidden variable (the *label*), starting from unsupervised data and given the ability to inductively reveal the label of single instances. It is hence a form of semi-supervised learning. The number of labels required to learn a model is part of the performance objective. The model is learned by induc-

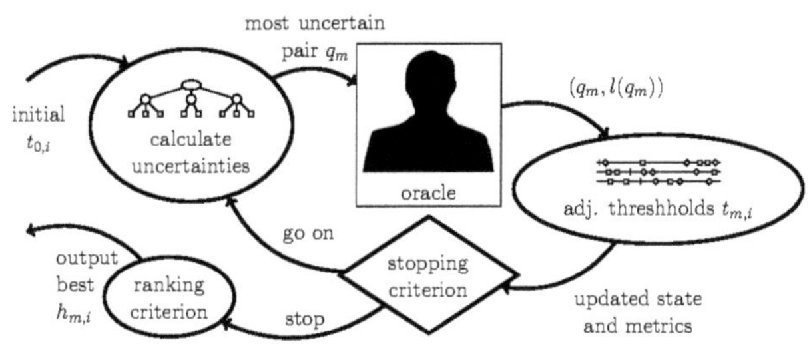

Figure 2: The process of Active String Matching

tively asking for single instances to be labeled, in a way that promises to help best in learning. In each iteration, the label for the new training instance is queried from an oracle such as a domain expert or a physical experiment.
The *query strategy* defines which instance to query next for a label, and is the core of any Active Learning algorithm. It depends on the classification model chosen and the characteristics of the classification problem. It may base its decision on unlabeled data and the few labeled data so far. Some general paradigms have proven very useful in designing such strategies. They are guided by principles that can shortly be described as follows: maximizing uncertainty of the label, minimizing the space of consistent (or likely) hypotheses, minimizing agreement among a committee of hypotheses or maximizing the gained information. See [18] for a general overview over Active Learning and a detailed account of different frameworks and paradigms.

3. ACTIVE STRING MATCHING

This section describes the *Active String Matching* approach proposed in this work. Its purpose is to learn with a least number of user queries a classification function for labeling pairs of strings as matches or non-matches.
We assume a scenario where initially no labels exist. To label the pairs of strings automatically we need a classification model. For this purpose, a user is successively queried to label a pair of strings whether they match or not. Each answer enlarges the training set for learning the model. Based on properties of this interim model, a next pair of strings is selected for labeling, or our algorithm decides to terminate this process. In that case, the algorithm outputs a prediction function (classifier) as its main result. This function can be subsequently used for tasks like similarity join or deduplication. Figure 2 shows the overall process.
The key components of our approach are the following. First, the *learning classifiers* component (Section 3.1) specifies how to optimize the thresholds of individual similarity measures w.r.t. F_1*-score* based on the set of currently known labels. From these, an aggregated prediction function is defined.
Secondly, the *query strategy* (Section 3.2 and Section 3.3) decides which string pair to query next, based on the current knowledge. Finally, the *stopping criterion* decides whether the quality of the learned model is sufficient, in which case it terminates the labeling process (Section 3.4).

We will use the following terms and notations (see Table 1). Let Q be the set of all string pairs that are considered for matching. We denote by m the number of finished iterations (which equals the number of answered queries). The symbol Q_m denotes the set of string pairs $q_1, \ldots, q_m$ which

Symbol	Definition
$m \in \mathbb{N}$	iteration number
Q	set of string pairs
$Q_m = \{q_1, .., q_m\}$	set of m queried string pairs
$l(q_1) \ldots, l(q_m)$	labels provided by the user
$F_1(T, p)$	F_1-score w.r.t. a predictor p and ground-truth of a set $T \subseteq Q$
$S = \{s_1, \ldots, s_n\}$	set of n similarity measures
$t_{m,i} \in \mathbb{R}$	threshold assigned to s_i in iteration m
$p_{m,i}$	predictor based on s_i and threshold $t_{m,i}$ (in iteration m)
p^*_m	best predictor found in iteration m

Table 1: Essential symbols used in Section 3.1

were labeled in iterations $1, \ldots, m$. We write $l(q_1), \ldots, l(q_m)$ for the labels assigned by the user to $q_1, \ldots, q_m$, respectively. In general, the function $l : Q \to \{0, 1\}$ represents the *ground-truth*, i.e. the labels assigned by the oracle. Here we identify the label *match* with 1 (or *positive*), and the label *non-match* with 0 (or *negative*).
Let $T \subseteq Q$ be a set of string pairs with known ground-truth and function p which predicts labels for elements in T. Then we denote by $F_1(T, p)$ the F_1-score computed over the ground-truth for T and labels assigned by p for all elements in T. In other words, $F_1(T, p)$ indicates the quality of predictions provided by p over string pairs in T.

3.1 Learning Classifiers

We first describe how, at the end of each iteration, a classification model for string matching is computed. Informally, our classifier is constructed as a string similarity measure $s : Q \to \mathbb{R}$ and a threshold $t \in \mathbb{R}$: if for a pair q of strings we have $s(q) \geq t$, then we predict the label *match*, otherwise *non-match*. We consider a collection of n such similarity measures and corresponding thresholds. Learning is performed after each new query by adjusting thresholds of all measures (Section 3.1.1), and identifying a best performing similarity measure (Section 3.1.2).
In detail, let S be a set of n similarity measures $s_1, \ldots, s_n$. For a fixed iteration number m let $t_{m,1}, \ldots, t_{m,n}$ denote real values used as thresholds. Then (for a specific m) we define n *prediction functions* or *predictors* $p_{m,1}, \ldots, p_{m,n}$ via:

$$p_{m,i}(q) = \begin{cases} 1 & \text{if } s_i(q) \geq t_{m,i} \\ 0 & \text{otherwise.} \end{cases} \qquad (1)$$

We denote as p^*_m the best predictor found in iteration m (characterized by a measure and its threshold). If our algorithm terminates at m, p^*_m becomes the overall output of the learning process.

3.1.1 Adjusting thresholds

The following procedure is outlined (for a generic quality metric) as the *straight-forward empirical method* to optimize thresholds in [3]. The values $l(q_1), \ldots, l(q_m)$ of labels queried in m first iterations are used as follows to find the thresholds $t_{m,1}, \ldots, t_{m,n}$. For a fixed similarity measure s_i we find an optimized threshold $t_{m,i}$ by evaluating the respective F_1-score for candidate threshold values t. How we find candidate values for t is described below. Let p be a predic-

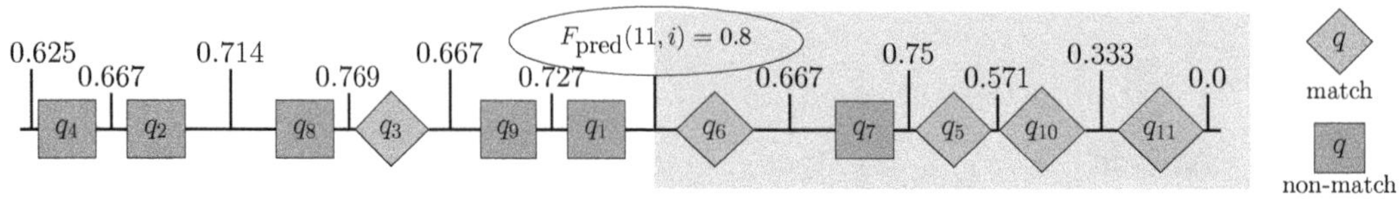

Figure 3: String pairs q_j are aligned according to their similarity value w.r.t to some similarity measure s_i (similarity values are not shown). Vertical lines indicate possible thresholds, labeled with their respective empirical F-measure. The right side of the optimal threshold is highlighted to indicate pairs that are predicted to be matches, the white area (on the left side) non-matches. Diamonds (red) indicate actual matches and squares (blue) indicate actual non-matches. Pairs without revealed labels are not shown for clarity.

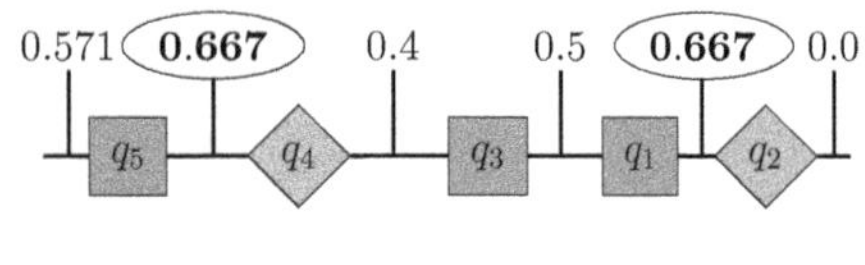

Figure 4: Maximum F_1-score values for a measure s_i may be achieved by multiple candidate thresholds

tor defined by Equation (1) for s_i and a fixed t. We compute the *empirical F-measure* of p, denoted as $F_1(Q_m, p)$, based on the known ground-truth for $Q_m = \{q_1, \ldots, q_m\}$. Among all candidate thresholds for s_i, we consider only those with the highest empirical F-measure. From these best threshold candidates we select only one as a threshold $t_{m,i}$ as described in Section 3.1.2.

The candidate thresholds for s_i are found as follows. We first compute the values $s_i(q_1), \ldots, s_i(q_m)$, that intersect the real number line in at most $m + 1$ intervals. The candidate thresholds are then the arithmetic means of each (closed) interval (and additionally the minimal value s_i and the maximal value plus a small constant $s_i + \epsilon$). Note that any point within one interval yields the same empirical F-measure for the corresponding candidate predictor.

Figure 3 illustrates this. There are 11 labeled pairs $q_1, \ldots, q_{11}$ that are aligned in a linear ordering, according to their similarity value as measured by s_i (increasing from left to right, not shown). The candidates for a new threshold $t_{11,i}$ for similarity measure s_i are the "middles" of each of the 12 intervals defined by $s_i(q_1), \ldots, s_i(q_{11})$. The vertical lines indicate these candidate thresholds; the corresponding empirical F-measures are shown in the text labels.

The interval defined by $s_i(q_1)$ and $s_i(q_6)$ gives rise to thresholds with empirical F-measure of 0.8. This is the best value, and so we use as a threshold $t_{m,i}$ for s_i the middle of this interval. All string pairs q with $s_i(q) \geq t_{m,i}$ are now classified by the resulting prediction function $p_{11,i}$ as matches (shaded or red area). Obviously, this prediction function errs on some of the queried pairs, namely q_3 (false negative) and q_7 (false positive).

3.1.2 Ranking of candidate predictors

There are two types of ambiguity when selecting p^*_m: (i) for each measure s_i several candidate thresholds might lead to the same empirical F-measure, and (ii) after all n thresholds are fixed, several predictors $p_{m,i}(q)$ $(i = 1, \ldots, n)$ might achieve the highest value $F^*_{\text{pred}}(m)$ of the empirical F-measure.

Ambiguities of type (i) are illustrated in Figures 3 (thresholds of the same interval are equivalent) and 4 (there may even be different equivalent intervals). We resolve those by selecting as the threshold $t_{m,i}$ for s_i the middle of the "rightmost" interval (i.e., containing the highest similarity values) among all these empirically optimal choices (e.g., between q_1 and q_2 in Figure 4). This choice has little impact on performance of the algorithm.

Ambiguity in case (ii) occurs since many predictors can have the same F-measure in a given iteration. As shown in the evaluation (Section 4), this becomes significantly less pronounced in later iterations. We devise here a simple secondary heuristic ranking to pick the best from these highest scoring predictors.

For each candidate predictor $p_{m,i}$ we inspect the interval containing the selected threshold for $p_{m,i}$: the lower the number of pairs with *unrevealed* labels in that interval, the higher the secondary ranking for the predictor. Our heuristic intuition is that the spread of these noisy pairs are expected to be more concentrated in good performing hypotheses, which leave few intermediate pairs unqueried.

3.2 Aggregated Prediction Function

In the following, we introduce an *aggregated prediction function* p_m that is computed in each iteration m. This function p_m is required by the query strategy described in Section 3.3. We describe how this is done in Sections 3.2.1 and 3.2.2. In Section 3.3, we explain how we define the most uncertain pair based on p.

In this paper, we use the term *hypothesis* as defined in [18]. A hypothesis is a classifier (or a configuration that is sufficient to identify one), that *explains* the data by generalizing the ground-truth. In our case, a hypothesis $h = (s, t)$ is determined by a specific similarity measure s from $S = \{s_1, \ldots, s_n\}$ and a corresponding threshold $t \in \mathbb{R}$. Consequently, the hypothesis space is $H = S \times \mathbb{R}$. Restating Equation (1), each hypothesis $h = (s, t)$ is assigned a prediction function defined by $p_h(q) = 1 :\Leftrightarrow s(q) \geq t$. We will write $h_{m,i}$ as shorthand for $(s_i, t_{m,i})$ and $p_{m,i}$ for $p_{h_{m,i}}$. We also define as $F_{\text{pred}}(m, i) := F_1\{Q_m, p_{m,i}\}$ the *empirical F_1-score* for hypothesis $h_{m,i}$ w.r.t. observed labels only (recall that Q_m is the set of already labeled string pairs).

3.2.1 Clustering of Similarity Measures

We account for redundancy among similarity measures by clustering measures that are mutually similar. It is important to notice about the hypotheses that they are not independent of one another. Some similarity measures may not even be defined similarly, but produce a very highly correlated ordering of pairs. In order to combine their predictions in a meaningful way, it is important to account for this redundancy. Otherwise some similarity measures might

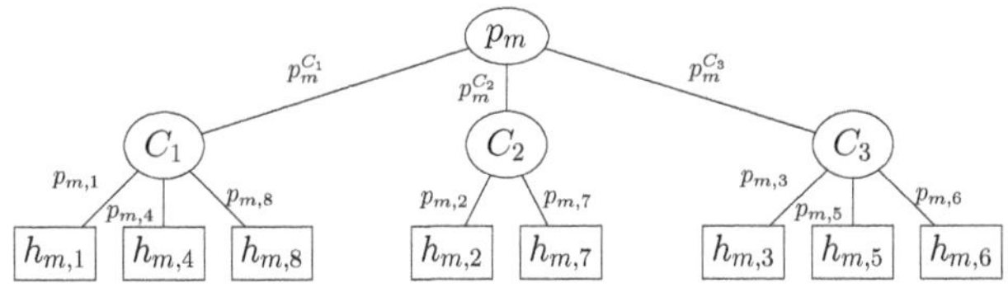

Figure 5: Structure of the aggregated prediction function p_m (a fictional example with $n = 8$)

Symbol	Definition
$F_{\text{pred}}(m, i) := F_1\{Q_m, p_{m,i}\}$	**empirical** F_1; the F_1 score for $h_{m,i}$ w.r.t. observed labels only
$C_1, \ldots, C_k \subseteq S$	k **clusters** of similarity measures
$p_{m,i} : Q \to \{0, 1\}$	**prediction function** of hypothesis $h_{m,i}$
$p_m^{C_j} : Q \to [0, 1]$	(intermediate) prediction function associated to cluster C_j
$p_m : Q \to [0, 1]$	**aggregated prediction function**
$w_{m,i}, w_m^{C_j}$	**weights** used in the aggregation
$p_m^{\text{target}} := 1 - r_m$	**target prediction** value

Table 2: Symbols used for the query strategy

be overrepresented and dominate the voting.
We represent similarity measures by the vector of similarity values, indexed by all considered string pairs. The redundancy among two similarity measures is then computed by their mutual Pearson correlation coefficient. Calculating the matrix of correlations between all pairs of similarity measures yields a weighted undirected graph. The nodes correspond to similarity measures and the weighted edges to the pairwise Pearson correlation. Clusters $C_1, \ldots, C_k$ in this graph correspond to sets of mutually similar similarity measures. We apply a graph clustering algorithm [16] that maximizes the so-called *modularity* of a graph clustering to achieve this. We used the implementation Linloglayout [1]. The clustering is computed once in the beginning and remains the same over the course of all iterations. In our experiments with a set of 24 similarity measures, k ranged from 2 to 5 and the cluster sizes from 1 to 12.

3.2.2 Aggregating

In the following, we explain how we combine in each iteration m the individual prediction functions $p_{m,i}$ to an overall prediction function p_m.
We do this in two steps, which we illustrate in Figure 5. The first step combines the prediction functions of hypotheses whose similarity measures are in the same cluster C to an intermediate prediction function p_m^C. The second step combines all predictions functions p_m^C to the overall prediction function p_m.
We estimate the predictive power of a prediction function $p_{m,i}$ with the F-measure on the seen labels. We assign weights $w_{m,i} = F_{\text{pred}}(m, i)$ to favour promising predictions over poor predictions. The prediction functions p_m^C are defined as follows:

$$p_m^C(q) := \left(\sum_{s_i \in C} w_{m,i}\right)^{-1} \cdot \left(\sum_{s_i \in C} p_{m,i}(q) \cdot w_{m,i}\right)$$

These prediction functions are then combined to the overall prediction function p_m:

$$p_m(q) := \left(\sum_{j=1}^{k} w_m^{C_j}\right)^{-1} \cdot \left(\sum_{j=1}^{k} p_m^{C_j}(q) \cdot w_m^{C_j}\right),$$

where $w_m^{C_j} = \frac{1}{|C|} \sum_{s_i \in C} F_{\text{pred}}(m, i)$.
The weights w_m^C for the functions p_m^C reflect how promising the hypotheses whose similarity measures belong to cluster C are on average.
The expression for $p_m(q)$ can be expanded and then simplified to the following:

$$p_m(q) = \left(\sum_{j=1}^{k} \sum_{s_i \in C_j} \frac{1}{|C_j|} w_{m,i}\right)^{-1} \cdot \left(\sum_{i=1}^{n} p_{m,i}(q) \cdot w_{m,i}\right)$$

3.3 Query Strategy

In terms of [18], the strategy can be described as an instance of uncertainty sampling. That is, the paradigm that is based on a prediction function for unseen labels and assigns a measure of certainty to each prediction. The basic insight is that there is little value in querying the instances whose labels can be predicted with high certainty. Conversely, the most gain for the learning progress can be expected from querying the most uncertain instances.
The prediction function $p_m : Q \to [0, 1]$ calculates a real value for each string pair. We now define our notion of uncertainty based on this function.
A clear prediction of $p_m(q) = 1.0$ implies that each hypothesis predicts the query to be a match. Conversely, $p_m(q) = 0.0$ means that each hypothesis predicts a non-match.
When the overall prediction $p_m(q)$ is equal to 0.5, the label of q is highly uncertain. This prediction can only occur if sufficiently highly-weighted or at least many hypotheses predict either label. This means that no matter which label will turn out to be true, a significant part of the hypotheses will see its prediction disproved. I.e., significant in the sense of a combination of the individual confidences. The first idea is hence to define the next query as

$$\text{argmin}_{q \in Q \setminus Q_{m-1}} |0.5 - p_m(q)|$$

Yet, to achieve fast convergence, we have to correct this notion of uncertainty to account for the overall prediction $p_m(q)$ which can be biased in early iterations. We will therefore replace the value 0.5 by a *target prediction*, denoted by $p_m^{\text{target}} \in [0, 1]$.
Since the thresholds have to be set to some initial setting, they are bound to be inappropriate in the beginning. Assume that the thresholds in iteration m are such that the functions $p_{m,i}$ are collectively biased towards predicting matches. That is, each function $p_{m,i}$ has a high false positive rate w.r.t. the whole ground-truth. Then the set of pairs that get a committee prediction close to 0.5 will consist of more non-matches than matches. So the label of such a pair is actually not most uncertain, when the hypotheses are collectively biased. The target prediction p_m^{target} for iteration m must be higher than 0.5 if the hypotheses are generally biased towards predicting matches. An analogous argument applies in the reverse situation.

We measure the current bias of the committee by calculating the ratio of match labels among the revealed labels. We define the target prediction p_m^{target} as the complement, or ratio of non-match labels among the seen labels:

$$p_m^{\text{target}} := 1 - r_m = \frac{1}{m-1} \sum_{n=1}^{m-1} 1 - l(q_n)$$

It will yield a value higher than 0.5, if the committee was biased towards matches in the past, as desired. This way the target prediction self-regulates until the thresholds adjust to the respective regions where the labels are truly uncertain. The next query is hence defined as follows:

$$q_m := \text{argmin}_{q \in Q \setminus Q_{m-1}} \left| p_m^{\text{target}} - p_m(q) \right|.$$

Note that the query q_m minimizing the expression above may not be uniquely defined. Therefore, we devised a secondary ranking of the pairs to further distinguish the pairs. This ensures that informative queries are done even when the prediction p_m is not (yet) well prepared to decide this. We measure the variance of ranks w.r.t. the different linear orderings that the similarity measures give. It can be calculated by unsupervised data. This is defined as follows.
For each pair, calculate the rank that it is assigned by each similarity measure s. That is, the pair q with the highest similarity value $s(q)$ will get rank 0 w.r.t. s, the pair with the second highest will get rank 1, and so on. Then calculate for each pair the variance with respect to its similarity rank across all similarity measures. The higher this variance is, the higher the pair be will appear in the secondary ranking for querying.

3.4 Stopping Criterion

In an approach using Active Learning it is useful to have a stopping criterion, i.e., a function indicating when the querying process can be terminated. It is important not to stop too early, when the solution is still improving. On the other hand, the algorithm should not issue additional queries after the solution is stable.
The stopping criterion can be designed independently of the query strategy and the ranking of candidate predictors. We tried a lot of other intuitive heuristics, but none seemed to be more successful than the one we will introduce now. The main problem in devising a stopping criterion is the scarcity of information that is inherent to Active Learning.
A trivial stopping criterion is a threshold on the number of queried labels. However, we noticed that the algorithm "progresses" at different speeds for different data sets. We measured the progress of the algorithm in terms of the *true F-measure* $F_{\text{true}}(m) := F(Q, p_m^*)$ of the currently best ranking prediction function p_m^* (for the ranking criterion, refer to Section 3.1.2). The true F-measure uses all hidden labels and can hence not be used by the algorithm.
However, (at least for the considered data sets) another measure seems to capture this progress well and does not require the hidden ground-truth. This measure is the total number of changes in thresholds that have occurred since the beginning of the algorithm:

$$TC_m := \sum_{i=1}^{n} \sum_{j=0}^{m-1} 1 - \delta(t_{j,i}, t_{j+1,i}),$$

where δ is equal to 1 if its arguments are equal and 0 otherwise. A stopping criterion can be devised as a condition that TC_m has exceeded a certain threshold. In Section 4.3 we compare different thresholds for TC_m in context of our data sets.

4. EVALUATION

In this section we evaluate our approach under several aspects. These include user labeling effort vs. accuracy (Section 4.3), convergence behavior (Section 4.4), impact of the stopping criterion (Section 4.5), and other aspects, such as impact of the predictor ranking (Section 4.6).

4.1 Experimental Setup

Data Sets. We use for the evaluation 17 data sets summarized in Table 3. Four data sets are created by us (marked with $^+$ in Table 3). To obtain the ground-truth we pursued a similar approach as [8], with a final manual review. We have also found and corrected errors in the ground-truth in 3 existing data sets (*business*, *animal*, and *bird2*). Details of these errors as well as all data sets can be downloaded from `http://pvs.ifi.uni-heidelberg.de/team/lb/`.

Similarity measures. In our experiments we use $n = 24$ similarity measures $s_1, \ldots, s_{24}$ taken from the library SecondString [2]. Some of these measures depend only on the two input strings, while others take into account frequencies of substrings across the whole data set. Our approach treats the similarity measures as black boxes.

Other parameters. Our experiments have shown that several parameters described in Section 3 do not have a notable impact on the behaviour of the algorithm. These include initial values of thresholds, and selecting the actual threshold value among several candidates with identical F_1-scores. Therefore, we report only the results obtained via implementation choices described above.

4.2 Evaluation metrics

We use in the following some symbols defined in Table 1. Recall that for a fixed iteration number m, the (intermediate) result of the learning process is the best predictor p_m^* (if m is the final iteration, p_m^* is the final result of the process). The following two metrics evaluate the convergence and accuracy of p_m^*. The *true* F_1, denoted as $F_{\text{true}}(m)$, is the F_1-score of the best predictor p_m^* taking into account the labels of *all* string pairs in Q (i.e., the complete ground-truth):

$$F_{\text{true}}(m) = F_1(Q, p_m^*).$$

This metric estimates the generalization capability of p_m^* since it takes into account all labels of the data set, not only the queried ones.
The *maximal* F_1 (symbol $F_{\max}$) is the F_1-score of the best possible prediction function across the hypothesis space $H = S \times \mathbb{R}$ w.r.t. the whole ground-truth, i.e.,

$$F_{\max} = \max_{h \in H} F_1(Q, p_h).$$

The *match ratio* in iteration m (denoted r_m) is the ratio of match labels versus non-match labels among the observed pairs. Finally, TC_m is the *total number of threshold changes*, which is the cumulative number of times when a threshold has changed for any similarity measure in any iteration.

Dataset name	domain	src 1	src 2	Original pairs	Original match	Reduced pairs	Reduced match	matches / pairs
string matching problems								
bird3[8]	common+scientific animal names	23	15	345	15	25	*14*	56.00%
USPresidents+	personal names	43	43	1,849	43	173	43	24.86%
ucdFolks[14]	personal names	45	45	2,025	45	184	45	24.46%
DBconferences+	names of database conferences	54	54	2,963	54	2441	54	2.21%
bird1[8]	common+scientific animal names	317	20	6,340	19	672	19	2.83%
faoMembers+	country names	194	194	37,636	194	2,633	*192*	7.29%
bird2[8]*	common animal names	914	68	62,152	64	4,089	64	1.57%
game[8]	names of computer games	798	105	83,790	41	4,276	41	0.96%
bird4[8]	common+scientific animal names	564	155	87,420	155	11,297	155	1.37%
park[8]	names of (national) parks	393	258	101,394	252	6,767	*250*	3.69%
census[9]	synthetic peronal names+addresses	449	392	176,008	329	18,438	*326*	1.77%
fodorZagrat[20]	restaurant names+addr+phone+style	532	331	176,092	114	73,657	*112*	0.15%
nobelLaureates+	personal names	839	839	703,921	839	27,011	*831*	3.08%
business[8]*	company names	1162	962	1,117,844	310	502,316	*309*	0.06%
animal[8]*	common animal names	4719	817	3,855,423	178	93,661	*175*	0.19%
string deduplication problems (single source)								
UVA[14]	institute names	116		6,670	280	2,932	*272*	9.28%
coraATDV[12]	publication references	956		456,490	7,766	453,987	7,766	1.71%

Table 3: Benchmark data sets (ordered by number of pairs) for string matching (upper part) and deduplication problems (lower part). Column "Reduced" shows effects of the indexing step. * indicates that ground-truth has been corrected; italic number of matches means false negatives due to indexing. +indicates new data sets. Summed entries in column "type" indicate concatenated strings of different types.

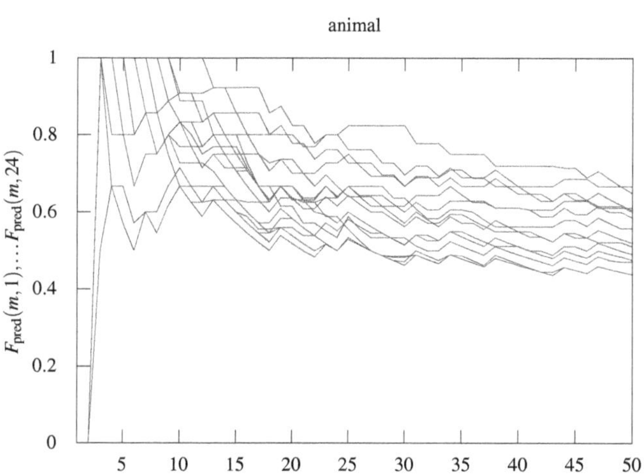

Figure 6: The empirical F_1-scores decrease with higher number of iterations.

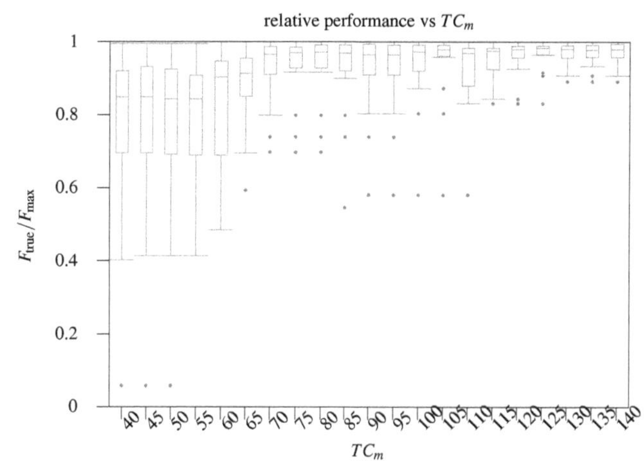

Figure 7: The ratio of true F_1-scores of the best predictor ($F_{\mathbf{true}}(m)$) to $F_{\mathbf{max}}$ vs. total number of threshold changes TC_m (each box/whisker plot shows distribution over all data sets).

4.3 User effort and predictor accuracy

Table 4 reports results for all data sets after learning prediction models with two different stopping criteria A: $TC_m \geq 75$ and B: $TC_m \geq 130$. For criterion A, the average number of queries (or iterations) is 7 and never exceeds 10, which shows that the labeling effort for the user is very low. At the same time, the ratios $F_{\mathbf{true}}/F_{\mathbf{max}}$ of solution quality (i.e. F_{true}) to maximum achievable quality (F_{max}, specific to a data set) are high. This indicates that the final matching prediction functions have been learned well.
In case of stopping criterion B, the ratios $F_{\mathbf{true}}/F_{\mathbf{max}}$ are in general higher, but not to a large degree. Also here the average number of iterations until stop is relatively low (around 15) which implies an acceptable labeling effort. Summarizing, we conclude that Active Learning performs very well, and allows minimizing user effort while achieving accurate prediction models.

4.4 Convergence behavior

Figure 8 gives more insight into convergence behavior of some selected representative data sets. While *animal* and *business* (top row) illustrate benign changes of $F_{\text{true}}(m)$ (the

		A: stop at $TC_m \geq 75$					B: stop at $TC_m \geq 130$				
Data set	$F_{\max}$	final m	s^*	t_m^*	F_{true}	$\frac{F_{\text{true}}}{F_{\max}}$	final m	s^*	t_m^*	F_{true}	$\frac{F_{\text{true}}}{F_{\max}}$
bird3	1.000	5	L2_JW	0.923	1.000	100.00%	15	TL	0.598	1.000	100.00%
USPres.	0.953	6	ST	0.403	0.925	96.98%	14	TL	0.778	0.943	98.85%
ucdFolks	1.000	5	ASD	0.342	0.917	91.67%	12	TL	0.643	0.989	98.90%
DBconf.	0.874	8	ME	0.779	0.851	97.45%	14	ME	0.840	0.845	96.75%
bird1	0.947	7	TFIDF	0.513	0.947	100.00%	16	TL	0.766	0.944	99.69%
faoMembers	0.961	9	L2_L	-0.300	0.958	99.70%	21	L2_ME	0.949	0.897	93.37%
bird2	0.944	7	JWT	0.982	0.918	97.25%	12	JC	0.633	0.929	98.42%
game	0.846	10	L2_JO	0.886	0.805	95.16%	20	L2_JO	0.927	0.827	97.70%
bird4	0.980	6	TL	0.615	0.951	96.96%	12	L2_JW	0.900	0.955	97.45%
park	0.970	7	SL	0.675	0.913	94.08%	15	ST	0.571	0.921	94.94%
census	0.899	6	A	0.609	0.665	73.94%	12	TL	0.816	0.817	90.80%
fodorZagrat	0.978	8	TL	0.751	0.959	98.09%	17	JWT	0.644	0.968	99.05%
nobelLaur.	0.989	7	JWT	0.399	0.790	79.93%	15	ST	0.443	0.882	89.21%
business	0.971	8	ASD	0.685	0.960	98.93%	16	ASD	0.663	0.964	99.30%
animal	0.926	8	M	0.495	0.891	96.24%	18	M	0.444	0.893	96.43%
UVA	0.907	7	JO	0.858	0.633	69.72%	13	TL	0.721	0.899	99.04%
coraATDV	0.800	6	ME	0.551	0.648	81.07%	15	L2_L	-0.675	0.736	92.07%
average		**7.06**				**92.29%**	**15.12**				**96.59%**

Table 4: Results after model learning with stopping criteria A: $TC_m \geq 75$ and B: $TC_m \geq 130$. Final m is the number of iterations, s^* is the best final similarity measure, and t_m^* the corresponding final threshold. $F_{\text{true}}/F_{\max}$ gives the ratio of solution quality (i.e. F_{true}) to maximum achievable quality ($F_{\max}$). Similarity measures: L2_*=*Level2, JW=*Jaro Winkler*, ST=*SourcedTFIDF*, ASD=*AveragedStringDistanceLearner*, ME=*MongeElkan*, L=*Levenstein*, JWT=*Jaro WinklerTFIDF*, JO=*Jaro*, TL=*TagLink*, SL=*ScaledLevenstein*, M=*Mixture*, JC=*Jaccard*. Note that thresholds may be negative.**

F_1-score of the best predictor, specific to iteration number m), *UVA* and *nobelLaureates* (bottom row) show less desirable behavior of $F_{\text{true}}(m)$. We also note that in the first iterations highest-ranked similarity measure changes frequently (indicated by vertical lines), while after 7 iterations the measure stabilizes. This is less pronounced for the "bad" cases *UVA* and *nobelLaureates*.

Figure 6 shows that the empirical F_1-scores $F_{\text{pred}}(m,i)$ decrease with growing iteration number m for all measures. This can be attributed to the fact that the uncovered labels come only from the "noisy" area that contains all hard-to-separate pairs. This also explains why $F^*_{\text{pred}}(m)$ decreases below the actual performance $F_{\text{true}}(m)$. So, the empirical F_1-scores do not approximate the true performance, but are sufficient to compare the quality of current predictors.

Note that the output prediction function p_m^* is chosen from the p_h (with $h \in H$). The aggregated prediction function p_m will not be output. It is only used to define the next query to the user. In fact, p_m performs significantly worse than the individual predictor p_m^* chosen in each time step by the algorithm. Our experiments showed that it is very unstable for most data sets (it does not converge) and shows worse F_1-scores most of the time; often significantly. A reason is that even a bad similarity measure s_i can achieve precision of r_m and recall of 1.0 by a small threshold (for $r_m = 0.3$ this equals $w_{m,i} = F_{\text{pred}}(m,i) = 0.462$). So p_m may always be somewhat influenced by inappropriate measures.

4.5 Stopping criterion

The choice of the stopping criterion determines the trade-off between user labeling effort and accuracy. Figure 8 shows that for *animal* and *business* the matching quality $F^*_{\text{pred}}(m)$ increases rapidly in the first few iterations and remains virtually unchanged after that. For *UVA* and *nobelLaureates* more than 10 iterations are needed in order to achieve a stable quality level (even not so in the case of UVA). This refines the findings from Section 4.3: for some data sets, less then 10 iterations are sufficient (i.e., stopping criterion A), while others require more labeling effort. Thus, the choice of a *universal* stopping criterion is hardly possible. Depending on the application, either low user effort (criterion A) or potentially higher accuracy (criterion B) must be preferred. Figure 9 shows on the right y-axis the values of TC_m used in our stopping criterion (i.e. cumulative number of threshold changes over all measures in S). More conclusive is Figure 7: we see that the variance of the true F_1-scores over all data sets decrease for TC_m values above 75, suggesting this as a potential threshold.

4.6 Other aspects

Figure 9 shows (on the left axis) the F_1-score of the best ranked predictor (line with crosses) among all predictors with maximal empirical F_1-scores in iteration m (shaded area). It illustrates the use of a secondary heuristic ranking explained in Section 3.1.2, especially when a lot of competing predictors (with the same best empirical F_1-scores) exist in the early iterations.

Figure 8 also shows that the match ratio r_m is very balanced, while tending towards lower values. Considering the skewed label distribution (see Table 3), this constitutes a very balanced sample. This indicates that the query strategy works well in terms of selecting string pairs with informative labels.

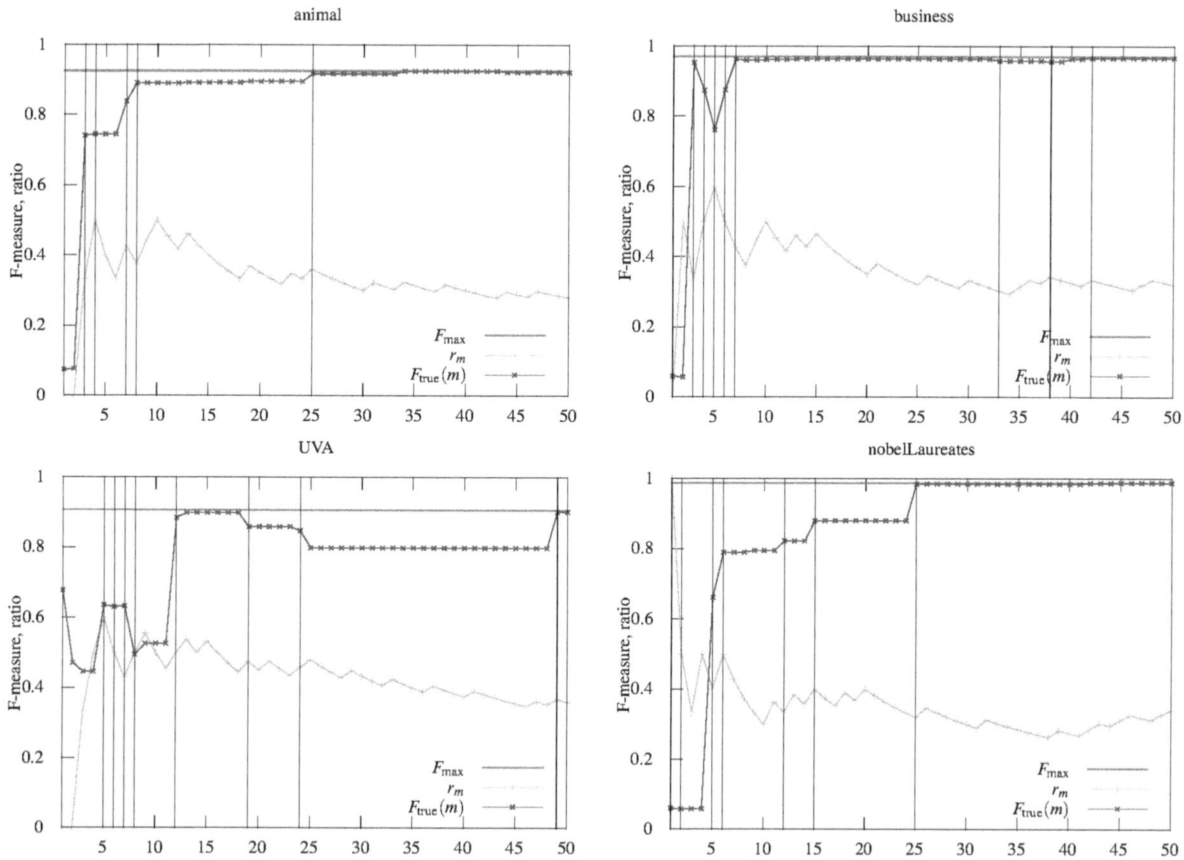

Figure 8: Convergence behavior for exemplary Active Learning runs. The x-axis shows the iteration number m. The values of F_{max}, r_m, and $F^*_{pred}(m)$ are plotted on the y-axis. Changes in $F^*_{pred}(m)$ result from adjusting thresholds and switching the best ranked similarity metric (latter changes are indicated by vertical bars).

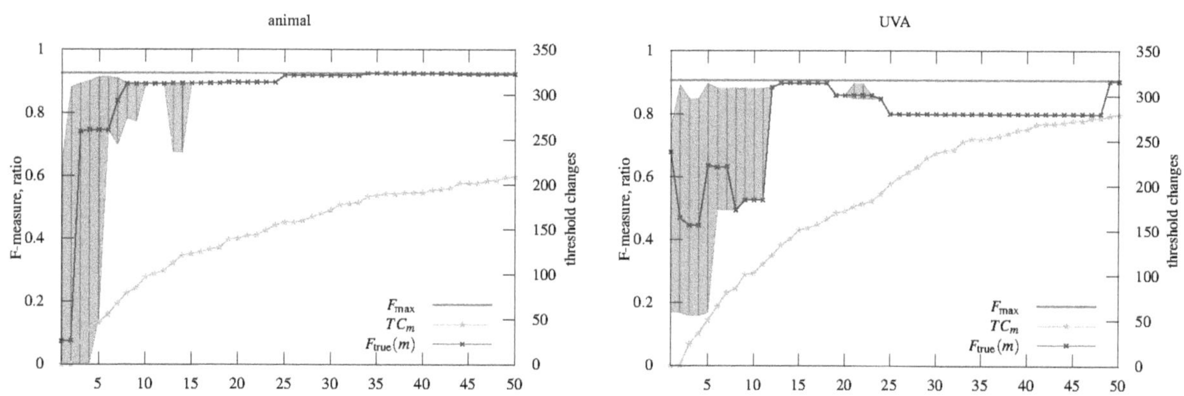

Figure 9: The x-axis shows the iteration number m. The left y-axis shows the F_1-scores, while the right y-axis reports the value of TC_m. The line labeled with $F_{true}(m)$ shows the true F_1-score of the best ranked predictor according to our ranking. The highlighted interval indicates the minimal and maximal true F_1-score among all predictors with maximal empirical F_1-scores.

5. RELATED WORK

We are aware of two works on optimizing threholds of similarity measures [3, 10]. Both approach this problem in the context of information retrieval. They consider query strings that are directed to a database of documents. The goal is to retrieve a ranked list of documents that contains relevant documents to a given query. A similarity measure is used to compare query strings to documents. A threshold decides, whether a document will be deemed relevant to the query. There can be many relevant documents to a query and the quality is measured in terms of the contingency table, e.g. in accuracy or F_1. Documents are usually very long strings. In [3], the authors describe a system that was implemented

to take part in a benchmark competition for text retrieval. It is trained online on a stream of queries. They introduce *score-distributional threshold optimization*, which uses a statistical model to estimate a threshold. The considered similarity measure is TFIDF with some preprocessing (like stemming and stop word removal). The approach works with any quality metric that is a function of the contingency table, like the F-measure. The paper outlines the *straightforward empirical method* to optimize thresholds w.r.t. a given quality metric, that exhaustively considers all thresholds on the present training data. The authors dismiss this simple approach, because of its drawbacks in their online problem setting. Most computations involved in their method can be updated incrementally. Also, it is able to produce a broad prediction for the threshold with only sparse supervised data. It is unclear, however, how score-distributional threshold optimization performs on only a few samples, since it is only evaluated in a very specific online setting. The approach is only evaluated on TFIDF and does not point out any method to compare several similarity measures.
The authors of [10] use the *straightforward empirical method* w.r.t. optimizing accuracy. Additionally, they formulate a statistical model with a bivariate Gaussian distribution. They show that this model captures the notion of an accuracy-optimal threshold well. Unfortunately, the evaluation of the optimization is not conclusive. Only one data set with artificial edit variations is used, and one similarity measure (Levenstein edit distance). The result suggests, that eventually the threshold arrives in the optimal interval. In the one experiment this happens close to 40 used samples. One sample corresponds to a ranking list which requires 8 labels (*relevant* or *irrelevant* to the query). The authors suggest to use clustering as an unsupervised method to approximate ground-truth to mitigate the labeling effort. The evaluation does not measure how good the intermediately approximated thresholds are, in terms of any quality metric. The sampling method for documents and queries is not described. Finally, a quality metric for similarity measures is introduced (arithmetic mean of accuracy and the size of the output interval of optimized thresholds). This metric is evaluated on eight similarity measures. The results show that this measure preserves the ranking by accuracy. Hence the empirical method for threshold optimization can also be used to compare similarity measures in terms of accuracy.

6. CONCLUSION

We have developed a novel method for finding a similarity measure and an appropriate threshold that work well specifically for given data, in order to solve the string matching problem. It requires no existing ground-truth and can be used by end-users. The experimental evaluation shows that good results can be achieved with only very few iterations. We propose two stopping criteria based on a notion of progress. Their thresholds have been determined empirically. The result of our proposed algorithm can directly be used in important applications like similarity join, record matching and schema matching.

7. REFERENCES

[1] https://code.google.com/p/linloglayout/.

[2] http://secondstring.sourceforge.net/.

[3] A. Arampatzis and A. van Hameran. The score-distributional threshold optimization for adaptive binary classification tasks. In *Proceedings of the 24th annual international ACM SIGIR conference on Research and development in information retrieval*, pages 285–293, 2001.

[4] J. Attenberg and F. Provost. Inactive learning?: difficulties employing active learning in practice. *ACM SIGKDD Explorations Newsletter*, 12(2):36–41, 2011.

[5] J. Bleiholder and F. Naumann. Data fusion. *ACM Computing Surveys (CSUR)*, 41(1):1, 2008.

[6] P. Christen. A comparison of personal name matching: Techniques and practical issues. In *ICDM Workshops*, 2006.

[7] P. Christen. *Data Matching*. 2012.

[8] W. W. Cohen. Data integration using similarity joins and a word-based information representation language. *ACM Transactions on Information Systems*, pages 288–321, July 2000.

[9] W. W. Cohen, P. D. Ravikumar, and S. E. Fienberg. A Comparison of String Distance Metrics for Name-Matching Tasks. In S. Kambhampati and C. A. Knoblock, editors, *Proceedings of IJCAI Workshop on Information Integration on the Web*, 2003.

[10] R. Da Silva, R. Stasiu, V. M. Orengo, and C. A. Heuser. Measuring quality of similarity functions in approximate data matching. *Journal of Informetrics*, 1(1):35–46, 2007.

[11] H. Koepcke and E. Rahm. Frameworks for entity matching: A comparison. *Data & Knowledge Engineering*, pages 197–210, Feb. 2010.

[12] A. McCallum, K. Nigam, and L. H. Ungar. Efficient clustering of high-dimensional data sets with application to reference matching. In *Proceedings of the sixth ACM SIGKDD international conference on Knowledge discovery and data mining*, 2000.

[13] D. Menestrina, S. E. Whang, and H. Garcia-Molina. Evaluating entity resolution results. *Proceedings of the VLDB Endowment*, 3(1-2):208–219, 2010.

[14] A. E. Monge, C. Elkan, and others. The Field Matching Problem: Algorithms and Applications. In *KDD*, pages 267–270, 1996.

[15] F. Naumann and M. Herschel. An introduction to duplicate detection. *Synthesis Lectures on Data Management*, 2(1):1–87, 2010.

[16] A. Noack. Modularity clustering is force-directed layout. *Physical Review E*, 79(2), 2009.

[17] E. Rahm and P. A. Bernstein. A survey of approaches to automatic schema matching. *the VLDB Journal*, 10(4):334–350, 2001.

[18] B. Settles. *Active Learning*. 2012.

[19] M. Stonebraker, I. F. Ilyas, S. Zdonik, G. Beskales, and A. Pagan. Data Curation at Scale: The Data Tamer System. *6th Biennial Conference on Innovative Data Systems Research*, 2013.

[20] S. Tejada, C. A. Knoblock, and S. Minton. Learning Object Identification Rules for Information Integration. *Information Systems*, 2001.

[21] C. Xiao, W. Wang, X. Lin, J. X. Yu, and G. Wang. Efficient similarity joins for near-duplicate detection. *ACM Transactions on Database Systems (TODS)*, 36(3):15, 2011.

A Unified Posterior Regularized Topic Model with Maximum Margin for Learning-to-Rank*

Shoaib Jameel[1], Wai Lam[2], Steven Schockaert[1], Lidong Bing[3]
[1]School of Computer Science and Informatics, Cardiff University.
[2]Dept. of Systems Engineering and Engineering Management, The Chinese University of Hong Kong.
[3]Machine Learning Department, Carnegie Mellon University.
{jameels1,schockaerts1}@cardiff.ac.uk wlam@se.cuhk.edu.hk lbing@cs.cmu.edu

ABSTRACT

While most methods for learning-to-rank documents only consider relevance scores as features, better results can often be obtained by taking into account the latent topic structure of the document collection. Existing approaches that consider latent topics follow a two-stage approach, in which topics are discovered in an unsupervised way, as usual, and then used as features for the learning-to-rank task. In contrast, we propose a learning-to-rank framework which integrates the supervised learning of a maximum margin classifier with the discovery of a suitable probabilistic topic model. In this way, the labelled data that is available for the learning-to-rank task can be exploited to identify the most appropriate topics. To this end, we use a unified constrained optimization framework, which can dynamically compute the latent topic similarity score between the query and the document. Our experimental results show a consistent improvement over the state-of-the-art learning-to-rank models.

Categories and Subject Descriptors

H.3 [**Information Storage and Retrieval**]: Information Search and Retrieval—*Clustering, Retrieval models, Search process*

Keywords

Learning-to-rank; Topic models; Maximum margin learning

*The work described in this paper is substantially supported by grants from the Research Grant Council of the Hong Kong Special Administrative Region, China (Project Codes: 413510 and 14203414) and the Direct Grant of the Faculty of Engineering, CUHK (Project Code: 4055034). This work is also affiliated with the CUHK MoE-Microsoft Key Laboratory of Human-centric Computing and Interface Technologies. Steven Schockaert has been supported by ERC Starting Grant 637277. This work was done when the first author was a Postdoctoral Fellow at The Chinese University of Hong Kong.

CIKM'15, October 19–23, 2015, Melbourne, Australia.
© 2015 ACM. ISBN 978-1-4503-3794-6/15/10 ...$15.00.
DOI: http://dx.doi.org/10.1145/2806416.2806482.

1. INTRODUCTION

The learning-to-rank (LTR) paradigm for information retrieval (IR) consists in the use of machine learning techniques for constructing suitable document ranking functions. Documents in this context are represented as vectors of features, capturing relevance w.r.t. the given query as well as query-independent statistics such as PageRank. LTR approaches can be distinguished in how they approach the ranking problem. In particular, pointwise (e.g. [22]), pairwise (e.g. [7]), and listwise (e.g. [8, 19, 31]) approaches are commonly considered, which respectively interpret ranking as a regression problem, a binary classification problem and an optimization problem.

In this paper, we will extend a maximum margin based LTR model, which is known to perform well on this task [22, 14, 1, 7], with information derived from a latent topic model, which has already proven beneficial in many IR tasks [30, 32, 10]. Several authors have already considered the use of latent topics for LTR. A common approach to do this is to adopt a two-stage "downstream" method [34], in which an existing topic model such as Latent Dirichlet Allocation (LDA) [6] is used to find the latent topics in the documents and queries. One can then compute a topic-based similarity between the query and a document, e.g. using cosine similarity or a likelihood based score [30]. By adding the resulting similarity scores as an additional feature, existing LTR models can be used to learn a ranking function for these topic-enriched feature vectors. For example, such a two-stage method has been used in [27] as a comparative method. However, since the mechanisms behind discovering the topics and learning the ranking are completely decoupled, this approach is inherently sub-optimal. Indeed, similar approaches have already been shown to perform unsatisfactorily in other prediction tasks [34, 27], as errors from one stage are propagated to the next.

The mechanism we propose in this paper is significantly different from these existing two-stage "downstream" approaches, as it is based on a tight coupling of latent topic detection and maximum margin classification. Specifically, we propose a unified constrained optimization framework, which is used to find a regularized posterior distribution of the predictive function in a space defined by the pairwise maximum margin constraints. The topic model component of the composite objective function is used to find the latent dimensions of the dataset, whereas the maximum margin component is used for label prediction. The advantage of this approach is that latent topic information can be chosen so as to aid the classification of data points around the decision boundary of a standard pairwise classifier, and more generally to prevent misclassifications. In particular, the proposed framework is capable of obtaining additional latent topic information to obtain a more discriminative representation of these hard data points. In this way, a more effective pairwise-based ranking classifier can be obtained, taking into account hidden topics that are automatically detected as part of the training process. After presenting the details of our model, we discuss a technique for solving the resulting optimization problem. Finally, we conduct extensive experiments on several benchmark datasets and show that our proposed model consistently improves the state-of-the-art approaches. We also present results related to the query-wise performance of our model in comparison to the comparative models and show that our model performs much better.

2. RELATED WORK

2.1 Learning-to-rank models

Maximum margin learning has already been successfully applied to LTR in a number of different ways [1, 14], in both pointwise [22] and pairwise [7] LTR models. For example, the latter approach uses `RankSVM` with a pairwise hinge loss function which is specifically adapted to the LTR task. Note that while [5] discusses the use of query topics in a maximum margin setting, it does not rely on a topic model for inferring these query topics. A large number of other learning-to-rank models have recently been proposed. For example, Gao et al. [13] presented a novel semi-supervised listwise LTR model to deal with domains for which no training data is available. A sparse learning-to-rank model for information retrieval has been proposed in [17]. Finally, Dang et al. [9] proposed a two-stage LTR framework to improve the performance in cases where many relevant documents are excluded from the ranking list by bag-of-words retrieval models. None of the above works consider latent topics for tackling the LTR problem.

2.2 Latent topic models

Unsupervised topic models such as Latent Dirichlet Allocation (`LDA`) [6] have proven very effective for ad-hoc information retrieval [30, 32, 10]. The usefulness of topic models in this context stems from the fact that latent topics can be used to better estimate the similarity between queries and documents when the overlap in actual content words is low [18, 12]. Existing approaches do not follow the LTR paradigm, but rather use the low-dimensional topic space to conduct traditional document retrieval under an unsupervised setting, without considering any other features.

Supervised models based on a latent semantic space have also been considered [18]. In [4], the authors have proposed a discriminative model, called supervised semantic indexing, which can compute query-document and document-document similarity in a semantic space. While the authors state that their model can easily be extended to an LTR setting, they have not developed such an extension. Gao et al. have proposed topic models which jointly consider the query and the title of a document, with the aim of improving document retrieval in a language modeling framework [12, 15]. Even though they also use posterior regularization, there are major differences with our approach; for instance, our model is designed for the LTR task. In addition, we introduce a novel interpretation to the optimization framework of the posterior distribution obtained using `LDA`, using a convex optimization technique, which leads to a novel formulation and inference algorithm.

There is another line of work that uses probabilistic topic modeling for document classification, which takes into account labeled training data during parameter estimation. One example is the supervised topic model from [21], which introduces a response variable in the topic modeling framework. The maximum margin entropy discrimination model, known as `MedLDA` [34], discriminatively learns a topic model for binary and multi-class document classification. A difference between our work and such maximum margin supervised topic models is that our model is designed for solving LTR tasks whereas the aforementioned models only consider document classification, which leads to a different optimization problem.

Note that both our model and the models proposed in [34, 35] are learned by solving a regularized Bayesian inference task. However, `MedLDA` and infinite latent `SVM` solve a different optimization problem. In particular, these models use the same input as text classification models, and use a latent linear discriminant function with a random weight vector that only encapsulates the topic feature weights, leading to an expected classifier with an effective discriminant function. Due to the use of a random weight vector, these models cannot directly take into account the non-random pre-computed features that are traditionally considered in the LTR task. Supervised text classification models also face problems when dealing with unbalanced data [22], where one class tends to dominate the training set, as is commonly the case for the class of non-relevant documents in information retrieval. Such unbalanced data leads to a classifier where the minority class is totally ignored by the text classification model [22]. Therefore, novel methodologies and algorithms are needed in order to solve the LTR task using topic models with pairwise maximum margin constraints.

2.3 Regularized posterior inference

Some probabilistic models have been proposed which make use of posterior inference with regularization, although latent topics have not previously been considered in such models. For example, in [11, 29] the authors proposed a probabilistic regularization framework for structured weakly supervised learning. They showed that by directly imposing decomposable regularization on the posterior moments of latent variables, the computational efficiency of the unconstrained model can be retained while ensuring that desired constraints hold in expectation. Supervised topic models discussed above such as [34, 16] also conduct posterior regularization.

3. BACKGROUND

3.1 Problem Definition

The learning-to-rank (LTR) paradigm aims to learn an optimal ranking function for a given set of available relevance features. Specifically, let a query set Q and document collection D be given, and assume that each query q_u from Q is associated with r_u documents. The learning algorithm is given x queries as training examples. The corresponding documents are typically retrieved from a search engine and will be denoted as $D_u = \{d_1^u, d_2^u, \cdots, d_{r_u}^u \in D\}$. Furthermore assume that in the training data, a discrete relevance label h_i^u is associated with each document d_i^u. Our objective is to learn a ranking function from this training data that can be used to rank documents for previously unseen queries.

As is typical in LTR settings, we assume that we have access to a mapping $\psi : Q \times D \rightarrow \mathbb{R}^n$ that maps each query-document pair to an n-dimensional feature vector. The training algorithm is then given labeled examples of the form $T = (T_1, T_2, \cdots, T_x)$, with each T_u of the form $T_u = ((\psi_1^u, h_1^u), (\psi_2^u, h_2^u), \cdots, (\psi_{r_u}^u, h_{r_u}^u))$ and $\psi_i^u = \psi(q_u, d_i^u)$. We then need to learn a real-valued function $f : \mathbb{R}^n \rightarrow \mathbb{R}$ such that $f(\psi(q, d_i)) > f(\psi(q, d_k))$ if document d_i is more relevant to query q than document d_k.

3.2 Pairwise Maximum Margin LTR

We will learn a linear ranking function, parametrized by a weight vector $\boldsymbol{\eta} \in \mathbb{R}^n$:

$$f_{\eta}(\psi) = \boldsymbol{\eta}^{\mathsf{T}}.\psi, \tag{1}$$

Our framework follows the pairwise approach to LTR. In other words, we treat LTR as a binary classification problem by constructing for each pair of documents (d_i^u, d_k^u), associated with a given query q_u, the vector $(\psi_i^u - \psi_k^u)$. The latter vector is assigned the class label y_{ik}^u defined as follows:

$$y_{ik}^u = \begin{cases} +1 & \text{if } d_i^u \text{ is ranked higher than } d_k^u \\ -1 & \text{otherwise.} \end{cases} \tag{2}$$

Let the set B_u of document index pairs, given a query q_u, be defined as follows:

$$B_u = \{(i,k) | h_i^u > h_k^u\} \tag{3}$$

In other words, $(i,k) \in B_u$ if d_i^u is more relevant than d_k^u.

Our framework is based on a maximum margin classifier model, similar to Support Vector Machines (SVM), which requires us to solve the following optimization problem:

$$\begin{aligned} \underset{\boldsymbol{\eta}}{\text{minimize}} \quad & \frac{1}{2}||\boldsymbol{\eta}||^2 + C\sum \xi_{ik} \\ \text{subject to} \quad & \xi_{ik} \geq 0 \\ & y_{ik}^u \boldsymbol{\eta}^{\mathsf{T}}(\psi_i^u - \psi_k^u) \geq 1 - \xi_{ik}, \forall u, i, k, \end{aligned} \tag{4}$$

where C is a regularization parameter and ξ_{ik} are the non-negative slack variables. It can be shown that solving this optimization problem is equivalent to minimizing the empirical hinge loss function, defined as follows:

$$L_h(B_u) = \sum_{(i,k)\in B_u} (1 - y_{ik}^u \boldsymbol{\eta}^{\mathsf{T}}(\psi_i^u - \psi_k^u)). \tag{5}$$

In our framework, we will consider a modified hinge loss function, which takes into account the difference in relevance degree and the different number of document pairs for different queries:

$$L'_h(B_u) = \frac{1}{|B_u|} \sum_{(i,k)\in B_u} [|h_i^u - h_k^u| - y_{ik}^u \boldsymbol{\eta}^{\mathsf{T}}(\psi_i^u - \psi_k^u)]. \tag{6}$$

Advantages of considering a query-level loss function have been discussed in [25, 1], where the relevance levels of different documents were also taken into account.

3.3 Topic Modeling

The topic modeling component of our framework is based on Latent Dirichlet Allocation (LDA). The aim of LDA is to represent the meaning of each document as a probability distribution over a set of latent topics. It assumes a generative process, in which each word in a document is generated by sampling a topic and then sampling a word. LDA assigns each word in the document collection to one of the latent topics (initially at random), and uses this assignment to estimate both the probability distribution over topics associated with each document and the probability distribution over words associated with each topics. These probability distributions are then used to improve the topic assignments of the words, and the whole process is repeated until convergence.

To apply LDA in our setting, we expand the document collection D with the set of queries from the training data Q, i.e. queries are treated as short documents to construct an aggregated document collection, denoted as $\mathbb{D}$. For any document d in $\mathbb{D}$, we let N^d denote the number of words in document d. Furthermore, we let $\boldsymbol{w}^d = \{w_n^d\}_{n=1}^{N^d}$ denote the words appearing in the each document and $\boldsymbol{W} = \{\boldsymbol{w}^d\}_{d=1}^{\mathbb{D}}$ the words in the entire aggregated document set. Let $\boldsymbol{z}^d = \{z_n^d\}_{n=1}^{N^d}$ denote the topic assignment of the words in document d and let $\boldsymbol{Z} = \{\boldsymbol{z}^d\}_{d=1}^{\mathbb{D}}$ denote the topic assignment of all words in $\mathbb{D}$. Let $\boldsymbol{\Theta} = \{\theta^d\}_{d=1}^{\mathbb{D}}$ be the topic distributions of all documents in $\mathbb{D}$. Let the number of topics be K. Let $\boldsymbol{\Phi} = \{\phi_1, \phi_2, \cdots, \phi_K\}$ be the $V \times K$ matrix of topic distribution parameters, where each ϕ_k parameterizes a topic-specific multinomial word distribution. V denotes the number of words in the vocabulary. The posterior distribution is then given by:

$$P(\boldsymbol{\Theta}, \boldsymbol{Z}, \boldsymbol{\Phi} | \boldsymbol{W}, \boldsymbol{\alpha}, \boldsymbol{\beta}) = \frac{P_0(\boldsymbol{\Theta}, \boldsymbol{Z}, \boldsymbol{\Phi} | \boldsymbol{\alpha}, \boldsymbol{\beta}) P(\boldsymbol{W} | \boldsymbol{\Theta}, \boldsymbol{Z}, \boldsymbol{\Phi})}{P(\boldsymbol{W} | \boldsymbol{\alpha}, \boldsymbol{\beta})}, \tag{7}$$

where $P_0(\boldsymbol{\Theta}, \boldsymbol{Z}, \boldsymbol{\Phi} | \boldsymbol{\alpha}, \boldsymbol{\beta})$ is the prior probability, with $\boldsymbol{\alpha}$ the parameter of the Dirichlet prior on the per-document topic distributions and $\boldsymbol{\beta}$ the parameter of the Dirichlet prior on the per-topic word distributions.

Zellner in [33] has extended Bayes' rule so that it can be used as a learning model. Specifically, Zellner has showed that Bayes' rule can be transformed into an optimization problem. In this way, it can be shown that the values for $\boldsymbol{\Theta}$, $\boldsymbol{Z}$ and $\boldsymbol{\Phi}$ which maximize the posterior distribution (7) can be found by solving the following optimization problem:

$$\begin{aligned} \underset{P(\boldsymbol{\Theta}, \boldsymbol{Z}, \boldsymbol{\Phi} | \boldsymbol{\alpha}, \boldsymbol{\beta}) \in \mathbb{P}}{\text{minimize}} \quad & \text{KL}[P(\boldsymbol{\Theta}, \boldsymbol{Z}, \boldsymbol{\Phi} | \boldsymbol{W}, \boldsymbol{\alpha}, \boldsymbol{\beta}) || P_0(\boldsymbol{\Theta}, \boldsymbol{Z}, \boldsymbol{\Phi} | \boldsymbol{\alpha}, \boldsymbol{\beta})] \\ & - \mathbb{E}_P[\log \text{P}(\boldsymbol{W} | \boldsymbol{\Theta}, \boldsymbol{Z}, \boldsymbol{\Phi})] \\ \text{subject to} \quad & P(\boldsymbol{\Theta}, \boldsymbol{Z}, \boldsymbol{\Phi} | \boldsymbol{W}, \boldsymbol{\alpha}, \boldsymbol{\beta}) \in \mathbb{P}, \end{aligned} \tag{8}$$

where $\mathbb{P}$ is the probability distribution space, $\text{KL}(P||P_0)$ is the Kullback-Leibler divergence from P to P_0, and $\mathbb{E}$ is the expected value operator. This interpretation of Bayes' theorem will be useful for designing our pairwise LTR model, which will be based on an extension of (8). Note that $P(\boldsymbol{W} | \boldsymbol{\alpha}, \boldsymbol{\beta})$ has been omitted because it does not depend on $\boldsymbol{\Theta}, \boldsymbol{Z}, \boldsymbol{\Phi}$.

4. DESCRIPTION OF OUR FRAMEWORK

The key characteristic of our framework is that maximum margin learning is tightly integrated with topic discovery. To this end, in Section 4.1, we extend the optimization problem from (4) with a latent topic model, similar to Latent Dirichlet Allocation (LDA). As we discuss in Section 4.2, solving the resulting optimization problem requires us to alternate between topic discovery (informed by the parameters of the maximum margin classifier) and maximum margin label prediction (informed by the latent topic structure).

4.1 Unified LTR Model

The optimization view of Zellner's interpretation of Bayes' rule in (8) can be extended to incorporate posterior constraints in Bayesian inference, by adding a convex function to (8). This leads to the introduction of some auxiliary free parameters, which can be slack variables. We will use the following formulation:

$$\begin{aligned}\underset{P(\boldsymbol{\Theta},\boldsymbol{Z},\boldsymbol{\Phi}|\boldsymbol{\alpha},\boldsymbol{\beta})\in\mathbb{P},\boldsymbol{\xi}}{\text{minimize}}\ & \mathrm{KL}[P(\boldsymbol{\Theta},\boldsymbol{Z},\boldsymbol{\Phi}|\boldsymbol{W},\boldsymbol{\alpha},\boldsymbol{\beta})||P_0(\boldsymbol{\Theta},\boldsymbol{Z},\boldsymbol{\Phi}|\boldsymbol{\alpha},\boldsymbol{\beta})]\\ & -\mathbb{E}_P[\log \mathrm{P}(\boldsymbol{W}|\boldsymbol{\Theta},\boldsymbol{Z},\boldsymbol{\Phi})]+M(\boldsymbol{\xi})\\ \text{subject to } & P(\boldsymbol{\Theta},\boldsymbol{Z},\boldsymbol{\Phi}|\boldsymbol{\alpha},\boldsymbol{\beta})\in\mathbb{P}_{\text{new}}(\boldsymbol{\xi}),\\ & \xi\geq 0\end{aligned} \tag{9}$$

where $\mathbb{P}_{\text{new}}(\boldsymbol{\xi})$ is the subspace of probability distributions satisfying the constraints that arise out of the optimization framework. The convex function $M(\boldsymbol{\xi})$ in our case will be based on the relevance-weighted pairwise query-level hinge loss defined in (6). Note that many other interesting extensions to Zellner's equation have been proposed in the past such as the MedLDA model [34].

To consider latent topics during maximum margin learning, the loss function in (6) needs to take into account the topic similarity between the query q_u and document d_i^u. If we denote this similarity by Υ_i^u, we can consider the following discriminant function:

$$\boldsymbol{\eta}^{\intercal}(\psi_i^u-\psi_k^u)+\eta_t(\Upsilon_i^u-\Upsilon_k^u). \tag{10}$$

where η_t is a parameter encoding the relative importance of the topic similarity Υ_i^u, which is calculated based on the topic document distribution $\boldsymbol{\Theta}$. Recall that in this distribution, a document (or query) d is represented as a $K\times 1$ vector $\vec{d_i^u}$, encoding for each latent topic z the corresponding probability $P(z|d)$. For document d_i^u associated with a query q_u, we define Υ_i^u as the cosine similarity between $\vec{d_i^u}$ and $\vec{q_u}$. Other metrics such as KL-divergence could also be used. The overall optimization problem we end up with is as follows:

$$\begin{aligned}\underset{\substack{P(\boldsymbol{\Theta},\boldsymbol{Z},\boldsymbol{\Phi}|\boldsymbol{\alpha},\boldsymbol{\beta}),\\ \boldsymbol{\eta},\eta_t,\boldsymbol{\xi}}}{\text{minimize}}\ & \mathrm{KL}[P(\boldsymbol{\Theta},\boldsymbol{Z},\boldsymbol{\Phi}|\boldsymbol{W},\boldsymbol{\alpha},\boldsymbol{\beta})||P_0(\boldsymbol{\Theta},\boldsymbol{Z},\boldsymbol{\Phi}|\boldsymbol{\alpha},\boldsymbol{\beta})]\\ & -\mathbb{E}_P[\log P(\boldsymbol{W}|\boldsymbol{\Theta},\boldsymbol{Z},\boldsymbol{\Phi})]+\frac{1}{2}(||\boldsymbol{\eta}||^2+\eta_t^2)\\ & +\frac{C}{x}\sum_{u=1}^{x}\frac{1}{|B_u|}\sum_{(i,k)\in B_u}\xi_{(i,k)}^u\\ \text{subject to } & \xi_{(i,k)}^u\geq|h_i^u-h_k^u|-y_{ik}^u\left[\boldsymbol{\eta}^{\intercal}(\psi_i^u-\psi_k^u)+\right.\\ & \left.\eta_t(\Upsilon_i^u-\Upsilon_k^u)\right],\ \forall u,i,k,\\ & P(\boldsymbol{\Theta},\boldsymbol{Z},\boldsymbol{\Phi}|\boldsymbol{\alpha},\boldsymbol{\beta})\in\mathbb{P}(\xi_{(i,k)}^u)\\ & \xi_{(i,k)}^u\geq 0,\ \forall u,i,k.\end{aligned} \tag{11}$$

Note that the latent topic similarities Υ_i^u and Υ_k^u are computed in the regularized topic space arising from the optimization component, which differentiates our approach from the two-stage heuristic methods described in Section 1. By directly regularizing the posterior distribution with the maximum margin constraint, we obtain a more powerful model, catered specifically to the pairwise LTR task. The usefulness of this approach stems from the fact that latent topics can be chosen specifically to help the maximum margin classifier, e.g. by preventing instances from being located near the margin.

4.2 Solving the Optimization Problem

As solving (11) exactly is intractable, we resort to a Monte Carlo method which alternates between two steps. In the first step, our goal is to find a maximum margin separation of the points, i.e. we determine $\boldsymbol{\eta}$ and η_t given $P(\boldsymbol{\Theta},\boldsymbol{Z},\boldsymbol{\Phi}|\boldsymbol{W},\boldsymbol{\alpha},\boldsymbol{\beta})$. As in the existing RankSVM algorithm, the optimum solution can be found by adopting the Lagrangian method. In the second step, we estimate $P(\boldsymbol{\Theta},\boldsymbol{Z},\boldsymbol{\Phi}|\boldsymbol{W},\boldsymbol{\alpha},\boldsymbol{\beta})$ given $(\boldsymbol{\eta},\eta_t)$, as explained below. Both steps are repeated for a given number of iterations or until the sampler converges to a steady state. As in traditional topic modeling, the procedure starts with a random initialization of the topic assignments. Note that this mechanism closely resembles the Expectation-Maximization (EM) algorithm. However, while EM maximizes the expected log-likelihood under the marginal distribution of the latent variables, we are minimizing the regularized loss.

To estimate $P(\boldsymbol{\Theta},\boldsymbol{Z},\boldsymbol{\Phi}|\boldsymbol{W},\boldsymbol{\alpha},\boldsymbol{\beta})$, we use collapsed Gibbs sampling, where our goal is to estimate the model parameters $\boldsymbol{\Theta}$ and $\boldsymbol{\Phi}$. We present a brief derivation of the collapsed Gibbs sampler with maximum margin constraints below. Let n_{zw} denote the number of times a word w is assigned to a topic z and let p_{dz} denote the number of times a word from document d has been assigned to topic z. We can start with the joint distribution of the model, which can be expressed as:

$$P(\boldsymbol{Z}|\boldsymbol{\alpha})\propto P(\boldsymbol{W},\boldsymbol{Z}|\boldsymbol{\alpha},\boldsymbol{\beta}) \tag{12}$$

When we incorporate the maximum margin framework in (12), we obtain the following model:

$$P(\boldsymbol{Z}|\boldsymbol{\alpha})\propto\frac{P(\boldsymbol{W},\boldsymbol{Z}|\boldsymbol{\alpha},\boldsymbol{\beta})}{\Omega}\cdot\mathrm{e}^{\frac{1}{2}\Delta-\Psi}. \tag{13}$$

where Ω is the normalization constant. The first factor in the right-hand side of (13) adopts the collapsed Gibbs sampling formulation. In this sampling scheme, we also compute the transition probabilities, which are used to iteratively find the word-topic and document-topic latent topic distributions. The second factor corresponds to the regularization effects of the pairwise maximum margin classifier. Let Γ denote the Gamma function where $\Gamma(x)=(x-1)!$. By integrating out $\boldsymbol{\Theta}$ and $\boldsymbol{\Phi}$, we get the marginalized posterior distribution:

$$\begin{aligned}P(\boldsymbol{Z}|\boldsymbol{\alpha})\propto&\prod_{z=1}^{K}\left(\frac{\Gamma(\sum_{s=1}^{|\boldsymbol{\beta}|}\beta_s)}{\prod_{s=1}^{|\boldsymbol{\beta}|}\Gamma(\beta_s)}\int\prod_{w=1}^{V}\phi_{zw}^{n_{zw}+\beta_w-1}\mathrm{d}\boldsymbol{\phi}_z\right)\cdot\\ &\prod_{d=1}^{\mathbb{D}}\left(\frac{\Gamma(\sum_{s=1}^{|\boldsymbol{\alpha}|}\alpha_s)}{\prod_{s=1}^{|\boldsymbol{\alpha}|}\Gamma(\alpha_s)}\int\prod_{z=1}^{K}\theta^{p_{dz}+\alpha_z-1}\mathrm{d}\boldsymbol{\theta}_d\cdot\mathrm{e}^{\frac{1}{2}\Delta-\Psi}\right)\end{aligned} \tag{14}$$

where Δ and Ψ are defined as follows

$$\Delta = \Bigg[\sum_{u=1}^{x} \sum_{(d,k)\in B_u} \sum_{\hat{u}=1}^{x} \sum_{(\hat{d}\hat{k})\in B_{\hat{u}}} \lambda^u_{dk} \lambda^{\hat{u}}_{\hat{d}\hat{k}} \cdot [(\psi^u_d - \psi^u_k) + (\Upsilon^u_d - \Upsilon^u_k)] \Bigg] \cdot [(\psi^{\hat{u}}_{\hat{d}} - \psi^{\hat{u}}_{\hat{k}}) + (\Upsilon^{\hat{u}}_{\hat{d}} - \Upsilon^{\hat{u}}_{\hat{k}})] \quad (15)$$

$$\Psi = \sum_{u=1}^{x} \sum_{(d,k)\in B_u} \lambda^u_{dk} (h^u_d - h^u_k) \quad (16)$$

with λ^u_{dk} and $\lambda^{\hat{u}}_{\hat{d}\hat{k}}$ the Lagrange multipliers, satisfying $0 \leq \lambda^u_{dk} \leq \frac{C}{x \times |B_u|}$ for all d, k and u. The above formulation can be used to derive the following updating rule for the Gibbs sampler, for one variable z^d_n given the others:

$$P(z^d_n = t | \boldsymbol{Z}_{\neg n}, w = v, \boldsymbol{W}_{\neg n}, \boldsymbol{\alpha}, \boldsymbol{\beta}) \quad (17)$$
$$\propto \left(\frac{n_{tv} + \beta_{w^d_n} - 1}{\left[\sum_{v=1}^{V} n_{tv} + \beta_v\right] - 1} \right) (p_{dt} + \alpha_t - 1) e^{\frac{1}{2}\Delta - \Psi}$$

In the above equation, the current word is excluded in the counts n_{zw} and p_{dz} which we denote with the symbol $\neg$. The parameters in the model can be estimated based on the following formulations:

$$\phi_{zv} = \frac{n_{zv} + \beta_v}{\left(\sum_{v=1}^{V} n_{zv} + \beta_v\right)} \quad (18)$$

$$\theta_{dz} = \frac{p_{dz} + \alpha_z}{\left(\sum_{z=1}^{K} p_{dz} + \alpha_z\right)} e^{\frac{1}{2}\Delta - \Psi} \quad (19)$$

4.3 Prediction on Unlabeled Data

To apply our LTR model on unseen data, we have to determine the latent dimensions of the unseen data using the regularized topic space that was learned from the training data. In addition, the model has to project the unseen data into the learned ranking space of the pairwise maximum margin classifier for label prediction. To this end, we use the point estimate of the topics computation procedure from the training data. After the Markov chain has reached a certain number of iterations, we draw J samples from it. Specifically, using the maximum a posteriori probability (MAP) estimation scheme, we obtain a new set of topic distributions $\boldsymbol{\Phi}$, which we write as $\hat{\boldsymbol{\Phi}}$. Using our collapsed Gibbs sampler, an estimate of $\hat{\boldsymbol{\Phi}}$ can be obtained as follows:

$$\hat{\phi}_{zw} \propto \frac{1}{J} \sum_{j=1}^{J} n^{(j)}_{zw} + \beta_w \quad (20)$$

The latent dimensions of an unseen document π can then be computed as follows:

$$P(z^\pi_n = t | \boldsymbol{Z}_{\neg n}) \propto \hat{\phi}_{tw^\pi_n} (p_{\pi t} + \alpha_t) \quad (21)$$

The above formulations can be used to separately compute the latent dimensions for the query and the documents. Let $\boldsymbol{\pi}$ denote a feature vector for π, containing the same features as those considered in the training set. The prediction formula for the pairwise maximum margin classifier can be expressed as:

$$F(\boldsymbol{\pi}) = \sum_{u=1}^{x} \sum_{(i,k)\in B_u} \lambda^u_{ik} [(\psi^u_i - \psi^u_k) + (\Upsilon^u_i - \Upsilon^u_k)] . \boldsymbol{\pi} \quad (22)$$

In the right-hand side of (22), the expression $\sum_{u=1}^{x} \sum_{(i,k)\in B_u} \lambda^u_{ik} [(\psi^u_i - \psi^u_k) + (\Upsilon^u_i - \Upsilon^u_k)]$ computes the feature weights for the new vector $\boldsymbol{\pi}$. The recipe is to alternately run, until convergence is reached, the topic prediction model depicted in (21) using the parameters of the trained regularized topic space, and then use the pairwise maximum margin formulations depicted in (22), which provides the pairwise regularization effect to the latent dimensions computed in the previous step, for predicting the labels. When (21) and (22) are combined together following the same paradigm as depicted in (13), the new documents are "folded-in" in the previously trained regularized topic space.

5. EXPERIMENTS AND RESULTS

5.1 Datasets

Many benchmark LTR collections have been released in the past, such as LETOR [24] and the Yahoo! LTR Challenge dataset. These collections contain pre-computed query-dependent and query-independent features but do not provide access to the corresponding documents, which means that the latent topic features cannot be computed. As a result, such existing public benchmark LTR collections cannot be used in our experiments. One exception is the LETOR OHSUMED [24] benchmark collection, whose text and queries are freely available[1]. In addition to LETOR OHSUMED, we will use three new collections, which we have built based on well-known TREC datasets. First, we have used AQUAINT, which is used in the TREC-HARD [2] track and contains a total of 50 queries[2]. The queries along with the corresponding annotations are provided on the TREC HARD disk. Second, we have used the WT2G dataset[3], consisting of 50 TREC queries[4]. Finally, we have used the ClueWeb09 Category B English documents collection. In particular, we used a list of 91 features from [3], where the authors have considered 150 TREC Web Track queries from 2009 to 2011.

Recently, Terrier v4.0 has introduced LTR in its distribution[5]. We used this open source search engine to create training, testing and validation sets for our two new datasets (AQUAINT and WT2G). We created the corresponding LTR datasets using all query-dependent and query-independent models currently available in Terrier v4.0. Note that Terrier v4.0 uses the "title" field from the TREC topics file to retrieve documents. The created datasets comprise 39 normalized features, which form a subset of the features described in [20]; all considered features fall in the WM and WMP classes described in [20]. Terrier v4.0 can be set to use its default `BM25` implementation to retrieve the top 1000 documents, which corresponds to what is used in the official LETOR [24] collections. We separately created the LTR dataset for ClueWeb09 because of two reasons. First, this dataset is extremely large for Terrier to handle on a standalone machine. Second, Terrier's implementation currently cannot compute the 91 considered features for the ClueWeb09 dataset. In all text collections,

[1] http://ir.ohsu.edu/ohsumed/
[2] Note that we use the term queries here whereas in TREC usually the term topics is used.
[3] http://ir.dcs.gla.ac.uk/test_collections/access_to_data.html
[4] http://trec.nist.gov/data/t8.web.html
[5] http://terrier.org/docs/current/learning.html

we used stemming (Porter stemmer) and stopword removal, as implemented in Terrier v4.0. Subsequently, we created five folds. Each fold has approx. 60% query-document pairs for training, approx. 20% query-document pairs for testing and the rest for validation. Note that the training, testing and validation sets do not share any queries. One can thus notice that we have followed the standard LTR dataset creation procedure as reported in the LETOR dataset documentation [24]. In our experiments, 42681 unique documents were retrieved by Terrier for the 50 queries in the AQUAINT collection. For the WT2G dataset, we retrieved 40773 unique documents, whereas the ClueWeb09 dataset consists of 42044 unique documents. Note that our implementation of topic modeling considers the complete documents, irrespective of different fields (e.g. TITLE) that may be present.

The publicly available LETOR OHSUMED dataset contains training (approx. 60% of query-document pairs), testing (approx. 20% of query-document pairs) and validation (approx. 20% of query-document pairs) splits in five folds. It consists of 14430 unique documents. More information about this dataset can be obtained from [1]. Each feature vector in the LETOR OHSUMED also contains the document identifier. This information can help us relate a document from the downloaded OHSUMED text documents with its corresponding feature vector in LETOR OHSUMED. LETOR OHSUMED also contains meta-information which allows us to relate text queries with their corresponding query identifiers.

5.2 Comparative Methods

Many popular models have been implemented in RankLib[6]: `Listnet`, `AdaRank-MAP`, `AdaRank-NDCG`, `Coordinate Ascent`, `LambdaMART` and `MART`, which belong to the listwise class of LTR models, as well as the pairwise models `RankNet`, `RankBoost` and `LambdaRank`, and the pointwise model `Linear Regression - L2 Norm` and `Random Forests`. Note that models implemented in RankLib have been used as strong state-of-the-art baselines in many recent works such as [26, 23]. We will compare our method against the aforementioned methods, as well as a number of other publicly available implementations: `SVMMAP`[7], a listwise model, `RankSVM-Struct`[8], a pairwise model, and the recently proposed `DirectRank`.

Finally, we will also compare our approach with a semantic search model similar to the one proposed in [4], which we have slightly modified to handle the feature instances needed for the LTR task; we will refer to this model as `Semantic Search`. Note that while the authors of [4] mention that their model can be adapted to incorporate LTR features, they have not included such an evaluation in their work. This model bears some resemblance to our proposed framework, in that both models are capable of generating latent topic similarity features dynamically. In particular, `Semantic Search` can be made to generate topic similarity with minor changes to the original model. However, a crucial difference is that we compute topic similarity in the regularized space, whereas `Semantic Search` computes topic similarity in a so-called "concept space", which is very similar to the space obtained by the latent semantic indexing (`LSI`) model. We have also experimented with a variant of `Semantic Search`, proposed in [12], but found its performance on LTR datasets to be very similar to, but slightly weaker than that of the model from [4]. Finally, note that we have not considered any unsupervised topic models for comparison, as such models cannot make use of relevance judgements during the training process, and can therefore not be competitive with LTR models in this context.

[6]http://people.cs.umass.edu/~vdang/ranklib.html

[7]http://projects.yisongyue.com/svmmap/

[8]http://research.microsoft.com/en-us/um/beijing/projects/letor/letor4.0/baselines/ranksvm-struct.html

5.3 Experimental Setup

Hyperparameter Values: We use the following symmetric hyperparameter values in the `LDA` topic model: $\alpha = \frac{50}{K}$ and $\beta = 0.01$, where K is the number of topics. This value is used throughout all experiments, for both our model and other approaches that use latent topics. These values have also been used e.g. in `LDA` for document retrieval [30]. We have experimented with different hyperparameter values, but did not obtain any significantly different results. We used the validation set for model selection, which is common for LETOR baselines [26, 19]. All NDCG results have been averaged across five folds.

Parameter tuning for comparative models: The parameters of the comparative LTR models in each fold were tuned using the validation set. To replicate the results for LETOR OHSUMED, we followed the official guidelines[9], which state: "*The validation set can only be used for model selection (setting hyper-parameters and model structure), but cannot be used for learning. Most baselines released in LETOR website use MAP on the validation set for model selection; you are encouraged to use the same strategy and should indicate if you use a different one.*" For consistency, we used the same rules for model selection in the three other datasets. Parameters were tuned for each fold separately, as is usual for the LTR setting.

Parameter tuning for our model: We need to tune the regularization parameter C, the learning rate and the number of topics K for each fold. In each fold, we varied C from 0.1 to 1 in steps of 0.1, and K from 10 to 1000 in steps of 10. The learning rate values that we experimented with are $\{10^{-2}, 10^{-3}, 10^{-4}, 10^{-5}, 10^{-6}\}$. The value of K was varied from 10 to 200 in steps of 10. The number of iterations of the Markov chain was set to 1000. Using these ranges for the parameters, as for the comparative models, we searched for the configuration that produced the best mean average precision (MAP) score on the validation set. Note that because we use regularized Bayesian inference, overfitting in our model is unlikely, despite using 1000 iterations for the Markov chain. Moreover, there is evidence that models based on Bayesian inference in general tend not to overfit [28].

Description of the experiments: We have conducted two types of experiments. First, we have compared our approach with the comparative models, using their default feature sets, as described in Section 5.1. The results of this experiment are discussed in Section 5.4.1. While this allows us to find out whether our approach can outperform the existing state-of-the-art LTR models, it should be noted that we are using a latent topic similarity feature, which other models do not have access to, and it might be that our model is performing better simply because it has access to better features. Therefore, in a second experiment, we have added

[9]http://research.microsoft.com/en-us/um/beijing/projects/letor//letor3baseline.aspx

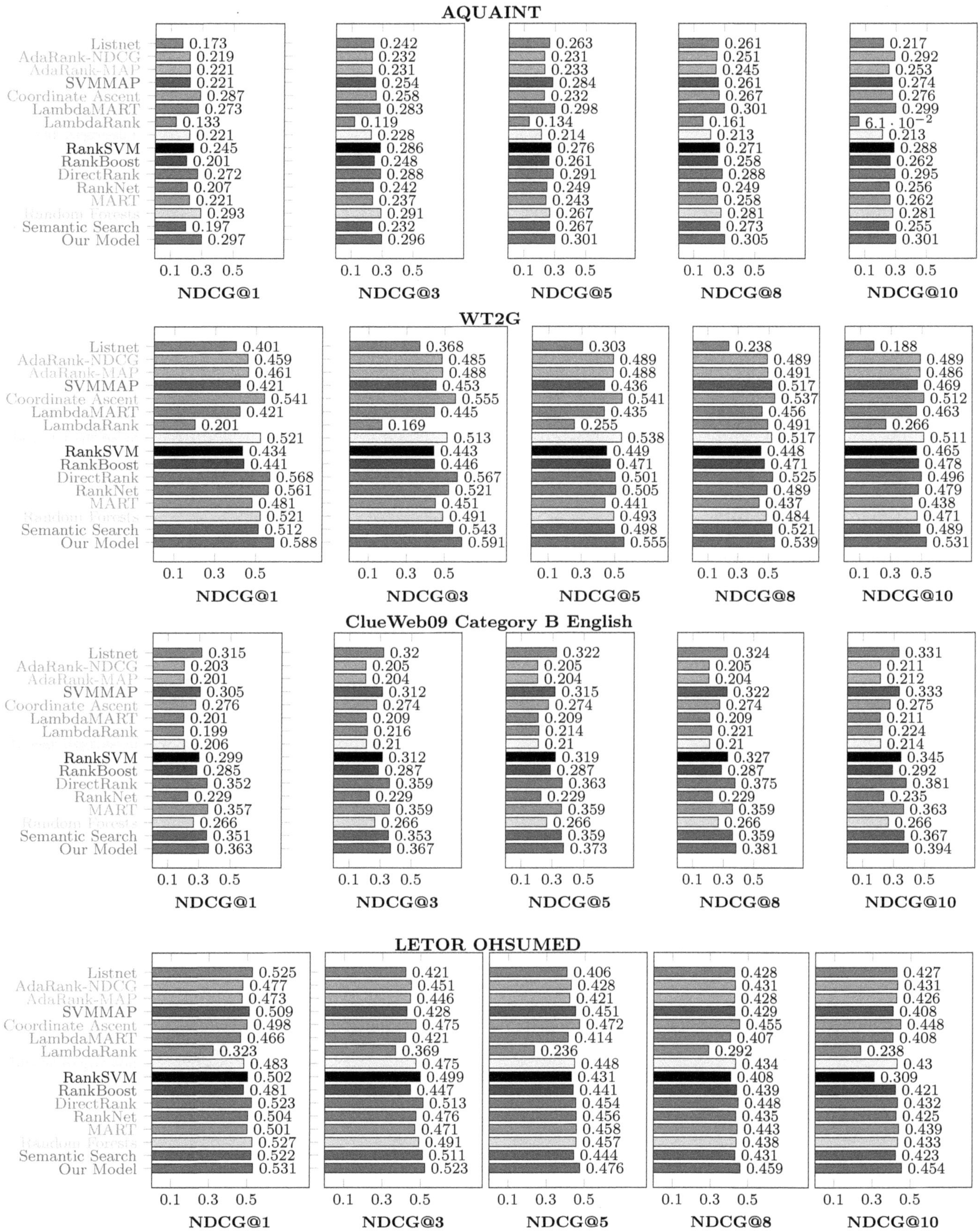

Figure 1: LTR results for four datasets.

the query-document latent topic similarity as an additional feature for the comparative models. In particular, we have used LDA, following the procedure described in [30] to independently compute query-document topic similarity. We also experimented with the cosine similarity for comparing queries and documents in the latent topic space, but the results were inferior to those of the method from [30]. As for our model, the number of latent topics K was automatically determined using the validation set by varying the number of topics from 10 to 200 in steps of 10. The number of iterations in the Gibbs sampler for computing the topic similarity using the method from [30] is 1000. This experiment will allow us to assess whether our integrated model has any benefits over models that simply use latent topics as one of the features. The results are presented in Section 5.4.2.

Evaluation metric: We have used the PERL evaluation tool available in LETOR 3.0 for evaluating all the models[10]. Our evaluation metric is NDCG which is popular for LTR evaluation; we refer to [1] for a definition of this metric. We will use NDCG@k to present our main results, where $k = 1, 3, 5, 8, 10$. We have tested for statistical significance using the paired t-test, as is usual for LTR experiments.

5.4 Experimental Results

5.4.1 Traditional LTR Comparison

Figure 1 presents the results for the considered datasets. As can be seen from the figure, our model consistently outperforms all the comparative models, for each of the datasets and NDCG cut-offs. The improvements against each of the comparative methods are statistically significant according to the paired t-test with $p < 0.05$. For the AQUAINT dataset, DirectRank, Semantic Search, Coordinate Ascent, and LambdaMART do much better than the other comparative models. For the WT2G dataset, LambdaRank performs very poorly, with our model being the only one that clearly differs. The results for ClueWeb09 and LETOR OHSUMED are consistent with the results for AQUAINT. In both cases, our model considerably outperforms the other, while DirectRank also shows good performance among the comparative models. These results confirm our intuition that integrating latent topic information with maximum margin learning is capable of outperforming the state-of-the-art approaches.

To better understand the differences in performance across different queries, Table 1 shows a winning number comparison. We refer to [19] for a detailed description of this metric, which has also been used in e.g. [26]. As we can see from the table, our model substantially outperforms all of the comparative models, with DirectRank again the best performer among the comparative methods.

5.4.2 Topic Enhanced Datasets Experiment

We present the results for the second experiment in Figure 2. As we can see from this figure, the performance of many comparative methods has slightly improved or has remained same as in the previous result. For example, in the AQUAINT dataset, performance of many comparative models has improved and none of the results have deteriorated. Therefore, in the majority of cases latent topic information leads to a slightly improved performance. However, even with the latent topic feature added, none of the comparative methods can outperform our approach. The improvement is still statistically significant for all datasets and all models, according to the paired t-test with $p < 0.05$, except at NDCG@8 in WT2G dataset where Coordinate Ascent model performs equally well. For the LETOR OHSUMED dataset, our model performs strictly better than each of the comparative methods, except at NDCG@8 where Coordinate Ascent performs equally well. Linear Regression model also shows good performance in this experiment. We can see that the performance gap between the comparative models and our model has slightly decreased compared to Figure 1. Table 2 presents the winning number results. Comparing this table with Table 1 clearly shows that the relative performance of the comparative methods has improved. This demonstrates that latent topic information is helpful, even when used as a standard feature in other LTR models. However, our approach still performs consistently better, confirming the benefit of using an integrated model.

When looking in more detail at the per-query performance in each dataset, we note that our model especially outperforms the comparative methods for long queries, e.g. consisting of two words or more. In Table 3, we present this comparison in terms of the percentage of winning numbers,

Models	N@1	N@3	N@5	N@8	N@10
ListNet	17	16	13	13	14
AdaRank-NDCG	12	14	16	17	18
AdaRank-MAP	15	12	14	11	12
SVMMAP	15	20	18	20	18
Coordinate Ascent	24	25	26	25	27
LambdaMART	21	23	21	19	22
LambdaRank	05	08	06	02	11
Linear Regression	18	19	15	18	20
RankSVM	18	15	19	15	15
RankBoost	16	12	13	18	15
DirectRank	30	34	31	32	34
RankNet	19	21	19	12	15
MART	18	18	22	16	15
Random Forests	25	20	21	20	18
Semantic Search	28	33	25	28	25
Our Model	**33**	**39**	**37**	**36**	**36**

Table 1: Winning number comparison.

Models	N@1	N@3	N@5	N@8	N@10
ListNet	19	17	14	16	18
AdaRank-NDCG	13	16	17	19	20
AdaRank-MAP	16	14	15	10	15
SVMMAP	16	21	20	19	20
Coordinate Ascent	27	26	24	20	23
LambdaMART	23	27	20	21	23
LambdaRank	02	04	03	05	12
Linear Regression	19	20	18	20	21
RankSVM	20	17	20	18	16
RankBoost	18	15	15	19	17
DirectRank	28	28	29	25	25
RankNet	19	18	21	18	19
MART	19	19	24	19	18
Random Forests	23	19	24	21	19
Semantic Search	25	31	26	23	22
Our Model	**30**	**33**	**31**	**28**	**27**

Table 2: Winning number comparison when the latent topic similarity feature is incorporated in the comparative methods.

[10]http://research.microsoft.com/en-us/um/beijing/projects/letor/letor3download.aspx

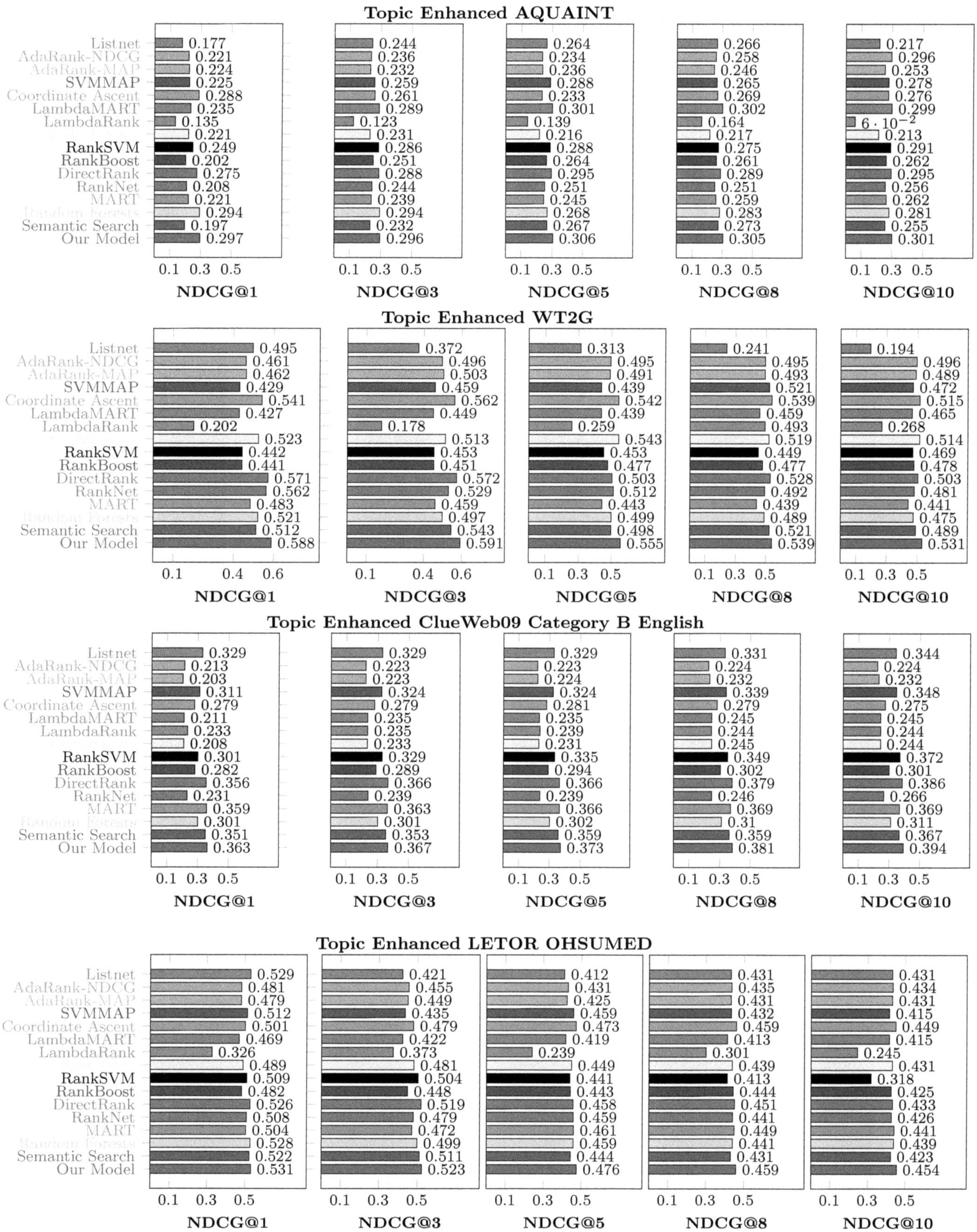

Figure 2: LTR results in topic enhanced datasets.

	1	2	3	>3
AQUAINT	54.33	59.74	69.12	78.66
WT2G	59.64	67.35	73.92	73.92
ClueWeb	61.23	72.98	79.76	83.21
LETOR OHSUMED	57.34	63.65	69.44	75.61

Table 3: Query level performance in terms of the percentage of winning numbers for different query lengths.

which shows that the relative performance also improves with longer queries. These comparisons are done by considering the latent topic feature in the comparative methods. This result is expected, as longer queries make it easier to assign meaningful topics to the query.

6. CONCLUSION

We have presented a novel LTR model that combines latent topic information with maximum margin learning in a unified way. In our model the latent topic representation is directly regularized with a pairwise maximum margin constraint, which leads to more informative latent topics. We have conducted extensive experiments using benchmark collections and have shown clear improvements over the state-of-the-art comparative methods. The main strength of our model stems from the fact that topic similarity is computed in the regularized latent topic space. This allows for a direct interplay between the pairwise maximum margin classifier and the topic model, which ensures that the topics which are learned are maximally informative for the prediction of labels. As our experiments show, such an integrated approach outperforms the existing two-stage de-coupled approach to incorporating latent topics for in LTR models. One interesting line for future work would be to look at different LTR tasks such as temporal LTR, for which the use of temporal topic models seems promising.

7. REFERENCES

[1] S. Agarwal and M. Collins. Maximum margin ranking algorithms for information retrieval. In *ECIR*, pages 332–343. 2010.

[2] J. Allan. HARD track overview in TREC 2003 high accuracy retrieval from documents. Technical report, DTIC Document, 2005.

[3] N. Asadi and J. Lin. Effectiveness/efficiency tradeoffs for candidate generation in multi-stage retrieval architectures. In *SIGIR*, pages 997–1000, 2013.

[4] B. Bai, J. Weston, D. Grangier, R. Collobert, K. Sadamasa, Y. Qi, O. Chapelle, and K. Weinberger. Learning to rank with (a lot of) word features. *IR*, 13(3):291–314, 2010.

[5] J. Bian, X. Li, F. Li, Z. Zheng, and H. Zha. Ranking specialization for web search: A divide-and-conquer approach by using topical RankSVM. In *WWW*, pages 131–140. ACM, 2010.

[6] D. M. Blei, A. Y. Ng, and M. I. Jordan. Latent Dirichlet Allocation. *JMLR*, 3:993–1022, 2003.

[7] Y. Cao, J. Xu, T.-Y. Liu, H. Li, Y. Huang, and H.-W. Hon. Adapting ranking SVM to document retrieval. In *SIGIR*, pages 186–193, 2006.

[8] Z. Cao, T. Qin, T.-Y. Liu, M.-F. Tsai, and H. Li. Learning to rank: from pairwise approach to listwise approach. In *ICML*, pages 129–136, 2007.

[9] V. Dang, M. Bendersky, and W. B. Croft. Two-stage learning to rank for Information Retrieval. In *ECIR*, pages 423–434. 2013.

[10] D. Duan, Y. Li, R. Li, R. Zhang, and A. Wen. RankTopic: Ranking based topic modeling. In *ICDM*, pages 211–220, 2012.

[11] K. Ganchev, J. Graça, J. Gillenwater, and B. Taskar. Posterior regularization for structured latent variable models. *JMLR*, 11:2001–2049, 2010.

[12] J. Gao, K. Toutanova, and W.-t. Yih. Clickthrough-based latent semantic models for Web search. In *SIGIR*, pages 675–684, 2011.

[13] W. Gao and P. Yang. Democracy is good for ranking: Towards multi-view rank learning and adaptation in web search. In *WSDM*, pages 63–72, 2014.

[14] R. Herbrich, T. Graepel, and K. Obermayer. Large margin rank boundaries for ordinal regression. *NIPS*, pages 115–132, 1999.

[15] J. Jagarlamudi and J. Gao. Modeling click-through based word-pairs for Web search. In *SIGIR*, pages 483–492, 2013.

[16] Q. Jiang, J. Zhu, M. Sun, and E. P. Xing. Monte Carlo methods for maximum margin supervised topic models. In *NIPS*, pages 1592–1600, 2012.

[17] H. Lai, Y. Pan, C. Liu, L. Lin, and J. Wu. Sparse learning-to-rank via an efficient primal-dual algorithm. *IEEE Transactions on Computers,*, 62(6):1221–1233, 2013.

[18] H. Li and J. Xu. Semantic matching in search. *FTIR*, 8, 2013.

[19] T.-Y. Liu. *Learning to rank for Information Retrieval.* Springer, 2011.

[20] C. Macdonald, R. L. Santos, and I. Ounis. The whens and hows of learning to rank for Web search. *IR*, 16(5):584–628, 2013.

[21] J. D. Mcauliffe and D. M. Blei. Supervised topic models. In *NIPS*, pages 121–128, 2008.

[22] R. Nallapati. Discriminative models for Information Retrieval. In *SIGIR*, pages 64–71, 2004.

[23] S. Niu, Y. Lan, J. Guo, X. Cheng, and X. Geng. What makes data robust: A data analysis in learning to rank. In *SIGIR*, pages 1191–1194, 2014.

[24] T. Qin, T.-Y. Liu, J. Xu, and H. Li. LETOR: A benchmark collection for research on learning to rank for Information Retrieval. *IR*, 13(4):346–374, 2010.

[25] T. Qin, X.-D. Zhang, M.-F. Tsai, D.-S. Wang, T.-Y. Liu, and H. Li. Query-level loss functions for Information Retrieval. *IPM*, 44(2):838–855, 2008.

[26] M. Tan, T. Xia, L. Guo, and S. Wang. Direct optimization of ranking measures for learning to rank models. In *KDD*, pages 856–864, 2013.

[27] J. Tang, N. Liu, J. Yan, Y. Shen, S. Guo, B. Gao, S. Yan, and M. Zhang. Learning to rank audience for behavioral targeting in display ads. In *CIKM*, pages 605–610, 2011.

[28] Y. W. Teh. Dirichlet process. In *Encyclopedia of Machine Learning*, pages 280–287. 2010.

[29] K. Vorontsov and A. Potapenko. Additive regularization of topic models. *ML*, pages 1–21, 2014.

[30] X. Wei and W. B. Croft. LDA-based document models for ad-hoc retrieval. In *SIGIR*, pages 178–185, 2006.

[31] F. Xia, T.-Y. Liu, J. Wang, W. Zhang, and H. Li. Listwise approach to learning to rank: Theory and algorithm. In *ICML*, pages 1192–1199, 2008.

[32] X. Yi and J. Allan. Evaluating topic models for Information Retrieval. In *CIKM*, pages 1431–1432, 2008.

[33] A. Zellner. Optimal information processing and Bayes's theorem. *The American Statistician*, 42(4):278–280, 1988.

[34] J. Zhu, A. Ahmed, and E. P. Xing. MedLDA: maximum margin supervised topic models. *JMLR*, 13(1):2237–2278, 2012.

[35] J. Zhu, N. Chen, and E. P. Xing. Bayesian inference with posterior regularization and applications to infinite latent SVMs. *JMLR*, 15:1799–1847, 2014.

Collaborating between Local and Global Learning for Distributed Online Multiple Tasks

Xin Jin[1,2], Ping Luo[1], Fuzhen Zhuang[1], Jia He[1,3] and Qing He[1]

[1]Key Lab of Intelligent Information Processing of Chinese Academy of Sciences (CAS), Institute of Computing Technology, CAS, Beijing 100190, jinxin11@huawei.com, luop@ict.ac.cn, {zhuangfz, hej, heq}@ics.ict.ac.cn

[2]Central Software Institute, Huawei Technologies Co. Ltd., Beijing 100085, China

[3]University of Chinese Academy of Sciences, Beijing 100049, China

ABSTRACT

This paper studies the novel learning scenarios of Distributed Online Multi-tasks (DOM), where the learning individuals with continuously arriving data are distributed separately and meanwhile they need to learn individual models collaboratively. It has three characteristics: distributed learning, online learning and multi-task learning. It is motivated by the emerging applications of wearable devices, which aim to provide intelligent monitoring services, such as health emergency alarming and movement recognition.

To the best of our knowledge, no previous work has been done for this kind of problems. Thus, in this paper a collaborative learning scheme is proposed for this problem. Specifically, it performs *local learning* and *global learning* alternately. First, each client performs online learning using the increasing data locally. Then, DOM switches to global learning on the server side when some condition is triggered by clients. Here, an asynchronous online multi-task learning method is proposed for global learning. In this step, only this client's model, which triggers the global learning, is updated with the support of the *difficult* local data instances and the other clients' models. The experiments from 4 applications show that the proposed method of global learning can improve local learning significantly. DOM framework is effective, since it can share knowledge among distributed tasks and obtain better models than learning them separately. It is also communication efficient, which only requires the clients send a small portion of raw data to the server.

Categories and Subject Descriptors

I.2.6 [**Artificial Intelligence**]: Learning—*Machine Learning*

Keywords

multi-task learning; online learning; distributed tasks;

CIKM'15, October 19-23, 2015, Melbourne, VIC, Australia.
Copyright 2015 ACM. ISBN 978-1-4503-3794-6/15/10 ...$15.00.
DOI: http://dx.doi.org/10.1145/2806416.2806553.

1. INTRODUCTION

Many real world problems include a number of related learning tasks, for which multi-task learning (MTL) [5, 9, 10, 29] methods are favorable, as they can learn multiple related tasks together so as to improve the performance of each task relative to learning them separately. In certain situations, the data are continually arriving, and online multi-task learning methods [6, 30] are useful to efficiently learn these data samples. All these methods require that the data are collected at a centralized place, so that a central learner can be used to learn all the tasks' prediction models. However, data and tasks are distributed on isolated clients in many problems. At the same time, data are continually arriving, which make them more challenging.

The emerging applications of wearable devices motivate these tasks. Wearable devices are becoming more and more prevalent these days. By various sensors these devices continuously collect the data from people and then provide some intelligent services, such as health monitor, emergency alarming, and movement recognition. The key component on wearable devices is the prediction model for these monitor services. However, the learning of the prediction models should consider the following challenges. First, the sensors on wearable devices usually have high sampling frequency, and the local data may increase dramatically. Thus, we need the online learning method for these models. Second, since different person may have different activity patterns, a distinct model should be learned for each user. Additionally, for the complex tasks the local model should leverage the knowledge from other devices for better prediction performance. Thus, the multi-task learning scheme should be adopted. Finally, since all these devices are distributed separately, we need to carefully consider the communication overhead involved in the collaborative learning due to the limited communication bandwidth and the shortage of device power.

By combining all these challenges, we actually face the learning scenarios of Distributed Online Multi-tasks (DOM), where the learning individuals with continuously arriving data are distributed separately and meanwhile they need to learn individual models collaboratively. Obviously, traditional centralized multi-task learning methods [5, 9, 10, 29] are not suitable for these problems since they require that all the data be collected to a central place and then do the learning in batch mode. Previous online multi-task learning methods [6, 30] can not be used for these problems because in the learning process of these methods, one task must use the raw training samples from all the other tasks, which is not feasible in our problem. Distributed online multi-task learning problems has also been studied [15], but the main focus of Dinuzzo et al. [15] is how to divided the overall computation into each client, so that the server can do learning more efficiently. The communication cost is too high for real distributed applications, because each client should send all their data to the server. Then, the server has to send all the data from all the clients to each client.

To solve this problem, we assume that a global server exists for coordinating the collaborative learning, and the clients can only communicate with this server. In this client-server setting, a collaborative scheme with local learning and global learning alternatively is proposed. First, it includes the local online learning on clients. Each client can learn from the local data and obtain a preliminary prediction model. Second, on the server side, to efficiently incorporate knowledge from multiple clients, an asynchronous multi-task learning method is proposed. Specifically, only the client's model, which triggers the global learning, is updated with the support of the *difficult* local data instances and the other clients' models. Compared to previous methods, this asynchronous global learning strategy is more efficient for computation and economical for communication. In these two alternate steps, local learning depends on global learning to obtain knowledge of other related clients, while global learning is based on the results of local learning to reduce the amount of raw training samples needed, which reduces communication cost.

The main contributions of this paper can be summarized as follows.

1. *Problem Definition:* we introduce a novel Distributed Online Multi-tasks (DOM) learning problem, which has three prominent characteristics.

2. *Framework:* a collaborative learning scheme is proposed, which performs *local learning* and *global learning* alternately.

3. *Algorithm:* an asynchronous online multi-task learning method is proposed for global learning, which is more suitable for DOM problem.

4. *Experiments:* it is tested on four real-world problems to show the effectiveness of the DOM framework.

2. PROBLEM DEFINITION AND PRELIMINARIES

Notations. In this paper, $[N : M]$ $(M > N)$ denotes a set of integers in the range of N to M inclusively. $\|\cdot\|$ represents the Frobenius norm of a matrix. I_l denotes the $l \times l$ identity matrix. Some specific notations used in the paper are summarized in Table 1.

Table 1: Notations Used in the Paper

Notation	Description
T	The number of clients (tasks)
n_t	Number of labeled training samples in client t
$x_{t,i}$	d dimension feature vector for the i-th sample in client t
$y_{t,i}$	Class label of the i-th sample in client t
d	Dimension of the feature vector for data samples
w_t	Weight vector represents the prediction model for client t
k	Clients' buffer size
l	Maximum number of samples a client can send to the server in one interaction
D_t	The collection of representative samples client t sent to the server in one interaction
A	A $T \times T$ symmetric matrix represents the relations between different tasks
a_t	The t-th column of A, represents the relations between the t-th task and other tasks

The Distributed Online Multi-task (DOM) learning problem can be formally described as follows. Let T be the number of clients (number of tasks), they are connected to a server, although different clients are not connected directly. For each client $t \in [1 : T]$, there are n_t data examples $\{(x_{t,i}, y_{t,i})\}_{i\in[1:n_t]}$ available, where $x_{t,i} \in \mathbb{R}^d$ represents the feature vector for the i-th example in the t-th task while $y_{t,i}$ is its label. The dimension of the feature vector is d. For simplicity, this paper only considers binary classification problems, i.e., $y_{t,i} \in \{-1, 1\}$. These data come in sequentially in time, i.e., the i-th example arrives before the $(i + 1)$-th example. This is a distributed learning problem, because each client does not have access to the data from other clients, and the clients can not transmit all their data to the server due to communication cost and privacy issues. The goal is to progressively train a distinct model with the continually arrived examples for each client, as different clients have distinct patterns. However, because these clients are related to each other, we need to devise a communication efficient method to share knowledge among them to obtain better models. Clients and tasks have the same meaning in this paper and they are used interchangeably in the paper.

3. OVERALL FRAMEWORK

3.1 Problem Analysis

In this paper, a simple form of linear predictor is used. The goal is to learn a distinct model $f_t(x) = w_t^\top x$ for each client t, which is a linear separator function parameterized by weight vector $w_t \in \mathbb{R}^d$.

After receiving the representative data and the local model for a client, the server will do global multi-task learning. Unlike in the centralized online multi-task learning [28], in the method proposed in this paper, the server only learns and updates the model for this client in this learning step while keeping other clients' models unchanged. This asynchronous learning method for multiple tasks has several advantages. First, only computing the new model for a single task each time can reduce the computation cost and make the algorithm more efficient. Second, in this way, multiple clients are more loosely coupled with each other. Each client only takes advantage of other clients models, not the frequently changing or even noisy training samples, which keep the learning process more robust. Third, to guarantee the models on clients and server are consistent, updating one model each time means that the server only need to send one model back to a client, which is more communication efficient. Also, clients request the server to do global learning asynchronously, so it is very natural to use this asynchronous update method.

3.2 Proposed Framework

The overall framework for the distributed online multi-task learning problem is shown in Figure 1. Clients make request to do global learning, and the server will send the updated models back to clients. The explicit interactions between clients and the server are shown in Figure 2. The communication flow between clients and the server is represented by black dashed arrows. The main works done by clients and the server are described in the following.

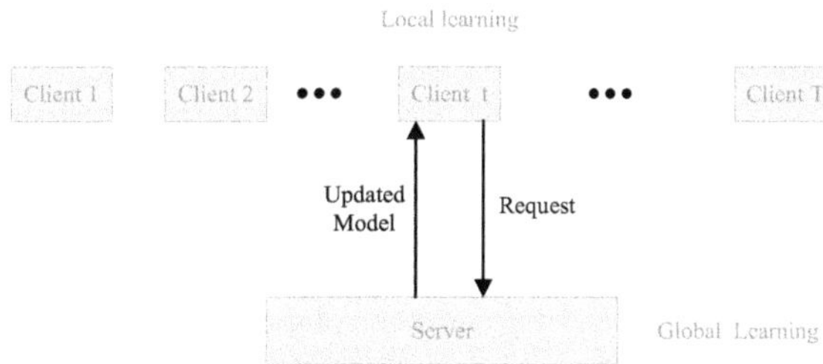

Figure 1: The Overall Framework for the Distributed Online Learning Problem

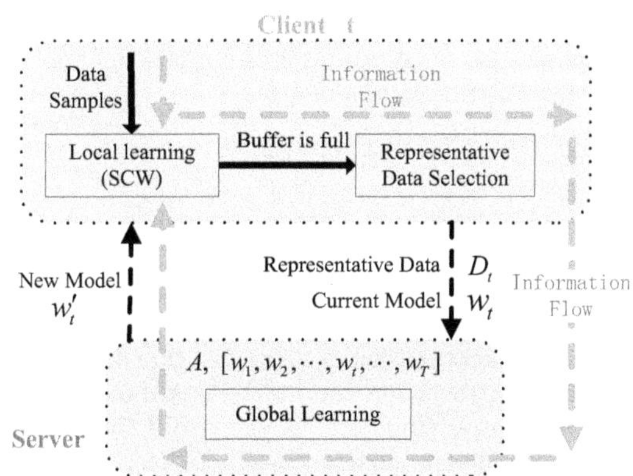

Figure 2: Communication between Client t and The Server

Learning on Clients. In this part, the simple, fast and state-of-the-art online learning method soft confidence-weighted classifier (SCW) [31] can be used by clients. Using this method, the learned model can be represented by a weight vector w_t, which is convenient to transmit between clients and the server. Although the data arrive continually in each client, to facilitate the manipulation of the data transmission process, clients interact with the server by dealing with the data block-by-block at the clients. It is supposed that each client contains a buffer with size k, which can store a small number of samples. After a whole block of samples are learned by the client, this client will obtain a newly updated prediction model. Then, to request the server to do global multi-task learning for it, a client need to send some representative data D_t and its current model w_t to the server. Usually, it is restricted that a maximum number l of samples can be sent for each block learning process.

Learning on The Server. For the server, it keeps all the clients' latest models $\{w_t\}_{t\in[1:T]}$ and their relations A. A is a $T \times T$ matrix, each of its element $a_{i,j}$ represents the correlation between the i-th and j-th tasks. We propose an asynchronous multi-task learning method for server. Upon request by a client, the server will conduct global online multi-task learning for this specific client, i.e., update the model for this client while keep other clients' models unchanged. The multi-task learning method should produce a linear prediction model, which the server will send back to the client to help client's later local learning process.

In summary, in our framework the local learning on clients and global learning on the server work collaboratively to improve the performance of distributed online multi-task learning problem, and efficiently alleviate the privacy-preserving concern and communication cost.

4. GLOBAL LEARNING ON THE SERVER

4.1 Global Multi-task Learning

Recall that the server maintains the latest models $\{w_t\}_{t\in[1:T]}$ for all the clients. When a client requests the server to do the global learning for it, it will send its new model w_t and some representative data $D_t = \{(x_{t,i}, y_{t,i})\}_{i\in[1:l_t]}$ to the server, where l_t is the number of samples.

To do online multi-task learning, it is important to correlate multiple tasks to let them collaborate with each other in the learning process. Usually, a correlation matrix $A \in R^{T\times T}$ is used to represent the relations between different tasks. Previous online multi-task learning method assumes that prior knowledge about task relations is available in the form of correlation matrix A [7]. In this paper, the more flexible way to adaptively learn the correlation matrix in the learning process is adopted. Also, different from previous works, the models for different tasks are updated asynchronously. Each time, it only updates the model for the client that requests the server to do the global learning. This update strategy is more computation efficient. Different clients only loosely couple with each other, which makes the algorithm more robust. In this paper, it is assumed that the correlation matrix A can have both positive and negative values, which means it can deal with both positively and negatively related tasks. The t-th column of A is denoted as $a_t = [a_{1,t}, a_{2,t}, \ldots, a_{T,t}]^\top$, where $a_{j,t}$ represents the relation of the j-th and t-th tasks. To sequentially learn each sample $(x_{t,i}, y_{t,i})$ for task t, the optimization problem is as follows:

$$\min_{w_t', a_t'} \left(-\sum_{j=1}^{T} a_{j,t}' {w_t'}^\top w_j \right) + \beta l(w_t', (x_{t,i}, y_{t,i})) + \gamma \|w_t'\|^2$$

$$\Rightarrow \min_{w_t', a_t'} -{w_t'}^\top W a_t' + \beta l(w_t', (x_{t,i}, y_{t,i})) + \gamma \|w_t'\|^2 \quad (1)$$

$$\text{subject to:} \quad a_{t,t}' = 1, \ \sum_{\substack{j=1 \\ j\neq t}}^{T} (a_{j,t}')^2 = \eta$$

where w_t' is the new model after update, a_t' is the updated correlations, the matrix $W = [w_1, w_2, \ldots, w_T]$, $l(w_t', (x_{t,i}, y_{t,i}))$ is the hinge loss function defined as follows:

$$l(w_t') = \begin{cases} 0 & \text{if} \ \ y_{t,i} {w_t'}^\top x_{t,i} \geq 1 \\ 1 - y_{t,i} {w_t'}^\top x_{t,i} & \text{otherwise} \end{cases} \quad (2)$$

The first term in the optimization problem (1) correlates multiple clients' models and let one task take advantage of other tasks. It implies that when $a_{j,t}'$ is large, the two tasks are strongly correlated and we expect ${w_t'}^\top w_j$ will also has a large value. $l(w_t', (x_{t,i}, y_{t,i}))$ is the hinge loss function to guarantee the correctness of the method. The last term is a regularization term to control the complexity of the model. The constraint $a_{t,t}' = 1$ suggests that each task is positively related with itself. Constraint $\sum_{j=1, j\neq t}^{T} (a_{j,t}')^2 = \eta$ is used to restrict the absolute values of the correlations between this client and other clients. These correlations are used in the optimization problem and their absolute values will determine how the other clients can influence a certain client that are currently being learned. The effect of other clients' models can be controlled by setting different values for η. The weight vector γ controls the complexity of the model. In this paper, it is fixed as $\gamma = \sum_{j=1}^{T} |a'_{j,t}|$. Initial value of the correlation matrix is set as $A = I_T$, which means at start we assume different tasks are irrelevant to avoid any error bias.

Simultaneously optimizing w'_t and a'_t in problem (1) is difficult, so we alternately optimize one variable while the other is fixed. Denote the objective function in problem (1) as F_t, when the loss is larger than zero, the objective function's derivative with respect to w'_t is:

$$\frac{\partial F_t}{\partial w'_t} = -W a'_t - \beta y_{t,i} x_{t,i} + 2\gamma w'_t. \tag{3}$$

When a'_t are fixed, and let the derivative in Eq.(3) equal to zero, the following solution can be obtained:

$$w'_t = \frac{\beta y_{t,i} x_{t,i} + W a'_t}{2\gamma}. \tag{4}$$

When w'_t is given, the optimization problem (1) becomes the following constrained optimization problem:

$$\min_{a'_t} -{w'_t}^{\top} W a'_t \tag{5}$$

$$\text{subject to:} \quad a'_{t,t} = 1, \ \sum_{\substack{j=1 \\ j \neq t}}^{T} (a'_{j,t})^2 = \eta$$

It can be solved using Lagrange method, which gives the solution:

$$a'_{j,t} = \frac{{w'_t}^{\top} w_j}{\sqrt{\sum_{\substack{j=1 \\ j\neq t}}^{T} \left(\left({w'_t}^{\top} w_j\right)^2 / \eta \right)}} \tag{6}$$

4.2 Communication Overhead

When a client requests the server to do the global multi-task learning, it will send its current model and some representative samples to the server. Then, server will send the newly updated model back to the client. So, in one interaction, a client sends one prediction model and l representative samples to the server, and the server sends a model back to the client. The communication cost in one interaction is $l+2$ vectors, each vector has the same size as a data sample. The total communication cost for the T clients and the server in the overall learning process is:

$$\sum_{t=1}^{T} \lceil \frac{n_t}{k} \rceil (l+2) \tag{7}$$

where $\lceil x \rceil$ represents rounding the number x to the nearest integer towards infinity, n_t is the number of training samples for task t, k is the buffer size. It can be seen that the communication cost can be easily controlled by changing the values of k and l.

In fact, in the distributed online learning scenario, even if the clients transmit all their data to the server and server do centralized online multi-task learning, the server should also repeatedly send the learned models to clients, so that clients can use the up-to-date models for prediction. So, the model transmission is unavoidable, and we mainly consider how to reduce the raw data transmitted to the server.

5. LOCAL LEARNING ON CLIENTS

Data are continually arriving at the clients, so the clients must be able to do the single task online learning. Also, to take advantage of the models of other clients, it should interact with the server to exchange knowledge among them. These interactions will cause communication cost and affect the learning process of the server and clients, which need special attentions.

5.1 Local Single Task Online Learning

One work of the clients is to do the local single task online learning to incrementally learn the classification models. In this part, the simple, fast and state-of-the-art online learning method soft confidence-weighted classifier (SCW) [31] is used. For each client t, SCW assumes a Gaussian distribution of weights with mean vector $w_t \in \mathbb{R}^d$ and covariance matrix $\Sigma_t \in \mathbb{R}^{d \times d}$. The mean w_t corresponds to the linear classifier as described in Section 3. When a new sample $(x_{t,i}, y_{t,i})$ comes in, SCW updates the model by solving the following optimization problem:

$$\min_{w'_t, \Sigma'_t} D_{KL}\left(N(w'_t, \Sigma'_t) \| N(w_t, \Sigma_t)\right) +$$
$$C \max\left(0, \phi\sqrt{x_{t,i}^{\top} \Sigma'_t x_{t,i}} - y_{t,i} {w'_t}^{\top} x_{t,i}\right), \tag{8}$$

where ϕ controls the confidence of each update, and C balances between conservativeness and aggressiveness. D_{KL} means the Kullback-Leibler divergence. Through minimizing the divergence between the newly estimated weight distribution and the previous one, it can avoid the parameters change dramatically in each update and keep the algorithm robust against noises. The second term guarantees the correctness of the algorithm.

This optimization problem has closed-form solution, which is expressed as follows:

$$w'_t = w_t + \alpha_t y_{t,i} \Sigma_t x_{t,i}, \quad \Sigma'_t = \Sigma_t - \beta_t \Sigma_t x_{t,i}^{\top} x_{t,i} \Sigma_t \tag{9}$$

where the updating coefficients are as follows:

$$\alpha_t = \min\{C, \max\{0, \frac{1}{\nu_t \zeta}(-m_t \psi + \sqrt{m_t^2 \frac{\phi^4}{4} + \nu_t \phi^2 \zeta})\}\} \tag{10}$$

$$\beta_t = \frac{\alpha_t \phi}{\sqrt{u_t} + \nu_t \alpha_t \phi} \tag{11}$$

where $u_t = \frac{1}{4}(-\alpha_t \nu_t \phi + \sqrt{\alpha_t^2 \nu_t^2 \phi^2 + 4\nu_t})^2$, $\nu_t = x_{t,i}^{\top} \Sigma_t x_{t,i}$, $m_t = y_{t,i} {w_t}^{\top} x_{t,i}$, $\phi = \Phi^{-1}(\eta)$, $\psi = 1 + \frac{\phi^2}{2}$ and $\zeta = 1 + \phi^2$. In this paper, the parameters for SCW are fixed as $C = 1$, $\eta = 0.6$ and $\phi = \Phi^{-1}(\eta)$.

SCW have many advantages. SCW improves over the original confidence-weighted (CW) [13] algorithm by adding the capability to handle the non-separable cases, and improves over adaptive regularization of weights (AROW) [14] by adding the adaptive margin property [31]. SCW also enjoys the large margin training and confidence weighting properties. It can achieve better predictive accuracy and is more computational efficient [31].

5.2 Trigger Conditions for Global Learning

Local learner SCW can obtain a prediction model represented by w_t and a covariance matrix $\Sigma_t \in \mathbb{R}^{d \times d}$ that captures the relations between different features. Although Σ_t is beneficial for the later learning process, it can not be transmitted to the server due to its large size. To simplify the interaction process, suppose each client has a buffer of size k. A client interacts with the server when its buffer is full. In each interaction, the client will select at most l representative samples from the buffer and send them to the server. The samples must be carefully selected so that the most useful samples are selected. In this paper, the samples that have the largest hinge loss are selected, as they are the most difficult for local model to discriminate. This trigger condition for global learning is called *Regular Trigger Condition* and it is the default trigger condition used in the paper. Although global learning is triggered when a client has learned a certain number of samples (buffer size), our DOM framework makes no special requirement that multiple tasks must be synchronized when do global learning. Since the data arrive at different nodes with different speeds, the clients may trigger the global learning for updating its own model at different time points. Thus, it is actually an asynchronous process.

After receiving the updated model, this client will take the newly learned model by the server as its current model and it is the starting point for its later learning. So, the server and clients must use the same prediction model formulation and they should be compatible with each other.

At the initial stage of the learning process, the models clients learned may not be so accurate. In this case, letting these clients learn from each other could even be harmful. So, in the beginning, a client will learn a certain number of samples before sending its model to the server to do the initial global learning. When it sends model to server, the model is at least a weak classifier.

Adaptive Trigger Condition. In the above, the trigger condition for global learning is easy to understand with clear analysis on communication cost. Compared with this Regular Trigger Condition, we can also dynamically trigger the global learning based on the number of misclassified instances by local learning. In other words, when more errors occur in local learning, we trigger the global learning more frequently. Specifically, client can store the samples that are misclassified by the local model in its buffer. When error number reaches a certain number l', client will send these l' samples to the server for global learning. We have tested the performance of this Adaptive Trigger Condition on all the datasets. However, the results are similar to the results with Regular Trigger Condition in terms of model accuracy and communication overhead. So, only the results with Regular Trigger Condition are given in Experiments section.

6. EXPERIMENTS

In this section, we evaluate the effectiveness of the proposed algorithm for the Distributed Online Multi-task (DOM) learning problem.

6.1 Datasets

Four real world datasets are used to test our algorithm, two of them are text datasets and the other two are image datasets. Some statistics of the datasets are summarized in Table 2, where n_p and n_n denote the number of positive and negative samples in each task, respectively. n_t is the number of labeled training samples in each task, and the rest samples are used as testing set.

Table 2: Description of the Datasets

Dataset	T	d	n_p	n_n	n_t
Email Spam	15	3000	200	200	250
Sentiment	4	3000	1000	1000	1000
NUS-WIDE Object	12	636	$327 \sim 481$	$321 \sim 951$	500
Imagenet	9	1000	$1400 \sim 2086$	$1117 \sim 1444$	1000

Email Spam: The first dataset is the ECML/PKDD 2006 email spam dataset [3]. It includes 15 persons' emails, each person has 400 emails, which form 15 tasks (clients). These emails are labeled as spam or not. The goal is to learn a distinct prediction model for each person to classify emails. The *tf-idf* weighting scheme is adopted to represent the samples. Also, we have normalized the features to ensure that each sample's feature vector has norm 1.

Sentiment: The Multi-Domain Sentiment Dataset contains product reviews taken from Amazon.com from four product types (tasks), namely, books, dvd, electronics and kitchen [4]. The reviews are split into two classes, positive and negative. The goal is to learn a distinct prediction model for each product type. The features used are *tf-idf* features.

NUS-WIDE Object: In NUS-WIDE Object web image database [11], each image is annotated by objects such as "cars","dog", and etc. We select the images only belonging to one class. Similarly, we have normalized the features to ensure that each sample's feature vector has norm 1. We randomly select 7 classes that have not too few samples to form 12 tasks, the goal is to classify different classes. The tasks are shown in Table 3.

Table 3: Tasks for NUS-WIDE Object Dataset

Task	T1	T2	T3	T4	T5	T6
Positive Class	cars	statue	leaf	cars	statue	leaf
Negative Class	elk	elk	elk	dog	dog	dog
Task	T7	T8	T9	T10	T11	T12
Positive Class	cars	statue	leaf	cars	statue	leaf
Negative Class	horses	horses	horses	cat	cat	cat

Imagenet: ImageNet[1] is an image database organized according to the WordNet hierarchy. For the images, the 1000-dimension bag-of-word representations [24] based on raw SIFT [25] features provided by the ImageNet are used. We have normalized the features to ensure that each sample's feature vector has norm 1. We randomly select 6 class to form 9 tasks, the goal is to classify different classes. The tasks are shown in Table 4.

Table 4: Tasks for Imagenet Dataset

Task	T1	T2	T3
Positive Class	leopard	lion	tiger
Negative Class	persimmon	persimmon	persimmon
Task	T4	T5	T6
Positive Class	leopard	lion	tiger
Negative Class	orange	orange	orange
Task	T7	T8	T9
Positive Class	leopard	lion	tiger
Negative Class	lemon	lemon	lemon

6.2 Experimental Settings

Previous multi-task learning methods cannot be used in the situation that data are distributed on different clients and at the same time, new data are continually arriving and real-time online learning is necessary. So, we compare our algorithm with the single task online learning algorithm SCW, which learns each task separately. This algorithm is

[1]http://image-net.org/download-features

also the local algorithm each client uses in our distributed online multi-task learning (DOM) algorithm.

OMT. Furthermore, we compare DOM algorithm with the centralized online multi-task learning (OMT) algorithm [7]. This algorithm requires the prior knowledge of task correlations, so the pairwise distance interaction matrix given in Eq.(4) in its original paper [7] are used. Although OMT collects all the data to a cental place and each task have access to the data from all the other tasks, it is not necessarily better than DOM which contains two collaborative learners.

MTRL. Multi-task relationship learning (MTRL) [34] is a centralized multi-task learning algorithm. It is not an online algorithm. Since in this algorithm, all the tasks have access to the data from all the other tasks, and they stored all the data from beginning to do learning in the batch mode, it is supposed that it can obtain better results than DOM algorithm. It is used as an baseline to shown whether DOM can obtain comparable results to MTRL algorithm. We have used cross validation methods to select the parameters λ_1 and λ_2 used in MTRL algorithm.

In these experiments, we want to show the effectiveness of DOM algorithm and how the parameters affect the performance and communication overhead. The effectiveness can be shown in two aspects. One is that whether DOM is better than only using SCW for each task separately and whether DOM obtains comparable or even better results than OMT and MTRL algorithms which require all the data be collected to a same place. The other one is that, within DOM algorithm, whether global learning can help improve the results of local learning.

In each experiment, we randomly held out a number of samples for testing. The remaining data are used as training set. To reduce the effect of randomness, for each dataset, 5 random permutations of the samples are used to test the algorithms, and the mean results are given. For comparison, we test the single task online leaning algorithm SCW and OMT algorithm at regular intervals of buffer size, and calculate the accuracy of its current model for the testing data.

At the start of the learning process of our multi-task learning, clients learn at least 30 training samples before requesting the server to do global learning. That is because global learning is the most beneficial when each client's model is not so bad. For all the problems, we set $\beta = 0.01$, the buffer size $k = 20$ and select $l = 2$ (10%) samples to send to the server in each interaction. η is set as 0.01 for Sentiment dataset and 0.001 for other datasets.

Table 5: Classification Accuracy for Four Problems

(a) NUS-WIDE Object

Task	T1	T2	T3	T4	T5	T6
SCW only	0.866	0.709	**0.842**	0.829	0.753	0.820
OMT	0.835	0.667	0.819	0.816	0.739	0.802
DOM	**0.874**	**0.720**	0.838	**0.847**	**0.773**	**0.839**
Task	T7	T8	T9	T10	T11	T12
SCW only	0.815	0.700	**0.857**	0.841	0.725	0.813
OMT	0.804	0.697	0.807	0.826	0.707	0.793
DOM	**0.833**	**0.728**	0.848	**0.849**	**0.741**	**0.818**

(b) Email Spam

Task	T1	T2	T3	T4	T5
SCW only	0.919	0.944	0.952	0.901	0.909
OMT	0.908	0.941	0.952	0.896	0.892
DOM	**0.959**	**0.963**	**0.975**	**0.932**	**0.928**
Task	T6	T7	T8	T9	T10
SCW only	0.928	0.820	0.907	0.931	0.888
OMT	0.925	0.847	0.905	0.912	0.911
DOM	**0.953**	**0.873**	**0.931**	**0.959**	**0.936**
Task	T11	T12	T13	T14	T15
SCW only	0.905	0.888	0.944	0.893	0.913
OMT	0.915	0.899	0.937	0.847	0.911
DOM	**0.931**	**0.943**	**0.969**	**0.904**	**0.949**

(c) Imagenet

Task	T1	T2	T3	T4	T5
SCW only	0.919	0.926	0.925	0.919	0.910
OMT	0.920	0.888	0.918	0.922	0.911
DOM	**0.929**	**0.937**	**0.936**	**0.930**	**0.931**
Task	T6	T7	T8	T9	
SCW only	0.922	0.930	0.927	0.930	
OMT	0.914	0.915	0.913	0.922	
DOM	**0.935**	**0.936**	**0.939**	**0.943**	

(d) Sentiment

Task	T1	T2	T3	T4
SCW only	0.781	0.805	0.826	0.843
OMT	0.734	0.771	0.789	0.804
DOM	**0.806**	**0.820**	**0.855**	**0.863**

6.3 Experiment Results

The number of training samples n_t for each data set is shown in Table 2. The mean classification accuracy for 5 runs are displayed in Table 5. It can be seen that, for NUS-WIDE Object dataset, for 10 out of 12 tasks, our DOM algorithm obtains improved results compared to learning each task separately. For every task in the other three datasets, DOM algorithm always obtains improved results compared to learn each task separately. So, DOM algorithm is superior to SCW algorithms, which demonstrates that our algorithm can effectively share knowledge among multiple tasks and obtain better prediction models. It is interesting to see that our DOM algorithm is also better than centralized online multi-task algorithm OMT, which require all the data be collected at a same place. The reason maybe that: (a) OMT requires prior knowledge about task correlations, and a fixed interaction matrix given in Eq.(4) in its original paper [7] may not reflect the real task correlations. (b) Our DOM algorithm contains two collaborative learners, which is more robust.

To show the incremental online learning process more explicitly, we display how the accuracy changes with the increasing training sample numbers in Figure 3. In DOM algorithm, if through sharing knowledge among multiple tasks, global learning obtains improved result compared to local learning in each interaction, a red bar is plotted, and its length represents the absolute accuracy improvement. Similarly, if global learning failed to improve the local learning results, a blue bar is plotted. Due to the space limit, for each problem, we only display the two tasks that DOM obtains the largest improvement and the smallest improvement compared to SCW algorithm according to the final results in Table 5. It can be seen that, for most tasks, our DOM algorithm is superior to the single task SCW algorithm in the whole learning process. In addition, these improvements are obtained at the cost of only transmitting 10% of the samples to the server, which is communication efficient. DOM is also better than the centralized online multi-task algorithm OMT, which require all the data be collected at a same place. MTRL is better than DOM in most cases. However, DOM can obtain comparable result with MTRL when the number of training samples is large. So, our alternately two-learner DOM algorithm is very effective for distributed multiple tasks. Global learning within DOM algorithm is very beneficial, as it can be seen that, in most cases, it can help improve the local models.

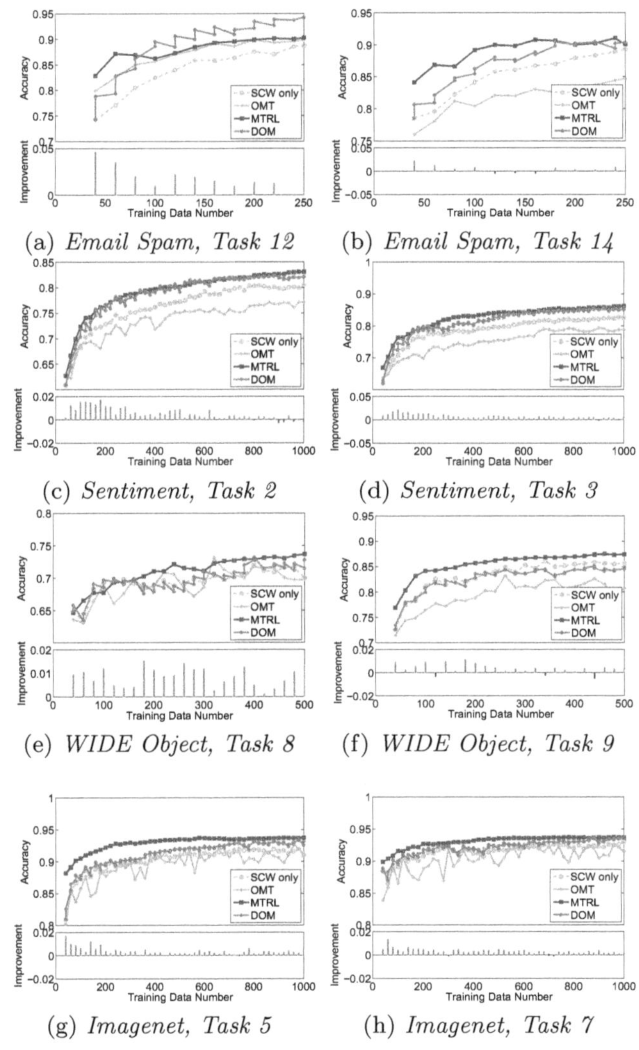

(a) *Email Spam, Task 12* (b) *Email Spam, Task 14*
(c) *Sentiment, Task 2* (d) *Sentiment, Task 3*
(e) *WIDE Object, Task 8* (f) *WIDE Object, Task 9*
(g) *Imagenet, Task 5* (h) *Imagenet, Task 7*

Figure 3: Classification Accuracy for Four Datasets

6.4 Parameter Analysis

Most of the parameters in DOM can be easily set, and only one parameter may need further tuning to obtain better results. Due to the space limitation, only the *results for the first task* in each problem are shown.

6.4.1 Number of Samples Sent to The Server

We first analyze the effect of parameter l, which is the number of samples that can be sent to the server in one interaction. The value of l controls the communication cost of our algorithm. We fix the buffer size k as 10, and set $l = \{1, 2, 4, 6, 8, 10\}$, respectively, which correspond to $\{10\%, 20\%, 40\%, 60\%, 80\%, 100\%\}$ of the data samples can be sent to the server. For each dataset, the first task's result is shown in Figure 4. It can be seen that, for Email Spam and Sentiment datasets, the accuracy slightly improves with the increasing number of l. The improvement is not so significant, especially when the number of total training samples is large. In this paper, to reduce communication cost, for all the datasets, only 10% of the data samples are sent to the server in each interaction.

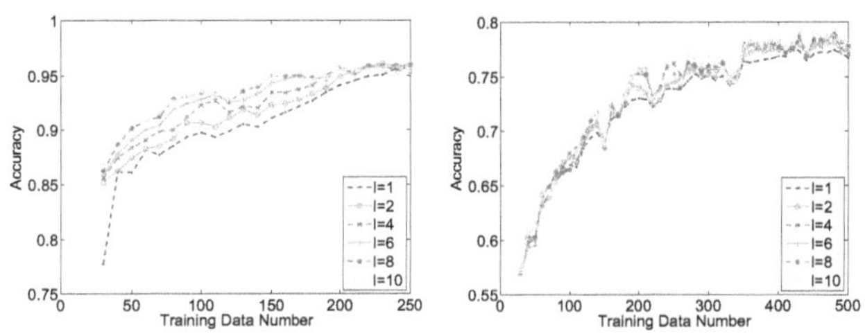

(a) *Email Spam* (b) *Sentiment*

Figure 4: Classification Accuracy against Different l

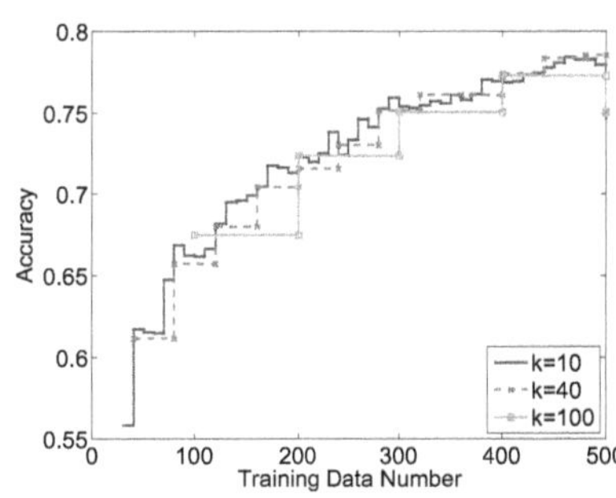

Figure 5: Different k for Sentiment Dataset

6.4.2 Buffer Size k

To analyze how buffer size influences the performance, we set $k = \{10, 40, 100\}$, respectively. We correspondingly set $l = 0.1k$. The results are given in Figure 5. In this comparison, since the value of l is fixed, the total number of data instances sent to the server is also fixed. Assume that the total number of training data on each client t is n_t. Then, the total number of instances sent to the server equals to $0.1n_t$. Each time a client only sends $0.1k$ instances to the server. Thus, the total number of times that a client send data equals to $\frac{n_t}{k}$ (This number is also the times for global learning triggered by client t). Therefore, the value of k actually controls the time when the data from clients arrive at the server. The smaller the value of k is, the earlier the data arrive at the server.

As shown in Figure 5, with different settings of k all the curves converge to the same value eventually. It indicates that the final model accuracy is not sensitive to k (since the total number of instances sent to the server is the same).

However, in the learning process smaller k outputs better performances since the data from the clients arrive at the server earlier to trigger the global learning.

6.4.3 Weighting Parameter β

Parameter β in Eq.(1) controls the importance of the training data. We set $\beta = \{1e-1, 1e-2, 1e-3, 1e-4, 1e-5, 1e-6\}$, respectively. The result are shown in Figure 6. It can be seen that, DOM algorithm's performance is relative stable with different β values used in this experiment, except for the NUS-WIDE Object dataset with $\beta = 0.1$. In this paper, we set $\beta = 0.01$ for all the datasets.

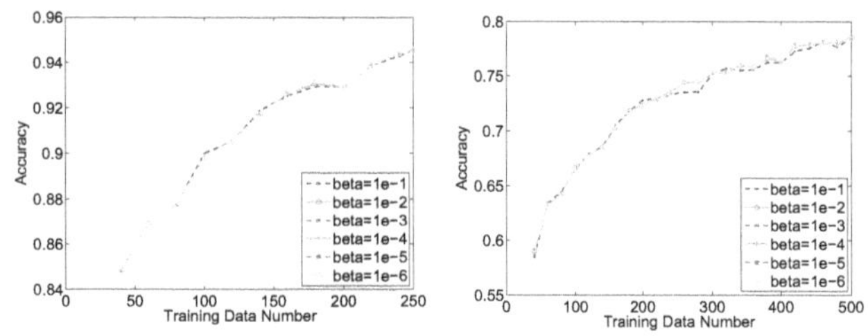

(a) *Email Spam* (b) *Sentiment*

Figure 6: Classification Accuracy against Different β

6.4.4 Constraint Parameter η

Parameter η in Eq.(1) constraint the correlations between different tasks and the influences of other tasks for a particular task. To analyze the effect of parameter η, we set $\eta = \{1e-1, 1e-2, 1e-3, 1e-4, 1e-5, 1e-6\}$, respectively. The accuracy is shown in Figure 7. It can be seen that, different η values affect the performance of DOM algorithm. So, parameter η need to be fine tuned to obtain better results.

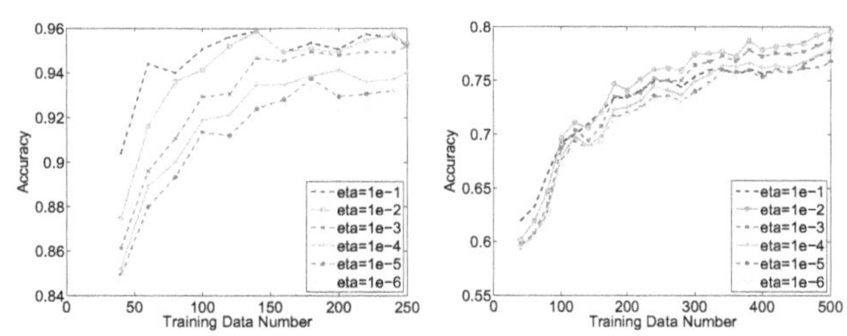

(a) *Email Spam* (b) *Sentiment*

Figure 7: Classification Accuracy against Different η

6.4.5 Minimum Number of Samples for Local Learning before Initial Global Learning

To guarantee the local models learned by clients are not so bad when they are sent to the server and be used by other clients, user may want the clients send their models to the server after they learned a certain number of samples and obtained good models. We want to know how the number of samples clients learned before initial global learning affects the performance of the algorithm. We set this number equals to $\{10, 30, 50, 70, 90, 110\}$, respectively. The results are shown in Figure 8. It can be seen that, for Sentiment dataset, it needs at least 30 samples to be learned by clients before doing global learning to obtain good results. The number of samples needed is very small. In this paper, we set the minimum number equal to 30 for all the datasets.

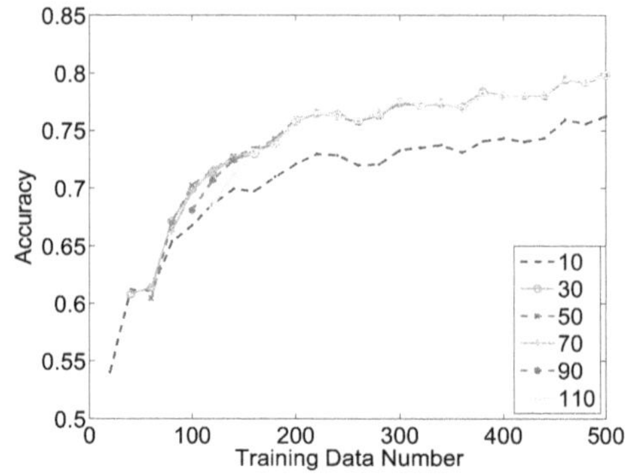

Figure 8: Classification Accuracy against Different Minimum Numbers of Samples before Initial Global Learning (Sentiment dataset)

To sum up, the buffer size k, number l of samples sent to the server in each interaction, minimum local sample number and weighting parameter β can be easily set and our algorithm can obtain good results in a wide range of parameter settings. Only the constraint parameter η need to be tuned by users.

7. RELATED WORKS

Online learning, multi-task learning and distributed data mining are three different learning scenarios. Traditionally, they are studied separately, some works also start to try to solve problems with more than one of these characteristics.

Online learning method [20, 36, 37] learns a set of data samples that arrive sequentially in time. At each time step, the algorithm processes an incoming sample and update the prediction model accordingly. The computation of online learning methods cannot be too complex, as they are efficient real-time learning algorithms. Online learning has also been applied to a wide range of applications [23]. Online learning has been thoroughly studied and a variety of online learning algorithms have been proposed. The first kind is the first-order algorithms include the classical Perceptron algorithm [26] and the well-known Passive-Aggressive algorithm [12]. Recently, second-order online learning algorithms are studied extensively. It has been shown that, by using parameter confidence information, second-order algorithms can improve online learning performance [8]. Confidence-weighted learning maintains a Gaussian distribution over the linear prediction models, which is also used to guide the model updating process [17]. However, due to its strict assumption that all the data samples are separable, it takes aggressive update rules and can cause overfit problem in certain situations. To improve this algorithm, Adaptive Regularization of Weights algorithm relaxes the separable assumption, which is capable to deal with noisy and non-separable data [14]. However, because it directly adds loss and confidence regularization, it loses the adaptive margin property [31]. In Soft Confidence-Weighted (SCW) learning method, the adaptive margin method assigns different margins for different instances via a probability formulation, which is more robust to handle noisy and non-separable data, and is also more effective and efficient [31]. Online sparse kernel learning has also been proposed to online learn a kernel classifier with a bounded number of support vectors [33]. SCW has the large margin, adaptive margin, confidence weighted properties and is able to deal with non-separable data. So, in this paper, it is taken as the local online learning method on the clients.

Multi-task learning (MTL) conducts multiple related learning tasks simultaneously so that the useful information in one task can be used for other tasks. Traditional MTL methods consider the centralized learning scenario that all the data are collected at a same place, where each task has access to all the data from other tasks, which is different from our problem settings. The earliest MTL method [5] learns a shared hidden layer representation for different tasks. Multi-task feature learning learns a low-dimensional representation which is shared across a set of multiple related tasks [2, 19]. The methods to learn predictive structures on hypothesis spaces from multiple learning tasks are also proposed [1, 9]. Supposing that all the tasks are similar, a regularization formulation is proposed for MTL [18]. MTL can be modeled by stochastic process methods, such as [29, 32]. To deal with outlier tasks, a robust multi-task learning algorithm is proposed [10]. MTDA algorithm [35] is a single view multi-task learning algorithm that can deal with learning tasks with different data representations. Multi-task learning with multiple views (MTMV) are also studied. CSL-MTMV [21] is a shared structure learning framework, which can learn shared predictive structures on common views from multiple related tasks, and use the consistency among different views to improve the performance. MAMUDA [22] can solve MTMV problems with heterogeneous tasks. All these algorithms are designed for centralized multi-task learning problems and they learn in the batch mode, that cannot do the real-time online learning.

Centralized multi-task learning under the online learning setting has also been studied. In online multi-domain learning [16], it first uses single task online learning method to learn a model for each task separately, and then proposes a method to combined all these models into a synthesized model. Cavallanti et al. [6] introduced new Perceptron-based algorithms for the online multi-task binary classification problem. They have proven that, under suitable regularity conditions, multi-task learning algorithms can improve on single task learning by a factor proportional to the number of tasks, which demonstrates the effectiveness of online multi-task learning. Saha et al. proposed an online multi-task learning algorithm that can adaptively learn task relationships [28]. It dose not assume fixed task relatedness, which makes it more flexible to deal with real world problems. Sun et al. proposed an online multi-task learning method to solve the human activity recognition problems [30]. Their major motivation for using online training algorithm is to speed up the training process. Instead of using batch training methods such as, steepest gradient descent, conjugate gradient descent, and limited-memory BFGS, they employed the online training method stochastic gradient descent to solve their problem. There are also efforts to solve multi-task learning in a lifelong learning setting [27]. All these algorithms are centralized learning algorithms, since not only the centered learner has access to all the data from all the tasks, each task can also obtains other tasks' data if it finds it is necessary. So, they are not suitable for our problems that the data are distributed stored and no one can obtain a whole copy of the data from all the tasks.

Dinuzzo et al. studied the online multi-task learning from distributed datasets [15]. They divided the overall computation into each client and the server can do learning more efficiently. Also, their method can preserve privacy of individual data. More specifically, although each client has access to the data from other clients, it does not know which client a particular data sample belongs to. However, the communication cost in this method is very high. Each client should send all their data to the server. Then, the server has to send all the data from all the clients to each client. Transmitting these huge amount of data between clients and the server is not possible in many real world applications. For example, a cell phone can not transmit all its data to the server or receive all other persons' data to help its local learning process.

8. CONCLUSIONS

In this paper, we formulated a new type of multi-task learning problem, i.e., distributed online multi-task learning problem. To solve it, a Distributed Online Multi-task (DOM) learning framework is proposed, which includes collaborative local learning and global learning. An asynchronous online multi-task learning method is proposed for the server, which is more efficient for computation and economical for communication. Our method can help the isolated clients to learn from each other and obtain better results than learn separately. There is no direct communication among different clients and the server does not transmit a client's data to other clients, so data privacy is perfectly conserved. Most of the parameters in the algorithm can be easily set. Also, experiments have proved the effectiveness of our method.

9. ACKNOWLEDGMENTS

This work is supported by the National Natural Science Foundation of China (No. 61473273, 61473274, 61175052, 61203297), National High-tech R&D Program of China (863 Program) (No.2014AA015105, 2013AA01A606).

10. REFERENCES

[1] R. K. Ando and T. Zhang. A framework for learning predictive structures from multiple tasks and unlabeled data. *JMLR*, 6:01, 2005.

[2] A. Argyriou, T. Evgeniou, and M. Pontil. Multi-task feature learning. In *Advances in Neural Information Processing Systems (NIPS)*, pages 41 – 48, Vancouver, BC, Canada, 2007.

[3] S. Bickel. Ecml-pkdd discovery challenge 2006 overview. In *ECML-PKDD Discovery Challenge Workshop*, pages 1–9, 2006.

[4] J. Blitzer, M. Dredze, and F. Pereira. Biographies, bollywood, boom-boxes and blenders: Domain adaptation for sentiment classification. In *ACL*, pages 440 – 447, Prague, Czech republic, 2007.

[5] R. Caruana. Multitask learning. *Machine learning*, 28(1):41–75, 1997.

[6] G. Cavallanti, N. Cesa-Bianchi, and C. Gentile. Linear algorithms for online multitask classification. *Journal of Machine Learning Research*, 11:2901 – 2934, 2010.

[7] G. Cavallanti, N. Cesa-Bianchi, and C. Gentile. Linear algorithms for online multitask classification. *Journal of Machine Learning Research*, 11:2901 – 2934, 2010.

[8] N. Cesa-Bianchi, A. Conconi, and C. Gentile. Second-order perceptron algorithm. *Siam Journal on Computing*, 34(3):640–668, 2005.

[9] J. Chen, L. Tang, J. Liu, and J. Ye. A convex formulation for learning shared structures from multiple tasks. In *ICML*, pages 137 – 144, Montreal, QC, Canada, 2009.

[10] J. Chen, J. Zhou, and J. Ye. Integrating low-rank and group-sparse structures for robust multi-task learning. In *ACM SIGKDD*, pages 42 – 50, San Diego, CA, United states, 2011.

[11] T.-S. Chua, J. Tang, R. Hong, H. Li, Z. Luo, and Y. Zheng. Nus-wide: A real-world web image database from national university of singapore. In *CIVR 2009 - Proceedings of the ACM International Conference on Image and Video Retrieval*, pages 368 – 375, Santorini Island, Greece, 2009.

[12] K. Crammer, O. Dekel, J. Keshet, S. Shalev-Shwartz, and Y. Singer. Online passive-aggressive algorithms. *Journal of Machine Learning Research*, 7:551 – 585, 2006.

[13] K. Crammer, M. Dredze, and F. Pereira. Exact convex confidence-weighted learning. In *NIPS*, pages 345 – 352, Vancouver, BC, Canada, 2009.

[14] K. Crammer, A. Kulesza, and M. Dredze. Adaptive regularization of weight vectors. *Machine Learning*, 91(2):155 – 187, 2013.

[15] F. Dinuzzo, G. Pillonetto, and G. De Nicolao. Client-server multitask learning from distributed datasets. *IEEE Transactions on Neural Networks*, 22(2):290 – 303, 2011.

[16] M. Dredze and K. Crammer. Online methods for multi-domain learning and adaptation. In *EMNLP*, pages 689 – 697, Honolulu, HI, United states, 2008.

[17] M. Dredze, K. Crammer, and F. Pereira. Confidence-weighted linear classification. In *ICML*, pages 264 – 271, Helsinki, Finland, 2008.

[18] T. Evgeniou and M. Pontil. Regularized multi-task learning. In *ACM SIGKDD*, pages 109 – 117, Seattle, WA, United states, 2004.

[19] A. Jalali, P. Ravikumar, S. Sanghavi, and C. Ruan. A dirty model for multi-task learning. In *NIPS*, Vancouver, BC, Canada, 2010.

[20] R. Jin, S. C. H. Hoi, and T. Yang. Online multiple kernel learning: Algorithms and mistake bounds. *Algorithmic Learning Theory*, 6331:390–404, 2010.

[21] X. Jin, F. Zhuang, S. Wang, Q. He, and Z. Shi. Shared structure learning for multiple tasks with multiple views. In *ECML PKDD 2013*, volume 8189 LNAI, pages 353 – 368, Prague, Czech republic, 2013.

[22] X. Jin, F. Zhuang, H. Xiong, C. Du, P. Luo, and Q. He. Multi-task multi-view learning for heterogeneous tasks. In *CIKM*, pages 441–450, New York, NY, USA, 2014. ACM.

[23] B. Li, P. Zhao, S. C. H. Hoi, and V. Gopalkrishnan. Pamr: Passive aggressive mean reversion strategy for portfolio selection. *Machine Learning*, 87(2):221–258, 2012.

[24] F.-F. Li and P. Perona. A bayesian hierarchical model for learning natural scene categories. In *CVPR*, volume II, pages 524 – 531, San Diego, CA, United states, 2005.

[25] D. G. Lowe. Distinctive image features from scale-invariant keypoints. *International Journal of Computer Vision*, 60(2):91 – 110, 2004.

[26] F. Rosenblatt. The perceptron: a probabilistic model for information storage and organization in the brain. *Psychological Review*, 65(6):386–408, 1958.

[27] P. Ruvolo and E. Eaton. Online multi-task learning via sparse dictionary optimization. In *AAAI*, volume 1, QuÃl'bec City, Canada, 2014.

[28] A. Saha, P. Rai, S. Venkatasubramanian, and H. Daume. Online learning of multiple tasks and their relationships. In *International Conference on Artificial Intelligence and Statistics*, pages 643–651, 2011.

[29] G. Skolidis and G. Sanguinetti. Bayesian multitask classification with gaussian process priors. *IEEE Transactions on Neural Networks*, 22(12):2011–2021, 2011.

[30] X. Sun, H. Kashima, and N. Ueda. Large-scale personalized human activity recognition using online multitask learning. *IEEE Transactions on Knowledge and Data Engineering*, 25(11):2551 – 2563, 2013.

[31] J. Wang, P. Zhao, and S. C. H. Hoi. Exact soft confidence-weighted learning. In *ICML*, volume 1, pages 121 – 128, Edinburgh, United kingdom, 2012.

[32] S. Yu, V. Tresp, and K. Yu. Robust multi-task learning with t-processes. In *Twenty-Fourth International Conference on Machine Learning (ICML)*, volume 227, pages 1103 – 1110, Corvalis, OR, United states, 2007.

[33] L. Zhang, J. Yi, R. Jin, M. Lin, and X. He. Online kernel learning with a near optimal sparsity bound. In *ICML*, number PART 2, pages 1658 – 1666, Atlanta, GA, United states, 2013.

[34] Y. Zhang and D.-Y. Yeung. A convex formulation for learning task relationships in multi-task learning. In *UAI 2010*, pages 733 – 742, Catalina Island, CA, United states, 2010.

[35] Y. Zhang and D.-Y. Yeung. Multi-task learning in heterogeneous feature spaces. In *AAAI*, volume 1, pages 574 – 579, San Francisco, CA, United states, 2011.

[36] P. Zhao, S. C. H. Hoi, and R. Jin. Double updating online learning. *Journal of Machine Learning Research (JMLR)*, 12:1587–1615, 2011.

[37] P. Zhao, S. C. H. Hoi, R. Jin, and T. Yang. Online auc maximization. In *Proceedings of the 28th International Conference on Machine Learning, ICML 2011*, pages 233 – 240, Bellevue, WA, United states, 2011.

Lifespan-based Partitioning of Index Structures for Time-travel Text Search

Animesh Nandi, Suriya Subramanian, Sriram Lakshminarasimhan, Prasad M Deshpande, Sriram Raghavan

IBM Research, Bangalore, India

ABSTRACT

Time-travel text search over a temporally evolving document collection is useful in various applications. Supporting a wide range of query classes demanded by these applications require different index layouts optimized for their respective query access patterns. The problem we tackle is how to efficiently handle different query classes using the same index layout.

Our approach is to use list intersections on single-attribute indexes of keywords and temporal attributes. Although joint predicate evaluation on single-attribute indexes is inefficient in general, we show that partitioning the index based on version lifespans coupled with exploiting the transaction-time ordering of record-identifiers, can significantly reduce the cost of list intersections.

We empirically evaluate different index partitioning alternatives on top of open-source Lucene, and show that our approach is the only technique that can simultaneously support a wide range of query classes efficiently, have high indexing throughput in a real-time ingestion setting, and also have negligible extra storage costs.

Categories and Subject Descriptors: H.3.3 [Information Search and Retrieval]: Search Process

Keywords: Time-travel Text Search; Index Partitioning; Lucene

1. INTRODUCTION

The ability to efficiently access historical data and analyze (*via keyword searches*) system states at a specific historic point (or range) in time is becoming essential for a number of web-scale applications. These applications include IT operational analytics, web crawling, and application provenance, where the data generated is typically in the form of unstructured text documents or partially structured key-value pairs (e.g. JSON data attributes). Each item or *document* gets created, undergoes multiple updates, creating a new *document version* each time, before finally getting deleted. Analytics used to derive insights from this *temporally evolving* data requires a platform that is capable of supporting efficient *time-travel text-searches* (i.e. queries with constraints on the temporal dimension and keyword matches) over a corpus of versioned documents.

To motivate this problem better, we take the specific example of IT operational analytics, where continuous monitoring, real-time problem detection and root cause diagnostics are required. The input data is a temporally evolving collection of machine-data documents, where each document captures the current state of a fine-grained machine entity. Examples of such entities can be a running process, a mounted disk partition, a network connection, installed packages, etc. Even a single machine can have several thousands of such machine-entities, and the document corresponding to each fine-grained machine entity evolves over time as its state changes. This stream of machine-data documents collected by the monitoring infrastructure arrive rapidly and need to indexed at real-time to be made readily available for query-driven analysis. The type of queries that power these analytics can vary as well – ranging from analyzing the state of the system at a historic point in time, analyzing the intersection (invariants) or difference (diffs) between datacenter state snapshots between two different points in time, to analyzing the entities that got updated within a historic time interval. Section 2.2 describes the different types of queries relevant to an IT operational analytics scenario. The key thing to observe is that queries can have arbitrary combinations of temporal and keyword predicates.

A system that can deliver high performance on time-travel text-searches has to overcome several challenges on the indexing, storage and query processing fronts. The indexer must be able to process document versions as they arrive in real time, rather than batch processing the entire document corpus that is available upfront. The incoming data must be indexed such that query execution is efficient across different classes of queries – queries with just keywords or only temporal constraints or combinations of both. Even as there is a need to support efficient execution on a wide variety of query classes, this cannot come at the cost of high storage overheads or substantial reduction in indexing throughput. A lightweight indexing solution is required, and replication of index structures to have different index layouts optimized for different query classes has to be avoided.

Prior works [1, 2, 4, 9] that support time-travel text search *partition* the document collection in different ways to enable queries to quickly narrow down on the document versions of interest. These techniques either have (a) have high storage costs due to replication of long-living document versions [4], or (b) are primarily designed for situations where the entire archival collection is available upfront since it incurs high periodic index-rebuilding costs in real-time ingestion settings [1], or (c) have performance degradation at high data rates and large datasets because of subtle dependencies of their partitioning technique on the expected available size of per-term memory buffers [2], or (d) have an index layout that is specifically optimized for the joint predicate (keyword+temporal) query and thereby cannot give good performance on other query classes (e.g. single-attribute queries) unless assumptions about the entire archival collection being available upfront hold [9].

In this paper, we make a number of design choices to improve the performance across a number of dimensions. Rather than creating nested or multi-dimensional indexes, we create single-attribute index structures that retain good performance on single-attribute queries (pure temporal or pure keyword). For the joint predicate queries, we focus on optimizing the list intersection performance. This is done by taking advantage of the implicit temporal encoding (chrono-

CIKM'15, October 19–23, 2015, Melbourne, Australia.

DOI: http://dx.doi.org/10.1145/2806416.2806442.

Name	Temporal component of query	Overall Query Predicate
keywordonly-search(k)	None	k
snapshot-search(k, t)	Snapshot S(t) of versions valid at t	$k \wedge (\textit{birthtime} \leq t) \wedge (\textit{deathtime} > t)$
alive-any-search(k, t_{min}, t_{max})	Valid at ANY point in interval $[t_{min}, t_{max}]$	$k \wedge (\textit{birthtime} \leq t_{max}) \wedge (\textit{deathtime} > t_{min})$
invariant-search(k, t_{min}, t_{max})	S$(t_{min}) \cap$ S(t_{max})	$k \wedge (\textit{birthtime} \leq t_{min}) \wedge (\textit{deathtime} > t_{max})$
born-search(k, t_{min}, t_{max})	Born at some point in interval $[t_{min}, t_{max}]$	$k \wedge (t_{min} \leq \textit{birthtime} \leq t_{max})$
died-search(k, t_{min}, t_{max})	Died at some point in interval $[t_{min}, t_{max}]$	$k \wedge (t_{min} \leq \textit{deathtime} \leq t_{max})$
positivediff-search(k, t_{min}, t_{max})	S$(t_{max}) \setminus$ S(t_{min})	$k \wedge (t_{min} \leq \textit{birthtime} \leq t_{max}) \wedge (\textit{deathtime} > t_{max})$
negativediff-search(k, t_{min}, t_{max})	S$(t_{min}) \setminus$ S(t_{max})	$k \wedge (\textit{birthtime} < t_{min}) \wedge (t_{min} \leq \textit{deathtime} \leq t_{max})$
transient-search(k, t_{min}, t_{max})	Transient in interval $[t_{min}, t_{max}]$	$k \wedge (t_{min} \leq \textit{birthtime} \leq t_{max}) \wedge (t_{min} \leq \textit{deathtime} \leq t_{max})$

Table 1: Example queries in IT-Operational analytics, as predicates on *birthtime* and *deathtime* and keyword expression k comprising AND/OR over multiple keywords. Note that temporal-only variants of these queries have k as a WILDCARD.

logical transaction time ordering) present in the record-identifiers of documents indexed by underlying indexing engine. This implicit ordering, coupled with partitioning based on lifespan allows us to effectively prune away index entries that do not satisfy the temporal constraints, resulting in good performance on the (keyword + temporal) query. With respect to storage overheads, we have disjoint partitions and every document version is present in exactly one partition, implying storage optimality. Last but not the least, given that the determination of which partition a document version should be part is a function of only the attributes of the version getting indexed (i.e. lifespan attribute) instead of a complex global optimization function, our approach is able to achieve low indexing overheads and also does not require any periodic re-organization of the index layout.

We implemented our approach on top of open-source Lucene [15], and empirically evaluated indexing, storage, and query evaluation costs using several real and synthetic datasets. Our indexing scheme adds negligible storage and indexing overhead on top of a regular keyword index, and can also work in a real-time ingestion setting. Our results demonstrate that our approach can efficiently support a wide variety of query classes demanded by emerging applications (e.g. IT operational analytics). For each query class, our approach gives query performance that is comparable (or superior) to the best performing indexing technique for that particular query class. In contrast, each of the prior index organization schemes is significantly worse than our approach on query classes for which the scheme was not optimized for.

Finally, would like to mention that although the IT operational analytics use-case influenced the design requirements of our time-travel text search engine, the study of a full-fledged datacenter management system built over our engine is outside the scope of this work[1]. Further, in order to demonstrate the generic value of our proposed technique, we have chosen *public* datasets that are not limited to machine-data in any way.

2. BACKGROUND AND MOTIVATION

2.1 Data model

Each version of a temporally evolving document entity is associated with a *validity interval* (i.e. [*birthtime*, *deathtime*)) which denotes the time-interval during which this version was valid. For a document that was successively updated at transaction times $t_0, t_1, \dots, t_n$ (in chronological time order), the document versions created are given by $v_0, v_1, \dots, v_n$, and the *validity intervals* of these successive versions are – $[t_0, t_1), [t_1, t_2), \dots, [t_n, \infty)$ respectively. The current unexpired version of the document is the one with *deathtime* set to the special value ∞. And, for a deleted document, the last version's *deathtime* attribute is the time of deletion.

2.2 Temporal search query classes

Our goal is to support a wide variety of query classes – searches comprising just keywords or only temporal constraints or combinations of both. Table 1 gives various instances of example query classes in our IT operational analytics use-case. The key observation here is that queries could span arbitrary unions/intersections over the *birthtime*, *deathtime*, and keyword predicates.

We will now give an example of how temporal search queries can enable valuable use-cases in IT operational analytics. Let's say a system administrator wants to identify machines that were potentially vulnerable to the heartbleed bug, by retrieving the list of machines where some affected application has been running over a vulnerable openssl package. This can be enabled by first indexing machine-data documents related to process entities, wherein each process document comprises process attributes like process.pid, process.command, process.libraries, process.hostmachine, etc. The administrator can then issue the *alive-any-search*(k, t_{min}, t_{max}) query with the keyword predicate k as (process.libraries: "openssl-1.0.1") and the temporal predicate attribute t_{min} set to the release date of the first vulnerable openssl version and t_{max} set to the date when all machines in the datacenter were patched with the openssl version having the security fix. This query would retrieve the list of potentially vulnerable process entities, and the machine documents corresponding to these entities could then be used to generate the list of *<application-type, host-machine>* tuples on which further forensic investigation would need to be done.

2.3 Temporal search query processing

Search index query processing leverages the standard *inverted index or postings lists* [24], wherein the search-index maintains a postings list for every distinct term. A term's postings list contains a list of *record-identifiers* assigned by the indexing engine to document versions that contain that term. To answer keyword-only queries with arbitrary conjunctions/disjunctions, the search engine performs intersections and unions on the respective term postings lists.

To answer joint predicate (keyword+temporal) queries, temporal search frameworks (e.g. [4]) extend the inverted-index structure to embed the validity interval (i.e. [*birthtime*, *deathtime*)) in the postings list *payload*. During query evaluation of the keyword predicates using standard postings list intersection/union operations, this payload information can then be used to check if the scanned postings list entries additionally satisfy the temporal predicate. The I/O cost is however proportional to the size of intermediate result set (i.e. satisfying keyword-only predicates), which could be substantially larger than the size of final result set. To address this, prior works have proposed techniques to divide term postings lists into *partitions* such that index-partitions that have no chance of satisfying the temporal predicates could be completely ignored, thereby avoiding wasteful disk I/O. Note that there could still be wasteful reads (i.e. versions scanned but not satisfying query's temporal predicates) in each partition since the partitioning is only at coarse granularity.

2.4 Index partitioning techniques

We use Figure 1 to highlight the pros and cons of different index-partitioning techniques. Figure 1(a) shows the *Simple Time-tiers* approach, wherein the index is split into disjoint collections along the

[1]This would require designing the types of machine-data to instrument and modelling the collected data into machine-documents.

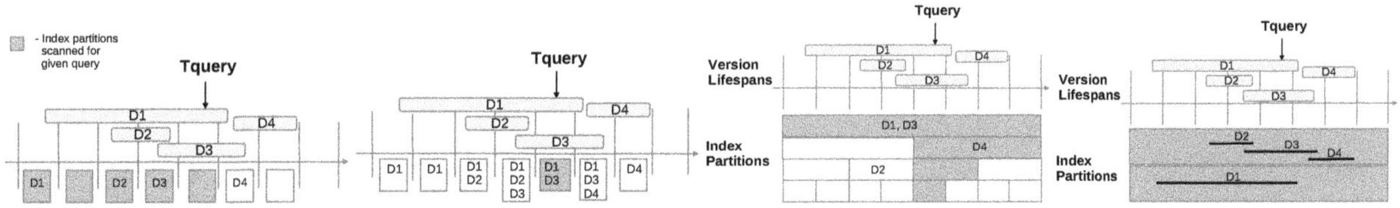

(a) Simple Time-Tiers (b) Replicated Time-Tiers (c) Interval-tree based (d) Staircase

Figure 1: Tradeoffs of index partitioning techniques. For the same lifespan distribution, we depict which index partitions store which versions. Taking the *snapshot-search*(k, t) query as example, we highlight (in blue) the index partitions accessed by query.

birthtime axis. With an ordering based only on *birthtime*, this layout becomes inefficient for *snapshot-search*(k, t) queries, since the desired results can comprise document versions that could have been born at any time between $[0, t)$ — meaning a large number of partitions would need to be accessed to answer the queries.

To overcome this query inefficiency, long-living versions can be replicated across the time-boundaries resulting in the *Replicated Time-tiers* technique [4], as illustrated in Figure 1(b). In this approach, the *snapshot-search*(k, t) query can be answered by accessing a single index-partition, i.e. the partition corresponding to the time t of the query. However, this query efficiency comes at the cost of considerable storage explosion (and corresponding increase in indexing time) that results from replication of long-living document versions across multiple partitions.

Interval Tree based partitioning is one alternative that can be to used to alleviate this storage explosion. Inspired from the temporal databases community [20], *Interval Tree* based partitioning, shown in Figure 1(c), partitions the text index into multi-level hierarchical partitions [9]. A version is made a part of the deepest partition (close to leaf level) whose time-boundaries fully encompass the version's validity interval. The *snapshot-search*(k, t) can thus be answered by querying logarithmic (of total time span) number of partitions that lie in the path-to-root for the query time t.

This index however has significant drawbacks for keyword-only queries due to high disk seek costs resulting from accessing all index-partitions, which are fragmented on disk. Similar drawbacks result for *wide* time-intervals in temporal-only and (keyword+temporal) queries. To alleviate this, fragments of a term's postings list can be *chained* together into consecutive disk blocks, which improves sequential access for multiple partitions. However, such techniques rely on the entire archival document collection being available upfront, and without apriori determination of the chaining order, periodic index-rebuilding costs become highly expensive. It is not applicable in our high data rate real-time ingestion setting.

One recent approach for time-travel text search has focused on partitioning the term index such that the unnecessary reads for each term is minimized. The *Staircase* technique [1, 2], shown in Figure 1(d), uses a greedy-algorithm to partition postings list entries such that no entry within a partition *subsumes* another entry. Validity interval v_1 is said to subsume v_2 when $((v_1.b < v_2.b)$ & $(v_1.d > v_2.d))$, where b and d denote *birthtime* and *deathtime* respectively. In Figure 1(d), D1 subsumes D2 and thereby needs to be separated out into different partitions, whereas {D2, D3, D4} satisfy staircase property.

With an *idealized* staircase sharding and sorted *birthtime* order on the posting list entries, it becomes simple to identify the starting and ending entries in each shard where the validity interval intersects with the query point. However, idealized sharding results in a large number of partitions because of increasing subsumption violations over time which degrades query performance. The hard subsumption constraint can be relaxed using cost-aware merging [1] and incremental sharding using bounded subsumptions [2], which balances the overall disk sequential read versus random seek costs. Because the merging technique is not suited for real-time processing, we compare our approach against an implementation of the latter. A limitation with the staircase partitioning in general is that it is specifically optimized for the *snapshot-search*(k, t) and *alive-any-search*(k, t_{min}, t_{max}) query in mind, and can result in unbounded amount of wasted reads for several query classes that cannot leverage the *birthtime* ordered shard layout.

2.5 Problem statement

Overcoming the limitations of the prior index partitioning techniques is a significant challenge that needs to be addressed. The goal of our work is to design an indexing system that for a wide variety of query classes, minimizes the number of fragmented partitions accessed by the query and also minimizes the amount of wasted reads in each partition. Further, we should be able to do this with minimal extra storage costs (i.e. not resorting to replication or different index layouts optimized for each query class). Further, the indexing logic must be applicable in a real-time ingestion setting and must be lightweight enough to cope with high incoming data rates.

3. DESIGN

This section describes the design of our proposed index partitioning technique and explains how it supports a wide variety of query classes with minimal storage or indexing overhead.

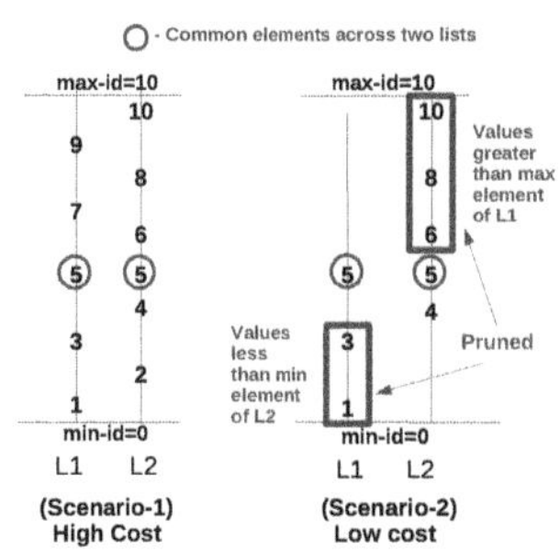

Figure 2: Factors affecting list intersection cost.

3.1 Assignment of temporal attributes

Our temporal search index is a simple layer on top of the popular text-search engine *Lucene* [15]. Our temporal search extensions handle the additional logic of maintaining *birthtime* and *deathtime* attributes and take document entities through their create, update, and delete life cycle. On receiving an update for a document entity with time-invariant key, our layer issues two API calls to the underlying indexing engine. First, it issues an *update* to the *deathtime* attribute of the latest version (if any), changing it from ∞ to the current time, while keeping the other attributes unchanged. Second, it also issues a *create* with *birthtime* attribute set to the current time, *deathtime* attribute set to the special time ∞ and the version's other attributes equal to the incoming content.

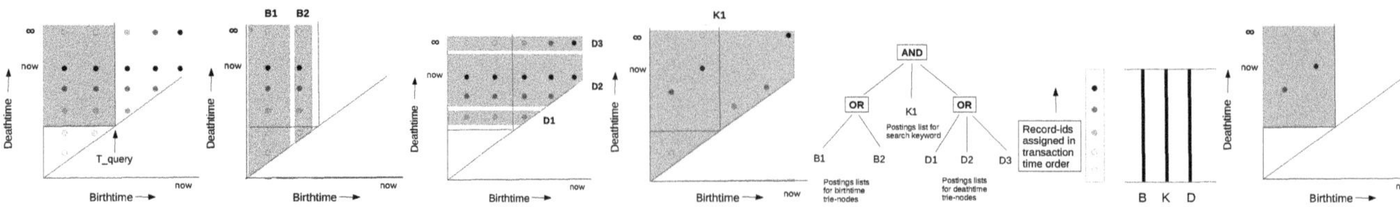

(a) Query region (b) Birthtime list (c) Deathtime list (d) Keyword list (e) Query plan (f) List Intersection (g) Result set

Figure 4: Snapshot search query evaluation in an append-only indexing system.

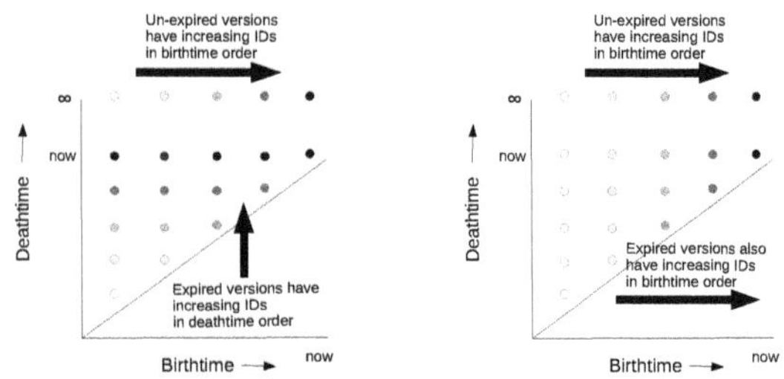

(a) Append-only (b) Update-in-place

Figure 3: Typical indexing engines assign *recordids* in transaction time order, going from lighter → darker shades of grey as time progresses.

3.2 Using single-attribute indexes

Our design objective is to avoid the limitations of prior works [1, 2, 4, 9] that organize the index layout based on apriori assumptions of specific query access patterns (e.g. *snapshot-search*(k, t) query). We avoid this approach since multi-attribute nested indexes are inefficient for single-attribute predicates like keyword-only queries as well as for keyword+temporal queries with a wide time-interval. To retain good performance on such queries, our approach is to explicitly index the *birthtime* and *deathtime* attributes and evaluate joint predicate queries by resorting to list unions and intersections on these single-attribute index structures for *birthtime*, *deathtime* and keywords.

Lucene indexes numerical attributes (here *birthtime* and *deathtime*) using *tries* [16]. Each trie-node of the multi-level trie-structure represents a contiguous numeric-range, with trie-nodes at the leaf-levels representing smaller ranges, while those towards the root representing larger ones. By assigning a distinct term to each trie-node, the search-index uses the postings list for a trie-node's term to track all the *recordids* whose numeric attribute falls within the trie-node's range.

The single-attribute indexes for each of *birthtime*, *deathtime* and keywords can thereby be realized using postings lists. Any query containing keyword and temporal predicates is evaluated via the standard keyword-search query evaluation plan that uses postings list unions and intersections.

3.3 Strawman approach: Using vanilla list intersection to evaluate joint predicates

Today's text search engines (e.g. Lucene) implement efficient algorithms/techniques [3] for intersecting postings lists maintained in sorted *recordid* order. In particular, they leverage an additional data-structure called *skip-list* that enables skipping portions of the list that are guaranteed to not be present in at least one other list being intersected with. Since no prior work in time-travel text search has explored this potential approach of leveraging list intersections with indexed temporal attributes, we now investigate whether a strawman approach of list intersection on these single-attribute indexes can efficiently answer the joint predicate *snapshot-search*(k, t) query.

The effectiveness of skipping in list intersection algorithms depends on the distribution of the values in the lists. Figure 2 depicts this dependence using two scenarios. The first, *Scenario-1*, demonstrates that in spite of the size of result set being small, the cost of list intersection is high if the values in the two lists interleave a lot. However, if the overlap between the ranges of values in the lists is low, as shown in *Scenario-2*, the cost of list intersection is only proportional to the overlap region since the other portions can be easily pruned away. The distribution of *recordid* in underlying postings lists has a significant impact on the cost of list intersection.

Figure 3 describes how typical search indexes such as Lucene assign *recordids* to documents. Each document version is depicted as a point, with the point's coordinates corresponding to its *birthtime* and *deathtime*, and the point's color/shade indicating its *recordid*. The current time is denoted as *now* and the special point ∞ on *deathtime* axis represents un-expired versions.

Although *recordids* are assigned in transaction time order, the distribution of *recordids* depends on whether the indexing engine uses an *append-only* or an *update-in-place* strategy. In update-in-place systems, updates to the attributes of an existing record are processed without changing the underlying *recordid* assigned to that record. As a result, *recordids* are in *birthtime* order, as shown in Figure 3(b). In contrast, append-only systems treat an *update* as a *delete* followed by a *create*. Thus, the *recordid* of its previous latest version is marked as deleted and a new document corresponding to the recently expired version is created with a new *recordid*. As a result, expired document version *recordids* are in *deathtime* order while unexpired version *recordids* are in *birthtime* order, as shown in Figure 3(a).

We will now examine how the underlying *recordid* assignment affects the list intersection cost of processing temporal search queries in our framework. Given that most indexing engines like Lucene adopt the append-only strategy for efficiency reasons, we take this indexing strategy as the default for our explanation below. Note however, that our proposed partitioning technique shows *similar* benefits for both append-only and update-in-place indexing systems, and is depicted in Figure 7.

Figure 4(a) highlights the region corresponding to the *snapshot-search*(k, t), which is specified via the temporal predicate ((*birthtime* $\leq t$) $\wedge$ (*deathtime* $> t$)). Out of all *recordids* lying in this region, only a subset of these satisfy the keyword predicate k, and this subset constitutes the result set as shown in Figure 4(g). Figure 4(b) and Figure 4(c) show the trie-node postings lists satisfying the query predicates for the *birthtime* and *deathtime* trie respectively, with the different widths being an illustration of these trie-nodes corresponding to different levels of the trie. Figure 4(d) shows the postings lists corresponding to keyword k.

To compute this result set, the search index performs list unions and intersections as per the query plan shown in Figure 4(e). The cost of the list intersection (i.e. "AND" at the root of query plan) is high since this scenario is similar to that of *Scenario-1* in Figure 2, wherein each of these three lists — *birthtime*, *deathtime* and keyword — span the entire range of *recordids* themselves, as depicted in Figure 4(f). As a consequence, skipping will *not* be effective, and all postings lists will be scanned from the beginning to the end, resulting in lots of wasted work.

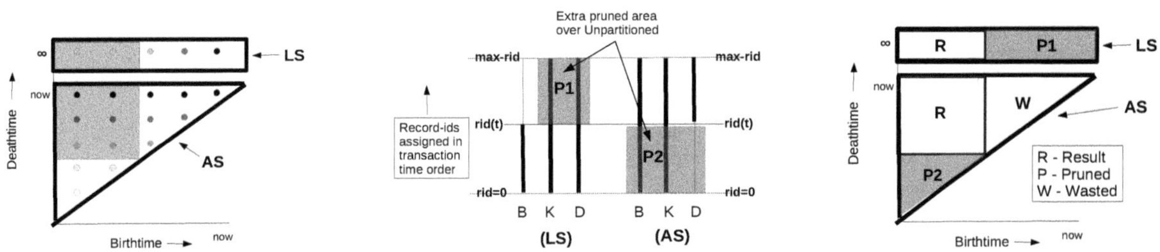

(a) Partition Boundaries (b) List Intersection (c) Pruned Regions

Figure 5: Pruning in LS+AS partitioned index.

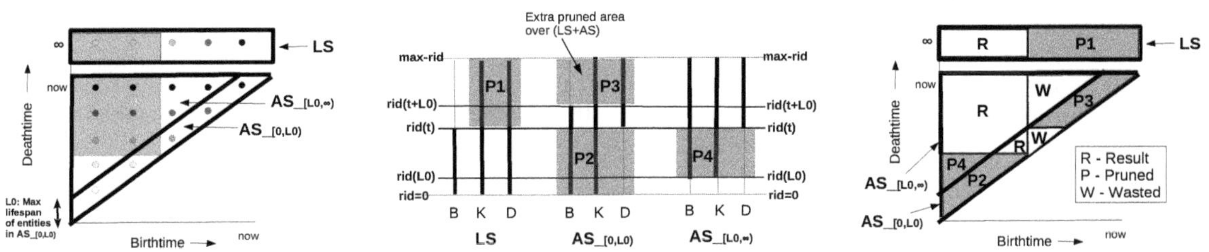

(a) Partition Boundaries (b) List Intersection (c) Pruned Regions

Figure 6: Pruning in LS+LogAS partitioned index.

3.4 Our proposal: Lifespan-based partitioning of postings lists

Our key insight is that we can exploit the temporal encoding in the *recordids* (i.e. fact that they are assigned in transaction time order), to partition the entire collection into *few disjoint partitions* to reduce the overlap between the postings list corresponding to *birthtime*, *deathtime* and keyword list, which will then translate to improving the skipping efficiency in the underlying list intersection.

To quantify the effectiveness of skipping/pruning, let us examine the interaction of the list intersection algorithm with the keyword postings list (K) in the *snapshot-search*(k, t). In particular, we categorize the *recordids* in the keyword's postings list into 3 parts – (a) *Result (R)* - This is the set of *recordids* whose temporal attributes satisfy the temporal component of the query and thus are in the result set, (b) *Pruned (P)* - This is the set of *recordids* whose temporal attributes do not satisfy the temporal predicates, but get easily pruned when doing the list intersection with the temporal (*birthtime/deathtime*) postings lists since they correspond to a non-overlapping region of Figure 2, and (c) *Wasted (W)* - This is essentially (K-R-P) and represents *recordids* that do not satisfy the temporal attributes of the query but were most likely examined by the list intersection algorithm since they belong to an overlapping region of Figure 2.

Our partitioning step 1: LS+AS partitioning

Our first intermediate partitioning step, referred to as *LS+AS*, simply divides the *recordid* space into two partitions; *latest* for current or unexpired versions which have *deathtime* set to ∞ and *archival* for archived versions which have a finite *deathtime* attribute, as shown in Figure 5(a). The final result is the union of versions satisfying the *snapshot-search*(k, t) in the two partitions. Note that since these partitions are disjoint, every query can simply aggregate the results from the two partitions without worrying about removal of duplicates.

This simple partitioning technique lowers query cost by reducing the overlap between the *birthtime* (B) , *deathtime* (D) and keyword (K) list. We will explain this using Figure 5(b). As described before, archival versions of a document have *recordids* in deathtime order, whereas unexpired (latest) versions have *recordids* in birthtime order. Lets say the *recordid* assigned at time t is *rid(t)*. Consequently, in the *latest* collection, the *recordids* in the *birthtime* list will range up to a maximum of rid(t). As a consequence, in spite of the *deathtime* and keyword list spanning the entire range of *recordids*, large portions of these lists having *recordid* values greater than rid(t) can be trivially pruned by the list intersection algorithm (since they correspond to *Scenario-2* of Figure 2. Similarly, in the *archival* collection, the *recordids* in the *deathtime* list will have a minimum value of rid(t). Consequently, in the *archival* collection, large portions of the *birthtime* and keyword postings list, having values less than rid(t) can be pruned away. The resulting benefits of pruning away these non-overlapping portions is depicted in Figure 5(c). The areas marked with P are the portions additionally pruned as compared to the basic unpartitioned approach where the entire region of the *recordid* space was examined by the list-intersection algorithm. As shown, the P1 region pruning benefits the *deathtime* and keyword posting lists, whereas P2 region pruning benefits the *birthtime* and keyword posting lists.

Our partitioning step 2: LS+LogAS partitioning

Our next partitioning step further sub-divides the *archival* partition based on the lifespan of document versions. This leads to more effective pruning and further reduction of the wasted (W) work, as illustrated in Figure 6. Let us first consider dividing the *archival* space into two partitions $AS_{[0,L_O)}$ and $AS_{[L_O,\infty)}$ as shown in Figure 6(a). $AS_{[0,L_O)}$ comprises of *short-lived* document versions with an maximum lifespan L_O, i.e. $lifespan$ = (*deathtime* − *birthtime*) $< L_O$. $AS_{[L_O,\infty)}$ comprises the remaining expired document versions with finite $lifespan \geqslant L_O$. $AS_{[0,L_O)}$ is the region between the two parallel lines *deathtime* = *birthtime* and *deathtime* = *birthtime* + L_O.

As before, assume that the *recordid* assigned at time t is *rid(t)*. In addition, assume that the *recordid* assigned at time $(t + L_O)$ is *rid(t+L_O)*. Consequently, in partition $AS_{[0,L_O)}$, the *recordids* in the *birthtime* list will range up to a maximum of rid(t+L_O), and the *recordids* in the *deathtime* list will have a minimum of rid(t), as shown in Figure 6(b). Consequently, in the $AS_{[0,L_O)}$ collection, the overlap between the lists is a small region of the *recordid* space in interval [rid(t), rid(t+L_O)], and this reduced overlap translates to large portions of these lists getting pruned away. The pruned areas shown in Figure 6(c) are more than those in the *LS+AS* strategy (Figure 5(c)).

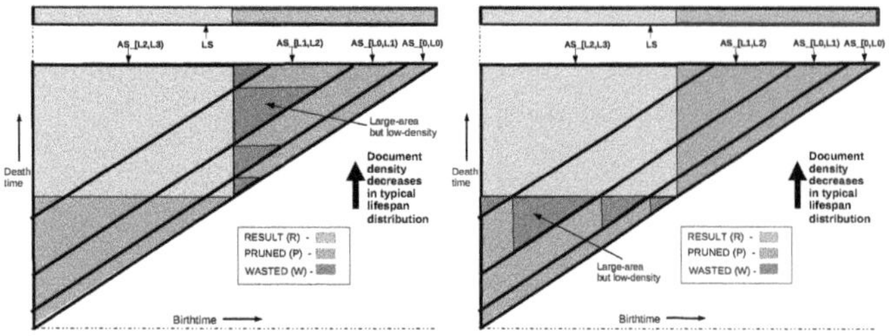

(a) Append-only (b) Update-in-place

Figure 7: Shape/Area/Density of wasted work in our lifespan partitioning approach

Extending the above idea, we can further reduce the amount of wasted work by further partitioning $AS_{[L_0,\infty)}$ in the same way. Specifically, we partition the archival space into a *logarithmic* (i.e. logarithmic of maximum lifespan or operational time-horizon of the indexing system) number of *partitions* based on the *lifespans* of versions. The logarithmic archival collections $AS_{[0,L_0)}$, $AS_{[L_0,L_1)}$, ..., $AS_{[L_{n-2},L_{n-1})}$ are created by using *exponentially increasing maximum lifespan* bounds (L_0, L_1, ..., L_{n-1}). The i-th lifespan-partition is denoted as $AS_{[l,u)}$, where $l = L_{i-1}$ and $u = L_i$, and this partition comprises of versions with lifespans in the interval $[l, u)$. Our justification of choosing such a scheme is inspired by our observation that several real-world datasets of temporally evolving data exhibit a *heavy-tail* distribution of lifespans. Under such a heavy-tail distributions, having exponentially larger lifespan intervals lead to partitions having similar number of documents. This enables a good trade-off between minimizing the number of index-partitions, yet minimizing the amount of wasted work.

Since lifespan-based partitioning relies on document versions arriving in transaction time order to efficiently answer queries, indexing documents out of order could affect query performance. However, arrival order does not affect the correctness of query results. In-order arrival could be violated in two scenarios — skew in arrival of data from multiple sources and batch upload of historical data. Slight skew does not affect query performance since *recordids* assigned around a time period will still be close to each other and temporally close document versions will map to the same or nearby disk blocks. Batch uploads on the other hand will not exhibit such a favorable *recordid* assignment. Our solution is to simply maintain a separate partition for batch data, and query this partition in addition to the others so that batch uploaded data does not affect query performance of the rest of the partitions.

Cost analysis

Figure 7 shows the unpruned/wasted regions (i.e. W regions) when performing list intersection on our proposed partitioning approach. While the *location* of the wasted work regions in the *birthtime / deathtime* two-dimensional space differ between the append-only and the update-in-place indexing systems, the *shape* and *area* of regions are identical.

Modulo boundary effects that show up when the query time is close to the start of the historic time span, the wasted work area W is smaller than that of the result set R in all partitions. Though W increases exponentially as the partition size increases, the heavy-tailed nature of lifespan density distribution ensures that the actual amount of wasted work done in terms of CPU computation or disk I/O, $cost(W) = area(W) * density(W)$, is approximately the same across all partitions.

Table 2 shows the average sizes of wasted work W and result sets R across different queries for various real and synthetic datasets. In order to get normalized results, we constructed datasets of equal sizes by sampling 100K document versions from the full datasets. We further removed latest state versions since wasted work in the latest state region is zero, and thereby only analyze the cost of queries made to the archival region. We issued *snapshot-search*(k, t) queries for a keyword with 1% selectivity for 100 evenly spaced query times t across the entire historic time span. The table reports the average wasted work W and average result size R across these 100 queries. The ratio W/R ranges from 0.34 to 1.14 across datasets showing that average cost per query ($W + R$) is around twice the optimal cost (i.e. result set size R).

Dataset	Dataset Size	Archival Size	Avg. W	Avg. R	Ratio W/R
Wikipedia	100 K	85 K	77	67	1.14
Linux	100 K	95 K	174	196	0.88
Log-normal	100 K	92 K	128	150	0.85
Pareto	100 K	68 K	70	90	0.78

Table 2: Average cost of wasted work W across datasets

Summary

Our lifespan-based partitioning ensures that we can answer joint predicate queries efficiently in spite of using single-attribute indexes. Our simple scheme has the following good properties – (a) *few partitions* - Having logarithmic number of partitions ensures low overhead of seek costs from accessing multiple index fragments in different partitions, (b) *disjoint partitions* - Having disjoint partitions implies no replication and thereby minimal extra storage overheads, and also enables trivial aggregation of results across all partitions, (c) *lightweight real-time aware indexing logic* - Since the decision of which partition a version should belong to is a function of *only* the version's self-attributes (i.e. *birthtime/deathtime*), our indexing logic does not require the entire archival collection to be available upfront, and neither does it require periodic re-organization of the index, and is thereby a perfect fit for the real-time ingestion setting.

4. IMPLEMENTATION

As described in Section 3, our temporal search index is a layer on top of the popular open-source Lucene [15] framework. This section describes the specifics of our index management.

4.1 Creating and maintaining index partitions

Our approach for implementing index-partitioning is inspired by how Lucene implements *tries* in order to support range queries on indexed numeric attributes [16]. On top of its default postings list abstraction, Lucene prefixes every numeric attribute's field name with a prefix value that corresponds to the trie-node that the numeric value should get indexed into. This results in *separate* postings lists for each trie-node, thereby emulating the desired effect of having a trie index.

This allows us to implement not only our proposed lifespan partitioning approach, but also the other comparative approaches as well. Our temporal-search layer prepends a *partition-prefix* to all field names of all document versions as they arrive into the system, which ensures that document versions get indexed in their respective partitions. At query time, the temporal search layer rewrites queries by prepending partition prefixes to field names and issuing queries to various partitions, as applicable for a particular query.

4.2 Query execution for numeric attributes

Efficient algorithms [3] to evaluate boolean queries involving conjunctions and disjunctions of attributes process all postings lists in the query tree in parallel, instead of first pre-computing the results of intermediate nodes. While Lucene evaluated non-numeric keyword queries using the former approach, we observed, to our surprise, that Lucene computed intermediate results for numeric range queries and was inefficient as a result. Hence, we changed Lucene's numeric query evaluation plan to also process postings lists in parallel, thus making it as efficient as keyword search queries.

4.3 Instrumenting low-level Lucene activities

We additionally instrumented portions of the Lucene source-code to report the number of *Lucene blocks* accessed during list intersection and union operations over postings lists. The skip-list data structure in Lucene operates at the granularity of a Lucene block consisting of 128 *recordids*. This instrumentation enabled us to verify that the end-to-end execution time of the query was indeed proportional to the number of Lucene blocks accessed, as reported in our evaluation.

5. EVALUATION

In this section, we evaluate our lifespan-based partitioning (i.e. *LS+LogAS*) approach of supporting time-travel text search against other approaches in terms of indexing throughput, storage costs, and query response time.

5.1 Datasets

Table 3 describes the datasets we used. We use two versions of the openly available Wikipedia corpus of articles [21]: *Wikipedia(s)* and *Wikipedia(l)*. The former is a 17 Million document revision subset whose uncompressed textual content totals 0.7 TB, and we index the *full content* of these document revisions (i.e. versions). With *Wikipedia(l)*, which comprises the entire 578M revision history of Wikipedia, we synthetically generate keywords with different popularities for each version (i.e. revision) and index these *synthetic keywords* in order to perform a large-scale controlled study. *Linux(r)* dataset is based on the git revision history of the Linux kernel [13], and is replicated to achieve the same size as Wikipedia(l). On observing that the Wikipedia and Linux datasets follow a *heavy-tailed distribution* (see Figure 8) with respect to their version lifespans – we additionally experimented with popular heavy-tailed distributions - *Log-normal* and *Pareto*, using the median lifespan of the Wikipedia dataset.

5.2 Setup and query methodology

To experiment with real-world scenarios, we used the Wikipedia(s) dataset and created the query workload for this dataset by sampling 10,000 queries from the AOL search logs with clicks to the Wikipedia domain. For each query, we extract its keywords and randomly associate it with different query classes, and also assign a temporal parameter to the query. We used a 12-core 2.40 GHz Intel Xeon E5645 server equipped with 32 GB of memory and a 2 TB SATA disk. At query time, we intentionally cap the OS physical memory (via boot settings) to 2 GB to ensure that queries are disk-bound.

In the absence of a real-world query workload for other datasets (Linux, Log-normal and Pareto), we indexed synthetic words with different term popularities and constructed a query workload by varying different configurable parameters such as the number of search terms, the query term's popularity (i.e. selectivity), and the temporal parameters. We ensured that we indexed a large number of terms per term-popularity at indexing time, so that successive queries issued with different randomly chosen terms of the desired term-popularity would result in fetching the term postings lists from disk rather than from memory. These experiments on all large (i.e. 578M) datasets were performed on cloud VMs with 2 GB of memory and connected to SAN disk drives with total capacity 8 TB.

5.3 Index partitioning strategies

Here, we highlight the relevant implementation details and configuration settings used for the approaches we compared against.

LS+LogAS Our technique is configured to use a leaf level partition having a lifespan of 1 day. With each successive level, the lifespan range increases by a factor of 10x, i.e. partition ranges being [0, 1 day), [1, 10 days) and so on.

Dataset	Size (Million)	Revs. per key	Time span
Wikipedia(l)	578	17.50	2001-2014
Wikipedia(s)	17	1070.20	2001-2014
Linux(r)	578	14.25	2005-2014
Log-normal	578	N/A	18 years
Pareto	578	N/A	18 years

Table 3: Dataset Characteristics

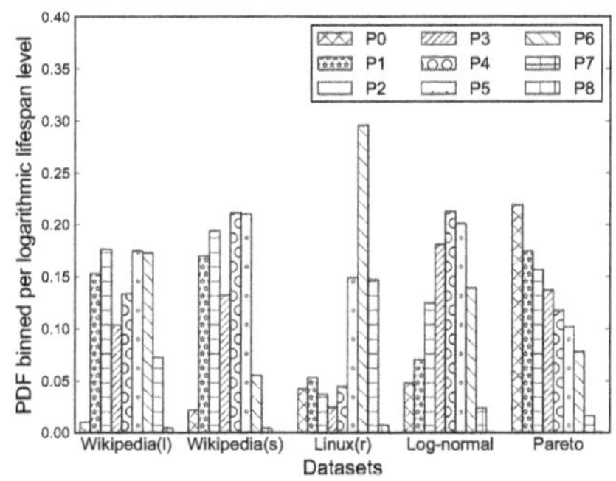

Figure 8: Lifespan distribution, as a fraction of total document versions, within partitions (P) of exponentially increasing lifespan durations (i.e. P0 = [0, 1 day), P1 = [1, 10 days), P2 = [10, 100 days), ...)

Optimized Lucene is the strawman approach described in Section 3.3. The optimization we did over vanilla Lucene, is the fix we made (described in Section 4.2) to Lucene's query evaluation plan for numeric attributes, which reduced the query execution times by a factor of $\approx$ 5x over vanilla Lucene.

Interval Tree is described in Section 2.4. We configured it with a partitioning granularity of 1 day at leaf level, and an arity of 10, similar to *LS+LogAS* approach. Our rational for choosing 1 day as the leaf level lifespan is to have sufficient fine-grained partitioning to cater to IT operational analytics use-cases where data volumes of TB / day are fairly common.

Optimized Staircase This is our *adaptation*[2] of the *Staircase* technique described in Section 2.4, in order to cope with high data rates. The number of partitions created by their algorithm is inversely proportional to the size of memory buffer per term-shard (η). At high data rates, the aggregate memory requirement of per-term buffers outgrows the machine's available memory, requiring periodic partial flushing of memory buffer entries. This effectively leads to operating at lower values of η, which in turn results in creation of a large number of partitions. To overcome this limitation, we do sharding at *document-level*, instead of a term-level. This completely eliminates the need for periodic buffer flushing, and also substantially (more than a factor of 10x) reduces indexing time since their algorithm is invoked on a per-document basis, instead of once per term in the document. We configured $\eta = 1000$, the recommended setting in [2] for disk-bound settings.

Replicated Time-tiers is described in Section 2.4. We configured *Replicated Time-tiers* with the same partitioning granularity of 1 day as with the other approaches.

5.4 Real-time indexing performance

Table 4 compares the indexing performance across techniques.

Indexing Throughput: We used the Wikipedia(s) to measure indexing throughput in terms of rate of indexing of actual raw content. The lightweight indexing logic of our *LS+LogAS* results in good indexing throughput of 2.48 TB / day, adding only 15.6% overhead compared to *Optimized Lucene*. In contrast, *Replicated Time-tiers*

[2]We verified the need of this adaptation in our high data rate setting with the first author of [2].

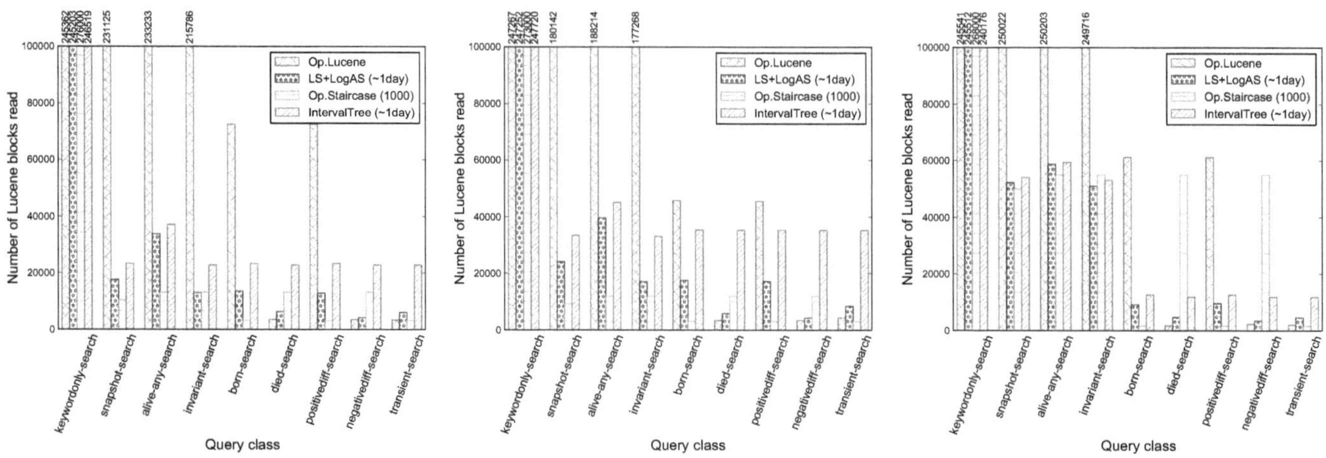

(a) Wikipedia(l) (578M) (b) Linux(r) (578M) (c) Pareto (578M)

Figure 9: Number of Lucene blocks read per query, as a function of varying query class, across different datasets

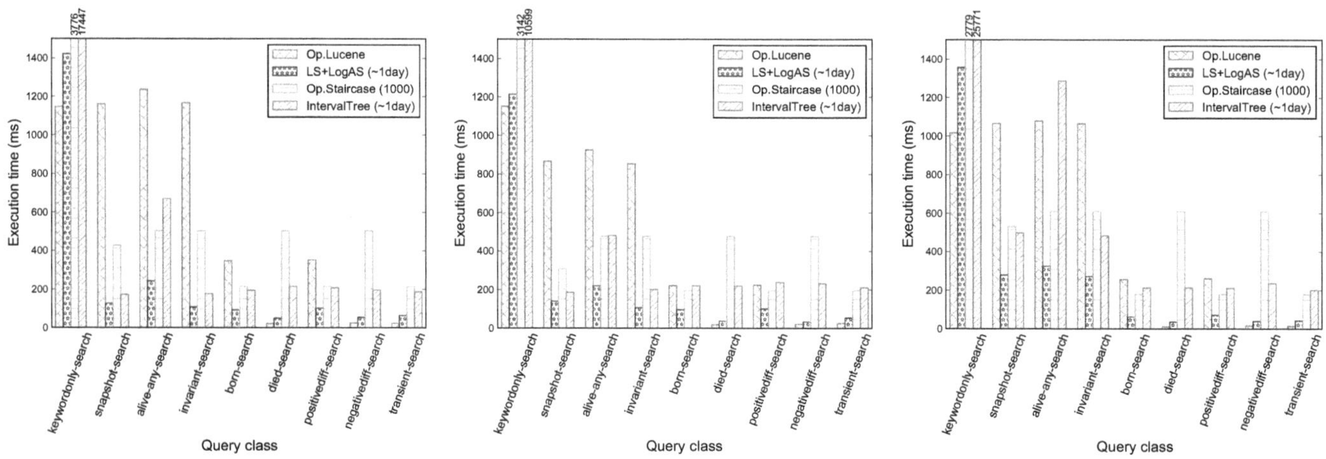

(a) Wikipedia(l) (578M) (b) Linux(r) (578M) (c) Pareto (578M)

Figure 10: End-to-end query execution time, as a function of varying query class, across different datasets

	ReplicatedTT	LS+LogAS	IntervalTree	OpStaircase
T	0.26	**2.48**	2.43	2.27
Δ(%)	-911.5	**-15.6**	-17.2	-22.9
S	1945	**183**	216	188
Δ(%)	+974.5	**+1.1**	+19.3	+3.8

Table 4: Indexing throughput (T) in TB / day and the size of the index (S) in GB on 17 million Wikipedia(s) article versions containing 0.7 TB of raw uncompressed content that needs to be indexed. Δ reflects the relative change (%) in metrics with respect to *Optimized Lucene*. For *Optimized Lucene*, S = 181 GB, T = 2.94 TB / day

has an order of magnitude (10x) greater overhead, as index entries have to replicated into multiple partitions, making it unsuitable in high data rate settings.

Index Size: Our *LS+LogAS* approach only has 1.1% storage overheads as compared to *Optimized Lucene*. As expected, *Replicated Time-tiers* has an order of magnitude more storage overhead (10x) compared to all the other approaches, and is completely impractical for high data rate settings. We thereby do not experiment with *Replicated Time-tiers* further on the larger 578M datasets.

5.5 Query performance: Controlled experiments

We measure the performance of different index partitioning techniques when subjected to the different query classes shown in Table 1. For each query class, we performed *controlled experiments* by varying the historic point in time t, the query time-interval, the number of keywords, and the selectivity (or popularity) of each individual keyword in the query. For brevity reasons, we present results for the following default setup — t is approximately midway into the historic past, time-interval is 1 month, individual keyword selectivity is 1%, and search query comprises 3 keywords. We experimented with all the four large 578M datasets (i.e. Wikipedia(l), Linux(r), Log-normal, and Pareto). For lack of space, we omit the depiction of Log-normal dataset results which were found to be very similar to the Wikipedia(l) dataset.

The overall end-to-end execution time of a query (reported in Figure 10) is a function of the number of partitions that the query needs to access (reported in Table 5) and the aggregate amount of index entries or Lucene blocks read across all the partitions (reported in Figure 9). We refer the reader to these charts to observe the relative query performance of different index partitioning techniques.

	OpLuc (all)	LS+LogAS (all)	OpStair (all)	IntervalTree tr=full	IntervalTree tr=0	IntervalTree tr=mo
Wikipedia(s)	1	6	36	5662	6	35
Wikipedia(l)	1	6	144	5662	6	35
Linux(r)	1	6	171	5662	6	35
Log-normal	1	6	143	5662	6	35
Pareto	1	6	123	5662	6	35

Table 5: The number of partitions accessed as a function of index-partitioning technique. For *Optimized Lucene*, *LS+LogAS*, and *Optimized Staircase*– the number of partitions accessed is the same for each query class. For the *Interval Tree*, the number of accessed partitions depends on the time range of the query. Except for *Optimized Staircase* where number of partitions is dataset dependent, other strategies have same value across datasets.

Firstly, observe that across all query classes, our *LS+LogAS* approach, with respect to overall execution time, is either the best performing technique, or comes very close to the best performing technique. In contrast, each of the other techniques performs badly for query classes that they are not designed for, as discussed below.

Optimized Lucene, which uses single-attribute index structures, has severely bad performance on the joint predicate *snapshot*, *alive-any-search*, and *invariant-search* queries because of very inefficient list intersection performance.

Interval Tree's performance deteriorates significantly with increased time-range in its queries or for the *keywordonly-search* query that effectively spans entire time range. This is because it needs to access increased number of index partitions, resulting in high disk seek costs (5662 partitions for *keywordonly-search* and 35 partitions for month queries). Further, since *Interval Tree* uses payload based post-filtering within each partition, it reads a similar number of Lucene blocks within each partition irrespective of overall query selectivity, and this value can be high at partitions closer to the root level.

Optimized Staircase technique suffers from the creation of lots of partitions ($\approx$150) on high popularity terms and larger datasets, which is a consequence of their greedy incremental sharding algorithm. Even for query classes that can leverage its *birthtime* ordered staircase layout within each partition (*snapshot-search*, *alive-any-search*, *born-search*, *positivediff-search*, and *transient-search*), the increased seek costs result in overall increased execution times. To add to this, query classes that cannot leverage their specific layout (*invariant-search*, *died-search* and *negativediff-search*), incur a high amount of wasted reads in each partition.

5.6 Query performance: Real-world query logs

Figure 11 compares the execution time of queries from the AOL search logs on the 17M Wikipedia(s) dataset where we indexed actual content of Wikipedia articles. We observe that the trends with query response times are similar to the previous controlled experiments, except that the relative gap between *Optimized Staircase* and *LS+LogAS* is lower. This is the expected behaviour of *Optimized Staircase*, wherein the number of partitions created is relatively much lesser for small datasets (here, 11 partitions for the 17M dataset) as compared to large datasets (144 partitions for the 578M dataset) – resulting in reduced disk seek costs for small datasets.

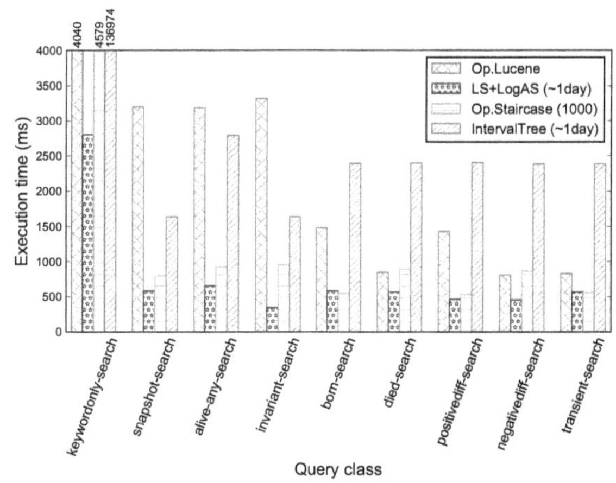

Figure 11: Query Performance on AOL Search Logs executed over the 17M Wikipedia(s) index

6. RELATED WORK

We organize the related work into the following categories.

6.1 Time-travel text-search

The focus of prior works in time-travel text search has been on devising index-partitioning techniques that can effectively prune away portions of the term postings-lists that do not satisfy the temporal predicate. Section 2.4 describes the limitations of prior works in detail, and is not summarized here for space reasons.

In addition to index-partitioning, a few works have explored approximate ranking techniques to reduce index storage costs by exploiting the typically high similarity in content that exists between successive temporal versions of the same document. These approaches typically index only the deltas [10, 11] or index a single representative version for a series of largely similar successive versions (i.e. temporal coalescing [4]). We aim to integrate with these works in the future.

6.2 Temporal databases

Works in temporal relational databases deal with management of temporally evolving data (see exhaustive survey by Salzberg and Tsotras [18]). Our work follows the notion of transaction-time model that was introduced in temporal databases, where changes can be made only to the latest version of a record. These versions (records) are identified by a primary key and the transaction-time is used to create the *implicit* validity intervals [*birthtime*, *deathtime*). In contrast to valid or bi-temporal time models, where validity intervals need *not* be related to create/update time, the notion of transaction-time directly applies in our IT operational analytics use case with real-time indexing. This notion enables us to design efficient update-friendly index structures.

The primary focus of work in this community is with the on-disk layout of the physical records and their associated *primary-index* for efficient retrieval via primary-key and/or time range predicates. The on-disk layouts that are typically aimed at supporting queries with pure time range predicates (e.g. append-only-tree [19], archival-time-index [20]), cannot efficiently answer queries containing a combination of time and primary-key range predicates. On the contrary, the more complex on-disk record layouts aimed at supporting a combination of time and primary-key range predicates (e.g. time-split B-tree index [14], nested ST-tree [7]), exhibit bad performance on queries with pure time predicates.

For a search-index application like ours, the focus is on efficiently supporting queries with multiple secondary attribute predicates, and our techniques optimize the on-disk layout of the *secondary-indexes* (i.e. postings lists) themselves. This stands in contrast with the work done in temporal databases, where the primary focus is on the layout of physical records. Although one might envision customizing these primary-index structures for use as secondary-index (e.g. adapting the nested ST-tree into AT-tree [7]), this community, to the best of our knowledge, did not explore the problem of how to perform efficient intersections on the results obtained from secondary indexes, across a wide range of query classes.

6.3 Geo-text index structures

One might think that treating *birthtime* and *deathtime* together as *(lat, long)* location tuple in geo-space, would enable us to leverage a wide range of geo-text indexes (see [5] for an exhaustive survey). Geo-text indexes capture geo-tagged objects containing both text descriptions and geo-locations, and answer queries involving spatial predicates (lat/long ranges) and text-keyword predicates. These approaches involve combinations of a spatial index (typically R-tree [8] or grid-file [17] based), along with a text index (postings-lists or bitmap based). Spatial and text index are coupled either loosely [23], or tightly [22] via aggregated structures in internal nodes to enable more pruning.

These index structures, however, are not applicable in our setting. While effective for certain classes of queries such as bounding-box queries in spatial dimension, these indexes cannot answer the *snapshot*(t) query, which has open intervals along each dimension of *birthtime* and *deathtime*. Second, they assume that queries contain both spatial and textual predicates, and thereby are designed to only cater to joint-predicate (spatial+text) query. These nested index structures are not designed to support single-attribute queries (spatial-only or text-only). For such queries they suffer from high I/O costs resulting from disk seeks to access the multiple fragmented index-partitions at the leaves of the nested index.

6.4 Improved clustering in postings lists

A few approaches have improved the performance of list intersection by employing intelligent *recordid* (or doc-id) assignment that makes skipping more effective. SFC-Quad [6] technique proposes assigning doc-ids to geo-objects based on their positions on a space-filling curve (Z-curve) spanning a spatial region, and then employ standard postings-list intersection techniques to answer geo-textual queries. The intuition behind this comes from the fact that geo-objects that are close by in the geographic space are *clustered* together in the doc-id space of the postings list. The work by Kane et. al [12] assigns doc-ids to documents based on content-similarity, thereby resulting in documents with similar terms getting assigned doc-ids that are closer in the doc-id space. However, these techniques are practical only in a setting where the entire collection is known in advance, since maintaining the postings-list in a sorted order as per the desired doc-id assignment/ordering scheme conflicts with the efficient append-only indexing operations on postings lists.

7. CONCLUSION

This paper presents lifespan-based partitioning of index structures to efficiently address the problem of time-travel text searches over massive datasets. Our scheme leverages temporal information embedded in the underlying *recordid* assignment and partitions the document space into a small number of disjoint partitions based on the lifespan of document versions. Rather than having an index layout that is optimized for a specific type of query, our solution uses list intersection on single-attribute indexes of keywords and temporal attributes to efficiently support a wide range of (keyword + temporal) queries. Our proposed technique significantly improves the list intersection skipping ability, and can efficiently narrow down to document versions that satisfy the temporal search predicates. As a result, our scheme supports a wide variety of query classes with performance comparable to the best solution for each query class, while simultaneously having an indexing logic that is lightweight enough to support high data rates in a real-time ingestion setting with negligible storage overheads.

8. ACKNOWLEDGMENT

We would like to thank Vasanth Bala for the motivating use-case of supporting keyword search on the historical state of the datacenter, Narendran Sachindran for discussions related to the design of our approach, Shai Erera for discussions related to internal implementation details of Apache Lucene, and Avishek Anand for clarifying our questions with respect to the related work on *Staircase* partitioning [1,2]. We would also like to thank the anonymous reviewers for their valuable feedback.

9. REFERENCES

[1] ANAND, A., BEDATHUR, S., BERBERICH, K., AND SCHENKEL, R. Temporal index sharding for space-time efficiency in archive search. In *SIGIR* (2011).

[2] ANAND, A., BEDATHUR, S., BERBERICH, K., AND SCHENKEL, R. Index maintenance for time-travel text search. In *SIGIR* (2012).

[3] BARBAY, J., LOPEZ-ORTIZ, A., LU, T., AND SALINGER, A. An experimental investigation of set intersection algorithms for text searching. In *Journal of Experimental Algorithmics (JEA), Volume 14* (2009).

[4] BERBERICH, K., BEDATHUR, S., NEUMANN, T., AND WEIKUM, G. A time machine for text search. In *SIGIR* (2007).

[5] CHEN, L., CONG, G., JENSEN, C. S., AND WU, D. Spatial keyword query processing: And experimental evaluation. In *VLDB* (2013).

[6] CHRISTOFORAKI, M., HE, J., DIMOPOULOS, C., MARKOWETZ, A., AND SUEL, T. Text vs. space: efficient geo-search query processing. In *CIKM* (2011).

[7] GUNADHI, H., AND SEGEV, A. Efficient indexing methods for temporal relations. In *TKDE* (1993).

[8] GUTTMAN, A. A dynamic index structure for spatial searching. In *SIGMOD* (1984).

[9] HE, J., AND SUEL, T. Faster temporal range queries over versioned text. In *SIGIR* (2011).

[10] HE, J., YAN, H., AND SUEL, T. Compact full-text indexing of versioned document collections. In *CIKM* (2009).

[11] HE, J., ZENG, J., AND SUEL, T. Improved index compression techniques for versioned document collections. In *CIKM* (2010).

[12] KANE, A., AND TOMPA, F. W. Skewed partial bitvectors for list intersection. In *SIGIR* (2014).

[13] Linux source code dataset. `https://www.kernel.org/`.

[14] LOMET, D., AND SALZBERG, B. Access methods for multiversion data. In *SIGMOD* (1989).

[15] Lucene. `www.lucene.apache.org`.

[16] Lucene numeric range query. `http://www.slideshare.net/VadimKirilchuk/numeric-rangequeries`.

[17] NIEVERGELT, J., HINTERBERGER, H., AND SEVCIK, K. C. The grid file: An adaptable, symmetric multikey file structure. In *TODS* (1984).

[18] SALZBERG, B., AND TSOTRAS, V. J. Comparison of access methods for time-evolving data. In *Proceedings of ACM Computing Surveys, Volume 31* (1999).

[19] SEGEV, A., AND GUNADHI, H. Event-join optimization in temporal relational databases. In *VLDB* (1989).

[20] VERMA, R., AND VARMAN, P. Efficient archival time index: A dynamic indexing scheme for temporal data. In *Proceedings of International Conference on Computer Systems and Education* (1994).

[21] Wikipedia dataset. `http://meta.wikimedia.org/wiki/Data_dumps`.

[22] WU, D., CONG, G., AND JENSEN, C. S. A framework for efficient spatial web object retrieval. In *VLDB* (2012).

[23] ZHOU, Y., XIE, X., WANG, C., GONG, Y., AND MA, W.-Y. Hybrid index structures for location-based web search. In *CIKM* (2005).

[24] ZOBEL, J., AND MOFFAT, A. Inverted files for text search engines. In *Proceedings of ACM Computing Surveys, Volume 38* (2006).

Contextual Text Understanding in Distributional Semantic Space *

Jianpeng Cheng †#,1 Zhongyuan Wang ‡†,2 Ji-Rong Wen ‡,3 Jun Yan †,4 Zheng Chen †,5

†Microsoft Research, Beijing, China #University of Oxford ‡Renmin University of China, Beijing, China

1jianpeng.ch,3jirong.wen@gmail.com 2zhy.wang,4junyan,5zhengc@microsoft.com

ABSTRACT

Representing discrete words in a continuous vector space turns out to be useful for natural language applications related to text understanding. Meanwhile, it poses extensive challenges, one of which is due to the polysemous nature of human language. A common solution (a.k.a word sense induction) is to separate each word into multiple senses and create a representation for each sense respectively. However, this approach is usually computationally expensive and prone to data sparsity, since each sense needs to be managed discriminatively. In this work, we propose a new framework for generating context-aware text representations without diving into the sense space. We model the concept space shared among senses, resulting in a framework that is efficient in both computation and storage. Specifically, the framework we propose is one that: i) projects both words and concepts into the same vector space; ii) obtains unambiguous word representations that not only preserve the uniqueness among words, but also reflect their context-appropriate meanings. We demonstrate the effectiveness of the framework in a number of tasks on text understanding, including word/phrase similarity measurements, paraphrase identification and question-answer relatedness classification.

Categories and Subject Descriptors

I.2.6 [**Artificial Intelligence**]: Learning; I.2.7 [**Artificial Intelligence**]: Natural Language Processing

General Terms

Algorithm, Application

Keywords

Information retrieval; Knowledge representation; Machine learning; Search engine

*This work was done at Microsoft Research Asia.

CIKM'15 October 19 - 23, 2015, Melbourne, VIC, Australia

ACM 978-1-4503-3794-6/15/10 ...$15.00.

DOI:http://dx.doi.org/10.1145/2806416.2806517.

1. INTRODUCTION

Native speakers of a language are able to make sense of sentences they have never seen or heard before. They understand words with more than one meaning in a given context, and how these combine to form meaningful utterances. While humans perform language understanding effortlessly, the task poses enormous challenges for machines. Discovering the meaning representations for texts is thus crucial for many natural language applications, such as web document classification and search query understanding [44, 43]. A common first approach is to translate words into a machine-understandable form, such as with vectors, which has led to the creation of distributional models.

The underlying idea of representing words as vectors dates back to the distributional hypothesis that "a word is characterized by the company it keeps" [15]. Under this assumption, the meaning of a word can be obtained empirically by examining the context in which the word appears. Ultimately, words are represented as vectors and their meanings are distributed across the dimensions of a semantic space. The points in space, therefore, represent semantic concepts in such a way that similar concepts are close to each other. The distributional models constitute a powerful representation framework in which the similarity of two meanings can be easily measured.

Traditional approaches to constructing a vector space rely on the explicit collection of co-occurrence statistics. Until recently, the idea has been reformed with the development of neural language models [2, 10, 29], in which the word vectors are treated as parameters to be optimized via the training of neural networks on unstructured text data. An advantage of the training based approach is that it produces salient word encodings in a dense and low-dimensional form (a.k.a word embeddings), proven to capture the semantic relationship among words [30].

Despite their effectiveness, generic distributional models, as suggested by their mathematical nature, suffer from low precision. One reason is due to the polysemous nature of human language. As a word reveals different senses as the context changes, it should be assigned more than one representation. For example, the word *apple* may either refer to "the name of an IT *company*" or "a type of *fruit*". Merging the two senses into a single vector may lead to inaccurate representation of either sense. Further consider two queries [*python zoo*] and [*python string*]. Humans can easily identify by context that the word *python* in the former query stands for an animal species while in the latter it means a type of *programming language*. Machines, however, are not generally equipped with this ability.

Previously solutions to address language polysemy in distributional models mainly focus on the creation of sense-specific embeddings. The idea was first proposed in the work of Schütze [38],

Table 1: Words, Senses and Concepts

Word	Sense	Concept
apple	the usually round, red or yellow, edible fruit of a small tree in the rose family	fruit
	an American multinational corporation that designs, develops, and sells consumer electronics	company
orange	the fruit of the citrus species in the family Rutaceae	fruit
	the colour of saffron, carrots, pumpkins and apricots, which is between red and yellow on the spectrum of light	colour

who obtain sense representations for a target word by collecting and clustering its context vectors. In the end, a sense is simply represented by the centroid of the corresponding cluster. Reisinger and Mooney [37] formalize the cluster-based model as a *multi-prototype vector space*, which has later been used in a series of tasks on word sense disambiguation [20, 21] and neural language modeling [18, 34]. The major limitation of the above works lies in the excessive computational cost induced by the clustering step, which has to be performed repeatedly for every word in the vocabulary.

Meanwhile, another line of research directly extends neural language models with the non-parametric Bayesian approach to learn sense embeddings [35, 1, 24]. Despite improved efficiency, there is no clear mapping between the senses learned from the data and the actual senses of a word. This becomes problematic for rare words or rare senses, for which there does not exist enough training context.

Following the above analysis and extending it a bit further, traditional approaches for modeling word senses in a vector space face the following challenges:

- Linguistic diversity: Each word in a vocabulary reveals different amounts of senses that vary with context.
- Data sparsity: Purely data-driven word sense induction methods require sufficient training contexts. In the case of rare words or rare senses, the representations will be underfit.
- Efficiency: Word sense induction aims to create as output a representation for each sense. This renders high cost in both computation and storage.

On the other hand, there exist many knowledge sources which contain rich linguistic knowledge, such as the relations between words. These knowledge sources can potentially help in the learning of word representations. Against this background, an interesting question we ask in the paper is as follows:

- Can we make use of additional knowledge sources to help learn contextual word representations in a unified manner, rather than partitioning each word into isolated senses and learning sense-specific representations given only a finite number of training contexts?

The solution we provide is based on the observation that different senses can share common concepts. Consider the two words *apple* and *orange*. While each has two distinct senses (as shown in Table 1), they share the same concept of *fruit*. To a certain extent, modeling the shared concepts among senses suffices to disambiguate a word meaning in a specific context. Motivated by this, we propose a novel framework for addressing language polysemy based on the concept space shared among senses. With the word-concept relations induced from an appropriate knowledge source, we train joint word-concept embeddings from a neural language model. As a result, each word is associated with an intrinsic vector that maintains the unique features of the word. Each concept is analogously assigned a vector that delivers an unambiguous meaning. We obtain the contextual representation of a word by combining its intrinsic vector and the most context-appropriate concept vector.

The main advantage of the proposed framework are in scalability, coverage and efficiency. The concept space has a much smaller and manageable size than the sense space while it emphasizes the commonality of senses. The proposed framework is completely general. Any meaningful concept space can be integrated with our neural language model, not limited to the one obtained from an explicit knowledge base.

An alternative to our approach is to utilize the word-concept relations outside embeddings. This involves a preprocessing step that replaces each word in the training text with a word-concept pair, after which a regular embedding training is applied. While this method violates our intention to avoid the memory cost and data sparsity issue in training sense embeddings, we refer to the method as *preprocessed* and use it as a baseline.

We perform extensive experiments to validate the effectiveness and efficiency of the proposed framework. In all experiments related to text understanding, including contextual word/phrase similarity measurements, paraphrase identification and question-answer relatedness classification. we achieve impressive results comparing to the state-of-art. The contextual embedding features computed from our framework have been used as important features to shift a commercial question-answering system.

The rest of this paper is organized as follows. Section 2 introduces neural skip-gram models, to which we extend train word-concept embeddings. Section 3 provides insights on the relationship between words and concepts. Section 4 details the topology and training aspects of the extended neural language model. Section 5 describes how context-aware representations can be created. The experiments and findings are described in Section 6. We present related work in Section 7 and conclude the paper in Section 8.

2. NEURAL SKIP-GRAM MODELS

Skip-gram [29] is an efficient neural language model for learning distributional word representations from unstructured text data. The training goal of Skip-gram is to find word representations that best predicate the existence of surrounding words (i.e, contextual words). Mathematically, the objective is to maximize the following average log probability:

$$\frac{1}{T}\sum_{i=1}^{T}\sum_{c=i-d,c\neq t}^{i+d}\log p(w_c|w_t) \quad (1)$$

where $w_1 ... w_T$ denotes the training text as a sequence of words, w_t and w_c represent the target word and the contextual word respectively, and d is the size of the context window centered at the target word. The standard way to compute the conditional probability $p(w_c|w_t)$ is to use a softmax function normalized over the entire vocabulary:

$$p(w_c|w_t) = \frac{\exp(s(\mathbf{w_c}, \mathbf{w_t}))}{\sum_{w_c \in W}\exp(s(\mathbf{w_t}, \mathbf{w_c}))} \quad (2)$$

where $\mathbf{w_t}$ and $\mathbf{w_c}$ are the respective vectors of the target word and the contextual word. W denotes the vocabulary. s is a scoring function for the pair $(\mathbf{w_t}, \mathbf{w_c})$. In a log-bilinear assumption, s is simply the dot product of the two word vectors.

Factorized Models. In the training of the above neural Skip-gram model, the time complexity induced in the softmax step is $O(|W|)$. One trick to reduce this excessive number is to factorize the vocabulary into *K* classes, such that every word belongs to exactly one class. As such, the problem of selecting a word from the whole vocabulary boils down to a two-step task: identifying the target class and selecting the word within the class. In other words, the conditional probability $p(w_c|w_t)$ is factorized as follows:

$$p(w_c|w_t) = p(s_c|w_t)p(w_c|w_t, s_c) \tag{3}$$

where s_c is the class that the word w_c belongs to. Since both terms $p(s_c|w_t)$ and $p(w_c|w_i, s_c)$ are normalized separately, the optimal time complexity of the softmax step can be reduced to $O(\sqrt{|W|})$.

In practice, a further reduction of the complexity can be achieved by repeatedly partitioning the vocabulary of a class into subclasses. The resulting tree structure is often called a *hierarchical softmax*. In general, factorized neural language models do not have any linguistic motivations behind them but are rather constructed for efficiency.

Noise Contrastive Normalization. Noise Contrastive Normalization (NCE) has previously been used as an *alternative* to factorization for speeding up the training of a neural language model. It is a technique that avoids evaluating the explicit normalization constant when computing gradients. The idea behind NCE is to convert the probability estimation problem into a binary classification task. Specifically, a binary classifier is defined to discriminate between samples drawn from the empirical distribution and those generated by a known noise distribution q, for example, a unigram distribution [33]. The objective replaces Equation (1) as:

$$\frac{1}{T}\sum_{i=1}^{T}\sum_{c=i-d,c\neq t}^{i+d}(\log p(D=1|w_t,w_c)+\sum_{n=1}^{N}\log p(D=0|w_t,\bar{w}_c)) \tag{4}$$

where N is the number of negative samples drawn from the noise distributions. In the above equation, the probability that a contextual word is generated from the empirical distribution given a target word is computed as follows.

$$\log p(D=1|w_t,w_c) = \frac{p(w_c|w_t)}{p(w_c|w_t) + Nq(w_c)} \tag{5}$$

Note the equation still involves the normalization constant in each term of $p(w_c|w_t)$, but here it is treated as a parameter to be optimized during training. In the work of Mnih and Teh [33], the authors discovered that fixing the normalization constants to 1 would not significant affect the model performance.

3. RELATIONS OF WORDS AND CONCEPTS

Before we extend the neural Skip-gram to account for both words and concepts, we provide some insights on the word-concept relations and how such relations can be obtained. The term *concept* is inherited from the context of the knowledge base, where it stands for the common hypernym of a group of hyponyms. For example, both *apple* and *pear* have the concept of *fruit*. Both *Microsoft* and *Google* hold the concept of *company*. In a broader sense, the term *concept* refers to the shared meaning of a group of words. The key idea behind our model is to obtain the word-concept relations and derive the respective embeddings for each word and each concept.

Table 2: Explicit and Implicit Word-Concept Relations

	Concept	Words
explicit	fruit	apple,pear,orange,peach,banana...
	company	microsoft,google,apple,amazon,sun...
	color	red, orange, green, yellow, grey...
implicit	class1	drugs,drug,medicine,body,abuse...
	class2	mind,thought,remember,memory,thinking...
	class3	school, students, schools, education, teacher...

Here, intrinsic word embeddings are local but ambiguous: every word has a unique representation, in which all senses get merged; concept embeddings are global but specific: a concept is shared by many words but conveys an unambiguous meaning. The complementary nature of word and concept embeddings suggests that better contextual representations of words can be derived by combining the two in the right manner. Consider for instance a target word w with a set of related concepts $c_1 \cdots c_n$. The contextual word representation for w is obtained with a compositional function f as follows:

$$\mathbf{w_x} = f(\mathbf{w}, \mathbf{c_i}) \tag{6}$$

where c_i is the most appropriate concept of the word in the given context.

A first step required by our model is to identify the *candidate* concepts for each word, after which we apply an algorithm to update the relevant concept vectors together with the word vectors during the training of a neural language model. In general, the term *concept* can be defined either explicitly or implicitly (see Table 2). On the one hand, explicit concepts of a word can be acquired from a knowledge base, such as Freebase [6] and Probase [46], where the word-concept relations are explicitly mentioned. On the other hand, implicit word-concept relations can be obtained with either supervised or unsupervised machine learning algorithms. Examples include topic models [5] and Brown clustering [12]. As we mentioned, the framework we propose is broadly applicable to any meaningful concept space. Next, we show how the word and concept embeddings can be jointly trained.

4. JOINTLY EMBEDDING WORDS AND CONCEPTS

We propose two classes of neural language models for co-training word-concept embeddings, based on the Skip-gram.

4.1 Parallel Word-Concept Skip-gram

The essence of a neural language model is to discover salient word representations that best interpret the co-occurrence relations among words. This is instantiated in the Skip-gram as updating the word representations so that the model can predict the likely contexts of a target word. An assumption made here is that words that appear often in similar contexts tend to have similar meanings, and hence should be assigned similar representations. Based on this assumption, we extend the Skip-gram by introducing concepts into the prediction. In the first model variant, we emphasize the co-occurrence relations between the target concept and the contextual words. The augmented objective function is to maximize the following average log probability:

$$\frac{1}{T}\sum_{i=1}^{T}\sum_{c=i-d,c\neq t}^{i+d}\log p(w_c|w_t)p(w_c|e_t) \tag{7}$$

Same as in Equation (1), $w_1, ...w_T$ denotes the entire training sequence. w_t and w_c represent the target word and contextual word respectively. e_t denotes the concept of w_t in the given context. The way e_t is selected from the candidate list will be discussed in a later section.

In the above model, the embeddings of a target word and its concept are updated in parallel; the two predictions $p(w_c|w_t)$ and $p(w_c|e_t)$ are decoupled but we want their values to be maximized at the same time. For the reason we call the model a variant of the Parallel Word-Concept Skip-gram (PWCS-1).

In the second variant of PWCS (PWCS-2), we use the target word to predict the concepts of the contextual words, with the following objective function:

$$\frac{1}{T}\sum_{i=1}^{T}\sum_{c=i-d,c\neq t}^{i+d}\log p(w_c|w_t)p(e_c|w_t) \tag{8}$$

Combining the above two model variants, we arrive at a more complete objective function embracing all possible predicative relationships:

$$\frac{1}{T}\sum_{i=1}^{T}\sum_{c=i-d,c\neq t}^{i+d}\log p(w_c|w_t)p(w_c|e_t)p(e_c|w_t)p(e_c|e_t) \tag{9}$$

The above model variant, which we name PWCS-3, depicts a complete bipartite graph between the target vertexes and the contextual vertexes, with a vertex representing a word or a concept. A pictorial interpretation of the three variants of PWCS is shown in Figure 1.

4.2 Generative Word-Concept Skip-gram

PWCS trains word-concept embeddings in a parallel fashion, where a word and its corresponding concept are assumed to be conditionally independent. A further question we pose is whether we can better emphasize the connections between a word and *its* concept within a single prediction process. As a *concept* refers to a collection of similar meanings, the task of choosing a word to fit in the context can be reduced to two steps: locating the right concept and then searching for a word underneath the chosen concept. This decomposed task can be integrated into a factorized neural language model, replacing the class s in Equation (3) with the concept e. The resulting objective function is

$$\frac{1}{T}\sum_{i=1}^{T}\sum_{c=i-d,c\neq t}^{i+d} logp(w_c|w_t)$$
$$p(w_c|w_t) = p(e_c|w_t)p(w_c|w_t, e_c) \tag{10}$$

We call the above model a variant of the Generative Word-Concept Skip-gram (GWCS-1) based on the generative nature. Note that the formulation of GWCS is in contrast to the conventional factorized neural language model, where factorization is only for efficiency concerns. Instead, we intend to extract the representation of a class as a summary of the word meanings underneath it. This in return injects linguistic motivations to the factorized neural language model. Also note that a word is allowed to be affiliated with multiple classes in GWCS.

GWCS-1 emphasizes the intrinsic relationship of a contextual word and its concept, but the concept of the target word is not included. Although it is hard to link the target word and its concept in a similar generative process, we can start from Equation (7) and extend each probabilistic term respectively:

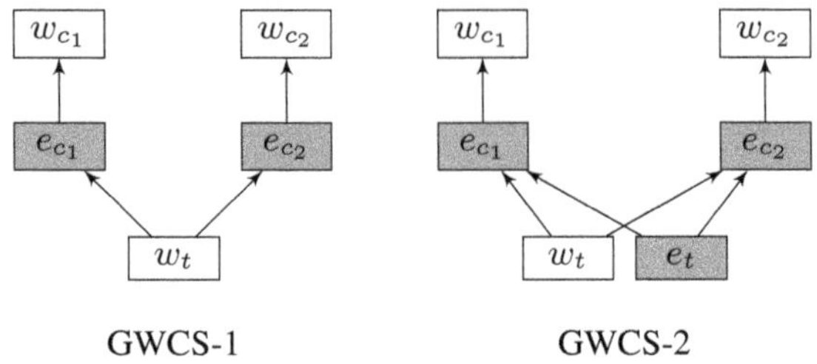

Figure 2: Generative Word-Concept Skip-grams

$$\frac{1}{T}\sum_{i=1}^{T}\sum_{c=i-d,c\neq t}^{i+d} logp(w_c|w_t)p(w_c|e_t)$$
$$p(w_c|w_t)p(w_c|e_t) = p(e_c|w_t)p(w_c|w_t, e_c)p(e_c|e_t)p(w_c|e_t, e_c) \tag{11}$$

We denote this model variant as GWCS-2. The topologies of GWCS-1 and GWCS-2 are depicted in Figure 2.

4.3 Speeding up the Training

In all variants of the extended neural Skip-gram models, computing the normalization constant for each probabilistic term can be expensive. Even for the factorized GWCSs, training can be slow if the number of concepts or the size of the class vocabulary is large. We therefore investigate methods to accelerate the training via term-wise noise contrastive estimation (NCE) [33]. Take the term $p(w_c|w_t, e_c)$ as an example, we show in the following how NCE can be applied.

With the notion of NCE described in Section 2, we define a binary classifier discriminating between samples drawn from the data distribution and those drawn from a uniform noise distribution of w_c, namely the distribution of words *within* a given class. The objective of maximizing the (log) likelihood of $p(w_c|w_t, e_c)$ is replaced as:

$$\log p(D=1|w_t, w_c, e_c) + \sum_{n=1,\bar{w}_c\sim q}^{N}\log p(D=0|w_t, \bar{w}_c, e_c) \tag{12}$$

By explicitly fixing the normalization constant to 1, we can estimate the probability as

$$p(D=1|w_t, w_c, e_c) = \frac{s(w_t, w_c, e_c)}{s(w_t, w_c, e_c) + Nq(w_c)} \tag{13}$$

where s is the scoring function as in Equation (2). By applying NCE to every term in the objective function by drawing samples from the noise distribution within the domain of interest, the training can be conducted much more efficiently.

4.4 Selecting the Right Concept to Update

Another question yet to be answered is how the context-appropriate concept of a word can be identified for updating. For example, when *apple* appears in the context of "*an apple engineer in america*", we hope that the majority of the concept updates are on the concept of *company*, since the other concept (*fruit*) is irrelevant. Formally, assuming a word w in a training sentence is associated with a set of candidate concepts C, the task can be recasted to that of finding the most suitable concept $c_i \in C$ for w_t to fit the current context.

The task of linking a word to its context-appropriate concept refers to *conceptualization* in the field of knowledge representa-

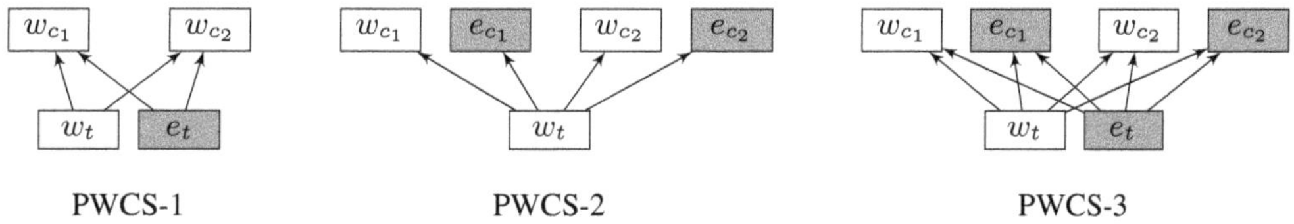

Figure 1: Parallel Word-Concept Skip-grams

tion and reasoning, which is considered an off-line task of unsupervised inference [42, 17, 45]. To save the excessive amount of time required in this preprocessing step, we propose using a softmax classifier and conceptualize each word "on the fly" of the training.

Specifically, for a word w occurring in a sentence $w_1, \cdots, w_m$ as context, we calculate the context representation as an average of the word vectors in the context:

$$\mathbf{x} = \frac{1}{m}\sum_{i=1}^{m} \mathbf{w_i} \tag{14}$$

where w_i is the representation of the ith contextual word. We are now able to estimate the probabilistic distribution of concepts of w_i based on the softmax function acting on the context representation:

$$p(e|x) = \frac{\exp(\mathbf{e} \cdot \mathbf{x})}{\sum_{e_i \in E(w)} \exp(\mathbf{e_i} \cdot \mathbf{x})} \tag{15}$$

where $E(w)$ is the set of candidate concepts for w.

Given the likelihood of each concept in the current context, the updates can be carried out in two ways. In a hard assignment, the concept that receives the highest score will be selected for updating:

$$e = \arg\max_{e_i \in E(w)} p(e_i|x) \tag{16}$$

Under a soft criterion, a weighted update of all candidate concepts is performed. Here, we redefine the error induced by the concept as a weighted sum error induced by all candidate concepts. Take Equation (7) as an example and assume we want to update parameters based on the error $J(e)$ induced when maximizing $p(w_c|e_t)$. We redefine $J(e)$ as

$$J_o(e) = \sum_{e_i \in E(w)} p(e_i|x) J(e_i) \tag{17}$$

Based on the above equation, we perform a weighted update of all candidate concepts. The soft update has been empirically found to ensure optimum performance in a "cold start" condition.

5. CONTEXTUAL REPRESENTATIONS

In this section, we discuss how the word-concept embeddings can be used to derive context-appropriate representations for words, phrases and sentences.

5.1 Contextual Representations for Words

In the proposed model, the intrinsic word embeddings preserve the unique features of each word, but theses representations are ambiguous. On the other hand, a concept is shared by a group of words, but it conveys a precise meaning. To obtain a better representation framework that is context aware, we combine the two types of embeddings in a compositional manner. Let $\mathbf{w_x}$ denote the contextual representation for word w, whose intrinsic embedding is $\mathbf{w}$. $\mathbf{c_x}$ denotes the current concept representation of w obtained either in a hard (selecting only one concept embedding) or a soft (weighing all concept embeddings) way based on Equation (15). Then

$$\mathbf{w_x} = f(\mathbf{w}, \mathbf{c_x}) \tag{18}$$

In the above equation, f stands for an arbitrary compositional function and we use weighted sum in this work. That is,

$$\mathbf{w_x} = \mathbf{w} + \lambda \mathbf{c_i} \tag{19}$$

where λ controls the relative importance between the two types of embeddings. The optimal value of λ can be decided via grid search in a small validation set.

5.2 Contextual Representations for Larger Text Units: A Brief Discussion

Distributional representations have proven successful at the word level. But in practice, the need for representations of larger text units is more evident. For example, in web searching, we are concerned with the representations of queries and documents. While this is not the main theme of the current paper, we provide a brief discussion on how the compositional representations can be obtained so as to be injected with the contextual component carried by the word representations.

Much work in research literature has been dedicated to exploring the compositional operations of words, ranging from simple algebraic operations [31] to more sophisticated neural networks [41, 19]. Among these approaches, the simplest one is vector addition, in which the representation of a piece of text s is obtained as the sum of all word representations w_i in the text:

$$\mathbf{s}(w_1 w_2 \cdots w_l) = \sum_{i=1}^{l} \mathbf{w_i} \tag{20}$$

The bag-of-words approach often constitutes a simple but effective baseline.

On the other hand, neural network based compositional models are evolving to become more important in compositionality [41, 19]. In these models, a neural network takes as input a pair of word vectors $\mathbf{w_1}, \mathbf{w_2}$ and returns a composite vector $\mathbf{y}$ as follows:

$$\mathbf{y} = f(\mathbf{t} \cdot \mathbf{w_{1:2}} + \mathbf{b}) \tag{21}$$

Here, $\mathbf{t}$ and $\mathbf{b}$ are model parameters and f represents the nonlinearity. During experiments, we find that a simple neural bigram model perform surprisingly well. The model refers to a convolutional neural network with one convolution layer (with a window of size 2) and one pooling layer that combines the compositional bigram features. This architecture is shown in Figure 3.

6. EXPERIMENTS

Three sets of experiments are conducted to evaluate the contextual word embeddings created in our framework. This section covers all experimental details, results and findings. We start by specifying aspects of the experimental set-up.

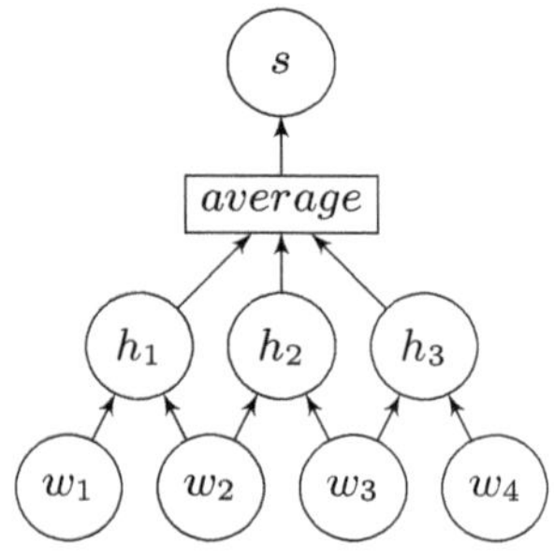

Figure 3: The architecture of a neural bigram sentence model.

6.1 Acquiring Concepts of Words

We explore two sets of word-concept relations, one obtained explicitly and the other implicitly.

Explicit Concepts. The explicit word-concept relations are retrieved from a large-scale probabilistic knowledge base, known as the Probase[1] [46]. As an advantage, Probase has a much richer concept space (with 2.7 million concepts) than other existing knowledge bases, such as Freebase (with 2,000 concepts) [6] and Cyc (with 120,000 concepts) [23]. The word-concept relationships in Probase are harvested from 1.68 billion web pages and two years of Microsoft Bing search logs [46, 22].

Overall, Probase contains a number of closely related concepts. For example, *apple* is associated with both concepts of *fruit* and *seasonal fruit*. To reduce the amount of overlapped concepts, we perform k-Medoids clustering [25] on the raw concepts of Probase. Eventually we get 4,819 concept clusters, with each centered at the most salient concept. We use the 4,819 concept clusters as the explicit concept space.

In Probase, every word-concept relationship has a typicality score indicating the importance of the concept to the word. After the K-Medoids clustering, we compute a similar score for each word-cluster by aggregating the scores between the word and every concept within the cluster. We then prune for each word the clusters with low scores. As a result, a polysemous word normally belongs to 3 to 10 clusters.

Implicit Concepts. The explicit word-concept relations usually have high accuracy but low coverage since many verbs and adjectives do not possess concepts in the knowledge base. We additionally explore implicit concepts obtained in a data-driven manner. Specifically, we perform Latent Dirichlet Allocation (LDA) [5], a well established topic model, with 3 million Wikipedia documents.

LDA is a hierarchical Bayesian model for text generation. In LDA, each document d is modeled as a distribution over K topics, each of which is then characterized by a distribution over words. The words in a document are generated by repeatedly sampling a topic based on the topic distribution and then sampling a single word from the selected topic.

Formally, given a corpus consisting of M documents, the generative process for a document d is defined as follows. First, the mixing proportion over topics θ_d is drawn from a Dirichlet prior with parameters α. Each document is then generated according to the topic distributions $z_{1:K}$ and word probabilities over topics β. The probability of a document d in a corpus is defined as:

$$p(d|\alpha,\beta) = \int_{\theta} p(\theta_d|\alpha)(\prod_{n=1}^{N}\sum_{z_k} p(z_k|\theta_d)p(w_n|z_k,\beta))d\theta \quad (22)$$

[1]Probase data is publicly available at http://probase.msra.cn/dataset.aspx

The central challenge in LDA is to compute the posterior distribution $p(\theta, z|d, \alpha, \beta)$ of the hidden variable z given a document d. Although this distribution is generally intractable, a variety of approximate inference algorithms have been proposed in the literature. In this work, we use a well-implemented variational inference for posterior estimation [36]. The number of topics is set to 500. As a result, we obtain 500 latent topics as implicit concepts. We prune for each word the topics that receive low probabilities.

6.2 Training

We train our neural language models on the "One Billion Word Language Modeling Benchmark" dataset [9] released by Google. All model variants are implemented in two respective concept spaces and the resulting embeddings are evaluated. In each model variant, a word is associated with two sets of vectors, assuming the same word as target and as context come from two distinct vocabularies [28]. For concepts we do not adopt this assumption since they are essentially shared among words. The dimension of all embeddings is set to 300. The code is written in C language as an extension of the efficient WORD2VEC toolkit [29]. All trainings are performed on a Windows Server 2008 with a 2.13 GHz Intel Xeon CPU (4 processors).

6.3 Similarities of Words and Phrases

The first set of experiments concerns the similarity of words and phrases as a generic evaluation of the vector space. We provide comparisons between the aforementioned model variants, as well as comparisons between our models and a few well-established baselines. To avoid overfitting, we adopt two datasets here, one at the word level and the other for phrases.

The word-level dataset refers to the Stanford Contextual Word Similarity Dataset (SCWS) of Huang et al. [18], which contains 2,003 pairs of words and their sentence contexts. For each pair of words, there are 10 human similarity scores provided. Our task is to evaluate by Spearman's correlation how the similarities computed from various models match those of human judgments. Note that the sentence contexts provided in the dataset enable us to create contextual word representations.

The phrase similarity dataset we use is the one of Mitchell and Lapata (M& L) [32]. This dataset consists of similarity judgments for 1,944 pairs of adjective-noun (A-N), noun-noun (N-N) and verb-object (V-O) phrases, respectively. (In total, there are 5,832 phrase pairs.) Similar to SCWS, each pair of phrases in M&L is annotated with a similarity score. Although there is no additional context provided for each phrase, the contextual representation of a word can be derived with its neighboring word in the phrase as context.

Hyper-parameters. At first, we consider the two forms of concept representations of a word in a given context. The *globalConcept* metric selects a single concept for the word based on the score computed from Equation (15). The *avgConcept* metric, on the other hand, derives the contextual concept representation as a sum of all concept embeddings weighed by their scores. We compare the two types of concept representations obtained by PWCS-1 with the explicit concept space. Meanwhile, we perform a grid search to decide the optimum value of λ in Equation (19).

From Figure 4, we observe that *avgConcept* generally outperforms *globalConcept*. In both metrics, the Spearman's correlation increases as the conceptual features start to be injected into the word embeddings. However, a further increase of λ will lead to some performance degradation in either case. One reason is that words need to maintain their unique features in order to discriminate one another; whereas the representations of two conceptually same words will be almost the same in the case of a large λ.

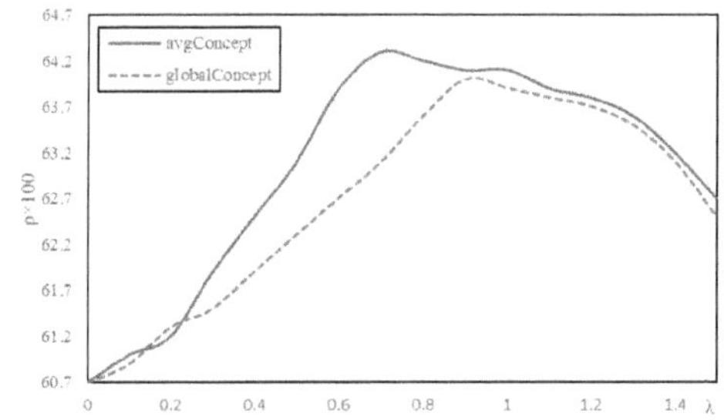

(a) SCWS

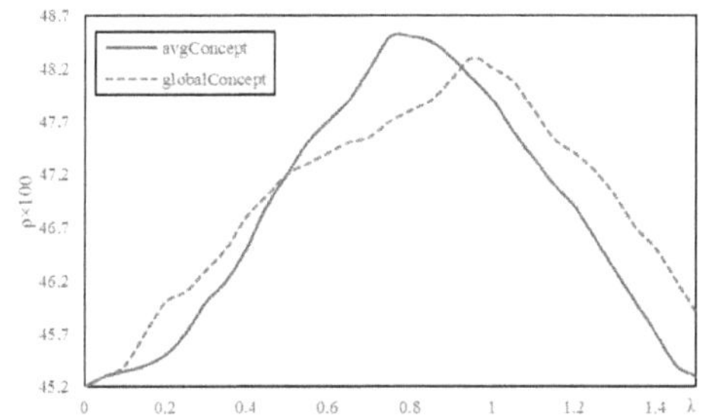

(b) A-N

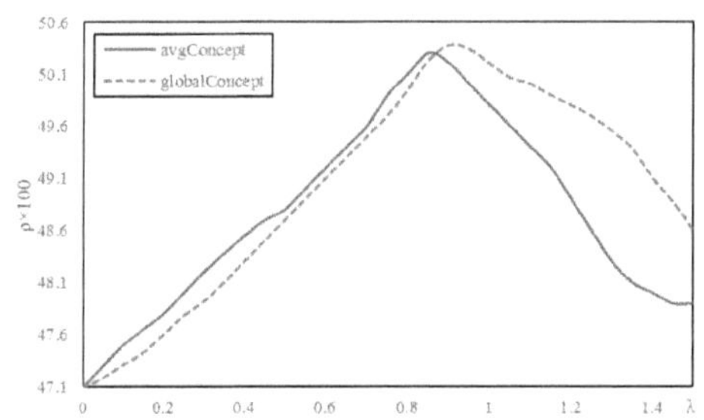

(c) N-N

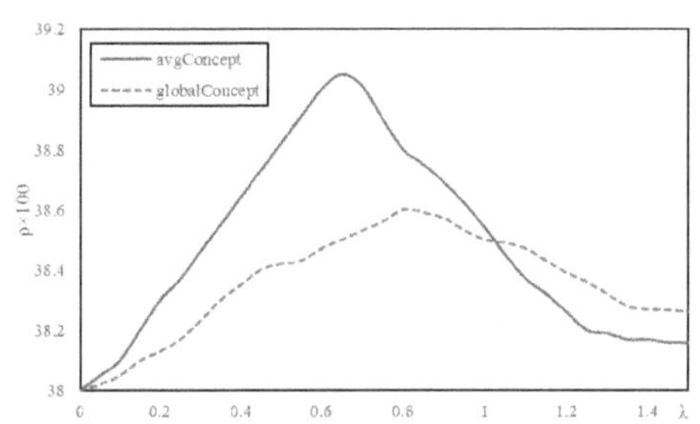

(d) V-O

Figure 4: Plot for Spearman's Correlation against λ.

For *avgConcept*, the best result is obtained when λ is between 0.5 to 0.8, while for *globalConcept* the optimum λ is between 0.8 to 1. The rest of the experiments will be based on *avgConcept* with lambda set to 0.75.

Comparison of Model Variants. In the next part, we evaluate the effectiveness of conceptual word representations against raw word embeddings. The comparison is respectively performed in each of the five model variants with the explicit concept space. The results are summarized in Table 3. As we can see, for all variants of PWCS and GWCS, representing words contextually brings significant performance gains. We further notice that GWCSs in general outperform PWCSs in terms of both types of embeddings. The finding indicates that taking into account the semantic relations within a neural architecture is helpful for the representation learning task.

		PWCS-1	PWCS-2	PWCS-3	GWCS-1	GWCS-2
SCWS	Raw	60.7	60.3	60.7	61.9	61.6
	Contextual	**63.5**	**63.4**	**64.1**	**65.7**	**64.5**
A-N	Raw	45.2	44.7	45.0	45.8	45.5
	Contextual	**48.5**	**48.1**	**49.3**	**50.4**	**49.2**
N-N	Raw	47.1	46.3	47.0	47.6	47.3
	Contextual	**50.3**	**50.5**	**50.6**	**53.1**	**51.3**
V-O	Raw	38.0	37.9	37.8	38.2	38.5
	Contextual	**38.9**	**38.2**	**38.9**	**39.7**	**38.6**

Table 3: Spearman's correlation $\rho \times 100$ of the variants of P-WCS and GWCS.

Comparison of Concept Spaces. Next, we compare the contextual word representations trained with the two concept spaces: explicit concepts based on the Probase and implicit concepts obtained via LDA. We use PWCS-3 and GWCS-1 in this evaluation. The results are shown in Table 4.

Comparing the numbers given by the two spaces, the explicit space shows superior performance on the similarity measure of noun-noun phrases, while the implicit space does better on the SCWS and verb-object tasks. One interpretation is that explicit concept mapping has higher accuracy but low "recalls": many words (such as verbs and adjectives) do not have any concept in the knowledge base. In this case, inducing implicit concepts provides a complement.

	Space	SCWS	A-N	N-N	V-O
	Explicit	64.1	49.3	**50.6**	38.9
PWCS-3	Implicit	**64.3**	**49.9**	49.2	**39.0**
	Explicit	65.7	**50.4**	**53.1**	39.7
GWCS-1	Implicit	**65.9**	50.0	52.5	**39.8**

Table 4: Spearman's correlation $\rho \times 100$ for contextual word representations in different concept spaces.

Comparison with Baselines and Published Results. Next, we compare the results of our models with a few well-established baselines in the SCWS task. These include the neural language model of Collobert and Weston (C&W) [10], the ordinary Skip-gram model trained with hierarchical softmax, and three sets of sense embedding models of Huang et al. [18] (*nClass*=3), Neelakantan et al. [34] and Bartunov et al. [1], respectively. These models were all trained with the code released by the authors. An additional baseline is *preprocessed*, in which the word-concept relations are used outside embeddings. In this method, the training words are preprocessed into *word-concept* pairs, after which the ordinary Skip-gram is applied. In terms of our models, we report the *best* number achieved with PWCS and GWCS respectively.

Overall, we see from Table 5 that the contextual word representations significantly outperform the word embedding baselines. The numbers given by sense embeddings are quite competitive without any consideration of efficiency in mind, but still the highest number is achieved by GWCS. Table 6 further compares the training time of various models *relative to* the Skip-gram. In terms of efficiency, our models have a clear advantage over Huang et al. [18], while they are slightly faster than the non-parametric methods of Neelakantan et al. [34] and Bartunov et al.[1], But note that we only need to store 4,819 explicit concept vectors or 500 implicit concept vectors, whereas the size of sense vectors is usually several times more than the size of the vocabulary (55,000).

	Model	$\rho \times 100$
Word Emb.	C&W	58.6
	Skip-gram	58.3
Sense Emb.	Huang et al. (2012)	62.9
	Neelakantan et al. (2014)	64.7
	Bartunov et al. (2015)	65.5
	preprocessed	63.5
Contextual Emb.	PWCS	64.3
	GWCS	**65.9**

Table 5: Spearman's correlation $\rho \times 100$ of various models in comparison.

Model	Time
Skip-gram	1
Huang et al. (2012)	117
Neelakantan et al. (2014)	3.9
Bartunov et al. (2015)	3.5
preprocessed	5
PWCS	3.4
GWCS	2.2

Table 6: Training time of various models relative to the Skip-gram.

Concept Assignments for Rare Words. In the end, we qualitatively evaluate the selected concepts by GWCS-1 for a few rare words in SCWS. In the concept-based disambiguation method, we can visualize directly the *exact* concept that a word is assigned to. However, in the sense-based models, we are unable to find out the exact meaning behind a sense.

Word	Context	Concept
Cambridge	Whittington , with the help of research students Derek Briggs and Simon Conway Morris of the University of **Cambridge** , began a thorough reassessment of the Burgess Shale , and revealed that the fauna represented were much more diverse and unusual than Walcott had recognized.	school:0.62 institution:0.27 spot:0.07 town:0.02 country:0.01 guide:0.01
placental	As a result, native Australian **placental** mammals, such as hopping mice, are more recent immigrants.	pregnancy outcome: 0.53 condition: 0.38 organ: 0.09
assimilation	Ethnic cohesiveness is a resistance strategy to **assimilation** and the accompanying cultural dissolution.	adaptation: 0.49 physiological process: 0.18 impact: 0.17 disturbance: 0.13 lifestyle change: 0.02 symptom:0.01
bootleg	Often , **bootleg** DVD copies of movies are available before the prints are officially released in cinemas.	motif: 0.77 work: 0.12 rarity: 0.07 brewery: 0.04

Table 7: Concept assignments for rare words in SCWS.

As the results in Table 7 suggest, rare words can be accurately mapped to the most context-appropriate concepts. We argue that the concept-based disambiguation method is superior in the sense that a concept representation is learnt with all words sharing that concept. This not only emphasizes the semantic interactions among words, but also provides an elegant solution to rare words whose senses are hard to induce the other way around.

6.4 Paraphrase Detection

Measuring the similarity of two words or phrases provides preliminary evidence on the quality of the contextual word representations. In the second experiment, we augment the evaluation by measuring the similarity of sentences. We use the Microsoft Research Paraphrase Corpus (MSRPC) introduced by Dolan et al. [11]. The MSRPC contains 5,801 sentence pairs (4,076 for training and 1,725 for test) and labels (0 or 1) indicating whether a pair of sentences has a paraphrase relationship. We explore the use of contextual features obtained with our models in the classification task and compare the results with various baselines and published numbers.

	Acc.	F1
Baselines		
Skip-gram + $\oplus$	71.9	81.3
Our Models		
PWCS + $\oplus$	74.5	82.7
PWCS + nn	75.0	**83.0**
GWCS + $\oplus$	74.3	82.5
GWCS + nn	**75.1**	82.9
Published Models		
LSA (Hassan,2011)	68.8	79.9
MSC (Mihalcea et al., 2006)	70.3	81.3
SSA (Hassan,2011)	72.5	81.4
SDS (Blacoe and Lapata, 2012)	73.0	82.3
RAE+DP (Socher et al., 2011)	76.8	83.6
MTM (Madnani et al., 2012)	**77.4**	**84.1**

Table 8: Results of the paraphrase identification.

Specifically, we use three sets of features here: 1) the cosine similarity of the pair of sentence vectors; 2) the number of shared concepts of the two sentences identified from our models; 3) the lengths and the co-occurring word counts of the two sentences. In the baselines, the second feature is not included. Note that the third set of features do not stem from our models but are used as a complement, since raw embeddings cannot capture subtle aspects of a sentence such as proper nouns. Similar features are also used in the studies of Blacoe and Lapata [4] and Socher et al. [40]. We follow Blacoe and Lapata [4] to use the liblinear classifier [13] in this task. Besides, we explore two ways to compose words into sentences: by vector addition ($\oplus$) and neural bigram model (nn) respectively.

As the results in Table 8 reveal, our models outperform most baselines and the published numbers which are based on distributional features [16, 4, 27]. Among the published models, the closest one to ours is the work of Blacoe and Lapata [4], who use a similar set of features except that their embeddings are based on co-occurrence statistics. Results demonstrate the superiority of our contextual embedding space. Still, there exist more sophisticated models that are successful in performing this task. For example, Socher et al. [40] apply dynamic pooling on the output of the recursive auto-encoder to create more faithful similarity features; and Madnani et al. [26] use a combination of eight machine translation metrics to achieve state-of-art results. Compared with these works, our features are much shallower yet we obtain close numbers.

6.5 Question-Answer Relatedness Classification

In the last experiment, we evaluate the effectiveness contextual word representations in a practical task. As an aid to open domain question-answering, the task is to decide whether a pair of question and answer are semantically related. The corresponding dataset contains 85,512 pairs of question-type queries and the corresponding answers retrieved from the search log of a commercial search engine. The semantic relatedness of each question and answer is scored by a group of professional annotators, after which a label (0 or 1) is assigned to each pair based on the average score. Our task here is to evaluate the quality of the embedding features by evaluating how the semantic relatedness computed in the vector space matches that of human judgment.We divide the dataset into

80% for training and 20% for testing. We train a logistic regression classifier that takes as input the cosine similarity of each question-answer and outputs the label. The representation of a question or an answer is obtained with vector addition excluding stop-words. The classification results of various models are shown in Table 9.

	Acc.
Baselines	
All positive	69.1
Skip-gram	76.8
Our models	
PWCS, Raw	77.8
PWCS, Contextual	**82.5**
GWCS, Raw	78.2
GWCS, Contextual	**83.1**

Table 9: Results of the Q-A relatedness classification.

We see a significant increase in the performance of contextual word representations with respect to raw word embeddings and baselines. In the presence of a large amount of training data, the experimental results provide stronger evidence on the effectiveness of our contextual word representations.

7. RELATED WORK

Word representations learnt from traditional distributional practices and neural language models are limited by their inability to handle polysemy. To solve the problem, several approaches have been proposed to create multi-sense word representations. The initial proposal was to obtain the sense vectors of a word by clustering the context vectors obtained in a normal distributional practice. This methodology has later been popularized by Reisinger and Mooney [37] and named as Multi-Prototype Vector Space (MPVS). Huang et al. [18] apply MPVS to pre-trained word embeddings to get neural sense representations. More recently, Neelakantan et al. [34] integrate the context clustering step into a Skip-gram, resulting in a unified model where all parameters are jointly optimized during training.

A common limitation of all the above work lies in the excessive amount of computational cost induced in the clustering step, which has to be applied to every word in the vocabulary.

There also exist several approaches to training sense embeddings directly from a neural language model, without considering any clustering step in mind. Pina and Johansson [35] use a naive Bayesian step for updating the most proper senses in a neural language model. Bartunov et al. [1] propose a non-parametric Bayesian extension of the Skip-gram. Their model is capable of learning not only sense embeddings but also the number of senses a word has. Meanwhile, Li and Jurafsky [24] use the non-parametric Chinese Restaurant Process for sense induction in a Skip-gram. Despite the improved efficiency of these models, they all require a significant amount of storage in the case of a large vocabulary, since every sense is associated with a vector which will be stored. Moreover, there is no clear mapping between the senses learned by these models and the actual senses of a word. This becomes problematic for rare words or rare senses, for which there does not exist enough training contexts for inference.

Another line of related research is on knowledge-powered word embeddings. Following the work of Bordes et al. [8], several methods have been proposed to represent entities of a knowledge base in the vectorial form [8, 7, 39]. The majority deal with the $< head\,entity, relation, tail\,entity>$ triplets and scores their relational plausibility with word embeddings. The scoring function ranges from simple spatial distance between entity embeddings transformed through the relation [8, 7] to more sophisticated Neural Tensor Networks [39]. Additionally, some works use relational information extracted from semantic lexicons as constrains in the training of neural language models [3], or in a post-processing step to refine pre-trained word vectors [14]. To the best of our knowledge, no previous work on embeddings deals with word-concept relations in a knowledge base.

8. CONCLUSION

Representing text well is crucial for machines to understand human language. In this paper, we propose a novel framework for representing text contextually in the distributional semantic space. The key idea is to utilize the conceptual information of words to disambiguate their meanings. In the proposed framework, words are assigned with dynamic representations which change with contexts. This framework differs from traditional "vector-space based word sense induction" in the sense that it does not create any sense-specific representations. Instead, it looks into the shared concepts among senses, resulting in a class of neural language models efficient in both computation and storage, and with improved applicability to rare words and rare senses. An interesting future direction would be incorporating the concept induction step within the training of a neural language model referencing Brown clustering [12].

9. ACKNOWLEDGMENTS

This work was partially supported by the National Key Basic Research Program (973 Program) of China under grant No. 2014CB340403 and the Fundamental Research Funds for the Central Universities & the Research Funds of Renmin University of China. The authors would like to acknowledge Haibo Shi for the initial discussions on this topic at Microsoft Research Asia.

10. REFERENCES

[1] S. Bartunov, D. Kondrashkin, A. Osokin, and D. Vetrov. Breaking sticks and ambiguities with adaptive skip-gram. *arXiv preprint arXiv:1502.07257*, 2015.

[2] Y. Bengio, R. Ducharme, P. Vincent, and C. Janvin. A neural probabilistic language model. *The Journal of Machine Learning Research*, 3:1137–1155, 2003.

[3] J. Bian, B. Gao, and T.-Y. Liu. Knowledge-powered deep learning for word embedding. In *Machine Learning and Knowledge Discovery in Databases*, pages 132–148. Springer, 2014.

[4] W. Blacoe and M. Lapata. A comparison of vector-based representations for semantic composition. In *EMNLP 2012*, pages 546–556. Association for Computational Linguistics, 2012.

[5] D. M. Blei, A. Y. Ng, and M. I. Jordan. Latent dirichlet allocation. *the Journal of machine Learning research*, 3:993–1022, 2003.

[6] K. Bollacker, C. Evans, P. Paritosh, T. Sturge, and J. Taylor. Freebase: a collaboratively created graph database for structuring human knowledge. In *SIGMOD 2008*, pages 1247–1250. ACM, 2008.

[7] A. Bordes, N. Usunier, A. Garcia-Duran, J. Weston, and O. Yakhnenko. Translating embeddings for modeling multi-relational data. In *Advances in Neural Information Processing Systems*, pages 2787–2795, 2013.

[8] A. Bordes, J. Weston, R. Collobert, and Y. Bengio. Learning structured embeddings of knowledge bases. In *Conference on Artificial Intelligence*, number EPFL-CONF-192344, 2011.

[9] C. Chelba, T. Mikolov, M. Schuster, Q. Ge, T. Brants, P. Koehn, and T. Robinson. One billion word benchmark for measuring progress in statistical language modeling. *arXiv preprint arXiv:1312.3005*, 2013.

[10] R. Collobert and J. Weston. A unified architecture for natural language processing: Deep neural networks with multitask learning. In *Proceedings of the 25th international conference on Machine learning*, pages 160–167. ACM, 2008.

[11] B. Dolan, C. Quirk, and C. Brockett. Unsupervised construction of large paraphrase corpora: Exploiting massively parallel news sources. In *Proceedings of the 20th international conference on Computational Linguistics*, page 350. Association for Computational Linguistics, 2004.

[12] M. B. Eisen, P. T. Spellman, P. O. Brown, and D. Botstein. Cluster analysis and display of genome-wide expression patterns. *Proceedings of the National Academy of Sciences*, 95(25):14863–14868, 1998.

[13] R.-E. Fan, K.-W. Chang, C.-J. Hsieh, X.-R. Wang, and C.-J. Lin. Liblinear: A library for large linear classification. *The Journal of Machine Learning Research*, 9:1871–1874, 2008.

[14] M. Faruqui, J. Dodge, S. K. Jauhar, C. Dyer, E. Hovy, and N. A. Smith. Retrofitting word vectors to semantic lexicons. *arXiv preprint arXiv:1411.4166*, 2014.

[15] Z. S. Harris. Distributional structure. *Word*, 1954.

[16] S. Hassan. *Measuring semantic relatedness using salient encyclopedic concepts*. University of North Texas, 2011.

[17] W. Hua, Z. Wang, H. Wang, K. Zheng, and X. Zhou. Short text understanding through lexical-semantic analysis. In *International Conference on Data Engineering (ICDE)*, 2015.

[18] E. H. Huang, R. Socher, C. D. Manning, and A. Y. Ng. Improving word representations via global context and multiple word prototypes. In *Proceedings of the 50th ACL*. Association for Computational Linguistics, 2012.

[19] N. Kalchbrenner, E. Grefenstette, and P. Blunsom. A convolutional neural network for modelling sentences. *arXiv preprint arXiv:1404.2188*, 2014.

[20] D. Kartsaklis, M. Sadrzadeh, et al. Prior disambiguation of word tensors for constructing sentence vectors. In *EMNLP*, pages 1590–1601, 2013.

[21] D. Kartsaklis, M. Sadrzadeh, and S. Pulman. Separating disambiguation from composition in distributional semantics. In *Proceedings of CoNLL*, pages 114–123, 2013.

[22] T. Lee, Z. Wang, H. Wang, and S.-w. Hwang. Attribute extraction and scoring: A probabilistic approach. 2013.

[23] D. B. Lenat. Cyc: A large-scale investment in knowledge infrastructure. *Communications of the ACM*, 38(11):33–38, 1995.

[24] J. Li and D. Jurafsky. Do multi-sense embeddings improve natural language understanding? *arXiv preprint arXiv:1506.01070*, 2015.

[25] P. Li, H. Wang, K. Q. Zhu, Z. Wang, and X. Wu. Computing term similarity by large probabilistic isa knowledge. In *CIKM*, 2013.

[26] N. Madnani, J. Tetreault, and M. Chodorow. Re-examining machine translation metrics for paraphrase identification. In *Proceedings of NAACL*, pages 182–190. Association for Computational Linguistics, 2012.

[27] R. Mihalcea, C. Corley, and C. Strapparava. Corpus-based and knowledge-based measures of text semantic similarity. In *AAAI*, volume 6, pages 775–780, 2006.

[28] T. Mikolov, Q. V. Le, and I. Sutskever. Exploiting similarities among languages for machine translation. *arXiv preprint arXiv:1309.4168*, 2013.

[29] T. Mikolov, I. Sutskever, K. Chen, G. S. Corrado, and J. Dean. Distributed representations of words and phrases and their compositionality. In *NIPS*, 2013.

[30] T. Mikolov, W.-t. Yih, and G. Zweig. Linguistic regularities in continuous space word representations. 2013.

[31] J. Mitchell and M. Lapata. Vector-based models of semantic composition. In *ACL*, pages 236–244, 2008.

[32] J. Mitchell and M. Lapata. Vector-based models of semantic composition. In *Proceedings of ACL-08: HLT*, pages 236–244, Columbus, Ohio, June 2008. Association for Computational Linguistics.

[33] A. Mnih and Y. W. Teh. A fast and simple algorithm for training neural probabilistic language models. *arXiv preprint arXiv:1206.6426*, 2012.

[34] A. Neelakantan, J. Shankar, A. Passos, and A. McCallum. Efficient nonparametric estimation of multiple embeddings per word in vector space. In *Proceedings of EMNLP*, 2014.

[35] L. N. Pina and R. Johansson. A simple and efficient method to generate word sense representations. *arXiv preprint arXiv:1412.6045*, 2014.

[36] D. Ramage, E. Rosen, J. Chuang, C. D. Manning, and D. A. McFarland. Topic modeling for the social sciences. In *Workshop on Applications for Topic Models, NIPS*, 2009.

[37] J. Reisinger and R. J. Mooney. Multi-prototype vector-space models of word meaning. In *NAACL 2010*, pages 109–117. Association for Computational Linguistics, 2010.

[38] H. Schütze. Automatic word sense discrimination. *Computational linguistics*, 24(1):97–123, 1998.

[39] R. Socher, D. Chen, C. D. Manning, and A. Ng. Reasoning with neural tensor networks for knowledge base completion. In *Advances in Neural Information Processing Systems*, pages 926–934, 2013.

[40] R. Socher, E. H. Huang, J. Pennin, C. D. Manning, and A. Y. Ng. Dynamic pooling and unfolding recursive autoencoders for paraphrase detection. In *Advances in Neural Information Processing Systems*, pages 801–809, 2011.

[41] R. Socher, C. C. Lin, C. Manning, and A. Y. Ng. Parsing natural scenes and natural language with recursive neural networks. In *Proceedings of (ICML-11)*, pages 129–136, 2011.

[42] Y. Song, H. Wang, Z. Wang, H. Li, and W. Chen. Short text conceptualization using a probabilistic knowledgebase. In *Proceedings of the Twenty-Second international joint conference on Artificial Intelligence-Volume Volume Three*, pages 2330–2336. AAAI Press, 2011.

[43] F. Wang, Z. Wang, Z. Li, and J.-R. Wen. Concept-based short text classification and ranking. In *ACM International Conference on Information and Knowledge Management (CIKM)*, October 2014.

[44] Z. Wang, H. Wang, and Z. Hu. Head, modifier, and constraint detection in short texts. In *IEEE 30th International Conference on Data Engineering (ICDE)*. IEEE, 2014.

[45] Z. Wang, K. Zhao, H. Wang, X. Meng, and J.-R. Wen. Query understanding through knowledge-based conceptualization. In *IJCAI*, 2015.

[46] W. Wu, H. Li, H. Wang, and K. Q. Zhu. Probase: A probabilistic taxonomy for text understanding. In *SIGMOD 2012*, pages 481–492. ACM, 2012.

External Knowledge and Query Strategies in Active Learning: a Study in Clinical Information Extraction

Mahnoosh Kholghi[1,2], Laurianne Sitbon[1], Guido Zuccon[1], Anthony Nguyen[2]
[1]Queensland University of Technology (QUT), Brisbane 4000, Queensland, Australia
[2]The Australian e-Health Research Centre, CSIRO, Brisbane 4029, Queensland, Australia
{m1.kholghi, laurianne.sitbon, g.zuccon}@qut.edu.au, anthony.nguyen@csiro.au

ABSTRACT

This paper presents a new active learning query strategy for information extraction, called Domain Knowledge Informativeness (DKI). Active learning is often used to reduce the amount of annotation effort required to obtain training data for machine learning algorithms. A key component of an active learning approach is the query strategy, which is used to iteratively select samples for annotation. Knowledge resources have been used in information extraction as a means to derive additional features for *sample representation*. DKI is, however, the first query strategy that exploits such resources to inform *sample selection*. To evaluate the merits of DKI, in particular with respect to the reduction in annotation effort that the new query strategy allows to achieve, we conduct a comprehensive empirical comparison of active learning query strategies for information extraction within the clinical domain. The clinical domain was chosen for this work because of the availability of extensive structured knowledge resources which have often been exploited for feature generation. In addition, the clinical domain offers a compelling use case for active learning because of the necessary high costs and hurdles associated with obtaining annotations in this domain. Our experimental findings demonstrated that (1) amongst existing query strategies, the ones based on the classification model's confidence are a better choice for clinical data as they perform equally well with a much lighter computational load, and (2) significant reductions in annotation effort are achievable by exploiting knowledge resources within active learning query strategies, with up to 14% less tokens and concepts to manually annotate than with state-of-the-art query strategies.

Categories and Subject Descriptors

I.2.7 [**Artificial Intelligence**]: Natural Language Processing – *text analysis.*

General Terms

Algorithms, Performance, Experimentation.

Keywords

Domain Knowledge; Active Learning; Concept Extraction; Clinical Free Text; Conditional Random Fields.

CIKM'15, October 19–23, 2015, Melbourne, VIC, Australia.

ACM 978-1-4503-3794-6/15/10…$15.00
http://dx.doi.org/10.1145/2806416.2806550

1. INTRODUCTION

Supervised machine learning (ML) algorithms can train powerful statistical models to effectively capture useful structured information from clinical free-text resources [19]. However, these algorithms require a large amount of annotated training data. Preparing high quality annotated data is a major obstacle to effective data analysis in many domains; this is even further exacerbated in the clinical domain as it requires significant efforts from highly trained, and costly, clinical professionals.

Active learning (AL) has been suggested as an effective solution for reducing the burden of manual annotations in automatic information extraction tasks [26]. In standard supervised learning, training samples are annotated at once. Active learning differs from this because the annotation is performed as an iterative process in which *informative* samples (i.e., those that contain useful information for the model) are selected from a pool of unlabeled data and provided to experts for annotation. The selection of informative samples takes place according to a query strategy, which thus represents a key component within AL approaches. In each iteration, after samples are selected and annotated, they are added to the labeled set of data, on which a refined supervised model is built [26]. It is possible to either fully retrain the model at each step, or incrementally update the model learnt in the preceding loop (see Figure 1).

AL approaches vary in the query strategies that are adopted, as well as in the supervised machine learning algorithm that is

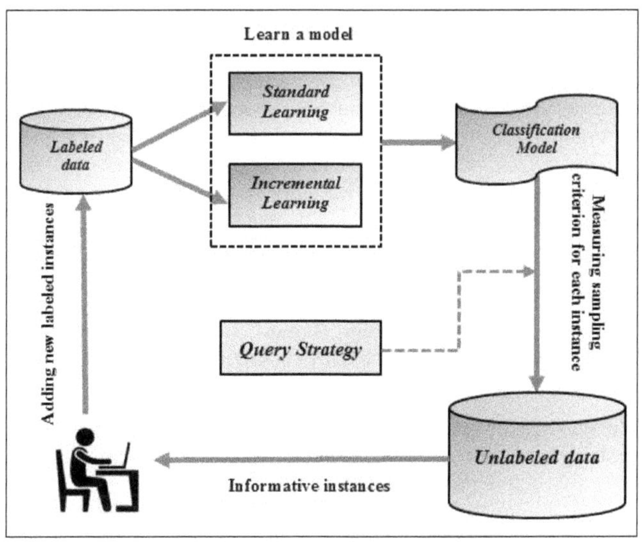

Figure 1. The active learning process.

employed throughout the iterations; as a result, AL has shown varying performance across different datasets [6].

Despite its practical benefits, active learning is not fully explored in clinical information extraction [19], in particular for the task of clinical concept extraction, which represents the focus of this paper. This task involves capturing natural language sequences (words or multi-words expressions) belonging to pre-determined semantic categories from unstructured free texts. These terms express meaningful concepts within a given domain (e.g. clinical problems, tests, and treatments) [8, 9]. Extracting clinical concepts is thus an important primary step in identifying meaningful information from clinical free texts.

The clinical domain is rich in terms of information resources. Clinical knowledge resources (e.g., the UMLS[1] [16] and the SNOMED CT[2] [4]) and tools (e.g., MetaMap [1], MedLEE [7], MedEx [35], cTAKES [24], and Medtex [18]) have been widely leveraged in combination with dictionary-, rule- and machine learning-based approaches in order to improve clinical concept extraction. The strong need for effective information extraction methods in the clinical domain has encouraged the development of shared datasets such as the i2b2 challenges [32-34] and the ShARe/CLEF eHealth Evaluation Lab [10, 31], which in turn have sparked the development of novel, more effective clinical information extraction methods. Specifically, a wide attention has been given to the engineering of powerful features obtained from domain knowledge resources to strengthen the supervised machine learning models and increase their effectiveness [21, 34].

While these resources have been used for data representation (i.e., features) both in supervised and active learning approaches [11], there is no study investigating the contributions these resources could have to improve current state-of-the-art query strategies within active learning methods for clinical information extraction.

In this paper, we address this gap and propose a novel active learning query strategy, called Domain Knowledge Informativeness (DKI), which leverages domain knowledge together with informativeness measures to select those samples that most strengthen the model obtained at the previous active learning iteration. We investigate the comparative performance of DKI and a wide range of state-of-the-art query strategies in terms of annotation effort savings in the clinical domain. The clinical domain is chosen for this work because of the already discussed availability of extensive structured knowledge resources. It also offers a compelling use case for active learning because of its intrinsic high costs and hurdles associated with obtaining annotations. To the best of our knowledge, DKI is the first query strategy which incorporates domain knowledge when querying samples within the active learning framework. The research questions we seek to tease out in this work are:

1. Which non-knowledge based query strategy is better suited to clinical data?
2. Can domain knowledge support a more effective query strategy that further reduces annotation efforts compared to state-of-the art AL approaches?

We find that, when comparing the current state-of-the-art query strategies, as well as a few novel strategies derived from existing ones for active learning, the confidence about the label of a sample as estimated by the classification model is a key factor for discovering informative samples in the clinical domain.

Our findings also suggest that domain knowledge can play an important role for enhancing active learning's performance by further reducing annotation effort. We also bring forward insights about how other machine learning approaches, such as semi-supervised learning, can be used to augment active learning.

The rest of this paper is organized as follows: Section 2 presents the problem definition. Section 3 introduces the query strategies. Section 4 describes our experimental and evaluation settings. Results are reported in Section 5. Section 6 briefly reviews related work and Section 7 concludes the paper by outlining directions of future investigation.

2. PROBLEM DEFINITION

Concept extraction (often referred to as entity extraction) can be modelled as a sequence labeling task. In this task, a label sequence $\vec{y} = (y_1, \dots, y_n)$ needs to be assigned to each observed sequence $\vec{x} = (x_1, \dots, x_n)$ in the dataset. Supervised machine learning models are applied to this task by casting the entity recognition problem to that of estimating the posterior probability of $\vec{y}$ given $\vec{x}$ under the model parameters θ. The output sequence with the highest posterior probability is the one that is chosen by the supervised models to annotate the input sequence.

Active learning approaches use supervised machine learning algorithms in an iterative process, where samples[3] from the dataset are successively selected to be annotated by an expert based on their "*informativeness*". Generally, samples are informative if they contain more useful information for the model compared to the rest of the samples in the unlabeled set. The intuition is that identifying and adding informative samples to the labeled set would lead to training a model that would achieve the highest effectiveness. One of the main scenarios in active learning is the pool-based approach (see Figure 2).

Under this paradigm, the active learning system has access to a pool of unlabeled data and, based on a query strategy, the system selects a batch of samples within successive interaction loops to add to the training set. This annotated data is then added to the training set and used to retrain the model [26]. A core issue when

Input:
$\mathcal{L}$: set of labelled samples
$\mathcal{U}$: set of unlabelled samples
$\emptyset$: classifier model
$\varphi(\vec{u}, \emptyset)$: query strategy where $\vec{u} \in \mathcal{U}$
B: number of samples to be selected in each iteration (batch size)

Procedure:
1- Randomly select an initial labeled set $\mathcal{L}$
2- Train a model $\emptyset$ on $\mathcal{L}$;
3- For all samples in the unlabeled set $\vec{u} \in \mathcal{U}$, calculate $\varphi(\vec{u}, \emptyset)$
4- Select a batch of samples (B) where $arg\,max_{\vec{u} \in \mathcal{U}}\ \varphi(\vec{u}, \emptyset)$ and ask the expert to label them;
5- Add samples from step 4 to labeled set $\mathcal{L}$ and remove them from the unlabeled set $\mathcal{U}$.
6- Repeat step 2 to 5.

Figure 2. Pool-based active learning algorithm.

[1] Unified Medical Language System

[2] Systematized Nomenclature of Medicine Clinical Terms

[3] In our experiments, a sample corresponds to a sequence of tokens or a sentence.

designing an active learning framework is: what query strategy should be used to estimate the informativeness of the samples that will be used to retrain or update the classification model? We discuss query strategies for active learning next.

3. Query Strategies

Active learning query strategies for sequence labeling tasks can be categorized in 3 groups of approaches: informativeness based, informativeness-similarity based, and model-independent. Within these categories we included a number of variations to commonly used query strategies (IDiv, IDD, MRD, and ALC).

In addition, we argue that a fourth group is formed by external knowledge-informed approaches, like DKI.

3.1 Informativeness Based Approaches

This group of approaches considers the uncertainty of a model about the label of a sample as a measure of informativeness. These approaches query samples where the learnt model is most uncertain about their label.

3.1.1 Least Confidence (LC)

Least confidence is a common query strategy for measuring informativeness [5]. This query strategy considers the confidence of a model $\emptyset$ with parameters θ about the label $\vec{y}$ of a sample $\vec{x}$. This confidence is estimated based on the posterior probability:

$$\varphi_{LC}(\vec{x}, \emptyset) = 1 - P_\theta(\vec{y}^* | \vec{x}) \quad (1)$$

The Viterbi algorithm is used to compute the most likely predicted label sequence $\vec{y}^*$.

3.1.2 Margin

Another uncertainty based strategy to measure the informativeness of a sample $\vec{x}$ is to consider the margin between the most likely ($\vec{y}_1^*$) and the second most likely ($\vec{y}_2^*$) label sequences [25]. To calculate the margin, the posterior probability of the two most likely label sequences is subtracted:

$$\varphi_{Margin}(\vec{x}, \emptyset) = -\left(P_\theta(\vec{y}_1^* | \vec{x}) - P_\theta(\vec{y}_2^* | \vec{x})\right) \quad (2)$$

The smaller the margin, the more difficult it is for the model to predict the label of a sample. Hence, according to this query strategy, that sample is an informative sample for the model. The first negative sign in Equation (2) ensures that φ_{Margin} acts as a maximizer to be used within the AL algorithm (Figure 2).

3.1.3 Sequence Entropy (SE)

Another way to estimate the informativeness is entropy [30]. Entropy is a measure of uncertainty that indicates the amount of information of a sequence. Sequence entropy [27] is a specialization of entropy for sequence labeling; this is used to find informative samples:

$$\varphi_{SE}(\vec{x}, \emptyset) = -\sum_{\acute{y}} P_\theta(\acute{y} | \vec{x}) log P_\theta(\acute{y} | \vec{x}) \quad (3)$$

where $\acute{y}$ includes all possible label sequences for an sample $\vec{x}$. The higher the entropy, the more informative the sample is.

3.1.4 Augmented Least Confidence

As described in Section 3.1.1, the least confidence (LC) approach uses the model's confidence about a sample's label to find informative samples, i.e., sample selection is based on those that have the lowest probability for the sample's label. To do so, the posterior probability of the model for all samples in the unlabeled set is computed and then samples are ranked accordingly.

The LC approach selects unlabeled samples that are characterized by low classification confidence. However, there are other samples that are characterized by high posterior probabilities, meaning that the model is confident about the samples' label. These samples can be automatically labeled by the model and added to the labeled set in each iteration, so as to provide further learning examples to the classifier. This approach is often referred to as semi-supervised learning [37]. To investigate whether this intuition can positively affect the active learning process, we modified step 4 in the active learning algorithm of Figure 2 as follows:

- Select a batch of samples where $arg\,max_{\vec{u}\in\mathcal{U}}\ \varphi_{LC}(\vec{u}, \emptyset)$ (Equation (1)) and ask the expert to label them. Then select those samples $\vec{u} \in \mathcal{U}$ where $P_\theta(\vec{y}|\vec{u}) > \tau$ (τ is a high probability used as decision threshold) and label them automatically using the current classification model.

We call this approach Augmented Least Confidence (ALC).

3.2 Informativeness-Similarity Based Approaches

The intuition behind informativeness-similarity based approaches is to consider similarity measures for the selection of both representative and diverse samples, in addition to informative ones, aiming to achieve a better coverage of the dataset characteristics.

3.2.1 Information Density (IDen)

Information Density [27] considers the representativeness of samples, along with their informativeness, to prevent outliers to be selected by the active learning process. IDen is computed according to:

$$\varphi_{IDen}(\vec{x}, \emptyset) = \varphi_{informative}(\vec{x}, \emptyset) \times \mathcal{R}_{representative}(\vec{x}) \quad (4)$$

where $\mathcal{R}_{\text{representative}}(\vec{x})$ corresponds to the representativeness of samples:

$$\mathcal{R}_{representative}(\vec{x}) = \frac{1}{U}\sum_{u=1}^{U} sim(\vec{x}, \vec{x}^{(U)}) \quad (5)$$

The average similarity between sample $\vec{x}$ and all other samples in the set of unlabeled samples ($\vec{x}^{(U)}$) indicates the representativeness of sample $\vec{x}$: the higher the similarity, the more representative the sample. Similarity is measured according to the cosine distance:

$$sim_{cos}(\vec{x}, \vec{x}^{(U)}) = \frac{\vec{\mathbf{x}}.\vec{\mathbf{x}}^{(U)}}{\|\vec{\mathbf{x}}\|.\,\|\vec{\mathbf{x}}^{(U)}\|} \quad (6)$$

where $\vec{\mathbf{x}}$ refers to the feature vector of sample $\vec{x}$. To measure the informativeness of samples ($\varphi_{informative}(\vec{x}, \emptyset)$), we use least confidence (Equation (1)). Therefore, according to this query strategy, those samples characterized by the least confidence and the highest similarity are those that are useful to the model.

3.2.2 Information Diversity (IDiv)

Differently from IDen, information diversity aims to take into account the diversity of the data within the process of querying samples; IDiv is formalized as follows:

$$\varphi_{IDiv}(\vec{x}, \emptyset) = \varphi_{informative}(\vec{x}, \emptyset) \times D_{diversity}(\vec{x}) \quad (7)$$

$D_{diversity}(\vec{x})$ is calculated based on how dissimilar a sample $\vec{x}$ is compared to already selected samples within the labeled set $\vec{x}^{(L)}$:

$$D_{diversity}(\vec{x}) = 1 - (\frac{1}{L}\sum_{l=1}^{L} sim(\vec{x}, \vec{x}^{(L)})) \quad (8)$$

Similarity is measured according to Equation (6). LC (Equation (1)) is also used as a measure of informativeness.

3.2.3 *Information Density and Diversity (IDD)*

One way to find both representative and diverse informative samples is to combine IDen and IDiv approaches as an IDD approach:

$$\varphi_{IDD}(\vec{x}) = \varphi_{informative}(\vec{x}) \times \mathcal{R}_{representative}(\vec{x}) \times D_{diversity}(\vec{x}) \quad (9)$$

3.3 A Model-Independent Approach

Both informativeness and informativeness-similarity based approaches are dependent on the model. In a real world active learning scenario, an expert should wait until a model is learnt on the current labeled set and then the next batch of samples are selected using one of the above-mentioned query strategies for labeling. This could introduce large time delays between expert annotations cycles due to the time required to train models. One way to prevent such a problem is to propose approaches that are independent from the model output.

3.3.1 *Maximum Representativeness-Diversity (MRD)*

Maximum representativeness-diversity is an approach which only relies on the similarity between a sample $\vec{x}$ and all other samples in the labeled ($\vec{x}^{(L)}$) and unlabeled ($\vec{x}^{(U)}$) sets:

$$\varphi_{MRD}(\vec{x}) = \mathcal{R}_{representative}(\vec{x}) \times D_{diversity}(\vec{x}) \quad (10)$$

$\mathcal{R}_{representative}(\vec{x})$ and $D_{diversity}(\vec{x})$ are calculated according to Equation (5) and (8), respectively. The most representative and diverse samples are labeled in the current batch and then added to the training set.

3.4 External Knowledge-Informed Approaches

External resources and ontologies are useful tools for extracting domain-specific features to represent samples and they have been shown to often enhance supervised machine learning models. However, there are no active learning query strategies that use external knowledge resources to drive the process of sample selection. Here, we tackle this gap and propose a novel query strategy called Domain Knowledge Informativeness.

3.4.1 *Domain Knowledge Informativeness (DKI)*

DKI is a query strategy to "inform" the model about unlabeled samples using external knowledge. We combine an informativeness based approach with domain knowledge to select samples for active learning:

$$\varphi_{DKI_t}(\vec{x}) = \frac{1}{|\vec{x}|} \times \sum_{\vec{x}} \left(K(x_i) \times \varphi_{informative}(x_i, \emptyset)\right) \quad (11)$$

Where $|\vec{x}|$ is the length of sequence $\vec{x}$, $K(x_i)$ is a function of the domain knowledge contained in the sequence (i.e., importance), and $\varphi_{informative}$ is the informativeness measure. φ_{DKI_t} measures the average importance of the tokens contained in a sequence based on their informativeness for the model as well as the importance of the domain knowledge they carry. A useful domain characteristic that can be extracted from domain knowledge resources is the semantic type that each token belongs to. This information has often been exploited to generate semantic features for sample representation in supervised models. Specifically, here we consider the distribution of semantic types as they appear in the target concept spans in the training set. We use this information to compute the Semantic Value (SV) of a semantic type as follows:

$$Semantic\ Value\ (semantic\ type) = \frac{\#\ semantic\ type\ appears\ in\ annotated\ target\ concept\ span}{\#\ semantic\ type\ appears\ in\ the\ whole\ training\ set} \quad (12)$$

Semantic Value is calculated based on the semantic types assigned to each token individually, without considering neighboring tokens. However, it is possible for a token to be a part of a longer concept span. For example, "*acute*" could be an adjective at the token level, but also part of the longer concept "*acute headache*" which is a disease, and should therefore be considered under this type instead. Since we model the concept extraction problem as a sequence labeling task, instead of considering the semantic types of each token separately, it is more appropriate to calculate the distribution of the semantic type assigned to the longest span that each token belongs to.

In this paper we consider a specific instantiation of DKI, where the domain knowledge contributes to the query strategy by means of the Longest Span Semantic Value (LSSV). Here, LSSV is used to find sequences with the maximum number of possible target concepts:

$$LSSV(semantic\ type) = \frac{\#\ semantic\ type\ appears\ in\ the\ longest\ span\ of\ annotated\ target\ concepts}{\#semantic\ type\ appears\ in\ the\ whole\ training\ set} \quad (13)$$

We use Equation (13) to calculate $K(x_i)$ in φ_{DKI_t} (Equation (11)). $K(x_i)$ is calculated for each token separately ($K(x_i)$, $\vec{x} = \{x_i | i = 0, \dots, |\vec{x}|\}$); informativeness is also measured per token:

$$\varphi_{info}(x_i, \emptyset) = 1 - P_\theta(y_j = y_j^* | x_i) \quad (14)$$

Where $P_\theta(y_j = y_j^* | x_i)$ is the marginal probability, y_j^* specifies the label at the corresponding position of the most likely label sequence $\vec{y}^*$.

Note that φ_{DKI_t} is normalized by the length of the sequence $\vec{x}$ ($1/|\vec{x}|$ in Equation (11) is the normalization factor). To encourage the selection of longer sequences as they usually contain more target concepts [27], we also propose a denormalized instantiation of DKI, termed the total token-based Domain Knowledge Informativeness (DKI_{tt}):

$$\varphi_{DKI_{tt}}(\vec{x}) = \sum_{\vec{x}} \left(K(x_i) \times \varphi_{informative}(x_i, \emptyset)\right) \quad (15)$$

4. EXPERIMENTAL SETUP

In this section we introduce the datasets and their preparation steps. We then elaborate on our supervised approach and active learning settings. Finally, our evaluation methodology is explained.

4.1 Dataset Description

We use the annotated training and testing sets for the concept extraction task in the i2b2/VA 2010 NLP challenge [34] and ShARe/CLEF 2013 eHealth Evaluation Lab (task 1) [20].

The i2b2/VA 2010 task requires the extraction of clinical problems, tests and treatments from clinical reports. These reports are a combination of discharge summaries and progress notes. They are organized as a collection of phrases and sentences.

The ShARe/CLEF 2013 eHealth Evaluation Lab (task 1) requires to extract and identify mentions of disorders from clinical free-text notes. The dataset consists of discharge summaries, electrocardiogram, echocardiogram, and radiology reports.

Table 1 reports the number of documents in the training and testing sets of the two datasets along with the number of sequences obtained after pre-processing.

Table 1. Document (#doc) and sequence (#seq) count in the training and testing sets of two considered datasets.

	Training Set		Testing Set	
	#doc	**#seq**	**#doc**	**#seq**
i2b2/VA 2010	349	30,673	477	45,025
ShARe/CLEF 2013	200	10,171	100	9,273

4.2 Dataset preparation

In this paper, a sample (in both supervised and active learning approaches) corresponds to a sequence of tokens or a sentence. In the i2b2/VA 2010 dataset, sentence boundaries are already identified as each line in a report file corresponds to a sentence. However, this is not the case for the ShARe/CLEF 2013 dataset. We then used the Leaman's sentence segmentation method [14] to derive sentences for this dataset.

After detecting sentence boundaries, the data was encoded into a representation format that clearly indicates the span of a concept within a sentence. The "BIO" format was leveraged to specify the beginning (B), inside (I), and outside (O) of a concept [23].

We employed a typical feature set, including linguistic (part-of-speech tags), orthographical (regular expression patterns), lexical and morphological (suffixes/prefixes and character n-grams), contextual (window of k words), and semantic features. The Medtex system [18] was leveraged to extract semantic features. Specifically, the UMLS and SNOMED CT (SCT) semantic types for each token were used as the domain knowledge. We leveraged this knowledge to distinguish target from non-target semantic types. A non-quantized value was assigned to each semantic type based on the distribution of each semantic type in the training set according to Equation (12).

4.3 Fully Supervised Approach

We use a tuned linear-chain Conditional Random Fields (CRFs) [12] as benchmark supervised ML algorithm as well as our base ML algorithm in the AL framework. CRFs [13] are the state-of-the-art supervised machine learning approach in clinical concept extraction tasks [20, 34].

The posterior probability of $\vec{y}$ given $\vec{x}$ is described by a linear-chain CRFs model with a set of parameters θ:

$$P_\theta(\vec{y}|\vec{x}) = \frac{1}{Z_\theta(\vec{x})}\exp\left(\sum_{i=1}^{n}\sum_{j=1}^{m}\lambda_j f_j(y_{i-1}, y_i, x_i)\right) \quad (16)$$

Here $Z_\theta(\vec{x})$ is the normalization factor. Each f_j is the transition feature function between label state $i-1$ and i on the sequence x at position i. The $\theta = (\lambda_1, \ldots, \lambda_m)$ represent the corresponding feature weights.

Our implementations of CRFs for supervised learning (Sup), both baselines, and all active learning (AL) approaches are based on the MALLET toolkit [17].

4.4 Active Learning Settings

Within this paper, we use an incremental, pool-based, active learning framework. In the incremental approach, a model is not trained from scratch at each iteration: instead, its parameters are updated in successive iterations [12]. As we aim to study how AL can contribute towards reducing the annotation effort compared to a supervised approach, we use supervised effectiveness as our target effectiveness. We use Medtex to extract the required knowledge for each sample $\vec{x}$ (Equation (13)) in the DKI query strategy.

Random sampling (RS) and longest sequence (LS) are two common baselines for analyzing the benefits of the AL framework. RS randomly selects samples; LS selects samples with the longest length (number of tokens).

For AL and the baseline approaches, the initial labeled set is formed by randomly selecting 1% of the training data. The batch size (B) is set to 200 for i2b2/VA 2010 and 100 for ShARe/CLEF 2013 across all experiments, leading to a total of 153 and 101 batches, respectively.

While in real settings AL would use human annotators to label informative samples at each iteration, here we simulate this process by using the annotations provided in the training set of the two datasets.

4.5 Evaluation Measures

In our evaluation, concept extraction effectiveness is measured by Precision, Recall and F1-measure. Evaluation metrics are computed on test data using MALLET's multi-segmentation evaluator[4]. Query strategies were analyzed and compared among each other and against the fully supervised method based on their learning curves across batches. Learning curves allow to associate model performance and annotation effort.

A core aspect of our evaluation is determining the first iteration at which AL strategies achieve an effectiveness comparable (i.e., equal or higher) to that of the supervised method. This allows to identify the *minimum amount of annotated data* the AL strategies require to achieve the same effectiveness of the supervised method (target effectiveness): this corresponds to the point of intersection between the AL learning curve and the target effectiveness.

We further analyze the results by considering the Annotation Rate

[4] The results obtained with this evaluator are not directly comparable to those reported using the i2b2 or ShARe/CLEF evaluation scripts.

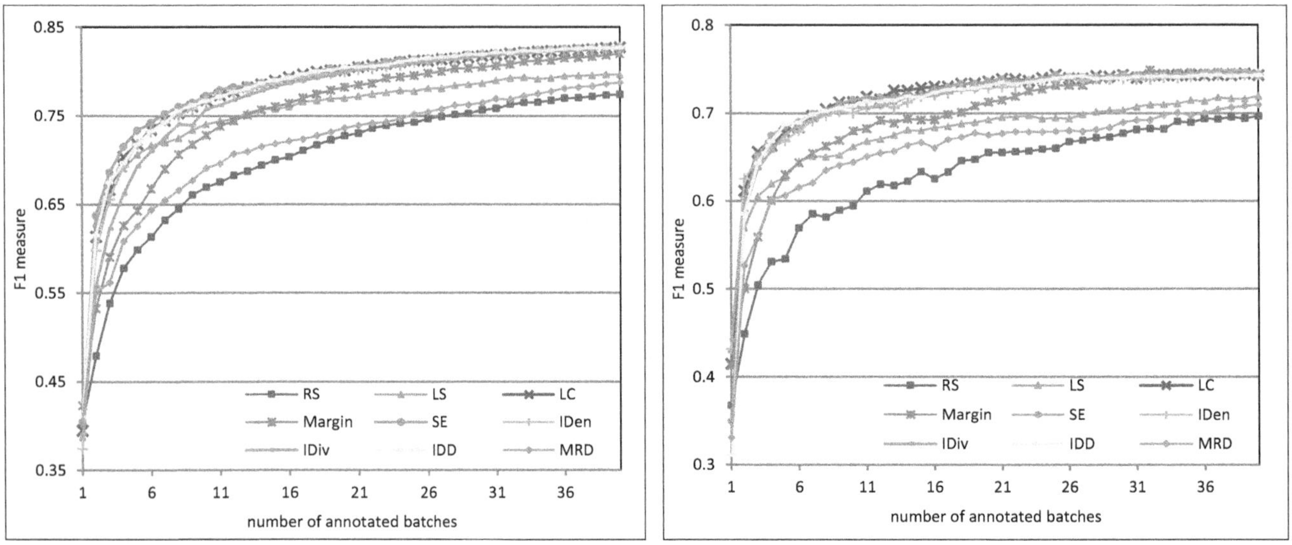

(a) (b)

Figure 3. The effectiveness of active learning approaches and baselines for the first 40 batches (a) i2b2/VA 2010 (b) ShARe/CLEF 2013.

(AR), which measures how much annotation effort is saved by an AL approach. AR is the number of labeled annotation units in terms of sequences (SAR), tokens (TAR) and concepts (CAR) used by AL to reach the target effectiveness, over the number of labeled annotation units used by the supervised method.

$$\text{AR} = \frac{\#\ labeled\ annotation\ units\ used\ by\ AL}{\#\ total\ labeled\ annotation\ units\ used\ by\ Sup} \quad (17)$$

The lower the AR, the less annotation effort is required. Note that here every annotation unit (sequence, token, and concept) is considered as having the same annotation cost (uniform annotation cost). While this setting may not be fully representative of real-world use cases [28], no annotation cost is distributed along with the considered datasets and the literature lacks of specific studies that consider annotation costs for clinical concept extraction.

5. RESULTS

We first study to what extent various active learning query strategies reduce the annotation effort for clinical data compared to a fully supervised approach: this serves to determine the state-of-the-art strategy for clinical concept extraction among those proposed in the literature. We then compare the best results from the state-of-the-art with our proposed query strategy to assess if domain knowledge based query strategies further reduce the burden of manual annotation in clinical settings.

5.1 Target Effectiveness for Active Learning

Table 2 presents the effectiveness of the fully supervised CRF model.

Table 2. Effectiveness of the fully supervised approach (Sup) (P = Precision, R = Recall, F1 = F1-measure).

	i2b2/VA 2010			ShARe/CLEF 2013		
	P	R	F1	P	R	F1
Sup	0.8409	0.8066	0.8234	0.8095	0.6804	0.7394

These results are used as the target effectiveness for determining the level of annotation effort savings contributed by different active learning approaches.

5.2 Analysis of AL Query Strategies on Clinical Data

5.2.1 Query Strategy Performance

Figure 3 shows the learning curves obtained with different active learning query strategies in the first 40 batches of the i2b2/VA 2010 and ShARe/CLEF 2013 datasets.

For both datasets, the learning curves of all query strategies are always well above the RS baseline, as expected. However, MRD always performs worse than the longest sequence baseline, suggesting that only relying on the similarity between samples to select subsequent batches in the AL loop is not effective. This further highlights that the similarity measure on its own is not enough to find useful samples for active learning. We hypothesize that this is because clinical data is partially characterized by the repetition of fairly similar patterns [11]. Although the diversity element prevents the MRD approach from selecting similar samples, it still fails to pick the most informative ones.

The fact that the learning curves of approaches that leverage informativeness in addition to similarity measures are higher than the learning curve of MRD demonstrates the importance of informativeness in selecting useful samples.

In i2b2/VA 2010, the LS baseline effectiveness is higher than IDiv in the first six batches (F1 = 0.7). The Margin strategy also performs poorly compared to the LS baseline in early batches, but outperforms LS after ten batches in i2b2/VA 2010 (F1 = 0.74) and six batches in ShARe/CLEF 2013 (F1 = 0.63). We hypothesize that this is because, in clinical datasets, longer sequences usually contain more concepts. Hence, by choosing the longest sequences, the effectiveness of LS increases quite sharply in early batches as it already reaches a reasonable effectiveness[5] compared to the

[5] i2b2/VA 2010, F1 ≈ 0.73 and ShARe/CLEF 2013, F1 ≈ 0.63.

Table 3. Annotation rates for all active learning query strategies and baselines.

		SAR(%)		TAR(%)		CAR(%)	
		i2b2/VA 2010	ShARe/CLEF 2013	i2b2/VA 2010	ShARe/CLEF 2013	i2b2/VA 2010	ShARe/CLEF 2013
Baselines	**RS**	90%	97%	90%	97%	90%	97.5%
	LS	58%	72.5%	88%	95%	92%	93.5%
Informativeness-based Approaches	**LC**	24%	24%	43%	38%	55%	63%
	Margin	30%	30%	50%	44%	60%	67.5%
	SE	22%	25%	43.5%	40.5%	54.5%	67%
Informativeness-Similarity Based Approaches	**IDen**	24%	26%	45%	42.5%	55%	67%
	IDiv	23%	24%	41%	38%	52%	63.5%
	IDD	22%	25%	41%	41%	51%	66%
Model-Independent Approaches	**MRD**	68%	74.5%	89%	94%	90%	91%

target effectiveness (Table 2) twice sooner than RS, and it is therefore a very strong baseline. However, after a few iterations the growth rate of the LS learning curve suddenly decreases: this is because the selected long sequences contain no more useful samples to train the model.

5.2.2 Active Learning and Annotation Effort

Annotation rates for all active learning query strategies and baselines are reported in Table 3. The top three approaches are highlighted.

Among the informativeness-based approaches, Least Confidence and Sequence Entropy are very close and outperform Margin.

By adding a similarity element to informativeness, annotation rates in terms of sequences, tokens, and concepts are reduced. However, the informativeness-similarity based approaches exhibit different behaviors across the two datasets. IDiv is the best method in ShARe/CLEF 2013, while IDD performs better than IDiv in i2b2/VA 2010, although differences are not significant.

Since token (TAR) and concept (CAR) annotation rates are more appropriate to measure the actual savings of annotation effort rather than the number of annotated sequences [11], we can conclude that IDD and LC are the most promising approaches for i2b2/VA 2010 and ShARe/CLEF 2013, respectively.

The advantage of LC compared to IDiv and IDD, is that LC is computationally more efficient. Indeed, informativeness-similarity based approaches generally require a considerably larger amount of computations. This is because $\mathcal{R}_{\text{representative}}(\vec{x})$ and $D_{diversity}(\vec{x})$ have to be computed for all samples in the unlabeled and labeled sets, respectively. Although these similarity computations for $\mathcal{R}_{\text{representative}}(\vec{x})$ can be performed prior to starting the active learning loop (as the unlabeled dataset is available upfront in pool-based active learning), $D_{diversity}(\vec{x})$ has to be computed at each iteration of active learning.

5.2.3 Least Confidence vs. Augmented Least Confidence

We now study how iteratively including samples to the labeled set $\mathcal{L}$ for which the model is very confident about their automatically assigned labels (Section 3.1.4) could lead to further annotation effort reduction. To identify these high confidence samples, we experiment with two thresholds, $\tau = 0.998$ and $\tau = 0.999$.

Based on the results reported in Table 4, we can observe that the ALC approach with $\tau = 0.999$ improved the results of LC (Table 3) in both datasets. However, when τ was set to 0.998, in the

Table 4. Annotation rates for ALC using two thresholds.

		ALC	
		$\tau = 0.998$	$\tau = 0.999$
i2b2/VA 2010	**SAR(%)**	24.5%	22.5%
	TAR(%)	44%	41.5%
	CAR(%)	55%	52.5%
ShARe/CLEF 2013	**SAR(%)**	25%	22.5%
	TAR(%)	40%	35%
	CAR(%)	67%	58.5%

ShARE/CLEF 2013 dataset ALC required more annotated data to reach the target effectiveness compared to LC.

5.2.4 Initial Labelled Set

While the longest sequence approach (LS) did not reach the target effectiveness much before having trained on all available batches, it is interesting to note that its effectiveness was comparable to the three best approaches (LC, IDD, and IDiv in Table 3) in the first five batches for both datasets. This suggests that long sequences in clinical reports often include useful information to train the classifier, even though its effectiveness increases at a slower rate after the initial batches. Hence, it may be preferable to consider the length of sequences in the early stages of the active learning process so as to select longer sequences first.

A possible way for achieving this is selecting long sequences as the initial labeled set instead of using random selection. Table 5 reports the results for LC, IDiv, IDD, and ALC ($\tau = 0.999$) approaches using the longest sequence approach (LS) for selecting the initial labeled set across both datasets.

Table 5. Annotation rates for LC, IDiv, IDD, and ALC ($\tau = 0.999$) using LS to produce the initial labeled set.

		LC	IDiv	IDD	ALC
i2b2/VA 2010	**SAR(%)**	23%	24%	24%	22.5%
	TAR(%)	42%	41.5%	40%	41%
	CAR(%)	52.5%	52%	53.5%	51%
ShARe/CLEF 2013	**SAR(%)**	26%	25%	22%	24%
	TAR(%)	43%	41%	39%	41.5%
	CAR(%)	67%	65%	60.5%	65%

Table 6. Annotation rates for baselines, benchmarks, and external knowledge based approaches.

		SAR(%)		TAR(%)		CAR(%)	
		i2b2/VA 2010	ShARe/CLEF 2013	i2b2/VA 2010	ShARe/CLEF 2013	i2b2/VA 2010	ShARe/CLEF 2013
Baselines	**RS**	90%	97%	90%	97%	90%	97.5%
	LS	58%	72.5%	88%	95%	92%	93.5%
Benchmarks	**LC**	24%	24%	43%	38%	55%	63%
	IDiv	23%	24%	41%	38%	52%	63.5%
	IDD	22%	25%	41%	41%	51%	66%
External Knowledge-based Approaches	**DKI_t**	22%	28%	39%	32%	51%	63%
	DKI_{tt}	21.5%	20%	27%	31%	37%	57%

Using the longest sequences as the initial labeled set did not show consistent results across datasets and query strategies. In fact, the annotation rates for IDD in ShARe/CLEF 2013, LC and ALC in i2b2/VA 2010 slightly decreased; but other query strategies do not exhibit improvements.

5.3 Domain Knowledge and Active Learning

The CAR results from Section 5.2.2 suggest that at least half of the concepts in the training set are required to be manually annotated before reaching the target effectiveness, even if the most effective AL approaches were used.

In this section, we compare the identified state-of-the-art approaches with the DKI query strategies to investigate how domain knowledge acquired from external resources can help to reduce the annotation effort on clinical data.

The results in Table 6 show that DKI based methods lead to a lower annotation rate compared to baselines and state-of-the-art AL methods. Token-based domain knowledge informativeness (DKI_t, Equation (11)) outperforms most baselines and benchmarks in the i2b2/VA dataset and is as good as IDD (the best approach so far). The results on the ShARe/CLEF 2013 dataset provide however less conclusive findings. If the length of the sequences is used when querying samples with DKI_{tt}, then significant reductions in token and concept annotation rates are achieved on both datasets. In the i2b2/VA 2010 dataset, DKI_{tt} reduces the concept and token annotation rates by 14% compared to IDD (the best state-of-the-art approach for this dataset, see Table 3). In the ShARe/CLEF 2013 dataset, DKI_{tt} reaches the target effectiveness using 6% less annotated concepts and 7% less annotated tokens than LC.

When the performance of DKI_t and DKI_{tt} are compared, it can be observed that the length of sequences has a significant contribution in the annotation effort savings. However, to achieve the best results, sequence length should be considered along with informativeness and domain knowledge, as it does not provide significant AR reductions when considered alone (i.e., LS).

An interesting result is the small difference in sequence annotation rate (SAR) between IDD and DKI_{tt} for the i2b2/VA 2010 dataset. The two approaches select almost the same number of sequences to reach the target effectiveness but with different characteristics (tokens and concepts); this leads to very different results when considering the number of tokens and concepts required to be annotated. This observation demonstrates that domain knowledge combined with a simple informativeness measure (marginal probability) can lead to a better selection of samples; and this is achieved without resorting to using similarity measures which are computationally costlier. DKI_{tt} shows a varied but significant range of savings in terms of required number of concepts to be annotated across the two datasets (37%-57%).

6. RELATED WORK

Active learning aims to achieve high effectiveness (at least comparable to that of supervised methods), while reducing annotation costs by minimizing the amount of data that is required to be annotated. Domains like the clinical one are characterized by high costs for obtaining (expert) annotations. In such domains, it becomes then critical to reduce the annotation effort while ensuring no loss of effectiveness for automated techniques.

One of the main challenges in active learning is identifying and querying samples that can better inform classification models [26]. Different strategies for selecting informative samples have been proposed, including: uncertainty sampling [15], query-by-committee [29], and information density [27]. Settles and Craven [27] performed an extensive empirical evaluation of different query selection strategies within active learning, using different corpora for sequence labeling tasks. They found that information density and sequence vote entropy outperform the state-of-the-art in active learning in most corpora. However, in this paper we found that diversity along with information density lead to better sample selection for concept extraction in the clinical domain. We speculate that this is because of the high similarity between sequences in clinical narratives. Hence, samples selected by information density are not useful for training classification model within the active learning process, while diversity allows to select more representative samples.

While the effectiveness of active learning methods has been conclusively demonstrated in many domains such as text classification, information extraction and speech recognition [26], as highlighted, clinical and biomedical natural language processing tasks have seen only limited use of active learning [19]. To demonstrate the key role of AL in reducing the burden of manual annotation, in previous work we built a preliminary active learning-based system and investigate the state-of-the-art AL methods (LC and IDen) for extracting medical concepts from clinical free text. The annotation effort saved by AL to achieve the target effectiveness (supervised effectiveness) was up to 54% of the total number of concepts (CAR) [11]. We also investigated the factors that influence the robustness and the effectiveness of models learnt within the active learning frameworks [12]. It was found that well selected feature set, the incremental learning setting, and the tuning of the supervised classifier parameters lead to more robust active learning models. Here we consider the same settings and parameters, and observe that the models are generally robust, as demonstrated by the learning curves (Figure 3).

Within the clinical domain, active learning has been used for classifying clinical concepts according to their assertions [3, 22] and co-reference resolution [36]. For assertion classification, Chen, et al. [3] introduced a "model change" sampling-based algorithm and found it performed better than random sampling, uncertainty sampling-based algorithms, and information density-based algorithm. Active learning has also been used for de-identifying Swedish clinical records [2]. There, the information extraction problem was treated as a classification task in which words belong to one of eight personal clinical information types or to the non-personal clinical information type. The most uncertain and the most certain sampling strategies were evaluated using the highest and lowest entropy, and it was found that these methods outperformed a random sampling baseline. Figueroa, et al. [6] analyzed the effectiveness of different active learning methods, including distance-based (DIST), diversity-based (DIV), and a combination of both (CMB), based on clinical data characteristics. However, this study focused on a clinical classification task and only applied a limited number of query strategies. They found that the effectiveness of DIV and DIST is strongly dependent on the dataset diversity and uncertainty, respectively. Rosales, et al. [22] presented a semi-supervised active learning framework based on query by committee and evaluated its effectiveness in a binary classification task, where concepts extracted from clinical free text are classified into two classes: present or absent/negated. Their framework is able to select both informative and representative samples.

7. CONCLUSION AND FUTURE WORK

This paper has introduced a new active learning query strategy, called domain knowledge informativeness (DKI). This novel query strategy leverages domain knowledge resources, such as ontologies and terminologies, for extracting concepts from text. DKI is instantiated and evaluated within the clinical domain for the task of clinical concept extraction. Our instantiation considers the longest span semantic value, as obtained from a clinical NLP tool, and the marginal probability of a text sequence, as assessed by a classification model. These are then used to query samples for selecting those that not only are informative but also contain useful concepts based on the external domain knowledge.

Our empirical evaluation highlights the promise of integrating domain knowledge within active learning query strategies, as indicated by the gains in annotation effort reduction achieved by DKI over state-of-the-art approaches.

We also found that, when analyzing the performance of active learning on clinical data, the confidence about samples' labels estimated by the classification model is a deciding factor in selecting effective samples.

Our study has two main limitations. First, all evaluation metrics used in this study cannot be directly translated into actual cost reduction. However, CAR and TAR values can be used to design a cost model for real world cases. Second, in real world settings the full training data is not available in advance for estimating the target effectiveness, thus making the decision of where to stop the active learning process is a challenging problem, which requires to consider a trade-off between cost and effectiveness.

In order to overcome these limitations, our future work will consider designing a cost model that uses the required number of annotated tokens and concepts. This cost model would constitute a step forward for precisely assessing the actual contribution of active learning in terms of cost reduction. At the same time, we plan to explore methods to determine a stopping point independently from the supervised effectiveness.

8. REFERENCES

[1] A. R. Aronson. Effective mapping of biomedical text to the UMLS Metathesaurus: the MetaMap program. In *Proceedings of the American Medical Informatics Association Annual Symposium*, 17-21, 2001.

[2] H. Boström and H. Dalianis. De-identifying health records by means of active learning. *Recall (micro)*, 97(97.55), 90-97, 2012.

[3] Y. Chen, S. Mani, and H. Xu. Applying active learning to assertion classification of concepts in clinical text. *Journal of Biomedical Informatics*, 45(2), 265-272, 2012.

[4] R. A. Cote and S. Robboy. Progress in medical information management. *Journal of the American Medical Association (JAMA)*, 243(8), 756-762, 1980.

[5] A. Culotta and A. McCallum. Reducing labeling effort for structured prediction tasks. In *Proceedings of the Twentieth National Conference on Artificial Intelligence (AAAI)*, 746–751, 2005.

[6] R. L. Figueroa, Q. Zeng-Treitler, L. H. Ngo, S. Goryachev, and E. P. Wiechmann. Active learning for clinical text classification: is it better than random sampling? *Journal of the American Medical Informatics Association (JAMIA)*, 19(5), 809-816, 2012.

[7] C. Friedman, L. Shagina, Y. Lussier, and G. Hripcsak. Automated encoding of clinical documents based on natural language processing. *Journal of the American Medical Informatics Association (JAMIA)*, 11(5), 392-402, 2004.

[8] H. Gurulingappa. Mining the medical and patent literature to support healthcare and pharmacovigilance, *Ph.D. dissertation*, University of Bonn, Bonn, Germany, 2012.

[9] M. Jiang, Y. Chen, M. Liu, S. T. Rosenbloom, S. Mani, J. C. Denny, and H. Xu. A study of machine-learning-based approaches to extract clinical entities and their assertions from discharge summaries. *Journal of the American Medical Informatics Association (JAMIA)*, 18(5), 601-606, 2011.

[10] L. Kelly, L. Goeuriot, H. Suominen, T. Schreck, G. Leroy, D. L. Mowery, S. Velupillai, W. W. Chapman, D. Martinez, and G. Zuccon. Overview of the share/clef ehealth evaluation lab 2014. In *Information Access Evaluation. Multilinguality, Multimodality, and Interaction*, 172-191, 2014.

[11] M. Kholghi, L. Sitbon, G. Zuccon, and A. Nguyen. Active learning: a step towards automating medical concept extraction. *Journal of the American Medical Informatics Association (JAMIA)*, 2015 [In Press].

[12] M. Kholghi, L. Sitbon, G. Zuccon, and A. Nguyen. Factors influencing robustness and effectiveness of conditional random fields in active learning frameworks. In *Proceedings of the 12th Australasian Data Mining Conference (AusDM 2014) (Vol. 158): Conferences in Research and Practice in Information Technology*, 2014.

[13] J. D. Lafferty, A. McCallum, and F. C. N. Pereira. Conditional Random Fields: Probabilistic Models for Segmenting and Labeling Sequence Data. In *Proceedings of the Eighteenth International Conference on Machine Learning (ICML)*, 282-289, 2001.

[14] R. Leaman, R. Khare, and Z. Lu. NCBI at 2013 ShARe/CLEF eHealth Shared Task: disorder normalization in clinical notes with DNorm. *Working Notes of the Conference and Labs of the Evaluation Forum (CLEF 2013)*, 2013.

[15] D. D. Lewis and J. Catlett. Heterogenous Uncertainty Sampling for Supervised Learning. In *Proceedings of the 18th International Conference on Machine Learning (ICML)*, 148-156, 1994.

[16] D. A. Lindberg, B. L. Humphreys, and A. T. McCray. The unified medical language system. *Methods of Information in Medicine*, 32(4), 281-291, 1993.

[17] A. K. McCallum. MALLET: A Machine Learning for Language Toolkit. http://mallet.cs.umass.edu, 2002.

[18] A. N. Nguyen, M. J. Lawley, D. P. Hansen, and S. Colquist. A simple pipeline application for identifying and negating SNOMED clinical terminology in free text. In *Proceedings of the Health Informatics Conference (HIC)*, 188-193, 2009.

[19] L. Ohno-Machado, P. Nadkarni, and K. Johnson. Natural language processing: algorithms and tools to extract computable information from EHRs and from the biomedical literature. *Journal of the American Medical Informatics Association (JAMIA)*, 20(5), 805, 2013.

[20] S. Pradhan, N. Elhadad, B. South, D. Martinez, L. Christensen, A. Vogel, H. Suominen, W. W. Chapman, and G. Savova. Task 1: ShARe/CLEF ehealth evaluation lab 2013. *CLEF 2013 Evaluation Labs and Workshops: Working Notes*, 2013.

[21] S. Pradhan, N. Elhadad, B. South, D. Martinez, L. Christensen, A. Vogel, H. Suominen, W. W. Chapman, and G. Savova. Evaluating the state of the art in disorder recognition and normalization of the clinical narrative. *Journal of the American Medical Informatics Association (JAMIA)*, 22(1), 143-154, 2015.

[22] R. Rosales, P. Krishnamurthy, and R. B. Rao. Semi-supervised active learning for modeling medical concepts from free text. In *Proceedings of the Sixth International Conference on Machine Learning and Applications*, 530-536, 2007.

[23] E. F. T. K. Sang and J. Veenstra. Representing text chunks. In *Proceedings of the ninth conference on European chapter of the Association for Computational Linguistics*, 173-179, 1999.

[24] G. K. Savova, J. J. Masanz, P. V. Ogren, J. Zheng, S. Sohn, K. C. Kipper-Schuler, and C. G. Chute. Mayo clinical Text Analysis and Knowledge Extraction System (cTAKES): architecture, component evaluation and applications. *Journal of the American Medical Informatics Association (JAMIA)*, 17(5), 507-513, 2010.

[25] T. Scheffer, C. Decomain, and S. Wrobel. Active hidden markov models for information extraction. In *Proceedings of the International Conference on Advances in Intelligent Data Analysis (CAIDA)*, 309-318, 2001.

[26] B. Settles. Active learning, (Vol. 6): Morgan & Claypool Publishers, 2012.

[27] B. Settles and M. Craven. An analysis of active learning strategies for sequence labeling tasks. In *Proceedings of the Conference on Empirical Methods in Natural Language Processing (EMNLP)*, 1070-1079, 2008.

[28] B. Settles, M. Craven, and L. Friedland. Active learning with real annotation costs. In *Proceedings of the NIPS Workshop on Cost-Sensitive Learning*, 1-10, 2008.

[29] H. S. Seung, M. Opper, and H. Sompolinsky. Query by committee. In *Proceedings of the fifth annual workshop on Computational learning theory*, 287-294, 1992.

[30] C. E. Shannon. A mathematical theory of communication. *Bell System Technical Journal*, 27, 379–423, 623–656, 1948.

[31] H. Suominen, S. Salanterä, S. Velupillai, W. W. Chapman, G. Savova, N. Elhadad, S. Pradhan, B. South, D. Mowery, G. F. Jones, J. Leveling, L. Kelly, L. Goeuriot, D. Martinez, and G. Zuccon. Overview of the ShARe/CLEF eHealth Evaluation Lab 2013. In *Information Access Evaluation. Multilinguality, Multimodality, and Visualization* (Vol. 8138), 212-231, 2013.

[32] Ö. Uzuner, I. Goldstein, Y. Luo, and I. Kohane. Identifying patient smoking status from medical discharge records. *Journal of the American Medical Informatics Association (JAMIA)*, 15(1), 14-24, 2008.

[33] Ö. Uzuner, I. Solti, and E. Cadag. Extracting medication information from clinical text. *Journal of the American Medical Informatics Association (JAMIA)*, 17(5), 514-518, 2010.

[34] Ö. Uzuner, B. R. South, S. Shen, and S. L. DuVall. 2010 i2b2/VA challenge on concepts, assertions, and relations in clinical text. *Journal of the American Medical Informatics Association (JAMIA)*, 18(5), 552-556, 2011.

[35] H. Xu, S. P. Stenner, S. Doan, K. B. Johnson, L. R. Waitman, and J. C. Denny. MedEx: a medication information extraction system for clinical narratives. *Journal of the American Medical Informatics Association (JAMIA)*, 17(1), 19-24, 2010.

[36] H.-T. Zhang, M.-L. Huang, and X.-Y. Zhu. A unified active learning framework for biomedical relation extraction. *Journal of Computer Science and Technology*, 27(6), 1302-1313, 2012.

[37] X. Zhu. Semi-supervised learning literature survey. *Technical Report 1530*: University of Wisconsin-Madison, 2007.

Ranking Deep Web Text Collections for Scalable Information Extraction

Pablo Barrio
Columbia University
New York, NY, USA
pjbarrio@cs.columbia.edu

Luis Gravano
Columbia University
New York, NY, USA
gravano@cs.columbia.edu

Chris Develder
Ghent University – iMinds
Ghent, Belgium
cdvelder@intec.ugent.be

ABSTRACT

Information extraction (IE) systems discover structured information from natural language text, to enable much richer querying and data mining than possible directly over the unstructured text. Unfortunately, IE is generally a computationally expensive process, and hence improving its efficiency, so that it scales over large volumes of text, is of critical importance. State-of-the-art approaches for scaling the IE process focus on one text collection at a time. These approaches prioritize the extraction effort by learning keyword queries to identify the "useful" documents for the IE task at hand, namely, those that lead to the extraction of structured "tuples." These approaches, however, do not attempt to predict which text collections are useful for the IE task—and hence merit further processing—and which ones will not contribute any useful output—and hence should be ignored altogether, for efficiency. In this paper, we focus on an especially valuable family of text sources, the so-called deep web collections, whose (remote) contents are only accessible via querying. Specifically, we introduce and study techniques for ranking deep web collections for an IE task, to prioritize the extraction effort by focusing on collections with substantial numbers of useful documents for the task. We study both (adaptations of) state-of-the-art resource selection strategies for distributed information retrieval, and IE-specific approaches. Our extensive experimental evaluation over realistic deep web collections, and for several different IE tasks, shows the merits and limitations of the alternative families of approaches, and provides a roadmap for addressing this critically important building block for efficient, scalable information extraction.

1. INTRODUCTION

A large body of today's knowledge is embedded in natural language text documents. Information extraction (IE) systems identify and extract information from text into a structured form, such as relational tables. For example, an IE system to extract an *Occurs-in*(*Natural Disaster*, *Location*) relation would extract the tuple ⟨earthquake, Mexico⟩ from the text fragment *"A powerful earthquake shook a wide area of Mexico."* Much richer querying and data mining are possible over structured information than over the unstructured text where it originates. Unfortunately, IE is generally a computationally expensive process [22], and hence improving its efficiency, so that it scales to large volumes of text, is of critical importance.

In this paper, we focus on IE over *deep web collections*, which are text document collections that are accessible only through a query interface and are hence not "crawlable" through traditional search engine crawlers [7,17,27,28]. Examples of such collections include the Federal Emergency Management Agency (FEMA) collection[1], a key up-to-date resource for natural disasters and other hazards in the United States; and PubMed[2], a well-known resource for life sciences and biomedical research with over 22 million abstracts and references to research papers. Deep web collections often host high-quality content and together span a broad range of topics. Furthermore, the collective content in deep web collections may exceed in volume, according to some estimates, that of the crawlable, or "surface" web [18,24].

To run an IE system over a deep web collection, a key challenge is effectively and efficiently retrieving its *useful* documents, namely, the documents from which the IE system manages to extract tuples. To address this challenge, techniques such as QXtract [2], PRDualRank [12], FactCrawl [8], and RSVM-IE and BAgg-IE [6] learn a collection-specific set of text queries (e.g., consisting of words and phrases) to target the useful documents and ignore the rest, thus reducing the overall extraction cost drastically. These techniques, however, do not attempt to predict which text collections are useful for the IE task—and hence merit further processing—and which ones will not contribute any useful output—and hence should be ignored, for efficiency.

In this paper, we introduce and address the problem of ranking deep web collections for an IE task, to prioritize the extraction effort by focusing on collections with substantial numbers of useful documents for the IE task. An approach for this task should rightfully conclude, for example, that FEMA is better for extracting *Occurs-in* tuples than PubMed. This collection ranking problem is related to the problem of resource selection in distributed information retrieval [29, Chapter 3], to identify topically relevant collections for a given user query. Unlike in distributed IR, though, our IE scenario requires that we identify collections

[1] `http://www.fema.gov/`

[2] `http://www.ncbi.nlm.nih.gov/pubmed`

CIKM'15, October 19–23, 2015, Melbourne, Australia.

DOI: http://dx.doi.org/10.1145/2806416.2806581.

with useful documents for the IE task, rather than documents that are topically relevant for a given query. Despite this difference in focus, we can adapt resource selection approaches to our IE scenario, as we will see, as well as develop alternative, IE-specific approaches.

To prioritize deep web collections for an IE task, we must identify the most useful collections, namely, the collections with the largest numbers of useful documents for the IE task. Therefore, we need to estimate the number of useful documents in each collection and, importantly, we need to do so efficiently (e.g., by issuing a relatively small number of queries to each collection). For this estimation problem, we could exploit state-of-the-art techniques for measuring certain deep web collection properties (e.g., their number of documents) [4, 34, 35]. Unfortunately, as we will see, such techniques can be prohibitively expensive for IE, because they may need to issue many queries to sufficiently cover the (often rare) useful documents for an IE task of interest.

To address the limitations of generic estimation techniques, and to effectively rank deep web collections for a given IE task, we develop approaches that target the useful documents for the IE task in question. We compare both (adaptations of) state-of-the-art resource selection strategies and IE-specific approaches in an extensive experimental evaluation over realistic deep web collections, and for several different IE tasks. In summary, our key contributions are:

- We introduce the problem of ranking deep web collections for efficient and scalable IE (Section 2).
- We study traditional as well as IE-specific approaches for estimating, for each deep web collection, the number of useful documents for a given IE task (Section 3).
- We report the results of an extensive evaluation of both (adaptations of) traditional approaches for distributed information retrieval and IE-specific approaches over real-world deep web collections and for several different IE tasks. Our results show the merits and limitations of the alternative families of approaches, and provide a roadmap for addressing this critically important building block for efficient, scalable information extraction (Sections 4 and 5).

2. PROBLEM DEFINITION

Our focus is on the efficiency and scalability of the IE process over deep web text collections, whose contents can only be accessed via querying and cannot be retrieved using traditional Web "crawlers." To run an IE system over the available deep web collections, a naïve, expensive approach could resort to state-of-the-art approaches for efficient query-based IE execution (e.g., [2,6,8,12]) over each deep web collection individually.[3] Such a naïve approach would be unnecessarily expensive, because not all collections contain any *useful* documents, or documents from which the IE system at hand manages to extract tuples. Therefore, to prioritize the IE effort, for efficiency, we focus on the problem of ranking deep web collections for an IE task of interest.

A related problem, *resource selection*, has been studied in the context of distributed information retrieval, to rank collections according to their topical relevance to a given user query [29]. Resource selection approaches generally consist of two steps: (1) *descriptor generation:* in an offline step,

[3]Our approach is not applicable over open information extraction scenarios (e.g., [3]) where documents frequently contribute tuples to the open-ended extraction task.

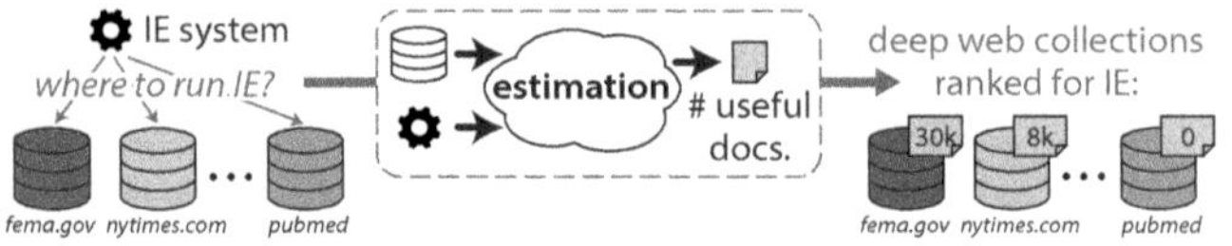

Figure 1: Collection ranking for IE over the deep web.

build a compact, representative collection summary (e.g., consisting of word frequency vectors [11, 15] or document samples [30,32]); (2) *relevance estimation:* to process a given query, use the collection descriptors to estimate the number of topically relevant documents in each collection, and rank the collections accordingly.

Unlike in distributed IR, our IE scenario requires that we identify collections with useful documents for the IE task, rather than collections with documents that are topically relevant to a given query. As a result, the collection descriptors will need to effectively capture the characteristics of the useful documents, a challenging proposition because of two critical reasons. First, the notion of document usefulness is, by definition, specific to a given IE task, so our collection ranking approaches—and the collection descriptors on which they rely—will have to be flexible to adapt to each given IE task. In particular, the "one-size-fits-all" descriptors adopted by resource selection approaches for distributed IR would not be appropriate for our IE scenario. Second, the fraction of documents in a collection that are useful for an IE task can many times be very small, so our collection ranking approaches—and the estimation techniques on which they rely—will have to effectively target the useful documents, to keep the ranking overhead to manageable levels. In particular, state-of-the-art techniques for estimating certain deep web collection properties [4,34,35], as discussed above, would be prohibitively expensive for our IE scenario.

We summarize the problem that we address as follows:

PROBLEM DEFINITION 1. *Consider a set of deep web collections and an information extraction task T with its corresponding (previously trained) information extraction system. Our goal is to rank the collections according to their number of useful documents for the IE task T (see Figure 1). Furthermore, the ranking process should be efficient (e.g., in terms of the number of queries issued to each collection), to keep its overhead to reasonable levels.*

Earlier efforts to identify collections for an extraction task (e.g., [1, 21]) have focused on examining the quality of the extraction output, rather than its volume. The (complementary) methods described in this paper can be adapted to consider quality (see Section 6).

3. ESTIMATING COLLECTION USEFULNESS

To prioritize the IE effort and rank deep web collections for an IE task, we need to estimate the number of useful documents for the IE task in each collection. Specifically, for each collection C, we will estimate the cardinality of C^U, the set of useful documents in C for the IE task at hand. In this section, we first provide an overview of three families of state-of-the-art estimation approaches that we can adapt for the task (Section 3.1) and then describe each method in detail (Sections 3.2 through 3.4).

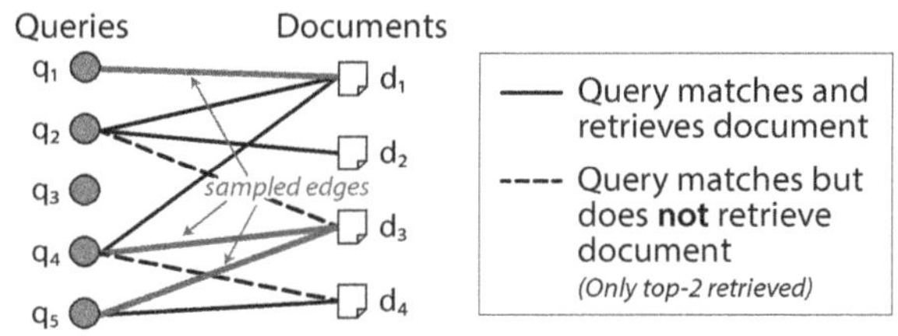

Figure 2: An example (query, document)-graph: the estimate contribution $f(d_1)$ from document d_1 has a $\frac{1}{3}$ weight (since its sampled degree is 3) and $f(d_3)$ is counted twice, each time with weight $\frac{1}{2}$.

Family	Technique (B or IE)	Collection	IE	
Surrogate	ReDDE (B)	Document sample + size estimate	Queries	
	Surrogate (IE)	Term-frequency map + size estimate	Document sample	
Query Pool-Based	PB (B)	In sum: - In avg: size estimate	In generic: -	In specific: query pool
	PB-W (IE)	In sum: - In avg: size estimate	In generic: weights	In specific: query pool + weights
Query Pool-Free	PF (B)	Query sample	-	
	PF-W (IE)	Query sample	Query sample	

Table 1: Summary of the characteristics of the baseline and IE-specific methods of Section 3.

3.1 Overview of Estimation Approaches

Given an IE task, we can cast the problem of estimating the number of useful documents for the task in a deep web collection as an instance of the generic task of estimating a "property" of interest for a deep web collection, which has been studied extensively in the research literature. Such a property F of a collection C is typically defined as an aggregate over a document-level function, say, $f(d)$. A simple example is the estimation of the number of documents in a deep web collection C: in this case, $f(d) = 1$ for every document d in C, and $F(C) = \sum_{d \in C} f(d)$. In our IE scenario, to estimate the number of useful documents we should define $f(d) = \mathbb{1}\{d \text{ is useful}\}$, that is, as the indicator function that returns 1 if d is useful and 0 otherwise. Various methods have been proposed to estimate properties of (queryable) document collections (e.g., collection size, number of documents relevant to a query, average document length) [4, 19, 34, 35], and these methods can be classified in three broad classes: (i) surrogate-based methods, (ii) query pool-based methods, and (iii) query pool-free methods.

Surrogate-based methods construct an approximate representation of the entire collection, and then use that surrogate to estimate the metric of interest, without further accessing the actual collection. A surrogate typically comprises a (relatively small) document sample (e.g., [30, 32]), or document frequency estimations for the terms occurring in the collection (e.g., [11, 15]). In resource selection for distributed IR, such representations have been widely used to estimate the number of documents relevant to a query (e.g., CORI [11], GlOSS [15], ReDDE [32], and Relax [30]). For example, ReDDE builds a random document sample S for each collection C, once and for all. Simply stated, to judge the relevance of C to a query q, ReDDE extrapolates the number of documents relevant to q in S to the entire collection.

Query pool-based methods pick queries from a predefined query pool Q (e.g., a dictionary of words or n-grams collected from extensive web crawls) to retrieve—from the collection at hand—documents from which to estimate the metric of interest. Unlike the collection-specific surrogates, the query pool can be shared across collections and can also be targeted specifically to the estimation task at hand. The query pool-based method in [23] aims at estimating collection size effectively but is inefficient: for large collections, the samples required to produce accurate estimates are very large. Subsequent (query pool-based) methods addressed this limitation, and sample random edges from a (query, document)-graph, as sketched in Figure 2: the graph vertices are queries $q \in Q$ and documents $d \in C$, and a solid edge (q, d) means that q retrieves d. For each sampled (q, d) pair, the measure $f(d)$ contributes to the estimation of $F(C)$ with a weight that is proportional to the probability of having sampled d (see Section 3.3). Pool-based methods work well, provided the query pool Q retrieves all documents of interest for the metric (i.e., for which $f(d) \neq 0$).

Query pool-free methods avoid relying on a query pool, and rather find the queries to issue "on the fly." These methods use a seed query (e.g., a common word or phrase) to retrieve a first set of documents and select the next query to issue from these documents. Thus, they issue queries and retrieve documents to perform a random walk on a graph where nodes are either queries or documents. To properly weigh the particular $f(d)$ value derived from visiting a node in such graph, these methods use the fact that the probability of visiting a node during a random walk is proportional to its number of incident edges.

In our IE scenario, we need to estimate the number of useful documents in a deep web collection for an IE task of interest. Unfortunately, only very few or no useful documents might be present in a truly random document sample from the collection, given that useful documents might be rare for an IE task. This poses a problem for all three families of estimation methods summarized above. The next subsections describe the existing approaches in detail and derive IE-specific estimators that effectively target useful documents. By aiming to collect documents for which $f(d) \neq 0$, our IE-specific methods are designed to have more non-zero terms in their estimation, thus alleviating the limitations of existing estimation techniques for other tasks. Each subsection first discusses a state-of-the-art baseline method and how we can apply it to our IE scenario; the second part introduces an IE-specific method, designed specifically for collection usefulness estimation. Table 1 summarizes the requirements of each method to handle collections and IE tasks.

3.2 Surrogate-Based Estimators

Baseline (ReDDE): Our first (baseline) estimator is an adaptation of ReDDE, a resource selection technique for distributed IR [31]. To estimate the number of topically relevant documents for a query q in a collection C, ReDDE predicts the relevance of a representative sample $S \subset C$ and scales it to the entire collection with a factor $SF = |C|/|S|$ to obtain a collection relevance metric $\text{Rel}(q, C)$. This metric relies on estimating (i) the collection size $|C|$ and (ii) the relevance of sample documents in S to the given query q. The size $|C|$ is query-independent and thus computed once and for all, while the query relevance for d is based on issuing q to a centralized global sample unifying all individual collection samples. To apply ReDDE to our IE scenario, we model the IE task as a set of high-performing queries Q_{IE}, which we can automatically learn (e.g., see QXtract [2]). We thus calculate collection relevance for the IE task as a sum of the ReDDE relevance metric, taken over the top-k queries from our set of IE-specific queries: $|\hat{C}^{\text{U}}| = \sum_{q \in \text{top}_k(Q_{\text{IE}})} \text{Rel}(q, C)$.

IE-specific (Surrogate): An alternative, IE-specific estimation approach is to collect a random sample S from a collection C, run the IE system over the documents in S, and extrapolate the number of useful documents to the full collection C as in ReDDE, namely, $|\hat{C}^{\text{U}}| = SF \cdot |S^{\text{U}}|$ with scaling factor $SF = |C|/|S|$. Unfortunately, a random sample might have very few or no useful documents because, as discussed, useful documents for an IE task are often rare. To address this problem, the document sample S should be then biased towards useful documents. This implies that we subsequently have to correct the scaling factor SF for that usefulness bias of S. The main idea is to look at document frequency differences of certain terms between the sample S and the full collection C. For a given term t, let $df(t, X)$ be the fraction of documents in X that contain t, and define the frequency ratio in the sample vs. in the full collection as $\alpha_t^S \triangleq \frac{df(t,S)}{df(t,C)}$. We propose to use the average of this ratio over *useful terms*, T^{U}, as a heuristic scaling factor: $SF = \mathbb{E}_{T^{\text{U}}}\left[1/\alpha_t^S\right]$, where useful terms are those that are (i) biased towards usefulness, in contrast to "neutral" terms that would appear equally in useful and useless documents; and (ii) overrepresented in the sample (i.e., $\alpha_t^S > 1$). The rationale for this choice of SF is that the overrepresentation of such useful terms in S compared to in C is a good proxy for the overrepresentation of useful documents. (We can find T^{U} through standard statistical significance tests.) Importantly, we assume that we know the document frequencies $df(t, C)$ in the complete collection, as well as the collection size $|C|$. We can estimate these values reliably once and for all for each collection (e.g., see [20] and [31]).

3.3 Query Pool-Based Estimators

Baseline (PB): We consider the method of Bar-Yossef *et al.* [4], which set the foundations for subsequent query pool-based estimators (e.g., [34]) and allows estimating any generic metric that can be expressed as a discrete integral over the documents in C: $\text{Int}_\pi(f) \triangleq \sum_{d \in C} f(d) \cdot \pi_D(d)$, where f is the target function of interest and π_D weighs documents as needed (e.g., $\pi_D(d) = 1$ if all documents contribute equally). As indicated in Section 3.1, documents $d \in C$ are obtained by issuing queries from a pool Q. Bar-Yossef *et al.*'s method relies on two core ideas: (i) extend π_D to a measure over the (query, document)-space $Q \times C$, and (ii) apply importance sampling to use a practical sampling strategy, selecting a (query, document)-pair with probability $p(q, d)$, rather than from the probability distribution induced by π_D, which is unfeasible to sample from. For (i), the extended measure is:

$$\pi(q, d) \triangleq \frac{\mathbb{1}\{d \in C_q\} \cdot \pi_D(d)}{\omega(d)},$$

where C_q is the set of documents that q retrieves from C and $\omega(d)$ is the degree of document d, defined as the number of queries in Q that retrieve d. For (ii), the practical sampling strategy is: (1) pick a random query q from the set of queries that return at least one document, noted as Q_+, and then (2) randomly pick one of the documents it retrieves:

$$p(q, d) \triangleq \frac{1}{|Q_+|} \cdot \frac{\mathbb{1}\{d \in C_q\}}{|C_q|}.$$

In importance sampling, $p(q, d)$ and $\pi(q, d)$ induce probability distributions referred to as the *trial* and *target* distributions, respectively, and define the importance weight as:

$$w(q, d) \triangleq \frac{\pi(q, d)}{p(q, d)} = \frac{\pi_D(d) \cdot |Q_+| \cdot |C_q|}{\omega(d)}.$$

Bar-Yossef *et al.* use an efficient estimator $u(q, d)$ of $w(q, d)$, defined as $u(q, d) = \pi_D(d) \cdot \text{PSE} \cdot |C_q| \cdot \text{IDE}(d)$, with a pool size estimator PSE for $|Q_+|$ and an inverse degree estimator $\text{IDE}(d)$ for $1/\omega(d)$, in turn, to calculate the approximate importance sampler (AIS): $\text{AIS}(q, d) \triangleq f(d) \cdot u(q, d)$. The authors show that if u approximates w well, and if the ratio u/w is uncorrelated with f, AIS remains largely unbiased.

A variant of the above estimator for sums [4] computes $\text{Avg}(f) = \sum_i (f(d) \cdot u(q_i, d_i)) / \sum_i u(q_i, d_i)$ (where the PSE factor cancels out) and obtains the estimator by multiplying $\text{Avg}(f)$ by the size of the collection. This collection size estimation can be done once and for all, and reused for different metrics (e.g., for the usefulness for different IE tasks), to amortize its cost.

However, directly using AIS in our IE scenario is problematic: (i) the number of queries to issue and subsequent IE-processing of returned documents to determine $f(d)$, to find some useful documents, may be high; and (ii) the estimation will have high variance because of the few non-zero $f(d)$ values.[4] To address the first limitation for the related problem of counting the frequency of a given word (e.g., "sports") in a collection, Zhang *et al.* identify the queries that are positively correlated with the word (e.g., query "golf") [34]. The query sampling process is then stratified over correlated and uncorrelated queries. Unfortunately, this approach still requires issuing a large number of queries.

IE-specific (PB-W): We adapt the Bar-Yossef *et al.* approach, with target and trial distributions that are aligned with $f(d)$ for usefulness: Our *target distribution* assigns probabilities greater than 0 only to useful documents:

$$\pi_{\text{U}}(q, d) \triangleq \frac{\mathbb{1}\{d \in C_q^{\text{U}}\} \cdot \pi_D(d)}{\omega(d)},$$

where C_q^{U} is the set of useful documents that q retrieves from C. Our *trial distribution*, accordingly, should (i) retrieve useful documents with high recall and precision, and (ii) be efficient to sample from. Specifically, for recall, we learn queries from a large, external text collection E that we can process once and for all. For precision, we learn the usefulness of queries with respect to the given IE task: (1) process E with the IE system at hand, (2) query E with all words in the documents, and (3) count the useful and useless documents within the top-k results for each query q, noted as $|E_q^{\text{U}}|$ and $|E_q^{\text{N}}|$, respectively. Finally, our trial distribution assigns a selection weight to each query q, defined as $w \cdot |E_q^{\text{U}}| + |E_q^{\text{N}}|$.[5]

Given these query weights, our trial process consists of two steps: (1) pick a useful query q proportionally to its weight,

[4]The variance can be reduced via Rao-Blackwellization, as suggested in [4], which requires running IE over all retrieved documents. We evaluate this version of the algorithm later in the experimental section.

[5]$|E_q^{\text{N}}|$ in the selection weight operates as a smoothing factor.

and (2) pick a document from q's useful results uniformly at random. This yields the following trial distribution:

$$p_{\text{U}}(q,d) \triangleq \frac{w \cdot |E_q^{\text{U}}| + |E_q^{\text{N}}|}{\mathbb{Z}_w} \cdot \frac{\mathbb{1}\{d \in C_q^{\text{U}}\}}{|C_q^{\text{U}}|}.$$

Here, $\mathbb{Z}_w = \sum_{q \in Q_+^{\text{U}}} w \cdot |E_q^{\text{U}}| + |E_q^{\text{N}}|$ is the normalization factor of the probability distribution induced by the queries that retrieve at least one useful document, Q_+^{U}. We can now obtain our importance weight function as:

$$w_{\text{U}}(q,d) \triangleq \frac{\pi_{\text{U}}(q,d)}{p_{\text{U}}(q,d)} = \frac{\mathbb{Z}_w \cdot \pi_D(d)}{\omega(d)} \cdot \frac{|C_q^{\text{U}}|}{w \cdot |E_q^{\text{U}}| + |E_q^{\text{N}}|},$$

which we need to compute only over the useful documents. Similarly to [4], we rely on an efficient estimator u_{U} of w_{U}, defined as:

$$u_{\text{U}}(d,q) \triangleq \frac{\text{NFE} \cdot \text{IDE}(d) \cdot \text{UE}(q) \cdot \pi_D(d)}{w \cdot |E_q^{\text{U}}| + |E_q^{\text{N}}|},$$

to keep estimation costs to reasonable levels. Here, NFE and UE(q) are estimators of normalization factor $\mathbb{Z}_w$ and number of useful documents retrieved by a query.

The key challenge in computing NFE is to account for the number of queries $|Q_+^{\text{U}}|$ and the distribution of their selection weight. We can compute them both on the fly while sampling during our trial process: Both factors can be computed by sampling according to the selection weight, instead of uniformly at random, as in Bar-Yossef *et al.*'s PSE. We compute NFE by keeping track of the fraction of sampled queries that retrieve at least one useful document, defined as α, and computing $\alpha \cdot \sum_{q \in Q}(w \cdot |E_q^{\text{U}}| + |E_q^{\text{N}}|)$.[6] To compute UE($q$), we proceed similarly to Bar-Yossef *et al.*'s IDE computation: we sample documents uniformly at random from C_q until we find a useful one; if we find the useful document after processing n documents, then $\text{UE}(q) = \frac{|C_q|}{n}$.

3.4 Query Pool-Free Estimators

Baseline (PF): We focus on the method introduced by Zhang *et al.* [35], using a query graph: (i) the nodes are h-grams[7] q that retrieve at least u documents[8] and (ii) undirected edges connect a node pair (q, q') if q' matches (i.e., appears in the text of) at least one of the documents that q retrieves, and vice versa. Since a random walk implies that a node q is visited with a probability proportional to its degree $d(q)$, each per-query estimate is weighted with $1/d(q)$ to agree with uniform sampling. The estimation of a function $F(C) = \sum_{d \in C} f(d)$ from sampled queries S in (query) graph Q is:

$$\hat{F}(C) = |\hat{Q}| \cdot \underbrace{\frac{\sum\limits_{q \in S} 1/d(q) \cdot \sum\limits_{d \in C_q} f(d)/\omega(d)}{\sum\limits_{q \in S} 1/d(q)}}_{\#\text{ useful documents per sampled query}}$$

$$= |V_c| \cdot \tilde{\lambda}(V_c) \cdot \frac{\sum\limits_{q \in S} 1/d(q) \cdot \sum\limits_{d \in C_q} f(d)/\omega(d)}{\sum\limits_{q \in S \cap V_C} 1/d(q)}. \quad (1)$$

[6]The $|E_q^{\text{U}}|$ and $|E_q^{\text{N}}|$ values in this formula are computed once and for all during the generation of the queries.

[7]Zhang *et al.* argue that $h = 1$ works well in practice.

[8]Parameter u controls the size and connectivity of the graph. Zhang *et al.* propose $u = 3$.

Here, $\omega(d)$ is the number of queries in Q that retrieve document d. Furthermore, the size of the query graph $|\hat{Q}|$ is estimated from a startup query collection V_C, which is a sample (e.g., obtained from the documents of another random walk, independent of S) of the vocabulary of h-grams appearing in the collection, and its estimated fraction $\tilde{\lambda}(V_C)$ that retrieve at least u documents when issued as a query.[9] While eliminating a potential coverage issue by avoiding an a priori query pool, the resulting estimation may still require many queries in the IE scenario, to find sufficiently many useful documents.

IE-specific (PF-W): To estimate the number of useful documents, we could restrict the graph to only useful queries (i.e., queries that retrieve at least one useful document and for which $f(d) = 1$). However, such graph could be largely disconnected and the random walk would be unable to fully explore it. Instead, we keep the original graph and modify the random walk process to favor visiting useful queries: We define a *weighted graph*, on which we perform a "weighted" random walk (i.e., edge e with weight $w(e)$ is selected from an edge set E with probability $w(e)/\sum_{e' \in E} w(e')$). We define an edge (q, q') to be *useful* if and only if both queries it connects retrieve at least one useful document. We assign useful edges weight w and the others 1. In Equation (1) we thus replace the original (unweighted) degree $d(q)$ with the weighted counterpart: $d_w(q) = w \cdot N_{\text{U}} + N_{\text{N}}$, where N_{U} is the number of q's useful incident edges (i.e., useful neighbors q') and $N_{\text{N}} = N_{\text{ALL}} - N_{\text{U}}$ (with $N_{\text{ALL}} = d(q)$). The definition of $\omega(d)$ (i.e., the number of queries that retrieve it) remains unchanged, thus we still estimate it using the method in [35].

To estimate the weighted degree $d_w(q)$ of a sampled query q we need (i) the number of all incident edges N_{ALL}, and (ii) the number of useful edges N_{U}. For N_{ALL} we proceed as in [35]. For N_{U} we proceed similarly, now counting the number of sampling attempts n_{U} we need to find a q' that both matches q and is useful, to estimate $\hat{N}_{\text{U}} = |Q'|/n_{\text{U}}$.[10] Thus, we calculate $\hat{d}_w(q) = w \cdot \hat{N}_{\text{U}} + (\hat{N}_{\text{ALL}} - \hat{N}_{\text{U}})$.

In this section, we described the baseline and IE-specific approaches that we study in this paper. We now describe the settings for our experimental evaluation of these techniques (Section 4) and report our results (Section 5).

4. EXPERIMENTAL SETTINGS

Collections: Our *test set* consists of 96 real web collections across different topics, collected using an approach similar to that in [16] over the Open Directory Project (ODP)[11]. Specifically, we first selected the 8 top-level ODP categories with the largest number of entries, namely, Business, Society, Arts, Science, Computers, Recreation, Shopping, and Sports. We then selected the 5 most popular subcategories in each of the 8 initial categories. In turn, we also picked the 5 most popular subsubcategories from each subcategory, for a total of 200 subsubcategories. For each subsubcategory, we then randomly chose 7 unique web collections that have a text search interface. Finally, we collected their contents using a state-of-the-art query-based sampler [10], issuing at most 20,000 queries and retrieving up to 1,000 documents for each. In our test set, we kept the collections that produced

[9]We correct an erroneous $1/|S|$ factor from [35, eq. (5)].

[10]Implementation-wise, we can get n_{ALL}, the sampling attempts for N_{ALL}, from the same sampling sequence as n_{U}.

[11]`http://www.dmoz.org/`

Relation	Useful documents	
	SSK	BONG
Person–Career	56.20%	55.95%
Natural Disaster–Location	2.03%	2.74%
Man Made Disaster–Location (*)	0.80%	0.87%
Person–Charge	1.55%	1.84%
Election–Winner	0.24%	0.84%

Table 2: Fraction of useful documents found in the TREC 1-5 collections for relations extracted using two IE systems, SSK and BONG. We use (*) only during tuning.

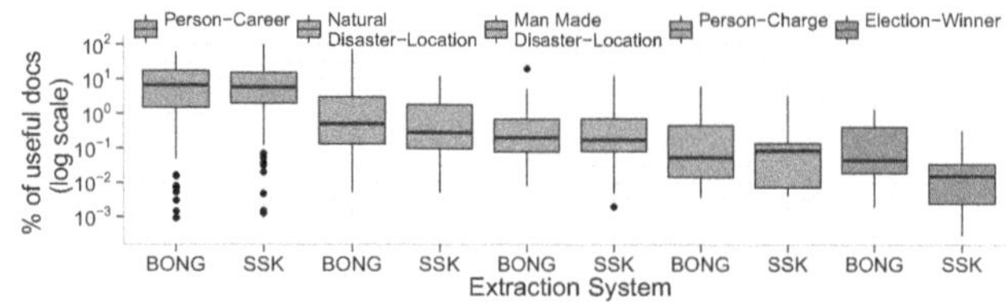

Figure 3: Fraction of useful documents for each relation across our 96 test collections. The box boundaries are the 25th and 75th percentiles, the bold horizontal line inside each box is the median, and the dots denote outliers.

at least 10,000 documents following this method, to focus the evaluation on collections with a substantial number of documents. Our *tuning set*, which we use for tuning parameters of the various techniques, consists of 40 collections selected randomly from among the collections under the above subsubcategories and not in the test set. We collected documents from these tuning collections using the Nutch Web crawler[12]. We indexed each collection, in both the tuning set and the test set, with the text retrieval toolkit Lucene[13], to emulate the query-only behavior of deep web collections and only access them through their query interface. We exhaustively processed the collections with our IE systems (see below) to obtain the real number of useful documents in each collection. We also used TREC 1-5 collections[14] for different operations (e.g., query pool construction), which we describe as needed throughout this section.

Information Extraction Systems: We evaluated a variety of IE systems and components for all relations in our experiments (see below) via 5-fold crossvalidation over a set of training documents, and selected the two best-performing combinations, namely, Subsequence Kernel (SSK) [9] and Bag of n-Grams (BONG) [14]. We implemented them using REEL[15] [5]. We also considered different named entity taggers and selected: for *person* and *location* entities, the pretrained conditional random fields (CRF) [26] from the StanfordNLP package[16]; for *natural disasters*, CRFs from the etxt2db framework[17]; for the remaining entities, maximum entropy markov models (MEMM) [25], also from etxt2db.

Relations: For a robust evaluation, we include 5 substantially different relations in the experiments (see Table 2). Four such relations, namely, Natural Disaster–Location, Man Made Disaster–Location, Person–Charge, and Election–Winner, are sparse, in that very few documents tend to be useful for them. In contrast, relation Person–Career is a dense relation. (Table 2 shows the percentage of useful documents for each relation in the TREC 1-5 collections for the two IE systems. Also, Figure 3 shows the distribution of useful documents over the collections in our test set.)

Technique Tuning: We tuned each technique over the tuning set and using the SSK IE system over Man Made Disaster–Location.

Surrogate-based methods (Section 3.2): (1) Baseline: We evaluated different query sets Q and numbers of queries k. For Q, we generated one-word queries using the SVM approach in [2] and two effective feature selection methods, namely, Information Gain and χ^2 test [36], over 10,000 documents (50% useful and 50% useless) from TREC 1-5; we kept the words that are discriminative of the useful class; also, and as suggested in [2], we evaluated a query set including all words in the documents and another one removing the tuple attribute values. We varied $k \in [10, 200]$ in intervals of 10. We built the document samples using the query-based sampling technique in [10], which produces nearly-random document samples from words collected from retrieved documents. *(2) IE-specific:* We compared (i) the query-based sampling technique in ReDDE; (ii) the bootstrapping-based sampling approach in [2], which starts from a set of seed tuples as queries that is iteratively expanded as it collects more useful documents and extracts tuples from them; (iii) a sampling technique that issues the queries in Q above based on their score. Finally, to find the useful terms and to asses term bias we used the Fisher exact test in [13] varying p-value $\in [0.01, 0.1]$.

Query pool-based methods (Section 3.3): We built two query pools of single words from TREC 1-5: (i) a generic query pool (G) of 4M words considering all documents; and (ii) an IE specific query pool (S) that only considers words from useful documents. We performed the estimation process with and without Rao-Blackwellization, suggested in the original paper for variance reduction [4]. We evaluated the sum and average approaches. For the IE-specific method, we also: (i) evaluated several different values for the weight $w \in [50, 500000]$; (ii) used the TREC 1-5 collections as our external collection; and (iii) varied the number of documents to retrieve $k \in [10, 1000]$ for weight computation.

Query pool-free methods (Section 3.4): We varied three parameters common to the baseline and IE-specific approach: (i) the number of sampled queries $|S| \in [10, 500]$, with increments of 10, (ii) the length of h-grams, $h \in \{1, 2, 3\}$, and (iii) the length of the burn-in of the random walk b before collecting the samples, $b \in [50, 500]$ with increments of 50. For the IE-specific method, we evaluated several different values for its weight $w \in [10, 5000]$.

Techniques for Comparison: We compared the following alternatives over the 96 collections in our test set, with the settings derived via tuning, as summarized below:

- *Baseline surrogate-based (ReDDE):* We generate the samples with the query-based document sampler in [10], issuing up to 300 queries and collecting (at most) 5 documents for each. We use the queries learned with χ^2 for Q and use the top-100 queries (i.e., $k = 100$).
- *IE-specific surrogate-based method (Surrogate):* For sampling, we derive Q using the χ^2 method and excluding tuple attributes. We considered the useful queries in order of χ^2.

[12]http://nutch.apache.org/
[13]http://lucene.apache.org/
[14]http://trec.nist.gov/data.html
[15]http://reel.cs.columbia.edu/
[16]http://nlp.stanford.edu/software/CRF-NER.shtml
[17]http://web.ist.utl.pt/rui.lageira/

Our sample S has at most 1000 documents. To select the useful terms T^{U}, we use p-value = 0.05 in the Fisher test.

- *Baseline query-pool-based (PB):* We use the sum (ABS) and average (AVG) methods using the G and Q query pools and applying Rao-Blackwellization. (The impact on efficiency of applying Rao-Blackwellization is low, because the number of documents processed with the IE system is small.)
- *IE-specific query-pool-based method (PB-W):* As with the baseline, we evaluate sum (ABS) and average (AVG) estimators using the G and S query pools and applying Rao-Blackwellization. We index our external collection using Lucene with default parameters. We use $k = 1000$ for the query weight computation and $w = 5000$.
- *Baseline query-pool-free (PF):* We use an English dictionary to randomly find an initial query for the estimation process. We use single terms as queries (i.e., $h = 1$) and only accept queries that retrieve at least $u = 3$ documents, as suggested in [35]. We collect 100 queries for V_c, the startup query path that can be shared across IE tasks, and at most 100 for the estimation sample queries S.
- *IE-specific query-pool-free method (PF-W):* We use a similar configuration to that in PF, but with $w = 1000$.

Additional Settings: Estimators issue at most 100 queries, and retrieve up to 50 documents per query. To account for randomness, we run each estimator five times and report average values over the five runs. Finally, note that all estimators contain some form of (weighted) averaging of a metric over samples S (e.g., for the pool-free estimator, we calculate the individual contribution of each q in the summation in the denominator of Equation (1)). We filter outliers from this average, using the outlier detection algorithm in [33, "Method I"] as implemented in the R[18] package "extremevalues": a value x is an outlier if it is outside the limit where less than 1 observation is expected, based on observed data within quantile limits $[\alpha, 1-\alpha]$. We evaluated every estimator with and without outlier removal (using $\alpha \in \{0.05, 0.1\}$). Removing outliers using $\alpha = 0.1$ performed best across all techniques. Thus, our final results include such removal.

Evaluation Metrics: We measure *ranking quality* and *estimation cost* with the following metrics:

- *Cumulative Gain (CG@k):* We measure the number of useful documents that we obtain by processing the collections in ranking order. If u_i is the number of useful documents in the ith collection, we define $\text{CG@}k = \sum_{i=1}^{k} u_i$. This metric focuses on absolute values of useful documents, which makes the comparison across relations problematic, and also does not fully capture "errors" in the ranking.
- *Normalized Discounted Cumulative Gain (nDCG@k):* nDCG@k alleviates the limitations above in a robust manner. Specifically, nDCG@k is defined as the normalized version of Discounted Cumulative Gain $\text{DCG@}k = u_1 + \sum_{i=2}^{k} \frac{u_i}{log_2(i)}$, which penalizes the errors in the ranking order.[19] Now, to normalize DCG@k—and obtain nDCG@k—, we need to calculate the DCG@k of an ideal ranking, namely, IDCG@k. Finally, $\text{nDCG@}k = \frac{\text{DCG@}k}{\text{IDCG@}k}$.
- *Processed Documents (PD) and Issued Queries (IQ):* We measure the efficiency of the IE process in terms of the number of issued queries and processed documents, and not running time. The reasons for this are twofold: (1) many factors (e.g., network traffic, collection responsiveness) can distort running times in the distributed environments on which we focus and are difficult to capture reliably; and (2) the number of issued queries and processed documents are good indicators of expected running time. Finally, we report these values only for the actual estimation process and ignore the initial, once-and-for-all processing (e.g., collection size estimation or random document sample generation) required by the techniques, which gets amortized over time.

[18] `http://www.r-project.org/`

[19] Variants of DCG@k exist in the literature; the version we use accounts for the distribution of useful documents.

5. EXPERIMENTAL RESULTS

We now evaluate the baseline and IE-specific ranking approaches of Section 3, with the settings of Section 4.

Quality of collection ranking approaches: We evaluate the ranking approaches over all relations and IE systems of Section 4. Figure 4 shows nDCG@k of all techniques over the entire rank of collections (i.e., $k \in [1, 96]$) for Natural Disaster–Location using the BONG IE system, and issuing at most 100 queries. (Other relations and IE systems—with the exception of Person–Career, which we study in detail later—yielded similar results. Also, we later vary the number of issued queries.) Figure 4a, for the surrogate and query pool-based methods, shows that the PF baseline outperforms PF-1000, its IE-specific counterpart, by almost 75%. PF-1000 requires on average more queries than PF to walk the random graph; for this reason, PF-1000 will rarely find useful documents at such small query budget. As we will see, when PF-1000 finds useful documents, its performance improves considerably, always overcoming its baseline counterpart. In contrast, among the surrogate methods, Surrogate outperforms ReDDE by almost 50%: the IE-specific document sample, although small, manages to include useful documents; also, ReDDE's collection descriptors do not accurately characterize the useful documents.

Figures 4b and 4c, for the query pool-based methods for sums and averages, show that the IE-specific versions also outperform the baseline counterparts. For sum, this difference is mainly based on the number of useful documents sampled during the estimation, because there are more non-zero components to include in the estimation. For this reason, PB-S-ABS-5K is best, with its weighted specific query pool highlighting potentially useful queries. For average, the quality of the ranking also depends on finding queries that retrieve a combination of useful and useless documents, as both types are crucial for computing the average in question. PB-S-AVG and PB-G-AVG-5K sample such queries and thus exhibit the highest quality in this family. Overall, and across families, the top contenders are Surrogate and the average pool-based estimators, which effectively exploit both useful and useless documents during estimation.

To understand the actual number of useful documents observed as we process collections in ranking order, Figure 5 shows CG@k for Natural Disaster–Location and Person Career using the BONG IE system, for a selection of high-quality techniques according to our experiments. For reference we also show the CG@k of an ideal ranking (labeled Ideal) and of a random ranking (noted as a dashed line). Figure 5 reveals substantial gains from prioritizing the collections for extraction. For Natural Disaster–Location, for example, Surrogate effectively identifies the collections containing 95% of the total useful documents within the top-10 collections. This would translate to an efficiency improvement of almost 90% if we were to only process these top-

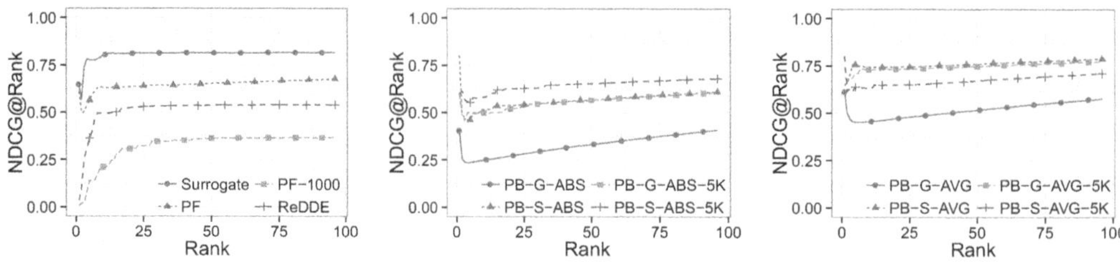

(a) Surrogate and pool-free (b) Pool-based (sum) (c) Pool-based (average)

Figure 4: nDCG@k for Natural Disaster–Location, for the BONG IE system and issuing (at most) 100 queries.

10 collections, because we would ignore 86 (out of 96) test collections. A noticeable benefit is also shown for Person–Career, which we discuss in detail later in this section, for Surrogate, ReDDE, and PB-G-AVG-5K.

Efficiency of collection ranking approaches: To understand the efficiency of the different approaches, we analyze the extraction cost and achieved ranking quality at different stages in the estimation process. Figures 6 and 7 show, respectively, the number of documents processed with the IE system and nDCG@10 for different numbers of issued queries, for Person–Charge using the SSK IE system. (Different relations and IE systems yielded analogous conclusions.) We show the same technique splits as in the above analysis, for clarity. Figure 6 shows that IE-specific techniques process on average more documents than their baseline counterpart. ReDDE is an exception: it does not incur querying or extraction costs during the estimation process.

The reasons as to why IE-specific approaches process more documents on average are manifold and differ for each family of techniques. Notably, for Surrogate (Figure 6a), the number of extracted documents grows with the size of the document sample, because all sampled documents need to be processed. For the pool-free family (also in Figure 6a), PF-1000 may need to process several documents before choosing the next "hop," due to its weighted walking strategy. In contrast, PF does not need this operation, since it navigates the graph only based on the document contents, without incurring additional extractions. However, these techniques may retrieve several hundred documents from each collection for graph construction, to extract h-grams from the documents.

Finally, for the pool-based families (Figures 6b and 6c), the extraction cost grows with the number of observed useful documents (from the sampled edges). In fact, after obtaining a useful document further operations take place: (i) for sum, the inverse degree estimator issues additional queries to the collection, although it avoids processing the documents with the IE system; the average estimators do not need inverse degree estimation and, therefore, more documents are often processed for the same query budget; and (ii) the Rao-Blackwellization method for variance reduction processes all documents that the current query retrieves; this increases the extraction cost, but this cost is comparable across the techniques we evaluated.

After analyzing the extraction cost, we also study the ranking quality associated with such costs. Figure 7 shows that the quality of the ranking improves with the number of issued queries: The estimators learn more—and more reliably—about the collections as the estimation progresses,

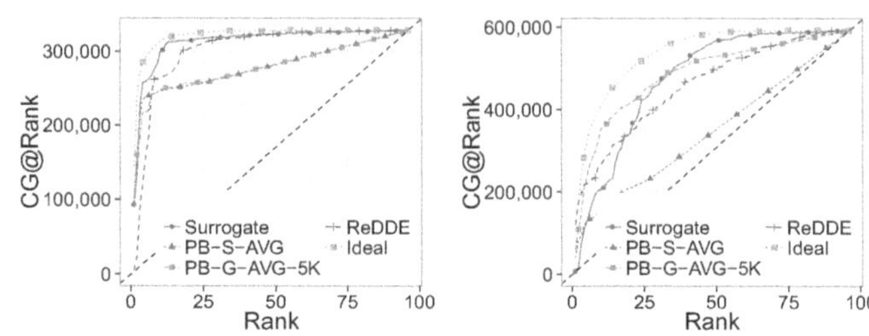

Figure 5: CG@k for Natural Disaster–Location (left) and Person–Career (right) for the BONG IE system and issuing (at most) 100 queries.

which is reflected in better estimations. These improvements, though, vary considerably across techniques: Surrogate, for instance, produces high-quality estimates even when issuing a small number of queries, whereas the remaining techniques improve their quality progressively, with a steeper gain for IE-specific than for baseline approaches. Furthermore, some IE-specific techniques yield higher quality rankings than other techniques at a fraction of their cost. For example, after issuing 25 queries, PB-G-ABS-5K and PB-G-AVG-5K exhibit comparable quality to PB-S-ABS and PB-S-AVG after issuing 100 queries, respectively.

Impact of collection characteristics: Deep web collections are rather heterogeneous, with substantial differences in size and contents. Notably, large collections are problematic for baseline approaches, as Figure 5a shows for Natural Disaster–Location, where the most useful collections were among the largest collections (350,000 documents on average). We showed the effectiveness of our IE-specific approaches for this case. Similarly, the collection contents also affect some of the other approaches: Pool-based approaches retrieved substantially fewer documents than pool-free approaches (see Figure 6), because many queries in the query pool were not topically relevant to the contents of the collections; pool-free approaches do not exhibit this problem.

Impact of IE-task characteristics: To understand the impact of relation characteristics, we now focus on a dense relation. Figure 8 shows nDCG@k over the entire rank of collections (i.e., $k \in [1, 96]$) for Person–Career using the BONG IE system, and for all techniques. We show the same technique splits as in the above analysis, for clarity. Figure 8a shows that Surrogate, PF, and PF-1000 exhibit comparable (low) quality: these techniques failed to correctly

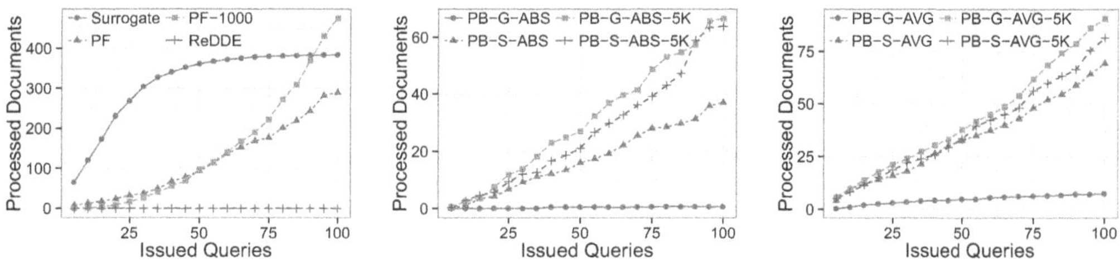

(a) Surrogate and pool-free (b) Pool-based (sum) (c) Pool-based (average)

Figure 6: Processed documents for Person–Charge, for the SSK IE system and different numbers of issued queries.

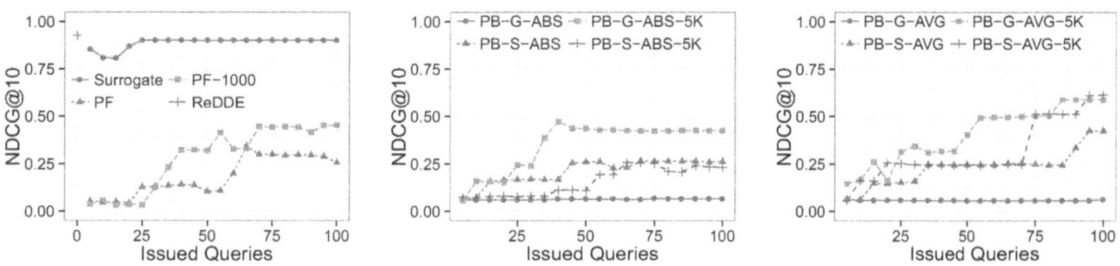

(a) Surrogate and pool-free (b) Pool-based (sum) (c) Pool-based (average)

Figure 7: nDCG@10 for Person–Charge, for the SSK IE system and different numbers of issued queries.

rank large collections with a large number—but a relatively low fraction—of useful documents. Specifically, Surrogate was unable to obtain discriminative terms for the estimation, since most sampled documents were useful. The pool-free approaches, on the other hand, were unable to reach many useful documents, because the useful documents in the top collections were a small fraction in each collection. The pool-based sum estimators in Figure 8b exhibit a trend similar to that of pool-free approaches. However, two sets of techniques performed relatively well, namely, ReDDE (Figure 8a) and the IE-specific pool-based AVG estimators (Figure 8c). These techniques benefited from the scaling to the entire collection, because the largest collections were among the top most useful collections.

Additional discussion: An orthogonal, interesting aspect to the discussion above concerns the overhead incurred by a ranking approach when new collections or IE tasks arrive. Table 1 summarized the collection- and IE-specific requirements of each ranking technique. For new collections, almost all techniques require some preprocessing (see collection column in Table 1). Deciding the approach to adopt will not only depend on the performance and overhead of the techniques but also on the number of IE systems that we will run over each (new) collection. Because size estimation and graph construction may take up to several thousand queries, approaches that rely on these will only be reasonable when many IE systems are involved, as the cost will amortize over time. In other cases, though, estimators that do not require additional information from the collection, such as pool-based estimators for sums, may be the best choice.

Similarly, for new IE tasks, almost all techniques also require some preprocessing (see IE column in Table 1). The most expensive process is, by far, producing a specific query pool (with or without query weights). The remaining processes, namely, learning queries for document sampling or for querying the descriptor in ReDDE and producing a query sample for the pool-free techniques, are relatively inexpensive. Therefore, and given our quality and efficiency results, surrogate methods (i.e., ReDDE or Surrogate) seem to be the most reasonable choice for new IE tasks. However, if new collections are expected to appear at high rates, it may be worthwhile building—and amortizing the construction of—a query pool, so that the estimation starts without overhead.

6. CONCLUSIONS AND FUTURE WORK

In this paper, we introduced and addressed the problem of ranking deep web collections for an IE task, to prioritize the extraction effort by focusing on collections with substantial numbers of useful documents for the IE task. Specifically, the problem is that of effectively and efficiently ranking a set of deep web collections according to their number of useful documents for a given IE task. We studied both (adaptations of) state-of-the-art resource selection strategies, and IE-specific approaches. We performed an extensive experimental evaluation over realistic deep web collections, and for several different IE tasks. Our evaluation focused on the quality and efficiency characteristics of the ranking approaches, with the following conclusions: (1) we found top contenders for each of these characteristics and provided insight on how to choose among them; (2) we analyzed which techniques are better suited for certain characteristics of the collections, such as their size and contents, and of the IE tasks, such as their sparsity; and (3) we discussed the overhead incurred by each technique in dynamic domains, where new collections or IE tasks may arrive. Overall, this paper provides a roadmap for addressing this critically important building block for efficient, scalable information extraction.

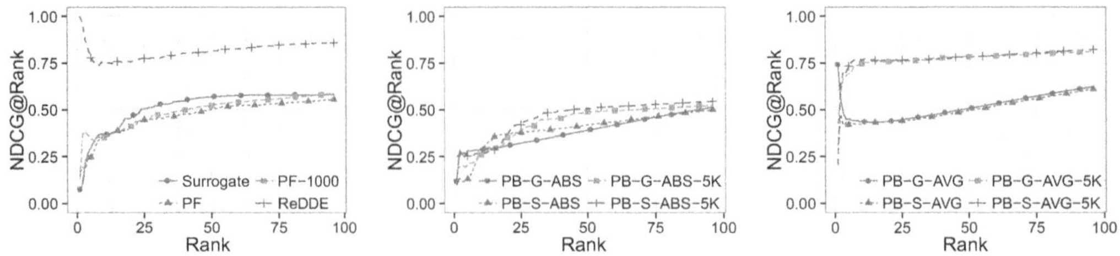

(a) Surrogate and pool-free (b) Pool-based (sum) (c) Pool-based (average)

Figure 8: nDCG@k for Person–Career, for the BONG IE system and issuing (at most) 100 queries.

As interesting future work, we will consider other factors for collection ranking, such as the quality, diversity, and novelty of the extraction output from the collections. Some of these factors (e.g., quality) just require defining an appropriate target measure f (e.g., as a function of the confidence scores of the tuples extracted from a document), as suggested in [4] and [35]. However, other factors (e.g., diversity and novelty) would also require analyzing the contents of multiple collections simultaneously, because the extraction output of one collection may be included in that of others.

Acknowledgments: This material is based upon work supported by the National Science Foundation under Grant IIS-08-11038 and by Bloomberg L.P. C. Develder was supported by a travel grant from the Research Foundation – Flanders (FWO). This work was also supported by the Intelligence Advanced Research Projects Activity (IARPA) via Department of Interior National Business Center (DoI/NBC) contract number D11PC20153. The U.S. Government is authorized to reproduce and distribute reprints for Governmental purposes notwithstanding any copyright annotation thereon. The views and conclusions contained herein are those of the authors and should not be interpreted as necessarily representing the official policies or endorsements, either expressed or implied, of IARPA, DoI/NBC, or the U.S. Government.

7. REFERENCES

[1] E. Agichtein and S. Cucerzan. Predicting accuracy of extracting information from unstructured text collections. In *CIKM*, 2005.

[2] E. Agichtein and L. Gravano. Querying text databases for efficient information extraction. In *ICDE*, 2003.

[3] M. Banko, M. J. Cafarella, S. Soderland, M. Broadhead, and O. Etzioni. Open information extraction from the web. In *IJCAI*, 2007.

[4] Z. Bar-Yossef and M. Gurevich. Efficient search engine measurements. *TWEB*, 5(4):18:1–18:48, 2011.

[5] P. Barrio, G. Simões, H. Galhardas, and L. Gravano. REEL: a relation extraction learning framework. In *JCDL*, 2014.

[6] P. Barrio, G. Simões, H. Galhardas, and L. Gravano. Learning to rank adaptively for scalable information extraction. In *EDBT*, 2015.

[7] M. K. Bergman. The deep web: surfacing hidden value. *JEP*, 7(1), 2001.

[8] C. Boden, A. Löser, C. Nagel, and S. Pieper. FactCrawl: A fact retrieval framework for full-text indices. In *WebDB*, 2011.

[9] R. C. Bunescu and R. J. Mooney. Subsequence kernels for relation extraction. In *NIPS*, 2005.

[10] J. Callan and M. Connell. Query-based sampling of text databases. *TOIS*, 19(2):97–130, 2001.

[11] J. P. Callan, Z. Lu, and W. B. Croft. Searching distributed collections with inference networks. In *SIGIR*, 1995.

[12] Y. Fang and K. C.-C. Chang. Searching patterns for relation extraction over the web: rediscovering the pattern-relation duality. In *WSDM*, 2011.

[13] R. A. Fisher. *Statistical methods for research workers*. Number 5. Genesis Publishing Pvt Ltd, 1936.

[14] C. Giuliano, A. Lavelli, and L. Romano. Exploiting shallow linguistic information for relation extraction from biomedical literature. In *EACL*, 2006.

[15] L. Gravano, H. García-Molina, and A. Tomasic. GlOSS: text-source discovery over the internet. *TODS*, 24(2):229–264, 1999.

[16] L. Gravano, P. G. Ipeirotis, and M. Sahami. QProber: A system for automatic classification of hidden-web databases. *TOIS*, 21(1):1–41, 2003.

[17] S. Gupta and K. K. Bhatia. A comparative study of hidden web crawlers. *IJCTT*, 12(3):111–118, 2014.

[18] B. He, M. Patel, Z. Zhang, and K. C.-C. Chang. Accessing the deep web. *CACM*, 50(5):94–101, 2007.

[19] D. Hong, L. Si, P. Bracke, M. Witt, and T. Juchcinski. A joint probabilistic classification model for resource selection. In *SIGIR*, 2010.

[20] P. G. Ipeirotis and L. Gravano. Classification-aware hidden-web text database selection. *TOIS*, 26(2):6:1–6:66, 2008.

[21] A. Jain and D. Srivastava. Exploring a few good tuples from text databases. In *ICDE*, 2009.

[22] S. Krause, H. Li, H. Uszkoreit, and F. Xu. Large-scale learning of relation-extraction rules with distant supervision from the web. In *ISWC*, 2012.

[23] K.-L. Liu, A. Santoso, C. Yu, and W. Meng. Discovering the representative of a search engine. In *CIKM*, 2001.

[24] J. Madhavan, S. R. Jeffery, S. Cohen, X. Dong, D. Ko, C. Yu, and A. Halevy. Web-scale data integration: You can only afford to pay as you go. In *CIDR*, 2007.

[25] A. McCallum, D. Freitag, and F. C. N. Pereira. Maximum entropy Markov models for information extraction and segmentation. In *ICML*, 2000.

[26] A. McCallum and W. Li. Early results for named entity recognition with conditional random fields, feature induction and web-enhanced lexicons. In *CONLL*, 2003.

[27] S. Raghavan and H. García-Molina. Crawling the hidden web. In *VLDB*, 2001.

[28] C. Sherman and G. Price. The invisible web: uncovering sources search engines can't see. *LIBT*, 52(2):282–298, 2003.

[29] M. Shokouhi and L. Si. Federated search. *FTIR*, 5(1):1–102, 2011.

[30] M. Shokouhi and J. Zobel. Federated text retrieval from uncooperative overlapped collections. In *SIGIR*, 2007.

[31] L. Si and J. Callan. Relevant document distribution estimation method for resource selection. In *SIGIR*, 2003.

[32] L. Si and J. Callan. Unified utility maximization framework for resource selection. In *CIKM*, 2004.

[33] M. van der Loo. Distribution based outlier detection for univariate data. Technical Report Discussion paper 10003, Statistics Netherlands, The Hague, 2010.

[34] M. Zhang, N. Zhang, and G. Das. Mining a search engine's corpus: Efficient yet unbiased sampling and aggregate estimation. In *SIGMOD*, 2011.

[35] M. Zhang, N. Zhang, and G. Das. Mining a search engine's corpus without a query pool. In *CIKM*, 2013.

[36] Z. Zheng, X. Wu, and R. Srihari. Feature selection for text categorization on imbalanced data. *SIGKDD Explorations*, 6(1):80–89, 2004.

Forming Online Support Groups for Internet and Behavior Related Addictions

Chih-Ya Shen[1], Hong-Han Shuai[2], De-Nian Yang[1], Yi-Feng Lan[3], Wang-Chien Lee[4], Philip S. Yu[5,6], Ming-Syan Chen[2]
[1]Academia Sinica, Taiwan
[2]National Taiwan University, Taiwan
[3]Tamkang University, Taiwan
[4]The Pennsylvania State University, USA
[5]University of Illinois at Chicago, USA
[6]Tsinghua University, China
chihya@citi.sinica.edu.tw, d99942020@ntu.edu.tw, dnyang@iis.sinica.edu.tw
carolyflan@gmail.com, wlee@cse.psu.edu, psyu@uic.edu, mschen@cc.ee.ntu.edu.tw

ABSTRACT

While online social networks have become a part of many people's daily lives, Internet and social network addictions (ISNAs) have been noted recently. With increased patients in addictive Internet use, clinicians often form support groups to help patients. This has become a trend because groups organized around therapeutic goals can effectively enrich members with insight and guidance while holding everyone accountable along the way. With the emergence of online social network services, there is a trend to form support groups online with the aid of mental health professionals. Nevertheless, it becomes impractical for a psychiatrist to manually select the group members because she faces an enormous number of candidates, while the selection criteria are also complicated since they span both the social and symptom dimensions. To effectively address the need of mental healthcare professionals, this paper makes the first attempt to study a new problem, namely Member Selection for Online Support Group (MSSG). The problem aims to maximize the similarity of the symptoms of all selected members, while ensuring that any two members are unacquainted to each other. We prove that MSSG is NP-Hard and inapproximable within any ratio, and design a 3-approximation algorithm with a guaranteed error bound. We evaluate MSSG via a user study with 11 mental health professionals, and the results manifest that MSSG can effectively find support group members satisfying the member selection criteria. Experimental results on large-scale real datasets also demonstrate that our proposed algorithm outperforms other baselines in terms of solution quality and efficiency.

CIKM'15, October 19–23, 2015, Melbourne, Australia.
© 2015 ACM. ISBN 978-1-4503-3794-6/15/10 ...$15.00.
DOI: http://dx.doi.org/10.1145/2806416.2806423.

Categories and Subject Descriptors

K.4.2 [**Computers and Society**]: Social Issues; F.2.2 [**Analysis of Algorithms and Problem Complexity**]: Non-numerical Algorithms and Problems

Keywords

social network; addictions; approximation algorithm

1. INTRODUCTION

Today, online social networks have become a part of many people's daily lives. While bringing many advantages, some *Internet and social network addictions (ISNAs)*, such as parasocial, information overloading, and net compulsion, have been noted recently [29]. Leading literature in mental health, such as American Journal of Psychiatry [8], has reported that the above addictions may incur excessive use, depression, social withdrawal, and negative repercussions. Traditional studies of addictions have mainly focused on drug dependence, which may alter the brain function. Recent studies point out that ISNAs may also incur negative impacts on the brain function. Note that the above addictive behavior triggers a reward system in the brain called Mesolimbic dopaminergic pathway, which most notably includes ventral tegmental area, ventral striatum, nucleus accumbens and other adjunct neurons close to the midline on the floor of the midbrain. The reward system leads to a thorny clinical disease, starting with physically over-stimulation of this system. The psychological euphoric effects then lead to repeat behavior, which gradually distorts a person's cognition. As a result, the person will be used to seek for euphoria without considering its outcome.

ISNAs, which represent excessive and uncontrolled behavior of using Internet and social apps, have been identified to have serious negative impacts on human behavior [28]: 1) *excessive use* of social networking and messaging apps – usually associated with a loss of the sense of time or a neglect of basic drives; 2) *withdrawal* – including feelings of anger, tension, and/or depression when the computer/apps are inaccessible; 3) *tolerance* – including the need for better computer equipment, more software and apps; and 4) *negative repercussions* – including arguments, lying, poor achievement, social isolation, and fatigue [8]. With increased patients in addictive Internet use, clinical interventions are considered as imperative as potential patients may suffer from social withdrawal, social impairment and emotional disturbances prospectively. Clinicians often provide an individual counseling session or a support group to help patients. In clinical settings, group therapy has become a trend because groups organized around therapeutic goals can effectively enrich members with insight and guidance [25], while holding everyone accountable along the way [1].

Recently, psychological researchers conclude that cognitive behavior therapy, in the form of group therapy plus other multi-modal school-based group therapy, is effective for ISNAs, particularly in improving emotional states and regulation ability, behavioral and self-management style [12, 24]. Effectively creating therapeutic recovery of emotion facilitation, it has been proved to be the predominant modality for treating addiction disorders [16, 19].

For a mental health professional to form a therapy group or support group (referred to as a *support group* hereafter) for ISNAs, three crucial criteria are usually considered: (i) *unfamiliarity* of patients, (ii) *similarity* of symptoms, and (iii) the *size* of a support group [10]. Unfamiliarity of patients and similarity of symptoms are two cornerstones for forming a therapy group. When the patients are unacquainted (unfamiliar) with each other, they are more inclined to share without hesitation, as private information and experiences are unlikely to spread among friends. With a similar symptom, patients are able to help each other better. Moreover, when the group is small, a patient will be less confident in receiving assistance from the group. However, traditional group therapy usually extracts patients from the same hospital or clinic. Due to a small pool of candidates, patients of different diseases are forced to group together. Otherwise, the formed group may have an insufficient number of patients. Not surprising, it will significantly deteriorate the quality of group therapy.

With the emergence of online social network services, there is a trend to form support groups online with the aid of mental health professionals, such as online group therapies in talkspace[1] and online group counseling[2]. Nevertheless, it becomes impractical for a psychiatrist to manually select the group members because she faces an enormous number of candidates. The task is challenging for a psychiatrist due to the careful examination required in two dimensions: 1) the social dimension – to guarantee unfamiliarity; and 2) the symptom dimension – to ensure similarity. Moreover, manually forming a group is inclined to introduce human bias and errors. To effectively address the need of mental healthcare professionals, this paper makes the first attempt to study a new problem, namely *Member Selection for Online Support Group (MSSG)*. The problem aims to maximize the similarity of the symptoms of all selected members, while ensuring that any two members are unacquainted to each other. MSSG can support psychiatrists and has a great potential to make a change on the current practice to avoid serious consequences caused by human bias and errors. To solve the problem, we design an algorithm, called *Support Group Member Selection (SGSel)*, which selects suitable members to form a support group. In addition, we provide a quantitative measure for the group quality.

The contributions of this paper are summarized as follows.

- To assist mental healthcare professionals forming online support groups effectively and efficiently, we formulate a new problem, namely, Member Selection for Online Support Group (MSSG), which aims to automatically form support groups by considering the *unfamiliarity of patients*, the *similarity of symptoms*, and the *group size*.
- We prove that the problem is NP-Hard and inapproximable within any ratio. The proposed Support Group Member Selection (SGSel) algorithm is a 3-approximation algorithm with a guaranteed error bound in the measure of group quality.
- To validate the usefulness of the problem and the provided solution, we invite a group of psychiatrists to conduct a user study. The psychiatrists agree that the proposed algorithm is helpful for them and can find better solutions.
- Extensive experiments are performed on real datasets to evaluate the proposed algorithm. The result shows that our algorithm outperforms the other baselines in terms of quality and efficiency.

The rest of this paper is organized as follows. Sec. 2 reviews the related works. Sec. 3 formulates Member Selection for Online Support Group (MSSG) problem, and proves that MSSG is NP-Hard and inapproximable within any factor. Sec. 4 details the proposed algorithm and Sec. 5 analyzes its performance. Sec. 6 introduces two pruning strategies to enhance the proposed algorithm. Sec. 7 presents a user study and experimental results. Finally, Sec. 8 concludes this paper.

2. RELATED WORK

Addictive disorders, a disease categorized in substance-related and addictive disorders in DSM-V (Diagnostic and Statistical Manual of Mental Disorders (5th Edition)) [4], is defined as a persistent and compulsive dependent on either substances or behavior. In most of the cases, the continuity of dependence often leads to reversible mood alerting [6]. Recent research works report a number of factors related to ISNAs. Barker [7] finds that collective self-esteem and group identification are correlated with peer group communication via social network services. Cheung et al. [11] assess the role of social presence, such as the recognition and endorsement from others. To effectively tackle this disease, self-help oriented, cognitive behavior oriented, and reality-therapy oriented group therapies have been studied. The cognitive behavior oriented therapy provides step-by-step approaches to stop compulsive behavior. Research shows that cognitive behavior group therapy is effective for adolescents with mental disorders [12, 24]. The reality-therapy oriented group, a therapeutic group model designed by choice theory to help individuals control their behavior, has been widely used as a treatment for addictive disorders [17, 21]. In addition, group therapy has been proved to be the predominant method for treating addiction disorders [16, 19] and thus widely adopted by mental healthcare professionals.

Various social cohesive measures have been proposed for finding dense social subgraphs, e.g., diameter, clique and its variations [23]. Although these social cohesive measures cover a wide range of application scenarios, they focus on deriving *socially tight* groups for team formation [18, 20] and activity planning [22, 27]. In contrast, the Member Selection for Online Support Group (MSSG) studied in this paper

[1]http://www.talkspace.com/public/forums-page.
[2]http://www.onlinecounselingfast.com/group-counseling/.

aims to extract a *sparse social group* and maximize the similarity in the symptoms of the group members, i.e., sparse in the social dimension but dense in the symptom dimension. Therefore, the problem formulation and hardness result are different from the previous ones. Most importantly, the above works and ideas are not applicable to MSSG due to the interplay of two dimensions, i.e., similarity of symptoms and unfamiliarity of the patients.

3. MEMBER SELECTION FOR ONLINE SUPPORT GROUP

Forming a support group online indeed provides more opportunities to choose proper patients. Nevertheless, it becomes much more challenging for a psychiatrist to manually select the group member since the social and symptom dimensions of a large number of candidates are necessary to be carefully examined. In this section, we study the *Member Selection for Online Support Group (MSSG)* problem that takes into account unfamiliarity of patients, similarity of symptoms, and the minimum size of a support group.

3.1 Problem Formulation

Specifically, we model the social network as a heterogeneous social graph $G = (V, E, S)$, where V is the set of individuals (including users with ISNAs and normal users), E is the set of *friend edges* denoting the existing social relationships, and S is the set of *similarity edges*. Each similarity edge is associated with a weight $w : S \rightarrow (0, 1]$. An individual v is associated with a set of symptom labels L_v. A score $s(l_{v,i}) \in [0, 1]$ for each symptom label $l_{v,i} \in L_v$ represents the severity level for v to be suffering from the symptom i. The symptom labels and the corresponding edge scores can be acquired by clinical counseling from mental health professionals or machine-learning approaches (discussed in [2]). Moreover, any two vertices u and v are connected by a similarity edge if L_u and L_v share at least one symptom. The vertex set V in G can be represented as $V = A \cup N$, where A is the set of users with ISNAs, and N is the set of normal users. We adopt Euclidean Distance as the similarity measure of users with ISNAs, i.e., $w[u, v] = \sqrt{\sum_{\forall i}(1 - |l_{v,i} - l_{u,i}|)^2}$, where i represents a symptom, and $w[u, v]$ is the similarity edge weight. We then normalize the similarity edge weights to $(0, 1]$. Euclidean Distance has been proved to be useful in grouping patients according to their symptoms [3].

Given a heterogeneous social graph $G = (V, E, S)$ described above, we formulate the *Member Selection for Online Support Group (MSSG)* problem to find a group F of patients from G to 1) maximize the similarity of symptoms in the group, i.e., the group has the largest average similarity edge weight among patients, 2) ensure the social unfamiliarity, i.e., any pair of members are not friends, and they do not have common friends,[3] and 3) ensure the size of the group at least p.[4] Given vertices $u, v \in F$, we denote $w(F)$ the total similarity of F, i.e., $w(F) = \sum_{u,v \in F} w[u, v]$, and $\alpha(F)$ is the *average similarity* of F, i.e., $\alpha(F) = \frac{w(F)}{|F|}$. In MSSG, a *similarity constraint* s is also incorporated, which excludes a vertex u from V if all of u's incident similarity edges have weights smaller than s. This similarity constraint avoids examining and including potential patients dissimilar to the others. Moreover, we refer to $G_f = (V, E)$ as the social graph representing the friendships of the individuals, and $G_m = (V, S)$ as the similarity graph denoting the similarity of the symptoms for individuals. The problem is formulated as follows.

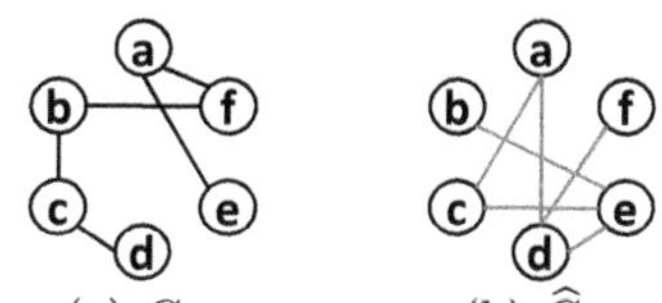

(a) G_f. (b) $\widehat{G}_f$.

Figure 1: Graph Transformation from G_f to $\widehat{G}_f$.

Problem: Member Selection for Online Support Group (MSSG)
Given: A social network $G = (V, E, S)$, size constraint p, and similarity constraint s.
Objective: Find an induced subgraph $F \subseteq G$ with maximum $\alpha(F)$ where i) each vertex in F is with ISNAs, i.e., $u \in A, \forall u \in F$, ii) $|F| \geq p$, iii) for any $u, v \in F$, $\nexists(u, v) \in E$, and $\nexists r \in V$ such that $(u, r), (r, v) \in E$, and iv) $\exists[u, v] \in S$ such that $w[u, v] \geq s, \forall u \in F$.

For any instance of $MSSG(G, p, s)$, we first transform the input graph $G = (V, E, S)$ into a complement graph $\widehat{G} = (V, \widehat{E}, S)$ in the social dimension. $\widehat{G}$ contains the same vertex set V and the same similarity edge set S. The transformed edge set $\widehat{E}$ is constructed by satisfying the following conditions. 1) For any $u, v \in V$, $(u, v) \in \widehat{E}$ if u and v are not friends. 2) If $\exists r \in V$ with r as the common friend of u and v, u and v do not share an edge in $\widehat{E}$.

Example. Fig. 1 is an example illustrating the transformation from $G_f = (V, E)$ (i.e., the original social graph) to $\widehat{G}_f = (V, \widehat{E})$ (i.e., the transformed social graph), where the original and the complement graphs are shown in Figs. 1(a) and 1(b), respectively. Any edge $(u, v) \in \widehat{E}$ is present if u and v does not share an edge in E. Moreover, (a, b), (b, d), and (c, f) do not appear in $\widehat{E}$ because each of them shares at least one common friend in G_f.

With $\widehat{G}$, it can be observed that a group F is the optimal solution to an instance of $MSSG(G, p, s)$ if and only if F is a *clique* in $\widehat{G}_f = (V, \widehat{E})$, while F has the same $\alpha(F)$ in both G and $\widehat{G}$. We now formulate the tackled problem on the transformed graph $\widehat{G}$, namely, *Complement Member Selection for Online Support Group (CMSSG)*. The problem is different from the traditional clique or social cohesive problems due to the similarity dimension incorporated.

Problem: Complement Member Selection for Online Support Group (CMSSG)
Given: A social network $\widehat{G} = (V, \widehat{E}, S)$, size constraint p, and similarity constraint s.
Objective: Find an induced subgraph $F \subseteq \widehat{G}$ with maximum $\alpha(F)$ where i) each vertex in F is with ISNAs, i.e., $u \in A, \forall u \in F$, ii) $|F| \geq p$, iii) $(u, v) \in \widehat{E}, \forall u, v \in F$, and iv) $\exists[u, v] \in S$ such that $w[u, v] \geq s, \forall u \in F$.

[3]The small world property of social network states that people are connected via a small number of friends. Therefore, randomly selecting members to form a support group may easily find acquaintances and friends' friend. MSSG aims to maximize the similarity among members while satisfying the unfamiliarity constraint simultaneously. This makes MSSG very challenging computationally.

[4]We do not consider the upper bound of group size $\widehat{p}$ here for simplicity. The proposed SGSel algorithm in Sec. 4 iteratively removes vertices from the graph to construct candidate groups. Thus it is not difficult to modify SGSel for finding the best group with size at most $\widehat{p}$.

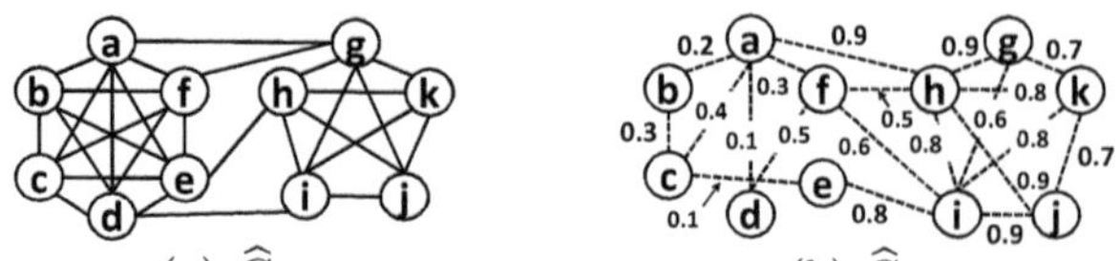

(a) $\widehat{G}_f$. (b) $\widehat{G}_m$.

Figure 2: Running Example for Algorithm SGSel.

Please note that, a group F is the optimal solution to $CMSSG(\widehat{G}, p, s)$ if and only if F is the optimal solution to its counterpart $MSSG(G, p, s)$. A straightforward approach for CMSSG is to handle the social and similarity dimensions in two separate phases: 1) It first finds the maximum clique K_{max} in the social graph $\widehat{G}_f = (V, \widehat{E})$. Maximum clique K_{max} ensures that every two vertices of K_{max} are connected by an edge in $\widehat{E}$ and maximizes the number of individuals in K_{max}. The maximum clique problem is NP-Hard. Thus, an approximation algorithm (e.g., [13]) can be adopted. 2) Afterward, if $|K_{max}| \geq p$, the second phase processes the similarity graph $\widehat{G}_m = (V, S)$ induced from only the individuals in K_{max}. Specifically, it finds the weighted dense k subgraph (DkS) on K_{max}. Weighted DkS finds a group $F' \subseteq K_{max}$ of exactly k vertices to maximize $k\alpha(F)$. In the second phase, weighted DkS iteratively considers $p \leq k \leq |K_{max}|$, and extracts the group with maximum similarity. The weighted DkS problem is also NP-Hard, and thus an approximation algorithm (e.g., [14]) can be adopted.

However, this straightforward approach has two serious pitfalls. 1) In the first phase, only one subgraph K_{max} in $\widehat{G}$ is examined, and the optimal solution of CMSSG may not be within K_{max} but located in another clique in $\widehat{G}$. In other words, the solution exploration space is very limited. 2) In the second phase, the best approximation ratio of weighted DkS is $O(|K_{max}|^{\frac{1}{3}} \log |K_{max}|)$ [14]. Therefore, even when a good subgraph K_{max} is acquired in the first phase, the second phase can only guarantee that $\alpha(F) \geq \alpha(OPT) \times \frac{1}{O(|K_{max}|^{\frac{1}{3}} \log |K_{max}|)}$, where OPT is the optimal solution. The performance bound on the similarity is practically useless because $|K_{max}|$ can be arbitrarily large.

Example. Consider the example in Fig. 2, where $\widehat{G}_f$ (i.e., the transformed social graph) and $\widehat{G}_m$ (i.e., the similarity graph) are shown in Fig. 2(a) and 2(b), respectively. Let $p = 4$. The straightforward approach first obtains the approximated maximum clique $K_{max} = \{a, b, c, d, e, f\}$, and then finds the approximated weighted DkS in K_{max} as $\widehat{F} = \{a, b, c, d, f\}$ with $\alpha(\widehat{F}) = 0.36$, which is far from the optimal solution $F^{OPT} = \{h, i, j, k, g\}$ with $\alpha(F^{OPT}) = 1.42$. This example manifests that the straightforward approach performs poorly.

3.2 Hardness Analysis

The above two-phase strategy indicates that CMSSG is very challenging because processing only one of the social and similarity dimensions is already very difficult. In the following, we prove that there exists no approximation algorithm for CMSSG due to the need to processes two dimensions simultaneously.

THEOREM 1. *CMSSG is NP-Hard and inapproximable within any factor unless $P = NP$.*

PROOF. Please refer to Appendix. □

4. ALGORITHM DESIGN FOR CMSSG

Although CMSSG has no approximation algorithm, we observe that there is a chance to approximate CMSSG after introducing a small error bound in F. By slightly relaxing the constraint to ensure a clique in $\widehat{G}_f$, it becomes possible to extract a group F with good similarity. Specifically, a clique is a graph with diameter as 1. We propose an algorithm, namely, *Support Group Member Selection (SGSel)*, which is a 3-approximation algorithm for CMSSG (proved in Sec. 5). SGSel returns a solution with guaranteed similarity $\alpha(F)$, while the shortest path distance of $u, v \in F$ in $\widehat{G}_f$ may exceed 1 but is always bounded by 2 (i.e., a small error bounded). Afterwards, a post-processing procedure is proposed (detailed in Sec. 6) to tailor the solution to ensure that F is still a clique. This relax-and-tailor strategy is very effective for handling difficult NP-Hard problems. It has been widely adopted by the research community of approximation algorithms [26].

SGSel first performs a pre-processing procedure to remove redundant vertices and edges from $\widehat{G}$, which will never appear in any feasible solution. Then, SGSel starts to process the remaining graph. Intuitively, the idea of algorithm SGSel is to target on *2-clique*, instead of 1-clique. Let $d_{\widehat{G}}^{\widehat{E}}(u, v)$ denote the shortest path distance between vertices $u, v \in \widehat{G}$ on $\widehat{E}$. In a k-clique C, the shortest path between any vertices $u, v \in C$ is k [23], i.e., $d_{\widehat{G}}^{\widehat{E}}(u, v) \leq k, \forall u, v \in C$. In SGSel, the shortest path distance between any vertices in a 2-clique is bounded by 2. Compared to 1-clique (i.e., the clique with an edge connecting any two vertices), 2-clique can be acquired more efficiently (explained later). SGSel includes two steps for each vertex v in $\widehat{G}_f = (V, \widehat{E})$: (i) *2-clique expansion* from v and (ii) *2-clique trimming*. For each vertex v, step (i) expands a 2-clique C_v from v. We ensure that if the maximum clique K_{max} includes v, C_v must include all vertices of K_{max}. This observation plays a crucial role in our proof of the approximation ratio in the next section. Then, step (ii) examines C_v and iteratively removes the vertices that are inclined to share small similarity with the others. The 2-clique trimming step produces a candidate solution for C_v. After every vertex v in $\widehat{G}_f$ is processed, SGSel extracts the best solution among all candidate solutions. Finally, the post processing in SGSel (detailed in Sec. 6) tailors the best solution to ensure that the returned solution satisfies the unfamiliarity requirement on the social graph.

Specifically, SGSel first performs a pre-processing procedure. Given $\widehat{G} = (V, \widehat{E}, S)$, SGSel removes from V all the normal users $u \in N$ because the resulting group includes only the patients. Then, to satisfy the similarity constraint s, SGSel removes from V each vertex v if all of v's incident similarity edges have weights smaller than s, i.e., v is removed from V if $w[u, v] < s, \forall [u, v] \in S$. Please note that, given an instance of CMSSG, the optimal solution remains the same before and after the pre-process procedure because we only remove the vertices and edges that will not appear in any feasible solution. Afterwards, 2-clique expansion and 2-clique trimming are performed as follows. To further improve the efficiency of SGSel, an effective pruning strategy for each of the above two steps will be proposed in Sec. 6.

2-clique Expansion. A 2-clique C_v is expanded from v by including every vertex u with $(u, v) \in \widehat{E}$. Therefore, every two vertices $u, t \in C_v$ must have $d_{\widehat{G}}^{\widehat{E}}(u, t) \leq 2$. If the optimal solution includes v, C_v must have all the vertices in the optimal solution. Note that finding the maximal clique K_{max} is NP-Hard and thus computationally intensive. By contrast, C_v can be generated in linear time. Moreover, if $|C_v| < p$, C_v can be discarded because no group extracted from the current C_v will satisfy the size constraint. Therefore, exploiting 2-clique, instead of 1-clique, is important for SGSel to process CMSSG efficiently.

To improve the processing speed of the 2-clique expansion step, let $I_M(v)$ denote the incident similarity of a vertex v in any subgraph $M \subseteq \widehat{G}$, where $I_M(v) = \sum_{u \in M} w[v, u]$. To find the set of 2-cliques containing different vertices, SGSel initially sorts the vertices in V according to their incident similarities. Then, it iteratively selects a vertex $v \in V$ with the maximum incident similarity as a *reference vertex*, and expands the 2-clique C_v from v.

2-clique Trimming. Next, the second step iteratively removes the vertices with small incident similarity within each C_v. More specifically, let Γ_{i+1} denote the graph after removing a vertex $\hat{v}_i$ from Γ_i in iteration i. Initially Γ_1 is set as C_v, and at iteration i, Γ_{i+1} represents the graph $\Gamma_i - \{\hat{v}_i\}$. The intuition behind is that truncating the vertices with low incident similarities is more likely to increase the average similarity of the remaining subgraph. During each iteration i, $\hat{v}_i$ is selected as the vertex with the lowest incident similarity in Γ_i, i.e., $\hat{v}_i = \arg\min_{u \in \Gamma_i} I_{\Gamma_i}(u)$. Then, $\hat{v}_i$ and its incident similarity edges are removed from Γ_i and the remaining graph is Γ_{i+1}. Then, Γ_{i+1} is processed in the next iteration $i+1$. The above procedure ends until Γ_i is empty. In the next section, we prove that this strategy can successfully achieve the approximation ratio.

In summary, to maximize the objective function $\alpha(F) = \frac{w(F)}{|F|}$, after a 2-clique C_v is processed, SGSel extracts the group $\Gamma_v^* = \arg\max_{1 \le i \le |C_v|, |\Gamma_i| \ge p} \alpha(\Gamma_i)$. If $\alpha(\Gamma_v^*) > \alpha(F^{APX})$, we replace F^{APX} with Γ_v^*. Then, SGSel continues to the next vertex v' to examine the corresponding 2-clique $C_{v'}$ until all vertices in V are examined. Finally, SGSel employs a post-processing procedure on F^{APX}, i.e., the best solution obtained in SGSel, to ensure that F^{APX} satisfies the unfamiliarity requirement and further maximizes $\alpha(F^{APX})$. Then, F^{APX} is output as the solution. Algorithm 1 presents the pseudo code of SGSel.

Example. Recall our running example in Fig. 2. After SGSel assigns h as the reference vertex and extracts $C_h = \{a, f, h, i, j, k, g\}$, SGSel sets Γ_1 as the 2-clique C_h and starts the trimming step. In iteration 1, $\hat{v}_1$ is chosen as a because a incurs the minimum $I_{\Gamma_1}(v), \forall v \in \Gamma_1$, i.e., $I_{\Gamma_1}(a) = 1.2$. Then, a is removed from Γ_1 to produce Γ_2. Similarly, $\hat{v}_2 = f$ is identified with $I_{\Gamma_2}(f) = 1.1$. Vertex f is removed from Γ_2 to produce Γ_3. The above procedure repeats until $\Gamma_8 = \varnothing$. SGSel then extracts $\Gamma_3 = \{h, i, j, k, g\}$ with $\alpha(\Gamma_3) = 1.42$, which is the maximum among all $\Gamma_i, \forall 1 \le i \le 8$. F^{APX} is set as Γ_3. SGSel then extracts the next reference vertex, i.e., i, and continues the above iterations to check if better solutions can be obtained until all vertices in $\widehat{G}$ are examined. Finally, SGSel performs the post processing and returns the solution $F^{APX} = \{h, i, j, k, g\}$. Please note that $\alpha(F^{APX}) = 1.42$, which outperforms the straightforward approach with $\widehat{F} = \{a, b, c, d, f\}$ and $\alpha(\widehat{F}) = 0.36$.

Algorithm 1 Support Group Member Selection (SGSel)

Require: Graph $\widehat{G} = (V, \widehat{E}, S)$, size constraint p, and similarity constraint s

```
V ← A, remove v from V if all of v's incident similarity
    edges have edge weight smaller than s
T ← V        ▷ T is the set of vertices that have not been
    selected as reference vertices yet
F^APX ← ∅
while T ≠ ∅ do
    v ← arg max_{u∈T} I_Ĝ(u), T ← T − {v}
    let C_v be the 2-clique with reference vertex v
    if |C_v| < p then
        continue;
    let Γ_1 ← C_v
    for i ← 1 to |C_v| do
        v̂_i ← arg min_{u∈Γ_i} I_{Γ_i}(u)
        Γ_{i+1} ← Γ_i − {v̂_i}
    end for
    let Γ*_v be the Γ_i with maximum α(Γ_i) and |Γ_i| ≥ p
    if α(Γ*_v) > α(F^APX) then
        F^APX ← Γ*_v
PostProcessing(F^APX)
return F^APX
```

5. THEORETICAL ANALYSIS

In the following, for each vertex v and the corresponding 2-clique C_v in the 2-clique expansion step, we first prove that there exists a subgraph $U \subseteq C_v$ such that $3 \cdot w(U)$ is an upper bound of F_v^{OPT}, which is the optimal solution of CMSSG on only C_v. Next, we prove that the average similarity $\alpha(\Gamma_v^*)$ of Γ_v^* returned from the 2-clique trimming step for v is at least $\frac{1}{3}\alpha(F_v^{OPT})$. Finally, after processing each vertex $v \in \widehat{G}$, we prove that the proposed algorithm is a 3-approximation algorithm with guaranteed error bound to CMSSG.

In Lemma 1, we first prove that there exists a subgraph $U \subseteq C_v$, which has the property $I_U(u) \ge \frac{2}{3}\alpha(F_v^{OPT}), \forall u \in U$. With U, we can derive an upper bound on the total similarity of the optimal solution in C_v, i.e., $w(F_v^{OPT})$.

LEMMA 1. *There exists a subgraph $U \subseteq C_v$ such that $I_U(u) \ge \frac{2}{3}\alpha(F_v^{OPT}), \forall u \in U$ holds.*

PROOF. Since $F_v^{OPT} \subseteq C_v$, we prove the existence of U in C_v by trimming F_v^{OPT}. Let X_1 be F_v^{OPT}. At each step j, $1 \le j \le |F_v^{OPT}|$, we remove a vertex $\hat{v}_j$ and its incident similarity edges from X_j to produce X_{j+1}, where $\hat{v}_j$ is identified as the vertex with the minimum $I_{X_j}(\hat{v}_j)$ in X_j. Then, there exists an X_k for some $k \in [1, |F_v^{OPT}|]$ such that $I_{X_k}(\hat{v}_k) \ge \frac{2}{3}\alpha(F_v^{OPT})$. We prove the above statement by contradiction. If such k does not exist, then $\max_{\forall j} I_{X_j}(\hat{v}_j) < \frac{2}{3}\alpha(F_v^{OPT})$ must hold. Nevertheless, during the above procedure, the total similarity of F_v^{OPT} is $\sum_{j=1}^{|F_v^{OPT}|} I_{X_j}(\hat{v}_j)$, because when removing $\hat{v}_j$ from X_j, the corresponding incident similarity edges are also trimmed from X_j. Therefore,

$$w(F_v^{OPT}) = \sum_{j=1}^{|F_v^{OPT}|} I_{X_j}(\hat{v}_j) \le |F_v^{OPT}| \cdot \max_{\forall j} I_{X_j}(\hat{v}_j)$$

$$< |F_v^{OPT}| \cdot \frac{2}{3}\alpha(F_v^{OPT}) = \frac{2}{3} w(F_v^{OPT}),$$

which is a contradiction. Therefore, set $U = X_k \subseteq F_v^{OPT} \subseteq C_v$ with $I_{X_k}(\hat{v}_k) \ge \frac{2}{3}\alpha(F_v^{OPT})$ exists, and $I_{X_k}(u) \ge \frac{2}{3}\alpha(F_v^{OPT})$, $\forall u \in X_k$, because $I_{X_k}(\hat{v}_k) \le I_{X_k}(u)$. The lemma follows. □

The above lemma states that $U \neq \varnothing$. We then derive an upper bound of $w(F_v^{OPT})$, i.e., $3 \cdot w(U) > w(F_v^{OPT})$.

LEMMA 2. *$w(F_v^{OPT})$ is upper bounded by $3 \cdot w(U)$, i.e., $3 \cdot w(U) > w(F_v^{OPT})$.*

PROOF. In Lemma 1, we have $w(F_v^{OPT}) = \sum_{j=1}^{|F_v^{OPT}|} I_{X_j}(\hat{v}_j)$. Let step k denote the earliest step such that the selected $\hat{v}_k$ satisfies $I_{X_k}(\hat{v}_k) \geq \frac{2}{3}\alpha(F_v^{OPT})$. Then, $\sum_{j=1}^{|F_v^{OPT}|} I_{X_j}(\hat{v}_j)$ can be written as $\sum_{j=1}^{k-1} I_{X_j}(\hat{v}_j) + \sum_{j=k}^{|F_v^{OPT}|} I_{X_j}(\hat{v}_j)$ according to k. For each $1 \leq j \leq (k-1)$, $I_{X_j}(\hat{v}_j) < \frac{2}{3}\alpha(F_v^{OPT})$ holds because $\hat{v}_k$ is the first vertex selected during the steps which has $I_{X_k}(\hat{v}_k) \geq \frac{2}{3}\alpha(F_v^{OPT})$. Therefore, $\sum_{j=1}^{k-1} I_{X_j}(\hat{v}_j) < k \cdot \frac{2}{3}\alpha(F_v^{OPT}) \leq |F_v^{OPT}| \cdot \frac{2}{3}\alpha(F_v^{OPT})$. On the other hand, $\sum_{j=k}^{|F_v^{OPT}|} I_{X_j}(\hat{v}_j) = w(X_k)$, and we have

$$w(F_v^{OPT}) = \sum_{j=1}^{|F_v^{OPT}|} I_{X_j}(\hat{v}_j) < |F_v^{OPT}| \cdot \frac{2}{3}\alpha(F_v^{OPT}) + w(X_k),$$

which implies that $w(U) = w(X_k) > \frac{1}{3}w(F_v^{OPT})$. The lemma follows. □

In the above lemmas, we extract U from the optimal solution F_v^{OPT}. The following lemma compares U and Γ_i derived by the 2-clique trimming step.

LEMMA 3. *For each C_v, if step i is the earliest step such that the extracted $\hat{v}_i$ from Γ_i is also in U, then $I_{\Gamma_i}(u) \geq \frac{2}{3}\alpha(F_v^{OPT})$, $\forall u \in \Gamma_i$.*

PROOF. If $\hat{v}_i$ represents the first trimmed vertex from U, $U \subseteq \Gamma_i$ holds because in each previous step j of SGSel with $1 \leq j \leq (i-1)$, no $\hat{v}_j$ is in U due to smaller incident similarity. Moreover, since $I_U(u) \geq \frac{2}{3}\alpha(F_v^{OPT})$ for $\forall u \in U$, $I_U(\hat{v}_i) \geq \frac{2}{3}\alpha(F_v^{OPT})$. Because $U \subseteq \Gamma_i$, $I_{\Gamma_i}(\hat{v}_i) \geq I_U(\hat{v}_i) \geq \frac{2}{3}\alpha(F_v^{OPT})$ holds. In addition, $\hat{v}_i$ is selected due to the minimum $I_{\Gamma_i}(\hat{v}_i)$ in Γ_i. Therefore, $I_{\Gamma_i}(u) \geq \frac{2}{3}\alpha(F_v^{OPT})$, $\forall u \in \Gamma_i$. □

With $I_{\Gamma_i(u)} \geq \frac{2}{3}\alpha(F_v^{OPT})$, we derive the lower bound on $\alpha(\Gamma_v^*)$, i.e., $\alpha(\Gamma_v^*) \geq \frac{1}{3}\alpha(F_v^{OPT})$. Afterward, we prove that $\alpha(F^{APX}) \geq \max_{v \in \widehat{G}} \alpha(\Gamma_v^*) \geq \frac{1}{3}\alpha(F^{OPT})$, where F^{OPT} is the optimal solution of CMSSG on $\widehat{G}$. This indicates that SGSel is a 3-approximation algorithm. We also prove that SGSel has a guaranteed error bound.

THEOREM 2. *For each C_v, if step i is the earliest step such that $\hat{v}_i$ satisfies $I_{\Gamma_i}(\hat{v}_i) \geq \frac{2}{3}\alpha(F_v^{OPT})$, then $\alpha(\Gamma_v^*) \geq \frac{1}{3}\alpha(F_v^{OPT})$. Moreover, SGSel returns the solution F^{APX} with $\alpha(F^{APX}) \geq \frac{\alpha(F^{OPT})}{3}$, and $d_{\widehat{G}}^{\widehat{E}}(u,v) \leq 2$, $\forall u, v \in F^{APX}$.*

PROOF. Since $I_{\Gamma_i}(\hat{v}_i) \geq \frac{2}{3}\alpha(F_v^{OPT})$, each $u \in \Gamma_i$ must satisfy $I_{\Gamma_i}(u) \geq \frac{2}{3}\alpha(F_v^{OPT})$. Recall that the average similarity $\alpha(\Gamma_i) = \frac{1}{2|\Gamma_i|}\sum_{u \in \Gamma_i} I_{\Gamma_i}(u)$. Therefore, $\alpha(\Gamma_i) \geq \frac{1}{2|\Gamma_i|} \cdot |\Gamma_i| \cdot \frac{2}{3}\alpha(F_v^{OPT}) = \frac{1}{3}\alpha(F_v^{OPT})$. If $|\Gamma_i| \geq p$, then $\alpha(\Gamma_v^*) \geq \frac{1}{3}\alpha(F_v^{OPT})$ holds because Γ_i is a candidate of Γ_v^*. If $|\Gamma_i| < p$, then there must exist a Γ_j with $j < i$ and $|\Gamma_j| = p$ (i.e., Γ_j is derived earlier than Γ_i, and thus $\Gamma_i \subseteq \Gamma_j$). Therefore, $\alpha(\Gamma_j) = \frac{w(\Gamma_j)}{p} \geq \frac{w(\Gamma_i)}{p} \geq \frac{w(U)}{p} > \frac{1}{3 \cdot p}w(F_v^{OPT})$. Because $|F_v^{OPT}| \geq p$, $\frac{1}{3 \cdot p}w(F_v^{OPT}) \geq \frac{w(F_v^{OPT})}{3 \cdot |F_v^{OPT}|} = \frac{1}{3}\alpha(F_v^{OPT})$. Therefore, if $|\Gamma_i| < p$, $\alpha(\Gamma_v^*) \geq \frac{1}{3}\alpha(F_v^{OPT})$ also holds because Γ_j is a candidate of Γ_v^*. Since $\alpha(F^{OPT}) = \max_{v \in \widehat{G}} \alpha(F_v^{OPT})$ and $\alpha(F^{APX}) = \max_{v \in \widehat{G}} \alpha(\Gamma_v^*)$ hold, $\alpha(F^{APX}) \geq \frac{\max_{v \in \widehat{G}} \alpha(F_v^{OPT})}{3}$ holds. This implies that $\alpha(F^{APX}) \geq \frac{\alpha(F^{OPT})}{3}$. On the other hand, $d_{\widehat{G}}^{\widehat{E}}(u,v), \forall u, v \in F^{APX}$ is bounded by 2 since the shortest path distance from the reference vertex of F^{APX} to any other vertex is at most 1. The theorem follows. □

6. PRUNING STRATEGIES AND POST PROCESSING

Although the proposed SGSel algorithm can find the solution in polynomial time, it still involves redundant examination of the vertices and 2-cliques. In the following, we propose two pruning strategies to effectively improve the efficiency of SGSel. The first pruning strategy, namely *2-Clique Pruning*, removes unnecessary 2-cliques during the 2-clique expansion step, such that not every C_v needs to be expanded. For the remaining 2-cliques, the second pruning strategy, namely *Incident Similarity Pruning (ISP)*, trims redundant vertices in each 2-clique to further improve the efficiency in the 2-clique trimming step.

Specifically, to improve the processing speed of the 2-clique expansion step, the 2-Clique Pruning strategy effectively removes redundant 2-cliques that will never generate better solutions. Let F^{APX} denote the best solution (obtained from another 2-clique) so far. If half of the maximum incident similarity among the vertices u in C_v, i.e., $(1/2) \cdot \max_{u \in C_v} I_{C_v}(u)$, does not exceed $\alpha(F^{APX})$, we observe that no solution in C_v can outperform $\alpha(F^{APX})$, and C_v can be trimmed.

PROPOSITION 1. ***2-Clique Pruning.*** *Given a 2-clique C_v, if $\frac{1}{2} \cdot \max_{u \in C_v} I_{C_v}(u) \leq \alpha(F^{APX})$ holds, C_v can be pruned.*

PROOF. For any subgraph $C' \subseteq C_v$, the average similarity $\alpha(C') = \frac{\sum_{t \in C'} I_{C'}(t)}{2|C'|} \leq \frac{\max_{u \in C_v} I_{C_v}(u) \cdot |C'|}{2|C'|} = \frac{\max_{u \in C_v} I_{C_v}(u)}{2}$. If $\frac{1}{2} \cdot \max_{u \in C_v} I_{C_v}(u) \leq \alpha(F^{APX})$ holds, C_v does not contain any subgraph which has larger average similarity than $\alpha(F^{APX})$. Therefore, C_v can be pruned. □

Afterward, to improve the processing speed of the 2-clique trimming step, assume that the current best solution is F^{APX} with the average similarity $\alpha(F^{APX})$. The second pruning strategy carefully examines the incident similarity of each vertex in C_v to filter out unqualified vertices which will never belong to any solution better than F^{APX}. For any 2-clique C_v with a vertex $u \in C_v$, since incident similarity $I_{C_v}(u)$ represents the contribution of u to the total similarity in C_v, it can be used to derive a powerful pruning strategy for SGSel. Specifically, let $y = \alpha(F^{APX})$. Given a 2-clique C_v and any subgraph $H \subseteq C_v$ with $\alpha(H) \geq y$, let $X \subseteq C_v$ denote the set of vertices such that the incident similarity of each vertex in X is smaller than y, i.e., $I_{C_v}(u) < y, \forall u \in X$. Then, the following lemma states that, adding any subset $\widehat{X} \subseteq X$ to H is not able to generate an improved solution, i.e., $\alpha(H \cup \widehat{X}) \leq \alpha(H)$.

LEMMA 4. *Given any subgraph $H \subseteq C_v$ with $\alpha(H) \geq y$, a set of vertices $X \subseteq C_v$ with $I_{C_v}(u) < y, \forall u \in X$, for every subgraph $\widehat{X} \subseteq X$, $\alpha(H \cup \widehat{X}) \leq \alpha(H)$ always holds.*

PROOF. We prove this lemma by induction. We first consider the case when adding exactly one vertex $u \in X$ to H, i.e., $\widehat{X} = \{u\}$. Then, the difference of the average similarity is: $\alpha(H) - \alpha(H \cup \{v\}) = \frac{w(H)}{|H|} - \frac{w(H \cup \{v\})}{|H|+1} \geq \frac{w(H)}{|H|} - \frac{w(H)+I_{C_v}(u)}{|H|+1}$. Since $I_{C_v}(u) < y$, $\frac{w(H)}{|H|} - \frac{w(H)+I_{C_v}(u)}{|H|+1} \geq \frac{w(H)}{|H|} -$

$\frac{w(H)+y}{|H|+1} = \frac{w(H)-y\cdot|H|}{|H|\cdot(|H|+1)}$. Because $\alpha(H) \geq y$, $w(H) \geq |H| \cdot y$ holds. Therefore, $\alpha(H) - \alpha(H \cup \{v\}) \geq 0$, and this lemma holds when combining exactly one vertex in X with H.

Assume that the lemma holds when adding any k vertices in X to H. That is, let $\widehat{X} \subseteq X$ with $|\widehat{X}| = k$ and $\widehat{H} = (H \cup \widehat{X})$. We have $\alpha(\widehat{H}) \leq \alpha(H)$. Then, for any vertex $u \in X - \widehat{H}$, we have $\alpha(\widehat{H} \cup \{u\}) \leq \frac{w(\widehat{H})+I_{C_v}(u)}{|H|+k+1} \leq \frac{w(\widehat{H})+y}{|H|+k+1}$. Since $\alpha(\widehat{H}) \leq \alpha(H)$, $w(\widehat{H}) \leq \frac{(|H|+k)\cdot w(H)}{|H|}$ holds. Therefore, $\alpha(\widehat{H}\cup\{u\}) \leq \frac{(|H|+k)\cdot w(H)+|H|\cdot y}{|H|\cdot(|H|+K+1)}$. Hence, $\alpha(H)-\alpha(\widehat{H}\cup\{v\}) \geq \frac{w(H)}{|H|} - \frac{(|H|+k)\cdot w(H)+|H|\cdot y}{|H|\cdot(|H|+k+1)} = \frac{w(H)-|H|\cdot y}{|H|\cdot(|H|+K+1)}$. Since $\alpha(H) \geq y$ implies $w(H) \geq |H| \cdot y$, as a result, $\alpha(H) - \alpha(\widehat{H} \cup \{u\}) \geq \frac{|H|\cdot y-|H|\cdot y}{|H|\cdot(|H|+k+1)} = 0$. The lemma follows. □

In addition to the case $\alpha(H) \geq y$, the following lemma further points out that, if $\alpha(H) < y$, $(H \cup \widehat{X})$ does not need to be examined.

LEMMA 5. *Given any subgraph $H \subseteq C_v$ with $\alpha(H) < y$, a set of vertices $X \subseteq C_v$ with $I_{C_v}(u) < y, \forall u \in X$, for every subgraph $\widehat{X} \subseteq X$, $\alpha(H \cup \widehat{X}) < y$ always holds.*

PROOF. We prove this lemma by induction. We first consider the case when adding exactly one vertex $u \in X$ to H, i.e., $\widehat{X} = \{u\}$. Then, $\alpha(H\cup\{u\}) = \frac{w(H\cup\{u\})}{|H|+1} \leq \frac{w(H)+I_{C_v}(u)}{|H|+1} < \frac{w(H)+y}{|H|+1}$. Since $\alpha(H) < y$ holds, $w(H) < |H| \cdot y$ also holds. Therefore, $\alpha(H \cup \{u\}) < \frac{|H|\cdot y+y}{|H|+1} = y$.

Assume that the lemma holds when adding any k vertices in X to H. That is, let $\widehat{X} \subseteq X$ with $|\widehat{X}| = k$ and $\widehat{H} = (H\cup\widehat{X})$. We have $\alpha(\widehat{H}) < y$. Then, for any vertex $u \in X-\widehat{H}$, $\alpha(\widehat{H}\cup\{u\}) < y$ holds. We have $\alpha(\widehat{H}\cup\{u\}) \leq \frac{w(\widehat{H})+I_{C_v}(u)}{|H|+k+1} < \frac{w(\widehat{H})+y}{|H|+k+1}$. Since $\alpha(\widehat{H}) < y$ implies that $w(\widehat{H}) < (|H| + k) \cdot y$ holds, $\alpha(\widehat{H}\cup\{u\}) < \frac{(|H|+k)\cdot y+y}{|H|+k+1} = y$. The lemma follows. □

From the above two lemmas, we conclude that given the current best solution F^{APX} with $\alpha(F^{APX}) = y$ and a 2-clique C_v, any vertex u with $I_{C_v}(u) < y$ can be safely removed from the 2-clique C_v if the size constraint is not employed, i.e., $p = 0$. However, if $p > 0$, more detailed cases are necessary to be examined. Specifically, let $\widehat{C}_v$ denote the 2-clique after removing each vertex u with $I_{C_v}(u) < y$ from the original C_v. Then, 1) if $|\widehat{C}_v| \geq p$, we start the 2-clique Trimming step directly from $\widehat{C}_v$, i.e., those vertices u with $I_{C_v}(u) < y$ are pruned from C_v. 2) If $|\widehat{C}_v| < p$, and $\alpha(\widehat{C}_v) < y$, then the whole C_v can be pruned without performing 2-clique Trimming step on $\widehat{C}_v$ because there will never exist a subgraph $H \subseteq C_v$ with $\alpha(H) \geq y$. 3) Finally, if $|\widehat{C}_v| < p$ but $\alpha(\widehat{C}_v) \geq y$ holds, it is still necessary to perform 2-clique Trimming on the original C_v to find out if there is a better solution than F^{APX}.

PROPOSITION 2. ***Incident Similarity Pruning.*** *Given the current best solution F^{APX} with $\alpha(F^{APX}) = y$ and a 2-clique C_v, let $\widehat{C}_v$ be the 2-clique after removing each vertex u with $I_{C_v}(u) < y$ from the original C_v. 1) If $|\widehat{C}_v| \geq p$, SGSel can start 2-clique Trimming step directly on $\widehat{C}_v$. 2) If $|\widehat{C}_v| < p$, and $\alpha(\widehat{C}_v) < y$, the whole C_v can be pruned without performing 2-clique Trimming step.*

It is worth noting that the incident similarity of each vertex u in a 2-clique C_v can be pre-computed before SGSel starts. Therefore, Incident Similarity Pruning can be performed very efficiently. Moreover, more vertices in each C_v are inclined to be pruned because $\alpha(F^{APX})$ will increase as the algorithm proceeds. Moreover, as discussed above, 2-Clique Pruning and Incident Similarity Pruning only trim the 2-cliques and vertices that never generate better solutions than F^{APX}. Therefore, the performance bound in Theorem 2 still holds.

Post Processing. We propose a post-processing procedure to tailor F^{APX} from 2-clique for meeting the unfamiliarity requirement of the MSSG. Given F^{APX} obtained in SGSel, we first define the *violating set* Ω of vertices in F^{APX}. A vertex u in F^{APX} is a violating vertex if there exists at least one other vertex v in F^{APX} such that $(u, v) \notin \widehat{E}$. The post processing includes three adjustment steps. 1) Swap: a violating vertex u can be swapped with a vertex $v \in (V\backslash F^{APX})$ if $|\Omega|$ is reduced and $\alpha(F^{APX})$ does not decrease. Note that $V \subseteq A$ here because the pre-processing procedure has already removed all the normal users from V. If there are many u and v satisfying the requirements, we give priority to the u and v which maximize $\alpha((F^{APX} - \{u\}) \cup \{v\})$. 2) Expand: a vertex $v \in (V\backslash F^{APX})$ can be added into F^{APX} if adding v does not increase $|\Omega|$ but increases $\alpha(F^{APX})$. We also give priority to the v which maximizes $\alpha(F^{APX} \cup \{v\})$. 3) Shrink: given a violating vertex $u \in \Omega$, u can be safely removed if after removing u from F^{APX}, $|\Omega|$ decreases but $\alpha(F^{APX})$ does not. Similar to 1), we give priority to the u that maximizes $\alpha(F^{APX} - \{u\})$. Note that the above post-processing procedure minimizes the number of $u, v \in V$ with $(u, v) \notin \widehat{E}$ while improving $\alpha(F^{APX})$. Therefore, after post processing, the performance bound in Theorem 2 still holds.

7. EXPERIMENTAL RESULTS

To evaluate the proposed MSSG problem and SGSel algorithm, a user study is performed by inviting 11 professional psychiatrists (4 psychiatrists and 7 clinical psychologists)[5] to compare the support groups selected by themselves and by SGSel, respectively. Each psychiatrist and clinical psychologist (psychiatrist for short) is given 5 tasks of support group formation. For each task, we randomly select 12 to 18 candidates from a user study dataset, FB_Small [2], in which we randomly hire 500 Internet and social network users, where 146 of them are ISNA patients. These patients are identified based on the standard diagnosis rules [5, 29] employed by professional psychiatrists.

Specifically, in dataset FB_Small, three types of ISNAs are identified [29]: 1) *Cyber-Relationship (CR) Addiction.* This includes the addictions to social networking, checking and messaging to the point where social relationships to virtual and online friends become more important than real-life ones with family and friends; 2) *Net Compulsion (NC).* This includes compulsive online social gaming or gambling; and 3) *Information Overload (IO).* This includes compulsive surfing of user status and news feeds, leading to lower work productivity and less social interactions with family and friends offline. Among the 146 ISNA patients, there are 41% with CR, 3% with NC, and 56% with IO.

[5]They are from California School of Professional Psychology, Taipei City Hospital, Nat'l Taipei Univ., Nat'l Yang-Ming Univ., psychiatric clinics, etc.

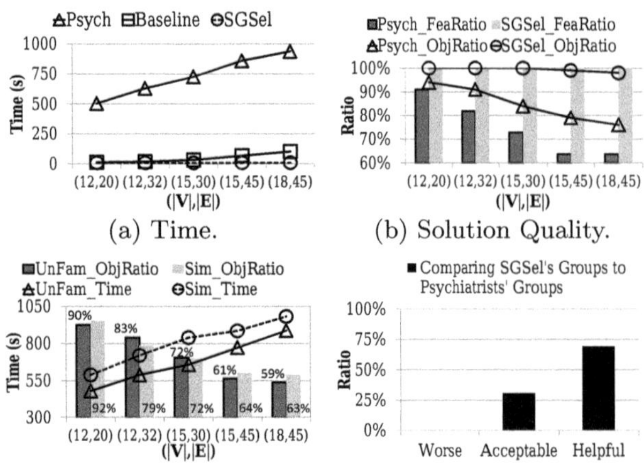

(a) Time. (b) Solution Quality.

(c) Diff. Strategies. (d) Surveyed Opinions.

Figure 3: User Study Results.

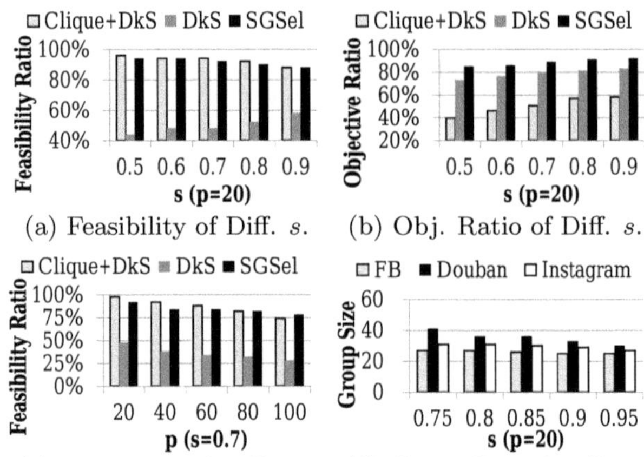

(a) Feasibility of Diff. s. (b) Obj. Ratio of Diff. s.

(c) Feasibility of Diff. p. (d) Group Size of Diff. s.

Figure 4: Comparisons of Different Approaches.

In addition to FB_Small, we also acquire large-scale datasets from Facebook (63K nodes, and 1.5M edges),[6] Instagram (1.7M media associated to 2K users, with 9M tags, 1200M likes, and 41M comments) [15], and Douban (5M nodes and 86M edges)[7] to evaluate SGSel. Since ISNA information of each person in the above three datasets is not available, a simple approach is to randomly assign the scores in accordance with the distribution of 500 individuals of user study. However, ISNA distributions may not be consistent in each social network. Therefore, a machine learning approach [2] is employed to find the potential patients in the three OSNs accordingly. The individuals in the datasets are classified into *ISNA* or *normal*. For each ISNA user, she is further associated with three ISNA labels, i.e., Cyber-Relationship (CR) addictions, Information Overload (IO), and Net Compulsion (NC) (note that a person may belong to multiple types of ISNAs). A score in $[0, 1]$ is associated with each label to indicate the ISNA users' severity of the specific type of ISNAs. The ratios of users with ISNAs to normal users are 0.24, 0.16, and 0.18 in Facebook, Instagram, and Douban, respectively. We evaluate the quality of the solution groups obtained by SGSel using the above three datasets. We extract the social relationships and the similarities of users, and similarity edge weights are assigned according to Sec. 3.

We compare SGSel with three algorithms, namely, Baseline, DkS, and Clique+DkS. Baseline finds the optimal solution of CMSSG by enumerating all the subgraphs satisfying the constraints. Clique+DkS, as introduced in Sec. 3, first finds the approximated maximum clique K_{max} [13] and then iteratively employs the weighted DkS [14] to extract the group $\widehat{F}$ with the maximum $\alpha(\widehat{F})$, $|\widehat{F}| \geq p$. Moreover, DkS employs the approximated weighted DkS algorithm on $\widehat{G}$ directly to obtain a group of size p. For fair comparison, before these algorithms start, we first trim the graph $\widehat{G}$ by removing normal users and the similarity edges with weights smaller than the similarity constraint s. The algorithms are implemented in an IBM 3650 server with Quadcore Intel X5450 3.0 GHz CPUs. Each result is averaged by 50 samples.

7.1 User Study

We first compare the solution groups returned by psychiatrists and clinical psychologists (psychiatrists for short) and SGSel with $p = 7$, $s = 0$. The result shows that, among the 55 groups formed by the psychiatrists, 32 of them are identical to SGSel's choices, while 9 of them have only 1 different patient from SGSel's. It is worth noting that the average similarity of SGSel is 16% better than psychiatrists' in the 9 groups. Therefore, MSSG is able to meet the patient selection criteria adopted by mental health psychiatrists. On average, the groups formed by psychiatrists include 27%, 4% and 69% of CR, NC, and IO addicts, respectively. The ratio of CR addicts in these groups is smaller than that in the user study dataset because CR addicts are more likely to be friends with other CR addicts. Thus, it is difficult to satisfy the unfamiliarity requirement. Fig. 3(a) presents the time spent by psychiatrists (Psych), Baseline, and SGSel to find the solution groups, while Fig. 3(b) compares the solution quality among psychiatrists and SGSel. Here, Psych_FeaRaio and SGSel_FeaRatio denote the ratios of feasible solutions (i.e., satisfying the unfamiliarity constraint) obtained by psychiatrists and SGSel, respectively. Similarly, Psych_ObjRatio and SGSel_ObjRatio indicate the ratios of the average similarity of the groups formed by psychiatrists and SGSel to that of the optimal solutions. As the number of candidate patients and friendships increases, it becomes more difficult for the psychiatrists to obtain the solutions. Thus, the time they spend increases, but Psych_ObjRatio and Psych_FeaRatio drop rapidly. By contrast, the groups formed by SGSel are all feasible solutions and their objective values are very close to the optimal solutions.

We further investigate the strategies of psychiatrists for selecting the groups. 45% psychiatrists examine the unfamiliarity of the members first (UnFam), while the other 55% consider the similarity of the members first (Sim). As shown in Fig. 3(c), the psychiatrists who consider similarity first obtain slightly better ObjRatio but spend more time since 1) there are so many candidates for psychiatrists to extract similar ones, and 2) it is difficult to find a group with a high similarity score after considering the unfamiliarity. Psychiatrists are inclined to iteratively adjust the group members to ensure the unfamiliarity and improve the similarity, and thus need much more time. Fig. 3(d) presents the surveyed opinions of the psychiatrists upon SGSel's solutions. All the psychiatrists agree that the groups obtained by SGSel are either helpful (69%) or acceptable (31%). Moreover, as the number of candidate patients increases, more psychiatrists

[6] http://tinyurl.com/pv52des

[7] http://tinyurl.com/lq9fjsx

agree that SGSel is helpful to find a support group effectively and efficiently.

7.2 Performance Evaluations

We evaluate SGSel and three alternative approaches, i.e., Baseline, Clique+DkS, and DkS, using the large Instagram, Facebook, and Douban datasets. Here, *Feasibility Ratio* denotes the ratio of solution feasibility (the portion of solutions which are cliques on $\widehat{G}_f$). *Objective Ratio* denotes the ratio of $\alpha(F)$ in the solution obtained by the algorithms to that of the optimal solution.

Group Quality. We first compare SGSel with Baseline, Clique+DkS and DkS on FB_Small. Fig. 4(a) and Fig. 4(b) compare the Feasibility and Objective Ratios of different algorithms, respectively. When s decreases, Feasibility Ratio of SGSel increases because in this case the post processing procedure has more choices to better tailor the solution. SGSel achieves higher Objective Ratio because it extracts the solution F^{APX} with the maximum $\alpha(F^{APX})$ among various subgraphs in different C_v to strike a good balance between similarity and group sizes. In the groups obtained by SGSel, on average, the ratios of the group members with CR, NC, and IO users are 0.29, 0.07, and 0.64, respectively, different from the ratios in FB_Small (i.e., 0.41, 0.03, and 0.56). The proportion of group members with CR is much smaller than that in FB_Small, because each user with CR has a large number of friends in OSNs. Moreover, they usually have other users with CR as friends – this phenomenon has been described as *loneliness propagates* [9]. Therefore, SGSel selects fewer users with CR to maintain the unfamiliarity requirement. Users with IO usually share high similarity but have comparatively fewer online friends. Therefore, SGSel is inclined to choose more IO users to maximize the similarity of the group while fulfilling the unfamiliarity requirement.

In contrast, although Clique+DkS has high Feasibility Ratios in Fig. 4(a), its Objective Ratios are poor as shown in Fig. 4(b) because it only considers a small subgraph of $\widehat{G}$. Moreover, Feasibility Ratios of Clique+DkS are not always 100%, especially when s becomes larger. This is because in some cases the sizes of returned maximum cliques are smaller than p. Objective Ratio of DkS is better than Clique+DkS because DkS considers the whole graph $\widehat{G}$. However, it is worth noting that DkS has very poor Feasibility Ratio because it ignores the unfamiliarity of the potential patients.

Fig. 4(c) compares Feasibility Ratios of the algorithms with different p. When p increases, Feasibility Ratios drop because larger groups are difficult to obtain, and the possibility that at least one member violates the unfamiliarity constraint increases. We also evaluate SGSel on large datasets, i.e., Facebook, Douban, and Instagram in Fig. 4(d). Fig. 4(d) manifests that the sizes of the returned groups grow when s decreases especially in Douban which is a social application for people with the same interests to share information, because the friendship relation in Douban plays a less important role as compared to other social applications, such as Faebook. Therefore, Douban contains many large densely connected components in $\widehat{G}_f$.

Running Time. To evaluate the scalability of SGSel, Figs. 5(a) and 5(b) compare the execution time of SGSel and other approaches in Douban (5M vertices). Baseline is not included because it takes more than one day to find a solution. SGSel is able to obtain solutions mostly within 5 minutes. The execution time is smaller when s increases because more vertices with low incident similarities are effectively removed in this case. Similarly, when p increases, the execution time also drops because more unnecessary 2-cliques (with sizes smaller than p.) are skipped by SGSel.

Fig. 5(c) compares the pruning strategies proposed in this paper in Douban. Both SGSel with only Incident Similarity Pruning (Only_ISP) and SGSel with only 2-Clique Pruning (Only_2-CP) outperform SGSel without pruning (NoPruning) because the pruning strategies effectively remove redundant vertices and 2-cliques. Only_ISP performs better than Only_2-CP because the pruning condition of 2-CP is more difficult to satisfy, even though 2-CP can prune the whole 2-clique at once. When s increases, the power of the pruning strategies drops because the edges in the similarity graph are of larger weights, and the conditions of either pruning strategies are thus more difficult to satisfy.

Fig. 5(d) further compares the execution time reduction by employing either pruning strategies in the three real datasets. The variance of the vertices' incident similarities is the largest in Douban, i.e., there are many dense and sparse components in the similarity graph. Therefore, the pruning strategies perform better because they effectively remove a larger number of vertices and 2-cliques with small incident similarities (i.e., sparse components). In contrast, the variance of incident similarities is the smallest in FB because FB has a large number of CR and IO addicts, who are usually similar to each other. In this case, the incident similarities of these vertices are usually high. Therefore, the pruning strategies can only prune a smaller number of vertices and 2-cliques in FB. Finally, Fig. 5(e) compares the execution time of different approaches in FB_Small. The execution time of Baseline grows exponentially as s decreases because Baseline needs to consider more cases when s is small. By contrast, the execution time of SGSel is tiny because the 2-cliques and the pruning strategies effectively trim the search space.

8. CONCLUSION

With the emergence of online support groups, this paper aims to address the need of mental health professionals and formulates a new problem, namely, Member Selection for Online Support Group (MSSG). MSSG is to find a support group that maximizes the similarity of the symptoms of all selected members, while ensuring that any two members are unacquainted to each other. We prove that MSSG is NP-Hard and inapproximable within any factor. Moreover, we develop a 3-approximation algorithm, namely SGSel, with a guaranteed error bound. A user study on psychiatrists and clinical psychologists manifests that the proposed algorithm is helpful for them and can find better solutions. Extensive experiments on real datasets show that our algorithm outperforms the other baselines in terms of both quality and efficiency.

9. ACKNOWLEDGMENTS

This work is supported in part by NSF through grant CNS-1115234, USA, and by Ministry of Science and Technology through grants MOST 103-2221-E-002-286-MY2, MOST 101-2628-E-001-003-MY3, and MOST 103-2221-E-001-005-MY2, Taiwan.

10. REFERENCES

[1] American Psychological Association. `http://www.apa.org/helpcenter/group-therapy.aspx`.

[2] Detecting social network mental disorders via social network Data. `https://goo.gl/FgCNpy`.

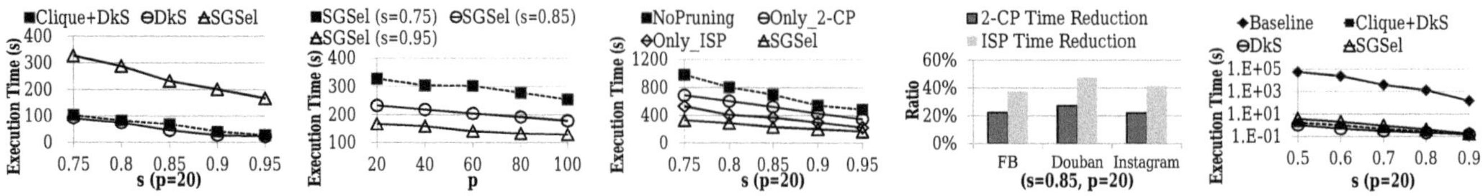

(a) Diff. s in Douban. (b) Diff. p in Douban. (c) Pruning of Diff. s. (d) Diff. Datasets. (e) Time on FB_Small.

Figure 5: Comparisons of Execution Time.

[3] J. Abramowitz, M. Franklin, S. Schwartz, and J. Furr. Symptom presentation and outcome of cognitive-behavioral therapy of obsessive-compulsive disorder. *J. Consult. Clin. Psych.*, 2003.

[4] American Psychiatric Association. Diagnostic and statistical manual of mental disorders (5th ed.), 2013.

[5] C. Andreassen, T. Torsheim, G. Brunborg, and S. Pallesen. Development of a facebook addiction scale. *Psycho. Rep.*, 2012.

[6] D. Angres and K. Bettinardi-Angres. The disease of addiction: origins, treatment and recovery. *Disease-a-Month*, 2008.

[7] V. Barker. Older adolescents' motivations for social network site use: the influence of gender, group identity, and collective self-esteem. *CyberPsychol. Behav.*, 2009.

[8] J. Block. Issues for DSM-V: internet addiction. *Am. J. of Psychiat.*, 2008.

[9] J. Cacioppo, J. Fowler, and N. Christakis. Alone in the crowd: the structure and spread of loneliness in a large social network. *J. Pers. Soc. Psychol.*, 2009.

[10] Center for substance abuse treatment. Substance abuse treatment: group therapy. *Treatment improvement protocol (TIP) series 41*, 2005.

[11] C. Cheung, P. Chiu, and M. Lee. Online social networks: why do students use facebook? *Comput. Hum. Behav.*, 2010.

[12] Y. Du, W. Jiang, and A. Vance. Longer term effect of randomized, controlled group cognitive behavioral therapy for internet addiction in adolescent students in Shanghai. *Aust. N. Z. J. Psychiat.*, 2010.

[13] U. Feige. Approximating maximum clique by removing subgraphs. *SIAM J. Discrete Math*, 2004.

[14] U. Feige, G. Kortsarz, and D. Peleg. The dense k-subgraph problem. *Algorithmica*, 2001.

[15] E. Ferrara, R. Interdonato, A. Tagarelli. Online popularity and topical interests through the lens of instagram. *HT*, 2014.

[16] G. Fisher and T. Harrison. Substance abuse: information for school counselors, social workers, therapists, and counselors. *Boston: Allyn & Bacon*, 1997.

[17] W. Howatt. Choice theory: a core addiction recovery tool. *Int. J. Reality Therapy*, 2003.

[18] M. Kargar and A. An. Discovering top-k teams of experts with/without a leader in social networks. *CIKM*, 2011.

[19] J. Kim. The effect of a R/T group counseling program on the internet addiction level and self-esteem of internet addiction university students. *In. J. Reality Therapy*, 2008.

[20] T. Lappas, K. Liu, and E. Terzi. Finding a team of experts in social networks. *KDD*, 2009.

[21] J. Lewis and J. Carlson. Reality therapy for addictions with robert wubboling. New York, NY: Prentice Hall, 2003.

[22] K. Li, W. Lu, S. Bhagat, L. Lakshmanan, and C. Yu. On social event organization. *KDD*, 2014.

[23] R. Mokken. Cliques, clubs and clans. *Quality and Quantity: International Journal of Methodology*, 1979.

[24] J. Saisan, M. Smith, L. Robinson, and J. Segal. Internet and computer addiction: signs, symptoms, and help for balancing your time online and off. Available online: `http://www.helpguide.org/articles/addiction/internet-and-computer-addiction.htm`.

[25] S. Scheidlinger. The group psychotherapy movement at the millennium: some historical perspectives. *Int. J. Group Psychother.*, 2000.

[26] D. Williamson and D. Shmoys. The design of approximation algorithms. *Cambridge University Press*, 2011.

[27] D. Yang, Y. Chen, W. Lee, and M. Chen. On social-temporal group query with acquaintance constraint. *VLDB*, 2011.

[28] K. Young. Internet addiction: the emergence of a new clinical disorder, *Cyberpsychol. Behav.*, 1998.

[29] K. Young, M. Pistner, J. O'Mara, and J. Buchanan. Cyber disorders: the mental health concern for the new millennium. *Cyberpsychol. Behav.*, 1999.

APPENDIX

THEOREM 1. *CMSSG is NP-Hard and inapproximable within any factor unless $P = NP$.*

PROOF. We prove this theorem with the reduction from the maximum clique problem. Decision problem of maximum clique, given a graph $G_c = (V_c, E_c)$, decides from the graph if there exists a clique of size no smaller than q, i.e., a complete graph with at least q vertices and with an edge connecting every two vertices. In the input graph of CMSSG, i.e., $\widehat{G} = (V, \widehat{E}, S)$, let $A = V = V_c$ (all individuals are with ISNAs), $\widehat{E} = E_c$, and $p = q$. The similarity edge set S and the corresponding edge weights are set arbitrarily. CMSSG finds a feasible solution F of size no smaller than p if and only if the maximum clique problem returns TRUE, i.e., there is a clique of size at least q. Therefore, CMSSG is NP-Hard.

Note that CMSSG returns $\alpha(F) = 0$ if $F = \varnothing$, i.e., no feasible solution exists for CMSSG. Given the instance of $CMSSG(\widehat{G}, p, s)$ mentioned above, the solution of CMSSG, i.e., F, is a clique with size no smaller than p. Therefore, if CMSSG has a polynomial-time approximation algorithm with an arbitrarily large ratio $\rho < \infty$, then the following statements hold: 1) the algorithm finds a feasible solution for CMSSG if the maximum clique returns TRUE, and 2) any CMSSG instance with the algorithm returning a feasible solution implies that the corresponding instance in maximum clique is TRUE. In other words, the ρ-approximation algorithm can solve the maximum clique problem in polynomial time, implying that $P = NP$, which is widely deemed incorrect. Therefore, CMSSG has no polynomial-time approximation algorithm, i.e., CMSSG is inapproximable within any factor unless $P = NP$. $\square$

Concept-Based Relevance Models for Medical and Semantic Information Retrieval

Chunye Wang
Technology and Information Management
University of California Santa Cruz
Santa Cruz, CA, USA
cwang@soe.ucsc.edu

Ramakrishna Akella
School of Information, TIM
University of California
Berkeley and Santa Cruz, CA, USA
akella@ischool.berkeley.edu

ABSTRACT

Relevance models provide an important approach for estimating probabilities of words in the relevant class. However, the associated bag-of-words assumption breaks dependencies between words, especially between those within a phrase. If such dependencies could be preserved, it would permit matching the query terms with document terms having the same dependencies. Additionally, during the estimation of relevance, relevance models are unable to distinguish relevant and non-relevant information in a feedback document, and hence take the entire document into account, which potentially hurts the accuracy of estimation. In this paper, we define the notion of "concept", and design a concept-based information retrieval framework. Using this framework, we transform documents and queries from term space into concept space, and propose a concept-based relevance model for improved estimation of relevance. Our approach has three advantages. First, this approach only assumes independence between concepts, so is able to keep the strong dependencies between the words of a concept. Second, it unifies synonyms or different surface forms of a concept, leading to reduced dimensionality of the space, increased sample size of a concept, and consequently more accurate and reliable estimates of the relevance. Third, when knowledge bases are available, our approach enables the semantic analysis of query concepts, and thus identifies concepts related to the query, from which a more accurate distribution of relevance can be estimated. This work is aligned with semantic search methods.

We apply our concept-based relevance model to information retrieval in the medical domain, where concepts are abundant and their variations are numerous. We compare with relevance models, BM25 with pseudo relevance feedback, and the state of the art conceptual language models, on several data collections. The proposed model demonstrates consistent and statistically significant improvements across collections, outperforming top benchmark conceptual language models by at least 9% and up to 20% on a number of metrics.

Categories and Subject Descriptors

H.3.3 [**Information Storage and Retrieval**]: Information Search and Retrieval

CIKM'15, October 19-23, 2015, Melbourne, VIC, Australia
 ISBN 978-1-4503-3794-6/15/10...$15.00
DOI: http://dx.doi.org/10.1145/2806416.2806497

Keywords

Information retrieval; concepts; term dependency; relevance; concept relevance models; semantic search; ontology; UMLS

1. INTRODUCTION

Relevance has always been fundamental to information retrieval. In the research community, however, there are many different views of relevance. Jones, Robertson, et al. argued that relevance should be explicitly recognized in any formal models [1], since it is the key notion in retrieval. The classical Probabilistic Model, which is derived from the Probabilistic Ranking Principle, does this straightforwardly [2]. The Vector Space Model assumes that some of the points in the multi-dimensional information space of a retrieval system represent relevant documents. However, the early Language Modeling (LM) approach works differently. Instead of modeling relevance directly, LM presumes that if it is highly probable that the document generates the query, then the content of the document is more likely to be relevant to the information need underlying the user's request. Therefore, it uses as the ranking function the probability that a language model that generated the document would generate the query [3]. To answer the question "Where's the relevance?" in LM, Laffety and Zhai [4] provided a theoretical justification for LM that the language modeling approach and the traditional probabilistic model can be interpreted within the same probabilistic framework based on a generative relevance model, but these two models are not equivalent from a statistical point of view, since the factorization and estimation are different.

To bridge the gap between relevance and LM, Lavrenko and Croft [5] proposed the Relevance-based Language Models (or Relevance Models, RM), which seek to estimate a more generalized notion of relevance. This approach assumes that there exists an ideal, accurate model of relevance, and both the relevant documents and the query are random samples from it. This relevance model can be estimated from relevant documents, or in a pseudo relevance feedback fashion, if training documents are unavailable. RM proved very effective in the field. It achieved the best results on the TREC 2005 and 2006 Terabyte tracks, respectively [8, 12]. Recent research trends show that the relevance model formalism has established a foothold in the research in IR community, based on which new models and algorithms are continuously built and developed [6, 7, 8, 12].

Like most statistical retrieval models, RM assumes words are independent of each other in a document. This is a compromise due to the infeasibility of estimating the general term dependencies from sparse data. As we all know, for example, when we read the phrase "information retrieval and knowledge management" in a CIKM proceeding, the association between "information" and "retrieval", or between "knowledge" and "management" is much stronger than that between "retrieval" and "and", or "and" and "knowledge". In this circumstance, if modeling all the dependencies is infeasible, at least one should attempt to keep the highly dependent words such as "information retrieval" or "knowledge management" together. Towards this end, we make our initial effort by proposing and modeling the notion of concept. We define a concept as a word or a multi-word phrase that represents a single but complete meaning in context. We argue that the dependencies within the words of a concept (if more than one), should be preserved; therefore, given a document, independence only exists between concepts; and it would be beneficial to conduct the estimation of model components in concept space, rather than in term space. In this paper, we will show how concept-based relevance can be estimated without the bag-of-words assumption, and how the relevance model can be developed to the Concept-based Relevance Model (CRM). There are three primary advantages of our model.

First, CRM replaces the bag-of-words assumption of RM with the bag-of-concepts assumption, in order to retain term dependencies within a concept. Usually, term dependencies inside a concept are stronger than those outside of it. Preserving inside dependencies will provide retrieval systems extra information to better match query concepts and document concepts with the same dependencies. Following the above example, when users query "knowledge management" in a system, matching the entire concept could enable a retrieval system to rank the text "information retrieval and knowledge management" higher than "domain knowledge in project management". In order to present more relevant documents to users, such association among query terms should be considered. In the meanwhile, we assume independence between concepts, so the joint probability of concepts can be decomposed and estimated conveniently.

Next, CRM provides an advanced approach to estimating relevance. It improves estimation from two perspectives. During the concept extraction, with the aid of information extraction and natural language processing (NLP), the synonyms and other different surface forms of a concept (e.g. "heart attack", "myocardial infarction", "MI", "infarction of heart", and "cardiac infarction") will be identified and unified under the same concept. This consequently reduces the dimensionality of the concept space and increases the sample size of a concept to be estimated, essentially helping solve the synonym problem and the data sparsity issue in information retrieval. The estimation performed in such a denser space is more accurate and reliable. In fact, previous work has shown that increasing density helps improve the estimation. Diaz and Metzler [16] accomplished this by incorporating more data from large external corpora, while in this study we seek to find an alternative by better mining the data itself. In addition, some noisy text and non-relevant information, such as author's affiliations, privacy notices, and advertisements, will be pruned during concept extraction, which makes the content transformed to concept space more relevant and consistent.

Finally, if knowledge base is available, CRM allows semantic analysis to further improve relevance estimation. By modeling semantic types of query concepts, CRM is able to find concepts that are semantically related to query concepts in feedback documents. Estimating on these relevant concepts yields a more accurate distribution of relevance. Note this could be termed semantic search, since it is aligned with methods in that area.

The remainder of the paper is structured as follows. In Section 2, we briefly survey the IR models considering term dependencies and using concepts. In Section 3, we construct and estimate the simple concept-based relevance models. Section 4 shows how we develop a full concept-based relevance models by semantic analysis and modeling concept semantic types. We elaborate the experimental setup and results in Section 5, discuss the reason for significant improvements in Section 6, and conclude in Section 7.

2. RELATED WORK

Many recent studies in IR consider query terms associated with each other. Most of them have focused on the term proximity. N-gram models consider n word sequences to expand the radius of matching [15], but it is yet hard to determine the optimal n, and the complexity usually grows exponentially with the growth of n. Some work integrates word proximity or term location information into probabilistic weighting models in a heuristic manner [7, 18]. Other models have been proposed to capture the exact dependencies between more than two terms. Despite the more complex nature, they have been shown to produce little or no improvements in effectiveness. As mentioned in [23, 24], most previous term dependence models have failed to show robust, significant improvements over baseline bag-of-words models, with only a few exceptions such as the dependence language models [25] and the Markov random fields (MRF) model [24, 27]. The dependence language models require computing a link structure for each query, which is not straightforward. As a query expansion technique, the Latent Concept Expansion (LCE) derived from MRF shows significant improvements over relevance models on MAP across different data sets, but only small, insignificant improvements on precision at 5, 10, and 20 [27]. One problem of LCE is that it adds new words to a concept based on word statistics regardless of the semantics and syntax of the expanded concepts. This results in expanded concepts inconsistent with common language usage and unnatural to human understanding. For example, "two hubble space" and "telescope shuttle" will be generated from the query "hubble telescope achievements". Learning from the above studies, we do not plan to model term dependencies directly in this paper. Instead, we intend to extract concepts that are naturally expressed in documents and queries, so that the strong term dependencies will be preserved in the concept. In fact, as the authors pointed out, the inability to improve performance by expanding two-word concepts using LCE indicates that two-word concepts already consist of two highly dependent terms [27], so it is difficult to find additional terms that would make the concept more effective to retrieval. This finding potentially supports our hypothesis of using the stronger dependencies inside of natural concepts and skipping the weaker dependencies outside.

For concept-based IR, some empirical studies show that retrieval models using only concepts have inconsistent results, since not all documents and queries could be effectively represented using concepts. Different methods are investigated to combine relevance scores from both word and concept retrievals in [9, 10, 20]. Explicit Semantic Analysis (ESA) represents and analyzes text as vectors in a high-dimensional space of natural concepts derived from Wikipedia [21]. In this model, a concept is actually represented by a document, the Wikipedia article. An inverted index is built to store the *tf-idf* word-concept association. Then the text-concept strength (the entry of the above vector) can be calculated by the weighted sum of *tf-idf* scores of all words occurring in the text. Ranking these strengths yields the most related concepts of that text. According to its nature of characterizing information by concept vectors, ESA is a vector space retrieval model.

Table 1: Notation of random variables.

w: A term in term space
D: A document in term space
$Q = q_1 \dots q_l$: A query in term space, composed of l terms $q_1 \dots q_l$
R_C: A concept relevance model
c: A concept in R_C
D_C: A relevant document in concept space
$Q_C = q_{C1} \dots q_{Ck}$: The query Q in concept space, composed of k concepts $q_{C1} \dots q_{Ck}$
$U_C = D_{C1}, D_{C2}, \dots D_{CM}$: The collection of M relevant documents

In the LM framework, Conceptual Language Models (CLM) have been proposed to enrich the representation of a textual query with information carried by concepts [22]. This model does not extract concepts from text, but uses metadata or keywords assigned to abstracts of scientific papers (only 11 human-annotated concepts per document on average), so the concepts used by the model are limited in number and do not represent the content of documents, while our model will recognize hundreds to even thousands of concepts from the entire document for estimation. Besides, concepts in CLM are merely used as a pivot language to help estimate textual terms from pseudo relevant documents, but the word expression of concepts is not used in estimation or retrieval. The final expanded query is still in the bag-of-words representation, leaving the term dependency issue unresolved. However, CLM would be an appropriate baseline to compare with our models, considering the same LM framework, but different approaches to dealing with concepts.

3. SIMPLE CONCEPT-BASED RELEVANCE MODELS

To obviate the limitations described above in related work, we model and use concepts in a novel, simple, and effective manner. We propose a concept-based relevance model for information retrieval. Figure 1 shows the role and steps of our novel CRM in a retrieval process. A more detailed workflow of CRM retrieval algorithm is described later in Figure 4. CRM is derived from the idea of Lavrenko's RM, but unique in four respects (shown as shaded boxes in Figure 1): (1) We perform *concept extraction and estimation* in concept space, while performing query expansion in term space, with appropriate weights for both regular query terms and the word expression of estimated concepts; (2) We make a *new assumption* concerning the generative process for relevance, which is more pertinent to the criteria used by judges to assess relevance, and subsequently validate this new assumption; (3) We develop the model by proposing *semantic analysis* to identify concepts relevant to queries; and (4) We propose a *new estimation method* of document models using such relevant concepts. In this section, we mainly focus on extracting concepts and developing a simple CRM. The full CRM with semantic analysis and new estimation method will be presented in Section 4.

3.1 Concept Extraction

In our current study, we set the retrieval environment to the medical domain, because there are abundantly many concepts and numerous concept variations in medical documents [17], and rich domain resources available to exploit. There are many existing algorithms and tools for medical concept extraction. Our research focus in this paper is information retrieval, rather than the investigation of high accuracy information extraction algorithms; the influence of concept extraction on retrieval performance may

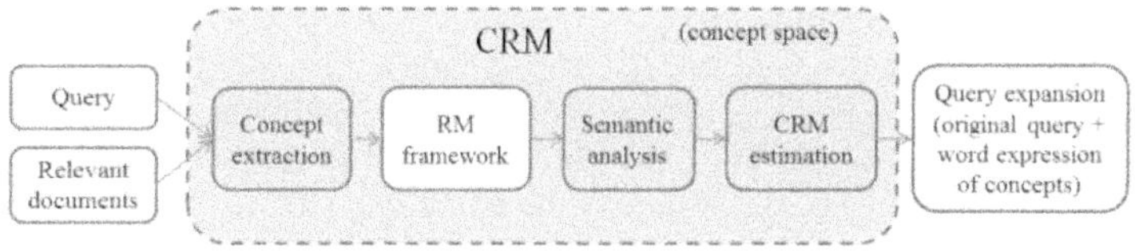

Figure 1: The role and basic steps of CRM in retrieval.

comprise our future work. Instead, we adopt an unsupervised, ontology-based extraction method to identify concepts in medical documents. To be specific, we employ the tool of MetaMap[1] to map biomedical text to concepts defined in the Unified Medical Language System[2] (UMLS) ontologies. The UMLS comprises over 1 million biomedical concepts and 5 million concept names, from over 130 lexicons and thesauri in clinical care, public health, and epidemiology. It is produced and updated by the National Library of Medicine with the purpose of assisting computer systems to "understand" the language of biomedicine and health. For a particular concept, the UMLS provides a list of synonyms, concept semantic types, and their semantic relationships to other concepts and types. In our work, we use MetaMap to interact with the UMLS to discover concepts referred to in text. The NLP and computational linguistic techniques used in MetaMap, such as shallow parsing, noun phrase chunking, and lexicon lookup, enable it to achieve a 0.909 precision and a 0.554 recall in medical concept extraction task [28], which are fairly good results for unsupervised algorithms.

3.2 Simple Concept-Based Relevance Models

Once we extract concepts from documents and queries, the entire modeling process can be transformed into a concept space. In this space, queries, documents, user's information need, and any other type of information are represented in the form of concepts (see Table 1 for the definition of random variables). We assume that there is an underlying concept relevance model R_C for every information need, which is a multinomial distribution over concepts. Assume that a concept c in D_C is sampled from R_C by the probability $P(c|R_C)$, and a query Q_C is sampled from R_C by the probability $P(Q_C|R_C)$. Both the D_C and the query Q_C are random samples from the distribution $P(c|R_C)$, but they do not necessarily follow the same sampling process.

Considering a query $Q_C = q_{C1} \dots q_{Ck}$ which provides the only available samples observed about the unknown process R_C, the best guess for the probability of observing c from R_C is naturally related to the conditional probability of observing c given $q_{C1} \dots q_{Ck}$:

$$P(c|R_C) \approx P(c|q_{C1} \dots q_{Ck}) = \frac{P(c, q_{C1} \dots q_{Ck})}{P(q_{C1} \dots q_{Ck})} \qquad (1)$$

The challenge then becomes estimating the joint probability of observing the concept c together with query concepts $q_{C1} \dots q_{Ck}$. Lavrenko and Croft proposed two methods for estimating the joint probability of RM [5]. The first method assumes that the query words and the words in relevant documents are sampled identically and independently from a unigram distribution. This is a simple but very strong independence assumption so that makes the estimation not as good as the other method [5]. We choose the other method, the conditional sampling, to estimate our model.

Given a specific concept c, we pick a document $D_C \in U_C$ according to $P(D_C|c)$, then sample the query concept q_{Ci} from D_C

[1] http://metamap.nlm.nih.gov/

[2] http://www.nlm.nih.gov/research/umls/

with the probability $P(q_{Ci}|D_C)$, and repeat this process k times to generate the whole query Q_C. This sampling strategy assumes the query concepts $q_{C1} \dots q_{Ck}$ are independent of each other, but keep their dependence on c. Here U_C is a set of documents that are relevant or pseudo relevant to the initial query Q. In the pseudo relevant case, they are the top ranked documents for query Q. Following this sampling process, the joint distribution can be expressed as below:

$$P(c, q_{C1} \dots q_{Ck}) = P(c) \prod_{i=1}^{k} P(q_{Ci}|c)$$

$$= P(c) \prod_{i=1}^{k} \sum_{D_C \in U_C} P(q_{Ci}|D_C)\, P(D_C|c) \quad (2)$$

The prior $P(c)$ can be estimated from the concept in every relevant document in U_C.

$$P(c) = \sum_{D_C \in U_C} P(c|D_C) P(D_C) \quad (3)$$

The conditional probability of picking D_C given the concept c can be expressed as below using Bayes' rule:

$$P(D_C|c) = \frac{P(c|D_C)P(D_C)}{P(c)} \quad (4)$$

The document prior $P(D_C)$ is assumed to be uniform over U_C. Then, the only unknown term is the critical document model $P(c|D_C)$. We employ RM's estimation method for it in this section, but will propose a much more effective method later.

$$P(c|D_C) = (1-\lambda) \cdot \frac{n(c, D_C)}{|D_C|} + \lambda \cdot P(c|coll) \quad (5)$$

where $n(c, D_C)$ is the frequency of c in D_C, $|D_C|$ is the total number of concepts in D_C, $P(c|coll)$ is the frequency of c in the collection divided by the total number of concepts in the collection, and $\lambda \in [0,1]$ is the smoothing parameter.

We are able to calculate the joint probability by plugging Eq. (3)-(5) into Eq. (2), and then estimate $P(c|R_C)$ in Eq. (1). This approach can be seen as an extension of RM in concept space, therefore we name it the Simple Concept-based Relevance Model (s-CRM). We will show how we incorporate semantic information to develop the full CRM in the next section.

4. FULL CONCEPT-BASED RELEVANCE MODELS

The process of concept extraction not only annotates medical concepts in documents, but also provides semantic types of concepts, and semantic relations between them. Such additional information motivates us to improve the estimation of $P(c|R_C)$ under a new assumption.

4.1 A New Assumption

The assumption in Section 3.2 is equivalent to that used in RM, based on which RM generates the query and the *entire relevant document*. However, we are aware that this assumption is not consistent with the prevailing TREC standard used to create relevance judgments, which was described by Voorhees in [13]:

"*To define relevance for the assessors, the assessors are told to assume that they are writing a report on the subject of the topic statement. If they would use any information contained in the document in the report, then the (entire) document should be marked relevant, otherwise it should be marked irrelevant.*"

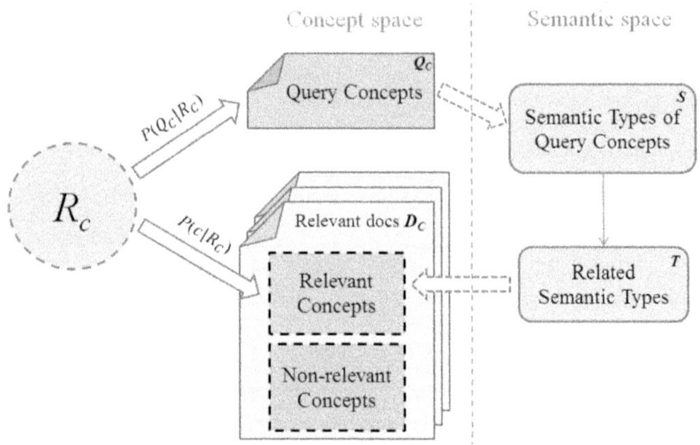

Figure 2: The generative process of concept relevance.

We can see that a document is relevant to a topic if part of it is relevant. This actually coincides with van Rijsbergen's definition of relevance judgment [14]:

"*A document is relevant to an information need if and only if it contains at least one sentence which is relevant to that need.*"

These definitions can be seen as a practical guideline to make the process of assigning relevance judgments more executable. But apparently it results in obstacles to the estimation of relevance. Now that a relevant document may contain only a small piece of information that is really pertinent to the information need, using the entire document to estimate relevance appears inefficient, sometimes even ineffective.

For this reason, we are motivated to make a new assumption that R_C generates the query Q_C but only the *relevant concepts* in a relevant document D_C (instead of the entire D_C). In this situation, a relevant document comprises two subsets: the relevant concepts (with regard to the query) and the non-relevant concepts, where only the relevant concepts are generated from R_C. Their relationships are represented in Figure 2 left side. We argue that this assumption is more consistent with the prevailing standard of relevance judgments, though it may not be the only valid assumption or even optimal.

Such a change in the assumption is very important, because it directly reformulates the scope of information we will use to estimate the model, and eventually makes a considerable impact on the accuracy of estimated relevance. The right side of Figure 2 briefly shows the process we intend to perform through semantic analysis, which will be detailed next.

Table 2: Notation of random variables on semantic types

s: A semantic type
s_c: The semantic type of concept c
$S = \{s_{q_{C1}}, \dots, s_{q_{Ck}}\}$: The set of semantic types of query Q_C
$L(s, s')$: if a semantic relation between two semantic types has been defined in the Sematic Network, $L(s, s') = 1$; otherwise 0.

4.2 Semantic Analysis

In its Semantic Network, the UMLS defines: (1) a set of broad subject categories, or semantic types, that provide a consistent categorization of all concepts represented in it; (2) a set of useful and important relationships, or semantic relations, that exist between semantic types. The semantic types are the nodes in the network, and the semantic relations between them are the links. In current version, the Semantic Network contains 133 semantic types and 54 relations. A small portion of concepts may have more than one semantic type. During concept extraction, MetaMap will determine which one fits such a concept best in the context. Table 2 shows the definition of random variables on semantic types and relations.

From the semantic point of view, it is reasonable to assume that a concept a is unlikely to be relevant to concept b, if the category of a does not interact from any perspective with the category of b on a hyper semantic level. On the other hand, if a and b are related in certain manner, s_a and s_b should have been linked in the Sematic Network. Based on this assumption, we define the concepts that are relevant to query Q_C as:

$$relevant\ concepts = \{c: s_c \in T\} \quad (6)$$

$$\text{where } T = \{s: \exists s' \in S, L(s, s') = 1\} \quad (7)$$

T is actually the set of all semantic types that are related to query semantic types.

The identification of relevant concepts can be illustrated with an example in Figure 3. We extract and present all concepts in the cloud. To determine the relevant concepts of "scar tissue", we map all concepts to their semantic types (rectangular boxes) in the semantic space. If there is a defined relation (solid edge) between a semantic type and "Pathologic Function", the semantic type of "scar tissue", all concepts mapped to that type will be treated as relevant to "scar tissue". To make it clearer, we mark yellow all boxes that have certain relation with "Pathologic Function", and then mark red all concepts mapped to these yellow boxes. They are the relevant concepts of "scar tissue", from which a more accurate relevance model of "scar tissue" will be estimated. On the contrary, the concepts detected as non-relevant are some spatial concepts, quantitative concepts, and conceptual entities. They are probably not what users want to know, therefore will deteriorate the estimation if not filtered out. If a query contains multiple concepts, we will repeat this process for every concept.

It is worth mentioning that semantic relations are inheritable from parent nodes. In spite of no direct edge between "Pathologic Function" and "Body Substance", since "Pathologic Function" is a child node of "Biologic Function" (defined by "is a" relation), it inherits the "produces" relation between "Biologic Function" and "Body Substance". If "Pathologic Function" has child nodes, this relation is further transitive to them as well.

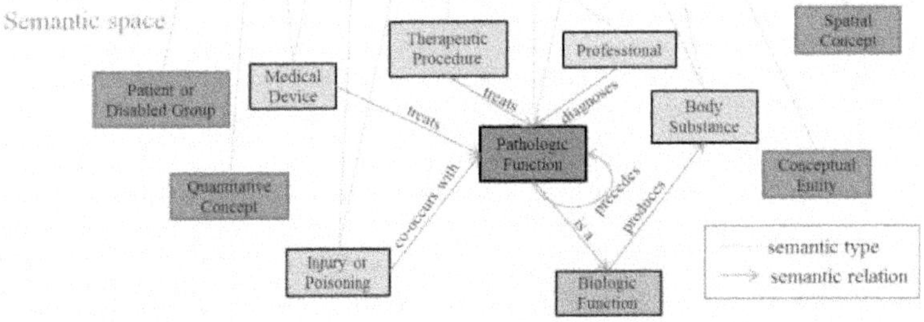

Figure 3: The process of semantic analysis to identify concepts relevant to the query "scar tissue".

4.3 Modeling Semantic Types

We assume that there is a multinomial distribution of concepts for any semantic type in a document. We model the document as a mixture of concept distributions of different semantic types. Given a concept c and a relevant document D_C, we first pick a semantic type s by the probability $P(s|D_C)$, and then sample the concept c from s by the probability $P(c|s, D_C)$. Following this process, we propose a new method to estimate the document model $P(c|D_C)$, instead of using Eq. (5) in RM framework.

$$P(c|D_C) = \sum_s P(s|D_C)P(c|s, D_C) \quad (8)$$

where $P(s|D_C)$ can be treated as the importance of a semantic type in D_C, and $P(c|s, D_C)$ is the concept distribution of this semantic type in D_C.

We are able to estimate $P(c|s, D_C)$ by the maximum likelihood estimation of c in this semantic type, and then smoothed by the collection background model.

$$P(c|s, D_C) = (1-\lambda) \cdot \frac{n(c, D_C)\boldsymbol{I}(s_c = s)}{\sum_{c'} n(c', D_C)\boldsymbol{I}(s_{c'} = s)} + \lambda \cdot P(c|s, coll) \quad (9)$$

where $\boldsymbol{I}$ is the indicator function and $P(c|s, coll)$ is

$$P(c|s, coll) = \frac{\sum_{D_C} n(c, D_C)\boldsymbol{I}(s_c = s)}{\sum_{D_C}\sum_{c'} n(c', D_C)\boldsymbol{I}(s_{c'} = s)} \quad (10)$$

For $P(s|D_C)$, ideally, users could specify what types of information and how much of them they would like to see in a retrieved document. For example, the document should mainly present the "Disease or Syndrome" description, the "Therapeutic Procedure", or a certain combination of both. However, without user input, we are unable to obtain such prior information. In this situation, the best guess for user's need on semantic types is naturally related to estimating it from pseudo relevant documents. Intuitively, the weight of a semantic type depends on the frequency of concepts of this semantic type in the document. On the other hand, according to our new assumption, only the semantic types belonging to T should be taken into account in relevance estimation. Consequently, we propose the following formula to estimate $P(s|D_C)$.

$$P(s|D_C) = \frac{\sum_c n(c, D_C)\boldsymbol{I}(s_c = s)\boldsymbol{I}(s \in T)}{\sum_{s' \in T}\sum_c n(c, D_C)\boldsymbol{I}(s_c = s')} \quad (11)$$

In this formula, the weight of a semantic type from T is proportional to the occurrence of all concepts in this type in the document. Semantic types that are absent from T will receive a null weight, which makes concepts in such semantic types have a null $P(c|D_C)$, and eventually a null $P(c|R_C)$. In other words, R_C will be composed of relevant concepts shown in Eq. (6) only. We name the $P(c|R_C)$ estimated using this approach the Full Concept-based Relevance Model (f-CRM). Both s-CRM and f-CRM may be referred to as CRM or CRMs later.

4.4 Retrieval Using CRM

We describe the workflow of CRM retrieval algorithm in Figure 4. Estimating CRM requires obtaining U_C, a set of pseudo relevant documents. We employ the query likelihood model with a Dirichlet prior for this purpose. Its ranking function is

$$P(Q|D) = \prod_{w \in Q}\left[\frac{n(w, D) + \mu \cdot P(w|coll)}{|D| + \mu}\right]^{n(w,Q)} \quad (12)$$

where $n(w,Q)$ is the frequency of w in Q, $P(w|D)$ is estimated by the maximum likelihood of w in D with Dirichlet smoothing, $P(w|coll)$ is the frequency of w in the collection divided by the total number of terms in the collection, and μ is the smoothing parameter from Dirichlet prior. We set μ to the average document length for each individual data collection [22]. The top M documents ranked by the query likelihood model will be incorporated in U_C.

Relevance models capture the behavior of returned documents but may drift from the original query. In practice, they are usually employed for query expansion to achieve better retrieval results [9, 10, 19]. We carry out the similar procedure for CRM by linearly interpolating it with the maximum likelihood query estimate. Then we obtain the final expanded query model Q_C'.

$$P(c|Q_C') = (1-\omega)\cdot P(c|Q_C) + \omega \cdot P(c|R_C) \qquad (13)$$

where $\omega \in [0,1]$ controls the weight of concepts from CRM. For computational efficiency, we truncate and normalize using the concepts with the highest probabilities [10, 22]. Concepts are sorted in the descending order of $P(c|R_C)$, the top N concepts are selected, and their probabilities are normalized to sum to one.

We utilize the Indri retrieval model for document retrieval in our work. This model combines the language modeling and inference network approaches, and enables modeling structured queries[3] with language modeling estimates in the network [26], and is therefore able to evaluate structured queries derived based on Eq. (7). We will discuss the specific approach to formulating structured queries using the word expression of estimated concepts in Section 5.1.3.

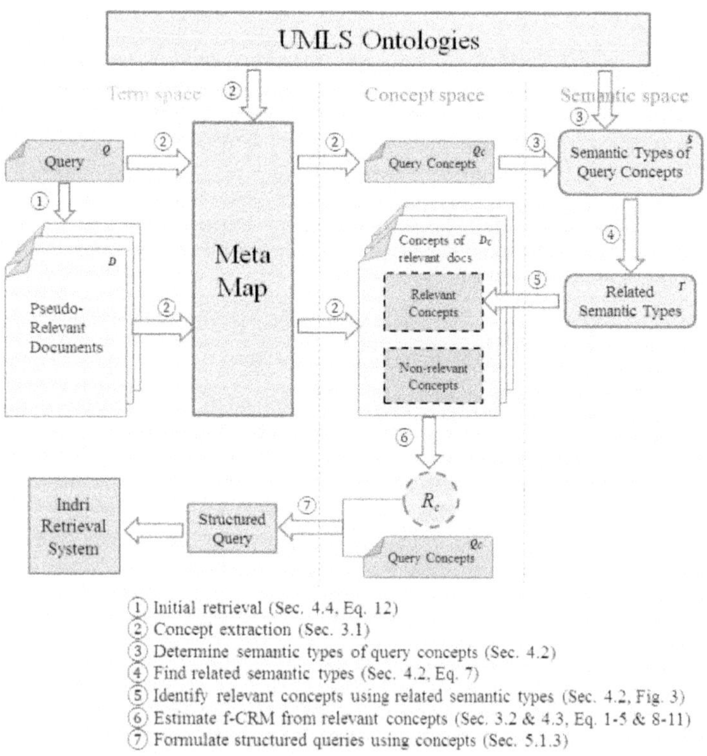

Figure 4: The workflow of the f-CRM retrieval algorithm.

[3] The "structure" typically refers to operators that are used to express constraints between the words in the retrieved documents, such as Boolean and proximity operators [26].

5. EXPERIMENTS

5.1 Experimental Setup

5.1.1 Data Collections

In order to better understand the strengths and weaknesses of CRM, we carefully pick three data collections for evaluation, TREC Genomics 2006, CLEF2013, and OHSUMED. All of them are designed for medical information retrieval, but have quite different characteristics (full-text articles, web pages, and article abstracts). Table 3 provides a summary of these.

The document collection for the TREC 2006 Genomics ad-hoc search task [29] consists of full-text scientific papers from 49 biomedical journals. Its original topics follow the pre-defined templates, such as "What is the role of [**gene**] in [**disease**]?" We derive the topics used in our experiments by only extracting bold-faced terms and discarding the remainder of the template [22]. The relevance is assessed at the document, passage, and aspect level. We only use the judgments at the document level. Two topics without any relevant documents are not used in evaluation.

The CLEF2013 collection comes from the information retrieval task of the eHealth Challenge in the Conference and Labs of the Evaluation Forum 2013 [30]. It is a large web collection covering a broad range of health topics from several online sources, including websites certified by Health on the Net Foundation, as well as other commonly used health and medicine websites (e.g. ClinicalTrial.gov, Diagnosia, and Drugbank). 50 topics are created based on questions that patients realistically posed after reading their discharge summaries. We preprocess the HTML files by extracting textual content using Boilerpipe library.

Apart from the above two collections with relatively long documents, we are also interested in the performance of CRM on short documents, which are assumed to challenge the model by providing a limited amount of data points and decreased sample size of concepts. For this reason, we choose OHSUMED, a collection of titles and abstracts of MEDLINE articles over a five-year period [31]. Its relevance judgments are definitely relevant, partially relevant, or irrelevant. We count both the definitely relevant and the partially relevant as relevant to be consistent with other studies. Five topics without any relevant documents are not used in evaluation. PubMed stopwords list and Porter stemming are applied to all three collections. In all experiments, only the title portion from the original topics is used to construct queries.

5.1.2 Concept Extraction

We use the query likelihood model to acquire pseudo relevant documents. The top 100 documents of each query are gathered and sent to MetaMap for concept extraction. To avoid losing any information during the transformation from Q to Q_C, if any query term (other than stopwords) cannot be mapped to a concept, we will manually extract it as a concept and add to MetaMap, so that such term will be identified by MetaMap in pseudo relevant documents. We find nine such terms in all queries. Most of extracted concepts contain two words (47%), then one word (35%), three words (14%), and less than 5% over three words. In Table 4, we show the statistics of feedback document subsets, and compare them between term space and concept space.

5.1.3 Query Formulation

We use the Indri retrieval system from the Lemur project for indexing and retrieval. Indri has flexible query language and provides multiple operators for us to express concepts in structured queries. The "#1(...)" operator restricts the words of a concept to appear in the exact order. The "#weight(...)" operator assigns different weights to expressions in it. The "#syn(...)"

Table 3: Statistics of three data collections.

	TREC2006	CLEF2013	OHSUMED
Documents	162,259	1,628,533	348,566
Total terms	1,071,091,488	1,459,450,141	35,028,334
Uniq. terms	2,335,219	9,722,143	129,188
Topics	28	50	106
Rel. docs/top.	52	37	45
Doc length	6601	896	100
Query length	7.3	3.4	5.2

Table 4: Statistics of feedback subsets in term space and concept space.

	TREC2006		CLEF2013		OHSUMED	
	Term	Concept	Term	Concept	Term	Concept
Documents	2,277	2,277	4,790	4,790	9,214	9,214
Total terms	17,624,538	7,848,578	11,296,756	4,300,160	1,012,793	760,334
Uniq. terms	205,193	57,076	109,240	26,689	30,273	18,295
Term freq.	86	138	103	161	33	42
Doc length	7,740	3,447	2,358	898	110	83
Qry length	7.3	3.8	3.4	2.0	5.2	3.6

Table 5: Comparison of different CRMs with relevance models (RM), BM25 with pseudo relevance feedback (BM25-FB), and Conceptual Language Model (CLM).

(a) Experimental results on TREC Genomics 2006

	P@5		P@10		nDCG@5		nDCG@10		MAP	
CLM	0.585^{γ}	-	0.504	-	0.612	-	0.572	-	0.401	-
RM	0.569	-2.6%	0.489	-3.0%	0.615	-0.6%	0.568	-0.6%	0.392	-2.2%
BM25-FB	0.531	-9.2%	0.496	-1.5%	0.567	-7.3%	0.552	-3.4%	0.410	2.3%
s-CRM	$0.623^{\beta\gamma}$	6.6%	$0.531^{\alpha\beta\gamma}$	5.4%	$0.674^{\alpha\beta\gamma}$	10.2%	$0.626^{\alpha\beta\gamma}$	9.5%	$0.453^{\alpha\beta\gamma}$	12.9%
f-CRM	$\mathbf{0.662}^{\alpha\beta\gamma}$	13.2%	$\mathbf{0.569}^{\alpha\beta\gamma\delta}$	13.0%	$\mathbf{0.712}^{\alpha\beta\gamma}$	16.5%	$\mathbf{0.668}^{\alpha\beta\gamma\delta}$	16.7%	$\mathbf{0.473}^{\alpha\beta\gamma}$	17.8%

(b) Experimental results on CLEF2013

	P@5		P@10		nDCG@5		nDCG@10		MAP	
CLM	0.500^{β}	-	0.478^{γ}	-	0.503	-	0.494^{γ}	-	0.335^{γ}	-
RM	0.460	-8.0%	0.478^{γ}	0%	0.471	-6.4%	0.483	-2.2%	0.332^{γ}	-0.7%
BM25-FB	0.472	-5.6%	0.432	-9.6%	0.478	-5.1%	0.451	-8.8%	0.282	-15.7%
s-CRM	$0.564^{\alpha\beta\gamma}$	12.8%	$0.548^{\alpha\beta\gamma}$	14.6%	$0.573^{\alpha\beta\gamma}$	13.8%	$0.568^{\alpha\beta\gamma}$	15.0%	$0.364^{\alpha\beta\gamma}$	8.7%
f-CRM	$\mathbf{0.572}^{\alpha\beta\gamma}$	14.4%	$\mathbf{0.572}^{\alpha\beta\gamma\delta}$	19.7%	$\mathbf{0.584}^{\alpha\beta\gamma}$	15.9%	$\mathbf{0.587}^{\alpha\beta\gamma\delta}$	18.9%	$\mathbf{0.369}^{\alpha\beta\gamma}$	10.2%

(c) Experimental results on OHSUMED

	P@5		P@10		nDCG@5		nDCG@10		MAP	
CLM	0.517	-	0.464	-	0.524	-	0.495	-	0.320	-
RM	0.521	0.8%	0.460	-0.9%	0.538	2.7%	0.500	1.1%	0.345^{α}	7.7%
BM25-FB	0.503	-2.7%	0.476	2.5%	0.511	-2.5%	0.498	0.5%	0.342^{α}	6.9%
s-CRM	$0.547^{\alpha\gamma}$	5.7%	$0.501^{\alpha\beta\gamma}$	7.9%	$0.554^{\alpha\gamma}$	5.7%	$0.530^{\alpha\beta\gamma}$	7.2%	$0.355^{\alpha\gamma}$	11.0%
f-CRM	$\mathbf{0.566}^{\alpha\beta\gamma\delta}$	9.6%	$\mathbf{0.514}^{\alpha\beta\gamma\delta}$	10.7%	$\mathbf{0.572}^{\alpha\gamma\delta}$	9.2%	$\mathbf{0.545}^{\alpha\beta\gamma\delta}$	10.1%	$\mathbf{0.356}^{\alpha\gamma}$	11.2%

operator treats all expressions in it as synonyms. The expanded query in Eq. (7) can be implemented by creating a structured query of the form:

$$\#weight(\ (1-\omega)\ EXP_1\ \omega\ EXP_2\ )\ \text{ where}$$

$$EXP_1 = \#weight(\ P(q_{C1}|Q_C)\ \#1(q_{C1}) \ldots P(q_{Ck}|Q_C)\ \#1(q_{Ck})\ )$$

$$EXP_2 = \#weight(\ P(c_1|R_C)\ \#1(c_1) \ldots P(c_N|R_C)\ \#1(c_N)\ ))$$

If a concept c_i has B surface forms $c_i = \{c_{ij}, j = 1 \ldots B\}$, we will replace $\#1(c_i)$ above by $\#syn(\ \#1(c_{i1}) \ldots \#1(c_{iB})\ )$ to include all synonyms.

5.2 Retrieval Results

We now investigate the effectiveness of our models in practice. Two CRMs (s-CRM and f-CRM) are compared with relevance models (RM-3 version) from language modeling framework, and Okapi BM25 with pseudo relevance feedback (BM25-FB) from probabilistic ranking framework, and the state of the art Conceptual Language Models (CLM, the baseline) [22]. Both CRMs and CLM will use the same U_C from the initial retrieval. We follow the same setting of parameters in [22] to estimate the parsimonious language model in CLM. Retrieval performance is evaluated using a variety of metrics, including precision at 5 and 10, nDCG at 5 and 10, and MAP (cutoff at 1000). In order to obtain a fair comparison, we pursue five-fold cross-validation on all models, and then compare their cross-validation performance. We randomize and separate queries into five partitions as evenly as possible. For the k-th (k=1,2,3,4,5) set of queries, we tune the parameters to optimize MAP for the other four sets, and use such parameters to test on the k-th set of queries. The cross-validation performance is the average performance on the five test query sets.

The free parameters trained in cross-validation include: (1) for all models, the number of pseudo relevant documents and the number of expansion terms/concepts in [1,50], with 1 increment in [1,30] and 5 in [30,50], and the expansion weight in [0,1] with 0.1 increment; (2) for CLM, RM, and CRMs, smoothing parameter in [0,1] with 0.1 increment; (3) for CLM, $|\mathcal{C}| \in [1,100]$, with 1 increment in [1,30] and 5 in [30,100]; (4) for BM25-FB, $k_1 \in [1,5]$ with 0.1 increment and $b \in [0,1]$ with 0.05 increment.

Table 5 shows the experimental results of different models on three data collections. The percentage changes over the baseline CLM are listed in the second column. We also conduct one million times randomization tests to compute the significance of the improvements [11]. The superscripts α, β, γ, and δ indicate statistically significant improvements over CLM, RM, BM25-FB, and s-CRM for p<0.05. The best result under each metric is bold.

From the results, two CRM retrieval algorithms consistently outperform CLM, RM and BM25-FB algorithms on all metrics across three data sets. And the improvements are all statistically significant over these three models, except on P@5 from TREC2006 and few metrics from OHSUMED. In general, BM25-

FB performs worse than RM, which is caused by its high sensitivity to parameter selection. We will address this problem in next section. CLM performs better than RM on TREC2006 and CLEF2013, while not as well as RM on OHSUMED because of the small average document length. This observation is consistent with the experiment results on other data sets of short documents reported in [22]. In all five models, f-CRM achieves the best results, substantially improving P@5 by 10%, P@10 by 11%, nDCG@5 by 9%, nDCG@10 by 10%, and MAP by 10%, at least.

CLM in our experiments is able to use hundreds of concepts extracted from the entire document for model estimation, which is quite different from the environment in [22] that only a limited number of concepts assigned to the abstract are available. We compare the results on TREC2006 reported in [22] with those in our experiments (experiment settings are slightly different though). Unsurprisingly, using more concepts for model estimation improves retrieval performance substantially. This confirms the positive effect of concept extraction in our work.

Comparing f-CRM with s-CRM, we find that the full CRM with semantic information consistently produces better results, with an extra 5% improvement over s-CRM on average. In addition, such improvement is statistically significant on most metrics. This validates our new assumption on relevance generation and the approach to modeling semantic types.

We also compare our results with the official best results from data collection campaigns. For CLEF2013, there is no single best model dominating on every metric [30], but f-CRM improves over the best reported results by 8%, 10%, 21%, 26%, and 18% on P@5, P@10, nDCG@5, nDCG@10, and MAP. On TREC2006, the best model reported a 0.5439 document-level MAP, but it was actually calculated using top ranked passages instead of documents [29], which is different from the standard evaluation method we used, and thus makes the results incomparable. However, this best TREC2006 model successfully conducted fine-grained preprocessing [32], such as Greek letter conversion, conditional stemming, and gene symbol handling, to customize algorithms for this particular gene data set, which can also be incorporated in our CRMs for further improvement.

5.3 Parameter Sensitivity

We explore the empirical settings of four parameters: the smoothing parameter λ, the interpolation parameter ω, the number of feedback documents M, and the number of concepts used in query N. In addition to the cross-validation parameters, we run models over all queries and search for their global optimal parameters that yield the best MAP. We investigate parameter sensitivities, and why some models perform well and some not.

5.3.1 Smoothing and Interpolation Parameters

Smoothing is a critical component of any system based on language modeling. The smoothing parameter λ in Eq. (9) controls how much of the background estimate will be used in $P(c|s, D_C)$. The interpolation parameter ω in Eq. (13) controls how much weight will be assigned to CRM concepts in the interpolation with the original query. We plot the performance simplex and contours of the f-CRM in Figure 5 to show the sensitivity of λ and ω on TREC2006. Figures on other collections show similar patterns, so we skip them in the interest of space. In general, λ is not sensitive and has less impact to MAP. [0.2, 0.6] appears a safe interval. However, ω influences the performance significantly. Choosing a small value will relegate CRM to the query likelihood model, while choosing a large value will underestimate the original query. On all data sets, ω in [0.2, 0.8] could yield results better than RM, and in [0.4, 0.6] yields satisfactory results.

5.3.2 Feedback Document Size and Concept Size

M is the number of pseudo relevant documents in U_C. Setting M too small leads to insufficient relevant information for estimation; setting M too large brings in more interference from non-relevant content. N is the number of top-ranked concepts used for retrieval. Ideally, we would like to use all of them; however running thousands of concepts in a query is computationally very expensive. We plot the performance simplex and contours of the f-CRM in Figure 6 to show the sensitivity of M and N on TREC2006. Typically, these two parameters have less sensitivity than the interpolation parameter ω, though very small values of M and N will hurt the performance. For M, the empirical recommendation [6,15] produce satisfactory results on all data sets. For N, initially, the more concepts are added, the better the results become; however, once reaching certain level, the results stay stable. This can be explained by the insight that the concepts added later have a low probability $P(c|R_C)$, which results in a negligible impact on the entire query once it is small enough. The optimal value of N varies from 20 to 50 for different data sets. However, when examining $P(c|R_C)$ of the N-th concept, we find that it is around 0.0047 on every data set. In practice, we can truncate R_C with $P(c|R_C)$>0.0047 for retrieval.

5.3.3 Parameters Estimated from Cross-Validation

For CRMs, all five sets of parameters trained from cross-validation are very consistent with their global optimal parameters, with more than 80% identical and the rest very close. Therefore, CRMs could achieve relatively high cross-validation performance (e.g. MAP 0.473 vs. the global optimal 0.484). The similar trend on parameters can be observed from CLM and RM as well. We attribute this to the reduced parameter sensitivity and good generalization capability of language modeling framework. By way of contrast, BM25-FB appears more sensitive to parameters. Its parameters obtained from each partition in cross-validation are quite different from each other, and the model performs worse on test data using trained parameters.

6. DISCUSSION

In this section we aim to develop a deeper understanding why CRM achieves such significant improvements. First, let us review Table 4 more closely. There are obvious differences on data representation between term space and concept space. For the same data set, the number of unique concepts is much smaller than the number of unique words. This indicates that the dimensionality of concept space is significantly reduced. Besides, the average concept frequency is higher than the average word frequency. Higher concept frequency means that more samples are available for concept estimation. From above observations we conclude that working on concepts yields a denser space for relevance estimation, which should theoretically produce better estimates.

Then, we would like to examine the quality of the empirical distribution of relevance estimated by CRM. Table 6 lists the top10 relevant words or concepts and their probabilities to a given query. We observe that: (1) RM and CLM could obtain some relevant words, but also includes quite a few noisy and non-relevant words such as "et", "al", "usa", and "about.com", which can be pruned by CRM; (2) RM and CLM are unable to keep necessary term dependencies, so that it estimates fuzzy relevance, which comprises of individual words without complete meanings; for example, despite "white", "blood", and "cells" are captured by RM, the meaning they convey is not as precise as the entire concept "white blood cells"; using such relevance for retrieval is prone to erroneously matching documents containing "white

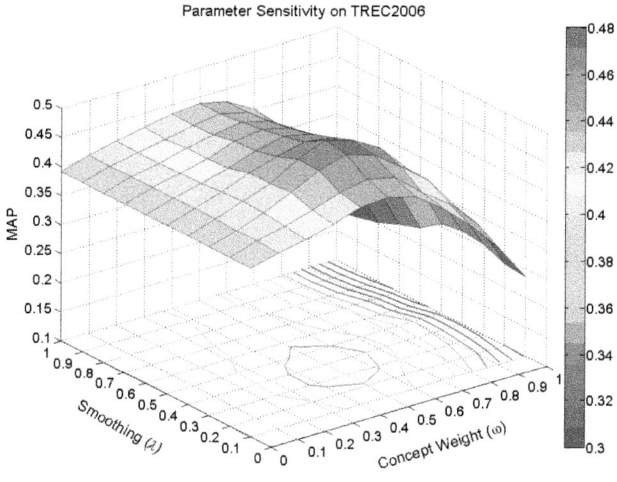

Figure 5: Sensitivity of smoothing parameter λ and concept weight ω to MAP in f-CRM.

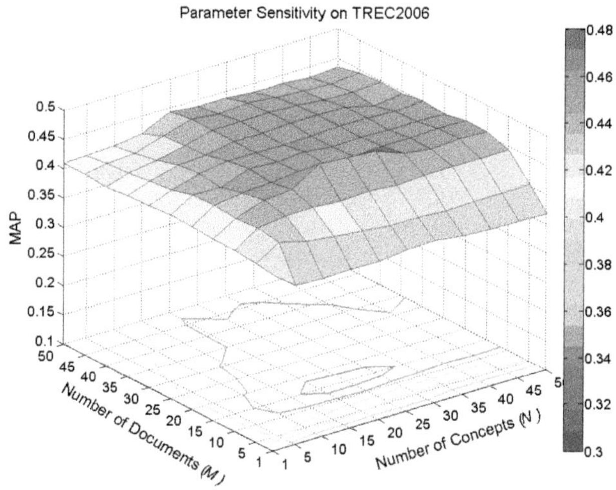

Figure 6: Sensitivity of pseudo relevant document size M and concept size N to MAP in f-CRM.

Table 6: Relevant words or concepts and probabilities estimated from a query by RM, CLM, s-CRM, and f-CRM.

(a) Query: "asystolic arrest"

RM		CLM		Simple CRM		Full CRM	
0.0183	cardiac	0.0193	cardiac	0.0292	cardiac arrest	0.1200	cardiac arrest
0.0163	arrest	0.0173	arrest	0.0193	patient	0.0399	cpr
0.0119	patient	0.0079	resuscitation	0.0154	study	0.0249	ventricular fibrillation
0.0076	al	0.0062	hospital	0.0123	cpr	0.0245	treatment
0.0072	usa	0.0036	epinephrine	0.0089	drug	0.0216	defibrillation
0.0068	et	0.0035	al	0.0086	hospital	0.0202	circulator
0.0061	study	0.0035	et	0.0081	result	0.0185	study
0.0057	resuscitation	0.0035	cpr	0.0081	ventricular fibrillation	0.0181	resuscitation
0.0053	lipid	0.0033	cardiopulmonary	0.0077	treatment	0.0166	first aid
0.0051	heart	0.0029	ventricular	0.0074	resuscitation	0.0127	adrenaline

(b) Query: "white blood cells and bacteria"

RM		CLM		Simple CRM		Full CRM	
0.0328	cells	0.0354	cells	0.0212	white blood cells	0.1028	white blood cells
0.0275	white	0.0215	blood	0.0190	health	0.0569	treatment
0.0267	blood	0.0117	white	0.0142	colon cancer	0.0326	human body
0.0205	colon	0.0064	cancer	0.0133	cells	0.0315	neutrophil
0.0151	cancer	0.0058	colon	0.0119	disease	0.0308	blood
0.0134	about.com	0.0055	immune	0.0112	treatment	0.0297	cells
0.0104	health	0.0039	basophil	0.0110	infection	0.0257	bacteria
0.0077	killer	0.0039	wbc	0.0110	human body	0.0220	thymus-dependent lymphocyte
0.0074	bacteria	0.0032	com	0.0097	blood	0.0216	immune system
0.0073	leukocyte	0.0032	body	0.0086	acute myeloblastic leukaemia	0.0200	bone marrow

people" and "red blood cells"; (3) CRM is able to deliver explicit relevance with natural concepts, which conforms to human language and comprehension; (4) CRM is able to deliver more accurate relevance, by providing more concepts closely related to the query; (5) CRM assigns higher probabilities to relevant concepts, due to the increased sample size and the reduced dimensionality of the space; (6) semantic analysis further refines concepts by removing those not directly related to the query, e.g. "patient", "hospital", and "health". All these observations empirically demonstrate CRM indeed produces better relevance. Query expansion resulting from such relevance will better represent user's underlying search intent. And retrieval using these expanded concepts would precisely match document terms with the same dependencies. All these factors together eventually improve the retrieval performance by a significant degree.

Despite both CLM and CRM are LM-based models that are built on concepts, they have major differences in modeling concepts. In CLM, concepts serve as an intermediate form to connect pseudo relevant documents, document terms, and queries, where the important information such as word expression of concepts and term dependencies within concepts is ignored. However, in our work, CRM is proposed to model and utilize such information from the beginning, and factors in the semantic information in the domain. Experimental results demonstrate that all this information is critical to retrieval results, and should be formally included by future concept-based retrieval models.

Another interesting finding is that, CRMs perform even better on TREC2006 and CLEF2013 than on OHSUMED, which is in accordance with our conjecture and the observation on CLM. The documents in the first two sets are full-text articles and web pages, much longer than the abstracts in OHSUMED, so they provide sufficient data points for accurate statistical estimation. This again supports our motivation of modeling relevance by constructing a denser, more relevant concept space. It is encouraging to observe that CRMs also work effectively on short documents.

7. CONCLUSSION

We have presented a concept-based relevance model for improved estimation of relevance. Our method models natural concepts, so is able to keep the strong dependencies inside of a concept, generate the explicit expression of relevance, and precisely match terms with the same dependencies. The empirical relevance distribution estimated by CRMs confirms that CRMs unify synonyms or different surface forms of a concept, leading to reduced dimensionality of the space, increased sample size of a concept, and eventually more accurate and reliable estimates of the relevance. We show that, when semantic analysis is enabled, f-CRM is able to further improve relevance estimation by modeling semantic types and relevant concepts.

We evaluate the effectiveness of CRMs for information retrieval on different types of data sets. Experimental results demonstrate that the models are highly effective. They completely and consistently dominate conceptual language models, relevance models, and BM25 with pseudo relevance feedback across data sets. In fact, f-CRM achieves statistically significant improvement over conceptual language models by at least 9% on any metric of precision@5, precision@10, nDCG@5, nDCG@10, and MAP.

In future work, we would like to experiment CRM on generic or other domain data sets. It would be interesting to use the publicly available Wikipedia concepts in CRM, where ample contextual information is available for new exploration. A potential improvement can be made by estimating a query-specific ω, so that concept weights will be customized for each query. We are also interested in expanding our research on CRM to the probabilistic ranking framework.

8. REFERENCES

[1] K. S. Jones, S. Robertson, D. Hiemstra, and H. Zaragoza. Language modelling and relevance. In *Language Modeling for Information Retrieval*, pp. 57-71, 2003.

[2] K. S. Jones, S. Walker, and S. Robertson, A probabilistic model of information retrieval: development and comparative experiments, Part 1. *Information Processing and Management*, 36, no. 6, pp. 779-808, 2000.

[3] J. M. Ponte and W. B. Croft. A language modeling approach to information retrieval. In *Proc. of SIGIR*, 275-281, 1998.

[4] L. Lafferty and C. Zhai. Probabalistic relevance models based on document and query generation. In *Language Modeling for Information Retrieval*, pp. 1-10, 2003.

[5] V. Lavrenko and W. B. Croft. Relevance-based language models. In *Proceedings of SIGIR*, pp. 120-127, 2001.

[6] S. Vargas, P. Castells, and D. Vallet. Explicit relevance models in intent-oriented information retrieval diversification. In *Proceedings of SIGIR*, pp. 75-84, 2012.

[7] Y. Lv and C. Zhai. Positional relevance model for pseudo-relevance feedback. In *Proc. of SIGIR*, pp. 579-586, 2010.

[8] D. Metzler, T. Strohman, Y. Zhou, and W.B. Croft. Indri at TREC 2005: Terabyte Track. In *Proceedings of TREC*, 2005.

[9] D. Trieschnigg, D. Hiemstra,F. de Jong, and W. Kraaij. A cross-lingual framework for monolingual biomedical information retrieval. In *Proc. of CIKM*, pp. 169-178, 2010.

[10] N. Limsopatham, C. MacDonald, and I. Ounis. Learning to combine representations for medical records search. In *Proceedings of SIGIR*, pp. 833-836, 2013.

[11] M. D. Smucker, J. Allan, and B. Carterette. A comparison of statistical significance tests for information retrieval evaluation. In *Proceedings of CIKM*, pp. 623-632, 2007.

[12] J. Li and H. Yan. Peking University at the TREC 2006 Terabyte Track. In *Proceedings of TREC*, 2006.

[13] E. Voorhees. Overview of TREC 2003. In *Proceedings of TREC*, pp. 1-13, 2003.

[14] C.J. van Rijsbergen. Information Retrieval. Butterworths, London, England, 1979.

[15] F. Ahmed and A. Nurnberger. Evaluation of n-gram conflation approaches for Arabic text retrieval. *Journal of Amer. Soc. Inf. Sci. Technology*, 60, no. 7, 1448-1465, 2009.

[16] F. Diaz and D. Metzler. Improving the estimation of relevance models using large external corpora. In *Proceedings of SIGIR*, pp. 154-161, 2006.

[17] C. Wang and R. Akella. A hybrid approach to extracting disorder mentions from clinical notes. In *Proc. of AMIA Joint Summits on Translational Science*, pp. 183-187, 2015.

[18] B. He, J.X. Huang, and X. Zhou. Modeling term proximity for probabilistic information retrieval models. *Journal of Information Science* 181, no. 14, pp. 3017–3031, 2011.

[19] A.-J. Nasreen, J. Allan, W.B. Croft, et al. UMass at TREC 2004: Novelty and HARD. In *Proceedings of TREC*, 2004.

[20] P. Castells, M. Fernandez, and D. Vallet. An adaptation of the vector-space model for ontology-based information retrieval. *IEEE Transactions on Knowledge and Data Engineering*, 19(2):261–272, 2007.

[21] O. Egozi, S. Markovitch, and,E. Gabrilovich. Concept-based information retrieval using explicit semantic analysis. *ACM Transactions on Information Systems* 29, no. 2, 2011.

[22] E. Meij, D. Trieschnigg, M. de Rijke, and W. Kraaij. Conceptual language models for domain-specific retrieval. *Information Processing and Management* 46:448-469, 2010.

[23] T. Tao and C. Zhai. An exploration of proximity measures in information retrieval. In *Proc. of SIGIR*, pp. 295-302, 2007.

[24] D. Metzler. Automatic feature selection in the Markov random field model for information retrieval. In *Proceedings of CIKM*, pp. 253-262, 2007.

[25] J. Gao, J.-Y. Nie, et al. Dependence language model for information retrieval. In *Proc. of SIGIR*, pp. 170-177, 2004.

[26] D. Metzler and W.B. Croft. Combining the language model and inference network approaches to retrieval. *Information Processing and Management*, 40(5): 735-750, 2004.

[27] D. Metzler and W. B. Croft. Latent concept expansion using Markov random fields. In *Proc. of SIGIR*, pp. 311-318, 2007.

[28] J. Osborne, B. Gyawali, and T. Solorio. Evaluation of YTEX and MetaMap for clinical concept recognition. *Working Notes of the CLEF Evaluation Labs and Workshop*, 2013.

[29] W. Hersh, A. Cohen, P. Roberts, et al. TREC 2006 genomics track overview. In *Proceedings of TREC*, 2006.

[30] H. Suominen, S. Salantera, et al. Overview of the ShARe/CLEF eHealthEvaluation Lab 2013. *Information Access Evaluation, LNCS*, 8138: 212-231, 2013.

[31] W. Hersh, C. Buckley, T. Leone, et al. OHSUMED: An interactive retrieval evaluation and new large test collection for research. In *Proceedings of SIGIR*, pp. 192-201, 1994.

[32] W. Zhou, C. Yu, et al. A concept-based framework for passage retrieval in genomics. In *Proc. of TREC*, 2006.

PlateClick: Bootstrapping Food Preferences Through an Adaptive Visual Interface

Longqi Yang[†,‡], Yin Cui[†,‡], Fan Zhang[†,‡], John P. Pollak[‡], Serge Belongie[†,‡], Deborah Estrin[†,‡]
[†]Department of Computer Science, Cornell University; [‡]Cornell Tech
{ylongqi, ycui, fanz}@cs.cornell.edu; {jpp9, sjb344, de226}@cornell.edu

ABSTRACT

Food preference learning is an important component of wellness applications and restaurant recommender systems as it provides personalized information for effective food targeting and suggestions. However, existing systems require some form of food journaling to create a historical record of an individual's meal selections. In addition, current interfaces for food or restaurant preference elicitation rely extensively on text-based descriptions and rating methods, which can impose high cognitive load, thereby hampering wide adoption.

In this paper, we propose *PlateClick*, a novel system that bootstraps food preference using a simple, visual quiz-based user interface. We leverage a pairwise comparison approach with only visual content. Using over 10,028 recipes collected from Yummly, we design a deep convolutional neural network (CNN) to learn the similarity distance metric between food images. Our model is shown to outperform state-of-the-art CNN by 4 times in terms of mean Average Precision. We explore a novel online learning framework that is suitable for learning users' preferences across a large scale dataset based on a small number of interactions (≤ 15). Our online learning approach balances exploitation-exploration and takes advantage of food similarities using preference-propagation in locally connected graphs.

We evaluated our system in a field study of *227* anonymous users. The results demonstrate that our method outperforms other baselines by a significant margin, and the learning process can be completed in less than one minute. In summary, *PlateClick* provides a light-weight, immersive user experience for efficient food preference elicitation.

Categories and Subject Descriptors

H.4.m [**Information Systems Applications**]: Miscellaneous; I.2.6 [**Artificial Intelligence**]: Learning

Keywords

Food preference elicitation; visual interface; online learning

CIKM '15 19-23 October, 2015 Melbourne, Australia
© 2015 ACM. ISBN 978-1-4503-3794-6/15/10 ...$15.00.
DOI: http://dx.doi.org/10.1145/2806416.2806544.

1. INTRODUCTION

The problem of capturing and understanding people's food preferences has attracted substantial attention from industry (e.g., Yelp and Foursquare) and academia [12,13,17,38]. Food preferences guide our diet choices [32] which in turn have a strong effect on our personal health and social lives [32]. A recipe advice system [13,27] could more effectively coach users to prepare healthier meals at home if alternative food suggestions provided were appealing to them. This is important because healthy diet recommendations are of no benefit if users don't adopt them. Another application area that could leverage user preferences is commercial restaurant recommender systems like Yelp and Foursquare. The recommendations will be more accurate and personalized if the system output is tuned to the user's diet profile. However, food preference is notoriously difficult to learn because of its dependence on context (e.g., evolving personal goals). Existing systems and algorithms suffer from several limitations that interfere with efficient learning and wide user adoption:

Data sparsity. Current food preference learning systems require longitudinal records of the meals that users have eaten [12,13,17,38]. These historical data traces [11] typically come from location sensing, which is not always related to food preference, or burdensome food journaling, which is often abandoned after short periods of adoption [9]. As a result, data points are too sparse to provide enough food preference information.

High cognitive load. Preference elicitation [29], in which users are asked to rate different food items explicitly (on a scale from 1 to 5) [12,17], is an approach that is complementary to the above longitudinal methods. While text-based instruments and rating methods [5,10,35,43] effectively address the *cold-start* problem [23,34,42] in movie recommender systems, the counterpart for food preference is especially hard for users [9] as it is time consuming [28] and presents a high cognitive load [8].

Insufficient Visual Understanding. Traditional methods mainly use food tags and other metadata for learning tasks [12,17]. However, as people's diet decisions are greatly influenced by visual appearances of meals [9], analysis of image features can provide a valuable signal for diet profiling and food preference elicitation.

In this paper, we propose ***PlateClick*, a novel system for efficient food preference elicitation using a simple, visual quiz-based user interface**. *PlateClick* alleviates the limitations mentioned above with deep understanding of food images and a user-friendly visual interface. To

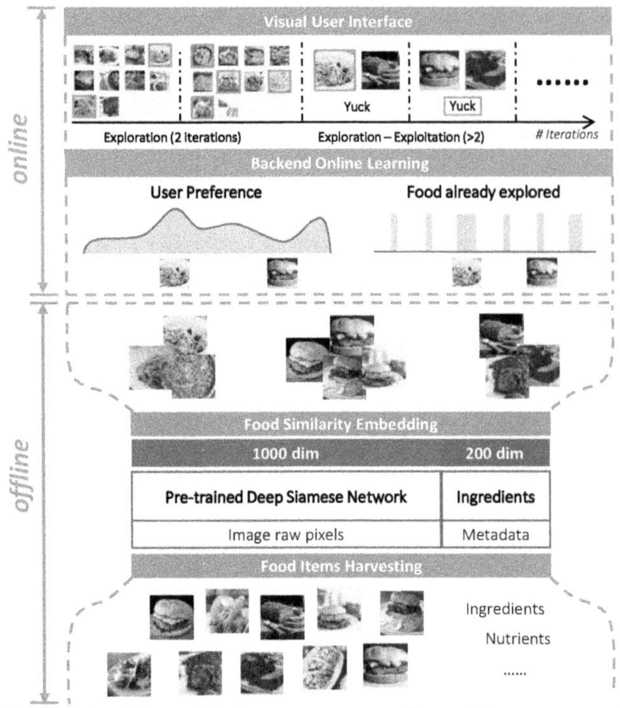

Figure 1: *PlateClick* system pipeline. The system is divided into two major parts: *Offline preprocessing*, which is surrounded by *green dotted line* and *Online preference learning*, which is surrounded by *blue dotted line.*

the best of our knowledge, this is the first system and algorithm that learns users' food preferences through real-time interactions without any requirements of diet history. We developed this system as a lightweight, easily accessible web service that can be completed within 60 seconds. Through a field study with *227* anonymous users in the wild, we show that our system is able to predict the food items that a user likes/dislikes with high accuracy. The system pipeline of *PlateClick* is shown in Fig. 1, which consists of offline and online stages with several components, as follows.

Food Items Harvesting. We pulled 12,000 main dish recipes with their images and metadata (ingredients, nutrients, tastes, etc.) via the Yummly API [1] and filter out image outliers. The final dataset has 10,028 food items across various cuisines (American, Asian, Mexican, Italian, etc.)

Food Similarity Embedding. In order to tame a large number of food items and facilitate image understanding, we learn the image similarity distance metric based on labels from the Food-101 dataset [4] using a deep Siamese network [7]. With the trained network, we extract *1,000 dim* visual features for each food image. The method we propose improves the performance of other state-of-the-art visual feature extraction approaches. We append *200 dim* ingredients features to visual features, resulting in an embedding of the food items into a *1,200 dim* space in which similar items are nearby one another and dissimilar ones are farther away.

Visual User Interface. The process of our food preference elicitation consists of several iterations. We explore the advantages of image picking and pairwise comparison in interface design, both of which offer a potentially improved user experience [8,28]. In each of the first two iterations, we present ten images and users are asked to tap on *all the ones they like*. In each subsequent iteration, we present a pair of food images and ask users either to tap on *whichever they prefer* or click *yuck*, indicating a preference for neither.

Backend Online Learning. The backend of our system consists of a novel online learning algorithm that explores the similarity between food items. Our algorithm is inspired by label propagation [44] in locally connected graphs and the Exponentiated Gradient Algorithm for bandit settings (EXP3) [2]. We demonstrate that this algorithm is more effective in our proposed workflow than other baselines.

Compared to traditional food preference learning systems, our work offers 3 major contributions and points of novelty.

- We get rid of the requirements for users' historical diet records and completely bootstrap food preference from scratch. This design enables *context aware preference learning* that adapts preference information in various conditions.
- We propose a novel image similarity measure that significantly outperforms state-of-the-art algorithms. By leveraging an improved embedding of food items, we simplify the UI by making it completely image based. This offers opportunities for personal interpretation [28] and can provide an immersive experience with personalized, adaptive information [9].
- We design a novel online learning algorithm that can support real-time elicitation of food preference from modest number (≤ 15) of pairwise comparisons on a large scale food image database ($> 10,000$ instances). The pairwise comparison method is known to have lower cognitive load [15], and our system is thus more user-friendly.

We envision that *PlateClick*, a light-weight and efficient food preference elicitation system, will provide a personalized user experience capable of fueling a wide range of applications in domains including health care, diet planning, and restaurant recommendation.

2. RELATED WORK

Collaborative Filtering. As one of the most popular algorithms adopted in current recommender systems, collaborative filtering (CF) [18] has been widely studied in a variety of applications. The main idea of this method is to predict and learn a user's preferences based on similarity measures such as user-based CF [18] and item-based CF [33]. It has also been shown that latent factor models [21] and matrix factorization [31] are promising to predict users' ratings for previously unobserved items.

A major limitation of collaborative filtering is its requirement for historical user data. Although several techniques have been proposed to address the cold-start problem [23, 42], the performance of CF is still largely dependent on the number of active users, availability of contextual information [42] and observed ratings for different items [23]. In the case of food preference learning, it's typically difficult to get access to a user's diet history since meal journaling is burdensome [9]. Therefore, in the design of *PlateClick*, we don't assume any prior knowledge of the users.

Preference elicitation. To alleviate the cold-start problem mentioned above, several models of *preference elicitation* have been proposed in recent years. The most prevalent method of elicitation is to train decision trees to poll users

[1]http://developer.yummly.com

in a structured fashion [10,14,30,35,45]. These questions are either generated in advance and remain static [30] or change dynamically based on real-time user feedback [10,14,35,45]. In addition, another previous work explores the possibility of eliciting item ratings directly from the user [5,43]. This process can either be carried at item-level [43] or within-category (e.g., movies) [5].

The preference elicitation methods we mentioned above largely focus on the domain of movie recommendations [5, 30, 35, 43] and visual commerce [10] (e.g., cars, cameras) where items can be categorized based on readily available metadata. When it comes to real dishes, however, categorical data (e.g., cuisines) and other associated information (e.g., cooking time) possess a much weaker connection to a user's food preferences. Through the design of *PlateClick*, we leverage the visual representation of each meal so as to better capture the process through which people make diet decisions.

Food preference learning system. Most existing food preference learning approaches are hybrids of historical record mining and rating elicitation [12,13,17,38,40]. To avail oneself of these systems to promote healthy eating, one is often required to record daily meal intake and provide this information as a bootstrapping resource to a diet recommender system [12,13,38]. After that, several food items are selected for display based on matching scores between meal metadata and the user's previous choices. For each item provided, the user is prompted to enter a rating on a scale from 1 to 5.

To the best of our knowledge, no existing systems take visual features – arguably one of the most important factors in assisting people's daily food choices [9] – into consideration. Additionally, the most common methods adopted in food preference elicitation (i.e. text based interface and numerical rating scale) impose a high cognitive load on the user [8] and are susceptible to noisy and unreliable responses. Inspired by elicitation strategies in other domains (e.g. crowdsourcing [6], housing [15]), we propose a simplified, purely visual interface that presents users with simple pairwise comparisons. Through our field study with anonymous users, we show that this lightweight interface can promote efficient food preference learning.

3. METADATA PREPROCESSING

For 12,000 main dishes recipes pulled from Yummly API, we filter out entries with unrelated (or missing) image content, resulting in a final dataset $\mathcal{S}$ containing 10,028 food items, i.e., $\mathcal{S} = \{s_1, s_2, ..., s_{10028}\}$. As illustrated in Fig.1, apart from visual features, we append *200 dim* ingredient features as the representation of each food image. The ingredient feature vector is calculated according to the following pre-processing steps:

1. *Keyword extraction and lemmatization.* For each ingredient appearing in the metadata, we extract keywords from its description and apply lemmatization; see Table 1.

2. *Aggregation and Filtering.* We aggregate and count the occurrences of each ingredient appearing in our dataset. We select top 200 most frequent ingredients [2] as our list of ingredient features.

3. *Feature Vector Calculation.* For each food item $s_i \in \mathcal{S}$, its d_{ingr} = *200 dim* normalized ingredient feature vector $\boldsymbol{g}^{s_i} = [g_1^{s_i}, ..., g_{d_{ingr}}^{s_i}]$ is finally calculated based on whether ingredient j appears in food item s_i's ingredient list $Ingr\{s_i\}$, as Equation (1) shows:

$$g_j^{s_i} = \begin{cases} 1 \,/\, |Ingr\{s_i\}| & : j \in Ingr\{s_i\} \\ 0 & : j \notin Ingr\{s_i\} \end{cases} \quad (1)$$

original ingredient	filtered ingredient
low moisture ***mozzarella***	***mozzarella***
fresh ***mozzarella***	***mozzarella***
less sodium ***beef broth***	***beef broth***
lower sodium ***beef broth***	***beef broth***
chicken ***egg***s	***egg***
soft-boiled ***egg***	***egg***

Table 1: Keyword extraction and lemmatization.

4. FOOD SIMILARITY EMBEDDING

4.1 Training the Deep Siamese Network

Recent advances in similarity metric learning with Deep Convolutional Neural Networks (CNNs) have resulted in breakthroughs in areas including Face Verification [37], Image Retrieval [41], Geo-localization [24] and Product Design [3]. The CNN architectures in these works are based on the Siamese Network [7], which is trained on a large number of paired inputs of similar and dissimilar examples. In light of the prior efforts mentioned above, we adopt this approach to generate a distance embedding for meals.

The proposed CNN architecture (Food-CNN) is illustrated in Fig. 2. The inputs of Food-CNN are a pair of color food images $x, y \in \mathcal{S}$, each of size $227 \times 227 \times 3$. Then, each image proceeds through an identical feature extraction CNN containing several layers from Convolution to Batch Normalization. Finally, the outputs of the last layer are used as their low-dimensional feature embeddings $f(x), f(y)$. The architecture from the first Convolution layer to the last Fully Connected layer (i.e. layers in dashed line bounding box in Fig.2) is the same as the architecture that achieved state-of-the-art image classification performance on ImageNet [22]. For each of the layers, the numbers at the top specify its window size and step size (Convolution and Max Pooling); the numbers at the bottom specify the size of its output feature map. For example, the first convolution layer takes a $227 \times 227 \times 3$ color image from image data layer as the input and convolves it with 96 filters. Each filter has a size of $11 \times 11 \times 3$ and convolves the image on a grid with step size 4×4. In this sense, the output of the first Convolution layer is a 55×55 feature map with 96 channels. We add a final Batch Normalization layer to normalize the *1000 dim* feature vector so that each dimension has zero mean and unit variance within a training batch. Batch Normalization provides a faster convergence rate and higher accuracy in practice [19].

Our goal of Food-CNN is to learn a low dimensional feature embedding that pulls similar food items together and pushes dissimilar food items far away. Specifically, we want $f(x)$ and $f(y)$ to have small distance (close to 0) if x and y are similar items; otherwise, they should have distance larger than a margin m. Therefore, we choose Contrastive

[2]We will incorporate more sophisticated methods such as *tf-idf* and homonyms/synonyms handling in the future.

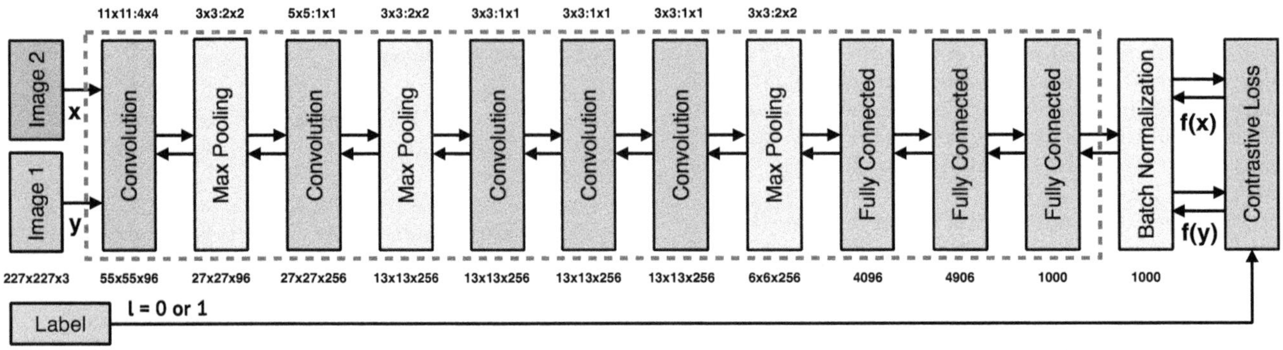

Figure 2: Food-CNN architecture for supervised food similarity distance metric learning.

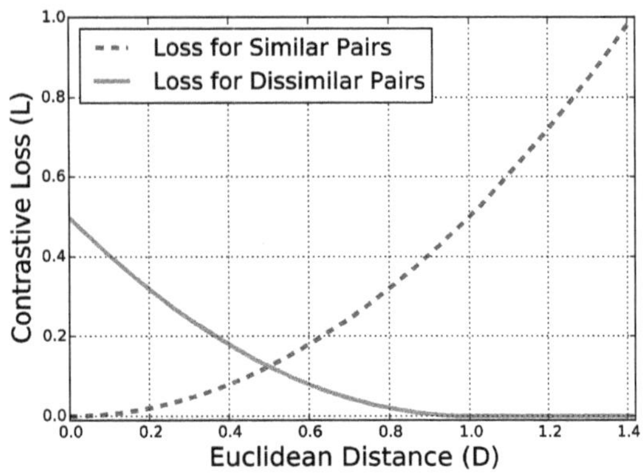

Figure 3: Contrastive Loss function with $m = 1$.

Loss proposed in [16] as the loss function to optimize Food-CNN, which can be expressed as:

$$\mathcal{L}(x, y, l) = \frac{1}{2} l D^2 + \frac{1}{2}(1 - l) \max(0, m - D)^2 \qquad (2)$$

where similarity label $l \in \{0, 1\}$ indicates whether the input pair of food items x, y are similar or not ($l = 1$ for similar, $l = 0$ for dissimilar), $m > 0$ is the margin for dissimilar items and $D = \|f(x) - f(y)\|_2$ is the Euclidean Distance between $f(x)$ and $f(y)$ in embedding space.

As illustrated in Fig. 3, Contrastive Loss function exactly matches our goal. Minimizing the loss in Eqn. (2) pulls similar food images closer and pushes dissimilar ones apart as it penalizes similar pairs by their distances quadratically and dissimilar pairs by their squared differences of the distances to the margin m if they are smaller than m.

Training a deep Siamese Network usually requires huge amount of training data that can't fit in memory. To address this problem, we adopt Nesterov's Accelerated Gradient Descent method [26] with Momentum algorithm [36]. We use back-propagation to compute the gradient of the loss with respect to the parameters of each layer. Suppose we have an n-layer CNN:

$$f(x) = g_n(g_{n-1}(\dots g_i(\dots g_1(x)\dots))) \qquad (3)$$

where $g_i(.)$ represents the computation of i-th layer (e.g., convolution, pooling etc.), x, y and $f(x), f(y)$ represent the input and output pairs of the Siamese Network, respectively. We adopt function $\mathcal{L}(.)$ to calculate the loss of the input pairs x, y as $\mathcal{L}(x, y, l)$. To minimize loss by updating parameters W_i of i-th layer, we need the gradient of the loss with respect to W_i: $\frac{\partial \mathcal{L}(.)}{\partial W_i} = \frac{\partial \mathcal{L}(.)}{\partial g_i} \times \frac{\partial g_i}{\partial W_i}$. Using back-propagation, $\frac{\partial \mathcal{L}(.)}{\partial g_i}$ can be calculated with the chain rule: $\frac{\partial \mathcal{L}(.)}{\partial g_i} = \frac{\partial \mathcal{L}(.)}{\partial g_n} \times \frac{\partial g_n(.)}{\partial g_{n-1}} \times \dots \times \frac{\partial g_{i+1}(.)}{\partial g_i}$. Therefore, for k-th layer $g_k(.)$, we only need to calculate $\frac{\partial g_k(.)}{\partial g_{k-1}}$ and $\frac{\partial g_k(.)}{\partial W_k}$. We use the implementation of gradient descent and back-propagation in Caffe [20], an open source deep learning framework.

Since the food dataset $\mathcal{S}$ pulled from Yummly doesn't include categorical similarity annotations, we trained Food-CNN on the Food-101 dataset [4], which is the largest food image dataset so far and contains 101 food categories and 101,000 food images. We sampled 75,750 same pairs and 757,500 different pairs from the training set to train our Food-CNN.

4.2 Feature Extraction

After the training process, we use the pre-trained Food-CNN to extract visual features from images in our dataset. For each item $s_i \in \mathcal{S}$, we feed the food image to pre-trained feature extraction layers (i.e. layers in blue dashed line bounding box in Fig. 2) and get the feature vector $\tilde{\boldsymbol{v}}^{s_i}$. We normalize $\tilde{\boldsymbol{v}}^{s_i}$ so that it has unit ℓ_1 norm: $v_i^{s_i} = \tilde{v}_i^{s_i} / (\sum_{i=1}^{d_{vis}} |\tilde{v}_i^{s_i}|)$, where $\tilde{\boldsymbol{v}}^{s_i} = [\tilde{v}_1^{s_i}, \dots, \tilde{v}_{d_{vis}}^{s_i}]^T$ and $\boldsymbol{v}^{s_i} = [f_1^{s_i}, \dots, f_{d_{vis}}^{s_i}]^T$ are the feature vectors before and after normalization, respectively; $d_{vis} = 1,000$ is the dimension of visual features.

We then concatenate the visual features $\boldsymbol{v}^{s_i}$ with ingredient features $\boldsymbol{g}^{s_i}$ to create a *1,200 dim* feature embedding $\boldsymbol{f}^{s_i} = [\boldsymbol{v}^{s_i}, \boldsymbol{g}^{s_i}]$ for each food item $s_i \in \mathcal{S}$.

5. ONLINE PREFERENCE LEARNING

5.1 Online Settings and Framework

As discussed in previous sections, each food item $s_i \in \mathcal{S}$ has a *1,200 dim* feature vector $\boldsymbol{f}^{s_i}$ in the embedding space. Building upon the offline feature extraction results, we model the interaction between user and our backend system at iteration $t, (t \in \mathcal{R}^+, t = 1, 2, ..., T)$ as Fig. 4 shows. The symbols that will be used in our algorithms are defined as follows:

$\mathcal{K}_t$: Set of food items that are presented to user at iteration t ($\mathcal{K}_0 = \emptyset$). $\forall k \in \mathcal{K}_t$, $k \in \mathcal{S}$;

$\mathcal{L}_{t-1}$: Set of food items that user *prefer(select)* among $\{k | k \in \mathcal{K}_{t-1}\}$. $\mathcal{L}_{t-1} \subseteq \mathcal{K}_{t-1}$;

$\boldsymbol{p}^t = [p_1^t, ..., p_{|\mathcal{S}|}^t]$: User's preference distribution on all food items $s_i (i = 1, ..., |\mathcal{S}|)$, where $\|\boldsymbol{p}^t\|_1 = 1$. $\boldsymbol{p}^0$ is initialized as $p_i^0 = \frac{1}{|\mathcal{S}|}$;

$\mathcal{B}_t$: Set of food images that have been already explored until iteration t ($\mathcal{B}_0 = \emptyset$). $\mathcal{B}_i \subseteq \mathcal{B}_j (i < j)$;

Based on the workflow depicted in Fig. 4, for each iteration t, backend system updates vector $\boldsymbol{p}^{t-1}$ to $\boldsymbol{p}^t$ and set

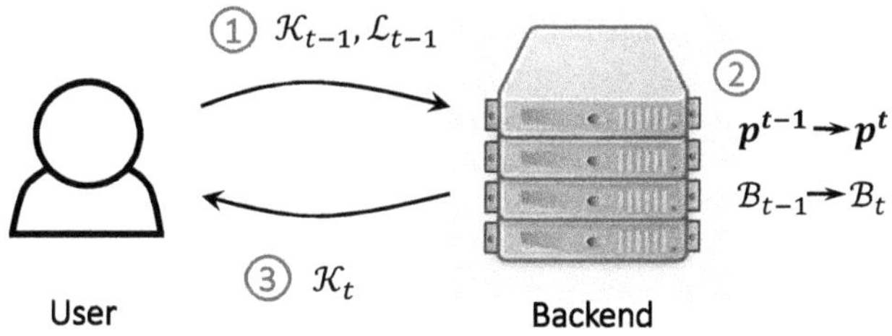

Figure 4: User-system interaction at iteration t.

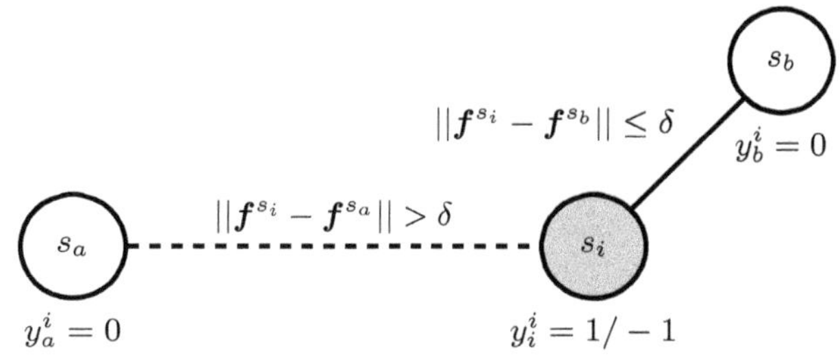

Figure 5: Locally connected graph with item s_i.

$\mathcal{B}_{t-1}$ to $\mathcal{B}_t$ based on users' selections $\mathcal{L}_{t-1}$ and previous image set $\mathcal{K}_{t-1}$. After that, it decides the set of images that will be immediately presented to the user (i.e., $\mathcal{K}_t$). Our food preference elicitation framework can be formalized in Algorithm. 1. The core procedures are *update* and *select*, which will be described in the following subsections for more details.

Algorithm 1: Food Preference Elicitation Framework

Data: $\mathcal{S} = \{s_1, ..., s_{10028}\}$, $\mathcal{F} = \{\boldsymbol{f}^{s_1}, ..., \boldsymbol{f}^{s_{10028}}\}$
Result: $\boldsymbol{p}^T$

```
B_0 = ∅, K_0 = ∅, L_0 = ∅, p^0 = [1/|S|, ..., 1/|S|] ;
for t ← 1 to T do
    [B_t, p^t] ← update(K_{t-1}, L_{t-1}, B_{t-1}, p^{t-1}) ;
    K_t ← select(t, B_t, p_t) ;
    if t equals T then
        return p^T
    else
        ShowToUser(K_t) ;
        L_t ← WaitForSelection() ;
```

5.2 User State Update

Based on user's selections $\mathcal{L}_{t-1}$ and the image set $\mathcal{K}_{t-1}$, the *update* module renews user's state from $\{\mathcal{B}_{t-1}, \boldsymbol{p}^{t-1}\}$ to $\{\mathcal{B}_t, \boldsymbol{p}^t\}$. Our intuition and assumption behind following algorithm design is that people tend to have close preferences for similar food items in *1,200 dim* space.

5.2.1 Preference vector $\boldsymbol{p}^t$

Our strategy of updating preference vector $\boldsymbol{p}^t$ is inspired by Exponentiated Gradient Algorithm in bandit settings (EXP3) [2]. Specifically, at iteration t, each p^t_i in vector $\boldsymbol{p}^t$ is updated by:

$$p^t_i \leftarrow p^{t-1}_i \times e^{\frac{\beta u^{t-1}_i}{p^{t-1}_i}} \tag{4}$$

where β is the exponentiated coefficient that controls update speed and $\boldsymbol{u}^{t-1} = \{u^{t-1}_1, ..., u^{t-1}_{|\mathcal{S}|}\}$ is the update vector used to adjust each preference value.

In order to calculate update vector $\boldsymbol{u}$, we formalize user's selection process as a data labeling problem [44] where for $s_i \in \mathcal{L}_{t-1}$, label $y^{t-1}_i = 1$ and for $s_j \in \mathcal{K}_{t-1} \backslash \mathcal{L}_{t-1}$, label $y^{t-1}_j = -1$. Thus, the label vector $\boldsymbol{y}^{t-1} = \{y^{t-1}_1, ..., y^{t-1}_{|\mathcal{S}|}\}$ provided by user is:

$$y^{t-1}_i = \begin{cases} 1 & : s_i \in \mathcal{L}_{t-1} \\ 0 & : s_i \notin \mathcal{K}_{t-1} \\ -1 & : s_i \in \mathcal{K}_{t-1} \backslash \mathcal{L}_{t-1} \end{cases} \tag{5}$$

For update vector $\boldsymbol{u}$, we expect that it is close to label vector $\boldsymbol{y}$ but with smooth propagation of label values to nearby neighbors (For convenience, we omit superscript that denotes current iteration). The update vector $\boldsymbol{u}$ can be regarded as a soften label vector compared with $\boldsymbol{y}$. To make the solution more computationally tractable, for each item s_i with $y_i \neq 0$, we construct a locally connected undirected graph G^i as Fig. 5 shows: $\forall s_j \in \mathcal{S}$, add an edge (s_i, s_j) if $\|\boldsymbol{f}^{s_i} - \boldsymbol{f}^{s_j}\| \le \delta$ ($\delta = 35$ in our implementation). The labels $\boldsymbol{y}^i$ for vertices s_j in graph G^i are calculated as $y^i_j = 0 (j = 1, \ldots, |\mathcal{S}| \setminus i), y^i_i = y_i$.

For each locally connected graph G^i, we fix u^i_i value as $u^i_i = y^i_i$ and propose the following regularized optimization method to compute other elements ($\forall u^i_j, j \neq i$) of update vector $\boldsymbol{u}^i$, which is inspired by the traditional label propagation method [44]. Consider the problem of minimizing following objective function $Q(\boldsymbol{u}^i)$:

$$\min_{\boldsymbol{u}^i} \sum_{j=1, j\neq i}^{|\mathcal{S}|} w_{ij}(y^i_i - u^i_j)^2 + \sum_{j=1, j\neq i}^{|\mathcal{S}|} (1 - w_{ij})(u^i_j - y^i_j)^2 \tag{6}$$

In Eqn. (6), w_{ij} represents the similarity measure between food item s_i and s_j:

$$w_{ij} = \begin{cases} e^{-\frac{1}{2\alpha^2}\|\boldsymbol{f}^{s_i} - \boldsymbol{f}^{s_j}\|^2} & : \|\boldsymbol{f}^{s_i} - \boldsymbol{f}^{s_j}\| \le \delta \\ 0 & : \|\boldsymbol{f}^{s_i} - \boldsymbol{f}^{s_j}\| > \delta \end{cases} \tag{7}$$

where $\alpha^2 = \frac{1}{|\mathcal{S}|^2} \sum_{i,j \in \mathcal{S}} \|\boldsymbol{f}^{s_i} - \boldsymbol{f}^{s_j}\|^2$.

The first term of the objective function $Q(\boldsymbol{u}^i)$ is the *smoothness constraint* as the update value for similar food items should not change too much. The second term is the *fitting constraint*, which makes $\boldsymbol{u}^i$ close to the initial labeling assigned by user (i.e. $\boldsymbol{y}^i$). However, unlike [44], in our algorithm, the trade-off between these two constraints is dynamically adjusted by the similarity between item s_i and s_j where similar pairs are weighed more with smoothness and dissimilar pairs are forced to be close to initial labeling.

With Eqn. (6) being defined, we can take the partial derivative of $Q(\boldsymbol{u}^i)$ with respect to different u^i_j as follows:

$$\frac{\partial Q(\boldsymbol{u}^i)}{u^i_{j, j\neq i}} = 2w_{ij}(u^i_j - u^i_i) + 2(1 - w_{ij})(u^i_j - y^i_j) = 0 \tag{8}$$

As $u^i_i = y^i_i$, then:

$$u^i_j = w_{ij} u^i_i = w_{ij} y^i_i (j = 1, 2, ..., \mid \mathcal{S} \mid) \tag{9}$$

After all $\boldsymbol{u}^i$ are calculated, the original update vector $\boldsymbol{u}$ is then the sum of $\boldsymbol{u}^i$, i.e. $\boldsymbol{u} = \sum_i \boldsymbol{u}^i$. The pseudo code for the algorithm of updating preference vector is shown in Algorithm.2 for details.

5.2.2 *Explored food image set* $\mathcal{B}_t$

In order to balance the *exploitation* and *exploration* in image selection phase, we maintain a set $\mathcal{B}_t$ that keeps track of all similar food items that have already been visited by user and the updating rule for $\mathcal{B}_t$ is as follows:

$$\mathcal{B}_t \leftarrow \mathcal{B}_{t-1} \cup \{s_i \in \mathcal{S} | min_{s_j \in \mathcal{K}_{t-1}} \|\boldsymbol{f}^{s_i} - \boldsymbol{f}^{s_j}\| \leq \delta\} \quad (10)$$

With the algorithms designed for updating preference vector $\boldsymbol{p}^t$ and explored image set $\mathcal{B}_t$, the overall functionality of procedure *update* is shown in Algorithm.2.

Algorithm 2: User state update Algorithm - *update*

Function `update`($\mathcal{K}_{t-1}, \mathcal{L}_{t-1}, \mathcal{B}_{t-1}, \boldsymbol{p}^{t-1}$)
  input : $\mathcal{K}_{t-1}, \mathcal{L}_{t-1}, \mathcal{B}_{t-1}, \boldsymbol{p}^{t-1}$
  output: $\mathcal{B}_t, \boldsymbol{p}^t$
  $\boldsymbol{u} = [0, ..., 0], \mathcal{B}_t = \mathcal{B}_{t-1}, \boldsymbol{p}^t = \boldsymbol{p}^{t-1}$
  for $i \leftarrow 1$ **to** $|\mathcal{S}|$ **do**
    // preference update
    for s_j *in* $\mathcal{K}_{t-1}$ **do**
      $u_i \leftarrow u_i + (-1)^{(s_j \in \mathcal{L}_{t-1})-1} w_{ij}$
    $p_i^t = p_i^{t-1} e^{\frac{\beta u_i}{p_i^{t-1}}}$
    // explored image set update
    if `min`($\|\boldsymbol{f}^{s_i} - \boldsymbol{f}^{s_j}\|, \forall s_j \in \mathcal{K}_{t-1}$) $\leq \delta$ **then**
      $\mathcal{B}_t \leftarrow \mathcal{B}_t \cup \{s_i\}$
  // normalize p^t s.t. $\|p^t\|_1 = 1$
  `normalize`($\boldsymbol{p}^t$)

Algorithm 3: Kmeans++ Algorithm for Exploration

Function `k-means-pp`($\mathcal{S}$, n)
  input : $\mathcal{S}, n$
  output: $\mathcal{K}_t$
  $\mathcal{K}_t$=`random`($\mathcal{S}$)
  while $|\mathcal{K}_t| < n$ **do**
    prob $\leftarrow [0, ..., 0]_{|\mathcal{S}|}$
    for $i \leftarrow 1$ **to** $|\mathcal{S}|$ **do**
      $\text{prob}_i \leftarrow min(\|\boldsymbol{f}^{s_i} - \boldsymbol{f}^{s_j}\|^2 | \forall s_j \in \mathcal{K}_t)$
    sample $s_m \in \mathcal{S}$ with probability $\propto \text{prob}_m$
    $\mathcal{K}_t \leftarrow \mathcal{K}_t \cup \{s_m\}$

5.3 Images Selection

After updating user state, the *select* module then picks food images that will be presented in the next round. In order to trade-off between exploration and exploitation in our algorithm, we propose different images selection strategies based on current iteration t.

5.3.1 *Food Exploration*

For each of the first two iterations, we select ten different food images by using *K-means++* [1] algorithm, which is a seeding method used in *K-means clustering* and can guarantee that selected items are evenly distributed in the feature space. For our use case, *K-means++* algorithm is summarized in Algorithm.3.

5.3.2 *Food Exploitation-Exploration*

Starting from the third iteration, users are asked to make pairwise comparisons between food images. To balance the Exploitation and Exploration in our algorithm design, we always select one image from the area with higher preference value based on current $\boldsymbol{p}^t$ and another one from *unexplored* area, i.e. $\mathcal{S} \backslash \mathcal{B}_t$. (Both selections are **random** in a given subset of food items). With above explanations, the image selection method we propose in this application is shown in Algorithm 4.

Algorithm 4: Images Selection Algorithm - *select*

Function `select`($t, \mathcal{B}_t, \boldsymbol{p}^t$)
  input : $t, \mathcal{B}_t, \boldsymbol{p}^t$
  output: $\mathcal{K}_t$
  $\mathcal{K}_t = \emptyset$
  if $t \leq 2$ **then**
    $\mathcal{K}_t \leftarrow$ `k-means-pp`($\mathcal{S}$, *10*) // K-means++
  else
    // 99th percentile (top 1%)
    threshold $\leftarrow$ `percentile`($\boldsymbol{p}^t$, *99*)
    topSet $\leftarrow \{s_i \in \mathcal{S} | p_i^t \geq \text{threshold}\}$
    $\mathcal{K}_t \leftarrow$ [`random`(*topSet*), `random`($\mathcal{S} \backslash \mathcal{B}^t$)]

6. EXPERIMENTAL EVALUATION

6.1 Food Similarity Embedding

We examine and evaluate the clustering performance of Food-CNN model on Food-101 [4] dataset, where each image is tagged with a categorical label. We first extract *1,000 dim* visual feature for each food image in the test set. After that, we explore k, where $k = 1, 2, \ldots, N$ (N is the size of the test set), nearest neighbors of each food image and calculate the Precision and Recall values for each k:

Suppose $\mathcal{N}_k^i$ is the set of k nearest neighbors of item i under category $\mathcal{C}_i$, then the Precision and Recall values are:

$$Precision = \frac{|\{j | \forall j \in \mathcal{N}_k^i \wedge j \in \mathcal{C}_i\}|}{|\mathcal{N}_k^i|} \quad (11)$$

$$Recall = \frac{|\{j | \forall j \in \mathcal{N}_k^i \wedge j \in \mathcal{C}_i\}|}{|\mathcal{C}_i|} \quad (12)$$

In order to measure the overall performance of our embedding method on Food-101 test set, we average the Precision/Recall values over all food images for each method and plot Precision-Recall Curve (PR Curve) as Fig. 6 shows. We use mean Average Precision (mAP), which corresponds to the area under PR Curve, as the quantitative comparison metric. The mAP value of the ideal algorithm is equal to 1.

We compare our Food-CNN model with several state-of-the-art feature extraction methods: 1. *Pretrained AlexNet deep neural network*: This is the state-of-the-art feature extraction method using pretrained AlexNet [22]. We take *1,000 dim* feature representation from the output of the last fully-connected layer. 2. *SIFT+Bag of visual Words(BoW)*: As the most popular method among hand-crafted feature representations, SIFT [25] has been shown to be effective in several applications. We extract visual features using 1000

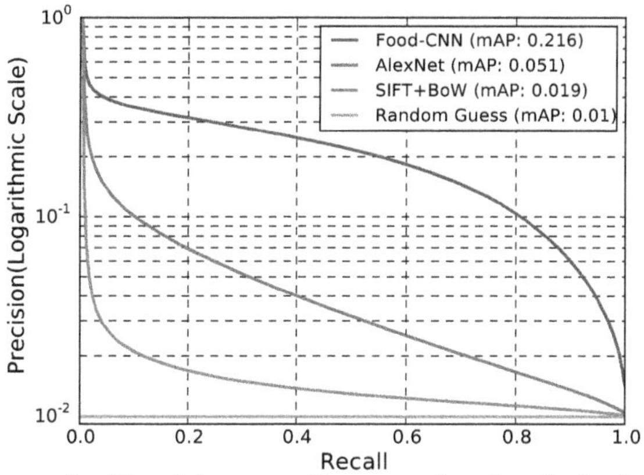

Figure 6: Precision-recall curve for food similarity embedding(*mAP:* mean Average Precision, which represents area under each curve).

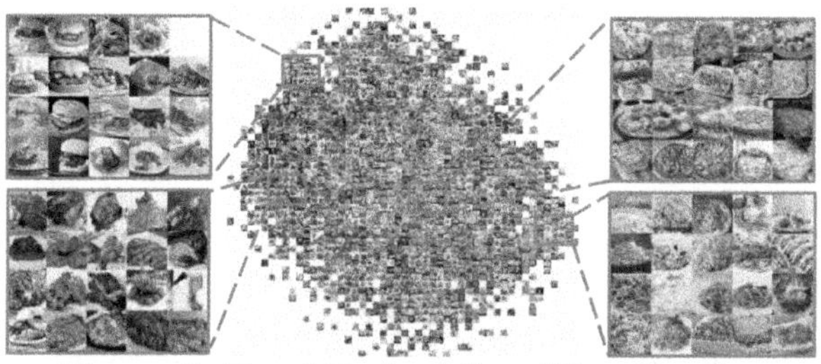

Figure 7: Food Embedding Visualization.

words so as to guarantee that it has the same feature dimension with our Food-CNN.

As can be seen in our results, although *SIFT+BOW* and *AlexNet* greatly outperform random guess baseline, they lack discriminative power for food images because these models are mainly designed for the general clustering purpose. With Food-CNN, we can achieve 4 times performance improvements over state-of-the-art models in terms of mAP value. Algorithm that with much better clustering power can help the whole system understand visual content and thus improve the efficiency of online preference learning.

To further verify and visualize the generalization power of our system, for each of the recipe images that collected from Yummly, we embed it into *1200 dim* feature space by first using Food-CNN to extract *1000 dim* visual representation and then concatenate it with *200 dim* ingredients feature. We project all image representations to 2-D plane by using t-Distributed Stochastic Neighbor Embedding(t-SNE) [39] method. As shown in Fig. 7, we divide the 2-D plane into several blocks and for each block, we sample a representative food image resides in that area. The final embedding results clearly show that our method can effectively group similar food items (recipes) together and push dissimilar items away based on their visual appearances and ingredients metadata. For example, in Fig. 7, we show that burgers, noodles, pizzas, and meat are grouped in different areas of the feature space.

6.2 Online user study

We conducted field study among 227 anonymous users that recruited from social networks and university mailing lists. The experiment was approved by Institutional Review Board (ID: 1411005129) at Cornell University. All participants were required to use this system independently for three times. Each time the study consisted of following two phases:

Training Phase. Users played with *PlateClick* for the first T iterations and the system learnt and elicited preference vector $\boldsymbol{p}^T$ based on the algorithms proposed in this paper or baseline methods, which will be discussed later. We randomly picked T from set $\{5, 10, 15\}$ at the beginning but made sure that each user experienced different values of T only once.

Testing Phase. After T iterations of training, users entered the testing phase, which consisted of 10 rounds of pairwise comparisons. We picked testing images based on preference vector $\boldsymbol{p}^T$ that learnt from online interactions: One of them was selected from food area that user liked (i.e. item with top 1% preference value) and the other one from the area that user disliked (i.e. item with bottom 1% preference value) Both of the images were picked **randomly** among **unexplored** food items.

6.2.1 Prediction accuracy

In order to show the learning performance of our algorithm, we compare it with several combinatorial baselines that mentioned next. Users encountered these online learning algorithms **randomly** when they logged into the system:

LE+EE: This is the online learning algorithm proposed in this paper that combines the ideas of **L**abel propagation, **E**xponentiated Gradient algorithm for user state update and **E**xploitation-**E**xploration strategy for images selection.

LE+RS: This algorithm retains our method for user state update (**LE**) but **R**andom **S**elect images to present to user without any exploitation or exploration.

OP+EE: As each item is represented by *1200 dim* feature vector, we can adopt the idea of regression to tackle this online learning problem (i.e. learning weight vector $\boldsymbol{w}$ such that $\boldsymbol{w}\boldsymbol{f}^{s_i}$ is higher for item s_i that user prefer). Hence, we compare our method with **O**nline **P**erceptron algorithm that updates $\boldsymbol{w}$ whenever it makes error, i.e. if $y_i\boldsymbol{w}\boldsymbol{f}^{s_i} \leq 0$, assign $\boldsymbol{w} \leftarrow \boldsymbol{w} + y_i\boldsymbol{w}\boldsymbol{f}^{s_i}$, where y_i is the label for item s_i (pairwise comparison is regarded as binary classification such that the food item that user select is labeled as +1 and otherwise -1). In this algorithm, we retain our strategy of images selection (i.e. **EE**).

OP+RS: The last algorithm is the **O**nline **P**erceptron that mentioned above but with **R**andom images **S**election strategy.

Among 227 participants in our study, 58 of them finally used algorithm **LE+EE**, 57 used **OP+RS**. For the rest of users (112), half of them (56) tested **OP+EE** and the other half (56) tested **LE+RS**. Overall, the participants for different algorithms are totally random so that the performances of different models are directly comparable.

After all users going through training and testing phases, we calculate the prediction accuracy of each **individual user** and aggregate them based on the context that they encountered (i.e. the number of training iterations T and the algorithm settings that mentioned above). The prediction accuracies and their cumulative distributions are shown in Fig. 8, 9 and 10 respectively.

Length effects of training iterations. As can be seen in Fig. 8 and Fig. 9, the prediction accuracies of our online learning algorithm are all significantly higher than the baselines.The algorithm performance is further improved with longer training period. As is clearly shown in Fig. 9, when

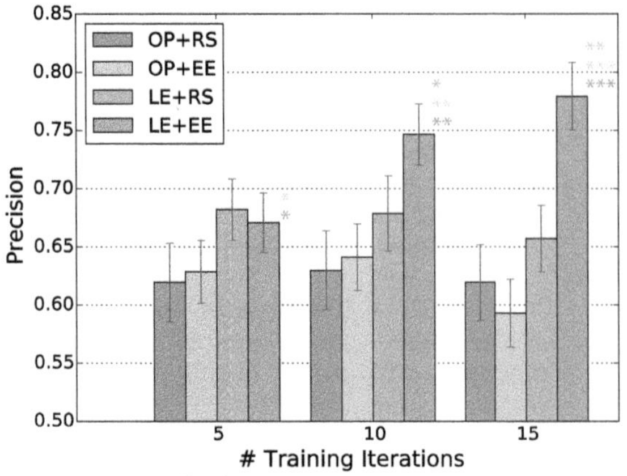

Figure 8: Prediction accuracy for different algorithms in various training settings (asterisks represent different levels of statistical significance: $***$: $p < 0.001$, $**$: $p < 0.01$, $*$: $p < 0.05$).

the number of training iterations reaches *15*, about half of the users will experience the prediction accuracy that exceeds 80%, which is fairly promising and decent considering small number of interactions that system elicited from scratch. The results above justify that *PlateClick*, as an online preference learning system, can adjust itself to explore users' preference area as more information is available from their choices. For the task of item-based food preference bootstrapping, our system can efficiently balance the exploration-exploitation while providing reasonably accurate predictions.

Comparison across different algorithms. As mentioned previously, we compared our algorithm with some obvious alternatives. Unfortunately, according to the results shown in Fig. 8 and Fig. 10, none of these algorithms works very well and the accuracy of prediction is actually decreasing as the user provides more information. Additionally, as is shown in Fig. 10, our algorithm has particular advantages when users are making progress (i.e. the number of training iterations reaches 15). The reasons why these techniques are not suited for our application is mainly due to the following limitations:

Random Selection. Within a limited number of interactions, random selection can not maintain the knowledge that it has already learned about the user (exploitation), nor explore unknown areas (exploration). In addition, it's more likely that the system will choose food items that are very similar to each other and thus hard for the user to make decisions. Therefore, after short periods of interactions, the system is messed up, and the performance degrades.

Underfitting. The algorithm that will possibly have the underfitting problem is the online perceptron (**OP**). For our application, each food item is represented by *1200 dim* feature vector and **OP** is trying to learn a separate hyperplane based on a limited number of training data. As each single feature is directly derived from deep neural network, the linearity assumptions made by perceptron might yield wrong predictions for the dishes that haven't been explored before.

6.2.2 System efficiency

As another two aspects of online preference elicitation system, computing efficiency and user experience are also very important metrics for system evaluation. Therefore, we recorded the program execution time and user response

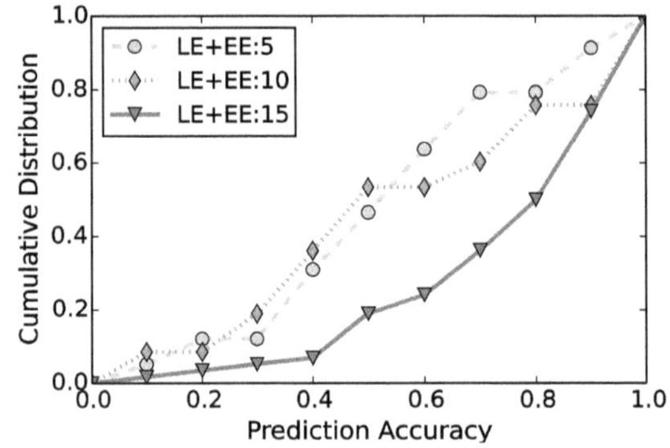

Figure 9: Cumulative distribution of prediction accuracy for *LE+EE* algorithm (Numbers in the legend represent the values of T through training phase).

time as a lens into the real-time performance of *PlateClick*. As shown in Fig. 11(b), the program execution time is about $0.35s$ for the first two iterations and less than $0.025s$ for the iterations afterwards[3]. Also, according to Fig. 11(a), the majority of users can make their decisions in less than $15s$ for the task of comparison among ten food images while the payload for the pairwise comparison is less than $2-3s$. As a final cumulative metric for the system overhead, it is shown in Table 2 that even for 15 iterations of training, users can typically complete the whole process within 53 seconds, which further justify that *PlateClick* is a light-weight user-friendly visual interface for efficient food preference elicitation.

# Iter: 5	# Iter: 10	# Iter: 15
28.75s	39.74s	53.22s

Table 2: Average time to complete training phase.

6.2.3 User Behavior

An interesting phenomenon that we observed from our field study is that there exists obvious correlation between *total user response time* and *Precision* of our model: Preference learning of *PlateClick* tends to be more accurate if the user made decisions within shorter period of time. As is shown in Fig. 12, we plot scatter diagram that contains all data points that users generated when they used *PlateClick* under **LE+EE** algorithm setting and with 15 number of training iterations ($T = 15$). Apparently, most of the points (blue ones) are above the dotted line in Fig. 12 and the expected total response time is higher for those users with lower prediction accuracy. The possible reason behind this result is that if food pairs are hard to be distinguished with each other, the responses from user will likely to have large noise and uncertainty,[4] which in turn affects the performance of online learning system.

7. DISCUSSION

In this section we discuss limitations and future directions for *PlateClick*.

[3]Our web system implementation is based on Amazon EC2 t2-micro Linux 64-bit instance

[4]User engagement is a critical issue in our application. We will conduct studies/interviews on the effects of human behavior in the future.

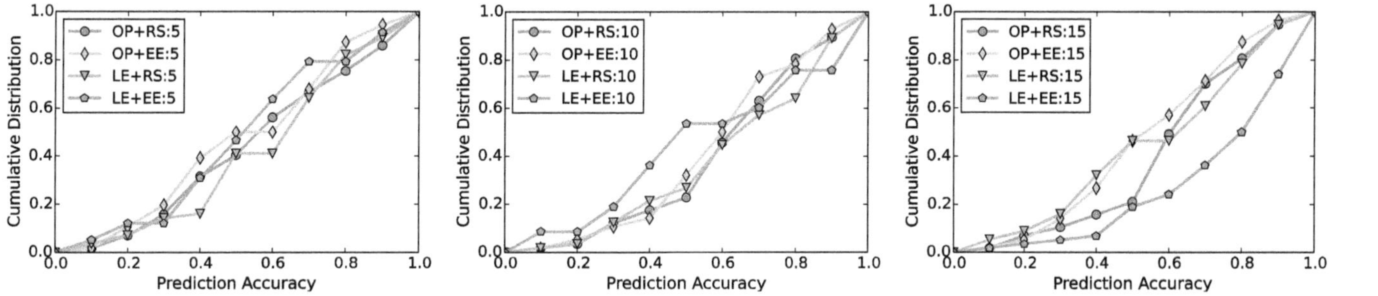

(a) # training iterations: 5 (b) # training iterations: 10 (c) # training iterations: 15

Figure 10: Comparison of cumulative distribution of prediction accuracy across algorithms.

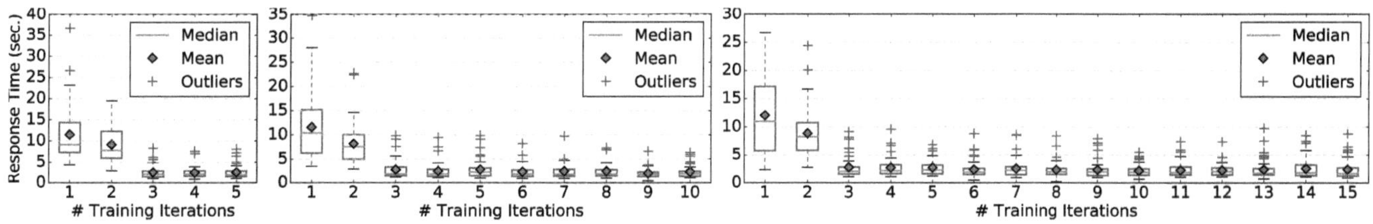

(a) User Response Time

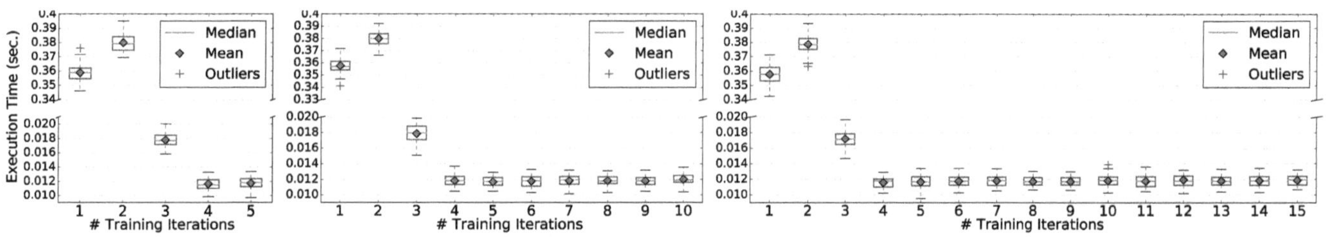

(b) System Execution Time

Figure 11: Timestamp records for user response and system execution.

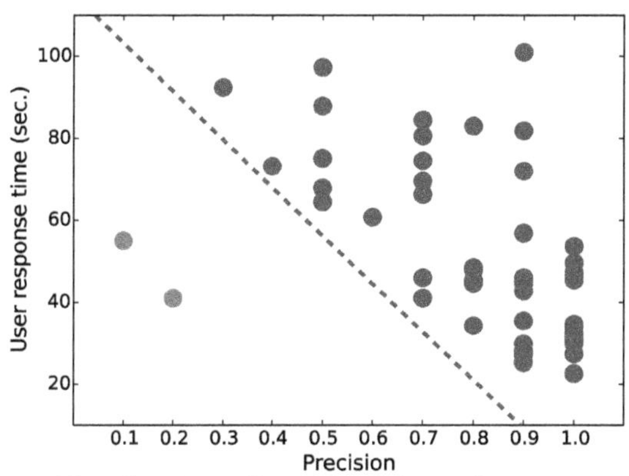

Figure 12: Scatter diagram of total user response time under different precision of model prediction (Points in the graph represent experimental results under LE+EE algorithm setting and with 15 number of training iterations).

Special diets. We noticed in the user study that our current system can not be efficiently used by people with special diets (e.g., vegetarian, vegan, kosher and halal) due to the limits of our image corpus. It's very unlikely that the system will select anything such a user would like from the current main-dishes dataset. It will degrade user experience to repeatedly show dishes that are not to their taste. In the future, we need to consider different diets and curate special food datasets accordingly.

Food courses and diversity. People's food preferences are highly dependent on context as determined by factors such as time of day. It is unnecessarily difficult and possibly confounding to compare dishes across different courses (e.g., between desserts and dinner). In our current system, we mainly focus on food items from main dishes, which conveniently constrains the space of choices available to the user. Future work will incorporate dishes across different courses (e.g., breakfast and lunch) and enrich the diversity of our dataset.

Healthy recommendation. One of the most important applications that could build on *PlateClick* is a healthy food recommendation system. Combining a user's diet profile and recipe nutrient metadata, we could recommend appealing but healthier food alternatives to users so that they are more likely to follow the system's advice in their daily lives and choices. Suggestions guided by people's preferences will be more effective and persuasive than a traditional strategy that lack awareness of what a given person actually likes. This was our initial motivation for developing *PlateClick* and we hope to pursue integration with existing nutritional behavior change apps.

8. CONCLUSION

In this work, we introduced *PlateClick*, a novel visual interface for real-time food preference elicitation from scratch. Compared with previous solutions and online learning systems, we don't assume any prior knowledge of the user. In addition, we greatly simplify the elicitation user interface by replacing traditional text-based instruments with visual contents and leveraging a pairwise comparison method. We demonstrated that these design choices reduce user burden and cognitive load when using the elicitation system.

Although our algorithmic framework was originally designed for visual content based food preference learning, the techniques proposed in this paper could be used to enhance the interplay between human hedonic and content similarities in solving general *human-in-the-loop* problems. We envision that *PlateClick*, an efficient and user-friendly food preference learning system, could be used to capture personal diet profiles and fuel a wide range of applications in healthcare and commercial recommender systems.

9. ACKNOWLEDGMENTS

We would like to thank Dr. Curtis Cole for suggesting the development of food preference modeling and Dr. Thorsten Joachims for discussion of ML algorithms. Also, we appreciate the anonymous reviewers for insightful comments. This research is partly funded by AOL-Program for Connected Experiences, NSF grant IIS-1344587 and further supported by the small data lab at Cornell Tech which receives funding from UnitedHealth Group, Google, Pfizer, RWJF, NIH and NSF.

10. REFERENCES

[1] D. Arthur and S. Vassilvitskii. k-means++: The advantages of careful seeding. In *ACM-SIAM symposium on Discrete algorithms*, 2007.

[2] P. Auer, N. Cesa-Bianchi, Y. Freund, and R. E. Schapire. The nonstochastic multiarmed bandit problem. *SIAM Journal on Computing*, 2002.

[3] S. Bell and K. Bala. Learning visual similarity for product design with convolutional neural networks. *ACM Trans. on Graphics*, 2015.

[4] L. Bossard, M. Guillaumin, and L. Van Gool. Food-101 – mining discriminative components with random forests. In *ECCV*, 2014.

[5] S. Chang, F. M. Harper, and L. Terveen. Using groups of items for preference elicitation in recommender systems. In *CSCW*, 2015.

[6] X. Chen, P. N. Bennett, K. Collins-Thompson, and E. Horvitz. Pairwise ranking aggregation in a crowdsourced setting. In *WSDM*, 2013.

[7] S. Chopra, R. Hadsell, and Y. LeCun. Learning a similarity metric discriminatively, with application to face verification. In *CVPR*, 2005.

[8] V. Conitzer. Eliciting single-peaked preferences using comparison queries. In *AAMAS*, 2007.

[9] F. Cordeiro, E. Bales, E. Cherry, and J. Fogarty. Rethinking the mobile food journal: Exploring opportunities for lightweight photo-based capture. In *CHI*, 2015.

[10] M. Das, G. De Francisci Morales, A. Gionis, and I. Weber. Learning to question: leveraging user preferences for shopping advice. In *KDD*, 2013.

[11] D. Estrin. Small data, where n = me. *Commun. ACM*, 57(4):32–34, Apr. 2014.

[12] J. Freyne and S. Berkovsky. Intelligent food planning: personalized recipe recommendation. In *ACM IUI*, 2010.

[13] G. Geleijnse, P. Nachtigall, P. van Kaam, and L. Wijgergangs. A personalized recipe advice system to promote healthful choices. In *ACM IUI*, 2011.

[14] N. Golbandi, Y. Koren, and R. Lempel. Adaptive bootstrapping of recommender systems using decision trees. In *WSDM*, 2011.

[15] S. Guo and S. Sanner. Real-time multiattribute bayesian preference elicitation with pairwise comparison queries. In *AISTATS*, 2010.

[16] R. Hadsell, S. Chopra, and Y. LeCun. Dimensionality reduction by learning an invariant mapping. In *CVPR*, 2006.

[17] M. Harvey, B. Ludwig, and D. Elsweiler. Learning user tastes: a first step to generating healthy meal plans? In *International Workshop on Recommendation Technologies for Lifestyle Change*, 2012.

[18] J. L. Herlocker, J. A. Konstan, A. Borchers, and J. Riedl. An algorithmic framework for performing collaborative filtering. In *SIGIR*, 1999.

[19] S. Ioffe and C. Szegedy. Batch normalization: Accelerating deep network training by reducing internal covariate shift. *arXiv preprint arXiv:1502.03167*, 2015.

[20] Y. Jia, E. Shelhamer, J. Donahue, S. Karayev, J. Long, R. Girshick, S. Guadarrama, and T. Darrell. Caffe: Convolutional architecture for fast feature embedding. *arXiv preprint arXiv:1408.5093*, 2014.

[21] Y. Koren. Factorization meets the neighborhood: a multifaceted collaborative filtering model. In *KDD*, 2008.

[22] A. Krizhevsky, I. Sutskever, and G. E. Hinton. Imagenet classification with deep convolutional neural networks. In *NIPS*, 2012.

[23] J. Li and W. Zhang. Conditional restricted boltzmann machines for cold start recommendations. *arXiv preprint arXiv:1408.0096*, 2014.

[24] T.-Y. Lin, Y. Cui, S. Belongie, and J. Hays. Learning deep representations for ground-to-aerial geolocalization. In *CVPR*, 2015.

[25] D. G. Lowe. Distinctive image features from scale-invariant keypoints. *IJCV*, 2004.

[26] Y. Nesterov. A method of solving a convex programming problem with convergence rate o (1/sqrt(k)). In *Soviet Mathematics Doklady*, 1983.

[27] J. Noronha, E. Hysen, H. Zhang, and K. Z. Gajos. Platemate: crowdsourcing nutritional analysis from food photographs. In *Proceedings of the 24th annual ACM symposium on User interface software and technology*. ACM, 2011.

[28] J. P. Pollak, P. Adams, and G. Gay. Pam: a photographic affect meter for frequent, in situ measurement of affect. In *CHI*, 2011.

[29] P. Pu and L. Chen. User-involved preference elicitation for product search and recommender systems. *AI magazine*, 2009.

[30] A. M. Rashid, I. Albert, D. Cosley, S. K. Lam, S. M. McNee, J. A. Konstan, and J. Riedl. Getting to know you: learning new user preferences in recommender systems. In *ACM IUI*, 2002.

[31] J. D. Rennie and N. Srebro. Fast maximum margin matrix factorization for collaborative prediction. In *ICML*, 2005.

[32] P. Rozin, C. Fischler, S. Imada, A. Sarubin, and A. Wrzesniewski. Attitudes to food and the role of food in life in the usa, japan, flemish belgium and france: Possible implications for the diet–health debate. *Appetite*, 1999.

[33] B. Sarwar, G. Karypis, J. Konstan, and J. Riedl. Item-based collaborative filtering recommendation algorithms. In *WWW*, 2001.

[34] A. I. Schein, A. Popescul, L. H. Ungar, and D. M. Pennock. Methods and metrics for cold-start recommendations. In *SIGIR*, 2002.

[35] M. Sun, F. Li, J. Lee, K. Zhou, G. Lebanon, and H. Zha. Learning multiple-question decision trees for cold-start recommendation. In *WSDM*, 2013.

[36] I. Sutskever, J. Martens, G. Dahl, and G. Hinton. On the importance of initialization and momentum in deep learning. In *ICML*, 2013.

[37] Y. Taigman, M. Yang, M. Ranzato, and L. Wolf. Deepface: Closing the gap to human-level performance in face verification. In *CVPR*, 2014.

[38] C.-Y. Teng, Y.-R. Lin, and L. A. Adamic. Recipe recommendation using ingredient networks. In *Annual ACM Web Science Conference*, 2012.

[39] L. Van der Maaten and G. Hinton. Visualizing data using t-sne. *JMLR*, 2008.

[40] Y. van Pinxteren, G. Geleijnse, and P. Kamsteeg. Deriving a recipe similarity measure for recommending healthful meals. In *ACM IUI*, 2011.

[41] J. Wang, T. Leung, C. Rosenberg, J. Wang, J. Philbin, B. Chen, Y. Wu, et al. Learning fine-grained image similarity with deep ranking. *arXiv preprint arXiv:1404.4661*, 2014.

[42] M. Zhang, J. Tang, X. Zhang, and X. Xue. Addressing cold start in recommender systems: A semi-supervised co-training algorithm. In *SIGIR*, 2014.

[43] X. Zhang, J. Cheng, S. Qiu, G. Zhu, and H. Lu. Dualds: A dual discriminative rating elicitation framework for cold start recommendation. *Knowledge-Based Systems*, 2015.

[44] D. Zhou, O. Bousquet, T. N. Lal, J. Weston, and B. Schölkopf. Learning with local and global consistency. *NIPS*, 2004.

[45] K. Zhou, S.-H. Yang, and H. Zha. Functional matrix factorizations for cold-start recommendation. In *SIGIR*, 2011.

Data Driven Water Pipe Failure Prediction: A Bayesian Nonparametric Approach

Peng Lin
NICTA & UNSW
peng.lin@nicta.com.au

Bang Zhang
NICTA
bang.zhang@nicta.com.au

Yi Wang
NICTA & UNSW
yi.wang@nicta.com.au

Zhidong Li
NICTA
zhidong.li@nicta.com.au

Bin Li
NICTA
bin.li@nicta.com.au

Yang Wang
NICTA
yang.wang@nicta.com.au

Fang Chen
NICTA & UNSW
fang.chen@nicta.com.au

ABSTRACT

Water pipe failures can cause significant economic and social costs, hence have become the primary challenge to water utilities. In this paper, we propose a Bayesian nonparametric approach, namely the Dirichlet process mixture of hierarchical beta process model, for water pipe failure prediction. It can select high-risk pipes for physical condition assessment, thereby preventing disastrous failures proactively.

The proposed method is adaptable to the diversity of failure patterns. Its model structure and complexity can automatically adjust according to observed data. Additionally, the sparse failure data problem that often occurs in real-world data is tackled by the proposed method via flexible pipe grouping and failure data sharing. An approximated yet computational efficient Metropolis-within-Gibbs sampling method is developed with the exploitation of the failure data sparsity for model parameter inference.

The proposed method has been applied to a metropolitan water supply network. The details of the application context are also presented for demonstrating its real-life impact. The comparison experiments conducted on the metropolitan water pipe data show that the proposed approach significantly outperforms the state-of-the-art prediction methods, and it is capable of bringing enormous economic and social savings to water utilities.

Categories and Subject Descriptors

I.5.1 [**Models**]: Statistical

Keywords

Water pipe failure prediction; Bayesian nonparametric approach; beta process; Dirichlet process.

CIKM'15, October 19–23, 2015, Melbourne, Australia.

ACM 978-1-4503-3794-6/15/10 ...$15.00.
DOI: http://dx.doi.org/10.1145/2806416.2806509 .

Figure 1: Scenes of water pipe failures.

1. INTRODUCTION

Water supply networks are valuable urban infrastructure assets that are responsible for reliable water resource distributions. However, as urbanization trends continue and urban populations rise, water utilities find it increasingly difficult to meet growing water demand with aging and failing water pipe networks. Water pipe failures, which can cause tremendous economic and social costs, as illustrated in Fig. 1, have become the primary challenge to water utilities. In order to tackle the problem in a financially viable way, preventative risk management strategies are widely adopted by water utilities to prevent disastrous failures. The basic idea of the strategies is to identify high-risk pipes proactively and renew them in time to avoid potential failures. Meanwhile, it is also required to avert any replacements of pipes that are still in healthy condition. Therefore, the strategies consist of two main steps accordingly: (1) high-risk pipe prioritization, in which pipes are ranked based on their risks of failures, and (2) physical condition assessment, in which physical inspections are conducted on highly rated pipes to confirm their actual conditions for replacements. The pipes, which are not identified as high-risk pipes at the prioritization step, will only be renewed reactively. Hence, the success of the strategies heavily relies on the prioritization step. For making accurate selections of high-risk pipes, the prioritization step requires a failure prediction method that can give a precise estimation of pipe failure likelihood, based on which the estimated failure cost and renewal cost can be readily obtained.

The mechanisms of water pipe failures have been studied for many decades, and two main research avenues exist for water pipe failure prediction, namely physical modeling and statistical modeling. For physical modeling, a variety of models has been proposed for explaining and predicting the deterioration processes of water pipes, such as pipe-soil interaction analysis, residual structural resistance, corrosion status index and hydraulic characteristics modeling. A comprehensive review can be found in [14]. For statistical modeling, it considers historical failure records, pipe attributes and environmental factors together for making predictions. It assumes that pipes with similar intrinsic attributes and environmental factors share similar failure patterns, and that failure patterns which appeared before are likely to reappear in the future.

Although physical models can help understand the mechanisms of water pipe failures, they have strong limitations when being applied to large-scale pipe networks for failure prediction due to the following reasons: (1) Physical models need a large amount of physical factor data to support their modeling and prediction. The data can only be obtained by intrusive investigations, which can cause water supply interruptions. (2) Expensive equipment and manpower are required for collecting physical factor data, which makes physical models financially unviable. (3) Furthermore, physical factors usually interact with each other to make impacts on pipe failures. It is difficult for a single physical model to consider all the potential factors, whereas statistical modeling can readily take into account all the available factors. All these issues make physical models only suitable for inspecting a small number of pipes rather than making predictions for large-scale pipe networks. In contrast, statistical models require significantly fewer resources, which make themselves suitable for high-risk pipe prioritization on large-scale networks. Moreover, because of the rapid development of information technology, enormous water pipe failure data has been accumulated and becomes available, making advanced statistical modeling feasible.

In order to improve high-risk pipe prioritization for large-scale metropolitan pipe networks, we propose a Bayesian nonparametric statistical approach, namely the Dirichlet process mixture of hierarchical beta process model, for water pipe failure prediction. Unlike parametric approaches, the structure and complexity of the proposed model can grow as the amount of observed data increases. It makes the model invulnerable to faulty assumptions of model forms and adaptable to various failure patterns, thereby leading to more accurate predictions for different application scenarios.

It is worth noting that water pipe failure data is extremely sparse in reality. Very few pipes have failure records during the observation period. Such sparsity makes traditional failure prediction methods incompetent for accurate pipe failure prediction since most pipes do not have failure data for training. The proposed approach deals with this issue by sharing failure data via a flexible hierarchical modeling of failure behaviours. The key component of the hierarchical modeling is a flexible grouping scheme. It clusters similar pipes together for modeling so that failure data can be shared by similar pipes for training. Additionally, the failure data sparsity is exploited for developing an approximated yet computationally efficient Metropolis-within-Gibbs sampling method for model parameter inference.

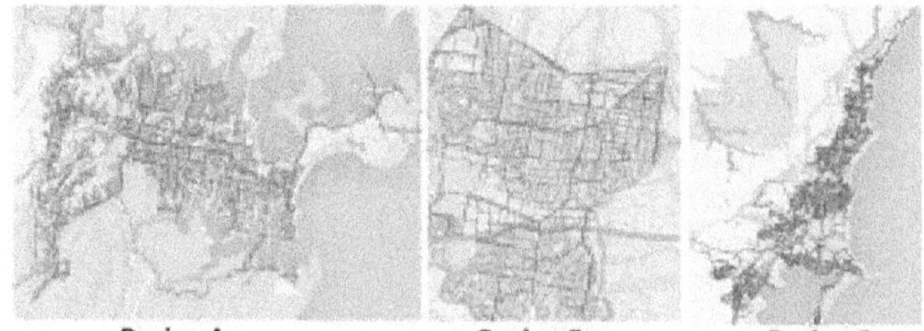

Figure 2: Water supply networks in the selected regions.

The proposed method has been applied to the water supply network of an international metropolis that has a total population of near five million people. In this work, three representative regions are selected from the metropolis for comparison experiments. The regions and the networks are shown in Fig. 2. As we can see, the water supply network is constituted of two main categories of water pipes, critical water main (CWM) indicated by red lines and reticulation water main (RWM) indicated by blue lines. CWMs have larger diameters (300 millimeters and above), and RWMs have smaller diameters (smaller than 300 millimeters). Each water pipe is composed of a set of pipe segments connected in series. Failure records can be precisely matched with pipe segments, allowing the proposed method to model failure behaviours of pipe segments.

Although CWM only takes a small portion of the network, it plays a more important role than RWM. The consequences caused by CWM failures are significantly more severe than RWM failures. Given the large scale of the network and the high cost of physical inspection, it is infeasible to inspect both types of pipes physically. Thus, the preventative risk management strategy just focuses on preventing CWM failures in practice. Accordingly, in this work, the proposed approach is compared with other state-of-the-art prediction methods for predicting CWM failures, of which the data sparsity is even more significant. The experimental results obtained from the real-world pipe data demonstrate the superiority of the proposed approach over the others.

The rest of the paper is organized as follows. Section 2 reviews the related work. Section 3 describes the details of the proposed method. Empirical studies are shown in Section 4, and the conclusions are drawn in Section 5.

2. RELATED WORK

In this section, we briefly review the related work on statistical water pipe failure prediction methods and Bayesian nonparametric approaches.

2.1 Statistical Failure Prediction Methods

In recent decades, many statistical models have been proposed for water pipe failure prediction. In the early stages, various of methods were developed for modeling the relationship between pipe age and pipe failure rate. For instance, the work in [15] proposed a time-exponential model, which formulates the number of failures per unit length per year as an exponential function of pipe age. Similarly, time-power model [12] and time-linear model [9] were developed with comparable performances.

Later on, multivariate probabilistic models were suggested. They make predictions based on a variety of pipe attributes, such as age, material, length and diameter. One of the most popular multivariate approaches is the Cox proportional hazards model [3]. It is a semi-parametric method, in which the baseline hazard function has an arbitrary form and the pipe attributes alter the baseline hazard function via an exponential function multiplicatively. The Weibull model and its variants [2, 8] are also widely adopted in practice. They utilize either a Weibull distribution or a Weibull process for modeling pipe failure behaviours.

Recently, a ranking-based method [18] was proposed for predicting water pipe failures. It treats failure prediction as a ranking problem. Pipes are ranked based on their failure risk. The method performs failure prediction via a real-valued ranking function rather than an estimation of failure probability.

2.2 Bayesian Nonparametric Approaches

All the aforementioned methods are parametric or semi-parametric, which means the forms of the methods are pre-defined and fixed during the training process. If the assumptions made on the model form are not satisfied, accurate predictions cannot be achieved. In contrast, Bayesian nonparametric approaches do not make assumptions about the model structure. Instead, their model complexities grow as the amount of observed data increases, endowing Bayesian nonparametric approaches with flexibility for modeling complex real-world data.

Beta process [5] and Dirichlet process [4] are two Bayesian nonparametric approaches that were developed recently with tremendous success in a variety of domains. They have become the cornerstones for building more sophisticated Bayesian nonparametric models.

Beta process was originally developed for survival analysis on life history data. It was utilized as a prior distribution over the space of cumulative hazard function. Later, the work in [17] extended beta process to more general spaces for different applications, such as factor analysis [13], image reconstruction [20, 21], image interpolation and document analysis [17]. One of its variants was also applied to water pipe failure prediction [10, 11].

Dirichlet process [4] is a flexible Bayesian nonparametric prior for data clustering. It does not set any assumptions on the number of clusters. Instead, it allows the number of clusters to grow as the number of data points increases. It is the foundation of many nonparametric mixture models, and has been widely adopted in various applications, such as document analysis [16], musical similarity analysis [6] image annotation [19] and DNA sequence analysis [7].

3. THE PROPOSED METHOD

The proposed Dirichlet process mixture of hierarchical beta process model consists of two main components working with each other interactively: a hierarchical representation of water pipe failure behaviours and a flexible pipe grouping scheme. The grouping scheme generates a set of groups, on each of which the hierarchical representation can be constructed. The hierarchical representation provides a precise modeling of each group's failure behaviours, hence acts as the basis of grouping.

The two main components are described in Section 3.1 and Section 3.2 respectively. The details of the proposed model are given in Section 3.3. The inference algorithm is developed in Section 3.4.

3.1 Hierarchical Modeling of Water Pipe Failure Behaviours

The hierarchical beta process is adopted in this work as the hierarchical modeling of water pipe failure behaviours. We first briefly introduce the beta-Bernoulli process for modeling failure event and failure probability in Section 3.1.1 and Section 3.1.2. Then the details of the hierarchical modeling are given in Section 3.1.3.

3.1.1 Beta Process

On a measurable space Ω, a beta process H is defined as a positive Levy process, a positive random measure whose masses on disjoint subsets of Ω are independent. It is parameterized by a positive concentration function c and a base measure H_0, which is also defined on space Ω. In simplified cases, where function $c(\omega_i)$ becomes a constant, we call c concentration parameter.

For disjoint infinitesimal partitions of Ω, the beta process can be generated as:

$$H(B_k) \backsim Beta(cH_0(B_k), c(1 - H_0(B_k)), \tag{1}$$

where B_k indicates a partition, and $k \in \{1, \cdots, K\}$ is the index. The process can be denoted as $H \backsim BP(c, H_0)$.

When the base measure H_0 is discrete and has a set function form of $H_0 = \sum_i p_i \delta_{\omega_i}$, H turns to have atoms at the same locations as H_0's and can be written in a set function form accordingly as:

$$\begin{gathered} H(\omega) = \sum_i \pi_i \delta_{\omega_i}(\omega) \\ \pi_i \backsim Beta(cq_i, c(1 - q_i)) \end{gathered} \tag{2}$$

where $\delta_{\omega_i}(\omega) = 1$ when $\omega = \omega_i$ and 0 otherwise.

As defined in a general space Ω, beta process provides us a flexible Bayesian nonparametric prior for water pipe failure events which themselves can be modeled by Bernoulli process.

3.1.2 Bernoulli Process

For a Bernoulli process $BeP(H)$, each of its draws X_j is again a measure on space Ω. j represents the draw index. H indicates a beta process on Ω, as defined before. It acts as the prior of the Bernoulli process. A draw of the Bernoulli process can also be represented via a set function form as:

$$\begin{gathered} X_j(\omega) = \sum_i x_{ij} \delta_{\omega_i}(\omega) \\ x_{i,j} \backsim Bernoulli(\pi_i) \end{gathered} \tag{3}$$

where δ_{ω_i} corresponds to the same atom location of H. The random variable x_{ij} is generated from a Bernoulli distribution parameterized by π_i which is defined as Eq. 2. With x_{ij} as its elements, an infinite binary column vector, also denoted by X_j, can be used for representing a draw of the Bernoulli process. Then the draws of the Bernoulli process can form an infinite binary matrix X, with X_j representing a column and j representing the column index. Each row of the matrix corresponds to an atom location δ_{ω_i}. We can see that the beta process appears to be a proper Bayesian nonparametric prior for such infinite binary matrices.

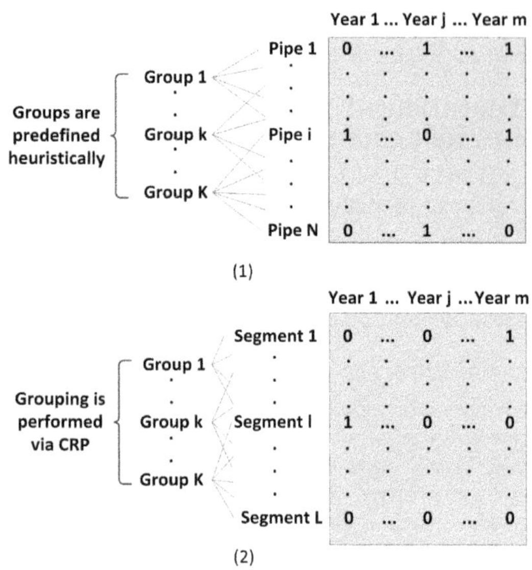

Figure 3: Binary failure matrices for pipes and pipe segments

It is worth noting that beta process is a conjugate prior of Bernoulli process. Given a beta process prior $H \backsim BP(c, H_0)$, and a set of m observations drawn from a Bernoulli process $X_j \backsim BeP(H)$, the posterior is again a beta process, with parameters updated as follow:

$$H|X_{1,\cdots,m} \backsim BP(c+m, \frac{c}{c+m}H_0 + \frac{1}{c+m}\sum_{j=1}^{m} X_j) \quad (4)$$

The conjugacy significantly simplifies the inference procedure for parameter estimation.

3.1.3 Hierarchical Modeling

With the aid of beta-Bernoulli process, a hierarchical representation can be developed for modeling water pipe failure behaviours. Firstly, failure events can be modeled by a Bernoulli process $BeP(H)$. Let an infinite binary matrix X, as illustrated in Fig. 3 (1), represent failure records of pipes. Each of its columns, X_j, can be treated as a draw from the Bernoulli process $BeP(H)$. It is an infinite binary column vector with the i-th element $x_{i,j}$ generated from $x_{i,j} \backsim Bernoulli(\pi_i)$. $x_{i,j} = 1$ means pipe i failed in year j, and $x_{i,j} = 0$ otherwise. Then the beta process, $H \backsim BP(c, H_0)$, defined as a positive Levy process on pipe space Ω, can be used as a prior of failure events, namely failure probability. Its set function form is defined as Eq. 3.

With beta process H as a prior, each row of the matrix X corresponds to an atom location δ_{ω_i} in the pipe space Ω, which can be infinitely large. We assume that two pipes share the same failure patterns if they have the same intrinsic attributes and environmental factors. Hence, we treat such two pipes as the same in the pipe space Ω. Considering all the possible combinations of pipe attributes and environmental factors, the number of "unique" pipes in the pipe space becomes infinite. Therefore, each column of the matrix X is an infinite binary vector that is drawn from a Bernoulli process. The beta process H is then a conjugate prior of the infinite binary matrix X. It models the failure probabilities of pipes via π_i.

While beta-Bernoulli process is capable of modelling failure behaviours as described above, there are two issues of adopting it in practice. Firstly, the number of failures is extremely small compared with the number of pipes, especially for CWMs. Only a small portion of CWMs have failure records since most of CWMs did not fail during the observation period. Thus, the majority of CWMs have no failure data for model training. Secondly, in addition to pipe failure histories, pipe attributes and environmental factors are also crucial for estimating failure probabilities. However, they are not properly considered in beta-Bernoulli process. The fact that the pipes with similar intrinsic attributes and environmental factors often share similar failure patterns is ignored by beta-Bernoulli process.

In order to address these issues, the hierarchical beta process (HBP) model [11, 17] can be adopted as a hierarchical modeling of water pipe failure behaviours. Given a water pipe grouping, *e.g.*, grouping by intrinsic attributes, one more beta process can be added into the model hierarchy for modeling the failure behaviours of groups. The new beta process is on top of the existing beta process, serving as the prior of its mean parameter. The graphical model in Fig. 4 (1) illustrates the HBP model. It can also be described as the followings:

$$\begin{aligned} q_k &\backsim Beta(c_0 q_0, c_0(1-q_0)), \ k \in [1, \cdots, K], \\ \pi_i &\backsim Beta(c_k q_k, c_k(1-q_k)), \ i \in [1, \cdots, N], \\ x_{i,j} &\backsim Bernoulli(\pi_i), \qquad j \in [1, \cdots, m_i], \end{aligned} \quad (5)$$

where π_i and x_{ij} are defined as before, modeling the failure probability of pipe i and failure history of pipe i in year j respectively. q_k and c_k are the mean and concentration parameters for group k. q_k can be regarded as modeling the failure rate of group k. q_0 and c_0 are the hyper parameters.

By adding one more hierarchy level, the HBP model estimates failure probabilities through the inferences on both group level and pipe level. Group level inference estimates the group failure rate q_k, and pipe level inference estimates the pipe failure probability π_i. Failure data can be shared by the same group of pipes for estimating group failure rate q_k. It helps to solve the failure data sparsity problem. The failure patterns that are shared by similar pipes are captured at the group level since the pipes within the same group share the same q_k. At the pipe level, the pipe failure probability π_i is estimated by considering not only the failure observations x_{ij}, but also the group similarity through the group failure rate q_k.

3.2 Flexible Water Pipe Grouping

Real world data is complicated and often demonstrates multi-modality property, which is the case for water pipe failures. Consequently, single-modality models become insufficient in such circumstances for modeling the whole data corpora. Mixture model is a widely adopted probabilistic approach for modeling the data arising from different modalities. It assumes that the final model consists of a set of mixture components, each of which can accurately model a portion of data.

For conventional parametric mixture models, the number of mixture components is required to be known in advance, which is unrealistic for many real world applications, such as water pipe grouping. Therefore, we adopt Dirichlet process (DP), a nonparametric approach, for pipe grouping. It serves as a flexible prior for data partitioning and sets no assumptions on the number of partitions. Correspondingly, the Dirichlet process mixture model, which is built based on Dirichlet process, can comprise a countably infinite number of components and adjust itself for fitting observed data.

In order to adopt DP as the prior of pipe grouping, we use the Chinese restaurant process (CRP) [1] as the constructive representation of DP. It exhibits the clustering property of DP via the following metaphor. Suppose there is a Chines restaurant that has an infinite number of tables. A sequence of customers enter and select a table to sit. The first customer sits at the first table. The following customers sit at tables with a guide:

$$p(z_l = r|z_{-l}, \alpha) \propto \begin{cases} \frac{n_r}{n-1+\alpha} & \text{if } r \leqslant k \\ \frac{\alpha}{n-1+\alpha} & \text{if } r = k+1. \end{cases} \tag{6}$$

z_l indicates a customer, z_{-l} denotes all the customers that appeared before z_l, r indicates a cluster index, and k represents the current number of clusters. n_r is the number of customers in cluster r and α is the concentration parameter for CRP, controlling the probability that a customer is assigned to an unoccupied table.

The CRP offers an exchangeable distribution over the table assignments z_l. The joint distribution is invariant to the order of customers. The procedure of assigning a table for a customer can be performed as he or she is the last customer entering the restaurant. As described by Eq. 6, the i-th customer sits at an occupied table with a probability proportional to the number of customers who are already sitting at that table. He or she sits at an unoccupied table with a probability proportional to the concentration parameter α. In this metaphor, customers correspond to data points and tables correspond to clusters. Fig. 4 (2) shows the Dirichlet process mixture model with the CRP as the constructive definition. Each data point x_i is drawn from a component of the mixture model. z_i is the component indicator for x_i. θ_k represents the parameter for component k.

With the aid of the CRP, we can group pipes adaptively for fitting data observations. As a result, pipes with similar failure behaviours are grouped together. Moreover, the CRP helps to integrate the grouping process and the failure modeling process for achieving accurate performance.

3.3 Dirichlet Process Mixture of Hierarchical Beta Process

In this section, we give the detailed description of the proposed Dirichlet process mixture of hierarchical beta process (DPMHBP) model for water pipe failure prediction.

For the proposed DPMHBP model, a water pipe is treated as a set of pipe segments that are connected in series. The failure probability of a pipe segment is modeled by a beta process. It is different from the HBP model [11] where beta process is used for modeling failure probabilities of pipes.

Pipe length is an important attribute for estimating failure probability. The intuition is that longer pipes tend to have higher failure probabilities if other attributes and external factors are the same. However, the HBP model ignores the impact of the length attribute when estimating failure probabilities. It only focuses on pipe age attribute and failure histories. The significant variance of pipe lengths is neglected. In order to tackle the problem, the proposed approach suggests to model the failure probabilities of pipe segments whose lengths are relatively constant with a very small variance.

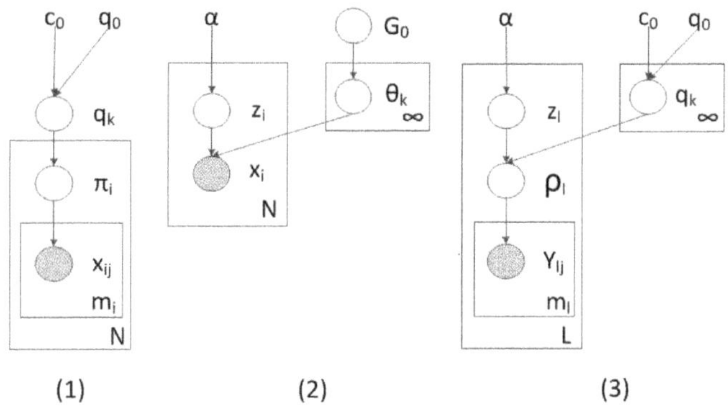

Figure 4: Graphical models for (1) Hierarchical Beta process, (2) Dirichlet process mixture model (with Chinese restaurant process as the constructive definition), (3) Dirichlet process mixture of hierarchical beta process.

Another difference between the HBP model and the proposed DPMHBP model is that the HBP model groups pipes based on heuristic domain information *e.g.*, pipe age. Its grouping is predefined and fixed during the inference process. The number of the groups is also required to be set beforehand, which can be heuristic. In contrast, for the proposed DPMHBP method, the grouping process is integrated with the inference process via the DP mixture model. They interact with each other for achieving an optimal model. The number of groups is not fixed and can grow as the size of the training data increases.

Considering all the issues mentioned above, the DPMHBP model can finally be given as follows:

$$\begin{aligned} q_k &\backsim Beta(c_0 q_0, c_0(1-q_0)), && k \in [1, \cdots, K], \\ z_l &\backsim CRP(\alpha), && z_l \in [1, \cdots, K], \\ \rho_l &\backsim Beta(c_{z_l} q_{z_l}, c_{z_l}(1-q_{z_l})), && l \in [1, \cdots, L], \\ y_{l,j} &\backsim Bernoulli(\rho_l), && j \in [1, \cdots, m_l], \\ \pi_i &= 1 - \prod_{l=1}^{s_i}(1-\rho_l), && l \in [1, \cdots, s_i]. \end{aligned} \tag{7}$$

The failure probability estimation is conducted on three levels: segment group level, segment level and pipe level. The failure events are recorded for segments rather than pipes. The grouping is performed on segments via the CRP, as illustrated by Fig. 3 (2). At segment group level, q_k denotes the failure rate of segment group k. z_l represents the group index for segment l. At segment level, ρ_l indicates the failure probability of segment l. Once the segment level estimation is obtained, pipe failure probability π_i can be readily computed via the failure probability of a series of connected segments. Fig. 4 (3) shows the graphical model of the DPMHBP model.

It is worth noting that Bernoulli process is more suitable for modeling segment failures than modeling pipe failures because it is very rare for a segment to fail twice in a year.

3.4 Inference Algorithm

In this section, we describe the inference algorithm for the proposed DPMHBP model. Suppose we are given: (1) a set of pipes, $\{u_i\}_{i=1}^N$, (2) the segment composition $\{v_l\}_{l=1}^{s_i}$ for each pipe u_i, and (3) m-year failure records for segments,

$\{y_{l,j}\}_{l\in[1,L],j\in[1,m]}$. The aim of the inference is to estimate pipe failure probabilities $\{\pi_i\}_{i=1}^N$, which are required for both physical condition assessment and proactive replacement. In order to achieve the goal, we need to estimate the variables $\{q_k\}_{k=1}^K$, $\{z_l\}_{l=1}^L$ and $\{\rho_l\}_{l=1}^L$.

Since no analytical solution is available for the proposed model, we use Markov chain Monte Carlo (MCMC) sampling algorithm for inference. Gibbs sampling is the MCMC-based method that has been widely used for DP mixture models when conjugacy exists between prior and likelihood. However, for the DPMHBP model, such conjugacy is broken by the extra hierarchy of the HBP model. Therefore, we choose to utilize Metropolis-within-Gibbs sampling method for inference.

For Metropolis-within-Gibbs sampling method, model variables are updated one by one iteratively until convergence as Gibbs sampling does. However, for each update step, Metropolis-Hastings sampling is used if the conditional distribution of a model variable is not available for sampling. It is the case for $\{q_k\}_{k=1}^K$ and $\{z_l\}_{l=1}^L$.

In order to use Metropolis-Hastings method for sampling a variable w, a proposal distribution $q(w^*|w)$ is required for generating a candidate state w^*. The candidate state is accepted with the acceptance probability:

$$a(w^*, w) = \min\left(1, \frac{q(w|w^*)\tau(w^*)}{q(w^*|w)\tau(w)}\right), \tag{8}$$

where $\tau(w)$ can be any unnormalized distribution measuring the probability of w. $\frac{q(w|w^*)\tau(w^*)}{q(w^*|w)\tau(w)}$ is often called acceptance ratio.

Now we give the details of how to update model variables. Because no conjugate prior exists, we use Metropolis-Hastings sampling method to update group index z_l. The CRP conditional prior of z_l, defined by Eq. 6, is used as the proposal distribution for generating a candidate z_l^*. As a result, we can find that this factor cancels when computing the acceptance probability defined in Eq. 8 , leaving the acceptance ratio as:

$$r_{z_l} = \frac{p(y_{l,1\ldots m}|q_{z_l^*}, c_{z_l^*})}{p(y_{l,1\ldots m}|q_{z_l}, c_{z_l})}. \tag{9}$$

For the CRP conditional prior of z_l, defined in Eq. 6, k indicates the current number of segment groups, r denotes group index, α is the concentration parameter for CRP, n_r indicates the number of segments in group r, and z_{-l} represents all the z's with z_l removed. Non-informative prior is used for c_k's.

The likelihood function in r_{z_l} can be obtained by marginalizing out ρ_l:

$$\begin{aligned} & p(y_{l,1\ldots m}|q_{z_l}, c_{z_l}) \\ = & \int p(y_{l,1\ldots m}|\rho_l)p(\rho_l|q_{z_l}, c_{z_l})d\rho_l \\ = & \int p(\rho_l|q_{z_l}, c_{z_l})\prod_{j=1}^{m} p(y_{l,j}|\rho_l)d\rho_l \\ = & \frac{\Gamma(c_{z_l})\Gamma(c_{z_l}q_{z_l}+\sum_{j=1}^m y_{l,j})}{\Gamma(c_{z_l}q_{z_l})\Gamma(c_{z_l}(1-q_{z_l}))} * \\ & \frac{\Gamma(c_{z_l}(1-q_{z_l})+m-\sum_{j=1}^m y_{l,j})}{\Gamma(c_{z_l}+m)} \end{aligned} \tag{10}$$

Similar to z_l, Metropolis-Hastings sampling can be used for updating q_k. We use the normal distribution with the current value of q_k as mean for proposing a new candidate q_k^*. Hence, the Metropolis-Hastings sampling reduces to Metropolis sampling because of the symmetric proposal distribution. The acceptance ratio, r_{q_k}, can be calculated accordingly as:

$$r_{q_k} = \frac{p(q_k^*)p(\{y_{l,1\ldots m}\}_{z_l=k}|q_k^*, c_k, \{z_l\}=k)}{p(q_k)p(\{y_{l,1\ldots m}\}_{z_l=k}|q_k, c_k, \{z_l\}=k)}. \tag{11}$$

The likelihood function in r_{q_k} can be computed by marginalizing out $\{\rho_l\}_{z_l=k}$ as:

$$\begin{aligned} & p(\{y_{l,1\ldots m}\}_{z_l=k}|q_k, c_k, \{z_l\}=k) \\ = & \prod_{l,z_l=k}\left[\int p(\rho_l|q_k, c_k, \{z_l\}=k)\prod_{j=1}^m p(y_{l,j}|\rho_l)d\rho_l\right] \\ = & \prod_{l,z_l=k}\left[\frac{\Gamma(c_k)\Gamma(c_kq_k+\sum_{j=1}^m y_{l,j})}{\Gamma(c_kq_k)\Gamma(c_k(1-q_k))}\right. \\ & \left.\cdot\frac{\Gamma(c_k(1-q_k)+m-\sum_{j=1}^m y_{l,j})}{\Gamma(c_k+m)}\right] \end{aligned} \tag{12}$$

Although the Metropolis sampling approach can sample new q_k, it is much less efficient than Gibbs sampling. Therefore, we derive an approximated Gibbs sampling step for updating q_k, in favour of the inference for large-scale datasets.

$$\begin{aligned} & p(q_k|c_k, \{z_l\}=k, \{y_{l,1\ldots m}\}_{z_l=k}) \\ \propto & \; p(q_k, \{y_{l,1\ldots m}\}_{z_l=k}|c_k, \{z_l\}=k) \\ = & \; p(q_k)p(\{y_{l,1\ldots m}\}_{z_l=k}|q_k, c_k, \{z_l\}=k) \\ \approx & \; \frac{\Gamma(c_0)}{\Gamma(c_0q_0)\Gamma(c_0(1-q_0))}q_k^{c_0q_0-1}(1-q_k)^{c_0(1-q_0)-1} \\ & \cdot\prod_{l,z_l=k}\left[\frac{(c_kq_k)^{s_l}\prod_{t=0}^{m-s_l-1}(c_k(1-q_k)+t)}{\prod_{t=0}^{m-1}(c_k+t)}\right] \end{aligned} \tag{13}$$

The approximation made on the last step of Eq. 13 is based on the sparse nature of the pipe failure prediction problem. For water supply networks, most of the pipe segments never fail during the observation period. It is even more rare for a pipe segment to have more than one failures during the observation period. Therefore, the number of failures for a segment, $s_l = \sum_j y_{l,j}$, satisfies $s_l \le 1$, which leads to the approximation in Eq. 13.

By applying Taylor expansion, the posterior distribution in Eq. 13 can be further approximated as:

$$\begin{aligned} & p(q_k|c_k, \{z_l\}=k, \{y_{l,1\ldots m}\}_{z_l=k}) \\ \propto & \; q_k^{c_0q_0-1}(1-q_k)^{c_0(1-q_0)-1} \\ & \cdot\prod_{l,z_l=k}\left[\left(\frac{c_kq_k}{c_k+m-1}\right)^{s_l}(1-q_k)^{\sum_{t=0}^{m-s_l-1}\frac{c_k}{c_k+t}}\right] \end{aligned} \tag{14}$$

Based on Eq. 14, we can see that the posterior of q_k can finally be approximated by a beta distribution:

$$\begin{aligned} & p(q_k|c_k, \{z_l\}=k, \{y_{l,1\ldots m}\}_{z_l=k}) \backsim \\ & \text{Beta}\left(c_0q_0+\sum_l s_l, c_0(1-q_0)+\sum_l\sum_t^{m-s_l-1}\frac{c_k}{c_k+t}\right) \end{aligned} \tag{15}$$

It dramatically improves the efficiency of the updates for q_k.

For updating ρ_l, we can directly sample a new value from its conditional distribution given the other variables:

$$p(\rho_l|q_{z_l}, z_l, c_{z_l}, y_{l,1\ldots m}) \backsim \text{Beta}(c_{z_l}q_{z_l} + \sum_{j=1}^{m} y_{l,j}, c_{z_l}(1 - q_{z_l}) + m - \sum_{j=1}^{m} y_{l,j}). \quad (16)$$

Once, ρ_l is obtained, pipe failure probability π_i can be readily calculated via $\pi_i = 1 - \prod_l (1 - \rho_l)$, $l \in [1, \cdots, s_i]$.

All the updating steps described above are performed iteratively until convergence is reached. Then the estimations for the model variables can be obtained by taking means of the sampled variable values, with burn-in samples omitted.

4. EXPERIMENTS

In this section, we conduct comparison experiments on the metropolitan water supply network data to demonstrate the superiority of the proposed DPMHBP model. We first introduce the pipe network data and the failure data in Section 4.1. The features used in the experiments are explained in Section 4.2. Then the compared methods are listed in Section 4.3. Finally, we give the comparison results and discuss the impact of the proposed method in Section 4.4.

4.1 Data Collection

Three representative regions from the metropolis are selected to perform the experiments. Region A is a local government area with a population around 210, 000, which is one of the most populous local government areas in its state. Its population density is 629 people per km^2. Region B is a local government area with a high population density of 2, 374 people per km^2. Its population is about 182, 000. Region C is a low density suburban local government area, which has a population of 205, 000 and a population density of 300 people per km^2.

For each region, both network data and failure data are collected. Network data consists of pipe IDs, pipe attributes, pipe locations and environmental factors. Pipe location is represented as a set of connected line segments, each of which corresponds to a pipe segment. Failure data contains pipe IDs, failure dates and failure locations.

Pipe amount, failure amount, laid year range and observation period are summarized for different pipe types in Table 1. As we can see, CWMs only take a small portion of the network, 24.97% for region A, 20.76% for region B, and 28.00% for region C. The ratio between CWM failures and all the failures is even more smaller, 12.71% for region A, 11.70% for region B, and 12.74% for region C.

The observation period covers 12 years, spanning from 1998 to 2009. It is short compared with pipe life span which can be more than 100 years as shown in Table 1. The majority of the pipes did not fail or just failed once during the observation period. If considering pipe segment failures, the failure events are even more sparse. Hence, the sparsity assumption holds for the proposed approximated sampling algorithm.

Failure locations are used for matching failures with pipe segments. It enables the proposed DPHBP model to work on pipe segment level for estimating failure probabilities.

As mentioned before, we focus on CWMs for comparison experiments since both physical condition assessment and proactive replacement are conducted for CWMs. For comparing the performances of different approaches, we use the first 11 years' failure records as training data and the last year's failure records as testing data. All the compared methods have the same setting for fair comparison.

4.2 Feature Description

In this section, we describe the pipe attributes and the environmental factors that we used in the experiments. There are five pipe attributes utilized in the experiments including protective coating, diameter, length, laid date, and material. Two types of environmental factors are considered in the experiments. One is the surrounding soil condition, and the other is the distance between pipe segment and its closest traffic intersection. These features are summarized in Table 2.

For pipe attributes, protective coating and material are categorical features indicating the type of coating and material. Typical protective coatings are polyethylene sleeve and tar coating. Typical materials are cast iron cement lined (CICL) and polyvinyl chloride (PVC). Diameter, length, and laid date are continuous features.

Surrounding soil condition is one of the most complex and important environmental factors for water pipe failure prediction. It puts direct impact on pipe degradation process. In the experiments, four different soil features are considered including soil corrosiveness, soil expansiveness, soil geology and soil map. They depict different perspectives of soil characteristics.

Soil corrosiveness describes the risk of pipe pitting (metal corrosion) which is essentially an electrical phenomenon and can be measured by linear polarization resistance test. Soil expansiveness describes the shrinking and swelling of expansive clays in response to moisture content change. It is a phenomenon that affects clay soil and can be measured by shrink swell test. Soil geology depicts the information of rocks, *e.g.*, sandstone and shale. Soil map represents the landscape information, *e.g.*, fluvial, colluvial and erosional. It also include the information of the soil types that are associated with different landscapes.

Each soil factor is a categorical feature containing several distinct values. The selected local government areas are partitioned into small regions according to the distinct values of soil factors. Pipe segments falling into the same region share the same soil factor value.

A large portion of CWMs are buried underneath roads. It makes the change of road surface pressure another important environmental factor for estimating water pipe failures. It has been shown that frequent pressure changes can lead to high failure rate. One of the main sources causing road surface pressure change comes from traffic intersections due to the frequent vehicle starting and stopping. In order to measure the impact of road surface pressure change, we calculate the distance between each pipe segment and its closest traffic intersection. The obtained continuous value is regarded as a feature of the pipe segment for predicting its failure probability.

4.3 Compared Approaches

In order to evaluate the proposed approach, four state-of-the-art methods are compared in the experiments including Cox proportional hazard model, Weibull model, HBP model and support vector machine (SVM) based ranking method. Additionally, different grouping methods are used with HBP

		# Pipes	# Failures	Laid years	Observation period
Region A	All	15189	4093	1930 – 1997	1998 – 2009
	CWM	3793	520	1930 – 1997	1998 – 2009
Region B	All	11836	3694	1888 – 1997	1998 – 2009
	CWM	2457	432	1888 – 1997	1998 – 2009
Region C	All	18001	4421	1913 – 1997	1998 – 2009
	CWM	5041	563	1913 – 1997	1998 – 2009

Table 1: Summary of pipe network data and pipe failure data .

Property and factors	Description
Protective coating	Categorical value indicating the type of coating
Diameter	Continuous value indicating pipe diameter.
Length	Continuous value indicating pipe length
Laid date	Laid date for pipe
Material	Categorical value indicating the type of pipe material
Soil corrosiveness Soil expansiveness Soil geology Soil map	Categorical value indicating soil property for the corresponding soil factor
Distance to traffic intersection	Continuous value indicating the distance between pipe segment and the closest traffic intersection

Table 2: Pipe attributes and environmental factors

model as comparisons for demonstrating the advantage of the grouping scheme of the proposed approach.

The Cox proportional hazard model [3] is one of the most popular approaches for survival analysis. It is a semi-parametric approach, in which the form of the baseline hazard function can be arbitrary, and the explanatory features put impacts on the baseline hazard function via an exponential function multiplicatively. Formally, the Cox proportional hazard model can be described as:

$$h(t, z) = h_0(t)e^{b^T z}, \tag{17}$$

where h_0 indicates the baseline hazard function, z indicates the explanatory features of water pipe, and b is the parameter vector that can be learned from training data via a partial likelihood maximization procedure.

For Weibull model [2, 8], water pipe failures are modeled as a set of stochastic events governed by a time dependent stochastic process, namely the Weibull process. It can be regarded as a nonhomogeneous Poisson process whose intensity varies as time changes. The intensity function can be formally given as:

$$\lambda(t) = \alpha\beta t^{\beta-1}, \tag{18}$$

where t represents pipe age, α and β are parameters that need to be learned from training data. Similar to Cox proportional hazard model, the explanatory features can also be utilized via an exponential function multiplicatively.

Analogous to the method proposed in [18], an SVM-based ranking approach is compared. This approach formulates pipe failure prediction as a ranking problem. It ranks pipes according to their failure risks without estimating their actual failure probability. It learns a real-valued ranking function H that maximizes the objective function:

$$\sum_{z\in P, z'\in N} \frac{I(H(z) > H(z'))}{|P| \cdot |N|}, \tag{19}$$

where P and N represent the positive class dataset (failure dataset) and negative class dataset respectively. $I(\cdot)$ is the indicator function. $|P|$ and $|N|$ indicate the numbers of data points in the positive and negative class datasets respectively.

The HBP model proposed by [11] is also compared. In order to evaluate the grouping scheme of the proposed approach, three different grouping methods are integrated with HBP model for comparisons. They group pipes based on pipe attributes according to domain expert suggestion. Specifically, pipes are grouped based on material, diameter and laid year.

For fair comparison, the features described in the previous section are used for all the compared methods. For HBP and DPMHBP, the features are applied multiplicatively similar to Cox proportional hazard model and Weibull model. A linear kernel is used for the SVM-based ranking approach.

4.4 Prediction Results and Real Life Impact

In this section, we compare the prediction results to demonstrate the superiority of the proposed approach. As mentioned before, the historical failure data from 1998 to 2008 is used for training and the failures occurred in 2009 are used for testing. Water pipes are ranked by different methods based on their estimated failure risks. The failure prediction results are shown in Fig. 5. The x-axis represents the cumulative percentage of the inspected water pipes, and the y-axis indicates the percentage of the detected pipe failures.

Besides, we calculate AUC for measuring the performances of different approaches. The results are shown in Table 3. Statistical significance tests, particularly the one-sided paired t-test at 5% level of significance, are performed on AUC to evaluate the significance of the performance differences. The results are shown in Table 4. For Table 3 and Table 4, only the results from the best groupings are shown for the HBP model.

As we can see from Fig. 5 and Table 3, the proposed DPMHBP model consistently gives the most accurate prediction for all the three regions, whereas the other methods only perform accurately for some of the regions. It demonstrates the adaptability of the proposed approach to the diversity of failure patterns. The significance test results, listed in Table 4, show that the proposed model significantly outperforms the other methods.

In addition to the comparison studies shown above, we also demonstrate the real-life impact of the proposed method by showing its improvements in its real-world application. Different from the standard performance measurement, do-

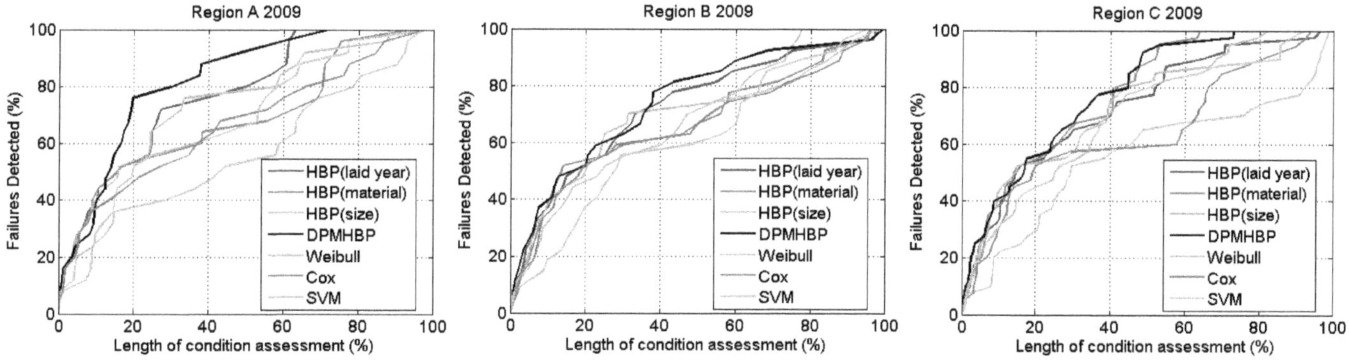

Figure 5: Failure prediction results for the selected regions by different models.

	Region A			Region B			Region C		
	DPMHBP Cox	HBP SVM	Weibull	DPMHBP Cox	HBP SVM	Weibull	DPMHBP Cox	HBP SVM	Weibull
AUC(100%)	**82.67%** 66.91%	77.05% 56.45%	68.44%	**74.51%** 65.53%	72.56% 61.90%	65.20%	**78.37%** 64.50%	73.54% 69.48%	55.84%
AUC(1%)	**8.09‱** 4.67‱	5.64‱ 4.32‱	5.84‱	**4.21‱** 2.46‱	3.60‱ 3.41‱	2.70‱	**5.11‱** 2.50‱	2.48‱ 1.73‱	2.98‱

Table 3: AUC of different approaches. The second row shows the AUC when 100% of CWMs are inspected. The third row shows the AUC when 1% of CWMs are inspected. The best performance is in bold.

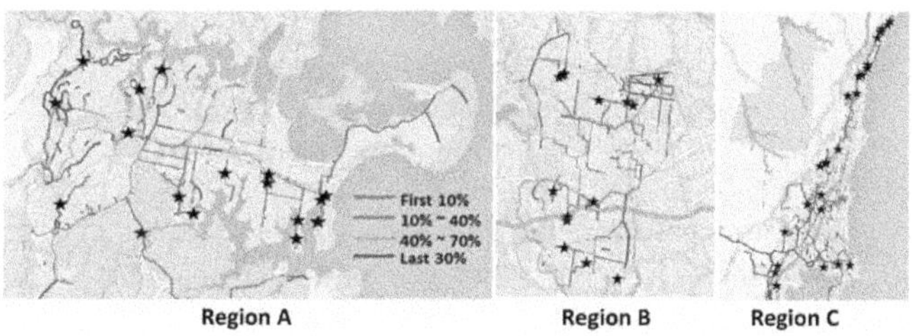

Figure 7: Risk maps for the selected three regions

main experts often adopt evaluation criteria that can reflect the constraints encountered in reality. In the context of water pipe failure prediction, as mentioned before, only a small portion of the pipes can be physically inspected each year. Specifically, due to budget constraint, only 1% of the total CWMs can be inspected every year. Therefore, we show the performance curves with 1% of CWMs inspected in Fig. 6. AUC and significance test results are also given in Table 3 and Table 4 for the situation of inspecting 1% of CWMs. As we can see, the proposed approach significantly outperforms the other methods for all the three regions. In region C, the proposed approach nearly doubles the number of detected failures compared with the second best method.

A risk map, as shown in Fig. 7, is another widely used method for visualizing real-life impact. As illustrated in the figure, the prioritization of pipes is coded by different colours. For instance, red lines indicate the top 10% high-risk pipes predicted by our method. Black stars in the figure denote the failures which occurred in the testing year. As we can see, many failures could be prevented and significant economic and social savings could be brought to the water utility if the proposed method were applied.

5. CONCLUSIONS

In this paper, we present the Dirichlet process mixture of hierarchical beta process model for water pipe failure prediction. The model demonstrates high adaptability to the diversity of failure patterns. Its structure and complexity can grow as the number of data points increases. It tackles the sparse failure data problem by sharing failure data through pipe grouping. An efficient Metropolis-within-Gibbs sampling algorithm is also proposed for handling large-scale datasets. The empirical studies conducted on the real water pipe data verifies the superiority of the proposed approach.

6. ACKNOWLEDGMENTS

National ICT Australia (NICTA) is funded by the Australian Government as represented by the Department of Broadband, Communications and the Digital Economy and the Australian Research Council through the ICT Centre of Excellence program.

7. REFERENCES

[1] D. J. Aldous. *Exchangeability and related topics.* Springer, 1985.

[2] A. G. Constantine. Pipeline reliability: Stochastic models in engineering technology and management. Singapore: World Scientific, 1996.

[3] D. R. Cox. Regression models and life-tables. In *Journal of the Royal Statistical Society*, pages 187–220. Series B Methodological, 1972.

[4] T. S. Ferguson. A bayesian analysis of some nonparametric problems. *The annals of statistics*, pages 209–230, 1973.

[5] N. L. Hjort. Nonparametric bayes estimators based on beta processes in models for life history data. *The Annals of Statistics*, pages 1259–1294, 1990.

	Region A		Region B		Region C	
	vs.HBP	vs.Weibull	vs.HBP	vs.Weibull	vs.HBP	vs.Weibull
	vs.Cox	vs.SVM	vs.Cox	vs.SVM	vs.Cox	vs.SVM
AUC(100%)	2.56(= 0.08)	9.37(< 0.05)	3.12(= 0.05)	22.01(< 0.05)	7.83(< 0.05)	43.55(< 0.05)
	10.58(< 0.05)	18.88(< 0.05)	21.17(< 0.05)	30.11(< 0.05)	26.08(< 0.05)	15.63(< 0.05)
AUC(1%)	44.29(< 0.05)	40.46(< 0.05)	1.26(< 0.05)	4.64(< 0.05)	65.90(< 0.05)	53.43(< 0.05)
	62.44(< 0.05)	69.01(< 0.05)	5.53(< 0.05)	1.99(< 0.05)	65.43(< 0.05)	61.72(< 0.05)

Table 4: Statistical significance test (t-test) results for the proposed method and the others. The second row shows the results when 100% of CWMs are inspected. The third row shows the results when 1% of CWMs are inspected.

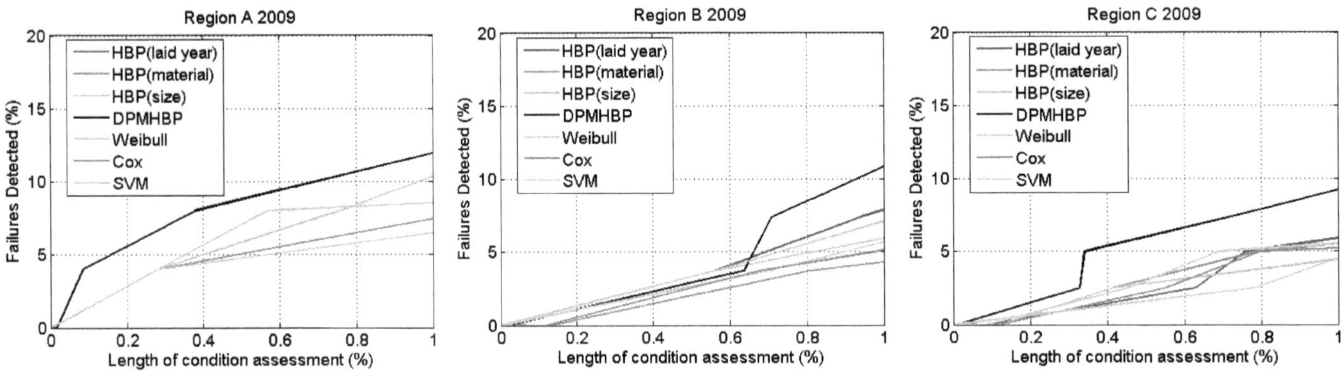

Figure 6: The detection results with 1% of pipe network length inspected.

[6] M. D. Hoffman, D. M. Blei, and P. R. Cook. Content-based musical similarity computation using the hierarchical dirichlet process. In *ISMIR*, pages 349–354, 2008.

[7] J. P. Huelsenbeck, S. Jain, S. W. Frost, and S. L. K. Pond. A dirichlet process model for detecting positive selection in protein-coding dna sequences. *Proceedings of the National Academy of Sciences*, 103(16):6263–6268, 2006.

[8] J. G. Ibrahim, M.-H. Chen, and D. Sinha. *Bayesian survival analysis*. Wiley Online Library, 2005.

[9] A. Kettler and I. Goulter. An analysis of pipe breakage in urban water distribution networks. *Canadian Journal of Civil Engineering*, 12(2):286–293, 1985.

[10] B. Li, B. Zhang, Z. Li, Y. Wang, F. Chen, and D. Vitanage. Prioritising water pipes for condition assessment with data analytics. *OzWater*, 2015.

[11] Z. Li, B. Zhang, Y. Wang, F. Chen, R. Taib, V. Whiffin, and Y. Wang. Water pipe condition assessment: a hierarchical beta process approach for sparse incident data. *Machine learning*, 95(1):11–26, 2014.

[12] K. Mavin. Predicting the failure performance of individual water mains. *Urban Water Research Association of Australia*, (114), 1996.

[13] J. Paisley and L. Carin. Nonparametric factor analysis with beta process priors. In *Proceedings of the 26th Annual International Conference on Machine Learning*, pages 777–784. ACM, 2009.

[14] B. Rajani and Y. Kleiner. Comprehensive review of structural deterioration of water mains: physically based models. *Urban water*, 3(3):151–164, 2001.

[15] U. Shamir and C. Howard. An analytic approach to scheduling pipe replacement. pages 71(5),248–258, 1979.

[16] Y. W. Teh, M. I. Jordan, M. J. Beal, and D. M. Blei. Hierarchical dirichlet processes. *Journal of the american statistical association*, 101(476), 2006.

[17] R. Thibaux and M. I. Jordan. Hierarchical beta processes and the indian buffet process. In *International conference on artificial intelligence and statistics*, pages 564–571, 2007.

[18] R. Wang, W. Dong, Y. Wang, K. Tang, and X. Yao. Pipe failure prediction: A data mining method. In *Data Engineering (ICDE), 2013 IEEE 29th International Conference on*, pages 1208–1218. IEEE, 2013.

[19] O. Yakhnenko and V. Honavar. Annotating images and image objects using a hierarchical dirichlet process model. In *Proceedings of the 9th International Workshop on Multimedia Data Mining: held in conjunction with the ACM SIGKDD 2008*, pages 1–7. ACM, 2008.

[20] M. Zhou, H. Chen, L. Ren, G. Sapiro, L. Carin, and J. W. Paisley. Non-parametric bayesian dictionary learning for sparse image representations. In *Advances in neural information processing systems*, pages 2295–2303, 2009.

[21] M. Zhou, H. Yang, G. Sapiro, D. B. Dunson, and L. Carin. Dependent hierarchical beta process for image interpolation and denoising. In *International conference on artificial intelligence and statistics*, pages 883–891, 2011.

Tumblr Blog Recommendation with Boosted Inductive Matrix Completion

Donghyuk Shin
Dept. of Computer Science
University of Texas at Austin
dshin@cs.utexas.edu

Suleyman Cetintas
Advertising Sciences Group
Yahoo Labs, Sunnyvale, CA
cetintas@yahoo-inc.com

Kuang-Chih Lee
Advertising Sciences Group
Yahoo Labs, Sunnyvale, CA
kclee@yahoo-inc.com

Inderjit S. Dhillon
Dept. of Computer Science
University of Texas at Austin
inderjit@cs.utexas.edu

ABSTRACT

Popular microblogging sites such as Tumblr have attracted hundreds of millions of users as a content sharing platform, where users can create rich content in the form of posts that are shared with other users who follow them. Due to the sheer amount of posts created on such services, an important task is to make quality recommendations of blogs for users to follow. Apart from traditional recommender system settings where the follower graph is the main data source, additional side-information of users and blogs such as user activity (e.g., like and reblog) and rich content (e.g., text and images) are also available to be exploited for enhanced recommendation performance. In this paper, we propose a novel boosted inductive matrix completion method (BIMC) for blog recommendation. BIMC is an additive low-rank model for user-blog preferences consisting of two components; one component captures the low-rank structure of follow relationships and the other captures the latent structure using side-information. Our model formulation combines the power of the recently proposed inductive matrix completion (IMC) model (for side-information) together with a standard matrix completion (MC) model (for low-rank structure). Furthermore, we utilize recently developed deep learning techniques to obtain semantically rich feature representations of text and images that are incorporated in BIMC. Experiments on a large-scale real-world dataset from Tumblr illustrate the effectiveness of the proposed BIMC method.

Categories and Subject Descriptors

H.2.8 [**Database Management**]: Database Applications—*Data Mining*; H.3.3 [**Information Search and Retrieval**]: Information Filtering

CIKM'15, October 19–23, 2015, Melbourne, VIC, Australia.

DOI: http://dx.doi.org/10.1145/2806416.2806578.

(a) Blog recommendation module in Tumblr (b) Example post with high note count.

Figure 1: The blog recommendation module (a) and an example post (b) with high note count (i.e., like and reblog count) in Tumblr.

Keywords

Blog Recommendation, Inductive Matrix Completion, Deep Learning Features

1. INTRODUCTION

Microblogging services have emerged as a leading content sharing and communication platform combining both traditional blogging and social networking characteristics. Tumblr[1] is one of the most popular microblogging services with more than 230 million users, where users can create and share posts with the followers of their blogs. Conversely, users consume shared content by following blogs of interest, which has become an overwhelming task due to the sheer number of options. Thus, one of the core problems in microblogging sites is predicting whether a user will follow a blog or not. Improved blog recommendations would not only lead to higher user engagement by assisting users to discover interesting content, but also attract more appealing followers for sponsored or advertisers blogs. Figure 1(a) shows the blog recommendation module in Tumblr.

The problem of recommending blogs differs from traditional collaborative filtering settings, such as the Netflix rating prediction problem [3], in two main aspects. First, in-

[1] `www.tumblr.com`

teractions between users and blogs are *binary* in the form of follows and there is no explicit rating information available about user preferences. The "follow" information can be represented as a unidirectional unweighted graph and popular proximity measures based on the structural properties of the graph can then be applied to the problem [36]. Secondly, an important but beneficial difference is that blog recommendation inherently entails rich *side information* in addition to the conventional user-item matrix (i.e., follower graph). There are two main categories of side information: (1) *user generated content* such as images, tags and text (e.g., Figure 1(b)) and (2) *user activity* including likes and reblogs. In the case of Tumblr, incorporating image features is crucial as majority of posts contain photos. Text data is also rich in Tumblr, since posts have no limitation in length, compared to other microblogging sites such as Twitter[2]. While such user generated content characterizes various blogs, user activity is a more direct and informative signal of user preference as users can explicitly express their interests by liking and reblogging a post. This implies that users who liked or reblogged the same posts are likely to follow similar blogs. In fact, as shown in many existing studies, such side information not only improves recommendation quality, but also alleviates sparsity issues in the user-item matrix [26, 14, 31].

On the other hand, rigorous approaches for incorporating side-information in a recommender system setting are lacking. Consider the standard matrix completion (MC), one of the most widely used and theoretically well-studied method for recommendation tasks, for which there have been several rigorous guarantees established in the recent past [20, 5, 17, 7]. However, MC is exposed to data sparsity issues and restricted to the transductive setting, i.e., predictions can only be made for existing users/items, as it only considers observations from the user-item matrix. More recently, the inductive matrix completion (IMC) was proposed and theoretically analyzed by [16] motivated by settings where side information of users/items is available in the form of feature vectors. However, IMC assumes that observed entries are fully explained by such features, which is not always the case especially with noisy features that do not support the user-item matrix. Furthermore, IMC cannot make meaningful recommendations for users or items without any features, which is often the case in Tumblr (see Section 3).

To this end, we propose a novel Boosted Inductive Matrix Completion (BIMC) model for blog recommendation that combines the power of an inductive matrix completion model together with a standard matrix completion model via boosting. Specifically, BIMC first applies the MC model to smooth the input matrix and reduce the noise level by low-rank approximation, and then further models the residual of the approximation with the IMC model. That is, BIMC captures both the low-rank structure of follow relationships as well as the latent structure using side-information of users and items in an additive manner capturing entries in the follower graph where MC fails to learn.

By incorporating user/blog features, BIMC is also capable of making recommendations in the *inductive* setting, i.e., make predictions for users or blogs *not seen at training time*, which includes cold-start cases[3]. This is particularly important for Tumblr as users and blogs often have very few or no links in the follower graph as shown in Section 3. Experiments on large-scale real-world proprietary data from Tumblr show that our proposed BIMC significantly outperforms MC, IMC and several other standard methods for the blog recommendation task.

Lastly, an important issue is how to effectively represent the three side-information sources (image, text and activity) as features. Recently, deep learning approaches have emerged as a powerful class of models that understand semantic content of images, giving state-of-the-art performance on image recognition tasks [24, 9, 19]. This is also the case for text data, where vectorial representations of words capturing semantic relations between them are learned from neural networks [27, 35]. Encouraged by these results, we employ deep learning features for both images and tags/text as a useful and robust representation of users and blogs. For activity features, we represent likes and reblogs as a weighted graph similar to the follower graph and we compute principal components of the activity graph as features. To our knowledge, we are the first to consider image as well as activity features. Furthermore, adopting deep learned features for recommender systems is still unexplored.

Our contributions are summarized as follows:

- We propose a Boosted Inductive Matrix Completion based blog recommendation system that combines the power of an inductive matrix completion model together with a standard matrix completion model.
- We represent users and blogs with an extensive set of side information sources such as the user activity, text/tags, and images; and extract a comprehensive set of features using state-of-the-art deep learning methods.
- We show that the proposed BIMC model effectively combines heterogeneous user and blog features from multiple sources for more accurate recommendations.
- We conduct extensive experiments as well as detailed analysis on large-scale real-world data from Tumblr, and demonstrate the superiority of the proposed BIMC method over several state-of-the-art baselines.

The rest of the paper is organized as follows. In Section 2, we review some closely related work. Then we analyze the Tumblr data and study some of its important characteristics in Section 3. Next we present our proposed blog recommendation method in Section 4 and give details of user and blog feature extraction in Section 5. Experimental results are given in Section 6 followed by conclusions in Section 7.

2. RELATED WORK

In general, various sources of information additional to the traditional user-item matrix can boost recommendation performance. Recommender systems with side information is by no means new and numerous methods have been proposed based on the type of side information they utilize, such as user generated content [22, 38, 13, 28, 25, 2], user/item profile or attribute [1, 4], social network [18, 26] and context information [29]. A recent comprehensive survey of the state-of-the-art methods can be found in [31].

One of the main approaches that extend MC with side information is the Collective Matrix Completion (CMC) model [33, 4], where the goal is to jointly recover a collection of matrices with shared low-rank structure. In [38], the user-item matrix and the user-user similarity matrix based on tags information are jointly factorized to facilitate better recommendations. Recent work on CMC provides consis-

[2]`www.twitter.com`; posts (or tweets) are restricted to 140 characters.

[3]Cold-start refers to users or items without any known entries in the user-item matrix.

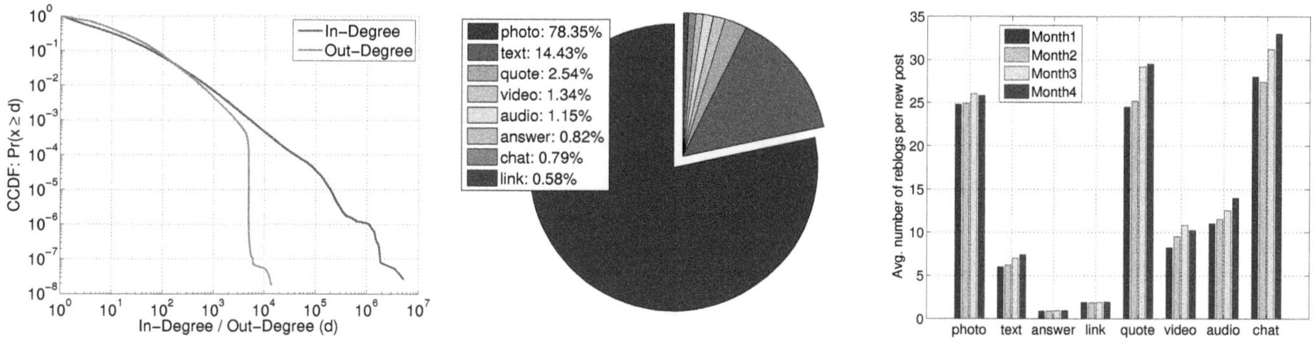

(a) In/out degree distribution of the follower graph. (b) Distribution of different post types. (c) Average number of reblogs per new post for each post type.

Figure 2: Statistics of Tumblr data.

tency guarantees under certain assumptions [11], which can be restrictive due to imposing a common structure. Recommender systems with social networks are mostly based on the latent factor model with additional constraints in the objective such as latent factors being similar between connected users [18, 26]. Another approach is the regression-based latent factor model proposed by [1], where attribute information is integrated into the model. However, the proposed method does not scale well to large datasets. Graph-based methods have also been extended to incorporate side information. For example, [22] constructs a multi-partite graph with social and tag information, which does not scale well with additional side-information or when features are represented as a dense matrix. Lastly, user generated content, such as reviews and comments, have been exploited by analyzing sentiment information [28, 25]. In most cases, methods are either specialized for a particular source of information or do not scale well with large number of features and lack theoretical guarantees.

Closely related to Tumblr blog recommendation is the Who-To-Follow system in Twitter [12]. Previous approaches for followee recommendation include a probabilistic model based on probabilistic latent semantic analysis proposed by [21]. In [37], a community-based approach is proposed, where matrix factorization is applied independently to each of the discovered communities. However, both methods do not consider any other explicit user/blog features. In [13], follower/followee as well as content (tweets) information is used to represent users in a similarity-based collaborative filtering method. Similarly, [2] first identifies a list of candidate followees, which are the 2-hop neighbors in the follower graph, and then refines the list using content-based profiles of users. Graph-based methods that use proximity measures between nodes have also been applied to followee recommendation [36]. One major drawback is that these methods can not efficiently deal with the inductive setting. Furthermore, none of the existing methods consider images nor user activity information, which is also available in Twitter.

There has been limited work on employing deep learning methods for recommender systems. One exception is the music recommendation method proposed by [30]. In [30], the traditional matrix factorization is combined with a deep convolutional neural network to learn a function that maps music content features to corresponding latent factors. Another exception is the work by [10], where a recurrent neural network is trained to capture semantics of text documents that is used in a content-based recommender system. Both studies have shown deep learning as a promising approach for recommender systems.

3. DATASET CHARACTERISTICS

In this section, we analyze some important characteristics of different aspects of the Tumblr data[4]. As a social network service, Tumblr users can follow blogs of interest without mutual confirmation similar to Twitter, but different from Facebook[5]. The follow information can be represented as a directed bipartite graph where nodes correspond to users and blogs and an edge from node i to j represents user i following blog j. We use a snapshot of the follower graph sampled from June 2014, which consists of 76.86 million nodes with 2.27 billion edges. We find similar characteristics as in [6] including the in/out degree distributions shown in Figure 2(a). The in-degree follows a power-law distribution, while the out-degree does not and shows a sharp drop when the out-degree is around 5,000, which is the maximum number of blogs a user can follow in Tumblr. About 50% of nodes are without any followers (i.e., 0 in-degree) and the maximum in-degree is 5.22 million, while about 25% of nodes are not following any blogs (i.e., 0 out-degree) and the maximum out-degree is 14,208.

As a microblogging platform, Tumblr provides useful tools close to that of traditional blogging sites for creating longer, richer and higher quality content. Specifically, it allows users to create 8 different types of posts: *photo*, *text*, *answer*, *link*, *quote*, *video*, *audio* and *chat*. Furthermore, posts in Tumblr have no limitation in length unlike other microblogging sites such as Twitter, which is restricted to 140 characters per post. It also supports the use of *tags* for each post, which are separate from the post content. Lastly, users can *like* a post or re-broadcast the post to its own followers by *reblogging*. While these two activities have different intentions to the user, both directly reflect the user's interest which should be utilized for better recommendation quality.

We processed 5 months of Tumblr data, where each month contains about 1.5 TB of sampled records of posts created, reblogged and liked. Note that we restrict to users with at least 5 records in each month. On average, there are more than 150 million newly created posts, 2.5 billion reblogged posts and 2 billion likes per month. We show the

[4]The reported datasets and results are deliberately incomplete and subject to anonymization, and thus do not necessarily reflect the real portfolio at any particular time.

[5]www.facebook.com

distribution of each post type in Figure 2(b). Almost 80% of posts are *photo* posts suggesting image features are a crucial component for analyzing posts. Figure 2(c) reports the average number of reblogs a new post gets for each post type. We can see in the figure that photo, quote and chat posts are reblogged significantly more than other types of posts. Overall, a new post gets reblogged more than 15 times on average illustrating the high sharing activity in Tumblr. We have also found that about 8.3% of users do not have any posts and about 12.2% of users do not have any activity information. More detailed analysis of the Tumblr data can be found in [6].

4. METHODS

In this section, we describe a natural way of combining various user/blog features and the follower graph to enable the inductive setting, i.e., recommendations for new users and blogs. We first describe the Inductive Matrix Completion method for blog recommendation, which is based on the proposition that user-blog follow behavior arises from applying a low-rank matrix to user and blog features. Next we motivate and present our proposed Boosted Inductive Matrix Completion method. We briefly establish the notation used before describing our proposed approaches.

Notation: We denote the follower graph by $\mathcal{G} = (\mathcal{V}_1, \mathcal{V}_2, \mathcal{E})$, where $\mathcal{V}_1$ ($m = |\mathcal{V}_1|$) and $\mathcal{V}_2$ ($n = |\mathcal{V}_2|$) is the set of users and blogs, respectively; $\mathcal{E} = \{e_{ij} | i \in \mathcal{V}_1, j \in \mathcal{V}_2\}$ is the set of edges indicating user i follows blog j. Let $A \in \mathbb{R}^{m \times n}$ be the adjacency matrix of $\mathcal{G}$, where each row corresponds to a user and each column corresponds to a blog, such that $A_{ij} = 1$, if user i is following blog j and 0 otherwise. That is, we treat missing values as zeros. Note that $\mathcal{G}$ is a directed graph, i.e., A is non-symmetric. Let $X \in \mathbb{R}^{m \times f_u}$ and $Y \in \mathbb{R}^{n \times f_b}$ denote the user and blog feature matrices, respectively.

4.1 Matrix Completion

The low rank matrix completion (MC) approach is one of the most popular and successful collaborative filtering methods for recommender systems [23]. The goal is to recover the underlying low rank matrix by using the observed entries of A, which is typically formulated as follows:

$$\min_{U,V} \sum_{(i,j)\in\Omega} (A_{ij} - (UV^T)_{ij})^2 + \frac{\lambda}{2}(\|U\|_F^2 + \|V\|_F^2), \quad (1)$$

where $U \in \mathbb{R}^{m \times r}$ and $V \in \mathbb{R}^{n \times r}$ with r being the dimension of the latent feature space; $\Omega \in [m] \times [n]$ is the set of observed entries; λ is a regularization parameter. Note that matrix completion only utilizes samples from the follower graph A and ignores the side information that might be present in the system.

4.2 Inductive Matrix Completion

The standard matrix completion formulation is restricted to the transductive setting, i.e., predictions can only be made for existing users and items without re-training for latent factors of new users or items. Furthermore, the standard formulation suffers performance with extreme sparsity in the data, which is the case for Tumblr as about 50% of users do not have any followers and about 25% of users are not following any blogs. One simple way to make predictions for such users is to use a popularity based global ranking of blogs and recommend the top ranked ones. In order to make meaningful predictions, one would need more information about users and blogs. For Tumblr, such information can be obtained from rich content (photos, text) and activity (reblog, like) information.

Recently, a novel inductive matrix completion (IMC) approach was proposed and theoretically analyzed by [16] to alleviate data sparsity issues as well as enable predictions for new users and items by incorporating side information of users and items given in the form of feature vectors. The main idea is to model A_{ij} using user i's feature vector $\mathbf{x}_i \in \mathbb{R}^{f_u}$, item j's feature vector $\mathbf{y}_j \in \mathbb{R}^{f_b}$ and a low-rank matrix $Z \in \mathbb{R}^{f_u \times f_b}$ as

$$A_{ij} = \mathbf{x}_i^T Z \mathbf{y}_j. \quad (2)$$

That is, the interaction between user i and item j is generated by applying their respective feature vectors to Z. For a new item b, the predictions A_{ib} for each user i can be calculated with the feature vector $\mathbf{y}_b$ available.

By factoring $Z = WH^T$, the goal of IMC is to recover $W \in \mathbb{R}^{f_u \times r}$ and $H \in \mathbb{R}^{f_b \times r}$ using the observed entries in A. The IMC objective is given as

$$\min_{W,H} \sum_{(i,j)\in\Omega} \ell(A_{ij}, \mathbf{x}_i^T W H^T \mathbf{y}_j) + \frac{\lambda}{2}(\|W\|_F^2 + \|H\|_F^2),$$

for some loss function ℓ that measures the difference between the observations and predictions, e.g., squared loss $\ell_s(a,b) = (a-b)^2$ or logistic loss $\ell_l(a,b) = \log(1+e^{-ab})$. The number of parameters to learn is $(f_u + f_b) \times r$ depending only on the number of user and item features, whereas there are $(m+n) \times r$ parameters in the standard matrix completion. Note that matrix completion is a special case of IMC when $X = I$ and $Y = I$.

For a convex loss function ℓ, the above IMC objective becomes a convex function when either W or H is fixed (similar to the standard matrix completion case). The computational cost to solve the optimization problem differs based on the choice of the loss function ℓ. In our experiments, we use the squared loss in the objective and employ the alternative minimization approach in [15]. Under this setting, the computational cost for each step is $O((nnz(A)+mf_u+nf_b)r^2c)$, where $nnz(A)$ is the number of non-zeros in A and c is a small constant. In our experiments, f_u, f_b and r are very small (few hundreds) and the solution converges in less than 10 iterations.

4.3 Boosted Inductive Matrix Completion

Next we present our method called Boosted Inductive Matrix Completion (BIMC). One issue with IMC is that the model is too rigid as it heavily depends on the user features X and item features Y. That is, user and item features from different sources should support the underlying structure of the follower graph A in order to make good predictions. Let $X = U_X \Sigma_X V_X^T$, where $U_X \Sigma_X V_X^T$ is the SVD of X. Similarly, let $Y = U_Y \Sigma_Y V_Y^T$ be the SVD of Y. From the IMC formulation, we have

$$A = XZY^T = U_X(\Sigma_X V_X^T Z V_Y \Sigma_Y)U_Y^T = U_X \hat{Z} U_Y^T,$$

where $\hat{Z} = \Sigma_X V_X^T Z V_Y \Sigma_Y$. Thus, the subspace spanned by U_X must have significant overlap with that of A to achieve small error. For example, like and reblog activity features can be quite helpful as a direct reflection of user interest. Similar arguments can be made for Y as well.

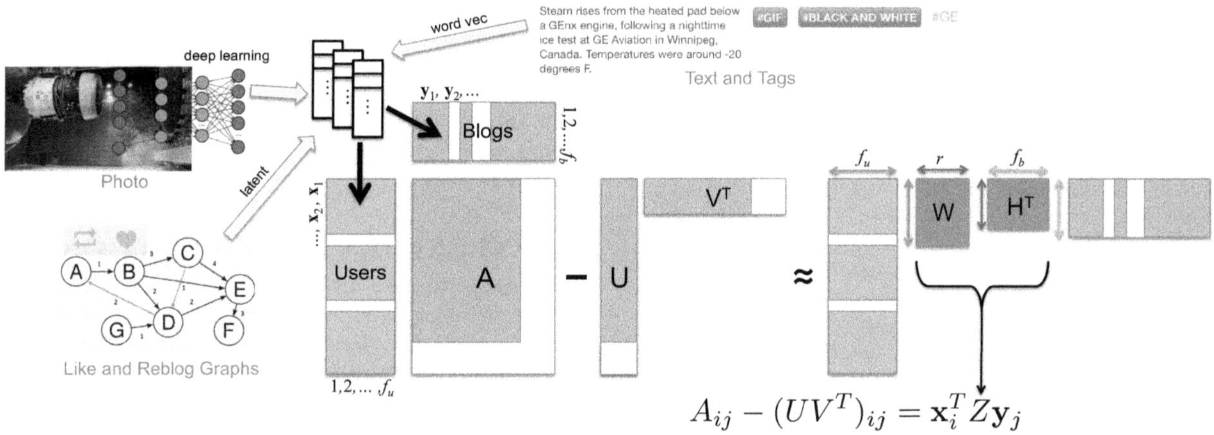

Figure 3: Boosted Inductive Matrix Completion model. Shaded areas represent available information.

However, features from various sources may not always support the matrix A and IMC can suffer performance significantly in such case. For instance, text data in Tumblr is extremely sparse and noisy, and thus may not directly reveal user preference. Moreover, it is not always the case that all users and items have features (as shown in Section 3), in which IMC would not be able to make any predictions.

To address these problems, we propose to combine both standard matrix completion and inductive matrix completion, and thereby better utilize the power of both approaches. That is, we combine the power of MC to reduce the noise level in the input data as well as the advantage of IMC to incorporate side information of users and items. Our idea is to model A_{ij} as

$$A_{ij} = (UV^T)_{ij} + \alpha \mathbf{x}_i^T Z \mathbf{y}_j, \tag{3}$$

where the parameter α adjusts the contribution of features in the final prediction. Choosing a good α is crucial for both performance and solving the optimization problem, which can be difficult to tune. Furthermore, simultaneously solving for all four latent factor matrices U, V, W and H will lead to slower convergence due to the increased number of parameters.

Thus, our strategy is to first learn the latent factor matrices U and V of the MC model as in (1). The resulting approximation error or residual matrix $R = A - UV^T$ represents links in the follower graph that MC could not fully capture. Then we model R_{ij} with IMC as

$$R_{ij} = A_{ij} - (UV^T)_{ij} = \mathbf{x}_i^T Z \mathbf{y}_j. \tag{4}$$

In other words, we first try to find the support of the follower graph A with the latent factors U and V and focus on the part that it can not accurately model using IMC. This is especially useful when the norm of the residual from (1) is large, which suggests a significant deviation from low rank structure in A. Our objective is

$$\min_{W,H} \sum_{(i,j)\in\Omega} \ell(A_{ij} - (UV^T)_{ij}, \mathbf{x}_i^T W H^T \mathbf{y}_j) + \frac{\lambda}{2}(\|W\|_F^2 + \|H\|_F^2).$$

With ℓ being the squared loss and fixing H, the gradient of the above objective in matrix form is given as

$$X^T(A - UV^T - XWH^TY)Y^TH + \lambda W.$$

Note that we do not have to explicitly form $A - UV^T$, which would be a dense matrix and infeasible to store in memory.

Our approach eliminates the need to fine tune the parameter α. Furthermore, existing efficient solvers for MC and IMC with theoretical guarantees [17, 15] can be directly applied. An overview of our proposed BIMC model can be found in Figure 3, where we can see that BIMC can handle both sparsity in A as well as users/items without features. Given a user i with features $\mathbf{x}_i$ and blog j with features $\mathbf{y}_j$, we use (3) to obtain predictions with the learned factors and α set to 1. Finally, we note that a converse approach can also be used, i.e., learn the IMC model first, and then train the MC model on the resulting residual matrix; we found the results to be comparable, so we only present results for the former.

We illustrate the advantages of BIMC compared to IMC when features are noisy with the following experiment on the MovieLens-100K dataset[6]. We compute the rank-20 SVD of the user-movie matrix $A = U_A \Sigma_A V_A^T$ and set $X = U_A$ and $Y = V_A$, i.e., the left and right singular vectors of A to be the user and movie features, respectively. Then we perturb the columns of X by adding noise and measure the relative approximation error for IMC: $\|A - XWH^TY^T\|_F / \|A\|_F$ and for BIMC: $\|A - UV^T - XWH^TY^T\|_F / \|A\|_F$. Results are given in Figure 4 confirming that BIMC achieves lower approximation error rates than IMC due to modeling the residual matrix R as in (4). This shows that BIMC is robust to noisy features whereas IMC suffers performance as the noise level increases in the user features X.

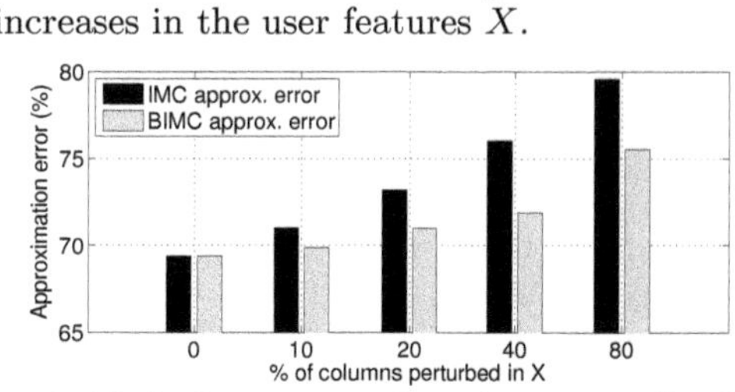

Figure 4: Relative approximation error for IMC and BIMC with different levels of noise in features.

5. FEATURE EXTRACTION

As described in Section 3, Tumblr data contains three main sources of side information of users and blogs: (1) likes and reblogs, (2) tags and text, and (3) images. Extracting

[6] 100,000 ratings from 1,000 users on 1,700 movies; http://grouplens.org/datasets/movielens/

useful features from these sources is a crucial step of the recommender system. We discuss the details of how we extract these user and blog features as follows.

User Activity: For user activity information, we use likes and reblogs from Tumblr of the 1 million sampled users and blogs. Both like and reblog activities can be represented as a weighted graph similar to the follower graph A, where the edge weight between a user i and blog j is set to be the number of liked and reblogged posts of blog j by user i. The edge weights in both cases follow a power-law distribution. Each user likes or reblogs about 340 posts from 27 blogs and each blog gets a total of 410 likes or reblogs on average. In the experiments, we aggregate like and reblog graphs to a single activity graph from the training data and use a log-scale of the edge weights. One way to obtain useful and robust features is to consider the principal components of the adjacency matrix corresponding to the activity graph. That is, we compute p principal components and use them as latent user and blog features for IMC. Thus, we have $f_u = f_b = p$ user activity features for users and blogs, where we empirically set $p = 500$ in the experiments.

Tags and Text: Tags and text used in posts of Tumblr are extremely sparse and noisy. There are an average of 28.7 words and 4.8 tags per post. Furthermore, tags are unconstrained in Tumblr, where a user can put in any arbitrary text. Existing models based on bag-of-words (e.g., LSA, LDA) can suffer from such issues. Therefore, we utilize word2vec, which is a recent neural network inspired method that learns word embeddings in the vector space [27]. word2vec utilizes the technique called skip-gram with negative samples, which tries to represent each of the words by a vector such that words in similar contexts are close to each other. This representation is accomplished by maximizing the predicted probability of words co-occurring in the training corpus. In our work, we first compute d-dimensional vector representations of each word using word2vec, and then cluster these words into c clusters by the k-means algorithm. Using the cluster information, we finally create a histogram of word clusters for each post as a compact representation of tags and text used in that blog. We set $d = 300$ and $c = 1,000$ and processed both textual features for each month in the training data.

Images: Images are an important part of Tumblr data as shown in Section 3. We randomly sampled about 800K images per month from blogs that appear in the training data. We trained a convolutional neural network (CNN) [24, 9] on 1.5M Flickr images with labels due to the unavailability of image labels for the Tumblr dataset. The CNN is composed of seven hidden layers, which consist of five successive convolutional layers followed by two fully connected layers, plus a final soft-max layer. The nonlinearity of each neuron in this CNN is modeled by Rectified Linear Units (ReLUs) $f(x) = \max(0, x)$, which accelerates learning compared with saturating nonlinearity such as tanh units. The CNN takes a 224 × 224 pixel RGB image as input. Each convolutional layer convolves the output of its previous layer with a set of learned kernels, followed by ReLU non-linearity, and two optional layers, local response normalization and max pooling. The local response normalization layer is applied across feature channels, and the max pooling layer is applied over neighboring neurons. The output of the 7th layer is fed into the last soft-max layer, which outputs confidence scores over the pre-defined 958 categories for a given input image. Using the neural network, we extracted deep learning features from the sampled Tumblr images. For users, we averaged the resulting feature vector over all images that the user posted, liked and reblogged. For blogs, only posted and reblogged images were considered as reblogged posts also become a post of the blog.

6. EXPERIMENTAL EVALUATION

In this section, we present the experimental setup used to evaluate our proposed method BIMC in comparison to IMC as well as several other baseline methods on the Tumblr dataset for blog recommendation with additional side information of users and blogs. From the Tumblr follower graph, we randomly sampled 1 million users and blogs resulting in about 12 million follows, i.e., nonzero elements in A. Both user activity and user generated content information were collected over a 5 month period from Tumblr post data.

6.1 Baselines and Evaluation Metrics

We perform both offline and temporal evaluations. For the offline evaluation, we use 10-fold cross-validation. Temporal evaluation is used to simulate online evaluations, where we use data from preceding 4 months as training and the remaining month as testing.

In both cases, we compare BIMC against the standard matrix completion formulation (MC) and the Singular Value Decomposition (SVD), which has been shown to perform well for top-N recommendation tasks [8]. We also compare with methods that incorporate side information including the inductive matrix completion (IMC). Another popular approach is the collective matrix completion (CMC) [33, 4]. The goal of CMC is to jointly recover a collection of matrices with shared low rank structure, which is different from IMC. Specifically, given user-item matrix A, user features X and item features Y, CMC finds a joint factorization as:

$$A = UV^T, \quad X = UP^T \text{ and } Y = VQ^T.$$

That is, the shared user latent factor matrix U is obtained from both A and X (similarly V is obtained from A and Y). Recent work by [11] provides consistency guarantees for CMC, thus we use the algorithm presented in [11]. The Katz measure [34, 32], which is one of the most successful proximity measures for link prediction, is also included in the comparison as a graph-based approach. We compute Katz scores[7] between users and blogs on the combined (symmetric) matrix $C = \begin{bmatrix} S_u & A \\ A^T & S_b \end{bmatrix}$, where S_u and S_b are similarity matrices between users and blogs, respectively, computed from their features. Lastly, we report results of using a simple global popularity ranking (Global) for recommendation as a baseline, where blogs are ranked by the number of followers. We use rank $r = 10$ for MC and SVD, rank $r = 100$ for CMC, IMC and BIMC, and set $\lambda = 0.1$ for all methods, which are determined using cross-validation.

We measure the recommendation performance using precision (PRC@10) and recall (RCL@10) at top-10 generated by each method, which is the region of practical interest for recommender systems. We also report the AUC (area under the ROC curve) of each method for completeness.

[7] The Katz measure is defined as $\sum_{i=1}^{\infty} \beta^i C^i$. We set $\beta = 10^{-6}$.

Table 1: Offline evaluation results of the proposed Boosted Inductive Matrix Completion method (BIMC) in comparison to several baselines.

Method	PRC@10	RCL@10	AUC
Global	1.03%	4.80%	0.8687
SVD	1.28%	5.10%	0.8530
MC	1.28%	5.07%	0.8515
Katz	1.90%	8.15%	0.9209
CMC	0.49%	2.41%	0.8996
IMC	2.93%	11.33%	0.9075
BIMC	**3.21%**	**12.28%**	**0.9221**

Table 2: Temporal evaluation results of the proposed Boosted Inductive Matrix Completion method (BIMC) in comparison to several baselines.

Method	PRC@10	RCL@10	AUC
Global	1.01%	4.70%	0.8626
SVD	1.24%	4.82%	0.8479
MC	1.19%	4.53%	0.8464
Katz	1.33%	5.69%	0.9125
CMC	0.46%	1.81%	0.8932
IMC	2.85%	10.38%	0.8953
BIMC	**3.12%**	**11.32%**	**0.9129**

6.2 Experimental Results

Results of the proposed BIMC method with user and blog features are shown in comparison to the baselines: Global, SVD, MC, Katz, CMC, and IMC for PRC@10, RCL@10 and AUC in Table 1 for the offline evaluation and Table 2 for the temporal evaluation (that simulated A/B testing conditions).

6.2.1 *Performance comparison*

It is very interesting to see in Table 1 that the simple Global method outperforms both SVD and MC baselines in terms of AUC. This can be explained by the facts that most users follow highly popular blogs such as institutions or celebrities [6] and that both SVD and MC suffer from data sparsity. Yet, it is important to note that Global is outperformed by both SVD and MC for precision and recall results. Table 1 also shows that our proposed method, BIMC, achieves the best performance in all three evaluation metrics out of all methods. Note that the two best performing methods, BIMC and IMC, both utilize side information of users and blogs. This implies that such information is crucial to improve the recommendation quality.

In contrast, CMC performs the worst in the top-k list as seen in Table 1 showing that there does not exist significant shared low-rank structure between the follower graph and user/item features. Moreover, textual features in Tumblr are extremely sparse and noisy, which makes the CMC formulation more problematic. This clearly demonstrates that BIMC and IMC incorporate user/item features more effectively in a robust manner. Nonetheless, CMC still achieves similar AUC results compared with IMC. Katz performs comparably to BIMC in terms of AUC, but not in the top-k list, which can also be explained by the fact that similarities in S_u and S_b are affected by noisy features. In sum, we can see that BIMC achieves superior performance than other methods by successfully incorporating rich user and blog features.

Table 3: AUC results for different groups of users of the proposed Boosted Inductive Matrix Completion method (BIMC) in comparison to several baselines.

Method	Low	Medium	High
Global	0.8639	0.8623	0.8403
SVD	0.8488	0.8782	0.8715
MC	0.8473	0.8767	0.8709
Katz	0.9199	0.9304	0.9194
CMC	0.8978	0.9063	0.9058
IMC	0.9040	0.9299	0.9162
BIMC	**0.9209**	**0.9316**	**0.9198**

6.2.2 *Temporal evaluation*

Although cross-validation is a widely accepted evaluation methodology, it can produce biased results when temporal effects are not considered when splitting the data into training and testing sets. Thus, we evaluated all methods using another dataset divided into training and testing using a fixed date and time. Specifically, we use data from a 4-month period as training and the following 5th month data as testing. This evaluation is more similar than the offline-evaluation to A/B testing, which is broadly used in industry. Results for the temporal evaluation is given in Table 2, in which we can observe very similar results to the offline case in Table 1. This suggests that our proposed methods would also perform well in production settings.

6.2.3 *Performance for users and items with different levels of sparsity*

In order to better understand the effect of utilizing rich information about users and items in BIMC, we divide users as well as blogs into different categories based on the number of people they follow and the number of people who follow them. In other words, user and blog segmentation is done based on the number of nonzero elements in A, to examine how the methods perform under different levels of sparsity in the data. Specifically, users are partitioned into three groups based on the number of followees n_f: $n_f \leq 40$ (Low), $40 < n_f \leq 100$ (Medium) and $n_f > 100$ (High), where each group consists of about 89.36%, 7.81% and 2.83% of users. Similarly, we also partition the blog dimension (with the same thresholds), where each group consists of about 95.12%, 3.26% and 1.63% blogs respectively.

For each user category, we present Recall@k in Figure 5 for $k = 1, 2, \cdots, 20$. As shown in Figure 5, BIMC outperforms all other baselines for all user groups in terms of Recall@k. The second best method is IMC followed by Katz. This explicitly shows that utilizing both user and item features significantly helps in dealing with different sparsity conditions including cold-start. For the Low user group in Figure 5, it is interesting to see that SVD and MC suffers from severe sparsity and therefore perform comparably with the Global baseline. Note that the performance decreases for all methods as we move from Low to High user groups. This can be explained by the facts that users who already follow many popular blogs would need to be recommended more diverse blogs in the long-tail, which is generally a much harder task. Table 3 presents AUC results on all three user groups, where we can see that BIMC achieves the largest AUC values across all user categories. As discussed in Section 6.2.1, CMC is not able to make any good predictions in the top-

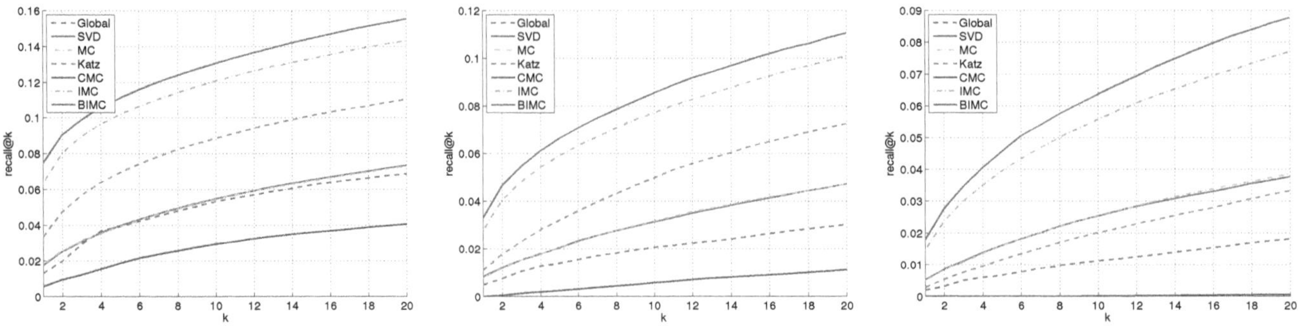

(a) Users with low activity (b) Users with medium activity (c) Users with high activity

Figure 5: Recall@k results for user groups with different activity levels (low/medium/high) the proposed Boosted Inductive Matrix Completion method (i.e., BIMC) in comparison to several baselines ($k = 1, 2, \cdots, 20$).

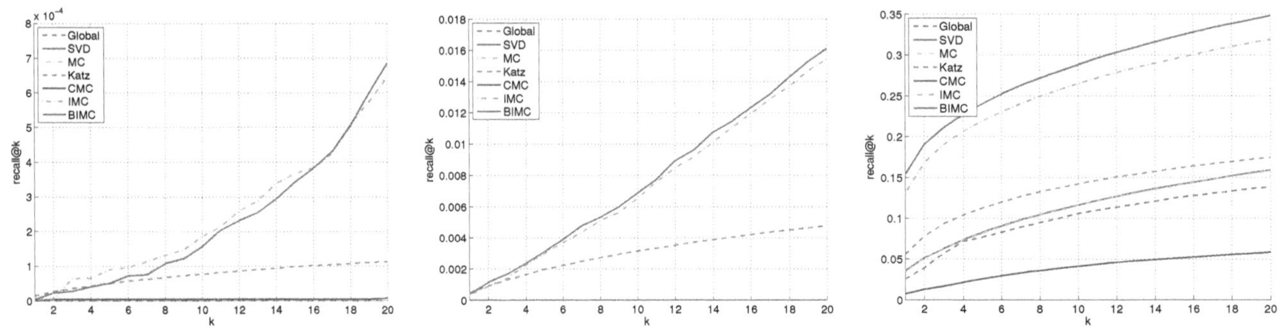

(a) Blogs with low popularity (b) Blogs with medium popularity (c) Blogs with high popularity

Figure 6: Recall@k results for blog groups with different popularity levels (low/medium/high) of the proposed Boosted Inductive Matrix Completion method (i.e., BIMC) in comparison to several baselines ($k = 1, 2, \cdots, 20$).

k list, but still achieves reasonable AUC levels as shown in Table 3. This set of results shows that BIMC successfully handles data sparsity by incorporating rich user and blog features, and significantly improves over other methods.

Next, we analyze the performance of all methods for blog groups with different popularity levels as shown in Figure 6, where we can observe similar trends as found in Figure 5 with different user groups. It can be seen in Figure 6 that BIMC and IMC outperforms all other baselines for all blog groups in terms of Recall@k, while all other baselines suffer from data sparsity, and cannot make any correct retrieval. For blogs with high popularity, their performances are much better. For this group, SVD and MC perform slightly better than the Global, but still much worse than BIMC and IMC. Another set of interesting results is the fact that IMC performs comparably with BIMC for items with low and medium popularity. This can be explained by the fact that the MC step in BIMC is suffering from data sparsity in both of these cases, and is not helping the BIMC as much as in the case of items with high popularity.

Finally, we analyze the performance of all methods for user groups and item groups jointly. Specifically, Figures 7 and 8 show the performances of all methods for all user and item groups jointly in terms of Precision@k and Recall@k respectively. It can be observed that both precision and recall increases significantly for users and items with high activity/popularity. For users with low and medium activity, all methods other than BIMC and IMC severely suffer from data sparsity. For users with high activity, BIMC outperforms IMC, both of which significantly outperform other baselines. Another interesting result is the fact that IMC outperforms or performs comparably with BIMC for user and items with low activity/popularity, showing that the the MC step in BIMC suffers from data sparsity and cannot effectively help IMC, in which case all prediction from BIMC depends on IMC step alone. Overall, this set of experiments clearly demonstrate the power of BIMC over IMC, as well as utilizing rich set of user and item features in BIMC and IMC over other baselines.

7. CONCLUSIONS

Recommending blogs to follow is one of the core tasks for online microblogging sites such as Tumblr for improving user engagement as well as advertising revenue. In this paper, we propose a novel boosted inductive matrix completion (BIMC) model for the task that combines the power of an inductive matrix completion model together with a standard matrix completion model. the proposed BIMC model focuses on the residual matrix that is calculated from the approximation matrix of a standard matrix completion (MC) model, and learns an inductive matrix completion model (IMC) to effectively utilize the rich side information of users and blogs to learn the missing links in the follower graph where a standard MC fails to learn. We utilize state-of-the art deep learning methods such as word2vec and convolutional neural networks to extract a comprehensive set of features. An extensive set of experiments conducted on large-scale real-world data from Tumblr demonstrate the effectiveness of the proposed BIMC over MC and IMC methods as well as several other baselines.

8. REFERENCES

[1] D. Agarwal and B.-C. Chen. Regression-based latent factor models. In *SIGKDD*, pages 19–28, 2009.

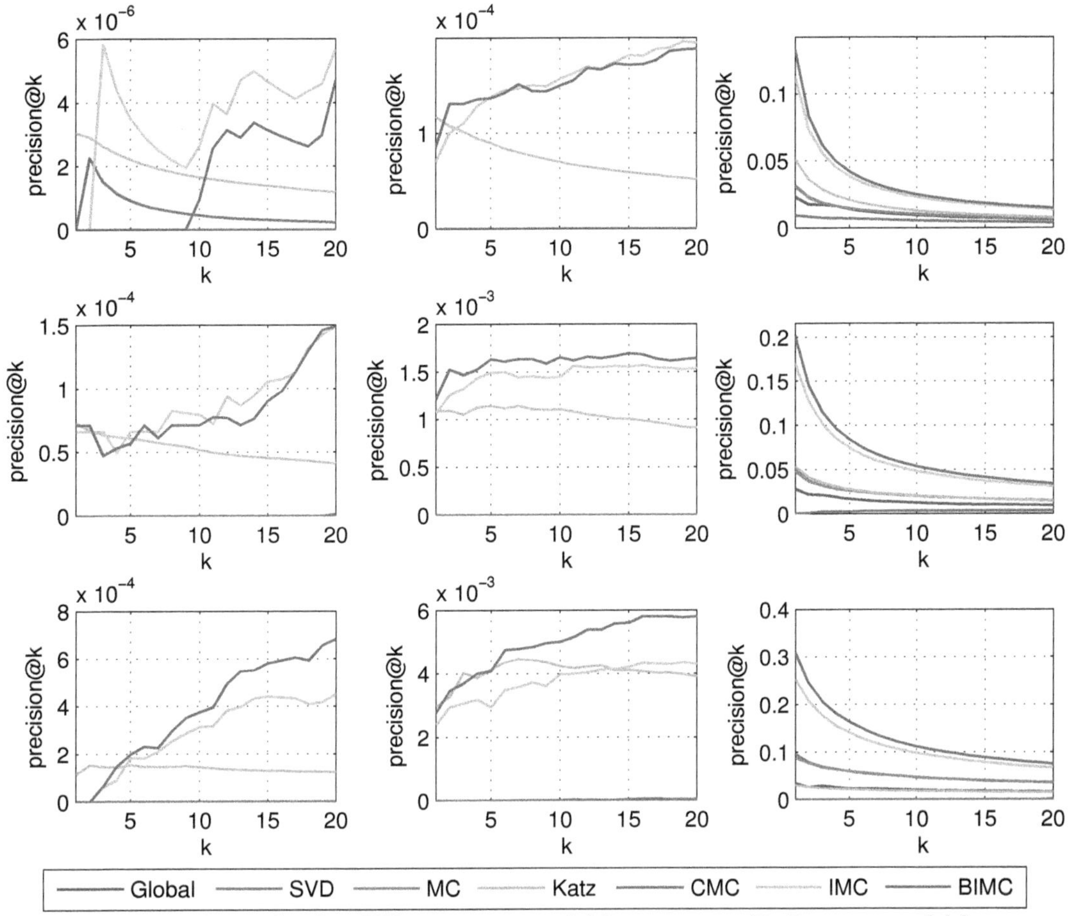

Figure 7: Precision at top-k results for different user and blog groups. Both users and blogs are divided into three groups (n_d: the number of links): (1) $n_d \leq 40$, (2) $40 < n_d \leq 100$, and (3) $n_d > 100$. From left to right are blog groups 1, 2 and 3, and from top to bottom are user groups 1, 2 and 3. BIMC outperforms other methods in most user-blog group combinations.

[2] M. G. Armentano, D. Godoy, and A. A. Amandi. Followee recommendation based on text analysis of micro-blogging activity. *Information Systems*, 38(8):1116–1127, 2013.

[3] R. M. Bell and Y. Koren. Lessons from the Netflix Prize Challenge. *SIGKDD Explor. Newsl.*, 9(2):75–79, 2007.

[4] G. Bouchard, D. Yin, and S. Guo. Convex collective matrix factorization. In *AISTATS*, pages 144–152, 2013.

[5] E. Candès and B. Recht. Exact matrix completion via convex optimization. *CACM*, 55(6):111–119, 2012.

[6] Y. Chang, L. Tang, Y. Inagaki, and Y. Liu. What is Tumblr: A statistical overview and comparison. *SIGKDD Explor. Newsl.*, 16(1):21–29, 2014.

[7] Y. Chen, S. Bhojanapalli, S. Sanghavi, and R. Ward. Coherent matrix completion. In *ICML*, pages 674–682, 2014.

[8] P. Cremonesi, Y. Koren, and R. Turrin. Performance of recommender algorithms on top-N recommendation tasks. In *RecSys*, pages 39–46, 2010.

[9] J. Donahue, Y. Jia, O. Vinyals, J. Hoffman, N. Zhang, E. Tzeng, and T. Darrell. DeCAF: A deep convolutional activation feature for generic visual recognition. In *ICML*, pages 647–655, 2014.

[10] O. U. Florez and L. Nachman. Deep learning of semantic word representations to implement a content-based recommender for the RecSys Challenge'14. In *ESWC*, 2014.

[11] S. Gunasekar, M. Yamada, D. Yin, and Y. Chang. Consistent collective matrix completion under joint low rank structure. In *AISTATS*, pages 306–314, 2015.

[12] P. Gupta, A. Goel, J. Lin, A. Sharma, D. Wang, and R. Zadeh. WTF: The Who to Follow service at Twitter. In *WWW*, pages 505–514, 2013.

[13] J. Hannon, M. Bennett, and B. Smyth. Recommending Twitter users to follow using content and collaborative filtering approaches. In *RecSys*, pages 199–206, 2010.

[14] L. Hong, A. S. Doumith, and B. D. Davison. Co-factorization machines: modeling user interests and predicting individual decisions in Twitter. In *WSDM*, pages 557–566, 2013.

[15] Y. Hsiang-Fu, P. Jain, P. Kar, and I. S. Dhillon. Large-scale multi-label learning with missing labels. In *ICML*, pages 593–601, 2014.

[16] P. Jain and I. S. Dhillon. Provable inductive matrix completion. *CoRR*, abs/1306.0626, 2013.

[17] P. Jain, P. Netrapalli, and S. Sanghavi. Low-rank matrix completion using alternating minimization. In *STOC*, pages 665–674, 2013.

[18] M. Jamali and M. Ester. A matrix factorization technique with trust propagation for recommendation in social networks. In *RecSys*, pages 135–142, 2010.

[19] A. Karpathy, G. Toderici, S. Shetty, T. Leung, R. Sukthankar, and L. Fei-Fei. Large-scale video classification with convolutional neural networks. In *CVPR*, pages 1725–1732, 2014.

[20] R. H. Keshavan, A. Montanari, and S. Oh. Matrix completion from noisy entries. *JMLR*, 11:2057–2078, 2010.

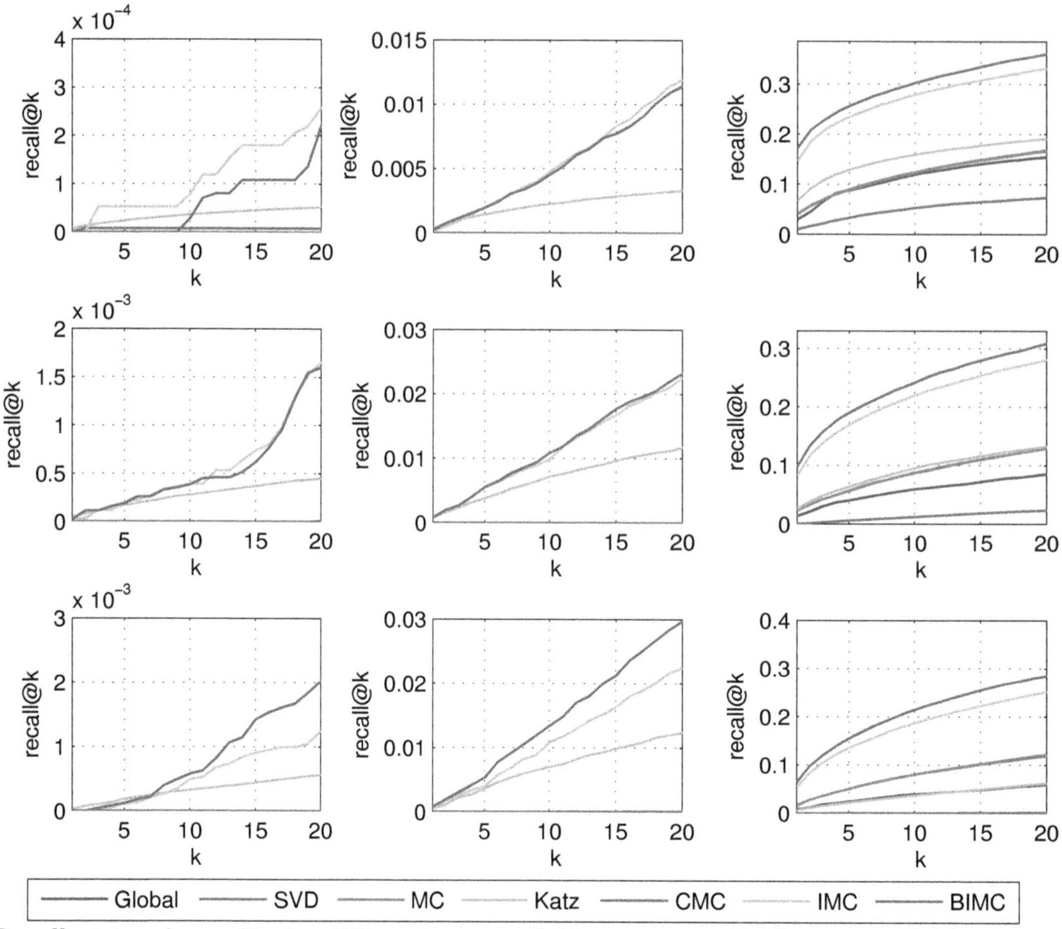

Figure 8: Recall at top-k results for different user and blog groups. Both users and blogs are divided into three groups (n_d: the number of links): (1) $n_d \leq 40$, (2) $40 < n_d \leq 100$, and (3) $n_d > 100$. From left to right are blog groups 1, 2 and 3, and from top to bottom are user groups 1, 2 and 3. BIMC outperforms other methods in most user-blog group combinations.

[21] Y. Kim and K. Shim. Twitobi: A recommendation system for Twitter using probabilistic modeling. In *ICDM*, pages 340–349, 2011.

[22] I. Konstas, V. Stathopoulos, and J. M. Jose. On social networks and collaborative recommendation. In *SIGIR*, pages 195–202, 2009.

[23] Y. Koren, R. Bell, and C. Volinsky. Matrix factorization techniques for recommender systems. *Computer*, 42(8):30–37, 2009.

[24] A. Krizhevsky, I. Sutskever, and G. Hinton. Imagenet classification with deep convolutional neural networks. In *NIPS*, pages 1097–1105, 2012.

[25] A. Levi, O. Mokryn, C. Diot, and N. Taft. Finding a needle in a haystack of reviews: Cold start context-based hotel recommender system. In *RecSys*, pages 115–122, 2012.

[26] H. Ma, D. Zhou, C. Liu, M. R. Lyu, and I. King. Recommender systems with social regularization. In *WSDM*, pages 287–296, 2011.

[27] T. Mikolov, I. Sutskever, K. Chen, G. S. Corrado, and J. Dean. Distributed representations of words and phrases and their compositionality. In *NIPS*, pages 3111–3119, 2013.

[28] Y. Moshfeghi, B. Piwowarski, and J. M. Jose. Handling data sparsity in collaborative filtering using emotion and semantic based features. In *SIGIR*, pages 625–634, 2011.

[29] N. Natarajan, D. Shin, and I. S. Dhillon. Which app will you use next? collaborative filtering with interactional context. In *RecSys*, pages 201–208, 2013.

[30] A. Oord, S. Dieleman, and B. Schrauwen. Deep content-based music recommendation. In *NIPS*, pages 2643–2651, 2013.

[31] Y. Shi, M. Larson, and A. Hanjalic. Collaborative filtering beyond the user-item matrix: A survey of the state of the art and future challenges. *ACM Comput. Surv.*, 47(1):3:1–3:45, 2014.

[32] D. Shin, S. Si, and I. S. Dhillon. Multi-scale link prediction. In *CIKM*, pages 215–224, 2012.

[33] A. P. Singh and G. J. Gordon. Relational learning via collective matrix factorization. In *SIGKDD*, pages 650–658, 2008.

[34] V. Vasuki, N. Natarajan, Z. Lu, B. Savas, and I. S. Dhillon. Scalable affiliation recommendation using auxiliary networks. *ACM TIST*, 3(1):3:1–3:20, 2011.

[35] J. Weston, S. Chopra, and K. Adams. #TagSpace: Semantic embeddings from hashtags. In *EMNLP*, pages 1822–1827, 2014.

[36] D. Yin, L. Hong, and B. D. Davison. Structural link analysis and prediction in microblogs. In *CIKM*, pages 1163–1168, 2011.

[37] G. Zhao, M. L. Lee, W. Hsu, W. Chen, and H. Hu. Community-based user recommendation in uni-directional social networks. In *CIKM*, pages 189–198, 2013.

[38] Y. Zhen, W.-J. Li, and D.-Y. Yeung. Tagicofi: Tag informed collaborative filtering. In *RecSys*, pages 69–76, 2009.

BiasWatch: A Lightweight System for Discovering and Tracking Topic-Sensitive Opinion Bias in Social Media

Haokai Lu
Texas A&M University
hlu@cse.tamu.edu

James Caverlee
Texas A&M University
caverlee@cse.tamu.edu

Wei Niu
Texas A&M University
weiniu.2010@gmail.com

ABSTRACT

We propose a lightweight system for (i) semi-automatically discovering and tracking bias themes associated with opposing sides of a topic; (ii) identifying strong partisans who drive the online discussion; and (iii) inferring the opinion bias of "regular" participants. By taking just two hand-picked seeds to characterize the topic-space (e.g., "pro-choice" and "pro-life") as *weak labels*, we develop an efficient optimization-based opinion bias propagation method over the social/information network. We show how this approach leads to a 20% accuracy improvement versus a next-best alternative for bias estimation, as well as uncovering the opinion leaders and evolving themes associated with these topics. We also demonstrate how the inferred opinion bias can be integrated into user recommendation, leading to a 26% improvement in precision.

Categories and Subject Descriptors

H.3.4 [**Information Storage and Retrieval**]: Systems and Software—*Information networks*

Keywords

opinion analysis; bias; social media

1. INTRODUCTION

Social media has increasingly become a popular and important platform for "regular" people to express their opinions, without the need to rely on expensive and fundamentally limited conduits like newspapers and broadcast television. These opinions can be expressed on a variety of themes including politically-charged topics like abortion and gun control as well as fun (but heated) rivalries like android vs. iOS and Cowboys vs. 49ers. Our interest in this paper is in creating a flexible tool for discovering and tracking the themes of opinion bias around these topics, the strong partisans who drive the online discussion, and the degree of opinion bias of "regular" social media participants, to determine to what degree particular participants support or oppose a topic of interest.

However, assessing topic-sensitive opinion bias is challenging. First, the opinion bias of "regular" users may not be as pronounced as prominent figures, so discerning this bias will require special care. Second, how opinion bias manifests will inevitably vary by topic, so a system should be adaptable to each topic. Third, the themes by which people express their opinions may change over time depending on the circumstances (e.g., gun control debates may take different forms based on the ebb and flow of elections, recent shooting incidents, and so forth). As a result, assessing bias should be adaptive to these temporal changes.

CIKM'15, October 19–23, 2015, Melbourne, VIC, Australia.
© 2015 ACM. ISBN 978-1-4503-3794-6/15/10 ...$15.00.
DOI: http://dx.doi.org/10.1145/2806416.2806573.

Hence in this paper, we develop a lightweight system – BiasWatch – for discovering and tracking opinion bias in social media. BiasWatch begins by taking just two hand-picked seeds to characterize the topic-space (e.g., "pro-choice" and "pro-life" for abortion) as *weak labels* to bootstrap the opinion bias framework. Concretely, we leverage these hand-picked seeds to identify other emerging (and often unknown) themes in social media, reflecting changes in discourse as new arguments and issues arise and fade from public view (e.g., an upcoming election, a contentious news story). We propose and evaluate two approaches for expanding the hand-picked seeds in the context of Twitter to identify supporting and opposing hashtags – one based on co-occurrence and one on signed information gain. We use these discovered hashtags to identify strong topic-based partisans (what we dub *anchors*). Based on the social and information networks around these anchors, we propose an efficient opinion-bias propagation method to determine user's opinion bias – based on both content and retweeting similarity – and embed this method in an optimization framework for estimating the topic-sensitive bias of social media participants. In summary, this paper makes the following contributions:

- First, we build a systematic framework – BiasWatch – to discover biased themes and estimate user-based opinion bias quantitatively under the context of controversial topics in social media. We propose an efficient optimization scheme – called User-guided Opinion Propagation [UOP] – to propagate opinion bias. By feeding just two opposing hashtags, the system can discover bias-related hashtags, find bias anchors, and assess the degree of bias for "regular" users who tweet about controversial topics.
- Second, we evaluate the estimation of users' opinion bias by comparing the quality of the proposed opinion bias approach versus several alternative approaches over multiple Twitter datasets. Overall, we see a significant improvement of 20.0% in accuracy and 28.6% in AUC on average over the next-best method.
- Third, we study the effect of different approaches for biased theme discovery to measure the impact of newly discovered biased hashtags as additional supervision. We observe that the newly discovered hashtags are often associated with the underlying community of similar opinion bias, and that they temporally fluctuate due to the impact of new controversial events.
- Finally, we demonstrate how these inferred opinion bias scores can be integrated into user recommendation by giving similar-minded users a higher ranking. We show that the integration

can improve the recommendation performance by 26.3% in precision@20 and 13.8% in MAP@20. This result implicitly confirms the principle of homophily in the context of opinion bias, and demonstrates how topic-sensitive opinion bias can enrich user modeling in social media.

2. RELATED WORK

There has been considerable research effort devoted to exploring political polarization, assessing media bias of major news outlets, and assessing user sentiment towards particular topics.

Political polarization. Political polarization has been a topic of great interest in the past decade and studied in news articles [33], online forums [3] and social media [1, 5, 6, 7, 11, 16, 23]. Adamic and Glance [1] demonstrated the divided community structure in the citation network of political blogs. Conover et al. [7] and Livne et al. [16] showed that there exists a highly segregated network structure using modularity. Guerra et al. [11] compared polarized and non-polarized networks and proposed a new measure to determine whether a network is polarized given that the network is also modular. Since knowing users' political orientation can be of great importance for understanding the overall political landscape, many approaches have been proposed to classify a user's political identity. Conover et al. [6] and Pennacchiotti and Popescu [23] exploit text and network features for classification. Akoglu [3] proposed to use signed bipartite opinion networks for the classification and ranking of user's political polarity on forum data. Zhou et al. [33] applied semi-supervised learning methods to classify news articles and users' political standing. Cohen et al. [5] employ supervised methods to classify political users into groups with different political activities, and conclude that it is hard to infer "ordinary" users' political orientation. In our work, instead of simply focusing on the classification of user's political orientation, we are interested in developing a flexible tool to explore controversial themes and discover their underlying users' degree of opinion bias on a topic basis. We show that user's opinion bias can be leveraged to improve other applications such as user recommendation.

Media bias. Apart from user-oriented political orientation, some works have explored media bias. Groseclose et al. [10] proposed a new measure to quantify media bias by comparing the number of citations to think tanks and policy groups to those of Congress members. Gentzkow et al. [9] also proposed a media bias measure which considers the frequency of phrases quoted by Congressional members of Republican and Democratic parties in newspapers. Lin et al. [15] focused on the measure of coverage quantity to compare the extent of bias between blogs and news media. Wong et al. [29] quantified the political leanings of media outlets on Twitter using aggregated retweeting statistics. Our work differs from these in that we target the opinion bias of "regular" users instead of prominent media, and with respect to different controversial topics instead of only political leanings.

User sentiment. There are also prior works which infer user's sentiment toward a topic in social media or online forums. Tan et al. [26] proposed a semi-supervised approach to inferring users' sentiment using social network information. Kim et al. [12] and Gao et al. [8] proposed to use a collaborative filtering like approach to estimate user-level sentiment. Lu et al. [17] proposed to use content and social interactions to discover opinion networks in forum discussions. However, our work has two differences from these and other sentiment-oriented approaches. The first is that many of these works require a significant amount of manually labelled tweets or users as ground truth. In our work, we develop automatic approaches using crowdsourced hashtags as seeds to substantially reduce manual labor. The second is that we focus on intrinsic opinion bias instead of sentiment. Sentiment [22] centers around users' attitude or emotional state, usually reflected by the use of emotional words. However, opinion bias can also be reflected by the news or factual information she chooses to post, which may lack any prominent emotional words.

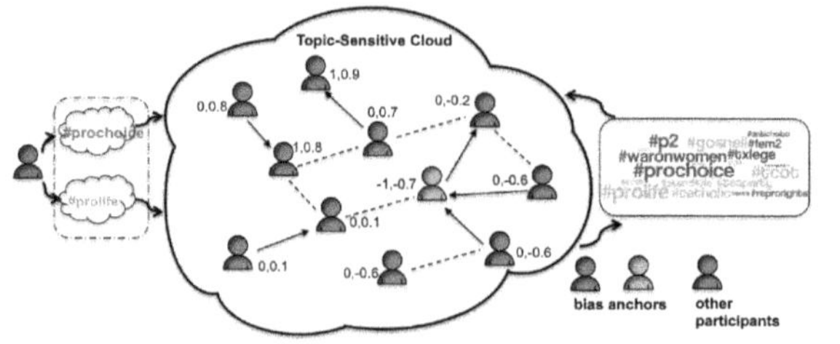

Figure 1: Overall BiasWatch Framework

3. LIGHTWEIGHT BIAS DISCOVERY

Problem Statement. We assume there exists a set of users $U = \{u_1, u_2, ..., u_n\}$ sampled from Twitter. Each user has their corresponding tweets $D = \{d_1, d_2, ..., d_n\}$ related to a controversial topic T, where d_i is a collection of tweets by u_i. Since a person's opinion bias represents the intrinsic tendency that she chooses to support or oppose a concept under a controversial context, we choose to quantize the degree of her opinion bias by a numeric score ranging from -1 to 1. Specifically, we assign $B = \{b_1, b_2, ..., b_n\}$ for each user in U, respectively, where $b_i \in [-1, 1]$. When b_i is close to 1, it denotes that user u_i has a strong positive standing toward the topic; when b_i is close to -1, it represents the opposite. Thus, given a controversial topic T, a sampled set of users U and their on-topic tweets D, we identify the following tasks of the system framework: (i) Discovering biased themes that are discussed by opposing sides of users. We denote P as the set of positive themes and N as the set of negative themes; (ii) Finding bias anchors who show strong degree of opinion bias, which we denote as U_{anchor}; (iii) Determining "regular" participants' opinion bias B.

Overall Approach. In order to tackle these tasks, we propose a lightweight framework that propagates opinion bias scores based only on a few hand-picked seeds that characterize the topic-space (e.g., "pro-choice" and "pro-life" for abortion). The BiasWatch framework, illustrated in Figure 1, takes as input these hand-picked seeds and then proceeds through the following three key steps:

- **Finding Bias Anchors.** This first step identifies topic-based partisans whose opinion bias is strongly revealed through their choice of hashtags. We develop two automatic approaches to: (i) identify biased themes in the form of hashtags through initial seeds; (ii) expand the pools of bias anchors with these identified biased themes.
- **Propagating Bias.** This second step builds a user similarity network around these expanded anchors and other "regular" participants, and propagates bias along this network. The edges here measure the similarities of two users through content and link features from tweets.
- **Noise-Aware Optimization.** Lastly, we propose to embed the previous two steps into a noise-aware optimization framework where anchors' opinion bias can be effectively propagated to each "regular" participant throughout the network. A key facet is that this optimization is tolerant of noisy labels on the initial bias anchors, so that initial errors made in identifying bias anchors need not lead to cascading errors in "regular" participants.

3.1 Finding Bias Anchors

Our first challenge is to identify strong topic-based partisans (what we dub *anchors*). These anchors serve as the basis for propa-

Table 1: Top ten themes at different times for "fracking" discovered by seed expansion; red for pro-fracking; blue for anti-fracking.

Dec 2012	Mar 2013	June 2013	Sept 2013
#shale	#dontfrackny	#shale	#balcombe
#natgas	#shale	#energy	#shale
#oil	#energy	#natgas	#frackoff
#energy	#oil	#oil	#energy
#gas	#gas	#gas	#greatgasgala
#tcot	#natgas	#banfracking	#natgas
#jobs	#frack	#fracked	#banfracking
#frack	#banfracking	#frack	#gas
#marcellus	#nokxl	#tcot	#oil
#naturalgas	#tcot	#dontfrackny	#frack

gating opinion bias throughout the social and information network. One reasonable method for identifying anchors is to manually label a number of users, among whom we hope that there exist a portion of users whose opinion bias is clearly shown. However, there are two disadvantages of this approach: (i) it is potentially expensive and time-consuming; and (ii) because of the random nature of labeling, typically, we have to label many users whose opinion bias is not clear or neutral in order to obtain anchors.

To overcome these difficulties, we propose to exploit crowd-generated hashtags in Twitter. Hashtags are often used to tag tweets with a specific topic for better discoverability or to indicate the community to which the tweets are posted [30]. Some hashtags may be viewed as a rich source of expressing opinions [28], potentially indicating user's opinion bias. For example, some most popular hashtags for "gun control" include #guncontrolnow and #2ndamendment, which reveal strong user bias, with the former often used by supporters of gun control and the latter by opponents. Hashtags of this nature can be essentially considered as *weak labels* of the polarity of tweets with respect to a controversial topic. Hence, to find bias anchors we first seek to identify a candidate set of hashtags that provide support for the topic and a candidate set of hashtags that express opposition. Since the hashtags used to express an opinion may change over time as new issues arise and fade from public view (e.g., an upcoming election, a contentious news story) and as new arguments are reflected in online discourse, we leverage these seeds to identify emerging themes in social media via seed expansion. To show a concrete example, Table 1 lists top ranking opposing and supporting themes at different times for the topic "fracking" after seed expansion is performed. We can see that new biased themes emerge as controversial events occur. In the following, we consider two approaches for expanding the hand-picked seeds to identify supporting and opposing hashtags:

Seed Expansion via Co-Occurrence. The first approach relies on hashtag co-occurrence statistics to find other hashtags used by users with similar opinion bias. The intuition is that if two hashtags are often used together by different users (whether in the same tweet or different tweets with respect to a topic), these two hashtags are likely to indicate the same opinion bias. Here, hashtag co-occurrence is based on users instead of tweets, considering that a user's opinion bias is not likely to change. Thus, for hashtags which occur in different tweets, as long as they are used by the same user, they are still considered to occur together.

Let f_i and f_j represent the frequency of the hashtag h_i and h_j related to a topic, respectively. Let f_+ and f_- represent the frequency of the pro-seed h_+ and the anti-seed h_-, respectively. The similarity between two hashtags, denoted as $\sigma(h_i, h_j)$, is computed by *Jaccard coefficient (JC)* as:

$$\sigma(h_i, h_j) = \frac{f_{h_i \cap h_j}}{f_{h_i \cup h_j}}$$

where $f_{h_i \cap h_j}$ represents the co-occurrence frequency of h_i and h_j, and $f_{h_i \cup h_j}$ represents the total occurrence frequency of either h_i or h_j. Thus, $\sigma(h_+, h_i)$ and $\sigma(h_-, h_i)$ represents the similarity of h_i to the pro-seed and anti-seed, respectively. We select top hashtags with the largest similarity to the pro-seed and anti-seed as the candidate set C_+ and C_-. However, since some hashtags, for example, "#guncontrol", are generic and co-occur with both the pro-seed and anti-seed, these hashtags do not indicate any opinion bias. To filter out common hashtags like these, we impose the following constraint on hashtag from C_+ for pro-seed:

$$\sigma(h_+, h_i)/\sigma(h_-, h_i) > \epsilon$$

where a large ϵ reflects more correlation with the pro-seed; similar constraint can also be imposed to filter hashtags in C_-. We then use the resulting m top hashtags for pro-seed as positive theme set P, and m top hashtags for anti-seed as negative theme set N.

Seed Expansion via Signed Information Gain. Although the approach above does find other biased hashtags, there are two disadvantages: (i) it often gives niche hashtags which are only used by a small number of participants; (ii) it often misses event-related short-lasting biased hashtags. In light of these issues, we propose the second approach which relies on weak supervision to select the most distinguishing hashtags for each side. Specifically, we perform the following procedure:

1. Training with pro-seed and anti-seed. First, we aggregate a user's tweets and use a bag-of-words model to compute TFIDF for each user. Users who have tweeted with at least one hashtag are then selected and used. From these users, we treat users with only pro-seed as positive class c_+, users with only anti-seed as negative class c_-, and the rest for prediction. Finally, an SVM classifier is learned on the training data and used to predict the polarity of users which are left. We now have an expanded set of users who are positive, and an expanded set of users who are negative.

2. Selecting hashtags. From the expanded sets of users, we use *signed information gain (SIG)* proposed by Zheng et al. [31] as the measure to select hashtags for pro-seed and anti-seed, respectively.

$$SIG(h_i, c) = sign(AD - BC) \cdot \sum_{c \in \{c_+, c_-\}} \sum_{h \in \{h_i, \bar{h}_i\}} p(h, c) \cdot log \frac{p(h, c)}{p(h) \cdot p(c)}$$

where A is the number of users with h_i and in class c_+, B is the number of users with h_i and in class c_-, C is the number of users without h_i and in class c_+ and D is the number of users without h_i and in class c_-. Also, $\bar{h}_i$ represents hashtags other than h_i. Here, the probability p is obtained by maximum likelihood estimation. We select m hashtags with the largest SIG as the finalized hashtag set P for pro-seed, and m hashtags with the smallest SIG as the finalized hashtag set N for anti-seed.

As a result, this approach can not only filter out common hashtags used by both sides of users without manually specifying any extra parameters, but also can discover popular yet distinguished biased hashtags.

Bias Anchors. Given the expanded set of hashtags (both supporting and opposing a particular topic), we identify as our strong partisans users who consistently adopt hashtags from only one opinion standpoint, which we denote as U_{anchor}. We assign an initial bias score $\tilde{b_i}$ to these anchors as follows:

$$\tilde{b_i} = \begin{cases} +1, & \text{if } u_i \in U_P \\ -1, & \text{if } u_i \in U_N \end{cases} \tag{1}$$

where U_P and U_N is the set of anchors adopting hashtags from P and N, respectively, and $U_{anchor} = U_P \cup U_N$. These opinion bias anchors serve as the basis for propagating bias throughout the social and information network, which we tackle next.

3.2 Bias Propagation Network

After the discovery of bias anchors, how do we determine the opinion bias of those remaining participants? We propose to build a propagation network where two users are only connected if their similarity passes a threshold. In the following, we adopt both content and link features to determine user similarity.

Content-Based Propagation. The assumption of content induced propagation is that if two users have a high textual similarity in their posts, it is likely that they may share similar opinion bias. To compute the content similarity of two users, we aggregate each user's topic-related tweets and treat each user as a document. Thus, content similarity of two users can be computed with document similarity. Here, we adopt cosine similarity of the TFIDF of the two documents with a standard bi-gram model. Tokenization of tweets is done through the tool provided by Owoputi et al. [21] for its robustness. Hashtags and mentions are also included in the model as features. To reduce the size of feature dimensions, we performed stop-word removal and kept only unigrams and bi-grams with occurrence frequency greater than two. The content similarity between u_i and u_j can be written as:

$$w_{ij}^{content} = \begin{cases} C_{ij}, & \text{if } u_j \in \mathcal{N}^c(u_i) \\ 0, & \text{if } u_j \notin \mathcal{N}^c(u_i) \end{cases} \quad (2)$$

where C_{ij} is the cosine similarity of u_i and u_j. To reduce the propagation complexity, we construct a sparse network by only considering k-nearest neighbors $\mathcal{N}^c(u_i)$ for each user u_i. We choose k to be 10 for its efficiency without compromising much accuracy in experiments.

Link-Based Propagation. Retweeting can be considered a form of endorsement for users in Twitter [4, 7]. Based on this observation, it is expected that if a user retweets another user on a topic, both users tend to share similar opinion bias. Thus, we define the link similarity between u_i and u_j as follows:

$$w_{ij}^{link} = \begin{cases} 1, & \text{if } u_j \in \mathcal{N}^l(u_i) \\ 0, & \text{if } u_j \notin \mathcal{N}^l(u_i) \end{cases} \quad (3)$$

where u_j is in the neighbors of u_i if u_j retweeted u_i or u_i retweeted u_j. Besides retweeting links, we can also take advantage of the follower/following network information in Twitter. Here, we choose not to use it since following link is not as strong a signal as retweeting. One reason is that a user whose opinion is on one side may choose to follow someone on the opposite side for the purpose of receiving any topic related statuses or refuting their arguments. Furthermore, we notice that the resource of retweeting activities is usually sparse so that the propagation network constituted only from retweeting links is separated into many isolated networks. Thus, a retweeting-based propagation is not enough to be treated by itself but needs to be combined with content-based propagation, leading to the following fusion of similarity between users:

$$w_{ij} = w_{ij}^{content} + \lambda w_{ij}^{link} \quad (4)$$

where λ is a weighting parameter for content and link similarity.

3.3 Optimization Framework

Finally, we embed the discovered anchors and bias propagation network into an optimization setting to propagate the opinion-bias score of all users more effectively. Since the initial input to the approach is a set of weak labels (two user-specified opposite hashtags), we call this optimization *User-guided Opinion Propagation [UOP]*. Specifically, by allowing each user's true opinion bias b_i to change as an optimization variable, we force the following conditions: (i) for bias anchors, b_i should be as close to the bias indicated by adopting biased hashtags (Eqn. 1); (ii) for other participants, b_i and b_j should be close to the degree indicated by their content and link similarity (Eqn. 4). Their opinion bias is initialized randomly between $[-1, 1]$ and can now be iteratively propagated through optimization. Thus, we have the following objective function:

$$\begin{aligned} \min_{b_i \in B} \quad & f = \sum_{u_i \in U_{anchor}} (b_i - \tilde{b_i})^2 + \mu_1 \sum_{i=1}^{n} \sum_{j=i+1}^{n} w_{ij}(b_i - b_j)^2 \\ \text{subject to} \quad & -1 \leq b_i \leq 1 \qquad \forall i \in \{1, ..., n\} \end{aligned} \quad (5)$$

where μ_1 is the tradeoff weight for different components. Thus, by solving this optimization, each user's opinion bias is propagated through the network in an optimized fashion. Since the objective function is convex, we can use the standard L-BFGS method with constraints to solve it efficiently. Another advantage of this framework is that other similarity signals such as location, profile demographics, and so on can be easily incorporated into Equation 5.

Handling Noisy Bias Anchors. The essence of the above optimization framework is that we propagate users' opinion bias which we know with confidence to other users who we have seldom knowledge of. We can see that anchor's opinion bias $\tilde{b_i}$ is treated as the golden truth and stays unchanged. However, a prominent issue is that users who consistently adopt hashtags from either P or N are not guaranteed to have the corresponding opinion bias. To give an example, one user's tweet reads, "#Gosnell certainly a tragedy, also cautionary tale, but not an argument against abortion rights in the US. Want more Gosnells? Ban abortion." This sarcastic pro-choice user adopted the hashtag #Gosnell, as we can observe from many tweets, is a primary hashtag pro-life users would use. Hence, according to Equation 1, this user is falsely identified as a pro-life anchor. Without manual inspection of user's profile and their related tweets, it is very hard to judge whether a bias anchor determined from Equation 1 is correctly identified. To relieve this problem, we introduce another variable y_i for $u_i \in U_{anchor}$ as the ideal opinion bias. Intuitively, it should satisfy: (i) y_i should be close to the opinion bias inferred from neighbors; (ii) most y_i should be consistent with $\tilde{b_i}$, with a few of them being noisy. Inspired by the annotation of noisy web images in [27], we propose a modified minimization function as follows:

$$\begin{aligned} \min_{b_i \in B} \quad & f = \sum_{u_i \in U_{anchor}} (b_i - y_i)^2 + \mu_1 \sum_{i=1}^{n} \sum_{j=i+1}^{n} w_{ij}(b_i - b_j)^2 \\ & \quad + \mu_2 \sum_{u_i \in U_{anchor}} |y_i - \tilde{b_i}| \\ \text{subject to} \quad & -1 \leq b_i \leq 1 \quad -1 \leq y_i \leq 1 \quad \forall i \in \{1, ..., n\} \end{aligned} \quad (6)$$

where μ_1 and μ_2 are the weighting parameters. We use l-1 norm to constrain the ideal variable y_i to $\tilde{b_i}$ since normally, only a small portion of bias anchors are noisy and l-1 norm could force most anchors to stay as biased. We solve the above minimization through the following steps:

(i) Initialize y_i to $\tilde{b_i}$ and solve Equation 5 to obtain b_i.

(ii) Solve the following sub-minimization problem with b_i to obtain y_i:

$$\begin{aligned} \min_{b_i \in B} \quad & f = \sum_{u_i \in U_{anchor}} (b_i - y_i)^2 + \mu_2 |y_i - \tilde{b_i}| \\ \text{subject to} \quad & -1 \leq y_i \leq 1 \qquad \forall i \in \{1, ..., n\} \end{aligned} \quad (7)$$

We employ the package L1 General [24] to solve the problem.

(iii) Replace $\tilde{b_i}$ with y_i in Equation 5 to get final b_i. We could repeat step (i) and (ii) for several times for further optimization but

Table 2: Datasets

Topic	Users	Tweets	Retweets
gun control	70,387	117,679	60,293
abortion	119,664	173,236	93,690
obamacare	67,937	123,320	70,008
vaccine	27,362	36,822	13,108
fracking	22,231	34,485	14,524

usually two to three iterations are enough shown by experiments. In this way, errors made in identifying bias anchors can be mitigated, leading to more accurate opinion bias estimation.

4. EXPERIMENTAL EVALUATION

In this section, we perform several sets of experiments to evaluate the BiasWatch framework for topic-sensitive opinion bias discovery. We investigate the impact of seed expansion, the quality of bias propagation via both content and retweeting links, and compare the performance versus alternative opinion bias approaches. We couple this study with an application of the system on two more controversial datasets.

4.1 Data

The datasets that we use are collected with Twitter's streaming API from October 2011 to September 2013. To create topic-related datasets for opinion discovery, we selected three controversial topics: "gun control", "abortion" and "obamacare". We select these topics because they are popular controversial topics discussed by a large number of Twitter users with both opposing sides of opinion expressed in the time period. For each topic, we extracted a base set of tweets (and their corresponding users) containing at least one topic-related keyword: for "gun control": *gun control, gun right, pro gun, anti gun, gun free, gun law, gun safety, gun violence*; for "abortion": *abortion, prolife, prochoice, anti-abortion, pro-abortion, planned parenthood*; and for "obamacare": *obamacare, #aca*. Additionally, we created another two datasets on the topics "vaccine" and "fracking" for demonstration. We select these two topics for further evaluation because they are relatively recent controversial topics compared to the previous ones, and also their opposing sides may not be fully entrenched in traditional left/right party politics. To extract "vaccine" related tweets, we use the following keywords: *vaccine, vaccination, vaccinate, #vaxfax*; for "fracking", we use: *fracking, #frack, hydraulic fracturing, shale, horizontal drilling*. We summarize the datasets in Table 2.

4.2 Gathering Ground Truth

In order to evaluate the framework, we need to know the true opinion of a randomly sampled user set against which we can compare the optimization results. Without direct access to user's bias and considering the inherent difficulty of knowing a user's bias degree with respect to a controversial topic, we rely on an external labeling scheme using Amazon Mechanical Turk. Since the bias score obtained from Equation 5 is continuous, we discretize the opinion bias of a Twitter user into the following five categories: strong support [+2], some support [+1], neutral or no evidence [0], some opposition [-1], strong opposition [-2].

Thus, we can map the continuous range into the above categories for evaluation. For each topic, we randomly selected 504 Twitter users from the total users in Table 2, and assigned eight users in each human intelligence task (HIT), then ask the turkers (human labeler) to select the most appropriate category for these users. For each user, we show her twitter user ID and her topic related tweets for each turker to examine. We also highlight the hyperlinks embedded in the tweets and make them clickable. To ensure good quality of assessment, we follow the suggestions by Marshall and Shipman [18]. For each human intelligence task, we put two additional users in random positions, making a total of ten users in one HIT. Those users' bias are already known through experts, which we refer to as the golden users. If the label given by a turker for any of these golden users is very different from that by experts, we discard the entire answer by this turker for the HIT. Moreover, we ask five turkers to label one user and take the majority vote as the final label for the user. The results are shown in Table 3.

Table 3: Turker labeling results of HITs

topic	Number of users for each category				
	+2	+1	0	-1	-2
gun control	116	40	60	54	234
abortion	115	54	55	26	254
obamacare	82	26	33	26	337

Agreement of Opinion Bias Labels. To measure the reliability of the above human labeling tasks, we investigate the inter-rater agreement of the obtained assessment with Fleiss' κ statistic. Specifically, we obtained the 5-category κ statistic of 0.264, 0.393 and 0.418 for "gun control", "abortion" and "obamacare", respectively. These values lie in the interpretation of fair agreement by Landis and Koch [13]. In addition, we also adopt the accuracy of agreement provided by Nowak [20] and adapt it into the following formula since each user is assessed by more than two turkers:

$$accuracy = \frac{1}{N}\sum_{i=1}^{N}\frac{\text{\# of votes of the majority category for user i}}{\text{\# of votes for user i}}$$

where N is the total number of users to be assessed by turkers for each topic. The accuracy ranges from 0.304 when the majority is obtained by chance to 1 when every user's bias category is agreed by all turkers. The lower bound 0.304 is obtained by calculating the average number of people in a majority out of five when they select one category from five by chance. Hence, an accuracy of 0.6, for example, means that on average, 3 out of 5 turkers agree on a category. The accuracy for "gun control", "abortion" and "obamacare" is 0.646, 0.727 and 0.788, respectively, which means, on average, at least 3 turkers agree on the majority category.

Furthermore, we aggregated the same polarity into one category, namely, category [+1] and [+2] are combined to one category and vice versa. The 3-category κ statistic increases to 0.461, 0.588 and 0.649, correspondingly, while the accuracy increases to 0.811, 0.857 and 0.906. The κ values can now be interpreted as moderate agreement. The accuracy now means at least four out of five people agree on the majority bias polarity on average. This indicates that humans are more capable of discerning the polarity of users' opinion bias than determining the extent of users' bias.

In the following, we choose to use the 3 bias categories as ground truth since it has the most consistent and reliable performance by human labelers. We additionally consider only the support and opposition categories (ignoring the minority of users who are neutral or do not show evidence, namely, category [0]) so we can cast the evaluation as a binary class problem. We adopt the standard classification measures of accuracy and area under the curve (AUC).

4.3 Alternative Opinion Bias Estimators

To evaluate our approach of determining users' opinion bias, we consider the following alternative opinion bias estimators:

- **SentiWordNet [SWN]**. This is a simple sentiment detection approach, where we assign a sentiment score to each user's tweets according to SentiWordNet and classify each user's opinion bias with the relative portion of positive and negative tweets. Specifically, for each tweet d_i of user u_i, we classify it positive if

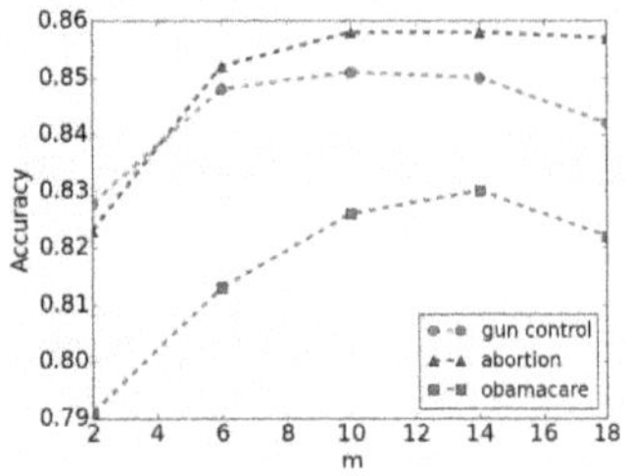

Figure 2: Effect of m for seed expansion via SIG.

$\sum_{w_j \in d_i} pos(w_j) > \sum_{w_j \in d_i} neg(w_j)$, and vice versa. We then classify user u_i as positive if the number of positive tweets is greater than the number of negative tweets, and vice versa.

- **User Clustering with Content [uCC]**. In this baseline, we construct a user graph and perform user clustering with tweets. The nodes of the graph are users and the edges are constructed based on k nearest neighbors with the largest content similarities of tweets. We choose to use cosine similarity of the TFIDF of bi-grams as the similarity measure. To perform graph clustering, we apply normalized cuts for graph partitioning by Shi and Malik [25] due to its simplicity and good performance. This is essentially a max-cut problem explored in [2, 19] to partition news-group and online debates into opposite positions, respectively. The purpose of using this unsupervised baseline is to examine whether the selected biased hashtags as a form of weak supervision can provide much improvement.
- **User Clustering with Content and Links [uCCL]**. This baseline is the modified version of uCC in which the edge weight combines both content and link similarity. Specifically, if there exists a retweeting link between two users, we add a constant to its content similarity, i.e., $w = w^{content} + \theta * w^{link}$, where θ is used to balance the weights. The purpose of this baseline is to examine if retweeting links can help distinguish opposing sides of users' opinion bias compared to uCC.
- **Weakly-supervised SVM [wSVM]**. We train an SVM with a bi-gram model of bias anchors' tweets, which is then used to classify the test dataset. The parameters of SVM are determined through 5-fold cross-validation. We denote the trained classifier with bias anchors found through initial seeds (IS) as *wSVM+IS*, and the other two classifiers trained on seed expansions as *wSVM+JC* and *wSVM+SIG*. Here, wSVM+IS is treated as the baseline, and the other two as our improved versions.
- **Local Consistency Global Consistency [LCGC]**. This is a semi-supervised method proposed by Zhou et al. [32] and applied in [33] for the classification of the political learning of news articles. This method optimizes the tradeoff between local consistency and global consistency among node labels. Here, we use Equation 4 as the affinity between nodes for the method and adapt LCGC into our own version by incorporating seed expansion from SIG, denoted as *LCGC+SIG*.
- **UOP***. This is the framework in which we only consider content based bias propagation without handling noisy bias anchors.
- **UOP†**. This is the framework in which we consider both content and link based bias propagation without handling noisy bias anchors, indicated by Equation 5.
- **UOP**. This is the full blown-approach indicated by Equation 6.

4.4 Biased Theme Discovery

Before experiments, we first select the following pro-seed and anti-seed manually as the input to the system: #guncontrolnow and #2ndamendment for "gun control"; #prochoice and #prolife for "abortion"; #ilikeobamacare and #defundobamacare for "obamacare". We later show in the experiments the effect of different seed selections.

We then highlight the seed expansion methods – both hashtag co-occurrence (JC) and signed information gain (SIG) – used to identify biased hashtags adopted by users with similar opinion bias. For seed expansion via SIG, we need to determine the value of parameter m. To study the influence of this parameter, we adopt the method UOP* to evaluate performance changes with values from $\{2, 6, 10, 14, 18\}$. Figure 2 shows that the accuracy is highest when m is approximately at 10 for "gun control" and "abortion", and is slightly larger for "obamacare". After those values, accuracy levels or even decreases, possibly because the additional discovered hashtags are noisy or do not imply much opinion bias. Thus, in the following experiments, m is fixed at 10 for all topics. For seed expansion via co-occurrence, we choose m to be 10 using the similar approach, and empirically set ϵ to 3. The expanded hashtags, as we observed from the output, can be approximately categorized as:

(i) *Sentiment-oriented.* These hashtags can be easily discerned and used directly by participants to show opinion bias, such as #nowaynra for "gun control" and #dontfundit for "obamacare".

(ii) *Community identification.* These hashtags indicate personal or political identities and are often used in a community, such as #p2, #tcot, #teaparty and #fem2 (for feminists);

(iii) *Thematic.* These hashtags often indicate arguments used by participants to express their opinion. For example, gun control antagonists say #gunrights as a constitutional right protected by #2ndamendment (also #2a); abortion protagonists may emphasize #reprorights or #reprojustice in their arguments;

(iv) *Action-oriented.* Examples include #momsdemandaction, #stand4life, #standwithcruz (stand with Ted Cruz), #swtw (stand with Texas women) and #demandaplan (as in "#demandaplan to end gun violence");

Overall, we can conclude that seed expansion through our proposed approaches is able to find other biased hashtags which are used by people with similar opinion bias. The above categorization also serves as guidance for users to pick initial opposing seeds as input to the system. Now that we have discovered the biased themes related to each side of polarity for different controversial topics, can we leverage those to determine "regular" participants' opinion bias? Specifically, we ask the following questions:

(i) Can these newly discovered biased hashtags help to identify user's opinion bias? If so, how much better can they do?

(ii) Do different pro-seed and anti-seed selections affect performance? If so, can seed expansion help us with the selection?

(iii) Can social ties, in the form of retweeting links, help us determine user's opinion bias?

Effect of Seed Expansion. To evaluate the performance of these expanded hashtags, we use wSVM and UOP* as the base methods since both of them only rely on the information provided by bias anchors and content. For UOP*, the weight parameter μ_1 in Equation 5, is empirically determined to be 0.1.

We now compare the performance between the version when opinion bias is propagated only through initial seeds and the version when the seeds are expanded. Since the result of accuracy is similar with AUC, we only show AUC in Figure 3. We can see that both seed expansion approaches outperform initial seeds, with seed expansion via SIG giving the best performance. Specifically, AUC from seed expansion via SIG gives a 19.5% and 6.8% improvement over IS and JC for wSVM, respectively, while the improvement is 12.5% and 5.6% for UOP*, respectively. This shows that (i) the newly discovered hashtag set through seed expansion provides additional amount of bias information for users; and (ii) the quality of

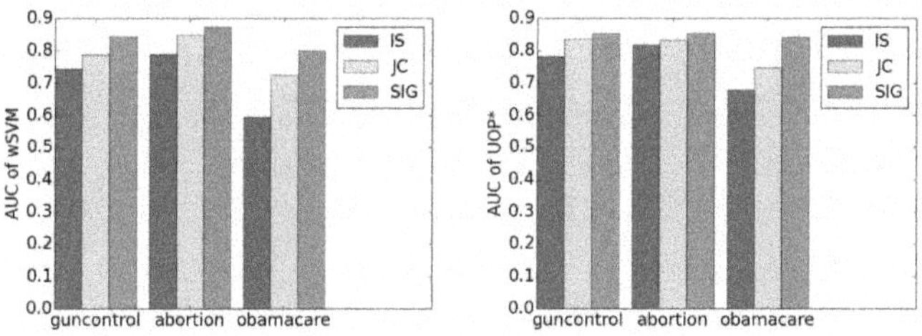

Figure 3: Effect of seed expansion.

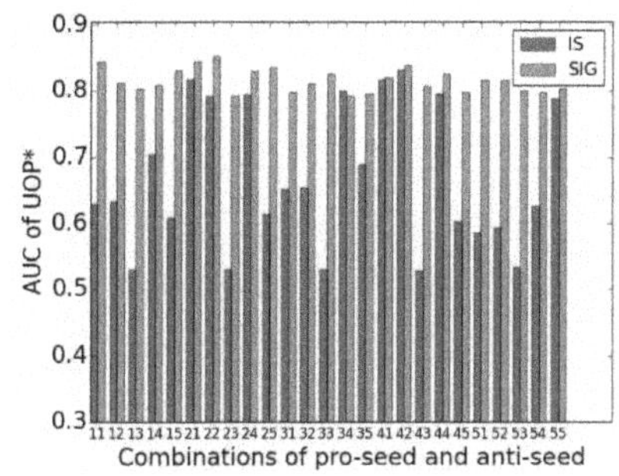

Figure 4: Performance for 25 pro-seed and anti-seed combinations.

expanded hashtag set via SIG is generally the best, i.e., it is able to discover higher quality of biased themes.

Effect of Different Seeds. Here, we are interested in studying the influence of different choices of initial seeds to the system. To that end, we first rank hashtags by occurrence frequency and then manually select top five pro-seeds and top five anti-seeds for "gun control" by observing tweets with those hashtags. The top five pro-seeds are: 1. #nowaynra; 2. #guncontrolnow; 3. #demandaplan; 4. #newtown; 5. #whatwillittake. The top five anti-seeds are: 1. #tcot; 2. #2ndamendment; 3. #nj2as; 4. #2a; 5. #gunrights. We represent a pro-seed and anti-seed combination with their corresponding number. For example, "12" represents the combination "#nowaynra #2ndamendment". We then use the method UOP* to evaluate the performance of each combination for two cases: one with initial seeds; the other with seed expansion via SIG. The results are shown in Figure 4. Overall, we can see that for different choices of input seeds, the performance without seed expansion is very sensitive to the choices, while it gives consistent high accuracy for seed expansion with SIG. We can also observe that #nj2as is not a good anti-seed choice since all combinations with #nj2as performs bad. Also, all combinations with #gunrights give unsatisfactory results except "55". These results indicate that it is difficult to choose the most effective seed combinations, since very often a single pair of seeds can be noisy and do not cover enough bias related themes. However, seed expansion can mitigate this effect by introducing other and often more complete biased hashtags for bias propagation. Hence, even though the initial seeds are not well selected, the final performance does not suffer much due to the benefits of seed expansion. For other topics, similar results are observed, and thus are not reported due to the space limit.

Effect of Social Ties. Here, we evaluate the effect of social ties in the form of retweeting links for different seed expansion approaches. The retweeting links are randomly sampled for ten times for each fraction since a different sample of retweeting links gives a different propagation network. Here, we adopt UOP† for the evaluation, with the weight given to the link-based propagation λ in

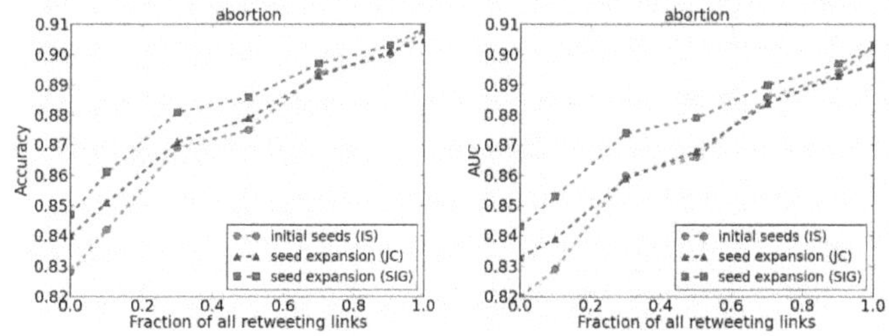

Figure 5: Performance for different seed expansion approaches with respect to different fraction of retweeting links for abortion.

Equation 4 empirically chosen to be 1. The final results are averaged and plotted in Figure 5. We only show the results for abortion since it is similar with other topics. We can see that as more retweeting links are added for propagation, the performance increases for all three approaches, which confirms the assumption that users linked via retweeting tend to share similar opinion bias.

Furthermore, among these three approaches, the performance obtained via SIG is always the best for different fractions of retweeting links at all topics. As the fraction gets larger, the improvement generally gets smaller. This indicates that the effect of seed expansion gets reduced when the fraction increases. For seed expansion via JC, the performance is generally better than that of initial seeds when the fraction is small. However, this initial improvement gets reduced or even disappears when retweeting link is abundant, hence, making the extra hashtags obtained via co-occurrence less effective. This is probably because of the noisiness of those extra hashtags. Though beneficial at a small number of retweeting links, they prevent the correct bias from being propagated when more of them are added for optimization. This shows again that the key of seed expansion is that not only more biased hashtags should be discovered, but also they should be of high quality.

4.5 Comparison with Baselines

In this section, we compare our proposed BiasWatch framework with the alternative opinion bias estimators. For uCCL, the weight-balancing parameter θ is selected from $\{0.05, 0.1, 0.15, 0.2, 0.25\}$ to be 0.1 for best performance. For LCGC+SIG, we use the same parameter setting as in [33]. Other parameter settings in UOP*, UOP† and UOP are the same as in previous experiments. For μ_2 in Equation 6, we empirically set it to 0.2 for handling noisy bias anchors. We choose the best seed expansion approach (via SIG) for all methods. The final results are shown in Table 4.

Overall, user-guided approaches give much better performance than unsupervised methods, indicating that by just a small amount of human guidance — two opposite seed hashtags, the performance can be boosted significantly. Moreover, UOP gives the best performance, reaching an average accuracy and AUC of 0.923 and 0.913, respectively (an improvement of 20.0% and 28.6% over supervised baseline wSVM+IS). Note that the sentiment based approach SWN gives unsatisfactory results, probably because user's opinion bias is multifaceted and can be reflected by the topical arguments or factual information published by the user. For example, one of the anti-obamacare tweets reads, "Double Down: Obamacare Will Increase Avg. Individual-Market Insurance Premiums By 99% For Men, 62% For Women. #Forbes". Also, we can see that UOP† gives better results than LCGC+SIG, indicating that our framework works better in capturing user's opinion bias. UOP, however, gives better performance than UOP†, confirming that initial bias anchors determined through biased hashtags are noisy, and that UOP is able to correct some wrongly determined bias anchors due to the l-1 norm regularization on ideal bias scores.

Table 4: Comparison of performance with alternative opinion bias estimators. Boldface: the best result for each topic among all methods. '$*$' marks statistically significant difference against the best of alternative opinion bias estimators (with two sample t-test for $p \leq 0.05$).

Method	Accuracy				AUC			
	gun control	abortion	obamacare	average	gun control	abortion	obamacare	average
SWN	0.560	0.527	0.465	0.517	0.570	0.531	0.541	0.547
uCC	0.534	0.537	0.516	0.529	0.533	0.527	0.522	0.527
uCCL	0.586	0.530	0.520	0.545	0.584	0.531	0.546	0.554
wSVM+IS	0.696	0.825	0.786	0.769	0.745	0.790	0.594	0.710
wSVM+SIG	0.860	0.884	0.727	0.824	0.844	0.874	0.800	0.839
UOP*	0.851	0.847	0.826	0.841	0.853	0.843	0.842	0.846
LCGC+SIG	0.858	0.900	0.811	0.856	0.857	0.900	0.864	0.874
UOP†	0.881	0.906	0.894	0.894	0.861	0.903	0.915	0.893
UOP	**0.908***	**0.915**	**0.945***	**0.923***	**0.883***	**0.910**	**0.945***	**0.913***

Furthermore, we see from the table that UOP† has an improvement of 0.053 and 0.047 for accuracy and AUC over UOP*, respectively. Compared to the corresponding improvement of 0.016 and 0.027 by uCCL over uCC, it is considerably higher. This indicates that retweeting links are more effective in contributing to bias propagation with the help of bias anchors. When some users are correctly "labeled" by discovered biased hashtags, opinion bias can be propagated more effectively through retweeting links.

4.6 Multi-Category Classification

In previous experiments, we mainly evaluate our framework as a binary class problem. However, in this way, we lose the finer granularity of the inferred opinion bias score by ignoring users who are neutral or do not show evidence. This category of users can not only be beneficial to our understanding of the general landscape of controversial topics, but also can be targeted by polarized activists to influence their bias. Thus, in this section, we are interested in a finer level of evaluation by casting it as a three-class problem. Here, instead of combining the category +1 and +2, and the category -1 and -2, we aggregate users in the category of +1, 0 and -1 into one neutral category 0 for a relatively larger pool of users in the middle. We then partition the datasets into 50% for training and 50% for testing, and compare the performance of wSWM+SIG, LCGC+SIG, UOP† and UOP. We are interested to see how these methods perform in the recall defined by $\frac{1}{3}\sum_i \frac{tp_i}{tp_i+fn_i}$. This measure indicates the ability of finding out the correct user category in a three-category setting for different methods.

For wSVM+SIG, we adopt the one-vs-rest multi-class implementation. For LCGC, we modified it to consider three labels. For UOP based methods, we select two optimal thresholds as boundaries: θ_p, used to distinguish category +2 and 0 and θ_n, used to distinguish category -2 and 0. These thresholds are selected by searching the range (-1,1) with a step of 0.05 with the training data. For UOP, θ_n and θ_p are determined as -0.25 and 0.2 for "gun control", -0.35 and 0.35 for "abortion", -0.2 and 0.2 for "obamacare". The final results are shown in Table 5. As we can see, UOP gives the best performance of all, indicating that it is the most capable in finding out users who are polarized and neutral. wSVM and LCGC perform worse, probably because of the small amount of training samples for category 0. UOP based methods are able to mitigate this effect by propagating constrained bias score without explicit consideration of neutral users and only with bias anchors. Thus, we can conclude that UOP is effective in representing the degree of user's opinion bias under the controversial topics.

4.7 Case Study: Fracking and Vaccines

Now that we have demonstrated the effectiveness of the system in finding general users' opinion bias, we would like to test the framework further in another two datasets: "fracking" and "vaccine". Since these two topics are relatively new compared to the above politically-driven well-known topics, it would be interesting to discover what is being posted and debated by opinionated users of both sides. For "fracking", we pick the seeds #dontfrackny and #jobs as the input to the system. We select #jobs as the pro-seed for "fracking" because protagonists tend to emphasize the benefit of creating jobs as one of the arguments for "fracking". For "vaccine", we pick the seeds #health and #autism as the input to the system. Again, we select #autism as the anti-seed because antagonists tend to focus the negative effect of vaccination. Overall, selection of input seeds is intuitive due to the recognizability of some of the crowd-generated tags and thus does not require much human effort.

We first demonstrate the biased themes discovered via SIG. Table 1 shows the top-ranking biased hashtags for different time periods. We can see that some themes such as #natgas and #frack remain constantly used by users supporting and opposing fracking, respectively; some other themes, such as #dontfrackny and #balcombe, arise and fade as related controversial events occur. For example, the occurrence of #dontfrackny corresponds with a rally of New Yorkers in the mid February 2013 to urge Governor Cuomo to resist fracking in the state of New York; the occurrence of #balcombe corresponds with a protest against a license to drill near Balcombe in England granted by Environment Agency. These changing themes indicate a strong degree of opinion bias and emerge as a group of users start to use them together, making them a very use-

Table 5: Multi-category classification performance.

Method	gun control	abortion	obamacare
wSVM+SIG	0.611	0.592	0.573
LCGC+SIG	0.632	0.657	0.646
UOP†	0.690	0.699	0.673
UOP	0.705	0.701	0.716

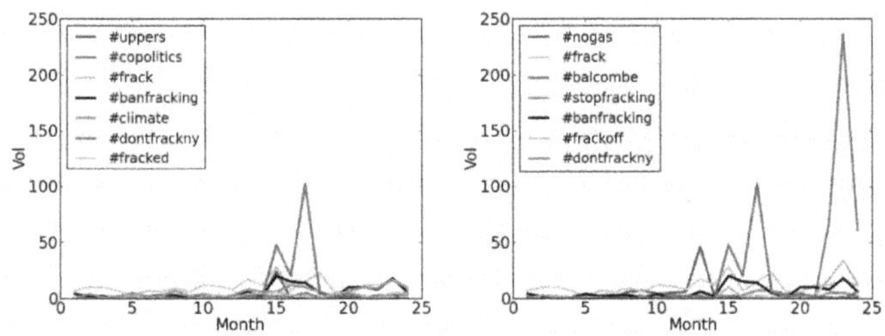

Figure 6: Temporal volumes of top anti-fracking themes for seed expansions via co-occurrence (Left) and via SIG (Right).

Table 6: Top ten themes at different times for "vaccine"; red for pro-vaccine; blue for anti-vaccine.

Feb 2012	June 2012	Nov 2012	Apr 2013
#vaxfax	#health	#health	#vaccineswork
#health	#vaxfax	#vaxfax	#health
#flu	#polio	#flu	#measles
#polio	#hpv	#autism	#mmr
#hpv	#vaccineswork	#news	#hiv
#autism	#pakistan	#polio	#autism
#thrillers	#autism	#hiv	#vaxfax
#measles	#news	#suspense	#polio
#action	#suspense	#thrillers	#flu
#flushot	#action	#hpv	#news

ful signal to determine and propagate user's opinion bias. Furthermore, the transient property of these changing themes also makes the approach of seed expansion via co-occurrence less effective. Figure 6 illustrates the temporal characteristics of discovered anti-fracking themes for different seed expansion approaches. We can see that seed expansion via co-occurrence failed discovering #balcombe and #nogas, as both of these hashtags do not co-occur with #dontfrackny. In contrast, SIG tackles the problem by tapping into the power of content to discover more related biased themes. Table 6 shows the top-ranking biased hashtags at different time periods for the dataset "vaccine". To illustrate how the system can uncover strong partisans, Table 7 shows two uncovered bias anchors – @Energy21, a pro-fracking account from the Institute for 21st Century Energy, and @Duffernutter, an anti-fracking account associated with TheEnvironmentTV.

5. INTEGRATING OPINION BIAS INTO USER RECOMMENDATION

In this section, we demonstrate the application of integrating opinion bias for user recommendation in social media. The principle of homophily, observed both in political blogosphere [1] and social media [7], states that people tend to associate with others who are like-minded. Thus, when social media services recommend users to follow, it is natural to consider recommending users who have similar opinion bias on shared topic interests. User recommendation can also be considered as a task of link prediction in graphs, and there has already exist many works [14] which specifically address this task, mostly taking advantage of graph structure. Here, our goal is to demonstrate how opinion bias can be utilized for user recommendation as a different dimension.

The task can be formally described as follows: Given a controversial topic T, a sampled set of users U and their corresponding on-topic tweets D, recommend k friends to follow for the target user. Note that we have only tweets to rely on to determine the recommendations. We provide two approaches for the task.

Content-Based approach. In this collaborative filtering approach, users with the highest content similarities to the target user are recommended. Specifically, we aggregated the corresponding tweets for each user and applied vector space model (VSM) with unigrams and bi-grams, with the similarity computed by cosine measure.

Opinion-Weighted (OW) approach. Here, user similarity is considered as a weighted sum of content similarity and opinion similarity. The content similarity is computed in the same way as VSM. The opinion similarity is obtained as follows. First, user's opinion bias score is obtained through UOP. Then, we characterize the opinion similarity of two users as:

$$sim_{opi}(u_i, u_j) = 1 - |f(b_i) - f(b_j)|$$

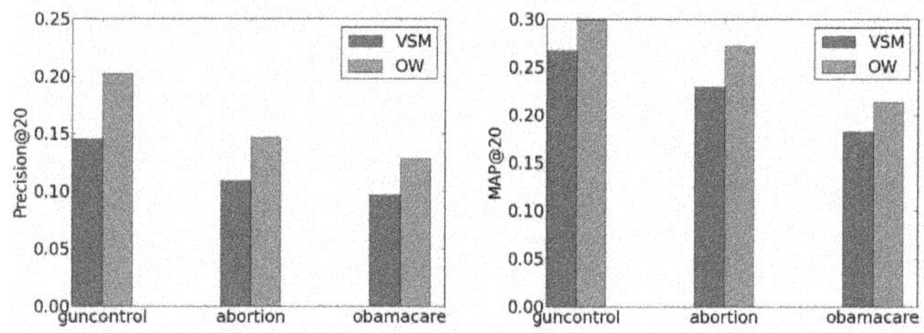

Figure 7: Performance comparison for VSM and OW.

where $f(x)$ is a normalizing function with the form as $\frac{1}{1+e^{-c \cdot x}}$. The value of parameter c should be chosen to make b's transition to opposite sign steep enough, so that two bias scores with small difference but opposite signs can still result in large difference after transformation. Also, when b_i and b_j have the same sign, they can have a relatively large opinion similarity. To this end, c is chosen to be 5. The final similarity is computed as the weighted sum (α is the weighting parameter), which we use for ranking users:

$$sim(u_i, u_j) = \alpha sim_{vsm}(u_i, u_j) + (1 - \alpha) sim_{opi}(u_i, u_j)$$

5.1 Evaluating User Recommendation

For evaluation, we additionally crawled following links for the dataset "gun control", "abortion" and "obamacare". These following links are used as the ground truth in our experiments. We randomly sampled 500 users who have at least 20 followees for each topic and used the following metrics to evaluate: (i) precision@K: which measures the percent of the correct followees out of the top K recommended users; and (ii) mean average precision@K: which is the average of the precision at the position of each correct followee out of the top K recommended users. This measure considers the positions of the recommended users. K is chosen to be 20.

Figure 7 shows the performance comparisons between the two approaches. Here, α is set to 0.5. For both metrics, the OW approach has a better performance than the vanilla VSM for each topic. On average, it gives an improvement of 26.3% in precision@20 and 13.8% in MAP@20. These results indicate that user's opinion similarity boosted the rank of some of the true followees who have similar opinion bias as the target user, while lowering the similarity with users who hold different opinion. Hence, it implicitly confirms the principle of homophily that people tend to make friends who share similar opinions.

In Figure 8, we also show the performance at different values of α. As we can see, the best performance is achieved neither at $\alpha = 0$ or 1 for all topics, but at a mixed weight between content and opinion similarity. Even when the weight given to opinion similarity is small, i.e., when $\alpha = 0.9$, the improvement can reach 20.2% for precision@20 and 9.2% for MAP@20 on average. The figure shows that the performance is not very sensitive to the value of α when α is approximately in the range of (0.2, 0.8), indicating it does not require fine tuning to reach a better performance.

6. CONCLUSION AND NEXT STEPS

We have seen how the BiasWatch system can lead to an improvement of 20% in accuracy over the next-best alternative for bias estimation, as well as uncover opinion leaders and bias themes that may evolve over time. We also demonstrated how the inferred opinion bias can be integrated into user recommendation and showed that it gives a performance improvement of 26% in precision. While our investigation has focused on textual and relational features, it does not limit us from integrating new signals such as location and profile demographics for better performance in future work. We are also interested in incorporating opinion bias into a

Table 7: Sample opinionated users and their corresponding tweets for "fracking"; positive bias score represents pro-fracking.

users	bias anchor	bias score	tweets
@Energy21	yes	0.91	Four real-life examples of how #shale #energy is creating #jobs and improving the economy: via @FreeEnterprise.
@Duffernutter	yes	-0.92	RT @ABFalecbaldwin: Together we can help @NYGovCuomo see there is no place for #fracking in NY. RT to let him know #DontFrackNY.
@IntellisysUK	no	0.15	RT @JimWoodsUK: Provocative article from @James_BG on New Environmentalism. Worth remembering fracking has reduced US CO2 emissions.
@janet_ewan	no	-0.39	RT @IshtarsGate: A 5.7-magnitude earthquake linked to fracking in Oklahoma in 2011 knocked down 14 homes and injured two people.

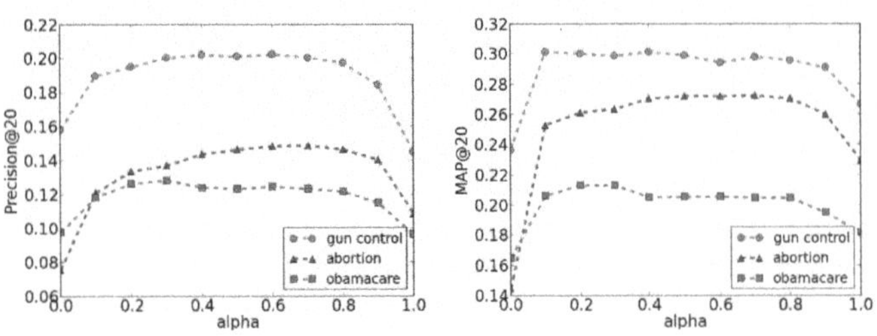

Figure 8: Performance at different values of parameter α.

social media dashboard, so that participants can be aware of their own opinion dynamics as well as those of others.

7. ACKNOWLEDGMENTS

This work was supported in part by AFOSR grant FA9550-12-1-0363 and NSF grant IIS-1149383. Any opinions, findings and conclusions or recommendations expressed in this material are the author(s) and do not necessarily reflect those of the sponsors.

8. REFERENCES

[1] L. Adamic and N. Glance. The political blogosphere and the 2004 u.s. election: Divided they blog. In *LinkKDD*, 2005.

[2] R. Agrawal, S. Rajagopalan, R. Srikant, and Y. Xu. Mining newsgroups using networks arising from social behavior. In *WWW*, 2003.

[3] L. Akoglu. Quantifying political polarity based on bipartite opinion networks. In *ICWSM*, 2014.

[4] D. Boyd, S. Golder, and G. Lotan. Tweet, tweet, retweet: Conversational aspects of retweeting on twitter. In *HICSS*, 2010.

[5] R. Cohen and D. Ruths. Classifying political orientation on twitter: It's not easy! In *ICWSM*, 2013.

[6] M. Conover, B. Gonçalves, J. Ratkiewicz, A. Flammini, and F. Menczer. Predicting the political alignment of twitter users. In *SocialCom*, 2011.

[7] M. Conover, J. Ratkiewicz, M. Francisco, B. Gonçalves, A. Flammini, and F. Menczer. Political polarization on twitter. In *ICWSM*, 2011.

[8] H. Gao, J. Mahmud, J. Chen, J. Nichols, and M. Zhou. Modeling user attitude toward controversial topics in online social media. In *ICWSM*, 2014.

[9] M. Gentzkow and J. Shapiro. *What Drives Media Slant? Evidence from US Daily Newspapers*. National Bureau of Economic Research Cambridge, Mass., USA, 2006.

[10] T. Groseclose and J. Milyo. A measure of media bias. *The Quarterly Journal of Economics*, 2005.

[11] P. Calais Guerra, W. Meira Jr., C. Cardie, and R. Kleinberg. A measure of polarization on social media networks based on community boundaries. In *ICWSM*, 2013.

[12] J. Kim, J. Yoo, H. Lim, H. Qiu, Z. Kozareva, and A. Galstyan. Sentiment prediction using collaborative filtering. In *ICWSM*, 2013.

[13] J. Landis and G. Koch. The measurement of observer agreement for categorical data. *Biometrics*, 1977.

[14] D. Liben-Nowell and J. Kleinberg. The link-prediction problem for social networks. *Journal of the American society for information science and technology*, 2007.

[15] Y. Lin, J. Bagrow, and D. Lazer. Quantifying bias in social and mainstream media. *SIGWEB Newsl.*, 2012.

[16] A. Livne, M. Simmons, E. Adar, and L. Adamic. The party is over here: Structure and content in the 2010 election. In *ICWSM*, 2011.

[17] Y. Lu, H. Wang, C. Zhai, and D. Roth. Unsupervised discovery of opposing opinion networks from forum discussions. In *CIKM*, 2012.

[18] C. Marshall and F. Shipman. Experiences surveying the crowd: Reflections on methods, participation, and reliability. In *WebSci*, 2013.

[19] A. Murakami and R. Raymond. Support or oppose?: Classifying positions in online debates from reply activities and opinion expressions. In *COLING*, 2010.

[20] S. Nowak and S. Rüger. How reliable are annotations via crowdsourcing: A study about inter-annotator agreement for multi-label image annotation. In *MIR*, 2010.

[21] O. Owoputi, B. O'Connor, C. Dyer, K. Gimpel, N. Schneider, and N. Smith. Improved part-of-speech tagging for online conversational text with word clusters. In *NAACL*, 2013.

[22] B. Pang and L. Lee. Opinion mining and sentiment analysis. *Foundations and trends in information retrieval*, 2008.

[23] M. Pennacchiotti and A. Popescu. Democrats, republicans and starbucks afficionados: User classification in twitter. In *SIGKDD*, 2011.

[24] Mark Schmidt. L1 general, May 2015.

[25] J. Shi and J. Malik. Normalized cuts and image segmentation. *Pattern Analysis and Machine Intelligence, IEEE Transactions on*, 2000.

[26] C. Tan, L. Lee, J. Tang, L. Jiang, M. Zhou, and P. Li. User-level sentiment analysis incorporating social networks. In *SIGKDD*, 2011.

[27] J. Tang, R. Hong, S. Yan, T. Chua, G. Qi, and R. Jain. Image annotation by knn-sparse graph-based label propagation over noisily tagged web images. *ACM TIST*, 2011.

[28] X. Wang, F. Wei, X. Liu, M. Zhou, and M. Zhang. Topic sentiment analysis in twitter: a graph-based hashtag sentiment classification approach. In *CIKM*, 2011.

[29] F. Wong, C. Tan, S. Sen, and M. Chiang. Quantifying political leaning from tweets and retweets. In *ICWSM*, 2013.

[30] L. Yang, T. Sun, M. Zhang, and Q. Mei. We know what@ you# tag: does the dual role affect hashtag adoption? In *WWW*, 2012.

[31] Z. Zheng, X. Wu, and R. Srihari. Feature selection for text categorization on imbalanced data. *SIGKDD Explor. Newsl.*, 2004.

[32] D. Zhou, O. Bousquet, T. Lal, J. Weston, and B. Schölkopf. Learning with local and global consistency. In *NIPS*, 2004.

[33] X. Zhou, P. Resnick, and Q. Mei. Classifying the political leaning of news articles and users from user votes. In *ICWSM*, 2011.

Knowlywood: Mining Activity Knowledge From Hollywood Narratives

Niket Tandon
Max Planck Institute for Informatics
ntandon@mpi-inf.mpg.de

Gerard de Melo
Tsinghua University, China
demelo@tsinghua.edu.cn

Abir De
IIT Kharagpur, India
abir.de@cse.iitkgp.ernet.in

Gerhard Weikum
Max Planck Institute for Informatics
weikum@mpi-inf.mpg.de

ABSTRACT

Despite the success of large knowledge bases, one kind of knowledge that has not received attention so far is that of human activities. An example of such an activity is proposing to someone (to get married). For the computer, knowing that this involves two adults, often but not necessarily a woman and a man, that it often takes place in some romantic location, that it typically involves flowers or jewelry, and that it is usually followed by kissing, is a valuable asset for tasks like natural language dialog, scene understanding, or video search.

This corresponds to the challenging task of acquiring semantic frames that capture human activities, their participating agents, and their typical spatio-temporal contexts. This paper presents a novel approach that taps into movie scripts and other narrative texts. We develop a pipeline for semantic parsing and knowledge distillation, to systematically compile semantically refined activity frames.

The resulting knowledge base contains hundreds of thousands of activity frames, mined from about two million scenes of movies, TV series, and novels. A manual assessment study, with extensive sampling and statistical significance tests, shows that the frames and their attribute values have an accuracy of at least 80 percent. We also demonstrate the usefulness of activity knowledge by the extrinsic use case of movie scene search.

Categories and Subject Descriptors

I.2.7 [**Natural Language Processing**]: Text Analysis

Keywords

Activity Knowledge; Commonsense Knowledge Acquisition

1. INTRODUCTION

Motivation and Problem. Knowledge graphs like DBpedia, Freebase, or Yago [2, 5, 40] have become major assets for enriching the Web towards more semantic search and recommendations. They are heavily used at large companies such as Baidu, Facebook, Google, Microsoft, and others. The emphasis in these settings is on individual entities like people, organizations, and products or creative works, with focus on *factual knowledge* about such entities (e.g., songs and awards of an artist, CEOs and products of companies, cities and restaurants visited by friends, etc.).

Recently, however, with ground-breaking new products like Amazon Echo as well as assistants like Google Now, Microsoft's Cortana, and Apple's Siri, there is a strong need for commonsense knowledge enabling smart interpretation of queries relating to *everyday human activities*.

Unfortunately, fact-oriented knowledge graphs do not provide detailed knowledge of human activities. The same holds for more commonsense-oriented knowledge bases, from the seminal projects Cyc [22] and WordNet [15] to more recent endeavors such as ConceptNet [17], WebChild [41], and NEIL [9]. While these contain millions of assertions between general concepts, referring to predicates like *isPartOf* (e.g., *engine isPartOf car*), *usedFor* (e.g., *car usedFor transportation*, *hasTaste* (e.g., *chocolate hasTaste sweet*), *hasShape* (e.g., *apple hasShape round*), *occursInScene* (e.g., *car occursInScene streetTraffic*), and more, they do not deliver fine-grained information about large numbers of specific activities.

In this paper, we fill this void by automatically compiling large amounts of knowledge about human activities from narrative text. For example, `climbing a mountain` should be a known activity, along with attributes like participating agents — a human, especially a climber, typical location, and time of day. This knowledge should be organized in a frame-style representation, as illustrated in Figure 1. Further, the activities must be semantically grouped (here with hiking up a hill), and these semantic groups must be hierarchically arranged. These activity groups should also be temporally linked to typical previous and next activities. Having this sort of data can greatly improve computer behavior in tasks like natural language dialog, scene understanding, or video search.

While parts of our approach could be applied to other genres, we focus on narrative text because it possesses some attractive yet under-utilized properties. Rather than being limited to newsworthy events, narrative text may include descriptions of common, rather mundane everyday activities. These are often described in a very detailed way and in chronological order with marked boundaries. For instance, we may find that one often unlocks a door before entering a building. Finally, we wish to connect our knowledge to visual content in movies, which enables several new applications, including the ones we consider later in Section 7.

Recent work in computer vision [34] has manually compiled a small collection of activity scripts, based on short videos about cooking. This contains about 65 different activities such as *melting butter* or *cooking pasta*, with attributes *tool=pan* or *tool=sieve*. Our goal is to broaden and automate the construction of these kinds of semantic frames, in order to populate a comprehensive *activity knowledge base*, in which, all concepts are sense-disambiguated

CIKM'15, October 19–23, 2015, Melbourne, Australia.
© 2015 ACM. ISBN 978-1-4503-3794-6/15/10 ...$15.00.
DOI: http://dx.doi.org/10.1145/2806416.2806583.

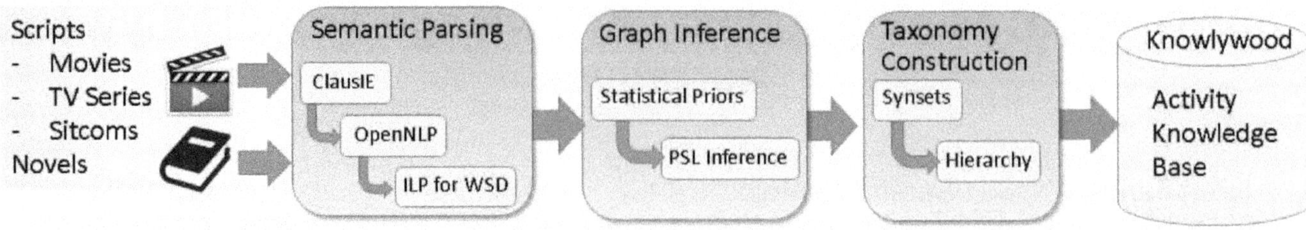

Figure 2: Knowlywood System Overview

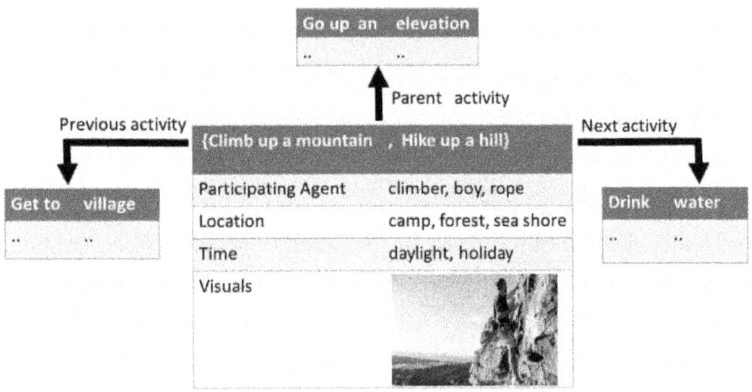

Figure 1: Activity Frame Example

and thus canonicalized with regard to high-quality linguistic resources like WordNet or VerbNet [36, 18].

Approach and Contribution. We have developed an advanced pipeline for semantic parsing and knowledge distillation, which allows us to systematically compile semantically refined activity frames from scripts and novels. We have processed nearly 2 million scenes from 560 movies, 460 TV series, and 100 books, and constructed a high-quality activity knowledge base with almost one million frames. Specifically, we represent activities as JSON objects which gives us typed attributes (also known as slots in knowledge representation terminology) and set-valued entries for attributes (also known as values or fillers). JSON is a popular format for data export/import. Our frames can also be easily cast into RDF triples. Overall, our contributions are:

- The first system, called Knowlywood, that automatically acquires detailed knowledge about activities, by tapping into movie/TV scripts and narrative texts and combining semantic parsing techniques for candidate generation with probabilistic inference and graph algorithms for candidate cleaning.
- New techniques for sense disambiguation of multi-word phrases (mapping them to WordNet) and taxonomy induction for activities, as building blocks of our construction pipeline.
- A large knowledge collection with nearly one million activities in the form of semantic frames, and with linkage to visual contents where activities occur. This Knowlywood collection will be made publicly accessible.[1] Its high quality has been confirmed by manual assessment with extensive sampling.

Our activity frames are valuable for use-cases such as video search, provide background knowledge for human-computer dialog, and can aid tasks like video scene understanding and the generation of textual descriptions for visual contents. Note also that the developed methodology is general and can be applied to other input sources if available, for example, personal diaries or travel logs.

[1] http://tinyurl.com/knowlywood

2. SYSTEM OVERVIEW

Figure 2 illustrates the Knowlywood pipeline of methods and tools. For automatically building the Knowlywood KB, we take the following main steps:

- **Semantic Parsing:** We first apply information extraction techniques on our input sources and then feed the output into a novel technique for semantic parsing, based on identifying clauses, mapping words and phrases to WordNet and VerbNet, and using integer linear programming (ILP) for the final disambiguation and construction of candidate activity frames.
- **Graph Inference:** We use the output data of the first stage to construct a preliminary activity knowledge graph, with noise and false positives. We then use Probabilistic Soft Logic (PSL) for efficient inference to construct a cleaner graph as consistent, high-quality output.
- **Taxonomy Construction:** We merge activities into equivalence classes, so-called *synsets* in the terminology of lexical resources (e.g., WordNet). An example is merging activity *propose to girlfriend* with *propose to fiancee*. Finally, we construct a subsumption hierarchy of activity synsets, which connects activities by the *hasType* relation. An example is: *propose to girlfriend* hasType *propose to someone*.

We additionally attach video frames to activities. To align scenes in movie scripts with their respective video frames, we exploit timestamp information in subtitle data.

Computational Model. The input to our methods is primarily scripts about movies or episodes of TV series. Figure 3 shows an example from the movie "Sex and the City" (obtained from the website `imsdb.com`). Although this is in a free format, there is some structure that we can exploit. Specifically, there are cues for detecting scene boundaries, we can identify speakers, and we can extract short descriptions about the setting of a scene that typically precede the actual dialog. Also, there are short narrative texts in between dialogs. Our methods are primarily geared for narrative snippets such as "Big proposes to Carrie" or "Big and Carrie kiss". Section 3 discusses how to further process these snippets and extract semantically cleaner information.

Obviously, individual scripts may be too noisy for automated methods to extract any meaningful information. Our method leverages that certain cues for activities appear in several scenes of different movies. Further, our scope is beyond movie scripts, including sitcoms, TV series, and novels, providing us with a broad spectrum of activities and higher redundancy.

We treat *verbal phrases* in narrative snippets as surface expressions for activity candidates. Using NLP techniques , this gives us cues such as "propose to a woman" and "kiss someone". Generally, we extract *verb-object* pairs, where the verb can have a preposition (e.g., "propose to") and the object is a noun phrase, potentially a multi-word phrase. Initially, these are still ambiguous words that may have many different meanings. Our methods map both verb and object to unambiguous senses, so-called *synsets* in the WordNet lexical thesaurus [15]. This is crucial for semantic interpretation, and also key to being able to combine cues from different scenes and to organize activities in a clean taxonomy. In the example, we would obtain *propose#5 woman#1* where #5 and #1 are the WordNet sense numbers of the ambiguous words "propose" and "woman". The result of this sense disambiguation forms the core of an activity frame.

Definition 1. *An* activity *is a pair* (v, o) *where* v *is a WordNet synset for a verb or verb phrase and* o *is a WordNet synset for a noun or noun phrase.*

Activities are then enriched by *attributes* (or frame slots) about location, time, and involved participants. The latter includes both the humans in an activity (e.g., man, woman, judge) and objects or props that play role in the activity (e.g., diamond or ring). We obtain cues for the location and time attribute values using NLP techniques as well as from the scene description (before the dialog starts), e.g., "apartment", "courthouse", "spring", "day". For the participants attributes, we extract cues from both the characters in a scene and noun phrases in narrative snippets or dialogs. All these will also be sense-disambiguated in the output for the KB.

Definition 2. *An* activity frame *is an activity enhanced with attribute values for location, time, and participants.*

- *For location, the allowed values are WordNet senses that are hyponyms (specialization) of the WordNet sense* location#1.
- *For time, the allowed values are hyponyms of the sense* time period#1 *or* event#1.
- *For participants, the allowed values are hyponyms of* living thing#1 *or* physical object#1.

Each attribute can have zero, one or multiple values.

Finally, as we may extract activity candidates from each scene, we can relate activities from successive scenes (if there is a typical pattern found in several movies). To this end, we introduce frame attributes *prev* for a previous activity and *next* for a following activity. This way we link different activity frames to form entire chains. In the example, *propose#5 woman#1* would be *next*-linked to *kiss#1 someone#1*.

Definition 3. *An* activity chain *is a sequence of temporally related activities connected by* prev *and* next *links.* A.next = B *and B.prev = A denote that activity A is often followed by activity B.*

3. SEMANTIC PARSING

We have devised a customized pipeline for semantic parsing that starts with the input scripts and extracts and disambiguates constituents, all the way to constructing a frame structure for candidate activities.

Consider the input sentence *He shot a video in the moving bus*. The output frame for this input is shown in the last column of Table 1. The activity name is given by the verb followed by an object (i.e., shoot#4;video#1). Note that the words in this frame are mapped to disambiguated *WordNet senses* [15], denoted by the numbers after the # symbols. If a phrase is absent in WordNet, e.g. *moving bus*, then we merely map its head word (*bus*). The other columns in

235 INT. PENTHOUSE APARTMENT – LATER – SPRING
Carrie and Big are on the carpeted floor.
Big proposes to Carrie.
BIG (CONT'D)
Carrie Bradshaw
love of my life -
will you marry me?

She nods. Speechless. Overcome. He smiles.

BIG (CONT'D)
See, this is why
there's a diamond.

236 INT. COURTHOUSE/ROOM – DAY – SPRING

Carrie stands with Big in front of a JUDGE.
JUDGE
By the power vested in me, by
the state of New York, I now
pronounce you husband and wife.
You may now kiss the bride

Big and Carrie kiss.

Figure 3: Excerpt from Movie Script

Table 1: Semantic parsing example

Phrase	WordNet Mapping	VerbNet Mapping	Output Frame
the man	man#1	Agent . animate	Agent: man#1
began to shoot	shoot#4	shoot#vn#3	Action: shoot#4
a video	video#1	Patient . solid	Patient:video#1
in	in	PP . in	
the moving bus	bus#1	NP . Location . solid	Location: moving bus#1

Table 1 show the input phrases (after chunking) and their mappings to WordNet senses and entries in VerbNet [18], as discussed below.

Sentence Analysis. We first use ClausIE [11] to decompose sentences into shorter clauses, whenever possible. These are then further decomposed by applying the OpenNLP (*opennlp.sourceforge.net*) maximum entropy model for chunking the text of each individual clause. In the example in Table 1, this results in the sentence being split as shown in the first column.

Sense and Argument Analysis. Understanding the verb is the most critical task for semantic interpretation. We address this by mapping the verb or verb phrase to its proper sense in WordNet [15], which in turn is linked with VerbNet [18], a manually curated linguistic resource for English verbs. For each verb class, VerbNet lists relevant thematic roles, semantic restrictions on the arguments, and syntactic frames. For example, for the main predicate verb *shoot* in our example sentence, VerbNet lists multiple candidate senses, and for the first of these, `shoot#vn#1`, it provides, among others, the following syntactic frame:

Agent.animate V Patient.animate PP Instrument.solid

This would match *He shot the man with a gun*. Here, several roles are accompanied by a semantic constraint, known as a *selectional restriction*. A selectional restriction such as `animate` for the patient requires that this patient be a living being when used in the given syntactic frame. This can guide the choice of the proper WordNet mappings for the objects and for other words. For instance, *the man* in our example sentence could be disambiguated as `man#1`, which in turn is in a *hasInheritedHypernym* relationship with `living_thing#1`, which leads us to the `animate` label from VerbNet, and helps us find the right VerbNet sense for the verb.

These dependencies are captured as constraints in our joint disambiguation method, based on Integer Linear Programming (ILP) — discussed below. The ILP method uses prior weights obtained from simpler heuristics for word sense disambiguation (WSD) — discussed next.

WSD Priors. For an initial disambiguation of individual words and phrases, we use the state-of-the-art WSD system It-Makes-Sense (IMS) [43], which relies on supervised learning. We obtain the following scores for mapping a word i to sense j:

$$\tau_{ij} = \begin{cases} \text{score of IMS} & \text{for } j \in S_{\text{W}} \\ \sum_{j'} \tau_{ij'} & \text{for } j \in S_{\text{V}} \text{ linked to } j' \in S_{\text{W}} \end{cases}$$

Here, S_{W} denotes the set of candidate WordNet senses for the verbs and S_{V} denotes the set of candidate VerbNet senses. Note that VerbNet is much smaller and thus coarser-grained than WordNet, hence the summation over all WordNet senses linked with the same VerbNet verb.

An additional feature used in the ILP later are the most-frequent-sense ranks that WordNet provides, based on manual annotation of a large news corpus:

$$\theta_{ij} = \begin{cases} \text{1/rank(j for i)} & \text{for } j \in S_{\text{W}} \\ \sum_{j'} \theta_{ij'} & \text{for } j \in S_{\text{V}} \text{ linked to } j' \in S_{\text{W}} \end{cases}$$

Finally, we compute syntactic and semantic priors based on how well the input verb matches a VerbNet entry:

syn_{ij} frame match score for word i and VerbNet sense j
sem_{ij} selectional restriction score of the roles in a VerbNet frame j for word i

ILP Model. For the *joint* disambiguation of all words in the input sentence, we have devised an ILP with *binary decision variables* x_{ij} set to 1 if word i is mapped to sense j (in WordNet and/or VerbNet). V denotes the set of all input words or phrases i that are verb chunks. Our ILP is defined as follows:

maximize

$$\sum_{i,j} x_{ij}(\alpha\tau_{ij} + \beta_1\theta_{ij} + \beta_2\text{syn}_{ij} + \beta_3\text{sem}_{ij})$$

subject to

$$\begin{array}{lll} \sum_{j \in S_{\text{V}}} x_{ij} & \leq 1 & \forall i \in V \\ x_{ij} & \leq x_{ij'} & \forall i \in V, j \in S_{\text{W}}, \\ & & j \textit{ mapped to } j' \in S_{\text{V}} \\ x_{i_0 j_0} & \leq x_{ij} & \forall i_0 \in V, j \in S_{\text{V}}, \\ & & x_{ij} \in \textit{role-restr}(x_{i_0 j_0}) \\ \sum_j x_{ij} & \leq 1 & \forall i \notin V \\ x_{ij} & \in \{0,1\} & \end{array}$$

The objective function combines the various prior scores, with coefficients tuned on withheld training sentences that are manually labeled. The first constraint ensures that at most one VerbNet sense is chosen for each verb. The second one ensures consistency between choices of WordNet senses and corresponding VerbNet ones. The third constraint covers the selectional restrictions described earlier. The fourth constraint ensures that at most one sense is chosen for each non-verb word. We instantiate a separate ILP for every sentence, and thus the ILP size and complexity remain tractable.

4. GRAPH INFERENCE

Based on the output frames of the semantic parsing phase, we derive connections between different activity frames: parent types (hypernyms), semantic similarity edges, and temporal order (previous/next). We cast this as a graph inference problem, denoting the three types of connections as T, S, and P (previous) edges. We tackle this task using the Probabilistic Soft Logic (PSL) framework [6] for relational learning and inference.

For each frame, the activity name is either a single word that is directly mapped to a WordNet/VerbNet sense, or it is a multi-word phrase. In the latter case, we only map the head word of the phrase to WordNet or VerbNet. For an activity a, we denote the mapped part as $h(a)$ and the remaining part as $\bar{h}(a)$ ($\bar{h}(a) = \emptyset$ for single-word activity names).

Edge Priors. We define an activity as a (verb-sense,noun-sense) pair. This allows us to leverage WordNet's taxonomic hierarchy to estimate parent types and similarities between activities.

Our model starts off with prior probabilities for each of the three kinds of edges. The prior for T (parent type) edges between two pairs (v_1, n_1), (v_2, n_2) is calculated as a multiplicative score $\mathtt{t}(v_1, v_2) \cdot \mathtt{t}(n_1, n_2)$. For the noun senses, we use the WordNet hypernymy: The score is 1 if parent and child are connected by hypernymy, and 0 otherwise. For the verb senses, we check both WordNet hypernymy and VerbNet verb hierarchy.

Finally, we derive edges from the subsumption of activity participants, retrieved from WordNet, e.g. between *drinking tea* and *drinking beverage*.

We create S (similarTo) edges based on the similarity between (v_1, n_1), (v_2, n_2) using the multiplicative score: $\text{sim}(v_1, v_2) \cdot \text{sim}(n_1, n_2)$. The taxonomic relatedness score between two noun senses n_1, n_2 is computed using a WordNet path similarity measure [30]. Scores between two verb senses v_1, v_2 are computed using WordNet verb groups and VerbNet class membership [36].

P (previous) edges: Scripts come with scene boundaries. We assume that the activity sequences that occur in a scene are temporally alignable. While an exact sequence of activity does not bring much redundancy, a gap-enabled sequence of activities can have rich statistics. Secondly, generalizing activities to potential parent nodes brings more redundancy, and hence richer statistics. We use a generalized sequence mining algorithm, GSP [38], perfectly suitable to our scenario. We define two parameters: minimum support=3 and maximum gap = 4. We use GSP to efficiently determine P edges. We provide priors to P edges according to the following. An activity a_1 precedes a_2 with probability proportional to the support $\frac{\text{freq}(a_1 \text{ prev } a_2)}{\text{freq}(a_1)\,\text{freq}(a_2)}$.

Inference. Based on the initial prior scores for T, S, P, our task is to compute a cleaner graph of T, S, and P edges with scores reflecting their joint dependencies. These dependencies are captured in our PSL model with the following soft first-order logic rules. Since these are soft rules, they do not need to hold universally. The model automatically determines to what extent they should contribute to the final solution.

1. Parents often inherit prev. (P) edges from their children: $P(a, b) \wedge T(a, a') \wedge T(b, b') \Rightarrow P(a', b')$.
2. Similar activities are likely to share parent types $S(a, b) \wedge T(b, b_0) \Rightarrow T(a, b_0)$.
3. Likely mutual exclusion between edge types: $T(a, b) \wedge S(a, b) \Rightarrow \neg P(a, b)$.
4. Siblings are likely to be similar: $T(a, c) \wedge T(b, c) \Rightarrow S(a, b)$.

5. Similarity is often transitive:
   $S(a,b) \wedge S(b,c) \Rightarrow S(a,c)$.

6. Similarity is normally symmetric:
   $S(a,b) \Rightarrow S(b,a)$.

The inference weights w_i are tuned based on withheld data, using the PSL system's weight learning module.

5. TAXONOMY CONSTRUCTION

Activity Merging. The previous steps of our pipeline yield fairly clean activity frames, but may produce overly specific activities such as "embrace spouse", "hug wife", "hug partner", "caress someone", etc. These are sufficiently similar to be grouped together into a single frame (with slightly generalized semantics). Thus, the relation S from the previous step provides a pruned starting point for activity merging.

Definition 4. *An* activity synset *is a group of activities with highly related semantics. For a synset* $\{(v_1, o_1), (v_2, o_2), \dots\}$ *of verb-sense/object-sense pairs, we require that* $a_i = (v_i, o_i)$ *and* $a_j = (v_j, o_j)$ *have a semantic distance in WordNet below a certain threshold.*

Specifically, we consider *WordNet path similarity* [30] as a measure of semantic distance. To this end, we construct a graph between activity frames based on the synset (i.e., equivalence) and hypernym/hyponym relations in WordNet. The edges in this graph could be weighted by relatedness strength, such as gloss overlap [3], but we simply used uniform weights,i.e. simple path lengths $dist(v_i, v_j)$. For two activities a_i, a_j, we compute

$$\frac{1}{2}\left(\frac{1}{1+\text{dist}(v_i,v_j)} + \frac{1}{1+\text{dist}(o_i,o_j)}\right).$$

In addition, we consider the participants sets P_i, P_j in the frames of a_i,a_j, respectively. Recall that each P_i is a set of WordNet noun-phrase senses. We compute the WordNet path similarity for each element in $P_i \times P_j$, and aggregate them into an overall measure by taking the maximum (or alternatively the average). The final distance between a_i and a_j is the average of the verb-sense/object-sense distance and the participants distance.

The threshold for merging two activities into a synset is determined by manually grouping a small sample of activities and computing the threshold that achieves the synsets in the sample. We transitively merge activities whenever their distance is below that tuned threshold. We perform a transitive closure on this pruned neighborhood to allow grouping of activities.

Hierarchy Induction. The above techniques provide us with a suitably grained but still flat collection of activity synsets. However, some of these may semantically subsume others. For example, *divorce husband* is subsumed by *break up with a partner*. Again, the relation T from the previous step provides a pruned starting point for hierarchy induction.

Definition 5. *An* activity taxonomy *is a DAG (directed acyclic graph) of activity synsets such that* $a_i \sqsubset a_j$ *is an edge in the DAG if* a_i *is semantically subsumed by* a_j*. That is, the verb or object of* a_j *is more general than that of* a_i*.*

To construct the hierarchy, we again use WordNet path similarity but consider only *hypernym* relations now (i.e., disregard hyponyms). For this asymmetric measure, we again tune a threshold by manually assessing a small sample. The resulting taxonomy graph initially contains all subsumption pairs with semantic distance below the threshold. As this may create cycles, we finally break cycles by greedily removing low-weight edges. In building the Knowlywood KB, we had to eliminate only few cycles.

6. RESULTS

To evaluate our approach, we conducted a series of experiments to thoroughly examine our pipeline for semantic parsing and knowledge distillation, as well as the resultant Knowlywood activity frames.

Data Processing. Knowlywood is constructed by processing 1.89 million scenes from several sources:

- 560 movie scripts, scripts of 290 TV series, and scripts of 179 sitcoms. We crawled this data from Web sites like `wikia.com` and `dailyscript.com`.
- The Novels dataset comprises 103 novels from Project Gutenberg [14].
- Crowdsourcing: We use the data from [34], which consists of textual descriptions of videos portraying humans engaging in cooking related activities.

6.1 System Components

Semantic Parsing. In order to gain deep insights about our system, we had human judges annotate at least 250 random samples of the outputs of the different stages in our semantic parsing method, i.e., sentence extraction by pre-processing datasets, clause level splitting, the basic NLP pipeline (tagging, chunking, etc.), and finally disambiguation and VerbNet-based role assignment. Table 2 presents the resulting precision scores with statistical significance given as Wilson score intervals for $\alpha = 95\%$ [7].

We observe that most of the errors stem from the NLP pipeline, especially chunking. This could be addressed by using more advanced NLP tools, which, however, tend to be slower. Processing the sitcom and TV series data is the most challenging and error-prone due to the nature of these texts: the sentences are long and often filled with slang (e.g., "hold'em"). Some errors are also introduced at the early stage of pre-processing movie scripts, where we rely on regular expressions to parse the semi-structured text files (e.g., the introductory text for each scene which introduces the location, time, etc.).

Graph Inference. Next, we evaluate the PSL-based graph inference. Our findings indicate that it was instrumental in cleaning the candidate relations between activities and also in acquiring new edges between them. Table 3 shows the precision and size of the graph before and after the inference step. For example, from the P edge between `acquire#1; cutting knife#1` and `use#1; cutting knife#1`, a new P edge is derived from `acquire#1; knife#1` to `use#1; knife#1`. The transitive closure on the S relationships adds new edges. Thus, our graph inference increases Knowlywood's coverage and accuracy by inferring missing edges and removing inconsistent ones.

Table 3: Effect of PSL inference

	Before inference		After inference	
	Precision	#Edges	Precision	#Edges
T	0.77±0.04	1,906,520	0.87±0.03	4,511,203
S	0.84±0.02	1,022,700	0.85±0.04	3,421,210
P	0.78±0.04	116,186	0.84±0.09	205,678

Table 2: Evaluation of the semantic parsing

	sentence	clause	NLP	senses	participant roles	overall
Movie scripts	0.79 ±0.11	0.84 ±0.07	0.87 ±0.06	0.96 ±0.04	0.96 ±0.03	0.91 ±0.03
TV series	0.90 ±0.06	0.96 ±0.04	0.40 ±0.10	0.65 ±0.10	0.79 ±0.08	0.74 ±0.04
Sitcoms	0.91 ±0.07	0.93 ±0.06	0.38 ±0.12	0.67 ±0.12	0.72 ±0.11	0.73 ±0.05
Novels	0.94 ±0.05	0.91 ±0.07	0.74 ±0.12	0.85 ±0.09	0.93 ±0.06	0.90 ±0.04
Crowdsourcing	0.96 ±0.04	0.96 ±0.04	0.86 ±0.09	0.75 ±0.11	0.91 ±0.07	0.91 ±0.03

Synset and Hierarchy Construction. We performed a static analysis of the hierarchy as well as an empirical evaluation. There were 543 cycles in the graph. These were of a very small length (average length 3). After breaking the cycles, the DAG consists of 505,788 synset nodes without any cycles. The maximum depth of the graph is 5.

Over a random sample of 119 activity synsets, human judges were asked if the edge between random synset members was indeed a synonymy relation, i.e. semantically equivalent activities. To evaluate the hierarchy, in a similar way, human judges were asked if the edge between two activity synsets was one of hypernymy, i.e. subsuming activity synsets.

The synset grouping achieved a very high accuracy of 0.976±0.02 (Wilson score intervals for $\alpha = 95\%$ [7]). One of the reasons for this high accuracy was the tight threshold for taxonomic similarities. We had empirically chosen a high threshold of 0.40 for the synset similarity.

The hierarchy grouping achieved a high accuracy of 0.911±0.04 (Wilson score intervals for $\alpha = 95\%$). An example error case was *walk with a fly* having a hypernymy link to *travel with a beast*. This is because *animal* and *beast* are synonymous. Such mildly incorrect cases led to a slightly lower precision.

6.2 Knowlywood KB Evaluation

In total, the Knowlywood pipeline produced 964,758 unique activity instances, grouped into 505,788 activity synsets. In addition to the edges mentioned above, we also obtain 581,438 `location`, 71,346 `time`, and 5,196,156 `participant` attribute entries over all activities.

Quality. To evaluate the quality of these activity frames, we compiled a random sample of 119 activities from the KB, each as a full frame with values for all attributes (participants, location, time, previous and next activity, etc.). We relied on expert human annotators to judge each attribute for each of these activities. An entry was marked as correct if it made sense to the annotator as typical knowledge for the activity. The judgement were aggregated separately for each attribute, and we computed the precision as $\frac{c}{c+i}$, where c and i are the counts of correct and incorrect attribute values, respectively. For statistical significance, we again computed Wilson score intervals for $\alpha = 95\%$. The per-attribute results are reported in Table 4. The inter-annotator agreement for three judges in terms of Fleiss' κ is 0.77.

We can observe from these assessments that Knowlywood achieves good precision on most of the attributes. In some datasets like the Crowdsourcing collection, no information on time or location is available. This accounts for the low scores.

Examples. Fig. 4 presents anecdotal examples of Knowlywood's activity frames, with specific sense numbers from WordNet.

Comparison with ConceptNet. There is no direct competitor that provides frames of semantically refined activities. We thus compared Knowlywood with ConceptNet 5 (CN), the closest available

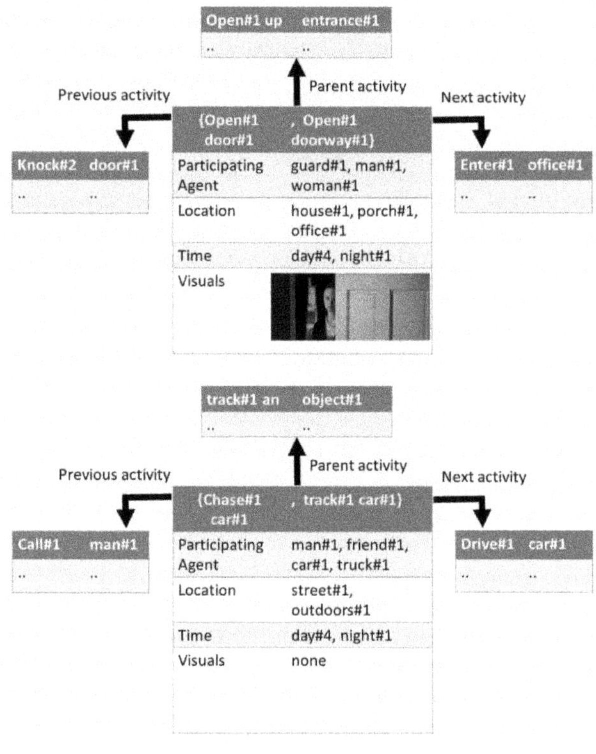

Figure 4: Anecdotal Examples

resource, assuming that any concept name matching the pattern *verb [article] object* is an activity. We mapped CN's relations to our notion of activity attributes as follows:

- IsA, InheritsFrom → type,
- Causes, ReceivesAction, RelatedTo, CapableOf, UsedFor → agent,
- HasPrerequisite, HasFirstSubevent, HasSubevent, HasLastSubevent, MotivatedByGoal → prev/next,
- SimilarTo, Synonym → similarTo,
- AtLocation, LocationOfAction, LocatedNear → location.

The activities derived this way from CN were manually assessed by the same pool of annotators that assessed the Knowlywood frames. We randomly sample 100 activities from CN and take all their relations but adding further relationships if we encountered too few of any one relationship type. The last row of Table 4 shows the results — both coverage and precision. We see that CN works well for eliciting previous/next activities. Here its quality exceeds that of Knowlywood. CN's crowdsourcing-based knowledge acquisition leads to fine-grained temporal knowledge that is rather difficult to mine from narrative texts (e.g., that riding a horse is preceded by keeping your heel down, and followed by your bottom getting sore).

Table 4: Knowlywood coverage and precision

Source	#Input Scripts	#Scenes	#Unique Activities	Parent	Participant	Prev	Next	Loc.	Time	Avg.
Movie scripts	560	148,296	244,789	0.87	0.86	0.78	0.85	0.79	0.79	0.84
TV series	290	886,724	565,394	0.89	0.85	0.81	0.84	0.82	0.84	0.86
Sitcoms	179	286,266	200,550	0.88	0.85	0.81	0.87	0.81	0.83	0.87
Novels	103	383,795	137,365	0.84	0.84	0.78	0.88	0.85	0.72	0.84
Crowdsrc.	25	3,701	9,575	0.82	0.91	0.91	0.87	0.74	0.40	0.86
Knowlywood	1,157	1,708,782	964,758	0.87	0.86	0.84	0.85	0.78	0.84	**0.85±0.01**
ConceptNet 5	-	-	4,757	0.15	0.81	0.92	0.91	0.33	N/A	**0.46±0.02**

However, these high precision values also result from the specific nature of CN's knowledge representation. Since CN's concepts are essentially strings (not word senses), we instructed our annotators to evaluate an attribute value as correct even if it holds true for just one possible interpretation of the concept names, ignoring ambiguity. The data also contains duplicates (e.g. "you open your wallet", "open your wallet", "open wallet", ...) that were all judged as correct as predecessors of "taking out money". CN's less formalized nature is particularly apparent from the fact that the parent type attribute obtains a precision of only 15%. Generally, except for the temporal ordering of activities, the precision of CN is substantially below that of Knowlywood.

Most importantly, Knowlywood's coverage of activities dwarfs that of CN. CN merely provides 4,757 activities, most of which are also included in Knowlywood, while the latter additionally contains nearly a million activity frames.

Comparison with ReVerb. We also compare Knowlywood with ReVerb [12], the most widely used system for broad-coverage open information extraction. Open information extraction aims at mining all possible subject-predicate-object triples from text. We mine activity knowledge from these triples such that the subject is an agent, and the predicate and object together form an activity, e.g. *drink + coffee*.

For role assignment, we mine `MovieClips.com` to obtain mappings from words to labels. MovieClips contains high-quality human-annotated and categorized tags for nearly 30,000 movie scenes (e.g. "action:singing", "prop:violin", "setting:theater"). These tags have a direct correspondence to our attributes (see Table 6). The tag co-occurrence statistics can be used to create a Bayesian classifier as $P(\text{class}|\text{word}) = \frac{P(\text{class,word})}{\sum_{w_i} P(\text{class},w_i)}$, relying on the joint probabilities for classes and words from `MovieClips.com`. One may also consider using semantic role labeling systems as an alternative. However, they cannot solve our semantic parsing task because they require large amounts of domain-specific labeled training data. Moreover, they suffer from poor scalability.

We consider two different datasets as input to ReVerb. First, all the input Script data that we used for our system (setup called ReVerbMCS). Second, all of ClueWeb09 dataset (setup called ReVerbClue). ReVerb extractions over ClueWeb09 are already available in the form of a publicly available dataset [12], consisting of 15 million unique SVO (Subject Verb Object) triples. The ReVerbClue data does not contain enough context to use the MovieClips-based role classifier because it consists of only SVO triples.

Since both ReVerbMCS and ReVerbClue extractions are strings (not word senses), we leniently evaluated an attribute value as correct if it holds true for any possible sense of the concept. This is thus a much easier task than Knowlywood's, for which we required the correct sense disambiguation.

Table 5: ReVerb baselines (counts and precision scores)

	Activities	Participant	Location	Time
ReVerbMCS	0.37M	0.37M, 0.77	0.17M, 0.83	0.05M, 0.66
ReVerbClue	0.86M	1.47M, 0.41	0.055M , -	0.008M, -

Table 6: Mappings between MovieClips.com and Knowlywood

MovieClips tag	Knowlywood attributes	Example
action	activity.v	cut
prop	activity.o	knife
setting	location	bar
occasion	time	thanksgiving
charactertype	participant	policeman

In Table 5, we list the number of activities as well as numbers and precision of several roles. The precision values are obtained by evaluating the frames corresponding to the activities overlapping with the Knowlywood test set of 119 activities resulting in more than 400 attribute triples. Knowlywood outperforms both the ReVerb based baselines (compare to Table 4), in terms of both precision and counts. The role labels score in ReVerbMCS reflect the rich statistics (though limited in size) obtained from the manually curated MovieClips. We also see that extractions from ClueWeb09 data, which is an order of magnitude larger than our scripts data, did not entail better quality.

Multimodal Content. By automatically aligning the movie scripts with subtitled videos, we were also able to associate 27,473 video frames with Knowlywood's activities. We believe that this will be an important asset for computer vision, because existing systems for activity detection in videos suffer from a lack of training data and background knowledge, and hence have been quite limited in their coverage.

7. USE CASES

7.1 Movie Scene Tagging

In order to evaluate the usefulness of the Knowlywood KB extrinsically, we introduce the task of predicting the activity portrayed in a movie clip, without task-specific training data, given only the location and participants in the corresponding scene.

As ground truth, we consider `Movieclips.com`, which contains high quality, manually curated categorized tags for nearly

30,000 movie clips/ scenes. Examples of these include: "location/setting: cemetery", "participating object/prop: rose", "action: obituary speech". By analyzing the co-occurrence statistics over the tags of these clips, we obtain a scored list of activities for a given [participant(s), location(s), time(s)]. We randomly select 1,000 clips from this gold data.

The evaluation task is to assess Knowlywood's (or any baseline activity KB's) top-k activity recommendations given only [participant(s), location(s), time(s)]. This task is more complex than a simple tag recommendation which would ignore any tag categories. As KBs, we use the Knowlywood KB, and the various baselines: ConceptNet, ReverbMCS, and ReverbClue.

Table 7: Movie Scene Tagging evaluation

	MRR	Hit rate
ReVerbClue	0.070	0.180
ConceptNet	0.143	0.345
ReVerbMCS	0.254	0.415
Knowlywood	0.327	0.610

The evaluation is based on a comparison of the predicted top-k activity list with the ranked gold list of activities. We report the standard IR-metric [21] Mean Reciprocal Rank (MRR) that rewards early hits in the predictions. We also report Hit-Rate metric which is one whenever the top-10 results contain atleast one good tag.

We then evaluated the various KBs on the movie scene tagging task. This is an automated evaluation, as the ground truth gold data is already available. For both the KBs and the gold-set, we uniformly set k=10, i.e. we compare the top-10 predictions against the top-10 ground truth rankings. The results in Table 7 demonstrate that although Knowlywood has not been trained or mined from `Movieclips.com` tags at all, the system is able to outperform the baselines by a large margin both on MRR and Hit rate. ReverbMCS outperforms other baselines because the role label classifer in ReverbMCS uses `Movieclips.com` statistics already. Knowlywood also yields a much better coverage in terms of the hit rate.

7.2 Scene Search

For a second extrinsic evaluation, we use Knowlywood to build a search platform over the corpus, which again comprises movie scripts, the Crowdsourcing dataset, TV series, sitcoms, and novels. This search system takes a text query q as input, which is expected to correspond to some activity. Examples of such queries are *animal attacks man, kissing during a romantic dinner.* As output, we expect a ranked list of scenes over the indexed corpus.

Approach. We use the textual (not visual) content of the scenes to obtain the score of a scene s for a given query.

Given an activity $a \in K$, where K denotes the Knowlywood knowledge base, let a_p be the set of

participants according to K and $A_p = \bigcup_{a \in K} a_p$ be the set of all participants associated

with activities in K. We derived a query-likelihood statistical language model as follows.

The probability that the scene s generates a query q is given by

$$P(q|s_t) = \sum_{a \in K} \sum_{p \in A_p} P(q|a) \cdot P(a|p) \cdot P(p|s_t)$$

- s_t is the textual representation of the scene,
- $P(p|s_t)$ is the probability that the scene generates participant p of an activity (e.g., girl, ring, etc.), estimated from noun-phrase occurrences in t with corpus smoothing,
- $P(a|p)$ is the probability that participant p generates activity a, again with smoothing, and
- $P(q|a)$ is the query likelihood of activity a, estimated by the occurrences of the verb-object words of a in the query, once more with smoothing.

Table 8: Query Frames.

Frame	Semantic restriction
S	WN physical entity
V	WN verb (compulsory)
O_1	WN physical entity
O_2	WN physical entity
L	WN location or WN physical entity
T	WN time-period

Table 9: Performance of the two search methods.

Algorithm	NDCG	MAP	Precision@5	MRR
Knowlywood	0.8972	0.9512	0.8809	0.9840
Text retrieval	0.0772	0.0696	0.0404	0.0730

Experimental Setup. As there is no similar activity search system or evaluation dataset, we construct a benchmark dataset by gathering 100 queries of a predefined frame (`S V O1 O2 Location Time`), such as, *man kissed the girl on the cheek at the movie theater in the evening.* For this, we relied on a user interface as in Table 8, asking two people (one outsider and one of the authors) to enter arbitrary queries of their choice, as long as it fit the template. Further examples of these gathered queries include *frying onion* and *killing a bird.*

For this set of 100 queries, we generate search results using our generative model over the Movie script, Crowdsourcing, Sitcom, TV series, and Novels datasets.

For comparison, we also obtain the search results using a text-retrieval baseline, in particular, a statistical language model with Dirichlet smoothing, as implemented in the well-known INDRI system [39].

Two annotators evaluated the top-10 results for each of these queries both for the baseline and the Knowlywood search system. Each result was scored between 1 (irrelevant) to 5 (perfectly relevant). The final rating for each result is given by the average of the ratings by the two annotators.

The annotation ratings were then used to compute four widely-used IR evaluation metrics, namely NDCG, Precision@k, MAP, and MRR [21].

Scene Search Results. Table 9 gives a comparative analysis of the NDCG, MAP, Precision@5, and MRR scores for both search methods. Since MAP, Precision@5, and MRR involve binary notions of relevance, we assume that those scenes that are rated with a score of at least 3 are the only relevant scenes.

We observe that for all four metrics, the Knowlywood search method performs best. We observed that the text retrieval engine often returns scenes with script text that closely matches the words in the query, while Knowlywood achieves a higher level of abstraction. For example, given the query *man climbs mountain*, the text engine favors scenes with many occurrences of the keywords *mountain* and *climb*, but not used in the specific sense of climbing mountains. The Knowlywood search method, on the other hand, uncovers those scenes that portray the activity, even if they do not contain the word *mountain* explicitly, but just semantically related expressions such as *hiking up a hill* etc. The Knowlywood search also

Table 10: Anecdotal examples for Scene Search results

Query	Knowlywood based scheme	Text based retrieval scheme
man climbs mountain	.. following Jack , and helps him **climb a mountain** and find a crystal that will transport Jack home both... from TV series: **Samurai Jack**	.. from deep in the **mountains** ... had entered the **Mountain** ...carried deeper into the **mountain** . .... **climbs** out of the river... looking for the **Mountain** of Skulls as well...turns his attention to Lysinka and the others down the **mountain** .. from Novel: **Conan**
man shoots video	.. While **shooting Dixons music video** , Silver gets a call from the fertility clinic informing her that the IVF procedure has been moved up to the next day .. from Beverly Hills, 90210	.. the woman **shoots Alex with a video game gun** as the woman traps her in the game that the.. from TV series: **Totally Spies**
kill a bird	..mark go hunting with sophie 's dad. jeremy go hunting with sophie 's dad. mark tries to **kill a bird** . the man injures it simply. the man tries to break its neck.. from Sitcom: Peep Show	.. Carlos and Susan are still painting over the graffiti on the wall as those people discuss **To Kill a Mocking Bird** , however , while talking , .. from TV series: Desperate Housewives

correctly identifies the true meaning of an activity even if it contains verbs with ambiguous meaning. For example, the query *shoot a video* is often interpreted wrongly by the text retrieval engine and therefore it returns irrelevant snippets referring to shooting with a gun, etc. Table 10 provides some anecdotal examples of queries and scene search results by the two competitors.

8. RELATED WORK

Large-scale knowledge graphs have become a major trend both in academia (DBpedia, NELL, Yago, etc.) and industry (Google, Microsoft, etc.). However, these are focused on facts about individual entities, rather than commonsense. Commonsense KBs like ConceptNet [17], VerbOcean [10], or WebChild [41], on the other hand, focus on simpler relationships between concepts such as *partOf*, *usedFor*, *hasColor*, *hasShape*, etc.

Formal upper-level ontologies such as Cyc [22] and SUMO [26] contain some activity knowledge like agents involved in concepts expressed by verbs. For example, SUMO knows that kissing involves two humans as agents and their lips. However, this is manually modeled and the amount of activity knowledge in these ontologies is tiny compared to what Knowlywood captures. Also, these ontologies focus on knowledge that is expressible in first-order logics, and lack commonsense knowledge offered by Knowlywood such as typical locations, times, prev./next chains, and participants.

Interest in human activities goes back to Schank and Abelson's early work on scripts [35], where procedural knowledge was gathered manually. More recently, such knowledge has been crowdsourced via Amazon Mechanical Turk [32], but this data only covers 22 stereotypical scenarios. Other research has developed ways to mine activity knowledge from the Web using text analysis [8] and deep neural networks [23]. These methods aim at solving small temporal ordering tasks, which is different from our goal of producing a large KB. [37] analyze a collection of event similarity data, but do not construct any new activities.

Regarding multimodal data, [9] attempt to mine a large-scale collection of simple conceptual knowledge from images, e.g. that wheels are parts of cars. However, this work does not recognize activities. [33] relate crowdsourced activity descriptions to videos. However, this is a very small collection of only 26 activity types. Activities play an important role in different domains. [42] present a KB of object affordances for robotics, but cover only 250 objects.

Semantic parsing has received much attention in computational linguistics recently; see [1] and references there. So far it has been applied only to specific use-cases like natural-language question answering [4, 13] or understanding temporal expressions [19]. We believe that our work is the first to apply semantic parsing to large amounts of narrative text for KB construction. Our methodology uses techniques like ILP and graphical models that have been previously used in natural language analysis. However, applying them to the huge input in our setting requires judicious design decisions that are not straightforward at all.

Semantic role labeling (SRL) [16, 28] is highly related to semantic parsing, the goal being to fill the slots of a pre-defined frame with arguments from a sentence. However, state-of-the-art methods are slow and do not work well for our task of activity knowledge acquisition. Moreover, SRL methods typically consider Propbank [27] as a backbone, and Propbank lacks the semantic organization of verbs that VerbNet provides.

Word sense disambiguation (WSD) [25] is another component in semantic parsing and semantic role labeling. We use the state-of-the-art tool IMS (It-Makes-Sense) [43] as a WSD prior for our joint disambiguation ILP. Note, though, that WSD alone focuses on the lexical semantics of individual words – this is still far from full-fledged semantic parsing for populating an activity KB.

Taxonomy induction has a rich body of prior work in NLP and AI. However, this is primarily for hypernymy (isa, subclasses) between general concepts (classes, noun senses) (see, e.g., [31, 29] and references given there). There is little research on taxonomy induction for verbal phrases [20, 10, 24]. But this line of work does not consider rich attributes for actions, and is about general verbs rather than focused on human activities.

9. CONCLUSION

We have presented Knowlywood, the first comprehensive KB of human activities. It provides a semantically refined hierarchy of activity types, participating agents, spatio-temporal information, information about activity sequences, as well as links to visual contents. Our algorithms ensure that the entries are fully disambiguated and that inconsistent attributes are removed. Our experiments show that Knowlywood compares favorably to several baselines, including in use cases such as tag recommendations. We believe that the resulting collection of around one million activity frames is an important asset for a variety of applications such as image and video understanding.

10. REFERENCES

[1] Yoav Artzi, Nicholas FitzGerald, and Luke S Zettlemoyer. Semantic parsing with combinatory categorial grammars. In *ACL*, 2013.

[2] S. Auer, C. Bizer, J. Lehmann, G. Kobilarov, R. Cyganiak, and Z. Ives. DBpedia: A nucleus for a web of open data. In *In ISWC/ASWC*, 2007.

[3] Satanjeev Banerjee and Ted Pedersen. Extended gloss overlaps as a measure of semantic relatedness. In *IJCAI*, 2003.

[4] Jonathan Berant, Andrew Chou, Roy Frostig, and Percy Liang. Semantic parsing on freebase from question-answer pairs. In *EMNLP*, 2013.

[5] Kurt Bollacker, Colin Evans, Praveen Paritosh, Tim Sturge, and Jamie Taylor. Freebase: A collaboratively created graph database for structuring human knowledge. In *SIGMOD*, 2008.

[6] Matthias Brocheler, Lilyana Mihalkova, and Lise Getoor. Probabilistic similarity logic. *arXiv 1203.3469*, 2012.

[7] Lawrence D. Brown, T. Tony Cai, and Anirban DasGupta. Interval estimation for a binomial proportion. *Statistical Science*, 16(2):101–133, 2001.

[8] Nathanael Chambers and Dan Jurafsky. Unsupervised learning of narrative schemas and their participants. In *ACL*, 2009.

[9] Xinlei Chen, Abhinav Shrivastava, and Abhinav Gupta. Neil: Extracting visual knowledge from web data. In *ICCV*, 2013.

[10] Timothy Chklovski and Patrick Pantel. VerbOcean: Mining the web for fine-grained semantic verb relations. In *EMNLP*, 2004.

[11] Luciano Del Corro and Rainer Gemulla. ClausIE: Clause-based open information extraction. 2013.

[12] Anthony Fader, Stephen Soderland, and Oren Etzioni. Identifying relations for open information extraction. In *Proc. EMNLP*, 2011.

[13] Anthony Fader, Luke Zettlemoyer, and Oren Etzioni. Open question answering over curated and extracted knowledge bases. In *SIGKDD*, 2014.

[14] Manaal Faruqui and Sebastian Pado. Towards a model of formal and informal address in english. In *EACL*, April 2012.

[15] Christiane Fellbaum, editor. *WordNet: An Electronic Lexical Database*. The MIT Press, 1998.

[16] Daniel Gildea and Daniel Jurafsky. Automatic labeling of semantic roles. *Comput. Linguist.*, 28(3):245–288, 2002.

[17] Catherine Havasi, Robert Speer, and Jason Alonso. ConceptNet 3: a flexible, multilingual semantic network for common sense knowledge. In *RANLP*, 2007.

[18] Karen Kipper, Anna Korhonen, Neville Ryant, and Martha Palmer. Extending VerbNet with novel verb classes. In *LREC*, 2006.

[19] Kenton Lee, Yoav Artzi, Jesse Dodge, and Luke Zettlemoyer. Context-dependent semantic parsing for time expressions. In *ACL*, 2014.

[20] Dekang Lin and Patrick Pantel. Dirt@ sbt@ discovery of inference rules from text. In *KDD*, 2001.

[21] Christopher D Manning, Prabhakar Raghavan, and Hinrich Schütze. *Introduction to information retrieval*, volume 1. Cambridge University Press, 2008.

[22] C. Matuszek, M. Witbrock, R.C. Kahlert, J. Cabral, D. Schneider, P. Shah, and D. Lenat. Searching for common sense: Populating Cyc from the Web. In *AAAI*, 2005.

[23] Ashutosh Modi and Ivan Titov. Inducing neural models of script knowledge. In *CoNLL*, Baltimore, MD, USA, 2014.

[24] Ndapandula Nakashole, Gerhard Weikum, and Fabian Suchanek. PATTY: A taxonomy of relational patterns with semantic types. In *EMNLP/CONLL*, 2012.

[25] Roberto Navigli. Word Sense Disambiguation: a survey. *ACM Computing Surveys*, 41(2):1–69, 2009.

[26] Ian Niles and Adam Pease. Towards a standard upper ontology. In *FOIS*, 2001.

[27] Martha Palmer, Daniel Gildea, and Paul Kingsbury. The Proposition Bank: An annotated corpus of semantic roles. *Computational linguistics*, 31(1):71–106, 2005.

[28] Martha Palmer, Daniel Gildea, and Nianwen Xue. Semantic role labeling. *Synthesis Lectures on Human Language Technologies*, 3(1):1–103, 2010.

[29] Marius Pasca. Acquisition of open-domain classes via intersective semantics. In *Proc. WWW*, pages 551–562, 2014.

[30] Ted Pedersen, Siddharth Patwardhan, and Jason Michelizzi. WordNet::Similarity: Measuring the relatedness of concepts. In *NAACL*, 2004.

[31] Simone Paolo Ponzetto and Michael Strube. Taxonomy induction based on a collaboratively built knowledge repository. *Artificial Intelligence*, 175(9-10), 2011.

[32] Michaela Regneri, Alexander Koller, and Manfred Pinkal. Learning script knowledge with web experiments. In *ACL*, 2010.

[33] Michaela Regneri, Marcus Rohrbach, Dominikus Wetzel, Stefan Thater, Bernt Schiele, and Manfred Pinkal. Grounding action descriptions in videos. *TACL*, 1:25–36, 2013.

[34] Marcus Rohrbach, Sikandar Amin, Mykhaylo Andriluka, and Bernt Schiele. A database for fine grained activity detection of cooking activities. In *CVPR*, 2012.

[35] R. Schank and R. Abelson. *Scripts, plans, goals and understanding: An inquiry into human knowledge structures.* Hillsdale, NJ., 1977.

[36] Karin Kipper Schuler, Anna Korhonen, and Susan Windisch Brown. VerbNet overview, extensions, mappings and applications. In *HLT-NAACL*, 2009.

[37] Tomohide Shibata and Sadao Kurohashi. Acquiring strongly-related events using predicate-argument co-occurring statistics and case frames. In *IJCNLP*, 2011.

[38] Ramakrishnan Srikant and Rakesh Agrawal. *Mining sequential patterns: Generalizations and performance improvements*. Springer, 1996.

[39] Trevor Strohman, Donald Metzler, Howard Turtle, and W Bruce Croft. Indri: A language model-based search engine for complex queries. In *International Conference on Intelligent Analysis*, 2005.

[40] Fabian M. Suchanek, Gjergji Kasneci, and Gerhard Weikum. Yago: A Core of Semantic Knowledge. In *WWW*, 2007.

[41] Niket Tandon, Gerard de Melo, Fabian Suchanek, and Gerhard Weikum. Webchild: Harvesting and organizing commonsense knowledge from the web. In *WSDM*, 2014.

[42] Karthik Mahesh Varadarajan and Markus Vincze. Afnet: The affordance network. In *ACCV (1)*. Springer, 2012.

[43] Zhi Zhong and Hwee Tou Ng. It makes sense: A wide-coverage word sense disambiguation system for free text. In *ACL*, 2010.

Entity and Aspect Extraction for Organizing News Comments

Radityo Eko Prasojo
Free University of Bozen-Bolzano
Dominikanterplatz 3
39100 Bolzano, Italy
radityoeko.prasojo@stud-inf.unibz.it

Mouna Kacimi
Free University of Bozen-Bolzano
Dominikanterplatz 3
39100 Bolzano, Italy
mouna.kacimi@unibz.it

Werner Nutt
Free University of Bozen-Bolzano
Dominikanterplatz 3
39100 Bolzano, Italy
nutt@inf.unibz.it

ABSTRACT

News websites give their users the opportunity to participate in discussions about published articles, by writing comments. Typically, these comments are unstructured making it hard to understand the flow of user discussions. Thus, there is a need for organizing comments to help users to (1) gain more insights about news topics, and (2) have an easy access to comments that trigger their interests. In this work, we address the above problem by organizing comments around the entities and the aspects they discuss. More specifically, we propose an approach for entity and aspect extraction from user comments through the following contributions. First, we extend traditional Named-Entity Recognition approaches, using coreference resolution and external knowledge bases, to detect more occurrences of entities in comments. Second, we exploit part-of-speech tag, dependency tag, and lexical databases to extract explicit and implicit aspects around discussed entities. Third, we evaluate our entity and aspect extraction approach, on manually annotated data, showing that it highly increases precision and recall compared to baseline approaches.

Categories and Subject Descriptors

H.3.3 [**Information Storage and Retrieval**]: Information Search and Retrieval; I.2.7 [**Artificial Intelligence**]: Natural Language Processing

Keywords

entity extraction; aspect extraction; text mining

1. INTRODUCTION

Media platforms, like CNN[1] and Al Jazeera[2], deliver the latest breaking news on various topics about everyday events. Moreover, they provide the possibility to write comments about any published article and engage in discussions with other users. Figure 1 shows an example of a news article about the Scottisch independence referendum, published at Al Jazeera on September 19, 2014. On this article, users started several threads of discussions about *"Scots origin"*, *"Benefit of terrorists from Scottisch independence"*, *"The results of the vote"*, and other subjects. Although user comments form such well-defined discussions, they are displayed in an unstructured way, listed based on time and date information, as shown in Figure 1. Consequently, it is hard for the reader to catch the flow of discussions and to understand their main points of agreement and disagreement. Thus, there is a need for organizing user comments to (1) have a better understanding of the viewpoints related to each topic and (2) facilitate the participation in discussions and thus increase the chance of acquiring new viewpoints. A natural way to summarize and organize comments is to cluster those that contain similar discussions. In other words, they talk about the same entities and argue about the same aspects of those entities. To achieve this task, we need to extract entities and aspects from user comments.

The core problem of our work is entity and aspect extraction from unstructured text. Several techniques for Named Entity Recognition (NER) have been proposed in the literature [1, 3, 5–7, 11, 12, 19–21], including supervised, semi-supervised, and unsupervised techniques. Similarly, several approaches have been proposed for aspect extraction from user reviews about products [22]. Exploiting existing approaches to extract entities and aspects from user comments brings new challenges: (1) a user comment can refer to other comments when talking about entities, which requires the integration of coreference resolution strategies and tailored techniques for identifying the context of a comment; (2) user comments are informal and might include noisy information such as abbreviations and misspellings, which make entity extraction difficult; (3) aspect extraction techniques limit aspects to attributes and components of entities and thus do not cover other forms of aspects related to entities that are not objects, such as people or events.

In this paper, we propose an approach for entity and aspect extraction from user comments on news media platforms, tackling the problems above. The main contributions of this paper are summarized as follows:

1. We extend traditional Named Entity Recognition (NER) approaches to detect more occurrences of enti-

[1] www.cnn.com
[2] www.aljazeera.com

CIKM '15, October 19–23, 2015, Melbourne, Australia
© 2015 ACM. ISBN 978-1-4503-3794-6/15/10 ...$15.00.
DOI: http://dx.doi.org/10.1145/2806416.2806576.

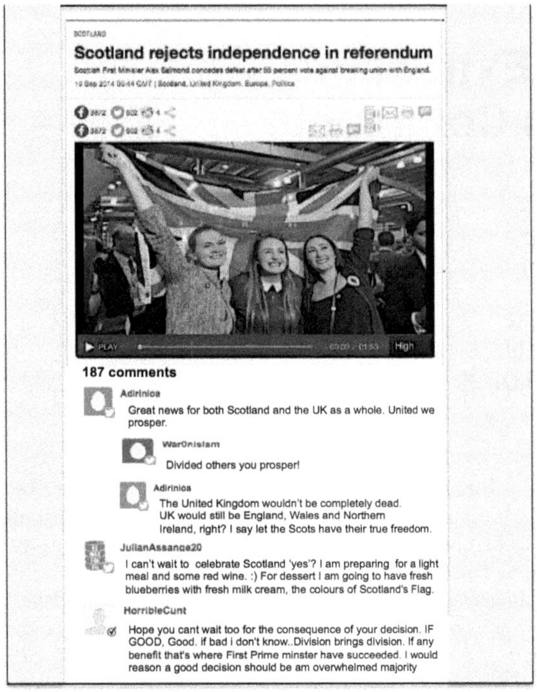

Figure 1: User comments on a news article

ties in a given comment. To achieve that, we use coreference resolution techniques to detect entities from comments that are not self-contained. Furthermore, we exploit external knowledge bases to solve the problem of abbreviations and misspellings.

2. We propose an aspect extraction approach to detect both explicit and implicit aspects around discussed entities. To handle aspect extraction, we exploit part-of-speech tags, dependency tags, and lexical databases.

3. We evaluate our entity and aspect extraction approach, on manually annotated data, showing that it highly increases precision and recall compared to the AIDA, Zemanta, and NERD approaches.

The rest of this paper is organized as follows. Section 2 presents related work. Section 3 introduces the problem we are tackling in this work. Section 4 presents the extensions we propose for entity extraction tools. Section 5 describes our approach for extracting explicit and implicit aspects. Section 6 presents and discusses experiment results, and finally Section 7 concludes the paper.

2. RELATED WORK

Our work falls into the category of Text Mining. To the best of our knowledge, we are the first to touch the area of organizing opinionated texts from user-generated content using a domain-independent approach for entity and aspect extraction. One of the most similar works to ours was done by Hu et al. [8,10]. They extract product features that are commented on by the user, then they group up review sentences commenting on the same features. This work was later improved by Poria et al. [15] who developed an unsupervised technique of product feature extraction and summarization using handcrafted rules. The difference between these approaches and our work is that they completely break down user comments into small sentences and they lose connection to the original user comments, whereas we want to preserve this information. Moreover, they are domain-specific while our work is more general. In terms of beautiful visualization of text summary, the Word Cloud[3] may be one of the best work available. It emphasizes important terms, however, it does not preserve semantic relations between terms. Some other similar works are those focusing on the area of topic mining [9,14]. Pons-Poratta et al. [14] explored a topic discovery system to browse and select topics of interest. Similarly to topic classification approaches, our work aims at maintaining relationships between entities and aspects. The main difference is that the relationships we build are not only semantic but they depend also on the co-occurences of terms in user comments.

Directly related to our work is research in Named Entity Recognition (NER) [20]. The first class of approaches is supervised and consists in learning classifiers from training data for entity recognition [1,3,5,6,11,19]. One of the most well-known open tools for supervised learning of NER is the StanfordNLP[4], which is based on the CRF classifier [7]. To address the difficulty of obtaining manually-annotated data for training, a second class of approaches was proposed. It relies on a semi-supervised learning technique called "bootstraping" [12]. Typically, this approach uses a small initial set of seeds as a start of the learning process, and then it searches for the occurrence of the seed in the sentences and identifies common contextual clues of the initial seeds. Then, the technique proceeds to find new instances of the seeds that have similar context.

The third class of approaches to NER uses unsupervised learning techniques, typically by making use of open knowledge bases such as DBpedia.[5] Some of the unsupervised NER tools are available online, such as AIDA,[6] AlchemyAPI,[7] NERD,[8] Zemanta,[9] and Wikifier.[10] In addition to detecting entities, they also employ entity linking/disambiguation, which is the ability to correctly disambiguate entities that have the same name (to some extent). These tools have been evaluated to have good performances [17]. However, their application in our work raises several problems. First, they do not have a common agreement of what an entity is and thus they provide, in some cases, unreliable results. For example, AIDA does not recognize "Tories", the british political party, as an entity, while NERD returns "true freedom" as an entity, which is subjective. This problem makes it hard to decide which NER tool to use for our purpose. Second, they do not cover all forms of occurrences of entities, including coreferences, which is crucial for user comments. In our work, we address these issues to discover more occurrences of entities and reduce the amount of noise involved in the process.

[3] http://www.wordle.net/
[4] http://nlp.stanford.edu/
[5] http://dbpedia.org/
[6] https://gate.d5.mpi-inf.mpg.de/webaida/
[7] http://www.alchemyapi.com/
[8] http://nerd.eurecom.fr/
[9] http://www.zemanta.com/
[10] http://cogcomp.cs.illinois.edu/page/demo_view/Wikifier

Aspect extraction has also gained attention in the product review domain [22]. These approaches define aspects as the components and the attributes of a given entity. Moreover, they rely on the presence of sentiments to detect aspects. Thus, the process of identifying and extracting aspects and entities is limited to evaluative texts. However, in our work, we want to extend the definition of aspects so that (1) it includes other forms than attributes or components and (2) the extraction does not rely solely on the presence of sentiments.

3. PROBLEM DEFINITION

User comments talk about entities and argue about specific aspects of those entities. An *entity* can be either a person, an organization, a location, or any well-defined concept such as languages, nationalities, or wars. By contrast, an *aspect* is all what is arguable about an entity. Consider the following example:

> *"I'm all for Scottish independence. This vote is about continuing to depend on the UK without having to bear the responsibilities."*

This comment talks about the entities *"Scottish"* and *"UK"*, and argues about the aspect *"independence"* of the entity *"Scottish"* and the aspect *"responsibility"* related to the entity *"UK"*. In this work, our task is to extract from each comment the set of entities it talks about, and the aspects related to each entity.

Entity extraction from user comments brings new challenges to traditional NER. First, existing NER tools provide, in some cases, results that do not correspond to our entity definition, such as *"true freedom"*. Note that an entity must refer to an objective concept since subjective concepts are subject to discussion among users and they need to be extracted as aspects. Distinguishing entities from aspects is important for an accurate representation of the various view points of users about a given entity. Second and more importantly, a comment is typically a part of a discussion which implies that entities are not always explicitly mentioned but appear as coreferences. Note that limiting the entity extraction process only to occurrences that mention the name will not allow having a wide coverage of the aspects of an entity. Third, comments are informal in nature and might contain grammatical errors, misspellings, abbreviations, and unreliable capitalization.

To address the above problems, we need first to filter the outcome of NER tools to have only entities of the types we have defined. Second, we need to extract the context of each comment from its related comments and eventually from the news article itself. The underlying structure of comments in news sites is a tree, where users can post a standalone comment, a reply to a standalone comment, or a reply to another reply. Figure 2 shows the two largest sub-trees of the full tree of comments on the Scottish independence news article. The largest contains 28 comments discussing about terrorism, and the other one has 17 comments discussing about Scots origin. Generally, the full tree has a news article as a root, and comments as either intermediate nodes or leaves. Based on this structure, the context of a comment is given by its ancestors. Having context information would then help resolving entities that occur as coreferences and ambiguity related to abbreviations and missspellings.

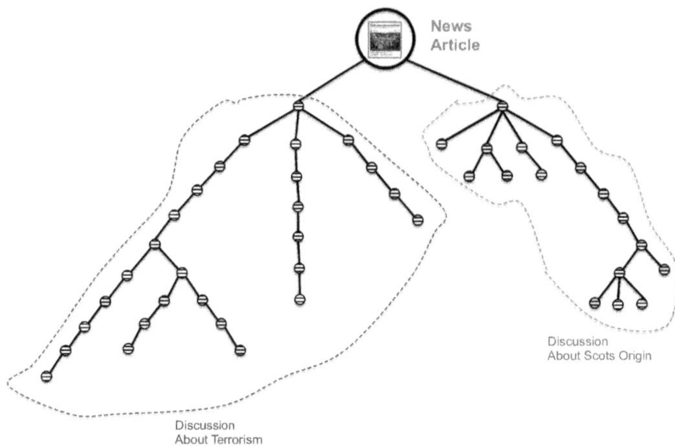

Figure 2: Example of Comment Trees

After extracting entities from comments, we need to extract for each entity its corresponding aspects. Aspects occur in the text as noun phrases. Thus, aspect extraction consists in finding noun phrases that have a grammatical relationship with the extracted entities. Consider the following example:

> *"Scots love to spout nonsense about independence."*

In this comment, there is a dependency between the noun phrase *"independence"* and the nominal subject of the sentence which is the entity *"Scots"*. Thus, the noun phrase *"independence"* is extracted as aspect for the entity *"Scots"*. The main challenge is that aspects are not always explicitly mentioned in the text. Consider the following example:

> *"You live in the British Isles. The largest is Great Britain. Some of you are Irish, Scottish, and English. Some of you claim to be Welsh."*

The sentence *"The largest is Great Britain"* talks about the aspect *"Isle"* of the entity *"Great Britain"* even though it is not explicitly mentioned. In other cases, aspects can be semi-implicit. Consider the following example:

> *"Scotland can vote however it wants, it's the Scottish peoples right."*

This comment talks about the aspect *"voting"* of the entity *"Scotland"*. In this case, the aspect can be derived from explicitly mentioned words in the sentence such as verbs and adjectives. To tackle the problem of aspect extraction from user comments, we propose in this paper tailored techniques for each case of explicit, implicit, and semi-implicit aspects This involves the exploitation of context information to find frequent co-occurrences of noun phrases with verbs and adjectives. .

4. ENTITY EXTRACTION

Our aim is to exploit an existing NER tool for extracting entities from user comments. However, there are a number of limitations raised by the structure and the nature of user comments as described earlier. In this section we tackle these limitations through the following strategies.

4.1 Entity Filtering

We have defined an entity to be either a person, an organisation, a location, or any well-defined concept such as languages. According to this definition, an entity is an individual of a class. A class is not an entity because it describes a very general concept. The issue with existing tools is that they do not have an agreement on what an entity is. As a consequence, entity filtering is not implemented in any of them. Consider the following example:

> *"I say let the Scots have their true freedom. Don't be afraid of Rasmussen or NATO, this is none of their business. If he ends up sending USS Ronald Reagan aircraft carrier to the coast of Scotland, then he should have done the same to Crimea."*

From this comment, AIDA[21] does not recognize *"Crimea"* as an entity whereas NERD[17] does. Moreover, NERD extracts *"aircraft carrier"* and *"true freedom"* as entities. However, *"aircraft carrier"* is a class and *"true freedom"* is not an instance of a class but an aspect which is arguable.

Our entity filtering approach consists in exploiting a knowledge base to check whether a given noun phrase is an entity or not. To this end, we choose DBpedia [2], a large scale knowledge base extracted from Wikipedia. DBpedia is a graph database that uses the RDF[11] format. It represents Wikipedia categories as resources and uses the *rdf:type* predicate to state whether a resource is a class or an individual of a class. Using this property, entity filtering removes all results produced by NER tools that have no property *rdf:type* in DBpedia.

In the previous example, NERD extracts as entities: *"Scots"*, *"true freedom"*, *"NATO"*, *"USS Ronald Reagan"*, *"aircraft carrier"*, *"Scotland"*, and *"Crimea"*. It provides, for each extracted entity, a link to Wikipedia. We then convert the Wikipedia link to its corresponding DBpedia *URI*, and check whether the object represented in the *URI* has property `rdf:type` other than `owl:class` and `owl:thing`. In this example, because *"true freedom"* and *"aircraft carrier"* do not have any `rdf:type` property, they are removed. All other entities have types other than `owl:class` and `owl:thing` and thus they are kept.

4.2 Name Normalization

When writing comments, users tend not to write the full name of entities. They use abbreviations, or only last names of people, and sometimes they misspell names. We call all variations of the name of an entity an *"alias"*. Interestingly, traditional NER tools are not always able to recognize entities from aliases. Thus, we introduce a name normalization technique that converts all aliases to normalized names to facilitate entity extraction. To begin, we extract entities from the news article and all its related comments using the entity filtering technique described earlier. For entities of type *Person*, we set as aliases first names, middle names, and last names. For other types, we find possible aliases using a knowledge base. In DBpedia, there are two properties that are very useful for finding aliases.

1. `dbpedia-owl:wikiPageDisambiguates`: represents the disambiguation page of Wikipedia. For example, by using this property, we know that *"UK"* is an alias for *"United Kingdom"*.
2. `dbpedia-owl:wikiPageRedirects`: stores less common aliases than the first property does, including some frequent typos of the entity, which can be useful in detecting typos to some extent. For example, the Wikipedia *URL* corresponding to *"United Kingdon"* is directed to the Wikipedia page of *"United Kingdom"* and thus we can resolve the misspelling.

[11]http://www.w3.org/RDF/

Once we have all entities with their aliases, we proceed as follows. For each unresolved alias s in comment c, we check if c contains an entity e that has s as alias. If e exists then we replace s by e. Otherwise, we look for e in the parent comment of c. We recursively run this procedure until we find the entity that has s as alias. Formally the algorithm is given as follows. In some cases (although rare), we

Data: s: unresolved alias, c: comment containing s
Result: e: entity for which s is an alias
FindEntity(s,c)
begin
  if $c = \emptyset$ **then**
    return null;
  end
  $E \leftarrow getEntities(c)$;
  $e \leftarrow getEntityForAlias(E, s)$;
  if $e \neq \emptyset$ **then**
    return e;
  end
  $FindEntity(s, Parent(c))$;
end

may encounter an alias that refers to multiple normalized names. In this work, we use a coin toss to decide which normalized name to choose. Considering that *"Rasmussen"* is not extracted as an entity in the previous example, we run our algorithm and if *"'Anders Fogh Rasmussen"* is mentioned in one of the ancestors of the comment, then we replace the string *"Rasmussen"* by *"Anders Fogh Rasmussen"*.

4.3 Coreference Resolution

NER approaches are not designed to detect entities that appear as coreferences. This is a problem for our work since we need to extract aspects related to each entity and thus all types of occurrences of an entity should be taken into account. Let us consider the following example:

> *"If the Scots pull out it leaves the rest of the UK to themselves where the Tories will be the dominant party. They have promised an IN/Out referendum on EU membership."*

From this comment, NER does not recognize the pronoun *"they"* as an occurrence of the entity *"Tories"*. Consequently, *"IN/Out referendum"* and *"EU membership"* cannot be extracted as aspects related to *"Toris"*. To solve this problem we apply the Stanford Deterministic Coreference Resolution System [16] to map coreferences to their corresponding entities. The difference that our work makes is that comments are not independent from each other. In this case, a coreference can be related to an entity mentioned in another comment or in the news article itself. To handle this problem we propose an *Intertextual Coreference Resolution* approach that finds the context of comments to resolve coreferences.

The approach works as follows. For each unresolved coreference, we take the phrase that contains it and append it to the parent of the comment. Then, we apply the Stanford Coreference Resolution[16]. If the coreference is not resolved, we recursively extend the context to the ancestors until we find the referent or reach the root of the tree. The algorithm of intertextual coreference resolution is formally given by:

Data: r: unresolved coreference, p: phrase containing r,
c: comment that gives the context for r, initially set to the parent of the comment where r occurs.

ICR(r,p,c)
begin
  if $c! = null$ **then**
    $context = c.append(p)$;
    $ApplyStanfordCorNLP(context)$;
    if r *is not resolved* **then**
      $ICR(r, p, Parent(c))$;
    end
  end
end

Note that in practice, the referent often belongs to the parent comment or the news article. The reason is that a comment either replies to its parent or comments directly on the content of the news article.

4.4 Context-related Entity Search

Comments might contain aliases that refer to entities which are not mentioned in the news article. If we take the previous example:

> *"Don't be afraid of Rasmussen or NATO, this is none of their business."*

and we suppose that the name "Anders Fogh Rasmussen" is not mentioned in the news article, then applying the name normalization would not work. We call entities mentioned in the news article *explicit entities*, while we call *implicit entities* those that are not mentioned in the news article but brought up by users in their comments. To be able to detect implicit entities, we proceed with a context-related entity search. We start by extracting all explicit entities using a traditional NER tool and the name normalization technique. Further, for each explicit entity, we search the set of entities that are related to it by some arbitrary property in Dbpedia. Note that we use the entity filtering method to remove all implicit entities that do not have the property *rdf:type*. In this work, we do the search only by one step to reduce noise and the running time. However, it might be the case that in the knowledge base implicit entities are connected to explicit entities multiple steps away. The result of this search is then used to extend the entity alias mapping by including the aliases of implicit entities. If we

Figure 3: Example of entities extracted by context search

take the previous example, we find that the entity *"NATO"* is related to the entity *"Anders Fogh Rasmussen"* via the relationship *dbprop:leaderName* as shown in Figure 3. Note that *"Anders Fogh Rasmussen"* was the Secretary General of *"NATO"*. After finding the entity *"Anders Fogh Rasmussen"*, we set all its possible aliases including *"Anders"*, *"Fogh"* and *"Rasmussen"*. Thus, when *"Rasmussen"* is encountered in a given comment, it is normalized using the name of the implicit entity. In case a comment mentions *"McGarr"*, we need to do a two-step search to find the entity *"Pearson Center"*, then from that entity we find the entity *"Kevin McGarr"* as shown in Figure 3.

5. ASPECT EXTRACTION

We divide aspects into three categories: (1) *Explicit Aspects*, (2) *Implicit Aspects*, and (3) *Semi-Implicit Aspects*. Explicit aspects appear explicitly as noun phrases, implicit aspects are derived from the context, while semi-implicit aspects are inferred from other part-of-speech tags. In the following, we describe in more detail each type of aspect and present our approach to extracting it.

5.1 Explicit Aspect Extraction

An explicit aspect of an entity e appears as a noun phrase that has a relationship with e. We use the dependency grammar to identify this relationship. Explicit aspect extraction parses comments using the part-of-speech tagging and the dependency grammar, and then selects noun phrases that have a specific grammatical dependency to e. We exploit the following types of dependencies:

Prepositional Dependency. We extract as explicit aspects, for an entity e, all noun phrases that have a relationship with e using prepositions, such as *"of"*, *"at"*, or *"in"*.

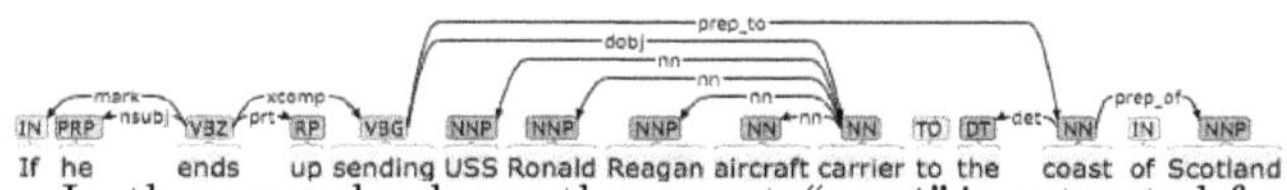

In the example above, the aspect *"coast"* is extracted for the entity *"Scotland"* using the propositional dependency *"of"*.

Possessive Dependency. We extract as explicit aspects, for an entity e, all noun phrases that have a possessive dependency to e.

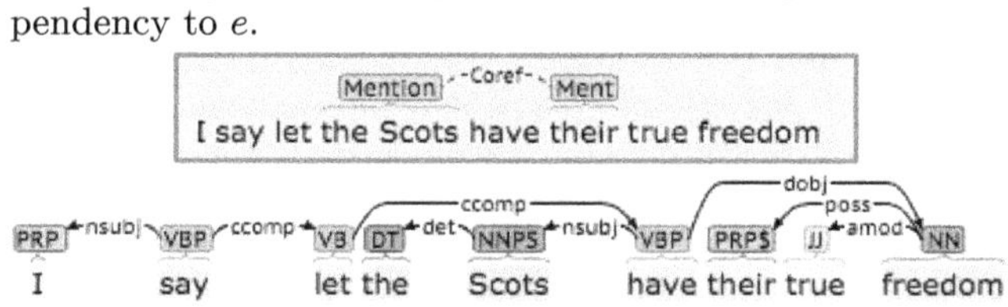

In the example above, the aspect of *"freedom"* is extracted for the entity *"Scots"* by applying possessive dependency, combined with the coreference resolution described in section 4.3. We can see that *"their"* is detected as a coreference for the entity *"Scots"*. Moreover, the noun phrase *"freedom"* has a possessive dependency to the coreference *'their'*. Thus, *"freedom"* has a possessive dependency to *"Scots"*.

Verb Dependency. We extract as explicit aspects, for an entity e, all noun phrases connected to e using a verb that has dependencies to both of the aspects and the entity e. In the following example the aspect *"Queen"* is extracted for the entity *"Scots"* using verb dependency. The clausal complement of the verb *"want to keep"* has a dependency on both *"Scots"* and *"Queen"*.

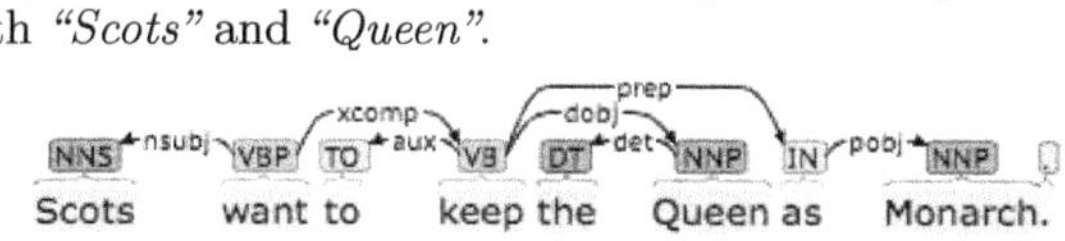

The dependencies described above are very precise and thus they rarely fail to extract explicit aspects. However, they only cover a small portion of possible occurrences of aspects in a comment because most of them appear implicitly. Therefore, implicit aspect extraction is needed.

5.2 Implicit Aspect Extraction

To deal with the problem of extracting aspects that are implicit in the text, we propose two approaches. The first approach exploits mappings between adjectives and aspects that co-occur frequently. By contrast, the second approach deals with word-sense disambiguation and lemmatization over implicit aspects.

5.2.1 Adjective-to-aspect Mapping

The extraction rules described in Section 5.1 do not rely on the occurrence of any opinionated word, which makes them different from previous work of explicit aspect extraction [22]. However, the occurrence of an opinionated word is in fact still useful to help extracting some implicit aspects. In this work, we identify the occurrence of words containing sentiment, typically adjectives[12], to build a mapping from pairs of entity and adjective to some explicit aspects.

From all comments, we extract the set of pairs $P = \{\langle e_i, adj_k \rangle\}$ where e_i is an entity, and adj_k is an adjective that has a dependency to entity e_i. To each pair $\langle e_i, adj_k \rangle$, we associate the set of aspects $S_{ik} = \{a_1, ..., a_n\}$ that have a dependency to entity e_i and adjective adj_k. Whenever a pair of entity e_i and adjective adj_k is found in a comment without any occurrence of an explicit aspect, we use adjective-to-aspect mapping. We extract as implicit aspect of e_i, the aspect a_j of S_{ik} which has the highest frequency of occurrence with the pair $\langle e_i, adj_k \rangle$. In the case of multiple aspects that share the value of highest frequency, we use word-sense disambiguation to choose the most appropriate aspect as described in the next section.

> *"Tesco is large! Of course many of the jobs it offers are in shops, transport etc. Those would stay regardless of 'yes' or 'no'."*

In the first sentence of the above comment, *"Tesco"* is an entity and *"large"* is an adjective associated to it. Moreover there is no explicit aspect related to *"Tesco"*. In this case, we check the adjective-to-aspect mapping and we find three occurrences of explicit aspects with the adjective *"large"* and the entity *"Tesco"*: {employer (2), back office (1), call centre operation (1)}. Among these three aspects, we assign to the entity *"Tesco"* the aspect *"employer"*, which has the highest number of occurrences. The aspect *"employer"* was implicitly referred to by the sentence.

5.2.2 Lexical Adjective-to-aspect Mapping

Adjective-to-aspect mapping might lead to ambiguity when there are multiple aspects that have the highest frequency with respect to a given entity and adjective. To address this issue, we exploit a lexical database, more specifically WordNet[13] for word-sense disambiguation. We do this in two steps. First, we increase the coverage of adjectives in the mapping by including other similar adjectives. Take the following example:

> *"Tesco is big!"*

Because *"big"* is an adjective similar to *"large"*, the aspect *"employer"* was implicitly referred to by the sentence. The similarity between adjectives in WordNet is captured by the *similar to* lexical relation, which is symmetric. In WordNet, adjectives *"huge"* and *"great"* are also *similar to "large"*. To reduce noise, we do the lexical relation search only by one step.

Second, if a pair of an entity and an adjective is related to multiple aspects having the highest frequency of occurrences, then we use the similarity measures of WordNet to choose the aspect which is most similar to the context of the entity and its adjective. The context is defined by the sentences around the entity and the adjective. Formally, we define a context c as a set of words $\{w_1, w_2, ..., w_m\}$. The similarity between an aspect a and a context c is computed as follows:

$$Sim(a, c) = \frac{\sum_{i=1}^{m} Wordnet::Similarity(a, w_i)}{|c|}$$

where $Wordnet::Similarity$ is a quantitative measure of the degree to which two word senses are related, provided by WordNet. Basically, for each aspect a we compute the average similarity between a and the words of context c. Then, we choose the aspect with the highest similarity to c.

5.3 Aspect Enrichment

We have seen so far how to extract explicit and implicit aspects from comments. Explicit aspects are extracted from prepositions, possessions, and verbs, while implicit aspects are inferred based on adjectives. An explicit aspect extracted using verb dependency is typically the subject or the object of the verb. By contrast, an implicit aspect is always something that is described by an adjective. Let us take the previous example on verb dependency:

> *"Scots want to keep the Queen as Monarch."*

We note that *"Queen"* is an explicit aspect of *"Scots"* and it is also the object of the verb *"keep"*. Similarly, we take the example of implicit aspects:

> *"Tesco is large!"*

Recall that the implicit aspect *"employer"* was extracted for the entity *"Tesco"*, and in fact this aspect is described by the adjective *"large"*.

The two types of aspects described above can be enhanced with complementary information. The goal is to give more meaning to the aspects discussed about entities. The first comment talks about the aspect *"Queen"* of the entity *"Scots"* and more specifically about *"Keeping the Queen"*. In the same way, the second comment talks about *"Tesco"* being *"large"* and more specifically about being a *"large employer"*. We present in the following our approach for enhancing explicit and implicit aspects.

5.3.1 Explicit Aspect Enrichment

We focus here on aspects extracted using verb dependency. To have complimentary information about an explicit aspect, we convert to a noun the verb to which the explicit aspect is related. In the previous example we convert the verb *"keep"* to *"keeping"*. Then, we concatenate the resulting noun to the explicit aspect, so it becomes *"Keeping the Queen"*.

[12] We consider adjective to be the only form of the opinionated words, as we do not focus on investigating a sophisticated sentiment analysis.

[13] https://wordnet.princeton.edu

5.3.2 *Implicit Aspect Enrichment*

To have complementary information about an implicit aspect, we convert to a noun the adjective which is related to the aspect. In the example above, *"large"* is converted to *"largeness"*. Then we concatenate the resulting noun to the implicit aspect, so it becomes *"employer largeness"*.

5.3.3 *Semi-implicit Aspect Extraction*

In some cases, entities are not related to any explicit or implicit aspect, but they are related to an action or described as a whole without referring to a specific side. Let us take the following example:

> *"Scotland can vote however it wants, it's the Scottish peoples right."*

The first sentence of this comment talks solely about *"Scotland"* voting. Consider another example:

> *"I would love to visit Scotland again—hopefully an independent one—it is a very beautiful country and the Scots are so honest."*

Here we can see that the entity *"Scots"* as a whole is described as honest. To generalize, if an entity (1) has a dependency to a verb and (2) the verb is not related to an explicit or implicit aspect, then we convert the verb to a noun and use it as an aspect for the entity. The same thing applies for adjectives. Applying this rule, we would have from the two previous examples the aspect *"voting (or vote)"* assigned to *"Scotland"* and the aspect *"honesty"* assigned to *"Scots"*.

To convert verbs and adjectives into nouns, we use WordNet, which returns for each word a list of nouns that are lexically related. There are different relations that can be exploited such as *"synonym"*, *"similar to"*, and *"derivationally related form"* to find the noun form of a verb or an adjective. Among the returned nouns, we choose the one most similar to the input, using the *Wordnet::Similarity* function.

6. EXPERIMENTS

In this section, we describe the setup of our experiments, then we present and discuss the results.

6.1 Setup

Dataset. We have crawled comments on 10 different news articles from the Al Jazeera and CNN websites. For each news article, we have selected the 100 longest comments. For each comment we have added the set of its ancestor comments to keep track of its context. This process resulted in 1087 comments on the 10 news articles. We have chosen the articles from three different categories: *Politics*, *Sport*, and *Techs*. The reason of this choice is to reflect the various types of user comments. Comments on sport category have a high tendency to introduce entities that are not mentioned in the article. Comments on techs category have the same characteristic of sport comments and in addition they have the tendency to use slang language. Finally, comments on politics are highly controversial and discuss a variety of aspects regarding the same entity. Besides the ancestor comments, the distribution of comments on the three categories is: 400 comments in politics, 300 comments in techs, and 300 in Sport

Annotation. The collected dataset of 1087 comments was annotated by five first-year bachelor students who are not involved in this project. Their task was to extract from each comment the set of entities and aspects using the following guidelines:[14]

1. An entity is either a person, an organisation, a location, or a well-defined concept (non arguable or subjective) such as languages.
2. An explicit aspect is a noun phrase that has a grammatical dependency on an entity.
3. An implicit aspect is referred to by an adjective that has a dependency to an entity.
4. A semi-implicit aspect is the noun form of a verb or adjective that have a dependency to an entity

It is important to mention that the students had the freedom to extract the implicit aspects based on what they understood from the comment, decide the suitable noun form of the verb or the adjective, and decide whether something is a well-defined concept or not. The results of these annotations were use as our ground truth data.

Baselines. We have used three baseline approaches for entity extraction: NERD and Zemanta, which are two of the best NER tools [17,18], and AIDA, which has been demonstrated to have an accuracy competitive to the very best named-entity disambiguation (NED) systems [4]. We do not use the Stanford NER as our baseline because it does not provide us with the necessary information, that is URI for extracted entities, to run our improvements.

We have used the baseline approaches to extract entities from user comments. Then, we applied the different approaches we have proposed to assess their impact on the results. Regarding aspect extraction, there is no existing work that is really comparable to ours, because all work on aspect extraction has mainly focused on product reviews [15]. More importantly, they assume the input text to be always about a single entity, whereas texts in our dataset may contain multiple entities. Thus, they perform poorly.

Metrics. To assess the performance of our approach, we use three evaluation metrics: *precision*, *recall*, and F_1 score. Precision is given by:

$$Precision = \frac{truePositives}{truePositives + falsePositives}$$

recall is given by:

$$Recall = \frac{truePostives}{truePositives + falseNegatives}$$

and F_1 score is given by:

$$F_1 = \frac{2 \cdot Precision \cdot Recall}{Precision + Recall}$$

6.2 Results

We have tested separately entity extraction and aspect extraction techniques and the results are described in the following.

6.2.1 *Entity Extraction*

The overall results are shown in Table 1. We can see the approach we have proposed for extending existing NER improves substantially both precision and recall. We note that precision is improved by 22% for Zemanta, and 30% for NERD. Similarly, the recall is improved by 34% for Zemanta and 25% for NERD. Although we slightly improved

[14]they are also provided with an extended, comprehensive guidelines

	Underlying NER			Our Proposed Extensions		
	Prec.	*Recall*	F_1	*Prec.*	*Recall*	F_1
NERD	56.94	52.13	54.43	**86.18**	**77.50**	**81.61**
Zemanta	72.74	50.35	59.51	**90.09**	**74.94**	**81.82**
AIDA	81.67	56.93	67.10	**82.08**	**72.34**	**76.90**

Table 1: Overall Precision and Recall (in percent) for Entity Extraction

	Zemanta (baseline)		+Entity Filtering		+Name Normalization		+Context Search		+Coreference Resolution	
	Prec.	*Recall*	*Prec.*	*Recall*	*Prec.*	*Recall*	*Prec.*	*Recall*	*Prec.*	*Recall*
Politics	70.01	59.17	89.33	58.83	89.23	67.43	89.22	71.99	89.07	81.31
Techs	74.10	52.33	94.52	52.31	94.51	53.09	94.51	54.98	89.43	61.62
Sport	75.04	36.61	96.11	36.61	96.09	40.68	95.89	70.61	92.08	79.81
Average.	72.74	50.35	92.92	50.21	92.88	55.06	92.81	66.75	90.09	74.94

Table 2: Precision and Recall (in percent) for Entity Extraction based on Zemanta

the precision of AIDA, we have significantly improved its recall by 15% mainly by detecting more forms of occurrences of entities. More details about the impact of each proposed technique to enhance existing NER are shown in Tables 2, 3, and 4. They report the overall precision and recall together with the average values for each category of user comments including politics, techs, and sport. The different techniques we have proposed, in this paper, are applied incrementally from the leftmost one (traditional NER tool as baseline) to the rightmost one (coreference resolution). Therefore, the numbers listed in the coreference resolution are obtained after applying all the techniques in order. The results for each technique are presented in the following.

Entity Filtering. After applying entity filtering, the precision of all baselines is boosted for a little drawback on recall. If we use Zemanta, the entity filtering increases the precision by 27%, but reduces the recall by 0.5% for all categories, while when we use NERD, the precision increases by 64% and the recall is reduced by 0.4%. Note that the precision of NERD increases more than the one of Zemanta because NERD produces more noise. Regarding AIDA, it returns as entities instances of classes thus the improvement is very small.

Name Normalization. The improvement that name normalization brings is on the recall. This is natural since its goal is to detect more occurrences of entities. While precision values are almost the same for entity filtering and after applying name normalization, recall has an overall increase of 4% for both Zemanta and NERD and less than 3% for AIDA. We note that the increase depends on the category of comments. For techs, it is around 4% and for politics is two times higher. This is due to the fact that typically techs entities are not mentioned using aliases while in politics they are. We note that AIDA behaves differently because it already performs labeling people, organization, and country names in abbreviation. However, we provide an additional improvement of 3% on its precision and recall values

Context Search. The same observation holds for context search which improves the recall keeping the values of precision stable. We can note an additional improvement of 11% in overall recall for both Zemanta and NERD. It is interesting to see that the improvement depends on the category of comments. For example, in the techs category, the recall improves by 2% at most while in sports is of 30%. This huge difference is due to the fact that sport comments often talk about entities that are not mentioned in the news article. For example, a comment may mention members of a football team while the article talks on the team as a whole, without using specific names. In this case, context search is more evident helps extracting these implicit entities and thus we can see the impact clearly in sport comments. This strategy penalizes slightly the precision which is natural, since we collect from the knowledge base extra information that can contain some noise. However, the decrease in precision is negligible. Although AIDA performs also context search, our approach provides additional improvement of 4% on the recall.

Coreference Resolution. After applying coreference resolution, we complete the integration of all the methods we have proposed in the entity extraction process. We provide an additional improvement in recall of more than 9% for Zemanta, NERD, and AIDA while we have a slight decrease in precision of less than 3%. This is because coreference resolution extracts more occurrences of entities, but sometimes it infers the wrong entity which penalizes the precision.

We also evaluate the Stanford Coreference Resolution on our annotated data using the pairwise metric [23]. It has precision of 74.12% and recall of 46.86%. This result is similar to the one presented in [16].

6.2.2 *Aspect Extraction from Clean Data*

In this section, we present the experiment results for our aspect extraction approach based on our annotated dataset. This means that we take the annotated entities as starting point. The reason is to analyze the performance of our approach independently from the influence of external tools. The results are shown in Table 5. We can see that the combination of explicit, implicit, and semi-implicit techniques provide the best trade-off between precision and recall. The details of the performance of each technique are presented in the following.

Explicit Aspect Extraction. This technique achieves a very high precision of 90.88% because the extraction rules are designed to correctly capture all explicit aspects. However it fails, in very few cases, when figurative language is used. For example, consider the sentence *"This game is a*

	NERD (baseline)		+Entity Filtering		+Name Normalization		+Context Search		+Coreference Resolution	
	Prec.	*Recall*	*Prec.*	*Recall*	*Prec.*	*Recall*	*Prec.*	*Recall*	*Prec.*	*Recall*
Politics	52.21	61.21	86.47	60.95	86.39	67.74	86.38	73.66	86.19	83.58
Techs	59.43	54.18	90.48	54.16	90.47	55.01	90.46	55.97	85.70	63.26
Sport	60.27	37.96	90.52	37.95	90.50	42.16	90.15	73.18	86.69	83.91
Average	56.94	52.13	88.90	52.01	88.86	56.17	88.75	68.13	86.18	77.50

Table 3: Precision and Recall (in percent) for Entity Extraction based on NERD

	AIDA (baseline)		+Entity Filtering		+Name Normalization		+Context Search		+Coreference Resolution	
	Prec.	*Recall*	*Prec.*	*Recall*	*Prec.*	*Recall*	*Prec.*	*Recall*	*Prec.*	*Recall*
Politics	77.82	66.35	78.08	66.34	80.21	67.88	80.17	68.51	80.01	77.56
Techs	83.51	69.33	83.75	69.33	88.37	75.75	87.33	76.07	83.30	85.98
Sport	91.55	31.97	91.89	31.95	91.89	32.44	90.86	45.64	86.67	51.74
Average	81.67	56.93	81.93	56.92	84.73	59.61	84.19	63.92	82.08	72.34

Table 4: Precision and Recall (in percent) for Entity Extraction based on AIDA

piece of cake for Arsenal? Our approach will extract *"piece of cake"* as an aspect of *"Arsenal"* because of the presence of a prepositional dependency between them, while in fact, the term *"piece of cake"* is an idiom that suggests an aspect of *"easiness"*. In contrast, the recall of this technique is very low because most aspects appear implicitly.

Explicit + Implicit Aspect Extraction. We can see in Table 5 that adjective-to-aspect mapping is not very useful when tested on our annotated data. It increases the recall by less than 3% while it decreases the precision by 14%. The reason is that choosing implicit aspect based on the highest frequency of occurrences may create a bias which negatively influences precision and recall. However, when we use the lexical adjective-to-aspect mapping, we improve both precision and recall values because the use of aspect disambiguation decreases the likelihood of bias.

Explicit + Semi-implicit Aspect Extraction. Using semi-implicit aspect extraction together with explicit aspect extraction increases the recall from 23.50% to 65.62%, which is substantial. The precision is deceased because of the inaccuracies of choosing the best aspects using the lexical relations and similarity measures. The *Wordnet::Similarity* itself is not optimized for comparing similarity between synsets other than nouns and verbs [13], therefore the drawback in precision is understandable.

6.2.3 Aspect Extraction from Noisy Data

To assess the effectiveness of our aspect extraction approach, we use the set of entities provided by the baseline approaches after applying the extension techniques as shown in section 6.2.1. The set of entities would contain noisy information and the goal is to analyze the impact of this noisy information on the precision and recall of aspect extraction. The results are shown in Table 6. We can observe that using NER tools decreases both precision and recall compared to ground truth data which is obvious. The interesting observation is that AIDA is the one performing worse causing a decrease of 12% in precision and 22% in recall. The best in terms of precision is Zemanta, and the best in term of recall is NERD. These results are very consistent with the entity extraction findings where AIDA is the worst, while Zemanta and NERD provide the best precision and recall values.

	Prec.	Recall	F_1
Ground Truth	73.12	73.82	73.47
Zemanta	66.33	56.37	60.95
NERD	63.36	58.48	60.82
AIDA	60.69	55.63	58.05

Table 6: Aspect Extraction from noisy data

6.3 Discussion

We have shown that our proposed techniques for extending NER tools improve significantly precision and recall values. Interestingly, AIDA performs best when we do not apply any extension. This is because it already provides similar strategies to what we have proposed for entity filtering, name normalization, and context search. However, Zemanta and NERD, which are relatively much simpler, perform better than AIDA when we extend them with our proposed techniques. There are two benefits from this result: (1) we do not depend on one NER tool but can use different tools to cover diverse types of entities while still guaranteeing high quality results; and (2) we can improve the performance of a simple NER tool using our light-weight extension techniques and outperform more sophisticated tools such as AIDA. The simplicity of our approach makes the results more effective and the computation time faster.

Another important point to consider is that AIDA uses Stanford NER which is supervised, while NERD and Zemanta are unsupervised. In our work, we aim at giving more room to unsupervised techniques because in news domain, new types of entities continue to emerge and we want to have a system that can handle that. For example, AIDA does not detect entities of type product, so we need to be able to use another NER to extract this type of entities.

Regarding aspect extraction, we have seen that we achieve 73% on recall and precision on the ground truth data. This result is very encouraging. We can also see that if the input is noisy, aspect extraction provides less accurate results because of the decrease in recall and precision of extracted entities. This is also due to some specific reasoning that NER tools perform on entities, such as AIDA that labels *"Scotland"* as *"United Kingdom"*, *"ISIS"* as random entities, and *"Ukraine* as Russian Empire.Inaccurate labelling would then lead to inaccurate aspects.

	Precision	Recall	F_1
Explicit	**90.88**	23.50	37.34
Explicit + Implicit (frequent mapping)	76.87	26.12	38.99
Explicit + Implicit (lexical mapping)	87.07	32.72	47.56
Explicit + Semi-Implicit	71.31	64.62	67.80
Explicit + Implicit+ Semi-Implicit	73.12	**73.82**	**73.47**

Table 5: Overall Precision and Recall (in percent) for Aspect Extraction

7. CONCLUSIONS

We have presented, in this paper, a new approach for entity and aspect extraction from user comments. We have introduced light-wight techniques to extend existing NER tools using coreference resolution and comment context information. We have defined new forms of aspects that can be either explicit or implicit and proposed extraction techniques for each type. The experiments results have shown that our approach is promising giving new insights about information extraction from user-generated content. In future work, we aim at testing our approaches on larger datasets, which is a tedious task because of manual annotation. Moreover, we would like to investigate *concept extraction* to also be able to handle news articles talking about general concept, like vaccination or human rights. Furthermore, we need to investigate aspect extraction techniques to improve their performance. Some of our ideas include aspect normalization and figurative language analysis in aspect extraction.

Acknowledgements

This work has been funded by the to-KNOW project and the European Master's Program in Computational Logic.

8. REFERENCES

[1] M. Asahara and Y. Matsumoto. Japanese named entity extraction with redundant morphological analysis. In *Conference of the North American. ACL, 2003.*

[2] S. Auer, C. Bizer, G. Kobilarov, J. Lehmann, R. Cyganiak, and Z. Ives. *Dbpedia: A nucleus for a web of open data.* Springer, 2007.

[3] D. M. Bikel, S. Miller, R. Schwartz, and R. Weischedel. Nymble: a high-performance learning name-finder. In *5th conference on Applied natural language processing.* ACL, 1997.

[4] C. Bizer, T. Heath, S. Auer, and T. Berners-Lee, editors. *Workshop on Linked Data on the Web (WWW)*, 2014.

[5] A. Borthwick, J. Sterling, E. Agichtein, and R. Grishman. Exploiting diverse knowledge sources via maximum entropy in named entity recognition. In *The Sixth Workshop on Very Large Corpora*, 1998.

[6] H. L. Chieu and H. T. Ng. Named entity recognition: a maximum entropy approach using global information. In *The 19th international conference on Computational linguistics.* ACL, 2002.

[7] J. R. Finkel, T. Grenager, and C. Manning. Incorporating non-local information into information extraction systems by gibbs sampling. In *The 43rd Annual Meeting on Association for Computational Linguistics.* ACL, 2005.

[8] M. Hu and B. Liu. Mining and summarizing customer reviews. In *ACM SIGKDD*, 2004.

[9] D. Kitayama, N. Oda, and K. Sumiya. Organizing user comments in a social video sharing system by temporal duration and pointing region. INGS'08, 2008.

[10] B. Liu, M. Hu, and J. Cheng. Opinion observer: analyzing and comparing opinions on the web. *WWW*, 2005.

[11] A. McCallum and W. Li. Early results for named entity recognition with conditional random fields, feature induction and web-enhanced lexicons. In *7th Conference on Natural language learning at HLT-NAACL.* ACL, 2003.

[12] D. Nadeau and S. Sekine. A survey of named entity recognition and classification. *Lingvisticae Investigationes*, 2007.

[13] T. Pedersen, S. Patwardhan, and J. Michelizzi. Wordnet:: Similarity: measuring the relatedness of concepts. In *Demonstration Papers at HLT-NAACL 2004.* ACL, 2004.

[14] A. Pons-Porrata, R. Berlanga-Llavori, and J. Ruiz-Shulcloper. Topic discovery based on text mining techniques. *Information processing & management*, 2007.

[15] S. Poria, E. Cambria, L.-W. Ku, C. Gui, and A. Gelbukh. A rule-based approach to aspect extraction from product reviews. *SocialNLP 2014*, page 28, 2014.

[16] K. Raghunathan, H. Lee, S. Rangarajan, N. Chambers, M. Surdeanu, D. Jurafsky, and C. Manning. A multi-pass sieve for coreference resolution. In *The 2010 Conference on Empirical Methods in Natural Language Processing.* ACL, 2010.

[17] G. Rizzo and R. Troncy. Nerd: evaluating named entity recognition tools in the web of data. In *Proceedings of ISWC*, 2011.

[18] G. Rizzo, R. Troncy, S. Hellmann, and M. Bruemmer. Nerd meets nif: Lifting nlp extraction results to the linked data cloud. *LDOW*, 937, 2012.

[19] S. Sekine, R. Grishman, and H. Shinnou. A decision tree method for finding and classifying names in japanese texts. In *6th Workshop on Very Large Corpora*, 1998.

[20] S. Sekine and C. Nobata. Definition, dictionaries and tagger for extended named entity hierarchy. In *LREC*, 2004.

[21] M. A. Yosef, J. Hoffart, I. Bordino, M. Spaniol, and G. Weikum. AIDA: an online tool for accurate disambiguation of named entities in text and tables. *PVLDB*, 4(12):1450–1453, 2011.

[22] L. Zhang and B. Liu. Aspect and entity extraction for opinion mining. In *Data Mining and Knowledge Discovery for Big Data*, Springer, 2014.

[23] J. Gosh. Scalable clustering methods for data mining. In N. Ye, editors, *The Handbook of Data Mining*, Lawrence Erlbaum Associates, 2003.

HDRF: Stream-Based Partitioning for Power-Law Graphs*

Fabio Petroni
Department of Computer Control and Management Engineering Antonio Ruberti
Sapienza University of Rome
petroni@dis.uniroma1.it

Leonardo Querzoni
Department of Computer Control and Management Engineering Antonio Ruberti
Sapienza University of Rome
querzoni@dis.uniroma1.it

Khuzaima Daudjee
David R. Cheriton School of Computer Science
University of Waterloo
kdaudjee@uwaterloo.ca

Shahin Kamali
David R. Cheriton School of Computer Science
University of Waterloo
s3kamali@uwaterloo.ca

Giorgio Iacoboni
Department of Computer Control and Management Engineering Antonio Ruberti
Sapienza University of Rome
g.iacoboni@gmail.com

ABSTRACT

Balanced graph partitioning is a fundamental problem that is receiving growing attention with the emergence of distributed graph-computing (DGC) frameworks. In these frameworks, the partitioning strategy plays an important role since it drives the communication cost and the workload balance among computing nodes, thereby affecting system performance. However, existing solutions only partially exploit a key characteristic of natural graphs commonly found in the real-world: their highly skewed power-law degree distributions. In this paper, we propose High-Degree (are) Replicated First (*HDRF*), a novel streaming vertex-cut graph partitioning algorithm that effectively exploits skewed degree distributions by explicitly taking into account vertex degree in the placement decision. We analytically and experimentally evaluate *HDRF* on both synthetic and real-world graphs and show that it outperforms all existing algorithms in partitioning quality.

Categories and Subject Descriptors

E.1 [**Data Structures**]: Graphs and Networks

Keywords

Graph Partitioning; Streaming Algorithms; Distributed Graph-Computing Frameworks; Replication; Load Balancing.

*This work has been partially supported by the TENACE PRIN Project (n. 20103P34XC) funded by the Italian Ministry of Education, University and Research.

CIKM'15, October 19-23, 2015, Melbourne, VIC, Australia.
©2015 ACM. ISBN 978-1-4503-3794-6/15/10 ...$15.00.
DOI: http://dx.doi.org/10.1145/2806416.2806424.

1. INTRODUCTION

The last few years have witnessed a huge growth in information production. Some corporations like IBM estimate that "2.5 quintillion bytes of data are created every day", amounting to 90% of the data in the world today having been created in the last two years [10]. On the face of this growth, researchers from both academia and industry have focussed their efforts on the design of new, efficient, approaches for parallel data analysis able to withstand the deluge of data expected in forthcoming years.

Given the proliferation of data which can be represented as graphs of interconnected vertices, a graph-based computation paradigm provides a nice, suitable, abstraction to perform computation on it. Large amounts of data, particularly scale-free graphs or power-law graphs[1], fall within this paradigm. An example is recommendation systems where the input data is usually provided in the form of votes (edges) that users (vertices) express on products (vertices). Additionally, graph-based computation finds application in many diverse and important fields such as social networks, computational biology, chemistry, and computer security. A key problem in graph computation is that it is often difficult to scale with increasing input data sizes as graphs are not easily partitionable into independent subgraphs that can be computed in parallel.

To be able to work on large datasets, distributed graph-computing (DGC) frameworks (such as GraphLab [18] or Pregel [20]) forcibly partition the input graph by placing its constituting elements, be they either vertices or edges, in distinct partitions, one for each available computing resource. During the partitioning phase, data elements that share connections with other elements already placed in other partitions result in having remote connections amongst them. Since these partitions are usually placed on different machines, this can incur unnecessary or excessive network and computation costs. To address this issue, one frequently used technique is to create and locally place replicas of remotely connected data among these partitions. While this reduces the access cost, replicated data elements must be synchronized during computation so as to avoid replica states

[1]We use scale-free and power-law graphs synonymously.

from diverging and generating meaningless computation results. This synchronization can significantly hinder performance as it forces replicas to coordinate and exchange data several times during computation.

The way the input dataset is partitioned has a large impact on the performance of the graph computation. A naive partitioning strategy may end up replicating a large fraction of the input elements on several partitions, severely hampering performance by inducing a large replica synchronization overhead during the computation phase. Furthermore, the partitioning phase should produce evenly balanced partitions (i.e. partitions with similar sizes) to avoid possible load skews in a cluster of machines over which the data is partitioned. Several recent approaches have looked at this problem. Here we focus our attention on *stream-based* graph partitioning algorithms, i.e. algorithms that partition incoming elements one at a time on the basis of only the current element properties and on previous assignments to partitions (no global knowledge on the input graph). Furthermore, these algorithms are usually *one-pass*, i.e. they refrain from changing the assignment of a data element to a partition once this has been done. These algorithms are the ideal candidates in settings where input data size and constraints on available resources restrict the type of solutions that can be employed.

Other characteristics of input data also play an important role in partitioning. It has been shown that vertex-cut algorithms are the best approach to deal with input graphs characterized by power-law degree distributions [1, 12]. This previous work also clearly outlined the important role high-degree nodes play from a partitioning quality standpoint. Nevertheless, few algorithms take this aspect into account [27, 24]. Understandably, this is a challenging problem to solve for stream-based approaches due to their *one-pass* nature.

In this paper, we leverage the idea that a partitioning algorithm should do its best to cut, i.e., *replicate*, high-degree vertices. In particular, we introduce High Degree (are) Replicated First (*HDRF*), a stream-based graph partitioning algorithm based on a greedy vertex-cut approach that leverages information on vertex degrees.

HDRF is characterized by the following desirable properties: (i) it outputs partitions with the smallest average replication factor among all competing solutions when applied on power-law graphs (Figure 2) while (ii) providing close to optimal load balancing (Figure 3). The former is obtained by greedily replicating vertices with larger degrees, while the latter is provided by a parametrizable balancing term whose impact can be tuned to adapt the algorithm behavior to any data input order. On the one hand, lowering the average replication factor is important to reduce network bandwidth cost, memory usage and replica synchronization overhead at computation time. A fair distribution of load on partitions, on the other hand, allows a more efficient usage of available computing resources. HDRF takes into account both of these aspects in an integrated way, significantly reducing the time needed to perform computations on large-scale graphs.

Summing up, this paper provides the following contributions:

- a novel stream-based graph partitioning algorithm, namely *HDRF*, that performs better than any competing solution (i.e. processes less vertex-cuts while balancing the load) when applied on power-law graphs;
- a theoretical analysis of *HDRF* that provides an average-case upper bound for the vertex replication factor;
- a comprehensive experimental evaluation based both on simulations and on a working prototype integrated with GraphLab [19] that shows how a system using *HDRF* achieves up to 2× speedup than adopting a standard greedy placement, and close to 3× speedup than using a constrained solution.

The rest of this paper is organized as follows: we define the problem in Section 2; we briefly describe existing solutions in Section 3; we introduce *HDRF* in Section 4; we show theoretical bounds for *HDRF* in Section 5; we present the results of an extensive experimental evaluation in Section 6 and we conclude the paper in Section 7.

2. PROBLEM DEFINITION

The problem of optimally partitioning a graph to minimize vertex-cuts while maintaining load balance is a fundamental problem in parallel and distributed applications as input placement significantly affects the efficiency of algorithm execution [25]. An edge-cut partitioning scheme results in partitions that are vertex disjoint while a vertex-cut approach results in partitions that are edge disjoint. Both variants are known to be NP-Hard [16, 11, 2] but have different characteristics and difficulties [16]; for instance, one fundamental difference between the two is that a vertex can be cut in multiple ways and span several partitions while an edge can only connect two partitions.

One characteristic observed in real-world graphs from social networks or the Web is their skewed power-law degree distribution: most vertices have relatively few connections while a few vertices have many. It has been shown that vertex-cut techniques perform better than edge-cut ones on such graphs (i.e., create less storage and network overhead) [12]. For this reason modern graph parallel processing frameworks, like GraphLab [19], adopt a vertex-cut approach to partition the input data over a cluster of computing nodes. The focus of this paper is on streaming vertex-cut partitioning schemes able to efficiently handle graphs with skewed power-law degree distribution.

Notation — Consider a graph $G = (V, E)$, where $V = (v_1, \cdots, v_n)$ is the set of vertices and $E = (e_1, \cdots, e_m)$ the set of edges. We define a partition of edges $P = (p_1, .., p_k)$ to be a family of pairwise disjoint sets of edges (i.e. $p_i, p_j \subseteq E$, $p_i \cap p_j = \emptyset$ for every $i \neq j$). Let $A(v) \subseteq P$ be the set of partitions each vertex $v \in V$ is replicated. The size $|p|$ of each partition $p \in P$ is defined as its edge cardinality, because computation steps are usually associated with edges. Since we consider G having a power-law degree distribution, the probability that a vertex has degree d is $P(d) \propto d^{-\alpha}$, where α is a positive constant that controls the "skewness" of the degree distribution, i.e. the smaller the value of α, the more skewed the distribution.

Balanced k-way vertex-cut problem — The problem consists in defining a partition of edges such that (i) the average number of vertex replicas (i.e. the number of partitions each vertex is associated to as a consequence of edge partitioning) is minimized and (ii) the partition load (i.e. the number of edges associated to a partition) is within a given bound from the theoretical optimum (i.e. $|E|/|P|$) [2].

More formally, the balanced $|P|$-way vertex-cut partitioning problem aims at solving the following optimization problem:

$$\min \frac{1}{|V|} \sum_{v \in V} |A(v)| \quad s.t. \quad \max_{p \in P} |p| < \sigma \frac{|E|}{|P|} \tag{1}$$

where $\sigma \geq 1$ is a small constant that defines the system tolerance to load imbalance. The objective function (Equation (1)) is called *replication factor* (*RF*), which is the average number of replicas per vertex.

Streaming setting — Without loss of generality, here we assume that the input data is a list of edges, each identified by the two connecting vertices and characterized by some application-related data. We consider algorithms that consume this list in a streaming fashion, requiring only a single pass. This is a common choice for several reasons: (i) it handles situations in which the input data is large enough that fitting it completely in the main memory of a single computing node is impractical; (ii) it can efficiently process dynamic graphs; (iii) it imposes the minimum overhead in time and (iv) it's scalable, providing for straightforward parallel and distributed implementations. A limitation of this approach is that the assignment decision taken on an input element (i.e., an edge) can be based only on previously analyzed data and cannot be later changed.

3. STREAMING ALGORITHMS

Balanced graph partitioning is a well known NP-hard problem with a wide range of applications in different domains. We do not discuss offline and edge-cut partitioning techniques since they are out of the scope of the paper. It is possible to divide existing streaming vertex-cut partitioning techniques in two main families: hashing and constrained partitioning algorithms and greedy partitioning algorithms.

Hashing and constrained partitioning algorithms — All of these algorithms ignore the history of the edge assignments and rely on the presence of a predefined hash function $h : \mathbb{N} \rightarrow \mathbb{N}$. The input of the hash function h can be either the unique identifier of a vertex or of an edge. All these algorithms can be applied in a streaming setting and achieve good load balance if h guarantees uniformity. Four well-known existing heuristics to solve the partitioning problem belong to this family: *hashing*, *DBH*, *grid* and *PDS*. The simplest solution is given by the *hashing* technique that (pseudo-)randomly assigns each edge to a partition: for each input edge $e \in E$, $A(e) = h(e) \bmod |P|$ is the identifier of the target partition. This heuristic results in a large number of vertex-cuts in general and performs poorly on power-law graphs [12]. A recent paper describes the *Degree-Based Hashing* (*DBH*) algorithm [27], a variation of the *hashing* heuristic that explicitly considers the degree of the vertices for the placement decision. *DBH* leverages some of the same intuition as *HDRF* by cutting vertices with higher degrees to obtain better performance. Concretely, when processing edge $e \in E$ connecting vertices $v_i, v_j \in V$ with degrees d_i and d_j, *DBH* defines the hash function $h(e)$ as follows:

$$h(e) = \begin{cases} h(v_i), & \text{if } d_i < d_j \\ h(v_j), & \text{otherwise} \end{cases}$$

Then, it operates as the *hashing* algorithm.

The *grid* and *PDS* techniques belong to the *constrained partitioning* family of algorithms [14]. The general idea of these solutions is to allow each vertex $v \in V$ to be replicated only in a small subset of partitions $S(v) \subset P$ that is called the *constrained set* of v. The constrained set must guarantees some properties; in particular, for each $v_i, v_j \in V$: (i) $S(v_i) \cap S(v_j) \neq \emptyset$; (ii) $S(v_i) \not\subseteq S(v_j)$ and $S(v_j) \not\subseteq S(v_i)$; (iii) $|S(v_i)| = |S(v_j)|$. It is easy to observe that this approach naturally imposes an upper bound on the replication factor. To position a new edge e connecting vertices v_i and v_j, it picks a partition from the intersection between $S(v_i)$ and $S(v_j)$ either randomly or by choosing the least loaded one. Different solutions differ in the composition of the vertex constrained sets. The *grid* solution arranges partitions in a $X \times Y$ matrix such that $|P| = XY$. It maps each vertex v to a matrix cell using a hash function h, then $S(v)$ is the set of all the partitions in the corresponding row and column. It this way each constrained sets pair has at least two partitions in their intersection. *PDS* generates constrained sets using *Perfect Difference Sets* [13]. This ensure that each pair of constrained sets has exactly one partition in the intersection. *PDS* can be applied only if $|P| = x^2 + x + 1$, where x is a prime number.

Greedy partitioning algorithms — This family of methods uses the entire history of the edge assignments to make the next decision. The standard *greedy* approach [12] breaks the randomness of the hashing and constrained solutions by maintaining some global status information. In particular, the system stores the set of partitions $A(v)$ to which each already observed vertex v has been assigned and the current partition sizes. Concretely, when processing edge $e \in E$ connecting vertices $v_i, v_j \in V$, the *greedy* technique follows this simple set of rules:

Case 1: If neither v_i nor v_j have been assigned to a partition, then e is placed in the partition with the smallest size in P.

Case 2: If only one of the two vertices has been already assigned (without loss of generality assume that v_i is the assigned vertex) then e is placed in the partition with the smallest size in $A(v_i)$.

Case 3: If $A(v_i) \cap A(v_j) \neq \emptyset$, then edge e is placed in the partition with the smallest size in $A(v_i) \cap A(v_j)$.

Case 4: If $A(v_i) \neq \emptyset$, $A(v_j) \neq \emptyset$ and $A(v_i) \cap A(v_j) = \emptyset$, then e is placed in the partition with the smallest size in $A(v_i) \cup A(v_j)$ and a new vertex replica is created accordingly.

Symmetry is broken with random choices. An equivalent formulation consists of computing a score $C^{\text{greedy}}(v_i, v_j, p)$ for all partitions $p \in P$, and then assigning e to the partition p^* that maximizes C^{greedy}. The score consists of two elements: (i) a replication term $C^{\text{greedy}}_{\text{REP}}(v_i, v_j, p)$ and (ii) a balance term $C^{\text{greedy}}_{\text{BAL}}(p)$. It is defined as follows:

$$C^{\text{greedy}}(v_i, v_j, p) = C^{\text{greedy}}_{\text{REP}}(v_i, v_j, p) + C^{\text{greedy}}_{\text{BAL}}(p) \tag{2}$$

$$C^{\text{greedy}}_{\text{REP}}(v_i, v_j, p) = f(v_i, p) + f(v_j, p) \tag{3}$$

$$f(v, p) = \begin{cases} 1, & \text{if } p \in A(v) \\ 0, & \text{otherwise} \end{cases}$$

$$C^{\text{greedy}}_{\text{BAL}}(p) = \frac{\text{maxsize} - |p|}{\epsilon + \text{maxsize} - \text{minsize}} \tag{4}$$

where *maxsize* is the maximum partition size, *minsize* is the minimum partition size, and ϵ is a small constant value.

A recent paper [24] proposes an hybrid solution that tries to combine both edge-cut and vertex-cut approaches together. The resulting heuristic, called *Ginger*, aims at optimizing the partitioning in a DGC framework. However, *Ginger* is not a streaming solution, since it needs extra re-assignment phases after the original streaming graph partitioning.

We remark there are other facets of graph partitioning that may affect performance of a DGC framework and have been addressed in other works. For example, some applications are based on dynamic graphs and provided a hashing-based partitioning solution to manage such type of input [21]. Another aspect is the use of other metrics for optimization. For example [28] proposes a solution aimed at aggressively replicating vertices to improve the performance of queries on the graph and to keep them local to each single partition as much as possible. Further contributions along these lines are orthogonal and out of the scope of this paper.

4. THE HDRF ALGORITHM

In this section, we present *HDRF*, a greedy algorithm tailored for skewed power-law graphs.

In the context of robustness to network failure, Cohen et al. [7, 8] and Callaway et al [6] have analytically shown that if only a few high-degree vertices (hubs) are removed from a power-law graph then it is turned into a set of isolated clusters. Moreover, in power-law graphs, the clustering coefficient distribution decreases with increase in the vertex degree [9]. This implies that low-degree vertices often belong to very dense sub-graphs and those sub-graphs are connected to each other through high-degree vertices.

Our partitioning scheme leverages these properties by focusing on the locality of low-degree vertices. In particular, it tries to place each strongly connected component with low-degree vertices into a single partition by cutting high-degree vertices and replicating them on a large number of partitions. As the number of high-degree vertices in power-law graphs is very low, encouraging replication for only these vertices leads to an overall reduction of the replication factor.

Concretely, when *HDRF* creates a replica, it does so for the vertex with the highest degree. However, obtaining degrees of vertices for a graph that is consumed in a streaming fashion is not trivial. To avoid the overhead of a pre-processing step (where the input graph should be fully scanned to calculate the vertex exact degrees), a table with partial degrees of the vertices can be maintained that is continuously updated while input is analyzed. As each new edge is considered in the input, the degree values for the corresponding vertices are updated in the table. The partial degree values collected at runtime are usually a good indicator for the actual degree of a vertex since it is more likely that an observed edge belongs to a high-degree vertex rather than to a low-degree one.[2]

More formally, when processing edge $e \in E$ connecting vertices v_i and v_j, the *HDRF* algorithm retrieves their partial degrees and increments them by one. Let $\delta(v_i)$ be the partial degree of v_i and $\delta(v_j)$ be the partial degree of v_j. The degree values are then normalized such that they sum up to one:

$$\theta(v_i) = \frac{\delta(v_i)}{\delta(v_i) + \delta(v_j)} = 1 - \theta(v_j) \tag{5}$$

As for the greedy heuristic, the *HDRF* algorithm computes a score $C^{\text{HDRF}}(v_i, v_j, p)$ for all partitions $p \in P$, and then assigns e to the partition p^* that maximizes C^{HDRF}. The score for each partition $p \in P$ is defined as follows:

$$C^{\text{HDRF}}(v_i, v_j, p) = C^{\text{HDRF}}_{\text{REP}}(v_i, v_j, p) + C^{\text{HDRF}}_{\text{BAL}}(p) \tag{6}$$

$$C^{\text{HDRF}}_{\text{REP}}(v_i, v_j, p) = g(v_i, p) + g(v_j, p) \tag{7}$$

$$g(v,p) = \begin{cases} 1 + (1 - \theta(v)), & \text{if } p \in A(v) \\ 0, & \text{otherwise} \end{cases}$$

$$C^{\text{HDRF}}_{\text{BAL}}(p) = \lambda \cdot C^{\text{greedy}}_{\text{BAL}}(p) = \lambda \cdot \frac{\text{maxsize} - |p|}{\epsilon + \text{maxsize} - \text{minsize}} \tag{8}$$

The λ parameter allows control of the extent of partition size imbalance in the score computation. We introduced this parameter because the standard *greedy* heuristic may result in highly imbalanced partition sizes, especially when the input is ordered somehow. To see this problem note that $C^{\text{greedy}}_{\text{BAL}}(p)$ (Equation 4) is always smaller than one, while $C^{\text{greedy}}_{\text{REP}}$ and $C^{\text{HDRF}}_{\text{REP}}$ are either zero or greater than one. For this reason, the balance term C_{BAL} in the *greedy* algorithm or when $0 < \lambda \leq 1$ is used only to choose among partitions that exhibit the same value for the replication term C_{REP}, thereby breaking symmetry.

However, this may not be enough to ensure load balance. For instance, if the stream of edges is ordered according to some visit order on the graph (e.g., breadth first search or depth first search), when processing edge $e \in E$ connecting vertices v_i and v_j there is always a single partition p^* with $C^{\text{greedy}}_{\text{REP}}(v_i, v_j, p^*) \geq 1$ (resp. $C^{\text{HDRF}}_{\text{REP}}(v_i, v_j, p^*) > 1$) and all the other partitions $p \in P$ s.t. $p \neq p^*$ have $C^{\text{greedy}}_{\text{REP}}(v_i, v_j, p) = 0$ (resp. $C^{\text{HDRF}}_{\text{REP}}(v_i, v_j, p) = 0$). In this case, the balance term is useless as there is no symmetry to break, and the heuristic ends up placing all edges in a single partition p^*. This problem can be solved by setting a value for $\lambda > 1$. In our evaluation (Section 6), we empirically studied the trend of the replication factor and the load balance by varying λ (Figure 6). Moreover, note that when $\lambda \to \infty$ the algorithm resembles a random heuristic, where past observations are ignored and it only matters to have partitions with equal size. The following summarizes the behavior of the *HDRF* algorithm with respect to the λ parameter:

$$\begin{cases} \lambda = 0, & \text{agnostic of the load balance} \\ 0 < \lambda \leq 1, & \text{balance used to break the symmetry} \\ \lambda > 1, & \text{balance importance proportional to } \lambda \\ \lambda \to \infty, & \text{random edge assignment} \end{cases}$$

When $\lambda = 1$ the *HDRF* algorithm can be represented by a set of simple rules, exactly as in *greedy*, with the exception of *Case 4* that is modified as follows:

Case 4 If $A(v_i) \neq \emptyset$, $A(v_j) \neq \emptyset$ and $A(v_i) \cap A(v_j) = \emptyset$, then
- if $\delta(v_i) < \delta(v_j)$, e is assigned to the partition with the smallest size $p^* \in A(v_i)$ and a new replica of v_j is created in p^*;

[2]During experiments, we noticed no significant improvements in the algorithm performance when using exact degrees instead of their approximate values.

- if $\delta(v_j) < \delta(v_i)$, e is assigned to the partition with the smallest size $p^* \in A(v_j)$ and a new replica of v_i is created in p^*.

HDRF can be run as a single process or in parallel instances to speed up the partitioning phase. As with *greedy*, *HDRF* also needs some state to be shared among parallel instances during partitioning. In particular, we noticed that sharing the values of $A(v)$, $\forall v \in V$ is sufficient to let *HDRF* perform at its best. Note that optimizing the execution time of *HDRF* was a goal beyond the scope of this work; we will consider it as part of our future work.

5. THEORETICAL ANALYSIS

In this section we characterize the *HDRF* algorithm behavior from a theoretical perspective, focussing on the vertex replication factor. In particular we are interested in an average-case analysis of *HDRF*. A worst-case analysis would provide poor performance, as expected for any similar greedy algorithm, while failing to capture the typical behavior of *HDRF* in real cases. In the rest of this section we assume $\lambda = 1$ for the sake of simplicity.

Cohen et al. [8] considered the problem of a scale-free network (characterized as a power-law graph) attacked by an adversary able to remove a fraction c of vertices with the largest degrees. In particular they characterized the approximate maximum degree $\tilde{M}$ observable in the graph's largest component after the attack. If $|V| \gg 1/c$ this value can be approximated by the following equation:

$$\tilde{M} = mc^{1/(1-\alpha)} \tag{9}$$

where m is the (global) minimum vertex degree and α is the parameter characterizing the initial vertex degree distribution.

Let us now consider the algorithm *aHDRF* as an approximation of *HDRF*: *aHDRF* performs exactly as *HDRF*, but for the fact that we assume it knows the exact degree of each input vertex (and not the observed degree as for *HDRF*).

THEOREM 1. *Algorithm* aHDRF *achieves a replication factor, when applied to partition a graph with $|V|$ vertices on $|P|$ partitions, that can be bounded by:*

$$RF \le \tau|P| + \frac{1}{|V|(1-\tau)} \sum_{i=0}^{|V|(1-\tau)-1} \left[1 + m\left(\tau + \frac{i}{|V|}\right)^{\frac{1}{1-\alpha}}\right]$$

$$\tau = \left(\frac{|P|-1}{m}\right)^{1-\alpha}$$

PROOF. The replication factor bound is the sum of two distinct parts. The first part considers the fraction τ of vertices with the largest degrees in the graph, referred to as *hubs*. The worst case for hubs is to be replicated in all the partitions, with a corresponding replication factor of $\tau|P|$. τ represents the fraction of vertices that must be removed from the graph such that the maximum vertex degree in the remaining graph is $|P|-1$; this value is obtainable through Equation (9) by imposing $\tilde{M} = |P|-1$.

The second part of the equation consider the contribution to the replication factor from non-hub vertices, i.e. all vertices whose degree is expected to be smaller than $|P|-1$ after the τ vertices with the largest degrees have been removed from the graph (together with their edges). When *aHDRF* processes an edge connecting a hub vertex with a non-hub vertices, it always favors the replication the hub vertex (that has a larger degree) and replicates the non-hub vertex only if executes *Case 1* or *Case 2*, that is only if it is the first time it observes that vertex. Since the degree of non-hub vertices, ignoring the connections with hub vertices, is bounded by $m\tau^{1/(1-\alpha)}$, and since the connections with hub vertices can produce at most one replica, the worst case replication factor for non-hub vertices is bounded by:

$$\frac{1}{|V|(1-\tau)}\left(1 + m\tau^{\frac{1}{1-\alpha}}\right)$$

This bound can be further improved by considering what happens to the graph once the non-hub vertex v_0 with the largest degree is removed. The previous bound is valid for v_0. However, the removal of v_0 from the graph will change the degree distribution, thus also reducing the bound for the next non-hub vertex with the largest degree. Using this consideration, it is possible to iteratively bound the degree of each non-hub vertex v_i with $m(\tau + i/|V|)^{1/(1-\alpha)}$ where $0 \le i \le |V|(1-\tau)-1$. Hence, the total worst case replication factor for non-hub vertices, is bounded by:

$$\frac{1}{|V|(1-\tau)} \sum_{i=0}^{|V|(1-\tau)-1} \left[1 + m\left(\tau + \frac{i}{|V|}\right)^{\frac{1}{1-\alpha}}\right]$$

□

If edges arrive in random order, *aHDRF* gives an approximation of *HDRF*. In this case, the observed values for vertex degrees are a good estimate for the actual degrees. We can conclude that, assuming random order arrival for edges, *HDRF* is expected to achieve a replication factor, when applied to partition a graph with $|V|$ vertices on $|P|$ partitions, of at most *RF* of Theorem 1.

For example, consider a graph with $\alpha = 2.2$, $|P| = 128$, $m = 1$ and 1M vertices. The average-case upper bound for the replication factor of *HDRF* is ≈ 5.12 while the actual result it achieves is ≈ 1.37. The bounds for *DBH* and *hashing* [12, 27] with this configuration are respectively ≈ 5.54 and ≈ 5.88, while the actual results they achieve are ≈ 1.89 and ≈ 2.52.

The upper bound given by Theorem 1 cannot be extended to other algorithms (e.g., *greedy*). Informally, *HDRF breaks* network at hubs by replicating a small fraction of vertices with large degrees. In contrast, *greedy* and other algorithms are agnostic to the degree of vertices when replicating them. Intuitively, these algorithms try to break network by removing *random* vertices. Unfortunately, power-law graphs are resilient against removing random vertices (see [7] for details). This implies that, in order to fragment a scale-free network, a very large number of random vertices should be removed. In other words, *greedy* and other algorithms tend to replicate a large number of vertices in different partitions. This intuition is verified in our experiments (see Section 6).

6. EVALUATION

This section presents experimental results for the *HDRF* partitioning algorithm. The evaluation was performed on real-world graphs by running the proposed algorithm both in a stand-alone partitioner (useful for scaling up to large partition numbers) and running an implementation of *HDRF*

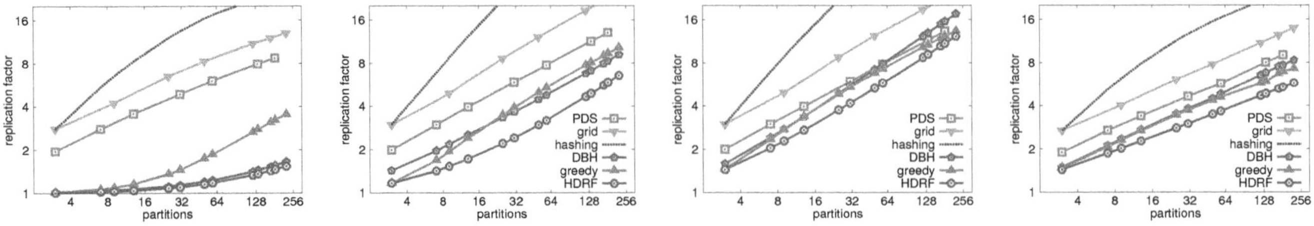

(a) Tencent Weibo (b) Netflix (c) MovieLens 10M (d) twitter-2010

Figure 1: Replication factor varying the number of target partitions (log-log scale).

Dataset	$\|V\|$	$\|E\|$
Tencent Weibo	1.4M	140M
Netflix	497.9K	100.4M
MovieLens 10M	80.6K	10M
twitter-2010	41.7M	1.47B

Table 1: Statistics for real-world graphs.

integrated into GraphLab[3]. The evaluation also reports experiments on synthetic graphs generated randomly with increasingly skewed distributions to study the extent to which *HDRF* performance is sensitive to workload characteristics.

6.1 Experimental Settings and Test Datasets

Evaluation Metrics — We evaluate the performance of *HDRF* by measuring the following metrics:

Replication factor: is the average number of replicas per vertex. This metric is a good measure of the synchronization overhead and should be minimized.

Load relative standard deviation: is the relative standard deviation of the number of edges hosted in target partitions. An optimal partitioning strategy should have a value for this metric close to 0.

Max partition size: is the number of either vertices or edges hosted in the largest partition. We consider this metric with respect to both vertices and edges as each conveys different information. Edges are the main input for the computation phase, thus more edges in a partition mean more computation for the computing node hosting it; conversely, the number of vertices in the system, and, therefore, in the largest partition, also depends on the number of replicas generated by the partitioning algorithm.

Execution time: is the number of seconds needed by the DGC framework to perform the indicated computation on the whole input graph. Better partitioning, by reducing the number of replicas, is expected to reduce the synchronization overhead at runtime and thus reduce the execution time as well.

Datasets — In our evaluation, we used as datasets both synthetic power-law graphs and real-word graphs. The former were used to study how *HDRF* performance vary when the degree distribution skewness of the input graph gradually increases. In particular, each synthetic graph was generated with 1M vertices, minimum degree of 5 and edges using a power law distribution with α ranging from 1.8 to 4.0. Therefore, the number of edges in the graphs ranges from $\sim$ 60M ($\alpha = 1.8$) to $\sim$ 3M ($\alpha = 4$). Graphs were generated with *gengraph* [26]. We also tested the performance of *HDRF* on real-world graphs: *twitter-2010* from LAW (Laboratory for Web Algorithmics) [5, 4], *Tencent Weibo* from the KDD-Cup 2012 [22], *Netflix* from the Netflix Prize [3] and *MovieLens 10M* from the GroupLens research lab (`http://grouplens.org`). Table 1 reports some statistics for these 4 datasets.

System Setup — We implemented a stand-alone version of a graph partitioner that captures the behavior of a DGC framework during the graph loading and partitioning phase. Within our partitioner, we implemented the five different algorithms described so far: *hashing*, *DBH*, *grid*, *PDS*, *greedy* and *HDRF*. Furthermore, we compared our solution against two offline methods: *Ginger* [24] and METIS [15], a well-known edge-cut partitioning algorithm. To compute the replication factor delivered by METIS, we used the same strategy of [12]: every edge-cut forces the two spanned partitions in maintaining a replica of both vertices and a copy of the edge data. To run realistic tests needed to measure execution time, we implemented and integrated *HDRF* into GraphLab v2.2. Experiments with GraphLab where conducted on a cluster consisting of 8 machines with dual 16-core *Intel Xeon* CPUs and *128GB* of memory each. We experimented with 32, 64 and 128 partitions by running multiple instances on a single machine.

Data input order — Since the input dataset is consumed as a stream of edges, the input order can affect the performance of the partitioning algorithm. We considered three different stream orders as in [25]: *random*, where edges arrive according to a random permutation; *BFS*, where the edge order is generated by selecting a vertex uniformly at random and performing a breadth first search visit starting from that vertex; *DFS*, that works as *BFS* except for the visit algorithm that is depth-first search. All reported results are based on a *random* input order unless otherwise mentioned in the text.

6.2 Performance Evaluation

The experimental results reported in this section are organized as follows: we first report on experiments that show the ability of *HDRF* to deliver the best overall performance in terms of execution time with the smallest overhead (replication factor) and close to optimal load balance when executed on real-world graphs. We then study how *HDRF* performance is affected by changes in the characteristics of the input dataset and changes in the target number of partitions. Finally, the last set of results analyze the sensitivity of *HDRF* to input stream ordering.

[3]The stand-alone software and the GraphLab patch are available at `https://github.com/fabiopetroni/VGP`.

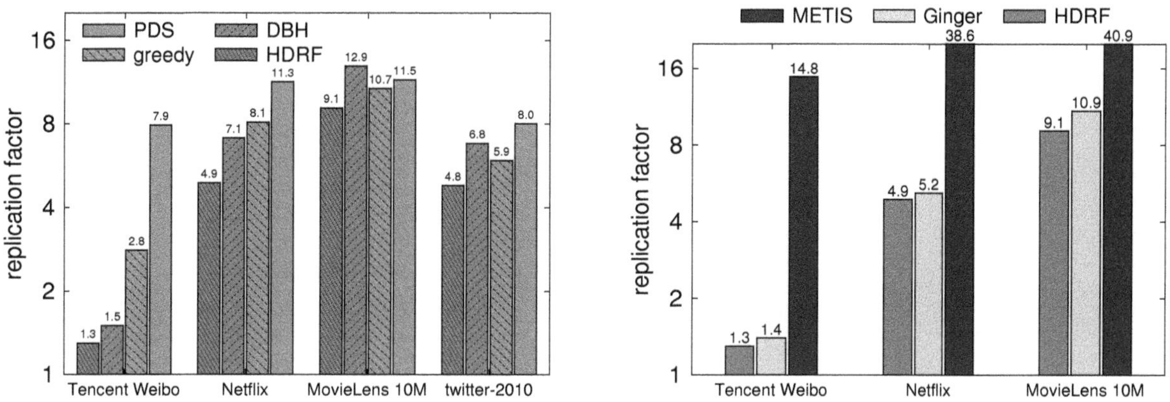

(a) Streaming algorithms

(b) Offline algorithms

Figure 2: Replication factor (log scale) with $|P| = 133$. *HDRF* is compared against streaming (a) and offline (b) solutions.

6.2.1 *Runtime comparison*

We first measured *HDRF* performance against other streaming partitioning algorithms on our set of real-world graphs. These experiments were run by partitioning the input graphs on a set of target partitions in the range $[3, 256]$ with our stand-alone partitioner. Figure 1 reports the replication factor that the considered partitioning algorithms achieve on different input graphs[4]. Moreover, Figure 2a provides a snapshot of the evaluation, by setting the number of target partition to 133, a number compliant with PDS constraints. It can be observed that *HDRF* is the algorithm that provides the smallest replication factor for all the considered datasets.

In particular, for the Weibo dataset, characterized by large edge count differences among high-degree and low-degree vertices, it is possible to observe how *HDRF* and *DBH* are the best performers as they both exploit vertex degrees. In all the other datasets *HDRF* is always the best performer, albeit with larger absolute RF values. Summarizing, on the considered datasets *HDRF* achieves on average a replication factor about 40% smaller than DBH, more than 50% smaller than *greedy*, almost 3× smaller than *PDS*, more than 4× smaller than *grid* and almost 14× smaller than *hashing*. We experimented with other datasets as well (i.e. *arabic-2005*, *uk-2002*, *indochina-2004* from LAW, and *Yahoo! Music* from the KDD-Cup 2011). In all our test *HDRF* outperforms competing solutions, simultaneously guaranteeing close to perfect load balance (results omitted due to space constraints).

Next, we compared *HDRF* against two offline partitioning algorithms: *Ginger* and *METIS*. Note that these offline solutions have full knowledge of the input graph that can be exploited to drive their partitioning choices. Figure 2b compares the replication factor achieved by these two solutions and *HDRF* (we maintain $|P| = 133$ to be coherent with Figure 2a). We do not report the results for the *twitter-2010* dataset since *METIS* produced greatly unbalanced partitions[5], making a comparison on this dataset unfair. The poor performance of *METIS* was an expected result since it has been proved that edge-cut approaches perform worse than vertex-cut ones on power-law graphs [12]. However, *HDRF* outperforms *Ginger* as well, by reducing its replication factor by 10% on average. In addition, *HDRF* has the clear advantage of consuming the graph in a one-pass fashion while *Ginger* needs several passes over the input data to converge. These results show that *HDRF* is always able to provide a smaller average replication factor with respect to all other algorithms, both streaming and offline, when used to partition graphs with power-law degree distributions.

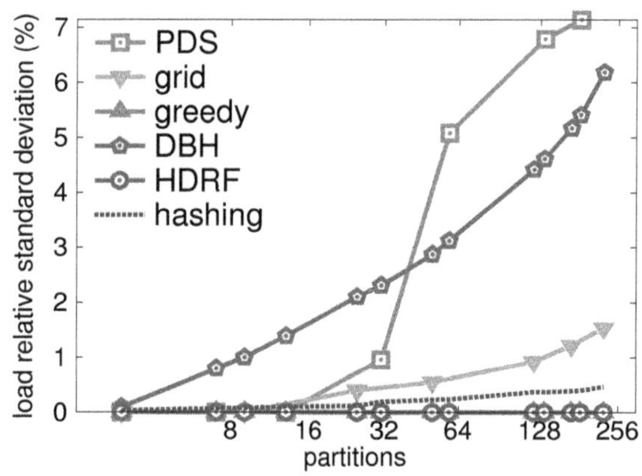

Figure 3: Load relative standard deviation produced by different partitioning algorithms on the MovieLens 10M dataset.

Figure 3 reports the load relative standard deviation produced by the tested streaming algorithms when run on the *MovieLens 10M* dataset with a variable number of target partitions (results for other datasets showed similar behavior so we omit them). The curves show that *HDRF* and *greedy* provide the best performance as the number of target partitions grows. As expected, *hashing* provides well bal-

[4]Due to specific constraints imposed by the *PDS* and *grid* algorithms on the total number of partitions, their data points are not aligned with those of the other algorithms.

[5]Note that the scope of Metis is to balance vertex load among partitions.

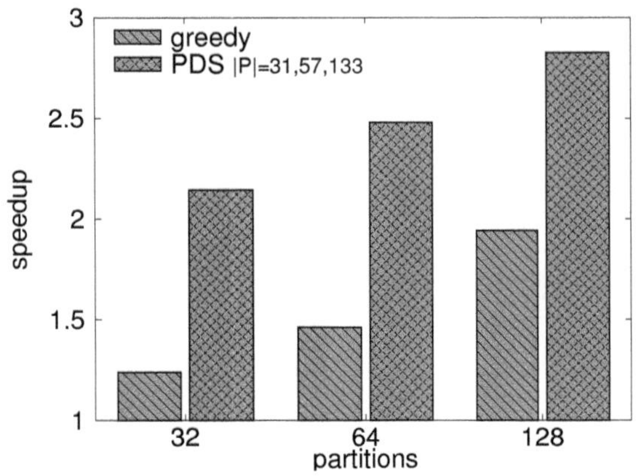

Figure 4: Speedup in the execution time for the SGD algorithm on the *Tencent Weibo* dataset by applying *HDRF* with respect to *greedy* and *PDS*, with 32, 64 and 128 partitions.

anced partitions, but it still performs worse that the other algorithms as its expected behavior with respect to load balancing is only probabilistic. *Grid* performs similarly, even if its more complex constraints induce some skew in load. *DBH* and *PDS* are the worse performers, with load skew growing at a fast pace as the number of target partitions grows. Note that replication factor reflects communication cost, and edge-imbalance reflects workload-imbalance; providing good performance with these two metrics means that *HDRF* can provide partitioning results that make the execution of application algorithms more efficient.

To this end, we studied how much all of this translates to a performance improvement with respect to the execution time. Since a DGC framework has to periodically synchronize all the vertex replicas, having fewer replicas in the system is expected to provide an advantage and to speed up the execution time. To investigate the impact of the different partitioning techniques we ran the Stochastic Gradient Descent (SGD) algorithm for matrix completion [17, 23] on GraphLab, using the *Tencent Weibo* dataset and 100 latent factors, with 32, 64 and 128 partitions respectively. Figure 4 reports the measured speed-up, obtained by using *HDRF* to partition the input over *greedy* and *PDS*[6]. The SGD algorithm runs up to 2× faster using *HDRF* as input partitioner with respect to *greedy*, and close to 3× faster than *PDS*. The actual improvement is larger as the number of target partitions grows. Moreover, the speedup is proportional to the gain in RF (see Figure 1a) and, as already shown in [12], halving the replication factor approximately halves runtime. Furthermore, having partitions with fewer replicas also help SGD to converge faster [23].

We tested the speedup for other datasets and algorithms as well, namely Single Source Shortest Path (SSSP), Weakly Connected Components (WCC), Page Rank (PR) and Alternating Least Squares (ALS). The results (not reported here due to space constraints) confirmed our intuitions: the speedup is proportional to both the advantage in replication factor and the actual network usage of the algorithm. The speedup it is larger for IO-intensive algorithms (e.g. SGD, ALS and PR) and smaller for algorithm with less network IO (SSSP and WCC). None of the tests we conducted with *HDRF* showed a slowdown with respect to other solutions.

Our results show that *HDRF* is the best solution to partition input graphs characterized by skewed power-law degree distributions. *HDRF* achieves the smallest replication factor with close to optimal load balance. These two characteristics combined make application algorithms execute more efficiently in the DGC framework.

6.2.2 *Performance sensitivity to input shape*

We next analyze how the input graph degree distribution affects *HDRF* performance. To this end, we used *HDRF* to partition a set of synthetic power-law graphs. In doing so, we experimentally characterize the sensitivity of the average replication factor on the power-law shape parameter α, and on the number of partitions. Figure 5a reports the replication factor improvement for *HDRF* with respect to other algorithms, expressed as a multiplicative factor, by varying α in the range $[1.8, 4.0]$ with $|P| = 128$ target partitions ($|P| = 133$ and $|P| = 121$ for *PDS* and *grid* respectively). The curves show two important aspects of *HDRF* behavior: (1) with highly skewed degree distributions (i.e. small values of α), its performance is significantly better than *greedy* and other algorithms (with the exception of DBH); (2) with less skewed degree distributions, the performance of *HDRF* approaches that provided by *greedy*, while all the other solutions (including *DBH*) perform worse. These results show how *HDRF* behavior approximates *greedy*'s behavior as the number of high degree vertices in the input graph grows as in this case making a different partitioning choice on high-degree vertices is less useful (as there are a lot of them). Note that Gonzalez et al. [12] showed that the effective gain of a vertex-cut approach relative to an edge-cut approach actually increases with smaller α. Our solution boosts this gain, not only with respect to constrained techniques but also over the *greedy* algorithm. Figure 5b reports the replication factor, and clearly shows that *HDRF* is able to outperform all competing algorithms for all values of α. At the extremes, *HDRF* is better than *DBH* when α is very small and performs slightly better than *greedy* when α is very large.

6.2.3 *Performance sensitivity to input order*

A shortcoming of the standard *greedy* algorithm is its inability to effectively handle streams of input edges when they are ordered. If the input stream is ordered such that two subsequent edges always share a vertex, *greedy* always places all the edges and their adjacent vertices in a single partition, whatever the target partition number is. The final result is clearly far from being desirable as all of the computation load will be incurred by a single node in the computing cluster.

To overcome this limitation, we explicitly introduced the parameter λ in the computation of the score for each partition in *HDRF* (Equations (6) and (8)), that defines the importance of the load balance in the edge placement decision (Section 4). Figure 6 shows the result of an experiment run on the Netflix dataset, where the input stream of edges is ordered according to either a *depth-first-search* (DFS) or a *breadth-first-search* (BFS) visit on the graph. The figure shows the average replication factor (Figure 6a), the size of the largest partition expressed as number of contained edges (Figure 6b) and the size of the largest partition ex-

[6]We needed to use respectively 31, 57 and 133 partitions, to fit *PDS* constraints.

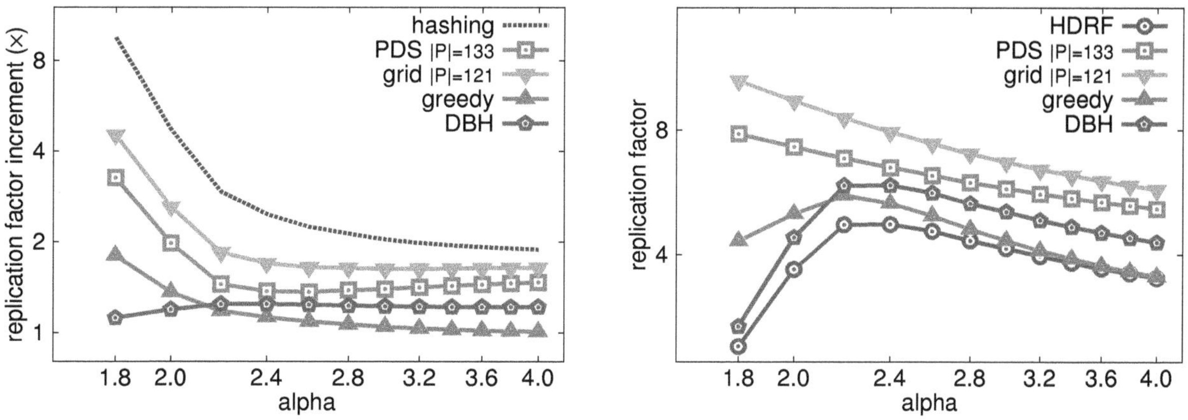

(a) RF increment varying α (*HDRF*= 1)

(b) RF varying α

Figure 5: Replication factor improvement for *HDRF* in synthetically generated graphs (log-log scale). Figure (a) reports the replication factor increment and Figure (b) the actual replication factor when α grows ($|P| = 128$ except for *PDS*, where $|P| = 133$, and *grid*, where $|P| = 121$). For Figure (a) *HDRF* represents the baseline.

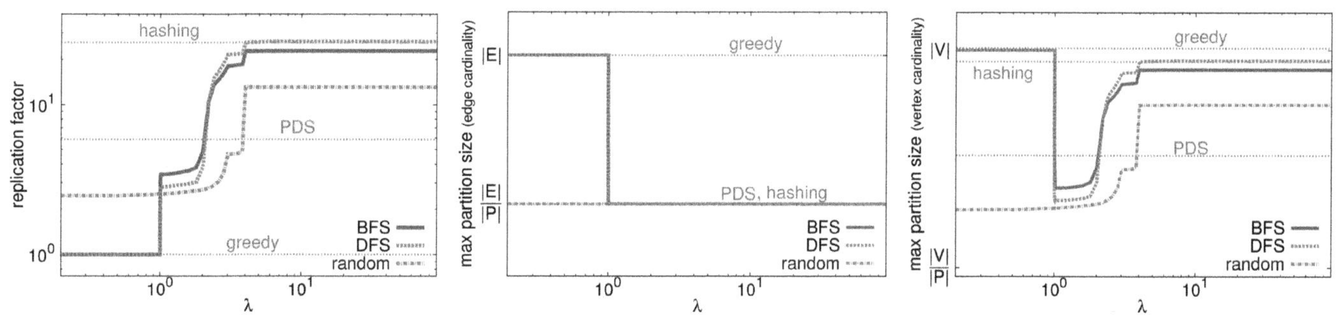

(a) replication factor

(b) max edge cardinality

(c) max vertex cardinality

Figure 6: *HDRF* behavior on the Netflix dataset varying λ, with input edge stream either random or ordered (DFS or BFS graph visits). Reference grey lines represent *greedy*, *hashing* and *PDS* performance.

pressed as number of contained vertices (Figure 6c) all while varying the value of λ in the range $[0.1, 100]$ (log-log axes). All three figures report the performance obtained with the *greedy*, *hashing* and *PDS* algorithms as horizontal grey lines for reference.

With $\lambda \leq 1$ *HDRF* behaves exactly as *greedy* (curves BFS and DFS): all edges are placed in a single partition and no vertex is replicated. This behavior is confirmed by the size of the largest partition that in this case contains exactly $|E|$ edges and $|V|$ vertices (Figures 6b and 6c). For $\lambda > 1$ the C_{BAL} factor starts to play a fundamental role in balancing the load among the available partitions: the average replication factor for *HDRF* with both DFS and BFS inputs is just slightly larger than what is achievable with a random input[7] and still substantially lower than what is achievable with *PDS* or *hashing* (Figure 6a). At the same time, the size of the largest partition drops to its minimum (Figures 6b and 6c) indicating that the algorithm immediately delivers close to perfect load balancing (i.e. $|E|/|P|$ edges per partition), while the number of vertices hosted in the largest partition reaches its minimum. By further increasing λ toward larger values, the effect of C_{BAL} dominates the *HDRF* score computation and the algorithms behavior quickly approaches the behavior typical of *hashing*: large average replication factor, with close to perfect load balancing.

These results show that i) the C_{BAL} term in *HDRF* score computation plays an effective role in providing close-to-perfect load balancing among partitions while keeping a low average replication factor, and ii) by setting the value of λ slightly larger than 1, it is possible to let *HDRF* work at a "sweet spot" where it can deliver the best performance, even when working on an ordered stream of edges. This last point makes *HDRF* particularly suitable for application settings where it is not possible to randomize the input stream before feeding it to the graph partitioning algorithm.

7. CONCLUSION

Distributed graph-computing frameworks provide programmers with convenient abstractions to enable computation on large datasets. In these frameworks, system performance is often determined by the graph data partitioning strategy, which impacts the communication cost and the workload balance among compute resources. In this paper, we pro-

[7]The difference is due to *HDRF*'s usage of partial information on vertex degrees. Such values are not a good proxy of real vertex degrees if the input stream is not random.

posed *HDRF*, a novel stream-based graph partitioning algorithm for distributed graph-computing frameworks. *HDRF* is based on a greedy vertex-cut approach that leverages information on vertex degrees. Through a theoretical analysis and an extensive experimental evaluation on real-world as well as synthetic graphs using both a stand-alone partitioner and implementation of *HDRF* in GraphLab, we showed that HDRF is overall the best performing partitioning algorithm for graphs characterized by power-law degree distributions. In particular, *HDRF* provides the smallest average replication factor with close to optimal load balance. These two characteristics put together allow *HDRF* to significantly reduce the time needed to perform computation on graphs and makes it the best choice for partitioning graph data.

8. REFERENCES

[1] R. Albert, H. Jeong, and A.-L. Barabási. Error and attack tolerance of complex networks. *Nature*, 406(6794):378–382, 2000.

[2] K. Andreev and H. Räcke. Balanced graph partitioning. In *Proceedings of the 16th Annual ACM Symposium on Parallelism in Algorithms and Architectures*, 2004.

[3] J. Bennett and S. Lanning. The netflix prize. In *Proceedings of KDD cup and workshop*, 2007.

[4] P. Boldi, M. Rosa, M. Santini, and S. Vigna. Layered label propagation: A multiresolution coordinate-free ordering for compressing social networks. In *Proceedings of the 20th international conference on World Wide Web*, 2011.

[5] P. Boldi and S. Vigna. The webgraph framework i: compression techniques. In *Proceedings of the 13th international conference on World Wide Web*, 2004.

[6] D. S. Callaway, M. E. Newman, S. H. Strogatz, and D. J. Watts. Network robustness and fragility: Percolation on random graphs. *Physical review letters*, 85(25):5468, 2000.

[7] R. Cohen, K. Erez, D. Ben-Avraham, and S. Havlin. Resilience of the internet to random breakdowns. *Physical review letters*, 85(21):4626, 2000.

[8] R. Cohen, K. Erez, D. Ben-Avraham, and S. Havlin. Breakdown of the internet under intentional attack. *Physical review letters*, 86(16):3682, 2001.

[9] S. N. Dorogovtsev and J. F. Mendes. Evolution of networks. *Advances in physics*, 51(4):1079–1187, 2002.

[10] C. Eaton, D. Deroos, T. Deutsch, G. Lapis, and P. Zikopoulos. *Understanding Big Data*. Mc Graw Hill, 2012.

[11] U. Feige, M. Hajiaghayi, and J. R. Lee. Improved approximation algorithms for minimum weight vertex separators. *SIAM Journal on Computing*, 38(2):629–657, 2008.

[12] J. E. Gonzalez, Y. Low, H. Gu, D. Bickson, and C. Guestrin. Powergraph: Distributed graph-parallel computation on natural graphs. In *Proceedings of the 10th USENIX Symposium on Operating Systems Design and Implementation*, 2012.

[13] H. Halberstam and R. Laxton. Perfect difference sets. In *Proceedings of the Glasgow Mathematical Association*, 1964.

[14] N. Jain, G. Liao, and T. L. Willke. Graphbuilder: Scalable graph etl framework. In *1st International Workshop on Graph Data Management Experiences and Systems*, 2013.

[15] G. Karypis and V. Kumar. A fast and high quality multilevel scheme for partitioning irregular graphs. *SIAM Journal on scientific Computing*, 20(1):359–392, 1998.

[16] M. Kim and K. S. Candan. SBV-Cut: Vertex-cut based graph partitioning using structural balance vertices. *Data & Knowledge Engineering*, 72:285–303, 2012.

[17] Y. Koren, R. Bell, and C. Volinsky. Matrix factorization techniques for recommender systems. *Computer*, 42(8):30–37, 2009.

[18] Y. Low, D. Bickson, J. Gonzalez, C. Guestrin, A. Kyrola, and J. M. Hellerstein. Distributed graphlab: a framework for machine learning and data mining in the cloud. *Proceedings of the VLDB Endowment*, 5(8):716–727, 2012.

[19] Y. Low, J. Gonzalez, A. Kyrola, D. Bickson, C. Guestrin, and J. M. Hellerstein. Graphlab: A new framework for parallel machine learning. In *Proceedings of the 26th Conference on Uncertainty in Artificial Intelligence*, 2010.

[20] G. Malewicz, M. H. Austern, A. J. Bik, J. C. Dehnert, I. Horn, N. Leiser, and G. Czajkowski. Pregel: a system for large-scale graph processing. In *Proceedings of the 2010 ACM SIGMOD International Conference on Management of data*, 2010.

[21] J. Mondal and A. Deshpande. Managing large dynamic graphs efficiently. In *Proceedings of the 2012 ACM SIGMOD International Conference on Management of Data*, 2012.

[22] Y. Niu, Y. Wang, G. Sun, A. Yue, B. Dalessandro, C. Perlich, and B. Hamner. The tencent dataset and kdd-cup'12. In *KDD-Cup Workshop*, 2012.

[23] F. Petroni and L. Querzoni. Gasgd: stochastic gradient descent for distributed asynchronous matrix completion via graph partitioning. In *Proceedings of the 8th ACM Conference on Recommender systems*, 2014.

[24] Y. C. R. Chen, J. Shi and H. Chen. Powerlyra: Differentiated graph computation and partitioning on skewed graphs. In *Proceedings of the 10th ACM SIGOPS European Conference on Computer Systems*, 2015.

[25] C. Tsourakakis, C. Gkantsidis, B. Radunovic, and M. Vojnovic. Fennel: Streaming graph partitioning for massive scale graphs. In *Proceedings of the 7th ACM international conference on Web search and data mining*, 2014.

[26] F. Viger and M. Latapy. Efficient and simple generation of random simple connected graphs with prescribed degree sequence. In *Computing and Combinatorics*. Springer, 2005.

[27] C. Xie, L. Yan, W.-J. Li, and Z. Zhang. Distributed power-law graph computing: Theoretical and empirical analysis. In *Advances in Neural Information Processing Systems*, 2014.

[28] S. Yang, X. Yan, B. Zong, and A. Khan. Towards effective partition management for large graphs. In *Proceedings of the 2012 ACM SIGMOD International Conference on Management of Data*, 2012.

Towards Scale-out Capability on Social Graphs

Haichuan Shang[‡†] Xiang Zhao[§] Uday Kiran[‡†] Masaru Kitsuregawa[¶†]

[‡] National Institute of Information and Communications Technology, Japan
[†] University of Tokyo, Japan
[§] National University of Defense Technology, China
[¶] National Institute of Informatics, Japan
[†]{shang, uday_rage, kitsure}@tkl.iis.u-tokyo.ac.jp [§]xiangzhao@nudt.edu.cn

ABSTRACT

The development of cloud storage and computing has facilitated the rise of various big data applications. As a representative high performance computing (HPC) workload, graph processing is becoming a part of cloud computing. However, scalable computing on large graphs is still dominated by HPC solutions, which require high performance all-to-all collective operations over torus (or mesh) networking. Implementing those torus-based algorithms on commodity clusters, e.g., cloud computing infrastructures, can result in great latency due to inefficient communication. Moreover, designing a highly scalable system for large social graphs, is far from being trivial, as intrinsic features of social graphs, e.g., degree skewness and lacking of locality, often profoundly limit the extent of parallelism.

To resolve the challenges, we explore the iceberg of developing a scalable system for processing large social graphs on commodity clusters. In particular, we focus on the scale-out capability of the system. We propose a novel separator-combiner based query processing engine which provides native load-balancing and very low communication overhead, such that increasinglylarger graphs can be simply addressed by adding more computing nodes to the cluster.The proposed system achieves remarkable scale-out capability in processing large social graphs with skew degree distributions, while providing many critical features for big data analytics, such as easy-to-use API, fault-tolerance and recovery. We implement the system as a portable and easily configurable library, and conduct comprehensive experimental studies to demonstrate its effectiveness and efficiency.

Categories and Subject Descriptors

H.2.4 [**Database Management**]: Systems

General Terms

Algorithms; Experimentation; Performance

CIKM'15, October 19-23, 2015, Melbourne, VIC, Australia
ACM 978-1-4503-3794-6/15/10.
http://dx.doi.org/10.1145/2806416.2806420.

Keywords

Graph Databases; Distributed Databases; Social Networks

1. INTRODUCTION

In an era of information explosion, big data analytics have become an increasingly important component of industry, which focuses on developing special parallel computational platforms to analyze various forms of massive data. The widespread usage of these platforms has changed the landscape of scalable parallel computing, which was long dominated by High Performance Computing (HPC) applications. The big data platforms support applications, different from those solved by HPC before in that (1) big data platforms rely on commodity cluster-based execution and storage infrastructure like MapReduce; and (2) the utility computing model introduced by cloud computing makes computing resources available to the customer as needed, such that large scale-out capability is mandatory for the systems on cloud.

As one of the most popular data-intensive applications, the rapidly growing social networks require an efficient and scalable graph processing platform. Unfortunately, MapReduce, the de-facto big data processing model, and its associated technologies such as Pig [19] and Hive [31] are often ill-suited for iterative computing problems on large graphs. As a result, several graph-parallel projects [1, 17, 18, 22, 24, 27, 30, 32, 36], have been proposed to facilitate data analysis on large graphs. These projects can be generally classified into two categories:

- The first category is 1D partitioning methods, which means that the vertices of a graph are divided into partitions along with their outgoing edges. 1D partitioning is widely adopted by graph-parallel projects. Different from its predecessor Parallel BGL [10] which exposes a whole graph to user-code as the interface, Pregel [18] introduces an easy-to-use interface, named vertex-centric *Bulk Synchronous Parallel* (BSP) [34] model. This model is similar to a BSP model which consists of a sequence of supersteps separated by global synchronization points until the algorithm terminates. In every superstep, a user-programmable function *vertex.compute()* is called exactly once for each vertex. The function *vertex.compute()* receives messages via the incoming edges from the previous superstep, processes the messages such as an aggregation, and sends messages via the outgoing edges for the next superstep. Pregel inspires several research and open-source projects [1, 22, 24, 27, 30, 32, 36].

Advantage. The advantage of these projects is providing an easy-to-use infrastructure to reduce the costs of implementing distributed graph algorithms in terms of human time and effort, because the man-hour spent on developing well-optimized native code is usually unaffordable to enterprise IT infrastructure.

Disadvantage. Real-world graphs typically follow power law degree distributions [3, 5, 8, 23]. The systems based on 1D partitioning cannot scale-out to a large number of computing nodes when processing massive power law graphs, because the workers (i.e. the instances of an algorithm running on a computing node) in charge of the high degree vertices will take longer query processing time than the others, and thus exceedingly slow down the overall response time. In other words, increasing the number of computing nodes in a cluster cannot further reduce overall response time, because the elapsed time in which a worker processes the vertex with the highest degree determines the overall response time.

- The second category is 2D partitioning methods [7, 37], in which every vertex is managed by a group of computing nodes. In each superstep, the computing nodes in the same group communicate with one another to aggregate the received messages, and then send messages to the other groups along outgoing edges to the next superstep. The communication among the computing nodes in the same group is implemented by either *AllReduce* [37] or *AllGather* [7]. A scalable system based on the 2D partitioning approach is usually supported by special HPC hardware such as torus (or mesh) networking. For example, a 2D torus configuration places 16 computing nodes in a 4×4 grid. Each of the 16 computing nodes is directly linked to its four nearest-neighbors. Initially, the vertices of a graph is partitioned into four non-overlapping subsets. Each row of the computing nodes in the torus manages a subset of the vertices. The outgoing edges from a subset of the vertices are further partitioned into four edge subsets by their targets, and each edge subset is handled by a computing node. In a typical computation, every worker communicates vertically (**Fold**) to send messages along outgoing edges, and performs *AllReduce* or *AllGather* horizontally (**Expand**) to aggregate received messages for the same group of vertices.

  Advantage. This approach is highly scale-out-capable to more than sixty thousand computing nodes [2] on HPC.

  Disadvantage. This approach tackles degree-skew and scale-out capability as a trade-off of communication cost. Indeed, the communication cost of the **Fold** step is equal to 1D partitioning's total communication cost in terms of total message size. The communication cost of the **Expand** step is the price we pay extra for load-balancing and scalability. The high-performance implementation [6, 20] of row-wise and column-wise collective communication including *AllReduce* and *AllGather* is critical to the scale-out capability. Due to lacking torus networking and high-performance implementation of *AllGather* operation, implementing this approach on commodity clusters can lead to inefficiency in the form of inefficient communication. In addition, it is fairly expensive to implement 2D graph algorithms, in terms of human time and effort, which conflict with the "ease-of-use" concept of big data.

Briefly, the existing systems provide the following choices to process large graphs.

1. Relying on the existing systems which are based on vertex-centric BSP model or MapReduce platforms. The systems, such as Apache Giraph [1] on Hadoop [35] and GraphX [36] on Spark[38], are very easy to use, but cannot handle large degree-skewed graphs derived from massive social networks.
2. Adopting the HPC solutions which provide high performance on large-scale clusters, but needs expensive HPC clusters with torus (or mesh) networking.
3. Extending collective communication to commodity clusters. These systems [9, 11] alleviate the effect of degree-skew on small-scale clusters, but the impact of concurrent network transactions can be significant for collective communication on large-scale clusters, and thus degrades the performance of these systems in processing large graphs.

	Degree-skew	Commodity	Scale-out
1D (Commodity)	✗	✓	✓
2D (HPC)	✓	✗	✓
2D (Commodity)	✓	✓	✗

Table 1: Existing systems against requirements

Developing a system for processing large social graphs on large-scale commodity clusters means satisfying three requirements: **1. Degree-skew**: the partitioning method is load-balanced when processing graphs with skew degree distributions; **2. Commodity**: the system does not rely on costly networking such as torus; and **3. Scale-out**: larger graphs can be addressed by simply adding more computing nodes to the system. As shown in Table 1, none of the existing approaches satisfy the above three requirements.

Motivated by this, we propose a novel system, named GraphSlice. GraphSlice's query processing is based on a Separator-Combiner BSP model. We demonstrate that the above three requirements can be satisfied simultaneously by an elegantly designed query processing engine by which massive social graphs can be efficiently processed on commodity clusters. This system provides the following features.

1. Capturing the common patterns of graph algorithms such that API's are sufficient to express a wide range of graph algorithms.
2. Achieving scalable performance in processing large graphs with skew degree distributions.
3. Synchronizing supersteps without all-collective communication which elegantly fit large-scale commodity clusters where the impact of concurrent network transactions is serious.
4. Relying on one-to-one communication in a BSP model, such that the proposed system is highly reliable and

fault-tolerant on commodity clusters and is able to be seamlessly integrated with existing commodity cluster-based infrastructures such as MapReduce.

The rest of this paper is organized as follows. Section 2 introduces the background knowledge. Section 3 gives the framework of our approach. Section 4 describes the query processing engine. Section 5 presents API of our system. Section 6 discusses system implementation. Section 7 reports the experimental results. The related work and conclusion is given in Section 8 and 9, respectively.

2. PRELIMINARIES

In this section, we briefly introduce the background knowledge on 1D partitioning and vertex-centric BSP model.

2.1 1D partitioning

The 1D partitioning (a.k.a. distributed adjacency list, source-vertex partitioning and horizontal partitioning) is the most popular partitioning method for graph processing in distributed environments. The vertices are partitioned to workers along with their outgoing edges. Figure 1 (a) and (b) illustrate the partitions of an example graph and its distributed adjacency list, respectively. In this example, the vertices are partitioned into three partitions $\{A, B, C\}$, $\{D, E, F\}$ and $\{G, H, I\}$ along with their outgoing edges.

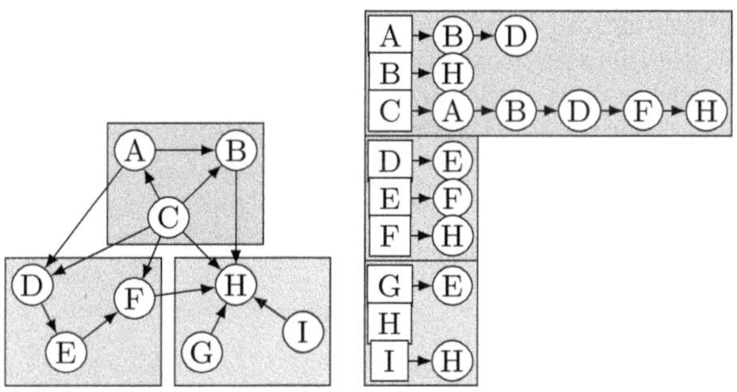

(a) Distributed graph (b) Distributed adjacency list

Figure 1: 1D partitioning

2.2 BSP model

In a BSP model [34], the superstep concept is used for synchronizing the parallel execution of workers. A superstep typically consists of three parts.

- Computation: Every worker executes computation for the vertices it owns.
- Communication: The worker sends messages on behalf of the vertices it owns to the neighboring vertices.
- Barrier: The worker waits until all other workers have finished their computation and communication.

Then the algorithm moves to the next superstep. An algorithm may involves several supersteps which are executed one after another.

For example, a simple BFS algorithm on 1D partitions is illustrated in Figure 2. The BFS begins at the root vertex 'C' which is initialized by the vertex value '0' as its distance to the root. In the *Superstep 1*, the worker, which owns the vertex 'C' , sends the messages that contains the value '1' as the distance of frontiers, along the outgoing edges. Every vertex which has received messages from the vertex 'C' updates its vertex value to '1', and sends the messages that contains the value '2' for the next superstep. The algorithm iteratively updates vertex values if the received value is smaller than the current vertex value, and sends messages which contain the updated value plus '1'. The algorithm terminates when there is no update in a superstep.

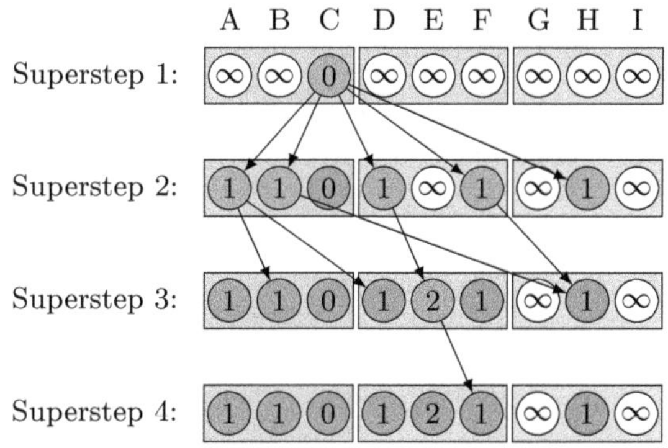

Figure 2: A simple BFS algorithm on 1D partitions

Algorithm 1 The Vertex API foundations of Pregel

```
template <VertexType, EdgeType, MessageType>
class Vertex {
  virtual void Compute(MessageIterator msgs);
  string vertexID();
  boolean isSource(string vertexID);
  int superstep();
  VertexType getVertexValue();
  void setVertexValue(VertexType value);
  OutEdgeIterator getOutEdgeIterator();
  void SendMessageTo(string dest_vertex, MessageType
  message);
  void VoteToHalt();
}
```

2.3 Vertex-centric API

Pregel [18] proposes a vertex-centric API on BSP model, abbreviated as *vertex-centric BSP*. Writing a vertex-centric BSP program usually means overriding the virtual *Compute()* function in the **Vertex** class as shown in Algorithm 1, which will be executed at each active vertex in every superstep. The template defines three value types which are associated with vertices, edges and messages. The vertex-centric BSP model exposes all outgoing edges of a vertex to the *Compute()* function by providing an **OutEdgeIterator**.

A vertex-centric BSP implementation of Single Source Shortest Path (SSSP) algorithm is shown in Algorithm 2. The **ShortestPathVertex** class inherits from **Vertex** class and implements the *Compute()* function. The vertex value with each vertex is initialized to a constant INF which is larger than any feasible distance. In each superstep, each vertex first receives messages via its incoming edges, and calculates the minimum value among the received messages. If the minimum is less than the current vertex value, this vertex updates it value and sends the updated value via the outgoing edges, consisting of the updated vertex value added

Algorithm 2 Single Source Shortest Path (SSSP)

```
class ShortestPathVertex extends Vertex <int, int, int>
{
  void compute(MessageIterator msgs) {
    int mindist = isSource(vertexID()) ? 0 : INF;
    For (;!msgs.Done();msgs.Next())
      mindist = min(mindist, msgs.Value());
    If (mindist < getVertexValue()) {
      setVertexValue(mindist);
      OutEdgeIterator iter= getOutEdgeIterator();
      For(;!iter.Done();iter.Next())        SendMessage(
      iter.Target(), iter.getEdgeValue() + mindist);
    }else{
      VoteToHalt();
    }
  }
}
```

to the edge weight. The algorithm terminates when there is no new updates in a superstep, after that the value of each vertex denotes the distance from the source to that vertex. This algorithm is amenable to optimization using a combiner as discussed in [18], which is omitted here due to the interest of space.

3. FRAMEWORK

In this paper, we propose a system GraphSlice that employs novel partitioning and query processing methods to tackle degree-skew and scale-out problems, while providing an easy-to-use API to the users. It consists of three parts:

1. **Partitioning.** The partitioning is managed by Separators which are containers of a subset of edges outgoing from a same vertex.
2. **Query Processing.** The query processing is based on a Separator-Combiner BSP model.
3. **API.** The API provides an easy Vertex-and-Edge view, while the concept of Separator and Combiner is usually hidden from the users.

The next three sections will introduce the system details.

4. PARTITIONING AND QUERY PROCESSING

In this section, we introduce the basic idea of the partitioning method, followed by the query processing model. More implementation details will be given in Section 6.

4.1 Parititioning

The vertices are firstly partitioned to workers according to a user-defined Hash function. Then, edge parititioning is managed by **Separators** which are containers of a subset of edges outgoing from a same vertex. We provide two types of Separators to manage the outgoing edges of every vertex: PreSeparator and PostSeparator which are abbreviated for pre-communication separator and post-communication separator respectively. Every vertex's outgoing edges are managed by either PreSeparator or PostSeparator. In particular, there is an underlying degree-based mechanism which manages high degree vertices by PostSeparators and low degree vertices by PreSeparators.

PreSeparator is very similar to the existing 1D paritition-ing method. It is hosted by the worker which owns the source vertex of the PreSeparator. PostSeparator is more tricky. If a vertex v is managed by PostSeparator, it is indeed managed by at most N PostSeparators on N different workers where N is the total number of workers in the system. Each PostSeparator on a worker manages a subset of the outgoing edges of v which emanate to the vertices owned by that worker.

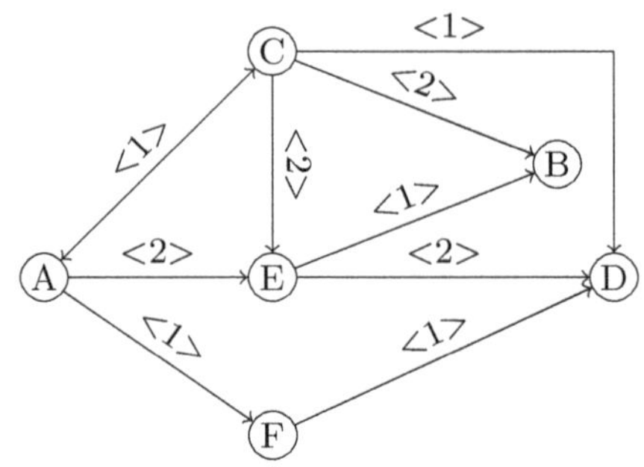

Figure 3: A sample graph

For example, a weighted directed graph is shown in Figure 3. A user-defined hash function firstly divides the vertices into two partitions: {A,B,C} and {D,E,F}. The system estimates the degree of every vertex to determine the type of Separators. In this example, the vertex 'C', whose out-degree is four, is managed by PostSeparator, while the others are managed by PreSeparator. In particular, 'C' is managed by two PostSeparators, one for edges {'CA', 'CB'} and the other for {'CD', 'CE'}. It is worth-noting that these subsets are classified by the target vertex of each edge. For instance, the edges 'CA' and 'CB' are partitioned into the same subset, as the target vertices 'A' and 'B' are owned by the first worker. It is similar that the edges 'CD' and 'CE' are on the second worker which owns vertices 'D' and 'E'.

4.2 Query Processing

The query processing engine employs a Separator-Combiner BSP model (SC-BSP). A **Combiner** is an instance of an aggregation function that aggregates the messages emanating to a same vertex. We illustrate the query processing procedure by an example of the SSSP algorithm on the graph in the previous example. The SSSP algorithm starts with a root at vertex 'A'. In Superstep 1, the distance of root vertex 'A' is initialized to '0' ; the root vertex 'A' sends messages to its neighbors 'C', 'E' and 'F'; and finally these three neighbors update their distances to '1', '2' and '1', respectively. We omit the execution of Superstep 1, but enlarge the details of the execution of Superstep 2 in Figure 4. There are two workers as depicted by the large gray rectangles. One of them contains the vertices 'A', 'B' and 'C', while the other contains the vertices 'D', 'E' and 'F'. In Superstep 2, the vertices 'C', 'E' and 'F' are the frontiers which are marked in red color, as their distances have just been updated in Superstep 1.

As shown in the example in Figure 4, the low degree vertices 'E' and 'F' are managed by PreSeparators, while the high degree vertex 'C' is controlled by two PostSeparators {'CA', 'CB'} and {'CD', 'CE'}.

A superstep consists of three parts: pre-computation, communication and post-computation. In the pre-computation of Superstep 2, the vertex 'C' broadcasts its value '1' to

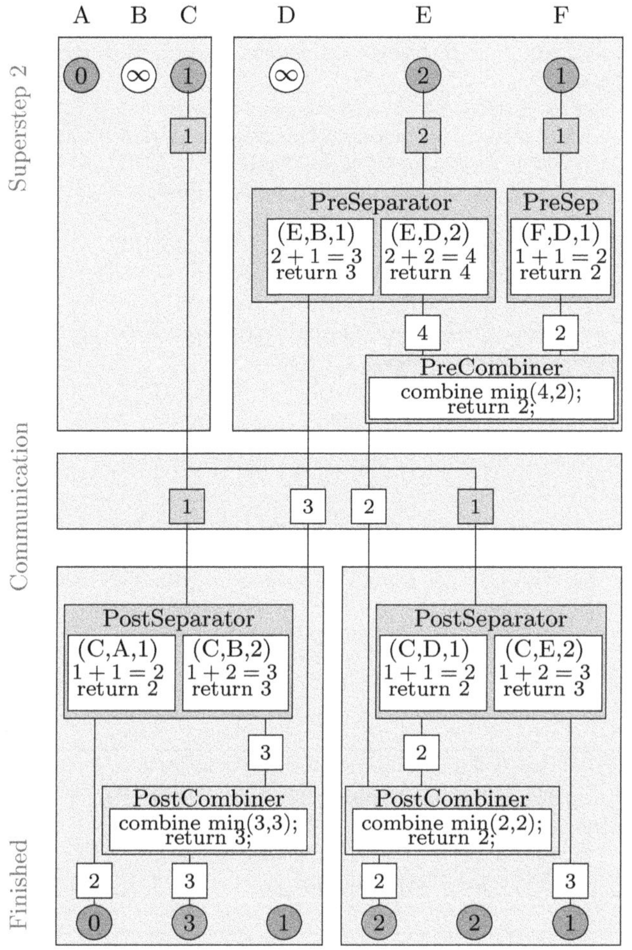

Figure 4: The query processing of Separator-Combiner BSP model: a sample superstep in the SSSP algorithm

all the workers since it is manged by PostSeparators. In the meanwhile, the vertices 'E' and 'F' call their PreSeparators to conduct **edgeCompute()** function (the API will be discussed in the next section). In the SSSP algorithm, **edgeCompute()** function adds the edge weight to the vertex value, and sends the sum to the target vertex of the edge. As the two edges 'ED' and 'FD' have the same target vertex 'D', the PreCombiner is called after the PreSeparators to combine the two messages. For the SSSP algorithm, the **MinValueCominber** merges the messages by selecting the minimum value. Then, the communication part exchanges the fours messages among two workers.

In the post-computation of Superstep 2, the PostSeparators of vertex 'C' traverse the outgoing edges of 'C' in which **edgeCompute()** function is called to add the edge weight to the vertex value for every edge. The messages produced by PostSeparators are combined by their destinations in the PostCombiners. Then, these combined messages are sent to vertices in the next superstep. In the beginning of Superstep 3, the distances of vertices 'B' and 'D' are updated, and these two vertices will become the new frontiers.

The degree threshold, which determines whether a vertex is manged by PreSeparator or PostSeparator, is user-configurable. By default, the threshold is the number of workers. The default setting can minimize the total message size in communication for most applications. We observe that there are some existing graph algorithms which are optimized by degrees. The one which is similar to our proposal is [28]. Compared with the existing algorithm, our contribution is designing a degree-based mechanism in a parallel graph processing engine, while the complexity of the design is hidden from users. Users can use GraphSlice's API to develop graph algorithms without an understanding of the underlying degree-based mechanism.

5. GRAPHSLICE'S API

In this section, we present an overview of GraphSlice's API which includes the major classes and functions. The focus of GraphSlice's API is providing an easy **Vertex-and-Edge** view to users, while the underlying degree-based mechanism for **Separator** and **Combiner** is hidden.

5.1 Basic API

The **Vertex** class of GraphSlice introduces three new features to the vertex-centric BSP model: (1) the **enum Path** which describes the message-passing paths between the vertices, (2) the template argument **SeparationType** which defines a user-specified value type for intermediate results, and (3) the concept of edge compute and **EdgeHandler** class which handles edge compute.

As shown in Algorithm 3, users override the virtual **vertexCompute()** method, which will be executed at each active vertex in every superstep. The **SendMessage()** method allows vertexCompute() to send messages to other vertices, and these messages will be received by the other vertices via **MessageIterator** in their next superstep. **SendMessage()** contains three arguments: (1) **enum Path**, which describes the destinations of this message, either the target vertex of the outgoing edges of the current vertex or all vertices in the graph, (2) **SeparationType**, which is the value type that will be passed to **EdgeHandler**, and (3) a user-defined subclass of the **EdgeHandler** class.

Algorithm 3 The Vertex API foundations

```
template <VertexType, EdgeType, MessageType,
SeparationType>
class Vertex {
  virtual void vertexCompute(MessageIterator msgs);
  long vertexID();
  boolean isSource(long vertexID);
  int superstep();
  VertexType getVertexValue();
  void setVertexValue(VertexType value);
  enum Path {OutgoingEdges, AllVertices}
  void SendMessage(Path path, SeparationType separation, Class<? extends EdgeHandler > edgeHandler);
  void VoteToHalt();
  int getNumofOutgoingEdges();
  int getNumofIncomingEdges();
  OutEdgeIterator getOutEdgeIterator();
  OutEdgeIterator getInEdgeIterator();
}
```

The **EdgeHandler** class is shown in Algorithm 4. Instead of exposing all outgoing edges in the **Vertex** class, the **EdgeHandler** class is responsible for edge compute. Users override the virtual **edgeCompute()** method which receives a **SeparationType** value from its source vertex, produces a **MessageType** value and sends the **MessageType** value to its target vertex.

Algorithm 4 The Edge API foundations

```
template <EdgeType, MessageType, SeparationType>
class EdgeHandler {
  virtual MessageType edgeCompute(SeparationType
  separation);
  int superstep();
  EdgeType getEdgeValue();
  void setEdgeValue(EdgeType value);
}
```

An example of implementing the SSSP algorithm by overriding the **Vertex** class and the **EdgeHandler** class is illustrated in Algorithm 5. For representation simplicity, we set **VertexType**, **EdgeType**, **MessageType** and **SeparationType** to **int** which is abbreviated for Integer. By overriding the **vertexCompute()** function, the algorithm firstly calls the **isSource(**long VertexID) function to get an initial value for the distance. The distance is initialized to zero if the vertex is the source (i.e. root) of the algorithm, otherwise it is assigned with a constant INF which is larger than any feasible distance. In each superstep, every vertex processes the received messages to calculate the minimum value among all the messages. If the minimum value is less than the current vertex value, the vertex updates its value and sends the updated value via the outgoing edges by specifying **OutgoingEdges** as the **Path** in the **SendMessage** method. The class type **ShortestPathEdge.class** is also specified to indicate the **EdgeHandler** of this message.

The **ShortestPathEdge** class is the **EdgeHandler** in the SSSP algorithm. It adds the vertex distance to the edge weight, and returns the sum. By default, the returned value will be sent to the target vertex of the current edge as a received message in the next superstep. The algorithm terminates when there is no update to any vertex in a superstep, at which point the value of each vertex indicates the distance from the source to that vertex.

As shown in Algorithm 6, the **Combiner** class is usually used for reducing the communication of an algorithm. A combiner combines the messages which are sent to the same vertex. For example, in the SSSP algorithm, only the minimum value of the messages is useful to the vertex. The combiner has been proposed in Pregel. But the GraphSlice's Combiner API is different from that of Pregel's, due to their difference in query processing engines. In Pregel's API, the combiner exposes all the messages, which are sent to the same vertex, as an iterator of messages to users. However, GraphSlice's API in Algorithm 6 provides a **combine()** function which always combines the original message and a newly arrived message, because its SC-BSP based query processing engine combines messages in both pre-computation and post-computation.

An example of the minimum value combiner for the SSSP algorithm is shown in Algorithm 7. If the value of a newly arrived message **msgToCombine** is less than the original message **originalMsg**, the value of the original message will be replaced by the value of the newly arrived message.

5.2 Advanced API

In consideration of ease-of-use, the **Separator** class is usually hidden from users. We provide in Algorithm 8 a default **separate()** which is usually applicable for most applications. The default **separate()** function iterates the edges in the subset, calls the **edgeCompute()** function of each edge, and sends the returned **MessageType** value to the target of each edge.

Algorithm 5 Single Source Shortest Path(SSSP)

```
class ShortestPathVertex extends Vertex <int, int, int,
int> {
  void vertexCompute(MessageIterator msgs) {
    int mindist = isSource(this.VertexID()) ? 0 : INF;
    For (;!msgs.Done();msgs.Next()) {
      mindist = min(mindist, msgs.Value());
    }
    If (superstep()==1) setVertexValue(INF);
    If (mindist < getVertexValue()) {
      setVertexValue(mindist);
      SendMessage(OutgoingEdges, mindist, Shortest-
      PathEdge.class);
    }else{
      VoteToHalt();
    }
  }
}
class ShortestPathEdge extends EdgeHandler <int, int,
int> {
  MessageType edgeCompute(SeparationType source)
  {
    return source + getEdgeValue();
  }
}
```

Algorithm 6 The Combiner API foundations

```
template <MessageType>
class Combiner {
  virtual void combine(MessageType originalMsg, Mes-
  sageType msgToCombine);
}
```

Advanced users may override the **separate()** function to implement advanced algorithms. The **Separator** class provides a set of functions to users for implementing complicated algorithms. We briefly introduce some important functions. The **getSourceVertexID()** function returns the **VertexID** of the source vertex of this subset of edges. The **isPreSeparator()** function provides the type of the separator which can be either PreSeparator (**true**) or PostSeparator (**false**). The **getNumOfSubsets()** and **getSubsetID()** functions return the number of subsets which are responsible for the same source vertex and the ID of this subset, respectively.

6. IMPLEMENTATION

We are dedicated to implementing GraphSlice as an easy-to-use, easily maintainable and scale-out capabile system on commodity clusters.

Indexing of Graph Structure. GraphSlice organizes the graph structure in the distributed memory of workers. The vertices are distributed to workers according to a user-defined Hash function. The distributed memory holds PreSepara-

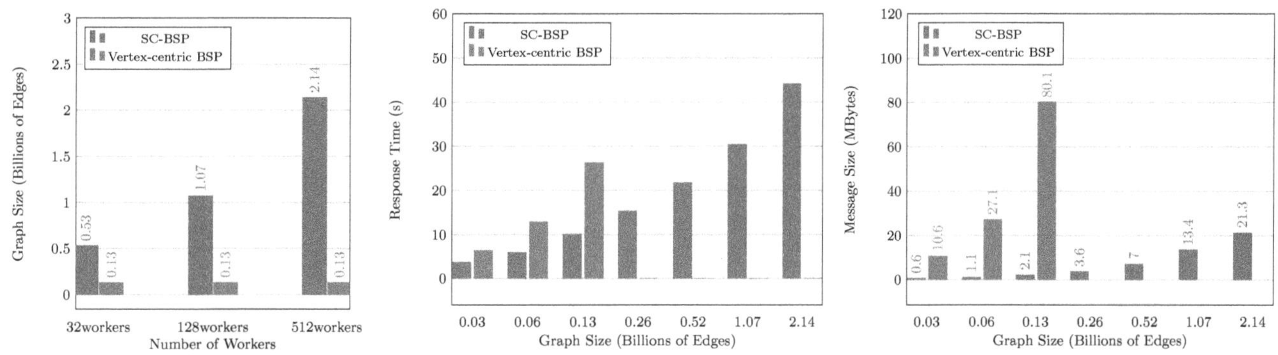

(a) Scale-out (b) Response Time (c) Communication

Figure 5: SC-BSP model *vs* vertex-centric BSP model

Algorithm 7 Minimum Value Combiner

```
class MinValueCombiner extends Combiner <int> {
  void combine(int originalMsg, int msgToCombine) {
    If (originalMsg > msgToCombine) {
      originalMsg.setValue(msgToCombine.getValue());
    }
  }
}
```

Algorithm 8 The Separator API foundations

```
template <EdgeType, MessageType ,SeparationType>
class Separator {
  void separate(EdgeIterator edges, SeparationType separation) {
    For (;!edges.Done();edges.Next()) {
      EdgeHandler edge = edges.Value();
      MessageType msg=edge.edgeCompute(separation);
      sendMessageToVertex(edge.target, msg);
    }
  }
  long getSourceVertexID();
  boolean isPreSeparator();
  long getNumOfSubsets();
  long getSubsetID();
  void sendMessageToVertex(long VertexID, MessageType msg);
}
```

tors and PostSeparators with corresponding B-tree indexes respectively. Iterating all vertices, iterating all PreSeparators and iterating all PostSeparators on a worker are also supported for advanced users. This capability enables users to develop "think like a graph" algorithms [32].

Communication. There are two alternative implementations of PostSeparators. The first is indexing the workers in which a high degree vertex has PostSeparators, and sending **SeparationType** value to the indexed workers. The second is broadcasting the **SeparationType** value of a high degree vertex to all the workers. When the outgoing edges of a high degree vertex are distributed across more workers, the efficiency produced by such indexes will be reduced. We implement the prototype of PostSeparators as a broadcasting method in order to make the code easily readable and easily maintainable.

Online Updating. Some graph mining algorithms may need to change the graph's topology in their algorithms. Online update of graph structure is supported with some constraints. GraphSlice supports setVertexValue, addVertex, removeVertex, addEdge and removeEdge functions in **Vertex** class. It also supports setEdgeValue function in **EdgeHandler** class.

Persistent Storage. GraphSlice accesses persistent storage only for input, output and checkpoints. Either general graph formats or a specific partitioned graph format can be used as an input. General graph formats are user-configurable, which include adjacency lists, edge lists and etc. When general graph formats are used as the input, GraphSlice needs to estimate the degree of every vertex to determine the type of separators. The estimation is typically calculated by randomly sampling of edges. After the estimation step, the graph structure are loaded into distributed memory, while the corresponding in-memory indexes are built on the fly.

GraphSlice is able to write the graph structure on disk in either general graph formats or the specific partitioned graph format. The specific partitioned graph format organizes the graph structure into two parts: vertices and separators. It directly writes the separators on each worker's local disk. This format is used as the format in checkpointing for fault tolerance and recovery.

Fault Tolerance and Recovery. As the query processing of GraphSlice uses a BSP model, the mechanism of fault tolerance and recovery is based on checkpointing, which is similar to Pregel's. According to a user-defined parameter T_{CP}, we make check points every T_{CP} supersteps. In these check points, the modified graph data and the buffered messages are written to the persistent file system for failure recovery. The persistent file system adopts the hadoop distributed file system (HDFS) with a configurable replication factor; that is, the file content is replicated on the storage of multiple computing nodes for reliability.

7. EXPERIMENTS

We conduct comprehensive experiments to evaluate the performance of the proposed SC-BSP model against the vertex-centric BSP model on massive degree-skewed graphs. We implement both two models as an in-memory system based on Hadoop, Netty and Giraph on an existing HDFS cluster with 128 physical machines each of which is configured with two Intel Xeon E5530 2.4GHz CPUs, 24GB memory and four 500GB SSDs. In the default settings, the number of workers is fixed to 512 such that each physical machine runs four instances of an SSSP algorithm.

We adopt the HPC benchmark Graph500 [2] with default settings to generate graphs with skewed distributions. The graph generator is a Kronecker generator [5]. The generated graphs are highly degree-skewed. For example, when the graph contains one billion vertices, the maximum out-degree of a vertex will be more than half billion.

Scale-Out Capability. The experiments in Figure 5 (a) evaluate the scale-out capability on degree-skewed social graphs. Scale-out capability means that larger graphs can be addressed by simply adding more workers to a system.

Both SC-BSP model and vertex-centric BSP model are initially allocated with 32 workers with 4GB memory on each worker. With 32 workers, SC-BSP can process graphs up to 0.5 billion edges. In contrast, vertex-centric BSP model only can process graphs up to 0.1 billion edges. Although both of the two systems own the same amount $32 \times 4\text{GB} = 128\text{GB}$ of distributed memory, SC-BSP model can process larger graph than vertex-centric BSP model because of its native load-balancing technique. As the maximum degree vertex emanates more than 10% of edges, the vertex-centric BSP model needs to keep these edges in a single worker's memory due to its vertex-centric property. SC-BSP model deploys **PostSeparators** as a container of edges, such that edges emanating from the maximum degree vertex are managed by the **PostSeparators** on different workers.

We increase the number of workers to examine if the system can address larger graphs. Vertex-centric BSP model fails to process any larger graph, as the maximum degree vertex consumes too much memory on a single worker. On the contrary, SC-BSP model can address larger graphs by simply adding more workers to the system. With 512 workers, SC-BSP model can process a graph with up to 2.1 billion edges.

Response Time. The response time is illustrated in Figure 5 (b). Because vertex-centric BSP model cannot process any graph larger than 0.13 billion edges, we only report its performance until this graph size. Within graph size they can address, both two systems shows scalable response time with respect to the number of edges.

Communication. The communication is measured by the average message size produced by each worker. Figure 5 (c) reports the comparison between two BSP models. It is not surprising that performance gap is up to 40 times, even when the graph size is relatively small. The **PreSeparators** of the SC-BSP model produce the same amount of messages as the vertex-centric BSP model. However, the **PostSeparators** exceedingly reduce the amount of messages that are produced by high degree vertices, because only the **SeperationType** value will be transfered in communication and all messages along with outgoing edges will be processed by **PostSeparators** in a same worker. In power law graphs, when increasing the size of graph, more and more edges will be connected to the existing high degree vertices. These increased edges do not produce extra messages in the SC-BSP model, thus the performance gap drastically increases with the graph size. We observe that the message size increases sublinearly with the graph size in the SC-BSP model.

Dynamic SC-BSP. When graphs are relatively small, allocating a large amount of workers may introduce cost overhead. We propose a simple optimization to reduce the cost overhead. This optimization dynamically determines the number of workers according to the graph size. In this experiment, we intuitively set this ratio to 2 million edges per worker. Therefore, we allocate 16 workers to the graph with 0.03 billion edges and 512 worker to the graph with 1.07 billion edges. For the graph with 2.14 billion edges, we still allocate 512 workers due to reaching the constraint on the maximal number of workers. Figure 6 shows Dynamic SC-BSP can reduce up to three-fourth of the response time on relatively small graphs.

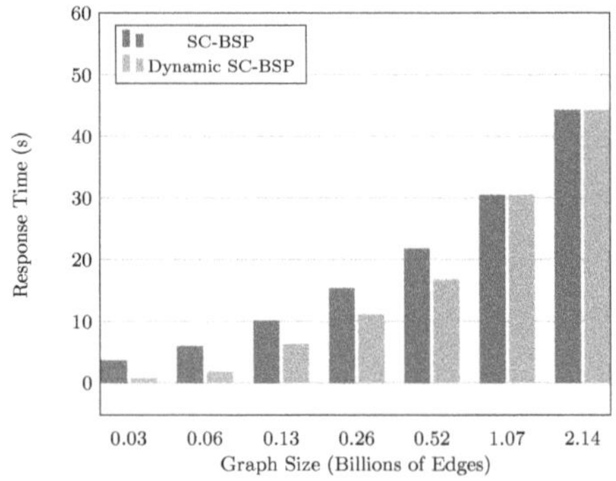

Figure 6: Dynamic worker allocation

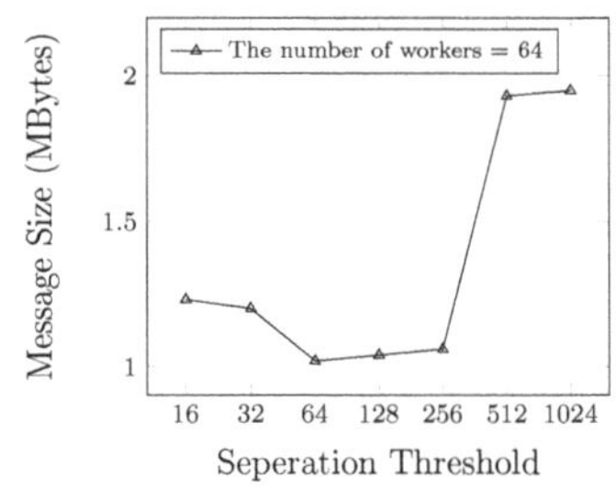

Figure 7: Varying threshold

Degree threshold. The experiments in Figure 7 verify the choice of the threshold to determine whether a vertex is managed by **PreSeparator** or **PostSeparator**. The result shows that the minimum message size is achieved when the threshold is equal to the number of workers, which is the default setting in our system.

8. RELATED WORK

This section discusses existing literature on graph-parallel computing systems, with a focus on partitioning methods of graphs and corresponding communication models of messages. As real-life graphs are often too huge to be loaded into the memory of single machines, graph-parallel computing systems divide the graph into partitions. Every worker loads a partition of the graph into its own memory, and communicates with the other workers to execute a parallel graph algorithm. Next, we organize the related work into two categories according to their partitioning methods.

8.1 1D Partitioning

Parallel BGL [10] is a generic C++ library for research. It implements 1D partitioning method on Boost Graph Library, and uses MPI for communication in a BSP model.

Pregel [18] is currently the most popular large graph processing framework. In Pregel, master is primarily responsible for coordinating workers, and also participates in the computation of *aggregators*, which is a mechanism for global communication. GPS [24] extended aggregator to a master compute mechanism, which was later adopted by Giraph [1]. In Giraph's API, the **MasterCompute** class has a `compute()` function, in which users are able to read and change aggregated values from the previous superstep; additionally, each aggregator is assigned to one of the workers such that master does not have to perform any aggregation. [25] proposed to monitor the size of the subgraph of active vertices. When the active subgraph becomes small enough, it is sent to the master to perform the remaining computation serially. [25] also discusses the optimization techniques including merging vertices to supervertices, cleaning edges on demand, etc.

It has been noted that the vertex-centric BSP model is unsuitable for the graph applications that require coordination, e.g., graph coloring. Lately, Giraphx [30] presented a modification to the BSP model to meet the aforementioned requirement by categorizing vertices as border and internal vertices. The modification allows the direct read to worker's memory for internal vertices. For border vertices, additional synchronization is implemented by adopting two alternative coordination mechanisms, e.g., dinning philosophers and token ring.

The vertex-centric BSP model is easy to program, but sacrifices the flexibility of a vertex being able to access the other vertices in the same worker. Two recent studies, Giraph++ [32] and VB-Partitioner [14], exploited the idea of sharing information in the same worker to improve efficiency. In particular, vertices in the same worker are processed in a `compute()` function together. Remarkable performance improvements can be achieved by carefully designing the algorithms, with, however, a trade-off of the ease-of-use.

High-degree vertices in a single worker are likely impose a bottleneck when processing power-law graphs, which are commonly seen in real world. The PowerGraph [9, 16] proposed to use a randomized edge partitioning approach to balance workloads. As the outgoing edges of each vertex are stored across workers, a synchronization mechanism aggregates the vertex values across all workers for all vertices in the graph. Since the aggregation is an all-to-all collective communication and the size of aggregators is proportional to the number of vertices, the scale-out capability to the number of computing nodes is hence limited.

Among others, Trinity [29] and Facebook's TAO [4] are data models for serving online queries on a large-scale graph. These systems answer graph queries with low read latency and high read availability. The applications of Trinity and TAO are quite different from the other systems which focus on high throughput offline processing. In contrast to the BSP models, [12] proposed an asynchronous model for graph processing. A comprehensive performance comparison and analysis can be found in [26].

8.2 2D Partitioning

2D partitioning was first proposed in [37] and adopted by [7, 33]. In 2D partitioning, the outgoing edges of a set of vertices are collectively owned by all the computing nodes in a row of mesh networking. We employ a level-synchronous BFS algorithm to describe how graph algorithms run on 2D partitioning. A 2D-BFS algorithm contains two steps in each superstep: (1) **Expand**: Every computing node sends the current frontier of vertices that it owns to other computing nodes in the same column as an *AllGather* operation, and inspects the outgoing edges of vertices which belong to the gathered frontier set; and (2) **Fold**: Every computing node exchanges newly-discovered vertices with the other computing nodes in the same row, and constructs the new frontiers for the next superstep.

The 2D solution handles load-balancing and scalability with a trade-off of communication cost. Indeed, the communication cost of the **Fold** step is equal to 1D partitioning's total communication cost in terms of total number of messages. The communication cost of the **Expand** step is the price we pay extra for load-balancing and scalability. Due to lacking torus networking and the a high-performance implementation of *AllGather* operation, deploying these algorithms on commodity clusters and cloud computing infrastructures can lead to inefficiency in the form of expensive communication. Moreover, implementing 2D graph algorithms requires great human effort, conflicting with the "ease-of-use" concept of big data analytics.

Note that there is another line of research on graph computation on MapReduce. This category of systems, such as Pegasus [13], Cloud9 [15], Pig Latin [19], Hive [31] and SGC [21], rely on Map and Reduce tasks for graph processing. MapReduce is often ill-suited for graph computation problems [18], and consequently can lead to suboptimal performance and usability issues. Therefore, MapReduce-based systems are beyond the scope of this paper.

9. CONCLUSION

We introduce a parallel system called GraphSlice for large-scale graph processing on commodity clusters and cloud computing infrastructures. The major contribution of this system is enabling high parallelism and scale-out capability for graph processing in real-world applications, where graphs typically have power law degree distributions. The other usability aspects such as the easy-to-use API, fault-tolenrance, recovery and portability make GraphSlice easily configurable and usable on an existing Hadoop cluster. The performance, scalability and scale-out capability of GraphSlice have been experimentally demonstrated, which is able to meet the requirements of large-scale graph processing.

10. REFERENCES

[1] Apache giraph: http://giraph.apache.org/.

[2] The graph 500 list,http://www.graph500.org/.

[3] A. Z. Broder, R. Kumar, F. Maghoul, P. Raghavan, S. Rajagopalan, R. Stata, A. Tomkins, and J. L. Wiener. Graph structure in the web. *Computer Networks*, 33(1-6):309–320, 2000.

[4] N. Bronson, Z. Amsden, G. Cabrera, P. Chakka, P. Dimov, H. Ding, J. Ferris, A. Giardullo, S. Kulkarni, H. Li, M. Marchukov, D. Petrov, L. Puzar, Y. J. Song, and V. Venkataramani. Tao: Facebook's distributed data store for the social graph. In *Presented as part of the 2013 USENIX ATC*, pages 49–60, 2013.

[5] D. Chakrabarti, Y. Zhan, and C. Faloutsos. R-mat: A recursive model for graph mining. In *SDM*, pages 442–446, 2004.

[6] E. Chan, M. Heimlich, A. Purkayastha, and R. van de Geijn. Collective communication: Theory, practice, and experience: Research articles. *Concurr. Comput. : Pract. Exper.*, 19(13):1749–1783, Sept. 2007.

[7] F. Checconi and F. Petrini. Massive data analytics: The graph 500 on ibm blue gene/q. *IBM Journal of Research and Development*, 57(1/2):10, 2013.

[8] M. Faloutsos, P. Faloutsos, and C. Faloutsos. On power-law relationships of the internet topology. In *SIGCOMM*, pages 251–262, 1999.

[9] J. E. Gonzalez, Y. Low, H. Gu, D. Bickson, and C. Guestrin. Powergraph: Distributed graph-parallel computation on natural graphs. In *Proceedings of the 10th USENIX Conference on OSDI*, pages 17–30, 2012.

[10] D. Gregor and A. Lumsdaine. The parallel bgl: A generic library for distributed graph computations. In *Parallel Object-Oriented Scientific Computing*, 2005.

[11] T. Gunarathne, J. Qiu, and D. Gannon. Towards a collective layer in the big data stack. In *CCGrid*, pages 236–245, 2014.

[12] M. Han and K. Daudjee. Giraph unchained: Barrierless asynchronous parallel execution in pregel-like graph processing systems. *PVLDB*, 8(9):950 – 961, 2015.

[13] U. Kang, C. E. Tsourakakis, and C. Faloutsos. Pegasus: mining peta-scale graphs. *Knowl. Inf. Syst.*, 27(2):303–325, 2011.

[14] K. Lee and L. Liu. Efficient data partitioning model for heterogeneous graphs in the cloud. In *SC*, page 46, 2013.

[15] J. Lin and C. Dyer. *Data-Intensive Text Processing with MapReduce.* Synthesis Lectures on Human Language Technologies. Morgan & Claypool Publishers, 2010.

[16] Y. Low, J. Gonzalez, A. Kyrola, D. Bickson, C. Guestrin, and J. M. Hellerstein. Graphlab: A new parallel framework for machine learning. In *Conference on Uncertainty in Artificial Intelligence (UAI)*, 2010.

[17] Y. Low, J. Gonzalez, A. Kyrola, D. Bickson, C. Guestrin, and J. M. Hellerstein. Distributed graphlab: A framework for machine learning in the cloud. *CoRR*, abs/1204.6078, 2012.

[18] G. Malewicz, M. H. Austern, A. J. C. Bik, J. C. Dehnert, I. Horn, N. Leiser, and G. Czajkowski. Pregel: a system for large-scale graph processing. In *SIGMOD Conference*, pages 135–146, 2010.

[19] C. Olston, B. Reed, U. Srivastava, R. Kumar, and A. Tomkins. Pig latin: a not-so-foreign language for data processing. In *SIGMOD Conference*, pages 1099–1110, 2008.

[20] J. Pjesivac-Grbovic, T. Angskun, G. Bosilca, G. E. Fagg, E. Gabriel, and J. Dongarra. Performance analysis of mpi collective operations. pages 127–143, 2007.

[21] L. Qin, J. Yu, L. Chang, H. Cheng, C. Zhang, and X. Lin. Scalable big graph processing in mapreduce. In *SIGMOD Conference*, pages 827–838, 2014.

[22] M. Redekopp, Y. Simmhan, and V. K. Prasanna. Optimizations and analysis of bsp graph processing models on public clouds. *Parallel and Distributed Processing Symposium, International*, 0:203–214, 2013.

[23] S. Redner. How popular is your paper? an empirical study of the citation distribution. *European Physical Journal B*, 4(2):131–134, Aug. 1998.

[24] S. Salihoglu and J. Widom. Gps: A graph processing system. In *SSDBM*, 2013.

[25] S. Salihoglu and J. Widom. Optimizing graph algorithms on pregel-like systems. In *PVLDB*, 2014.

[26] N. Satish, N. Sundaram, M. M. A. Patwary, J. Seo, J. Park, M. A. Hassaan, S. Sengupta, Z. Yin, and P. Dubey. Navigating the maze of graph analytics frameworks using massive graph datasets. In *SIGMOD Conference*, pages 979–990, 2014.

[27] S. Seo, E. J. Yoon, J. Kim, S. Jin, J.-S. Kim, and S. Maeng. Hama: An efficient matrix computation with the mapreduce framework. In *CloudCom*, pages 721–726, 2010.

[28] H. Shang and M. Kitsuregawa. Efficient breadth-first search on large graphs with skewed degree distributions. In *Joint 2013 EDBT/ICDT Conferences*, pages 311–322, 2013.

[29] B. Shao, H. Wang, and Y. Li. Trinity: A distributed graph engine on a memory cloud. In *SIGMOD Conference*, pages 505–516, 2013.

[30] S. Tasci and M. Demirbas. Giraphx: Parallel yet serializable large-scale graph processing. In *Proceedings of the 19th International Conference on Parallel Processing*, Euro-Par'13, pages 458–469, Berlin, Heidelberg, 2013. Springer-Verlag.

[31] A. Thusoo, J. S. Sarma, N. Jain, Z. Shao, P. Chakka, N. Zhang, S. Anthony, H. Liu, and R. Murthy. Hive - a petabyte scale data warehouse using hadoop. In *ICDE*, pages 996–1005, 2010.

[32] Y. Tian, A. Balmin, S. A. Corsten, S. Tatikonda, and J. McPherson. From "think like a vertex" to "think like a graph". *PVLDB*, 7(3):193–204, 2013.

[33] K. Ueno and T. Suzumura. 2d partitioning based graph search for the graph500 benchmark. In *IPDPS Workshops*, pages 1925–1931, 2012.

[34] L. G. Valiant. A bridging model for parallel computation. *Commun. ACM*, 33(8):103–111, Aug. 1990.

[35] T. White. *Hadoop - The Definitive Guide: Storage and Analysis at Internet Scale.* O'Reilly, 2012.

[36] R. S. Xin, J. E. Gonzalez, M. J. Franklin, and I. Stoica. Graphx: a resilient distributed graph system on spark. In *GRADES*, page 2, 2013.

[37] A. Yoo, E. Chow, K. W. Henderson, W. M. III, B. Hendrickson, and Ü. V. Çatalyürek. A scalable distributed parallel breadth-first search algorithm on bluegene/l. In *SC*, page 25, 2005.

[38] M. Zaharia, M. Chowdhury, M. J. Franklin, S. Shenker, and I. Stoica. Spark: Cluster computing with working sets. In *Proceedings of the 2Nd USENIX Conference on HotCloud*, pages 10–10, 2010.

Identifying Top-k Structural Hole Spanners in Large-Scale Social Networks

Mojtaba Rezvani[†] Weifa Liang[†] Wenzheng Xu[†‡] Chengfei Liu[¶]

† Australian National University, Canberra, ACT 0200, Australia
‡ Sichuan University, Chengdu, P. R. China
¶ Swinburne University of Technology, Melbourne, VIC, Australia
mojtaba.rezvani@anu.edu.au, wliang@cs.anu.edu.au, wenzheng.xu3@gmail.com, cliu@swin.edu.au

ABSTRACT

Recent studies have shown that in social networks, users who bridge different communities, known as structural hole spanners, have great potentials to acquire available resources from these communities and gain access to multiple sources of information flow. Structural hole spanners are crucial in many applications such as community detections, diffusion controls, and viral marketing. In spite of their importance, not much attention has been paid to them. Particularly, how to characterize the structural hole spanner properties and how to devise efficient yet scalable algorithms to find them are fundamental issues. In this paper, we formulate the problem as the top-k structural hole spanner problem. Specifically, we first provide a generic model to measure the quality of structural hole spanners, by exploring their properties, and show that the problem is NP-hard. We then devise efficient and scalable algorithms, by exploiting the bounded inverse closeness centralities of vertices and making use of articulation points of the network. We finally evaluate the performance of the proposed algorithms through extensive experiments on real and synthetic datasets, and validate the effectiveness of the proposed model. Our experimental results demonstrate that the proposed model can capture the characteristics of structural hole spanners accurately, and the proposed algorithms are very promising.

Categories and Subject Descriptors

H.2.8 [**Database Management**]: Database Applications; J.4 [**Social and Behavioral Sciences**]: Miscellaneous

Keywords

Social networks, Top-k structural hole spanners, Linear-time algorithms, Inverse closeness centrality, Articulation points

1. INTRODUCTION

The last decade experienced an exponential growth of a variety of large-scale networks such as social networks, citation networks, biological networks, wireless networks, etc. Thus, there are high demands for developing efficient algorithms to explore some unique properties of such networks. Most social networks exhibit the so-called community structure property, that is, the vertices in a network can be grouped into different sets of cohesive groups (communities) [10], where vertices in the same community share similar attributes. The communities play a significant role in information diffusion within the network, information within a community circulates very quickly and diffuses to other communities through community boundaries or bridges. On the other hand, there is a consensus among social scientists [7] that a person who plays a bridge role between different communities can acquire more potential resources from these communities and has more control over the information that is being transmitted. Burt [7] studied social structures of many organizations and introduced the notion of *structural holes* as positions that can bridge diverse groups and bring benefits to the beholder. It is shown that information within a single community tends to be homogeneous. Non-redundant information is often obtained through the contacts between different communities [23]. Therefore, a person who develops relations with people from multiple communities will gain more benefits. *Structural hole spanners* were studied initially by Lou *et al.* [19], as a few people who fill the structural holes can bridge different communities. For example, a community in an academic collaboration network represents the group of people with the similar research interests, and people (structural hole spanners) who bridge different communities are more potent to combine ideas from different research groups and create interdisciplinary works. Structural hole spanners have a wide range of applications. For example, in community detection, identifying central hubs that connect different groups can help isolate and identify communities [2, 29]. In Epidemic diseases and rumors spreading, quarantining structural hole spanners can stop the spread of infection and rumors into other communities [6, 12, 20]. In viral marketing, the most influential structural hole spanners can speed-up the new product marketings to different groups [15, 26, 25, 31].

Since structural hole spanners are fundamental in many applications, several models have been proposed for it [11, 17, 19, 24]. For example, Lou *et al.* [19] introduced a model for structural hole spanners, and proposed two algorithms based on the model, by assuming that communities are given already. However, their work relies on communities while finding communities in a large-scale network is painstaking. Moreover, the quality of the solution delivered by their algo-

CIKM'15, October 19–23, 2015, Melbourne, Australia.
ACM 978-1-4503-3794-6/15/10.
DOI: http://dx.doi.org/10.1145/2806416.2806431.

rithm is determined by the chosen communities. There are other studies that aim to discover the structural hole spanners from a social network, using the topological structure of the network. Goyal *et al.* [11] considered a structural hole spanner as a vertex that lies on a large number of shortest paths, which is similar to betweenness centrality. Tang *et al.* [24] formulated structural hole spanners as the vertices which lie on a large number of shortest paths of length two only. These models however failed to capture some essential properties of structural hole spanners, which is illustrated by Fig. 1. As can be seen, vertex v_1, rather than vertex v_2, lies on a large number of shortest paths of length two, vertex v_2, instead of vertex v_1 is a better structural hole spanner as it bridges more communities.

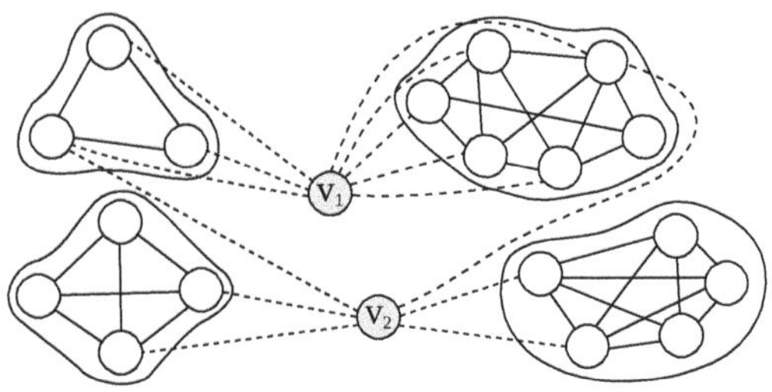

Figure 1: Illustration of structural hole spanners; each closed area represents a community, and vertices v_1, v_2 represent structural hole spanners that span multiple communities.

One of the implications of structural hole spanners is that they bridge different communities and the shortest paths between those communities go through them. Therefore, their removal will increase the length of shortest path between other vertices. For example, vertex v_1 in Fig. 1 plays a key role in the shortest paths between the nodes in different communities and its removal can significantly change the length between the other nodes, while the impact of the removal of other vertices on shortest paths is insignificant. In this paper, we propose a model based on the *mean distance* of the network [5] for modeling the structural hole spanners, which is the average of the lengths of all pairs of vertices in the network. We consider the structural hole spanners problem as a set of vertices whose removal will result in the maximum increase on the mean distance of the network, and we term *the top-k structural holes problem* as the problem of finding a set of k vertices whose removal will make the increase on the mean distance maximized. To the best of our knowledge, this is the first time that a novel, top-k structural hole spanner problem is formulated and its NP-hardness is proven. Unlike most existing works that assume that either all communities are given or rely on community detection algorithms to find them first, our model relies on the network topological structure only.

The main contributions of this paper are as follows. We study the top-k structural hole spanner problem in a large-scale social network. We first formulate the problem as an optimization problem and show its NP-hardness. We then devise two efficient, yet scalable algorithms, by exploiting the small-world phenomenon and using the bounded inverse of closeness centrality of vertices and using articulation points in the network. We finally evaluate the performance of the proposed algorithms by extensive experiments on real and synthetic datasets. Experimental results show that the structural hole spanners delivered by the proposed algorithms can connect more and larger communities in comparison with that by other existing methods in real datasets. Moreover, using a synthetic datasets, we show that the proposed algorithms can accurately find the structural hole spanners. Furthermore, our evaluations show that the proposed algorithms outperform the other heuristics in terms of accuracy and running time.

The rest of this paper is organized as follows. Section 2 introduces basic notations, and the problem definition. Section 3 shows the NP-hardness of the problem. Section 4 proposes algorithms for the problem. Section 5 evaluates the performance of the proposed algorithms, using real and synthetic datasets. Section 6 reviews related works on structural hole spanners, and Section 7 concludes the paper.

2. PRELIMINARIES AND DEFINITIONS

2.1 Network Model

A social network can be modeled as an undirected connected graph $G = (V, E)$, where V is the set of vertices representing individuals and E is the set of edges representing the relationships between individuals. Let $n = |V|$ and $m = |E|$. The degree of a vertex v is the number of its neighbors, denoted by $\deg(v)$. Maximum degree of vertices in G is denoted by $\Delta(G)$.

Given two vertices $u, v \in V$, the *vertex connectivity* $\kappa^G(u, v)$ in G between them is the minimum number of vertex-disjoint paths. Vertices u and v are referred to as *k-vertex-connected* if they are still connected after the removal of no more than k vertices from G. A graph G is *k-vertex-connected* if any pair of vertices in it is k-vertex-connected. A vertex is an *articulation point* of G if its removal will disconnect the graph.

As G is an unweighted graph, we assume that each edge has a weight of 1, and we term each edge $e \in E$ as a *real edge*. The distance d^G_{uv} between two vertices u and v in G is the length of the shortest path between them. We assume that $d^G_{vv} = 0$ for any vertex $v \in V$. Given a subset V_S of V, let $G[V \setminus V_S]$ be the induced subgraph of G by the vertices in $V \setminus V_S$. We abbreviate $G[V \setminus V_S]$ by $G \setminus V_S$. The *inverse closeness centrality* of a vertex v in G is the average distance between vertex v and other vertices [5], i.e.,

$$c(v) = \frac{\sum_{u \in V} d^G_{uv}}{n-1}. \tag{1}$$

The mean distance of a graph G thus is defined as follows.

$$c(G) = \frac{\sum_{v \in V} c(v)}{|V|} = \frac{\sum_{v \in V}\sum_{u \in V} d^G_{uv}}{(n-1)|V|} = \frac{\sum_{v \in V}\sum_{u \in V} d^G_{uv}}{n(n-1)}. \tag{2}$$

The sum of lengths of all pairs shortest paths in G is

$$C(G) = \sum_{u \in V}\sum_{v \in V} d^G_{uv} = n(n-1)c(G). \tag{3}$$

Note that if G is disconnected, to make the mean distance of G still be valid, the distance between two vertices not in the same connected component is defined by a sufficiently large value ζ to avoid the infinite distance. This value should be larger than the sum of lengths of all pairs of shortest paths in any connected component of G, e.g., $\zeta = n^3$, as the upper bound on the sum of lengths of all pairs shortest paths in a n-vertex graph is no more than $\zeta/3$ [22].

2.2 Problem Definition

Given a social network $G = (V, E)$ and a positive integer k, the top-k *structural hole spanner problem* in G is to find a subset of vertices V_S ($V_S \subset V$) with $|V_S| = k$, such that the removal of the vertices in V_S from G will result in the maximum increase on the sum of the lengths of all pairs of shortest paths among the vertices in the induced subgraph $G \setminus V_S$, i.e., the problem objective is to

$$\max_{V_S \subset V,\ |V_S|=k} \{C(G \setminus V_S) - C(G)\}, \quad (4)$$

which is equivalent to

$$\max_{V_S \subset V,\ |V_S|=k} \{C(G \setminus V_S)\}. \quad (5)$$

Since communities are dense, the distance between vertices within each community is small and the member removal does not change the distance between the other members considerably. In contrast, the removal of top-k structural hole spanners in a network will result in the maximum number of communities disconnected in comparison with other k-vertex removals, thereby significantly increasing the mean distance of network. Fig. 1 illustrates the impact of removal of structural hole spanners on the distances. Specifically, the proposed model captures three important characteristics of structural hole spanners.

1. Given an individual u who bridges multiple communities and another individual v who contacts with people only in his/her community, individual u is considered by the model to be a better structural hole spanner than individual v, since the connections among individuals within the communities to which individual v belongs are strong, and the absence of v only slightly increases the distance among other individuals in the network. In contrast, individual u connects people who are in different communities, thus the absence of u can dramatically increase the distance between them, as they are loosely connected.
2. Given an individual u who bridges large communities and an individual v who bridges small communities, individual u is considered to be a better structural hole spanner than individual v, since the removal of u will disconnect more people in the network.
3. Given an individual u who bridges many communities and an individual v who bridges only a few, individual u is considered to be a better structural hole spanner, since the removal of u can increase the distance between more communities (even if they are smaller).

3. NP-HARDNESS

In this section we show that the top-k structural hole spanner problem is NP-hard by a reduction from an NP-hard problem - the *Most Vital Node Problem* (MVNP) [4], defined as follows. Given an undirected graph $G = (V \cup \{s, t\}, E)$, a pair of nodes s and t, and a positive integer k, assume that there is no edge in G connecting vertices s and t and the vertex connectivity $\kappa^G(s, t)$ between vertices s and t is no less than $k + 1$, the problem is to find a subset V_S of V with $|V_S| = k$ such that the length of the shortest path between s and t in subgraph $G[(V \setminus V_S) \cup \{s, t\}]$ of G is maximized. The rest is to show that the problem is NP-hard by a reduction from the MVNP by the following theorem.

THEOREM 1. *The top-k structural hole spanner problem is NP-hard.*

SKETCH OF THE PROOF. Given an instance of MVNP in an undirected graph $G = (V \cup \{s, t\}, E)$ with $n = |V \cup \{s, t\}|$, a pair of vertices s and t in G, and a positive integer k, an instance of top-k structural hole spanner problem in another undirected graph $G' = (V \cup S \cup T, E')$ can be constructed as follows. Let $l = 4n^6$. Sets of vertices S and T are obtained by duplicating vertices s and t, each l times, i.e., $S = \{s_1, s_2, \ldots, s_l\}$ and $T = \{t_1, t_2, \ldots, t_l\}$. For any two different vertices $u, v \in V$, an edge (u, v) is added to E' if an edge $(u, v) \in E$. For each vertex $v \in V$, l edges $(v, s_1), (v, s_2), \ldots,$ and (v, s_l) (or $(v, t_1), (v, t_2), \ldots,$ and (v, t_l)) are added to E' if edge (v, s) (or (v, t)) is contained in E. The construction of G' is illustrated in Fig. 2. Clearly, it can be verified that $\kappa^{G'}(s_j, t_j) = \kappa^G(s, t)$ for any vertex $s_j \in S$ and any vertex $t_j \in T$ and $d^{G'}_{uv} = d^G_{uv}$ for every pair of vertices u and v.

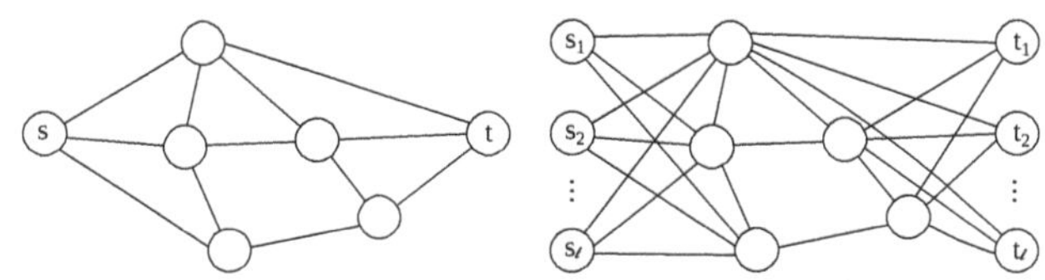

Figure 2: G' is constructed from G by replicating vertices s and t and their incident edges l times.

The MVNP in $G = (V \cup \{s, t\}, E)$ can be reduced to the structural hole spanner problem in G' as follows. We first show that the optimal solution to the problem in G' does not contain any vertex s_i or t_i. We prove so by showing that for every given solution V_S of the problem for G', if V_S contains a vertex s_i or t_j, we can construct another set V'_S such that the mean distance of $G' \setminus V'_S$ is strictly larger than $G \setminus V_S$. Since, $\kappa^{G'}(s_i, t_j) > k$, therefore, there exist at least one path from s_i to t_j in $G' \setminus V_S$, thus we replace one s_i or t_j in V_S by a vertex that lies on the shortest path between s_i and t_j in $G \setminus V_S$ to obtain V'_S. We then prove that every feasible solution V_S of the MVNP problem is optimal if and only if it is the optimal solution for the problem in G', otherwise, we show a contradiction to the optimality by finding another set V'_S such that $d^{G \setminus V'_S}_{st} > d^{G \setminus V_S}_{st}$.

Due to space limit, the detailed version of the proof is deferred to the full version of this paper. □

4. ALGORITHMS FOR TOP-k STRUCTURAL HOLE SPANNER PROBLEM

In this section, we devise efficient algorithms for the top-k structural hole spanner problem. We first consider a greedy approach for the problem and improve the efficiency by simplifying the objective function. We start with a basic algorithm, using the inverse closeness centrality of vertices. We then develop a faster algorithm, by exploring the bounded inverse closeness centrality of vertices. We finally propose a fast, scalable algorithm by utilizing both articulation points and the bounded inverse closeness centrality of vertices.

4.1 The basic Algorithm

A structural hole spanner in a social network usually spans multiple communities, thus the sum of distances between the spanner and the other vertices should not be larger than the sum of distances between an ordinary vertex and the other members in the network. The mean distance of the network after the removal of a vertex $v \in V$ thus is

$$c(G \setminus \{v\}) = \frac{n(n-1)c(G) - 2\sum_{u \in V} d^G_{uv}}{(n-1)(n-2)} + \frac{\sum_{u,w \in V} (d^{G\setminus\{v\}}_{uw} - d^G_{uw})}{(n-1)(n-2)}, \quad (6)$$

where the value of $n(n-1)c(G)$ is the same for every vertex in G. If we only consider the first term in Eq. (6) as the dominant term, it can be implied that the shorter the distance between v and others, the more likely vertex v is to maximize the mean distance in the graph - the inverse closeness centrality of a vertex. We will use this metric as a measure to find the top-k structural hole spanners in G. Specifically, the algorithm proceeds iteratively. The set of hole spanners V_S is empty initially, within each iteration, a new hole spanner $v \in V \setminus V_S$ is found and added to V_S, if its inverse closeness centrality $c(v)$ is the smallest among vertices in $V \setminus V_S$. This procedure continues until the number of vertices in V_S becomes k. The detailed algorithm is described as follows.

Algorithm 1 `ICC`

Input: $G = (V, E), k$
Output: The set V_S of top-k structural hole spanners

$V_S \leftarrow \emptyset$;
build a priority queue Q of top k hole spanners with the key of each element in Q; is its inverse closeness centrality;
for each vertex $v \in V$ **do**
  calculate the inverse closeness centrality $c(v)$ of v;
  if $|Q| < k$ **then**
    add v to Q;
  else if $c(v)$ is less than the largest key in Q **then**
    remove the largest key element from Q;
    add v to Q;
$V_S \leftarrow Q$.

We refer to Algorithm 1 based the Inverse Closeness Centrality of vertices as Algorithm `ICC` for short.

The dominant running time of Algorithm 1 is to find a single source shortest path tree for each source vertex $v \in V$, which takes $O(m + n)$ time, using the BFS traversal on G. Algorithm 1 thus takes $O(nm + n \log k) = O(mn)$ time, where the $\log k$ factor in the second term is the time of each priority operation in priority queue Q. Despite Algorithm 1 is efficient, its time complexity is still quite high for a large-scale network that contains millions or billion of vertices. A challenging question then is whether this time complexity can be further significantly improved, e.g. a linear-time complexity, while the solution quality is not inversely compromised. In the following we answer this question affirmatively by devising two efficient algorithms for the problem.

4.2 Algorithm based on the bounded inverse closeness centrality

Most real world social networks follow two important facts: one is the sparsity. The number of neighbors of each vertex is constant, which does not proportionally grow with the network size [3]; another follows the small world law: the expected distance between any pair of vertices is a small constant, not proportional to the network size [16, 30]. Thus, instead of finding the single source shortest path tree for each vertex that includes all vertices in G, it suffices to find a *partial shortest path tree* for the vertex that reaches up to a given level of neighbors, where the neighbors of a vertex is its *level-1 neighbors*, the neighbors of its neighbors is its level-2 neighbors, and so on. We term the partial shortest path tree spanning up to level-l neighbors of v as the *l-bounded shortest tree* $T_l(v)$, and the *l-bounded inverse closeness centrality* of v thus is defined as

$$c_l(v) = \sum_{u \in T_l(v)} d^G_{uv}/(n-1). \quad (7)$$

We here adopt the similar metric as Algorithm 1, the only difference between this algorithm and Algorithm 1 is to choose K vertices with top-K *largest* l-bounded inverse closeness centrality, rather than the k vertices with top-k *smallest* inverse closeness centralities in Algorithm 1, assuming that $K \geq k$. The rationale behind is that if a vertex (as a source) can reach a larger portion of vertices in a network within a small distance l, then its average distance to other vertices is shorter. To explore the diversity among vertices and to mitigate two neighbors to be chosen as the top-k structural hole spanners at the same time, the number of candidates K for the top-k hole spanners can be larger than k, e.g., $K = ck$ ($c \geq 1$). We then calculate the inverse closeness centralities of these K vertices in G, and choose the top-k smallest ones as the top-k structural hole spanners of the network. Specifically, the proposed algorithm proceeds as follows.

Algorithm 2 `BICC`

Input: $G = (V, E), k, K, l$
Output: The set of top-k structural hope spanners V_S

build a priority queue H with the bounded inverse closeness as the key of each element in H;
build a priority queue V_S with the inverse closeness as the key of each element in V_S;
for each vertex $v \in V$ **do**
  calculate the bounded inverse closeness centrality $c_l(v)$ of v, using BFS search;
  if $|H| < K$ **then**
    add v to H;
  else if $c_l(v)$ is larger than the smallest key in H **then**
    remove the smallest key element from H;
    add v to H;
for each vertex $v \in H$ **do**
  calculate the inverse closeness centrality $c(v)$ of v;
  if $|V_S| < k$ **then**
    add v to V_S;
  else if $c(v)$ is less than the largest key in V_S **then**
    remove the largest key element from V_S;
    add v to V_S;
return V_S.

It first identifies K vertices with top-K largest l-bounded inverse closeness centralities, starting at each vertex $v \in V$, using the BFS traversal on G. Assume that $c_l(v)$ is the sum of the lengths of shortest paths from each vertex within the l-neighborhood of vertex v. Let H be the set of top-K vertices with top-K largest bounded inverse closeness centralities. It then calculates the inverse closeness centrality $c(v)$ of v, for each vertex $v \in H$, using the BFS technique on G. It finally identifies the k vertices from the K chosen vertices with top-k smallest inverse closeness centralities of the vertices. We refer to Algorithm 2 based the Bounded Inverse Closeness Centrality of vertices as algorithm `BICC` for short. The rest is to analyze its time complexity by the following theorem.

THEOREM 2. *Given an undirected connected graph $G = (V, E)$ with constant maximum degree and positive integers k and l, there is a fast, scalable algorithm, Algorithm 2, for the bounded inverse closeness centrality in G, which takes $O(m+n)$ time, where $n = |V|$ and $m = |E|$.*

PROOF. Assume that G is represented by adjacency lists of its vertices. Following Algorithm 2, it first constructs a partial shortest path tree $T_l(v)$ rooted at v for each vertex $v \in V$ using BFS, which takes $O(\sum_{i=1}^{l} d_{max}^{i}) = O(d_{max}^{l+1})$ time, where d_{max} is the maximum degree of vertices in G. It then identifies the top-K vertices with the largest bounded inverse closeness centrality, which takes $O(\log K)$ time for each vertex insertion into the priority queue H. Therefore, it takes $O(nd_{max}^{l+1}) = O(m+n)$ time for finding the set H as both d_{max} and l are small constants, in comparison with the network size n. Identifying set V_S takes $O(K(n+m)+K\log k)$ time, due to the BFS search in G for each candidate vertex in H, and the addition of the candidate vertex to set V_S, where V_S is maintained as a priority queue. Therefore, the time complexity of Algorithm 2 is $O(K(n+m)+K\log K) = O(m+n)$ as $K = ck$ usually is constant. □

Note that in real social networks the number of neighbours of an individual is a small constant which is not proportional to the network size.

4.3 A fast and scalable algorithm

So far, we have provided an algorithm based on the inverse closeness centrality and devised an efficient algorithm by approximating the inverse closeness centrality of each vertex, through the introduction of l-bounded inverse closeness centrality concept. In the following, we take the second term of Eq. (6) into account and devise another efficient algorithm which further speeds up the running time in practice, by exploring articulation points of G.

One of the instinct properties of structural hole spanners in most real social networks is their tendency to connect multiple isolated communities. Such hole spanners are referred to the *articulation points* in graph theory. Thus, a top-k structural hole spanner usually is an articulation point too. However, the number of articulation points in real social networks is quite large, e.g., the number of articulation points in each network of Table 1 is at least 10% of the number of vertices in the network. How to identify top-k structural hole spanners from all articulation points in a large-scale network is a challenging issue. In the following, we shall devise a fast yet scalable algorithm for the top-k structural hole spanner problem, by exploring the articulation points and using the bounded inverse closeness centrality of vertices.

LEMMA 1. *[22] Let G be an unweighted graph $G = (V, E)$ with $n = |V|$ vertices, then the sum of lengths of all pairs shortest paths in G is no more than $n^3/3$.*

Given two vertices u and v that are not in the same connected component of G, we assume that there is a *virtual edge* in G between them with weight larger than the sum of lengths of all pairs of shortest paths in G, and we assign this virtual edge with a weight $w(u, v) = cn^3$ with $c \geq 1/3$. For the sake of convenience, we set $c = 1$ in the rest of discussion. Assume that v is an articulation point in G, we distinguish into two cases as follows.

Case one: if the removal of v results in two connected components CC_1 and CC_2. Let CC_i contain n_i vertices. The weighted sum of all virtual edges resulting from the removal of v is $n_1 \times (n-n_1)cn^3 + n_2 \times (n-n_2)cn^3 = cn^3(nn_1 + nn_2 - n_1^2 - n_2^2)$. Clearly, when $n_1 \approx n_2$, the weighted sum is maximized. This implies that an articulation point is likely to be a top-k hole spanner if its removal results in two large connected components.

Case two: if the removal of v results in l connected components $CC_1, CC_2, \ldots, CC_l$ with $l > 2$. Let CC_i contain n_i vertices ($1 \leq i \leq l$). Let $n = \sum_{i=1}^{l} n_i$. Then, the weighted sum of virtual edges between vertices in CC_i and CC_j is $\sum_{i=1}^{l}\sum_{j=1}^{l} n_i n_j cn^3 = cn^3 \sum_{i=1}^{l} n_i(n-n_i)$, which is maximized when all components have roughly equal sizes.

Following the analysis of these two cases, it can be seen that an articulation point in G is likely to be one of top-k structural hole spanner if its inverse closeness centrality is maximized, which approximately equals the weighted sum of virtual edges resulting from its removal, since the sum of all pairs shortest paths in each connected component is much less than the weight of each virtual edge. We now propose a fast, scalable algorithm by exploring the inverse closeness centralities of articulation points. Specifically, the algorithm consists of two stages. Let A be the set of articulation points in G. If $|A| < k$, the algorithm will proceed the second stage after the first stage. Within the first stage, there is a number of iterations. An articulation point within each iteration will be chosen as a top-k hole spanner. In the second stage, Algorithm 2 will be invoked to find the rest of top-k structural hole spanners. The detailed algorithm is described in Algorithm 3.

Algorithm 3 AP_BICC

Input: $G = (V, E), k, K, l$
Output: The set of top-k structural hole spanners V_S

```
build a priority queue V_S of top-K approximate inverse closeness candidates with the key of each element in V_S;
let A be the set of articulation points in G, which can be found by invoking Procedure 1;
for each vertex v ∈ A do
    find the approximate inverse closeness centrality c'(v);
    if |V_S| < k then
        add v to V_S;
    else if c'(v) is larger than the smallest key in V_S then
        remove the smallest key element from V_S;
        add v to V_S;
if |V_S| < k then /* the number of APs is less than k */
    U ← V \ A;
    k' ← k − |V_S|;
    build a priority queue Q of K elements with the key of each element in U being its l-bounded inverse closeness centrality;
while |V_S| ≠ k do
    extract the the element v with largest key from Q;
    add v to V_S;
return V_S.
```

We refer to Algorithm 3 based on Articulation Points and Bounded Inverse Closeness Centrality of vertices as Algorithm AP_BICC for short. We now show the articulation point finding and their approximate inverse closeness centrality, $c'(v)$, for each $v \in A$ can be efficiently calculated, using a Depth-First Search (DFS) traversal on G.

Let v be an articulation point of G, in the DFS tree construction starting from a vertex v, assume that $u_1, u_2, \ldots, u_p$ be the children of vertex v in the DFS tree. Let V_i be the set of vertices in the subtree T_i rooted at u_i and CC_i the connected component of G induced by the vertices in V_i with

$1 \leq i \leq p$. Let CC_0 be the connected component containing the ancestors of v in the DFS tree. Following the DFS search property, all edges in G can be partitioned into "tree edges" and "non-tree edges", respectively. And all non-tree edges are "back edges", which means that one endpoint of the edge is a descendant while another endpoint of the edge is a proper ancestor of v in the DFS tree. Clearly, there is no edges between any two connected components CC_i and CC_j with $i \neq j$ and $1 \leq i, j \leq p$, by the DFS traversal property. If there is a back edge between a vertex in V_i and a vertex in CC_0, then both CC_i and CC_0 are the same connected component when the removal of v from G, $1 \leq i \leq p$. An illustration of this case is shown in Fig 3.

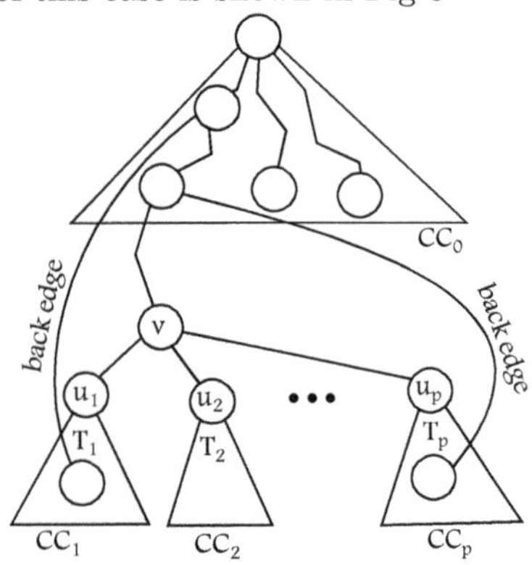

Figure 3: An illustration of exploring an articulation point v and its p children $u_1, u_2, \ldots, u_p$ during a DFS traversal on G.

Assume that there are p' CCs among the p CCs derived from p children of v have back edges. Then, the removal of v will result in $p - p'$ CCs. For the sake of convenience, we assume that these $p-p'$ CCs are $CC'_1, CC'_2, \ldots, CC'_{p-p'}$ with each having n'_i vertices. The approximate inverse closeness centrality of v then is

$$c'(v) \approx \sum_{i=1}^{p-p'} |CC'_i| \cdot (n - |CC'_i| - 1) \cdot n^3. \quad (8)$$

The linear-time procedure of detecting each articulation point and the calculation of its approximate inverse closeness centrality is then detailed as follows. A vertex v is identified as an articulation point of G if a subtree rooted at one of its children does not contain any back edges. The induced subgraph by the set of vertices in this subtree is a connected component after the removal of vertex v from G. The number of vertices contained in each such connected component is the number of descendants of that child in the DFS tree. To keep track of the number of descendants of each vertex when performing the DFS traversal on G and to identify those children of the vertex without any back edges, the approximate inverse closeness centrality of v (as an articulation point) can be easily calculated. The detailed implementation of this is given in Procedure 1 and Procedure 2.

THEOREM 3. *Given a graph $G(V, E)$ with constant maximum degree and an integer $k > 0$, Algorithm 3 takes time $O(n \log k + m) = O(m + n)$ as k is a constant.*

PROOF. Following Algorithm 3, the detection of all articulation points and the calculation of their approximate inverse closeness centralities takes $O(n + m)$ time by Procedure 1.

Procedure 1 Articulation points and their approximate inverse closeness centrality calculation

```
for each vertex u ∈ V do
    /* the number of children of u */
    u.child ← 0;
    /* each vertex has 3 colors white/grey/black */
    u.color ← white;
    c'(u) ← 0;
time ← 0;
for each vertex u ∈ V do
    if u.color == white then
        call Modified-DFS(G,u) /* Procedure 2 */;
```

Procedure 2 Modified-DFS(G, u)

```
u.color ← black;
time ← time + 1;
/* the discovered time of vertex u */
u.discovered ← time;
/* the smallest discovered time of any neighbor of u's descen-
dants (through a back-edge) */
u.lowest ← time;
/* the number of vertices in CC0 after removing u */
cc0 ← n;
/* the number of descendants of u in DFS tree */
u.descendant ← 0;
for all (u, v) ∈ E do
    if u.color == white then
        u.color ← grey;
        v.π ← u /* u is the parent of v */;
        u.child ← u.child + 1;
        call Modified-DFS(G,v);
        u.descendant ← u.descendant + v.descendant;
        u.lowest ← min (u.lowest, v.lowest);
        if (v.lowest ≥ u.discovered) OR (u is root AND
        u.child > 1) then
            /* v will be disconnected without u */
            c'(u) ← c'(u)+(v.descendant×(n−v.descendant−
            1));
            cc0 ← cc0 − v.descendant /* subtree of v is not
            part of CC0 */;
    else if v ≠ u.π then
        u.lowest ← min (u.lowest, v.discovered);
c'(u) ← c'(u) + (cc0 × (n − cc0 − 1)).
```

For each vertex u, its adjacency list is traversed exactly once and the number of descendants and children are calculated in the post-traversal in DFS. The maintenance of the priority queue Q takes $O(|A| \log k) = O(n \log k)$ time, where A is the set of all articulation points in G. The total amount of time for calculating the number of descendants of each vertex in the DFS tree is $O(n)$. Thus, the time complexity of Algorithm 3 is $O(n + m)$. □

5. PERFORMANCE EVALUATION

In this section we evaluate the performance of the proposed algorithms for the structural hole spanner problem, using different datasets. We start with the experimental environment settings, we then investigate the effectiveness of the proposed models of structural hole spanners, compared with other models using both real and synthetic datasets. We finally study the performance of the proposed algorithms and the impacts of parameters on the performance using the datasets in Table 1 and in the end, we discuss the results.

5.1 Experimental environment setting

To evaluate the performance of the proposed algorithms, we adopt the real-world datasets, which are listed in Table 1, where GR-QC is the collaboration network from arXiv[1], covering collaborations between authors of papers submitted to General Relativity and Quantum Cosmology category. Epinions is an online social network of a general consumer review site Epinions[2]. The Twitter dataset was obtained from [19]. Email-EuAll is the anonymous email network of a large European research institution for an 18-month period [18]. The DBLP-2011 dataset is the collaboration network obtained from the DBLP web site[3], and the LiveJournal dataset describes the social network of free on-line blogging community[4].

Recall that Algorithms 1, 2, 3 are denoted by ICC, BICC and AP_BICC, respectively. To evaluate their performance on the mentioned datasets, we will use the following state-of-the-art algorithms for benchmark purposes.

- Algorithm PathCount [11] is similar to betweenness centrality and assigns each vertex a score that is the average number of shortest paths (between all pairs of vertices) on which the vertex lies, then selects the top-k vertices with the highest scores.
- Algorithm 2-Step [24] assigns each vertex a score that is the number of pairs of its neighbors without edges between them, then selects the top-k highest scores.
- Algorithm PageRank [21] assigns each vertex v a PageRank score $r(v)$ that is the visiting probability of v by a random surfer, $r(v) = 1/n$ initially. The algorithm then updates $r(v)$ with a new value $r(v) = (1-\alpha)/n + \alpha \sum_{(u,v)\in E} r(u)/\deg(u)$, where $\alpha = 0.85$ is the random jump parameter. It finally chooses the top-k vertices with the highest PageRank scores.
- Algorithm MaxD [19] is to find a set of k vertices such that the minimum cut of communities will be reduced significantly, after removing these vertices, assuming that l communities are given. For any pair of communities, the algorithm selects $\lceil 2k/(l(l-1)) \rceil$ vertices as structural hole spanners using a greedy strategy. In each round, it chooses the vertex whose removal will result in a maximum decrease of the minimum cut.
- Algorithm HIS [19] assigns each vertex v a score that simulates the likelihood of v as a structural hole spanner across the given subset of communities, assuming that l communities are given.

Notice that all our experiments were conducted based on a Linux desktop with GenuineIntel Core i7-3370 (3.40GHz) CPU and 8GB main memory.

Dateset	$\|V\|$	$\|E\|$	% APs	$\Delta(G)$	Diam
GR-QC	5,242	28,980	15%	81	17
Epinions	75,879	508,837	14%	1,551	14
Twitter	92,180	188,971	14%	233	26
Email-euAll	265,214	420,045	2%	7,636	14
DBLP-2011	986,324	6,707,236	9%	979	12
LiveJournal	5,363,260	79,023,142	16%	2,469	14

Table 1: Six different real datasets, where APs stands for Articulation Points in the corresponding network and Diam stands for Diameter.

[1]http://arxiv.org/
[2]http://epinions.com/
[3]http://www.informatik.uni-trier.de/~ley/db/
[4]http://livejournal.com/

5.2 Effectiveness of the proposed model

We first evaluate the effectiveness of the proposed model using the definition proposed by Burt [7] such as: (1) the size of communities that each individual spans, (2) the number of communities and (3) the number of neighbours of that individuals. Burt [7] suggested that a good structural hole spanner is connected to many communities, but to be influential, the ratio of the number of its communities to the number of its neighbors should be large. This definition implies a metric for evaluating the structural hole spanners in a setting where the communities are given in advance. Given a graph $G = (V, E)$, suppose S is the set of structural holes found by an algorithm, then, the quality of the solution S is

$$\rho(S) = \frac{\sum_{v\in S} \frac{\text{\# of communities that } v \text{ is connected to}}{\deg(v)}}{|S|}. \tag{9}$$

We evaluate the performance of different algorithms using this metric in order to find out the degree to which our model maps the real structural hole spanners. We use the DBLP dataset which has been used for the same purpose in [19]. The communities in this network are publication venues, e.g, journal or conference; authors who published to a certain journal or conference form a community. We evaluate two algorithms by MaxD and HIS proposed by Lou *et al.* [19].

Fig. 4(a) shows that Algorithm AP_BICC significantly outperforms all the other algorithms in terms of the average community size by varying k. Fig. 4(a) verifies our claim in Section 2.2 that our model can identify the vertices connecting with larger communities. Similarly, it can be observed in Fig. 4(b) that algorithm AP_BICC outperforms the other algorithms in the benchmark at least 50%, using the metric in Eq. (9). In a nutshell, Algorithm AP_BICC can guarantee to find efficient structural hole spanners connecting to larger communities in this dataset while the other algorithms produce the results with less number of communities compared to the number of their neighbors. Also, the running time of Algorithm AP_BICC is a few milliseconds, while Algorithm MaxD takes minutes and Algorithm HIS takes a few seconds.

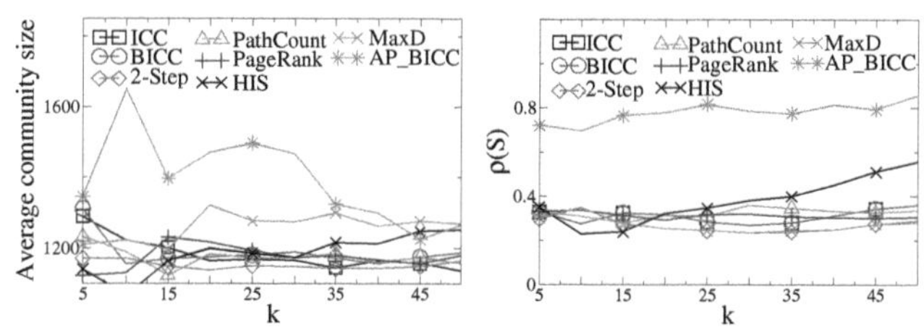

(a) Average community size (b) Community membership

Figure 4: Effectiveness of different algorithms on dataset DBLP using different quality metrics.

5.3 Performance on synthetic datasets

We then evaluate the quality of structural hole spanners found by different algorithms. We generate a random graph of 2^{11} vertices using SSCA method[5]. SSCA generates cliques of random size with average size 2^7 and random inter-clique edges. We then place a ground-truth structural hole spanner s_i for every clique i. For every edge (u, v), such that u is in clique i and v is in clique j, we replace it with two edges (u, s_i) and (s_i, v). Fig. 5 shows the performance improvement made by Algorithm AP_BICC in empirical results.

[5]http://www.cse.psu.edu/~madduri/software/GTgraph/

Fig. 5 demonstrates that the solution accuracy delivered by Algorithm AP_BICC is at least 20% of the others for $k > 5$. The reason for such significant improvement is that algorithm AP_BICC finds more meaningful structural hole spanners that play a significant role in the connectivity of communities (cliques) and vertices in the network.

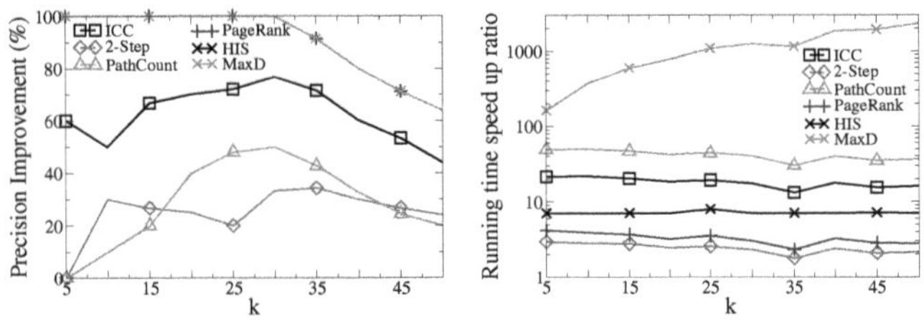

(a) Precision improvement (b) Speed up ratio

Figure 5: Running time and precision improvement by Algorithm AP_BICC using synthetic dataset.

5.4 Performance on real datasets

We thirdly evaluate the performance of the proposed algorithms ICC, BICC, and AP_BICC, against benchmark structure-based algorithms PathCount, PageRank, and 2-Step against different datasets listed in Table 1. We avoid comparing community-based algorithms MaxD and HIS, since using any community detection method is subject to unfairness.

Fig. 6 and Fig. 7 show the performance of different algorithms in terms of the optimization objective in Eq. (4), i.e., $C(G \setminus S) - C(G)$ and their running times. Specifically, it can be seen from Fig. 6(a) that Algorithm AP_BICC significantly outperforms all the other algorithms by at least 100% for dataset GR-QC, while its running time is only 6% of the best of the three benchmark algorithms as shown in Fig. 7(a). It can be observed from Fig. 6(e) to Fig. 6(f) that Algorithm AP_BICC has the similar performance and running time for other datasets. That is, it outperforms all the other algorithms at least 50% while its running time is only around 7% and 65% of the fastest benchmark algorithm for datasets DBLP-2011 and LiveJournal, respectively. Fig. 6(b) and Fig. 6(d) show that it is superior in comparison with benchmark algorithms such as PageRank and PathCount on both performance and running time for datasets Epinions and Email-EuAll when k is small ($k < 20$). With the increase of k, the performance gap between Algorithm AP_BICC and other algorithms increases, too. Furthermore, it can be seen from Fig. 7(b) and Fig. 7(d) that the running time of Algorithm AP_BICC is less than 7% of the fastest benchmark Algorithm PageRank and 0.01% of Algorithms ICC and PathCount for dataset DBLP-2011 as shown in Fig. 7(e). Moreover, Algorithm AP_BICC significantly outperforms Algorithm BICC, which means that the second term in Eq. (6) is dominant. Furthermore, since the number of articulation points is large, Algorithm AP_BICC never reaches to the second phase, causing it to run considerably faster than Algorithm BICC.

5.5 Impact of parameters on the performance

We finally evaluate the impact of parameters on the performance of the proposed Algorithms AP_BICC and BICC. As the number of articulation points in each mentioned dataset is far larger than k, the second stage of Algorithm AP_BICC, the bounded inverse closeness centrality of vertices will not be invoked. Therefore, we only investigate the impact of parameters l and K on the performance of algorithm BICC.

Fig. 8 plots the performance curves of Algorithm BICC by varying the value of l, based on two representative large datasets LiveJournal and DBLP-2011 in Table 1. As the experimental results indicate that algorithm BICC will deliver the similar performance for other datasets, we focus only on these two large datasets. Fig. 8(b) implies that when l is small with $2 \leq l \leq 6$, Algorithm BICC has the best performance for dataset LiveJournal. It also exhibits similar behavior for dataset DBLP-2011 as shown in Fig. 8(a). However, its performance degrades chromatically when $l = 6$, i.e., its performance decreases by at least 80% compared with its performance when $l = 2$. This implies that its performance dramatically drops with the growth of l. The reason behind is that algorithm BICC always chooses the top-K vertices with the largest l-bounded inverse closeness $c_l(v)$. By continuously increasing the value of l, the value of $c_l(v)$ will be closer to the value of its inverse closeness centrality $c(v)$. Since the top-K vertices with the "largest" l-bounded inverse closeness centrality (that is indeed almost the same as inverse closeness centrality for large l) will be chosen, the algorithm performance drops. Fig. 8 suggests that the value of l in practice should be small, otherwise the quality of the solution is not promising, this further verifies the small-world phenomenon that causes l-bounded closeness centrality to be very close to inverse closeness centrality, since the small-world phenomenon states that the largest distance in the network is expected to be a constant. Fig. 8(d) plots the running times of algorithm BICC for different k using dataset LiveJournal, from which it can be seen that it takes more time on finding a solution with the growth of l. Specifically, its running time when $l = 2$ is a tiny fraction of its running time when $l = 10$ (0.001%). Fig. 8(c) further shows that it has the similar behavior for dataset DBLP-2011.

Fig. 9(a) shows that the performance of algorithm BICC for dataset DBLP is stable, with the increase of K. The rationale behind is that social networks follow the small-world law that individuals can reach each other with a few number of hops, thus the l-bounded inverse closeness centrality of vertices can approximately represent closeness centrality. Fig. 9(b) demonstrates that algorithm BICC leads to a better performance for dataset LiveJournal with the growth of K. Fig. 9(d) shows its running time, using different values of K for dataset LiveJournal, from which it can be seen that the running time of algorithm BICC linearly increases, with the growth of K. The reason is that by increasing the value of K, algorithm BICC will examine more candidate vertices.

5.6 Discussion

We now turn to the discussion of the experimental results. Fig. 6 shows that in co-authorship datasets GR-QC and DBLP-2011, the performance gain of Algorithm AP_BICC over Algorithm PageRank is significant. The reason is that Algorithm AP_BICC finds the individuals who bridge different communities, while Algorithm PageRank detects the individuals with high reputation. In other words, within co-authorship networks, opinion leaders have a high reputation as they collaborate with many people in their own community, however, the structural hole spanners connect different communities and their absence is more tangible. Similarly, in dataset LiveJournal, bloggers produce contents within a few subjects gain high reputation. The bloggers who publish in multiple subjects however, have a wider perspective, more sources of information and hold more significant positions.

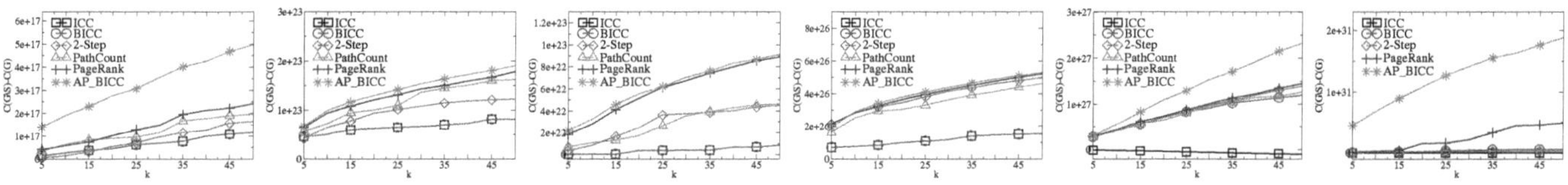

(a) GR-QC (b) Epinions (c) Twitter (d) Email-EuAll (e) DBLP-2011 (f) LiveJournal

Figure 6: Performance of various algorithms, using different datasets.

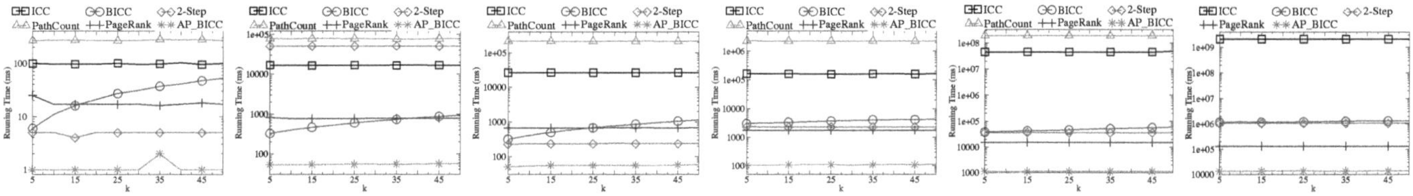

(a) GR-QC (b) Epinions (c) Twitter (d) Email-EuAll (e) DBLP-2011 (f) LiveJournal

Figure 7: Running times of various algorithms, using different datasets.

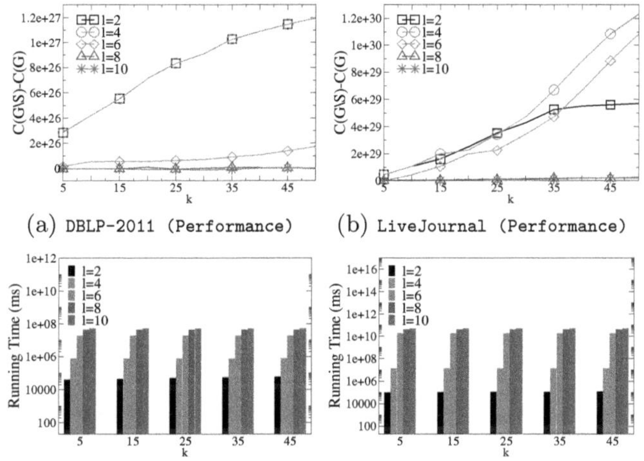

(a) DBLP-2011 (Performance) (b) LiveJournal (Performance)

(c) DBLP-2011 (Time) (d) LiveJournal (Time)

Figure 8: Impact of parameter l on performance of algorithm BICC.

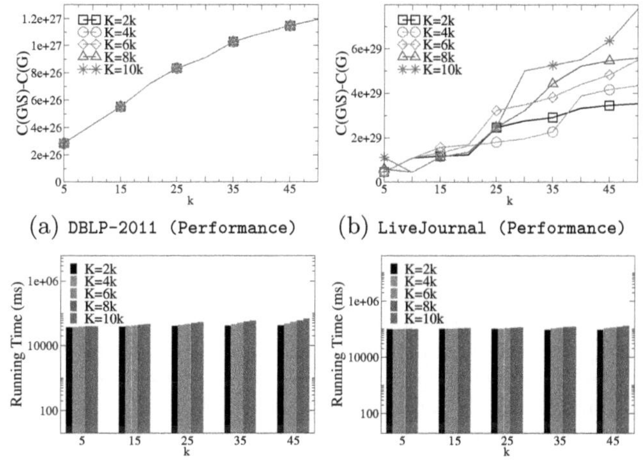

(a) DBLP-2011 (Performance) (b) LiveJournal (Performance)

(c) DBLP-2011 (Time) (d) LiveJournal (Time)

Figure 9: Impact of parameter K on performance of algorithm BICC.

Moreover, Fig. 6 shows that the performance of Algorithm **AP_BICC** is similar to **PageRank** for dataset **Email-EuAll**. Dataset **Email-EuAll** is the email network of an organization in which high level managers gain a high reputation. The high level managers communicate with the operation managers in each separate division and act as the only communication link between each separate division. Thus, they are also structural hole spanners. A similar explanation can be applied to dataset **Twitter**, where people who have higher reputation are directly followed by a larger portion of users and their content is forwarded by their followers.

6. RELATED WORK

Over last few years, the size of real networks has increased enormously, developing efficient algorithms for finding influential individuals in such large-scale networks with unique properties such as structural hole spanners has become a challenging task. Moreover, building accurate models that truly reflect the properties of structural hole spanners is crucial to identify such individuals. Nevertheless, researchers take lots of effort towards this aim.

The notion of structural hole spanners was first introduced by Burt [7] to find the key employees in organizations for integrating operations across functional and business boundaries. This concept later was further refined in [1, 8, 9]. A few studies have exploited the concept of structural holes in order to design strategic games for network formation [11, 17]. Goyal *et al.* [11] presented a network formation model that a vertex u serves as an intermediary between many vertices. However, this strategy leads to the star network and real networks do not follow a star topology. In order to tackle this problem, Kleinberg *et al.* [17] designed a game by building a model of the payoffs that arise from filling structural holes. This payoff is a decreasing function of the number of paths with length two between each pair of neighbors to avoid the star topology. One of the limitations of the model presented by Kleinberg *et al.* [17] is that this model needs careful tuning of parameters such as the link maintenance cost that is not easily achieved in large-scale networks. Another line of research in computer science is to find structural hole spanners in order to incorporate them in contagion, and can be divided in two categories as follows.

Structural-based Models: Goyal *et al.* [11] formulated a structural hole spanner as a vertex that resides on more shortest paths between different pairs of vertices. Since counting the number of shortest paths in large networks is time-consuming, Tang *et al.* [24] proposed to only count the number of shortest paths with length two on which a vertex lies. In this model, any shortest path of length greater than two will be ignored, thus the model suggests candidates that are connected to smaller rather than larger, richer and more influential communities. A fairly common case under this model is its failure of finding good quality structural hole spanners when a vertex is densely connected to two communities. For example, in Fig. 1, vertex v_1 forms more length-2 paths than that of v_2, while v_2 is connected to more communities and is a better structural hole based on Burt's theory [7]. However, this model suggests v_1 as a better structural hole spanner. In order to address this problem, Ugander *et al.* [28] defined the *structural diversity* of an individual as the number of connected components in its contact neighborhood, which is a similar notion as structural hole spanners, and studied the role of structural diversity in contagion of information within real social networks. Huang *et al.* [14] studied the top-k structural diversity search in large networks and developed efficient algorithms for massive dynamic networks. However, only a small number of vertices in each community can be part of contact neighborhood, and they can form multiple connected components. Similarly, Tong *et al.* [27] defined the gateway-ness of a vertex v, proportional to the paths between source vertices S and target vertices T, on which v lies. In addition, each path is given a score, which is inversely proportional to its length. Yang *et al.* [31] studied the role of structural holes in diffusion.

Community-based Models: Lou *et al.* [19] proposed a model to find structural holes in a network, assuming that communities in the network are given. The objective in their model is to maximize a utility function that measures the degree to which vertices span communities. One instantiation is to find a set of vertices whose removal leads to the maximum decreases on the number of inter-community edges. One major concern about this model is that communities usually are not known, thus the quality of the solution relies on the quality of communities found. Moreover in Fig. 1, the removal of v_1 decreases the number of inter-community edges by 8 and the removal v_2 decreases the inter-community edges by 6. Therefore, this model implies v_1 as the preferred structural hole spanner. However, v_2 should be a better structural hole as it bridges more communities.

7. CONCLUSION

In this paper we studied the top-k structural hole spanner problem in a large-scale social network. We first proposed a novel model to measure the quality of structural holes. We then formulated a novel top-k structural hole spanner problem and showed its NP-hardness. We thirdly devised two fast yet scalable linear-time algorithms for the problem by using both the bounded inverse closeness centrality of vertices and articulation points of the network. We finally evaluated the performance of the proposed algorithms and validated the effectiveness of the proposed model through extensive experiments on real and synthetic datasets. Experimental results demonstrated that the proposed model can capture the characteristics of structural hole spanners, and the proposed algorithms outperform several other heuristics.

8. ACKNOWLEDGMENTS

This work is supported by the grant of Australian Research Council Discovery Project No. DP120102627.

9. REFERENCES

[1] G. Ahuja. Collaboration Networks, Structural Holes, and Innovation: A Longitudinal Study. *Administrative science quarterly*, vol. 45, pp. 425–455, 2000.

[2] R. Andersen, and K. J. Lang. Communities from Seed Sets. *WWW'06*, pp. 223–232, ACM, 2006.

[3] A-L. Barabási, and R. Albert. Emergence of Scaling in Random Networks. *Science 286*, pp. 509–512, 1999.

[4] A. Bar-Noy, S. Khuller, and B. Schieber. The Complexity of Finding Most Vital Arcs and Nodes. *Univ. of Maryland Institute for Advanced Computer Studies Report No. UMIACS-TR-95-96*, 1998.

[5] M. A. Beauchamp. An Improved Index of Centrality. *Behavioral Science* , vol. 10, pp. 161–163, 1965.

[6] C. Budak, D. Agrawal, and A. El Abbadi. Limiting the Spread of Misinformation in Social Networks. *WWW'11*, pp. 665–674, ACM, 2011.

[7] R. S. Burt. Structural holes: The Social Structure of Competition. *Harvard university press*, 1992.

[8] R. S. Burt. Structural Holes and Good Ideas. *American Journal of Sociology*, vol. 110, pp. 349–399, 2004.

[9] R. S. Burt. Secondhand Brokerage: Evidence on the Importance of Local Structure for Managers, Bankers, and Analysts. *Academy of Management Journal*, vol. 50, pp. 119–148, 2007.

[10] N. Girvan, and M. E. Newman. Community Structure in Social and Biological Networks. *Proc. Natl. Acad. Sci.* , vol. 99, pp. 7821–7826, 2002.

[11] S. Goyal, and F. Vega-Redondo. Structural Holes in Social Networks. *Journal of Economic Theory*, vol. 137, pp. 460–492, Elsevier, 2007.

[12] A. Guille, H. Hacid, C. Favre, and D. A. Zighed. Information Diffusion in Online Social Networks: A Survey. *ACM SIGMOD Record*, vol. 42(2), pp. 17–28, 2013.

[13] J. Hopcroft, T. Lou, and J. Tang. Who Will Follow You Back? : Reciprocal Relationship Prediction. *CIKM'11*, pp. 1137–1146, ACM, 2011.

[14] X. Huang, H. Cheng, R. Li, L. Qin, and J. X. Yu. Top-*K* Structural Diversity Search in Large Networks. *VLDB'13*, vol. 6, pp. 1618–1629, 2013.

[15] D. Kempe, J. Kleinberg, and É. Tardos. Maximizing the Spread of Influence through a Social Network. *SIGKDD'03*, pp. 137–146, ACM, 2003.

[16] J. Kleinberg. Navigation in a Small World. *Nature*, vol. 406, pp. 845–845, 2000.

[17] J. Kleinberg, S. Suri, É. Tardos, and T. Wexler. Strategic Network Formation with Structural Holes. *EC'08*, pp. 284–293, 2008.

[18] J. Leskovec, A. Krevl. SNAP Datasets: Stanford Large Network Dataset Collection. *http://snap.stanford.edu*, 2014.

[19] T. Lou, and J. Tang. Mining Structural Hole Spanners through Information Diffusion in Social Networks. *WWW'13*, pp. 825–836, 2013.

[20] M. Marathe, and A. K. S. Vullikanti. Computational Epidemiology. *SIGKDD'14*, pp. 1969–1969, 2014.

[21] L. Page, S. Brin, R. Motwani, and T. Winograd. The PageRank Citation Ranking: Bringing Order to the Web. *Stanford InfoLab*, 1999.

[22] J. Plesník. On the Sum of All Distances in a Graph or Digraph. *Journal of Graph Theory*, vol. 8, 1984.

[23] E. J. Rinia, T. N. Van Leeuwen, E. E. Bruins, H. G. Van Vuren, and A. F. Van Raan. Citation Delay in Interdisciplinary Knowledge Exchange. *Scientometrics*, vol. 51, pp. 293–309, Springer, 2001.

[24] J. Tang, T. Lou, and J. Kleinberg. Inferring Social Ties Across Heterogenous Networks. *WSDM'12*, 2012.

[25] J. Tang, S. Wu, and J. Sun. Confluence: Conformity Influence in Large Social Networks. *SIGKDD'13*, pp. 347–355, 2013.

[26] Y. Tang, X. Xiao, and Y. Shi. Influence Maximization: Near-Optimal Time Complexity Meets Practical Efficiency. *SIGMOD'14*, pp. 75–86, ACM, 2014.

[27] H. Tong, S. Papadimitriou, C. Faloutsos, P. S. Yu, and T. Eliassi-Rad. Gateway Finder in Large Graphs: Problem Definitions and Fast Solutions. *Information retrieval*, vol. 15, pp. 391–411, Springer, 2012.

[28] J. Ugander, L. Backstrom, C. Marlow, and J. Kleinberg. Structural Diversity in Social Contagion. *Proc. Natl. Acad. Sci.* , vol. 109, pp. 5962–5966, 2012.

[29] L. Wang, T. Lou, J. Tang, and J. E. Hopcroft. Detecting Community Kernels in Large Social Networks. *ICDM'11*, 2011.

[30] D. Watts, and S. Strogatz. Collective Dynamics of 'Small-World' Networks. *Nature*, vol. 393, pp. 440–442, 1998.

[31] Y. Yang, J. Tang, C. Leung, Y. Sun, Q. Chen, J. Li, and Q. Yang. RAIN: Social Rrole-Aware Information Diffusion. *AAAI'15*, 2015.

Scalable Facility Location for Massive Graphs on Pregel-like Systems

Kiran Garimella
Aalto University
kiran.garimella@aalto.fi

Gianmarco De Francisci Morales
Aalto University
gdfm@acm.org

Aristides Gionis*
Aalto University
aristides.gionis@aalto.fi

Mauro Sozio†
Télécom ParisTech, CNRS LTCI
sozio@telecom-paristech.fr

ABSTRACT

We propose a new scalable algorithm for the facility-location problem. We study the *graph setting*, where the cost of serving a client from a facility is represented by the shortest-path distance on a graph. This setting is applicable to various problems arising in the Web and social media, and allows to leverage the inherent sparsity of such graphs.

To obtain truly scalable performance, we design a parallel algorithm that operates on clusters of shared-nothing machines. In particular, we target modern Pregel-like architectures, and we implement our algorithm on Apache Giraph.

Our work builds upon previous results: a facility location algorithm for the PRAM model, a recent distance-sketching method for massive graphs, and a parallel algorithm to finding maximal independent sets. The main challenge is to adapt those building blocks to the distributed graph setting, while maintaining the approximation guarantee and limiting the amount of distributed communication. Extensive experimental results show that our algorithm scales gracefully to graphs with billions of edges, while, in terms of quality, being competitive with state-of-the-art sequential algorithms.

1. INTRODUCTION

Facility location is a classic combinatorial-optimization problem. It has been widely studied in *operations research* [31, 39] and *theoretical computer science* [1, 11, 30, 48], and it has many different applications, e.g., in data compression [9], grammar inference [23], information retrieval [49], and design of communication networks [43]. In the most basic setting of the problem, we are given a set of facilities F, a set of clients C, and costs $c(f)$ for *opening* a facility $f \in F$ and $d(c, f)$ for *serving* a client $c \in C$ with a facility $f \in F$. The goal is to select a subset of facilities to open so that all clients are served by an open facility and the total cost of opening the facilities plus serving the clients is minimized.

*This work was supported by a Yahoo! Faculty Research and Engagement Program (FREP) award.

†This work was partially funded by a Google Faculty Award.

CIKM'15, October 19–23, 2015, Melbourne, VIC, Australia

ACM 978-1-4503-3794-6/15/10 $15.00 DOI: http://dx.doi.org/10.1145/2806416.2806508.

Modern applications related to web graphs, large social networks, and other such massive-scale datasets, whose size may far exceed the memory of a single machine, could also benefit from facility location as a general-purpose optimization mechanism. Examples of such applications include placing caches for content delivery on the Internet [24], placement of shopping centers on a road network, finding central nodes in a social network [7]. Similar objective functions arise in outbreak detection in networks [34].

We study the facility location problem in the graph setting, where the input consists of a graph with clients and facilities being represented by vertices while the cost of serving a client from a facility is represented by their shortest-path distance on the graph. Our goal is to develop efficient distributed algorithms for this problem setting.

Several sequential approximation algorithms [1, 11, 30, 48], as well as parallel/distributed algorithms [13, 4] have been devised for the facility location problem. Alas, adapting existing methods to the distributed graph setting is challenging, as the known algorithms present at least one of the following shortcomings: (*i*) they assume the input to be the full distance matrix between facilities and clients, which requires $\Omega(n^2)$ space and time to be materialized (where n is the number of vertices in the graph); (*ii*) they are sequential and assume that the input data reside in main memory.

In this paper, we present the first algorithm for the facility-location problem that addresses both issues outlined above. Our algorithm is designed for the Pregel model of computation [38]. In particular, we implement our algorithm on Giraph [12], thus adding facility location to the toolbox of optimization problems that can be solved for very large datasets on modern computer clusters.

Graph setting. Most works in the the area of theoretical computer science focus on the classical formulation of the facility-location problem, where the input consists of the full $|F| \times |C|$ set of distances [46]. Unfortunately, in this setting even algorithms with linear running time (in the size of input) are not practical when both $|F|$ and $|C|$ are large.

In many real-world problems the input for facility location can be represented as a graph $G = (V, E)$, where F and C are vertices of G. Typically, the number of edges $m = |E|$ is much smaller than $|F||C|$, i.e., the graph is sparse. A client $c \in C$ can be served by a facility $f \in F$ even if $(c, f) \notin E$, provided that there is a path in the graph from c to f, and the cost $d(c, f)$ is the *induced shortest-path distance*. Hence, in this so-called *graph-setting*, we do not need to represent the full $|F| \times |C|$ set of distances. This setting poses non-trivial challenges, as such distances have to be computed throughout the execution of the algorithm. However, it is crucial to leverage the sparsity of a massive input graph.

Our approach is designed for this graph-based setting. We require that the time and space requirements of our algorithm be quasilinear functions of $|E|$. If the graph is sparse, as most real-world datasets are, this leads to a significantly more scalable algorithm. Thorup [48] has proposed the only previous (sequential) algorithm for the graph setting.

Pregel model. To cope with large problem sizes modern applications take advantage of distributed systems, such as MapReduce [19] and Hadoop, or of variants targeted to graph data, such as Pregel [38] and its open-source clones, Giraph [12] and GraphLab [36]. Such systems offer several advantages, among which, high scalability and a simple programming interface.

Our algorithm targets a parallel shared-nothing computing environment. While other parallel algorithms have been proposed in the literature, our approach is the first one to target modern clusters. In particular, Blelloch and Tangwongsan [4] proposed a parallel facility-location approximation algorithm for the PRAM model. Our work extends this parallel algorithm to the more scalable Pregel model.

Algorithm summary. Our approach has three phases: (*i*) *neighborhood sketching*, (*ii*) *facility opening*, and (*iii*) *facility selection*. All three phases are fully implemented in Giraph, and the code is open-source.[1]

The first phase builds an all-distances sketch (ADS) that estimates the neighborhood function of each vertex. This sketch is used in the second phase to decide when to open a facility. Our sketch relies on the historic inverse probability (HIP) estimator, recently proposed by Cohen [15].

The facility-opening phase expands balls around facilities in parallel. It decides which facilities to open depending on the number of clients that reside within the facility-centered balls. To estimate the number of clients inside the balls, we use the sketch created in the previous phase.

Finally, the facility-selection phase removes duplicate assignments of a client to more than one facility that might have been created due to the parallel nature of the algorithm. To accomplish this task, we need to compute a maximal independent set (MIS) on the 2-hop graph of the open facilities. For this sub-problem, we design a distributed version of a recent greedy approximation algorithm [5].

Our main challenge is to adapt and combine previous results to the distributed graph setting, while maintaining the approximation guarantee of the algorithm, and limiting the amount of distributed communication. Concretely, the contributions of this paper are as follows:

- we provide the first Pregel solution for the facility-location problem – our algorithm, unlike previous sequential and PRAM ones, is deployable on clusters available in modern computing environments;
- at the same time, we do not compromise on accuracy – our algorithm provides an approximation guarantee similar to previous PRAM and sequential ones;
- our solution uses the sparse graph-based representation of the facility-location problem, which improves significantly the scalability of the method;
- our algorithm employs fundamental subproblems, all-distances sketch and maximal independent set, for which we provide the first implementations in the Pregel model;
- we provide an extensive experimental evaluation that shows the scalability of our methods on very large datasets.

[1] `https://github.com/gvrkiran/giraph-facility-location`

The rest of the paper is organized as follows. In Section 2 we formally define our problem, and discuss the background techniques needed for our approach. Our algorithm, comprising of the three phases outlined above, is detailed in Section 3, while an experimental evaluation of the different components of our method is presented in Section 4. In Section 5 we place our work in the context of relevant research, while Section 6 is a short conclusion.

2. PRELIMINARIES

Problem definition. In the *metric uncapacitated facility-location problem*, we are given a set of facilities F and a set of clients C. For each facility $f \in F$ and client $c \in C$, there is a cost $c(f)$ for *opening* the facility f, and a cost $d(c, f)$ for *serving* client c with facility f. The objective is to select a set of facilities $S \subseteq F$ to *open* in order to minimize the objective function

$$\sum_{f \in S} c(f) + \sum_{c \in C} d(c, S),$$

where $d(c, S)$ is the distance of client $c \in C$ to its *closest* open facility, i.e., $d(c, S) = \min_{f \in S} d(c, f)$.

In this paper, we are interested in the *graph setting* of the facility-location problem, where we are also given a weighted graph $G = (V, E, w)$, with $w : E \to \mathbb{R}_+$ a weight function on the edges of the graph. The sets of facilities and clients are subsets of the graph vertices ($F, C \subseteq V$). The distance between clients and facilities is given by the shortest-path distance on the weighted graph. We assume that facility costs and edge weights be polynomial in $|V|$.

We focus on the graph setting of the facility-location problem so as to leverage the sparsity of real-world graphs, such as web graphs and social networks. This allows us to develop practical and scalable algorithms, with running time being quasilinear in the size of the input graph. Previous algorithms for our problem, are sequential or require all pairwise vertex distances which is not practical for large graphs.

We consider both directed and undirected graphs. For the case of undirected graphs our algorithm offers a provable approximation guarantee, while for the case of directed graphs the algorithm provides a practical heuristic. We focus on the case when $F = C = V$, although all our claims hold for the more general case when $F, C \subseteq V$.

The Giraph platform. The algorithms presented in this paper are designed for the Giraph platform [12], an Apache implementation of the Pregel computational paradigm. Pregel is based on the Bulk Synchronous Parallel (BSP) computation model, and can be summarized by the motto "think like a vertex" [38]. At the beginning of the computation, the vertices of the graph are distributed across worker tasks running on different machines on a cluster. Computation proceeds as a sequence of iterations called supersteps. Algorithms are expressed in a vertex-centric fashion inside a `vertex.compute()` function, which gets called on each vertex exactly once in every superstep. The computation involves three activities: receiving messages from the previous superstep, updating the local value of the vertex, and sending messages to other vertices.

Algorithm 1: Build ADS sequentially

```
  Input: Graph G(V, E)
  Output: ADS of G
1 for v ∈ V do
2 |  ADS(v) = ∅
3 |  BKMH(v) = ∅ // Bottom-k min-hash
4 for v ∈ V and u ∈ {V sorted by d(v)} do
  |  // list vertices in incr. distance from v
5 |  if r(u) < max_r(BKMH(v)) then
  |  |  // r(u) is the hash of u
6 |  |  ADS(v) ← ADS(v) ∪ (u, d(v, u))
7 |  |  BKMH(v) ← bottomK(BKMH(v) ∪ u)
8 return ADS
```

Pregel also provides *aggregators*, a mechanism used for coordination and monitoring, as well as for computing global statistics. Each vertex can write a value to an aggregator in superstep t, the system combines those values via a reduction operator, and the resulting value is made available to all vertices in superstep $t+1$.

Giraph adds an optional `master.compute()` to the Pregel model. This function performs centralized computation, and is executed by a single master task before each superstep. Aggregators written by workers are read by the master in the following superstep, while aggregators written by the master are read by workers in the same superstep. We employ this feature in our implementation (see Section 3.5).

Approximate neighborhoods (ADS). The all-distances sketch (ADS) is a probabilistic data structure for approximating the neighborhood function of a graph [15]. ADS aims to answer the query *"how many vertices are within distance d from vertex v?"*. ADS maintains a logarithmic-size sketch for each vertex. In the sequential computational model, the total time to build the ADS is quasilinear in the number of graph edges. ADS-based techniques have been used to estimate efficiently graph properties, such as the distance distribution, effective diameter, and vertex similarities [6, 16].

The ADS of a vertex v consists of a random sample of vertices. The probability that a vertex u is included in the sketch of vertex v decreases with the distance $d(u,v)$. The sketch contains not only the vertex u but also the distance $d(u,v)$. The ADS can be thought as an extension of the simpler *min-hash* sketch [8, 14], which has been used for approximate distinct counting [14, 20, 21], and for similarity estimation [8, 14]. The ADS of v is simply the union of the min-hash sketches of all the sets of the ℓ closest vertices to v, for each possible value of ℓ. Min-hash sketches have a parameter k that controls the trade-off between size and accuracy: a larger k entails a better approximation at the expense of a larger sketch. The size of the ADS is $\mathcal{O}(k \log n)$.

Our algorithm relies heavily on a recently-proposed ADS structure, the historic inverse probability (HIP) estimator [15], which extends significantly previous variants and offers novel estimation capabilities. In particular, HIP can be used to answer neighborhood queries for both *unweighted* and *weighted* graphs. It can also be used to answer *predicated* neighborhood queries, that is, to approximate the number of vertices in a neighborhood that satisfy a certain predicate on vertex attributes. We use this latter feature in to exclude already served clients from the estimation of the number of clients within a ball (see Section 3).

Algorithm 2: ADS in Giraph. `Vertex.Compute()`

```
   Input: vertex value v, edge values E, messages M
   Output: updated vertex value v'
   Data: ADS = ∅; BKMH = ∅
   // state variables are stored in the vertex v
1  OutMsgs = ∅
2  for m ∈ M do
   |  // the message contains the entries of the
   |  // ADS of neighbors that were updated in
   |  // the previous super step
3  |  for (u, d) ∈ m.getEntries() do
   |  |  // u is the vertex.id and d its distance
4  |  |  if r(u) < max_r(BKMH) then
   |  |  |  // if u has already reached v before,
   |  |  |  // it will not be considered again
5  |  |  |  ADS ← ADS ∪ (u, d)
6  |  |  |  CleanUp(ADS(u), d) // for each
   |  |  |      distance, remove an entry from
   |  |  |      ADS(u) if its hash is not in the
   |  |  |      bottom-k for that distance
7  |  |  |  BKMH ← bottomK(BKMH ∪ u)
8  |  |  |  OutMsgs ← OutMsgs ∪ (u, d + e(u, v))
   |  |  |  // for unweighted graphs
   |  |  |  // e(u, v) is 1
   |  |  |  // for weighted graphs, its the weight
   |  |  |      of the edge between u and v
9  for e ∈ E do
10 |  sendMsgTo(e, OutMsgs)
```

The sequential version of ADS is presented in Algorithm 1, and our adaptation for Giraph is shown in Algorithm 2. The algorithm works for both weighted and unweighted graphs. A cleanup operation is performed in line 6, which removes those entries for which the hash is not in the bottom-k min-hashes for a given distance (this may happen only for weighted graphs, when the vertices processed by ADS are discovered by a BFS and are not sorted by their distance from a given vertex). While the cleanup step can be time-consuming, we do not need to perform it in each superstep, but only periodically when the size of the ADS becomes too large. For unweighted graphs the cleanup is not needed.

3. ALGORITHM

As discussed earlier, our algorithm consists of three phases: (*i*) *neighborhood sketching*, (*ii*) *facility opening*, and (*iii*) *facility selection*. This section presents the main body of the algorithm: phases (*ii*) and (*iii*). In the pseudocode presented henceforward, `for` and `while` loops are meant to be *parallel* i.e., executed by all vertices in parallel.

3.1 PRAM algorithm for facility location

Our method is inspired by the algorithm of Blelloch and Tangwongsan [4], which is developed for the PRAM model. We adapt this algorithm to a Pregel-like platform, and also extend it to the graph setting, as discussed in Section 2.

The algorithm operates in two phases: facility opening, and facility selection. It starts with all facilities being *unopened* and all clients being *unfrozen*.

The algorithm maintains a graph H that represents the connections between clients and open facilities. Initially, H has F and C as vertices and an empty set of edges. During the execution of the algorithm, if a client c is to be served by a facility f, the edge (c, f) is added in H. During the facility-opening phase, it is possible for a client to be connected to more than one facility. However, in the facility-selection phase, redundant facilities are closed and it is ensured that each client is connected to exactly one facility.

In the facility-opening phase, each client tries to reach a facility by expanding a ball with radius α, in parallel. The expansion phase is iterative, and in each iteration the radius grows by a factor of $(1+\epsilon)$, where ϵ is a parameter that provides an accuracy-efficiency trade-off.

The radius of the ball of a client c is denoted by $\alpha(c)$. If a client c is unfrozen, the radius of its corresponding ball is set to the current global value α, while if a client c gets frozen it does not increase the radius of its ball anymore. When a facility f is reached by a sufficiently large number of clients it is declared *open*. In particular, a facility f is opened when

$$\sum_{c \in C} \max\{0, (1+\epsilon)\alpha(c) - d(c, f)\} \geq c(f). \tag{1}$$

For a newly opened facility f, all clients c within radius α from f are frozen, and the edges (c, f) are added in H. The facility-opening phase continues as long as there is at least one unopened facility and at least one unfrozen client.

At this point, as mentioned earlier, a client may be served by more than one facility. In the facility-selection phase, the algorithm closes the facilities that are not necessary, as their clients can be served by other nearby facilities. This step relies on computing a maximal independent set (MIS) in an appropriately-defined graph $\overline{H}$: the open facilities are the vertices of $\overline{H}$ and there is an edge between two facilities f_a, f_b if and only if there is a client c that is connected to both f_a and f_b. It is easy to see that a maximal independent set S in $\overline{H}$ has the property that each client c is connected to exactly one facility. Clients whose facility is not in S are assigned to the nearest open facility.

To complete the description of the algorithm, the initial ball radius is set to $\alpha_0 = \frac{\gamma}{m^2}(1+\epsilon)$, where $m = |F||C|$ and γ is defined as follows. For each client $c \in C$ we set

$$\gamma_c = \min_{f \in F} \{c(f) + d(c, f)\},$$

and then $\gamma = \max_{c \in C} \gamma_c$. Blelloch and Tangwongsan [4] prove the following theorem on the quality of approximation.

Theorem 1 ([4]). *For any $\epsilon > 0$, the algorithm of Blelloch and Tangwongsan has an approximation guarantee of $3+\epsilon$, while the total number of parallel iterations is $\mathcal{O}(\frac{1}{\epsilon}\log(|F||C|))$.*

3.2 Pregel-like algorithm for facility location

We now discuss how to adapt the algorithm of Blelloch and Tangwongsan to the graph setting discussed in Section 2, as well as in a Pregel-like platform, such as Apache Giraph, discussed in Section 2. The main challenges we need to tackle are the following:

- leverage the sparsity of the graph $G = (V, E)$ to avoid a quadratic blowup of distance computations between facilities and clients;
- compute efficiently, in a distributed manner, a maximal independent set on the graph $\overline{H}$. In particular, as the graphs H and $\overline{H}$ may be dense, it is desirable to compute a MIS of $\overline{H}$ without materializing H nor $\overline{H}$ explicitly.

The first challenge, i.e., exploiting the sparsity of the graph, boils down to being able to check whether Equation (1) is satisfied so as to decide when to open a facility.

To this end, we rearrange the left-hand side of Equation (1), so as to be able to evaluate it by means of the ADS algorithm discussed in Section 2. Observe that the α's take values in the range $R = \{\alpha_0, (1+\epsilon)\alpha_0, (1+\epsilon)^2\alpha_0, \dots\}$.

For every facility f, let $N(f, d)$ be the number of clients within distance d from f, while let $n(f, d)$ be the number of clients whose distance from f is in the range $(d/(1+\epsilon), d]$. Suppose that all clients within distance $\alpha \in R$ from facility f are unfrozen. In this case, we know that for all these unfrozen clients $\alpha(c) = \alpha$, so we can rewrite the left-hand side of Equation (1) as follows:

$$\sum_{c \in C | d(c,f) \leq \alpha} \max\{0, (1+\epsilon)\alpha(c) - d(c, f)\} =$$

$$\sum_{d \in R | d \leq \alpha} n(f, d) \cdot \max\{0, (1+\epsilon)\alpha - d\},$$

where we replace $\alpha(c)$'s with α and rearrange the terms of the summation by grouping terms with the same value.

If some clients within distance α from f are frozen, the former claim might not hold anymore, and we need a more sophisticated solution. Our goal is then to maintain an approximation of the the left-hand side of Equation (1) incrementally. Let $q(f)$ denote the current approximation computed by our algorithm. Also, for each facility f, let $\hat{N}(f, d)$ be the number of *unfrozen* clients within distance d from f, while let $\hat{n}(f, d)$ be the number of *unfrozen* clients at distance in the range $(d/(1+\epsilon), d]$. At each iteration of the ball-expansion phase, we add a term $t(f, \alpha)$ to $q(f)$. This term accounts for the increase in contribution to $q(f)$ due to the newly-reached unfrozen clients, while subtracting excess contribution due to previous iterations.

The increase in contribution $t(f, \alpha)$ is defined as

$$\sum_{d \in R | d \leq \alpha} \hat{n}(f, d) \cdot \max\{0, (1+\epsilon)\alpha - d\}, \tag{2}$$

if $\alpha = \alpha_0$ (no excess contribution to be subtracted), and

$$\sum_{d \in R | d \leq \alpha} \hat{n}(f, d) \cdot (\max\{0, (1+\epsilon)\alpha - d\} - \max\{0, \alpha - d\}), \tag{3}$$

otherwise. The term $t(f, \alpha)$ is added to $q(f)$ in each iteration of the algorithm for the current value of radius α.

The terms $\hat{N}(f, d)$ can be computed efficiently in a distributed fashion by employing the ADS. Given that $\hat{n}(f, d) = \hat{N}(f, d) - \hat{N}(f, d/(1+\epsilon))$, it follows that also the left-hand side of Equation (1) can be computed efficiently in a distributed fashion. To show the validity of our approximation we need the following definition.

Definition 2. *Given real numbers $a, b, \epsilon > 0$, we say that a approximates b with accuracy ϵ, and write $a \approx_\epsilon b$, if $a \in [(1+\epsilon)^{-1}b, (1+\epsilon)b]$.*

Our approximation is quantified with the following Lemma, whose proof is omitted from due to space limitations.

Lemma 3. *Given $\epsilon > 0$, consider the quantity $q(f)$ computed as described above, for $f \in F$. Let α be the ball radius at the current step of the algorithm. The following holds:*

$$q(f) \approx_\epsilon \sum_{c \in C} \max\{0, (1+\epsilon)\alpha(c) - d(c, f)\}.$$

Algorithm 3: Pregel-like algorithm for facility location (graph setting)

Input: Graph $G = (V, E, d)$, facilities $F \subseteq V$, clients $C \subseteq V$, facility opening cost $c(\cdot)$, accuracy ϵ
Output: Subset of opened facilities S

$O \leftarrow \emptyset$ `// opened facilities`
$U \leftarrow C$ `// Unfrozen clients`
$\alpha \leftarrow \alpha_0 \leftarrow \frac{\gamma}{m^2}(1+\epsilon)$ `// Initial ball radius`
$q(f) \leftarrow 0$ for each $f \in F$
`// next one is a sequential while`
while $(O \neq F)$ *and* $(U \neq \emptyset)$ **do**
  $\alpha \leftarrow \alpha(1+\epsilon)$ `// Increase ball radius`
  $\alpha(c) \leftarrow \alpha$ for each $c \in U$
  $\overline{O} \leftarrow$ OpenFacilities$(G, F \setminus O, U, c(\cdot), \alpha, \alpha(\cdot), q(\cdot))$
  for $f \in \bar{O}$ **do**
    send(f, α,"FreezeClient") `// f sends a "FreezeClient" message to all vertices within distance` α
  for $c \in U$ **do**
    if *c receives a "FreezeClient" message* **then**
      $U \leftarrow U \setminus \{c\}$
  $O \leftarrow O \cup \overline{O}$
if $O = F$ *and* $U \neq \emptyset$ **then**
  for $c \in U$ **do**
    $\alpha(c) \leftarrow \arg\min_f d(c, f)$
$S = \text{MIS}\overline{\text{H}}(G, O, C, \alpha(\cdot))$ `// Computing a MIS of` $\overline{H}$ `without building` H `nor` $\overline{H}$
return S

Algorithm 4: OpenFacilities$(G, D, U, c(\cdot), \alpha, \alpha(\cdot), q(\cdot))$

Input: Graph $G = (V, E)$, unopened facilities D, unfrozen clients U, facility opening cost $c(\cdot)$, current radius α, radius for frozen clients and opened facilities $\alpha(\cdot)$, facility contribution from clients $q(\cdot)$
Output: Newly opened facilities $\overline{O}$

for $f \in D$ `// For each unopened facility`
do
  `// use ADS Algorithm 2`
  Compute $\hat{n}(d, f)$ for each $f \in F$ and $d \in R$
  if $\alpha = \alpha_0$ **then**
    Compute $t(f, \alpha)$ as in Equation (2)
  else
    Compute $t(f, \alpha)$ as in Equation (3)
  $q(f) \leftarrow q(f) + t(f, \alpha)$
  if $q(f) \geq c(f)$ **then**
    add f in $\overline{O}$
    `// α's allow not to materialize` H `nor` $\overline{H}$
    $\alpha(f) \leftarrow \alpha$
return $\overline{O}$

Pseudocode for our method is shown in Algorithm 3. It consists of two building blocks: an algorithm for deciding which facilities to open (Algorithm 4), and an algorithm for computing a maximal independent set of the graph $\overline{H}$ without explicitly building such a graph (Algorithm 5). The pseudocode for distributing messages in the graph (denoted by the `send` procedure) is omitted for brevity.

During the execution of the algorithm, for each open facility f we let $\alpha(f)$ be the value of α when f is opened. Observe that there is an edge (c, f) in H only if (1) $\alpha(c) = \alpha(f)$, (2) c is within distance $(1+\epsilon)\alpha(c)$ from f, and (3) f is open. Therefore, storing the values for $\alpha(f)$ and $\alpha(c)$ allows us not to materialize $\overline{H}$, which might be very costly.

3.3 Maximal independent set

Salihoglu and Widom [45] recently proposed an implementation of the classic Luby's algorithm [37] for computing the MIS in a Pregel-like system such as Giraph. In our approach, we need to compute a MIS of $\overline{H}$ which is essentially the graph H^2 after removing all unopened facilities (and their edges) from H^2. As we do not materialize H nor $\overline{H}$, even computing the degree of a vertex in $\overline{H}$ (which is needed in Luby's algorithm) might require to exchange a large number of messages. Therefore, we resort to another algorithm developed by Blelloch et al. [5] and which works as follows.

Initially, all vertices are *active* and a unique ID is assigned randomly to each of them. Let $\pi(f)$ be the ID for facility f. Then, in parallel, each active vertex v checks whether its ID is the minimum among its neighbors. If this is the case, v is included in the maximal independent set and all its neighbors become *inactive*. This process is iterated $O(\log^2 n)$ times. It can be shown that, with high probability, the selected vertices induce a maximal independent set.

As we do not materialize H nor $\overline{H}$, we need to slightly modify the algorithm by Blelloch et al. [5]. Recall that there is an edge (c, f) in $E(H)$ only if (1) $\alpha(c) = \alpha(f)$, (2) c is within distance $(1+\epsilon)\alpha(c)$ from f, and (3) f is open. Moreover, there is an edge (f_a, f_b) in $E(\overline{H})$ if there exist $c \in C$ such that (c, f_a) and $(c, f_b) \in E(H)$. After determining its ID $\pi(f)$, each facility f sends a message $(\pi(f), \alpha(f))$ to all vertices within distance $(1+\epsilon)\alpha(f)$ from f. Each client c collects all messages $(\pi(f), \alpha(f))$, and retains only the pairs $(\pi(f), \alpha(f))$ corresponding to the facilities f that c is connected. Then, each client computes the minimum ID $\pi_{\min}$ among all the facilities it is connected to, and sends back a message containing $\pi_{\min}$ to all such facilities. Each facility f is included in the maximal independent set if an only if $\pi_{\min} = \pi(f)$, in which case it sends $\pi_{\min}$ to all neighboring facilities (in $\overline{H}$) so that they are removed from the set of active vertices. The last step is performed by letting each facility f send $\pi_{\min}$ to all clients c within distance $(1+\epsilon)\alpha(f)$, which in turn deliver such message to all facilities within distance $(1+\epsilon)\alpha(c)$. For pseudocode see Algorithm 5.

In Section 4, we evaluate the proposed algorithms against the algorithm proposed by Salihoglu and Widom [45].

3.4 Approximation guarantee and running time

Combining Theorem 1, Lemma 3, and the fact that ADS provides an approximation to the values of $\hat{n}(f, d)$, we can show an approximation guarantee for our algorithm.

Theorem 4. *For any $\epsilon > 0$ and any integer $k \geq 1$, Algorithm 3 has an approximation guarantee of $3 + o(1) + \epsilon$. The total number of parallel iterations is $\mathcal{O}(\frac{\delta}{\epsilon}\log^2(n))$, while the total number of messages exchanged by vertices is $\mathcal{O}(m)$, with each message requiring $\mathcal{O}(k \log n)$ bits.*

The parameter k is related to the bottom-k in ADS. Observe that we are able to derive the same approximation guarantees of Thorup [48], but in a distributed setting.

Algorithm 5: $\mathrm{MIS\overline{H}}(G, O, C, \alpha(\cdot))$

$S \leftarrow \emptyset, A \leftarrow O$
for $f \in A$ **do**
  $\pi(f) \leftarrow RAND([1, n^3])$
// next one is a sequential for
for $i = 1, \ldots, \lceil \log^2 n \rceil$ **do**
  for $f \in A$ **do**
    $\mathrm{send}(f, (1+\epsilon)\alpha(f), (\pi(f), \alpha(f)))$
  for $c \in C$ **do**
    $\pi_{\min} = \min_{(\pi(f),\alpha(f)):\alpha(f)=\alpha(c)} \pi(f)$
    $\mathrm{send}(c, (1+\epsilon)\alpha(c), \pi_{\min})$
  for $f \in A$ **do**
    if $\pi_{\min} = \pi(f)$ **then**
      $S \leftarrow S \cup \{f\}$
      $A \leftarrow A \setminus \{f\}$
      $\mathrm{send}(f, (1+\epsilon)\alpha(f), \pi_{min})$
  for $c \in C$ **do**
    if c receives $\pi_{\min}$, $\mathrm{send}(c, (1+\epsilon)\alpha(c), \pi_{min})$
  for $f \in A$ **do**
    if $\pi_{\min} < \pi(f)$, $A \leftarrow A \setminus \{f\}$
return S

Theorem 4 holds only for undirected graphs. For directed graphs our guarantee does not hold, even though our algorithm can be adapted in a straightforward manner. In our experiments we have used directed graphs as well, and the performance of the algorithm is equally good.

With respect to the running time, the overall number of supersteps required by the algorithm is proportional to the diameter δ of the graph. This follows from the hop-by-hop communication between clients and facilities. Thus, as typically real-world graphs have small diameter, we expect our algorithm to terminate in a small number of supersteps.

3.5 Implementation in Giraph

The facility-opening phase consists of two subroutines, *ball expansion* and *client freezing*, which are implemented by the vertices and masters compute functions. Initially, the algorithm expands the balls around the potential facilities in parallel. When one of the balls encompasses a large enough number of clients, the facility at the center of the ball opens. At this point, all clients within the ball freeze, via the `FreezeClients` subroutine. The algorithm then resumes expanding the balls in parallel until another facility opens. This phase terminates when no unfrozen client remains, condition monitored by the master via a `sum` aggregator. By the end of the algorithm, vertices are either open facilities, or frozen clients with at least one facility serving them. Clients may have multiple facilities serving them as a result of concurrent openings or intersecting balls.

We now describe in detail the implementation of this phase of the algorithm in Giraph. The communication and coordination between the two main subroutines is particularly interesting. In Giraph, the communication between master and workers happens via aggregators.

How to "call a subroutine"? While expanding the balls, we use a boolean aggregator called `SwitchState` to monitor if any facility was opened in the current superstep. Every vertex can write a boolean value to this aggregator, and the master can read the boolean `and` of all the values in its next superstep. The value of the aggregator is computed efficiently in parallel via a tree-like reduction. If `SwitchState` is true, the master writes to another aggregator `State` that represents the current function being computed. By setting the value of `State` to `FreezeClients`, the master can communicate to the vertices to switch their computation, effectively mimicking a subroutine call.

How does `FreezeClients` work? The vertices execute different subroutines by switching on the `State` aggregator. When `FreezeClients` is executed, each facility opened in the last superstep sends a "FreezeClient" message to all the clients within the current radius of the ball. This message contains the ID of the facility, and the distance it needs to reach, i.e., the radius. Each client that receives this message gets activated modifies its state to frozen by the facility whose ID is in the message, and propagates the message to its own neighbors, as explained next. When a vertex deactivates, it writes true on the `SwitchState` aggregator. When all the vertices terminate and deactivate, the master's `SwitchState` aggregator (which is a boolean `and`) becomes true. The master can then resume the `OpenFacilities` routine by writing on the `State` aggregator.

How to send a message to all vertices at distance d? In Giraph, messages are usually propagated along the graph, hop-by-hop. A vertex v that wants to send a message $\mathcal{M}$ to all veritces within distance d, sends to each neighbor u a message containing $\mathcal{M}$, as well as, the remaining distance $d - d(v, u)$, if such a distance is larger than zero. The message is then in turn propagated by u to its neighbors if the remaining distance is larger than zero. If a vertex receives multiple copies of the same message $\mathcal{M}$ it propagates only the one with maximum remaining distance. This subroutine takes several supersteps to complete, proportional to the distance to reach, and sends a number of messages proportional to the number of edges within distance d.

How to estimate the number of unfrozen clients? We employ ADS to estimate $N(f_i, d)$, i.e., the number of unfrozen clients within distance d from f_i. We achieve this by using the *predicated* query feature of ADS. Given that ADS is composed by a sample of the vertices in a graph (for each possible distance), we can obtain an unbiased sample of a subset of the vertices that satisfy a predicate simply by filtering the ADS with such predicate. That is, we can apply the condition *a posteriori*, after having built the ADS.

However, there is another issue to solve in our setting. The predicate we want to compute (unfrozen) is dynamic, as clients are frozen continuously while the algorithm is running. Therefore, we implement this predicate by maintaining explicitly the set of frozen clients. Whenever a client is frozen, it writes its own ID to a custom aggregator which computes the set union of all the values written in it. At the next superstep, each facility has access to this set, and can use it to filter the ADS for the following query. Notice that, even though this set can grow quite large, it can be approximated by using a Bloom filter at the cost of decreased accuracy in the estimate. Our experiments are not affected by this issue, so for simplicity we do not explore the use of Bloom filters, and defer its study to a later work.

4. EXPERIMENTS

We test our approach using several datasets on a shared Giraph cluster containing up to 500 machines. We design our experiments to answer the following questions:

Table 1: Datasets.

Name	$\|V\|$	$\|E\|$	Description
FF10K	10k	712k	Forest Fire random graphs
FF100K	100k	11M	
FF1M	1M	232M	
FF10M	10M	1.6B	
RMAT10K	2^{13}	3M	R-MAT random graphs
RMAT100K	2^{17}	5M	
RMAT1M	2^{20}	30M	
RMAT10M	2^{23}	500M	
ORKUT	3M	117M	Orkut social network
TUMBLR	10M	166M	Tumblr reblog network
USROAD	23M	58M	Complete road network of the USA
UK2005	39M	1.4B	Web graph of the .uk domain
FRND	65M	1.8B	Friendster social network

Q1: What is the performance of ADS and how does it affect the main algorithm? (Section 4.1)

Q2: How does our algorithm compare with state-of-the-art sequential ones, in terms of quality? (Section 4.2)

Q3: What is the scalability of our approach in terms of time and space? (Section 4.3)

Q4: How do the two implementations of MIS compare with each other? (Section 4.4)

Parameters. There are two parameters of interest in our approach: the parameter k of the bottom-k min-hash, which regulates the space-accuracy trade-off of ADS, and the parameter ϵ, which regulates the time-accuracy trade-off in the facility-location algorithm.

Datasets. Table 1 summarizes the datasets used in our experiments. We use both synthetic and real-world datasets. We use two types of synthetic datasets and create instances with exponentially increasing sizes to test the scalability of our approach. We choose graph-generation models that resemble real-world graphs. The first type of synthetic graphs is generated using the Forest Fire (FF) model [33], where the forward burning probability is set equal to 0.3 and the backward equal to 0.4. The second type of synthetic graphs uses the recursive matrix model (RMAT) [10] with parameters $a = 0.45$, $b = 0.15$, $c = 0.15$, and $d = 0.25$.[2] This model can only generate graphs with a number of vertices that is a power of 2. For weighted graphs, we assign weights between 1 and 100, uniformly at random.

4.1 Evaluation of ADS

We perform experiments to assess the quality of the ADS estimates. To the best of our knowledge, we are the first to implement and test ADS on Giraph on a large scale. First, we evaluate the quality of ADS approximation by comparing against exact neighborhood sizes. Then, we experiment with the time taken for computing the ADS as a function of k.

Accuracy vs. k: To evaluate the accuracy of the estimates produced by ADS, we need to compute exact neighborhood sizes. Since such computation is infeasible for large graphs, we compute exact neighborhood sizes on a sample of vertices. For each neighborhood distance (from 1 to 20 for unweighted graphs, and from 100 to 2000, at increments of 100, for weighted graphs), we sample 100 random vertices and compute their exact neighborhood sizes. For each sampled vertex and each distance, we compute the relative error as $|S_E - S_{\text{ADS}}|/S_E$, where S_E is the exact neighborhood size and S_{ADS} the ADS estimate. Relative error averages and variances across the 2000 samples are reported in Figure 1 (unweighted) and Figure 2 (weighted).

[2]For both models, FF and RMAT, we use the default parameters that the data generators come with.

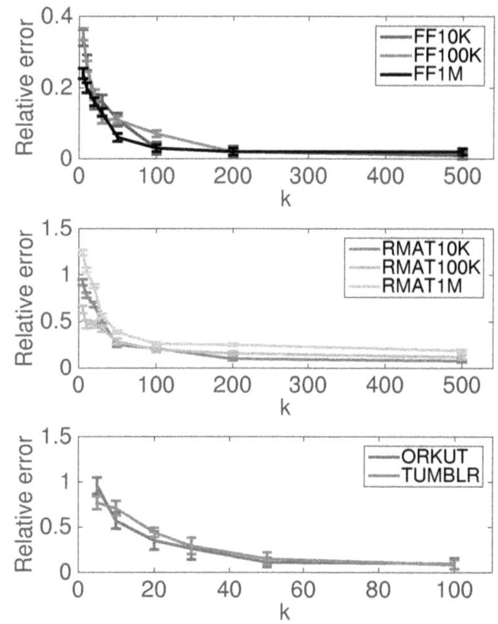

Figure 1: ADS relative error vs. k (unweighted graphs).

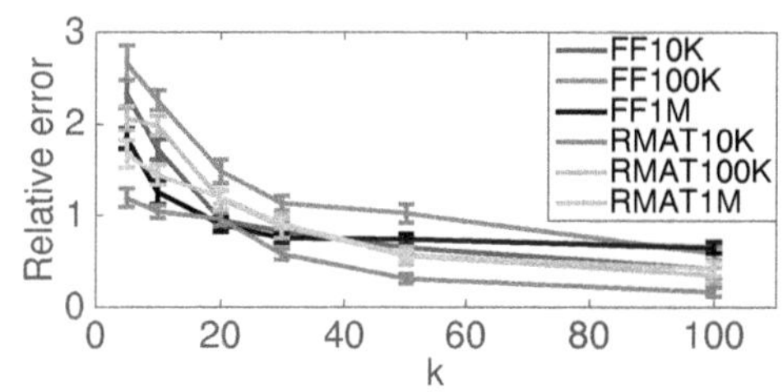

Figure 2: ADS relative error vs. k (weighted graphs).

We can see that the estimates are of high quality. In most cases, even for small values of k, the average relative error is less than 50%. The variance is also small.

Time vs. k: Next, we measure the time taken to compute the ADS as a function of k, as shown in Figure 3. We clearly see that even for graphs with 1 million vertices and k as large as 500, the algorithm finishes in less than 800 seconds.

Space requirements: Since increasing the value of k does not increase the time taken by the algoritom, one would assume that we could use a very high value of k in order to improve the quality of approximation of ADS. The bottleneck, though, is the size of the ADS, which is proportional to k. In our setting, we have a limitation of 3.5 GB of memory per machine, which makes it infeasible to store an ADS for large graphs with very large values of k (say, $n > 10$m and $k > 200$). Recall, however, that the size of the ADS is proportional to $nk \log n$, thus, the value of k can increase linearly with the number of available machines.

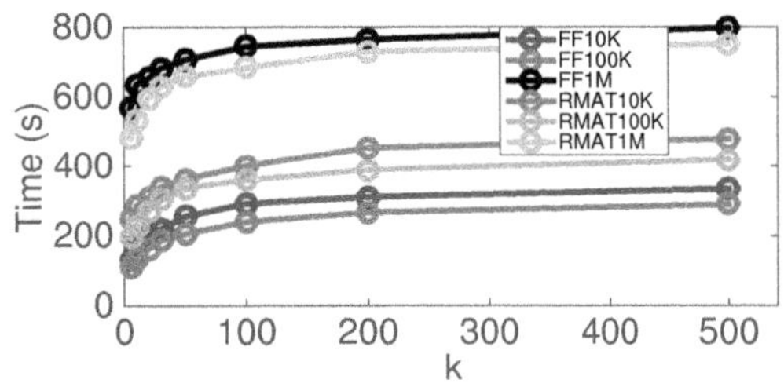

Figure 3: ADS time taken vs. k (unweighted graphs).

Table 2: Relative cost of the Giraph algorithm against the sequential one ($k = 200$).

Type	$\|V\|$	$\|E\|$	$\epsilon = 0.01$	$\epsilon = 0.1$	$\epsilon = 1$
FF	1k	11k	1.21	1.46	2.56
FF	2k	25k	1.15	1.60	2.45
FF	3k	60k	1.07	1.75	2.47
FF	4k	67k	1.08	1.48	2.16
FF	5k	121k	1.05	1.5	2.13
FF	6k	206k	1.01	1.41	2.02
FF	7k	268k	1.03	1.33	1.67
FF	8k	380k	1.03	1.25	1.55
FF	9k	520k	1.01	1.18	1.41
FF	10k	712k	1.02	1.09	1.43
RMAT	2^{10}	100k	1.08	1.55	1.88
RMAT	2^{11}	200k	1.06	1.36	1.7
RMAT	2^{12}	500k	1.05	1.35	1.73
RMAT	2^{13}	800k	1.05	1.24	1.44
RMAT	2^{14}	1000k	1.02	1.14	1.39

4.2 Facility-location algorithm

We evaluate the quality of the solutions produced by our distributed algorithm by comparing against a simple sequential baseline. We evaluate the performance and the running time of the algorithm as a function of ϵ.

Comparison with sequential algorithm: As a baseline we use the sequential approximation algorithm by Charikar and Guha [11], which achieves an approximation ratio of $(2.414+\epsilon)$ and has running time of $\tilde{\mathcal{O}}(n^2/\epsilon)$. The sequential algorithm assumes the availability of all-pairs shortest path distances, which is very expensive to compute, even for small graphs. Therefore, we perform our evaluation with graphs consisting of no more than 10 K vertices.

Table 2 shows the results of the comparison in terms of *relative cost*, which is defined as the cost of the sequential algorithm divided by the cost of our algorithm, for different values of ϵ. A smaller value means that our algorithm is competitive with the baseline. We can see that our algorithm performs quite well, even for large values of ϵ.

Cost vs. accuracy (ϵ): Table 2 shows the relative cost of our algorithm (compared again to the sequential algorithm) with respect to the accuracy. As expected, we get better solutions for smaller values of ϵ, but the solution does not get much worse even for large values of ϵ.

Running time vs. accuracy (ϵ): Figure 4 shows the time taken by our algorithm as a function of ϵ. We see that, as expected, our algorithm scales linearly with respect to the size of the graph,[3] and is faster for larger values of ϵ.

[3]A linear fit gives R^2 values between 0.8 and 0.9.

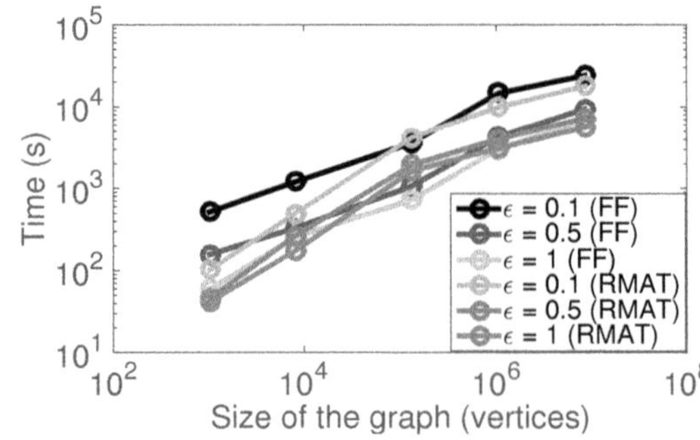

Figure 4: Time taken by the algorithm for different values of ϵ on several graphs.

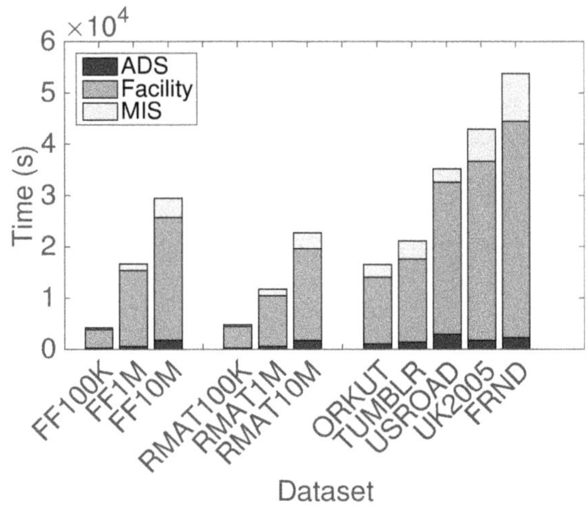

Figure 5: Time taken by each phase of the algorithm.

4.3 Scalability

Next, we examine the scalability of the different phases of our algorithm. Recall that the three phases of our algorithm are (*i*) ADS computation (pre-processing), (*ii*) facility-location algorithm, and (*iii*) MIS computation (post-processing). Figure 5 presents the time taken, for different datasets, broken down by phase. The total running time, for various graph sizes, is also shown in Figure 6.

For the results shown in Figure 5, we used $k = 20$, $\epsilon = 0.1$, and 200 machines. Since the running time on a distributed cluster depends on various factors, such as the current load of the machines, we repeat all experiments three times and report the median running time.

Next, we vary the size of the graph and the number of machines, keeping the number of vertices per machine constant and test the time taken by our algorithm. The results are presented in Figure 7. We can clearly see that the time taken almost remains constant, indicating the scalability of our approach to large graphs.

4.4 Luby's vs. parallel MIS

As discussed above, we implement two methods for finding the maximal independent set (MIS): Luby's [37], which was also implemented recently by Salihoglu and Widom [45], and a recent algorithm by Blelloch et al. [5]. We compare the two methods in terms of total time taken and number of supersteps needed to converge. Table 3 shows the results. We see that our parallel MIS algorithm implementation is at least 3 to 5 times faster than Luby's algorithm.

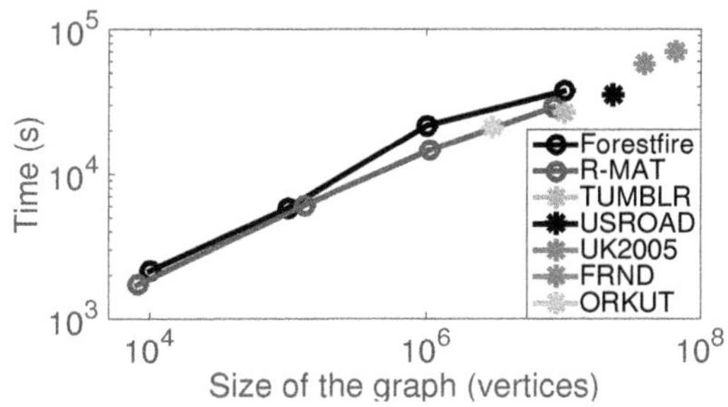

Figure 6: Total time taken by the algorithm.

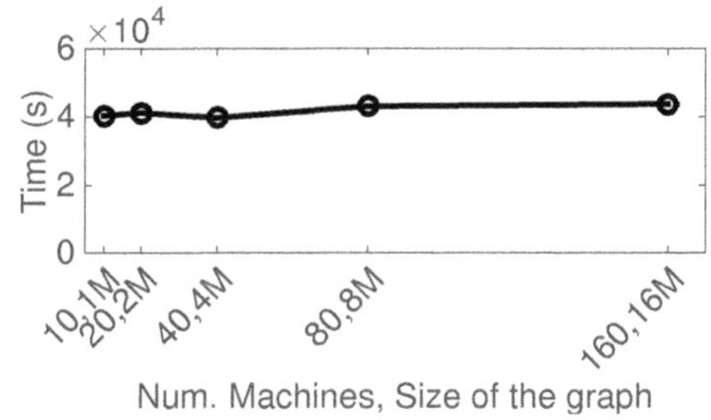

Figure 7: Total time taken by our algorithm for different number of machines for different sized graphs.

5. RELATED WORK

Facility location. Facility location is a classic optimization problem. The traditional formulation (metric uncapacitated facility location) is **NP**-hard, and so are many of its variants. Existing algorithms rely on techniques such as LP rounding, local search, primal dual, and greedy. The greedy heuristic obtains a solution with an approximation guarantee of $(1 + \log|\mathcal{D}|)$ [29], while constant-factor approximation algorithms have also been introduced [1, 11]. The approximation algorithm with the best factor so far (1.488) is very close to the approximability lower bound (1.463) [35].

Differently from most previous work, the input to our algorithm is a sparse graph representing potential facilities and clients and their distances, rather than the full bipartite graph of distances between facilities and clients. Note that building the full bipartite graph requires computing all-pairs of distances and implies an $\Omega(n^2)$ algorithm. Thorup [48] considers a setting similar to ours, and provides a fast sequential algorithm $\tilde{\mathcal{O}}(n + m)$.

Blelloch and Tangwongsan [4] propose a parallel approximation algorithm for facility location in the PRAM model. In this work, we extend the former algorithm to work in a more realistic shared-nothing Pregel-like model. Other parallel algorithms have also been proposed [25, 41, 42].

Applications. Facility location is a flexible model that has been applied successfully in many domains, such as city planning, telecommunications, electronics, and others. For an overview of applications, please refer to the textbook of Hamacher and Drezner [28].

Large-scale graph processing. MapReduce [19] is one of the most popular paradigms used for mining massive datasets. Many algorithms have been proposed for various graph problems, such as counting triangles [47], matching [18, 32, 40], building similarity graphs [3, 17], and finding densest subgraphs [2].

Table 3: Comparison of two implementations of MIS, in terms of supersteps and time taken (median over three runs).

Graph	Supersteps		Time (s)	
	Luby's	MIS	Luby's	MIS
FF10K	750	29	730	104
FF100K	3473	85	1869	296
FF1M	6119	325	6155	1205
FF10M	20 154	1613	11 744	3711
RMAT10K	645	17	616	87
RMAT100K	3200	73	1576	319
RMAT1M	5832	285	4109	1232
RMAT10M	17 557	1533	9492	3181

However, given the iterative nature of most graph algorithms, MapReduce is often not the most efficient solution. Pregel [38] is large-scale graph processing platform that supports a vertex-centric programming paradigm and uses the bulk synchronous parallel (BSP) model of computation. Giraph [12] is an open-source clone of Pregel. It is the platform that we use in this work. Other distributed systems for graph processing have recently been proposed, for instance, GraphLab [36], PowerGraph [26], GPS [44], and GraphX [27]. Most of the APIs of these system follow the gather-apply-scatter (GAS) paradigm, which can be readily used to express our algorithm. However, the BSP model is still used due to its simplicity and ease of use.

Algorithms. Our work takes advantage of a number of successful algorithmic techniques. We use the all-distance-sketches (ADS) and the historic inverse probability (HIP) estimator by Cohen [15] to estimate the number of vertices within certain distance from a given vertex. HIP is a cardinality estimator similar to HyperLogLog counters [22] and Flajolet-Martin counters [21]. HyperANF [6] is a related algorithm that approximates the global neighborhood function of the graph by using HyperLogLog counters, but it is not directly usable in our case as we need separate neighborhood functions for each vertex.

6. CONCLUSIONS

We have shown how to tackle the facility-location problem at scale by using Pregel-like systems. In particular, we addressed the graph setting of the problem, which allows to represent the input in sparse format as a graph. We leveraged graph sparsity to tackle problem instances whose size is much larger than previously possible.

Our algorithm is composed by three phases: (*i*) *neighborhood sketching*, (*ii*) *facility opening*, and (*iii*) *facility selection*. We implemented all three phases in Giraph, and published the code as open-source software. For the first phase, we showed how to use ADS with HIP, a recent graph-sketching technique. We adapted an existing PRAM algorithm with approximation guarantees for the second phase. Finally, for the third phase we proposed a new Giraph algorithm for the maximal independent set (MIS), which is much faster than the previous state-of-the-art. Our approach was able to scale to graphs with millions of vertices and billions of edges, thus adding facility location to the tool set of algorithms available for large-scale problems.

This work opens up several new research questions. From

the point of view of the practitioner, this algorithm enables to solve large-scale facility-location problems, thus is a candidate for real-world applications in Web and social-network analysis. A more general question is whether better algorithms exist for the setting we consider. Also, it would be interesting to know whether there are any primitives that the system could offer to develop better algorithms.

7. REFERENCES

[1] K. Aardal, D. Shmoys, and E. Tardos. Approximation algorithms for facility location problems. In *STOC*, 1997.

[2] B. Bahmani, R. Kumar, and S. Vassilvitskii. Densest Subgraph in Streaming and MapReduce. *PVLDB*, 5(5), 2012.

[3] R. Baraglia, G. De Francisci Morales, and C. Lucchese. Document similarity self-join with MapReduce. In *ICDM*, 2010.

[4] G. E. Blelloch and K. Tangwongsan. Parallel approximation algorithms for facility-location problems. In *SPAA*, 2010.

[5] G. E. Blelloch, J. T. Fineman, and J. Shun. Greedy sequential maximal independent set and matching are parallel on average. In *SPAA*, 2012.

[6] P. Boldi, M. Rosa, and S. Vigna. HyperANF: Approximating the neighbourhood function of very large graphs on a budget. In *WWW*, 2011.

[7] U. Brandes and T. Erlebach. *Network analysis: methodological foundations*, volume 3418. Springer, 2005.

[8] A. Broder. On the resemblance and containment of documents. In *SEQUENCES*, 1997.

[9] A. L. Buchsbaum, D. F. Caldwell, K. W. Church, G. S. Fowler, and S. Muthukrishnan. Engineering the compression of massive tables: an experimental approach. In *SODA*, 2000.

[10] D. Chakrabarti, Y. Zhan, and C. Faloutsos. R-MAT: A recursive model for graph mining. In *SDM*, 2004.

[11] M. Charikar and S. Guha. Improved combinatorial algorithms for the facility location and k-median problems. In *FOCS*, 1999.

[12] A. Ching and C. Kunz. Giraph: Large-scale graph processing infrastructure on Hadoop. *Hadoop Summit*, 2011.

[13] F. Chudak, T. Erlebach, A. Panconesi, and M. Sozio. Primal-dual distributed algorithms for covering and facility location problems. *Unpublished Manuscript*, 2, 2005.

[14] E. Cohen. Size-estimation framework with applications to transitive closure and reachability. *Journal of Computer and System Sciences*, 55(3), 1997.

[15] E. Cohen. All-distances sketches, revisited: HIP estimators for massive graphs analysis. In *PODS*, 2014.

[16] E. Cohen, D. Delling, F. Fuchs, A. V. Goldberg, M. Goldszmidt, and R. F. Werneck. Scalable similarity estimation in social networks: Closeness, node labels, and random edge length. In *COSN*, 2013.

[17] G. De Francisci Morales, C. Lucchese, and R. Baraglia. Scaling Out All Pairs Similarity Search with MapReduce. In *LSDS-IR*, 2010.

[18] G. De Francisci Morales, A. Gionis, and M. Sozio. Social Content Matching in MapReduce. *PVLDB*, 4(7), 2011.

[19] J. Dean and S. Ghemawat. MapReduce: Simplified Data Processing on Large Clusters. In *OSDI*, 2004.

[20] M. Durand and P. Flajolet. Loglog counting of large cardinalities. In *ESA*, 2003.

[21] P. Flajolet and G. N. Martin. Probabilistic counting algorithms for data base applications. *Journal of Computer and System Sciences*, 31(2), 1985.

[22] P. Flajolet, E. Fusy, O. Gandouet, and F. Meunier. HyperLogLog: the analysis of a near-optimal cardinality estimation algorithm. In *AofA*, 2007.

[23] M. Garofalakis, A. Gionis, R. Rastogi, S. Seshadri, and K. Shim. XTRACT: a system for extracting document type descriptors from XML documents. *SIGMOD Record*, 29(2), 2000.

[24] B. Gavish. Topological design of telecommunication networks-local access design methods. *Annals of Operations Research*, 33(1):17–71, 1991.

[25] J. Gehweiler, C. Lammersen, and C. Sohler. A distributed $O(1)$-approximation algorithm for the uniform facility location problem. In *SPAA*, 2006.

[26] J. Gonzalez, Y. Low, H. Gu, D. Bickson, and C. Guestrin. PowerGraph: Distributed Graph-Parallel Computation on Natural Graphs. In *OSDI*, 2012.

[27] J. Gonzalez, R. Xin, and A. Dave. GraphX: Graph processing in a distributed dataflow framework. In *OSDI*, 2014.

[28] H. W. Hamacher and Z. Drezner. *Facility location: applications and theory*. Springer, 2002.

[29] D. S. Hochbaum. Heuristics for the fixed cost median problem. *Mathematical Programming*, 22(1), 1982.

[30] K. Jain, M. Mahdian, E. Markakis, A. Saberi, and V. Vazirani. Greedy facility location algorithms analyzed using dual fitting with factor-revealing LP. *JACM*, 50(6), 2003.

[31] A. Kuehn and M. Hamburger. A heuristic program for locating warehouses. *Management science*, 9(4), 1963.

[32] S. Lattanzi, B. Moseley, S. Suri, and S. Vassilvitskii. Filtering: A method for solving graph problems in MapReduce. In *SPAA*, 2011.

[33] J. Leskovec, J. Kleinberg, and C. Faloutsos. Graph evolution: Densification and shrinking diameters. *TKDD*, 1 (1), 2007.

[34] J. Leskovec, A. Krause, C. Guestrin, C. Faloutsos, J. VanBriesen, and N. Glance. Cost-effective outbreak detection in networks. In *KDD*, 2007.

[35] S. Li. A 1.488 approximation algorithm for the uncapacitated facility location problem. In *ICALP*, 2011.

[36] Y. Low, D. Bickson, and J. Gonzalez. Distributed GraphLab: a framework for machine learning and data mining in the cloud. *PVLDB*, 5(8), 2012.

[37] M. Luby. A simple parallel algorithm for the maximal independent set problem. *SIAM J. on Comp.*, 15(4), 1986.

[38] G. Malewicz, M. H. Austern, A. J. C. Bik, J. C. Dehnert, I. Horn, N. Leiser, and G. Czajkowski. Pregel: A system for large-scale graph processing. In *SIGMOD*, 2010.

[39] A. Manne. Plant location under economies-of-scale-decentralization and computation. *Management Science*, 11(2), 1964.

[40] F. M. Manshadi, B. Awerbuch, R. Gemula, R. Khandekar, J. Mestre, and M. Sozio. A distributed algorithm for large-scale generalized matching. *PVLDB*, 6(9), 2013.

[41] T. Moscibroda and R. Wattenhofer. Facility location: distributed approximation. In *PODC*, 2005.

[42] S. Pandit and S. Pemmaraju. Return of the primal-dual: distributed metric facility location. In *PODC*, 2009.

[43] L. Qiu, V. Padmanabhan, and G. Voelker. On the placement of web server replicas. In *INFOCOM*, 2001.

[44] S. Salihoglu and J. Widom. GPS: A graph processing system. In *SSDBM*, 2013.

[45] S. Salihoglu and J. Widom. Optimizing graph algorithms on pregel-like systems. *PVLDB*, 7(7), 2014.

[46] D. B. Shmoys. Approximation Algorithms for Facility Location Problems. *AACO*, 1913, 2000.

[47] S. Suri and S. Vassilvitskii. Counting triangles and the curse of the last reducer. In *WWW*, 2011.

[48] M. Thorup. Quick k-median, k-center, and facility location for sparse graphs. In *ICALP*, 2001.

[49] G. Zuccon, L. Azzopardi, D. Zhang, and J. Wang. Top-k retrieval using facility-location analysis. In *ECIR*, 2012.

Rank by Time or by Relevance? Revisiting Email Search

David Carmel[1], Guy Halawi[2], Liane Lewin-Eytan[2], Yoelle Maarek[1], Ariel Raviv[2]
Yahoo Labs, MATAM Park
Haifa, 31905, Israel
[1]{david.carmel,yoelle}@ymail.com, [2]{ghalawi,liane,arielr}@yahoo-inc.com

ABSTRACT

With Web mail services offering larger and larger storage capacity, most users do not feel the need to systematically delete messages anymore and inboxes keep growing. It is quite surprising that in spite of the huge progress of relevance ranking in Web Search, mail search results are still typically ranked by date. This can probably be explained by the fact that users demand perfect recall in order to "re-find" a previously seen message, and would not trust relevance ranking. Yet mail search is still considered a difficult and frustrating task, especially when trying to locate older messages. In this paper, we study the current search traffic of *Yahoo mail*, a major Web commercial mail service, and discuss the limitations of ranking search results by date. We argue that this sort-by-date paradigm needs to be revisited in order to account for the specific structure and nature of mail messages, as well as the high-recall needs of users. We describe a two-phase ranking approach, in which the first phase is geared towards maximizing recall and the second phase follows a learning-to-rank approach that considers a rich set of mail-specific features to maintain precision. We present our results obtained on real mail search query traffic, for three different datasets, via manual as well as automatic evaluation. We demonstrate that the default time-driven ranking can be significantly improved in terms of both recall and precision, by taking into consideration time recency and textual similarity to the query, as well as mail-specific signals such as users' actions.

Categories and Subject Descriptors: H.3.3 [Information Search and Retrieval]: Retrieval models

General Terms: Algorithms, Experimentation

Keywords: Email Search, Ranking

1. INTRODUCTION

Recent market analysis studies have shown that in spite of the rise of communications through social media, email traffic keeps increasing [21]. In addition, Web mail services offer more free storage than in the past, with quotas that range from 15GB for Gmail to 1TB for Yahoo Mail. For most users, cleaning up inboxes is not compulsory anymore, and they adopt the "lazy" approach of rarely deleting messages. We have verified over 2 months of users' activities in Yahoo Web mail service, that 82% of users never deleted a single message. Thus, mailboxes have grown and will keep growing, storing together with useless messages, such as hotel newsletters or obsolete personal exchanges, critical information such as e-tickets or invoices that users will want to re-access at some point. Indeed, mailboxes have been used for data archiving of personal communications for more than a decade [26], and more recently for storing important machine-generated messages [12]. Folders are not of much assistance for discovering past mail, as demonstrated by a study conducted by Whittaker et al [25]. It is even worse in the context of Web email, in which it has been shown that more than 70% of users never define a single folder [14], and among those who do define folders, less than 10% are actually using them [12]. Therefore, the default discovery paradigm for retrieving past messages or attachments is search.

Unfortunately, email search remains "frequently difficult, time-consuming and frustrating" [11]. Some possible reasons for this is that email search mechanisms have not been sufficiently tailored to the specific needs of email users and to the specific structure of email messages. The task is clearly challenging as users, unlike in Web search but very much like in desktop search, will know when a relevant message has not been returned. Indeed, in email search, users usually want perfect recall as they are looking for *stuff they've seen*, to paraphrase the pioneering work by Dumais et al. on desktop search [8]. Email search strategies and email searchers' behavior have both been studied in depth [6, 23, 11, 25, 12, 13]. Yet to the best of our knowledge, there has not been any large study of email search ranking mechanisms in major Web email services. As an example, it is not clear why by default, all existing services display search results in reverse chronological order, and how this impacts precision and recall, as well as the user search behavior. Note that this "sorting by time" default view is critical since it has been shown that email searchers almost never re-sort search results [11].

In this paper, we challenge the prevalent ranked-by-time search result view in Web email and investigate whether an email-specific ranked-by-relevance view could bring value to users. Note that relevance is not totally absent from Web email search. Yahoo Mail for instance allows users to change the search results sort view from time to relevance. Yet, the

CIKM'15, October 19–23, 2015, Melbourne, Australia.
© 2015 ACM. ISBN 978-1-4503-3794-6/15/10 ...$15.00.
DOI: http://dx.doi.org/10.1145/2806416.2806471.

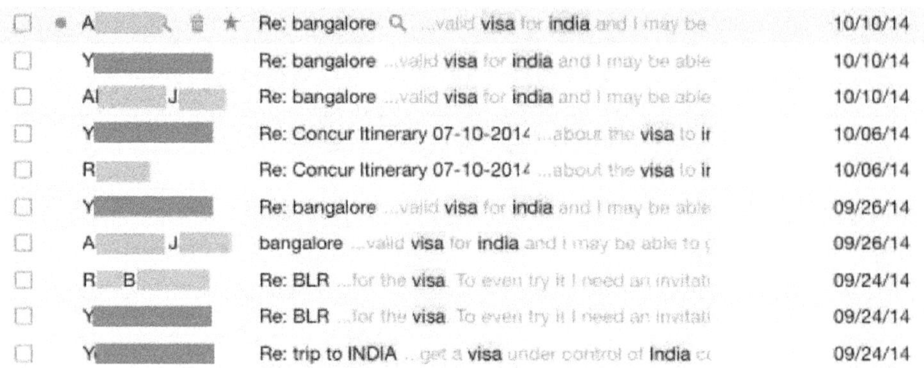

Figure 1: Time-sorted results for the query "visa to india"

sort preference toggling is quite hidden, and it most probable that the majority of users never changes the default order. Google exposes relevance ranking in small results sets: one example is the Gmail autocomplete search box [19], which dynamically predicts a few relevant messages as the user types the query; a more recent example is Inbox for Gmail[1], which lists a few "top results" ranked by relevance above the usual ranked by time of "all results". None of the major Web email services have divulged how their search mechanisms operate. However, one can safely assume that a two-stage approach is applied in which a pool of results that pass a certain relevant threshold is first identified, and then, in a second stage, these results are sorted by recency so as to rank fresher messages higher.

The main drawbacks of the chronological ordering of the results are twofold. First, it makes the discovery of older messages even harder. The older the message, the more difficult it is to remember characteristic attributes (such as its senders or differentiating terms). More specifically, Elsweiler et al. [10] have demonstrated that re-finding older email is notably difficult and that "specific support is required when the user is looking for older information". Second, chronological ordering imposes quite strict constraints for messages to qualify as relevant in the first phase. This is necessary in order to avoid embarrassing, non-relevant yet recent results from being displayed at the top of the list. As a result, recall is often degraded, contradicting the requirement for high recall, possibly at the cost of lower precision in a re-find scenario. Finding the "perfect query" for older messages becomes even harder.

Consider this motivating example taken from one of the authors' mailboxes. The searcher, to whom we refer as Y, is trying to recover the visa application form that he sent to his travel agency the last time he traveled to India. He does not remember which travel agent he worked with, nor his exact time of travel. When he issues the query "visa to india", using the default mail search ranking of his Web mail, he gets the results shown in Figure 1. Note that all personal information was obfuscated in this screen capture, as well as the mail system logo, for obvious privacy and anonymization reasons. These results match the terms "visa" and "india", in the body of the message, as indicated by the snippet match in grey, yet none satisfy his intent. They are all recent inquiries from friends and colleagues who are discussing with Y their own travel to India. In order to recover his old form, Y will need to try several reformulations, or advanced structured operator such as, "from":" or "has attachment", etc. We will revisit this example in Section 4.

In this work, we aim at demonstrating that while freshness remains indeed important in email search, ranking by time is not the optimal solution for satisfying users' needs. We argue that with a proper time and email-domain aware relevance estimation, relevance ranking will achieve better results. We investigate whether relaxing the match requirements in the first phase can improve recall, while improving precision during the second phase via a novel Learning-to-Rank (LTR) approach that considers a rich set of email-specific features. The latter range from features related to the query, the message, and the sender, to more traditional text-similarity features between candidate messages and the query.

More specifically, we pay special attention to the following types of features. First, we recognize email messages as structured documents, composed of a body and a header, where the header includes a subject line, and other fields such as sender, recipient(s) and date, as per the standard Internet message format[2].. Textual similarity between the query and a message is obviously key to relevance, yet query terms might appear in several textual fields of the message. Relevance should be affected by the type of field in which the query terms appear. To this effect, we take into account the message structure by using the BM25f score [22], which has been specifically designed for structured documents, in addition to other traditional similarity scores. Second, we propose to fully integrate in our relevance estimation the recency of a message, which we refer to as *freshness*, rather than using recency as a sorting mechanism. In addition, in the same way that usage data such as page clicks and dwell time has been shown to be critical in Web search [3], we propose to consider email actions performed by the user on each message (e.g., read, reply, forward, mark, etc.). Finally, we investigate whether more static signals, such as sender global email activity and the strength of the sender correspondence with the user, bring value to message ranking.

The contributions of our paper are three-fold:

1. We revisit email search, considering it as an independent search domain that requires its own ranking model.

[1]See the "Find emails" section in Google Support `https://support.google.com/inbox/answer/6067584`

[2]See Internet Message Format, RFC2822 and RFC6854

We challenge the traditional chronological ranking commonly used in email search, and argue that using a new email relevance model is better adapted to the user "re-find" needs.

2. We introduce REX (Relevance Extended), a novel email relevance ranking algorithm, that makes use of a wide variety of features relevant to email search, including freshness, under a learning-to-rank approach.

3. We describe a full evaluation system and report our offline as well as online experiments conducted on the Yahoo Web mail system. We report on qualitative judgments conducted by professional editors on their own mailboxes as well as automatic evaluation results in a large scale privacy-preserving experiment. This is to the best of our knowledge the first experiment of that scale.

2. RELATED WORK

Email search in general, and email ranking in particular, have not received much attention by the IR research community, probably due to the lack of publicly available benchmarks of email data, which is too private and too sensitive to be widely exposed. One exception is the TREC Enterprise track dataset [6, 23], which contains about 200K email messages crawled from the W3C public mailing list archive `lists.w3.org`. In the known-item search task of the TREC 2005 enterprise track, participants were challenged with (query, message-id) pairs where their task was to rank the given message at the top of their search results. Participants took different approaches at integrating the message text with the message meta-data, as well as balancing between the various message fields. Macdonald et al. [17] combined Web features with email features using a field-based weighting model, investigating the retrieval performance attainable by each field and whether field evidences should be combined or not. Craswell et al [7] applied the BM25f formula [22] in order to account for the message meta-data in the final message score. Ogilvie and Callan [18] took a language model approach in order to combine evidences from the text of the message, the subject, the text of the thread in which the message occurs, and the text of messages that are in reply to the message. A comprehensive overview of this track can be found in [6].

The same dataset was also utilized in the email discussion search task of the TREC 2006 enterprise track [23]. In this task, participants searched for email discussions that are relevant to a given topic and added pro or con arguments.

The W3C dataset was also used in a few more studies. Yahyaei and Montz [27], showed that maximum entropy can be successfully applied in order to estimate feature weights in known-item email retrieval, leading to statistically significant improvements over several baselines. Weerkamp et al.[24] studied the usage of contextual information to improving email search. They expanded queries using several sources, such as threads and mailing lists. Additionally, their experiments showed that using query-independent features (email length, thread size, text quality), implemented as priors, resulted in further improvements.

Abdelrahman et al. [1] experimented with email search over the Enron corpus[3], an enterprise email corpus dating from 2003 that was released by the Federal Energy Regulatory Commission after the Enron investigation. They proposed a scoring function that derived information from the email subject, content, and sender. However since the Enron dataset does not include queries and relevance judgments, the authors generated 300 synthetic queries (using topic words related to Enron) and used a sample of 35 queries for testing. Relevance was estimated by three judges according to given guidelines. This approach is clearly far from a real life scenario as both queries and relevance judgments were not originated from the mailbox owners.

None of the previous work described above investigate ranking methods in a real online setting, and in particular in commercial Web email services, which serve hundreds of millions of users. A rare exception to this, is the work by Aberdeen et al. [2] on Gmail priority inbox. The authors predict the "importance" of a message, which is defined as the likelihood that a user will act on it. Their learning procedure considers social features that are based on the degree of interaction between the sender and the recipient, content features that identify important terms in the message, thread features that measure the user's interaction with the message thread, and label features which examine the labels that the user applies to the message. Recently, Kooti et al. [13] tried to predict the reply time and length for email messages, based on the stage of the conversation, user demographics, and use of portable devices. They found that as users receive more email messages in a day, they reply to a smaller fraction of them, while using shorter replies. However, their responsiveness remains intact, and they may even reply to emails faster.

While these recent works do not directly pertain to email ranking, the message importance score [2], or the predicted reply time [13], could potentially be utilized as additional features for message ranking. Similar to these works, we do consider content, sender, and action features, but in a different flavor, as our task is drastically different. To the best of our knowledge, our work is the first that discusses email ranking in the context of a large Web mail service, and experiments with real queries and real messages, considering not only editorial judgments (conducted by professional editors on their own mailboxes) but also real-user implicit satisfaction derived from clicks.

3. RANKING MODEL

Our model is based on a standard two-phase retrieval process. In the first phase, that we refer to as the "matching phase", we retrieve a pool of messages qualified as potentially relevant to the query. We use here standard IR text matching mechanisms and do not differentiate between candidates within the pool. The second phase ranks these messages using a rich set of features. The goal of the first phase is to improve performance, so that not all messages in the inbox need to be considered by the more expensive relevance estimation of the second phase.

We will get back to the first phase at the end of the section, and focus in the meantime on the second phase, the ranking phase that introduces a new mail-specific relevance estimation. Our ranking model is based on a large set of features covering the message (body and meta-data), its similarity to the query, and characteristics of the participants involved in the mail correspondence (sender and recipients). We de-

[3] `http://www.cs.cmu.edu/~enron/`

scribe next the set of features used by the ranking function as well as our LTR approach.

3.1 Ranking features

We detail below the four types of features that we consider, which relate to an individual message, senders, recipients, and the message/query similarity. These features are listed in a summarized view in Table 1.

3.1.1 Message

The retrieval unit we consider here is a single message. We could not consider a thread as a retrieval unit as the current version of Yahoo Web mail service that hosted our experiments does not support such a feature. Note however that we do recognize whether or not a message is part of a thread and reflect this fact in a message feature as discussed later.

Message features describe message characteristics that are independent from the query. One critical type of message features is the message freshness that we account for in different time units. An important characteristic of our work is to consider message freshness as a set of features in our relevance model, rather than as a sorting criterion. As shown in many other domains, temporal aspects of the documents can significantly impact their relevance to many query types [16, 9].

More specifically, we consider the freshness of a message in days, weeks, months and years, using the formula given below. We define

$$fresh_g(M) = e^{-\tau_g \cdot age(M)}, \quad (1)$$

where τ_g is a tunable decay factor and $age(M)$ is the message age measured in seconds. The different values of τ_g are set according to the granularity g of the message age with $g \in \{days, weeks, months, years\}$.

The second set of message features reflects the user's actions on a message. More specifically, we consider *replied, forwarded, draft, flagged, seen (read), spam, ham,* as binary features that denote whether or not the user conducted the respective action on the message.

An additional set of features corresponds to message attachments when they exist. The attachment features reflect the type of the attached object (e.g. document, image, audio, video, calendar invitation, etc.) and size range. An additional set of feature, that we refer to as "folder", indicate the type of folder to which the message belongs, where the message can belong to a predefined system folder such as inbox, sent, draft, trash, spam, chats, etc., or to a personal user-defined folder (we do not differ here between different user-defined folders as this data was not available in our experiment settings). Finally, the last set of message features represents its "exchange type", reflecting whether the message is a reply or a forwarded message, and whether or not it is part of a thread correspondence (clearly, a message can be both a reply/forward, as well as part of a thread).

3.1.2 Sender

We detail here features that relate to the sender of the message. The sender features are divided into two sub-types, that we refer to "vertical" when the feature pertains to the sender activity with respect to the user's mailbox, and as "horizontal" when it pertains to the sender activity across all users' mailboxes. We use a single vertical sender feature that represents the volume of communication between the user and the sender. The more frequent and the more recent (as per a decay factor we discuss later) the communication is, the higher the value of this feature. We compute it per user, as a same sender will have different exchange patterns with different users. We define it as:

$$P_u(s) \cong \frac{M^T_{u,s}}{M^T_u} \cdot \frac{M^O_{u,s}}{M^O_u} \quad (2)$$

The score $P_u(s)$ to sender s is thus relative to user u, where $M^T_{u,s}$ counts the total number of messages between u and s (both inbound and outbound), M^T_u counts the total number of messages between u and all its contacts (both inbound and outbound), $M^O_{u,s}$ counts the total number of outbound messages from u to s, and M^O_u counts the total number of outbound messages from u. The intuition here is that the user's outbound messages is a valuable signal in estimating the importance of a sender. Taking it into account prevents us from assigning an overwhelmingly high score to a mass sender (e.g. a robot sending a hotel newsletter for instance).

In addition, we decrease the influence of a message on the different counters in Equation 2, as it gets older, by using a decay factor. A recent message will contribute a score of 1 to the relevant counters, however, an old message will contribute only $\alpha^{age(M)}$, where $0 < \alpha < 1$ is a tunable parameter (we empirically set α to 0.92 in our experiments).

A special case of sender-user connection is reflected in the so-called "self correspondence" that indicates whether the sender is the user himself. Note that such cases are not rare, since as mentioned before, mailboxes have been used for long for data archiving.

The horizontal sender features are computed across all users, and relate to the global activity of the sender. Features in this set account for the volume of the sender inbound and outbound traffic (where the sender traffic is measured with respect to the entire user population in the system), the average number of URLs appearing in the sender messages, and the average number of recipients of these messages. In addition, we aggregate mail actions performed on the sender's messages over all users. For each action type, we provide the ratio of the sender messages triggering this action. Examples of action types include *delete, read, reply, forward, move-to-folder, mark-ham/spam, flag/star,* etc. We note that a large part of the horizontal sender features are good indicators as whether the sender is a robot sending a machine-generated message or a human actually composing the messages. For example, messages addressed to a very large number of recipients, or containing a high amount of URLs in their content, are likely to be machine generated, while messages triggering reply actions are commonly sent by humans.

3.1.3 Recipient

Recipient features aim at capturing the strength of the connection between the recipient and the message. These features differentiate between messages that are targeted to the user as the sole recipient, or as a part of a larger distribution list, under the intuition that a message sent only to the user might be more important to him/her. We parse the message header fields, namely `To:`, `CC:`, `BCC:` and reflect this information in the following recipient features: *isInTo*, *isInCC* and *isInGroup*.

Type	Sub-Type	Feature (or features set) Name	Description
Message	Freshness	time by days/weeks/months/years	message age by respective resolution
	User Actions	replied	message was replied
		forwarded	message was forwarded
		draft	message is saved as draft
		flagged	message is flagged by star
		seen	message was read
		spam	message was marked as Spam
		ham	message was marked as Ham
	Attachment	has attachment	message has an attachment
		attachment type	set of binary features for attachment type
		attachment size	set of binary features for attachment size range
	Folder	folder type	set of binary features indicating the folder of the message (specific system folder or a personal folder)
	Exchange Type	reply/forward	binary features indicating if message is a reply or a forward
		in thread	message is part of a thread correspondence
Recipient		in To/Cc/Group	set of binary features corresponding to wether recipient is in To/Cc/Group (group is Bcc or mailing list)
Sender	Vertical	sender-user connection	strength of correspondence between sender and user
		self correspondence	sender is the user (binary, message was sent from the user to himself)
	Horizontal (over all users)	sender outbound/inbound traffic	set of binary features for sender's outbound/inbound traffic range
		sender urls	set of binary features for range of urls num in sender's messages
		sender recipients num	set of binary features for range of recipients num in sender's messages
		sender-users actions	ratio of the sender's messages on which a specific action was performed
Query Similarity		BM25f	BM25f similarity between message and query
		tf-idf	tf-idf similarity between message fields and query
		coord	fraction of query terms found in the message

Table 1: Set of features used by the ranking function.

3.1.4 Message-Query Similarity

We consider three main features for representing the connection between the message and the query, all evaluating the textual similarity between the two: $BM25f$, $tf.idf$, and *coord* as defined below.

BM25f [22], is a state-of-the-art ranking function that measures the textual similarity between a query Q and a structured document D that consists of several textual fields. It is defined as

$$BM25f(Q,D) = \sum_{q \in Q} idf(q) * \frac{\hat{tf}(q,D)}{k + \hat{tf}(q,D)}$$
$$\hat{tf}(q,D) = \sum_{f \in F} w_f \frac{tf(q,D_f)}{(1-b_f) + b_f \frac{l_{D_f}}{avl_f}}, \quad (3)$$

where $idf(q)$ is the inverse document frequency of the query term q in the user mailbox, and k is a tunable parameter. F is the set of document fields, $tf(q, D_f)$ is the term frequency of the query term within the field D_f, l_{D_f} and $avgl_f$ are the document field length, and the average document field length, over all documents respectively. Finally b_f and w_f are the field parameters. We consider both unigrams and bigrams as query terms. We extend here the definition of a bigram, and consider it both as two consecutive query terms, as well as two consecutive query terms found (unordered) within a window of 5 terms in the respective field. Each of these cases, consecutive or within a window, is reflected as a separate term in the sum.

In our context, D represents as message, and the fields f are its textual message fields. More specifically, we consider the header fields (i.e., `Subject, From, To, CC`), the attachment name and the attachment content when appropriate, and the body of the message. The scoring function also leverages, for each field f, its relative importance weight w_f and the normalization parameter b_f. For each message field f, we tune the pair (w_f, b_f). In addition, the k parameter is used to normalize the term frequency scores $\hat{tf}$. All parameters of the $BM25$ formula were tuned using a small random subset of the datasets we experimented with.

The second feature is **tf.idf** that we use under the following variant:

$$tf.idf(Q, D_f) = \frac{\sum_{q \in Q} tf(q, D_f) \cdot idf(q)}{l_{D_f}} \quad (4)$$

where l_{D_f} is the length of the message field.

There is a major difference between $BM25f$ and $tf.idf$. The first weights the query terms based on their distribution over the message fields, while the second measures the similarity of each field to the query independently of the others. We provide the $BM25f$ score of the whole message, and the independent $tf.idf$ scores of all message fields, as input to the LTR learning module that we describe below.

Lastly, we consider the **coord** feature, reusing Lucene (`http://lucene.apache.org/`) terminology, which defines *coord*(Q, D) as the fraction of query terms in query Q that occur at least once in the message D, in any of its textual fields.

3.2 Learning to Rank

Our LTR procedure is an online variant of SVMRank [4], which searches for a linear weight vector that aims to rank, for each training query, the clicked message higher than other top scored messages of the query. Our training dataset consists of a large scale random sample of real user queries issued on Yahoo Web mail service, as described in Section 4. All users voluntarily opted-in for being part of such a research experiment. For each query, we retrieve in the first phase of our model, up to 100 candidate messages from the searcher's mailbox, as well as the messages clicked by the searcher[4].

The training algorithm begins with a zero-weight vector and updates it for each example using the AROW online learning procedure [5], which showed comparable performance to SVMRank. Specifically, for each example, our algorithm first ranks the retrieved messages using the current scoring function. Then, it selects message pairs consisting of the feature vector v_c of the clicked message and of the feature vector v_m of each of the top K ranked messages. Following the original SVMRank algorithm, for each such pair, the algorithm generates the difference vector $v_c - v_m$, as a training example for the linear ranker.

The optimized parameters we used, based on an independent validation set, are the following: 5 training rounds, K set to 10, and the AROW hyper-parameter r set to 1.

3.3 First Matching Phase

The search process begins with the first phase, which retrieves a pool of candidate messages that match the user's query. We consider two approaches for the first matching phase. In the first approach, we demand a strict match between the query and the message: all query terms are required to appear in at least one of the message fields. This is also the default approach that is currently used by the live mail system on which we conducted our experiments. In the second approach we relax the matching constraints by requiring only a partial match between the query and the message: at least one query term should appear in the message content.

The strict match seems to be preferred when a chronological sort is applied in the second stage. Otherwise, partial match may end with non-relevant messages containing only a few insignificant query terms that will be ranked high due to their recency. Our hope here is that with an appropriate second stage ranking based on relevance estimation, no embarrassing cases would surface to the top of the list, even when applying the relaxed first matching phase.

In the second phase, the messages are ranked and returned as results to the user. The ranking method we experimented with is based on the trained ranking function learned by our LTR process over the training data. Our ranking score, which we coin REX (Relevance Extended), uses the tuned weight vector in order to linearly combine all message feature scores into a final message score used to rank the list of messages. We will discuss later the effectiveness of REX in both types of first-phase approaches.

4. EXPERIMENTS

In this section we present the large scale experiments we carried on Yahoo Web mail service. We describe the experiments setup, the datasets we used, as well as the results we achieved. We divide our experiments in two parts. The first part consists of a quantitative automatic evaluation, comparing our ranking to the current time-based ranking in the production system which we use as baseline. For both systems, the same strict match approach is used to generate the pool of candidates, which allows us to evaluate the contribution of the second phase of reranking. This automatic evaluation was performed using two datasets extracted from Yahoo email service query log; the Web dataset contain email queries of regular users while the Corporate dataset contain queries of Yahoo employees.

The second experimental part consists of a qualitative editorial evaluation that was performed on the Corporate dataset by professional editors who conducted judgments on their own corporate mailboxes. In this second set of experiments, we relaxed the matching constraints of the first phase before applying our REX ranking.

4.1 Automatic evaluation

The automatic evaluation was performed in order to evaluate the performance of REX, our relevance ranking algorithm, as compared to the default chronological ranking view deployed in production of the Yahoo Web mail service. Both ranking methods (REX and chronological) were run on the same system, where the matching process conducted in the first phase required a strict match between the query and the message as mentioned at Section 3.

Due to the different nature of the two datasets, learning was performed separately for each, using the same system and set of features. Furthermore, there is a major difference between the search activity of users in these domains. For the Corporate email dataset, we followed the corporate privacy guidelines and could collect a large dataset of 100,000 queries from a few thousands opt-in users. For the Web mail dataset, due to privacy limitations, we collected queries only from users who opted in for the research study. This limited us to 10,000 queries originating from these opt-in users. In both datasets the queries were collected over a period of one month.

For the Corporate dataset, LTR was performed over a training set of 75,000 queries randomly selected (leaving the rest for testing), while for the Web email dataset, LTR was performed over 10,000 queries, using 10-fold cross validation, due the smaller size of the dataset.

Our goal here is to evaluate the quality of our re-ranking process as compared to the default chronological ranking. Precision is evaluated using two performance measures: MRR and *success@k*. The MRR measure stands for the Mean Reciprocal Rank score across all queries, that is, $\frac{1}{|Q|}\sum_{i=1}^{|Q|}\frac{1}{r_i}$, where Q is the set of all queries, and r_i is the rank of the clicked message for query i. The *success@k* measure is the percentage of the queries for which the clicked message was ranked within the top-k results.

The baseline established for our evaluation is the time-based ranking used in production by the leading Web mail service, referred as *Time*. In order to evaluate the contribution of the different features we used for relevance ranking, we divided them into different sets, adding them one after the other to the learning process. For each additional set of features added to the system, new weights were learned following the LTR procedure and performance measures were derived following an additional evaluation round. The feature sets were added by order of direct relation to the message, from its content, through actions it triggered, and up to features related to its sender. More precisely, the features were divided into four sets:

- *freshness* (see Table 1, message/freshness). Taking this set only results in a ranking very close to that of *Time*.

[4]When several messages were clicked by the searcher we only consider the most recent clicked one while ignoring the rest.

Algo	*MRR (+lift %)*	*success@1*	*success@3*	*success@5*	*success@10*
	Corporate email dataset				
Time	0.3722	0.2238	0.4213	0.5416	0.7037
REX$(fresh. + sim.)$	0.4261 (+14.48%)	0.2748	0.4887	0.6028	0.7509
REX$(fresh. + sim. + actions)$	0.4550 (+22.24%)	0.2999	0.5253	0.6421	0.781
REX$(fresh. + sim. + actions + sender)$	0.4548 (+22.19%)	0.2994	0.5263	0.6419	0.7837
	Web email dataset				
Time	0.3717	0.2282	0.4290	0.5264	0.6783
*****REX***$(fresh. + sim.)$	0.3785 (+1.81%)	0.2316	0.4406	0.5419	0.6909
REX$(fresh. + sim. + actions)$	0.4238 (+14%)	0.2711	0.4925	0.6004	0.7436
REX$(fresh. + sim. + actions + sender)$	0.4258 (+14.55%)	0.2731	0.4959	0.6000	0.7427

Table 2: Automatic evaluation on the Corporate and Web email datasets: MRR and success@k values for search result sets ≥ 30. The MRR lift for REX is computed with respect to the chronological ranking baseline. All *REX* results, except those in the line marked by asterisk, are statistically significant better than Time results (two-tailed paired t-test, $p < 1.0e\text{-}8$).

- *message-query similarity*, which contains features based on the textual similarity between the query and the message, taking into account both the content of the message and its metadata fields (see Table 1, query similarity). Taking freshness and this feature set together results in a ranking model that is very close in spirit to previous work on email ranking [7, 17] which mostly integrated textual similarity and message freshness.

- *user actions*, which corresponds to the various actions the user performed on the message, which should reflect its importance to the user (see Table 1, message/user actions).

- *sender*, which characterizes the sender via horizontal features computed across the whole set of users (see Table 1, sender/horizontal), as well as the vertical features representing the correspondence between the sender and the user (see Table 1, sender/vertical).

The evaluation results of both datasets are summarized in Table 2. Each row for the REX algorithm takes into account an additional set of features, as denoted in the table. We experimented with only queries that generate a match pool of at least 30 results in the first phase, in order to verify the effect of reranking, which are clearly less visible in very short result sets.

In the next experiment we considered smaller as well as larger match pools. We used different thresholds τ for the minimal size of the search results, where τ ranges over the values $\{10, 20, 30, 40, 50\}$. That is, for each value of τ, we performed an evaluation round over 10,000 queries with search result sets of size $\geq \tau$. The performance of REX, with full feature set, and the chronological ranking, as a function of τ which controls the minimal size of the search results, are summarized in Figure 2.

4.2 Discussion

There are several interesting insights that can be derived from the experimental results. At first, it is clear that the REX ranker significantly outperforms the existing chronological ranker for email search results, both in the Corporate and in the Web email datasets. The improvement in both domains, based on the automatic evaluation on a large-scale test set, is statistically significant, and is larger than 22% in MRR, in the Corporate domain, and larger than 14% in the Web domain. Moreover, as Figure 2 shows, the relative

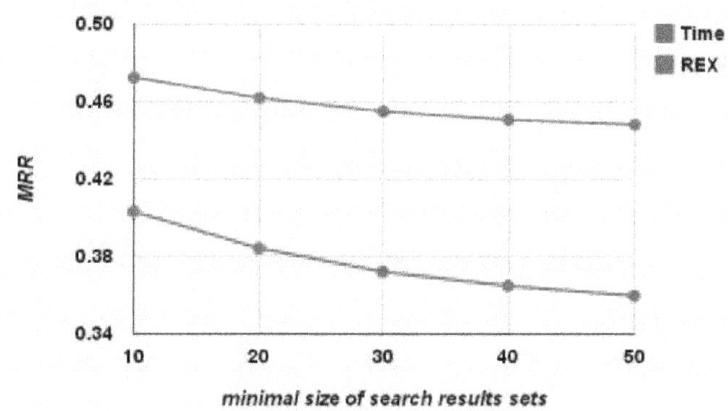

Figure 2: MRR of REX and Time, as a function of τ, in the corporate email dataset.

improvement increases as more messages in the user mailbox match the query, growing from 17% for small result sets of at least 10 messages, to 24% for result sets with at least 50 messages. Note that the MRR naturally decreases as the result set grows, yet it does not deteriorate as fast as with time-sorted results.

The relative contribution of the feature sets to ranking can be seen in Table 2. While the similarity features give an increase in MRR of more than 14% in the Corporate domain (on top of the freshness features), they almost do not contribute to the Web mail dataset, probably due to noisier content that is typical to that domain.

The user actions features contribute an additional increase of 8% in the Corporate domain, and of 12% in the Web domain. This can be easily explained by the large difference in the activity levels of the users in both sets. For example, more than 50% of the messages in the Corporate email dataset are reply messages, compared to less than 30% in the Web email domain. This is partly due to the larger number of threads in Corporate dataset compared to the Web dataset: about 30% of the messages in the Corporate dataset were part of threads, compared to less than 20% in the Web dataset.

Surprisingly, the sender features do not bring further improvement in both domains. This is counter-intuitive as we expected these features, which represent the sender characteristics and its relation with the user, to have a significant impact on relevance estimation. As noted in Section 3, many of the sender features are good indicators as whether the message is machine generated or personally composed (i.e., the sender is a robot or a human). One interpretation could be that some senders send a mix of important and not important messages. Yet, we believe it is worth continuing exploring other models for sender representation, maybe at finer levels of granularity, and reserve this for future work.

Other features listed in Table 1, that did not bring much value, include the message exchange type, message attachment and message folder features, as well as the set of recipient features. Considering for example the recipient features, one could have expected that user appearance in the `To:`, rather than in the `CC/BCC:` fields of a message, would impact the message importance. However, this is not the case, as it seems that important information that the user would like to re-access can equally be found in messages that were not addressed directly and personally to him. An interesting difference arises from this feature, with respect to the nature of the two domains. While in the Web domain the user appears in more than 60% of the messages in the `To:` field (and only in 5% in the `CC:` field), in the Corporate domain the user appears in only 40% of the messages in the `To:` field in (and in 14% in the `CC:` field).

Looking at the REX ranking models learned in both domains, we can see that both models are very similar in terms of the relative weights assigned to the model features. In both models the freshness features are the most important, as expected, then user actions, followed by the textual similarity to the query, and finally the sender features. For freshness, the most important feature is the message age in years, then in months, weeks and days. For the user actions features, the most important one is *Seen* (whether the message was opened), then *Forwarded, Spam, Flagged, Replied, Draft*, and *Ham*. For the similarity features, *Coord* is the most significant one, then the *tf.idf* similarity of the fields *From, Body, Subject, Attachment*, and the *To* fields. Finally the $BM25f$ similarity score.

Interestingly, different natures of search usage can also be observed when looking at the fields similarity in both domains. For example, the `From:` field was relevant to the query in almost 30% of the messages in our Web dataset, while being relevant in less than 20% of the messages in the Corporate dataset. This could indicate that in Web email, users use more often the name of a contact to retrieve a message from the respective sender. On the other hand, we observe a larger number of hits on the subject field in the Corporate dataset compared to the Web email dataset (22% compared to 17%). Finally, the low significance of the sender features for ranking is also reflected by their low relative weights in both domains.

4.3 Editorial evaluation

Given that the first matching phase has a direct impact on recall, we decided to explore a less strict matching policy. As discussed earlier, relaxing matching constraints, when using pure chronological ranking, would have negative effects on quality – non-relevant recent messages containing only a few query terms may be pushed on top of the list. However, our hope is that we can allow softer constraints and still not hurt quality thanks to our REX ranking method.

To this effect, we conducted a manual evaluation, with the help of professional editors who were given directives on searching their own mailboxes in the corporate settings. Our editorial evaluation included 20 professional editors. They were all asked to issue 25 queries on their own mailboxes. Each of the 25 queries had to match a given pattern, which specified the number of terms as well as their type (e.g., **<sender name>, <subject word>, <body word>**). The patterns were defined so as to cover most possible query scenarios as found in our query log. Editors were directed to formulate their own queries, in full freedom, as long they match one of the required patterns. In addition, they were asked to add a description of the associated intent, in order to describe the message they wish to re-find, before issuing their queries.

Using searcher-generated queries is a key requirement in the context of email search, as only the mailbox owner knows what his or her mailbox might cover. This differentiates our work from previous work such as [1], which uses synthetic queries over the Enron corpus. Examples of query patterns are given in Table 3, while examples of real editorial queries instantiating these patterns with associated intents are shown in the three left columns of Figure 3. Note that the editor queries may include misspelled or redundant words. We allowed such queries as they do happen in mail search and are a common source of frustration when no results are returned.

Query Pattern Examples
<sender name>
<sender name> <body word>
<subject word>
<subject word> <subject word>
<subject word> <subject word> <body word>
<sender name> <subject word> <body word>
to:<recipient name> <subject word>
from:<sender name> <body word>
<sender name> <subject word> <redundant word>

Table 3: Editorial evaluation - query patterns

Each query was run on two systems: one using the existing chronological ranking deployed in the Yahoo Web mail system we experiment with, and the other using REX, on top of the relaxed first phase match we evaluate here. Note that due to environment constraints in our Web mail system, we could not change the ranking in the live system. Instead, we compared the two systems as a whole, the existing live time-based ranking, vs. REX on top of a relaxed phase one.

For each system, the editors had to identify the rank of the most relevant result, if any, hopefully the message the editor had in mind at query time. In addition they were asked to judge other relevant results, if any. Each message was labeled according to three relevance levels: most significant (assigned to at most one result), related, and unrelated. Examples of result assessments made by editors for their own queries are presented in the right-side columns of Figure 3.

The ranking algorithms were evaluated using MRR and *success@k*, as before. Furthermore, the identification of the relevance level of the results allowed us to use two additional measures: NDCG@k (Normalized Discounted Cumulative Gain), and *p@k*. The NDCG@10 measure was computed over the 10 first results, using 3 relevance scores $\{0, 1, 3\}$ for, unrelated, related and most significant results, respectively. Tables 4 and 5 summarize the results of the editorial

Pattern	Query	Intent Description	Algo A Most relevant	Algo A Related	Algo B Most relevant	Algo B Related
<sender name> <body word>	Lila dress	Searching for the disscussion with Lila about the dress of the party	4	1,2,3,5	1	2,3,4,5,6
<subject word>	Reports	Trying to pull up my most recent weekly report to copy as a template	4	1,2,3,5,6,7	>10	1,2,3,4,5,6,7,8,9,10
<subject word> <body word>	Top Holiday	Looking for the spreadsheet for the Top Holiday	>10	1, 3, 4, 5, 6, 7, 8, 9, 10	3	1, 2, 4, 5, 6, 7, 8, 9, 10
to:<recipient name> <subject word>	to:spence KE	Invite to KE meeting	Not found	1,2,3	4	1,2,3,5,6,7,10
from:<sender name> <body word>	from:Gaylon highest-priority	Want to know which project was the highest priority	2	1	2	5
<sender name>	Christina	Looking for the most recent email from Christina	1	2, 3, 4, 7, 8	1	2, 3, 4, 6, 8, 9, 10
<sender name> <body word> <body word>	Marta terri schedule	Want to know when did Marta schedule training for LL	2	1	2	1,3,4,5,6

Figure 3: Examples of real editorial queries and ranking results

evaluation. All measures show significant and sustainable improvement of *REX* over *Time* (40.6% improvement in MRR and 34.6% improvement in NDCG@10).

Algo	*MRR* (+lift %)	*succ@1*	*succ@3*	*succ@5*	*succ@10*
Time	0.3629	0.2360	0.4140	0.5280	0.6560
REX	0.5105 (+40.65%)	0.3580	0.6000	0.7020	0.8260

Table 4: Editorial evaluation - MRR and success@k values of Time and REX. All *REX* results, are statistically significant better than Time results (two-tailed paired t-test, $p < 0.05$).

Algo	*NDCG@10* (+lift %)	*p@1*	*p@3*	*p@5*	*p@10*
Time	0.4936	0.5540	0.4420	0.3920	0.2962
REX	0.6647 (+34.66%)	0.6960	0.6073	0.5352	0.4244

Table 5: Editorial evaluation - NDCG and p@k values of Time and Rex. All *REX* results are statistically significant better than Time results (two-tailed paired t-test, $p < 0.05$).

In addition to providing relevance judgments, the editors were given an opportunity to provide some feedback on their own impression from the two ranking systems. Most of the returned responses were very positive regarding the REX ranker. Examples include "... Sometimes, I had the feeling that Algo. B was really reading my mind to put in the first place exactly the email message I was thinking of", and "...Today, after I ran it again, it was not that much impressive, but still I have the feeling it was the type of search that gave me the best results...". Given how experienced these editors are with email search and with assessing search results, we found their feedback to be most encouraging.

4.4 Revisiting our Motivating Example

We revisit here our motivating example shown in Figure 1 in the Introduction. User Y issued the same query "visa to india" on his mailbox, but this time selecting our REX relevance ranking instead of the default time ranking. Note that at the time of writing, the REX ranking on top of the strict matching phase is fully implemented in production, but not deployed yet to all users, in our Web mail service. However it can be invoked on demand via a hidden parameter for experimentation purposes. A screen capture of the results Y obtained is shown in Figure 4. We note that older results from 2013 suddenly pop up. The third one, which contains an attachment as indicated by the paper clip icon, turns out to be the perfect one containing the actual visa form that Y was seeking. The signals that played a significant role here were the previous actions of Y on this message (reading, replying, folding), the textual similarity between the query and the subject field, and the existing attachment. Note also that there was no noticeable difference in response time between the default existing time-based search and the REX-based experimental search, as our ranking model naturally scales to Web mail requirements, thanks to its two-phase approach.

5. CONCLUSIONS AND FUTURE WORK

While some leading Web mail services return search results sorted by relevance, either in short "top results" like in Gmail, or as a non-too-visible feature in Yahoo mail, search results are still predominantly ranked by default by time in the leading Web mail services. In this paper, we challenge this chronological sort, as a sort of anachronism in light of the progress in relevance ranking. Yet, we do recognize the importance of freshness by integrating it in a mail-specific relevance model. While the set of features we introduce are not all novel (freshness for instance has been used in Web ranking), this is, to the best of our knowledge, the first time a mail-specific relevance model is described publicly, applied and evaluated, in production in a real Web mail service, under the hard performance requirements of Web-scale mail systems.

We detailed the experiments we conducted with real users and demonstrated that our model performs significantly better in terms of quality, as compared to the default existing time-based ranking in the Web mail service. We showed significant improvements in multiple settings, using the same system with Web mail users as well as corporate users of the same service, including professional editors. We shared the insights we derived from our extensive study and experiments. Some were expected such as the importance of textual similarity across message fields and of actions conducted on message. Others were more surprising such the poor influence of the message sender importance. We were particularly pleased by the evidence that the larger the result set, the more significant the improvement is.

This encourages us to believe that now is the time to depart from the old date sort in favor of more modern relevance ranking. We believe that Web mail users should be able to re-find past messages without having to play with advanced operators, which, like in Web search, are typically ignored by the overwhelming majority of Web mail users.

We plan to continue improving our model considering more signals as they become available, investigating the handling of threads as full-fledge retrieval units. We would also like to verify whether personalizing the ranking models, either by user, or by type of user, in case of sparse data, would bring value. We hope that this work will open new research directions for mail research, especially around the impact of such ranking on user engagement. Chronological ranking

Figure 4: REX-sorted results for the query "visa to india"

dictates users to re-find their target in traversal mode that is based on the message submission time, while relevance ranking might educate users to better express their information needs. In the long term, after mail searchers get sufficiently used to such relevance ranking, we would like to verify whether it affects the way query formulation, users' search strategy, as well as the overall way users interact with the mail system.

6. REFERENCES

[1] S. AbdelRahman, B. Hassan, and R. Bahgat. A new email retrieval ranking approach. *International Journal of Computer Science & Information Technology*, 2(5), 2010.

[2] D. Aberdeen, O. Pacovsky, and A. Slater. The learning behind gmail priority inbox. In *LCCC: NIPS 2010 Workshop on Learning on Cores, Clusters and Clouds*, Vancouver, BC, Canada, Dec 2010.

[3] R. Baeza-Yates and Y. Maarek. (big) usage data in web search. In *Proceedings of SIGIR*, Portland, Oregon, USA, 2012.

[4] Y. Cao, J. Xu, T.-Y. Liu, H. Li, Y. Huang, and H.-W. Hon. Adapting ranking SVM to document retrieval. In *Proceedings of SIGIR*, Seattle,WA, Aug 2006.

[5] K. Crammer, A. Kulesza, and M. Dredze. Adaptive regularization of weight vectors. *Machine Learning*, 91(2):155–187, 2013.

[6] N. Craswell, A. P. de Vries, and I. Soboroff. Overview of the trec 2005 enterprise track. In *TREC*, volume 5, pages 199–205, 2005.

[7] N. Craswell, H. Zaragoza, and S. Robertson. Microsoft cambridge at trec 14: Enterprise track. In *TREC*, 2005.

[8] S. Dumais, E. Cutrell, J. Cadiz, G. Jancke, R. Sarin, and D. C. Robbins. Stuff I've seen: A system for personal information retrieval and re-use. In *Proceedings of SIGIR*, Toronto, Canada, 2003.

[9] M. Efron and G. Golovchinsky. Estimation methods for ranking recent information. In *Proceedings of SIGIR*, pages 495–504. ACM, 2011.

[10] D. Elsweiler, M. Baillie, and I. Ruthven. What makes re-finding information difficult? a study of email re-finding. In *Proceedings of ECIR*, Dublin, Ireland, 2011.

[11] D. Elsweiler, M. Harvey, and M. Hacker. Understanding re-finding behavior in naturalistic email interaction logs. In *Proceedings of SIGIR*, Beijing, China, 2011.

[12] M. Grbovic, G. Halawi, Z. Karnin, and Y. Maarek. How many folders do you really need? classifying email into a handful of categories. In *Proceedings of CIKM*, Shanghai, China, 2014.

[13] F. Kooti, L. M. Aiello, M. Grbovic, K. Lerman, and A. Mantrach. Evolution of conversations in the age of email overload. In *Proceedings of WWW*, 2015.

[14] Y. Koren, E. Liberty, Y. Maarek, and R. Sandler. Automatically tagging email by leveraging other users' folders. In *Proceedings of KDD*, San-Diego,CA, Aug 2011.

[15] B. Leiba. Update to internet message format to allow group syntax in the "from:" and "sender:" header fields, RFC 6854, March 2013.

[16] X. Li and W. B. Croft. Time-based language models. In *Proceedings of CIKM*, pages 469–475. ACM, 2003.

[17] C. Macdonald and I. Ounis. Combining fields in known-item email search. In *Proceedings of SIGIR*, Seattle, WA, Aug 2006.

[18] P. Ogilvie and J. Callan. Experiments with language models for known-item finding of e-mail messages. 2005.

[19] D. Olanoff. Gmail search autocomplete gets smarter predictions, using past searches to help you find things. Techcrunch, April 2013.

[20] E. P. Resnick. Internet message format, RFC 2822, April 2001.

[21] S. Radicati and J. Levenstein. Email market, 2013-2017, Nov 2013.

[22] S. Robertson, H. Zaragoza, and M. Taylor. Simple BM25 extension to multiple weighted fields. In *Proceedings of CIKM*, pages 42–49. ACM, 2004.

[23] I. Soboroff, A. P. de Vries, and N. Craswell. Overview of the trec 2006 enterprise track. In *TREC*, 2006.

[24] W. Weerkamp, K. Balog, and M. De Rijke. Using contextual information to improve search in email archives. In *Advances in Information Retrieval*, pages 400–411. Springer, 2009.

[25] S. Whittaker, T. Matthews, J. Cerruti, H. Badenes, and J. Tang. Am I wasting my time organizing email?: A study of email refinding. In *Proceedings of CHI*, Vancouver, BC, Canada, 2011.

[26] S. Whittaker and C. Sidner. Email overload: Exploring personal information management of email. In *Proceedings of CHI*, Vancouver, BC, Canada, 1996.

[27] S. Yahyaei and C. Monz. Applying maximum entropy to known-item email retrieval. In *Advances in Information Retrieval*, pages 406–413. Springer, 2008.

On the Cost of Extracting Proximity Features for Term-Dependency Models

Xiaolu Lu
RMIT University
Melbourne, Australia
xiaolu.lu@rmit.edu.au

Alistair Moffat
The University of Melbourne
Melbourne, Australia
ammoffat@unimelb.edu.au

J. Shane Culpepper
RMIT University
Melbourne, Australia
shane.culpepper@rmit.edu.au

ABSTRACT

Sophisticated ranking mechanisms make use of term dependency features in order to compute similarity scores for documents. These features often include exact phrase occurrences, and term proximity estimates. Both cases build on the intuition that if multiple query terms appear near each other, the document is more likely to be relevant to the query. In this paper we examine the processes used to compute these statistics. Two distinct input structures can be used – inverted files and direct files. Inverted files must store the position offsets of the terms, while "direct" files represent each document as a sequence of preprocessed term identifiers. Based on these two input modalities, a number of algorithms can be used to compute proximity statistics. Until now, these algorithms have been described in terms of a single set of query terms. But similarity computations such as the Full Dependency Model compute proximity statistics for a collection of related term sets. We present a new approach in which such collections are processed holistically in time that is much less than would be the case if each subquery were to be evaluated independently. The benefits of the new method are demonstrated by a comprehensive experimental study.

Categories and Subject Descriptors

H.3.4 [**Information Storage and Retrieval**]: Systems and Software—*Performance evaluation*

Keywords

Experimentation; Measurement; Dependency Ranking Models

1. INTRODUCTION

A range of sophisticated ranking mechanisms have been proposed that make use of term dependency features in order to compute similarity scores for documents [16, 17, 19, 21]. The features that get used include exact phrase occurrences, in which a sequence of words appear consecutively; term bigram co-occurrences; and more generalized term proximity estimates. Intuitively, these methods build on the belief that if multiple query terms appear next to, or nearby each other, it can be inferred that the document in question has an increased probability of being relevant to the query compared to a document in which the occurrences are separated by many intervening words.

Here we examine the processes that are used to compute the necessary frequency statistics, with an emphasis on generalized term proximity features. For example, the "unordered window" attribute is based on, for each document being ranked, the number of distinct intervals of some specified length within the document in which all of the listed query terms appear. Two distinct input structures can be used to compute proximity features – inverted files, in which term positional information is retained as part of the posting associated with each terms' presence in the document; and the "direct" files that are constructed by some retrieval systems, in which each document is represented by a surrogate consisting of a sequence of preprocessed term identifiers.

A number of algorithms have been described for computing proximity statistics using these two input structures. These approaches include the plane-sweep and divide-and-conquer methods described by Sadakane and Imai [18], and other similar approaches described by Huston [12] and Clarke et al. [8]. All of the algorithms are presented in terms of a single set of query terms, with the objective being to compute a list of minimal intervals in the given document within which each query term appears at least once. But similarity computations such as the Full Dependency Model (FDM) [16] involve the computation of proximity statistics for a collection of related term sets, because every subset of terms from the underlying query is permitted to influence the final score. That is, multiple related queries of the form considered by Sadakane and Imai must be evaluated as part of scoring each document of the collection in a ranked retrieval environment. These considerations lead us to two research questions.

RQ 1 *Do inverted lists consistently offer advantages for computing proximity statistics when compared to direct files?*

RQ 2 *Is it possible to compute multiple related proximity statistics within a single evaluation?*

In this paper we present a new approach in which a suite of related general proximity queries can be computed *in a single pass*, generating significant execution time savings compared to the alternative of evaluating each subset of the terms independently. By exploiting a key insight in the way optimal subquery intervals must be formed, we show how to dramatically reduce the cost of computing all of the intervals for all query term combinations. We show that FDM-like scoring can be carried out holistically in time that is much less than would be the case with independent subquery evaluations, thereby answering the second question in the affirmative. The experimental study we have undertaken also provides evidence that while inverted lists are often superior to direct files, this is not always the case.

CIKM'15, October 19–23 2015, Melbourne, VIC, Australia

ACM 978-1-4503-3794-6/15/10 ...$15.00.
http://dx.doi.org/10.1145/2806416.2806467.

2. BACKGROUND

Phrases and proximity in IR Many of the recent ranking models in information retrieval include proximity features, such as term-pairs, phrases or unordered windows. Early models such as INQUERY [6] considered both phrases and proximity features, and a number of studies have been carried out to better understand their relative contributions. For example, Hawking and Thistlewaite [10] investigated the value of phrase-only queries and showed that documents that score higher using only phrase features may in fact be less relevant, and that phrase features may not be sufficient to reliably increase effectiveness. Tao and Zhai [20] compare several different term proximity models to determine which combination of k-term proximities can best improve query effectiveness. After comparing all possible proximity feature mappings in a BM25 ranking model, they conclude that term-pair proximity is sufficient to obtain a statistically significant improvement in effectiveness.

The common thread in using either phrases or proximity is that effectiveness can be improved some of the time, but predicting which method works best is difficult. Based on this insight, Metzler and Croft [16] proposed a Markov Random Field (MRF) model that incorporates both types of dependency relations into a single weighted model. Term dependencies in the SDM (Sequential Dependency Model) and FDM (Full Dependency Model) are represented as matches against ordered or unordered windows, using the Indri[1] operators #owλ and #uwλ. The basic MRF model improves effectiveness over a bag-of-words model, especially on large collections and long queries [14]. Effectiveness can be further improved by using a Weighted Sequential Dependency Model where concept weightings are determined in a supervised manner instead of using a fixed configuration [2, 13]. Huston and Croft [13] found that k-term proximity improves effectiveness for some queries, but not all. The exact interaction of term-pair versus k-term concept weightings remains inconclusive and an interesting area of further study.

Computing proximity features Extracting all proximity features is a computationally expensive task. As a consequence, most efficiency studies consider only term-pair proximity, since term co-occurrences can easily be computed on the fly, or pre-indexed. Asadi and Lin [1] show that extracting BM25 and all two-term dependency features requires longer (20.6 microseconds per document) than only considering unigram BM25 features (14.6 microseconds per document). Term co-occurrences can also be pre-computed without the size of the index increasing too much. Based on ranking models proposed by Büttcher et al. [4], Broschart and Schenkel [3] designed a combined index structure for both terms and term-pairs. Their index can be tuned to balance efficiency and effectiveness. Yan et al. [22] also index term co-occurrences, but use a different ranking model and consider only term-pairs within a fixed distance. They also incorporated early termination techniques to improve efficiency when scoring documents. Rather than keeping exact position information in the index, Elsayed et al. [9] only store approximated counts for various term-pair features. They segment documents into different buckets and use a membership query to determine if two query terms appear in adjacent buckets. Elsayed et al. also examine several different strategies to partition documents, and different encodings to reduce the total index size.

Relatively few methods have been described for computing k-word proximity features when k is larger than two. Asadi and Lin [1] suggest that the problem of matching #owλ and #uwλ can be formulated as a set intersection and evaluated using the *small adaptive* algorithm, but then mainly focus on extracting term co-occurrence features. Two $O(N \log N)$ approaches for finding optimal intervals in an N-word document that include a set of k query terms were proposed by Sadakane and Imai [18]: a method that they denoted as *plane-sweep*; and a method that they categorized as *divide-and-conquer*. Experiments conducted on data indexed using both suffix arrays and inverted files showed that unless one query term has a much lower term frequency (TF), plane-sweep is the best approach. Sadakane and Imai suggest that performance could be improved by selectively choosing plane-sweep or divide-and-conquer based on the relative term frequency, but do not explore this option in detail.

[1]`http://www.lemurproject.org/indri.php`

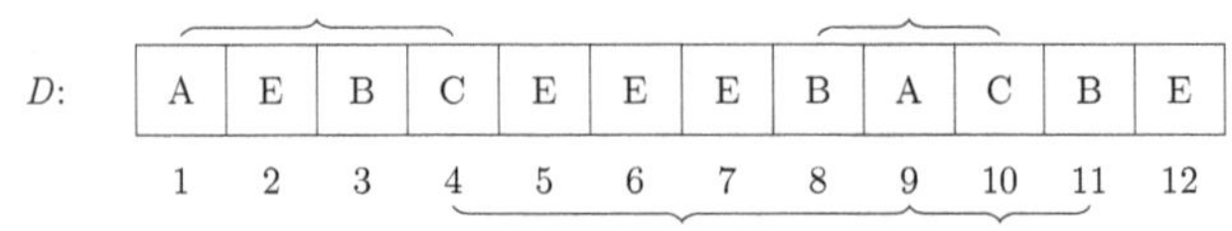

Figure 1: For document D and query $Q = \{\mathrm{A}, \mathrm{B}, \mathrm{C}\}$ there are four optimal 3-intervals: 1...4, 4...9, 8...10 and 9...11. The interval 3...9 is not optimal because it has 4...9 as a proper subset.

Contribution We focus on how to efficiently compute term proximity features for queries of $k \geq 3$ terms, assuming a context in which the $2^k - k - 1$ non-empty subsets of those terms must all be treated as *subqueries* for which term statistics are to be computed. This point of view allows us to develop efficient approaches to the holistic generation of *sets* of data for use in ranking computations, covering all of the requirements of an overarching k-term query. As is demonstrated in the development below, that point of view provides more efficient document scoring than is possible if standard interval-finding techniques are used in an iterative manner, processing each subquery separately.

We first revisit the problem of calculating k-word proximity by formalizing the problem. We next review current solutions according to their corresponding input structure – inverted indexes, or direct files. In the new work, we then discuss how to compute all k-intervals using a single-pass strategy in Section 4; and demonstrate the efficacy of those methods in Section 5.

Definitions First we define what is meant by an optimal k-word proximity interval, relative to a query $Q = \{q_1, q_2, \ldots, q_k\}$ with k query terms, and relative to a document $D[1..N]$ containing a sequence of N words:

DEFINITION 1 (OPTIMAL k-INTERVAL). *An interval $p_l ... p_r$ bounded by left position p_l and right position p_r is optimal if all k terms in Q appear in $D[p_l ... p_r]$, and there is no proper subset of $D[p_l ... p_r]$ with the same property.*

Figure 1 shows an example document, and lists the four optimal 3-intervals induced by the query $\{\mathrm{A}, \mathrm{B}, \mathrm{C}\}$.

Markov Random Field term dependency implementations use the operator #uwλ to match windows containing all specified query terms within a distance λ [15]. In these models, all non-empty subqueries of Q are formed, and proximity statistics computed for each subquery. For example, the query $Q = \{\mathrm{A}, \mathrm{B}, \mathrm{C}, \mathrm{D}\}$ gives rise to one 4-item subquery; four 3-item subqueries; and six 2-item subqueries. The total number of subqueries induced by a k-term query is given by $2^k - k - 1$. The rapid growth as a function of k means that methods that compute intervals for all proximity statistics in a single pass are of interest, and gives rise to the challenge we consider:

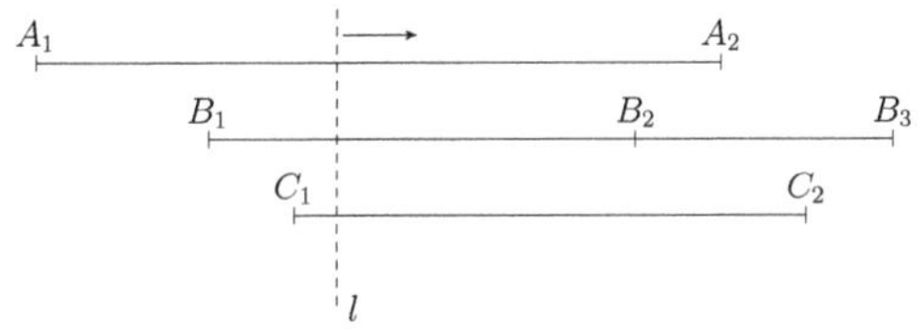

Figure 2: The plane-sweep algorithm checks whether the interval formed by the current leftmost representative and its next appearance encloses all the representatives. A virtual line l sweeps from left to right, with term positions determined using position offsets from an inverted file, or by sequentially processing a direct file.

PROBLEM 1 (OPTIMAL k-INTERVAL ENUMERATION). *For document $D[1\ldots N]$ and query $Q = \{q_1, q_2 \ldots, q_k\}$, find all optimal $|Q'|$-intervals in D for all non-empty subqueries $Q' \subseteq Q$ in which $|Q'| \geq 2$.*

For example, for the query $Q = \{\text{A}, \text{B}, \text{C}\}$ shown in Figure 1, the complete set of answer intervals required consists of optimal 2-intervals for $\{\text{A}, \text{B}\}$, $\{\text{A}, \text{C}\}$, and $\{\text{B}, \text{C}\}$, plus the optimal 3-intervals for $\{\text{A}, \text{B}, \text{C}\}$ that have already been described.

Our goal in this paper is to compute the intervals for all of the subqueries in a single pass over the input structures, rather than require one pass per subquery.

3. SINGLE-QUERY INTERVAL FINDING

As a prelude to considering Problem 1, we describe methods for computing optimal k-intervals for one-off sets of terms.

Input representations Two alternative representations of positional information are used in IR systems. In a *direct file*, a surrogate for each document is maintained, with terms represented in document appearance order by their mapped identifiers. Each document in the collection has a contiguous section of the direct file allocated to it; and for each document that is to be scored in response to a query, that segment is identified and processed. The other option is to make use of a *positional inverted index*, which contains a postings list for each term in the collection. In this representation, the position offsets for each term are stored relative to either the start of the collection, or relative to the start of the enclosing document. Query processing is done via the postings lists, and only when a set of documents comprising the query's answer has been determined is it necessary to access documents or their parsed surrogates. Both representations can be used to support phrase and proximity operations. For example, Terrier[2] uses a direct file to support operators beyond bag-of-words computations, while Indri uses a merge operation over position offsets stored in an inverted file to support similar operations.

Despite considerable early work on the role of proximity in effectiveness computations [7, 10, 11], few studies have explored efficient computation techniques, and those that do mostly focus on the case where k is 2 or 3 [5, 8]. Sadakane and Imai [18] considered k in the unbounded case, and compared the efficiency of several different methods. One of the approaches they evaluated is the *plane-sweep* algorithm; if the input is assumed to be provided as postings lists, then plane-sweep outperformed the alternative *divide and conquer* approach.

Eager Plane Sweep (EPS) The plane-sweep approach processes terms in document order, checking whether the interval formed by the current leftmost term encloses all of the other endpoints. For example, consider the scenario shown in Figure 2. The interval $A_1 \ldots A_2$ contains B_1 and C_1. Therefore, $A_1 \ldots C_1$ is an optimal 3-interval. The leftmost term (in the example, A_1) is then discarded, and B_1 becomes the leftmost term. Now the interval $B_1 \ldots B_2$ does not contain both of the remaining terms, so B_1 is discarded, and C_1 becomes the leftmost term. As it turns out, this is the left-hand anchor point of another optimal 3-interval, through to A_2.

The plane-sweep approach can be visualized as sweeping a line from left to right across term positions in the document, hence the name. If the positions are represented using positional postings lists, then next-leftmost representatives are easily selected as are their successors, and all of the required information can be kept up to date with relatively little effort. We call this the *eager* version of plane-sweep; Algorithm 1 presents it in detail.

Algorithm 1 Eager Plane Sweep, Single Interval (EPS-IF-S)

Input: A query Q of k terms, and sorted position lists of all terms $\{P_1, P_2, \ldots, P_k\}$
Output: A set of intervals $\mathcal{I}$
$\mathcal{I} \leftarrow \{\}$
for $i \leftarrow 1$ **to** k **do**
curr_occ$[i] \leftarrow$ FIRST(P_i)
end for
5: **while** $(\max_{1 \leq i \leq k} \textit{curr\_occ}[i]) < \infty$ **do**
lsym $\leftarrow \text{argmin}_{1 \leq i \leq k}\{\textit{curr\_occ}[i]\}$
rsym $\leftarrow \text{argmax}_{1 \leq i \leq k}\{\textit{curr\_occ}[i]\}$
lpos $\leftarrow$ NEXT(P_{lsym}) // returns ∞ if P_{lsym} is exhausted
if *lpos* $>$ *curr_occ*[*rsym*] **then**
10: $\mathcal{I} \leftarrow \mathcal{I} \cup \langle Q, \textit{curr\_occ}[\textit{lsym}] \ldots \textit{curr\_occ}[\textit{rsym}] \rangle$
end if
curr_occ[*lsym*] $\leftarrow$ *lpos*
end while
return $\mathcal{I}$

The inverted index is presumed to support the two usual access operations: FIRST and NEXT. Both return the position of a term in the current document being processed. The k-element array *curr_occ* is used to track the current positions of all terms in the query. In addition, *lpos* maintains the next position of *lsym*. If *lpos* is greater than *curr_occ*[*rsym*], the current interval is emitted. Finally in each iteration, *curr_occ*[*lsym*] is updated to the new most recent position, *lpos*. When any of the position lists is exhausted, the algorithm terminates. Figure 3 gives a concrete example of this process, matching the schematic shown in Figure 2. As already described, an interval is identified in the first iteration, but not in the second iteration.

Since each of the postings lists in the inverted index is already sorted by term positions, Algorithm 1 requires $O(\log k)$ time per iteration, using two heaps of k items to identify maximal and minimal representatives at steps 6 and 7 respectively. All other operations require $O(1)$ time each. Hence, over the k terms, there is a total of $T_{Q,D} = \sum_{i=1}^{k} |P_i| \leq N$ postings to be processed, and the total execution time is $O(T_{Q,D} \log k) = O(N \log N)$ [18].

Lazy Plane Sweep (LPS) In the EPS approach, the leftmost position is used as a pivot, and the next occurrence of that term is used to determine if the pivot is the leftmost end of an interval. However if the input format is a direct file, the NEXT operation cannot be carried out in $O(1)$ time per call, making the eager updating of *curr_occ* possibly costly.

Instead, in the *Lazy Plane Sweep* approach the direct file is sequentially scanned, and intervals are formed as their right-hand ex-

[2] `http://terrier.org/`

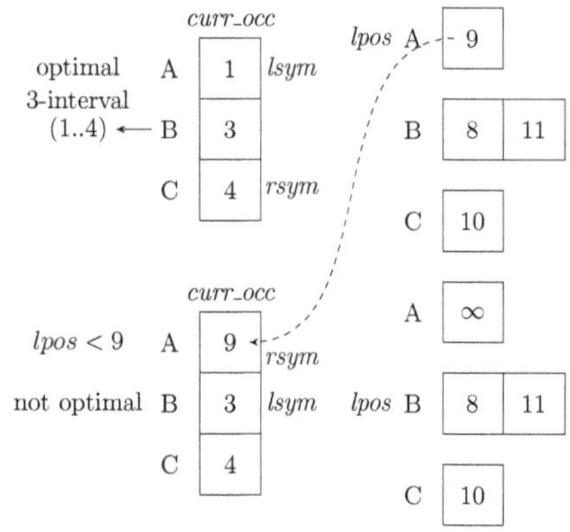

Figure 3: An example of Eager Plane Sweep. The array *curr_occ* records the current representative of each postings list. When $lpos > curr\_occ[rsym]$, as shown in the first configuration, an optimal 3-interval has been identified. The lower half then shows the following configuration, which does not generate an interval.

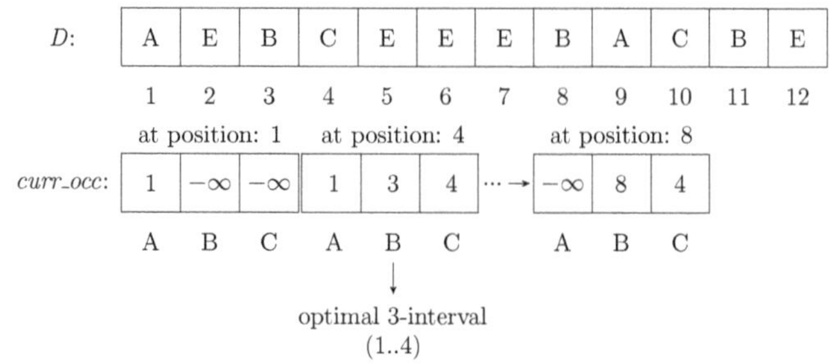

Figure 4: The LPS approach. Array *last_occ* of size k tracks the last position of each query term. When the minimum value in *last_occ* is $-\infty$, an optimal k-interval has not yet been formed. In the bottom array, an optimal k-interval has been formed, so the interval can be added into the result set based on the two endpoints.

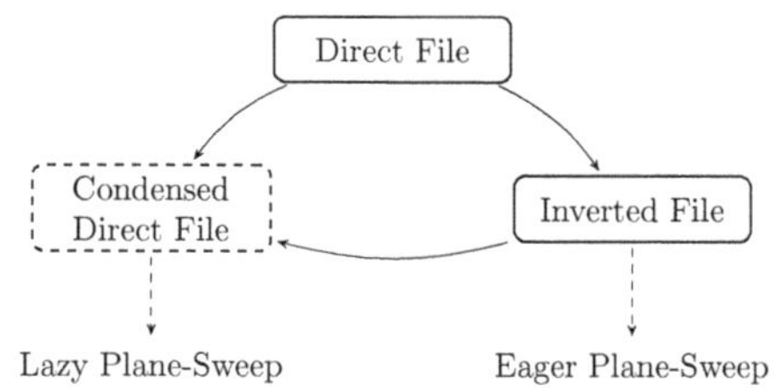

Figure 5: Input representations. A *condensed direct file* is a direct file restricted to the terms that appear in the query; it can be derived from a direct file in $O(N)$ time, or from an inverted file containing term positions in $O(T_{Q,D} \log k)$ time, where $T_{Q,D}$ is the total number of occurrences of query terms from Q in document D.

trema is processed. As with the EPS implementation, the most recent occurrence of each term is tracked in *curr_occ*. A sentinel value of $-\infty$ is used to indicate the absence of a term, and an interval can be formed only when a usable occurrence of each term is defined within the scope. That is, intervals are identified and emitted when the right-hand end of the interval is reached. If an interval is identified, the smallest of the values in *curr_occ* is then voided, as a signal that the next interval must contain a new instance of that term.

Algorithm 2 Lazy Plane Sweep, Single Interval (LPS-DF-S)

Input: A query Q of k terms, and a direct file $D[1 \ldots N]$
Output: A set of intervals $\mathcal{I}$

```
    I ← {}
    for i ← 1 to k do
        curr_occ[i] ← −∞
    end for
5:  for rpos ← 1 to N do
        curr_occ[term_map(D[rpos])] ← rpos
        lsym ← argmin_{1≤i≤k}{curr_occ[i]}
        if curr_occ[lsym] > −∞ then
            I ← I ∪ ⟨Q, curr_occ[lsym]...rpos⟩
10:         curr_occ[lsym] ← −∞
        end if
    end for
    return I
```

Algorithm 2 provides details. Now it is the N values in the direct file corresponding to the document that are processed. At each iteration the next term (or non-term) $D[rpos]$ is considered (step 6). A mapping to query terms (denoted *term_map*() in the pseudo-code) is used to convert raw term numbers across the whole collection to restricted values pertinent to this query, with instances of the k query terms being converted (uniquely) to values in $1 \ldots k$, and instances of non-query terms being converted to (say) $k+1$. At each cycle, if inclusion of the symbol in $D[rpos]$ means that all of the k positions in *curr_occ* have positive values, then the right-hand end of an interval has been located. If that happens, the interval is saved, and then the left-hand symbol of it interval is voided (step 10), since it cannot take part in any further intervals.

Step 7 in Algorithm 2 makes use of an "argmin" operator over k values, and is presented this way in order to draw out the symmetry between the EPS and LPS implementations. Step 7 does not, however, require a heap and $O(\log k)$ time per execution. That cost can be avoided by maintaining an *lpos* index into D, and advancing it to the right (at step 7) when necessary, bypassing any non-query terms. Each time *lsym* is required, it can then be computed as *term_map*(D[*lpos*]). In total, over the whole of Algorithm 2, advancing *lpos* can require at most $O(N)$ time, and hence in an amortized sense, it is $O(1)$ time per loop iteration. The only other possible concern in Algorithm 2 is the cost of the term mapping *term_map*(); but it can be implemented as a hash-table lookup with expected time $O(1)$ per call. Hence, Algorithm 2 requires $O(N)$ time. Its correctness follows directly from the correctness of the eager plane-sweep approach [18].

Comparing Input Structures As has been noted, the two most common input representations are direct files and inverted indexes. Input via an inverted index is the "natural" arrangement for the eager plane-sweep process; conversely, the lazy plane-sweep approach was presented assuming input from a direct file. But the lazy mechanism can also be coupled with an inverted file – all that is required is to merge the postings lists for the query terms, and construct an intermediate form we call a *condensed direct file*, as shown in Figure 5. For query Q of k terms, and postings lists P_1 to P_k, the cost of doing the merge is given by $O(T_{Q,D} \log k)$, where $T_{Q,D} = \sum_{i=1}^{k} |P_k|$ is the sum of the lengths of the postings lists for D. So, the cost of generating the condensed direct file is the same as the cost of running EPS (Algorithm 1) starting with an inverted file. Note that the condensed direct file is query specific, and for that reason cannot be precomputed and stored.

Starting with a direct file, the specific condensed direct file for a query Q can be constructed in $O(N)$ time. Then, once the condensed direct file has been constructed, the EPS mechanism (Algorithm 2) can be executed in $O(T_{Q,D})$ time. Which of these various computation pathways should be chosen depends in no small part on the relative scale of $T_{Q,D}$, k, and N. For example, a short query of rare terms against a long document will favor the use of an inverted file/EPS approach; whereas a long query that includes one or more frequent terms is likely to execute more quickly using the direct file/LPS approach.

Either way, in the case of proximity queries in the context of FDM and similar retrieval models, multiple related subqueries must be evaluated. This need brings further tradeoffs, because it means that the cost of generating a condensed direct file can be amortized over the subqueries. This is one of the themes that is addressed in the next section.

4. EXTRACTING MULTIPLE INTERVALS

We now turn our attention to Problem 1, the larger task of computing interval statistics for a query Q and all of its subqueries Q', where $Q' \subseteq Q$ and $|Q'| \geq 2$.

Repeated Computation If a query has k terms, then there are $2^k - k - 1$ non-empty non-singleton term subsets possible: four, for a 3-term query; eleven, for a 4-term query, and so on. Hence, one obvious way of computing an all-subqueries solution is to iterate over the subsets, applying either Algorithm 1 or Algorithm 2 the requisite number of times. But this approach has the potential to be very expensive, and it would be better if the running time for generating a solution was dominated by polynomial functions of k and N, rather than being exponential in k. Moreover, in an ideal situation the size of the computed output set $\mathcal{I}$ should also be a factor that bounds the cost of the computation. That is, a useful algorithm is one that does the amount of work necessary to generate the required output, in this case $|\mathcal{I}|$, with an overhead cost as a function of N (or $T_{Q,D}$) and k that is additive rather than multiplicative.

One way in which time can be saved when multiple related subqueries Q' are being evaluated against the same document D has already been noted at the end of Section 3 – the formation of a query-specific condensed direct file (CDF) which retains only (and exactly) the positions of the terms in Q that appear in D. The cost of constructing the CDF is the same as running a single-query interval finding mechanism: $O(T_{Q,D} \log k)$ time if the input is an inverted file, or $O(N)$ time if the starting point is a direct file of length N, meaning that there is little point to the conversion operation for the single-interval task. On the other hand, the conversion cost can be amortized over multiple executions for the all-subqueries task, and allows a more flexible range of options. Hence, we can consider two relatively obvious baseline mechanisms for Problem 1, based on the two methods presented in Section 3:

- EPS-IF-S*: starting with an inverted file, apply Algorithm 1 a total of $2^k - k - 1$ times, reinitializing the postings list pointers and starting a fresh computation at each iteration.
- LPS-CDF-S*: starting with an inverted file or a direct file, construct a condensed direct file; then, using the CDF, apply Algorithm 2 a total of $2^k - k - 1$ times.

Both of these methods are used as reference points in the experimentation reported in Section 5 .

A Critical Observation Consider again the arrangement shown in Figure 2, and the occurrences of term B, marked by B_1, B_2, and B_3. Focusing on B_2, consider its relationship to the other two terms, A and C. Because there are no instances of term A that appear between B_1 and B_2, occurrence B_2 cannot be the right-hand end of an $\{A, B\}$ interval. On the other hand, the appearance of C_1 between B_1 and B_2 means that B_2 is the right-hand endpoint of a $\{B, C\}$ interval, spanning $C_1 \ldots B_2$.

Similarly, consider A_2, the next possible right-hand point for intervals encountered during the plane-sweep process. The previous occurrence of A is at A_1. There is no possible benefit from considering B_1 as a possible left-hand partner for A_1, because there is another instance of B between A_1 and A_2 that "shadows" it. Only the most recent instance of each symbol needs to be regarded as "interesting"; and B_2 is the instance of B that fits this definition, and defines the left-hand end of an $\{A, B\}$ interval. Position C_1 is also interesting, because it is the rightmost C prior to A_2, and hence can potentially be pinned at the left-hand end of intervals stretching through to A_2. Once that range $C_1 \ldots A_2$ is established as a viable one, all subsets of the set of distinct items strictly contained within that range need to be used to create intervals. In the example, B_2 lies between C_1 and A_2, and hence there are two subsets to be considered, $\{\}$ and $\{B_2\}$, and thus two intervals that span $C_1 \ldots A_2$: $\{A, C\}$ and $\{A, B, C\}$ respectively. In total, three intervals are identified while the focus is on A_2.

Shifting the focus to the next point in the sweep, C_2, then opens up A_2 and B_2 as potential left-hand partners. The interval $\{A, C\}$ is first identified while A_2 is being evaluated as a left-hand partner; and then $\{B, C\}$ and $\{A, B, C\}$ both emerge when it is B_2 that is being considered as a left-hand partner for C_2, covering $B_2 \ldots C_2$.

Lazy All Interval Querying, LPS-IF-A More generally, each time an item *rsym* at position *rpos* becomes the right-hand focus of the sweep, all right-most instances of other terms that lie between *rpos* and the prior occurrence of *rsym* can be used as the left-hand partners for intervals that terminate at *rpos*. The endpoints of that range define an interval over two terms; other intervals using the same range get added as a result of the need to include not just the endpoint items, but every combination of other terms that lies between them. Algorithm 3 captures these ideas.

The main loop in Algorithm 3 iterates over potential interval right-hand ends in variable *rpos*, drawing them out of a merging process on the terms' posting lists, as was also the case in Algorithm 1. The term identifier that matches this right-hand pivot value is stored as *rsym*. For any particular right-hand pivot point at *rpos*, there are at most $k - 1$ corresponding left-hand partners to be considered; moreover, to be interesting, the most recent occurrence of the candidate must fall between *rpos* and the previous appearance of *rsym*. That "last occurrence" location for each symbol in the query is maintained throughout the computation in the array *curr_occ*[*rsym*], with all values initialized to $-\infty$. If such an intervening symbol *lsym* is found, then its position *lpos* forms an interval with *rpos*, and a two-element interval can be emitted. Once a two-element interval has been identified, every distinct item that occurs between *lpos* and *rpos* can also be (or not be) a member of an interval with the same bounding endpoints. To accommodate that requirement, the set of in-between items is accumulated in S, and then every subsets $s \subseteq S$ is combined with the fixed endpoints *lpos* and *rpos* to create valid intervals. The whole process completes when all occurrences of all terms have been consumed out of the postings lists. This occurs when every *next_occ*[i] value is $+\infty$. Note that the pseudo-code shows all output information be-

Algorithm 3 Lazy Plane Sweep, All Intervals (LPS-IF-A)

```
Input: A query Q of k terms, and sorted position lists of all terms
    {P_1, P_2, ..., P_k}
Output: A set of intervals I for Q and all subqueries of Q
    I ← { }
    for i ← 1 to k do
        curr_occ[i] ← −∞
        next_occ[i] ← FIRST(P_i)
    end for
    while (min_{1≤i≤k} next_occ[i]) < ∞ do
        rsym ← arg min_{1≤i≤k}{next_occ[i]}
        rpos ← next_occ[rsym]
        for lsym ←1 to k do
            if curr_occ[lsym] > curr_occ[rsym] then
                // lpos can be LH end of intervals ending at rpos
                lpos ← curr_occ[lsym]
                S ← {i | 1 ≤ i ≤ k and lpos < curr_occ[i]}
                for all subsets s of S, including the empty set do
                    elems ← s ∪ {lsym, rsym}
                    I ← I ∪ ⟨elems, lpos...rpos⟩
                end for
            end if
        end for
        curr_occ[rsym] ← rpos
        next_occ[rsym] ← NEXT(P_rsym)
    end while
```

Algorithm 4 Eager Plane Sweep, All Intervals (EPS-CDF-A)

```
Input: A query Q of k terms, and sorted position lists of all terms
    {P_1, P_2, ..., P_k}
Output: A set of intervals I for Q and all subqueries of Q
    (D', T_{Q,D}) ← BUILD_CDF({P_1, P_2, ..., P_k})
    I ← { }
    for i ←1 to k do
        seen[i] ← 0
5:  end for
    for lpos ←1 to T_{Q,D} − 1 do
        lsym ← D'[lpos]
        rpos ← lpos + 1 with lsym at left-hand end
        rsym ← D'[rpos]
10:     while rpos ≤ T_{Q,D} and lsym ≠ rsym do
            if seen[rsym] = 0 then
                // rpos can be RH end of intervals starting at lpos
                S ← {i | 1 ≤ i ≤ k and seen[i] = 1}
                for all subsets s of S, including the empty set do
15:                 elems ← s ∪ {lsym, rsym}
                    I ← I ∪ ⟨elems, lpos...rpos⟩
                end for
                seen[rsym] = 1
            end if
20:         rpos ← rpos + 1
            rsym ← D'[rpos]
        end while
        // reset seen to previous state
        for i ← lpos to rpos do
25:         seen[D'[i]] ← 0
        end for
    end for
```

ing accumulated into one stream $\mathcal{I}$, but that separate streams can also be generated if required, one per occurring subquery.

Eager All Interval Querying, EPS-CDF-A Algorithm 3 is a "lazy" implementation of the new approach; Algorithm 4 shows that the same idea can also be implemented in an eager manner using a condensed direct file. Now the primary loop iterates over potential left-hand positions, via variable *lpos*. For each value of *lpos* a forward scan is made using *rpos*, and *rsym*, building intervals of increasing size until $lsym = rsym$ and the bounding range for intervals whose left-hand end is at *lpos* has been found. The remainder of the process is similar between the two implementations – within the range *lpos*. . .*rpos*, all possible subsets of intervening items are used to form intervals. One important difference is that in Algorithm 4 terms are considered in position order, and the use of bitvector *seen* allows set S to be implemented as a stack when the pseudocode is translated into an actual program. On the other hand, in Algorithm 3, set S is rebuilt each time it is required by iterating over k possibilities, a factor that influences the relative execution times of the two methods in some situations.

Finally, note that while Algorithm 4 is presented assuming that an inverted file data structure is being used, it can also readily be executed starting with a direct file.

Correctness The discussion above already introduced the key notion that ensures that the two new algorithms are correct: *any optimal interval* $l \ldots r$ *that ends with some symbol* x *cannot contain any other instances of* x. To see the truth of this claim, suppose that some v exists such that $l < v < r$ and (making use of the notation employed for the direct file) $D[v] = x$. Now consider the interval $l \ldots r - 1$. Only one symbol, $D[r] = x$, has been excluded relative to the original interval, $l \ldots r$, and hence x is the only term that could possibly not also appear in $l \ldots r - 1$. But there is another location v with $l < v \leq r - 1$ for which $D[v] = x$. Hence, $l \ldots r - 1$ must be optimal for the same subset of terms as $l \ldots r$, contradicting the assumption that $l \ldots r$ is optimal. A similar argument shows that if $D[l] = x$, and $l \ldots r$ is optimal, then there cannot be any occurrence of x in $D[l + 1 \ldots r]$.

In both Algorithms 3 and 4 all possible intervals that do not violate this requirement are identified, and all possible subsets of intervening items within such intervals are considered. Hence both algorithms correctly generate all optimal intervals for the query Q and all of its subqueries $Q' \subseteq Q$ for which $|Q'| \geq 2$.

Analysis We consider Algorithm 4 first. The main loop at step 6 iterates $T_{Q,D}$ times, where $T_{Q,D}$ is the size of the CDF D', and is equal to the sum of the lengths of the terms' postings lists. The inner loop at step 10 then iterates a variable number of times, hunting forwards through D' for the next occurrence of *lsym*, the symbol at $D'[lpos]$. In total, for each of the query terms, the loop at step 10 iterates at most $T_{Q,D}$ times, since each rightward scan starts at one occurrence of *lsym*, and stops when it reaches the next, forming a telescoping sum. In aggregate, step 11 is executed at most $k \cdot T_{Q,D}$ times over all values of *lpos*.

As already noted, S need not be re-evaluated each time step 13 is reached, because intervening symbols are added to it and never removed, allowing it to be stored compactly in a k-element array. Once S is formed, each iteration of the inner loop at step 14 takes $O(1)$ time, and adds one item to $\mathcal{I}$. Over all iterations of all loops, the total time spent in the loop commencing at step 14 is thus $O(|\mathcal{I}|)$.

The only other cost is at step 1; as already discussed, this requires $O(T_{Q,D} \log k)$ time if a heap is used to convert a set of postings lists to a CDF, or $O(N)$ time if the input is from a direct file. Note that in a pragmatic implementation, with k unlikely to be larger

Queries	Description
Set A	500 queries sampled from the 2007–2008 MQT logs, with exactly 100 queries for each length $k = 3, 5, 7, 8$, and 10
Set B	1,000 queries sampled from the 2007 MQT log, with a natural distribution of query lengths $3 \le k \le 12$

Table 1: Summary of the two sampled query sets generated from the TREC 2007–2008 Million Query Track topics and the TREC GOV2 document collection.

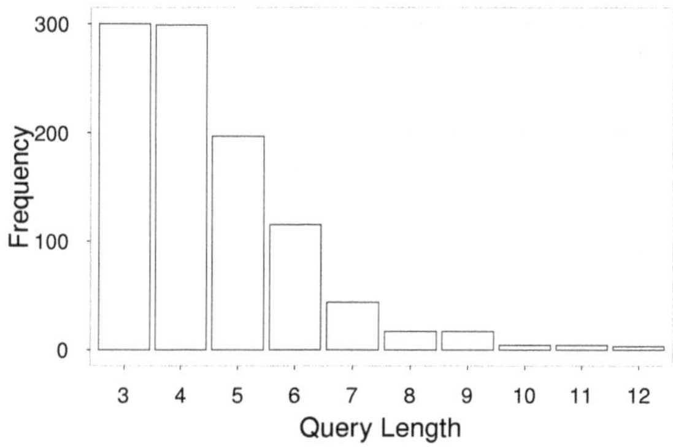

Figure 6: Length distribution for query Set B.

than around 10 or 15, an array (rather than a heap) is also a plausible choice for use during the IF to CDF conversion process, taking $O(T_{Q,D}k)$ time.

Summed over all components, the execution time of Algorithm 4 is thus $O(T_{Q,D}k + |\mathcal{I}|)$ when the input is provided as an inverted file, and $O(T_{Q,D}k + |\mathcal{I}| + N)$ if the input is a direct file.

Algorithm 3 is harder to analyze. The loop at step 6 iterates $T_{Q,D}$ times, with $O(T_{Q,D}k)$ or $O(T_{Q,D} \log k)$ time spent merging postings pointers, depending on the data structure used. For each iteration the loop at step 9 executes exactly k times and some number – possibly as many as all – of those executions makes it past the test at step 10, to execute the block of statements starting at step 11. At step 11, the process of constructing S requires $O(k)$ time, because *curr_occ* is not ordered. Finally, step 14 requires $O(1)$ time per interval that is generated, as was also the case with Algorithm 4. Putting all of these parts together, it is possible that on some inputs Algorithm 3 requires as much as $O(T_{Q,D}k^2)$ time. That worst-case bound could be reduced by maintaining *curr_occ* in sorted order via a permutation vector, paying an overhead cost to rearrange it every time it changes. As is shown below, for typical inputs the extra expense of that rearrangement is not warranted in terms of average case performance, but not doing it does indeed introduce the risk of more costly behavior on some queries.

5. EXPERIMENTS

Experimental Setup All experiments are performed on a machine using an Intel Xeon E5 CPU with 256 GB RAM running RHEL-v6.3 Linux, implemented in C++, and compiled using GCC 4.8.1 with –O2 optimization enabled, with execution times measured in milliseconds (msec) per document. All experiments use the TREC GOV2 collection. We also performed a similar series of experiments using the TREC ClueWeb09A data collection and obtained consistent results. Since our experiments focus on the set of top-ranked retrieved documents for each query, the results are influenced primarily by the nature of the documents retrieved, and agnostic to the overall collection composition.

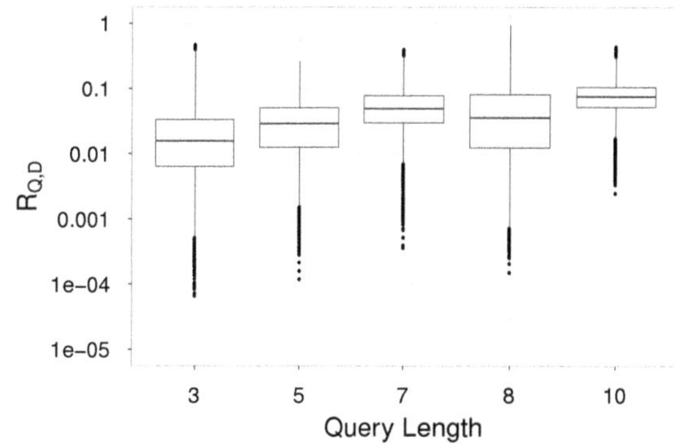

Figure 7: Distribution of $R_{Q,D}$ for Set A as a function of k.

The primary prerequisite to performing accurate comparisons of the algorithms we present is that a range of query lengths and document lengths be employed. To that end, two different query samples were created using the topics from the 2007–2008 Million Query Track (MQT) tasks. Table 1 summarizes the composition of the two query sets. Set A was developed in order to compare performance characteristics as a function of query length, with a focus on longer queries, and a minimum of 100 queries of each length. The MQT did not contain 100 queries of length 9. We also generated a second query set containing 1,000 randomly selected queries with $3 \le k \le 12$, in order to capture the query distribution in a real query stream. Longer queries exist in the MQT log, but did not emerge as part of our sample. We refer to this second set as Set B, and use it to compare performance characteristics when the sample distribution is representative of a real query stream, with short queries more probable than longer ones. The distribution of lengths in Set B is shown in Figure 6.

Each query in each set was then evaluated against GOV2 using Indri 4.7 with Krovetz stemming and a simple bag-of-words language model ranking, an out-of-the-box configuration, with stop words retained in the index. The 100 top-ranked documents for each query were retrieved, and used in conjunction with it as a query-specific pool of 100 documents against which the interval-finding algorithms might be plausibly applied in an operational setting, and against which execution times could be measured.

As discussed in Section 3, proximity evaluation depends on two key problem parameters – the length of the document, N, and the number of postings that must be processed, $T_{Q,D} = \sum_{i=1}^{k} |P_i|$. The *term density ratio* for a document D in respect of a query Q, defined as $R_{Q,D} = T_{Q,D}/N$, captures the relationship between these quantities. The direct file-based approaches are likely to be most useful when $T_{Q,D}$ is high, and many of the terms in a document are also in the query. The $R_{Q,D}$ distributions of the 50,000 documents extracted from GOV2 using Set A are shown in Figure 7. There is a slight trend for longer queries to be denser across the documents that they retrieve.

Single-Query Interval Finding We first compare the cost of direct files and inverted files. As previously discussed, EPS is most amenable to an inverted file input, and LPS to direct file input. But LPS can also be coupled with IF input – a condensed direct file can

k	LPS-DF-S		EPS-IF-S		LPS-IF-S	
	med.	max.	med.	max.	med.	max.
3	0.019	0.611	0.003	2.335	0.002	2.304
5	0.033	0.765	0.004	2.263	0.004	3.147
7	0.055	1.224	0.008	5.428	0.013	5.869
8	0.066	1.054	0.011	9.350	0.020	9.626
10	0.085	1.139	0.014	6.628	0.029	7.778

Table 2: Median and maximum time (msec/doc) spent finding optimal k-intervals using Set A.

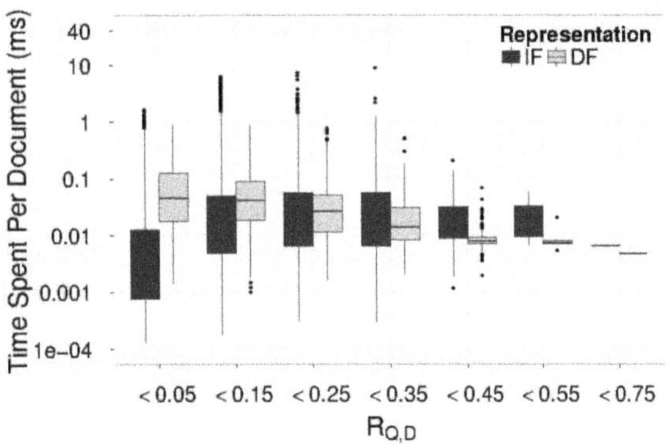

Figure 8: Time spent (msec/doc) constructing the condensed direct file, starting with an IF or a DF, using the Set A documents. There were no queries in the $0.55 \leq R_{Q,D} < 0.65$ range.

be implicitly constructed from position lists without affecting the asymptotic cost of the interval-finding task, allowing an LPS-IF-S combination to also be tested.

Table 2 lists optimal k-interval finding for the Set A queries for these three methods, with the -S suffix used to denote standard queries, without subquery intervals also being generated. The two IF-based methods exhibit similar behavior, but with EPS-IF-S consistently a little faster than LPS-IF-S. Both IF-based methods are faster than LPS-DF-S for most queries. However, LPS-DF-S is better in the worst case than both IF-based approaches, at all query lengths – situations in which $R_{Q,D}$ is high. When this happens, locality of access in the DF works better than iterating across several postings lists. Conversely, when $R_{Q,D}$ is small, the skips induced from the postings lists outperform a sequential scan of the direct file for most query-document combinations.

Consider two queries, as a concrete examples. In the three word query: "`mental health counselors`", all three terms tend to have a similar within-document term frequencies (around 200), and all of the optimal k-intervals appear close to each other. In this case, EPS-IF-S performs unnecessary comparisons and exchanges when trying to identify the rightmost position in the interval. However, in longer queries, such as "`what were the roles of african males in africa 1700s`" (recall that stop words are included) method LPS-IF-S performs poorly (7.64 msec). The same query on the same document is much faster with LPS-DF-S, taking 1.10 msec, with $R_{Q,D} = 0.16$.

Figure 8 captures these tensions, plotting the relative cost of constructing a condensed inverted file as a function of $R_{Q,D}$ for Set A. As expected, when $R_{Q,D}$ is small, it is much faster to start with an IF representation, whereas when $R_{Q,D}$ is large, the condensed file format can be created more efficiently starting with the DF format.

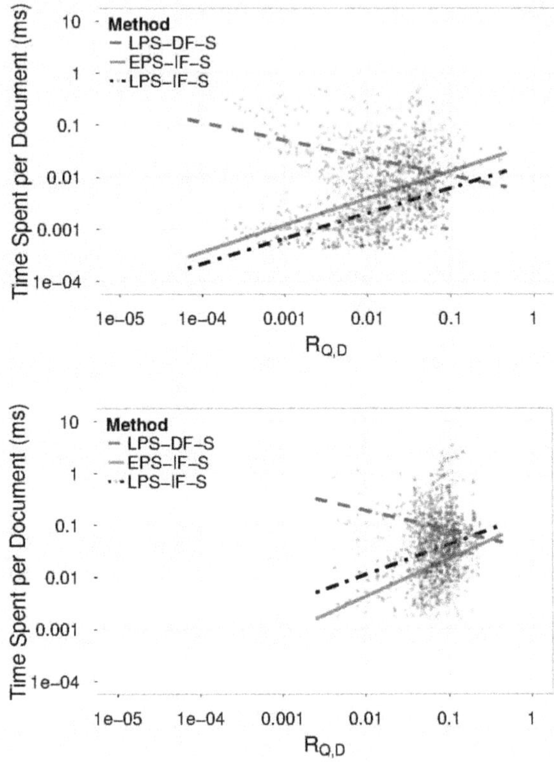

Figure 9: Time (msec/doc), as a function of $R_{Q,D}$ for Set A. The dashed blue regression line represents the LPS-DF-S method. The top figure shows results for $k = 3$ term queries, and the bottom one shows the results for $k = 10$ word queries. The plotted points represent a sample of 5% of the total data in each graph.

So, it seems conceivable that a query-sensitive mechanism might be devised to determine which input modality to use on a per-query basis if both formats were available at query time.

We now turn our attention to the performance of the interval-finding algorithms relative to $R_{Q,D}$ and query length. Figure 9 plots interval-finding time as a function of $R_{Q,D}$ for queries of length $k = 3$ (top) and $k = 10$ (bottom). The trend line for LPS-DF-S shows that query evaluation cost tends to decrease as $R_{Q,D}$ increases; whereas for EPS-IF-S and LPS-IF-S the trend is for cost to increase. For example, the three term query "`effingham county ga`" with $R_{Q,D} = 0.35$ performs poorly with both LPS-IF-S and EPS-IF-S, and is much more efficient with LPS-DF-S. The ten word query "`what was the population of the united states in 2000`" with $R_{Q,D} = 0.19$ exhibits similar behavior. Comparing the top panel to the bottom one, it can be seen that the "cloud" of points is shifted to the right in the $k = 10$ diagram, confirming that the LPS-DF-S approach is more likely to become superior as query lengths increase.

In general, our experiments for single-query interval finding show that an inverted file with position offsets is a better choice than a direct file representation. However, the worst case, while rare, is worth careful consideration. We will see shortly that the worst case costs are additive, and can have a significant impact when multiple interval computations are needed.

Computing All intervals for a Query The results in the previous experiments suggest that a direct file input representation is better in a limited set of cases, but that the majority of the time, an inverted file starting point is most efficient. However, the potential for an additive worst case means we should proceed with care.

As shown in Section 4, the problem of enumerating optimal k-intervals for all possible subqueries can be solved in a single pass using either a Lazy or Eager evaluation strategy. In addition, there are a couple of other confounding factors. It is possible to create a condensed direct file representation once, and amortize the cost of the merge from an inverted file across multiple "single-interval query" computations.

In Table 3, two different approaches are considered when enumerating all of the possible $2^k - k - 1$ term patterns. The first approach is what systems currently do, compute each interval separately. Method LPS-IF-S* runs Algorithm 1 multiple times, starting each time with the postings lists, with the -S* suffix intended to indicate that the single-query process is run multiple times. Method LPS-CDF-S* takes a different approach. It first creates a CDF by merging the position offsets from the inverted files. The CDF is then processed $2^k - k - 1$ times, each pass making use of Algorithm 2 to compute the intervals for one of the possible subqueries. The contrast between these two algorithms is captured by comparing the median execution time, and the worst-case execution time. For most query-document combinations EPS-IF-S* is the best choice. However, the additive worst case is very bad, taking a full 3 seconds for one of the 10 word queries on a *single* document. The one-off cost of computing the CDF dramatically decreases the worst-case performance, but it can still be inefficient.

We can greatly boost the overall performance in both cases by computing all $2^k - k - 1$ possible subquery results in a single pass using either Lazy or Eager evaluation as described by Algorithms 3 and 4 in Section 4. The LPS-IF-A algorithm makes a single traversal using an inverted file as the initial input, with suffix -A indicating that all subquery intervals are found in a single pass. The EPS-CDF-A algorithm computes the CDF once by merging the position offsets from the inverted file. The CDF is then used to make a single pass using eager evaluation.

An important point to note about input representations with LPS and EPS based single pass algorithms is that either can benefit from computing the CDF. For a single-query interval, we demonstrated that the eager processing strategy is best suited for IF-structured input. However, this is not true when enumerating all intervals, because the corner case of having a huge gap between the current and next position for a term is offset by the fact that it is very likely that several of the subquery intervals will be formed even if the k-term interval has not formed yet. The extra work in resetting the left interval boundary often results in a subquery interval being emitted. In practical terms, this means that the performance profile for EPS-CDF-S* and LPS-CDF-S* is almost identical.

The key message in Table 3 is that performing the optimal k-interval enumeration process in a single pass is dramatically more efficient than either of the two multi-pass strategies, and, as expected, the gap becomes more pronounced as the query length increases. Although there are some small differences, the two -A plane-sweep approaches exhibit similar average performance when generating intervals for all subqueries. The key difference is again related to the worst-case. The tension between amortizing the creation of the CDF once and benefiting from locality of access, versus the cost of hitting a rare long document with many occurrences of the terms, separates the two approaches in the worst case.

Figure 10 shows the relative performance of multiple-pass and single-pass approaches. Note the use of a log scale. The upper panel shows the average performance for all 10,000 document-query combinations in Set B. Each boxplot summarizes the time

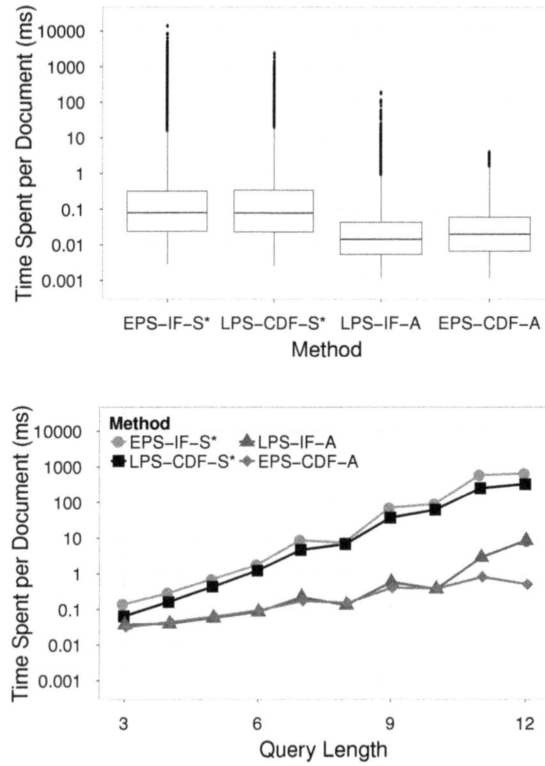

Figure 10: Time (msec/doc) to extract the optimal k-intervals for all subqueries using Set B. The top panel gives an overview of the per-query variation, incorporating all of the queries; the bottom panel shows the average time cost for each method broken down by query length. Note the log vertical scale on both graphs.

values as follows: the solid horizontal line indicates the median; the box shows the 25th and 75th percentiles; and the whiskers show the range, up to a maximum of 1.5 times the interquartile range, with outliers beyond this shown as separate points. In the overall performance comparison for all Set B queries, the LPS-IF-A algorithm appears to be slightly better than EPS-CDF-A, but a t-test shows that EPS-CDF-A is in fact significantly better with $p = 0.01$. This is largely due to the fact that the variance in query performance is more tightly bound for EPS-CDF-A than for LPS-IF-A. The bottom panel in Figure 10 shows the average (mean) processing cost in milliseconds per document as a function of query length. The two single-pass methods enjoy a near two-fold performance improvement for queries of length $k = 3$, and a more than 1000-fold improvement when $k = 12$.

The experiments we have described in this section leave absolutely no room for ambiguity. All-subqueries interval-finding is greatly accelerated by our two new methods, even when queries have as few as $k = 3$ terms in them.

6. CONCLUSION AND FUTURE WORK

We have explored two different questions. First, we considered two different approaches to efficiently compute an optimal k-interval based on input representation. We found that in most cases, starting with position offsets in an inverted file is more efficient than using a direct file. However, some query-document combinations can induce very bad behavior in k-interval computa-

k	EPS-IF-S*		LPS-CDF-S*		LPS-IF-A		EPS-CDF-A	
	med.	max.	med.	max.	med.	max.	med.	max.
3	0.011	7.300	0.011	1.307	0.006	2.821	0.007	0.986
5	0.089	37.770	0.104	8.757	0.018	3.758	0.024	1.790
7	0.778	344.800	1.113	59.060	0.060	7.037	0.071	3.282
8	2.104	1303.000	3.102	142.600	0.098	18.640	0.108	5.016
10	9.315	3397.000	17.160	801.600	0.175	46.350	0.191	9.222

Table 3: Median and maximum time (msec/doc) to find the optimal k-intervals for all subqueries for each query in Set A.

tions. By exploring the efficiency of the algorithms as a function of the term density ratio, we were able to isolate exactly when each evaluation strategy and input format is preferable.

In our second research question, we explored novel approaches to computing all term combination intervals in a single-pass. By exploiting a key insight in to the way intervals must be formed in subqueries, we showed how to significantly increase the performance of proximity computations. The performance gap between current approaches and our approach increases as query length increases, making it a viable tool in real search engines wishing to incorporate proximity computations into current ranking functions.

In future work, we will explore the impact on various interpretations of how intervals should be defined in IR ranking functions. Our current approach is more general than current FDM- and SDM-based ranking functions, which employed fixed-width window sizes, rather than optimal intervals. But note that the algorithms described in this paper can be adapted to also support fixed window sizes by counting only intervals that are less that a particular threshold.

Acknowledgment This work was supported by the Australian Research Council's *Discovery Projects* Scheme (DP140101587 and DP140103256). Shane Culpepper is the recipient of an Australian Research Council DECRA Research Fellowship (DE140100275).

References

[1] N. Asadi and J. Lin. Document vector representations for feature extraction in multi-stage document ranking. *Inf. Retr.*, 16(6):747–768, 2013.

[2] M. Bendersky, D. Metzler, and W. B. Croft. Parameterized concept weighting in verbose queries. In *Proc. SIGIR*, pages 605–614, 2011.

[3] A. Broschart and R. Schenkel. High-performance processing of text queries with tunable pruned term and term pair indexes. *ACM Trans. Information Systems*, 30(1):1–32, 2012.

[4] S. Büttcher, C. L. A. Clarke, and B. Lushman. Term proximity scoring for ad-hoc retrieval on very large text collections. In *Proc. SIGIR*, pages 621–622, 2006.

[5] S. Büttcher, C. L. A. Clarke, and G. V. Cormack. *Information Retrieval: Implementing and Evaluating Search Engines*. MIT Press, 2010.

[6] J. P. Callan, W. B. Croft, and S. M. Harding. The INQUERY retrieval system. In *Database and Expert Systems Applications*, pages 78–83. Springer, 1992.

[7] C. L. A. Clarke, G. Cormack, and F. J. Burkowski. Shortest substring ranking (multitext experiments for TREC-4). In *Proc. TREC*, pages 295–304, 1995.

[8] C. L. A. Clarke, G. V. Cormack, and E. A. Tudhope. Relevance ranking for one to three term queries. *Inf. Proc. & Man.*, 36(2):291–311, 2000.

[9] T. Elsayed, J. Lin, and D. Metzler. When close enough is good enough: approximate positional indexes for efficient ranked retrieval. In *Proc. CIKM*, pages 1993–1996, 2011.

[10] D. Hawking and P. Thistlewaite. Proximity operators-so near and yet so far. In *Proc. TREC*, pages 131–143, 1995.

[11] D. Hawking and P. Thistlewaite. Relevance weighting using distance between term occurrences. Technical Report TR-CS-96-08, Department of Computer Science, The Australian National University, 1996.

[12] S. Huston. *Indexing Proximity-Based Dependencies for Information Retrieval*. PhD thesis, University of Massachusetts, Amherst, 2014.

[13] S. Huston and W. B. Croft. A comparison of retrieval models using term dependencies. In *Proc. CIKM*, pages 111–120, 2014.

[14] D. Metzler. *Beyond Bags of Words: Effectively Modeling Dependence and Features in Information Retrieval*. PhD thesis, University of Massachusetts, Amherst, 2007.

[15] D. Metzler and W. B. Croft. Combining the language model and inference network approaches to retrieval. *Inf. Proc. & Man.*, 40(5): 735–750, 2004.

[16] D. Metzler and W. B. Croft. A Markov random field model for term dependencies. In *Proc. SIGIR*, pages 472–479, 2005.

[17] J. Peng, C. Macdonald, B. He, V. Plachouras, and I. Ounis. Incorporating term dependency in the DFR framework. In *Proc. SIGIR*, pages 843–844, 2007.

[18] K. Sadakane and H. Imai. Text retrieval by using k-word proximity search. In *Proc. Symp. Database Appl. Non-Trad. Envs.*, pages 183–188, 1999.

[19] R. Schenkel, A. Broschart, S. Hwang, M. Theobald, and G. Weikum. Efficient text proximity search. In *Proc. SPIRE*, pages 287–299, 2007.

[20] T. Tao and C. Zhai. An exploration of proximity measures in information retrieval. In *Proc. SIGIR*, pages 295–302, 2007.

[21] J. B. P. Vuurens and A. P. de Vries. Distance matters! Cumulative proximity expansions for ranking documents. *Inf. Retr.*, 17(4):380–406, 2014.

[22] H. Yan, S. Shi, F. Zhang, T. Suel, and J.-R. Wen. Efficient term proximity search with term-pair indexes. In *Proc. CIKM*, pages 1229–1238, 2010.

An Optimization Framework for Merging Multiple Result Lists

Chia-Jung Lee *, Qingyao Ai *, W. Bruce Croft and Daniel Sheldon
College of Information and Computer Sciences, University of Massachusetts Amherst
Amherst, MA, USA
{cjlee, aiqy, croft, sheldon}@cs.umass.edu

ABSTRACT

Developing effective methods for fusing multiple ranked lists of documents is crucial to many applications. Federated web search, for instance, has become a common practice where a query is issued to different verticals and a single ranked list of blended results is created. While federated search is regarded as collection fusion, data fusion techniques aim at improving search coverage and precision by combining multiple search runs on a single document collection. In this paper, we study in depth and extend a neural network-based approach, LambdaMerge [32], for merging results of ranked lists drawn from one (i.e., data fusion) or more (i.e., collection fusion) verticals. The proposed model considers the impact of the quality of documents, ranked lists and verticals for producing the final merged result in an optimization framework. We further investigate the potential of incorporating deep structures into the model with an aim of determining better combinations of different evidence. In the experiments on collection fusion and data fusion, the proposed approach significantly outperforms several standard baselines and state-of-the-art learning-based approaches.

Categories and Subject Descriptors

H.3.3 [**Information Systems**]: Information Search and Retrieval

Keywords

Data fusion; collection fusion; learning to merge; deep neural network

1. INTRODUCTION

Developing effective methods for fusing multiple result lists into one is beneficial to many applications such as web-scale federated search. A large body of fusing techniques has been widely studied, and can be broadly categorized into two tasks, namely data fusion and collection fusion. While both tasks seek an optimal blending of results from different lists, collection fusion has a focus on merging results retrieved simultaneously from multiple collections. Collection fusion, often referred to interchangeably as federated search, is preferred over centralized search alternatives for reasons such as efficiency [35]. In addition, federated search systems can search the content of the hidden web without crawling, producing results comprised of answers returned from multiple verticals [35]. Collection fusion techniques are mostly concentrated on approximating comparable document scores from different repositories [9, 38, 36]. In recent years, the TREC federated web search track established reusable test sets from real web search engines of different verticals [13, 14]. Better performing approaches for the result merging task in this track take into account combined signals such as the number of engines containing a document [31] and text similarity [18].

Data fusion, on the other hand, often refers to tasks where the aim is to merge results retrieved from a single document collection. Compared with individual ranking systems, data fusion provides the advantage that the merged list usually has a higher precision and recall [12]. Known as the *chorus effect* [39], many effective fusion methods are based on the premise that documents that are highly ranked in many of the lists are likely to be relevant [1, 2, 17, 24]. Recent developments in data fusion algorithms rely on using training queries to better estimate the probability of relevance using signals such as document ranks and scores [25, 34, 26].

Recent work [32] on results fusion presents the first attempt that uses relevance judgments to directly optimize retrieval performance metrics such as MAP or NDCG. In particular, Sheldon et al [32] merged results from multiple query reformulations to improve search while mitigating risks such as query topic drift. This approach, LambdaMerge (or λ-Merge), can be classified as a data fusion technique since search runs from different reformulations are conducted on the equivalent of a single collection[1]. λ-Merge learns a scoring function to rank documents by combining features indicating document relevance (e.g., retrieval score or rank of a document) with features indicating the quality of the reformulation and its results (e.g., query clarity and drift).

While λ-Merge has demonstrated strong performance in data fusion, it is unclear how an effective adaption to collection fusion can be carried out. In web-scale federated search, it is beneficial to understand the right medium and identify appropriate verticals for a query. System efficiency,

[1]The industrial level of document indices should be distributed, but experiments conducted in λ-Merge assumes the presence of every document in every list.

CIKM'15, October 19-23, 2015, Melbourne, VIC, Australia
© 2015 ACM. ISBN 978-1-4503-3794-6/15/10...$15.00
DOI: http://dx.doi.org/10.1145/2806416.2806489 [* equal contribution].

for instance, can be improved when a query is only issued to a number of top verticals. Ranking can further be guided by preferring certain verticals among those selected, resulting in better search performance[2]. In this paper, we address the task of result merging and extend λ-Merge in a way that the new model accommodates and considers the impact of drawing results from different verticals. Specifically, the proposed approach learns a scoring function characterized by not only the quality of documents and resources (i.e., ranked lists produced by different search engines), but verticals that contain the most relevant content. The final ranking of blended results is determined by directly optimizing the overall retrieval effectiveness.

Inspired by the recent success of deep structures [5, 16, 20], our model further investigates the potential of combining different ranking evidence using this approach. In particular, we incorporate a deep neural network (DNN) for learning the scoring function. The structure of a DNN is highly simple and generative, and can be applied to most classification and optimization problems given proper design of the loss function in the output layer. We note that the focus of previous studies is mostly around learning representation [15, 20, 29]; we propose to apply deep structured models to the fusion task.

We conduct extensive experiments in a variety of fusion scenarios. Specifically, we use two recent collections from the TREC federated web search track, FedWeb13 and FedWeb14, for testing collection fusion. For data fusion, it is typical to use existing runs submitted to TREC based on which a merged list is created. We experiment with two years of TREC Web Track data, WebTrack09 and WebTrack10, where measures capturing both precision and diversity (e.g., α-NDCG@k) of a ranked list can be evaluated using the sub-topic relevance judgments. The experimental results demonstrate that integrating vertical signals significantly improves retrieval effectiveness for collection fusion. We further show that, for both fusion scenarios, the performance of models with deep structures consistently outperforms standard baselines [17], state-of-the-art approaches [11, 7, 41], and models with shallow structures.

Since λ-Merge focuses on combining results from different query reformulations, features that quantify reformulation quality and topic drift are unavailable in a more general fusion scenario (i.e., only a singe query is present). One contribution of our work is to introduce new effective features that are able to characterize the quality of ranked lists. The features we use are also more semantically informative (e.g., aggregated retrieval scores), compared with the coarse features (e.g., bi-grams or tri-grams) used in other deep structured work [15, 20]. Although the amount of training instances in our experiments is relatively small, the higher-level definition of our features can make learning an effective deep model possible.

After a discussion of related work, we describe in detail the merging framework in Section 3. We then introduce the tested environments along with the features devised for these collections in Section 4. Section 5 shows the results of fusion experiments using a variety of baselines and the proposed models. We discuss and conclude the paper in Section 6.

[2]For instance, vertical *Game* may be preferred to *Entertainment* for query *Mine Craft* although both are deemed relevant.

2. RELATED WORK

This paper presents a merging framework that uses deep structures. This section first discusses general related work on merging multiple result lists, followed by a brief introduction to the applications of deep structures in the information retrieval field.

2.1 Merging Multiple Result Lists

Data Fusion

Methodologies for fusing multiple search results into a single one can be broadly categorized into two families: data fusion and collection fusion. Data fusion refers to tasks where a query is sent to multiple retrieval models that have access to the same document collection, and the rankings from different models are merged into a final single list [12, 39, 42]. One main advantage of data fusion is that often the merged list will have greater relevance than the output of any individual system [3]. Fox and Shaw [17] suggested several combination methods; among these, CombSUM and CombMNZ showed better effectiveness by fusing results based on normalized document scores and the number of systems containing a document. A follow-up work [24] modified CombMNZ by replacing document scores with ranks. Aslam and Montague [1] proposed to merge documents using the probability of relevance estimated for documents at given ranks. Bordafuse [2] also merged documents based on the ranks and no training data is required.

More recent developments in data fusion have laid an emphasis on techniques that use training queries to estimate scores assigned to documents. ProbFuse [25] divides each result list into equal length segments, and uses training queries to estimate the probability that a document returned in a particular segment is relevant. SegFuse [34] takes a similar approach and modifies ProbFuse by allowing variant size of segments. Building on these techniques, SlideFuse [26] introduces a sliding window to estimate relevance probability. A recent cluster-based fusion approach [22] considers inter-document similarities created across the lists to improve merging effectiveness.

Collection Fusion

Collection fusion focuses on a related yet somewhat different task. In particular, queries are issued to document collections that are disjoint or partially overlapped, and the returned results are integrated and merged into a single list [10, 40]. Result merging is a challenging task as different retrieval algorithms may be applied to different collections that may have different lexicon statistics. Earlier approaches to collection fusion [9] used simple heuristics to normalize collection-specific document scores for ranking. More recent methods approximate comparable document scores with higher accuracy. A semi-supervised learning method proposed by Si and Callan [38] trained a regression model for each collection, which is used to map document scores into their global merging scores. Shokouhi and Zobel [36] assumed that the ranking of sampled documents is a subranking of the original collection, and estimated the merging scores by applying curve fitting to the sub-ranking.

Collection fusion and federated search have been often used interchangeably [35]. Web-scale federated search has recently drawn much attention and become a common practice. To promote related research, the TREC federated web search track established reusable test sets from real world search engines and their results [13, 14]. In a web setting, a query is issued to a selected subset of engines (or verticals); this is regarded as the task of *resource selection*. The *result merging* step then merges the returned results from the selected resources into a single list. We only focus on the result merging task in this paper. In TREC FedWeb 2013, the best performing approach [31] fuses results by adapting the reciprocal rank fusion approach [11]. For FedWeb 2014, the best performing approach was submitted by the ICTNET group [18] where they fused documents by combining signals such as ranks and text similarity.

2.2 Deep Structure Learning

Deep structured models have been successfully applied to many language related applications such as speech recognition (SR), natural language processing (NLP) and information retrieval (IR) [4, 5, 20, 33]. Deep learning techniques can learn high level abstractions from training data which has been shown useful for both classification tasks and semantic analysis. General structures of supervised deep networks include the recurrent neural network (RNN), deep stacking network (DSN), deep neural network (DNN) and convolutional neural network (CNN) [16]. RNN describes a network that recurrently combines former activation states of hidden neurons with current input layer features to predict the next output. It has been widely used in SR and NLP tasks [27, 29], but not as much in IR. Most deep learning applications in IR focus on the generation of semantic representations for queries and documents. Deng et al. [15] first reported positive results with DSN models. The semantic representations extracted with DSN have higher retrieval performance than traditional learning to rank algorithms. Huang et al. [20] developed a DNN based architecture to learn semantic models with clickthrough data. Huang's model, namely the Deep Structured Semantic Model (DSSM), achieved significant improvements compared to many state-of-the-art latent semantic models. Shen et al. [29] further extended Huang's model with a layer of convolution and max-pooling (which is the main idea of CNN) and obtained even better performance than DSSM.

In our work, we choose the general structure of DNN as the network for the fusion task. Compared with other deep learning models, DNN has a structure that is simple and generative. With proper design of the loss function in the output layer, DNN can be applied to most classification and optimization problems, and it is easier to train than DSN. CNN showed better performance than DNN in tasks of latent semantic analysis; however, it does not fit our problem since our training instances consist of features that have a fixed number of dimensions as opposed to a sequential structure. Similar to CNN, RNN is also not appropriate for our task, which leaves DNN as our best choice.

3. MERGING MULTIPLE RESULT LISTS

Developing effective methods for fusing multiple ranked lists of documents is crucial to many applications. Conventionally, unsupervised approaches use retrieval scores or ranks to determine the final ranking of documents in a merged list. These methods have merits that they require no training examples. It is, however, often the case that learning-based approaches achieve better effectiveness, partly because additional features are easy to incorporate and customized objectives can be derived and optimized. This section first introduces an existing learning-to-merge framework, λ-Merge. We then describe our extension by introducing vertical estimation and deep structures.

3.1 Preliminaries of λ-Merge

The λ-Merge approach is the first proposed merging method that is trained using relevance judgments to directly optimize retrieval metrics such as NDCG or MAP [32]. λ-Merge considers, for a query q, a set of reformulations $\{q_1, q_2, \cdots, q_N\}$ (including the original q), and the goal is to fuse the corresponding output result lists $\{D_1, D_2, \cdots, D_N\}$ into a single one. For each document d in the ith result list, λ-Merge utilizes multiple *query-document* features x_i^d to capture how relevant d is to query q_i. In addition, for the ith result list returned of the ith reformulation, a vector of *query-list* features z_i is created to estimate the quality of that ranked list. These query-list features mostly focused on characterizing each query reformulation's difficulty and drift, including features such as query clarity score or the distance between original and rewrite queries (e.g., random walk probabilities between queries).

The core components of λ-Merge consist of a scoring function $f(x_i^d; \theta)$ and a gating function $g(z_i; \eta)$, based on which the parameters θ for features x_i^d as well as η for features z_i can be learned. The model defines the final score of a document d by re-weighting $f(x_i^d; \theta)$ with the gating component as in Equation 1, where L is the total number of lists.

$$s_d = \sum_{i=1}^{L} g_i \cdot f(x_i^d; \theta) \tag{1}$$

In the implementation of λ-Merge, the scoring function $f(x_i^d; \theta)$ is carried out using a fully connected neural network with a *single* hidden layer of four neurons, each having a *tanh* activation function. The hidden units are connected to an output unit, which is then re-weighted by the linear gating function g_i. The objective of λ-Merge is to produce a single fused list with NDCG optimized. The training is done by taking partial derivatives of s_d with respect to the network parameters θ and η.

3.2 The Proposed Framework

Now we introduce our extensions of λ-Merge. To apply λ-Merge to collection fusion, we incorporate an extra component that captures the quality of a vertical into the framework. The idea is that the quality of a vertical in which a document exists can affect the overall relevance of this document to a query. Figure 1 shows the structure of our framework. Suppose that, for a query q, we have L search engines drawn from a set of V verticals, each search engine producing one ranked list in response to q. Typically we have $V < L$, meaning that multiple engines are adopted for a vertical. The framework in Figure 1 first considers the feature function $f(x_{i,j}^d; \theta)$ derived for a document d that is in the ith ranked list belonging to the jth vertical. The model then re-weights f by g_i, which is defined as the *softmax* output of the feature function $g(z_i; \eta)$ that measures the quality of a ranked list. Finally, we incorporate the estimation for vertical quality by combining $g_i \cdot f$ with h_j. The weight h_j stands for the *softmax* output of feature function $h(y_j; \phi)$ that captures the goodness of a vertical given the current

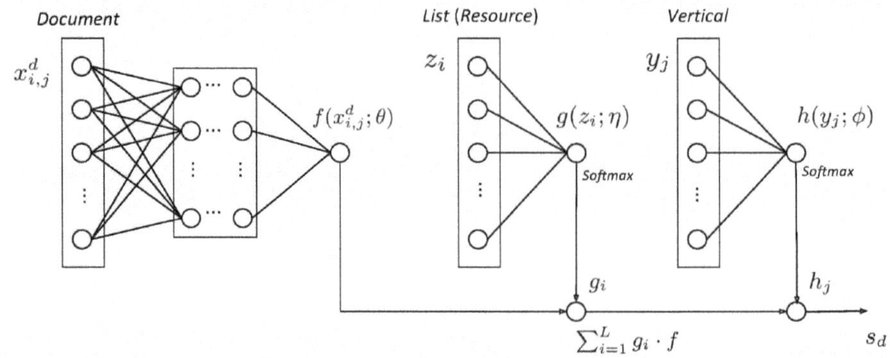

Figure 1: The proposed framework for merging results from multiple lists. The final score of a document is determined by the document, list, and vertical feature functions based on a DNN structure.

search context. Overall, the model produces the final document score s_d in the merged list using Equation 2.

$$s_d = \sum_{j=1}^{V} h_j \Big(\sum_{i=1}^{L} g_i \cdot f(x^d_{i,j};\theta) \Big) \tag{2}$$

Inspired by the widely reported effectiveness of deep models, our second extension investigates the potential of incorporating multiple hidden layers in an artificial neural network for the fusion task. We take the definition of deep structures to include properties that (1.) multiple layers of nonlinear processing units are incorporated and (2.) the supervised or unsupervised learning of feature representations takes place in each layer, with the layers forming a hierarchy from low-level to high-level features [16]. As shown in Figure 1, the implementation of the feature function $f(x^d_{i,j};\theta)$ is based on a DNN structure.

Feature functions for scoring

We implement the scoring function $f(x^d_{i,j};\theta)$ using a standard feed-forward artificial neural network that incorporates two or more layers of hidden neurons. Formally, denoting l_k as the input of intermediate hidden layer k and o as the output of neural network, the projection process can be described as in Equation 3. Here W_k and b_k are the projection matrix and bias term for hidden layer k, and a denotes the activation function. The parameter space is therefore $\theta = \{W_k, b_k : \forall k\}$.

$$\begin{aligned} l_1 &= W_1 x^d_{i,j} \\ l_k &= a(W_k l_{k-1} + b_k), k = 2, 3, ..., N-1 \\ o &= a(W_N l_{N-1} + b_N) \end{aligned} \tag{3}$$

We test the activation function a with both *tanh* and *sigmoid*. In practice, no substantial difference was observed and we opt for *tanh* in each neuron:

$$a(x) = \frac{1 - e^{-2x}}{1 + e^{-2x}} \tag{4}$$

Similar to the implementation of f, we design a neural network structure separately for the list feature function $g(z_i;\eta) = \eta^T z_i$ and the vertical feature function $h(y_j;\phi) = \phi^T y_j$. The two networks both follow a standard feed-forward propagation, and respectively taking query-list features z_i and query-vertical features y_j as input layer signals. To determine the re-weighting component g_i, we propagate $g(z_i;\eta)$ through a *softmax* smoothing function as shown in Equation 5, where L denotes the number of input rank lists. The same is done for h_j using Equation 6. In theory, these two weighting networks can incorporate deep structures as in the document scoring network $f(x^d_{i,j};\theta)$. This will require considerably more training data since list and vertical features are sparser than document ones; we thus choose to leave it as a shallow network.

$$g_i = \frac{exp(g(z_i;\eta))}{\sum_{k=1}^{L} exp(g(z_k;\eta))} \tag{5}$$

search context. Overall, the model produces the final docu-

$$h_j = \frac{exp(h(y_j;\phi))}{\sum_{k=1}^{V} exp(h(y_k;\phi))} \tag{6}$$

Optimizing retrieval performance

The result merging task seeks a single ranked list by fusing multiple ones with an aim of achieving retrieval effectiveness as high as possible. Accordingly, we train the model parameters θ, η and ϕ to directly optimize NDCG@20 of the fused list using a gradient-based approach. We note that other measures such as MAP or Precision@k can be used.

A problem that arises with the direct optimization of search effectiveness is that the retrieval metrics are discontinuous with respect to document scores[3]. To overcome the discontinuity of the objective, Burges et al [6] suggests it is sufficient to define the λ functions for which some objective C exists (as opposed to defining C directly). This technique is also used by the λ-Merge model. In our framework, it is sufficient to learn the model by implementing the gradients with respect to the model parameters θ, η and ϕ; that is, our goals are to compute $\frac{\partial C}{\partial \theta_k}$, $\frac{\partial C}{\partial \eta_k}$ and $\frac{\partial C}{\partial \phi_k}$.

The computation for these gradients can be decomposed using chain rule. Take θ_k as an example; we compute $\frac{\partial C}{\partial \theta_k} = \frac{\partial C}{\partial s_d} \cdot \frac{\partial s_d}{\partial \theta_k}$ where the index d is summed over. The former part $\frac{\partial C}{\partial s_d}$ can be solved by the λ functions in LambdaRank [8] as in Equation 7. Here, $d \succ j$ denotes that d has a larger relevance label than j, meaning that d should be ranked

[3]Metrics are determined by the ranks sorted by scores rather than the actual scores.

above j. $|\Delta_{NDCG@20}|$ denotes the variation in NDCG@20 when the two documents d and j are swapped.

$$\frac{\partial C}{\partial s_d} = \sum_{j;d \succ j} \frac{-1}{1 + e^{(s_d - s_j)}} |\Delta_{NDCG@20}| \tag{7}$$

To solve $\frac{\partial C}{\partial \theta_k}$, we further need to calculate the latter part $\frac{\partial s_d}{\partial \theta_k}$ of the decomposition. Taking the fact that only the document scoring network involves θ, the gradients can be done as in Equation 8. The update process of $\frac{\partial f(x_{i,j}^d;\theta)}{\partial \theta_k}$ follows the general algorithm of back-propagation (BP).

$$\frac{\partial C}{\partial \theta_k} = \frac{\partial C}{\partial s_d} \cdot \frac{\partial s_d}{\partial \theta_k} = \frac{\partial C}{\partial s_d} \cdot \sum_{j=1}^{V} h_j (\sum_{i=1}^{L} g_i \cdot \frac{\partial f(x_{i,j}^d;\theta)}{\partial \theta_k}) \tag{8}$$

Likewise, for $\frac{\partial C}{\partial \eta_k}$ and $\frac{\partial C}{\partial \phi_k}$, we need to solve $\frac{\partial s_d}{\partial \eta_k}$ and $\frac{\partial s_d}{\partial \phi_k}$ as we already know $\frac{\partial C}{\partial s_d}$. The computation can be done as in Equations 9 and 10.

$$\frac{\partial s_d}{\partial \eta_k} = \sum_{j=1}^{V} h_j (\sum_{i=1}^{L} \frac{\partial g_i}{\partial \eta_k} \cdot f(x_{i,j}^d;\theta)) \tag{9}$$

$$\frac{\partial s_d}{\partial \phi_k} = \sum_{j=1}^{V} \frac{\partial h_j}{\partial \phi_k} (\sum_{i=1}^{L} g_i \cdot f(x_{i,j}^d;\theta)) \tag{10}$$

Since the output of re-weighting network $g(z_i;\eta)$ goes through a *softmax* smoothing before being incorporated into the model, the partial differential equations are transformed according to Equation 11, where $\frac{\partial g(z_i;\eta)}{\partial \eta_k}$ can be inferred through the process of BP. Similar computation can be done for $\frac{\partial h_j}{\partial \phi_k}$ by replacing Equation 11 with the corresponding parameters.

$$\frac{\partial g_i}{\partial \eta_k} = \frac{\beta_i \frac{\partial g(z_i;\eta)}{\partial \eta_k} \sum_{j=1}^{L} \beta_j - \beta_i \sum_{j=1}^{L} \beta_j \frac{\partial g(z_j;\eta)}{\partial \eta_k}}{(\sum_{j=1}^{L} \beta_j)^2} \tag{11}$$
$$\beta_i = exp(g(z_i;\eta))$$

4. TEST BEDS AND FEATURES

Our experiments are conducted in both collection and data fusion environments. This section describes the selected test sets for each environment, and discusses the features in detail.

4.1 Collection Fusion Test Sets

Collection fusion refers to search tasks where a query is issued to disjoint or low overlap document collections, and a single ranked list of blended results is created. To this end, we use test sets derived from the TREC federated web search track in years 2013 and 2014. The main reason for using FedWeb collections is that the track provides test sets in a more realistic web setting. Specifically, the documents were collected from real web search engines as opposed to artificial ones such as those created by dividing existing TREC collections by topic or source [19]. The test sets contain the actual results of approximately 150 real web search engines drawn from a fixed set of 24 verticals, each providing their own retrieval method and heterogeneous content types such as news, travel, social etc. In each year, 50 official queries for the result merging task were created, and up to 10 ranked results were crawled and stored from each of the search engines[4]. We note that only the ranks are stored and no score information is available. Graded relevance judgments are gathered for these queries, following the conventions used in TREC web tracks, in 5 levels {Nav, Key, HRel, Rel, NRel}. The main evaluation metric used in the FedWeb track is NDCG@20.

For both years of data, one characteristic of the document collections is that search engines can return duplicate documents, although stored as different document identifiers. This can happen even within a search engine, meaning that this engine unexpectedly returned the same documents. To prevent rewarding merged search results containing duplicate (relevant) content, we pre-process the document collections using two steps. First, for each ranked list, we keep only one copy of a document and discard any subsequent duplicates. The remaining documents are sequentially moved to lower ranks following the original order. After the first pass of processing, we check if duplicates exist across different ranked lists for a given query. We assign the inter-list duplicates the same document identifier so as to let the merging framework know that they are actually the same. The official lists of duplicate documents can be obtained from TREC FedWeb13 and FedWeb14 sites, which were produced based on a number of heuristics such as identical smoothed URLs.

4.2 Data Fusion Test Sets

Data fusion techniques combine the ranked lists of multiple document retrieval systems to improve search coverage and precision. Different from collection fusion, the retrieval systems operate on the same set of documents in general, and thus the overlap rate across lists is much higher. Conventionally, existing runs submitted to TREC are used to evaluate this task. We experiment with two years of TREC Web Track data, WebTrack09 and WebTrack10. Using these newer data sets for experiments provides the advantage that we are able to evaluate not only precision but also the diversity of a ranked list based on the sub-topic relevance judgments. The test set of each year consists of 50 queries; 71 and 56 runs were submitted to 2009 and 2010 respectively. We randomly sampled 30 ranked lists from each year for the merging experiments.

4.3 Features

Our framework inherits the property of λ-Merge where features approximating document relevance and list quality are employed together for predicting document scores. We further incorporate vertical features in addition to those two categories. Table 1 shows an overview of the feature set used for the experiments, which we describe in detail below.

Document features.

Denoted as $x_{i,j}^d$, document features are used to describe the relation between a query and a document. In Table 1, the rank features correspond to positions where a document is assigned in a list. Reciprocal rank score $1/(60 + rank)$ is incorporated for its reported effectiveness [11].

Typically a document should be promoted in the final ranked list if more search systems deem it relevant. As such,

[4]FedWeb13 stores both snippets and documents of results while FedWeb14 only stores snippets

Table 1: **Document, list and vertical features used for learning to merge results. Partial features are only applicable to either FedWeb (F) or WebTrack (W). N denotes the total number of documents in a result list.**

Feature	Descriptions	Avail
	query-document feature	
Rank	rank, 1/(60+rank)	F, W
Co-exist	number of lists a document exists	F, W
Exist	exist-within/original-length	F
Score	retrieval scores, normalized retrieval scores, weighted scores	F, W
	query-list feature	
mCo-exist	mean of document co-exist scores of entire list	F, W
mCo-exist-k	mean of document co-exist scores of top k results, $k \in \{10, 20, 30\}$	W
mScore	mean of document (normalized) scores	F, W
Ratio-1	ratio of documents with co-exist > 1 to N	F, W
Ratio-k%	ratio of docs with co-exist $> k\%$ of retrieval systems to N, $k \in \{20, 40, 60, 80\}$	W
RatioRet	ratio of number of returned results to number requested	F
RatioDup	ratio of number of remained documents after de-duplication to number returned	F
	query-vertical feature	
vmScore	mean of mScore of the ranked lists a vertical has for a query	F
vmCo-exist	mean of mCo-exist of the ranked lists a vertical has for a query	F
vRatio-1	mean of Ratio-1 of the ranked lists a vertical has for a query	F

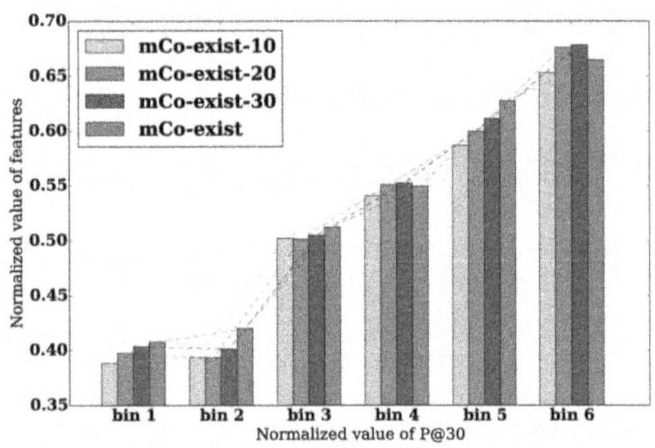

Figure 2: Relation between aggregated document co-exist scores and list performance using WebTrack09.

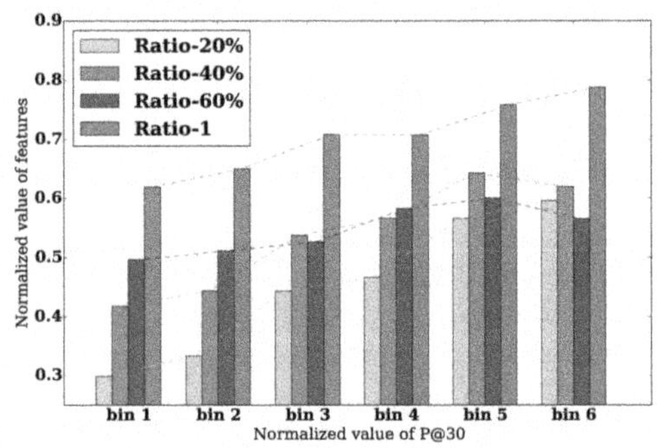

Figure 3: Relation between list ratio scores and list performance using WebTrack09.

the *co-exist* feature counts the number of result lists (i.e., search systems) in which a document appears. In the special case of FedWeb test sets, we also consider the property that a document can appear more than once in a list. The number of duplicates of document in a list divided by the original list length is included as a feature, which is denoted as the *exist* feature.

The score features reflect how relevant a ranker believes a document is to a query. We use two retrieval systems to estimate the score, including a query likelihood model and a sequential dependency model [28]. We also consider the zero-one normalized scores, and the weighted scores computed by taking products of *co-exist* and normalized scores. Finally, the same computation applies to scores from runs submitted to TREC when available.

List features.

Since the focus of λ-Merge is to combine results from different query reformulations, the emphasis for list features is mostly around the reformulation quality and its drift from original query, which is seldom available in a more general fusion setting. To propose more features that may be useful for quantifying list quality, we conduct a preliminary analysis on the retrieval effectiveness of different ranked lists. We hypothesize that better effectiveness of a list is related to whether the documents in that list are also returned by other search systems frequently. In particular, we compute the average *co-exist* scores of documents in a list, and plots its relation to the retrieval performance of the corresponding lists, as shown in Figure 2. The x-axis is constructed by bucketing the normalized P@30 scores for all ranked lists, and the y-axis shows the corresponding average *co-exist* scores for lists in that bin. The same is done for the top k results, where $k \in \{10, 20, 30\}$. Figure 2 shows consistently strong evidence that better performing ranked lists usually have more documents that appear across multiple lists. We accordingly incorporate *mCo-exist* and *mCo-exist-k* into the query-list features set. Note that we compute *mCo-exist-k* only for WebTrack since a ranked list from FedWeb only has up to 10 results.

Based on a similar idea, we correlate the percentage of documents that appear in more than one search engine (i.e., documents with *co-exist* > 1) with the performance of ranked lists, as shown in Figure 3. We observe that retrieval performance is higher when a larger set of documents appear in more than one ranked list (see *Ratio-1*). We further inspect how the trend changes w.r.t. the coverage over search systems. That is, in addition to examining documents with *co-exist* > 1, we conduct the same analysis for *co-exist* larger than k percent of total number of search systems (e.g., we count documents with *co-exist* > 6 given 30 ranked lists and $k = 20\%$). Compared with *Ratio-1*, *Ratio-k%* in general shows a similar trend but the gaps between performance buckets appear larger, indicating a higher potential of distinguishing ranked list quality. When k grows to 40% or 60%, we see it is not always true that best performing lists have the largest *Ratio-k%*. This may imply that the list performance, while being highly positively correlated, is not solely determined by co-existence.

We adopt the mean score features (i.e., *mScore*) as in the λ-Merge work[5]. Lastly, for the FedWeb test sets, we include two additional features for quantifying the quality of ranked lists. Although FedWeb was created by requesting 10 results per search engine, there are cases where less than required were returned, which we hope to capture by the *RatioRet* feature. Recall that duplicates can be returned by the same engine for a query. *RatioDup* computes the ratio of number of remained documents after de-duplication to the number returned. These two features are designed to reflect the stability of the black box search engines.

Vertical features.

Intuitively, the quality of a vertical depends on the quality of the ranked lists it contains for a query. We accordingly devise features that take the average of list features across the ranked lists a vertical includes. Deriving vertical features is highly related to the task of vertical selection introduced in FewdWeb 2014 [14], where the goal is to classify each query into a fixed set of 24 verticals. The top performing systems of this task assembled together the results of different techniques; for example, the similarity of vertical and query terms [18] and matching WordNet synonyms for queries and verticals [21]. As our focus is to investigate the utility of incorporating vertical estimates rather than exhausting all possible features, we leave more exploration of feature design as future work.

5. EXPERIMENTS

This section first introduces the setup for the experiments, followed by a detailed presentation of evaluation results tested under a variety of scenarios.

5.1 Experimental Setup and Baselines

Our experiments are conducted using four TREC collections as mentioned in Section 4. In each test case, a total number of 50 queries with associated graded relevance judgments are available. When learning is needed, we split training and test data into 5 folds and perform cross-validation. We evaluate using NDCG@K, as well as α-NDCG@k when sub-topic relevance judgments are available. We train all neural-based models for 25 epochs with learning rate $5 \cdot 10^{-3}$. Pairwise t-test is conducted when appropriate.

[5]Other moments such as variance, skewness or kurtosis could be considered; we excluded those due to lower effectiveness in our experiments.

We compare the results of our framework with three categories of baselines:

- *Score fusion.* CombSUM and CombMNZ proposed by Fox and Shaw [17] serve as standard baselines with which new algorithms are compared [11, 22]. We consider CombMNZ as our baseline since it often outperforms CombSUM. Equation 12 computes CombMNZ that considers the product of the number of lists containing d and the summation of normalized scores from each ranking.

$$CombMNZ = |\{k : d \in D_k\}| \cdot \sum_{k:d \in D_k} NScore(d) \quad (12)$$

- *Rank fusion.* Cormack et al. [11] proposed a simple and yet very effective method, reciprocal rank fusion (RRF), for combing searches. RRF sorts the documents using the formula given in Equation 13, where $c = 60$ is fixed during their pilot investigation. Simple as is, RRF was shown to invariably improve the best of the combined results (including runs with learning-to-rank methods), and outperformed established meta-ranking standards Condorcet Fuse [30] and CombMNZ. The best performing approach in FedWeb 2013 [31] is based on modifying RRF with logarithm and square transformation. We use RRF as a strong baseline.

$$RRFscore = \sum_{k:d \in D_k} \frac{1}{c + rank(d : D_k)} \quad (13)$$

- *Learning to rank.* The merging problem can also be cast as a learning to rank problem. A general LTR setting requires one representation per document; however, in a merging environment, documents can appear as several copies in different ranked lists. To address this, we transform the feature representation from the fusion task by taking the average of feature values for documents that have several copies. With the transformed feature vector, we can easily use any existing LTR method to sort the documents. In particular, we adopt the original gradient decent approach, RankNet [7], and its state-of-the-art variant, LambdaMART [41], in our experiments.

5.2 Performance on TREC FedWeb

Table 2 shows the retrieval performance tested on the FedWeb 2013 and 2014 collections. We denote our approach as LTM-Deep for that it is essentially a framework for learning to merge using deep structures. In each year's data, we compare the proposed framework with a number of baseline approaches, including two runs of CombMNZ that are generated based on normalized query likelihood or sequential dependency model [28] scores[6]. Among the baselines, we see that RRF is very competitive, even though its core idea is rather simple and it requires no training examples. The LTR group tends to perform better in NDCG@20, which is both the main evaluation metric in the track and the chosen optimization metric. In general, LambdaMART appears more effective than RankNet.

[6]Recall that no score information is available in FedWeb; we use two retrieval systems as alternatives.

Table 2: **Performance of tested techniques on FedWeb 2013 and FedWeb 2014 test sets. The source includes document (D), list (L) and vertical (V) features. The best results are marked bold. The improvement percentage and pairwise t-test are applied when comparing LTM-Deep (D+L+V) to the rest of approaches († is denoted for p-value < 0.05).**

TREC FedWeb 2013					
Source	Method	NDCG@10	NDCG@20	$\Delta_{N@10\%}$	$\Delta_{N@20\%}$
D	CombMNZ-QL	0.545†	0.476†	7.38%	20.49%
	CombMNZ-SD	0.547†	0.475†	6.89%	20.84%
	RRF	0.572	0.508†	2.27%	12.95%
D+L	LTR-RankNet	0.526†	0.483†	11.28%	18.77%
	LTR-LambdaMART	0.515†	0.491†	13.59%	17.00%
	LTM-Shallow	0.553†	0.567	5.88%	1.31%
	LTM-Deep	0.565	0.573	3.54%	0.17%
D+L+V	LTR-RankNet	0.570	0.573	2.63%	0.17%
	LTR-LambdaMART	0.556†	0.572	5.22%	0.35%
	LTM-Shallow	0.574	0.572	1.88%	0.31%
	LTM-Deep	**0.585**	**0.574**	-	-
TREC FedWeb 2014					
Source	Method	NDCG@10	NDCG@20	$\Delta_{N@10\%}$	$\Delta_{N@20\%}$
D	CombMNZ-QL	0.577†	0.485†	8.63%	23.17%
	CombMNZ-SD	0.580†	0.481†	8.05%	24.25%
	RRF	0.594†	0.504†	5.48%	18.50%
D+L	LTR-RankNet	0.554†	0.503†	13.26%	18.74%
	LTR-LambdaMART	0.550†	0.515†	13.92%	15.85%
	LTM-Shallow	0.583†	0.574†	7.57%	4.08%
	LTM-Deep	0.599†	0.574†	4.76%	4.08%
D+L+V	LTR-RankNet	0.601†	0.572†	4.33%	4.37%
	LTR-LambdaMART	0.602	0.576	4.15%	3.65%
	LTM-Shallow	0.624	0.565†	0.56%	5.65%
	LTM-Deep	**0.627**	**0.597**	-	-

For LTM-Deep in FedWeb 2014, the results suggest that incorporating vertical signals (i.e., D+L+V) improves significantly the performance compared to that without (i.e., D+L). The trend is similar in FedWeb 2013. For other learning-based approaches, including the LTR group and LTM-Shallow, it is clear that the model with vertical estimate consistently achieves better performance, confirming our hypothesis that vertical quality helps improve the fusion task.

LTM-Deep further outperforms LTM-Shallow in most cases, and the improvement in NDCG@20 is significant in FedWeb 2014. Despite the scarcity of training data, the results show that merging ranked lists with deep structures can be a promising direction, and we expect the improvement will be more evident with more training data. Overall, LTM-Deep shows the best performance across different baselines, measures and collections.

5.3 Performance on TREC WebTrack

The experimental results for WebTrack 2009 and 2010 are shown in Table 3. In addition to NDCG@k, we evaluate the results using the diversity measure α-NDCG@k based on sub-topic relevance judgments. The vertical component is omitted for data fusion experiments since all ranked lists are from the same vertical. Here, CombMNZ is generated using the normalized scores from runs submitted to TREC. In WebTrack09, RRF and LambdaMART again demonstrate better effectiveness among the baselines, while the RankNet method also appears highly effective in terms of precision.

The LTM group demonstrates overall the most effective results compared with the standard baselines and the LTR group. The LTM-Deep approach further achieves better performance than LTM-Shallow in terms of precision and diversity for both years. The improvement is significant in Web Track 2010. Similar to the results in collection fusion, LTM-Deep shows the best performance across different baselines, measures and collections.

5.4 Discussions

Model Design. The framework in this paper models simultaneously the impact of the quality of documents, ranked lists and verticals[7] for result merging. The experimental results suggest that modeling the diverse aspects of federated search improves ranking in general. The design may further include the features derived from specific types of documents. Tweets, for instance, can be extracted with features that represent recency or popularity, while for a CQA posting, it can be helpful to include authority signals such as the overall rating of an answer. In such cases, the document scoring network $f(x^k_{i,j}; \theta, \pi_1, \pi_2, ..., \pi_N)$ will be paramterized on θ for shared features (e.g., ranks and scores) and π_i for non-shared features, where N indicates the number of types of documents. Since the FedWeb test collections were compiled to conform to a uniform style, it will be necessary to get additional data that describes the characteristics of different types of documents for evaluating this design. As

[7]We note that vertical features are only available in a federated search scenario.

Table 3: Performance of tested techniques on Web Track 2009 and Web Track 2010 test sets. The source includes document (D) abd list (L) features. The best results are marked bold. The improvement percentage and pairwise t-test are applied when comparing LTM-Deep to the rest of approaches († is denoted for p-value < 0.05).

TREC Web Track 2009							
Source	Method	NDCG@10	NDCG@20	α-NDCG@10	α-NDCG@20	$\Delta_{N@20\%}$	$\Delta_{\alpha-N@20\%}$
D	CombMNZ	0.309†	0.288†	0.201†	0.227†	20.22%	22.47%
	RRF	0.337†	0.323†	0.229†	0.263†	7.05%	5.70%
D+L	LTR-RankNet	0.324†	0.309†	0.215†	0.243†	12.05%	14.40%
	LTR-LambdaMART	0.314†	0.307†	0.240	**0.290**	12.59%	-4.14%
	LTM-Shallow	0.352	0.340	0.238	0.274	1.88%	1.46%
	LTM-Deep	**0.360**	**0.346**	**0.243**	0.278	-	-
TREC Web Track 2010							
Source	Method	NDCG@10	NDCG@20	α-NDCG@10	α-NDCG@20	$\Delta_{N@20\%}$	$\Delta_{\alpha-N@20\%}$
D	CombMNZ	0.289†	0.281†	0.415†	0.451†	10.83%	5.76%
	RRF	0.295†	0.296†	0.428†	0.465	5.17%	2.58%
D+L	LTR-RankNet	0.306	0.299	0.304†	0.340†	39.4%	40.29%
	LTR-LambdaMART	0.289†	0.285†	0.404†	0.448†	9.20%	6.47%
	LTM-Shallow	0.301	0.299†	0.421†	0.452†	4.15%	5.53%
	LTM-Deep	**0.312**	**0.311**	**0.443**	**0.477**	-	-

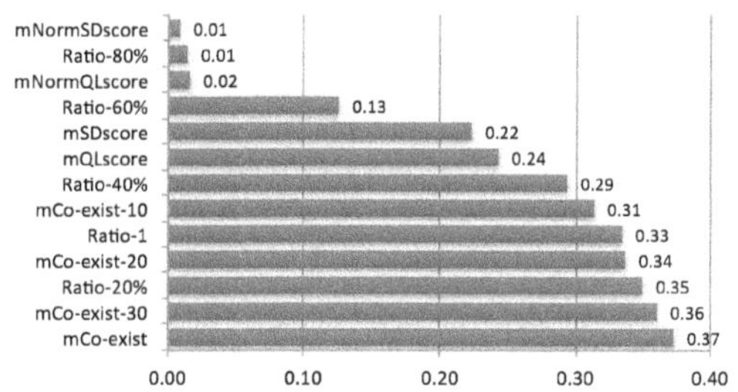

Figure 4: Pearson correlation coefficient ρ between list goodness and *query-list* features on WebTrack10.

aforementioned, the deep structures are also possible in the re-weighting networks for list and vertical features. This will require obtaining additional training data.

Feature Design. One reason behind the success of our framework, we believe, is the introduction of additional query-list features. As mentioned in [32], query-list features such as the mean and standard deviation of retrieval scores showed only small improvements, while the more effective features (e.g., reformulation scores) are not available in a general fusion task. Indeed, computing the Pearson correlation coefficient between feature values and list goodness[8], Figure 4 shows that the newly introduced features usually have a higher correlation. In addition, applying the same correlation analysis between document labels and query-document features, we re-confirm that the *co-exist* feature is the most effective in the data fusion environment. For the collection fusion environments, *co-exist* is far less correlated with ground-truth since the overlap rate between collections is approximately only 3% (as reported in [31]). Interestingly, although *co-exist* independently is not effective enough, the aggregated query-list feature *mCo-exist* is highly correlated with list goodness with $\rho = 0.7$ in both FedWeb 2013 and 2014.

[8]We use the average of document labels in a list as a surrogate to approximate list goodness.

Effective features are critical to system performance. We may explore the feasibility of incorporating the findings from the large body of literature on query performance prediction. In particular, post-retrieval predictors attempt to predict the performance of a ranked list using strategies such as measuring the divergence between the list and the entire collection [23, 37]. Again, since the FedWeb collections use search engines as a black box service, additional access to the entire collection statistics may be required.

6. CONCLUSIONS

In this paper, we explored the task of result merging in an optimization framework. The proposed model incorporated vertical signals on the top of the feature functions for documents and ranked lists, and learned to fuse results by optimizing the retrieval performance of the final list. The model further investigated the potential of applying deep neural networks to estimating the document feature function. We also developed a set of general query-list features that are effective and available for a general fusion task, compensating for the absence of specific reformulation features (e.g., query clarity and drift) used in λ-Merge.

We evaluated our model using two TREC FedWeb test sets for collection fusion, and two TREC Web Track test sets for data fusion. The results demonstrated that incorporating the vertical signals consistently improves the performance using only document and list feature functions. The results further showed that the LTM-Deep approach can significantly outperform standard baselines and state-of-art techniques.

Developing an effective optimization framework for result merging is a complex problem. While our experiments have shown promising results, it will be important for us to consider different possibilities in infrastructure and feature design as discussed in Section 5.4. Since the effectiveness of deep structures depends on the quality and quantity of training data, using larger test sets such as query search logs will be important, and we expect the performance can be further improved.

Acknowledgements

This work was supported in part by the Center for Intelligent Information Retrieval and in part by NSF IIS-1160894. Any opinions, findings and conclusions or recommendations expressed in this material are those of the authors and do not necessarily reflect those of the sponsor.

7. REFERENCES

[1] J. A. Aslam and M. Montague. Bayes optimal metasearch: A probabilistic model for combining the results of multiple retrieval systems (poster session). In *Proceedings of SIGIR*, SIGIR '00, pages 379–381, 2000.

[2] J. A. Aslam and M. Montague. Models for metasearch. In *Proceedings of SIGIR*, SIGIR '01, pages 276–284, 2001.

[3] S. M. Beitzel, E. C. Jensen, A. Chowdhury, D. Grossman, O. Frieder, and N. Goharian. On fusion of effective retrieval strategies in the same information retrieval system. *JASIST*, 55:859–868, 2004.

[4] Y. Bengio. Learning deep architectures for ai. *Found. Trends Mach. Learn.*, 2(1):1–127, Jan. 2009.

[5] Y. Bengio. Practical recommendations for gradient-based training of deep architectures. In *Neural Networks: Tricks of the Trade*, pages 437–478. Springer, 2012.

[6] C. Burges, R. Ragno, and Q. Le. Learning to rank with non-smooth cost functions. In *Advances in Neural Information Processing Systems 19*, January 2007.

[7] C. Burges, T. Shaked, E. Renshaw, A. Lazier, M. Deeds, N. Hamilton, and G. Hullender. Learning to rank using gradient descent. In *Proceedings of ICML*, ICML '05, pages 89–96, 2005.

[8] C. J. Burges. From ranknet to lambdarank to lambdamart: An overview. Technical report, June 2010.

[9] J. Callan. Distributed information retrieval. In *In: Advances in Information Retrieval*, pages 127–150. Kluwer Academic Publishers, 2000.

[10] J. P. Callan, Z. Lu, and W. B. Croft. Searching distributed collections with inference networks. In *Proceedings of SIGIR*, SIGIR '95, pages 21–28, 1995.

[11] G. V. Cormack, C. L. A. Clarke, and S. Buettcher. Reciprocal rank fusion outperforms condorcet and individual rank learning methods. In *Proceedings of SIGIR*, SIGIR '09, pages 758–759, 2009.

[12] W. B. Croft. Combining approaches to information retrieval. *Advances in Information Retrieval, Chapter 1, The Information Retrieval Series*, 7:1–36, 2000.

[13] T. Demeester, D. Trieschnigg, D. Nguyen, and D. Hiemstra. Overview of the trec 2013 federated web search track. In *Proceedings of TREC*, 2013.

[14] T. Demeester, D. Trieschnigg, D. Nguyen, Z. K., and D. Hiemstra. Overview of the trec 2014 federated web search track. In *Proceedings of TREC*, 2014.

[15] L. Deng, X. He, and J. Gao. Deep stacking networks for information retrieval. In *Acoustics, Speech and Signal Processing (ICASSP), 2013 IEEE International Conference on*, pages 3153–3157, May 2013.

[16] L. Deng and D. Yu. Deep learning: Methods and applications. Technical Report MSR-TR-2014-21, January 2014.

[17] E. A. Fox and J. A. Shaw. Combination of multiple searches. In *The Second Text REtrieval Conference (TREC-2)*, pages 243–252, 1994.

[18] F. Guan, S. Zhang, C. Liu, X. Yu, Y. Liu, and X. Cheng. Ictnet at federated web search track 2014. In *Proceedings of TREC*, 2014.

[19] D. Hawking and P. Thomas. Server selection methods in hybrid portal search. In *Proceedings of SIGIR*, SIGIR '05, pages 75–82, 2005.

[20] P.-S. Huang, X. He, J. Gao, L. Deng, A. Acero, and L. Heck. Learning deep structured semantic models for web search using clickthrough data. In *Proceedings of CIKM*, CIKM '13, pages 2333–2338, 2013.

[21] S. Jin and M. Lan. Simple may be best - a simple and effective method for federated web search via search engine impact factor estimation. In *Proceedings of TREC*, 2014.

[22] A. Khudyak Kozorovitsky and O. Kurland. Cluster-based fusion of retrieved lists. In *Proceedings of SIGIR*, SIGIR '11, pages 893–902, 2011.

[23] O. Kurland, A. Shtok, D. Carmel, and S. Hummel. A unified framework for post-retrieval query-performance prediction. In *Proceedings of ICTIR*, ICTIR'11, pages 15–26, 2011.

[24] J. H. Lee. Analyses of multiple evidence combination. In *Proceedings of SIGIR*, SIGIR '97, pages 267–276, 1997.

[25] D. Lillis, F. Toolan, R. Collier, and J. Dunnion. Probabilistic data fusion on a large document collection. *Artif. Intell. Rev.*, 26(1-2):23–34, Oct. 2006.

[26] D. Lillis, F. Toolan, R. Collier, and J. Dunnion. Extending probabilistic data fusion using sliding windows. In *Proceedings of ECIR*, ECIR'08, pages 358–369, 2008.

[27] G. Mesnil, X. He, L. Deng, and Y. Bengio. Investigation of recurrent-neural-network architectures and learning methods for spoken language understanding. In *INTERSPEECH*, pages 3771–3775, 2013.

[28] D. Metzler and W. B. Croft. A markov random field model for term dependencies. In *Proceedings of SIGIR*, SIGIR '05, pages 472–479, 2005.

[29] T. Mikolov, W.-t. Yih, and G. Zweig. Linguistic regularities in continuous space word representations. In *HLT-NAACL*, pages 746–751. Citeseer, 2013.

[30] M. Montague and J. A. Aslam. Condorcet fusion for improved retrieval. In *Proceedings of CIKM*, CIKM '02, pages 538–548, 2002.

[31] A. Mourao, F. Martins, and J. Magalhaes. Novasearch at trec 2013 federated web search track: Experiments with rank fusion. In *The 22nd Text Retrieval Conference*, TREC 13, 2013.

[32] D. Sheldon, M. Shokouhi, M. Szummer, and N. Craswell. Lambdamerge: Merging the results of query reformulations. In *Proceedings of WSDM*, WSDM '11, pages 795–804, 2011.

[33] Y. Shen, X. He, J. Gao, L. Deng, and G. Mesnil. A latent semantic model with convolutional-pooling structure for information retrieval. In *Proceedings of CIKM*, CIKM '14, pages 101–110, 2014.

[34] M. Shokouhi. Segmentation of search engine results for effective data-fusion. In *Proceedings of ECIR*, ECIR'07, pages 185–197, 2007.

[35] M. Shokouhi and L. Si. Federated search. *Found. Trends Inf. Retr.*, 5(1):1–102, Jan. 2011.

[36] M. Shokouhi and J. Zobel. Robust result merging using sample-based score estimates. *ACM Trans. Inf. Syst.*, 27(3):14:1–14:29, May 2009.

[37] A. Shtok, O. Kurland, D. Carmel, F. Raiber, and G. Markovits. Predicting query performance by query-drift estimation. *ACM Trans. Inf. Syst.*, 30(2):11:1–11:35, May 2012.

[38] L. Si and J. Callan. A semisupervised learning method to merge search engine results. *ACM Trans. Inf. Syst.*, 21(4):457–491, Oct. 2003.

[39] C. C. Vogt and G. W. Cottrell. Fusion via a linear combination of scores. *Inf. Retr.*, 1(3):151–173, Oct. 1999.

[40] E. M. Voorhees, N. K. Gupta, and B. Johnson-laird. The collection fusion problem. In *Proceedings of the TREC*, pages 95–104, 1995.

[41] Q. Wu, C. J. Burges, K. M. Svore, and J. Gao. Adapting boosting for information retrieval measures. *Inf. Retr.*, 13(3):254–270, June 2010.

[42] S. Wu and S. McClean. Performance prediction of data fusion for information retrieval. *Inf. Process. Manage.*, 42(4):899–915, July 2006.

Searching and Stopping: An Analysis of Stopping Rules and Strategies

David Maxwell and Leif Azzopardi
School of Computing Science
University of Glasgow
Glasgow, Scotland
d.maxwell.1@research.gla.ac.uk
Leif.Azzopardi@Glasgow.ac.uk

Kalervo Järvelin and Heikki Keskustalo
School of Information Sciences
University of Tampere
Tampere, Finland
kalervo.jarvelin@uta.fi
heikki.keskustalo@uta.fi

ABSTRACT

Searching naturally involves stopping points, both at a query level *(how far down the ranked list should I go?)* and at a session level *(how many queries should I issue?)*. Understanding when searchers stop has been of much interest to the community because it is fundamental to how we evaluate search behaviour and performance. Research has shown that searchers find it difficult to formalise stopping criteria, and typically resort to their intuition of what is *"good enough"*. While various heuristics and stopping criteria have been proposed, little work has investigated how well they perform, and whether searchers actually conform to any of these rules. In this paper, we undertake the first large scale study of stopping rules, investigating how they influence overall session performance, and which rules best match actual stopping behaviour. Our work is focused on stopping at the query level in the context of ad-hoc topic retrieval, where searchers undertake search tasks within a fixed time period. We show that stopping strategies based upon the *disgust* or *frustration point* rules - both of which capture a searcher's tolerance to non-relevance - typically result in *(i)* the best overall performance, and *(ii)* provide the closest approximation to actual searcher behaviour, although a fixed depth approach also performs remarkably well. Findings from this study have implications regarding how we build measures, and how we conduct simulations of search behaviours.

Categories and Subject Descriptors

H.3.3 [**Information Storage and Retrieval**]: Information Search and Retrieval: Search Process; H.3.4 [**Information Storage and Retrieval**]: Systems and Software: Performance Evaluation

General Terms

Theory, Experimentation, Simulation, Human Factors

Keywords

Retrieval Strategies, Search Behavior, Evaluation

CIKM'15, October 19 - 23, 2015, Melbourne, VIC, Australia

ACM 978-1-4503-3794-6/15/10 ...$15.00
DOI: http://dx.doi.org/10.1145/2806416.2806476

1. INTRODUCTION

Interactive Information Retrieval (IIR) is a non-trivial process where searchers issue numerous queries and examine a varying number of snippets and documents per query [14]. During the search process, searchers need to decide when they should abandon the current query (and thus issue a new query after examining the current results list), and when to curtail their search (stopping the search session altogether). Knowing when to stop is considered a fundamental aspect of human behaviour [26]. Stop too early, and important information may be missed. Stop too late, and time and effort is wasted. Worse still, the examination of fruitless result lists will mean not having time to examine other lists which may potentially contain greater yields for the searcher.

While important, research into stopping behaviours when searching has been relatively sparse. Of the studies undertaken in this area, many have concluded that the decision to stop is based upon a searcher's intuition - or the feeling that what they have found is *"good enough"* [36]. However, past research has revealed that certain factors impact upon stopping behaviour. Examples include a searcher's prior knowledge of the domain being searched [33], their knowledge and search experience, how they interpret the cues/snippets presented on the *Search Engine Results Page (SERP)* [35], their understanding of the given information need, and their feeling of *enough*. To quantify this feeling of *"good enough"*, various researchers have proposed an array of stopping rules and heuristics that try to encode this intuition [6, 9, 19, 26]. These proposals are detailed in Section 2.

In this paper, we aim to catalogue and evaluate a range of proposed stopping rules. Specifically, we focus on rules regarding when a searcher should stop examining the results for the current query, and move onto the next query (i.e. query stopping, rather than session stopping). Once catalogued, we operationalise and implement these rules. We then perform a large scale simulated analysis over two ad-hoc *TREC* test collections, exploring:

RQ1 how performance varies due to each stopping rule; and

RQ2 which stopping rule delivers the best overall performance.

We then conduct an analysis comparing the search stopping behaviour of 48 searchers to the set of stopping rules defined, exploring:

RQ3 which stopping rule(s) best reflect actual stopping behaviour; and

RQ4 whether different stopping rule(s) would lead to improved performance.

This work represents one of the first attempts to enumerate and encode the various stopping rules, and empirically test their validity in the context of ad-hoc topic retrieval. Our findings show that stopping strategies based upon the *frustration point rule* [9] and *disgust rule* [19], where searchers stop after examining a given number of non-relevant documents, delivers the best overall performance during simulations. These stopping strategies also best approximated when actual searchers stopped. However, a fixed depth stopping strategy - where searchers stopped after examining 13 documents - also provided a good approximation of actual stopping behaviour. These findings suggest that simulations can be improved upon and made more realistic if they encode a stopping strategy based upon the frustration point and disgust rules. However, our findings also suggest that measures and models using a fixed depth stopping strategy provide a good approximation on average.

Next, we provide an overview of the background related to stopping rules before operationalising these rules into a number of strategies that we can implement and evaluate in Section 3. Our methodology, which consists of both a simulated comparison - and a comparison with data taken from a previous user study - is then described in Section 4. Results follow in Section 5. A summary of our findings and directions for future work then concludes this paper.

2. RELATED WORK

In *Information Retrieval (IR)*, research into stopping rules and stopping behaviour has been approached from two main perspectives. *User-sided research* focuses on how and why searchers stop, and often formulate motivations, heuristics and guidelines regarding stopping behaviour [11, 28, 31, 34, 35]. Additionally, *system-sided research* focuses on encoding stopping models into measures and models to evaluate IR system performance [9, 15, 24], and/or conduct simulations of user interaction [1, 4]. However, when people stop is considered a fundamental aspect of human behaviour [26], and as such has been considered more broadly from cognitive and decision-making perspectives [7, 19]. Determining when to stop is an inherently difficult task. This is due to the fact that the decision is usually instrumented by a series of internal factors of the decision maker's thinking [26]. This therefore makes the concept of stopping an extremely difficult phenomenon to model effectively.

Wu et al. [35] explain that a majority of studies examining stopping behaviours have been conducted with a series of interviews. This was to obtain an understanding of why people decide to stop. Many of these studies [11, 28, 31, 36] have often concluded that the decision to stop searching is based on intuition, or the *"feeling of good enough"* (termed *satisficing*) [36]. A small number of information-seeking and retrieval studies have also shown that stopping decisions are dependent upon the task type being undertaken, the time constraints imposed upon them, and a range of more specific, internally constructed stopping rules [28, 36]. For example, Prabha et al. [28] found that time constraints reduced how many documents were examined, whereas Zach [36] found that decision makers often stopped their searching earlier because they were satisfied with what they had found, even though they believed more information was available.

As highlighted by Marchionini [21], these internal stopping rules are dependent upon the searcher's task domain knowledge and information-seeking ability. Wu and Kelly [34] more recently undertook a study where subjects performed a series of search tasks. Subjects were then interviewed about their query stopping and task stopping behaviours. Results from this study showed that query stopping decisions were taken primarily on the face of search results, queries and search tasks. Task stopping decisions were determined by the subject's overall goal for each task, the content examined (and their subjective perceptions on the examined content), and the study constraints imposed upon them (e.g. imposed time constraints, and the search interface used).

Despite the difficulties associated with the modelling of stopping behaviours, researchers have proposed numerous stopping rules which are *believed* to quantify/explain when searchers stop searching. Proposed rules tend to be high-level descriptions of when a search should be stopped, and may apply to stopping at the query level, the session/task level, or both. Two of the earliest stopping rules proposed were devised by Cooper [9], who presented:

- the frustration point rule, where a searcher stops after examining a certain number of non-relevant documents; and
- the *satisfaction stopping rule*, where searchers would stop only when a certain number of relevant documents were found.

Kraft and Lee [19] also presented three stopping rules which were devised for measuring the expected *search length* (the number of snippets scanned in a ranked list). The *satiation rule* borrowed the underlying theory of the satisfaction stopping rule [9], where searchers would stop after being *satiated* by finding a desired number of relevant documents. In addition, the disgust rule borrowed the underlying theory from the frustration point rule of Cooper [9]. The *combination rule* is the final rule introduced by Kraft and Lee [19]. This rule combines both the satiation and disgust rules into one. Here, searchers would stop if they are satisfied with what has been found, or disgusted by having examined too many non-relevant documents - whichever condition is met first. Kraft and Lee [19] further demonstrated that the expected search length could be approximated using each of their stopping rules by considering the size of the retrieval set, the number of relevant documents a searcher wished to obtain, and the number of non-relevant documents a searcher would be willing to tolerate. The number of documents required to consider a search successful is dependent upon whether the search task is high-precision (stopping comparatively early) or high-recall (stopping comparatively later), as hypothesised by Bates [5].

In addition to the rules posited by Cooper [9] and Kraft and Lee [19], Nickles [26] proposed four cognitive rules investigating the sufficiency of information:

- the *mental list rule*, where searchers construct a mental list of criteria about a given item (such as the number of seats and engine displacement in a car) that must be satisfied before stopping;
- the *representational stability rule*, where a searcher continues to examine information until the underlying mental model that they possess of the topic in question begins to stabilise;

- the *difference threshold rule*, where a searcher sets an *a priori* difference level to gauge when he or she is not learning anything new; and
- the *magnitude threshold rule*, where a searcher has a cumulative amount of information that must be found before he or she stops searching. In this rule, the focus is attaining 'enough' information.

A further fifth rule, the *single criterion rule*, was proposed by Browne et al. [6]. Here, searchers would examine documents for information on a single criterion, stopping when enough information had been collected about said criterion.

A decision-theoretic approach using utility theory was proposed by Cooper [10]. This approach posited that searchers will stop examining documents once the effort of conducting a new search outweighs the benefit of any new information that may be obtained. Similarly, the economic model of search proposed by Azzopardi [1] suggests that a searcher should stop when the marginal gain equals the marginal cost. Related to these approaches is the *patch model* from *Information Foraging Theory (IFT)* [27] to predict when a searcher should stop examining a ranked list. Applying *Charnov's Marginal Value Theorem* [8] to search, Pirolli and Card's theory suggests that a searcher should stop when the rate of gain from a given result falls below the average rate of gain experienced by the searcher [27].

In previous work, we performed an initial analysis comparing a fixed depth stopping strategy against two implementations of the frustration point/disgust rules [23]. The fixed depth stopping strategy assumed that the searcher would stop at a particular document n in the ranked list, regardless of whether previous documents were considered relevant or non-relevant. This strategy assumed the same stopping model as encoded in many IR evaluation measures, such as *Precision-at-k (P@k)* and *Normalised Discounted Cumulative Gain (NDCG)* [15]. Our implementation of the frustration point rule consisted of counting the number of non-relevant documents seen in the ranked list at position k. If the total number of non-relevant documents exceeded a given threshold, the searcher would then stop. A similar implementation of this rule was also examined by Lin and Smucker [20], but in the context of document browsing. Our second implementation of the frustration point rule considered that if the total number of non-relevant documents observed *contiguously* exceeded some threshold, then the searcher would stop. The initial findings from the simulation we conducted showed that our implementations of the frustration point rule resulted in higher levels of gain per second across a number of different querying strategies. In this paper, we go beyond our initial study. We implement more sophisticated stopping rules and evaluate them across two TREC test collections, before comparing the rules to actual observed searcher behaviour.

As previously mentioned, retrieval measures also encode stopping models that dictate the likelihood of a searcher stopping at a particular rank [25]. For example, $P@k$ assumes that a searcher will stop at rank k. However, more sophisticated measures exist, such as *Rank-Biased Precision* [24]. This measure has a patience/persistence parameter that determines whether a searcher is more likely to go further down a ranked list (if they are patient), or less likely (if they are impatient). Indeed, Moffat et al. [25] argue that all measures have an implicit stopping model, and show how the stopping model used can be derived from a number of common measures. Consequently, forming a better understanding of how and why searchers stop is quintessential to the development of IR measures.

In terms of modelling search and stopping behaviours, numerous studies have been performed that simulate session-based IIR. Studies examining click models implicitly employ the use of stopping probabilities which determine the likelihood of how far down a searcher will examine a ranked list of results [12, 13, 32]. However, in many other studies, it has been assumed that for a given query, a searcher will go to a prescribed and fixed depth for each query issued during the session [1, 3, 17, 18]. This is clearly a major limitation as actual searcher behaviour varies according to a number of factors. Consequently, finding and selecting a stopping rule that is more in line with the actual stopping behaviour of searchers will result in more realistic simulations.

3. STOPPING RULES

In the previous section, we outlined a number of stopping rules defined in the literature. In this section, we take a subset of these rules and propose a number of ways in which we can operationalise them, such that we can subsequently implement them. The implemented stopping strategies fit into the wider simulated searcher model, illustrated in Figure 1 (where key decision points are denoted with a *?* marker). The model is explained in detail in Section 4.2.

The first rule (and baseline) for this study is the fixed depth stopping rule.

SS1 ***(Fixed Depth)*** Under this stopping strategy, the simulated searcher will stop once they have observed x_1 snippets, regardless of their relevance to the given topic.

This represents the typical approach taken in most simulations, and represents the basic stopping searcher model in $P@k$ measures. On average, this rule makes sense, but when result lists are of varying quality, it is not a very sensible approach. For example, consider the situation where a searcher submits a poor query that returns no relevant information. Naïvely examining ten snippets (where $x_1 = 10$) - and potentially some documents along the way - is by and large a waste of the searcher's time.

Thus, we derive two further stopping strategies and their subsequent variants - ***SS2*** and ***SS3*** - based upon the frustration point and disgust stopping rules, as defined by Cooper [9] and Kraft and Lee [19].

SS2 ***(Total Non-Relevant)*** Under this stopping strategy, the searcher will stop once they have observed x_2 non-relevant snippets. If a snippet has been previously seen in the search session and was considered non-relevant, it is included in the count.

SS3 ***(Contiguous Non-Relevant)*** Similar to ***SS2*** above, the searcher will stop once they have observed x_3 non-relevant snippets in a row (contiguously). As with ***SS2***, previously seen non-relevant snippets within the search session are included in the count.

Intuitively, these strategies will mean that the simulated searcher adapts their interaction with a ranked list of results depending upon the performance of the underlying query. For example, a ranked list is judged by a simulated searcher

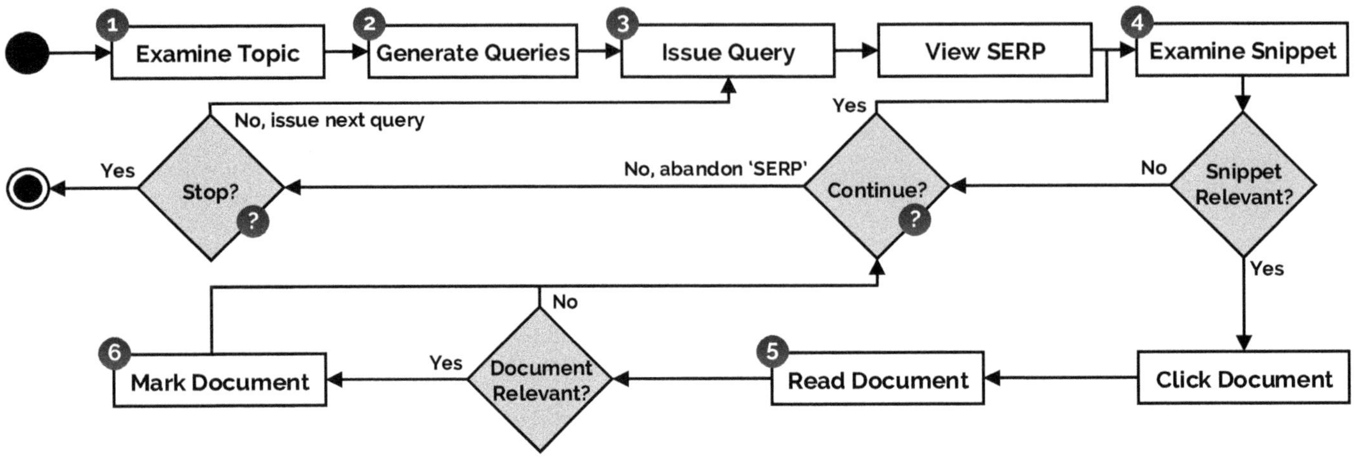

Figure 1: A flowchart of decisions (shown in grey) and tasks (shown in white) undertaken by simulated searchers 'participating' in this study. The model is adapted from Baskaya et al. [4] and Thomas et al. [30]. Numbers associated with tasks correspond to the steps detailed in Section 4.2. The two *?* markers indicate the decisions that are encoded within each implemented stopping strategy (refer to Section 4.5).

as [R,N,N,R,N,N,N], where R and N[1] denote relevant and non-relevant items respectively. Under ***SS2***, with $x_2 = x_3 = 3$, the simulated searcher would stop at rank five. Under ***SS3***, the simulated searcher would stop at rank seven.

Since documents are examined when the associated snippet is considered relevant (see Figure 1), a simulated searcher may revise their opinion of the amount of relevant information observed once they see the document. A simulated searcher may for example inspect the first snippet thinking it is relevant, and then examine the document. The document is subsequently considered non-relevant, meaning the initial R is changed to a N. This updates the count, so that under a stopping strategy with *revised relevance*, simulated searchers would stop at rank three in the list shown above using ***SS2***, and similarly for ***SS3***. This therefore introduces two variants of ***SS2*** and ***SS3***, which were found in a pilot study to perform slightly better. Therefore, we only report the revised relevance variants of ***SS2*** and ***SS3*** in this paper.

The next two stopping strategies are based upon the difference threshold rule [26]. To operationalise this rule, we consider the difference between the text of the current snippet and the text of previously examined snippets. Here, the idea is that as simulated searchers examine snippets, they may encounter a snippet that is not sufficiently different from what they already have observed, meaning that they are unlikely to find new information. The searcher therefore stops and issues a new query. From this rule, we devised two separate stopping strategies where we computed the difference based upon *term overlap* and *KL-Divergence* scores.

SS4 ***(Term Overlap Difference)*** This stopping strategy compares the occurrences of terms in a given snippet against all terms in previously examined snippets. The more terms that overlap, the greater the chance that the new snippet does not contain any new information. If $\frac{|s_{curr} \cap s_{prev}|}{|s_{curr}|} > x_4$, the new snippet is considered too similar to previously examined content. The simulated searcher then moves to the next query. Here, s_{curr} denotes the terms of the current snippet, s_{prev} denotes terms from all previously observed snippets, and x_4 is the threshold at which the simulated searcher stops.

SS5 ***(KL-Divergence Difference)*** This stopping strategy compares a given snippet against previously seen snippets using the KL-Divergence measure. If the resulting value is less than threshold x_5, then the snippet is considered too similar to previously seen content, and the simulated searcher stops, moving to the next query.

When implementing ***SS4*** and ***SS5***, we considered the *per-query difference* and the *per-session difference*. For the per-query variant, previously observed text consisted of the first snippet, thus meaning that the simulated searcher always considers at least two snippets before stopping. For the per-session variant, all previously seen snippets over the simulated search session are used. In this paper, we will only report the per-query variants of ***SS4*** and ***SS5***, as both performed somewhat better than their per-session variants in a pilot study. A number of other variants were also considered but not explored, such as using the document and snippet text, and using only text from snippets considered relevant. To compute the KL-Divergence, we used a *Maximum Likelihood Estimate (MLE)* of the term distribution given the new snippet, and all the previously examined snippets. We also explored smoothing the distribution with the probabilities of each collection used. However, this approach was not used; performance was not increased, only complexity.

The final stopping strategy that we implemented was based upon IFT to represent utility-based approaches.

SS6 ***(IFT)*** With this stopping strategy, a searcher is assumed to have some idea of the average rate of gain (denoted as x_6). If the rate of gain from the observed documents thus far does not exceed x_6, the searcher then stops and proceeds to issue the next query.

To determine the rate of gain at the current snippet, we first computed the *Discounted Cumulative Gain (DCG)* g received from the observed documents up to that point in the ranked list at position i. We then divided g by the total time taken, i.e. $i * t_d + t_q$, where i represents the rank,

[1]NB: Judgements R and N do not (necessarily) represent TREC relevance judgements. Instead, they represent the decision taken by the simulated searcher as to whether snippets are relevant (or non-relevant) to the given topic.

t_d is the time taken to examine a document, and t_q is the time taken to issue a query. This estimate is very dependent upon the first document. For example, if the first document is non-relevant, then the gain is zero, and thus the simulated searcher would immediately stop when $x_6 > 0$. We also included another parameter which specifies how many snippets they should first consider before making their decision based on the rate of gain[2]. This would essentially mean that the simulated searcher would look at y_6 snippets/documents, and then decide to continue with the current query.

Stopping strategies ***SS1-SS6*** represent a subset of the rules that we have catalogued in Section 2. It should be noted that we have not selected rules which are based upon satisfaction or satiation because the task we are investigating is ad-hoc topic retrieval, where the goal is to find as many relevant documents as possible in a given period of time. The satisfaction/satiation rules therefore do not seem particularly applicable in this context. Furthermore, rules such as the mental list rule seem to be more topic specific, requiring a searcher to know in advance all the criteria that they need to check off in their head *a priori*. However, these criteria are largely unknown in ad-hoc circumstances.

4. EXPERIMENTAL METHOD

To address research questions **RQ1-RQ4** as posed in Section 1, we conducted a large scale simulation to compare a total of six stopping strategies based upon four stopping rules. Each stopping strategy was then compared against the actual stopping behaviour of 48 subjects, all of whom took part in our previously conducted user study [22].

4.1 Corpora, Topics, System and Users

We used two test collections: TREC *AQUAINT* with the TREC *2005 Robust Track* topic set, and TREC *WT2g* with the TREC *Ad-Hoc and Small Web* topic set. The topic sets contain a total of 50 topics each, all of which were used for our stopping strategy comparisons. Both collections were indexed using the *Whoosh* IR toolkit[3], where stopwords[4] were removed with Porter stemming applied. The retrieval model used for all simulations was PL2 ($c = 10.0$).

In the user study we performed [22], 48 undergraduate subjects were recruited to undertake ad-hoc topic retrieval over two 2005 Robust Track topics, №. 347 and №. 435. For each topic, subjects had a total of 1200 seconds (20 minutes) to complete each task using the same system and setup as defined above. For each query submitted, we recorded various interactions that subjects undertook. Of particular interest for this study is the data that report the documents that each subject clicked on, what documents they marked as relevant, the depth to which they hovered on each SERP (inferred from mouseover events), and the depth of the last document that they clicked. This data were used to first ground our simulations (refer to Section 4.3), and then to evaluate the different stopping strategies against each other.

4.2 Implemented Searcher Model

Figure 1 presents a flowchart of the operations that simulated searchers undertook during a simulated search session. The processes are largely based upon the simulation framework used by Baskaya et al. [4], but includes additional decision points as suggested by Thomas et al. [30].

Essentially, the simulated searcher begins by ***(1)*** examining the given topic and title description. From the title and description, the simulated searcher then ***(2)*** generates a series of queries[5] which are issued to the underlying search engine. The simulated searcher then ***(3)*** issues a query from the generated list, and then ***(4)*** proceeds to examine the first/next snippet in the ranked list provided. The simulated searcher can also decide to issue a new query, thus returning to *(3)*. If the snippet is considered relevant by the simulated searcher, ***(5)*** the document is then examined in full. If the document is also considered relevant, ***(6)*** the document is then marked relevant. If either the snippet or document are considered non-relevant, the simulated searcher then returns to *(4)* with the document unmarked. The gain for each marked document is determined from TREC relevance judgements. A marked document can score either *0* (non-relevant), *1* (somewhat relevant), or *2* (very relevant).

For the purposes of this study, we assume that *(i)* there is only one 'SERP', consisting of a maximum of 75 results (thus meaning no pagination and associated interaction costs), and *(ii)* the results in the 'SERP' are examined using the *cascade* assumption [16], meaning examination of a results list top-down in sequential order.

The searcher model detailed above is encoded within our simulator. It was developed as a highly modularised framework to allow for the easy experimentation of different simulated searchers, test collections, querying strategies, stopping strategies, and more[6]. Below, we describe how the components in the framework were instantiated.

4.3 Interaction Times and Probabilities

To ground our simulations, we computed the interaction probabilities and the times it took subjects to perform various actions when undertaking our user study [22]. Average times for each action simulated are reported in Table 1. For each action that a simulated searcher performed during a simulated run, the time spent was accumulated given the times reported in Table 1 until the time limit of 1200 seconds was exceeded. After reaching this limit, the simulated search session ended. The interaction probabilities, associated with clicking snippets and marking documents when TREC relevant/non-relevant, are reported in Table 2.

Since the simulation is stochastic based upon the interaction probabilities, this means that for different runs (i.e. stopping strategies and different thresholds), the same document can be considered relevant in one run and non-relevant in another. To ensure a fair comparison, we used a set of pre-rolled outcomes. For each snippet/document, we pre-computed the probabilities, and stored these in *action judgement files* - one related to the action of clicking on a snippet, another related to the action of marking a document. If a document was judged as relevant in one run, then by pre-computing these actions in advance, the same document would be considered relevant in other runs. We repeated this process ten times, so that for each particular stopping strategy and threshold value, we performed ten trials (in which documents could be marked as either relevant or non-

[2]This parameter was set to 2 for this study - refer to Section 4.5.

[3]Whoosh is available at `https://pypi.python.org/pypi/Whoosh`.

[4]Fox's classical stopword list was used. Refer to `http://git.io/vT3So` for the complete list.

[5]Refer to Section 4.4 for more information on the query generation strategy used for this study.

[6]The simulator is open-source, and freely available for download from *GitHub* at `http://git.io/vOBLz`.

Table 1: A summary of the interaction times (in seconds) used for all simulations in this study. Values are obtained from the user study conducted by Maxwell and Azzopardi [22].

Time Required to...	Seconds
...issue a query	15.1
...undertake an initial SERP examination	1.1
...examine an individual snippet	1.3
...examine a document	21.45
...mark a document as relevant	2.57

Table 2: The four probabilities used in all simulations run as part of this study. Probabilities are derived from the user study conducted by Maxwell and Azzopardi [22].

Probability	Value
$P(C\|R_s)$ (Clicking a relevant snippet)	0.36
$P(C\|N_s)$ (Clicking a non-relevant snippet)	0.21
$P(M\|R_d)$ (Marking a relevant document)	0.71
$P(M\|N_d)$ (Marking a non-relevant document)	0.53

relevant). This meant a fairer and paired comparison could be undertaken within runs. The action judgement files for each trial were produced with different seeded probabilities, allowing for reproducible results[7]. For each run, we report the average over all trials.

4.4 Query Generation Strategy

To successfully run our simulations, we required a component to generate a series of queries to be issued to the underlying search engine. We followed two approaches to query selection: automatically generating queries with a given, *idealised querying strategy*, and using the queries from our user study [22] to provide a direct comparison between real-world and simulated searcher behaviours. This section provides details of the automatic query generation component.

Keskustalo et al. [18] and Baskaya [2] defined and analysed five prototypical querying strategies, each of which represented an idealised subset of searcher behaviours [18]. Of particular interest to us were the two querying strategies which yielded the worst (***QS1***) and best performance (***QS3***). These are briefly explained below. Our explanations use the following notation, where Q_n represents query n within a search session, with t_n representing term n from a list of terms available to formulate queries.

QS1 ***(Single Term)*** This strategy generated a series of single term queries, e.g.:

$$\mathbf{Q_1}\ t_1 \rightarrow \mathbf{Q_2}\ t_2 \rightarrow \mathbf{Q_3}\ t_3$$

QS3 ***(Three-Term)*** Here, queries are produced with two *pivot* terms and one other term. The first two terms therefore remain constant, with the third term changing for each subsequent query, e.g.:

$$\mathbf{Q_1}\ t_1t_2t_3 \rightarrow \mathbf{Q_2}\ t_1t_2t_4 \rightarrow \mathbf{Q_3}\ t_1t_2t_5$$

For this study, we implemented a blended querying strategy, ***QS1+3***, where a single term from ***QS1*** is issued, followed by a three-term query from ***QS3***. This is repeated until the generated queries are exhausted. All stopping strategy comparison simulations in this study use querying strategy ***QS1+3***. The blended querying strategy provided a balance between good queries (generated by ***QS3***) and poor queries (generated by ***QS1***) in terms of performance (see Table 3). This would allow us to determine the robustness of each stopping strategy when faced with a poor set of results. Interleaving good and bad queries poses a key challenge to stopping strategies: to spot a poor performing query and subsequently stop early, thus saving time.

Queries for the two underlying strategies ***QS1*** and ***QS3*** were generated as follows. For each topic used, the title and description were used to create a MLE language model, i.e. $p(term|topic)$. For ***QS1***, we then extracted a list of all single terms, ranking them according to this probability. For ***QS3***, we took all two-word combinations of the title terms, and selected the pair with the highest joint probability to act as the two pivot terms as described above. A list of three-term candidate queries, q, was then constructed by appending another term from the topic to the pivot terms. These three-term queries were then ranked according to $p(q|topic)$.

4.5 Stopping Strategies

For stopping strategies ***SS1***, ***SS2*** and ***SS3***, we set the associated thresholds (x_1, x_2 and x_3 respectively) to explore a range of values, from 1-20 in steps of 1, and 25-50 in steps of 5. The final threshold value of 50 was sufficiently deep such that if a simulated searcher only issued one query and examined all documents, they would reach their 1200-second time limit. Note that for ***SS1***, x_1 corresponds to the *maximum depth per query*, whereas for ***SS2*** and ***SS3***, x_2 and x_3 represent the *minimum depth per query*. For example, when $x_2 = 3$, a searcher is willing to tolerate three non-relevant snippets. However, they may see two relevant snippets in the process, and thus stop at a depth of five. Section 3 also provides a further example of this scenario.

For our difference rule-based stopping strategies ***SS4*** and ***SS5***, we explored a different threshold range for both. For ***SS4***, which considered term overlap differences, we explored a threshold range where $x_4 = 0.0$ to $x_4 = 1.0$ in steps of 0.05. The lower the threshold, the less similar the content. For ***SS5*** which utilised KL-Divergence, the threshold range varied between $x_5 = 3.0$ to $x_5 = 8.0$ in steps of 0.5. A small scale pilot study revealed that the majority of KL-Divergence scores for both the AQUAINT and WT2g collections fell within this range.

Finally, for IFT-based ***SS6***, we experimented with manipulating the gain threshold parameter and the number of documents first viewed before estimating the gain. From this pilot study, we observed that ***SS6*** was very sensitive when the number of documents first viewed was set to one. This was due to the fact that if the first document was non-relevant, the searcher would always stop. We found that basing the estimate on two snippets was much less sensitive and resulted in better performance. Thus, we report findings based upon that value. For x_6 (i.e. the average rate of gain that needed to be exceeded to continue searching), we explored the range 0.002 to 0.03 in steps of 0.002.

4.6 Searcher Comparisons

To determine which stopping strategy best approximated when people stopped searching, we evaluated each strategy against actual searcher stopping behaviour. For each

[7]Configuration files required to run the experiments reported in this paper can be obtained by contacting the lead author.

of the 48 subjects who undertook our previously discussed user study [22], we extracted from the corresponding log file all of the queries that the subjects issued across the two AQUAINT topics (№. 347 and №. 435). We issued the queries to the same search engine that the subjects used during the user study, and then computed when each stopping strategy said they would stop (for each threshold). To determine which stopping strategy/threshold best approximated the subjects of the user study, we calculated the *mean squared error (MSE)* between the actual observed subject/searcher behaviour and the simulated searcher's behaviours (as defined by the stopping strategy). This was calculated for both click depth (the last document clicked) and hover depth (the last document hovered over). The mean ± standard deviation for the click depth of the last document was 9.6 ± 15.8, while the mean ± standard deviation of the last snippet hovered over was 13.5 ± 17.5.

5. RESULTS

We present our results over two main sections. Section 5.1 provides results for our stopping strategy comparison simulations. Section 5.2 provides the key findings for comparing the stopping behaviour of 48 subjects against the six implemented stopping strategies (***SS1-SS6***).

5.1 Stopping Strategy Comparison

Figure 2 provides an overview of the simulation results over both the AQUAINT and WT2g collections. The two plots show how the mean *Cumulative Gain (CG)* varies across each of the six stopping strategies (***SS1-SS6***) versus the mean depth per query, given the threshold values used. All results presented in this section are averaged out over the 50 topics used for the associated collection, and over the ten times each simulation was run (refer to Section 4.3). The plots in Figure 2 show how the performance of the six stopping strategies ***SS1-SS6*** vary, thus answering **RQ1**. Table 4 reports the best performing threshold - complete with corresponding CG and depth per query values - across the two collections used and all six stopping strategies. This therefore provides an answer to **RQ2**.

By inspecting the plots in Figure 2, we first note that the two stopping strategies ***SS2*** and ***SS3*** - both of which are based upon the frustration point/disgust rules - both perform very well, especially at lower depths per query. Indeed, ***SS3*** generally outperforms all of the other stopping strategies over both the AQUAINT and WT2g collections. ***SS3*** also achieves the highest CG (8.6 ± 1.1) over AQUAINT, at a depth per query of 14.2, where $x_3 = 5$. The counterpart stopping strategy to ***SS3***, ***SS2***, also performs very well, close to the baseline fixed depth stopping strategy ***SS1***. Interestingly, ***SS1*** marginally attained the highest level of CG over the WT2g collection, with a value of 5.6 ± 1.2, at a depth per query of 22.2, with $x_1 = 40$. ***SS2*** and ***SS3*** attained CG values of 5.55 ± 0.9 and 5.48 ± 0.7 respectively. Recall the difference between these two stopping strategies: ***SS2*** considers the total number of non-relevant documents observed, while ***SS3*** considers a certain number of non-relevant documents observed contiguously. The fixed depth stopping strategy ***SS1*** results in good performance when a sufficiently high threshold is selected, resulting in a depth of approximately 21-22 documents per query. The utility-based stopping strategy ***SS6*** also performed reasonably well. Simulated searchers examined to comparatively

Table 3: Mean (±) standard deviations of the performance of the three simulated querying strategies used (*QS1*, *QS1+3* and *QS3*) over both the AQUAINT (AQ.) and WT2g (WT.) collections.

		QS1	*QS1+3*	*QS3*
AQ.	***P@10***	0.02 ± 0.09	0.14 ± 0.24	0.25 ± 0.28
	P@20	0.02 ± 0.08	0.13 ± 0.22	0.24 ± 0.26
WT.	***P@10***	0.03 ± 0.12	0.17 ± 0.25	0.32 ± 0.27
	P@20	0.03 ± 0.10	0.16 ± 0.22	0.28 ± 0.24

Table 4: Summary of the best performing thresholds (x_n) for the six stopping strategies *SS1-SS6*, along with the corresponding CG values (± standard deviations) and depths per query. Results are presented for both the AQUAINT and WT2g collections.

		Threshold	CG	Depth/Query
AQUAINT	*SS1*	$x_1 = 35$	8.3 ± 1.5	20.9
	SS2	$x_2 = 25$	8.3 ± 1.3	21.4
	SS3	$\mathbf{x_3 = 5}$	**8.6 ± 1.1**	**14.2**
	SS4	$x_4 = 0.95$	6.9 ± 1.3	27.4
	SS5	$x_5 = 3$	6.3 ± 1.2	17.7
	SS6	$x_6 = 0.004$	7.3 ± 1.5	17.3
WT2g	*SS1*	$\mathbf{x_1 = 40}$	**5.6 ± 1.2**	**22.2**
	SS2	$x_2 = 19$	5.6 ± 0.9	18.9
	SS3	$x_3 = 6$	5.5 ± 0.7	19.7
	SS4	$x_4 = 1$	4.3 ± 0.8	33.2
	SS5	$x_5 = 3$	3.9 ± 0.8	9.6
	SS6	$x_6 = 0.004$	4.8 ± 1.1	19.7

lower depths per query (17.3 and 19.7 for AQUAINT and WT2g respectively), yet still attained a respectable level of CG. The general trend of lower CG over the WT2g collection confirms an underlying concept of IFT. If the rate of gain experienced is lower, searchers will examine result lists to greater depths. This suggests that ***SS6*** is somewhat less adaptive when experienced performance is low (on average). However, further simulations are required to confirm this and are left for future work. Finally, difference-based stopping strategies ***SS4*** and ***SS5*** consistently performed poorly. As thresholds x_4 and x_5 decreased (i.e. less overlap, more difference), simulated searchers went deeper. This did not however translate into substantially higher returns in gain.

The baseline stopping strategy ***SS1*** - which is commonly used in IR simulations and is employed in many IR measures - perhaps surprisingly performed well. To determine the difference between the baseline and other stopping strategies, we performed a series of paired t-tests. For each stopping strategy, we took the best performing threshold and assumed that there was a significant difference in total CG when compared against that of ***SS1*** when $p < 0.05$. Over AQUAINT, the frustration point/disgust-based stopping strategies ***SS2*** ($p = 0.1$) and ***SS3*** ($p = 0.8$) were not statistically significant from the CG attained by ***SS1***. However, ***SS4*** ($p = 0.003$), ***SS5*** ($p = 0.0004$) and ***SS6*** ($p = 0.0008$) all attained significantly lower levels of CG. A similar trend was found over WT2g, where the frustration point/disgust-based stopping strategies ***SS2*** ($p = 0.07$) and ***SS3*** ($p = 0.2$) were not statistically significant when compared to the CG value of ***SS1***.

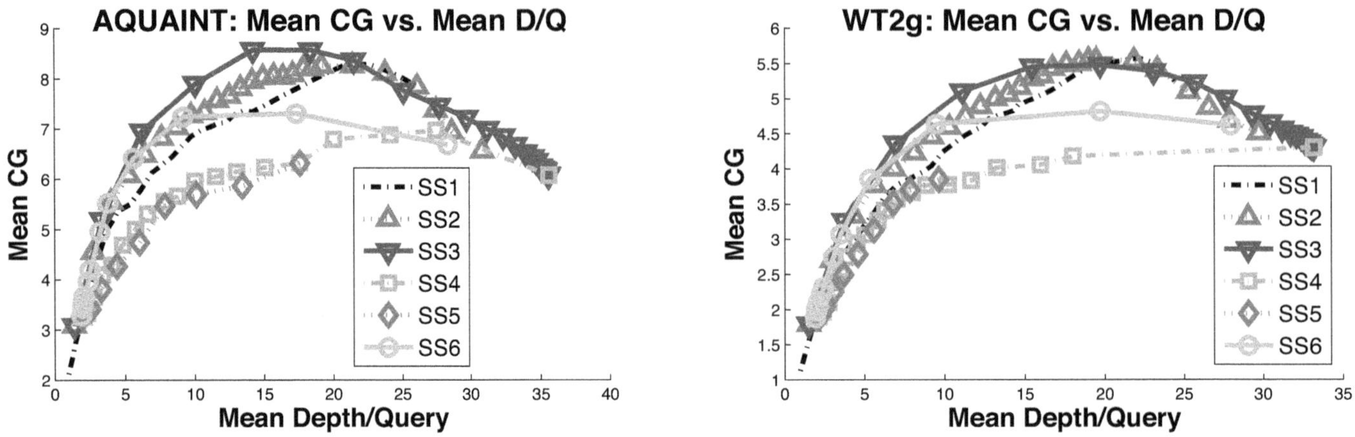

Figure 2: Plots showing the mean CG attained versus the mean depth per query, for both the AQUAINT (left) and WT2g (right) collections. Note the particularly strong performance of our baseline, *SS1*.

In addition, ***SS4*** ($p = 0.001$), ***SS5*** ($p = 0.0005$) and ***SS6*** ($p = 0.001$) were all significantly lower when compared to ***SS1***.

Table 3 reports the mean retrieval performance metrics (P@10 and P@20) over both the AQUAINT and WT2g collections, examining each individual querying strategy (***QS1***, ***QS1+3*** and ***QS3***) as detailed in Section 4.4. As expected, we find that queries generated by ***QS1*** generally performed poorly, while queries generated by ***QS3*** performed substantially better. The performance of blended querying strategy ***QS1+3*** was roughly the average of querying strategies ***QS1*** and ***QS3***. However, this hides the bimodal distribution of performance that would be experienced during searching. We posit that this may have been very detrimental to the difference-based strategies ***SS4*** and ***SS5***. This is due to the fact that for single term queries, the diversity of the results are likely to be much greater than for three term queries. Consequently, for single term queries, which provide little gain, the simulated searcher is likely to go far deeper. This means that the searcher wastes time, getting little gain in return. The plots in Figure 2 confirm this, showing that performance barely increases past a depth of 10. As a result, this suggests that such difference methods would need to consider the length of the query and expected diversity of the results, with the stopping threshold set accordingly. Similarly for the utility-based strategy ***SS6***, between-topic variation would mean that the rate of gain experienced from topic to topic will be quite different. Ultimately, this means that a more adaptive threshold for ***SS6*** may be more appropriate. For example, the threshold set could be updated based upon the performance of the queries issued by searchers. Therefore, if the issued queries are delivering a high rate of gain, the threshold could then be increased - and conversely for a low rate of gain. These directions are left for future work.

5.2 Real-World Searcher Analysis

As previously explained in Section 4.6, we used the MSE to measure the difference between the search behaviours of subjects and their simulated counterparts. This was realised for each implemented stopping strategy (***SS1-SS6***). For our analysis, we used two behavioural aspects of the real-world searchers - their click depths and their hover depths. Regarding our simulated searchers, the click depth was the last document observed by the searcher, irrespective of whether it was considered relevant or non-relevant. The hover depth was operationalised as the last snippet that was inspected before the stopping threshold criteria was met or exceeded.

Figure 3 plots the MSE for the click depths (top) and hover depths (bottom) for all six stopping strategies (***SS1-SS6***) across the depth per query (given the thresholds used; refer to Section 4.5). Table 5 reports the MSE for the best threshold over each stopping strategy, both for click depths and hover depths, broken down across topics (complete with a mean over the two topics used). On inspecting the MSE plots, we can see that the frustration point/disgust-based stopping strategies ***SS2*** and ***SS3*** both tend to result in lower MSE values across all depths (thresholds), with the baseline fixed depth stopping strategy ***SS1*** close behind. On average, the click and hover depths were best approximated when $x_2 = 9$. These findings therefore provide an answer to **RQ3**. Utility-based stopping strategy ***SS6*** then followed, performing consistently well. As with the findings reported in Section 5.1, lower thresholds for ***SS6*** yielded a closer approximation to actual searcher behaviour. This suggests real-world searchers may be attuned to obtaining small increases of gain between snippets and documents. However, it is likely that the way in which we calculated the gain (approximated as the rate of gain) and the lack of adaptive thresholds impacted the accuracy of results for ***SS6***. Furthermore, difference-based stopping strategies ***SS4*** and ***SS5*** consistently performed poorly. Despite comparatively poor approximations, we posit that the difference methods would improve with longer queries. The queries posed by the 48 real-world subjects typically were around 2-4 terms in length. It should also be noted that ***SS2*** generally outperformed its counterpart ***SS3*** in this scenario. This suggests that real-world searchers are more sensitive to the total amount of non-relevant information encountered per query. In addition, note that ***SS1-SS6*** all provided better approximations for click depths than hover depths, with click depth approximations yielding a lower MSE.

The thresholds yielding the lowest MSE for click depth for ***SS1-SS6*** were then used as the basis for Table 6. This is because those thresholds best approximated actual searcher stopping behaviour. Here, we report the mean CG that would have resulted from the queries issued by subjects if they had followed exactly each of the six stopping strategies - and the actual mean CG attained by the subjects (denoted as **RW**). Both frustration point/disgust-based stopping strategies ***SS2*** and ***SS3*** again performed well, with

Table 5: The lowest observed MSE values for each stopping strategy (*SS1*-*SS6*) along with the threshold at which the value was obtained (x_n). Values are reported for both topics examined, and the mean.

		Topic №. 347		Topic №. 435		Mean	
		MSE	x_n	MSE	x_n	MSE	x_n
Click Depth	*SS1*	335.4	13	166.4	13	250.2	13
	SS2	328.9	10	**159.7**	**9**	**244.4**	**9**
	SS3	**319.7**	**5**	164.7	4	253.3	5
	SS4	366.3	0.5	193.6	0.45	279.3	0.5
	SS5	392.6	5	211.5	5	301.3	5
	SS6	357.1	0.01	198.4	0.01	277.1	0.01
Hover Depth	*SS1*	397.3	14	219.3	13	307.9	13
	SS2	386.2	10	**210.3**	**9**	**298.4**	**9**
	SS3	**383.2**	**5**	213.7	4	302.4	4
	SS4	444.1	0.5	259.2	0.6	351.1	0.55
	SS5	480.6	4.5	301.3	4.5	390.2	4.5
	SS6	436.7	0.006	281.8	0.006	358.6	0.006

Table 6: The mean CG $\pm$ standard deviations for each implemented stopping strategy (*SS1*-*SS6*). CG values reported are attained at threshold x_n which attained the lowest MSE for click depths, as reported in Table 5. Also included is the mean CG actually attained by the real-world (RW) searchers.

	Topic №. 347		Topic №. 435		Mean	
	CG	x_n	CG	x_n	CG	x_n
RW	11.7 ± 8.9	-	13.5 ± 7.9	-	12.6 ± 8.5	-
SS1	13.1 ± 8.2	13	17 ± 7.9	13	15 ± 8.3	13
SS2	14.4 ± 8.9	10	18.2 ± 8.8	9	15.8 ± 9	9
SS3	15.9 ± 10.8	5	17.8 ± 10.2	4	19.6 ± 11.8	5
SS4	9.7 ± 6.7	0.5	9.6 ± 4.7	0.45	10.6 ± 6.1	0.5
SS5	6.7 ± 4.9	5	6.9 ± 3.9	5	6.8 ± 4.4	5
SS6	5.4 ± 5.1	0.01	8.2 ± 5.4	0.01	6.8 ± 5.4	0.01

SS3 attaining the highest mean CG (19.6). ***SS2*** followed with 15.8, with ***SS1*** attaining 15. Interestingly, ***SS1*-*SS3*** all attained a higher mean CG (15-19.6) than the subjects of the user study (at 12.6). This answers **RQ4**. Of note, ***SS1*** performed very well with a fixed depth ($x_1 = 13$) slightly deeper than what is typically assumed (i.e. $x_1 = 10$ for P@10). However, the high levels of variance observed will motivate further work to examine whether these findings hold at an individual searcher level.

6. DISCUSSION AND CONCLUSION

In this paper, we have examined a series of stopping rules and transformed them into stopping strategies that can be implemented and evaluated. In the context of ad-hoc topic retrieval, we found that stopping strategies ***SS1*** and ***SS3*** delivered the best overall performance. ***SS3*** was not however significantly better than a well chosen fixed depth threshold. Intuitively, an adaptive strategy appears much more realistic, and more in line with what searchers are likely to adopt. Indeed, our simulations confirmed this hypothesis, with frustration point/disgust-based ***SS2*** consistently providing the best approximation for actual searcher behaviour. In all cases however, the fixed depth baseline stopping strategy ***SS1*** performed remarkably well.

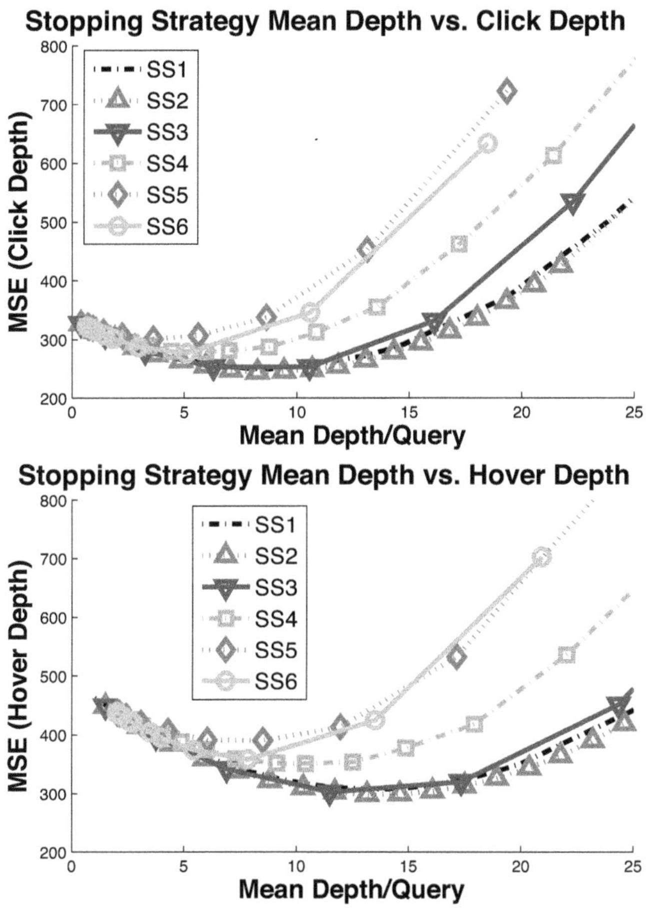

Figure 3: The MSE plots for each stopping strategy (*SS1*-*SS6*) across the mean depth per query. The plot at the top compares click depths, with hover depths at the bottom. Smaller MSE values indicate a closer approximation to actual searcher behaviour. Both plots indicate that *SS1*-*SS3* are closer to actual searcher behaviour at reasonable depths.

Our findings are both reassuring and promising. Firstly, they are reassuring in the sense that past simulations and various measures that are employed which assume a fixed depth (i.e. ***SS1***) are reasonable approximations for actual observed stopping behaviour. However, this is only in terms of the *average* stopping distance, and not the variance. A caveat here is that we have selected the best fixed depth. Therefore, an open question is how to determine this value in advance. Using the average stopping distance provides a very strong baseline to which we can improve upon. The results we have obtained from this study are promising as we have examined only a subset of possible stopping rules, and explored only a small number of possible implementations. An obvious direction for future work would be to explore this area further and consider how more adaptive variants of the proposed stopping strategies would fare. This would allow us to provide more accurate estimates of when searchers stop examining search results.

Aspects that we did not vary were the interaction probabilities and times which vary according to the veracity and expertise of the searchers. It is likely that these probabilities and times will influence which stopping strategy is employed and which stopping strategy yields the highest gains. For example, assessment strategies such as *"fast and liberal"* or *"slow and neutral"* [29] which characterise different types of searchers when assessing are likely to impact upon the depth to which they search. On the other hand, the utility-based stopping strategy ***SS6*** is sensitive to the time spent examining snippets and documents. Accounting for and encoding these values on a group or per-searcher basis would result in a deeper understanding of how such factors influence stopping behaviour. We leave these directions for future work.

In conclusion, we have examined a range of stopping strategies and have found that strategies based upon the frustration point/disgust rules generally provide the best overall performance under simulated conditions. Furthermore, a frustration point/disgust-based strategy also closely approximated actual stopping behaviour. However, a well chosen depth with a fixed depth strategy also provided a very close approximation to actual stopping behaviour. Nevertheless, searchers can obtain markedly better performance by adopting an adaptive strategy based upon the frustration point/disgust rules. This work opens up a number of interesting lines of investigation regarding stopping rules and strategies which will be the subject of future work.

Acknowledgments: Funding for this project was provided by the MUMIA Cost Action, ref `ECOST-STSM-IC1002-080914-049840`. Funding was also provided by the ACM SIGIR for the lead author to attend the conference. We'd also like to thank the three anonymous reviewers and Alastair Maxwell for their feedback. Their comments greatly improved the clarity of this work.

References

[1] L. Azzopardi. The economics in interactive information retrieval. In *Proc. 34th ACM SIGIR*, pages 15–24, 2011.

[2] F. Baskaya. *Simulating Search Sessions in Interactive Information Retrieval Evaluation.* PhD thesis, University of Tampere, School of Information Sciences, Finland, 2014.

[3] F. Baskaya, H. Keskustalo, and K. Järvelin. Time drives interaction: Simulating sessions in diverse searching environments. In *Proc. 35th ACM SIGIR*, pages 105–114, 2012.

[4] F. Baskaya, H. Keskustalo, and K. Järvelin. Modeling behavioral factors in interactive information retrieval. In *Proc. 22nd ACM CIKM*, pages 2297–2302, 2013.

[5] M.J. Bates. The fallacy of the perfect thirty-item online search. *RQ*, 24(1):pp. 43–50, 1984.

[6] G.J. Browne, M.G. Pitts, and J.C. Wetherbe. Stopping rule use during web-based search. In *Proc. HICSS-38*, page 271b, 2005.

[7] G.J. Browne, M.G. Pitts, and J.C. Wetherbe. Cognitive stopping rules for terminating information search in online tasks. *MIS Quarterly*, 31(1):89–104, 2007.

[8] E.L. Charnov. Optimal foraging, the Marginal Value Theorem. *Theoretical Population Biology*, 9(2):129–136, 1976.

[9] W.S. Cooper. On selecting a measure of retrieval effectiveness part ii. implementation of the philosophy. *J. of the American Soc. for Info. Sci.*, 24(6):413–424, 1973.

[10] W.S. Cooper. The paradoxical role of unexamined documents in the evaluation of retrieval effectiveness. *Info. Processing and Management*, 12(6):367 – 375, 1976.

[11] M. Dostert and D. Kelly. Users' stopping behaviors and estimates of recall. In *Proc. 32nd ACM SIGIR*, pages 820–821, 2009.

[12] F. Guo, C. Liu, A. Kannan, T. Minka, M. Taylor, Y. Wang, and C. Faloutsos. Click chain model in web search. In *Proc. 18th WWW*, pages 11–20, 2009.

[13] K. Hofmann. Fast and reliable online learning to rank for information retrieval. *SIGIR Forum*, 47(2):140–140, 2013.

[14] P. Ingwersen and K. Järvelin. *The Turn: Integration of Information Seeking and Retrieval in Context (The Information Retrieval Series).* 2005.

[15] K. Järvelin and J. Kekäläinen. Cumulative gain-based evaluation of IR techniques. *ACM TOIS*, 20(4):422–446, 2002.

[16] T. Joachims, L. Granka, B. Pan, H. Hembrooke, F. Radlinski, and G. Gay. Evaluating the accuracy of implicit feedback from clicks and query reformulations in web search. *ACM Trans. on Info. Systems*, 25(2), 2007.

[17] H. Keskustalo, K. Järvelin, and A. Pirkola. Evaluating the effectiveness of relevance feedback based on a user simulation model: Effects of a user scenario on cumulated gain value. *Information Retrieval*, 11(3):209–228, 2008.

[18] H. Keskustalo, K. Järvelin, A. Pirkola, T. Sharma, and M. Lykke. Test collection-based ir evaluation needs extension toward sessions — a case of extremely short queries. In *Proc. 5th AIRS*, pages 63–74, 2009.

[19] D.H. Kraft and T. Lee. Stopping rules and their effect on expected search length. *IPM*, 15(1):47 – 58, 1979.

[20] J. Lin and M.D. Smucker. How do users find things with pubmed?: Towards automatic utility evaluation with user simulations. In *Proc. 31st ACM SIGIR*, pages 19–26, 2008.

[21] G. Marchionini. *Information Seeking in Electronic Environments.* Cambridge University Press, 1995.

[22] D. Maxwell and L. Azzopardi. Stuck in traffic: How temporal delays affect search behaviour. In *Proc. 5th IIiX*, pages 155–164, 2014.

[23] D. Maxwell, L. Azzopardi, K. Järvelin, and H. Keskustalo. An initial investigation into fixed and adaptive stopping strategies. In *Proc. 38th ACM SIGIR*, pages 903–906, 2015.

[24] A. Moffat and J. Zobel. Rank-biased precision for measurement of retrieval effectiveness. *ACM Trans. on Info. Systems*, 27(1):2:1–2:27, 2008.

[25] A. Moffat, P. Thomas, and F. Scholer. Users versus models: What observation tells us about effectiveness metrics. In *Proc. 22nd ACM CIKM*, pages 659–668, 2013.

[26] K.R. Nickles. *Judgment-based and reasoning-based stopping rules in decision making under uncertainty.* PhD thesis, University of Minnesota, 1995.

[27] P. Pirolli and S.K. Card. Information foraging. *Psychological Review*, 106:643–675, 1999.

[28] C. Prabha, L.S. Connaway, L. Olszewski, and L.R. Jenkins. What is enough? Satisficing information needs. *J. of Documentation*, 63(1):74–89, 2007.

[29] M.D. Smucker. An analysis of user strategies for examining and processing ranked lists of documents. In *Proc. of 5th HCIR*, 2011.

[30] P. Thomas, A. Moffat, P. Bailey, and F. Scholer. Modeling decision points in user search behavior. In *Proc. 5th IIiX*, pages 239–242, 2014.

[31] E.G. Toms and L. Freund. Predicting stopping behaviour: A preliminary analysis. In *Proc. 32nd ACM SIGIR*, pages 750–751, 2009.

[32] S. Verberne, M. Sappelli, K. Järvelin, and W. Kraaij. User simulations for interactive search: Evaluating personalized query suggestion. In *Advances in Information Retrieval*, volume 9022 of *LNCS*. 2015.

[33] R.W. White, S.T. Dumais, and J. Teevan. Characterizing the influence of domain expertise on web search behavior. In *Proc 2nd ACM WSDM*, pages 132–141, 2009.

[34] W. Wu and D. Kelly. Online Search Stopping Behaviors: An Investigation of Query Abandonment and Task Stopping. In *77th ASIS&T Annual Meeting*, 2014.

[35] W. Wu, D. Kelly, and A. Sud. Using information scent and need for cognition to understand online search behavior. In *Proc 37th ACM SIGIR*, pages 557–566, 2014.

[36] L. Zach. When is "enough" enough? modeling the information-seeking and stopping behavior of senior arts administrators: Research articles. *J. American Soc. for Info. Sci. and Tech.*, 56(1):23–35, 2005.

Automated News Suggestions for Populating Wikipedia Entity Pages

Besnik Fetahu[†], Katja Markert[†‡], Avishek Anand[†]

[†]L3S Research Center, Leibniz University of Hannover
Hannover, Germany

[‡]School of Computing, University of Leeds
United Kingdom

{fetahu,markert,anand}@L3S.de

ABSTRACT

Wikipedia entity pages are a valuable source of information for direct consumption and for knowledge-base construction, update and maintenance. Facts in these entity pages are typically supported by references. Recent studies show that as much as 20% of the references are from online news sources. However, many entity pages are incomplete even if relevant information is already available in existing news articles. Even for the already present references, there is often a delay between the news article publication time and the reference time. In this work, we therefore look at Wikipedia through the lens of news and propose a novel news-article suggestion task to improve news coverage in Wikipedia, and reduce the lag of newsworthy references. Our work finds direct application, as a precursor, to Wikipedia page generation and knowledge-base acceleration tasks that rely on relevant and high quality input sources.

We propose a two-stage supervised approach for suggesting news articles to entity pages for a given state of Wikipedia. First, we suggest news articles to Wikipedia entities (article-entity placement) relying on a rich set of features which take into account the *salience* and *relative authority* of entities, and the *novelty* of news articles to entity pages. Second, we determine the exact section in the entity page for the input article (article-section placement) guided by class-based section templates. We perform an extensive evaluation of our approach based on ground-truth data that is extracted from external references in Wikipedia. We achieve a high precision value of up to 93% in the *article-entity* suggestion stage and upto 84% for the *article-section placement*. Finally, we compare our approach against competitive baselines and show significant improvements.

Categories and Subject Descriptors

H3.3 [**Information Systems**]: Information Storage and Retrieval—*Information Search and Retrieval*

1. INTRODUCTION

Wikipedia is the largest source of open and collaboratively curated knowledge in the world. Introduced in 2001, it has evolved into a reference work with around 5m pages for the English Wikipedia alone. In addition, entities and event pages are updated quickly via collaborative editing and all edits are encouraged to include source citations, creating a knowledge base which aims at being both timely as well as authoritative. As a result, it has become the preferred source of information consumption about entities and events[1]. Moreso, this knowledge is harvested and utilized in building knowledge bases like YAGO [19] and DBpedia [4], and used in applications like text categorization [24], entity disambiguation [11], entity ranking [13] and distant supervision [20, 14].

However, not all Wikipedia pages referring to entities (entity pages) are comprehensive: relevant information can either be *missing* or added with a *delay*. Consider the city of *New Orleans* and the state of *Odisha* which were severely affected by cyclones *Hurricane Katrina* and *Odisha Cyclone*, respectively. While *Katrina* finds extensive mention in the entity page for *New Orleans*, *Odisha Cyclone* which has 5 times more human casualties (cf. Figure 1) is not mentioned in the page for *Odisha*. Arguably *Katrina* and *New Orleans* are more popular entities, but *Odisha Cyclone* was also reported extensively in national and international news outlets. This highlights the lack of important facts in trunk and long-tail entity pages, even in the presence of relevant sources. In addition, previ-

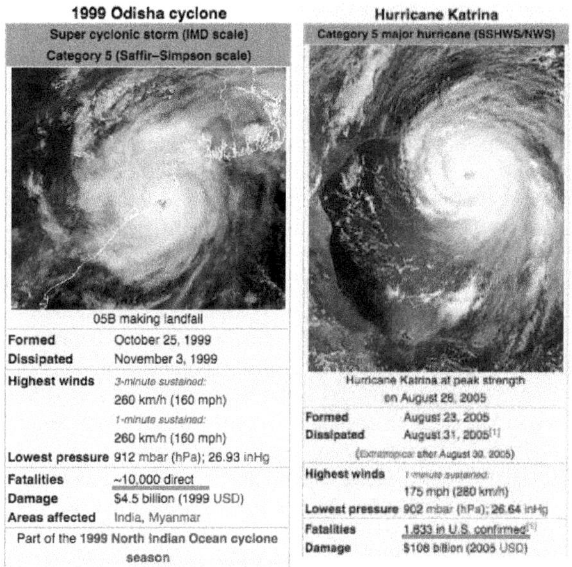

Figure 1: Comparing how cyclones are reported in Wikipedia entity pages.

[1]Wikipedia is one of the Top 10 viewed page sites and the top reference site according to Alexa Internet ranking `www.alexa.com`.

CIKM'15, October 19–23, 2015, Melbourne, Australia.
© 2015 ACM. ISBN 978-1-4503-3794-6/15/10 ...$15.00.
DOI: http://dx.doi.org/10.1145/2806416.2806531.

ous studies have shown that there is an inherent delay or lag when facts are added to entity pages [10].

To remedy these problems, it is important to identify information sources that contain novel and salient facts to a given entity page. However, not all information sources are equal. The online presence of major news outlets is an authoritative source due to active editorial control and their articles are also a timely container of facts. In addition, their use is in line with current Wikipedia editing practice, as is shown in [10] that almost 20% of current citations in all entity pages are news articles. We therefore propose *news suggestion* as a novel task that enhances entity pages and reduces delay while keeping its pages authoritative.

Existing efforts to populate Wikipedia [18] start from an entity page and then generate candidate documents about this entity using an external search engine (and then post-process them). However, such an approach lacks in (a) reproducibility since rankings vary with time with obvious bias to recent news (b) maintainability since document acquisition for each entity has to be periodically performed. To this effect, our news suggestion considers a news article as input, and determines if it is valuable for Wikipedia. Specifically, given an input news article n and a state of Wikipedia, the news suggestion problem identifies the entities mentioned in n whose entity pages can improve upon suggesting n. Most of the works on knowledge base acceleration [2, 1, 8], or Wikipedia page generation [18] rely on high quality input sources which are then utilized to extract textual facts for Wikipedia page population. In this work, we do not suggest snippets or paraphrases but rather entire articles which have a high potential importance for entity pages. These suggested news articles could be consequently used for extraction, summarization or population either manually or automatically – all of which rely on high quality and relevant input sources.

We identify four properties of good news recommendations: *salience*, *relative authority*, *novelty* and *placement*. First, we need to identify the most salient entities in a news article. This is done to avoid pollution of entity pages with only marginally related news. Second, we need to determine whether the news is important to the entity as only the most relevant news should be added to a precise reference work. To do this, we compute the *relative authority* of all entities in the news article: we call an entity more authoritative than another if it is more popular or noteworthy in the real world. Entities with very high authority have many news items associated with them and only the most relevant of these should be included in Wikipedia whereas for entities of lower authority the threshold for inclusion of a news article will be lower. Third, a good recommendation should be able to identify *novel* news by minimizing redundancy coming from multiple news articles. Finally, addition of facts is facilitated if the recommendations are fine-grained, i.e., recommendations are made on the section level rather than the page level (*placement*).

Approach and Contributions. We propose a two-stage news suggestion approach to entity pages. In the first stage, we determine whether a news article should be suggested for an entity, based on the entity's *salience* in the news article, its *relative authority* and the *novelty* of the article to the entity page. The second stage takes into account the class of the entity for which the news is suggested and constructs *section templates* from entities of the same class. The generation of such templates has the advantage of suggesting and expanding entity pages that do not have a complete section structure in Wikipedia, explicitly addressing long-tail and trunk entities. Afterwards, based on the constructed template our method determines the best fit for the news article with one of the sections.

We evaluate the proposed approach on a news corpus consisting of 351,982 articles crawled from the *news* external references in Wikipedia from 73,734 entity pages. Given the Wikipedia snapshot at a given year (in our case [2009-2014]), we suggest news articles that might be cited in the coming years. The existing news references in the entity pages along with their reference date act as our ground-truth to evaluate our approach. In summary, we make the following contributions.

- we propose a two-stage news suggestion approach for Wikipedia entity pages.
- we adopt and address the problem of determining whether a news article should be referenced to an entity considering the entity *salience*, *relative authority* and *novelty* of the article for the entity page.
- we are able to place articles in a specific section of the entity page. Through *section templates*, we address the problems of entities with a limited section structure by class-based generalization i.e. we can expand entity pages with sections that come from entities of a similar class.
- an extensive evaluation on 351,982 news articles and 73,734 entity pages, using their state for the years [2009-2013].

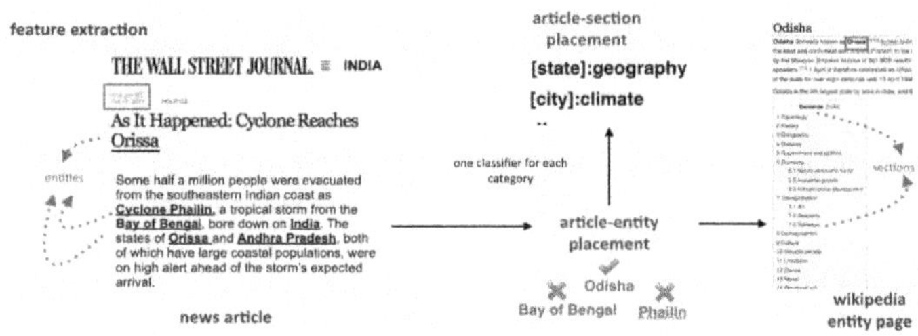

Figure 2: News suggestion approach overview.

2. RELATED WORK

As we suggest a new problem there is no current work addressing exactly the same task. However, our task has similarities to Wikipedia page generation and knowledge base acceleration. In addition, we take inspiration from Natural Language Processing (NLP) methods for salience detection.

Wikipedia Page Generation is the problem of populating Wikipedia pages with content coming from external sources. Sauper and Barzilay [18] propose an approach for automatically generating whole entity pages for specific entity classes. The approach is trained on already-populated entity pages of a given class (e.g. '*Diseases*') by learning templates about the entity page structure (e.g. diseases have a *treatment* section). For a new entity page, first, they extract documents via Web search using the entity title and the section title as a query, for example '*Lung Cancer*'+'*Treatment*'. As already discussed in the introduction, this has problems with reproducibility and maintainability. However, their main focus is on identifying the best paragraphs extracted from the collected documents. They rank the paragraphs via an optimized supervised *perceptron model* for finding the most representative paragraph that is the least similar to paragraphs in other sections. This paragraph is then included in the newly generated entity page. Taneva and Weikum [21] propose an approach that constructs short summaries for the long tail. The summaries are called '*gems*' and the size of a '*gem*' can be user defined. They focus on generating summaries that are novel and diverse. However, they do not consider any structure of entities, which is present in Wikipedia.

In contrast to [18] and [21], we actually focus on suggesting entire documents to Wikipedia entity pages. These are authoritative documents (news), which are highly relevant for the entity, novel for the entity and in which the entity is salient. Whereas relevance in Sauper and Barzilay is implicitly computed by web page ranking we solve that problem by looking at relative authority and salience of an entity, using the news article and entity page only. As Sauper and Barzilay concentrate on empty entity pages, the problem of novelty of their content is not an issue in their work whereas it is in our case which focuses more on updating entities. Updating entities will be more and more important the bigger an existing reference work is. Both the approaches in [18] and [21] (finding paragraphs and summarization) could then be used to process the documents we suggest further. Our concentration on news is also novel.

Knowledge Base Acceleration. In this task, given specific information extraction templates, a given corpus is analyzed in order to find worthwhile mentions of an entity or snippets that match the templates. Balog [2, 1] recommend news citations for an entity. Prior to that, the news articles are classified for their appropriateness for an entity, where as features for the classification task they use entity, document, entity-document and temporal features. The best performing features are those that measure similarity between an entity and the news document. West et al. [25] consider the problem of knowledge base completion, through question answering and complete missing facts in Freebase based on templates, i.e. *Frank_Zappa* `bornIn` *Baltymore, Maryland*.

In contrast, we do not extract facts for pre-defined templates but rather suggest news articles based on their relevance to an entity. In cases of long-tail entities, we can suggest to add a novel section through our abstraction and generation of section templates at entity class level.

Entity Salience. Determining which entities are prominent or salient in a given text has a long history in NLP, sparked by the linguistic theory of Centering [23]. Salience has been used in pronoun and co-reference resolution [15], or to predict which entities will be included in an abstract of an article [8]. Frequent features to measure salience include the frequency of an entity in a document, positioning of an entity, grammatical function or internal entity structure (POS tags, head nouns etc.). These approaches are not currently aimed at knowledge base generation or Wikipedia coverage extension but we postulate that an entity's salience in a news article is a prerequisite to the news article being relevant enough to be included in an entity page. We therefore use the salience features in [8] as part of our model. However, these features are document-internal — we will show that they are not sufficient to predict news inclusion into an entity page and add features of entity authority, news authority and novelty that measure the relations between several entities, between entity and news article as well as between several competing news articles.

3. PROBLEM DEFINITION AND APPROACH OUTLINE

3.1 Terminology and Problem Definition

We are interested in named entities mentioned in documents. An entity e can be identified by a canonical name, and can be *mentioned* differently in text via different *surface forms*. We canonicalize these mentions to entity pages in Wikipedia, a method typically known as *entity linking*. We denote the set of canonicalized entities extracted and linked from a news article n as $\varphi(n)$. For example, in Figure 2, entities are canonicalized into Wikipedia entity pages (e.g. *Odisha* is canonicalized to the corresponding article[2]). For a collection of news articles $\mathbf{N}$, we further denote the resulting set of entities by $\mathbf{E} = \cup_{n \in \mathbf{N}} \{e_i\}$.

Information in an entity page is organized into sections and evolves with time as more content is added. We refer to the state of Wikipedia at a time t as $\mathscr{W}_t$ and the set of sections for an entity page e as its *entity profile* $S_e(t)$. Unlike news articles, text in Wikipedia could be explicitly linked to entity pages through anchors. The set of entities explicitly referred in text from section $s \in S_e(t)$ is defined as $\gamma(s)$. Furthermore, Wikipedia induces a category structure over its entities, which is exploited by knowledge bases like YAGO (e.g. *Barack_Obama* `isA` `Person`). Consequently, each entity page belongs to one or more entity categories or classes c. Now we can define our news suggestion problem below:

DEFINITION 1 (NEWS SUGGESTION PROBLEM). *Given a set of news articles* $\mathbf{N} = \{n_1, \dots, n_k\}$ *and set of Wikipedia entity pages* $\mathbf{E} = \{e_1, \dots, e_m\}$ *(from* $\mathscr{W}_t$*) we intend to suggest a news article* n *published at time* $t_i > t$ *to entity page* e *and additionally to the most relevant section for the entity page* $s \in S_e(t)$.

3.2 Approach Overview

We approach the news suggestion problem by decomposing it into two tasks:

1. *AEP*: *Article–Entity* placement
2. *ASP*: *Article–Section* placement

In this first step, for a given entity-news pair $\langle n, e \rangle$, we determine whether the given news article $n \in \mathbf{N}$ should be suggested (we will refer to this as *'relevant'*) to entity $e \in \mathbf{E}$. To generate such $\langle n, e \rangle$ pairs, we perform the *entity linking* process, $\varphi(n)$, for n.

The *article–entity* placement task (described in detail in Section 4.1) for a pair $\langle n, e \rangle$ outputs a binary label (either *'non-relevant'* or *'relevant'*) and is formalized in Equation 1.

$$AEP : \langle e, n \rangle \rightarrow \{0, 1\}, \ \forall e \in \varphi(n) \wedge n \in \mathbf{N} \tag{1}$$

In the second step, we take into account all *'relevant'* pairs $\langle n, e \rangle$ and find the correct *section* for article n in entity e, respectively its profile $S_e(t)$ (see Section 4.2). The *article–section* placement task, determines the correct section for the triple $\langle n, e, S_e(t) \rangle$, and is formalized in Equation 2.

$$ASP : \langle e, n, S_e(t) \rangle \rightarrow \{s_1, \dots, s_k\}, \ s \in S_e(t) \tag{2}$$

In the subsequent sections we describe in details how we approach the two tasks for suggesting news articles to entity pages.

4. NEWS ARTICLE SUGGESTION

In this section, we provide an overview of the *news suggestion* approach to Wikipedia entity pages (see Figure 2). The approach is split into two tasks: (i) *article-entity* (*AEP*) and (ii) *article-section* (*ASP*) placement. For a Wikipedia snapshot $\mathscr{W}_t$ and a news corpus $\mathbf{N}$, we first determine which news articles should be suggested to an entity e. We will denote our approach for *AEP* by $\mathscr{F}_e$. Finally, we determine the most appropriate section for the *ASP* task and we denote our approach with $\mathscr{F}_s$.

In the following, we describe the process of learning the functions $\mathscr{F}_e$ and $\mathscr{F}_s$. We introduce features for the learning process, which encode information regarding the entity *salience*, *relative authority* and *novelty* in the case of AEP task. For the *ASP* task, we measure the *overall fit* of an article to the entity sections, with the entity being an input from *AEP* task. Additionally, considering that the entity profiles $S_e(t)$ are incomplete, in the case of a missing section we suggest and expand the entity profiles based on *section templates* generated from entities of the same class c (see Section 4.2.1).

[2]`http://en.wikipedia.org/wiki/Odisha`

4.1 Article–Entity Placement

In this step we learn the function $\mathcal{F}_e$ to correctly determine whether n should be suggested for e, basically a binary classification model (0=*'non-relevant'* and 1=*'relevant'*). Note that we are mainly interested in finding the *relevant* pairs in this task. For every news article, the number of disambiguated entities is around 30 (but n is suggested for only two of them on average). Therefore, the distribution of *'non-relevant'* and *'relevant'* pairs is skewed towards the earlier, and by simply choosing the *'non-relevant'* label we can achieve a high accuracy for $\mathcal{F}_e$. Finding the relevant pairs is therefore a considerable challenge.

An article n is suggested to e by our function $\mathcal{F}_e$ if it fulfills the following properties. The entity e is *salient* in n (a central concept), therefore ensuring that n is about e and that e is important for n. Next, given the fact there might be many articles in which e is *salient*, we also look at the reverse property, namely whether n is important for e. We do this by comparing the *authority* of e (which is a measure of popularity of an entity, such as its frequency of mention in a whole corpus) with the authority of its co-occurring entities in $\varphi(n)$, leading to a feature we call *relative authority*. The intuition is that for an entity that has overall lower authority than its co-occurring entities, a news article is more easily of importance.[3] Finally, if the article we are about to suggest is already covered in the entity profile $S_e(t)$, we do not wish to suggest *redundant* information, hence the *novelty*. Therefore, the learning objective of $\mathcal{F}_e$ should fulfill the following properties. Table 1 shows a summary of the computed features for $\mathcal{F}_e$.

1. **Salience:** entity e should be a *salient* entity in news article n
2. **Relative Authority:** the set of entities $e' \in \varphi(n)$ with which e co-occurs should have higher *authority* than e, making n important for e
3. **Novelty:** news article n should provide *novel* information for entity e taking into account its profile $S_e(t-1)$

feature	description	
$\Phi(e,n)$	the relative frequency of e in news article n.	*salience*
`Baseline Features`	set of features as proposed by Dunietz and Gillick [8]	
$\hat{\Gamma}(e\|\varphi(n))$	relative authority as the score of entities that have higher authority than e and that co-occur in n.	*authority*
$P(D)$	measures the news domain authority.	
$\mathcal{N}(n\|e)$	measures the novelty of a news article n for a given entity e	*novelty*

Table 1: *Article–Entity* placement feature summary.

4.1.1 Salience-based features

Baseline Features. As discussed in Section 2, a variety of features that measure salience of an entity in text are available from the NLP community. We reimplemented the ones in Dunietz and Gillick [8]. This includes a variety of features, e.g. positional features, occurrence frequency and the internal POS structure of the entity and the sentence it occurs in. Table 2 in [8] gives details.

Relative Entity Frequency. Although frequency of mention and positional features play some role in baseline features, their interaction is not modeled by a single feature nor do the positional features encode more than sentence position. We therefore suggest a novel feature called *relative entity frequency*, $\Phi(e,n)$, that has three properties.: (i) It rewards entities for occurring throughout the text instead of only in some parts of the text, measured by the number of paragraphs it occurs in (ii) it rewards entities that occur more frequently in the opening paragraphs of an article as we model $\Phi(e,n)$ as an *exponential decay* function. The decay corresponds to the positional index of the news paragraph. This is inspired by the news-specific discourse structure that tends to give short summaries of the most important facts and entities in the opening paragraphs. (iii) it compares entity frequency to the frequency of its co-occurring mentions as the weight of an entity appearing in a specific paragraph, normalized by the sum of the frequencies of other entities in $\varphi(n)$.

$$\Phi(e,n) = \frac{|p(e,n)|}{|p(n)|} \sum_{p \in p(n)} \left(\frac{tf(e,p)}{\sum\limits_{e' \neq e} tf(e',p)} \right)^{\frac{1}{p}} \tag{3}$$

where, p represents a news paragraph from n, and with $p(n)$ we indicate the set of all paragraphs in n. The frequency of e in a paragraph p is denoted by $tf(e,p)$. With $|p(e,n)|$ and $|p(n)|$ we indicate the number of paragraphs in which entity e occurs, and the total number of paragraphs, respectively.

4.1.2 Authority-based features

Relative Authority. In this case, we consider the comparative relevance of the news article to the different entities occurring in it. As an example, let us consider the meeting of the Sudanese bishop *Elias Taban*[4] with *Hillary Clinton*[5]. Both entities are salient for the meeting. However, in Taban's Wikipedia page, this meeting is discussed prominently with a corresponding news reference[6], whereas in Hillary Clinton's Wikipedia page it is not reported at all. We believe this is not just an omission in Clinton's page but mirrors the fact that for the lesser known Taban the meeting is big news whereas for the more famous Clinton these kind of meetings are a regular occurrence, not all of which can be reported in what is supposed to be a selection of the most important events for her. Therefore, if two entities co-occur, the news is more relevant for the entity with the lower a priori authority.

The *a priori authority* of an entity (denoted by $\Gamma(e)$) can be measured in several ways. We opt for two approaches: (i) probability of entity e occurring in the corpus $\mathbf{N}$, and (ii) authority assessed through centrality measures like PageRank [16]. For the second case we construct the graph $G = (V,E)$ consisting of entities in $\mathbf{E}$ and news articles in $\mathbf{N}$ as *vertices*. The *edges* are established between n and entities in $\varphi(n)$, that is $\langle n \rightarrow \varphi(n) \rangle$, and the out-links from e, that is $\langle e \rightarrow \gamma(s_(t-1)) \rangle$ (arrows present the *edge* direction).

Starting from a priori authority, we proceed to *relative authority* by comparing the a priori authority of co-occurring entities in $\varphi(n)$. We define the *relative authority* of e as the proportion of co-occurring entities $e' \in \varphi(n)$ that have a higher a priori authority than e (see Equation 4.

$$\hat{\Gamma}(e|\varphi(n)) = \frac{1}{|\varphi(n)|} \sum_{e' \in \varphi(n)} \mathbb{1}_{\Gamma(e') > \Gamma(e)} \tag{4}$$

As we might run the danger of not suggesting any news articles for entities with very high a priori authority (such as Clinton) due to the strict inequality constraint, we can relax the constraint such that the authority of co-occurring entities is above a certain threshold.

[3] This is why people occurring infrequently in the news keep any press cutting mentioning them.

[4] `http://en.wikipedia.org/wiki/Elias_Taban`

[5] `http://en.wikipedia.org/wiki/Hillary_Clinton`

[6] `http://tinyurl.com/mshf7j2`

News Domain Authority. The news domain authority addresses two main aspects. Firstly, if bundled together with the *relative authority* feature, we can ensure that dependent on the entity authority, we suggest news from authoritative sources, hence ensuring the quality of suggested articles. The second aspect is in a news streaming scenario where multiple news domains report the same event — ideally only articles coming from authoritative sources would fulfill the conditions for the news suggestion task.

The *news domain* authority is computed based on the number of news references in Wikipedia coming from a particular *news domain* D. This represents a simple prior that a news article n is from domain D in corpus $\mathbf{N}$. We extract the domains by taking the base URLs from the news article URLs.

4.1.3 Novelty-based features

An important feature when suggesting an article n to an entity e is the *novelty* of n w.r.t the already existing entity profile $S_e(t-1)$. Studies [3] have shown that on comparable collections to ours (TREC GOV2) the number of duplicates can go up to 17%. This figure is likely higher for major events concerning highly authoritative entities on which all news media will report.

Given an entity e and the already added news references $N_{t-1} = \{n_1, \ldots, n_k\}$ up to year $t-1$, the *novelty* of n_{k+1} at year t is measured by the KL divergence between the language model of n_{k+1} and articles in N_{t-1}. We combine this measure with the *entity* overlap of n_{k+1} and $n' \in N_{t-1}$. The *novelty* value of n_{k+1} is given by the minimal divergence value. Low scores indicate low novelty for the entity profile $S_e(t)$.

$$\mathcal{N}(n|e) = \min_{n' \in N_{t-1}} \{\lambda \cdot D_{KL}\left(\theta(n')||\theta(n)\right) + (1-\lambda) \cdot jaccard\left(\varphi(n'), \varphi(n)\right)\} \quad (5)$$

where D_{KL} is the KL divergence of the language models ($\theta(n)$ and $\theta(n')$), whereas λ is the mixing weight ($\lambda = \{0, \ldots, 1\}$) between the language models D_{KL} and the entity overlap in n and n'.

4.2 Article–Section Placement

We model the *ASP* placement task as a successor of the *AEP* task. For all the *'relevant'* news entity pairs, the task is to determine the correct entity section. Each section in a Wikipedia entity page represents a different topic. For example, *Barack Obama* has the sections *'Early Life'*, *'Presidency'*, *'Family and Personal Life'* etc. However, many entity pages have an incomplete section structure. Incomplete or missing sections are due to two Wikipedia properties. First, long-tail entities miss information and sections due to their lack of popularity. Second, for all entities whether popular or not, certain sections might occur for the first time due to real world developments. As an example, the entity *Germanwings* did not have an *'Accidents'* section before this year's disaster, which was the first in the history of the airline.

Even if sections are missing for certain entities, similar sections usually occur in other entities of the same class (e.g. other airlines had disasters and therefore their pages have an accidents section). We exploit such homogeneity of section structure and construct templates that we use to expand entity profiles. The learning objective for $\mathcal{F}_s$ takes into account the following properties:

1. **Section-templates:** account for incomplete section structure for an entity profile $S_e(t)$ by constructing section templates $\widehat{S}_c$ from an entity class c
2. **Overall fit:** measures the overall fit of a news article to sections in the section templates $\widehat{S}_c$

4.2.1 Section-Template Generation

Given the fact that *entity profiles* are often incomplete, we construct *section templates* for every *entity class*. We group entities based on their class c and construct *section templates* $\widehat{S}_c$. For different entity classes, e.g. `Person` and `Location`, the section structure and the information represented in those section varies heavily. Therefore, the section templates are with respect to the individual classes in our experimental setup (see Figure 3).

$$\widehat{S}_c = \{s_1, \ldots, s_k\}, \forall S_e(t) \in \mathbf{E} \wedge e \texttt{ typeOf } c \quad (6)$$

Generating *section templates* has two main advantages. Firstly, by considering class-based profiles, we can overcome the problem of incomplete individual entity profiles and thereby are able to suggest news articles to sections that do not yet exist in a specific entity $S_e(t)$. The second advantage is that we are able to canonicalize the sections, i.e. *'Early Life'* and *'Early Life and Childhood'* would be treated similarly.

To generate the section template $\widehat{S}_c$, we extract all sections from entities of a given type c at year t. Next, we cluster the entity sections, based on an extended version of *k–means* clustering [12], namely *x–means* clustering introduced in Pelleg et al. which estimates the number of clusters efficiently [17]. As a similarity metric we use the cosine similarity computed based on the *tf–idf* models of the sections. Using the *x–means* algorithm we overcome the requirement to provide the number of clusters k beforehand. *x–means* extends the *k–means* algorithm, such that a user only specifies a range $[K_{min}, K_{max}]$ that the number of clusters may reasonably lie in.

4.2.2 News-section fit

The learning objective of $\mathcal{F}_s$ is to determine the overall fit of a news article n to one of the sections in a given section template $\widehat{S}_c$. The template is pre-determined by the class of the entity for which the news is suggested as relevant by $\mathcal{F}_e$. In all cases, we measure how well n fits each of the sections $s \in \widehat{S}_c(t-1)$ as well as the specific entity section $s' \in S_e(t-1)$. The section profiles in $\widehat{S}_c(t-1)$ represent the aggregated entity profiles from all entities of class c at year $t-1$.

To learn $\mathcal{F}_s$ we rely on a variety of features that consider several similarity aspects as shown in Table 2. For the sake of simplicity we do not make the distinction in Table 2 between the individual entity section and class-based section similarities, $s_e(t-1)$ and $s(t-1)$, respectively. Bear in mind that an entity section s_e might be present at year t but not at year $t-1$ (see for more details the discussion on entity profile expansion in Section 6.2.4).

Topic. We use topic similarities to ensure (i) that the content of n fits topic-wise with a specific section text and (ii) that it has a similar topic to previously referred news articles in that section. In a pre-processing stage we compute the topic models for the news articles, entity sections $S_e(t-1)$ and the aggregated class-based sections in $\widehat{S}_c$. The topic models are computed using LDA [5]. We only computed a single topic per article/section as we are only interested in topic term overlaps between article and sections. We distinguish two main features: the first feature measures the overlap of topic terms between n and the entity section $s_e(t-1)$ and $s(t-1) \in \widehat{S}_c$, and the second feature measures the overlap of the topic model of n against referred news articles in N_{t-1} at time $t-1$.

Syntactic. These features represent a mechanism for conveying the importance of a specific text snippet, solely based on the frequency of specific POS tags (i.e. `NNP`, `CD` etc.), as commonly used in text summarization tasks. Following the same intuition as in [18], we weigh the importance of articles by the count of specific

feature type	feature	description
Topic	$jaccard(LDA(n), LDA(s(t-1)))$ $jaccard(LDA(n), N_{t-1})$	Topic similarity between an article n and the (entity) section text, and with already referenced news articles in a given entity section.
Syntactic	$POS - sim$	POS tag overlap (uni/bi/trigrams) between a news article and the section text.
Lexical	$jaccard(title(n), s(t-1))$ $D_{KL}(\theta(p(k)) \| \| \theta(s(t-1)))$ $cos(p(n), s(t-1))$	News title and top–k paragraphs ($k = 1 \ldots 5$) similarity with (entity) section text.
Entity-based	$jaccard(\varphi(n), \gamma(s, t-1))$ $jaccard(\texttt{typeOf}(\varphi(n)), \texttt{typeOf}(\gamma(s(t-1))))$	Entity and entity class overlap between the news article and entities appearing in a specific entity section.
Frequency	`#POS`, `#paragraphs`, $\|n\|$, $\|\varphi(n)\|$ `top-`$k(e)$, `top-`k(`typeOf`(e))	Frequency based features of the different POS tags, number of paragraphs, entities that are found in a news article

Table 2: Feature types used in $\mathscr{F}_s$ for suggesting news articles into the entity sections. We compute the features for all $s \in \widehat{S}_c(t-1)$ as well as $s_e(t-1)$.

POS tags. We expect that for different sections, the importance of POS tags will vary. We measure the similarity of POS tags in a news article against the section text. Additionally, we consider *bi-gram* and *tri-gram* POS tag overlap. This exploits similarity in syntactical patterns between the news and section text.

Lexical. As *lexical* features, we measure the similarity of n against the entity section text $s_e(t-1)$ and the aggregate section text $s(t-1)$. Further, we distinguish between the overall similarity of n and that of the different news paragraphs ($p(n)$ which denotes the paragraphs of n up to the 5th paragraph). A higher similarity on the first paragraphs represents a more confident indicator that n should be suggested to a specific section s. We measure the similarity based on two metrics: (i) the KL-divergence between the computed *language models* and (ii) *cosine* similarity of the corresponding paragraph text $p(n)$ and section text.

Entity-based. Another feature set we consider is the overlap of *named entities* and their corresponding *entity classes*. For different entity sections, we expect to find a particular set of entity classes that will correlate with the section, e.g. '*Early Life*' contains mostly entities related to family, school, universities etc.

Frequency. Finally, we gather statistics about the number of entities, paragraphs, news article length, top–k entities and entity classes, and the frequency of different POS tags. Here we try to capture patterns of articles that are usually cited in specific sections.

5. DATASETS AND PRE-PROCESSING

5.1 Evaluation Plan

In this section we outline the evaluation plan to verify the effectiveness of our learning approaches. To evaluate the news suggestion problem we are faced with two challenges.

- *What comprises the ground truth for such a task ?*
- *How do we construct training and test splits given that entity pages consists of text added at different points in time ?*

Consider the ground truth challenge. Evaluating if an arbitrary news article should be included in Wikipedia is both subjective and difficult for a human if she is not an expert. An invasive approach, which was proposed by Barzilay and Sauper [18], adds content directly to Wikipedia and expects the editors or other users to redact irrelevant content over a period of time. The limitations of such an evaluation technique is that content added to long-tail entities might not be evaluated by informed users or editors in the experiment time frame. It is hard to estimate how much time the added content should be left on the entity page. A more non-invasive approach could involve crowdsourcing of entity and news article pairs in an IR style relevance assessment setup. The problem of such an approach is again finding knowledgeable users or experts for long-tail entities. Thus the notion of *relevance* of a news recommendation is challenging to evaluate in a crowd setup.

We take a slightly different approach by making an assumption that the news articles already present in Wikipedia entity pages are relevant. To this extent, we extract a dataset comprising of all news articles referenced in entity pages (details in Section 5.2). At the expense of not evaluating the space comprising of news articles absent in Wikipedia, we succeed in (i) avoiding restrictive assumptions about the quality of human judgments, (ii) being invasive and polluting Wikipedia, and (iii) deriving a reusable test bed for quicker experimentation.

The second challenge of construction of training and test set separation is slightly easier and is addressed in Section 5.4.

5.2 Datasets

The datasets we use for our experimental evaluation are directly extracted from the Wikipedia entity pages and their revision history. The generated data represents one of the contributions of our paper.[7] The datasets are the following:

Entity Classes. We focus on a manually predetermined set of *entity classes* for which we expect to have news coverage. The number of analyzed *entity classes* is 27, including 73,734 entities with at least one news reference. The *entity classes* were selected from the DBpedia class ontology. Figure 3 shows the number of entities per class for the years (2009-2014).

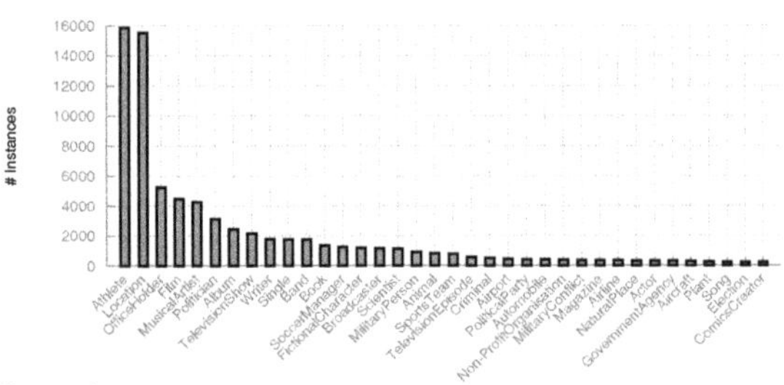

Figure 3: Number of entities with at least one news reference for different entity classes.

News Articles. We extract all news references from the collected Wikipedia entity pages.[8] The extracted news references are associated with the sections in which they appear. In total there were 411,673 news references, and after crawling we end up with 351,982 successfully crawled news articles. The details of the news

[7] `http://l3s.de/~fetahu/cikm2015/data/`

[8] A news reference in Wikipedia is denoted by the template `{cite type='news' | url=''}`

article distribution, and the number of entities and sections from which they are referred are shown in Table 3.

year	#news	#entities	#sections
2009	42707	13550	3510
2010	78328	24953	8416
2011	73491	23144	6581
2012	81473	25980	8455
2013	69079	22121	8183
2014	29961	11088	4694

Table 3: News articles, entities and sections distribution across years.

Article-Entity Ground-truth. The dataset comprises of the news and entity pairs $\langle n,e\rangle \rightarrow \{0,1\}$. News-entity pairs are relevant if the news article is referenced in the entity page. Non-relevant pairs (i.e. negative training examples) consist of news articles that contain an entity but are not referenced in that entity's page. If a news article n is referred from e at year t, the features are computed taking into account the entity profiles at year $S_e(t-1)$.

Article-Section Ground-truth. The dataset consists of the triple $\langle n,e,s\rangle$, where $s \in \widehat{S_c}$, where we assume that $\langle n,e\rangle$ has already been determined as relevant. We therefore have a multi-class classification problem where we need to determine the section of e where n is cited. Similar to the *article-entity* ground truth, here too the features compute the similarity between n, $S_e(t-1)$ and $\widehat{S_c}(t-1)$.

5.3 Data Pre-Processing

We POS-tag the news articles and entity profiles $S_e(t)$ with the Stanford tagger [22]. For entity linking the news articles, we use TagMe![9] with a confidence score of 0.3. On a manual inspection of a random sample of 1000 disambiguated entities, the accuracy is above 0.9. On average, the number of entities per news article is approximately 30. For entity linking the entity profiles, we simply follow the *anchor* text that refers to Wikipedia entities.

5.4 Train and Testing Evaluation Setup

We evaluate the generated supervised models for the two tasks, *AEP* and *ASP*, by splitting the train and testing instances. It is important to note that for the pairs $\langle n,e\rangle$ and the triple $\langle n,e,\widehat{S_c}\rangle$, the news article n is referenced at time t by entity e, while the features take into account the entity profile at time $t-1$. This avoids any 'overlapping' content between the news article and the entity page, which could affect the learning task of the functions $\mathscr{F}_e$ and $\mathscr{F}_s$. Table 4 shows the statistics of train and test instances. We learn the functions at year t and test on instances for the years greater than t. Please note that we do not show the performance for year 2014 as we do not have data for 2015 for evaluation.

	$\mathscr{F}_e$		$\mathscr{F}_s$	
	train	test	train	test
2009	74,005	469,386	19,399	218,757
2010	190,409	382,085	70,486	167,670
2011	286,588	292,398	115,286	122,870
2012	386,647	177,755	170,682	67,474
2013	471,209	59,172	218,538	19,618

Table 4: Number of instances for train and test in the *AEP* and *ASP* tasks.

6. RESULTS AND DISCUSSION

6.1 Article–Entity Placement

Here we introduce the evaluation setup and analyze the results for the *article–entity (AEP)* placement task. We only report the evaluation metrics for the *'relevant'* news-entity pairs. A detailed explanation on why we focus on the *'relevant'* pairs is provided in Section 4.1.

6.1.1 Evaluation Setup

Baselines. We consider the following baselines for this task.

- **B1.** The first baseline uses only the salience-based features by Dunietz and Gillick [8].
- **B2.** The second baseline assigns the value *relevant* to a pair $\langle n,e\rangle$, if and only if e appears in the title of n.

Learning Models. We use *Random Forests* (RF) [6].[9] We learn the RF on all computed features in Table 1. The optimization on RF is done by splitting the feature space into multiple trees that are considered as ensemble classifiers. Consequently, for each classifier it computes the margin function as a measure of the average count of predicting the correct class in contrast to any other class. The higher the margin score the more robust the model.

Metrics. We compute *precision* P, *recall* R and F1 score for the *relevant* class. For example, precision is the number of news-entity pairs we correctly labeled as relevant compared to our ground truth divided by the number of all news-entity pairs we labeled as relevant.

6.1.2 Approach Effectiveness

The following results measure the effectiveness of our approach in three main aspects: (i) overall *performance* of $\mathscr{F}_e$ and comparison to baselines, (ii) *robustness* across the years, and (iii) *optimal* model for the *AEP* placement task.

Performance. Figure 4 shows the results for the years 2009 and 2013, where we optimized the learning objective with instances from year t and evaluate on the years $t_i > t$ (see Section 5.4).[10] The results show the *precision–recall* curve. The *red* curve shows baseline **B1** [8], and the *blue* one shows the performance of $\mathscr{F}_e$. The curve shows for varying *confidence scores* (high to low) the precision on labeling the pair $\langle e,n\rangle$ as *'relevant'*. In addition, at each *confidence score* we can compute the corresponding recall for the *'relevant'* label. For high confidence scores on labeling the news-entity pairs, the baseline **B1** achieves on average a precision score of P=0.50, while $\mathscr{F}_e$ has P=0.93. We note that with the drop in the confidence score the corresponding precision and recall values drop too, and the overall F1 score for **B1** is around F1=0.2, in contrast we achieve an average score of F1=0.67.

It is evident from Figure 4 that for the years 2009 and 2013, $\mathscr{F}_e$ significantly outperforms the baseline **B1**. We measure the significance through the *t-test* statistic and get a *p-value* of $2.2e-16$. The improvement we achieve over **B1** in absolute numbers, ΔP=+0.5 in terms of precision for the years between 2009 and 2014, and a similar improvement in terms of F1 score. The improvement for recall is Δ R=+0.4. The relative improvement over **B1** for P and F1 is almost 1.8 times better, while for recall we are 3.5 times better. In Table 5 we show the overall scores for the evaluation metrics for **B1** and $\mathscr{F}_e$. Finally, for **B2** we achieve much poorer performance, with average scores of P=0.21, R=0.20 and F1=0.21.

Robustness. In Table 5, we show the overall performance for the years between 2009 and 2013. An interesting observation we make is that we have a very robust performance and the results are stable across the years. If we consider the experimental setup,

[9]Our emphasis in this paper is not a comparison of learning models but of course other classifiers can be used for this task.

[10]We only show the first year 2009 and the last year 2013, since the difference to the other years is marginal.

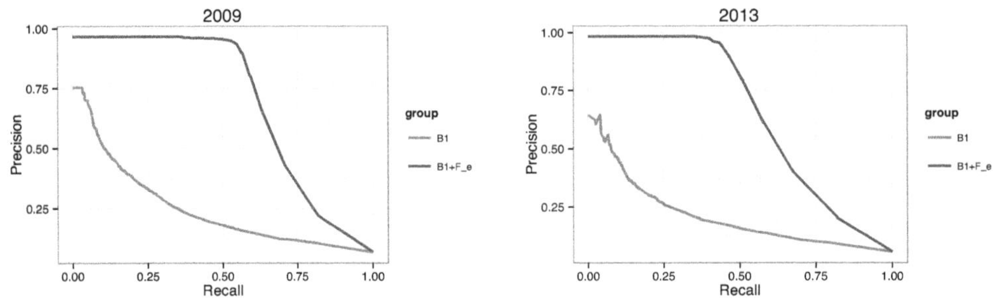

(a) 2009 (b) 2013

Figure 4: Precision-Recall curve for the *article–entity* placement task, in *blue* is shown $\mathscr{F}_e$, and in *red* is the baseline **B1**.

where for year $t = 2009$ we optimize the learning objective with only 74k training instances and evaluate on the rest of the instances, it achieves a very good performance. We predict with F1=0.68 the remaining 469k instances for the years $t \in (2009, 2014]$.

The results are particularly promising considering the fact that the distribution between our two classes is highly skewed. On average the number of *'relevant'* pairs account for only around $4-6\%$ of all pairs. A good indicator to support such a statement is the *kappa* (denoted by κ) statistic. κ measures agreement between the algorithm and the gold standard on both labels while correcting for chance agreement (often expected due to extreme distributions). The κ scores for **B1** across the years is on average 0.19, while for $\mathscr{F}_e$ we achieve a score of 0.65 (the maximum score for κ is 1).

year	P		R		F1	
	B1	$\mathscr{F}_e$	**B1**	$\mathscr{F}_e$	**B1**	$\mathscr{F}_e$
2009	0.450	0.930	0.143	0.550	0.216	0.691
2010	0.503	0.939	0.128	0.540	0.204	0.685
2011	0.475	0.937	0.133	0.520	0.208	0.669
2012	0.476	0.935	0.110	0.515	0.177	0.664
2013	0.407	0.939	0.116	0.445	0.181	0.674

Table 5: *Article–Entity* placement task performance.

6.1.3 *Feature Analysis*

In Figure 5 we show the impact of the individual feature groups that contribute to the superior performance in comparison to the baselines. *Relative entity frequency* from the *salience* feature, models the entity salience as an exponentially decaying function based on the positional index of the paragraph where the entity appears. The performance of $\mathscr{F}_e$ with *relative entity frequency* from the *salience* feature group is close to that of all the features combined. The *authority* and *novelty* features account to a further improvement in terms of precision, by adding roughly a 7%-10% increase. However, if both feature groups are considered separately, they significantly outperform the baseline **B1**.

6.2 Article-Section Placement

Here we show the evaluation setup for *ASP* task and discuss the results with a focus on three main aspects, (i) the overall performance across the years, (ii) the *entity class* specific performance, and (iii) the impact on *entity profile* expansion by suggesting missing sections to entities based on the pre-computed templates.

6.2.1 *Evaluation Setup*

Baselines. To the best of our knowledge, we are not aware of any comparable approach for this task. Therefore, the baselines we consider are the following:

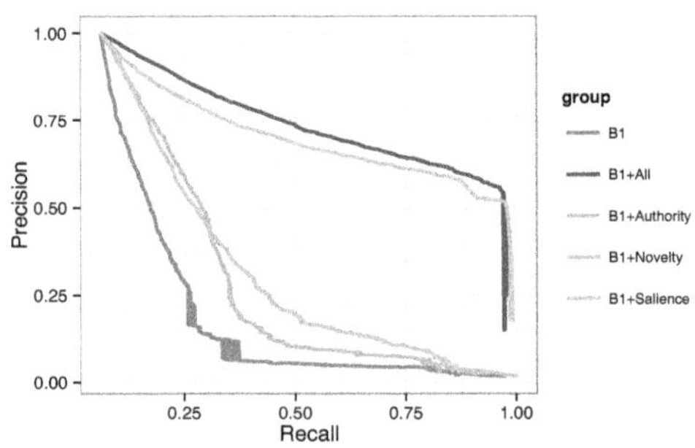

Figure 5: Feature analysis for the *AEP* placement task for $t = 2009$.

- **S1**: Pick the section from template $\widehat{S}_c$ with the highest lexical similarity to n: **S1**= $\text{argmax}_{s \in \widehat{S}_c(t-1)} \langle n, e, s \rangle$
- **S2**: Place the news into the most frequent section in $\widehat{S}_c$

Learning Models. We use *Random Forests* (RF) [6] and *Support Vector Machines* (SVM) [7]. The models are optimized taking into account the features in Table 2. In contrast to the *AEP* task, here the scale of the number of instances allows us to learn the SVM models. The SVM model is optimized using the $\varepsilon - SVR$ *loss* function and uses the *Gaussian* kernels.

Metrics. We compute *precision* P as the ratio of news for which we pick a section s from $\widehat{S}_c$ and s conforms to the one in our ground-truth (see Section 5.2). The definition of *recall* R and F1 score follows from that of precision.

6.2.2 *Overall Article-Section Performance*

Figure 6 shows the overall performance and a comparison of our approach (when $\mathscr{F}_s$ is optimized using SVM) against the best performing baseline **S2**. With the increase in the number of training instances for the *ASP* task the performance is a monotonically non-decreasing function. For the year 2009, we optimize the learning objective of $\mathscr{F}_s$ with around 8% of the total instances, and evaluate on the rest. The performance on average is around P=0.66 across all classes. Even though for many classes the performance is already stable (as we will see in the next section), for some classes we improve further. If we take into account the years between 2010 and 2012, we have an increase of ΔP=0.17, with around 70% of instances used for training and the remainder for evaluation. For the remaining years the total improvement is ΔP=0.18 in contrast to the performance at year 2009.

On the other hand, the baseline **S1** has an average precision of P=0.12. The performance across the years varies slightly, with the year 2011 having the highest average precision of P=0.13. Always picking the most frequent section as in **S2**, as shown in Figure 6, results in an average precision of P=0.17, with a uniform distribution across the years.

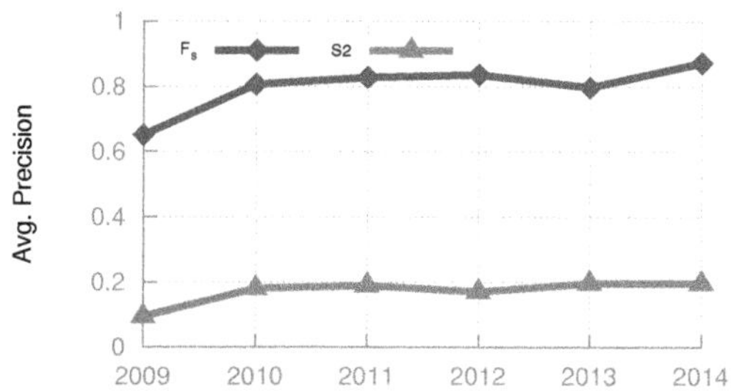

Figure 6: *Article-Section* performance averaged for all entity classes for $\mathscr{F}_s$ (using SVM) and **S2**.

6.2.3 *Article-Section Performance per Entity Class*

Here we show the performance of $\mathscr{F}_s$ decomposed for the different entity classes. Specifically we analyze the 27 classes in Figure 3. In Table 6, we show the results for a range of years (we omit showing all years due to space constraints). For illustration purposes only, we group them into four main classes ({ `Person`, `Organization`, `Location`, `Event`}) and into the specific sub-classes shown in the second column in Table 6. For instance, the entity classes `OfficeHolder` and `Politician` are aggregated into `Person–Politics`.

It is evident that in the first year the performance is lower in contrast to the later years. This is due to the fact that as we proceed, we can better generalize and accurately determine the correct *fit* of an article n into one of the sections from the pre-computed *templates* $\widehat{S_c}$. The results are already stable for the year range (2009,2012]. For a few `Person` sub-classes, e.g. `Politics`, `Entertainment`, we achieve an F1 score above 0.9. These additionally represent classes with a sufficient number of training instances for the years [2009,2012]. The lowest F1 score is for the `Criminal` and `Television` classes. However, this is directly correlated with the insufficient number of instances.

The baseline approaches for the *ASP* task perform poorly. **S1**, based on *lexical similarity*, has a varying performance for different entity classes. The best performance is achieved for the class `Person - Politics`, with P=0.43. This highlights the importance of our feature choice and that the *ASP* cannot be considered as a *linear function*, where the maximum similarity yields the best results. For different entity classes different features and combination of features is necessary. Considering that **S2** is the overall best performing baseline, through our approach $\mathscr{F}_s$ we have a significant improvement of over ΔP=+0.64.

The models we learn are very robust and obtain high accuracy, fulfilling our pre-condition for accurate news suggestions into the entity sections. We measure the robustness of $\mathscr{F}_s$ through the κ statistic. In this case, we have a model with roughly 10 labels (corresponding to the number of sections in a template $\widehat{S_c}$). The score we achieve shows that our model predicts with high confidence with $\kappa = 0.64$.

6.2.4 *Entity Profile Expansion*

The last analysis is the impact we have on *expanding* entity profiles $S_e(t)$ with new sections. Figure 7 shows the ratio of sections for which we correctly suggest an article n to the right section in the section template $\widehat{S_c}(t)$. The ratio here corresponds to sections that are not present in the entity profile at year $t-1$, that is $s \notin S_e(t-1)$. However, given the generated templates $\widehat{S_c}(t-1)$, we can expand the entity profile $S_e(t-1)$ with a new section at time t. In details, in the absence of a section at time t, our model trains well on similar sections from the section template $\widehat{S_c}(t-1)$, hence we can predict accurately the section and in this case suggest its addition to the entity profile. With time, it is obvious that the expansion rate decreases at later years as the entity profiles become more 'complete'.

This is particularly interesting for expanding the entity profiles of long-tail entities as well as updating entities with real-world emerging events that are added constantly. In many cases such missing sections are present at one of the entities of the respective entity class c. An obvious case is the example taken in Section 4.1, where the *'Accidents'* is rather common for entities of type `Airline`. However, it is non-existent for some specific entity instances, i.e *Germanwings* airline.

Through our *ASP* approach $\mathscr{F}_s$, we are able to expand both *long-tail* and *trunk* entities. We distinguish between the two types of entities by simply measuring their section text length. The real distribution in the ground truth (see Section 5.2) is 27% and 73% are *long-tail* and *trunk* entities, respectively. We are able to expand the entity profiles for both cases and all entity classes without a significant difference, with the only exception being the class `Creative Work`, where we expand significantly more *trunk* entities.

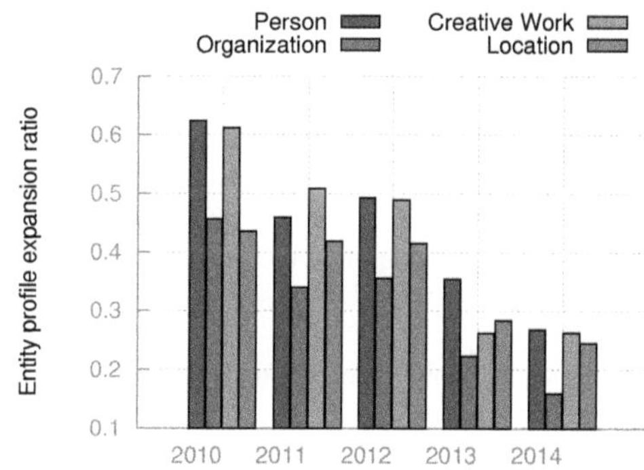

Figure 7: Correctly suggested news articles for $s \in S_e(t) \wedge s \notin S_e(t-1)$.

7. CONCLUSION AND FUTURE WORK

In this work, we have proposed an automated approach for the novel task of suggesting news articles to Wikipedia entity pages to facilitate Wikipedia updating. The process consists of two stages. In the first stage, *article–entity* placement, we suggest news articles to entity pages by considering three main factors, such as *entity salience* in a news article, *relative authority* and *novelty* of news articles for an entity page. In the second stage, *article–section* placement, we determine the best fitting section in an entity page. Here, we remedy the problem of incomplete entity section profiles by constructing section templates for specific entity classes. This allows us to add missing sections to entity pages. We carry out an extensive experimental evaluation on 351,983 news articles and 73,734 entities coming from 27 distinct entity classes. For the first stage, we achieve an overall performance with P=0.93, R=0.514 and F1=0.676, outperforming our baseline competitors significantly. For the second stage, we show that we can learn incrementally to determine the correct section for a news article based on section templates. The overall performance across different classes is P=0.844, R=0.885 and F1=0.860.

In the future, we will enhance our work by extracting facts from the suggested news articles. Results suggest that the news content

Entity class	Sub-Class	2009			(2009,2012]			(2012,2014]		
		P	R	F1	P	R	F1	P	R	F1
Person	Entertainment	0.737	0.815	0.764	0.912	0.941	0.923	0.963	0.976	0.969
	Politics	0.916	0.943	0.930	0.923	0.948	0.933	0.936	0.958	0.946
	Scientists	0.467	0.681	0.554	0.890	0.940	0.914	0.931	0.951	0.938
	Sports	0.820	0.872	0.836	0.868	0.912	0.885	0.929	0.955	0.941
	Military	0.688	0.779	0.721	0.842	0.908	0.871	0.882	0.928	0.903
	Criminal	0.647	0.764	0.682	0.758	0.704	0.698	0.693	0.816	0.743
Organization	Organization	0.567	0.649	0.586	0.794	0.855	0.817	0.832	0.869	0.843
Creative Work	Television	0.528	0.650	0.563	0.745	0.732	0.709	0.732	0.772	0.745
	Music	0.598	0.620	0.591	0.860	0.748	0.762	0.897	0.936	0.914
	Written Work	0.657	0.765	0.695	0.733	0.829	0.772	0.722	0.791	0.743
Location	Location	0.781	0.763	0.715	0.857	0.898	0.872	0.922	0.956	0.938
Event	Event	0.560	0.682	0.611	0.858	0.865	0.853	0.693	0.716	0.694
	average	0.663	0.748	0.687	0.836	0.856	0.834	0.844	0.885	0.860

Table 6: *Article-Section* placement performance (with $\mathscr{F}_s$ learned through SVM) for the different *entity classes*. The results show the standard **P/R/F1**.

cited in entity pages comes from the first paragraphs. However, challenging task such as the canonicalization and chronological ordering of facts, still remain.

Acknowledgements. This work is funded by the ERC Advanced Grant ALEXANDRIA (grant no. 339233).

8. REFERENCES

[1] K. Balog and H. Ramampiaro. Cumulative citation recommendation: classification vs. ranking. In *36th ACM SIGIR, Dublin, Ireland, 2013*, pages 941–944.

[2] K. Balog, H. Ramampiaro, N. Takhirov, and K. Nørvåg. Multi-step classification approaches to cumulative citation recommendation. In *OAIR, Lisbon, Portugal, 2013*, pages 121–128.

[3] Y. Bernstein and J. Zobel. Redundant documents and search effectiveness. In *14th ACM CIKM*, pages 736–743, New York, USA, 2005.

[4] C. Bizer, J. Lehmann, G. Kobilarov, S. Auer, C. Becker, R. Cyganiak, and S. Hellmann. DBpedia - a crystallization point for the web of data. *J. Web Sem.*, 7(3), Sept. 2009.

[5] D. M. Blei, A. Y. Ng, and M. I. Jordan. Latent dirichlet allocation. *J. Mach. Learn. Res.*, 3:993–1022, Mar. 2003.

[6] L. Breiman. Random forests. *Machine Learning*, 45(1):5–32, 2001.

[7] C.-C. Chang and C.-J. Lin. Libsvm: a library for support vector machines. *ACM TIST*, 2(3):27, 2011.

[8] J. Dunietz and D. Gillick. A new entity salience task with millions of training examples. In *14th EACL, Gothenburg, Sweden*, pages 205–209, 2014.

[9] P. Ferragina and U. Scaiella. Fast and accurate annotation of short texts with wikipedia pages. *IEEE Software*, 29(1):70–75, 2012.

[10] B. Fetahu, A. Anand, and A. Anand. How much is wikipedia lagging behind news? In *WebSci '15, Oxford, UK*, 2015.

[11] J. Hoffart, M. A. Yosef, I. Bordino, H. Fürstenau, M. Pinkal, M. Spaniol, B. Taneva, S. Thater, and G. Weikum. Robust disambiguation of named entities in text. In *2011 EMNLP*, Stroudsburg, PA, USA, 2011.

[12] T. Kanungo, D. M. Mount, N. S. Netanyahu, C. D. Piatko, R. Silverman, and A. Y. Wu. An efficient k-means clustering algorithm: Analysis and implementation. *IEEE Trans. Pattern Anal. Mach. Intell.*, 24(7):881–892, 2002.

[13] R. Kaptein, P. Serdyukov, A. De Vries, and J. Kamps. Entity ranking using wikipedia as a pivot. In *19th ACM CIKM*, New York, USA, 2010.

[14] M. Mintz, S. Bills, R. Snow, and D. Jurafsky. Distant supervision for relation extraction without labeled data. In *47th ACL and the 4th AFNLP*, pages 1003–1011, Stroudsburg, PA, USA, 2009.

[15] V. Ng. Supervised noun phrase coreference research: The first fifteen years. In *48th ACL, 2010, Uppsala, Sweden*, pages 1396–1411.

[16] L. Page, S. Brin, R. Motwani, and T. Winograd. The pagerank citation ranking: Bringing order to the web. 1999.

[17] D. Pelleg, A. W. Moore, et al. X-means: Extending k-means with efficient estimation of the number of clusters. In *ICML*, pages 727–734, 2000.

[18] C. Sauper and R. Barzilay. Automatically generating wikipedia articles: A structure-aware approach. In *47th ACL, 2009, Singapore*, pages 208–216.

[19] F. M. Suchanek, G. Kasneci, and G. Weikum. Yago: A core of semantic knowledge. In *16th WWW*, New York, USA, 2007.

[20] M. Surdeanu, D. McClosky, J. Tibshirani, J. Bauer, A. X. Chang, V. I. Spitkovsky, and C. D. Manning. A simple distant supervision approach for the tac-kbp slot filling task. In *Text Analysis Conference 2010 Workshop*.

[21] B. Taneva and G. Weikum. Gem-based entity-knowledge maintenance. In *22nd ACM CIKM*, pages 149–158, New York, USA, 2013.

[22] K. Toutanova, D. Klein, C. D. Manning, and Y. Singer. Feature-rich part-of-speech tagging with a cyclic dependency network. In *NAACL*, pages 173–180, Stroudsburg, USA, 2003.

[23] M. A. Walker, A. K. Joshi, and E. F. Prince. *Centering theory in discourse*. Oxford University Press, 1998.

[24] P. Wang and C. Domeniconi. Building semantic kernels for text classification using wikipedia. In *14th ACM SIGKDD*, New York, USA, 2008.

[25] R. West, E. Gabrilovich, K. Murphy, S. Sun, R. Gupta, and D. Lin. Knowledge base completion via search-based question answering. In *23rd WWW, Seoul, Korea*, pages 515–526, 2014.

Mining Coordinated Intent Representation for Entity Search and Recommendation

Huizhong Duan
WalmartLabs
860 W California Ave, Sunnyvale CA 94086
hduan@walmartlabs.com

ChengXiang Zhai
University of Illinois at Urbana-Champaign
201 N Goodwin Ave, Urbana, IL 61801
czhai@illinois.edu

ABSTRACT

We study the problem of learning query intent representation for an entity search task such as product retrieval, where a user would use a keyword query to retrieve entities based on their structured attribute value descriptions. Existing intent representation has been mostly based on the query space. These methods overlook the critical information from the entity space and the connection in between. Consequently, when such representation methods are used in intent mining from user engagement logs in entity search, they cannot fully discover the comprehensive knowledge of user preference, which is essential for improving the effectiveness of entity search and recommendation, as well as many applications such as business intelligence.

To address this problem, we propose a novel Coordinated Intent Representation, where each user intent is represented collectively in both the query space and the entity space. Specifically, a coordinated intent representation consists of a language model to capture typical query terms used for search and a series of probabilistic distributions on entity attributes and attribute values to characterize the preferred features of entities for the corresponding intent. We propose a novel generative model to discover coordinated intent representations from the entity search logs. Evaluation in the domain of product search shows that the proposed model is effective for discovering meaningful coordinated shopping intents, and the discovered intent representation can be directly used for improving the accuracy of product search and recommendation.

Categories and Subject Descriptors

H.2.8 [**DATABASE MANAGEMENT**]: Database applications—*Data mining*; H.3.3 [**INFORMATION STORAGE AND RETRIEVAL**]: Information Search and Retrieval

General Terms

Algorithms, Performance, Experimentation

CIKM'15, October 19–23, 2015, Melbourne, Australia.
© 2015 ACM. ISBN 978-1-4503-3794-6/15/10 ...$15.00.
DOI: http://dx.doi.org/10.1145/2806416.2806557.

Keywords

Intent representation; intent mining; product search; product recommendation; coordinated representation; joint mixture model

1. INTRODUCTION

In many application domains, there is a need to rank entities in a database in response to a preference keyword query, which we refer to as entity search. Often times, the databases of entities are naturally available as in the case of product search or medical record search, where detailed descriptions of entities are manually added to a database with clearly defined attributes. A database of entities can also be constructed automatically or semi-automatically by using information extraction techniques to extract entities and their attribute values from unstructured text data; for example, genes, along with their regulation relations and associated species, can be automatically extracted from biology literature. In the most general setting, databases of entities may be formed by merging manually created databases with automatically extracted structured data.

Such databases are very different from the traditional transactional databases in that the application needs are dramatically different. Particularly, in entity datases, there is a need for supporting keyword queries to help users find relevant items by providing a ranked list of entities in descending order of likelihood of matching the user's query. A good example of such application system is product search engine for e-commerce, which is an integral and indispensable part of e-commerce websites such as *walmart.com*[1], *amazon.com*[2] and *ebay.com*[3]. These product search engines answer a gigantic volume of queries every day and are essential for people who shop online. Naturally, their accuracy affects the productivity and quality of our lives.

While general Web search has been studied extensively, research on entity search (as we defined) has just started with only a few studies [7, 8], which have mainly focused on developing effective probabilistic retrieval models. As in all search engines and recommender systems, understanding users' search intent is of critical importance and largely determines the accuracy of the application. For example, in product search, users' search intents directly relate to their purchasing activities. Rather than having an information need as in the case of Web search, a user's product search intent primarily reveals his/her shopping preferences. Clearly, understanding such preferences is very useful for optimizing the product search and recommendation accuracy. In this paper, we study how to model and discover users' search intents in an entity search

[1]http://www.walmart.com
[2]http://www.amazon.com
[3]http://www.ebay.com

system and explore applications of the discovered intent models in improving entity search and recommendation.

Intent understanding has been widely studied in the context of document retrieval and Web search. Existing work use predefined taxonomies, automatically determined topics or concepts mined from knowledge base to represent user intents[14]. A major limitation of these methods is that the intent representations are only based on the query space with little or no connection with the entity space. Due to such disconnection, when used in intent mining from user engagement logs in entity search, these methods cannot fully utilize the data and discover the comprehensive user preferences. It is also difficult to leverage such inferred intents to directly improve retrieval accuracy due to the gap between the query space representation and the entity space representation. Although similar issue also exists in traditional document search, the problem is amplified in the entity search scenario, where the concepts in query space do not naturally map into the target entity space, creating a severe vocabulary gap.

To address this problem, we propose a novel Coordinated Intent Representation, where the intent is represented in both the query space and the entity space. Specifically, a coordinated intent representation consists of a language model to characterize the user preferred query terms and a series of probabilistic distributions on entity attributes and attribute values to characterize the preferred entity features for the intent. Each intent is thus "collaboratively" captured in the vocabularies of both the query space and the entity space.

Such a dual-space intent representation is well suited for entity search because we can leverage the structures of entities to obtain another layer of understanding of user intents, which will allow us to drill down to what users actually look for in the target entity space directly, rather than "superficially" understanding the semantic meanings of queries as the current intent representation does. By coordinating the understanding of user intents in both query and entity space, we can achieve a holistic view of intents, which will enable/improve many important analytical tasks.

Further, we stress that compared with existing work on query space intent representation, the proposed coordinated intent representation provides more complete information, which are necessary for disambiguating search intents and are therefore useful for improving the accuracy of entity search. As an illustrating example, Figure 1 shows three users having different purchasing intents in buying laptops. Two users issue the same query "lightweight laptop", but they are looking for different types of products: the first user is looking for an inexpensive lightweight laptop used for web browsing (*Processor=Atom & Price<$250*); the second user is looking for a portable but high performance laptop with more capabilities (*Processor=Core i3*), and price is not the primary concern (*Price>$500*). Yet another user is having a similar preference as the first user (searching for "netbook"), but he/she ended up buying a different laptop. In this example we can see using either query space representation or entity space representation alone would not be sufficient to differentiate the subtle differences among intents.

In the proposed coordinated representation, we capture both query space and entity space with several probabilistic distributions. Specifically, we use an attribute distribution to capture the importance of attributes (e.g. *Processor*), a feature distribution for each attribute to capture user preferences on that attribute (e.g. *Processor=Atom*), and a word distribution to capture users' choice of search terms (e.g. "netbook").

Once we can infer the coordinated intent representation for a query, we can leverage it to improve accuracy of entity search and recommendation. Take product search for example. It is often that users use different keywords to search for similar or same products because their perception and knowledge about the product varies. For instance, the queries "camera stick", "camera pole", "selfie holder", "selfie kit" are used to search for the same type of products. Separately optimizing each query based on text matching is clearly not the ideal solution, especially for a conversion-centric product search engine. On the other hand, different users may also use the same query to search for distinct products. For instance, users with the query "camera kit" may be either looking for tripods, cleaning tools or even camera lens for phones. With a good intent model, we can interpret a query based on the users' potential shopping preferences and rank products based on how likely they can satisfy such preferences. In this way, search queries can be optimized in semantic groups, rather than each individually. As a result, semantic level matching can be achieved. A successful intent model will not only improve search accuracy, but also largely benefit the search experience as a whole. For instance, when the user query is too specific (e.g. directly copied from product titles elsewhere), matching zero or few products, we can provide recommendations based on the inferred intents and/or matching products of the query. On the other hand, when a user query is too broad or ambiguous, we can diversify the results according to the potential user intent, so that representative products of different intents are showed first.

The benefit of understanding and modeling entity search intent goes beyond optimizing search and recommendation. For example, accurate understanding of user's shopping intent provides a platform for multiple business intelligence purposes. Also, a successful intent model would be able to predict the demands of product features, so that we can optimize for inventory and even for manufacture.

To automatically discover coordinated intent representations, we propose a novel joint mixture model to learn such intent representations from entity search logs. The proposed model assumes the following generative process for modeling a user's query and the attribute values of the entities liked by the user simultaneously. First, the user chooses an intent from a mixture of search intent. The user then composes a query according to the word distribution of the chosen intent model. Upon receiving the search results, the user decides which product to engage with by generating the entities by sampling the features on each of its attributes. Particularly, the user first selects an attribute based on the attribute preference distribution, and then samples a value based on the feature value distribution of the attribute. In order to estimate the joint mixture model, we use an expectation-maximization (EM) algorithm to maximize the data likelihood of a search log.

To demonstrate the utility of the proposed coordinated representation, we apply it to product search and empirically evaluate the fitted models on several large domains in online shopping. Examination of representative queries, terms and product features of popular intents in three large online shopping categories show that the proposed method can accurately detect the distinct intents and predict their popularities. Further, we apply the intent model in product search and product recommendation. We show the model can be easily incorporated into the language modeling framework. With the combination of the intent model and the language model, we can achieve significant improvement in search accuracy. When used in recommendation, the intent model enables semantic matching between products even though they may not share the exact same features. Experiment results confirm the effectiveness of our model in both the applications. Although not studied in this paper, the intent model can also be applied to many other related applications such as query suggestion and search result diversification.

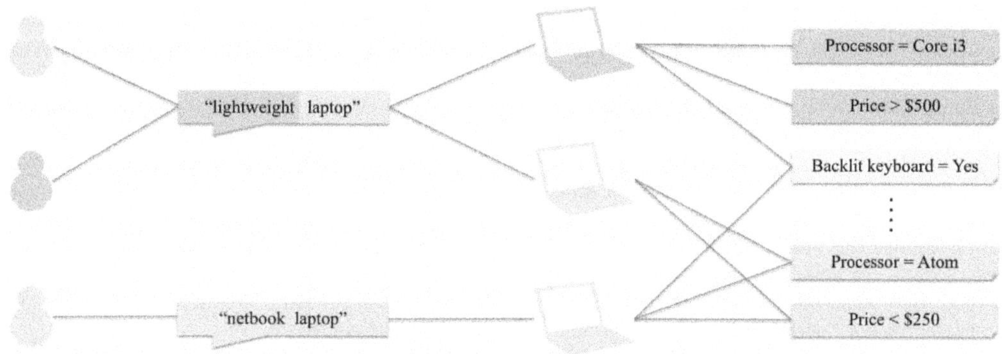

Figure 1: Example of Search Intent

2. RELATED WORK

Intent modeling in search systems has been studied in recent years mostly in the context of document retrieval and Web search. Much work has been done on categorizing search intent into the general stereotypes of navigational, informational and transactional intent [1, 16, 22, 15, 17]. Nguyen et al. propose to capture user intent based on three components including context, interests and preferences [20]. Guo and Agichitein propose to explore mouse movements for enhancing query intent detection [10]. But due to the lack of structure in documents, it is usually difficult to appropriately represent intent, hence difficult to gain insights in intent understanding. Personalization studies user specific intent modeling. Work in this area typically explore the search and browse history of a user in order to obtain a better understanding of the user's preferences [21, 23, 4]. The problem of intent representation and intent discovery in entity search is very different from the existing work on document retrieval. As we have seen in the examples in Section 1, understanding search intent on the text level is not sufficient and leveraging the structure information of entities is critical for successful intent modeling.

Our work also falls into the general category of query log mining. Query log mining has provided opportunities to improve search and many other applications. The data driven methods based on query log mining have been shown to be effective in these applications. Cui et al. mine search logs for query expansion [6]. Zhang and Nasraoui mine search logs for query recommendation [26]. Hassan et al. mine from user behaviors to detect success of search [11]. Our work in terms of query log mining is unique and important in several ways. In particular, we study entity search log, which is very different from ordinary document search log as the data consists of both unstructured and structured data. There has been only few studies on product search log, and no previous work has explored the dual space of queries and entities in entity search log to represent and discover user intent.

Click modeling is a special branch of query log mining and analysis. The goal of click modeling is to extract reliable evidence for relevancy. Early work study how to reduce the position bias from click logs [9, 2, 5]. Hu et al. propose an intent hypothesis to capture the search intent and query formulation bias to complement the existing click models that only consider position and relevance bias [13]. Wang et al. propose a content-aware model of relevance in dealing with click data, where the dependencies among documents are taken into account [24]. In general, click modeling can be the building block for almost all query log analysis. Because the main focus of this work is the modeling of user intent, the discussion of click modeling techniques falls out of the scope of the paper. However, it is clear that these techniques can be incorporated into the proposed intent modeling method and potentially improve the performance. We plan to explore them in our future work.

Our work is also related to applications such as product search and product recommendation, as the discovered intent models can be directly applied to improve these applications. Work has been done to adapt document retrieval models on structured data [3]. It has also been studied in the form of keyword search in databases where the emphasis is on the efficiency and problem of matching keywords across different tables [19]. In this paper, we focus on studying the benefits of intent modeling in product search, which is novel and has not been explored in either area. Duan et al. study the problem of vocabulary gap between user queries and structured product information in product search [7, 8]. Probabilistic retrieval models are proposed to leverage search logs and product reviews, in order to align product features with word descriptors. Although these methods can transform specific query intent into data level representations, they cannot discover and model the popular user intent in product search, which is the research problem we study in this paper.

3. COORDINATED INTENT REPRESENTATION

Understanding a user's search intent is necessary in order to optimize search accuracy. However, it is not immediately clear what is exactly an intent. In some existing work, an intent is characterized by categories (e.g., one intent can be "travel" and another can be "shopping", or even more broader categories such as "navigational" vs. "informational" queries) [1, 15, 18]. Such a coarse representation is clearly insufficient for optimizing the search accuracy for a specific query. In general, the existing work has either not been able to explicitly capture an intent or only represented an intent using the information from the query space. While such kind of representation is natural and meaningful to a certain extent, it has the limitation of being disconnected from the information items, which in our case, are entities in the collection. Such a disconnection creates a gap between the intent representation and the representation of entities, thus making it difficult to directly use the inferred intents to optimize retrieval accuracy.

We observe that in general, a search intent can be viewed from two different perspectives. One perspective is how a user describes an intent, i.e., what kind of query terms the user would likely use to search in order to fulfill the intent. This naturally correlates to a query-space representation. The other perspective is what entities or entity features the user is looking for with such an intent. This leads to an entity-space representation. We argue that a more appropriate and useful representation of search intent should capture an intent in both the query space and the entity space, i.e., obtaining a dual-space intent representation. Based on this idea, we propose a Coordinated Intent Representation for entity search.

Compared with the existing intent representation methods, the coordinated intent representation has three major advantages. First, it bridges the vocabulary gap between a user's query and the entity data. Therefore, the inferred intents of a query can be directly used to optimize entity search results. This is significant for entity search tasks because in entity search, the keywords that users search for do not naturally translate into what entities they are looking for. For example, a user searching for "performance laptop" is actually looking for some specific types of CPUs and/or graphics cards. Second, because such an intent representation is more meaningful and interpretable, it enables interesting analytical applications to provide business intelligence for product manufacturers and answer questions such as what features of products are important to users.

In the following we describe the coordinated intent representation in more detail. We use three distributions to characterize entity search intent. Formally, let I be a set of intent models, let k be the size of I and I_i be the ith intent in I. We have

$$I_i = \{\psi_i, \Gamma_i, \Theta_i\}$$

where ψ_i is a multinomial distribution over search terms W, capturing the importance of each term in describing the intent. For example, given a shopping intent for *portable TV set*, words such as "potable" and "compact" will likely have high probabilities, while words such as "signal" and "wifi" may have relatively low probabilities. $\Gamma_i = \{\gamma_{i,a}|a \in A\}$ is a set of Bernoulli distributions over each attribute a from the entire attribute set A in the entity data. $\gamma_{i,a}$ captures how likely the corresponding attribute a (e.g. *Color*) is concerned in the intent I_i (vs. in the generic intent). A small $\gamma_{i,a}$ value corresponds to a high probability that users want to impose a preference on the attribute, rather than complying with the popular preference. For example, in the *portable TV set* intent, the *Size* attribute will have a very high probability, possibly close to 1, meaning that users have specific requirements on TV size; whereas other attributes like *Refresh Rate* and *Warranty* will have low probabilities, meaning that users do not care much about these properties as long as their values comply with the popular choices. The third parameter Θ_i is a set of multinomial distributions, also defined on the entity attributes. Each $\theta_{i,a} \in \Theta_i$ is a multinomial distribution over possible values of attribute a, capturing the preference on that given attribute. In the same *portable TV set* intent example, on the *Size* attribute, it will have high probabilities on the small sizes such as *Size=10"* and *Size=18"*, and low probabilities on large sizes. In the following, we introduce how such intent models can be automatically discovered from user engagements in entity search logs.

4. JOINT MIXTURE MODEL FOR INTENT DISCOVERY

The coordinated intent representation simultaneously captures a user intent in the dual space, i.e. the query space and entity space. Each intent model encodes comprehensive information to distinguish it from other intents. However, it is no easy task to automatically discover a set of distinct intents, as user intents are not directly observable. In entity search, users are not able to explicitly reveal their search intents. Rather, their intents are embodied in the search activities, which are ambiguous in several ways. On one hand, users with different intents may have overlap behaviors on the choices of search queries and entities they engage with (see example in Figure 1). On the other hand, users with the same intent may as well use semantically the same but verbally quite different queries and examine similar but different entities. To overcome these ambiguities in observation, and to automatically discover the set of popular and distinguishable entity search intent, we propose and explore a generative process, which "produces" the observations of user activities in entity search based on a set of intent models. This is referred to as the joint mixture model. We then propose an EM (Expectation-Maximization) algorithm to infer the underlying intents based on the observed user behaviors by maximizing the likelihood of the data. Below we present the joint mixture model and the EM algorithm.

Notations. For the convenience of discussion, we introduce a set of notations and will use them throughout the rest of the paper. We use E to denote a set of entities. Each entity is represented by a feature vector in a predefined attribute space A. For an entity $e \in E$, its value on attribute $a \in A$ is denoted as $v_{e,a}$. We use S to denote a set of sessions acquired from entity search logs, where each session $s \in S$ consists of a query q_s and a set of engaged entities E_s. Each query q consists of a set of keywords, i.e. $q = \{w|w \in W\}$, where W is the word vocabulary.

Note that our definition of "session" is different from the typical definition of session, as each session contains only one query. The notion here is merely to encapsulate all user behaviors in response to the search results of one query. Conceptualizing user behaviors in this way ensures the assumption that a user's search intent remains invariant during one session.

4.1 Joint Mixture Model

Given an entity search log, We assume a generative process that explains the observations of user behaviors. At the beginning of any session s, the user chooses an intent I_i by sampling from a mixture of intent. Upon choosing an intent, the user will follow the encoded behaviors in its intent model $\{\psi_i, \Gamma_i, \Theta_i\}$ to determine how he/she interacts with the search system. In particular, this will determine the query q_s and the set of entities the user will engage with, i.e. E_s.

More specifically, the user first selects a query q_s by repeatedly sampling a word from the word distribution ψ_i. Note that although a specific intent model has been selected, the user still has the freedom of choice to either select a topic specific word or a more general word from the generic word distribution ψ_G. Then each entity $e \in E_s$ is generated in the following way. On each attribute, the user first decides whether he/she has strong preference on the features of the attribute, as compared to the general popular preference on that attribute. For this the user chooses between the selected intent model I_i and the generic intent model I_G by sampling a binary variable from the Bernoulli distribution $\gamma_{i,a}$. If the intent specific preference is selected, the value $v_{e,a}$ will be generated by the intent model's value distribution $\theta_{i,a}$. Otherwise, it will be sampled from the generic value distribution $\theta_{G,a}$. To further understand this, consider in product search a user is searching for large TV set. Given this intent, the user may have strong preference on certain attributes, such as *TV size* and *Price range*. The user may also have preference on some less obvious attributes, such as *TV technology* as some technology (e.g. LED vs. Plasma) might be more suitable for larger TV sets. These could be very different preferences from the general preferences on TVs and are unique to this intent. Therefore, the Bernoulli distribution γ on these attributes will reflect such preferences by having a higher probability on choosing the intent specific feature distribution. On the other hand, on certain attributes, such as *Warranty*, the users searching for large TV sets do not have a distinguishable preference than users who are searching for TV sets in general. In all cases, users are likely to prefer longer warranty on the product. In this case, this intent model will have a lower probability on selecting the intent specific value distribution, therefore a higher probability selecting the general value distribution on the *Warranty* attribute.

The joint mixture model has many advantages. First, compared with alternative generative processes where users may select intent models to generate queries and entities separately, the proposed joint mixture model generates both queries and all attribute values for the engaged entities using the same intent model. This is consistent with our intuition that user's general intent (e.g. shopping) remains unchanged throughout a single search query. Therefore, it is more likely to produce meaningful intents. Second, because the joint mixture model accounts for both the query and the entities in a user engaged session, the intent models discovered in this way will be coherent and less likely to be affected by users' behavioral ambiguity in choosing queries and engaging with entities. Finally, the joint mixture model utilizes the structure of entities in modeling intent. The feature value generation process is modeled separately on different attributes. Compared to an alternative model which generates the values using an all-in-one distribution similar to generating words, the proposed solution is more consistent with the entity search behaviors. More importantly, it ensures that the estimation of one feature probability will not affect other features on different attributes, i.e. values on different attributes do not need to "fight" for the same probability mass. The intent models is therefore more meaningful and interpretable.

4.2 Model Estimation

To infer the underlying intents from a set of observed sessions S in search log, we follow the generative process of the joint mixture model and maximize the likelihood of the data:

$$\mathcal{L} = \sum_{s \in S} \log \left[\sum_{i=1}^{k} p(I_i|s) \prod_{w \in q_s} \Big((1-\lambda) p(w|\psi_i) + \lambda p(w|\psi_G) \Big) \cdot \prod_{e \in E_s} \prod_{a \in A} \Big((1-\gamma_{i,a}) p(v_{e,a}|\theta_{i,a}) + \gamma_{i,a} p(v_{e,a}|\theta_{G,a}) \Big) \right] \quad (1)$$

To estimate the intent models, we employ an EM algorithm. The algorithm maximizes the likelihood by iteratively applying an expectation step (E-step) and a maximization step (M-step).

In the E-step, the algorithms computes the expectation of the likelihood by inferring the identity variables:

$$p(z_i = 1|s) = \frac{\tilde{p}(z_i = 1|s)}{\sum_{i'=1}^{k} \tilde{p}(z_{i'} = 1|s)} \quad (2)$$

$$p(z_G = 1|s, e, a, I_i) = \frac{\gamma_{i,a} p(v_{e,a}|\theta_{G,a})}{(1-\gamma_{i,a}) p(v_{e,a}|\theta_i) + \gamma_{i,a} p(v_{e,a}|\theta_{G,a})} \quad (3)$$

$$p(\xi_G = 1|s, w, I_i) = \frac{\lambda p(w|\psi_G)}{(1-\lambda) p(w|\psi_i) + \lambda p(w|\psi_G)} \quad (4)$$

where

$$\tilde{p}(z_i = 1|s) = p(I_i|s) \prod_{w \in q_s} \Big((1-\lambda) p(w|\psi_i) + \lambda p(w|\psi_G) \Big) \cdot \prod_{e \in E_s} \prod_{a \in A} \Big((1-\gamma_{i,a}) p(v_{e,a}|\theta_i) + \gamma_{i,a} p(v_{e,a}|\theta_{G,a}) \Big) \quad (5)$$

Here ψ_G is a generic word preference distribution and $\theta_{G,a}$ is a generic value preference distributions on attribute a. Both can be estimated using the entire collection data. z_i, z_G and ξ_G are indicator variables. If $z_i = 1$, the ith intent, i.e. I_i, will be selected. If $z_G = 1$, the generic intent model will be used to generate the feature value; if $z_G = 0$, the selected intent model I_i will be used instead. The same semantic is applied to ξ_G for generating words.

In the M-Step, the algorithm reestimate the model parameters based on the values of the latent variables inferred in the previous iteration:

$$p(v|\theta_{i,a}) = \frac{\sum_{s \in S} \sum_{e \in E_s} \delta(v_{e,a}, v)(1 - p(z_G = 1|s, e, a, I_i)) p(z_i = 1|s)}{\sum_{s \in S} \sum_{e \in E_s} (1 - p(z_G = 1|s, e, a, I_i)) p(z_i = 1|s)} \quad (6)$$

$$\gamma_{i,a} = \frac{\sum_{s \in S} p(z_i = 1|s) \sum_{e \in E_s} p(z_G = 1|s, e, a, I_i)}{\sum_{s \in S} p(z_i = 1|s)|E_s|} \quad (7)$$

$$p(w|\psi_i) = \frac{\sum_{s \in S} c(w, s)(1 - p(\xi_G = 1|s, w, I_i)) p(z_i = 1|s)}{\sum_{w' \in V} \sum_{s \in S} c(w', s)(1 - p(\xi_G = 1|s, w', I_i)) p(z_i = 1|s)} \quad (8)$$

$$p(I_i|s) = p(z_i = 1|s) \quad (9)$$

where $\delta(v_1, v_2)$ is an indicator function assigning value 1 if $v_1 = v_2$, and 0 otherwise.

In the previous discussions, we fix the number of intents to k. In fact, we can determine the number of intent models dynamically by using a relatively large k and eventually combine similar intent models. This can be done by applying a similarity measure on intent models. In this work, we use the KL-Divergence of the word distributions as the similarity function. With this method, we can combine overlapping intents and obtain the final intent set.

5. APPLICATIONS OF COORDINATED INTENT DISCOVERY

Interpretability is one of the advantages of the coordinated intent representation. We will demonstrate this in more details in Section 6.1 where we empirically evaluate the quality of discovered intents. As such it is also clear that the intents discovered from real user activities will largely benefit business related analytical tasks. But beyond these, one primary goal of intent discovery is to reapply it to entity search to optimize the overall search experience. As discussed earlier, this includes a number of applications, such as entity search, entity recommendation, query suggestion, result diversification, etc. In this work, we will demonstrate the utility of intent discovery in optimizing the accuracy of entity search and entity recommendation. We will further explore its utility in other applications in our future work.

5.1 Improving Entity Search Accuracy

Previous work have shown that a good understanding of search intent will improve the accuracy of search. Existing methods utilizing search intent are to augment the search queries using categories and concepts, etc [14]. However, these methods are limited by the incomplete intent representations that emphasizes only the query space. Based on the coordinated intent representation, in this work we propose an intent-based language model for entity search, where each intent is evaluated based on how likely it generates the search query, and entities are ranked according to how likely they are generated from the most suitable intents for the query. The model bridges queries and entities with the intents, and therefore enables semantic matching between terms and entity features.

More specifically, we integrate the discovered intent models with the KL-Divergence language model. In this model, the scoring function is essentially given by the negative KL-Divergence of the query language model and the document language model (entity model in our case):

$$score(q,e) = \sum_{w \in W} p(w|q) \log p(w|e) \tag{10}$$

Without assumption of any feedback data, the query language model is estimated using the query itself. In the regular keyword-based language model, the document language model is typically estimated by the content of the document, and smoothed by the collection language model. In the case of entity search, we can use entity information (i.e. words describing each feature) for estimating the entity language model.

In the intent-based language model, rather than generating query terms directly from the distinct entity space, we first sample an intent from the entity, and then use the intent's word distribution to generate the query. Formally, in the intent-based language model, we reuse the scoring function and redefine $p(w|e)$ as follows:

$$p(w|e) = \sum_{i=1}^{k} p(w|I_i)p(I_i|e) \tag{11}$$

where

$$p(I_i|e) = \frac{p(e|I_i)p(I_i)}{\sum_{j=0}^{k} p(e|I_j)p(I_j)} \tag{12}$$

where

$$p(e|I_i) = \prod_{a \in A} (1 - \gamma_{i,a})p(v_{e,a}|\theta_i) + \gamma_{i,a}p(v_{e,a}|\theta_{G,a}) \tag{13}$$

The intent-based language model avoids the vocabulary problem between queries and entities. Therefore, it can match between what user searches for (the query) and what user is indeed intended for (the target entity). It also constructs an "intent map" of the query, so that results are optimized for the intents, rather than for separate queries. For example, the results of "selfie kit" and "camera stick" will be similar as they are from the same intent.

Despite the advantage of semantic matching, sometimes keyword matching still provides the most reliable evidence of relevance. Because the intent-based language model deemphasized keyword matching, we can complement the effect by combining the regular keyword based language model with it. Given the two separately estimated language models (typical LM and intent model augmented LM), there are two possible ways to combine them. We can either combine them into one probabilistic model, or perform separate rankings and combine the final scores for each item. Interestingly, we find the latter method tend to outperform the former. Therefore in practice we linearly interpolate the two language models and set the interpolation parameter using cross validation.

5.2 Improving Entity Recommendation

Recommending entities based on a given entity is an important application to enrich the overall entity search experience. For instance, product recommendation in online shopping is an important way for users to explore product inventory. To make good recommendations, we need to be able to measure the similarity of two products.

Typically, the similarity can be measured by comparing product features. Products having more overlapping features are deemed to be more relevant. Such a method does not account for the similarities between attributes. For instance, 65 inch TVs are more recommendable if the user is considering a 60 inch TV, as compared to a 40 inch TV. Further, the method does not distinguish the importance of different attributes. A match on TV size is clearly more important than matching on length of warranty. To overcome these issues, a typical solution is to cluster related features. For instance, in a session based clustering method, if two brands are constantly examined together in the same sessions, then products with these brands are more likely to be similar, therefore the brands are clustered and treated as a match.

In this work, we apply the proposed intent model to product recommendation. From Section 6.1 we see that the intent modeling method serves as a principled way to simultaneously cluster query terms and product features. It also naturally provides a similarity measurement for products. Intuitively, if two products can be derived from the same intent model (with high probabilities), they are likely good recommendations for each other. Based on these considerations, we derive the similarity function within the probabilistic framework. Specifically, the similarity of two products e_1 and e_2 are measured by their joint probability:

$$p(e_1, e_2) = \sum_{i=0}^{k} p(e_1|I_i)p(e_2|I_i)p(I_i) \tag{14}$$

where k is the total number of intents we discovered, $p(e|I_i)$ is computed using Equation 13 and $p(I_i)$ is computed using Equation 15. Here we assume the generation of two products is independent from each other given a specific intent I_i.

Because $p(I_i)$ captures the popularity of the intent I_i, the entities matching on more popular intents are more "similar", i.e. more recommendable for each other. The similarity metric can therefore produce more meaningful entity recommendations. We will evaluate the proposed metric with existing methods in more detail in Section 6.3, in the context of product recommendation.

6. EVALUATION

In this section, we apply coordinated intent discovery to the domain of product search, and empirically evaluate its utility, both qualitatively and quantitatively. In particular, we first examine the quality of the discovered intents in three major online shopping domains, and also demonstrate the interpretability of the coordinated intent representation. We then apply the discovered intents to product search and recommendation, to evaluate their effect in improving search experience.

6.1 Automatically Discovered Product Shopping Intent

By fitting the joint mixture model to a product search log, we can automatically discover a set of popular shopping intent in the form of coordinated representation. In this section, we empirically examine the discovered intent models using search engagement logs from *Walmart.com*[4], an established e-commercial website with large search volume. For demonstration we use three large categories in online shopping, "Computer Laptops", "TVs" and "Cameras". We obtain a month's search logs and extract engagements

[4]http://www.walmart.com

Table 1: Corpora statistics

	Laptop	TV	Camera
#Session	9633	25489	10819
#Engagement	35808	97995	42269
#Engagement per session	3.7	3.8	3.9

for the three categories separately by matching the engaged product entities to the corresponding category's database. In total, we have more than 9K sessions for the "Computer Laptops" category with user engagements (each session containing one query), more than 25K sessions for the "TVs" category and more than 10K sessions for the "Cameras" category. On average there are 3.8 engagements per session. The detailed statistics of the corpora are summarized in Table 1.

Obtaining useful information using intent models. The intent models we discover are probabilistic models that contain comprehensive information about search intent. While these raw probability distributions are informative, they can also be used to obtain more interpretable knowledge. In the following, we demonstrate this by computing intent popularity and representative queries, both of which can help us better understand user intent.

Intent popularity. Intent popularity is an important piece of information that can help us draw insights from the discovered intent models. Knowing how likely users have certain intent has clear impact on e-commerce business. Formally, given the ith intent I_i, its popularity is captured by $p(I_i)$, which can be computed by marginalizing over the joint mixture model parameter $p(I_i|s)$:

$$p(I_i) = \sum_{s \in S} p(I_i|s)p(s) \tag{15}$$

Since we don't have any prior knowledge on each session, it is reasonable to assume $p(s)$ is uniformly distributed. $p(I_i)$ reflects the popularity of an intent.

Representative queries. Both the word distribution and the feature distribution in the intent models are very informative, but they can also be used to obtain more directly interpretable information, e.g. representative queries.

There are many ways to select meaningful queries given the intent models. In our case, we prefer queries that are both representative and discriminative. In order to be representative, a query should have high probability being generated from the intent model. Meanwhile, we also want the selected queries to be exclusively generated from the given intent. That is, the query should have low probability being generated by all other intent models. Following this idea, we use the conditional probability $p(I_i|q)$ to rank queries:

$$p(I_i|q) = \frac{p(q|I_i)p(I_i)}{\sum_j p(q|I_j)p(I_j)} \tag{16}$$

where $p(I_i)$ is the intent popularity computed by Equation 15, and $p(q|I_i)$ is the probability of generating query q from the intent model of I_i, which is computed as:

$$p(q|I_i) = \prod_{w \in q} ((1-\gamma)p(w|\psi_i) + \gamma p(w|\psi_B)) \tag{17}$$

Given intent I_i, $p(I_i|q)$ provides a balance between representativeness and discriminativeness. Queries with high $p(I_i|q)$ tend to be meaningful and uniquely characterizing the intent. In this order, we select queries to cover a desired probability mass in the term distribution for each intent.

With this additional information, we summarize the discovered most popular intent models in the categories "Laptop", "TV" and "Camera" in Table 2, Table 3 and Table 4, respectively. For each intent model I_i, we first show the probability $p(I_i)$ as an indication of intent popularity. We then show the representative queries, the top 5 words in ψ_i, the top 5 attributes ranked by $1 - \gamma_{i,a}$, and up to 3 top feature values on each attribute a according to θ_i (values with probabilities smaller than 0.01 are ignored).

Table 2: Top discovered intent models in "Laptop" category

Intent 1. $p(I) = 0.52$		
Queries	laptop bundle	
Words	laptop, computer, bundle, gateway, refurbished	
Features	Type	Bundle
	Processor	Celeron, Core 2 Duo, Core i3
	RAM	2GB, 4GB
	Screen size	11"-14", 17" & larger, 15"-16"
	Brand	Dell, Acer, HP
Intent 2. $p(I) = 0.11$		
Queries	netbook, hp mini, acer netbook, hp netbook, mini laptop	
Words	laptop, netbook, acer, computer, mini	
Features	Processor	Atom
	RAM	1GB, 2GB
	Screen size	10" & under, 11"-14"
	Type	Netbook, Bundle
	Hard Drive	250GB-640GB, 250GB&under
Intent 3. $p(I) = 0.10$		
Queries	pink laptop, sony vaio, sony, sony laptop	
Words	laptop, sony, pink, computer, vaio	
Features	Processor	Core i5, Core i3, Core i7
	Brand	Sony, HP
	Color	White, Silver, Pink
	RAM	8GB, 4GB, 6GB
	Screen size	11"-14", 15"-16", 17"&larger

Judging from the representative queries in Table 2, we can see that the top intent models in "Laptop" category can be interpreted as "laptop bundles" and "netbook laptop", with "laptop bundles" being the most dominating intent. Looking into the words and features, we can see the three intent models are clearly different from each other. The first one is mostly concerned with the "bundle" feature; the second has emphases on a particular type of processor and the size of the laptop; the third intent model prefers high end CPUs and specific brands and colors. From the discovered intent models in the "TV" category, we can see that the user difference is mostly captured by the screen sizes. Different intent models have distinct preferences on the "Price" and the "Screen Size". For "Camera" category, the top 3 intent models are clearly different in the "Type" attribute, each preferring "Point Shoot", "Ultra-zoom" or "DSLR". Each intent also has a unique price range.

Overall, we can see that the proposed intent modeling method can successfully capture the user behavioral difference and generate meaningful intent models as well as interpretable representations. The queries selected based on the proposed query selection procedure can effectively capture the preferences.

6.2 Evaluating Product Search

To evaluate the performance of product search, we created an evaluation set by randomly selecting queries and asking experienced industrial annotators to label the returned products from the search engine into 5 relevance degrees. In total we obtain 96 queries for the "Laptop" category, 146 for "TV" and 98 for the "Camera"

Table 3: Top discovered intent models in "TV" category

Intent 1. $p(I) = 0.21$		
Queries	vizio 47, vizio 47 class, vizio 42 class, vizio 47 class theater, vizio 3d	
Words	tv, vizio, 3d, led, smart	
Features	Price	\$500-\$750, \$250-\$500, \$750-\$1k
	Screen Size	40"-49", 50"-59"
	Resolution	1080p
	Brand	Vizio, LG, RCA
	Refresh	120Hz, 60Hz
Intent 2. $p(I) = 0.18$		
Queries	32 inch tv, 32 tv, pink tv, 32 inch, 32 in tv, 32 class, sceptre	
Words	tv, 32, vizio, inch, lcd	
Features	Price	\$200-\$250, \$250-\$500, \$150-\$200
	Screen Size	30"-39", 21"-29"
	Brand	Sceptre, Vizio, RCA
	Refresh	60Hz
	Technology	LCD, LED
Intent 3. $p(I) = 0.11$		
Queries	19 inch tv, tv with dvd, 19 inch flat screen tv, 22 tv, 22 inch tv, vizio 22	
Words	tv, dvd, vizio,with, combo	
Features	Price	\$100-\$150, \$150-\$200, \$200-\$250
	Screen Size	21"-29", 20"&Smaller, 30"-39"
	Brand	Vizio, RCA, Emerson
	Technology	LED, LCD
	Refresh	60Hz, 120Hz

Table 4: Top discovered intent models in "Camera" category

Intent 1. $p(I) = 0.19$		
Queries	canon powershot, nikon coolpix, point shoot camera	
Words	camera, digital, canon, shoot, point	
Features	Type	Point Shoot, Ultra Zoom
	Price	\$50-\$100, \$100-\$150, \$150-\$200
	Features	Image Stabilization, HD Video, Face Detection
	Optical	2x - 8x, 9x - 18x
	Brand	Canon, Nikon, Samsung
Intent 2. $p(I) = 0.15$		
Queries	ultra-zoom camera, olympus, ge camera	
Words	camera, ultra-zoom, dslr, digital, olympus	
Features	Price	\$150-\$200, \$100-\$150, \$200-\$250
	Type	Ultra Zoom, DSLR, Point Shoot
	Optical	20x & Up, 9x - 18x
	Features	HD Video, Image Stabilization
	Brand	GE, Olympus, Samsung
Intent 3. $p(I) = 0.14$		
Queries	nikon d5100, nikon d3100, nikon d3200, canon t3i, nikon dslr	
Words	nikon, camera, dslr, d5100, d3100	
Features	Price	\$500-\$750, \$250-\$500, \$750-\$1000
	Type	DSLR, Ultra Zoom
	Features	HD Video, Image Stabilization
	Color	Black
	Brand	Nikon, Canon

Table 5: Evaluation of product search

Category	Method	NDCG@3	NDCG@10
Laptop	Base.LM	0.275	0.161
	FB.LM	$0.387^{\dagger}$	$0.222^{\dagger}$
	UInt.LM	$0.383^{\dagger}$	$0.218^{\dagger}$
	Int.LM	$0.390^{\dagger}$	$0.223^{\dagger}$
	Base+Int.LM	$\mathbf{0.409}^{\ddagger}$	$\mathbf{0.240}^{\ddagger}$
TV	Base.LM	0.527	0.366
	FB.LM	$0.640^{\dagger}$	$0.439^{\dagger}$
	UInt.LM	$0.641^{\dagger}$	$0.442^{\dagger}$
	Int.LM	$0.647^{\dagger}$	$0.445^{\dagger}$
	Base+Int.LM	$\mathbf{0.661}^{\ddagger}$	$\mathbf{0.461}^{\ddagger}$
Camera	Base.LM	0.512	0.395
	FB.LM	$0.593^{\dagger}$	$0.463^{\dagger}$
	UInt.LM	$0.588^{\dagger}$	$0.459^{\dagger}$
	Int.LM	$0.597^{\dagger}$	$0.461^{\dagger}$
	Base+Int.LM	$\mathbf{0.607}^{\ddagger}$	$\mathbf{0.477}^{\ddagger}$

category. We evaluate the search systems based on NDCG@3 and NDCG@10.

We show the experiment results on product search accuracy in Table 5. For comparison we implement three baseline systems. The first baseline is a regular KL divergence language model approach, Base.LM, where the product language models are estimated based on the keywords from the product feature descriptions. The second baseline method is language model with relevance feedback (FB.LM). This method is implemented according to Zhai and Lafferty [25]. We include this feedback method as a baseline method because the proposed intent modeling method uses product search logs for estimation, so they are indirectly using relevance feedback information. The third baseline is an unstructured intent model (UInt.LM) wherein we eliminate the use of product structure in estimating search intents. In practice this is achieved by fixing the γ_{ia} to a constant value in the joint mixture model in Section 4 (same as λ). In effect this produces co-clusters of terms-product features. We compare the performance of these three baseline methods with our proposed intent modeling method (Int.LM) and the interpolated model with baseline language model (Base+Int.LM). We perform statistical significant test to compare our methods with Base.LM, FB.LM and Uint.LM. Values showing significant improvement (p-value<0.05) over Base.LM are marked by †. Values showing significant improvement over all three baseline methods are marked by ‡.

From Table 5 we see that all other methods outperform Base.LM. This is expected because these methods use search log data, therefore leveraging the relevance feedback information directly or indirectly. We also observe that Int.LM almost always outperforms the regular feedback method FB.LM. This shows that the intent modeling method is a better way of utilizing user feedback. Through intent modeling, we can generalize the knowledge from feedback information, whereas the existing method FB.LM only use the feedback information for each individual query (i.e. queries with no feedback will not be affected). Compared with UInt.LM, Int.LM has consistent advantages in all three categories. This is because by modeling product feature structures, we can achieve more accurate and representative intent models. Finally, we find that the search accuracy could be further boosted by combining Int.LM with the Base.LM model. While Intent model captures the generalized feedback knowledge, the keyword language model produces more direct evidences for matching against query terms and such

Table 6: Intent similarity vs. topic similarity for product recommendation

Laptop			
Method	Precision	Recall	F1
Feat.Sim	0.131	0.203	0.159
Feat+Clu.Sim	0.126	0.204	0.156
Feat+Int.Sim	0.135	0.202	0.162
TV			
Method	Precision	Recall	F1
Feat.Sim	0.119	0.247	0.162
Feat+Clu.Sim	0.132	0.285	0.181
Feat+Int.Sim	0.147	0.310	0.200
Camera			
Method	Precision	Recall	F1
Feat.Sim	0.138	0.282	0.136
Feat+Clu.Sim	0.141	0.277	0.187
Feat+Int.Sim	0.144	0.299	0.194

Table 7: Intent similarity vs. co-occurrence counting for product recommendation

Laptop			
Method	Precision	Recall	F1
Co.Cnt	0.103	0.195	0.136
Feat+Int.Sim	0.135	0.202	0.162
Feat+Int.Sim+Co.Cnt	**0.166**	**0.272**	**0.207**
TV			
Method	Precision	Recall	F1
Co.Cnt	0.103	0.207	0.138
Feat+Int.Sim	0.147	0.310	0.200
Feat+Int.Sim+Co.Cnt	**0.152**	**0.329**	**0.207**
Camera			
Method	Precision	Recall	F1
Co.Cnt	0.174	0.325	0.227
Feat+Int.Sim	0.144	0.299	0.194
Feat+Int.Sim+Co.Cnt	**0.197**	**0.402**	**0.264**

evidences should not be neglected. By combining the effects from the two types of language models, the best performance is achieved by Base+Int.LM in all three categories.

6.3 Evaluating Product Recommendation

To evaluate product recommendation, we create an evaluation set by extracting products that co-occur frequently in user engagement in search log. To avoid bias, for estimating intent models we use a different time duration from the search log used in evaluation. The two sets of logs are half a year apart. We set a high threshold so that only confident candidates are selected. On average, each queried product has 2.8 recommendations. We select top 5 products for each method and measure the precision, recall and F1 score.

In Table 6, we show results for the evaluation of product recommendation. For comparison we implement two baseline methods, one based on feature matching (Feat.Sim) and the other based on clustering of product features (Clu.Sim). A generative clustering algorithm similar to PLSA [12] is used for this purpose. The proposed method based on intent model is denoted by "Int.Sim". From Table 6, we can see that in general clustering product features has a positive effect in recommendation, though the precision decreased in "Laptop" category. With the intent based similarity, there is a consistent improvement on precision and recall compared to both baseline methods. This is because our intent model can more precisely capture the important user preferences. Products matching on these dimensions are likely better recommendations for each other.

To further understand the effect of the intent model in product recommendation, we further compare it with the co-occurrence counting method (Co.Cnt). Note that co-occurrence counting is the same method we use for generating the ground truth data, except here we use a different set of session logs (half a year before) and a relatively low threshold to ensure coverage.

As compared to the intent model based similarity method, we can see the co-occurrence counting method performs inconsistently across different categories. One explanation is that some categories update inventories faster than others. For categories that constantly have new products coming out, the co-occurrence counting method would not work well as it cannot recommend unseen products. It lacks the ability to generalize from observations. We further combined the two methods, i.e. co-occurrence counting and the proposed similarity measurement method based on intent modeling. This is denoted as Feat+Int.Sim+Co.Cnt. We see that the results are consistently better in all three categories compared to either of the method used alone. While co-occurrence counting captures the more direct and confident recommendation signals, the intent model provides more coverage by successfully generalizing from the search session data.

7. CONCLUSION AND FUTURE WORK

In this paper, we study the problem of mining coordinated intent representation from entity search logs. To comprehensively characterize users' search intent, we propose a novel coordinated representation, where each intent is collectively represented by users' preference in query terms, entity attributes and targeting features (i.e. values on the attributes). We propose a novel joint mixture model and employ an EM algorithm to automatically discover the representative intents from an entity search log. Our intent representation and modeling methods can successfully mine the unique knowledge from entity search logs, where queries and entities typically have very different structures.

We propose and study how to utilize the coordinated intent representations to improve entity search and recommendation. We apply coordinated intent discovery to the domain of product search and evaluate the quality of discovered intents and their utility in optimizing search applications. Evaluation results show that the proposed method is effective for discovering distinct, coherent and interpretable shopping intents. The discovered intents are meaningful and representative. Quantitative evaluation on product search and product recommendation also demonstrate the benefits of leveraging the proposed intent modeling method in both applications.

This work opens many interesting future directions. First, the intent model we proposed in entity search will enable/improve many practical applications. Because the represented intents are highly interpretable, they can be easily used in market analysis and user analysis. Further use of the model can help improve business intelligence applications such as inventory planning and pricing optimization. Second, the results are also encouraging to new ideas in search intent modeling in general, where good intent representation is key for improvement. In the future, we plan to enhance the intent discovery by utilizing all types of user engagements and investigate into its value in more critical applications in business intelligence.

8. REFERENCES

[1] A. Broder. A taxonomy of web search. In *ACM Sigir forum*, volume 36, pages 3–10. ACM, 2002.

[2] O. Chapelle and Y. Zhang. A dynamic bayesian network click model for web search ranking. In *Proceedings of the 18th International Conference on World Wide Web*, WWW '09, pages 1–10, New York, NY, USA, 2009. ACM.

[3] S. Chaudhuri, G. Das, V. Hristidis, and G. Weikum. Probabilistic information retrieval approach for ranking of database query results. *ACM Trans. Database Syst.*, 31(3), 2006.

[4] K. Collins-Thompson, P. N. Bennett, R. W. White, S. de la Chica, and D. Sontag. Personalizing web search results by reading level. In *CIKM'11*, pages 403–412. ACM, 2011.

[5] N. Craswell, O. Zoeter, M. Taylor, and B. Ramsey. An experimental comparison of click position-bias models. In *Proceedings of the 2008 International Conference on Web Search and Data Mining*, WSDM '08, pages 87–94, New York, NY, USA, 2008. ACM.

[6] H. Cui, J.-R. Wen, J.-Y. Nie, and W.-Y. Ma. Query expansion by mining user logs. *Knowledge and Data Engineering, IEEE Transactions on*, 15(4):829–839, 2003.

[7] H. Duan, C. Zhai, J. Cheng, and A. Gattani. A probabilistic mixture model for mining and analyzing product search log. In *Proceedings of the 22Nd ACM International Conference on Conference on Information & Knowledge Management*, CIKM '13, pages 2179–2188, New York, NY, USA, 2013. ACM.

[8] H. Duan, C. Zhai, J. Cheng, and A. Gattani. Supporting keyword search in product database: A probabilistic approach. *PVLDB*, 6(14):1786–1797, 2013.

[9] G. E. Dupret and B. Piwowarski. A user browsing model to predict search engine click data from past observations. In *Proceedings of the 31st Annual International ACM SIGIR Conference on Research and Development in Information Retrieval*, SIGIR '08, pages 331–338, New York, NY, USA, 2008. ACM.

[10] Q. Guo and E. Agichtein. Ready to buy or just browsing?: Detecting web searcher goals from interaction data. In *Proceedings of the 33rd International ACM SIGIR Conference on Research and Development in Information Retrieval*, SIGIR '10, pages 130–137, New York, NY, USA, 2010. ACM.

[11] A. Hassan, R. Jones, and K. L. Klinkner. Beyond dcg: User behavior as a predictor of a successful search. In *Proceedings of the Third ACM International Conference on Web Search and Data Mining*, WSDM '10, pages 221–230, New York, NY, USA, 2010. ACM.

[12] T. Hofmann. Probabilistic latent semantic analysis. In *Proceedings of the Fifteenth conference on Uncertainty in artificial intelligence*. Morgan Kaufmann Publishers Inc., 1999.

[13] B. Hu, Y. Zhang, W. Chen, G. Wang, and Q. Yang. Characterizing search intent diversity into click models. In *Proceedings of the 20th International Conference on World Wide Web*, WWW '11, pages 17–26, New York, NY, USA, 2011. ACM.

[14] J. Hu, G. Wang, F. Lochovsky, J.-t. Sun, and Z. Chen. Understanding user's query intent with wikipedia. In *Proceedings of the 18th International Conference on World Wide Web*, WWW '09, pages 471–480, New York, NY, USA, 2009. ACM.

[15] B. J. Jansen, D. L. Booth, and A. Spink. Determining the user intent of web search engine queries. In *Proceedings of the 16th International Conference on World Wide Web*, WWW '07, pages 1149–1150, New York, NY, USA, 2007. ACM.

[16] B. J. Jansen, D. L. Booth, and A. Spink. Determining the informational, navigational, and transactional intent of web queries. *Information Processing & Management*, 44(3):1251–1266, 2008.

[17] U. Lee, Z. Liu, and J. Cho. Automatic identification of user goals in web search. In *Proceedings of the 14th International Conference on World Wide Web*, WWW '05, pages 391–400, New York, NY, USA, 2005. ACM.

[18] X. Li, Y.-Y. Wang, and A. Acero. Learning query intent from regularized click graphs. In *Proceedings of the 31st Annual International ACM SIGIR Conference on Research and Development in Information Retrieval*, SIGIR '08, pages 339–346, New York, NY, USA, 2008. ACM.

[19] F. Liu, C. Yu, W. Meng, and A. Chowdhury. Effective keyword search in relational databases. In *Proceedings of the 2006 ACM SIGMOD International Conference on Management of Data*, SIGMOD '06, pages 563–574, New York, NY, USA, 2006. ACM.

[20] H. Nguyen, E. Santos, Q. Zhao, and H. Wang. Capturing user intent for information retrieval. In *Proceedings of the Human Factors and Ergonomics Society Annual Meeting*, volume 48, pages 371–375. SAGE Publications, 2004.

[21] F. Qiu and J. Cho. Automatic identification of user interest for personalized search. In *Proceedings of the 15th International Conference on World Wide Web*, WWW '06, pages 727–736, New York, NY, USA, 2006. ACM.

[22] D. E. Rose and D. Levinson. Understanding user goals in web search. In *Proceedings of the 13th International Conference on World Wide Web*, WWW '04, pages 13–19, New York, NY, USA, 2004. ACM.

[23] A. Sieg, B. Mobasher, and R. Burke. Web search personalization with ontological user profiles. In *Proceedings of the Sixteenth ACM Conference on Conference on Information and Knowledge Management*, CIKM '07, pages 525–534, New York, NY, USA, 2007. ACM.

[24] H. Wang, C. Zhai, A. Dong, and Y. Chang. Content-aware click modeling. In *Proceedings of the 22Nd International Conference on World Wide Web*, WWW '13, pages 1365–1376, Republic and Canton of Geneva, Switzerland, 2013. International World Wide Web Conferences Steering Committee.

[25] C. Zhai and J. Lafferty. Model-based feedback in the language modeling approach to information retrieval. In *Proceedings of the Tenth International Conference on Information and Knowledge Management*, CIKM '01, pages 403–410, New York, NY, USA, 2001. ACM.

[26] Z. Zhang and O. Nasraoui. Mining search engine query logs for query recommendation. In *Proceedings of the 15th International Conference on World Wide Web*, WWW '06, pages 1039–1040, New York, NY, USA, 2006. ACM.

Sentiment Extraction by Leveraging Aspect-Opinion Association Structure

Li Zhao, Minlie Huang, Jiashen Sun*, Hengliang Luo*, Xiankai Yang, Xiaoyan Zhu
State Key Lab. of Intelligent Technology and Systems
Tsinghua National Laboratory for Information Science and Technology
Dept. of Computer Science and Technology, Tsinghua University, Beijing 100084, PR China
*Samsung R&D Institute China - Beijing
zhaoli19881113@126.com aihuang@tsinghua.edu.cn

ABSTRACT

Sentiment extraction aims to extract and group aspect and opinion words from online reviews. Previous works usually extract aspect and opinion words by leveraging association between a single pair of aspect and opinion word[5] [14] [9] [4][11], but the structure of aspect and opinion word clusters has not been fully exploited.

In this paper, we investigate the *aspect-opinion association structure*, and propose a "first clustering, then extracting" unsupervised model to leverage properties of the structure for sentiment extraction. For the clustering purpose, we formalise a novel concept *syntactic distribution consistency* as soft constraint in the framework of posterior regularization; for the extraction purpose, we extract aspect and opinion words based on cluster-cluster association. In comparison to traditional word-word association, we show that cluster-cluster association is a much stronger signal to distinguish aspect (opinion) words from non-aspect (non-opinion) words. Extensive experiments demonstrate the effectiveness of the proposed approach and the advantages against state-of-the-art baselines.

Categories and Subject Descriptors

I.2.7 [**Natural language processing—Text Analysis**]

Keywords

Sentiment Analysis; Opinion Mining; Sentiment Extraction; Information Extraction

1. INTRODUCTION

Sentiment extraction is the task of extracting and grouping aspect words and opinion words from online reviews. This task is important because, on top of extracted aspects and opinions, we can aggregate various opinions according to a product's aspects (or attributes), and provide much detailed, complete, and in-depth summaries of a large number of reviews. More specifically, aspect words refer to a product's or service's properties (or attributes) which people have expressed opinion upon, such as *battery, screen*, and so on. While opinion words are words that people use to express sentiment, such as *amazing*, and *interesting*. Since aspect/opinion is usually expressed by different synonymous aspect/opinion words, we need to group aspect/opinion words into clusters.

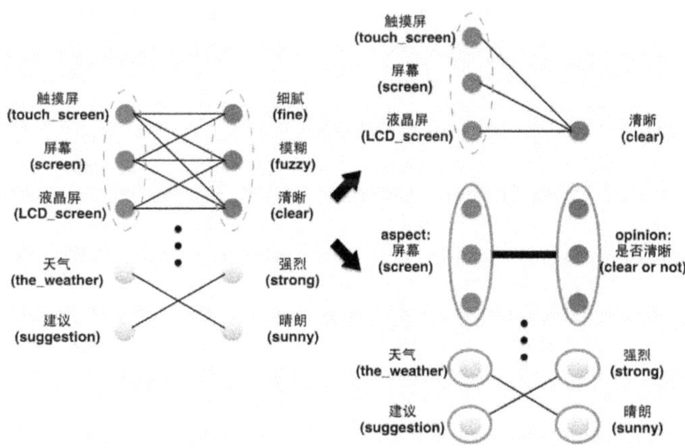

Figure 1: Aspect-opinion association structure. As shown in the figure, "touch-screen", "screen" and "LCD-screen" are synonymous aspect words, while "fine", "fuzzy" and "clear" are synonymous/antonymous opinion words. The rest words are non-aspect/non-opinion words. An edge represents the association between a pair of aspect and opinion word candidate. The picture shows that synonymous aspect words("touch-screen", "screen" and "LCD-screen") are modified by the same opinion word "clear", and vice versa; and that, the associations between aspect and opinion clusters are stronger and less prone to noises than word level associations.

Previous works for sentiment extraction focus on modeling the association between an aspect word and an opinion word [5] [14] [9] [4][11]. The central assumption lies in that, if a word is likely to be an opinion word, the words which has strong association with the word will be more possible to be aspect words, and vice versa. The word-word association has been modeled by nearest neighbor rule [5], manually designed dependency pattern[14], word alignment model [9], and statistical correlation such as likelihood ratio test[4]. Despite the success of previous works, they may discover some "False Opinion Relations"(false word-word as-

CIKM'15, October 19–23, 2015, Melbourne, Australia.
© 2015 ACM. ISBN 978-1-4503-3794-6/15/10 ...$15.00.
DOI: http://dx.doi.org/10.1145/2806416.2806525.

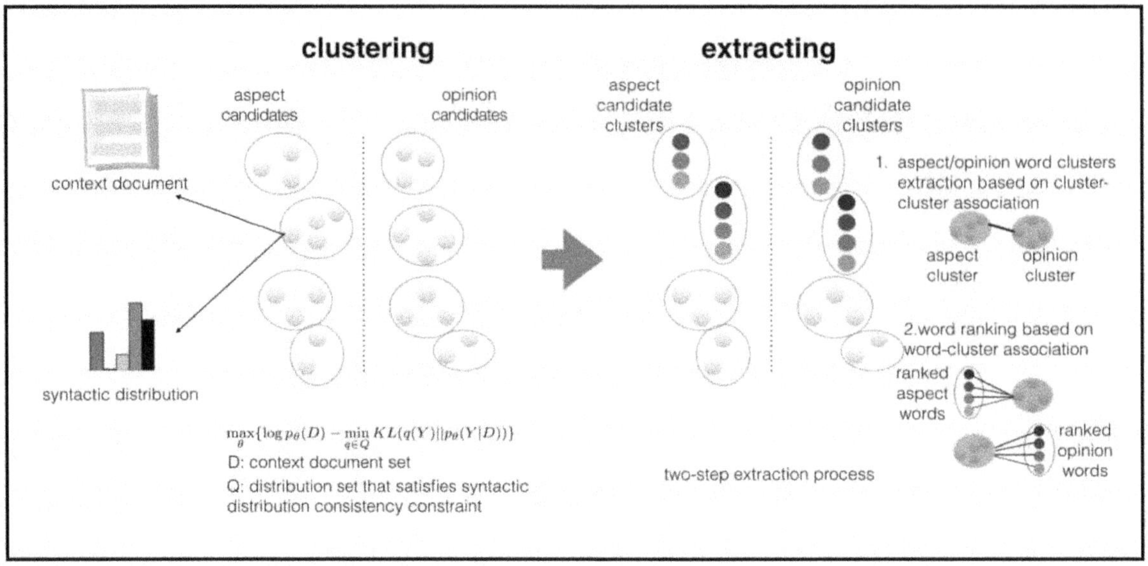

Figure 2: The framework of our model. Our model consists of two components: clustering and extracting. Firstly, aspect/opinion word candidates are clustered based on both context information and syntactic distribution. Secondly, we extract aspect/opinion word clusters based on cluster-cluster association. For each extracted cluster, we further rank each word based on word-cluster association. Points with darker color represent words with higher confidence to be aspect/opinion words. Blue/red denotes aspect/opinion, respectively.

sociations) as discussed in [16]. For example, the phrase "autofocus camera" can be matched by a dependency pattern "Adj-amod-Noun", which is widely used in previous works[16][14]. But this phrase doesn't bear any sentiment orientation. The mined association between "autofocus" and "camera" is a false word-word association. Besides, we also find that previous works cannot fully employ the structure of the constructed graph, which is actually very useful for both extracting and clustering as we will show later.

Aspect-opinion association structure(Fig. 1) refers to the structure that the bipartite graph is particularly dense, nearly complete with regard to an associated pair of aspect and opinion. In other words, considering the subgraph which contains an associated pair of aspect and opinion word cluster, the bipartite subgraph is very dense and nearly complete. As shown in Fig.1, consider all the aspect words in aspect cluster "screen", and all the opinion words in opinion cluster "clear(or not)". Since most synonymous words can be used exchangeably, we observe that there is a very dense connection structure between words in aspect cluster "screen" and words in opinion cluster "clear(or not)".

From the perspective of sentiment extraction, *aspect-opinion association structure* preserves two properties: 1. Synonymous aspect words are likely to be modified by the same opinion word, and vice versa. 2. The associations between aspect and opinion clusters are stronger and less prone to noises than word-word association.

The first property is useful for clustering aspect/opinion word candidates. This property leads to our *syntactic distribution consistency* assumption, assuming that *synonymous aspect words are likely to be connected to the same opinion word through same dependency relation.* This assumption is further formulated as constraint to guide the clustering process. Our clustering model is especially useful for distinguishing words with similar contexts but different syntactic distributions. For example, "market" and "price" are somehow semantic-related and may have similar context. But they are modified by different opinion word candidates. With the help of syntactic distribution, we can assign them to different clusters. As a result, our clustering model can produce more pure clusters.

Inspired by the second property, we extract aspect and opinion by leveraging the association between an aspect candidate cluster and an opinion candidate cluster. Strongly associated cluster pairs are extracted as pairs of aspect and opinion. The extraction rule is illustrated as follows. As mentioned above, the resultant clusters can boost the association between an aspect word and an opinion word by exploiting cluster-cluster association. Now consider the non-aspect/non-opinion words, such as "suggestion" and "strong". Non-aspect/non-opinion words usually don't have that much synonymous words as aspect/opinion words do. Ideally, many non-aspect/non-opinion clusters would contain few words (as shown in Fig. 1). Thus the clustering process will not enhance the association of those cluster pairs. Therefore, the association between a pair of aspect and opinion is much stronger than that of non-aspect/non-opinion pairs.

In practice, the non-aspect/non-opinion clusters usually contains several words. But our assumption still holds well, and this is verified by our clustering results. The association between a pair of aspect cluster(with more than 10 aspect words) and opinion cluster(with more than 10 opinion words) is 6.8 times as much as the association between other cluster pairs on average.

To leverage the two properties of *aspect-opinion association structure*, we propose a "first clustering, then extracting" unsupervised model for sentiment extraction. Firstly, we cluster all aspect and opinion word candidates based on both context information and syntactic information. Secondly, we extract aspect and opinion by constructing a graph to model association between aspect and opinion candidate clusters.

Our contributions are listed as follows:

- We propose a "first clustering, then extracting" model for sentiment extraction by leveraging properties of *aspect-opinion association structure.*
- For the clustering component, we propose *syntactic distribution consistency* assumption and formulate this assumption as data-driven constraint. This constraint is further integrated into a context-based probabilistic model to guide the clustering process.
- For the extraction component, we propose a novel ranking algorithm by leveraging cluster-cluster association. Unlike word-word association, cluster-cluster association is a much stronger signal to distinguish aspect (opinion) words from non-aspect (non-opinion) words. As a result, our extraction method can promote the extraction performance.

The rest of this paper is organized as follows. We introduce the framework of our methodology in Section 2, along with the clustering model in Section 2.1, and the extraction model in Section 2.2. We present experiment results in Section 3. In Section 4, we survey related work. We summarize our work in Section 5.

2. METHODOLOGY

To extract and cluster aspect and opinion words from reviews, we propose a "first clustering, then extracting" framework, as shown in Fig. 2. Our model consists of two components as follows:

1) The Clustering component(Section 2.1) aims to cluster aspect/opinion candidates separately into word clusters. In this paper, we select nouns/adjectives to be aspect/opinion candidates. We cluster those candidates by leveraging both context information and syntactic information.

2) The Extracting component(Section 2.2) aims to extract aspect/opinion clusters from all candidate clusters. For each extracted cluster, we further rank each word of the cluster to find aspect or opinion words. We extract aspect/opinion clusters based on cluster-cluster association, and rank words in a cluster based on word-cluster association.

2.1 Clustering Based on Syntactic Distribution Consistency

In this section, we firstly present the *syntactic distribution consistency* assumption and show how to model it as constraint. Then, this constraint is integrated into a context-based probabilistic model(Multinomial Naive Bayes) under the framework of Posterior Regularization (PR).

We present our method only from the perspective of aspect word candidates. The process for opinion word candidates is similar. We use ac to represent an aspect word candidate, and acc to represent a golden aspect candidate cluster.

2.1.1 Syntactic Distribution Consistency

In this subsection, we describe *syntactic distribution consistency* formally, and show how to use it robustly on unbalanced data.

We propose a novel corpus-level syntactic representation for each aspect word candidate, by simply counting how many times the word is connected to each opinion word candidate through each direct dependency relation in the corpus. Taking aspect word candidate "screen" for example, its syntactic representation is

$$\begin{aligned} &Syn(ac = screen)\\ &=(Count(\overset{nsubj}{\longleftarrow} clear), Count(\overset{nsubj}{\longleftarrow} fine),\\ &..., Count(\overset{rcmod}{\longrightarrow} expensive), ...)^T\\ &=(73, 31, ..., 0, ...)^T \end{aligned} \quad (1)$$

For an aspect candidate cluster, we simply add all syntactic vectors of the cluster's members together.

Given an ideal cluster acc_i, let us consider its syntactic representation. In a large review dataset, aspect words in cluster acc_i could be modified by different opinion words through different dependency relations many times. Each time can be viewed as a trial, and the syntactic vector of candidate cluster acc_i follows a certain multinominal distribution $\vec{p_i}$, which is the syntactic distribution of acc_i.

$$Syn(acc_i) \sim Multinomial(n_i, \vec{p_i}) \quad (2)$$

where n_i is calculated by adding all elements in vector $Syn(acc_i)$ together.

Based on the syntactic representation, we further assume that syntactic vector of candidate word ac_j follows the same distribution that its cluster follows. This leads to our *syntactic distribution consistency* assumption:

- ***Syntactic Distribution Consistency*** : The syntactic distribution of *aspect word candidate* is the same as that of the corresponding *aspect candidate cluster.* Formally, for any aspect word candidate $ac_j \in$ aspect candidate cluster acc_i, $Syn(ac_j) \sim Multinomial(n_j, \vec{p_i})$.

n_j is calculated by adding all elements in vector $Syn(ac_j)$.This assumption is verified on our dataset.

However, the frequencies of aspect word candidates could vary from very small to very large, making the estimate of these distributions unstable. As shown in Fig 3 [1], the estimated syntactic distribution of frequent word is reliable, and our assumption holds well. But for less frequent words, their estimated distributions are different from that of their clusters due to insufficient observations.

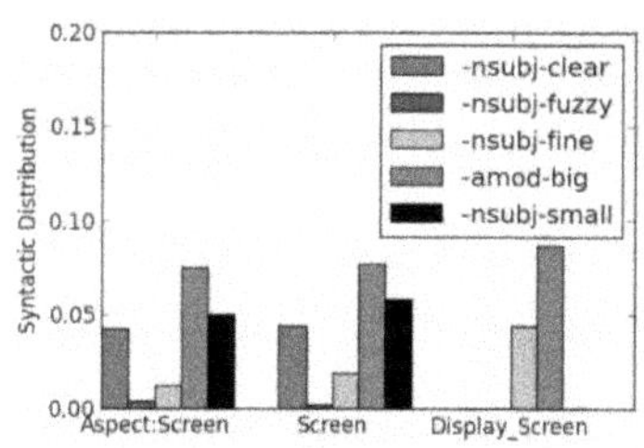

	Count
Aspect:Screen	3,267
Screen	1,670
Display-Screen	23

Figure 3: Estimated syntactic distribution of Aspect:Screen and its aspect word "Screen" and "Display-Screen".

[1]We calculate the syntactic distribution on the laptop domain. For simplicity, we only show probability on 5 dependency-opinion features. A frequent aspect candidate could be connected to tens of opinion candidates in total.

We employ *Pearson's chi-squared test* to judge whether this difference between the expected distribution and observed candidate syntactic distribution is due to sampling variation, or differs significantly. The chi-square statistic is a summary measure of how well the observed frequencies of categorical data match the frequencies that would be expected under certain multinomial distribution. In our case, we want to measure how well $Syn(ac_j)$ match $\vec{p_i}$, which is the syntactic distribution of acc_i. According to *Pearson's chi-squared test*, we have the following equation.

$$\chi^2(acc_i, ac_j) = \sum_{k=1}^{k=dim(\vec{p_i})} \frac{(n_j\vec{p_i}^{(k)} - Syn(ac_j)^{(k)})^2}{n_j\vec{p_i}^{(k)}} \leq \chi^2_{dim(\vec{p_i})-1,\alpha} \quad (3)$$

$dim(\vec{p_i})$ represents the dimension of vector $\vec{p_i}$, and α corresponds to a certain confidence level. We look up the chi-square distribution table to find the right threshold corresponding to a certain confidence level(such as 95%, $\alpha = 0.05$) with the freedom of $dim(p_i) - 1$. If aspect candidate ac_j belongs to aspect candidate cluster acc_i, then we are confident that the above equation holds. In other words, if the above equation doesn't hold, we are confident that $ac_j \notin acc_i$ according to our assumption.

We introduce an indicator variable z_{ij} to represent whether aspect candidate ac_j belongs to aspect candidate cluster acc_i, as follows:

$$z_{ij} = \begin{cases} 1 & ;\text{if } ac_j \in acc_i \\ 0 & ;\text{otherwise} \end{cases} \quad (4)$$

This leads to our *syntactic distribution consistency(SDC)* constraint function.

$$z_{ij}\chi^2(acc_i, ac_j) \leq \chi^2_{dim(\vec{p_i})-1,\alpha} \quad (5)$$

Thus, we can leverage syntactic information for both frequent words and less frequent words in a very robust way. Only when we have enough observations for ac_j and the reliable estimated syntactic distribution of ac_j is really different from that of acc_i, we apply $ac_j \notin acc_i$.

2.1.2 *Syntactic Distribution Consistency Regularized Multinomial Naive Bayes (SDC-MNB)*

In this section, we present our probabilistic model which employs both context information and syntactic distribution.

First of all, we extract a context document d to represent each candidate, by collecting the preceding and following t words of a candidate in each review. We use D to represent the document collection for all aspect word candidates. Assuming that the documents in D are independent and identically distributed, the probability of generating D is then given by:

$$p_\theta(D) = \prod_{j=1}^{|D|} p_\theta(d_j) = \prod_{j=1}^{|D|} \sum_{y_j} p_\theta(d_j, y_j) \quad (6)$$

where y_j is a latent variable indicating the cluster label for aspect word candidate ac_j, and θ is the model parameter.

In our problem, we are actually more interested in the posterior distribution over cluster label, i.e., $p_\theta(y_j|d_j)$. Once the learned parameter θ is obtained, we can get our clustering result from $p_\theta(y_j|d_j)$, by assigning cluster label acc_i with the largest posterior to aspect word candidate ac_j. We can also enforce SDC-constraint in expectation(on posterior p_θ). We use $q(Y)$ to denote the valid posterior distribution that satisfy our SDC-constraint, and Q to denote the valid posterior distribution space, as follows:

$$Q = \{q(Y) : E_q[z_{ij}\chi^2(acc_i, ac_j)] \leq \chi^2_{dim(\vec{p_i})-1,\alpha}, \forall i, j\}. \quad (7)$$

Since posterior plays such an important role in joining the context model and SDC-constraint, we formulate our problem in the framework of Posterior Regularization (PR). PR is an efficient framework to inject constraints on the posteriors of latent variables. Instead of restricting p_θ directly, which might not be feasible, PR penalizes the distance of p_θ to the constraint set Q. The posterior-regularized objective is termed as follows:

$$\max_\theta\{\log p_\theta(D) - \min_{q \in Q} KL(q(Y)||p_\theta(Y|D))\} \quad (8)$$

By trading off the data likelihood of the observed context documents (as defined in the first term), and the KL divergence of the posteriors($p_\theta(Y|D)$) to the valid posterior subspace(Q) defined by SDC-constraint (as defined in the second term), the objective encourages model with both desired posterior distribution and data likelihood. In essence, the model attempts to maximize data likelihood of context subject (softly) to SDC-constraint.

Multinomial Naive Bayes.

In spirit to [19], we use Multinomial Naive Bayes (MNB) to model the context document. Let $w_{d_j,k}$ denotes the kth word in document d_j, where each word is from the vocabulary $V = \{w_1, w_2, ..., w_{|V|}\}$. For each aspect phrase f_j, the probability of its latent aspect cluster label being acc_i and generating context document d_j is

$$p_\theta(d_j, y_j = acc_i) = p(acc_i) \prod_{k=1}^{|d_j|} p(w_{d_j,k}|acc_i) \quad (9)$$

where $p(acc_i)$ and $p(w_{d_j,k}|acc_i)$ are parameters of this model. Each word $w_{d_j,k}$ is conditionally independent of all other words given the cluster label acc_i.

The optimization algorithm for our model is an EM-like algorithm, which can be easily implemented as described in [3]. So we omit the algorithm here. After each E-step, the syntactic distribution of each cluster is updated by adding and normalizing all syntactic vectors of the cluster's candidates together according to the current posterior distribution q.

2.2 Extraction Based on Cluster-Cluster Association

Our extraction model consists of two steps: 1. We extract aspect cluster and opinion cluster based on cluster-cluster association. 2. Since clustering results may not be perfect and each cluster may still contain some noisy words, we propose a word ranking algorithm based on word-cluster association. At the end of this section, we also present an in-depth comparison between our model and models based on word-word association.

2.2.1 *Association-based Cluster Extraction*

As mentioned earlier, the clustering process leads to dramatic boosting on the association between associated pairs of aspect and opinion, and little or no boosting on the association of other cluster pairs. This leads to our following assumption,

Assumption: If a pair of clusters have strong association, the two clusters are likely to be a pair of aspect cluster and opinion cluster.

In spirit to [4], we adopt the Likelihood Ratio Test (LRT) statistics to measure cluster-cluster association. LRT computes a contingency table of aspect candidate cluster AC_i and opinion candidate cluster OC_j, derived from corpus statistics, as given in Table 1. $k_1(AC_i, OC_j)$ is the number of times that words in AC_i and words in OC_j is connected by an direct dependency relation. $k_2(AC_i, \overline{OC_j})$ is the number of dependency relation connected pair that contains words in AC_i but not words in OC_j. $k_3(\overline{AC_i}, OC_j)$ is the number of dependency relation connected pair that contains words in OC_j but not words in AC_i. $k_4(\overline{AC_i}, \overline{OC_j})$ is the number of dependency relation connected pair that contains neither words in AC_i nor words in OC_j. Note that our purpose here is to measure how strongly pair-wise clusters are associated with each other given the corpus statistics, rather than performing an actual statistics test.

Corpus statistics	AC_i	$\overline{AC_i}$
OC_j	$k_1(AC_i, OC_j)$	$k_2(AC_i, \overline{OC_j})$
$\overline{OC_j}$	$k_3(\overline{AC_i}, OC_j)$	$k_4(\overline{AC_i}, \overline{OC_j})$

Table 1: Contingency table for aspect candidate cluster AC_i and opinion candidate cluster OC_j

Based on the corpus statistics shown in Table 1, the LRT model captures the statistical association between aspect candidate cluster AC_i and opinion candidate cluster OC_j by employing the following function:

$$\begin{aligned} LRT(AC_i, OC_j) =& f(k_1, k_2, k_3, k_4) \\ =& 2[logL(p1, k1, n1) + logL(p2, k2, n2) \\ & - logL(p, k1, n1) - logL(p, k2, n2)] \end{aligned} \quad (10)$$

where,

$$L(p, k, n) = p^k(1-p)^{n-k}; n_1 = k_1 + k_3;$$
$$n_2 = k_2 + k_4; p_1 = k_1/n_1; p_2 = k_2/n_2;$$
$$p = (k_1 + k_2)/(n_1 + n_2;)$$

The larger the quantity $LRT(AC_i, OC_j)$ is, the stronger the statistical association between aspect candidate cluster AC_i and opinion candidate cluster OC_j. We rank all cluster pairs by the LRT score, and top ranked pairs are extracted as aspect clusters and opinion clusters.

2.2.2 *Association-based Word Ranking*

After cluster level extraction, we get pairs such as "Aspect:Screen" - "Opinion:Clear(or not)". However, there might be some noisy words in the "Aspect:Screen" cluster or "Opinion:Clear(or not)" cluster. For each word in the "Aspect:Screen" cluster, the stronger the association of the word to the "Opinion:Clear(or not)" cluster, the more likely the word is an aspect word in "Aspect:Screen".

This motivates our word ranking method. For an extracted aspect/opinion cluster, we select its corresponding opinion/aspect cluster with the strongest association, and calculate the association between each word with the corresponding cluster. The higher the association score is, the word is more likely to be the aspect/opinion word of this cluster. The word-cluster association is also calculated by LRT, based on the corpus statistics shown in Table 2 [2]

Corpus statistics	C_i	$\overline{C_i}$
T_j	$k_1(C_i, T_j)$	$k_2(C_i, \overline{T_j})$
$\overline{T_j}$	$k_3(\overline{C_i}, T_j)$	$k_4(\overline{C_i}, \overline{T_j})$

Table 2: Contingency table for term T_j and cluster C_i

First of all, for each selected aspect/opinion cluster, we selected the opinion/aspect cluster with the largest LRT score as the corresponding paired cluster. Then, for each word T_j in the aspect/opinion cluster, we calculate the LRT score $LRT(T_j, C_i)$ between the word and its cluster's corresponding paired cluster C_i. Finally, each word is ranked by the LRT score. The higher the LRT score is, the word is more likely to be an aspect/opinion word of the cluster.

2.2.3 *Key Difference to Word-word Association based Models*

As mentioned above, existing models based on word level association may discover some "False Opinion Relations"(false word-word associations) as discussed in [16]. We will show that our cluster level associations are more robust and less prone to noises than word level associations.

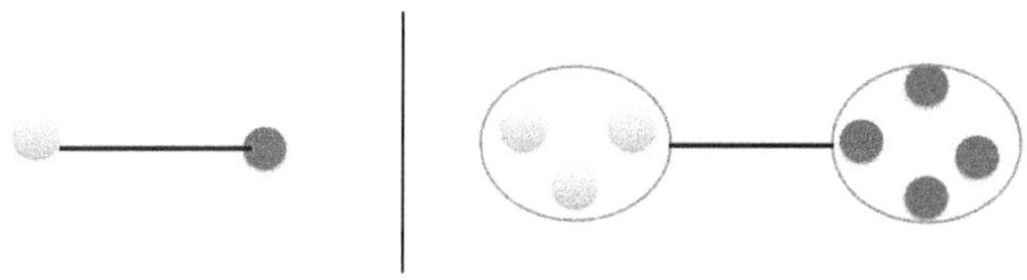

Figure 4: Left is a false association where a non-aspect word na connects an opinion word o. Right is the cluster-cluster association between the cluster of na and that of o.

As shown in Fig. 4, there is a false association that connects a non-aspect word na and an opinion word o. This non-aspect word na may be extracted as "aspect word" by word-word association based models. In our model, we examine the association between the cluster of the non-aspect word na and the cluster of the opinion word o. The association between this two clusters will be much weaker than that between a real pair of aspect and opinion cluster. Thus this pair of clusters will not be extracted by our cluster-cluster association based method. In practice, our method is also better at filtering non-aspect/non-opinion words.

Another important difference is that we not only extract but also cluster aspect/opinion words, while existing models that leverage word-word association only extract aspect/opinion words. For instance, for the aspect "picture", the model extracts opinion clusters "clear(or not)", "bright(or not)" and "good(or not)" as shown in Table 5 in experiment.

3. EXPERIMENTS

In this section, we evaluate our approach on reviews from various domains. To assess the effectiveness of our approach, we conduct three experiments on the task of aspect extraction, clustering, aspect and opinion word extraction.

[2]The corpus statistics is calculated in a similar way as in Table 1.

- ***Aspect Extraction***: Aspect extraction refers to the task of extracting and clustering aspect words simultaneously. We compare our model with existing knowledge-based topic models.
- ***Clustering***: Aspect/opinion word candidate clustering is a key component in our model. We compare our unsupervised, syntactic distribution consistency inspired clustering model with other unsupervised clustering models.
- ***Aspect and Opinion Word Extraction***: Aspect and opinion word extraction aims at extracting opinion targets (e.g., *battery*) and opinion words (e.g., *amazing*). In this task, we don't care about which cluster each word belongs to. Two state-of-art methods are selected as baselines.

Since there is no prior work on clustering opinion words, the result of opinion word clustering is qualitatively evaluated in this paper.

3.1 Datasets and Evaluation Metrics

We evaluate our method on a large Chinese review corpus, as used in [21]. This dataset contains reviews from four domains: *Camera*, *Cellphone*, *Laptop*, and *MP3/MP4*. The statistics of the corpus are present in Table 3.

We create a gold standard for aspect/opinion word extraction and clustering.[3] Since the dataset is very large, it is impossible to go through every review and label each word manually. Therefore, we select all nouns with frequency larger than 3 (5 for the cellphone domain) as aspect candidates, and all adjectives as opinion candidates. We go through every candidate word, and read sampled reviews which contain this candidate to judge whether it's an aspect/opinion word or not. Since it is impossible to discover all the aspect/opinion words, it is infeasible to evaluate the recall measure.

	Camera	Cellphone	Laptop	MP3/MP4
#Products	449	694	702	329
#Reviews	101,235	579,402	102,439	129,471
#Aspect Candidates	3,686	6,360	4,373	3,724
#Aspect Words	894	1,321	993	930
#Aspect	27	26	25	27
#Opinion Candidates	1,614	2,235	1,657	1,617
#Opinion Words	806	880	791	792
#Opinion	28	28	28	28

Table 3: Statistics of the review corpus. # denotes the size.

Evaluation Metrics: Similar to previous work [2] [13] we adopt precision@k (or p@k), where k is the rank position to compare different approaches. As just mentioned, recall is not applicable in our settings.

3.2 Evaluation on Aspect Extraction

Aspect extraction refers to the task of extracting and clustering aspect words simultaneously. Existing models for aspect extraction are all topic-model based methods[1][2][13].

In this section, we compare our model with three topic-model based aspect extraction methods: Latent Dirichlet allocation(**LDA**), Seeded Aspect and Sentiment model(**SAS**)[13] and topic modeling with Automatically generated Must-links and Cannot-links(**AMC**)[1]. Those baselines represent three types of topic models: unsupervised, semi-supervised, self-learning.

[3]We will release our gold standard later.

- ***LDA***: We implement LDA as suggested in [2]. Each sentence is treated as a document.
- ***SAS***: SAS is implemented as suggested in [13]. For SAS, we randomly sample 15 topics as labeled topics, and provide 5 seeds for each labeled topic.
- ***AMC***: AMC is a self-learning topic model, which learns knowledge from other similar domains. This method requires many similar domains to work well. Since our dataset only contains 4 domains, we randomly split data in each domain into 5 pieces, and each piece is treated as a "domain" in AMC. Each sentence is treated as a document. We use the code provided by [4][1].

Settings:

The parameter of all topic models are set to $\alpha = 1$, $\beta = 0.1$. For LDA and AMC, each sentence is treated as a document.

Setting the number of topics/aspects is often tricky. We follow the approach in [13] and assume that we already know the gold aspect number.

Note that the topic models used in our experiments are also with only candidate words but not with all words without filtering. The filtering process always promotes the performance of these topic models. We believe this configuration makes it more fair to compare our method with topic model baselines.

For our method, we set the cluster number to be 100, and the extracted aspect number to be the gold aspect number. For clustering, we set the window size to be 4 to extract contexts, and set α to be 0.05 to get the chi-squared threshold. Since our method depends on the random initiation, we use the average result of 5 runs as the final result.

3.2.1 Quantitative Results

We follow the evaluation methods in [2]. For each topic (or cluster in our setting), we judge it as a "good topic" if the top 15 words contain at least 5 synonymous aspect words. If so, we also assign the corresponding aspect to this topic.

For each good topic, we evaluate whether the top-ranked words belong to the corresponding aspect of the topic in terms of precision@k (or p@k).

	Camera	Cellphone	Laptop	MP3/MP4
LDA	3.8/27	4.0/26	6.8/25	4.8/27
AMC	8.6/27	11.4/26	13.8/25	11.8/27
SAS	6.0/27	6.0/26	15.0/25	9.0/27
Ours	**16.8**/27	**15.6**/26	**15.4**/25	**18.0**/27

Table 4: Comparison with topic model baselines : each cell denotes the number of good topics/ all extracted topics.

Experiment results are shown in Table 4 and Fig.5. We can see that our approach can extract more good topics with better precision than all baselines on all domains. The merits of our approach may come from the following facts:

- We have an explicit extraction process and filter many non-aspect words. While in knowledge based topic models, they attempt to rank aspect words higher and generate less noisy topics. But since all non-aspect

[4]https://github.com/czyuan/AMC.git

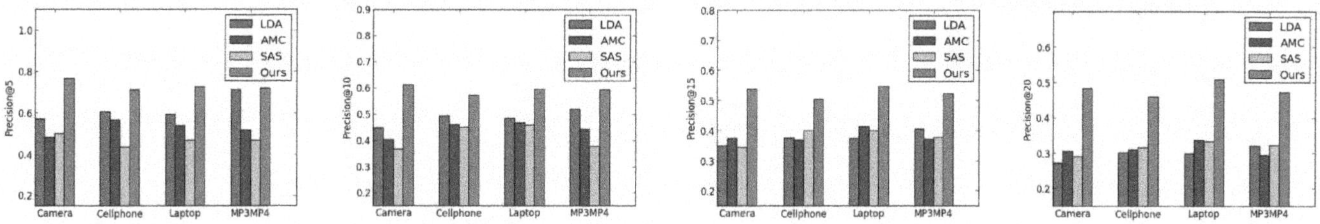

Figure 5: Comparison with topic model baselines : p@k of good topics across different domains. k = 5,10,15,20.

Our Method						
Aspect	Opinion			Aspect	Opinion	
Picture	Clear	Bright	Good	Battery	Good	Long-lasting
画面 (picture)	清晰 (clear)	艳丽 (bright)	好 (good)	时间 (time)	好 (good)	耐用 (durable)
图像 (picture)	细腻 (fine)	亮丽 (bright)	差 (bad)	寿命 (life)	差 (bad)	持久 (long-lasting)
画质 (picture)	清楚 (clear)	逼真 (lifelike)	棒 (good)	周期 (period)	棒 (good)	强悍 (powerful)
图象 (image)	柔和 (soft)	饱满 (full)	烂 (suck)	待机 (standby)	烂 (suck)	强劲 (powerful)
影像 (picture)	顺畅 (smooth)	淡 (light)	完美 (perfect)	续航 (life)	完美 (perfect)	受用 (powerful)
字迹 (writing)	满 (full)	锐利 (sharp)	一般 (ordinary)	电力 (electricity)	一般 (ordinary)	长久 (long)
色彩 (color)	过瘾 (fun)	鲜明 (bright)	差劲 (poor)	使用 (usage)	差劲 (poor)	猛 (powerful)
图画 (picture)	快活 (happy)	鲜活 (bright)	理想 (ideal)	用量 (amount)	理想 (ideal)	凶猛 (powerful)
画片 (picture)	壮观 (great)	鲜艳 (bright)	糟糕 (bad)	研究 (study)	糟糕 (bad)	充沛 (abundant)
图案 (picture)	生动 (vivid)	黯淡 (dim)	可靠 (reliable)	供电 (power)	可靠 (reliable)	弱 (weak)

SAS				AMC		LDA	
Picture		Battery		Battery		Battery	
Aspect	Opinion	Aspect	Opinion	Aspect	Opinion	Aspect	Opinion
画面 (picture)	大 (big)	时间 (time)	长 (long)	待机 (standby)	短 (short)	时间 (time)	长 (long)
显示 (display)	清晰 (clear)	小时 (hour)	耐用 (durable)	时间 (time)	长 (long)	电池 (battery)	耐用 (durable)
效果 (effect)	好 (good)	待机 (standby)	好 (good)	小时 (hour)	耐用 (durable)	小时 (hour)	短 (short)
视频 (video)	不错 (good)	使用 (usage)	不错 (good)	电池 (battery)	坏 (bad)	待机 (standby)	强 (strong)
色彩 (color)	高 (high)	能力 (ability)	短 (short)	续航 (life)	粘 (sticky)	续航 (life)	低 (low)
感觉 (feel)	小 (small)	充电 (charge)	强 (strong)	能力 (ability)	最大 (biggest)	能力 (ability)	清楚 (clear)
清晰度 (sharpness)	低 (low)	电量 (power)	行 (ok)	充电 (charge)	好看 (good-looking)	电量 (power)	太多 (too much)
图像 (image)	清楚 (clear)	播放 (broadcast)	久 (long)	使用 (usage)	次 (bad)	充电 (charge)	实际 (actual)
角度 (angle)	差 (suck)	电影 (movie)	次 (bad)	CPU (CPU)	可惜 (pity)	颜色 (color)	不错 (good)
电影 (movie)	细腻 (fine)	容量 (capacity)	差 (bad)	温度 (temparater)	耐磨 (wear-resisting)	选择 (choice)	麻烦 (troublesome)

Table 5: Qualitative results on aspect extraction and opinion extraction in MP3/MP4 domain.

Aspect	Camera			Cellphone			Laptop			MP3/MP4		
	DP	LRT	Ours	DP	LRT	Ours	DP	LRT	Ours	DP	LRT	Ours
P@100	0.830	0.810	**0.872**	0.780	0.710	**0.846**	0.820	0.810	**0.858**	0.820	0.810	**0.899**
P@200	0.695	0.695	**0.764**	0.655	0.645	**0.677**	0.710	0.685	**0.767**	0.715	0.685	**0.777**
P@300	0.620	0.607	**0.649**	0.592	0.583	**0.593**	0.646	0.633	**0.651**	0.626	0.603	**0.691**
P@400	0.580	0.560	**0.595**	**0.550**	0.543	0.529	**0.595**	0.585	0.584	0.588	0.575	**0.615**
P@500	0.532	0.516	**0.550**	0.496	0.492	**0.499**	**0.552**	0.542	0.543	0.556	0.550	**0.588**
Opinion	Camera			Cellphone			Laptop			MP3/MP4		
	DP	LRT	Ours	DP	LRT	Ours	DP	LRT	Ours	DP	LRT	Ours
P@100	0.900	0.890	**0.968**	0.890	0.880	**0.906**	0.890	0.880	**0.926**	0.870	0.880	**0.929**
P@200	0.835	0.780	**0.909**	0.815	0.810	**0.905**	0.805	0.785	**0.869**	0.830	0.805	**0.881**
P@300	0.796	0.770	**0.855**	0.783	0.760	**0.873**	0.760	0.740	**0.817**	0.786	0.766	**0.841**
P@400	0.770	0.757	**0.788**	0.767	0.735	**0.833**	0.747	0.740	**0.774**	0.770	0.737	**0.788**
P@500	0.748	0.726	**0.758**	0.756	0.716	**0.792**	**0.740**	0.712	0.728	0.746	0.730	**0.749**

Table 6: Comparison on aspect and opinion word extraction across different domains.

words are still in their ranking list, it's hard to low-rank frequent non-aspect words.

- We leverage both context information and syntactic information to generate aspect word clusters. While in knowledge based topic models, they only use context information. As discussed above, our method can distinguish words with similar contexts but different syntactic distributions, leading to better clustering performance.
- In knowledge based topic models, there are topics which contain different aspects. Knowledge-based topic models are good at extracting coarse-grained aspects, while our model is good at extracting fine-grained aspects.
- SAS and AMC are better than LDA, which demonstrates the effectiveness of human-provided knowledge and self-learning.

3.2.2 *Qualitative Results*

Table 5 shows two example aspects ("picture" and "battery") and its top 10 words produced by each methods in MP3/MP4 domain. From Table 5, we can see that our method discovers more correct and meaningful aspect words at the top positions. While AMC and LDA fail to discover fine-grained aspect "picture".

Compared with topic-model based methods, our method can extract aspect cluster and opinion cluster simultaneously. As a result, our methods can capture the many-to-many association between aspect clusters and opinion clusters. For example, opinion "good(or not)" is related to both aspect "picture" and aspect "battery" in our extraction result. Our method can also extract and distinguish fine-grained opinion cluster. For aspect "picture", we extract three related fine-grained opinion clusters: "clear(or not)", "bright(or not)" and "good(or not)". While topic model based methods can only extract one mixed opinion topic for each aspect topic.

We believe that extracting fine-grained opinion clusters has potential value for generating fine-grained opinion summary. For example, we may want to know more detailed opinions about "picture", i.e., whether it's "clear(or not)", "bright(or not)", or generic opinions such as "good(or not)".

We can also see that some opinion cluster contains both synonymous and antonymous opinion words. Separating positive opinion words and negative opinion words is beyond the scope of this paper.

3.3 Evaluation on Clustering

In this section, we want to evaluate the effectiveness of leveraging syntactic distribution consistency in the clustering component. We conduct an extrinsic experiment that evaluate the final aspect extraction performance, by changing the clustering component. We compare our clustering model with two simple clustering methods: **Kmeans** and **MNB-EM**.

- ***Kmeans***: Kmeans is the most popular clustering algorithm, and is also used as baseline in previous work[21]. Here we use the context distributional similarity (cosine similarity) as the similarity measure.
- ***MNB-EM***: MNB-EM is our clustering model without the *syntactic distribution consistency* constraint. Compared with MNB-EM, we can see clearly the effectiveness of leveraging syntactic distribution consistency.

The result is shown in Fig.6. We can see that our SDC-MNB clustering model can extract more good topics with better or comparable precision than baselines, which demonstrates the merits of syntactic distribution consistency in the clustering component. Besides, our extraction model with kmeans is comparable to topic model baselines, which demonstrates the effectiveness of our "first clustering, then extracting" framework.

	Camera	Cellphone	Laptop	MP3/MP4
Kmeans	8.4/27	10.4/26	9.4/25	10.6/27
MNB-EM	14.0/27	14.2/26	11.2/25	17.8/27
SDC-MNB	**16.8**/27	**15.6**/26	**15.4**/25	**18.0**/27

Table 7: Comparison with clustering baselines : each cell denotes the number of good topics/ all extracted topics.

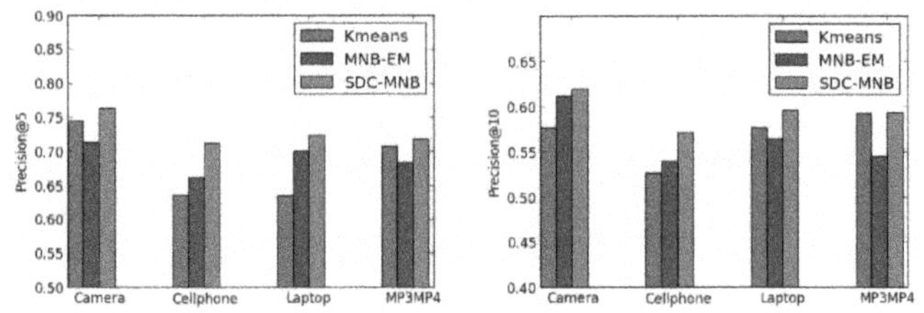

Figure 6: Comparison with clustering baselines : p@k of good topics across different domains. k = 5,10.

3.4 Evaluation on Aspect and Opinion Word Extraction

In this section, we evaluate our method on the aspect and opinion word extraction task. In this task, we don't care about which cluster each word belongs to. An extracted word is correct, as long as it's an aspect/opinion word. We choose precision@k as evaluation measure. We compare our method with two strong baselines: **DP** and **LRT**.

- ***DP***: DP uses syntax-based patterns to capture word-word associations in sentences, and then uses a bootstrapping process to extract aspect/opinion words [14].
- ***LRT***: LRT captures associations using co-occurrence statistics. They employ these statistics to extract opinion words/targets in a bootstrapping framework[4].

Extracted aspect/opinion words are ranked by frequency in DP and LRT.

The result is shown in Table 6. We can see that our method outperforms two baselines for most cases. This result demonstrates that, based on candidate clustering result, our simple ranking method works well for aspect and opinion word extraction task.

We also find that our method works especially well for smaller k in term of p@k. As k increases, the performance of our method drops only slightly. The reason is as follows: In the first step of extraction, we extract aspect/opinion cluster. If the extracted cluster number is small, then the extracted clusters may not cover all aspect/opinion words. So our method doesn't perform well for aspect/opinion word extraction in terms of p@k for larger k. However, since we don't care about the aspect number in this task, a larger cluster number could solve this problem.

4. RELATED WORK

Sentiment extraction is an important task for aspect-level sentiment analysis. Previous works can be divided into two categories: sentence level extraction and corpus level extraction.

For sentence-level extraction, previous methods mainly aimed to identify all opinion target/word mentions in sentences by supervised learning[15] [12][7] [17]. They regarded it as a sequence labeling task, where several classical models were used. Jin and Ho applied a lexicalized HMM model to learn patterns to extract aspects and opinion expressions[6]. Li et al. integrated two CRF variations, i.e., Skip-CRF and Tree-CRF, to extract aspects and also opinions[7].

This paper falls into corpus level extraction, and aims to generate an aspect/opinion cluster list rather than to identify mentions in sentence. Previous corpus level extraction methods can be divided into two categories: knowledge-based topic models that leverage word-word co-occurrence information implicitly, and graph-based models that model the association between aspect and opinion candidates explicitly.

Knowledge-based topic models performed aspect term extraction and clustering simultaneously by leveraging word-word co-occurrence information implicitly. To generate coherent topics, several knowledge-based topic models, have been proposed. Mukherjee and Liu proposed Seeded Aspect and Sentiment model(SAS) by using human-generated seeds to learn coherent topics[13]. Chen et al. proposed MC-LDA to leverage both must-sets and cannot-sets[2]. Chen et al. also proposed AMC to learning knowledge from other domain[1].

Our method is similar to topic models in terms of discovering aspect and opinion based on word co-occurrence. The key difference is that topic models can't distinguish aspect words and background(or non-aspect) words based on word association in an unsupervised manner, but our model can. Topic models such as ME-LDA[22] includes a word classification module, which classifies words into three categories: aspect, opinion, and background. But they need heavy annotation. Topic models such as SAS work in a weakly supervised manner. But they treat all words as either aspect or opinion words. Since not all words are aspect words or opinion words, the learned topic must contains some background words. If a background word is frequent, it's usually hard to filter it. While our method can filter frequent non-aspect words based on cluster-cluster association.

Graph-based models extracted aspect and opinion terms by modeling association between aspect and opinion candidates explicitly. Those models usually started from seeds and propagate label on a graph. The word-word association has been studied by many researchers. Hu and Liu exploited nearest neighbor rules to mine association among words[5]. Qiu et al. designed syntactic patterns to perform this task[14]. Liu et al. employed word alignment model to capture word-word association rather than syntactic parsing[9][8][10]. Hai et al. explore robust statistical correlation in a bootstrapping framework[4].

Our method is similar to graph-based models in terms of employing association strength for extraction. However, our method extract aspect and opinion by leveraging cluster-cluster association, while graph-based models employ word-word association. We found that the bond between aspect and opinion clusters are stronger and less prone to noises than word level associations.

Another line of work focused on clustering aspect terms based on context information. Several weakly supervised models has been proposed. Zhai et al. proposed an EM-based semi-supervised learning method to group aspect expressions into user-specified aspects[18]. They employed lexical knowledge to provide a better initialization for EM. In Zhai et al.[19], an EM-based unsupervised version was proposed. The so-called L-EM model first generated softly labeled data by grouping feature expressions that share words in common, and then merged the groups by lexical similarity. Zhai et al.[20] proposed a LDA-based method that incorporates must-link and cannot-link constraints. Zhao et al. proposed an EM-based unsupervised method by leveraging data-driven sentiment consistency constraint[21].

Compared with previous work, our model has two advantages: 1. Our model can extract aspect and opinion based on cluster-cluster association. 2. Our model is totally unsupervised, doesn't need any labeled data, human-generated knowledge, or seeds.

5. CONCLUSION

In this paper, we propose a novel sentiment extraction method by leveraging *aspect-opinion association structure*. First, we cluster all aspect candidates and opinion candidates by our *syntactic distribution consistency* inspired model. Second, we extract aspect and opinion word clusters based on cluster-cluster association. Compared with existing topic-model based aspect extraction methods, our method performs an explicit extraction process and filter many non-aspect/non-opinion candidates. Compared with existing graph-based methods that extract aspect words and opinion words, our method can extract aspect and opinion at cluster level. Experiments show that our approach outperforms state-of-the-art baselines remarkably.

6. ACKNOWLEDGEMENT

This work was partly supported by the National Basic Research Program (973 Program) under grant No.2012CB316301 /2013CB329403, the National Science Foundation of China under grant No.61272227/61332007, and the Beijing Higher Education Young Elite Teacher Project. The work was also supported by Tsinghua University Beijing Samsung Telecom R&D Center Joint Laboratory for Intelligent Media Computing.

7. REFERENCES

[1] Z. Chen and B. Liu. Mining topics in documents: Standing on the shoulders of big data. In *Proceedings of the 20th ACM SIGKDD International Conference on Knowledge Discovery and Data Mining*, KDD '14, pages 1116–1125, New York, NY, USA, 2014. ACM.

[2] Z. Chen, A. Mukherjee, B. Liu, M. Hsu, M. Castellanos, and R. Ghosh. Exploiting domain knowledge in aspect extraction. In *EMNLP*, pages 1655–1667. ACL, 2013.

[3] J. V. Graca, L. Inesc-id, K. Ganchev, B. Taskar, J. V. Graça, L. F. Inesc-id, K. Ganchev, and B. Taskar. Expectation maximization and posterior constraints. In *In Advances in NIPS*, pages 569–576, 2007.

[4] Z. Hai, K. Chang, and G. Cong. One seed to find them all: Mining opinion features via association. In *Proceedings of the 21st ACM International Conference on Information and Knowledge Management*, CIKM '12, pages 255–264, New York, NY, USA, 2012. ACM.

[5] M. Hu and B. Liu. Mining opinion features in customer reviews. In *Proceedings of the 19th National Conference on Artifical Intelligence*, AAAI'04, pages 755–760. AAAI Press, 2004.

[6] W. Jin and H. H. Ho. A novel lexicalized hmm-based learning framework for web opinion miningnote from acm: A joint acm conference committee has determined that the authors of this article violated acm's publication policy on simultaneous submissions. therefore acm has shut off access to this paper. In *Proceedings of the 26th Annual International Conference on Machine Learning*, ICML '09, pages 465–472, New York, NY, USA, 2009. ACM.

[7] F. Li, C. Han, M. Huang, X. Zhu, Y.-J. Xia, S. Zhang, and H. Yu. Structure-aware review mining and summarization. In *Proceedings of the 23rd International Conference on Computational Linguistics*, COLING '10, pages 653–661, Stroudsburg, PA, USA, 2010. Association for Computational Linguistics.

[8] K. Liu, L. Xu, Y. Liu, and J. Zhao. Opinion target extraction using partially-supervised word alignment model. In *Proceedings of the Twenty-Third International Joint Conference on Artificial Intelligence*, IJCAI '13, pages 2134–2140. AAAI Press, 2013.

[9] K. Liu, L. Xu, and J. Zhao. Opinion target extraction using word-based translation model. In *Proceedings of the 2012 Joint Conference on Empirical Methods in Natural Language Processing and Computational Natural Language Learning*, EMNLP-CoNLL '12, pages 1346–1356, Stroudsburg, PA, USA, 2012. Association for Computational Linguistics.

[10] K. Liu, L. Xu, and J. Zhao. Syntactic patterns versus word alignment: Extracting opinion targets from online reviews. In *Proceedings of the 51st Annual Meeting of the Association for Computational Linguistics (Volume 1: Long Papers)*, pages 1754–1763, Sofia, Bulgaria, August 2013. Association for Computational Linguistics.

[11] K. Liu, L. Xu, and J. Zhao. Extracting opinion targets and opinion words from online reviews with graph co-ranking. In *Proceedings of the 52nd Annual Meeting of the Association for Computational Linguistics (Volume 1: Long Papers)*, pages 314–324, Baltimore, Maryland, June 2014. Association for Computational Linguistics.

[12] T. Ma and X. Wan. Opinion target extraction in chinese news comments. In *Proceedings of the 23rd International Conference on Computational Linguistics: Posters*, COLING '10, pages 782–790, Stroudsburg, PA, USA, 2010. Association for Computational Linguistics.

[13] A. Mukherjee and B. Liu. Aspect extraction through semi-supervised modeling. In *Proceedings of the 50th Annual Meeting of the Association for Computational Linguistics: Long Papers - Volume 1*, ACL '12, pages 339–348, Stroudsburg, PA, USA, 2012. Association for Computational Linguistics.

[14] G. Qiu, B. Liu, J. Bu, and C. Chen. Opinion word expansion and target extraction through double propagation. *Comput. Linguist.*, 37(1):9–27, Mar. 2011.

[15] Y. Wu, Q. Zhang, X. Huang, and L. Wu. Phrase dependency parsing for opinion mining. In *Proceedings of the 2009 Conference on Empirical Methods in Natural Language Processing: Volume 3 - Volume 3*, EMNLP '09, pages 1533–1541, Stroudsburg, PA, USA, 2009. Association for Computational Linguistics.

[16] L. Xu, K. Liu, S. Lai, Y. Chen, and J. Zhao. Mining opinion words and opinion targets in a two-stage framework. In *Proceedings of the 51st Annual Meeting of the Association for Computational Linguistics, ACL 2013, 4-9 August 2013, Sofia, Bulgaria, Volume 1: Long Papers*, pages 1764–1773, 2013.

[17] B. Yang and C. Cardie. Joint inference for fine-grained opinion extraction. In *Proceedings of the 51st Annual Meeting of the Association for Computational Linguistics (Volume 1: Long Papers)*, pages 1640–1649, Sofia, Bulgaria, August 2013. Association for Computational Linguistics.

[18] Z. Zhai, B. Liu, H. Xu, and P. Jia. Grouping product features using semi-supervised learning with soft-constraints. In *Proceedings of the 23rd International Conference on Computational Linguistics*, COLING '10, pages 1272–1280, Stroudsburg, PA, USA, 2010. Association for Computational Linguistics.

[19] Z. Zhai, B. Liu, H. Xu, and P. Jia. Clustering product features for opinion mining. In *Proceedings of the Fourth ACM International Conference on Web Search and Data Mining*, WSDM '11, pages 347–354, New York, NY, USA, 2011. ACM.

[20] Z. Zhai, B. Liu, H. Xu, and P. Jia. Constrained lda for grouping product features in opinion mining. In *Proceedings of the 15th Pacific-Asia Conference on Advances in Knowledge Discovery and Data Mining - Volume Part I*, PAKDD'11, pages 448–459, Berlin, Heidelberg, 2011. Springer-Verlag.

[21] L. Zhao, M. Huang, H. Chen, J. Cheng, and X. Zhu. Clustering aspect-related phrases by leveraging sentiment distribution consistency. In *Proceedings of the 2014 Conference on Empirical Methods in Natural Language Processing (EMNLP)*, pages 1614–1623, Doha, Qatar, October 2014. Association for Computational Linguistics.

[22] W. X. Zhao, J. Jiang, H. Yan, and X. Li. Jointly modeling aspects and opinions with a maxent-lda hybrid. In *Proceedings of the 2010 Conference on Empirical Methods in Natural Language Processing*, EMNLP '10, pages 56–65, Stroudsburg, PA, USA, 2010. Association for Computational Linguistics.

Leveraging Joint Interactions for Credibility Analysis in News Communities

Subhabrata Mukherjee Gerhard Weikum
Max Planck Institute for Informatics
{smukherjee, weikum}@mpi-inf.mpg.de

Abstract

Media seems to have become more partisan, often providing a biased coverage of news catering to the interest of specific groups. It is therefore essential to identify *credible* information content that provides an objective narrative of an event. News communities such as digg, reddit, or newstrust offer recommendations, reviews, quality ratings, and further insights on journalistic works. However, there is a complex *interaction* between different factors in such online communities: fairness and style of reporting, language clarity and objectivity, topical perspectives (like political viewpoint), expertise and bias of community members, and more.

This paper presents a model to systematically analyze the different interactions in a news community between users, news, and sources. We develop a probabilistic graphical model that leverages this *joint* interaction to identify 1) highly *credible* news articles, 2) *trustworthy* news sources, and 3) *expert* users who perform the role of "citizen journalists" in the community. Our method extends CRF models to incorporate real-valued ratings, as some communities have very fine-grained scales that cannot be easily discretized without losing information. To the best of our knowledge, this paper is the first full-fledged analysis of credibility, trust, and expertise in news communities.

Categories and Subject Descriptors

H.3.3 [**Information Storage and Retrieval**]: Information Search and Retrieval - *Information Filtering*; I.2.7 [**Computing Methodologies**]: Artificial Intelligence - *Natural Language Processing*

Keywords

Credibility; News Community; Probabilistic Graphical Models

1. INTRODUCTION

Motivation: Media plays a crucial role in the public dissemination of information about events. Many people find online information and blogs as useful as TV or magazines. At the same time, however, people also believe that there is substantial media bias in news coverage [24, 8], especially in view of inter-dependencies and cross-ownerships of media companies and other industries (like energy).

Several factors affect the coverage and presentation of news in media incorporating potentially biased information induced via the fairness and style of reporting. News are often presented in a polarized way depending on the political viewpoint of the media source (newspapers, TV stations, etc.). In addition, other source-specific properties like *viewpoint, expertise, and format* of news may also be indicators of information credibility.

In this paper, we embark on an in-depth study and formal modeling of these factors and inter-dependencies within *news communities* for *credibility analysis*. A news community is a news aggregator site (e.g., reddit.com, digg.com, newstrust.net) where users can give explicit feedback (e.g., rate, review, share) on the quality of news and can interact (e.g., comment, vote) with each other. Users can rate and review news, point out differences, bias in perspectives, unverified claims etc. However, this adds user subjectivity to the evaluation process, as users incorporate their own bias and perspectives in the framework. Controversial topics create polarization among users which influence their ratings. [30, 6] state that online ratings are one of the most trusted sources of user feedback; however they are systematically *biased* and easily manipulated.

Problem Statement: Given a set of news sources generating news articles, and users reviewing those articles on different qualitative aspects with mutual interactions — our objective is to *jointly* rank the sources, articles, and users based on their trustworthiness, credibility, and expertise respectively.

In this process, we want to analyze the influence of various factors like the writing style of a news article, its topic distribution, type of media and format of news, political viewpoint and expertise, and other user traits on the *credibility analysis* of the community.

Our Approach: To analyze the factors and inter-dependencies in a news community, we have developed a sophisticated probabilistic graphical model, specifically a Continuous Conditional Random Field (CCRF) model, which exploits several *moderate* signals of interaction *jointly* between the following factors to derive a *strong* signal for information credibility (refer to Figures 1a and 1b). In particular, the model captures the following factors.

- *Language and credibility of a news article*: *objectivity*, rationality, and general quality of language in the news article. Objectivity is the quality of the news to be free from emotion, bias and prejudice of the author. The *credibility* of a news article refers to presenting an unbiased, informative and balanced narrative of an event.
- *Properties and trustworthiness of a news source*: *trustworthiness* of a news source in the sense of generating credible articles based on source properties like viewpoint, expertise and format of news.
- *Expertise of users and review ratings*: *expertise* of a user, in the news community, in properly judging the credibility of news articles. Expert users should provide objective evaluations – by reviews and/or ratings – of news articles, corroborating with the evaluations of other expert users. This can be used to identify potential "citizen journalists" [17] in the community.

We show that the CCRF performs better than sophisticated col-

CIKM'15, October 19-23, 2015, Melbourne, VIC, Australia
 ISBN 978-1-4503-3794-6/15/10 ...$15.00.
DOI: http://dx.doi.org/10.1145/2806416.2806537

laborative filtering approaches based on latent factor models, and regression methods that do not consider all these interactions.

Although this work is focused on news communities, the framework can also be used for instance, in health communities (e.g. `healthboards.com`) where users write posts on drug usage — the objective being to *jointly* rank posts, drug side-effects, and users based on their quality, credibility, and trustworthiness respectively.

In this work, the attributes *credibility* and *trustworthiness* are always associated with a news article and a news source, respectively. The joint interaction between several factors also captures that a source garners trustworthiness by generating credible news articles, which are highly rated by expert users. Similarly, the likelihood of a news article being credible increases if it is generated by a trustworthy source.

Some communities offer users *fine-grained scales for rating* different aspects of news articles and news sources. For example, the *newstrust.net* community analyzes an article on 15 aspects like insightful, fairness, style and factual. These are aggregated into an overall *real-valued* rating after weighing the aspects based on their importance, expertise of the user, feedback from the community, and more. This setting cannot be easily discretized without blow-up or risking to lose information. Therefore, we model ratings as real-valued variables in our CCRF.

Contributions: The paper introduces the following novel elements:

- A continuous CRF that captures the mutual dependencies between credibility of articles, trustworthiness of sources, expertise of users, and expresses real-valued ratings.
- An inference method for the CCRF that allows us to *jointly* (a) predict ratings; and (b) rank articles, sources, and users by their credibility, trustworthiness, and expertise, respectively.
- A large experimental study with data from *newstrust.net*, one of the most sophisticated news communities with a focus on quality journalism.

The rest of the paper is organized as follows. Section 2 presents how we model news communities, and which factors we include in the model. Section 3 develops the CCRF that captures the interaction between all the factors. Section 4 introduces the dataset that we use for experimental evaluation and further studies. Section 5 presents our experimental results followed by discussion.

2. MODELING NEWS COMMUNITIES

Our approach exploits the rich interaction taking place between the different factors in a news community. We propose a *probabilistic graphical model* that leverages the interplay between news credibility, language objectivity, source trustworthiness, and user expertise. Refer to Figure 1 for the following discussion.

Consider a set of news sources $\langle s \rangle$ (e.g., s_1 in Figure 1c) generating articles $\langle d \rangle$ which are reviewed and analyzed by users $\langle u \rangle$ for their credibility. Consider r_{ij} to be the review by user u_j on article d_i. The overall article rating of d_i is given by y_i.

In our model, each news source, news article, user and her rating or review, and overall article rating is associated with a continuous random variable $r.v. \in [1 \dots 5]$, that indicates its trustworthiness, objectivity, expertise, and credibility, respectively. 5 indicates the best quality that an item can obtain, and 1 is the worst. Discrete ratings, being a special case of this setting, can be easily handled.

Each node is associated with a set of observed features that are extracted from the news community. For example, a news source has properties like topic specific expertise, viewpoint and format of news; a news article has features like topics, and style of writing from the usage of discourse markers and subjective words in the article. For users we extract their topical perspectives and expertise, engagement features (like the number of questions, replies,

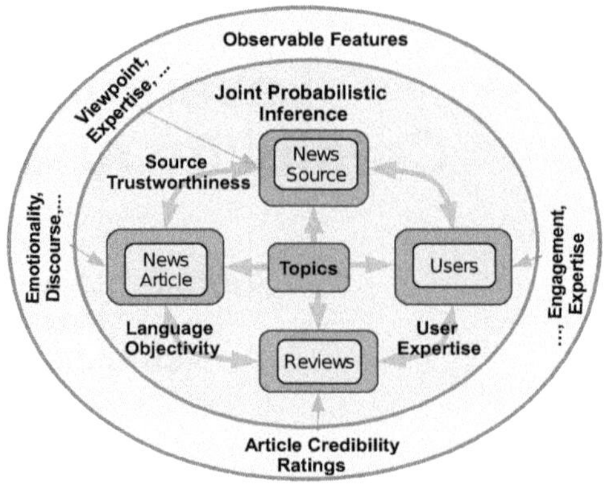

(a) Interactions between source trustworthiness, article credibility, language objectivity, and user expertise.

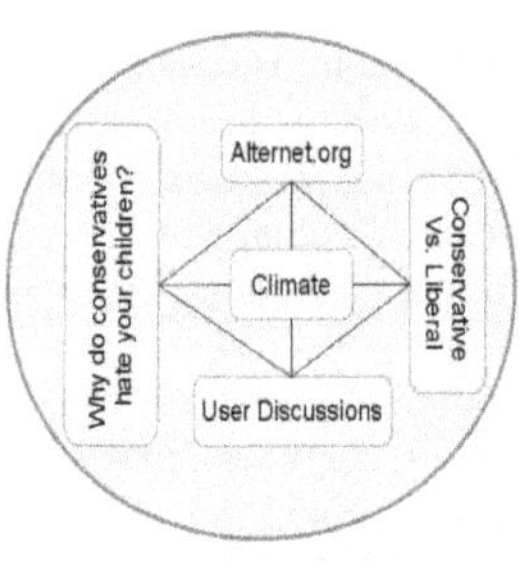

(b) Sample instantiation.

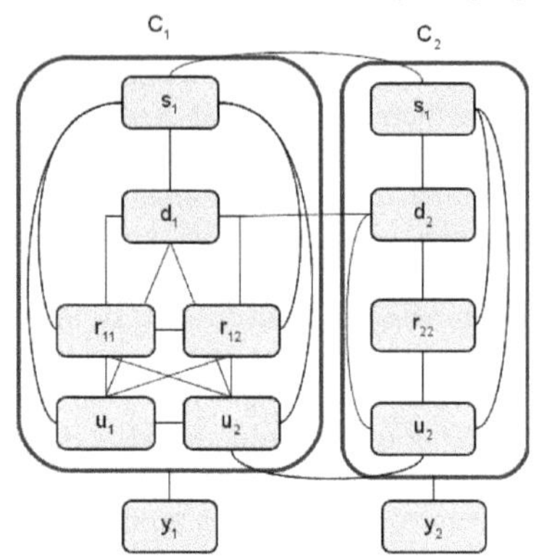

(c) Clique representation.

Figure 1: Graphical model representation.

reviews posted) and various interactions with other users (like upvotes/downvotes) and news sources in the community.

The objective of our model is to predict credibility ratings $\langle y \rangle$ of news articles $\langle d \rangle$ by exploiting the mutual interactions between different variables. The following edges between the variables capture their interplay:

- Each news article is connected to the news source from where it is extracted (e.g., $s_1 - d_1, s_1 - d_2$)
- Each news article is connected to its review or rating by a user (e.g., $d_1 - r_{11}, d_1 - r_{12}, d_2 - r_{22}$)
- Each user is connected to all her reviews (e.g., $u_1 - r_{11}, u_2 - r_{12}, u_2 - r_{22}$)
- Each user is connected to all news articles rated by her (e.g., $u_1 - d_1, u_2 - d_1, u_2 - d_2$)
- Each source is connected to all the users who rated its articles (e.g., $s_1 - u_1, s_1 - u_2$)
- Each source is connected to all the reviews of its articles (e.g., $s_1 - r_{11}, s_1 - r_{12}, s_1 - r_{22}$)
- For each article, all the users and all their reviews on the article are inter-connected (e.g., $u_1 - r_{12}, u_2 - r_{11}, u_1 - u_2$). This captures user-user interactions (e.g., u_1 upvoting/downvoting u_2's rating on d_1) influencing the overall article rating.

Therefore, a *clique* (e.g., C_1) is formed between a news article, its source, users and their reviews on the article. Multiple such cliques (e.g., C_1 and C_2) share information via their common news sources (e.g., s_1) and users (e.g., u_2).

News *topics* play a significant role on information credibility. Individual users in community (and news sources) have their own perspectives and expertise on various topics (e.g., environmental politics). Modeling user-specific topical perspectives explicitly captures credibility judgment better than a user-independent model. However, many articles do not have explicit topic tags. Hence we use Latent

Dirichlet Allocation (LDA) [1] in conjunction with Support Vector Regression (SVR) [4] to learn words associated to each (latent) topic, and user (and source) perspectives for the topics. Documents are assumed to have a distribution over topics as latent variables, with words as observables. Inference is by Gibbs sampling. This LDA model is a component of the overall model, discussed next.

We use a probabilistic graphical model, specifically a Conditional Random Field (CRF), to model all factors jointly. The modeling approach is related to the prior work of [23]. However, unlike that work and traditional CRF models, our problem setting requires a *continuous* version of the CRF (CCRF) to deal with real-valued ratings instead of discrete labels. In this work, we follow an approach similar to [26, 27, 32] in learning the parameters of the CCRF. We use Support Vector Regression [4] to learn the elements of the feature vector for the CCRF.

The inference is centered around cliques of the form $\langle$ source, article, $\langle$ users $\rangle$, $\langle$ reviews $\rangle\rangle$. An example is the two cliques $C_1 : s_1 - d_1 - \langle u_1, u_2 \rangle - \langle r_{11}, r_{12} \rangle$ and $C_2 : s_1 - d_2 - u_2 - r_{22}$ in the instance graph of Figure 1c. This captures the "cross-talk" between different cliques sharing nodes. A news source garners trustworthiness by generating multiple credible articles. Users attain expertise by correctly identifying credible articles that corroborate with other expert users. Inability to do so brings down their expertise. Similarly, an article attains credibility if it is generated by a trustworthy source and highly rated by an expert user. The inference algorithm for the CCRF is discussed in detail in Section 3.

In the following subsections, we discuss the various feature groups that are considered in our CCRF model.

2.1 Articles and their Stylistic Features

The style in which news is presented to the reader plays a pivotal role in understanding its credibility. The desired property for news is to be objective and unbiased. In this section, we examine the different stylistic indicators of news credibility. All the lexicons used in this section are compiled from [28, 23].

Assertives: Assertive verbs (e.g., "claim") complement and modify a proposition in a sentence. They capture the degree of certainty to which a proposition holds.

Factives: Factive verbs (e.g., "indicate") pre-suppose the truth of a proposition in a sentence.

Hedges: These are mitigating words (e.g., "may") to soften the degree of commitment to a proposition.

Implicatives: These words trigger pre-supposition in an utterance. For example, usage of the word *complicit* indicates participation in an activity in an unlawful way.

Report verbs: These verbs (e.g., "argue") are used to indicate the attitude towards the source, or report what someone said more accurately, rather than using just *say* and *tell.*

Discourse markers: These capture the degree of confidence, perspective, and certainty in the set of propositions made. For instance, strong modals (e.g., "could"), probabilistic adverbs (e.g., "maybe"), and conditionals (e.g., "if") depict a high degree of uncertainty and hypothetical situations, whereas weak modals (e.g., "should") and inferential conjunctions (e.g., "therefore") depict certainty.

Subjectivity and bias: News is supposed to be objective: writers should not convey their own opinions, feelings or prejudices in their stories. For example, a news titled "Why do conservatives hate your children?" is not considered objective journalism. We use a subjectivity lexicon[1], a list of positive and negative opinionated words[2], and an affective lexicon[3] to detect subjective clues in articles. The *affective features* capture the state of mind (like attitude and emotions) of the writer while writing an article or post (e.g., anxiousness, confidence, depression, favor, malice, sympathy etc.).

Latent Topics	Topic Words
Obama admin.	obama, republican, party, election, president, senate, gop, vote
Citizen journ.	cjr, journalism, writers, cjrs, marx, hutchins, reporting, liberty, guides
US military	iraq, war, military, iran, china, nuclear, obama, russia, weapons
AmyGoodman	democracy, military, civil, activist, protests, killing, navajo, amanda
Alternet	media, politics, world news, activism, world, civil, visions, economy
Climate	energy, climate, power, water, change, global, nuclear, fuel, warming

Table 1: Latent topics (with illustrative labels) and their words.

We additionally harness a lexicon of bias-inducing words extracted from the Wikipedia edit history from [28] exploiting its Neutral Point of View Policy to keep its articles "fairly, proportionately, and as far as possible without bias, all significant views that have been published by reliable sources on a *topic*".

Feature vector construction: For each stylistic feature type f_i and each news article d_j, we compute the relative frequency of words of type f_i occurring in d_j, thus constructing a feature vector $F^L(d_j) = \langle freq_{ij} = \#(words\ in\ f_i)\ /\ length(d_j)\rangle$. Consider the review $r_{j,k}$ written by user u_k on the article d_j. For each such review, analogous to the per-article stylistic feature vector $\langle F^L(d_j)\rangle$, we construct a *per-review* feature vector $\langle F^L(r_{j,k})\rangle$.

2.2 Articles and their Topics

Topic tags for news articles play an important role in user-perceived prominence, bias and credibility, in accordance to the Prominence-Interpretation theory [7]. For example, the tag *Politics* is often viewed as an indicator of potential bias and individual differences; whereas tags like *Energy* or *Environment* are perceived as more neutral news and therefore invoke higher agreement in the community on the associated articles' credibility. Obviously, this can be misleading as there is a significant influence of Politics on all topics in all format of news.

Certain users have topic-specific expertise that make them rate articles on those topics better than others. News sources also have expertise on specific topics and provide a better coverage of news on those topics than others. For example, National Geographic provides a good coverage of news related to *environment*, whereas The Wall Street Journal provides a good coverage on *economic* policies.

However, many news articles do not have any explicit topic tag. In order to automatically identify the underlying theme of the article, we use Latent Dirichlet Allocation (LDA) [1] to learn the latent topic distribution in the corpus. LDA assumes a document to have a distribution over a set of topics, and each topic to have a distribution over words. Table 1 shows an excerpt of the top topic words in each topic, where we manually added illustrative labels for the topics. The latent topics also capture some subtle themes not detected by the explicit tags. For example, *Amy Goodman* is an American broadcast journalist, syndicated columnist and investigative reporter who is considered highly credible in the community. Also, associated with that topic cluster is *Amanda Blackhorse*, a Navajo activist and plaintiff in the Washington Redskins case.

Feature vector construction: For each document d_j and each of its review $r_{j,k}$, we create feature vectors $\langle F^T(d_j)\rangle$ and $\langle F^T(r_{j,k})\rangle$ respectively, using the learned *latent* topic distributions, as well as the *explicit* topic tags. Section 3.1 discusses our method to learn the topic distributions.

2.3 News Sources

A news source is considered *trustworthy* if it generates highly *credible* articles. We examine the effect of different features of a news source on its trustworthiness based on user assigned ratings

[1] http://mpqa.cs.pitt.edu/lexicons/subj_lexicon/
[2] http://www.cs.uic.edu/ liub/FBS/opinion-lexicon-English.rar
[3] http://wndomains.fbk.eu/wnaffect.html

Category	Elements
Media	newspaper, blog, radio, magazine, online
Format	editorial, investigative report, news, research
Scope	local, state, regional, national, international
Viewpoint	far left, left, center, right, neutral
Top Topics	politics, weather, war, science,, U.S. military
Expertise on Topics	U.S. congress, Middle East, crime, presidential election, Bush administration, global warming

Table 2: Features for source trustworthiness.

in the community. We consider the following source features (summarized in Table 2): the type of *media* (e.g., online, newspaper, tv, blog), *format* of news (e.g., news analysis, opinion, special report, news report, investigative report), (political) *viewpoint* (e.g., left, center, right), *scope* (e.g., international, national, local), the top *topics* covered by the source, and their topic-specific *expertise*.

Feature vector construction: For each news source s_l, we create a feature vector $\langle F^S(s_l)\rangle$ using features in Table 2. Each element $f_i^S(s_l)$ is 1 or 0 indicating presence or absence of a feature. Note that above features include the top (explicit) topics covered by any source, and its topic-specific expertise for a subset of those topics.

2.4 Users, Ratings and Interactions

A user's expertise in judging news credibility depends on many factors. [5] discusses the following traits for recognizing an expert.

Community Engagement of the user is an obvious measure for judging the user authority in the community. We capture this with different features: number of answers, ratings given, comments, ratings received, disagreement and number of raters.

Inter-User Agreement: Expert users typically agree on what constitutes a credible article. This is inherently captured in the proposed graphical model, where a user gains expertise by assigning credibility ratings to articles that corroborate with other expert users.

Topical Perspective and Expertise: The potential for harvesting user preference and expertise in topics for rating prediction of reviews has been demonstrated in [22, 21]. For credibility analysis the model needs to capture the user's *perspective* and *bias* towards certain topics based on their political inclination that bias their ratings, and their topic-specific *expertise* that allows them to evaluate articles on certain topics better as "Subject Matter Experts". These are captured as *per-user* feature weights for the stylistic indicators and topic words in the language of user-contributed reviews.

Interactions: In a community, users can upvote (*digg, like, rate*) the ratings of users that they appreciate, and downvote the ones they do not agree with. High review ratings from expert users increase the value of a user; whereas low ratings bring down her expertise. Similar to this *user-user* interaction, there can be *user-article*, *user-source* and *source-article* interactions which are captured as edges in our graphical model (by construction). Consider the following anecdotal example in the community showing an expert in nuclear energy *downvoting* another user's rating on nuclear radiation: *"Non-expert: Interesting opinion about health risks of nuclear radiation, from a physicist at Oxford University. He makes some reasonable points ...*
Low rating by expert to above review: Is it fair to assume that you have no background in biology or anything medical? While this story is definitely very important, it contains enough inaccurate and/or misleading statements..."

Feature vector construction: For each user u_k, we create an engagement feature vector $\langle F^E(u_k)\rangle$. In order to capture user *subjectivity*, in terms of different stylistic indicators of credibility, we consider the *per-review* language feature vector $\langle F^L(r_{j,k})\rangle$ of user u_k (refer to Section 2.1). To capture *user perspective and expertise* on different topics, we consider the *per-review* topic feature vector $\langle F^T(r_{j,k})\rangle$ of each user u_k.

Variables	Type	Description
d_j	Vector	Document with sequence of words $\langle w\rangle$
s	Vector	Sources
u	Vector	Users
$r_{j,k}$	Vector	Review by user u_k on document d_j with sequence of words $\langle w\rangle$
$y_{j,k}$	Real Number	Rating of $r_{j,k}$
z	Vector	Sequence of topic assignments for $\langle w\rangle$
SVR_{u_k}, SVR_{s_i} SVR_L, SVR_T	Real Number $\in [1\dots5]$	SVR prediction for users, sources, language, and topics
$\Psi = f(\langle\psi_j\rangle)$	Real Number	Clique potential with $\psi_j = \langle y_j, s_i, d_j, \langle u_k\rangle, \langle r_{j,k}\rangle\rangle$ for clique of d_j
$\lambda = \langle\alpha_u, \beta_s, \gamma_1, \gamma_2\rangle$	Vector	Combination weights for users $\langle u\rangle$, sources $\langle s\rangle$, language and topic models
$y_{n\times1}$	Vector	Credibility rating of documents $\langle d\rangle$
$X_{n\times m}$	Matrix	Feature matrix with $m = \lvert U\rvert + \lvert S\rvert + 2$
$Q_{n\times n}$	Diagonal Matrix	$f(\lambda)$
$b_{n\times1}$	Vector	$f(\lambda, X)$
$\Sigma_{n\times n}$	CovarianceMatrix	$f(\lambda)$
$\mu_{n\times1}$	Mean Vector	$f(\lambda, X)$

Table 3: Symbol table.

3. JOINT PROBABILISTIC INFERENCE

In this section we incorporate the discussed features and insights into a joint probabilistic graphical model. The task is to identify credible news articles, trustworthy news sources, and expert users *jointly* in a news community. Table 3 summarizes the important notations used in this section.

3.1 Topic Model

Consider an article d consisting of a sequence of $\{N_d\}$ words denoted by $w_1, w_2, ...w_{N_d}$. Each word is drawn from a vocabulary V having unique words indexed by $1, 2, ...V$. Consider a set of topic assignments $z = \{z_1, z_2, ...z_K\}$ for d, where each topic z_i can be from a set of K possible topics.

LDA [1] assumes each document d to be associated with a multinomial distribution θ_d over topics Z with a symmetric dirichlet prior ρ. $\theta_d(z)$ denotes the probability of occurrence of topic z in document d. Topics have a multinomial distribution ϕ_z over words drawn from a vocabulary V with a symmetric dirichlet prior ζ. $\phi_z(w)$ denotes the probability of the word w belonging to the topic z. Exact inference is not possible due to intractable coupling between Θ and Φ. We use Gibbs sampling for approximate inference.

Let $n(d, z, w)$ denote the count of the word w occurring in document d belonging to the topic z. In the following equation, (.) at any position in the above count indicates marginalization, i.e., summing up the counts over all values for the corresponding position in $n(d, z, w)$. The conditional distribution for the latent variable z (with components z_1 to z_K) is given by:

$$P(z_i = k | w_i = w, z_{-i}, w_{-i}) \propto \frac{n(d,k,.) + \rho}{\sum_k n(d,k,.) + K\rho} \times \frac{n(.,k,w) + \zeta}{\sum_w n(.,k,w) + V\zeta} \quad (1)$$

Let $\langle T^E\rangle$ and $\langle T^L\rangle$ be the set of explicit topic tags and latent topic dimensions, respectively. The topic feature vector $\langle F^T\rangle$ for an article or review combines both explicit tags and latent topics and is constructed as follows:

$$F_t^T(d) = \begin{cases} \#freq(w,d), & \text{if } T_{t'}^E = F_t^T \\ \#freq(w,d) \times \phi_{T_{t'}^L}(w), & \text{if } T_{t'}^L = F_t^T \text{ and } \phi_{T_{t'}^L}(w) > \delta \\ 0 & \text{otherwise} \end{cases}$$

So for any word in the document matching an explicit topic tag, the corresponding element in the feature vector $\langle F^T\rangle$ is set to its occurrence count in the document. If the word belongs to any latent topic with probability greater than threshold δ, the probability of the word belonging to that topic ($\phi_t(w)$) is added to the corresponding element in the feature vector, and set to 0 otherwise.

3.2 Support Vector Regression

We use Support Vector Regression (SVR) [4] to combine the different features discussed in Section 2. SVR is an extension of the max-margin framework for SVM classification to the regression problem. It solves the following optimization problem to learn weights w for features F:

$$\min_{w} \frac{1}{2} w^T w + C \times \sum_{d=1}^{N} (max(0, |y_d - w^T F| - \epsilon))^2 \tag{2}$$

Article Stylistic Model: We learn a stylistic regression model SVR_L using the *per-article* stylistic feature vector $\langle F^L(d_j) \rangle$ for article d_j (or, $\langle F^L(r_{j,k}) \rangle$ for review $r_{j,k}$), with the overall article rating y_j (or, $y_{j,k}$) as the response variable.

Article Topic Model: Similarly, we learn a topic regression model SVR_T using the *per-article* topic feature vector $\langle F^T(d_j) \rangle$ for article d_j (or, $\langle F^T(r_{j,k}) \rangle$ for review $r_{j,k}$), with the overall article rating y_j (or, $y_{j,k}$) as the response variable.

Source Model: We learn a source regression model SVR_{s_i} using the *per-source* feature vector $\langle F^S(s_i) \rangle$ for source s_i, with the overall source rating as the response variable .

User Model: For each user u_k, we learn a user regression model SVR_{u_k} with her *per-review* stylistic and topic feature vectors $\langle F^L(r_{j,k}) \cup F^T(r_{j,k}) \rangle$ for review $r_{j,k}$ for article d_j, with her overall review rating $y_{j,k}$ as the response variable.

Note that we use overall article rating to train article stylistic and topic models. For the user model, however, we take user assigned article ratings and per-user features. This model captures user subjectivity and topic perspective. The source models are trained on news-source specific meta-data and its ground-truth ratings.

3.3 Continuous Conditional Random Field

We model our learning task as a Conditional Random Field (CRF), where the random variables are the ratings of news articles $\langle d_j \rangle$, news sources $\langle s_i \rangle$, users $\langle u_k \rangle$, and reviews $\langle r_{j,k} \rangle$. The objective is to predict the credibility ratings $\langle y_j \rangle$ of the articles $\langle d_j \rangle$.

The cliques in the CRF consist of an article d_j, its source s_i, set of users $\langle u_k \rangle$ reviewing it, and the corresponding user reviews $\langle r_{j,k} \rangle$ — where $r_{j,k}$ denotes the review by user u_k on article d_j. Different cliques are connected via the common news sources, and users. There are as many cliques as the number of news articles.

Let $\psi_j(y_j, s_i, d_j, \langle u_k \rangle, \langle r_{j,k} \rangle)$ be a potential function for clique j. Each clique has a set of associated *vertex* feature functions. In our problem setting, we associate features to each vertex.The features constituted by the stylistic, topic, source and user features explained in Section 2 are: $F^L(d_j) \cup F^T(d_j) \cup F^S(s_i) \cup_k (F^E(u_k) \cup F^L(r_{j,k}) \cup F^T(r_{j,k}))$.

A traditional CRF model allows us to have a *binary* decision if a news article is *credible* ($y_j = 1$) or not ($y_j = 0$), by estimating the conditional distribution with the probability *mass* function of the discrete random variable y:

$$Pr(y|D, S, U, R) = \frac{\prod_{j=1}^{n} exp(\psi_j(y_j, s_i, d_j, \langle u_k \rangle, \langle r_{j,k} \rangle))}{\sum_y \prod_{j=1}^{n} exp(\psi_j(y_j, s_i, d_j, \langle u_k \rangle, \langle r_{j,k} \rangle))} \tag{3}$$

But in our problem setting, we want to estimate the credibility *rating* of an article. Therefore, we need to estimate the conditional distribution with the probability *density* function of the continuous random variable y:

$$Pr(y|D, S, U, R) = \frac{\prod_{j=1}^{n} exp(\psi_j(y_j, s_i, d_j, \langle u_k \rangle, \langle r_{j,k} \rangle))}{\int_{-\infty}^{\infty} \prod_{j=1}^{n} exp(\psi_j(y_j, s_i, d_j, \langle u_k \rangle, \langle r_{j,k} \rangle))dy} \tag{4}$$

Given a news article d_j, its source id s_i, and a set of user ids $\langle u_k \rangle$ who reviewed the article, the regression models $\text{SVR}_L(d_j)$, $\text{SVR}_T(d_j)$, SVR_{s_i}, $\langle \text{SVR}_{u_k}(d_j) \rangle$ (discussed in Section 3.2) predict rating of d_j. For notational brevity, hereafter, we drop the argument d_j from the SVR function. These SVR predictors are for separate feature groups and independent of each other. Now we combine the different SVR models to capture mutual interactions, such that the weight for each SVR model reflects our confidence on its quality. Errors by an SVR are penalized by the squared loss between the predicted article rating and the ground-truth rating. There is an additional constraint that for any clique *only* the regression models corresponding to the news-source and users present in it should be activated. This can be thought of as partitioning the input feature space into subsets, with the features inside a clique capturing *local* interactions, and the *global* weights capture the overall quality of the random variables via the shared information between the cliques (in terms of common sources, users, topics and language features) — an ideal setting for using a CRF. Equation 5 shows one such linear combination. Energy function of an individual clique is given by:

$$\psi_j(y_j, s_i, d_j, \langle u_k \rangle, \langle r_{j,k} \rangle) = -\sum_{k=1}^{k=U} \alpha_k \mathbb{I}_{u_k}(d_j)(y_j - \text{SVR}_{u_k})^2$$
$$-\sum_{i=1}^{i=S} \beta_i \mathbb{I}_{s_i}(d_j)(y_j - \text{SVR}_{s_i})^2 - \gamma_1 (y_j - \text{SVR}_L)^2 - \gamma_2 (y_j - \text{SVR}_T)^2 \tag{5}$$

Indicator functions $\mathbb{I}_{u_k}(d_j)$ and $\mathbb{I}_{s_i}(d_j)$ are 1 if u_k is a reviewer and s_i is the source of article d_j respectively, and are 0 otherwise.

As the output of the SVR is used as an input to the CCRF in Equation 5, each element of the input feature vector is already predicting the output variable. The learned parameters $\lambda = \langle \alpha, \beta, \gamma_1, \gamma_2 \rangle$ (with dimension(λ) $= |U| + |S| + 2$) of the linear combination of the above features depict how much to trust individual predictors. Large λ_k on a particular predictor places large penalty on the mistakes committed by it, and therefore depicts a higher quality for that predictor. α_u corresponding to user u can be taken as a proxy for that user's *expertise*, allowing us to obtain a ranked list of expert users. Similarly, β_s corresponding to news source s can be taken as a proxy for that source's *trustworthiness*, allowing us to obtain a ranked list of trustworthy news sources.

Overall energy function of all cliques is given by:

$$\Psi = \sum_{j=1}^{n} \psi_j(y_j, s_i, d_j, \langle u_k \rangle, \langle r_{j,k} \rangle)$$

(Substituting ψ_j from Equation 5 and re-organizing terms)

$$\Psi = \sum_{j=1}^{n} (-\sum_{k=1}^{k=U} \alpha_k \mathbb{I}_{u_k}(d_j)(y_j - \text{SVR}_{u_k})^2$$
$$-\sum_{i=1}^{i=S} \beta_i \mathbb{I}_{s_i}(d_j)(y_j - \text{SVR}_{s_i})^2 - \gamma_1 (y_j - \text{SVR}_L)^2 - \gamma_2 (y_j - \text{SVR}_T)^2)$$
$$= -\sum_{j=1}^{n} y_j^2 [\sum_{k=1}^{k=U} \alpha_k \mathbb{I}_{u_k}(d_j) + \sum_{i=1}^{i=S} \beta_i \mathbb{I}_{s_i}(d_j) + \gamma_1 + \gamma_2]$$
$$+ \sum_{j=1}^{n} 2 y_j [\sum_{k=1}^{k=U} \alpha_k \mathbb{I}_{u_k}(d_j) \text{SVR}_{u_k} + \sum_{i=1}^{i=S} \beta_i \mathbb{I}_{s_i}(d_j) \text{SVR}_{s_i} + \gamma_1 \text{SVR}_L$$
$$+ \gamma_2 \text{SVR}_T] - \sum_{j=1}^{n} [\sum_{k=1}^{k=U} \alpha_k \mathbb{I}_{u_k}(d_j) \text{SVR}_{u_k}^2 + \sum_{i=1}^{i=S} \beta_i \mathbb{I}_{s_i}(d_j) \text{SVR}_{s_i}^2$$
$$+ \gamma_1 \text{SVR}_L^2 + \gamma_2 \text{SVR}_T^2]$$

Organizing the bracketed terms into variables as follows:

$$Q_{i,j} = \begin{cases} \sum_{k=1}^{k=U} \alpha_k \mathbb{I}_{u_k}(d_i) + \sum_{l=1}^{l=S} \beta_l \mathbb{I}_{s_l}(d_i) + \gamma_1 + \gamma_2 & i = j \\ 0 & i \neq j \end{cases}$$

$$b_i = 2[\sum_{k=1}^{k=U} \alpha_k \mathbb{I}_{u_k}(d_i)\text{SVR}_{u_k} + \sum_{l=1}^{l=S} \beta_l \mathbb{I}_{s_l}(d_i)\text{SVR}_{s_l} + \gamma_1 \text{SVR}_L + \gamma_2 \text{SVR}_T]$$

$$c = \sum_{j=1}^{n}[\sum_{k=1}^{k=U} \alpha_k \mathbb{I}_{u_k}(d_j)\text{SVR}_{u_k}^2 + \sum_{i=1}^{i=S} \beta_i \mathbb{I}_{s_i}(d_j)\text{SVR}_{s_i}^2 + \gamma_1 \text{SVR}_L^2 + \gamma_2 \text{SVR}_T^2]$$

We can derive:

$$\Psi = -y^T Q y + y^T b - c \tag{6}$$

Substituting Ψ in Equation 4:

$$\begin{aligned} P(y|X) &= \frac{\prod_{j=1}^{n} exp(\psi_j)}{\int_{-\infty}^{\infty} \prod_{j=1}^{n} exp(\psi_j) dy} \\ &= \frac{exp(\Psi)}{\int_{-\infty}^{\infty} exp(\Psi) dy} \\ &= \frac{exp(-y^T Q y + y^T b)}{\int_{-\infty}^{\infty} exp(-y^T Q y + y^T b) dy} \\ &= \frac{exp(-\frac{1}{2} y^T \Sigma^{-1} y + y^T \Sigma^{-1} \mu)}{\int_{-\infty}^{\infty} exp(-\frac{1}{2} y^T \Sigma^{-1} y + y^T \Sigma^{-1} \mu) dy} \\ &\quad (\text{Substituting } Q = \tfrac{1}{2}\Sigma^{-1}, b = \Sigma^{-1}\mu) \end{aligned} \tag{7}$$

Equation 7 can be transformed into a multivariate Gaussian distribution after substituting $\int_{-\infty}^{\infty} exp(-\frac{1}{2} y^T \Sigma^{-1} y + y^T \Sigma^{-1} \mu) dy = \frac{(2\pi)^{n/2}}{|\Sigma^{-1}|^{\frac{1}{2}}} exp(\frac{1}{2} \mu^T \Sigma^{-1} \mu)$. Therefore obtaining,

$$P(y|X) = \frac{1}{(2\pi)^{\frac{n}{2}} |\Sigma|^{\frac{1}{2}}} exp(-\frac{1}{2}(y-\mu)^T \Sigma^{-1} (y-\mu)) \tag{8}$$

Q represents the contribution of λ to the covariance matrix Σ. Each row of the vector b and matrix Q corresponds to one training instance, representing the *active* contribution of features present in it. To ensure Equation 8 represents a valid Gaussian distribution, the covariance matrix Σ needs to be positive definite for its inverse to exist. For that the diagonal matrix Q needs to be a positive semi-definite matrix. This can be ensured by making all the diagonal elements in Q greater than 0, by constraining $\lambda_k > 0$.

Since this is a constrained optimization problem, gradient ascent cannot be directly used. We follow the approach similar to [27] and maximize log-likelihood with respect to $log\ \lambda_k$, instead of λ_k as in standard gradient ascent, making the optimization problem unconstrained as:

$$\frac{\partial logP(y|X)}{\partial log\lambda_k} = \alpha_k(\frac{\partial logP(y|X)}{\partial \lambda_k}) \tag{9}$$

Taking partial derivative of the log of Equation 8 w.r.t λ_k:

$$\frac{\partial logP(y|X)}{\partial \lambda_k} = \frac{1}{2}\frac{\partial}{\partial \lambda_k}(-y^T \Sigma^{-1} y + 2y^T \Sigma^{-1} \mu - \mu^T \Sigma^{-1} \mu + log|\Sigma^{-1}| + Constant) \tag{10}$$

Substituting the following in the above equation:

$$\begin{aligned} \frac{\partial \Sigma^{-1}}{\partial \lambda_k} &= 2\frac{\partial Q}{\partial \lambda_k} \\ &= 2I \\ \frac{\partial \Sigma^{-1}\mu}{\partial \lambda_k} &= \frac{\partial b}{\partial \lambda_k} \quad [\because \mu = \Sigma b] \\ &= 2X_{(.),k} \end{aligned}$$

where, $X_{(.),k}$ indicates the kth column of the feature matrix X.

$$\begin{aligned} \frac{\partial \Sigma}{\partial \lambda_k} &= -\Sigma \frac{\partial \Sigma^{-1}}{\partial \lambda_k} \Sigma \\ &= -2\Sigma\Sigma \\ \frac{\partial}{\partial \lambda_k}(\mu^T \Sigma^{-1} \mu) &= \frac{\partial}{\partial \lambda_k}(b^T \Sigma b) \\ &= b^T \frac{\partial \Sigma b}{\partial \lambda_k} + \frac{\partial b^T}{\partial \lambda_k} \Sigma b \\ &= b^T(\Sigma \frac{\partial b}{\partial \lambda_k} + \frac{\partial \Sigma}{\partial \lambda_k} b) + \frac{\partial b^T}{\partial \lambda_k} \Sigma b \\ &= 4X_{(.),k} \Sigma b - 2b^T \Sigma\Sigma b \\ &= 4X_{(.),k} \mu - 2\mu^T \mu \\ \frac{\partial log|\Sigma^{-1}|}{\partial \lambda_k} &= \frac{1}{|\Sigma^{-1}|} \text{Trace}(|\Sigma^{-1}| \Sigma \frac{\partial \Sigma^{-1}}{\partial \lambda_k}) \\ &= 2\text{Trace}(\Sigma) \end{aligned}$$

We can derive the gradient vector:

$$\frac{\partial logP(y|X)}{\partial \lambda_k} = -y^T y + 2y^T X_{(.),k} - 2X_{(.),k}^T \mu + \mu^T \mu + \text{Trace}(\Sigma) \tag{11}$$

Let η denote the learning rate. The update equation is given by:

$$log\lambda_k^{new} = log\lambda_k^{old} + \eta \frac{\partial logP(y|X)}{\partial log\lambda_k} \tag{12}$$

Once the model parameters are learned using gradient ascent, the inference for the prediction y of the article credibility rating is straightforward. As we assume the distribution to be Gaussian, the prediction is the expected value of the function, given by the mean of the distribution: $y\prime = argmax_y\ P(y|X) = \mu = \Sigma b$.
Note that Σ and b are both a function of $\lambda = \langle \alpha, \beta, \gamma_1, \gamma_2 \rangle$ which represents the combination weights of various factors to capture mutual interactions. The optimization problem determines the optimal λ for reducing the error in prediction.

4. USE CASE: NEWSTRUST

We performed experiments with data from a typical news community: *newstrust.net*[4]. This community is similar to *digg.com* and *reddit.com*, but has more refined ratings and interactions. We chose NewsTrust because of the availability of *ground-truth* ratings for credibility analysis of news articles; such ground-truth is not available for the other communities.

We collected *stories* from NewsTrust from May, 2006 to May, 2014. Each such story features a *news article* from a source (E.g. BBC, CNN, Wall Street Journal) that is posted by a member, and reviewed by other members, many of whom are *professional journalists* and *content experts*[5]. We crawled all the stories with their explicit topic tags and other associated meta-data. We crawled all the *news articles* from their original sources that were featured in any NewsTrust story. The earliest story dates back to May 1, 1939 and the latest one is in May 9, 2014.

We collected all *member profiles* containing information about the demographics, occupation and expertise of the members along with their activity in the community in terms of the posts, reviews and ratings; as well as *interaction* with other members. The members in the community can also rate each others' ratings. The earliest story rating by a member dates back to May, 2006 and the most recent one

[4]Code and data available at
http://www.mpi-inf.mpg.de/impact/credibilityanalysis/
[5]http://www.newstrust.net/help#about_newstrust

Factors	Count
Unique news articles reviewed in NewsTrust	62,064
NewsTrust stories on news articles	84,704
NewsTrust stories with $\geq$ 1 reviews	43,107
NewsTrust stories with $\geq$ 3 reviews	18,521
NewsTrust member reviews of news articles	134,407
News articles extracted from original sources	47,565
NewsTrust stories on extracted news articles	52,579
News sources	5,658
Journalists who wrote news articles	19,236
Timestamps (month and year) of posted news articles	3,122
NewsTrust members who reviewed news articles	7,114
NewsTrust members who posted news articles	1,580
News sources reviewed by NewsTrust members	668
Explicit topic tags	456
Latent topics extracted	300

Table 4: Dataset statistics.

Factors	Count	Factors	Count
Nodes	181,364	No. of weakly connected components	12
Sources	1,704	Diameter	8
Members	6,906	Average path length	47
News articles	42,204	Average degree	6.641
Reviews	130,550	Average clustering coefficient	0.884
Edges	602,239	Modularity	0.516
Total triangles	521,630		

Table 5: Graph statistics.

is in Feb, 2014. In addition, we collected information on member evaluation of news sources, and other information (e.g., type of media, scope, viewpoint, topic specific expertise) about source from its *meta data*.

Crawled dataset: Table 4 shows the dataset statistics. In total 62K unique news articles were reviewed in NewsTrust in the given period, out of which we were able to extract 47K full articles from the original sources like New York Times, TruthDig, ScientificAmerican etc — a total of 5.6K distinct sources. The remaining articles were not available for crawling. There are 84.7K stories featured in NewsTrust for all the above articles, out of which $52.5K$ stories refer to the news articles we managed to extract from their original sources. The average number of reviews per story is 1.59. For general analysis we use the entire dataset. For experimental evaluation of the CCRF and hypotheses testing, we use only those stories (18.5K) with a *minimum of* 3 *reviews* that refer to the news articles we were able to extract from original sources.

Generated graph: Table 5 shows the statistics of the graph constructed by the method of Section 2.

Ground-Truth for evaluation: The members in the community can rate the credibility of a news article on a scale from 1 to 5 regarding 15 qualitative aspects like facts, fairness, writing style and insight, and popularity aspects like recommendation, credibility and views. Members give an overall *recommendation* for the article explained to them as: *"... Is this quality journalism? Would you recommend this story to a friend or colleague? ... This question is similar to the up and down arrows of popular social news sites like Digg and Reddit, but with a focus on quality journalism."* Each article's aspect ratings by different members are weighted (and aggregated) by NewsTrust based on findings of [16], and the member expertise and member level (described below). This overall article rating is taken as the ground-truth for the article *credibility* rating in our work. A user's member level is calculated by NewsTrust based on her community engagement, experience, other users' feedback on her ratings, profile transparency and validation by NewsTrust staff. This member level is taken as the proxy for user *expertise* in our work. Members rate news sources while reviewing an article. These ratings are aggregated for each source, and taken as a proxy for the source *trustworthiness* in our work.

Model	MSE
Latent Factor Models (LFM)	
Simple LFM [15]	0.95
Experience-based LFM [21]	0.85
Text-based LFM [20]	0.78
Our Model: User SVR	0.60

Table 6: MSE comparison of models for predicting users' credibility rating behavior with 10-fold cross-validation. Improvements are statistically significant with *P-value* < 0.0001.

Model	Only Title MSE	Title & Text MSE
Language Model: SVR		
Language (Bias and Subjectivity)	3.89	0.72
Explicit Topics	1.74	1.74
Explicit + Latent Topics	1.68	1.01
All Topics (Explicit + Latent) + Language	1.57	0.61
News Source Features and Language Model: SVR		
News Source	1.69	1.69
News Source + All Topics + Language	0.91	0.46
Aggregated Model: SVR		
Users + All Topics + Language + News Source	0.43	0.41
Our Model: CCRF+SVR		
User + All Topics + Language + News Source	0.36	0.33

Table 7: MSE comparison of models for predicting aggregated article credibility rating with 10-fold cross-validation. Improvements are statistically significant with *P-value* < 0.0001.

Training data: We perform 10-fold cross-validation on the news articles. During training on any 9-folds of the data, the algorithm learns the user, source, language and topic models from user-assigned ratings to articles and sources present in the train split. We combine sources with less than 5 articles and users with less than 5 reviews into background models for sources and users, respectively. This is to avoid modeling from sparse observations, and to reduce dimensionality of the feature space. However, while testing on the remaining *blind* 1-fold we use *only the ids* of sources and users reviewing the article; we do not use any user-assigned ratings of sources or articles. For a new user and a new source, we draw parameters from the user or source background model. The results are averaged by 10-fold cross-validation, and presented in the next section.

Experimental settings: In the first two experiments we want to find the power of the CCRF in predicting user rating behavior, and credibility rating of articles. Therefore, the evaluation measure is taken as the *Mean Squared Error* (MSE) between the prediction and the actual ground-rating in the community. For the latter experiments in finding expert users (and, trustworthy sources) there is no absolute measure for predicting user (and, source) quality; it only makes sense to find the relative ranking of users (and, sources) in terms of their expertise (and, trustworthiness). Therefore, the evaluation measure is taken as the *Normalized Discounted Cumulative Gain* (NDCG) [13] between the ranked list of users (and, sources) obtained from CCRF and their actual ranking in the community.

5. EXPERIMENTS

5.1 Predicting User Ratings of Articles

First we evaluate how good our model can predict the credibility ratings that users assign to news articles using the *Mean Squared Error* (MSE) between the prediction and the actual rating.

Model	NDCG
Experience LFM [21]	0.80
PageRank	0.83
CCRF	0.86

Table 8: NDCG scores for ranking trustworthy sources.

Model	NDCG
Experience LFM [21]	0.81
Member Ratings	0.85
CCRF	0.91

Table 9: NDCG scores for ranking expert users.

Baselines: We consider the following baselines for comparison:
1. *Latent Factor Recommendation Model* (LFM) [15]: LFM considers the tuple $\langle userId, itemId, rating\rangle$, and models each user and item as a vector of latent factors which are learned by minimizing the MSE between the rating and the product of the user-item latent factors. In our setting, each news article is considered an item and rating refers to the credibility rating assigned by a user to an article.
2. *Experience-based LFM* [21]: This model incorporates *experience* of a user in rating an item in the LFM. The model builds on the hypothesis that users at similar levels of experience have similar rating behaviors which evolve with *time*. The model has an extra dimension: the *time* of rating an item which is not used in our SVR model. Note the analogy between the *experience* of a user in this model, and the notion of user *expertise* in the SVR model. However, these models ignore the text of the reviews.
3. *Text-based LFM* [20]: This model incorporates text in the LFM by combining the latent factors associated to items in LFM with latent topics in text from topic models like LDA.
4. *Support Vector Regression* (SVR) [4]: We train an SVR model SVR_{u_k} for *each* user u_k (refer to Section 3.2) based on her reviews $\langle r_{j,k}\rangle$ with language and topic features $\langle F^L(r_{j,k}) \cup F^T(r_{j,k})\rangle$, with the user's article ratings $\langle y_{j,k}\rangle$ as the response variable. We also incorporate the article language features and the topic features, as well as source-specific features to train the user model for this task. The other models ignore the stylistic features, and other fine-grained *user-item* interactions in the community.

Table 6 shows the MSE comparison between the different methods. Our model (User SVR) achieved the lowest MSE and thus performed best.

5.2 Finding Credible Articles

As a second part of the evaluation, we investigate the predictive power of different models in order to find credible news articles based on the *aggregated ratings from all users*. The above LFM models, unaware of the *user cliques*, cannot be used directly for this task, as each news article has multiple reviews from different users which need to be aggregated. We find the *Mean Squared Error* (MSE) between the estimated overall article rating, and the ground-truth article rating. We consider stories with *at least 3 ratings* about a news article. We compare the CCRF against the following baselines:
1. *Support Vector Regression* (SVR) [4]: We consider an SVR model with features on language (bag-of-all-words, subjectivity, bias etc.), topics (explicit tags as well as latent dimensions), and news-source-specific features. The language model uses all the lexicons derived and used in [28, 23]. The source model also includes topic features in terms of the top topics covered by the source, and its topic-specific expertise for a subset of the topics.
2. *Aggregated Model* (SVR) [4]: As explained earlier, the user features cannot be directly used in the baseline model, which is agnostic of the user *cliques*. Therefore, we adopt a simple aggregation approach by taking the *average* rating of all the user ratings $\frac{\text{SVR}_{u_k}(d_j)}{|u_k|}$ for an article d_j as a feature. Note that, in contrast to this simple average used here, our CCRF model learns the weights $\langle\alpha_u\rangle$ *per-user* to combine their overall ratings for an article.

Table 7 shows the MSE comparison of the different models.

MSE Comparison: The first two models in Table 6 ignore the textual content of news articles, and reviews, and perform worse than the ones that incorporate full text. The text-based LFM considers title and text, and performs better than its predecessors. However, the User SVR model considers richer features and interactions, and attains 23% MSE reduction over the best performing LFM baselines.

The baselines in Table 7 show the model performance after incorporating different features in two different settings: 1) with news article *titles* only as text, and 2) with titles and the *first few paragraphs* of an article. The language model, especially the bias and subjectivity features, is less effective using only the article titles due to sparseness. On the other hand, using the entire article text may lead to very noisy features. So including the first few paragraphs of an article is the "sweet spot". For this, we made an ad-hoc decision and included the first 1000 characters of each article. With this setting, the language features made a substantial contribution to reducing the MSE.

The aggregated SVR model further brings in the *user* features, and achieves the lowest MSE among the baselines. This shows that a user-aware credibility model performs better than user-independent ones. Our CCRF model combines all features in a more sophisticated manner, which results in 19.5% MSE reduction over the most competitive baseline (aggregated SVR). This is empirical evidence that the *joint* interactions between the different factors in a news community are indeed important to consider for identifying highly credible articles.

5.3 Finding Trustworthy Sources

We shift the focus to two use cases: 1) identifying the most trustworthy sources, and 2) identifying expert users in the community who can play the role of "citizen journalists".

Using the model of Section 3, we rank all news sources in the community according to the learned $\langle\beta_{s_i}\rangle$ in Equation 5. The baseline is taken as the *PageRank* scores of news sources in the Web graph. In the experience-based LFM we can consider the sources to be users, and articles generated by them to be items. This allows us to obtain a ranking of the sources based on their overall authority. This is the second baseline against which we compare the CCRF.

We measure the quality of the ranked lists in terms of *NDCG* using the actual ranking of the news sources in the community as ground-truth. NDCG gives geometrically decreasing weights to predictions at the various positions of the ranked list:

$NDCG_p = \frac{DCG_p}{IDCG_p}$ where $DCG_p = rel_1 + \sum_{i=2}^{p} \frac{rel_i}{\log_2 i}$

Table 8 shows the NDCG scores for the different methods.

5.4 Finding Expert Users

Similar to news sources, we rank users according to the learned $\langle\alpha_{u_k}\rangle$ in Equation 5. The baseline is the average rating received by a user from other members in the community. We compute the NDCG score for the ranked lists of users by our method. We also compare against the ranked list of users from the experience-aware LFM [21]. Table 9 shows the NDCG scores for different methods.

5.5 Discussion

Hypothesis Testing: We test various hypotheses under the influence of the feature groups using explicit labels, and ratings available in the NewsTrust community. A summary of the tests is presented in Table 10 showing a *moderate* correlation between various factors which are put together in the CCRF to have a *strong* indicator for information credibility.

Language: The stylistic features (factor (a) in Table 10) like *assertives, hedges, implicatives, factives, discourse* and *affective* play a significant role in the credibility detection of news, in conjunction with other language features like *topics*.

Factors	Corr.
a) Stylistic Indicators Vs. Article Credibility Rating	
Insightful (Is it well reasoned? thoughtful?)	0.77
Fairness (Is it impartial? or biased?)	0.75
Style (Is this story clear? concise? well-written?)	0.65
Responsibility (Are claims valid, ethical, unbiased?)	0.72
Balance (Does this story represent diverse viewpoints?)	0.49
b) Influence of Politics Vs. Disagreement	0.11
c) Expertise (Moderate, High) Vs. Disagreement	-0.10, -0.31
Interactions	
d) User Expertise Vs. User-User Rating	0.40
e) Source Trustworthiness Vs. Article Credibility Rating	0.47
f) User Expertise Vs. MSE in Article Rating Prediction	-0.29

Table 10: Pearson's product-moment correlation between various factors (with *P-value* < 0.0001 for each test).

Money - Politics	War in Iraq	Media - Politics	Green Technology
Most Trusted			
rollingstone.com	nybooks.com	consortiumnews	discovermagazine.com
truthdig.com	consortiumnews	thenation.com	nature.com
democracynow.org	truthout.org	thedailyshow.com	scientificamerican.com
Least Trusted			
firedoglake.com	crooksandliars	rushlimbaugh.com	
suntimes.com	timesonline	rightwingnews.com	
trueslant.com	suntimes.com	foxnews.com	

Table 11: Most and least trusted sources on sample topics.

Topics: Topics are an important indicator for news credibility. We measured the influence of the *Politics* tag on other topics by their co-occurrence frequency in the explicit tag sets over all the news articles. We found significant influence of Politics on all topics, with an average measure of association of 54% to any topic, and 62% for the overall news article. The community gets polarized due to different perspectives on topical aspects of news. A moderate correlation (factor (b) in Table 10) indicates a weak trend of disagreement, measured by the standard deviation in article credibility rating among users, increasing with its political content. In general, we find that community disagreement for different viewpoints are as follows: Right (0.80) > Left(0.78) > Center(0.65) > Neutral (0.63).
Users: User engagement features are strong indicators of expertise. Although credibility is ultimately subjective, experts show moderate agreement (factor (c) in Table 10) on highly credible news. There is a moderate correlation (factor (d) in Table 10) between feedback received by a user on his ratings from community, and his expertise.
Sources: Various traits of a news source like viewpoint, format and topic expertise are strong indicators of trustworthiness. In general, science and technology websites (e.g., discovermagazine.com, nature.com, scientificamerican.com), investigative reporting and non-partisan sources (e.g., truthout.org, truthdig.com, cfr.org), book sites (e.g., nybooks.com, editorandpublisher.com), encyclopedia (e.g., Wikipedia) and fact checking sites (e.g., factcheck.org) rank among the top trusted sources. Table 11 shows the most and least trusted sources on four sample topics. Overall, news sources are considered trustworthy with an average rating of 3.46 and variance of 0.15. Tables 12 and 13 show the most and least trusted sources on different viewpoints and media types respectively. Contents from *blogs* are most likely to be posted followed by newspaper, magazine and other online sources. Contents from *wire service, TV* and *radio* are deemed the most trustworthy, although they have the least subscription, followed by *magazines*.
Interactions: In principle, there is a moderate correlation between *trustworthy* sources generating *credible* articles (factor (e) in Table 10) identified by *expert* users (factor (f) in Table 10). A negative sign of correlation indicates decrease in disagreement or MSE with increase in expertise. In a news community, we can observe *moderate* signals of interaction between various factors that characterize users, articles, and sources. Our CCRF model brings all these features together to build a *strong* signal for news credibility.

Left	Right	Center	Neutral
Most	**Trusted**		
democracynow, truthdig.com, rollingstone.com	courant.com, opinionjournal.com, townhall.com	armedforces-journal.com, bostonreview.net	spiegel.de,cfr.org, editorandpublisher.com
Least	**Trusted**		
crooksandliars, suntimes.com, washingtonmonthly.com	rightwingnews, foxnews.com, weeklystandard.com	sltrib.com, examiner.com, spectator.org	msnbc.msn.com, online.wsj.com, techcrunch.com

Table 12: Most and least trusted sources with different viewpoints.

Magazine	Online	Newspaper	Blog
Most Trusted Sources			
rollingstone.com	truthdig.com	nytimes.com	juancole.com
nybooks.com	cfr.org	nola.com	dailykos.com
thenation.com	consortiumnews	seattletimes	huffingtonpost
Least Trusted Sources			
weeklystandard.com	investigativevoice	suntimes.com	rightwingnews
commentarymagazine	northbaltimore	nydailynews.com	firedoglake.com
nationalreview.com	hosted.ap.org	dailymail.co.uk	crooksandliars

Table 13: Most and least trusted sources on different types of media.

6. RELATED WORK

Rating prediction in online communities: Collaborative filtering based approaches [15] for rating prediction exploit user and item similarities by latent factors. [21] further studies the temporal evolution of users and their rating behavior in this framework. Recent works [20, 22] also tap into user review texts to generate user-specific ratings of reviews. Other papers have studied temporal issues for anomaly detection [10].Prior work that tapped user review texts focused on other issues. Sentiment analysis over reviews aimed to learn latent topics [18], latent aspects and their ratings [35], and user-user interactions [36]. Our model unifies several dimensions to jointly study the role of language, users, topics, and interactions for information credibility.
Information credibility in social media: [3] analyzes micro-blog postings in Twitter related to trending topics, and classifies them as credible or not based on features from user posting and re-posting behavior. [14] focuses on credibility of users, harnessing the dynamics of information flow in the underlying social graph and tweet content. [2] analyzes both topical content of information sources and social network structure to find credible information sources in social networks. Information credibility in tweets has been studied in [11]. [33] conducts a *user study* to analyze various factors like contrasting viewpoints and expertise affecting the truthfulness of controversial claims. However, none of these prior works analyze the interplay between *sources, language, topics,* and *users*.

The works closest to our problem and approach are [34, 23]. [34] presents an algorithm for propagating trust scores in a heterogeneous network of claims, sources, and documents. [23] proposes a method to jointly learn user trustworthiness, statement credibility, and language objectivity in online health communities. However, these works do not analyze the role of *topics, language bias, user perspective, expertise,* and fine-grained interactions in community.
Bias in social communities and media: The use of biased language in Wikipedia and similar collaborative communities has been studied in [9, 28]. Even more broadly, the task of characterizing

subjective language has been addressed, among others, in [37, 19]. The influence of different kinds of bias in online user ratings has been studied in [30, 6]. [6] proposes an approach to handle users who might be subjectively different or strategically dishonest.
Citizen journalism: [29] defines citizen journalism as "the act of a citizen or group of citizens playing an active role in the process of collecting, reporting, analyzing and dissemination of news and information to provide independent, reliable, accurate, wide-ranging and relevant information that a democracy requires." [31] focuses on user activities like blogging in community news websites. Although the potential of citizen journalism is greatly highlighted in the recent Arab Spring [12], misinformation can be quite dangerous when relying on users as news sources (e.g., the reporting of the Boston Bombings in 2013 [25]).

7. CONCLUSIONS

In this work, we analyzed the effect of different factors like *language, topics* and *perspectives* on the credibility rating of articles in a news community. These factors and their mutual interactions are the features of a novel model for jointly capturing *credibility* of news articles, *trustworthiness* of news sources and *expertise* of users. From an application perspective, we demonstrated that our method can reliably identify credible articles, trustworthy sources and expert users in the community.

As future work, we plan to model and analyze the *temporal* evolution of the factors associated with each of the components in our model. We have a strong intuition that time has a significant influence on the trustworthiness of sources and credibility of news.

8. REFERENCES

[1] D. M. Blei, A. Y. Ng, and M. I. Jordan. Latent dirichlet allocation. *J. Mach. Learn. Res.*, 3, 2003.

[2] K. R. Canini, B. Suh, and P. Pirolli. Finding credible information sources in social networks based on content and social structure. In *PASSAT*, 2011.

[3] C. Castillo, M. Mendoza, and B. Poblete. Information credibility on twitter. In *WWW*, 2011.

[4] H. Drucker, C. J. C. Burges, L. Kaufman, A. J. Smola, and V. Vapnik. Support vector regression machines. In *NIPS*, 1996.

[5] H. J. Einhorn, R. M. Hogarth, and E. Klempner. Quality of group judgment. *Psychological Bulletin*, 1977.

[6] H. Fang, J. Zhang, and N. Magnenat Thalmann. Subjectivity grouping: Learning from users' rating behavior. In *AAMAS*, 2014.

[7] B. J. Fogg. Prominence-interpretation theory: explaining how people assess credibility online. In *CHI*, 2003.

[8] Gallup.com. Americans' confidence in newspapers continues to erode. http://www.gallup.com/poll/163097/americans-confidence-newspapers-continues-erode.aspx. Accessed: 2015-05-07.

[9] S. Greene and P. Resnik. More than words: Syntactic packaging and implicit sentiment. In *NAACL*, 2009.

[10] S. Günnemann, N. Günnemann, and C. Faloutsos. Detecting anomalies in dynamic rating data: A robust probabilistic model for rating evolution. KDD, 2014.

[11] A. Gupta and P. Kumaraguru. Credibility ranking of tweets during high impact events. In *PSOSM*, 2012.

[12] P. N. Howard, A. Duffy, D. Freelon, M. Hussain, W. Mari, and M. Mazaid. Opening closed regimes: What was the role of social media during the arab spring? 2011.

[13] K. Järvelin and J. Kekäläinen. Cumulated gain-based evaluation of IR techniques. *ACM Trans. Inf. Syst.*, 20(4), 2002.

[14] B. Kang, J. O'Donovan, and T. Höllerer. Modeling topic specific credibility on twitter. In *IUI*, 2012.

[15] Y. Koren. Factorization meets the neighborhood: A multifaceted collaborative filtering model. KDD, 2008.

[16] C. Lampe and R. K. Garrett. It's all news to me: The effect of instruments on ratings provision. In *HICSS*, 2007.

[17] S. C. Lewis, K. Kaufhold, and D. L. Lasorsa. Thinking about citizen journalism: The philosophical and practical challenges of user-generated content for community newspapers. *Journalism Practice*, 4(2), 2010.

[18] C. Lin and Y. He. Joint sentiment/topic model for sentiment analysis. CIKM, 2009.

[19] C. Lin, Y. He, and R. Everson. Sentence subjectivity detection with weakly-supervised learning. In *IJCNLP*, 2011.

[20] J. McAuley and J. Leskovec. Hidden factors and hidden topics: Understanding rating dimensions with review text. RecSys, 2013.

[21] J. J. McAuley and J. Leskovec. From amateurs to connoisseurs: modeling the evolution of user expertise through online reviews. In *WWW*, 2013.

[22] S. Mukherjee, G. Basu, and S. Joshi. Joint author sentiment topic model. In *SDM*, 2014.

[23] S. Mukherjee, G. Weikum, and C. Danescu-Niculescu-Mizil. People on drugs: Credibility of user statements in health communities. KDD, 2014.

[24] Nber.org. Media bias and voting. http://www.nber.org/digest/oct06/w12169.html. Accessed: 2015-05-07.

[25] Nytimes.com. Should reddit be blamed for the spreading of a smear? http://www.nytimes.com/2013/07/28/magazine/should-reddit-be-blamed-for-the-spreading-of-a-smear.html. Accessed: 2015-05-07.

[26] T. Qin, T. Liu, X. Zhang, D. Wang, and H. Li. Global ranking using continuous conditional random fields. NIPS, 2008.

[27] V. Radosavljevic, S. Vucetic, and Z. Obradovic. Continuous conditional random fields for regression in remote sensing. ECAI, 2010.

[28] M. Recasens, C. Danescu-Niculescu-Mizil, and D. Jurafsky. Linguistic models for analyzing and detecting biased language. In *ACL*, 2013.

[29] B. Shayne and W. Chris. We media: How audiences are shaping the future of news and information. 2003.

[30] Sloanreview.mit.edu. The problem with online ratings. http://sloanreview.mit.edu/article/the-problem-with-online-ratings-2/ . Accessed: 2015-05-07.

[31] A. Stuart. Citizen journalism and the rise of 'mass self-communication': Reporting the london bombings. *Global Media*, 1(1), 2007.

[32] B. Tadas, P. Robinson, and L. Morency. Continuous conditional neural fields for structured regression. In *ECCV*, 2014.

[33] V. Vydiswaran et al. BiasTrust: Teaching biased users about controversial topics. CIKM, 2012.

[34] V. V. Vydiswaran, C. Zhai, and D. Roth. Content-driven trust propagation framework. In *KDD*, 2011.

[35] H. Wang et al. Latent aspect rating analysis without aspect keyword supervision. KDD, 2011.

[36] R. West, H. S. Paskov, J. Leskovec, and C. Potts. Exploiting social network structure for person-to-person sentiment analysis. *TACL*, 2(2), 2014.

[37] J. Wiebe and E. Riloff. Creating subjective and objective sentence classifiers from unannotated texts. In *CICLing*, 2005.

Clustering-based Active Learning on Sensor Type Classification in Buildings

Dezhi Hong, Hongning Wang, Kamin Whitehouse
Department of Computer Science, University of Virginia, VA USA
{hong, hw5x, whitehouse}@virginia.edu

ABSTRACT

Commercial and industrial buildings account for a considerable portion of all energy consumed in the U.S., and thus reducing this energy consumption is a national grand challenge. Based on the large deployment of sensors in modern commercial buildings, many organizations are applying data analytic solutions to the thousands of sensing and control points to detect wasteful and incorrect operations for energy savings. Scaling this approach is challenging, however, because the metadata about these sensing and control points is inconsistent between buildings, or even missing altogether. Moreover, normalizing the metadata requires significant integration effort.

In this work, we demonstrate a first step towards an automatic metadata normalization solution that requires minimal human intervention. We propose a clustering-based active learning algorithm to differentiate sensors in buildings by type, e.g., temperature v.s. humidity. Our algorithm exploits data clustering structure and propagates labels to their nearby unlabeled neighbors to accelerate the learning process. We perform a comprehensive study on metadata collected from over 20 different sensor types and 2,500 sensor streams in three commercial buildings. Our approach is able to achieve more than 92% accuracy for type classification with much less labeled examples than baselines. As a proof-of-concept, we also demonstrate a typical analytic application enabled by the normalized metadata.

Categories and Subject Descriptors

H.4 [**Information Systems Applications**]: Miscellaneous

General Terms

Algorithms, Performance, Experimentation

Keywords

Active learning, Clustering, Metadata normalization

CIKM'15, October 19–23, 2015, Melbourne, Australia.
© 2015 ACM. ISBN 978-1-4503-3794-6/15/10 ...$15.00.
DOI: http://dx.doi.org/10.1145/2806416.2806574.

1. INTRODUCTION

According to recent reports from U.S. Department of Energy [27, 17], commercial and industrial buildings in the U.S. account for almost 20 percent of the country's total energy use and a good 30 percent of that energy is used "inefficiently or unnecessarily." Reducing this energy usage is a national grand challenge: in 2011, the U.S. government launched the Better Buildings Challenge to make these buildings at least 20 percent more efficient by 2020 [10]. To achieve this goal, many organizations are applying data analytics to the thousands of sensing and control points in a typical commercial building to detect wasteful and incorrect operations.

The analytic-based approach is highly effective but very difficult to scale because the metadata about the type, location, and relationships between the sensing and control units are inconsistent between buildings, or even missing altogether. Generally, the sensing and control points in a building are intended to be used for manual inspection or by handcrafted control loops in a building automation system (BAS); they are not designed for automatic extraction and consumption by external software. As a result, mapping the sensor streams to the inputs of a data analytic engine requires significant integration effort and anecdotally takes about a week or longer for each commercial building. For large organizations that are applying this approach to hundreds or more buildings, such as Microsoft's 88 Acres project [28], this process can take years. Even if this highly manual process is performed once, the need for additional mapping is not necessarily eliminated. New types of metadata will be required as the building is modified or renovated, as the equipment is upgraded, or as new conditions and algorithms are added to the analytics engine.

Building	Point Name
A	`Zone Temp 2 RMI204`
	`spaceTemperature 1st Floor Area1`
B	`SDH_SF1_R282_RMT`
	`SDH_S1-01_ROOM_TEMP`
C	`SODA1R300__ART`
	`SODA1R410B_ART`

Table 1: Example point names for temperature sensors from three different buildings.

In modern commercial buildings, a sensing or control "point" is a sensor measurement, a controller, or a software value, e.g., a temperature sensor installed in an office room. The metadata about the point indicates the physical location, the type of sensor or controller, how the sensor or controller relates to the mechanical systems, and other important contextual information. Most of the time, the metadata is encoded as a "point name", which is usually a short text string with several concatenated abbreviations. Table 1 lists a few point names of sensors in three different building management systems contracted by Trane[1], Siemens[2] and Barrington Controls[3]. For example, the point name `SDH_SF1_R282_RMT` is constructed as a concatenation of the name of the building (`SDH`), the supply fan unit identifier (`SF1`), the room number (`R282`) and the sensor type (`RMT`, room temperature). As the name indicates, this sensor stream measures the temperature in a specific room; and it also reveals the control unit that can affect the temperature in this room. Unfortunately, different naming conventions are used in most buildings due to different equipment, vendors, manufacturers, and contractors being used. As shown in the table, the notion of *room temperature* is encoded with different abbreviations in these three buildings: `Temp`, `RMT` and `ART`. Similar variation exists between buildings on a single commercial campus and even between buildings with the same contractor.

We envision a system that will allow an advanced analytic engine to quickly connect to and analyze the data from a commercial building. It would extract or infer metadata values about sensing and control points to a normalized metadata standard. Such a tool would not only save time but also allow building managers to experiment with many different kinds of analytic engines. Nevertheless, there is limited work on this topic. Bhattarcharya et al. [4] exploit a programming language based solution, where they derive a set of regular expressions from a handful of labeled examples to normalize the point name of sensors. This approach assumes a consistent format for all point names and one single pattern for each type, which is not the case in practice, as shown in Table 1. Schumann et al. [22] develop a probabilistic framework to classify sensor types based on the similarity of a raw point name to the entries in a manually constructed dictionary. However, the performance of this method is limited by the coverage and diversity of entries in the dictionary, and the dictionary size becomes intractable when there exist a lot of variations of the same type, or conflicting definitions of a dictionary entry in different buildings.

In this work, we demonstrate a first step towards an automatic metadata normalization solution that requires minimal human intervention. We focus on a key category of metadata: the type of sensor associated with a sensing point. In contrast to the aforementioned methods, where the annotation process is isolated from model training, we develop a novel active learning based solution to integrate these two processes so as to minimize the manual labeling effort throughout the metadata normalization process. Beyond the traditional active learning solutions [24, 6, 5], we further accelerate the learning process by exploiting the clustering structure of point names. We should note that although the naming schemata vary significantly across buildings, there will be definite variants within the same building, given there are only finite types of sensors deployed in a building. As a result, during active learning, unlabeled examples can be clustered; those in the same cluster are more likely to share the same label and hence do not need to be queried repeatedly. Moreover, the acquired labels can be further propagated to the unlabeled neighbors in the same cluster to expedite classifier training. In our solution, the examples selected for labeling are chosen based on both their representativeness in the cluster and the informativeness of the cluster itself. A Gaussian Mixture Model with Dirichlet Process Prior [20] is used to cluster the instances on the fly to accommodate the dynamic nature of active learning. Label propagation is performed with respect to the connectivity of labeled examples' neighborhood in an adaptive manner.

To investigate the effectiveness of the proposed solution for sensor type classification, we performed extensive experimental comparisons against the state-of-the-art active learning algorithms on a large collection of real sensor stream data, which includes over 20 different sensor types and 2,500 sensors in three different commercial buildings. Our method achieved increased classification performance with reduced amount of manual labels.

Our main contributions in this paper can be summarized as follows:

- We propose a novel, effective yet general active learning approach by exploiting the clustering structure of instances and label propagation to unlabeled neighbors, in order to achieve better convergence rate.
- We evaluate our proposed solution in sensor type classification based on real metadata containing 20 different sensor types and 2,500 sensors in three different commercial buildings; and our solution achieved more than 92% accuracy with at least 16% less manual labels than the state-of-the-art active learning algorithms.
- We also illustrate how data analytics can be performed on top of the automatically normalized building metadata with an example of keyword-based search.

2. RELATED WORK

To the best of our knowledge, there is few existing work addressing the sensor metadata normalization problem studied in this paper. Besides [4, 22] discussed before, there are two major bodies of related work to ours, i.e., active learning in machine learning and schema matching in database.

The main idea behind active learning is that a machine learning algorithm can achieve greater accuracy with fewer labeled training instances if it is allowed to choose the data from which it learns [24]. Therefore, the key research question in active learning is evaluating the informativeness of unlabeled instances for querying. Various solutions have been proposed from different perspectives, including uncertainty reduction [6], query by committee [12], and expected error reduction [2]. In particular, Nguyen and Smeulders also incorporated clustering idea into active learning to select the most informative examples [16]. Their proposed query strategy gives priority to instances that are close to both classification boundary and cluster centroid. Dasgupta and Hsu utilized a hierarchical clustering structure to alleviate sampling bias and improve learning efficiency [7]. They present an algorithm that is statistically consistent and guarantees to have better label complexity than supervised learning. However, in those two methods clustering is performed in an ad-hoc manner, e.g., with predefined cluster size; and neither of them considers the label proximity between adja-

[1]`http://www.trane.com/`
[2]`http://www.siemens.com/`
[3]The company is no longer in business.

cent examples or propagates labels to reduce the amount of labels required for model training.

Automatic schema matching [19] is a classical problem in the database community where correspondences between elements of two schemata are identified as part of the data integration process. Many techniques have been proposed to achieve a partial automation of the match operation for specific application domains. Doan et al. ask a user to provide semantic mappings for a small set of data sources and then train a set of learners with existing machine learning approaches to find the mappings for new data sources [9]. Dhamankar et al. extend [9] to a semi-supervised setting, where domain-specific knowledge is introduced for complex expressions learning [8]. Madhavan et al. exploit a large collection of schemata with known mappings to learn a prior distribution of the elements and their properties [14]. The learned prior distribution is then used as constraints to help a suite of base learners to complete the matching. Though adapting learning techniques, these works mostly focus on offline supervised settings and do not emphasize the efficiency of learning methods, i.e., to reduce manual efforts throughout the learning procedure.

3. METHODOLOGY

In this work, we develop a novel active learning based solution to perform automated sensor type classification in commercial buildings. Because in practice one can get direct access to all point names in a target building, our approach adopts the *pool-based* sampling setting, which selects the most informative instances from the entire collection of unlabeled data points. The data clustering structure is exploited to aid manual labeling of instances and to avoid repeated selection of similar instances. In addition, the acquired labels are propagated to their unlabeled neighbors to accelerate the training process. To accommodate the dynamic nature of active learning, we appeal to a non-parametric Bayesian approach to identify the clustering structure, and perform label propagation in an adaptive manner.

3.1 Clustering-based Active Learning

Formally, the problem of using active learning for automated sensor type classification can be described as follows. For a given collection of unlabeled point names $\mathcal{D} = \{x_1, x_2, \ldots, x_n\}$, in which the text string of point name x_i is represented as a d dimensional feature vector, we aim at learning a classifier $f : f(x) \rightarrow y$, with respect to a set of labeled instances $\mathcal{D}_l = \{(x_1, y_1), (x_2, y_2), \ldots, (x_n, y_n)\}$ acquired during classifier training. In particular, y_i is the true sensor type for the point name x_i and takes value from a set of predefined labels. Our goal of learning is to maximize $f(x)$'s classification accuracy on the future testing data while minimizing the size of $\mathcal{D}_l$. We should note that our proposed solution has no assumption about the classifier $f(x)$; any supervised multi-class classifier can be used in our method.

Conventional active learning methods mostly focus on efficient search through the hypothesis space. Each time a new label is added to $\mathcal{D}_l$, the set of hypothesis space shrinks, e.g., filters the classifiers that are inconsistent with the labels seen so far. Great research attention has been devoted onto designing effective query strategies for label acquisition. Typical solutions include uncertainty-based sampling [6], query by committee [12], and expected model change [2].

However, such solutions implicitly assume unlabeled instances are independent, and thus fail to exploit any information conveyed in the density of data, i.e., the marginal distribution of $p(x)$ is assumed to be uniform. However, if the unlabeled instances in $\mathcal{D}$ form clusters, i.e., their clustering membership is consistent with the underlying class labels, one will only need one label from each cluster to estimate a perfect classifier. Although this example is overly optimistic, the clustering structure can still unveil the representativeness of instances with respect to their neighborhood. Hence special emphasis should be given to those most representative instances while labeling them. In addition, because instances in the same cluster are more likely to share the same label [31], one can accelerate active learning by avoiding labeling instances from the same cluster and propagating labels to the nearby unlabeled instances.

In our solution, the density of unlabeled instances, i.e., $p(x)$, is exploited via its clustering structure. In particular, we use a probabilistic mixture model to identify the latent clusters, e.g., $p(x) = \sum_c p(x|c)p(c)$, where c denotes a cluster label. The detailed instantiation of this mixture model, e.g., how to decide the cluster size and the specification of cluster conditional likelihood, will be discussed in Section 3.3. With the identified clustering structure at hand, we devise a divide-and-conquer strategy for selecting the query instances: 1) it should come from the most *informative* cluster; and 2) it should be *representative* in that cluster. This query strategy focuses on the entire input space; comparing to those individual instance based selection methods, it can thus help to avoid querying outliers or repeatedly querying similar instances.

To quantify the "informativeness" of a cluster, we exploit an information theoretic metric - class entropy $H(c)$. For every cluster c, we apply $f(x)$ to predict the labels for all the unlabeled instances in it. Then based on these predicted labels, we compute the class entropy for this cluster as,

$$H(c_i) = -\sum_{y \in Y_{c_i}} p(y) \log p(y) \quad (1)$$

where Y_{c_i} is the set of unique labels in cluster c_i predicted by classifier $f(x)$.

A cluster with larger class entropy indicates increased discrepancy between the current classifier's prediction and clustering structure inferred from the density of unlabeled instances. Therefore instances from such a cluster are considered potentially more helpful in introducing new information to classifier training. In addition, the size of a cluster is also an important criterion for measuring its informativeness. When multiple clusters have similar class entropy, a larger cluster will indicate more uncertainty of class labels in it. Hence acquiring a label for such a cluster can mostly reduce the classifier's uncertainty on a larger portion of instances. Combining these two aspects, we locate the cluster of choice by the product of cluster proportion $p(c)$ and class entropy $H(c)$ as follows,

$$\hat{c} = \arg\max_c p(c)H(c) \quad (2)$$

Once we locate the candidate cluster $\hat{c}$, we need to choose the most "representative" instance from it for labeling. We use the conditional likelihood $p(x|\hat{c})$ over all the unlabeled instances to select such an instance. The intuition behind this choice is that the instance with the maximum conditional likelihood best captures the homogeneity of instances in the selected cluster, such that knowing its label will provide a substantial boost for the classifier to predict the class labels within this cluster.

In addition, we also view high class entropy in the selected cluster as an indication of low resolution of clustering results in that local region: classification boundary goes inside the cluster. To reduce this divergence between predicted classes and clustering results, we need to further separate this cluster into finer clusters. The benefit of this sub-clustering is that the class distribution estimated by the classifier is introduced into clustering; this helps generate more homogeneous clusters for later instance selection.

3.2 Label Propagation

The basic assumption in our clustering-based active learning solution is that instances in the same cluster tend to share the same class label. The query strategy described in the previous section exploits this assumption to avoid repeated selection of similar instances. In this section, we will further capitalize on this assumption to propagate the acquired labels to their nearby unlabeled neighbors to reinforce our current knowledge about the underlying class distribution.

The idea of label propagation is popularized in transductive learning [31, 30, 3], where class labels are propagated from the labeled instances to their unlabeled neighbors based on the structure of data manifold. In practice, the data manifold is approximated by the nearest neighbors of each instance derived from data features. To empirically validate the feasibility of applying label propagation in our problem, we randomly selected a small portion of labeled sensor point names in our evaluation corpus, computed the Euclidean distance between all pairs of instances based on their feature vectors, and grouped them into pairs from the same class and different classes. We plot the cumulative distributions of those three types of distances in Figure 1.

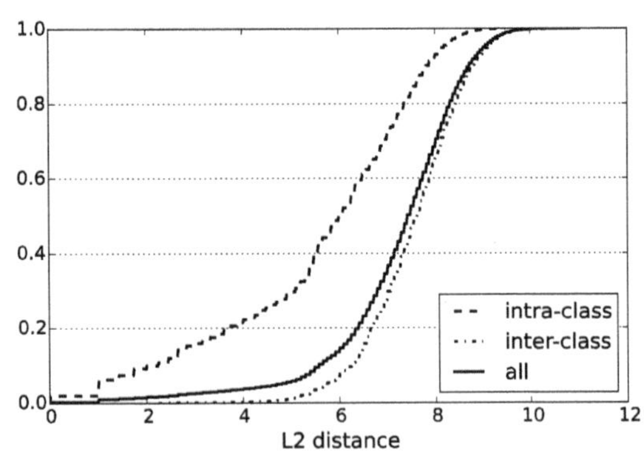

Figure 1: Distribution of pairwise distance between instances from the same class and different classes.

As we can clearly notice from the results, there is a clear gap between the cumulative distribution of distances between instances from the same class and those from different classes. This result also confirms our assumption in the proposed clustering-based active learning that nearby instances tend to share the same class label. Therefore, with proper choice in constructing the data manifold, we can confidently propagate the labels to their closest unlabeled neighbors and use them to update the classifier. This label propagation will amplify the importance of acquired labels and better avoid repeatedly querying of similar instances.

A typical approach to construct the data manifold for label propagation in transductive learning is to look for the k nearest neighbors of each instance. However, in our solution it is challenging to find a universal setting of k. To accommodate the clustering structure, label propagation should only be performed within the same cluster. However, since the resulting clusters vary and change across iterations, a fixed setting of k might lead to inconsistency between the data manifold and clustering results. To address this issue, we introduce a distance threshold r to define the data manifold for label propagation in our active learning process. When the label y is acquired for instance x, all the unlabeled instances located within the distance r to x will be assigned the same label y. Those instances will be then removed from $\mathcal{D}$ and added to a collection of propagated label set $\mathcal{D}_p$ for later classifier training.

The optimal threshold r should be the minimum inter-class distance between any pair of instances. However, it is impossible to calculate without knowing the true class labels. In our solution, we keep an estimation of r from all the labeled instances in $\mathcal{D}_l$ during active learning,

$$r = \underset{(x_i,y_i),(x_j,y_j)\in\mathcal{D}_l}{\arg\min} \frac{d(x_i,x_j)}{2}, \ \textit{with}\ y_i \neq y_j \tag{3}$$

$d(x_i, x_j)$ is the Euclidean distance between x_i and x_j.

We divide the minimum distance by 2 to avoid possible overlapping of label propagation between two labeled instances. The adaptive estimation of distance threshold defined in Eq (3) will shrink during active learning and therefore refines the propagated labels. Accordingly, we need to correct previously propagated labels where the estimation of r was less accurate. In particular, when we have a new estimation of r, we will remove instances from $\mathcal{D}_p$ that fall outside the region defined by the latest r to any closest labeled neighbors with the same label, and put them back into the unlabeled set $\mathcal{D}$. This correction happens before the new round of classifier training.

3.3 Clustering with Non-parametric Bayesian

In our proposed clustering-based active learning, data density is exploited via its latent clustering structure. Since we assume instances in the same cluster tend to share the same class label, we choose Gaussian Mixture Model (GMM) [32], a partitional clustering algorithm, to perform the clustering.

In GMM, the cluster label for every instance is treated as a latent variable, which is drawn from a multinomial distribution $p(c)$, i.e., $p(c) \propto \alpha_c$, where $\forall c, \alpha_c \geq 0$ and $\sum_c \alpha_c = 1$. In any given cluster c, the conditional data likelihood of an instance x is specified by a multivariate Gaussian distribution. To reduce the number of parameters to be estimated, we choose the isotropic Gaussian in our solution,

$$p(x|c) = (2\pi\sigma^2)^{-d/2} \exp -\frac{(x-\mu_c)^\mathsf{T}(x-\mu_c)}{2\sigma^2} \tag{4}$$

where the variance σ^2 is shared by all the clusters. $\{\alpha_c, \mu_c\}_{c=1}^k$ and σ are considered as model parameters in GMM.

However, in GMM, we need to manually specify the number of clusters for a given input data set; and the clustering result of GMM is very sensitive to such setting. More importantly, in our solution, we also need to perform sub-clustering whenever we encounter a cluster contradicting with the current classifier's prediction. It is impossible for us to predefine the size of those sub-clusters during active learning. To make clustering feasible in our solution, we appeal to a non-parametric Bayesian solution: we assume the model parameters (α, μ) in each cluster are random variables, which are drawn from a Dirichlet Process prior [11].

A Dirichlet Process $DP(G_0, \eta)$ with a base distribution G_0 and a scaling parameter η is a distribution over distributions [11]. The base distribution G_0 specifies the prior distribution of model parameters, e.g., mean parameter μ in each cluster, and the scaling parameter η specifies the concentration of samples drawn from DP, e.g., cluster proportion $p(c)$. An important property of the DP is that though the draws from a DP have countably infinite size, they are discrete with probability one, which leads to a probability distribution on partitions of data. The number of unique draws, i.e.,the number of clusters, varies with respect to the data and therefore is random, instead of being pre-specified.

As a result, with the introduced $DP(G_0, \eta)$ prior, data density in a given collection of instances can be expressed using a stick-breaking representation [23]:

$$p(x) = \sum_{c=1}^{\infty} \alpha_c \mathcal{N}(x|\mu_c, \sigma) p(\mu_c|G_0) \tag{5}$$

where $\alpha = \alpha_{c=1}^{\infty} \sim Stick(\eta)$ represents the proportion of clusters in the whole collection. The stick-breaking process $Stick(\eta)$ for the cluster proportion parameter α is defined as: $\alpha'_c \sim Beta(1, \eta), \alpha_c = \alpha'_c \prod_{i=1}^{c-1}(1 - \alpha'_i)$. Since the variance σ^2 is fixed in all clusters, we use a conjugate prior for μ in G_0, i.e., for $\forall c, \mu_{ci} \sim \mathcal{N}(a, b)$, with the assumption that each dimension in μ_c is independently drawn from a univariate Gaussian. This will greatly simplify the later on inference procedure.

Because the data density distribution defined in Eq (5) only has finite support at the points of $\{\alpha_c, \mu_c\}_{c=1}^{k}$, we can calculate the posterior distribution of latent cluster labels in each unlabeled instance to discover the clustering structure for active learning. Following the sampling scheme proposed in [15], we appeal to a Gibbs sampling method to infer the posterior of cluster membership. Detailed specifications of this sampling algorithm can be found in [15]. In particular, we use the same hyper-parameter setting of (a, b) in G_0 and η for initial clustering and subsequent sub-clustering during our cluster-based active learning process.

Putting it all together: Algorithm 1 summarizes our clustering-based active learning solution for the sensor type classification problem. In each iteration, we select the most "informative" cluster measured by the class entropy of predicted labels by the classifier. We acquire a label for the instance centered in the selected cluster, and propagate the newly obtained label to its unlabeled neighbors within an estimated distance. At the end of this iteration, we perform sub-clustering on the selected cluster to refine its local clustering structure for later instance selection.

Algorithm 1: Clustering-based Active Learning

Input: point names $\mathcal{D} = \{x_1, x_2, \ldots, x_n\}$, and label budget B
Output: predicted labels of the point names Y
Initialize: Generate clusters with $DP(G_0, \eta)$ on $\mathcal{D}$, reset the labeled instance set $\mathcal{D}_l$ and propagated label set $\mathcal{D}_p$ to empty
while $B > 0$ **do**
    Train the classifier $f(x) \rightarrow y$ based on $\mathcal{D}_l$ and $\mathcal{D}_p$;
    Apply $f(x)$ to all instances in $\mathcal{D}$;
    Compute class entropy $H(c)$ defined in Eq (2) for each cluster c;
    Retrieve a cluster by $\hat{c} = \arg\max_c p(c)H(c)$;
    Acquire label $\hat{y}$ for example $\hat{x}$ given by $\arg\max_{x \in \mathcal{D}} Pr(x|\hat{c})$, and move $(\hat{x}, \hat{y})$ from $\mathcal{D}$ to $\mathcal{D}_l$;
    Update the distance threshold r by Eq (3);
    Update all previous propagated label in $\mathcal{D}_p$ with new threshold r;
    Assign $\hat{y}$ to all unlabeled examples x_u, where $x_u \in \hat{c}$ and $d(x_u, \hat{x}) < r$;
    Move (x_u, y) from $\mathcal{D}$ to $\mathcal{D}_p$;
    Perform sub-clustering with $DP(G_0, \eta)$ in $\hat{c}$;
end

3.4 Discussion

Comparing to the existing solutions for the sensor type classification, our proposed algorithm addresses the problem from a totally different perspective. As we discussed before, because existing solutions [4, 22] isolated the annotation process from model training, it likely leads to wasted effort in data annotation. With active learning, we can restrict our effort to a smaller set of instances that are the most helpful for classifier training. A practical benefit of this learning approach is that we can rapidly bootstrap the building analytic software across different sites. Instead of going back and forth for several rounds of blind annotation, a building manager only needs to interact with the system for several iterations on the fly to achieve immediate satisfactory results.

Comparing to the other active learning algorithms, our proposed method focuses on exploiting information conveyed in the data clustering structure. Based on the assumption that nearby instances are more likely to share the same class label, we select the instances for labeling based on the identified latent clustering structure of instances and propagate the labels to their adjacent unlabeled neighbors. This helps us avoid repeatedly querying similar instances and enhance the importance of labeled instances. In addition, the clustering structure and label propagation strategy are adapted in an online fashion. In Nguyen and Smeulders's work [16], clustering is also exploited for active learning; but their clustering structure is static and no label propagation is performed. In Dasgupta and Hsu's work [7], hierarchical clustering is used to provide a more flexible and dynamic clustering structure, but no label propagation is performed as well. We should note this proposed active learning algorithm is general, it only assumes the proximity of label distribution in nearby instances. Therefore, this algorithm can also be applied in a broader context, e.g., document categorization [26] and image retrieval [25].

4. EVALUATION

To demonstrate the effectiveness of our proposed solution in addressing sensor type classification, we evaluate our clustering-based active learning algorithm on point names collected from three distinct buildings. Extensive experimental comparisons confirm that our method achieved the

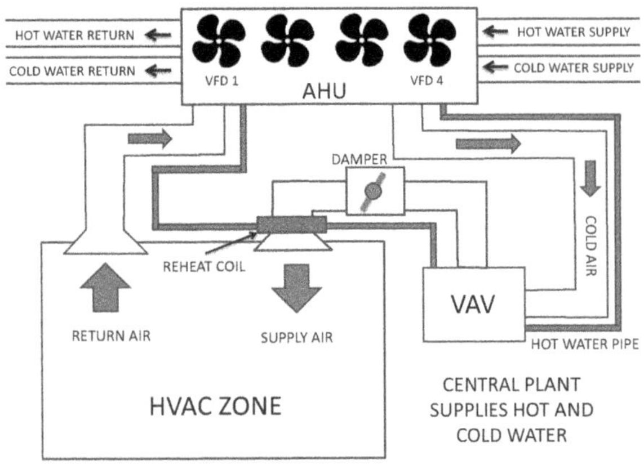

Figure 2: A typical HVAC system consisting of an air handler unit (AHU), several variable air volume boxes (VAV), water-based heating/cooling pipes and air circulation ducts. (Figure used with permission from the authors of [1].)

same classification accuracy with much fewer labeled examples than all the baseline methods. We also demonstrate how metadata normalization can enable meaningful analytic applications with the raw sensor streams under the context of commercial building energy control and comfort assessment.

4.1 Background & Building Sensor Taxonomy

Figure 2 illustrates a typical heating, ventilation, and air conditioning (HVAC) system deployed in modern commercial buildings. An HVAC system usually uses a combination of hot and cold water pipes in conjunction with air handler units (AHU) to maintain the appropriate thermal environment within the building. An HVAC system usually consists of several AHUs and each AHU is responsible for a physical zone in the building. An AHU consists of variable speed drives that supply cold air (cooled by the supplied cold water) using ducts to VAV boxes distributed throughout the building. The hot water loop is also connected to these VAV boxes using separate pipes. Each VAV box controls the amount of air to be let into an HVAC zone using dampers, whose opening angle can be programmed. A reheat coil, which uses supplied hot water, is used to heat the air to meet the appropriate HVAC settings for each zone.

Our evaluation data set is collected from sensor streams from over 2,500 sensors of more than 20 different types deployed in three commercial buildings. Specially, Building A uses a building management system contracted with Trane and building B comprises deployment by KETI[4] and Siemens, while building C uses an archaic system by Barrington Controls.

Table 2 summarizes all the types of sensors evaluated in these three buildings and the number of sensors of each type. For example, "room temperature" measures the temperature in room and for a better understanding, all the other temperature measurements on water circulation and air ventilation are illustrated in Figure 2. For setpoints, we assign only one general type which includes all set points for every actuator configured in the building.

[4]`http://www.keti.re.kr/e-keti/`

	Building		
Type	A	B	C
CO_2	16	52	0
Humidity	54	52	0
Air Pressure	142	216	215
Room Temp	159	231	208
Facility Operation Status	59	72	41
Facility Control	0	138	403
Setpoint	140	486	229
Air Flow Volume	14	172	9
Damper Position	0	290	10
Fan Speed	0	25	15
HW Supply Temp	27	1	0
HW Return Temp	15	1	0
CW Supply Temp	18	2	11
CW Return Temp	15	3	10
Supply Air Temp	20	17	3
Return Air Temp	6	2	4
Mixed Air Temp	5	2	3
Ice Tank Entering Temp	1	2	0
Ice Tank Leaving Temp	1	4	0
Occupancy	25	52	0
Timer	0	0	15
Sum	575	1124	1166

Table 2: Number of points by type for the 3 test buildings. "Temp" stands for "temperature", "HW" for "hot water" and "CW" for "cold water".

4.2 Feature Construction

The sensor point names are the input of our active learning algorithm. As shown in our motivating example in Table 1, the point names are short text strings with several concatenated abbreviations. To represent the primitive point names as feature vectors for classifier training, we first convert all point names to lower cases and trim out the numerical characters, resulting in a series of words, e.g., `Zone Temp 2 RMI204` becomes `{zone, temp, rmi}`. To capture possible variants of abbreviations in point names, e.g., "tmp" and "temp" for temperature, we adopt k-mers [13] as our features. The term k-mer refers to all the possible substrings of length k, which are contained in a string. This feature is popularly used in protein and gene sequence analysis in bioinformatics. And it helps measure sequence similarity without alignment. In our case, we limit the k-mers computation only within a word boundary. In general, having too small a k will increase the chance of overlapping k-mers, making the points less differentiable. Therefore, we compute k-mers of length 3 and 4 for all point names. For example, `{zone, temp, rmi}` will yield a set `{zon, one, tem, emp, rmi}` with k=3. A dictionary of k-mers is constructed with all the k-mers generated from each point name. Each point name is then converted into a feature vector based on the frequency of k-mers in it. For example, a set of k-mers `{zon, tem, emp, zon}` will be transformed into a vector of `(2,0,1,1,0)` with the dictionary `{zon, one, tem, emp, rmi}`. This feature representation will be used in our later evaluations.

4.3 Baselines

To evaluate the performance of our proposed algorithm, we adopt four active learning algorithms as baselines.

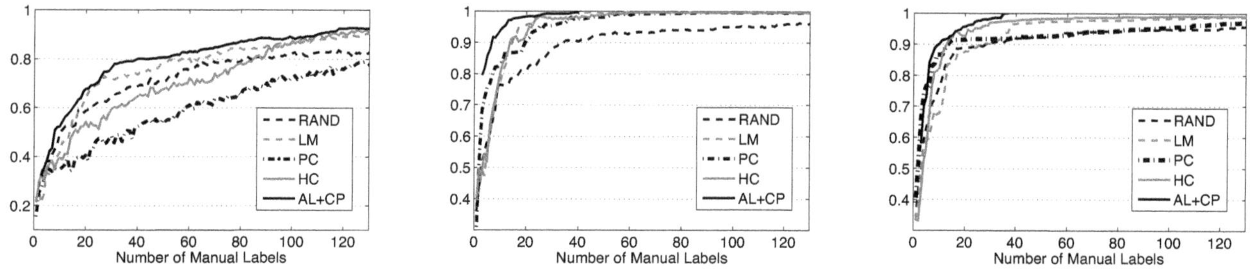

(a) Building A (b) Building B (c) Building C

Figure 3: Classification accuracy on three different buildings: comparing to the baselines, our method (AL+CP) is able to achieve better accuracy on all buildings with less labeled examples.

	Building A			Building B			Building C		
Labeled Percentage	1%	5%	10%	1%	5%	10%	1%	5%	10%
RAND	0.204	0.582	0.696	0.711	0.933	0.970	0.795	0.915	0.937
LM	0.222	0.572	0.769	0.736	0.995	0.995	0.835	0.980	0.988
PC	0.232	0.515	0.581	0.752	0.958	0.968	0.762	0.862	0.987
HC	0.326	0.516	0.669	0.829	0.993	0.996	0.867	0.977	0.987
AL+CP	**0.416***	**0.765***	**0.819***	**0.919***	**1.000***	**1.000***	**0.890***	**1.000***	**1.000***

*p-value<0.01

Table 3: Weighted macro F1 score of classification on three buildings with different labeling budgets. Our method (AL+CP) converges with less than 5% examples being labeled in Building B and C. It consistently outperforms the baselines in all cases.

Random (RAND): this method selects an example at random uniformly from the unlabeled set in each iteration.

Least Margin (LM) [21]: this method adopts the a simple yet effective sampling strategy, which queries the instances for labeling with least confidence measured by the difference of posterior probability of the first and second most probable class labels predicted by the classifier:

$$x_M^* = \arg\min_x \; p(\hat{y}_1|x) - p(\hat{y}_2|x),$$

where $\hat{y}_1$ and $\hat{y}_2$ are the first and second most probable predicted class labels, respectively. We compute the class prediction probability by SVM based on the method proposed in [18].

Pre-clustering (PC) [16]: this method pre-clusters the instances and selects the example for querying satisfying two criteria: 1) locate at the classification boundary and 2) representative of dense clusters. The clusters are constructed by the same Gaussian Mixture Model with Dirichlet Process prior as used in our method.

Hierarchical Clustering (HC) [7]: this method leverages a hierarchical clustering structure, which is represented as a binary tree, and estimates the purity of labels for each cluster node. The algorithm iteratively selects examples from a subtree whose size is significantly large or the impurity of labels is high.

In all baselines, and our method, a linear SVM model is used as the classifier.

We measure the overall classification accuracy of each active learning algorithm with different amount of manual labels, and examine how many examples are needed by each method to reach a required accuracy level. Besides classification accuracy, we also compute the weighted macro F1 score of each method given different labeling budgets (e.g., 5%, 10%, etc of the entire unlabeled set) in each building.

In our experiments, to reduce possible bias introduced by training/testing split, we perform 10-fold cross validation for each active learning method, and repeat it 10 times with different random seeds. The average performance of 10 runs from each method is reported.

4.4 Classification Results

In Figure 3, we illustrate the comparison results of sensor type classification accuracy from all three buildings over all methods. In all three buildings, our method performed the best against all the baselines. In particular, our method consistently requires the least amount of manual labels to achieve a satisfactory and converged accuracy. In building A, to achieve the accuracy of 90%, our clustering based active learning method (denoted as AL+CP) requires 105 labeled examples while HC needs 110, which is the best among all baselines. LM takes 127 labeled examples and the other two baselines take a hundred more labeled examples to obtain the same accuracy. In building B, both our method and LM reach the accuracy of 99% with 26 examples, while it takes 51, 61 and more than 200 examples, respectively, for the HC, PC and RAND baselines. In building C, our method achieves 99% accuracy with 35 labels while HC and LM requires 101 and 135 labels, respectively, for the same accuracy. Again, PC and RAND require much more labeled examples to get the same performance.

On all three buildings, RAND performs reasonably on initial iterations (e.g., before 20) but becomes the worst later on. This is because of imbalanced class distribution in our three data sets. RAND selects more examples from larger classes at the beginning and quickly gets a fraction of the major classes correctly classified. However, in later iterations, RAND has a lower chance in picking examples from smaller classes and converges to a local optimal quickly.

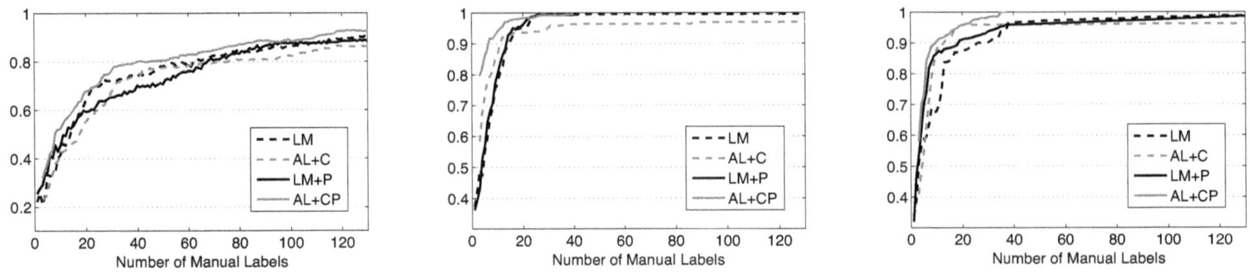

(a) Building A (b) Building B (c) Building C

Figure 4: Comparison of margin-based active learning (LM), clustering-based active learning without label propagation (AL+C), margin-based active learning with label propagation (LM+P), and clustering with label propagation based active learning (AL+CP). The label propagation significantly improves the performance of learning with clustering only.

The PC baseline, which also exploits data clustering structure, performs significantly worse than other baselines for Building A. PC gives priority to the examples that are: 1) close to the decision boundary, and 2) representative in a cluster. Such criteria are very similar to those in our method. Further inspection reveals that examples selected by the PC baseline were neither informative nor representative enough to distinguish different types of instances. This stems from the fact that for building A, the initial clusters from GMM fairly overlap with each other. This biases the PC baseline to select more examples with relatively high uncertainty but less representative in a cluster.

The HC baseline is quite effective in avoiding querying similar examples from dense areas. However, because HC does not perform label propagation, after all clusters become roughly equally pure with sufficient sampling, it will start repeatedly querying previously sampled areas, which results in a long plateau for building B and C. For building A, the larger classes contain a few variations in their point names, therefore when HC avoids sampling from the same dense area at first, it misses important informative examples and is only able to pick them up in later iterations.

Moreover, we notice that, for all methods, the convergence rate on building B and building C is much better than building A, despite the fact that there are more points in those two buildings. The reason is that the point names in these two buildings share stronger regularities - the last segment always indicates the sensor type. Recall the examples shown in Table 1: `SDH_SF1_R282_RMT` from building B and `SODA1R410B_ART` from building C. Both of them adhere to the same order of segment categories - **`building name-air handler/supply fan identifier-room number-sensor type`**, only with a slightly different set of delimiters. Our string feature captures such regularity and helps the learning algorithm converge faster. However, the same rule doesn't apply to building A because there the type information can be encoded in any segment in a point name. For instance, a temperature measurement can be named in many conventions, such as `averageSpaceTemperature 1st Floor Area1`, `East Space Temperature scc2UIP33` or `RM511A Zone Temp`. With such variety in the naming conventions, the learning algorithms need to explore all possible variants of point names for convergence in building A.

On such imbalanced data sets, investigation of accuracy only is not enough. We also measure the weighted macro F1 score of classification for each method with different labeling budgets, i.e., different percentage of total instances that can be labeled. We examine the F1 score at three different labeling budgets, 1%, 5% and 10%. The weighted macro F1 score is an altered version of macro F1 score [29], which calculates the F1 score for each class, where "one-versus-all" binary classification is performed, and weight the resulting F1 of each class by support (the number of true instances for each label). Paired two sample t-test is performed to validate the statistical significance of improvement from our method over the best-performing baseline. The results are shown in Table 3. In general, more labeled examples leads to better classification performance over all classes; and our method performed the best in all cases. As we discussed earlier, all methods converge much faster in building B and C than in building A. In those two buildings, our method can achieve an 100% classification accuracy with slightly more than 1% of total examples being labeled.

In addition, to investigate the contributions of data clustering and label propagation in our proposed active learning algorithm, we also conduct experiments by disabling data clustering and label propagation in our method. From the results in Figure 4, we can observe that with clustering only, the performance of our method is no better than margin-based active learning; and beyond a certain point, the performance plateaus because the classification boundary converges to the clustering structure, and no more new examples could be selected for labeling. However, we do observe some improvement from clustering only over margin-based active learning for building B and building C in early iterations. This is because the same type of points in these two buildings contain few variations and these initial examples at the center of relatively pure clusters are more representative for a dense region. Interestingly, after adding label propagation, we clearly see a boost in the performance than performing clustering only. We attribute the improvement of our method to label propagation which considerably amplifies the amount of available labeled examples for classifier training, and therefore helps to estimate a better classifier.

Besides, we also examine how the label propagation alone can help active learning in general. We adopt the same distance threshold estimation method as defined in Eq (3) to introduce propagated labels in the margin-based baseline and denote it as LM+P in Figure 4. On building A, the inclusion of label propagation makes LM even worse, because in early stage the estimated threshold r in LM+P is not accurate enough, and it mistakenly propagates the labels. Only when more labels are acquired in later stages, the estimation of distance threshold r improves and therefore LM receives propagated labels with improved quality. In our method, because of data clustering, the labeled examples in the early stage are more representative; it in turns helps better estimate the distance threshold r. As a conclusion, data clustering and label propagation complement with each other in our proposed method, and help active learning acquire more informative examples quickly.

4.5 Proof-of-Concept Study

As a first step towards automated metadata normalization, our algorithm is able to classify and transform the type information in the primitive metadata into a normalized name space. It provides a better opportunity for running uniform analysis on heterogeneous metadata across buildings with different management systems. As a proof-of-concept, we demonstrate an illustrative example, in which we search over the normalized metadata for different types of sensors that are in the same room under the application context of building comfort assessment and energy control.

Ideally, with the occupancy information of spaces considered, a properly configured building should automatically stop conditioning unoccupied rooms and areas. However, one typical problem plaguing buildings that incurs energy waste is unoccupied room being conditioned. For a building manager to inspect the building and locate such spots for better scheduling, he should be able to run simple keyword based searches over the metadata to look for different types of streams, such as room temperature and occupancy streams. With the desired types of streams returned, he can match different types of streams by room location to perform further examination, e.g., which room is still comfortable during unoccupied periods.

To accomplish the task, we first classify the sensor streams by type with both our method and the best baseline (LM). Then based on the predicted sensor type for each stream, we normalize each type of sensors into a common name space, e.g., all the streams predicted as room temperature are named as "room temperature". With the type information normalized, we can simply retrieve all the streams of a certain type with one keyword, e.g, using "temperature" to search for temperature streams. The next step is to match different types of sensors by room location. In particular, we derive a few regular expressions to find the segment indicating room location in the point names of each sensor.

In this experiment, we search for four types of sensors - occupancy, temperature, humidity and CO_2 - by simply using these type names as the keywords. Then we match the room location of these four groups with regular expressions on their original primitive point names. Specifically, we examine the accuracy of three searches: 1) occupancy and temperature in the same room; 2) occupancy, temperature and humidity in the same room; and 3) occupancy, temperature, humidity and CO_2 in the same room, given these combinations are usually used to assess the comfort of a room or identify potential waste in unoccupied rooms.

Table 4 illustrates the performance of basic searches on building A for occupancy (O), temperature (T), humidity (H) and CO_2 (C). Our method can return better results with both higher recall and precision because of better predictions on type class for the streams. Given the four returned groups of streams, we further run regular expression

	AL+CP		LM	
	Precision	Recall	Precision	Recall
O	0.930	1.000	1.000	0.688
T	0.892	0.935	0.635	0.975
H	0.962	1.000	0.778	0.519
C	0.556	0.833	0.222	0.286

Table 4: The performance of searches over the normalized metadata with our method (AL+CP) and the best baseline (margin based active learning, LM). We search for four specific types of streams: occupancy (O), temperature (T), humidity (H) and CO_2 (C).

	AL+CP		LM	
	Precision	Recall	Precision	Recall
O+T	0.832	1.000	1.000	0.900
O+T+H	0.926	1.000	1.000	0.400
O+T+H+C	0.375	0.833	1.000	0.125

Table 5: The performance of searches for different types of streams that are in the same room. We consider the pair of occupancy and temperature (O+T), the combination of occupancy, temperature and humidity (O+T+H), and also the combination of occupancy, temperature, humidity along with CO_2 (O+T+H+C).

based matching on the primitive metadata to find the pairs in the same room. For instance, we first identify the room location of each returned occupancy stream with regular expressions, then we search for the temperature stream with the same room number as each of these occupancy streams. Similarly, we search for humidity and CO_2 streams in the same room. With these different types of streams grouped into the same room, a building manager can compare the actual data against some standards to decide if a room is problematic or not. We summarize the search results in Table 5. In general, the normalized metadata by our method produces search results with higher recall and slightly lower precision. Such results are expected considering the practical demand from building managers - it is acceptable to return some unexpected results (false positives) while not missing the expected ones (false negatives), where he can manually examine a much smaller group of candidates and filter out the incorrect ones. We conclude that with normalized metadata for a building, people such as a building manager can more easily retrieve expected streams and conduct meaningful analysis to identify problems in a building.

5. CONCLUSION & FUTURE WORK

In this paper, as a first step towards automated sensor metadata normalization, we investigate the problem of building sensor type classification and introduce a novel, effective yet general active learning method to address the problem. Following the assumption that similar instances are more likely to share the same class label, our solution exploits the data clustering structure and propagates the labels to their nearby unlabeled examples to accelerate the learning process. Extensive experimental comparisons are performed against several state-of-the-art active learning algorithms with over 20 different sensor types and 2,500 sensor streams collected from three buildings. Our proposed solution is able to achieve satisfactory classification accuracy with much less labeled examples than the baseline algorithms. In addition, we also demonstrate that the normalized metadata can potentially enable meaningful analytic applications with the raw sensor streams under the context of commercial building comfort assessment and energy control.

Our proposed active learning algorithm is general, and therefore it is applicable in a broader context, e.g., document categorization [26] and image retrieval [25]. In our current metadata normalization process, only the text features from point names are utilized. However, another important aspect of the sensor streams is the actual data from the sensor readings. Features constructed from such raw signals can also be introduced to characterize the stream. Such feature becomes vital when the point names are missing or corrupted. In addition, our current problem setting is limited to one building; it is necessary for us to solve the normalization problem across buildings, e.g., classification model learned in one building can be used to bootstrap the learning in another building.

6. REFERENCES

[1] B. Balaji, J. Xu, A. Nwokafor, R. Gupta, and Y. Agarwal. Sentinel: Occupancy based hvac actuation using existing wifi infrastructure within commercial buildings. In *Proceedings of the 11th ACM Conference on Embedded Networked Sensor Systems*, SenSys '13, pages 17:1–17:14, 2013.

[2] M.-F. Balcan, A. Broder, and T. Zhang. Margin based active learning. In *Proceedings of the 20th Annual Conference on Learning Theory*, COLT'07, pages 35–50, Berlin, Heidelberg, 2007. Springer-Verlag.

[3] M. Belkin, P. Niyogi, and V. Sindhwani. Manifold regularization: A geometric framework for learning from labeled and unlabeled examples. *The Journal of Machine Learning Research*, 7, 2006.

[4] A. Bhattacharya, D. E. Culler, J. Ortiz, D. Hong, and K. Whitehouse. Enabling portable building applications through automated metadata transformation. Technical Report UCB/EECS-2014-159, EECS Department, University of California, Berkeley, Aug 2014.

[5] D. Cohn, L. Atlas, and R. Ladner. Improving generalization with active learning. *Machine learning*, 15(2), 1994.

[6] D. A. Cohn, Z. Ghahramani, and M. I. Jordan. Active learning with statistical models. *J. Artif. Int. Res.*, 4(1):129–145, Mar. 1996.

[7] S. Dasgupta and D. Hsu. Hierarchical sampling for active learning. In *Proceedings of the 25th International Conference on Machine Learning*, ICML '08, pages 208–215, New York, NY, USA, 2008. ACM.

[8] R. Dhamankar, Y. Lee, A. Doan, A. Halevy, and P. Domingos. imap: Discovering complex semantic matches between database schemas. In *Proceedings of the 2004 ACM SIGMOD International Conference on Management of Data*, SIGMOD '04, pages 383–394, New York, NY, USA, 2004. ACM.

[9] A. Doan, P. Domingos, and A. Y. Halevy. Reconciling schemas of disparate data sources: A machine-learning approach. In *Proceedings of the 2001 ACM SIGMOD International Conference on Management of Data*, SIGMOD '01, pages 509–520, New York, NY, USA, 2001. ACM.

[10] U. DOE. Better buildings challenge. *http://www4.eere.energy.gov/challenge/sites/default /files/uploaded-files/may-recognition-fs-052013.pdf (Feb. 26, 2014)*, 2013.

[11] T. S. Ferguson. A Bayesian Analysis of Some Nonparametric Problems. *The Annals of Statistics*, 1, 1973.

[12] Y. Freund, H. Seung, E. Shamir, and N. Tishby. Selective sampling using the query by committee algorithm. *Machine Learning*, 28(2-3):133–168, 1997.

[13] C. S. Leslie, E. Eskin, A. Cohen, J. Weston, and W. S. Noble. Mismatch string kernels for discriminative protein classification. *Bioinformatics*, 20(4), 2004.

[14] J. Madhavan, P. A. Bernstein, A. Doan, and A. Halevy. Corpus-based schema matching. In *Proceedings of the 21st International Conference on Data Engineering*, ICDE '05, pages 57–68, Washington, DC, USA, 2005. IEEE Computer Society.

[15] R. Neal. Markov chain sampling methods for dirichlet process mixture models. *Journal of computational and graphical statistics*, 9(2), 2000.

[16] H. T. Nguyen and A. Smeulders. Active learning using pre-clustering. In *Proceedings of the Twenty-first International Conference on Machine Learning*, ICML '04, pages 79–86, New York, NY, USA, 2004. ACM.

[17] U. D. of Energy Better Buildings program. Total annual cost of energy in the commercial and industrial sector. Mar. 2015.

[18] J. C. Platt. Probabilistic outputs for support vector machines and comparisons to regularized likelihood methods. In *ADVANCES IN LARGE MARGIN CLASSIFIERS*. MIT Press, 1999.

[19] E. Rahm and P. A. Bernstein. A survey of approaches to automatic schema matching. *the VLDB Journal*, 10(4), 2001.

[20] C. E. Rasmussen. The infinite gaussian mixture model. In *NIPS*, volume 12, 1999.

[21] T. Scheffer, C. Decomain, and S. Wrobel. Active hidden markov models for information extraction. In *Advances in Intelligent Data Analysis*. Springer, 2001.

[22] A. Schumann, J. Ploennigs, and B. Gorman. Towards automating the deployment of energy saving approaches in buildings. In *Proceedings of the 1st ACM Conference on Embedded Systems for Energy-Efficient Buildings*, BuildSys '14, pages 164–167, New York, NY, USA, 2014. ACM.

[23] J. Sethuraman. A constructive definition of dirichlet priors. *Statistica Sinica*, 4, 1994.

[24] B. Settles. Active learning literature survey. Computer Sciences Technical Report 1648, University of Wisconsin–Madison, 2009.

[25] S. Tong and E. Chang. Support vector machine active learning for image retrieval. In *Proceedings of the ninth ACM international conference on Multimedia*. ACM, 2001.

[26] S. Tong and D. Koller. Support vector machine active learning with applications to text classification. *The Journal of Machine Learning Research*, 2, 2002.

[27] E. S. p. U.S. Environmental Protection Agency. Useful facts and figures. June 2007.

[28] J. Warnick. 88 acres: How microsoft quietly built the city of the future. *http://www.microsoft.com/en-us/stories/88acres/88-acres-how-microsoft-quietly-built-the-city-of-the-future-chapter-1.aspx (May 8, 2015)*, 2012.

[29] Y. Yang. An evaluation of statistical approaches to text categorization. *Inf. Retr.*, 1, 1999.

[30] D. Zhou, O. Bousquet, T. N. Lal, J. Weston, and B. Schölkopf. Learning with local and global consistency. *Advances in neural information processing systems*, 16(16), 2004.

[31] X. Zhu, Z. Ghahramani, J. Lafferty, et al. Semi-supervised learning using gaussian fields and harmonic functions. In *ICML*, volume 3, 2003.

[32] Z. Zivkovic. Improved adaptive gaussian mixture model for background subtraction. In *Pattern Recognition, 2004. ICPR 2004. Proceedings of the 17th International Conference on*, volume 2. IEEE, 2004.

gSparsify: Graph Motif Based Sparsification for Graph Clustering

Peixiang Zhao
Department of Computer Science
Florida State University, Tallahassee, FL 32306
zhao@cs.fsu.edu

ABSTRACT

Graph clustering is a fundamental problem that partitions vertices of a graph into clusters with an objective to optimize the intuitive notions of *intra-cluster density* and *inter-cluster sparsity*. In many real-world applications, however, the sheer sizes and inherent complexity of graphs may render existing graph clustering methods inefficient or incapable of yielding quality graph clusters. In this paper, we propose gSparsify, a graph sparsification method, to preferentially retain a small subset of edges from a graph which are more likely to be within clusters, while eliminating others with less or no structure correlation to clusters. The resultant simplified graph is succinct in size with core cluster structures well preserved, thus enabling faster graph clustering without a compromise to clustering quality. We consider a quantitative approach to modeling the evidence that edges within densely knitted clusters are frequently involved in small-size graph motifs, which are adopted as prime features to differentiate edges with varied cluster significance. Path-based indexes and path-join algorithms are further designed to compute graph-motif based cluster significance of edges for graph sparsification. We perform experimental studies in real-world graphs, and results demonstrate that gSparsify can bring significant speedup to existing graph clustering methods with an improvement to graph clustering quality.

Categories and Subject Descriptors

I.5.3 [**Clustering**]: Algorithms; G.2.2 [**Graph Theory**]: Graph Algorithms

Keywords

Graph Sparsification; Graph Clustering; Graph Motif

1. INTRODUCTION

Recent years have witnessed a growing trend in business intelligence and scientific exploration that models and interprets structured data as graphs [1, 9]. As a ubiquitous abstraction depicting relationships among entities, graphs have become an increasingly common focus of data sciences, and have fused a wide range of applications in social networks, biological networks, and the Web. Out of many graph analytical and mining tasks, *graph clustering* is a fundamental building block with extensive applications in community detection [13], network visualization [31], ranking [38], and keyword search [11], to name a few. The objective of graph clustering is to partition vertices of a graph into clusters such that vertices within the same cluster are densely connected, while those in different clusters are sparsely interlinked. As a result, there have been an array of graph clustering methods toward optimizing the intuitive notions of *intra-cluster density* and *inter-cluster sparsity* for graph clusters [14, 33].

However, the problem of graph clustering remains challenging due in particular to the following reasons. First, graphs drawn from real-world applications become massive in scale. The sheer sizes of graphs may hinder a direct application of existing graph clustering methods that are mainly applicable to small or medium-size graphs. Second, and more interestingly, when graphs get larger and more complex, a great percentage of interactions (edges) have been witnessed accompanying redundant and spurious information [32]. The existence of extremely tangled, noisy edges can easily obfuscate intrinsic properties of graphs, thus leading to low-quality graph clusters on the one hand, and inducing fruitless computation on the other.

To address the aforementioned issues, we design in this paper a new graph sparsification method, gSparsify. The goal of gSparsify is to simplify a graph G in a way that the *cluster-significant* edges (*w.r.t.* the graph clustering objectives) are well retained, while edges with little or no cluster structure insight can be filtered without sacrificing the clustering quality significantly. This way, the salient structures of G are approximately preserved, or even enhanced, in the sparsified graph G', which is much smaller and more amenable to effective graph clustering. gSparsify can be employed as a pre-processing step for existing graph clustering methods with significant speedup (2x to 37x in our experimental studies) and no compromise on the quality of graph clusters. gSparsify is also of practical interest as an individual tool in many graph analytical tasks, such as graph summarization, graph backbone detection, and large-scale graph visualization.

EXAMP E 1. *Figure 1a illustrates the famous karate club social network with* 34 *vertices and* 78 *edges. We further add random edges to complicate the graph structure with* 127 *edges in total. The graph exhibits a "hair-ball" structure*

CIKM'15, October 19–23, 2015, Melbourne, Australia.
© 2015 ACM. ISBN 978-1-4503-3794-6/15/10 ...$15.00.
DOI: http://dx.doi.org/10.1145/2806416.2806543.

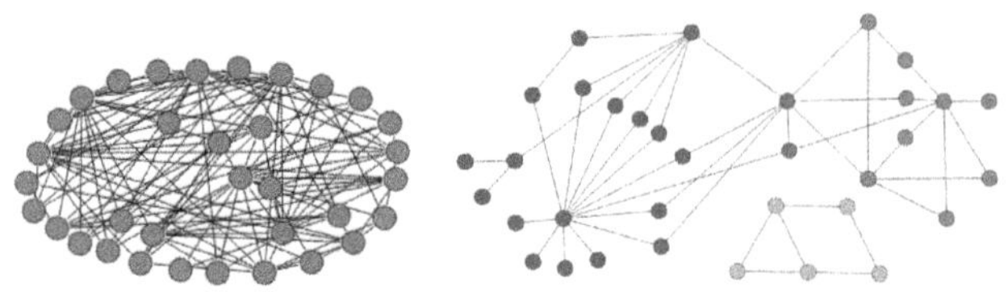

(a) Karate Club Network (b) The Sparsified Graph

Figure 1: Sparsifying the Karate Club Network with 34 Vertices and 127 Edges into a Simplified Graph with 48 edges Exhibiting 4 Clusters.

which is hard to cluster. After applying the proposed graph sparsification method, gSparsify, *we get a sparsified graph (Figure 1b) with* 48 *edges* (62.2% *edge reduction). It is immediately clear that there exist* 4 *clusters in the graph.* □

To accurately identify cluster-significant edges that need to be retained during graph sparsification, we propose a quantitative approach to associating each edge $e = (u, v)$ with *structure-aware* weights denoting the degrees of relevance of two constituent vertices, u and v, to be in the same cluster. We start our reasoning with an important observation that vertices of an *intra-cluster* edge e are usually densely connected within a cluster. As a result, e is frequently involved in many basic, localized graph primitives, termed as *graph motifs*. Graph motifs are small, connected subgraphs occurring in significantly higher frequencies than would be expected in random graphs [28], and thus play a key role in uncovering structural design principles from real-world graphs. We examine a series of small-size graph motifs, and select short-length cycles as prime features to quantify cluster significance for edges. Specifically, a vector of *cluster-significance scores* is associated with each edge $e \in E$, with each component representing the number (or ratio) of every pre-selected cycle motif e lies in. Cluster-significance scores can be further aggregated to synthesize the collective significance of e in participating in and forming all specified graph motifs. The higher the cluster-significance scores of e, the more occurrences of e witnessed in graph motifs, and thus more probably e is an intra-cluster edge that should be preserved in graph sparsification.

To compute the cluster-significance scores of an edge $e = (u, v)$ in terms of short-length cycle motifs, we need enumerate all cycles encompassing e as a constituent edge, which turns out to be very time-consuming. We design a path-based indexing approach to maintaining short-length paths emanating from vertices. This way the cycle-motif enumeration problem boils down to a set of *path-join* operations on all indexed paths originated from u and v, respectively. We further use another level of inverted index to facilitate path-join evaluation, thus resulting in fast enumeration of cycle motifs in large graphs. Specifically, the contribution of our work is summarized as follows,

1. We propose a graph sparsification principle based on graph motifs with an objective to improve the efficiency and quality for graph clustering in real-world graphs. We justify the effectiveness of graph motifs, more specifically short-length cycle motifs, in encoding local cluster information of graphs, and propose a motif-based approach to computing cluster significance of edges in graphs (Section 4);
2. We design a path-based indexing approach to enumerating all short-length cycles for the computation of cluster-significance scores of edges in graphs. This approach is efficient and can be extended to enumerate other graph motifs in large graphs (Section 5);
3. We design the motif-based graph sparsification algorithm, gSparsify, to simplify real-world graphs. The experimental studies demonstrate that gSparsify can improve state-of-the-art graph clustering methods, in terms of clustering efficiency and quality (Section 6,7).

The remainder of this paper is organized as follows. We first elaborate on the related work in Section 2, then define preliminary concepts and notations in Section 3. Section 4 examines graph motifs, more specifically short length-cycles, in quantifying cluster significance of edges in graphs. In Section 5 we discuss a path-based indexing approach to enumerating short-length cycles for computing cluster significance of edges. Section 6 summarizes the graph sparsification algorithm, gSparsify. We discuss experimental studies in Section 7, and provide concluding remarks in Section 8.

2. RELATED WORK

In this section, we discuss related work for graph clustering, graph sparsification, and graph motifs. We then brief an existing graph sparsification method, L-Spar [32], with similar goals as gSparsify.

Graph clustering, also referred to as *community detection* in the social network community, has been extensively studied, and there exist rich literature on a wide range of graph clustering methods, including network flow based approaches [29], spectral clustering approaches [25], modularity based approaches [34], hierarchical graph partitioning approaches [21, 12], and local clustering approaches [10, 36, 16] (see surveys [14, 33] for a comprehensive list of graph clustering algorithms). Most of existing graph clustering solutions aim to optimize intra-cluster density, or inter-cluster sparsity, or both, based on various definitions of "density" and "sparsity" of graph clusters. Note that gSparsify is not restricted to any specific graph clustering method. Instead, it is to complement existing graph clustering methods.

Graph sparsification is to approximate a graph $G = (V, E)$ by another sparse graph $G' = (V, E')$ in achieving desired graph metrics within reasonable error bounds. As $|E'| \ll |E|$, the computation cost of related problems upon G', as opposed to G, is expected to be cheaper. Cut sparsifiers [15] are simplified graphs in which the weight of every cut agrees up to a multiplicative factor of $(1 \pm \epsilon)$ with that of the corresponding cut in the original graph. Graph spanners [7] are sparsified graphs to approximate pairwise distances of vertices. Spectral sparsifiers [3, 35] are to approximate eigenvalues to an arbitrarily small multiplicative error. SPINE [26] is to identify backbones of graphs for information propagation. However, existing graph sparsification methods are not primarily proposed to optimize graph clustering, which is the goal of our work.

Graph motifs, also known as *graphlets*, are small subgraphs defined as interaction patterns occurring at numbers significantly higher than those in randomized graphs [28]. As elementary structures of complex networks, graph motifs carry out key functionalities and represent a broad range of natural phenomena. Triangles [4] and related clustering coefficients [23] are used to detect the presence of spamming ac-

$G = (V, E)$	An input graph
$G' = (V, E')$	The sparsified graph
$\mathcal{C} = \{c_1, c_2, \dots, c_k\}$	A clustering of k graph clusters
l_0	The user-specified length threshold
l-path	A path with l edges
l-cycle	A cycle with l edges
d_u	The degree of the vertex $u \in V$
d	The maximum degree of vertices in G
$\mathbb{F}(\cdot)$	An aggregate function
γ	The local sparsification exponent
$\varphi(c)$	The graph conductance of the cluster c

Table 1: A Primer of Notations

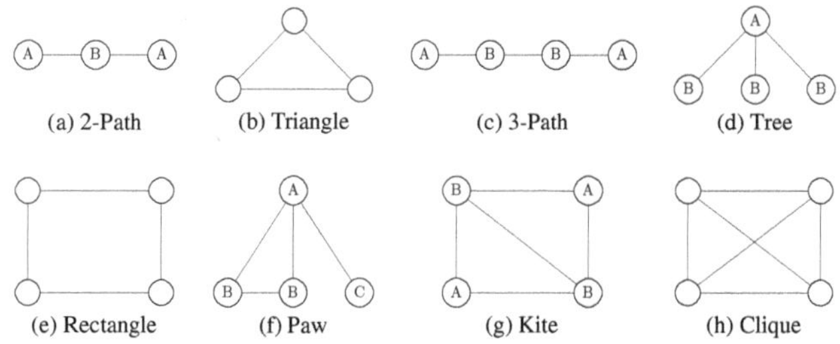

Figure 2: Graph Motifs with 3 and 4 Vertices. Different Non-isomorphic Positions of Vertices in Graph Motifs are Marked by Different Alphabet Letters.

tivities in large-scale Web graphs. The distribution of graph motifs in which a vertex is part of is used as an indicator for network classification [27]. Graph motifs are also used to analyze protein-protein interaction networks [8]. However, to the best of our knowledge, there is no existing work that considers graph motifs for promoting the efficiency and effectiveness of graphs clustering.

Enumerating graph motifs is nontrivial in large graphs [18]. Both exact and approximate solutions have been proposed under various paradigms including exact counting [41], sampling [28], frequent pattern mining [8], and color coding [17]. Specifically, triangle enumeration has been extensively studied, including memory-resident algorithms [24] with the optimal complexity of $O(|E|^{3/2})$ in the worst case, and disk-resident algorithms [30, 22] for massive graphs. Counting the number of short-length cycles can be accomplished in $O(|V|^{\omega})$ where $\omega < 2.376$ is the exponent for matrix multiplication [2]. Enumerating maximal cliques from a graph has proven to be optimal in $O(3^{|V|/3})$ in the worst-case [39].

L-Spar [32] (short for **L**ocal **Spar**sifier) is most similar to our method, gSparsify, for graph sparsification. L-Spar takes advantage of a similarity-based heuristic that an edge $e = (u, v)$ that is a part of many triangles is probably an intra-cluster edge [19]. L-Spar adopts Jaccard coefficient, $|\Gamma(u) \cap \Gamma(v)|/|\Gamma(u) \cup \Gamma(v)|$, where $\Gamma(\cdot)$ is the adjacency list of a given vertex, to model this heuristic and uses minwise hashing [5] to approximate Jaccard coefficient, thus achieving excellent scalability for graph sparsification. The key difference between gSparsify and L-Spar is two-fold. First, instead of using a single triangle motif, gSparsify considers a group of short-length cycle motifs including triangles (a special kind of cycle motif of length 3), to model cluster significance of edges. Evaluation based on multiple graph motifs can help identify intra-cluster edges that are not necessarily involved solely in triangles, and will significantly enhance the effectiveness of graph sparsification. From this perspective, L-Spar is just a special case of gSparsify. Second, the modeling of Jaccard coefficient and minwise hashing in L-Spar fails to generalize if non-triangle motifs are considered for graph sparsification. As a result, we propose a path-based indexing approach in gSparsify to enumerate all short-length cycles based on path-join operations. This path-join method can also be extended to enumerate other graph motifs in large graphs.

3. PRELIMINARIES

We consider in this paper the graph sparsification problem on simple, undirected, and connected graphs, while the proposed algorithms can be easily extended to other types of graphs.

Given a graph $G = (V, E)$, we consider some basic structures that are of special interest for graph motifs and graph sparsification. A *path* $p = (v_1, \dots, v_{l+1})$ is a sequence of vertices where $(v_i, v_{i+1}) \in E, 1 \leq i \leq l$. When the context is clear, we consider p a *simple path* in which all vertices are distinct and can be indexed and represented by $p[i], 1 \leq i \leq l+1$. A path containing $l+1$ vertices, or l edges, is of length l, denoted as an l-path for brevity. If $v_1 = v_{l+1}$, the path p is *closed* and it turns out to be a *cycle*. A cycle containing l vertices (edges) is denoted as an l-cycle. The shortest cycles are 3-cycles, also known as *triangles*. Table 1 summarizes the key notations in this paper.

4. GRAPH MOTIF-BASED CLUSTER SIGNIFICANCE

The goal of graph sparsification towards optimizing graph clustering is to preferentially retain intra-cluster edges of a graph, such that cluster structures can be well preserved in the resultant spersified graph. The critical problem is to accurately identify edges that are more likely to be intra-cluster edges. In this section, we discuss how graph motifs can be used as prime features to encode cluster structures of graphs and help identify intra-cluster edges from a graph.

In comparison to global features of graphs, such as degree distributions, diameters, and community structures [6], graph motifs are small, connected graphs captured in the local vicinity of vertices or edges, and are primarily used as elementary features representing key functionalities of graphs. Figure 2 illustrates graph motifs with 3 and 4 vertices, which can be broadly classified into two categories. The *position-sensitive* graph motifs contain vertices in different equivalence classes *w.r.t.* graph isomorphism. For example, in Figure 2, paths ((a) and (c)), tree (d), paw (f), and kite (g) are position-sensitive motifs, and the alphabet letters denote different equivalence classes of vertices *w.r.t.* graph isomorphism. In contrast, in *position-insensitive* graph motifs, all vertices are isomorphic to each other. For example, in Figure 2, cycles ((b) and (e)) and clique (h) are position-insensitive motifs.

Based on the intuitive definition of graph clustering, we note that clusters of a graph are relatively dense subgraphs. Therefore, the chances of small-size graph motifs occurring in a graph cluster are high. Equivalently, an intra-cluster edge $e \in E$ is very likely to lie frequently in different graph motifs. As a result, we evaluate the *cluster significance* of e by examining the distribution of graph motifs that include e as a constituent edge. The higher the cluster-significance value of e is, the more probably e is involved in a closely knitted local structure, and hence e is more likely to be an intra-cluster edge in the graph.

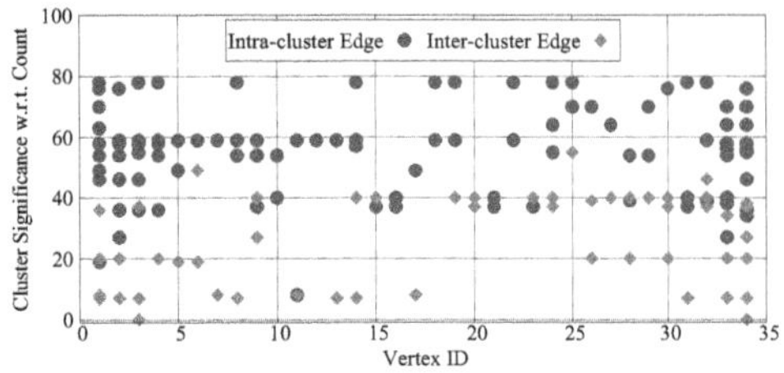

(a) Cluster Significance *w.r.t.* Count

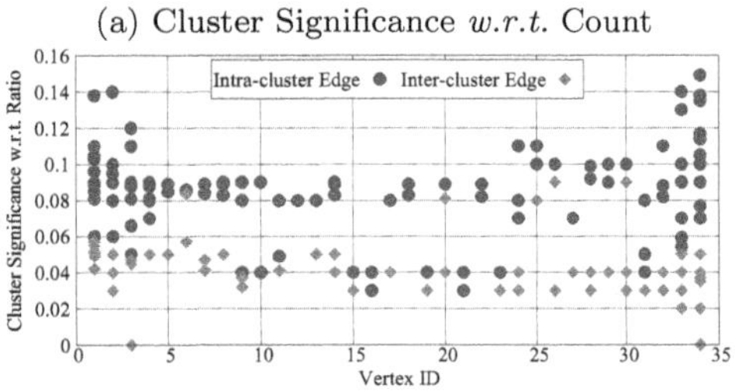

(b) Cluster Significance *w.r.t.* Ratio

Figure 3: Cluster Significance Scores of Edges in the Karate Club Network.

However, not all graph motifs play an equal role in representing local cluster structures of graphs. Path motifs (Figure 2(a) and (c)) are often used to identify cuts in sparse regions of graphs [20]. Similarly, all the edges of tree motifs (Figure 2(d)) and the singular edge (A, C) of the paw motif (Figure 2(f)) are likely to be cuts straddling different clusters. We therefore consider short-length *cycle motifs* as prime features for cluster significance evaluation in that:

1. Graph clusters are characterized by a high density of edges, so it is reasonable to expect that intra-cluster edges form a significant number of *closed* graph structures like short-length cycles. In contrast, edges across different clusters are hardly part of cycles. It turns out that edges within many cycles are more likely to be intra-cluster edges than inter-cluster ones;
2. Cycles are the simplest position-insensitive graph motifs, so edges within a cycle can be treated uniformly *w.r.t.* graph isomorphism. We thus can design graph sparsification algorithms irrespective of the exact position an edge lies in cycles;
3. For other complex position-insensitive graph motifs such as cliques, they can be treated approximately as a composition of cycle motifs. For instance, the fact that an edge e is in a 4-clique can be simulated as e is both in two triangles (length-3 cycles) and in two rectangles (length-4 cycles).

EXAMP E 2. *We consider the four clusters in the karate club network in Example* 1 *(Figure 1). Each edge in the original graph G can be classified as intra-cluster edges if two end-vertices are in the same cluster, or inter-cluster edges otherwise. We quantify the cluster significance of an edge e in two different ways: (1)* ***Count:*** *we compute the absolute number of* 3*-cycles (triangles),* 4*-cycles (quadrangles) and* 5*-cycles (pentagons) in the graph containing e in these cycles; (2)* ***Ratio:*** *we compute the accumulative ratio of* 3*-cycles,* 4*-cycles, and* 5*-cycles containing e relative to* 3*-paths,* 4*-paths, and* 5*-paths, respectively, which go through e. For each vertex in G, its incident edges are sorted non-increasingly in terms of cluster-significance scores, and results are shown in Figure 3a and Figure 3b, respectively. Note that intra-cluster edges (blue circles) are consistently ranked higher than, and well separated from, inter-cluster edges (red diamonds), because intra-cluster edges are more frequently involved in short-length cycles. Therefore, short-length cycle motifs lend themselves well as representative candidates to model cluster significance of edges in graphs.* □

Henceforth, we focus on short-length cycles as prime graph motifs to evaluate the cluster significance of edges. We first define the notion of "cluster significance" upon which edges can be ranked *w.r.t.* short-length cycle motifs. Given a graph $G = (V, E)$ and an edge $e \in E$, if $c^l(e)$ denotes the number of l-cycles ($l \geq 3$), each of which includes e as a constituent edge, we define the *cluster significance* of e *w.r.t. the l-cycle motif* as

$$CS^l_{\mathbb{C}}(e) = c^l(e) \tag{1}$$

Here the subscript $\mathbb{C}$ stands for *absolute counting.* Given a user-specified cycle length threshold $l_0 \geq 3$, we can further maintain a *cluster-significance vector* for the edge e as

$$CSV_{\mathbb{C}}(e) = (CS^3_{\mathbb{C}}(e), \ldots, CS^{l_0}_{\mathbb{C}}(e)) \tag{2}$$

$CSV_{\mathbb{C}}(e)$ is a vector of $(l_0 - 2)$ cluster-significance scores of e *w.r.t.* a set of cycles of lengths ranging from 3 up to l_0. We further define the *cluster significance* of e *w.r.t.* counting as

EFINITION 1 **(CS *w.r.t.* COUNTING)**. *Given $e \in E$ and a cycle length threshold l_0, the cluster significance of e* w.r.t. *counting is an aggregation of $CSV_{\mathbb{C}}(e)$:*

$$CS_{\mathbb{C}}(e) = \mathbb{F}(CS^3_{\mathbb{C}}(e), \ldots, CS^{l_0}_{\mathbb{C}}(e)) \tag{3}$$

where $\mathbb{F}(\cdot)$ is an aggregate function like SUM *or* AVG.

Alternatively, if $p^l(e)$ denotes the number of l-paths, each of which passes through the edge e, and we allow *closed paths, i.e.,* vertices within paths can occur repeatedly, we define the *cluster significance* of e *w.r.t.* l-cycle motif as

$$CS^l_{\mathbb{R}}(e) = \frac{c^l(e)}{p^l(e)} \tag{4}$$

Here the subscript $\mathbb{R}$ stands for *ratio.* Analogously, we can define the cluster-significance vector $CSV_{\mathbb{R}}(e)$ as

$$CSV_{\mathbb{R}}(e) = (CS^3_{\mathbb{R}}(e), \ldots, CS^{l_0}_{\mathbb{R}}(e)) \tag{5}$$

The cluster-significance *w.r.t.* ratio can be defined as

EFINITION 2 **(CS *w.r.t.* RATIO)**. *Given $e \in E$ and a cycle length threshold l_0, the cluster significance of e* w.r.t. *ratio is an aggregation of $CSV_{\mathbb{R}}(e)$:*

$$CS_{\mathbb{R}}(e) = \mathbb{F}(CS^3_{\mathbb{R}}(e), \ldots, CS^{l_0}_{\mathbb{R}}(e)) \tag{6}$$

EXAMP E 3. *We consider a sample graph shown in Figure 4, the cycle motif length threshold $l_0 = 5$, and the aggregate function is SUM$(\cdot)$. For the edge $(1, 2)$, the cluster-significance vector* w.r.t. *counting is $CSV_{\mathbb{C}}(1, 2) = (2, 4, 4)$, meaning that the edge $(1, 2)$ is contained in two* 3*-cycles, four* 4*-cycles, and four* 5*-cycles. So the cluster significance of $(1, 2)$* w.r.t. *counting, $CS_{\mathbb{C}}(1, 2)$, is* 10. *Similarly, the cluster-significance vector* w.r.t. *ratio is $CSV_{\mathbb{R}}(1, 2) = ($*0.167, 0.1, 0.036*$)$, and the cluster significance of $(1, 2)$* w.r.t. *ratio, $CS_{\mathbb{R}}(1, 2)$, is* 0.303*. If we consider the edge $(5, 6)$, both*

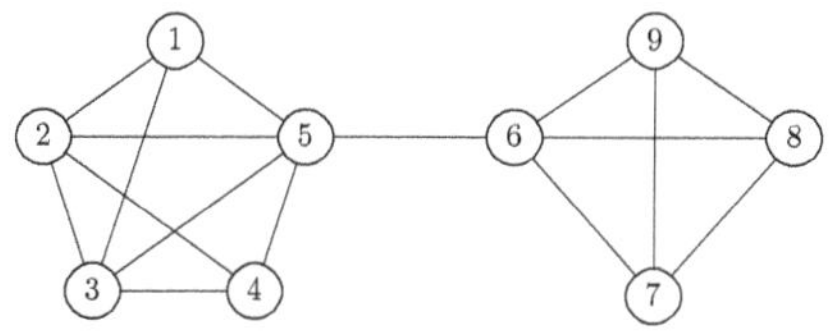

Figure 4: A Sample Graph G

$CS_{\mathbb{C}}(5,6)$ and $CS_{\mathbb{R}}(5,6)$ are 0. It means that this edge is not contained in any cycle motifs, and most probably it is an inter-cluster edge. □

5. COMPUTING CLUSTER SIGNIFICANCE

In this section, we discuss the computation of cluster-significance scores for edges in a graph. For either the count-based model, $CS_{\mathbb{C}}(e)$, or the ratio-based model, $CS_{\mathbb{R}}(e)$, we need enumerate all short-length cycles that contain e as a constituent edge. However, even enumerating the simplest triangle motifs turns out to be time-consuming in large graphs. We thus design an efficient path-based indexing approach to facilitating the computation.

Consider an edge $e = (u, v) \in E$, any cycle including e as a constituent edge can be decomposed into three sub-parts: a path $p_1 = (u, \ldots, w)$ originating from u, another path $p_2 = (v, \ldots, w)$ originating from v, and the edge $e = (u, v)$, where p_1 and p_2 are two vertex-disjoint paths except that they share one common end-vertex $w \in V$. Specifically, we choose w as the median point to u and v in the cycle, such that either $|p_1| = |p_2|$ or $|p_1| = |p_2| \pm 1$. As a result, an l-cycle that contains the edge $e = (u, v)$ can be identified as follows. We enumerate every path p_1 of length $\lceil \frac{l-1}{2} \rceil$ emanating from u, and every path p_2 of length $\lfloor \frac{l-1}{2} \rfloor$ emanating from v, respectively. if p_1 and p_2 share no common vertices except the end-vertex other than u and v, a cycle is identified from the graph. We formulate this idea based on the notion of *path join*, as follows,

EFINITION 3 **(PATH JOIN)**. *For an edge $e = (u, v)$, l-cycles containing e can be identified by joining two paths p_1 and p_2, $p_1 \bowtie_\theta p_2$, where the join condition θ is*

1. $|p_1| = \lceil \frac{l-1}{2} \rceil$, $|p_2| = \lfloor \frac{l-1}{2} \rfloor$;
2. $p_1[1] = u$, $p_2[1] = v$ *(p_1 and p_2 originate from u and v, respectively);*
3. $p_1[\lceil \frac{l-1}{2} \rceil] = p_2[\lfloor \frac{l-1}{2} \rfloor]$ *(p_1 and p_2 share one common end-vertex, other than u and v);*
4. $p_1[i] \neq p_2[j]$ *for* $1 < i < \lceil \frac{l-1}{2} \rceil$, $1 < j < \lfloor \frac{l-1}{2} \rfloor$ *(p_1 and p_2 are vertex-disjoint).*

THEOREM 1. *All cycle motifs of length l containing the edge $e = (u, v) \in E$ as an constituent edge can be enumerated based on path join, as defined in Definition 3.*

EXAMP E 4. *Figure 5 illustrates two examples for enumerating cycle motifs that contain the edge (u, v) (in thick black color), based on path join. In Figure 5a, we enumerate all 4-cycles. The 2-paths emanating from u (color in red), and 1-paths enumerating from v (color in blue) are joined together, thus resulting in three 4-cycles. In Figure 5b, we enumerate all 5-cycles. The 2-paths emanating from u and v, respectively, are considered for path join, thus resulting in seven 5-cycles. Note that the paths (u, d, w) and (v, d, w) fail to join as both share a common intermediate vertex d, so the path-join condition does not hold.* □

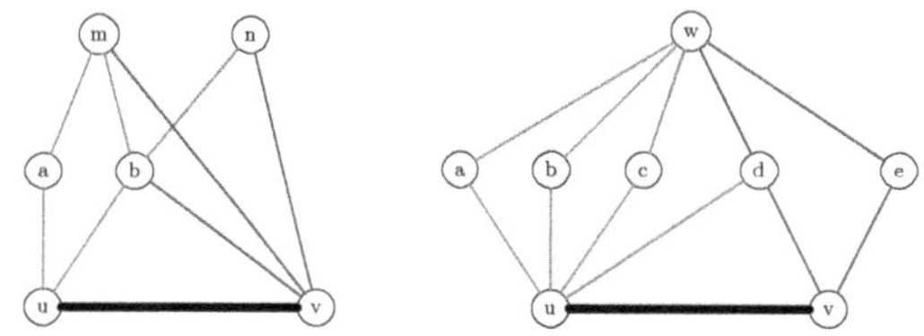

(a) 4-cycles (b) 5-cycles

Figure 5: Enumerating Cycle Motifs for the Edge (u, v)

Algorithm 1: Computing $CS^l_{\mathbb{C}}(e)$

Input: An edge $e = (u, v) \in E$, the motif length l
Output: The cluster-significance score $CS^l_{\mathbb{C}}(e)$

begin
  for $w \in V$ **do**
    $\mathcal{H}_1(w) \leftarrow \emptyset$; $\mathcal{H}_2(w) \leftarrow \emptyset$;
  for $p_i \in \mathcal{P}_{\lceil \frac{l-1}{2} \rceil}(u)$ **do**
    $\mathcal{H}_1(p_i[\lceil \frac{l-1}{2} \rceil]) \leftarrow \mathcal{H}_1(p_i[\lceil \frac{l-1}{2} \rceil]) \cup \{i\}$;
  for $p_j \in \mathcal{P}_{\lfloor \frac{l-1}{2} \rfloor}(v)$ **do**
    $\mathcal{H}_2(p_j[\lfloor \frac{l-1}{2} \rfloor]) \leftarrow \mathcal{H}_2(p_i[\lfloor \frac{l-1}{2} \rfloor]) \cup \{j\}$;
  $CS^l_{\mathbb{C}}(e) \leftarrow 0$;
  for $w \in V$ **do**
    if $\mathcal{H}_1(w) \neq \emptyset$ **and** $\mathcal{H}_2(w) \neq \emptyset$ **then**
      for $i \in \mathcal{H}_1(w)$ **do**
        for $j \in \mathcal{H}_2(w)$ **do**
          if $\theta : (p_i \bowtie_\theta p_j)$ **then**
            $CS^l_{\mathbb{C}}(e) \leftarrow CS^l_{\mathbb{C}}(e) + 1$;
  return $CS^l_{\mathbb{C}}(e)$;

To this end, we design a path-based indexing approach to computing cluster significance of edges in G. Given the motif length threshold, $l_0 \geq 3$, we maintain, for each vertex $v \in V$, all distinct l-paths emanating from v into a vector, $\mathcal{P}_l(v)$, where $1 \leq l \leq \lceil \frac{l_0-1}{2} \rceil$. Specifically, $\mathcal{P}_1(v)$ is just the adjacency list of v. If the maximum degree of vertices in G is denoted d, both the time and space complexity for path-based index construction are $O(d^{\lceil \frac{l_0-1}{2} \rceil} \cdot |V|)$. Note that real-world graphs often follow power-law degree distributions, so in practice a majority of vertices have degrees that are significantly smaller than d. Another important factor is that, the length threshold of cycle motifs, l_0, is often set small, as longer cycles in cluster-significance evaluation will bring marginal improvement for graph sparsification. Therefore, this path-based index can be pre-built offline effectively in the index construction phase.

Based on Theorem 1, in order to enumerate all cycle motifs of length l ($l \leq l_0$) containing an edge $e = (u, v)$, we employ all pre-indexed paths $p_i \in \mathcal{P}_{\lceil \frac{l-1}{2} \rceil}(u)$ and $p_j \in \mathcal{P}_{\lfloor \frac{l-1}{2} \rfloor}(v)$ to perform a path join, $p_i \bowtie_\theta p_j$, as detailed in Algorithm 1. To facilitate the evaluation of path join, we maintain an inverted index $\mathcal{H}_1(\cdot) : V \longmapsto 2^{\mathbb{N}}$, such that for each vertex $w \in V$, if w is the last end-vertex (other

Algorithm 2: gSparsify

Input: Graph $G = (V, E)$, the motif length threshold l_0, the local sparsification exponent γ, an aggregate function $\mathbb{F}(\cdot)$

Output: Sparsified graph G'

1 **begin**
2 $\quad G' \leftarrow \emptyset$;
3 $\quad$ **for** $e = (u, v) \in E$ **do**
4 $\quad\quad CS_{\mathbb{C}}(e) \leftarrow 0$; $\quad CS_{\mathbb{P}}(e) \leftarrow 0$;
5 $\quad\quad$ **foreach** $l : 3 \leq l \leq l_0$ **do**
6 $\quad\quad\quad$ compute $CS^l_{\mathbb{C}}(e)$ (Algorithm 1);
7 $\quad\quad\quad$ compute $CS^l_{\mathbb{R}}(e)$ (Equation 7);
8 $\quad\quad CS_{\mathbb{C}}(e) \leftarrow \mathbb{F}(CS^3_{\mathbb{C}}(e), \ldots, CS^{l_0}_{\mathbb{C}}(e))$;
$\quad\quad CS_{\mathbb{R}}(e) \leftarrow \mathbb{F}(CS^3_{\mathbb{R}}(e), \ldots, CS^{l_0}_{\mathbb{R}}(e))$;
9 $\quad$ **foreach** $u \in V$ **do**
10 $\quad\quad$ Sort all incident edges $e = (u, v) \in E$ by $CS_{\mathbb{C}}(e)$ (or by $CS_{\mathbb{R}}(e)$);
11 $\quad\quad$ Add top d^{γ}_u edges to G';
12 $\quad$ **return** G';

than u) of a path $p_i \in \mathcal{P}_{\lceil \frac{l-1}{2} \rceil}(u)$, then w together with the path index i of p_i are stored into $\mathcal{H}_1(w)$. This way, all the paths of $\mathcal{P}_{\lceil \frac{l-1}{2} \rceil}(u)$ that share a common end-vertex, w, are grouped together. Analogously, we build another inverted index $\mathcal{H}_2(\cdot)$, in which all paths of $\mathcal{P}_{\lfloor \frac{l-1}{2} \rfloor}(v)$ sharing common end-vertices (other than v) are grouped together. Both inverted indexes are first initialized (Lines 2-3), and updated in terms of the last end-vertex of each path in $\mathcal{P}_{\lceil \frac{l-1}{2} \rceil}(u)$ and $\mathcal{P}_{\lfloor \frac{l-1}{2} \rfloor}(v)$, respectively (Lines 4-7). To compute the cluster significance *w.r.t.* counting, $CS^l_{\mathbb{C}}(e)$, we consider the paths $p_i \in \mathcal{P}_{\lceil \frac{l-1}{2} \rceil}(u)$, and $p_j \in \mathcal{P}_{\lfloor \frac{l-1}{2} \rfloor}(v)$, both of which sharing a common end-vertex (Line 10). If p_i and p_j satisfy the path-join condition θ, as defined in Definition 3, we successfully identify an l-cycle from the graph (Lines 13-14).

Assume paths originating from u may end at any vertex of G, then $|\mathcal{H}_1(\cdot)| = |\mathcal{P}_{\lceil \frac{l-1}{2} \rceil}(u)|/|V|$. Similarly, $|\mathcal{H}_2(\cdot)| = |\mathcal{P}_{\lfloor \frac{l-1}{2} \rfloor}(v)|/|V|$. The time complexity of Algorithm 1 turns out to be $O(|\mathcal{P}_{\lceil \frac{l-1}{2} \rceil}(u)| \cdot |\mathcal{P}_{\lfloor \frac{l-1}{2} \rfloor}(v)| \cdot ((l-1)/2)^2/|V|)$, where the term $((l-1)/2)^2)$ denotes the time to evaluate the path-join condition θ for p_i and p_j. Note that $|\mathcal{P}_{\lceil \frac{l-1}{2} \rceil}(u)|$ is the number of $(\lceil \frac{l-1}{2} \rceil)$-paths originating from u, bounded up by $d^{\lceil \frac{l-1}{2} \rceil}$, so the worst-case complexity of Algorithm 1 is $O(\frac{d^l}{|V|})$.

Once the cluster significance *w.r.t.* counting, $CS^l_{\mathbb{C}}(e)$, has been computed, it is straightforward to derive the cluster significance *w.r.t.* ratio, $CS^l_{\mathbb{R}}(e)$, which is to normalize $CS^l_{\mathbb{C}}(e)$ by considering all possible paths passing through e:

$$CS^l_{\mathbb{R}}(e) = \frac{CS^l_{\mathbb{C}}(e)}{|\mathcal{P}_{\lceil \frac{l-1}{2} \rceil}(u)| \cdot |\mathcal{P}_{\lfloor \frac{l-1}{2} \rfloor}(v)|} \quad (7)$$

Note that all $(\lceil \frac{l-1}{2} \rceil)$-paths originating from u are maintained in the index $\mathcal{P}_{\lceil \frac{l-1}{2} \rceil}(u)$, and analogously all $(\lfloor \frac{l-1}{2} \rfloor)$-paths originating from v are maintained in $\mathcal{P}_{\lfloor \frac{l-1}{2} \rfloor}(v)$. Once $CS^l_{\mathbb{C}}(e)$ is known, $CS^l_{\mathbb{P}}(e)$ can be computed in $O(1)$.

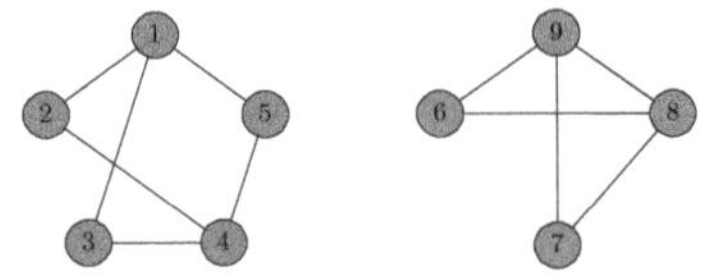

Figure 6: The Sparsified Graph, G'

6. GRAPH SPARSIFICATION: gSparsify

In this section, we detail our graph motif-based sparsification method, gSparsify, which uses short-length cycle motifs to model the cluster significance of edges. The edges with highly ranked cluster-significance scores are preferably retained. This way, the core cluster structures can be well preserved in the sparsified graph.

Algorithm 2 describes the whole process for graph sparsification. The sparsified graph, G', is first initialized as an empty graph (Line 2). For each edge $e \in G$, we compute its cluster-significance scores, $CS_{\mathbb{C}}(e)$ and $CS_{\mathbb{R}}(e)$, based on Algorithm 1 (Lines 3-8). We further choose an aggregate function, $\mathbb{F}$, to synthesize cluster-significance scores of edges based on a series of cycle motifs. After that, a localized, *vertex-centric* sparsification approach is employed to retain edges with high cluster significance in the neighborhood of vertices. Specifically, for each vertex u of the graph G, we select the top d^{γ}_u $(0 \leq \gamma < 1)$ incident edges, ranked on either $CS_{\mathbb{C}}(e)$ or $CS_{\mathbb{R}}(e)$, where d_u is the degree of u, into G' for sparsification (Lines 9-11). In principle, we sparsify high-degree vertices more aggressively than low-degree ones, because high-degree vertices are more likely to be hubs that tend to connect multiple clusters. As a result, their incident edges are likely to be inter-cluster edges. In implementation, we choose a strictly concave function, d^{γ}_u, for graph sparsification. When $\gamma \to 0$, the sparsified graph G' contains very few edges but each vertex u still preserves at least one edge, making the resultant cluster containing u connected. When $\gamma \to 1$, the sparsified graph G' is almost identical to G as most edges are retained.

The complexity of Algorithm 2 is formulated with two components. The first is to compute cluster significance of edges in the graph, which is $O(d^{l_0}|E|/|V|)$. The second is to sort, for each vertex, its incident edges based on cluster-significance scores, which is $\sum_u O(d_u \log d_u) \leq \sum_u O(d_u \log d) = O(\log d \cdot |E|)$. So the overall complexity of Algorithm 2 is $O(d^{l_0}|E|/|V| + \log d \cdot |E|)$.

EXAMP E 5. *We apply the graph sparsification algorithm,* gSparsify*, on the sample graph G shown in Figure 4 by setting* $l_0 = 5$, $\gamma = 0.1$, *and* $\mathbb{F} =$ SUM. *The sparsified graph* G' *is illustrated in Figure 6.* G' *contains* 11 *edges, so* 5 *edges of G are filtered out during graph sparsification. It can be witnessed that there are two clusters (colored in red and blue, respectively) in the sparsified graph* G'. □

7. EXPERIMENTS

In this section, we present our experimental studies for gSparsify. We make use of gSparsify as a pre-processing step to sparsify a series of real-world graphs, and examine both the benefit and cost of gSparsify toward improving the effectiveness and efficiency of state-of-the-art graph clustering methods. We implement gSparsify in C and compile it with GCC 4.4.7. All experiments were carried out in a Linux machine running RedHat Enterprise Server 6.5, with 12 AMD Opteron 2.3GHz CPUs and 96GB of memory.

7.1 Datasets

We consider three real-world graphs in our experimental studies, including a protein-protein interaction network, a co-authorship network, and a social network:

1. **Yeast PPI Network:** This is a protein-protein interaction (PPI) network in the BioGrid database [37]. This graph contains 4,531 vertices representing yeast genes, and 22,736 edges depicting protein interactions. The average degree of vertices is 10 and the maximum degree is 1,549. We cluster this graph into 450 clusters, each of which contains approximately 10 vertices in average, because the sizes of most protein complexes are in the range of 5 to 15;

2. **DBLP**[1]**:** This is a co-authorship graph where two authors are connected if they publish as co-authors at least one paper. This co-authorship graph contains 317,080 vertices and 1,049,866 edges. The publication venues, *e.g.*, journals or conferences, define the ground-truth clusters. We consider 5,000 clusters in the experiments;

3. **Orkut**[2]**:** This is an online social network where vertices represent anonymized individuals, and edges illustrate friendship relations between individuals. The graph has 3,072,441 vertices and 117,185,083 edges. Orkut allows users to form groups, which are used as ground-truth clusters. We consider 5,000 clusters in the experiments.

7.2 Graph Clustering Methods

We consider three well-known graph clustering methods in our experimental studies:

1. **METIS**[21] is a high-quality graph partitioning toolkit implemented based on multilevel recursive-bisection, multilevel k-way, and constraint-based graph partitioning schemes. We used METIS 5.1.0 with default parameter settings;

2. **Graclus**[12] is a fast graph clustering tool that computes normalized cut and ratio association for a graph without costly eigenvector computation. We use Graclus 1.2 and choose the default parameter settings for graph clustering;

3. **MCL**[40] is a scalable graph clustering method based on simulation of stochastic flows in graphs. Note that the number of clusters are indirectly controlled by the inflation parameter. By tuning this parameter, we can generate the desired number of graph clusters in the experiments.

It is worth noting that gSparsify is not restricted to the above-mentioned graph clustering algorithms. Any graph clustering technique toward optimizing the notions of intra-cluster density and inter-cluster sparsity of graph clusters can benefit from the proposed method, gSparsify.

[1]DBLP datasets: http://snap.stanford.edu/data/index.html
[2]Orkut datasets: http://snap.stanford.edu/data/index.html

Dataset	Graph Motif Length					
	$l_0 = 3$		$l_0 = 4$		$l_0 = 5$	
	Time	Space	Time	Space	Time	Space
Yeast	0	0.22	0.11	2.66	0.13	2.93
DBLP	0	10.93	47.3	349.5	49.2	371.5
Orkut	0	762.1	1,159	2,716	1,174	2,755

Table 2: Index Construction Cost of gSparsify (Time in Seconds, and Space in Megabytes).

7.3 Evaluation Metrics

We evaluate the graph sparsification method from multiple perspectives. The foremost evaluation is to examine to what extent gSparsify can help improve the graph clustering effectiveness. We apply graph clustering algorithms on the original graph G, and the sparsified graph G', respectively, and assess the clustering quality *w.r.t.* ground truth or graph clustering metrics.

If we have ground truth for clusters, $\mathcal{C} = \{c_1, c_2, \ldots, c_k\}$ (*e.g.*, in DBLP and Orkut), we evaluate clustering quality based on the *average F-score* of graph clusters. The F-score of a predicted graph cluster $\bar{c}$ *w.r.t.* a ground-truth cluster $c_i \in \mathcal{C}$, denoted $F(\bar{c})|_{c_i}$, is the harmonic mean of the precision and recall. Furthermore, the F-score of $\bar{c}$ is

$$F(\bar{c}) = \max_{c_i \in \mathcal{C}} F(\bar{c})|_{c_i} \quad \forall i : 1 \leq i \leq k$$

It is the F-score of the predicted cluster $\bar{c}$ *w.r.t.* the ground truth cluster $c^* \in \mathcal{C}$ to which $\bar{c}$ approximates best. The average F-score of all the predicted clusters is the weighted average of all F-scores, each of which is weighted by the cluster size. Empirically, the higher the average F-score, the better the clustering quality.

We also consider the *average graph conductance* to evaluate the quality of graph clusters in all graph datasets. Given a cluster $c \in \mathcal{C}$ of G, the graph conductance of c is

$$\varphi(c) = \frac{\sum_{i \in c, j \in G/c} I_{ij}}{\min(I(c), I(G/c))} \quad \forall i, j \in V$$

where I_{ij} is an indicator function that equals 1 if there exists an edge (i, j) between vertices i and j, and 0 otherwise, and

$$I(c) = \sum_{i \in c} \sum_{j \in V} I_{ij}$$

Graph conductance lies between 0 and 1 with lower values indicating better clustering quality. The average graph conductance is the average of $\varphi(c)$ for all clusters $c \in \mathcal{C}$. Note that the evaluation of clustering quality based on graph conductance should be performed on the original graph G. That is, for clusters derived from the sparsified graph G', we need map all such clusters back into G and compute graph conductance in G. This way, it will reflect how well graph sparsification can retain the cluster structures of G.

Another evaluation metric is the speedup gSparsify offers for graph clustering. We apply different graph clustering methods on the original graph G and the sparsified graph G', respectively, and examine the runtime performance gain gSparsify provides. As G' is much smaller than G, clustering on G' is expected to be significantly faster.

There exist several critical parameters for gSparsify, including the cycle length threshold l_0, the local sparsification exponent γ, and the aggregate function $\mathbb{F}$. We also examine how these parameters regulate the performance of graph sparsification. If not specified otherwise, we choose the cluster significance *w.r.t.* ratio, $CS_{\mathbb{R}}$, as the default model for

Metis									
Dataset	Original			Sparse Ratio	Speedup	L-Spar		gSparsify	
	F-score	φ	Time(s)			F-score	φ	F-score	φ
Yeast	N.A.	0.89	2.47	**0.26**	**21x**	N.A.	0.84	**N.A.**	**0.76**
DBLP	16.04	0.65	116.45	**0.21**	**18x**	16.67	0.65	**18.83**	**0.60**
Orkut	11.08	0.85	13,858	**0.17**	**37x**	10.97	0.79	**15.45**	**0.72**

Table 3: Graph Clustering Using METIS

Graclus									
Dataset	Original			Sparse Ratio	Speedup	L-Spar		gSparsify	
	F-score	φ	Time(s)			F-score	φ	F-score	φ
Yeast	N.A.	0.83	0.25	**0.26**	**2x**	N.A.	0.80	**N.A.**	**0.73**
DBLP	16.72	0.61	73.9	**0.21**	**13x**	17.15	0.55	**17.36**	**0.59**

Table 4: Graph Clustering Using Graclus

MCL									
Dataset	Original			Sparse Ratio	Speedup	L-Spar		gSparsify	
	F-score	φ	Time(s)			F-score	φ	F-score	φ
Yeast	N.A.	0.84	6.56	**0.26**	**18x**	N.A.	0.83	**N.A.**	**0.74**
DBLP	16.50	0.77	133.79	**0.21**	**17x**	16.52	0.75	**18.04**	**0.67**
Orkut	11.65	0.72	20,519	**0.17**	**21x**	10.79	0.81	**12.85**	**0.66**

Table 5: Graph Clustering Using MCL

graph sparsification, and set the key parameters with the following default values: $l_0 = 5$, $\gamma = 0.5$ and $\mathbb{F} = \mathsf{AVG}(\cdot)$. Meanwhile, as an indexing approach, gSparsify needs to build path-based indexes and inverted indexes, we also evaluate the time and space cost of index construction in the experimental studies.

We compare gSparsify with L-Spar [32] that only uses the triangle motif for graph sparsification. The results will demonstrate that gSparsify is a generalized method where a series of graph motifs can be incorporated together to improve the clustering quality of real-world graphs.

7.4 Index Construction Cost

We first report the index construction cost of gSparsify in different graph datasets, shown in Table 2. We choose different lengths of cycle motifs ranging from 3 to 5. When $l_0 = 3$, only the one-level neighborhood index $\mathcal{P}_1$, *i.e.*, the adjacency list, is built. When $l_0 = 4$, we need to build the path index $\mathcal{P}_2$ and use the inverted index $\mathcal{H}_1$, and when $l_0 = 5$, both the path index $\mathcal{P}_2$ and inverted indexes of all vertices are required. When the graph is small, for example, in the Yeast dataset, the index can be constructed efficiently with very small memory consumption. When the graph becomes excessively large, for example, in the Orkut dataset, the index construction needs more time and memory. However, this path-based index is constructed offline only once. Such cost is much affordable compared with the performance gain obtained for graph sparsification.

7.5 Improvement on Graph Clustering

We consider both gSparsify and L-Spar to sparsify the three graph datasets, and examine the clustering quality and speedup by applying three graph clustering algorithms on the original graph G and the sparsified graph G', respectively. As to the clustering quality, we evaluate both average F-scores, if graphs have ground truth for clusters, and the average graph conductance. For speedup, we consider the runtime cost of graph clustering on G' against G. The graph sparsification ratio, $|E'|/|E|$, is controlled by tuning the local sparsification exponent, γ.

The experimental results of using METIS are shown in Table 3. For all the three datasets, gSparsify provides better clustering quality results than the plain graph clustering method applied on the original graph, in terms of both F-scores and the graph conductance. gSparsify also outperforms L-Spar by offering better clustering quality results. For example, in the largest Orkut dataset, the F-score is enhanced from 10.97 to 15.45, and the graph conductance is further reduced from 0.79 to 0.72, both indicating that gSparsify preserves more intra-cluster edges during graph sparsification. The main reason is that gSparsify leverages short-length cycle motifs for cluster significance quantification, such that intra-cluster edges can be effectively identified from within large graphs. However, L-Spar only uses the 3-cycle motif, thus leading to less effective results. Another benefit of graph sparsification is the speedup it offers for graph clustering. We apply METIS on the original graph G, and the sparsified graph G', which is about $1/4$ to $1/5$ the size of G. The speedups for graph clustering are 21x, 18x, and 37x, respectively, for the Yeast, DBLP and Orkut datasets. This indicates that, gSparsify can significantly speedup graph clustering on large graphs while preserving, or even enhancing, the clustering quality.

We perform the same experimental studies using Graclus and MCL clustering algorithms, and the results are presented in Table 4, and Table 5, respectively. Note that Graclus cannot finish successfully in the largest Orkut dataset, so the results are not included. Our graph sparsification method, gSparsify, can improve clustering quality in different graph datasets. Specifically, gSparsify results in better clustering quality than L-Spar, in terms of both F-scores and the graph conductance. Meanwhile, gSparsify brings significant speedup for these two clustering methods. This is important because clustering in large graphs is very resource-intensive and time-consuming, while graph sparsification is an effective means to shorten the gap of the application of many graph clustering solutions that are designed mainly for small or medium-size graphs.

7.6 Parametric Analysis

The graph sparsification algorithm, gSparsify, is critical to a series of algorithmic parameters. We then perform experimental studies to examine how these key parameters affect the overall graph sparsification performance.

7.6.1 Graph Spasification w.r.t. l_0

We first examine the motif length threshold, l_0. By tuning the values of l_0, we adopt different short-length cycle motifs for graph sparsification. For example, if $l_0 = 3$, we only use 3-cycles in graph sparsification, while if $l_0 = 4$, both 3-cycles and 4-cycles will be employed. As shown in Figure 7a and Figure 7b, we choose l_0 ranging from 3 to 5 and evaluate the clustering quality *w.r.t.* F-scores and the graph conductance, respectively, using the METIS method. When more short-length cycle motifs are considered, intra-cluster edges are more likely to be identified during graph sparsification, and thus improve the graph clustering quality. We perform the same experiments and witness similar evidences using the MCL method, and the results are illustrated in Figure 7c and Figure 7d, corresponding to F-scores and the graph conductance, respectively.

However, when l_0 is set high, we have to take more time for graph sparsification. Figure 8 illustrates the sparsification time for three different datasets, in terms of l_0. Here a common trade-off needs to be made between sparsification time and effectiveness. Considering graph sparsification can be performed offline, we still can afford more time for graph sparsification to trade better graph clustering quality, which is the goal of our work.

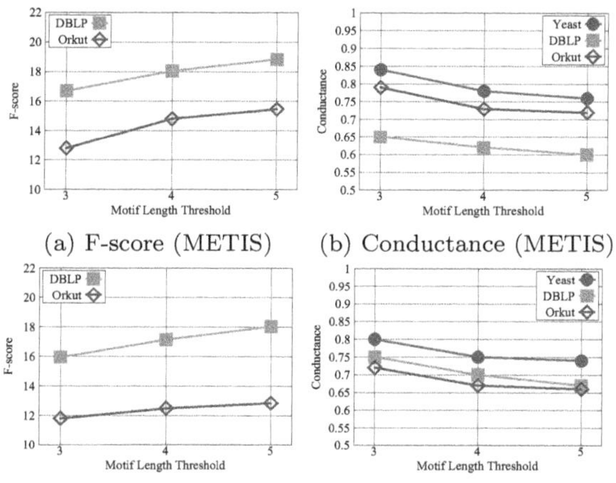

(a) F-score (METIS) (b) Conductance (METIS)

(c) F-score (MCL) (d) Conductance (MCL)

Figure 7: Graph Clustering Quality *w.r.t.* l_0

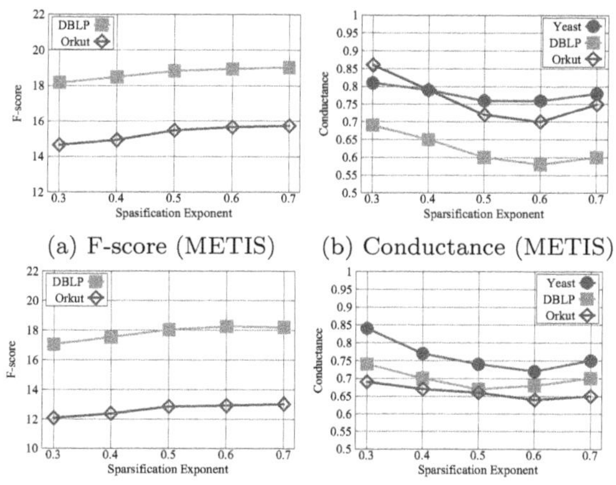

(a) F-score (METIS) (b) Conductance (METIS)

(c) F-score (MCL) (d) Conductance (MCL)

Figure 9: Graph Clustering Quality *w.r.t.* γ

7.6.2 *Graph Spasification* w.r.t. γ

We then examine the local sparsification exponent, γ, which controls the number of top ranked edges to be retained during graph sparsification. By tuning $0 \leq \gamma < 1$, we can derive a series of sparsified graphs with varied sizes. As shown in Figure 9a, we generate five different sparsified graphs for the graph datasets by choosing different γ ranging from 0.3 to 0.7, and evaluate clustering quality using METIS. We note that, in terms of F-scores, if we retain more edges during graph sparsification ($\gamma = 0.7$), the clustering quality can be slightly improved. If we sparsify the graph avidly be setting $\gamma = 0.3$, more edges will be filtered thus resulting in a slightly worse clustering result. However, the F-score for $\gamma = 0.3$ is still better than that generated from the original graph. It indicates that although we filter out most edges from G and retain about 10% of the edges into the sparsified graph G', the core cluster structures are still largely preserved with most of the noisy edges eliminated.

Similarly, we evaluate the clustering quality *w.r.t.* the graph conductance, and results are shown in Figure 9b. When γ is set low ($\gamma = 0.3$), we filter out many edges that may hurt the clustering effectiveness. However, when γ is set high ($\gamma = 0.7$), many noisy edges are retained in G', which also bring side effects for graph clustering and lead to inferior results. We conduct the same experiments using MCL, and results are shown in Figure 9c and Figure 9d, respectively. The patterns between the clustering quality and γ are very similar to the cases where METIS is adopted.

7.6.3 *Graph Spasification* w.r.t. $\mathbb{F}$

If multiple short-length cycle motifs are adopted to quantify the cluster significance of edges, we use an aggregate function $\mathbb{F}$ to synthesize cluster-significance scores. In this experiment, we choose two aggregate functions, SUM and AVG, and examine the effect of such aggregate functions for graph sparsification. Note that with different aggregate functions, the top ranked edges that are to be retained during graph sparsification will be different, and thus the final sparsified graph G' may vary. We test the clustering quality results, in terms of both F-scores and the graph conductance, on the DBLP dataset, as shown in Figure 10. For different graph clustering methods, AVG offers better clustering quality results than SUM in most cases. Note that it is inappropriate to choose MIN or MAX as the aggregate function in our framework, as they only choose the cluster-significance score based on one type of cycle motifs, which usually offers inferior sparsification results.

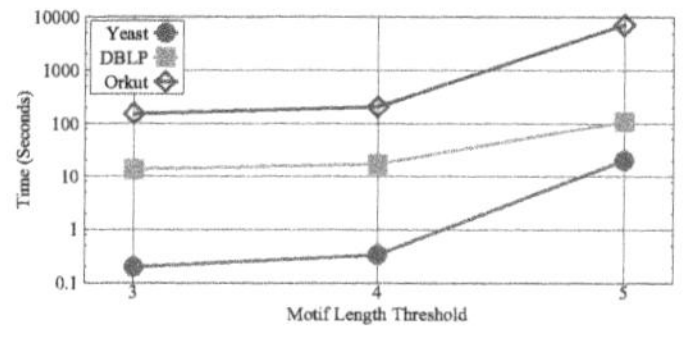

Figure 8: Graph Sparsification Time *w.r.t.* l_0

7.6.4 $CS_{\mathbb{C}}$ vs. $CS_{\mathbb{R}}$

When modeling cluster significance of edges in a graph, we consider two approaches: $CS_{\mathbb{C}}$ and $CS_{\mathbb{R}}$. The first one counts the absolute number of motifs that contain the edge to be examined, while the second one computes the relative ratio *w.r.t.* the total number of possible paths passing through the edge. We perform another experiment to evaluate these two models, each of which is chosen as the underlying method for the computation of cluster-significance scores of edges. We apply gSparsify with $CS_{\mathbb{C}}$, termed as COUNT, and gSparsify with $CS_{\mathbb{R}}$, termed as RATIO, in the DBLP dataset and examine the clustering quality of different graph clustering methods. The results are shown in Figure 11. We notice that RATIO provides consistently better quality results than COUNT, in terms of both F-scores and the graph conductance. This is especially true when dealing with edges incident to high-degree vertices.

8. CONCLUSIONS

In this paper, we designed a new graph sparsification method, gSparsify, toward enabling efficient and cost-effective graph clustering on real-world graphs. The goal of gSparsify is to identify and preferentially retain cluster-significance edges of a graph G into a sparsified graph G', such that edges with little or no cluster structure insight can be effectively pruned before costly graph clustering is performed. The main idea of gSparsify is to make use of a group of short-length cycle motifs to model cluster significance of edges. To facilitate the computation of cluster significance, we devised a path-based indexing approach such that the costly graph-motif enumeration can be cast into a systemic path-join process. Our experimental studies demonstrated that, gSparsify generalizes and outperforms the state-of-the-art graph spar-

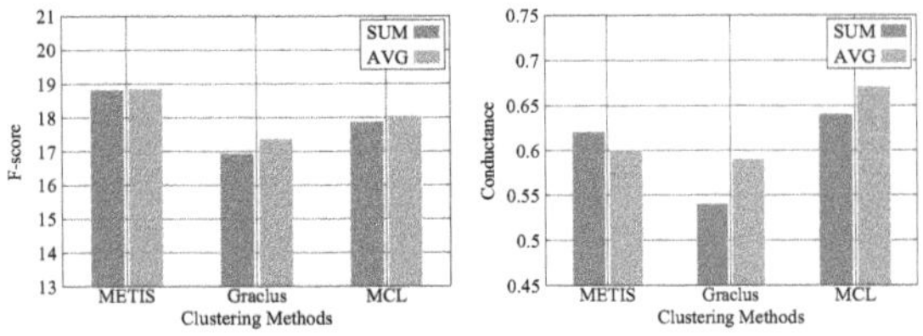

(a) F-score (DBLP) (b) Conductance (DBLP)

Figure 10: Graph Clustering Quality *w.r.t.* $\mathbb{F}$

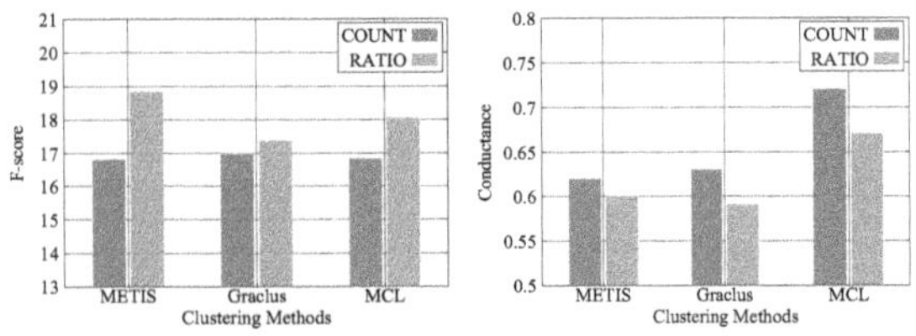

(a) F-score (DBLP) (b) Conductance (DBLP)

Figure 11: Graph Clustering Quality *w.r.t.* Cluster-significance Modeling

sification method, L-Spar. More importantly, gSparsify enables more efficient graph clustering without a compromise of clustering quality, and therefore can be effectively employed to cluster real-world large graphs.

9. REFERENCES

[1] C. C. Aggarwal and H. Wang. *Managing and Mining Graph Data*. Springer, 2010.

[2] N. Alon, R. Yuster, and U. Zwick. Finding and counting given length cycles. In *ESA'94*, pages 354–364, 1994.

[3] J. Batson, D. A. Spielman, N. Srivastava, and S.-H. Teng. Spectral sparsification of graphs: Theory and algorithms. *Commun. ACM*, 56(8):87–94, 2013.

[4] L. Becchetti, P. Boldi, C. Castillo, and A. Gionis. Efficient algorithms for large-scale local triangle counting. *ACM Trans. Knowl. Discov. Data*, 4(3):13:1–13:28, 2010.

[5] A. Z. Broder, M. Charikar, A. M. Frieze, and M. Mitzenmacher. Min-wise independent permutations. In *STOC'98*, pages 327–336, 1998.

[6] D. Chakrabarti and C. Faloutsos. Graph mining: Laws, generators, and algorithms. *ACM Comput. Surv.*, 38(1), 2006.

[7] S. Chechik, M. Langberg, D. Peleg, and L. Roditty. Fault-tolerant spanners for general graphs. In *STOC'09*, pages 435–444, 2009.

[8] J. Chen, W. Hsu, M. L. Lee, and S.-K. Ng. Nemofinder: Dissecting genome-wide protein-protein interactions with meso-scale network motifs. In *KDD'06*, pages 106–115, 2006.

[9] D. J. Cook and L. B. Holder. *Mining Graph Data*. John Wiley & Sons, 2006.

[10] W. Cui, Y. Xiao, H. Wang, and W. Wang. Local search of communities in large graphs. In *SIGMOD'14*, pages 991–1002, 2014.

[11] B. B. Dalvi, M. Kshirsagar, and S. Sudarshan. Keyword search on external memory data graphs. *Proc. VLDB Endow.*, 1(1):1189–1204, 2008.

[12] I. S. Dhillon, Y. Guan, and B. Kulis. Weighted graph cuts without eigenvectors: A multilevel approach. *IEEE Trans. Pattern Anal. Mach. Intell.*, 29(11):1944–1957, 2007.

[13] H. N. Djidjev and M. Onus. Scalable and accurate graph clustering and community structure detection. *IEEE Trans. Parallel Distrib. Syst.*, 24(5):1022–1029, 2013.

[14] S. Fortunato. Community detection in graphs. *CoRR*, 2009.

[15] W. S. Fung, R. Hariharan, N. J. Harvey, and D. Panigrahi. A general framework for graph sparsification. In *STOC '11*, pages 71–80, 2011.

[16] D. F. Gleich and C. Seshadhri. Vertex neighborhoods, low conductance cuts, and good seeds for local community methods. In *KDD'12*, pages 597–605, 2012.

[17] M. Gonen and Y. Shavitt. Approximating the number of network motifs. In *WAW'09*, pages 13–24, 2009.

[18] J. A. Grochow and M. Kellis. Network motif discovery using subgraph enumeration and symmetry-breaking. In *RECOMB'07*, pages 92–106, 2007.

[19] R. Gupta, T. Roughgarden, and C. Seshadhri. Decompositions of triangle-dense graphs. In *ITCS '14*, pages 471–482, 2014.

[20] M. Haghir Chehreghani. Effective co-betweenness centrality computation. In *WSDM'14*, pages 423–432, 2014.

[21] G. Karypis and V. Kumar. A fast and high quality multilevel scheme for partitioning irregular graphs. *SIAM J. Sci. Comput.*, 20(1):359–392, 1998.

[22] J. Kim, W.-S. Han, S. Lee, K. Park, and H. Yu. OPT: A new framework for overlapped and parallel triangulation in large-scale graphs. In *SIGMOD'14*, pages 637–648, 2014.

[23] K. Kutzkov and R. Pagh. On the streaming complexity of computing local clustering coefficients. In *WSDM'13*, pages 677–686, 2013.

[24] M. Latapy. Main-memory triangle computations for very large (sparse (power-law)) graphs. *Theor. Comput. Sci.*, 407(1-3):458–473, 2008.

[25] J. Liu, C. Wang, M. Danilevsky, and J. Han. Large-scale spectral clustering on graphs. In *IJCAI'13*, pages 1486–1492, 2013.

[26] M. Mathioudakis, F. Bonchi, C. Castillo, A. Gionis, and A. Ukkonen. Sparsification of influence networks. In *KDD'11*, pages 529–537, 2011.

[27] T. Milenkovic and N. Przulj. Uncovering biological network function via graphlet degree signatures. *Cancer Inform.*, 6:257–273, 2008.

[28] R. Milo and et al. Network motifs: simple building blocks of complex networks. *Science*, 298(5595):824–827, 2002.

[29] L. Orecchia and Z. A. Zhu. Flow-based algorithms for local graph clustering. In *SODA'14*, 2014.

[30] R. Pagh and F. Silvestri. The input/output complexity of triangle enumeration. In *PODS'14*, pages 224–233, 2014.

[31] T. Praneenararat, T. Takagi, and W. Iwasaki. Interactive, multiscale navigation of large and complicated biological networks. *Bioinformatics*, 27(8):1121–1127, 2011.

[32] V. Satuluri, S. Parthasarathy, and Y. Ruan. Local graph sparsification for scalable clustering. In *SIGMOD '11*, pages 721–732, 2011.

[33] S. E. Schaeffer. Survey: Graph clustering. *Comput. Sci. Rev.*, 1(1):27–64, 2007.

[34] H. Shiokawa, Y. Fujiwara, and M. Onizuka. Fast algorithm for modularity-based graph clustering. In *AAAI'13*, 2013.

[35] D. A. Spielman and N. Srivastava. Graph sparsification by effective resistances. In *STOC'08*, pages 563–568, 2008.

[36] D. A. Spielman and S.-H. Teng. A local clustering algorithm for massive graphs and its application to nearly linear time graph partitioning. *SIAM J. Comput.*, 42(1):1–26, 2013.

[37] C. Stark, B.-J. Breitkreutz, T. Reguly, L. Boucher, A. Breitkreutz, and M. Tyers. BioGRID: a general repository for interaction datasets. *Nucleic Acids Research*, 34:535–539, 2006.

[38] Y. Sun, J. Han, P. Zhao, Z. Yin, H. Cheng, and T. Wu. RankClus: Integrating clustering with ranking for heterogeneous information network analysis. In *EDBT '09*, pages 565–576, 2009.

[39] E. Tomita, A. Tanaka, and H. Takahashi. The worst-case time complexity for generating all maximal cliques and computational experiments. *Theor. Comput. Sci.*, 363(1):28–42, 2006.

[40] S. van Dongen. *Graph Clustering by Flow Simulation*. PhD thesis, University of Utrecht, 2000.

[41] S. Wernicke. Efficient detection of network motifs. *IEEE/ACM Trans. Comput. Biol. Bioinformatics*, 3(4):347–359, 2006.

Incomplete Multi-view Clustering via Subspace Learning

Qiyue Yin, Shu Wu, Liang Wang
Center for Research on Intelligent Perception and Computing (CRIPAC)
National Laboratory of Pattern Recognition (NLPR)
Institute of Automation, Chinese Academy of Sciences, Beijing 100190, China
{qyyin, shu.wu, wangliang}@nlpr.ia.ac.cn

ABSTRACT

Multi-view clustering, which explores complementary information between multiple distinct feature sets for better clustering, has a wide range of applications, e.g., knowledge management and information retrieval. Traditional multi-view clustering methods usually assume that all examples have complete feature sets. However, in real applications, it is often the case that some examples lose some feature sets, **which results in incomplete multi-view data** and notable performance degeneration. In this paper, a novel incomplete multi-view clustering method is therefore developed, which learns unified latent representations and projection matrices for the incomplete multi-view data. To approximate the high level scaled indicator matrix defined to represent class label matrix, the latent representations are expected to be non-negative and column orthogonal. Besides, since data are often with high dimensional and noisy features, the projection matrices are enforced to be sparse so as to select relevant features when learning the latent space. Furthermore, the inter-view and intra-view data structure is preserved to further enhance the clustering performance. To these ends, an objective is developed with efficient optimization strategy and convergence analysis. Extensive experiments demonstrate that our model performs better than the state-of-the-art multi-view clustering methods in various settings.

Categories and Subject Descriptors

H.3.3 [**Information Storage and Retrieval**]: Information Search and Retrieval—*Clustering*; I.5.3 [**Pattern Recognition**]: Clustering—*Algorithms*

Keywords

Multi-view clustering; Incomplete multi-view data; Feature selection; Subspace learning; Graph regularization

CIKM'15, October 19–23, 2015, Melbourne, Australia.

DOI: http://dx.doi.org/10.1145/2806416.2806526.

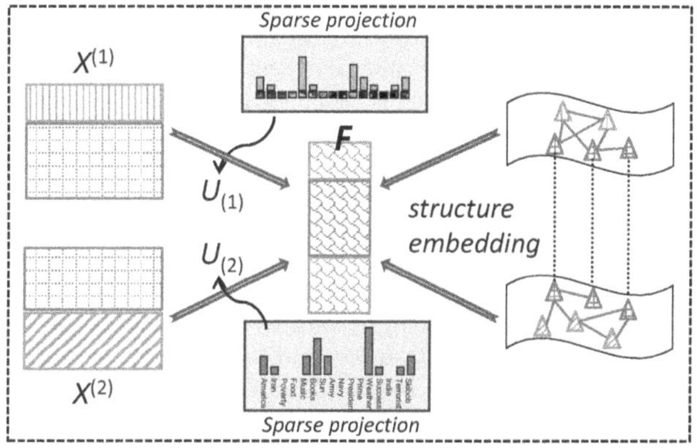

Figure 1: The overview of the proposed method. X_1 and X_2 are incomplete multi-view data with the red rectangular indicating examples with complete feature sets. We learn projection matrices $U_{(1)}$ and $U_{(2)}$ and the unified latent representations F (non-negative and column orthogonal) for multi-view data. Here we constrain the projection matrix to be sparse so as to select relevant features from the possibly high dimensional and noisy feature sets. Besides, the inter-view and intra-view data structure is preserved when learning the latent space. Finally, the clustering results are obtained by performing the k-means algorithm on F.

1. INTRODUCTION

Various kinds of real-world data appear in multiple modalities or come from multiple channels. For example, a web page can be described by both images and texts, and an image can be encoded by different visual features such as SIFT and GIST. We call such data multi-view data with each view representing a type of feature set. Usually, multiple views provide complementary information for the semantically same data, which leads to the development of multi-view learning. By exploiting the complementary characteristics between multi-view data, multi-view learning can obtain better performance of learning tasks than relying on just one single view [27]. Till now, multi-view learning has been widely studied in a variety of areas, such as knowledge management, data mining, multimedia and information retrieval [18, 27].

Multi-view clustering, as one of basic tasks of multi-view learning, provides a natural way to cluster multi-view datasets. Generally, the main challenge lies in the mining of the complementary information among multiple sources of information. Fortunately, a number of promising approaches have been proposed, which can be roughly classified into four categories [27, 31, 8]. Methods in the first category are subspace based ones [5, 15, 16, 29, 28], which learn a latent space so that different views are comparable in that space. On the other hand, some methods are co-training based algorithms [1, 14, 33], which obtain the clustering results in an iterative clustering manner. The third category is called late fusion [3, 10, 13], which combines the clustering results of different views by voting or other fusion strategies. The last category learns a unified similarity matrix among multi-view data [32, 19, 30], which serves as an affinity matrix for final clustering. For more details on multi-view clustering, please refer to Section 2.

It should be noted that previous multi-view clustering methods usually assume that all the examples have complete information of all views, i.e., each example in the database has complete feature sets. However, in real applications, it is often the case that some views suffer from missing information. For example, in image clustering based on visual and textual features, some images have only visual or textual information with only a part of the data sharing both feature sets. We call such dataset incomplete multi-view data. When traditional multi-view clustering methods confront the above scenarios, a naive approach may remove the data examples that are incomplete. However, this strategy is contradicting with our goal that groups all data examples into their corresponding clusters.

Recently, a few attempts have been made concentrating on multi-view clustering with incomplete views, which may be classified into two major categories. The first strategy preprocesses incomplete views by filling missing information. Piyush et al. [23] and Shao et al. [24] provided to complete the kernel matrices of the incomplete views and then used kernel-based clustering methods for final clustering. However, these two methods can only deal with the kernel-based multi-view clustering algorithms, which greatly limit their extension to more widely used subspace-based multi-view clustering methods. Recently, Li et al. [34] claimed that the methods in the first category are not a good choice for incomplete multi-view clustering and accordingly proposed a nonnegative matrix factorization based method (PVC), which proved to be effective for document clustering. But, there are also some limitations about the PVC method. Firstly, since data are now often with high dimensional and noisy features, it becomes urgent to select relevant and discriminative features when performing clustering. Secondly, PVC utilizes nonnegative matrix factorization to learn latent representations of data, which cannot well deal with data with negative feature representations.

In this paper, we propose a novel incomplete multi-view clustering method based on joint feature selection and subspace learning (as shown in Figure 1). Firstly, we utilize a regression-like objective to learn a subspace, in which data examples from different views can be compared irrespective of the heterogeneity between feature sets. To directly explore the complementary characteristics among different views, the latent representations of data examples with complete views are expected to be the same. Besides, since the features for different views may be high dimensional and even noisy, feature selection is performed to select relevant features for latent space learning. At last, a graph regularization is utilized to further explore the inter-view and intra-view relationship of the data examples. To these ends, we develop an objective to achieve all the above goals, and accordingly propose an alternating minimization algorithm to find an efficient solution. Extensive experiments demonstrate that our method outperforms the state-of-the-art multi-view clustering methods.

Main contributions: 1) We propose a novel incomplete multi-view clustering method, which incorporates feature selection, subspace learning and inter-view and intra-view similarity preserving into a unified objective. 2) We develop an iterative optimization algorithm to efficiently solve the proposed objective, and theoretical analysis is provided to guarantee its convergence. 3) We validate our proposed method with extensive experiments under two settings on four databases, achieving better performance than the state-of-the-art methods.

The rest of the paper is organized as follows. In Section 2, we briefly review multi-view clustering methods. Then our incomplete multi-view clustering algorithm is elaborated in Section 3. Section 4 shows experimental results and analysis. Finally, Section 5 concludes the paper.

2. RELATED WORK

Multi-view learning deals with data represented by multiple distinct feature sets and aims at boosting the learning performance [27]. Till now, plenty of methods have been developed with sound theories and multi-view learning has become a hot topic with widespread applicability [20, 26]. For example, the co-training method [2], one of the most famous multi-view learning frameworks, has been widely applied for webpage classification. When multi-view learning meets the unsupervised clustering task, multi-view clustering is accordingly developed to extend traditional single view clustering to the multi-view case.

Generally, multi-view clustering can be roughly classified into four categories. Algorithms in the first category find a unified low-dimensional space, in which the learned embedding of data can well explore the complementary information among different views [5, 15, 16, 29, 11]. These methods obtain final clustering results through a single view clustering method performed on the learned embedding. Kamalika et al. [5] obtained the low-dimensional subspace of multi-view data through the widely used canonical correlation analysis technique. Kumar et al. [15] proposed two objectives to regularize the Laplacian embeddings between different views to be similar and spectral analysis is employed for parameter learning. Liu et al. [16] developed a multi-view non-negative matrix factorization based method to gain a consensus embedding of the original data, which is further developed by He et al. [12] using various co-regularization forms. Recently, Wang et al. [29] proposed a regression-like objective, which conducts multi-view clustering and feature selection at the same time. Tang et al. [28] utilized unsupervised feature selection to cluster multi-view social media, and Qian and Zhai [22] also resorted to the above technique to obtain a low dimensional embedding of multi-view web news data.

Methods in the second category integrate multiple sources of information in the clustering process. Typical examples are the co-training and co-EM based multi-view clustering methods [1, 14, 33]. Kumar et al. [14] resorted to co-training, a popular semi-supervised tool, to develop the first co-training based multi-view clustering algorithm. Furthermore, Zhan et al. [33] proposed a more sophisticated multi-view clustering algorithm by combining LDA, k-means and the co-training framework. The third category is late fusion, which integrates the clustering results obtained from each view by voting or other fusion strategies [3, 10, 13]. Long et al. [17] proposed to learn the best clusters by fusing the clusters from each view through mapping functions. Greene et al. [10] utilized the matrix factorization based method to obtain optimal clusters. The last category aims to learn a unified similarity matrix among multi-view data, which serves as affinity matrix for final clustering [32, 19, 30, 4]. Muthukrishnan et al. [19] combined multiple similarity matrices by using a regularization framework to obtain a better similarity graph. Furthermore, Yin et al. [32] resorted to subspace clustering to obtain comparable similarity matrices through pairwise co-regularization.

The existing multi-view clustering methods mainly focus on the data with complete views, i.e., each data example has complete feature sets. However, in real applications, some data examples possibly lose some views. To handle this scenario, a few works have been developed [23, 24, 34]. Piyush et al. [23] proposed a spectral-based multi-view clustering method, which can deal with the scenario that at least one view is complete. They use the similarity matrix of the complete view to fill the kernel matrices of incomplete views through Laplacian regularization. Furthermore, Shao et al. [24] improved [23] by dealing with situations where no views are complete. They collectively fill all the kernel matrices by optimizing the alignment of shared data examples in the database. To sum up, both methods are based on the kernel matrices and can only adapt to kernel-based multi-view clustering. Recently, Li et al. [34] proved that the above methods are not a good choice for incomplete multi-view clustering and proposed a subspace based method using nonnegative matrix factorization (PVC). However, PVC has some limitations restricting its applications. Firstly, multi-view data are often high dimensional and noisy, and it may be necessary to select discriminative features when learning the latent subspace. Secondly, PVC utilizes nonnegative matrix factorization to learn latent representations of the data, which limits it applications to data with negative feature sets.

3. METHOD

3.1 Notations

For the sake of introducing our model, we discuss a dataset with two views and it is straight-forward to extend our model to the dataset with more views. Assume the two views of data are represented as $X^{(1)}$ and $X^{(2)}$ respectively. In the traditional multi-view clustering setting, a complete database $X = \{X^{(1)}, X^{(2)}\} = \{(X_i^{(1)}, X_i^{(2)}), i = 1, ..., N\}$ is given, where N is the number of data examples. However, in the incomplete view setting, we are given data $\hat{X} = \{\hat{X}^{(1,2)}, \hat{X}^{(1)}, \hat{X}^{(2)}\}$, where $\hat{X}^{(1,2)} = \{(X_i^{(1)}, X_i^{(2)}), i = 1, ..., c\}$, $\hat{X}^{(1)} = \{(X_i^{(1)}), i = c+1, ..., c+m\}$ and $\hat{X}^{(2)} = \{(X_i^{(2)}), i = c+m+1, ..., c+m+n\}$ represent data examples having complete views, only the first view and only the second view with the number of examples being c, m and n respectively. In total, we have $c+m+n$ examples in the database.

We denote $X_c^{(1)} \in R^{d_1 \times c}$ and $X_c^{(2)} \in R^{d_2 \times c}$ the examples having both views with d_1 and d_2 being the dimensionality of the two feature sets. Then $X_c^{(1)}$ and $\hat{X}^{(1)}$ consist of the examples in the first view, as denoted as $\bar{X}^{(1)} = [X_c^{(1)}, \hat{X}^{(1)}] \in R^{d_1 \times (c+m)}$. Similarly, we have the examples of the second view represented as $\bar{X}^{(2)} = [X_c^{(2)}, \hat{X}^{(2)}] \in R^{d_2 \times (c+n)}$. Our task is to group the incomplete multi-view data into their corresponding groups.

3.2 Formulation

Generally, multi-view data consist of heterogeneous feature sets representing the same object, and therefore they share the same class labels. We denote $Y = [Y_1, ..., Y_{c+m+n}]^T \in \{0,1\}^{(c+m+n)\times k}$ the class index of the incomplete multi-view database, where $Y_i \in \{0,1\}^{k\times 1}$ is the class indicator vector for the i-th example and k is the number of clusters. Then the scaled indicator matrix F is defined as $F = [F_1, ..., F_{c+m+n}]^T = Y(Y^TY)^{-1/2}$ [28] with the property $F^TF = I_k$, where I_k is an identity matrix with a size of k.

In our objective, we aim to find a F satisfying the above properties for multi-view clustering and the advantages are listed as follows. Firstly, F reflects the class indicator of the multi-view data, which is a higher level semantic representation of data. Even though data consist of multiple heterogeneous features, they should share the same semantic information. By introducing this semantic space, we construct a bridge for different heterogeneous feature sets. Furthermore, using such an indictor matrix, we can learn the projection matrix for each view and perform feature selection in a supervised manner, which will be described later.

To learn the indictor matrix, we learn a projection matrix for each view to project their original space to such a semantic space. The objective is then formulated as:

$$\begin{aligned} \min \; & ||[X_c^{(1)}, \hat{X}^{(1)}]^T U_{(1)} - [F^c; \hat{F}^{(1)}]||^2 + \beta \|U_{(1)}\|_{21} \\ & + ||[X_c^{(2)}, \hat{X}^{(2)}]^T U_{(2)} - [F^c; \hat{F}^{(2)}]||^2 + \beta \|U_{(2)}\|_{21} \\ s.t. \; & F^TF = I_k, F \geq 0 \end{aligned} \quad (1)$$

where $U_{(1)} \in R^{d_1\times k}$ and $U_{(2)} \in R^{d_2\times k}$ are projection matrices for the two views. $F^c \in R^{c\times k}$, $\hat{F}^{(1)} \in R^{m\times k}$ and $\hat{F}^{(2)} \in R^{n\times k}$ are the learned latent representations for data examples with complete views, only the first view and only the second view, respectively. It can be seen that we explore the relationship between the two views by enforcing the data examples with complete feature sets to have the same latent representation. $||U_{(1)}||_{21} = \sum_i ||U_{(1)}(i,:)||$, where $U_{(1)}(i,:)$ is the i-th row of $U_{(1)}$. The $\ell 21$-norms imposed on the projection matrices result in relevant features being selected for each view as always done by supervised feature selection [21]. β is a regularization parameter controlling the degree of the sparsity of projection matrices. When β is big, only a small subset of features will be selected, otherwise a large subset of features will be selected. $F = [F^c; \hat{F}^{(1)}; \hat{F}^{(2)}] \in R^{(c+m+n)\times k}$ is the learned latent representations for all the data examples, and $F^TF = I_k$ and $F \geq 0$ are used to constrain the latent representation to be consistent with the indicator matrix of the database.

In Equation 1, we project different feature sets into the same latent space and the relationship between different views is explored on such space in a direct manner. In the following part, we add extra regularization constraints on the projection matrices to further dig the relationship between data examples in each view and between the two views to model the structure of the multi-view data. More specifically, we hope to preserve the intra-view similarity and the inter-view similarity relationships in the dataset. Their details are listed as follows.

1) Intra-view similarity relationship: to preserve the local structure of data examples in each view, we constrain the neighborhood relationship between data points under each view also hold in the learned latent space. Generally, the neighborhood structure can be obtained by using a Gaussian based kernel matrix. we denote the matrices as $W^{(1)}$ and $W^{(2)}$ for the two views respectively and the entities in the matrix indicate the similarity between two data examples under a specific view. The detailed formulation is:

$$W_{ij}^{(t)} = \begin{cases} \exp(-z_{ij}^{(t)}/2\sigma^2), \bar{X}_i^{(t)} \in N_k(\bar{X}_j^{(t)}) \text{or} \bar{X}_j^{(t)} \in N_k(\bar{X}_i^{(t)}) \\ 0, \quad \text{otherwise} \end{cases} \tag{2}$$

where $z_{ij}^{(t)}$ is the Euclidean distance between data examples $X_i^{(t)}$ and $X_j^{(t)}$ and $N_k(X_i^{(t)})$ indicates the examples of k nearest neighbors of $X_i^{(t)}$.

2) Inter-view similarity relationship: although different views of data have different feature sets, they share the same semantics if they represent the same content or topic. To preserve such inter-view similarity when learning the projection matrices, we construct similarity matrices $W^{(12)}$ and $W^{(21)}$ for view 1 to view 2 and view 2 to view 1 respectively. Under the incomplete view setting $W^{(12)} = (W^{(21)})^T$ and they are defined as:

$$W_{ij}^{(12)} = \begin{cases} 1, \text{ if } \bar{X}_i^{(1)} \text{and } \bar{X}_j^{(2)} \text{have same semantics} \\ 0, \quad \text{otherwise} \end{cases} \tag{3}$$

Using the inter-view and intra-view similarities, we define the overall similarity matrix W as:

$$W = \begin{bmatrix} W^{(1)} & W^{(12)} \\ W^{(21)} & W^{(2)} \end{bmatrix} \tag{4}$$

Based on this similarity, we define the regularization on the projection matrices as :

$$\begin{aligned} \Omega(U_{(1)}, U_{(2)}) = & \sum_{ij} W_{ij}^{(1)} \|U_{(1)}^T \bar{X}_i^{(1)} - U_{(1)}^T \bar{X}_j^{(1)}\|^2 \\ & + \sum_{ij} W_{ij}^{(2)} \|U_{(2)}^T \bar{X}_i^{(2)} - U_{(2)}^T \bar{X}_j^{(2)}\|^2 \\ & + \sum_{ij} W_{ij}^{(12)} \|U_{(1)}^T \bar{X}_i^{(1)} - U_{(2)}^T \bar{X}_j^{(2)}\|^2 \\ & + \sum_{ij} W_{ij}^{(21)} \|U_{(2)}^T \bar{X}_i^{(2)} - U_{(1)}^T \bar{X}_j^{(1)}\|^2 \end{aligned} \tag{5}$$

and it is further rewritten as:

$$\Omega(U_{(1)}, U_{(2)}) = \sum_{s=1}^{2} \sum_{t=1}^{2} Tr(U_{(s)}^T \bar{X}^{(s)} L_{st} (\bar{X}^{(t)})^T U_{(t)}) \tag{6}$$

where $L = D - W$ is the Laplacian matrix and D is a diagonal matrix with its i-th diagonal element defined as the sum of the i-th row of W. Tr is the trace of a matrx.

Adding this regularization constraint to Equation 1, we obtain the final objective as:

$$\begin{aligned} \min_{U,F} & \|[X_c^{(1)}, \hat{X}^{(1)}]^T U_{(1)} - [F^c; \hat{F}^{(1)}]\|^2 + \beta \|U_{(1)}\|_{21} \\ & + \|[X_c^{(2)}, \hat{X}^{(2)}]^T U_{(2)} - [F^c; \hat{F}^{(2)}]\|^2 + \beta \|U_{(2)}\|_{21} \\ & + \gamma \sum_{s=1}^{2} \sum_{t=1}^{2} Tr(U_{(s)}^T \bar{X}^{(s)} L_{st} (\bar{X}^{(t)})^T U_{(t)}) \\ s.t. \quad & F^T F = I_k, \ F \geq 0 \end{aligned} \tag{7}$$

In our objective, we have three terms: using the projection matrix to project each incomplete view to the latent space defined by F; feature selection for each view using the $\ell 21$-norm based constraint and the inter-view and intra-view similarity preserving term defined by the Laplacian matrix. Besides, the constraints imposed on F guarantee that each example only belongs to one group.

3.3 Optimization

In this section, we propose to optimize the objective as described in Equation 7. Since the variables, such as the projection matrix and the latent representation, are coupled together, it may be difficult to optimize them at the same time. Hence, we propose to alternatively optimize the variables to obtain a local solution.

1) Optimize F with fixed U: the constraints on F in Equation 7 make the optimization not an easy problem, especially different views only have part of all the latent representations, i.e., $[F^c; \hat{F}^{(1)}]$ and $[F^c; \hat{F}^{(2)}]$ are only part of F. To handle this, we optimize F^c, $\hat{F}^{(1)}$ and $\hat{F}^{(2)}$ separately and relax the constraints to the following form:

$$(F^c)^T F^c = I_k, F \geq 0 \tag{8}$$

Even though the orthogonal constraint on F^c may not be rigorous when data examples with complete feature sets do not have all kinds of class labels. We ignore this slight influence. In turn, it makes our optimization very compact. As for $\hat{F}^{(k)}, (k = 1, 2)$, since examples in the same view share the same projection matrix and these examples follow the same data distribution, $\hat{F}^{(k)}$ will have similar characteristic with F^c. In summary, the relaxed constraints will have almost the same effect with that of the original ones and can make the optimization more succinct.

We denote the objective in Equation 7 as O. Then minimizing O over F^c, $\hat{F}^{(1)}$ and $\hat{F}^{(2)}$ are simplified as:

$$\begin{aligned} \min_{F^c} & \|(X_c^{(1)})^T U_{(1)} - F^c\|^2 + \|(X_c^{(2)})^T U_{(2)} - F^c\|^2 \\ s.t. \quad & (F^c)^T F^c = I_k, F^c \geq 0 \end{aligned} \tag{9}$$

$$\begin{aligned} & \min_{\hat{F}^{(1)} \geq 0} \|(\hat{X}^{(1)})^T U_{(1)} - \hat{F}^{(1)}\|^2 \\ & \min_{\hat{F}^{(2)} \geq 0} \|(\hat{X}^{(2)})^T U_{(2)} - \hat{F}^{(2)}\|^2 \end{aligned} \tag{10}$$

To optimize F^c, we bring in Lagrangian function as:

$$\begin{aligned} L(F^c) = & Tr(\Gamma((F^c)^T F^c - I_k)) \\ & - Tr(\Lambda F^c) + \sum_{i=1,2} Tr(-2A_i^T F^c + (F^c)^T F) \end{aligned} \tag{11}$$

where Γ and Λ are Lagrangian multipliers of the above function and $A_i = (X_c^{(i)})^T U_{(i)}$. Applying KKT condition, i.e., $\Lambda(s,t) F^c(s,t) = 0$, we obtain:

$$\left(\sum_{i=1,2} (-A_i + F^c) + F^c \Gamma\right)(s,t) \, F^c(s,t) = 0 \tag{12}$$

and we can obtain the following updating rule for F^c:

$$F^c(s,t) = F^c(s,t) \sqrt{\frac{(\sum_{i=1,2} A_i^+ + F^c \Gamma^-)(s,t)}{(\sum_{i=1,2} (A_i^- + F^c) + F^c \Gamma^+)(s,t)}} \tag{13}$$

where for a matrix C, $C^+(s,t) = (|C(s,t)| + C(s,t))/2$, $C^-(s,t) = (|C(s,t)| - C(s,t))/2$ and $C = C^+ - C^-$. As for Γ, its diagonal elements are obtained by summing s: $\Gamma(s,s) = \sum_{i=1,2}((F^c)^T A_i - I_k)(s,s)$. And the off-diagonal elements of Γ are approximated by ignoring the non-negative values of F^c: $\Gamma(s,t) = \sum_{i=1,2}((F^c)^T A_i - I_k)(s,t)$. In summary, Γ is calculated by $\Gamma = \sum_{i=1,2}((F^c)^T A_i - I_k)$.

To optimize $\hat{F}^{(1)}$ and $\hat{F}^{(2)}$, we directly obtain their gradients and the updating rule is:

$$\hat{F}^{(i)} = \max((X_c^{(i)})^T U_{(i)}, 0), \quad i = 1,2 \tag{14}$$

2) Optimize U with fixed F: Minimizing the objective O in Equation 7 with respect to $U_{(1)}$ and $U_{(2)}$ are rewritten as:

$$\begin{aligned}\min_{U_{(s)}} \sum_{s=1,2} ||(\bar{X}^{(s)})^T U_{(s)} - \bar{F}^{(s)}||^2 + \beta \sum_{s=1,2} ||U_{(s)}||_{21} \\ +\gamma \sum_{s=1}^{2} \sum_{t=1}^{2} Tr(U_{(s)}^T \bar{X}^{(s)} L_{st} (\bar{X}^{(t)})^T U_{(t)})\end{aligned} \tag{15}$$

where $\bar{X}^{(s)}, (s = 1,2)$ and $\bar{F}^{(s)}, (s = 1,2)$ are the feature matrix and the latent representation for one view as described before. They consist of the data examples with both feature sets and only with the s-th feature set.

Differentiating the objective function in Equation 15 with respect to $U_{(s)}$ and setting it to zero, we have the following equation:

$$\begin{aligned}&\bar{X}^{(s)}((\bar{X}^{(s)})^T U_{(s)} - \bar{F}^{(s)}) + \beta D_{(s)} U_{(s)} \\ &+\gamma \bar{X}^{(s)} L_{ss} (\bar{X}^{(s)})^T U_{(s)} + \gamma \sum_{t \neq s} \bar{X}^{(s)} L_{st} (\bar{X}^{(t)})^T U_{(t)} = 0\end{aligned} \tag{16}$$

where $D_{(s)}$ is a diagonal matrix with its i-th diagonal element calculated as $D_{(s)}(i,i) = 1/(2||U_{(s)}(i,:)||)$, and $U_{(s)}(i,:)$ is the i-th row of $U_{(s)}$. Practically, $D_{(s)}(i,i)$ is calculated by[1]:

$$D_{(s)}(i,i) = \frac{1}{2\sqrt{||U_{(s)}(i,:)||^2 + \varepsilon}} \tag{17}$$

where ε is a smoothing term, which is usually set to be a small positive value.

Then Equation 16 is further written as:

$$\begin{aligned}&(\bar{X}^{(s)}(\bar{X}^{(s)})^T + \beta D_{(s)} + \gamma \bar{X}^{(s)} L_{ss} (\bar{X}^{(s)})^T) U_{(s)} \\ &= \bar{X}^{(s)} \bar{F}^{(s)} - \gamma \sum_{t \neq s} \bar{X}^{(s)} L_{st} (\bar{X}^{(t)})^T U_{(t)}\end{aligned} \tag{18}$$

The objective can be optimized using the following equation:

$$\begin{aligned}U_{(s)} = &(\bar{X}^{(s)}(\bar{X}^{(s)})^T + \beta D_{(s)} + \gamma \bar{X}^{(s)} L_{ss} (\bar{X}^{(s)})^T)^{-1} \\ &(\bar{X}^{(s)} \bar{F}^{(s)} - \gamma \sum_{t \neq s} \bar{X}^{(s)} L_{st} (\bar{X}^{(t)})^T U_{(t)})\end{aligned} \tag{19}$$

Algorithm 1 gives the overall optimization for equation 7. In Step 3, we calculate the latent representation for the incomplete multi-view dataset. In Steps 4 and 5, we optimize the projection matrices $U_{(s)}, (s = 1,2)$. Finally Steps 3, 4 and 5 are repeated until convergence. Based on the latent representation, the final clustering results can be obtained by using regular clustering algorithms, e.g., k-means. The overall clustering algorithm is summarized in Algorithm 2.

[1] $||U_{(s)}(i,:)||$ can be zero, which cannot guarantee the convergence of the algorithm. Similar to [9], we add a smoothing term as in Equation 17.

Algorithm 1 Solving Equation 7 to obtain the latent representation of the incomplete multi-view dataset

Input:
Incomplete multi-view dataset $\{\bar{X}^{(1)}, \bar{X}^{(2)}\}$, parameter β and γ, the number of classes.

1: $t = 1$. Initialize $U_{(s)}, (s = 1,2)$ and F randomly;
2: **while** not converge **do**
3: Calculate F^c, $\hat{F}^{(1)}$ and $\hat{F}^{(2)}$ using Equation 13 and 14 respectively;
4: Solve $D_{(s)}, (s = 1,2)$ using Equation 17;
5: Calculate $U_{(s)}, (s = 1,2)$ using Equation 19 respectively;
6: **end while**

Output:
The latent representation for the incomplete multi-view dataset $F = [F^c; \hat{F}^{(1)}; \hat{F}^{(2)}]$.

Algorithm 2 Clustering procedure for the incomplete multi-view dataset

Input:
Incomplete multi-view dataset $\{\bar{X}^{(1)}, \bar{X}^{(2)}\}$, parameter β and γ, the number of classes.

1: Obtain the latent representation F of all the data by using Algorithm 1.
2: Perform k-means clustering on F to obtain the clustering results.

Output:
Groups of the incomplete multi-view dataset

3.4 Convergence and complexity analysis

In this section, we prove that Algorithm 1 converges to a local minima.

Theorem 1. *The proposed iterative optimization strategy in Algorithm 1 will monotonically decrease the objective function in Equation 7 in each iteration until convergence.*

a) In Step 3 of Algorithm 1, we will resort to auxiliary function approach [7] to validate that the updating rule for F^c will monotonically decrease the objective value. As for the updating rule for $\hat{F}^{(1)}$ and $\hat{F}^{(2)}$, it is easy to verify that their objectives are convex and their optimization methods can decrease the objective function monotonically.

Let

$$\begin{aligned}H(F^c) = Tr(&\sum_{i=1,2}(-2A_i^T F^c + (F^c)^T F^c) \\ &+\Gamma((F^c)^T F^c - I_k))\end{aligned} \tag{20}$$

and it is further rewritten as:

$$\begin{aligned}H(F^c) = &Tr(\sum_{i=1,2}(2(A_i^-)^T F^c + (F^c)^T F^c) + \Gamma^+ (F^c)^T F^c \\ &-Tr(\sum_{i=1,2}(2(A_i^+)^T F^c + \Gamma^- (F^c)^T F^c)\end{aligned} \tag{21}$$

Then the following function

$$\begin{aligned}&h(F^c, \tilde{F}^c) = \\ &\sum_{i,s,t}(A_i^-(s,t)\frac{F^c(s,t)^2 + \tilde{F}^c(s,t)^2}{\tilde{F}^c(s,t)} + \frac{\tilde{F}^c(s,t) F^c(s,t)^2}{\tilde{F}^c(s,t)}) \\ &-\sum_{st}(\sum_i 2A_i(s,t))\tilde{F}^c(s,t)(1 + \log\frac{F^c(s,t)}{\tilde{F}^c(s,t)}) \\ &+\sum_{st}\frac{(\tilde{F}^c\Gamma^+)(s,t) F^c(s,t)^2}{\tilde{F}^c(s,t)} \\ &+\sum_{ist}\Gamma^-(s,t)\tilde{F}^c(i,s)\tilde{F}^c(i,t)(1 + \log\frac{F^c(i,s) F^c(i,t)}{\tilde{F}^c(i,s)\tilde{F}^c(i,t)})\end{aligned} \tag{22}$$

ia an auxiliary function of $H(F^c)$. Besides, it is easy to verify that the Hessian matrix of $h(F^c, \tilde{F}^c)$ is a positive definite matrix, thus, $h(F^c, \tilde{F}^c)$ is convex and its global minimum is obtained as in Equation 13.

Through the definition of the auxiliary function and the above derivation, we can obtain the following inequality:

$$H(F_0^c) = h(F_0^c, F_0^c) \geq h(F_0^c, F_1^c) \geq H(F_1^c)... \quad (23)$$

Thus, the updating rule for F^c will monotonically decrease the objective value.

b) In Step 5 of Algorithm 1, we will prove that the updating rule in Equation 19 for $U_{(s)}, (s = 1, 2)$ will decrease the objective monotonically.

Taking $U_{(1)}$ as an example, we can derive that:

$$U_{(1)}^{t+1} = \min_{U_{(1)}} ||(\bar{X}^{(1)})^T U_{(1)} - \bar{F}^{(1)}||^2 + \beta tr(U_{(1)}^T D_{(1)}^{t+1} U_{(1)}) + \gamma \sum_{s=1}^{2} Tr(U_{(1)}^T \bar{X}^{(1)} L_{1s} (\bar{X}^{(s)})^T U_{(s)}) \quad (24)$$

and Equation 19 is the analytic solution of the above function. Then we have:

$$L_{t+1} + \beta tr((U_{(1)}^T)^{t+1} D_{(1)}^{t+1} U_{(1)}^{t+1}) \leq L_t + \beta tr((U_{(1)}^T)^t D_{(1)}^{t+1} U_{(1)}^t) \quad (25)$$

where

$$\begin{aligned} L_{t+1} = & |(\bar{X}^{(1)})^T U_{(1)}^{t+1} - \bar{F}^{(1)}||^2 \\ & + \gamma Tr((U_{(1)}^T)^{t+1} \bar{X}^{(1)} L_{11} (\bar{X}^{(1)})^T U_{(1)}^{t+1}) \\ & + \gamma Tr((U_{(1)}^T)^{t+1} \bar{X}^{(1)} L_{12} (\bar{X}^{(2)})^T U_{(2)}^t) \end{aligned} \quad (26)$$

Substituting $D_{(1)}^{t+1}$ into the above inequality, we have:

$$\begin{aligned} & L_{t+1} + \sum_i \sum_j \frac{U_{(1)}^{t+1}(i,j) U_{(1)}^{t+1}(i,j)}{2||U_{(1)}^t(i,:)||} \\ & \leq L_t + \sum_i \sum_j \frac{U_{(1)}^t(i,j) U_{(1)}^t(i,j)}{2||U_{(1)}^t(i,:)||} \end{aligned} \quad (27)$$

Here we introduce a function $f(x) = x - x^2/(2a)$, which satisfies $\{\forall x \in R, f(x) \leq f(a) | a > 0\}$. Then we make x and a be $||U_{(1)}^{t+1}(i,:)||$ and $||U_{(1)}^t(i,:)||$ respectively, we have the following inequality:

$$\begin{aligned} & ||U_{(1)}^{t+1}(i,:)|| - \sum_j \frac{U_{(1)}^{t+1}(i,j) U_{(1)}^{t+1}(i,j)}{2||U_{(1)}^t(i,:)||} \\ & \leq \sum_j ||U_{(1)}^t(i,:)|| - \frac{U_{(1)}^t(i,j) U_{(1)}^t(i,j)}{2||U_{(1)}^t(i,:)||} \end{aligned} \quad (28)$$

Add both sides of the above inequality to Equation 27, we obtain the following inequality:

$$L_{t+1} + \beta ||U_{(1)}^{t+1}||_{21} \leq L_t + \beta ||U_{(1)}^t||_{21} \quad (29)$$

Thus the updating rule for U will decrease the objective function monotonically.

Combining the above derivation, we prove that Algorithm 1 converges to a local minimum.

Complexity analysis: We briefly discuss the computational complexity of our algorithm. As for the optimization of F, the main computation lies in the updating for F^c as in Equation 13, which mainly consists of some matrix multiplication operations. When optimizing U, we need to compute the overall multi-view similarity matrix, whose complexity is about $O(d_m N_m^2)$, where $d_m N_m^2$ being the product of the dimensionality and the square of the number of examples for the m-th view is the largest one among all views. However, it is a constant matrix and can be computed before the optimization of the variables. Besides, we need to use Equation 19 to calculate U, which solves an inverse problem. Instead, we can update the projection matrices by solving a linear system for $O(\hat{d}^2)(\hat{d} = \max(d_1, d_2))$.

4. EXPERIMENTS

4.1 Datasets

We report experiments on four widely used multi-view datasets and their descriptions are summarized in Table 1.

Dataset	# size	# view	# cluster	# feature size
USPS	2,000	2	10	76+216
Cora	2,708	2	7	2,708+1,433
BBC	2,012	2	5	822+840
WebKB	1,051	2	2	1,840+3,000

Table 1: Information of the multi-view datasets. # feature size means the dimensionality of the two feature sets of the database.

UCI Handwritten Digit Dataset[2] It consists of feature sets of handwritten numerals (0-9) extracted from Dutch utility maps. The database has 2,000 examples even-distributed in ten categories and is represented in terms of six visual features. Being same in [15], we use the 76 Fourier coefficients of the character shapes and the 216 profile correlations as two views.

Cora Dataset[3] It contains 2,708 scientific publications divided into 7 classes (Neural_Networks, Rule_Learning, Reinforcement_Learning, Probabilistic_Methods, Theory, Genetic_Algorithms, Case_Based). Two heterogeneous feature sets, i.e., citations and content are utilized here for experiments, where the content feature is represented by 0/1-valued word vector indicating the absence/presence of the corresponding word from the 1,433 words constructed dictionary.

BBC Dataset[4] It is a synthetic multi-view text database, which is constructed using single view BBC and BBCSport corpora. In total, it consists of 2,012 data examples categorized into 5 classes. The two views used here are the segments representations of the same document with the dimensions being 6,838 and 6,790 respectively. We use principal component analysis (PCA) to preprocess the data and the dimension is selected based on the eigenvalues of the covariance matrix obtained from the data.

WebKB Datasets[5] It is a webpage dataset from the computer science departments of four universities. The dataset consists of two categories, i.e., course and non-course with two heterogeneous feature sets, namely the textual content of the webpage and the link representation. Here the link representation is the anchortext on links in the other webpages linking to the current webpage.

4.2 Settings

To simulate the incomplete multi-view datasets, we randomly select part of examples to have only one single feature

[2]http://archive.ics.uci.edu/ml/datasets/Multiple+Features
[3]http://lig-membres.imag.fr/grimal/data.html
[4]http://mlg.ucd.ie/datasets/segment.html
[5]http://vikas.sindhwani.org/manifoldregularization.html

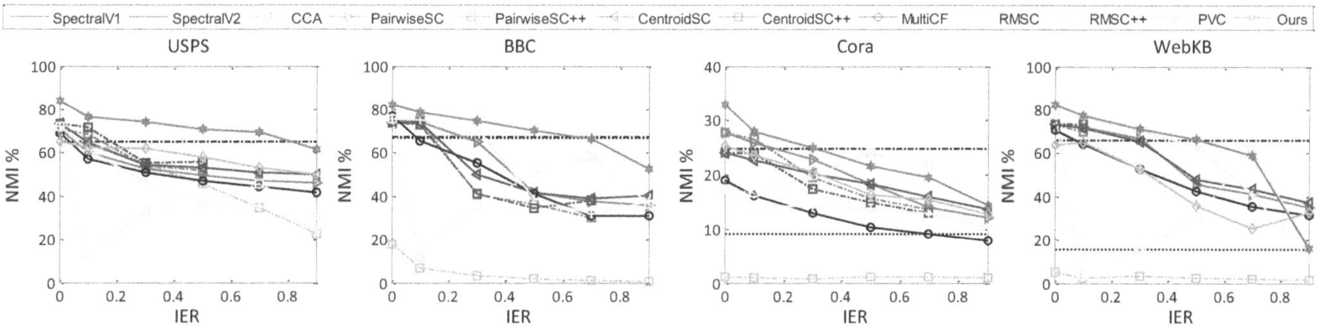

Figure 2: The NMI results on the four databases when both views suffer from the loss of examples. IER (incomplete example ratio) is the ratio of examples with only one feature set.

set. Similar to [34], two different settings are considered and listed as follows.

As described in Section 3, we denote m and n the numbers of examples appearing only in the first view and only in the second view respectively.

1) the first setting: $m > 0, n > 0$, namely both views do not contain all the examples in the database.

2) the second setting: either $m = 0$ or $n = 0$, namely at least one view is complete.

For the above two settings, we randomly select 10% to 90% of the total examples, with 20% as interval, to have only one feature set. And this process is repeated 10 times with the average to be reported. Besides, as for the first setting, we evenly distribute the number of examples for the two views for simplicity.

4.3 Compared methods

We compare our algorithm with several representative multi-view clustering methods, which consist of three subspace learning based methods and three kernel matrix based methods and their modifications.

SingleV1, SingleV2: We run spectral clustering [25] on the two views under the condition that all views have complete data examples.

CCA: We use canonical correlation analysis to obtain the latent representation of multi-view data and then apply k-means on the obtained representation.

PairwiseSC, CentroidSC: The multi-view spectral clustering methods based on two regularization frameworks developed by Kumar et al. [15].

MultiCF: Wang et al. [29] proposed a structure sparsity based unsupervised feature selection method for the task of multi-view clustering.

RMSC: Xia et al. [30] developed a multi-view spectral clustering method, which is based on low rank and sparse decomposition of the transition matrix.

PVC: Li et al. [34] proposed probably the only incomplete multi-view clustering method without filling the missing information.

PairwiseSC++, CentroidSC++, RMSC++: For the kernel based multi-view clustering algorithms, Piyush et al. [23] proposed to fill the kernel matrix of the view with incomplete examples using the kernel matrix of the view with complete examples. So in our second setting that one view is complete, we can use this method to fill the incomplete kernel matrix. Then the modified PairwiseSC, CentroidSC and RMSC methods may obtain better clustering results. Moreover, Shao et al. [24] proposed to fill the kernel matrices even there are no views with complete examples. Then in our first setting, we may promote PairwiseSC, CentroidSC and RMSC methods using this method. We denote the PairwiseSC, CentroidSC and RMSC methods with the preprocessing of the kernel matrix under the two settings as PairwiseSC++, CentroidSC++, RMSC++ respectively.

For the compared methods that are not designed for incomplete multi-view clustering, i.e., CCA, PairwiseSC, CentroidSC, MultiCF and RMSC, we just use zeros to replace incomplete feature sets. This may be a little arbitrary, but we find possibly no methods can well fill various types of features at the same time, e.g., visual features and textual features. Besides, it may be fair enough since our method do not preprocess the data at all. For PairwiseSC, CentroidSC, RMSC and PVC methods, we use the codes the authors have released to achieve their best performance and the method CCA is achieved using the LSCCA package[6]. As for MultiCF, we implement the method and follow the authors' suggestions to achieve the clustering results. For our method, we use KNN based Gaussian kernel to construct the intra-view similarity matrix and the number of the KNN neighbors and the width parameter for Gaussian kernel are empirically selected as ten percent of the total examples of the database and one respectively in all the experiments. As for the trade off parameters β and γ, they are empirically selected to achieve the best clustering results. We will test their effects in the parameter study part. Since k-means is used in all the experiments, it is run 20 times with random initialization and the mean value is reported.

Finally, by following [34], the normalized mutual information (NMI), as one of the most famous clustering evaluation measures, is utilized. Users can refer to [6] for more details on its definition.

4.4 Experimental results

4.4.1 *Experimental results under the first setting*

Figure 2 shows the clustering results of all the methods under the first setting, i.e., both views suffer from information loss. *IER* (incomplete example ratio) indicates the percentage of examples having only one feature set. Besides, the results of all methods with *IER* being zero are also reported as the upper bound of each method. Overall, it can be seen that our method performs better than all the com-

[6]http://www.public.asu.edu/jye02/Software/CCA/ index.html

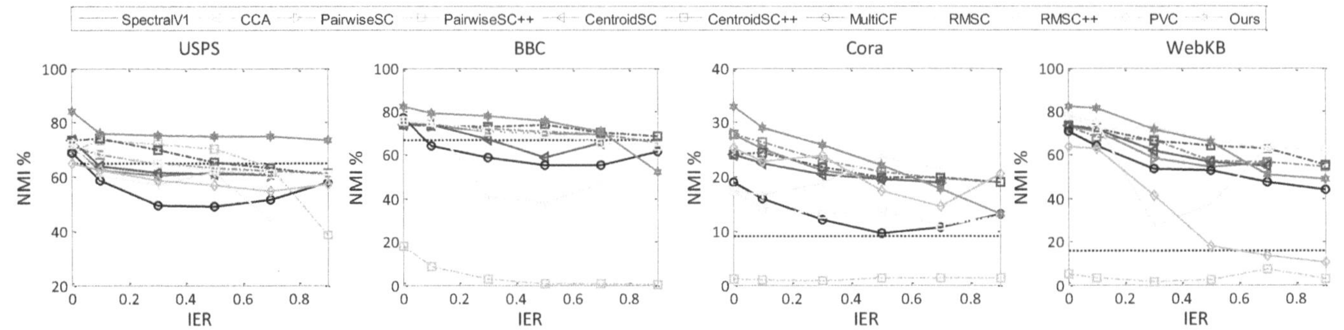

Figure 3: The NMI results on the four databases when the first view suffer from the loss of examples. IER (incomplete example ratio) is the ratio of examples with only one feature set.

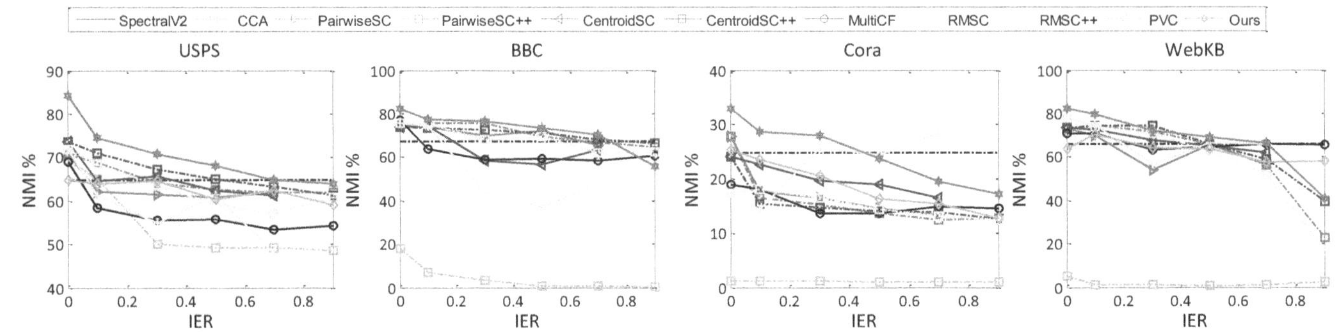

Figure 4: The NMI results on the four databases when the second view suffer from the loss of examples. IER (incomplete example ratio) is the ratio of examples with only one feature set.

peting methods under different incomplete example ratios on the four databases.

Compared with the results of SingleV1 and SingleV2 methods, our method performs better even with up to 50% of examples only appearing in one feature set on the USPS, Cora and WebKB datasets. This is an inspiring result, which indicates that our method can well explore the multi-view complementary information even in relatively large incomplete example ratios.

As for PairwiseSC, CentroidSC and RMSC, we utilize the method proposed in [24] to fill the kernel matrices of the incomplete views and accordingly PairwiseSC++, CentroidSC++, RMSC++ are developed. From Figure 2, they perform better in some databases and the performance gain seems not very considerable especially when *IER* being large. In summary, our method performs better although these kernel based multi-view clustering methods preprocess to fill the lost information.

As for PVC, it uses non-negative matrix factorization to find a unified low dimensional space and constrains the examples with complete views sharing the same representations to deal with the incomplete multi-view data. Compared with it, we also apply feature selection to select relevant features when learning the low dimensional subspace, which works confronting the high dimensional and noisy features. Besides, the multi-view data structure is also explored in the proposed method. Thus our method performs better than PVC.

One of the major differences between our method and the MultiCF method under complete views is the constraint imposed on the learned latent representation. We add the non-negative constraint, which is more reasonable to approach the normalized indictor matrix and this may be the reason that our method performs better when the incomplete example ratio is zero. Since MultiCF is not designed for incomplete multi-view data, our method also outperforms it when *IER* is greater than zero.

4.4.2 Experimental results under the second setting

Figures 3 and 4 display the clustering performance under the second setting with the first and second view suffering from incomplete examples respectively. It should be noted that we apply the method in [23] to fill the kernel matrix of the incomplete view using that of the complete view for PairwiseSC, CentroidSC and RMSC to obtain the PairwiseSC++, CentroidSC++, RMSC++ methods.

It can be seen that similar results are obtained as in Figure 2 except that all the methods obtain relatively better performance compared with that in the first setting under the same incomplete example ratio. This may be because there exists one complete view to aid the multi-view clustering and it may be more useful compared with the scenario of no complete views. Overall, our method still obtains the best clustering performance almost on all the datasets under this setting.

4.5 Parameter study

In our proposed model as in Equation 7, there are two parameters β and γ balancing the effect of feature projection term, $\ell21$-norm based feature selection term and graph regularization based structure preserving term. In this section, we investigate how the performance varies with the changes of the above two parameters. Due to space limitation, we conduct experiments on the four databases under the first setting and the incomplete example ratios are selected as 0 and 0.3 respectively. It should be noted that similar results can be obtained under the second setting. The results are shown in Figure 5.

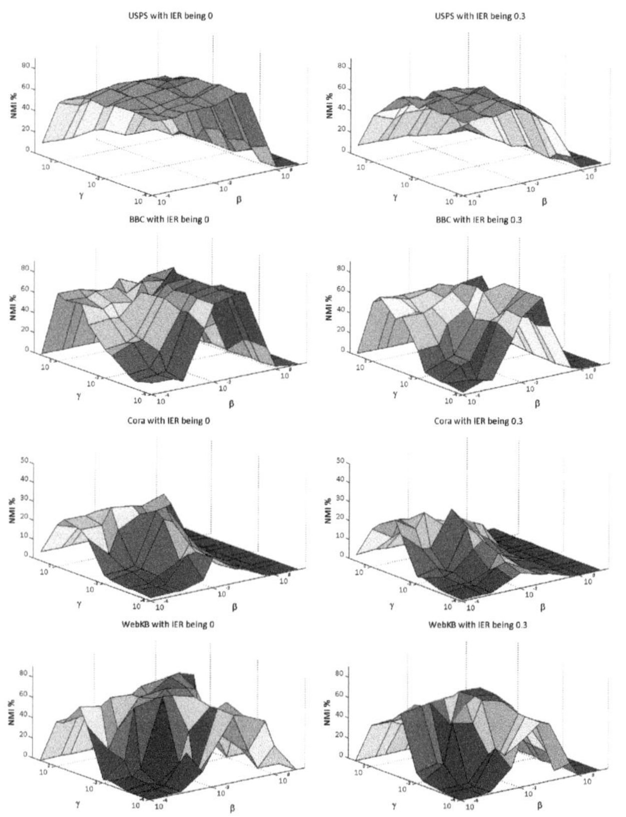

Figure 5: The NMI results on the four databases under the first setting with the incomplete example ratio being 0 and 0.3 respectively.

β controls the sparsity of the projection matrices. When it is small, the constraint will lose the effect of feature selection. In the case when β is too big, the sparse characteristic will lead to the loss of useful features and harm the learned latent representations. γ is the weight for the graph regularization term, which keeps the inter-view and intra-view data structure of the original spaces in the learned space. When it is too big, it may rely on too much of the neighborhood relationship obtained using the similarity metric and this may harm the intrinsical data structure because of the possible inaccuracy of the calculated similarity matrix. In summary, β and γ should be carefully selected and [0.001,0.01] is an optimal interval when the multi-view data is normalized.

4.6 Convergence study

As discussed in Section 3.4, the optimization strategy converges to a local minima. In this section, we give the convergence and the corresponding NMI curves with the varying updating iterations. Due to space limitation, we only give the results under the first setting with incomplete example ratio being 30% and similar results can be achieved under the second setting. From Figure 6, it can be seen that the objective function converges fast, and the clustering performance needs about 100 iterations to reach the best results. This may because the initial values of the variables in Algorithm 1 are randomly set. In the future, we may consider a nice initialization method to reduce the number of iterations.

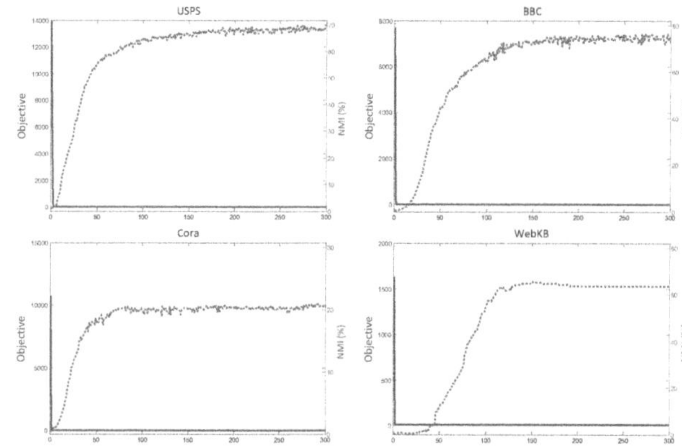

Figure 6: Convergence and the corresponding NMI curves for the four databases under the first setting with incomplete example ratio being 0.3.

5. CONCLUSION AND FUTURE WORK

In this paper, we have proposed a novel incomplete multi-view clustering algorithm to cluster incomplete multi-view data. In our model, we learn a latent representation of the data examples, which serves as an approximation of the normalized indictor matrix. Besides, the complementary information between different views is explored by enforcing examples with complete views sharing the same representations. Through the $\ell 21$-norm based constraint, relevant features are selected for the projection to the latent space. Furthermore, we add a graph regularization term to preserve the inter-view and intra-view data structure, which further promotes the clustering performance. Extensive experiments have validated the effectiveness of the proposed method compared with the state-of-the-art methods. Since it is practical to obtain partial label or must-link and cannot-link information between data examples, we may consider adding such information to promote clustering in the future.

Acknowledgments

This work is jointly supported by National Basic Research Program of China (2012CB316300), and National Natural Science Foundation of China (61175003, 61420106015, U1435221, 61403390).

6. REFERENCES

[1] S. Bickel and T. Scheffer. Multi-view clustering. *International Conference on Data Mining*, 4:19–26, 2004.

[2] A. Blum and T. Mitchell. Combining labeled and unlabeled data with co-training. *Annual Conference on Computational Learning Theory*, pages 92–100, 1998.

[3] E. Bruno and S. Marchand-Maillet. Multiview clustering: a late fusion approach using latent models. *ACM SIGIR Conference on Research and*

Development in Information Retrieval, pages 736–737, 2009.

[4] X. Cao, C. Zhang, H. Fu, S. Liu, and H. Zhang. Diversity-induced multi-view subspace clustering. *IEEE Conference on Computer Vision and Pattern Recognition*, 2015.

[5] K. Chaudhuri, S. M. Kakade, K. Livescu, and K. Sridharan. Multi-view clustering via canonical correlation analysis. *International Conference on Machine Learning*, pages 129–136, 2009.

[6] W.-Y. Chen, Y. Song, H. Bai, C.-J. Lin, and E. Y. Chang. Parallel spectral clustering in distributed systems. *IEEE Transactions on Pattern Analysis and Machine Intelligence*, 33(3):568–586, 2011.

[7] C. Ding, T. Li, and M. I. Jordan. Convex and semi-nonnegative matrix factorizations. *IEEE Transactions on Pattern Analysis and Machine Intelligence*, 32(1):45–55, 2010.

[8] X. Dong, P. Frossard, P. Vandergheynst, and N. Nefedov. Clustering on multi-layer graphs via subspace analysis on grassmann manifolds. *IEEE Transactions on Signal Processing*, 62(4):905–918, 2014.

[9] I. F. Gorodnitsky and B. D. Rao. Sparse signal reconstruction from limited data using focuss: a re-weighted minimum norm algorithm. *IEEE Transactions on Signal Processing*, 45(3):600–616, 1997.

[10] D. Greene and P. Cunningham. A matrix factorization approach for integrating multiple data views. *Machine Learning and Knowledge Discovery in Databases*, pages 423–438, 2009.

[11] Y. Guo. Convex subspace representation learning from multi-view data. *AAAI Conference on Artificial Intelligence*, 1:2, 2013.

[12] X. He, M.-Y. Kan, P. Xie, and X. Chen. Comment-based multi-view clustering of web 2.0 items. *International Conference on World Wide Web*, pages 771–782, 2014.

[13] S. F. Hussain, M. Mushtaq, and Z. Halim. Multi-view document clustering via ensemble method. *Journal of Intelligent Information Systems*, 43(1):81–99, 2014.

[14] A. Kumar and H. Daumé. A co-training approach for multi-view spectral clustering. *International Conference on Machine Learning*, pages 393–400, 2011.

[15] A. Kumar, P. Rai, and H. Daume. Co-regularized multi-view spectral clustering. *Advances in Neural Information Processing Systems*, pages 1413–1421, 2011.

[16] J. Liu, C. Wang, J. Gao, and J. Han. Multi-view clustering via joint nonnegative matrix factorization. *SIAM International Conference on Data Mining*, 13:252–260, 2013.

[17] B. Long, S. Y. Philip, and Z. M. Zhang. A general model for multiple view unsupervised learning. *SIAM International Conference on Data Mining*, pages 822–833, 2008.

[18] E. Muller, S. Gunnemann, I. Farber, and T. Seidl. Discovering multiple clustering solutions: grouping objects in different views of the data. *International Conference on Data Engineering*, pages 1207–1210, 2012.

[19] P. Muthukrishnan, D. Radev, and Q. Mei. Edge weight regularization over multiple graphs for similarity learning. *International Conference on Data Mining*, pages 374–383, 2010.

[20] J. Ngiam, A. Khosla, M. Kim, J. Nam, H. Lee, and A. Y. Ng. Multimodal deep learning. *International Conference on Machine Learning*, pages 689–696, 2011.

[21] F. Nie, H. Huang, X. Cai, and C. H. Ding. Efficient and robust feature selection via joint l21-norms minimization. *Advances in neural information processing systems*, pages 1813–1821, 2010.

[22] M. Qian and C. Zhai. Unsupervised feature selection for multi-view clustering on text-image web news data. *ACM International Conference on Information and Knowledge Management*, pages 1963–1966, 2014.

[23] P. Rai, A. Trivedi, H. Daumé III, and S. L. DuVall. Multiview clustering with incomplete views. *NIPS Workshop on Machine Learning for Social Computing*, 2010.

[24] W. Shao, X. Shi, and P. S. Yu. Clustering on multiple incomplete datasets via collective kernel learning. *International Conference on Data Mining*, pages 1181–1186, 2013.

[25] J. Shi and J. Malik. Normalized cuts and image segmentation. *IEEE Transactions on Pattern Analysis and Machine Intelligence*, 22(8):888–905, 2000.

[26] N. Srivastava and R. R. Salakhutdinov. Multimodal learning with deep boltzmann machines. *Advances in Neural Information Processing Systems*, pages 2222–2230, 2012.

[27] S. Sun. A survey of multi-view machine learning. *Neural Computing and Applications*, 23(7-8):2031–2038, 2013.

[28] J. Tang, X. Hu, H. Gao, and H. Liu. Unsupervised feature selection for multi-view data in social media. *SIAM International Conference on Data Mining*, pages 270–278, 2013.

[29] H. Wang, F. Nie, and H. Huang. Multi-view clustering and feature learning via structured sparsity. *International Conference on Machine Learning*, pages 352–360, 2013.

[30] R. Xia, Y. Pan, L. Du, and J. Yin. Robust multi-view spectral clustering via low-rank and sparse decomposition. *AAAI Conference on Artificial Intelligence*, 2014.

[31] C. Xu, D. Tao, and C. Xu. A survey on multi-view learning. *arXiv:1304.5634*, 2013.

[32] Q. Yin, S. Wu, R. He, and L. Wang. Multi-view clustering via pairwise sparse subspace representation. *Neurocomputing*, 156:12–21, 2015.

[33] X. Zhao, N. Evans, and J.-L. Dugelay. A subspace co-training framework for multi-view clustering. *Pattern Recognition Letters*, 41:73–82, 2014.

[34] S.-Y. L. Y. J. Zhi and H. Zhou. Partial multi-view clustering. *AAAI Conference on Artificial Intelligence*, 2014.

Robust Subspace Clustering via Tighter Rank Approximation

Zhao Kang
Computer Science Dept.
Southern Illinois University
Carbondale, IL, USA
zhao.kang@siu.edu

Chong Peng
Computer Science Dept.
Southern Illinois University
Carbondale, IL, USA
pchong@siu.edu

Qiang Cheng
Computer Science Dept.
Southern Illinois University
Carbondale, IL, USA
qcheng@cs.siu.edu

ABSTRACT

Matrix rank minimization problem is in general NP-hard. The nuclear norm is used to substitute the rank function in many recent studies. Nevertheless, the nuclear norm approximation adds all singular values together and the approximation error may depend heavily on the magnitudes of singular values. This might restrict its capability in dealing with many practical problems. In this paper, an arctangent function is used as a tighter approximation to the rank function. We use it on the challenging subspace clustering problem. For this nonconvex minimization problem, we develop an effective optimization procedure based on a type of augmented Lagrange multipliers (ALM) method. Extensive experiments on face clustering and motion segmentation show that the proposed method is effective for rank approximation.

Categories and Subject Descriptors

I.5 [**Pattern recognition**]: Clustering—*Algorithm*; G.1.6 [**Optimization**]: Constrained optimization

Keywords

Subspace Clustering; Rank Minimization; Nuclear Norm; Nonconvex Optimization

1. INTRODUCTION

Matrix rank minimization arises in control, machine learning, signal processing and other areas [43]. It is difficult to solve due to the discontinuity and nonconvexity of the rank function. Existing algorithms are largely based on the nuclear norm heuristic, i.e., to replace the rank by the nuclear norm [11]. The nuclear norm of a matrix X, denoted by $\|X\|_*$, is the sum of all its singular values, i.e., $\|X\|_* = \sum_i \sigma_i(X)$. Under some conditions, the solution to the nuclear norm heuristic coincides with the minimum rank solution [31, 32]. However, since the nuclear norm is the convex envelop of rank(X) over the unit ball $\{X : \|X\|_2 \leq 1\}$, it may deviate from the rank of X in many circumstances [4, 3]. The rank function counts the number of nonvanishing singular values, while the nuclear norm sums their amplitudes. As a result, the nuclear norm may be dominated by a few very large singular values. Variations of standard nuclear norm are shown to be promising in some recent research [14, 2, 29]. A number of nonconvex surrogate functions have come up to better approximate the rank function, such as Logarithm Determinant [11, 16], Schatten-p norm [26], truncated nuclear norm [14] and others [24]. In general, they are to solve the following low-rank minimization problem:

$$\min_Z \sum_{i=1}^{\min(m,n)} h(\sigma_i(Z)) + \lambda g(Z), \tag{1}$$

where $\sigma_i(Z)$ denotes the i-th singular value of $Z \in \mathcal{R}^{m\times n}$, $h(\cdot)$ is a potentially nonconvex, nonsmooth function, and $g(\cdot)$ is a loss function. By choosing $h(z) = z$, the summation of the first term in (1) goes back to the nuclear norm $\|Z\|_*$, problem (1) becomes the well known convex relaxation of the rank minimization problem:

$$\min_Z \|Z\|_* + \lambda g(Z). \tag{2}$$

In this paper, we will propose a new nonconvex rank approximation and consider subspace clustering as a specific application.

1.1 Previous Work on Subspace Clustering

In many real-world applications, high-dimensional data reside in a union of multiple low-dimensional subspaces rather than one single low-dimensional subspace [7]. Subspace clustering deals with exactly this structure by clustering data points according to their underlying subspaces. It has numerous applications in computer vision [30] and image processing [25]. Therefore subspace clustering has drawn significant attention in recent years [36]. In practice, the underlying subspace structure is often corrupted by noise and outliers, and thus the data may deviate from the original subspaces. It is necessary to develop robust estimation techniques.

A number of approaches to subspace clustering have been proposed in the past two decades. According to the survey in [36], they can be roughly divided into four categories: 1) algebraic methods; 2) iterative methods; 3) statistical methods; and 4) spectral clustering-based methods. Among them, spectral clustering-based methods have obtained state-of-the-art results, including sparse subspace clustering (SSC) [9], and low rank representation (LRR) [21].

CIKM'15, October 19–23, 2015, Melbourne, Australia.
© 2015 ACM. ISBN 978-1-4503-3794-6/15/10 ...$15.00.
DOI: http://dx.doi.org/10.1145/2806416.2806506.

They perform subspace clustering in two steps: first, learning an affinity matrix that encodes the subspace membership information, and then applying spectral clustering algorithms [33, 28] to the learned affinity matrix to obtain the final clustering results. Their main difference is how to obtain a good affinity matrix.

SSC assumes that each data point can be represented as a sparse linear combination of other points. The popular l_1-norm heuristic is used to capture the sparsity. It enjoys great performance for face clustering and motion segmentation data. Now we have a good theoretical understanding about SSC. For instance, [8] shows that disjoint subspaces can be exactly recovered under certain conditions; geometric analysis of SSC [34] significantly broadens the scope of SSC to intersecting subspaces. However, the data points are assumed to be lying exactly in the subspace. This assumption may be violated in the presence of corrupted data. [38] extends SSC by adding adversarial or random noise. However, SSC's solution might be too sparse, thus the affinity graph from a single subspace will not be a fully connected body [27]. To address the above issue, another regularization term is introduced to promote connectivity of the graph [9].

LRR also represents each data point as a linear combination of other points. It is to find the lowest rank representation Z of all data points jointly, where the nuclear norm is used as a common surrogate of the rank function. In the presence of noise or outliers, LRR solves the following problem:

$$\min_{Z,E} \|Z\|_* + \lambda \|E\|_l \quad s.t. \quad X = XZ + E, \tag{3}$$

where λ balances the effects of the low rank representation and errors, $X = [x_1, \cdots, x_n] \in \mathcal{R}^{m\times n}$ is a set of m-dimensional data vectors drawn from the union of k subspaces $\{S_i\}_{i=1}^k$, and $\|\cdot\|_l$ characterizes certain corruptions E. For example, when E represents Gaussian noise, squared Frobenius norm $\|E\|_F^2 = \sum_{i=1}^m \sum_{j=1}^n E_{ij}^2$ is used; when E denotes random corruptions, l_1 norm $\|E\|_1 = \sum_{i=1}^m \sum_{j=1}^n |E_{ij}|$ is appropriate; when E indicates the sample-specific corruptions, $l_{2,1}$ norm is adopted, where $\|E\|_{2,1} = \sum_{j=1}^n \sqrt{\sum_{i=1}^m E_{ij}^2}$. The low rank as well as sparsity requirement may help counteract corruptions. A variant of LRR works even in the presence of some arbitrarily large outliers [23]. However, LRR has never been shown to succeed other than under strong "independent subspace" condition [15].

In view of the issues with the nuclear norm mentioned in the beginning, we propose the use of an arctangent function instead in this work. We demonstrate the enhanced performance of the proposed algorithm on benchmark data sets.

1.2 Our Contributions

In summary, the main contributions of this paper are threefold:

- More accurate rank approximation is proposed to obtain the low-rank representation of high-dimensional data.
- An efficient optimization procedure is developed for arctangent rank minimization (ARM) problem. Theoretical analysis shows that our algorithm converges to a stationary point.
- The superiority of the proposed method to various state-of-the-art subspace clustering algorithms is verified with significantly and consistently lower error rates of ARM on popular datasets.

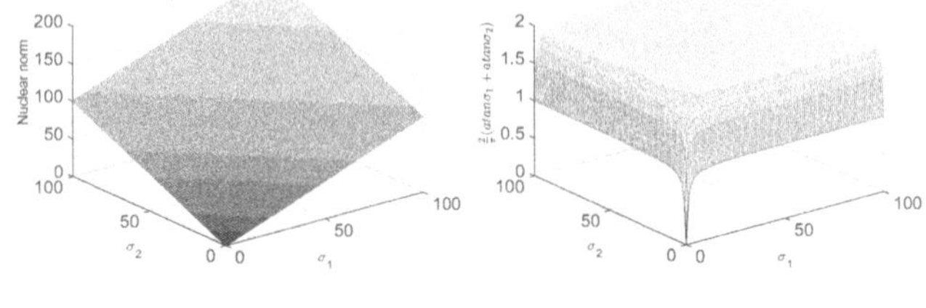

Figure 1: Comparison of approximation for rank 2.

2. SUBSPACE CLUSTERING BY ARM

In this work, we demonstrate the application of $F(Z) = f \circ \sigma(Z)$, where $f(x) = \sum_i \arctan(|x_i|)$ for any $x \in \mathcal{R}^n$ (for high dimensional data usually $m >> n$ which is the case we suppose in the paper), as a rank approximation of matrix Z in subspace clustering setting. There are three advantages of this approximation function. First, it approximates rank(Z) much better than the nuclear norm does, i.e., as $\sigma_i \in [0, \infty]$, $\frac{2}{\pi}\arctan(\sigma_i) \in [0, 1]$. Figure 1 shows the rank approximation value of the two approaches for rank 2 situation. We can clearly see that arctangent reflects the real rank pretty well on a broad range of singular values. Second, f is differentiable, concave and monotonically increasing on $[0, \infty]^n$, by defining the gradient of f at 0 as $\frac{\partial}{\partial x_i} f(0) = \lim_{x_i \to 0^+} \frac{1}{1+x_i^2} = 1$. Third, F is unitarily invariant and f is absolutely symmetric, i.e., $f(x)$ is invariant under arbitrary permutation and sign changes of the components of x. Based on these properties, we have the following theorems, which is proved in Appendix A.

THEOREM 2.1. *For $\mu > 0$ and $A \in \mathcal{R}^{m\times n}$, the following problem*

$$Z^* = \arg\min_Z F(Z) + \frac{\mu}{2}\|Z - A\|_F^2 \tag{4}$$

is solved by the vector minimization

$$\sigma^* = \arg\min_{\sigma \geq 0} f(\sigma) + \frac{\mu}{2}\|\sigma - \sigma_A\|_2^2, \tag{5}$$

so that $Z^* = Udiag(\sigma^*)V^T$ with the SVD of A being $Udiag(\sigma_A)V^T$.

2.1 Arctangent Rank Minimization

To demonstrate the effectiveness of the arctangent rank approximation, we consider its application in the challenging subspace clustering problem. We propose the following arctangent rank minimization (ARM) problem:

$$\min_{Z,E} \sum_{i=1}^n arctan(\sigma_i(Z)) + \lambda \|E\|_l \quad s.t. \quad X = XZ + E. \tag{6}$$

It is difficult to solve (6) directly because the objective function is neither convex nor concave. We convert it to the following equivalent problem:

$$\min_{Z,E,J} \sum_{i=1}^{n} arctan(\sigma_i(J)) + \lambda \|E\|_l \; s.t. X = XZ + E, Z = J. \tag{7}$$

Now we resort to a type of augmented Lagrange multipliers (ALM) [20] method to solve (7). For simplicity of notation, we denote $\sigma_i = \sigma_i(J)$ and $\sigma_i^t = \sigma_i(J^t)$. The corresponding augmented Lagrangian function is:

$$\begin{aligned} L(E, J, Y_1, Y_2, Z, \mu) &= \sum_{i=1}^{n} arctan(\sigma_i) + \lambda \|E\|_l \\ &+ Tr(Y_1^T(X - XZ - E)) + Tr(Y_2^T(J - Z)) \\ &+ \frac{\mu}{2}(\|X - XZ - E\|_F^2 + \|J - Z\|_F^2), \end{aligned} \tag{8}$$

where $\mu > 0$ is a penalty parameter and Y_1, Y_2 are Lagrangian multipliers. The variables E, J, and Z can be updated alternatively, one at each step, while keeping the other two fixed. For the $(t + 1)$th iteration, the iterative scheme is given as follows.

For Z^{t+1}, by fixing E^t, J^t, Y_1^t and Y_2^t, we have:

$$\begin{aligned} Z^{t+1} = \arg\min_Z \; & Tr[(Y_1^t)^T(X - XZ - E^t)]+ \\ & Tr[(Y_2^t)^T(J^t - Z)]+ \\ & \frac{\mu^t}{2}(\|X - XZ - E^t\|_F^2 + \|J^t - Z\|_F^2). \end{aligned} \tag{9}$$

It is evident that the objective function of (9) is a strongly convex quadratic function which can be solved directly. By setting the first derivative of it to zero, we have:

$$Z^{t+1} = (I+X^TX)^{-1}[X^T(X-E^t)+J^t+\frac{X^TY_1^t + Y_2^t}{\mu^t}], \tag{10}$$

where $I \in \mathcal{R}^{n\times n}$ is the identity matrix.

For J^{t+1}, we have:

$$J^{t+1} = \arg\min_J \; \sum_{i=1}^{n} arctan(\sigma_i) + \frac{\mu^t}{2}\|J - (Z^{t+1} - \frac{1}{\mu^t}Y_2^t)\|_F^2. \tag{11}$$

Then we can convert it to problem (5). The first term in (5) is concave while the second term convex in σ, so we can apply difference of convex (DC) [13] (vector) optimization method. A linear approximation is used at each iteration of DC programing. At iteration $k + 1$,

$$\sigma_{k+1} = \arg\min_{\sigma\geq 0} \; \langle w_k, \sigma\rangle + \frac{\mu^t}{2}\|\sigma - \sigma_A\|_2^2, \tag{12}$$

whose closed-form solution is

$$\sigma_{k+1} = (\sigma_A - \frac{\omega_k}{\mu^t})_+, \tag{13}$$

where $\omega_k = \partial f(\sigma_k)$ is the gradient of $f(\cdot)$ at σ_k and the SVD of $Z^{t+1} - \frac{Y_2^t}{\mu^t}$ is $Udiag\{\sigma_A\}V^T$. Finally, it converges to a local optimal point σ^*. Then $J^{t+1} = Udiag\{\sigma^*\}V^T$.

For E^{t+1}, we have the following subproblem:

$$\begin{aligned} E^{t+1} = \arg\min_E \; & \lambda \|E\|_l + \frac{\mu^t}{2}\|X - XZ^{t+1} - E\|_F^2 \\ & + Tr[(Y_1^t)^T(X - XZ^{t+1} - E)]. \end{aligned} \tag{14}$$

Algorithm 1 Arctan Rank Minimization

Input: data matrix $X \in \mathcal{R}^{m\times n}$, parameters $\lambda > 0, \mu^0 > 0$, and $\rho > 1$.
Initialize: $J = I \in \mathcal{R}^{n\times n}$, $E = 0$, $Y_1 = Y_2 = 0$.
REPEAT
1: Update Z by (10).
2: Solve (11).
3: Solve E by either (15), (16) or (17) according to l.
4: Update Y_1 by (18) and Y_2 by (19).
5: Update μ by $\mu^{t+1} = \rho\mu^t$.
UNTIL stopping criterion is met.

Depending on different regularization strategies, we have different closed-form solutions. For squared Forbenius norm, it is again a quadratic problem,

$$E^{t+1} = \frac{Y_1^t + \mu^t(X - XZ^{t+1})}{\mu^t + 2\lambda}. \tag{15}$$

For l_1 and $l_{2,1}$ norm, we use the lemmas from Appendix B. Let $Q = X - XZ^{t+1} + \frac{Y_1^t}{\mu^t}$, we can solve E element-wisely as below:

$$E_{ij}^{t+1} = \begin{cases} Q_{ij} - \frac{\lambda}{\mu^t} sgn(Q_{ij}), & \text{if } |Q_{ij}| < \frac{\lambda}{\mu^t}; \\ 0, & \text{otherwise.} \end{cases} \tag{16}$$

In the case of $l_{2,1}$ norm, we have

$$[E^{t+1}]_{:,i} = \begin{cases} \frac{\|Q_{:,i}\|_2 - \frac{\lambda}{\mu^t}}{\|Q_{:,i}\|_2} Q_{:,i}, & \text{if } \|Q_{:,i}\|_2 > \frac{\lambda}{\mu^t}; \\ 0, & \text{otherwise.} \end{cases} \tag{17}$$

The update of Lagrange multipliers is:

$$Y_1^{t+1} = Y_1^t + \mu^t(X - XZ^{t+1} - E^{t+1}), \tag{18}$$

$$Y_2^{t+1} = Y_2^t + \mu^t(J^{t+1} - Z^{t+1}). \tag{19}$$

The procedure is outlined in Algorithm 1.

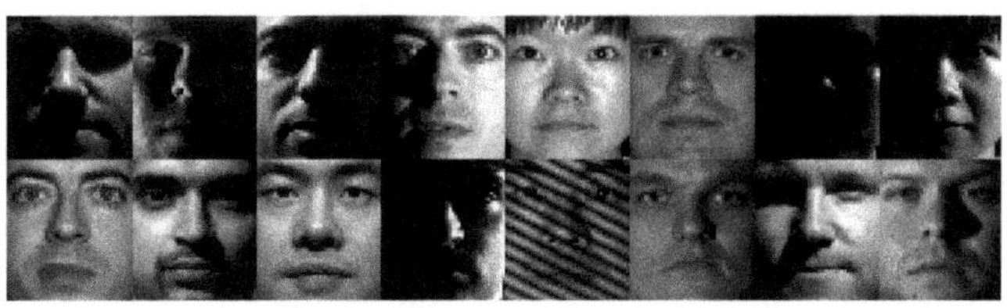

Figure 2: Sample face images in Extended Yale B.

2.2 Affinity Graph Construction

After obtaining optimal Z^*, we can build the similarity graph matrix W. As argued in [9], some postprocessing of the coefficient matrix can improve the clustering performance. Following the angular information based technique of [21], we define $\widetilde{U} = U\Sigma^{1/2}$, where U and Σ are from the skinny SVD of $Z^* = U\Sigma V^T$. Inspired by [17], we define W as follows:

$$W_{ij} = (\frac{\widetilde{u}_i^T \widetilde{u}_j}{\|\widetilde{u}_i\|_2 \|\widetilde{u}_j\|_2})^{2\alpha}, \tag{20}$$

where $\widetilde{u}_i$ and $\widetilde{u}_j$ denote the i-th and j-th columns of $\widetilde{U}$, and $\alpha \in \mathcal{N}^*$ controls the sharpness of the affinity between two

Algorithm 2 Subspace Clustering by ARM

Input: data matrix X, number of subspaces k.

Do

Obtain optimal Z^* by solving (7).

Compute the skinny SVD $Z^* = U\Sigma V^T$.

Calculate $\widetilde{U} = U(\Sigma)^{1/2}$.

Construct the affinity graph matrix W by (20).

Perform NCuts on W.

points. Increasing the power α enhances the separation ability in the presence of noise. However, an excessively large α would break affinities between points of the same group. In order to compare with LRR[1], we use $\alpha = 2$ in our experiments, then we have the same postprocessing procedure as LRR. After obtaining W, we directly utilize a spectral clustering algorithm NCuts [33] to cluster the samples. Algorithm 2 summarizes the complete subspace clustering steps of the proposed method.

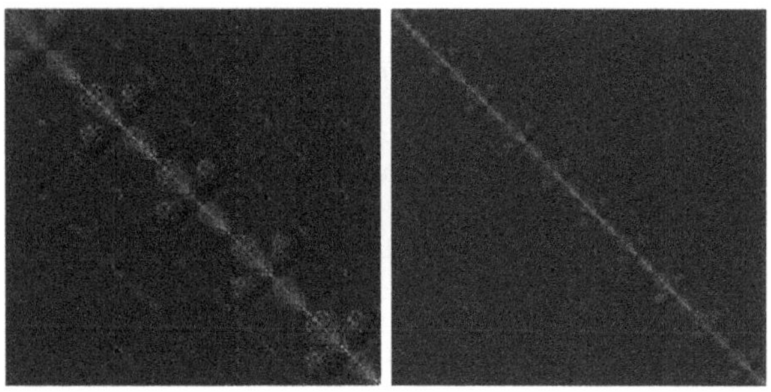

Figure 3: Affinity graph matrix W with five and ten subjects.

3. CONVERGENCE ANALYSIS

Since the objective function (6) is nonconvex, it would not be easy to prove the convergence in theory. In this paper, we mathematically prove that our optimization algorithm has at least a convergent subsequence which converges to an accumulation point, and moreover, any accumulation point of our algorithm is a stationary point. Although the final solution might be a local optimum, our results are superior to the global optimal solution from convex approaches. Some previous work also reports similar observations [39, 12, 42].

We will show the proof in the case of $\|E\|_1$. Let's first reformulate our objective function:

$$G(J,Z,E) = F(J) + \lambda\|E\|_1 \quad s.t. \quad Z = J, \quad X = XZ + E, \tag{21}$$

$$L(J,Z,E,Y_1,Y_2,\mu) = G(J,Z,E) + \langle Y_1, X - XZ - E\rangle + \langle Y_2, J - Z\rangle + \frac{\mu}{2}(\|J - Z\|_F^2 + \|X - XZ - E\|_F^2). \tag{22}$$

LEMMA 3.1. *The sequences of $\{Y_1^t\}$ and $\{Y_2^t\}$ are bounded.*

[1]As we confirmed with an author of [21], the power 2 of its equation (12) is a typo, which should be 4.

PROOF. J^{t+1} satisfies the first-order necessary local optimality condition,

$$\begin{aligned} &\partial_J L\left(J, Z^{t+1}, E^t, Y_1^t, Y_2^t, \mu^t\right)|_{J^{t+1}} \\ =&\partial_J F(J)|_{J^{t+1}} + \mu^t\left(J^{t+1} - Z^{t+1} + \frac{Y_2^t}{\mu^t}\right) \\ =&\partial_J F(J)|_{J^{t+1}} + Y_2^{t+1} \\ =&0. \end{aligned} \tag{23}$$

Let's define $\theta_i = \frac{1}{1+(\sigma_i)^2}$ if $\sigma_i \neq 0$; otherwise, it is 1. According to (41) in Appendix B,

$$U diag(\theta) V^T = \partial_J F(J)|_{J^{t+1}}, \tag{24}$$

and $0 < \frac{1}{1+(\sigma_i^{t+1})^2} \leq 1$, $\partial_J F(J)|_{J^{t+1}}$ is bounded. From (23), we conclude that Y_2^{t+1} is bounded.

Similarly, for E^{t+1}

$$\begin{aligned} 0 \in\, &\partial_E L\left(J^{t+1}, Z^{t+1}, E, Y_1^t, Y_2^t, \mu^t\right)|_{E^{t+1}} \\ &= \partial_E \lambda(\|E\|_1)|_{E^{t+1}} - Y_1^t \\ &- \mu^t\left(X - XZ^{t+1} - E^{t+1}\right) \\ &= \partial_E \lambda(\|E\|_1)|_{E^{t+1}} + Y_1^{t+1}. \end{aligned} \tag{25}$$

Here ∂_E denotes the subgradient operator [6]. Because $||E||_1$ is nonsmooth only at $E_{ij} = 0$, we define $[\partial_E\|E\|_1]_{ij} = 0$ if $E_{ij} = 0$. Then $0 \leq \|\partial_E\|E\|_1\|_F^2 \leq mn$ is bounded. Therefore, $\{Y_1^{t+1}\}$ is bounded. □

LEMMA 3.2. *$\{J^t\}$, $\{E^t\}$ and $\{Z^t\}$ are bounded if $\sum \frac{\mu^{t+1}}{(\mu^t)^2} < \infty$, $\sum \frac{1}{\mu^t} < \infty$ and X^TX is invertible.*

PROOF.

$$\begin{aligned} &L\left(J^t, Z^t, E^t, Y_1^t, Y_2^t, \mu^t\right) \\ &= L\left(J^t, Z^t, E^t, Y_1^{t-1}, Y_2^{t-1}, \mu^{t-1}\right) + \\ &\frac{\mu^t - \mu^{t-1}}{2}(\|J^t - Z^t\|_F^2 + \|X - XZ^t - E^t\|_F^2) \\ &+ Tr((Y_1^t - Y_1^{t-1})(X - XZ^t - E^t)) \\ &+ Tr((Y_2^t - Y_2^{t-1})(J^t - Z^t)) \\ &= L\left(J^t, Z^t, E^t, Y_1^{t-1}, Y_2^{t-1}, \mu^{t-1}\right) + \\ &\frac{\mu^t + \mu^{t-1}}{2(\mu^{t-1})^2}(\|Y_1^t - Y_1^{t-1}\|_F^2 + \|Y_2^t - Y_2^{t-1}\|_F^2). \end{aligned} \tag{26}$$

$$\begin{aligned} &L\left(J^{t+1}, Z^{t+1}, E^{t+1}, Y_1^t, Y_2^t, \mu^t\right) \\ &\leq L(J^{t+1}, Z^{t+1}, E^t, Y_1^t, Y_2^t, \mu^t) \\ &\leq L(J^t, Z^{t+1}, E^t, Y_1^t, Y_2^t, \mu^t) \\ &\leq L\left(J^t, Z^t, E^t, Y_1^t, Y_2^t, \mu^t\right) \\ &\leq L\left(J^t, Z^t, E^t, Y_1^{t-1}, Y_2^{t-1}\mu^{t-1}\right) + \\ &\frac{\mu^t + \mu^{t-1}}{2(\mu^{t-1})^2}(\|Y_1^t - Y_1^{t-1}\|_F^2 + \|Y_2^t - Y_2^{t-1}\|_F^2). \end{aligned} \tag{27}$$

Iterating the inequality (27) gives that

$$\begin{aligned} &L(J^{t+1}, Z^{t+1}, E^{t+1}, Y_1^t, Y_2^t, \mu^t) \\ &\leq L\left(J^1, Z^1, E^1, Y_1^0, Y_2^0, \mu^0\right) + \\ &\sum_{i=1}^{t} \frac{\mu^i + \mu^{i-1}}{2(\mu^{i-1})^2}(\|Y_1^i - Y_1^{i-1}\|_F^2 \\ &+ \|Y_2^i - Y_2^{i-1}\|_F^2). \end{aligned} \tag{28}$$

Under the given conditions on $\{\mu^t\}$, both terms on the right-hand side of the above inequality are bounded, thus $L\left(J^{t+1}, Z^{t+1}, E^{t+1}, Y_1^t, Y_2^t, \mu^t\right)$ is bounded. In addition,

$$\begin{aligned} & L\left(J^{t+1}, Z^{t+1}, E^{t+1}, Y_1^t, Y_2^t, \mu^t\right) + \\ & \frac{1}{2\mu^t}(\|Y_1^t\|_F^2 + \|Y_2^t\|_F^2) \\ & = F(J^{t+1}) + \lambda\|E^{t+1}\|_1 + \\ & \frac{\mu^t}{2}\|J^{t+1} - Z^{t+1} + \frac{Y_2^t}{\mu^t}\|_F^2 + \\ & \frac{\mu^t}{2}\|X - E^{t+1} - XZ^{t+1} + \frac{Y_1^t}{\mu^t}\|_F^2. \end{aligned} \tag{29}$$

The left-hand side in the above equation is bounded and each term on the right-hand side is nonnegative, so each term is bounded. Therefore, E^{t+1} is bounded. XZ^{t+1} is bounded according to the last term on the right-hand side of (29), and thus after multiplying a constant matrix X^T, we have X^TXZ^{t+1} is bounded. Under the condition that X^TX is invertible, by multiplying a constant matrix $(X^TX)^{-1}$, we have that $(X^TX)^{-1}X^TXZ^{t+1} = Z^{t+1}$ is bounded. Finally, J^{t+1} is bounded because the second to the last term is bounded. Therefore, $\{J^t\}$, $\{E^t\}$ and $\{Z^t\}$ are bounded. □

THEOREM 3.1. *The sequence $\{J^t, E^t, Z^t, Y_1^t, Y_2^t\}$ generated by Algorithm 1 has at least one accumulation point, under the conditions that $\sum \frac{\mu^{t+1}}{(\mu^t)^2} < \infty$, $\sum \frac{1}{\mu^t} < \infty$ and X^TX is invertible. For any accumulation point $\{J^*, E^*, Z^*, Y_1^*, Y_2^*\}$, $\{J^*, E^*, Z^*\}$ is a stationary point of optimization problem (21), under the conditions that $\mu^t(J^{t+1} - J^t) \to 0$, and $\mu^t(E^{t+1} - E^t) \to 0$.*

PROOF. Based on the conditions on the penalty parameter sequence $\{\mu^t\}$ and X^TX, Algorithm 1 generates a bounded sequence $\{J^t, E^t, Z^t, Y_1^t, Y_2^t\}$ by Lemma (3.1) and (3.2) . By the Bolzano-Weierstrass theorem, at least one accumulation point exists, e.g., $\{J^*, E^*, Z^*, Y_1^*, Y_2^*\}$. Without loss of generality, we assume that $\{J^t, E^t, Z^t, Y_1^t, Y_2^t\}$ itself converges to $\{J^*, E^*, Z^*, Y_1^*, Y_2^*\}$. As shown below, $\{J^*, E^*, Z^*\}$ is a stationary point of problem (21), under additional conditions that $\mu_t(E^{t+1} - E^t) \to 0$ and $\mu_t(J^{t+1} - J^t) \to 0$.

Since $J^t - Z^t = \frac{Y_2^t - Y_2^{t-1}}{\mu^{t-1}}$ and $\mu^t \to \infty$, we have $J^t - Z^t \to 0$. Therefore, $J^* = Z^*$.

Similarly, by $X - XZ^t - E^t = \frac{Y_1^t - Y_1^{t-1}}{\mu^{t-1}}$, we have $E^* = X - XZ^*$.

For Z^{t+1}, the first-order optimality condition is

$$\begin{aligned} & \nabla_Z L\left(J^t, Z, E^t, Y_1^t, Y_2^t, \mu^t\right)|_{Z^{t+1}} \\ & = -Y_2^t - X^TY_1^t - \mu^t\left(J^t - Z^{t+1}\right) \\ & - \mu^tX^T\left(X - E^t - XZ^{t+1}\right) \\ & = -Y_2^t - X^TY_1^t - \mu^t\left(J^{t+1} - Z^{t+1} + J^t - J^{t+1}\right) \\ & - \mu^tX^T\left(X - E^{t+1} - XZ^{t+1} - E^t + E^{t+1}\right) \\ & = -Y_2^{t+1} + \mu^t\left(J^{t+1} - J^t\right) - X^TY_1^{t+1} \\ & - \mu^tX^T\left(E^{t+1} - E^t\right) \\ & = 0. \end{aligned}$$

If $\mu^t(J^{t+1} - J^t) \to 0$ and $\mu^t(E^{t+1} - E^t) \to 0$, we have $X^TY_2^t + Y_1^t \to 0$, i.e., $-X^TY_2^* = Y_1^*$. It is easy to verify $\partial_E L\left(J, Z, E, Y_1, Y_2, \mu\right)|_{E^*} = 0$. Therefore, $\{J^*, E^*, Z^*, Y_1^*, Y_2^*\}$ satisfies the KKT conditions of $L(J, E, Z, Y_1, Y_2)$ and thus $\{J^*, E^*, Z^*\}$ is a stationary point of (21). □

4. EXPERIMENTS

This section presents experiments with the proposed algorithm on the Extended Yale B (EYaleB) [18] and Hopkins 155 databases [35]. They are standard tests for robust subspace clustering algorithms. As shown in [9], the challenge in the Hopkins 155 dataset is due to the small principal angles between subspaces. For EYaleB, the challenge lies in the small principal angles and another factor that data points from different subspaces are close. Our results are compared with several state-of-the-art subspace clustering algorithms, including LRR [21], SSC [9], LRSC [10, 37], spectral curvature clustering (SCC) [5], and local subspace affinity (LSA) [40], in terms of misclassification rate. For fair comparison, we follow the experimental setup in [9] and obtain the results.

As other methods do, we tune our parameters to obtain the best results. In general, the value of λ depends on prior knowledge of the noise level of the data. If the noise is heavy, a small λ should be adopted. μ^0 and ρ affect the convergence speed. The larger their values are, the fewer iterations are required for the algorithm to converge, but meanwhile we may lose some precision of the final objective function value. In the literature, the value of ρ is often chosen between 1 and 1.1. The iteration stops at a relative normed difference of 10^{-5} between two successive iterations, or a maximum of 150 iterations.

4.1 Face Clustering

Face clustering refers to partitioning a set of face images from multiple individuals to multiple subspaces according to the identity of each individual. The face images are heavily contaminated by sparse gross errors due to varying lighting conditions, as shown in Figure 2. Therefore, $\|E\|_1$ is used to model the errors in our experiment. The EYaleB database contains cropped face images of 38 individuals taken under 64 different illumination conditions. The 38 subjects were divided into four groups as follows: subjects 1 to 10, 11 to 20, 21 to 30, and 31 to 38. All choices of $n \in \{2, 3, 5, 8, 10\}$ are considered for each of the first three groups, and all choices of $n \in \{2, 3, 5, 8\}$ are considered for the last group. As a result, there are $\{163, 416, 812, 136, 3\}$ combinations corresponding to different n. Each image is downsampled to 48×42 and is vectorized to a 2016-dimensional vector. $\lambda = 10^{-5}$, $\mu^0 = 1.7$ and $\gamma = 1.03$ are used in this experiment.

Table 1 provides the best performance of each method. As shown in the table, our proposed method has the lowest mean clustering error rates in all five settings. In particular, in the most challenging case of 10 subjects, the mean clustering error rate is as low as 3.85%. The improvement is significant compared with other low rank representation based subspace clustering, i.e., LRR and LRSC. For example, 19% and 11% improvement over LRR can be observed in the cases of 10 and 8 subjects, respectively. This demonstrates the importance of accurate rank approximation. In addition, the error of LSA is large maybe because LSA is based on MSE. Since the MSE is quite sensitive to outliers, LSA will fail to deal with large outliers.

Figure 3 shows the obtained affinity graph matrix W for the five and ten subjects scenarios. We can see a distinct block-diagonal structure, which means that each cluster be-

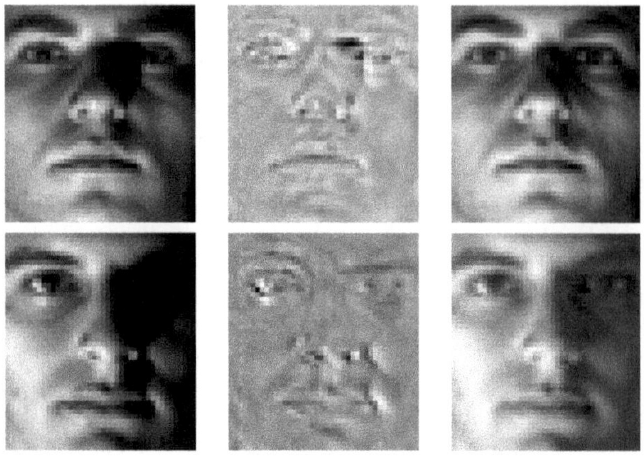

Figure 4: **Recovery results of two face images. The three columns from left to right are the original image (X), the error matrix (E) and the recovered image (XZ), respectively.**

Table 1: Clustering error rates (%) on the EYaleB database.

Algorithm	LRR	SSC	LSA	LRSC	SCC	ARM
2 Subjects						
Mean	2.54	1.86	32.80	5.32	16.62	**1.51**
Median	0.78	**0.00**	47.66	4.69	7.82	0.78
3 Subjects						
Mean	4.21	3.10	52.29	8.47	38.16	**2.26**
Median	2.60	**1.04**	50.00	7.81	39.06	1.56
5 Subjects						
Mean	6.90	4.31	58.02	12.24	58.90	**3.06**
Median	5.63	**2.50**	56.87	11.25	59.38	**2.50**
8 Subjects						
Mean	14.34	5.85	59.19	23.72	66.11	**3.70**
Median	10.06	4.49	58.59	28.03	64.65	**3.32**
10 Subjects						
Mean	22.92	10.94	60.42	30.36	73.02	**3.85**
Median	23.59	5.63	57.50	28.75	75.78	**2.97**

comes highly compact and different subjects are well separated.

In Figure 4, we present the recovery results of some sample faces from the 10-subject clustering case. We can see that the proposed algorithm has the benefit of removing the corruptions in data.

Figure 5 plots the progress of objective function values of (6). It is observed that with more iterations, the value of objective function decreases monotonically. This empirically verifies the convergence of our optimization method.

We compare the average computational time of LRR, SSC, and ARM as a function of the number of subjects in Figure 6. All the experiments are conducted and timed on the same machine with an Intel Xeon E3-1240 3.40GHz CPU that has 4 cores and 8GB memory, running Ubuntu and Matlab (R2014a). We can observe that the computational time of SSC is higher than LRR and ARM, while ARM is a little slower than LRR in most cases.

4.2 Motion Segmentation

Motion segmentation involves segmenting a video sequence of multiple moving objects into multiple spatiotemporal regions corresponding to different motions. These motion sequences can be divided into three main categories: checkerboard, traffic, and articulated or non-rigid motion sequences. The Hopkins 155 dataset includes 155 video sequences of 2 or 3 motions, corresponding to 2 or 3 low-dimensional subspaces of the ambient space. Each sequence represents a data set and so there are 155 motion segmentation problems in total. Several example frames are shown in Figure 7. The trajectories are extracted automatically by a tracker, so they are slightly corrupted by noise. As in [21, 22], $\|E\|_{2,1}$ is adopted in the model. In this experiment, $\lambda = 2$, $\mu^0 = 10$ and $\gamma = 1.05$.

We use the original 2F-dimensional feature trajectories in our experiment. We show the clustering error rates of different algorithms in Table 2. ARM outperforms other algorithms in mean error rate. Especially, its all mean error rates are around 1.5%. This again demonstrates the effectiveness of using arctangent as a rank approximation.

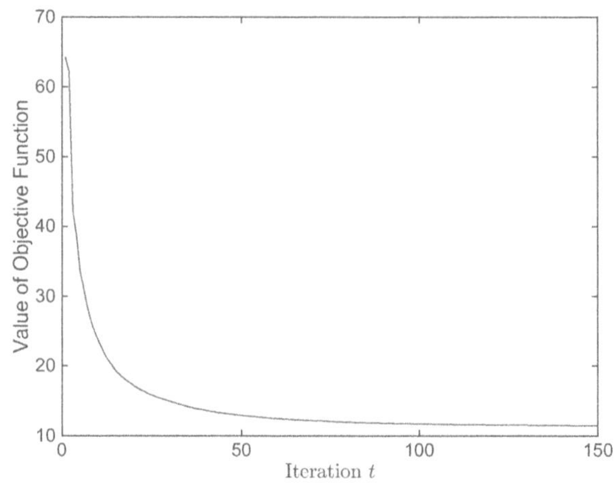

Figure 5: Convergence curve of the objective function value in (6).

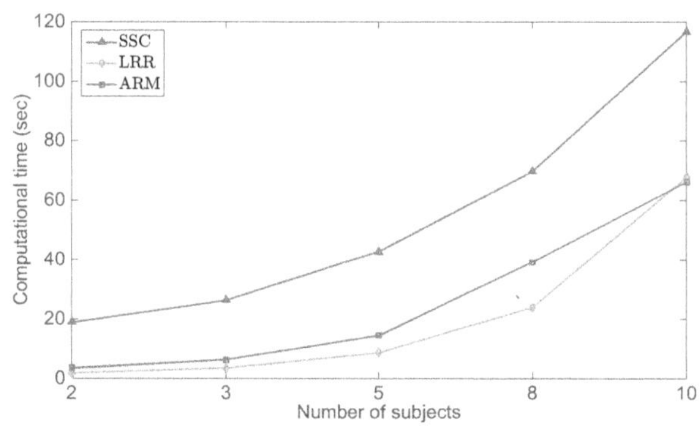

Figure 6: Average computational time (sec) of the algorithms on the EYaleB database as a function of the number of subjects.

Figure 7: Example frames from two video sequences of the Hopkins 155 database with traced feature points.

Table 2: Segmentation error rates (%) on the Hopkins 155 Dataset.

ALGORITHM	LRR	SSC	LSA	LRSC	SCC	ARM
2 MOTIONS						
MEAN	2.13	1.52	4.23	3.69	2.89	**1.48**
MEDIAN	**0.00**	**0.00**	0.56	0.29	**0.00**	**0.00**
3 MOTIONS						
MEAN	4.03	4.40	7.02	7.69	8.25	**1.49**
MEDIAN	1.43	0.56	1.45	3.80	**0.24**	0.84
ALL						
MEAN	2.56	2.18	4.86	4.59	4.10	**1.48**
MEDIAN	**0.00**	**0.00**	0.89	0.60	**0.00**	**0.00**

Figure 8 shows the culstering error rate of ARM for different λ over all 155 sequences. When λ is between 1 and 3, the clustering error rate varies between 1.48% and 2.19%. This demonstrates that ARM performs well under a pretty wide range of values of λ. This is another advantage of ARM over LRR [21].

5. CONCLUSION

In this work, we propose to use arctangent as a concave rank approximation function. It has some nice properties compared with the standard nuclear norm. We apply this function to the low rank representation-based subspace clustering problem and develop an iterative algorithm for optimizing the associated objective function. Extensive experimental results demonstrate that, compared to many state-of-the-art algorithms, the proposed algorithm gives the lowest clustering error rates on many benchmark datasets. This fully demonstrates the significance of accurate rank approximation. Interesting future work includes other applications of the arctangent rank approximation; for example, matrix completion. Since LRR can only ensure its validity for independent subspace segmentation, it is worthwhile to investigate somewhat dependent yet possibly disjoint subspace clustering.

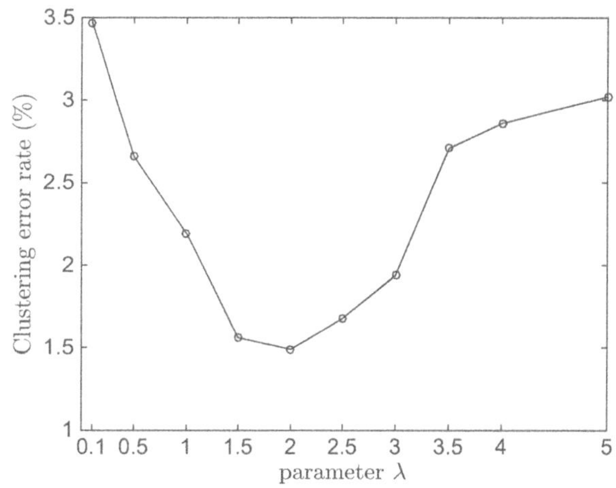

Figure 8: The influence of parameter λ of ARM on clustering error of Hopkins 155 database.

6. ACKNOWLEDGMENTS

This work is supported by US National Science Foundation Grants IIS 1218712. The corresponding author is Qiang Cheng.

7. REFERENCES

[1] A. Beck and M. Teboulle. A fast iterative shrinkage-thresholding algorithm for linear inverse problems. *SIAM Journal on Imaging Sciences*, 2(1):183–202, 2009.

[2] J.-F. Cai, E. J. Candès, and Z. Shen. A singular value thresholding algorithm for matrix completion. *SIAM Journal on Optimization*, 20(4):1956–1982, 2010.

[3] E. J. Candès and B. Recht. Exact matrix completion via convex optimization. *Foundations of Computational mathematics*, 9(6):717–772, 2009.

[4] E. J. Candès and T. Tao. The power of convex relaxation: Near-optimal matrix completion. *Information Theory, IEEE Transactions on*, 56(5):2053–2080, 2010.

[5] G. Chen and G. Lerman. Spectral curvature clustering (scc). *International Journal of Computer Vision*, 81(3):317–330, 2009.

[6] F. H. Clarke. *Optimization and nonsmooth analysis*, volume 5. Siam, 1990.

[7] E. Elhamifar and R. Vidal. Sparse subspace clustering. In *Computer Vision and Pattern Recognition, 2009. CVPR 2009. IEEE Conference on*, pages 2790–2797. IEEE, 2009.

[8] E. Elhamifar and R. Vidal. Clustering disjoint subspaces via sparse representation. In *Acoustics Speech and Signal Processing (ICASSP), 2010 IEEE International Conference on*, pages 1926–1929. IEEE, 2010.

[9] E. Elhamifar and R. Vidal. Sparse subspace clustering: Algorithm, theory, and applications. *Pattern Analysis and Machine Intelligence, IEEE Transactions on*, 35(11):2765–2781, 2013.

[10] P. Favaro, R. Vidal, and A. Ravichandran. A closed form solution to robust subspace estimation and clustering. In *Computer Vision and Pattern Recognition (CVPR), 2011 IEEE Conference on*, pages 1801–1807. IEEE, 2011.

[11] M. Fazel. *Matrix rank minimization with applications.* PhD thesis, PhD thesis, Stanford University, 2002.

[12] P. Gong, J. Ye, and C.-s. Zhang. Multi-stage multi-task feature learning. In *Advances in Neural Information Processing Systems*, pages 1988–1996, 2012.

[13] R. Horst and N. V. Thoai. Dc programming: overview. *Journal of Optimization Theory and Applications*, 103(1):1–43, 1999.

[14] Y. Hu, D. Zhang, J. Ye, X. Li, and X. He. Fast and accurate matrix completion via truncated nuclear norm regularization. *Pattern Analysis and Machine Intelligence, IEEE Transactions on*, 35(9):2117–2130, 2013.

[15] K. Kanatani. Motion segmentation by subspace separation and model selection. In *Computer Vision, 2001. ICCV 2001. Proceedings. Eighth IEEE International Conference on*, volume 2, pages 586–591, 2001.

[16] Z. Kang, C. Peng, J. Cheng, and Q. Cheng. Logdet rank minimization with application to subspace clustering. *Computational Intelligence and Neuroscience*, 2015, 2015.

[17] F. Lauer and C. Schnorr. Spectral clustering of linear subspaces for motion segmentation. In *Computer Vision, 2009 IEEE 12th International Conference on*, pages 678–685. IEEE, 2009.

[18] K.-C. Lee, J. Ho, and D. Kriegman. Acquiring linear subspaces for face recognition under variable lighting. *Pattern Analysis and Machine Intelligence, IEEE Transactions on*, 27(5):684–698, 2005.

[19] A. S. Lewis and H. S. Sendov. Nonsmooth analysis of singular values. part i: Theory. *Set-Valued Analysis*, 13(3):213–241, 2005.

[20] Z. Lin, R. Liu, and Z. Su. Linearized alternating direction method with adaptive penalty for low-rank representation. In *Advances in neural information processing systems*, pages 612–620, 2011.

[21] G. Liu, Z. Lin, S. Yan, J. Sun, Y. Yu, and Y. Ma. Robust recovery of subspace structures by low-rank representation. *Pattern Analysis and Machine Intelligence, IEEE Transactions on*, 35(1):171–184, 2013.

[22] G. Liu, Z. Lin, and Y. Yu. Robust subspace segmentation by low-rank representation. In *Proceedings of the 27th International Conference on Machine Learning (ICML-10)*, pages 663–670, 2010.

[23] G. Liu, H. Xu, and S. Yan. Exact subspace segmentation and outlier detection by low-rank representation. In *AISTATS*, pages 703–711, 2012.

[24] C. Lu, J. Tang, S. Y. Yan, and Z. Lin. Generalized nonconvex nonsmooth low-rank minimization. In *IEEE International Conference on Computer Vision and Pattern Recognition*. IEEE, 2014.

[25] Y. Ma, H. Derksen, W. Hong, and J. Wright. Segmentation of multivariate mixed data via lossy data coding and compression. *Pattern Analysis and Machine Intelligence, IEEE Transactions on*, 29(9):1546–1562, 2007.

[26] K. Mohan and M. Fazel. Iterative reweighted algorithms for matrix rank minimization. *The Journal of Machine Learning Research*, 13(1):3441–3473, 2012.

[27] B. Nasihatkon and R. Hartley. Graph connectivity in sparse subspace clustering. In *Computer Vision and Pattern Recognition (CVPR), 2011 IEEE Conference on*, pages 2137–2144. IEEE, 2011.

[28] A. Y. Ng, M. I. Jordan, Y. Weiss, et al. On spectral clustering: Analysis and an algorithm. *Advances in neural information processing systems*, 2:849–856, 2002.

[29] F. Nie, H. Huang, and C. H. Ding. Low-rank matrix recovery via efficient schatten p-norm minimization. In *AAAI*, 2012.

[30] S. Rao, R. Tron, R. Vidal, and Y. Ma. Motion segmentation in the presence of outlying, incomplete, or corrupted trajectories. *Pattern Analysis and Machine Intelligence, IEEE Transactions on*, 32(10):1832–1845, 2010.

[31] B. Recht, M. Fazel, and P. A. Parrilo. Guaranteed minimum-rank solutions of linear matrix equations via nuclear norm minimization. *SIAM review*, 52(3):471–501, 2010.

[32] B. Recht, W. Xu, and B. Hassibi. Null space conditions and thresholds for rank minimization. *Mathematical programming*, 127(1):175–202, 2011.

[33] J. Shi and J. Malik. Normalized cuts and image segmentation. *Pattern Analysis and Machine Intelligence, IEEE Transactions on*, 22(8):888–905, 2000.

[34] M. Soltanolkotabi, E. J. Candes, et al. A geometric analysis of subspace clustering with outliers. *The Annals of Statistics*, 40(4):2195–2238, 2012.

[35] R. Tron and R. Vidal. A benchmark for the comparison of 3-d motion segmentation algorithms. In *Computer Vision and Pattern Recognition, 2007. CVPR'07. IEEE Conference on*, pages 1–8. IEEE, 2007.

[36] R. Vidal. A tutorial on subspace clustering. *IEEE Signal Processing Magazine*, 28(2):52–68, 2010.

[37] R. Vidal and P. Favaro. Low rank subspace clustering (lrsc). *Pattern Recognition Letters*, 43:47–61, 2014.

[38] Y.-X. Wang and H. Xu. Noisy sparse subspace clustering. In *Proceedings of The 30th International Conference on Machine Learning*, pages 89–97, 2013.

[39] S. Xiang, X. Tong, and J. Ye. Efficient sparse group feature selection via nonconvex optimization. In *Proceedings of the 30th International Conference on Machine Learning (ICML-13)*, pages 284–292, 2013.

[40] J. Yan and M. Pollefeys. A general framework for motion segmentation: Independent, articulated, rigid, non-rigid, degenerate and non-degenerate. In *Computer Vision–ECCV 2006*, pages 94–106. Springer, 2006.

[41] J. Yang, W. Yin, Y. Zhang, and Y. Wang. A fast algorithm for edge-preserving variational multichannel image restoration. *SIAM Journal on Imaging Sciences*, 2(2):569–592, 2009.

[42] Z. Zhang and B. Tu. Nonconvex penalization using laplace exponents and concave conjugates. In *Advances in Neural Information Processing Systems*, pages 611–619, 2012.

[43] Y.-B. Zhao. An approximation theory of matrix rank minimization and its application to quadratic equations. *Linear Algebra and its Applications*, 437(1):77–93, 2012.

APPENDIX

A. PROOF

THEOREM A.1. *For $\mu > 0$ and $A \in \mathcal{R}^{m\times n}$, the following problem*

$$Z^* = \arg\min_{Z} F(Z) + \frac{\mu}{2}\|Z - A\|_F^2 \tag{30}$$

is solved by the vector minimization

$$\sigma^* = \arg\min_{\sigma\geq 0} f(\sigma) + \frac{\mu}{2}\|\sigma - \sigma_A\|_2^2, \tag{31}$$

so that $Z^* = Udiag(\sigma^*)V^T$ with the SVD of A being $Udiag(\sigma_A^*)V^T$.

PROOF. Let $A = U\Sigma_A V^T$ be the skinny SVD of A, then $\Sigma_A = U^T AV$. Denoting $X = U^T ZV$ which has exactly the same singular values as Z, we have

$$F(Z) + \frac{\mu}{2}\|Z - A\|_F^2 \tag{32}$$
$$= F(X) + \frac{\mu}{2}\|X - \Sigma_A\|_F^2, \tag{33}$$
$$= F(\Sigma_X) + \frac{\mu}{2}\|X - \Sigma_A\|_F^2, \tag{34}$$
$$= F(\Sigma_X) + \frac{\mu}{2}\left(\|X\|_F^2 + \|\Sigma_A\|_F^2 - 2\langle X, \Sigma_A\rangle\right), \tag{35}$$
$$\geq F(\Sigma_X) + \frac{\mu}{2}\left(\|\Sigma_X\|_F^2 + \|\Sigma_A\|_F^2 - 2\langle \Sigma_X, \Sigma_A\rangle\right), \tag{36}$$
$$= F(\Sigma_X) + \frac{\mu}{2}\|\Sigma_X - \Sigma_A\|_F^2, \tag{37}$$
$$= F(\Sigma_Z) + \frac{\mu}{2}\|\Sigma_Z - \Sigma_A\|_F^2, \tag{38}$$
$$= f(\sigma) + \frac{\mu}{2}\|\sigma - \sigma_A\|_2^2, \tag{39}$$
$$\geq f(\sigma^*) + \frac{\mu}{2}\|\sigma^* - \sigma_A\|_2^2. \tag{40}$$

In the above, (33) holds because the Frobenius norm is unitarily invariant; (34) holds because $F(X)$ is unitarily invariant; (36) is true by von Neumann's trace inequality; and (38) holds because of the definition of X. Therefore, (38) is a lower bound of (32). Note that the equality in (36) is attained if $X = \Sigma_X$. Because $\Sigma_Z = \Sigma_X = X = U^T ZV$, the SVD of Z is $Z = U\Sigma_Z V^T$. By minimizing (39), we get σ^*. Therefore, eventually we get $Z^* = Udiag(\sigma^*)V^T$, which is the minimizer of problem (30). □

B. THEOREM AND LEMMAS

THEOREM B.1. *[19] Suppose $F : \mathcal{R}^{m\times n} \to \mathcal{R}$ is represented as $F(X) = f \circ \sigma(X)$, and $f : \mathcal{R}^n \to \mathcal{R}$ is absolutely symmetric and differentiable, where $X \in \mathcal{R}^{m\times n}$ with SVD $X = Udiag(\sigma)V^T$, the gradient of $F(X)$ at X is*

$$\frac{\partial F(X)}{\partial X} = Udiag(\theta)V^T, \tag{41}$$

where $\theta = \frac{\partial f(y)}{\partial y}|_{y=\sigma(X)}$.

LEMMA B.1. *[1] For $\mu > 0$, and $K \in \mathcal{R}^{s\times t}$, the solution of the problem*

$$\min_L \mu\|L\|_1 + \frac{1}{2}\|L - K\|_F^2,$$

is given by $L_\mu(K)$, which is defined component-wisely by

$$[L_\mu(K)]_{ij} = max\{|K_{ij}| - \mu, 0\} \cdot sign(K_{ij}).$$

LEMMA B.2. *[41] Let H be a given matrix. If the optimal solution to*

$$\min_W \alpha\|W\|_{2,1} + \frac{1}{2}\|W - H\|_F^2$$

is W^*, then the i-th column of W^* is

$$[W^*]_{:,i} = \begin{cases} \frac{\|H_{:,i}\|_2 - \alpha}{\|H_{:,i}\|_2} H_{:,i}, & \text{if } \|H_{:,i}\|_2 > \alpha; \\ 0, & \text{otherwise.} \end{cases}$$

Interactive User Group Analysis

Behrooz Omidvar-Tehrani
Université Grenoble Alpes - LIG, CNRS
Grenoble, France
behrooz.omidvar-tehrani@imag.fr

Sihem Amer-Yahia
Université Grenoble Alpes - LIG, CNRS
Grenoble, France
sihem.amer-yahia@imag.fr

Alexandre Termier
University of Rennes 1, IRISA/INRIA
Rennes, France
alexandre.termier@irisa.fr

ABSTRACT

User data is becoming increasingly available in multiple domains ranging from phone usage traces to data on the social Web. The analysis of user data is appealing to scientists who work on population studies, recommendations, and large-scale data analytics. We argue for the need for an interactive analysis to understand the multiple facets of user data and address different analytics scenarios. Since user data is often sparse and noisy, we propose to produce *labeled groups* that describe users with common properties and develop IUGA, an interactive framework based on *group discovery* primitives to explore the user space. At each step of IUGA, an analyst visualizes group members and may take an action on the group (add/remove members) and choose an operation (exploit/explore) to discover more groups and hence more users. Each discovery operation results in *k most relevant and diverse groups.* We formulate group exploitation and exploration as optimization problems and devise greedy algorithms to enable efficient group discovery. Finally, we design a principled validation methodology and run extensive experiments that validate the effectiveness of IUGA on large datasets for different user space analysis scenarios.

Categories and Subject Descriptors: H.2.8 [**Database management**]: Database Application; Data Mining.
General Terms: Algorithms.
Keywords: User Data; Interactive Analysis; Validation.

1. INTRODUCTION

One of the major applications of data-driven research is the analysis of *user data*. User data is the conjunction of a profile made of several attributes (e.g., age, occupation, location), and of user interests via activity data (e.g., application usage on smartphones, researchers' publications, movie ratings, exercise and eating habits). Building *labeled user groups* instead of focusing on individual data enables new findings and addresses issues raised by the peculiarities of user data such as noise and sparsity.[1] The discovery of user groups bears similarities to the *redescription mining* problem [21]: one wants to find groups of users that have identical values for some profile attributes (e.g. *gender* = `female` $\wedge$ *country* = `US`) and that exhibit common activity data (e.g. *keywords* = {`databases, social networks`} and *publish_in* = {`WWW, VLDB`}). The large number of possible groups hinders user data analysis. In this paper, we advocate an exploratory navigation of the space of groups and develop IUGA, an interactive user data analysis framework that provides analysts with the ability to incrementally discover user groups efficiently.

There exist numerous approaches that could be used for the discovery of user groups, many of which are based on *pattern mining* such as frequent itemset discovery [2] or subspace clustering [1]. The main limitation of those approaches is that, on real data, they can output millions of labeled groups inside which it is hard to know a priori which ones are of interest to the analyst. To alleviate that, a large body of work has been dedicated to providing knowledgeable analysts with the ability to specify *constraints* on groups of interest [6, 7]. However, that is not adapted to exploratory scenarios where only limited knowledge is available on the dataset and the analyst does not necessarily know which subset of the data is of interest. The same argument applies to expressing queries on raw data, e.g. using SQL [10]. SQL being declarative in nature, it is difficult to use it to express an exploration scenario which is iterative in nature: e.g., finding a set of groups with a SQL query then asking to find "related" groups. Other work proposed to reduce the output of a pattern mining algorithm to a *representative pattern set* of limited size (typically tens of labeled groups) [23]. However, resulting groups may be too coarse and miss groups that contain users of interest. Group granularity may be reduced with parameter relaxation but the number of resulting groups is bound to increase and quickly become hard to manage by the analyst.

When faced with the daunting task of analyzing large amounts of user data, an analyst may have different goals in mind. In this paper, we focus on helping analysts find one or several users of interest by exploring relevant groups until she reaches her target users. More specifically, an analyst may want to *discover and gather several users* who may be scattered in different groups of interest. An analyst may also be interested in *finding a specific group member*, i.e., a user, for whom she remembers some but not all information. We illustrate these variants in the following two realistic examples.

EXAMPLE 1 (A MULTI-TARGET EXAMPLE). *Martin is a PC Chair looking to build a program committee formed by geographically distributed male and female researchers with different seniority levels and different expertise. Figure 1 shows a simplified scenario for the* WEBDB *2014*[2] *PC.*

As is often the case, PC chairs think of a set of potential members first. In this case, G. Fletcher, M. Theobald, S. Michel and X.

[1] *http://www.wired.com/2014/04/forget-the-quantified-self-we-need-to-build-the-quantified-us/; https://jawbone.com/blog/napa-earthquake-effect-on-sleep/*

[2] *http://webdb2014.eecs.umich.edu*

CIKM'15, October 19-23, 2015, Melbourne, VIC, Australia
 ISBN 978-1-4503-3794-6/15/10 ...$15.00
DOI: http://dx.doi.org/10.1145/2806416.2806519.

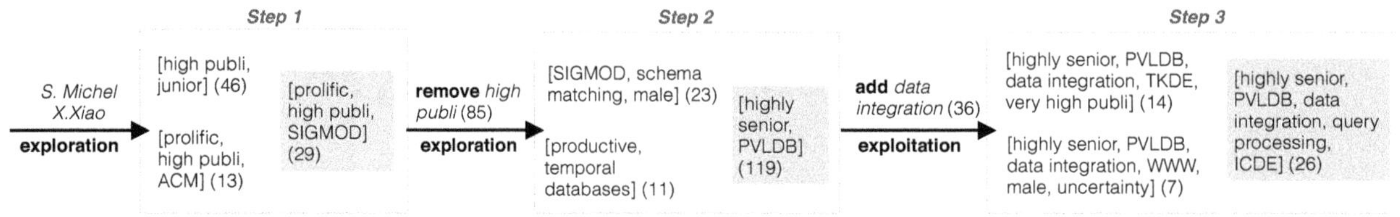

Figure 1: Discovering Several Users (WEBDB 2014 Program Committee)

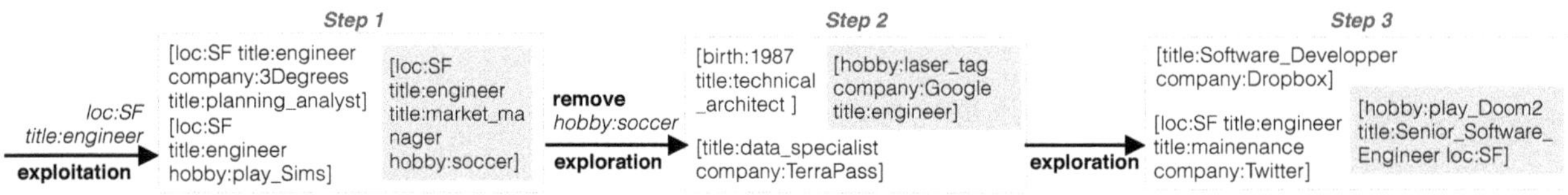

Figure 2: Finding a Specific User

Xiao are 4 initial members. Martin decides to use S. Michel and X. Xiao as seeds because they are junior and prolific (high frequency of annual publications). The action of keeping those 2 researchers is followed by an exploration which delivers 3 groups each of which containing one of S. Michel or X. Xiao (Step1). He then decides to keep the highlighted one: `prolific, high publications` *and publishing at* `SIGMOD` *(with which* WEBDB *is associated.) The selected group contains 29 researchers out of which 4 geographically distributed (L. Popa, A. Doan, M. Benedikt, S. Amer-Yahia). In order to find more users related to that group, Martin decides to perform an action that removes the predicate* `high publi`*, because it has been investigated before.*

Step 2 is explores the resulting group and outputs 3 diverse groups. Martin ignores the first group because he has already seen enough male candidates. He notices that the highlighted group contains 119 highly senior researchers who published in PVLDB (which is related to WEBDB*). Therefore, he decides to get more information about that group by first adding the predicate* `data integration` *to specialize it and asking to split it into 3 groups. Step 3 shows the result of this exploitation operation. In particular, the group labeled with* `query processing`, `PVLDB` *and* `ICDE` *contains 26 senior researchers out of which 8 are of interest to the PC chairs (J. Wang, F. Bonchi, K. Chakrabarti, P. Fratenali, D. Barbosa, F. Naumann, Y. Velegrakis and X. Zhou). At this stage, Martin covered 80% of the* WEBDB *PC.* □

EXAMPLE 2 (A SINGLE TARGET EXAMPLE). *Nicole liked a person she met at last night's party in Cole Valley, San Francisco, but she doesn't remember his name and has lost his phone number. She only knows that he lived in the same neighborhood as Mike, the party host, and works as an engineer. Nicole asks Mike to have access to his social network which contains some of his friends' information: job title(s), company, location, birth year, and hobby(ies).*

Mike is an avid Facebook user and has over 800 friends, most of which are computer engineers and live in San Francisco (SF). Thus no querying mechanism could lead Nicole directly to the person she is looking for. Also, advanced search tools (e.g., Facebook Graph Search[3]) can only show similar people based on an input query. Nicole needs a tool for her navigational analysis of Mike's friends. She first uses the query `loc:SF` *and* `title:engineer` *which returns 3 different user groups among Mike's friends that are highly related to her query (Step 1 in Figure 2). Nicole remembers that the person was talking about "website design", thus he shouldn't be working for* `3Degrees` *which is a renewable energy certificate provider. She also remembers that he mentioned he only likes "shooting" computer games thus he should not belong to the group labeled with* `Sims`*, a life simulation computer game. So she prefers to select the group labeled* `loc:SF`, `title: engineer`, `title:market manager` *and* `hobby: soccer` *as a seed. As Nicole doesn't remember any discussion about sports, she prefers to remove the attribute* `hobby:soccer` *to widen her navigation scope. The tool then finds 3 other groups in Step 2.*

Nicole is sure the person she met is at least 30 years old. This eliminates the first group with `birth:1987`*. Also, she herself works for* `TerraPass` *and knows the person does not work there. Also being a fan of shooting games, the group with* `hobby:laser tag` *and* `company:Google` *would be the best choice. Now, the tool returns 3 other user groups in step 3. The title "Senior Software Engineer" captures her attention as she remembers he said he was a manager. This group contains 3 users among whom Kevin Systrom, co-founder of Instagram and Mike's friend, is the one she was searching for.* □

Acknowledging the limitations of previous solutions, a recent line of work based on *interactive data mining* is being developed.[4] Such work is based on providing operations on the result of pattern mining in order to help the analyst navigate in the space of labeled groups and find groups and group members she is most interested in [5]. Existing work in this area is mainly a description of systems that have been designed to show the potential of interactive approaches. In this paper, we propose two important contributions to further advance the state of the art of interactive data mining with a focus on interactive user data analysis:

1. IUGA, a formalization of interactive user data analysis based on simple yet powerful *group discovery* primitives that enable an exploratory navigation of user groups.

2. A principled validation methodology. To the best of our knowledge, there exists no such methodology.

IUGA is *an optimization-based interactive framework where analysts are free to select any group of interest at each step and use it as a seed for further optimization.* It is based on 3 key principles:

[3] *https://www.facebook.com/graphsearcher*

[4] *http://poloclub.gatech.edu/idea2013/; http://poloclub.gatech.edu/idea2014/*

P1: The analyst must be able to explore different groups and not be overwhelmed with analysis options. The analysis process is broken into successive steps during which an analyst chooses a seed group, examines the users it contains, takes actions such as remove/add users, and continues with a group discovery operation.

P2: Groups offered to the analyst must be of high quality. The analysis process must help the analyst cover the space of groups of interest. We propose a "holistic" measure that finds k groups that are relevant to the seed group and are as diverse as possible.

P3: The train of thought of the analyst must not be lost. Each interactive group discovery step must be fast.

Our examples show that with simple group discovery operations, an analyst can navigate a good proportion of the space of users of interest. In this work, we formalize two such operations: *opExplore()* that finds groups *outside of the seed group*, and *opExploit()* that finds groups *inside*. The examples also show that before applying group discovery operations to a seed group, an analyst may want to transform that group using *actions* that remove or add specific users (in our example by modifying group labels).

Devising an efficient multi-step group discovery approach is a challenge due to the large number of available groups. We hence propose to formulate group exploration and exploitation as optimization problems that find relevant and diverse groups at each step of the interaction. Both operations discover k diverse groups that have some relevance to the seed group, i.e., users in common. In the case of exploration, diversity aims to cover *as many different users as possible* outside of the seed group. For exploitation, diversity aims to *cover the seed group* while providing *distinct options* inside that group. We show that both problems are NP-complete by reductions from the MAXIMUM EDGE SUBGRAPH PROBLEM and the MAXIMUM COVERAGE PROBLEM respectively. We design GROUPDISCOVERY, a greedy algorithm to solve those problems.

Our last challenge is to devise a principled methodology that validates the need for an interactive multi-step group discovery approach. In particular, since our focus is to solve the multi-target and single-target search questions, we validated IUGA on two real use cases, namely, Program Committee (PC) formation by building a dataset from DBLP, and a single target scenario by building a synthetic dataset. Our results show that IUGA leads analysts to their target(s) in a small number of steps regardless of their starting points and their level of expertise.

The outline of the paper is as follows: in Section 2 we give necessary definitions and formalize the GROUPDISCOVERY operations as well as the Interactive User Group Analysis problem. In Section 3 we describe the IUGA algorithm. Section 4 presents detailed experiments. The related work is provided in Section 5. Last, we conclude and give some perspectives for future work in Section 6.

2. MODEL AND PROBLEM DEFINITION

We model user data as a set of users $\mathcal{U}$, a set of items I, and a database D of tuples $\langle u, i\rangle$ where $u \in \mathcal{U}$ and $i \in I$. A tuple $\langle u, i\rangle$ represents the action of u (such as *authored*, *recorded*, *rated*, *purchased*, *tagged*, *voted*, etc.) on i.

Each user u is also described with attributes drawn from a set of attributes A representing demographics information such as *gender* and *age*. We refer to each attribute in A as a_i and to its values as v_j^i. The domain of values of attribute a_i is D_{a_i} with $D_A = \cup D_{a_i}$. For example, if we use a_1 to refer to *gender*, it takes two values v_1^1 and v_2^1 representing *male* and *female* respectively.

A large number of datasets could be modeled in this manner. In the case of scientists, items are conferences they publish in and keywords they contribute on. For online collaborative rating sites, items are movies or restaurants they rate. The choice of what constitutes a user attribute or a user action depends on the application and does not affect our problem and solution.

Due to the sparsity of user data, we propose to analyze it based on forming user groups and providing a framework to the analyst to discover groups in a step-by-step fashion. We first define the notion of user group followed by the GROUPDISCOVERY Problem and finally, IUGA, our interactive user data analysis framework.

DEFINITION 1. **User Group.** *A user group g, is a subset of $\mathcal{U}$ to which is associated a label $l_g = [P_g, I_g]$ where P_g is a conjunction of predicates on user attribute $(a_1 = v_j^1) \wedge \ldots \wedge (a_n = v_j^n)$, and $I_g \subseteq I$ a set of items. Each user in g must satisfy P_g and have an action on each item in I_g. More formally, $\forall u \in g, P_g$ is true and $\forall u \in g, \forall i \in I_g, \langle u, i\rangle \in D$.*

In the case of a movie rating site, the group of reviewers defined by the label [(*age*=`25`) ∧ (*occupation*=`student`), {`Terminator 2`, `The Matrix`}] is the set of 25-year old students who rated both movies. Similarly, [(*seniority*=`junior`) ∧ (*gender*=`female`) ∧ (*pub rate*=`productive`), {`Algorithms`, `Data Mining`}] is the set of junior young female researchers who are productive and have expertise in algorithms and data mining.

To simplify readability, we will use a simplified representation for labels in the remainder of the paper. For example, [(*age*=`25`) ∧ (*occupation*=`student`), {`Terminator 2`, `The Matrix`}] becomes [`25`, `student`, `Terminator 2`, `The Matrix`].

We use $\mathcal{G}$ to refer to the set of all user groups formed by predicates on A and items in I. $\mathcal{G}$ is very large even with a small number of attribute values and items.

2.1 Group Discovery Operations

We now introduce our formalization of group discovery operations and actions that form building blocks of IUGA. We first define the *exploration* operation that allows to "navigate the group space in an outward way" starting from a set of users, it discovers groups containing new users.

DEFINITION 2. **Group Exploration.** *We define a function $gExplore(U, \mathcal{G}, \mu)$ that takes a set of users $U \subseteq \mathcal{U}$ and finds all groups in $\mathcal{G}$ that overlap with U with at least μ, a given threshold. More formally, $gExplore(U, \mathcal{G}, \mu) = \{(g, overlap(U, g)) | g \in \mathcal{G} \wedge g \neq U \wedge overlap(U, g) \geq \mu\}$ where $overlap(U, g) = \frac{|U \cap g|}{|U \cup g|}$ (i.e. Jaccard similarity coefficient).*

The overlap condition provides a progressive exploration of the space, which helps the analyst build an understanding of the underlying data. Figure 1 illustrates several steps in IUGA used to build the WEBDB 2014 PC. At the beginning, the analyst (here a PC chair) has two "seed members" in mind: S. Michel and X. Xiao. She then performs an exploration step over these two researchers, which produces (among other) three groups: a group of 46 researchers labeled as [`junior`, `high publi`], a group of 13 researchers labeled as [`prolific`, `high publi`, `ACM`], and a group of 29 researchers labeled as [`prolific`, `high publi`, `SIGMOD`]. All these groups lead to different research communities, the third one is most adapted to a database workshop.

When an interesting group is found, another important operation is *exploitation*, i.e., an operation that "drills down" into the most interesting subgroups contained in a seed group.

DEFINITION 3. **Group Exploitation.** *We define a function $gExploit(U, \mathcal{G})$ that takes a set of users $U \subseteq \mathcal{U}$ and finds all groups* *in $\mathcal{G}$ that are contained in U. More formally, $gExploit(U, \mathcal{G}) = \{g \in \mathcal{G} | g \subseteq U\}$.*

Figure 1 shows the result of applying *gExploit()* on the group labeled [`highly senior`, `PVLDB`, `data integration`] (Step 3). That results in 3 subgroups: one formed by 26 experts in query processing who publish in ICDE, the other by 14 prolific researchers who publish in TKDE, and the last one by 7 male researchers who work on uncertainty in databases. All 3 groups contain solely highly senior researchers who publish in PVLDB and work in the area of data integration. This example clearly illustrates that 32 out of 36 users of the selected group are covered.

2.2 Group Discovery Problem

The discovery of new groups relies on the two functions, *gExplore()* and *gExploit()* (Definitions 2 and 3 respectively), that are applied to a seed set of users. In order to comply with principles **P1** and **P2**, the number of groups returned to the analyst at each step must be limited, and output groups must exhibit diversity. Hence, we define the GROUPDISCOVERY Problem as follows: given a set of users $U \subseteq \mathcal{U}$, an overlap threshold μ, the GROUPDISCOVERY Problem returns k groups in $\mathcal{G}$, referred to as $\mathcal{G}_U$ and is expressed either as an exploration or an exploitation problem depending on an analyst's needs.

For exploration, we define $opExplore(U, \mathcal{G}, \mu, k)$ that must satisfy the following conditions:

1. $\mathcal{G}_U \subseteq gExplore(U, \mathcal{G}, \mu)$
2. $|\mathcal{G}_U| = k$
3. $diversity(\mathcal{G}_U)$ is maximized.

where $diversity(\mathcal{G}_U)$ is defined as follows:
$diversity(\mathcal{G}_U) = \Sigma_{\{g_i, g_j\} \subseteq \mathcal{G}_U | g_i \neq g_j} (1 - overlap(g_i, g_j))$

In exploration, the aim is to start from a seed set of users of interest U, and find k groups that have some relevance to U, using $gExplore(U, \mathcal{G}, \mu)$, and that have maximal diversity (as little overlap as possible with each other).

For exploitation, we define $opExploit(U, \mathcal{G}, k)$ that must satisfy the following conditions:

1. $\mathcal{G}_U \subseteq gExploit(U, \mathcal{G})$
2. $|\mathcal{G}_U| = k$
3. $divCoverage(\mathcal{G}_U)$ is maximized.

where $divCoverage(\mathcal{G}_U)$ is defined as follows:

$$divCoverage(\mathcal{G}_U) = diversity(\mathcal{G}_U) \times (|\bigcup_{g \in \mathcal{G}_U} g| / |U|) \quad (1)$$

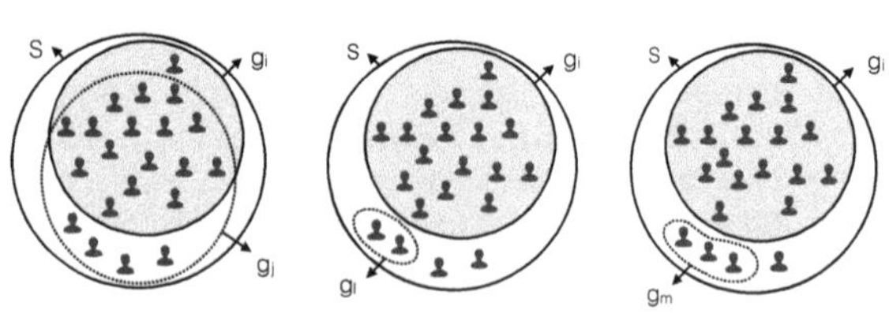

Figure 3: Illustrations of $diversity()$ and $divCoverage()$

In exploitation, the aim is to find k groups that maximize coverage of the seed set U. Choosing k groups that have the highest coverage may potentially cause high overlap between those groups. Figure 3 left illustrates that, with $k = 2$ and two highly overlapping groups g_i and g_j. Therefore, in the case of exploitation, we revisit the definition of diversity in a way that it prioritizes k diverse groups which cover as many users as possible in U. In [16], it is shown that there does not exist a unique optimal solution for both diversity maximization and coverage maximization. Therefore, the diversity formula is modified by adding $(|\bigcup_{g \in G_U} g| / |U|)$ (see Equation 1). For example, in Figure 3, $diversity(\{g_i, g_l\}) = diversity(\{g_i, g_m\}) = 1$. Thus for *opExplore()*, both g_l and g_m can be chosen with g_i. However, for *opExploit()*, g_m is preferred because $divCoverage(\{g_i, g_m\}) > divCoverage(\{g_i, g_l\})$.

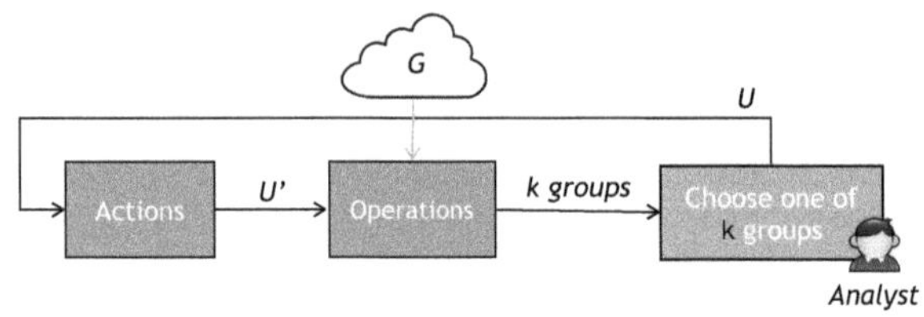

Figure 4: GROUPDISCOVERY within IUGA

2.3 Interactive User Group Analysis (IUGA)

IUGA builds on the GROUPDISCOVERY operations letting an analyst apply one of *opExplore()* or *opExploit()* on a set of users U and obtain k groups that constitute further analysis options. Figure 4 illustrates that process. In order to comply with principle **P3**, IUGA introduces a time limit parameter. Each step of IUGA solves the GROUPDISCOVERY Problem and returns the best possible k groups within a given time limit.

In addition to *opExplore()* and *opExploit()*, the analyst is provided with a set of actions that could be performed on a chosen group to transform it according to his/her needs. The analyst examines the set of k groups at each step and chooses a new seed group on which one of 3 actions could be performed: *actKeepUsers(U,U')*, *actModifyLabel(U,l)*, and *actUndo()* to undo the previous step. Table 1 summarizes each action. *actKeepUsers(U,U')* allows the analyst to mark which users to keep for the next step. *actModifyLabel(U,l)* is used to remove/add predicates or items to l_U, the label of U, resulting in new seed users.

Action	Description
actKeepUsers(U,U')	keeps U' users in U
actModifyLabel(U,l)	replaces l_U with a new label l
actUndo()	back-tracks to the previous step

Table 1: IUGA Actions

The ability to "manipulate group membership" using actions on a seed group, provides additional flexibility at each step. For example, as illustrated in Figure 1, in order to narrow down the set of 119 senior researchers who publish in PVLDB, the analyst adds the predicate `data integration` and obtains 36 researchers as the new seed set to analyze. Also in Figure 2, the analyst removes the predicate `hobby:soccer` to direct the navigation towards her preferences.

3. GROUP DISCOVERY ALGORITHM

Our GROUPDISCOVERY Problem requires to develop an efficient algorithm for dynamically finding and comparing user groups.

We have proved that GROUPDISCOVERY Problem is NP-complete by reductions from the MAXIMUM EDGE SUBGRAPH Problem [12] for *opExplore()* and from the MAXIMUM COVERAGE Problem [17] for *opExploit()*. Proofs are available in [19].

Our overall approach operates in two steps: an off-line process to produce initial user groups $\mathcal{G}$ and an online iterative process during which the analyst chooses a selected group for which k groups are discovered.

In the off-line process, a set of groups $\mathcal{G}$ are generated using the LCM closed frequent pattern mining algorithm [24] given a minimum support σ. Each frequent pattern corresponds to a user group, which has at least σ users. To feed LCM, we convert predicates in group labels into an item. For instance, the predicates (*gender* = `male`) and (*gender* = `female`) become two independent items. In addition, in order to speedup computing group relevance, we pre-compute an inverted index for each user group $g \in \mathcal{G}$ (as is commonly done in Web search). Each index $\mathcal{L}^g$ stores all other groups in $\mathcal{G}$ in decreasing order of their overlap with g. Thanks to the parameter μ, we only partially materialize the indices. In the case of datasets we used in our experiment, we only materialize in average 10% of the whole index size.

Algorithm 1 summarizes a single greedy procedure that solves the GROUPDISCOVERY Problem, be it exploration or exploitation. It is called at each step of IUGA (as described in Figure 4). The algorithm admits as input a user group g, an operation *op* (*gExplore()* or *gExploit()*), an overlap threshold μ, k, and a time limit $tlimit$, and returns the best k groups denoted $\mathcal{G}_g$. Line 1 selects the most overlapping groups with g by simply retrieving the k highest ranking groups in $\mathcal{L}^g$. Function $getNext(\mathcal{L}^g)$ (Line 2) returns the next group g_{in} in $\mathcal{L}^g$ in sequential order. Lines 3 to 11 iterate over the inverted indices to determine if other groups should be considered to increase diversity while staying within the time limit and not violating the overlap threshold with the selected group. Since groups in $\mathcal{L}^g$ are sorted on decreasing overlap with g, the algorithm can safely stop as soon as the overlap condition is violated (or if the time limit is exceeded).

Algorithm 1: GROUPDISCOVERY Algorithm

Input: $g \in \mathcal{G}$, *op*, μ, k, $tlimit$
Output: $\mathcal{G}_g$

```
1  G_g ← topk(L^g)
2  g_out ← getNext(L^g)
3  while (tlimit not exceeded ∧ overlap(g, g_out) ≥ μ) do
4      for g_in ∈ G_g do
5          if betterDiv(G_g, g_out, g_in, op) then
6              G_g ← replace(G_g, g_out, g_in)
7              break
8          end
9      end
10     g_out ← getNext(L^g)
11 end
12 return G_g
```

The algorithm then looks for a candidate group $g_{out} \in \mathcal{G}_g$ to replace in order to increase diversity. The boolean function $betterDiv()$ (Line 5) checks if by replacing g_{out} by g_{in} in $\mathcal{G}_U$, the overall diversity of the new $\mathcal{G}_U$ increases. Obviously, the diversity of a group set $\mathcal{G}_k$ depends on the operation *op*.

The number of diversity improvement loops (lines 3 to 11) is $|\mathcal{L}^g| = |\mathcal{G}|$ in worst case. For each group $g_{in} \in \mathcal{G}_g$, we verify if the diversity score is improved by $betterDiv()$, hence $\mathcal{O}(k^2)$. The time complexity of the algorithm is then $\mathcal{O}(k^2.|\mathcal{G}|)$.

Attribute	Description & Values
Seniority	Number of years since the author's first publication in DBLP with values "starting" (1 to 8), "junior" (9 to 12), "senior" (13 to 15), "highly senior" (16 to 21) and "confirmed" (22 and higher)
# publications	With values "very few" (3 to 14), "few" (15 to 28), "fair" (29 to 53), "high" (54 to 107) and "very high" (108 and higher)
Publication rate	Average number of publications per year with values "active" (0.18 to 1.47), "very active" (1.48 to 2.48), "productive" (2.49 to 3.71), "very productive" (3.72 to 6.0) and "prolific" (6.1 and higher)
Venues	set of all conferences and journals where the author published in, at least once
Topics	Set of topics extracted from the author's publications using the LDA topic model [4]
Gender	Based on matching the author's first name to an NLP resource with 54,915 names.[7]

Table 2: Researcher Attributes

4. EXPERIMENTS

Our experiments aim to validate the usability and efficiency of interactive analysis and the quality of discovered groups at each step. All experiments are implemented in C on a 2.4GHz Intel Core i5 machine with an 8GB main memory, running OS X 10.9.2.

Summary of Results: In our first experiments, we observe that IUGA leads a knowledgable analyst to cover most PCs of major data management conferences in 12 steps (multi-target scenario). We also show that IUGA arrives sooner to target than its competitors (single-target scenario). Our second experiment is a user study of the quality of groups found by GROUPDISCOVERY in each step of IUGA. We find that most participants prefer IUGA to other options mainly because it helps them better understand the landscape of user groups.

4.1 Datasets

We use 2 real datasets for our experiments: DM-AUTHORS and MOVIELENS and one synthetic dataset with the same characteristics as MOVIELENS. DM-AUTHORS and the synthetic dataset are used to validate the interactive analysis and MOVIELENS is used to validate group quality.

The MOVIELENS 1M dataset[5] contains 1,000,209 ratings of 3,952 movies by 6,040 users. For each user, gender, age-group, occupation and zip-code are also provided. DM-AUTHORS contains 4907 researchers who have at least 3 publications in WWW, KDD, SIGMOD, CIKM, ICWSM, EDBT, ICDM, ICDE, RecSys, SIGIR or VLDB. Authors were crawled in October 2014 from DBLP[6] for years between 2000 and 2014. For each researcher, we compute the attributes summarized in Table 2. Values of the first 3 attributes are discretized using equal-frequency binning [13].

Table 3 summarizes the real datasets. It contains the number of user groups ($|\mathcal{G}|$) with at least σ users. For DM-AUTHORS, σ is set to a very low value because smaller groups are of interest

[5] *http://www.grouplens.org/node/73*
[6] *http://dblp.uni-trier.de/db/*

	MovieLens	DM-Authors
# users	6,040	4,907
# items	3,952	11,890
# attributes	4	4
# predicates	80	18
avg index size $\lvert\mathcal{L}\rvert$	485	79,127
# groups $\lvert\mathcal{G}\rvert$	4,918	790,017
σ	450	3
μ	0.1	0.01

Table 3: Real Datasets

(e.g., 976 researchers are associated to `high publi` predicate, but only 28 researchers have published both in `WWW` and in `CIKM`). For MovieLens, we set σ to 7% of all users in order to obtain an adequate number of groups for our group quality validation. In both datasets, we set μ in a way that each group overlaps with 10% of groups in $\mathcal{G}$, hence pruning around 90% of inverted indices.

Our synthetic dataset is generated by initializing a binary matrix of users and items M with *0* and then randomly adding some initial groups $\mathcal{G}_{initial}$, i.e., rectangles in M that are completely filled with *1*. For each group in $\mathcal{G}_{initial}$, we randomize its number of users (between 10 and 2000) and items (between 5 and 50 items). Then we mark $\lvert\mathcal{G}_{target}\rvert$ groups as target. We mine M with a minimum support threshold σ to obtain the group set $\mathcal{G}$. More details are presented in Table 4. All parameters are chosen in a way to mimic MovieLens with a larger number of users.

# users	10,000	$maxlenght$	50
# items	3000	$tlimit$	20 ms
$\lvert\mathcal{G}_{target}\rvert$	50	σ	10
$\lvert\mathcal{G}_{initial}\rvert$	500	μ	0.06

Table 4: Synthetic Dataset

4.2 Interactive Analysis Validation

We validate the effectiveness of our interactive analysis IUGA by addressing the two motivating scenarios described in Section 1. We first verify the utility of IUGA for building a program committee on DM-Authors (multi-target). Then, we describe a thorough validation of IUGA using our synthetic dataset that mimics MovieLens (single-target). In both cases, *tlimit* is set to $20ms$.

4.2.1 Multi-Target Scenario

We study the effectiveness of IUGA with a realistic task of interactively building the PC of major conferences/workshops in data management. We first start with an experiment with many PCs then we delve into the details of WebDB 2014.

Summary of Many PCs.

Figure 6 illustrates the results of interactively building the PCs of the following conferences in 2014: SIGMOD, VLDB[8], WebDB and CIKM[9]. For a given PC, we start from 5% of its members and use IUGA to find the remaining ones. Target PC members should be discovered in user groups proposed in different steps of IUGA. The figure reports the number of steps to discover 50% and 80% of PC members as the average of 50 runs of IUGA for each PC.

We can observe that any PC selection can be done in 12.04 steps on average. CIKM's PC is the hardest to discover and WebDB's the easiest. Our conjecture is two key factors influence that: PC *size* and PC *diversity*. Indeed, the PCs of VLDB, CIKM and SIGMOD contain over 100 members while WebDB is smaller. This is why the former require a higher number of steps to cover 50% of their members (6.7, 6.5 and 5.9 steps respectively). In addition, the average pairwise Jaccard similarity[10] between PC members of CIKM is 7.35 . This high diversity results in more steps to reach 80% of their PCs (8.3 and 8.1 steps respectively). SIGMOD has the least heterogeneous PC which leads to 4.8 steps to reach 80% of its PC.

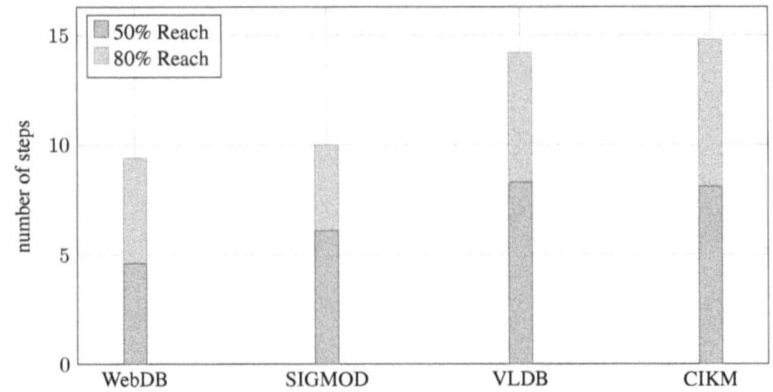

Figure 6: Number of Steps in IUGA for PC Selection

Focus on one PC.

We now have a closer look to the WebDB 2014 PC selection. Our detailed illustration will show the following facts: **F1**: how the analysis of user groups is more useful than analyzing individual users; **F2**: how our actions and operations (defined in Section 2) are *adequate* and *necessary* in interactive analysis; **F3**: which users are reachable or not, depending on their similarity to other users; **F4**: how *relevance* and *diversity* contribute to the analysis.

We characterize different scenarios based on the *analyst's expertise* and the analysis *starting points*. We assume 5 virtual analyst summarized in Table 5. To measure the effect of expertise, we consider two cases where the analyst is *knowledgeable* about PC selection and the case where she is *a novice PC chair*. We also examine different starting points to build the PC: a subset of the final PC, a subset of the previous year's PC (i.e., WebDB 2013), or a set of arbitrary researchers outside the PC. Figure 6 shows that the average number of steps to cover 80% of the PC is 9.4. At each analysis step, $k = 3$. Figures 7 and 8 illustrate the results. Notation is simplified by replacing *actKeepUsers()* with **keep** and *actModifyLabel()* with **add/remove**.

Scenario	Analyst	Starting Point
KnowIn	Knowledgeable	Inside WebDB 2014
KnowOut	Knowledgeable	Outside WebDB
Know13	Knowledgeable	Inside WebDB 2013
NonExpertIn	Non-expert	Inside WebDB 2014
NonExpertOut	Non-expert	Outside WebDB

Table 5: Validation Scenarios

In the KnowIn scenario (Figure 7), a knowledgeable analyst starts with a subset of the final PC, i.e., G. Fletcher, M. Theobald, S. Michel, and X. Xiao, and selects the last two as a seed group (because they are prolific young researchers with a high number of publications.) Exploring this group results in 3 groups out of

[8] *We only considered* Review Board *members for VLDB*

[9] *We only considered the* knowledge management *track for CIKM*

[10] *Computed based on the profile of researchers containing attributes defined in Section 4.1.*

Figure 5: Word Frequency Cloud for Jian Li (left) and the Whole WEBDB 2014 PC (right)

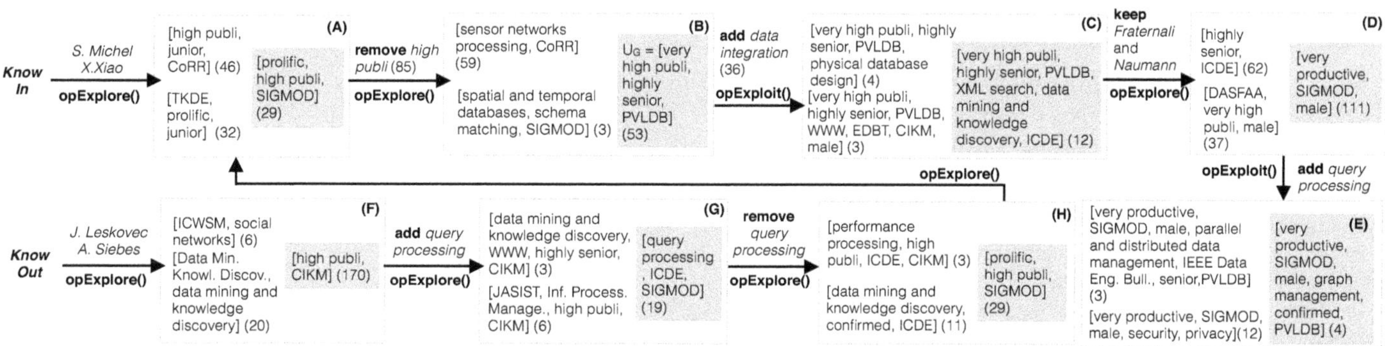

Figure 7: Scenarios KNOWIN (top) and KNOWOUT (bottom)

which the one labeled with SIGMOD (the conference that hosts WEBDB) contains 4 researchers of interest (L. Popa, A. Doan, Benedikt and S. Amer-Yahia). This already shows the advantage of user group analysis (fact **F1**) where in one single step, 4 PC members are retrieved. The analyst then uses *actModifyLabel()* to replace the predicate `high publi` with `data integration` (i.e., the WEBDB main theme in 2014) and decides to exploit the resulting group. In step D, the analyst keeps only P. Fraternali and F. Naumann among 12 group members using *actKeepUsers()* action. This action makes it easier to reach groups containing items like SIGMOD (P. Fraternali and F. Naumann have 9 and 6 SIGMOD publications respectively) and ICDE (e.g., F. Naumann has 14 ICDE publications). This shows the necessity of actions, confirming fact **F2**. Up to step E, the analyst is able to find 14 out of 15 PC members. The missing PC member is Jian Li. We compare Li's word cloud in Figure 5 containing all his publication title words, conferences and journals, with the cloud for all WEBDB 2014 PC members. This shows that Li's research areas differ significantly. This is an observation of the fact **F3** that shows the limitation of interactive analysis.

In KNOWOUT (Figure 7), the knowledgeable analyst starts with J. Leskovec and A. Siebes, two researchers outside the final WEBDB PC. The *opExplore()* operation first finds k related groups that expand possible candidates. In step H, the analyst encounters the same group as in step A of scenario KNOWIN. This shows that in this case, a knowledgeable analyst only needs 2 more steps to reach relevant groups from a random departure point. Step H is also an illustration of fact **F4** and shows that all 3 returned groups are *relevant* and *diverse* leading the analyst to pick the group labeled with SIGMOD.

We verified another scenario KNOW13 where the analyst starts from a subset of the WEBDB 2013[11] PC which has 10 researchers in common with 2014. Due to lack of space, we do not illustrate it. We observed that KNOW13 is very similar to KNOWIN.

In NONEXPERTIN (Figure 8), we consider a junior PC. The aim is to observe the effect of *analyst expertise* by comparing this scenario with KNOWIN. We will see that in the case of poor expertise, the analysis is done mostly by exploration. We also observe a tendency to manipulate group labels rather than group membership (specific researchers in groups). The analyst starts with 4 given researchers and applies *opExplore()* to expand the analysis scope. The analyst finds a group of 138 researchers labeled with `query processing`, SIGMOD and ICDE, and decides to expand that group by removing `query processing`. The analyst then navigates up to step L, where she does not find any helpful group. Thus she commands an *actUndo()* action. Up to step O, she finds 12 out of 15 PC members. Compared to KNOWIN, the number of useless steps (without any PC member discovery) has increased.

Finally, in NONEXPERTOUT, we examine the case where a non-expert analyst starts with researchers outside the final PC. In this scenario, the analyst may abandon a path and start again with different groups. She may need to repeat that until a satisfying starting point is found. In our experiment, a non-expert analyst jumps 4 times to land at step K, the first step of NONEXEPERTIN.

4.2.2 Single-Target Scenario

The previous experiment showed how effective our interactive analysis is in building a program committee by "gathering" members of interest along the way during the analysis. In this experiment, we focus on validating the effectiveness of IUGA in finding a single target as described in Example 2 in Section 1. We use our synthetic dataset that was generated to scale up MOVIELENS. Our dataset is a matrix M with 3×10^7 cells, where squares with at least 10 users (i.e., minimum support σ) filled with 1, represent user groups. We propose a measure called AVERAGE TARGET AR-

[11] *http://webdb2013.lille.inria.fr*

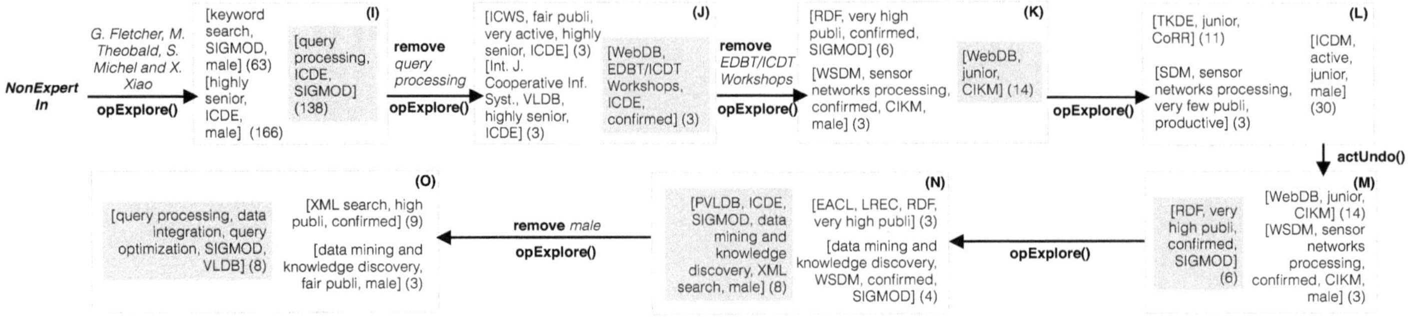

Figure 8: Scenario NONEXPERTIN

RIVAL (ATA), i.e., the average number of iterations to reach a group containing a target group starting from a non-target group. We randomly mark 50 groups as targets and compute ATA for those groups (we refer to target groups as $\mathcal{G}_{target}$). We compare IUGA with two different baselines: *unsupervised* and *interactive*. Briefly, if m_1 and m_2 are two different methods and ATA(m_1) < ATA(m_2), then m_1 is considered faster. Note that the concept of ATA differs significantly from finding the shortest path. For the latter, we assume the starting and target points are known, while this is not the case in the interactive analysis.

Algorithm 2: Experimental ATA Protocol $ATAalg$

Input: $\mathcal{G}$, $\mathcal{G}_{target}$, k, μ, g, len, $method$, $maxlen$
Output: length of navigation path
if $g \in \mathcal{G}_{target}$ **then return** len
if $len > maxlen$ **then return** *-1* // lost path
$\mathcal{G}_k \leftarrow choose(opExplore(g, \mathcal{G}, \mu, k, method), opExploit(g, \mathcal{G}, k, method))$
foreach $g \in \mathcal{G}_k$ **do**
  $ATAalg(\mathcal{G}, \mathcal{G}_{target}, k, \mu, g, len + 1, method, maxlen)$
end

Algorithm 2 illustrates how ATA is computed. We designed 200 different sessions each of which has a different synthetic dataset and is repeated 100 times for each method. Hence, we compute 20,000 ATA values for each one of the interactive analysis methods we defined. For a random group g_{rnd}, k groups are returned using *method*, and a random choice between *opExplore()* and *opExploit()* (the algorithm starts always with an *opExplore()). Each of* the k groups becomes the new seed. This depth-first recursive call terminates either when one group in $\mathcal{G}_{target}$ is found or when a path of length 50 has been built (*maxlength* in Table 4). These recursive calls form paths inside the group space. A path is called *valid* if its last group belongs to $\mathcal{G}_{target}$. The ATA is computed as the average of valid path lengths for each method.

Unsupervised Baseline Comparison.

This experiment compares IUGA to a variant of k-MEANS with *Jaccard* as the distance measure. k-MEANS is the representative of offline clustering algorithms with a constraint on the number of clusters (k). At each step, both IUGA and k-MEANS return k groups while respecting *timelimit*. Any number of iterations is allowed for k-MEANS within *timelimit*. We then report ATA for both methods. For k-MEANS, we randomly add/remove attributes at each step i so that a new set of k clusters is obtained in step $i+1$. Presence or absence of an attribute changes the clusters' membership, as the *Jaccard* distance between users varies. For instance, adding a specific value of `age` reduces the distance between two users having the same age.

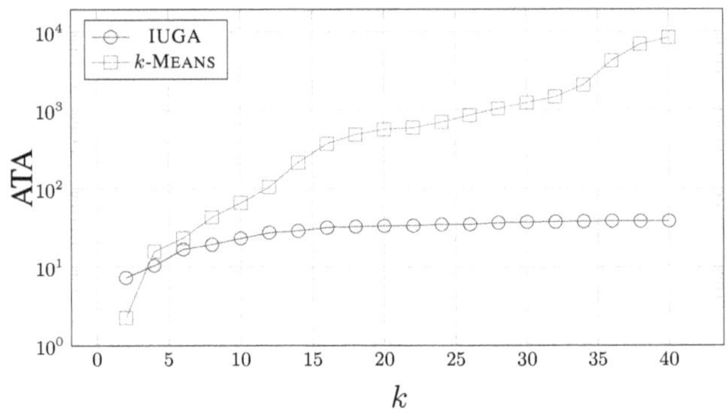

Figure 9: IUGA **Comparison with Clustering Algorithm**

Figure 9 illustrates ATAs for IUGA and k-MEANS in log scale. We vary k from 2 to 40 and observe how ATA for both algorithms evolves. While k-MEANS performs better for very small values of k, IUGA outperforms it by two orders of magnitude for higher values of k. When k is very small, clusters are huge. Thus most of the time, there exists a cluster that contains all users of a target group. For larger values of k, more clusters with smaller size are generated and more steps are needed to finally reach the target. We can conclude that the superiority of IUGA over unsupervised methods comes from the use of diversity at each step in order to cover as many users as possible.

Interactive Analysis Baseline Comparison.

We compare IUGA with some interactive analysis baselines: DIVRAND, RANDOM, EXHAUSTIVE and ILP. At each step, DIVRAND randomly generates as many sets of k groups as possible within *tlimit* and returns the one with the highest diversity. RANDOM navigates randomly in the space of groups and does not respect *tlimit*. EXHAUSTIVE generates all possible k among n groups in $\mathcal{G}$, i.e., $C\binom{n}{r}$ and chooses the one with the highest diversity. ILP returns k groups with maximal diversity using an integer linear programming formulation (using CHOCO 3.0 solver[12]).

Table 6 illustrates ATA and execution times for IUGA and optimal methods. Since both EXHAUSTIVE and ILP generate optimal paths, their ATA are very close. However, their execution times are different. This experiment shows that IUGA is faster than EX-

[12] *http://choco-solver.org/?q=Choco3*

HAUSTIVE and ILP (3.49 minutes faster than ILP) while maintaining a comparable ATA.

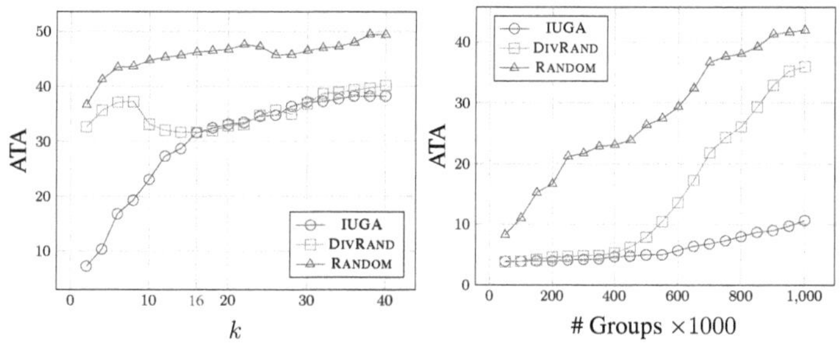

Figure 10: ATA as a Function of k and # Groups

Figure 10 illustrates ATA for all heuristic-based methods: IUGA, DIVRAND and RANDOM by varying k from 2 to 40, and varying # groups from 50,000 to 1,000,000. Optimal methods (EXHAUSTIVE and ILP) do not terminate for this experiment. In general, we observe that IUGA has much lower ATA for $k \leq 16$ and $k \geq 30$. This simply shows that considering relevance and diversity at each step reduces ATA by an average of 15.91 steps.

	EXHAUSTIVE	ILP	IUGA
ATA	9.90	9.91	10.13
Time (sec)	862.47	213.12	3.35

Table 6: IUGA vs Optimal Methods

For $k \in [16, 30]$, DIVRAND and IUGA have close results. This shows that although the *relevance* component, i.e., the difference between DIVRAND and IUGA, is shown to be very useful in general, it is less effective for large values of k. In [5, 25], it is shown that in a context with too many options and no hint for further navigation, *long* jumps are preferred to *short* jumps. In our case, *relevance* tends to favor *short* directed jumps in the space of groups while DIVRAND does not. This is why when few options are available, IUGA performs better and DIVRAND performs as well as IUGA for larger values of k. In another research[13], it has been shown that people faced with numerous choices, whether good or bad, find it difficult to stay focused on a task. Choosing a small value of k is hence better both for performance and effectiveness.

We observe that increasing the number of groups has a huge effect on DIVRAND. When the number of groups increases, the target groups are more likely to be diverse. Thus, precision (ratio of valid paths over all navigated paths) decreases for all methods, while thanks to relevance, the decrease is negligible for IUGA.

4.3 Quality of Discovered Groups

Our last experiment focuses on a single step of IUGA by evaluating the quality of obtained groups at each iteration of GROUPDISCOVERY. We ask participants in a user study to compare the top 5 groups obtained by GROUPDISCOVERY with some competitive methods. We use MOVIELENS because people are usually familiar with movies and their attributes. We setup a questionnaire which was answered anonymously by 35 participants. The evaluation consists of a *comparative evaluation* where results of competitive methods are evaluated together, and an *individual evaluation* where each set of top 5 groups is evaluated separately.

[13] *Too many choices (good or bad) can be mentally exhausting: http://phys.org/news127404469.html*

In the comparative evaluation, we compare the top-5 groups obtained by GROUPDISCOVERY with those returned by 4 baselines: *Largest Groups*, *Most Overlapping*, *Least Overlapping* and *Most Concise* (groups which have the shortest description). Those baselines were designed using interestingness measures commonly used in pattern evaluation [14]. Each question contains an input group (e.g. [`Total Recall`, `Star Wars IV`] in MovieLens dataset) and sets of top-5 groups corresponding to each method. Participants chose the method that offers the most satisfying top-5 groups. Also, participants were instructed to select a justification for their preferred method: *it helps better understand who does what*, *it helps to discover new users*, *it helps to discover new group labels*.

Figure 11 illustrates the average percentages of responses for each analysis option. In this part, participants have mostly preferred the results of GROUPDISCOVERY followed by *Most Concise* groups. Also, they have mostly justified their responses as *it helps better understand who does what* (52.75%). The choice of *Most Concise* groups reveals that people prefer groups with short labels.

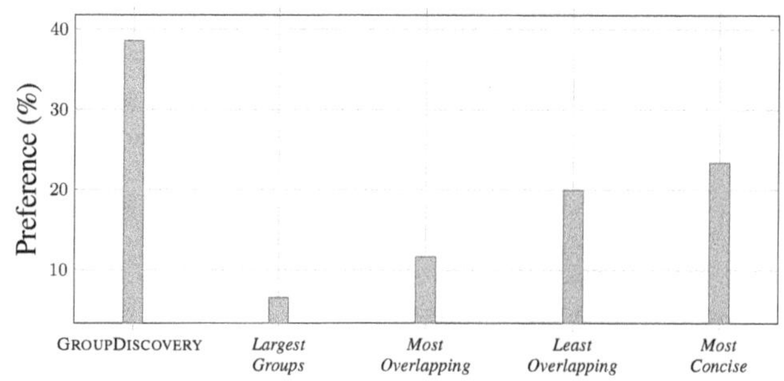

Figure 11: User Preference Results for Set Evaluation

In the *individual* evaluation, we compare each of top 5 groups of GROUPDISCOVERY with *Most Overlapping* and *Least Overlapping* groups, i.e. two extremes. Participants have preferred groups of GROUPDISCOVERY in 51.79% of cases, *Most Overlapping* in 33.12% and *Least Overlapping* in 15.09%. They justified their responses as follows: *Justification 1*: *understand the selected group*, *Justification 2*: *discover new users* or *Justification 3*: *understand the whole data*. Whenever our solution was selected, *Justification 1* was chosen by 56% of participants on average, followed by *Justification 2* (34.22%). In general, 63% of participants mentioned that their preferred group helps better understand the selected group (*Justification 1*), followed by 28% who believe the preferred group helps discover new users (*Justification 2*).

5. RELATED WORK

To the best of our knowledge, no approach has proposed and formalized an interactive group analysis framework. Recent studies [14] have shown an interest in reporting statistics about pre-defined groups, as opposed to our work where we look to discover users. Our work does relate to a number of others in functionality, interactivity/visualization and diversity.

Constrained-based Mining: IUGA bears similarity to constrained mining [6, 7], but the latter heavily relies on the analyst having some knowledge about the underlying data to be able to formalize constraints, as opposed to our data-driven work where relevant and diverse options are suggested to the analyst.

Interactive and Visual Analysis: Interactive pattern analysis approaches [3, 5] focus on learning the subjective measure in the

[14] *http://blog.testmunk.com/how-teens-really-use-apps/*

mind of the analyst to guide pattern exploration. For example, ONECLICK [5] is a personalized interactive navigation approach that learns an interestingness function based on patterns that were *liked* or *unliked* by the analyst in previous steps. In IUGA, we adopt an approach based on exploration or exploitation and let the analyst choose which operation to apply at each step. The ability to *personalize* the navigation as in ONECLICK is an interesting direction for future work. Semi-automatic PC construction has been addressed in [8]. The proposed approach requires the definition of *quality* and *cost* values for each researcher. This is a subjective and challenging task that assumes full knowledge of researchers' profiles which is not always the case in out analysis tasks.

While visualization [22, 18] and interactive exploration differ in focus, there exist a few efforts that combine both. Few examples are data mining suites like RAPIDMINER, KNIME, and MIME [15]. These approaches develop a toolbox to manipulate and visualize patterns according to preferences specified by the analyst at each step. In MIME, analysts can refine discovered patterns on the fly by selecting additional items. These methods do not provide semantics for exploration or exploitation nor do they rely on an optimization framework to cover the space of patterns.

Diversity: Diversity is a widely studied subject that finds its roots in Web search with a goal similar to ours. In [9], the concept of diversity in text retrieval and summarization is introduced to balance document relevance and novelty. Most approaches fall into two cases: *content-based* (e.g. [9]) and *intent-based* [11]. Our algorithm, GROUPDISCOVERY, is based on a greedy approach similar to content-based diversification.

6. CONCLUSION

We introduced IUGA, the first interactive user data analysis framework that is based on a simple and intuitive optimization formulation: the GROUPDISCOVERY Problem that finds the k most diverse and relevant user groups a seed group. IUGA relies on two group discovery operations: exploration and exploitation. We prove the hardness of our problem and devise greedy algorithms to help analysts navigate in the space of groups and reach one or several target users. Our extensive experiments on real and synthetic datasets show the utility of relevance and diversity in group discovery and in finding users of interest in different scenarios. We are currently pursing two improvements: (i) expressing group discovery as a multi-objective optimization problem and (ii) incorporating the *abstraction* operator defined in [20] to better summarize found groups.

Acknowledgments. Parts of this research was supported by grants PEPS FAAAWS and ANR-13-CORD-0020.

7. REFERENCES

[1] R. Agrawal, J. Gehrke, D. Gunopulos, and P. Raghavan. *Automatic subspace clustering of high dimensional data for data mining applications*, volume 27. ACM, 1998.

[2] R. Agrawal, T. Imielinski, and A. N. Swami. Mining association rules between sets of items in large databases. In *SIGMOD*, pages 207–216, 1993.

[3] M. Bhuiyan, S. Mukhopadhyay, and M. A. Hasan. Interactive pattern mining on hidden data: a sampling-based solution. In *CIKM*, pages 95–104, 2012.

[4] D. M. Blei, A. Y. Ng, and M. I. Jordan. Latent dirichlet allocation. *the Journal of machine Learning research*, 3:993–1022, 2003.

[5] M. Boley, B. Kang, P. Tokmakov, M. Mampaey, and S. Wrobel. One click mining: Interactive local pattern discovery through implicit preference and performance learning. *IDEAS (ACM SIGKDD Workshop)*, 2013.

[6] F. Bonchi, F. Giannotti, A. Mazzanti, and D. Pedreschi. Exante: Anticipated data reduction in constrained pattern mining. In *PKDD*, pages 59–70, 2003.

[7] C. Bucila, J. Gehrke, D. Kifer, and W. M. White. Dualminer: a dual-pruning algorithm for itemsets with constraints. In *Knowledge Discovery and Data Mining*, pages 42–51, 2002.

[8] C. C. Cao, J. She, Y. Tong, and L. Chen. Whom to ask?: jury selection for decision making tasks on micro-blog services. *VLDB*, 2012.

[9] J. G. Carbonell and J. Goldstein. The use of MMR, diversity-based reranking for reordering documents and producing summaries. In *Research and Development in Information Retrieval*, pages 335–336, 1998.

[10] U. Cetintemel, M. Cherniack, J. DeBrabant, Y. Diao, K. Dimitriadou, A. Kalinin, O. Papaemmanouil, and S. B. Zdonik. Query steering for interactive data exploration. In *CIDR*, 2013.

[11] O. Chapelle, S. Ji, C. Liao, E. Velipasaoglu, L. Lai, and S.-L. Wu. Intent-based diversification of web search results: metrics and algorithms. *Information Retrieval*, 14(6):572–592, 2011.

[12] U. Feige, G. Kortsarz, and D. Peleg. The dense k-subgraph problem. *Algorithmica*, 29(3):410–421, 2001.

[13] N. Friedman, M. Goldszmidt, et al. Discretizing continuous attributes while learning bayesian networks. In *ICML*, pages 157–165, 1996.

[14] L. Geng and H. J. Hamilton. Interestingness measures for data mining: A survey. *ACM Computing Surveys (CSUR)*, 38(3):9, 2006.

[15] B. Goethals, S. Moens, and J. Vreeken. Mime: A framework for interactive visual pattern mining. In *PKDD*, 2011.

[16] P. Indyk, S. Mahabadi, M. Mahdian, and V. S. Mirrokni. Composable core-sets for diversity and coverage maximization. In *ACM SIGMOD SIGART*, pages 100–108. ACM, 2014.

[17] D. S. Johnson. Approximation algorithms for combinatorial problems. In *Proceedings of the fifth annual ACM symposium on Theory of computing*, pages 38–49. ACM, 1973.

[18] A. Leuski and J. Allan. Strategy-based interactive cluster visualization for information retrieval. *International Journal on Digital Libraries*, 3:170–184, 2000.

[19] B. Omidvar-Tehrani, S. Amer-Yahia, and A. Termier. Interactive user group analysis. Research Report RR-LIG-048, LIG, Grenoble, France, 2015.

[20] B. Omidvar-Tehrani, S. Amer-Yahia, A. Termier, A. Bertaux, E. Gaussier, and M.-C. Rousset. Towards a framework for semantic exploration of frequent patterns. *IMMoA*, 2013.

[21] L. Parida. Redescription mining: Structure theory and algorithms. In *In Proc. AAAI'05*, pages 837–844, 2005.

[22] C. K. sang Leung, P. P. Irani, and C. L. Carmichael. WiFIsViz: Effective Visualization of Frequent Itemsets. In *ICDM*, 2008.

[23] A. Siebes, J. Vreeken, and M. van Leeuwen. Item sets that compress. In *SDM*, volume 6, pages 393–404. SIAM, 2006.

[24] T. Uno, M. Kiyomi, and H. Arimura. Lcm ver. 2: Efficient mining algorithms for frequent/closed/maximal itemsets. In *FIMI*, 2004.

[25] R. West and J. Leskovec. Automatic versus human navigation in information networks. In *ICWSM*, 2012.

Viewability Prediction for Online Display Ads

Chong Wang
Information Systems Dept.
New Jersey Institute of Technology
Newark, NJ 07102, USA
cw87@njit.edu

Achir Kalra*
Forbes Media
499 Washington Blvd
Jersey City, NJ 07310
akalra@forbes.com

Cristian Borcea
Computer Science Dept.
New Jersey Institute of Technology
Newark, NJ 07102, USA
borcea@njit.edu

Yi Chen
School of Management
New Jersey Institute of Technology
Newark, NJ 07102, USA
yi.chen@njit.edu

ABSTRACT

As a massive industry, display advertising delivers advertisers' marketing messages to attract customers through graphic banners on webpages. Advertisers are charged by ad serving, where their ads are shown in web pages. However, recent studies show that about half of the ads were actually never seen by users because they do not scroll deep enough to bring the ads in-view. Thus, the ad pricing standards are shifting to a new model: ads are paid if they are in view, not just being served. To the best of our knowledge, this paper is the first to address the important problem of ad viewability prediction which can improve the performance of guaranteed ad delivery, real-time bidding, as well as recommender systems. We analyze a real-life dataset from a large publisher, identify a number of features that impact the scroll depth for a given user and a page, and propose a probabilistic latent class model that predicts the viewability of any given scroll depth for a user-page pair. The experiments demonstrate that our model outperforms comparison systems based on singular value decomposition and logistic regression, in terms of prediction quality and training time.

Categories and Subject Descriptors

H.3.5 [**Information Storage and Retrieval**]: Online Information Services—*Commercial services, Web-based services*

General Terms

Algorithms, Performance, Economics, Experimentation, Human Factors

*Author is also with the Computer Science Department, New Jersey Institute of Technology, USA.

CIKM'15, October 19–23, 2015, Melbourne, Australia.
 ISBN 978-1-4503-3794-6/15/10 ...$15.00.
DOI: http://dx.doi.org/10.1145/2806416.2806536.

Keywords

Computational Advertising; Viewability Prediction; User Behavior

1. INTRODUCTION

Online display advertising has emerged as one of the most popular forms of advertising. Studies [16] show that display advertising is generating earnings of over $63.2 billions in 2015. Online advertising involves a publisher, who integrates ads into its online content, and an advertiser, who provides ads to be displayed. Display ads can be seen in a wide range of different formats and contain items such as text, images, Flash, video, and audio. A typical display ad is shown in Figure 1: an advertiser, e.g., Audi, pays a publisher, e.g., Forbes, for space on webpages to display a banner during page views in order to attract visitors that are interested in its products. A page view happens each time a webpage is requested by a user and displayed in a browser. One display of an ad in a page view is called an ad impression, and it is considered the basic unit of ad delivery. For instance, one view of the page in Figure 1 contains one ad impression.

Figure 1: An Example of Display Ads

Advertisers pay for ad impressions with the expectation that their ads will be viewed, clicked on, or converted by users (e.g., the ad results in a purchase). Traditional display ad compensation is mainly based on user clicks and conversion, because they bring direct profits to the advertisers. Much research has been done for predicting click rate and conversion rate [7, 20], bid optimization [25], auctions [6], and audience selection [13].

Recently, there is growing interest by advertisers to use online display ads to raise brand awareness and to promote the visibility of the company and their products. Indeed, users like to purchase products from the brands that they recognize and trust. Display ads can create emotional experience that gets users excited about a brand and builds trust. However, users do not typically click this type of ads, rendering the traditional form of pricing structure based on clicks or conversion to be ineffective.

To address this problem, another pricing model, which pays ads by the number of impressions that a publisher has served, has become popular in the display advertising market. However, a recent study [10] shows that more than half of the impressions are actually not viewed by users because they do not scroll down a page enough to view the ads. Low viewability leads to ineffective brand promotion.

Therefore, a new pricing model is emerging: pricing ads by the number of impressions that can be *viewed* by a user, instead of just being served [18]. This avoids the frustration of advertisers, who are concerned about paying for ads that were served but not seen by users.

Not surprisingly, ads placed at different page depths have different likelihood of being viewed by a user [9]. Therefore, it is important to predict the probability that an ad at a given page depth will be shown on a user's screen, and thus be considered as *viewed*. The vertical page depth that a user scrolls to is defined as the scroll depth. Many web analytics platforms, e.g., Google Analytics, provide plugins to measure user scroll depth.

Viewability prediction is important for many applications: *Guaranteed impression delivery.* One of main ad selling methods is guaranteed delivery, in which advertisers contract publishers to buy guaranteed advertising campaigns. The contracts may fix the number of impressions, targeting criteria, price, etc. As the industry moves toward transacting on viewable impressions, advertisers may propose contracts that specify the number of impressions that will be viewed. Predicting ad viewability helps publishers to fulfill such contracts by placing the ads in the right impressions.

Real-time impression bidding. Advertisers can also buy impressions through real-time bidding. Given the impression context, including the user, the page, and the ad position, advertisers desire to know the probability that the ad will be in-view. Based on the viewability, advertisers can adjust the bidding price for an impression and improve ad investment effectiveness. Specifically, they can bid higher for impressions with high predicted viewability. In addition, publishers can also benefit from ad viewability prediction by adjusting the minimum prices for impressions which are offered for bidding.

Webpage layout selection. With the ad pricing standards shifting to ad viewability, viewability will become a crucial factor in page layout design, which may impact ad revenue [8]. Publishers are exploring personalized page layouts that can balance ad viewability and user experience. For example, if a user will not scroll deep, the ad slot at the bottom may be moved higher, while considering the impact on user experience.

Recommender Systems. Dwell time (i.e., the time a user spends on a page) has been regarded as a significant indicator of user interest. Recommender systems can also employ scroll depth prediction as another critical metric of user interest.

In this paper, we study the problem of predicting the probability that a user scrolls to a page depth where an ad may be placed, thus the ad can be *in-view*. To the best of our knowledge, this is the first work that tries to address viewability prediction.

Scroll depth viewability prediction is challenging. First, most users visit only several webpages on a website. It is challenging to detect user interests based on such a sparse history of user-page interaction. Second, it is challenging to select significant webpage and user features related to user scrolling. Intuitively, page topics and user interests are regarded as influential factors. But it is non-trivial to explicitly model these features. Naturally, we may resort to latent models that utilize latent features. However, a commonly used latent model, Singular Value Decomposition (SVD), is not suitable to give probabilistic predictions on a full spectrum of scroll depths. Specifically, an SVD model can be trained with data consisting of users, pages, and whether a certain scroll depth is in-view in individual page views, and then be used to predict the viewability for that specific scroll depth. But one SVD has to be trained for each possible scroll depth. Another option is to train an SVD model with data consisting of users, pages, and the maximum page depth that a user scrolls to on a page. The predicted maximum page depth can help give a binary decision for any given scroll depth (i.e., in-view or not), but it cannot give a probabilistic value for a scroll depth to be in-view, which is important to determine pricing. As a webpage typically have multiple ad slots at different page depths (and sometimes ad positions may be even dynamically determined), it may be costly to build one SVD model for every single depth.

In this paper, we first analyze a real-life dataset from a large publisher to understand user scrolling behavior. Then, in order to find out how probable a specific user is to scroll to any given page depth, we propose a viewability prediction model based on the probabilistic latent class model (PLC). Our model utilizes latent user classes and webpage classes as well as an observed scroll distribution to overcome the data sparsity issue. The output of the model is the probability that a given scroll depth is in view. Compared with a binary decision, i.e. in-view or not, a probabilistic output is very useful in optimization problems, e.g., page layout selection.

PLC has been experimentally compared with three systems: SVD, Logistic Regression (LR), and a deterministic method. The experiments show that, on average, PLC achieves a higher F1-score for both in-view and not in-view classes than the other systems. PLC has also a significantly lower prediction error than the comparison systems. Also, unlike LR and SVD, one trained PLC model can predict the viewability of any scroll depth. Thus, PLC is less costly. In addition, PLC can make predictions fast enough to be usable in real-time. Finally, PLC works well for different training datasets, with a 10-day window resulting in the optimal balance between training time and prediction accuracy.

To the best of our knowledge, this is the first work that studies the problem of ad viewability prediction. Our contribution is summarized in the following: 1) We define the problem of viewability prediction for any scroll depth. 2) We present an empirical study of scrolling behavior using a real-life dataset. 3) We propose a novel statistical model based on PLC to predict the probability that a scroll depth will be in view. (4) We demonstrate experimentally that PLC outperforms three comparison systems.

The rest of the paper is organized as follows. Section 2 discusses the related work. Section 3 presents the results and analysis of the empirical study for scroll behavior, and describes the proposed PLC model for viewability prediction. Experimental results and insights are presented in Section 4. The paper concludes in Section 5.

2. RELATED WORK

Researchers have investigated scrolling behavior and viewability for webpage usability evaluation. In [22, 17, 9], the authors discovered that users spend more time looking at information on the upper half of the page than the lower half. Also, the distribution of the percentage of content viewed by users follows a normal distribution, which is also observed in our data presented in Section 3. We differ from these works in our main goal, which is viewability prediction.

Existing work [2, 12] collects scrolling behavior and uses it as an implicit indicator of user interest to measure the quality of webpage design and content. In contrast, we design an algorithm to predict the scrolling behavior for any user-webpage pair.

Several studies have attempted to predict user browsing behavior, including click [7, 21, 5, 1] and dwell time [15, 23]. For click prediction, one important application is sponsored search, i.e., ads are selected based on user queries submitted to the search engine and shown along with the search results. Chen et al. [7] propose a factor model to predict if an ad shown together with search results at a specific position will be clicked on. However, this prediction is made for a given position and a query-ad pair, but does not consider the individual user as a factor. In contrast, our method makes predictions that are tailored for individual users and pages.

Wang et al. [21] learn user's click behavior from server logs in order to predict if a user will click an ad shown for the query. The authors use features extracted from the queries to represent the user search intent. In our case, search queries, which can explicitly reflect user interest, are not available. Most of the work on click prediction [5, 1] is done on the advertiser side, based on high-dimensional features about users (e.g., private profiles), ad campaigns (e.g., ad content), and impression context. However, such data is not accessible at the publisher side. Our goal is to use the publisher data to predict page viewability.

For dwell time prediction, Liu et al. [15] fit the dwell time data with Weibull distributions and demonstrate the possibility of predicting webpage dwell time distribution from page-level features. Yi et al. [23] predict dwell time through Support Vector Regression, using the context of the webpage as features. Both methods do not consider individual user characteristics, an important factor of scrolling prediction.

In summary, there is no existing research attempt to predict the maximum scroll depth of a user/page pair and to predict ad viewability. In addition, existing methods for user behavior prediction cannot be easily adapted to solve the scroll depth prediction problem.

3. VIEWABILITY PREDICTION

In this section, we formally define the research problem, present the analysis of user scrolling behavior using a dataset from a large publisher which reveals several features that impact the scroll depth, and finally describe our novel viewability prediction model.

3.1 Problem Definition

Let us first introduce several important concepts used in the problem definition: 1) The *scroll depth* is the percentage of a webpage content vertically scrolled by a user. 2) The *maximum scroll depth* of a page view is how far down the page the user has scrolled during that view. The maximum scroll depth that a user u will scroll on a webpage a is denoted as x_{ua}. 3) The *target scroll depth*, denoted as X, is the page depth whose viewability an advertiser or publisher wants to predict. For instance, a publisher wants to predict the probability that an ad is in-view in a page view. In this case, the target scroll depth can be the percentage of the webpage that contains at least half of the ad. [1]

Our problem is to estimate how likely a user will be to scroll down to a target scroll depth of a webpage. Specifically, the prediction should be personalized to individual users and webpages. The proposed approach is a supervised learning technique. The inputs of the training module are historical user logs that contain the context of page views. The output is our viewability prediction model. The inputs of the prediction model are a target page depth X and a given pair of user u and webpage a, while the output is the viewability probability of X in the page view.

Problem Definition. *Given a page view, i.e., a user u and a webpage a, our goal is to predict the probability that the max scroll depth, denoted by x_{ua}, will be no less than X, i.e., $P(x_{ua} \geq X|u, a)$.*

3.2 Real-Life Dataset

We use a proprietary dataset collected over one and a half months on a large publisher's website. It contains more than 1.2 million page views and 100 thousand unique users. The dataset consists of logs of user browsing behavior captured via Javascript events. These scripts send the data to a server. This type of client-side approach accurately captures users' behavior even in multi-tabbed modern browsers [23].

The scroll depth is recorded according to the last row of pixels on users' screens. In this paper, we adopt 1% as the minimum unit of scroll depth; thus, the range of scroll depth is from 0% to 100%. Once a user stops scrolling and stays at a position for one second, the scroll depth is recorded in the user log. Figure 2 shows an example, in which the bottom of the user screen is at the 50% of the whole page. Thus, the scroll depth at the moment is 50%.

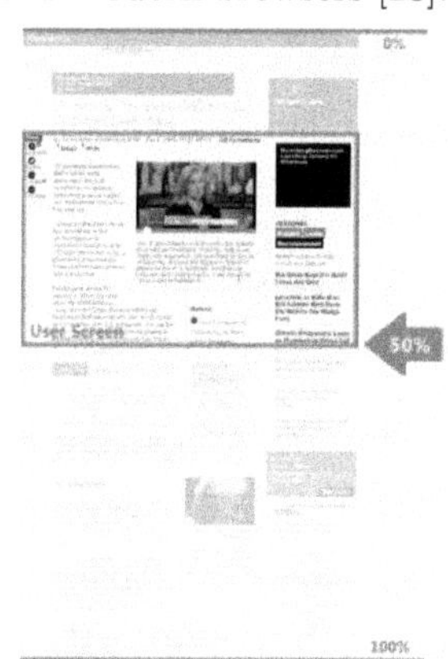

Figure 2: An Example of a Scroll Depth

The user log of this project includes user IDs, URLs, user agents, user geo-locations and maximum scroll depths of page views. Individual users are identified by cookies. Table 1 shows some of the important attributes captured in the log. Each row corresponds to a page view. For instance, the max scroll depth of the first page view is 72% and that of the second page view is 66%.

Figure 3 illustrates the distribution of max scroll depths in our user log. We observe that the distribution of the max scroll depth generally follows a normal distribution. It can also be noticed that there are very few page views whose

[1]This is in line with the definition suggested by the Interactive Advertising Bureau: a viewable display ad impression requires that a minimum of 50% of pixels be in-view for a minimum of 1 second. We do not consider the one second in-view duration.

Table 1: Example of User Log

User ID	IP	URL	Max Scroll Depth	GMT Time
001	1.3.4.5	/abc	72%	11/23/2014 11:00:00
002	7.6.9.2	/bcd	66%	11/23/2014 11:01:33

scroll depths are less than 10%. The main reason is that the the top 10% of most webpages can be loaded on the first screen, especially on desktops. In this case, the viewability of the first 10% of webpages is almost always 1. Therefore, in this research, we mainly focus on the viewability prediction for the page depths greater than 10%.

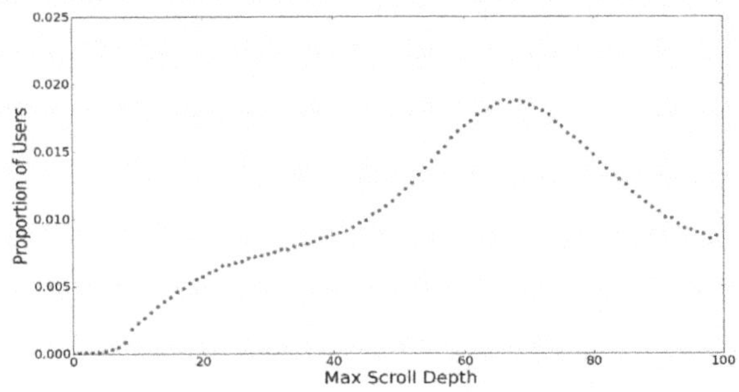

Figure 3: The Distribution of Max Scroll Depth

3.3 Features Impacting the Max Scroll Depth

We analyzed the dataset to understand which log attributes influence the scroll depth the most, with the aim of selecting these attributes as features in our prediction model.

3.3.1 Scroll Depth vs. Device Type

The reason that we adopted page percentage, rather than pixels, as a measure of scroll depth is because it provides a relative measure independent of device types (i.e., different devices have different screen sizes). If a user reads 50% of a page on a mobile device, while another user reads 50% of the same page on a desktop, it can be assumed that they read the same content of the page. However, this does not deny a hypothesis that devices may affect user behavior which may further influence the max scroll depth. For instance, when reading on mobile phones, users may not have enough patience and may leave the page with little scrolling.

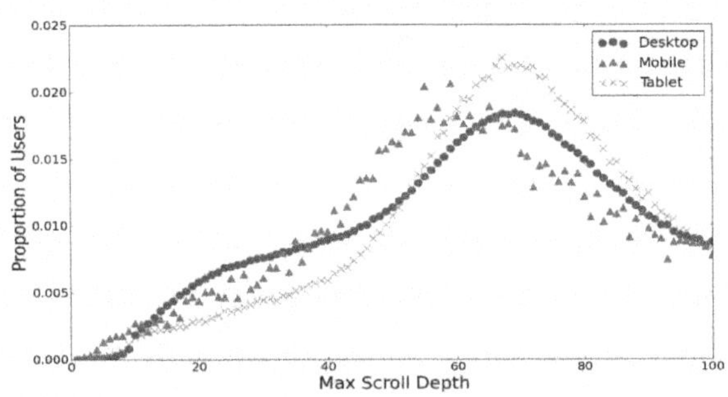

Figure 4: Distribution of Max Scroll Depth across Devices

Figure 4 illustrates the distribution of the max scroll depth across multiple devices, i.e., desktop, mobile/phone, and tablet. The device type is detected from the user agent attribute. The average max scroll depth is highest on the tablets (65.7%), followed by desktops (61.6%), and mobiles (60.2%). The possible reasons for the overall similar results across devices are: 1) The publisher's webpages are displayed in a mobile-friendly manner; 2) Flicking fingers on the screen is as easy as scrolling the wheel of a mouse [14]. Finally, we notice that mobiles, as expected, have certain page views with max scroll depth under 15%. This is very rare for desktops. The reasons for such low percentages are: 1) some pages are very long on the mobiles; 2) users close the browser tabs with loaded pages before they view these pages or stop loading the pages before they are shown, in which case the max scroll depth is zero. Although generally similar, the results exhibit a number of differences, and thus we consider the device type as a feature in our model.

3.3.2 Scroll Depth vs. Geo-location

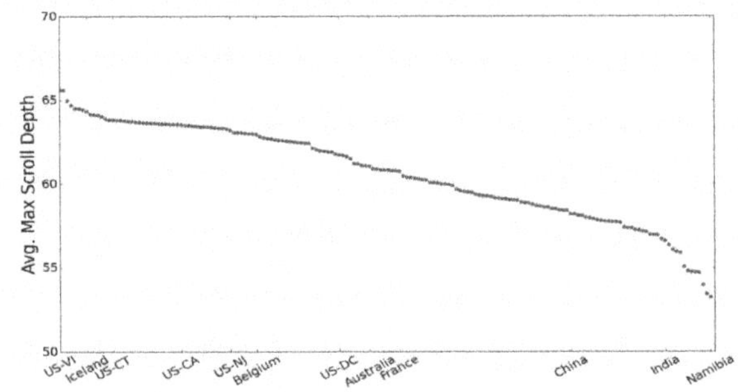

Figure 5: Average Max Scroll Depth as a Function of User Geo-location

Our user log records the countries from which the visitors connect and the US states if the visitors are from US. We filtered out the locations with sample page view sizes less than 1000. Figure 5 shows that most of the top 50 locations for max scroll depth are US states. Interestingly, visitors from U.S. Virgin Islands (65.62%) view pages the deepest, followed by New York State (65.60%) and Texas (65.49%). On the other hand, user from Namibia read the least (53.23%). In addition to user interests and reading habits, user geo-locations may also determine the connection speed, the distance from the publishers' host servers, etc. These factors, independent of users and webpages, may directly play a role on how users engage with the content. Since user geo-location is a significant factor, we consider it in our prediction model.

3.3.3 Scroll Depth vs. Day of the Week

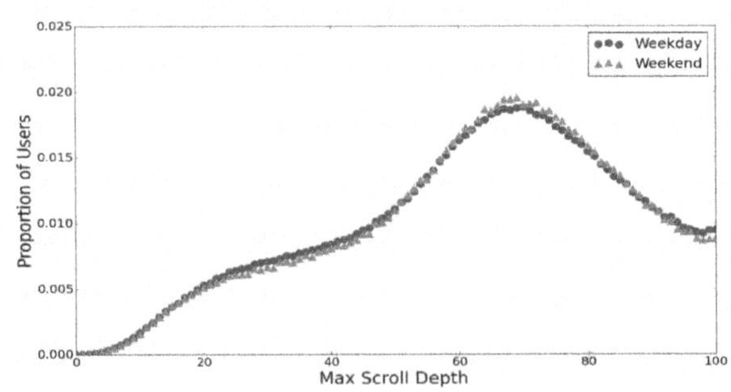

Figure 6: Distribution of Max Scroll Depth for Week Days

The day of the week and hour of the day are calculated using the local time of the user which is inferred from the user's IPs and the GMT time in the user log. Figure 6 shows that the day of the week does not have a significant impact on the scroll depth. This result contradicts past research [24] which revealed that the day of week determines the impression volume. Thus, we do not consider the day of the week in the prediction model.

3.3.4 Scroll Depth vs. Hour of the Day

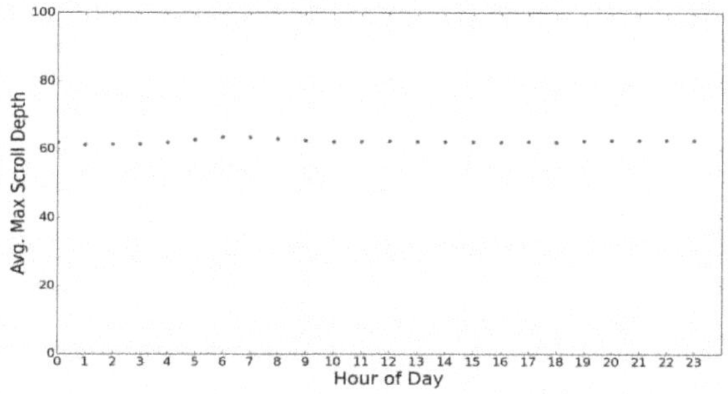

Figure 7: Distribution of Max Scroll Depth of Different Hours of the Day

One plausible hypothesis is that users may scroll deepest in the evening, after work. However, surprisingly, Figure 7 demonstrates that users seemingly perform very similar at different hours of the day. Thus, the hour of the day is not a significant factor to predict max scroll depth.

3.4 Max Scroll Depth Prediction Model

Our primary task is to infer the max scroll depth of a page view, x_{ua}, where u is the user and a is the webpage.

It is intuitive that the characteristics of individual users and webpages can be utilized to improve the performance of max scroll depth prediction models. For example, users who prefer to scroll far down on most webpages would have a higher probability to scroll down the current page. Also, features such as the ones identified in Section 3.3 (i.e., device type and geo-location) are easy to be modeled.

However, some other significant features are very hard to be captured due to lack of data and the ambiguity of user-webpage interaction. For example, pages with popular content and good design may motivate users to scroll more. But accurately modeling topic popularity and design is difficult. Other examples include user interest and psychology. Therefore, depending solely on explicit features will not lead to an accurate prediction.

In addition to feature modeling, data sparsity is another challenge. While a large publisher usually has tens of thousands of webpages, one user only visits several. Likewise, one page may be visited by a small subset of the entire user population. As a result, the user-page interaction employed in prediction could be extremely large and sparse, which brings about challenges in the prediction performance. A widely-used solution is grouping similar users and similar webpages together and inferring the prediction for a user/page pair using the known data of similar user/page pairs.

To overcome these issues, we use a latent class model [4, 3] to discover classes of users and webpages. Specifically, we build a probabilistic latent class model (PLC). The intuition behind PLC is that different latent classes of webpages and users tend to generate different levels of max scroll depths. PLC can detect classes of users and webpages that share similar patterns of max scroll depth. The class membership of each user and webpage are learned from the user log. PLC outputs the probability $P(x_{ua}|u,a)$, where x_ua is the max scroll depth that a user u reaches in a page a.

In addition, PLC incorporates our finding that max scroll depths of page views follow a normal distribution, as shown in Figure 3. Particularly, given a latent user class and a webpage class, we specify the outputted max scroll depth to follow a normal distribution by modeling the conditional probability as the probability density function of the normal distribution. Formally, PLC works as follow:

$$P(x_{ua}|u,a) = \sum_{i=1}^{N_s}\sum_{j=1}^{N_p} P(s_i|u)P(p_j|a)P(x_{ua}|s_i,p_j) \quad (1)$$

where x_{ua} is the max scroll depth of a page view. N_s is the number of latent user classes, and N_p is the number of latent webpage classes. Both N_s and N_p are pre-defined as model parameters. The optimal values for these parameters can be explored by cross validation. $P(s_i|u)$ is the probability that user u belongs to the latent user class s_i, while $P(p_j|a)$ is the probability that webpage a belongs to the latent webpage class p_j. The last term, $P(x_{ua}|s_i,p_j)$, represents the probability that the max scroll depth of the page view is x_{ua}, given the latent user class s_i and webpage class p_j.

As mentioned above, the last term can be approximated by the probability density function of the normal distribution (Equation 2).

$$P(x_{ua}|s_i,p_j) = \frac{1}{\sigma_{s_ip_j}\cdot\sqrt{2\pi}} * \exp\left(-\frac{(x_{ua}-\mu_{ua})^2}{2\sigma_{s_ip_j}^2}\right) \quad (2)$$

The right side of Equation 2 is developed based on the probability density function of a normal distribution, i.e., $\frac{1}{\sigma\sqrt{2\pi}}\cdot\exp(-\frac{(x-\mu)^2}{2\sigma^2})$. The mean of the distribution, μ_{ua}, can be modeled by a regression whose features are extracted from the history of u and a as well as the context of the page view, i.e., $\mu_{ua} = \sum_m^M w_{spm} f_m^{ua}$. f_m^{ua} is the mth feature and w_{spm} is the weight of the mth feature. Each pair of latent user class s_i and latent webpage class p_j has a set of $w_{s_ip_j*}$ and $\sigma_{s_ip_j}$. M is the total number of the features.

Based on the observations presented so far, we consider seven features:

- User Features:
  1) The mean max scroll depth of all page views of u. This feature captures user browsing habits.
  2) The most recent three max scroll depths of u. This feature captures the recent scroll behavior of the user.
- Webpage Features:
  3) The mean max scroll depth of a by all users. This feature captures the overall popularity of the webpage.
  4) The most recent three max scroll depths of page views of a. This feature captures the recent scroll behavior for this webpage.
- Interaction of User and Webpage:
  5) Interaction of the mean max scroll depth of u and that of a, i.e., the product of features 1 and 3. This is a commonly-used method in statistics to capture the joint effect of two input variables, i.e., for a particular user and a page, the scrolling behavior depends on both.
- Page View Context:
  6) User geo-locations, which were shown to be important by our analysis of the dataset.[2]

[2]There are 172 locations in our dataset. The number of dimensions are reduced to 20 by Principal Component Anal-

7) Device Type (i.e., desktop, mobile, or tablet), also shown to have a certain relevance by our analysis.

These features are used to train the normal distribution of each pair of latent user class s_i and webpage class p_j. Let $\mathbf{W}$ be the collection of the weight vectors w_{sp*} of all latent user classes s and webpage classes p. $\boldsymbol{\sigma}$ is the collection of the standard deviations σ_{sp*} of all latent user classes s and webpage classes p. Specifically, the features help to iteratively determine $\mathbf{W}$ and $\boldsymbol{\sigma}$.

In Equation 1 and 2, there are several parameters ($P(s|u)$, $P(p|a)$, $\mathbf{W}$, $\boldsymbol{\sigma}$). They can be calculated by maximizing the following likelihood function:[3]

$$l\left(P(s|u), P(p|a), \mathbf{W}, \boldsymbol{\sigma}\right) =$$
$$\sum_{u,a} \log\left(\sum_{i=1}^{N_s}\sum_{j=1}^{N_p} P(s_i|u)P(p_j|a)P(x_{ua}|s_i,p_j)\right) \quad (3)$$

Maximizing equation 3 determines the set of parameters. To maximize it, we adopt the Expectation Maximization (EM) algorithm, which is is widely used to solve the maximum-likelihood parameter estimation problem. The EM algorithm performs an expectation step (E-step) and a maximization step (M-step) alternatively. The E-step creates a function for the expectation of Equation 3. This function, i.e., Equation 4, is evaluated using the current estimates of the parameters. The initial values of the parameters are randomly generated.

$$P(s_i, p_j|u, a, x_{ua}) =$$
$$P(s_i|u)P(p_j|a)\cdot\frac{1}{\sigma_{s_ip_j}\cdot\sqrt{2\pi}}\cdot$$
$$\exp\left(-\frac{(x_{ua}-\sum_m^M w_{s_ip_jm}f_m^{ua})^2}{2\sigma_{s_ip_j}^2}\right) \quad (4)$$

The M-step updates the parameters in Equation 4, which can maximize Equation 3. The M-step updates the value of each parameter based on the result of the E-step of each iteration. The updated $w_{s_ip_j}{}^*$ of each iteration in Equation 7 can be determined by Limited-memory BFGS (L-BFGS), an optimization algorithm in the family of quasi-Newton methods. Equation 8 is the closed form of standard deviation of normal distributions.

$$P(s_i|u)^* \propto \sum_{p,a} P(s_i,p|u,a,x_{ua}) \quad (5)$$

$$P(p_j|a)^* \propto \sum_{s,u} P(s_j,p|u,a,x_{ua}) \quad (6)$$

$$w_{s_ip_j*}^* \propto \underset{w_{s_ip_j}}{argmax}\{-\sum_{u,a} P(s_i|u)P(p_j|a)\cdot$$
$$[\frac{(x_{ua}-\sum_m^M w_{s_ip_jm}f_m^{ua})^2}{2\sigma_{s_ip_j}^2} + \log\sigma_{s_ip_j} + \log\sqrt{2\pi}]\} \quad (7)$$

$$\sigma_{s_ip_j}^* \propto \sqrt{\frac{\sum_{ua} P(s_i|u)P(p_j|a)(x_{ua}-\sum_m^M w_{s_jp_jm}f_m^{ua})^2}{\sum_{ua} P(s_i|u)P(p_j|a)}} \quad (8)$$

The EM iterations stop if the max ratio defined below is not greater than a pre-defined threshold, which is set to 10^{-3} in our experiments. For each m in M,

$$\left|w_{s_ip_jm,t} - w_{s_ip_jm,t-1}\right| / w_{s_ip_jm,t} < 10^{-3} \quad (9)$$

After convergence, the PLC model with the optimal parameters can predict $P(x_{ua}|u,a)$, i.e., the probability of any target max scroll depth x_{ua} of a user/webpage pair. Section 3.5 uses this probability to predict the viewability of any target scroll depth. Similarly, this model can be applied to recommender systems, as mentioned in Section 1. The predicted max scroll depth x_{ua} reflects the interest of the user u in the webpage a.

3.5 Viewability Prediction for a Target Scroll Depth

Given a target scroll depth X and a user/webpage pair, the trained PLC model computes the probability that the max scroll depth will be X, i.e., $P(x_{ua} = X|u,a)$. As stated in the problem definition, the goal of this project is to predict the probability that a given scroll depth will be in view, i.e., $P(x_{ua} \geq X|u,a)$. Therefore, we integrate $P(x_{ua}|u,a)$ from X to 100%, as shown in Equation 10. The result is the probability that the max scroll depth of the page view will be greater or equal to the target scroll depth X. This means the max scroll depth x_{ua} is at a page percentage no less than X. The upper bound of the max scroll depth is 100%, i.e., the bottom of a page.

$$P(x_{ua} \geq X|u,a) = \int_X^{100\%} P(x_{ua}|u,a)dx_{ua} \quad (10)$$

4. EXPERIMENTAL EVALUATION

4.1 Experiment Datasets

To evaluate the proposed method, we use Forbes' user browsing log as described in Section 3. The user log is split into three sets of training and testing data, as shown in Table 2. This was done to avoid bias. The experimental results are reported by taking the average over the the three sets. On average, there are 31K+ unique users who generated 300K+ page views in a 10 days training set and 23K+ page views in a 2 days testing set. We run the experiments on a computer with Intel Core i7 3.6GHz and 32GB of memory.

Table 2: Training and Test Data Partitioning

Set#	Training Data (10d)	Testing Data (2d)
1	11/01/2014-11/10/2014	11/11/2014-11/12/2014
2	11/13/2014-11/22/2014	11/23/2014-11/24/2014
3	11/25/2014-12/04/2014	12/05/2014-12/6/2014

4.2 Comparison Systems

We compare the performance of the proposed model (PLC) with three other system described below: a deterministic method, a logistic regression (LR) system, and a singular value decomposition (SVD) system. implement several comparison systems. PLC and LR are implemented in Java, while SVD is built in C++. We use MongoDB to store pre-processed user logs.

ysis (PCA). We also tried feature hashing, which generates similar performance.

[3]Since Equation 2 is an exponential function, we do a log transformation in the likelihood function in order to approximate the parameters. Note that there is no loss of information in using a log transformation because the log is a one-to-one function.

Deterministic Method (DET): We compute the proportion of the page views whose max scroll depths are greater or equal to the target scroll depth X in each training set. This proportion is the prediction for all page views given X. For instance, $P(x_{ua} \geq 30\%|u, a)$ is 0.8953 means that the viewability x_{ua} for all test page views is 0.8953. Formally:

$$P(x_{ua} \geq X|u, a) = \frac{\#pageviews\ whose\ x_{ua} \geq X}{\#pageviews}$$

Logistic Regression (LR): We build an LR model based on the Stanford NLP API. Since one LR model cannot predict for every given target scroll depth, we train an LR model for each target scroll depth. We use the same set of input features as those used to train PLC. The target variable is 1 or 0, i.e., if a page scroll x_{ua} is not less than X, then target variable is 1; otherwise it is 0. When testing, given the features vector of a test page view, the LR model outputs the probability that X is in-view, i.e., $P(x_{ua} \geq X|u, a)$. This probability can be further converted into a binary decision.

Singular Value Decomposition (SVD): In addition to dimension reduction, SVD is often used to predict a target variable based on historical data. For any $M*N$ matrix A of rank r, SVD can decompose it as $A = U\sum V^T$. U is a $M*M$ orthogonal matrix that spans the "column space". V is a $N*N$ orthogonal matrix that spans the "row space". $\sum$ is a $M*N$ diagonal matrix whose first r entries are the nonzero singular values of A. Using matrix factorization, SVD maps both row items (e.g., users) and column items (e.g., pages) to a joint latent factor space, such that the interactions of row items and column items are modeled as inner products in that space. In our case, it generates a vector to represent each user or page. The dot product of a user vector and a webpage vector is the prediction of their interaction. Unlike PLC, SVD does not utilize the distribution of max scroll depth and the explicit features of page views.

Our SVD model implementation is based on libFM [19]. The number of factors is set to 8, as suggested in the manual. The matrix A is a user-webpage matrix. Each cell value is either 1 or 0, i.e., whether X is in-view or not. The output for a page view is a value between 0 and 1, which is treated as the probability that X is in-view. This probability can be converted into a binary decision. Similar to LR, we build an SVD model for each X.

4.3 Metrics

The main metrics we adopt are the Root-Mean-Square Deviation (RMSD) and the F1-score of class 0 (i.e., given scroll depth not in-view) and class 1 (i.e., given scroll depth in-view). We also compare the methods using the precision and recall metrics.

RMSD: The RMSD measures the differences between the values predicted by a model, $\hat{y}_i$, and the values actually observed, y_i. It is widely used in various research fields and is defined as the square root of the mean square error:

$$RMSD = \sqrt{\frac{\sum_{i=1}^{N}(\hat{y}_i - y_i)^2}{N}}$$

where N is the number of test page views. y_i is the ground truth of the ith page view. If the target scroll depth X is in-view, $y_i = 1$; otherwise, $y_i = 0$. $\hat{y}_i$ is the probabilistic prediction of the ith page view, i.e., $\hat{y}_i \in [0, 1]$. RMSD serves to aggregate the magnitudes of the errors in predictions for various times into a single measure of the predictive power of a method. Thus, the lower RMSD is, the better the prediction performance.

Precision, Recall and F1-score: The probability that X is in-view can be converted to 0 or 1, i.e., if it is greater or equal to 0.5, then X is in-view; otherwise, X is not in-view. Thus, the probabilistic prediction problem can be considered a binary classification problem as well. Hence, precision, recall, and F1-score can be used to compare the models. The precision of a class is the number of page views correctly labelled as belonging to the class divided by the total number of page views labelled as belonging to the class. High precision means high true positive rate and low false positive rate. The recall of a class is the number of page views correctly labelled as belonging to the class divided by the total number of page views that belong to the class. High recall means high true positive rate and low false negative rate. The F1-score of a class is the harmonic mean of the precision and recall of the corresponding class.

4.4 Effect of Parameter Combination

We investigate the performance of PLC with different combinations of the two parameters, N_s and N_p, shown in Equation 1. N_s is the number of latent user classes, while N_p is the number of latent webpage classes. Since there is an ad slot located at the 60% page depth on the real webpages analyzed, we take 60% as the target scroll depth X. We adopt grid search and random search to find the optimal parameters. For the grid search, we try all combinations of $N_s \in [2, 12]$ and $N_p \in [2, 12]$. For the random search, we try 20 combinations of $N_s \in [2, 30]$ and $N_s \in [2, 30]$ which are not included in the grid search. The range of obtained RMSDs is [0.3637, 0.3683].

Table 3: RMSDs of Different Parameter Pairs

RMSD	N_p=4	N_p=5	N_p=6	N_p=7	N_p=8	N_p=9
N_s=4	0.3681	0.3672	0.3678	0.3678	0.3676	0.3659
N_s=5	0.3671	**0.3691**	0.3678	0.3686	0.3675	0.3663
N_s=6	0.3679	0.3676	0.3678	0.3679	0.3671	0.3659
N_s=7	0.3674	0.3679	0.3672	0.3672	0.3645	0.3656
N_s=8	0.3675	0.3678	0.3663	0.3640	0.3672	0.3660
N_s=9	0.3678	0.3671	0.3652	0.3652	0.3638	0.3663
N_s=10	0.3671	0.3673	0.3649	0.3639	0.3644	0.3646
N_s=11	0.3657	0.3644	0.3637	**0.3631**	0.3638	0.3643
N_s=12	0.3640	0.3637	0.3634	0.3636	0.3645	0.3644

Table 3 shows the 5-fold cross validation RMSD results for different N_s and N_p combinations. For the sake of brevity, we only present partial results which contain the best and the worst performance. We observe that different combinations do not largely influence the performance, with the difference between the best and the worst results being only 0.006. Most parameter combinations generate similar values for precision, recall, and F1-score, respectively.

4.5 RMSD Comparison

The goal of this experiment is to test the performance of the models with different target scroll depths. Since generally the top 10% of a page can be shown in the first screen without the user performing any scrolling, we set the range of the target scroll depth to the interval [0.1, 1].

Figure 8 plots the RMSD comparison for the four systems. The results show that PLC significantly outperforms the three comparison systems. The RMSD performance of PLC at all Xs is averagely 10%, and 17% at maximum,

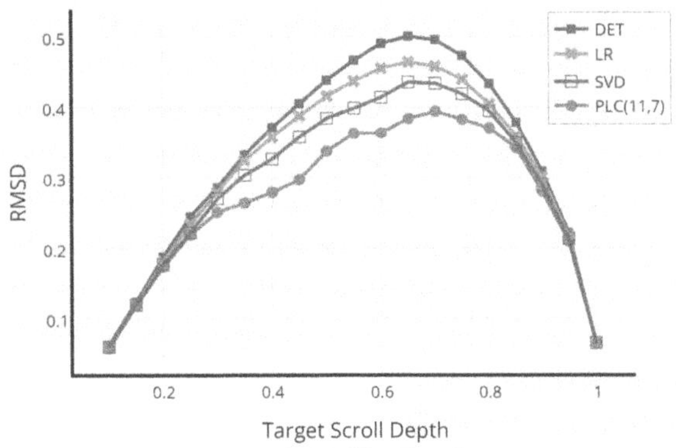

Figure 8: RMSD Performance

better than the second best system, SVD. All models have better performance near the top and bottom of a webpage than in the middle. The reasons for the top of the pages is that most pages are in-view at scroll depths such as [0.1, 0.2]. Being trained by such skewed data, most probabilistic outputs of the models are closer to 0 than 1. Although they may commit mistakes on the cases that are not in-view, the average RMSDs are still relatively low.

The prediction becomes harder with X moving toward the middle of the pages. Intuitively, the models are more prone to making incorrect predictions. Thus, RMSDs in this interval are higher than those in the two tails. Nevertheless, PLC performs substantially better than the other systems within this challenging interval. Due to the difficulty of capturing all the significant features, logistic regression does not perform as well as SVD and PLC, which identify latent features or latent classes, respectively.

Although RMSD reflects the deviation between probabilistic prediction and ground truth, it cannot tell the whole story of the performance. For example, let us assume there are 100 page views. Given a certain X, the ground truth tells that 99 belong to the not-in-view class and one belongs to the in-view class. A naive model makes the same prediction, which is 0, all the time. Thus, RMSD for this naive model at X is 0.1, which looks decent. However, such a good RMSD hides the inability of the model to recognize in-view instances. To overcome this issue, we adopt precision, recall, and F1-score to further evaluate our model.

4.6 Precision, Recall, and F1-score Comparison

Avoiding both false positives and false negatives can improve investment effectiveness for advertisers and increase the ad revenue for publishers. Therefore, identifying both in-view and not in-view impressions is equally important. Two practical examples illustrate this goal: (1) since the viewability of the page bottoms tends to be low, it is important to recognize when the page bottoms are actually in-view; (2) relatively high viewability of the page tops leads to expectations that ads at top are always in-view; however, this is not always the case, and it is very helpful to identify those pages whose tops are not in-view.

Figure 9 shows the precision, recall, and F1 score of both class 0 and 1 (i.e., not in-view and in-view). Overall, PLC performs the best among the four systems. The performance for class 1 is high when X is set in the interval [0.1, 0.6] because the top of most pages are in-view. Although it is more challenging to recognize the page views whose top is not in-view, PLC classifies these page views the best because its precision and recall for class 0 in the interval [0.1, 0.6] are the highest. Likewise, although it is difficult to detect the page views whose bottoms are in-view, PLC has the highest precision and recall for class 1 within [0.6, 1].

PLC has relatively low recall for class 1 in the interval [0.3 0.6] because it tends to boldly classify more page views to class 0 than the other systems. Most of these predictions are correct, (i.e., true negatives), while just a few are wrong (i.e., false negatives). The correct predictions increase the precision and recall for class 0, but the wrong predictions inevitably decrease the recall for class 1 since fewer page views are classified into class 1. This also explains why PLC's precision for class 1 is the highest in the interval [0.3, 0.6]. In the interval [0.6, 1], these observations are even more apparent. At the cost of sacrificing the recall for class 0, PLC achieves decent performance on the precision for both classes as well as the recall for class 1.

The differences among the models in Figure 9 are not as substantial as those in Figure 8 because RMSD is a more sensitive metric. For instance, given a page view whose X is in-view according to the ground truth, the probabilistic prediction of PLC is 0.8, while that of LR is 0.6. Both methods have the same evaluation results on the classification metrics because the outputs are greater than 0.5. But their performance can be distinguished when looking at RMSD: PLC's RMSD is 0.2, while LR's is 0.4.

LR, SVD, and PLC do not have precision results for class 1 in the interval [0.9, 1] because no page view is classified into class 1. Thus, a precision value cannot be calculated because the number of page views labeled in class 1 acts as the denominator in the precision formula and is 0 in this case. For the same reason, the recall for class 1 is 0 in this interval and no F1-score for class 1 can be computed for this interval. A similar behavior happens for class 0 in the interval [0.1, 0.2].

The reason that no page view is classified into class 1 within [0.9, 1] is that the distributions of the two classes are very skewed in the interval. Particularly, a large majority of page views are not in-view. Such imbalanced data precludes statistical methods like ours to work appropriately [11]. Essentially, the classifiers cannot learn well from the skewed data because the training examples are scarce. To overcome this issue, we have tried simple under/over-sampling. But inevitably, the precision has largely decreased. Therefore, mitigating data imbalance remains a task for future work.

Note that DET is not impacted by imbalanced data because it always makes the same decision for all test page views given an X. It works as well as the other methods in the interval [0.1, 0.2] and [0.9, 1]. Since DET is much simpler and faster, a practical suggestion on viewability prediction is to use DET to predict the viewability of scroll depths in [0.1, 0.2] and [0.9, 1] intervals, while PLC should be employed to predict in [0.2, 0.8] interval.

4.7 Runtime Comparison

Figure 10 shows the runtime comparison for PLC, LR, and SVD. In this experiment, we build one PLC model to predict the viewability of all target scroll depths from 10% to 100%. (step = 5%, so 19 scroll depths). However, for LR and SVD, we build 19 models (the step is 5% for the interval 10% to 100%). Therefore, the time for PLC includes one training, while the time for LR and SVD is the sum of 19 trainings. We do not include DET because it does not involve training

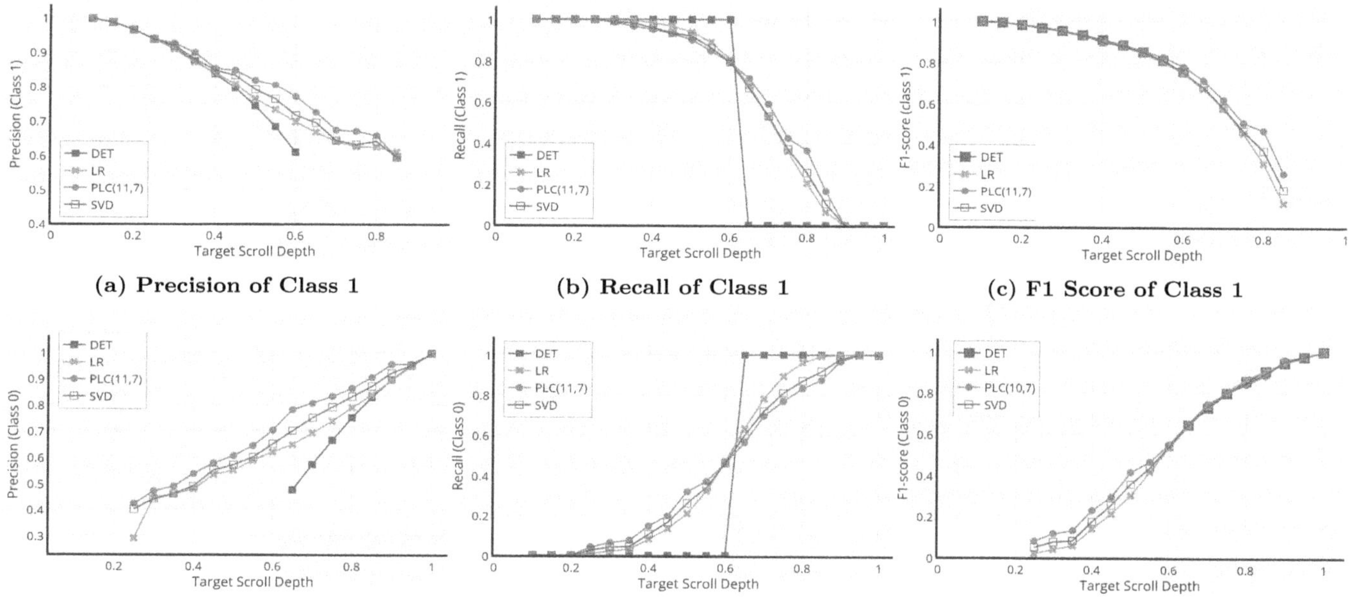

(a) Precision of Class 1 (b) Recall of Class 1 (c) F1 Score of Class 1

(d) Precision of Class 0 (e) Recall of Class 0 (f) F1 Score of Class 0

Figure 9: Classification Performance Comparison

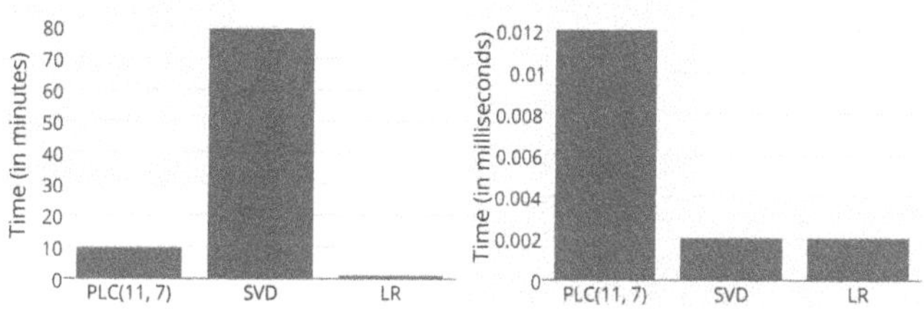

(a) Avg. Training Time for Entire Training Set **(b) Avg. Testing Time for One Test Page View**

Figure 10: Runtime Comparison

and makes consistent predictions for all page views for a given X (i.e.. its training and testing runtime are almost 0).

The results show that the training time of LR is much lower than those of PLC and SVD because LR does not have to learn any latent patterns from data. Intuitively, learning and applying more latent user classes and webpage classes takes more time. Since PLC performs better in terms of prediction accuracy, its training time is reasonable, especially compared to SVD. Let us also note that training can be done offline.

The results also show that PLC needs more time to make a prediction. However, the absolute value is very low (i.e., 0.012 ms). As an exchange-sold ad is often sold in 200 milliseconds, the PLC prediction time can easily be afforded for real-time predictions of incoming pages.

4.8 PLC Performance on Different Training Data Sizes

Table 4: Dataset Partitions with Different Sizes

Training Data	Testing Data (2d)
11/10/2014 (1d)	11/11/2014-11/12/2014
11/01/2014-11/10/2014 (10d)	
10/22/2014-11/10/2014 (20d)	
10/12/2014-11/10/2014 (30d)	

To test the impact of different training data sizes on PLC's performance, we re-partition the dataset by fixing the testing dates and varying the training data sizes, as shown in Table 4. All models share the common parameter pair, $N_s = 11$ and $N_p = 7$ According to Figure 11, the PLC results are almost the same for F1 scores. However, the results are distinguishable for RMSD, as this is a more sensitive metric. RMSD for PLC(30d) is slightly worse than the others. A possible reason is that the user interest may change over a longer period of time and subsequently hurts the prediction performance. The performance of PLC(1d) is not as good as those of PLC(10d) and PLC(20d) because it utilizes much less user and webpage history. Generally, PLC(10d) and PLC(20d) have very similar performance. The former should be preferred in practice because less data are required for training.

5. CONCLUSIONS

This paper initiates the study of predicting the viewability probability for a given scroll depth and a user/webpage pair. Solving this problem is of great value to online advertisers and publishers because it will allow them to invest more effectively in advertising and to increase their revenue, respectively. We presented PLC, a probabilistic latent class model, that is trained only once to predict the viewability for any given scroll depth. The model includes a number of features identified from our analysis of a dataset from a large online publisher that have significant impact on the maximum scroll depth, such as user geo-location and device type. The experimental results show that PLC has higher prediction accuracy than three system used for comparison. The results also demonstrate that PLC can be used in real-time and works well for different training datasets.

In future work, we plan to collect data about webpage content, investigate its effect on viewability, and incorporate this information in our model for viewability prediction. We will also continue improving the proposed model to handle unbalanced data.

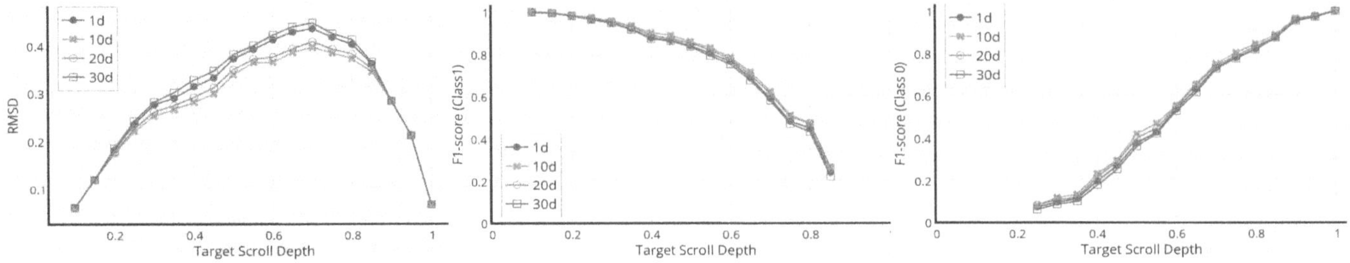

(a) RMSD **(b) F1 Score for Class 1** **(c) F1 Score for Class 0**

Figure 11: Performance Comparison of Different Training Data Sizes

Acknowledgement

This work is partially supported by National Science Foundation (NSF) CAREER Award IIS-0845647, NSF Grant No. CNS 1409523, Google Cloud Service Award and the Leir Charitable Foundations. Any opinions, findings, and conclusions or recommendations expressed in this material are those of the authors and do not necessarily reflect the views of the funding agencies.

6. REFERENCES

[1] D. Agarwal, B. Long, J. Traupman, D. Xin, and L. Zhang. Laser: a scalable response prediction platform for online advertising. In *ACM WSDM'14*, pages 173–182, 2014.

[2] E. Agichtein, E. Brill, and S. Dumais. Improving web search ranking by incorporating user behavior information. In *ACM SIGIR'06*, pages 19–26, 2006.

[3] S. Cetintas, D. Chen, and L. Si. Forecasting user visits for online display advertising. *Information retrieval*, 16(3):369–390, 2013.

[4] S. Cetintas, D. Chen, L. Si, B. Shen, and Z. Datbayev. Forecasting counts of user visits for online display advertising with probabilistic latent class models. In *ACM SIGIR'11*, pages 1217–1218, 2011.

[5] O. Chapelle, E. Manavoglu, and R. Rosales. Simple and scalable response prediction for display advertising. *ACM Transactions on Intelligent Systems and Technology (TIST)*, 5(4):61, 2014.

[6] W. Chen, D. He, T.-Y. Liu, T. Qin, Y. Tao, and L. Wang. Generalized second price auction with probabilistic broad match. In *ACM EC'14*, pages 39–56, 2014.

[7] Y. Chen and T. W. Yan. Position-normalized click prediction in search advertising. In *Proceedings of the 18th ACM SIGKDD*, pages 795–803, 2012.

[8] H. Cheng, E. Manavoglu, Y. Cui, R. Zhang, and J. Mao. Dynamic ad layout revenue optimization for display advertising. In *Proceedings of the Sixth International Workshop on Data Mining for Online Advertising and Internet Economy*, page 9, 2012.

[9] S. Flosi, G. Fulgoni, and A. Vollman. if an advertisement runs online and no one sees it, is it still an ad? *Journal of Advertising Research*, 2013.

[10] Google. The importance of being seen. http://think.storage.googleapis.com/docs/the-importance-of-being-seen_study.pdf.

[11] H. He and E. A. Garcia. Learning from imbalanced data. *IEEE Transactions on Knowledge and Data Engineering*, 21(9):1263–1284, 2009.

[12] M. Holub and M. Bielikova. Estimation of user interest in visited web page. In *WWW'10*, pages 1111–1112, 2010.

[13] B. Kanagal, A. Ahmed, S. Pandey, V. Josifovski, L. Garcia-Pueyo, and J. Yuan. Focused matrix factorization for audience selection in display advertising. In *IEEE ICDE'13*, pages 386–397, 2013.

[14] S. Kyle. Experimenting in loyalty conversion with wnyc: Achieving mobile-desktop parity. http://blog.chartbeat.com/2013/10/07/experimenting-loyalty-conversion-wnyc-achieving-mobile-desktop-parity/.

[15] C. Liu, R. W. White, and S. Dumais. Understanding web browsing behaviors through weibull analysis of dwell time. In *ACM SIGIR'10*, pages 379–386, 2010.

[16] I. Lunden. Internet ad spend to reach $121b in 2014. http://techcrunch.com/2014/04/07/internet-ad-spend-to-reach-121b-in-2014-23-of-537b-total-ad-spend-ad-tech-gives-display-a-boost-over-search/.

[17] F. Manjoo. You won't finish this article. *Slate*, 2013.

[18] M. Mareck. Is online audience measurement coming of age? *Research World*, 2015(51):16–19, 2015.

[19] S. Rendle. Factorization machines with libfm. *ACM Transactions on Intelligent Systems and Technology (TIST)*, 3(3):57, 2012.

[20] R. Rosales, H. Cheng, and E. Manavoglu. Post-click conversion modeling and analysis for non-guaranteed delivery display advertising. In *ACM WSDM'12*, pages 293–302, 2012.

[21] C.-J. Wang and H.-H. Chen. Learning user behaviors for advertisements click prediction. In *ACM SIGIR'11 Workshop on Internet Advertising*, pages 1–6, 2011.

[22] H. Weinreich, H. Obendorf, E. Herder, and M. Mayer. Not quite the average: An empirical study of web use. *ACM Transactions on the Web (TWEB)*, 2(1):5, 2008.

[23] X. Yi, L. Hong, E. Zhong, N. N. Liu, and S. Rajan. Beyond clicks: dwell time for personalization. In *ACM Recsys'15*, pages 113–120, 2014.

[24] S. Yuan, J. Wang, and X. Zhao. Real-time bidding for online advertising: measurement and analysis. In *Proceedings of the Seventh International Workshop on Data Mining for Online Advertising*, page 3, 2013.

[25] W. Zhang, S. Yuan, and J. Wang. Optimal real-time bidding for display advertising. In *ACM SIGKDD'14*, pages 1077–1086, 2014.

10 Bits of Surprise: Detecting Malicious Users with Minimum Information

Reza Zafarani
Department of EECS
Syracuse University
reza@zafarani.net

Huan Liu
Computer Science and Engineering
Arizona State University
huan.liu@asu.edu

ABSTRACT

Malicious users are a threat to many sites and defending against them demands innovative countermeasures. When malicious users join sites, they provide limited information about themselves. With this limited information, sites can find it difficult to distinguish between a malicious user and a normal user. In this study, we develop a methodology that identifies malicious users with limited information. As information provided by malicious users can vary, the proposed methodology utilizes **minimum information** to identify malicious users. It is shown that as little as **10 bits** of information can help greatly in this challenging task. The experiments results verify that this methodology is effective in identifying malicious users in the realistic scenario of limited information availability.

Categories and Subject Descriptors

H.2.8 [**Database Management**]: Database Applications—*Data mining*

Keywords

Malicious User Detection; Minimum Information; Information Verification; Behavior Analysis

1. INTRODUCTION

Social media sites are inundated with malicious users. In June 2012, Facebook reported that 8.7% – or 83 million – of its user accounts are fake [35]; that is roughly the size of Egypt's population and larger than the population of 230 countries in the world [37]. Facebook also reported that of that 8.7%, **1.5%** are "undesirable" accounts that are created for malicious purposes [35]. Twitter faces similar challenges. In its security filings, Twitter claims that 5% of its users are fake [10]; however, researchers estimate the percentage of its fake accounts to be as high as 10% [10]. These fake accounts are mostly sold on black market for as low as $0.05 and are used for malicious activities [10].

CIKM'15, October 19–23, 2015, Melbourne, Australia.
© 2015 ACM. ISBN 978-1-4503-3794-6/15/10 ...$15.00.
http://dx.doi.org/10.1145/2806416.2806535.

Malicious accounts may be created for different purposes. According to Cao et al. [4], some malicious accounts are created for profitable activities, such as click fraud, identity fraud, and malware distribution. Others are created for social purposes such as pranks, stalking, cyberbullying, or identity concealing. Online service providers find detecting and subsequently, suspending malicious accounts vital in order to protect their normal users against external threats.

Detecting malicious accounts dates back to the onset of social media. Comprehensive feature-based techniques, human-in-the-loop approaches, or techniques that use social-graphs are devised (see a review in Section 2). These techniques assume that a good amount of information about malicious users has been gathered. This information includes (1) the content that malicious users generate, (2) the users they befriend, or (3) the malicious activities they have exhibited. In short, their *content*, *links*, or *activities*. However, malicious users often do not have an incentive to generate content or befriend others and detecting them after they have exhibited malicious activities is not useful. Hence, malicious users need to be detected using their often limited content or link (i.e., friends) information. Even the limited information that malicious users provide can vary. Therefore, to detect malicious users with different levels of information, one needs to be able to detect malicious users even when there is **minimum information** available.

In this paper, we aim to detect malicious users with minimum information. We make the following contributions:

1. We introduce the first methodology to detect malicious users with minimum information. This methodology can be used as the first line of combat against malicious users on the Web.
2. We identify five general characteristics of malicious users and demonstrate how one can identify these characteristics in user-generated content online.
3. We demonstrate that with as little as **10 bits** of information, one can distinguish between normal and malicious users.
4. We show via experiments that the methodology is robust and at least as effective as techniques that have access to more information.

In Section 2, we review the malicious user detection literature. We formally define the malicious user detection problem with minimum information in Section 3. We detail characteristics of malicious users and how one can identify such characteristics in user content in Section 4. We detail our experiments in Section 5. Finally, we conclude in Section 6 with directions for future work.

2. LITERATURE ON MALICIOUS USER DETECTION

While detecting malicious users with minimum information is unexplored, identifying malicious users in general is not a new topic. Often, to identify malicious users, (1) feature-based techniques, (2) human-in-the-loop techniques, or (3) techniques that use social graphs are used. We review representative techniques for each category and discuss how the current work relates to these techniques.

I. Feature-based Techniques. In feature-based methods, different features are constructed to capture the behavior of the malicious user. These features are then used to construct a dataset that is trained by a supervised learning framework. For instance, Xie et al. [39], develop the *AutoRe* framework that identifies botnet campaigns. Their framework identifies traffic that is (1) bursty and (2) distributed. These features of traffic help identify botnets. The bursty and distributed nature of unwanted content is also used in detecting malicious posts on Facebook [12]. Wang [34] introduces a method that detects spam on Twitter using network features such as the number of followers or friends and content features such as duplicated tweets. Feature-based techniques have been discussed extensively for detecting unwanted content in social tagging systems [20,24], social networks [29], email [21], online videos [3], and microblogging sites [2,43]. Our work differs from the existing work in two aspects. First, current techniques for identifying malicious users often employ content or link information. Thus, one often needs a large collection of data instances to obtain guaranteed performances. Our approach employs minimum information across sites. Second, current literature is often context-dependent (e.g., site specific). Our method employs the minimum information that is universally available across sites and is robust even when information is collected from multiple sites.

II. Human-in-the-loop Methods. One approach of identifying malicious users is to employ human experts. Humans can naturally identify malicious users by their activities. Alternatively, one can combat malicious activities by technologies such as CAPTCHAs [33] or photo-based authentications [4] that are only solvable by humans. Although specific attacks are proposed for human-in-the-loop methods [26,41], they are in general considered effective. Unfortunately, verifying accounts by humans is time consuming. For example, Tuenti, a Spain-based social networking service, hires humans to investigate reported users and block malicious ones [4]. An employee can only process 250 to 300 reports an hour from the daily 12,000 reports received. This issue makes human-in-the-loop processes infeasible for large-scale networks. Our approach in this paper is automatic and can easily scale to billions of users.

III. Social Graph-based Techniques. In social graph-based methods, the information about the links (i.e., friendships) that the malicious individual has created helps detect the malicious user. For instance, Yang and colleagues [42] detect more than 100,000 fake accounts using social network features on RenRen social network. In particular, they find that invitation frequency, outgoing requests accepted, incoming requests accepted, and network clustering coefficient can help identify fake accounts. In other works, probabilistic, combinatorial, or random walk models have been applied to network information to identify malicious users. Examples include, *Sybilguard* [45], *Gatekeeper* [31], *SybilInfer* [7], *SumUp* [30], and *Sybillimit* [44]. These methods or variants can be applied on sites such as Twitter to identify malicious users [13]. Mislove et al. [32] show that most techniques in this area function by finding local communities around trusted nodes. Assuming the existence of a social graph is a strong assumption. One often requires specific privacy permission to obtain such graphs and in specific cases, this graph is not available. In cases where there is no social graph, our methodology is still easily applicable.

3. MALICIOUS USER DETECTION WITH MINIMUM INFORMATION

Who is a malicious user? The definition varies in the literature from users that harass other users to users that jeopardize the privacy of others [4]. We consider malicious users on a site, those whom normal users consider malicious. Clearly, the opinion of normal users can be subjective and has to be verified by experts. In section 5.1, we demonstrate how such human-verified data can be collected. Humans are known to be accurate in detecting malicious users on social media [15,16,27]. However, as discussed in our literature review, human-in-the-loop approaches are time consuming and expensive for large-scale networks. Hence, by investigating how humans detect malicious users, one can not only scale detection of malicious users, but can also protect against a wide spectrum of malicious activities that humans are able to detect on social media [4,5].

Our goal in this paper is to identify such malicious users. Malicious users often provide little or no information. Hence, a method that can be universally employed on different sites is constrained to use the minimum information available on all sites. *Usernames* are the minimum information available on all social media sites [46]. Often, usernames are alphanumeric strings or email addresses, without which users cannot join sites. Because of their unique characteristics, usernames are shown to be surprisingly effective for identifying individuals [46]. We formalize our problem using usernames as the minimum information available on all sites. Other content or link information such as user profile information or friends, when added to usernames, should help better identify malicious individuals. However, the lack of consistency in the availability of such information on all social media sites, directs us toward formulating our problem with usernames.

When using usernames, the goal is to detect malicious users from their usernames. Hence, one can learn a function $\mathbf{M}(.)$ that given a username u, predicts whether the username belongs to a malicious user or not. We denote the $\mathbf{M}$ function as the *malicious user detection* function. Formally,

Definition. ***Malicious User Detection.*** *Given a username u, a malicious user detection method attempts to learn a malicious user detection function $\mathbf{M}(.)$ such that*

$$\mathbf{M}(u) = \begin{cases} 1 & \textit{If } u \textit{ belongs to a malicious user;} \\ 0 & \textit{Otherwise.} \end{cases}$$

Malicious users have distinctive characteristics. These characteristics leave traces in the usernames of malicious users. These traces can be captured using data features. Following the common machine learning and data mining practice, the malicious user detection function can be learned using a supervised learning algorithm that utilizes these features and *labeled data*. In our problem, labeled data includes usernames that are known to be malicious or normal.

Supervised learning can be performed using classification or regression. Depending on the malicious user detection task at hand, one can even learn the probability that a username is malicious, generalizing our binary $\mathbf{M}$ function to a probabilistic one ($\mathbf{M}(u) = p$). This probability can help select the most likely malicious username. The learning of the malicious user detection function is the most straightforward. Therefore, we next elaborate on different characteristics of malicious users and how features can be constructed to capture traces introduced in usernames due to these characteristics. Note that the designed features may or may not help in the learning framework and are included as as long as they could be computed from usernames. Later on in Section 5, we will analyze the effectiveness of all features, and if it is necessary to find as many features as possible.

In summary, to detect malicious users, we (1) identify characteristics of malicious users, (2) construct features to identify traces of these characteristics in usernames, and (3) train a learning model to detect malicious users. Due to the interdependent nature of these user characteristics and feature construction, we discuss them together next.

4. CHARACTERISTICS OF MALICIOUS USERS

Humans detect malicious users on social media by their characteristics. By reviewing related literature from computer science, security, criminology, among other fields [4, 11, 29, 32, 39, 42], we identified five general characteristics of malicious users. Malicious users can have one (or a combination) of these characteristics. As researchers identify more characteristics of malicious users, our methodology can be extended with these characteristics and the corresponding features that can capture traces left by them in usernames.

4.1 Malicious Users are Complex and Diverse

Malicious users often generate (1) *complex* and (2) *diverse* information to ensure their anonymity.

I. Complexity. To measure complexity of usernames, it is natural to borrow techniques from complexity theory. We employ Kolmogorov complexity [22] to determine the complexity of a username. Kolmogorov complexity of a username is defined as the length of the shortest program capable of reproducing the username on a universal computer such as a Turing Machine. Hence, Kolmogorov complexity is the minimum quantity of information required to reproduce the username and measures its complexity.

For username u, let $K(u)$ denote its Kolmogorov complexity. While $K(u)$ defines the complexity of username u, it is well-known that its exact value cannot be computed [19]. Nonetheless, the following theorem helps compute the expected Kolmogorov complexity. Assume that usernames such as u are distributed as a random variable U, called *username space*, with probability distribution P.

THEOREM 1. *(from Li and Vitányi [22]) For random variable U, expected Kolmogorov complexity $\mathbb{E}(K(U))$ equals its entropy $H(U)$, plus a constant term that depends only on P.*

Hence, by computing the entropy of the username space, one can approximate the expected Kolmogorov complexity in usernames. However, the theorem discusses the entropy of the username space and it is not clear how one can connect this theorem to a specific username. For connecting properties of specific usernames to the entropy of the username space, we can use the concept of *information surprise* [6].

For username u, let $p(u)$ denote the probability of observing u. Information surprise for u is defined as

$$I(u) = -\log_2(p(u)). \qquad (1)$$

Hence, for a rare username u with a small observation probability $p(u)$, information surprise $I(u)$ is much higher than that of a common username with a higher observation probability. It is well-known that information surprise is deeply connected to entropy:

THEOREM 2. *(from Cover and Thomas [6]) The expected information surprise $\mathbb{E}(I(U))$ for username space U (i.e., random variable U) is equivalent to its entropy $H(U)$.*

So, by combining Theorems 1 and 2, one can approximate the expected Kolmogorov complexity of usernames by computing the expected information surprise in them. The information surprise for a username u is computed by measuring $I(u) = -\log_2(p(u))$, which requires the probability of observing username u. The probability of observing username u, denoted in characters as $u = c_1c_2 \dots c_n$, is

$$p(u) = \Pi_{i=1}^{n} p(c_i|c_1c_2 \dots c_{i-1}). \qquad (2)$$

We approximate this probability using an n-gram model,

$$p(u) \approx \Pi_{i=1}^{n} p(c_i|c_{i-(n-1)} \dots c_{i-1}). \qquad (3)$$

Often, to denote the beginning and the end of a word special symbols are added such as $\star$ and $\bullet$. So, for username `sara`, the probability approximated using a 2-gram model is

$$p(sara) \approx p(s|\star)p(a|s)p(r|a)p(a|r)p(\bullet|a). \qquad (4)$$

To estimate the probability of a username using an n-gram model, one needs to compute the probability of its comprising n-grams. The probability of these n-grams can be computed using a large set of usernames. For that, we use a dataset of 158 million Facebook usernames (later discussed in Section 5.1) to train a 6-gram model. This n-gram model was employed to compute the probability of a username and in turn, its information surprise.

Being able to compute information surprise, we obtain its values for a set of 33 million usernames. The set contains both normal and malicious users. The process followed to collect these usernames is later discussed in Section 5.1. For both normal and malicious users, we estimate the empirical probability density function using Kaplan-Meier estimate. Figure 1 plots the empirical probability density function of information surprise values for normal and malicious users.

The thick solid line in Figure 1 demonstrates the distribution of surprise values for normal usernames and the thin solid line depicts the distribution for malicious usernames. As shown in the figure, malicious usernames are more complex with the expected information surprise (i.e., expected Kolmogorov complexity) value of 23.11 bits and more diverse, ranging from 4.14 bits to 232.64 bits.

Unlike malicious usernames, normal usernames are less surprising and more concentrated around a mean value, with a mean of 12.49 bits and the information surprise value ranging from 3.90 to 31.93 bits. The figure shows that these

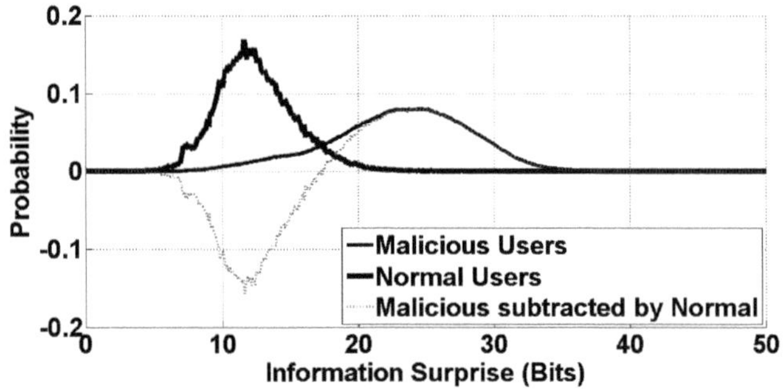

Figure 1: Probability Density Function for Information Surprise Values of Malicious and Normal Users.

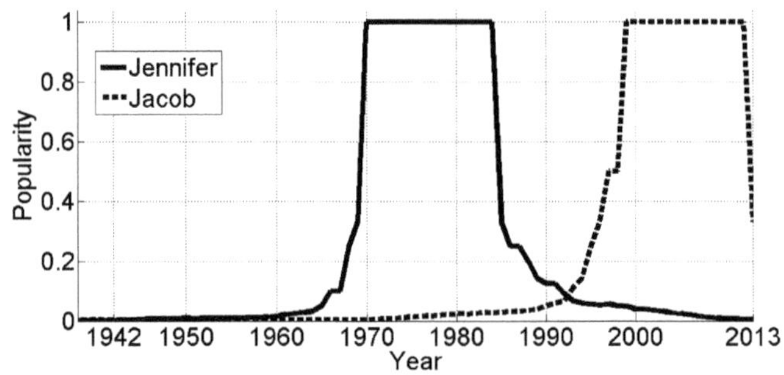

Figure 2: Popularity of names: *Jennifer* and *Jacob* over time. Higher values shows more popularity.

distributions are well separated indicating that by using the information surprise of a username, one might be able to accurately classify usernames into malicious or normal.

In Figure 1, the dashed line depicts the curve for the malicious usernames subtracted by the curve for the the normal usernames. Hence, when this gray line is above zero, it shows that for a specific information surprise value, the username is more likely to be malicious and whenever the gray line is below zero, we observe the opposite. We notice that for values between 3.91 and 17.96 the curve is below the zero line, showing usernames are more likely to be normal. In this range, the mean value is 10.9 bits. Thus, when the information surprise for a username is approximately 10 bits, the username is more likely to be normal. The title of this paper is inspired by this observation.

Hence, we include the information surprise of the username (i.e., its complexity) as another feature in our dataset.

II. Diversity. To create diverse information, malicious users often generate usernames that include digits. Therefore, we include the number of digits in the username as a feature. We also include the proportion of digits in the username as another feature in our feature set.

4.2 Malicious Users are Demographically Biased

In the criminology literature [11], it is well-known that crime correlates with demographic information. Thus, one expects to better detect malicious users by determining their demographics. Following the *diffusion of innovations* terminology [23], a malicious user has internal demographic attributes, external demographic attributes, or a combination of internal and external (i.e., mixed) attributes.

Internal attributes are endogenous attributes that the user has no control over such as his or her age. External attributes are attributes due to the environment that the malicious user lives in such as the language that the malicious user speaks. The level of knowledge that the malicious user has is an example of a user attribute that is mixed (internal+external). This is because it depends on both the environment that the malicious user lives in and on the internal attributes of a user such as his interests. To concretely profile a malicious user, one has to consider all these attributes. We select gender from internal attributes, language from external attributes, and knowledge (i.e., vocabulary size) from mixed demographic attributes to be predicted from usernames. Clearly, with more internal/external/mixed demographic attributes, one should better profile malicious users.

We leave that as a future direction for this work. But, how can we detect gender, language, or other attributes of individuals from their usernames?

Psychological studies [14] show that users leave traces of their personal information and attributes in the information they generate such as their usernames. For example, our analysis of popular names by birth year of US social security records[1] since 1879 shows us that the frequency of different names change over time. For instance, in Figure 2, we depict the popularity of first names: *Jennifer* and *Jacob* over time. For each year, the popularity of each name is shown on a scale of [0,1], 1 being the most popular name and 0 being the least popular. Jennifer was the most popular female name between [1970-1984] whereas Jacob has been the most popular male name for [1991-2012]. Similar patterns can be observed for different English and non-English names given the diversity of the US population. Hence, given a name, one can estimate the most likely age. Names, interests, as well as other personal attributes are often abbreviated or used in usernames [46]. We use these information traces in usernames to predict gender, language, among other attributes.

I. Malicious User Gender. To predict gender from usernames, we train a classifier. The classifier decomposes a username into character n-grams and estimates the gender likelihood based on these n-grams. This classifier is trained on the n-grams of a labeled dataset of usernames, in which the gender for each username is known. We collect our labeled dataset from Facebook. Our labeled dataset contains a set of 4 millions usernames with their corresponding gender. The classifier predicts the gender of a username with up to 80% accuracy. Notice that because malicious users tend to hide their identity and gender; instead of the actual prediction, we include the classifier's confidence in the predicted gender as the feature.

II. Malicious User Language. To detect the language of the username, we train an n-gram statistical language detector [9] over the European Parliament Proceedings Parallel Corpus[2], which consists of text in 21 European languages (*Bulgarian, Czech, Danish, German, Greek, English, Spanish, Estonian, Finnish, French, Hungarian, Italian, Lithuanian, Latvian, Dutch, Polish, Portuguese, Romanian, Slovak, Slovene,* and *Swedish*) from 1996-2006 with more than 40 million words per language. The trained model detects the username's language, which is a feature in our feature

[1] http://www.ssa.gov/oact/babynames/

[2] http://www.statmt.org/europarl/

set. The *detected language* feature is limited to European languages. Our language detector will not detect other languages. The language detector is also challenged when dealing with words that may not follow the statistical patterns of a language, such as location names, etc. This issue can be tackled by including the distribution of alphabet letters in usernames as features [46]. Thus, in addition to predicted language, we include the alphabet distribution of the username as a feature.

III. Malicious User Knowledge. To approximate the level of knowledge of a malicious user, we can compute his or her vocabulary size. The vocabulary size can be computed by counting the number of words in a large dictionary that are substrings of the username [46]. This approach captures different possible interpretations of the username and approximates the level of knowledge of the malicious user. We include the vocabulary size as a feature. As this is a rough approximation, we will determine the efficiency of this feature in our feature importance analysis in Section 5.5.

4.3 Malicious Users are Anonymous

Malicious activity often requires a level of anonymity [1]. Theoretically, the maximum level of anonymity is achieved when a username has the maximum entropy [40]. We compute the entropy of the alphabet distribution of the username as well as the normalized entropy of the username to measure its level of anonymity. To normalize entropy, we divide it by $\log n$, where n is the number of unique alphabet letters used in the username. In addition, we also measure the uniqueness of letters in the username – that is, the number of unique letters used in the username divided by the username length. We include entropy, normalized entropy, and uniqueness as features.

4.4 Malicious Users are Similar

Malicious users tend to be similar. For instance, individuals marketing an illegal product `Dangerous-Pill` all share the name of the product `Dangerous-Pill` in their marketing content. This malicious content similarity can be captured in usernames by identifying specific (1) language patterns and (2) words in the usernames.

4.4.1 Language Patterns

To find finer grain language patterns of users, we employ character-level n-grams. Character-level n-grams have shown to be effective in detecting unwanted content [17, 18] and connecting users across social media sites [28]. We compute the normalized character-level bigrams of usernames and include them as features. Bigram features are normalized using TF-IDF. Bigrams allow for a language-agnostic solution [46] that can detect common patterns of malicious users conveniently.

For coarser grain language patterns, we investigate common habits of malicious users. For instance, it is known that the use of digits is an indication of unwanted content [20]. In particular, we notice that malicious users tend to start their usernames with digits; therefore, we include the number of digits at the beginning of the username as a feature. We also notice that malicious users repeat character letters more often that normal users. This strategy allows them to circumvent widely used statistical malware blockers [38]. Hence, we include the maximum number of times a letter has been repeated in the username as another feature.

4.4.2 Word Patterns

A well-known approach to identify malicious users or content is by finding specific keywords in the content generated by these users. Hence, we denote the existence of these specific keywords in usernames as an indication of malicious activity. We utilize two dictionaries, one containing keywords related to malicious activities and the other for offensive keywords[3] For each dictionary, we count the number of words in the dictionary that appear as the substring of the username. We include these two counts for the aforementioned two dictionaries as features.

4.5 Malicious Users are Efficient

In contrast with complex malicious users (Section 4.1), some malicious users demand efficiency. This is because the malicious user is interested in performing the malicious activity frequently, quickly, and at large-scale. For instance, when performing click-fraud, the malicious user is interested in creating many accounts, each clicking on specific ads. This efficiency can be observed in usernames in terms of (1) the username length; and (2) the number of unique alphabet letters in usernames. We include both as features. In addition, we can observe efficiency by determining the typing patterns of the malicious user.

Most people use one of the two well-known DVORAK and QWERTY keyboards, or slight variants such as QWERTZ or AZERTY [36]. It has been shown that the keyboard layout significantly impacts how random usernames are selected [8]. For example, `qwer1234` and `aoeusnth` are two well-known passwords commonly selected by QWERTY and DVORAK users, respectively. To model typing patterns of malicious users, for each username we construct the following 15 features for each keyboard layout (a total of 30 for both keyboard layouts),

1. (1 feature) The percentage of keys typed using the *same hand* that was used for the previous key. The higher this percentage the less users had to change hands for typing.
2. (1 feature) The percentage of keys typed using the *same finger* that was used for the previous key.
3. (8 features) The percentage of keys typed using each finger. Thumbs are not included.
4. (4 features) The percentage of keys pressed on rows: Top Row, Home Row, Bottom Row, and Number Row. Space bar is not included.
5. (1 feature) The approximate *distance* (in meters) traveled for typing a username. Normal typing keys are assumed to be $(1.8\text{cm})^2$ (including gap between keys).

We construct $15 \times 2 = 30$ features that capture the typing patterns of usernames for both keyboards and include them in our feature set.

We have detailed how characteristics of malicious users can be captured by meaningful features. These features help identify traces of malicious activities in usernames. Overall, for each username, we construct 1,413 features.

Clearly, not all characteristics of malicious users are covered by our features, and with more theories on characteristics of malicious users, more features can be constructed. We will empirically study if it is necessary to use all features and the effect of using different features on learning performance of detecting malicious users.

[3] All data available at: http://reza.zafarani.net/data/10bits

Following our approach, we compute the feature values over labeled data, and verify the effectiveness of our methodology by learning the malicious user detection function. Next, experiments for evaluating our methodology are detailed.

5. EXPERIMENTS

We evaluate our methodology to detect malicious users in this section. First, we verify if our proposed approach can identify malicious users well. Next, we verify if different learning algorithms can influence the prediction task. Then, we determine the sensitivity of our approach to different conditions. Finally, we perform feature importance analysis and determine how features designed for each characteristic of malicious users influence the detection outcome. Before we present the experiment details, we detail how experimental data was collected for this research.

5.1 Data Preparation

Our approach to detect malicious users employs a supervised learning framework. Hence, labeled data is required. This labeled data consists of usernames and their corresponding label: malicious or normal. To construct this labeled data and for our experiments, we collect four datasets.

I. Malicious Users (negative examples). We collect malicious usernames from sites such as dronebl.org, ahbl.org, among others (for a complete list see [25]). These sites gather lists of usernames that have been reported by other normal users for malicious purposes. Once reported, these accounts are manually verified by domain owners to be malicious. These lists are published to help sites promote their security. We collect a set of 32 million usernames that are manually reported as malicious by users on different sites. This set forms our negative examples.

II. Normal Users (positive examples). For collecting normal users, we require users that are manually labeled as normal. For that, we refer to Twitter verified accounts, all manually verified by Twitter employees. These accounts are all followed by the Twitter handle `verified`[4]. By crawling all the users this account follows, we collect a set of 45,953 usernames guaranteed to be normal. These usernames form our positive examples.

III. Facebook Users (positive+negative examples). To diversify the types of usernames we have collected, we also collect a set of 158 million usernames from Facebook, that is, 1 in 9 Facebook users in the world are included in our dataset. Note that the Facebook dataset is not completely normal as Facebook expects around 1.5% to be malicious. We employ this dataset for analyzing the sensitivity of our approach to different conditions (Section 5.4.2).

IV. Gender Dataset. We collect a different set of 4 million Facebook usernames for which we have the gender information. This dataset was used to train our gender prediction classifier in Section 4.2 to predict gender from usernames.

After collecting these four datasets of usernames[5], we compute the corresponding 1,413 features for all datasets and employ them in our experiments.

[4]http://twitter.com/verified

[5]We ensure that the alphabet used in both sets of usernames match. To avoid site-enforced specific patterns on how usernames should be created, we filter out usernames that are not in ASCII or alphanumeric. Our experiments show that this procedure does not influence our results.

Table 1: Malicious User Detection Performance.

Technique	AUC	F1
Our Approach	0.9932	0.9644
Baseline b_1: Keyword Detection	0.51	0.66
Baseline b_2: Username Randomness	0.70	≈ 0
Baseline b_3: Letter Repetition	0.61	≈ 0
Reference Point r_1: *Markines et al.* [24]	0.984	0.983
Reference Point r_2: *Gao et al.* [12]	0.945	–
Reference Point r_3: *Wang* [34]	0.917	0.917

5.2 Learning the Malicious User Detection Function

Once the negative and positive examples are prepared, learning the malicious user detection function can be achieved by training a classifier. Because our collected negative examples are more, we subsample the negative examples to have the same size as the positive examples. This way we create a dataset that has 50% positive examples and 50% negative ones. Using this dataset, we train a classifier. The random prediction on this dataset cannot achieve more than 50% accuracy. We train an ℓ_2-Regularized Logistic Regression using 10-fold cross validation and obtain an accuracy of 96.42%, an AUC of 0.9932, and an F1-measure of 0.9644.

As there are no comparable methods, we evaluate the effectiveness of our approach by devising three baseline methods for comparison. When individuals are asked to detect malicious users based on their usernames, they often look for specific "keywords", verify if the username looks "random", or look for "repetition of letters". Hence, they form our three baselines b_1, b_2, and b_3:

- **Baseline b_1: Keyword Detection.** We consider a username malicious if it contains a specific keyword. We use the same set of keywords used in Section 4.4.2 and train a classifier based on the single feature. b_1 results in an AUC of 0.5140 and F1-measure of 0.66.
- **Baseline b_2: Username Randomness.** For finding username randomness, b_2 uses the entropy of the username as a feature. Using our data labels, we perform logistic regression. b_2 achieves an AUC of 0.700 and F1-measure of ≈ 0.
- **Baseline b_3: Letter Repetition.** Similar to the procedure followed in baseline b_2, in b_3, we use the maximum number of times a letter is repeated in the username as a feature and train a logistic regression model using our data labels. b_3 achieves an AUC of 0.61 and an F1-measure of ≈ 0.

While the baseline performances demonstrate the difficulty of our problem, the proposed approach outperforms all baselines by at least 41%. The performance for our approach, and baselines are summarized in Table 1. As reference points, we also include in the table the performance of recent state-of-the-art techniques for detecting malicious users. These techniques have access to more information compared to our methodology and do not employ usernames; therefore, no improvement percentage will be reported. Our approach, with usernames only, outperforms these techniques. Next, we investigate if different learning algorithms can further improve the learning performance.

Table 2: **Malicious User Detection Performance for Different Classification Techniques.**

Technique	AUC	Accuracy
ℓ_2-Regularized ℓ_1-Loss SVM	0.9966	97.05%
ℓ_2-Regularized ℓ_2-Loss SVM	0.9913	96.05%
ℓ_2-Regularized Logistic Regression	0.9923	96.25%
ℓ_1-Regularized Logistic Regression	0.9971	**97.26%**

5.3 Choice of Learning Algorithm

To evaluate the choice of learning algorithm, we perform the classification task using a range of learning algorithms and 10-fold cross validation. The AUCs and accuracy rates are available in Table 2. These algorithms have different learning biases, and one expects to observe different performances for the same task. While we observe a slight increase in the performance, as shown in the table, results are not significantly different across algorithms. This shows that when sufficient information is available in features, the performance is not sensitive to the choice of learning algorithm.

In our experiments, ℓ_1-Regularized Logistic Regression is shown to be the most accurate method; therefore, we use it in the following experiments as the method of choice.

In our previous experiments, we assumed that there is no class imbalance between malicious and normal users. In reality this distribution is skewed. Furthermore, unlike our malicious users, all of our normal users are from one source (Twitter). Thus, we need to verify how this decision influences our results. We analyze the sensitivity of our approach to class imbalance and the distribution of normal users next.

5.4 Sensitivity Analysis

5.4.1 *Sensitivity to Class Imbalance*

In real-world networks such as Facebook and Twitter, the percentage of malicious users in the population is approximated to be at most 10% [10,35]. In other words, for every 9 normal users there exists at most 1 malicious user. This rate could be different across networks. Thus, we perform a sensitivity analysis with respect to different ratios of malicious users. We construct datasets, where α percent of the dataset consists of malicious users and change α in the range $5 \leq \alpha \leq 50$. Values larger than 50 were not selected, because then we are assuming that malicious users are more than the normal ones.

Because we collected more negative examples, we sample the negative examples many times to guarantee that each negative example is seen at least once. Thus, for each α, many datasets are created. For each one of these datasets, we perform classification and average the performance metrics over all datasets created for a specific α.

Figure 3 depicts the average performance (accuracy, AUC, and F1-measure) of our methodology with different percentages of malicious users. As shown in the Figure, as the number of malicious users increase, AUC remains stable and F1-measure and accuracy slightly drop, but in all cases, all measures stay above 0.97.

5.4.2 *Sensitivity to the Distribution of Normal Users*

To determine the sensitivity of our classifier to different normal users, we use samples of Facebook users instead

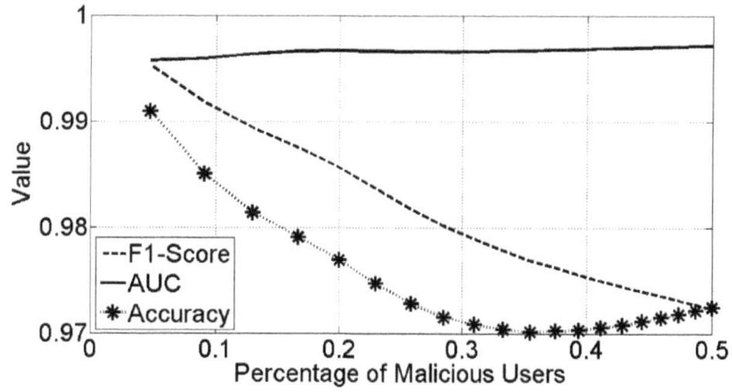

Figure 3: Performance (AUC, F1, and Accuracy) of our methodology for Different Percentages of Malicious Users.

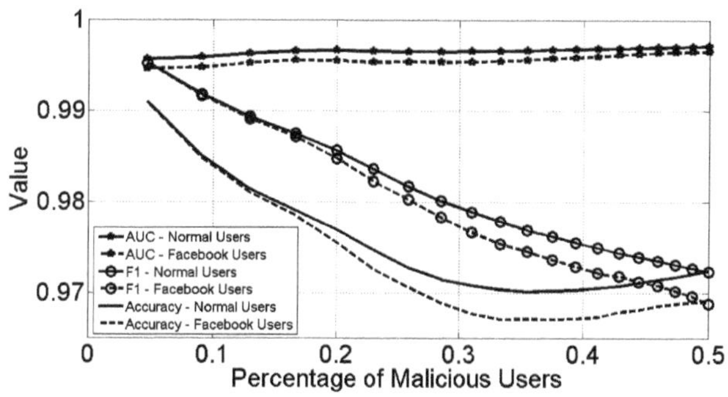

Figure 4: Performance Measures (F1, AUC, and Accuracy) of our Methodology for Different Percentages of Malicious Users when Facebook Identities were used instead of Normal Users.

of our normal users in training. Facebook users are not completely normal and Facebook approximates that around 1.5% of its users are malicious [35]. If our classifier can detect Facebook malicious users, some positive instances (Facebook users) will be classified as negative (malicious). Hence, the performance is expected to slightly decrease. In theory, for all datasets that have at most 50% negative examples (malicious users) and Facebook users as positive examples, one expects at most a $50\% \times 1.5\% = 0.0075$ decrease in accuracy. Our experiments verify this expectation. Figure 4 plots the performance (accuracy, AUC, F1-measure) of the algorithm with different percentages of malicious users and using Facebook users as positive examples. We notice a slight drop in performance for all measures, but the performance remains high and is never below 0.9671. For comparison, we include the performance measures with the original normal users. Comparing the performance measures with those of normal users, we notice that the accuracy drops by at most 0.0035 (less than the expected maximum: 0.0075), AUC drops by at most 0.0012, and F1-measure drops by at most 0.0036.

In our experiments, we employ all 1,413 features to detect malicious users. Designing 1,413 features and computing their values is computationally expensive. Hence, we empirically determine whether all features are necessary next.

5.5 Feature Importance Analysis

Here, we analyze how important different features are in learning the malicious user detection function. In other

Table 3: Malicious User Detection Performance for Different Groups of Features.

Feature Groups	AUC	Accuracy
Complexity-based	0.8032	83.16%
Demographic-based	0.9342	86.78%
Anonymity-based	0.7219	63.26%
Similarity-based	**0.9933**	**95.86%**
Efficiency-based	0.9299	87.19%

words, we find features that contribute the most to the classification task. This can be performed by standard feature selection measures such as Information Gain, χ^2, among others. Here, we use the χ^2 statistic to find the top features. The top 10 features in decreasing order of importance are:

1. The information surprise of the username
2. The number of digits used in the username.
3. The percentage of keys pressed on the top row of a QWERTY keyboard when typing the username.
4. The percentage of keys pressed on the top row of a DVORAK keyboard when typing the username.
5. The proportion of digits used in the username.
6. The approximate distance (in meters) traveled for typing a username with a DVORAK keyboard.
7. The percentage of keys pressed on the home row of QWERTY keyboard when typing the username.
8. The approximate distance (in meters) traveled for typing a username with a QWERTY keyboard.
9. The percentage of keys pressed on the bottom row of a DVORAK keyboard when typing the username.
10. Entropy of the username.

We notice that the complexity of the username is the most important feature and that 6 of the top 10 features are features that capture typing patterns. Using only these 10 features, we trained a logistic regression model and achieved an accuracy of 92.95% and an AUC of 0.973.

We also determine groups of features that contribute most to the classification. We divide features into groups based on the characteristic of malicious users they represent. We denote these features based on the discussion in Section 4 as (1) Complexity-based, (2) Demographic-based, (3) Anonymity-based, (4) Similarity-based, and (5) Efficiency-based. Table 3 summarizes the classification performance obtained using only these groups of features.

We observe that similarity-based features work the best and anonymity-based features are least effective. Note that similarity-based features are in general hard to construct as they require n-gram constructions. Surprisingly, efficiency-based or complexity-based features that are easier to compute, can classify malicious users accurately, with up to 87% accuracy. Our observations in this section allows users with limited time and resources to take informed decisions on the features and groups of features to construct.

6. CONCLUSIONS AND FUTURE WORK

In this research, we have introduced a methodology that can identify malicious users with minimum information. Our methodology looks into different characteristics of malicious users and systematically constructs features that can capture traces of malicious behaviors. With new theories on characteristics of malicious users, new features can be introduced into our methodology.

We categorize characteristics of malicious users into 5 general categories. In particular, malicious users can be (1) complex and diverse, (2) demographically biased, (3) anonymous, (4) self-similar, and (5) efficient. A malicious user can exhibit one or a combination of these characteristics. By introducing comprehensive features across these five categories, we train a learning framework that can detect malicious users. The evaluation of this framework demonstrates the effectiveness of this systematic approach.

We notice some interesting observations. First, we notice that usernames that carry approximately 10 bits of information surprise, are more likely owned by normal users. Second, with only minimum information, one can achieve an accuracy of 97%, an AUC of 0.9971, and robust performances with different class imbalances and irrespective of the learning algorithm. Finally, we identify that in case of limited time or resources, one can implement a limited set of features and obtain reasonable accuracy rates.

The findings in this paper have many implications. First, we note that our methodology is in general easy to implement with minimum dependency on the availability of information. Second, our methodology works with usernames from different sites. This is empirically shown in our experiments with usernames collected from a variety of sites. Finally, our methodology performs with reasonable accuracy, compared to state-of-the-art techniques that have access to additional information.

Future work of this research includes integrating additional information available across sites in a principled manner. However, this extension requires considering the heterogeneity of data available across sites. In addition, similar to the observation we had regarding the information surprise values of usernames, we are interested in how surprise values change for other content generated by users.

Acknowledgments. The authors would like to thank Fred Morstatter, Shamanth Kumar, and Ashwin Rajadesingan for valuable suggestions. This work was supported, in part, by the Office of Naval Research grant: N000141410095.

7. REFERENCES

[1] Anne Barron. Understanding spam: A macro-textual analysis. *Journal of Pragmatics*, 38(6):880–904, 2006.

[2] Fabrıcio Benevenuto, Gabriel Magno, Tiago Rodrigues, and Virgılio Almeida. Detecting spammers on twitter. In *CEAS*, volume 6, page 12, 2010.

[3] Fabricio Benevenuto, Tiago Rodrigues, Virgilio Almeida, Jussara Almeida, Chao Zhang, and Keith Ross. Identifying video spammers in online social networks. In *Proceedings of the 4th international workshop on Adversarial information retrieval on the web*, pages 45–52. ACM, 2008.

[4] Qiang Cao, Michael Sirivianos, Xiaowei Yang, and Tiago Pregueiro. Aiding the detection of fake accounts in large scale social online services. In *NSDI*, 2012.

[5] Zi Chu, Steven Gianvecchio, Haining Wang, and Sushil Jajodia. Who is tweeting on twitter: human, bot, or cyborg? In *ACSAC*, pages 21–30, 2010.

[6] Thomas M Cover and Joy A Thomas. *Elements of information theory*. John Wiley & Sons, 2012.

[7] George Danezis and Prateek Mittal. Sybilinfer: Detecting sybil nodes using social networks. In *NDSS*, 2009.

[8] C. Doctorow. Preliminary Analysis of LinkedIn User Passwords. `http://bit.ly/L5AHo3`.

[9] T. Dunning. *Statistical Identification of Language*. CR Lab, New Mexico State University, 1994.

[10] J. Elder. Inside a Twitter Robot Factory. `http://on.wsj.com/1bdQbEI`.

[11] Lee Ellis, Kevin M Beaver, and John Wright. *Handbook of crime correlates*. Academic Press, 2009.

[12] Hongyu Gao, Jun Hu, Christo Wilson, Zhichun Li, Yan Chen, and Ben Y Zhao. Detecting and characterizing social spam campaigns. In *IMC*, pages 35–47. ACM, 2010.

[13] Saptarshi Ghosh, Bimal Viswanath, Farshad Kooti, Naveen Kumar Sharma, Gautam Korlam, Fabricio Benevenuto, Niloy Ganguly, and Krishna Phani Gummadi. Understanding and combating link farming in the twitter social network. In *WWW*, pages 61–70. ACM, 2012.

[14] Sam Gosling. *Snoop: What your stuff says about you*. Basic Books, 2009.

[15] C Harris. Detecting deceptive opinion spam using human computation. In *Workshops at AAAI on Artificial Intelligence*, 2012.

[16] Muhammad Asim Jamshed, Wonho Kim, and KyoungSoo Park. Suppressing bot traffic with accurate human attestation. In *Proceedings of the 1st ACM asia-pacific Workshop on systems*, pages 43–48, 2010.

[17] Ioannis Kanaris, Konstantinos Kanaris, Ioannis Houvardas, and Efstathios Stamatatos. Words versus character n-grams for anti-spam filtering. *International Journal on Artificial Intelligence Tools*, 16(06):1047–1067, 2007.

[18] Ioannis Kanaris, Konstantinos Kanaris, and Efstathios Stamatatos. Spam detection using character n-grams. In *Advances in Artificial Intelligence*, pages 95–104. Springer, 2006.

[19] Eamonn Keogh, Stefano Lonardi, and Chotirat Ann Ratanamahatana. Towards parameter-free data mining. In *SIGKDD*, pages 206–215. ACM, 2004.

[20] Beate Krause, Christoph Schmitz, Andreas Hotho, and Gerd Stumme. The anti-social tagger: detecting spam in social bookmarking systems. In *Proceedings of the 4th international workshop on Adversarial information retrieval on the web*, pages 61–68. ACM, 2008.

[21] Ho-Yu Lam. *A learning approach to spam detection based on social networks*. PhD thesis, HKUST, 2007.

[22] Ming Li and Paul MB Vitányi. *An introduction to Kolmogorov complexity and its applications*. Springer, 2009.

[23] Vijay Mahajan and Robert A Peterson. *Models for innovation diffusion*, volume 48. Sage, 1985.

[24] Benjamin Markines, Ciro Cattuto, and Filippo Menczer. Social spam detection. In *Proceedings of the 5th International Workshop on Adversarial Information Retrieval on the Web*, pages 41–48, 2009.

[25] MediaWiki. Combating Spam - List of Proxy and Spambot IPs. `bit.ly/1mwUqml`.

[26] Greg Mori and Jitendra Malik. Recognizing objects in adversarial clutter: Breaking a visual captcha. In *CVPR*, volume 1, pages I–134. IEEE, 2003.

[27] Terri Oda and Tony White. Increasing the accuracy of a spam-detecting artificial immune system. In *CEC*, volume 1, pages 390–396. IEEE, 2003.

[28] Daniele Perito, Claude Castelluccia, Mohamed Ali Kaafar, and Pere Manils. How unique and traceable are usernames? In *PET*, pages 1–17. Springer, 2011.

[29] Gianluca Stringhini, Christopher Kruegel, and Giovanni Vigna. Detecting spammers on social networks. In *ACSAC*, pages 1–9. ACM, 2010.

[30] Dinh Nguyen Tran, Bonan Min, Jinyang Li, and Lakshminarayanan Subramanian. Sybil-resilient online content voting. In *NSDI*, volume 9, pages 15–28, 2009.

[31] Nguyen Tran, Jinyang Li, Lakshminarayanan Subramanian, and Sherman SM Chow. Optimal sybil-resilient node admission control. In *INFOCOM*, pages 3218–3226, 2011.

[32] Bimal Viswanath, Ansley Post, Krishna P Gummadi, and Alan Mislove. An analysis of social network-based sybil defenses. *SIGCOMM Computer Communication Review*, 41(4):363–374, 2011.

[33] Luis Von Ahn, Manuel Blum, Nicholas J Hopper, and John Langford. Captcha: Using hard ai problems for security. In *EUROCRYPT 2003*, pages 294–311. Springer, 2003.

[34] Alex Hai Wang. Don't follow me: Spam detection in twitter. In *SECRYPT*, pages 1–10. IEEE, 2010.

[35] T. Wasserman. 83 Million Facebook Accounts Are Fake. `http://on.mash.to/1hdze2B`.

[36] Wikipedia. Keyboard Layouts. `http://bit.ly/kXso`.

[37] Wikipedia. List of countries by population. `http://bit.ly/1eTTUHe`.

[38] Gregory L Wittel and Shyhtsun Felix Wu. On attacking statistical spam filters. In *CEAS*, 2004.

[39] Yinglian Xie, Fang Yu, Kannan Achan, Rina Panigrahy, Geoff Hulten, and Ivan Osipkov. Spamming botnets: signatures and characteristics. *Computer Communication Review*, 38(4):171–182, 2008.

[40] J. Yan, A. Blackwell, R. Anderson, and A. Grant. The Memorability and Security of Passwords-Some Empirical Results. *U. of Cambridge Tech. Rep.*, 2000.

[41] Jeff Yan and Ahmad Salah El Ahmad. A low-cost attack on a microsoft captcha. In *Proceedings of the 15th ACM conference on Computer and communications security*, pages 543–554. ACM, 2008.

[42] Zhi Yang, Christo Wilson, Xiao Wang, Tingting Gao, Ben Y Zhao, and Yafei Dai. Uncovering social network sybils in the wild. In *IMC*, pages 259–268. ACM, 2011.

[43] Sarita Yardi, Daniel Romero, Grant Schoenebeck, et al. Detecting spam in a twitter network. *First Monday*, 15(1), 2009.

[44] Haifeng Yu, Phillip B Gibbons, Michael Kaminsky, and Feng Xiao. Sybillimit: A near-optimal social network defense against sybil attacks. In *Security and Privacy*, pages 3–17, 2008.

[45] Haifeng Yu, Michael Kaminsky, Phillip B Gibbons, and Abraham Flaxman. Sybilguard: defending against sybil attacks via social networks. *Computer Communication Review*, 36(4):267–278, 2006.

[46] Reza Zafarani and Huan Liu. Connecting users across social media sites: a behavioral-modeling approach. In *SIGKDD*, pages 41–49. ACM, 2013.

MAPer: A Multi-scale Adaptive Personalized Model for Temporal Human Behavior Prediction

Sarah Masud Preum
University of Virginia
Charlottesville, Virginia 22904
preum@virginia.edu

John A. Stankovic
University of Virginia
Charlottesville, Virginia 22904
jas9f@virginia.edu

Yanjun Qi
University of Virginia
Charlottesville, Virginia 22904
yq2h@virginia.edu

ABSTRACT

The primary objective of this research is to develop a simple and interpretable predictive framework to perform temporal modeling of individual user's behavior traits based on each person's past observed traits/behavior. Individual-level human behavior patterns are possibly influenced by various temporal features (e.g., lag, cycle) and vary across temporal scales (e.g., hour of the day, day of the week). Most of the existing forecasting models do not capture such multi-scale adaptive regularity of human behavior or lack interpretability due to relying on hidden variables. Hence, we build a **multi-scale adaptive personalized (MAPer)** model that quantifies the effect of both lag and behavior cycle for predicting future behavior. MAper includes a novel basis vector to adaptively learn behavior patterns and capture the variation of lag and cycle across multi-scale temporal contexts. We also extend MAPer to capture the interaction among multiple behaviors to improve the prediction performance.

We demonstrate the effectiveness of MAPer on four real datasets representing different behavior domains, including, habitual behavior collected from Twitter, need based behavior collected from search logs, and activities of daily living collected from a single resident and a multi-resident home. Experimental results indicate that MAPer significantly improves upon the state-of-the-art and baseline methods and at the same time is able to explain the temporal dynamics of individual-level human behavior.

Keywords

Time series prediction; Temporal human behavior modeling

1. INTRODUCTION

Regular human behaviors are constantly being captured in virtual platforms (e.g., social media, search logs) as well as in physical platforms (e.g., smart phone, smart watch) [16]. The vast amount of individual user data generated by these platforms facilitates modeling the temporal footprint

CIKM'15, October 19–23, 2015, Melbourne, Australia.
© 2015 ACM. ISBN 978-1-4503-3794-6/15/10 ...$15.00.
DOI: http://dx.doi.org/10.1145/2806416.2806562.

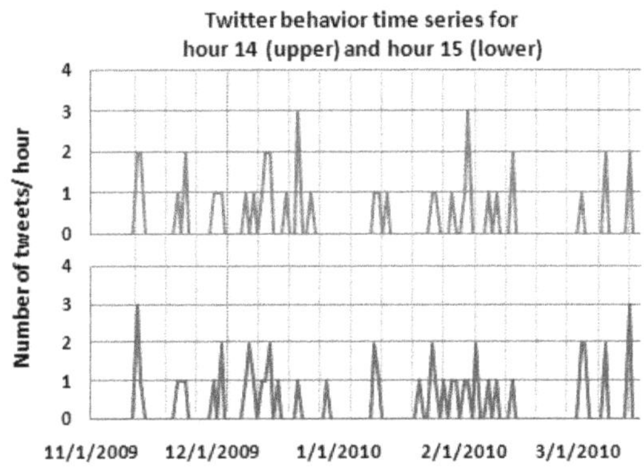

Figure 1: A Twitter user often tweets at hour 14 and hour 15 at the same day. This depiction from real data suggests an impact of lag on tweeting behavior, i.e., the behavior at hour 14 is followed by the behavior at hour 15.

of different human behaviors. Accurate and explanatory temporal behavior models can serve as the building block of several useful applications.

For example, predicting when an online user is going to be active (e.g., searching a query, posting a tweet) can be useful for targeted advertising (e.g., finding peak *social* hours to maximize visibility of content among target audience) [6], churn prediction (i.e., predicting users who are likely to leave a service provider) [27], and temporal user profiling [1, 11]. Similarly, a predictive model that can model human behaviors in the context of daily activities (e.g., sleeping, cooking, or eating) is extremely useful for functional assessment of elderly people [9] and designing behavior intervention for rehabilitation [26]. Scott et al. demonstrated that dynamically predicting room occupancy and energy usage patterns of its residents enable efficient designing of smart thermostats and thus save energy costs significantly [23]. Explanatory predictive models can serve end users who use smart phones and smart watches for self monitoring: a sleep monitoring application that builds explanatory predictive models of sleep pattern can help the user to detect sleep anomaly and suggest sleep time.

This paper focuses on a data-driven modeling of temporal human behavior at a single individual level. Our goal is to build an accurate and interpretable temporal behavior model that can serve as a building block for the motivating examples presented above.

Individual-level temporal behavior is often influenced by three major temporal features: (1) temporal smoothness (i.e., lag), (2) behavior rhythms (i.e., cycle), and (3) interaction among multiple behaviors. Temporal smoothness refers to lag phenomenon: behavior at time t can be influenced by the behavior at time $(t-1)$ (Figure 1). Behavior rhythm refers to the repetitive habits of a human. For instance, some online users frequently post tweets on Friday night (i.e., cycle length is 7 days). Moreover, often the interaction among multiple behavior traits/activities needs to be captured to model a single behavior, e.g., watching TV until late night can delay sleep time. Quantifying the effects of these features on a specific behavior of an individual is challenging, because they vary with multi-scale temporal contexts (e.g., specific hour of the day or day of the week). Such as, working people may prefer watching TV for a longer duration during weekend nights rather than during weekday mornings. Here, the lag length is changing due to the change in temporal context from a weekday morning to a weekend night. To address such personalized temporal dynamics, we need a modeling approach that dynamically adapts with such variation of features over multiple time scales.

The existing time series prediction models are too general to be applicable in this context. With regard to the computational behavior modeling methods, the most relevant existing study is from Zhu et al. where they predict user activity level in social media [27]. But their modeling of temporal behavior dynamics is limited to reducing the impact of out-of-date training data. Another work uses Bayesian networks to predict future activity based on current activity in a home setting [20]. Neither of these works quantify the effect of variation of the temporal features across multi-scale temporal contexts (e.g., daily, weekly).

The main contributions of this paper are following. (i) We build a **multi-scale adaptive personalized** model, namely **MAPer**, that models regular temporal human behavior by capturing the effects of three temporal features: lag, cycle, and interaction among multiple behaviors. (ii) We introduce a novel approach to capture the variation of these behavior features across multi-scale temporal contexts and learn adaptively. (iii) Our performance analysis demonstrates the overall effectiveness of MAPer as compared to multiple baselines and a state-of-art time series prediction model (SARIMA). Using behavior data collected from Twitter [7], search logs [21], and two smart homes [3, 13], we show the effectiveness of the key parts of the model, demonstrate the value of personalization, and perform a sensitivity analysis along three dimensions: training set size, temporal scale, and order of lag. These experiments show MAPer reduces prediction error by about 15%, 31% and 10% over the state-of-art SARIMA model for Twitter, search log, and a single resident smart home data, respectively. (iv) Another key value of our solution is its explanatory capability. As MAPer uses a linear model for prediction based on only observed behavior, it has higher interpretability over other predictive models that are non-linear or rely on unobserved variables (e.g., state space model or hidden Markov model).

2. PROBLEM FORMULATION

2.1 Extracting Discrete Time Series from Temporal Behavior Data Stream

We use $H(t)$ to represent a given behavior data with corresponding time stamp spanning over a total stream length T. We divide T into a set of n equal length time intervals $t_1, t_2, \ldots, t_i, \ldots, t_n$. Then we summarize $H(t)$ over each in-

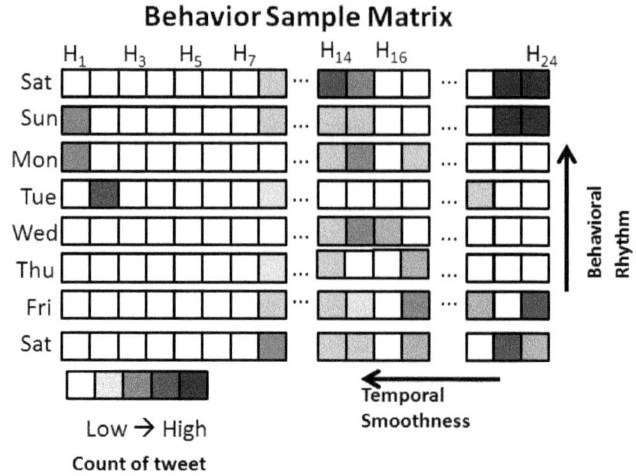

Figure 2: An example of behavior sample matrix representation: demonstrating lag and cycle for modeling an individual user's behavior in the context of Twitter usage. The cells are darkened in proportion to the number of tweets at the corresponding time interval.

terval to obtain behavior sample $Hs(s, t_i)$, such that Hs applies a summarizing process s over the behavior of interval t_i. The summarizing process s can be frequency/average/length of some countable behavior measure. With this process we get a discrete series of n behavior samples: $Hs(s, t_1)$, $Hs(s, t_2)$,..., $Hs(s, t_n)$ For example, consider a set of tweets from a Twitter user u, where each tweet has its corresponding time stamp. After sorting the tweets according to their increasing time stamp, we find the total window length T that spans from the starting time stamp to the ending time stamp. Assume there are n different days in T. Next, we divide T into hourly/daily/weekly intervals. If the chosen interval is *hour* and the chosen summarizing process is *total count of tweets* then the behavior sample will be *total count of tweets per hour*. In this case, the length of the behavior sample time series will be $n \times 24$, since we divide each day into 24 hours. The choices of interval and summarizing process depend on a specific application requirement.

We denote the time series $Hs(s, t_i)$ as y_i in the rest of the paper. In addition, we denote y_i for an activity[1] k of a user (e.g., an activity of daily living) as y_t^k. Our goal is to predict y_i^k based on it's previous values i.e., $y_1^k, y_2^k, \ldots, y_{i-1}^k$.

Essentially, a more accurate notation would be $y_t^{k,u}$ to indicate modeling specific activity k from an individual u. Instead, we use the simplified notation y_t^k since we do not consider interaction among multiple users for predicting future activity of a single user.

2.2 Behavior Sample Matrix Generation

After generating the discrete time series from historical longitudinal behavior data of a user (u^k), we create corresponding behavior-sample matrix (M) to extract features corresponding to lag, cycle, and interaction with other behaviors. This matrix representation encodes the temporal patterns of behavior concisely. Specifically, each row of M represents a day (d_i) and each column of M represents an hour (h_j). The content of a cell $M_{i,j}^k$ is the sample of a

[1]We use the terms activity and behavior interchangeably in this paper.

behavior k from a user u on day d_i and hour h_j. In other words, $M_{i,j}^k$ represents the intensity of overall activity level of the user at the j-th hour of the i-th day.

Figure 2 demonstrates a Twitter behavior sample matrix where the behavior sample is the count of tweets per hour. It appears this particular user is most active during weekend nights. Tweets generated at hour 14 might act as a lag feature to tweets generated at hour 15. The Twitter user usually tweets on hour 24 during weekends. So there is a possible cycle of this behavior that repeats on weekends. As shown in Figure 2, the contents of same columns contribute to behavior rhythm or cycle and the contents of same rows contribute to temporal smoothness or lag.

This matrix representation highlights the lag and cycle properties of regular human behavior and is easily generalizable to represent more coarse or granular time scales. After generating behavior sample matrix, we build a general temporal model for behavior prediction that extracts the temporal features from this matrix.

3. MULTI-SCALE ADAPTIVE PERSONALIZED MODEL

In this section we present incrementally the formation of the MAPer model. Since MAPer combines lag, cycle, and interaction among multiple behaviors across multiple temporal scales, we first describe extracting lag feature(s) and then incrementally add features culminating in the complete model in Section 3.1.4.

3.1 Extracting Features for Temporal Behavior Prediction

3.1.1 Temporal Smoothness/Lag Features

For the purpose of forecasting the lag features can be represented using auto regression (**AR**), a standard linear time series forecasting technique. An l-th order auto-regressive model for predicting the t-th item of a behavior time series time series is described as,

$$\hat{y}_t = \sum_{i=1}^{l} \alpha_i \cdot y_{t-i} + c + \epsilon \quad (1)$$

where $\alpha_1, \alpha_2, \ldots, \alpha_l$ are lag parameters to learn, c is a constant, and the random variable ϵ represents white noise [12]. The coefficient value of α_i quantifies the effect of the i-th lag component for the current time point. Referring to Figure 2, for a cell $M_{i,j}^k$ in a behavior time series matrix M^k, we consider $M_{i,j-1}^k$ as the lag of order 1, $M_{i,j-2}^k$ as the lag of order 2, and so on. We also wrap the matrix to extract lag features for early hours of a day. Such as, when predicting for hour 1 of a day and considering a lag of order 4, we extract lag features from hour 21 to hour 24 of the past day.

3.1.2 Behavioral Rhythm/Cycle Features

Human behaviors often demonstrate cyclic pattern, such as, cooking meal on every Friday night (i.e., the cycle is 7 days). To capture the behavior rhythm effect, we add a cycle component in Equation 1. The derived model for a single individual is presented below.

$$\hat{y}_t = \sum_{i=1}^{l} \alpha_i \cdot y_{t-i} + \sum_{j=1}^{c} \beta_j \cdot y_{t-c_j} + c' + \epsilon \quad (2)$$

Here, the value of the coefficient β_j quantifies the effect of j-th cyclic component on the current time point of interest. If the cycle of a behavior time series is found to be 7 days, we will use $M_{3,16}^k$ as a cycle feature to predict the value of $M_{10,16}^k$. We describe the method of selecting cycles of a behavior time series in Section 3.2.

In the rest of the paper, we refer to the model corresponding to Equation 2 as the auto regression with cycle component (**AR-C**) model.

3.1.3 Interaction Features

So far for predicting future values of time series of activity k (i.e., y_t^k), we have extracted features from only the time series y_t^k. But often time series of one activity can influence another from the same user as the corresponding activities interact with each other. We define such interaction of human behaviors/activities in terms of co-occurrence. We hypothesize that, if two activities are frequently observed consecutively, the former activities can influence the prediction of the later for which they *interact*. For instance, watching TV and using internet until late night often delay sleeping. In this case, *watching TV* and *using internet* are interacting with *sleeping*. Similarly, having a meal is usually followed by washing dishes. To consider such interactions among activity k and other activities, we update equation 2 as below.

$$\hat{y}_t{}^k \approx \sum_{i=1}^{L_k} \alpha_i^k \cdot y_{t-i}^k + \sum_{j=1}^{C_k} \beta_j^k \cdot y_{t-c_j}^k + \sum_{k' \in S} \sum_{l'=1}^{L_{k'}} W_{l'}^{(k,k')} \cdot y_{t-l'}^{k'} \quad (3)$$

Here, S is a set of activities of a user u and $k \neq k'$ such that activity k' precedes activity k and interacts with it. $L_{k'}$ refers to the length of lag that we are considering for the behavior time series $y_t^{k'}$. Note that we omit $c'' + \epsilon$ from Equation 5 and subsequent equations to simplify notations.

Unlike Equation 2, Equation 3 models an individual's single activity k using historical values of k and a set of other activities (i.e., k's) that influence k.

3.1.4 Multi-scale Adaptive Features

For regular daily human behavior the two most common temporal contexts of behavior are day of the week and hour of the day. Often behavior varies over such multi-scale temporal contexts. The lag length, cycle, and amount of interaction vary with the temporal contexts too. Such as, the order of lag of watching TV is likely to vary from morning to night for working class people, as they have to leave home early in the morning. Here the lag is varying with hour of the day. Similarly, it can vary with day of the week. Therefore, we need a feature representation to encode such multi-scale variation and adapt the prediction model dynamically.

Hence, we introduce a discrete binary vector representation describing multi-scale temporal contexts whose length is determined by the corresponding scale (e.g., hour of the day or day of the week) and whose value is determined by the current time stamp. Specifically, hour i can be represented as a 24-dimensional binary vector with a series of $(i-1)$ zeroes followed by an one and $(24-i)$ zeroes. Thus, hour 3 can be represented by a series of two zeroes followed by an one and 21 zeroes. The corresponding vector B_3 is $[00100\ldots0]$, where $|B_3| = 24$. Similarly, we obtain a basis vector representation describing different days of the week.

We denote the combination of daily basis vector and weekly basis vector as $\vec{B_d}, \vec{B_w}$. We add this basis vector representation in Equation 3 to represent the multi-scale temporal context.

$$\hat{y_t}^k \approx \sum_{i=1}^{L_k} \alpha_i^k \cdot y_{t-i}^k + \sum_{j=1}^{C_k} \beta_j^k \cdot y_{t-c_j}^k + \gamma^k \cdot (\vec{B_d}, \vec{B_w}) + \sum_{k' \in S} \sum_{l'=1}^{L_{k'}} W_{l'}^{(k,k')} \cdot y_{t-l'}^{k'} \quad (4)$$

We use the model corresponding to Equation 4 when we consider interaction between multiple streams of behavior. Otherwise, we use the following model.

$$\hat{y_t}^k \approx \sum_{i=1}^{L_k} \alpha_i^k \cdot y_{t-i}^k + \sum_{j=1}^{C_k} \beta_j^k \cdot y_{t-c_j}^k + \gamma^k \cdot (\vec{B_d}, \vec{B_w}) \quad (5)$$

It should be noted that unlike lag and cycle features, the value of $(\vec{B_d}, \vec{B_w})$ is not unique for all y_t where $t \in 1, 2, \ldots, n$. $(\vec{B_d}, \vec{B_w})$ is same for y_i and y_j if they represent same day of the week and same hour of the day. This is necessary to encode the temporal context of behavior: behavior samples from similar context share similar features. Equation 4 captures the effect of temporal smoothness, behavior rhythm, interaction, and multi-scale temporal contexts using parameters α_i, β_j, γ, and basis vectors $(\vec{B_d}, \vec{B_w})$, respectively. This model is personalized for each user and is customized for each activity of the user. In addition, the basis vector representation enables the model to learn adaptively across multi-scale temporal contexts. Hence we denote the model corresponding to Equation 4 as the **M**ulti-scale **A**daptive **Per**sonalized (**MAPer**) model.

With different combination of basis vectors, we have two variations of MAPer: (i) daily scale adaptive personalized (**DAPer**) model that uses only daily basis vector ($\vec{B_d}$) and (ii) weekly scale adaptive personalized (**WAPer**) model that uses only weekly basis vector ($\vec{B_w}$). MAPer uses both daily and weekly basis vectors. MAPer can be also generalized to add more coarse/granular temporal contexts.

3.2 Feature Selection

Cycle Features: The cycle of a behavior can vary across individual users and individual activities. We extract the cycle length of a behavior time series by applying discrete Fast Fourier Transform (FFT) analysis, a spectral decomposition technique where we treat the time series as an input signal. Although there are other time series decomposition techniques including piecewise polynomial, symbolic, wavelets, etc. [24], they are out of scope of this paper. We derive a set of frequencies from the FFT analysis and choose the highest C frequencies as the relevant cycle features, where the frequencies are sorted according to their amplitudes. We plug in these C frequencies as the cycle features in the models corresponding to Equation 2 to Equation 5.

Interaction Features: Considering all activities for modeling interaction can introduce noise rather than signal and increase the feature space prohibitively, since only a subset of behaviors interact with each other usually. To select a subset of activities that interact with our target activity k, we propose a frequent item-set mining approach. Specifically, for each day we sample every two hours and create an itemset of activities that took place during that window. We empirically set the window length to two hours. We do not use a strict window to create itemsets as (i) it results into large number of unique itemsets (i.e., occur only once), (ii) it can not capture fluctuation of routine: one may frequently have dinner at anytime between 7.30pm to 8.30pm. After all the itemsets are generated over the training set, we generate the closed itemsets[2] using ECLAT [5], a fast algorithm for frequent item set mining. For each activity of our interest, we sort other activities that appear in the closed itemsets based on how frequently they co-occur. Finally, for each activity k we use the top three activities derived from the closed item set such that they precede the k-th activity. The interaction features for activity k are extracted from these three activities according to Equation 4. Using frequent itemset mining for interaction features is scalable as the number of candidates (i.e., ADLs) for interaction is limited in our case.

4. CONNECTING TO PAST STUDIES

Although the exact problem we are trying to solve is unique in the literature, there are various relevant areas of existing research as presented below.

Time series forecasting: For the task of time series prediction, the existing algorithms can be broadly categorized as parametric and non-parametric approaches. Parametric approaches assume the underlying stationary process has a structure which can be estimated using a number of parameters. Hence, these methods normally fit a statistical model on the time series data and have better interpretability. The Autoregressive Integrated Moving Average (**ARIMA**) model [15] is used to forecast a stationary time series[3]. The ARIMA model predicts a stationary time series (y_t) using lags of the dependent variable (y_{t-l}) and lags of forecasting error ($e_t = y_t - \hat{y_t}$). A non seasonal ARIMA model is expressed as ARIMA(p,d,q) where p,d, and q are the model parameters corresponding to the number of auto-regressive terms, the number of nonseasonal differences needed for stationarity, and the number of lagged forecast errors used in the prediction equation. Suppose Y_t denotes the d-th difference of y_t, i.e., if $d = 0$ then $Y_t = y_t$, if $d = 1$ then $Y_t = y_t - y_{t-1}$, and so on. Then the general forecasting equation for the ARIMA model is

$$\hat{Y_t} \approx \mu + \sum_{i=1}^{l} \phi_i \cdot Y_{t-i} + \sum_{i=1}^{l} \theta_i \cdot e_{t-i} \quad (6)$$

The ARIMA model is one of the most general time series forecasting models as many forecasting models are merely a special case of ARIMA model. For instance, ARIMA(l,0,0) is the l-th order auto-regressive model expressed as Equation 1. A seasonal ARIMA (SARIMA) model is a state-of-art parametric model of time series forecasting. It uses seasonal lag and differencing to fit the seasonal pattern. The SARIMA model can be expressed as ARIMA (p,d,q) × (P,D,Q), where P, D, and Q denote the number of seasonal autoregressive terms, the number of seasonal differencing, and the number of seasonal moving-average terms.

[2] An itemset is closed if none of its immediate supersets has the same support as the itemset.

[3] A time series is stationary if its statistical properties are constant over time. A non stationary time series can be made stationary by differencing and non-linear transformation (if required).

On the other hand, nonparametric approaches (e.g., neural network based local forecasting models) approximate the underlying structure of the stationary process that generates the time series without making any structural assumption. A comprehensive survey on time series forecasting can be found in [8]. There are also several variations of vector autoregressive methods that aim at multi-dimensional time series forecasting [18].

Activity Prediction: Although a lot of works from computer vision and sensing community focus on activity recognition, the problem of daily activity prediction is largely unexplored. A recent work [20] proposes an activity prediction approach using Bayesian network. Unlike us, they model the problem as a multi-label classification and predict activity label and relative start time using current activity label, location, and temporal context. Although they consider daily and weekly context of behavior, their approach does not quantify the effect of different temporal features and lacks explanatory power. Pentland et al. propose that some human behaviors (e.g., driving, running) can be described as a set of dynamic models (e.g., Kalman filters) sequenced together by a Markov chain. However, as their application domain involves more granular behavior, it does not require quantifying the effect of cycle on behavior or how lag/cycle varies with multi-scale temporal contexts.

Zhu et al. focus on predicting user activity level in social networks to facilitate churn prediction (i.e., identify users who are likely to leave a service) [27]. They build a personalized and socially regularized time decay model based on logistic regression to capture effects of user diversity, social influence on future activity level. A novel approach of activity prediction was proposed in [25]. They predict a set of future popular activities by analyzing textual content of Twitter posts using keyword matching. Unlike other works [20, 27], they focus on aggregated behavior rather than individual behavior. Although these research focus on behavior prediction, unlike us they do not explicitly quantify the effect of different temporal factors (e.g., lag, cycle) on regular human behavior.

Modeling Temporal Behavior: Recently, the temporal modeling of online user population has been extensively studied in order to improve query search performance [22, 4, 17], to understand and model content generation in social networking sites [1, 2], and to model mobile behavior of users [10, 19].

For example, aiming to improve the query auto-suggestion and the ranking results, Radinsky et al. recently developed a temporal modeling framework that predicts temporal patterns of aggregated web search behavior [22]. Specifically, they model temporal features, like, trend, periodicity, and sudden spikes of queries by using dynamic state space models. Although their work is similar to ours in terms of modeling behavior based on temporal features, they focus on temporal modeling of search queries, while our study focuses on directly modeling the temporal behavior of humans. Baskaya et al. analyzed the effects of a set of search-related human behaviors (e.g., formulate a query, scan, click a link) on retrieval performance [4]. In [17] the authors studied how search behaviors of users evolve over time, e.g., long term users demonstrate more complex behavior than newbies.

In addition to improving query based content-search, temporal modeling has also been explored to analyze user behavior in social media or on content sharing platforms. Abel et al. demonstrated how temporal profiling of Twitter users based on their shared contents facilitates personalized news article recommendation [1]. Although these previous studies mostly analyzed user generated textual contents for modeling the temporal dynamics, our proposed temporal modeling of individual-level human behavior could facilitate their goals as well.

Name	Entities	Span	Domain
Search log	1307 users	3 months	Need based behavior
Twitter	1274 users	5 months	Habitual behavior
ARAS	27 ADLs	1 month	Multi-resident home
HOLMES	14 ADLs	3 months	Single-resident home

Table 1: Summary of datasets used for evaluation.

5. EXPERIMENTAL SETUP

5.1 Data

To evaluate the effectiveness and generality of our model we use four benchmark datasets each representing different aspects of human behavior. The datasets are summarized in Table 1. The details are described below[4].

Search Log Data Representing Need Based Behavior

We use AOL search log data [21] for predicting temporal query search behavior. This dataset consists of around 20M web queries collected from 650k users. The data was collected for over three months starting from March 2006 to May 2006. The dataset includes anonymized user ID, search query, time stamp of query, and click information (whether a search result was clicked or not). The data is sorted by anonymous user ID and is sequentially arranged according to their time stamps. We have used a subset of this dataset containing 1307 unique users so that each user has a search log spanning 60 days. In our sampled dataset there are 449,423 unique queries in total. However, from our experiments we discover that our modeling approach is generalizable to other cases where the training phase is as small as 2 weeks (Section 6.3.1).

We consider number of unique queries per hour as the behavior sample and generate a normalized behavior sample matrix as described in Section 2.2. Other choices of behavior samples include number of queries, number of clicks, duration of a session. Also, the temporal resolution of the interval (i.e., hour) can be adjusted to different granularity (e.g., week, day).

Twitter Data Representing Habitual Behavior

We use a Twitter dataset [7] for predicting users' temporal social media behavior. It consists of 121,022 users and more than 9 million time-stamped tweets that were collected from September 2009 to January 2010. However, it does not include any re-tweet and follow relationships. We sample the dataset to obtain the users who have Twitter posts spanning over at least 120 days. In total we obtain 1,275,709 tweets from 1,274 Twitter users for evaluating our predictive model.

We consider number of tweets per hour as the behavior sample. Alternatively, one can use number of Twitter messages, number of re-tweets, duration of Twitter session, or a weighted combination of these as a behavior sample. The

[4]The datasets are available here: https://goo.gl/Za0YIs

generation of a Twitter behavior sample matrix is similar to the generation of a search log behavior sample matrix.

ARAS: ADL Data from a Multi Resident Setting

We consider Activities of Daily Living (ADL) data as the behavior captured from physical world where each activity corresponds to a behavior.

We use the ARAS smart home project [3] dataset as a multi-resident ADL dataset. It contains labelled sensor data from a system deployed in a smart home of 2 residents. This dataset has 27 annotated activities of daily living for each user. It contains start time and end time of each activity. With a preference to model and predict health related behaviors, we focus on 5 behaviors from each user. They are: sleeping, snacking, having breakfast, lunch, and dinner. However, for resident 2, the number of samples for having breakfast, lunch and dinner are too few. So we model 7 activities for 2 users in total: sleeping of both residents, snacking of both residents, and breakfast, lunch, and dinner of resident 1.

HOLMES: ADL Data from a Single Resident Setting

We use HOLMES dataset as a single resident ADL dataset [13]. We use three months data from this dataset. It contains 15 annotated activities from which we model the following health related activities: sleeping, breakfast, lunch, dinner, snack, shower, and cooking.

While in case of the Twitter data and the search log data we model each user separately, in case of the ADL data we perform forecasting of each activity of each user separately[5]. Unlike the Twitter or search log data, we use the duration of an activity as the behavior sample instead of count of activity since most of the ADL take place only once per interval. We sample each activity duration every half an hour for each day to form a time series of duration of each activity. Later, we vary the temporal resolution/scale to demonstrate the effect of temporal resolution on the prediction accuracy. We normalize the behavior sample matrix, M such that if activity k takes place over the whole span of interval j on day i, then $M^k_{i,j}$ contains 1; if activity a^k takes place over half of the span of interval j of day i, then $M^k_{i,j}$ contains 0.5 and so on.

5.2 Comparing with Baseline Methods

1. Moving Average (MA): As one of the simplest time series forecasting method, the moving average method predicts average of l lag values as the next value. We modify the original moving average model to include the effect of cycle. Specifically, the prediction at y_t is the average of all l lag components and all c cyclic components. Using our behavior sample matrix, the lag components are selected from l previous columns of the same row and the cycle components are selected from c previous rows of the same column. Mathematically,

$$\hat{y_t} \approx 0.5 \times \left(\frac{\sum_{i=1}^{l} y_{t-i}}{l} + \frac{\sum_{i=1}^{c} y_{(t-i*24)}}{c} \right).$$

In our experiments we set $l = 4$ hours and $c = 14$ days. To compare the performance of MAPer with a non-parametric baseline method that considers both lag and cycle, we use this method.

2. Auto regression with Cycle Component (AR-C): Equation 2 refers to this baseline method.

To compare the performance of MAPer with a parametric baseline method that considers both lag and cycle, we use this method. It is also used to highlight the effectiveness of adaptive learning.

5.3 Comparing with state-of-art

We compare MAPer with the SARIMA model, a parametric state-of-art forecasting model described in Section 4. We use an R implementation of SARIMA model provided in [14]. For parameter estimation of SARIMA model, we use a function that conducts a search over all possible models and return the best model according to AIC value. We use this model to explore the predictive power of MAPer across different behavior domains.

For the SARIMA model and MAPer, we perform two parameter estimation settings: global and local. In general, we divide a chronologically sorted behavior dataset into training and testing sets. For global parameter estimation, we estimate the parameters only once using the full training set. But for local parameter estimation, we take a sliding window approach to form a separate training set for each point of test set. Specifically, for predicting i-th point in the test set, we construct the training set from $(i - w)$ to $(i - 1)$ point where w is the length of the sliding window.

5.4 Response Variable and Metrics

We evaluate our model mainly in a regression setting to predict the future intensity of a behavior marker based on its historical samples. In this setting, the content of each cell of behavior sample matrix acts as a response variable (y_i) where $y_i \in [\,0, 1]$. The features described in Section 3 act as the predictor variables. We measure the performance in terms of two standard evaluation metrics: mean square error (MSE) of prediction and Pearson correlation (PC) between the actual y and the predicted y.

We compare the baselines described in Section 5.2 with MAPer and show how effective the various features (described in Section 3) of MAPer are. We also evaluate the effectiveness of (i) multi-scale adaptive features, (ii) personalized modeling, and (iii) interaction among activities. While comparing different methods, we set the corresponding parameters to default values. Later, we perform sensitivity analysis by varying its hyper-parameters.

6. EXPERIMENTAL RESULTS

6.1 Effectiveness of MAPer

6.1.1 Comparing with Baseline Methods

In this section we compare the performance of MAPer with two baseline methods (Section 5.2). Referring to **Tables 2** and **3**, MAPer outperforms all baseline methods in terms of MSE for search log, Twitter, and HOLMES data. MAPer increases the Pearson Correlation at least 1.5 times when compared to the baseline methods for all of the datasets. This highlights the significance of using temporally adaptive learning method where the significance of lag and cycle features varies over time.

[5]Given a Twitter dataset that annotates different activities of a user (e.g., tweeting, re-tweeting, sending message), we can model each activity of a Twitter user separately too.

	Baseline Methods		state-of-art		Multi-scale Adaptive Methods		% Improvement
Dataset	MA	AR-C	Global SARIMA	Local SARIMA	Global MAPer	Local MAPer	over state-of-art
Search log	0.046	0.045	0.065	0.048	0.045	**0.041**	14.6
Twitter	0.056	0.052	0.073	0.065	0.049	**0.045**	30.7
ARAS	0.032	0.017	0.042	**0.011**	0.018	0.016	-
HOLMES	0.021	0.001	0.082	0.001	0.001	**0.0009**	10

Table 2: Comparing different methods in terms of mean **MSE**. The best performing (statistically significant) results are shown in bold. The right-most column shows the performance improvement of MAPer over the state-of-art (Local SARIMA). Local models outperforms global models and MAPer results into the lowest prediction error.

	Baseline Methods		state-of-art		Multi-scale Adaptive Methods		% Improvement
Dataset	MA	AR-C	Global SARIMA	Local SARIMA	Global MAPer	Local MAPer	over state-of-art
Search log	0.180	0.165	0.098	**0.479**	0.228	0.337	-
Twitter	0.277	0.330	0.079	0.254	0.410	**0.491**	93.3
ARAS	0.239	0.384	0.204	0.7166	0.446	**0.782**	9
HOLMES	0.296	0.104	0.136	0.340	0.277	**0.583**	71.5

Table 3: Comparing different methods in terms of mean **Pearson Correlation**. MAPer outperforms the SARIMA model for all datasets except the search log data.

6.1.2 Comparing with SARIMA

Tables 2 and **3** demonstrate that the local model outperforms the global model for all four datasets in case of both the SARIMA model and MAPer. This highlights the dynamic pattern of human behavior. In subsequent sections we use only the local estimation approach, i.e., MAPer refers to local MAPer.

In terms of MSE, MAPer with local parameter estimation outperforms SARIMA for both online behavior dataset and for HOLMES dataset. Specifically, it reduces MSE from the SARIMA model by 14.6%, 30.7%, and 10% for search log, Twitter, and HOLMES dataset, respectively. This performance improvement is statistically significant at 95% confidence interval as found in a pair wise t-test. In terms of Pearson correlation, MAPer increases the performance by about 93.3%, 9%, and 71.5% for Twitter, ARAS, and HOLMES data, respectively. The local SARIMA model performs better than MAPer in terms of Pearson correlation for search log data. Because, issuing search query is a need based behavior and MAPer performs better in case of predicting habitual behavior.

Overall, MAPer demonstrates better or at least equal predictive power to SARIMA model for all four datsets. In case of Twitter, MAPer significantly outperforms the SARIMA model as Twitter behavior is habitual and MAPer is designed to capture the dynamics of habitual behavior over multi-scale temporal contexts. Among the ADL datasets, MAPer performs at least as good as the SARIMA model. The ground truth suggests more regular activity pattern for the HOLMES dataset rather than the ARAS data. So MAPer outperforms the SARIMA in terms of both performance metrics for HOLMES dataset.

6.1.3 Effect of Multi-scale Temporal Adaptive Features

We measure the effectiveness of using multi-scale adaptive features. Specifically, we compare performances of daily scale adaptive (DAPer), weekly scale adaptive (WAPer), and multi-scale adptive (MAPer) models (Table 4). For search log and Twitter, MAPer shows better prediction performance as it has lower MSE and higher Pearson correlation. For the two activities of daily living (ADL) datasets, DAPer results in better performance. These results suggest for online behavior considering both hour of the day and day of the week as potential temporal contexts results in better performance and for ADL behavior considering only the hour of the day results in better performance in this case. It should be noted that for both of the ADL datasets, most of the activities have very low number of samples when compared to the number of samples of online behavior datasets. Hence it is more difficult to capture behavior variation across weekly scale for the ADL datasets.

	Pearson Correlation			Mean Square Error		
Dataset	DAPer	WAPer	MAPer	DAPer	WAPer	MAPer
Search log	0.33	0.21	**0.34**	0.041	0.044	**0.041**
Twitter	0.49	0.40	**0.49**	0.045	0.048	**0.045**
ARAS	**0.78**	0.68	0.78	0.016	0.019	0.016
HOLMES	**0.58**	0.33	0.58	0.0009	0.0009	0.0009

Table 4: Analyzing the effect of using multi-scale adaptive features: the best performing statistically significant results are shown in bold. For online behavior, considering both daily and weekly contexts results in better prediction result while for activities of daily living considering only daily context yields better results.

6.1.4 Effect of Personalization

So far we have assumed to predict individual level behavior we need to estimate the model parameters from corresponding individual user's data. In this section we compare personalized modeling approach with aggregated modeling approach. In case of aggregated approach we estimate model parameters using aggregated behavior data and then use those parameters for individual level prediction. Following Table 5, personalization drastically increases performance of prediction for both search log and Twitter behavior: Pearson correlation increases more than 2.5 times for both datasets and MSE decreases by as much as 64%. Improvement of search log data is higher than the improvement of Twitter data. We perform this experiment only for online behavior data as for the ADL datasets we have no more than two individuals.

6.1.5 Effect of Interaction

In this section we present the results of analysing interaction among activities and the effect of interaction on prediction. Table 6 presents the set of interactive activities for each activity that we want to model in case of the ARAS

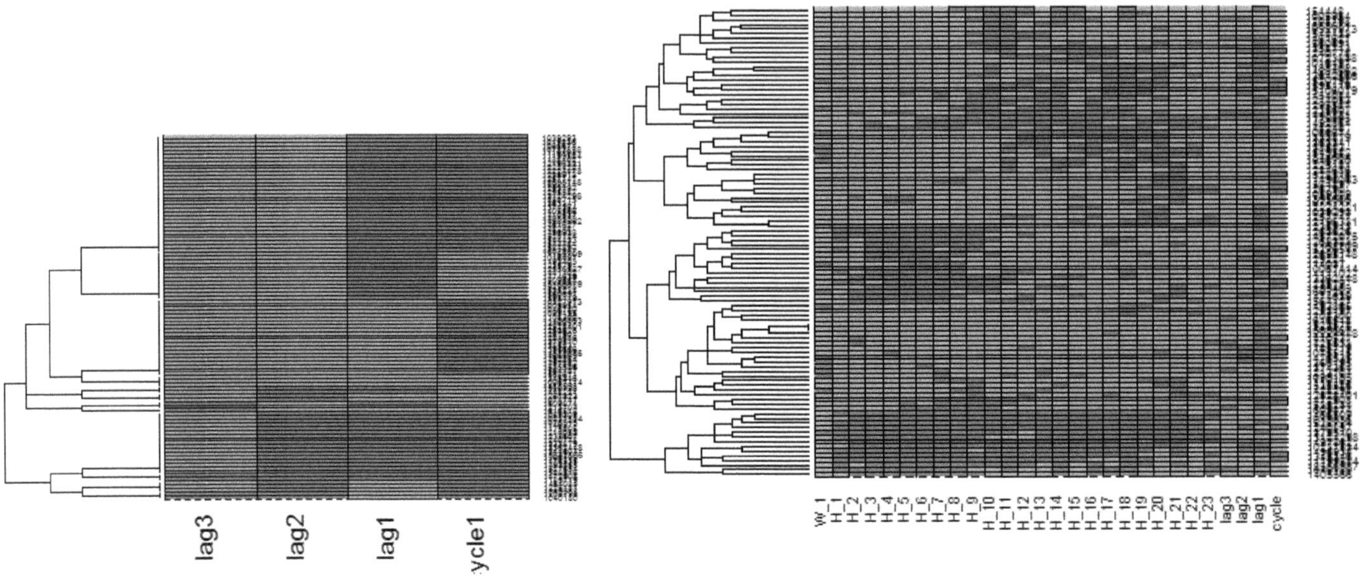

(a) AR-C model

(b) MAPer model

Figure 3: Demonstrating how our modeling approach explains effect of different parameters using heatmap for randomly chosen 100 search log users. Each row represents a user and each column of a row represents the significance of a parameter for modeling the users behavior. Red (the darker shade) and green indicate significance and insignificance of corresponding parameters, respectively. Users who are similar in terms of their behavior model (i.e., set of learned parameters from training model), are clustered together.

	Pearson Correlation		Mean Square Error	
	Search log	Twitter	Search log	Twitter
Personalized	**0.337**	**0.491**	**0.041**	**0.045**
Aggregated	0.127	0.192	0.114	0.064
Improvement	2.65 times	2.56 times	64%	30%

Table 5: Personalized models for each user significantly improve the prediction performance for both Twitter and search log datasets.

dataset. We found these interactive activities by adopting a frequent itemset mining approach (as described in Section 3.2). It indicates both residents 1 and 2 watch TV before going to sleep. Both of the residents are found to watch TV while having snacks. Resident 1 is found to talk on the phone before having lunch or dinner. These are also confirmed in the actual dataset. Although resident 1 washes dishes often before / after breakfast and lunch, resident 2 washes dishes frequently after dinner and before going to bed. Hence, for resident 2 washing dishes influences sleep time. Due to space limitation, we are not showing the interactive activities found in HOLMES dataset.

When we consider interaction among activities as features of prediction we find an increase in prediction performance of MAPer. The percent improvement of performance due to adding interaction is presented in Table 7. For example, in case of HOLMES dataset, the Pearson correlation of MAPer without interaction (Equation 5) and MAPer with interaction (Equation 4) are 0.385 and 0.583, respectively. So adding interaction features increases Pearson Correlation by 51% for HOLMES dataset.

6.2 Explanatory Power of MAPer

MAPer is an explanatory model as it uses the features that are relevant and specific to desirable human behavior.

Activity	**Influential Activities**
R1:sleep	brushing teeth, using internet, watching TV
R2:sleep	brushing teeth, watching TV, washing dishes
R1:snack	watching TV, using internet, talking on the phone
R2:snack	watching TV, having shower, using internet
R1:breakfast	preparing breakfast, using internet, watching TV
R1:lunch	preparing lunch, talking on the phone, watching TV
R1:dinner	talking on the phone, watching TV, preparing dinner

Table 6: Interaction among different activities of ARAS dataset: the left column contains the activities we want to predict and the right column contains the activities that interact with them.

Therefore each of the model parameters quantifies the effect of corresponding feature on the behavior. This is demonstrated in Figure 3 (a-b) using heatmap representation. Here we present two heatmaps of model parameters corresponding to the AR-C model and MAPer model for a set of randomly chosen 100 search log users. Figure 3 (a) demonstrates the lag and cycle features that are significant in the AR-C model for the 100 users. Figure 3 (b) demonstrates the lag, cycle, and multi-scale adaptive features that are significant in the MAPer model for the same set of users. Each row of a heatmap represents a user and each column of a row represent significance of a parameter (in terms of p-value) in the behavior model of that user. Here the red cells correspond to the significant parameters. Users who are similar in terms of their behavior model (i.e., set of learned parameters

	Pearson Correlation		Mean Square Error	
	ARAS	HOLMES	ARAS	HOLMES
MAPer w/o Interaction	0.7169	0.385	0.0184	0.0009
MAPer	0.782	0.583	0.016	0.0009
%Improvement	9	51	15	-

Table 7: Increase in performance due to adding interaction features.

Parameter	Range	
	Online Behavior	Offline Behavior
Scale (hours)	**1**,2,4,6	**1/2**,1,2,4
Training set size (weeks)	2,**4**,6,8	NA[6]
Lag (hours)	2,3,**4**,6,8	1/2,1,**2**,3,4

Table 8: The range of different parameters used in experiments. The default values of parameters are shown in bold.

from training model), are clustered together using hierarchical agglomerative clustering algorithm. The explanatory power of MAPer is multi-fold.

Firstly, when comparing the two figures, we see that MAPer does not only capture the significance of lag and cycle, but also the significance of hour of the day and day of the week. This can serve as a useful behavior model for the end users. As MAPer not only predicts future behavior but also provide a set of temporal contexts when the prediction accuracy of behavior is higher.

Secondly, from Figures 3a and 3b, MAPer has much higher number of clusters. Here a cluster represents a set of users who have similar model parameter and thus presumably similar temporal behavior. So, MAPer essentially detects similar users in a more granular scale than the AR-C model. This is useful for detecting user community based on temporal behavior and finding an equivalent class of users.

Thirdly, unlike several existing methods MAPer directly quantifies the effect of a feature in behavior modeling. For instance, from Figure 3b, the feature corresponding to lag of order 3 is significant for only a handful of users. Thus we can infer which parameter is more important under different temporal contexts for the behavior modeling of an individual.

6.3 Sensitivity Analysis

Here we evaluate our model by varying its hyper-parameters: temporal scale, training set size, and lag length (l). The default value and range of each parameter are presented in Table 8.

6.3.1 Varying Training Set Size

Methods	Pearson Correlation		Mean Square Error	
	Search log	**Twitter**	**Search log**	**Twitter**
2 weeks	**0.4**	**0.52**	**0.039**	**0.044**
4 weeks	0.34	0.49	0.041	0.045
6 weeks	0.31	0.45	0.042	0.048
8 weeks	-	0.44	-	0.048
% Improvement	31	18	7	8

Table 9: Training set with more recent data results into better prediction.

In the previous sections we have used a dynamic training approach where for each data point in test set, we consider behavior data from the immediate previous 4 weeks as the training set. In this section we vary the training set size according to Table 9 and analyze its effect on prediction performance.

For search log data we vary training set size as 2, 4, and 6 weeks. For Twitter data, we vary training set size as 2, 4, 6, and 8 weeks. In both cases, smaller training set size results into smaller MSE and higher Pearson correlation. This indicates that human behavior changes over time and recent behavior is a better predictor of future behavior.

6.3.2 Varying Temporal Scale

Scale	Pearson Correlation		Mean Square Error	
	Search log	**Twitter**	**Search log**	**Twitter**
1 hour	0.337	0.49	0.041	0.045
2 hours	0.38	0.45	0.022	0.0261
4 hours	0.427	0.49	0.011	0.0138
6 hours	**0.431**	**0.50**	**0.008**	**0.0094**
Improvement	27%	11%	5 times	4.7 times

Table 10: Varying temporal scale: larger scale results into better prediction performance for online behavior data.

So far, we have analyzed performance of different baseline methods and MAPer by keeping the temporal scale 1 hour for search log and Twitter data and half hour for ADL data. In this experiment we vary the temporal scale according to Table 8 and investigate its effect on prediction performance. We fix the other parameters in their default values.

For search log and Twitter data, higher temporal scale results into lower MSE and higher Pearson correlation (PC) (Table 10). Specifically, as we move from 1 hour to 6 hours' scale, MSE decreases by about 5 times for both datasets. In terms of PC, with an increase in temporal scale there is 27% and 11% improvement in case of search log and Twitter data, respectively. This is because as we move to larger temporal scale the sparsity of data reduces and the task of parameter estimation gets less difficult.

On the other hand, in case of both of the ADL datasets the results vary with different scales without conforming to any particular trend. Because different temporal scales are suitable for modeling different activities. For example, while predicting *sleep*, half hourly scale results in better performance. But for predicting dinner, breakfast, and lunch, 2 hourly scale is more effective as the start time of these activities slightly vary across different days. On average, there is 45% and 42% performance improvement due to scale variation in terms of Pearson correlation and mean square error, respectively. Due to space limit we are not tabulating the results from the two ADL datasets.

6.3.3 Varying Order of Lag

In this experiment we vary the lag length as described in Table 8 while keeping the other parameters in their default values. The MSE values decrease very slightly with increase of lag for all four datasets. The Pearson correlation increases by 6.5%, 8.4%, 2% and 3% with increase of lag for search log, Twitter, ARAS, and HOLMES dataset, respectively. Over all the effect of changing lag is limited for all datasets. Due to space limitation, we are skipping the detailed results here.

7. DISCUSSION

Our extensive experiments with four real world behavior data suggest that by using a combination of lag, cy-

[6]As the sample size for most of the activities of both ADL dataset is too small to vary training period, this experiment was performed only on online behavior data

cle, and interaction of activities, MAPer improves prediction performance significantly. They also demonstrate the effectiveness of using an adaptive learning approach that adapts with multi-scale temporal contexts. These features enable MAPer to perform equally or better than the parametric state-of-art SARIMA model. From an extensive sensitivity analysis, we discover that (i) using only 2 weeks data can result in higher accuracy for most of the online users, (ii) using recent training data is more useful as human behavior changes over time, and (iii) the suitable temporal scale vary over activities. In addition, MAPer yields explanatory results which can be useful for several interesting applications. Such as, detecting user community or recommending friends based on similarity of temporal behavior as explained in Section 6.2. MAPer can be paired with text mining approaches to provide personalized information retrieval, i.e., retrieving entertainment related queries during weekends. Other potential application domains where our model is applicable include personalized human activity understanding, temporal user profiling, or social recommendations from an individual user's online behavior.

We also find that MAPer is not generalizable to all human behavior as it assumes regularity in behavior. Hence, it's performance is limited in case of predicting the need based behavior (e.g., issuing search query) or random behavior. In addition, using more granular temporal scales like minutes instead of hours can incur significant computational cost. Finally, evaluation using longer ADL datasets can yield more comprehensive results.

8. CONCLUSION

With the surge of easy online access and ubiquitous sensing, abundant data contents have been generated that capture the individual human behavior over time. In spite of having great potentials to provide real-time insights, personalized temporal modeling of human behavior patterns remains largely unexplored. In this work, we introduce a multi-scale adaptive personalized **MAPer** model, an easy-to-interpret and simple-to-build predictive method for modeling the temporal dynamics of human behavior. Through results obtained from four real datasets of multiple individuals' behavior records over time, our model yields statistically significantly better predictions than a parametric state-of-art method (SARIMA model). Specifically, MAPer reduces the mean square error of the SARIMA model by about 15%, 31%, and 10% for the Twitter, ARAS, and HOLMES datasets, respectively.

Currently we are using only temporal footprint of activities. In the future, we want to model behavior by extracting textual features from user generated contents. We also want to combine virtual and physical world behaviors of an individual using smart devices.

9. ACKNOWLEDGMENTS

This paper was supported, in part, by NSF grant CNS-1319302.

10. REFERENCES

[1] F. Abel, Q. Gao, G.-J. Houben, and K. Tao. Analyzing user modeling on twitter for personalized news recommendations. In *User Modeling, Adaption and Personalization*, pages 1–12. Springer, 2011.

[2] E. Adar, D. S. Weld, B. N. Bershad, and S. S. Gribble. Why we search: visualizing and predicting user behavior. In *Proceedings of the 16th international conference on World Wide Web (WWW)*, pages 161–170. ACM, 2007.

[3] H. Alerndar, H. Ertan, O. D. Incel, and C. Ersoy. Aras human activity datasets in multiple homes with multiple residents. In *IEEE PervasiveHealth*, 2013.

[4] F. Baskaya, H. Keskustalo, and K. Järvelin. Modeling behavioral factors ininteractive information retrieval. In *Proceedings of the 22nd ACM international conference on information & knowledge management (CIKM)*, pages 2297–2302. ACM, 2013.

[5] C. Borgelt. Frequent item set mining. *Wiley Interdisciplinary Reviews: Data Mining and Knowledge Discovery*, 2(6):437–456, 2012.

[6] Y. Chen, D. Pavlov, and J. F. Canny. Large-scale behavioral targeting. In *ACM SIGKDD*, 2009.

[7] Z. Cheng, J. Caverlee, and K. Lee. You are where you tweet: a content-based approach to geo-locating twitter users. In *ACM SIGKDD*, 2010.

[8] M. Clements and D. Hendry. *Forecasting economic time series.* Cambridge University Press, 1998.

[9] J. F. Desforges, W. B. Applegate, J. P. Blass, and T. F. Williams. Instruments for the functional assessment of older patients. *New England Journal of Medicine*, 322(17):1207–1214, 1990.

[10] H. Gao, J. Tang, X. Hu, and H. Liu. Modeling temporal effects of human mobile behavior on location-based social networks. In *ACM CIKM*, 2013.

[11] S. A. Golder, D. M. Wilkinson, and B. A. Huberman. Rhythms of social interaction: Messaging within a massive online network. In *Communities and Technologies 2007*, pages 41–66. Springer, 2007.

[12] J. D. Hamilton. *Time series analysis*, volume 2. Princeton university press Princeton, 1994.

[13] E. Hoque, R. F. Dickerson, S. M. Preum, M. Hanson, A. Barth, and J. A. Stankovic. Holmes: A comprehensive anomaly detection system for daily in-home activities. In *Proceedings of the 11th IEEE international conference on distributed computing in sensor systems*, 2015.

[14] R. J. Hyndman, Y. Khandakar, et al. Automatic time series for forecasting: the forecast package for r. Technical report, Monash University, Department of Econometrics and Business Statistics, 2007.

[15] M. G. Kendall and J. K. Ord. *Time-series*, volume 296. Edward Arnold London, 1990.

[16] J. R. Kwapisz, G. M. Weiss, and S. A. Moore. Activity recognition using cell phone accelerometers. *ACM SigKDD Explorations Newsletter*, 12(2):74–82, 2011.

[17] J. Liu, Y. Liu, M. Zhang, and S. Ma. How do users grow up along with search engines?: a study of long-term users' behavior. In *ACM CIKM*, 2013.

[18] H. Lütkepohl. *Vector autoregressive models.* Springer, 2011.

[19] M. Naaman, A. X. Zhang, S. Brody, and G. Lotan. On the study of diurnal urban routines on twitter. In *ICWSM*, 2012.

[20] E. Nazerfard and D. J. Cook. Using bayesian networks for daily activity prediction. In *AAAI Workshop: Plan, Activity, and Intent Recognition*, 2013.

[21] G. Pass, A. Chowdhury, and C. Torgeson. A picture of search. In *InfoScale*, volume 152, page 1. Citeseer, 2006.

[22] K. Radinsky, K. Svore, S. Dumais, J. Teevan, A. Bocharov, and E. Horvitz. Modeling and predicting behavioral dynamics on the web. In *ACM WWW*, 2012.

[23] J. Scott, A. Bernheim Brush, J. Krumm, B. Meyers, M. Hazas, S. Hodges, and N. Villar. Preheat: controlling home heating using occupancy prediction. In *Proceedings of the 13th international conference on Ubiquitous computing*, pages 281–290. ACM, 2011.

[24] P. V. Senin. Literature review on time series indexing. 2009.

[25] W. Weerkamp and M. De Rijke. Activity prediction: A twitter-based exploration. In *SIGIR Workshop on Time-aware Information Access*, 2012.

[26] M. Ylvisaker and T. J. Feeney. *Collaborative brain injury intervention: Positive everyday routines.* Singular Publishing Group, 1998.

[27] Y. Zhu, E. Zhong, S. J. Pan, X. Wang, M. Zhou, and Q. Yang. Predicting user activity level in social networks. In *ACM CIKM*, 2013.

Classification with Active Learning and Meta-paths in Heterogeneous Information Networks

Chang Wan†, Xiang Li†, Ben Kao†, Xiao Yu‡, Quanquan Gu‡, David Cheung†, Jiawei Han‡
† The University of Hong Kong, Pokfulam Road, Hong Kong
‡ University of Illinois at Urbana-Champaign, Urbana, IL, USA
† {cwan, xli2, kao, dcheung}@cs.hku.hk ‡ {xiaoyu1, qgu3, hanj}@illinois.edu

ABSTRACT

A heterogeneous information network (HIN) is used to model objects of different types and their relationships. Meta-paths are sequences of object types. They are used to represent complex relationships between objects beyond what links in a homogeneous network capture. We study the problem of classifying objects in an HIN. We propose *class-level meta-paths* and study how they can be used to (1) build more accurate classifiers and (2) improve active learning in identifying objects for which training labels should be obtained. We show that class-level meta-paths and object classification exhibit interesting synergy. Our experimental results show that the use of class-level meta-paths results in very effective active learning and good classification performance in HINs.

Categories and Subject Descriptors

H.2.8 [**Database Management**]: Database Applications—*Data Mining*

Keywords

heterogeneous information network; classification; meta-path; active learning

1. INTRODUCTION

Networks (or graphs) model real world entities and their relationships by objects and links[1]. Traditional networks are *homogeneous* in the sense that objects represent entities of the same type and links represent one type of relationship. For example, Figure 1(a) shows a network of *authors* (of research papers) with the *co-authorship* relationships represented by links in the network.

[Heterogeneous Information Network (HIN)] Homogeneous networks, although popular, are limited in representing more complex information that involves objects of different types. A heterogeneous information network (HIN), on the other hand, is a network whose objects are of different types and whose links represent different kinds of relationships. As an example, Figure 1(b) shows a simple bibliographic information network represented by an HIN. In the figure, we see five types of objects: author (A □), organization (O ○), paper (P ◇), venue (V ⬡) and tag (T ⬠), as well as four types of links (or relationships): authorship (A–P), affiliation (A–O), description (P–T) and publication (P–V). Comparing Figures 1(a) and 1(b), we see that the HIN is a much richer source of information — not only can the co-authorship relationship (Figure 1(a)) be derived, it also captures information that can hardly be represented by the simple network. For example, the HIN shows that the three co-authorship relationships among A1, A2 and A3 (as shown by the three links in Figure 1(a)) come from one co-authored paper (P1) instead of from three separate papers.

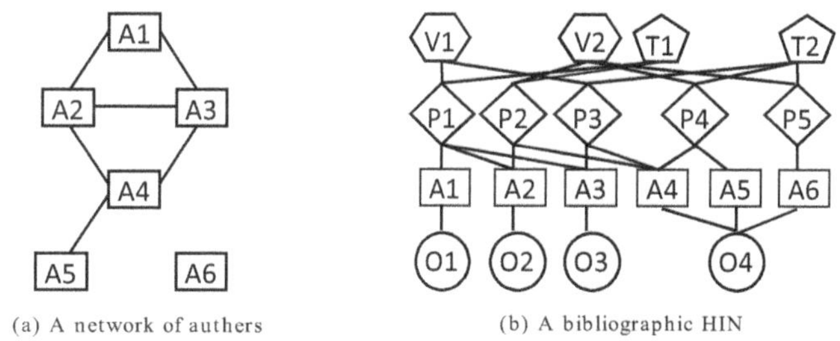

Figure 1: Homogeneous vs. heterogeneous information network

[Meta-paths] An interesting feature of an HIN is that *meta-paths* can be defined on it to further enrich the representation of relationships among objects in the network [21]. A meta-path is a sequence of object types that expresses a binary relationship between two objects in an HIN. For example, the meta-path "author-paper-author" (denoted by APA) expresses the *co-authorship* relationship. Specifically, two author objects, say A1 and A2[2], satisfy the co-authorship relationship if there is some paper, say P1, such that A1 and A2 are connected via a path A1-P1-A2 in the HIN. Similarly, the meta-path APVPA expresses a relationship between two authors who have published in the same publication venue. Meta-paths are a powerful way to abstract relationships on an HIN and there have been recent works on applying them to improve various data mining tasks. Meta-paths can be obtained either from domain experts or through an automatic extraction process [23].

[Classification] Classification is one of the most important and fundamental data mining tasks. Classifying objects in an HIN has found many interesting applications, especially those related to object recommendation, link prediction, and community detection.

[1]In this paper, we use the terms "vertex" and "object" interchangeably, and the terms "edge" and "link" interchangeably.

[2]In this paper we use capital letters, e.g., A, P, to represent object types, and we use numbered capital letters, e.g., A1, P3, to represent objects of the corresponding types.

CIKM'15, October 19–23, 2015, Melbourne, VIC, Australia.
© 2015 ACM. ISBN 978-1-4503-3794-6/15/10 ...$15.00.
DOI: http://dx.doi.org/10.1145/2806416.2806507.

For example, consider an HIN modeling the Facebook network, which consists of various object types such as users, messages, product pages, interest groups, advertisements and photos. If one can classify these objects into their topics of interest (e.g., music (rock, jazz, etc.), sports (football, tennis, etc.), shopping (fashion, electronics, etc.)) accurately, one can perform very effective recommendation (e.g., recommending a relevant product to a user), link prediction (e.g., measuring the likelihood that two users will become friends) and community detection (e.g., detecting a community of users with shared interest for target marketing). The problem of classifying objects in an HIN has been studied [7, 8, 29]. However, many of these classifiers do not consider meta-paths. As we have argued, meta-paths are a powerful tool to express objects' relationships. They are thus very useful in determining object correlation and therefore in object classification. A major objective of this paper is to derive an effective HIN object classifier that uses meta-paths. Our classifier is based on two ideas: (1) we derive a learning model to *weigh* meta-paths, and (2) we propose the use of *class-level meta-paths*. Figure 2 helps us to illustrate these ideas in the following discussion.

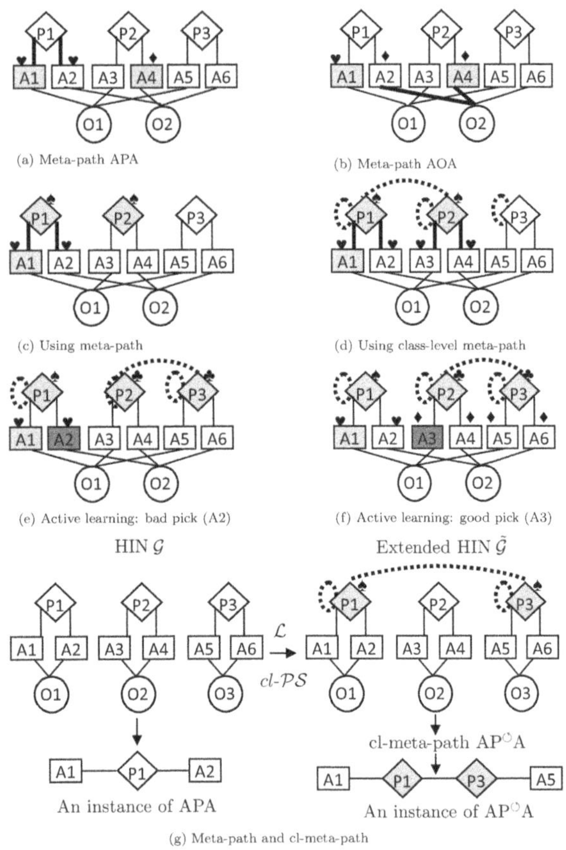

Figure 2: Illustrative examples of meta-path weighing ((a), (b)), class-level meta-paths ((c), (d)), active learning ((e), (f)), and path instances (g). Jumps are shown as dotted lines.

[Weighing meta-paths] There could be many meta-paths derived for an HIN, especially when the meta-paths are automatically extracted (e.g., using the technique described in [23]). Some meta-paths may be better than others for a given classification task. For example, consider Figure 2(a), which shows a small bibliographic network. (For simplicity, we only show objects of types organization (O), author (A) and paper (P).) In the figure, two objects A1 and A4 are shaded to denote that their class labels are already known. Let's say their labels are ♥ and ◆ (which are the symbols shown next to the objects). Now consider two meta-paths APA and AOA. The former expresses co-authorship and the latter expresses co-workership. If we apply the meta-path APA to deduce object correlation then we will classify object A2 to the same class (♥) of A1 because A1 and A2 are connected by an *instance* of the meta-path APA. (This path instance is highlighted in Figure 2(a) with thick edges.) On the other hand, if we use the meta-path AOA instead, then object A2 will be given A4's class label (◆) because A2 and A4 are connected by an instance of AOA (path highlighted in Figure 2(b)). Which classification result is more likely to be correct depends on the classification task. For example, if the task is to label objects with a research area (say AI, DB), then the co-authorship meta-path APA would be more relevant than the co-workership meta-path AOA. (Two researchers from the same university can work in different areas.) This example illustrates that a mechanism for selecting meta-paths is important in constructing a classifier. As we will show later, our algorithm automatically assigns weights to meta-paths so that those that are more relevant to a given classification task will be given higher weights over the less relevant meta-paths.

[Class-level meta-paths] We extend meta-path to class-level meta-path in capturing object correlation to achieve better classification results. We have briefly discussed how meta-paths can help construct classifiers. The classifiers, in return, can help us derive *class-level meta-paths* (or cl-meta-path for short) in the following way. Consider again the co-authorship meta-path APA. Suppose we have the HIN shown in Figure 2(c) in which three objects P1, P2, A1 are already given labels (they are shaded in the figure). If we consider only the meta-path APA, we can only relate author A2 to the labeled author A1; the other authors are not related to A1 via the meta-path. Hence, we can only deduce the label of author A2 and give it the same label (♥) of A1. Now, from the meta-path APA we derive a cl-meta-path AP$^{\circlearrowleft}$A. We use the notation X$^{\circlearrowleft}$ to refer to a *jump* from an object X1 to an object X2 if (1) both objects are of type X and (2) both are given the same class label. In Figure 2(d), an instance of the jump P$^{\circlearrowleft}$ is P1 to P2 because they are given the same label. This jump instance is illustrated by a dotted edge (P1→P2) in the figure. Conceptually, two authors A1 and A2 are connected by the cl-meta-path AP$^{\circlearrowleft}$A if we can traverse from A1 to A2 in the HIN following edges and jumps specified by the cl-meta-path. For example, from Figure 2(d), we see that A1 is connected to A3 via (A1→P1⇢P2→A3), which matches the cl-meta-path AP$^{\circlearrowleft}$A. Likewise, A1 is connected to A2 and A4 as well. w.r.t. AP$^{\circlearrowleft}$A. Hence, all these three authors can be labeled by the class of A1. Intuitively, if two authors have published papers on the same topic, they are likely to be in the same research area, even if they have not co-authored papers before. This example illustrates the advantage of cl-meta-paths over meta-paths in deriving objects' correlation.

[Active learning] Typical HINs are huge. For example, Facebook has more than 1 billion users and there are more than 2 million publications on DBLP. Obtaining the class labels of enough objects to form an effective training set is costly. Active learning is about wisely selecting objects for which labels are sought so that accurate classifiers are built. Due to the large sizes of HINs, a good active learning strategy is essential. We remark that cl-meta-paths, which express objects' correlation, can facilitate active learning on HINs. But how exactly shall cl-meta-paths and active learning be integrated? To illustrate, consider the HIN shown in Figure 2(e). Let us use the cl-meta-path AP$^{\circlearrowleft}$A. Four (lightly-shaded) objects, P1, P2, P3, A1 are already labeled. Suppose we want to add one more object to the training set, which object shall we pick so that we can, say, classify more author objects? Note that picking A2 (darkly shaded in Figure 2(e)) to label is a bad choice. This is because the cl-meta-path only connects A2 to A1, and A1 is already labeled. Intuitively, a good choice should be an object that is connected to many unlabeled objects and not so to labeled objects. In our example, A3 is a good choice (see Figure 2(f)). Note that A2 can be labeled because it is connected to (an already labeled object) A1 via $AP^{\cup}A$, and A4, A5, A6 can be labeled because they are connected to the new addition (A3) of the training set via $AP^{\cup}A$. A major objective of this work is to study how meta-paths and active learning are integrated in constructing HIN classifier. In particular, we investigate (1) how to automatically choose good cl-meta-paths from a cl-meta-path set, and (2) how to design an active learning strategy given a set of cl-meta-paths.

We further show the usefulness of object classification on an HIN using Yago as a motivating example. YAGO[3] is a semantic knowledge base of objects and their relationships. It consolidates information derived from Wikipedia, WordNet and GeoNames. Currently, Yago has knowledge of more than 10 million objects (e.g., people, organizations, cities, locations, etc.) and more than 120 million relationships about these objects. This information on objects and relationships can be conceptually viewed as an HIN.

An interesting kind of relationship of a Yago object is called "*type*", which relates the object to other descriptive conceptual objects (e.g., scientist, actor, politician, etc.). Each such conceptual object is expressed either by a word from WordNet or by a category from Wikipedia. These conceptual objects form hierarchies, e.g., "American economist" is a subconcept of "economist", which in turn, is a subconcept of a person. One can consider such conceptual objects (e.g., mathematician) as "labels" of an object (e.g., Knuth). The list of descriptive labels given to an object on Yago is not quite complete. For example, someone working at a university on scientific studies may be given the type "scientist" but not "professor"; the scientist might also not be given a type that describes his area of research (e.g., "database", "discrete geometry").

The incompleteness in an object's description weakens the effectiveness of searching and logical deductions on a knowledge base. For example, to identify all database professors of Stanford University, we need the labels "database" and "professor" be given to the appropriate person objects on Yago. However, while some professors at Stanford are given the "professor" type/label on Yago, others are not. Since it is infeasible to exhaustively assign labels to objects on a knowledge base, automatic classification techniques on an HIN is thus highly desirable. Our work therefore would be highly applicable in knowledge base deduction.

Note that in our HIN model links are not labeled. For example, with the bibliographic HIN, a link between an author object and a paper object is assumed to represent the authorship relationship. On Yago, links are labeled with semantic properties (such as "isA" and "worksAt"). We remark that our approach can be easily adapted to handle HINs for which multiple links of different semantic between objects are possible. A straightforward way is to add *relationship objects*. For example, the labeled link Knuth $\xrightarrow{worksAt}$ Stanford, can be modeled by a path Knuth → worksAt → Stanford, where "worksAt" is considered a vertex in the graph.

In this paper we put forward the idea of meta-path and cl-meta-path to capture complex relationships among objects to facilitate object classification. This idea can be applied to a knowledge base like Yago. E.g., the meta-path $X \xrightarrow{advisedBy} Y \xrightarrow{advises} Z$, where X, Y, Z are person objects, captures the relationship that X and Z share the same academic advisor. They are therefore likely to be scholars of the same research area. Hence, knowing the class label of one (e.g., mathematician) allows us to deduce the label of another.

[3]http://www.mpi-inf.mpg.de/yago-naga/yago/

Here we summarize our contributions in this paper:

- We propose to use meta-paths of an HIN to derive object correlation in the construction of classifiers. Moreover, we propose the idea of cl-meta-path which is an extension of meta-path to further capture object relationships by exploiting objects' labels.
- We study how active learning should be applied to facilitate HIN object classification. In particular, we put forward an algorithm that integrates cl-meta-paths into various active learning strategies.
- We propose a method of training a model that automatically assigns weights to meta-paths such that meta-paths that are more relevant to a classification task are given higher weights. Our training model provides an adaptive strategy that leads to more effective active learning and more accurate classifiers.
- We conduct experiments on real datasets to evaluate our classifiers and our active learning algorithm. We show that our classifiers that use cl-meta-paths can achieve high classification accuracy. We also show that our active learning algorithm is highly effective.

The rest of our paper is organized as follows. We review related works in Section 2. In Section 3 we formally define various concepts and the problem being studied. In Section 4 we present our classification and active learning algorithms. Experimental results are shown in Section 5. Finally, we conclude our work in Section 6.

2. RELATED WORK

There are a number of works studying various data mining tasks on HINs. These works include object clustering [24, 23, 17, 4], link prediction [19, 27, 26, 18], search [20] and object ranking [6, 22, 7, 2]. Some of these works use meta-paths, which were first proposed in [21], to derive object similarity. There is also work, such as [14], which models textual data using heterogeneous networks and focuses on text classification.

Some representative studies on active learning techniques for general classifiers include [10, 16, 3]. To select objects for which labels are to be obtained, [10] employs *uncertainty sampling* (US). US evaluates each object in terms of how confident the classifier is in deducing the object's label. Objects that the classifier is the least confident about are picked. Our HIN active learning method is based on uncertainty sampling. In particular, we study how cl-meta-paths can be integrated nicely with US to achieve very effective active learning. In [16], an active learning method that employs the idea of *query-by-committee* (QBC) is given. Given a number of classifiers, objects for which the classifiers disagree most are selected. A disadvantage of the QBC approach is that it needs multiple classifiers as well as a "disagreement measure". In [3], each object is assessed in terms of how much the expected error of a classifier would be reduced if the object is assigned a label. Objects that lead to the largest error reductions are picked. Typically, error-reduction-methods are computationally much more expensive than US and QBC methods.

The problem of classifying objects in traditional (homogeneous) networks have been studied extensively. Collective classification [11, 28, 15, 12] is a general technique that classifies an object based on the labels of the object's neighbors in the network. As an example, LLGC [28] builds an *affinity matrix* A that reflects the "closeness" (e.g., in terms of path lengths) of any two objects in the network. The affinity matrix derives a classifier F. LLGC follows the intuition that objects that are close according to A should be given the same class label. So, if there are objects whose labels assigned by F violate the intuition, F is updated to resolve the conflict between F and A. The updating step repeats until F converges. Although

LLGC is designed to classify homogeneous network objects, we can apply it to classify HIN objects by disregarding object types.

RankClass [7] integrates object ranking with classification in an HIN. The intuition behind the method is that higher-ranked objects in a network should play a bigger role in classifier construction[4]. For each class label k, RankClass assigns a *class-k rank score* $P(x_p|k)$ for each object x_p. Also, if there is a link e_{pq} between two objects x_p and x_q, the algorithm assigns a class-k weight $S(e_{pq}|k)$ to the link. The algorithm performs an iterative authority propagation on the network to determine the rank scores and link weights such that: (1) if an object x_p connects to many neighbors with large class-k rank scores through heavyweight links, then $P(x_p|k)$ is large; (2) if a link e_{pq} connects two objects with large class-k rank scores, then $S(e_{pq}|k)$ is large. After the rank scores and link weights converge through the iterative procedure, the algorithm calculates a posterior probability $Prob(k|x_p)$ to make class prediction.

In [8] a graph-based regularization framework, GNetMine, is proposed. GNetMine first constructs a predictive function $f^k_{t_i}$ for each object type t_i and class label k. It then derives an objective function that aims to minimize two values: (1) for any two highly correlated objects x_p and x_q, the difference between their predictive values $f^k_{t_i}(x_p)$ and $f^k_{t_i}(x_q)$, and (2) for any labeled object, x_r, the difference between its predictive value $f^k_{t_i}(x_r)$ and its true class-induced value, which is 1 if x_r's label is k; 0 otherwise. The predictive functions $f^k_{t_i}$'s are trained by optimizing the objective function. Finally, GNetMine makes class predictions based on the $f^k_{t_i}$'s.

In [29], the AEClass algorithm for classifying objects in an HIN is proposed. Given an HIN G and a set of objects in G for which class labels are to be assigned, AEClass first constructs a *collaboration graph CG*. For example, if we want to label authors with their research areas, CG can be constructed by the co-authorship relationship. Then, CG is augmented by considering the various *activities* that relate the objects. For example, these activities could be *conferences* that the authors have published in, or the *terms* that appear in the authors' papers. By first labeling the activities through classification, objects' similarities under each label are derived. These similarities are then used to assign labels to the objects. A strong requirement of AEClass is that for a given set of objects in an HIN to be labeled, associated activities can be derived from the HIN. Moreover, the labels of such activities need to be of the same kind as those of the objects to be classified.

Our classification algorithm differs from the above methods in that we utilize meta-paths (or cl-meta-paths) to further derive object relationships. In particular, our algorithm recognizes the different link types (e.g., we distinguish a paper-venue link from a paper-author link when extracting instances of a meta-path), while the other methods regard all links as an expression of the simple neighbor relationship.

In [9], a meta-path-based collective classification algorithm, HCC, is proposed. While traditional collective classification algorithms use links to define an object's neighbors, HCC extends that by using meta-paths. Our algorithm differs from HCC in two aspects: (1) our algorithm derives cl-meta-paths from meta-paths and use cl-meta-paths to train the classifiers, and (2) our algorithm automatically assigns weights to different meta-paths so that meta-paths that are more relevant to the classification tasks are given higher weights. This avoids the issue of irrelevant meta-paths adversely affecting the quality of the classifiers. Moreover, we integrate active learning into our HIN object classification, which is not done in other previous works.

[4]An object ranks high if it connects to many other highly-ranked objects.

Table 1: Descriptions of symbols

Notation	Description
t_h	An object type
$\mathcal{T}, m$	$\mathcal{T}$ is a set of m object types
$\mathcal{G}, \mathcal{V}, \mathcal{E}$	$\mathcal{G}$ is a HIN with object set $\mathcal{V}$ and link set $\mathcal{E}$
$\tilde{\mathcal{G}}$	$\tilde{\mathcal{G}}$ is the extended HIN of $\mathcal{G}$
x	An object
$T(x)$	Type of object x
$x_i^{t_h}$	The i-th type-t_h object
n	$\lvert\mathcal{V}\rvert$
$\mathcal{X}_h$	Objects that are of type t_h
n_h	$\lvert\mathcal{X}_h\rvert$
$p, \mathcal{P}, \tilde{\mathcal{P}}$	Path p, meta-path $\mathcal{P}$, cl-meta-path $\tilde{\mathcal{P}}$
$\mathcal{PS}$,	The set of meta-paths
$cl\text{-}\mathcal{PS}$	The set of cl-meta-paths
$p \vdash \mathcal{P}$	p is an instance of $\mathcal{P}$
$l_{h,j}$, CL_h	CL_h is the set of labels $l_{h,j}$'s of type-t_h objects
$\mathcal{L}$, $L(x)$	Training set $\mathcal{L}$; $L(x)$ = label of object x if $x \in \mathcal{L}$
$\mathcal{J}$	Set of jumps
B	Budget
N_s	Number of Objects to label per iteration

3. PROBLEM DEFINITION

In this section we define the problem of active learning in HIN object classification. For simplicity, we use O, A, P to denote various object types and A5, O2, P3, etc. to denote objects of the corresponding types. Table 1 lists the symbols used in the paper.

DEFINITION 1 (HETEROGENEOUS INFORMATION NETWORK (HIN)). *Let $\mathcal{T} = \{t_1, \ldots, t_m\}$ be a set of m object types. Let $\mathcal{V}$ be a set of n objects. Each object $x \in \mathcal{V}$ has a unique type, denoted by $T(x)$. We use $\mathcal{X}_h$ to denote the set of all objects of type t_h, i.e., $\mathcal{X}_h = \{x \in \mathcal{V} \mid T(x) = t_h\}$ and $\mathcal{V} = \cup_{h=1}^m \mathcal{X}_h$. Let $n_h = |\mathcal{X}_h|$. Let $\mathcal{E}$ be a set of links, which represents a binary relation between objects in $\mathcal{V}$. An object x_i is related to another object x_j iff $(x_i, x_j) \in \mathcal{E}$. An HIN $\mathcal{G} = \langle \mathcal{V}, \mathcal{E} \rangle$ is a set of objects $\mathcal{V}$ and a set of links $\mathcal{E}$.* □

For simplicity, we assume that objects are ordered. We use x_i to denote the i-th object in $\mathcal{V}$. Similarly, we use $x_i^{t_h}$ to denote the i-th type-t_h object.

DEFINITION 2 (META-PATH). *A meta-path $\mathcal{P} = t_{i_1} \ldots t_{i_d}$ is a sequence of object types. We use $\mathcal{P}[j]$ to denote the j-th object type (t_{i_j}) specified in the meta-path $\mathcal{P}$. Given an HIN $\mathcal{G}$ and a path p in $\mathcal{G}$, let $|p|$ be the length (as measured by the number of objects) of path p and $p[j]$ be the j-th object in p. Path p is an* instance *of $\mathcal{P}$, denoted by $p \vdash \mathcal{P}$ iff p and $\mathcal{P}$ are of the same length and the types of the objects in p match those specified in $\mathcal{P}$. Formally, $p \vdash \mathcal{P}$ iff (1) $|p| = d$ and (2) $T(p[j]) = \mathcal{P}[j]$ $\forall 1 \leq j \leq d$.* □

EXAMPLE 1. *Consider the HIN $\mathcal{G}$ shown in Figure 2(g) and the meta-path APA. The path A1-P1-A2 in $\mathcal{G}$ is an instance of meta-path APA because objects A1 and A2 are of type author (A) and P1 is of type paper (P).* □

Each object type t_h is associated with a set of class labels $CL_h = \{l_{h,1}, \ldots, l_{h,|CL_h|}\}$. We assume that the class labels of different object types do not overlap[5]. An object x_i of type t_h may be assigned a label $l_{h,j} \in CL_h$. If so, we say x_i is *labeled* and we write $L(x_i) = l_{h,j}$. If x_i has not been assigned any label, we write $L(x_i) = NA$. We call $L()$ the label function, which is straightforwardly derived from a training set $\mathcal{L}$ of labeled objects.

[5]For example, the labels of author objects could be {DB-Author, AI-Author, ...} while the labels of paper objects could be {Transaction-processing-paper, Planning-paper, ... }.

DEFINITION 3 (JUMP AND EXTENDED HIN). *Given an HIN $\mathcal{G} = \langle \mathcal{V}, \mathcal{E} \rangle$ and a training set of labeled objects $\mathcal{L}$ (and hence the label function L()), a* jump *is a link between two objects x_i and x_j if either (1) $x_i = x_j$ (i.e., they are the same object) or (2) $L(x_i) = L(x_j) \neq NA$ (i.e., they share the same label). We denote the set of all jumps by $\mathcal{J}$. An extended HIN $\tilde{\mathcal{G}} = \{\mathcal{V}, \mathcal{E}, \mathcal{J}\}$ is obtained from the HIN $\mathcal{G}$ by including $\mathcal{J}$ as another type of links in the network.* □

EXAMPLE 2. *Figure 2(g) shows an extended HIN $\tilde{\mathcal{G}}$. Jumps are shown as dotted lines in the figure. For clarity, only jumps involving papers (P) are shown. Note that (1) every object is connected to itself by a jump, and (2) P1 and P3 are connected by a jump because they share the same label.*

DEFINITION 4 (CLASS-LEVEL META-PATH (CL-META-PATH)). *Given a length-d meta-path $\mathcal{P}$, we construct a length-d cl-meta-path $\tilde{\mathcal{P}}$ by replacing every object type t mentioned in $\mathcal{P}$ by the symbol $t^{\cup}$, except for the beginning and the ending object types in $\mathcal{P}$. That is (1) $\tilde{\mathcal{P}}[1] = \mathcal{P}[1]$, (2) $\tilde{\mathcal{P}}[d] = \mathcal{P}[d]$, and (3) ($\tilde{\mathcal{P}}[i] = t^{\cup}$ if $\mathcal{P}[i] = t$) $\forall 2 \leq i \leq d-1$. For example, from the meta-path APVPA we obtain the cl-meta-path $AP^{\cup}V^{\cup}P^{\cup}A$.* □

DEFINITION 5 (PATH INSTANCE). *Given an extended HIN $\tilde{\mathcal{G}} = \{\mathcal{V}, \mathcal{E}, \mathcal{J}\}$, conceptually, a path p in $\tilde{\mathcal{G}}$ is an instance of a cl-meta-path $\tilde{\mathcal{P}}$, denoted by $p \vdash \tilde{\mathcal{P}}$, if (1) the objects visited in p follow the sequence of types specified in $\tilde{\mathcal{P}}$ and (2) a jump $Xi \rightarrow Xj$ is taken whenever we encounter an $X^{\cup}$ in $\tilde{\mathcal{P}}$. For example, consider the cl-meta-path $AP^{\cup}A$. The path $A1 \rightarrow P1 \xrightarrow{jump} P3 \rightarrow A5$ shown in Figure 2(g) is an instance because we start with an author object, follow a link to a paper object, take a jump to another paper object, and follow another link to an author object. Formally, $p \vdash \tilde{\mathcal{P}}$ iff (1) $|p| = (|\tilde{\mathcal{P}}| - 2) \times 2 + 2$, (2) $T(p[\lfloor i/2 \rfloor + 1]) = \tilde{\mathcal{P}}[i]$ $\forall 1 \leq i \leq |p|$, (3) $(p[i], p[i+1]) \in \mathcal{E}$ $\forall$ odd $1 \leq i \leq |p| - 1$, (4) $(p[i], p[i+1]) \in \mathcal{J}$ $\forall$ even $1 \leq i \leq |p| - 1$.*

Given two objects $x_i, x_j \in \tilde{\mathcal{G}}$, we say that a length-d path p relates *x_i and x_j if p starts from x_i and ends at x_j, i.e., if $(p[1] = x_i) \wedge (p[d] = x_j)$.* □

Our objective is to integrate meta-paths (and hence cl-meta-paths) into classifier construction and active learning to get more accurate classification results. The goal of the latter is to wisely select objects to be included into the training set to achieve good classifier accuracy despite the training set is limited in size (e.g., by a labeling budget).

DEFINITION 6. *(Active Learning for HIN Object Classification (ALHOC)): Given an HIN $\mathcal{G} = \langle \mathcal{V}, \mathcal{E} \rangle$ of m object types $\mathcal{T}$, the set of class labels CL_h for each object type $t_h \in \mathcal{T}$, a training set of labeled objects $\mathcal{L}$, a set of meta-paths $\mathcal{PS}$, and a budget B, the ALHOC problem is (1) to select B unlabeled objects in $\mathcal{V}$ to obtain their labels (and thus to update $\mathcal{L}$), and (2) to construct m accurate classifiers $f_h : X_h \mapsto CL_h, 1 \leq h \leq m$.* □

4. ALGORITHM

In this section we describe our algorithm HINAL for classifying objects in HINs using meta-paths and active learning. We assume that a budget B is given, which is the number of objects we can select in active learning for labeling. We first give an overview of HINAL before we explain the technical details later in this section. Figure 3 abstracts the 7 major steps of HINAL.

Given an HIN $\mathcal{G}$ and a set of meta-paths $\mathcal{PS}$, we first derive a set of cl-meta-paths $cl\text{-}\mathcal{PS}$ (Step 1). Given the set of labeled objects $\mathcal{L}$ and $cl\text{-}\mathcal{PS}$, we determine jumps and construct an extended HIN $\tilde{\mathcal{G}}$ (Step 2). From $\tilde{\mathcal{G}}$ we determine the relative weights $\theta_{\tilde{\mathcal{P}}}$ of each cl-meta-paths $\tilde{\mathcal{P}}$ in $cl\text{-}\mathcal{PS}$ (Step 3). Intuitively, a *heavier* cl-meta-path is more relevant to the classification task. Since a cl-meta-path expresses a relationship between objects, we derive a correlation matrix $W^{\tilde{\mathcal{P}}}$ for each $\tilde{\mathcal{P}}$ in $cl\text{-}\mathcal{PS}$ (Step 4). If two objects are related by many instances of $\tilde{\mathcal{P}}$, then they are highly correlated w.r.t. $\tilde{\mathcal{P}}$ and so the entry in $W^{\tilde{\mathcal{P}}}$ corresponding to the object pair will be large. The correlation matrices $W^{\tilde{\mathcal{P}}}$'s and their weights $\theta_{\tilde{\mathcal{P}}}$'s are used in two ways. First, they are used to train m SVM classifiers f_h's (one for each object type $t_h \in \mathcal{T}$) (Step 5). Second, if the budget B is not exhausted, then the matrices, together with the classifiers, are used to perform active learning (Step 6). After objects are selected to label, we update $\mathcal{L}$ and $\tilde{\mathcal{G}}$ (Step 7). The training process is then repeated until the labeling budget B is exhausted. Next, we give more details on Steps 3-6.

4.1 Computing cl-meta-path weights $\theta_{\tilde{\mathcal{P}}}$ and correlation matrices $W^{\tilde{\mathcal{P}}}$ (Steps 3 and 4)

For each cl-meta-path $\tilde{\mathcal{P}}$, its correlation matrix $W^{\tilde{\mathcal{P}}}$ is an n-by-n matrix ($n = |\mathcal{V}|$) that measures how correlated any two objects are w.r.t. $\tilde{\mathcal{P}}$. We measure this correlation between two objects x_i and x_j by the number of path instances of $\tilde{\mathcal{P}}$ that relate x_i and x_j, i.e.,

$$W^{\tilde{\mathcal{P}}}[i,j] = \left|\{(p \mid (p \vdash \tilde{\mathcal{P}}) \wedge (p \text{ relates } x_i \text{ and } x_j)\}\right|. \quad (1)$$

Each cl-meta-path $\tilde{\mathcal{P}}$ is given a weight $\theta_{\tilde{\mathcal{P}}}$. We learn the weights $\Theta = \{\theta_{\tilde{\mathcal{P}}} \mid \tilde{\mathcal{P}} \in cl\text{-}\mathcal{PS}\}$ by optimizing an objective function O based on the training data set $\mathcal{L}$. The idea is to maximize the correlations of objects that share the same labels and to minimize the correlations of objects that are given different labels:

$$O = \max_{\Theta} \sum_{x_i, x_j \in \mathcal{L}} \left(\text{sgn}(x_i, x_j) \cdot \sum_{\tilde{\mathcal{P}} \in cl\text{-}\mathcal{PS}} \theta_{\tilde{\mathcal{P}}} W^{\tilde{\mathcal{P}}}[i,j] \right) - \lambda \|\Theta\|_2^2, \quad (2)$$

where λ is a regularization parameter, $\|\cdot\|_2$ is the L_2 norm, and sgn() is a sign function: $\text{sgn}(x_i,x_j) = 1$ if x_i and x_j share the same label; it is -1 if the objects have different labels[6]. To learn Θ, we take partial derivative w.r.t. each $\theta_{\tilde{\mathcal{P}}}$, set those derivatives to 0, and obtain

$$\theta_{\tilde{\mathcal{P}}} = \frac{1}{2\lambda} \sum_{x_i, x_j \in \mathcal{L}} \left(\text{sgn}(x_i, x_j) \cdot W^{\tilde{\mathcal{P}}}[i,j] \right). \quad (3)$$

4.2 Training classifiers (Step 5)

We train an SVM classifier $f_h : X_h \mapsto CL_h$ for each object type $t_h \in \mathcal{T}$. We first describe how to construct the feature vector v_{x_i} for each object $x_i \in \mathcal{V}$. Then, we describe how we learn the parameters of the SVM classifier f_h.

Consider the set of cl-meta-paths $cl\text{-}\mathcal{PS}$. Let N_{clmp} be the number of cl-meta-paths. The feature vector v_{x_i} consists of N_{clmp} segments, each corresponds to a cl-meta-path. Specifically, for each cl-meta-path $\tilde{\mathcal{P}}$, the segment is obtained by extracting the row in the correlation matrix $W^{\tilde{\mathcal{P}}}$ that corresponds to object x_i, weighted with $\theta_{\tilde{\mathcal{P}}}$. We denote this segment of x_i's feature vector $v_{x_i}^{\tilde{\mathcal{P}}}$, i.e., $v_{x_i}^{\tilde{\mathcal{P}}} = \theta_{\tilde{\mathcal{P}}} \cdot W^{\tilde{\mathcal{P}}}[i,:]$, and v_{x_i} is the concatenation of $v_{x_i}^{\tilde{\mathcal{P}}}$'s $\forall \tilde{\mathcal{P}} \in cl\text{-}\mathcal{PS}$. After we have constructed the feature vectors of all objects $x_i \in X_h$, we normalize all the feature vectors' entries into the range [0,1].

[6]Since we assume different object types have disjoint label sets, $\text{sgn}(x_i,x_j) = 1$ if x_i and x_j are of the same type. One can extend the definition of sgn() to model the similarity of labels of different object types. E.g., the author label DB-author and the paper label Transaction-processing-paper share some similarity. Therefore objects of these two labels could be given a positive sign() value.

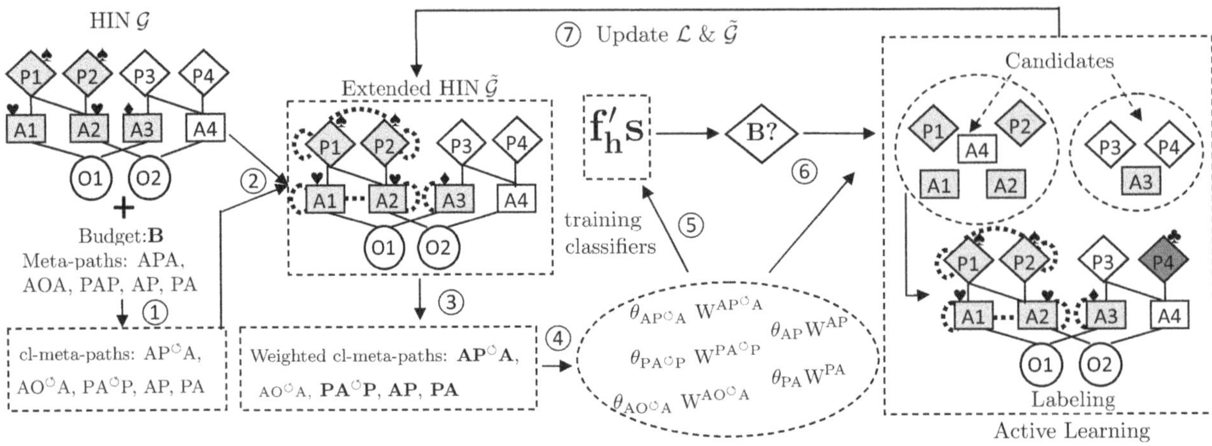

Figure 3: HINAL's framework

Next, we build a multi-class SVM classifier f_h[7]. For each label $l_{h,j} \in CL_h$, we define the predictive function $\hat{f}_{h,j}$ by

$$\hat{f}_{h,j}(x_i) = \sum_{\tilde{\mathcal{P}} \in cl\text{-}\mathcal{PS}} \left(\mathbf{w}_{h,j}^{\tilde{\mathcal{P}}} \cdot \Phi(v_{x_i}^{\tilde{\mathcal{P}}}) \right) + b_{h,j}, \tag{4}$$

where Φ is a mapping function, and $\mathbf{w}_{h,j}^{\tilde{\mathcal{P}}}$ (for $\tilde{\mathcal{P}} \in cl\text{-}\mathcal{PS}$) and $b_{h,j}$ are parameters to be learned using soft-margin SVM [1]. With the predictive functions of all the labels in CL_h, a type-t_h object is classified to the label $l_{h,j}$ whose predictive function $\hat{f}_{h,j}$ gives the largest value among all labels in CL_h. The classifier f_h is given by,

$$f_h(x_i) = \arg\max_{l_{h,j} \in CL_h} \hat{f}_{h,j}(x_i) \qquad \forall x_i \in \mathcal{X}_h. \tag{5}$$

4.3 Active learning (Step 6)

We perform iterative active learning to select objects to label. In each iteration, we pick N_s objects for which labels are obtained, after which the training set $\mathcal{L}$ and hence the extended HIN $\tilde{\mathcal{G}}$ are updated. This is repeated until the budget B is exhausted.

An active learning iteration consists of two parts. First, we select a set of candidate unlabeled objects C. Second, N_s objects from C are selected based on uncertainty sampling (see Section 2). Intuitively, if two objects are highly correlated, labeling one of them is enough for us to infer the label of another. In other words, labeling both of them is redundant. Hence, we want the objects in the candidate set C not being strongly correlated. To achieve that, we cluster objects so that highly correlated objects are put into the same cluster. By picking our candidates across these clusters, we avoid putting many highly-correlated (and thus redundant) candidates in the candidate set C. (see Figure 3 for an illustration).

To perform clustering, we need a distance measure between objects. For that, we use a global correlation matrix W, which is given by the weighted sum of all the cl-meta-paths' correlation matrices:

$$W = \sum_{\tilde{\mathcal{P}} \in cl\text{-}\mathcal{PS}} \theta_{\tilde{\mathcal{P}}} W^{\tilde{\mathcal{P}}}. \tag{6}$$

We perform two touch-ups on W: (1) We normalize the entries in W to the range [0,1]. (2) For any labeled object pair $x_i, x_j \in \mathcal{L}$, we update the entry $W[i,j]$ to 1 if x_i and x_j are given the same label; or to 0 if they are given different labels. This update is a well-known method to construct constraints for graph clustering [30]. The objects are clustered using KASP [25], which is a fast approximation algorithm of spectral clustering.

We select one candidate from each cluster. Intuitively, a candidate x_i is good if (1) it is highly correlated to many unlabeled objects (so that labeling x_i allows us to infer the labels of many other unlabeled objects), and (2) it is not highly correlated to many labeled objects (so that labeling x_i is not redundant). This idea can be quantitatively measured by the following score:

$$\text{goodness}(x_i) = \sum_{x_j \in \mathcal{V}-\mathcal{L}} W[i,j] - \sum_{x_k \in \mathcal{L}} W[i,k]. \tag{7}$$

The object in each cluster with the best score is then added to the candidate set C[8].

To finally pick the N_S objects to label, we conduct uncertainty sampling [5]. We briefly give an outline of the procedure. For each unlabeled object x_u, let t_h be its type. Object x_u's *label distribution* is given by $[\hat{f}_{h,1}(x_u), \hat{f}_{h,2}(x_u) \ldots, \hat{f}_{h,|CL_h|}(x_u)]$, where $\hat{f}_{h,k}(x_u)$ is the predictive function of x_u being of class label $l_{h,k} \in CL_h$ (see Equation 4). We denote the entropy of the distribution by $E(x_u|\mathcal{L})$. (We put the training set $\mathcal{L}$ in the entropy notation because the predictive functions are trained based on $\mathcal{L}$.) Now, for each candidate object $x \in C$, if we add it to the training set and give it a label y, the training set is expanded. Let $\mathcal{L}_{+(x,y)}$ denote this expanded training set. We compute the entropies $E(x_u|\mathcal{L}_{+(x,y)})$'s for all possible labels y of x, and aggregate them into an *expected entropy*, denoted by $E(x_u|\mathcal{L}_{+(x,*)})$[9]. The sum over all unlabeled objects x_u, i.e., $\sum_{x_u \in \mathcal{V}-\mathcal{L}} E(x_u|\mathcal{L}_{+(x,*)})$, measures the overall expected entropy of all unlabeled objects if x is added to the training set $\mathcal{L}$. The results of the active learning is to select from C, N_S candidates that give the smallest overall expected entropies. Algorithm 1 summarizes our algorithm HINAL.

5. EXPERIMENTS

In this section we present experimental results to evaluate HINAL. Our experiments consist of two parts. First, we study the performance of the SVM classifiers that are trained using cl-meta-paths (see Section 4.2). In particular, we show that our way of learning the cl-meta-paths' weights is very effective. This allows

[7]We use a linear kernel in the experiment.

[8]One can also add the top few objects from each cluster to C, just to allow more candidates to be considered.

[9]We employ an incremental SVM algorithm to train the classifiers when we modify $\mathcal{L}$.

Algorithm 1 HINAL

Input: $\mathcal{G} = \langle \mathcal{V}, \mathcal{E} \rangle, \mathcal{T}, \mathcal{L}, \mathcal{PS}, B, N_S, N_C$: # of clusters.
Output: f_h, $1 \le h \le |\mathcal{T}|$: classifier for object type t_h.
1: Derive *cl*-$\mathcal{PS}$ from $\mathcal{PS}$; ▷ Get class-level meta-paths
2: **while** Budget $B > N_S$ **do** ▷ Enough budget?
3: Construct $\tilde{\mathcal{G}}$ from $\mathcal{G}$, $\mathcal{L}$, *cl*-$\mathcal{PS}$;
4: Compute $W^{\tilde{\mathcal{P}}}$'s based on Eq. 1;
5: Learn Θ based on Eq. 2; ▷ Learn $\theta_{\tilde{\mathcal{P}}}$
6: Train SVM classifiers f_h's based on Eqs. 4 and 5;
7: Compute correlation matrix W based on Eq. 6;
8: Cluster objects into N_C clusters;
9: Pick candidates from clusters to form candidate set C based on Eq. 7;
10: Select a set A of N_S objects from C using uncertainty sampling;
11: $\mathcal{L} \leftarrow \mathcal{L} \cup A$; $B \leftarrow B - N_S$;
12: **end while**
13: **return** f_h's;

HINAL to automatically use the most effective cl-meta-paths in classifier construction. Second, we evaluate the effectiveness of our active learning technique. We show that the three steps taken in HINAL's active learning phase, namely, *clustering*, *candidate selection*, and *uncertainty sampling* (see Section 4.3) work very well together. This results in much more effective active learning compared to other approaches.

5.1 Data

We collected two real data sets `DBLP` and `IMDB` to conduct our experiments. Both of them represent HINs.

DBLP[10] is a bibliographic information network. We extracted objects related to four research areas: *database*, *data mining*, *information retrieval*, and *artificial intelligence* to form the `DBLP` dataset. The dataset contains 14,376 papers (P), 20 publication venues (V), 14,475 authors (A), and 8,920 terms (T)[11]. There are in total 170,794 direct links of three types: P-V, P-A, and P-T. We have labeled 4,057 authors and all 20 conferences as ground truth. The classification task is to classify authors and venues by research areas. Similar to [23], we consider the meta-path set $\mathcal{PS}$ = {VPTPV, VPAPV, APA, APTPA, APAPA, APVPA, APV, APAPV}.

IMDB[12] is a movie information database. We extracted objects that are related to movies of three genres: *sci-fi*, *comedy*, and *horror* to form the `IMDB` dataset. The dataset contains 11,430 actors (A), 5,612 movies (M), 3,092 directors (D), and 5,067 keywords (K). There are 53,030 links of three types: M-A, M-D, and M-K. The classification task is to classify actors and directors by their genres. We labeled all actor and director objects as ground truth. We consider the meta-path set $\mathcal{PS}$ = {DMKMD, DMAMD, AMA, AMKMA, AMAMA, AMDMA, AMD, AMAMD}.

5.2 Classification Algorithms

We study the performance of HINAL's SVM classifiers, which are constructed using the cl-meta-paths derived from the set $\mathcal{PS}$. We turn off active learning (Step 6) and assume that all our budget B is spent on getting an initial training set $\mathcal{L}$.

We compare HINAL with four other classification algorithms: LLGC, GNetMine, HCC, and KEY. We have already described the first three in Section 2. Here, we further describe LLGC and KEY and explain how they are applied to our classification problem.

- LLGC is designed for homogeneous networks. To apply it on an HIN $\mathcal{G}$, we transform $\mathcal{G}$ into a homogeneous network first. For example, to build a classifier for authors in DBLP, we need an *author network*. We get this network by establishing a link between two authors if they are related by the co-authorship relationship, which is equivalent to the relationship expressed by the meta-path APA. Figure 1(a) shows an example network derived from the HIN in Figure 1(b). Similarly, for the task of classifying venues in DBLP, under LLGC, we construct the venue network based on VPAPV. For IMDB, we use meta-paths AMA and DMAMD for constructing the networks of actors and directors, respectively.
- KEY is a keyword-based classifier. KEY uses the same classifier (SVM) as HINAL but it differs at how the feature vector of each node is constructed. Under KEY, the feature vector of an object is composed of the keywords (or terms) that are associated with the object. For example, in DBLP, the feature of an author is all the terms mentioned in the papers written by the author. In other words, authors' feature vectors are derived from the meta-path APT. Similarly, we use VPT to derive venue's feature vectors (the terms mentioned in all the papers of a conference). For IMDB, we use meta-paths AMK and DMK to extract keywords for classifying actors and directors, respectively.

Table 2: Classifier accuracy (DBLP)

(a%, v%) of authors and venues labeled	LLGC	HCC	KEY	GNetMine	HINAL
(0.14%, 40%)	25.5%	38.9%	46.9%	66.8%	**77.3%**
(0.28%, 50%)	29.3%	48.1%	52.4%	79.6%	**88.8%**
(0.42%, 60%)	33.3%	58.6%	58.7%	78.9%	**89.9%**
(0.56%, 70%)	37.5%	64.4%	62.6%	88.7%	**90.9%**
(0.70%, 80%)	40.2%	68.3%	65.9%	90.1%	**91.5%**

Table 3: Classifier accuracy (IMDB)

(a%, d%) of actors and directors labeled	LLGC	HCC	KEY	GNetMine	HINAL
(1%, 1%)	42.7%	33.8%	43.6%	59.5%	**66.6%**
(2%, 2%)	43.6%	34.5%	44.5%	61.6%	**68.0%**
(3%, 3%)	43.8%	35.6%	44.9%	63.0%	**68.5%**
(4%, 4%)	44.3%	36.1%	45.1%	64.5%	**69.2%**
(5%, 5%)	44.6%	36.8%	45.8%	65.5%	**69.5%**

Tables 2 and 3 show the classifiers' accuracies for DBLP and IMDB, respectively, as the size of the training set ($\mathcal{L}$) changes[13]. We use (a%, v%) to represent that $\mathcal{L}$ contains a% of author objects and v% of venue objects in the DBLP experiment. Since there are much more authors than venues, the author objects in $\mathcal{L}$ represent a fairly small fraction of the total author population. Similarly, we use (a%, d%) to represent that $\mathcal{L}$ contains a% of actor objects and d% of director objects in the IMDB experiment. From the tables, we observe that (1) a larger $\mathcal{L}$ generally gives more accurate classifiers, and (2) HINAL gives much higher accuracies than other algorithms under all cases.

An important feature of HINAL is that it automatically learns the weights $\theta_{\tilde{\mathcal{P}}}$'s of the meta-paths. This weighting mechanism is important for HINAL to distinguish meta-paths that are very effective to the classification task from those that are not. Before we give

[10] http://www.informatik.uni-trier.de/ ley/db/
[11] A term is a keyword listed in a paper.
[12] http://www.imdb.com/
[13] We randomly generated 10 $\mathcal{L}$'s for each training set size. The reported values are averages of the accuracies obtained over 10 runs.

an in-depth comparison study of the classifiers, let us first evaluate how well HINAL learns those weights. As will become clear later, our discussion on meta-path effectiveness can help us understand the relative performance of the various classification algorithms.

Consider the task of classifying authors in DBLP. Figure 4 shows HINAL's classifier accuracy vs. $\mathcal{L}$ given different meta-path sets. For simplicity, we consider only four meta-paths as shown in the figure. The curve labeled APA, for example, refers to the case $\mathcal{PS}$ = {APA}, likewise for the other curves labeled APAPA, APTPA, and APVPA. The curve labeled ALL4 refers to the case in which $\mathcal{PS}$ consists of all four meta-paths.

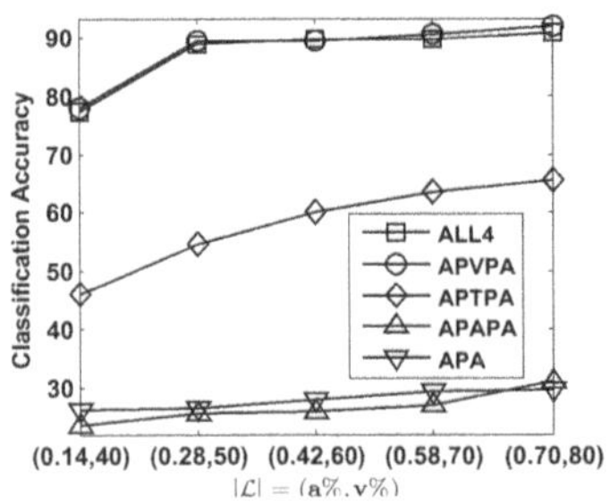

Figure 4: Author classification vs. $|\mathcal{L}|$ under various $\mathcal{PS}$

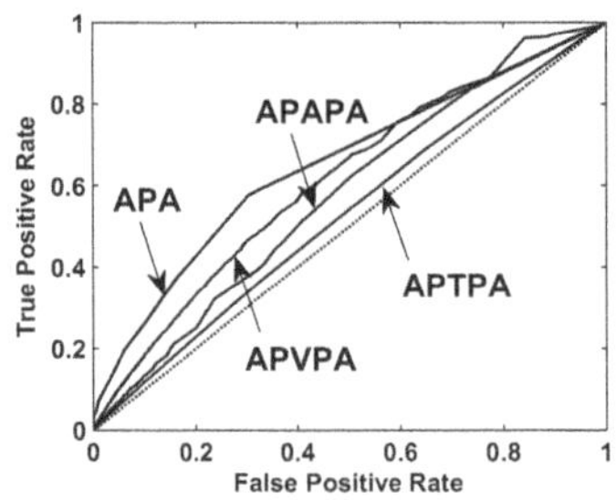

Figure 5: ROC curves

Comparing the individual meta-paths, Figure 4 shows that the meta-path APVPA is highly effective, leading to a high accuracy even when it is the only meta-path HINAL uses. Meta-path APTPA is less effective but it is better than APAPA and APA. Also, we see that when HINAL is given all four meta-paths to work with, its performance is very close to that of APVPA, which is the most effective of the given four. This indicates that HINAL is able to adjust to the most effective meta-paths. In fact, the relative weights of the meta-paths HINAL learned are APA (0.47), APAPA (0.59), APTPA (3.71), APVPA (8.33) when $|\mathcal{L}|$ = (0.14%, 40%). The weight of APVPA is about 18 times that of APA.

The relative effectiveness of the meta-paths may look counterintuitive. After all, two authors co-authoring a paper is a strong indicator that they work in the same research area. So, wouldn't APA be the best meta-path for classifying authors instead of the worst as shown in Figure 4? To answer that question, let us consider the weighted correlation matrix $\theta_{\mathcal{P}} W^{\mathcal{P}}$ derived from each meta-path $\mathcal{P}$. Now, for a threshold value α and two labeled author objects A1 and A2 such that $\theta_{\mathcal{P}} W^{\mathcal{P}}[A1, A2] \geq \alpha$, we say that (A1, A2) form a "true positive" if they share the same labels; they form a "false positive" otherwise. This true/false positive measures how well the correlation derived from $\mathcal{P}$ helps predict authors' labels. In Figure 5, we show the ROC curves of the true/false positive values derived from the various meta-paths. We see that APA (with the largest AUC) indeed is the best relationship for inferring author label. The problem with APA is that the relationship has a very small *reach*, i.e., the number of co-authors of a given (labeled) author is very limited and so we can infer very few author labels via the APA relationship. Consider the case when $\mathcal{L}$ = (0.14%,40%), Table 4 shows, on average, the percentage of author objects that can be reached from an author object via a (class-level) meta-path. We see that the *reach* of APA is too small for the meta-path to build an effective classifier. Combining the *reach* factor with our discussion based on the ROC curves, one can easily understand the relative effectiveness of the four meta-paths as shown in Figure 4.

Now, let's go back to Table 2. As we have mentioned earlier in this section, LLGC is essentially using the APA meta-path to derive the co-authorship network. As we have explained, APA is a poor meta-path for classifying authors due to its poor reach. This explains why LLGC performance is so poor. HCC uses meta-paths to classify HIN objects. However, it treats all meta-paths equally. Its performance is thus dragged down by the ineffective meta-paths (such as APA and APAPA, as illustrated in Figure 4). KEY derives an object's feature by keywords (or terms) through the relationship APT. So, two authors are "similar" under KEY if they have written papers that share common terms. KEY thus effectively correlates authors through the APTPA meta-paths, which is shown to be mediocre in Figure 4. Although GNetMine does not use meta-paths, its classifier uses all links provided by an HIN. The information GNetMine uses to classify objects is therefore quite rich, which results in its coming second in classifier accuracy. Our algorithm HINAL uses meta-paths, which are information rich. Its ability to learn the weights of meta-paths allows it to adapt to the most effective meta-paths. Our results show that HINAL significantly outperforms the other classifiers. We have also conducted experiments on HINAL using meta-paths instead of cl-meta-paths. Our results show that using cl-meta-paths (i.e., with jumps) gives better performance than using meta-paths. This shows the significance of jumps in object classification.

Table 4: Fraction of authors reachable from a given author via a cl-meta-path

percentage of labeled data	APA	APAPA	APTPA	APVPA
(0.14%, 40%)	0.07%	0.25%	78.52%	34.21%
(0.28%, 50%)	0.07%	0.27%	78.52%	34.68%
(0.42%, 60%)	0.07%	0.29%	78.52%	35.92%
(0.56%, 70%)	0.07%	0.31%	78.52%	38.75%
(0.70%, 80%)	0.07%	0.35%	78.52%	40.25%

5.3 Active Learners

In this section we study the effectiveness of HINAL's active learning component. Recall that HINAL performs active learning with three sub-steps: (1) Clustering — which groups objects into clusters so as to avoid picking *redundant* objects to label. (2) GenC — which picks candidates from each cluster that give the best *goodness* scores (Equation 7) to form the candidate set C. (3) US — which performs uncertainty sampling to select objects from C to label. Also, given a budget B, HINAL iterates B/N_S times, picking N_S objects to label in each iteration. After each iteration, the classifiers are re-trained (Figure 3). We call this *iterative refinement*. We study the significance of these steps by modifying HINAL with the following active learning strategies:

- *Random*: Randomly pick N_S unlabeled objects to label. This is equivalent to HINAL with all three sub-steps turned off. This strategy serves as a baseline for comparison.
- *Label Selection Based on Clustering (LSC)* [13]: Group objects into N_C clusters and then randomly select N_S/N_C unlabeled objects from each cluster to label. This strategy is equivalent to HINAL with GenC and US turned off.
- *Goodness*: Evaluate the goodness score for every unlabeled object and pick the top-N_S of them with the highest scores to label. This is equivalent to HINAL with clustering and US turned off.
- *Uncertainty Sampling (US)* [5]: Perform uncertainty sampling directly on all unlabeled objects to pick N_S objects to label. This is equivalent to HINAL with Clustering and GenC turned off.

- *HINAL without Iterative Refinement (HINAL-noIR)*: This is HINAL with $N_S = B$, the whole budget. So all objects to be labeled are selected within one iteration.

Figure 6 shows the classifier accuracy under the various active learners as the budget B varies. Two figures are shown, one for DBLP and the other for IMDB. Note that the algorithms differ only by the active learning strategy employed. Classifiers are still built based on HINAL's cl-meta-path-based approach. The initial training set for DBLP contains 8 labeled authors and 4 labeled venues. For IMDB, it is 16 actors and 4 directors. We set $N_S = 1$ and 5 for the experiments on DBLP and IMDB, respectively.

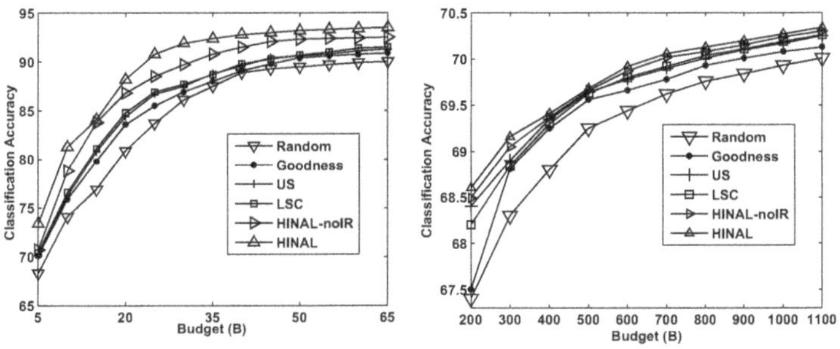

(a) DBLP (b) IMDB

Figure 6: Active Learner Comparison

From Figure 6(a), we see that, for DBLP, the trivial Random strategy performs worst compared with other active learners. LSC, Goodness, and US, which apply one of the three sub-steps of HINAL each, show comparable performance and they are clearly better than Random. This shows that all of the three sub-steps, namely, clustering, goodness measure, and uncertainty sampling are useful. Also, we see that HINAL significantly outperforms the others. This shows that the improvements brought about by the three sub-steps are additive. If we compare HINAL and Random, we see that the performance gap between them are wider when B is smaller. Hence, it is very important that we have a good active learning component when we have a tight labeling budget. HINAL-noIR also performs very well because it does all three sub-steps. However, by picking objects in one shot, HINAL-noIR misses the opportunity to perform active learning with more refined classifiers. This results in a slightly worse performance compared with the iterative HINAL. Similar conclusions can be drawn for the IMDB experiment (Figure 6(b)).

Tables 5(a) and (b) show the budget B needed to achieve certain classifier accuracy for DBLP and IMDB, respectively. We see that HINAL requires a much smaller budget than the other active learners, especially when compared against Random. The savings are particularly significant for IMDB. This is because IMDB objects are harder to classify (as reflected by the classifier accuracy values) and so it is even more important that a good training set (as obtained through a good active learning strategy) is used.

5.4 Yago

We end this section with a brief description of a case study in which we applied HINAL to classify objects on Yago. As we have discussed in the introduction, it is important that objects in a knowledge base are given descriptive labels to facilitate effective information retrieval and logic deductions. However, such labelings require a lot of manual efforts and so are often incomplete. As an example, Yago contains about 60,000 movie objects, some of which are labeled with their genres (such as *comedy*, *action*, *sci-fi*, etc.). These labelings, however, are incomplete. For example, the movie "The Lord of the Rings: The Return of the King" is given the label *fantasy* on Yago. However, the movie is categorized by Freebase (another collaborative knowledge base) as *fantasy* and *adventure*. In fact, we inspected a good fraction of Yago's 60,000 movie objects. We found that, among them, about 1/3 are not labeled with any genre (we marked them as *unlabeled*); about 1/2 of them are only *partially labeled*, meaning that the genre labels given to each of those movies form only a proper subset of the labels given to the corresponding movie on Freebase; and only about 1/6 of the movies on Yago are *completely labeled*. As a further example, we inspected the movie objects on Yago that are categorized as *comedy* on Freebase. We found that about 47.5% of them are not given the *comedy* label on Yago.

Table 5: Budget needed to achieve certain accuracy

(a) DBLP

Active Learner	B					
	65%	70%	75%	80%	85%	90%
Random	4	6	11	19	28	61
Goodness	3	5	10	16	24	47
US	2	5	10	14	21	43
LSC	2	5	9	13	21	42
HINAL-noIR	2	4	8	11	18	31
HINAL	2	4	6	9	16	23

(b) IMDB

Active Learner	B					
	60%	62%	64%	66%	68%	70%
Random	15	40	75	120	275	1055
Goodness	15	35	65	110	230	865
US	10	30	65	105	185	785
LSC	10	30	60	100	195	765
HINAL-noIR	10	25	55	90	170	675
HINAL	10	25	50	85	155	615

We investigate how HINAL helps a knowledge base acquire object labels, especially when only a small fraction of the objects have already been properly labeled. As an illustrative example, we consider a very simple binary classification task — to label each movie object on Yago as either *comedy* or *non-comedy*.

We randomly selected 530 movie objects on Yago as our training data (which is about 0.9% of all movies on Yago). We consulted Freebase and labeled each movie object in the training data as either *comedy* or *non-comedy*. We then applied HINAL on the Yago information network to infer the label (*comedy*, *non-comedy*) of the movie objects. We used the meta-path set $\mathcal{PS}$ = { MAM, MDM, MPM, MUM, MAMAM, MPMPM, MUMUM }, where the symbols denote (M)ovie, (A)ctor/actress, (D)irector, (P)roducer, and m(U)sician. These seven meta-paths connect two movies via the following relationships: (1) they share an actor, (2) they are directed by the same director, (3) they are produced by the same producer, (4) they share a music composer, (5) they have actors that have co-acted in a movie, (6) they are produced by producers who have co-produced a movie, (7) they have musicians that have contributed to the music of the same movie.

Note that some of these meta-paths (and the cl-meta-paths they derive) may not be useful in the classification task. Their relative effectiveness is automatically determined by HINAL via its weight-assignment mechanism. Table 6 shows the weights of the meta-paths HINAL assigned. We see that the longer meta-paths (e.g., MAMAM and MPMPM) received higher weights than the shorter ones (e.g., MAM, MPM). This is again due to the *reach* issue.

Table 6: Weights of meta-paths

Path	MAM	MDM	MPM	MUM
Weight	0.0825	0.0269	0.0288	0.0163
Path	MAMAM	MPMPM	MUMUM	
Weight	2.9681	0.3844	0.1169	

Our experiment results show that HINAL is quite effective in identifying comedy movies on Yago. Specifically, the precision and recall for the comedy class is 94.8% and 73.3%, respectively. Note that the classification task is an asymmetric one. That is, while movies on the knowledge base that are identified as comedy should be marked (*comedy*), those that are non-comedy would not be physically given the (non-comedy) label. Instead, other classification tasks could have been done to determine whether those movies are *sci-fi* or *action* movies, etc.

We remark that in the experiment, a very small training set was used (which is about 0.9% of all movie objects). Yet, based on this small set of training examples and the meta-paths (and their derived cl-meta-paths), HINAL was able to identify 73.3% of all comedy movies. This number is significantly larger than what Yago currently knows (47.5%). This experiment thus further illustrates the applicability of HINAL in improving knowledge bases.

6. CONCLUSION

In this paper we studied the problem of classifying objects in heterogeneous information networks. We proposed to use meta-paths to derive correlations between objects so as to build better classifiers. In particular, we proposed class-level meta-paths and put forward a method to determine the relative weights of cl-meta-paths through a learning process. The correlations derived from cl-meta-paths allow us to achieve two objectives. One is to construct object feature vectors for classifiers construction. The other is to perform active learning by which objects are picked to form the training set. We presented a comprehensive study on our algorithm HINAL by experiments. Our results show that HINAL outperforms existing classification algorithms for HINs. Its active learning component is also very effective, beating other approaches. In the future, we plan to apply our method to more networks to evaluate its effectiveness. On the other hand, we can analyze more general classification problem in heterogeneous information networks, in which an object could have more than one class label. This makes sense since a venue could be related to both database and information retrieval on DBLP data set. It would be more interesting if we could model it as a multi-label classification problem and output a class distribution over each object.

7. ACKNOWLEDGMENTS

This research is supported by Hong Kong Research Grants Council GRF grant HKU712712E.

8. REFERENCES

[1] C. Cortes and V. Vapnik. Support-vector networks. *Machine Learning*, 1995.

[2] H. Deng et al. Modeling and exploiting heterogeneous bibliographic networks for expertise ranking. In *JCDL*, 2012.

[3] Q. Gu and J. Han. Towards active learning on graphs: An error bound minimization approach. In *ICDM*, 2012.

[4] M. Gupta et al. Evolutionary clustering and analysis of bibliographic networks. In *ASONAM*, 2011.

[5] A. Holub and P. P. M. Burl. Entropy-based active learning for object recognition. In *CVPR*, 2008.

[6] H. Huang, A. Zubiaga, et al. Tweet ranking based on heterogeneous networks. In *COLING*, 2012.

[7] M. Ji et al. Ranking-based classification of heterogeneous information networks. In *KDD*, 2011.

[8] M. Ji, Y. Sun, M. Danilevsky, J. Han, and J. Gao. Graph regularized transductive classification on heterogeneous information networks. In *ECML-PKDD*, 2010.

[9] X. Kong, P. S. Yu, Y. Ding, and D. J. Wild. Meta path-based collective classification in heterogeneous information networks. In *CIKM*, 2012.

[10] D. D. Lewis and W. A. Gale. A sequential algorithm for training text classifiers. In *SIGIR*, 1994.

[11] Q. Lu and L. Getoor. Link-based classification. In *ICML*, 2003.

[12] J. Neville and D. Jensen. Relational dependency networks. *JMLR*, 2007.

[13] D. Pfeffermann and C. Rao. *Sample Surveys*. Handbook of Statistics. 2009.

[14] R. G. Rossi, A. A. Lopes, and S. O. Rezende. A parameter-free label propagation algorithm using bipartite heterogeneous networks for text classification. In *SAC*, 2014.

[15] P. Sen, G. Namata, et al. Collective classification in network data. *Artificial Intelligence Magazine*, 2008.

[16] H. S. Seung, M. Opper, and H. Sompolinsky. Query by committee. In *COLT*, 1992.

[17] Y. Sun, C. C. Aggarwal, and J. Han. Relation strength-aware clustering of heterogeneous information networks with incomplete attributes. *PVLDB*, 2012.

[18] Y. Sun et al. Co-author relationship prediction in heterogeneous bibliographic networks. In *ASONAM*, 2011.

[19] Y. Sun et al. When will it happen?: relationship prediction in heterogeneous information networks. In *WSDM*, 2012.

[20] Y. Sun and J. Han. Meta-path-based search and mining in heterogeneous information networks. In *Tsinghua Science and Technology*, 2013.

[21] Y. Sun, J. Han, X. Yan, P. S. Yu, and T. Wu. Pathsim: Meta path-based top-k similarity search in heterogeneous information networks. *PVLDB*, 2011.

[22] Y. Sun, J. Han, P. Zhao, Z. Yin, H. Cheng, and T. Wu. Rankclus: integrating clustering with ranking for heterogeneous information network analysis. In *EDBT*, 2009.

[23] Y. Sun, B. Norick, et al. Integrating meta-path selection with user-guided object clustering in heterogeneous information networks. In *KDD*, 2012.

[24] Y. Sun, Y. Yu, and J. Han. Ranking-based clustering of heterogeneous information networks with star network schema. In *KDD*, 2009.

[25] D. Yan, L. Huang, and M. I. Jordan. Fast approximate spectral clustering. In *KDD*, 2009.

[26] Y. Yang et al. Predicting links in multi-relational and heterogeneous networks. In *ICDM*, 2012.

[27] X. Yu, Q. Gu, M. Zhou, and J. Han. Citation prediction in heterogeneous bibliographic networks. In *SDM*, 2012.

[28] D. Zhou et al. Learning with local and global consistency. In *NIPS*, 2003.

[29] Y. Zhou and L. Liu. Activity-edge centric multi-label classification for mining heterogeneous information networks. In *KDD*, 2014.

[30] X. Zhu. *Semi-supervised learning with graphs*. PhD thesis, 2005.

Semantic Path based Personalized Recommendation on Weighted Heterogeneous Information Networks

Chuan Shi
Beijing University of Posts and Telecommunications
Beijing, China
shichuan@bupt.edu.cn

Zhiqiang Zhang
Beijing University of Posts and Telecommunications
Beijing, China
zzqsmall@gmail.com

Ping Luo
Institute of Computing Technology, CAS
Beijing, China
luop@ict.ac.cn

Philip S. Yu
University of Illinois at Chicago
IL,USA
psyu@cs.uic.edu

Yading Yue
Tencent Corporation
Shenzhen, China
adenyue@tencent.com

Bin Wu
Beijing University of Posts and Telecommunications
Beijing, China
wubin@bupt.edu.cn

ABSTRACT

Recently heterogeneous information network (HIN) analysis has attracted a lot of attention, and many data mining tasks have been exploited on HIN. As an important data mining task, recommender system includes a lot of object types (e.g., users, movies, actors, and interest groups in movie recommendation) and the rich relations among object types, which naturally constitute a HIN. The comprehensive information integration and rich semantic information of HIN make it promising to generate better recommendations. However, conventional HINs do not consider the attribute values on links, and the widely used meta path in HIN may fail to accurately capture semantic relations among objects, due to the existence of rating scores (usually ranging from 1 to 5) between users and items in recommender system. In this paper, we are the first to propose the weighted HIN and weighted meta path concepts to subtly depict the path semantics through distinguishing different link attribute values. Furthermore, we propose a semantic path based personalized recommendation method SemRec to predict the rating scores of users on items. Through setting meta paths, SemRec not only flexibly integrates heterogeneous information but also obtains prioritized and personalized weights representing user preferences on paths. Experiments on two real datasets illustrate that SemRec achieves better recommendation performance through flexibly integrating information with the help of weighted meta paths.

Categories and Subject Descriptors

H.2.8 [**Database Management**]: Database applications-Data Mining

CIKM'15, October 19–23, 2015, Melbourne, VIC, Australia.

DOI: http://dx.doi.org/10.1145/2806416.2806528.

Keywords

heterogeneous information network, recommendation, similarity, meta path

1. INTRODUCTION

In recent years, there is a surge of research on Heterogeneous Information Network (HIN) in which objects are of different types and links among objects represent different relations [11]. The heterogeneity and rich relation of information network make it a better data representation in many scenarios. As a unique characteristics of HIN, the meta path [12, 15], connecting two objects through a sequence of relations between object types, is widely used to exploit rich semantic information. Many meta path based data mining tasks have been done in the past couple of years, including similarity search [12, 10], clustering [13], and classification [3] etc.

More recently, some works [2, 7, 15] have taken notice of the benefits of HIN for recommendation, where the objects and their relations in recommender system constitute a HIN. Fig. 1 shows such an example. The HIN not only contains different types of objects in movie recommendation (e.g., users and movies) but also illustrates all kinds of relations among objects, such as viewing information, social relations, and attribute information. Constructing heterogeneous networks for recommendation can effectively integrate all kinds of informations, which can be potentially utilized for recommendation. Moreover, the objects and relations in the networks have different semantics, which can be explored to reveal subtle relations among objects. For example, the meta path "User-Movie-User" in Fig. 1 means users viewing the same movies, and can be used to find the similar users according to viewing records. If we recommend movies following this meta path, it will recommend the movies that are seen by users having the same viewing records with the given user. It corresponds to the collaborative filtering model in essence. Similarly, the "User-Interest Group-User" path can find the similar users with similar interests. This path corresponds to the member recommendation [16]. So we can directly recommend items based on the similar users generated by different meta paths connecting users. Moreover, it can realize different recommendation models through properly

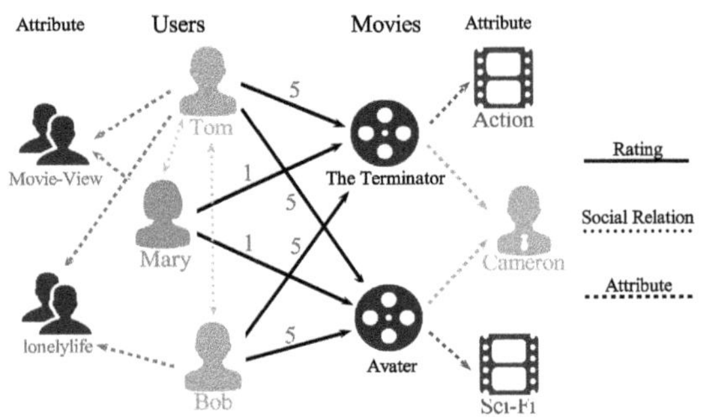

Figure 1: The objects and relations in movie recommender system is organized as a weighted heterogeneous information network.

setting meta paths. However, this idea faces the following two challenges.

Firstly, conventional HIN and meta path cannot be directly applied to recommender system. As we know, conventional HIN and meta path do not consider the attribute values on links. However, this movie recommendation network can contain attribute values on links. Concretely, in recommender system, the users can provide a rating score to each movie viewed. The rating scores usually range from 1 to 5 as indicated on the link between user and movie in Fig. 1, where higher score means stronger preference. Ignoring the rating scores may result in bad similarity discovery on users. For example, according to the path "User-Movie-User", Tom has the same similarity with Mary and Bob, since they view the same movies. However, they may have totally different tastes due to different rating scores. In fact, Tom and Bob should be more similar, since they both like the same movies very much with high scores. Mary may have totally different tastes, because she does not like these movies at all. The conventional meta path does not allow links to have attribute values (e.g., rating scores in the above example) [12, 15], and hence it cannot reveal this subtle difference. However, this difference is very important, especially in recommender system, to more accurately reveal relations of objects. So we need to extend existing HIN and meta path for considering attribute values on links. Moreover, the new similarity measures are urgently needed for development.

Secondly, it is difficult to effectively combine information from multiple meta paths for recommendation. As we have said, different types of similar users will be generated through different meta paths, and these different types of similar users will recommend different items. A weight learning method can be designed to combine these recommendations and each path can be assigned with a learned weight preference. A good weight learning method should obtain prioritized and personalized weights. That is, the learned weights can represent the importance of paths, and each user should have personalized weights to embody his preferences on paths. The prioritized and personalized weights are very important for recommendation, since they can deeply reveal the characteristics of users. Much more than this, it makes the recommendation more explainable, since meta paths contain semantics. For example, if a user has high weight preference on the "User-Interest Group-User" path, we can explain that the recommendation results stem from movies viewed by users in the interest groups he joined in. Unfortunately, the personalized weights may suffer from the rating sparsity problem, especially for users with little rating information. The reasons lie in that so many parameters are needed to be learned and rating information are usually not sufficient.

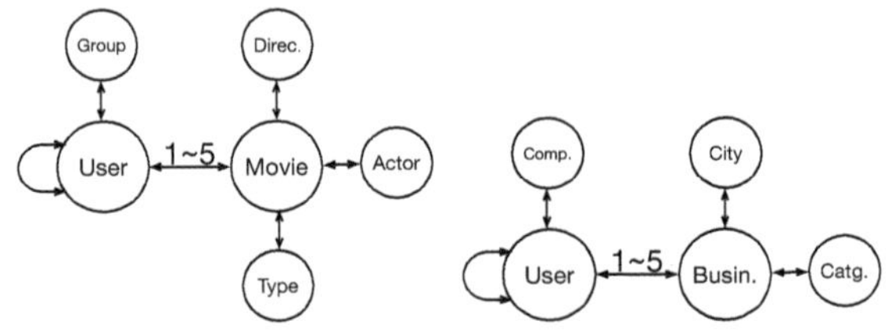

(a) Douban (b) Yelp

Figure 2: Network schema of weighted heterogeneous information networks constituted by two datasets.

In this paper, we extend HIN and meta path for widely-existing attribute values on links in information networks, and firstly propose the weighted HIN and weighted meta path concepts to more subtly reveal object relations through distinguishing link attribute values. Instead of designing an ad hoc similarity measure for weighted meta paths, we design a novel similarity computation strategy that can make existing path-based similarity measures still usable. Furthermore, the semantic path based personalized recommendation method SemRec is proposed to flexibly integrate heterogeneous information through setting meta paths. In SemRec, we design a novel weight regularization term to obtain personalized weight preferences on paths and alleviate the rating sparsity through employing the consistency rule of weight preferences of similar users. The datasets and codes can be downloaded from the web [1]. The major contributions of this paper are summarized as follows:

- To the best of our knowledge, we are the first to propose weighted HIN and weighted meta path to consider attribute values on links in information networks. Furthermore, we propose the similarity measure strategy on weighted meta path.
- We design a novel SemRec method, which not only effectively integrates all kinds of information contained in recommender system but also flexibly represents different kinds of recommendation models through properly setting meta paths. In addition, SemRec can obtain the prioritized and personalized weight preferences on paths, which are important for real applications, e.g., user characteristics analysis and recommendation explanation.
- Empirical studies on two real datasets, Douban and Yelp, demonstrate the power of SemRec. SemRec outperforms the state of the arts, especially for cold-start users and items, and the personalized weights learned by SemRec are able to reflect user preferences on paths. In addition, SemRec can achieve better performances with the help of weighted meta paths.

2. HETEROGENEOUS NETWORK FRAMEWORK FOR RECOMMENDATION

In this section, we describe notations used in this paper and present some preliminary knowledge.

[1]https://github.com/zzqsmall/SemRec

2.1 Basic concepts

A HIN is a special type of information network with the underneath data structure as a directed graph, which either contains multiple types of objects or multiple types of links. Traditionally, HIN does not consider the attribute values on links. However, many real networks contain attribute values on links. For example, users usually rate movies with a score from 1 to 5 in movie recommender system, and the "author of" relations between authors and papers in bibliographic networks can take values (e.g., 1, 2, 3) which means the order of authors in the paper. In this paper, we formally propose the weighted heterogeneous information network concept to handle this condition.

DEFINITION 1. ***Weighted Information Network.*** *Given a schema $S = (\mathcal{A}, \mathcal{R}, \mathcal{W})$ which consists of a set of object types $\mathcal{A} = \{A\}$, a set of relations connecting object pairs $\mathcal{R} = \{R\}$, and a set of attribute values on relations $\mathcal{W} = \{W\}$, a* ***weighted information network*** *is defined as a directed graph $G = (V, E, W)$ with an object type mapping function $\varphi : V \to \mathcal{A}$, a link type mapping function $\psi : E \to \mathcal{R}$, and an attribute value type mapping function $\theta : W \to \mathcal{W}$. Each object $v \in V$ belongs to one particular object type $\varphi(v) \in \mathcal{A}$, each link $e \in E$ belongs to a particular relation $\psi(e) \in \mathcal{R}$, and each attribute value $w \in W$ belongs to a particular attribute value type $\theta(w) \in \mathcal{W}$. When the types of objects $|\mathcal{A}| = 1$ and the types of relations $|\mathcal{R}| = 1$, it is a* ***homogeneous information network****. When the types of objects $|\mathcal{A}| > 1$ (or the types of relations $|\mathcal{R}| > 1$) and the types of attribute values $|\mathcal{W}| = 0$, the network is called* ***unweighted heterogeneous information network****. When the types of objects $|\mathcal{A}| > 1$ (or the types of relations $|\mathcal{R}| > 1$) and the types of attribute values $|\mathcal{W}| > 0$, the network is called* ***weighted heterogeneous information network*** *(WHIN).*

Conventional HIN is an unweighted HIN, where there are no attribute values on relations or we do not consider them. For a WHIN, there are attribute values on some relation types, and these attribute values may be discrete or continuous values.

EXAMPLE 1. *A movie recommender system can be organized as a weighted heterogeneous information network, whose network schema is shown in Fig. 2(a). The network contains objects from six types of entities (e.g., users, movies, groups, actors) and relations between them. Links between objects represent different relations. For example, links exist between users and users denoting the friendship relations, between users and movies denoting rating and rated relations. In addition, the network also contains one type of attribute value on the rating relation between users and movies, which take values from 1 to 5.*

Two objects in a HIN can be connected via different paths and these paths have different meanings. As an example shown in Fig. 2(a), users can be connected via "User-User" (UU) path, "User-Group-User" (UGU) path, "User-Movie-User" (UMU) and so on. These paths are called meta paths that are the combination of a sequence of relations between object types. Although meta path is widely used to reveal semantics among objects [11], it fails to distinguish the attribute values between two objects in WHIN. For example, if ignoring the different rating scores of users on items in above movie recommendation, we may obtain incorrect results. Consider a scenario that we use the UMU path to find the similar users of Tom according to their viewing records in Fig. 1. We can infer that Tom is very similar to Mary and Bob, since they have the same viewing records. However, it is obvious that Tom and Mary have totally different tastes. So the UMU path cannot subtly reveal the different ratings of users on the same movies. In order to effectively exploit semantics in WHIN, we extend the conventional meta path to consider attribute values on relations. Without loss of generality, we assume the attribute values on relations in WHIN are discrete. For continuous attribute values on relations, we can convert the continuous attribute values into discrete ones.

DEFINITION 2. ***Extended meta path on WHIN.*** *Extended meta path is a meta path based on a certain attribute value constraint on relations, which is denoted as $A_1 \xrightarrow{\delta_1(R_1)} A_2 \xrightarrow{\delta_2(R_2)} \cdots \xrightarrow{\delta_l(R_l)} A_{l+1}|\mathcal{C}$ (also denoted as $A_1(\delta_1(R_1)) A_2(\delta_2(R_2)) \cdots (\delta_l(R_l))A_{l+1}|\mathcal{C}$). If the relation R has attribute values on links, the attribute value function $\delta(R)$ is a set of values from the attribute value range of relation R, else $\delta(R)$ is an empty set. $A_i \xrightarrow{\delta_i(R_i)} A_{i+1}$ represents the relation R_i between A_i and A_{i+1} based on the attribute values $\delta_i(R_i)$. The constraint $\mathcal{C}$ on attribute value functions is a set of correlation constraints among attribute value functions. If all attribute value functions in a meta path are empty set (the corresponding constraint $\mathcal{C}$ is also an empty set), the path is called an* ***unweighted meta path****, else the path is called a* ***weighted meta path****.*

Note that, the conventional meta path is an unweighted meta path that can be considered as the special case of a weighted meta path.

EXAMPLE 2. *Taking Fig. 2(a) as an example, the rating relation between users U and movies M can take scores from 1 to 5. the weighted meta path $U \xrightarrow{1} M$ (i.e., $U(1)M$) means movies rated by users with score 1, which implies that users dislike the movies. The weighted meta path $U \xrightarrow{1,2} M \xrightarrow{1,2} U$ (i.e., $U(1,2)M(1,2)U$) means users disliking the same movies as the target user, while the unweighted meta path UMU can only reflect that users have the same viewing records. Furthermore, we can flexibly set the correlation constraints of attribute value functions on different relations in weighted meta paths. For example, the path $U(i)M(j)U|i = j$ means users having exactly the same ratings on some movies as the target user. Under this path, we can easily find that, in Fig. 1, Tom is very similar to Bob, while they are totally dissimilar to Mary.*

2.2 Recommendation on heterogeneous networks

For a target user, recommender systems usually recommend items according to his similar users. In HIN, there are a number of meta paths connecting users, such as "User-User" and "User-Moive-User". Based on these paths, users have different similarities. Here we define the path based similarity as follows.

DEFINITION 3. ***Path based similarity.*** *In HIN, the path based similarity of two objects is the similarity evaluation based on the given meta path connecting these two objects.*

Table 1: The meanings and corresponding recommendation models of meta paths.

No.	Meta Path	Semantic Meaning	Recommendation Model
1	UU	friends of the target user	Social recommendation
2	UGU	users in the same group of the target user	Member recommendation
3	UMU	users who view the same movies with the target user	Collaborative recommendation
4	UMTMU	users who view the movies having the same types with that of the target user	Content recommendation

After obtaining the path based similarity of users, we can recommend items according to the similar users of the target user. More importantly, the meta paths connecting users have different semantics, which can represent different recommendation models. As an example shown in Fig. 2(a), "User-User" (UU) means friends of the target user. If we recommend movies according to the similarity of users generated by that path, it will recommend the movies viewed by friends of the target user. Indeed, it is the social recommendation. Another example is that "User-Movie-User" (UMU) means users who view the same movies with the target user. Following that path, it will recommend the movies viewed by users having the similar viewing records with the target user. it is collaborative recommendation in essential. Table 1 shows the other representative paths and the corresponding recommendation models. Based on the HIN framework, we can flexibly represent different recommendation models through properly setting meta paths.

2.3 Similarity measure based on weighted meta path

Similarity measure on meta paths have been well studied, and several path based similarity measures have been proposed on HIN, such as PathSim [12], PCRW [4], and HeteSim [10]. However, these similarity measures cannot be directly applied to weighted meta path, because they do not consider the attribute value constraint on relations. As we know, the essential of the path based similarity measure is to evaluate the proportion of the number of paths connecting two objects on all possible paths along the meta path [12], so the paths along a weighted meta path must satisfy the attribute value constraint. Moreover, the attribute value on relations may be a variable, even correlated. Taking the U(i)M(j)U$|i=j$ path as an example, the attribute values i and j are variables from 1 to 5, and they satisfy constraint $i=j$. For this kind of paths, existing path based similarity measures cannot handle it.

In order to address the variable, even correlated, attribute value constraints in a weighted meta path, we extend the meta path concept and propose a general strategy to make existing path based similarity measure still usable, instead of proposing an ad hot similarity measure. Specifically, we can decompose the weighted meta path into a group of atomic meta paths with fixed attribute value constraint. For an atomic meta path, the existing path based similarity measures can be used directly.

DEFINITION 4. ***Atomic meta path.*** *If all attribute value functions $\delta(R)$ in a weighted meta path take a specific value, the path is called an* ***atomic meta path****. A weighted meta path is* ***a group of atomic meta paths*** *which contain all atomic meta paths that satisfy the constraint $\mathcal{C}$.*

EXAMPLE 3. *Taking Fig. 2(a) as an example, $U(1)M(1)U$ and $U(1)M(2)U$ both are atomic meta paths. The weighted meta path $U(i)M(j)U|i=j$ is a group of five atomic meta paths (e.g., $U(1)M(1)U$ and $U(2)M(2)U$).*

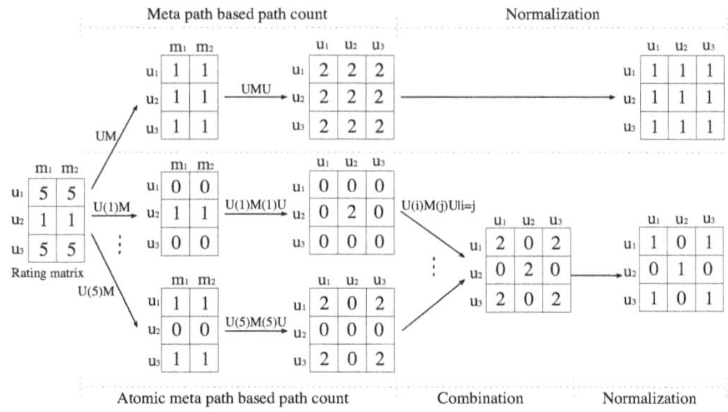

Figure 3: PathSim similarity measure based on conventional and weighted meta path.

Since a weighted meta path is a group of corresponding atomic meta paths, the similarity measure based on a weighted meta path can be considered as the sum of the similarity measure based on the corresponding atomic meta paths. So the similarity measure based on a weighted meta path can be evaluated based on the following two steps: (1) evaluate the similarity based on each atomic meta path with existing path based measures; (2) sum up the similarities on all atomic meta paths in the weighted meta path. Note that, the similarity measure needs to consider the effect of the normalized term existing in some path based similarity measures, such as PathSim [12] and HeteSim [10]. Taking PathSim as an example, we illustrate its calculation process along conventional and weighted meta path in Fig. 3, where the rating matrix between 3 users and 2 movies are from Fig. 1. We know that PathSim counts the number of path instances connecting two objects along conventional meta path with a normalized term (shown in the upper half of Fig. 3), and thus it regards that the users all are the same. As shown in the lower half of Fig. 3, PathSim along weighted meta path firstly counts the number of path instances along each atomic meta path, and then sums up the the number of path instances along all atomic meta paths before normalization. And thus it can more accurately discover that only u_1 and u_3 are similar, since they have the same tastes in movies.

3. THE SEMREC SOLUTION

3.1 Basic Idea

In this section, we proposed a **Sem**antic path based personalized **Rec**ommendation method (**SemRec**) to predict the scores of items. Specifically, SemRec first evaluates the similarity of users based on weighted or unweighted meta paths, and then infers the predicted scores on items according to the rating scores of similar users. Under different meta paths, the users can obtain different recommendation results. How to effectively combine these recommendations generated by different meta paths is challenging. We need to put different preferences on the various meta paths. This results in assigning preference weight to each meta path. We abbreviate the preference weight as weight when the context is clear without confusion with the link weight in the weighted meta path. There are two aspects of difficulties on learning the weights. (1) Prioritized weights. That is, the weights learned should embody the importance of paths and reflect users' preferences. However, the similarity evaluations based on different paths have significant bias, which makes path preference hard to reflect the path importances. For example, the similarity evaluations may all be high based on a path with dense relations, while the similarity evaluations may all be low based on another path with sparse relations. So the similarity evaluations based on different paths cannot reflect the similarity of two objects. SemRec designs a normalized rating intensity operation to eliminate the similarity bias, which makes the weight better reflect path importances. (2) Personalized weights. That is, it is better to learn weight preferences for each user. However, personalized weight learning may suffer from the rating sparsity problem, since many users have little rating informations. In order to alleviate the rating sparsity problem for personalized weight learning, we propose *the consistency rule of weight preferences of similar users.* That is, we assume that two similar users have consistent weight preferences on meta paths. While it is reasonable, it is seldom used before. Two users are similar based on a path, which implies the path has similar impacts on these two users. That is to say, these users have the consistent preferences on the path. Following this principle, we design a novel weight regularization term, which effectively alleviate rating sparsity in personalized weight learning.

In following sections, we firstly design the basic recommendation method based on a single path. And then we propose three levels of personalized recommendation methods based on multiple paths: unified weights for all users, personalized weights for each user, and personalized weights with weight regularization.

3.2 Recommendation with single path

Based on the path based similarity of users, we can find the similar users of a target user under a given path, and then the rating score of the target user on an item can be inferred according to the rating scores of his similar users on the item. Assume that the range of rating scores are from 1 to N (e.g., 5); $\mathcal{P}$ is a set of unweighted or weighted meta paths; $R \in \mathbf{R}^{|U|\times|I|}$ is the rating matrix, where $R_{u,i}$ denotes the rating score of user u on item i; and $S \in \mathbf{R}^{|U|\times|U|}$ is the path based similarity matrix of users, where $S^{(l)}_{u,v}$ is the similarity of users u and v under path $\mathcal{P}_l$. Here we define the *rating intensity* $Q \in \mathbf{R}^{|U|\times|I|\times N}$, where $Q^{(l)}_{u,i,r}$ represents the intensity of user u rating item i with score r given path $\mathcal{P}_l$. $Q^{(l)}_{u,i,r}$ is determined by two aspects: the number of similar users rating the item i with score r, and the similarity of users. So we calculate $Q^{(l)}_{u,i,r}$ as the sum of similarity of users rating i with r.

$$Q^{(l)}_{u,i,r} = \sum_v S^{(l)}_{u,v} \times E_{v,i,r}$$
$$E_{v,i,r} = \begin{cases} 1 & R_{v,i} = r \\ 0 & \text{others,} \end{cases} \tag{1}$$

where $E_{v,i,r}$ indicates whether user v rates item i with score r.

Under a meta path $\mathcal{P}_l$, the rating of a user u on an item i range from 1 to N with different rating intensity $Q^{(l)}_{u,i,r}$. So the *predicted rating score*, denoted as $\hat{R}^{(l)}_{u,i}$, of user u on item i under the path $\mathcal{P}_l$ can be the average of rating scores weighted by corresponding normalized intensity.

$$\hat{R}^{(l)}_{u,i} = \sum_{r=1}^{N} r \times \frac{Q^{(l)}_{u,i,r}}{\sum_{k=1}^{N} Q^{(l)}_{u,i,k}}, \tag{2}$$

and $\hat{R}^{(l)} \in \mathbf{R}^{|U|\times|I|}$ means the predicted rating matrix under path $\mathcal{P}_l$.

According to Eq. (2), we can predict the rating score of a user on an item under a given path, and then recommend the item with the high score for a target user. Moreover, the Eq. (2) has an additional advantage that it eliminates the similarity bias existing in different meta paths. As we know, the similarity of users under different meta paths have different scales, which makes similarity evaluation and rating intensity incomparable among different paths. The normalized rating intensity in Eq. (2) is able to eliminate those scale differences.

3.3 Recommendation with multiple paths

Under different meta paths, there are different predicted rating scores. In order to calculate the compositive score, we propose three different weight learning methods corresponding to different levels of personalized weights of users.

3.3.1 Unified weight learning for all users

For all users, we assign each meta path with a unified weight, which means the user preference on the path. This weight vector is denoted as $\boldsymbol{w} \in \mathbf{R}^{1\times|\mathcal{P}|}$, and $\boldsymbol{w}^{(l)}$ means the weight on path $\mathcal{P}_l$. The final predicted rating score under all meta paths, denoted as $\hat{R}_{u,i}$, can be the weighted sum of predicted rating score under each meta path.

$$\hat{R}_{u,i} = \sum_{l=1}^{|\mathcal{P}|} \boldsymbol{w}^{(l)} \times \hat{R}^{(l)}_{u,i}. \tag{3}$$

Hopefully, the predicted rating matrix $\hat{R} \in \mathbf{R}^{|U|\times|I|}$ should be as close as to the real rating matrix R. So a direct optimization objective can be defined as the square error between the real scores and the predicted scores.

$$\begin{aligned} \min_{\boldsymbol{w}} \mathcal{L}_1(\boldsymbol{w}) &= \tfrac{1}{2}||Y \odot (R - \textstyle\sum_{l=1}^{|\mathcal{P}|} \boldsymbol{w}^{(l)}\hat{R}^{(l)})||_2^2 \\ &+ \tfrac{\lambda_0}{2}||\boldsymbol{w}||_2^2 \\ s.t. \quad & \boldsymbol{w} \geq 0, \end{aligned} \tag{4}$$

where the notation $\odot$ is the Hadamard product (also know as the entrywise product) between matrices, and $||\cdot||_p$ is the matrix L^p-norm. Y is an indicator matrix with $Y_{u,i} = 1$ if user u rated item i, and otherwise $Y_{u,i} = 0$.

3.3.2 Personalized weight learning for individual user

The above optimization objective has a basic assumption: all users have the same path preferences. However, in many real applications, each user has his personal interest preferences. Unified weights cannot provide personalized recommendations for users. To realize personalized recommendation, each user is assigned with weight vector on meta paths. The weight matrix is denoted as $W \in \mathbf{R}^{|U|\times|\mathcal{P}|}$, in which each entry, denoted as $W^{(l)}_u$, means the preference weight of user u on path $\mathcal{P}_l$. The column vector $W^{(l)} \in \mathbf{R}^{|U|\times 1}$

means the weight vector of all users on path $\mathcal{P}_l$. So the predicted rating $\hat{R}_{u,i}$ of user u rating item i under all paths is as follow.

$$\hat{R}_{u,i} = \sum_{l=1}^{|\mathcal{P}|} W_u^{(l)} \times \hat{R}_{u,i}^{(l)}. \tag{5}$$

Similarly, we can define the optimization objective as follows.

$$\begin{aligned} \min_W \mathcal{L}_2(W) &= \tfrac{1}{2}\|Y \odot (R - \sum_{l=1}^{|\mathcal{P}|} diag(W^{(l)})\hat{R}^{(l)})\|_2^2 \\ &+ \tfrac{\lambda_0}{2}\|W\|_2^2 \\ s.t. \quad & W \geq 0, \end{aligned} \tag{6}$$

where $diag(W^{(l)})$ means the diagonal matrix transformed from a vector $W^{(l)}$.

3.3.3 Personalized weight learning with weight regularization

Although Eq. (6) consider user's personalized weights, it may be hard to effectively learn weights for those users that have little rating information. There are $|U| \times |\mathcal{P}|$ weight parameters to learn, while the training samples are usually much smaller than $|U| \times |I|$. The training samples are usually not sufficient for the weight learning, specially for those cold-start users and items. According to the consistency rule of weight preferences of similar users mentioned above, the path weights of a user should be consistent to that of his similar users. For users with little rating information, their path weights can be learnt from the weights of their similar users, since the similarity information of users are more available through meta paths. So we design a weight regularization term as follows, which compels the weights of a user consistent to the average of weights of his similar users.

$$\sum_{u=1}^{|U|}\sum_{l=1}^{|\mathcal{P}|}(W_u^{(l)} - \sum_{v=1}^{|U|} \bar{S}_{u,v}^{(l)} W_v^{(l)})^2, \tag{7}$$

where $\bar{S}_{u,v}^{(l)} = \frac{S_{u,v}^{(l)}}{\sum_v S_{u,v}^{(l)}}$ is the normalized user similarity based on path $\mathcal{P}_l$. For convenience, the weight regularization term can be written as the following matrix format.

$$\sum_{l=1}^{|\mathcal{P}|} \|W^{(l)} - \bar{S}^{(l)}W^{(l)}\|_2^2. \tag{8}$$

And thus the optimization objective is defined as follows.

$$\begin{aligned} \min_W \mathcal{L}_3(W) &= \tfrac{1}{2}\|Y \odot (R - \sum_{l=1}^{|\mathcal{P}|} diag(W^{(l)})\hat{R}^{(l)})\|_2^2 \\ &+ \tfrac{\lambda_1}{2}\sum_{l=1}^{|\mathcal{P}|}\|W^{(l)} - \bar{S}^{(l)}W^{(l)}\|_2^2 + \tfrac{\lambda_0}{2}\|W\|_2^2 \\ s.t. \quad & W \geq 0. \end{aligned} \tag{9}$$

The above optimization objective is a non-negative quadratic programming problem, a simple special case of non-negative matrix factorization. Projected gradient method for non-negative bound-constrained optimization [5] can be applied to solve this problem. The gradient of Eq. (9) with respect to $W_u^{(l)}$ can be calculated as follows,

$$\begin{aligned} \frac{\partial \mathcal{L}_3(W)}{\partial W_u^{(l)}} &= -(Y_u \odot (R_u - \sum_{l=1}^{|\mathcal{P}|} W_u^{(l)}\hat{R}_u^{(l)}))\hat{R}_u^{(l)T} + \lambda_0 W_u^{(l)} \\ &+ \lambda_1(W_u^{(l)} - \bar{S}_u^{(l)}W^{(l)}) - \lambda_1 \bar{S}_u^{(l)T}(W^{(l)} - \bar{S}^{(l)}W^{(l)}). \end{aligned} \tag{10}$$

$W_u^{(l)}$ can be updated as follows,

$$W_u^{(l)} = max(0, W_u^{(l)} - \alpha\frac{\partial \mathcal{L}_3(W)}{\partial W_u^{(l)}}), \tag{11}$$

where α is the step size and can be set according to [5]. Algorithm 1 shows the framework of this version of SemRec.

Algorithm 1 Framework of SemRec

Input:
G: weighted heterogeneous information network
$\mathcal{P}$: meta paths connecting users
λ_0 and λ_1: controlling parameter
α: step size for updating parameters
ϵ: convergence tolerance
Output:
W: the weight matrix of all users on all paths.

1: **for** $\mathcal{P}_l \in \mathcal{P}$ **do**
2: Evaluate user similarity $S^{(l)}$
3: Calculate rating intensity $Q^{(l)}$ with Eq. (1)
4: Calculate predicted rating score $\hat{R}^{(l)}$ with Eq. (2)
5: **end for**
6: Initialize $W > 0$
7: **repeat**
8: $W_{old} := W$
9: Calculate $\frac{\partial \mathcal{L}_3(W)}{\partial W}$ with Eq. (10)
10: $W := max(0, W - \alpha\frac{\partial \mathcal{L}_3(W)}{\partial W})$
11: **until** $|W - W_{old}| < \epsilon$

3.4 Discussion

From the optimization objectives, we find that the unified weight learning method ($\mathcal{L}_1$ in Eq. (4)) is a special case of personalized weight learning ($\mathcal{L}_2$ in Eq. (6)), when the weights of all users on path $\mathcal{P}_l$ (i.e., $W^{(l)}$) have the same value. Furthermore, they both are the special cases of personalized weight learning with weight regularization. The objective $\mathcal{L}_3$ converts to $\mathcal{L}_2$ when λ_1 is 0, and $\mathcal{L}_3$ converts to $\mathcal{L}_1$ when λ_1 converges to $+\infty$. So the λ_1 parameter controls the personalized level in fact. The smaller λ_1 means the more personalized weights for users, while it may lead to more difficult learning task. So a proper λ_1 is needed to be set in real applications. Algorithm 1 is a flexible algorithm framework. Through setting different meta paths (weighted or unweighted), SemRec can flexibly realize different recommendation models and generate different recommendations complying with path semantics.

The time complexity of SemRec is analyzed as follows. As shown in Algorithm 1, SemRec includes two main parts: (1) Calculation of basic information (Lines 1-5). The main time-consuming component lies in similarity evaluation, while it can be done offline and many strategies [10] and parallel computing can speed it up. (2) Weight learning (Lines 6-11). It is an quadratic programming problem with complexity $O((|R| + |U|^2) \times |\mathcal{P}|)$.

Table 2: Statistics of Douban/Yelp Datasets

Dataset	Relations (A-B)	Number of A	Number of B	Number of (A-B)	Ave. Degrees of A/B
Douban	User-Movie	13367	12677	1068278	79.9/84.3
	User-User	2440	2294	4085	1.7/1.8
	User-Group	13337	2753	570047	42.7/207.1
	Movie-Director	10179	2449	11276	1.1/4.6
	Movie-Actor	11718	6311	33587	2.9/5.3
	Movie-Type	12676	38	27668	2.2/728.1
Yelp	User-Business	16239	14284	198397	12.2/13.9
	User-User	10580	10580	158590	15.0/15.0
	User-Compliment	14411	11	76875	5.3/6988.6
	Business-City	14267	47	14267	1.0/303.6
	Business-Category	14180	511	40009	2.8/78.3

4. EXPERIMENTS

In this section, extensive experiments on two real datasets illustrate the traits of SemRec from five aspects. We first validate the effectiveness of SemRec, especially for cold-start problem. Then we thoroughly explore the meanings of weights learned and validate the benefits of the proposed weighted meta path. Finally, we illustrate the effect of λ_1 on performances.

4.1 Datasets

In order to get more comprehensive heterogeneous information, we crawled a new dataset from Douban [2], a well known social media network in China. The dataset includes 13367 users and 12677 movies with 1068278 movie ratings ranging from 1 to 5. The dataset includes the social relation among users and the attribute information of users and movies. Another dataset is the Yelp challenge dataset [3]. This dataset contains user ratings on local business and attribute information of users and businesses. The dataset includes 16239 users and 14284 local businesses with 198397 ratings from 1 to 5. The detailed description of these two datasets can be seen in Table 2, and their network schemas are shown in Fig. 2. We can find that these two datasets have different properties. The Douban dataset has dense rating relations but sparse social relations, while the Yelp dataset has sparse rating relations but dense social relations.

4.2 Metrics

We use two widely used metrics, Root Mean Square Error (RMSE) and Mean Absolute Error (MAE), to measure the rating prediction quantity.

$$RMSE = \sqrt{\frac{\sum_{(u,i)\in R_{test}} (R_{u,i} - \hat{R}_{u,i})^2}{|R_{test}|}}, \quad (12)$$

$$MAE = \frac{\sum_{(u,i)\in R_{test}} |R_{u,i} - \hat{R}_{u,i}|}{|R_{test}|}. \quad (13)$$

where R_{test} denotes the whole test set. A smaller MAE or RMSE means a better performance.

4.3 Comparison Methods

In order to show the effectiveness of the proposed SemRec, we compare four variations of SemRec with the state of the arts. Besides the personalized weight learning method with weight regularization (called $\text{SemRec}_{\text{Reg}}$), we include three special cases of SemRec: single path based method (called $\text{SemRec}_{\text{Sgl}}$), unified weight learning method for all

[2]http://movie.douban.com/

[3]http://www.yelp.com/dataset_challenge/

Table 3: Meta Paths used in Experiments

Douban	Yelp
UGU	UU
U(i)M(j)U$\|i=j$	UCoU
U(i)MDM(j)U$\|i=j$	U(i)B(j)U$\|i=j$
U(i)MAM(j)U$\|i=j$	U(i)BCaB(j)U$\|i=j$
U(i)MTM(j)U$\|i=j$	U(i)BCiB(j)U$\|i=j$

users (called $\text{SemRec}_{\text{All}}$), and personalized weight learning method for individual user (called $\text{SemRec}_{\text{Ind}}$). As the baselines, four representative rating predication methods are illustrated as follows. Note that the top k recommendation methods [15, 2] are not included here, since they solve different problems.

- PMF [9]: It is the basic matrix factorization method using only user-item matrix for recommendations.
- SMF [8]: It adds the social regularization term into PMF, which aims at getting the users' latent factor closer to their friends' latent factors.
- CMF [6]: A collective matrix factorization method, which factorizes all relations in HIN and shares the latent factor of same object types in different relations.
- HeteMF [14]: A matrix factorization method with entity similarity regularization, which also utilizes the relations in HIN.

We employ 5 meaningful meta paths whose lengths are not longer than 4 for both datasets, since the longer meta paths are not meaningful and they fail to produce good similarity measures [12]. Table 3 shows those paths which include the weighted and unweighted meta paths. For SemRec, we use PathSim [12] as the similarity measure to calculate the similarity between users. The parameter λ_0 in SemRec is 0.01 and λ_1 is 10^3 for the best performance. The parameters in other methods are set with the best performances on these datasets.

4.4 Effectiveness Experiments

For Douban dataset, we use different training data settings (20%, 40%, 60%, 80%) to show the comparison results in different data sparseness. Training data 20%, for example, means that 20% of the ratings from user-item rating matrix is randomly selected as the training data to predict the remaining 80%. From Table 2, we can find that the Douban dataset has dense rating relations, while Yelp has very sparse rating relations. So we utilize more training data (60%, 70%, 80%, 90%) on Yelp. The random selection was repeated 10 times independently and the average results are reported in Table 4. Note that $\text{SemRec}_{\text{Sgl}}$ reports the best performances on these five paths.

From the results, we can observe that all versions of SemRec outperform other approaches in most conditions. Particularly, $\text{SemRec}_{\text{Reg}}$ always achieves the best performances on all conditions. For example, on 20% training set of Douban, $\text{SemRec}_{\text{Reg}}$ outperforms PMF up to 19.55% on RSME and 15.89% on MAE. As compared to PMF, CMF improves the recommendation performances through integrating heterogeneous information with matrix factorization. However, its performances are much worse than the proposed SemRec on all conditions, especially on less training set. As the most similar method to SemRec, HeteMF also has good performances, while its performances are still worse than the proposed $\text{SemRec}_{\text{Reg}}$. These all imply that

Table 4: Experimental Results of Effectiveness (The improvement is based on PMF)

Dataset	Training Settings	PMF RMSE	PMF MAE	SMF RMSE	SMF MAE	CMF RMSE	CMF MAE	HeteMF RMSE	HeteMF MAE	$\text{SemRec}_{\text{Sgl}}$ RMSE	$\text{SemRec}_{\text{Sgl}}$ MAE	$\text{SemRec}_{\text{All}}$ RMSE	$\text{SemRec}_{\text{All}}$ MAE	$\text{SemRec}_{\text{Ind}}$ RMSE	$\text{SemRec}_{\text{Ind}}$ MAE	$\text{SemRec}_{\text{Reg}}$ RMSE	$\text{SemRec}_{\text{Reg}}$ MAE
Douban	20%	0.9750	0.7198	0.9743	0.7192	0.9285	0.6971	0.8513	0.6342	0.8434	0.6506	0.8125	0.6309	0.8753	0.6412	**0.7844**	**0.6054**
				0.07%	0.08%	4.77%	3.15%	12.69%	11.89%	13.50%	9.61%	16.67%	12.35%	10.23%	10.92%	19.55%	15.89%
	40%	0.8455	0.6319	0.8449	0.6313	0.8273	0.6263	0.7796	0.5927	0.8138	0.6351	0.7814	0.6149	0.8083	0.6032	**0.7452**	**0.5808**
				0.07%	0.09%	2.15%	0.89%	7.79%	6.20%	3.75%	-0.51%	7.58%	2.69%	4.40%	4.54%	11.86%	8.09%
	60%	0.7975	0.6010	0.7967	0.6002	0.8042	0.6090	0.7601	0.5800	0.7937	0.6172	0.7709	0.6098	0.7729	0.5840	**0.7296**	**0.5698**
				0.10%	0.13%	-0.84%	-1.33%	4.69%	3.49%	0.48%	-2.70%	3.34%	-1.46%	3.08%	2.83%	8.51%	5.19%
	80%	0.7673	0.5812	0.7674	0.5815	0.7741	0.5900	0.7550	0.5758	0.7846	0.6142	0.7656	0.6072	0.7540	0.5739	**0.7216**	**0.5639**
				-0.01%	-0.05%	-0.89%	-1.51%	1.60%	0.93%	-2.25%	-5.68%	0.22%	-4.47%	1.73%	1.26%	5.96%	2.98%
	Time(s)	260.25		266.78		509.31		736.85		0		1.44		155.98		293.14	
Yelp	60%	1.6779	1.2997	1.4843	1.0830	1.6161	1.2628	1.2333	0.9268	1.3252	0.9657	1.2166	0.9040	1.3654	1.0029	**1.2025**	**0.8901**
				11.54%	16.67%	3.68%	2.84%	26.50%	28.69%	21.02%	25.70%	27.49%	30.45%	18.62%	22.84%	28.33%	31.51%
	70%	1.5931	1.2262	1.4017	1.0547	1.5731	1.2224	1.2090	0.9107	1.2889	0.9420	1.1906	0.8873	1.3229	0.9728	**1.1760**	**0.8696**
				12.01%	13.99%	1.26%	0.31%	24.11%	25.73%	19.09%	23.18%	25.27%	27.64%	16.96%	20.67%	26.18%	29.08%
	80%	1.5323	1.1740	1.3678	1.0282	1.5194	1.1740	1.1895	0.8969	1.2576	0.9224	1.1665	0.8723	1.2922	0.9517	**1.1559**	**0.8548**
				10.74%	12.42%	0.84%	0.00%	22.37%	23.60%	17.93%	21.43%	23.87%	25.70%	15.67%	18.94%	24.56%	27.19%
	90%	1.4833	1.1324	1.3377	1.0085	1.4793	1.1405	1.1755	0.8878	1.2331	0.9067	1.1496	0.8616	1.2658	0.9322	**1.1423**	**0.8442**
				9.82%	10.94%	0.27%	-0.72%	20.75%	21.60%	16.87%	19.93%	22.50%	23.91%	14.66%	17.68%	22.99%	25.45%
	Time(s)	31.80		51.19		375.38		619.25		0		0.25		57.22		374.57	

the proposed SemRec has better mechanism to integrate heterogeneous information.

In addition, different versions of SemRec have different performances. Generally, SemRec with multiple paths (e.g., $\text{SemRec}_{\text{All}}$, and $\text{SemRec}_{\text{Reg}}$) have better performances than SemRec with single path (i.e., $\text{SemRec}_{\text{Sgl}}$) except $\text{SemRec}_{\text{Ind}}$, which indicates that the weight learning of SemRec can effectively integrate the similarity information generated by different paths. Because of rating sparsity, $\text{SemRec}_{\text{Ind}}$ has worse performances than $\text{SemRec}_{\text{All}}$ on most conditions. In addition, the better performances of $\text{SemRec}_{\text{Rec}}$ over $\text{SemRec}_{\text{Ind}}$ confirm the benefit of the weight regularization term. In all, $\text{SemRec}_{\text{Reg}}$ always achieves best performances in all conditions. The reason lies in that $\text{SemRec}_{\text{Reg}}$ not only realizes personalized weight learning for all users but also avoids the rating sparsity through the weight regularization in it.

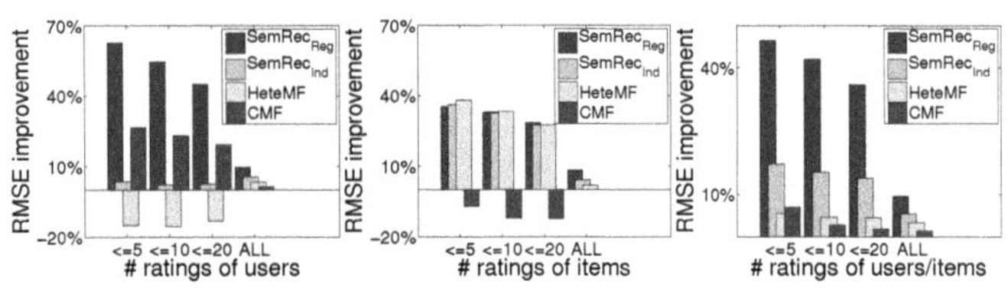

(a) Users (b) Items (c) Users&Items

Figure 4: Performance improvements of three HIN methods against PMF on different levels and types of cold-start problems.

Furthermore, we record the average running time of these methods on the learning process. For two similarity based methods (e.g., SemRec and HeteMF), we do not consider the running time on similarity evaluation, since it can be done offline beforehand. For the four versions of SemRec, their running times increase when the weight learning tasks become more complex. Both $\text{SemRec}_{\text{Sgl}}$ and $\text{SemRec}_{\text{All}}$ are very fast, which can be applied for online learning. The running times of $\text{SemRec}_{\text{Ind}}$ and $\text{SemRec}_{\text{Reg}}$ are still acceptable when comparing to CMF and HeteMF. We can select a proper model through balancing the efficiency and effectiveness of SemRec in real applications.

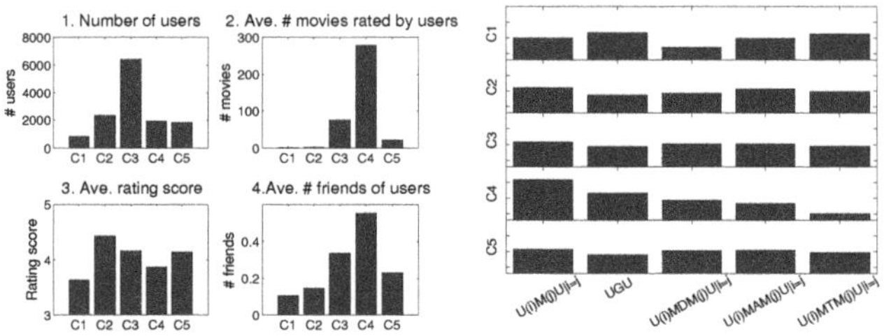

(a) Statistics of clusters (b) Weights on meta paths

Figure 5: Analysis of clusters' characteristics and path preferences of results returned by $\text{SemRec}_{\text{Reg}}$ on Douban dataset. C1-C5 represents the index of five clusters.

4.5 Study on Cold-Start Problem

The above results also show that SemRec has more obvious superiority with less training set, which implies that SemRec has the potential to alleviate the cold-start problem. In this section, we will exploit the ability of SemRec on alleviating the cold-start problem through observing its performances on different levels of cold-start users and items. We run PMF, CMF, HeteMF, $\text{SemRec}_{\text{Ind}}$, and $\text{SemRec}_{\text{Reg}}$ on Douban dataset with users having the different numbers of rated movies. We select four types of users: three types of cold-start users with different numbers of rated movies (e.g., users with the number of rated movies no more than 5, denoted as ≤ 5 in Fig. 4) and all users (called ALL in Fig. 4). In addition, we also do the similar experiments on cold-start items and users&items (contain both cold-start users and items). We record the RMSE performance improvement of other four algorithms against PMF in Fig. 4.

It is clear that $\text{SemRec}_{\text{Reg}}$ always achieves the best performance improvements on almost all conditions, and its superiority is more significant for less rating information. On the contrary, CMF only achieves improvements on cold-start users and HeteMF's improvements are only on items. We think the reason lies in that the collective matrix factorization of all relations in CMF may introduce much noises, especially for items. HeteMF only utilizes the similarity information of items, ignoring that of users. Generally, integrating heterogeneous information is helpful for alleviating cold-start problem (see Fig. 4(c)), while the integrating mechanisms may have different impact on cold-start items and users. The overall performance improvements of $\text{SemRec}_{\text{Reg}}$ are attributed to multiple meta paths that not only contain rich attribute information but also provide comprehensive and complementary similarity evaluation of users and items. In addition, the better performances of $\text{SemRec}_{\text{Reg}}$ over $\text{SemRec}_{\text{Ind}}$ further validate that the weight regularization term employed in $\text{SemRec}_{\text{Reg}}$ is really helpful for the weight learning of cold-start users from similar users.

4.6 Study of Weight Preferences

In this section, we illustrate the meanings of weights learned by SemRec through a case study. Based on the results of $\text{SemRec}_{\text{Reg}}$ on Douban dataset with 60% training data in the above experiments, we cluster users' weight vectors into 5 groups using K-means, and then show the statistics information of users in five clusters in Fig. 5(a). Moreover, the weight preferences of the five cluster centers on 5 meta paths are also shown in Fig. 5(b).

Let's observe the relationship of the statistics information of users in different clusters and their weight preferences on paths from Fig. 5(a) and (b). As we know, Douban is a unique social media platform in China, in which the major active users are young people who love culture and arts. As the typical and major users in Douban, the users in C3 view a good number of movies, give relatively good rating scores, and have a moderate number of friends. So they also have close weight preferences on all paths. As the top movie fans, the users in C4 view a great many movies, tend to give lower rating scores due to critical attitude, and have many friends. And they obviously like to get recommendation from viewing records of other users (i.e., UMU) and interest group (i.e., UGU), but less paying attentions to movies' content (e.g., UMTMU and UMAMU). In addition, the users in C1 and C2 are two types of inactive users, and they view few movies and have few friends. Because of not being fond of movies, these users tend to give much high or low rating scores. These users comparatively prefer to follow movie content (e.g., UMTMU and UMAMU). The picky users in C1 is more likely to get recommendation from interest group (i.e., UGU), while the idealess users in C2 give more preferences to viewing records of other users (i.e., UMU).

In all, the weights of paths learned by SemRec can reflect the users' path preferences, and these path preferences are able to reveal the users' characteristics to a large extent. More importantly, the meaningful weight preferences are very useful for recommendation explanation. We know that the meta path has semantics, so we can tell users the recommendation reason according to the path semantics of the high weight path. Although some weight learning methods on paths have been proposed [7, 15], their weights fail to reflect users' preferences on paths. We think two strategies adopted in RecSem contribute to its good properties. (1) We design the predicted rating score in Eq. (2), which can eliminate the similarity bias on different meta paths by the adoption of normalized rating intensity. (2) We employ the weight regularization term in Eq. (9) according to the consistency rule of weight preferences of similar users. The consistency rule makes similar users have similar weight preferences. In other words, weights also reveal users' similarity and preferences.

4.7 Study on Weighted Meta Path

In this section, we study the effectiveness of weighted meta path on improving the performances of SemRec through more accurately revealing relations among objects. For the meta path UMU, we design two weighted paths $U(i)M(j)U|i = j$ and $U(i)M(j)U||i - j| \leq 1$. $U(i)M(j)U|i = j$ means users rating the exact same scores on the same movies, while $U(i)M(j)U||i - j| \leq 1$ means users rating close scores. Similarly, we design two corresponding weighted paths for UMDMU, UMAMU, and UMTMU. Based on the similarity generated by these meta paths, we employ $\text{SemRec}_{\text{Sgl}}$ to make recommendations. We compare the performances of $\text{SemRec}_{\text{Sgl}}$ with different paths and record the results in Fig. 6.

The experimental results on all four paths clearly show that SemRec with weighted meta paths (e.g., $U(i)M(j)U|i = j$ and $U(i)M(j)U||i - j| \leq 1$) significantly outperform SemRec with unweighted meta paths (e.g., UMU). Let's take the UMU path as an example to analyze the reasons. Failing to distinguish the different rating scores of users on the same movies, UMU cannot accurately reveal user similarity, so it has bad performances. The path $U(i)M(j)U|i = j$ and $U(i)M(j)U||i - j| \leq 1$ not only consider the differences of rating scores but also keep dense relations, so they can achieve better performances than UMU. Compared to $U(i)M(j)U|i = j$, the relatively bad performances of $U(i)M(j)U||i - j| \leq 1$ may be attributed to the noise introduced by some improper relation constraints (e.g., U(3)M(4)U, and U(4)M(3)U). The experiments illustrate that the weighted meta paths are really helpful to improve recommendation performances by more accurately revealing object relations.

5. RELATED WORK

Recently there are a lot of research on HIN in which objects are of different types and links among objects represent different relations [11]. Many meta path based data mining tasks have been done in the past couple of years, including clustering [13], and classification [3] etc. Among these tasks, similarity measure in HIN is an important and basic function. Several path-based similarity measures have been proposed. For example, Sun et al. proposed PathSim [12] on symmetrical meta paths, and Shi et al. proposed a symmetric measure HeteSim [10] on arbitrary meta paths. Conventional HIN does not consider the link attribute values, which makes that meta path fails to subtly and accurately capture the relation of objects.

Some researchers have began to be aware of the importance of heterogeneous information for recommendations. Jamali and Lakshmanan [2] proposed HETEROMF to integrate a general latent factor and context-dependent latent factors. Wang et al. [1] proposed the OptRank method to alleviate the cold start problem by utilizing heterogeneous information contained in social tagging system. Lippert et al. [6] proposed a collective matrix factorization method which shares the latent factor of same object types in different relations. Yu et al. [14] proposed a matrix factorization method with entity similarity regularization. More recently, Luo et al. [7] proposed a collaborative filtering-based social recommendation method using heterogeneous relations. These methods usually focus on integrating heterogeneous information and only consider partial information available in HIN. The proposed SemRec considers more comprehensive information and focuses on exploiting path semantics.

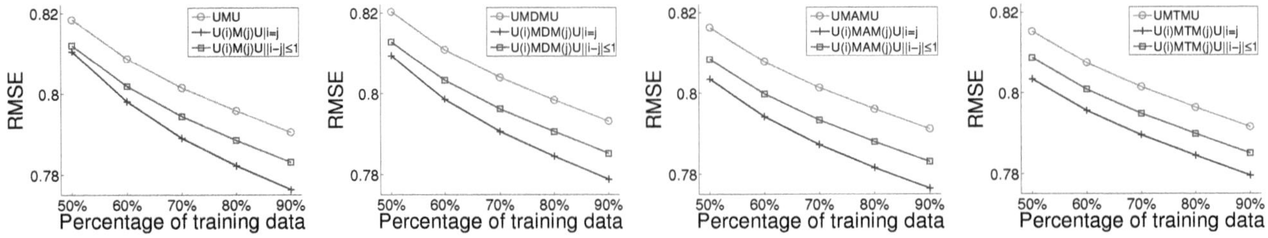

(a) UMU (b) UMDMU (c) UMAMU (d) UMTMU

Figure 6: The performances of SemRec with different weighted meta paths.

The most similar work is HeteRec proposed by Yu et al. [15] which employs an implicit feedback recommendation model with systematically extracted latent features from heterogeneous network. However, it is different from SemRec in many aspects. In order to solve the top k recommendation problem, HeteRec adopts the Bayesian ranking optimization technique to realize the personalized recommendation, and utilizes the meta path to capture path semantics. In order to solve the rating score prediction problem, SemRec employs the novel weight regularization to realize personalized recommendation and avoid the rating sparsity. More importantly, SemRec firstly applies the proposed weighted meta path to delicately depict the path semantics.

6. CONCLUSION

In this paper, we extend conventional HIN and meta path for information networks with attribute values on links, and apply them on recommender system. We propose weighted HIN and weighted meta path to more subtly depict object relations through distinguishing link attribute values, and put forwards the similarity measure strategy based on weighted meta path. Furthermore, we design a novel semantic path based personalized recommendation method SemRec. The SemRec method not only flexibly integrates heterogeneous information through setting meta paths, but also obtains the prioritized and personalized weights representing user preferences on paths. Extensive experiments illustrate the effectiveness of SemRec.

7. ACKNOWLEDGMENTS

This work is supported in part by National Key Basic Research and Department (973) Program of China (No. 2013CB329606), the National Natural Science Foundation of China (No. 61375058, 71231002), the National High-tech R&D Program (863 Program 2015AA050203, 2015AA050204), and the CCF-Tencent Open Fund.

8. REFERENCES

[1] W. Feng and J. Wang. Incorporating heterogeneous information for personalized tag recommendation in social tagging systems. In *KDD*, pages 1276–1284, 2012.

[2] M. Jamali and L. V. Lakshmanan. Heteromf: Recommendation in heterogeneous information networks using context dependent factor models. In *WWW*, pages 643–653, 2013.

[3] M. Ji, J. Han, and M. Danilevsky. Ranking-based classification of heterogeneous information networks. In *KDD*, pages 1298–1306, 2011.

[4] N. Lao and W. Cohen. Fast query execution for retrieval models based on path constrained random walks. In *KDD*, pages 881–888, 2010.

[5] C. J. Lin. Projected gradient methods for non-negative matrix factorization. In *Neural Computation*, pages 2756–2279, 2007.

[6] C. Lippert, S. H. Weber, Y. Huang, V. Tresp, M. Schubert, and H. P. Kriegel. Relation prediction in multi-relational domains using matrix factorization. In *NIPS Workshop on Structured Input Structure Output*, 2008.

[7] C. Luo, W. Pang, Z. Wang, and C. Lin. Hete-cf: Social-based collaborative filtering recommendation using heterogeneous relations. In *ICDM*, pages 917–922, 2014.

[8] H. Ma, D. Zhou, C. Liu, M. R. Lyu, and I. King. Recommender systems with social regularization. In *WSDM*, pages 287–296, 2011.

[9] R. Salakhutdinov and A. Mnih. Probabilistic matrix factorization. In *NIPS*, volume 20, 2008.

[10] C. Shi, X. Kong, Y. Huang, P. S. Yu, and B. Wu. Hetesim: A general framework for relevance measure in heterogeneous networks. *IEEE Transactions on Knowledge and Data Engineering*, 26(10):2479–2492, 2014.

[11] Y. Sun and J. Han. Mining heterogeneous information networks: A structural analysis approach. *SIGKDD Explorations*, 14(2):20–28, 2012.

[12] Y. Sun, J. Han, X. Yan, P. Yu, and T. Wu. Pathsim: Meta path-based top-k similarity search in heterogeneous information networks. In *VLDB*, pages 992–1003, 2011.

[13] Y. Sun, B. Norick, J. Han, X. Yan, P. S. Yu, and X. Yu. Integrating meta-path selection with user guided object clustering in heterogeneous information networks. In *KDD*, pages 1348–1356, 2012.

[14] X. Yu, X. Ren, Q. Gu, Y. Sun, and J.Han. Collaborative filtering with entity similarity regularization in heterogeneous information networks. In *IJCAI HINA*, 2013.

[15] X. Yu, X. Ren, Y. Sun, Q. Gu, B. Sturt, U. Khandelwal, B. Norick, and J. Han. Personalized entity recommendation: A heterogeneous information network approach. In *WSDM*, pages 283–292, 2014.

[16] Q. Yuan, L. Chen, and S. Zhao. Factorization vs. regularization: fusing heterogeneous social relationships in top-n recommendation. In *RecSys*, pages 245–252, 2011.

A Graph-based Recommendation across Heterogeneous Domains

Deqing Yang[§]*, Jingrui He[‡], Huazheng Qin[§] Yanghua Xiao[§], Wei Wang[§]
[§]School of Computer Science, Shanghai Key Laboratory of Data Science
[§]Fudan University, Shanghai, 200433, China P. R.
[§]{yangdeqing, huazhengqin13, shawyh, weiwang1}@fudan.edu.cn
Arizona State University, AZ, USA, [‡]jingrui.he@gmail.com

ABSTRACT

Given the users from a social network site, who have been tagged with a set of terms, how can we recommend the movies tagged with a completely different set of terms hosted by another website? Given the users from a website dedicated to Type I and Type II diabetes, how can we recommend the discussion threads from another website dedicated to gestational diabetes, where the keywords used in the two websites might be quite diverse? In other words, how can we recommend across heterogeneous domains characterized by barely overlapping feature sets?

Despite the vast amount of existing work devoted to recommendation within homogeneous domains (e.g., with the same set of features), or collaborative filtering, emerging applications call for new techniques to address the problem of recommendation across heterogeneous domains, such as recommending movies hosted by one website to users from another website with barely overlapping tags. To this end, in this paper, we propose a graph-based approach for recommendation across heterogeneous domains. Specifically, for each domain, we use a bipartite graph to represent the relationships between its entities and features. Furthermore, to bridge the gap among multiple heterogeneous domains with barely overlapping sets of features, we propose to infer their semantic relatedness through concept-based interpretation distilled from online encyclopedias, e.g., Wikipedia and Baike. Finally, we propose an efficient propagation algorithm to obtain the similarity between entities from heterogeneous domains. Experimental results on both Weibo-Douban data set and Diabetes data set demonstrate the effectiveness and efficiency of our algorithm.

Categories and Subject Descriptors

H.3.5 [**Information Storage and Retrieval**]: On-line Information Services-Web-based services; H.2.8 [**Database Management**]: Database applications-Data mining; I.2.4 [**Artificial Intelligence**]: Knowledge Representation Formalisms and Methods-Semantic networks

*Corresponding author.

CIKM'15, October 19-23, 2015, Melbourne, VIC, Australia
© 2015 ACM. ISBN 978-1-4503-3794-6/15/10 ...$15.00.
DOI: http://dx.doi.org/10.1145/2806416.2806523.

Keywords

cross-domain recommendation, heterogenous domains, graph propagation, semantic matching

1. INTRODUCTION

Up until now, recommender systems have been successfully applied to a variety of domains, ranging from movies to research papers, from online friends to social tags. Existing techniques for recommender systems can be mainly categorized into three different groups: *collaborative filtering (CF for short)* [15, 16], *content-based filtering* [3,6], and *hybrid recommender systems* [5]. Most of these techniques focus on a single domain [27,36]. In other words, the users and the items come from the same website.

More recently, researchers have studied cross-domain recommendation [19,21,24,32], where the users and the items come from different websites. The main goal of cross-domain recommendation is to alleviate the cold start problem, such that the matching between users and items across different domains is satisfactory in the beginning. Notice that, most, if not all, of existing techniques for cross-domain recommendation work best if different domains share a large number of features. In this way, the relevance between users from one domain and items from another can be naturally obtained based on the common features. Please refer to Section 4 for a detailed review of related works.

1.1 Applications

Nowadays, with the emergence of various e-commerce websites, a natural question is: how can we recommend items across *heterogeneous* domains, i.e., the different domains sharing very few features? Take Weibo (Chinese version of Twitter, `http://www.weibo.com`) and Douban (the largest Chinese movie database, `http://www.douban.com`) as an example. The tags used by Weibo users are quite different from those used to specify movies on Douban, which is illustrated by the tag clouds in Figure 1. From this figure, we can see that the common Weibo tags include 'music', 'movie', 'food', '80s', which generally characterize a Weibo user's hobby, age, constellation, etc. In contrast, Douban tags are generally used to specify a movie's nation, year and genre, such as 'USA', 'Japan', 'animation', 'classic', etc. For this case, existing techniques for cross-domain recommendation may not be able to accurately identify the movies from Douban that may be of potential interest to Weibo users. Another example is the recommendation of articles across different websites. In particular, among the various social network websites dedicated to diabetes patients, some of them might be open to all types of diabetes patients, such as `http://www.tudiabetes.org` (denoted by

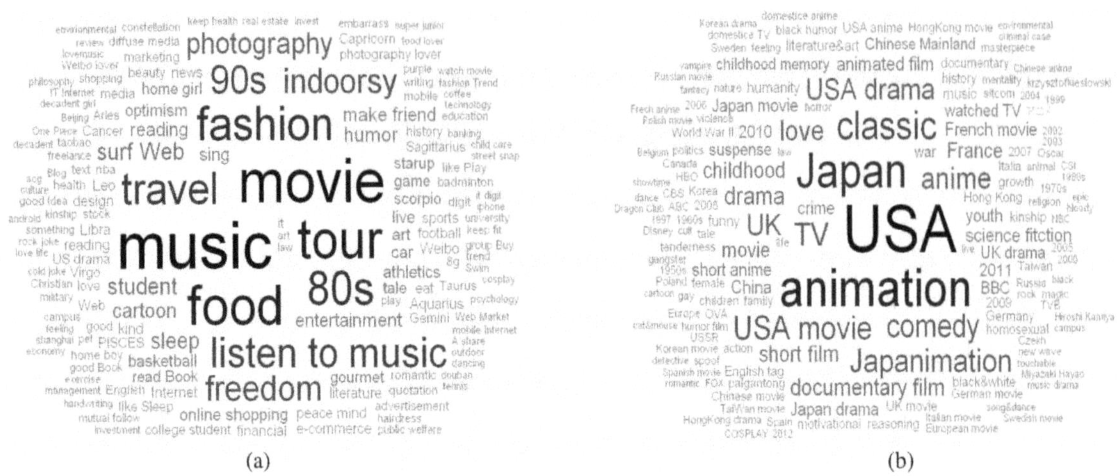

Figure 1: Tag clouds of Weibo users (a) and Douban movies (b). These tags can be viewed as the features specifying Weibo users and Douban movies to be used for recommendation. However, seldom tags are shared in these two groups.

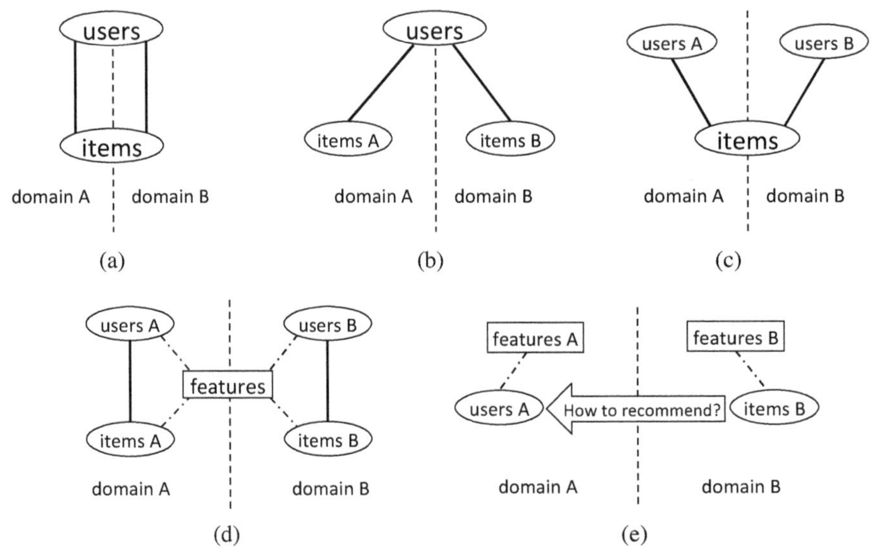

Figure 2: Different settings of cross-domain recommendation. The solid lines between users and items represent user-item interactive relations such as ratings, reviews and so on. In subfigure (a)∼(c), shared users or items can be found in both two domains. Furthermore, in subfigure (d), common features exist. In subfigure (a)∼(d), user-item relations can be found in both domains. All this abundant information can be used to discover the relations between the two domains. In this paper, we focus the setting of subfigure (e) which is more challenging than the formers because neither user-item relations nor common features across the domains can be obtained.

Diabetes1), which is for patients of Type I, Type II, and prediabetes. And some of them might focus on a specific type of diabetes patients, such as `https://diabetessisters.org` (denoted by Diabetes2), which is for female diabetes patients, especially for those with gestational diabetes. In this case, due to the different vocabulary used by the different websites, existing techniques for cross-domain recommendation may not be able to effectively recommend discussion threads from Diabetes2 to the users of Diabetes1 who are not aware of the other website.

1.2 Challenges

The main difference between our concern of recommendation across heterogeneous domains and traditional cross-domain recommendation is demonstrated in Figure 2. Previous solutions mainly focused on two typical cross-domain settings. In the first setting, either users or items are shared in both domains. For example, in [24], there is an one-one mapping between the users and items of the two domains. It indicates that the two domains have the same groups of users and items as depicted in Figure 2(a). As depicted in Figure 2(b) and (c), the two domains share either users or items [7, 21]. The second setting is illustrated in Figure 2(d), both users and items are disjoint, but the relations between the two domains can be derived through the shared features, such as the same tag space [32,37] or similar user-item interactive patterns [19]. Furthermore, in the preceding four cases, the user-item interactive relations (the solid lines in the figures) such as rating, review or purchase exist in each domain. However, all the solutions for these cases obviously can not be directly used to solve the problem setting as shown in Figure 2(e), where domain A only contains users and domain B only contains items and no shared features can be used to establish the links between the users in domain A and the items in domain B.

However, the heterogenous cross-domain recommendation scenario of Figure 2(e) is a popular and valuable setting in real world. For example, it will create a lot of business opportunities if we can accurately recommend products in eBay to a user in Tweet or Facebook. Therefore, in this paper, we focus on the challenging problem of recommendation across heterogeneous domains. In general, this new problem setting poses two challenges.

1. The first challenge is the sparsity of shared features across heterogeneous domains, which makes the discovery of the connections among the non-shared features non-trivial. Recall the tags of Weibo users and Douban movies, correlating different tags across the two domains is critical for recommending Douban movie to Weibo users. However, discovering such connections is not a trivial task.

2. The second challenge is designing an effective and efficient model for inferring the similarity of entities across heterogeneous domains, especially when the numbers of entities and features are very large. Recall the setting of Figure 2(e), even when the connections between the features of the two domains are discovered, inferring the similarity between users and items is also challenging.

1.3 Basic Idea and Organization

To overcome these challenges, we propose to use bipartite graphs to represent the relationships between entities and their features, and build the connection between heterogeneous domains through semantic matching of features. Based on the composite multi-partite graph, we propose an effective and efficient propagation algorithm to infer the global similarity between entities across different domains. The major contributions of this paper can be summarized as follows.

1. We propose a novel recommendation approach based on a multi-partite graph representation and an efficient propagation algorithm. Furthermore, we justify the optimization of our algorithm.

2. We conduct extensive experiments on two real applications: Douban movie recommendation for Weibo users, article recommendation across different diabetes social networks, to verify the effectiveness of our solution for recommendation across heterogenous domains.

The rest of this paper is organized as follows. In Section 2, we introduce our graph-based approach for recommendation across heterogeneous domains including the semantic matching between different tags/keywords. In Section 3, we evaluate the performance of our approach against existing techniques. Finally, we survey the related works in Section 4 and conclude our paper in Section 5.

2. GRAPH-BASED APPROACH FOR CROSS-DOMAIN RECOMMENDATION

Different from traditional CF-based methods, in this paper, we target a more challenging problem of cross-domain recommendation, i.e., recommending the items from one domain to the users from another heterogenous domain. This problem essentially boils down to inferring the similarity between different types of objects (users and items) from multiple domains. In this section, we present our graph-based method: we first start with some notations, followed by the introduction of the global similarity and the efficient computation of the relevance vectors, and finally discuss semantic matching for inducing cross-domain correlation.

2.1 Notation

Without loss of generality, in this paper, we consider 2 different domains, although the proposed method can be easily generalized to multiple domains. Formally, for the ith domain (i=1,2), we use a bi-partite graph $G_i = \{V_i, E_i\}$ to represent the relationships between the objects in this domain and their characterizing features, where V_i is the set of nodes in this graph, and E_i is a set of undirected edges. Let n_i denote the number of objects in the ith domain, and m_i denote the number of features. Therefore, V_i consists of two types of nodes: n_i object nodes, and m_i feature nodes. Notice that in E_i, an edge only exists between different types of nodes, i.e., between an object node and a feature node, and the edge weights are set to the feature value of the corresponding object. Let $\boldsymbol{X}_i$, $n_i \times m_i$, denote the connectivity matrix between the two types of nodes, whose elements are set to be the edge weights.

In cross-domain recommendation where only a small fraction of features are shared across different domains, a critical question is how to build the connection between the bi-partite graphs for different domains. To address this problem, in our method, we propose the following matching graph between features from the two domains. Let $G_0 = \{V_0, E_0\}$ denote such a bi-partite matching graph, where V_0 includes all the feature nodes from the two domains, and E_0 denotes the set of edges connecting features from different domains. Based on this graph, we define connectivity matrix $\boldsymbol{X}_0$, $(m_1 + m_2) \times (m_1 + m_2)$, whose elements measure the similarity between features from different domains. Details of learning the connectivity matrix $\boldsymbol{X}_0$ based on semantic matching will be discussed in Subsec. 2.4.

Putting all above graphs together, we get a multi-partite graph $G = \{V, E\}$ as shown in Figure 3, where $V = V_1 \bigcup V_2$, and $E = E_1 \bigcup E_2 \bigcup E_0$. Then, we define an *affinity matrix* $\boldsymbol{X}$ for this graph. $\boldsymbol{X}$ is an $(n_1 + n_2 + m_1 + m_2) \times (n_1 + n_2 + m_1 + m_2)$ matrix and is represented as,

$$\boldsymbol{X} = \begin{bmatrix} \mathbf{0}_{n_1 \times n_1} & \mathbf{0}_{n_1 \times n_2} & \boldsymbol{X}_1 & \mathbf{0}_{n_1 \times m_2} \\ \mathbf{0}_{n_2 \times n_1} & \mathbf{0}_{n_2 \times n_2} & \mathbf{0}_{n_2 \times m_1} & \boldsymbol{X}_2 \\ \boldsymbol{X}_1^T & \mathbf{0}_{m_1 \times n_2} & \mathbf{0}_{m_1 \times m_1} & \boldsymbol{X}_0 \\ \mathbf{0}_{m_2 \times n_1} & \boldsymbol{X}_2^T & \boldsymbol{X}_0^T & \mathbf{0}_{m_2 \times m_2} \end{bmatrix}$$

where $(\cdot)^T$ denotes matrix transpose and $\mathbf{0}$ is a zero matrix. Based on this graph, our goal is to infer the similarity between object nodes from different domains.

2.2 Global Similarity between Objects

In graph G, the direct connections between object nodes from different domains are absent, e.g., between user nodes and item nodes in Figure 3. Thus, we will measure their similarity based on graph propagation. To be specific, we first normalize the affinity matrix $\boldsymbol{X}$ as follows.

$$\begin{aligned} \boldsymbol{S} &= \boldsymbol{D}^{-\frac{1}{2}} \boldsymbol{X} \boldsymbol{D}^{-\frac{1}{2}} \\ &= \begin{bmatrix} \mathbf{0}_{n_1 \times n_1} & \mathbf{0}_{n_1 \times n_2} & \boldsymbol{S}_1 & \mathbf{0}_{n_1 \times m_2} \\ \mathbf{0}_{n_2 \times n_1} & \mathbf{0}_{n_2 \times n_2} & \mathbf{0}_{n_2 \times m_1} & \boldsymbol{S}_2 \\ \boldsymbol{S}_1^T & \mathbf{0}_{m_1 \times n_2} & \mathbf{0}_{m_1 \times m_1} & \boldsymbol{S}_0 \\ \mathbf{0}_{m_2 \times n_1} & \boldsymbol{S}_2^T & \boldsymbol{S}_0^T & \mathbf{0}_{m_2 \times m_2} \end{bmatrix} \end{aligned} \quad (1)$$

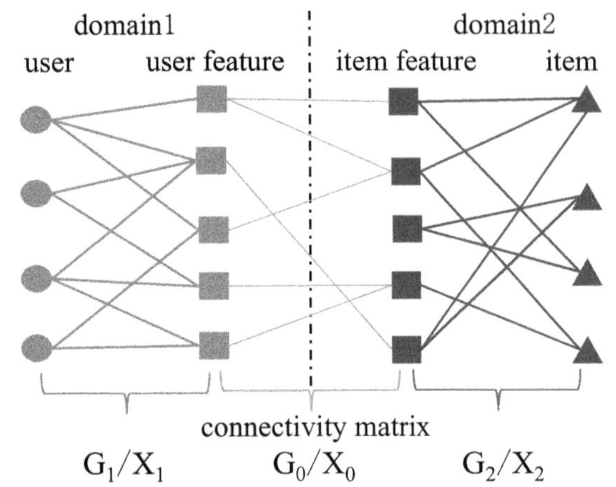

Figure 3: A multi-partite graph across two domains. Red lines are user-feature edges in domain 1 and blue lines are item-feature edges in domain 2. The green lines between red rectangles and blue rectangles are the edges between user features and item features, which can be established by the semantic similarity of features.

where $\boldsymbol{D}$ is a diagonal matrix with each element equal to the row sum of $\boldsymbol{X}$; $\boldsymbol{S}_1$, $\boldsymbol{S}_2$, and $\boldsymbol{S}_0$ are normalized versions of $\boldsymbol{X}_1$, $\boldsymbol{X}_2$, and $\boldsymbol{X}_0$, respectively.

In order to compute the global similarity between the ith node and all the other nodes in the composite multi-partite graph, we use $\boldsymbol{v}_i$ to denote the $(n_1+n_2+m_1+m_2)$ dimensional vector, whose i^{th} element is 1 and all the others are 0. Using the manifold ranking algorithm proposed in [35], the global similarity vector with respect to the ith node can be written as $(\boldsymbol{I}-\alpha\boldsymbol{S})^{-1}\boldsymbol{v}_i$, where $\boldsymbol{I}$ is an $(n_1+n_2+m_1+m_2)\times(n_1+n_2+m_1+m_2)$ identity matrix, and α is a positive scalar whose value is close to 1. Putting all these vectors together, we have the following $(n_1+n_2+m_1+m_2)\times(n_1+n_2+m_1+m_2)$ global similarity matrix $\boldsymbol{K}$,

$$\boldsymbol{K}=(\boldsymbol{I}-\alpha\boldsymbol{S})^{-1}[\boldsymbol{v}_1,\ldots,\boldsymbol{v}_{n_1+n_2+m_1+m_2}]=(\boldsymbol{I}-\alpha\boldsymbol{S})^{-1} \tag{2}$$

Each element in $\boldsymbol{K}$ measures the global similarity between each pair of nodes. The property of the global similarity matrix $\boldsymbol{K}$ can be interpreted using Taylor expansion [14], i.e., $\boldsymbol{K}=\sum_{i=0}^{\infty}(\alpha\boldsymbol{S})^i$. Notice that the ith term measures the weighted i^{th}-step similarity on the multi-partite graph, and its impact on the overall similarity decreases exponentially with respect to i.

It is easy to see that $\boldsymbol{K}$ has the following block structure.

$$\boldsymbol{K}=\left(\begin{bmatrix}\boldsymbol{A} & \boldsymbol{B}\\ \boldsymbol{B}^T & \boldsymbol{C}\end{bmatrix}\right)^{-1}=\begin{bmatrix}\boldsymbol{K}_1 & \boldsymbol{K}_2\\ \boldsymbol{K}_2^T & \boldsymbol{K}_3\end{bmatrix}$$

According to Equation 2, we conclude that, $\boldsymbol{A}=\begin{bmatrix}\boldsymbol{I}-\boldsymbol{0}_{n_1\times n_1} & \boldsymbol{0}_{n_1\times n_2}\\ \boldsymbol{0}_{n_2\times n_1} & \boldsymbol{I}-\boldsymbol{0}_{n_2\times n_2}\end{bmatrix}$, $\boldsymbol{B}=\begin{bmatrix}-\alpha\boldsymbol{S}_1 & \boldsymbol{0}_{n_1\times m_2}\\ \boldsymbol{0}_{n_2\times m_1} & -\alpha\boldsymbol{S}_2\end{bmatrix}$, and $\boldsymbol{C}=\begin{bmatrix}\boldsymbol{I} & -\alpha\boldsymbol{S}_0\\ -\alpha\boldsymbol{S}_0^T & \boldsymbol{I}\end{bmatrix}$. $\boldsymbol{K}_1$, $\boldsymbol{K}_2$, and $\boldsymbol{K}_3$ are submatrices of $\boldsymbol{K}$, which are of the same dimensionality as $\boldsymbol{A}$, $\boldsymbol{B}$, and $\boldsymbol{C}$ respectively. Since we are only interested in the similarity among objects from different domains, instead of the whole matrix $\boldsymbol{K}$, we only compute the submatrix $\boldsymbol{K}_1$, $(n_1+n_2)\times(n_1+n_2)$, which has the following closed form solution.

LEMMA 1.

$$\boldsymbol{K}_1=\left(\boldsymbol{I}-\boldsymbol{B}\boldsymbol{C}^{-1}\boldsymbol{B}^T\right)^{-1} \tag{3}$$

Proof. Lemma 1 can proved by applying the Woodbury formula [25] on Equation 2, and leveraging the block structure of both $\boldsymbol{K}^{-1}$ and $\boldsymbol{K}$.■

Notice that the inverse of both $\boldsymbol{C}$ and $\boldsymbol{B}\boldsymbol{C}^{-1}\boldsymbol{B}^T$ exists. This is because $\boldsymbol{K}_1$ is part of $\boldsymbol{K}$, which is the inverse of the symmetric positive definite matrix $\boldsymbol{I}-\alpha\boldsymbol{S}$.

Based on $\boldsymbol{K}_1$, if the objects in the first domain are users, and the objects in the second domain are items, the relevance between the kth user and all the items can be obtained from the kth row or column of $\boldsymbol{K}$, since $\boldsymbol{K}_1$ is a symmetric matrix. In other words, the *relevance vector* can be written as $\boldsymbol{s}_i=\boldsymbol{K}_1\boldsymbol{u}_i$, where $\boldsymbol{u}_i$ is an n_1+n_2 dimensional vector. The elements of $\boldsymbol{u}_i$ are 0 except the ith one, which is set to 1.

2.3 Efficient Computation of Relevance Vector

In this subsection, we focus on the efficient computation of the relevance vector, which is summarized in Algorithm 1. It takes as input matrices $\boldsymbol{B}$ and $\boldsymbol{C}$, the query vector $\boldsymbol{u}$ (with only one non-zero entry), α and the number of iterations n_{iter}. The output is the relevance vector $\boldsymbol{s}$ with respect to $\boldsymbol{u}$. Here we define $\tilde{\boldsymbol{S}}_0=\begin{bmatrix}\boldsymbol{0} & \boldsymbol{S}_0\\ \boldsymbol{S}_0^T & \boldsymbol{0}\end{bmatrix}$. In this way, matrix $\boldsymbol{C}$ has the following equivalent form $\boldsymbol{C}=I-\alpha\tilde{\boldsymbol{S}}_0$.

The algorithm works as follows. In Step 1, we initialize the relevance vector to be the query vector $\boldsymbol{u}$. In the outer loop starting from Step 2, we set $\boldsymbol{w}$ to be $\boldsymbol{B}^T\boldsymbol{s}$ in Step 3, initialize $\boldsymbol{r}$ to be $\boldsymbol{w}$ in Step 4, and pass both vectors to the inner loop starting from Step 5. In the inner loop, we update $\boldsymbol{r}$ in Step 6 n_{iter} times. Finally, in the outer loop, we re-scale $\boldsymbol{r}$ in Step 8, based on which we obtain the current estimate of the relevance vector $\boldsymbol{s}$.

Algorithm 1 Graph-based Recommendation across Heterogeneous Domains

Input: $\boldsymbol{B}, \boldsymbol{C}, \boldsymbol{u}, \alpha, n_{iter}$
Output: $\boldsymbol{s}$
1: Initialize $\boldsymbol{s}$ to be $\boldsymbol{u}$
2: **for** $i=1$ to n_{iter} **do**
3: $\quad\boldsymbol{w}\leftarrow\boldsymbol{B}^T\boldsymbol{s}$
4: $\quad$Initialize $\boldsymbol{r}$ to be $\boldsymbol{w}$
5: $\quad$**for** $j=1$ to n_{iter} **do**
6: $\quad\quad\boldsymbol{r}\leftarrow\alpha\tilde{\boldsymbol{S}}_0\boldsymbol{r}+(1-\alpha)\boldsymbol{w}$
7: $\quad$**end for**
8: $\quad\boldsymbol{r}\leftarrow\frac{1}{1-\alpha}\boldsymbol{r}$
9: $\quad\boldsymbol{s}\leftarrow\boldsymbol{B}\boldsymbol{r}+(1-\alpha)\boldsymbol{u}$
10: **end for**

The convergence property of Algorithm 1 is presented in the following theorem.

THEOREM 1. *As n_{iter} goes to infinity, $\boldsymbol{s}$ returned by Algorithm 1 converges to $(1-\alpha)\boldsymbol{K}_1\boldsymbol{u}$.*

Proof. We prove Theorem 1 via the following two steps. In the first step, we analyze the convergence property of the inner loop between Step 5 and Step 7 of Algorithm 1; then in the second step, we analyze the convergence property of the outer loop between Step 2 and step 10.

First, the following lemma shows the convergence property of the inner loop.

LEMMA 2. *Given $\boldsymbol{w}$, as n_{iter} goes to infinity, in the inner loop of Algorithm 1, $\boldsymbol{r}$ converges to $(1-\alpha)\boldsymbol{C}^{-1}\boldsymbol{w}$.*

Proof. To prove Lemma 2, simply observe that upon convergence, $\boldsymbol{r} = \alpha\tilde{\boldsymbol{S}}_0\boldsymbol{r} + (1-\alpha)\boldsymbol{w}$. Therefore, $(\boldsymbol{I} - \alpha\tilde{\boldsymbol{S}}_0)\boldsymbol{r} = (1-\alpha)\boldsymbol{w}$. Together with the fact that $\boldsymbol{C} = I - \alpha\tilde{\boldsymbol{S}}_0$, we conclude the proof for Lemma 2.■

Based on Lemma 2, we can see that the inner loop provides an efficient way of computing $\boldsymbol{r} = (1-\alpha)\boldsymbol{C}^{-1}\boldsymbol{w}$. Combined with Step 2 and Step 8 of Algorithm 1, we can see that in Step 9, the vector $\boldsymbol{r}$ is equal to $\boldsymbol{C}^{-1}\boldsymbol{B}^T\boldsymbol{s}$. Upon convergence, $\boldsymbol{s} = \boldsymbol{B}\boldsymbol{C}^{-1}\boldsymbol{B}^T\boldsymbol{s} + (1-\alpha)\boldsymbol{u}$. Therefore, $(\boldsymbol{I} - \boldsymbol{B}\boldsymbol{C}^{-1}\boldsymbol{B}^T)\boldsymbol{s} = (1-\alpha)\boldsymbol{u}$. Together with the definition of $\boldsymbol{K}_1$ in Equation (3), we conclude our proof for Theorem 1. ■

Comparing Algorithm 1 with direct computation of $\boldsymbol{s} = (\boldsymbol{I} - \boldsymbol{B}\boldsymbol{C}^{-1}\boldsymbol{B}^T)^{-1}\boldsymbol{u}$, the major advantage is its time efficiency. In our applications, it is often the case that both $\boldsymbol{B}$ and $\tilde{\boldsymbol{S}}_0$ are very sparse. Let $l_{\boldsymbol{B}}$ and $l_{\tilde{\boldsymbol{S}}_0}$ denote the number of non-zero elements in $\boldsymbol{B}$ and $\tilde{\boldsymbol{S}}_0$ respectively. The time complexity of Algorithm 1 can be shown as follows.

LEMMA 3. *The time complexity of Algorithm 1 is $O(l_{\boldsymbol{B}} + l_{\tilde{\boldsymbol{S}}_0})$.*

Proof. It is easy to see that the major computation in Algorithm is matrix vector multiplication. Since both $\boldsymbol{B}$ and $\tilde{\boldsymbol{S}}_0$ are very sparse, the computational complexity of $\tilde{\boldsymbol{S}}_0\boldsymbol{r}$ is $O(l_{\tilde{\boldsymbol{S}}_0})$, and the computational complexity of $\boldsymbol{B}$ is $O(l_{\boldsymbol{B}})$, which completes the proof.■

Therefore, Algorithm 1 scales to large data sets since its time complexity is linear with respect to the number of non-zeros elements in $\boldsymbol{B}$ and $\tilde{\boldsymbol{S}}_0$. On the other hand, for direct computation of $\boldsymbol{s}$ via matrix inversion, the typical time complexity is $O((n_1 + n_2)^{2.373})$ using optimized CW-like algorithms [12], which is prohibitive for large data sets.

2.4 Semantic Matching

According to our algorithm, some relationships between features should be established in order to discover the similarity of objects in the two domains, i.e., inferring E_0 in G_0. In this subsection, we introduce how to find the relationships between different features from two heterogeneous domains, respectively. For a better interpretation, we use the case where the features are represented by tags to illustrate our method.

2.4.1 Basic Idea

As we declared before, most tags coming from heterogenous domains are different, which demands us to correlate two tags on semantic level rather than lexical level. In general, semantic matching requires more context information of tags. To accomplish it, we try to discover hyper-links existing among millions of concepts in online encyclopedias.

Most prior works on computing semantic relatedness resorted to some well-defined lexical resources, such as WordNet [18]. However, lexical resources require lexicographic expertise and only cover a small fraction of language lexicons. As we observed, the tags adopted by Weibo users contain many proper names, neologisms, and etc., which are seldom included in current lexical resources. The authors in [11, 22] used substantial semantic information of online encyclopedias, e.g., Wikipedia, to enrich the semantic representation of terms. In this paper, we also utilize online encyclopedias to achieve the semantic matching of tags. Concretely, we adopt Wikipedia and Baike (`http://baike.baidu.com`) for English tags and Chinese tags, respectively.

As we known, an online encyclopedia contains millions of concepts including person, location, organization, hobby and etc. There exists an article page describing the fact about each concept. As well, there are many hyper-links linking to other concepts on each article page to enrich its semantic description. According to the principle of previous Wikipedia based methods [11,22], two terms, i.e., two concepts, are considered semantically related if they cooccur as hyper-links in one article page. The more such article pages can be found, the more semantically related the two terms are.

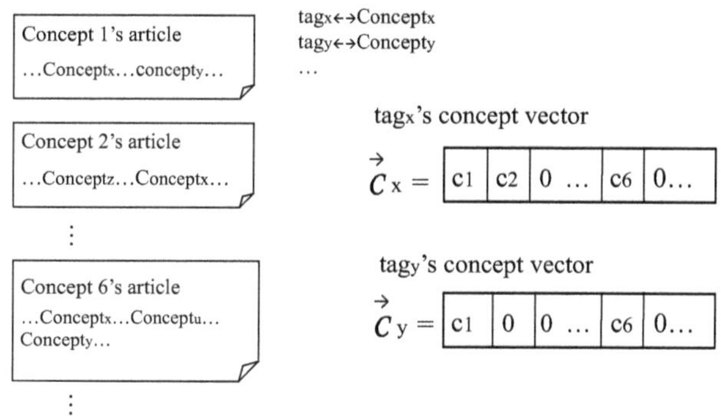

Figure 4: The articles in online encyclopedias derive the concept vectors of tags. The left part display some articles in the online encyclopedia. In this case, tag_x and tag_y are mapped into $Concept_x$ and $Concept_y$ respectively, and then tag_x is semantically related to tag_y through some encyclopedia concepts although they are not represented by the same term.

2.4.2 Interpreting Semantic Reslationships

Then, we formalize the semantic interpretation of a tag. In order to represent the semantics of a tag through the contexts provided by the encyclopedia, we should first map a tag into an article entry (i.e., a concept) of the encyclopedia. Given a tag i and a concept c, we map i into c if i and c are exactly same or c's string is a maximal substring of i's string. Under this mapping scheme, we can find a mapped concepts for nearly 90% of tags. As depicted in Figure 4, tag_x and tag_y are first mapped into $Concpet_x$ and $Concpet_y$, respectively. Then, we can find that $Concept_x$ and $Concept_y$ cooccur in the article page of Concept 1, indicating their semantic relatedness. Similarly, we may find another evidence, i.e., Concept 6's article page. Therefore, although $Concept_x$ and $Concept_y$ are not same, they are still semantically related. Clearly, the indirect matching through the contexts provided by concepts' article pages in online encyclopedia rather than lexical matching, is exactly what we expect in the semantic matching for two tags.

According to *Explicit Semantic Analysis (ESA for short)*'s basic idea [11], the semantic interpretation of a tag i can be represented by a *concept vector* which is formally defined as $\vec{C_i} = [c_1, ..., c_C] \in \mathbb{R}^C$. C is the total number of concepts in the encyclopedia and $c_j (1 \le j \le C)$ represents the semantic relevance of concept j to tag i, i.e., the TF-IDF score of concept i's occurrence in concept j's article. Figure 4 describes the compositions of $\vec{C_x}$ and $\vec{C_y}$. Thus, the semantic similarity between tag x and tag y can be represented as the cosine similarity of $\vec{C_x}$ and $\vec{C_y}$, namely $cos(\vec{C_x}, \vec{C_y})$. To establish the links between user tags and item tags, i.e., E_0 in the bi-partite graph G_0, we can set a threshold λ. Then, the edge between x and y is created if $cos(\vec{C_x}, \vec{C_y}) \ge \lambda$. As well,

$cos(\vec{C}_x, \vec{C}_y)$ is set as the element of connectivity matrix $\boldsymbol{X}_0$ (refer to Figure 3). Accordingly, λ decides the density of $\boldsymbol{X}_0$. In our experiments, we will display how λ affects on the performance of our recommendation algorithm.

3. EXPERIMENTS

In this section, we evaluate the performance of our proposed graph-based algorithm through two applications of recommendation across heterogeneous domains.

3.1 Experiment Setup

We first present some experiment settings including data sets, baseline methods and performance metrics.

3.1.1 Data sets

To demonstrate the performance of our algorithm, we focus on the following two different types of data sets in our evaluation experiments.

1. Weibo-Douban Data Set.

The first data set is collected from two Chinese websites: Weibo and Douban. Weibo is the largest Chinese Twitter which has more than 0.6 billion accounts and 90 million active users per day. Recommending various products to Weibo users can create plenty of business opportunities. On the other hand, Douban is a famous Chinese website of movie reviews. Although both Weibo users and Douban movies are profiled by a set of tags, the tags in these two websites are quite different (recall to Figure 1 in Section 1). Thus, recommending Douban movies to Weibo users is a typical recommendation problem across heterogeneous domains. To construct the bi-partite graphs for this problem, we define the edge weight between an object node and a feature node (the weight of E_i, i=1,2) by a *tag score*, which quantifies the extent to which a tag can characterize the user/movie. For a Weibo user, the tag score is computed by a local tag propagation algorithm proposed in [33]. For a Douban movie, the score of a tag is its tagging frequency for this movie which can be fetched directly from Douban website. From Douban website, we totally collected 4,028 movies whose average rating scores are above 7.5 (10 is the best) and review numbers are greater than 2000. Since most Weibo tags and Douban tags are both written in Chinese, we used Baike encyclopedia to explore the semantic similarity of these tags.

2. Diabetes Data Set.

The second data set is collected from two diabetes social network websites, i.e., Diabetes1 and Diabetes2 introduced in Section 1. It can be obtained from our Lab's website (`http://gdm.fudan.edu.cn/GDMWiki/Wiki.jsp?page=Network%20DataSet`). The former is dedicated to diabetes patients of Type I, Type II, and pre-diabetes, whereas the latter focuses on female diabetes patients, especially those with gestational diabetes. Our goal is to recommend discussion threads from Diabetes2 to the users of Diabetes1. Due to the different vocabulary used by the different websites, we can also regard this problem as recommendation across heterogeneous domains. In this data set, we randomly collected 5,000 users from Diabetes1. Each user is profiled by a set of keywords extracted from his/her historical posts on this website. From Diabetes2, we collected 2,790 posts (threads) each of which is also characterized by a set of keywords. Furthermore, to fully demonstrate the effectiveness of our proposed approach, we removed some tags shared by the two forums as a pre-processing step. When we constructed the bi-partite graphs, we set the edge weights of E_i (i=1,2) as the TF-IDF scores of the keywords for each user/post.

3.1.2 The Ground Truth of Recommendation

Then, we introduce how to capture the ground truths of the two cross-domain recommendation tasks in our experiments.

1. Douban Movie Recommendation.

Unlike some famous movie recommendation data set such as *MovieLens* (`https://movielens.org.`), there are no explicit rating/review data of Weibo users on Douban movies, it is difficult to directly obtain the ground truth of Weibo users' preferences on Douban movies. Therefore, we have to rely on human assessments for generating ground truth of Douban movie recommendation. Specifically, we randomly selected 100 Weibo users from our data set as volunteers, to whom we recommended some Douban movies generated by the tested approaches. Then we asked each volunteer whether to accept the recommended movies or not. Each volunteer can give one of three answers, i.e., *yes*, *no* and *unknown*. We only took the move of *yes* as a *hit* recommendation. We took their average acceptance rates as the performance measure of the tested approaches.

2. Diabetes Post Recommendation.

To generate the ground truth of a diabetes patient's preferred posts, we first generated a representative vector for each Diabetes1's user and Diabetes2's post. Given a Diabetes1's user, we collected all his/her published posts as a corpus from which a set of keywords were extracted. Each element of the user vector is the TF-IDF score of one keyword. So does a Diabetes2's post vector. Then, we ranked all posts according to the cosine similarity of the user vector and the post vectors. Finally, we assume that the user will only accept top 30% of the posts whose cosine similarity is greater than 0. These posts were considered as recommendation ground truth of the user. Since all Diabetes keywords are English words, we used Wikipedia's concepts to compute the semantic similarity of keywords.

3.1.3 Baselines

To emphasize the effectiveness of our approach, we also compared the performance of some state-of-the-art baselines.

1. Random Recommendation.

It is the most naive method for recommendation. To let this baseline be more competitive, we randomly recommended items from some filtered candidates. In this naive baseline, for Douban movie recommendation, we randomly selected movies from those having more than 15,000 reviews and more than 8.8 rating scores. For Diabetes recommendation, we randomly recommended the posts from those having more than 2 keywords shared with the users. We denote this baseline as RAND.

2. Lexical Matching.

It measures the similarity between a user and an item by computing the cosine similarity of their feature (tag/keyword) vectors. This recommendation scheme can be further divided into two baselines, i.e., LEXIC1 and LEXIC2. In LEXIC1, the vector's element is set as 1 if the user/item has the corresponding feature, otherwise as 0. In LEXIC2, each element of the vector equals to the corresponding feature's score to the user/item. Obviously, an item will not be recommended to a user by this method if they do not share any common feature.

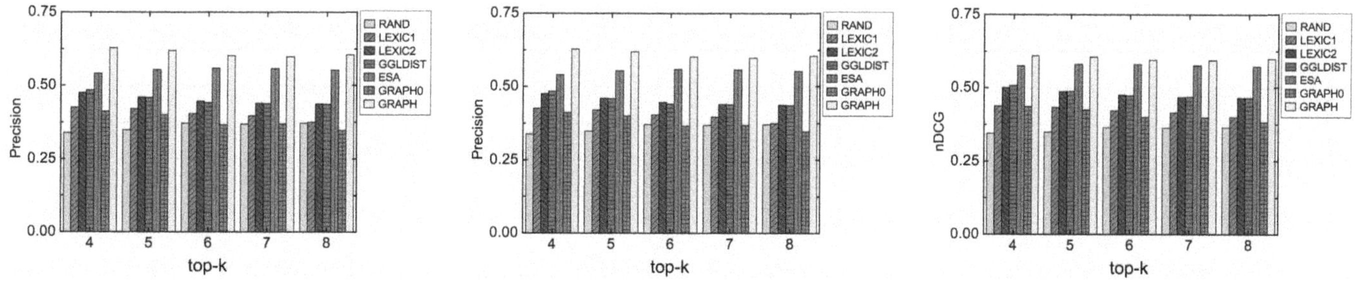

(a) Precision score (b) Average Precision score (c) nDCG score

Figure 5: Human assessment performance of Douban movie recommendation. Each column represents a competitor method. The X-axis represents the number of recommended movies. It shows that our method (GRAPH) beats all baselines in each top-k cases.

3. ESA Matching.

To highlight the effectiveness of our graph propagation approach, we adopted ESA scheme [11] as a baseline. Specifically, a user or an item are characterized by a profile vector that is the sum of concept vectors of user/item's features. Then, we measure the similarity between a user and an item by the cosine similarity of their profile vectors.

4. Google Distance.

Besides ESA, Normalized Google Distance (NGD for short) [9] is also an effective measure on two terms' semantic relatedness. For recommendation, the similarity between a user and an item can be represented by the NGD of their feature (tag/keyword) sets. Specifically, given a user u and an item v, suppose T_u is the in-neighbor concept set of u's features in the encyclopedia hyper-link graph, so is T_v for v's features. Then the NGD similarity of u and v is computed as

$$GS(u,v) = 1 - \frac{max\{log|T_u|, log|T_v|\} - log|T_u \cap T_v|}{logN - min\{log|T_u|, log|T_v|\}} \quad (4)$$

where N is the total number of concepts in the encyclopedia. We denote this baseline as GGLDIST.

3.1.4 Performance Metrics

In our experiments, we use the following three metrics to quantify the acceptance rate of the users (Weibo users or diabetes users) to the top-k recommended items (Douban movies or diabetes posts). The results of these metrics directly reflect the performance of all recommendation methods.

Precision at rank k (Pr). It is defined as the proportion of top-k recommended items that are accepted by the users.

Average Precision at rank k (AP). It is the *average precision score* of top-k recommended items and is defined as:

$$AP = \frac{\sum_{i=1}^{k}(P(i) \times rel(i))}{M} \quad (5)$$

where $rel(i)$ is an indicator function. It equals to 1 if the i-th recommended item is accepted, otherwise 0. $P(i)$ is the accepted proportion of top-i items and M is the total number of accepted items in all top-k items. Compared with Pr, AP is more accurate to measure ranking performance.

Normailzed Discounted Cumulative Gain (nDCG). It is another popular metric to measure relevance level of search results to the query in IR systems [17]. For a set of top-k recommended items, the nDCG score can be calculated as:

$$nDCG = \frac{1}{Z}\sum_{i=1}^{k}\frac{2^{rel(i)} - 1}{log_2(i+1)} \quad (6)$$

where $rel(i)$ is same as Eq. (5) and Z is a normalized factor. Compared with AP, nDCG is more sensitive to rank position of recommended items. In general, a user pays less attention to the items listed behind, hence nDCG is better to evaluate recommendation performance.

3.2 Evaluation Results

Next, we present our experimental results. In particular, we use Precision, Average Precision and nDCG as evaluation metrics to quantify the acceptance rate of the users to the top-k recommended items, i.e., movies and posts. Note that we set the α in Equation (2) to 0.99 when running our algorithm in the experiments. Small variations of α will not affect the comparative performance of our approach versus the competitors. We also study the impact of the parameter λ on the overall performance, which is used to construct the connectivity matrix based on semantic matching.

3.2.1 Douban Movie Recommendation

For Douban movie recommendation task, as mentioned before, the performance results were evaluated by surveying the 100 volunteers who have Weibo accounts in our data set. In order to highlight our graph-based approach's superiority, we compared our approach with all baselines for this recommendation task. Furthermore, we selected an optimal value of λ (=0.01) in our algorithm. The parameter study of λ will be introduced in the following subsection.

Figure 5(a)~(c) display the average scores of all competitors' performance under the three metrics including the performance of recommending top-4 to top-8 movies. We only list the results from top-4 to top-8 due to the space limitation of the figures. The results of other top-k recommendations also highlight our method's superiority. In the figures, our graph-based method is denoted as GRAPH. GRAPH0 is a variation of our method where the weights of $E_i (i = 0, 1, 2)$ are set to 1 or 0 instead of concrete feature score (for E_1 and E_2) or semantic similarity value of two terms (for E_0). From the results we find that all methods perform best when recommending top-4 movies. Naturally, good recommendation methods should rank the *hit* items to priority positions. Compared with other competitors, GRAPH almost always performs the best. The superiority of GRAPH over GRAPH0 justifies the advantage of fine-grained edge weight in the multi-partite graph. The superiority of ESA and GRAPH over LEXIC1/2 justifies the effec-

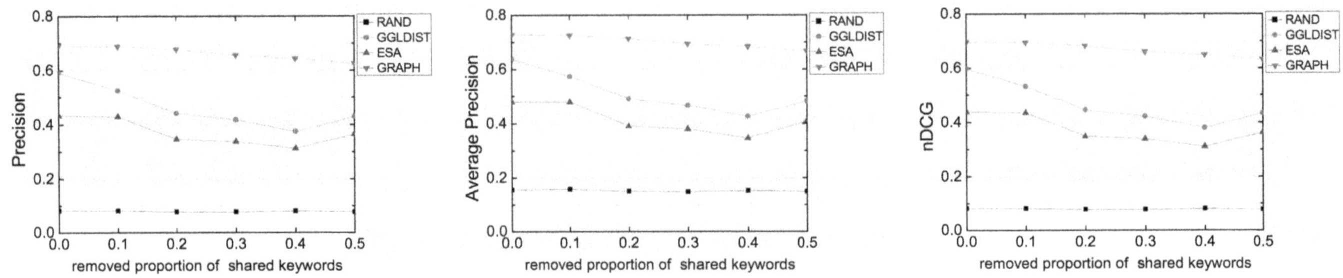

(a) Precision score (b) Average Precision score (c) nDCG score

Figure 6: The performance of all competitors on recommending top-4 diabetes posts. It shows that our method (GRAPH) outperforms the baselines no matter how many shared keywords across domains are removed.

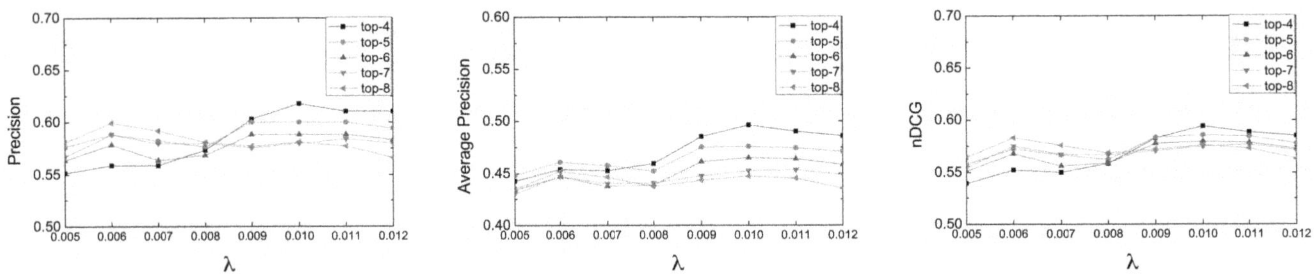

(a) Precision score (b) Average Precision score (c) nDCG score

Figure 7: Human assessment performance of graph-based method in different λs. Each line depicts a top-k Douban movie recommendation, showing that 0.01 is the best threshold to decide the sparsity of E_O in the bi-partite graph.

tiveness of concept-based semantic interpretation w.r.t. uncovering the latent relationships between users and items. The superiority of GRAPH over LEXIC1/2, GGLDIST and ESA indicates that, our graph-based method can discover more similarities between users and items that are originally neglected due to the gap of heterogenous domains. The outperformance of our approach over these baselines should be mainly attributed to graph propagation principle.

3.2.2 *Diabetes Post Recommendation*

By statistics, we found that there are many shared keywords across the two diabetes domains. Specifically, the Jaccard coefficient of the keyword sets of two domains is 0.221. As a result, we first removed a fraction of shared keywords before running the algorithms in order to simulate the setting of cross-heterogenous-domain recommendation, i.e., few common keywords can be found in the two domains. Then, we tested the algorithms under different situations when a specific proportion of shared keywords are deleted. As introduced in Subsec. 3.1.2, the ground truth of diabetes post recommendation were generated according to the principle of LEXIC2. Consequently, we only compared GRAPH with RAND, GGLDIST and ESA for this recommendation task. Referring to the results of Douban movie recommendation, we only list the performance of top-4 diabetes posts since all approaches perform best when recommending top-4 items. The other top-k results will not affect the comparative performance of our proposed approach versus the competitors.

Figure 6(a)$\sim$(c) depict performance scores of the competitors as the function of removed proportion of shared keywords where the proportion varies from 0% to 50%. From the figures we can find that, although the performance of all methods except for RAND decays evidently as more shared keywords are removed, GRAPH only decays a bit. Even when 50% of shared keywords are removed, our method's performance can still stay above 0.6. It indicates that the graph-based method is more qualified for recommendation across heterogenous domains with rarely shared features.

3.2.3 *Parameter Study*

As mentioned before, the parameter λ in our algorithm decides the sparsity of E_O in the bi-partite graph G_O. That is, for two feature nodes belonging to two different domains respectively, an edge linking them is established only when the semantic similarity of the two features is bigger than λ. Then, how does it affect the performance of our graph-based algorithm? To answer this question, we tested the performance of our approach when the λ is set to different values.

Figure 7(a)$\sim$(c) show our approach's performance as the function of λ on Douban movie recommendation. In the figures, each line corresponds the performance of a top-k recommendation where k varies from 4 to 8. From the figures we can see the performance of our proposed approach is robust with respect to small variations in the value of λ. In particular, our approach gains the best performance in all metrics when $\lambda = 0.01$. The results of other k's values also agree this point. On one hand, it is obvious that too sparse edges in G_O (larger λ) are not beneficial to the recommendation performance because fewer connections across two domains can be derived through them. On the other hand, our experiment results indicate that more edges in G_O (smaller λ) between user features and item features will not improve the recommendation performance either because potential noises will be imported by the additional edges with lower weights in G_O.

4. RELATED WORK

In this section, we survey the research works related to our work through the following three categories.

4.1 Social and Cross-domain Recommendation

By now, *Social Recommender Systems* have become the main part of recommender systems including content-based and structure-based mechanisms. Hannon et al. [13] proposed content-based user profiling based on CF for recommending new friends in Twitter. In [1], users are first represented by a frequency vector of hashtags and entities in tweets and then are recommended to with the URLs having similar profile vectors. In [3], consumers are recommended to based on the analysis of product reviews. For structure-based mechanism, the authors in [4, 8] emphasized that the structure of social links is an important clue to recommend new users. The social clues are effective on mitigating cold start problem in CF.

More recently, *cross-domain recommendation* has been a hot spot in recommendation field. Ignacio et al. [10] made a survey of emerged solutions for cross-domain recommendation and emphasized two major tasks. One is to exploit knowledge about the users and the items in the source domain for improving recommendation quality for the items in the target domain. The second task is to make joint recommendations for the items belonging to different domains. Many previous works on cross-domain recommendation focus on improving CF-based scheme. For example, the authors in [19,32] tried to migrate the rating data from a dense auxiliary domain to alleviate the cold start problem in a sparse target domain resulting in the improvement of recommendation performance in the target domain. Besides, [2, 29] merged user profiles distributed in different domains for better recommendation. The settings in above works are different from our problem setting. The cross-domain setting of Zhang et al.'s work [34] is similar to ours. But they correlated Facebook users to eBay products through Facebook's page categories and eBay taxonomy other than the semantic similarities between features in the heterogenous domains.

4.2 Transfer Learning across Heterogenous Domains

Transfer learning has been extensively studied in the past decade. It aims to improve a learning task in a target domain by using the knowledge transferred from other domain in which a related task is known [23]. Recently, transfer learning techniques have been widely applied to mitigate the sparsity problem of collaborative filtering in cross-domain recommendation.

In [19], Li et al. proposed a transfer learning approach that performs a co-clustering strategy on the rating matrix of an auxiliary domain with high rating density, and discovers rating patterns at the cluster level. Assuming that user rating behavior is similar in two domains, the approach establishes relations between domains based on the found rating patterns. In their other work [20], Li et al. extended the previous approach by means of a probabilistic model in which a user or item belonging to a particular cluster is not binary, but is described in terms of probability density function. In this case a common model is built from the ratings of all the considered domains, without requiring a dense source domain. Also addressing the sparsity problem in CF-based recommendation, W. Pan et al. [24] transferred the rating knowledge from some auxiliary data source in binary form to a target numerical rating matrix through a novel framework of transfer by collective factorization. In all above works, the user-item relations, i.e., users' ratings on items exist in both domains which is different to our scenario. Y. Zhu et al. [37] also applied transfer learning method to learn image classification by using the knowledge of document/image labels in auxiliary domains. In this work, relations between documents and images are captured by their co-occur tags. B. Cao et al. [7] proposed a non-parametric Bayesian framework for solving the collective link prediction, which allows knowledge to be adaptively transferred across heterogeneous tasks while taking into account the similarities between tasks. These methods are not suitable to be applied in our setting, where we aim to build the connections between heterogeneous entities across different domains instead of learning multiple models.

4.3 Semantic Relatedness Measurement

In NLP, measuring semantic relatedness of two terms or entities is an important task. Many prior works utilized the lexical concepts in WordNet's taxonomy [18] based on the deepest point in the taxonomy [31] or information content [26]. To expand concept coverage, many researchers took Wikipedia as the knowledge base of semantic interpretation. M. Strube et al. [28] and D.Milne et al. [22] used the taxonomy and the Normalized Google Distance [9] in Wikipedia to compute semantic relatedness, respectively. E.Gabrilovich et al. [11] proposed a widely applied model of semantic interpretation, i.e., Explicit Semantic Analysis which is also based on the relations between concepts in online encyclopedia. More recently, T. Mikolov et al. [30] proposed *word embedding* which learns a distributed representation for a word through neural network. Then the semantic relatedness of two words can be computed by the distance of two word vectors. This approach is effective but costly in computation and depends training corpus.

5. CONCLUSION

In this paper, we address a new challenging problem of recommendation across heterogenous domains. That is, recommending the items in one domain to the users in another domain when the features of the two domains rarely overlap, as well as no user-item interactive relations in each domain can be obtained. To this end, we first capture the semantic relations between user features and item features (tags/keywords) through ESA-based concept interpretation from online encyclopedias. Then, we propose a novel graph-based algorithm to discover the hidden similarity between two entities (users/items) via propagation principle. We not only exploit our algorithm with solid proofs, but also justify our approach's performance superiority over the state-of-the-art competitors through extensive evaluations. The results demonstrate our approach's merits to many real world applications of cross-domain recommendation.

6. ACKNOWLEDGEMENTS

This paper was supported by the National NSFC (No.61472085, 61171132, 61033010), by National Key Basic Research Program of China under No.2015CB358800, by Basic research project of Shanghai science and technology innovation action plan under No.15JC1400900, and by Shanghai Science and Technology Development Funds (13dz2260200, 13511504300). This paper was also partially supported by an IBM Faculty Award.

7. REFERENCES

[1] F. Abel, Q. Gao, G.-J. Houben, and K. Tao. Analyzing temporal dynamics in twitter profiles for personalized recommendations in the social web. In *Proc. of WebSci*, 2011.

[2] F. Abel, E. Herder, G.-J. Houben, N. Henze, and D. Krause. Cross-system user modeling and personalization on the social web. In *Proc. of UMUAI*, 2013.
[3] S. Aciar, D. Zhang, S. Simoff, and J. Debenham. Recommender system based on consumer product reviews. In *Proc. of WI*, 2006.
[4] M. J. Brzozowski and D. M. Romero. Who should i follow? recommending people in directed social networks. In *Proc. of CSCW*, 2011.
[5] R. Burke. Hybrid web recommender systems. *LNCS*, 4321:377–408, 2007.
[6] I. Cantador, A. Bellogin, and D. Vallet. Content-based recommendation in social tagging systems. In *Proc. of Recommender System*, 2010.
[7] B. Cao, N. N. Liu, and Q. Yang. Transfer learning for collective link prediction in multiple heterogenous domains. In *Proc. of ICML*, 2010.
[8] J. Chen, W. Geyer, C. Dugan, M. Muller, and I. Guy. Make new friends but keep the old, recommending people on social networking sites. In *Proc. of CHI*, 2009.
[9] R. L. Cilibrasi and P. M. Vitanyi. The google similarity distance. *Knowledge and Data Engineering, IEEE Transactions on*, 19(3):370–383, 2007.
[10] I. Fernandez-Tobias, I. Cantador, M. Kaminskas, and F. Ricci. Cross-domain recommender systems: A survey of the state of the art. 2011.
[11] E. Gabrilovich and S. Markovitch. Computing semantic relatedness using wikipedia-based explicit semantic analysis. In *Proc. of IJCAI*, 2007.
[12] L. Gall and François. Powers of tensors and fast matrix multiplication. In *Proc. of ISSAC*, 2014.
[13] J. Hannon, M. Bennett, and B. Smyth. Recommending twitter users to follow using content and collaborative filtering approaches. In *Proc. of RecSys*, 2010.
[14] Hazewinkel and Michiel. *Taylor series*. Encyclopedia of Mathematics, Springer, 2001.
[15] T. Hofmann. Collaborative filtering via gaussian probabilistic latent semantic analysis. In *Proc. of SIGIR*, 2003.
[16] T. Hofmann. Latent semantic models for collaborative filtering. *ACM Transactions on Information Systems*, 2:89 - 115, 2004.
[17] K. JÍarvelin and J. KekÍalÍainen. Cumulated gain-based evaluation of ir techniques. *ACM Transactions on Information Systems*, 20:422-446, 2002.
[18] F. L., G. E., and Matias. *WordNet: An Electronic Lexical Database*. MIT Press, Cambridge, MA., 1998.
[19] B. Li, Q. Yang, and X. Xue. Can movies and books collaborate? cross-domain collaborative filtering for sparsity reduction. In *Proc. of IJCAI*, 2009.
[20] B. Li, Q. Yang, and X. Xue. Transfer learning for collaborative filtering via a rating-matrix generative model. In *Proc. of ICML*, 2009.
[21] Z. Lu, E. Zhong, L. Zhao, E. Xiang, W. Pan, and Q. Yang. Selective transfer learning for cross domain recommendation. In *Proc. of SDM*, 2013.
[22] D. Milne and I. H. Witten. An effective, low-cost measure of semantic relatedness obtained from wikipedia links. In *Proc. of AAAI*, 2008.
[23] S. J. Pan and Q. Yang. A survey on transfer learning. *IEEE TKDE*, 22(10):1345 - 1359, 2010.
[24] W. Pan, N. N. Liu, E. W. Xiang, and Q. Yang. Transfer learning to predict missing ratings via heterogeneous user feedbacks. In *Proc. of IJCAI*, 2011.
[25] W. H. Press, S. A. Teukolsky, W. T. Vetterling, and B. P. Flannery. *Numerical Recipes: The Art of Scientific Computing*. Cambridge University Press, 2007.
[26] P. Resnick. Using information content to evaluate semantic similarity in a taxonomy. In *Proc. of IJCAI*, 1995.
[27] S. Sen, J. Vig, and J. Riedl. Tagommenders: Connecting users to items through tags. In *Proc. of WWW*, 2009.
[28] M. Strube and S. P. Ponzetto. Wikirelate! computing semantic relatedness using wikipedia. In *Proc. of AAAI*, 2006.
[29] M. Szomszor, H. Alani, I. Cantador, K. OHara, and N. Shadbolt. Semantic modelling of user interests based on cross-folksonomy analysis. In *Proc. of ISWC*, 2008.
[30] M. Tomas, S. Ilya, C. Kai, C. Greg, and D. Jeffrey. Distributed representations of words and phrases and their compositionality. In *arXiv:1310.4546*, 2013.
[31] Z. Wu and M. Palmer. Verb semantics and lexical selection. In *Proc. of ACL*, 1994.
[32] W. C. Wynne, H. Mong, and L. Lee. Making recommendations from multiple domains. In *Proc. of SIGKDD*, 2013.
[33] D. Yang, Y. Xiao, H. Tong, J. Zhang, and W. Wang. An integrated tag recommendation algorithm towards weibo user profiling. In *Proc. of DASFAA*, 2015.
[34] Y. Zhang and M. Pennacchiotti. Predicting purchase behaviors from social media. In *Proc. of WWW*, 2013.
[35] D. Zhou, J. Weston, A.Gretton, O.Bousquet, and B. Scholkopf. Ranking on data manifolds. In *Proc. of NIPS*, 2003.
[36] T. C. Zhou, H. Ma, M. R. Lyu, and I. King. Userrec: A user recommendation framework in social tagging systems. In *Proc. of AAAI*, 2010.
[37] Y. Zhu, Y. Chen, Z. Lu, S. J. Pan, G.-R. Xue, Y. Yu, and Q. Yang. Heterogeneous transfer learning for image classification. In *Proc. of AAAI*, 2011.

Query Relaxation across Heterogeneous Data Sources

Verena Kantere
University of Geneva
Switzerland
verena.kantere@unige.ch

George Orfanoudakis
National Technical University
of Athens, Greece
gorfas@ece.ntua.gr

Anastasios
Kementsietsidis
Google Inc.
akement@google.com

Timos Sellis
RMIT University, Australia
timos.sellis@rmit.edu.au

ABSTRACT

The fundamental assumption for query rewriting in heterogeneous environments is that the mappings used for the rewriting are *complete*, i.e., *every* relation and attribute mentioned in the query is associated, through mappings, to relations and attributes in the schema of the source that the query is rewritten. In reality, it is rarely the case that such complete sets of mappings exist between sources, and the presence of partial mappings is the norm rather than the exception. So, practically, existing query answering algorithms fail to generate any rewriting in the majority of cases. The question is then whether we can somehow relax queries that cannot be rewritten as such (due to insufficient mappings), and whether we can identify the interesting query relaxations, given the mappings at hand.

In this paper, we propose a technique to compute query relaxations of an input query that can be rewritten and evaluated in an environment of collaborating autonomous and heterogeneous data sources. We extend traditional techniques for query rewriting, and we propose both an exhaustive and an optimized heuristic algorithm to compute and evaluate these relaxations. Our technique works with input of any query similarity measure. The experimental study proves the effectiveness and efficiency of our technique.

Categories and Subject Descriptors

H.2.5 [**Database Management**]: Heterogeneous Databases

Keywords

big heterogeneous data; approximate querying; query relaxation

1. INTRODUCTION

In typical data exchange [9], integration [13], and sharing [24] settings, schema mappings (often in the form of Local-As-View (LAV) mappings [13]) are commonly used to alleviate the heterogeneity across *pairs* of autonomous sources (or sets of sources in general). In the case of data exchange, such mappings are used for instance generation, i.e., to generate instances of a *target* schema based on those of the *source* schema. In data integration and sharing, the mappings are used during query evaluation, i.e., to *translate* or *rewrite* queries that are posed over a source schema to new queries that can be evaluated over the constructs (schemas and attributes) of a target schema.

CIKM'15, October 19–23, 2015, Melbourne, Australia.
© 2015 ACM. ISBN 978-1-4503-3794-6/15/10 ...$15.00.
DOI: http://dx.doi.org/10.1145/2806416.2806529.

```
VacPackage (vacid, fno, hid, from, until)
Flights (fno, depart, return, carrier, origin, dest, price)
Hotels (hid, chkin, chkout, name, location, served, rate)
```

(a) The iTravel.com schema

```
SELECT *
FROM   VacPackage V, Flights F, Hotels H
WHERE  V.fno = F.fno AND V.from = F.depart AND V.until = F.return AND
       F.depart = "11/01" AND F.return = "11/09" AND F.origin = "NYC" AND
       F.depart = H.chkin AND F.return = H.chkout AND F.dest = H.served AND
       V.hid = H.hid AND H.location = "Hana"
```

(b) Planning a vacation to Hana, Hawaii

```
iAirline.com: Segment (fno, depart, return, origin, dest, price)
iHotel.com:   Locations (location, served, rate)
iInn.com:     Inn (name, chkin, chkout, served, rate)
```

(c) Related travel sources

```
Segment (fno, dep, ret, org, dst, pr) :- Flights (fno, dep, ret, car, org, dst, pr)
Locations (loc, srv, pr) :- Hotels (hid, chkin, chkout, nm, loc, srv, pr)
Inn (nm, ckin, ckout, srv, pr) :- Hotels (hid, ckin, ckout, nm, loc, srv, pr)
```

(d) Local-as-view Mappings

Figure 1: Querying the iTravel.com

Here, we focus on the query rewriting problem and on the techniques that have been developed to this end. Classical rewriting algorithms, like Inverse Rules [8], Bucket [15] and MiniCon [23] have already addressed some of the fundamental issues in this area, both in terms of computing complete or maximally-contained rewritings (given an input query and a set of mappings), and in terms of doing so efficiently. Yet, a common assumption in all these algorithms is that the set of available mappings should provide at least one combination that *fully* rewrites the query. If this is not the case, that is, if the input query refers to a relation or to an attribute that does not participate in any of the input mappings, then the rewriting *fails* (no output is produced). In what follows, we argue that in many practical settings, the mappings are inherently incomplete and that the assumption of existing algorithms is rather restrictive.

Consider a travel web-site iTravel.com offering services similar to the ones found in web-sites like Expedia or Travelocity. Like these web-sites, a user can go to iTravel.com and enter (a) the origin; (b) the destination; and (c) the dates of the vacation; and the system can generate candidate vacation packages that include the flight(s) and hotel room(s) for the duration of the vacation. Conceptually, one can think of this as a single query over iTravel.com database, as illustrated in Figure 1(a). The database includes three relations (with key attributes underlined in each). Relation VacPackage stores for each vacation package its id (vacid), the associated flight (fno) and hotel (hid), as well as the dates the package is available (from and until). Relation Flights includes a flight number (fno), the depart and return dates, as well as the flight carrier, origin, dest ination and ticket price. Relation Hotels includes the identifier (hid), hotel name, location and closest airport (served), as well as the check-in and check-out dates (chkin and chkout) and room rate.

Consider a user looking for vacation packages between the 1st and 9th of November, flying out of New York to the city of Hana, Hawaii. Figure 1(b) shows the equivalent SQL query over the schema of iTravel.com. The query joins the three relations on the fno and hid attributes, as well as on the corresponding date attributes (to ensure that the right flight and hotel are selected for the vacation period). Notice that the flight and hotel relations are also joined (term F.dest = H.served) to ensure that the flight lands into an airport that serves the hotel. Web-sites like iTravel.com usually act as brokers. They do not store the latest information for flight and hotel prices (or availability). Instead, they often access the airline and hotel databases (at query-time) to get the latest data. Figures 1(c) and (d) show three such databases along with their corresponding mappings to the iTravel.com schema (expressed as LAV mappings).

Notice that the user query in Figure 1(b) *cannot* be rewritten using the above mappings. For one thing, there is no mapping for VacPackage since none of the individual sources stores information for vacation packages. Also, identifiers like vacid and hid are internal to the iTravel.com database and cannot be mapped to any of the attributes of the individual sources. As well, the join on these identifiers is also not *covered* by any combination of mappings. Any of the classical algorithms on query rewriting will fail to provide a rewriting. Yet, it is not hard to see that the individual sources provide us with enough information to *reconstruct* vacation packages since the *important* attributes, like the dates, origin and destination of flights, and the check-in and check-out dates of hotels, are present in the sources. Indeed, it is not hard to see that the following two queries can be computed by *relaxing* (removing the join with VacPackage) the query in Figure 1(b):

```
SELECT *
FROM   Segment S, Locations L
WHERE  S.depart = "11/01" AND S.return = "11/09" AND S.origin = "NYC"
       AND S.dest = L.served AND L.location = "Hana"
SELECT *
FROM   Segment S, Inn I
WHERE  S.depart = "11/01" AND S.return = "11/09" AND S.origin = "NYC"
       AND S.depart = I.chkin AND S.return = I.chkout
       AND S.dest = I.served
```

The first query identifies flight/hotel combinations where the user gets to stay in a hotel, while in the second the user gets to stay in an inn. Given an input query and a set of mappings there are *multiple* possible relaxations and not all relaxations are equally *good*.

• How can we efficiently compute the set of possible relaxations of an input query, given a set of mappings?
• How can we examine the *best* query relaxations first?

Detailed contributions. In response to the above challenges, we propose a technique for approximate query answering in an environment of autonomous data sources. To the best of our knowledge, this is the first work towards this direction.

• We build a new technique that performs query relaxation and approximate rewriting of the originally posed query. This technique complements and reuses existing traditional query answering algorithms using LAV mappings.
• The search space considered by the approximate rewriting technique is represented such that: (i) it is smaller than the number of possible approximate rewritings (ii) it increases at a slow rate with respect to the query size, and (iii) it accepts heuristics.
• An exhaustive algorithm is presented for approximate query rewriting that searches the space in an efficient way, such that, the *best* possible approximations are considered first. It is proved that the algorithm is complete, i.e. it finds the optimal approximation. Furthermore, an optimized heuristic algorithm is proposed, that trades a much higher efficiency for a very low approximation error. The algorithms take as input a user-defined query similarity function.
• The algorithms are enhanced with a preprocess that unifies LAV mappings in more generalized ones that can rewrite query parts which could not be rewritten otherwise.
• The experimental evaluation proves the substantial efficiency and scalability of the proposed algorithms compared to a straightforward solution that employs traditional query rewriting and their effectiveness on the solution of the query relaxation and, in general, the approximate query answering problem.

We note here that the problem of defining the notion of query similarity and defining query similarity measures is orthogonal to the problem of finding approximate query versions with respect to such measures, and is out of the scope of this work. Query similarity and respective measures are investigated and proposed in [3, 6, 11, 12] and other works. The algorithms proposed here work with input of any similarity measure as a 'black box'.

In the rest of the paper, Section 2 summarizes related work and Section 3 gives an overview and introduces preliminary notions. Section 4 discusses the cases of query approximation and Section 5 describes the approximate query answering algorithms. Section 6 presents our experimental study and Section 7 concludes the paper.

2. RELATED WORK

Approximation in query answering has been extensively studied from several aspects. A big trend has been the effort to reduce response time by seeking approximate query answers. Some techniques compute approximate answers based on data summaries, statistics or histograms [22]. A noticeable work is [21], which discusses summarization of XML data. The AQAX system [1, 25] aims to fast generation of approximate results, in order to improve efficiency. Towards the same end, the work in [7] introduces approximate data exchange. The aim is to produce fast approximate answers and exact answers later. The motivation is on trees that are semi-consistent. For this kind of problems it offers a solution that relaxes in a restricted way the data request.

Another trend is query answering in inconsistent databases. The work in [10] is a solution that provides consistent query answers on inconsistent databases with respect to some integrity constraints. Many other works focus on query answering in incomplete databases. The work in [27] presents the QPIAD framework, which focuses on the retrieval of tuples that miss values on constrained attributes. Their approach is based on attribute correlations. The work in [20] deals with answering imprecise queries, with respect to the schema on which they are posed. The focus is on the retrieval of not only the precise answers, but also imprecise ones, with respect to some similarity of the imprecise answers to the precise query. The technique reasons on the data and relaxes the query according to estimation of the similarity between values binding categorical attributes. In the same spirit, but focusing on vocabulary and semantics, the work in [4] deals with the problem of approximate query mapping. The interest is on Boolean query constraints in heterogeneous sources and there is a discussion on closeness and its quantification with respect to precision and recall.

Furthermore, there is some interest on the problem of query relaxation. The work in [5] studies the problem of approximation of

Input: set of views $\mathcal{V}$, query Q_{orig}, query similarity function M_{sim}
Output: best approx. rewriting Q^{best}_{apprx} and its M_{sim} value
begin
  Set $Q^{best}_{apprx} = Q_{orig}$;
  Set $MaxSim = max$;
  Unify views in $\mathcal{V}$ if possible;
  while *no query rewriting* $Q^{best}_{apprx_R}$ **do**
    Run classical query rewriting on Q^{best}_{apprx};
    if no rewriting $Q^{best}_{apprx_R}$ **then**
      create set $\mathcal{F}(Q^{best}_{apprx}, \mathcal{V})$;
      Explore possible query approximations guided by $\mathcal{F}$;
      Set new Q^{best}_{apprx} and new $MaxSim$;
  return $Q^{best}_{apprx_R}$, $MaxSim$;

Figure 2: Approximate query rewriting

Datalog queries with a union of conjunctive ones. It calls the similarity of approximations "easiness" or "goodness" and proposes the notion of upper and lower envelopes that characterize the containment of a conjunctive query in a Datalog one. The work in [19] focuses on queries that failed to get an answer and discusses the notion of similar queries. It proposes a query relaxation method for producing query versions that succeed in retrieving similar tuples. This approach is based on training the system beforehand on part of the data. The interest is on queries with conjunctions or disjunctions of atoms and the relaxation procedure is based on bayesian networks, targeting the approximation of domain knowledge.

In spite of the numerous works in approximate query answering, the problem of producing query approximations that can be rewritten on autonomous and heterogeneous databases with respect to a set of mappings has not been tackled. Our work aims to an efficient and practical solution of this problem, that can be employed in several application settings of autonomous databases.

3. OVERVIEW AND PRELIMINARIES

A classical query rewriting algorithm takes as input a query and a set of views, and outputs a rewritten query version (usually the maximally contained version [13]). If the available views are not adequate to form a combination that rewrites the query completely, then no output is produced. Our aim is to offer such a rewriting technique that outputs a rewritten query employing in the *best* way the available views, even if a complete rewriting is not possible.

This work presents a query rewriting technique that produces approximate rewritings or equivalently, rewritings of approximations, of an originally posed query employing a set of Local-As-View (LAV [13, 14]) views, $\mathcal{V}$. Hereafter we refer to the query input to the approximate rewriting algorithm as Q_{orig}, to an approximation of it as Q_{apprx} and to a rewritten version of the approximation as Q_{apprx_R}. We are interested in SQL queries of the SPJ form (plus comparisons and value conditions), which can be written in conjunctive form. Whenever not clear from the context we note as Q^{SQL} and as Q^{conj} the SQL and conjunctive form, respectively, of Q. Roughly, a user poses Q_{orig} in the local database which should be approximated to Q_{apprx} so that it can be rewritten as Q_{apprx_R} and answered on a remote database through a set of mappings (in general, chain of mappings [17]).

We define the search space of possible approximations through the removal of distinct query parts. This is a smaller search space than the one that considers arbitrary approximate versions of a query. Furthermore, the size of the selected space not only increases slower than the size of the space of arbitrary approximations, but it also lends itself nicely to efficient pruning heuristics.

VacPackage (vacid, fno, hid, from, until)
Flights (fno, depart, return, carrier, origin, dest, price)
HotelsCheck (hid, chkin, chkout, name, location, rate)
Hotels (name, room#, rate, lowestprice)
Rooms (room#, floor#)
HotelLocation (name, lowestprice, location)
Airport (aid, location, distance)
SeasonPrices (season, lowestprice)

Figure 3: The extended iTravel.com schema

We develop an exhaustive algorithm that operates on this search space. The input of the algorithm is Q_{orig}, a set of available views $\mathcal{V}$ and a query similarity function M_{sim}, used as a black box. The latter is formed by the user and quantifies the quality of the possible approximate rewritings. Naturally, the exhaustive algorithm finds the optimal approximation with respect to the similarity function. Furthermore, we propose a heuristic that proves to prune the space efficiently, with a small trade of approximation error.

Users are assumed to express their queries and expect answers in SQL form, since it is more intuitive and user-friendly. Existing query rewriting algorithms, however, take as input queries and output rewritten versions of them in conjunctive form. A SQL query is considered to be a set of *elements*, one for each 'select' attribute and one for each 'where' condition. The transformation of Q^{SQL}_{orig} to Q^{conj}_{orig} is unique; moreover, the transformation of $Q^{conj}_{apprx_R}$ to $Q^{SQL}_{apprx_R}$ is unique with respect to the elements of Q^{SQL}_{orig}.

A conjunctive query is of the form: $Q(X) : -R_1(X_1)...R_n(X_n)$, where Q and R_i, $i = 1, \ldots, n$ are names of predicates (i.e. relations) and X_i, $i = 1, \ldots, n$ are tuples (i.e. each is an ordered set of attribute variables or constants). $Q(X)$ is the *head* and $\cup_{i=1,\ldots,n} R_i$ the *body* of the query. The R_is, $i = 1, \ldots, n$ are called the *subgoals* of the query Q. The variables in X are called *distinguished* and the variables in R_is that do not appear in the query head are called *existential*. Conjunctive queries can have comparisons as subgoals; if $R_i(X_i)$ is a comparison subgoal, any variables in X_i must also appear in X. A query is *safe* is all variables in X appear in $\cup_{i=1,\ldots,n} X_i$. A mapping or as called a *homomorphism* of a query $Q(X) : -R_1(X_1) \ldots R_n(X_n)$ on a view $V(Y) : -S_1(Y_1) \ldots S_m(Y_m)$ is the mapping of query predicates $R_1, \ldots, R_n$ on the view predicates $S_1, \ldots, S_m$ and variables $X, X_1, \ldots, X_n$ on variables $Y, Y_1, \ldots, Y_m$.

The proposed approximate rewriting technique takes advantage of the existing literature on classical query rewriting using LAV views [8, 15, 16, 18, 23] in order to perform the actual rewriting. Specifically, when the algorithm finds an approximation, Q_{apprx}, of the original query, which can be thoroughly rewritten using the set of views in hand $\mathcal{V}$, it rewrites it to Q_{apprx_R} in the classical manner. Figure 2 is a coarse summary of the technique. Classical query rewriting algorithms [8, 15, 16, 18, 23] rewrite the query to a query in which the subgoals are no more R_is, but the head of views $V_i \in \mathcal{V}$ or they are new comparison subgoals. In general, the algorithms start from mapping some of the head variables X of Q on some of the head variables Y of V, and proceed by mapping a subset of subgoals R_is to a subset of subgoals S_is progressively, such that the whole query body is finally mapped on (or as said *covered by*) one or more views. If there are subgoals that are covered by more than one views, then the check for query containment is performed in order to see if the rewritten query can be reduced to a version the answers of which are contained in the answers of the original query. Figure 3 shows an extended version of the iTravel.com schema, used in the examples throughout the rest of the paper.

Assume that Q^{SQL}_{orig} is:

Q^{SQL}_{orig}: **SELECT** H. name, H. room#
FROM Hotels H, HotelLocation HL
WHERE H.rate = "300" **AND** H.name = HL.name
AND HL.location = "sea"

The conjunctive query form Q^{conj}_{orig} is:

Q^{conj}_{orig}(name, room#) :- Hotels(name, room#, '300', lowestprice1) HotelLocation(name, lowestprice2, 'sea')

Assume a view:

V(name, rate) :- Hotels(name, room#, rate, lowestprice)

A rewriting algorithm creates the following partial query mapping on the view (starting from the head and moving on to the body):

Q^{conj}_{orig}.name → V.name

Q^{conj}_{orig}.Hotels → V.Hotels

Q^{conj}_{orig}.Hotels.room# → V.Hotels.room#

Q^{conj}_{orig}.Hotels.'300'→ V.Hotels.rate

Q^{conj}_{orig}.Hotels.lowestprice1 → V.Hotels.lowestprice

Namely, three very well know classical rewriting algorithms, Inverse Rules [8], Bucket [15] and MiniCon [23] work as follows: Inverse Rules inverses the views such that the subgoals of the views become the heads of rules the subgoal of which is the view head; the inversed rules are matched with the query subgoals to find out a set of rules that covers all of them. The Bucket Algorithm [15] creates a bucket for each subgoal and puts in each bucket the views that can cover this subgoal. It then tries to find a minimal combination of views (one from each bucket). The MiniCon algorithm [23] works similarly to the Bucket algorithm, but instead of creating a bucket for each subgoal and then trying to combine views from within the buckets, it matches each view with as many as possible query subgoals following join chains. When no more subgoals can be matched, the algortihm tries to match another view with as many as possible from the rest such that the two views can be joined in the rewritten query body. This procedure is performed until all subgoals are covered by a set of views.

Overall, all three algorithms have two coarse steps:

1. Map the query on the view in the least restrictive manner (in terms of homomorphism).

2. Combine view mappings produced in the previous step so that all query subgoals are covered in a non-redundant manner.

In the following we refer to query rewriting employing an algorithm based on query containment, such as the above, as *classical* or *complete* query rewriting. Also, we use interchangeably: the terms *rewriting* and *answering* (since answering is performed through rewriting); the terms of query element *mapping*, *covering* and *satisfaction*; query *conditions* and *constraints* (usually the first term is used for SQL and the second for conjunctive forms), *relaxation* and *approximation* (the latter is a broader term than the first and covers cases of query versions that may not only be relaxed but have additional elements - the proposed technique works in case of such query approximation). A complete mapping of query variables on view variables is denoted with $\phi(.)$.

4. APPROXIMATE QUERY ANSWERING

Our approximate rewriting technique searches the optimal approximation based on the removed query elements from Q_{orig}. The algorithm is based on a structure called F (from 'failure') that records the query rewriting procedure at the point of failure, indicating which query part should be removed in order to create an approximation of the Q_{orig}, Q_{apprx}, and try to rewrite the latter with possible success. Since the traditional query rewriting algorithms proceed in two coarse steps (described informally in Section 3), failure of rewriting, and, therefore, creation of a new instance of F, can occur in any one of the two steps.

4.1 Creation of Fs

With respect to a view $V \in \mathcal{V}$ and the query Q, an instance of F records the failure of mapping V on Q. The latter can either be the originally posed query Q_{orig}, or an approximate version of it. The definition of F is:

Definition 1 *A failure F for a view V and a query Q is the set $F(Q,V) = (h_P, \phi_P, G_P, D)$ where:*
-h_P is a head homomorphism on V
- ϕ_P is a partial mapping from the subgoal variables of Q to the subgoal variables of $h_P(V)$
- G_P is the subset of the subgoals in Q which are covered by some subgoal in $h_P(V)$ using the mapping ϕ_P,
- $D = \{x\}$, where x is a (a) join, (b) comparison, (c) constant, (d) variable or (e) subgoal of Q.

An instance of F for a query Q and a view V is created when the mapping of the view on the query fails. The D part of F consists of the part of Q that constitutes the point of failure of the extension of h_P, ϕ_P or G_P. Naturally, the creation of a F can be terminated prematurely because of several mismatches in the mapping process of V on Q. Moreover, even if there is no failure in the mapping of a view V on a query Q, the creation of F is possible in the case that the mapping of V cannot be combined with the mapping of other views in order to rewrite Q as a whole. A F is created in the following situations, either during the mapping of V on Q or the combination of the mapping of one view V and another view V'.

4.1.1 *Creation of a single* F

Failure of mapping V on a query Q and, therefore, the creation of $F(Q,V)$, can occur in the following cases:

Case 1: Query head variables are mapped to variables in the view, but the latter are not distinguished, thus they cannot be exposed to the rewriting algorithm. Formally: If there is a query head variable x which is in the domain of the view mapping ϕ_P of V on Q but is not in h_p, then: $D = \{x\}$. F indicates the elimination of x.

Example 1 *Assume the query Q_{orig}(room#, floor#):-Rooms (room#, floor#) and the view V(room#):-Rooms (room#, floor#). Then the head variable floor# should be eliminated in order to avoid view mapping failure, thus D = {floor#}*

Case 2: A query subgoal is mapped on the view but a join between variables within the subgoal is neither mapped, nor the respective mapped variables in the view are distiguished. Formally: If a homomorphism cannot be created or extended on V, in order to satisfy a join in a query subgoal $g.x = g.y$, then: $D = \{g.x = g.y\}$. The homomorphism on V is needed to satisfy a query join and F indicates the elimination of this join.

Example 2 *Assume the query Q_{orig}(name, room#):- Hotels (name, room#, price, price) and the view V(name, room#):- Hotels (name, room#, rate, lowestprice). Then the join Hotels.rate = Hotels.lowestprice should be eliminated in order to avoid the failure; thus D = {Hotels.rate = Hotels.lowestprice}.*

Case 3: A variable present in a set of query subgoals is mapped on V as an existential variable, but not all of these subgoals are mapped on V. Formally: If x is a variable in a query subgoal g, and ϕ_P is extended to contain the mapping of x but cannot be extended to contain g, then: $D = \{g\}$. The requirement for the mapping extension is due to a query join. F indicates the elimination of this join in case that the mapping ϕ_P cannot be extended or g cannot be satisfied by V.

Example 3 *Assume the query that asks for the location with the lowest price for a specific period:* Q_{orig}*(location):- HotelsCheck (hid, '03/11', '04/11', name, location, rate1) Hotels (name, room#, rate2, lowestprice) HotelLocation (name, lowestprice, location) and the view V (location):- HotelsCheck (hid, chkin, chkout, name, location, rate1) Hotels (name, room#, rate2, lowestprice). The subgoal HotelLocation should be eliminated to avoid failure; thus D = {HotelLocation}.*

Case 4: Query subgoals are mapped on V but joins between these subgoals are neither mapped in V nor respective variables in V are distinguished, so that the join can be enforced there. Formally: If a set of query subgoals $\mathcal{G}$ is satisfied by V, but there is a query variable $x \in g, \forall g \in \mathcal{G}$ such that ϕ_P cannot be extended to contain $\phi_P(x)$; then for any two subgoals $g_1, g_2 \in \mathcal{G}$: $D = \{g1.x = g2.x\}$. The reason for this failure is the incapability of V to rewrite a query join. F indicates the elimination of this join. (Checks for rewriting head variables as well as constant and comparison constraints are treated separately).

Example 4 *Assume a query that asks for hotel names and lowest prices by the sea, but double checks the validity of information in both HotelLocation and Hotels,* Q_{orig}*(name, lowestprice):- HotelLocation (name, lowestprice, 'sea') Hotels (name, room#, rate, lowestprice) and the view V(name, rate):- HotelLocation (name, rate, 'sea') Hotels(name, room#, rate, lowestprice). Then there is no appropriate homomorphism for the view and the join HotelLocation.lowestprice = Hotels.lowestprice should be eliminated in order to avoid failure; thus D = {HotelLocation.lowestprice = Hotels. lowestprice}*

Case 5: Query variables involved in comparison subgoals are not mapped on V. Formally: If x, y are a query variables, $y \in g$ and there is a subgoal $x.y$, where . is a comparison predicate, $\phi_P(x)$ is an existential variable, but ϕ_P cannot be extended to contain $\phi_P(y)$, then: $D = \{x.y\}$. F indicates the elimination of the comparison atom in case that ϕ_P cannot be extended or a subgoal g cannot be satisfied by V. (Equivalent to case 3).

Example 5 *Assume the query* Q_{orig}*(name, lowestprice1):- Hotels (name, room#, rate, lowestprice1) SeasonPrices (season, lowestprice2) rate ≤ lowestprice2 and the view V(name, lowestprice):- Hotels (name, room#, rate, lowestprice). Since V does not include the subgoal SeasonPrices the comparison cannot be satisfied and D = {rate ≤ lowestprice2}.*

Case 6: Query variables in a comparison subgoal are mapped on variables of V that are not distinguished and the comparison subgoal is not mapped in V. Formally: If x, y are a query variables, $y \in g$ and there is a comparison subgoal $x.y$, where . is a comparison predicate, $\phi_P(x)$ and/or $\phi_P(y)$ are existential variables, but ϕ_P cannot be extended to contain $\phi_P(x.y)$, then : $D = \{x.y\}$. V is incapable to satisfy the query comparison, thus, F indicates the elimination of the respective subgoal. (Equivalent to case 4).

Example 6 *Assume the query* Q_{orig}*(name1, lowestprice1):- Hotels (name1, room#1, rate1, lowestprice1) Hotels (name2, room#2, rate2, lowestprice2) lowestprice1 ≤ lowestprice2 and the view V(name):-Hotels (name, room#, rate, lowestprice). The view does not export sufficient information (distringuished variables) in order for the query comparison to be produced.*

Case 7: A query constant is either mapped in a variable of V that is not distinguished, or it is not mapped at all. Formally: If a is a query constant, but $\phi_P(a)$ is neither the constant a nor it is in h_p, then: $D = \{a\}$. F indicates the elimination of a.

Example 7 *Assume the query* Q_{orig}*(name):- HotelLocation (name, lowestprice, 'sea') and the view V(name):- HotelLocation (name, lowestprice, location). A rewriting failure occurs because the view does not make the specialization location = 'sea'. To avoid failure the constant constraint should be removed: D = {'sea' }.*

4.1.2 *Creation of multiple Fs*

Even if $F(Q, V)$ is not created while the rewriting algorithm is mapping V on Q, it can be created later on, while the algorithm tries to combine the mapping $\phi(V)$ of V, with the mapping $\phi(V')$ of another view V' (in which case the mappings are complete)[1].

Case 8: Views are covering overlapping query subgoals. Formally: If $\mathcal{V}$ is the set of views for which there is no $F(Q, V), \forall V \in \mathcal{V}$, then, if $\forall \mathcal{V}' \subseteq \mathcal{V}$ there is a set of overlapping query subgoals $\mathcal{G}$ mapped on $\mathcal{V}'$, then $\forall g \in \mathcal{G}$ and $\forall V \in \mathcal{V}'$ such that g is satisfied in all $V \in \mathcal{V}'$, an $F(V)$ is created, such that: $D = \{g\}$. The extension of G satisfied by a view is caused by query joins and variable comparisons. $\mathcal{F}$ is created, such that $\forall F \in \mathcal{F}$, F indicates the elimination of one join or one variable comparison.

Example 8 *Assume the query* Q_{orig}*(lowestprice, distance):- Hotels (name, room#, rate, lowestprice) HotelLocation (name, lowestprice, location) Airport (aid, location, distance) and the views* V_1*(lowestprice, location):- Hotels (name, room#, rate, lowestprice) HotelLocation (name, lowestprice, location) and* V_2*(name, distance):- HotelLocation (name, lowestprice, location) Airport (aid, location, distance).* V_1 *and* V_2 *cannot be combined due to overlapping subgoals.*

Case 9: Views have contradictory constant constraints. Formally: If for $\mathcal{V}$ there is no $F(Q, V) \forall V \in \mathcal{V}$, then if there are $V_1, V_2 \in \mathcal{V}$ with contradictory constant constraints, i.e. $\phi(V_1.x) = a \neq b = \phi(V_2.x)$, then $\mathcal{F}_1 \equiv \mathcal{F}(Q, V_1)$ and $\mathcal{F}_2 \equiv \mathcal{F}(Q, V_2)$ are created such that each $F \in \mathcal{F}_1$ and $F \in \mathcal{F}_2$ eliminates a query join such that the mapping of x is not in $\phi_P(V_1), \phi_P(V_2)$.

Example 9 *Assume the query* Q_{orig}*(name, location):- Hotels (name, room#, rate, lowestprice) HotelLocation (name, lowestprice, location) and the views* V_1*(name):- Hotels (name, room#, rate, '500') and* V_2 *(name, location):- HotelLocation (name, '300', location).* V_1 *and* V_2 *cannot be combined due to contradictory constants.*

Case 10: Views have contradictory comparison constraints. Formally: If $\mathcal{V}$ is the set of views for which there is no $F(Q, V) \forall V \in \mathcal{V}$, then if there are $V_1, V_2 \in \mathcal{V}$ with contradictory comparison constraints, i.e. $\phi(V_1.(x.y)) \neq \phi(V_2.(x.y))$, then $\mathcal{F}_1 \equiv \mathcal{F}(Q, V_1)$ and $\mathcal{F}_2 \equiv \mathcal{F}(Q, V_2)$ are created such that each $F \in \mathcal{F}_1$ and $F \in \mathcal{F}_2$ eliminates a query join or a comparison so thatthe mapping of $x.y$ is not in $\phi_P(V_1), \phi_P(V_2)$.

Example 10 *Assume* Q_{orig}*(fno, carrier):- Flights(fno, depart, return, carrier, org, dest, price) and the views* V_1*(fno):- Flights (fno, depart, return, carrier, org, dest, price), price < '400',* V_2*(fno, carrier):- Flights(fno, depart, return, carrier, org, dest, price), price > '400'.* V_1 *and* V_2 *cannot be combined due to contradictory comparisons.*

Figures 4 and 5 show the procedures that produce the Fs.

4.2 Unification of views

The unification of LAV mappings is an optimization integrated in the procedure that preprocesses and rewrites the query. The classical query rewriting algorithms that employ LAV mappings require that each query subgoal has to be translated by a single mapping. Therefore, if this requirement cannot be satisfied, then the subgoal has to be eliminated from the query; however, it may be that a combination of LAV mappings can rewrite this subgoal.

We have developed a procedure that overcomes this kind of situations by combining LAV mappings that can, as a set, rewrite the

[1] Although ϕ and ϕ_P are formally defined for query subgoal variables, for simplicity of presentation, we use it loosely with other arguments too, such as a subgoal g and view V, meaning the overall mapping of g and V, respectively

Input: set of views $\mathcal{V}$, query Q
Output: set of Fs
begin
  $\mathcal{F} = \emptyset$;
  foreach *subgoal* $g \in Q$ **do**
    foreach *view* $V \in \mathcal{V}$ **do**
      foreach *subgoal* $u \in V$ **do**
        Let h be the least restrictive head homomorphism on V s.t. $\exists\, \phi | \phi(g) = h(u)$;
        if $h = null$ **then**
          foreach *join in which g participates and is not mapped in V* **do**
            Create F (case 1); $\mathcal{F} \cup F$;
        else Let $G = \{g\}$;
          Let the mapping until this point be ϕ;
          repeat
            if $necessary$ conditions hold, (Sec. 4.1.1) **then**
              Create Fs in the order (w.r.t. Sec. 4.1.1):;
              case 6; case 7; case 5; case 4; case 3; case 2;
              Create h_P;Create ϕ_P; Create G_P;
              Create D;$\mathcal{F} \cup F$;
          until *No extensions can be made*;
  return $\mathcal{F}$;

Figure 4: Create Fs for failed view mappings on the query

Input: set of views $\mathcal{V}$, query Q
Output: set of Fs $\mathcal{F}$
begin
  $\mathcal{F} = \emptyset$;
  foreach $\mathcal{V}' \subset \mathcal{V}$ *s.t. views in* $\mathcal{V}'$ *cover all Q-subgoals* **do**
    foreach $V_i, V_j \in \mathcal{V}', i \neq j$ **do**
      if V_i, V_j do not have overlapping subgoals **then**
        If V_i, V_j have compatible constants **then**
          If V_i, V_j have compatible comparisons**then**
            Consider V_i, V_j compatible;
          else Create $\mathcal{F}' = F_1, .., F_n$ (case 10);$\mathcal{F} \cup \mathcal{F}'$;
        else Create $\mathcal{F}' = F_1, .., F_n$ (case 9);$\mathcal{F} \cup \mathcal{F}'$;
      else Create $\mathcal{F}' = F_1, .., F_n$ (case 8);$\mathcal{F} \cup \mathcal{F}'$;
  return $\mathcal{F}$;

Figure 5: Create Fs for failed combinations of complete view mappings on the query

query subgoal. In detail, this procedure searches for LAV mappings, the head of which encompasses the key attributes of the subgoal. In this case, a simple join between the found LAV mappings can produce a new mapping that rewrites the complete subgoal. Figure 6 delineates the steps of this procedure. The unification of LAV mappings not only enables approximate query rewriting, but also *extends* classical query rewriting for the particular case in which a set of views can be completely mapped on the posed query, but the views cover overlapping subgoals, which can be joined on their key. Multiple occurrences of these subgoals are eliminated, as shown in the following example.

Example 11 *Assume a SQL query with a star select clause, written as follows in conjunctive form:*
Q^{conj}_{orig}*(vacid,fno, hid, from, until):- VacPackage(vacid,fno, hid, from, until)*
and the available views are:
V_1*(vacid, fno, hid):- VacPackage(vacid, fno, hid, from, until)*
V_2*(vacid, from, until):- VacPackage(vacid, fno, hid, from, until)*
The classical rewriting algorithms do not rewrite the above query, since the query subgoal is covered by both views. However, with view unification, the following view is produced:
$V_{1,2}$*(vacid,fno, hid, from, until) :-* V_1*(vacid, fno, hid)* V_2*(vacid, from, until)*
The above view can rewrite the query. The expansion of the view has a repeated subgoal self-joined on the key. Thus, the rewritten query is a classical rewriting.

Input: set of views $\mathcal{V}$, query Q_{orig}
Output: set of views $\mathcal{V}$
begin
  foreach *subgoal* g *of* Q_{orig} **do**
    $V_g = \emptyset$;
    $X_g = \emptyset$;
    foreach $V in \mathcal{V}$ **do**
      if the primary key of g is distinguished in V **then**
        Add V to V_g;
        foreach *attribute* x *of* g *in* Q^{SQL}_{orig} **do**
          if x is distinguished in V **then**
            Add x to X_g;
    Create subsets of V_g, V_{g_i}, for some i, such that:
    - All $V \in V_{g_i}$ have compatible constraints.;
    - Distinguished attributes of all $V \in V_{g_i}$ cover as many as possible attributes in X_g;
    foreach V_{g_i} **do**
      if $|V_{g_i}| > 1$ **then**
        Create new view $V_{new_i} = null$;
        Add to the distinguished variables of V_{new_i} all the distinguished variables of all $V \in V_{g_i}$;
        Add to the body of V_{new_i} the bodies of all $V \in V_{g_i}$;
        Merge (w.r.t. constraints) subgoals with the same predicate;
        Remove duplicate subgoals from V_{new_i};
    Add V_{new_i} to $\mathcal{V}$;
  return $\mathcal{V}$;

Figure 6: Unification of views

4.3 Approximate rewriting for comparisons

Solving the containment, and therefore, the rewriting of queries with comparison subgoals has been a challenging issue [2]. As stated in [23], there are some cases of queries with comparison predicates that can be rewritten using the available views, but are not, since the respective containment check fails. Specifically, these are the cases that even though the comparison cannot be rewritten by the available views (i.e. no appropriate distinguished variables or comparison predicates in the views), the comparison constraint is satisfied; Actually, the view entails a specific case of the comparison, i.e. a contained rewriting. These situations occur if the comparison includes an equation. Intuitively, an equation reduces the comparison to a join, which can be satisfied by the view. Classical query rewriting cannot make this reduction. However, the proposed approximate query answering technique, achieves to include this reduction, by relaxing the requirement for the comparison satisfaction. Even with this relaxation, the joins in the considered view may be able to rewrite the equation.

Example 12 *A query requests vacation packages the information of which is correct in the database, meaning that the 'from' date is before or on the 'until' date:* Q_{orig}*(vacid):- VacPackage(vacid, fno, hid, from, until), from* $\leq$ *until (let us assume that dates can be compared). Assume the following view that gives packages for one day is available to rewrite the query: V(vacid):- VacPackage(vacid, fno, hid, from, until) VacPackage(vacid fno, hid, until, from).*
Classical algorithms cannot rewrite Q_{orig} *using V because the comparison constraint cannot be satisfied. The approximate rewriting technique, however, relaxes the query by removing the comparison, and achieves to produce the classically contained rewriting:*
Q_{orig}*(vacid):- V(vacid)*

5. THE ALGORITHMS

In the following the algorithms that produce and rewrite the best Q_{apprx} of Q_{orig} with respect to a set of views $\mathcal{V}$ are presented.

```
Input: set of views V, query Q_orig
Output: best approx. rewriting Q^best_apprx and its M_sim value
begin
    Q^best_apprx = null;
    MaxSim = −∞;
    queue = ∅;
    Add Q_orig to queue;
    while queue ≠ ∅ do
        minQ_apprx = Q_apprx with min uncovered subgoals;
        Dequeue minQ_apprx;
        Run classical query rewriting for minQ_apprx;
        if minQ_apprx can be rewritten then
            if M_sim(Q_orig, minQ_apprx) > MaxSim then
                Q^best_apprx = minQ_apprx;
                MaxSim = M_sim(Q_orig, minQ_apprx);
        else
            foreach F created do
                Create the corresponding query Q_apprx_apprx;
                Add Q_apprx_apprx to queue;
    return Q^best_apprx, MaxSim;
```

Figure 7: The F Exhaustive algorithm

5.1 Exploring approximations

In order to produce an approximate rewriting of Q_{orig} it is necessary to navigate through the possible approximate versions of it. Imagine a tree of approximate versions of Q_{orig} where each node has one query element less than its father. Specifically, the root of the tree is Q_{orig}; the children of the root correspond to approximations of Q_{orig} where a single query element is missing. The number of the nodes of the 1st level is equal to the number of query elements in Q_{orig}. Each one corresponds to a Q_{apprx} which contains all the elements of Q_{orig} minus 1. Similarly, the children of the kth level contain $n-k-1$ elements of Q_{orig}, which are all the elements of their father minus 1. The total number of nodes on the kth level is $n!/(n-k)!$. The total number of nodes is quite big with respect to n: $e\Gamma(n+1,1)$. Leaf nodes correspond to empty Q_{apprx}. It is obvious that more than one tree nodes correspond to the same Q_{apprx}. Consequently, there are subtrees that are repeated in the tree. Pruning the repeated subtrees results in a (non-balanced) tree with 2^n nodes for a Q_{orig} with n elements.

A straightforward approach in order to explore query approximations and their rewritings, is to create the tree of approximations and run a classical rewriting algorithm for each of the distinct nodes of this tree. Then, we can compare the rewritings produced by each such execution and find the best approximation Q_{apprx}. In detail, for a Q_{orig} of n subgoals, the employment of a classical rewriting algorithm in the above manner has to check $O(2^n)$ Q_{apprx} versions, as follows: (1) produce all possible Q_{apprx}, (2) order them in descending manner with respect to their similarity to Q_{orig}, and (3) check them iteratively until an output, i.e. a complete rewriting, can be produced. We call this the *Simple Exhaustive* algorithm and we use it as a reference for comparison to the algorithms that are proposed in the following and that are guided by the creation of F structures, as shown in Figure 2. *Simple Exhaustive* is quite expensive, mainly because of step (1), which has to produce all the nodes of the search tree described above and prune repeated subtrees. The complexity of *Simple Exhaustive* is $O(e \cdot \Gamma(n+1,1))$.

5.2 The F Exhaustive algorithm

Employing the structures Fs, we can explore the tree of possible query approximations, such that far fewer nodes are visited than those that are visited in a straightforward manner with the *Simple Exhaustive* algorithm. Essentially, Fs can guide the exploration to the subtrees that contain approximations which are (a) possible with respect to the available views as well as (b) necessary with respect to the failures of mapping the available views on the query. Exploration is cheaper (i.e. it visits fewer tree nodes) because guided by Fs we can prune the subtrees such that approximated queries that are missing elements which can be rewritten by combinations of complete view mappings are not visited. Figure 7 presents the F *Exhaustive* algorithm that explores the possible approximations guided by Fs. Briefly, the algorithm proceeds as follows: First the algorithm computes the initial set of complete view mappings; if this set of views is not able to thoroughly rewrite Q_{orig}, it creates the tree of Fs (and not the tree of possible approximations). Each edge of this tree corresponds to a F and each node to the Q_{apprx} produced by the path of Fs that leads to it from the root. The tree is created as follows: Initially, the approximation similarity $MaxSim$ is set to minimum and all the necessary Fs are created and form the set $\mathcal{F}$. For each $F \in \mathcal{F}$ the respective Q_{apprx} is created and if its similarity is higher than the current value of $MaxSim$, search explores more this possible approximation. The algorithm iterates on this F by reseting the set $\mathcal{V}$ and running a classical rewriting algorithm on Q_{apprx} (note that steps 6-9 of Figure 2 are suitably merged for efficiency). In case of failure, the procedure starts from the beginning by computing the new Fs and adding them to $\mathcal{F}$. Since F *Exhaustive* searches guided by the F tree and not by the tree of approximations, its complexity is $O(|\mathcal{F}|)$, where $\mathcal{F}$ is the set of possible Fs. The latter are far fewer than the number of possible approximations and in general it holds that their number is proportional to the number of available views $|\mathcal{F}| \propto |\mathcal{V}|$. In practice the number of views is far smaller than the size of the approximation tree, thus, $O(|\mathcal{V}|) < O(e \cdot \Gamma(n+1,1))$, or the number of possible approximations.

Theorem 1 *The search space of* F Exhaustive *is a subset of the search space of* Simple Exhaustive.

Sketch of proof: Assume a Q_{apprx} that corresponds to a F with some $D = \{x\}$. Then Q_{apprx} is missing a query element corresponding to x. x represents the point of failure during the mapping of a view $V \in \mathcal{V}$ and to a query Q that is either Q_{orig} or an approximation of it Q'_{apprx}. Q'_{apprx} has a subset of the query elements of Q_{orig}. Thus, the mapping of V on Q'_{apprx} can fail in a subset of the possible points of failure of the mapping of V on Q_{orig}. The possible points of failure of the mapping of V created for Q_{orig} correspond to a subset of all the query elements; let us call it $\mathcal{E}_V$. The union of the $\mathcal{E}_V$ for all $V \in \mathcal{V}$, called $\mathcal{E}_\mathcal{V}$ is a subset of all the query elements of Q_{orig}. Therefore, if a Q_{apprx} is missing an element that is not in $\mathcal{E}_\mathcal{V}$, it is not in the search space of F *Exhaustive*. On the opposite, the search space of *Simple Exhaustive* contains all the possible Q_{apprx}.

Intuitively, the search space of F *Exhaustive* is much smaller than that of *Simple Exhaustive* because the first contains only the Q_{apprx} that are missing query elements that cannot be rewritten employing the available views, whereas the second contains all the possible Q_{apprx}. The following is an intuitive example.

Example 13 *Assume the query:*

Q^{SQL}_{orig}: ***SELECT*** H. name
FROM Hotels H, HotelLocation HL, SeasonPrices SP
WHERE H.name = HL.name ***AND*** HL.lowestprice = SP.lowestprice
AND SP.season = "spring" ***AND*** HL.location = "sea"

written in conjunctive form as:
Q^{conj}_{orig} *(name):- Hotels (name, room#, rate, lowestprice1) HotelLocation (name, lowestprice, 'sea') SeasonPrices('spring', lowestprice).*
Q^{SQL}_{orig} *has 5 elements and therefore the total number of distinct*

```
Input: set of views 𝒱, query Q_orig
Output: best approx. rewriting Q^best_apprx and its M_sim value
begin
  Q^best_apprx = null;
  MaxSim = −∞;
  queue = ∅;
  queue_children = ∅;
  Add Q_orig to queue;
  while queue ≠ ∅ do
    𝒬_apprx = all Q_apprx with min uncovered subgoals;
    while 𝒬_apprx ≠ ∅ do
      Select minQ_apprx with max M_sim(Q_orig, Q_apprx);
      Remove minQ_apprx from 𝒬_apprx;
      Run classical query rewriting for minQ_apprx;
      if M_sim(Q_orig, minQ_apprx) > MaxSim then
        if minQ_apprx can be rewritten by MiniCon then
          Q^best_apprx = minQ_apprx;
          MaxSim = M_sim(Qorig, minQ_apprx);
          return Q^best_apprx, MaxSim;
        else foreach F created do
          Create the corresponding query Q_apprx_apprx;
          Add Q_apprx_apprx to queue_children;
    queue = queue_children;
    queue_children = ∅;
  return Q^best_apprx, MaxSim;
```

Figure 8: The F $B\&B$ algorithm

approximations is 32 *and the size of the approximation tree is* 205. *Assume that the available views are:*

V_1 (name, lowestprice) :- Hotels (name, room#, rate, lowestprice) HotelLocation (name, lowestprice, 'sea') and

V_2 (lowestprice) :- SeasonPrices (season, lowestprice).

V_1 has a complete mapping on Q and therefore we do not need to examine approximations that miss elements that can be satisfied by V_1, i.e. the 'select' attribute, the condition $HL.location =$ "sea" and the join $H.name = HL.name$. V_2 has a partial mapping that creates an F with $D = \{$"spring"$\}$. This is the only F created, and examined for produced approximations, since the combination of the complete mapping of V_1 and the partial mapping of V_2 cover the remaining element $HL.lowestprice = SP.lowestprice$.

Theorem 2 F Exhaustive *is complete, i.e. it finds the Q_{apprx} with the maximal $MaxSim$.*

Sketch of proof: We have to prove that the Q_{apprx} with the maximal $MaxSim$ is in the search space of *F Exhaustive*. Assume that Q_{apprx_1} and Q_{apprx_2} are the approximate queries with the maximal $MaxSim$ in the search space of *F Exhaustive* and *Simple Exhaustive*, respectively. If $Q_{apprx_1} \not\equiv Q_{apprx_2}$, then Q_{apprx_1} is missing a query element $E \in \mathcal{E}_{orig}$ and therefore E corresponds to a $D = \{x\}$ of a $F \in \mathcal{F}$. Thus, F has been considered by *F Exhaustive* and the best approximate query following F has been compared to Q_{apprx_1} and rejected. Therefore if E is in Q_{apprx_2} then E is in Q_{apprx_1}. The opposite holds because Q_{apprx_2} is by default the best possible approximation. Therefore $Q_{apprx_1} \equiv Q_{apprx_2}$.

Intuitively, *F Exhaustive* is complete because the best Q_{apprx} is missing only elements of Q_{orig} that constitute points of failure of mapping views on Q_{orig}; all of these points are explored by the produced Fs. Thus, the best Q_{apprx} is in the search space of the algorithm. Since the latter is exhaustive, it finds the best Q_{apprx}.

The set of $\mathcal{F}$ in *F Exhaustive* is augmented in each iteration and one $F \in \mathcal{F}$ is selected for examination. To improve efficiency, we reorder the $\mathcal{F}$ before each iteration with respect to a heuristic criterion that is based on the notion of *uncovered subgoals*:

Definition 2 *With respect to a set of views $\mathcal{V}$ and their complete mappings $\phi(\mathcal{V})$ on the query Q_{orig}, the* uncovered subgoals *of Q_{orig} is the set of the subgoals that cannot be covered by any mapping in $\phi(\mathcal{V})$.*

The heuristic criterion Cr_1 is defined as follows:

Definition 3 *Create an ascending order of all $F \in \mathcal{F}$ with respect to the number of uncovered subgoals of Q_{orig} that cannot be covered by each F.*

Criterion Cr_1 dictates that the more *uncovered subgoals* can be covered by the considered F, the greater the possibility that the view mapping to be created after relaxing the query according to F will achieve the rewriting of currently not covered subgoals of Q_{orig}. The F that does not cover few *uncovered subgoals* leads to a view mapping on the respective Q_{apprx} that covers many of the query elements that cannot be covered by all existing mappings $\phi(\mathcal{V})$ for Q_{orig}. The more these query elements are, the fewer are left that could not be covered by the available views and demand the exploration of approximations. Using Cr_1 *F Exhaustive* achieves to explore the Q_{apprx} with a high $MaxSim$ first, such that a big part of the F tree is not visited, making the algorithm very efficient as shown in Section 6.

5.3 The F $B\&B$ algorithm

Even though the search space of the *F Exhaustive* is much smaller than that of the *Simple Exhaustive*, the exhaustive traversal of the F tree can be very expensive. Thus, we propose a method that prunes the tree such that a partial traversal of it is still eligible to produce a Q_{apprx} close, in terms of query similarity, to the best possible one. The following heuristic criterion, Cr_2, is used complementary to criterion Cr_1 so that such a pruning is achieved.

Definition 4 *Create a descending order of all $F \in \mathcal{F}$ with respect to the similarity of Q_{apprx} to Q_{orig}, where Q_{apprx} is the approximation produced employing F.*

Orthogonally to Cr_1, Cr_2 denotes that the better the approximation of Q_{orig} produced according to the considered F, the bigger the possibility that F leads to the production of the best approximation of Q_{orig}. Oppositely to Cr_1, Cr_2 is optimistic and judges the possibility of achieving the approximate query rewriting based on the query elements that *are* covered by the considered F.

The combination of Cr_1 and Cr_2 forms the branch-and-bound version of the *F Exhaustive*, that we call the *F B&B* algorithm. This algorithm is presented in Figure 8 and, briefly, it proceeds as follows: At each iteration that a view mapping fails, the children nodes corresponding to appropriate Fs are created and are ordered based on the values of Cr_1; The Fs that lead to query approximations that are of different similarity to Q_{orig} but are in the same partial order according to Cr_1, are ordered based on Cr_2. The combination of Cr_1 and Cr_2 that gives the lead to the first and refines the search with the second is adequate to guarantee a near-optimal query rewriting approximation, as shown in Section 6.

6. EXPERIMENTAL STUDY

In what follows, we present the experimental evaluation of producing approximate versions of Q_{orig} using a set of views $\mathcal{V}$.

6.1 Experimental Setup

Methodology. The proposed algorithms, *F Exhaustive* and *F B&B*, are compared against *Simple Exhaustive* with respect to their execution time. For *F B&B* the similarity difference (denoted as "approximation error") of the computed approximation against the optimal approximation, (computed by both *F Exhaustive* and *Simple*

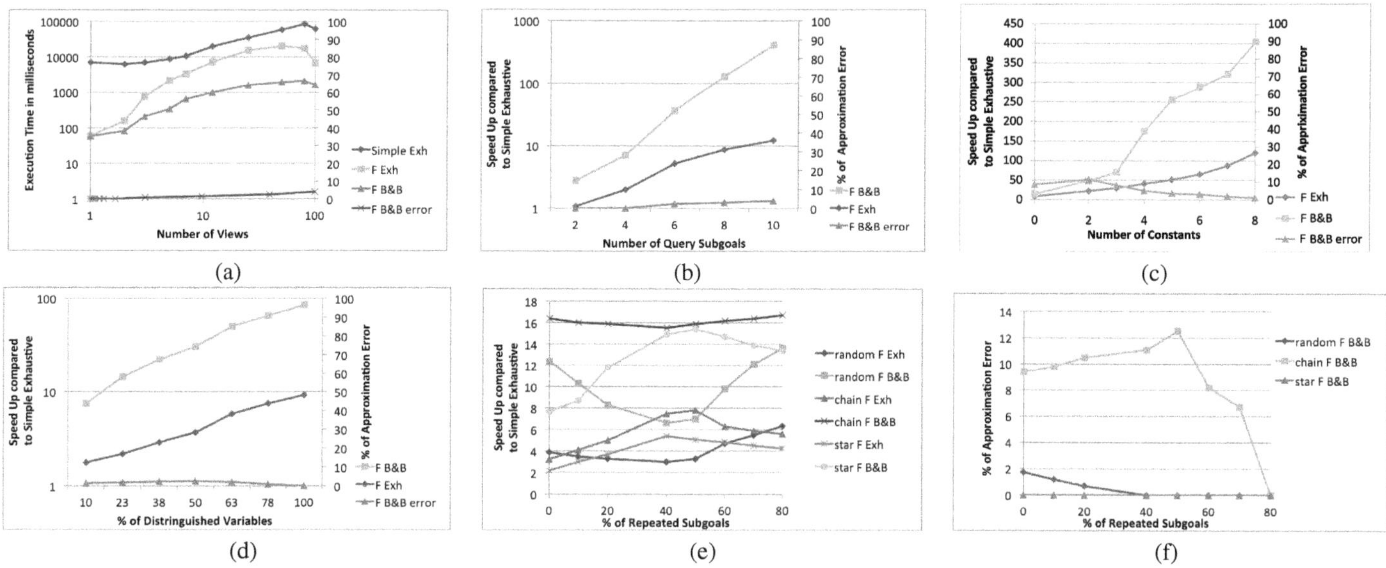

Figure 9: Results for execution time of F *B&B* and F *Exhaustive* and approximation error of F *B&B*

Exhaustive) is measured. In the graphs, the "F *B&B* error" lines refer to the scale on the right and the rest lines refer to the scale on the left (if there are two vertical axes). Among all classical query rewriting algorithms we have used for the implementation of the algorithms and the experimentation with the proposed approximate query rewriting technique the MiniCon algorithm [23], which is the latest and most efficient of the well-known ones. As stated before, defining a query similarity measure is an orthogonal problem to finding query approximations. In the experiments we employ one of the query similarity measures presented in [11] as follows:

$$M_{sim_1}(Q_{orig}, Q_{apprx}) = \sum w_i \cdot |sat(E_i, E_i')| / \sum w_i \quad (1)$$

This measure confines the similarity of two queries by the similarity of their elements. E_i's are elements ('select' values or 'where' conditions) of Q_{orig}, E_i''s are the respective elements of Q_{apprx}, and $\sum w_i = 1$. The function $sat(E_i, E_i')$ captures the notion of E_i represented by E_i' and for this work is either 0 or 1.

Datasets. The experiments are performed on synthetic data, following the example of works in query rewriting using views [16, 23, 26]. Synthetic data give the opportunity to control the form/size of Q_{orig} and the set of views $\mathcal{V}$; therefore, it enables the case-study of a big variety of query-views combinations, that cannot be found in real datasets. The parameters of the algorithms are plenty. For both the query and the views: number of subgoals, number of distinguished variables, number of repeated subgoals, shape (random, star and chain queries for repeated subgoals), presence of arithmetic comparisons; More parameters are: the number of views, query-views shape and size combinations, as well as different similarity functions. The number of parameters prohibits the presentation of the thorough experimental study due to lack of space. In the following the most important and interesting experiments are described. If not fluctuated, the following parameter values are used. Number of: relations = 10, views = 10, view subgoals = 4, query subgoals = 5, repeated query subgoals = 2, query constants = 1, view distinguished variables = 2, view joins = 3, view constants = 3, view comparisons = 3; query form = "random", query distinguished variables = 20%, .

6.2 Experimental Results

Figure 9 shows graphically the experimental results, which are commented in the following.

6.2.1 *Number of views*

Figure 9(a) shows the results for random queries and views as the number of views increases. F *Exhaustive* starts with being 100 times faster from *Simple Exhaustive*, and this difference shrinks but remains substantial for bigger number of views. F *Exhaustive* performs exceptionally for a low number of views compared to *Simple Exhaustive*, because the search in F *Exhaustive* is guided by the views, (i.e. only query parts that cannot be rewritten based on the (few) views are examined for elimination), whereas *Simple Exhaustive*, is guided by approximate query versions; even though it checks approximation with increasing approximation cost, the small number of views results in the consideration of many query elements for elimination, and therefore, of an exponential number of approximate query versions. Since the rewriting of a query based only on a few (less than 5) views is expected to be a common case in real situations, using F *Exhaustive* gives a big advantage. Both algorithms perform much better for a very big (> 90) number of views. The reason is that in this case, most frequently, the query can be rewritten with very few eliminations. The relative performance of F *Exhaustive* increases because it easily finds the appropriate eliminations. F *B&B* is steadily 1000 faster than *Simple Exhaustive* achieving a very low approximations error ($< 4\%$), which makes it very competitive to F *Exhaustive*.

6.2.2 *Number of query elements*

Figures 9(b), (c) and (d) shows the results varying the number of query elements, i.e. the distinguished variables (the 'select' attributes) and the constraints (i.e. where conditions: joins and variable comparisons, comparisons with constants). Overall, the efficiency of the algorithms steadily increases as the query size increases. *Simple Exhaustive* is affected exponentially by the query size, since each additional element adds combinations with all the rest to the set of possible approximations. However, since the creation of Fs is not based on query elements, but on query - view combinations, the number of Fs is not affected so radically by the increase in the number of query elements. Both algorithms become more efficient for larger queries.

Number of subgoals. Figure 9(b) shows the results for random queries and views as the number of query subgoals increases. The efficiency of both the F algorithms increases with the number of subgoals. The approximation error of F *B&B* increases with an ex-

tremely low rate with the number of subgoals. Naturally, the bigger the number of subgoals the bigger the number of joins, which slightly but consistently affects the refined pruning of *B&B*.
Number of constants. Figure 9(c) shows the results while increasing the number of constants in the query. The efficiency of the algorithms increases with a slightly bigger rate than the respective rate for increasing number of subgoals. The satisfaction of constant constraints is uncorrelated to the satisfaction or not of the rest of the constraints (joins between subgoals), because they do not participate in join pools. *F B&B* shows a very small approximation error that is reduced as the number of constants increases.
Number of distinguished variables Similarly, the results for increasing number of distinguished variables, (Figure 9(d)), show an even bigger rate of efficiency increment: the satisfaction of a distinguished variable is independent from the satisfaction of the rest query elements. Thus, the algorithms insist on specific search paths and examine a restricted number of Fs. The behavior of the approximation cost is between the one for increasing number of constants and the one for subgoals. *F B&B* is really benefitted by the independence of the satisfaction of distinguished variables.

6.2.3 Number of repeated subgoals

Figures 9(e),(f) present the results for queries with a constant number of elements, but with increasing repeated subgoals (i.e. self-joins). These experiments focus on the role of the query shape: random, chain and star [23,26]. Overall, repeated subgoals increase the dependency of query constraints: because of the self-joins, a view may be able to rewrite a big number of query elements if it satisfies one of them, or the opposite.
Random queries. The results for random queries show that a percentage of 40% of repeated subgoals affects negatively the efficiency of the algorithms: they have to satisfy a big number of tightly dependent subgoals and a similar number of non-related to them subgoals. On the opposite, a small or big percentage of repeated subgoals either weakens or strengthens the effect of their dependance, leading the algorithm either to shortly leave a bad or stick to a good search path. *F B&B* achieves a zero approximation error for queries with more than 25% repeated subgoals.
Star queries. The results for star queries are harsher than in the case of random queries. Star queries indicate intensively to Fs which constraints should be eliminated. The presence of repeated subgoals reinforces the possible choice of a subset of approximations, reducing the occurrences of backtracking in search space.
Chain queries. Oppositely to star, chain queries may create more approximations, because the satisfaction of constraints is primarily led by the join chain, which gradually indicates the options for approximation in each algorithm iteration. Efficiency results are smoother than those for random or star queries. Repeated subgoals, reinforce some of the approximation options and reduce the error.

6.2.4 Overall experimental conclusions

Overall, *F Exhaustive* is considerably faster than *Simple Exhaustive* and their speed difference is substantial for the important situations of few views or big queries (in terms of number of elements). *F B&B* is much faster than *F Exhaustive* and keeps a steady or even increasing rate of speed up with respect to *Simple Exhaustive*. The heuristic of *F B&B* is very efficient and the approximation error is generally much lower than 10%. Chain queries are the hardest to handle with *F B&B*.

7. CONCLUSIONS

We tackle the problem of approximate query answering in environments of autonomous and heterogeneous sources and we propose a query relaxation technique that extends traditional query answering. The technique comprises algorithms that search for the best approximation and employ as a black box a query similarity function. The experiments prove the efficiency of the algorithms.

Acknowledgments

This research has funding from the EU Seventh Framework Programme (FP7/2007-2013), Grant Agreement n° 619706 ASAP.

8. REFERENCES

[1] S. Acharya, P. B. Gibbons, V. Poosala, and S. Ramaswamy. The aqua approximate query answering system. In *SIGMOD*, 1999.
[2] F. Afrati, C. Li, and P. Mitra. Answering Queries Using Views with Arithmentic Comparisons. In *21th ACM PODS*, 2002.
[3] S. Agrawal, S. Chaudhuri, G. Das, and A. Gionis. Automated Ranking of Database Query Results. In *CIDR*, 2003.
[4] K. C.-C. Chang and H. Garcia-Molina. Approximate query mapping: Accounting for translation closeness. *VLDB J.*, 10(2-3), 2001.
[5] S. Chaudhuri and P. G. Kolaitis. Can datalog be approximated? In *PODS*, 1994.
[6] W. Cohen. Integration of Heterogeneous Databases Without Common Domains Using Queries Based on Textual Similarity. In *SIGMOD*, 1998.
[7] M. de Rougemont and A. Vieilleribière. Approximate data exchange. In *ICDT*, pages 44–58, 2007.
[8] O. M. Duschka and M. R. Genesereth. Answering Recursive Queries Using Views. In *16th ACM PODS*, 1997.
[9] R. Fagin, P. G. Kolaitis, R. J. Miller, and L. Popa. Data exchange: semantics and query answering. *Theor. Comput. Sci.*, 336(1), 2005.
[10] A. Fuxman and R. J. Miller. First-order query rewriting for inconsistent databases. *J. Comput. Syst. Sci.*, 73(4):610–635, 2007.
[11] V. Kantere, D. Tsoumakos, T. Sellis, and N. Roussopoulos. Groupeer: Dynamic clustering of p2p databases. *Inf. Syst.*, 34(1):62–86, 2009.
[12] W. Kieling and G. Kostner. Preference SQL - Design, Implementation, Experiences . In *VLDB*, 2002.
[13] M. Lenzerini. Data Integration: A Theoretical Perspective. In *21th ACM PODS*, 2002.
[14] A. Y. Levy. Answering Queries Using Views: A Survey. In *VLDB Journal*, 2001.
[15] A. Y. Levy, A. Rajaraman, and J. O. Ordille. Query-answering Algorithms for Information Agents. In *13th International Conference on Artificila Intelligence*, 1996.
[16] V. Lín, V. Vassalos, and P. Malakasiotis. Minicount: Efficient rewriting of count-queries using views. In *ICDE*, page 1, 2006.
[17] J. Madhavan and A. Y. Halevy. Composing mappings among data sources. In *VLDB*, pages 572–583, 2003.
[18] P. Mitra. An Algorithm for Answering Queries Efficiently Using Views. In *Australesian Database Conference*, 2001.
[19] I. Muslea and T. J. Lee. Online query relaxation via bayesian causal structures discovery. In *AAAI*, pages 831–836, 2005.
[20] U. Nambiar and S. Kambhampati. Answering imprecise queries over autonomous web databases. In *ICDE*, page 45, 2006.
[21] N. Polyzotis, M. N. Garofalakis, and Y. E. Ioannidis. Approximate xml query answers. In *SIGMOD Conference*, pages 263–274, 2004.
[22] V. Poosala and V. Ganti. Fast approximate query answering using precomputed statistics. In *ICDE*, page 252, 1999.
[23] R. Pottinger and A. Levy. A Scalable Algorithm for Answering Queries Using Views. In *VLDB*, 2000.
[24] P. Rodríguez-Gianolli, A. Kementsietsidis, M. Garzetti, I. Kiringa, L. Jiang, M. Masud, R. J. Miller, and J. Mylopoulos. Data sharing in the hyperion peer database system. In *VLDB*, 2005.
[25] J. Spiegel, E. D. Pontikakis, S. Budalakoti, and N. Polyzotis. Aqax: A system for approximate xml query answers. In *VLDB*, pages 1159–1162, 2006.
[26] M. Steinbrunn, G. Moerkotte, and A. Kemper. Heuristic and randomized optimization for the join ordering problem. *VLDB J.*, 6(3):191–208, 1997.
[27] G. Wolf, H. Khatri, B. Chokshi, J. Fan, Y. Chen, and S. Kambhampati. Query processing over incomplete autonomous databases. In *VLDB*, pages 651–662, 2007.

Approximated Summarization of Data Provenance

Eleanor Ainy
Tel Aviv University
eleanora@mail.tau.ac.il

Pierre Bourhis
CNRS CRIsTAL UMR 9189
pierre.bourhis@univ-lille1.fr

Susan B. Davidson
University of Pennsylvania
susan@cis.upenn.edu

Daniel Deutch
Tel Aviv University
danielde@post.tau.ac.il

Tova Milo
Tel Aviv University
milo@post.tau.ac.il

ABSTRACT

Many modern applications involve collecting large amounts of data from multiple sources, and then aggregating and manipulating it in intricate ways. The complexity of such applications, combined with the size of the collected data, makes it difficult to understand how the resulting information was derived. *Data provenance* has proven helpful in this respect, however, maintaining and presenting the full and exact provenance information may be infeasible due to its size and complexity. We therefore introduce the notion of *approximated summarized provenance*, which provides a compact representation of the provenance at the possible cost of information loss. Based on this notion, we present a novel provenance summarization algorithm which, based on the semantics of the underlying data and the intended use of provenance, outputs a summary of the input provenance. Experiments measure the conciseness and accuracy of the resulting provenance summaries, and improvement in provenance usage time.

Categories and Subject Descriptors

H.2 [**Database Management**]: Miscellaneous; I.1.1 [**Symbolic and Algebraic Manipulation**]: Expressions and Their Representation—*representations (general and polynomial), simplification of expressions*

Keywords

Provenance;Provisioning;Crowd-sourcing applications

1. INTRODUCTION

Complex applications that collect, store and aggregate large-scale data, and interact with a large number of users, are found in a wide variety of domains. Notable examples are *crowd-sourcing applications* such as Wikipedia, social tagging systems for images, traffic information aggregators such as Waze, or hotel and movie ratings such as TripAdvisor and IMDb.

In the context of such applications, several questions arise related to *how data was derived*. As a user of the information, what is the basis for trusting it? How do contributions vary among crowd members based on characteristics such as age or gender? If some contribution seems wrong, how does the information change if we discard it? These questions are fundamentally important to better understand the application and its results.

At its core, the answer to these questions is based on the *provenance* of the collected data and resulting information, that is, *who* provided the data in *what* context and *how* the information was derived. However, provenance goes well beyond simply providing a log of the application execution. In particular, the algebraic model of provenance based on semirings of [21, 7] can be used to *explain* results by correlating input with output data, and tracking important details of the computational process that took place. As shown in [17], it can also be used to *provision* the result with respect to hypothetical scenarios, i.e. to observe changes to the result based on changes to the input without re-running the process. Detailed tracking of provenance is therefore an essential vehicle for the applications mentioned above.

As an example, consider a crowd-sourced application for movie reviews, where the number of movies, and number of reviews for each movie, may be very large. An *aggregated score* for each movie is computed by combining the scores of multiple different users, possibly accounting for their previous reviews and for their preferences. These features, and the way in which they are used in the computation, should all be reflected in the provenance. In turn, this provenance may be presented to explain results such as the computed recommendations of movies, or to provision them, e.g. to determine how the average movie rating would change if we ignore ratings by some group of users.

Unfortunately, the large amount of data and complexity of processing the data means that the resulting detailed provenance information can be overwhelming. Presenting it in full, as an explanation for a computation, may make it extremely hard for users to understand. In this paper we therefore introduce the notion of *approximated summarized provenance*, which provides a compact representation of provenance at the possible cost of information loss. This compact representation will enable the user to see trends, for example that women aged 20-25 tended to rate a particular movie more highly than men aged 20-25.

CIKM'15, October 19–23, 2015, Melbourne, VIC, Australia.
© 2015 ACM. ISBN 978-1-4503-3794-6/15/10 ...$15.00.
DOI: http://dx.doi.org/10.1145/2806416.2806429.

Contributions. We present a novel algorithm that provides approximated summarization of provenance information for complex applications. The summarization is based in part on the semantics of the underlying data (such as gender, age or occupation of users), where annotations of "similar" data items are intuitively more amenable to be grouped together. More importantly, it is also geared towards the intended use of provenance (namely explanation and/or provisioning): we define a distance function between provenance expressions that is based on the intended use, and optimizing this distance while still obtaining small expressions guides the summarization. We have conducted experiments with three datasets - MovieLens, Wikipedia and DDP (Data Dependent Process), in which we compared our algorithm to other approaches and showed that our approach gives better summarizations in terms of distance and size.

Paper Organization. The rest of the paper is organized as follows. Section 2 describes workflow provenance and the provenance model. Section 3 describes the notion of provenance summarization through mappings and the quality measurements for such summarization. In section 4 we present a few propositions that, combined together, lead to our summarization algorithm. We end this section with an example of the full algorithm flow. Section 5 describes the datasets we used and also includes interesting use cases. We later describe our experimental results in section 6. Finally, related work and conclusions are discussed in Section 7.

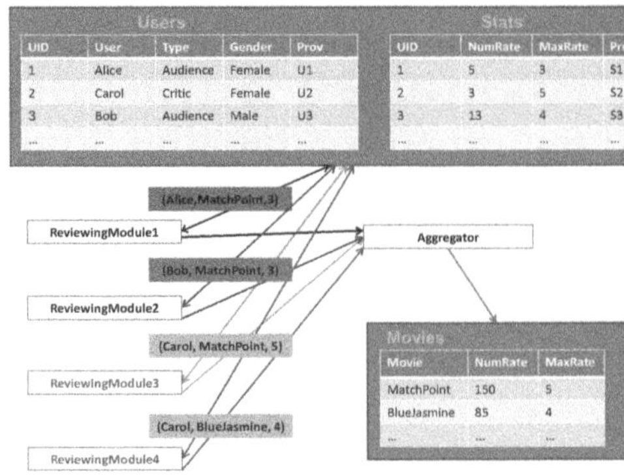

Figure 1: Example Workflow

2. MODEL DESCRIPTION

We now give an overview of the semiring provenance model of [21], and its extension to queries with aggregates in [8, 7]. This will serve as the basis for our work.

2.1 Workflows

We capture applications logic by a standard notion of workflows. One possible model for workflow [15, 7] consists of a specification and an associated set of executions. The specification can be thought of as an FSM (Finite State Machine), in which modules represent processing steps and edges indicate potential dataflow between the output port of one module to the input port of another module. In the model of [7], the workflow operates in the context of some global persistent state, i.e. some underlying database. Modules may be atomic, meaning that they are a query on the inputs to the module as well as the underlying database. Modules can also update the underlying database. A workflow *execution* (or "run") is a repeated application of modules, which are ordered according to the workflow specification. [1]

EXAMPLE 2.1. *Consider a movie rating application, in which users rate movies and the ratings are aggregated using the application logic described by the workflow in Figure 1.*

Certain information about users is known, such as gender and type (movie critic, director, audience, etc.), and stored in the Users *table in the underlying database.*

Reviews are collected by different reviewing modules, which crawl different reviewing platforms such as IMDb and newspaper web-sites. Each such module updates statistics in the Stats *table in the underlying database, e.g. how many reviews the user has submitted (*NumRate*), what their max score is (*MaxRate*), etc. (alternatively, we could use sum or any other aggregation function). A reviewing module also consults* Stats *to output a* sanitized review *by implementing some logic. The sanitized reviews are then fed to an aggregator, which computes an aggregate movies scores.*

There are many plausible logics for the reviewing modules; we exemplify one in which each module sanitizes the reviews by joining the users and statistics relations (depending on the module), keeping only reviews of users listed under the corresponding role (audience/critic) and who are "active", i.e. who have submitted more than 2 reviews. The aggregator combines the reviews obtained from all modules to compute overall movie ratings (num, max).

[1]This departs from the representation of executions and their provenance as multigraphs in [15]

2.2 Provenance Model

We next explain in general what a provenance model is and then use examples to illustrate the concepts described. We start by fixing a finite set *Ann* of *provenance annotations*, corresponding to the basic units of data manipulated by the application, and which can be thought of as abstract variables identifying the data. Depending on the application, these annotations may correspond to different tuples in a database, to different users, to different questions, etc.

A correspondence between data manipulation and algebraic operations in the structure of a *commutative semiring* can then be defined. A *commutative semiring* is a structure $(K, +_K, \cdot_K, 0_K, 1_K)$ where $(K, +_K, 0_K)$ and $(K, \cdot_K, 1_K)$ are commutative monoids. This means that the operations are associative and commutative with 0 and 1 standing for the neutral elements for addition and multiplication, respectively. In addition, $\cdot_K$ is distributive over $+_K$, and $a \cdot_K 0_K = 0 \cdot_K a = 0_K$.

Given our set *Ann* of basic provenance annotations, the *provenance semiring* is the semiring of polynomials with natural coefficients, with indeterminates from the set *Ann*. It is denoted $(N[Ann], +, \cdot, 0, 1)$, and was shown in [21] to capture provenance for positive relational queries. Intuitively, the $+$ operation corresponds to the *alternative use* of data (as in union and projection) and $\cdot$ to the *joint use* of data (as in join); 1 annotates data that is present, and 0 annotates data that is absent.

To capture aggregate queries, K-relations were further generalized by extending their data domain with *aggregated values* [8]. In this extended framework, relations have provenance also as part of their values, rather than just in the tuple annotations. Such a value is a *formal sum* $\sum_i t_i \otimes v_i$, where v_i is the value of the aggregated attribute in the ith tuple, while t_i is the provenance of that tuple. We can think of $\otimes$ as an operation that pairs values (from a monoid M) with provenance annotations. Each such pair is called a *tensor*. The formal sum, presented by the $\oplus$ operation is used to capture the aggregation function.

In [8, 17] the framework was also used to define provenance for *nested aggregates* and *negation* by introducing equation and inequality elements. Intuitively an equation such as $[(d_1 \cdot d_2) \otimes m > 3]$ is kept as an abstract token and can be used in conjunction with other semiring elements. Given concrete values for d_1, d_2 and m one may test the truth value of the equality and replace the equation by the truth value [2]. A precise algebraic treatment of aggregated values and the equivalence laws that govern them is based on semimodules and is described in [8]. We will focus, for simplicity, on the case where the values monoid M is that of real numbers with numbers addition and 0.

EXAMPLE 2.2. *The basic provenance annotation set Ann consists here of* $U_1, ..., S_1, ...$
The provenance-aware value stored as MaxRate *in the aggregator's output table, the Movies table, for the "MatchPoint" tuple would be:*

$$\boldsymbol{P} = U_1 \cdot [S_1 \cdot U_1 \otimes 5 > 2] \otimes (3,1) \oplus$$
$$U_2 \cdot [S_2 \cdot U_2 \otimes 3 > 2] \otimes (5,1) \oplus$$
$$U_3 \cdot [S_3 \cdot U_3 \otimes 13 > 2] \otimes (3,1) \oplus ...$$

where U_i is a user identifier, S_i is the provenance of the user's Stats tuple, and as aggregation we use a monoid of pairs to capture the aggregated rating (MAX with value 3 in the first tensor) and how many users contributed to this value (1 per tensor here but we will next show examples with other values). Intuitively, each rating is associated with the provenance of the tuple obtained as the output of the reviewing module, namely the U_i annotation identifying the user. Each such sub-expression is multiplied by an inequality term serving as a conditional guard, indicating that the number of reviews recorded for the user is above the threshold of 2. Applying aggregation then results in coupling values (numeric reviews) with annotations to form the expression above.

2.3 Valuations and Provisioning

An important use of semiring provenance is for *provisioning*, i.e. examining changes to the application's execution that are the result of some hypothetical modifications to the data (e.g. "How would the movie ratings change if we ignore some reviews suspected as spam?"). This is formalized in [21] through the notion of *truth valuations* applied to annotations. Intuitively, specifying that U_1 is a spammer corresponds to mapping it to $false$ (and that U_1 is reliable to mapping it to $true$), and recomputing the derived value w.r.t this valuation. Such valuation can again be extended in the standard way to a valuation $V : N[Ann] \mapsto \{true, false\}$ using the following intuitive rules: (1) $0 \otimes m$ is interpreted as 0; (2) $1 \otimes m$ is interpreted as m; and (3) A comparison expression is interpreted as 1 if satisfied and as 0 otherwise.

Note that given a truth valuation for annotations, we obtain a real number for the expression by simply performing the substitution as defined above, and applying the basic semiring axioms [3].

[2]The obtained semiring is denoted by K^M in [8]. For simplicity we will abuse notation here and just use K

[3]Similarly, the provenance can capture scores of multiple movies and valuation then leads to a vector of values.

EXAMPLE 2.3. *Consider the provenance expression P of Example 2.2 and partial truth valuation that maps S_1 to 0 and U_1 to 1. Then $U_1 \cdot [S_1 \cdot U_1 \otimes 5 > 2] \otimes (3,1)$ maps to $0 \otimes (3,1) \equiv 0$: Although U_1 is mapped to 1, $S_1 \cdot U_1 \otimes 5$ is mapped to 0 and so the inequality does not hold, and the inequality expression is mapped to 0. In contrast, if S_1 is mapped to 1 then the condition would hold and we would have $(1 \cdot 1) \otimes (3,1) \equiv 3$ (notice that $(3,1) \equiv 3$ since we apply aggregation on a single user with score 3). Intuitively the second case corresponds to keeping the review, while the first one corresponds to discarding it.*

3. PROVENANCE SUMMARIZATION

The provenance model described in the previous section provides full documentation of the transformations that took place. Since the resulting expression may be extremely long and complex, we would like to summarize the provenance expression, at the possible cost of information loss. We start by formalizing summarization through a notion of *mappings*, and then discuss how to quantify the quality of a summary.

3.1 Summarization Through Mappings

Let Ann be a domain of annotations (for the $N[Ann]$ semiring) and Ann' be a domain of annotation summaries. Typically, we expect that $| Ann' | << | Ann |$. We then define a mapping $h : Ann \mapsto Ann'$ which maps each annotation to a corresponding summary. Abusing notation, this extends naturally to a homomorphism $h : N[Ann] \mapsto N[Ann]'$, i.e. define $h(a + b) = h(a) + h(b)$ and $h(a \cdot b) = h(a) \cdot h(b)$. This further extends to $N[Ann]' \otimes M$ by the standard construction $h(k \otimes m) = h(k) \otimes m$. Essentially, to apply h to a provenance expression p, each occurrence of $a \in Ann$ in p is replaced by $h(a)$. The mapped expression, $h(p)$, is a summary of the real provenance, in the sense that we lose track of some exact annotations and summarize the provenance using the abstract annotations in Ann'.

EXAMPLE 3.1. *Consider the provenance-aware expression P obtained in Example 2.2. To simplify the example we focus on the reviews of users U_1, U_2, U_3 for the movie "Match Point", and map all S_i annotations to 1 so we can discard the inequality terms. We thus obtain a simplified version of the provenance expression P:*

$$\boldsymbol{P_s} = U_1 \otimes (3,1) \oplus U_2 \otimes (5,1) \oplus U_3 \otimes (3,1)$$

Next, we map user annotations to annotation summaries that intuitively reflect values of attributes of the corresponding users. Mapping U_1 and U_2 to an annotation summary called "Female" [4]*, and applying congruences in the tensor structure, we obtain an expression that includes a maximum score of 5 collected from two female users:*

$$\boldsymbol{P'_s} = Female \otimes (5,2) \oplus U_3 \otimes (3,1)$$

Another summary results from mapping annotations U_1 and U_3 to the annotation "Audience":

$$\boldsymbol{P''_s} = Audience \otimes (3,2) \oplus U_2 \otimes (5,1)$$

In the example, we used two possible mappings h that combine reviews based on gender or role. In general there may be many possible mappings and the challenge is, given a provenance expression p, to (a) define what a good mapping h is (correspondingly, what is a good summary $h(p)$), and (b) find such good h.

[4]We later describe which mappings are possible and which are preferable to ours.

3.2 Quantifying Summary Quality

Several, possibly competing, considerations need to be combined in quantifying the quality of a summary.

Provenance size. Since the goal of summarization is to reduce the provenance size (measured as the number of annotations), it is natural to use the size of the obtained expression (after simplifications) as a measure of its quality.

Semantic Constraints. The provenance expression obtained may be of little use if it is constructed by identifying multiple unrelated annotations. It is thus natural to impose constraints on which annotations may be grouped together. One simple example of such a constraint is to allow two annotations $a, b \in Ann$ to be mapped to the same annotation in Ann' (or to 0 or 1) only if they annotate tuples in the *same input table*, intuitively meaning that they belong to the same domain. Other constraints may be specified in the form of *taxonomies*, where available. Taxonomies give semantic relations between the underlying objects (users, movie, etc.), and are used to constrain homomorphisms by requiring that all annotations that are grouped together by mapping to the same annotation share a common ancestor.

Additional constraints involve restricting mappings based on the original input data, by requiring that annotations that are mapped together reference tuples that share values in some (or one of some) specified attributes. For example, we may specify that users that are grouped together must share a common attribute out of gender, age group, etc. This allows us to give a meaningful name to the new annotation for presentation purposes, based on the joint attribute.

Taxonomic information may also be useful for deciding between choices of mappings, and may be incorporated as part of the computation. For example, we may take into account the taxonomic distance between annotations and the annotation they are mapped to by using the MAX or SUM of these distances, and prefer mappings of annotations to a new annotation that is relatively close to them (e.g. mapping user annotations to annotation 'Guitarist' is preferable to mapping them to annotation 'Person').

Distance. Depending on the *intended use* of provenance, we may *quantify the distance* between the original and summary expressions. For that we again use the notion of valuations, and define distances with respect to a set $\mathcal{V}_{Ann}$ of valuations to the original annotations Ann.

EXAMPLE 3.2. *Consider a distance function designed to use provenance for provisioning in the presence of spammers. To simplify the example, we assume that there is a single spammer. In this case, the class of valuations considered consists of those assigning* 0 *to a single user annotation, and* 1 *to all others. A concrete aggregated value for each movie may then be computed by simply canceling every summand in which the mapped annotation is* 0*, and taking the aggregate values for the rest. (We use here the congruences* $0 \otimes m \equiv 0$, $1 \otimes m \equiv m$*, and the ability to embed the result in* M*, see [8].)*

A central issue is how we transform a valuation in $\mathcal{V}_{Ann}$, on the original annotations to one in $\mathcal{V}_{Ann'}$, on the new annotation summaries. We propose that this will be given by a combiner function ϕ that sets a boolean value to $a' \in Ann'$ based on the truth values assigned to a annotations that were mapped to it. For example, if ϕ is a disjunction of the truth values, then intuitively an annotation summary is cancelled only if all of the annotations it summarizes are cancelled. More formally, let Ann, Ann' be two domains of annotations and let $h : Ann \mapsto Ann'$. Further let $\phi : Ann' \mapsto N[Ann]$ be a function such that for every $a' \in Ann'$, $\phi(a')$ is a polynomial *only* in elements of $\{a \in Ann \mid h(a) = a'\}$. In a sense, ϕ complements h, by specifying how the elements that are mapped to an annotation a' should be combined. Now, any valuation $v_{Ann} \in \mathcal{V}_{Ann}$ uniquely extends to a valuation $v_{Ann'} \in \mathcal{V}_{Ann'}$ by defining $v_{Ann'}(a') = v_{Ann}(\phi(a'))$; note that the use of v_{Ann} refers to its extension to the domain of $N[Ann]$. We use $v^{h,\phi}$ to denote the valuation obtained in such a way from a valuation v and mappings h, ϕ.

We next define the distance between a provenance expression p and its summary $h(p)$ as an average over all truth valuations, of some property of p, $h(p)$, and the valuation. This property is based on yet another function we call `VAL-FUNC`, whose choice depends on the intended provenance use. We only require that it is a computable function fed as an additional input to the algorithm.

DEFINITION 3.3. *Let* p *be a provenance expression over a set of annotations Ann, and let* $p' = h(p)$*, we define:*

$$dist^{h,\phi}(p,p') = \frac{\sum_{v \in \mathcal{V}_{Ann}} \texttt{VAL-FUNC}(v, v^{h,\phi}, p, p')}{\mid \mathcal{V}_{Ann} \mid}$$

where `VAL-FUNC` *is some function measuring a property of the effect of the valuation over the two polynomials.*

`VAL-FUNC` *functions.* We next give examples for natural choices of `VAL-FUNC`(v, v', p, p'). In all examples $w(v)$ is some weighting over the valuation, e.g. the joint probability of the truth values it defines.

(1) **Expected error**: $w(v) \cdot \mid v(p) - v'(p') \mid$. Using $w(v) = 1$ leads to comparing the overall error over all truth valuations out of the given set. This scenario makes sense when provenance is likely to be performed for multiple valuations, and it is all right to suffer some small error in each computation.

(2) **Weighted fraction of disagreeing valuations**: 0 if $v(p) = v'(p')$ and w(v) otherwise. Using $w(v) = 1$ would be a reasonable choice if the user is to uniformly sample valuations and is interested in the probability of obtaining a correct/incorrect answer.

(3) **Euclidean distance**: `euclidean-dist`$(v(p), v(p'))$. This is well-defined when v(p) and v(p') are aggregation vectors rather than aggregation values (e.g. a vector of aggregated ratings of different movies of same genre).

EXAMPLE 3.4. *Observe that using* $\mid v(p) - v'(p') \mid$ *as the* `VAL-FUNC`, P_s'' *is at distance* 0 *from* P_s *w.r.t. valuations that map only a single user annotation to False. All these valuations yield the same value w.r.t. the two provenance expressions – if* U_2 *is mapped to True then the aggregated MAX value is* 5 *regardless of other truth values, and otherwise both* U_1 *and* U_3 *are mapped to True and so is Audience. In contrast,* P_s' *differs from* P_s *for the valuation that maps* U_2 *to False and the rest to True.*

Putting it all together. In addition to obtaining a provenance summary with small distance, we of course wish to minimize the provenance expression size. The distance and size measurements are combined together to form a weighted average, where the weights are given as input parameters, that is used as a score given to candidate mappings. We later describe how this score is used in our summarization algorithm and also how taxonomy distances are incorporated in the computation.

DEFINITION 3.5. *Let p_0 be an input provenance expression and let $p_{cand} = h(p_0)$. Also, let $wDist$ and $wSize$ be user-defined weights ($wDist + wSize = 1$), $rDist$ the approximated distance rank of p_{cand} and $rSize$ its size rank. We define a candidate mapping score as follows:*
$CandidateScore^{h,\phi}(p_0, p_{cand}) =$
$wDist \times rDist^{h,\phi}(p_0, p_{cand}) + wSize \times rSize(p_{cand})$

Computational problems. Given a provenance expression p_0 with a set of annotations Ann, ϕ and VAL-FUNC functions, our goal is to explore the tradeoff between distance and size. This is studied in three flavors:
(1) using input weights for size and distance, for obtaining a homomorphic expression p', in each algorithm iteration, that minimizes the function CandidateScore.
(2) minimizing the distance while obtaining a summary p' of size less than some size bound TARGET-SIZE.
(3) minimizing the size while obtaining a summary p' of distance less than some distance bound TARGET-DIST.
These three flavors are all studied using the summarization algorithm. To use the first flavor the user can choose weights and bounds according to her preferences. For the second flavor, the user must set the distance weight to 1 and TARGET-DIST to the maximal distance (1). For the third flavor, the user must set the size weight to 1 and TARGET-SIZE to the minimal size (1). We study both a variant where the distance is computed with respect to all possible valuations (and then V_{Ann} is not an explicitly given input) as well as a variant where a subset V_{Ann} of valuations is given as input.

4. COMPUTING PROVENANCE SUMMARIZATIONS

There are two main building blocks in a solution that summarizes a provenance expression. The first is, given a summary, compute its quality based on the measurements discussed above. The second is a search algorithm that explores multiple possible expressions, uses the first building block to compute the quality for each, and aims at finding the best ones. We next detail the two components.

4.1 Computing Summary Quality

Recall that a summary quality was defined through the notion of distance. Let **DIST-COMP** be the problem of computing the exact distance (w.r.t. all possible valuations) between two provenance expressions p and p'=h(p), given input p, h, ϕ and VAL-FUNC.

PROPOSITION 4.1. ***DIST-COMP*** *is $\sharp$P-hard in the size of the input provenance p. This is true even if p includes no tensor elements.*

The proof (in [2]) is by reduction from $\sharp$-DNF. On the other hand, approximating the distance is feasible.

PROPOSITION 4.2. *Given a provenance expression p and a homomorphism h on its annotations, and given $0 < \epsilon, 0 < \delta < 1$, one can compute d' such that $Prob(\mid d' - dist(p, h(p)) \mid > \epsilon) < 1 - \delta$. The computation of d' may be performed in polynomial time with respect to $\mid p \mid$, δ, and $\frac{1}{\epsilon}$.*

The proof (in [2]) is constructive in the sense that it involves a simple sampling-based approximation algorithm, that will be used as a building block in our summarization algorithm.

4.2 Finding a Summarization

Towards a summarization algorithm, we recall that the set of truth valuations V_{Ann} may be restricted, guided by the intended use (in the sequel we will assume that V_{Ann} is given as input). In this case, we observe that V_{Ann} may already dictate some simplifications that may be performed (see below).

PROPOSITION 4.3. *Given a provenance expression p, finding a minimal p' such that $distance(p, p') = 0$ is in PTIME in p and in V_{Ann}.*

Equivalence Classes. The proof for the above proposition (in [2]) is based on computing equivalence classes of annotations with respect to a set of valuations, with every two annotations being equivalent if they agree for *every* valuation in the set. The intuition is that there is no need to maintain these different annotations, since they in any case may not be differentiated. Replacing them by ("mapping them to") the same annotation will further allow simplifications of the expression based on the algebraic identities. This calls for a first step in the summarization algorithm, grouping together provenance annotations that are equivalent. Of course, this may still yield expressions of large size; we will thus perform a A^*-like search ([26]) of expressions, motivated by the next proposition.

Input: A provenance expression p_0 with a set of annotations Ann, ϕ and VAL-FUNC functions, distance and size weights, size bound TARGET-SIZE and distance bound TARGET-DIST
Output: Summary provenance expression p_1

$p' := GroupEquivalent(p_0, V_{Ann})$;
while $Size(p') >$ *TARGET-SIZE or* $ApproxDistance(p_0, p', V_{Ann}) <$ *TARGET-DIST* **do**
  for *every* $h \in CandidateHom(p')$ **do**
    $p_{cand} := h(p')$;
    if $CandidateScore^{h,\phi}(p_0, p_{cand})$ *is minimal* **then**
      $p'_{prev} := p'$;
      $p' := p_{cand}$;
    end
  end
end
if $ApproxDistance(p_0, p', V_{Ann}) \geq$ *TARGET-DIST* **then**
  return p'_{prev};
end
return p' ;

Algorithm 1: Provenance Summarization Algorithm

Monotonicity. Let $p_0, p_1, ..., p_n$ be provenance expressions such that $p_i = h_i(p_{i-1})$ for some sequence of homomorphisms h_i. We define monotonicity of the distance and size functions, as follows: the distance function is increasing monotone iff for all $i > j$: $distance(p_0, p_i) \geq distance(p_0, p_j)$ and the size function is decreasing monotone iff for all $i > j$: $size(p_i) \leq size(p_j)$.

PROPOSITION 4.4. *All the VAL-FUNC functions described in section 3 yield increasing monotone distance and decreasing monotone size functions.*

Naturally, not every choice of VAL-FUNC leads to monotonicity, e.g. a function that returns alternating constants, but, as the above proposition indicates, natural choices of functions do.

Provenance Summarization Algorithm. The above proposition (proof in [2]) leads to Algorithm 1. Starting from the original set of annotations Ann and the given provenance expression p_0, the heuristic algorithm constructs the homomorphism h gradually, essentially by deciding on grouping of annotations. First, we obtain p' by grouping annotations that are equivalent w.r.t. the set of truth valuations (GroupEquivalent in line 1), as indicated by Proposition 4.3. Then, we iterate and in each step examine a set of possible single-step mappings (in $CandidateHom$) of two annotations to the same, new annotation name (line 3). For each such mapping we apply the obtained homomorphism to the current expression, computing $h(p')$ (line 4) and approximating the distance between p_0 and $p_{cand} = h(p')$. The p_{cand} with the smallest `CandidateScore` value is chosen (lines 5-8) and the process repeats until the stop condition is met. The stop condition for `TARGET-SIZE` (`TARGET-DIST`) is when the expression meets the size (resp. distance) bound (line 2).

If multiple candidates have minimal candidate scores, input taxonomies, if given as input, are used to break ties. For each such candidate, the taxonomy distances of the annotations from the new annotation they are mapped to are computed and the MAX (or SUM) of these distances is computed. The candidate that minimizes this value is chosen. If no taxonomies are given as input, we arbitrarily choose a candidate with minimal score.

EXAMPLE 4.5. *Returning to our running example, assume now that the Movies table also includes a movie genre column. Further assume that the user would like to view scores of movies of certain genres and so the aggregator now aggregates multiple movies of the same user-specified genre. We next exemplify the algorithm flow, using the following provenance expression for the movies "Match Point" and "Blue Jasmine":* $\boldsymbol{P_0} = P_{MP} \oplus_M P_{BJ}$ *where* $P_{MP} = P_s$ *is the provenance expression from Example 3.1 that consists of the three user reviews for the movie "Match Point",* $P_{BJ} = U_2 \otimes (4, 1)$ *is the added review for the movie "Blue Jasmine" and* $\oplus_M$ *is a formal sum for combining reviews of different movies (we will later see how this formal sum is used).*

In each step, the algorithm examines the set of possible mappings of two annotations to the same new annotation. The mappings $U_1, U_2 \to Female$ *and* $U_1, U_3 \to Audience$ *discussed in Example 3.1 are such possible single-step mappings that are examined by the algorithm. For simplicity, assume these are the only possible mappings. The algorithm computes the new provenance expressions that the candidate mappings yield:*
$\boldsymbol{P_0'} = P'_{MP} \oplus_M P'_{BJ} = Female \otimes (5, 2) \oplus U_3 \otimes (3, 1) \oplus_M Female \otimes (4, 1)$
$\boldsymbol{P_0''} = P''_{MP} \oplus_M P''_{BJ} = Audience \otimes (3, 2) \oplus U_2 \otimes (5, 1) \oplus_M U_2 \otimes (4, 1)$
Also, a candidate score for each such candidate is computed. Assuming $wDist = 1$ *and* $wSize = 0$*, the candidate that is chosen in each step in the one that minimizes the distance from the original provenance* P_0.

Assume we compute the distance w.r.t. the class of valuations that cancel a single annotation and the euclidean distance VAL-FUNC. Keep in mind that evaluating a valuation on this kind of provenance, that consists of reviews for different movies, results in a vector of aggregated ratings where each coordinate holds the aggregated rating of a certain movie. In this setting, P_0'' *is at distance 0 from* P_0 *while* P_0' *differs from* P_0 *for the valuation that cancels* U_2*. This is due to the fact that by canceling* U_2 *in* P_0 *we cancel the maximum rating for "Match Point" and the only rating for "Blue Jasmine". Canceling* U_2 *in* P_0' *does not have a similar effect since we use a disjunction of the truth values (of* U_1, U_2*) as our* ϕ *function, and so the new annotation "Female" is assigned the value true. Obviously, the euclidean distance between the aggregation vectors that are the result of evaluating this valuation on* P_0 *and* P_0' *is greater than zero and so the overall distance over all considered valuations is greater than zero. This leads to the conclusion that the algorithm would choose* P_0'' *over* P_0' *so the provenance for the next algorithm iteration is* $P_1 = P_0''$ *and so the algorithm continues.*

5. DATASETS AND USE CASES

We next describe the three provenance datasets that we used and show provenance examples for these datasets.

Datasets. We used three datasets: (1) MovieLens dataset, that includes ratings of different movies by users of MovieLens movie recommender that is based on collaborative filtering ([1]). (2) Wikipedia dataset - collected using the MediaWiki web API which is a Web service that provides convenient access to wiki features, data, and meta-data over HTTP. We also used YAGO Taxonomy ([5]) that contains rdfs:subClassOf facts derived from Wikipedia and WordNet. This taxonomy was used in our provenance summarization algorithm in order to improve the choices made by the algorithm when the input is a Wikipedia provenance expression. We used Wu-Palmer method for measuring semantic relatedness ([28]) in order to compute the distance between WordNet concepts in the taxonomy. (3) Data-Dependent Processes (DDP's) dataset - we generated provenance expressions that represent data-dependent processes based on the structure described in [17].

EXAMPLE 5.1. *A Wikipedia provenance expression represents different user edits of Wikipedia pages that belong to different categories. Each user edit can either be minor (0) or major (1). Consider the following provenance expression:*
$\boldsymbol{P_0} = (SalubriousToxin \cdot Adele) \otimes (0, 1) \oplus$
$(Dubulge \cdot CelineDion) \otimes (1, 1) \oplus$
$(Dr.\ Back\text{-}In\text{-}The\text{-}Street \cdot LoriBlack) \otimes (1, 1) \oplus$
$(JaspertheFriendlyPunk \cdot AlecBaillie) \otimes (1, 1)$.
This provenance includes 3 major (Dubulge, Dr. Back-In-The-Street and Jasper the Friendly Punk) and 1 minor (Salubrious Toxin) user edits of 4 Wikipedia pages - 2 pages whose title is a famous singer (Adele and Celine Dion) and 2 whose title is a famous guitarist (Lori Black and Alec Baillie).

To simplify the example, assume we only map user annotations to the same annotation if the associated users have a similar number of edits and then the new annotation would describe their contribution level, e.g. "Top-Contributor" and "Reviewer". Also assume we map Wikipedia pages to a new annotation only if the corresponding pages have the same parent WordNet concept in the taxonomy. Moreover, assume we use SUM aggregation and that we compute the distance w.r.t. $\phi = \vee$ *and the class of valuations that cancel a single annotation and are consistent with the taxonomy. A valuation is considered to be inconsistent if it assigns false to a Wikipedia category/WordNet concept A, but assigns true to a Wikipedia category/WordNet concept B s.t. B is a child of A in the taxonomy. A summarization is:*

$\boldsymbol{P'} = (\textit{Top-Contributor} \cdot \textit{<wordnet\_guitarist>}) \otimes (2,2) \oplus (\textit{Reviewer} \cdot \textit{<wordnet\_singer>}) \otimes (1,2)$.
According to the summary, two users that are top contributors edited Wikipedia pages of guitarists (one major edit each) and two simple reviewers edited Wikipedia pages of singers (one major edit and the other minor).

By obtaining such a provenance summary it is easier to answer questions such as: what are the most controversial or interesting topics, what are relatively popular topics among top contributors, do top contributors make more major edits relative to other users, etc (e.g. obtaining a summary similar to the above summary for many Wikipedia users might lead us to the conclusion that top contributors prefer to edit guitarist pages than singer pages). These are questions that are much harder to answer using the original long provenance expression. We can also present such summaries in a ui that makes it easier for the user to understand the summary and get insights on the underlying data.

EXAMPLE 5.2. *A DDP (Data Dependent Process), described in [17], models an application whose control flow is guided by a finite state machine, as well as by the state of an underlying database. DDP provenance expressions are summaries of executions where an execution is a multiplication of transitions. Each transition is either based on a user's choice or on a database query result. A user dependent transition is of the form* $\langle c_k, 1\rangle$ *where* c_k *is the cost associated with the transition (the user's effort). A database dependent transition is of the form* $\langle 0, [d_i \cdot d_j] \neq 0\rangle$ *or* $\langle 0, [d_i \cdot d_j] = 0\rangle$. *Consider the following DDP provenance example of two executions (each consisting of two transitions):*
$\langle c_1, 1\rangle \cdot \langle 0, [d_1 \cdot d_2] \neq 0\rangle + \langle 0, [d_2 \cdot d_3] = 0\rangle \cdot \langle c_2, 1\rangle$.

The aggregation function used is based on the semirings described in [17]. The "attributes" that are used as constraints here are the mappings of different database variables to new database variables and the mappings of cost variables to new cost variables. If two database variables are mapped to a single one, it means that either both tuples need to be present for the database query to be satisfied or both should be missing. Similarily, if we know that user transitions have more or less the same cost, it is possible to map the two cost variables to a new cost variable. Also, assume we use the "Cancel Single Attribute" class of valuations.

The following is a possible summary for the above provenance, obtained by mapping d_1, d_3 *to* D_1 *and* c_1, c_2 *to* C_1:
$\langle C_1, 1\rangle \cdot \langle 0, [D_1 \cdot d_2] \neq 0\rangle + \langle 0, [d_2 \cdot D_1] \neq 0\rangle \cdot \langle C_1, 1\rangle$
which is equal to: $\langle C_1, 1\rangle \cdot \langle 0, [D_1 \cdot d_2] \neq 0\rangle$.
This final summary represents a single execution that consists of two transitions - one user dependent transition and one database dependent transition.

By summarizing this kind of provenance, analysts can test and explore the effect of hypothetical modifications to a DDP's state machine and/or to the underlying database (e.g. using the above summary, analysts can explore the effect of removing the database dependent transition). Exploring the effect of such modifications using the original provenance expression can be much more complicated.

6. EXPERIMENTS

The main purpose of our experiments was to examine the effectiveness of our summarization algorithm, compared to other approaches, in terms of: (1) conciseness of the obtained provenance expression (measured by size), (2) accuracy of evaluations (measured by distance from original provenance), (3) faster provenance usage ("Usage Time" experiment) and (4) feasibility of summarization ("Summarization Time" experiment). The first two were examined as functions of the wDist weight (wDist experiment), and of the `TARGET-DIST` and `TARGET-SIZE` stop conditions (`TARGET-DIST` and `TARGET-SIZE` experiments). This covers the three computational problems that we have presented in section 3. Each experiment was conducted for the three datasets - MovieLens, Wikipedia and DDP. For each dataset, we generated multiple input provenance expressions, executed the experiments and averaged the results.

Algorithms Examined. In each experiment that we conducted, we executed the following algorithms for each dataset and compared different parameters of the result summary provenance: (1) Prov-Approx (Algorithm 1) - our provenance summarization algorithm. (2) Clustering - using only the MovieLens and Wikipedia datasets, since the DDP dataset is not suitable for the clustering experiment (it is not clear how to construct feature vectors to be used as input to the clustering algorithm). (3) Random - in which every pair of annotations was chosen randomly from the list of pairs that satisfy the mapping constraints. All three algorithms take into account the user-specified size and distance bounds (`TARGET-SIZE` and `TARGET-DIST`) and stop if and when they reach these bounds.

Clustering Algorithm. We used a library for hierarchical agglomerative clustering called HAC ([4]). This library supports the following linkage criteria (i.e. a criteria that determines the distance between sets of observations as a function of the pairwise distances): Single Linkage, Average Linkage, Centroid Linkage, Complete Linkage, Median Linkage, Ward Linkage and Weighted Average, described in [13]. All linkage criteria were examined in the experiments, but since they all yield similar results compared to our approach we present the "Single Linkage" results. Next we describe how the clustering approach was implemented for the MovieLens dataset. Similarly, it was also implemented for the Wikipedia dataset. Not all provenance datasets are suitable for a Clustering algorithm, e.g. our DDP dataset. Each user, that rated k movies, was associated with a feature vector of the following form:
$(UID, Gender, AgeRange, Occupation, ZipCode, (MovieTitle_1 = Rating_1, ..., MovieTitle_k = Rating_k))$, e.g. $(UID278, M, 45-49, tradesman/craftsman, 60482,$

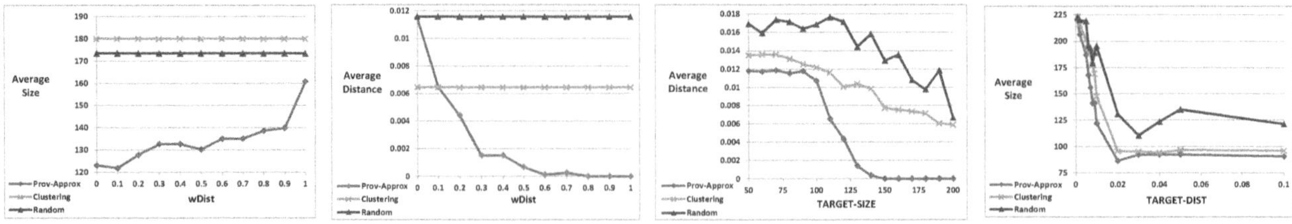

(a) Size-wDist (b) Dist-wDist (c) Dist-TARGET-SIZE (d) Size-TARGET-DIST

Figure 2: Average Distance as a Function of wDist and `TARGET-SIZE` and Average Size as a Function of wDist and `TARGET-DIST` (MovieLens Dataset)

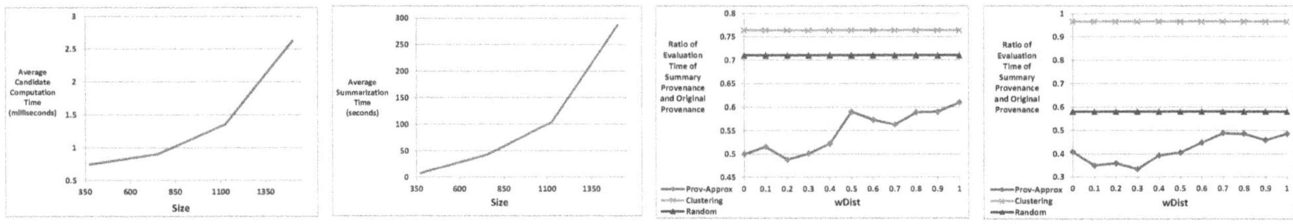

(a) Time Per Candidate (b) Summarization Time (c) Ratio of Usage Time of Summary Provenance and Original Provenance (Using 20 Steps) (d) Ratio of Usage Time of Summary Provenance and Original Provenance (Using 30 steps)

Figure 3: Summarization and Candidate Computation Time (MovieLens Dataset)

$(TheFury = 4.0, NearDark = 4.0))$.
In addition, we implemented a dissimilarity measure for computing the distance between each pair of feature vectors. We used Pearson Correlation Coefficient as a measure of similarity between the ratings vectors, that the feature vectors include as a single feature. Moreover, we added our mapping constraints to the clustering algorithm so that both our algorithm and the clustering algorithm would take into account the same constraints (we do not allow two clusters to merge if the users that belong to these clusters do not have at least one attribute in common).

We next describe how we obtain the Clustering's provenance summary in order to compare its quality to ours. Similarily to our summarization algorithm, each step of the Clustering algorithm, in which two clusters are merged, corresponds to a mapping of 2 annotations to an annotation summary. According to this mapping, we compute the obtained provenance expression and use it to check the stop conditions - `TARGET-DIST`, `TARGET-SIZE`, etc.

Experimental Settings. The experiments were conducted for different combinations of datasets, valuation classes and aggregation functions and all combintaions have similar results. Specifically, two valuation classes were examined: (1) "Cancel Single Annotation" - each valuation in this class cancels a single annotation by assigning it *false* and assigning *true* to the rest. (2) "Cancel Single Attribute" - the class of valuations that cancel all annotations that share the same attribute and assigns *true* to the rest (e.g. the valuation that cancels all Male users). For space constraints, we present a set of representative results. It is important to note that the distance values we present, represent average error over all valuations, which we divide by the maximum possible error in order to normalize to [0,1]. Presenting the un-normalized distances results in the same graph trends.

We next describe our experimental results for the MovieLens dataset. Later we show some experimental results for the other two datasets.

6.1 wDist Experiment

The purpose of this experiment is to check the effect of the wDist and wSize weights on the summary distance and size. For that purpose, we bounded the maximum number of algorithm steps, the `TARGET-DIST` was set to 1 (max distance) and the `TARGET-SIZE` was set to 1 also (minimum size) so that they would have no effect as stop conditions. Figures 2a and 2b show the results for the MovieLens dataset using "Cancel Single Attribute" valuation class, MAX aggregation and at most 20 steps. As expected, using Prov-Approx, greater values of wDist yield smaller distance values and greater size values. The wDist has no effect on the Clustering and Random approaches (they do not take this parameter into account) so we averaged their results for different wDist values. As the wDist used increases, Prov-Approx yields smaller distance compared to the Clustering (starting from wDist = 0.1 as presented in the graph), as expected. Also, the Clustering approach yields greater size compared to our approach. The Random approach yields much greater distance and size values.

6.2 TARGET-SIZE Experiment

This experiment checks the problem variant in which the user aims to reach a certain `TARGET-SIZE` value while keeping the result relatively "close" to the original provenance. For that purpose, we set the wDist and `TARGET-DIST` values to 1. Figure 2c shows the results of the experiment for the MovieLens dataset. As expected, since the wDist was set to 1, our approach gave better distance values compared to the Clustering and Random approaches. The Random approach gave the worst results. For the Prov-Approx and the Clustering algorithms, as the `TARGET-SIZE` increases, the

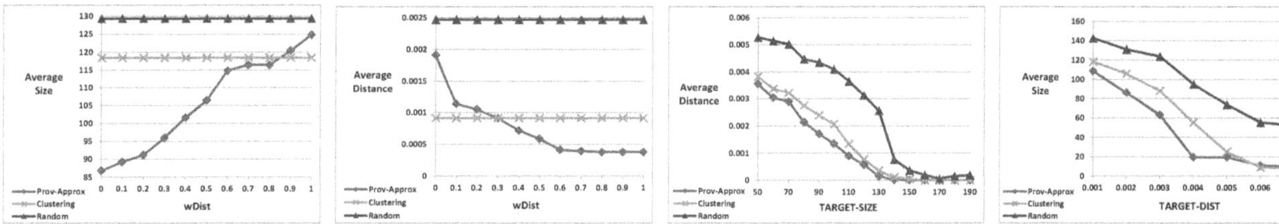

(a) Size-wDist (b) Dist-wDist (c) Dist-TARGET-SIZE (d) Size-TARGET-DIST

Figure 4: Average Distance as a Function of wDist and TARGET-SIZE and Average Size as a Function of wDist and TARGET-DIST (Wikipedia Dataset)

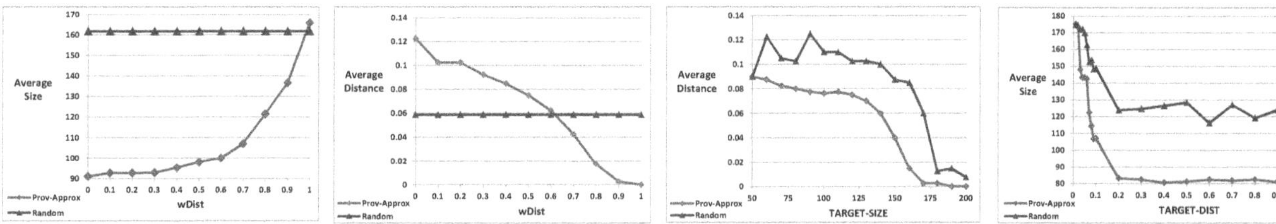

(a) Size-wDist (b) Dist-wDist (c) Dist-TARGET-SIZE (d) Size-TARGET-DIST

Figure 5: Average Distance as a Function of wDist and TARGET-SIZE and Average Size as a Function of wDist and TARGET-DIST (DDP Dataset)

size increases (the algorithms stop earlier) and as a result the distance is smaller. This is not always the case for the Random approach. Since this approach does not make the same choices for all the TARGET-SIZE values but just randomly chooses a pair, there could be better distance choices made when smaller TARGET-SIZE values are used (e.g. the distance that Random achieved using TARGET-SIZE 130 is actually smaller than the one achieved using 140).

6.3 TARGET-DIST Experiment

This experiment checks another variant, in which the user wishes to bound the distance with the TARGET-DIST value while obtaining a small provenance expression. For that reason, wDist was set to 0 and TARGET-SIZE was set to 1 also. Figure 2d shows the results of the experiment for the MovieLens dataset. As expected, as the TARGET-DIST increases the size decreases until we reach a point from where we cannot decrease the size further. Moreover, as a result of using wDist = 0 the choices made were the ones that minimize the next expression's size and that reflects in the results, where our approach reaches the smallest size values. Random gives the worst results. Also, Random does not make the same choices for all TARGET-DIST values, so it is also possible that it would make better choices for smaller TARGET-DIST values and that would yield better size, just like in TARGET-DIST 0.03.

6.4 Usage Time Experiment

This experiment examines the ratio between the average evaluation time of valuations on the summary and original expressions, as a function of wDist. Figures 3c and 3d show the results for the MovieLens dataset using 20 and 30 maximum number of steps respectively. The TARGET-DIST was set to 1 and the TARGET-SIZE to 1 so that the only relevant stop condition would be the number of steps. The experiment was conducted as follows: we randomly chose 10 valuations, evaluated these valuations on the original and summary expressions for the three approaches and examined the ratio of evaluation time. As expected, using Prov-Approx, as the wDist increases, the result's size is greater and the distance is smaller. For that reason, the expression is closer to the original expression and so the ratio in evaluation time is greater. Also, using more algorithm steps, the ratio is smaller; using 30 steps the range is 0.3-0.5 (30% - 50% improvement in evaluation time) compared to 0.45-0.65, when using 20 steps. To conclude, the summary usage time is faster than the original provenance usage time. In addition, the Random and Clustering approaches are not affected by wDist, so we averaged the results for all the wDist values. As expected, our approach yields smaller ratio compared to the Random approach using smaller wDist values. The Clustering approach yields much greater ratio than ours for all wDist values (less improvement in usage time).

6.5 Summarization and Candidate Computation Time Experiment

This experiment examines the summarization time and also the average candidate computation time (distance and size computation for a candidate pair of annotations) as functions of provenance size. Figures 3a and 3b show the results for the MovieLens dataset, wDist weight set to 1 and 50 maximum number of steps. As expected, as the expression size decreases, the number of pairs to consider in each step decreases and so the number of distance calculations decreases and as a result the summarization time decreases. Also, as the expression size decreases, the distance computation is faster, as expected.

6.6 Other Datasets

All the figures so far show results for the MovieLens dataset; we next describe results for the other two datasets. Figures 4a, 4b, 5a and 5b show the results of the wDist experiment conducted on the Wikipedia and DDP datasets using 20 and 10 maximum number of steps respectively. Figures 4c, 4d, 5c and 5d show the results of the TARGET-SIZE and TARGET-DIST experiments for these datasets, using "Cancel

Single Annotation" valuation class and sum aggregation for the Wikipedia dataset and "Cancel Single Attribute" for the DDP dataset. All results are similar to those obtained for the MovieLens dataset. Note that the DDP dataset is the only one that wasn't compared to the Clustering approach since it's unclear how to construct a Clustering competitor for this complex-structured data provenance.

7. RELATED WORK AND CONCLUSIONS

Provenance models have been extensively studied in multiple lines of research such as provenance for database transformations (see e.g. [18, 11, 9, 21, 10, 12]), for workflows (see e.g. [16, 14, 6, 22, 19, 27, 23]), for the web [3], for data mining applications [20], and many others, but typically full and exact provenance is presented (sometimes in an optimized form, e.g. factorized as in [24]). Provenance views have been proposed in context of workflows (see e.g.[16]), but the summarization obtained through these views is based on a notion of granularity levels, and is lossless rather than approximate. A notion of approximate provenance was proposed in [25], and somewhat resembles ours, but is limited to UCQs (and in particular allows no aggregates), geared towards probabilistic computation, and does not account for semantic constraints. Our notion of mapping to summarized annotations is also reminiscent of clustering, however the function that we optimize is one that depends on the provenance expression itself and its intended uses, which leads to different design choices and to different results.

We have studied in this paper summarization of provenance information. We have identified three desiderata for the assessment of candidate summaries: conciseness, semantic constraints satisfaction and small distance from original provenance. This has led us to the development of our summarization algorithm that finds an "optimal" summary according to these quality measurements. After comparing our approach to other approaches (Clustering and Random) by conducting different experiments using different provenance datasets, we conclude that our approach is indeed better - it finds better quality summaries compared to the others and allows the user to control the desired tradeoff between distance (that affects evaluation accuracy) and size (that affects presentation and usage time). As future work, we intend to explore a generalized version of the algorithm in which in each iteration we map k annotations to a new annotation rather than just 2. An additional line of future work is to acheive further theoretical bounds on the algorithm's performance and output quality.

8. ACKNOWLEDGMENTS

This work has been partially funded by the European Research Council under the FP7, ERC grant MoDaS, agreement 291071, by the Broadcom Foundation and Tel Aviv University Authentication Initiative, by the Israeli Science Foundation (Grant No. 1636/13), by the National Science Foundation Institute (NSF), Information and Intelligent Systems (IIS) Division (Grant No. 1302212) and by the French National Research Agency (ANR), Aggreg project.

9. REFERENCES

[1] Movielens site. https://movielens.org/.
[2] Paper's online version. http://bit.ly/1ceBKEC.
[3] Provenance working group. http://www.w3.org/2011/prov/.
[4] Sape research group. http://sape.inf.usi.ch/hac.
[5] Yago knowledge base. http://www.mpi-inf.mpg.de/departments/databases-and-information-systems/research/yago-naga/yago/.
[6] A. Ailamaki, Y. E. Ioannidis, and M. Livny. Scientific workflow management by database management. In *SSDBM*, 1998.
[7] Y. Amsterdamer, S. B. Davidson, D. Deutch, T. Milo, J. Stoyanovich, and V. Tannen. Putting Lipstick on Pig: Enabling Database-style Workflow Provenance. *PVLDB*, 2012.
[8] Y. Amsterdamer, D. Deutch, and V. Tannen. Provenance for aggregate queries. In *PODS*, 2011.
[9] O. Benjelloun, A. Sarma, A. Halevy, M. Theobald, and J. Widom. Databases with uncertainty and lineage. *VLDB J.*, 17, 2008.
[10] P. Buneman, J. Cheney, and S. Vansummeren. On the expressiveness of implicit provenance in query and update languages. *ACM Trans. Database Syst.*, 33(4), 2008.
[11] P. Buneman, S. Khanna, and W. Tan. Why and where: A characterization of data provenance. In *ICDT*, 2001.
[12] J. Cheney, L. Chiticariu, and W. C. Tan. Provenance in databases: Why, how, and where. *Foundations and Trends in Databases*, 1(4):379–474, 2009.
[13] P. R. Christopher D. Manning and H. SchÃijtze. *Introduction to Information Retrieval*. Cambridge University Press, 2008.
[14] D. Cohn and R. Hull. Business artifacts: A data-centric approach to modeling business operations and processes. *IEEE Data Eng. Bull.*, 32(3), 2009.
[15] S. B. Davidson, S. C. Boulakia, A. Eyal, B. Ludäscher, T. M. McPhillips, S. Bowers, M. K. Anand, and J. Freire. Provenance in scientific workflow systems. *IEEE Data Eng. Bull.*, 30(4):44–50, 2007.
[16] S. B. Davidson and J. Freire. Provenance and scientific workflows: challenges and opportunities. In *SIGMOD Conference*, pages 1345–1350, 2008.
[17] D. Deutch, Y. Moskovitch, and V. Tannen. A provenance framework for data-dependent process analysis. *PVLDB*, 7(6):457–468, 2014.
[18] R. Fink, L. Han, and D. Olteanu. Aggregation in probabilistic databases via knowledge compilation. *PVLDB*, 5(5), 2012.
[19] I. Foster, J. Vockler, M. Wilde, and A. Zhao. Chimera: A virtual data system for representing, querying, and automating data derivation. *SSDBM*, 2002.
[20] B. Glavic, J. Siddique, P. Andritsos, and R. J. Miller. Provenance for Data Mining. In *Theory and Practice of Provenance (TAPP)*, 2013.
[21] T. J. Green, G. Karvounarakis, and V. Tannen. Provenance semirings. In *PODS*, pages 31–40, 2007.
[22] D. Hull, K. Wolstencroft, R. Stevens, C. Goble, M. Pocock, P. Li, and T. Oinn. Taverna: a tool for building and running workflows of services. *Nucleic Acids Res.*, 34, 2006.
[23] P. Missier, N. Paton, and K. Belhajjame. Fine-grained and efficient lineage querying of collection-based workflow provenance. In *EDBT*, 2010.
[24] D. Olteanu and J. Zavodny. Factorised representations of query results: size bounds and readability. In *ICDT*, pages 285–298, 2012.
[25] C. Ré and D. Suciu. Approximate lineage for probabilistic databases. *PVLDB*, 1(1):797–808, 2008.
[26] S. Russell and P. Norvig. *Artificial Intelligence: A Modern Approach*. Pearson, 2009.
[27] Y. L. Simhan, B. Plale, and D. Gammon. Karma2: Provenance management for data-driven workflows. *Int. J. Web Service Res.*, 5(2), 2008.
[28] Z. Wu and M. Palmer. Verb semantics and lexical selection. In *Proc. of 32nd Annual meeting of the Associations for Computational Linguistics*, pages 133–138, 1994.

An Integrated Bayesian Approach for Effective Multi-Truth Discovery

Xianzhi Wang,
Quan Z. Sheng,
Xiu Susie Fang, Lina Yao
School of Computer Science
The University of Adelaide
Adelaide, SA 5005, Australia
xianzhi.wang@adelaide.edu.au

Xiaofei Xu
School of Computer Science and Technology
Harbin Institute of Technology
Harbin 150001, China
xiaofei@hit.edu.cn

Xue Li
School of IT and Electrical Engineering
The University of Queensland
Brisbane, QLD 4072, Australia
xueli@itee.uq.edu.au

ABSTRACT

Truth-finding is the fundamental technique for corroborating reports from multiple sources in both data integration and collective intelligent applications. Traditional truth-finding methods assume a single true value for each data item and therefore cannot deal will multiple true values (i.e., the *multi-truth-finding* problem). So far, the existing approaches handle the multi-truth-finding problem in the same way as the single-truth-finding problems. Unfortunately, the multi-truth-finding problem has its unique features, such as the involvement of sets of values in claims, different implications of inter-value mutual exclusion, and larger source profiles. Considering these features could provide new opportunities for obtaining more accurate truth-finding results. Based on this insight, we propose an integrated Bayesian approach to the multi-truth-finding problem, by taking these features into account. To improve the truth-finding efficiency, we reformulate the multi-truth-finding problem model based on the mappings between sources and (sets of) values. New mutual exclusive relations are defined to reflect the possible co-existence of multiple true values. A finer-grained copy detection method is also proposed to deal with sources with large profiles. The experimental results on three real-world datasets show the effectiveness of our approach.

Categories and Subject Descriptors

H.2.8 [**Information Systems**]: Database Management—*Data Mining*; I.2.m [**Computing Methodologies**]: Artificial Intelligence—*Miscellaneous*

General Terms

Models; Algorithms; Experimentation; Measurement

CIKM'15, October 19–23, 2015, Melbourne, Australia.
© 2015 ACM. ISBN 978-1-4503-3794-6/15/10 ...$15.00.
DOI: http://dx.doi.org/10.1145/2806416.2806443.

Keywords

Truth discovery; multi-truth-finding features; Bayesian model; data source dependence

1. INTRODUCTION

Integrating data from multiple sources has been increasingly becoming a commonplace in both Web and the emerging Internet of Things (IoT) applications to support collective intelligence and collaborative decision making [4]. Unfortunately, it is not unusual that the information about a single item comes from different sources, which might be noisy, out-of-date, or even erroneous. It is therefore of paramount importance to resolve such conflicts among the data and to find out which piece of information is more reliable [15]. For example, in a recent controversy on Obama's birthplace[1], some people rumored Kenya, while others insisted on Hawaii. Clearly, such conflicts can be extremely disturbing and misleading to the users who want to find the specific facts on something or somebody they concern [12]. Solutions to this challenge are generally recognized as *truth-finders*. Different from methods that seek non-factual truth (e.g., aggregating users' rating on a product, or analyzing people's opinions on a recent event), truth-finders aim at discovering the factual truth, such as the birthplace of Obama and the capital city of the United States.

While the *single-truth-finding problem* (STF)—which aims at finding the single true value for an item—has been widely studied, a more general case, where multiple true values (or multi-truth) might exist for a single item, is rarely explored [24]. In fact, multi-truth scenarios commonly exist in our real lives. For example, a book is usually authored by several people; a conference may have several deadlines; and the presidents of the United States involve a long list of names. We recognize the discovery of multiple true values (for either one or multiple data items) as the *multi-truth-finding problem* (MTF), of which STF can be treated as a special case. We identify the main challenges on solving MTF as follows:

- *Unknown quality on data sources.* The quality of data sources (e.g., trustworthiness) varies and is usually unknown *a priori* to truth-finding methods. For example, no website guarantees how much information it

[1]http://beforeitsnews.com/obama-birthplace-controversy/

publishes is accurate. Without assessing and differentiating the quality of data sources, truth-finding approaches could be easily misled by low quality and dependent sources[2].

- *Poor availability of the ground truth.* Obtaining the ground truth is a nontrivial task by itself due to the possibly numerous sources and data items involved. For example, it took tremendous efforts to setup a gold standard for the experimental book-author dataset—by manually checking the covers of each book [21], not to mention the more practical tasks like consolidating millions of book records from different libraries. The difficulty in obtaining the ground truth suggests an *unsupervised* approach to the truth-finding problem.

- *Unique multi-truth-finding features.* The multi-truth-finding problem (MTF) has unique features that should be properly addressed. For instance, instead of being totally different or exactly the same, the values claimed by different sources may overlap. Also, claiming one value for an item does not necessarily imply disclaiming all the other values for the item, because the claimed value may only cover the truth partially. All these features require special consideration when developing truth-finding solutions.

In this paper, we propose an integrated Bayesian approach to address the above challenges. In a nutshell, we make the following main contributions:

- We propose to reformulate the problem model for multi-truth discovery based on the relations between sources and values, and present corresponding methods for grouping sources and values to enable the reformulation. The reformulation can significantly reduce the computation load when solving the multi-truth-finding problem, without sacrificing the accuracy of the truth-finding results.

- We develop an integrated Bayesian model, which comprehensively incorporates novel methods on three key aspects, namely *source/value grouping*, *source dependency*, and *inter-value mutual exclusion*, to solve MTF. In particular, we define a method for calculating the effect of mutual exclusion between different values, by taking into account the agreement occurring by chance, similar to what *Kappa coefficient* does [6]. We also develop a finer-grained copy detection method to infer source dependencies. The new method is more efficient and especially suitable for sources with large profiles (i.e., sources that claim lots of values).

- We empirically show that our approach outperforms traditional methods using three large real-world datasets. We also study the impact on the effectiveness of the proposed approach of the three technical aspects in the Bayesian model.

The rest of the paper is structured as follows. Section 2 reviews the related work. Section 3 reformulates the multi-truth-finding problem. Section 4 presents the details of our solution, including the integrated Bayesian model and the related algorithms. Section 5 reports our experimental results. Finally, Section 6 provides some concluding remarks.

[2]Dependent sources are those sources that rely on other sources to provide data, e.g., copiers or aggregators.

2. RELATED WORK

Over the last few years, truth finding has become an active research area [21, 3, 5, 24, 9, 11]. Early truth-finding methods either take the *mean* or *median* (for numerical data) or employ the *majority voting* (for categorical data) to predict the truth. These methods treat every source equally and neglect their quality differences [1]. Recent approaches differentiate sources by giving more credit to trustworthy sources and propose solutions for the quality estimation of data sources. TruthFinder [21] alternately computes two measures, the *confidence of fact* (here, facts refer to values) and the *trustworthiness of source*, from each other through an iterative procedure. Pasternack et al. [16] propose *Average-Log*, *Investment* and *PooledInvestment* to avoid overestimating the trustworthiness of those sources that make more claims. Galland et al. [5] propose *Cosine* and *2-Estimates* to incorporate the mutual exclusion between categorical values. In [5], the authors refine the *2-Estimates* algorithm by introducing a new measure, *hardness of fact*, to estimate how hard in obtaining each fact. Truth-finding has also been modeled as optimization problems. The Conflict Resolution on Heterogeneous Data (CRH) framework recently proposed by Li *et al.* [11] models truth-finding as the problem of minimizing the weighted deviation of multi-source inputs from the estimated truth. Yin and Tan [22] employ a different optimization model and propose a semi-supervised solution.

Most above approaches have the disadvantage that a single evaluation result (e.g., the *confidence of fact* of a value) alone cannot indicate whether the value is true, which is also the reason that we have to adapt some of the existing methods in Section 5.2 for MTF. For better interpretation of evaluation results, Bayesian analysis [3] is introduced as a principled approach to the truth-finding problem, which yields explicit probabilistic estimations. Most current Bayesian-based approaches assume a prior distribution of latent variables, such as a uniform distribution over a single type of values (e.g., false values) [3] or distributions of all latent variables [7, 23, 24, 9]. Many of them develop probabilistic graphical models for handling categorical values [24], numerical values [23], ordinal values [9] and knowledge base triples [7]. Waguih *et al.* [20] summarize and experimentally evaluate these truth-finding methods.

Despite these efforts, most existing studies focus on single-truth-finding, yet little attention has been paid to the more general multi-truth-finding problem (MTF). The only work that we are aware of dealing with MTF is the Latent Truth Model (LTM) proposed in [24]. Based on a probabilistic graphical model, LTM makes strong assumptions on the prior distributions of latent variables, rendering the modeled problem intractable and inhibitive to incorporating various considerations. Distinguishing from previous approaches, our approach features an integrated Bayesian model based on a reformulated MTF model. Besides considering the unique features of MTF, our work also differs from the LTM approach [24] in two aspects: i) no assumption on prior distribution of latent variables and ii) new measures for better data source quality estimation. Both the reformulation model and no requirement of prior distribution of latent variables help reduce the computational load, which has been validated in our experimental studies (see Section 5).

3. MULTI-TRUTH-FINDING PROBLEM

3.1 The Problem Model

In general, a multi-truth-finding problem (MTF) involves four basic inputs: i) *data items*, the true values of which are to be discovered, e.g., the author-names of a book, ii) *sources*, which provide values on data items, e.g., a website that publishes the information on books and authors, iii) *values*, e.g., the author-names published by a website, and iv) *mappings* among the above elements, e.g., which websites publish which author's which books.

For each data item, MTF aims at identifying an optimal subset of values from the multi-source inputs to approximate the truth. Multi-truth-finding differs from single-truth-finding in that each source may claim multiple values—instead of a single value—on a single item, and multiple true values may hold on a single item.

Suppose m sources, $\mathcal{S} = \{s_1, s_2, \ldots, s_m\}$, provide values on n items, $\mathcal{O} = \{o_1, o_2, \ldots, o_n\}$. We denote by $\mathcal{S}_i$ the sources that provide values on item o_i, $\mathcal{O}(s_i)$ the items on which a source s_i provides values, and $\mathcal{V}_{ij}$ the values provided by source s_i on item o_j. To describe the mappings between sources and values, we further denote by $\mathcal{S}_i(v)$ the data sources that provide a specific value v on item o_i, and $\mathcal{V}_i(s)$ the values provided by a specific source s on item o_i.

3.2 Reformulating the Problem Model

MTF is inherently difficult and prohibitive to be solved directly. Given a set of possible true values $\mathcal{V}$, any element of the power set of $\mathcal{V}$, instead of any single value of $\mathcal{V}$ in STF, could be the actual truth in MTF. Intuitively, MTF can be first transformed into its single-truth counterparts to be solvable by the existing approaches. However, a direct transformation could excessively expand the problem scale and the unique features of MTF may not be preserved.

To address these problems, we propose to reformulate the MTF model by grouping sources and values based on their mapping relationships over all data items. For ease of illustration, we depict the source-value mappings under different models of MTF with respect to a single data item in Figure 1. Each subfigure shows a bipartite graph/hypergraph that maps sources (or sets of sources) and values (or sets of values) via edges. The three models are as the following:

- The *multi-mapping* model (Figure 1a): A many-to-one mapping between sources and sets of values, which represents the original MTF model as described in Section 3.1.
- The *single-mapping* model (Figure 1b): A many-to-many mapping between sources and values, which represents the result of casting an MTF directly to its single-truth counterparts.
- The *group-mapping* model (Figure 1c): A many-to-many mapping between groups of sources and groups of values, which represents our reformulated model.

Under the single-mapping model (Figure 1b), edges between sources and sets of values can be simply replaced with the edges between sources and individual values (e.g., the three edges between data source s_2 and values v_3, v_4, v_5). Interestingly, the single-truth-finding problem (STF), which is a many-to-one mapping between sources and values on a

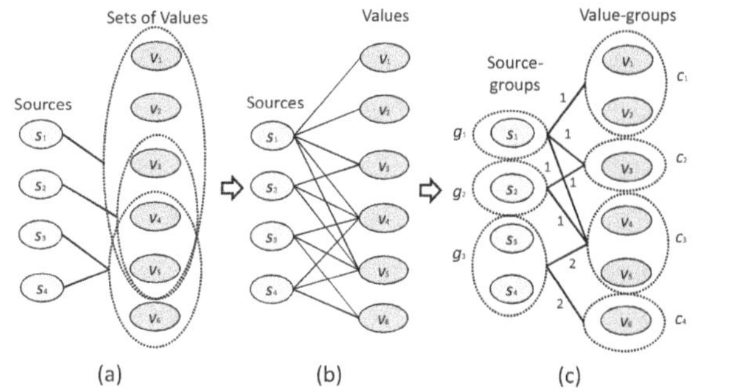

Figure 1: An example illustrating four sources claiming six potential true values under different models of the multi-truth-finding problem.

single item, immediately transforms to the single-mapping model when multiple items are concerned. This explains why the single-mapping model can be directly solved by existing single-truth-finding methods.

Though viable, transforming an MTF directly to the single-mapping model tends to result in an exploded problem scale, represented by a multiplied number of nodes in the resulting graph. This could in turn complicate the computation load of the truth-finding methods. As an example, the three nodes in the right side of Figure 1a—which are actually three overlapping sets of values—are decomposed into six nodes in Figure 1b. To reduce the resulting problem scale, instead of decomposing each set into single values, we group the sources (resp., values) that share the same mapping schema in Figure 1b. Each source-group represents the maximum number of sources that claim the same set of values. Similarly, each value-group represents the maximum number of values that are claimed by the same set of sources. As an example, sources s_3 and s_4 in Figure 1c claim the same set of values $\{v_4, v_5, v_6\}$, so s_3 and s_4 are grouped together as a source-group g_3. While v_6 is solely claimed by s_3 and s_4, v_1 and v_2 are claimed by s_1, so, v_1 and v_2 are grouped together as a value group c_1, and v_6 alone as a group c_4. We can see that after the grouping, the node size is reduced from 10 (4:6) in Figure 1b to 7 (3:4) in Figure 1c.

We introduce new concepts of *source-group* and *value-group* to define our reformulated problem model. In particular, we denote by $\mathcal{G}$ the set of source-groups, $\mathcal{C}$ the set of value-groups, $\mathcal{G}_n$ the source-groups that claim values on item o_n, $\mathcal{O}(g_k)$ the items on which a source group g_k claims values, and $\mathcal{C}_{kn}$ the value-groups claimed by the source-group g_k on item o_n. To describe the mapping, we further denote by $\mathcal{G}_n(c)$ the source-groups that claim a specific value-group c on item o_n, and $\mathcal{C}_n(g)$ the value-groups claimed by a specific source-group g on item o_n.

Different from value-groups, each source-group represents the joint strength of all the member sources. To represent this joint strength, we add weights to the edges associated with source-groups in Figure 1c. Given a data item o_n, we define the weight on the edge between source-group g and an associated value-group c as $\omega(g, c) = |g|$, where $c \in \mathcal{C}_n(g)$, $|g|$ is the number of sources contained in g. For the example in Figure 1c, both the edges associated with g_3 should be weighted by 2 because g_3 contains two sources. All the other edges are weighted by 1 because they each contains only one source. After the weighting, each source-group and each value-group will be considered as a single node in the subsequent truth-finding process.

4. THE TRUTH-FINDING MODEL

In this section, we introduce the details of our approach, including the methods on grouping sources and values, the integrated Bayesian framework and the corresponding algorithms. The main notations used in this paper are summarized in Table 1.

4.1 Grouping Sources and Values

Grouping methods aim at reducing the scale of the truth discovery problems. To this end, we expect each group to be as large as possible, to maximally reduce the computation load. Meanwhile, we expect the elements in each group to be as similar as possible, so as to keep the computation simple.

In our approach, we group sources directly based on the multi-mapping model for all data items, which is similar to Figure 1a, but involves multiple data items. We first map all distinct values to a Hash table, and then calculate the sum of hash values regarding each source. If two sums turn out equal, the corresponding sources are further compared with respective to their claimed values. In this way, we gradually assemble similar sources until all sources associated with the same set of values are grouped together. In case the hash values are non-additive, we designate a unique sequence over all the different values, and group those sources that map to the same subsequences. Values are grouped with respect to each data item in three steps based on the resulting source-groups. First, we transform the multi-mapping into the single-mapping model, and then transform the source-value mapping in the single-mapping model into the mapping between source-groups and values. Finally, the values are grouped in the similar way as we group sources. The time complexity of the grouping methods is $O(|\mathcal{S}||\mathcal{V}|)$.

4.2 Integrated Bayesian Model

The Bayesian model estimates the *a posteriori* veracity of values (i.e., latent variables) based on sources' trustworthiness (i.e., model parameters) and sources' reports on potential true values (i.e., observations) by Eq.(1). The sources' trustworthiness can in turn be assessed by the estimated veracity.

$$\mathcal{P}(a(c)|\mathcal{X}) = \frac{\mathcal{P}(\mathcal{X}|a(c))\mathcal{P}(a(c))}{\sum_{a\in\{a(c),\bar{a}(c)\}} \mathcal{P}(\mathcal{X}|a)\mathcal{P}(a)} \quad (1)$$

Both the *a priori* veracity and sources' trustworthiness are manually defined, and the conditional probabilities are calculated by:

$$\mathcal{P}(\mathcal{X}|a) = \prod_{g\in G^+(a)} \tau(g) \prod_{g'\in\mathcal{G}^-(a)} (1-\tau(g')) \quad (2)$$

In our approach, we extend the basic Bayesian model by incorporating the following considerations:

- *Degree of claim*, $w(g,c)$, represents the weights on the edges of the bipartite graph (defined in Section 3.2). The concept is the co-product of reducing the problem scale by using the source-grouping method.

- *Confidence score*, $\mu(g,c)$, is used to quantify the impact of mutual exclusive relation between different categorical values on multi-truth-discovery. We develop the corresponding methods to characterize the multi-truth features (to be detailed in Section 4.3).

- *Independence score*, $\mathcal{I}(g,c)$, is specified to quantify the impact of source dependency to multi-truth-discovery. We develop a finer-grained copy detection method to deal with sources with large profiles (to be detailed in Section 4.4).

In addition, since combining positive and negative perspectives can help better distinguish between sources with truth-sensitive and fault-sensitive behavioral features, we use *positive precision* (τ_{pp})—precision on true samples, and *negative precision* (τ_{np})—precision on false samples, to replace τ in Eq.(2). We define the above two measures based on the *veracity score* ($\sigma(c)$) of value-groups as follows:

$$\begin{cases} \tau_{pp}(g) = \frac{\sum_{o_n\in\mathcal{O}}\sum_{c\in\mathcal{C}_n(g)}\sigma(c)}{\sum_{o_n\in\mathcal{O}}|\mathcal{C}_n(g)|} \\ \tau_{np}(g) = \frac{\sum_{o_n\in\mathcal{O}}\sum_{c'\in\mathcal{C}_n(g)}(1-\sigma(c'))}{\sum_{o_n\in\mathcal{O}}|\mathcal{C}_n\setminus\mathcal{C}_n(g)|} \end{cases} \quad (3)$$

We compute *veracity score* as the truth probability of value-groups using the extended Bayesian model. We find the *degree of claim* naturally resides over quality measures as powers in the Bayesian model and should not be normalized—the Bayesian model calculates the joint effect of sources by multiplying their respective effects, and the multiplication turns into a power function when all sources have equal effect. Indeed, the Bayesian model requires modeling all factors as powers because simple multipliers will be eliminated during calculation. Therefore, we model above parameters as powers over the quality measures in our model. Here, we simply take the product of the different scores to represent their joint effect, but leave more sophisticated combinations of the scores to our future work. For simplicity, we synthesize the parameters into four factors:

$$\begin{cases} f(g,c) = \tau_{pp}(g)^{\omega(g,c)\mathcal{I}(g,c)\mu(g,c)} \\ \mathcal{J}(g,c) = (1-\tau_{np}(g))^{\omega(g,c)\mathcal{I}(g,c)\mu(g,c)} \\ \hat{f}(g,c) = (1-\tau_{pp}(g))^{\omega(g,c)\mathcal{I}(g,c)\mu(g,c)} \\ \hat{\mathcal{J}}(g,c) = \tau_{np}(g)^{\omega(g,c)\mathcal{I}(g,c)\mu(g,c)} \end{cases} \quad (4)$$

Given a value-group c, we define the likelihood of $\mathcal{X}$ under different assumptions on the truthfulness[3] of c:

$$\begin{cases} \mathcal{P}(\mathcal{X}|a(c)) = \prod_{g\in\mathcal{G}^+(a(c))} f(g,c) \prod_{g'\in\mathcal{G}^-(a(c))} \mathcal{J}(g',c) \\ \mathcal{P}(\mathcal{X}|\bar{a}(c)) = \prod_{g'\in\mathcal{G}^+(\bar{a}(c))} \hat{\mathcal{J}}(g',c) \prod_{g\in\mathcal{G}^-(\bar{a}(c))} \hat{f}(g,c) \end{cases} \quad (5)$$

The source-groups that support or oppose the same assertions should have the following relations:

$$\mathcal{G}^+(a(c)) = \mathcal{G}^-(\bar{a}(c)), \mathcal{G}^-(a(c)) = \mathcal{G}^+(\bar{a}(c)) \quad (6)$$

By substituting Eq.(5) into Eq.(1) and adopting Eq.(6), we have:

$$\mathcal{P}(a(c)|\mathcal{X}) = \frac{1}{1+\frac{\mathcal{P}(\bar{a}(c))}{\mathcal{P}(a(c))}\prod_{g\in\mathcal{G}^+(a(c))}\frac{\hat{f}(g,c)}{f(g,c)}\prod_{g'\in\mathcal{G}^-(a(c))}\frac{\hat{\mathcal{J}}(g',c)}{\mathcal{J}(g',c)}} \quad (7)$$

4.3 Calculating Confidence Scores

Since most truth-finding methods tend to favor sources with large profiles, incorporating the mutual exclusive relation can significantly neutralize this effect and therefore improve truth discovery accuracy on categorical data. An example of mutual exclusion is that, by claiming *Washington, D.C.* as the capital city of the United States, a source

[3] Truthfulness could be either true or false.

Table 1: Notations used in the paper

Notation	Explanation
s, g	A source (resp., source-group)
v, c	A value (resp., value-group)
$\mathcal{S}$, $\mathcal{G}$	The set of all sources (resp., all source-groups)
$\mathcal{V}$, $\mathcal{C}$	The set of all values (resp., all value-groups)
$\mathcal{G}(c)$, $\mathcal{S}(c)$	The set of all source-groups (resp., sources) that claim a specific value-group
$\mathcal{C}(g)$	The set of all value-groups claimed by a specific source-group
$a(c)$, $\bar{a}(c)$	The assertion that a specific value-group is true (resp., false)
$\mathcal{G}^+(a)$, $\mathcal{G}^-(a)$	The set of all source-groups that supports (resp., oppose) an assertion $a \in \{a(c), \bar{a}(c)\}$
$\omega(g, c)$	The degree of the claims made by a source-group on a value-group
$\mathcal{I}(g, c)$, $\mathcal{I}(s, c)$	The independence score of a source-group (resp., a source) on a value-group
$\mu(g, c)$	The confidence score of a source-group on a value-group
$\tau(g)$	The trustworthiness of a source-group
$\tau_{pp}(g)$, $\tau_{np}(g)$	The positive precision (resp., negative precision) of a source-group
$\sigma(c)$	The veracity (i.e., the probability of being true) of a value-group
ρ	The probability of a source-group copying from other source-groups
ρ_t, ρ_f	The probability of a source-group copying a true (resp. false) value-group from other source-groups
$\mathcal{X}$	The observation of which source-groups claim which value-groups
Ψ_c	The observation that two source-groups claim the same specific value-group

implicates that all other cities are not. Similarly, we can define mutual exclusion between sets of values for MTF. However, traditional truth-finding methods assume that a source always supports or opposes an assertion by its full credit. In fact, in MTF, a claimed value does not strictly reject the unclaimed values because each source could provide only partial true values. We use the *confidence score*, $\mu(g, c)$, to quantify the strength that a source-group supports or opposes an assertion. Similar to the *Kappa coefficient* [6], the idea is to exclude the effect of random guess in determining the strength. More specifically, given a set of value-groups $\mathcal{C}$, if a source-group g claims a subset $\mathcal{C}(g) \subseteq \mathcal{C}$, the *confidence score* of g on each value-group c is calculated as:

$$\mu(g,c) = \begin{cases} \dfrac{1}{|\mathcal{C}(g)|}\left(1 - \dfrac{1}{|\mathcal{C}|}\right), & c \in \mathcal{C}(g) \quad \text{(8a)} \\ \dfrac{1}{|\mathcal{C} \backslash \mathcal{C}(g)|} \dfrac{1}{|\mathcal{C}|}, & c \in \mathcal{C} \backslash \mathcal{C}(g) \quad \text{(8b)} \end{cases}$$

Based on above definition, by claiming certain value-groups, a source-group supports each claimed value-group and opposes each unclaimed value-group at the same time with the *confidence scores* defined by Eq.(8a) and Eq.(8b), respectively. All the *confidence scores* regarding the same source-group sum up to 1, where each score $\mu(g, c) \in (0, 1]$.

Generally, the *confidence score* has the following interesting properties:

- Given a fixed set of value-groups, the more (resp., less) value-groups a source-group claims, the less (resp., more) confidence the source-group has on the claimed value-groups, and meanwhile the more (resp., less) confidence on the unclaimed value-groups.
- Given a fixed number of value-groups claimed by a source-group, the larger (resp., smaller) the set of value-groups are, the more (resp., less) confidence the source-group has on the claimed (resp., unclaimed) value-groups.

As an example, suppose a source-group claims a subset $\{v_1, v_3\}$ of $\{v_1, v_2, v_3, v_4, v_5\}$, the traditional method obtains the corresponding scores as $\{+1, -1, +1, -1, -1\}$. In contrast, our method would produce $\{\frac{+2}{5}, \frac{-1}{15}, \frac{+2}{5}, \frac{-1}{15}, \frac{-1}{15}\}$[4]. In particular, the values $\frac{2}{5}$ is calculated as $\frac{1}{2} \cdot (1 - \frac{1}{5})$ by using Eq. (8a) and $\frac{1}{15}$ is calculated as $\frac{1}{3} \cdot \frac{1}{5}$ by using Eq. (8b). Compare to the results of the traditional method, our results reflect a differentiation towards source-groups' confidence on the claimed and unclaimed value-groups, i.e., $\frac{2}{5}$ for the claimed and $\frac{1}{15}$ for the unclaimed value-groups, instead of 1 for both types of value-groups. This is important because disclaiming a value is no longer equivalent to disclaiming the value in the MTF's context. Besides, our results implicitly reflect a differentiation towards source-groups of different behavioral features. Following the above example, if a source-group claims another subset $\{v_1, v_3, v_4, v_5\}$, which is closer to the full set, our method would redeem the source-group as being more audacious than being cautious and therefore lower the confidence on the claimed value-groups (meanwhile increase the confidence on the unclaimed value-groups), as manifested by the new results $\{\frac{+1}{5}, \frac{-1}{5}, \frac{+1}{5}, \frac{+1}{5}, \frac{+1}{5}\}$.

[4]In both results, the positive (resp., negative) sign represents the source-group supports (resp., opposes) the assertion that the corresponding value is true.

4.4 Inferring Source Dependency

Although copying relation has been actively studied recently [3, 14, 19], existing copy detection techniques only calculate a global score for each source [13]. Thus, they can hardly be applied to cases with partial dependence and/or high-order dependence. Especially according to the long tail characteristics [10], a source may have an extremely large profile (e.g., the store *A1Books*, which is a source in the *book-author* dataset, published nearly 700 book records on *www.abebooks.com*). Under such condition, a global score cannot manifest the characteristics of all different parts of the source's data. In contrast, a finer-grained copy detection technique will produce better predictions.

Based on this insight, we introduce a new copy detection method to calculate the *independence score* for each (source-group, value-group) pair. Given such a pair (g, c), we first calculate a score, $\mathcal{I}(s, c)$, for each (source, value-group) pair (s, c), where $s \in g$, and then aggregate the above scores to derive to independence score for (g, c) as follows:

$$\mathcal{I}(g,c) = \frac{\sum_{s \in g} \mathcal{I}(s,c)}{|g|} \quad (9)$$

where $\mathcal{I}(g, c)$ is the independence score of source-group g on value-group c.

4.4.1 Calculating Independence Score

Copying only happens between sources that provide the same value-group. Based on this observation, we propose to calculate $\mathcal{I}(s,c)$ by examining the independence probability of s on every other sources that provide the same value-group c. Given Ψ_c, the observation that two sources provide the same value-group c, we denote by $\perp$ (resp., $\sim$) the independence (resp., copying) relation between sources on c, and $\rightarrow$ the former copies c from the latter. Note that, we omit parameterizing the above notations by c (except Ψ_c) for ease of description. For two arbitrary sources s and s_i ($s \neq s_i$), we have:

$$\begin{cases} \mathcal{P}(s \perp s_i|\Psi_c) + \mathcal{P}(s \sim s_i|\Psi_c) = 1 \\ \mathcal{P}(s_i \rightarrow s|\Psi_c) + \mathcal{P}(s \rightarrow s_i|\Psi_c) = \mathcal{P}(s \sim s_i|\Psi_c)) \end{cases} \quad (10)$$

Given a value-group c, and any source that claims c, $s \in \mathcal{S}(c)$, we define the independence score of s on c as the probability that s never copies c from other sources:

$$\mathcal{I}(s,c) = \prod_{s_i \in \mathcal{S}(c) \wedge s_i \neq s} 1 - \mathcal{P}(s \rightarrow s_i|\Psi_c) \quad (11)$$

We assume equal probability of the two directions of copying, i.e.,

$$\mathcal{P}(s_i \rightarrow s|\Psi_c) = \mathcal{P}(s \rightarrow s_i|\Psi_c) \quad (12)$$

By incorporating Eq.(10) and Eq.(12), we reform Eq.(11) into:

$$\mathcal{I}(s,c) = \prod_{s_i \in \mathcal{S}(c) \wedge s_i \neq s} \frac{1 + \mathcal{P}(s \perp s_i|\Psi_c)}{2} \quad (13)$$

4.4.2 Calculating Independence Probability

To calculate the probability of independence between two sources, we first define the likelihood of Ψ_c under different assumptions on source dependence and the truthfulness of c:

$$\begin{cases} \mathcal{P}(\Psi_c|s_1 \sim s_2, a(c)) = \mathcal{P}(\Psi_c|s_1 \sim s_2, \bar{a}(c)) = 1 \\ \mathcal{P}(\Psi_c|s_1 \perp s_2, a(c)) = \prod_{s \in \{s_1,s_2\}} \tau_{pp}(s) \prod_{s \in \{s_1,s_2\}} \theta \\ \mathcal{P}(\Psi_c|s_1 \perp s_2, \bar{a}(c)) = \prod_{s \in \{s_1,s_2\}} \tau_{np}(s) \prod_{s \in \{s_1,s_2\}} \eta \end{cases} \quad (14)$$

Here, θ=1 - $\tau_{np}(s)$ and η=1 - $\tau_{pp}(s)$. For any assumption $d \in \{s_1 \sim s_2, s_1 \perp s_2\}$, we develop Bayesian formulas to calculate the corresponding probability, where $a \in \{a(c), \bar{a}(c)\}$:

$$\begin{aligned} \mathcal{P}(d|\Psi_c) &= \frac{\mathcal{P}(\Psi_c|d)\mathcal{P}(d)}{\sum_{d'} \mathcal{P}(\Psi_c|d')\mathcal{P}(d')} \\ &= \frac{\sum_a \mathcal{P}(\Psi_c|d,a)\mathcal{P}(d|a)\mathcal{P}(a)}{\sum_{d'}\sum_{a'} \mathcal{P}(\Psi_c|d',a')\mathcal{P}(d'|a')\mathcal{P}(a')} \end{aligned} \quad (15)$$

In our approach, we distinguish between two types of copiers, namely *blind copiers* and *smart copiers*. The blind copiers assume independence between the veracity of values and sources' probability of copying, i.e., $\mathcal{P}(d|a) = \mathcal{P}(d)$. We can thereby rewrite Eq.(15) to:

$$\mathcal{P}(d|\Psi_c) = \frac{\mathcal{P}(d)\sum_a \mathcal{P}(\Psi_c|d,a)\mathcal{P}(a)}{\sum_{d'} \mathcal{P}(d')\sum_{a'} \mathcal{P}(\Psi_c|d',a')\mathcal{P}(a')} \quad (16)$$

Since blind copiers have no bias on copying true/false values, we define a single *copying probability* ρ for all sources and on all value-groups:

$$\begin{cases} (\mathcal{P}(s_1 \sim s_2) = \mathcal{P}(s_1 \rightarrow s_2) + \mathcal{P}(s_2 \rightarrow s_1) = 2\rho \\ \mathcal{P}(s_1 \perp s_2) = 1 - 2\rho \end{cases} \quad (17)$$

By substituting Eq.(14) and Eq.(17) into Eq.(16), we get:

$$\mathcal{P}(s_1 \perp s_2|\Psi_c) = \frac{(1-2\rho)\mathcal{P}_{sum}}{2\rho + (1-2\rho)\mathcal{P}_{sum}} \quad (18)$$

where $\mathcal{P}_{sum}$ denotes the sum term in the numerator of Eq.(16):

$$\begin{aligned} \mathcal{P}_{sum} =& \mathcal{P}(a(c))(\tau_{pp}(s_1)\tau_{pp}(s_2) + (1-\tau_{np}(s_1))(1-\tau_{np}(s_2))) \\ &+ \mathcal{P}(\bar{a}(c))(\tau_{np}(s_1)\tau_{np}(s_2) + (1-\tau_{pp}(s_1))(1-\tau_{pp}(s_2))) \end{aligned} \quad (19)$$

Without prior knowledge, we can initialize veracity as:

$$\forall c \in \mathcal{C},\ \mathcal{P}(a(c)) = \mathcal{P}(\bar{a}(c)) = 0.5$$

On the other hand, the smart copiers have some "smartness" that they are more likely to copy true value-groups than false value-groups. We define different conditional probabilities for the two cases to reflect the "smartness":

$$\mathcal{P}(s_1 \sim s_2|a(c)) = 2\rho_t,\ \mathcal{P}(s_1 \sim s_2|\bar{a}(c)) = 2\rho_f \quad (20)$$

It can be inferred from the above equations that:

$$\mathcal{P}(s_1 \perp s_2|a(c)) = 1 - 2\rho_t,\ \mathcal{P}(s_1 \perp s_2|\bar{a}(c)) = 1 - 2\rho_f \quad (21)$$

For copiers to be "smart", the probability of a source copying a true value-group should be larger than the probability of copying a false value-group, i.e., $\rho_t > \rho_f$. By substituting Eq.(14)(20)(21) into Eq.(15), we get:

$$\mathcal{P}(s_1 \perp s_2|\Psi_c) = \frac{\mathcal{P}_{over}}{2\rho_t\mathcal{P}(a(c)) + 2\rho_f\mathcal{P}(\bar{a}(c)) + \mathcal{P}_{over}} \quad (22)$$

where $\mathcal{P}_{over}$ denotes the numerator in Eq.(15):

$$\begin{aligned} \mathcal{P}_{over} =& (1-2\rho_t)\mathcal{P}(a(c)) \\ & (\tau_{pp}(s_1)\tau_{pp}(s_2) + (1-\tau_{np}(s_1))(1-\tau_{np}(s_2))) \\ &+ (1-2\rho_f)(1-\mathcal{P}(a(c))) \\ & (\tau_{np}(s_1)\tau_{np}(s_2) + (1-\tau_{pp}(s_1))(1-\tau_{pp}(s_2))) \end{aligned}$$

Because it is critical for smart copiers to acquire some prior knowledge in order to be "smart", we update the prior probability with the latest estimation of veracity scores after each cycle of the iteration:

$$\forall c \in \mathcal{C},\ \mathcal{P}(a(c)) \leftarrow \sigma(c), \mathcal{P}(\bar{a}(c)) \leftarrow 1 - \sigma(c) \quad (23)$$

This ensures that the smart copiers' perception on values' veracity keeps evolving with the truth-finding process.

4.5 The Algorithm

Various algorithms, such as the iteration algorithm [21, 3, 5, 17] and the Expectation Maximization (EM) algorithm [23, 2], can be applied to solve our model. Both algorithms belong to the category of *coordinate ascent algorithms*, which differ in the methods used for estimating the quality of data sources. In particular, the former defines linear or nonlinear functions to calculate sources' quality, while the latter infers sources' quality by maximizing the (lower bound of the logarithmic) likelihood of observations over all source-claimed values.

Here we present an iteration algorithm for our integrated Bayesian model, but omit the description of the EM algorithm, which is only slightly different from [18], due to the limited space. For the ease of illustration, we use a single notation to represent the copying probabilities of the two

Algorithm 1: Iterative Multi-Truth-Finding

Input: data items $\mathcal{O}$, value-groups $\mathcal{C} = \{\mathcal{C}_n | o_n \in \mathcal{O}\}$, source-groups $\mathcal{G}$, the mapping between source-groups and value-groups $\mathcal{G}_n(c)$ and $\mathcal{C}_n(g)$

Output: $\{v | v \in c \wedge \sigma(c) \geq 0.5\}$

1 $\rho \leftarrow$ default values;
2 **foreach** $g \in \mathcal{G}$ **do**
3     $\{\tau_{pp}(g), \tau_{np}(g)\} \leftarrow$ default values;
4 **foreach** $o_n \in \mathcal{O}$ *and* $c \in \mathcal{C}_n$ **do**
5     $\sigma(c) \leftarrow$ default values;
6 **foreach** $o_n \in \mathcal{O}$, $g \in \mathcal{G}_n(c)$, $c \in \mathcal{C}_n(g)$ **do**
7   compute $w_n(g, c)$, $u_n(g, c)$;
8 **repeat**
9   **foreach** $o_n \in \mathcal{O}$ *and* $c \in \mathcal{C}_n$ **do**
10   **foreach** $g \in \mathcal{G}_n(c)$ **do**
11             $f_n(g, c)$,$\hat{f}(g, c)$,$J_n(g, c)$, $\hat{J}_n(g, c) \leftarrow$Eq.(4);
12             $I_n(g, c) \leftarrow$Eq.(9) ;
13         $\sigma(c) \leftarrow$Eq.(7);
14   **foreach** $g \in \mathcal{G}$ **do**
15         $\tau_{pp}(g)$, $\tau_{np}(g) \leftarrow$Eq.(3);
16 **until** *convergence*;

types of copiers:

$$\rho = \begin{cases} \{\rho\}, & \textit{for blind copiers} \\ \{\rho_t, \rho_f\}, & \textit{for smart copiers} \end{cases}$$

The detailed procedure is described in Algorithm 1. In the initialization phase (Lines 1-7), the copying probabilities are defined *a priori* (Line 1). Sources' quality and values' veracity are initialized with default values (Lines 2-5). The algorithm then computes the *degree of claim* and *confidence score* for each pair of source-group and value-group (Lines 6-7). Both parameters and the copying probabilities remain unchanged until the algorithm terminates. For each cycle of the iteration (Line 8-16), the algorithm calculates the veracity scores (Lines 9-13) and sources' quality (Lines 14-15) in turn. For each data item, the veracity scores are calculated in two steps: i) calculates the synthesized factors (as defined by Eq.(4)) and *independence score* for each pair of source-group and value-group (Lines 10-12) and ii) updates the veracity scores for each value-group (Line 13). The iteration terminates when the algorithm converges (i.e., the algorithm's judgment on the truthfulness of all values remains unchanged for certain consecutive cycles) (Line 16). Logarithms are used in calculating the multiplication of small decimals to ensure accuracy.

5. EXPERIMENTS

In this section, we report our experimental studies on the comparison of our approach with the state-of-the-art algorithms and the impact on the performance of our approach of different key aspects in the Bayesian model.

5.1 The Datasets

We used three real-world datasets in our experiments. The *book-author dataset* [21] contains 33,971 book-author records crawled from *www.abebooks.com*. The records of the website are contributed by numerous book stores (i.e., sources), where each record represents a book store's claim on the author(s) of a book. We removed the invalid and duplicated records. To make the problem more challenging, we also excluded the records with only minor conflicts (i.e., the records related to those books on which less than two distinct lists of author-names are provided). Finally, we obtained 12,623 distinctive claims describing 649 sources (i.e., websites) that provide author-names on 664 books. On average, each book has 3.2 authors. The ground truth provided for the original dataset is used as gold standard.

Table 2: Evaluation of the major sources in the *movie-director* dataset.

Source	Record number	Positive precision	Negative precision
hkmdb.com	5265	0.91	0.87
rottentomatoes.com	4950	0.92	0.95
mrqe.com	4931	0.98	0.93
nowrunning.com	3433	0.83	0.81
imdb.com	2592	0.98	0.94
moviefone.com	2529	0.92	0.86
dvdmoviemenus.com	2208	0.87	0.69
abc.net.au	1563	0.99	0.84
nollywoodreinvented.com	1071	0.95	0.80
hoyts.com.au	1066	0.96	0.93

The *parent-children dataset* [16] contains 11,099,730 records about people's birth and death dates, the names of their parents/children and spouses, edited by different users (i.e., sources) on Wikipedia. We particularly extracted the records on the parent-children relations from this dataset. After eliminating the duplicates, we finally obtained 55,259 users claiming children for 2,579 persons. In the resulting dataset, each person has on average 2.45 children. We used the latest editing records as the ground truth.

We prepared the third dataset, the *movie-director dataset*, by crawling 33,194 records from 16 movie websites. We removed redundant records and finally obtained 6,402 movies, each on average having 1.2 directors. We sampled 200 movies and extracted their director information from *citwf.com* as the ground truth. Table 2 shows the top ten websites that provide the most records, with their quality values obtained by one of our methods MBM (see Section 5.2 for details). It should be noted that most datasets used in previous works for categorical truth discovery [12, 20] are not suitable for our multi-truth-finding problem. The three real datasets used in our work are comparable to those datasets in size.

5.2 Baselines and Metrics

We compared our approach with the following methods, which were modified, if necessary, to incorporate mutual exclusion.

- *Majority Voting.* This method regards a value as true if the proportion of the sources that claim the value exceeds a certain threshold.
- *Sums (Hubs and Authorities)* [8], *Average-Log* [16]. Both methods compute the total trustworthiness of all sources that claim and disclaim a value separately, and recognize the value as true if the former is larger than the latter.
- *TruthFinder* [21], *2-Estimates* [5], and *LTM* [24]. The three methods can be directly applied without modification, which recognize a value as true if its veracity score exceeds 0.5.

It should be noted that we excluded the comparison with several methods that are inapplicable to the multi-truth-finding problem. For example, the algorithms in [3] cannot be applied to our problem because they all assume the number of false values as a prior knowledge. The approach

Table 3: Comparison of different algorithms on the three datasets: the best and second best performance values are in bold; both *precision* and *recall* are in the range of [0,1].

Method	Book-author dataset			Parent-children dataset			Movie-director dataset		
	Precision	Recall	Time(s)	Precision	Recall	Time(s)	Precision	Recall	Time(s)
Majority voting	0.88	0.62	**0.03**	**1.00**	0.52	**1.25**	**1.00**	0.74	**0.07**
Sums	0.69	0.49	**0.10**	0.86	0.59	3.20	0.88	0.64	0.22
Average-Log	0.70	0.38	0.13	0.89	0.79	4.08	0.89	0.87	0.24
TruthFinder	0.73	0.80	**0.10**	0.86	**0.89**	**2.89**	0.87	**0.88**	0.27
2-Estimates	0.79	0.65	0.12	0.92	0.62	3.44	0.89	0.77	**0.21**
LTM	0.84	0.78	0.86	0.93	0.82	39.2	0.83	0.83	1.84
MBM	0.78	**0.87**	0.16	**0.97**	**0.87**	3.19	0.89	0.87	0.22
MBM-C	**0.88**	0.85	0.50	0.94	0.85	19.1	**0.93**	**0.92**	1.28
MBM-EM	**0.86**	**0.91**	0.26	0.92	0.84	6.87	0.92	**0.88**	0.72

in [16] requires normalizing the veracity of values, which is infeasible for the multi-truth-finding problem. Finally, the methods in [23, 11] focus on handling heterogeneous data, while our approach is proposed specially for categorical data.

To ensure fair comparisons, we first ran a series of experiments to decide the optimal parameter settings for the baseline methods. Since the parameter tuning for our methods are relatively more complicated, we simply used a generic parameter settings for all datasets, i.e., the copying probabilities of blind copiers ρ=0.8 and for smart copiers, ρ_t=0.85 and ρ_f=0.7. The initial source quality values do not usually affect the experimental results as long as they are not unreasonably large or small (as indicated in our experiments in Section 5.3.2), so we just initialized them as $\tau_{pp}(g)$=0.8 and $\tau_{np}(g)$=0.7.

To evaluate our approach under different implementations, we derived three variants of our approach:

- *MBM*: our (**M**ulti-truth) **B**ayesian **M**odel that adopts the grouping method and the new mutual exclusion definition.
- *MBM-C*: a variant of MBM that additionally incorporates our **C**opy detection method for blind copiers[5].
- *MBM-EM*: a variant of MBM that estimates sources' quality by performing the Maximum Likelihood Estimation using the **EM** algorithm, instead of Eq.(3).

We implemented all algorithms using Java SDK 7, and conducted experiments on a 64-bit Windows 7 PC with an octa-core 3.4GHz CPU and 8GB RAM.

5.3 The Results

5.3.1 Comparison of Truth-Finding Methods

Table 3 shows the performance of different algorithms on the three datasets in terms of *precision*, *recall*, and *computation time*. The computation time of our algorithms includes the time spent for both problem reformulation and Bayesian truth discovery. However, the results show the time spent on reformulation is minor when compared to that of main truth discovery process. Our three algorithms consistently achieved the best precision and recall among all the compared methods, except the *majority voting* which always achieved the best precision (in those cases, our algorithms still yielded the second best results). All the algorithms achieved lower precision on the *book-author* dataset due to the elimination of the records with minor conflicts.

[5]We only used blind copiers for the comparison because smart copiers tend to produce similar results. They will be specially compared via experiments in Section 5.3.2.

The *majority voting* achieved comparatively low recall (nearly always the lowest) on all datasets. This is because most sources tend to provide only a minor proportion of the entire truth. So when tuning the sources' trustworthiness as the prior parameters, only the precision of the method is optimized. Despite the low recall, the majority voting achieved nearly perfect precision—except on the *book-author* dataset where the approach is inapplicable. This may imply that the majority voting method is better used for generating the ground truth for semi-supervised truth-finding approaches, rather than for solving MTF, unless more comprehensive quality measures are considered in evaluating the sources.

Besides the majority voting, both LTM and 2-Estimates showed higher precision than the other baselines. All baselines except TruthFinder considered the mutual exclusive relation. However, these methods achieved lower recall when compared to TruthFinder or our methods. They identified only a small proportion of true values. This may be due to their neglect of the possibility of random guess in considering sources' claims—as opposed to the definition of mutual exclusive relation in our approach. This should explain why our methods achieve better recall than those methods. It should be noted that TruthFinder achieved better recall yet generally lower precision than the other baselines, which may attribute to its overestimation of veracity scores.

As for the efficiency, our MBM and all the baselines—except LTM—had comparable computation time on the three datasets. LTM and MBM-C always demanded the longest computation time. While the efficiency of LTM depends on the problem scale, MBM-C is more sensitive to datasets. Specially, MBM-C achieved significantly better efficiency than LTM on the *parent-children* dataset, because of the many source-groups and value-groups in this dataset. Overall, our three methods showed no significant difference in their truth-finding quality. However, MBM-C exhibited less stable performance, depending on the underlying dependence among sources in the datasets. MBM-EM always ranked in the middle of the three in term of efficiency.

5.3.2 Impact of Different Concerns

We also studied the impact of different aspects to our methods and report the findings in this section.

Grouping of sources/values. We exploited our methods to discover various source-groups and value-groups in the three datasets. Table 4 shows examples of three source-groups found in the *book-author* dataset. In the first example, six sources claim the same two authors for a book. In the third example, two sources claim the same author for each of the ten books. By grouping the sources , the number of sources in the three examples was reduced from 10

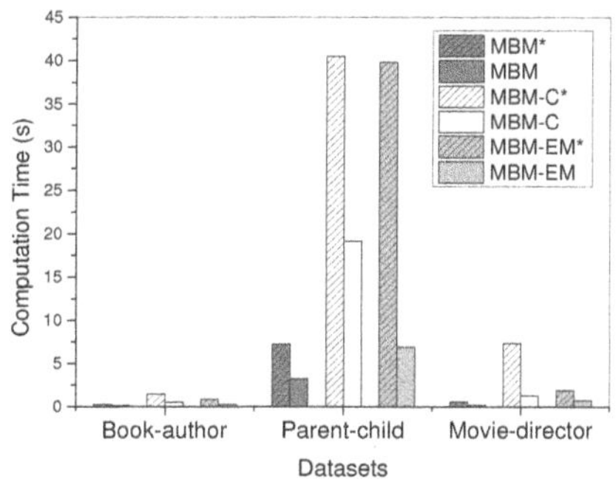

Figure 2: Performance comparison of the proposed algorithms between using and not using the grouping methods. The algorithms marked by asterisk are those without using the grouping methods.

to 3. After the grouping, the total number of sources (or joint sources) in the *book-author dataset* is reduced from 4,264 to 3,874. We found the *author-book dataset* contained more source-groups, while the *movie-director dataset* contains more value-groups. The *parent-children dataset* contains large numbers of both types of groups. A comparison of the three algorithms between using and not using the grouping methods (Figure 2) demonstrates the effectiveness of the grouping methods.

Mutual exclusion. In our datasets, each item has on average 1 to 4 different values, so the confidence scores stay in the range of $(0.08, 0.75)$ (calculated by Eq.(8a) and Eq.(8b)). To examine the effect of our defined confidence scores, we implemented our methods based on the traditional definition and our new definition of mutual exclusive relation, respectively, and compared the results. Figure 3a shows the comparison on the *movie-director* dataset, which demonstrates that our definition almost always brings better precision and recall. The results on the other two datasets are similar.

Table 4: An example of three source-groups in the *book-author* dataset.

Source (Website)	Item (ISBN)	Value (Authors)
bookscorner1 Jerome McCarthy Mybooklocator "Rare Finds Books, Music, Etc." Twice Read Books Shadow Books	0201489163	Campbell David Campbell Mary
bookmac Allen Williams Books	9780335216369	Alyson Simpson Angela Thomas Asha Jennifer Len Unsworth
Usedbooks123 Free Shipping Books	0201308207 0201325705 0201379538 0201379619 0201489295 0201489805 0201633957 0201657643 0201709147 0201711141	Denning Dorothy E Brent Callaghan Black Daryl P Jeffrey Rule S F John Lescher J Smedinghoff Thomas Bradner Scott Sharma Vivek Box Don Aviel D Rubin

Blind and smart copiers. We investigated the effect of incorporating copy detection by comparing MBM and MBM-C in the experiments. The results showed improved precision and recall of our approach by incorporating copy detection methods. We further studied the performance of our methods using blind copiers and smart copiers, respectively. We observed that using smart copiers led to slightly slower convergence but better results on the *movie-director* dataset (Figure 3b). As the copying probability grew, we observed an increase in both precision and recall of the methods using blind copiers on the movie-director dataset, until the probability became close to 0.8 (Figure 4a). Smart copiers also showed similar features (Figure 4b) on the movie-director dataset (Figure 4b). It is worth noting that, *recall* had some robustness on ρ_f. At certain points, increasing ρ_f could even yield a higher *recall*. The impact of initial parameters were similar for the other datasets.

Comprehensive source quality. We varied the initial values of source quality measures for our methods and observed similar results on all three datasets. This indicates that our approach is insensitive to the initial assumptions of source quality (as long as the initial values are not infeasible large or small, such as equal to one, or close to zero). Compared to the traditional measures, our source quality measures incurred similar computation time but higher recall on larger

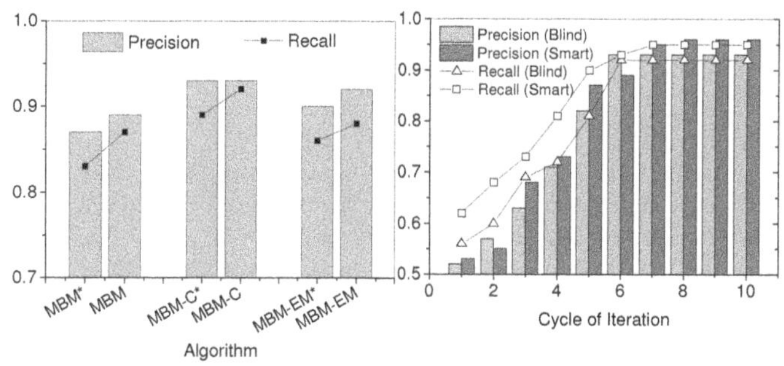

(a) (b)

Figure 3: (a) Performance comparison of the proposed algorithms between using the traditional definition and using our definition of mutual exclusion on the *movie-direct* dataset: the algorithms marked by asterisk are those adopting the traditional definition. (b) Performance comparison of MBM-C between using the blind copiers and using the smart copiers. Both blind copiers and smart copiers were configured with their optimal parameter settings and ran a fixed number of iterations, i.e., 10, regardless if they converge.

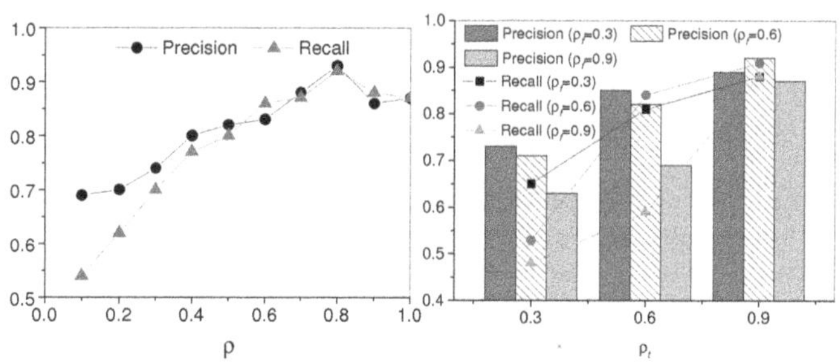

(a) (b)

Figure 4: (a) Performance of MBM-C under varying copying probability of blind copiers, i.e., ρ. (b) Performance of MBM-C under varying copying probabilities of smart copiers, i.e., ρ_t and ρ_f.

datasets (e.g., the *parent-children* dataset and the *movie-director* dataset), while the advantages on smaller datasets (e.g., the *book-author* dataset) was not obvious.

5.4 Discussion

In this section, we briefly review the important concepts incorporated in our approach via the *hardness of fact* to better understand the experimental results. The *hardness of fact* was first proposed in [5] to quantify the difficulty in determining the truthfulness of a value. It is used by paying the most trust on the sources that claim a more difficult value (which has a higher *hardness of fact*). We find that both the *smart copiers* and our mutual exclusion definition can be interpreted or inferred from the concept of *hardness of fact* in evaluating the sources. In particular, a smart copier prefers copying the values with higher veracity. Those values are usually claimed by more sources. In defining a higher probability of copying, the smart copier actually dampens the effect of those sources which jointly claim values with many other sources. This is exactly the effect of considering the hardness of fact in the truth-finding process. As for our proposed mutual exclusion definition, a claimed value would receive a higher confidence score if given a larger number of distinct values on a specific item. This can also be interpreted from the *hardness of fact*. Since it is more difficult to identify a true value from a larger set of different values, once a value is identified as true, the value should be more trusted based on the philosophy of the *hardness of fact*.

6. CONCLUSION

In this paper, we address the problem of discovering multiple true values from the multi-source data, which has rarely been studied in the previous works. We propose an integrated Bayesian approach, which comprehensively incorporates novel methods on three key aspects that characterize the multi-truth-finding problem (MTF), namely source-value mapping, mutual exclusive relation, and source dependency, to better solve the problem. In particular, we leverage the unique mapping features of MTF to reformulate the problem model in order to reduce the problem scale. We develop a new definition of mutual exclusion to reflect the inter-value implication under the MTF's context and a finer-grained copy detection method to cope with sources with large profiles. Experimental studies on three real-world datasets demonstrate the effectiveness of our approach. Our future work will focus on investigating more comprehensive ways for solving the MTF, e.g., by identifying and integrating more aspects to enhance the Bayesian model.

7. REFERENCES

[1] J. Bleiholder and F. Naumann. Conflict handling strategies in an integrated information system. In *IIWeb, held together with WWW*, 2006.

[2] A. P. Dempster, N. M. Laird, and D. B. Rubin. Maximum likelihood from incomplete data via the em algorithm. *J. Roy. Statist. Soc. Ser. B*, 39(1):1–38, 1977.

[3] X. L. Dong, L. Berti-Equille, and D. Srivastava. Integrating conflicting data: the role of source dependence. *PVLDB*, 2(1):550–561, 2009.

[4] X. L. Dong and D. Srivastava. Big data integration. In *ICDE*, pages 1245–1248, 2013.

[5] A. Galland, S. Abiteboul, A. Marian, and P. Senellart. Corroborating information from disagreeing views. In *WSDM*, pages 131–140, 2010.

[6] K. L. Gwet. *Handbook of inter-rater reliability: The definitive guide to measuring the extent of agreement among raters.* Advanced Analytics, LLC, 2014.

[7] G. Kasneci, J. V. Gael, D. Stern, and T. Graepel. Cobayes: bayesian knowledge corroboration with assessors of unknown areas of expertise. In *WSDM*, pages 465–474, 2011.

[8] J. M. Kleinberg. Authoritative sources in a hyperlinked environment. *JACM*, 46(5):604–632, 1999.

[9] B. Lakshminarayanan and Y. W. Teh. Inferring ground truth from multi-annotator ordinal data: a probabilistic approach. *arXiv preprint arXiv:1305.0015*, 2013.

[10] Q. Li, Y. Li, J. Gao, L. Su, B. Zhao, M. Demirbas, W. Fan, and J. Han. A confidence-aware approach for truth discovery on long-tail data. *PVLDB*, 8(4), 2014.

[11] Q. Li, Y. Li, J. Gao, B. Zhao, W. Fan, and J. Han. Resolving conflicts in heterogeneous data by truth discovery and source reliability estimation. In *SIGMOD*, pages 1187–1198, 2014.

[12] X. Li, X. L. Dong, K. Lyons, W. Meng, and D. Srivastava. Truth finding on the deep web: is the problem solved? *PVLDB*, 6(2):97–108, 2012.

[13] X. Li, X. L. Dong, K. B. Lyons, W. Meng, and D. Srivastava. Scaling up copy detection. In *ICDE*, 2015.

[14] X. Liu, X. L. Dong, B. C. Ooi, and D. Srivastava. Online data fusion. *PVLDB*, 4(11):932–943, 2011.

[15] A. Pal, V. Rastogi, A. Machanavajjhala, and P. Bohannon. Information integration over time in unreliable and uncertain environments. In *WWW*, pages 789–798, 2012.

[16] J. Pasternack and D. Roth. Knowing what to believe (when you already know something). In *COLING*, pages 877–885, 2010.

[17] J. Pasternack and D. Roth. Making better informed trust decisions with generalized fact-finding. In *IJCAI*, pages 2324–2329, 2011.

[18] J. Pasternack and D. Roth. Latent credibility analysis. In *WWW*, pages 1009–1020, 2013.

[19] R. Pochampally, A. D. Sarma, X. L. Dong, A. Meliou, and D. Srivastava. Fusing data with correlations. In *SIGMOD*, pages 433–444, 2014.

[20] D. A. Waguih and L. Berti-Equille. Truth discovery algorithms: An experimental evaluation. *arXiv preprint arXiv:1409.6428*, 2014.

[21] X. Yin, J. Han, and P. S. Yu. Truth discovery with multiple conflicting information providers on the web. *TKDE*, 20(6):796–808, 2008.

[22] X. Yin and W. Tan. Semi-supervised truth discovery. In *WWW*, pages 217–226, 2011.

[23] B. Zhao and J. Han. A probabilistic model for estimating real-valued truth from conflicting sources. In *QDB*, 2012.

[24] B. Zhao, B. I. Rubinstein, J. Gemmell, and J. Han. A bayesian approach to discovering truth from conflicting sources for data integration. *PVLDB*, 5(6):550–561, 2012.

Approximate Truth Discovery via Problem Scale Reduction

Xianzhi Wang[1], Quan Z. Sheng[1], Xiu Susie Fang[1], Xue Li[2], Xiaofei Xu[3], and Lina Yao[1]
[1]The University of Adelaide, Adelaide, SA 5005, Australia
[2]The University of Queensland, Brisbane, QLD 4072, Australia
[3]Harbin Institute of Technology, Harbin 150001, China
{xianzhi.wang, michael.sheng, xiu.fang, lina.yao}@adelaide.edu.au,
xiaofei@hit.edu.cn, xueli@itee.uq.edu.au

ABSTRACT

Many real-world applications rely on multiple data sources to provide information on their interested items. Due to the noises and uncertainty in data, given a specific item, the information from different sources may conflict. To make reliable decisions based on these data, it is important to identify the trustworthy information by resolving these conflicts, i.e., the truth discovery problem. Current solutions to this problem detect the veracity of each value jointly with the reliability of each source for every data item. In this way, the efficiency of truth discovery is strictly confined by the problem scale, which in turn limits truth discovery algorithms from being applicable on a large scale. To address this issue, we propose an approximate truth discovery approach, which divides sources and values into groups according to a user-specified approximation criterion. The groups are then used for efficient inter-value influence computation to improve the accuracy. Our approach is applicable to most existing truth discovery algorithms. Experiments on real-world datasets show that our approach improves the efficiency compared to existing algorithms while achieving similar or even better accuracy. The scalability is further demonstrated by experiments on large synthetic datasets.

Categories and Subject Descriptors

H.2.8 [**Information Systems**]: Database Management—*Data Mining*; I.2.m [**Computing Methodologies**]: Artificial Intelligence—*Miscellaneous*

Keywords

Truth discovery; problem scale reduction; recursive method; consistency assurance

1. INTRODUCTION

The increasing amount of data generated from the World Wide Web and the recently emerged Internet of Things (IoT) applications pose challenges to database research, characterized by the *volume*, *velocity*, *variety* and *veracity* features of Big Data. With advanced data extraction and collection technologies, information about a real-world entity can be obtained from various sources in both cyber and physical worlds. The data provided by distant sources are inherently unreliable, due to the uncertain data—noises, missing updates, missing values, transmission errors, or maliciously manipulated data. Thus, multi-source data for describing the same entity are liable to be conflicting. To support reliable decisions based on or to exploit the maximal value from multi-source data, it is critical to identify the trustworthy information from the multi-source inputs. This problem is non-trivial because the reliability of sources is often unknown *a priori* and ground truths are in most cases unavailable. To complicate the matter, the number of sources and entities in a truth discovery problem can be extremely large, which requires high scalability of truth discovery algorithms.

While the truth discovery problem has been studied from different perspectives [12], it remains inefficient. Waguih *et al.* [18] experimentally evaluated the performance of several truth discovery algorithms on three computing nodes on both real-world and synthetic datasets with various configurations, and concluded that most algorithms have efficiency problems. For example, both the algorithms based on Maximum Likelihood Estimation (MLE) and those on probabilistic graphical approaches were too computationally expensive to be applied to large scale problems. Moreover, to pursue higher accuracy, recent approaches incorporate more factors, such as the hardness of fact [7], the effect of random guess [16], and data sufficiency [10], making them increasingly complex and less efficient.

To the best of our knowledge, no studies have focused on improving the efficiency of truth discovery algorithms. We perceive that the issue in truth discovery is a hybrid technical problem, which inspires us to strategically reduce the problem scale and pursue approximate solutions in exchange for higher efficiency. Based on this insight, we propose an approximate approach focusing on reducing the problem scale. In a nutshell, we make the following contributions:

- We investigate the characteristics of real-world datasets and propose an approximate truth discovery approach, which groups sources and values to reduce the problem scale and considers the inter-group influence to improve truth discovery accuracy. The approach can achieve a personalized balance between the efficiency and accuracy of truth discovery algorithms according to a user-specified criterion.

CIKM'15, October 19–23, 2015, Melbourne, Australia.
© 2015 ACM. ISBN 978-1-4503-3794-6/15/10 ...$15.00.
DOI: http://dx.doi.org/10.1145/2806416.2806444.

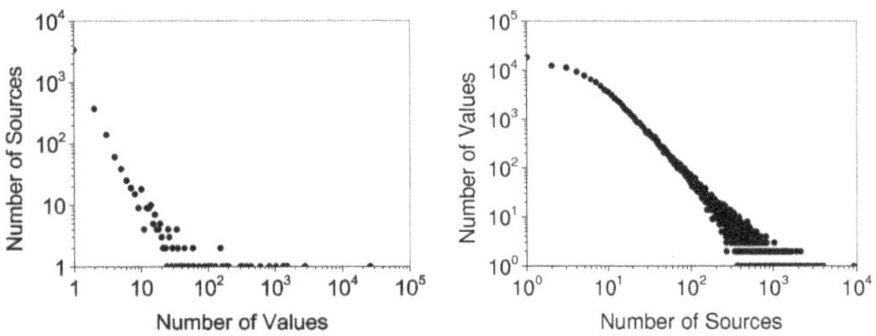

(a) Population Dataset (b) Biography Dataset

Figure 1: The number of values claimed by each source: most sources claim very few values.

- We propose a number of content-based and mapping-based methods for grouping sources and values, respectively, to reduce the problem scale. In particular, we model content-based grouping as an optimization problem and solve it by a recursive algorithm with the *branch and bound* strategy.
- We present the methods for improving the truth discovery accuracy, by amending the estimated veracity scores of values without manual intervention.
- We conduct experiments using both real-world and synthetic datasets to evaluate the proposed approaches, which show the significant improvements of the efficiency of existing truth discovery algorithms without necessarily sacrificing the accuracy.

The rest of the paper is organized as follows. We discuss the observations that motivate our work and define the truth discovery problem in Section 2. Section 3 introduces our approach. The experimental results are reported in Section 4. We discuss the related work in Section 5 and give some concluding remarks in Section 6.

2. PRELIMINARIES

2.1 Observations and the Motivation

This work is motivated by two sources of observations: real world datasets and existing truth discovery algorithms.

2.1.1 Real-World Datasets

We investigate the distribution of values on different sources and items in various real-world datasets (e.g., Figure 1 and Figure 2 show the results in *population* [14] and *biography* [14] datasets, respectively). We observe *long tail phenomenon* [10] in most investigated datasets, which has the following characteristics: i) most sources claim very few values and ii) most items have very few distinct values claimed.

Since the complexity of truth discovery is fundamentally determined by the problem scale—characterized by the number of links[1] between sources and values, an intuitive solution for improving truth discovery efficiency is to reduce the number of nodes (sources and values) and links. We focus on two types of nodes in developing our approach:

- *Sources that claim very few values.* While such sources make up a major portion of all sources, their association with values are sparse. This makes it more likely for different sources to claim the same set of values on the data items. Without extra information, truth discovery methods assess sources' reliability solely based on the sources' inputs. Hence, the sources that claim the same sets of values will always receive the same assessment results, and repetitively computing the reliability for each of those sources becomes unnecessary.
- *Items with large numbers of values.* Intuitively, when the values of an item become enormous, they easily become close. To verify this point, we investigate the value distribution of data items and observe varying distributions on different data items. For example, the claimed population sizes of *sarajevo* (Figure 3a) are distributed rather unevenly, with some values extremely close to each other and others well separated. In contrast, the claimed birth dates of *George W. Bush* (Figure 3b) are dominated by a single value. Indeed, in many practical cases, especially those where the optimal solution is difficult to reach, users do not usually care about the minor differences. Thus, we can provide approximate solutions and only offer more precise results per users' requests.

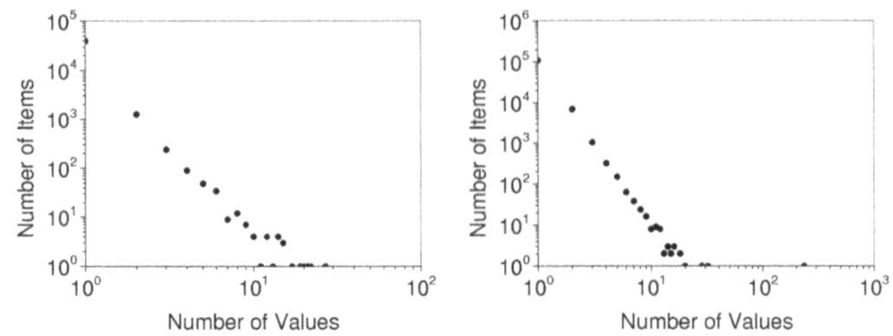

(a) Population Dataset (b) Biography Dataset

Figure 2: The number of values claimed for each item: some data items have large numbers of values claimed.

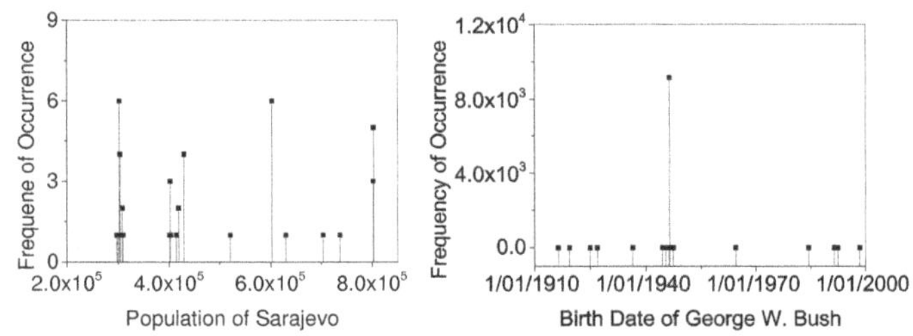

(a) (b)

Figure 3: Examples of value distribution of the *population* and *biography* datasets: varying distributions for different data items (Note that some values are not shown because they fall out of the range of display).

2.1.2 Truth Discovery Algorithms

We investigate the truth probability[2] distribution of existing truth discovery algorithms during each cycle of iteration, if the algorithms require iteration, to examine if they

[1] A link exists between a source and a value only when the source claims the value.

[2] *Truth probability* means the probability of being true, which is calculated by normalizing the evaluation results, or veracity score, of each distinct value.

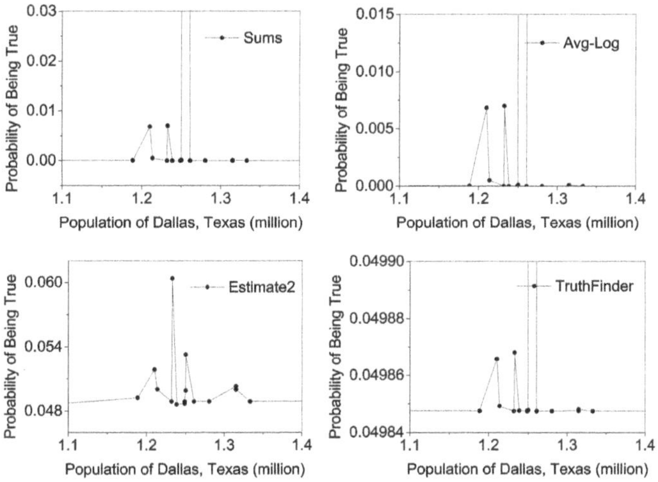

Figure 4: The distribution of truth probability achieved by four truth discovery algorithms during their third cycle of iteration over the different population sizes of Dallas, Texas.

produce consistent evaluation results. Here, by consistency, we mean *similar values should get similar truth probabilities*. For example, in determining a city's population size, two similar values, e.g., 8,390,482 and 8,416,535, should have similar truth probabilities. In contrast, the truth probability of 3,517,424 should be more different, since the value is less similar to the former two values. Enforcing consistent evaluation is crucial for ensuring the accuracy of truth discovery, as it improves the robustness of truth discovery algorithms in terms of smoothing the fluctuations and anomalies in the evaluation results. Intuitively, the truth discovery results cannot be justified without ensuring consistency because it would be insensible to assign very different truth probabilities to two values if they are extremely close.

Unfortunately, existing truth discovery algorithms lack consideration of such consistency, which obtain rather fluctuating truth probability distribution over the distinct values for the same item (as shown by the examples in Figure 4). Yin *et al.* [20] and Dong *et al.* [5] propose to improve the consistency by considering the inter-value influence in evaluating the values. They amend the evaluation results of an arbitrary value by:

$$\sigma^*(v) = \sigma(v) + \rho \cdot \sum_{v' \neq v} \sigma(v') \cdot sim(v', v) \qquad (1)$$

where v' and v are two different values for the same item, $sim(v', v) \in [0, 1]$ is their similarity; σ and σ^* are the veracity scores[3] of v before and after the amendment, respectively; $\rho \in (0, 1]$ is the influence factor which represents the influence strength.

Such amendment can significantly add to the computation load of truth discovery algorithms. It also requires manually defining the influence strength, which is sometimes tricky. Since in practice, we often regard a value as true as long as it is sufficiently close to the truth, a practical approximation may avail the amendment method in two aspects: i) reducing the computation load and ii) avoiding the necessity of manually determining the influence strength.

[3]Veracity score does not necessarily equal to the truth probability, but a higher score indicates a higher truth probability.

2.1.3 A Motivating Example

Based on above analysis and insights, we propose an approximate truth discovery approach, which groups sources and values to reduce the problem scale and considers the inter-group influence to improve the truth discovery accuracy. Now we illustrate our approach with an example.

EXAMPLE 1. *Suppose we want to corroborate the birth dates of some historical figures. Five data sources provide such information and only s_1 provided all the true values (Table 1). A naive voting would incur a computation load of $(6+5)+(6+4)*2 = 31$—for each of the three items (i.e., people), the algorithm performs two steps: i) scanning the six records to get the times of occurrence of each distinctive values, i.e., 5, 4, and 4 for the three items, respectively, and ii) checking through the five distinctive values to find out the most frequently occurring value as the estimated truth. The average accuracy is* 0.5.

By considering the inter-value influence, the computation load is increased to $(6 + P_2^5 + 5) + (6 + P_2^4 + 4) * 2 = 75$—between the two steps, the algorithm takes an additional step to calculate the mutual influence between each pair of different values, which is a permutation (denoted by P). The resulting accuracy is 1.

Now suppose a user only wants to know the birth years and months of these people instead of the exact dates. In this case, we can simply group the dates in the same year and month for each people, forming 3, 3, and 2 groups of dates for the three people, respectively. Moreover, we find s_2 and s_5 claim exactly the same groups of dates, so they can be grouped to form a joint source. Through such approximation, the computation load is decreased to $(5+3)*2+(5+2) = 23$ without veracity score amendment and $(5+P_2^3+3)*2+(5+P_2^2+2) = 37$ with amendment. The resulting accuracy is also 1. *For now even if the user still wants an exact date, the approximation approach can still deliver the true values with an accuracy of* 1*—by selecting the most promising date from the most promising group for each people using the naive voting method.*

Table 1: A motivating example: five sources provide information on the birth dates of three historical figures. Only s_1 provides all true values.

	e_1: G. Washington	e_2: A. Lincoln	e_3: N. Mandela
s_1	Feb. 22, 1732	Feb. 12, 1809	Jul. 18, 1918
s_2	Jul. 22, 1743	Feb. 20, 1809	Jul. 9, 1918
s_3	May 9, 1721	Jan. 20, 1813	Apr. 22, 1916
s_4	Feb. 27, 1732	Jan. 20, 1809	Apr. 16, 1916
s_5	Jul. 22, 1743	Feb. 12, 1809	Jul. 18, 1918
s_6	Feb. 15, 1732	Jan. 20, 1813	Jul. 18, 1918

2.2 Definitions and Notations

Let E be a set of entities. Each entity $e \in E$ is described by a set of attributes A.

Each pair (e, a), where $e \in E$, $a \in A$, represents a distinct data item.

Let S be a set of data sources. Each source $s \in S$ publish some values (that are potentially true) on a subset of attributes in A regarding a subset of the entities in E.

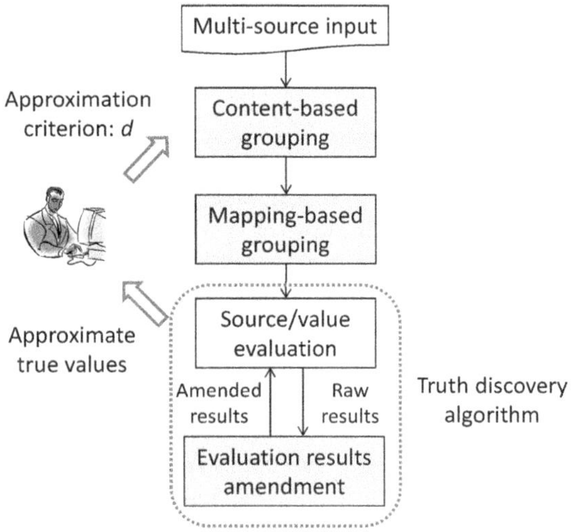

Figure 5: Approximate truth discovery

Let $V(e,a)$ be the set of all source-claimed values on data item (e,a). We consider the case where each item has only one true value, so at most one value in $V(e,a)$ can be true, while all the other values are false.

We denote by R a set of input records. Each record $r \in R$ describe a source's claim on a specific item (e,a), which is a 5-tuple: $< id, s, e, a, v >$, where id uniquely identifies the record and v is the value claimed by s on (e,a).

We assume all records from different sources have been transformed to a unified schema. Given a set of input records R published by a set of data sources S, the goal of truth discovery is to identify a single true value $v^* \in V(e,a)$, if the true value exists, for each attribute entity $e \in E$ and each attribute $a \in A$.

3. THE APPROACH

Our approach facilitates efficient truth discovery by reducing the problem scale and improves accuracy by enforcing consistent evaluation of the truth discovery results. It has three main components (as shaded in Figure 5) besides the truth discovery module: *content-based grouping*—for reducing the number of values, *mapping-based grouping*—for reducing the number of sources, and *veracity score amendment*—for enforcing consistency. The first two components are one-time jobs, while the last is incorporated into the truth discovery process.

- *Content-based grouping.* This component groups similar values according to a user-specified approximation criterion. Each resulting group will be regarded as a single value by truth discovery algorithms.
- *Mapping-based grouping.* This component groups the sources that claim the same portfolio of value-groups. Each resulting source-group will be regarded as a joint source by truth discovery algorithms.
- *Veracity score amendment.* This component amends the veracity scores of values by considering the inter-group influence of values. The amended results can be directly used for estimating the truth.

The following subsections will introduce each of the components, respectively.

3.1 Content-based Grouping

This component aims at reducing the problem scale by grouping similar values according to a user-specified approximation criterion. We assume user input as a personalized threshold (i.e., d in Figure 5) on the numerical distance between the true values estimated before and after using the content-based grouping methods, meaning any two values can be grouped together only when their distance is smaller than d. We notice that treating similar values as a group does not necessarily impair the truth discovery accuracy: i) the truth estimated based on single values may be inaccurate by itself and ii) due to the unreliable and unevenly distributed source inputs, the estimated true and false values could interleave in the spectrum of all values. Discovering truth based on the grouped values tends to be more robust in term of smoothing the local inconsistency and focusing on a global estimation. We also note that influence might still exists between the resulting value-groups. For example, Figure 6 shows an example of three values and the distances between them compared with the criterion d, where v_2 can be grouped with either v_1 or v_3. Whichever happens, the other value will still have an influence on v_2 from outside the group. In the worst case, if v_2 makes up a group of itself, it would be influenced by both the other values from outside of the group.

Referring to the philosophy of clustering, we expect each value to be maximally influenced by the (other) values of the same group while minimally influenced by the values of other groups, to preserve the accuracy of truth discovery. Therefore, we define the content-based grouping problem as follows: given a set of values V and the criterion d (which value is specific to each data item), find such a division of V, say $\boldsymbol{V_{opt}} = \{V_1, V_2, \ldots, V_n\}$, that:

$$Minimize \sum_{V_i, V_j \in \boldsymbol{V_{opt}}, i \neq j} inf(V_i \rightarrow V_j) \quad (2)$$

$$subject\ to: \ \forall v_x, v_y \in V_i \ (\in \boldsymbol{V_{opt}}), \ |v_x - v_y| < d.$$

where V_i is a value-group, v_x and v_y are individual values, $inf(V_i \rightarrow V_j)$ quantifies the influence of V_i on V_j. The parameter d enables users to make personalized decisions on the degree of approximation. Given a larger d, less groups would be formed, and *vice versa*.

We prove the NP-Completeness of the content-based grouping problem as follows.

PROOF. The NP-Completeness proof proceeds via an efficient reduction from the Balanced Graph Partitioning problem (BGP) [1]. BGP aims at partitioning graphs into equal sized components while minimizing the number of edges between different components. The number of components immediately transforms into d when the values for each single data item are evenly distributed in their domain. If we replace the optimization objective of "the number of edges between different components" into "the mutual influence between different sub-graphs", BGP immediately transforms into the content-based grouping problem. □

While clustering represents a technique for set division, we avoid considering clustering as an appropriate solution for three reasons: i) most clustering methods cannot determine the optimal cluster number based on a single input such as d, ii) some do not guarantee to obtain the optimal results, and iii) it is hard to apply optimization techniques

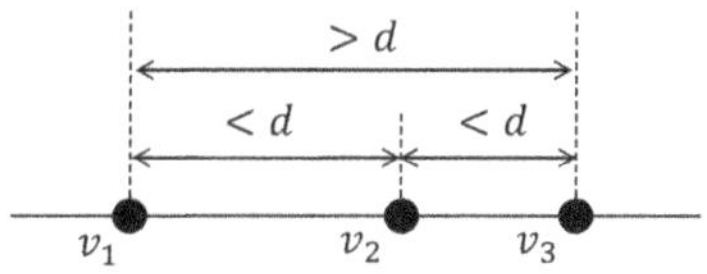

Figure 6: An example illustrating the circumstances that cause inter-group influence. Whichever another value (i.e., v_1 or v_3) v_2 is grouped with, or even v_2 makes up a group of itself, it will still be influenced by at least one other value from outside the group.

such as *branch and bound* to accelerate the clustering process. Another option would be based on graph models. We could take all distinctive values claimed for a specific data item as nodes to construct a complete graph. Then we can remove the edges longer than d (resulting in G) and partition G so that each resulting sub-graph is still a complete graph. In this way, the content-based grouping problem can be solved approximately by adopting existing solutions to the Maximum Clique Problem (MCP) [19]. Unfortunately, our problem differs from MCP in that, instead of pursuing the largest complete sub-graph, it pursues all complete sub-graphs and the minimal influence among those sub-graphs. Moreover, even if a MCP solution is applicable, we need to apply the MCP solution multiple times to find all the complete sub-graphs—by each time finding and removing the new maximum clique from the remaining graph. Besides severe computation load, this approach does not guarantee to produce the optimal grouping results.

Our problem is special in that all values are unidimensional and can thus be sorted for given specific data item. This enables us to employ novel heuristics to improve efficiency. We propose a recursive solution with *branch and bound* technique to optimally assign groups to the values. The components of this solution are described in Figure 7.

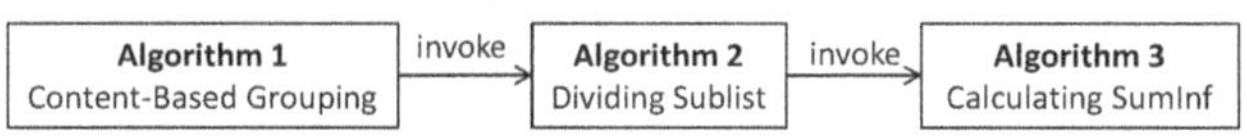

Figure 7: The invocation relation between the algorithms for content-based grouping.

Algorithm 1 is the entry of our content-based grouping solution. Given a specific data item, the algorithm first sorts the values for the item (line 1), and then compares the distance between each pair of adjacent values with the criterion d (lines 4-9). Whenever the distance between two values surpasses d, the list is divided in-between. Each sub-list is either regarded as a cluster of itself (if it contains a single value; lines 12-13) or applied the recursive method (otherwise; lines 14-18) to find the optimal group assignment. Since no influence exists between different sub-lists (due to the division criterion d), the grouping results for every sub-list together form the grouping results regarding the given data item.

Algorithm 2 recursively constructs the potentially optimal (and possibly partial) group division for the input sub-list. It takes a preorder and depth-first traversal of the tree-like search space. Given a (partial) group division solution, which is a (either complete or incomplete) list of groups formed from the sublist, the algorithm first checks whether the inter-group influence of this (partial) solution exceeds the historical best—that is the bounding condition, which

Algorithm 1: Content-Based Grouping

```
   Input: a set of possible true values V; a tolerable deviation
          from the true value for the item d.
   Output: a set of value-groups {V_k | V = ∪V_k}.
1  {v_1, v_2, ..., v_|V|} ←sort the elements of V;
   /* Split the list of sorted values into sub-lists            */
2  x ← 1 ;                           // x is the index for sub-list
3  L_x ← {v_1} ;                     // initialize the first sub-list
4  foreach i = 1, 2, ..., |V| − 1 do
5      if |v_{i+1} − v_i| ≤ d then
6          L_x ← L_x ∪ {v_{i+1}} ;   // add a value to the sub-list
7      else
8          x++;
9          L_x ← {v_{i+1}} ;         // initialize a new sub-list
   /* Find the optimal group division for each sub-list          */
10 LC ← ∅ ;                          // the grouping results
11 foreach L ∈ {L_1, L_2, ..., L_x} do
12     if |L| = 1 then
13         LC ← LC ∪ {L};
14     else
           /* The initial (partial) group of interest            */
15         C ← {v | v is the first element of L};
           /* The initial (partial) solution of interest         */
16         Solution_0 ← {C} ; // which is list of groups ordered
           by their time of addition to the list
17         L ← L\{v};
           /* initial as the maximal possible because no known
              solution currently exists                          */
18         B_best ← Max_Value;
           /* call Algorithm 2                                   */
19         LC ←
           LC∪DividingSublist(Solution_0, L, d(e, a), B_best);
```

is the minimal inter-group influence ever achieved by any complete group division solution. If it does, the solution will be abandoned; otherwise, the algorithm examines its completeness—whether the solution contains all the values of the sublist (line 2). The algorithm returns the solution and corresponding evaluation result when the solution is complete (line 4-5; $L = \emptyset$).

In case the solution is incomplete (line 6), the algorithm checks whether the first value of the sublist can be added to an existing group (line 10). If true, the process diverges into two branches: i) adding the value to the existing group (lines 11-14) and ii) setting up a new group for the value (lines 15-18). In the first case, Algorithm 2 invokes itself, taking the updated solution (with the new value added to the last group) and the updated sublist (with the first value removed) as inputs (line 12). If the solution returned by the self-invocation is not *null*—meaning the returned solution is better, the bounding condition (B_{best}) will be updated with the evaluation result of the returned solution. In the second case, Algorithm 2 invokes itself only under one condition: the distance between the new value (v) and the last element of the third last group in *Solution* is larger than d (line 17). In this case, Algorithm 2 takes the new solution (with a new group added) and the updated sublist (with the first value removed) as inputs (line 19). Differing from the first case, B_{best} will not be updated even if a better solution is found (the returned solution$\neq$ *null*)—information from the last branch can only be passed to its upper-layers (instead of its siblings) in the tree-like structure.

We prove that only under the condition specified in line 17 could the new solution possibly be optimal as follows.

Proof. Given a (partial) solution that consists of four consecutive groups, C_i, C_{i+1}, C_{i+2}, and C_{i+3}, suppose the minimal distance between the elements of C_i and C_{i+3} is

Algorithm 2: Dividing Sublist

```
Input: the current (partial) solution of interest Solution, an
       ordered list of ungrouped values L; a tolerable deviation
       from the true value for the item d, the best evaluation
       result of all currently known solutions B_best.
Output: a couple (Solution, B), where Solution is the
       obtained grouping result and B is the corresponding
       evaluation result.
1  B_current <- CalculatingSumInf(Solution) //call Algorithm 3
2  if B_current >= B_best then
3      Return null ;   // bound the branch with historical best
4  if L = ∅ then
5      Return (Solution, B_current) ;   // better solution found
6  else
7      v <- the first element (i.e., a value) of L;
       /* get the current cluster in formation */
8      Solution.last <- the last element (i.e., a set) of Solution;
9      v_lFirst <- the first element (i.e., a value) of Solution.last;
       /* get alternative solutions */
10     if |v - v_lFirst| <= d then
           /* Choice 1: add as the new last element/value of
              the existing cluster */
11         Solution.last <- Solution.last ∪ {v};
12         Result1 <- DividingSublist(Solution, L\{v},
           d(e, a), B_best);
           // Suppose Result1 = (Solution1, B1)
13         if Result1 ≠ null then
14             B_best <- B1 ;   // update known best result; new
               bounding condition is set
           /* Choice 2: initialize a new cluster by v */
15         Solution.thirdLast <- the third last element (i.e., a set)
           of Solution;
16         v_tlLast <- the last element (i.e., a value) of
           Solution.thirdLast;
17         if ∄v_tlLast ∨ |v - v_tlLast| > d then
18             Solution <- Solution ∪ {v} ;   // add as the new
               last element/cluster of Solution
19             Result2 <- DividingSublist(Solution, L\{v},
               d(e, a), B_best);
               // Suppose Result2 = (Solution2, B2)
20             if Result2 ≠ null then
21                 Return Result2 ;   // better solution found
22     else
           /* only have one choice here */
23         Solution.thirdLast <- the third last element (i.e., a set)
           of Solution;
24         v_tlLast <- the last element (i.e., a value) of
           Solution.thirdLast;
25         if ∄v_tlLast ∨ |v - v_tlLast| > d then
26             Solution <- Solution ∪ {v} ;   // add as the new
               last element/cluster of Solution
27             Result3 <- DividingSublist(Solution, L\{v},
               d(e, a), B_best);
               // Suppose Result3 = (Solution3, B3)
28             if Result3 ≠ null then
29                 Return Result3;
30 Return null.
```

smaller than d. We can easily get a better solution by merging C_{i+1} and C_{i+2}. Thus the given (partial) solution could not be the optimal (partial) solution. □

For the case that the value cannot be added to an existing group (line 22), it is tackled in the similar way as we tackle the second branch above (lines 23-29). Note that, in Algorithm 2, we intentionally put the first case before the second, i.e., greedy selection —the first case does not add to the total inter-group influence, but the second case does.

Algorithm 3 evaluates the (partial) grouping solution for a specific sub-list. Given a group within the solution, the algorithm calculates the influence of at most five groups on this group—two precedent groups (line 6), two succeeding groups (line 8), if they exist, and the group itself (line 4). The algorithm returns the extent (i.e., a ratio) to which the group is influenced by other groups (line 9). The conditions in line 17 and line 25 of Algorithm 2 ensure a group is influenced by at most four other groups according to the user-specified criterion d.

Algorithm 3: Calculating SumInf

```
Input: A (partial) group assignment solution
       Solution = {C_i | i = 1, 2, ..., |Solution|}, which is a
       ordered list of value-groups.
Output: SumInf, the sum of influence between all pairwise
       groups.
1  while C_i ∈ Solution do
2      sum_cur <- 0, sum_pre <- 0, sum_fol <- 0;
3      foreach v ∈ C_i do
           /* influence by values of the same cluster */
4          sum_cur <- sum_cur + Σ_{v' ∈ C_i ∧ v' ≠ v} inf(v' -> v);
           /* influence by values of other clusters */
5          if i > 1 then
6              sum_pre <- sum_pre + Σ_{v' ∈ C_{i-1}} inf(v' -> v);
7          if i > 2 then
8              sum_pre <- sum_pre + Σ_{v' ∈ C_{i-2}} inf(v' -> v);
9          if i < |LC| then
10             sum_fol <- sum_fol + Σ_{v' ∈ C_{i+1}} inf(v' -> v);
11         if i < |LC| - 1 then
12             sum_fol <- sum_fol + Σ_{v' ∈ C_{i+2}} inf(v' -> v);
13     SumInf <-
       (sum_pre + sum_fol)/(sum_pre + sum_cur + sum_fol);
```

In Algorithm 3, the influence between two values, e.g., v' on v, is calculated as follows:

$$\begin{cases} \sigma = d \\ inf(v' \to v) = \frac{1}{\sigma\sqrt{2\pi}} e^{-(v'-v)^2/2\sigma^2} \end{cases} \tag{3}$$

Different from traditional linear combination, we assume Gaussian density of the influences to a specific value. In this way, only the similar values would have a major influence on a value. In particular, for each item, Eq.(3) transforms d into an acceptable variable domain of Gaussian density function. We derive different influence domains to represent different levels of user confidence. For example, suppose a user proposes some d with a confidence degree of 0.8 ($\in [0, 1]$), which approximately equals to the Area Under the Curve (AUC) of Gaussian density function within the domain of $(-\sigma, +\sigma)$, we get a σ which is equal to d in Eq.(3). Given a full confidence of approximately 1, the resulting influence domain would turn into $(-3\sigma, +3\sigma)$.

3.2 Mapping-based Grouping

This component aims at reducing the problem scale by grouping sources according to their associations with the value-groups. The mapping-based grouping (Algorithm 4) involves two steps: i) extracting (line 1-5) and sorting (line 6) each source's claims and sorting sources by their claim sizes (line 7), and ii) grouping the sources that make the same set of claims (lines 8-23): the algorithm only compares adjacent sources in the sorted list and makes further comparison only when the sources have the same claim size (Line 12).

Table 2 shows two examples of the grouping results on the *population dataset* [14], where four Wikipedia users provide the same population size for *New Orleans* and another four

Algorithm 4: Mapping-Based Grouping

```
Input: a set of records regarding value-groups R' = {r' =<
       id, s, e, a, C > |s ∈ S, e ∈ E, a ∈ A, C ∈ Solution(e, a)}.
Output: {S_k|S_k ⊆ S, ⋃ S_k = S ∧ ⋂ S_k = ∅}
foreach s_i ∈ S do
    profile_i ← ∅ ;                          // Initialize claims of s_i
    foreach r' ∈ R' do
        if r'.s equals s_i then
            profile_i ← profile_i ∪ {<' r.e, r'.a, r'.C >};
    Sort triples of profile_i;
Sort s_i by {|profile_i|};
i ← 1; k ← 1 ;                       // Initialize source & group index
while i ≤ |S| do
    S_k ← {s_i}; k++ ;                       // Initialize a group
    j ← i + 1;
    while j ≤ |S| ∧ |profile_i| == |profile_j| do
        isIdentical ← true ; // If two profiles are identical
        foreach m = 1, 2, . . . , |profile_i| do
            /* t_{i,m} is the m-th triple in profile_i */
            if t_{i,m}.e ! = triple_{j,m}.e || t_{i,m}.a ! = t_{j,m}.a ||
            t_{i,m}.C ! = t_{j,m}.C then
                isIdentical ← false;
                break;
        if isIdentical then
            S_k ← S_k ∪ {profile_j};
            j++;
        else
            break;
    i ← j;
```

users for *Mexico City*. The mapping-based grouping method reduces the total number of sources (or joint source) of the dataset from 4264 to 3874. It should be noted that, the grouped sources do not only receive the same assessment, but also have the same effect as the group of individual sources do before they are grouped together in the truth discovery process.

Table 2: Two examples of the mapping-based grouping results on the population dataset [14]: each of the two cities has four contributors claiming the same population size.

Source	Item	Value
2442135: Mikelj 4444: Infrogmation 395740: ArielGold 2558878: Duece22	New Orleans, Louisiana	484674
240649: Rune.welsh 3093230: Kwsn 0 (71.104.219.117) 111478: Mixcoatl	Mexico City	8720916

3.3 Veracity Score Amendment

This component aims at improving the accuracy of truth discovery by enforcing consistent evaluation of value-groups. The amendment (Algorithm 5) relies on pre-computed inter-group influence matrix to update the veracity scores, where $c(C_x)$ and $\hat{c}(C_x)$ are the original and amended veracity scores of value-group C_x, respectively, and $inf(C_x \rightarrow C_i)$ is the influence of C_x on another group C_i. The matrix is calculated in a similar way as what Algorithm 3 does in calculating the inter-group influence. The only difference is that instead of summing up the influences of all groups, here we separately calculate the influence of different groups and store this information in a pentadiagonal matrix. Algorithm 5 calculates the veracity score of a value-group by linearly combining the veracity scores of all relevant groups using their influences on this value-group as weights. We are aware that there exist more compact ways to store these quintuples, but they are out of the scope of this paper.

Algorithm 5 reduces the time complexity of inter-value influence computing by an order. Suppose $\forall e \in E$, $\forall a \in A$, $|V(e,a)| = V$ and $|LC(e,a)| = G$, where $LC(e,a)$ is the set of all value-groups for data item (e,a). The time complexity of traditional methods is $O(L \cdot V) \leq O(|E||A| \cdot V^2)$, where L is the number of links between sources and values. In contrast, Algorithm 5 achieves a time complexity of $O(L') \leq O(|E||A| \cdot G)$, where L' is the number of links between source-groups and value-groups. Furthermore, Algorithm 5 does not require configuring additional parameters, such as ρ in Eq.(1), but automatically incorporates the influence of different groups based on probabilities. The amended veracity scores remain in the same range of the original scores, therefore require no additional efforts for normalization.

Algorithm 5: Veracity Score Amendment

```
Input: a set of value-groups LC(e, a), the correlation matrix for
       each item M_{e,a}[|V|][|LC|], where e ∈ E, a ∈ A; a set of
       veracity scores {c(C)|C ∈ LC(e, a)}.
Output: a set of amended scores for each item
       {ĉ(C)|C ∈ LC(e, a)}.
foreach e ∈ E and a ∈ A do
    foreach C_i ∈ LC(e, a) do
        ĉ(C_i) ← Σ_{x∈{i−1,i,i+1}} inf(C_x → C_i)c(C_x);
```

Our approach recommends the group with the highest veracity score as the estimated truth. But we can also estimate a single value as truth by using the weighted median method[4]. The procedure for weighting the values is similar to lines 2-12 in Algorithm 3: given each value v of the recommended group g, we calculate the influence of values on both inside and outside of the group, i.e., $inf^{(v)}_{inside}$ and $inf^{(v)}_{outside}$, respectively. Then, we assign v with weight $\frac{inf^{(v)}_{inside}}{inf^{(v)}_{inside}+inf^{(v)}_{outside}}$. After weighting and sorting the values, we can output the weighted median as the estimated truth.

4. EXPERIMENTS

In this section, we evaluate our approach using both real-world and synthetic datasets. We first discuss the experimental setup in Section 4.1 and then report the experimental results on real-world datasets in Section 4.2. Since the real-world datasets are limited in scale and diversity, we further evaluated the sensitivity and scalability of the proposed approach based on synthetic datasets.

4.1 Experimental Setup

We introduce the measures to evaluate the algorithms' performance and the baselines methods, respectively.

4.1.1 Performance Measures

We apply three measures to evaluate the performance. For all these measures, a smaller value indicates a better result.

[4]http://en.wikipedia.org/wiki/Weighted_median/

- *Mean Absolute Mean Error (MAE).* The absolute linear distance between the estimated truth and the ground truth.
- *Root Mean Square Error (RMSE).* Compared to MAE, RMSE amplifies and severely punishes large errors.
- *Computation Time.* The time required for the algorithm to produce a final result, which includes the time spent on possible pre-processing (such as source/value grouping), source/value evaluation, and possible post-processing (such as veracity score amendment).

4.1.2 Baselines

All the following algorithms are used in an unsupervised manner and compared on numerical datasets:

- *Voting*: for each item, outputs the value claimed by the most sources as the estimated truth.
- *Sums*: evaluates sources and values alternately from each other by iteration.
- *Avg-Log*: uses a non-linear function (a combination of logarithm and average functions) to assess sources.
- *Investment* [15]: evaluates values based on their contribution to the assessment of related sources.
- *2-Estimates* [7]: assumes that claiming one value indicates disclaiming (vote against) all unclaimed values.
- *TruthFinder* [20]: considers inter-value influence and evaluates each value by a probability.
- *AccuSim* [5]: evaluates a value by the *a posterior* probability and incorporating the inter-value influence.
- *Gaussian Truth Model (GTM)* [22]: applies generative models to estimate truths.

In this paper, we focus on discovering a single true value for each data item from the numerical data, but leave the incorporation of source dependency and other data types for future work. We implemented the algorithms in Java 7 and ran experiments on 3 PCs with Intel Core i7-5600 processor (3.20GH×8) and 16GB RAM.

4.2 Experiments on Real-World Datasets

4.2.1 Datasets

We employ two real-world datasets[5] in the experiments and use the ground truth provided by the original contributors as gold standards.

The population dataset [14] contains 51,761 records. Each record describes a user's answer to a city's population size. After eliminating duplication and ambiguity, we got records about 4,264 sources claiming 49,956 values on 41,197 data items.

The biography dataset [14] contains 11,099,730 records. Each record describes a user's answer to the birth or death date of a person. After removing the irrelevant, duplicated, and ambiguous records, we merged the birth and death dates of the same person made by the same user and got 1,148,644 users and 3,211,983 claims related to 116,499 people.

[5]Until now, these are the only two public numerical datasets, which are also used in recent works [22, 14].

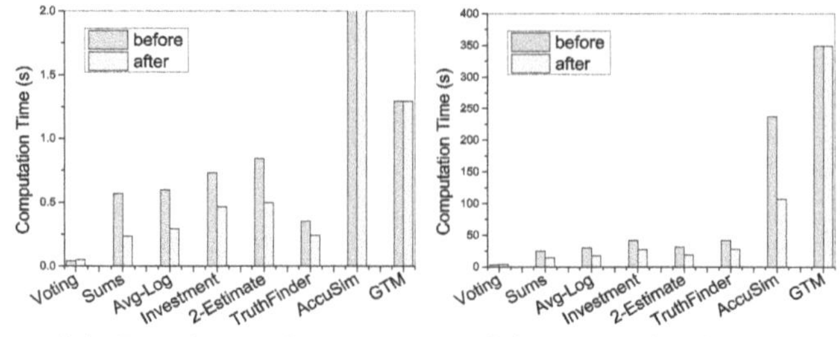

(a) *Population* dataset (b) *Biography* dataset

Figure 8: Comparison of computation time.

4.2.2 Comparison Results

Figue 8 shows the comparison of different algorithms in terms of their computation time before and after adopting our approach, based on the *population* and *biography datasets.* The results show that our approach reduces the computation time of the algorithms significantly, for some cases even by half. The effect is especially evident on the *population dataset*, where claims are sparse. Since our approach is not applicable to GTM, its computation time remains unchanged.

In Table 3 and Table 4, we summarize the performance of the algorithms before and after the adoption of our approach in terms of MAE and RMSE. The results show that our approach does not significantly decrease the truth discovery accuracy. Indeed, all algorithms achieve similar or even higher accuracy than their original implementations under the optimal configurations of d. This indicates that, if configured properly, our proposed approach does not only reduce the computation time, but also improves the truth discovery accuracy.

Table 3: Comparison on the *Population* dataset: the measures marked with asterisk represent the performance after adopting our approach; F# is the percentage of the estimated truths that have larger deviations from the actual truths than d.

Method	MAE	RMSE	MAE*	RMSE*	F#(%)
Voting	10327.2	126217.9	9823.4	124992.7	12.92
Sums	3026.25	17023.52	3008.47	17016.24	10.32
Avg-Log	2923.33	16923.36	2910.24	169431.3	9.21
Investment	1787.65	8797.43	1694.53	8634.38	13.84
2-Estimate	1652.29	8429.32	1609.98	**8339.99**	22.16
TruthFinder	1633.60	8824.09	1632.23	8823.09	**8.70**
AccuSim	1626.52	8718.10	**1498.59**	8596.26	9.26
GTM	**1523.29**	**8382.73**	1523.29	8382.73	8.87

Table 4: Comparison on the *biography* dataset: the meanings of the notations are the same as the ones in Table 3.

Method	MAE	RMSE	MAE*	RMSE*	F#(%)
Voting	237.35	4847.80	**213.53**	1772.63	22.65
Sums	396.69	5429.37	394.23	5427.46	18.23
Avg-Log	392.26	5296.62	382.33	5263.69	17.41
Investment	3858.90	26237.65	3294.73	24923.98	19.23
2-Estimate	234.42	**4723.53**	232.53	4694.97	20.83
TruthFinder	660.66	6959.72	661.39	6962.49	15.23
AccuSim	267.62	4844.46	253.28	**2823.53**	**11.46**
GTM	**228.19**	4831.53	228.19	4831.53	13.97

4.3 Experiments on Synthetic Datasets

4.3.1 Datasets Preparation

We generate synthetic data to evaluate the effectiveness of our approach on larger datasets. In particular, we generate synthetic records based on a real-world dataset, i.e., by adding new sources and data items to the *population dataset*.

We generate a new source by randomly selecting an existing source as reference—the new source will have exactly the same number of values on the same sets of items as the referred source. We then associate a source to the values in two steps: i) for each item, we divide the whole value range into a series of intervals, making sure each interval contains exactly one value. Given two adjacent intervals, their boundary is the average value of the two values that reside in the two intervals, respectively; ii) each time we add new association to a value: we first randomly select an interval which the value to be associated with are supposed to reside in, namely $\mathcal{I}$, and then associate the source with the existing value in $\mathcal{I}$ with a probability ρ, and with a random value within the interval $\mathcal{I}$ with a probability of $1 - \rho$. We assume a slight increase in the total number of sources associated with the original values by defining $\rho = 0.01 (> 0)$. Data items are generated in a similar way.

4.3.2 Scalability Experiments

We conduct experiments to investigate the effect of our approach on improving the algorithms' scalability. We first fix the number of data items and vary the number of sources from 1,000 to 10,000, thus increasing the number of values for each data item. Then we fix the number of sources and vary the number of data items. Figure 9 shows how the reduced amount of computation time changes as the number of sources and the number of data items grow, after applying our approach. The results show the reduction amount keeps increasing as the two numbers grow. Since d remains fixed in both above experiments, the number of value-groups formed by our approach does not significantly change. But generally the more sources considered, the larger the source-groups tend to be, as the sources has a higher chance to be merged into an existing group. Experiments with respect to both above numbers reveal that the reduced computation time grows at lease linearly with the increased record size.

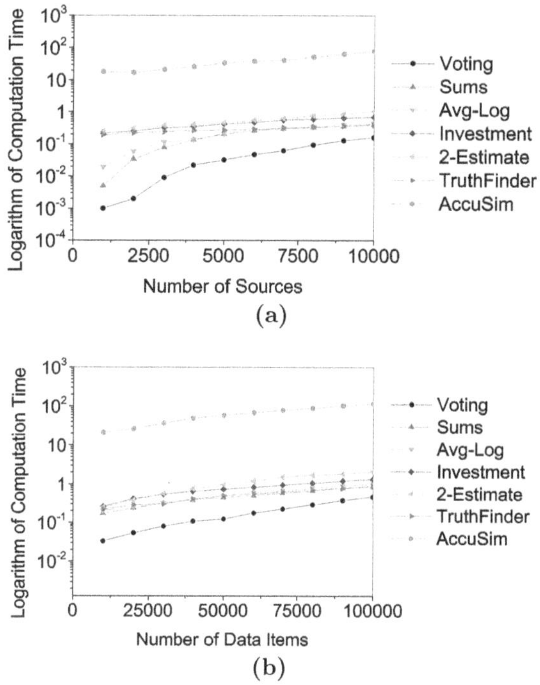

Figure 9: Computation time reduction under: (a) varying number of sources, (b) varying number of data items.

4.3.3 Sensitivity Experiments

We study the impact of d to the effectiveness of our approach based on a synthetic dataset of 10,000 sources and 45,000 data items, where each item has on average 1 to 1,000 distinct values. Figure 10 shows the algorithms' performance with respect to a varying d within the range of $[0, SD/10]$, where SD is the standard deviation of all values for each data item—therefore, each item will have no more than 100 groups. Specially, when $d = 0$, the problem degrades to the circumstance of estimating the truths without adopting any grouping methods. We observe an exponential decrease in the computation time of all algorithms as d grows. As for the error rates, both MAE and RMSE tend to be low when d is small, but gradually increase as d grows.

5. RELATED WORK

Truth discovery has been a longstanding problem in the data quality research community [4, 13]. We classify existing truth discovery approaches into four categories and review them in this section.

Primitive methods. These methods take the *mean*, *median*, or *majority voting* results of the values for each data time as estimated true values [3]. They are efficient but often inaccurate due to the neglect of varying reliabilities of sources in the real world.

Iterative algorithms. These methods jointly compute source reliability and confidence of value through an iterative procedure. Multiple ingredients, such as the inter-value influence [20], inter-value exclusion[7], source dependency [5], hardness of fact [7], as well as human knowledge [15] are incorporated to pursue more accurate estimation.

Probabilistic models. Many researchers model truths as latent variables in probabilistic graphical models to support truth discovery [16, 22]. Such models generally require tremendous computation time.

Optimization approaches. Yin and Tan [21] and Li *et al.* [11] respectively model the truth discovery problem as optimization problems and developed corresponding solutions.

Other related approaches include crowdsourcing [9] and web search [2, 17]. Crowdsourcing systems assess worker quality in accomplishing their crowdsourcing tasks while web search methods recommend trustworthy source links to answer user's queries. Truth discovery differs from crowdsourcing in pursuing only the factual truths and from web search in operating on well-formatted records instead of raw data.

The most related research is on source selection. Dong *et al.* [6] propose to select only partial sources for truth discovery, so as to reduce the integration cost while ensuring certain accuracy. Li *et al.* [9] present a framework for discovering the common characteristics of high quality workers, so as to facilitate the selection of high quality workers for future tasks. Gupta *et al.* [8] evaluate source quality and select only

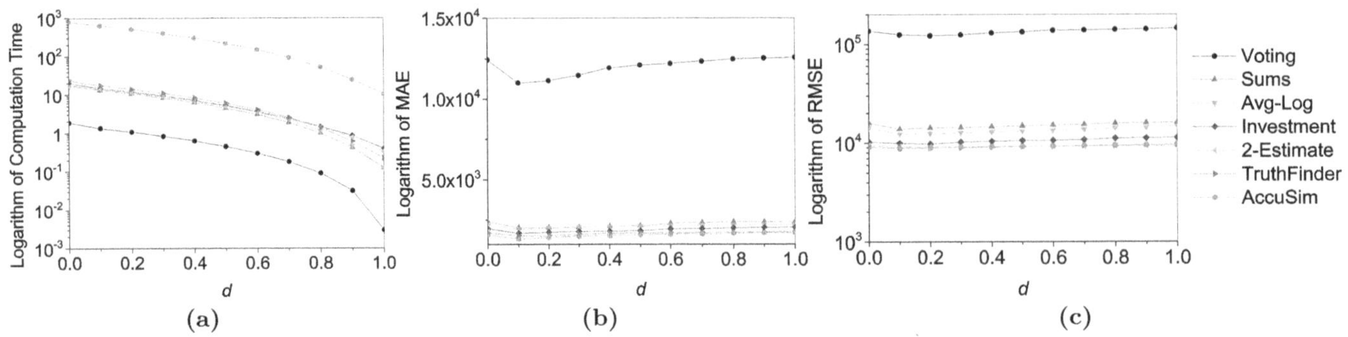

Figure 10: Comparison of algorithms' (a) computation time, (b) MAE, and (c) RMSE, under varying d.

trustworthy sources for each group of entities (obtained by clustering) to improve truth discovery accuracy. To the best of our knowledge, there is no previous work that specializes on improving the efficiency of truth discovery, nor utilizing grouping methods to reduce the problem size, which is the main contribution of this paper.

6. CONCLUSION

In this paper, we propose an approximate truth discovery approach, which improves the truth discovery efficiency via problem scale reduction. We develop content-based grouping and mapping-based grouping methods to reduce the sizes of sources and values, respectively. Veracity score amendment methods are used to improve the truth discovery accuracy with efficiency. The approach features approximate truth discovery according to a user-specified criterion, which can achieve a personalized balance between the efficiency and accuracy. The approach has been applied to several existing truth discovery algorithms. Experiments on both real-world and synthetic datasets demonstrate the effectiveness of our approach.

7. REFERENCES

[1] K. Andreev and H. Racke. Balanced graph partitioning. *Theory of Computing Systems*, 39(6):929–939, 2006.

[2] R. Balakrishnan and S. Kambhampati. Sourcerank: relevance and trust assessment for deep web sources based on inter-source agreement. In *WWW*, pages 227–236, 2011.

[3] J. Bleiholder and F. Naumann. Conflict handling strategies in an integrated information system. In *IJCAI Workshop on Information on the Web*, 2006.

[4] J. Bleiholder and F. Naumann. Data fusion. *CSUR*, 41(1):1–41, 2008.

[5] X. L. Dong, L. Berti-Equille, and D. Srivastava. Integrating conflicting data: the role of source dependence. *PVLDB*, 2(1):550–561, 2009.

[6] X. L. Dong, B. Saha, and D. Srivastava. Less is more: Selecting sources wisely for integration. *PVLDB*, 6(2):37–48, 2012.

[7] A. Galland, S. Abiteboul, A. Marian, and P. Senellart. Corroborating information from disagreeing views. In *WSDM*, pages 131–140, 2010.

[8] M. Gupta, Y. Sun, and J. Han. Trust analysis with clustering. In *WWW*, pages 53–54, 2011.

[9] H. Li, B. Zhao, and A. Fuxman. The wisdom of minority: discovering and targeting the right group of workers for crowdsourcing. In *WWW*, pages 165–176, 2014.

[10] Q. Li, Y. Li, J. Gao, L. Su, B. Zhao, M. Demirbas, W. Fan, and J. Han. A confidence-aware approach for truth discovery on long-tail data. *PVLDB*, 8(4):425–436, 2014.

[11] Q. Li, Y. Li, J. Gao, B. Zhao, W. Fan, and J. Han. Resolving conflicts in heterogeneous data by truth discovery and source reliability estimation. In *SIGMOD*, pages 1187–1198, 2014.

[12] X. Li, X. L. Dong, K. Lyons, W. Meng, and D. Srivastava. Truth finding on the deep web: is the problem solved? *PVLDB*, 6(2):97–108, 2012.

[13] F. Naumann, A. Bilke, J. Bleiholder, and M. Weis. Data fusion in three steps: Resolving schema, tuple, and value inconsistencies. *IEEE Data Engineering Bulletin*, 29(2):21–31, 2006.

[14] J. Pasternack and D. Roth. Knowing what to believe (when you already know something). In *COLING*, pages 877–885, 2010.

[15] J. Pasternack and D. Roth. Making better informed trust decisions with generalized fact-finding. In *IJCAI*, pages 2324–2329, 2011.

[16] J. Pasternack and D. Roth. Latent credibility analysis. In *WWW*, pages 1009–1020, 2013.

[17] V. Vydiswaran, C. Zhai, and D. Roth. Content-driven trust propagation framework. In *SIGKDD*, pages 974–982, 2011.

[18] D. A. Waguih and L. Berti-Equille. Truth discovery algorithms: An experimental evaluation. *arXiv preprint arXiv:1409.6428*, 2014.

[19] Q. Wu and J.-K. Hao. A review on algorithms for maximum clique problems. *EJOR*, 242(3):693–709, 2015.

[20] X. Yin, J. Han, and P. S. Yu. Truth discovery with multiple conflicting information providers on the web. *TKDE*, 20(6):796–808, 2008.

[21] X. Yin and W. Tan. Semi-supervised truth discovery. In *WWW*, pages 217–226, 2011.

[22] B. Zhao and J. Han. A probabilistic model for estimating real-valued truth from conflicting sources. In *QDB*, 2012.

Organic or Organized? Exploring URL Sharing Behavior

Cheng Cao
Texas A&M University
College Station, TX, USA
chengcao@cse.tamu.edu

James Caverlee
Texas A&M University
College Station, TX, USA
caverlee@cse.tamu.edu

Kyumin Lee
Utah State University
Logan, UT, USA
kyumin.lee@usu.edu

Hancheng Ge
Texas A&M University
College Station, TX, USA
hge@cse.tamu.edu

Jinwook Chung
Utah State University
Logan, UT, USA
jinwook.chung@usu.edu

ABSTRACT

URL sharing has become one of the most popular activities on many online social media platforms. Shared URLs are an avenue to interesting news articles, memes, photos, as well as low-quality content like spam, promotional ads, and phishing sites. While some URL sharing is organic, other sharing is strategically organized with a common purpose (e.g., aggressively promoting a website). In this paper, we investigate the individual-based and group-based user behavior of URL sharing in social media toward uncovering these organic versus organized user groups. Concretely, we propose a four-phase approach to model, identify, characterize, and classify organic and organized groups who engage in URL sharing. The key motivating insights of this approach are (i) that patterns of individual-based behavioral signals embedded in URL posting activities can uncover groups whose members engage in similar behaviors; and (ii) that group-level behavioral signals can distinguish between organic and organized user groups. Through extensive experiments, we find that levels of organized behavior vary by URL type and that the proposed approach achieves good performance – an F-measure of 0.836 and Area Under the Curve of 0.921.

Categories and Subject Descriptors

H.3.5 [**Online Information Services**]: Web-based services

Keywords

URL; URL Sharing; User Behavior; Social Media

1. INTRODUCTION

URL sharing is one of the most popular avenues to share information on Twitter. Users can enrich their inherently limited length postings by inserting a URL pointing to an external resource such as a blog, video, or image. By doing so, many different viewpoints and additional context can be expressed through URL sharing. In the early days of Twitter in 2007, Java et al. already saw that about 13% of a collection of 1.3 million tweets included a URL [14]. Recent studies have confirmed the ongoing popularity of URL sharing on Twitter. In 2010, Boyd et al. found 22% of a sample of 720,000 tweets included a URL [3]. And in 2011, Rodrigues et al. found that nearly a quarter of 1.7 billion tweets contained URLs [21].

While some URL sharing is organic, other sharing is strategically organized with a common (perhaps, nefarious) purpose. And the differences between these two extremes – organic and organized – is often not a simple distinction. Consider the following examples:

- Figure 1 shows three users who tweeted the same URL `bit.ly/1dtous`, linking to a YouTube webpage related to the boy band One Direction. They all express their affections for the band in their tweets. It seems very likely they are the fans of One Direction, which explains that they spontaneously posted the same link. This *common interest* in a subject related to a link leads to the coincidence of multiple organically posted URLs.
- Figure 2 shows four more users who posted the same One Direction YouTube URL – `bit.ly/1dtous`. In this case, however, we can deduce that the users are participating in a voting campaign to attract the band to their hometown. The users are somewhat linked in this common desire.
- Continuing this theme, Figure 3 shows four additional users who have all tweeted a "vote" for Boston to attract One Direction. In this case, the voting behavior is suspicious: the tweets have highly similar text, and the latter three tweets were posted on the same day and the accounts names are quite similar. Were they organized to post the same URL? Are these accounts controlled by the same person? Is the first account "innocent"?
- Finally, Figure 4 highlights three users who engage in a clear example of a somewhat sophisticated organized URL spamming. Each user posts slightly different text and different appearing URLs, though ultimately all of the URLs redirect to the same destination URL – an advertising webpage. This coordinated behavior of URL sharing is fundamentally different from the first case of organic URL sharing.[1]

These observations motivate us to investigate URL sharing in social media. Our goal in this paper, *in the context of URL sharing*, is to automatically (i) identify *user groups* in terms of similar URL-sharing behaviors; and (ii) differentiate strategically *organized* and genuinely *organic* user groups, through the development of a URL-posting behavior based model. Our study aims to bridge the gap in the research of social media between user behavior, URL sharing, and general user similarity. The key insight motivating our

[1]These accounts have been alive for more than two years, which suggests the official Twitter spam policy has limited impact on this type of coordinated URL-sharing behavior.

CIKM'15, October 19–23, 2015, Melbourne, Australia.

DOI: http://dx.doi.org/10.1145/2806416.2806572.

Figure 1: One example of three users who have organically posted the same URL: bit.ly/1dtous

Figure 2: Four users seemingly post URL for a voting campaign

Figure 3: Four users suspiciously cooperate to post the same URL

work is that the publicly available URL-posting information can help model users with similar behaviors of URL sharing, and that group-level behavioral signals can characterize a group of users as organic or organized.

Studying similar user behaviors in URL sharing has important applications, on both bright and dark sides. On the one hand, based on the historical URL-posting information, the service provider (e.g., Twitter, in this paper) can effectively target groups of users and promote them their interested links. On the other hand, to purify and improve the information quality on their platform, it becomes imperative that the service provider can detect those organized behaviors of URL-sharing, such as campaign-like advertising, spamming, and other adversarial propagandas.

Given a group of organized users, on the one hand, we expect those users – no matter whether managed by a command-and-control structure or not – post URLs toward a common goal. We do not argue the goal has to be malicious, like the example in Figure 3. On the other hand, we focus on *group-level* behavioral evidences that can reflect their coordination. For instance, the users in Figure 2 were seemingly participating in the same "voting campaign", but they actually have different goals (the targeting cities) and their tweet content are quite distant. Even the users in Figure 3 seem suspicious, we need more evidences and should design a systematic framework for detection.

Concretely, we propose a four-step approach. We first formulate URL sharing based on its three key factors: user, URL, and the posting activity. Based upon such a model, we design a similarity measurement of user behaviors in URL sharing. Then, given the pairwise similarity function, we build a user graph model from which we identify user groups each of which contains users with similar URL-sharing behaviors. Next, on the group level, we characterize the organic and organized user groups based on the URL-posting behaviors of their members. Finally, we embed those characteristics into a classification framework to systematically distinguish organic and organized groups of users.

Figure 4: Three users coordinate to post the same advertising URL

2. RELATED WORK

Many recent studies have investigated URL sharing in social media, with different goals. One thread is about sharing intention, i.e., why people share links in social media. Suh et al. found that embedding URLs is one of the most important factors for increasing the *retweetability* of a tweet [24]. Smith et al. found that Twitter users add URLs to their tweets when discussing controversial topics, toward spreading information instead of conversing [22].

Another thread focuses on what people spread through URLs in social media, e.g., [20, 1, 16, 18]. These efforts have mainly focused on grouping similar messages or grouping users, such that the URLs provide additional context that may reflect the interests of the people posting these URLs.

Recently, several efforts have mentioned the dark side of URL sharing in social media. Stringhini et al. examined spam campaigns on Twitter that posted messages with URLs pointing to the same site [23]. Grier et al. defined a spam campaign as the set of Twitter accounts that spammed at least one blacklisted URL in common [13], and so Gao et al. did on Facebook [11]. Ghosh et al. studied the *link farming* on Twitter and found many participants are sybil accounts. Among those top link farmers, 79% have URLs linking to their external webpages [12]. More recently, Nikiforakis et al. explored the ecosystem of ad-based URL shortening services, and the vulnerabilities made possible by these services [17].

Since 2006, there have been many social network-based sybil defense methods proposed such as SybilGuard [27], SybilLimit [26], and SybilInfer [7]. Viswanath et al. pointed out most of those approaches are essentially *graph partitioning* algorithms [25]. They all made certain assumptions of the social network topology, used ground-truth information of trusted users, ranked all users, and determined who are sybils based on some cutoff. Rather than exclusively focus on spammers or sybils, our interest is to reveal groups of strategically organized users who engage in URL sharing with a purpose: some of the groups will post spam, but many others spread propaganda, aggressively promote products or services, and generally engage in coordinated manipulation. Unlike spamming or subverting reputation, the users we consider can be genuine and legitimate, as in Figure 3. Additionally, our problem is more general in the sense that our approach can detect those "URL-posting based" sybils attacks or spam campaigns. We explicitly model and identify groups of users who have similar behaviors of URL sharing, and differentiate the organized and organic groups via a group-level classification framework.

3. INVESTIGATING URL SHARING

In this section, we propose our approach to explore similar user behaviors in URL sharing. In this context, our objective is to (i) formulate and collect user groups; and (ii) differentiate the organic and organized user groups. To tackle this problem, we formulate the concept of user group in the context of URL sharing, and focus exclusively on behavioral signals. We are interested in answering the following questions: How do we model user in URL sharing? How do we define and find user group? And how can we distinguish between organic and organized user group?

Toward answering these questions, our approach is structured in four steps. The main intuition is that the users from an organic group coincidently share similar interests on certain subjects so that they have similar behaviors of URL sharing. On the contrary, organized groups consist of users who plot to post URLs with a certain goal in common so that their behaviors conform to a notion of *co-operation* or *coordination*.

- First, we model the user in URL sharing, and design a similarity measurement to quantify similar behaviors between users.
- Second, we construct a user graph where nodes are users who have posted URLs and then identify user groups from the graph.
- Then, we extract group-level features to characterize organized user groups and organic user groups.
- Finally, we build a classifier for distinguishing organized and organic user groups.

We tackle each of these steps in turn, as follows.

3.1 Modeling URL Sharing

URL sharing on Twitter is fundamentally different from other popular activities such as *tweeting*, *re-tweeting*, and *following*. To systematically investigate users with similar behaviors of URL sharing, we model the three factors in URL sharing: the user, URL, and the action of posting. In the meanwhile, we need to pay attention on the following three issues. First, we should consider all URLs every user has ever posted on Twitter so that our model is general. Second, we should design a measurement that can quantify user similarity in URL sharing. Third, it should take the URL posting behavior into account. Such a measurement should be more specific towards URL sharing than other traditional user similarity based on profiles, social neighborhood, tweet content, and so forth. Therefore, we aim to model users engaged in URL sharing with two facets in mind: (i) Which URLs a user has ever posted; and (ii) How (s)he posted them.

3.1.1 User, URL, and Posting

Our key idea is that, in terms of the posting behaviors, a user can be characterized by all the URLs he has posted and how often he has posted them. For instance, a user who likes sports tends to share more URLs linking to sports websites than URLs of politics websites. A Japanese user is prone to post more URLs of Japanese websites than English websites. Two users who may have a realistic social relationship can have distinct tastes and preferences in URL sharing, but their posting behaviors (especially the posting frequency of different URLs) may reflect such a scenario. It is even more prominent for strategically organized users.

Formally, suppose we have a set of m users $\mathcal{U} = \{u_1, u_2, ..., u_m\}$. If u_i, in total, posted k different URLs $v_1, v_2, \ldots, v_k$, we define such an associated URL set of u_i as $\mathbf{p}_{u_i} = \{v_1, v_2, \ldots, v_k\}$. By aggregating all users, we get a URL set $\mathcal{V} = \{v_1, v_2, ..., v_n\} = \bigcup_{u_i \in \mathcal{U}} \mathbf{p}_{u_i}$. Therefore, each pair (u_i, v_j) can be seen as an action of posting a URL.

We introduce the function $f(u_i, v_j)$ that quantifies such a posting of v_j by u_i. Here, we give a straightforward definition $f(u_i, v_j) = PostingCount(u_i, v_j)$ where $PostingCount(u_i, v_j)$ represents the concrete *posting count* of every pair (u_i, v_j). Given a user $u_i \in \mathcal{U}$, we can represent u_i by an n-dimension vector $\mathbf{u_i} = (f(u_i, v_1), f(u_i, v_2), \ldots, f(u_i, v_n))$.

3.1.2 User Similarity in URL Sharing

We have two considerations to design a user similarity measure in URL sharing. On the one hand, if both users have posted overlapping URLs, the more intersections they have, the closer they are. On the other hand, we want to take the posting count into account. If two users posted the same URL many times, we reward the similarity between them. If not, we penalize them if they have quite distant posting counts for the same URL they have posted. Thus, we propose a measurement of user similarity defined as:

$$sim(u_i, u_j) = \sum_{k=1}^{n} \frac{ln(min(f(u_i, v_k), f(u_j, v_k)) + 1)}{|f(u_i, v_k) - f(u_j, v_k)| + 1} \quad (1)$$

We sum over all URLs to favor those pairs having posted many URLs in common. We pick the smaller posting count among two users ($min(f(u_i, v_k), f(u_j, v_k))$) as the pair-level scale of the posting count, and take the logarithm considering it can be quite large. We put the difference of posting counts as the denominator. We ensure a URL can contribute towards the similarity only if it was posted at least once by both users, yet it's different from traditional "cosine-like" measures as we explicitly emphasize the penalization.

3.2 Identifying User Groups

Given the definition of user similarity, the next question is how to find those users having similar behaviors of URL sharing. Given a set of users $\mathcal{U} = \{u_1, u_2, ..., u_m\}$, the task of *user group identification* is to find a collection of user groups $\mathcal{C} = \{\mathbf{c_0}, \mathbf{c_1}, \ldots, \mathbf{c_k}\}$ where $\forall \mathbf{c_i}, \mathbf{c_j} \in \mathcal{C}$, $\mathbf{c_i}, \mathbf{c_j} \subset \mathcal{U}$ and $\mathbf{c_i} \cap \mathbf{c_j} = \emptyset$.

The user similarity function can only locally measure the pairwise connection. Therefore, if we want to globally consider all possible users, adopting a graph structure is a natural choice. Extensive existing algorithms can partition a graph into *connected components*, which can fit our concept of user group here. In general, a *user graph* $G = (V, E)$ can be defined by $V = \mathcal{U}$ and $E = \{(u_i, u_j) | \forall u_i, u_j \in \mathcal{U}, weight(u_i, u_j) = sim(u_i, u_j)\}$. However, if we consider all possible user pairs, the resulting graph can be huge: it will have only one connected component where most connections are weak. Hence, we need a specific version of a user graph upon which we can extract our interested user groups.

3.2.1 The kNN User Graph

If we simply set a global threshold to filter out low-weight edges, we may lose important information. For example, the users from an organized group unnecessarily (and usually do not) post many URLs of popular websites — they have their own targets to spread. As a result, those users may be excluded from the graph due to the lack of overlapping URLs with others, and finally we may obtain only a few big components in which people share popular websites.

Since we are interested in those organized users, our graph model should be able to grasp those "abnormal connections". Organized users do not often share various URLs, whereas the nature of coordination leads to their locally firm neighborhoods within the group. To retain such "conspiracies" as much as possible, we require a model that emphasizes the mutually steady neighborhood. Thus, we adapt the model of *k nearest neighbor (kNN)* graph.

The kNN user graph connects u_i and u_j only if u_i is among the k-nearest neighbors of u_j. Such a restriction retains only those k strongest neighborhoods, with less emphasis on the edge weight. A formal definition of the kNN user graph $G = (V, E)$ is $V = \mathcal{U}$ and $E = \{(u_i, u_j) \mid \forall u_i \in knn(u_j), \forall u_j \in knn(u_i)\}$. Here, $knn(u_i)$ is a function defined as $\{u_j | \forall u_j \in neib(u_i), sim(u_i, u_j) \in max_k(\{sim(u_i, u_j) | \forall u_j \in neib(u_i)\})\}$, where $neib(u_i)$ is the set of u_i's neighbors and $max_k(\mathcal{S})$ returns the k largest elements given $\mathcal{S}$. Now, since any node can have k neighbors, a group of users who post unusual URLs can still form a big component.

3.2.2 *Extracting User Groups*

It is a non-trivial task to extract a collection of user groups from the user graph. The concept of *connected component* in *graph theory* naturally matches our concept of user group, but we need two more considerations. First, we require that every group should have a compact size. Hence, we discard those small connected components (e.g., fewer than five members), and decompose those large components into smaller ones. Second, we hope the partition algorithm to be general, i.e., having been proved effective and efficient on many different types of graphs. Thus, we choose the well-known *Louvain method* [2], which is one of the most widely-used algorithms in *community detection* [8].

The Louvain method is a greedy algorithm to maximize the *modularity* of a graph structure. It starts by locally optimizing modularity for small communities, and then iteratively repeats to aggregate until reaching a maximum of modularity. Though the modularity optimization problem is known as NP-hard, the Louvain algorithm can run in $O(n \log n)$ in most practical cases so that it already has many mature implementations. Its maximum modularity ensures it conservatively segments big components only when it does contain multiple modularities.

3.3 Characterization: Organized vs. Organic

Given a collection of user components (groups) that we have extracted, our ultimate goal is to systematically distinguish organized and organic user groups. But before that, we need to characterize these two types of groups. Suppose we have a group of users who have similar behaviors of URL sharing, we want to feature to what degree they have organized behaviors when posting URLs.

First, we should ensure our features build upon the group level. Our biggest interest is the collective user behavior, which is fundamentally different from individual spamming or sybil behavior. Second, our features should target the behavioral signals of posting. We have seen in Figure 4 how easily the posters manipulated their tweet content to disguise themselves. Moreover, they unnecessarily follow each other as long as they post the same URLs. So, our insight here is those traditional features based on either text content or network structure become vulnerable for the organized user group in our context. On the contrary, what they cannot cover are the URLs they posted (they hope more exposures after all), the time-stamps they posted (they have to leave the records anyway), and their own profiles (they use public profiles so that others can see their postings). Therefore, in this section, we introduce nine group-level features that cover three posting-related aspects: *posted URLs*, *posting time*, and *poster profile*.

3.3.1 *Posted URL-based Features*

Our motivation is that, intuitively, the users in an organized group usually have a clear goal of promoting certain URLs. Thus, they have a relatively narrow selection of URLs they post, and each URL gets high-volume postings. Instead, an organic group usually posts a variety of URLs each of which has reasonable amounts of exposures. Therefore, we come up with two group-level features that capture the diversity of the posted URLs.

Suppose we have a user group $\mathbf{c} = \{u_1, u_2, \ldots, u_k\}$, and we know the set of URLs posted by every member, i.e., $\mathbf{p_{u_i}}$. Thus, we can extend it to the group level, as well as the posting count $f(u_i, v_j)$. Both can be formulated as the following:

$$\mathbf{p_{c_i}} = \cup_{u_j \in \mathbf{c_i}} \mathbf{p_{u_j}} \tag{2}$$

$$f(\mathbf{c_i}, v_j) = \sum_{u_i \in \mathbf{c_i}} f(u_i, v_j) \tag{3}$$

Based upon these definitions, we provide the following two posted URL-based features:

- Average Posting Count. We can calculate the *average posting count* per URL by the ratio of $|\mathbf{p_c}|$ and $\sum_{v_j \in \mathbf{p_c}} f(\mathbf{c}, v_j)$. By our motivation explained above, we expect organized groups have higher values of such feature than organic ones.
- URL Posting Entropy. Entropy is an important measure of *uncertainty* in *information theory*. Here, in our case, to describe the diversity of posted URLs in a group, we extend it to *URL posting entropy*, computed as:

$$H(\mathbf{c}) = -\sum_{v_j \in \mathbf{p_c}} \frac{f(\mathbf{c}, v_j)}{\sum_{v_j \in \mathbf{p_c}} f(c, v_j)} log \frac{f(\mathbf{c}, v_j)}{\sum_{v_j \in \mathbf{p_c}} f(c, v_j)} \tag{4}$$

  And based on the same idea, we suppose that organic groups have larger URL posting entropy than organized .ones.

3.3.2 *Posting Time-based Features*

One of the most important posting behavioral signals is the *posting timestamp* of every tweet. The poster has no access to tamper such information, making it a potentially robust feature. For each poster, we can collect a *posting time series* so we can compute all the *posting intervals*, defined as the temporal differences between consecutive posting timestamps. Our motivation here is: with the goal of promoting or advocating, the users from an organized group usually post tweets in a similar frequency, and the intervals tend to be short as they are eager to rapidly increase the exposures of their URLs. Therefore, we propose two group-level posting interval related features, measuring both the quantity and the deviation.

- Posting Interval Median. For every user, we can always quantify the posting interval by some temporal unit. Then we get the *individual posting interval median* by taking the median among all intervals. We use median rather than mean mainly because it is more robust to outliers. Moreover, since we care more about the group level, we take a further median over all members in a group. As mentioned, we expect organized groups have shorter interval medians than organic ones.
- Posting Interval Deviation. As said, our inference is that the organized accounts have similar posting manners, or even are bots manipulated by the same person. Thus, we can compute the group-level *posting interval deviation* given the individual interval median. Since an organic group is likely to post more randomly, we expect organic groups have larger deviations.

3.3.3 Poster Profile-based Features

Compared to an organized group, our main motivation here is that the users in an organic group have more various demographics. Given a group of organized accounts, if their goal is improper (e.g., advertising, spamming), they are mostly managed (like sybils) or hired (like for-pay turkers) by the same agent so they have close demographics. Even if their goal is relatively legitimate (e.g., propaganda, voting), their conspiracy attributes their enthusiastic interests on some common subjects, which can be reflected on their profiles to certain degree, too.

The profile information is one of the best publicly-available resources we can utilize to infer the diversity of demographics. We reify it into three aspects: total number of posted tweets, account registration date, and followers (friends) count. We calculate the group-level deviation of the total number of tweets, of the followers counts, and measure the average interval of the registration time.

- Tweets Counts Deviation. We count the total number of tweets an account has posted ever since the beginning, and take the deviation among all accounts in a group. The larger deviation means the more variety, so we expect an organic group has a larger *tweets counts deviation* than an organized one.
- Followers Counts Deviation. We record the count of followers for every user in a group. The count can be dynamic over time so we take the median. Then we take the deviation among all members. We believe the count of followers is more reliable than of friends simply because it is more difficult to fabricate. Again, we expect organized groups have lower deviations.
- Registration Interval Median. It is similar to how we computed the *posting interval median*. We look into the registration date of each user so that we have a *registration time series* for every group, and then we take the median. Our idea is that the registration interval is one of the most direct evidences for those fabricated or hired accounts. We prefer median to mean because the latter one is too sensitive to outliers. We expect organized groups have smaller *registration interval medians* than organic groups, similar to the reason for the posting interval median.

Then, we come up with two more features related to the registration date. We define the *user lifespan* by counting the temporal span, in terms of days, from the day an account registered to his latest posting date in our dataset. The motivation here is that the user lifespan is one of the most important user profile information and it should be quite random for users from an organic group. Instead, the organized users are created for certain URL-promotion mission, so they all tend to have short lifespans. Another idea is that Twitter may already have detected the suspicious behaviors from organized users and suspended them, leading to short lifespans too. Hence, we provide two features to characterize the group-level user lifespan via the quantity and the deviation.

- Poster Lifespan Median. We take the median of all accounts' lifespans in a group. As said, we suppose an organized group generally has a shorter *poster lifespan median*.
- Poster Lifespan Deviation. Every member from a group has a lifespan so we can calculate the group-level deviation. We expect organic ones have larger *lifespan deviations*.

3.4 Classification: Organized vs. Organic

Recall that our ultimate goal is to automatically discern organized and organic user groups, in the context of URL sharing. Given the features in the previous section, it becomes quite natural that we embed them into a classification framework. To choose appropriate classification algorithms, we should guarantee: (i) the algorithm has been widely used and maturely implemented; and (ii) we need to test on multiple algorithms.

We choose 4 well-known classification algorithms in our framework: *Random Forest* [4], *Naive-Bayes Decision Tree* [15], *Sequential Minimal Optimization* [19], and *Additive Logistic Regression* [10]. We notate them *RandomForest*, *NBTree*, *SMO*, and *LogitBoost*, respectively. NBTree is a *decision tree learning* algorithm in which the tree leaves are naive Bayes classifiers. SMO algorithm is used for training the support vector classifier and has been implemented in many existing SVM libraries like LIBSVM [6]. LogitBoost can be seen as a variant of AdaBoost [9] that adapts *logistic regression* techniques. All of them have mature implemented packages. With different theoretical foundations, these four candidates can well-serve the testing algorithms in our experiment.

4. EXPERIMENTS

We present our experimental studies in this section. We first introduce our data. Then, we describe how we identified all the user groups we formulated. Third, we provide details how we collected the ground truth. Finally, we show our analysis results towards distinguishing organized versus organic user groups.

4.1 Data

We deployed a tweet crawler via the official Twitter Streaming API from October 2011 to October 2013. Since our main interest is URL sharing, we only collect tweets that contain URLs. The API provides a 1% sample of all published tweets, but our 24-month uninterrupted crawling gives us 1.6 billion *"raw URLs"* posted by 136 million accounts. Raw URLs are those URLs in their original format when posted, without any further processing (e.g., resolution) after being crawled. Due to either irregular typing or the URL shortening service, many raw URLs become inaccessible or actually link to the same webpage. For instance, we have both `WWw.TwiTtEr.com` and `tWITTER.com/` in our dataset, as well as `bit.ly/1a8jUOr` and `bitly.com` both of which direct to the same destination.

To address such an issue of *URL variants*, we need to resolve for all URLs. Since resolving billions of URLs can be expensive, we focus on URLs that appeared at least 50 times. We resolve through standard HTTP requests and record the landing long URLs. The summary of our dataset is shown in Table 1: 47 million accounts have shared 1.6 million raw URLs within 445 million tweets. 82% raw URLs get resolved to nearly 1.2 million distinct long URLs. 869 thousand accounts have generated at least 50 postings.

Given a resolved long URL, we ignore all its post parameters as a reasonable approximation to the URL. We call the remaining part *URL domain name* and we obtain 166,000 unique ones. Compared to a complete URL, we believe the domain name has better interpretability because it can conceptually represent a "website". For users, we exclude those who just occasionally share URLs, i.e., less than 50 postings. To model the user, we decide to also use URL domain name as the dimension. One reason is that using original long URL may result in extremely sparse user vector given enormous dimensions. Another reason is a user group can be better interpreted if each member corresponds to some "website" instead of a long HTML page link.

4.2 Collecting User Groups

To construct the kNN user graph, a non-trivial issue is how to choose an appropriate k. We adopt the idea in [5] to pick k roughly equal to $ln(|\mathcal{U}|)$. Thus, 869,571 users give us k of 14. In the end, we obtain a user graph containing 216,523 nodes and 3,862,116 edges. This graph contains 12,251 connected components most of

Table 1: Dataset Summary

# Raw URLs (Resolved)	# Tweets	# Unique long URLs	# Unique domain names	# Posters (Having at least 50 postings)
1,617,234 (1,327,729)	445 million	1,199,930	166,107	47,658,839 (869,571)

which are small: only 2,150 components have no less than 5 nodes and just 36 components are bigger than 100. We filter out those tiny components smaller than 5, and exhaustively decompose (if possible) large ones bigger than 100 to ensure maximal modularity. Eventually, we identify 2,775 groups, together including 192,719 users. Among those 2,775 groups, we find around 40% groups are smaller than 10, and nearly 90% groups are bounded by 100 users. The largest one has 14,080 users.

How can we find a way to see whether our identified user groups are "meaningful"? And how to interpret and measure it here? Naturally, the most direct evidence is our groups maintain closer manners of URL sharing behaviors than "a random user group", yet we need a way to measure it. The entropy of posted URLs in a group is one of the most typical properties that capture the similar URL sharing behavior, as explained in Section 3.3. Thus, first, we simulate a collection of user groups with the exact same sizes via randomly picking users from our dataset. Then, we compare the distributions of the URL posting entropy for our collected groups and the simulated ones. The result is in Figure 5, and we clearly see the difference. Around 20% of our groups have a zero entropy, i.e., all the members posted the same one URL all the time, and the median is about 1.5. On the contrary, none of the simulated groups have a 0 entropy, and the median is around 4 while 80% of our groups are below it.

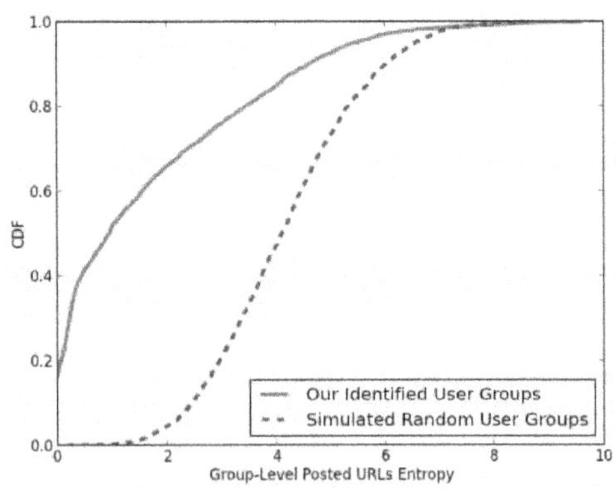

Figure 5: The URL posting entropy CDF of our collected user groups, compared with a collection of simulated random groups

Besides the natural evidence from those URL-posting related features, we hope to see more different evidences showing our collected groups are meaningful. Here, we adopt the group-level *language usage entropy* to measure certain "homophily" among all members in a group. The intuition is that if a set of users have similar selections of URLs (embedding in their tweets), then their language choice in their tweets should be similar. Conversely, two users who have distinct language backgrounds would hardly overlap many URLs. Therefore, for each group, we aggregate all the published tweets (with or without URLs, having valid language usage information), count the usage frequency, and calculate the entropy. To compare, again we simulate the user groups with the exactly same sizes. We compare their distributions in Figure 6, and find the contrast is apparent.

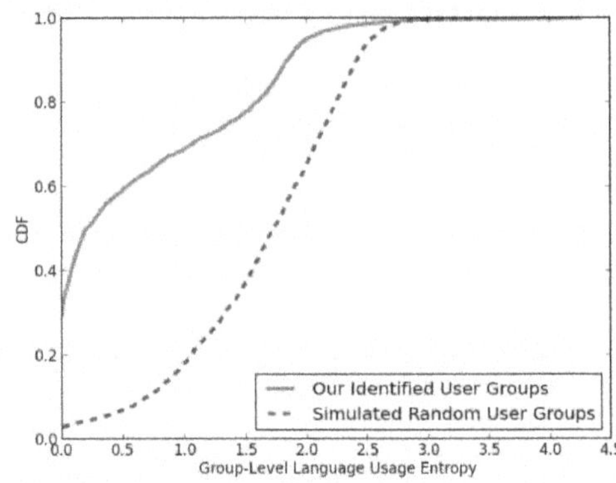

Figure 6: The language usage entropy CDF of our collected user groups, compared with a collection of simulated random groups

About 30% groups in our collection whose language entropy is 0, i.e., all members always use the same language writing tweets. 90% of our groups have entropies less than 2.0. In contrast, in the simulated collection, almost none have 0 entropy, and the median is between 1.5 to 2.0 where 80% of our groups are below it. This comparison shows the users in our identified groups have much similar language usages. Recall that our method of computing user groups has not used any user information on language usage, which demonstrates the potential of extending our approach into general problems related to user similarity.

4.3 Ground Truth

To test our proposed features in Section 3.3 on characterizing organized and organic groups, we need a set of groups with known labels of either organized or organic. Since there is no such existing ground truth, we randomly pick 1,000 of our identified groups, and manually check each of them as follows.

4.3.1 Manual Labeling Setup

Our labeling for each group is a two-tier task: (i) categorizing the content of the URLs the members posted and inferring the purpose that they posted URLs; (2) and rating to what degree we think their behaviors were organized or organic.

The rating task directly connects to our interest here, but the categorization task can help us interpreting the similar user behaviors. Our focus is to collectively seek for group-level evidence that reflects the coordinated behaviors of posting URLs, not just individually inspecting each account. In particular, we examine the accounts in each group through looking into their: (1) tweets (e.g., all the posted URLs, landing webpages, and tweets that contain URLs); (2) account profile (e.g., self-introduction, name, avatar, language, geo location); and (3) posting pattern (e.g., the URL shortening pattern, textual pattern in tweets, posting timeline pattern). If a group is too large, we randomly pick at least 5 users with accessible information to judge. Judges make decisions without knowledge of the proposed features in Section 3.3.

To measure to what extent a group is coordinating can be subtle. Our ratings will be the scores between 1 to 5, the larger the more

Figure 7: Example users whose group we categorize into "spam" and think is organized

Table 2: The distribution (percentage) of twelve categories that we have labeled for our user groups

advertising	spamming	app-auto-generated	entertainment	social-media	adult	news	blog	follow-back	public-information	propaganda	voting
318 (41%)	195 (25%)	171 (22%)	66 (8%)	33 (4%)	22 (3%)	20 (3%)	10 (1%)	8 (1%)	6 (0.8%)	6 (0.8%)	4 (0.5%)

suspicious towards an organized group. Then, we transform our scores to the label of either organized or organic. It is an organized group if its score is above 3, and organic if below 3. If its score is 3, we inspect it again. By such a 5-scale rating, we avoid curtly labeling a group is organized or organic.

We assign 3 annotators the exactly same set of 1,000 user groups, and separately ask them to manually label each group as organized or organic. Since the number of our annotators is odd, if the individual decisions of our 3 annotators have a clear "major voting", we take it as the final result. The rating usually has an obvious favor (below or above 3), and we accept a category if it has been mentioned by at least two annotators. Otherwise, a fourth annotator adds a label and a rating. We finalize a category or rating only when it has two or more endorsements, and count a user group has valid labels only if it finally obtains at least one category or rating.

4.3.2 *Categorizing a User Group*

As said, our categorization aims to infer the common intent of a group of users who have similar URL-sharing behaviors. The idea is that organized groups have a much clearer goal in common than organic groups, even though the purpose can be either improper (e.g., advertising, spamming) or legitimate (e.g., self-promoting, preaching). In practice, we do find sometimes speculating the intention is not obvious, so we change to summarize the content of posted URLs and tweets in this case. In the meanwhile, we find usually categorizing a group is more difficult than rating it, especially if the members post quite various subjects or many non-sense words. Finally, among all the 1,000 randomly picked groups we have judged, 773 ones have been labeled by at least one of the 12 categories in Table 2.

The category of *advertising* emphasizes the intention of posting URLs. It includes everything about absorbing viewer's attention on the URL, such as marketing, funds-raising, or even self-promotion of personal websites or uploads. We have seen instances that all members in a group shared URLs linking to the exactly same news articles or blogs. We still think such a group is suspicious to advertising. Moreover, the irrelevance between the content of tweets and the linked webpages can also indicate the poster is advertising, and one example is shown in Figure 8.

We make the assumption that Twitter's official suspension indicates *spamming* activities to some extent. In addition, if the browser or the shortening service warns when we click into a URL, we believe it is a spam URL. Other than that, we label spamming if the URL links to some typical spam webpage of "phishing" or "malware". For instance, we categorize a group full of users like the left-hand two in Figure 7 into spamming, because their posted URLs point to the phishing website shown in the rightmost subfigure.

Figure 8: Example users whose group is organized

App-auto-generated is a special category. All users in such a group posted tweets (containing URLs) automatically generated by some external app or service. Usually it happens when the poster is unconscious or at least not intentionally doing so, e.g., using own Twitter account to log in some mobile game. For *entertainment*, we find groups of fans who posted URLs about their supported artists like we have seen in Figure 1, 2, 3. Sometimes they can be *voting* (like in Figure 2 and 3), but many are just bonded by fan's passion. Other entertainment groups often talked about music, video game or anime. *News* are mostly about politics and technology. *Propaganda* usually relates to politics and religion.

Social-media and *blog* stress the source website. These websites can host various webpages, and typical examples are `youtube.com`, `instagram.com`, and `blogspot.com`, etc. This also explained we found many such groups. The groups of *public-information* posted links of public information like traffic or weather. The posters usually are accounts managed by regional institutions.

Among all these 12 categories, some are capturing the purpose of posting (e.g., advertising, spamming, propaganda), and some are summarizing the content of posting (e.g., entertainment, social-media, news). A user group can have more than one category, e.g., mixed with spam, adult, and advertising. In total, from Table 2 we can see advertising and spamming together take up 66% appearances of all categories. This observation reflects our idea that the kNN graph model, emphasizing the locally pairwise connection, can potentially retain many abnormal behaviors.

Another interesting finding is the category of app-auto-generated surprisingly occupied 22%. Its substantive existence leads to a new thread for future work: the *user-unconscious* posting behavior in social media, caused by some external application. What security issues could it raise? Do most posts contain URLs? If yes, can our study of URL sharing be an entry point?

4.3.3 Rating a User Group

For rating, what has been posted matters less, and we care more on who have posted and how. As mentioned, we look over the profiles of all accounts from the same group. We seek for similar patterns between them in self-introduction, name, avatar picture, etc. We rate above 3 if we see highly overlapped textual patterns in their tweets such as the posting date, hashtag, language and URL shortening. Figure 8 includes two accounts with identical posting timeline, tweets content, and similar names. Their group is the instance that we rate 5. It becomes even more dubious when the members always retweet each other's tweets. A typical "rate-5" example is in Figure 7. The users, who have extremely close posting timelines and names, always retweeted from the other account.

Our rating focuses on the collective behavioral evidences of coordination, independent with the posting purpose. For example, we find most groups of entertainment are users spontaneously talk about the subjects they like, but it becomes suspicious when the URLs link to the same music video page on Youtube. Most groups of public-information have fairly legitimate goal of posting, but naturally many accounts are centrally managed so they still have many common patterns.

If all members in a group have been suspended (and we label it as a spamming group), we cannot access their accounts so we conservatively leave them unrated. For those groups of app-auto-generated or social-media, we mainly judge their postings are whether advertising-oriented or unconscious, and we usually find most of them fall into the latter scenarios. The groups of news, social-media or blog often share popular news, blog article, and online forum. We rate them low except we find they advertised their own-related (person or institution) webpages.

4.4 Experiments: Organized vs. Organic

4.4.1 Analyzing Our Labeling

As introduced, we finalize the labeling result for each user group via adopting the major vote over our 3 annotators. We find 986 groups that have been labeled at least one of the categorization and rating results, and 602 ones that received both. The fourth annotator agreed on 871 (88.3%) and 520 (86.4%) ones, respectively. Finally, we obtain 815 groups with ratings where 325 (40%) are organized and 490 (60%) are organic.

Those 602 groups with both information of category and rating give us the opportunity to understand the following questions: Which subjects our collected groups mostly talked about? What kinds of content the organized groups and organic groups usually posted? Are they different? Can we see a relation between the levels of organized behavior and the types of URL?

We aggregate the average rating each group received by the group category, and plot the CDFs of our ratings for all 12 categories in Figure 9. We can see the distributions take on clear gradients. If we look at the median, 12 categories are evenly divided by the rate of 3. The groups of spamming, adult, and follow-back are most likely as organized, followed by advertising, public-information, and propaganda whose distributions are quite close. Then, blog, voting, entertainment and news have similar distributions, most of whose groups are organic. Social-media and app-auto-generated groups are the least likely organized (recall how we rate them). These observations reveal the connection between the level of organized behavior and the inherent content of different categories. For spamming, adult, follow-back, advertising, they essentially include those improper ingredients that motivate more organized behaviors. On the contrary, the category of app-auto-generated is user-unconscious, and blog, news, entertainment and social-media naturally contain more legitimate activities, so their groups tend to be more organic.

4.4.2 Classifying Organized and Organic Groups

We are ready to build the classifier. In terms of posting behaviors in URL sharing, can our proposed group-level features distinguish the organized and organic groups? Which features work best? Which classification algorithm performs best?

To address the issue of class imbalance, we give a hybrid solution that combines undersampling of the majority class and oversampling the rare one. In the end, we have 406 organic and 406 organized groups, and we normalize the values of each feature to the interval of 0 to 1. To evaluate, we do 10-fold cross validation and focus on precision, recall, F-measure, and ROC area. We first consider the two classes are equally important and take the average. The results are in Figure 10.

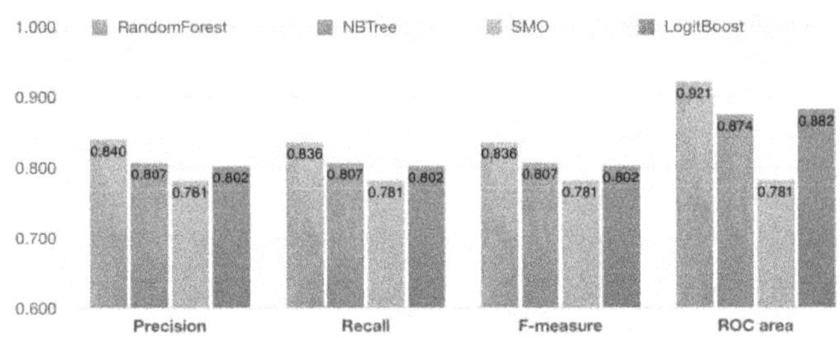

Figure 10: Evaluation results by four classification methods

The performance achieves around 0.8 no matter which method or measure we choose. RandomForest works best with high F-measure (0.836) and ROC area (0.921). All the results suggest the potential of our approach for distinguishing organized and organic user groups, purely based on behavioral signals in URL sharing.

In reality, detecting organized user groups becomes more important. We especially want to find out organized groups as many as possible, corresponding to the measure of recall. Thus, we further show the recall result for the class of organized in Figure 11. We see those two decision tree based algorithms outperform the other two, and even better than their own averaged results in Figure 10. This observation hints us we can prioritize decision tree based algorithms when we solve such a problem in practice.

Another investigation is the feature impact. We select two popular measures — *Chi-squared* and *Information gain* — to evaluate each feature with respect to the class. The full ranking is in Table 3. We see the rankings by chi-square and information gain are almost identical. We have 3 interesting discoveries. First, the two URLs-based features always rank the top 3. This suggests the URL-related property is the most reliable aspect when we study URL sharing. Second, if we have two features from the same type (e.g., lifespan deviation and median), the deviation feature always has more influence than the median one. One possible explanation is that the median value is too sensitive compared to the dispersion value. This tells us those features derived from a relative measure can be more robust than those from an absolute measure. Third,

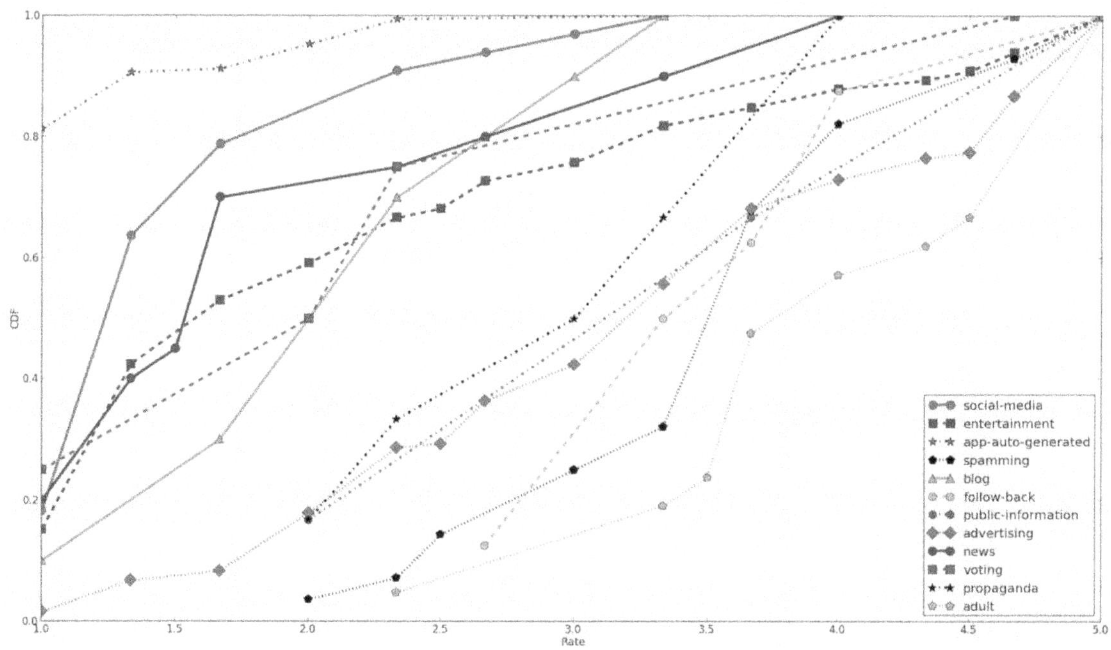

Figure 9: The CDFs of our ratings for all 12 types of group categories

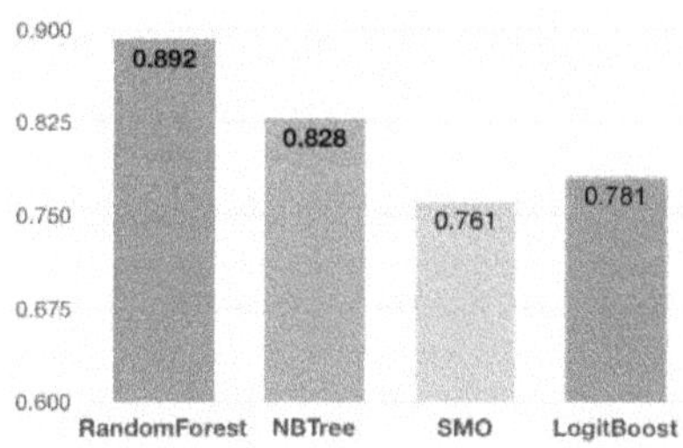

Figure 11: The Recall results for the class of organized group by four classification methods

the feature of poster lifespan deviation performs the best. It favors our intuition in Section 3.3: User lifespan is one of the strongest signals to capture the diversity of poster demographics.

Table 3: The rankings of the feature impact measured by Chi-Squared and Info Gain

Chi-Squared	Info Gain
Poster Lifespan Deviation	Poster Lifespan Deviation
Average Posting Count	Average Posting Count
URL Posting Entropy	URL Posting Entropy
Registration Interval Median	Registration Interval Median
Poster Lifespan Median	Tweets Counts Deviation
Tweets Counts Deviation	Poster Lifespan Median
Posting Interval Deviation	Posting Interval Deviation
Posting Interval Median	Posting Interval Median
Followers Counts Deviation	Followers Counts Deviation

We conduct two more informative comparisons of organic versus organized groups. One is about the number of distinct URL domains that a group has posted. Our idea is that organized groups tend to have a much tighter selection of URLs to post than organic groups, mainly due to their specific common goal of posting. In Figure 12, we find the significant gap between two classes. More than 20% of organic groups have mentioned at least 100 different URL domains in their tweets, and yet the median for organized groups is merely no more then 10. 20% of organized groups have posted only one kind of URL domain all along.

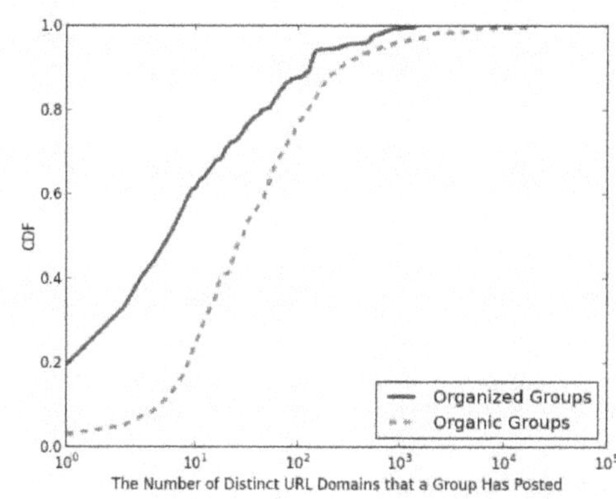

Figure 12: Organized vs. Organic: # URL domain names

The final exploration comes back to Twitter itself. We would like to see how the Twitter's official monitoring reacts for the two types of similar user behaviors in URL sharing. So, we calculate the *group-level suspension percentage* in each of our groups, i.e., how many accounts in a group have been suspended. Recall that we have excluded those groups whose members were all suspended. We have two interesting observations from Figure 13. On the one hand, the distributions of our two types of groups are quite discerning. We find 80% of organic groups have less than 10% suspension percentage, where 80% of organized groups are more than it in contrast. Twitter's suspension is for individuals, yet it still reflects on our user groups formulated through URL sharing. On the other hand, we find the official suspension still has limited impact on the organized posting behavior: the median is just around 30%. These findings suggest the complementary potential of our investigations on organized user behavior in URL sharing.

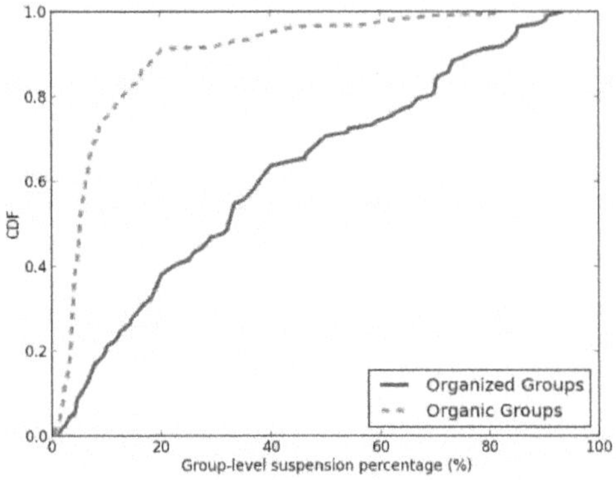

Figure 13: Organized vs. Organic: group-level suspension ratio

5. CONCLUSION

In this paper, we are interested in exploring users with similar behaviors when they share URLs on Twitter. While some users organically share common interests on certain websites, some are organized to aggressively promote the same URLs towards a common goal. This motivates us to tackle the problem of distinguishing organized and organic users in the context of URL sharing. Focusing on the behavioral signals of URL-posting, we propose a four-step approach to model, identify, characterize, and classify those two types of user groups. We test our approach on four different classification algorithms and in most cases it performs good in terms of precision, recall, F-measure, and ROC area. Random Forest algorithm works best with 0.921 ROC. Our experimental analysis demonstrated the capability of our approach for (i) understanding users with similar URL-sharing behaviors; and (ii) distinguishing the level of organized user behaviors in URL sharing.

6. ACKNOWLEDGMENT

This work was supported in part by AFOSR Grant FA9550-12-1-0363. Any opinions, findings and conclusions expressed in this material are the author(s) and do not necessarily reflect those of the sponsors.

7. REFERENCES

[1] E. Bakshy, I. Rosenn, C. Marlow, and L. Adamic. The role of social networks in information diffusion. In *WWW*, 2012.

[2] V. D. Blondel, J.-L. Guillaume, R. Lambiotte, and E. Lefebvre. Fast unfolding of communities in large networks. *Journal of Statistical Mechanics: Theory and Experiment*, 2008(10):P10008, 2008.

[3] D. Boyd, S. Golder, and G. Lotan. Tweet, tweet, retweet: Conversational aspects of retweeting on twitter. In *HICSS*, 2010.

[4] L. Breiman. Random forests. *Machine learning*, 45(1), 2001.

[5] M. Brito, E. Chavez, A. Quiroz, and J. Yukich. Connectivity of the mutual k-nearest-neighbor graph in clustering and outlier detection. *Statistics & Probability Letters*, 35(1):33–42, 1997.

[6] C.-C. Chang and C.-J. Lin. Libsvm: a library for support vector machines. *TIST*, 2(3), 2011.

[7] G. Danezis and P. Mittal. Sybilinfer: Detecting sybil nodes using social networks. In *NDSS*, 2009.

[8] S. Fortunato. Community detection in graphs. *Physics Reports*, 486(3), 2010.

[9] Y. Freund and R. E. Schapire. Experiments with a new boosting algorithm. In *ICML*, 1996.

[10] J. Friedman, T. Hastie, R. Tibshirani, et al. Additive logistic regression: a statistical view of boosting (with discussion and a rejoinder by the authors). *The annals of statistics*, 28(2), 2000.

[11] H. Gao, J. Hu, C. Wilson, Z. Li, Y. Chen, and B. Y. Zhao. Detecting and characterizing social spam campaigns. In *SIGCOMM*, 2010.

[12] S. Ghosh, B. Viswanath, F. Kooti, N. K. Sharma, G. Korlam, F. Benevenuto, N. Ganguly, and K. P. Gummadi. Understanding and combating link farming in the twitter social network. In *WWW*, 2012.

[13] C. Grier, K. Thomas, V. Paxson, and M. Zhang. @ spam: the underground on 140 characters or less. In *CCS*, 2010.

[14] A. Java, X. Song, T. Finin, and B. Tseng. Why we twitter: understanding microblogging usage and communities. In *Joint 9th WebKDD and 1st SNA-KDD Workshop*, 2007.

[15] R. Kohavi. Scaling up the accuracy of naive-bayes classifiers: A decision-tree hybrid. In *KDD*, 1996.

[16] J. Lehmann, C. Castillo, M. Lalmas, and E. Zuckerman. Transient news crowds in social media. In *ICWSM*, 2013.

[17] N. Nikiforakis, F. Maggi, G. Stringhini, M. Z. Rafique, W. Joosen, C. Kruegel, F. Piessens, G. Vigna, and S. Zanero. Stranger danger: exploring the ecosystem of ad-based url shortening services. In *WWW*, 2014.

[18] J. Park, M. Cha, H. Kim, and J. Jeong. Managing bad news in social media: A case study on domino's pizza crisis. In *ICWSM*, 2012.

[19] J. C. Platt. Fast training of support vector machines using sequential minimal optimization. In *Advances in kernel methods*. MIT press, 1999.

[20] J. Ratkiewicz, M. Conover, M. Meiss, B. Gonçalves, A. Flammini, and F. Menczer. Detecting and tracking political abuse in social media. In *ICWSM*, 2011.

[21] T. Rodrigues, F. Benevenuto, M. Cha, K. Gummadi, and V. Almeida. On word-of-mouth based discovery of the web. In *SIGCOMM*, 2011.

[22] L. M. Smith, L. Zhu, K. Lerman, and Z. Kozareva. The role of social media in the discussion of controversial topics. In *SocialCom*, 2013.

[23] G. Stringhini, C. Kruegel, and G. Vigna. Detecting spammers on social networks. In *ACSAC*, 2010.

[24] B. Suh, L. Hong, P. Pirolli, and E. H. Chi. Want to be retweeted? large scale analytics on factors impacting retweet in twitter network. In *SocialCom*, 2010.

[25] B. Viswanath, A. Post, K. P. Gummadi, and A. Mislove. An analysis of social network-based sybil defenses. *SIGCOMM Computer Communication Review*, 41(4), 2011.

[26] H. Yu, P. B. Gibbons, M. Kaminsky, and F. Xiao. Sybillimit: A near-optimal social network defense against sybil attacks. In *SP*, 2008.

[27] H. Yu, M. Kaminsky, P. B. Gibbons, and A. Flaxman. Sybilguard: defending against sybil attacks via social networks. In *SIGCOMM Computer Communication Review*, volume 36, 2006.

Mining Brokers in Dynamic Social Networks

Chonggang Song
School of Computing
National University of Singapore
a0095629@nus.edu.sg

Wynne Hsu
School of Computing
National University of Singapore
whsu@comp.nus.edu.sg

Mong Li Lee
School of Computing
National University of Singapore
leeml@comp.nus.edu.sg

ABSTRACT

The theory of brokerage in sociology suggests if contacts between two parties are enabled through a third party, the latter occupies a strategic position of controlling information flows. Such individuals are called *brokers* and they play a key role in disseminating information. However, there is no systematic approach to identify brokers in online social networks. In this paper, we formally define the problem of detecting top-k brokers given a social network and show that it is NP-hard. We develop a heuristic algorithm to find these brokers based on the weak tie theory. In order to handle the dynamic nature of online social networks, we design incremental algorithms: *WeakTie-Local* for unidirectional networks and *WeakTie-Bi* for bidirectional networks. We use two real world datasets, DBLP and Twitter, to evaluate the proposed methods. We also demonstrate how the detected brokers are useful in diffusing information across communities and propagating tweets to reach more distinct users.

Categories and Subject Descriptors

J.4 [**Social and Behavioral Sciences**]: Miscellaneous

General Terms

Algorithm, experimentation

Keywords

Broker, weak tie, social network analysis

1. INTRODUCTION

Social networks play significant roles in spreading news and opinions. Online social networks accelerate and expand the diffusion of information among web users [2, 13]. Sociologists have long recognized that users situated between otherwise disconnected or remote users possess advantageous positions [3]. On one hand, such users serve as bridges and enable the interaction between their neighbors; on the other hand, they can access remote information sources and control the information flow between them. These users are called *brokers*. A number of empirical studies have shown the significant roles played by brokers in disseminating information [19].

The work in [19] defines different types of brokers based on the direction of information flow and whether the end users are members in the same community. [14] assumes that the set of communities is known and proposes two methods to find users who connect different communities and are responsible for information diffusion across communities. They call these users *structural hole spanners* which is one type of brokers. In the first method *MaxD*, the idea is to remove one node at a time such that the removal of this node will lead to the maximum decrease in the minimum cut in the given set of communities. The second method *HIS* looks for nodes that are incident with "opinion leaders" in different communities. However, for most social networks, it is not easy to determine the number nor the boundaries of communities that exist in the networks.

In this paper, we examine a more general type of broker that is not defined based on communities. We define a broker as one whose removal would result in the greatest increase in the pairwise distance among the remaining users. The intuition behind this definition is to capture users who are situated between otherwise disconnected or distant users. We propose a community independent method to find the top-k brokers in online social networks. Formally, we have

DEFINITION 1. ***Top-k Brokers.*** *Let $G = (V, E)$ be a directed graph where each node $v \in V$ denotes a user, and each edge $(u, v) \in E$ denotes that user u follows user v. The top-k brokers are the set of users $H \subset V$, $|H| = k$, such that the utility function ϕ is maximized:*

$$\phi = \sum_{u,v \in V-H} \frac{1}{d(u,v)} - \sum_{u,v \in V-H} \frac{1}{d'(u,v)}, \quad (1)$$

where $d(u,v)$ and $d'(u,v)$ denote the distance between u and v in G and $G \backslash H$ respectively. $G \backslash H$ is the resultant subgraph of G having the nodes in H and their incident edges removed.

We believe brokers play a special role in the dissemination of information in social networks. Existing works have used different measures to identify nodes that are important in information diffusion. For example, [4, 18] design PageRank based algorithms to identify users with high degrees as seed nodes for viral marketing. Other works utilize the betweenness measure [8] to identify the users who have a large number of shortest paths that pass through them. These measures focus on the big clusters of users and tend to neglect the small clusters of remote users.

Consider the example social network in Figure 1. PageRank based algorithms will select u_7 because it is incident with other high-degree nodes. Methods that utilize betweenness measure will

CIKM '15, October 19-23, 2015, Melbourne, VIC, Australia
ACM 978-1-4503-3794-6/15/10 ...$15.00.
DOI: http://dx.doi.org/10.1145/2806416.2806468 .

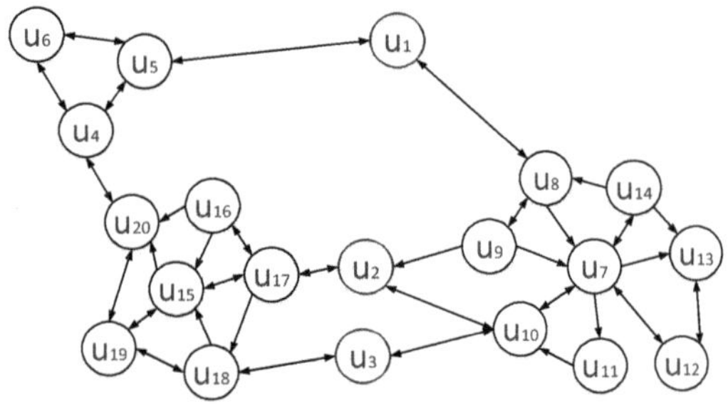

Figure 1: Example Social Network.

find u_2 since it carries the shortest paths between the two clusters of nodes. However, we note that the removal of u_2 or u_7 does not have much impact on their neighbors as the neighbours can still reach other users without significant increase in the distance.

On the other hand, the situation is different for u_1. We see that u_1 enables u_4, u_5 and u_6 to reach u_7 and its neighbours within 3 or 4 hops. However, when u_1 is removed, u_4, u_5 and u_6 need to travel a very long distance to reach u_7 and its neighbors. We say u_1 is the broker that brings remote nodes close to others. With the online social networks playing an increasingly significant role in spreading news and opinions, identifying such brokers is clearly advantageous. Information disseminated through these users have a much higher chance of reaching distant users whereas the centrality-based nodes may not reach those isolated individuals.

Finding top-k brokers is an NP-hard problem as it can be reduced from the k-densest subgraph problem (see Section 2). In order to tackle this problem, we design a heuristic solution to find the top-k brokers based on the theory of *weak ties* [6]. We propose a connection-aware scoring function and design an algorithm called *WeakTie* to find the top-k brokers. Further, to handle the highly dynamic nature of social networks, we also develop incremental algorithms: *WeakTie-Local* for unidirectional networks, and *WeakTie-Bi* for bidirectional networks. These algorithms are efficient as they recompute the scores based on the local views of these nodes.

Finally, we demonstrate how brokers can be useful in two information diffusion tasks: (a) structural hole spanner detection and (b) mention recommendation. We found that our detected brokers improve the precision of spanner detection by 35%. For mention recommendation, brokers can help diffuse a message to users located far away from the author and reach 23% more distinct users.

The contribution of this work is summarized as follows.

- We formally define the problem of detecting top-k brokers in social networks, and prove that this is an NP-hard problem.
- We utilize the theory of weak ties in our design of a heuristic solution to find top-k brokers.
- We develop two incremental algorithms, *WeakTie-Local* and *WeakTie-Bi* to identify brokers efficiently in dynamic social networks.
- Extensive experimental analysis on real world datasets demonstrate the effectiveness of the proposed approach. We show that the detected brokers are able to significantly improve the performance of structural hole spanner detection and mention recommendation applications.

The rest of this paper is organized as follows. Section 2 proves the NP-hardness of the problem. Section 3 presents our observations on weak ties and introduces our proposed approach based on the weak tie theory. Section 4 further introduces the incremental algorithms, WeakTie-Local and WeakTie-Bi to accelerate the computation in unidirectional and bidirectional networks respectively. In Section 5 we empirically evaluate our approaches and demonstrate the usefulness in two real world applications. Section 6 presents the related work and we conclude in Section 7.

2. PROBLEM ANALYSIS

In this section, we prove that the problem of finding top-k brokers is NP-hard.

THEOREM 1. *Identifying the top-k brokers in a directed graph is NP-hard.*

PROOF. The decision version of the top-k broker problem is stated as follow: Is there a subset of nodes H where $|H| = k$ such that the utility function ϕ in Equation 1 is greater than a given value s? To prove that the top-k broker problem is NP-hard, we first show that the decision version of top-k broker can be reduced from its function version in polynomial time and then we prove the decision version of top-k broker problem is NP-hard.

Suppose we have a graph with n nodes, the maximum distance between any pair of nodes is $(n-1)$ and there can be at most n^2 pairs of nodes. This implies that there are at most $n^2(n-1)$ possible values for ϕ. If we can solve the decision version in polynomial time, then the solution to the top-k broker problem is the set of nodes H that gives the largest s value which can be found in polynomial time.

Next, we prove that the top-k broker decision problem is NP-hard by showing that it can be reduced from the known NP-hard *k-densest subgraph* problem, namely, determining if there exists a k-node subgraph with at least p edges in a given graph [1].

Given an instance $I = \{G = (V, E), k, p\}$ of the k-densest subgraph problem, let $n = |V|$, and $m = |E|$. We can construct a directed graph $G' = (V', E')$ of $(n+m+1)$ nodes and $(n+2m)$ edges as follows. We first create a terminal node t in G'. For each node u in G, we create a corresponding node u' in G', and connect u' to t. For each edge $e(u, v)$ in G, let u' and v' in G' be the corresponding nodes of u and v respectively. We create a node e' in G', and connect e' to u' and v'. Let $Y_1 = \{e'_1, \cdots, e'_m\}$ and $Y_2 = \{u'_1, \cdots, u'_n\}$. Then $V' = Y_1 \cup Y_2 \cup \{t\}$.

Figure 2 shows an example graph G and the corresponding constructed graph G'. It is clear that the construction of G' can be done in polynomial time.

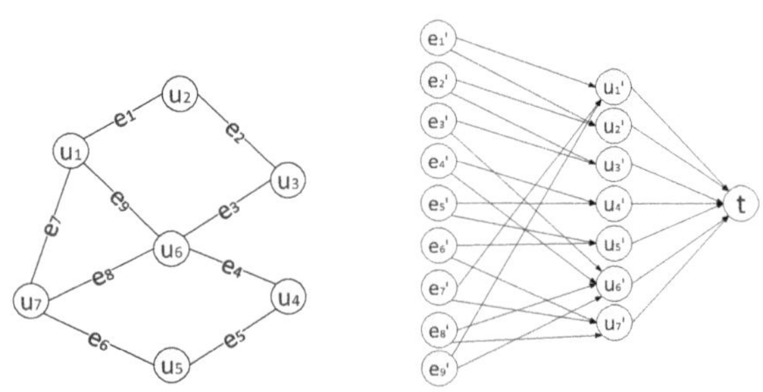

(a) Original graph G (b) Converted graph G'

Figure 2: Construction of G' from G.

Next, we prove that the k-densest subgraph instance I is satisfiable, *if and only if* there exists a subset $H \subseteq Y_2$ and $|H| = k$ such that $\phi \geq \frac{p}{2}$ in G'.

For the *only if* direction, suppose the k-densest subgraph instance I is satisfiable, that is, we have a subgraph with k nodes and at least p edges in G. Let $H \subseteq Y_2$ be the set of nodes in G' that correspond to these k nodes. When we remove H from G', there are at least $p \in Y_1$ nodes in G' that become isolated. These isolated nodes correspond to the p edges in the k-densest subgraph solution. Recall the utility function in Equation 1 which computes the difference in the sum of the inverse pairwise distance between G' and $G'\backslash H$. From the graph G' in Figure 2(b), we note that

$$d(u,v) = \begin{cases} 1 & u \in Y_1 \text{ and } v \in Y_2 \\ 1 & u \in Y_2 \text{ and } v = t \\ 2 & u \in Y_1 \text{ and } v = t \end{cases}.$$

Clearly, the p isolated nodes will cause a difference in the pairwise distances between the remaining nodes in G' and $G'\backslash H$. This is because these p nodes are able to reach the terminal node t in G' in 2 hops, but they can no longer reach t in $G'\backslash H$. Hence,

$$\begin{aligned} \phi &= \sum_{u,v \in V'-H} \frac{1}{d(u,v)} - \sum_{u,v \in V'-H} \frac{1}{d'(u,v)} \\ &= \sum_{u \in \{isolated\ nodes\}} \frac{1}{d(u,t)} \\ &\geq \frac{p}{2}. \end{aligned}$$

For the *if* direction, suppose the top-k broker decision instance is satisfiable, that is, there exists $H \subset V'$ such that $\phi \geq \frac{p}{2}$. As mentioned above, the utility function is affected when nodes that are previously reachable in G' are no longer reachable in $G'\backslash H$. This occurs when nodes in Y_2 are removed, leading to isolated nodes in Y_1. In this case, the number of nodes removed from Y_2 is $|H \cap Y_2| \leq k$. Since $\phi \geq \frac{p}{2}$, we have at least p isolated nodes in Y_1. These p nodes are edges in G whose end points correspond to the nodes in $H \cap Y_2$. Thus, we have found a subgraph with at most k nodes and at least p edges. In other words, the k-densest subgraph instance I is satisfiable. □

Given that the problem of detecting top-k brokers is NP-hard, we propose a solution that is based on the weak tie theory [6].

3. PROPOSED APPROACH

Granovetter [6] first introduced the concept of weak ties in social networks where the relationship between two users is weak when their number of overlapping friends is small. Bakshy et al. [2] showed that weak ties are important in the diffusion of novel information between remote users in Facebook while Burt [3] found that users with many weak ties are more likely to be placed in bridging positions.

We carry out preliminary experiments on the real world DBLP dataset to investigate the correlation between weak ties and brokers. Here, the authors are the nodes while co-authorships form the edges. The tie strength of an edge $(author1, author2)$ is given by the fraction of the number of common co-authors between $author1$ and $author2$ to the total number of co-authors they have. An edge is a weak tie if the tie strength is below some threshold. We consider authors who have served as PC members in only one research area as opinion leaders, and those who have served in multiple research areas as brokers.

We compute the number of weak ties that are incident to each author and sort the authors according to the number of weak ties. Figure 3 shows the percentage of opinion leaders and brokers with respect to the different ranges of weak ties. We observe that as the number of weak ties increases, the proportion of brokers increases significantly. This motivates us to develop an algorithm to find brokers based on the their number of incident weak ties.

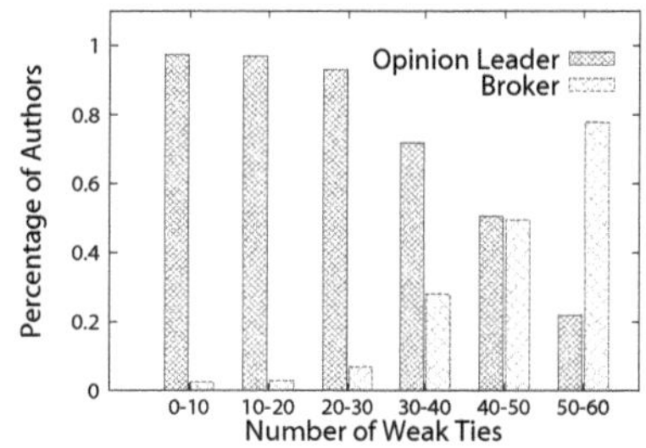

Figure 3: Percentage of opinion leaders and brokers versus weak ties in DBLP.

Although the experiment results show that a broker is correlated with the number of weak ties, simply counting the number of weak ties is not a good indicator of a node being a broker. Consider Figure 4 where a bold line denotes that two users have many overlapping friends, i.e. they have a *strong tie*. u_1 has a total of 4 weak ties while u_2 has 5. We observe that even though u_2 has more incident weak ties than u_1, u_1 is connected to more separate groups and is more likely to be a broker. A closer observation reveals that many of u_2's neighbours are, in fact, friends of each other's friends. Thus we need to take into account the connectedness among friends' friends.

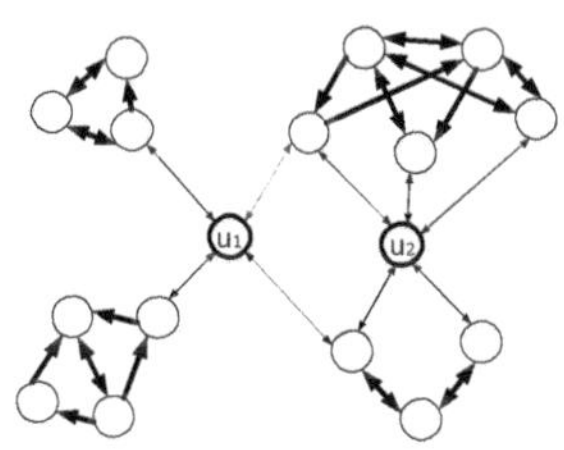

Figure 4: Example of two users with weak ties.

We first define the tie strength in a social network as follows:

DEFINITION 2. ***Tie Strength.*** *Let $G = (V, E)$ be a social network. For any edge $(u, v) \in E$, u is a follower of v and v is a followee of u. Let F_u denote the followees of u inclusive of u, and F_v denote the followees of v inclusive of v. Then the tie strength of the edge $(u, v) \in E$ is given by*

$$S_{uv} = \frac{| F_u \cap F_v |}{| F_u \cup F_v |}.$$

This implies that if the majority of u and v's followees are the same, S_{uv} will be close to 1. The edge from u to v is a weak tie if S_{uv} is below some threshold τ. Otherwise, it is a strong tie. Note that $S_{uv} = 0$ if u is not a follower of v.

A path from u to v is a sequence of directed edges that starts from u and ends at v. The strength of a path (*path strength*) is defined as the minimum tie strength among all the edges in the path. Now we define a strongly connected group as follows:

DEFINITION 3. ***Strongly Connected Group.*** *Given a social network $G = (V, E)$ and a tie threshold τ, a strongly connected group is a maximal subgraph of G such that for all pairs of nodes (u, v) in the subgraph, there exists a path from u to v with path strength greater than τ.*

Note that our strongly connected groups are in fact strongly connected components with the additional constraint on the minimum

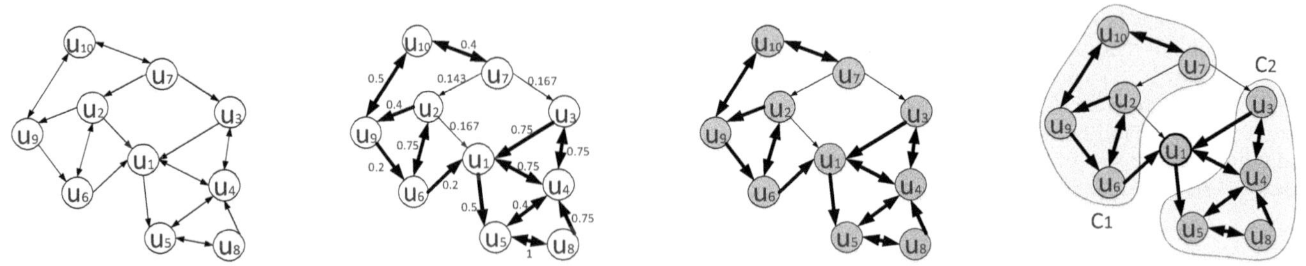

(a) Example network (b) Compute tie strengths ($\tau = 0.2$) (c) Strongly connected groups (d) Closeness of groups c_1 and c_2 to u_1

Figure 5: Illustration of *WeakTie* algorithm (best viewed in color).

path strength. We denote the set of strongly connected groups as C. Based on Definition 3, when two nodes u and v are in the same strongly connected group, there exists a path from u to v with path strength greater than τ and vice versa. This implies that all the nodes in the same strongly connected group form a cycle. Hence, the order of processing is irrelevant as we will still find the same set of strongly connected groups.

We define the *closeness* of a strongly connected group c to a node u as follows: Let N be the number of users in c whose tie strength to u is non-zero.

$$closeness(c, u) = \frac{\sum_{v \in c} S_{vu} - N \times \tau}{|c|}. \quad (2)$$

If $closeness(c, u) < 0$, this implies that u does not share many common followees with the users in c. In other words, u is more likely to be a broker connecting c to the rest of the network.

With this, we can assess the potential of a node u being a broker as follows:

$$score(u) = \begin{cases} \sum_{c \in \mathcal{C}} (-closeness(c, u)) & \mathcal{C} \neq \emptyset \\ 0 & otherwise \end{cases}, \quad (3)$$

where $\mathcal{C} \subset C$ denotes the set of strongly connected groups whose closeness with u is below 0. A large value of $score(u)$ indicates that u is connected to many largely non-overlapping groups. Hence, u is in a bridging position among these groups and plays an important role in bringing the users of these groups close to each other.

Given a social network $G = (V, E)$ and threshold τ, our proposed approach to find the top-k brokers in G consists of the following main steps:

1. For each directed edge $(u, v) \in E$, compute tie strength S_{uv};
2. Find the set of strongly connected groups C in G;
3. For each node $u \in V$, compute its $score(u)$;
4. Return the top-k nodes with the highest scores.

Step 2 utilizes the Tarjan's method [20], which is designed for detecting strongly connected *components*, to perform a depth-first traversal of the strong ties in G to obtain the set of strongly connected *groups*.

Figure 5 illustrates the proposed approach using a small network with 10 nodes. We first compute the tie strengths for all the edges. For example, the tie strength for edge (u_1, u_5) is 0.5 since we have $F_{u_1} = \{u_1, u_4, u_5\}$ while $F_{u_5} = \{u_4, u_5, u_8\}$, with u_4 and u_5 being the common followees out of 4. Figure 5(b) shows the weak and strong (bold arrows) ties in the example network when $\tau = 0.2$.

Next, we find all the strongly connected groups by applying Tarjan's algorithm [20] to traverse only the strong ties. Figure 5(c) shows two strongly connected groups obtained (marked in different colors). With this, we can compute the scores of all the nodes in the network. For example, node u_1 is connected to two strongly connected groups, c_1 and c_2 (see Figure 5(d)). We use Equation 2 to compute the closeness of each group to u_1 as follows:

$$closeness(c_1, u_1) = \frac{(S_{u_2u_1} + S_{u_6u_1} - 2 \times \tau)}{2} = -0.033,$$

$$closeness(c_2, u_1) = \frac{(S_{u_3u_1} + S_{u_4u_1} - 2 \times \tau)}{2} = 1.1.$$

Based on the above, we conclude that c_1 is not close to u_1 since the closeness is less than 0, while c_2 is close to u_1. Finally, we have score(u_1) = 0.033.

4. INCREMENTAL METHODS

Real world social networks are highly dynamic. In an evolving social network, there are many users joining (add node) and leaving (remove node) each day. Existing users may start new relationships (add edge) or they may break off their existing relationships (remove edge). These changes in relationships can all potentially affect the set of top-k brokers. Figure 6 shows the changes in the

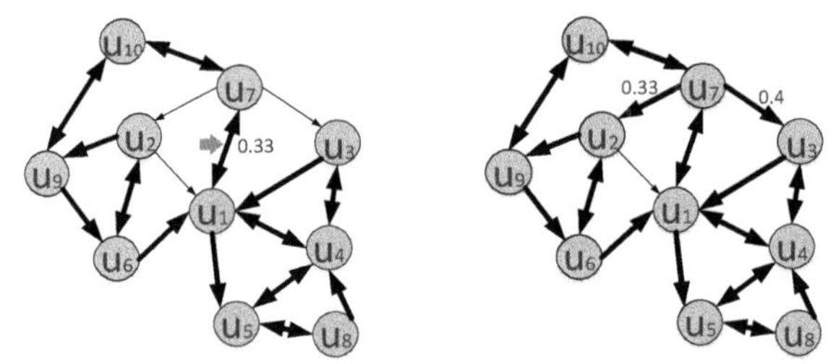

(a) (b)

Figure 6: Effect of Adding Edges (best viewed in color).

network after u_1 and u_7 start following each other. Note that when edges (u_1, u_7) and (u_7, u_1) are added, their tie strength is 0.33 and hence they are strongly connected to each other. Additionally, the tie strengths between their common followers increase and the edges (u_7, u_2) and (u_7, u_3) now become strong ties (see Figure 6(b)). Therefore, the entire network forms a single strongly connected group.

Recomputing the set of new top-k brokers when each update occurs is computationally expensive. Each update requires reapplying the Tarjan's algorithm on the entire graph to obtain the strongly connected groups. This has a complexity of $O(|V| + |E|)$ and is clearly not a practical solution for online social networks where the volume of updates is high. This motivates us to propose incremental algorithms to handle the dynamic nature of social networks.

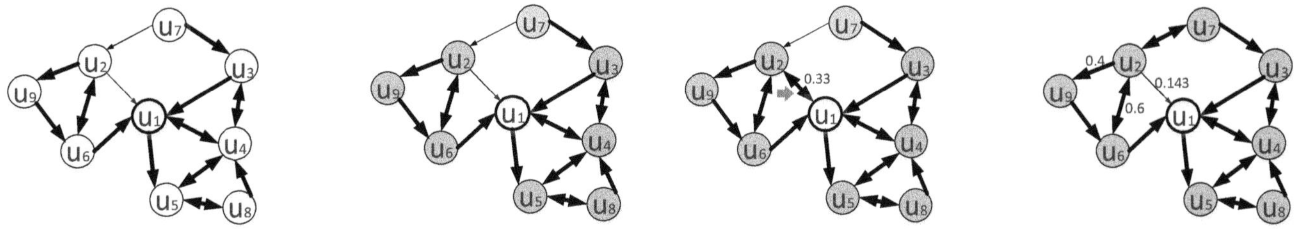

(a) 2-hop neighborhood of u_1 (b) Local groups of u_1 (c) Add edge (u_2, u_7) (d) New local groups of u_1

Figure 7: Illustration of *WeakTie-Local* algorithm (best viewed in color).

4.1 Algorithm WeakTie-Local

Updates in social networks are handled as either addition of new edges or removal of existing edges. This is because adding a node can be modelled as the addition of a list of edges between the new node and existing nodes; while removing an existing node is modelled as the removal of the edges associated with the removed node. Empirical investigation reveals changes to the strongly connected groups are often restricted to the 2-hop neighborhood of the affected nodes. This is because it is rarely the case that two users are connected by a chain of close friends and they do not know each other [9]. We design *WeakTie-Local* algorithm that utilizes the 2-hop neighborhood of an affected node to identify brokers.

Algorithm 1 gives the details. Suppose an edge (u, v) is added, Algorithm WeakTie-Local first creates the respective nodes if they do not exist and updates the tie strength S_{uv}. Since F_u has changed because of the addition/deletion of (u, v), for any neighbor w of u, we update S_{uw} or S_{wu} according to Definition 2 (Lines 14-15).

Let G_u be the 2-hop neighborhood of a node u and C_u be the set of strongly connected groups of nodes in G_u. From henceforth, we call C_u the local groups of u. We extract the 2-hop neighborhoods G_u and G_v. The scores of u and v are recomputed by calling the function *UpdateScore()* (Lines 1-8). For u's neighbor w, we need to recompute the $closeness(c, w)$ for $u \in c \wedge c \in C_w$ and update $score(w)$ (Lines 24-25). Further, adding the edge (u, v) may affect the local groups of the *common neighbors* of u and v. Hence, we also update the scores of these nodes (Lines 20-22). Similarly, when an edge is deleted, the corresponding 2-hop neighborhoods are extracted and we recompute the scores of the affected nodes.

Figure 7 illustrates the WeakTie-Local algorithm. Figure 7(a) is the 2-hop neighborhood of node u_1 and the tie strengths of the edges have been computed. We find all the local groups by applying Tarjan's algorithm [20] on the nodes in G_{u_1} considering the ties among them. Figure 7(b) shows the 3 local groups for u_1 and we compute the score of u_1. When the edge (u_2, u_7) is added (Figure 7(c)), u_2 has gained a new followee. This changes the tie strengths $S_{u_7u_2}$, $S_{u_2u_1}$, $S_{u_2u_6}$ and $S_{u_2u_9}$ and edge (u_7, u_2) now becomes a strong tie (Figure 7(d)). We then apply the Tarjan's algorithm to obtain the new set of local groups of u_1 and compute the updated score of u_1.

4.2 Algorithm WeakTie-Bi

For bidirectional social networks, we do not need to perform Tarjan's algorithm to find the new set of strongly connected groups whenever updates come. In most cases, as we will show soon, updating the score of an affected node takes linear time to the number of neighbors. The only case when we need to traverse the neighborhood is when the deleted edge causes a group to split into smaller groups. We present *WeakTie-Bi* algorithm to carefully exam the different cases in order to further accelerate broker detection in bidirectional networks.

Algorithm 1: WeakTie-Local

```
input : 1. Social network G = (V, E)
        2. Set of edges to be added E+
        3. Set of edges to be removed E−
        4. Tie strength threshold τ
output: Top-k Brokerss

1  Function UpdateScore(u, G)
2      Call Tarjan's algorithm to find the set of strongly connected
       groups C_u in G.
3      score(u) = 0;
4      foreach c ∈ C_u do
5          Compute closeness(c, u) with Equation 2;
6          if closeness(c, u) < 0 then
7              score(u) = score(u) − closeness(c, u);
8      Return score(u);
9  foreach (u, v) ∈ E+ ∪ E− do
10     if (u, v) ∈ E+ then
11         Create node u if u ∉ V;
12         Create node v if v ∉ V;
13         Compute S_uv;
14     foreach neighbor w of u do
15         Compute S_wu or S_uw;
16     Extract u, v's 2-hop neighborhood G_u, G_v;
17     score(u) = UpdateScore(u, G_u);
18     score(v) = UpdateScore(v, G_v);
19     foreach neighbor w of u do
20         if w is neighbor of v then
21             Extract w's 2-hop neighborhood G_w;
22             score(w) = UpdateScore(w, G_w);
23         else
24             Compute closeness(c, w)for u ∈ c ∧ c ∈ C_w with
               Equation 2;
25             Compute score(w) with Equation 3;
26 Return top-k nodes with highest scores.
```

Algorithm 2 gives the details. Lines 2-8 process the insertion of new edges. Given an edge (p, q), if either p or q does not exist, we create a new node (Line 3). Lines 4-7 update the friend lists of p and q as well as their tie strengths. Line 8 calls Algorithm 3 to handle the various cases for the addition of edges. Lines 10-13 process the deletion of edges. The updating of friend lists is done in Line 10 and the tie strengths are recomputed in lines 11 and 12. Line 13 calls Algorithm 4 to handle cases for the deletion of edges. The scores of the affected nodes are updated in lines 14-18. Finally, we return the top k nodes with the highest scores.

We enumerate the cases that may arise due to the insertion of an edge. The cases are illustrated using the network in Figure 8(a).

A1. New group formed.

This corresponds to the case when the edge (u_1, u_6) is added. Although u_6 was already a friend of u_2 prior to becoming friend of u_1, the tie between u_6 and u_2 is weak. Hence, a new group

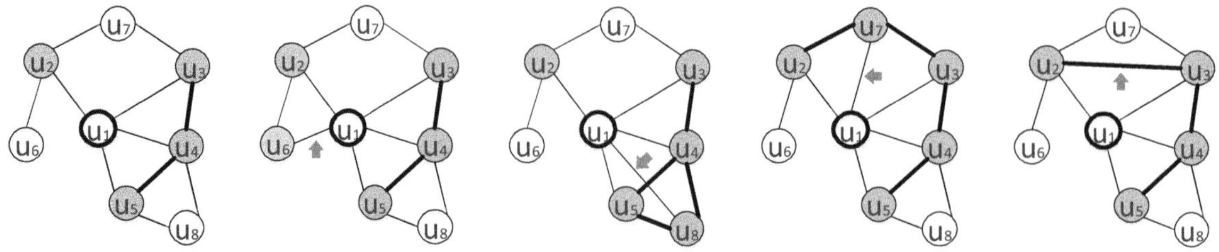

(a) Original network (b) Add (u_1, u_6) (c) Add (u_1, u_8) (d) Add (u_1, u_7) (e) Add (u_2, u_3)

Figure 8: Illustration of cases A1, A2 and A3 (best viewed in color). The new yellow group is formed in (b). The blue group is strengthened in (c). Blue group merge with green group in (d) and (e).

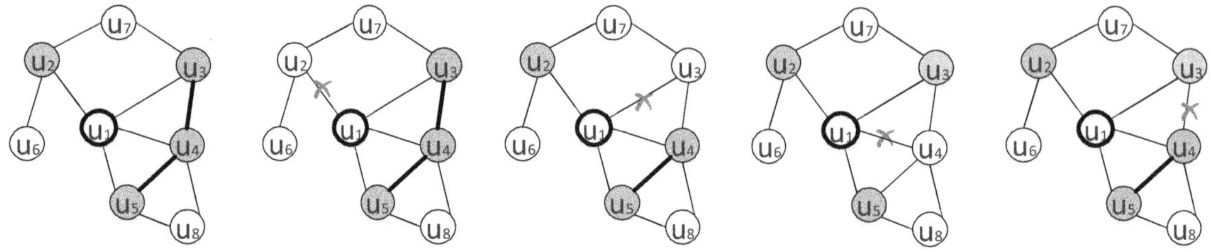

(a) Original network (b) Remove (u_1, u_2) (c) Remove (u_1, u_3) (d) Remove (u_1, u_4) (e) Remove (u_3, u_4)

Figure 9: Illustration of cases D1, D2 and D3 (best viewed in color). The green group is removed in (b). The blue group is weakened in (c). The blue group split into blue and yellow groups in (d) and (e).

Algorithm 2: WeakTie-Bi

```
input  : 1. Social network G = (V, E)
         2. Set of edges to be added E+
         3. Set of edges to be removed E-
         4. Tie strength threshold τ
output: Top-k Brokers
foreach (p, q) ∈ E+ ∪ E- do
    if (p, q) ∈ E+ then
        Create nodes p and q if p, q ∉ V;
        F_p = {q} ∪ F_p; F_q = {p} ∪ F_q;
        Compute S_pq;
        foreach w ∈ F_p ∪ F_q do
            Compute S_pw and S_qw;
        Call Algorithm AddCases (p, q);
    else
        F_p = F_p − {q}; F_q = F_q − {p};
        foreach w ∈ F_p ∪ F_q do
            Compute S_pw and S_qw;
        Call Algorithm RemoveCases(p, q);
    Update closeness between p and q and their local groups;
    Compute score(p) and score(q);
    foreach w ∈ F_p ∪ F_q do
        Update closeness between w and its local groups;
        Compute score(w);
Return top-k nodes with highest scores.
```

(colored in yellow) is formed (see Figure 8(b)). Lines 11-13 in Algorithm 3 deal with this case.

A2. Strengthen group.
Here, (u_1, u_8) has been added and u_8 is strongly connected with multiple friends of u_1 where all these friends are in the same group in blue (see Figure 8(c)). In this case, we simply include u_8 into the blue group and update the corresponding $closeness$. Lines 14 and 15 in Algorithm 3 handle this case.

A3. Merge groups.
This case corresponds to the addition of edge (u_1, u_7) or (u_2, u_3) (see Figure 8(d) and 8(e)). After adding the edge, u_1's local green group is now merged with the blue group to form the resultant group c_{new}. We compute $closeness(c_{new}, u_1)$. This case is handled in lines 6-10 and 16-19 of Algorithm 3.

Similarly, we enumerate the cases when an edge is removed.

D1. Remove group.
In this case, the edge removed is (u_1, u_2). u_2 has no other overlapping friends with u_1 and hence the strongly connected group in green consisting of only u_2 is dropped (see Figure 9(b)). Lines 10 and 11 in Algorithm 4 handle this case.

D2. Weaken group.
This case corresponds to the removal of edge (u_1, u_3). Here, u_3 has only one common neighbor with u_1. After the edge has been removed, the remaining users in the blue group are still strongly connected to each other (see Figure 9(c)). Lines 12-14 in Algorithm 4 deal with this case.

D3. Split group.
This case corresponds to the removal of (u_1, u_4) or (u_3, u_4). If (u_1, u_4) is removed, u_3 and u_5 are no longer strongly connected, or if (u_3, u_4) is removed, u_3 needs to form an individual group (see Figure 9(d) and 9(e)). As a result, two groups are formed and we compute the closeness of the two new groups. Lines 5-9 and 15-19 in Algorithm 4 handle this case.

We now analyze the efficiency of WeakTie-Local and WeakTie-Bi algorithms. Let d denote the degree of a node, where $0 \leq d \leq |V|$. Given that real world social networks are sparse, we have $d \ll |V|$ for most of the nodes. In WeakTie-Local, when an edge (u, v) is added or deleted, it takes $O(d^2)$ to find the local groups again. Hence, the time needed to recompute the scores for u and v is $O(d^2)$. For a neighbor w of u only, it needs to recompute the $closeness$ between each group and update the $score$, and this takes $O(|C_w|)$. For the common neighbors of u and v, WeakTie-

Algorithm 3: AddCases (e)

input : Edge e = (m,n)
output: Updated local groups
Let $C' = \emptyset$;
foreach $w \in F_m \cap F_n$ **do**
  Let c_w denote the local group that contains w;
  if $S_{nw} > \tau$ **then**
    $C' = C' \cup \{c_w\}$
  if $S_{mn} > \tau$ **then**
    Let $c_1, c_2 \in C_w$ be the local groups of m and n respectively;
    if $c_1 \neq c_2$ **then**
      $c_{new} = c_1 \cup c_2$;
      $C_w = (C_w - \{c_1, c_2\}) \cup \{c_{new}\}$;
if $|C'| = 0$ **then**
  Create new group $c_{new} = \{n\}$;
  $C_m = C_m \cup \{c_{new}\}$;
if $|C'| = 1$ *and* $C = \{c\}$ **then**
  $c = \{n\} \cup c$;
if $|C'| > 1$ **then**
  Merge all the groups in C' to form c_{new};
  $c_{new} = c_{new} \cup \{n\}$;
  $C_m = (C_m - C') \cup \{c_{new}\}$.

Algorithm 4: RemoveCases(e)

input : Edge e = (m,n)
output: Updated local groups
Let $N' = \emptyset$;
foreach $w \in F_m \cap F_n$ **do**
  if $S_{nw} > \tau$ **then**
    $N' = N' \cup \{w\}$
  if $S_{mn} > \tau$ **then**
    Let $c_1, c_2 \in C_w$ be the local groups of m and n respectively;
    if $c_1 = c_2$ **then**
      Regroup nodes in c to form new groups C_{new};
      $C_w = (C_w - \{c\}) \cup C_{new}$;
if $|N'| = 0$ **then**
  $C_m = C_m - \{n\}$;
if $|N'| = 1$ **then**
  Get n's local group $c \in C_m$;
  $c = c - \{n\}$;
if $|N'| > 1$ **then**
  Get n's local group c;
  $c = c - \{n\}$;
  Regroup nodes in c to form new groups C_{new};
  $C_m = (C_m - \{c\}) \cup C_{new}$.

Local needs to run the strongly connected group detection procedure in the neighborhood whose time complexity is $O(d^2)$ for each node. We have at most d such nodes, hence the time complexity for WeakTie-Local is $O(d^3)$. In WeakTie-Bi, when (u, v) is added, updating the scores for u and v takes $O(|C_u|)$ and $O(|C_v|)$ respectively since we need to recompute the *closeness* with each local group. Similarly for the a friend w of u or v, each friend takes $O(|C_w|)$ time to update its score. This requires a time complexity of $O(d|C_w|)$ as we have d friends. When (u, v) is deleted, both cases D1 and D2 require $O(d|C|)$ complexity. For case D3, the complexity is $O(d^3)$ as we have d nodes to apply depth-first search to find local groups again in their neighborhood.

5. EXPERIMENT STUDY

In this section we evaluate the effectiveness and efficiency of the weak tie based algorithms in identifying brokers. We also study how brokers can help information diffusion tasks. All the algorithms are implemented in Python 2.7, and the experiments are run on a Windows 7 PC with CPU 3.4GHz and 8 GB memory.

Datasets. We use two real world datasets, DBLP[1] and Twitter[2]. The DBLP dataset has 815,946 authors which form the nodes in the network. We extract a subset of authors from 4 research areas in computer science, namely Databases (DB), Information Retrieval (IR), Artificial Intelligence (AI) and Networks and Communication (NC). The resulting dataset has 219,815 authors and 1,089,793 co-authorships. The longest distance between any two authors is 20 and the average distance is 7.06.

The Twitter dataset contains 1.8 million users, including the active users in July 2009 and their neighbors. We prune out the accounts that have no posts and select the largest connected component, which consists of 542,798 users and 98,380,438 follow-relationships. The diameter is 59, and its average distance is 4.65. Table 1 summarizes the basic statistics of datasets.

Table 1: Dataset Summary

Dataset	#Nodes	#Edges	Diameter	Avg. Distance
DBLP	219,815	1,089,793	20	7.06
Twitter	542,798	98,380,438	59	4.65

5.1 Effectiveness Experiments

In this set of experiments, we evaluate the quality of the solutions given by the following methods:

- WeakTie: This method uses the entire graph to find the strongly connected groups.
- WeakTie-Local: Based on Algorithm *WeakTie*, this method utilizes the 2-hop neighborhood of a node to find local groups.
- WeakTie-Bi: This method is based on Algorithm *WeakTie-Local* and is optimized for undirected graphs.
- PageRank♯: In this method, each node's follower' PageRank scores [17] are summed up, and the k nodes with the highest scores are returned.
- Betweenness [8]: This returns the top k nodes that has the largest number of shortest paths passing through them.

We run WeakTie, PageRank♯ and Betweenness on both DBLP and Twitter datasets. Since DBLP is a bidirectional network while Twitter is a unidirectional network, we apply WeakTie-Bi on DBLP dataset and WeakTie-Local on Twitter dataset. We vary k from 100 to 700 and compute the utility function ϕ values obtained (see Equation 1).

Figure 10 shows that WeakTie is able to obtain the highest ϕ values for all k. WeakTie-Bi and WeakTie-Local suffer a slight decrease in quality as they only consider the local views of the affected nodes, and may not obtain the true picture of the connectedness among their friends. We observe that the Betweenness method performs well when k is small. This is because when we remove the nodes that have many shortest paths passing through them, the average distance between nodes will increase. However, as k increases, many of the nodes have alternate paths and the performance of the Betweennesss method decreases. Note that PageRank♯ performs worse in Twitter than in DBLP. This is because a user with many followers tends to have high PageRank♯ score. However, this user may not have any followee. As such, he/she ends up at the end of a path, and will not contribute much to the reduction of the average distance among other users.

5.2 Sensitivity Experiments

Next, we examine the effect of τ on the performance of the proposed methods. We set k = 500. Figure 11 shows the results. We

[1]http://aminer.org/billboard/structural-hole.html
[2]http://an.kaist.ac.kr/traces/www2010.html

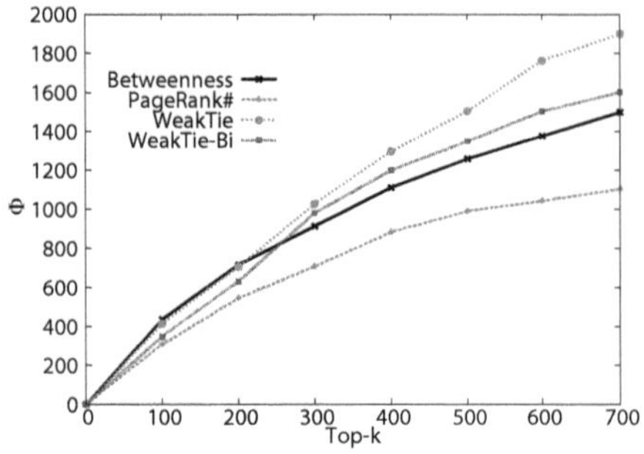

(a) DBLP

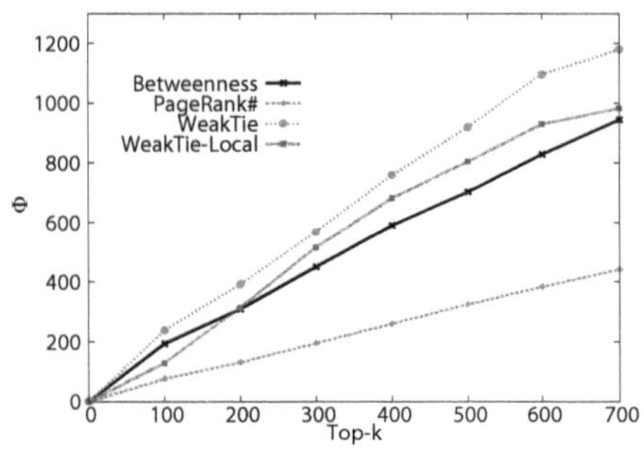

(b) Twitter

Figure 10: Quality of returned solutions.

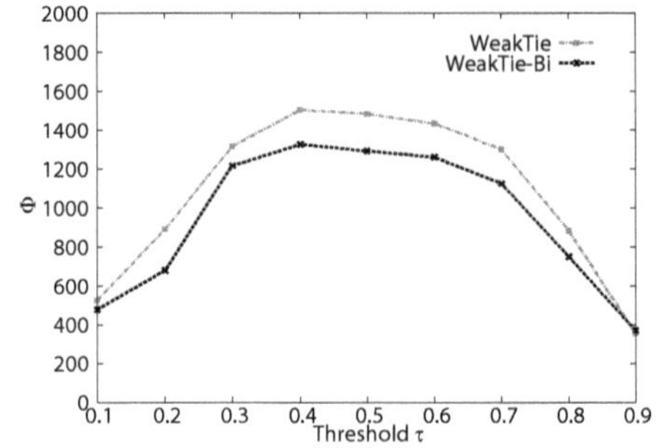

(a) DBLP

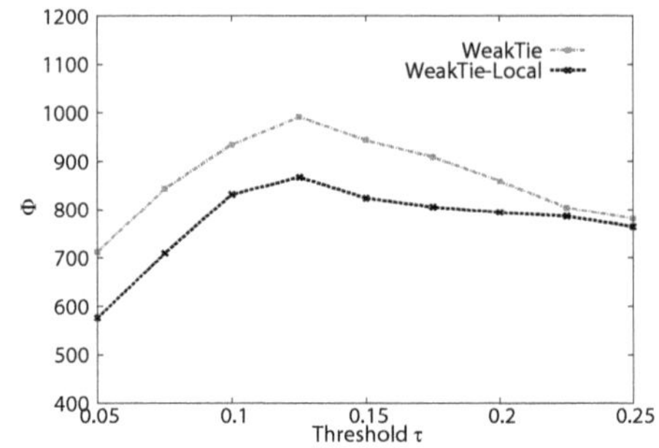

(b) Twitter

Figure 11: Effect of τ.

observe the performance of the proposed algorithms is dependent on τ. For the Twitter dataset, both methods perform best when $\tau = 0.125$. For the DBLP dataset, the best performance is achieved when τ is around 0.5. Clearly, τ is dependent on the overall connectedness of the users in the social network.

For Twitter-like network, users tend to follow a large set of users and the proportion of overlapping friends tends to be small. As a result, a small value of τ for the Twitter dataset is preferred. On the other hand, in the DBLP dataset, each paper has only a small number of co-authors resulting in relatively larger tie strengths, and hence a larger value of τ is appropriate. If τ is too large/small, almost all edges will be characterized as weak/strong ties, our proposed algorithms will not work well as they would not be able to distinguish between weak and strong ties. In all our experiments, we set τ as the *average tie strength* in the entire social network, which is 0.172 for Twitter and 0.486 for DBLP.

5.3 Scalability

We also compare the scalability of WeakTie, and incremental algorithms WeakTie-Local and WeakTie-Bi. We use the larger Twitter dataset for this experiment. Since WeakTie-Bi requires undirected graph, we convert each directed edge (u, v) in the Twitter dataset to an undirected edge by adding the edge (v, u) if it does not exist. We start with an initial size of 100k nodes and increase the dataset size by 100k nodes as well as their associated edges at each time step.

Figure 12 shows that WeakTie is the slowest since WeakTie has to re-run the algorithm on the entire graph when updates arrive. On the other hand, both WeakTie-Local and WeakTie-Bi only look at the local view of the affected nodes to handle the new updates, hence they run much faster than WeakTie as the dataset size increases. Furthermore, WeakTie-Bi eliminates the need to call Tarjan's algorithm in most cases and achieves the best performance.

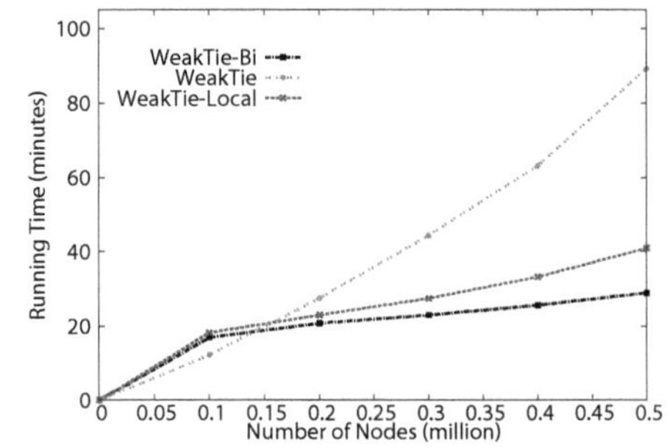

Figure 12: Scalability.

5.4 Applications of Brokers

5.4.1 Structural Hole Spanner Detection

In this set of experiments, we demonstrate the usefulness of brokers in diffusing information across communities. Lou and Tang [14] define structural hole spanners as users who have connections with different communities, and propose two models, MaxD and HIS to find the structural hole spanners. Given a set of communities **C**, MaxD iteratively finds a node such that removing this node leads to the largest reduction in the minimum cut of the communities in **C**. The first k nodes that are removed are the top-k spanners. In the HIS model, each user is assumed to have an importance score in each community. The structural hole score is the minimum value of a node's importance score in the different communities. The k nodes with highest structural hole scores are the spanners.

We adapt our WeakTie methods to detect the top-k spanners by finding the nodes that have connections to different communities with the highest WeakTie scores. Note that the spanners are a subset of the brokers we identify.

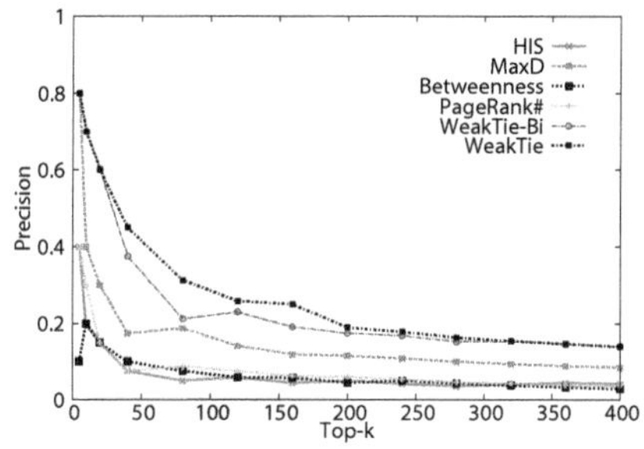

Figure 13: Precision of detected spanners in DBLP.

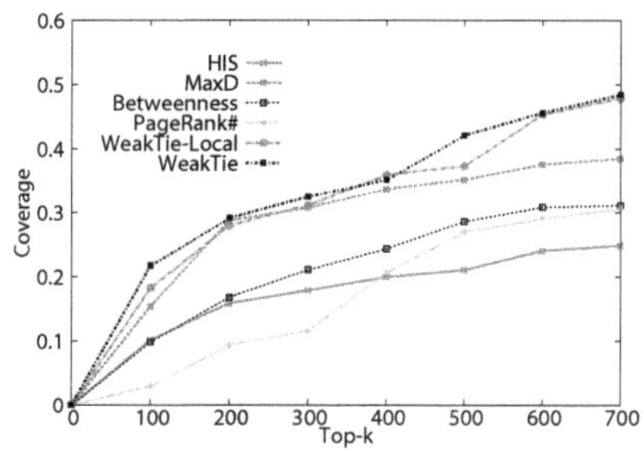

Figure 14: Coverage of detected spanners in Twitter.

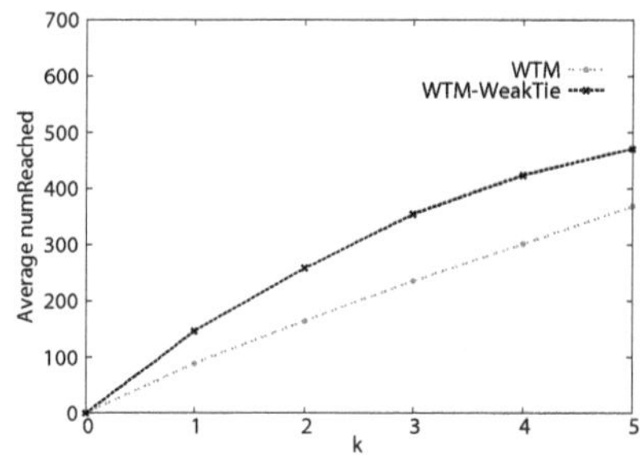

Figure 15: Number of users reached in Twitter.

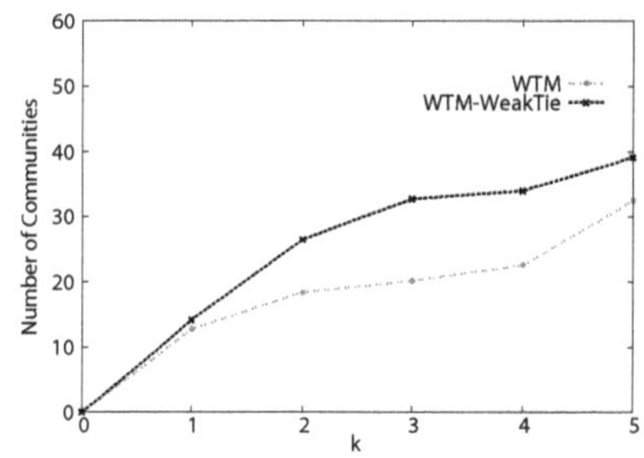

Figure 16: Number of communities reached in Twitter.

In the DBLP dataset, authors who have served as program committee members in conferences of different areas are considered as spanners [14]. Figure 13 shows the precision of the different approaches on this dataset. We observe that WeakTie significantly outperforms MaxD (+35%). Betweenness performs poorly, indicating spanners do not necessarily carry large numbers of shortest paths. HIS and PageRank♯ perform similarly as they both look for nodes that are incident with authority nodes but spanner authors do not merely establish cooperation with opinion leaders in different areas. WeakTie-Local performs slightly worse than WeakTie since it utilizes only the strongly connected groups in the local view.

For the Twitter dataset, since we do not have the ground truth, we examine the information diffusion paths instead. We divide Twitter dataset into 4 communities using Girvan-Newman's community detection method [16]. Let P be the set of paths that involve at least two users in different communities. Suppose S is the set of spanners found by a method. Let $P_S \subseteq P$ be the set of paths involving users in S. We define the coverage of a method as:

$$coverage = |P_S|/|P|.$$

A high coverage indicates that more information is being diffused across communities by the detected spanners. Figure 14 shows the coverage of the various methods in the Twitter dataset. We observe that WeakTie has the best performance, with WeakTie-Local being a close runner-up. On average, WeakTie outperforms the state-of-the-art method MaxD by more than 20%.

5.4.2 *Mention Recommendation*

Next, we discuss how top-k brokers can be used in mention recommendation to expand the spread of tweets. By adding "@username" in a tweet, the system will push the post to the mentioned user whose retweets could enable this post to reach more users. Note that for this mention recommendation task, since we need the retweet cascades as ground truth, we keep only tweets that have been retweeted more than 5 times. This prunes the Twitter dataset to 27,754 users, 1,285,097 edges and 35,480 paths.

The state-of-the-art mention recommendation method is WTM [22]. Given a tweet posted by a user u, WTM will rank the other users based on how well their interests match u's post, their interaction with u and how influential they are. In order to demonstrate how brokers are also useful in mention recommendation, we incorporate the WeakTie score into WTM's model of ranking the users. We call this model WTM-WeakTie.

We evaluate the effectiveness of WTM and WTM-WeakTie by the number of users reached using the top-k ranked users. The evaluation measure in [22] sums up the number of followers of the users in a cascade initiated by a recommended user regardless of whether these followers are duplicates. Based on this measure, we found that each tweet reaches 589 users on average for our Twitter dataset. However, if we consider only the distinct followers, each tweet actually reaches only 364 users on average. In order to present a more accurate picture of the actual number of people reached, we define the following measure $numReached$ which counts only the distinct followers.

Let L be the set of users who actually retweet, R_u denote the set of users involved in the retweet cascades initiated by a user u, and $Follower(w)$ denote the set of w's followers. We have:

$$numReached = |\cup_{u \in L} \cup_{w \in R_u} Follower(w)|. \qquad (4)$$

Figure 15 shows the results of WTM and WTM-WeakTie. We observe that after incorporating the WeakTie score, we have increased the number of users reached by 23% because brokers can help diffuse the tweet to users located far away from the author and initiate a cascade with more distinct users.

We further analyze the recommended users' ability to reach different parts of the network. We divide the dataset into 100 communities. Here we divide the dataset into smaller communities to avoid many retweets' cascades traveling within one big community. We consider that a user is able to reach a certain community if he/she has a follower from this community. Figure 16 shows the average number of communities the users in the recommendation list can reach. We observe that when $k > 1$, WTM-WeakTie can reach many more communities than WTM, indicating brokers are capable of broadcasting information to a wider range.

6. RELATED WORK

There has been much interest in social network analysis from both the sociology and computer science research communities. Sociologists have identified users who bridge otherwise disconnected, isolated or remote individuals as brokers and empirically verify their role in diffusing information [3, 19].

At the same time, computer scientists have tried to identify users who play significant roles in diffusing information in online social networks [4, 10]. The work in [10] analyzes different information diffusion models and identifies a set of influential users who can reach the maximum number of users. Extensions of their work include personalization [7] and scalability [13] of influence maximization algorithms. Other works employ centrality measures such as PageRank [11] or betweenness [8] to identify users that act as information sources and hence play an important role in disseminating information.

Tong et al. [21] finds the set of users whose removal would slow down the propagation of information in a network. They assume that information propagation follows some epidemic model in the form of a matrix whose first eigenvalue corresponds to the speed of propagation. Based on this, they iteratively remove a node at a time to minimize the first eigenvalue. Their method only applies to the specific diffusion model and does not show how these users are placed in the network.

Luo et al. [15] and Cui et al. [5] focus on identifying influential retweeters. They examine the author's followers' retweet history, active time and interest to identify influential retweeters who are able to accelerate the diffusion of information. However, the scope of influence of these retweeters is typically limited to a cluster of friends and do not try to reach remote users. In contrast, the brokers we have identified in this work are able to diffuse information to a larger pool of users, and to different parts of the network.

The work in [14] looks for structural hole spanners who can bridge the gap between different communities, thus enabling the diffusing of information across communities. However, the study in [12] shows that the best-expressed communities in real world networks are rather small, with only hundreds of nodes. Therefore, focusing only on the users between well-expressed communities is not practical for real world networks. In our work, we study the problem in a more general setting without the need of known communities. To the best of our knowledge, this paper is the first work that addresses the problem of finding top-k brokers in large online social networks.

7. CONCLUSION

In this paper, we have defined the problem of detecting brokers in social networks, and proved that the problem is NP-hard. We have also designed two incremental algorithms *WeakTie-Local* and *WeakTie-Bi* to deal with evolving social networks. Experiments on two real world datasets demonstrate the effectiveness and efficiency of the algorithms. We have also shown that utilizing brokers can improve the precision of spanner detection by 35% and help the mention recommendation task to reach 23% more distinct users. Future work includes applying the identified brokers in user recommendation and link prediction tasks.

8. REFERENCES

[1] Y. Asahiro, R. Hassin, and K. Iwama. Complexity of finding dense subgraphs. *Discrete Applied Mathematics*, 121(1):15–26, 2002.

[2] E. Bakshy, I. Rosenn, C. Marlow, and L. Adamic. The role of social networks in information diffusion. In *WWW*, 2012.

[3] R. S. Burt. Secondhand brokerage: Evidence on the importance of local structure for managers, bankers, and analysts. *Academy of Management Journal*, 50:119–148, 2007.

[4] S. Cheng, H. Shen, J. Huang, W. Chen, and X. Cheng. Imrank: Influence maximization via finding self-consistent ranking. In *SIGIR*, 2014.

[5] P. Cui, F. Wang, S. Liu, M. Ou, S. Yang, and L. Sun. Who should share what?: Item-level social influence prediction for users and posts ranking. In *SIGIR*, 2011.

[6] M. Granovetter. The Strength of Weak Ties. *The American Journal of Sociology*, 78(6):1360–1380, 1973.

[7] J. Guo, P. Zhang, C. Zhou, Y. Cao, and L. Guo. Personalized influence maximization on social networks. In *CIKM*, 2013.

[8] M. Haghir Chehreghani. An efficient algorithm for approximate betweenness centrality computation. In *CIKM*, 2013.

[9] E. Katz. The two-step flow of communication: An up-to-date report on an hypothesis. *Enis and Cox(eds.)*, Marketing Classisc(1):175–193, 1973.

[10] D. Kempe, J. Kleinberg, and E. Tardos. Maximizing the spread of influence through a social network. In *KDD*, 2003.

[11] O. Kurland and L. Lee. Respect my authority!: Hits without hyperlinks, utilizing cluster-based language models. In *SIGIR*, 2006.

[12] J. Leskovec, K. J. Lang, A. Dasgupta, and M. W. Mahoney. Statistical properties of community structure in large social and information networks. In *WWW*, 2008.

[13] Q. Liu, B. Xiang, E. Chen, H. Xiong, F. Tang, and J. X. Yu. Influence maximization over large-scale social networks: A bounded linear approach. In *CIKM*, 2014.

[14] T. Lou and J. Tang. Mining structural hole spanners through information diffusion in social networks. In *WWW*, 2013.

[15] Z. Luo, M. Osborne, J. Tang, and T. Wang. Who will retweet me?: Finding retweeters in twitter. In *SIGIR*, 2013.

[16] M. E. Newman. Fast algorithm for detecting community structure in networks. *Physical review E*, 2004.

[17] L. Page, S. Brin, R. Motwani, and T. Winograd. The pagerank citation ranking: Bringing order to the web. In *WWW*, 1998.

[18] A. Silva, S. Guimarães, W. Meira, Jr., and M. Zaki. Profilerank: Finding relevant content and influential users based on information diffusion. In *SNAKDD*, 2013.

[19] K. Stovel and L. Shaw. Brokerage. *Annual Review of Sociology*, 38(1):139–158, 2012.

[20] R. Tarjan. Depth-First Search and Linear Graph Algorithms. *SIAM Journal on Computing*, 1(2):146–160, 1972.

[21] H. Tong, B. A. Prakash, C. Tsourakakis, T. Eliassi-Rad, C. Faloutsos, and D. H. Chau. On the vulnerability of large graphs. In *ICDM*, 2010.

[22] B. Wang, C. Wang, J. Bu, C. Chen, W. V. Zhang, D. Cai, and X. He. Whom to mention: Expand the diffusion of tweets by @ recommendation on micro-blogging systems. In *WWW*, 2013.

Who Will You "@"?

Yeyun Gong, Qi Zhang, Xuyang Sun, Xuanjing Huang
Shanghai Key Laboratory of Data Science
School of Computer Science, Fudan University
825 Zhangheng Road, Shanghai, P.R.China
{12110240006, qz,13210240106, xjhuang}@fudan.edu.cn

ABSTRACT

In Twitter-like social networking services, people can use the "@" symbol to mention other users in tweets and send them a message or link to their profiles. In recent years, social media services are rapidly growing with thousands of millions of users participating in them every day. When the "@" symbol is entered, there should be an automatic suggestion function which recommends a small list of candidates in order to help users to easily identify and input usernames. In this paper, we present our work on building a recommendation system for the mention function in microblogging services. The recommendation strategy we used takes into consideration not only content of the microblog but also histories of candidate users. To better handle these textual information, we propose a novel method that extends the translation-based model. Experimental results on the dataset we collected from a real world microblogging service demonstrate that the proposed method outperforms state-of-the-art approaches.

Categories and Subject Descriptors

H.3.3 [**Information Storage and Retrieval**]: Information Search and Retrieval - Information Search and Retrieval; H.3.7 [**Digital Libraries**]: Collection, Systems Issues

Keywords

Microblog; Recommendation; Topical Model

1. INTRODUCTION

In Twitter-like services, the "@" symbol, which means what it appears to mean: "at", representing a connection, is one of the most important and common components. Once we put the "@" symbol in front of a username, an alert will be sent to that user signifying that a microblog is commenting directly to him. Since microblogging services have become one of the most important communication methods for people, there are a huge number of active users in real online services. According to a statistic on Twitter, there are 284 million monthly active users and the average number of followers for each account is 208[1]. Thus, if a recommendation system could recommend a smaller list of candidates, it would help users to efficiently identify and input usernames.

CIKM'15, October 19–23, 2015, Melbourne, Australia.
© 2015 ACM. ISBN 978-1-4503-3794-6/15/10 ...$15.00.
DOI: http://dx.doi.org/10.1145/2806416.2806458.

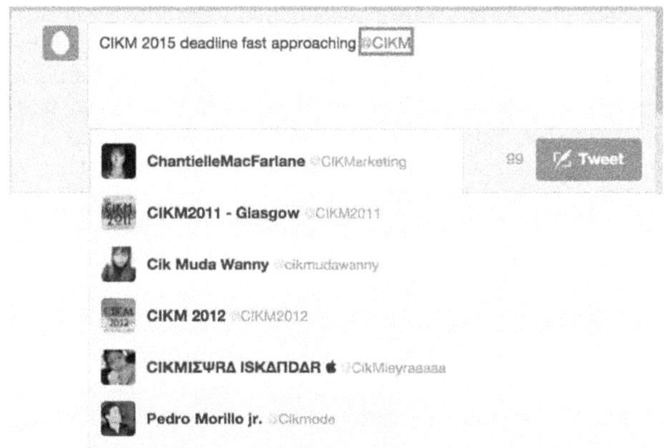

Figure 1: An example of username candidates given by Twitter.

Along with the development of social media, a variety of recommendation tasks have been proposed for different problems, such as content recommendation [4, 7, 11, 16, 35], community recommendation [22, 25, 27, 47], tag recommendation [8, 33], music recommendation [3, 15, 37], news recommendation [19, 38], and so on. Information used for recommendations can be roughly divided into the following types: textual information [8], structural information [16, 25], spatial information [36, 45], and temporal information [18, 46]. However, only a few of attention has been paid on the task of recommending usernames when users input the "@" in microblog posts [42]. The recommendations given by online microblogging services are usually based on either partial inputs or recent histories of users. Figure 1 illustrates an example of username candidates when user input "*CIKM*" after the "@" symbol. We can see that although the text input has clearly indicated the microblog to connect to CIKM 2015, the username "*CIKM2015*" is not in the top candidates.

[1]https://about.twitter.com/company

In this paper, we focus on the task of recommending usernames for users, when they try to use the "@" symbol to mention other users in their posts. To be able to make this task a reality we have to face several challenges. First, as we mentioned above, there are a huge number of active users in microblogging services. This means that the recommendation target space is extremely large. Second, personalization is an inherent requirement of this task. Since users have their specific preferences, different usernames should be recommended even when the microblog posts have the exact same content. Third, due to the limitation of character length in microblog posts, there is brevity in information and inadequate context and structure [6]. Wang et al. [42] formulated the task as a learning to rank problem and studied several features describing the interest of users, content-dependent user relationship, and user influence. However, the main aim of that work is to recommend the users who may retweet the microblog. Different from it, the aim of mention actions we focused on are not limited to the spread of a microblog. We analysed and evaluated on the microblogs posted by real online users.

Motivated by the advantage of translation based methods in capturing the content information in different recommendation tasks [14, 46], in this work, we also follow this framework and assume that the usernames and textual content in a microblog are parallel descriptions of the same thing in different languages. Hence, the username recommendation task can be regarded as a translation process from the content of microblogs to the usernames. Since the existing translation model is sometimes vague without the aid of background knowledge, we integrated latent topical information into the translation model to facilitate the translation process. As we mentioned above, users have their own preferences, histories of users are important factor in this task, so we also incorporated the posts of both the user and candidates into the model. To evaluate the proposed method, we constructed a dataset which contains more than 10 million microblogs from an online microblog service and selected a subset from it as golden standards. We compared the proposed method with several state-of-the-art methods on the constructed dataset. Experimental results demonstrate that the proposed approach can achieve significantly better performance than the other methods.

The contributions of this work can be summarized as follows:

- We proposed a novel topical translation-based method to predict the users who the authors try to mention. Both content of the microblog and histories of candidate users are taken into consideration.
- We constructed a large data set which contains more than ten million words. This dataset can also be used for other related tasks.
- Through various experiments in the real online dataset, we demonstrated the effectiveness of the proposed method.

2. RELATED WORK

The proposed method relates to the following two research areas: recommendation on social medias and topic model. In this section, we briefly describe the related works on these areas.

2.1 Recommendation on Social Medias

In twitter-like services, users usually have to scan microblogs presented in chronological order to find what they are interested in. Hence, the task of recommending microblogs has received considerable attentions in recent years [4, 7, 11, 16, 30, 35, 44]. Chen et al.[4] proposed to use collaborative ranking to capture personal interests. They incorporate the topics of tweets, social relations factors and some explicit features (such as authority of the publisher and quality of the tweet) to perfrom the task. Guy et al. [11] proposed to use both related people and related tags to recommend social media items. Pan et al.[30] introduced a joint model to combine collaborative filtering and diffusion processes for recommending microblogs. They also studied several diffusion features to capture the characteristic of diffusion processes. Graph based method was also proposed to perform the microblog recommendation task [44]. Microblogs and authors were ranked following a co-ranking algorithm.

Social interaction among people is the essential character of social media. To help users efficiently find their interested communities or friends, many studies have been proposed to perform the task [5, 22, 25, 27, 47]. Lo and Lin [22] proposed a weighted minimum-message ratio (WMR) method, which uses the real message interaction number among members, to generate personalized friend lists. Hao et al. [25] employed the opinions of trusted friends to make recommendations for the users under a probabilistic matrix factorization framework. In [47], the task of event-based group recommendation was introduced. They proposed a matrix factorization method, which considers location features, social features, and implicit patterns, to perform the task. Chen et al. [5] proposed a collaborative filtering based method to perform personalized community recommendations by considering multiple types of co-occurrences in social data at the same time.

Due to the usefulness of tag recommendation, a variety of methods have been proposed from different perspectives [12, 17, 34, 21, 8]. Heymann et al. [12] investigated the tag recommendation problem using the data collected from social bookmarking system. They introduced an entropy-based metric to capture the generality of a particular tag. In [39], a Poisson Mixture Model based method is introduced to perform the tag recommendation task. Krestel et al. [17] introduced a Latent Dirichlet Allocation to elicit a shared topical structure from the collaborative tagging effort of multiple users for recommending tags. Based on the observation that similar webpages tend to have the same tags, Lu et al. proposed a method taking both tag information and page content into account to perform the task [24]. Ding et al. proposed to use translation process to model this task [8]. They extended the translation based method and introduced a topic-specific translation model to process the various meanings of words in different topics. In [40], discriminative-term-weights were used to establish topic-term relationships, of which users' perception were learned to suggest suitable hashtags for users. To handle the vocabulary problem in keyphrase extraction task, Liu et al. proposed a topical word trigger model, which treated the keyphrase extraction problem as a translation process with latent topics [21].

The most similar work to ours is that of Wang et al. [42] which proposed the work of *whom-to-mention*. They

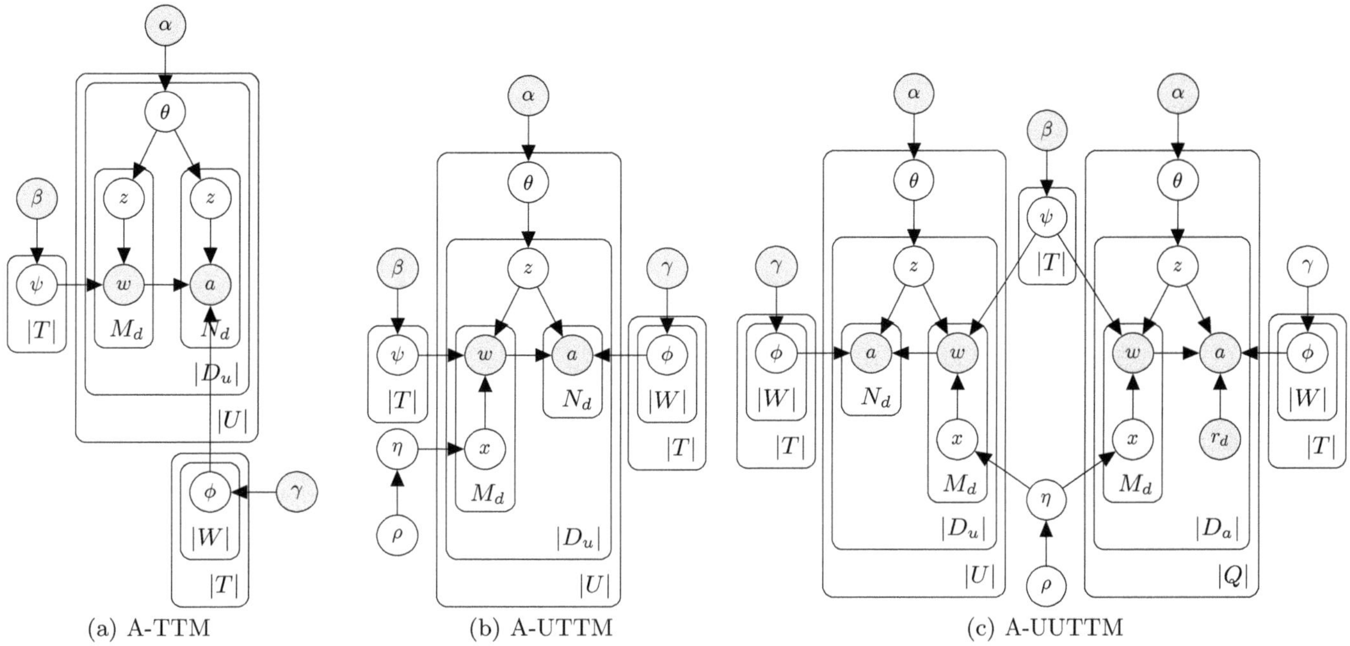

Figure 2: The graphical representation of the proposed model. Shaded circles are observations or constants. Unshaded ones are hidden variables.

try to find the users who have big influences and high probabilities to retweet the microblog. The main goal of their recommendation is to make the microblog to spread more quickly. Hence, they formulated the task as a learning to rank problem, and studied several features describing the interest of users, content-dependent user relationship, and user influence. Different from them, in this work, we use the microblogs which contain mention users and are posted by real users. Hence, we need to process different kinds of motivations when users input "@" in a microblog.

2.2 Topic Models

Topic models, such as probabilistic latent semantic indexing (pLSI) [13], latent Dirichlet allocation (LDA) [1], hierarchical dirichlet processes (HDP) [41], and so on, have proven to be useful in various tasks. In [1], latent Dirichlet allocation (LDA), a three-level hierarchical Bayesian model, was described for modeling collections of discrete data. Griffiths and Steyvers proposed a Markov chain Monte Carlo algorithm for inference LDA and used it to analyze abstracts of scientific papers [9]. Teh et al. [41] described Hierarchical dirichlet processes (HDP), a nonparametric approach, to model of groups of data. Each group was characterized by a mixture model and was desirable to allow mixture components to be shared between groups. Mcauliffe and Blei [26] introduced supervised latent Dirichlet allocation (sLDA) to model labelled documents.

Due to the capability of representing document themes, topic models have also been successfully used in natural language processing, image annotation, and various other applications [20, 32, 21, 8]. In [20], LDA-based image representation is proposed to classify the patches of the large image into the semantic concepts. To handle the vocabulary problem in keyphrase extraction task, Liu et al. [21] proposed a topical word trigger model, which treated the keyphrase extraction problem as a translation process with latent topics. Pennacchiotti and Gurumurthy [31] introduced a LDA based method to recommend friends with similar interests for users. For analysing text streams such as a sequence of posts from the same author, Wang et al. proposed Temporal-LDA to model the topic transitions that naturally arise in these data [43].

In this work, we also incorporate LDA with translation models to integrate topical information into them. The most similar work to ours is that of Lu et al. [23], which use translation methods to recommend citations. However, they did not take the topical information into consideration.

3. APPROACH

3.1 Preliminaries

Given a microblog d and its author u, the "@" recommendation task is to discover a list of candidate authors. In this work, we first use generative models to learn the joint distribution of the topics $\mathbf{z}$, the microblogs $\mathbf{w}$ and the mentioned users $\mathbf{a}$, $p(\mathbf{z}, \mathbf{w}, \mathbf{a})$. Then, we can use the probability $p(a|\mathbf{z}, w_d)$, which can be influenced based on the learned joint distribution, to generate candidate lists. The notations to be used throughout this paper are as follows. We use W and U to denote the word vocabulary set and the user set respectively. D_u denotes the set of microblogs posted by the user u. Q denotes the set of users who have been mentioned in one or more microblogs in the corpus. D_a is the set of microblogs which are posted by the mentioned user a, r_d is the rank of microblog d in the extracted microblogs which is based on the time of the microblog. Let T denote the topic set, and ψ_w^z be the probabilistic distribution over words for each topic. We use $\phi_a^{z,w}$ to denote the probabilistic distribution over users for each topic and each word which indexes the probability of a user being mentioned given a word and a topic. At the microblog level, we assume that each microblog has one topic and each user contains a mixture of topics. Let θ_u and θ_d denote the topic distribution of user u and topic distribution of microblog d respectively, $w_d = \{w_m\}_{m=1}^{M_d}$ are the words in microblog d, M_d is the number of words in microblog d. $a_d = \{a_n\}_{n=1}^{N_d}$ are the users mentioned in microblog d, N_d is the number of users mentioned in microblog d. $x_d = \{x_m\}_{m=1}^{M_d}$ are the topic word or background word indicate variables. Fig. 2 illustrates the graphical model representation of the proposed models.

3.2 A-TTM

The "At" Topic Translation Model (A-TTM) assumes that each microblog contains a mixture of topics. For the generation of the words in the microblog, each topic corresponds to a multinomial distribution over words. For the generation of the users mentioned in the microblog, each topic and word corresponds to a user distribution matrix $\phi^{z,w}$. The A-TTM is based on the following assumptions. When a user posts a microblog, she first chooses the words of the microblog and then selects the users she wants to mention. For each word, she first chooses a topic from the topic distribution and then chooses a word from the topic-word distribution. Finally, she chooses users to mention according to the topics and words in the microblog. The generation process of A-TTM is shown in Alg. 1.

Algorithm 1 The generation process of A-TTM model

```
for each topic z ∈ T do
  Draw ψ^z ~ Dir(β)
  for each word w ∈ W do
    Draw φ^{z,w} ~ Dir(γ)
  end for
end for
for each user u ∈ U: do
  for each microblog d ∈ D_u: do
    Draw θ_d ~ Dir(.|α)
    for each word in microblog d,w_m ∈ w_d: do
      Draw a topic z_m ~ Mult(.|θ_d)
      Draw a word from topic-word distribution w_m ~
      Mult(.|ψ^z)
    end for
    for each user mentioned in microblog d, a_n ∈ a_d: do
      Draw a topic z_n ~ Mult(.|θ_d)
      Draw a user a_n ~ p(.|z, w_d, φ^{z,w})
    end for
  end for
end for
```

3.3 A-UTTM

The A-TTM assumes that a microblog contains a mixture of topics, and each topic corresponds to a multinomial distribution over words. While this assumption is reasonable for long documents, for short microblog posts, a single post is most likely to be about a single topic. Therefore, in the "At" User Topic Translation Model (A-UTTM), we assume that a user contains a mixture of topics, represented by a topic distribution, and each microblog has a single topic label. The A-UTTM is based on the following assumptions. When a user posts a microblog, she first chooses a topic from her topic distribution and then chooses a sequence of words from the topic-word distribution or the background-word distribution one by one. Finally, she chooses a user to mention according to the topic and topic words in the microblog. The generation process of the A-UTTM is described in Alg. 2.

Algorithm 2 The generation process of A-UTTM

```
Draw ψ^B ~ Dir(β),η ~ Beta(ρ)
for each topic z ∈ T do
  Draw ψ^z ~ Dir(β)
  for each word w ∈ W do
    Draw φ^{z,w} ~ Dir(γ)
  end for
end for
for each user u ∈ U: do
  Draw θ_u ~ Dir(.|α)
  for each microblog d ∈ D_u: do
    Draw a topic z_d ~ Mult(.|θ_u)
    for each word in microblog d, w_m ∈ w_d: do
      Draw x_m ~ Bern(η)
      if x_m = 1 then
        Draw a word from topic-word distribution w_m ~
        Mult(.|ψ^z)
      else
        Draw a word from background-word distribution
        w_m ~ Mult(.|ψ^B)
      end if
    end for
    for each user mentioned in microblog d, a_n ∈ a_d: do
      Draw a user a_n ~ p(.|z_d, w_d, φ^{z,w})
    end for
  end for
end for
```

3.4 A-UUTTM

In the A-UTTM, we use a user level topic model to model the original microblogs. Although the A-UTTM takes into account the content of the original microblogs, usually the microblogs of the mentioned user are also important factors in influencing the mention behavior of the user. Hence, we incorporate the microblogs of the mentioned users into the A-UTTM, and we propose the "At" User-User Topic Translation Model (A-UUTTM). In the A-UUTTM, we assume that when a user posts a microblog, she first generates the words in the microblog. The generation process is similar as A-UTTM. She then chooses a user to mention based on not only the topic and topic words in the microblog, but also the microblogs of the mentioned user. The generation process of the A-UUTTM is described in Alg. 3.

3.5 Inference using Gibbs Sampling

To learn the parameters of all the models (A-TTM, A-UTTM and A-UUTTM), we use collapsed Gibbs sampling [10] to obtain samples of hidden variable assignment.

3.5.1 *Inference Estimation for A-TTM*

According to the generation process of Alg. 1, we can factorize the joint probability distribution of the topic $\mathbf{z}$, the microblog words $\mathbf{w}$ and the mentioned users $\mathbf{a}$ as follows:

$$p(\mathbf{w}, \mathbf{a}, \mathbf{z}|\alpha, \beta, \gamma) = p(\mathbf{z}|\alpha)p(\mathbf{w}|\mathbf{z}, \beta)p(\mathbf{a}|\mathbf{z}, \mathbf{w}, \gamma). \quad (1)$$

Algorithm 3 The generation process of A-UUTTM

Draw $\psi^B \sim Dir(\beta)$,$\eta \sim Beta(\rho)$
for each topic $z \in T$ **do**
  Draw $\psi^z \sim Dir(\beta)$
  for each word $w \in W$ **do**
    Draw $\phi^{z,w} \sim Dir(\gamma)$
  end for
end for
for each user mentioned in any microblog, $a \in Q$: **do**
  Draw $\theta_a \sim Dir(.|\alpha)$
  for each microblog $d \in D_a$: **do**
    Draw a topic $z_d \sim Mult(.|\theta_a)$
    for each word in microblog d, $w_i \in w_d$ **do**
      Draw $x_i \sim Bern(\eta)$
      if $x_i == 1$ **then**
        Draw a topic word $w_i \sim Mult(.|\psi^z)$
      else
        Draw a background word $w_i \sim Mult(.|\psi^B)$
      end if
    end for
    Draw $a \sim p(.|z_d, w_d, r_d, \phi^{z,w})$
  end for
end for
for each user $u \in U$: **do**
  Draw $\theta_u \sim Dir(.|\alpha)$
  for each microblog $d \in D_u$: **do**
    Draw a topic $z_d \sim Mult(.|\theta_u)$
    for each word in microblog d, $w_m \in w_d$: **do**
      Draw $x_m \sim Bern(\eta)$
      if $x_m == 1$ **then**
        Draw a topic word $w_m \sim Mult(.|\psi^z)$
      else
        Draw a background word $w_m \sim Mult(.|\psi^B)$
      end if
    end for
    for each user mentioned in microblog d, $a_n \in a_d$: **do**
      Draw a user $a_n \sim p(.|z_d, w_d, \phi^{z,w})$
    end for
  end for
end for

Let $N_z^{w,a}$ denote the number of co-occurrence times of user a and word w under topic z. According to the multinomial assumption on occurrences users, we obtain:

$$p(\mathbf{a}|\mathbf{z},\mathbf{w},\phi) = \prod_{u\in U}\prod_{d\in D_u}\prod_{a_n\in a_d} p(a_n|z_n,\mathbf{w_d}) = \prod_{z\in T}\prod_{a\in Q}\prod_{w\in W}(\phi_a^{z,w})^{N_z^{w,a}}, \tag{2}$$

where $\phi_a^{z,w}$ is proportional to the probability that user a to be mentioned with the topic z. The target posterior distribution for user generation, i.e. $p(\mathbf{a}|\mathbf{z},\mathbf{w},\gamma)$, can be obtained by integrating over all possible values of ϕ:

$$p(\mathbf{a}|\mathbf{z},\mathbf{w},\gamma) = \int \prod_{z\in T}\prod_{w\in W}\frac{1}{\Delta\gamma}\prod_{a\in Q}(\phi_a^{z,w})^{N_z^{w,a}+\gamma_a-1}d_{\phi^{z,w}} = \prod_{z\in T}\prod_{w\in W}\frac{\Delta(\mathbf{N}_{\phi^{\mathbf{z},\mathbf{w}}}+\gamma)}{\Delta(\gamma)}, \tag{3}$$

where $\Delta(\gamma) = \frac{\prod_{a=1}^{|Q|}\Gamma(\gamma_a)}{\Gamma(\sum_{a=1}^{|Q|}\gamma_a)}$ and $\mathbf{N}_{\phi^{\mathbf{z},\mathbf{w}}} = \{N_z^{w,a}\}_{a\in Q}$.

A similar derivation holds for $p(\mathbf{w}|\mathbf{z},\beta)$ and $p(\mathbf{z}|\alpha)$ leading to the expression for joint distribution:

$$p(\mathbf{w},\mathbf{a},\mathbf{z}|\alpha,\beta,\gamma) = \prod_{z\in T}\prod_{w\in W}\frac{\Delta(\mathbf{N}_{\phi^{\mathbf{z},\mathbf{w}}}+\gamma)}{\Delta(\gamma)} \prod_{z\in T}\frac{\Delta(\mathbf{N}_{\psi^{\mathbf{z}}}+\beta)}{\Delta(\beta)}\prod_{u\in U}\prod_{d\in D_u}\frac{\Delta(\mathbf{N_m}+\alpha)}{\Delta(\alpha)}. \tag{4}$$

For Gibbs sampler, we need to derive $p(z_i = k|\mathbf{z_{\neg i}},\mathbf{w},\mathbf{a})$, where $z_{\neg i}$ denotes the entire state space of z except the ith token and i iterates over each word in the corpus.

The sampling probability of a latent topic for word w_m in the microblog d of the user u is sampled from:

$$p(z_m = k|\mathbf{z_{\neg m}},\mathbf{w},\mathbf{a}) \propto \frac{N_{k,\neg m}^{w_m}+\beta}{N_{k,\neg m}^{(.)}+\beta|W|} \frac{N_{k,\neg m}+\alpha}{N_{(.),\neg m}+\alpha|T|}\prod_{a\in a_d}\frac{N_{k,\neg m}^{w_m,a}+\gamma}{N_{k,\neg m}^{w_m,(.)}+\gamma|U|}, \tag{5}$$

where $N_{k,\neg m}^{w_m}$ is the number of word w_m assigned to topic k. $N_{k,\neg m}^{w_m,a}$ is the number of word w_m and mentioned user a co-occurrence in the same microblog under the topic k. $N_{k,\neg m}$ is the total number of topic k. All the count with $\neg m$ is calculated without considering the current word w_m in the microblog d. And (.) represents the count is calculated of all conditions, for example, $N_{(.),\neg m} = \sum_{k\in T} N_{k,\neg m}$.

The sampling probability of a latent topic for the mentioned user a_n in the microblog d is sampled from:

$$p(z_n = k|\mathbf{z_{\neg n}},\mathbf{w},\mathbf{a}) \propto \frac{N_{k,\neg m}+\alpha}{N_{(.),\neg m}+\alpha|T|}\cdot(\sum_{w_m\in w_d}\frac{N_{k,\neg m}^{w_m,a_n}+\gamma}{N_{k,\neg m}^{(.),a_n}+\gamma|U|}). \tag{6}$$

3.5.2 Inference Estimation for A-UTTM

According to the generation process of Alg. 2, we can factorize the joint probability distribution of the topic $\mathbf{z}$, the microblog words $\mathbf{w}$, the topic or background word indicate variable $\mathbf{x}$ and the mentioned users $\mathbf{a}$ as follows:

$$p(\mathbf{w},\mathbf{a},\mathbf{z},\mathbf{x}|\alpha,\beta,\gamma,\rho) = p(\mathbf{z}|\alpha)p(\mathbf{x}|\rho)p(\mathbf{w}|\mathbf{z},\mathbf{x},\beta)p(\mathbf{a}|\mathbf{z},\mathbf{w},\mathbf{x},\gamma). \tag{7}$$

The derivation in previous section applies here which leads to following algebraic expression:

$$p(\mathbf{w},\mathbf{a},\mathbf{z},\mathbf{x}|\alpha,\beta,\gamma,\rho) = \frac{\Delta(\mathbf{N}_\eta+\rho)}{\Delta(\rho)}\prod_{z\in T}\frac{\Delta(\mathbf{N}_{\psi^{\mathbf{z}}}+\beta)}{\Delta(\beta)} \frac{\Delta(\mathbf{N}_{\psi^{\mathbf{B}}}+\beta)}{\Delta(\beta)}\prod_{z\in T}\prod_{w\in W}\frac{\Delta(\mathbf{N}_{\phi^{\mathbf{z},\mathbf{w}}}+\gamma)}{\Delta(\gamma)}\prod_{u\in U}\frac{\Delta(\mathbf{N_d}+\alpha)}{\Delta(\alpha)}. \tag{8}$$

Given the other variable state except the variable x_m, the sampling probability is calculated as follows:

$$p(x_m = p|\mathbf{w},\mathbf{a},\mathbf{z},\mathbf{x_{\neg m}}) \propto \frac{N_{\neg m,p}+\rho}{N_{\neg m,(.)}+2\rho}\cdot\frac{N_{\neg m,l}^{w_m}+\beta}{N_{\neg m,l}^{(.)}+\beta|W|}, \tag{9}$$

where $l = B$ if $p = 0$ and $l = z$ if $p = 1$. $N_{\neg m,1}$ is a count of topic words and $N_{\neg m,0}$ is a count of background words. $N_{\neg m,B}^{w_m}$ is the times of word w_m assigned to background word. $N_{\neg m,z}^{w_m}$ is the times of word w_m occurs as a topic word. $\neg m$ represents taking no account of the current word w_m.

Given the other variable state except the hidden topic z_d of microblog d in user u, the sampling probability is calculated as follows:

$$p(z_d = k|\mathbf{w}, \mathbf{a}, \mathbf{z_{\neg d}}, \mathbf{x}) \propto \frac{N^u_{k,\neg d} + \alpha}{N^u_{(\cdot),\neg d} + \alpha|T|} \prod_{w_m \in w_d} \frac{N^{w_m}_{k,\neg m} + \beta}{N^{(\cdot)}_{k,\neg m} + \beta|W|} \prod_{a_n \in a_d} \sum_{w_m \in w_d} \frac{N^{w_m,a_n}_{k,\neg d} + \gamma}{N^{w_m,(\cdot)}_{k,\neg d} + \gamma|Q|}, \quad (10)$$

where $N^u_{k,\neg d}$ is the number of microblogs assigned to topic k of user u. $\neg d$ denotes the count is calculated without taking account of the microblog d.

3.5.3 *Inference Estimation for A-UUTTM*

According to the generation process shown in Alg. 3, we can factorize the joint probability distribution of the topic $\mathbf{z}$, the microblog words $\mathbf{w}$, the topic or background word indicate variable $\mathbf{x}$ and the mentioned users $\mathbf{a}$ as follows:

$$p(\mathbf{w}, \mathbf{a}, \mathbf{z}, \mathbf{x}|\alpha, \beta, \gamma, \rho) = p(\mathbf{z}|\alpha)p(\mathbf{x}|\rho) p(\mathbf{w}|\mathbf{z}, \mathbf{x}, \beta)p_u(\mathbf{a}|\mathbf{z}, \mathbf{w}, \mathbf{x}, \gamma)p_a(\mathbf{a}|\mathbf{z}, \mathbf{w}, \mathbf{x}, \gamma). \quad (11)$$

The derivation in previous section applies here which leads to following algebraic expression:

$$p(\mathbf{w}, \mathbf{a}, \mathbf{z}, \mathbf{x}|\alpha, \beta, \gamma, \rho) = \frac{\Delta(\mathbf{N}_\eta + \rho)}{\Delta(\rho)} \frac{\Delta(\mathbf{N}_{\psi_\mathbf{B}} + \beta)}{\Delta(\beta)} \prod_{z \in T} \prod_{w \in W} \frac{\Delta(\mathbf{N}^\mathbf{U}_{\phi^\mathbf{z},\mathbf{w}} + \mathbf{N}^\mathbf{Q}_{\phi^\mathbf{z},\mathbf{w}} + \gamma)}{\Delta(\gamma)} \prod_{z \in T} \frac{\Delta(\mathbf{N}_{\psi^\mathbf{z}} + \beta)}{\Delta(\beta)} \prod_{u \in U} \frac{\Delta(\mathbf{N}^\mathbf{U}_\mathbf{d} + \alpha)}{\Delta(\alpha)} \prod_{a \in Q} \frac{\Delta(\mathbf{N}^\mathbf{Q}_\mathbf{d} + \alpha)}{\Delta(\alpha)}, \quad (12)$$

where $\mathbf{N}^\mathbf{U}_{\phi^\mathbf{z},\mathbf{w}} = \{N^{w,a}_z\}_{a \in Q}$ are the counts calculated in the original microblogs. $\mathbf{N}^\mathbf{Q}_{\phi^\mathbf{z},\mathbf{w}}$ are the counts calculated in the microblogs of mentioned users with decay factors, which can be calculated as follow:

$$\mathbf{N}^\mathbf{Q}_{\phi^\mathbf{z},\mathbf{w}} = \{\sum_{d \in D_a} N^d_w e^{-\frac{\tau_d}{\lambda}} \delta(z_d = z)\}_{a \in Q}, \quad (13)$$

where $N^d_{w_i}$ is the number of word w_i in microblog d. δ is the indicator function.

The inference process of A-UUTTM for the latent variables in the original microblogs is similar to A-UTTM model. Due to the space limit, we only show the inference process of the latent variables in the microblogs extracted from the mentioned users.

Given the other variable state except the variable $x_{\neg i}$, the sampling probability is calculated as follows:

$$p(x_i = p|\mathbf{w}, \mathbf{a}, \mathbf{z}, \mathbf{x_{\neg i}}) \propto \frac{N_{\neg i,p} + \rho}{N_{\neg i,(\cdot)} + 2\rho} \cdot \frac{N^{w_i}_{\neg i,l} + \beta}{N^{(\cdot)}_{\neg i,l} + \beta|W|}, \quad (14)$$

where $\neg i$ represents taking no account of the current word w_i.

Given the other variable state except the topic z_j of microblog j in user a, the sampling probability is calculated as follows:

$$p(z_j = k|\mathbf{w}, \mathbf{a}, \mathbf{z_{\neg j}}, \mathbf{x}) \propto \frac{N^a_{k,\neg j} + \alpha}{N^a_{(\cdot),\neg j} + \alpha|T|} \prod_{w_i \in w_j} \frac{N^{w_i}_{k,\neg i} + \beta}{N^{(\cdot)}_{k,\neg i} + \beta|W|} \sum_{w_i \in w_j} \frac{N^{w_i,a}_{U,k,\neg j} + N^{w_i,a}_{Q,k,\neg j} + \gamma}{N^{w_i,(\cdot)}_{U,k,\neg j} + N^{w_i,(\cdot)}_{Q,k,\neg j} + \gamma|Q|}, \quad (15)$$

where $N^{w_i,a}_{U,k}$ is the times of word w_i and user a co-occurrence under the topic k in the recommending users. $N^{w_i,a}_{Q,k}$ can be calculated by the equation $N^{w_i,a}_{Q,k} = \sum_{d \in D_a} N^d_{w_i} e^{-\frac{\tau_d}{\lambda}} \delta(z_d = k)$.

3.6 Prediction

We first run the inference algorithm of all the methods as described in previous section using the training set. Then we extend the Gibbs sampler state with the samples from the test set with following updates:

$$p(x_m = p|\mathbf{w}, \mathbf{a}, \mathbf{z}, \mathbf{x_{\neg m}}) \propto \frac{N^t_{\neg m,p} + N_{\neg m,p} + \rho}{N^t_{\neg m,(\cdot)} + N_{\neg m,(\cdot)} + 2\rho} \cdot \frac{N^{w^t_m}_{\neg m,l} + N^{w_m}_{\neg m,l} + \beta}{N^{(\cdot)^t}_{\neg m,l} + N^{(\cdot)}_{\neg m,l} + \beta|W|}, \quad (16)$$

where $(.^t)$ denotes the count calculated in the test set.

$$p(z_d = k|\mathbf{w}, \mathbf{a}, \mathbf{z_{\neg d}}, \mathbf{x}) \propto \frac{N^t_{k,\neg d} + N_{k,\neg d} + \alpha}{N^t_{(\cdot),\neg d} + N_{(\cdot),\neg d} + \alpha|T|} \prod_{w_m \in w_d} \frac{N^{w^t_m}_{k,\neg m} + N^{w_m}_{k,\neg m} + \beta}{N^{(\cdot)^t}_{k,\neg m} + N^{(\cdot)}_{k,\neg m} + \beta|W|}. \quad (17)$$

The parameters θ and ψ can be estimated as follows:

$$\theta^u_k = \frac{N^u_k + \alpha}{N^u_{(\cdot)} + \alpha|T|}; \psi^k_w = \frac{N^{w^t}_k + N^w_k + \beta}{N^{(\cdot)^t}_k + N^{(\cdot)}_k + \beta|W|}, \quad (18)$$

and the parameter ϕ can be obtained as:

$$\phi^{k,w}_a = \frac{N^{w,a^t}_k + N^{w,a}_{U,k} + N^{w,a}_{Q,k} + \gamma}{N^{w,(\cdot)^t}_k + N^{w,(\cdot)}_{U,k} + N^{w,(\cdot)}_{Q,k} + \gamma|Q|}. \quad (19)$$

The possibility table ϕ has a potential size of $|W| \cdot |Q| \cdot |T|$. The data sparsity problems may cause difficulties in estimating $\phi^{k,w}_a$. Hence, we employ a linear interpolation with the topic-free word alignment probability $p(a|w)$ to reduce the problem:

$$\Phi = \mu\phi + (1 - \mu)p(a|w). \quad (20)$$

To estimate the topic-free alignment probability $p(a|w)$, we explore IBM Model-1 [2] here. μ is trade-off of two probabilities ranging from 0.0 to 1.0. When $\mu = 0.0$, Φ will be reduce to topic-free word alignment probability; and when $\mu = 1.0$, there will be no smoothing in Φ.

In A-UUTTM, we perform the user recommendation as follows. Suppose a is the user to be mentioned and w_d are the words in the microblog d. We can calculate the score for user a by:

$$p(a|w_d) = \sum_{k \in T} p(a|k, w_d, \Phi) \int p(k|\theta^u) d\theta^u \propto \sum_{k \in T} \sum_{w_m \in w_d} \theta^u_k \Phi^{k,w}_a p(w_m|w_d), \quad (21)$$

where $p(w_m|w_d)$ is the weight of the word w_m in the microblog d, which we use the IDF score of the word. We can recommend the top-ranked users for the microblog according to the ranking scores.

4. EXPERIMENTS

4.1 Data sets and Settings

To examine the effectiveness of the proposed method, we constructed a dataset from Sina Weibo[2], which is one of the most popular websites providing a Twitter-like microblogging service in China. It also allows users to follow each other. If user A follows user B, user A is called the *follower* of B and B is called the *followee* of A. We collected both microblogs and *following-followee* relations of users. We constructed the dataset in the following way. First, we randomly selected 200 users as the *central* users. Then we collected the 2-*ego* network for all the central users based on their followees[3]. Through these steps, the crawling process produced a total of 2.07 million users and 299.6 billion following relationships. For each user, we collected the 2,000 most recent microblogs, resulting in 84.8 million microblogs in total.

In this paper, we focus on the "@" behavior. Hence, we randomly selected 10 users from the total sample of 200 central users. All of the microblogs were collected to construct the data set in accordance with the following requirements: 1) they were posted by the selected 10 central users or their followees; 2) the posting date lies between Jan. 1, 2013 and Dec. 31, 2013; 3) at least one "@username" is included in each microblog. Using these criteria, we gathered 178,841 microblogs. For each mentioned user in the set of microblogs, we extracted 4 microblogs matching the information of the mentioned user from the time line. Although the number of followees of the selected 10 central users is 1,286, there are in total 240,191 users involved in the constructed data set. Table 1 lists the statistics of the constructed dataset. We use the microblogs posted from Jan. 1, 2013 to Oct. 31, 2013 as training data. The others are used as test data.

Table 1: Statistics of the constructed data set

Data Set	#Users	#Relations	#Microblogs
SINA	240,191	383,639	178,841

For the evaluation metrics, we use Precision, Recall and F-score to evaluate the performance of user recommendation methods for the highest ranked result. To evaluate whether candidates with the top n highest scores contain the correct result, in this study, we use Hits@3 and Hits@5, which means percentage of usernames can be correctly identified from the top n results. Since the rank of the results is usually important, we use the common metrics detailed below to measure the rank of the results:

- **Mean Reciprocal Rank(MRR)**: The Reciprocal Rank (RR) calculates the reciprocal of the rank at which the first correct result occurs. The averaged RR across microblogs is called the MRR, which is calculated as follows:

$$\frac{1}{Z}\sum_{u\in U}\sum_{d\in D_u}\frac{1}{\text{rank}_d},$$

where Z is the total number of microblogs.

- **Binary Preference Measure(Bpref)**: For a microblog d, suppose an approach recommends a list of users A. J is a list of correctly recommended users in A. Let j be a correct recommendation and i be an incorrect recommendation. Bpref is defined as:

$$Bpref = \frac{1}{|J|}\sum_{j\in J}(1-\frac{|\text{i ranked higher than j}|}{|A|})$$

4.2 Baselines and Parameters Settings

For comparison with the proposed model, we evaluated the following methods on the constructed corpus:

- **Link-PLSA-LDA**: We implemented the method proposed in [28], where the microblogs content and the mentioned user information are incorporated under the topic model.
- **Frequency Descending (FD)**: We recommend user to the microblog depend on the rank of frequency of the candidates in the history. This method can recommend the user who is frequently mentioned by the author of the microblog.
- **Citation Translation Model (CTM)**: We implemented the method proposed in [14], which modifies the GIZA++ 1.07 [29] to learn translation probabilities using IBM Model-1. We set the number of training iterations equals to 10.
- **Ranking**: Following the approach proposed in [42], we also formalized the problem as a ranking problem and use support vector regression (SVR) [4] method to model it. We use same features set described in [42].

We run all of the topic-based models with 500 iterations of Gibbs sampling. We set the number of topics to 30 after trying a few different number of topics. We use $\alpha = 50.0/T$ and $\beta = 0.1$ as [10] suggested. We set parameter ρ to 0.01. The smoothing parameter μ is set to 0.8. For all compared methods, we use the parameter settings mentioned in Section 4.2, which are designed to give the best performance.

4.3 Results and Discussions

Table 2 shows the comparisons of the proposed method with the state-of-the-art methods on the constructed evaluation dataset. From the results, we observe that the A-UUTTM outperforms all the other methods on the dataset across the different evaluation metrics and significantly improves the user's recommendation robustly. The relative improvement of A-UUTTM over CTM is about 15.7% on MRR. The Precision, Recall and F-Score show us that the proposed method delivers the best result. The Bpref and MRR metrics show that the proposed method generates recommendations which are consistently ranked by users

[2]http://www.weibo.com

[3]According to Sina Weibo's constraints, we can get only the top 200 followees of each user.

[4]The toolkit scikit-learn 0.16.1 is used.

Table 2: Precision, Recall, F-Score, MRR, Bpref, Hits@3 and Hits@5 metrics on the dataset

Method	Precision	Recall	F-Score	MRR	Bpref	Hits@3	Hits@5
Link-PLSA-LDA	0.212	0.158	0.181	0.218	0.284	0.236	0.269
FD	0.340	0.253	0.290	0.341	0.385	0.309	0.341
Ranking	0.356	0.265	0.304	0.347	0.425	0.340	0.374
CTM	0.390	0.290	0.332	0.351	0.435	0.359	0.383
A-TTM	0.403	0.299	0.343	0.362	0.450	0.367	0.399
A-UTTM	0.424	0.315	0.362	0.385	0.482	0.394	0.426
A-UUTTM	**0.451**	**0.336**	**0.385**	**0.406**	**0.508**	**0.414**	**0.449**

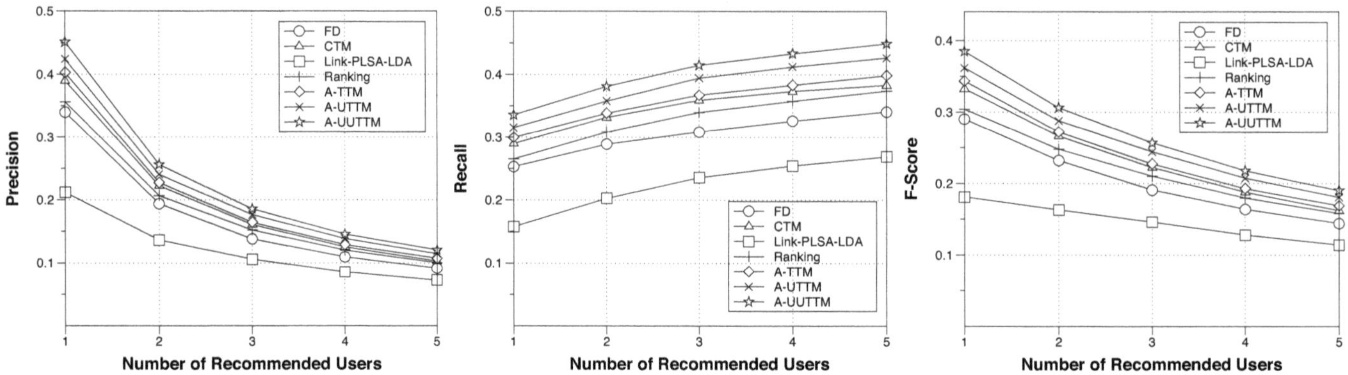

Figure 3: Precision, Recall and F-Score with recommended users varying from 1 to 5

as being superior. The results of Hits@3 and Hits@5 demonstrate that more than 41% of the original users can be found in the top 3 recommendations and around 45% of the original users can be found in the top 5 list.

From the results of CTM and Link-PLSA-LDA, we observe that the topic model and the translation model are effective for this task. Through comparing the results of the LDA-based model with CTM and Link-PLSA-LDA, we see that the A-TTM achieves better performance than either CTM or Link-PLSA-LDA on all the metrics. The results demonstrate that incorporating the topic into the translation model can impact the performance of the recommendation. The performances of ranking based method are worse than CTM. We think that the main reason may caused by the features which are more suitable for predicting who will retweet it. From the results of the A-TTM and A-UTTM, we observe that the A-TTM, based on the standard LDA, does not perform very well on the short microblogs. On the other hand, the A-UUTTM inherits the advantages of A-TTM and A-UTTM. Viewing the single microblog as one topic and each user corresponding to a topic distribution can improve LDA performance for short microblogs. Comparing the metrics of the A-UTTM with the A-UUTTM, we see that possessing the information of the candidates is helpful for the recommendation task.

Figure 3 shows the performance of different methods on Precision, Recall and F-Score varying with the number of recommended users by the various methods. In these figures, x-axis denotes the number of users recommended and the y-axis indicates the results of Precision, Recall, and F-Score respectively. From the results, we observe that the A-UUTTM achieves consistently better performance than the other methods with different number of recommendations.

Intuitively, since heavy social media users post a variety of microblogs and often mention other users in their microblogs, recommendation for them should be much more easily when then input "@" symbol in a microblog. To investigate this intuition, we split the users into three groups based on the number of occurrence of "@" in their microblogs. Group 1 consists of the users whom microblogs mentioned the other users less than 300 times. The users in whom microblogs the number of mentioned users is more than 300 times and less than 600 times are included in the Group 2. Group 3 includes heavy social media users whom microblogs contains more than 600 "@". Figure 4 shows the results of A-UUTTM on different groups. We see that the more frequently users mention others, the better performance the model can achieve. The relative improvement of A-UUTTM achieved in Group 3 over the results achieved in Group 1 is around 66.3% in MRR. The main possible reason is that the model can be better estimated with more training data.

4.4 Parameters Sensitive Analysis

In our model, there are two important parameters, the smoothing parameter μ and the number of topics $|T|$. In this section, we show how the performance of our model varies as μ changes from 0.0 $\sim$ 1.0 and $|T|$ changes from 10 $\sim$ 50. When analyzing one parameter, we keep other parameters fixed to the settings mentioned in the previous section. Experimental results validate that the proposed methods can achieve stable and superior performance under a wide range of parameter values.

Figure 5 shows the results of A-UUTTM when the smoothing parameter μ varies from 0.0 $\sim$ 1.0. From the figure, we observe that our model obtains the best

Figure 4: The results between heavy social media users and normal users.

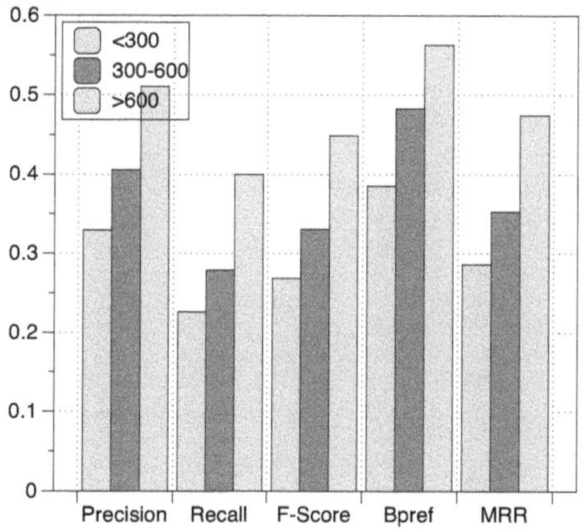

performance when $\mu = 0.8$. Furthermore, when the smoothing parameter μ is from $0.2 \sim 0.8$ we can achieve better performance than baseline methods. When μ equals to 1.0, the performance decrease. This demonstrates that it is necessary to reduce the sparsity problem by exploiting smoothing in our model. Table 3 shows the influences of topic number, we see that when the topic number changes from $10 \sim 30$, the performance of our model is much better than that of baseline methods, and we can obtain the best performance when $|T|$ is around 30. However, as the number of topics increases, the data sparsity problem will be more serious when estimating the topic-specific probability matrix ϕ, so the performance of our model will decrease accordingly. We can choose the topic number $|T|$ from $10 \sim 30$ and γ from $0.2 \sim 0.8$ to reduce the difficulty of parameter selection.

Table 3: The influence of topic number |T| in the A-UUTTM.

|T|	P	R	F	Bpref	MRR
10	0.445	0.331	0.380	0.505	0.402
20	0.446	0.332	0.381	0.506	0.403
30	**0.451**	**0.336**	**0.385**	**0.508**	**0.406**
40	0.434	0.323	0.370	0.488	0.390
50	0.422	0.314	0.360	0.477	0.382

Figure 6 shows the influence of the size of training data. According to the description, we used the posting date lies between Jan. 1, 2013 and Oct. 31, 2013 as training data. We trained A-UUTTM with several subsets selected based on the posting date. Comparing the result achieved by the model trained with the whole data set and part of it, we observe that A-UUTTM can achieve better performance with more training data. However, with only 2 months training data, A-UUTTM can achieve satisfactory results. This means that the more recent microblogs can make the greater contribution to the performance. Microblogs from more than 10 months ago offer little help for the recommendation. We also observe that the proposed method (A-UUTTM) achieves the best performance among all the methods when using only 5 months training microblogs.

Figure 5: The influence of the smoothing parameter μ in the A-UUTTM.

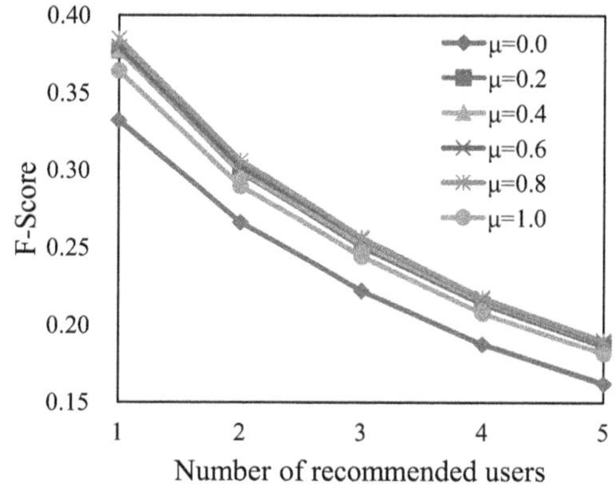

Figure 6: F-Score curve of different training size on this task.

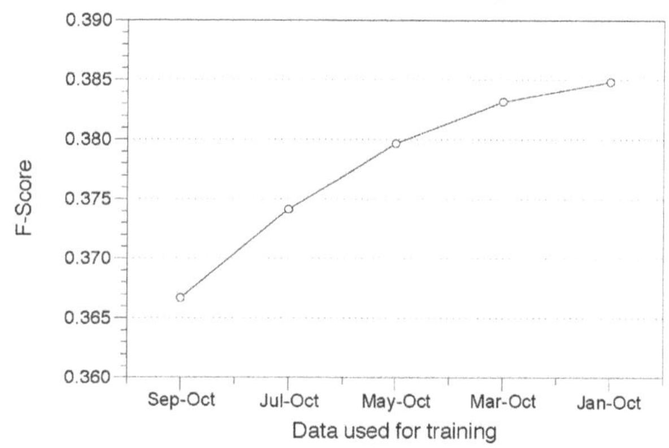

5. CONCLUSIONS

In this paper, we studied the task of recommending usernames when users input the "@" symbol in their microblogs. We incorporated both the content of the microblog and histories of candidate users into translation based methods to perform the task. A-TTM incorporated the topical information into the translation method. To tackle the short text problem, we proposed the A-UTTM model, which assumed that one microblog has a single topic and each user corresponds to a topic distribution. Furthermore, we proposed the A-UUTTM to incorporate the microblogs posted by the mentioned users. We evaluated the relative performance of the proposed methods based on a dataset collected from real world microblogging services. The experimental results demonstrated that our proposed algorithms can significantly outperform baseline methods.

6. ACKNOWLEDGEMENT

The authors wish to thank the anonymous reviewers for their helpful comments. This work was partially funded by National Natural Science Foundation of China (No. 61473092 and 61472088), the National High Technology Research and Development Program of China (No. 2015AA011802), and Shanghai Science and Technology Development Funds (13dz2260200ïijŇ13511504300).

7. REFERENCES

[1] D. M. Blei, A. Y. Ng, and M. I. Jordan. Latent dirichlet allocation. *J. Mach. Learn. Res.*, 3:993–1022, Mar. 2003.

[2] P. F. Brown, V. J. D. Pietra, S. A. D. Pietra, and R. L. Mercer. The mathematics of statistical machine translation: Parameter estimation. *Computational linguistics*, 1993.

[3] J. Bu, S. Tan, C. Chen, C. Wang, H. Wu, L. Zhang, and X. He. Music recommendation by unified hypergraph: combining social media information and music content. In *Proceedings of MM '10*, 2010.

[4] K. Chen, T. Chen, G. Zheng, O. Jin, E. Yao, and Y. Yu. Collaborative personalized tweet recommendation. In *Proceedings of SIGIR '12*, 2012.

[5] W.-Y. Chen, D. Zhang, and E. Y. Chang. Combinational collaborative filtering for personalized community recommendation. In *Proceedings of KDD '08*, 2008.

[6] A. Das and A. Kannan. Discovering topical aspects in microblogs. In *Proceedings of COLING 2014*, 2014.

[7] S. Debnath, N. Ganguly, and P. Mitra. Feature weighting in content based recommendation system using social network analysis. In *Proceedings of WWW'08*, 2008.

[8] Z. Ding, X. Qiu, Q. Zhang, and X. Huang. Learning topical translation model for microblog hashtag suggestion. In *Proceedings of IJCAI '13*, 2013.

[9] T. L. Griffiths and M. Steyvers. Finding scientific topics. *Proceedings of the National academy of Sciences of the United States of America*, 2004.

[10] T. L. Griffiths and M. Steyvers. Finding scientific topics. *Proceedings of the National Academy of Sciences*, 2004.

[11] I. Guy, N. Zwerdling, I. Ronen, D. Carmel, and E. Uziel. Social media recommendation based on people and tags. In *Proceedings of SIGIR' 10*, 2010.

[12] P. Heymann, D. Ramage, and H. Garcia-Molina. Social tag prediction. In *Proceedings of SIGIR '08*, 2008.

[13] T. Hofmann. Probabilistic latent semantic indexing. In *Proceedings of SIGIR '09*, 1999.

[14] W. Huang, S. Kataria, C. Caragea, P. Mitra, C. L. Giles, and L. Rokach. Recommending citations: translating papers into references. In *Proceedings of CIKM '12*, 2012.

[15] M. Kaminskas and F. Ricci. Contextual music information retrieval and recommendation: State of the art and challenges. *Computer Science Review*, 2012.

[16] I. Konstas, V. Stathopoulos, and J. M. Jose. On social networks and collaborative recommendation. In *Proceedings of SIGIR '09*, 2009.

[17] R. Krestel, P. Fankhauser, and W. Nejdl. Latent dirichlet allocation for tag recommendation. In *Proceedings of RecSys '09*, 2009.

[18] N. Lathia, S. Hailes, L. Capra, and X. Amatriain. Temporal diversity in recommender systems. In *Proceedings of SIGIR '10*, 2010.

[19] Q. Li, J. Wang, Y. P. Chen, and Z. Lin. User comments for news recommendation in forum-based social media. *Information Sciences*, 2010.

[20] M. Lienou, H. Maitre, and M. Datcu. Semantic annotation of satellite images using latent dirichlet allocation. *Geoscience and Remote Sensing Letters, IEEE*, 2010.

[21] Z. Liu, C. Liang, and M. Sun. Topical word trigger model for keyphrase extraction. In *Proceedings of COLING*, 2012.

[22] S. Lo and C. Lin. Wmr–a graph-based algorithm for friend recommendation. In *Proceedings of WI '06*, 2006.

[23] Y. Lu, J. He, D. Shan, and H. Yan. Recommending citations with translation model. In *Proceedings of CIKM '11*, 2011.

[24] Y.-T. Lu, S.-I. Yu, T.-C. Chang, and J. Y.-j. Hsu. A content-based method to enhance tag recommendation. In *Proceedings of IJCAI'09*, 2009.

[25] H. Ma, I. King, and M. R. Lyu. Learning to recommend with social trust ensemble. In *Proceedings of SIGIR '09*, 2009.

[26] J. D. Mcauliffe and D. M. Blei. Supervised topic models. In *Proceedings of NIPS*, 2008.

[27] M. Moricz, Y. Dosbayev, and M. Berlyant. Pymk: friend recommendation at myspace. In *Proceedings of SIGMOD '10*, 2010.

[28] R. Nallapati and W. Cohen. Link-plsa-lda: A new unsupervised model for topics and influence of blogs. In *AProceedings of AAAA '08*, 2008.

[29] F. J. Och and H. Ney. A systematic comparison of various statistical alignment models. *Computational Linguistics*, 2003.

[30] Y. Pan, F. Cong, K. Chen, and Y. Yu. Diffusion-aware personalized social update recommendation. In *Proceedings of RecSys '13*, 2013.

[31] M. Pennacchiotti and S. Gurumurthy. Investigating topic models for social media user recommendation. In *Proceedings of WWW '11*, 2011.

[32] D. Putthividhy, H. T. Attias, and S. S. Nagarajan. Topic regression multi-modal latent dirichlet allocation for image annotation. In *Proceedings of CVPR '10*, 2010.

[33] A. Rae, B. Sigurbjörnsson, and R. van Zwol. Improving tag recommendation using social networks. In *Proceedings of Adaptivity, Personalization and Fusion of Heterogeneous Information*, 2010.

[34] S. Rendle, L. Balby Marinho, A. Nanopoulos, and L. Schmidt-Thieme. Learning optimal ranking with tensor factorization for tag recommendation. In *Proceedings of KDD '09*, 2009.

[35] I. Ronen, I. Guy, E. Kravi, and M. Barnea. Recommending social media content to community owners. In *Proceedings of SIGIR '14*, 2014.

[36] T. Sakaki, M. Okazaki, and Y. Matsuo. Earthquake shakes twitter users: real-time event detection by social sensors. In *Proceedings of WWW '10*, 2010.

[37] M. Schedl and D. Schnitzer. Hybrid retrieval approaches to geospatial music recommendation. In *Proceedings of SIGIR '13*, 2013.

[38] E. Shmueli, A. Kagian, Y. Koren, and R. Lempel. Care to comment?: recommendations for commenting on news stories. In *Proceedings of WWW '12*, 2012.

[39] Y. Song, Z. Zhuang, H. Li, Q. Zhao, J. Li, W.-C. Lee, and C. L. Giles. Real-time automatic tag recommendation. In *Proceedings of SIGIR '08*, 2008.

[40] A. Tariq, A. Karim, F. Gomez, and H. Foroosh. Exploiting topical perceptions over multi-lingual text for hashtag suggestion on twitter. In *FLAIRS Conference*, 2013.

[41] Y. W. Teh, M. I. Jordan, M. J. Beal, and D. M. Blei. Hierarchical dirichlet processes. *Journal of the american statistical association*, 2006.

[42] B. Wang, C. Wang, J. Bu, C. Chen, W. V. Zhang, D. Cai, and X. He. Whom to mention: expand the diffusion of tweets by@ recommendation on micro-blogging systems. In *Proceedings of the 22nd international conference on World Wide Web*, pages 1331–1340. International World Wide Web Conferences Steering Committee, 2013.

[43] Y. Wang, E. Agichtein, and M. Benzi. Tm-lda: Efficient online modeling of latent topic transitions in social media. In *Proceedings of KDD '12*, 2012.

[44] R. Yan, M. Lapata, and X. Li. Tweet recommendation with graph co-ranking. In *Proceedings of ACL '12*, 2012.

[45] M. Ye, P. Yin, and W.-C. Lee. Location recommendation for location-based social networks. In *Proceedings of SIGSPATIAL '10*, 2010.

[46] Q. Zhang, Y. Gong, X. Sun, and X. Huang. Time-aware personalized hashtag recommendation on social media. In *Proceedings of COLING 2014*, 2014.

[47] W. Zhang, J. Wang, and W. Feng. Combining latent factor model with location features for event-based group recommendation. In *Proceedings of SIGKDD '13*, 2013.

Characterizing and Predicting Voice Query Reformulation

Ahmed Hassan Awadallah, Ranjitha Gurunath Kulkarni, Umut Ozertem and Rosie Jones
Microsoft Redmond, WA USA
{hassanam, raguruna, umuto, rosie.jones}@microsoft.com

ABSTRACT
Voice interactions are becoming more prevalent as the usage of voice search and intelligent assistants gains more popularity. Users frequently reformulate their requests in hope of getting better results either because the system was unable to recognize what they said or because it was able to recognize it but was unable to return the desired response. Query reformulation has been extensively studied in the context of text input. Many of the characteristics studied in the context of text query reformulation are potentially useful for voice query reformulation. However, voice query reformulation has its unique characteristics in terms of the reasons that lead users to reformulating their queries and how they reformulate them. In this paper, we study the problem of voice query reformulation. We perform a large scale human annotation study to collect thousands of labeled instances of voice reformulation and non-reformulation query pairs. We use this data to compare and contrast characteristics of reformulation and non-reformulation queries over a large a number of dimensions. We then train classifiers to distinguish between reformulation and non-reformulation query pairs and to predict the rationale behind reformulation. We demonstrate through experiments with the human labeled data that our classifiers achieve good performance in both tasks.

Categories and Subject Descriptors
H.3.3 [**Information Storage and Retrieval**]: Information Search and Retrieval – *selection process, search process.*

Keywords
Voice search, intelligent assistants, voice reformulation

1. INTRODUCTION
Voice-enabled interfaces are becoming a prevalent feature on both mobile and desktop devices. A voice-enabled interface makes human interaction with devices possible through issuing voice commands to the device. Voice-enabled interfaces are used in many scenarios including voice search and interaction with intelligent assistants. While voice interactions are useful and attractive for users, they pose new challenges in terms of understanding how they affect user behaviors that are widely understood with respect to text interfaces.

One such behavior that has been extensively studied in the context of Web search with text input is query reformulation [14]. Query reformulation is the act of submitting a query Q2 to modify a previous query Q1 in hope of getting better results [12]. When searchers experience difficulty in finding information, their struggle may be evident in their search behavior via different indicators such as query reformulation.

Query reformulation has been extensively studied in the literature from different angles including suggesting query reformulation, proposing taxonomies of query reformulation, proposing heuristics and regular expressions to identify different types of reformulation and automatically predicting query reformulation from log data. All this work has been focused on text input, and voice query reformulation has received little attention. Even though many of the studies performed on text queries can be useful for characterizing and predicting voice query reformulation, voice query reformulation has its unique characteristics in terms of the reasons that lead users to reformulate and how the queries are reformulated.

The end to end process of starting from user's search intent to the results that satisfy the user occasionally takes multiple search queries, and the entire process can be seen as a noisy channel problem. In text reformulations, the noisy channel tends to be the fingers -misspelling the search query- and sometimes cognitive errors, when the user cannot phrase the search intent well. Information retrieval literature is rich in spelling and query rewriting techniques to handle these. On the other hand, voice reformulations are different in nature, since the noisy channel is much more in the phonetic space, around the mistakes that the speech recognizer might typically make. This leads to reformulations that would rarely ever happen with text input, such as "ten issues"→"tennis shoes" or "youtube"→"U2".

In this paper, we present and evaluate methods to automatically identify voice query reformulation. Our focus is to characterize the difference between query pairs with and without reformulation. We study different signals that have been used before for predicting text query reformulation and show that many of them are useful for voice query reformulation. We also study several signals that are unique to voice query reformulation and show how they can be used to significantly improve the query reformulation prediction. We make the following contributions with this research:

- Characterize differences in the behavior associated with pairs of voice queries with and without reformulation including voice specific signals such as acoustic signals and statistics of the speech recognition process.
- Perform a large human annotation study to collect thousands of labeled instances of reformulation and non-reformulation query pairs.
- Develop methods to automatically identify voice query reformulations
- Develop methods to automatically identify some of the rationales that lead to voice query reformulation (speech recognition and relevance problems).

The remainder of the paper is structured as follows. In Section 2, we describe related work in query reformulation, query satisfaction and voice interactions. Section 3 describes the labeled data that we use in our analysis. We compare and contrast

CIKM'15, October 19 – 23, 2015, Melbourne, VIC, Australia.
 ISBN 978-1-4503-3794-6/15/10…$15.00
DOI: http://dx.doi.org/10.1145/2806416.2806491.

different characteristics of reformulation and non-reformulation query pairs in section 4. We describe our predictive models in Section 5. Our experiments and findings are summarized in Section 6 and we conclude in Section 7.

2. RELATED WORK

There are three areas of work related to the research presented in this paper: (i) query reformulation, (ii) search satisfaction, success, and frustration, (iii) voice search and intelligent assistants. We now describe previous work in each area in detail and discuss how our method and study extend this prior work.

Query Reformulation: Existing research has studied both how web search engines propose reformulations, and how people reformulate their own queries. Most of the research on the latter has focused on building taxonomies of query reformulation by examining a small set of query logs. Anick [2] classified a random sample of 100 reformulations by hand into eleven categories. Jensen et al. [17] identified 6 different kinds of reformulation states (New, Assistance, Content Change, Generalization, Reformulation, and Specialization) and provided heuristics for identifying them. They used the heuristics to predict when a user is most receptive to automatic query suggestions. The same categories were used in several other studies [10][22]. Huang and Efthimis [14] proposed another reformulation taxonomy. Their taxonomy was lexical in nature (e.g., word reorder, adding words, removing words, etc.). They also proposed the use of regular expressions to identify them. While studying re-finding behavior, Teevan et al. [27] constructed a taxonomy of query re-finding by manually examining query logs, and implemented algorithms to identify repeat queries, equal click queries and overlapping click queries. Another line of research focused on identifying reformulations using classifiers [12], heuristics [14] or regular expressions [17].

Another related problem focuses on the classification of the boundaries of the user search tasks within sessions in web search logs. Boldi et al. [5] presented the concept of the query-flow graph that represents chains of related queries in query logs. Arlitt [3] found session boundaries using a calculated timeout threshold. Murray et al. [23] extended this work by using hierarchical clustering to detect session boundaries. Jones and Klinkner [21] also addressed the problem of classifying the boundaries of the goals and missions in search logs. Lucchese et al. [23] used a similar set of features as [21], but uses clustering to group queries in the same task together. In this work, we extend previous work in that we focus on voice queries by understanding voice query reformulations and studying how we can build models for predicting the relation between pairs of voice queries.

Search Satisfaction: Extensive literature exists on deriving indicators of task success or failure from online user behavior. Fox et al. [8] used an instrumented browser to determine whether there was an association between explicit ratings of user satisfaction and implicit measures of user interest and identified the measures that were most strongly associated with user satisfaction. They found that there was a link between user activity and satisfaction ratings, and that clickthrough, dwell time, and session termination activity combined to make good predictors of satisfaction for Web pages. For example, they found out that a short dwell time is an indicator of dissatisfaction, while long dwell time is correlated more with satisfaction. Behavioral patterns were also used to predict user satisfaction for search sessions. Hassan et al. [20] developed models of user behavior to accurately estimate search success on a session level, independent of the relevance of documents retrieved by the search engine. Ageev et al. [1] proposed a formalization of different types of success for informational search, and presented a scalable game-like infrastructure for crowdsourcing search behavior studies, specifically targeted towards capturing and evaluating successful search strategies on informational tasks with known intent.. Feild et al. [7] developed methods to predict user frustration. They assigned users difficult information seeking tasks and monitored their degree of frustration via query logs and physical sensors. Our work is different from this work in that we focus on voice-activated interactions with search systems and intelligent assistants. We also do not focus on satisfaction, rather on reformulation which can then be used as an important signal for modeling satisfaction.

Voice Search and Intelligent Assistants: The research direction that's most related to our work is studying characteristics of voice search and its differences from text search. Jiang et al. presents results of a lab study with 20 participants to study query reformulation patterns with voice search, and reports that speech recognition errors significantly degrades performance and users tend to reformulate their queries by removing and substituting words [19]. In their follow up study, Jeng et al. reports that users usually find it difficult to use voice search due to misrecognitions resulting from various reasons [18]. Shokouhi et al. study query reformulations in mobile search, and compare them to reformulations in desktop search [26]. They show that users are less likely to switch between voice and text input methods unless they are starting a new task or correcting recognition errors. Our work extends this work in that it automatically extracts a large set of speech and acoustic features and uses them to build predictive models of voice query reformulation.

There has been significant amount of research on spoken dialog systems in the last two decades [28] and recently partially observable Markov decision processes (POMDP) have become the most commonly used method for managing dialogues [30]. In addition to speech input, intelligent assistants support other forms of input such as typing, or selecting displayed results, therefore regarded as multi-model conversational systems [29]. Recently, Jiang et al. present an automatic method from online data to evaluate intelligent assistants [13]. They build models to evaluate overall user satisfaction, as well as models to evaluate speech recognition and intent classification independently, and they also identify various behavioral patterns that relate to user satisfaction.

Contributions of Our Study: We extend previous research in a number of ways. First, we devise and evaluate methods to automatically identify voice query reformulation. Second, in contrast to prior work on query reformulation, we not only use text based features but also look at other signals unique to voice interactions like phonetic similarity, change in speaker emotions, speech rate, etc. Finally, we focus on identifying the rationales that lead the user to trying to reformulate the request providing useful insight that can help system developers improve the system performance and hence improve the overall user experience.

3. DATA & ANNOTATION GUIDELINES

In this section we describe the data we use in this study. We also describe the human annotation study we conducted to collect labels for this data.

3.1 Data

Our data consists of a sample of query pairs from the user logs of a major search engine. The data was sampled given the following conditions:

- Q1 is a voice query, Q2 can be of any input type (i.e. voice, text, autosuggest)
- The time difference between Q1 and Q2 is less than 5 minutes
- Q1 has received no clicks

The first condition is intended to focus on voice queries which are the main focus of this study. The remaining two conditions are intended to generate a high-recall low-precision filter that retrieves most of the reformulation pairs. This is following the work presented in [12] which showed that most query reformulations occur within 5 minutes of the original query and that the original query does not usually receive any clicks. Note that if we do not apply such filters before sampling, most of the sampled query pairs will not have a reformulation limiting our ability to study voice query reformulation [12]. Also note that once we build the query reformulation predictor, as will be described later, we can apply it freely to the logs without the need to apply such filters.

We randomly sampled such query pairs from user logs of a major search engine between June and December 2014. In order to remove variability caused by geographic and linguistic variation in search behavior, we only included queries generated in the English speaking United States locale. The query pairs were then labeled by human annotators. Annotators were recruited from the crowdsourcing service Clickworker.com, which provided access to crowd workers under contract. Annotators resided in the United States and were fluent in English. We collected human annotations on these query pairs along different dimensions: (1) speech recognition quality, (2) relevance of the results of Q1, and (3) whether Q2 is a reformulation, a related query, or an unrelated query. Each query pair was judged 5 times independently by different annotators and the majority label was used. We defined reformulation, related queries and unrelated queries as follows:

Definition: A *reformulation* is a query pair where the user is submitting a query Q2 to modify a query Q1 while still trying to satisfy the same information need as in Q1.

In voice queries, users opt to reformulate their queries if they think the results do not satisfy their original information need either due to a problem with the speech recognition or due to the retrieved results being not relevant. When users decide to reformulate their queries, they may issue another voice query with the exact words but pronounces it differently or speaks at a different pace. The user may also decide to type in what she said in Q1, fixing speech recognition errors, for example "watson's ministy"→"watson's manistee". Additionally, the user may decide to use different wording without changing the meaning, such as "pictures of kane's flowers"→"cannis flowers photos".

Definition: A *related query* is a query Q2 that has the same topic as Q1, but is not a reformulation of Q1.

Related queries are intended to satisfy a different information need and hence are not considered as a reformulation. Examples of related queries include "just dance"→"just dance videos", or "toyota corolla mpg"→"toyota yaris mpg".

Definition: An *unrelated query* is a query Q2 that is neither related to nor a reformulation of Q1.

3.2 Annotation Guidelines

The annotation task consists of listening to Q1 and examining the speech recognizer output for this voice query (and the same for Q2, if Q2 is also a voice query), and inspecting search result pages for both these queries, then answering three questions. To avoid overloading the annotator with all the information, the instructions are interleaved with the relevant questions, but the judge is encouraged to come back to the earlier questions at any time. Also the annotators are allowed to listen to the voice queries as many times as they like. In addition, to provide more context to the annotators, they were given the following information: the timestamps of each query, the search result pages of each query, the clicks the second query received and the fact that the first query received no clicks. The annotation process proceeded as follows:

1. The judge listens to audio of Q1 and examines the speech recognizer output for this query and answers Question 1 (SR quality): *Was Q1 recognized correctly*?
   PERFECT: if all the words are recognized correctly.
   GOOD: minor errors only, a word or two missed or misrecognized, but overall content is pretty well covered.
   BAD: a key word is missing or misrecognized
2. The judge is instructed to click on the recognized text of Q1, inspect search results and answer the second question. The judge can return and change the answer after listening to (or looking at) Q2: Question 2 (search relevance): *Did the user find what were they looking for in Q1?*
   PERFECT: the user found the required information
   GOOD: the user found some useful/relevant information
   BAD: the user did not find what he/she was looking for
3. The judge listens to Q2, and inspects the search results for Q2 and answers Question 3: *Is Q2 a reformulation of Q1?*
   YES: Q2 is a reformulation of Q1. Here note that this may be a reformulation, even if the recognized text for Q1 and/or Q2 do not correctly represent what the user said
   RELATED: Q2 is related to Q1, but not exactly the same information need
   NO: User is looking for something new

Our sample originally contained 7500 query pairs. After excluding query pairs that judges indicated have a problem with understanding the audio and they cannot provide a judgment, we ended up with 7322 labeled query pairs. When manually investigating these cases, we found out that these are cases where the audio is not intended for the speech recognizer, such as pocket dialing, or a child playing with the phone saying nothing intelligible.

4. CHARACTERIZATION OF VOICE REFOMULATION BEHAVIOR

In this section, we examine several characteristics of voice reformulation focusing on query similarity, speech quality, result quality and acoustic dimensions.

4.1 Query Similarity

At the outset of our analysis, we examine a number of different ways of measuring the similarity between a pair of queries and compare reformulation pairs to non-reformulation pairs. We might expect non-reformulation pairs to contain less overlap as people revise their queries to explore alternatives. We use three different methods for assessing the similarity between two queries: (1) lexical similarity, (2) semantic similarity, and (3) phonetic similarity.

Lexical Similarity: To measure the lexical similarity between pairs of queries, we begin by performing standard text normalization where we lowercase the query text, and remove stop words. Then we represent every query as a bag of non-stop word terms. The similarity between any two queries Qi and Qj is computed as follows:

$$\frac{|Qi \cap Qj|}{|Qi| + |Qj| - |Qi \cap Qj|}$$

where $|Qi|$ is the number of terms in query Qi, and $|Qi \cap Qj|$ is the number of matched terms in Qi and Qj. To calculate the number of matches in Qi and Qj ($Qi \cap Qj$), we consider two terms matched if: (1) the two terms match exactly, (2) to capture spelling variants and misspelling, we allow two terms to match if the Levenshtein edit distance between them is less than two, or (3) We match two terms if the lemmas of their tokens match. Lemmatization is the process of reducing an inflected spelling to its lexical root or lemma form.

Semantic Similarity: Latent semantic models, such as LSA, map text to a low-dimensional space where the similarity between two pieces of text is easily computed by measuring the distance between the vector representations of the two pieces of text. Recent developments in this area have used neural networks to learn vector representation of text, e.g. [24][15]. One use of these representations is to find semantic similarity between texts beyond what lexical bag-of-words representation can accomplish.

We used the model described in [15], to map each query to a vector space representation. The similarity between any two queries is then computed by measuring the cosine similarity of the two vectors

Phonetic Similarity: Voice query reformulation has unique characteristics compared to text query reformulation. There are multiple ways users reformulate their text queries [14]. One of the common ways people reformulate text queries is by introducing some lexical variations, e.g. "knoledge management" → "knowledge management", or a semantic variation, e.g. "barber" → "hair cut". In addition to these sources of errors, voice queries have a unique source of errors that result from mistakes made by the automatic speech recognition system, e.g. "u2" → "youtube". These cases cannot be identified using the lexical or semantic similarity measures and require special handling.

Philips [25] introduced an algorithm for reducing English words to their basic sounds. This allows us to index words by their pronunciation and hence identify query reformulations resulting from speech recognition errors. For example, a query "WhatsApp" may be incorrectly recognized as "what's up". Both lexical and semantic similarity will not find these two texts similar. However, the Metaphone code for both of them is "WTSP". In such cases, phonetic similarity can help identify query reformulations that happen in response to speech recognition errors. We transform the transcribed text of each query into Metaphone codes using [25]. We then compute the normalized Levenstein edit distance between the Metaphone representations to estimate the phonetic similarity.

In Figures Figure 1, Figure 2, and Figure 3, we plotted the distribution of the lexical, semantic and phonetic similarities for query pairs with and without reformulations. In all figures, the x-axis represent similarity values bins and the y-axis represent the percentages of query pairs in each bin. Since lexical and phonetic similarities are based on normalized Levenstein edit distances, their values range between 0 and 1 with 0 indicating a perfect match and 1 indicating no match at all. Since the semantic similarity is based on the cosine similarity between two vectors, it ranges between -1 and 1 denoting the weakest and the strongest similarity respectively. Note that the measure of lexical and phonetic similarity is a distance measure (i.e. the smaller, the more similar) while the measure of semantic similarity is a similarity measure (i.e. the larger, the more similar).

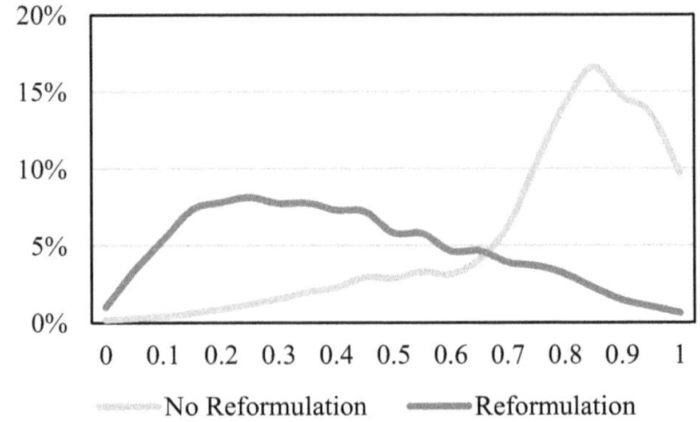

Figure 1. Lexical similarity in query pairs with and without reformulation

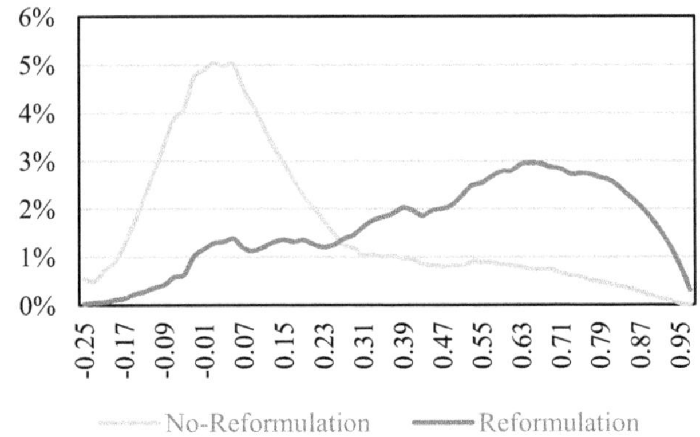

Figure 2. Semantic similarity in query pairs with and without reformulation

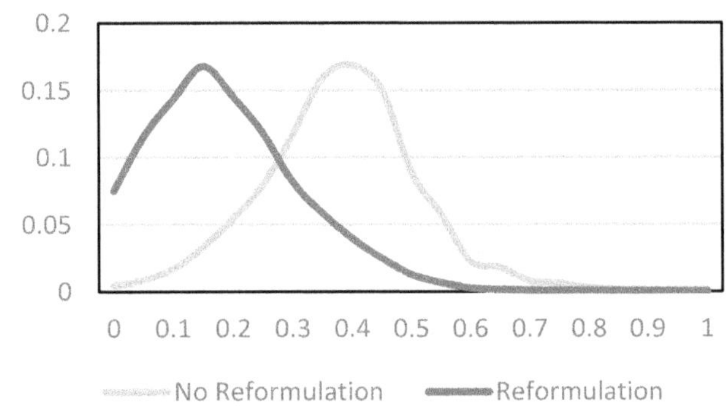

Figure 3. Phonetic similarity in query pairs with and without reformulation

Looking at the three figures, we notice that the distribution of all types of similarities is significantly different in the case of reformulation as opposed to the case of no reformulation. In all three cases, reformulation pairs had higher similarity/less distance. Note that the difference between the means for all three types of similarity with spastically significant ($p < 0.001$) using a two-tailed t-test. We will show later that the three types of similarities are also complementary in covering different types of query reformulation.

4.2 Speech recognition Quality

We now turn our attention to speech recognition quality with the objective of studying how it affects reformulations. We start by

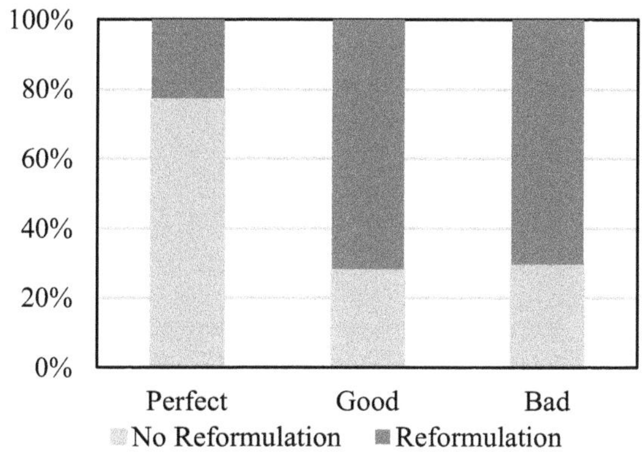

Figure 4. Relation between query reformulation and speech recognition quality as labeled by annotators

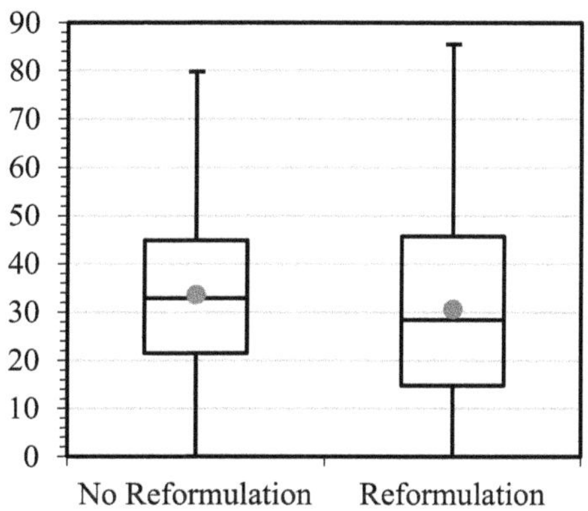

Figure 5. Box-and-whisker plot for speech recognition confidence for reformulation and no-reformulation cases. Mean is dot. Median is horizontal line.

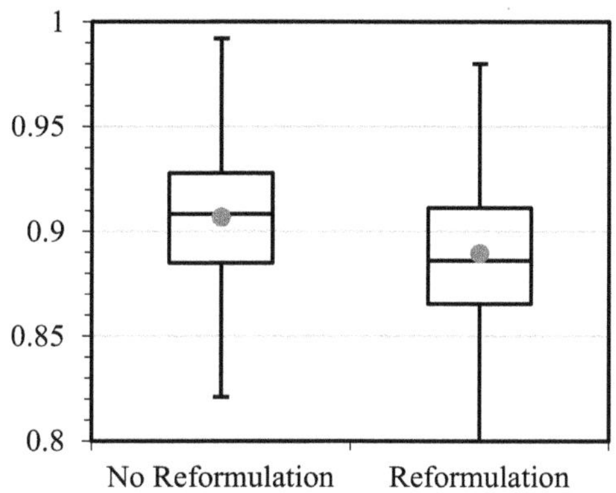

Figure 6. Box-and-whisker plot for language model score for reformulation and no-reformulation cases. Mean is dot. Median is horizontal line.

looking at speech recognition quality labels. Recall that we asked our annotator to judge the speech recognition quality on a 3-point scale (Perfect, Good, or Bad). We split the query pairs according to the speech recognition quality label of the first query. For every label$x$, we computed the proportion of queries that has been reformulated and the proportion of queries that has not. We show the results in Figure 4. Relation between query reformulation and speech recognition quality as labeled by annotators. We notice that only slightly over 20% of the queries are reformulated when the speech recognition is perfect. This quickly increases to almost 70% when the speech recognition quality is good or bad. This suggest that errors with speech recognition significantly increase the likelihood of the query being reformulated. It also shows that this happens both for minor and major speech recognition errors. Since human labeled assessment of speech recognition quality is available only for the labeled dataset, we now turn our attention to other properties of the speech recognition system that, while noisy, we suspect might be useful for use as a proxy for the speech recognition quality.

The first property we look at is the speech recognition system confidence. Confidence scores of automatic speech recognition system decoding [16]. In Figure 5, we show a box-and-whisker plot of the speech recognition confidence scores of recognizing the first query when it is followed by a reformulation and when it is not followed by a reformulation. The figure shows that queries that end up being reformulated typically have lower speech recognition confidence scores.

In addition to the speech recognition confidence score, we also use the language model score of the recognized text. Higher language model scores indicate higher relative likelihood of the recognized phrases given its context. A Box-and-whisker plot for language model score for reformulation and no-reformulation cases is shown in Figure 6. Like the speech recognition score, we notice that reformulated queries tend to have lower language model scores. The differences between the means for both speech recognition confidence and language model score were statistically significant ($p < 0.001$) using a two-tailed t-test.

4.3 Result Quality

Previous research [12] has shown that reformulation is a strong sign of dissatisfaction with the results of the current query. We asked our annotators to label the relevance of the results to the query on a 3-point scale (Perfect, Good, or Bad). Similar to what we did with the speech recognition quality labels, we split the query pairs according to the result quality label of the first query. For every label$x$, we compute the proportion of queries that has been reformulated and the proportion of queries that has not. We show the results in Figure 7. Confirming the findings of previous work, we see that the proportion of reformulated queries increasing as the quality of the results decrease showing that bad result quality is another factor, in addition to speech recognition quality, that can lead to query reformulation.

Since many queries can be satisfied by elements in the search result page (e.g. answers) without the need to click on any results, we looked at the time the user spends on the result page before entering the following query. Our hypothesis is that the time between queries in case of reformulation will be shorter than in case on no reformulation. To validate this hypothesis, we plot the distribution of time between queries in both reformulation and non-reformulation cases in Figure 8. We notice that it is indeed the case that users tend to spend less time between queries when the query is reformulated. This probably happens because the users quickly realize that the current results do not meet their needs and hence they decide to reformulate the query. On the other hand, when the query is not reformulated, the user may spend more time examining elements of the results page that may satisfy her information need (e.g. answers). This agrees with previous results reported on conventional (non-voice) search queries [12].

Finally, we look at the clicks received by the second query in cases where the second query was or was not a reformulation of the first query in Figure 9. Recall that our dataset was sampled such that all first queries have received no clicks. Hence, we only look at the second queries when studying clicks. Figure 9 shows that when the second query received a click, it is more likely to be a reformulation of the previous query. This probably happens because users find what they are looking for after reformulation.

4.4 Summary

In this section, we have characterized some key aspects of voice query reformulation. We have shown that there are several key differences between reformulation and non-reformulation queries. We have shown that previously studied query similarity measures, i.e. lexical similarity, is also effective for voice queries. We have also shown that other semantic similarity measures and similarity measures specific to voice queries, i.e. phonetic similarity, are also very effective. Additionally, we have shown that there are key characteristics related to the system performance, namely speech recognition quality and results quality, that play an important role in determining whether a query will be reformulated or not. Since these characteristics require human labeled data and are not readily available at production time, we have also shown that there are other system and user behavior signals that can be used as proxies for these properties and that also do differ between reformulation and non-reformulation queries. In the next section, we describe a model that leverages these features and others to distinguish between reformulation and non-reformulation query pairs.

5. REFORMULATION PREDICTION

In this section, we formally define our prediction task and then introduce the features used for prediction.

5.1 Problem Definition

As we stated earlier, voice Query Reformulation is the act of submitting a query Q2 to modify or repeat a previous search query Q1 in hope of avoiding misrecognition or retrieving better results. Hence, query reformulation is considered an indication of dissatisfaction with the previous query. For Q2 to be considered a reformulation of Q1, both queries must be intended to satisfy the same information need. A query reformulation happens when the user is not satisfied with the recognition of her query (e.g. speech recognition error), the results of the query or both.

Note that a related query on the same topic addressing a different information need is *not* considered as query reformulation for our purpose. Given a pair of queries, our objective is to predict whether the second query is a reformulation of the first query or not. For each query pair, we have the audio and recognized text of the first query and audio and recognized text of the second query if it was a voice query. Otherwise we have the text of the second query. Note that the first query is always a voice query, while the second could be either a voice query or a text query. We also have any clicks made by the user and the timestamps of all queries and clicks. Our second objective is to predict the rationale behind reformulation (speech recognition error or relevance issue) for queries that are known to be reformulated.

5.2 Features

Our predictive model uses the following groups of features:

Session features: These are the features that describe general characteristics of the current session such as the length of the two queries, the time between them, clicks etc. They also cover the input method and more particular any switches in the input method for voice to text. Note that the data is sampled such that all first queries are voice queries. Hence, we only used the input method of the second query as a feature.

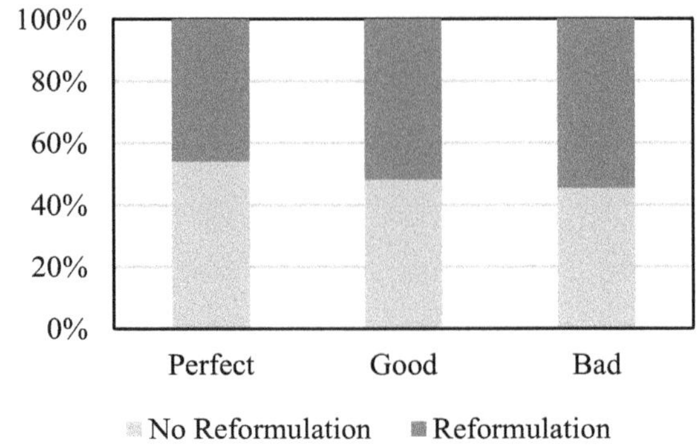

Figure 7. Relation between the relevance of the first query results and reformulation

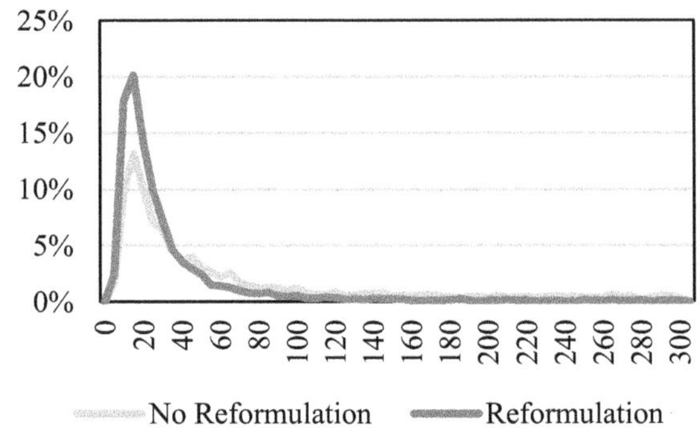

Figure 8. Time between queries for instances with and without reformulation

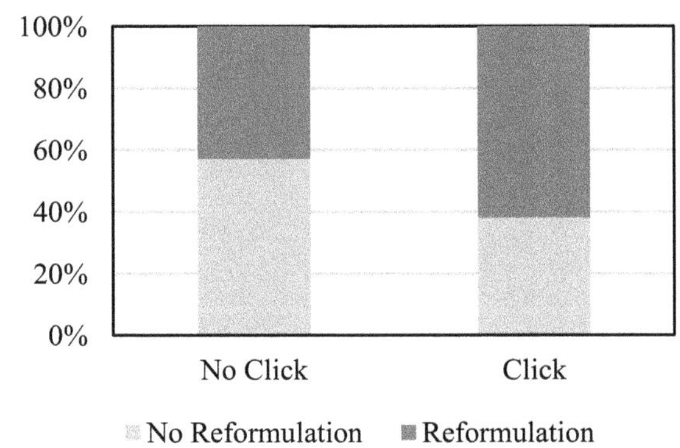

Figure 9. Relation between clicks on the second query

Lexical similarity features: The second group of features characterizes the lexical similarity between the two queries. Previous research, e.g. [21][12], has shown that reformulation query pairs are more likely to have higher lexical similarity than other consecutive query pairs. We characterize lexical similarity using a number of features including number of words in common, Jaccard coefficient between a bag of words representation of the two queries, whether the first query has been generalized (1+ terms are removed from the previous query) and whether the first query has been specified (1+ terms are added to the previous query). We also use a lexical similarity formula that combines edit distance and words in common as described in Section 4.1.

Phrase similarity features: As discussed earlier lexical similarity typically treats queries as a bag of words ignoring any structure in the text. Following previous work on text query reformulation [12], we introduce a number of features that take the phrase structure into consideration. Instead of the bag of words representation, queries are represented as a bag of keywords. For example, the query "weather in San Francisco" contains two keywords "weather" and "San Francisco". To build such a representation, we segment each query into keywords. Query segmentation is the process of taking a user's search query and dividing the tokens into individual phrases or semantic units [3]. Consider a query $x = \{x_1, x_2, \dots x_n\}$ consisting of n tokens. Query segmentation is the process of finding a mapping: $x \rightarrow y \in Y_n$, where y is a segmentation from the set Y_n. There are many approaches to query segmentation that have been presented in the literature. Some of them are supervised, e.g. [3], while others are unsupervised, e.g. [11]. We opt for using the unsupervised method presented in [11] especially since it has been shown it achieves similar performance to those that are trained on large labeled datasets. Once the phrase representation built, we extract a number of features similar to the lexical features including the total number of keywords in each query, and number of keywords in query 1/2 only. We also use the same similarity function that takes both edit distance and word overlap into consideration but applied to keywords rather than individual words.

Semantic similarity features: Lexical and phrase features cover the cases where the query is reformulated to add/remove terms or introduce some lexical variation to the original query. There are cases though where the user decides to use different terms, albeit semantically equivalent, to reformulate the query. We use the vector space representation described in Section 4.1 to represent each query as a vector and then use the cosine similarity to assess the semantic similarity between two queries by measure the cosine of the angle between their vector space representations.

Speech Features: Voice queries have the unique characteristic that the automatic speech recognition step adds another layer of noise between what the user says and what the system recognizes. This introduces a new reformulation pattern that arises from mistakes by the speech recognition engine. For example the speech recognition engine can easily mistake a search for the band "u2" as a search for the video sharing website "youtube". To capture such cases, we represent each query with the Metaphone representation and assess the *phonetic similarity* by the edit distance between the Metaphone representations of the queries.

We also add features that are motivated by our finding in Section 4.2 where we showed that reformulation is strongly dependent on the *speech recognition quality* as labeled by human judges. Since it is not feasible to have human judges label each voice query for its speech recognition quality, we instead use statistics of the speech recognition system that can act as a surrogate for the recognition quality. More specifically, we use the speech recognition confidence, the language model confidence and the recognition time. Since the speech recognition engine typically generates many candidate recognitions and then selects the most likely one, we also introduce features to assess the similarity between the reformulated query and the n best candidates generated by the speech recognition engine for the first query.

Finally, we add features to describe the acoustic characteristic of the utterances of the voice queries. We hypothesize that features of the acoustic signals of the utterance, as well as features characterizing the change in the acoustics from the first to the second query can be very useful for detecting query reformulation since users who select to reformulate their queries are likely to have a change in speed, loudness, pitch etc. as a way of showing frustration or partially emphasizing the words that where misrecognized. Partial emphasis, as labeled by human judges, have been shown earlier to correlate with reformulation [19]. Here, we automatically derive acoustic features that can act as a proxy for frustration, partial emphasis and other behaviors. To generate the pitch and loudness features, we use the openSmile toolkit [6]. openSmile is an open source large scale multimedia feature extraction toolkit that allows users to easily extract features from both audio and video files.

Table 1. Features used to distinguish between reformulation and non-reformulation query pairs. Features marked with an "*" were computed for both the first and the second query

Name	Description
Session Features	
CharQueryLen*	Query length in number of characters
WordQueryLen*	Query length in number of words
TimebetQueries	Time between queries
Query2Clciked	True if Q2 received any clicks
Voice2Text	True if user switched from voice input in Q1 to text input in Q2
Lexical Query Similarity Features	
AvgQuerySim	Similarity between queries (see Section 4.1)
WordsInCommon	Number of words in common
JaccardDistance	Jaccard distance between queries
Query2IsGen	1 if the second query has 1+ terms are removed from the previous query
Query2IsSpec	1 if the second query has 1+ terms are added to the previous query
Phrase/Keyword Similarity Features	
NumKWMatch	Number of keywords that match in both queries
NumKWinQuery*	Number of keywords in query
KWinQ1Only	Number of keywords in Q1 but not Q2
KWinQ2Only	Number of keywords in Q2 but not Q1
Semantic Similarity Features	
SemanticSim	Cosine similarity between semantic vector representations of the queries
Speech Features	
PhoneticSim	Levenstein distance between Metaphone representation of the two queries
SRConf	Speech recognition confidence
LMScore	Language model score
SRRecoTime	Speech recognition time
Q2NBestExactMatch	Q2 is in N best candidate recognitions of Q1 (exact match)
Q2NBestPartialMatch	Q2 is in N best candidate recognitions of Q1 (partial match)
DeltaWordRate	Diff. in speech rate (words/sec)
DeltaLoudness	Diff. in voice loudness
DeltaPitch	Diff. in voice pitch

5.3 Prediction Tasks

Using the features presented in the previous section, we build predictive models to tackle two main tasks. The first task is given a pair of queries, predict whether the second query is a reformulation of the first query or not. The second task focuses only on reformulation queries. There are multiple reasons that lead users to reformulate their queries. Two of the main reasons are speech recognition mistakes and relevance issues. To study this further, we collected additional labels, during the human annotation study described in Section 3, of whether there was a

Table 2. Voice reformulation prediction performance. * and + indicate statistical significance at $p < 0.05$ using paired t-tests compared to the B1 and B2 respectively. A majority baseline has a 53% accuracy.

		Accuracy	*Precision*	*Recall*	*F1*
1	**Lexical/Phrase**	72.93%	77.56%	69.65%	73.39%
2	**Semantic**	77.07%	79.34%	77.36%	78.34%
3	**Session**	64.47%	64.84%	73.63%	68.96%
4	**Speech**	79.47%	85.13%	74.75%	79.60%
5	**B1: Lexical/Phrase**	72.93%	77.56%	69.65%	73.39%
6	**B1 + Sem.**	81.27%*	82.48%*	82.59%*	82.53%*
7	**B1 + Speech**	85.13%*	85.91%*	86.44%*	86.17%*
8	**B2: B1+ Session**	81.67%	83.35%	82.21%	82.78%
9	**B2+ Semantic**	82.47%+	84.03%+	83.08%+	83.55%+
10	**B2 + Speech**	84.53%+	83.66%+	85.25%+	84.45%+
11	**All**	**86.27%**	**87.28%**	**87.6%**	**87.45%**

Table 3. Voice reformulation rationales (speech recognition and relevance issues) prediction performance. A majority baseline for speech recognition issues has a 68% accuracy and for relevance issues has a 79% accuracy.

		Accuracy	*Precision*	*Recall*	*F1*
1	**Speech Reco.**	83.96%	86.36%	92.65%	89.40%
2	**Relevance**	87.15%	89.70%	95.64%	92.57%

problem with the speech recognition or not and whether the results of the first query were relevant or not. Since the two issues are not mutually exclusive, we build separate predictive models for each. We discuss the details of these experiments and the experiments conducted to evaluate the reformulation predictive model in the next section.

6. EXPERIMENTS AND EVALUATION

In this section we describe the experimental setup and the results for the prediction experiments. We also include a detailed analysis of the performance of the features that were used in the prediction experiment.

6.1 Experimental Setup

We performed several experiments to study the performance of our predictive models. We conducted experiments using the data described in Section 3 which had 7322 labeled query pairs along with their audio file, if applicable, their timestamps and click information. We trained a classifier to distinguish between reformulation and non-reformulation query pairs. We also trained two other classifiers focusing on reformulated queries to predict whether there were issues with the speech recognition and/or relevance of the results of the first query.

In addition to using all the features we described in Section 5.2, we also experiment with several baselines that have access only to a subset of these features including the state-of-the-art features used for predicting query reformulation using text-input [12]. More specifically, we experimented with the following baselines:

Individual Feature Groups: The first set of baseline uses each feature group from Table 1 individually. This results in the following baselines: Lexical/Phrase, Semantic, Session, and Speech. Note that we treat lexical and phrase feature as one feature group and phonetic similarity and other speech signals as one feature group for simplicity.

Baseline 1 (Lexical/Phrase): This baselines implements all features from the literature that predict query reformulation bases on lexical and phrase similarity between the two queries.

Baseline 2 (Lex/Phrase + Session): This baseline adds session features to the previous baseline.

In addition to the baselines listed above, we experiment with adding each new feature group (semantic, and speech) to both baselines and finally, we show the performance with all features.

We used 10-fold cross validation for all experiments and Multiple Additive Regression Trees (MART) for classification [9].We experimented with other classifier (SVM and logistic regression), and MART yielded better performance.

6.2 Results and Findings

We now present the results of the prediction experiments. Table 2 presents the results of the reformulation prediction experiment. We report the performance of multiple classifiers corresponding to the different feature groupings we introduced in the previous section. For every classifier, we report accuracy, precision, recall and F1 measure. We also compare the classifiers to the majority baseline that always predicts the label of the dominant class.

We notice from the table that using only lexical and phrase features yields much better results than using marginal class distributions (53% accuracy). This shows the predictive power of the lexical and phrase features. This can be explained by the analysis we presented in Section 4.1 which shows that lexical query similarity is a clear distinguishing factor when it comes to telling reformulation query pairs apart from non-reformulation query pairs. This also shows that voice query reformulation is similar in some ways to text query reformulation and that there is a lot of room for improvement if we can find features that characterize the unique nature of voice query reformulation compared to text query reformulation.

We also notice that using semantic similarity features results in a performance that surpasses lexical and phrase similarity features (2nd row). This can also be explained by the analysis presented in Section 4.1 which highlighted the discriminative power of semantic features. Semantic features are particularly useful for cases where the user opts for using different words with the same meaning or even for cases where the user is still using the same words but with lexical variations that the edit distance measure fails to recognize.

As for the session features (3rd row), we notice that they are not as predictive as the similarity features. We also notice that they do a better job, in terms of F1 measure, in identifying the positive class (reformulation) compared to the negative class (no-reformulation). That said, they still yield better results than marginal class distributions (53% accuracy). Although session features are certainly useful, our data was collected in a way that makes the reformulation predicting task harder especially for session features since we restrict it to query pairs with no clicks on the first query.

The last feature group (4th row) contains all features that are unique to voice query reformulation like phonetic similarity, and other acoustic features. We notice from the table that this feature group performs significantly better than all other feature groups. They particular achieve very high precision showing that they can accurately identify reformulation cases. This supports the hypothesis we presented earlier that voice query reformulation

Table 4. Feature group importance.

Reformulation	Speech Reco.	Relevance
Speech	Speech	Semantic
Semantic	Semantic	Lexical
Session	Lexical	Session
Lexical	Phrase	Speech
Phrase	Session	Phrase

has different characteristics that cannot be captured by using session based features or features derived only from the text and ignoring the speech signal.

In the second part of the table (rows 5-7), we pivot on the lexical/phrase features as a baseline and study the effect of adding semantic and speech features to the baseline. Our objective is to understand whether the gains we are getting from the different feature groups are additive or not. Looking at rows 6 and 7, we see that adding both semantic and speech features improves the baseline with speech features resulting in a bigger gain compared to semantic features. All difference are statistically significant at $p < 0.05$ using a paired t-test. This is a desirable outcome as it shows that the gains from adding the semantic and speech features add up to the gains we get from the lexical/phrase baseline.

Moving on to the third part of the table (rows 8-10), we pivot on a second baseline which combines lexical, phrase and session features. These represent features from state-of-the-art work on reformulation prediction [12] and task boundary detection [21]. The table shows that, similar to the first baseline, adding the semantic and speech features to the second baseline also improves the performance. Also, we notice that adding speech feature results in a bigger gain than adding the semantic feature confirming that the speech feature do a better job in identifying voice reformulation. Finally, when we combine all features and train a single classifier (last row), we get a better performance than any other combination of features showing the usefulness of all feature groups in identifying voice reformulation.

We now move on to another set of experiments where we focused on reformulation queries and we tried to predict the rationale behind the reformulation. Recall that in our human annotation study, we collected labels for whether the user has faced any issues with the speech recognition quality and/or result relevance. These labels were collected on a 3 point scale. To build a binary classifier, we assigned the cases where no or few speech recognition errors were detected (and the case where results were relevant/somewhat relevant) to one class and the cases where many speech recognition errors were detected (and the cases where results were not relevant) to another class.

The results of these experiments are shown in Table 3. The table shows that we can predict the rationale behind reformulation with a high accuracy. Note that we do not claim that this is an exhaustive list of all the reasons that lead to query reformulation. Rather, we just focused on two of the main reasons that may lead users to reformulate their voice queries.

We now turn our attention to the features that contribute most to the prediction task. In order to assess the importance of the proposed features, we compute the information gain of all features. We do that by computing the error reduction for each feature at each node split using the squared loss function. We then aggregate the error reduction at all splits for every feature and use that as a measure of feature gain. We do not report feature gains at the individual feature level for space considerations. Instead, we report feature importance at the feature group level for groups in Table 1. Features used to distinguish between reformulation and non-reformulation query pairs. Features marked with an "*" were computed for both the first and the second query. We assigned every group a rank based on the average score of all its features in the top 10 list.

The results are shown in Table 4. It is clear from the table that speech and semantic features play the most important role. For predicting voice reformulation and speech recognition problems followed by the other feature groups. As for the relevance problems prediction, semantic and lexical features are ranked higher than other features. If we dig deeper into the speech feature group, we find out phonetic similarity, speech recognition confidence and acoustic features (change in word rate, loudness and pitch) contribute the most in the same order they were mentioned.

6.3 DISCUSSION AND IMPLICATIONS

Identifying pairs of reformulated queries is a very well-studied topic with multiple applications in text queries. However, this topic has received little attention when it comes to voice queries. A recent study[1], executed by Northstar Research and commissioned by Google, found out that 55% of U.S. teens use voice search every day and that 89% of teens and 85% of adults agree that voice search will be "very common" in the future. This shows the importance of studying and understanding important behaviors such as reformulation in the context of voice search. In this paper, we showed that we can build a classifier to identify voice query reformulation and the rationale behind them accurately. We also show that using speech related features significantly improves the prediction accuracy compared to features used for text queries.

There are at least two potential areas of future work that can increase the impact of the work in this paper. The first is improving the way by which the labels were collected for our data. The labels were assigned by third-party judges based on their consensus opinion of the two queries. While using the consensus may improve the reliability of the label, the fact that the judges were not those who submitted the queries may lead to unforeseen issues with the labels. Ways to address this shortcoming include soliciting judgments from the users in-situ at the time of their interaction with the system.

Second, we focused on how to build predictive models for predicting reformulation and the rationale behind it in this paper, and did not discuss its applications. Our contributions have potential implications on many applications. Detecting pairs of queries reformulated by the user is an important and necessary first step toward addressing the task of automatic query reformulation prediction. Query reformulation can be used to find chains of queries as constructed by the user. These chains provide us with labeled examples of how queries can be rewritten to improve the user experience. Using this labeled data, we can train system to automatically reformulate queries when it predicts that the user is/will not be satisfied with the current results. This has several applications ranging from learning to automatically rewrite queries or providing query suggestions in order to get the user to the correct results faster [2] or segmenting user queries into tasks [21].

[1] http://prn.to/1sfiQRr

Additionally, reformulation is a sign of struggle which has been shown in previous work to be one of the strongest factor behind user dissatisfaction [12]. This suggests that we can use our model for identifying cases where the users are dissatisfied with the system performance. This in turn can be used to generate such dissatisfaction cases that can be used by search systems developers to identify problems with their systems. This can be very useful when coupled with other predictive models that we developed that can decide whether the problem is with the speech recognition quality, the result relevance or both. Alternatively, it could also be used as a metric to compare different systems, and the rate of voice query reformulations can serve as a proxy for the quality of the user experience.

7. CONCLUSIONS

Reformulation is one of the clearest signs of struggle when interacting with a search system or an intelligent assistant. Although query reformulation has been extensively studied before in the context of Web search, voice query reformulation has not received as much attention. Voice query reformulation is similar to text query reformulation in many aspects. However, it also has unique characteristics in terms of the reasons that lead users to reformulation and the features that can be used to identify it. We have shown that there are differences in behavioral attributes such as phonetic query similarity, input method switching, etc., as well as system attributes such as speech recognition confidence, recognition time, etc. between reformulation and non-reformulation query pairs. These differences can be useful in distinguishing reformulation query pairs from other query pairs. We have also developed classifiers and showed that we can perform this prediction accuracy. We have also shown that we can accurately predict the reason behind query reformulation (e.g. speech recognition mistakes, non-relevant results or both). Future work involves the expansion of our research in this area to consider other applications of the predictors such as finding cases of dissatisfaction and helping users recover from such cases.

8. REFERENCES

[1] Ageev., M., Guo, Q., Lagun, D., and Agichtein, E. (2011). Find it if you can: a game for modeling different types of web search success using interaction data. In Proc. SIGIR, 345–354.

[2] Anick, P. (2003). Using terminological feedback for web search refinement:a log-based study. In Proc. SIGIR, 88–95.

[3] Arlitt, M. (2000). Characterizing Web user sessions. ACM SIGMETRICS Performance Eval Review, 28(2), 50–63.

[4] Bergsma, S., and Wang Q. I. (2007). Learning Noun Phrase Query Segmentation. In Proc. EMNLP, 819–826

[5] P. Boldi, F. Bonchi, C. Castillo, D. Donato, A. Gionis, and S. Vigna. (2008). The query-flow graph: model and applications. In Proc. CIKM, 609-618.

[6] F. Eyben, M. Wöllmer, and B. Schuller. openSMILE - The Munich Versatile and Fast Open-Source Audio Feature Extractor. In Proc. ACM'MM, 1459–1462.

[7] Feild, H., Allan, J., and Jones, R. (2010). Predicting searcher frustration. In Proc. SIGIR, 34–41.

[8] Fox, S., Karnawat, K., Mydland, M., Dumais, S.T., and White, T. (2005). Evaluating implicit measures to improve the search experience. ACM TOIS, 23(2), 147–168.

[9] Friedman, J.H., Hastie, T., and Tibshirani, R. (1998). Additive Logistic Regression: A Statistical View of Boosting. Technical Report, Stanford University.

[10] Guo, J., Xu, G., Li, H., and Cheng, X. (2008). A unified and discriminative model for query refinement. In Proc. SIGIR '08, 379-386.

[11] Hagen, M., Potthast, M. Stein, B, and Bräutigam, C. (2010). The Power of Naïve Query Segmentation. In Proc. SIGIR, 797–798.

[12] Hassan Awadallah, A., Shi, X., Craswell, N., and Ramsey, B. (2013). Beyond Clicks: Query reformulation as a predictor of search satisfaction. In Proc. CIKM, 2019–2028

[13] Jiang, J., Hassan Awadallah, A., Jones, R., Ozertem, U., Zitouni, I., Kulkarni, R. G., and Khan, O. Z. (2014) Automatic Online Evaluation of Intelligent Assistants. In Proc. WWW.

[14] Huang, J. and Efthimis N. (2009). Analyzing and evaluating query reformulation strategies in web search logs. In Proc. of CIKM, 77–86.

[15] Huang, P., He, X., Gao, J., Deng, L., Acero, A., and Heck, L. 2013. Learning deep structured semantic models for web search using clickthrough data. In Proc. CIKM,2333–2338.

[16] Huang, P.S., Kumar, K., Liu, C., Gong, Y. and Deng, L. (2013). Predicting speech recognition confidence using deep learning with word identity and score features. *Proc. ICASSP*, 7413–7417

[17] Jansen, B.J., Zhang, M., and Spink, A. (2007). Patterns and transitions of query reformulation during web searching.

[18] Jeng, W. Jiang, J., and He, D. (2013). Users' perceived difficulties and corresponding reformulation strategies in voice search. In Proc. HCIR, Vancouver, Canada

[19] Jiang, J., Jeng, W. and He, D. (2013). How do users respond to voice input errors? lexical and phonetic query reformula-tion in voice search. *Proc. SIGIR '13*, 143–152.

[20] Johnston, M., Bangalore, S., Vasireddy, G., Stent, A., Ehlen, P., Walker, M., Whittaker, S., and Maloor, P. (2002). MATCH: An architecture for multimodal dialogue systems Proc. AC, 376–383.

[21] Jones, R. and Klinkner, K.L. (2008) . Beyond the session timeout: automatic hierarchical segmentation of search topics in query logs. In Proc. CIKM.

[22] Lau, T. and Horvitz, E. (1999). Patterns of search: analyzing and modeling Web query refinement. In User Modeling '99, 119-128.

[23] C. Lucchese, S. Orlando, R. Perego, F. Silvestri and G. Tolomei. (2011). Identifying Task-based Sessions in Search Engine Query Logs. In Proc. WSDM 2011.

[24] Tomas Mikolov, Wen-tau Yih, and Geoffrey Zweig. Linguistic Regularities in Continuous Space Word Representations. In Proceedings of NAACL HLT, 2013.

[25] Lawrence Philips. Hanging on the Metaphone. Computer Language, 12(7), 39-43, 1990.

[26] Shokouhi, M., Jones, R., Ozertem, U., Raghunathan, K., Diaz, F. (2014) Mobile query reformulations. In Proc. SIGIR. 1011-1014.

[27] Teevan, J., Adar, E., Jones, R., and Potts, M. (2007) Information Re-Retrieval: Repeat Queries in Yahoo's Logs. In Proc. SIGIR.

[28] Tur, G., and De Mori, R. (2011). Spoken Language Understanding: Systems for extracting semantic information from speech. John Wiley & Sons.

[29] Wahlster, W. (2006). SmartKom: Foundations of multimodal dialogue systems. Springer.

[30] Young, S., Gasic, M., Thomson, B and Wiliams J. D. (2013). POMDP-based statistical spoken dialog systems: A review. Proc. IEEE, 101(5), 1160-1179.

A Hierarchical Recurrent Encoder-Decoder for Generative Context-Aware Query Suggestion

Alessandro Sordoni[f‡], Yoshua Bengio[f], Hossein Vahabi[g],
Christina Lioma[h], Jakob G. Simonsen[h], Jian-Yun Nie[f]
[f]DIRO, Université de Montréal, Québec
[g]Yahoo Labs, Barcelona, Spain
[h]Dept. Computer Science, University of Copenhagen, Denmark
[‡]sordonia@iro.umontreal.ca

ABSTRACT

Users may strive to formulate an adequate textual query for their information need. Search engines assist the users by presenting query suggestions. To preserve the original search intent, suggestions should be context-aware and account for the previous queries issued by the user. Achieving context awareness is challenging due to data sparsity. We present a novel hierarchical recurrent encoder-decoder architecture that makes possible to account for sequences of previous queries of arbitrary lengths. As a result, our suggestions are sensitive to the order of queries in the context while avoiding data sparsity. Additionally, our model can suggest for rare, or long-tail, queries. The produced suggestions are synthetic and are sampled one word at a time, using computationally cheap decoding techniques. This is in contrast to current synthetic suggestion models relying upon machine learning pipelines and hand-engineered feature sets. Results show that our model outperforms existing context-aware approaches in a next query prediction setting. In addition to query suggestion, our architecture is general enough to be used in a variety of other applications.

Categories and Subject Descriptors: H.3.3 [Information Search and Retrieval]: Query formulation

Keywords: Recurrent Neural Networks; Query Suggestion.

1. INTRODUCTION

Modern search engines heavily rely on query suggestions to support users during their search task. Query suggestions can be in the form of auto-completions or query reformulations. Auto-completion suggestions help users to complete their queries while they are typing in the search box. In this paper, we focus on query reformulation suggestions, that are produced after one or more queries have already been submitted to the search engine.

CIKM'15, October 19-23, 2015, Melbourne, VIC, Australia
© 2015 ACM. ISBN 978-1-4503-3794-6/15/10 ...$15.00.
DOI: http://dx.doi.org/10.1145/2806416.2806493.

Search query logs are an important resource to mine user reformulation behaviour. The query log is partitioned into query sessions, i.e. sequences of queries issued by a unique user and submitted within a short time interval. A query session contains the sequence of query reformulations issued by the user while attempting to complete the search mission. Therefore, query co-occurrence in the same session is a strong signal of query relatedness and can be straightforwardly used to produce suggestions.

Methods solely relying on query co-occurrence are prone to data sparsity and lack coverage for rare and *long-tail* queries, i.e. unseen in the training data. A suggestion system should be able to translate infrequent queries to more common and effective formulations based on similar queries that have been seen in the training data. Amongst the interesting models that have been proposed, some capture higher order collocations [7], consider additional resources [20, 41], move towards a word-level representation [8, 9] or describe queries using a rich feature space and apply learning to rank techniques to select meaningful candidates [28, 34].

An additional desirable property of a suggestion system is *context-awareness*. Pairwise suggestion systems operate by considering only the most recent query. However, previous submitted queries provide useful context to narrow down ambiguity in the current query and to produce more focused suggestions [22]. Equally important is the order in which past queries are submitted, as it denotes generalization or specification reformulation patterns [18]. A major hurdle for current context-aware models is dealing with the dramatic growth of diverse contexts, since it induces sparsity, and classical count-based models become unreliable [10, 15].

Finally, relatively unexplored for suggestion systems is the ability to produce *synthetic* suggestions. Typically, we assume that useful suggestions are already present in the training data. The assumption weakens for rare queries or complex information needs, for which it is possible that the best suggestion has not been previously seen [20, 40]. In these cases, synthetic suggestions can be leveraged to increase coverage and can be used as candidates in complex learning to rank models [28].

We present a generative probabilistic model capable of producing synthetic, context-aware suggestions not only for popular queries, but also for long tail queries. Given a sequence of queries as prefix, it predicts the most likely sequence of words that follow the prefix. Variable context lengths can be accounted for without strict built-in limits.

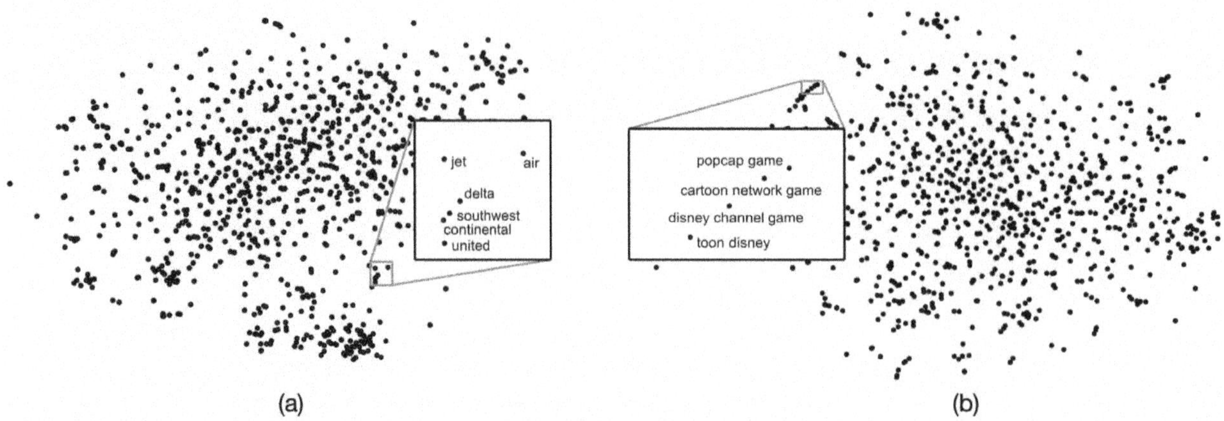

Figure 1: Projection of the (a) word and (b) query embeddings learnt by our neural network architecture. Topically similar terms and queries are close in the embedding space.

Query suggestions can be mined by sampling likely continuations given one or more queries as context. Prediction is efficient and can be performed using standard natural language processing word-level decoding techniques [23]. The model is robust to long-tail effects as the prefix is considered as a sequence of words that share statistical weight and not as a sequence of atomic queries.

As an example, given a user query session composed of two queries *cleveland gallery* → *lake erie art* issued sequentially, our model predicts sequentially the words *cleveland*, *indian*, *art* and ∘, where ∘ is a special end-of-query symbol that we artificially add to our vocabulary. As the end-of-query token has been reached, the suggestion given by our model is *cleveland indian art*. The suggestion is contextual as the concept of *cleveland* is justified by the first query thus the model does not merely rely on the most recent query only. Additionally, the produced suggestion is synthetic as it does not need to exist in the training set.

To endow our model with such capabilities, we rely on recent advances in generative natural language applications with neural networks [3, 11, 27]. We contribute with a new hierarchical neural network architecture, called hierarchical recurrent encoder-decoder (HRED), that allows to embed a complex distribution over sequences of sentences within a compact parameter space. Differently from count-based models, we avoid data sparsity by assigning single words, queries and sequences of queries to embeddings, i.e. dense vectors bearing syntactic and semantic characteristics (Figure 1) [4]. Our model is compact in memory and can be trained end-to-end on query sessions. We envision future applications to various tasks, such as query auto-completion, query next-word prediction and general language modeling.

2. KEY IDEA

Suggestion models need to capture the underlying similarities between queries. Vector representations of words and phrases, also known as *embeddings*, have been successfully used to encode syntactic or semantic characteristics thereof [3, 4, 25, 35]. We focus on how to capture query similarity and query term similarity by means of such embeddings. In Figure 1 (a) and (b), we plot a two-dimensional projection of the word and query embeddings learnt by our model. The vectors of topically similar terms or queries are close to each other in the vector space.

Vector representations for phrases can be obtained by averaging word vectors [25]. However, the order of terms in queries is usually important [38]. To obtain an order-sensitive representation of a query, we use a particular neural network architecture called Recurrent Neural Network (RNN) [3, 26]. For each word in the query, the RNN takes as input its embedding and updates an internal vector, called *recurrent* state, that can be viewed as an order-sensitive summary of all the information seen up to that word. The first recurrent state is usually set to the zero vector. After the last word has been processed, the recurrent state can be considered as a compact order-sensitive encoding of the query (Figure 2 (a)).

A RNN can also be trained to decode a sentence out of a given query encoding. Precisely, it parameterizes a conditional probability distribution on the space of possible queries given the input encoding. The process is illustrated in Figure 2 (b). The input encoding may be used as initialization of the recurrence. Then, each of the recurrent states is used to estimate the probability of the next word in the sequence. When a word is sampled, the recurrent state is updated to take into account the generated word. The process continues until the end-of-query symbol ∘ is produced.

The previous two use cases of RNNs can be pipelined into a single recurrent encoder-decoder, as proposed in [11, 39] for Machine Translation purposes. The architecture can be used to parameterize a mapping between sequences of words. This idea can be promptly casted in our framework by predicting the next query in a session given the previous one. With respect to our example, the query encoding estimated by the RNN in Figure 2 (a) can be used as input to the RNN in Figure 2 (b): the model learns a mapping between the consecutive queries *cleveland gallery* and *lake erie art*. At test time, the user query is encoded and then decoded into likely continuations that may be used as suggestions.

Although powerful, such mapping is pairwise, and as a result, most of the query context is lost. To condition the prediction of the next query on the previous queries in the session, we deploy an additional, session-level RNN on top of the query-level RNN encoder, thus forming a *hierarchy* of RNNs (Figure 3). The query-level RNN is responsible to

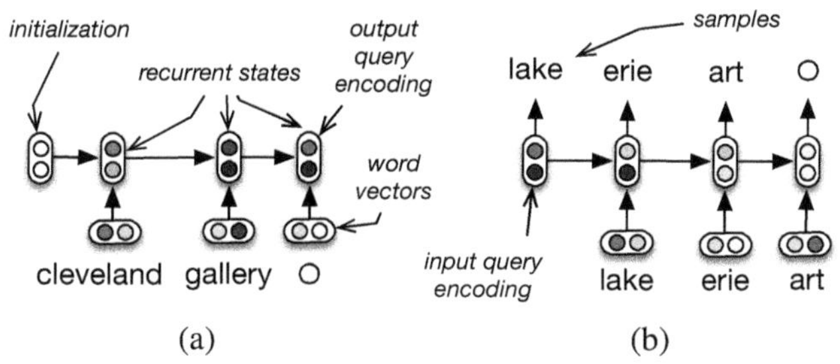

Figure 2: (a) An encoder RNN processing the query *cleveland gallery* followed by a special end-of-query symbol ∘. Each solid arrow represents a non-linear transformation. (b) A decoder RNN generating the next query in the session, *lake erie art*, from a query encoding as input.

encode a query. The session-level RNN takes as input the query encoding and updates its own recurrent state. At a given position in the session, the session-level recurrent state is a learnt summary of the past queries, keeping the information that is relevant to predict the next one. At this point, the decoder RNN takes as input the session-level recurrent state, thus making the next query prediction contextual.

The contribution of our hierarchical recurrent encoder-decoder is two-fold. The query-level encoder RNN maps similar queries to vectors close in the embedding space (Figure 1 (b)). The mapping generalizes to queries that have not been seen during training, as long as their words appear in the model vocabulary. This allows the model to map rare queries to more useful and general formulations, well beyond past co-occurred queries. The session-level RNN models the sequence of the previous queries, contextualizing the prediction of the next query. Similar contexts are mapped close to each other in the vector space. This property allows to avoid sparsity, and differently from count-based models [10, 15], to account for contexts of arbitrary length.

3. MATHEMATICAL FRAMEWORK

We start by presenting the technical details of the RNN architecture, which our model extends. We consider a query session as a sequence of M queries $S = \{Q_1, \dots, Q_M\}$ submitted by a user in chronological order, i.e. $Q_m <_t Q_{m+1}$ where $<_t$ is the total order generated by the submission time, and within a time frame, usually 30 minutes. A query Q_m is a sequence of words $Q_m = \{w_{m,1}, \dots, w_{m,N_m}\}$, where N_m is the length of query m. V is the size of the vocabulary.

3.1 Recurrent Neural Network

For each query word w_n, a RNN computes a dense vector called the *recurrent* state, denoted h_n, that combines w_n with the information that has already been processed, i.e. the recurrent state h_{n-1}. Formally:

$$h_n = f(h_{n-1}, w_n),\ h_0 = 0 \tag{1}$$

where $h_n \in \mathbb{R}^{d_h}$, d_h is the number of dimensions of the recurrent state, f is non-linear transformation and the recurrence is seeded with the 0 vector. The recurrent state h_n acts as a compact *summary* of the words seen up to position n.

Usually, f consists of a non-linear function, i.e. the logistic sigmoid or hyperbolic tangent, applied element-wise to a time-independent affine transformation [26]. The complexity of the function f has an impact on how accurately the RNN can represent sentence information for the task at hand. To reduce the fundamental difficulty in learning long-term dependencies [5], i.e. to store information for longer sequences, more complex functions have been proposed such as the Long Short-Term Memory (LSTM) [17] and the Gated Recurrent Unit (GRU) [11].

Once Eq. 1 has been run through the entire query, the recurrent states $h_1, \dots, h_N$ can be used in various ways. In an encoder RNN, the last state h_N may be viewed as an order-sensitive compact summary of the input query. In a decoder RNN, the recurrent states are used to predict the next word in a sequence [11, 26]. Specifically, the word at position n is predicted using h_{n-1}. The probability of seeing word v at position n is:

$$P(w_n = v | w_{1:n-1}) = \frac{\exp o_v^\top h_{n-1}}{\sum_k \exp o_k^\top h_{n-1}}, \tag{2}$$

where $o_i \in \mathbb{R}^{d_e}$ is a real-valued vector of dimensions d_e associated to word i, i.e. a word embedding, and the denominator is a normalization factor. A representation of the embeddings learnt by our model is given in Figure 1 (a). The semantics of Eq. 2 dictates that the probability of seeing word v at position n increases if its corresponding embedding vector o_v is "near" the context encoded in the vector h_{n-1}. The parameters of the RNN are learned by maximizing the likelihood of the sequence, computed using Eq. 2.

3.1.1 Gated Recurrent Unit

We choose to use the Gated Recurrent Unit (GRU) as our non-linear transformation f. GRUs have been demonstrated to achieve better performance than simpler parameterizations at an affordable computational cost [11]. This function reduces the difficulties in learning our model by easing the propagation of the gradients. We let w_n denote the one-hot representation of $w_n = v$, i.e. a vector of the size of the vocabulary with a 1 corresponding to the index of the query word v. The specific parameterization of f is given by:

$$\begin{aligned}
r_n &= \sigma(I_r w_n + H_r h_{n-1}), && \textit{(reset gate)} \\
u_n &= \sigma(I_u w_n + H_u h_{n-1}), && \textit{(update gate)} \\
\bar{h}_n &= \tanh(I w_n + H(r_n \cdot h_{n-1})), && \textit{(candidate update)} \\
h_n &= (1 - u_n) \cdot h_{n-1} + u_n \cdot \bar{h}_n, && \textit{(final update)}
\end{aligned} \tag{3}$$

where σ is the logistic sigmoid, $\sigma(x) \in [0, 1]$, $\cdot$ represents the element-wise scalar product between vectors, $I, I_u, I_r \in \mathbb{R}^{d_h \times V}$ and H, H_r, H_u are in $\mathbb{R}^{d_h \times d_h}$. The I matrices encode the word w_n while the H matrices specialize in retaining or forgetting the information in h_{n-1}. In the following, this function will be noted $GRU(h_{n-1}, w_n)$.

The gates r_n and u_n are computed in parallel. If, given the current word, it is preferable to forget information about the past, i.e. to reset parts of h_n, the elements of r_n will be pushed towards 0. The update gate u_n plays the opposite role, i.e. it judges whether the current word contains relevant information that should be stored in h_n. In the final update, if the elements of u_n are close to 0, the network discards the update $\bar{h}_n$ and keeps the last recurrent state h_{n-1}. The gating behaviour provides robustness to noise in the input sequence: this is particularly important for IR as

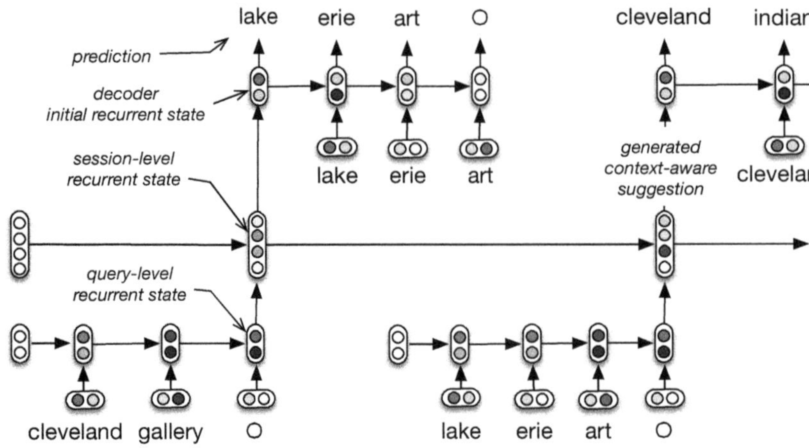

Figure 3: The hierarchical recurrent encoder-decoder (HRED). The user types *cleveland gallery* → *lake erie art*. During training, the model encodes *cleveland gallery*, updates the session-level recurrent state and maximize the probability of seeing the following query *lake erie art*. The process is repeated for all queries in the session. During testing, a contextual suggestion is generated by encoding the previous queries, by updating the session-level recurrent states accordingly and by sampling a new query from the last obtained session-level recurrent state. In the example, the generated contextual suggestion is *cleveland indian art*.

it allows, for example, to exclude from the summary non-discriminative terms appearing in the query.

3.2 Architecture

Our hierarchical recurrent encoder-decoder (HRED) is pictured in Figure 3. Given a query in the session, the model encodes the information seen up to that position and tries to predict the following query. The process is iterated throughout all the queries in the session. In the forward pass, the model computes the query-level encodings, the session-level recurrent states and the log-likelihood of each query in the session given the previous ones. In the backward pass, the gradients are computed and the parameters are updated.

3.2.1 Query-Level Encoding

For each query $Q_m = \{w_{m,1}, \dots, w_{m,N_m}\}$ in the training session S, the query-level RNN reads the words of the query sequentially and updates its hidden state according to:

$$h_{m,n} = GRU_{enc}(h_{m,n-1}, w_{m,n}), \quad n = 1, \dots, N_m, \tag{4}$$

where GRU_{enc} is the query-level encoder GRU function in Eq. 3, $h_{m,n} \in \mathbb{R}^{d_h}$ and $h_{m,0} = 0$, the null vector. The recurrent state h_{m,N_m} is a vector storing order-sensitive information about all the words in the query. To keep the notation uncluttered, we denote by $q_m \equiv h_{m,N_m}$ the vector for query m. In summary, the query-level RNN encoder maps a query to a fixed-length vector. Its parameters are shared across the queries. Therefore, the obtained query representation q_m is a general, acontextual representation of query m. The computation of the $q_1, \dots, q_M$ can be performed in parallel, thus lowering computational costs. A projection of the generated query vectors is provided in Figure 1 (b).

3.2.2 Session-Level Encoding

The session-level RNN takes as input the sequence of query representations $q_1, \dots, q_M$ and computes the sequence of session-level recurrent states. For the session-level RNN, we also use the GRU function:

$$s_m = GRU_{ses}(s_{m-1}, q_m), \quad m = 1, \dots, M, \tag{5}$$

where $s_m \in \mathbb{R}^{d_s}$ is the session-level recurrent state, d_s is its dimensionality and $s_0 = 0$. The number of session-level recurrent states s_m is M, the number of queries in the session.

The session-level recurrent state s_m summarizes the queries that have been processed up to position m. Each s_m bears a particularly powerful characteristic: it is sensitive to the order of previous queries and, as such, it can potentially encode order-dependent reformulation patterns such as generalization or specification of the previous queries [18]. Additionally, it inherits from the query vectors q_m the sensitivity to the order of words in the queries.

3.2.3 Next-Query Decoding

The RNN decoder is responsible to predict the next query Q_m given the previous queries $Q_{1:m-1}$, i.e. to estimate the probability:

$$P(Q_m|Q_{1:m-1}) = \prod_{n=1}^{N_m} P(w_n|w_{1:n-1}, Q_{1:m-1}). \tag{6}$$

The desired conditioning on previous queries is obtained by initializing the recurrence of the RNN decoder with a non-linear transformation of s_{m-1}:

$$d_{m,0} = \tanh(D_0 s_{m-1} + b_0), \tag{7}$$

where $d_{m,0} \in \mathbb{R}^{d_h}$ is the decoder initial recurrent state (depicted in Figure 3), $D_0 \in \mathbb{R}^{d_h \times d_s}$ projects the context summary into the decoder space and $b_0 \in \mathbb{R}^{d_h}$. This way, the information about previous queries is transferred to the decoder RNN. The recurrence takes the usual form:

$$d_{m,n} = GRU_{dec}(d_{m,n-1}, w_{m,n}), \quad n = 1, \dots, N_m, \tag{8}$$

where GRU_{dec} is the decoder GRU, $d_{m,n} \in \mathbb{R}^{d_h}$ [11]. In a RNN decoder, each recurrent state $d_{m,n-1}$ is used to compute the probability of the next word $w_{m,n}$. The probability of word $w_{m,n}$ given previous words and queries is:

$$P(w_{m,n} = v \mid w_{m,1:n-1}, Q_{1:m-1}) = \\ = \frac{\exp o_v^\top \omega(d_{m,n-1}, w_{m,n-1})}{\sum_k \exp o_k^\top \omega(d_{m,n-1}, w_{m,n-1})}, \quad (9)$$

where $o_v \in \mathbb{R}^{d_e}$ is the output embedding of word v and ω is a function of both the recurrent state at position n and the last input word:

$$\omega(d_{m,n-1}, w_{m,n-1}) = H_o\, d_{m,n-1} + E_o\, w_{m,n-1} + b_o, \quad (10)$$

where $H_o \in \mathbb{R}^{d_e \times d_h}$, $E_o \in \mathbb{R}^{d_e \times V}$ and $b_o \in \mathbb{R}^{d_e}$. To predict the first word of Q_m, we set $w_{m,0} = 0$, the 0 vector. Instead of using the recurrent state directly as in Eq. 2, we add another layer of linear transformation ω. The E_o parameter accentuates the responsibility of the previous word to predict the next one. This formulation has shown to be beneficial for language modelling tasks [29, 11, 26]. If o_v is "near" the vector $\omega(d_{m,n-1}, w_{m,n-1})$ the word v has high probability under the model.

3.3 Learning

The model parameters comprise the parameters of the three GRU functions, GRU_{enc}, GRU_{dec}, GRU_{ses}, the output parameters H_o, E_o, b_o and the V output vectors o_i. These are learned by maximizing the log-likelihood of a session S, defined by the probabilities estimated with Eq. 6 and Eq 9:

$$\mathcal{L}(S) = \sum_{m=1}^{M} \log P(Q_m | Q_{1:m-1}) \\ = \sum_{m=1}^{M} \sum_{n=1}^{N_m} \log P(w_{m,n} | w_{m,1:n-1}, Q_{1:m-1}). \quad (11)$$

The gradients of the objective function are computed using the back-propagation through time (BPTT) algorithm [32].

3.4 Generation and Rescoring

Generation. In our framework, the query suggestion task corresponds to an inference problem. A user submits the sequence of queries $S = \{Q_1, \ldots, Q_M\}$. A query suggestion is a query Q^* such that:

$$Q^* = \arg\max_{Q \in \mathcal{Q}} P(Q | Q_{1:M}), \quad (12)$$

where $\mathcal{Q}$ is the space of possible queries, i.e. the space of sentences ending by the end-of-query symbol. The solution to the problem can be approximated using standard word-level decoding techniques such as beam-search [11, 23]. We iteratively consider a set of k best prefixes up to length n as candidates and we extend each of them by sampling the most probable k words given the distribution in Eq. 9. We obtain k^2 queries of length $n+1$ and keep only the k best of them. The process ends when we obtain k well-formed queries containing the special end-of-query token $\circ$.

Example. Consider a user who submits the queries *cleveland gallery* → *lake erie artist*. The suggestion system proceeds as follows. We apply Eq. 4 to each query obtaining the query vectors $q_{\text{cleveland gallery}}$ and $q_{\text{lake erie art}}$. Then, we compute the session-level recurrent states by applying Eq. 5 to the query vectors. At this point, we obtain two session-level recurrent states, $s_{\text{cleveland gallery}}$ and $s_{\text{lake erie art}}$. To generate context-aware suggestions, we start by mapping the

Context	Synthetic Suggestions
ace series drive	ace hardware ace hard drive hp officejet drive ace hardware series
cleveland gallery → lake erie art	cleveland indian art lake erie art gallery lake erie picture gallery sandusky ohio art gallery

Table 1: HRED suggestions given the context.

last session-level recurrent state, $s_{\text{lake erie art}}$, into the initial decoder input d_0 using Eq. 7. We are ready to start the sampling of the suggestion. Let us assume that the beam-search size is 1. The probability of the first word w_1 in the suggestion is computed using Eq. 9 by using d_0 and $w_0 = 0$, the null vector. The word with the highest probability, i.e. *cleveland*, is added to the beam. The next decoder recurrent state d_1 is computed by means of Eq. 8 using d_0 and $w_1 =$ *cleveland*. Using d_1, we are able to pick $w_2 =$ *indian* as the second most likely word. The process repeats and the model selects *art* and $\circ$. As soon as the end-of-query symbol is sampled, the context-aware suggestion *cleveland indian art* is presented to the user. In Table 1 we give an idea of the generated suggestions for 2 contexts in our test set.

Rescoring. Our model can evaluate the likelihood of a given suggestion conditioned on the history of previous queries through Eq. 6. This makes our model integrable into more complex suggestion systems. In the next section, we choose to evaluate our model by adding the likelihood scores of candidate suggestions as additional features into a learning-to-rank system.

4. EXPERIMENTS

We test how well our query suggestion model can predict the next query in the session given the history of previous queries. This evaluation scenario aims at measuring the ability of a model to propose the target next query, which is assumed to be one desired by the user. We evaluate this with a learning-to-rank approach (explained in Section 4.3), similar to the one used in [27, 36] for query auto-completion and in [28, 34] for query suggestion. We first generate candidates using a co-occurrence based suggestion model. Then, we train a baseline ranker comprising a set of contextual features depending on the history of previous queries as well as pairwise features which depend only on the most recent query. The likelihood scores given by our model are used as additional features in the supervised ranker. At the end, we have three systems: (1) the original co-occurrence based ranking, denoted ADJ; (2) the supervised context-aware ranker, which we refer to as Baseline Ranker; and (3) a supervised ranker with our HRED feature. We evaluate the performance of the model and the baselines using mean reciprocal rank (MRR). This is common for tasks whose ground truth is only one instance [22, 27].

4.1 Dataset

We conduct our experiments on the well-known search log from AOL, which is the only available search log that is large enough to train our model and the baselines. The queries in this dataset were sampled between 1 March, 2006

Batches Seen	Training	Decoding (50)	Memory
135,350	44h 01m	$\sim$ 1s	301 Mb

Table 2: Full statistics about training time, memory impact and decoding time with a beam size of 50.

and 31 May, 2006. In total there are 16,946,938 queries submitted by 657,426 unique users. We remove all non-alphanumeric characters from the queries, apply a spelling corrector and lowercasing. After filtering, we sort the queries by timestamp and we use those submitted before 1 May, 2006 as our *background* data to estimate the proposed model and the baselines. The next two weeks of data are used as a *training* set for tuning the ranking models. The remaining two weeks are split into the *validation* and the *test* set. We define the end of a session by a 30 minute window of idle time [21]. After filtering, there are 1,708,224 sessions in the background set, 435,705 in the training set, 166,836 in the validation set and 230,359 in the test set.

4.2 Model Training

The most frequent $90K$ words in the background set form our vocabulary V. This is a common setting for RNN applied to language and allows to speed-up the repeated summations over V in Eq. 9 [11, 39]. Parameter optimization is done using mini-batch RMSPROP [13]. We normalize the gradients if their norm exceeds a threshold $c = 1$ [29]. The training stops if the likelihood of the validation set does not improve for 5 consecutive iterations. We train our model[1] using the Theano library [2, 6]. The dimensionality of the query-level RNN is set to $d_h = 1000$. To memorize complex information about previous queries, we ensure a high-capacity session-level RNN by setting $d_s = 1500$. The output word embeddings o_i are 300 dimensional vectors, i.e. $d_e = 300$. Our model is compact and can easily fit in memory (Table 2). The complexity of the decoding is largely dominated by the computation of the output probabilities, giving $O(nkVd_e)$, where n is the generated query length and k the beam size. In the future, the computational cost may be greatly reduced by employing locality sensitive hashing (LSH) based techniques [37].

4.3 Learning to Rank

Given a session $S = \{Q_1, \dots, Q_M\}$, we aim to predict the *target* query Q_M given the *context* $Q_1, \dots, Q_{M-1}$. Q_{M-1} is called the *anchor* query and will play a crucial role in the selection of the candidates to rerank. To probe different capabilities of our model, we predict the next query in three scenarios: (a) when the anchor query exists in the background data (Section 4.4); (b) when the context is perturbed with overly common queries (Section 4.5); (c) when the anchor is not present in the background data (Section 4.6).

For each session, we select a list of 20 possible candidates to rerank. The exact method used to produce the candidates will be discussed in the next sections. Once the candidates are extracted, we label the true target as relevant and all the others as non-relevant. We choose to use one of the state-of-the-art ranking algorithms LambdaMART as our supervised ranker, which is the winner in the Yahoo! Learning to Rank Challenge in 2010 [43]. We tune the LambdaMART model with 500 trees and the parameters are learnt using standard separate training and validation set.

We describe the set of pairwise and contextual features (17 in total) used to train a supervised baseline prediction model, denoted Baseline Ranker. The Baseline Ranker is a competitive system comprising features that are comparable with the ones described in the literature for query auto-completion [22, 27] and next-query prediction [15].

Pairwise and Suggestion Features. For each candidate suggestion, we count how many times it follows the anchor query in the background data and add this count as a feature. Additionally, we use the frequency of the anchor query in the background data. Following [22, 28] we also add the Levenshtein distance between the anchor and the suggestion. Suggestion features include: the suggestion length (characters and words) and its frequency in the background set.

Contextual Features. Similarly to [27, 36], we add 10 features corresponding to the character n-gram similarity between the suggestion and the 10 most recent queries in the context. We add the average Levenshtein distance between the suggestion and each query in the context [22]. We use the scores estimated using the context-aware Query Variable Markov Model (QVMM) [15] as an additional feature. QVMM models the context with a variable memory Markov model able to automatically back-off shorter query n-grams if the exact context is not found in the background data.

HRED Score. The proposed hierarchical recurrent encoder-decoder contributes one additional feature corresponding to the log-likelihood of the suggestion given the context, as detailed in Section 3.4.

4.4 Test Scenario 1: Next-Query Prediction

For each session in the training, validation and test set, we extract 20 queries that most likely follow the anchor query in the background data, i.e. with the highest ADJ score. The session is included if and only if at least 20 queries have been extracted and the target query appears in the candidate list. In that case, the target query is the positive candidate and the 19 other candidates are the negative examples. Note that a similar setting has been used in [22, 27] for query auto-completion. We have 18,882 sessions in the training set, 6,988 sessions in the validation set and 9,348 sessions in the

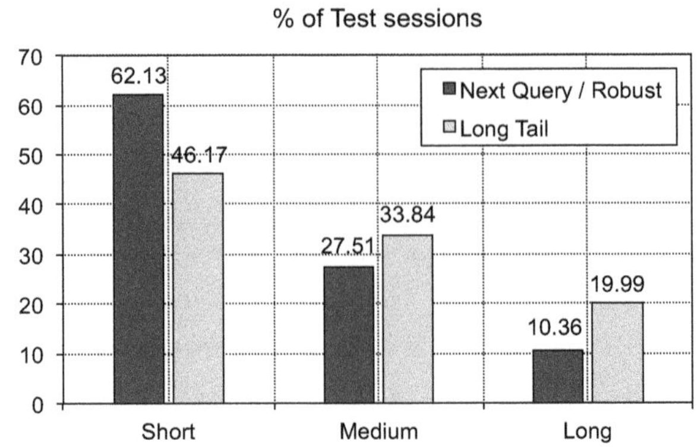

Figure 4: Proportion (%) of short (2 queries), medium (3 or 4 queries) and long (at least 5 queries) sessions in our test scenarios.

[1]An implementation of the model is available at `https://github.com/sordonia/hred-qs`.

Method	MRR	Δ%
ADJ	0.5334	-
Baseline Ranker	0.5563	*+4.3%*
+ HRED	**0.5749**	*+7.8%/+3.3%*

Table 3: Next-query prediction results. All improvements are significant by the t-test ($p < 0.01$).

test set. The distribution of the session length is reported in Figure 4. The scores obtained by the ADJ counts are used as an additional non-supervised baseline.

Main Result. Table 3 shows the MRR performance for our model and the baselines. Baseline Ranker achieves a relative improvement of 4.3% with respect to the ADJ model. We find that the HRED feature brings additional gains achieving 7.8% relative improvement over ADJ. The differences in performance with respect to ADJ and the Baseline Ranker are significant using a t-test with $p < 0.01$. In this general next-query prediction setting, HRED boosts the rank of the first relevant result.

Impact of Session Length. We expect the session length to have an impact on the performance of context-aware models. In Figure 5, we report separate results for short (2 queries), medium (3 or 4 queries) and long sessions (at least 5 queries). HRED brings statistically significant improvements across all the session lengths. For short sessions, the improvement is marginal but consistent even though only a short context is available in this case. The semantic mapping learnt by the model appears to be useful, even in the pairwise case. ADJ is affected by the lack of context-awareness and suffers a dramatic loss of performance with increasing session length. In the medium range, context-aware models account for previous queries and achieve the highest performance. The trend is not maintained for long sessions, seemingly the hardest for the Baseline Ranker. Long sessions can be the result of complex search tasks involving a topically broad information need or changes of search topics. Beyond the intrinsic difficulty in predicting the target query in these cases, exact context matches may be too coarse to infer the user need. Count-based methods such as QVMM meet their limitations due to data sparsity. In this difficult range, HRED achieves its highest relative improvement with respect to both ADJ (+15%) and the Baseline Ranker (+7%), thus showing robustness across different session lengths.

Impact of Context Length. We test whether the performance obtained by HRED on long sessions can be obtained using a shorter context. For each long session in our test set, we artificially truncate the context to make the prediction depend on the anchor query, Q_{M-1}, only (1 query), on Q_{M-2} and Q_{M-1} (2 queries), on 3 queries and on the entire context. When one query is considered, our model behaves similarly to a pairwise recurrent encoder-decoder model trained on consecutive queries. Figure 6 shows that when only one query is considered, the performance of HRED is similar to the Baseline Ranker (0.529) which uses the whole context. HRED appears to perform best when the whole context is considered. Additional gains can be obtained by considering more than 3 queries, which highlights the ability of our model to consider long contexts.

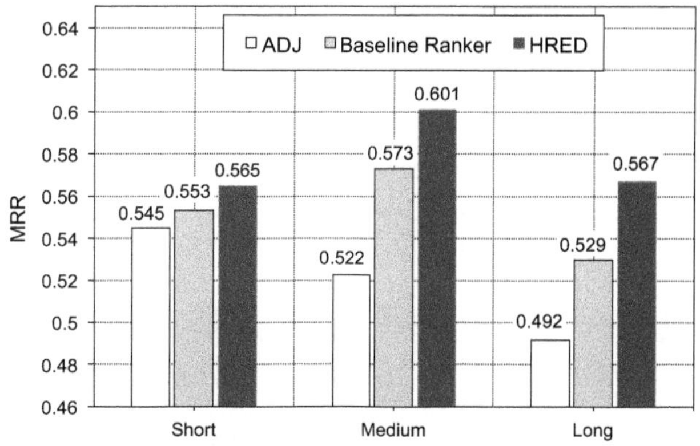

Figure 5: Next-query performance in short, medium and long sessions. All differences in MRR are statistically significant by the t-test ($p < 0.01$).

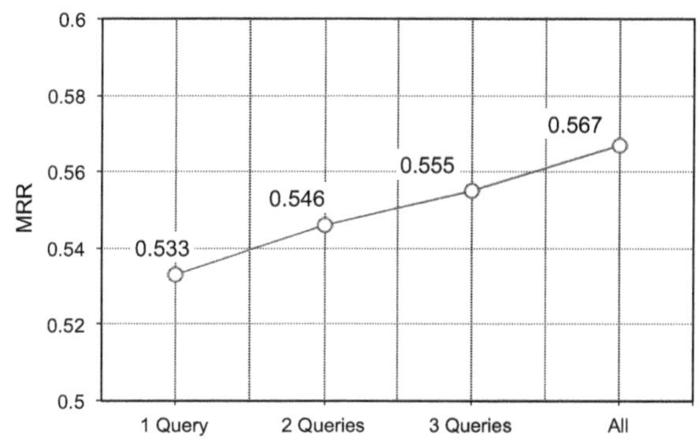

Figure 6: Variation of HRED performance with respect to the number of previous queries considered. The evolution is computed on long sessions.

4.5 Test Scenario 2: Robust Prediction

Query sessions contain a lot of common and navigational queries such as *google* or *facebook* which do not correspond to a specific search topic. A context-aware suggestion system should be *robust* to noisy queries and learn to discard them from the relevant history that should be retained. We propose to probe this capability by formulating an original robust prediction task as follows. We label the 100 most frequent queries in the background set as *noisy*[2]. For each entry in the training, validation and test set of the previous next-query prediction task, we corrupt its context by *inserting* a noisy query at a random position. The candidates and the target rest unchanged. The probability of sampling a noisy query is proportional to its frequency in the background set. For example, given the context *airlines → united airlines* and the true target *delta airlines*, the noisy sample *google* is inserted at a random position, forcing the models to predict the target given the corrupted context *airlines → united airlines → google*.

Main Result. Table 4 shows that corruption considerably affects the performance of ADJ. Cases in which the corruption occurred at the position of the anchor query severely harm pairwise models. The Baseline Ranker achieves significant gains over ADJ by leveraging context matches. Its

[2] A similar categorization has been proposed in [31].

Method	MRR	Δ%
ADJ	0.4507	-
Baseline Ranker	0.4831	*+7,2%*
+ HRED	**0.5309**	*+17,8%/+9.9%*

Table 4: Robust prediction results. The improvements are significant by the t-test ($p < 0.01$).

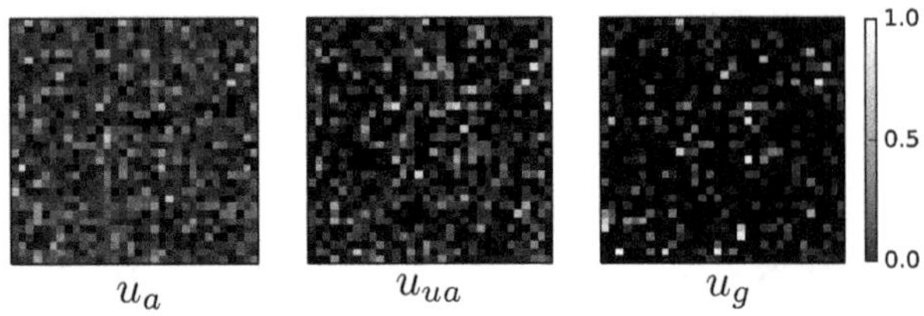

Figure 7: Magnitude of the elements in the session-level update gates. The darker the image, the more the model discards the current query. The vector corresponding to *google*, u_g, is darker, i.e. the network mainly keeps its previous recurrent state.

performance is inferior to the baseline ADJ performance in the next-query setting reported in Table 3 (0.5334). HRED appears to be particularly effective in this difficult setting achieving a relative improvement of 17.8% over ADJ and 9.9% over the Baseline Ranker, both statistically significant. Comparative to the next-query task, the improvements over ADJ and the Baseline Ranker are 2.5 and 3 times higher respectively. Our model appears to be more robust than the baselines in these extreme cases and can better reduce the impact of the noisy query.

Impact of the Hierarchical Structure. As noisy queries bring little information to predict future queries in the session, HRED may automatically learn to be robust to the noise at training time. The hierarchical structure allows to decide, for each query, if it is profitable to account for its contribution to predict future queries. This capability is sustained by the session-level GRU, which can ignore the noisy queries by "turning-off" the update gate u_n when they appear (see Section 3.1.1). Given the corrupted context *airlines* → *united airlines* → *google*, the session-level GRU computes three update gate vectors: u_a, u_{ua}, u_g, each corresponding to a position in the context. In Figure 7, we plot the magnitude of the elements in these vectors. As the model needs to memorize the initial information, u_a shows a significant number of non-zero (bright) entries. At this point, general topical information has already been stored in the first recurrent state. Hence, u_{ua} shows a larger number of zero (dark) entries. When *google* is processed, the network tends to keep past information in memory by further zeroing entries in the update gate. Interestingly, this mechanism may be used to address other search log related tasks such as session-boundary detection.

4.6 Test Scenario 3: Long-Tail Prediction

To analyze the performance of the models in the long-tail, we build our training, validation and test set by retaining the sessions for which the anchor query has not been seen in the background set, i.e. it is a long-tail query. In this case, we cannot leverage the ADJ score to select candidates

Method	MRR	Δ%
ADJ	0.3830	-
Baseline Ranker	0.6788	*+77.2%*
+ HRED	**0.7112**	*+85.3%/+5.6%*

Table 5: Long-tail prediction results. The improvements are significant by the t-test ($p < 0.01$).

to rerank. For each session, we iteratively shorten the anchor query by dropping terms until we have a query that appears in the background data. If a match is found, we proceed as described in the next-query prediction setting, that is, we guarantee that the target appears in the top 20 queries that have the highest ADJ scores given the anchor prefix. The statistics of the obtained dataset are reported in Figure 4. As expected, the distribution of lengths changes substantially with respect to the previous settings. Long-tail queries are likely to appear in medium and long sessions, in which the user strives to find an adequate textual query.

Main Result. Table 5 shows that, due to the anchor prefix matching, ADJ suffer a significant loss of performance. The performances of the models generally confirm our previous findings. HRED improves significantly by 5.6% over the Baseline Ranker and proves to be useful even for long-tail queries. Supervised models appear to achieve higher absolute scores in the long-tail setting than in the general next-query setting reported in Table 3. After analysis of the long-tail testing set, we found that only 8% of the session contexts contain at least one noisy query. In the general next-query prediction case, this number grows to 37%. Noisy queries generally harm performance of the models by increasing the ambiguity in the next query prediction task. This fact may explain why the Baseline Ranker and HRED perform better on long-tail queries than in the general case. It is interesting to see how the improvement of HRED with respect to the Baseline Ranker is larger for long-tail queries than in the general setup (5.6% to 3.3%). Although not explicitly reported, we analyzed the performance with respect to the session length in the long-tail setting. Similarly to the general next-query prediction setting, we found that the Baseline Ranker suffers significant losses for long sessions while our model appears robust to different session lengths.

4.7 User Study

The previous re-ranking setting does not allow to test the generative capabilities of our suggestion system. We perform an additional user study and ask human evaluators to assess the quality of synthetic suggestions. To avoid sampling bias towards overly common queries, we choose to generate suggestions for the 50 topics of the TREC Web Track 2011 [12]. The assessment was conducted by a group of 5 assessors. To palliate the lack of context information for TREC queries, we proceed as follows: for each TREC topic Q_M, we extract from the test set the sessions ending exactly with Q_M and we take their context $Q_1, \ldots, Q_{M-1}$. After contextualization, 19 TREC queries have one or more queries as context and the remaining are singletons. For HRED, we build synthetic queries following the generative procedure described in Section 3.4. In addition to QVMM and ADJ, we compare our model with two other baselines: CACB [10], which is similar to QVMM but builds clusters of queries to avoid sparsity,

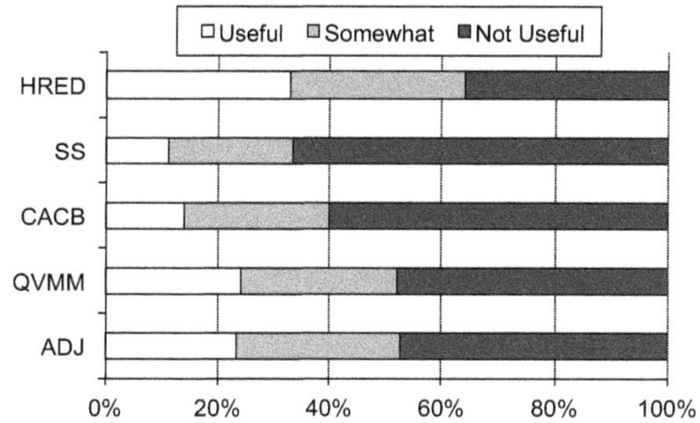

Figure 8: User study results, which compare the effectiveness of HRED with the baseline techniques.

and SS (Search Shortcuts) [9], which builds an index of the query sessions and extracts the last query of the most similar sessions to the source context. Note that we do not compare the output of the previous supervised rankers as this would not test the generative capability of our model. Each assessor was provided with a random query from the test bed, its context, if any, and a list of recommended queries (the top-5 for each of the methods) selected by the different methods. Recommendations were randomly shuffled, so that the assessors could not distinguish which method produced them. Each assessor was asked to judge each recommended query using the following scale: useful, somewhat useful, and not useful. The user study finished when each assessor had assessed all recommendations for all 50 queries in the test bed. Figure 8 reports the results of the user study averaged over all raters. Overall, for HRED, 64% of the recommendations were judged useful or somewhat useful. The quality of the queries recommended by HRED is higher than our baselines both in the somewhat and in the useful category.

5. RELATED WORKS

Query Suggestion. A notorious context-aware method was proposed by He et al. [15]. The authors use a Variable Memory Markov model (QVMM) and build a suffix tree to model the user query sequence. We used this model as a context-aware baseline feature in our supervised ranker. The method by Cao et al. [10] is similar but they build a suffix tree on clusters of queries and model the transitions between clusters. We didn't notice any improvements by adding this model as a feature in our case. For both models, the number of parameters increases with the depth of the tree inducing sparsity. Instead, our model can consider arbitrary length contexts with a fixed number of parameters. Jiang et al. [22] and Shokouhi et al. [36] propose context-aware approaches for query auto-completion. We adopted a similar framework for query suggestion and use our model as a feature to rank the next-query. Santos et al. [34] and Ozertem et al. [28] also use learning to rank approach for query suggestion. In those cases, the rankers are trained using pairwise features and do not consider previous queries. Interestingly, the authors model explicitly the usefulness of a suggestion by using click data and the result list.

Query suggestion algorithms use clustering methods to find similar queries so that they can be used as suggestions for one another [1, 42]. We demonstrated that our model exhibits similar clustering properties due to the embeddings learnt by the neural network. Other works build a Query Flow Graph (QFG) to capture high-order query co-occurrence [7, 33]. Operating at the query-level, these methods suffer from the long-tail problem. Bonchi et al. [8] propose a solution to these problems by introducing the Term-QFG (TQG), where single query terms are also included into the graph. However, suggestion requires repeated complex random walks with restart. Similarly, our model can handle rare queries as long as their words appear in the model vocabulary. Vahabi et al. [41] find suggestions to long-tail queries by comparing their search results. Although effective, the approach requires to have 100 results per query. A related approach is the Search Shortcut [9] which avoids the long-tail problem by means of a retrieval algorithm.

Few synthetic suggestion models have been proposed in the literature. Szpektor et al. [40] use a template generation method by leveraging WordNet. Jain et al. [20] combine different resources and use a machine learning approach to prune redundant suggestions. These methods achieve automatic addition, removal and substitution of related terms into the queries. By maximizing the likelihood of the session data, our model learns to perform similar modifications.

Neural Networks for NLP. Neural networks have found several applications in a variety of tasks, ranging from Information Retrieval (IR) [19, 35], Language Modeling (LM) [26, 30] and Machine Translation (MT) [11, 39]. Cho et al. [11] and Sutskever et al. [39] use a Recurrent Neural Network (RNN) for end-to-end MT. Our model bears similarities to these approaches but we contribute with the hierarchical structure. The idea of encoding hierarchical multi-scale representations is also explored in [16]. In IR, neural networks embeddings were used by Li et al [24]. The authors used deep feed-forward neural networks to use previous queries by the same user to boost document ranking. In [19, 35], the authors propose to use clickthrough data to learn a ranking model for ad-hoc IR. Recently, Grbovic et al. [14] used query embeddings to include session-based information for sponsor search. Our model shares similarities with the interesting recent work by Mitra [27]. The authors use the pairwise neural model described in [35] to measure similarity between queries. Context-awareness is achieved at ranking time, by measuring the similarity between the candidates and each query in the context. Our work has several key differences. First, we deploy a novel RNN architecture. Second, our model is generative. Third, we model the session context at training time. To our knowledge, this is the first work applying RNNs to an IR task.

6. CONCLUSION

In this paper, we formulated a novel hierarchical neural network architecture and used it to produce query suggestions. Our model is context-aware and it can handle rare queries. It can be trained end-to-end on query sessions by simple optimization procedures. Our experiments show that the scores provided by our model help improving MRR for next-query ranking. Additionally, it is generative by definition. We showed with a user study that the synthetic generated queries are better than the compared methods.

In future works, we aim to extend our model to explicitly capture the usefulness of a suggestion by exploiting user clicks [28]. Then, we plan to further study the synthetic generation by means of a large-scale automatic evaluation.

Currently, the synthetic suggestions tend to be *horizontal*, i.e. the model prefers to add or remove terms from the context queries and rarely proposes orthogonal but related reformulations [20, 41]. Future efforts may be dedicated to diversify the generated suggestions to account for this effect. Finally, the interactions of the user with previous suggestions can also be leveraged to better capture the behaviour of the user and to make better suggestions accordingly. We are the most excited about possible future applications beyond query suggestion: auto-completion, next-word prediction and other NLP tasks such as Language Modelling may be fit as possible candidates.

Acknowledgments

We would like to thank Jianfeng Gao, Çağlar Gülçehre and Bhaskar Mitra for their precious advice, enlightening discussions and invaluable moral support. We gratefully acknowledge the support of NVIDIA Corporation with the donation of the Tesla K40 GPU used for this research.

7. REFERENCES

[1] R. Baeza-Yates, C. Hurtado, and M. Mendoza. Query recommendation using query logs in search engines. In *In Proc. of Int. Conf. on Current Trends in Database Tech.*, pages 588–596, 2004.

[2] F. Bastien, P. Lamblin, R. Pascanu, J. Bergstra, I. J. Goodfellow, A. Bergeron, N. Bouchard, and Y. Bengio. Theano: new features and speed improvements. Deep Learning and Unsupervised Feature Learning NIPS 2012 Workshop, 2012.

[3] Y. Bengio. Deep learning of representations: Looking forward. *CoRR*, abs/1305.0445, 2013.

[4] Y. Bengio, R. Ducharme, and P. Vincent. A neural probabilistic language model. *Journal of Machine Learning Research*, 3:1137–1155, 2003.

[5] Y. Bengio, P. Simard, and P. Frasconi. Learning long-term dependencies with gradient descent is difficult. *IEEE Transactions on Neural Networks*, pages 157–166, 1994.

[6] J. Bergstra, O. Breuleux, F. Bastien, P. Lamblin, R. Pascanu, G. Desjardins, J. Turian, D. Warde-Farley, and Y. Bengio. Theano: a CPU and GPU math expression compiler. In *In Proc. of SciPy*, 2010.

[7] P. Boldi, F. Bonchi, C. Castillo, D. Donato, A. Gionis, and S. Vigna. The query-flow graph: Model and applications. In *In Proc. of CIKM*, pages 609–618, 2008.

[8] F. Bonchi, R. Perego, F. Silvestri, H. Vahabi, and R. Venturini. Efficient query recommendations in the long tail via center-piece subgraphs. In *In Proc. of SIGIR*, pages 345–354, 2012.

[9] D. Broccolo, L. Marcon, F. M. Nardini, R. Perego, and F. Silvestri. Generating suggestions for queries in the long tail with an inverted index. *Inf. Process. Manage.*, 48(2):326–339, 2012.

[10] H. Cao, D. Jiang, J. Pei, Q. He, Z. Liao, E. Chen, and H. Li. Context-aware query suggestion by mining click-through and session data. In *In Proc. of SIGKDD*, pages 875–883, 2008.

[11] K. Cho, B. Merrienboer, Ç. Gülçehre, F. Bougares, H. Schwenk, and Y. Bengio. Learning phrase representations using rnn encoder-decoder for statistical machine translation. *In Proc. of EMNLP*, 2014.

[12] C. LA Clarke, N. Craswell, I. Soboroff, and E. M Voorhees. Overview of the trec 2011 web track. *Proceedings of the 2011 Text Retrieval Conference (TREC 2011)*, 2011.

[13] A. Graves. Generating sequences with recurrent neural networks. *CoRR*, abs/1308.0850, 2013.

[14] M. Grbovic, N. Djuric, V. Radosavljevic, F. Silvestri, and N. Bhamidipati. Context- and content-aware embeddings for query rewriting in sponsored search. In *Proc. of SIGIR*. 2015.

[15] Q. He, D. Jiang, Z. Liao, S. C. H. Hoi, K. Chang, E. P. Lim, and H. Li. Web query recommendation via sequential query prediction. In *In Proc. of ICDE*, pages 1443–1454, 2009.

[16] S. El Hihi and Y. Bengio. Hierarchical recurrent neural networks for long-term dependencies. In *NIPS*, pages 493–499. Citeseer, 1995.

[17] S. Hochreiter and J. Schmidhuber. Long short-term memory. *Neural computation*, 9(8):1735–1780, 1997.

[18] J. Huang and E. N. Efthimiadis. Analyzing and evaluating query reformulation strategies in web search logs. In *In Proc. of CIKM*, pages 77–86, 2009.

[19] P. S. Huang, X. He, J. Gao, L. Deng, A. Acero, and L. Heck. Learning deep structured semantic models for web search using clickthrough data. In *In Proc. of CIKM*, pages 2333–2338, 2013.

[20] A. Jain, U. Ozertem, and E. Velipasaoglu. Synthesizing high utility suggestions for rare web search queries. In *In Proc. of SIGIR*, pages 805–814, 2011.

[21] B. J. Jansen, A. Spink, C. Blakely, and S. Koshman. Defining a session on web search engines: Research articles. *J. Am. Soc. Inf. Sci. Technol.*, 58(6):862–871, April 2007.

[22] J.Y. Jiang, Y.Y. Ke, P.Y. Chien, and P.J. Cheng. Learning user reformulation behavior for query auto-completion. In *In Proc. of SIGIR*, pages 445–454, 2014.

[23] P. Koehn. *Statistical machine translation.* Cambridge University Press, 2009.

[24] X. Li, C. Guo, W. Chu, Y.Y. Wang, and J. Shavlik. Deep learning powered in-session contextual ranking using clickthrough data. In *In Proc. of NIPS*, 2014.

[25] T. Mikolov, K. Chen, G. Corrado, and J. Dean. Efficient estimation of word representations in vector space. *arXiv preprint arXiv:1301.3781*, 2013.

[26] T. Mikolov, M. Karafiát, L. Burget, J. Cernocký, and S. Khudanpur. Recurrent neural network based language model. In *In Proc. of ACISCA*, pages 1045–1048, 2010.

[27] B. Mitra. Exploring session context using distributed representations of queries and reformulations. In *In Proc. of SIGIR*. To appear, 2015.

[28] U. Ozertem, O. Chapelle, P. Donmez, and E. Velipasaoglu. Learning to suggest: A machine learning framework for ranking query suggestions. In *In Proc. of SIGIR*, pages 25–34, 2012.

[29] R. Pascanu, C. Gulcehre, K. Cho, and Y. Bengio. How to construct deep recurrent neural networks. *arXiv preprint arXiv:1312.6026*, 2013.

[30] R. Pascanu, T. Mikolov, and Y. Bengio. On the difficulty of training recurrent neural networks. *In Proc. of ICML*, 2013.

[31] K. Raman, P. Bennett, and K. Collins-Thompson. Understanding intrinsic diversity in web search: Improving whole-session relevance. *ACM Trans. Inf. Syst.*, 32(4):20:1–20:45, October 2014.

[32] D. E Rumelhart, G. E Hinton, and R. J Williams. Learning representations by back-propagating errors. *Cognitive modeling*, 1988.

[33] E. Sadikov, J. Madhavan, L. Wang, and A. Halevy. Clustering query refinements by user intent. In *In Proc. of WWW*, pages 841–850, 2010.

[34] R. L.T. Santos, C. Macdonald, and I. Ounis. Learning to rank query suggestions for adhoc and diversity search. *Information Retrieval*, 16(4):429–451, 2013.

[35] Y. Shen, X. He, J. Gao, L. Deng, and G. Mesnil. A latent semantic model with convolutional-pooling structure for information retrieval. In *In Proc. of CIKM*, pages 101–110, 2014.

[36] M. Shokouhi. Learning to personalize query auto-completion. In *In Proc. of SIGIR*, pages 103–112, 2013.

[37] Anshumali Shrivastava and Ping Li. Asymmetric lsh (alsh) for sublinear time maximum inner product search (mips). In *In Proc. of NIPS*, pages 2321–2329, 2014.

[38] A. Sordoni, J.Y. Nie, and Y. Bengio. Modeling term dependencies with quantum language models for ir. In *In Proc. of SIGIR*, pages 653–662, 2013.

[39] I. Sutskever, O. Vinyals, and Q. V. V Le. Sequence to sequence learning with neural networks. In *In Proc. of NIPS*, pages 3104–3112. 2014.

[40] I. Szpektor, A. Gionis, and Y. Maarek. Improving recommendation for long-tail queries via templates. In *In Proc. of WWW*, pages 47–56, 2011.

[41] H. Vahabi, M. Ackerman, D. Loker, R. Baeza-Yates, and A. Lopez-Ortiz. Orthogonal query recommendation. In *In Proc. of RECSYS*, RecSys '13, pages 33–40. ACM, 2013.

[42] J.R. Wen, J.Y. Nie, and H.J. Zhang. Clustering user queries of a search engine. In *In Proc. of WWW*, pages 162–168. ACM, 2001.

[43] Q. Wu, C. J. Burges, K. M. Svore, and J. Gao. Adapting boosting for information retrieval measures. *Inf. Retr.*, 13(3):254–270, June 2010.

A Network-Aware Approach for Searching As-You-Type in Social Media

Paul Lagrée
Inria Saclay and Université Paris-Sud
Orsay, France
paul.lagree@u-psud.fr

Bogdan Cautis
Inria Saclay and Université Paris-Sud
Orsay, France
bogdan.cautis@u-psud.fr

Hossein Vahabi
Yahoo Labs
Barcelona, Spain
puya@yahoo-inc.com

ABSTRACT

We present in this paper a novel approach for as-you-type top-k keyword search over social media. We adopt a natural "network-aware" interpretation for information relevance, by which information produced by users who are closer to the seeker is considered more relevant. In practice, this query model poses new challenges for effectiveness and efficiency in online search, even when a complete query is given as input in one keystroke. This is mainly because it requires a joint exploration of the social space and classic IR indexes such as inverted lists. We describe a memory-efficient and incremental prefix-based retrieval algorithm, which also exhibits an anytime behavior, allowing to output the most likely answer within any chosen running-time limit. We evaluate it through extensive experiments for several applications and search scenarios, including searching for posts in micro-blogging (Twitter and Tumblr), as well as searching for businesses based on reviews in Yelp. They show that our solution is effective in answering real-time as-you-type searches over social media.

Categories and Subject Descriptors

H.3.3 [**Information Search and Retrieval**]

General Terms

Algorithms, Theory

Keywords

As-you-type search; network-aware search; social networks; microblogging applications.

1. INTRODUCTION

Information access on the Web, and in particular on the social Web, is, by and large, based on top-k keyword search. While we witnessed significant improvements on how to answer keyword queries on the Web in the most effective way (e.g., by exploiting the Web structure, user and contextual models, user feedback, semantics, etc), answering information needs in social applications requires often a significant departure from socially-agnostic approaches, which generally assume that the data being queried is decoupled from the users querying it. The rationale is that social links can be exploited in order to obtain more relevant results, valid not only with respect to the queried keywords but also with respect to the social context of the user who issued them.

While progress has been made in recent years to support this novel, social and *network-aware*, query paradigm – especially towards efficiency and scalability – more remains to be done in order to address information needs in real applications. In particular, providing the most *accurate* answers while the user is typing her query, *almost instantaneously*, can be extremely beneficial, in order to enhance the user experience and to guide the retrieval process.

In this paper, we adapt and extend to the as-you-type search scenario – one by now supported in most search applications, including Web search – existing algorithms for top-k retrieval over social data. Our solution, called TOPKS-ASYT (for TOP-k Social-aware search AS-You-Type), builds on the generic network-aware search approach of [21, 25] and deals with three systemic changes:

1. *Prefix matching:* answers must be computed following a query interpretation by which the last term in the query sequence can match tag / keyword prefixes.
2. *Incremental computation:* answers must be computed *incrementally*, instead of starting a computation from scratch. For a query representing a sequence of terms (keywords) $Q = [t_1, \ldots, t_r]$, we can follow an approach that exploits what has already been computed in the query session so far, i.e., for the query $Q' = [t_1, \ldots, t_{r-1}, t'_r]$, with t'_r being a one character shorter prefix of the term t_r.
3. *Anytime output:* answers, albeit approximate, must be ready to be outputted at any time, and in particular after any given time lapse (e.g., $50 - 100ms$ is generally accepted as a reasonable latency for as-you-type search).

We consider a generic setting common to a plethora of social applications, where users produce unstructured content (keywords) in relation to items, an activity we simply refer to as *social tagging*. More precisely, our core application data can be modelled as follows: (i) users form a social network, which may represent relationships such as similarity, friendship, following, etc, (ii) items from a public pool of items (e.g., posts, tweets, videos, URLs, news, or even users) are "tagged" by users with keywords, through various interactions and data publishing scenarios, and (iii) users search for some k most relevant items by keywords.

We devise a novel index structure for TOPKS-ASYT, denoted CT-IL, which is a combination of tries and inverted lists. While basic trie structures have been used in as-you-type search scenarios in the literature (e.g., see [18] and the references therein), ranked

CIKM'15, October 19–23, 2015, Melbourne, VIC, Australia.
© 2015 ACM. ISBN 978-1-4503-3794-6/15/10 ...$15.00.
DOI: http://dx.doi.org/10.1145/2806416.2806435.

access over inverted lists requires an approach that performs ranked completion more efficiently. Therefore, we rely on a trie structure tailored for the problem at hand, offering a good space-time tradeoff, namely the *completion trie* of [11], which is an adaptation of the well-known Patricia trie using priority queues. This data structure is used as the access layer over the inverted lists, allowing us to read in sorted order of relevance the possible keyword completions and the items for which they occur. Importantly, we use the completion trie not only as an index component over the database, but also as a key internal component of our algorithm, in order to speed-up the incremental computation of results.

In this as-you-type search setting, it is necessary to serve in a short (fixed) lapse of time, with each keystroke and in social-aware manner, top-k results matching the query in its current form, i.e., the terms $t_1, \ldots, t_{r-1}$, and all possible completions of the term t_r. This must be ensured independently of the execution configuration, data features, or scale. This is why we ensure that our algorithms have also an *anytime* behaviour, being able to output the most likely result based on all the preliminary information obtained until a given time limit for the TOPKS-ASYT run is reached.

Our algorithmic solution is validated by extensive experiments for effectiveness, feasibility, and scalability. Based on data from the Twitter and Tumblr micro-blogging platforms, two of the most popular social applications today, we illustrate the usefulness of our techniques for keyword search for microblogs. Based on reviews from Yelp, we also experiment with keyword search for businesses.

The paper is organised as follows. In Section 2 we discuss the main related works. We lay out our data and query model in Section 3. Our technical contribution is described in Section 4 and is evaluated experimentally in Section 5. We conclude and discuss follow-up research in Section 6. For space reasons, more experiments and discussions can be found in a technical report [15].

2. RELATED WORK

Top-k retrieval algorithms, such as the Threshold Algorithm (TA) and the No Random Access algorithm (NRA) [8], which are *early-termination*, have been adapted to network-aware query models for social applications, following the idea of biasing results by the social links, first in [31, 25], and then in [21] (for more details on personalized search in social media we refer the interested readers to the references within [21, 25]).

As-you-type (or typeahead) search and query auto-completion are two of the most important features in search engines today, and could be seen as facets of the same paradigm: providing accurate feedback to queries on-the-fly, i.e., as they are being typed (possibly with each keystroke). In as-you-type search, feedback comes in the form of the most relevant answers for the query typed so far, allowing some terms (usually, the last one in the query sequence) to be prefix-matched. In query auto-completion, a list of the most relevant query candidates is to be shown for selection, possibly with results for them. We discuss each of these directions separately.

The problem we study in this paper, namely top-k as-you-type search for multiple keywords, has been considered recently in [18], in the absence of a social dimension of the data. There, the authors consider various adaptations of the well-known TA/NRA top-k algorithms of [8], even in the presence of minor typing errors (fuzzy search), based on standard tries. A similar fuzzy interpretation for full-text search was followed in [12], yet not in a top-k setting. The techniques of [17] rely on precomputed materialisation of top-k results, for values of k known in advance. In [2, 3], the goal is finding all the query completions leading to results as well as listing these results, based on inverted list and suffix array adaptations; however, the search requires a full computation and then ranking of the results. For structured data instead of full text, type-ahead search has been considered in [9] (XML) and in [16] (relational data).

Query auto-completion is the second main direction for instant response to queries in the typing, by which some top query completions are presented to the user (see for example [27, 26, 4] and the references therein). This is done either by following a predictive approach, or by pre-computing completion candidates and storing them in trie structures. Probably the best known example today is the one of Google's instant search, which provides both query predictions (in the search box) and results for the top prediction. Query suggestion goes one step further by proposing alternative queries, which are not necessarily completions of the input one (see for instance [29, 13]). In comparison, our work does not focus on queries as first-class citizens, but on instant results to incomplete queries.

Person (or people) search represents another facet of "social search", related to this paper, as the task of finding highly relevant persons for a given seeker and keywords. Usually, the approach used in this type of application is to identify the most relevant users, and then to filter them by the query keywords [24, 1]. In this area, [6] describes the main aspects of the Unicorn system for search over the Facebook graph, including a typeahead feature for user search. A similar search problem, finding a sub-graph of the social network that connects two or more persons, is considered under the instant search paradigm in [30].

Several space-efficient trie data structures for ranked (top-k) completion have been studied recently in [11], offering various space-time tradeoffs, and we rely in this paper on one of them, namely the completion trie. In the same spirit, data structures for the more general problem of substring matching for top-k retrieval have been considered in [10].

3. MODEL

We adopt in this paper a well-known generic model of social relevance for information, previously considered among others in [19, 21, 31, 25]. In short, the social bias in scores reflects the social proximity of the producers of content with respect to the seeker (the user issuing a search query), where proximity is obtained by some aggregation of shortest paths (in the social space) from the seeker towards relevant pieces of information.

We consider a social setting, in which we have a set of items (could be text documents, blog posts, tweets, URLs, photos, etc) $\mathcal{I} = \{i_1, \ldots, i_m\}$, each tagged with one or more distinct tags from a tagging vocabulary $\mathcal{T} = \{t_1, t_2, \ldots, t_l\}$, by users from $\mathcal{U} = \{u_1, \ldots, u_n\}$. We denote our set of unique triples by $Tagged(v, i, t)$, each such triple saying that a user v tagged the item i with tag t. $Tagged$ encodes many-to-many relationships: in particular, any given item can be tagged by multiple users , and any given user can tag multiple items. We also assume that a user will tag a given item with a given tag at most once.

We assume that users form a social network, modeled for our purposes as an undirected weighted graph $G = (\mathcal{U}, E, \sigma)$, where nodes are users and the σ function associates to each edge $e = (u_1, u_2)$ a value in $(0, 1]$, called *the proximity* (social) score between u_1 and u_2. Proximity may come either from explicit social signals (e.g., friendship links, follower/followee links), or from implicit social signals (e.g., tagging similarity), or from combinations thereof. (Alternatively, our core social data can be seen as a tripartite tagging graph, superposed with an existing friendship network.)

In this setting, the classic keyword search problem can be formulated as follows: given a seeker user s, a keyword query $Q = \{t_1, \ldots, t_r\}$ (a set of r distinct terms/keywords) and a result size k, the top-k keyword search problem is to compute the (possibly ranked) list of the k items having the highest scores with respect to

s and the query Q. We rely on the following model ingredients to identify query results.

We model by $score(i \mid s, t)$, for a seeker s, an item i, and one tag t, the relevance of that item for the given seeker and query term t. Generally, we assume

$$score(i \mid s,t) = h(fr(i \mid s,t)), \tag{1}$$

where $fr(i \mid s,t)$ is the *frequency* of item i for seeker s and tag t, and h is a positive monotone function (e.g., could be based on inverse term frequency, BM25, etc).

Given a query $Q = (t_1, \ldots, t_r)$, the overall score of i for seeker s and Q is simply obtained by summing the per-tag scores:

$$score(i \mid s, Q) = \sum_{t_j \in Q} score(i \mid s, t_j). \tag{2}$$

(Note that this reflects an OR semantics, where items that do not necessarily match all the query tags may still be selected.)

Social relevance model. In an exclusively social interpretation, we can explicitate the $fr(i \mid s,t)$ measure by the *social frequency* for seeker s, item i, and one tag t, denoted $sf(i \mid s,t)$. This measure adapts the classic term frequency (tf) measure to account for the seeker and its social proximity to relevant taggers. We consider that each tagger brings her own weight (proximity) to an item's score, and we define social frequency as follows:

$$sf(i \mid s,t) = \sum_{v \in \{v \mid Tagged(v,i,t)\}} \sigma(s,v). \tag{3}$$

Note that, under the frequency definition of Eq. (1), we would follow a ranking approach by which information that may match the query terms but does not score on the social dimension (i.e., is disconnected from the seeker) is deemed entirely irrelevant.

Network-aware relevance model. A more generic relevance model, which does not solely depend on social proximity but is network-aware, is one that takes into account textual relevance scores as well. For this, we denote by $tf(t,i)$ the *term frequency* of t in i, i.e., the number of times i was tagged with t, and $IL(t)$ is the inverted list of items for term t, ordered by term frequency.

The frequency score $fr(i \mid s,t)$ is defined as a linear combination of the previously described social relevance and the textual score, with $\alpha \in [0,1]$, as follows:

$$fr(i \mid s,t) = \alpha \times tf(t,i) + (1-\alpha) \times sf(i \mid s,t). \tag{4}$$

(This formula thus combines the global popularity of the item with the one among people close to the seeker.)

Remark. We believe that this simple model of triples for social data is the right abstraction for quite diverse types of social media. Consider Tumblr [5]: one broadcasts posts to followers and rebroadcasts incoming posts; when doing so, the re-post is often tagged with chosen tags or short descriptions (hashtags). We can thus see a post and all its re-posted instances as representing one informational item, which may be tagged with various tags by the users broadcasting it. Text appearing in a blog post can also be interpreted as tags, provided either by the original author or by those who modified it during subsequent re-posts; it can also be exploited to uncover implicit tags, based on the co-occurrence of tags and keywords in text. Furthermore, a post that is clicked-on in response to a Tumblr search query can be seen as being effectively tagged (relevant) for that query's terms. All this data has obviously a social nature: e.g., besides existing follower/followee links, one can even use similarity-based links as social proximity indicators.

EXAMPLE 1. *We depict in Figure 1 a social network and the tagging activity of its users, for a running example based on popular tags from the fashion domain in Tumblr. There, for seeker Alice,*

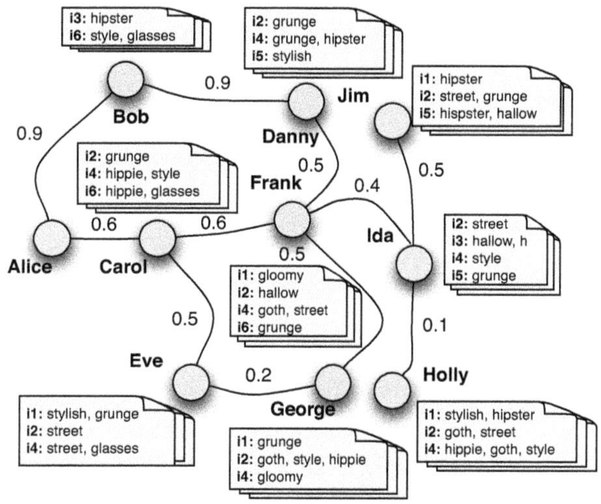

Figure 1: Running example: social proximity & tagging.

we have for instance, for $\alpha = 0.2$, $tf(glasses, i6) = 2$,

$$\begin{aligned} sf(i6 \mid Alice, glasses) &= \sigma(Alice, Bob) + \sigma(Alice, Carol) \\ &= 0.9 + 0.6 = 1.5 \\ fr(i6 \mid Alice, glasses) &= 0.8 \times 1.5 + 0.2 \times 2 \end{aligned}$$

Extended proximity. The model described so far takes into account only the immediate neighbourhood of the seeker (the users it connects to explicitly). In order to broaden the scope of the query and go beyond one's vicinity in the social network, we also account for users that are indirectly connected to the seeker, following a natural interpretation that user links and the query relevance they induce are (at least to some extent) transitive. To this end, we denote by σ^+ the resulting measure of *extended proximity*, which is to be computed from σ for any pair of users connected by at least one path in the network. Now, σ^+ can replace σ in the definition of social frequency Eq. (3).

For example, one natural way of obtaining extended proximity scores is by (i) multiplying the weights on a given path between the two users, and (ii) choosing the maximum value over all the possible paths. Another possible definition for σ^+ can rely on an aggregation that penalizes long paths, in a controllable way, via an *exponential decay* factor, in the style of the Katz measures for social proximity [14]. More generally, any aggregation function that is monotonically non-increasing over a path, can be used here. Under this monotonicity assumption, one can browse the network of users *on-the-fly* (at query time) and "sequentially", i.e., visiting them in the order of their proximity with the seeker.

Hereafter, when we talk about proximity, we refer to the extended one, and, for a given seeker s, the *proximity vector* of s is the list of users with non-zero proximity with respect to it, ordered decreasingly by proximity values (we stress that this vector is not necessarily known in advance).

EXAMPLE 2. *For example, for seeker Alice, when extended proximity between two users is defined as the maximal product of scores over paths linking them, the users ranked by proximity w.r.t. Alice are in order* $Bob : 0.9, Danny : 0.81, Carol : 0.6, Frank : 0.4, Eve : 0.3, George : 0.2, Ida : 0.16, Jim : 0.07, Holly : 0.01$.

The as-you-type search problem. We consider in this paper a more useful level of search service for practical purposes, in which queries are being answered *as they are typed*. Instead of assuming that the query terms are given all at once, a more

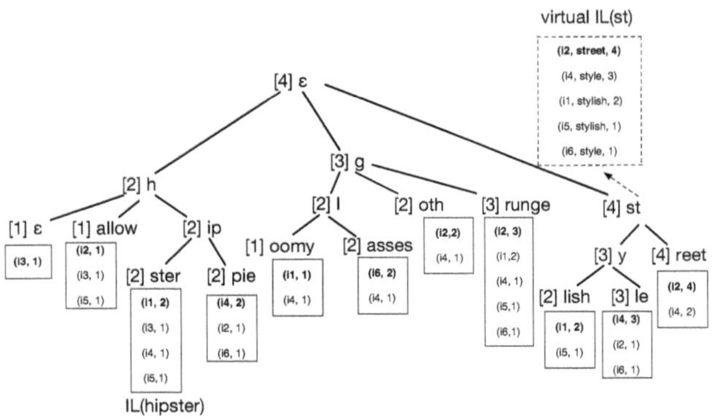

Figure 2: The CT-IL index.

realistic assumption is that input queries are sequences of terms $Q = [t_1, \dots, t_r]$, in which all terms but the last are to be matched exactly, whereas the last term t_r is to be interpreted as a tag potentially still in the writing, hence matched as a tag prefix.

We extend the query model in order to deal with tag prefixes p by defining an item's score for p as the maximal one over all possible completions of p:

$$sf(i \mid s, p) = \max_{t \in \{p's\ completions\}} sf(i \mid s, t) \quad (5)$$

$$tf(p, i) = \max_{t \in \{p's\ completions\}} tf(t, i) \quad (6)$$

(Note that when we compute the importance of an item, we might consider two different tag completions, for the social contribution and for the popularity one.)

EXAMPLE 3. *If Alice's query is* `hipster g`*, as* g *matches the tags* `gloomy`*,* `glasses`*,* `goth` *and* `grunge`*, we have*

$$\begin{aligned} sf(i4 \mid Alice, g) &= \max_{t \in \{g\ completions\}} sf(i4 \mid Alice, t) \\ &= \max[sf(i4 \mid Alice, \texttt{gloomy}), \\ &\quad sf(i4 \mid Alice, \texttt{glasses}), \\ &\quad sf(i4 \mid Alice, \texttt{grunge}), \\ &\quad sf(i4 \mid Alice, \texttt{goth})] \\ &= \max[0.2, 0.3, 0.81, 0.41] = 0.81 \end{aligned}$$

4. AS-YOU-TYPE SEARCH ALGORITHMS

We revisit here the network-aware retrieval approach of [21, 25], which belongs to the family of early termination top-k algorithms known as *threshold algorithms*, of which [8]'s TA (the Threshold Algorithm) and NRA (No Random-access Algorithm) are well-known examples.

In the social-aware retrieval setting, when social proximity determines relevance, the data exploration must jointly consider the network (starting from the seeker and visiting users in descending proximity order), the per-user/personal tagging spaces, and all available socially-agnostic index structures such as inverted lists. It is thus important for efficiency to explore the social network by order of relevance/proximity to the seeker, as to access all the necessary index structures, in a *sequential manner* as much as possible. We favor such an approach here, instead of an *incomplete* "one dimension at a time" one, which would first rely on one dimension to identify a set of candidate items, and then use the scores for the other dimension to re-rank or filter out some of the candidates.

4.1 Non-incremental algorithm

We first describe the TOPKS-ASYT approach for exclusively social relevance ($\alpha = 0$) and without incremental computation, namely when the full sequence of terms is given in one keystroke, with the last term possibly a prefix, as $Q = [t_1, \dots, t_r]$. We follow an early-termination approach that is "user-at-a-time": its main loop step visits a new user and the items that were tagged by her with query terms. Algorithm 1 gives the flow of TOPKS-ASYT.

Main inputs. For each user u and tag t, we assume a precomputed selection over the *Tagged* relation, giving the items tagged by u with t; we call these the *personal spaces* (in short, p-spaces). No particular order is assumed for the items appearing in a user list.

We also assume that, for each tag t, we have an inverted list $IL(t)$ giving the items i tagged by it, along with their term frequencies $tf(t, i)$[1], ordered descending by them. The lists can be seen as unpersonalized indexes. A completion trie over the set of tags represents the access layer to these lists. As in Patricia tries, a node can represent more than one character, and the scores corresponding to the heads of the lists are used for ranked completion: each leaf has the score of the current entry in the corresponding inverted list, and each internal node has the maximal score over its children (see example below). This index structure is denoted hereafter the CT-IL index.

EXAMPLE 4 (CT-IL INDEX). *We give in Figure 2 an illustration of the main components of* CT-IL*, for our running example. Each of the tags has below it the inverted list (the one of the* `hippie` *tag is explicitly indicated). The cursor positions in the lists are in bold. By storing the maximal score at each node (in brackets in Figure 2), the best (scoring) completions of a given prefix can be found by using a priority queue, which is initialized with the highest node matching that prefix. With each pop operation, either we get a completion of the prefix, or we advance towards one, and we insert in the queue the children of the popped node.*

For comparison, we also illustrate in Figure 3 the CT-IL *index that would allow us to process efficiently Alice's top-k queries, without the need to resort to accesses in social network and p-spaces. Obviously, building such an index for each potential seeker would not be feasible.*

While leaf nodes in the trie correspond to concrete inverted lists, we can also see each internal node of the trie and the corresponding keyword prefix as described by a "virtual inverted list", i.e., the ranked union of all inverted lists below that node. As defined in Eq. (6), (5), for such a union, for an item appearing in entries of several of the unioned lists, we keep only the highest-scoring entry. In particular, for the term t_r of the query, by $IL(t_r)$ we refer to the virtual inverted list corresponding to this tag prefix. There is one notable difference between the concrete inverted lists and the virtual ones: in the former, entries can be seen (and stored) as pairs $(item, score)$ (the tag being implied); in the latter, entries must be the form $(item, tag, score)$, since different tags (completions) may appear in such a list.

For each $t \in \{t_1, \dots, t_r\}$, we denote by $top\_item(t)$ the item present at the current (unconsumed) position of $IL(t)$, we use $top\_tf(t)$ as short notation for the term frequency associated with this item, and, for $IL(t_r)$, we also denote by $top\_tag(t_r)$ the t_r completion in the current entry.

EXAMPLE 5 (VIRTUAL LISTS). *The virtual inverted list for the prefix* `st` *is given in Fig. 2. The* $top\_tag(\texttt{st})$ *is* `street`*, for* $top\_item(\texttt{st})$ *being* $i2$*, for its entry scored* 4 *dominates the one scored only* 2*, hence with a* $top\_tf(\texttt{st})$ *of* 4*. A similar one, for the "personalized"* CT-IL *index for seeker Alice is given in Fig. 3.*

[1]Even when $\alpha = 0$, although social frequency does not depend directly on tf scores, we will exploit the inverted lists and the tf scores by which they are ordered, to better estimate score bounds.

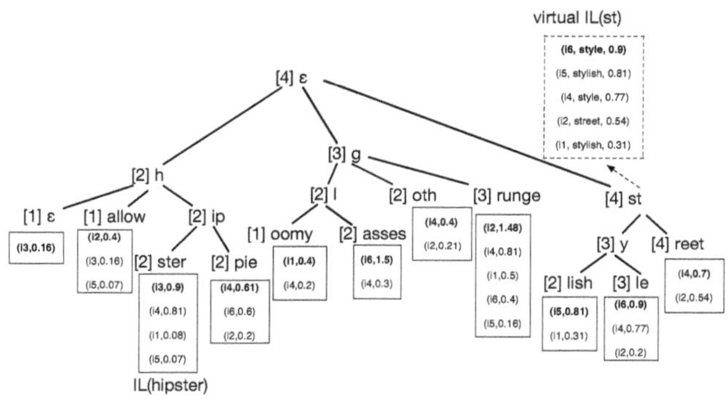

Figure 3: Alice's personalized CT-IL index.

Candidate buffers. For each tag $t \in \{t_1, \ldots, t_{r-1}\}$, we keep a list D_t of candidate items i, along with a sound score range: a lower-bound and an upper-bound for $sf(i \mid s, t)$ (to be explained hereafter). Similarly, in the case of t_r, for each completion t of t_r already encountered during the query execution in p-spaces (i.e., by triples (u, i, t) read in some u's p-space), we record in a D_t list the candidate items and their score ranges. Candidates in these D-buffers are sorted in descending order by their score lower-bounds.

An item becomes candidate and is included in D-buffers only when it is first met in a $Tagged$ triple matching a query term.

For uniformity of treatment, a special item $*$ denotes all the yet unseen items, and it implicitly appears in each of the D-lists; note that, in a given D_t buffer, $*$ represents both items which are not yet candidates, but also candidate items which may already be candidates but appear only in other D-buffers (for tags other than t).

Main algorithmic components. When accessing the CT-IL index, inverted list entries are consumed in some $IL(t)$ only when the items they refer to are candidates (they appear in at least one $D_{t'}$ buffer, which may not necessarily be D_t itself)[2]. We keep in lists called CIL_t (for *consumed IL entries*) the items read (hence known candidates) in the inverted lists (virtual or concrete), for t being either in $\{t_1, \ldots, t_{r-1}\}$ or a completion of t_r for which a triple $(item, t, score)$ was read in the virtual list of t_r. We also record by the set C all t_r completions encountered so far in p-spaces. We stress that the t_r completions encountered in p-spaces may not necessarily coincide with those encountered in $IL(t_r)$.

For each t being either in $\{t_1, \ldots, t_{r-1}\}$ or a completion of t_r already in C, by $unseen\_users(i, t)$ we denote the maximal number of yet unvisited users who may have tagged item i with tag t. This number is initially set to the maximal possible term frequency of t over all items. $unseen\_users(i, t)$ then reflects at any moment during the run of the algorithm the difference between the number of taggers of i with t already visited and one of either

- the value $tf(t, i)$, if this term frequency has been read already by accessing CT-IL, or otherwise
- the value $top\_tf(t)$, if $t \in \{t_1, \ldots, t_{r-1}\}$, or
- the value $top\_tf(t_r)$, if t is instead a completion of t_r.

During the algorithm's run, for known candidates i of some D_t, we accumulate in $sf(i \mid s, t)$ the social score (initially set to 0).

Each time we visit a user u having a triple (u, i, t) in her p-space (Algorithm 2), we can

1. update $sf(i \mid s, t)$ by adding $\sigma^+(s, u)$ to it, and
2. decrement $unseen\_users(i, t)$; when this value reaches 0, the social frequency value $sf(i \mid s, t)$ is final.

[2]The rationale is that our algorithm does not make any "wild guesses", avoiding reads that may prove to be irrelevant and thus leading to sub-optimal performance.

The maximal proximity score of yet to be visited users is denoted $max\_proximity$. With this proximity bound, a sound score range for candidates i in D_t buffers is computed and maintained as

- a score upper-bound (maximal score) $\text{MAXSCORE}(i \mid s, t)$, by $max\_proximity \times unseen\_users(i, t) + sf(i \mid s, t)$.
- a score lower-bound (minimal score), $\text{MINSCORE}(i \mid s, t)$, by assuming that the current social frequency $sf(i \mid s, t)$ is the final one (put otherwise, all remaining taggers u of i with t, which are yet to be encountered, have $\sigma^+(s, u) = 0$).

The interest of consuming the inverted list entries (Algorithm 3) in CT-IL, whenever top items become candidates, is to keep as accurate as possible the worst-case estimation on the number of unseen taggers. Indeed, when such a tuple $(i, t, score)$ is accessed, we can do some adjustments on score estimates:

1. if $i \in D_t$, we can mark the number of unseen taggers of i with t as no longer an estimate but an *exact* value; from this point on, the number of unseen users will only change whenever new users who tagged i with t are visited,
2. by advancing to the next best item in $IL(t)$, for $t \in \{t_1, \ldots, t_{r-1}\}$, we can refine the $unseen\_users(i', t)$ estimates for all candidate items i' for which the exact number of users who tagged them with t is yet unknown,
3. by advancing to the next best item in $IL(t_r)$, with some $t = top\_tag(t_r)$ completion of t_r, if $t \in C$, we can refine the estimates $unseen\_users(i', t)$ for all candidate items $i' \in D_t$ for which the exact number of users who tagged them with t is yet unknown.

Termination condition. From the per-tag D_t buffers, we can infer lower-bounds on the global score w.r.t. Q for a candidate item (as defined in Eq. (2)) by summing up its score lower-bounds from $D_{t_1}, \ldots, D_{t_{r-1}}$ and its maximal score lower-bound across all D_t lists, for completions t of t_r. Similarly, we can infer an upper-bound on the global score w.r.t. Q by summing up score upper-bounds from $D_{t_1}, \ldots, D_{t_{r-1}}$ and the maximal upper-bound across all D_t lists, for completions t.

After sorting the candidate items (the wildcard item included) by their global score lower-bounds, TOPKS-ASYT can terminate whenever (i) the wildcard item is not among the top-k ones, and (ii) the score upper-bounds of items not among the top-k ones are less than the score lower-bound of the kth item in this ordering (we know that the top-k can no longer change).

As in [21], it can be shown that TOPKS-ASYT visits users who may be relevant for the query in decreasing proximity order and, importantly, that it visits as few users as possible (it is *instance optimal* for this aspect, in the case of exclusively social relevance).

EXAMPLE 6. *Revisiting our running example, let us assume Alice requires the top-2 items for the query* $Q = [\texttt{style}, \texttt{gl}]$ *($\alpha = 0$). The first data access steps of* TOPKS-ASYT *are as follows: at the first execution of the main loop step, we visit Bob, get his p-space, adding i6 both to the* $D_{\texttt{style}}$ *buffer and to a* $D_{\texttt{glasses}}$ *one. There may be at most two other taggers of i6 with* `style` *($unseen\_users(i6, \texttt{style})$), and at most one other tagger of i6 with* `glasses` *($unseen\_users(i6, \texttt{glasses})$). No reading is done in* $IL(\texttt{style})$*, as its current entry gives the non-candidate item i4, but we can advance with one pop in the virtual list of the* `gl` *prefix, for candidate item i6. This clarifies that there is* exactly *one other tagger with* `glasses` *for i6. After this read in the virtual list of* `gl`*, we have* $top\_item(\texttt{gl}) = i1$ *(if we assume that items are also ordered by their ids). At this point* $max\_proximity$

Algorithm 1 TOPKS-ASYT (non-incremental, for $\alpha = 0$)

```
Require: seeker s, query Q = (t_1, ..., t_r)
1: for all users u do
2:     σ+(s, u) = −∞
3: end for
4: for all tags t ∈ {t_1, ..., t_{r−1}} do
5:     sf(i | s, t) = 0
6:     D_t = ∅, CIL_t = ∅
7:     set IL(t) position on first entry
8: end for
9: set IL(t_r) position on first entry
10: σ+(s, s) = 0;
11: C = ∅ (t_r completions)
12: H ← priority queue on users; init. {s}, computed on-the-fly
13: while H ≠ ∅ do
14:     u=EXTRACT_MAX(H);
15:     PROCESS_P_SPACE(u);
16:     PROCESS_CT-IL;
17:     if termination condition then
18:         break
19:     end if
20: end while
21: return top-k items
```

Algorithm 2 SUBROUTINE PROCESS_P_SPACE(u)

```
for all tags t ∈ {t_1, ..., t_{r−1}}, triples Tagged(u, i, t) do
    if i ∉ D_t then
        add i to D_t
        sf(i | s, t) ← 0
        unseen_users(i, t) ← top_tf(t)
    end if
    unseen_users(i, t) ← unseen_users(i, t) − 1
    sf(i | s, t) ← sf(i | s, t) + σ+(s, u)
end for
for all tags t completions of t_r, triples Tagged(u, i, t) do
    if t ∉ C then
        add t to C, D_t = ∅
    end if
    if i ∉ D_t then
        add i to D_t
        sf(i | s, t) ← 0
        unseen_users(i, t) ← top_tf(t)
    end if
    unseen_users(i, t) ← unseen_users(i, t) − 1
    sf(i | s, t) ← sf(i | s, t) + σ+(s, u)
end for
```

is 0.81. *Therefore, we have*

$$\begin{aligned} \text{MAXSCORE}(i6 \mid Alice, \texttt{style}) &= 0.81 \times 2 + 0.9 \\ \text{MINSCORE}(i6 \mid Alice, \texttt{style}) &= 0.9 \\ \text{MAXSCORE}(i6 \mid Alice, \texttt{glasses}) &= 0.81 \times 1 + 0.9 \\ \text{MINSCORE}(i6 \mid Alice, \texttt{glasses}) &= 0.9 \end{aligned}$$

We thus have that $score(i6|Alice, Q)$ *is between* 1.8 *and* 4.23.

At the second execution of the main loop step, we visit Danny, whose p-space does not contain relevant items for Q. A side-effect of this step is that $max\_proximity$ *becomes* 0.6, *affecting the upper-bound scores above:* $score(i6 \mid Alice, Q)$ *can now be estimated between* 1.8 *and* 3.6.

At the third execution of the main loop step, we visit $Carol$, *and find the relevant p-space entries for* $i4$ *(with tag* `style`*) and* $i6$ *(with tag* `glasses`*). Now* $max\_proximity$ *becomes* 0.4. *Also, we can advance with one pop in the inverted list of* `style`*. This clarifies that there are* exactly 2 *other taggers with* `style` *on* $i4$, *and now we have* $top\_item(\texttt{gl}) = i1$ *and* $top\_item(\texttt{style}) =$ 2. *This makes* $score(i6 \mid Alice, Q)$ *to be known precisely at* 2.4, $score(i4 \mid Alice, Q)$ *to be estimated between* 0.6 *and* $0.6 + 3 \times 0.4 = 1.8$, *and* $score(* \mid Alice, Q)$ *is at most* 0.8.

Algorithm 3 SUBROUTINE PROCESS_CT-IL

```
while ∃t ∈ Q s.t. i = top_item(t) ∈ ⋃_x D_x do
    if t ≠ t_r then
        tf(t, i) ← top_tf(t) (t's frequency in i is now known)
        advance IL(t) one position
        Δ ← tf(t, i) − top_tf(t) (the top_tf drop)
        add i to CIL_t
        for all items i' ∈ D_t \ CIL_t do
            unseen_users(i', t) ← unseen_users(i', t) − Δ
        end for
    end if
    if t = t_r then
        t' ← top_tag(t_r) (some t_r completion t')
        tf(t', i) ← top_tf(t_r) (t''s frequency in i known)
        advance IL(t_r) one position
        Δ ← tf(t', i) − top_tf(t_r) (the top_tf drop)
        add i to CIL_t' or set CIL_t' to {i} if previously empty
        for all t'' ∈ C and items i' ∈ D_t'' \ CIL_t'' do
            unseen_users(i', t'') ← unseen_users(i', t'') − Δ
        end for
    end if
end while
```

4.2 Adaptations for the network-aware case

Due to lack of space, we only sketch in this section the necessary extensions to Algorithm 1 for arbitrary α values, hence for any textual-social relevance balance. When $\alpha \in [0, 1]$, at each iteration, the algorithm can alternate between two possible execution branches: the *social branch* (the one detailed in Algorithm 1) and a *textual branch*, which is a direct adaptation of NRA over the CT-IL structure, reading in parallel in all the query term lists (concrete or virtual). Now, items can become candidates even without being encountered in p-spaces, when read in inverted lists during an execution of the textual branch. As before, each read from CT-IL is associated with updates on score estimates such as $unseen\_users$. For a given item i and tag t, the maximal possible fr-score can be obtained by adding to the previously seen maximal possible sf-score (weighted now by $1-\alpha$) the maximal possible value of $tf(t, i)$; the latter may be known (if read in CT-IL), or estimated as $top\_tf(t)$ otherwise. Symmetrically, the minimal possible value for $tf(t, i)$ is used for lower bounds; if not known, this can be estimated as the number of visited users who tagged i with t.

The choice between the two possible execution branches can rely on heuristics which estimate their utility w.r.t approaching the final result. Two such heuristics are explained in [21, 25], guiding this choice either by estimating the maximum potential score of each branch, or by choosing the branch that is the most likely to refine the score of the item outside the current top-k which has the highest estimated score (a choice that is likely to advance the run of the algorithm closer to termination).

4.3 Adaptations for incremental computation

We extended the approach described so far to perform the as-you-type computation *incrementally*, as follows:

1. when a new keyword is initiated (i.e., t_r is one character long), we take the following steps in order:
   (a) purge all D_t buffers for $t \in C$, except for $D_{t_{r-1}}$ (t_{r-1} is no longer a potential prefix, but a complete term),
   (b) reinitialize C to the empty set,
   (c) purge all CIL_t buffers for $t \notin \{t_1, \ldots, t_{r-1}\}$,
   (d) reinitialize the network exploration (the queue H) to start from the seeker, in order to visit again p-spaces looking for triples for the new prefix, t_r. (This amounts to the following changes in Algorithm 1: among its initialisation steps (1-12), the steps (4-8) are removed, and new steps for points (a) and (c) above are added.)

2. when the current t_r is augmented with one additional character (so t_r is at least two characters long), we take the following steps in order:
   (a) purge D_t buffers for $t \in C$ s.t. t is not a t_r completion
   (b) remove from C all ts which aren't completions for t_r,
   (c) purge all CIL_t buffers for $t \notin \{t_1, \ldots t_{r-1}\} \cup C$,
   (d) resume the network exploration.

   (This amounts to the following changes in Algorithm 1: among its initialisation steps (1-12), the steps (4-8) and (10-12) are removed, and new steps for points (a), (b), and (c) above are added.)

Note that, in the latter case, we can efficiently do the filtering operations by relying on a simple trie structure for directly accessing the data structures (D-lists, CIL-lists, the C subset) that remain valid for the new prefix.

4.4 Finding the most likely top-k anytime

As argued before, we also see as crucial for the as-you-type search approach to have an *anytime* behaviour, in the following sense: it should explore the social space and existing data structures / indexes in the most efficient manner, maintaining the candidate buffers, until a time limit is met or an external event occurs. Indeed, in practice, we can expect that *most searches will not meet the termination condition within the imposed time limit*; when this happens, we must output the most likely top-k result. In our case, this can be easily obtained from the intermediate result at any step in the TOPKS-ASYT computation, in particular the D-buffers, e.g., by adapting the more general SR-TA procedure (for Score-Ranges Threshold Algorithm) of [20], especially for the fact that we may have many D-buffers (if C is large). This calls for a different organization, which is "per-item" instead of "per-tag", for information in buffers D_t for $t \in C$. In short, for each item i, we can keep in a trie structure the t_r completions t for which triples $(user, i, t)$ have been encountered in p-spaces so far, with each leaf providing the score range for that item-tag pair. Further details are omitted here.

5. EXPERIMENTS

We evaluate in this section the effectiveness, scalability and efficiency of the TOPKS-ASYT algorithm. We used a Java implementation of our algorithms, on a low-end Intel Core i7 Linux machine with 16GB of RAM. We performed our experiments in an all-in-memory setting, for datasets of medium size (10-30 millions of tagging triples). We describe first the applications and datasets we used for evaluation.

5.1 Datasets

We used several popular social media platforms, namely Twitter, Tumblr, and Yelp, from which we built corresponding sets of (user, item, tag) triples. Table 1 reports some statistics about each dataset.

	Twitter	Tumblr	Yelp
Number of unique users	$458,117$	$612,425$	$29,293$
Number of unique items	$1.6M$	$1.4M$	$18,149$
Number of unique tags	$550,157$	$2.3M$	$177,286$
Number of triples	$13.9M$	$11.3M$	$30.3M$
Avg number of tags per item	8.4	7.9	685.7
Avg tag length	13.1	13.0	6.5

Table 1: Statistics on the datasets we used in our experiments.

Twitter. We used a collection of tweets extracted during Aug. 2012. As described in Section 3, we see each tweet and its re-tweet instances as one item, and the authors of the tweets/re-tweets as its taggers. We include both the text and the hashtags as tags.

Tumblr. We extracted a collection of Tumblr posts from Oct.-Nov. 2014, following the same interpretation on posts, taggers, and tags as in Twitter. Among the 6 different types of posts within Tumblr, we selected only the *default* type, which can contain text plus images. Moreover, in the case of Tumblr, we were able to access the follower-followee network and thus we extracted the induced follower-followee network for the selected taggers.

Yelp. Lastly, we considered a publicly available Yelp dataset, containing reviews for businesses and the induced follower-followee network.[3] In this case, in order to build the triples, we considered the business (e.g., restaurant) as the item, the author of the review as the tagger, and the keywords appearing in the review as the tags.

On Twitter and Tumblr datasets, in order to enrich the set of keywords associated to an item, we also expand each tag by the at most 5 most common keywords associated with it by a given user, i.e., by the tag-keyword co-occurrence. Finally, from the resulting sets of triples, we removed those corresponding to (i) items that were not tagged by at least two users, or (ii) users who did not tag at least two items.

To complete the data setting for our algorithm, we then constructed the user-to-user weighted networks that are exploited in the social-aware search. For this, we first used the underlying social network (when available). Specifically, for each user pair in Tumblr or Yelp, we computed the Dice coefficient corresponding to the common neighbors in the social network. To also study situation when such a network may not be available (as for Twitter), exploiting a thematic proximity instead of a social one, we built two other kinds of user similarity networks, based on the Dice coefficient over either (i) the item-tag pairs of the two users, or (ii) the tags of the two users. We considered the filtering of "noise" links, weighted below a given threshold (as discussed in Section 5.2).

5.2 Experimental results: effectiveness

We present in this section the results we obtained in our experiments for effectiveness, or "prediction power", with the purpose of validating the underlying as-you-type query model and the feasibility of our approach. In this framework, for all the data configurations we considered for effectiveness purposes, we imposed wall-clock time thresholds of $50ms$ per keystroke, which we see as appropriate for an interactive search experience.

To measure effectiveness, we followed an assumption used in recent literature, e.g. in [23, 21], namely that a user is likely to find his items – belonging to him or re-published by him – more interesting than random items from other users. For testing effectiveness, we randomly select triples (u,i,t) from each dataset. For each selected triple, we consider u as the seeker and t as the keyword issued by this user. The aim is to "get back" item i through search. The as-you-type scenario is simulated by considering that the user issues t one letter at a time. Note that an item may be retrieved back only if at least one user connected to the seeker tagged it. We picked randomly 800 such triples (we denote this selection as the set D), for tags having at least three letters. For each individual measurement, we gave as input a triple *(user, item, tag)* to be tested (after removing it from the dataset), and then we observed the ranking of *item* when *user* issues a query that is a prefix of *tag*.

Note that we tested effectiveness using single-word search for Twitter and Tumblr. On the contrary, for Yelp, due to its distinct features of having many triples per user, we did two-word search: given a query $q = (w_1, w_2)$, we first filtered items tagged by w_1, we then processed the remaining triples with query w_2 in the same manner as we did for Twitter and Tumblr.

[3]http://www.yelp.com/dataset_challenge

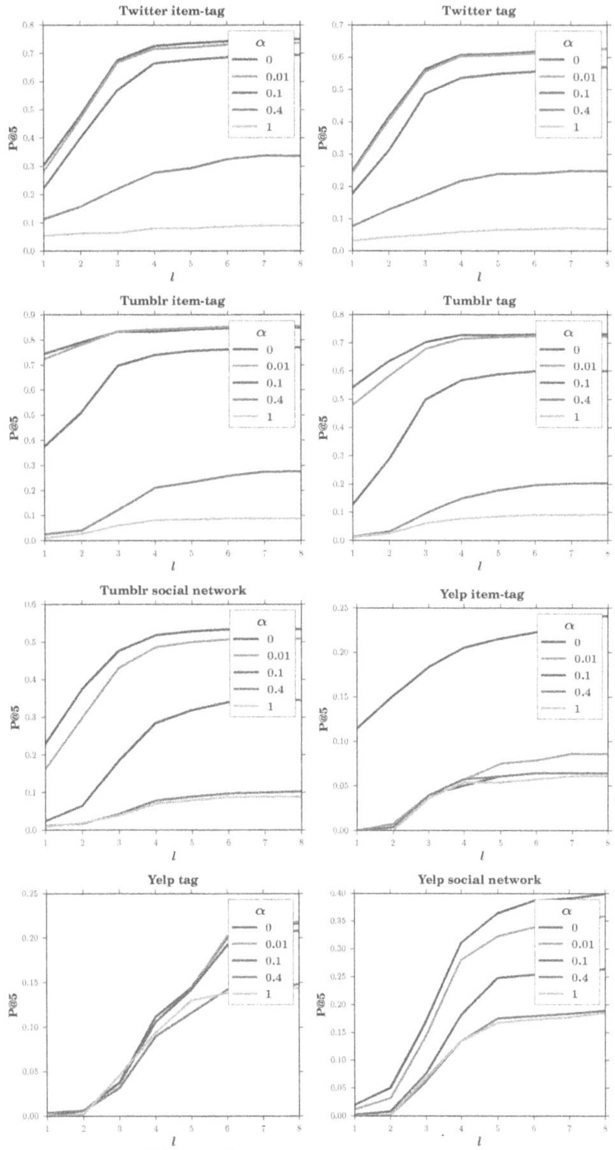

Figure 4: Impact of α on precision.

We define the precision $P@k$ for our selected set D as

$$P@k = \frac{\#\{triple \mid ranking < k, triple \in D\}}{\#D}$$

Since this precision can be seen as a function of the main parameters of our system, our goal was to understand how it is influenced by these parameters. We describe below the different parameters we took into account here.

- l, length of the prefix in the query (number of characters).
- θ, the threshold used to filter similarity links keeping only those having a score above.
- α, the social bias ($\alpha = 0$ for exclusively social score, $\alpha = 1$ for exclusively textual score).
- $\eta_i(u)$, the number of items tagged by user u, a user activeness indicator (for simplicity, hereafter referred to as η_i).
- $\eta_u(i)$, number of users who tagged item i, an item popularity indicator (η_u).

We present next the results we obtained for this experiment. (For space reasons, we only report here on $P@5$, but we performed

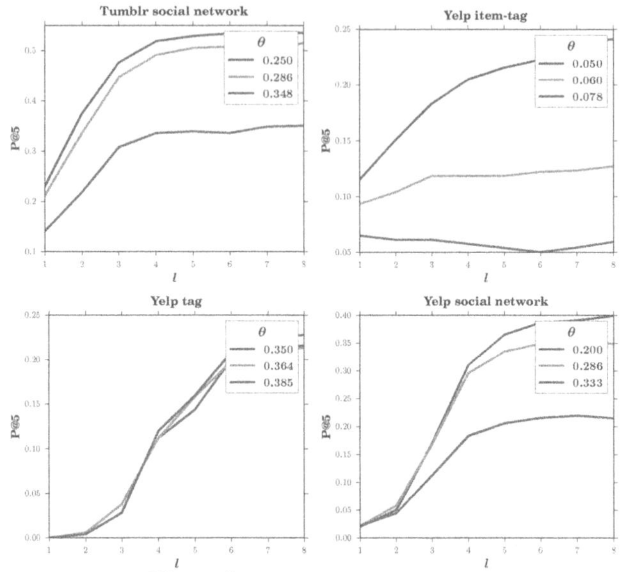

Figure 5: Impact of θ on precision.

test with $P@1$ and $P@20$ as well, which showcase similar evolution and improvement ratios, in the case of the latter, most often reaching precision levels of around 0.8-0.9.) When parameters are not variables of a figure, they take the following default values: $\alpha = 0$ (fully social bias), θ is assigned the lowest value of the tested dataset, η_i and η_u are associated to active users and popular items ($\eta_i \geq 3$ and $\eta_u \geq 10$).

Impact of α. As shown in Figure 4, α can have a major impact on precision. With a fully social bias ($\alpha = 0$), we obtained the best results for the three datasets and all the available similarity networks. Moreover, typing new characters to complete the prefix increases the precision. However, the evolution for $\alpha = 0$ can be quite slow, with the Tumblr or Yelp item-tag similarity network for witness. In this case, one likely reason is that these networks are quite rich in information, and the neighbors of the seeker are very likely to have the searched item, with the right tag, due to the way this network was built. This can also explain why the precision for the item-tag networks is higher in the case of Tumblr than those for tag and social similarity networks. The precision for the social similarity network is the lowest for Tumblr, while in the case of Yelp dataset the best results are obtained using the social network. Indeed, the tag and item-tag networks were built based on the same content we were testing on, whereas the social similarity network only uses the links between users to infer distances between them. Yelp exhibits lower precision levels overall, unsurprisingly, since it is a much denser dataset (number of triples per user).

Interestingly and supporting our thesis for social bias, we obtain good precisions levels with such networks of similarity in social links (the highest in the case of Yelp). For example, in the case of Tumblr, we can reach $P@5$ of around 0.82 for the item-tag similarity network, 0.7 for the tag one, and still 0.5 for the social one. This indicates that we can indeed find relevant information using a content-agnostic network using TOPKS-ASYT. Importantly, it also indicates that we can always search with the same social similarity network, even when the content evolves rather rapidly, with the same precision guarantees.

Impact of θ. In Figure 5, we can observe the impact of θ on the quality of results. We mention that the two highest θ values lead to 33% and 66% cuts on the total number of edges obtained with

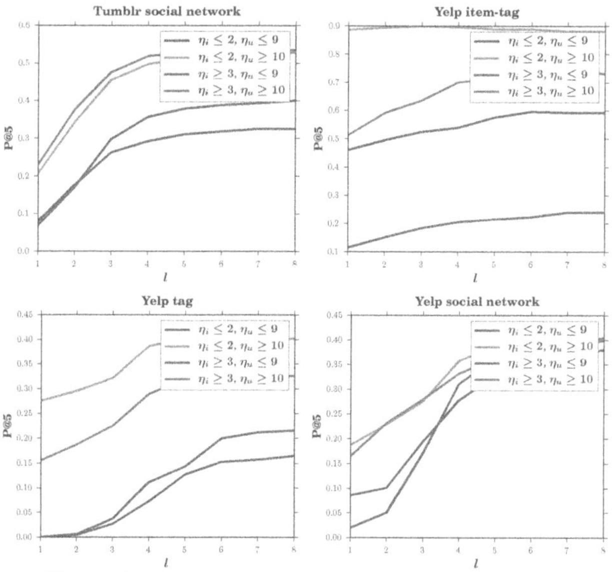

Figure 6: Precision for various types of users and items.

the lowest θ value. Unsurprisingly, removing connections between users decreases the precision. When using the similarity network filtered by the lowest θ value, the seeker is almost always connected to the network's largest connected component, and we can visit many users to retrieve back the targeted item. With higher θ values, the connectivity for certain seekers we tested with is broken, making some of the tested items unreachable.

Impact of popularity / activeness. We show in Figure 6 the effects of item popularity and user activity for Yelp and Tumblr. For all similarity networks, the precision is better for popular items (high η_u). This is to be expected, as a popular item is more likely to be found when visiting the graph, as it is expected that it will score high since it has many taggers. Along with item popularity, we can observe that user activeness has a different effect in both content-based and the social similarity networks. Active users yield a better precision score when similarity comes from social links, whereas it is the opposite with content-based similarity networks. Reasonably, retrieving back an item for a non-active seeker in a content-based network is easier since his similarity with neighbours is stronger (Dice coefficient computed on less content).

5.3 Experimental results: efficiency&scalability

In Figure 7, we display the evolution of NDCG@20 vs. time, for the densest dataset (Yelp), for different α values (where α is normalized to have similar social and textual scores in average). The NDCG is computed w.r.t. the exact top-k, that would be obtained running the algorithm on the entire similarity graph. This measure is an important indicator for the feasibility of social-aware as-you-type search, illustrating the accuracy levels reached under "typing latency", even when the termination conditions are not met. In this plot, we fixed the prefix length size to $l = 4$. The left plot is when a user searches with a random tag (not necessarily used by her previously), while the right plot follows the same selection methodology as in Section 5.2. Importantly, with α corresponding to an exclusively social or textual relevance, we reach the exact top-k faster than when combining these two contributions ($\alpha = 0.5$). Note also that this trend holds even when the user searches with random tags.

In Figure 8, similarly to the previous case, we show the evolution of NDCG@20 vs. time in Yelp, for different prefix lengths. (the left plot is for random tags). Results shows that with lower values of l we need more time to identify the right top-k. The reason

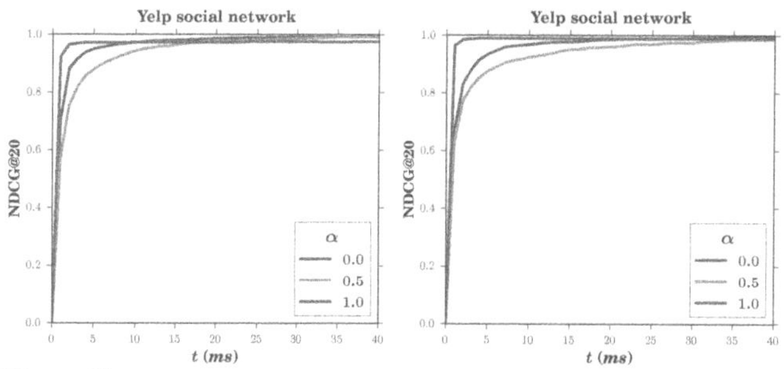

Figure 7: Impact of α on NDCG vs time for random search (left) and personal search (right).

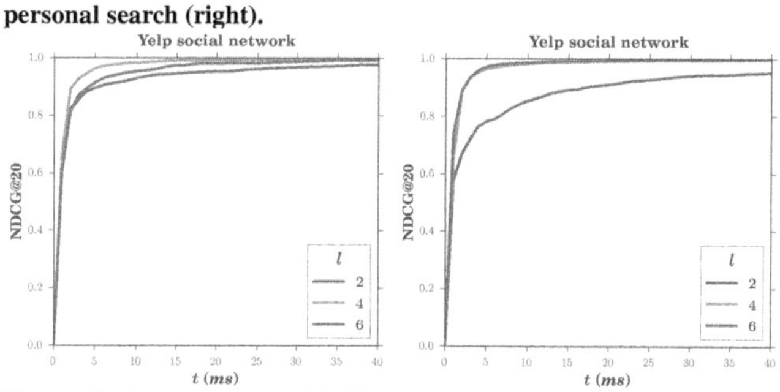

Figure 8: Impact of l on NDCG vs time for random search (left) and personal search (right).

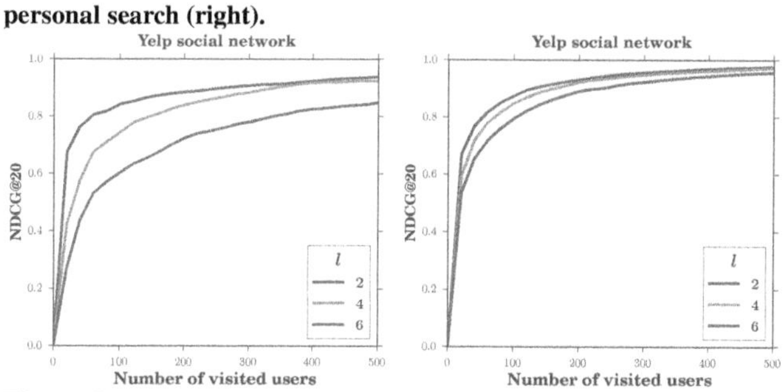

Figure 9: Impact of l on NDCG vs number of visited users for random search (left) and personal search (right).

is that shorter prefixes can have many potential (matching) items, therefore the item discrimination process evolves more slowly.

In Figure 9 we show the evolution of NDCG@20 when visiting a fixed number number of users. We show results for $l = 2, 4, 6$. As expected, the more users we visit the higher NDCG we reach. For longer prefixes, it is necessary to visit more users. For instance, when $l = 6$, after visiting 500 users, we reach an NDCG of 0.8 while for $l = 2$ the NDCG after 500 visits is 0.9.

Finally, in the experiment illustrated in Figure 10 we observed the time to reach the exact top-k for different dataset sizes. For that, we partitioned the Yelp triples sorted by time into five consecutive (20%) chunks. For each dataset we perform searches using prefixes of $l = 2, 3, 4, 5$. While the time to reach the exact top-k increases with bigger datasets and shorter prefixes, the algorithm scales adequately when l is more than 2. For instance, for $l = 3$, the time to reach the result over the complete dataset is just twice the time when considering only 20% of this dataset.

Main-memory vs. secondary memory considerations. We emphasize here that we performed our experiments in an all-in-memory setting, for datasets of medium size (tens of millions of tagging triples), in which the advantages of our approach may not be entirely observed. In practice, in real, large-scale applications such as Tumblr, one can no longer assume a direct and cheap access to p-spaces and inverted lists, even though some data dimensions such as the user network and the top levels of CT-IL – e.g., the trie

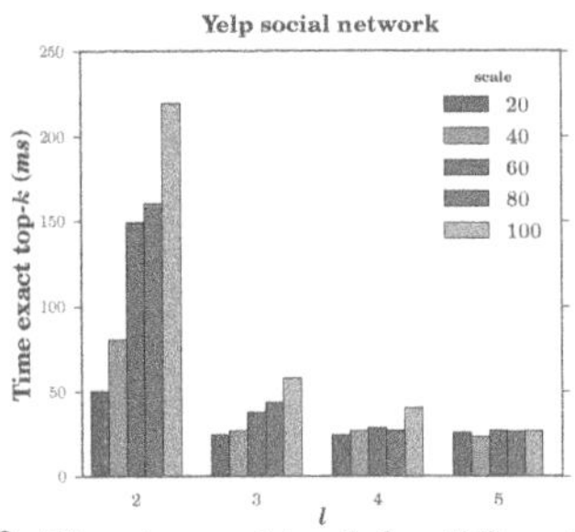

Figure 10: Time to exact top-k for different dataset sizes.

layer and possibly prefixes of the inverted lists – could still reside in main memory. In practice, with each visited user, the search might require a random access for her personal space, hence the interest for the sequential, user-at-a-time approach. Even when p-spaces may reside on disk, our last experiment shows that by retrieving a small number of them, less than 100, we can reach good precision levels; depending on disk latency, serving results in, for example, under $100ms$ seems within reach. One way to further alleviate such costs may be to cluster users having similar proximity vectors, and choose the layout of p-spaces on disk based on such clusters; this is an approach we intend to evaluate in the future, at larger scale.

6. CONCLUSION

We study in this paper as-you-type top-k retrieval in social tagging applications, under a network-aware query model by which information produced by users who are closer to the seeker can be given more weight. We formalize this problem and we describe the TOPKS-ASYT algorithm to solve it, based on a novel trie data structure, CT-IL, allowing ranked access over inverted lists. In several application scenarios, we perform extensive experiments for efficiency, effectiveness, and scalability, validating our techniques and the underlying query model. As a measure of efficiency, since as-accurate-as-possible answers must be provided while the query is being typed, we investigate how precision evolves with time and, in particular, under what circumstances acceptable precision levels are met within reasonable as-you-type latency (e.g., less than $50ms$). Also, as a measure of effectiveness, we analyse thoroughly the "prediction power" of the results produced by TOPKS-ASYT.

We see many promising directions for improving the TOPKS-ASYT algorithm. First, for optimising query execution over the CT-IL index structure, we intend to study how CT-IL can be enriched with certain pre-computed unions of inverted lists (materialised virtual lists). Assuming a fixed memory budget, this would be done for chosen nodes (prefixes) in the trie, in order to speed-up the sorted access time, leading to a memory-time tradeoff. While similar in spirit to the pre-computation of virtual lists of [18], a major difference for our setting is that we can rely on a materialization strategy guided by the social links and the tagging activity, instead of one guided by a known query workload. Also, one difficult case in our as-you-type scenario is the one in which t_r is the initial character, following a number of already completed query terms. One possible direction for optimisation in TOPKS-ASYT is to avoid revisiting users, by recording the accessed p-spaces for future reference. In short, within the memory budget, a naïve solution would be to keep these p-spaces as such (one per user). However, in order to speed-up the ranked retrieval, a more promising solution is to organise the p-spaces in a completion trie as well, which would allow us to access their entries by order of relevance.

Acknowledgements

This work was partially supported by the French research project ALICIA (ANR-13-CORD-0020) and by the EU research project LEADS (ICT-318809).

7. REFERENCES

[1] B. Bahmani and A. Goel. Partitioned multi-indexing: bringing order to social search. In *WWW*, 2012.

[2] H. Bast, C. W. Mortensen, and I. Weber. Output-sensitive autocompletion search. *Inf. Retr.*, 11(4):269–286, 2008.

[3] H. Bast and I. Weber. Type less, find more: Fast autocompletion search with a succinct index. In *SIGIR*, 2006.

[4] F. Cai, S. Liang, and M. de Rijke. Time-sensitive personalized query auto-completion. In *CIKM*, 2014.

[5] Y. Chang, L. Tang, Y. Inagaki, and Y. Liu. What is Tumblr: A statistical overview and comparison. *SIGKDD Expl.*, 16(1), 2014.

[6] M. Curtiss, I. Becker, T. Bosman, S. Doroshenko, L. Grijincu, T. Jackson, S. Kunnatur, S. Lassen, P. Pronin, S. Sankar, G. Shen, G. Woss, C. Yang, and N. Zhang. Unicorn: A system for searching the social graph. *VLDB*, 6(11), 2013.

[7] G. Das, D. Gunopulos, N. Koudas, and D. Tsirogiannis. Answering top-k queries using views. In *VLDB*, 2006.

[8] R. Fagin, A. Lotem, and M. Naor. Optimal aggregation algorithms for middleware. In *PODS*, 2001.

[9] J. Feng and G. Li. Efficient fuzzy type-ahead search in XML data. *IEEE Trans. on Knowl. and Data Eng.*, 24(5), 2012.

[10] W. Hon, R. Shah, and J. S. Vitter. Space-efficient framework for top-k string retrieval problems. In *FOCS*, 2009.

[11] B.-J. P. Hsu and G. Ottaviano. Space-efficient data structures for top-k completion. In *WWW*, 2013.

[12] S. Ji, G. Li, C. Li, and J. Feng. Efficient interactive fuzzy keyword search. In *WWW*, 2009.

[13] D. Jiang, K. W.-T. Leung, J. Vosecky, and W. Ng. Personalized query suggestion with diversity awareness. In *ICDE*, pages 400–411, 2014.

[14] L. Katz. *Psychometrika*, (1), Mar. 1953.

[15] P. Lagrée, B. Cautis, and H. Vahabi. A network-aware approach for searching as-you-type in social media - extended version. `http://arxiv.org/abs/1507.08107/`, 2015.

[16] G. Li, J. Feng, and C. Li. Supporting search-as-you-type using SQL in databases. *IEEE Trans. on Knowl. and Data Eng.*, 25(2), 2013.

[17] G. Li, S. Ji, C. Li, J. Wang, and J. Feng. Efficient fuzzy type-ahead search in tastier. In *In ICDE*, pages 1105–1108, 2010.

[18] G. Li, J. Wang, C. Li, and J. Feng. Supporting efficient top-k queries in type-ahead search. In *SIGIR*, 2012.

[19] S. Maniu and B. Cautis. Taagle: Efficient, personalized search in collaborative tagging networks. In *SIGMOD*, 2012.

[20] S. Maniu and B. Cautis. Context-aware top-k processing using views. In *CIKM*, 2013.

[21] S. Maniu and B. Cautis. Network-aware search in social tagging applications: Instance optimality versus efficiency. In *CIKM*, 2013.

[22] Q. Mei, D. Zhou, and K. Church. Query suggestion using hitting time. In *CIKM*, 2008.

[23] M. Pennacchiotti, F. Silvestri, H. Vahabi, and R. Venturini. Making your interests follow you on twitter. In *CIKM*, 2012.

[24] M. Potamias, F. Bonchi, C. Castillo, and A. Gionis. Fast shortest path distance estimation in large networks. In *CIKM*, 2009.

[25] R. Schenkel, T. Crecelius, M. Kacimi, S. Michel, T. Neumann, J. X. Parreira, and G. Weikum. Efficient top-k querying over social-tagging networks. In *SIGIR*, 2008.

[26] M. Shokouhi. Learning to personalize query auto-completion. In *SIGIR*, 2013.

[27] M. Shokouhi and K. Radinsky. Time-sensitive query auto-completion. In *SIGIR*, 2012.

[28] M. A. Soliman, I. F. Ilyas, and S. Ben-David. Supporting ranking queries on uncertain and incomplete data. *VLDBJ*, 19(4), 2010.

[29] H. Vahabi, M. Ackerman, D. Loker, R. Baeza-Yates, and A. Lopez-Ortiz. Orthogonal query recommendation. In *RecSys*, 2013.

[30] S. Wu, J. Tang, and B. Gao. Instant social graph search. In *PAKDD12*.

[31] S. Yahia, M. Benedikt, L. Lakshmanan, and J. Stoyanovich. Efficient network aware search in collaborative tagging sites. *VLDB*, 2008.

[32] J. Zobel and A. Moffat. Inverted files for text search engines. *ACM Comput. Surv.*, 38(2), 2006.

Improving Microblog Retrieval with Feedback Entity Model

Feifan Fan Runwei Qiang* Chao Lv Jianwu Yang†
{fanff, qiangrw, lvchao, yangjw}@pku.edu.cn
Institute of Computer Science and Technology
Peking University, Beijing 100871,China

ABSTRACT

When searching over the microblogging, users prefer using queries including terms that represent some specific entities. Meanwhile, tweets, though limited within 140 characters, are often generated with one or more entities. Entities, as an important part of tweets, usually convey rich information for modeling relevance from new perspectives. In this paper, we propose a feedback entity model and integrate it into an adaptive language modeling framework in order to improve the retrieval performance. The feedback entity model is estimated with the latest entity-associated tweets based upon a regularized maximum likelihood criterion. More specifically, we assume that the entity-associated tweets are generated by a mixture model, which consists of the entity model, the domain-specific language model and the collection language model. Experimental results on two public Text Retrieval Conference (TREC) Twitter corpora demonstrate the significant superiority of our approach over the state-of-the-art baselines.

Categories and Subject Descriptors

H.4 [**Information Systems Applications**]: Miscellaneous; H.3.3 [**Information Search and Retrieval**]: Information Search and Retrieval—*Retrieval models*

General Terms

Algorithms, Experimentation, Performance

Keywords

Microblog Retrieval; Language Modeling; Feedback Entity Model; Freebase

1. INTRODUCTION

With the rapid growth of microblogging, an increasing number of studies have paid much attention to the research on Information Retrieval (IR) in the context of microblogosphere, especially Twitter[1]. To explore the information seeking behavior in microblogosphere, TREC first introduced a temporally-anchored ad hoc search task in 2011 [18] to attract more studies on how to retrieve relevant tweets according to users' queries. In particular, the goal of the temporally-anchored ad hoc search task can be summarized as "*At time T, give me the most relevant tweets about topic Q*".

When searching over the microblogging, users tend to use entities in their queries to express the certain information need. Among the topics (i.e. queries) released by TREC[2] Microblog track [18, 23, 13], more than half of the topics include at least one named entities. Nevertheless, different people are likely to use alternative aliases to represent the same entity. Hence, the vocabulary gap between tweet-posters and the users who search tweets lies as a big challenge for effective IR over tweets. Moreover, as tweets are under the length limitation of 140 characters, the risk of mismatch between query terms and any word observed in relevant tweets is larger than that for traditional Web document retrieval.

Fortunately, we have observed that, while being not allowed to write long text in one tweet, users tend to leverage entities, usually regarding to specific real-world persons, organizations, and locations, to illustrate the topic of their tweets (See Figure 1 for example tweets about "Mila Kunis"). An analysis of a public Twitter corpus published by TREC has illustrated that more than 20% tweets contain at least one entity [18, 13].

Figure 1: Example tweets containing the entities.

Beyond the pure text, entities, as an important part of tweets, usually convey rich information for modeling relevance from new perspectives. Henceforth, to improve users' experience of surfing in microblogosphere, it becomes more necessary to explore how

*First two authors contribute to this work equally.
†Corresponding author.

[1]http://www.twitter.com
[2]http://trec.nist.gov

CIKM'15, October 19–23, 2015, Melbourne, Australia.
© 2015 ACM. ISBN 978-1-4503-3794-6/15/10 ...$15.00.
DOI: http://dx.doi.org/10.1145/2806416.2806461.

to take advantage of entity information from tweets to facilitate ad hoc search task in the microblogging context.

In this paper, we propose a novel feedback entity model and integrate it into an adaptive language modeling framework. Our new framework takes advantage of the rich entity information in Twitter to address the challenges in microblog retrieval. We first estimate the entity model using the entity-associated feedback tweets based upon a regularized maximum likelihood criterion. In particular, we take advantage of the domain information in an open-domain ontology (i.e. Freebase[3]) to filter domain-specific background noise in the estimation of the entity model. Then, by leveraging a language modeling based IR framework, it is quite natural to integrate the entity model into the whole IR framework via query expansion. Entity model can help update the estimation of the query language model based on the extra evidence carried by the entity-associated feedback tweets. Furthermore, with using our new method, different entity aliases referring to the same entity are likely to lead to similar entity models as they share a similar word context. This feature can also mitigate the vocabulary gap between different users to some extent.

The main contributions of this paper include: (1) we propose a feedback entity model and integrate it into the adaptive language modeling framework in order for a more effective IR in microblogging; (2) we use a generative model to estimate the entity model with entity-associated feedback tweets; (3) we perform a set of experiments on two public twitter test collections published by TREC to compare our proposed method with the state-of-the-art baseline systems. And, the experimental results demonstrate that our proposed approach can give rise to significantly better retrieval performance.

The rest of the paper is organized as follows. Section 2 gives an overview of the related work. Then, we describe our adaptive language modeling framework in Section 3. In Section 4, we present our proposed feedback entity model in details. The experimental results as well as the comparisons with the-state-of-arts are shown in Section 5. Finally, we conclude the paper and outline our future work in Section 6.

2. RELATED WORK

2.1 PRF-based Query Expansion

Query expansion (QE) based on pseudo-relevance feedback (PRF) [12, 14, 15, 27, 8] is widely used in microblog search to improve the retrieval performance. However, traditional PRF-based query expansion may not work well as it relies on the assumption that most of the frequent terms in the pseudo-relevance documents are useful [16]. Cao *et al.* [2] re-examined this assumption and showed that it does not always hold in reality – many expansion terms identified in traditional approaches are indeed unrelated to the query and harmful for the retrieval performance. They then integrated a term classification process to predict the effectiveness of expanded terms. Liang *et al.* [12] proposed a Real Time Ranking Model (RTRM), which utilized a two-stage pseudo-relevance feedback query expansion to estimate the query language model and expand documents with shortened URLs in microblog. In addition, RTRM can evaluate the temporal aspects of documents with the temporal re-ranking components. Miyanishi *et al.* [17] proposed a first-stage manual tweet selection feedback to improve the retrieval performance. They further used a two-stage PRF based on similarity of temporal profiles of the query and top retrieved tweets. However, this method sometimes fails due to the redundancy of selected tweets, which usually contain a significant number of meaningless words that may degrade search results. Just like Liang and Miyanishi, we attempt to improve the effectiveness of PRF based QE by utilizing a first stage query expansion.

Other works attempted to acquire knowledge from external sources to obtain additional query terms [5]. Li *et al.* [11] explored the possibilities of using Wikipedia's articles as an external corpus to expand ad-hoc queries and demonstrated that Wikipedia especially useful for the case of weak queries that PRF fails to improve. In their methods, expansion terms were extracted from the top ranked Wikipedia articles. Pan *et al.* [19] proposed using Dempster-Shafer's Evidence Theory to measure the certainty of expansion terms from the Freebase structure. Dalton *et al.* [3] proposed a new technique, called entity query feature expansion (EQFE) which enriches the query with features from entities and their links to knowledge bases, including structured attributes and text. In our study, we seek help from Freebase to guide estimating the domain background language model in feedback entity model estimation.

2.2 Entity-based Query Expansion

Entities have been well exploited in the search scenario, especially in short text retrieval, where entities represent important semantics. Sokes *et al.* [24] employed ontology-based (MeSH and Entrez Gene) query expansion and entity-based relevance feedback for genomics search. Their approach works by identifying potentially relevant entity instances in an initial set of retrieved candidate paragraphs. These entities are then directly added to the initial query with the aim of boasting the rank of passages containing lists of these entities.

Entities, not only real-world ones, but also user-generated ones (e.g. hashtags, user mentions), play a more important role in Twitter than in traditional documents due to the length limitation of tweets. Efron *et al.* [6] described the problem of "hashtag retrieval", a type of entity search. They leveraged the retrieved query-related hashtags in query expansion and achieved better retrieval performance. They assumed that hashtags often reflect some important aspects of a tweet such as its topic or its intended audience. However, some hashtags are very informal, so using hashtags as direct feedback words may lead to risky situations such as topic drift. Further analysis of the entity might gain some retrieval performance. To the best of our knowledge, entity models which model the entities with entity-associated feedback tweets, have not been adapted or leveraged in temporally-anchored search task yet, which might help a lot in retrieving relevant tweets.

2.3 Entity Recognition

To estimate and utilize the entity topic model, one important issue is to recognize entities in tweets and query. Many works have been attempted to extract entities in the microblogosphere. Among them, Ritter *et al.* [21] proposed a distantly supervised entity recognition approach. They first constructed large amounts of unlabeled data collection including large dictionaries of entities gathered from Freebase and information about an entity's context across its mentions, and then applied LabeledLDA [20] to leverage the unlabeled data. Their method has been reported with a good performance in named entity segmentation for tweets. In this study, we apply Ritter's method to recognize entities in tweets

The detection of the named entity in queries is even harder as queries tend to be very short. Guo *et al.* [7] first addressed the problem of Named Entity Recognition in Query (NERQ) and proposed taking a probabilistic approach to the task using query log data and Latent Dirichlet Allocation. It was found that keyword queries

[3]http://www.freebase.com

that people issue to retrieve information from Twitter are, on average, significantly shorter than queries submitted to traditional Web search engines (1.64 words vs. 3.08 words) [25]. Henceforth, in this paper, we adopt a two-stage entity match method to recognize entities in queries. This method works quite well for the short Twitter queries, most of which are entities themselves.

3. ADAPTIVE LANGUAGE MODELING FRAMEWORK

To address the ad hoc search task in the microblogosphere, we employ language modeling approach. In particular, we assume that a query Q is generated by the query language model $\hat{\theta}_Q$, while a document D is generated by the document language model $\hat{\theta}_D$. After estimating $\hat{\theta}_Q$ and $\hat{\theta}_D$ according to [9], the relevance score of D with respect to Q can be computed by the following negative KL-divergence function:

$$S(Q, D) = -KL(\hat{\theta}_Q || \hat{\theta}_D) \propto \sum_{w \in V} p(w|\hat{\theta}_Q) \cdot \log p(w|\hat{\theta}_D) \quad (1)$$

where V is the set of words in our vocabulary. To obtain an effective ranking function for IR in microblogosphere, it is critical to accurately estimate $\hat{\theta}_Q$ and $\hat{\theta}_D$, respectively.

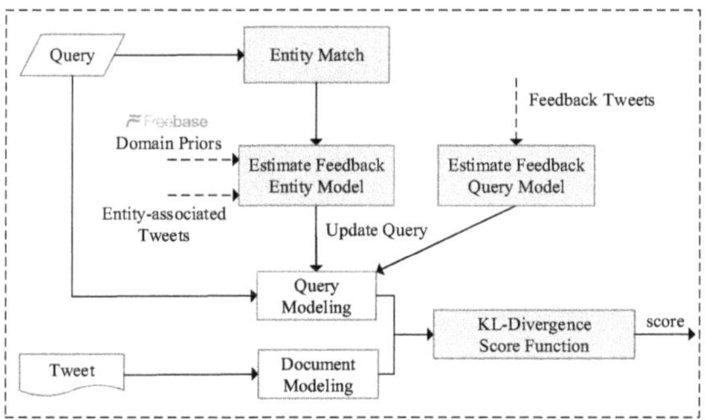

Figure 2: Overall architecture of the adaptive language modeling framework.

Figure 2 shows the overall architecture of our adaptive language modeling framework, which is based on the KL-divergence model and adopts a two-stage query expansion method.

When a new query comes, we first extract all the entities in the query. In our proposed system, we adopt a novel two-stage entity match method to recognize the named entities in the query:

- **Stage 1**: Tagging the entities in the query with an open source named entity recognition tool [4], which has been reported effective in twitter [21, 22].
- **Stage 2**: Taking another round of entity matching by adopting a maximum matching algorithm with a pre-generated entity dictionary. The entity dictionary is generated by combining all the entities extracted from the twitter corpus with the open source tool.

With the extracted entities, we estimate the feedback entity model with a generative model and update the original query model (i.e. first stage QE). Then, a traditional feedback query model is applied to further update the query model (i.e. second stage QE).

[4]https://github.com/aritter/twitter_nlp

3.1 Feedback Entity Model Based QE

To model the dynamics of microblogosphere, we propose to generate feedback entity model $\hat{\theta}_E$ for extracted entity in the query. Feedback entity model is a probabilistic distribution of words $\{p(w|\hat{\theta}_E)\}_{w \in V}$ and represents the common topics of a given entity. Section 4 will elaborated on the estimation of entity model. With the entity model $\hat{\theta}_E$, we are able to expand the original query language model, i.e. $\hat{\theta}_Q \rightarrow \hat{\theta}_{Q'}$ as query expansion. We take advantage of the linear interpolation for combining the original language model and the feedback entity model:

$$p(w|\hat{\theta}_{Q'}) = (1 - \alpha) \cdot p(w|\hat{\theta}_Q) + \alpha \cdot p(w|\hat{\theta}_E) \quad (2)$$

where $\alpha \in [0, 1]$ controls the influence of the entity model.

For the traditional feedback methods, the balance parameter α is usually set to a fixed value across all the queries. However, considering that entities in different queries may not have the same importance, an adaptive weighting parameter should be utilized to dynamically balance the original query and feedback entity information. In our method, our balance parameter takes the form of:

$$\alpha' = \alpha \times \frac{\sum_{w \in E} IDF(w)}{\sum_{w' \in Q} IDF(w')} \quad (3)$$

where E means the entities in the query Q, $\alpha \in [0, 1]$ is a fixed parameter and the IDF of terms in the entities can affect the final balance coefficient.

Note that, when there are more than one entities recognized in the query, we employ the weighted average of all entity models as the unified entity model to expand the corresponding query language model:

$$p(w|\hat{\theta}_E) = \frac{\sum_{i=1}^{n} IDF(E_i) \times p(w|\hat{\theta}_{E_i})}{\sum_{i=1}^{n} IDF(E_i)} \quad (4)$$

where n is the number of entities in the given query. $\hat{\theta}_{E_i}$ is the entity model for entity E_i, and $IDF(E_i)$ is the inverse document frequency for entity E_i. We suppose that an entity with a higher inverse document frequency is more important than that with a lower inverse document frequency. Taking the query "Hu Jintao visit to the United States" as an example, the entity "Hu Jintao" ($IDF = 5.7$) will have a higher weight compared with the entity "United States" ($IDF = 3.8$).

3.2 Feedback Query Model Based QE

When the query is expanded with the feedback entity model, our approach can retrieve more relevant documents at the top, which contain more accurate word distribution than by initial search result. Based on this hypothesis, we further utilize a model-based feedback to update the query representation. Note that the feedback tweets for model estimation are top ranked results using the language modeling framework with first stage QE. More specifically, we update the $\hat{\theta}_{Q'}$ using the feedback query model $\hat{\theta}_F$ which is widely used in the microblogging retrieval [27, 12].

$$p(w|\hat{\theta}_{Q''}) = (1 - \beta) \cdot p(w|\hat{\theta}_{Q'}) + \beta \cdot p(w|\hat{\theta}_F) \quad (5)$$

where $\beta \in [0, 1]$ is a parameter to control the weight of the model-based feedback.

The model-based feedback model generates a feedback document by mixing the feedback query model $\hat{\theta}_F$ with the collection language model $\hat{\theta}_C$. Under this simple mixture model (SMM), the log-likelihood of feedback documents F is:

$$\log p(F|\hat{\theta}_F) = \sum_w c(w, F) \cdot \log((1-\lambda) \cdot p(w|\hat{\theta}_F) + \lambda \cdot p(w|\hat{\theta}_C)) \quad (6)$$

where $c(w, F)$ denotes the count of word w occurred in the set of feedback documents F. Then, we follow the work of [12, 4] and implement the EM algorithm with the best tuned parameter λ.

4. FEEDBACK ENTITY MODEL

In this section, we describe the details of estimating the feedback entity model. We first propose a general method to estimate the feedback entity model with entity-associated feedback tweets (i.e. EF). Then, we discuss how to incorporate expert knowledge from Freebase into our model. Finally, we elaborate on two methods of fetching EF.

4.1 A Generative Entity Model of Feedback Tweets

A natural way to estimate a feedback entity model $\hat{\theta}_E$ is to assume that the EF is generated by a probabilistic model $p(EF \mid \theta)$. It is straightforward to leverage the unigram language model, which generates each word w in EF independently according to θ.

$$p(EF|\theta) = \prod_i \prod_w p(w|\theta)^{c(w,D_i)} \quad (7)$$

where $c(w, D_i)$ is the count of word w occurred in document D_i. This simple model would be reasonable if the feedback tweets only contain information relevant to the corresponding entity. However, the content in those feedback tweets is of high diversity, as it usually contains rich background information or even irrelevant topics. This problem is especially severe because of the redundancy of the tweet content. Therefore, it is extremely necessary to take advanced selection or filtration for these noisy feedbacks.

To address this problem, we propose a generative model to estimate the entity model using the observed EF based upon a regularized maximum likelihood criterion. The particular generative model we employ is a mixture of models, which incorporates not only the entity model, but also the collection language model and the domain-specific background language models. A graphical representation of the generative model is illustrated in Figure 3.

- Definition 1 (**Entity Model**): An entity model $\hat{\theta}_E$ in a twitter collection is a probabilistic distribution of words $\{p(w|\hat{\theta}_E)\}_{w \in V}$ and represents the common topics of the entity E. Clearly, we have $\sum_{w \in V} p(w|\hat{\theta}_E) = 1$.

- Definition 2 (**Collection Language Model**): A probabilistic distribution of words $\{p(w|\hat{\theta}_C)\}_{w \in V}$ is estimated based on the whole twitter collection. Also, we have $\sum_{w \in V} p(w|\hat{\theta}_C) = 1$.

- Definition 3 (**Domain-Specific Background Language Model**): A probabilistic distribution of words $\{p(w|\hat{\theta}_d)\}_{w \in V}$ is estimated based on the specific topic domain d, where $\sum_{w \in V} p(w|\hat{\theta}_d) = 1$. Here, you can think of domains as the sections in your favorite newspaper such as Business, Life Style, Arts and Economics, etc. And, the domain background language model is built for that specific domain. Note that we use the domain categories of Freebase in our approach.

By using the mixture model, the log-likelihood for the EF is:

$$\log p(EF|\hat{\theta}) = \sum_i \sum_w c(w, D_i) \cdot \log\{\lambda_E[(1-\lambda_C) \cdot p(w|\hat{\theta}_E) + \lambda_C \cdot p(w|\hat{\theta}_C)] + (1-\lambda_E) \sum_{d=1}^{k} \gamma_d p(w|\hat{\theta}_d)\} \quad (8)$$

where k is count of the corresponding domains for the entity E. Without prior expert knowledge of domains, we set k as the number of Freebase domain categories. $c(w, D_i)$ is the count of word w occurred in document D_i. Note that λ_C and λ_E are set empirically and represent the amounts of background noise and domain-specific background noise, respectively. Intuitively, when estimating the entity model, we try to "purify" the documents by eliminating some background noise along with the domain-specific background noise. The set of parameters includes:

- Entity model $\hat{\theta}_E$
- Domain-specific language models $\{\hat{\theta}_1, \ldots, \hat{\theta}_k\}$
- The domain mixture weights $\{\gamma_1, ..., \gamma_k\}$

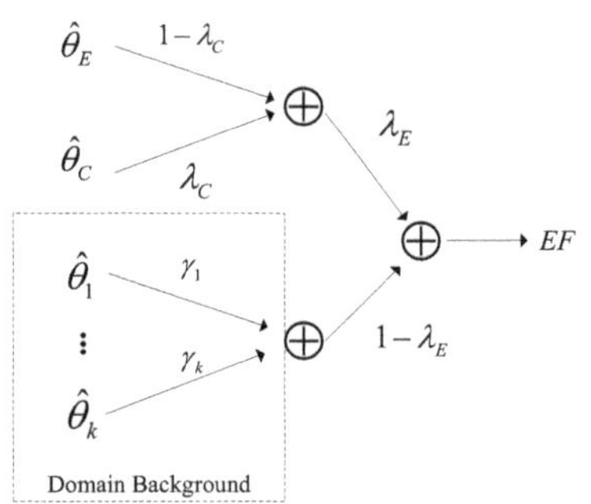

Figure 3: A graphical representation of the generative model.

We can apply EM algorithm [4] to compute a maximum likelihood estimate. The updating formulas are Eq.9-14.

4.2 Domain Priors Incorporation

Our framework aims at solving the problem with minimum supervision; however, if there exists prior expert knowledge on the structured semantics of entities, we also want to incorporate it into the model. Such prior knowledge, for example, can be obtained based on pseudo feedbacks [1] or click-through data [26] in the context of Web search. In our study, as an illustration, we seek help from Freebase, which provides a gold mine of knowledge for entities.

In Freebase, human knowledge is described by structured categories, which are also known as *types* and each type has a number of defined *properties*. Just as properties are grouped into types, types themselves are grouped into *domains*. Each entity in Freebase has been assigned into several specific domains according to expert's judgement. For instance, "Mila Kunis" is involved in seven specific Freebase domains (i.e. Film, TV, People etc.). Hence, we can set the domain number k in the mixture model as 7. In addition, we can use the type and property information of given domains to guide the discovering of domains by adding conjugate priors.

Specifically, we build a unigram language model $\{p(w|d)\}_{w \in V}$ for each pre-defined common domain d based on the information

$$t_d^{(n)}(w) = \frac{(1-\lambda_E)\gamma_d^{(n)} p^{(n)}(w|\hat{\theta}_d)}{\lambda_E[(1-\lambda_C)p^{(n)}(w|\hat{\theta}_E) + \lambda_C p(w|\hat{\theta}_C)] + (1-\lambda_E)\sum_{d'=1}^{k} \gamma_{d'}^{(n)} p^{(n)}(w|\hat{\theta}_{d'})} \tag{9}$$

$$s^{(n)}(w) = \frac{\lambda_E[(1-\lambda_C)p^{(n)}(w|\hat{\theta}_E) + \lambda_C p(w|\hat{\theta}_C)]}{\lambda_E[(1-\lambda_C)p^{(n)}(w|\hat{\theta}_E) + \lambda_C p(w|\hat{\theta}_C)] + (1-\lambda_E)\sum_{d=1}^{k} \gamma_d^{(n)} p^{(n)}(w|\hat{\theta}_d)} \tag{10}$$

$$r^{(n)}(w) = \frac{(1-\lambda_C)p^{(n)}(w|\hat{\theta}_E)}{(1-\lambda_C)p^{(n)}(w|\hat{\theta}_E) + \lambda_C p(w|\hat{\theta}_C)} \tag{11}$$

$$p^{(n+1)}(w|\hat{\theta}_d) = \frac{\sum_i c(w, D_i) \cdot t_d^{(n)}(w)}{\sum_{w'} \sum_i \sum_{d'=1}^{k} c(w', D_i) \cdot t_{d'}^{(n)}(w')} \tag{12}$$

$$p^{(n+1)}(w|\hat{\theta}_E) = \frac{\sum_i c(w, D_i) \cdot r^{(n)}(w) \cdot s^{(n)}(w)}{\sum_{w'} \sum_i c(w', D_i) \cdot r^{(n)}(w') \cdot s^{(n)}(w')} \tag{13}$$

$$\gamma_d^{(n+1)} = \frac{\sum_w \sum_i c(w, D_i) \cdot t_d^{(n)}(w)}{\sum_w \sum_i \sum_{d'=1}^{k} c(w, D_i) \cdot t_{d'}^{(n)}(w)} \tag{14}$$

of Freebase entites. We first recognize all the entities in the twitter collection with the entity recognition tool described in Section 3, and then link them to Freebase with the search API [5]. After that, we collect all the text from type names and the corresponding properties of these entities, and group the text according to their related domains. In this way, we could create a virtual document for each domain. A unigram domain language model can be built in each virtual document as:

$$p(w|d) = \frac{c(w, d)}{\sum_{w' \in V} c(w', d)} \tag{15}$$

where $c(w, d)$ is the count of word w occurred in the domain virtual document d. Table 1 shows the top occurred words for several typical domains in Freebase.

Table 1: Top words in several Freebase domains.

Domain	Top Words
TV	tv, program, episode, appear, series, contribute
Organization	organization, found, origin, leader, headquarter
Chemistry	chemical, compound, measure, element, identify
Astronomy	orbit, measure, relationship, star, object
Book	author, work, written, create, book
Location	locate, part, hud, area, place

Then, we could define a conjugate prior (i.e. Dirichlet prior) on each unigram language model, parameterized as:

$$Dir(\{\sigma_d \cdot p(w \mid d) + 1\}_{w \in V}) \tag{16}$$

where σ_d is a confidence parameter for the prior. Since we use a conjugate prior, σ_d can be interpreted as the *equivalent sample size* because the effect of adding the prior would be equivalent to adding $\sigma_d \cdot p(w \mid d)$ pseudo counts for word w when we estimate the specific domain language model. Basically, the prior serves as some *training data* to intentionally bias the domain language model estimation.

[5]https://developers.google.com/freebase/v1/search-overview

To this end, the prior for all the parameters is given by:

$$p(\theta) \propto \prod_w \prod_d p(w|\theta_d)^{\sigma_d \cdot p(w|d)} \tag{17}$$

where $\sigma_i = 0$ if we do not have prior knowledge for some domain d. Then, we can use the Maximum A Posteriori (MAP) estimator to estimate all the parameters as follows:

$$\hat{\theta} = \operatorname*{argmax}_{\theta} p(E|\theta)p(\theta) \tag{18}$$

The MAP estimate can be computed using the essentially same EM algorithm as presented above with slightly different updating formula for the component language models (Eq. 19).

4.3 Entity Feedback Acquisition

According to our proposed approach, EF yields a considerable influence on the feedback entity model. Two methods (i.e. *entity match* method and *entity query* method) are therefore proposed to collect the top M feedback tweets for each entity in a given query.

4.3.1 *Entity Match Method*

The entity match method first identifies all the entities from each tweet with the entity recognition tool described in Section 3. Then, we can obtain the feedback tweets by collecting all the tweets containing the very entity. To maintain the temporal characters of the feedback entity model, we can use the most recent M tweets containing that entity before query issue time T_Q.

4.3.2 *Entity Query Method*

In this method, we regard each entity as a new query and search related tweets with a temporal based language model [10]. To this end, we enhance the selection of feedback tweets by taking into account the features related to both temporal information and relevance. In contrast to the previous method, the feedback tweets may not have an exact match for a given entity. However, this method can give rise to flexibility of balancing the tradeoff between tweet recency and relevance. To build the time based language model, we leverage Eq.1 to incorporate a time prior for each document D:

$$p(D|T_D) = r \cdot e^{-r(T_Q - T_D)} \tag{20}$$

$$p^{(n+1)}(w|\hat{\theta}_d) = \frac{\sigma_d \cdot p(w|d) + \sum_i c(w, D_i) \cdot t_d^{(n)}(w)}{\sigma_d + \sum_{w'} \sum_i \sum_{d'=1}^{k} c(w', D_i) \cdot t_{d'}^{(n)}(w')} \quad (19)$$

where r is the exponential parameter that controls the temporal influence. T_Q is the query issue time and T_D is time when the tweet was posted. Both T_Q and T_D are measured in the granularity of days. Note that T_D is constantly less than T_Q as we cannot use the future evidence. Finally, we use the top ranked M tweets as the feedback set.

5. EXPERIMENTS

In this section, we conduct several experiments to evaluate the effectiveness of our proposed adaptive language modeling method enhanced by the feedback entity model. In these experiments, we also conduct corresponding analysis to investigate: (1) the influence of the various feedback entity model parameter settings on retrieval performance; (2) the effects of feedback tweets number; (3) the influence of the interpolation coefficient in query expansion and (4) a comparison of two different entity feedback acquisition methods.

5.1 Experimental Setup

In this section, we describe the experimental setup, including the dataset and evaluation methods which are adopted in TREC Microblog track [18, 23, 13].

5.1.1 Dataset

Two corpora (i.e. Tweets11 and Tweets13 collection) are used in our experiments. Instead of distributing the microblog corpus via physical or direct downloading, TREC organizers release a streaming API to participants [13]. Using the official API [6], we crawled a set of local copies of the canonical corpora. Our local Tweets11 collection has a sample of about 16 million tweets, ranging from January 24, 2011 to February 8, 2011 while Tweets13 collection contains about 259 million tweets, ranging from February 1, 2013 to March 31, 2013 (inclusive). In addition, we also crawled all the shortened URLs contained in Tweets11 and Tweets13 Corpora, and inferred their topic information to enrich the original tweets. In particular, we consider the topic information as the local context of the original tweets and combine it with the original tweets to form the tweet language model [12]. Tweets11 is used for evaluating the effectiveness of the proposed Twitter search systems over 50 official topics in the TREC 2011 Microblog track as well as 60 official topics in the TREC 2012 Microblog track, respectively. And, Tweets13 is used in evaluating the proposed Twitter search systems over 60 official topics in the TREC 2013 Microblog track. In our experiments, we only make use of those topics containing entities. The topics in TREC 2011 are used for tuning the parameters and then we use the best parameter setting to evaluate our methods with topics for TREC 2012 and TREC 2013. Table 2 summarizes basic statistics of the three years' topics. From the table, we can observe that half of the topics include entities, which is quite consistent with reality.

In our experiments, the tweets and their corresponding topic information would be preprocessed in several steps. First, we discarded those non-English tweets using a language detector with infinity-gram, named ldig[7]. After that, according to the Microblog

[6]https://github.com/lintool/twitter-tools

[7]http://github.com/shuyo/ldig

Table 2: Summary statistics of topics in TREC Microblog track.

Year	2011	2012	2013
Total number of topics	50	60	60
Topics including entities	36	36	34

track's guidelines, all simple retweets, i.e. tweets beginning with the string 'RT', were removed. Moreover, each tweet was stemmed using the Porter algorithm and stopwords were removed using the InQuery stopwords list. Table 3 summarizes basic statistics of the two corpora after all the steps of preprocessing. In TREC's temporally-anchored ad hoc search task, track organizers created several test topics, each of which contains query text Q and a timestamp T_Q. Only tweets posted prior to T_Q were assessed for relevance [18]. Thus for each query Q, we built a dynamic dataset consisting of tweets whose timestamps are prior to T_Q.

Table 3: Summary statistics of Tweets11 and Tweets13 corpora.

Corpus	Tweets11	Tweets13
Tweets after preprocessing	4,948,137	68,682,325
Tweets containing entities	1,422,292 (29%)	13,480,936 (20%)

5.1.2 Evaluation Metric

In TREC Microblog track, tweets are judged on the basis of the defined information using a three-point scale [18]: irrelevant (labeled as 0), minimally relevant (labeled as 1), and highly relevant (labeled as 2). In our experiments, we mainly leverage two widely-used evaluation metrics in IR, including Mean Average Precision (MAP) and Precision at N (P@N). Specifically, MAP for top 1000 ranked documents and P@30 with respect to *allrel* (i.e. tweet set labeled as 1 or 2) are the official main metrics for the temporally-anchored ad hoc search task in TREC, which are also used in this paper. Furthermore, we also do a query-by-query analysis and conduct t-test to determine whether the improvements on MAP and P@N are statistically significant.

5.2 Baselines

To demonstrate the superiority of our feedback entity model in query expansion for microblog retrieval, we compare our adaptive language model with several baseline methods.

1) The simple KL-divergence (denoted as **SimpleKL**) [28] is used as our first baseline. **SimpleKL** estimates both $\hat{\theta}_Q$ and $\hat{\theta}_D$ with empirical word distribution, in which we choose Dirichlet smoothing method for document model estimation. Throughout this paper, we set the Dirichlet smoothing parameter $\mu = 100$.

2) In addition, we implement Efron's hashtag-based relevance feedback method HFB1 [6] as an entity-based query expansion baseline (labeled as **QEHashtag**). The model parameter k is set as 25 and λ is set as 0.2.

3) To compare with the external query expansion method, we employ a Wikipedia-based query expansion method **QEWiki**, which is similar with the work of [11]. We downloaded a local copy of Wikipedia data for faster access and indexed the articles

using Lemur toolkit [8] (version 4.12). The expansion terms are derived from top ranked Wikipedia articles. In our experiments, we rank Wikipedia articles using language model (i.e. SimpleKL), and 10 terms with highest TFIDF scores are picked from the top 5 articles. Then we treat the terms as a new query and interpolate it with the original query with a weight of 0.5.

4) Simple Mixture Model [27] (denoted as **SimpleKL + SMM**) is used as another baseline. **SimpleKL + SMM** is reported with a relatively better retrieval performance among the state-of-the-art PRF-based query expansion methods [14]. The number of feedback documents is set as 5 and the number of terms in the feedback model is set as 7. The interpolation parameter β is set as 0.6. Note that the feedback tweets used for **SimpleKL + SMM** are derived from the initial search results, which often contain many irrelevant documents. Hence, we replace the feedback tweets with the top retrieval results using **QEHashtag** and **QEWiki**. In this way, we generate two additional baselines, i.e. **QEHashtag + SMM** and **QEWiki + SMM**.

5) Finally, we compare our approach with the state-of-the-art real-time ranking model (denoted as **RTRM**), proposed in [12]. **RTRM** also adopts a two-stage query expansion method like our proposed adaptive language model does. The first stage query expansion weight is set as 0.4. For the second stage query expansion, we extract the top 7 feedback terms from the top 5 tweets and set the interpolation weight as 0.6. In addition, it utilizes ranking position as temporal profile, and adopts the Gaussian temporal re-ranking function with $\sigma = 120$.

All the parameters of these baseline methods are tuned using TREC 2011 topics.

5.3 Experimental Results

In this section, we report the experimental results to demonstrate the effectiveness of our proposed feedback entity model based query expansion methods. In the following, we denote the KL-divergence retrieval model with feedback entity model based query expansion for query model $\hat{\theta}_{Q'}$ as **QEFEM**, and that for $\hat{\theta}_{Q''}$ as **QEFEM + SMM**. When estimating the entity model, we set feedback document count M as 50 with entity match method. The model parameter λ_E is set as 0.7 and λ_C is set as 0.5. The first interpolation coefficient α is set as 0.6 in Eq.3 for both **QEFEM** and **QEFEM + SMM**. For the simple mixture model, we use top 5 feedback documents, while setting β to 0.6 in Eq.5. For the adaptive language model with query model $\hat{\theta}_{Q'}$ and fixed interpolation coefficient α, we label it as **QEStaticFEM** and set $\alpha = 0.4$ for all queries in Eq.3. All these parameters are tuned using topics in TREC 2011.

5.3.1 Overall Results

Table 4 shows the MAP and P@30 performances of eight methods with statistical significance test results for *allrel* tweets. The best performances are marked in bold typeface. Note that all the methods listed in the table estimate the document model as **SimpleKL**.

We first examine the effectiveness of our adaptive language model using first stage query expansion (i.e. **QEFEM**). †, ‡ and ¶ indicate that the corresponding improvements over **SimpleKL**, **QEHashtag** and **QEWiki** are statistically significant ($p < 0.05$), respectively. It can be clearly observed from Table 4 that all these query expansion methods can result in improvements in terms of MAP compared with the **SimpleKL** method for both TREC 2012 and 2013 topics, which indicates the importance of query expansion in microblog search. Besides, **QEFEM** performs better than hashtag-based query expansion method **QEHashtag**, which indicates the importance of analyzing entities in twitter rather than simply using the entity terms. Moreover, **QEFEM** is better than the external expansion method **QEWiki** in terms of both MAP and P@30. This indicates that **QEFEM** can get purer entity-associated topic terms and thus leads to higher precision in top retrieved results. For TREC 2012 topics, **QEFEM** improves the P@30 and MAP scores significantly compared with the three baselines.

When the query is expanded with the feedback entity model, our approach can retrieve more relevant documents at the top, which contain more accurate word distribution than by initial search (i.e. search results by **SimpleKL**). Thus, we can further improve the retrieval performance by combining the model-based feedback method as second stage query expansion. Table 4 also shows all the performances using two-stage query expansion methods. §, △ and ▲ indicate that the corresponding improvements over **SimpleKL + SMM**, **QEHashtag + SMM** and **QEWiki + SMM** are statistically significant ($p < 0.05$), respectively. Note that our **QEFEM + SMM** method outperforms the baseline **SimpleKL + SMM** significantly. More specifically, for TREC 2012 topics, the **QEFEM + SMM** improves the MAP and P@30 over those of **SimpleKL + SMM** by 21.8% and 13.2%, respectively; while the corresponding increments for TREC 2013 topics are 9.5% and 6.5%, respectively. Besides, **QEFEM + SMM** also performs betther than the other two-stage query expansion method **QEHashtag + SMM** and **QEWiki + SMM**. This proves the superiority of our feedback entity model based query expansion method.

Table 5: Performance comparison of the adaptive language model with RTRM.

Topics	TREC 2012		TREC 2013	
Method	MAP	P@30	MAP	P@30
RTRM	0.3397	0.4356	0.3382	0.5207
QEFEM + SMM	**0.3471**	**0.4567**	**0.3519**	**0.5253**

Finally, we compare our adaptive language model with the state-of-the-art baseline **RTRM** in Table 5. RTRM is reported to acheive the best MAP score in TREC 2011 Microblog Track [12]. It can be clearly observed that **QEFEM + SMM** even performs better than **RTRM**, which demonstrates the effectiveness of our approach.

5.3.2 Effects of the Adaptive Weighting Parameter

In Table 6, we list the performances of our adaptive language model with both static weighting parameter (i.e. **QEStaticFEM**) and adaptive weighting parameter (i.e. **QEFEM**). From Table 6, we can observe that both of the methods perform well with respect to MAP and P@30. Besides, we can obtain additional performance improvement when using the adaptive weighting parameter α. This proves our assumption that entities in different queries have different influence, and thus we should adopt an adaptive parameter to balance the entity feedback and the original query.

Table 6: Performance comparison of the adaptive language model with both static weighting parameter and adaptive weighting parameter.

Topics	TREC 2012		TREC 2013	
Method	MAP	P@30	MAP	P@30
SimpleKL	0.2713	0.4067	0.3070	0.4931
QEStaticFEM	0.3053	0.4578	0.3130	0.4954
QEFEM	**0.3180**	**0.4611**	**0.3222**	**0.5057**

[8] http://www.lemurproject.org/lemur.php

Table 4: **Performance comparison of the proposed methods and baselines for allrel documents.**

Topics	TREC 2012		TREC 2013	
Method	**MAP**	**P@30**	**MAP**	**P@30**
SimpleKL	0.2713	0.4067	0.3070	0.4931
QEHashtag	0.2717	0.4122	0.3162	0.5034
QEWiki	0.2901	0.4244	0.3180	0.5023
QEFEM	0.3180 †‡¶	**0.4611** †‡¶	0.3222 †	0.5057 †
SimpleKL + SMM	0.2849	0.4033	0.3214	0.4931
QEHashtag + SMM	0.2831	0.4144	0.3293	0.5126
QEWiki + SMM	0.3267	0.4311	0.3331	0.5149
QEFEM + SMM	**0.3471** §△▲	0.4567 §△▲	**0.3519** §△▲	**0.5253** §

To further study what percentage of entity queries are enhanced by the adaptive weighting parameter, we conduct a query by query performance analysis using TREC 2012-2013 topics involving entities. Figure 4 shows the performance difference between **QEFEM** and **QEStaticFEM** in terms of MAP. It is apparent that using adaptive weighting parameter is effective for improving most queries containing entities.

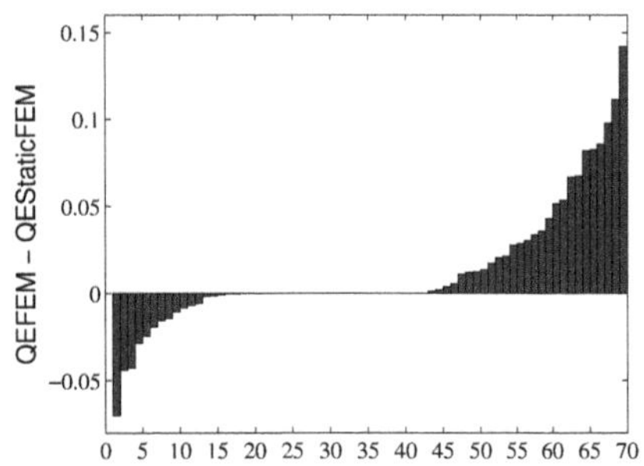

Figure 4: Difference in MAP between QEFEM and QEStaticFEM using the TREC 2012-2013 Microblog track topics.

5.4 Discussion

Many parameters in our proposed approach can affect the system performance. In this section, we analyze the robustness of the parameter setting in our adaptive language model. For the **QEFEM + SMM**, we expand the original query with feedback entity model as **QEFEM** does, and it also applies the traditional model-based feedback to further update the query. We set the second-stage query expansion parameter β as 0.6 and feedback document number as 5, which are reported with good retrieval performance in microblog search [12]. All these experiments in this section are run on TREC 2011 topics, which are used for parameter selection. Note that we first conduct a grid search on λ_C, λ_E, M and α in order to find the optimal parameters, then we check the sensitivity of each parameter when setting others as optimal values.

5.4.1 Effects of Feedback Entity Model Parameters

There are many parameters that may influence the effectiveness of feedback entity model in query expansion. To estimate the entity model, the parameter λ_E controls the amount of "domain background noise" while the parameter λ_C controls the amount of "collection background noise". The number of feedback documents for each entity is also very critical since it directly affects the available terms for the entity. In this section, for each query, we collect the latest 50 entity-associated feedback tweets, using entity match method for model estimation. When incorporating the domain prior information in Freebase, we simply set all the Dirichlet parameters $\sigma_i (i = 1, ..., k)$ as 1000.

To evaluate the sensitivity of retrieval performance to the two feedback model parameters λ_C and λ_E, we fix the interpolation coefficient α as 0.6. In the actual experiments, we truncated the estimated entity model by ignoring all terms whose probability is lower than 0.001, and renormalized it before interpolating. Then we conducted a grid search on λ_C and λ_E. Figure 5 shows the performance changes of the **QEFEM** and **QEFEM + SMM** against different λ_E while setting λ_C to a fixed value 0.5. A smaller λ_E can filter more domain background noise when estimating the entity model. However, from the figure, we can find that it might also decrease the retrieval performance when ignoring too many domain-specific words. In general, the performance change of the **QEFEM** with different λ_E is slight. However, if we set λ_E as 1 and totally ignore the domain-specific language models, the performance of **QEFEM** declines a lot in terms of MAP, which proves the importance of domain background noise filtration.

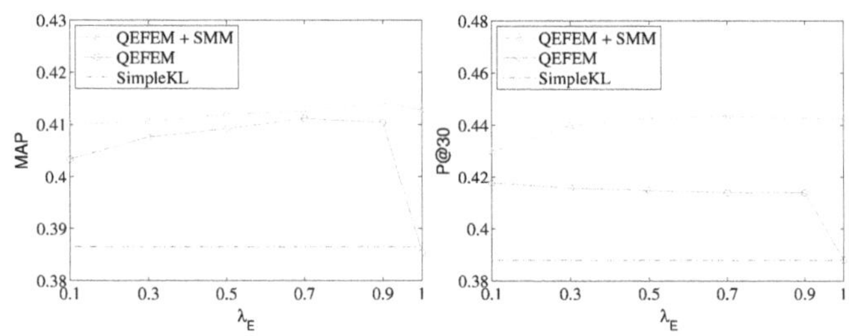

Figure 5: Sensitivity of retrieval performance to λ_E.

We also conduct an experiment to analyze the performance change of that **QEFEM** against different values of λ_C. Experimental results show the retrieval performance is not very sensitive to λ_C, while totally ignoring the collection background model would lead to a performance drop.

To further demonstrate the effectiveness of our mixture model, we compare the best tuned **QEFEM** (i.e. $\lambda_E = 0.7, \lambda_C = 0.5$, denoted as **QEFEM-Filtering**) with **QEFEM** without any noise filtration (i.e. $\lambda_E = 1, \lambda_C = 0$, denoted as **QEFEM-ML**). From Figure 6, we can observe that, after filtering the domain and background noise, we can increase both P@10 and P@30 scores, compared with the baseline method and the entity model without noise filtration.

5.4.2 Effects of Feedback Tweets Number

Another important parameter is the number of entity-associated feedback tweets for model estimation. Too few feedback tweets may not be adequate to summarize the entity, while too many entity related tweets may give rise to much noise for the entity model and

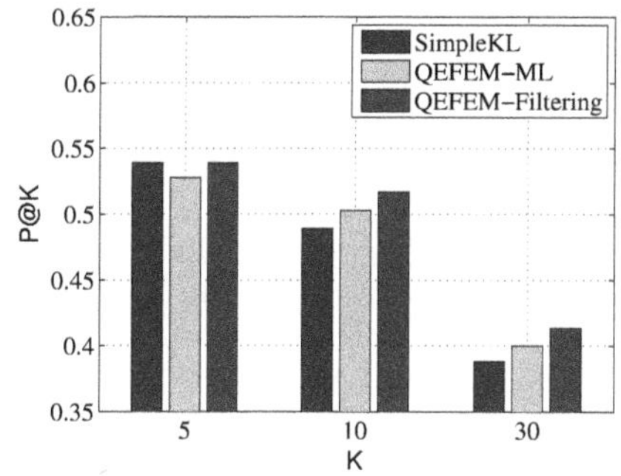

Figure 6: Precision at K for the methods of QEFEM-ML and QEFEM-Filtering.

it will decrease the efficiency if applying the EM algorithm. Figure 7 shows the performance change of **QEFEM** and **QEFEM + SMM** against different settings of the number of feedback tweets, i.e. M. From the figure, we can observe that either too small or too large M will lead to a performance drop of **QEFEM** in terms of MAP. This indicates the importance of choosing an appropriate M.

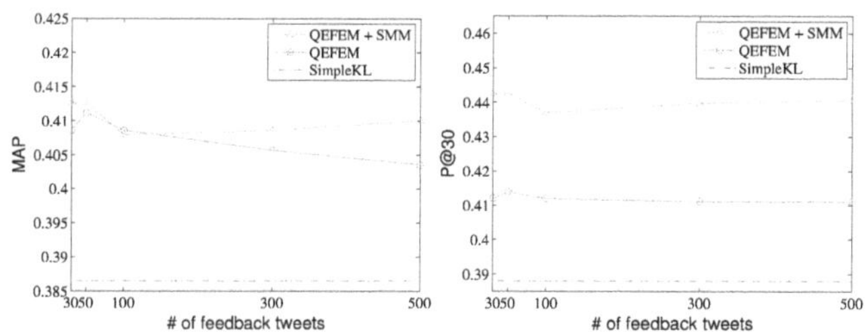

Figure 7: Sensitivity of retrieval performance to # of feedback tweets M.

5.4.3 *Effects of the Interpolation Coefficient*

Recall that we interpolate the estimated feedback entity model with the original maximum likelihood model estimated on the plain query text. The interpolation is controlled by an adaptive coefficient. When $\alpha = 0$, we only use the original query model (i.e. $\hat{\theta}_Q$); when $\alpha = 1$, our approach emphasizes the feedback entity model most. Actually, for queries which are entities themselves, our method of $\alpha = 1$ simply uses the entity model while ignoring the original query model (i.e. $\alpha' = 1$). For the feedback entity model estimation, we set λ_E as 0.7, λ_C as 0.5 and use the top 50 entity-associated tweets to estimate the model. Then, we evaluate the performance with different α varying from 0 to 1.

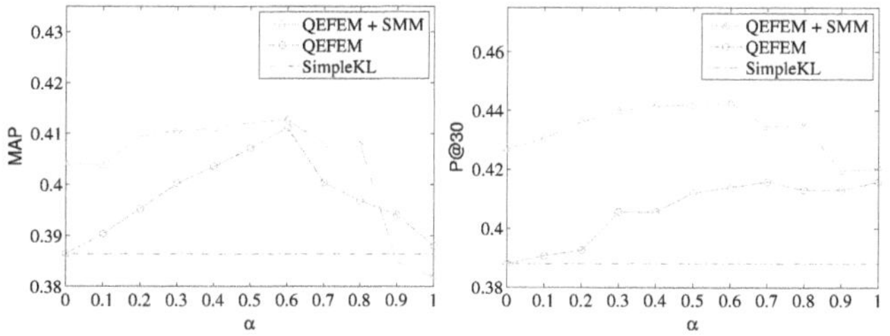

Figure 8: Sensitivity of retrieval performance to α.

Figure 8 shows the performance changes of **QEFEM** and **QEFEM + SMM** against different values of α. Note that, when $\alpha = 0$, **QEFEM** degenerates to the baseline method **SimpleKL**, while **QEFEM + SMM** degenerates to **SimpleKL + SMM**. From the figure, we can observe that the value of α yields a significant effect on the retrieval performance. It is important to choose an appropriate α. Since the entity model can only represent the entity part of the original query, setting α too large will result in a performance drop as it leads to much information loss about the original query. When setting α around 0.6, **QEFEM** and **QEFEM + SMM** can reach their optimal MAP scores. Besides, with the feedback entity model, the search engines can get more high-quality feedback tweets for the query. This could benefit the traditional PRF-based query expansion methods to gain additional performance improvements.

5.4.4 *Comparison of Entity Feedback Acquisition Methods*

Note that we propose two methods to fetch the feedback tweets, i.e. entity match method and entity query method. In the previous sections, we mainly use the entity match method. In the following, we take further discussion on the main differences between these two methods. First, when using the entity match method, those tweets which have an exact entity match can be fetched. When using the entity query method, we can get much more tweets since the partial match can also fetch back the related tweets. However, this could lead to a high probability of introducing irrelevant entities. Second, to reflect the temporal aspect of the entity model, the entity match method simply sorts the tweets by chronological order while the query match method incorporates the recency information into a temporal prior in the language modeling framework.

We evaluate the performance of **QEFEM** using entity match and entity query methods. Both of them use top 50 feedback tweets. The temporal prior r is set as 0.01 for the entity query method. The average and minimum count of feedback tweets fetched with different methods ($M = 50$) are summarized in Table 7. For the model estimation, we set parameter $\lambda_E = 0.7$ and $\lambda_C = 0.5$. The interpolation coefficient α is set as 0.6.

Table 7: Feedback tweets count analysis using different entity feedback acquisition methods.

Method	Average Count	Minimum Count
entity match	34	2
entity query	46	17

Table 8 shows the performance comparison of **QEFEM** using the two feedback acquisition methods. From the table, we can observe that both of the methods can improve the retrieval performance significantly compared with the baseline method. This indicates the effectiveness of both methods. Besides, the retrieval performances of the two methods are comparative across all the evaluation metrics.

Table 8: Performance comparison of different entity feedback acquisition methods.

Method	MAP	P@30	P@10
SimpleKL	0.3865	0.3880	0.4889
QEFEM with entity match	0.4112	0.4139	0.5167
QEFEM with entity query	0.4056	0.4111	0.5111

6. CONCLUSION AND FUTURE WORK

In this study, we propose to use feedback entity model to utilize the rich entity information in Twitter and solve the challenges such as the vocabulary mismatch problem in microblog search. By incorporating the feedback entity model into language modeling framework, the queries containing entities can be more comprehensible and thus more relevant documents can be retrieved. As a result, combining simple mixture model can gain further performance improvement as the feedback tweets contain more accurate word distribution than by initial search. Moreover, as we track the latest tweets containing the entity to build a feedback entity model, our method could also satisfy the real-time information need in microblog retrieval. Our thorough evaluation, using two standard TREC collections, demonstrates the effectiveness of the proposed method.

Many studies remain for the future work. (1) One of the most interesting directions is to generalize our method for topics not containing any entity by searching for top related entities (i.e. pseudo named entities of topics). (2) In this paper, we simply use the general entity model to update the query. In fact, entities can be ambiguous in different domains (e.g. apple in food and technology domains) and can have quite different word distribution in each domain. Thus, if we can recognize the concerning domain of the user query, we can use the domain-specific entity model to update the query. (3) Besides, when using entity model to update the query, we use an adaptive parameter α which only takes account of the IDF information of entity and query terms. However, due to the difference in the entities and entity-associated tweets, this balance parameter can be optimized for each entity and feedback tweets with a supervised method.

7. ACKNOWLEDGMENTS

The work reported in this paper is supported by the National Natural Science Foundation of China Grant 61370116. We thank anonymous reviewers for their beneficial comments. We also thank Jiang Bian, Lili Yao and Yue Fei for valuable suggestions related to this paper.

8. REFERENCES

[1] A. Z. Broder, M. Fontoura, E. Gabrilovich, A. Joshi, V. Josifovski, and T. Zhang. Robust classification of rare queries using web knowledge. In *SIGIR*, pages 231–238, New York, NY, USA, 2007. ACM.

[2] G. Cao, J.-Y. Nie, J. Gao, and S. Robertson. Selecting good expansion terms for pseudo-relevance feedback. In *SIGIR*, pages 243–250, 2008.

[3] J. Dalton, L. Dietz, and J. Allan. Entity query feature expansion using knowledge base links. 2014.

[4] A. Dempster, N. Laird, and D. Rubin. Maximum likelihood from incomplete data via the em algorithm. *Journal of the Royal Statistcal Society*, 39(B):1–38, 1977.

[5] F. Diaz and D. Metzler. Improving the estimation of relevance models using large external corpora. In *SIGIR*, pages 154–161. ACM, 2006.

[6] M. Efron. Hashtag retrieval in a microblogging environment. In *SIGIR*, pages 787–788, 2010.

[7] J. Guo, G. Xu, X. Cheng, and H. Li. Named entity recognition in query. In J. Allan, J. A. Aslam, M. Sanderson, C. Zhai, and J. Zobel, editors, *SIGIR*, pages 267–274. ACM, 2009.

[8] M. Keikha, S. Gerani, and F. Crestani. Time-based relevance models. In *SIGIR*, pages 1087–1088. ACM, 2011.

[9] J. D. Lafferty and C. Zhai. Document language models, query models, and risk minimization for information retrieval. In *SIGIR*, pages 111–119, 2001.

[10] X. Li and W. B. Croft. Time-based language models. In *CIKM*, pages 469–475, 2003.

[11] Y. Li, W. P. R. Luk, K. S. E. Ho, and F. L. K. Chung. Improving weak ad-hoc queries using wikipedia as external corpus. In *SIGIR*, pages 797–798, 2007.

[12] F. Liang, R. Qiang, and J. Yang. Exploiting real-time information retrieval in the microblogosphere. In *JCDL*, pages 267–276, 2012.

[13] J. Lin and M. Efron. Overview of the TREC-2013 Microblog Track. In *TREC'13*, 2014.

[14] Y. Lv and C. Zhai. A comparative study of methods for estimating query language models with pseudo feedback. In *CIKM*, pages 1895–1898, 2009.

[15] K. Massoudi, M. Tsagkias, M. de Rijke, and W. Weerkamp. Incorporating query expansion and quality indicators in searching microblog posts. In *ECIR*, volume 6611 of *Lecture Notes in Computer Science*, pages 362–367. Springer, 2011.

[16] M. Mitra, A. Singhal, and C. Buckley. Improving automatic query expansion. In *SIGIR*, pages 206–214. ACM, 1998.

[17] T. Miyanishi, K. Seki, and K. Uehara. Improving pseudo-relevance feedback via tweet selection. In *CIKM*, pages 439–448, 2013.

[18] I. Ounis, C. Macdonald, J. Lin, and I. Soboroff. Overview of the TREC-2011 Microblog Track. In *TREC'11*, 2012.

[19] D. Pan, P. Zhang, J. Li, D. Song, J.-R. Wen, Y. Hou, B. Hu, Y. Jia, and A. N. D. Roeck. Using dempster-shafer's evidence theory for query expansion based on freebase knowledge. In *AIRS*, volume 8281 of *Lecture Notes in Computer Science*, pages 121–132. Springer, 2013.

[20] D. Ramage, D. Hall, R. Nallapati, and C. D. Manning. Labeled lda: A supervised topic model for credit attribution in multi-labeled corpora. In *EMNLP*, pages 248–256. Association for Computational Linguistics, 2009.

[21] A. Ritter, S. Clark, Mausam, and O. Etzioni. Named entity recognition in tweets: An experimental study. In *EMNLP*, 2011.

[22] A. Ritter, Mausam, O. Etzioni, and S. Clark. Open domain event extraction from twitter. In *KDD*, 2012.

[23] I. Soboroff, I. Ounis, and J. Lin. Overview of the TREC-2012 Microblog Track. In *TREC'12*, 2013.

[24] N. Stokes, Y. Li, L. Cavedon, E. Huang, J. Rong, and J. Zobel. Entity-based relevance feedback for genomic list answer retrieval. In *TREC*, 2007.

[25] J. Teevan, D. Ramage, and M. R. Morris. #twittersearch: a comparison of microblog search and web search. In *WSDM*, pages 35–44, 2011.

[26] J.-R. Wen, H. Zhang, and J.-Y. Nie. Query clustering using content words and user feedback. In W. B. Croft, D. J. Harper, D. H. Kraft, and J. Zobel, editors, *SIGIR*, pages 442–443. ACM, 2001.

[27] C. Zhai and J. D. Lafferty. Model-based feedback in the language modeling approach to information retrieval. In *CIKM*, pages 403–410, 2001.

[28] C. Zhai and J. D. Lafferty. A study of smoothing methods for language models applied to ad hoc information retrieval. In *SIGIR*, pages 334–342, 2001.

Extracting Situational Information from Microblogs during Disaster Events: a Classification-Summarization Approach

Koustav Rudra
IIT Kharagpur, India

Subham Ghosh
IIT Kharagpur, India

Niloy Ganguly
IIT Kharagpur, India

Pawan Goyal
IIT Kharagpur, India

Saptarshi Ghosh
MPI-SWS, Germany
IIEST Shibpur, India

ABSTRACT

Microblogging sites like Twitter have become important sources of real-time information during disaster events. A significant amount of valuable *situational information* is available in these sites; however, this information is immersed among hundreds of thousands of tweets, mostly containing sentiments and opinion of the masses, that are posted during such events. To effectively utilize microblogging sites during disaster events, it is necessary to (i) extract the situational information from among the large amounts of sentiment and opinion, and (ii) summarize the situational information, to help decision-making processes when time is critical. In this paper, we develop a novel framework which first classifies tweets to extract situational information, and then summarizes the information. The proposed framework takes into consideration the typicalities pertaining to disaster events where (i) the same tweet often contains a mixture of situational and non-situational information, and (ii) certain numerical information, such as number of casualties, vary rapidly with time, and thus achieves superior performance compared to state-of-the-art tweet summarization approaches.

Categories and Subject Descriptors: H.3.3 [Information Search and Retrieval]: selection process; H.3.5 [On-line Information Services]: Web-based services

Keywords: Disaster events; Twitter; situational information; classification; summarization.

1. INTRODUCTION

In recent years, microblogging sites such as Twitter have become important sources of real-time information, especially during disaster events. Several recent research studies [1,12,17,19,26,28,30] have shown the importance of microblogging sites in enhancing situational awareness [20] during such events.

In a disaster situation, various types of information are posted by users in huge volume and at rapid rates, which include situational information, sentiment (e.g., sympathy for those affected by the disaster) and personal opinion (e.g., on the adequacy of relief operations). While different types of information have different utilities, *situational information* – information which helps the concerned authorities to gain a high-level understanding of the situation during disasters (including the actionable items [26] such as number of affected people) – is critical for the authorities to understand the situation and plan relief efforts accordingly. Hence it is important to develop automated methods to *extract microblogs / tweets which contribute to situational information* [27].[1] A related, yet different, challenge is to deal with the rapid rate at which microblogs are posted during such events – this calls for *summarization of the situational information.* Further, some of the situational information, such as the number of casualties or injured / stranded persons, changes rapidly with time, asking for special treatment. Since time is critical in a disaster situation, these tasks have to be performed in *near real-time*, so that the processed information is readily available to the authorities.

In this work, we observe that the tweets posted during disaster events have certain specific traits, which can be exploited for the above tasks. For instance, most of the important information is centered around a limited set of specific words, which we call *content words* (verbs, nouns, numerals). It is beneficial to focus on these content words while summarizing the situational tweets. Furthermore, a significant fraction of tweets posted during disasters have a mixture of situational and non-situational information within the same tweet (e.g., *'ayyo! not again! :(Blasts in Hyderabad, 7 Killed: tv reports'*). Again, many tweets contain partially overlapping information (e.g. an earlier tweet 'seven people died', followed by a later tweet 'seven died. high alert declared'). We show that separating out the different fragments of such tweets is vital for achieving good summarization.

The present work proposes a novel classification-summarization framework for extracting situational information from microblog streams posted during disaster scenarios. We develop a classifier which uses low-level lexical and syntactic features to distinguish between situational and non-situational information (Section 4). Using vocabulary-independent features enables our classifier to function accurately in cross-domain scenarios, e.g., when the classifier is trained over tweets posted during earlier disaster events and then deployed on tweets posted during a later disaster event. We

[1] Tweets which provide situational information are henceforth referred to as *situational* tweets, while the ones which do not are referred to as *non-situational* tweets.

CIKM'15, October 19–23, 2015, Melbourne, VIC, Australia.
 ISBN 978-1-4503-3794-6/15/10 ...$15.00.
DOI: http://dx.doi.org/10.1145/2806416.2806485.

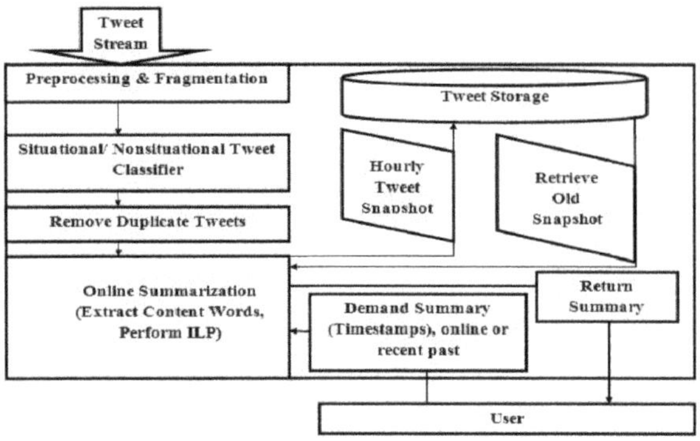

Figure 1: Overview of the classification and summarization methodology proposed in this paper.

then propose a novel content-word based summarization approach (COWTS) to summarize the situational tweet stream (Section 5) by optimizing the coverage of important content words in the summary, using an Integer Linear Programming (ILP) framework. We also devise a scheme where we utilize the direct objects of disaster-specific verbs (e.g., 'kill' or 'injure') to continuously update important, time-varying actionable items such as the number of casualties (Section 5.3).

Figure 1 gives an overview of our approach. First, the tweets are preprocessed and fragmented based on end-markers such as '!' and '?'. The fragmented tweets are classified to extract situational tweets. The situational tweet stream (after removing duplicate tweets) is then summarized using the content word based approach. To enable real-time summarization of long tweet streams (e.g., during disasters such as floods and typhoons, which can span several days), we maintain hourly snapshots of the tweets and the summaries generated previously, so that specific parts of the tweet stream can be summarized quickly when the user demands.

Experiments conducted over tweet streams related to four diverse disaster events show that the proposed classification model outperforms a vocabulary based approach [27] for various in-domain and cross-domain settings. The classification-summarization model also surpasses various state-of-the-art tweet summarization approaches [7, 8, 21, 31] in terms of ROUGE-1 Recall and F-scores over all the datasets (Section 6). Additionally, the proposed scheme is also deployed on tweets related to a recent (at the time of writing the paper) disaster event – the Nepal earthquake in April 2015 [11] – and it is found that the proposed scheme performs significantly better than several state-of-the-art summarization approaches.

As a final contribution, we make the tweet-ids of the tweets related to all these disaster events publicly available to the research community at `http://cse.iitkgp.ac.in/~krudra/disaster_dataset.html`.

2. RELATED WORK

Microblogging sites are serving as useful sources of situational information during disaster events [1, 12, 17, 19, 26, 28, 30]. However, for practical utility, such situational information has to be extracted from among a lot of conversational content, and summarized in near real-time. This section briefly discusses some recent studies on classification and summarization of tweets.

Classification of tweets during disaster events: Several studies have attempted to extract situational information during disaster events [26, 27]. Specifically, Verma *et al.* [27] observed that situational tweets are written in a more formal, objective, and impersonal linguistic style as compared to non-situational tweets, and used bag-of-words classifier models to classify tweets based on these features. However, as reported by Verma *et al.* themselves [27], this approach is heavily dependent on the vocabulary of a specific event, and does not work well in the practical cross-domain scenario where the classifier is trained on tweets of some past events and is used to classify tweets of a new disaster event. To overcome the limitations of bag-of-words model, this study uses low-level lexical and syntactic features of tweets to develop an event-independent classifier for situational and non-situational tweets, that outperforms the bag-of-words model.

Tweet summarization: Most of the prior research on tweet summarization has focused on summarizing sets of tweets, e.g., tweets posted during a sports event [2, 8, 22]. However, what is necessary during a disaster event is online / real-time summarization of continuous *tweet streams*, so that the government authorities can monitor the situation in real-time. A few approaches for online summarization of tweet streams have recently been proposed [13, 21, 31]. Shou *et al.* [21] proposed a scheme based on first clustering similar tweets and then selecting few representative tweets from each cluster, finally ranking these according to importance via a graph-based approach (LexRank) [4]. Olariu *et al.* [13] proposed a graph-based abstractive summarization scheme where bigrams extracted from the tweets are considered as the graph-nodes. Osborne *et al.* [14] proposed a real event tracking system using greedy summarization. Along with standard summarization approaches, a few recent studies [7] have also focused specifically on summarization of tweets posted during disaster events. The studies in the TREC temporal summarization track [24] also attempt to summarize information related to events such as disasters, but the focus is on summarization of sentences rather than tweets (which are likely to be written more informally).

Though there have been *separate* prior works on extracting situational information during disasters and on summarization of tweets (as discussed above), to our knowledge, no prior work has attempted to combine the two classical tasks. In this work, we show that summarization of tweets during disaster events can be better accomplished if different types of information (e.g., situational and non-situational) are first separated out, and then summarized separately. Additionally, the methodology proposed in this work separately identifies and summarizes time-varying actionable information such as the number of casualties, which constitute some of the most important information during disaster events, but has not been considered in any prior work.

3. DATASET

This section describes the datasets of tweets that are used to evaluate our classification–summarization approach.

3.1 Disaster events

We considered tweets posted during the following disaster events –
(i) **HDBlast** – two bomb blasts in the city of Hyderabad, India
(ii) **SHShoot** – an assailant killed 20 children and 6 adults at the Sandy Hook elementary school in Connecticut, USA
(iii) **UFlood** – devastating floods and landslides in the Uttaranchal state of India, and
(iv) **THagupit** – a strong cyclone code-named Typhoon Hagupit hit Philippines.
Note that the events are widely varied, including both man-made and natural disasters occurring in various regions of the world.

Hence, the vocabulary / linguistic style in the tweets can be expected to be diverse as well.

We collected relevant tweets posted during each event through the Twitter API [25] using keyword matching. For example, the keywords 'Hyderabad', 'bomb' and 'blast' were used to identify tweets related to the HDBlast event, while the keywords 'Sandyhook' and 'shooting' were used to collect tweets related to the SHShoot event. For each event, we selected the first 5,000 English tweets in chronological order. A tweet was considered to be in English if at least half of the words in the tweet (after removing @mentions and URLs) appeared in a standard English dictionary (similar to the approach in [6]). We make the tweet-ids of these tweets publicly available to the research community at `http://cse.iitkgp.ac.in/~krudra/disaster_dataset.html`.

3.2 Types of tweets posted during disasters

As stated earlier, tweets posted during a disaster event include both tweets contributing to situational awareness, and non-situational tweets. We employed human volunteers to observe the different categories of situational and non-situational tweets, and to annotate the tweets (details in Section 4). The different categories of tweets observed (which agrees with prior works [17]) are as follows. Some example tweets of each category are shown in Table 1.

Situational tweets: Tweets which contain situational information are primarily of the following two types: (i) *Status updates* – updates such as the number of casualties, and the current situation in various regions affected by the disaster, and (ii) *Helping relief operations* – information that can immediately help relief operations, e.g., phone numbers of nearby hospitals.

Non-situational Tweets: Non-situational tweets (which do not contribute to situational awareness) are generally of the following types: (i) *Sentiment / opinion* – sympathizing with the victims, or praising / criticizing the relief operations, opinion on how similar incidents can be prevented in future, (ii) *Event analysis* – post-analysis of how and why the disaster occurred, findings from police investigation in case of man-made disasters, and (iii) *Charities* – related to charities being organized to help the victims.

The next two sections discuss our proposed methodology of first separating the situational and non-situational information from tweet streams (Section 4), and then summarizing the situational information (Section 5).

4. CLASSIFICATION OF TWEETS

In this section, we focus on separating the situational and non-situational tweets by developing a supervised classifier. Since training such a classifier requires gold standard annotation for a set of tweets, we used human annotators to obtain this gold standard (details below). During annotation, it was observed that *a significant number of tweets posted during disaster events contain a mixture of situational and non-situational information.* Table 2 shows some examples of such tweets. This observation motivated us to preprocess the tweets in order to identify the different fragments, and then process the fragments separately for classification and summarization steps. This preprocessing stage is described next.

4.1 Preprocessing of Tweets

To effectively deal with tweets containing a mixture of situational and non-situational information, we perform the following preprocessing steps.

(1) We use the Twitter-specific part-of-speech (POS) tagger [15] to identify POS tags for each word in the tweet. Along with normal POS tags (nouns, verbs, etc.), this tagger also labels Twitter-specific keywords such as emoticons, retweets, and so on. We ignore the Twitter-specific words (that are assigned tag 'G' by the POS tagger [15]) because they represent abbreviations, foreign words, and symbols which do not contribute to meaningful information.

(2) We apply standard preprocessing steps like case-folding and lemmatization. Further, we use a standard abbreviation dictionary to replace contracted forms (such as *ppl, abt, shld, cud*) with their expanded versions. This is necessary since tweets often contain abbreviations due to the 140-character limit on their length. We also maintain uniformity across different representations of numeric information (e.g. '7' and 'seven').

(3) Subsequently, we focus on particular end-markers (e.g., '!', '.', '?') to split a tweet into multiple fragments. In case of the '.' end-marker, we break a tweet into two consecutive fragments if both the fragments possess their own verb; this prevents splitting a tweet at unnecessary breakpoints, such as the '.' in the tweet 'Upd Msg #31, Tropical Storm - Hagupit, NW Pacific Ocean, JTWC . [url]'.

As a result of these preprocessing steps, each tweet is decomposed into multiple fragments, and all the subsequent steps are carried out on these fragments.

4.2 Establishing Gold Standard

For training the classifier, we considered 1000 randomly selected tweet fragments related to each of the four events. Three human volunteers independently observed the tweet fragments, deciding whether they contribute to situational awareness.[2] Before the annotation task, the volunteers were acquainted with some examples of situational and non-situational tweets identified in prior works [27, 28]. We obtained unanimous agreement (i.e., all three volunteers labeled a fragment similarly) for 82% of the fragments, and majority opinion was considered for the rest of the fragments.

After this human annotation process, we obtained 416, 427, 432 and 453 tweet-fragments that were judged as situational, for the HDBlast, UFlood, SHShoot and THagupit events respectively. From each of these four datasets, we next selected an equal number of tweet-fragments that were judged non-situational, in order to construct balanced training sets for the classifier.

4.3 Classification features and performance

Prior research [27] has shown that the situational tweets are written in a more formal and less subjective style, and from a more impersonal viewpoint, as compared to the non-situational tweets. We consider a set of low-level lexical and syntactic features, as listed in Table 3, to identify the more complex notions of subjectivity and formality of tweets. Briefly, situational tweets / tweet-fragments are expected to have more numerical information, while non-situational tweets are expected to have more of those words which are used in sentimental or conversational text, such as subjective words, modal verbs, queries and intensifiers.

We use a Support Vector Machine (SVM) classifier – specifically, the LIBSVM package [3] with the default RBF kernel – to classify the fragmented tweets into two classes based on the features described in Table 3. We compare our classifier with a standard Bag-of-Words (BOW) model similar to that in [27], where the same SVM classifier is used considering as features – the frequency of every distinct unigram and bigram, POS tags, presence of strongly subjective words, and presence of personal pronouns.

We compare the performance of the two feature-sets (using the same classifier) under two scenarios — (i) *in-domain classification*,

[2]All volunteers are regular users of Twitter, have a good knowledge of the English language, and none of them is an author of this paper.

Table 1: Examples of various types of situational tweets (which contribute to situational awareness) and non-situational tweets.

Type	Event	Tweet text
		Situational tweets (which contribute to situational awareness)
Status updates	THagupit	typhoon now making landfall in eastern samar, with winds of 175 to 210 kph, and rainfall up to 30mm per hour
	SHShoot	state police are responding to a report of a shooting at an elementary school in newtown [url]
Help relief operations	UFlood	call bsnl numbers 1503, 09412024365 to find out last active location of bsnl mobiles of missing persons in uttarakhand
	SHShoot	If you want to donate blood, call 1-800-RED CROSS. @CTRedCross @redcrossbloodct
		Non-situational tweets
Sentiment / opinion	SHShoot	There was a shooting at an elementary school. I'm loosing all faith in humanity.
	THagupit	thoughts/prayers for everyone in the path of #typhoon hope lessons from #haiyan will save lives.
Event analysis	UFlood	#Deforestation in #Uttarakhand aggravated #flood impacts. Map showing how much forestland diverted [url]
	HDBlast	#HyderabadBlasts: Police suspect one of the bombs may have been kept on a motorcycle; the other in a tiffin box.
Charities	SHShoot	r.i.p to all of the connecticut shooting victims. for every rt this gets, we will donate $2 to the school and victims
	THagupit	1$ usd for a cause-super-typhoon hagupit, i'm raising money for eye care global fund, click to donate [url]

Table 2: Examples of tweets containing multiple fragments, some of which convey situational information while the other fragments are conversational in nature (in blue text).

ayyo! not again! :(Blasts in Hyderabad, 7 Killed: TV REPORTS
oh no !! unconfirmed reports that the incident in #newtown #ct may be a school shooting. police on the way
58 dead, over 58,000 trapped as rain batters Uttarakhand, UP.....may god save d rest....NO RAIN is a problem....RAIN is a bigger problem
@IvanCabreraTV: #Hagupit is forecast to be @ Super Typhoon strength as it nears Philippines. [url] Oh no! Not again!

where the classifier is trained and tested with the tweets of the same event using 10-fold cross validation, and (ii) *cross-domain classification*, where the classifier is trained with tweets of one event, and tested on another event. Table 4 shows the accuracies of the classifier using bag-of-words model (BOW) and the proposed features (PRO) on the fragmented tweets.

In-domain classification: BOW model performs well in the case of in-domain classification (diagonal entries in Table 4) due to the uniform vocabulary used during a particular event. However, the proposed features significantly outperform the BOW model. The result is specially significant since it shows that good classification can be achieved even without considering the event-specific words.

Cross-domain classification: The non-diagonal entries of Table 4 represent the accuracies, where the event stated on the left-hand side of the table represents the training event, and the event stated at the top represents the test event. The proposed classification model performs much better than the BOW model in such scenarios, since it is independent of the vocabulary of specific events.

Benefit of fragmentation and preprocessing before classification: As described earlier, our methodology consists of preprocessing and fragmenting the tweets before classification. A natural question that arises is whether the preprocessing and fragmentation steps help to improve the classification performance. To answer this question, we apply the same classifier as stated above on the *raw tweets*; the classification accuracies are reported in Table 5. Comparing the classification accuracies in Table 4 (on preprocessed and fragmented tweets) and Table 5 (on raw tweets), we can verify that the initial fragmentation and preprocessing steps help to improve the performance of both the BOW model as well as the proposed model. We shall also show later (in Section 6) that the preprocessing phase also helps in improving information coverage during the summarization process.

Thus the proposed classification scheme based on lexical and syntactic features performs significantly better than word-based classifiers [27] under various experimental settings. However, since the best achieved classification accuracy is still around 80%, a question naturally arises as to whether the 20% mis-classification would substantially impact the subsequent summarization step. We shall discuss the effect of mis-classification on summarization in Section 6.

4.4 Applying classifier on future disaster events

The good cross-domain performance of the proposed classification scheme (as stated above) implies that the selected low-level features can robustly distinguish between situational and non-situational tweets *irrespective of* the specific type of event under consideration, or the vocabulary / linguistic style related to specific events. Additionally, since we train our classifier using low-level patterns, we expect that the accuracy of the classifier will not vary significantly based on the size and diversity of training set (e.g., if multiple past disasters of various types are used to train the classifier).

To demonstrate this, we performed another set of experiments taking THagupit (the most recent of the four events under consideration) as the test event, and instead of training the classification model with only one event, we combined the remaining two / three events for training. The classifier achieved accuracy values of 79.24%, 79.47%, 78.97% and 80.46% respectively when trained on (HDBlast and UFlood), (HDBlast and SHShoot), (UFLood and SHShoot), and all three events taken together. These accuracy values show that as the classifier is trained on more patterns of expressing situational and non-situational information related to various types of disasters, the classifier's accuracy with cross-domain information becomes almost equal to that when it is trained with in-domain information. Thus, we conclude that the proposed classification framework can be trained over tweets related to one or more past disaster events, and then deployed to classify tweets posted during future events.

5. SUMMARIZATION OF TWEETS

After separating out situational tweets using the classifier described in the previous section, we attempt to summarize the situational tweet stream in real-time. For the summarization, we focus on some specific types of terms which give important information in disaster scenario – (i) numerals, (e.g., number of casualties or affected people, or emergency contact numbers), (ii) nouns (e.g., names of places, important context words like people, hospital etc.),

Table 3: Lexical and syntactic features used to classify between situational and non-situational tweets.

Feature	Explanation
Fraction of subjective words	Fraction of words listed as strongly subjective in a subjectivity lexicon for tweets [29]. Expected to be higher in non-situational tweets.
Count of personal pronouns	Number of commonly used personal pronouns in first-person (e.g., *I, me, myself, we*) and second-person (e.g., *you, yours*). Expected to be higher in non-situational tweets.
Count of numerals	Expected to be higher in situational tweets which contain information such as the number of casualties, emergency contact numbers.
Count of exclamations	Expected to be higher in non-situational tweets containing sentiment and exclamatory phrases (e.g., 'Oh My God!', 'Not Again!').
Count of question marks	Expected to be higher in non-situational tweets containing queries / grievances to the authorities (e.g., 'Can't they spend some of the #Coalgate cash for relief?').
Count of modal verbs	Expected to be higher in non-situational tweets containing opinion of people and event analysis (e.g., ('should', 'could', 'would', 'cud', 'shud').
Count of wh-words	Number of words such as 'why', 'when', etc. Expected to be higher in non-situational tweets containing queries of people, e.g., '*Why* don't you submit your coalgate scam money to disaster'.
Count of intensifiers	Number of frequently used intensifiers [18], more used in non-situational tweets to boost sentiment, e.g., 'My heart is *too* sad', 'Hyderabad blasts are *so* saddening'.
Count of non-situational words	We identify a set of words which appear *only* in non-situational tweets across all events, such as 'donate', 'condemn'. Then we count the number of such event-independent non-situational keywords.

Table 4: Classification accuracies of SVM on tweet-fragments, using (i) bag-of-words features (BOW), (ii) proposed features (PRO). Diagonal entries are for in-domain classification, while the non-diagonal entries are for cross-domain classification.

Train set	Test set							
	HDBlast		UFlood		SHShoot		THagupit	
	BOW	PRO	BOW	PRO	BOW	PRO	BOW	PRO
HDBlast	68.509%	78.245%	57.682%	**73.540%**	56.845%	**83.162%**	52.515%	**77.257%**
UFlood	56.704%	**75.600%**	61.928%	76.142%	55.715%	**78.111%**	53.485%	**78.476%**
SHShoot	54.385%	**77.163%**	57.139%	**74.428%**	65.162%	86.458%	55.897%	**78.697%**
THagupit	51.052%	**76.923%**	52.862%	**73.667%**	54.361%	**84.574%**	67.549%	81.898%

and (iii) main verbs (e.g., 'killed', 'injured', 'stranded'). We refer to these terms as *content words*. This section describes our proposed methodology, which we call COWTS (COntent Word-based Tweet Summarization).

5.1 Need for disaster-specific summarization approach

We observe a specific trend in case of situational tweets posted during disaster events, which is very different from tweet streams posted during other types of events. As tweets are seen in chronological order, the number of *distinct content words* increases very slowly with the number of tweets, in case of disaster events.

To demonstrate this, we compare tweet streams posted during disaster events with those posted during three political, sports, and technology-related events; these streams were made publicly available by [21]. Figure 2 plots the variation in the number of distinct content words seen across the first 5,000 tweets in these three tweet streams, as well as the situational tweet streams posted during three disaster events. It is evident that the number of distinct content words increases very slowly in case of the disaster events. We find that this is primarily due to (i) presence of huge number of retweets or near-duplicates of few important tweets, and (ii) presence of large number of tweets giving latest updates on some specific contexts, such as the number of people killed or stranded. This leads to heavy usage of some specific content-words (primarily, verbs) – such as 'killed', 'injured' and 'stranded' – and rapidly changing numerical information in the context of these content-words.

The above observations indicate that summarizing situational information in disaster scenarios requires a different approach, as compared to prior approaches developed for other types of events.

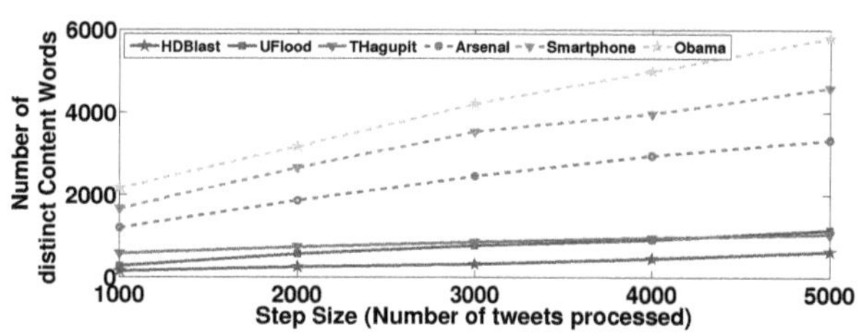

Figure 2: Variation in the number of distinct content words with the number of tweets in chronological order, shown for disaster events (lower three curves), and other types of events (upper three curves).

Hence, we (i) remove duplicate and near-duplicate tweets (using the techniques developed in [23]), (ii) focus on the content words during summarization (as described in Section 5.2), and (iii) adopt specific strategies for the heavily-repeated content words associated with frequently changing numerical information (described in Section 5.3).

5.2 Content word based summarization

The summarization framework we consider is as follows. Tweets relevant to the disaster event under consideration are continuously collected (e.g., via keyword matching), and situational tweets are extracted using the classifier. At any given point of time, the user may want a summary of the situational tweet stream, by specifying (i) the starting and ending timestamps of the part of the stream that is to be summarized, and (ii) a desired length L which is the number of words to be included in the summary.

Table 5: Classification accuracies of SVM on raw tweets, using (i) bag-of-words features (BOW), (ii) proposed features (PRO). Diagonal entries are for in-domain classification, while the non-diagonal entries are for cross-domain classification.

Train set	Test set							
	HDBlast		UFlood		SHShoot		THagupit	
	BOW	PRO	BOW	PRO	BOW	PRO	BOW	PRO
HDBlast	62.308%	75.862%	50%	**67.254%**	49.936%	**75.297%**	50.110%	**76.051%**
UFlood	50.063%	**70.498%**	58.969%	68.513%	50%	**77.976%**	49.963%	**74.258%**
SHShoot	48.375%	**71.295%**	50%	**68.010%**	64.369%	78.273%	50.063%	**75.728%**
THagupit	50%	**70.846%**	49.963%	**68.010%**	50.110%	**78.273%**	56.847%	81.717%

Table 6: Notations used in the summarization technique

Notation	Meaning
L	Desired summary length (number of words)
n	Number of tweets considered for summarization (in the time window specified by user)
m	Number of distinct content words included in the n tweets
i	index for tweets
j	index for content words
x_i	indicator variable for tweet i (1 if tweet i should be included in summary, 0 otherwise)
y_j	indicator variable for content word j
$Length(i)$	number of words present in tweet i
Score(j)	tf-idf score of content word j
T_j	set of tweets where content word j is present
C_i	set of content words present in tweet i

Considering that the important information in a disaster situation is often centered around content words, an effective way to attain good coverage of important information in the summary is by optimizing the coverage of *important content words* in the tweets included in the summary. The importance of a content-word is computed using the standard *tf-idf* score (with sub-linear *tf* scaling) considering the set of tweets containing it.

We use an Integer Linear Programming (ILP)-based technique [16] to optimize the coverage of the content words. Table 6 states the notations used. The summarization is achieved by optimizing the following ILP objective function:

$$max(\sum_{i=1}^{n} x_i + \sum_{j=1}^{m} Score(j).y_j) \quad (1)$$

subject to the constraints

$$\sum_{i=1}^{n} x_i \cdot Length(i) \leq L \quad (2)$$

$$\sum_{i \in T_j} x_i \geq y_j, j = [1 \cdots m] \quad (3)$$

$$\sum_{j \in C_i} y_j \geq |C_i| \times x_i, i = [1 \cdots n] \quad (4)$$

where the symbols are as explained in Table 6. The objective function considers both the number of tweets included in the summary (through the x_i variables) as well as the number of important content-words (through the y_j variables) included. The constraint in Eqn. 2 ensures that the total number of words contained in the tweets that get included in the summary is at most the desired length L (user-specified) while the constraint in Eqn. 3 ensures that if the content word j is selected to be included in the summary, i.e., if $y_j = 1$, then at least one tweet in which this content word is present is selected. Similarly, the constraint in Eqn. 4 ensures that if a particular tweet i is selected to be included in the summary, i.e., if $x_i = 1$, then the content words in that tweet are also selected.

We use GUROBI Optimizer [5] to solve the ILP. After solving this ILP, the set of tweets i such that $x_i = 1$ represents the summary at the current time.

Table 7: Variation in casualty information within a short time-span (less than 7 minutes), on the day of the Hyderabad blast (Feb 21, 2013)

Timestamp	Extract from tweet
14:13:55	seven killed in hyderabad blast [url]
14:16:18	at least 15 feared dead in hyderabad blast, follow live updates, [url]
14:19:01	10 killed in hyderabad blast more photos, [url]
14:20:56	hyderabad blast, 7 people are feared dead and 67 others are missing following a blast

5.3 Summarizing frequently changing information

As stated earlier, a special feature of the tweet streams posted during disaster events is that some of the numerical information, such as the reported number of victims or injured persons, changes rapidly with time. For instance, Table 7 shows how, during the HDBlast event, the reported number of victims / injured persons changed during a period of only seven minutes. Since such information is important and time-varying, we attempt to process such actionable information separately from summarizing the rest of the information. To our knowledge, none of the prior works on processing tweet streams during disaster events have attempted to deal with such rapidly changing (or even conflicting) information.[3]

Specifically, we consider particular disaster-specific key verbs like 'kill', 'die', 'injure', 'strand', etc., and report the different numerical values attached to them, coupled with the number of tweets reporting that number. For instance, considering the tweets in Table 7, the information forwarded would be: 'seven people killed' is supported by two tweets, while 'ten killed' and 'fifteen killed' is supported by one tweet each.

Assigning numeral values to keywords: It is often non-trivial to map numeral values to the context of a verb in a tweet. For instance, the number 'two' in *'PM visits blasts sites in hyderabad, three days after two powerful bombs killed'* is *not* related with the verb *'killed'*, as opposed to the number 'seven' in the tweet *'seven people were killed'*. Therefore, whenever the numeral is not directly associated with the main verb, we extract the direct object of the main verb and check whether (i) the numeral modifies the direct object, and (ii) the direct object is a living entity. We used the POS tagger and dependency parser for tweets [9] to capture this information. If a numeral is directly associated with a main verb (i.e., if an edge exists between numeral and the verb in the dependency

[3]Note that we only attempt to report all versions of such information; verifying which version is correct is beyond the scope of the current work.

Table 8: Comparison of ROUGE-1 F-scores (with classification, twitter specific tags, emoticons, hashtags, mentions, urls, removed and standard rouge stemming(-m) and stopwords(-s) option) for COWTS (the proposed methodology) and the four baseline methods (RTS, NAVTS, DIS, and Sumblr) on the same situational tweet stream, at breakpoints 1K, 2K, 3K, 4K and 5K tweets.

Step size	**ROUGE-1 F-score**																			
	HDBlast					UFlood					SHShoot					THagupit				
	COWTS	RTS	NAVTS	DIS	Sumblr	COWTS	RTS	NAVTS	DIS	Sumblr	COWTS	RTS	NAVTS	DIS	Sumblr	COWTS	RTS	NAVTS	DIS	Sumblr
0–1000	**0.88**	0.21	0.81	0.75	0.55	**0.71**	0.17	0.61	0.64	0.41	**0.85**	0.27	**0.85**	0.75	0.57	**0.68**	0.19	0.59	0.57	0.44
0–2000	**0.69**	0.18	0.62	0.65	0.51	**0.49**	0.18	0.43	0.45	0.34	**0.77**	0.25	0.73	0.74	0.51	**0.65**	0.17	0.58	0.56	0.35
0–3000	**0.61**	0.17	**0.61**	0.55	0.48	**0.57**	0.18	0.44	0.47	0.37	**0.71**	0.21	0.69	0.67	0.47	**0.66**	0.17	0.56	0.56	0.38
0–4000	**0.60**	0.17	0.51	0.54	0.42	**0.50**	0.11	0.45	0.45	0.35	**0.72**	0.23	0.70	0.67	0.49	**0.58**	0.14	0.51	0.49	0.37
0–5000	**0.54**	0.14	0.45	0.49	0.37	**0.52**	0.10	0.42	0.44	0.33	**0.72**	0.22	0.70	0.68	0.52	**0.51**	0.16	0.47	0.46	0.35

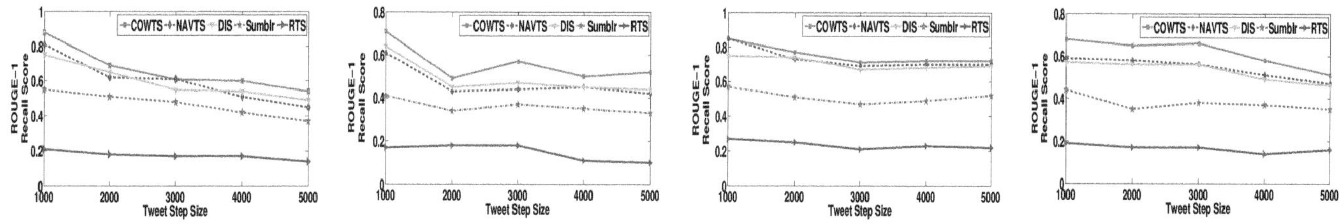

(a) HDBlast **(b) UFlood** **(c) SHShoot** **(d) THagupit**

Figure 3: ROUGE-1 recall scores of the summaries of different events, generated by the proposed methodology (COWTS) and the four baseline methods, at breakpoints 1K, 2K, 3K, 4K and 5K tweets.

tree), we associate that numeral with the verb (e.g., 'seven' with 'killed' in *'seven killed in hyderabad blast'*). The list of living-entity objects for disaster specific verbs was pruned manually from the exhaustive list obtained from Google syntactic n-grams (details omitted for brevity).[4] The performance of our methodology is discussed in the next section.

6. EXPERIMENTAL RESULTS

This section compares the performance of the proposed framework with that of four state-of-the-art summarization techniques (baselines). We first briefly describe the baseline techniques and the experimental settings, and then compare the performances.

6.1 Experiment settings: baselines & metrics

We considered the four disaster events described in Section 3 for the experiments. For each dataset, we considered the first 5000 tweet fragments in chronological order, extracted situational tweet-fragments using our classifier, and passed the situational tweets to the summarization modules. We considered five breakpoints at 1K, 2K, 3K, 4K and 5K tweets, i.e., the summaries were demanded at the corresponding time-instants.

Establishing gold standard summaries: At each of the breakpoints, three human volunteers (same as those involved in the classification stage) individually prepared summaries of length 30 tweets from the situational tweets. To prepare the final gold standard summary at a certain breakpoint, we first chose those tweets which were included in the individual summaries of all the volunteers, followed by those tweets which were included by the majority of the volunteers. Thus, we create a single gold-standard summary containing 30 tweets for each breakpoint, for each dataset.

Baseline approaches: We compare the performance of our proposed summarization scheme with that of four prior approaches, as described below. These include both generic tweet summarization approaches and disaster-specific approaches.

[4]Available at `http://commondatastorage.googleapis.com/books/syntactic-ngrams/index.html`.

(i) **Sumblr:** the online tweet summarization approach by Shou *et al.* [21] is taken as the first baseline with a simplifying assumption – whereas the original approach considers the popularity of the users posting specific tweets (based on certain complex functions), we give equal weightage to all the users.
(ii) **RTS:** the Real-Time Summarization approach by Zubiaga *et al.* [31]. We consider all words after removing hashtags, URLs, and Twitter-specific words, compute their weights, and prepare the final summary based on the ranking methodology of [31].
(iii) **DIS:** the methodology proposed by Kedzie *et al.* [7], meant for summarizing news articles posted during disaster events. In our experiment, we apply their technique over the processed tweet streams. DIS is a semi-supervised method, requiring some prior knowledge of what to include in the summary; for this purpose, we consider some of the tweets that were selected in multiple summaries generated by human volunteers (as described above).
(iv) **NAVTS:** Since COWTS considers nouns, numerals and main verbs as content words, a question arises as to whether this choice of content words is prudent. To verify this, we devise a competing baseline where noun, verbs and adjectives are taken as content words; these parts of speech were found to be important for tweet summarization (not online) in a prior study by Khan *et al.* [8].
We applied COWTS and all the above baseline methods on the same situational tweet stream (obtained after classification), and retrieved summaries of the same length, i.e. the number of words present in the 30 tweets of the gold standard summary for a certain breakpoint (described earlier). *To maintain fairness, the same situational tweet stream (after classification) was input to all the summarization approaches.*

Evaluation metrics: We used the standard ROUGE [10] metric for evaluating the quality of the summaries generated. Due to the informal nature of tweets, we actually considered the *recall and F-score* of the ROUGE-1 variant.

6.2 Performance Comparison

Table 8 and Figure 3 give the ROUGE-1 F-scores and recall for the five algorithms for the four datasets, at the various breakpoints respectively. It is evident that COWTS performs significantly better

Table 9: **Summary of length 100 words, generated from the first 300 situational tweets of the THagupit dataset by (i) COWTS (proposed methodology), (ii) DIS proposed in [7]. The tweets have been case-folder to lower case.**

Summary by COWTS	Summary by DIS
check out other emergency hotlines here, [url]	jtwc upgrades tropical depression of 22w to tropical storm 22w , hagupit , [url]
save and share, ndrrmc hotlines 0929 3356079 0917 5294438 0936 9108694 0929 3356077 0906 2042096	latest, ts hagupit has to intensify as a severe tropical storm in 24 hours & in 36 hours it will turn as typhoon
wp tropical storm hagupit advisory, 4, 45 kt/52 mph winds, 5.9 n 149.1 e, moving, wnw at 16 kt/18 mph tropics	Typhoon hagupit will bring heavy rain, destructive winds and storm surges close to the eye local warnings [url]
pagasa forecast models show either to make landfall or veer toward japan	class at all levels declared suspended by mayor dominador agahan of almeria on friday , december 5
jtwc sees becoming a super typhoon in 48 hours still split on track [url]	the hawaii-based joint typhoon warning center of the us navy on wednesday said hagupit will become a super typhoon in 48 hours
ndrrmc, dswd has 100,000 prepared family food packs regional offices have 30,000 in case of immediate response	now a typhoon 1,670 km east of mindanao and closing [url]
ndrrmc and pagasa released a list of areas deemed critical as typhoon approaches the country [url]	ruby, international name hagupit , intensifies into a tropical storm according to the us navy's joint typhoon [url]
as of december 3, 2014 at 5:04 pm class suspensions have been announced [url]	typhoon hagupit is a 100 knot , 115 mph , storm better hope gfs is right ecmwf could create devastating flooding [url]
if hagupit continues under projected track, an est 4.5 million people within the 65 km radius may be affected in 14 provinces in 4 regions	latest nasa satellite tracker typhoon hagupit curve north near philippine [url]

than all the baseline approaches. For instance, mean scores indicate an average improvement of more than 60% in terms of F-scores over Sumblr [21] which is a general-purpose (i.e., not disaster-specific) summarization scheme. The proposed methodology also performs better than the disaster-specific summarization technique DIS [7] in all cases – on an average, we obtain improvement of 20% for F-scores and 12% for recall over DIS. Further, the higher F-scores for COWTS than those for NAVTS indicate that our selected content words lead to better summarization. Figure 3 shows that the trend holds even if we increase the number of tweets for summarization.

To give an idea of the nature of the summaries generated by the methodologies, Table 9 shows summaries generated by COWTS and DIS (both disaster-specific methodologies) from the same tweet stream – the first 300 situational tweets posted during the THagupit event. The two summaries are quite distinct, with no tweet in common. We find that the summary returned by COWTS is more informative, and contains crucial information about hotline numbers, food packs, critical areas and information necessary for volunteers. On the other hand, the summary returned by DIS mostly contains the same information (about the nature or intensity of the storm) expressed in various ways.

Time taken for summarization: Since time is critical during disaster events, it is important that the summaries are generated in real-time. Hence, we analyze the execution times of the various techniques. At the breakpoints of 1K, 2K, 3K, 4K and 5K tweets, the proposed COWTS method takes 5.953, 8.084, 10.295, 12.627 and 15.135 seconds on average (over the four datasets) respectively to generate summaries. The time taken increases sub-linearly with the number of tweets and is comparable to those taken by the RTS and NAVTS baselines (on the same situational tweet streams), and significantly better than those taken by Sumblr and DIS. Specifically, DIS requires more time due to computation of large similarity matrices and execution of affinity propagation algorithm, whereas Sumblr requires large time due to the LexRank graph generation.

Benefit of classification before summarization: We verified that separating out situational tweets from non-situational ones significantly improves the quality of summaries. Considering all the four events together, the mean ROUGE F-score at breakpoint 1000 for COWTS was 0.61 *without* prior classification (i.e., when all tweets were input to the summarizer) as compared to 0.78 after classification. Table 10 gives the mean F-score of COWTS on classified and unclassified tweets, averaged over all the four events.

Effect of misclassification on summary recall: As stated in Section 4, the proposed classifier achieved around 80% accuracy in classifying between situational and non-situational tweets. We now investigate how the 20% error in classification affects the subsequent summarization of situational information.

Evidently, errors where a situational tweet is misclassified as non-situational are far more critical since they may impact the recall of the subsequent summarization step. We find that out of all classification errors, such errors account for only 8.09%, 10.94%, 7.25% and 9.69% for the four datasets respectively (in the order stated in Table 4). Thus, very few situational tweets are actually left out from the summarization process due to mis-classification.

We further checked what fraction of content-words are really missed out due to misclassification. Across all the four datasets, more than 84% of the content-words present in the *mis-classified tweets* are also covered by the correctly classified situational tweets; this implies that only a small fraction of the content-words are missed in the stream sent for summarization.

Effect of choice of content words: Choosing what type of words to focus on is important for achieving good summarization of tweet streams, as also observed in [8]. As stated in Section 5, we considered three types of content words – numerals, nouns, and verbs. From the comparison between COWTS and NAVTS, it has already been established that our choice of content words achieves better summarization for tweets posted during disaster events, than the information words proposed in [8].

We now analyze whether all the three chosen types of content words are effective for summarization. For this, we analyze the quality of the summaries generated in the *absence* of one of these types of content words. Figure 4 compares the F-scores (averaged over all four datasets) considering all three types of content words, with those obtained considering any two types of content words. It is clear that all three types of content words are important for the summarization quality, numerals and nouns being the most important ones (since the numeral-noun combination outperforms the

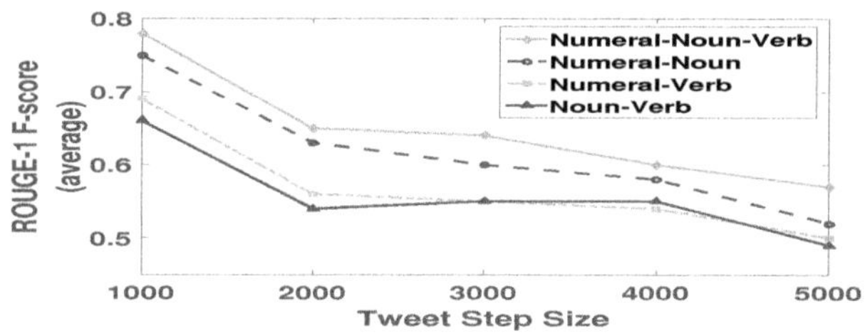

Figure 4: Effect of individual types of content words on summary

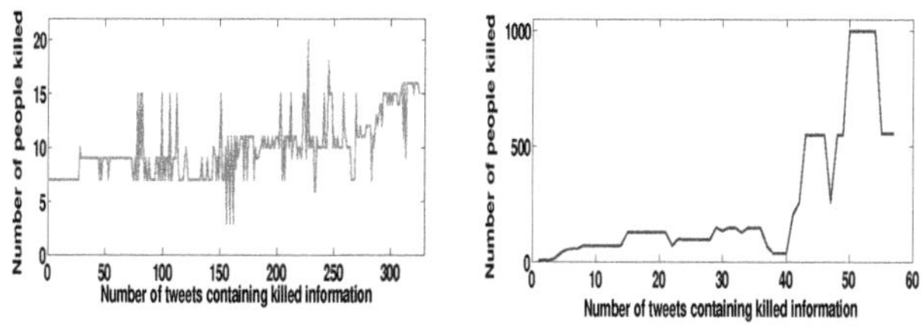

(a) HDBlast **(b) UFlood**

Figure 5: Variation in the reported number of people killed, during two disaster events. The x-axis represents the sequence of tweets which contain such information.

other 2-combinations). Side by side, as a sanity check, we have also included adjectives among the content words and run COWTS; we observed that the performance deteriorates noticeably.

Note that most of the earlier summarization frameworks *discarded* numerals contained in the tweets, whereas we show that numerals play a key role in tweets posted during disaster events, in not only identifying situational updates but also in summarizing frequently changing information (which we evaluate next).

Handling frequently changing numerals: Figure 5 shows how the numerical value associated with the key verb 'kill' changes with time (or sequence of tweets, as shown on the x-axis) during two different disaster events. Clearly, there is a lot of variation in the reported number of casualties, which shows the complexity in interpreting such numerical information.

We now evaluate the performance of our algorithm in relating such numerical information with the corresponding key verb (as detailed in Section 5.3). Specifically, we check what fraction of such numerical information could be correctly associated with the corresponding key verb. We compared the accuracy of our algorithm with a simple baseline algorithm where numerals occurring within a window of 3 words on either side of the verb were selected as being related to the verb. Considering all the four datasets together, the *baseline algorithm has a precision of 0.63, whereas our algorithm has a much higher precision of 0.95* – this shows the effectiveness of our strategy in extracting frequently changing numerical information.

6.3 Application on future disaster events

We envisage that the classification-summarization framework developed in the present work will be trained over tweets related to past disaster events, and then deployed to extract and summarize situational information from tweet streams posted during future events. In this final section, we demonstrate the utility of the framework by deploying it on tweets posted during a more recent disaster event – the earthquake in Nepal in April 2015 [11].

We collected related tweets using keyword matching, and then considered the first 1,000 matching tweets in chronological order. We trained our classifier model on the HDBlast dataset, then used

Table 10: ROUGE-1 F-score of COWTS on classified and unclassified tweets, averaged across four events.

Step size	ROUGE-1 F-score	
	Classified	Unclassified
1000	0.78	0.61
2000	0.65	0.52
3000	0.64	0.48
4000	0.60	0.43
5000	0.57	0.45

Table 11: Ranking by 5 volunteers for the summaries generated by various methods on the Nepal earthquake dataset.

Evaluator	Ranking			
	COWTS	NAVTS	Sumblr	RTS
1	1	2	3	4
2	1	2	2	3
3	1	2	3	4
4	1	2	3	4
5	1	2	3	4

the classifier to extract situational tweets, and then summarized the situational tweet stream. We also used the baseline methods NAVTS, Sumblr, and RTS on the same tweet stream in similar settings; however, the DIS method was not used since it is a semi-supervised method, requiring some prior knowledge about what to include in the summary.

Since for this dataset, we do not have any ground truth summary, we performed a manual evaluation of the summaries generated by all the different methods. Five human volunteers were asked to rank the summaries (anonymized, i.e., the volunteers were not told which summary was generated by which methodology) based on their informativeness. We tabulate the rankings given by the volunteers in Table 11. It is evident that all the volunteers ranked the summary produced by COWTS as the most informative.

Further, in order to test the scalability of COWTS, we considered the first 20,000 tweets related to the event in chronological order, and then summarized the situational tweet stream at the two breakpoints – 10,000 and 20,000 tweets. COWTS took 32.130 and 47.412 seconds respectively to summarize the tweets at the two breakpoints, and all the five human evaluators expressed satisfaction at the content of the summary. This experiment shows that COWTS is able to summarize tweet streams posted during new disaster events satisfactorily, and in near real-time.

6.4 Discussion on performance

A deeper look at various baseline techniques helps us to understand their shortcomings and the reasons behind the superior performance of COWTS. NAVTS, which is a variation of COWTS with different types of content words, brings out the importance of choosing proper content words for summarization. Out of the other baseline techniques, Sumblr and RTS [21, 31] do not discriminate among different types of POS tags. Additionally, RTS [31] suffers from potential redundancies – this methodology ranks tweets and selects the top-ranking ones for the summary, which may lead to redundancy if most of the top-ranking tweets have similar content. Sumblr [21] maintains clusters of related information and finally chooses one top scoring tweet from each cluster. If the desired summary length is not equal to the number of clusters, then it needs to be decided as to which clusters are important and should be selected for preparing the final summary. Similar types of tweet selection problem also arises in case of DIS [7], when we have large number of exemplar tweets. To resolve such issues, focusing on particular POS-tags and ILP-based technique (as used in COWTS) proves to be very handy.

To be fair to other methods, most of them are *not* specifically designed to summarize tweet streams posted during disaster-specific events, which have their own peculiarities. We observe that across all types of disaster events, numerals, nouns, and key verbs provide salient situational updates during disasters. Hence, we set our summarization objective to maximize the coverage of these parts of speech in the final summary, by using an ILP-based technique. The strong points in favor of COWTS is that it is completely unsupervised and can be applied to any type of disaster events.

7. CONCLUSION

This paper presents a novel classification-summarization framework for disaster-specific situational information on Twitter. We derive several key insights – (i) it is beneficial to work with tweet fragments rather than entire tweets, (ii) distinct lexical and syntactic features present in tweets can be used to separate out situational and non-situational tweets, which leads to significantly better summarization, (iii) content words are especially significant for summarization of disaster-specific tweet streams, and (iv) special arrangements are needed to deal with a small set of actionable keywords which have numerical qualifiers. We develop a domain-independent classifier which performs better than domain-dependent bag-of-words technique, and an ILP-based summarization framework that out-performs other summarization methods in summarizing the situational tweets.

We had several realizations during the course of this work. For instance, whereas some disasters are instantaneous and span short time durations (such as bomb blast, or shooting incidents), other events such as floods and hurricanes span much longer time periods. In such long ranging disasters, users may be interested both in current summaries (e.g., the last few hours) as well as historical summaries (e.g., the last week). Both these types of summaries can be generated by a minor modification of the underlying data structures of the present scheme. The Content Word Dictionary – which maintains the content words as well as the rate at which they are appearing in the tweets – can be created for each epoch, and accordingly both recent as well as historical summaries can be obtained as per user-requirement. We hope to formalize this in more detail in our future work, which includes deploying a live system. Further, the module which we develop to handle continuous updates of the actionable numerical items shows that conflicting numbers often get posted at the same time, and a robust technique needs to be developed to differentiate between rumours and authentic information. This would be another potential future work.

As a final note, we believe that our work is significant especially in developing countries, where government-sponsored sophisticated systems to monitor situational updates in disaster scenario is largely missing.

Acknowledgement: This research was partially supported by a grant from the Information Technology Research Academy (ITRA), DeITY, Government of India (Ref. No.: ITRA/15 (58)/ Mobile/ DISARM/ 05) Additionally, K. Rudra was supported by a fellowship from Tata Consultancy Services, and S. Ghosh was supported by a fellowship from the Alexander von Humboldt Foundation. K. Rudra would also like to thank Google and Flipkart for their travel support.

8. REFERENCES

[1] M. A. Cameron, R. Power, B. Robinson, and J. Yin. Emergency Situation Awareness from Twitter for Crisis Management. In *Proc. Conference on World Wide Web (WWW)*, 2012.

[2] D. Chakrabarti and K. Punera. Event summarization using tweets. In *Proc. AAAI ICWSM*, 2011.

[3] C.-C. Chang and C.-J. Lin. LIBSVM: A library for support vector machines. *ACM Transactions on Intelligent Systems and Technology*, 2:27:1–27:27, 2011.

[4] G. Erkan and D. R. Radev. LexRank:Graph-based lexical centrality as salience in text summarization. *Artificial Intelligence Research*, 22:457–479, 2004.

[5] Gurobi – The overall fastest and best supported solver available, 2015. http://www.gurobi.com/.

[6] A. Hannak, E. Anderson, L. F. Barrett, S. Lehmann, A. Mislove, and M. Riedewald. Tweetin' in the Rain: Exploring societal-scale effects of weather on mood. In *Proc. AAAI ICWSM*, 2012.

[7] C. Kedzie, K. McKeown, and F. Diaz. Summarizing Disasters Over Time. In *Proc. Bloomberg Workshop on Social Good (with SIGKDD)*, 2014.

[8] M. A. H. Khan, D. Bollegala, G. Liu, and K. Sezaki. Multi-Tweet Summarization of Real-Time Events. In *Proc. IEEE Socialcom*, 2013.

[9] L. Kong, N. Schneider, S. Swayamdipta, A. Bhatia, C. Dyer, and N. A. Smith. A Dependency Parser for Tweets. In *Proc. EMNLP*, 2014.

[10] C.-Y. Lin. ROUGE: A package for automatic evaluation of summaries. In *Proc. Workshop on Text Summarization Branches Out (with ACL)*, 2004.

[11] 2015 Nepal earthquake – Wikipedia, April 2015. http://en.wikipedia.org/wiki/2015_Nepal_earthquake.

[12] G. Neubig, Y. Matsubayashi, M. Hagiwara, and K. Murakami. Safety information mining – what can NLP do in a disaster. In *Proc. IJCNLP*, 2011.

[13] A. Olariu. Efficient online summarization of microblogging streams. In *Proc. EACL*, 2014.

[14] M. Osborne et al. Real-Time Detection, Tracking, and Monitoring of Automatically Discovered Events in Social Media. In *Proc. ACL*, 2014.

[15] O. Owoputi, B. O'Connor, C. Dyer, K. Gimpel, N. Schneider, and N. A. Smith. Improved part-of-speech tagging for online conversational text with word clusters. In *Proc. NAACL-HLT*, 2013.

[16] D. Parveen and M. Strube. Multi-document Summarization Using Bipartite Graphs. In *Proc. TextGraphs Workshop on Graph-based Methods for Natural Language Processing*, pages 15–24, October 2014.

[17] Y. Qu, C. Huang, P. Zhang, and J. Zhang. Microblogging After a Major Disaster in China: A Case Study of the 2010 Yushu Earthquake. In *Proc. ACM CSCW*, 2011.

[18] R. Quirk, S. Greenbaum, G. Leech, J. Svartvik, and D. Crystal. *A comprehensive grammar of the English language*, volume 397. Cambridge University Press, 1985.

[19] T. Sakaki, M. Okazaki, and Y. Matsuo. Earthquake shakes Twitter users: real-time event detection by social sensors. In *Proc. World Wide Web Conference (WWW)*, 2010.

[20] N. B. Sarter and D. D. Woods. Situation awareness: a critical but ill-defined phenomenon. *The International Journal of Aviation Psychology*, 1(1):45–57, 1991.

[21] L. Shou, Z. Wang, K. Chen, and G. Chen. Sumblr: Continuous summarization of evolving tweet streams. In *Proc. ACM SIGIR*, 2013.

[22] H. Takamura, H. Yokono, and M. Okumura. Summarizing a document stream. In *Proc. ECIR*, 2011.

[23] K. Tao, F. Abel, C. Hauff, G.-J. Houben, and U. Gadiraju. Groundhog Day: Near-duplicate Detection on Twitter. In *Proc. World Wide Web Conference (WWW)*, 2013.

[24] TREC Temporal Summarization, 2015. http://www.trec-ts.org/.

[25] REST API Resources, Twitter Developers. https://dev.twitter.com/docs/api.

[26] I. Varga, M. Sano, K. Torisawa, C. Hashimoto, K. Ohtake, T. Kawai, J.-H. Oh, and S. D. Saeger. Aid is out there: Looking for help from tweets during a large scale disaster. In *Proc. ACL*, 2013.

[27] S. Verma, S. Vieweg, W. J. Corvey, L. Palen, J. H. Martin, M. Palmer, A. Schram, and K. M. Anderson. Natural Language Processing to the Rescue? Extracting "Situational Awareness" Tweets During Mass Emergency. In *Proc. AAAI ICWSM*, 2011.

[28] S. Vieweg, A. L. Hughes, K. Starbird, and L. Palen. Microblogging During Two Natural Hazards Events: What Twitter May Contribute to Situational Awareness. In *Proc. ACM SIGCHI*, 2010.

[29] S. Volkova, T. Wilson, and D. Yarowsky. Exploring Sentiment in Social Media: Bootstrapping Subjectivity Clues from Multilingual Twitter Streams. In *Proc. ACL*, 2013.

[30] J. Yin, A. Lampert, M. Cameron, B. Robinson, and R. Power. Using Social Media to Enhance Emergency Situation Awareness. *IEEE Intelligent Systems*, 27(6):52–59, 2012.

[31] A. Zubiaga, D. Spina, E. Amigo, and J. Gonzalo. Towards Real-Time Summarization of Scheduled Events from Twitter Streams. In *Proc. ACM Hypertext*, 2012.

Profession-Based Person Search in Microblogs: Using Seed Sets to Find Journalists

Mossaab Bagdouri
Department of Computer Science
University of Maryland
College Park, MD, USA
mossaab@umd.edu

Douglas W. Oard
iSchool and UMIACS
University of Maryland
College Park, MD, USA
oard@umd.edu

ABSTRACT

We introduce the problem of searching for professionals in microblogging platforms. We describe a study of how a group of professional journalists with some common characteristics (e.g., works in a specific language, belongs to certain region, or specializes in a particular media) can be found. Starting from seed sets of different sizes, social network features and profile content features are used to find additional journalists. The results show that combining the social network features of the reciprocated mentions and a bidirectional friend/follower graph provides a signal stronger than either of them taken independently, that both social network and profile content features are useful, and that profile content features are able to find larger numbers of less prominent journalists. We apply our methods to find the Twitter accounts of British and Arab journalists.

Categories and Subject Descriptors:
H.3.3 [Information Storage and Retrieval]: Information Search and Retrieval

Keywords: Microblogs; Person Search; Journalists

1. INTRODUCTION

The variety in social media services induces a diversity of applications, ranging from personal communication and entertainment to professional networking and collaboration. Some of these services, such as LinkedIn, are, by design, more business-oriented than others. They are, perhaps, the most obvious places to search for some particular experts. Certain professionals, however, need regular communication with their public, and might opt for more engagement in other popular platforms such as Facebook or Twitter. We introduce the problem of finding journalists on Twitter, one type of profession-based person search.

One use of microblogging is to disseminate breaking news [17, 28]. The wide adoption of these social technologies has also enabled some news gathering, filtering and dissemination activity to be led by nonprofessionals who have come known as "citizen journalists" [5]. The mainstream media has responded by encouraging their audience to interact through some predefined hashtags, by maintaining a Twitter account to keep their followers up to date, by creating new positions such as social media editors [33], and by leading crowdsourcing efforts [10]. The impact of these changes on the professional activities of journalists in the United States has been the subject of some recent qualitative studies such as Parmelee et al. [26], and our ultimate interest is in conducting studies of this sort that focus on the Arab world, which is in the midst of some dramatic changes.

One prerequisite for such studies is the ability to identify a sufficiently large and representative set of members of the population to be studied. While such lists can sometimes be constructed from the membership of professional associations, that approach is more useful in some places than others. In the case of journalists who cover the Arab world, a group in which we are interested, only relatively small and incomplete lists can be found. Because we are interested in how these journalists use Twitter, it is natural to look to Twitter itself as a way to finding.

Our focus is therefore to design, build and evaluate an automated system that can find a large set of authentic Twitter accounts belonging to a group of journalists with specific characteristics. After surveying the state of the art of related work in Section 2, we present in Section 3 the input and the search space of our systems. In Section 4 we then describe two families of methods for finding fairly homogeneous groups of journalists, one based on social network features, and another based on profile content features. We first assess the potential of our approach using an existing fairly comprehensive list of British radio journalists (Section 5) before tackling the more challenging problem of finding Arab journalists, for which we must create manual annotations as a basis for evaluation (Sections 6 and 7). We conclude with a few remarks about future work in Section 8.

2. RELATED WORK

Our task is an instance of person search, which can be seen as a special case of the broader problem of prediction of a demographic characteristic of social media users. Our methods are an instance of partially supervised learning. In this section we review related work on those topics.

2.1 Person Search

Much of the work on person search has focused on finding people with expertise on some topic, a variant of the person search problem referred to as expert search. For example,

CIKM'15, October 19–23, 2015, Melbourne, VIC, Australia.

ACM 978-1-4503-3794-6/15/10 ...$15.00.
DOI: http://dx.doi.org/10.1145/2806416.2806466 .

Han et al. built an interactive system that searched for academic experts, finding that modeling the degree of the social connection offered useful evidence, even when relevance and authority had already been modeled [16]. Their experiments were limited to searching for few persons and their collection (a crawl of ACM papers) was not subject to the noise that characterizes online social media, but we leverage this insight that social connection features can be informative.

Focusing more specifically on Twitter, Ghosh et al. designed a method relying on the feature of Twitter lists that allow users to organize some profiles of interest into lists of common themes or topics [16, 14]. They mined the titles and descriptions of these lists to infer expertise on several topics among many millions of Twitter users. In follow-up work, they used the same method to find groups of people that include experts and seekers of information about some topic [4]. They note, however, that reliance on user-generated lists from non-authoritative sources may be vulnerable to manipulation by spammers [16]. For this reason, we begin with what we judge to be authoritative lists, thus limiting our approach to the use of at most a small number of lists.

Topic-based person search naturally tends to find both experts and interested parties, whereas for our task we seek to find journalists rather than others. For example, a political topic might find both politicians and political journalists, and a journalism topic might cluster together journalists with news organizations and with researchers who study journalism. Cheng et al. [7] sought to mitigate a similar problem by also using location features in order to balance between topical and local authority. Such features are promising, but only a small portion of the Twitter stream is reliably geocoded, and our work on location inference in Arabic is not yet at a stage where we can make broader use of such features. We therefore look instead to the literature on predicting user demographics for further inspiration, since we can view profession as a demographic characteristic.

2.2 Predicting User Demographics

A variety of recent work has tackled the task of predicting user demographics in microblogging platforms, of which profession classification is a special case. Rao et al. [30] introduced the problem of user classification in Twitter. They defined four tasks to classify hundreds of users from four balanced datasets based on their gender [12], age [25], regional origin [18] and political orientation [8], using different social and linguistic features for each task. Bergsma et al. [2] clustered names and locations using connections created by user mentions, finding improvements in the prediction of geolocation [15], language [3], gender, ethnicity and race of users [23]. Pennacchiotti et al. [27] demonstrated that improvements can be gained by incorporating additional features such as profile content, and statistics about followers, friends, tweeting rate, hashtags and URLs. Our work is, to the best of our knowledge, the first to consider detecting members of any specific profession among microbloggers as its focal prediction task. We make use of the insight of Pennacchiotti et al. that profile text can productively be used together with friend and follower features, and Bergsma et al.'s insight that mentions also yield a useful feature set.

2.3 Partially Supervised Learning

Finding documents similar to a given set of known positive documents is a text classification problem known as *PU classification* (Positive/Unlabeled) or *partially supervised learning* [20]. Unlike traditional text classification tasks in which two sets, ideally of comparable sizes, are given to a learner as positive and negative labels, partially supervised learning starts with a small set of positive instances and a larger unlabeled set. The challenge becomes then to find a subset of "good" (i.e., useful) negative examples within the unlabeled documents to be fed to the learner.

A wide range of approaches have been suggested for this problem. Qiu et al. [29] focused on finding the initial set of positive documents, starting from a keyword and then mining labels from Wikipedia hyperlinks. We avoid this challenge by starting with a manually generated seed list. Fung et al. [13] built two unigram models for a positive and an unlabeled set that they then used to generate a ranked list of *core vocabulary* associated with the positive documents, before extracting a set of *reliable negative examples.* Sadamitsu et al. [31] proposed a method to expand a set of entities using topic models. Mordelet and Vert [24] suggested building several binary classifiers with the same known positive documents and different random samples from the unlabeled set as artificial negative instances. Bagging was then used to aggregate over the trained models. Our approach to using profile content, described in Section 4.2 most closely resembles the focus of Fung et al. on leveraging core vocabulary, although our approach to normalization differs somewhat, and we need only positive examples.

A technique that is close in spirit to the way we perform PU classification is Pseudo-Relevance Feedback (PRF), in which the basic approach is to enrich a one-sided query representation and then to rank the content to be searched without any reliance on negative examples [9]. The usual approach is to find some highly ranked documents using an initial query, and then to extract some terms from those documents and add them to the original query. Miyanishi et al. [22] proposed a two-stage PRF method for Twitter that consists of selecting a single tweet from the original ranked list, followed by a temporal query expansion relevance model. Wang et al. [21] used a related approach, expanding a query targeting short texts by issuing the query to a commercial search engine and exploiting the returned set to gather more terms. A rather different approach, similar in spirit, is based on the observation that URLs are sometimes the core information in the text of a tweet. Rather than expanding based on topical similarity, extends traditional PRF with expansion based on embedded hyperlinks [11]. While these techniques are widely used when improving search is the goal, we are not aware of any Twitter research using PRF in which searching for specific entity types (as with our interest in journalists) has been the goal.

3. SEED AND CANDIDATE JOURNALISTS

While some professionals such as physicians, engineers and lawyers acquire their titles after graduating from an appropriate school, some journalists become so by practicing journalism, rather than by taking classes. This can make it difficult to even assess whether somebody is a journalist. Wikipedia[1] defines a journalist as "a person who collects, writes or distributes news or other current information." In practice, it would be difficult to identify journalists based only on this definition. For example, while an act as simple

[1] `http://en.wikipedia.org/wiki/Journalist`

Figure 1: The self-identified journalist @youssefkuw shares an article of @fdalqabandi who lakes a profile description.

as retweeting a story is a way of distributing it, it is hard to believe that merely retweeting news stories would make one a journalist. On the other hand, some non-professionals play such an active role in collecting news that they consider themselves to be "citizen journalists." Instead of relying solely on any normative a priori definition, we therefore decided to adopt a descriptive approach, starting with a set of people who are authoritatively asserted to be journalists. This approach yields two benefits. First, we begin to develop and refine annotation guidelines that span a diverse range of members of the profession. Second, we can adopt this set as a "seed" from which we can find additional journalists.

Our "seed journalists" are some set of journalists who share some common characteristics that define the population we ultimately wish (in future work) to study (e.g., they work in a specific language, are from certain region, or specialize in a particular media). When such a seed set is not readily available, we can build one at some annotation cost, as we show in Section 6. Our goal in this paper is then to apply an automated method for finding additional journalists with similar characteristics.

To do this, we first need to define some search space. We do this by assuming that many journalists with similar characteristics will share some types of social connections. We thus consider two social graphs that are built from our seed journalists. The first graph relies on the network of followers (i.e., accounts that follow a seed journalist) and friends (i.e., accounts that the journalist follows). We observe that some journalists are very well known, with millions of followers. The density of journalists within such a large set of followers would be expected to be rather low, however. Similarly, journalists might be expected to follow many types of accounts that are not necessarily journalists (e.g. @BarakObama). With a goal of high precision in mind, we therefore restrict our friend/follower graph to bidirectional relationships. We collect this graph by querying Twitter API for both friends and followers of each account in the seed set, then intersecting these friends and followers.

The second graph we consider is constructed from mentions. A user can draw the attention of another user by including her screen name preceded by the '@' sign. We therefore also build a mention graph by connecting edges to accounts having reciprocated mentions with any of our seed journalists. Gathering this set is not as trivial as with the friend/follower graph because the Twitter API lacks a feature that allows retrieving the list of users who have ever mentioned a given account. We therefore begin by using the API to crawl all of the available tweets from the "timeline" (i.e., the sequential listing of tweets) of each of the seed journalists. The API returns up to 3,200 of the most recent Tweets.[2] We then similarly crawl all of the available tweets of accounts that have been mentioned in any tweet of any seed journalist. We search this collection to find any mentions of any seed journalist. The 3,200-tweet API limit means that we may miss some mentions by prolific accounts.

4. METHODS

We present three approaches for finding journalists based on one or both social graphs, and one based on profile text.

4.1 Social Graph

We use identical methods to rank candidates using the friend/follower and the mention graphs, and then we combine the two resulting rankings to produce an integrated ranking based on both sources of evidence.

4.1.1 Follows and Mentions

Kang and Lerman [19] demonstrated the effect of homophily in Twitter, which is the tendency of individuals to connect to similar others. We illustrate this observation for the mentions graph in Figure 1. The a-priori known journalist *@youssefkuw* mentions his colleague *@fdalqabandi*, whose profile does not indiate any occupation, while sharing his article. The latter mentions him back in a thank-you note. Reciprocal connections can be noisy, as some users tend to follow/mention back each incoming follow/mention. We can reduce this noise by enlarging the number of distinct journalists a candidate user is connected to. We therefore want to rank candidate accounts by their connectivity to the seed journalists.

Formally, let G be a set of vertices partitioned into S and V, corresponding to the sets of seed and candidate vertices respectively. E is the adjacency matrix of V and G. That is, for two vertices v and g in V and G respectively, $e(v, g) \in E$ has a value of 1 if a connection exists between v and g, and 0 otherwise. For a given vertex v in V, and the set of seed vertices S, we define a connectivity measure as a function of all the weights of the edges connecting v to S. In this paper we use two connectivity measures:

- Raw count, which is an integer between 0 and $|S|$: $c(v, S) = \sum_{s \in S} e(v, s)$
- Relative density, a rational number between 0 and 1: $d(v, S) = (\sum_{s \in S} e(v, s))/(\sum_{g \in G} e(v, g))$

We sort the candidate set in a decreasing order by raw count, breaking ties by sorting by decreasing relative density.

We apply this to the follows and mentions graphs independently. We denote by S-Follows and S-Mentions the associated approaches, respectively. We leave the study of other graphs such as hashtags, retweets and replies to future work.

4.1.2 Intersection-Based Reranking

Combining two ranked lists can yield a new ranking that is sometimes better than either. Algorithm 1 describes a

[2] http://dev.twitter.com/rest/reference/get/statuses/user_timeline

Algorithm 1 *Combine*(L_0, L_1)

input: L_0, L_1
output: L // Combined list
$L \leftarrow \{\}$
$l_0, l_1 \leftarrow \{\}$ // Elements seen in L_0 and L_1
for iteration i in 1 .. $Max(|L_0|, |L_1|)$ **do**
  for j in $0, 1$ **do**
    $e_j \leftarrow L_j.get(i)$
    if $e_j \in l_{1-j}$ **then** $L.add(e_j)$
    else $l_j.add(e_j)$
  if $e_0, e_1 \in L$ **and** $L_1.index(e_0) < L_0.index(e_1)$ **then**
    $L.swap(e_0, e_1)$

method that combines two lists ranked by the approaches S-Follows and S-Mentions introduced in the previous section. At any iteration i, we look at the i-th elements of the input lists L_0 and L_1. If either of these two elements has already been seen in another list, then we add it to the combined list L. Otherwise we hold it in a temporary list l_i for future lookup. If both of these two elements are to be added to L, then we sort them according to which of them was seen first. This algorithm is illustrated in Table 1.

4.2 PU Classification

We expect a language model built on top of text describing a set of homogeneous journalists to contain a signal that differentiates that set from the language model corresponding to a set of accounts in which these journalists constitute a minority. Based on this assumption, we can rank any given account based on its similarity to the language model of the set of known journalists.

Drawing from the work on text classification without negative examples [13], we denote by $DF(w_G)$ the document frequency of a word w_G from the set of Twitter accounts G, where a document is a text associated with a Twitter account. $DF(w_G)$ is, thus, the count of accounts in which w_G appears in the corresponding document. We then scale $DF(w_G)$ to a value between 0 and 1 as:

$$df(w_G) = \frac{DF(w_G) - \min_{w'_G \in G} DF(w'_G)}{\max_{w'_G \in G} DF(w'_G) - \min_{w'_G \in G} DF(w'_G)}$$

For a word w that appears in both the seed set S and the candidates set V, we denote by H the value $H(w) = df(w_S) - df(w_V)$. This value gives higher credit to words that are more frequent in the seed set than in the candidates set. In other words H defines a ranking of words by their relatedness to the documents associated with the journalist accounts. To avoid noise that could be generated by the words ranked at the bottom of this list, we define a threshold θ above which we truncate this list H into a sublist H':

$$\theta = |W_S|^{-1} \sum_{w \in S} H(w),$$

where $|W_S|$ is the count of unique words in the documents associated with the seed set S. Finally, each element h_w in H' has a rank r_w that we use to define the unnormalized positive referencing power p_w as:

$$p_w = exp(-r/|H'|)$$

For a given Twitter account g in G with a corresponding document d_g, we want to sum over all $p_{w \in d_g}$ to compute the similarity score. This sum, however, needs to be normalized with respect to the document length l_{d_g}, which is the count of unique words in d_g. If we normalize naively by dividing the sum over l_{d_g}, we risk giving a high rank to documents with a single noisy word (i.e., a word that undesirably has a high p_w value). Instead, we dampen the document length logarithmically. Finally, we score the document d_g based on the text features as:

$$t(d_g) = (\sum_{w \in d_g} p_w)/log(1 + l_{d_g})$$

Several document types can be associated with a Twitter account, such as the set of all hashtags and the concatenation of all or the most recent tweets. We limit our experiments in this paper to the description field appearing in the user profile. We denote by T-Desc this method that is based on the text features of the description field. We limit the set of journalists to be ranked by T-Desc to the candidates that are found by at least one of the social graphs with the same seed set, and that are not missing a profile description. In addition to the computational convenience, this restriction increases the precision by limiting the false positives. As an example, some of the Arab journalists that we focus on in Section 7 use some French and English words (e.g., producer) in their description in lieu of their Arabic counterparts (e.g., منتج). As a consequence, some of these foreign words would get a high rank in the core vocabulary. Had we not made this restriction, a higher number of English and French speaking journalists would thus likely be retrieved.

Table 1: Example of combining two ranked lists. At step i, there is no intersection between the two lists. At step ii, element F appears in List 1. We add it to the top of the combined list because we have already seen it in List 0. The next intersection involves element B at step iv. At step v, both element D and G are added to the combined list, but we start with G because it was seen first at step ii. List 1 is exhausted, but List 0 still has element H which has been seen at step iv. We append it to the combined list.

Step	List 0	List 1	Combined
i	F	B	-
ii	G	F	F
iii	A	D	-
iv	B	H	B
v	D	G	G, D
vi	H	-	H

5. FORMATIVE EVALUATION RESULTS

We begin our experiments by exploring the performance of our methods with a set of British radio journalists that is large enough to be divided into training and test sets. Our goal in this first set of experiments is to find out to what extent our algorithms can exploit a seed subset of these journalists to find others from the full set.

The website `Media.info` collects a list of contacts of media organizations and journalists from the United Kingdom (UK), Ireland (IE) and Gibraltar (GI). The profiles are of either a person (P) or an organization (O), and are distributed across radio stations, TV channels, newspapers and magazines. We consider only profiles that have at least one Twitter account. A profile can belong to more than one organization type and region (e.g., a journalist may have worked

Table 2: Distribution of Twitter accounts in media.info. P and O correspond respectively to accounts of persons (i.e., journalists) and news organizations.

	Magazine		Newspaper		**Radio**		Television	
	P	O	P	O	**P**	O	P	O
UK	83	311	314	290	**1529**	579	433	154
IE	4	22	112	40	222	83	19	11
GI	1	4	5	6	8	3	2	2

in a UK magazine before moving to an IE TV channel). We found that five Twitter accounts belong to both personal and organizational profiles. We consider these to be errors in the dataset and we exclude them. Table 2 shows the distribution of the remaining 4,137 Twitter accounts. For our experiments we consider positive examples to be Twitter accounts of the 1,529 British radio journalists (i.e, UK Radio P), including those who have also worked in other venues, and as negative examples the other 2,608 Twitter accounts within this dataset. Examples of such negative accounts include the Twitter accounts of a UK radio station, a UK newspaper editor, and a GI radio broadcaster. We chose that positive/negative split for two reasons. First, this task is more focused than that of finding any English speaking or even British journalists. If we succeed at our narrower task, we would expect to also succeed at more general tasks. Second, the number of British radio journalists is the largest subset identified in Table 2. This allows us to explore the impact of the broadest range of seed set sizes.

We want to evaluate our four algorithms using the labels of this dataset. We also want to keep track of the impact of the seed-set size on the performance of the systems. Two evaluation design issues need to be addressed. First, we need to choose a measure that relies only on known labels. Inspired by the work of Sakai [32], in which he defines $AveP'$ as the average precision on a ranked list after removing documents with unknown judgements, we define $P'@N$ as the precision at rank N on a list that has all of the unknown accounts removed. $P'@N$ is exactly $P@N$ when we know the labels of all of the first N accounts. The fewer unknown accounts we have, the closer $P'@N$ will likely be to $P@N$. We wish to keep $P'@N$ close to $P@N$, which is the measure we really care about. Thus, we avoid choosing a high value for N (even though we will want to retrieve hundreds of journalists in our ultimate application), as doing so would increase the number of unknown accounts excluded from the measurement. Hence, we use $P'@10$. Second, we need to measure on a stable test set if we are to compare results from different seed-set sizes. We therefore randomly draw a single held out test set and sweep across seed sets drawn from the remaining items.

As our test set we first randomly draw 500 accounts (without replacement) from the set of all 4,137 Twitter accounts. About 185 of these will typically be positive examples, leaving at most just over 1,300 positive examples for training. We then randomly order these remaining positive examples, and draw 27 nested samples with sizes between 5 and 1,300 as seed sets of British radio journalists. We then run our person search algorithms, obtaining one ranked list for each seed-set size from each algorithm. These ranked lists will typically find many Twitter accounts from outside the test set. Rather than judging those results manually, we evaluate each ranked list by going down the ranked list from the top

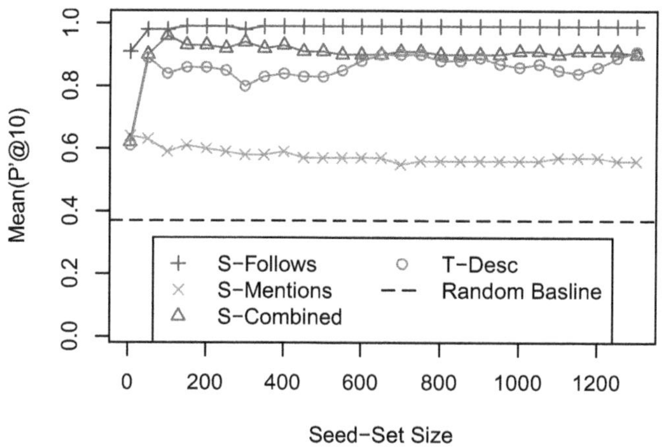

Figure 2: The mean of the precisions at 10, across ten random runs, for 27 seed-set sizes, using only the labels of accounts within test sets of size 500.

until 10 accounts that exist in the test set have been found, ignoring all other unknown accounts. If 10 known accounts are not found, we stop at the maximum number of accounts returned. We then compute the precision on just these first 10 known accounts. For cases in which fewer than 10 known positive examples are found anywhere in the ranked list, we still divide the number found by 10. This results in a single decile score (0.0, 0.1, 0.2, ..., 1.0) for each seed-set size and every algorithm. To obtain more fine-grained scores, we repeat the entire process—randomly drawing another test, randomly ordering the remaining positive examples, forming the 27 nested seed sets, running every algorithm for every seed set, and scoring the results—a total of ten times. We then average the resulting $P'@10$ values across the ten repetitions for each seed-set size and every algorithm.

Figure 2 depicts the results for each of our four person search algorithms. For reference, we plot a baseline $P'@10$ at 0.37, which is what would result from simply selecting 10 random accounts from the test set. We observe that S-Follows, S-Combined and T-Desc all yield fairly good results (mean $P'@10 \geq 0.8$) for seed-set sizes of at least 50. S-Mentions does least well, retrieving the largest number of detected false positives. To characterize the effect of ignoring unknown accounts, we can compute the mean of the ranks at which the first 10 known items in the test set were found. We take this mean across both the 10 items and the 10 repetitions. The lowest possible value for this mean is $avg(1..10) = 5.5$, which would be achieved if all of the top 10 accounts were in the test set. Taking a seed-set size of 200 as an example, the (rounded) average depths are 48, 49, 93 and 217 for S-follows, S-Combined, S-mentions, and T-Desc, respectively. We thus see that our three methods that rely on social features seem to behave more similarly than our one method (T-Desc) that relies on profile content features. Our results for Arabic in Section 7 help to explain this observation. To foreshadow that result, we believe that T-Desc is better able to find less prominent journalists than are our methods that are based on social features.

These formative evaluation results suggest that both social and profile content features can be useful. We therefore next evaluate our algorithms using a seed set of Arab journalists and newly created annotations.

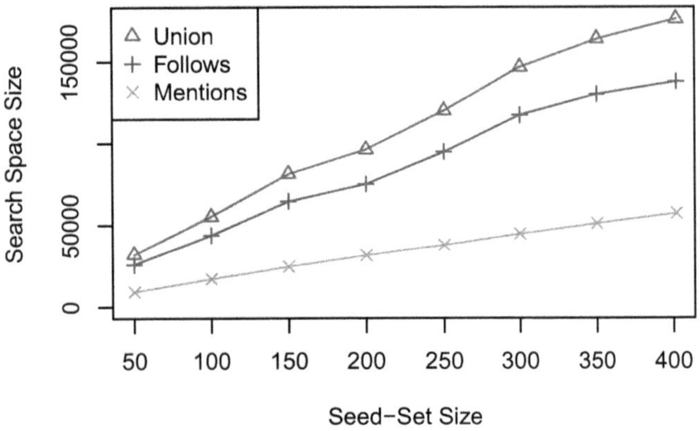

Figure 3: The average size of the search space as a function of the seed-set size. The limit of 3,200 tweets per account enforced by Twitter API makes the search space size of the mentions graph grow linearly but slowly. It grows at a higher speed for the follows graph, but with a diminishing return.

6. ARAB JOURNALISTS COLLECTION

Although Twitter accounts of many British radio journalists had been conveniently found, no such lists exist for Arab journalists. Twitter does allow users to construct lists of Twitter accounts, and several English news outlets do take advantage of this feature. For example, CNN maintains a list of 272 Twitter accounts, apparently of its own journalists[3] and Associated Press maintains a general list of 866 AP staff,[4] along with several more focused lists (e.g., of 73 AP photographers.[5]). Aljazeera Arabic, by contrast, offers no such list.[6] We therefore manually collected a seed set of Arab journalists, relying mainly on Wikipedia. After running our algorithms to find additional Arab journalists, we hired three annotators to evaluate our results.

6.1 Seed Journalists and Search Space

To build the seed set of Arab journalists, the first author looked at all names appearing under the category "Arab journalists" (including all its subcategories) in the Arabic version of Wikipedia.[7] We restricted our list to people who are still alive. The resulting set includes persons for whom Wikipedia indicates more than one title, such as writers, poets, politicians who are editing partisan newspapers, professors who are also newspaper columnists, news anchors, TV reporters, and retired journalists. Some pages contain direct links to a journalist's official website or Twitter account. If found, the first author visited the link to assess the authenticity of the account. Otherwise, two queries were issued to a commercial search engine that supports transliteration: (1) *name* site:twitter.com, and (2) *name* تويتر.[8] Because the name of a journalist might be shared with many other people, we sometimes needed to examine as many as 30 results, although often the candidate was found in the first 10.

[3]`http://twitter.com/CNN/lists/cnn-news`
[4]`http://twitter.com/AP/lists/ap-staff`
[5]`http://twitter.com/AP/lists/ap-photographers`
[6]`twitter.com/AlJazeera/lists/al-jazeera-arabic` contains only two organizational accounts.
[7]`http://ar.wikipedia.org/wiki/`تصنيف:صحفيون_عرب
[8]Twitter in Arabic

Table 3: List of labels available to the annotators to choose from. If the exact label was difficult to assess, a catch-all label for each category could be used (i.e., other).

Category	Labels
Journalist	Editor, photojournalist, magazine writer, news producer, broadcaster, correspondent, columnist, editor-in-chief, TV/radio host, other journalist
Cannot decide	Cannot verify (media person), cannot verify (other), account unavailable
Not a journalist	Writer, activist, oppositionist, poet, artist, spokesperson, blogger, politician, fan, bot, fake account, newspaper, station, channel, news org., news aggregator, other organization, other non-journalist

Table 4: Number of accounts assessed by both the first author, and each of the three independent annotators, with the corresponding Cohen's Kappa value.

	A1	A2	A3
Accounts /	317	418	20
Cohen's κ	0.78	0.75	0.78

To assess whether an account is actually associated with a specific journalist, rather than with a fan or with someone else with the same name, we relied on factors such as the name, the username, the profile content and picture, the number of tweets, the content of the most recent tweets (including links embedded in those tweets), the number of followers, a match between the age of the journalist as indicated by Wikipedia and by the profile, and an indication by Twitter that the account has been verified. No strict rules were set for any of these criteria. Instead, the first author made an individualized judgment in each case. Occasionally, in an ad-hoc way, he also considered some accounts that were followed by a journalist's account (e.g., their colleagues) as a way of expanding the list of journalists. The final result was a set of 402 Twitter accounts that we believe are quite clearly owned by Arab journalists. We use this set only for training; our evaluation data has been judged by independent annotators.

The union of the two bidirectional graphs of followers and mentions contains a set of 175,643 unique Twitter accounts. To study the effect of the seed-set size on the methods we describe below, we also define some nested subsets of our 402-journalist seed set. We do this by randomly sampling 50 journalists without replacement, then adding another 50, then another, and so on, up to 350. We repeat the graph construction process for each seed set, generating a subset of the full graph for each of the smaller seed sets. We perform this process three times, and we average our reported results over the three random sets. As an example of this process, Figure 3 shows how the average number of Twitter accounts in each graph grows with the seed set size.[9]

6.2 Annotations

To conduct our experiments we generated a pool of 1,441 annotations from the output of various systems and configurations (Section 4). We then hired three independent anno-

[9]These results are actually averaged over 10 points in each case because no annotation is required; results in Section 7 are averaged over three points to limit annotation costs.

tators (who are not aware of any details of our algorithms). We refer to these annotators as A1, A2 and A3; they assessed 710, 646 and 123 Twitter accounts, respectively. We asked them to judge whether an account is a journalist, and whether it is an Arab. To help them more consistently judge whether an account is a journalist, we gave them a list of labels, partitioned into three categories (journalist, cannot decide, not a journalist) that we allowed to grow incrementally based on their feedback (Table 3). For the results reported in this paper we consider as positive all accounts under the category journalist, and as negative all the other accounts. We asked the annotators to verify whether an account does actually belong to the corresponding person (by examining the profile and by running a Web search), and whether that person had ever practiced journalism (in a manner described by any of the provided titles). We emphasized that confusing labels within the same category was tolerable, but they were strongly encouraged to try their best not to confuse labels across different categories. It took, on average, three minutes to assess an account.

To compute inter-annotator agreement, the first author of this paper also annotated 723 accounts, doing so before examining the results of the independent annotators. Table 4 shows that there is high agreement with each annotator, with Cohen's chance-corrected Kappa values between 0.75 and 0.78. The first author's annotations were used only to compute inter-annotator agreement; the results in Section 7 are based solely on the independent annotations. In the few cases in which more than one independent annotator annotated the same account, we chose annotations from A1 or A3 over those of A2 for use as the gold standard.

7. EXPERIMENTS

We present our experiment design and discuss the results with respect to the number of journalists found, the diversity of retrieved accounts, and the trade-off between gathering a large seed set and annotating more retrieved accounts.

7.1 Baselines

We propose two baselines that a user who is trying to find Arab journalists might reasonably have tried. The first one is a keyword search: we issue a query through Twitter API to search for users using the word "journalist" in Arabic (صحفي). We name this method T-Baseline. The second method relies on Twitter's who-to-follow recommendations. For a given seed set, we create a Twitter account and configure its country to be Egypt, and its timezone to be that of Cairo (UTC +2 hours). We then set it to follow the accounts in the full 402-journalist seed set. To allow adequate time for any background processing performed by Twitter, we wait 24 hours before crawling the page of recommendations. We denote this method S-Baseline.

7.2 Performance

As described in Section 6, we sample nested subsets from the full seed set, repeating the process three times. We run our four systems on each subset and for the full set. We run S-Baseline only on the full set, and T-Baseline independently from any seed set. We then pool the top 50 accounts retrieved by each system and run, removing duplicates, ordering randomly, and partitioning arbitrarily among the three annotators. As our principal evaluation measure, we use precision at 50 (averaged, for the subsets, over the three

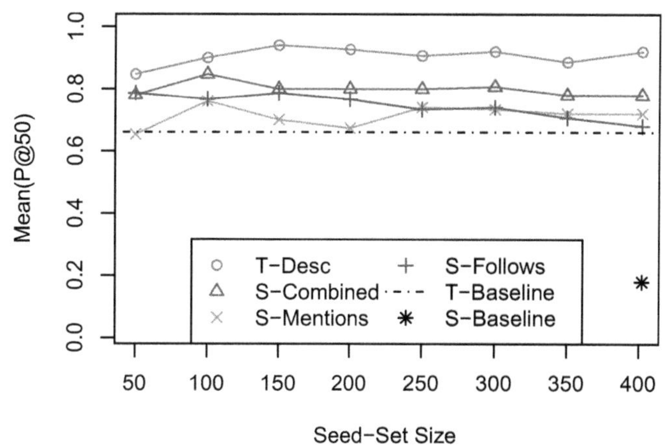

Figure 4: The mean, across three random runs, of the P@50 for our four methods (S-Follows, S-Mentions, S-Combined and T-Desc) on eight nested seed sets. The baselines are computed over one run, on seed-set size 402 for S-Baseline, and independently from the seed sets for T-Baseline.

samples) because annotations to depth 50 are sure from this process to be available. Figure 4 shows these results.

We observe that all four methods are relatively insensitive to the seed set size, although S-Follows seems to be slowly decreasing as the seed-set size increases, perhaps because its search space is increasing the most quickly (Figure 3). No clear preference between S-Mentions and S-Follows is evident, but intersection-based reranking (S-Combined) does indeed seem to be doing better than either of the methods that it combines. The clear winner, however, is T-Desc, which achieves outstanding results (precision at 50 of 0.94 at a seed-set size of 150, with only 3/50 false positives). This method does indeed extract a core vocabulary that one would expect to be related to Arab journalists such as *writer*, *journalist*, *editor*, *Sky* and *Arabia*, in addition to terms that we did not anticipate such as *opinions* and *endorsement*, which are often used when journalists want to separate their personal opinions from their employers, or emphasize that retweets are not endorsements.

For reference, we plot the precision at 50 for each of the proposed baselines. The keyword based baseline (T-Baseline), which is independent of the seed set, finds 33 Arab journalists in the top 50. This is markedly worse than our text based method (T-Desc) which finds, on average, no less than 42 journalists (which is the average value for a seed set size of 50). This baseline is close to what S-Mentions and S-Follows find, but is outperformed by S-Combined. The Twitter who-to-follow baseline (S-Baseline) finds nine Arab journalists in the top eleven retrieved accounts, and then starts to recommend accounts of celebrities and organizations in the region where we ran our experiments. This suggests that the eleven recommendations are based on the network of friends, while the other ones are recommended given the IP address of our machine. We do not know whether Twitter could have recommended additional journalists, but even if it were to have done so at the same rate (9/11=0.81) down to rank 50 (which seems to us a bit optimistic), it still would have been beaten by T-Desc.

P@50 is a useful measure of how accurate a method is, but to characterize completeness we need to look deeper in the

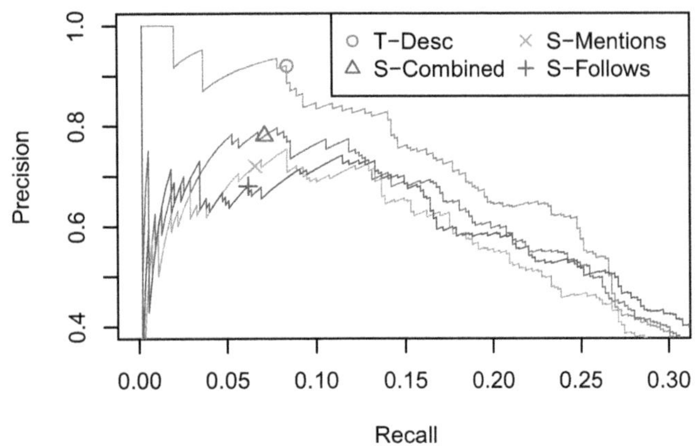

Figure 5: A recall / precision curve for the full seed set. We use all of the known annotations generated for three random runs, eight seed-set sizes and four systems. We assume all of the unassessed accounts to be negative.

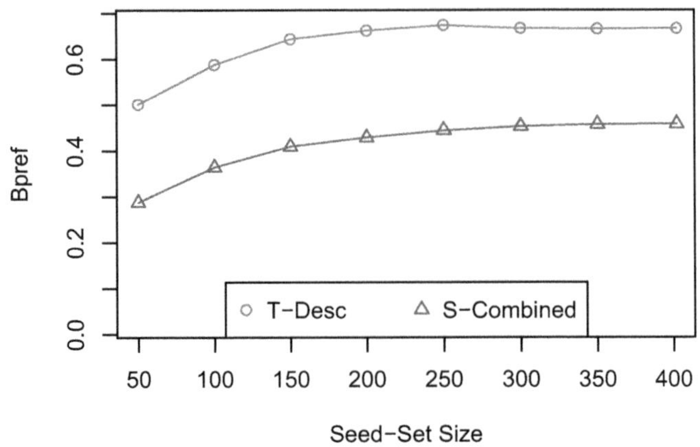

Figure 6: The mean of *bpref*, across three random runs, for eight seed-set sizes, using all of the annotations of the first 50 accounts, in addition to the annotations of seven accounts centered around the depths 50, 100, 250, 500, 750 and 1000.

ranked list. We can do this by computing a precision-recall plot. As is usual in such cases, we make the simplifying assumption that any unannotated account (i.e., any account that was never in the top 50 for any result set) is not a journalist. This tends to understate both precision and recall, but at relatively low computed recall levels (e.g, below 0.25) relative comparisons should remain reasonably accurate. In Figure 5, T-Desc is dominant over S-Combined over a large region, and there is almost no region in which S-Combined is dominated by either S-Mentions or S-Follows. For the remainder of this paper, we therefore focus on T-Desc and S-Combined.

Another way of looking deeper in the ranked list is to compute *bpref*, a ranked retrieval measure that is suitable for making system comparisons with incomplete judgments [6]. *bpref* is a ranking measure that scores a system based on its ability to rank known relevant items above the known irrelevant items; it is defined as:

$$bpref = \frac{1}{J}\sum_{j} 1 - \frac{|j \text{ ranked higher than } n|}{min(J,N)},$$

where j is an account retrieved from the set of known Arab journalists of size J, and n is retrieved from the set of accounts known to be not of Arab journalists (of size N).

On the positive side, *bpref* is able to consider the entirety of each ranked list; on the negative side its numerical value is not as easily interpreted as, for example, precision or recall. For computing *bpref* we also use the additional "point precision" annotations that we describe below in Section 7.4. Figure 6 illustrates the average *bpref* across three random runs for eight seed-set sizes, including annotations gathered at lower depths. Consistent with our other results, T-Desc does better at ranking journalists ahead of other accounts than S-Combined with any of the seed-set sizes that we tried, but they both tend to plateau at a seed-set size of about 250.

7.3 Retrieval Diversity

The results in Section 7.2 clearly indicate that between T-Desc and S-Combined, T-Desc is the better choice. This is, however, a false choice, since T-Desc and S-Combined find largely disjoint sets of journalists. To see this, we first look at the journalists retrieved by both methods based on the complete seed set (i.e., with 402 accounts). We find that T-Desc and S-Combined retrieve 46 and 39 journalists respectively within the first 50 accounts returned. Interestingly, only one journalist is returned by both of them. That is, out all of the top 50 journalists we can find with each method based on this seed set, only 1.19% are returned by both of these methods. Next, for each method independently, we look at all of the journalists retrieved using any of the eight seed sets and the three random runs. T-Desc finds a total of 261 journalists, while S-Combined finds 153. Only 12 journalists are retrieved by both. That is, less than 3%. Finally, we do not limit ourselves to the top 50 accounts, and we go as deep as we can (we cut off our analysis at 1000 returned accounts); for this analysis we also use the additional "point precision" annotations that we describe below in Section 7.4. We find that the intersection of the 660 and 541 journalists retrieved by T-Desc and S-Combined respectively is 260, 27.63% of the total.

Clearly, T-Desc and S-Combined are not finding the same journalists. This observation leads us to investigate the differences in the populations of journalists returned by these two methods. Figure 7 plots, on a log scale, some attribute values for the first 50 accounts returned using the full seed set. The filled circles and triangles correspond to the Arab journalists correctly retrieved by T-Desc or S-Combined, respectively (true positives), while the empty symbols correspond to the accounts retrieved that are not Arab journalists (false positives). We selected these attributes as indicators of the presence and activity of the accounts. As the top three plots for the Listed, Followers, and Favorites features show, journalists correctly found by S-Combined are more prominent than the ones returned by T-Desc.[10] Taking Followers as example, the median number of followers for journalists correctly detected by T-Desc is 1,328, while it is 53,540 for journalists correctly detected by S-combined.

These results suggest that different goals in the creation of lists of journalists may call for different methods. If the goal is to maximize the number of journalists, both techniques

[10] Listed counts the number of lists to which the account was added by other users; lists are a way of organizing tweets. Favorites counts how many times a journalist "favorites" another users' tweet as a way of calling attention to it.

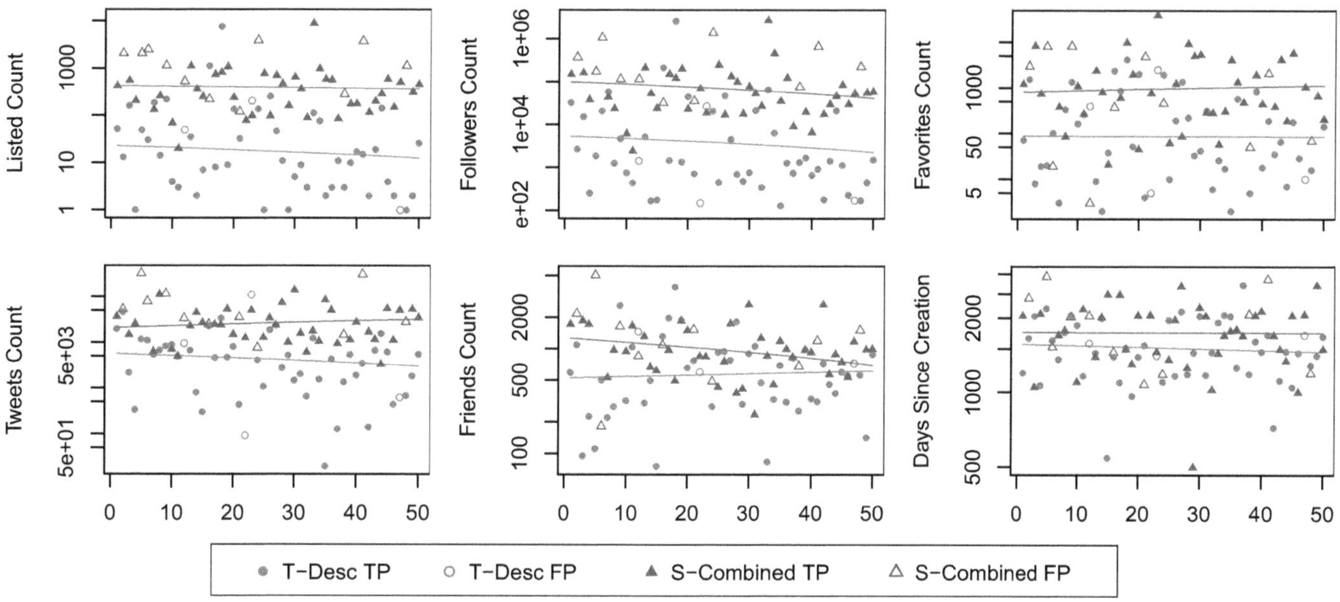

Figure 7: Numerical features of retrieved accounts (in a log scale) as a function of the retrieval rank (x-axis) and the ranking method. The retrieved accounts are either true or false journalists (TP and FP respectively). The fitting line are plotted after excluding the false journalists as well as the outliers (which are values outside the range $[q_1 - 1.5 \times IQR, q_3 + 1.5 \times IQR]$, where IQR is the difference between the first and the third quartiles q_1 and q_3 respectively).

should be used. If, however, the goal is to find journalists who are representative of a broad population, T-Desc alone may be the better choice because using S-Combined risks biasing the set in favor of prominent and prolific journalists. Of course, it is prominent journalists that we wish to study, then S-Combined would be an excellent choice.

7.4 Annotation Cost

We have so far focused on the performance of the various systems ignoring the cost of obtaining the initial seed set. Indeed, if this set was freely accessible and known a priori to be accurate, then focusing on the precision and yield (recall × cutoff) of the resulting systems would suffice. However, if this seed were to be expensive to gather and manually check, then we might be better off acquiring a smaller seed set and annotating more deeply in the ranked list. We now turn to the question of how best to balance annotation costs and the quality of the results. This is particularly useful when we want to find some minimum number of journalists, across the seed set and retrieved list. Here we model cost by annotation time using, for example, the average of three minutes per annotation that we reported above in Section 6.2.

We formalize this trade-off by estimating the number of retrieved journalists at any depth (down to 1000), as a function of the seed-set size. For each of a list of five seed-set sizes between 50 and 402, we compute the "point precision" (i.e., the precision near some point in the ranked list) at 50, 100, 250, 500, 750 and 1000. We do so by computing the ratio of accounts that are journalists within a radius of 3 of these specific points in the ranked list (i.e., count(journalists) / 7). The area under the curve defined by these depths and the corresponding point precisions approximates the number of retrieved journalists down to the depth 1000.

Figure 8 shows one way in which we can use these results, looking in this case at the estimated yield in the top 1000.

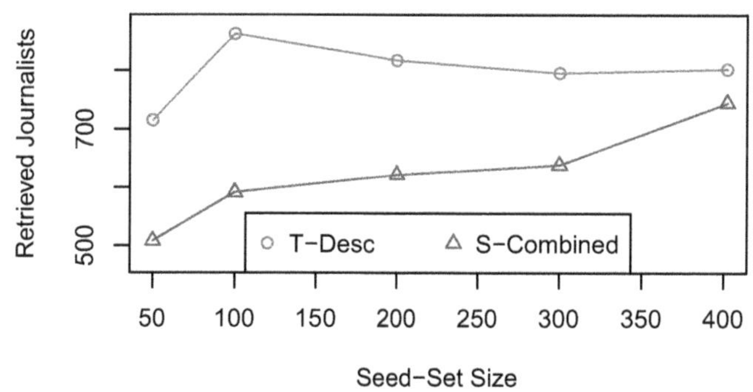

Figure 8: Number of retrieved journalists at depth 1000. For a given seed-set size, we estimate this number by computing the point precision at depths 50, 100, 250, 500, 750 and 1000, and calculating the area under the curve of the precision = f (depth). We then average over three random runs.

As with our earlier results for precision at 50, there is no evidence beyond seed set sizes of 100 that T-Desc does better with larger seed-set sizes. It appears that the core vocabulary words are learned adequately with even smaller seed-set sizes. On the other hand, S-combined does find more journalists as the seed set size increases, but with a diminishing return. Curves of this type, computed at different depths, can serve as a guide for balancing between training (i.e., acquiring more seed journalists) and testing (i.e., gathering more journalists by applying the ranking method) when the cost of training annotations is significant [1].

8. CONCLUSIONS AND FUTURE WORK

We have introduced the problem of using a seed set to find journalists in Twitter. We suggested two families of methods to solve this problem. The first relies on the bidirectional social links of friends/followers or mentions which, when combined, tends to retrieve prominent journalists with high precision. The second, based on text features from the profile description, retrieves journalists that are less active on Twitter, with even higher precision. As we have discussed, the preference for one approach over the other, or for using both, depends on the characteristics of the set of journalists that we wish to construct. Considering the total annotation budget for both building the seed set and assessing the retrieved ranked list, our results clearly indicate that we can get along rather well with fairly small seed sets.

This work can be extended in several directions. First, our Institutional Review Board approval to conduct this research and to disseminate our annotated list of Arab journalists requires us to reverify that each account that we identify in this way is associated with a public attribution of the account as being owned by a journalist. We were able to satisfy this condition for 1,1231 out of the 1,231 journalists in our seed set or for which we have independent annotations.[11]

Other sources of text features might also be exploited in future work (e.g., tweet content, hashtag use, or URL content). Other types of social relationships (e.g., physical proximity) might also be tried. In addition, we can extend the search space to the two-hop neighbors of the seed-set. We might also productively explore other ways of combining social evidence, and of combining social and content evidence. One more aspect that needs examination is the geographical and topical distribution of the journalists in the seed-set. A diversified sampling can lead to results different from simple random sampling, or using Wikipedia to construct the seed-set. Finally, we might also try these ideas with other populations. We expect to find that some professions (e.g., professors) might yield results quite like that which we have seen with journalists, while perhaps for others (e.g., airline pilots) with different patterns of Twitterati fame, we might see very different results.

ACKNOWLEDGMENT

This work was made possible by NPRP grant# NPRP 6-1377-1-257 from the Qatar National Research Fund (a member of Qatar Foundation). The statements made herein are solely the responsibility of the authors.

9. REFERENCES

[1] M. Bagdouri, W. Webber, D. D. Lewis, and D. W. Oard. Towards minimizing the annotation cost of certified text classification. In *CIKM*, 2013.
[2] S. Bergsma, M. Dredze, B. V. Durme, T. Wilson, and D. Yarowsky. Broadly improving user classification via communication-based name and location clustering on Twitter. In *NAACL*, 2013.
[3] S. Bergsma, P. McNamee, M. Bagdouri, C. Fink, and T. Wilson. Language identification for creating language-specific Twitter collections. In *LSM*, 2012.
[4] P. Bhattacharya, S. Ghosh, J. Kulshrestha, M. Mondal, M. B. Zafar, N. Ganguly, and K. P. Gummadi. Deep Twitter diving: Exploring topical groups in microblogs at scale. In *CSCW*, 2014.
[5] S. Bowman and C. Willis. We media: How audiences are shaping the future of news and information. `hypergene.net/wemedia`, 2003. Accessed: 2015-01-19.
[6] C. Buckley and E. M. Voorhees. Retrieval evaluation with incomplete information. In *SIGIR*, 2004.

[11] `http://cs.umd.edu/~mossaab/files/arab-journalists.tgz`

[7] Z. Cheng, J. Caverlee, H. Barthwal, and V. Bachani. Who is the barbecue king of Texas?: A geo-spatial approach to finding local experts on Twitter. In *SIGIR*, 2014.
[8] R. Cohen and D. Ruths. Classifying political orientation on Twitter: It's not easy! In *ICWSM*, 2013.
[9] W. B. Croft and D. J. Harper. Using probabilistic models of document retrieval without relevance information. *JDoc*, 35(4), 1979.
[10] D. Dailey and K. Starbird. Journalists as crowdsourcerers: Responding to crisis by reporting with a crowd. *CSCW*, 23(4-6), 2014.
[11] T. El-Ganainy, W. Magdy, and A. Rafea. Hyperlink-extended pseudo relevance feedback for improved microblog retrieval. In *SoMeRA*, 2014.
[12] C. Fink, J. Kopecky, and M. Morawski. Inferring gender from the content of tweets: A region specific example. In *ICWSM*, 2012.
[13] G. P. C. Fung, J. X. Yu, H. Lu, and P. S. Yu. Text classification without negative examples revisit. *TKDE*, 18(1), 2006.
[14] S. Ghosh, M. B. Zafar, P. Bhattacharya, N. Sharma, N. Ganguly, and K. Gummadi. On sampling the wisdom of crowds: Random vs. expert sampling of the Twitter stream. In *CIKM*, 2013.
[15] B. Han, P. Cook, and T. Baldwin. Text-based Twitter user geolocation prediction. *JAIR*, 2014.
[16] S. Han, D. He, J. Jiang, and Z. Yue. Supporting exploratory people search: A study of factor transparency and user control. In *CIKM*, 2013.
[17] M. Hu, S. Liu, F. Wei, Y. Wu, J. Stasko, and K.-L. Ma. Breaking news on Twitter. In *CHI*, 2012.
[18] W. Huang, I. Weber, and S. Vieweg. Inferring nationalities of Twitter users and studying international linking. In *HT*, 2014.
[19] J.-H. Kang and K. Lerman. Using lists to measure homophily on Twitter. In *ITWP*, 2012.
[20] B. Liu, W. S. Lee, P. S. Yu, and X. Li. Partially supervised classification of text documents. In *ICML*, 2002.
[21] W. Meng, L. Lanfen, W. Jing, Y. Penghua, L. Jiaolong, and X. Fei. Improving short text classification using public search engines. In *IUKM*, volume 8032. Springer, 2013.
[22] T. Miyanishi, K. Seki, and K. Uehara. Improving pseudo-relevance feedback via tweet selection. In *CIKM*, 2013.
[23] E. Mohammady and A. Culotta. Using county demographics to infer attributes of Twitter users. In *Joint Workshop on Social Dynamics and Personal Attributes in Social Media*, 2014.
[24] F. Mordelet and J. P. Vert. A bagging SVM to learn from positive and unlabeled examples. *PRL*, 2014.
[25] D. Nguyen, R. Gravel, D. Trieschnigg, and T. Meder. "How old do you think I am?" a study of language and age in Twitter. In *ICWSM*, 2013.
[26] J. H. Parmelee. Political journalists and Twitter: Influences on norms and practices. *JMP*, 14(4), 2013.
[27] M. Pennacchiotti and A.-M. Popescu. A machine learning approach to Twitter user classification. In *ICWSM*, 2011.
[28] S. Phuvipadawat and T. Murata. Breaking news detection and tracking in Twitter. In *WI-IAT*, 2010.
[29] Q. Qiu, Y. Zhang, J. Zhu, and W. Qu. Building a text classifier by a keyword and Wikipedia knowledge. In *ADMA*, 2009.
[30] D. Rao, D. Yarowsky, A. Shreevats, and M. Gupta. Classifying latent user attributes in Twitter. In *SMUC*, 2010.
[31] K. Sadamitsu, K. Saito, K. Imamura, and G. Kikui. Entity set expansion using topic information. In *HLT*, 2011.
[32] T. Sakai. Alternatives to bpref. In *SIGIR*, 2007.
[33] E. Zak. 4 questions with Liz Heron, the New York Times social media editor. `adweek.com/fishbowlny/-/250679`, 2012. Accessed: 2015-01-13.

Learning Entity Types from Query Logs via Graph-Based Modeling

Jingyuan Zhang[†], Luo Jie[*], Altaf Rahman[*], Sihong Xie[†], Yi Chang[*] and Philip S. Yu[†,‡]
[†]Department of Computer Science, University of Illinois at Chicago, Chicago, IL, USA
[‡]Institute for Data Science, Tsinghua University, Beijing, China
[*]Yahoo! Labs, Sunnyvale, CA, USA
{jzhan8, sxie6, psyu}@uic.edu, luoj.roger@yahoo.com, {altafr, yichang}@yahoo-inc.com

ABSTRACT

Entities (e.g., person, movie or place) play an important role in real-world applications and learning entity types has attracted much attention in recent years. Most conventional automatic techniques use large corpora, such as news articles, to learn types of entities. However, such text corpora focus on general knowledge about entities in an objective way. Hence, it is difficult to satisfy those users with specific and personalized needs for an entity. Recent years have witnessed an explosive expansion in the mining of search query logs, which contain billions of entities. The word patterns and click-throughs in search logs are not found in text corpora, thus providing a complemental source for discovering entity types based on user behaviors. In this paper, we study the problem of learning entity types from search query logs and address the following challenges: (1) queries are short texts, and information related to entities is usually very sparse; (2) large amounts of irrelevant information exists in search logs, bringing noise in detecting entity types. In this paper, we first model query logs using a bipartite graph with entities and their auxiliary information, such as contextual words and clicked URLs. Then we propose a graph-based framework called ELP (**E**nsemble framework based on **L**able **P**ropagation) to simultaneously learn the types of both entities and auxiliary signals. In ELP, two separate strategies are designed to fix the problems of sparsity and noise in query logs. Extensive empirical studies are conducted on real search logs to evaluate the effectiveness of the proposed ELP framework.

Categories and Subject Descriptors

H.2.8 [**Database management**]: Database applications-Data mining

Keywords

Query; Entity; Graph

CIKM'15, October 19–23, 2015, Melbourne, Australia.
© 2015 ACM. ISBN 978-1-4503-3794-6/15/10 ...$15.00.
DOI: http://dx.doi.org/10.1145/2806416.2806498.

1. INTRODUCTION

An *entity* is something that exists in itself, actually or potentially, concretely or abstractly, physically or not [1]. Entities are forming the building block for various web applications. Yelp [2] is building on top of a corpus of *local* class entities (*e.g.*, the restaurant entity "The French Laundry", the Point of Interest entity "Golden Gate Bridge", etc.) associated with user reviews. IMDB [3] has a large corpus of *movie* and *actor* class entities. Modern search engines like Bing, Google and Yahoo! start building Knowledge Graph containing a large collection of diverse types of entities. When a user issues a question about an entity (*e.g.*, "net worth of Bill Gates" or "phone number of Gary Danko"), the search engine can retrieve results directly from the knowledge graph, satisfying the user's need and providing better user experience. Recent study shows that around 70% of the queries contain entity information [31, 22]. Hence, the coverage of entities is very important for these applications. Moreover, knowing the exact types of entities can help the application decide the best way in presenting results to users.

Various entity repositories, ranging from the more general collaborative knowledge bases such as Wikipedia and Freebase to the domain-specific corpora such as IMDB and Yelp, are widely used to extract entity information and aggregate the information into a comprehensive knowledge graph. However, there are several problems with this approach: (a) *coverage*: it is one of the key metric in measuring the quality of knowledge. Knowledge bases like Wikipedia and Freebase primary focus on popular entities from a few limited types, while other domain-specific corpora are more expensive to obtain. Plus, little information exists in knowledge bases for many less popular entities or newly generated entities, such as a new music title. It is difficult to identify and extract such entities in time; (b) *ambiguity*: multiple types of entity are often associated with the same string collected from the same or different sources. For example, the token "Chicago" is not only a city entity, but also a movie entity or a rock band entity. How to separate them apart in case little is known about the types of the entities, and how to rank these entities according to the *popularity* and/or user intent, are both quite challenging; (c) *discrepancy*: errors may exist due to user-generated contents via crowdsourcing, thus information extracted from these sources may be noisy and inconsistent.

[1] `http://en.wikipedia.org/wiki/Entity`
[2] `http://www.yelp.com/`
[3] `http://www.imdb.com/`

User	Query	Clicked URL	Click Times
A	home sales in New York	www.zillow.com/homedetails/	4
B	real estate in Maxwell	www.zillow.com/homedetails/	5
C	albums of Maxwell	www.songkick.com/artists/	3
D	songs by Taylor Swift	www.songkick.com/artists/	5

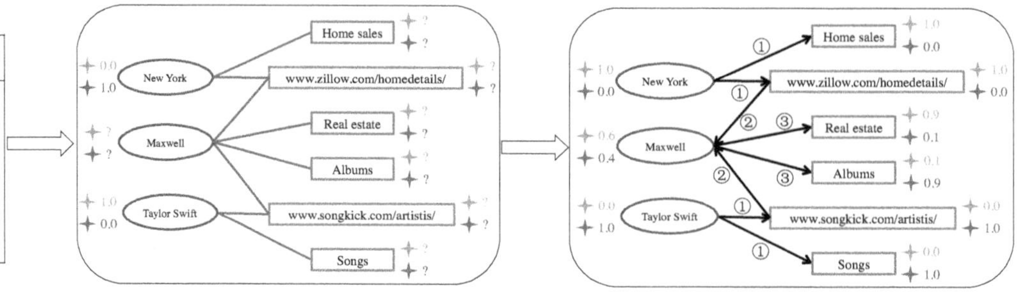

(a) Search query logs (b) Graph construction (c) Learning steps

Figure 1: An intuitive example of learning entity types from search query logs. In (b), the four-pointed orange and blue stars mean the person and place types, respectively. The number next to a star shows the probability of a node belonging to a type. "1.0" means the type is already known and "?" means that we need to learn the type from search query logs. In (c), each black arrowed line shows the propagation direction and the circled number on each line represents the order of the propagation process.

A lot of research work in the literature tries to overcome the above challenges from different perspectives. The existing knowledge bases could only cover a fraction of the whole entity space. In order to expand the size of knowledge bases, many automatic techniques have been proposed to discover entities and their types from different large corpora, such as news articles and web pages [3, 9, 30]. In addition, disambiguating entities from news reports is also studied in [14, 20]. Other sources such as search query logs can also be leveraged to extract and disambiguate entities. Since the search engine has become the main information source for most people to look for information, search query logs can be a nice complementary source for extracting new entity information as well as learning entity popularity and disambiguating entities. A few state-of-the-art approaches are proposed to classify and disambiguate entities in query logs [16, 26, 6]. For instance, intent-based Model (IM) [26] predicts entity type distributions by jointly modeling user intent and entity types via probabilistic inference in a graphical manner. Fast Entity Linker (FEL) is proposed in [6] to disambiguate entities by linking queries to entities in a knowledge base. However, these methods do not fully explore the importance of auxiliary signals in query logs, i.e. the structural language patterns (contextual word patterns) in queries and the clicked domains from relevant web URL results. For example, given the query "menu of Purple Pig" and a user's clicked domain URL "yelp.com", both the pattern "menu of" and the clicked URL help predicting "Purple Pig" as a local restaurant entity. Therefore, knowing the types of these important signals can help mining entity types from query logs more effectively.

In this paper, we model search query logs into a bipartite graph to encode relations between entities and important signals. Two kinds of nodes, entities and their auxiliary information, are contained in the constructed bipartite graph shown in Figure 1 (b). With such a bipartite graph, we can take advantage of the encoded relations [35] to learn entity types. Moreover, the type information can also be assigned to auxiliary nodes, thereby helping disambiguating entities via user-generated texts (*e.g.*, contextual words) and user feedbacks (*e.g.*, clicked URLs). In this paper, we apply a graph-based **L**abel **P**ropagation (LP) method to simultaneously learn types of both entities and auxiliary signals. Figure 1 (c) shows the steps of LP in an intuitive way. Given a small number of prior-known entities, the types of these entities are first propagated to the connected auxiliary nodes, and then the types are propagated back from auxiliary nodes to unknown entities. Despite the simple idea, mining entity types from the built graph is still a challenging task due to the following reasons:

- Queries are short texts, and information related to entities is usually very sparse. It is non-trivial to explore the hidden connections among entities and auxiliary information in search logs.
- Large amounts of irrelevant information exists in search logs, bringing noise in detecting entity types. It is difficult to discover and remove such noisy information from search logs.

In order to address these two issues, we propose an **E**nsemble framework based on **L**abel **P**ropagation (ELP) to simultaneously learn types of both entities and auxiliary signals. Specifically, we design two separate strategies to fix the problems of sparsity and noise in query logs, respectively.

In summary, our contributions are as follows:

- We represent query logs as a bipartite graph about entities and their auxiliary signals. We leverage such interconnected relationships between entities and their auxiliary signals to learn both entity types and auxiliary node types together.
- We propose an **E**nsemble framework based on **L**abel **P**ropagation (ELP) and design two separate strategies in ELP to effectively learn node types from search query logs.
- We conduct extensive empirical studies on search logs from a real-world search engine to demonstrate the effectiveness of the proposed ELP framework. In addition, some case studies show that ELP can learn important word patterns for different types of entities, as well as disambiguating entities via the connected auxiliary informaiton.

2. BACKGROUND

In this section, we first introduce several related concepts and notations. Then, we will formally define the problem of learning node types from a bipartite entity-auxiliary graph extracted from query logs.

Definition 1. **A Bipartite Entity-Auxiliary (EA) Graph**: A bipartite entity-auxiliary (EA) graph is represented as an undirected graph $\mathcal{G} = (\mathcal{V}, \mathcal{E})$. $\mathcal{V}$ is the set of nodes (objects), including two types of objects, i.e., entities $E = \{e_1, ..., e_M\}$ and auxiliary signals $A = \{a_1, ..., a_N\}$. $\mathcal{E} \subseteq E \times A$ is the set of links (relations) between the nodes in V, which involves the *associatedWith* link between entities and auxiliary signals. Let $\mathcal{W}$ denote an $M \times N$ weight matrix, in which element w_{ij} equals the frequency associating e_i and a_j.

Figure 1 (b) shows an example of a bipartite EA graph extracted from the search query logs in Figure 1 (a). Three entities are connected with six auxiliary signals, including four contextual words and two clicked URLs.

In EA graph, each entity has at least one type (label) in reality. We assume there are K labels for entities ($K \geq 2$) and represent entity types as $\mathcal{Y} \in \mathbb{R}^{M \times K}$. $y_{ik} \in \mathcal{Y}$ is a non-negative real number indicating the probability that entity e_i belongs to label k. In practice, a small set of entities (seed entities) in the graph may be manually labeled with their types. We denote the labeled entity set as E_L. In Figure 1 (b), both "New York" and "Taylor Swift" are considered as seed entities. We use $\mathcal{Y}^0$ to denote an instantiation of $\mathcal{Y}$ that is consistent with the seed labels. Given an entity $e_i \in E_L$ with n labels ($n \geq 1$), we set y_{ik}^0 as $1.0/n$ if e_i has label k, otherwise 0. Given the entity $e_i \in E \backslash E_L$ without labels, we have $y_{ik}^0 = 0$ for any label k.

From the existing search logs D, we can extract a bipartite graph $\mathcal{G} = (\mathcal{V}, \mathcal{E})$ and get $\mathcal{Y}^0$ according to some seed entities E_L. Our goal is to learn entity types $\mathcal{Y}$ from $\mathcal{G}$. Since the auxiliary nodes can also carry labels with them to indicate the important interconnections between entities and the auxiliary signals, another goal is to assign labels to those auxiliary nodes in $\mathcal{G}$. We use $\mathcal{Z} \in \mathbb{R}^{N \times K}$ as labels of auxiliary nodes, where the element z_{jk} is a non-negative real number indicating the probability that a_j relates to label k. Thus our ultimate goal becomes to estimate $\mathcal{Y}$ and $\mathcal{Z}$ given $\mathcal{G}$ and E_L. In order to solve this problem, we apply a graph-based **L**abel **P**ropagation (LP) method to leverage these important auxiliary signals via their connections with the target entities as shown in Figure 1 (c).

3. PROPOSED METHOD

In this section, we propose an **E**nsemble framework based on **LP** (ELP) to simultaneously learn types of both entities and auxiliary signals from query logs. Before proceeding, we first introduce how to build the entity-auxiliary graph from real-world search logs.

3.1 Graph Construction

Given search logs, we first have to extract entities from queries. Several methods are applied to find entities in this paper. First, we use a part-of-speech tagger [1] to extract contiguous words of proper nouns, common nouns and capitalized words [16, 17] to form noun phrases. Second, we match the extracted noun phrases according to a dictionary of entities built from knowledge bases, such as Wikipedia, Freebase and Yelp. We do not use the type information in those knowledge bases. We assume that the types of entities are unknown in the experiments. These methods help us detect entities in high precision. Besides, we can use a more complex model in [10] to identify the entity and the background part (i.e., contextual words). In the example of the search logs in Figure 1 (a), we extract "New York", "Maxwell" and "Taylor Swift" as entities. Thus, "home sales", "real estate", "albums" and "songs" are considered as contextual words. In our experiments, we use both the uni-gram and binary-grams of contexts as auxiliary nodes. The stop-word nodes are removed from our graph.

In search logs, clicked URLs are also very important for learning entity types. Since each clicked URL may have several levels of domain names to point to a certain webpage, there will be too many redundant nodes of clicked URLs in the constructed graph. Therefore, we group a set of URLs into a single auxiliary node if they have exactly the same top- and second-level domain names. In Figure 1 (a), we only show the first two domain names for the clicked URLs. We use the frequencies of entities and auxiliary nodes appearing together in the query logs as weights of corresponding edges.

Such a bipartite graph helps encode relations between entities and important auxiliary signals from search query logs. We can take advantage of the encoded relations to discover entity types by applying the graph-based LP method. However, directly applying LP may not be satisfying due to the following issues in query logs:

1. Queries are short texts, and information related to entities is usually very sparse. LP may not propagate labels adequately. Therefore, it is necessary to explore the hidden connections in EA graph.

2. Large amounts of irrelevant information exists in search logs, bringing noise in detecting entity types. LP may propagate errors out and enlarge the error information due to the noise. Hence, it is imperative to discover and remove such noisy information from the EA graph.

In the following, we first focus our attention on how to apply LP on the built graph to learn types of both entities and auxiliary signals simultaneously. Then we introduce two separate strategies LPA and LPD to address the problem of sparsity and noise in the EA graph respectively. After that, we describe the proposed ELP framework that takes advantage of the LPA and LPD strategies.

3.2 Methodology

3.2.1 The LP Method

The problem of learning with labeled and unlabeled data from graphs has been investigated in [36, 37, 18, 33, 11]. The objective and algorithm of the LP method used in this paper are heavily influenced by the works of [36, 18]. Given the collection of search log data D, we can extract an entity-auxiliary graph $\mathcal{G} = (\mathcal{V}, \mathcal{E})$ with a weight matrix $\mathcal{W}$ as introduced in Section 2. With a small set of seed entities E_L, we can initialize $\mathcal{Y}^0$. Our goal is to automatically estimate $\mathcal{Y}$ for entities and $\mathcal{Z}$ for auxiliary nodes according to $\mathcal{W}$ and $\mathcal{Y}^0$. We define a normalized frequency matrix as follows:

$$\mathcal{N} = \mathcal{D}^{-1/2}\mathcal{W}, \tag{1}$$

where $\mathcal{D}$ is a diagonal matrix and each element $d_{ii} \in \mathcal{D}$ is the sum of all the elements in the ith row (or column) of $\mathcal{W}\mathcal{W}^\top$. Intuitively, d_{ii} can be interpreted as the volume of all length-of-two paths that start at e_i. The reason we use such a normalization is to guarantee the convergence of LP as shown in [18].

Algorithm 1 The LP algorithm

Input: Search query log D, a set of seed entities E_L and a trade-off parameter α

Output: Label matrices $\mathcal{Y}$ and $\mathcal{Z}$

1: *//graph construction step*
Build an entity-auxiliary graph $\mathcal{G} = (\mathcal{V}, \mathcal{E})$ from D
2: *//initialization step*
Initialize $\mathcal{Y}$ as $\mathcal{Y}^0$ according to E_L
3: Compute the weight matrix $\mathcal{W}$ from $\mathcal{G}$
4: Compute $\mathcal{N}$ from $\mathcal{W}$ according to Equation (1)
5: *//iterative computation step*
6: **while** NOT converged **do**
7: *//propagation step from entities to auxiliary nodes*
Compute $\mathcal{Z}^t$ according to Equation (2)
8: *//propagation step from auxiliary nodes to entities*
Compute $\mathcal{Y}^t$ according to Equation (3)
9: **end while**
10: Normalize $\mathcal{Y}$ and $\mathcal{Z}$ according to Equation (5)

With the above definitions and notations, LP iteratively updates $\mathcal{Y}$ and $\mathcal{Z}$. For the t-th iteration, it first propagates the types of entities to the connected auxiliary nodes:

$$\mathcal{Z}^t = \mathcal{N}^\top \mathcal{Y}^{t-1}. \tag{2}$$

Then it propagates the types back to entities from the auxiliary nodes as follows:

$$\mathcal{Y}^t = \alpha \mathcal{N} \mathcal{Z}^t + (1-\alpha)\mathcal{Y}^0, \tag{3}$$

where α is a parameter to trade off the label consistency between the intrinsic graph structure and the seed entities. It has been shown in [18] that the sequence of $\mathcal{Y}^t$ asymptotically converges to:

$$\mathcal{Y}^* = (1-\alpha)(\mathbf{1} - \alpha \mathcal{D}^{-1/2}\mathcal{W}\mathcal{W}^\top \mathcal{D}^{-1/2})^{-1}\mathcal{Y}^0. \tag{4}$$

The time complexity of LP is $O(T|\mathcal{E}|)$, where T is the iteration number and $|\mathcal{E}|$ is the number of connections in the EA graph. Through our experiments, the algorithm converges after no more than 20 rounds in most cases. The LP method is summarized in Algorithm 1.

Once $\mathcal{Y}$ and $\mathcal{Z}$ are obtained, we normalize their elements to get the posterior probabilities $p(k|e_i)$ for $i = 1, ..., M$ and $p(k|a_j)$ for $j = 1, ..., N$ as follows:

$$\begin{aligned} p(k|e_i) &= y_{ik} / \sum_{l=1}^{k} y_{il}, \\ p(k|a_j) &= z_{jk} / \sum_{l=1}^{k} z_{jl}. \end{aligned} \tag{5}$$

3.2.2 The Proposed LPA Strategy

Directly applying LP may not be satisfying because the connections extracted from query logs are very sparse and LP cannot propagate labels adequately. Therefore, we propose a strategy LPA (**L**abel **P**ropagation after **A**dding more connections) to explore the hidden connections in the EA graph. We take advantage of the word2vec tool [4] to connect entities with more contextual words and help the LP model propagate labels more effectively.

[4]`https://code.google.com/p/word2vec/`

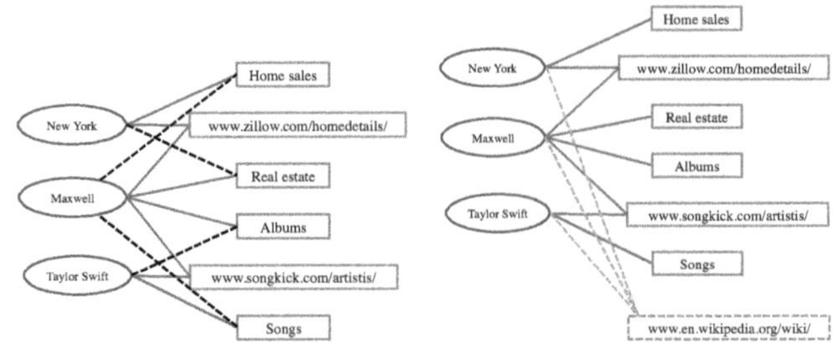

(a) The LPA strategy (b) The LPD strategy

Figure 2: Two seperate intuitive examples of the updated graphs obtained from the LPA and LPD strategies. The dashed black edges in (a) represent the hidden connections explored by LPA. In (b), the dashed box of the auxiliary node means that the node is multi-type, and the dashed orange edges represent the connections we should get rid of according to LPD.

The intuition behind LPA is that, if one entity e connects with one auxiliary node a_1 and a_1 has a high similarity with another auxiliary node a_2, we should connect e with a_2 to expand the connections in the bipartite EA graph. Hence, we need to measure the similarities among auxiliary nodes first. In this paper, we focus on contextual words and measure their similarities according to the semantic meanings by the word2vec tool. The word2vec tool provides an efficient implementation of the continuous bag-of-words and skip-gram architectures for computing vector representations of words [23, 24, 25]. By calculating the distance between two vector representations, we can obtain the similarity value for two words. Hence, given the auxiliary node set $A = \{a_j\}_{j=1}^N$, we could get a similarity matrix $\mathcal{S} \in \mathbb{R}^{N \times N}$, where each element $s_{ij} \in \mathcal{S}$ denotes the similarity value between a_i and a_j. The above exploration of connections can be formulated as follows:

$$\mathcal{W}_\mathcal{A} = \mathcal{W} \times \mathcal{S}, \tag{6}$$

where $\mathcal{W}_\mathcal{A}$ is the updated weight matrix according to LPA. Intuitively, $w_{ij} \in \mathcal{W}_\mathcal{A}$ can be interpreted as the weight aggregation of all length-of-two paths from e_i to a_j via every $a_{j'} \in A$. Given the search logs in Figure 1 (a), we show an intuitive example of the updated graph according to LPA in Figure 2 (a). We assume that the contextual words "home sales" and "real estate" are very similar so we connect "New York" with "real estate" in Figure 2 (a). With such a denser graph, we could run the LP algorithm to propagate labels more effectively. We denote the node types learned from LPA as $\mathcal{Y}_\mathcal{A}$ and $\mathcal{Z}_\mathcal{A}$ for entities and auxiliary nodes, respectively.

3.2.3 The Proposed LPD Strategy

Another issue of directly applying LP is that noise may exist in the built EA graph so that LP may propagate errors out and enlarge the error information. Therefore, we propose a strategy LPD (**L**abel **P**ropagation after **D**eleting noisy nodes) to discover and get rid of noisy information in the EA graph.

The basic idea of LPD is to discover some multi-type auxiliary nodes and delete them with their corresponding connections in the constructed EA graph. Here multi-type nodes mean contextual words or clicked URLs that cover several types of entities. For example, "picture" relates to several entity types, such as media, location, and person. Hence, it is not informative to take such contextual word into consideration. We apply a similar approach in [2] to get rid of some multi-type auxiliary nodes and update the graph accordingly. Specifically, we start by calculating the similarity (e.g., cosine similarity) between two entities according to the bag-of-word representations of their auxiliary nodes. Low similarity pairs are more likely to represent entities with different types. Hence, auxiliary nodes involved with such entities are not likely to be very specific. So we can consider low similarity pairs as voters and let the auxiliary nodes be the candidates. Each pair votes for its auxiliary nodes they share. The more votes an auxiliary node gets, the higher probability of multi-type it is. We can then apply a threshold to get rid of some auxiliary nodes and update the EA graph accordingly. Figure 2 (b) gives an intuitive example of the updated graph according to LPD. In this figure, we assume the clicked URL "www.en.wikipedia.org/wiki/" is a multi-type node and delete it with its corresponding edges from the graph. Then we can run LP on such a cleaner graph so that the error information can be propagated out as little as possible. We denote the node types learned from LPD as $\mathcal{Y}_\mathcal{D}$ and $\mathcal{Z}_\mathcal{D}$ for entities and auxiliary nodes, respectively.

3.2.4 The Proposed ELP Framework

Given the proposed LPA and LPD strategies, we can simply combine them together to derive another two strategies, LPAD and LPDA. LPAD updates the graph by first adding more connections and then deleting noisy nodes. The node types learned from LPAD are denoted as $\mathcal{Y}_{\mathcal{AD}}$ and $\mathcal{Z}_{\mathcal{AD}}$ for entities and auxiliary nodes, respectively. LPDA updates the graph in an opposite way, i.e., first deleting noisy nodes and then adding connections based on the remaining nodes. We denote the node types learned from LPDA as $\mathcal{Y}_{\mathcal{DA}}$ and $\mathcal{Z}_{\mathcal{DA}}$ for entities and auxiliary nodes, respectively.

Since each strategy has its advantage, we propose an **E**nsemble framework based on **LP** (ELP) to combine them together and maximize the margin [12]. We run each strategy separately and select the best one as the final result for each node as follows:

$$\begin{aligned} \mathcal{Y} &= max\{\mathcal{Y}_\mathcal{A}, \mathcal{Y}_\mathcal{D}, \mathcal{Y}_{\mathcal{AD}}, \mathcal{Y}_{\mathcal{DA}}\}, \\ \mathcal{Z} &= max\{\mathcal{Z}_\mathcal{A}, \mathcal{Z}_\mathcal{D}, \mathcal{Z}_{\mathcal{AD}}, \mathcal{Z}_{\mathcal{DA}}\}. \end{aligned} \quad (7)$$

In practice, we can also use the weighted results of the four strategies as the final solution. Since it would bring several weight parameters for these strategies, we calculate the results of ELP according to Equation (7) for simplicity in the experiments.

4. EXPERIMENTS

In this section, we conduct extensive experiments to evaluate the proposed ELP framework. After introducing the datasets and the experimental settings, we compare different baseline methods.

4.1 Data Processing

We collect a large set of click-through data (denoted as a system set) over a continuous period of time from a real-world search engine. Then a small number of click-through data are sampled from the system set and denoted as a gold set. We manually labeled entities from queries of the gold set with correct types. The labeled data are only used for seed

Table 1: Statistics of the collected query data.

Dataset	#Queries	#Clicked URLs
Gold	16,903	2,369,618
System	217,223,831	1,556,499,551

Table 2: Statistics of the entity-auxiliary graphs. "EC Links" means the entity-context links and "EU Links" means the entity-URL links.

		#Auxiliary nodes		#Links	
Dataset	#Entities	#Contexts	#URLs	#EC Links	#EU Links
Gold	934	1,445	10,059	3,323	36,475
System	10,722	39,279	24,107	514,489	221,668

Table 3: Distributions of labels for entities.

	Labels		
Dataset	Local	Media	Person
Gold	36.6%	36.4%	27.0%
System	33.5%	33.7%	32.8%

selections and performance evaluations in the experiments. The basis statistics of these two datasets are shown in Table 1.

In the experiments, we focus on 3 target types of classes, namely Local, Media and Person. By following the extraction rules in Section 3.1, we get entities and related auxiliary signals belonging to these 3 target types. In order to build a compact and reliable graph, we apply a threshold to get rid of some infrequent nodes. For example, we set the threshold as 1 for the gold dataset and filter out those nodes appearing only 1 time. The basic statistics of nodes and links in the entity-auxiliary graphs are represented in Table 2. The distributions of the 3 target labels for entities are shown in Table 3.

4.2 Compared Methods

In order to show that the LP model fits the constructed graph very well, we compare LP with several traditional classification methods. Given the bipartite EA graph, we consider the connected auxiliary nodes as features for each entity and the frequencies (the edge weights) as feature values. We focus on the following methods:

- SVM: **S**upport **V**ector **M**achine (SVM) is a popular classification method. Since non-linear RBF kernel is widely used in SVM models, we apply SVM (RBF) on the constructed bipartite EA graph.
- KNN: We compare with the **K**-**N**earest **N**eighbors method (KNN) to show the effectiveness of the LP method. We denote the KNN method using n neighbors as KNN-n.
- DT: The **D**ecision **T**ree method (DT) is applied on features extracted from the EA graph.
- NB: We apply the **N**aive **B**ayers (NB) on features of entities extracted from the built EA graph.
- LP: The original **L**abel **P**ropagation method (LP) is applied on the EA graph without the feature extraction.

In addition, in order to show the effectiveness of the proposed ELP framework, we compare with different variations of the LP model. Since both contextual words and clicked URLs can be considered as auxiliary information for entities in search query logs, we can construct three different bipartite graphs. They are the **E**ntity-**C**ontext (EC) graph, the **E**ntity-clicked **U**RL (EU) graph and the **E**ntity-**A**uxiliary (EA) graph. The EA graph considers both the contexts and clicked URLs as the auxiliary information in search query logs, so it contains more information than the EC and EU graphs. We can apply our proposed strategies on these different graphs and we summarize them as follows:

- LP: There are three versions for LP. They are LP (C), LP (U) and LP (A). LP (C) focuses on the EC graph. Similarly, LP (U) applies on the EU graph and LP (A) runs on the EA graph.

- LPA: We derive two baselines from LPA. The first one is LPA (C), which applies the LPA strategy on the bipartite EC graph. The other one is LPA (A) on the EA graph. The effectiveness of using more auxiliary information from search query logs can be demonstrated by comparing LPA (C) with LPA (A). Since the LPA strategy focuses on expanding the hidden connections between entities and contextual words, we cannot apply it on the EU graph.

- LPD: Three baselines can be generated from LPD. They are LPD (C), LPD (U) and LPD (A) on the EC, EU and EA graphs respectively. In particular, LPD (C) means that we first get rid of the top k multi-type contextual words and then apply the LP method on the updated EC graph. LPD (U) is derived in a similar way. For LPD (A), we first find the top k multi-type contextual words from the EC graph and the top k multi-type clicked URLs from the EU graph. After that we delete these contextual words and clicked URLs from the EA graph and apply LP on the updated graph. In this way, we guarantee that the most ambiguous auxiliary nodes (both contextual words and clicked URLs) are removed from the EA graph.

- LPAD: There are two baselines based on LPAD. They are LPAD (C) and LPAD (A). Specifically, LPAD (C) contains three steps: (1) expand connections and update the EC graph; (2) delete multi-type nodes in the denser EC graph; (3) run LP on the latest EC graph. LPAD (A) executes in a similar way.

- LPDA: We generate LPDA (C) and LPDA (A) from LPDA. LPDA (C) updates the EC graph by first deleting multi-type contextual words and then expanding hidden connections between entities and the remaining contextual words. LPDA (A) updates the EA graph in a similar way.

- ELP: We also derive two versions for ELP. They are ELP (C) and ELP (A). ELP (C) combines LPA (C), LPD (C), LPAD (C) and LPDA (C) in an ensemble way while ELP (A) ensembles LPA (A), LPD (A), LPAD (A) and LPDA (A) together to achieve a better performance.

For a fair comparison, we use the same parameter settings for the baselines related to the LP method. Specifically, we test with different α values for LP and find that $\alpha \in (0.5, 0.9)$ yields similar good results. So we set the parameter α to be 0.75 as in [18]. In order to get the similarities among contextual words, we use a pre-trained vectors[5] on about 100 billion words and phrases from various news articles. For the number of auxiliary nodes that should be deleted, we set it to be 10 in the experiments. In addition, we use SVM (RBF) with optimized parameters and other traditional classifiers with default parameters in our experiments. For each node, we can get a list of non-negative real numbers from LP indicating the posterior probabilities that the node relates to a label. We clamp these probabilities to 0/1 values for simplicity.

In order to evaluate the results, we focus on the labeled data and use accuracy and weighted average of the F1 score of each class (abbreviated as "weighted-F1") as the performance measures for entities. Weighted-F1 means that we calculate the F1 score for each label and find their average value weighted by the number of true instances for each label. This metric takes the label imbalance into consideration. For an entity with multi-labels, if the learned label matches with one of its multiple labels, we consider it as a correct prediction. Since we do not have ground truth for the auxiliary information, we will not present the quantitative analysis on the auxiliary information. We only show some qualitative analysis in Section 4.4. In the experiments, we randomly select a certain portion (e.g., 10%) of the entities as seeds for 10 times and report the average performances for models related to LP. We use the same seed entities as the training data for the traditional classification models.

4.3 Performance Evaluation

In this subsection, we show the performances of the proposed ELP framework. We first demonstrate that how the LP method takes advantage of the constructed bipartite EA graph compared with some traditional classification models. Due to space limit, we only show the performances on the EC graph of the gold dataset in Table 4. Similar performances can be obtained for other graphs.

It can be observed from Table 4 that LP consistently outperforms other classification methods on accuracy and weighted-F1 scores for different amounts of seed entities (training data). It illustrates that the constructed graph helps the LP method propagate the label information out very well. Since all the other classifiers ignore the graph structure, important information may be missing and the performances are not so well compared with the LP method that takes advantage of the graph structure. In addition, when the amount of seed entities increases, the performances become better for almost all classifiers except the SVM method with the RBF kernel. It seems that more training data does not help SVM (RBF) very much. However, in reality, more seed entities means more annotations and human labelings. With large volumes of new queries, extracting such supervised information from search query logs can be very expensive and time consuming. In Table 4, LP can only achieve 45% of accuracy when 1% of data are selected as seeds. The performance should be improved if we explore the hidden connections and get rid of multi-type nodes in the constructed graph as in the proposed ELP framework. So in the following, we focus on the gold dataset with 1% of seed entities to show the effectiveness of ELP.

[5]freebase-vectors-skipgram1000-en.bin.gz. It can be downloaded from `https://code.google.com/p/word2vec/`.

Table 4: Average performances with different amounts of seed entities for 10 times on the EC graph of the gold dataset. The results are reported as "average performance + (rank)". "↑" indicates that the larger the value the better the performance.

Metric	Method	Percentages of seed entities					
		1%	10%	20%	30%	40%	50%
Accuracy ↑	SVM (RBF)	0.3720 (3)	0.3876 (5)	0.3853 (5)	0.3763 (5)	0.4139 (5)	0.4206 (5)
	KNN-1	0.3610 (5)	0.4617 (4)	0.5100 (4)	0.5406 (4)	0.5591 (4)	0.5779 (4)
	DT	0.3688 (4)	0.4995 (3)	0.5568 (3)	0.5818 (3)	0.5989 (3)	0.6036 (3)
	NB	0.3752 (2)	0.5713 (2)	0.6106 (2)	0.6317 (2)	0.6271 (2)	0.6318 (2)
	LP	**0.4544** (1)	**0.6959** (1)	**0.7204** (1)	**0.7313** (1)	**0.7350** (1)	**0.7386** (1)
Weighted-F1 ↑	SVM (RBF)	0.2278 (3)	0.2445 (5)	0.2353 (5)	0.2206 (5)	0.2858 (5)	0.2918 (5)
	KNN-1	0.2248 (4)	0.4190 (4)	0.4987 (4)	0.5304 (4)	0.5522 (4)	0.5755 (4)
	DT	0.2231 (5)	0.4608 (3)	0.5404 (3)	0.5702 (3)	0.5903 (3)	0.5977 (3)
	NB	0.2789 (2)	0.5643 (2)	0.6066 (2)	0.6295 (2)	0.6233 (2)	0.6293 (2)
	LP	**0.3904** (1)	**0.6910** (1)	**0.7188** (1)	**0.7308** (1)	**0.7346** (1)	**0.7385** (1)

The results of different methods based on LP are shown in Table 5. It can be observed that ELP (A) outperforms other baseline methods on both accuracy and weighted-F1 and ELP (C) can also achieve a very good performance. ELP (A) outperforms ELP (C) with an improvement of 21% on the accuracy. It shows that more auxiliary nodes help ELP achieve a better performance on learning entity types from search query logs.

In particular, due to the noisy information in search query logs, directly applying the LP method on the constructed EA graph may reduce the performance as shown in Table 5. However, the results can be improved if we better build the graph as introduced in LPA and LPD. We can observe that the performance of LPA (LPD) on the EA graph are better than those on the EC and EU graphs. It demonstrates that using more high-quality auxiliary nodes can provide more important information and facilitate the process of LPA or LPD. Moreover, compared with the original LP method, both LPA and LPD can improve the performances for all the constructed bipartite graphs (i.e., EC, EU and EA). For example, LPA (A) significantly outperforms LP (A) with improvements of 45% and 104% on accuracy and weighted-F1, respectively. Furthermore, LPA seems more powerful than LPD on both the EC and EA graphs. It shows that exploring hidden connections among the sparse graph plays a more important role in learning entity types from search query logs.

Though LPA and LPD perform better than LP, our proposed ELP framework achieves better results than the LPA and LPD strategies. Specifically, ELP (A) outperforms LPA (A) with an improvement of 22% on the weighted-F1 score. In addition, ELP also performs better than LPAD and LPDA with an average improvement of 18% on the weighted-F1 score as shown in Table 5. It implies that ELP can maximize the effectiveness of combining different strategies together. Simply combining LPA and LPD together (e.g., LPAD and LPDA) may not make full use of the operations of adding more connections and deleting the noisy nodes.

In summary, with the help of exploring hidden connections and getting rid of noisy nodes, the proposed ELP framework can achieve an accuracy of 68% on the EA graph with only 1% of entities as seeds. From Table 4, we can see that the LP method needs around 10% of seed entities to get the same accuracy score. Therefore, ELP can help significantly reduce the cost of human labeling in learning entity types from search query logs.

We further show the effectiveness of the proposed ELP framework on the larger system set. Only 0.1% of seed entities are used in the experiments to test the power of ELP. Since we only labeled entities in the gold set and these entities are included in the system set, we calculate the accuracy and weighted-F1 scores on the labeled entities in the system set. The performances are presented in Table 6. We can get similar observations for the system set.

Table 5: Average performances with 1% of seed entities for 10 times on the gold dataset. The results are reported as "average performance + (rank)". "↑" indicates that the larger the value the better the performance.

Graph	Method	Metric	
		Accuracy ↑	Weighted-F1 ↑
EC	LP (C)	0.45 (8)	0.39 (8)
	LPA (C)	0.53 (5)	0.49 (5)
	LPD (C)	0.50 (7)	0.45 (6)
	LPAD (C)	0.53 (5)	0.49 (5)
	LPDA (C)	0.54 (4)	0.50 (4)
	ELP (C)	0.56 (3)	0.56 (2)
EU	LP (U)	0.39 (10)	0.26 (10)
	LPD (U)	0.52 (6)	0.44 (7)
EA	LP (A)	0.40 (9)	0.27 (9)
	LPA (A)	0.58 (2)	0.55 (3)
	LPD (A)	0.53 (5)	0.45 (6)
	LPAD (A)	0.58 (2)	0.55 (3)
	LPDA (A)	0.58 (2)	0.55 (3)
	ELP (A)	**0.68** (1)	**0.67** (1)

Table 6: Average performances with 0.1% of seed entities for 10 times on the system dataset. The results are reported as "average performance + (rank)". "↑" indicates that the larger the value the better the performance.

Graph	Method	Metric	
		Accuracy ↑	Weighted-F1 ↑
EC	LP (C)	0.44 (6)	0.32 (8)
	LPA (C)	0.45 (5)	0.37 (5)
	LPD (C)	0.50 (4)	0.41 (4)
	LPAD (C)	0.45 (5)	0.37 (5)
	LPDA (C)	0.45 (5)	0.37 (5)
	ELP (C)	0.57 (2)	0.56 (2)
EU	LP (U)	0.40 (9)	0.27 (10)
	LPD (U)	0.43 (7)	0.34 (7)
EA	LP (A)	0.42 (8)	0.30 (9)
	LPA (A)	0.55 (3)	0.51 (3)
	LPD (A)	0.44 (6)	0.36 (6)
	LPAD (A)	0.55 (3)	0.51 (3)
	LPDA (A)	0.55 (3)	0.51 (3)
	ELP (A)	**0.59** (1)	**0.58** (1)

4.4 Case Study

In this subsection, we present several case studies to show the effectiveness of the proposed ELP framework. We first show the most popular auxiliary nodes with their labels learned from ELP and explain how such auxiliary information can help detect new entities from search query logs. Then we give some examples of the hidden connections we explored in LPA. After that, we list several multi-type auxiliary nodes discovered in LPD. At the end, we will analyze

Table 7: **The most popular auxiliary information learned from ELP (A) on the gold dataset.**

		Auxiliary Information	
Label	Top k	Contextual Word	Clicked URL
Local	1	high school	hamptoninn3.hilton.com/en/
	2	Sale in	www.homes.com/Real_Estate
	3	IL	www.wunderground.com/weather-forcast/
	4	Orlando	www.accuweather.com/en/
	5	Coupons	www.city-data.com/city/
Media	1	Watch	www.tv.com/shows/
	2	Cast	tv.yahoo.com/shows/
	3	Season	tv.msn.com/tv/
	4	Songs	tv.yahoo.com/news/
	5	Episode	yidio.com/show/
Person	1	Biography	www.theguardian.com/film/
	2	Site	marquee.blogs.cnn.com/2014/
	3	Naked	images.fanpop.com/images/
	4	Nude	movies.msn.com/movies/
	5	Divorce	www.tmz.com/2014/

the potential to disambiguate multi-label entities in the proposed ELP framework.

4.4.1 Popular Auxiliary Information

Given the gold dataset, we first randomly select 1% of entities as seeds and run ELP on the EA graph. Then we apply a threshold (e.g., larger than 10) to select the most popular contextual words and clicked URLs separately. After that, we group the auxiliary nodes according to their learned types and rank nodes in each group by the learned probability value in a decreasing order. Due to space limit, we only show the top 5 related auxiliary information learned from ELP (A) for the gold dataset in Table 7. We can observe that people care about the education, real estate and weather very much when they search about local entities.

4.4.2 New Entity Discovery

With the learned types of auxiliary nodes in Table 7, we can discover new entities easily. For example, if a new TV series is released, we can detect it as a new entity when people search with the word "episode". In our experiments, we consider those entities appearing few times (≤ 2) as new entities and ELP can learn their types correctly. For instance, "Pogo" (an online game) appears only twice and ELP detects it as a media entity because its connected contextual words are "app" and "ipad". However, "Pogo" refers to a musical artist and a comic strip in Wikipedia. Therefore, the ELP method helps us discover "Pogo" as a new media entity, and we can add such information to the current knowledge graph.

4.4.3 Hidden Connections

Now we analyze how the hidden connections we explored help LPA fully propagate labels. We focus on those entities with few connected contextual words and give some examples of the entities with their hidden connections we discovered from the gold dataset as shown in Table 8. It can be observed that the hidden connections provide complementary and discriminative information for learning entity types. For example, given the entity "Big Brother" and its connected contextual word "CBS", the word "showtime" help predict "Big Brother" as an entity of media with more confidence. In addition, the hidden connections can help learn entity types more correctly. Take the entity "George Clooney" as an instance. The connected contexts "movie" and "new" are a bit ambiguous and "George Clooney" may be considered as an entity of media because "movie" is more related to media.

Table 8: Some entities and their connected contextual words from query logs. The hidden connected contextual words explored by LPA are also shown in the last column.

		Contextual Word	
Label	Entity	Existing word	Hidden word
Media	Big Brother	CBS	Showtime
Person	George Clooney	Movie, New	Wedding
Media	Haunted	Taylor Swift	Music, Video
Person	Sarah McLachlan	Song	Single
Local	Starbucks	free, coffee	open, free shipping, zip code

Table 9: The multi-type auxiliary information discovered from LPD on the gold dataset.

	Auxiliary Information	
Top k	Contextual Word	Clicked URL
1	Online	en.wikipedia.org/wiki/
2	Lyrics	geo.yahoo.com/t/
3	News	video.search.yahoo.com/video/
4	Free	video.search.yahoo.com/search/
5	Hotels	images.search.yahoo.com/search/
6	Movie	search.yahoo.com/
7	Newspaper	news.search.yahoo.com/
8	Weather	www.imdb.com/title/
9	Map	www.youtube.com/
10	Jobs	news.yahoo.com/photos/

However, if we connect "George Clooney" with "wedding", we can easily learn that "George Clooney" is an entity of person. Therefore, exploring the hidden connections in query logs can help learn entity types more accurately.

4.4.4 Multi-type Auxiliary Information

Here we analyze the effectiveness of discovering and removing the multi-type auxiliary information from LPD. We list the 10 most ambiguous auxiliary nodes discovered from the gold dataset in Table 9. It can be observed that these auxiliary nodes are related to different types of entities and getting rid of them can help propagate labels more accurately in LP. For example, the contextual word "Online" can refer to the online information of a place, a movie and a person. In addition, the clicked URL "en.wikipedia.org/wiki/" is related to a navigational website that contains diverse information. It is difficult to detect the type of an entity if such URLs are connected with the target entity. Therefore, we identify the ambiguous auxiliary nodes and remove them from our constructed graph.

4.4.5 Entity Disambiguation

According to the proposed ELP framework, we can get a list of non-negative real numbers indicating the probabilities that an entity relates to a type. We clamp these probabilities to 0/1 values for simplicity in the performance evaluation. However, in reality, a lot of entities have more than one type. In this subsection, we analyze the potential of ELP to disambiguate multi-label entities.

We first analyze those entities without ambiguity. From our experimental results, ELP gives high probability values to the types of these entities. For example, given the entity "Gold Digger", ELP learns a probability value of 0.94 for the media type. Similarly, "'Walt Disney World" has a probability value of 0.80 for the local type.

We also focus on those multi-type entities to see whether it is easy to disambiguate them in our experiments. We take the entity "Maxwell" as an example. ELP learns it as a local entity with a probability of 0.48 and a person entity with a probability of 0.37. Table 10 shows some connected

Table 10: Some auxiliary nodes for a multi-label entity "Maxwell". We group them according to their types learned from ELP.

		Auxiliary Information	
Label	Top k	Contextual Word	Clicked URL
Local	1	Real estate	www.zillow.com/homedetails/
	2	Weather forecast	www.realtor.com/realestateandhomes/
	3	Map of	www.healthgrades.com/physician/
	4	Sale in	www.homes.com/Real_Estate/
	5	Homes for sale	www.wunderground.com/weather-forecast/
Person	1	New album	www.allmusic.com/artist/
	2	Discography	www.jango.com/music/
	3	Songs by	www.oldies.com/artist-songs/
	4	Albums	www.songkick.com/artists/
	5	Full album	www.mtv.com/artists/

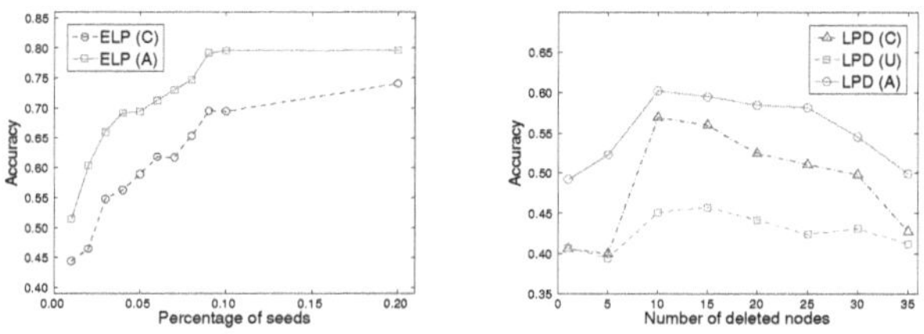

(a) Effect of seed entites (b) Effect of deleted nodes

Figure 3: Parameter analysis on the gold dataset.

auxiliary nodes for "Maxwell". We group them according to their labels learned from ELP and rank them by their probability values in a decreasing order. It can be observed that the auxiliary nodes for "Maxwell" as a local entity and a person entity are very different. Hence, ELP provides the potential for us to further split the entity node "Maxwell" into two nodes to better build the entity-auxiliary graph from search query logs.

4.5 Sensitivity Analysis

In this subsection, we assess the benefit of ELP with different amounts of seed entities. We focus on the EC and EA graphs extracted from the gold dataset and fix other parameters. Figure 3 (a) shows the classification accuracies. We find that the performances become better when we increase the seed entities. Moreover, the results stabilize when we use more than 10% of seed entities.

We also demonstrate the effect of the numbers of deleted nodes in Figure 3 (b). Here we fix 1% of seed entities and other parameters, but vary the numbers of deleted nodes. It can be observed that the best accuracy is achieved when we remove 10 multi-type auxiliary nodes. The noise may still exist if we get rid of too few nodes and the performance cannot be improved dramatically. However, information may be imcomplete if we delete too many nodes as shown in Figure 3 (b). So in our experiments, we set the number of deleted nodes as 10.

5. RELATED WORK

Entity extraction and classification have rapidly developed over the past few years [1, 5, 26]. Several methods are proposed to extract entities from web documents [3, 30] and the disambiguation of entities from news articles is studied in [14, 20]. In recent years, the extraction and classification of entities over query logs receive a lot of attention [27, 26, 16, 1, 17] and disambiguating entities in queries is also investigated in [6]. However, all these existing methods do not fully explore the importance of the auxiliary information related to entities. Our study is different since we encode entities and the important auxiliary information together into a bipartite graph and learn the types of both entities and auxiliary nodes simultaneously.

The graph-based label propagation method is also very popular in information retrieval tasks [18, 33]. Li et al. use click graphs, a bipartite-graph representation of click-through data from search query logs, to improve query intent classifiers [18]. Spam webpages are detected using the link structure of the click-through bipartite graph in [33]. It propagates spam scores iteratively between queries and URLs from a few seed pages/sites. In our work, we focus on learning entity types from search query logs, which differs from the task in [18, 33]. In addition, these models do not consider the sparsity and noise issues in search query logs. Our work proposes two separate strategies to explore hidden connections in the constructed bipartite graph and detect noisy information in query logs.

Besides the label propagation, many other learning methods, including Markov random walks [15], learning with local and global consistency [36, 8] and manifold regularization [4], are based on graphs. Furthermore, Chang et al. [7] proposed an unsupervised embedding scheme on graphs with heterogeneous components. Their method systematically captures network similarity between pairwise nodes by a deep learning framework. Though these models differ in their optimization objectives, they all share the same underlying assumption that if two samples are close in the intrinsic geometry of an input space, their conditional distributions will be similar.

The entity-oriented analysis of query data is also related to our work [13, 32]. For example, class attributes are extracted from search query logs for entities in [29, 28] as a complement source for existing knowledge bases. Based on the attributes, synonymous query intent templates are identified in [19]. In addition, entity-related search actions, annotations, and recommendation systems are studied in [22, 21, 34], respectively. However, our work is different from them since we study the problem of detecting entity types from search query logs.

6. CONCLUSION

In this paper, we study the problem of discovering entity types from search query logs. In order to take advantage of word patterns and user feedbacks (e.g., clicked URLs) from query logs, we construct a bipartite graph to encode entities and the important auxiliary information together. Based on this, the framework ELP is proposed to simultaneously learn types of both entities and auxiliary signals. In order to effectively learn node types, two separate strategies LPA and LPD are proposed and incorporated into ELP. Extensive empirical studies are conducted on real-world search logs to evaluate the effectiveness of the proposed ELP framework.

There are several interesting directions for future work. Since the constructed bipartite graph from search query logs reflects the most popular trending of entities, it can provide complementary information for the current knowledge bases. One direction of our future work is to explore the possibility of incorporating the built graph to the current knowledge bases. Another potential direction is to further disambiguate multi-label entities effectively based on the built bipartite graph, which is a hot but challenging problem in recent years.

Acknowledgement

This work is supported in part by NSF through grant CNS-1115234, Yahoo, and the Pinnacle Lab at Singapore Management University.

7. REFERENCES

[1] A. Alasiry, M. Levene, and A. Poulovassilis. Detecting candidate named entities in search queries. In *SIGIR*, 2012.

[2] R. Baeza-Yates and A. Tiberi. Extracting semantic relations from query logs. In *ACM SIGKDD*, 2007.

[3] M. Banko, M. Cafarella, S. Soderland, M. Broadhead, and O. Etzioni. Open information extraction for the web. In *IJCAI*, 2007.

[4] M. Belkin, P. Niyogi, and V. Sindhwani. Manifold regularization: A geometric framework for learning from labeled and unlabeled examples. *JMLR*, 7, 2006.

[5] K. Bellare, C. Curino, A. Machanavajihala, P. Mika, M. Rahurkar, and A. Sane. Woo: A scalable and multi-tenant platform for continuous knowledge base synthesis. *VLDB Endowment*, 6(11), 2013.

[6] R. Blanco, G. Ottaviano, and E. Meij. Fast and space-efficient entity linking in queries. In *WSDM*, 2015.

[7] S. Chang, W. Han, J. Tang, G.-J. Qi, C. C. Aggarwal, and T. S. Huang. Heterogeneous network embedding via deep architectures. In *ACM SIGKDD*, 2015.

[8] S. Chang, G.-J. Qi, C. C. Aggarwal, J. Zhou, M. Wang, and T. S. Huang. Factorized similarity learning in networks. In *ICDM*, 2014.

[9] S. Chaudhuri, V. Ganti, and D. Xin. Exploiting web search to generate synonyms for entities. In *WWW*, 2009.

[10] N. Dalvi, M. Olteanu, M. Raghavan, and P. Bohannon. Deduplicating a places database. In *WWW*, 2014.

[11] C. Ding, T. Li, and D. Wang. Label propagation on k-partite graphs. In *ICMLA*, 2009.

[12] A. Grove and D. Schuurmans. Boosting in the limit: Maximizing the margin of learned ensembles. In *AAAI*, 1998.

[13] D. Hakkani-Tür, A. Celikyilmaz, L. Heck, and G. Tür. A weakly-supervised approach for discovering new user intents from search query logs. In *INTERSPEECH*, 2013.

[14] J. Hoffart, Y. Altun, and G. Weikum. Discovering emerging entities with ambiguous names. In *WWW*, 2014.

[15] M. Jaakkola and M. Szummer. Partially labeled classification with markov random walks. In *NIPS*, 2002.

[16] A. Jain and M. Pennacchiotti. Open entity extraction from web search query logs. In *ACL*, 2010.

[17] A. Jain and M. Pennacchiotti. Domain-independent entity extraction from web search query logs. In *WWW*, 2011.

[18] X. Li, Y. Wang, and A. Acero. Learning query intent from regularized click graphs. In *SIGIR*, 2008.

[19] Y. Li, B. Hsu, and C. Zhai. Unsupervised identification of synonymous query intent templates for attribute intents. In *CIKM*, 2013.

[20] Y. Li, C. Wang, F. Han, J. Han, D. Roth, and X. Yan. Mining evidences for named entity disambiguation. In *ACM SIGKDD*, 2013.

[21] G. Limaye, S. Sarawagi, and S. Chakrabarti. Annotating and searching web tables using entities, types and relationships. *VLDB Endowment*, 3(1-2), 2010.

[22] T. Lin, P. Pantel, M. Gamon, A. Kannan, and A. Fuxman. Active objects: Actions for entity-centric search. In *WWW*, 2012.

[23] T. Mikolov, K. Chen, G. Corrado, and J. Dean. Efficient estimation of word representations in vector space. In *ICLR Workshop*, 2013.

[24] T. Mikolov, I. Sutskever, K. Chen, G. Corrado, and J. Dean. Distributed representations of words and phrases and their compositionality. In *NIPS*, 2013.

[25] T. Mikolov, W. Yih, and G. Zweig. Linguistic regularities in continuous space word representations. In *HLT-NAACL*, 2013.

[26] P. Pantel, T. Lin, and M. Gamon. Mining entity types from query logs via user intent modeling. In *ACL*, 2012.

[27] M. Paşca. Weakly-supervised discovery of named entities using web search queries. In *CIKM*, 2007.

[28] M. Paşca. Attribute extraction from conjectural queries. In *COLING*, 2012.

[29] M. Paşca and B. V. Durme. What you seek is what you get: Extraction of class attributes from query logs. In *IJCAI*, 2007.

[30] M. Pennacchiotti and P. Pantel. Entity extraction via ensemble semantics. In *EMNLP*, 2009.

[31] J. Pound, P. Mika, and H. Zaragoza. Ad-hoc object retrieval in the web of data. In *WWW*, 2010.

[32] J. Reisinger and M. Paşca. Fine-grained class label markup of search queries. In *ACL*, 2011.

[33] C. Wei, Y. Liu, M. Zhang, S. Ma, L. Ru, and K. Zhang. Fighting against web spam: a novel propagation method based on click-through data. In *SIGIR*, 2012.

[34] X. Yu, H. Ma, B. Hsu, and J. Han. On building entity recommender systems using user click log and freebase knowledge. In *WSDM*, 2014.

[35] J. Zhang, X. Kong, L. Jie, Y. Chang, and P. Yu. Ncr: A scalable network-based approach to co-ranking in question-and-answer sites. In *CIKM*, 2014.

[36] D. Zhou, O. Bousquet, T. Lal, J. Weston, and B. Schölkopf. Learning with local and global consistency. In *NIPS*, 2004.

[37] X. Zhu and Z. Ghahramani. Learning from labeled and unlabeled data with label propagation. Technical report, Technical Report CMU-CALD-02-107, 2002.

Collaborative Prediction for Multi-entity Interaction With Hierarchical Representation

Qiang Liu, Shu Wu, Liang Wang
Center for Research on Intelligent Perception and Computing
National Laboratory of Pattern Recognition
Institute of Automation, Chinese Academy of Sciences
{qiang.liu, shu.wu, wangliang}@nlpr.ia.ac.cn

ABSTRACT

With the rapid growth of Internet applications, there are more and more entities in interaction scenarios, and thus collaborative prediction for multi-entity interaction is becoming a significant problem. The state-of-the-art methods, e.g., tensor factorization and factorization machine, predict multi-entity interaction based on calculating the similarity among all entities. However, these methods are usually not able to reveal the joint characteristics of entities in the interaction. Besides, some methods may succeed in one specific application, but they can not be extended effectively for other applications or interaction scenarios with more entities. In this work, we propose a Hierarchical Interaction Representation (HIR) model, which models the mutual action among different entities as a joint representation. We generate the interaction representation of two entities via tensor multiplication, which is preformed iteratively to construct a hierarchical structure among all entities. Moreover, we employ several hidden layers to reveal the underlying properties of this interaction and enhance the model performance. After generating final representation, the prediction can be calculated using a variety of machine learning methods according to different tasks (i.e., linear regression for regression tasks, pair-wise ranking for ranking tasks and logistic regression for classification tasks). Experimental results show that our proposed HIR model yields significant improvements over the competitive compared methods in four different application scenarios (i.e., general recommendation, context-aware recommendation, latent collaborative retrieval and click-through rate prediction).

Categories and Subject Descriptors

H.3 [**Information Storage and Retrieval**]: Information Filtering

CIKM'15, October 19–23, 2015, Melbourne, Australia.
 ISBN 978-1-4503-3794-6/15/10 ...$15.00.
DOI: http://dx.doi.org/10.1145/2806416.2806530.

Keywords

Collaborative Prediction, Multi-Entity, Factorization Model, Hierarchical Representation

1. INTRODUCTION

Nowadays, collaborative prediction plays an important role in many real-world applications, e.g., recommender systems, information retrieval and social network analysis. With the rapid growth of web applications, there are more and more entities in one interaction scenario. For example, there are three entities in tag recommendation (i.e., user, item and tag) [25, 17, 20] and latent collaborative retrieval (i.e., user, query and document) [27, 2], and three or more entities in context-aware recommendation (i.e., user, query and several contexts) [4, 19, 21, 10]. Moreover, in some probability prediction applications, e.g., click-through rate prediction [12, 29, 14], there are even more entities in an interaction situation (e.g., device, website, application, advertisement and position). Accordingly, it is necessary to model joint characteristics of entities and collaboratively predict interaction among multiple entities.

Matrix factorization [13, 8] is widely used for interaction prediction between two entities, e.g., users and items in general recommendation. And matrix factorization based methods have been extensively studied, some of which, e.g., tensor factorization [28] and factorization machine [16], are implemented for predicting multi-entity interaction, e.g., user, query and document in latent collaborative retrieval. Both tensor factorization and factorization machine predict the interaction based on the similarity among all entities, which seems intuitive and reasonable. However, this does not conform to situations of various applications. Using latent collaborative retrieval as an example, both tensor factorization and factorization machine compute the similarity among user, query and document to predict their interaction. However, the similarity between the user and the query does not contribute to document selection of this user, and final selection is not merely based on the similarity between the user and the document or the similarity between the query and the document. We should measure the correlation between the document and the joint representation of user and query. In addition, there is another disadvantage of conventional methods. They only compute the similarity based on corresponding dimensional values in the latent vectors, which does not allow rich high-order calculation among values of different dimensions. Therefore, to be general, we provide a latent representation for a multi-entity interaction, which describes how these entities would act being together with

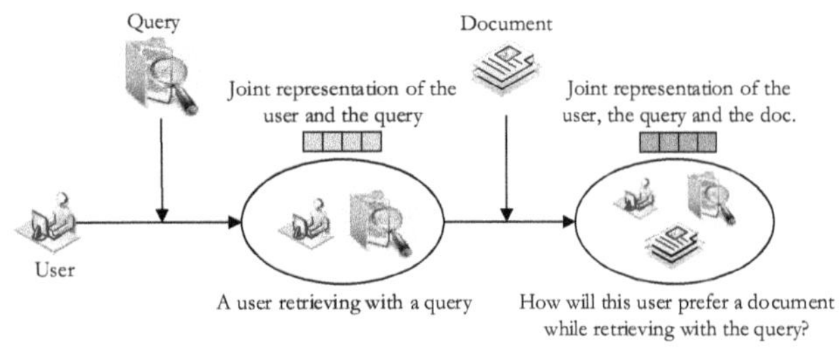

Figure 1: Illustration of the hierarchical structure of multi-entity interaction, using latent collaborative retrieval as an example.

each other and can reveal their high-order relation. As illustrated in Figure 1, when a user retrieves with a query, capturing the mutual action of the user and the query, a joint representation is generated. Similarly, when the user views a document, there will be a joint representation of user, query and document, which indicates how this user will prefer a document while retrieving with the query. Based on this joint representation, we could make prediction for the multi-entity interaction.

Recent studies on representation learning [1] in different areas give us great inspiration. Recently, joint representation of entities is employed for linked data [9] and structured data [24]. In recent works of natural language processing, using tensor multiplication, neural tensor networks are successfully used in learning the representation of two entities for knowledge base completion [22] and the representation of a sentence for semantic compositionality [23]. Tensor multiplication is also used in modeling contextual representation for context-aware recommendation [21, 10].

In this paper, we present a novel method to learn a Hierarchical Interaction Representation (HIR) model for predicting interaction among multiple entities. In our method, each entity is represented as a latent vector. And we use three-dimensional tensor multiplication to capture the joint characteristics of two entities. Tensor multiplication allows high-order calculation between these two entities. Moreover, rather than achieving a score of the interaction in conventional methods, HIR generates an interaction representation, which allows interacting with the next entity and can be widely implemented for various tasks. In a multi-entity interaction scenario with n entities, this tensor multiplying procedure can be performed iteratively, which forms a hierarchical architecture with n layers. The ith layer presents the interaction representation of the first i entities. The nth layer is the final representation of all the entities, which describes their joint characteristics. With such a hierarchical structure, we can also add new entities directly without re-training the former representations. Based on the final representation, we could select learning methods according to different application tasks for collaborative prediction (i.e., linear regression for regression tasks, pair-wise ranking method for ranking tasks and logistic regression for classification tasks).

The main contributions of this work are listed as follows:

- We model the joint representation of multiple types of entities in an interaction scenario, which presents a novel perspective on collaboratively modeling and predicting the entity interaction.
- Using the tensor multiplication, HIR allows high-order calculation among different types of entities, which reveals the underlying properties and relations among entities.
- Experiments conducted on four different tasks show that HIR is effective and clearly outperforms both general methods and state-of-the-art task-specific methods.

The rest of the paper is organized as follows. In section 2, we review some related work on both general methods and task-specific methods. Section 3 details our HIR model. In section 4, we introduce the learning methods of the HIR model. In section 5, we report experimental results in terms of four tasks and compare with several state-of-the-art methods. Section 6 concludes our work and discusses future research.

2. RELATED WORK

In this section, we briefly review related work on both general and task-specific methods, i.e., context-aware recommendation, latent collaborative retrieval, tag recommendation and click-through rate prediction.

2.1 General Methods

Matrix Factorization (MF) [13, 8] has become one of the state-of-the-art approaches to collaborative prediction. The basic objective of MF is to factorize a matrix into two low rank matrices, each of which represents the latent factors of entities, e.g., users and items in general recommendation. The original matrix can be approximated via the multiplying calculation. However, MF is not able to be implemented directly for collaborative prediction problem of multiple entities.

MF has been extended nowadays. Tensor Factorization (TF) [28] extends MF from two dimensions to three or even higher dimensions, which can be utilized for predicting multi-entity interaction. And Factorization Machine (FM) [16] gives a further extension of TF by modeling all interactions between pairs of entities. FM is a flexible model, and other state-of-the-art factorization models including TF, SVD++ [5] and timeSVD++ [6] can be implemented using FM by defining the input data or features [16]. Both TF and FM are successfully used in tag recommendation [25, 17, 20] and context-aware recommendation [4, 19]. FM also leads great improvement in click-through rate prediction [14]. However, predicting multi-entity interaction based on simply calculating the similarity among all entities, TF and FM are not able to better reveal the joint characteristics of interacting entities. Moreover, because FM uses the pair-wise interaction between entities to model the prediction of multi-entity interaction, this brings FM another disadvantage that the number of pairs grows exponentially with the number of entities.

2.2 Task-Specific Methods

In this subsection, we introduce some research works in different tasks that are related to the collaborative prediction for multi-entity interaction.

The context modeling approaches have made significant improvement for context-aware recommendation, which contains three or more entities (i.e., user, query and several contexts). Recent works on context modeling have focused on integrating contextual information with user-item rating matrix and building factorization models. Incorporating tensor factorization, multiverse recommendation [4] represents the user-item rating matrix with contextual information as a user-item-context rating tensor, which is factorized with Tucker decomposition [26]. And FM is applicable to a variety of contexts by specifying only the input data [19]. Random decision trees are also been applied here, in which contexts are split and general matrix factorization is performed on each leaf [11]. Furthermore, the work of [30] considers user attributes as priors for user latent vectors, and a transfer matrix is used to generate latent vectors from original ones. Similarly, Heterogeneous Matrix Factorization (HeteroMF) [3] generates context-specific latent vectors of entities using a context-dependent transfer matrix and the original latent vectors of entities. CARS2 [21] and Contextual Operating Tensor (COT) [10] model represents entities in a specific context using contextual representation and outperform previous methods in context-aware recommendation. Both of them model contexts as latent vectors, and generate contextual representations of users and items using tensor multiplication.

Recently, modeling the interaction among user, query and document, Latent Collaborative Retrieval (LCR) [27] has been proposed and extended to social network [2]. LCR represents a user with a matrix and generates the joint representation of user and query via multiplication. Then the prediction is given based on the inner product of latent representation of query and joint representation of user and query. Modeling the interaction among user, item and tag, tag recommendation can also be viewed as a LCR problem, in which a user retrieves tags with an item. Treating user, item and tag as three dimensions of a tensor, TF has been successfully used in this problem [25, 17]. As an extended version of TF, FM is also applied in tag recommendation and has become one of the state-of-the-art methods [20].

In the complex click-through rate (CTR) prediction problem, there may exist several entities such as user, device, website, application, advertisement, position and so on. Due to its ease of implementation and promising performance, Logistic regression (LR) has been widely used for CTR prediction, especially in industrial systems [12, 29]. LR can be used for the multi-entity interaction prediction with one-hot representation of each entity. However, LR or other classifiers have difficulties in discovering latent relation among entities, and the final prediction of LR could be viewed as the sum of biases of all the entities. Recently, as a representative method of factorization models, FM is applied for CTR prediction and brings a great improvement [14].

The methods mentioned above achieve delightful results in respective applications, which also greatly motivates our work. But they are unable to be extended effectively for other applications or interaction with more entities.

3. REPRESENTATION OF MULTI-ENTITY INTERACTION

In this section, we introduce our proposed hierarchical interaction representation. We introduce the definition and notations of our problem at first. Then we present the interaction representation of two entities, followed by the hierarchical representation of more entities. Finally, we show how to enhance the model via employing hidden layers.

3.1 Problem Definition

The problem we study in this paper can be described as follows. In an interaction scenario, suppose that we have an interaction prediction task with n types of entities denoted by $\{E^{(1)}, ..., E^{(n)}\}$. For each type of entity, we have $E^{(m)} = \{e_1^{(m)}, e_2^{(m)}, ...\}$, where $e_i^{(m)} \in \mathbb{R}^d$ and $m \in \{1, ..., n\}$. In the multi-entity interaction, the relation among $e_{k_1}^{(1)}, ..., e_{k_n}^{(n)}$ is denoted by $y_{k_1,...,k_n}$. The task of collaborative prediction for multi-entity interaction is to give a prediction $\hat{y}_{k_1,...,k_n}$ based on all the entities $e_{k_1}^{(1)}, ..., e_{k_n}^{(n)}$.

Here, using latent collaborative retrieval as an example, there will be three types of entities (i.e., user, query, document) denoted by $\{E^{(1)}, E^{(2)}, E^{(3)}\}$. Specifically, users, queries and documents are denoted by $E^{(1)} = \{e_1^{(1)}, e_2^{(1)}, ...\}$, $E^{(2)} = \{e_1^{(2)}, e_2^{(2)}, ...\}$ and $E^{(3)} = \{e_1^{(3)}, e_2^{(3)}, ...\}$ respectively. Each user, query and document are denoted as $e_i^{(1)} \in \mathbb{R}^d$, $e_i^{(2)} \in \mathbb{R}^d$ and $e_i^{(3)} \in \mathbb{R}^d$. Then the relation among user, query and document is denoted as y_{k_1,k_2,k_3}.

In this work, we would jointly model all the entities with an interaction representation $r_{k_1,...,k_n}^{(n)}$, and m-subset of the entities with an interaction representation $r_{k_1,...,k_m}^{(m)}$. The interaction representation describes the joint characteristics of entities. We could make prediction of their interaction based on this representation using various learning methods (i.e., linear regression, logistic regression and pair-wise ranking).

3.2 Interaction Representation

We first introduce the case with two entities. To get the joint representation of two entities, we need to employ an interaction function that satisfies:

$$r_{k_1,k_2}^{(2)} = f^{(2)}\left(e_{k_1}^{(1)}, e_{k_2}^{(2)}\right) , \tag{1}$$

where $f^{(2)}(\cdot)$ denotes an interaction function of two entities. Latent vector $r_{k_1,k_2}^{(2)}$ describes how the two entities would behave being together in an interaction scenario. For instance, if there are user and movie as two entities, their joint representation captures the characteristics of a user watching a movie, and models how much he or she likes the movie.

To capture the high-order relation between two entities, we use tensor multiplication, as shown in the bottom square of Figure 2. Here, we compute the interaction representation as:

$$r_{k_1,k_2}^{(2)} = \left[\left(e_{k_2}^{(2)}\right)^T T^{(1)}\right] e_{k_1}^{(1)} , \tag{2}$$

where $T^{(1)}$ is a $d \times d \times d$ tensor, modeling the interaction of these two entities. The tensor multiplication $\left(e_{k_2}^{(2)}\right)^T T^{(1)}$ can be defined as:

$$\left(e_{k_2}^{(2)}\right)^T T^{(1)} = \begin{bmatrix} \left(e_{k_2}^{(2)}\right)^T T_1^{(1)} \\ \cdots \\ \left(e_{k_2}^{(2)}\right)^T T_d^{(1)} \end{bmatrix} , \tag{3}$$

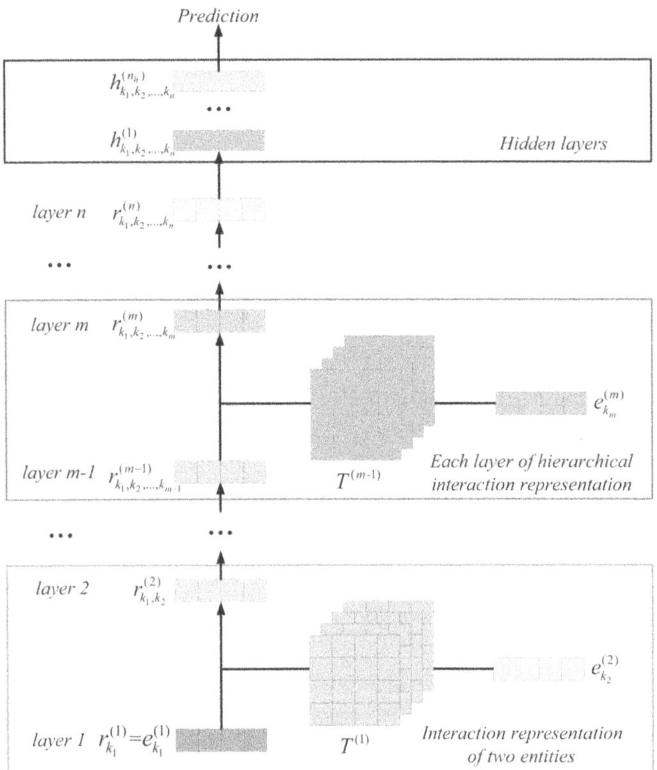

Figure 2: Overview of the learning procedure of HIR. Interaction representation of two entities is shown in the bottom square. Each layer of HIR is shown in the middle square. The top part illustrates hidden layers between interaction representation and prediction.

and Equation 2 can be calculated as:

$$r^{(2)}_{k_1,k_2} = \begin{bmatrix} \left(e^{(2)}_{k_2}\right)^T T^{(1)}_1 e^{(1)}_{k_1} \\ \cdots \\ \left(e^{(2)}_{k_2}\right)^T T^{(1)}_d e^{(1)}_{k_1} \end{bmatrix}, \tag{4}$$

where $T^{(1)}_m$ denotes the mth slice of the tensor $T^{(1)}$, and each slice is a $d \times d$ matrix.

With such computation, the tensor can model the rich high-order relation between entities. Each slice of the tensor can capture a specific type of relation between these entities.

Now, to predict the interaction of the two entities, we can use a simple linear regression, which can be concluded as:

$$\hat{y}_{k_1,k_2} = W^T \left[\left(e^{(2)}_{k_2}\right)^T T^{(1)}\right] e^{(1)}_{k_1}, \tag{5}$$

where W is a n-dimensional vector denoting the weights of regression.

3.3 Hierarchical Interaction Representation

After introducing the joint representation of two entities, we would model the joint representation of more entities in general cases. For more entities, we need another interaction function that satisfies:

$$r^{(n)}_{k_1,\ldots,k_n} = f^{(n)}\left(e^{(1)}_{k_1}, \ldots, e^{(n)}_{k_n}\right), \tag{6}$$

where $f^{(n)}(\cdot)$ denotes an interaction function of n entities. $r^{(n)}_{k_1,\ldots,k_n}$ describes the joint characteristics of all the entities in an interaction scenario.

To generate the interaction representation of n entities, we perform the tensor multiplication iteratively, which forms a hierarchical structure with n layers. These procedures can be concluded as:

$$\begin{cases} r^{(1)}_{k_1} = e^{(1)}_{k_1} \\ r^{(m)}_{k_1,\ldots,k_m} = \left[\left(e^{(m)}_{k_m}\right)^T T^{(m-1)}\right] r^{(m-1)}_{k_1,\ldots,k_{m-1}} \end{cases}, \tag{7}$$

where $1 < m \leq n$, and $T^{(m-1)}$ is a $d \times d \times d$ tensor, generating the interaction representation in the mth layer. Each layer of HIR is illustrated in the middle square of Figure 2. Thus, the joint representation of all entities can be calculated as:

$$r^{(n)}_{k_1,\ldots,k_n} = \prod_{i=2}^{n} \left[\left(e^{(i)}_{k_i}\right)^T T^{(i-1)}\right] e^{(1)}_{k_1}. \tag{8}$$

Taking latent collaborative retrieval for an example, there are three entities, i.e., user, query and document. Their interaction representation captures how a user prefers a document while retrieving with a query, which can be calculated as:

$$r^{(3)}_{k_1,k_2,k_3} = \left[\left(e^{(3)}_{k_3}\right)^T T^{(2)}\right] [\left(e^{(2)}_{k_2}\right)^T T^{(1)}] e^{(1)}_{k_1}. \tag{9}$$

With the joint representation, we can compute the collaborative prediction. A variety of machine learning methods can be used according to the specific task. For example, with a linear regression method, the prediction of multi-entity interaction can be generated as:

$$\hat{y}_{k_1,\ldots,k_n} = W^T \prod_{i=2}^{n} \left[\left(e^{(i)}_{k_i}\right)^T T^{(i-1)}\right] e^{(1)}_{k_1}, \tag{10}$$

where W is a n-dimensional vector denoting the weights of regression. Moreover, in the task of latent collaborative retrieval, the prediction can be generated as:

$$\hat{y}_{k_1,k_2,k_3} = W^T \left[\left(e^{(3)}_{k_3}\right)^T T^{(2)}\right] \left[\left(e^{(2)}_{k_2}\right)^T T^{(1)}\right] e^{(1)}_{k_1}. \tag{11}$$

3.4 Multiple Hidden Layers

Deep models with multiple layers have shown delightful performance in different areas [1]. As shown in the top square of Figure 2, to enhance the ability of representation and to improve the performance of our model, we can add several hidden layers between the joint representation $r^{(n)}_{k_1,\ldots,k_n}$ and the prediction $\hat{y}_{k_1,\ldots,k_n}$.

Suppose we add n_h hidden layers between the final representation and the prediction. With each hidden layer modeled by a matrix, the joint representation after hidden layers can be calculated iteratively as:

$$\begin{cases} h^{(0)}_{k_1,k_2,\ldots,k_n} = r^{(n)}_{k_1,k_2,\ldots,k_n} \\ h^{(m_h)}_{k_1,k_2,\ldots,k_n} = H_{m_h} h^{(m_h-1)}_{k_1,k_2,\ldots,k_n} \end{cases}, \tag{12}$$

where $1 \leq m_h \leq n_h$, $h^{(m_h)}_{k_1,k_2,\ldots,k_n}$ denotes the joint representation after m_h hidden layers, and H_{m_h} is a $d \times d$ matrix of the m_hth hidden layer. Combining interaction layers and hidden layers, the overall formulation generating the joint representation becomes:

$$h^{(n_h)}_{k_1,\ldots,k_n} = \prod_{i=1}^{n_h} H_i \prod_{i=2}^{n} \left[\left(e^{(i)}_{k_i}\right)^T T^{(i-1)} \right] e^{(1)}_{k_1} . \quad (13)$$

Furthermore, with a linear regression method, the final prediction can be made via:

$$\hat{y}_{k_1,\ldots,k_n} = W^T \prod_{i=1}^{n_h} H_i \prod_{i=2}^{n} \left[\left(e^{(i)}_{k_i}\right)^T T^{(i-1)} \right] e^{(1)}_{k_1} , \quad (14)$$

4. LEARNING FOR DIFFERENT TASKS

In this section, we introduce the learning process of the HIR model in three different tasks, i.e., personalised recommendation, personalised ranking and click-through rate prediction.

4.1 Collaborative Recommendation

In recommender systems with explicit rating values, the interaction prediction in HIR becomes rating prediction, which can be modeled as a regression problem. The model can be calculated via a linear regression:

$$\hat{y}_{k_1,\ldots,k_n} = W^T h^{(n_h)}_{k_1,\ldots,k_n} , \quad (15)$$

where W denotes the weights of linear regression. Therefore, HIR can be learned by minimizing the squared error [8], and the objective function can be written as:

$$\begin{aligned} J &= \sum (y_{k_1,\ldots,k_n} - \hat{y}_{k_1,\ldots,k_n})^2 + \frac{\lambda}{2} \|\Theta\|^2 \\ &= \sum (y_{k_1,\ldots,k_n} - W^T h^{(n_h)}_{k_1,\ldots,k_n})^2 + \frac{\lambda}{2} \|\Theta\|^2 \end{aligned} , \quad (16)$$

where $\Theta = \{E, T, H, W\}$ denotes all the parameters to be estimated, and λ is a parameter to control the power of regularization.

The derivations of J with respect to the parameters can be calculated as:

$$\frac{\partial J}{\partial W} = -2 \sum (y_{k_1,\ldots,k_n} - W^T h^{(n_h)}_{k_1,\ldots,k_n}) h^{(n_h)}_{k_1,\ldots,k_n} + \lambda W ,$$

$$\frac{\partial J}{\partial h^{(n_h)}_{k_1,\ldots,k_n}} = -2 \sum (y_{k_1,\ldots,k_n} - W^T h^{(n_h)}_{k_1,\ldots,k_n}) W + \lambda h^{(n_h)}_{k_1,\ldots,k_n} .$$

4.2 Personalized Ranking

In recommender systems and information retrieval, different from scenarios with explicit feedbacks, scenarios with implicit feedbacks (i.e., a binary signal such as click, buy, view, etc) are more common in real-world applications. This can be treated as a ranking problem. Bayesian Personalized Ranking (BPR) [18] is a state-of-the-art pairwise ranking method for the implicit feedback data. The basic assumption of BPR is that a user prefers a selected item than a negative item. So, using HIR in the BPR framework, we need to maximize the following function:

$$p(k_n \succ_{k_1,k_2,\ldots} k'_n) = g(\hat{y}_{k_1,k_2,\ldots,k_n} - \hat{y}_{k_1,k_2,\ldots,k'_n}) , \quad (17)$$

where k_n denotes a positive sample, k'_n denotes a negative sample, and $g(x)$ is a nonlinear function which we select as $g(x) = 1/(1 + exp(-x))$. Note that, the prediction here is based on linear regression as shown in Equation 15. Incorporating the negative log likelihood, we can solve the following objective function equivalently:

$$\begin{aligned} J &= -\sum \ln(p(k_n \succ_{k_1,k_2,\ldots} k'_n)) + \frac{\lambda}{2} \|\Theta\|^2 \\ &= -\sum \ln\left(\frac{1}{1 + \exp(-y(k_n \succ_{k_1,k_2,\ldots} k'_n))}\right) + \frac{\lambda}{2} \|\Theta\|^2 \\ &= \sum \ln(1 + \exp(-y(k_n \succ_{k_1,k_2,\ldots} k'_n)) + \frac{\lambda}{2} \|\Theta\|^2 \\ &= \sum \ln(1 + \exp(-W^T h(k_n \succ_{k_1,k_2,\ldots} k'_n))) + \frac{\lambda}{2} \|\Theta\|^2 \end{aligned} , \quad (18)$$

where

$$y(k_n \succ_{k_1,k_2,\ldots} k'_n) = \hat{y}_{k_1,k_2,\ldots,k_n} - \hat{y}_{k_1,k_2,\ldots,k'_n} ,$$

$$h(k_n \succ_{k_1,k_2,\ldots} k'_n) = h^{(n_h)}_{k_1,k_2,\ldots,k_n} - h^{(n_h)}_{k_1,k_2,\ldots,k'_n} .$$

The derivations of J with respect to the parameters can be calculated as:

$$\frac{\partial J}{\partial W} = -\sum q(k_n \succ_{k_1,k_2,\ldots} k'_n) h(k_n \succ_{k_1,k_2,\ldots} k'_n) + \lambda W ,$$

$$\frac{\partial J}{\partial h^{(n_h)}_{k_1,k_2,\ldots,k_n}} = -\sum q(k_n \succ_{k_1,k_2,\ldots} k'_n) W + \lambda h^{(n_h)}_{k_1,k_2,\ldots,k_n} ,$$

$$\frac{\partial J}{\partial h^{(n_h)}_{k_1,k_2,\ldots,k'_n}} = \sum q(k_n \succ_{k_1,k_2,\ldots} k'_n) W + \lambda h^{(n_h)}_{k_1,k_2,\ldots,k'_n} ,$$

where

$$q(k_n \succ_{k_1,k_2,\ldots} k'_n) = \frac{\exp(-W^T h(k_n \succ_{k_1,k_2,\ldots} k'_n))}{1 + \exp(-W^T h(k_n \succ_{k_1,k_2,\ldots} k'_n))} .$$

4.3 Click-Through Rate Prediction

Predicting the probability of clicking under a specific context, click-through rate prediction can be treated as a classification problem. As regular models for CTR prediction [12, 29], we incorporate logistic regression, and the prediction becomes:

$$\hat{y}_{k_1,\ldots,k_n} = \frac{1}{1 + exp(-W^T h^{(n_h)}_{k_1,\ldots,k_n})} , \quad (19)$$

where W denotes the weights of logistic regression. As in regular logistic regression, we use the negative log likelihood for model learning. The objective function can be written as:

$$\begin{aligned} J &= -\sum (1 - y_{k_1,k_2,\ldots,k_n}) \ln (1 - \hat{y}_{k_1,k_2,\ldots,k_n}) \\ &\quad - \sum y_{k_1,k_2,\ldots,k_n} \ln (\hat{y}_{k_1,k_2,\ldots,k_n}) + \frac{\lambda}{2} \|\Theta\|^2 \\ &= \sum \ln(1 + \exp(-W^T h^{(n_h)}_{k_1,\ldots,k_n})) \\ &\quad + \sum (1 - y_{k_1,k_2,\ldots,k_n}) W^T h^{(n_h)}_{k_1,\ldots,k_n} + \frac{\lambda}{2} \|\Theta\|^2 \end{aligned} . \quad (20)$$

The derivations of J with respect to the parameters can be calculated as:

$$\begin{aligned} \frac{\partial J}{\partial W} &= -\sum \frac{\exp(-W^T h^{(n_h)}_{k_1,\ldots,k_n})}{1 + \exp(-W^T h^{(n_h)}_{k_1,\ldots,k_n})} h^{(n_h)}_{k_1,\ldots,k_n} \\ &\quad + \sum (1 - \hat{y}_{k_1,k_2,\ldots,k_n}) + \lambda W \end{aligned} ,$$

$$\frac{\partial J}{\partial h^{(n_h)}_{k_1,\dots,k_n}} = -\sum \frac{\exp(-W^T h^{(n_h)}_{k_1,\dots,k_n})}{1+\exp(-W^T h^{(n_h)}_{k_1,\dots,k_n})} W + \sum (1-\hat{y}_{k_1,k_2,\dots,k_n}) + \lambda h^{(n_h)}_{k_1,\dots,k_n} .$$

4.4 Iterative Parameter Learning

In three tasks mentioned above, the derivation $\frac{\partial J}{\partial h^{(n_h)}_{k_1,\dots,k_n}}$ has been calculated. Based on this derivation, we can calculate the derivations of hidden layers and joint representation iteratively. Suppose we have $\frac{\partial J}{\partial h^{(m_h)}_{k_1,\dots,k_m}}$ of the m_hth ($0 < m_h \le n_h$) hidden layer, we can calculate the derivations of parameters on this layer as:

$$\frac{\partial J}{\partial H_{m_h}} = \frac{\partial J}{\partial h^{(m_h)}_{k_1,k_2,\dots,k_n}} h^{(m_h-1)}_{k_1,k_2,\dots,k_n} ,$$

$$\frac{\partial J}{\partial h^{(m_h-1)}_{k_1,k_2,\dots,k_n}} = H^T_{m_h} \frac{\partial J}{\partial h^{(m_h)}_{k_1,k_2,\dots,k_n}} .$$

On the first hidden layer, we can obtain the derivation of the joint representation:

$$\frac{\partial J}{\partial r^{(n)}_{k_1,\dots,k_n}} = \frac{\partial J}{\partial h^{(0)}_{k_1,\dots,k_n}} .$$

Now, with the derivation of the joint representation $\frac{\partial J}{\partial r^{(n)}_{k_1,\dots,k_n}}$, we can calculate all the derivations iteratively. Suppose we have $\frac{\partial J}{\partial r^{(m)}_{k_1,\dots,k_m}}$ of the mth ($1 < m \le n$) layer, we can calculate the derivations of parameters on this layer as:

$$\frac{\partial J}{\partial r^{(m-1)}_{k_1,\dots,k_{m-1}}} = \left[\left(e^{(m)}_{k_m}\right)^T T^{(m-1)}\right]^T \frac{\partial J}{\partial r^{(m)}_{k_1,\dots,k_n}} ,$$

$$\frac{\partial J}{\partial e^{(m)}_{k_m}} = \left[(r^{(m-1)}_{k_1,\dots,k_{m-1}})^T (T^{(m-1)})^T\right]^T \frac{\partial J}{\partial r^{(m)}_{k_1,\dots,k_n}} ,$$

$$\frac{\partial J}{\partial T^{(m-1)}_i} = e^{(m)}_{k_m} \left(r^{(m-1)}_{k_1,\dots,k_{m-1}}\right)^T \left(\frac{\partial J}{\partial r^{(m)}_{k_1,\dots,k_n}}\right)_i .$$

On the first layer, we can obtain the derivation of the first entity:

$$\frac{\partial J}{\partial e^{(1)}_{k_1}} = \frac{\partial J}{\partial r^{(1)}_{k_1}} .$$

After calculating all the derivations, a solution of learning HIR can be obtained by using stochastic gradient descent (SGD), which has been widely employed [8, 7]. Note that, the learning method can be changed according to different applications.

5. EXPERIMENTS

In this section, we empirically investigate the performance of HIR. As shown in Table 1, we conduct our experiments in four tasks: **general recommendation** with *user* and *movie*, **context-aware recommendation** with *user*, *item* and *context*, **latent collaborative retrieval** with *user*, *URL* and *tag*, and **click-through rate prediction** with *device*, *website*, *application*, *advertisement* and *position*. In all experiments, we implement HIR with 0, 1 and 2 hidden layers, denoted as HIR, HIR+ and HIR++ respectively. Then we analyze the impact of the dimensionality of latent representations and examine the interacting order of entities in context-aware recommendation and latent collaborative retrieval. Finally, we visualize representations in latent collaborative retrieval.

5.1 Experimental Settings

Our experiments are conducted on four real datasets for different applications:

- **Movielens-10M**[1] is a widely used dataset for rating prediction in recommender systems, which can be used for performance evaluation for general recommendation. There are two entities in the dataset: *user* and *movie*, with $10M$ observations.
- **Food** [15] is a dataset for rating prediction with contextual information. It is a suitable dataset for context-aware recommendation and has been used in previous works [4, 19, 21, 10]. This dataset contains three entities: *user*, *item* and *context*, with $6.3k$ observations. The contextual information captures the user's hunger degree and whether the user's feeling about hunger is real or virtual.
- **Delicious**[2] contains three entities: *user*, *URL* and *tag*, with about $0.4M$ observations. This dataset can be used for latent collaborative retrieval when considering *URL* as query and *tag* as document, which means a *user* retrieves *tags* for an untagged *URL*. Similar to [17], we use *p*-core[3] for filtering the dataset and p is chosen as 10.
- **Avazu**[4] is a dataset for click-through rate prediction, in which we extract five entities: *device*, *website*, *application*, *advertisement* and *position*, with $24M$ observations. We conduct two experiments on this dataset with the only difference of whether the entity *position* is included.

For all the datasets, we use 70% for training, 20% for testing, and the remaining 10% data as the validation set for tuning parameters, i.e., the dimensions of latent representations. And the regulation parameter is set as $\lambda = 0.01$. Moreover, we have different evaluation metrics for different tasks:

- **Root Mean Square Error (RMSE)** and **Mean Average Error (MAE)** are the most popular metrics for rating prediction. We use them for general recommendation and context-aware recommendation. The smaller the value, the better the performance.
- **Recall@k**, **Precision@k** and **F1-score@k** are three important metrics for ranking tasks. We use them for latent collaborative retrieval. The evaluation score for a given *user*-*URL*-*tag* triple is computed according to

[1]http://grouplens.org/datasets/movielens/
[2]http://grouplens.org/datasets/hetrec-2011/
[3]The *p*-core of the dataset is the largest subset of the dataset with the property that every user, every item and every tag has to occur in at least p posts.
[4]https://www.kaggle.com/c/avazu-ctr-prediction/data

Table 1: Experimental summarization

task	problem	dataset	#entities	entities	compared methods	evaluation metrics
recommendation	regression	Movielen-10M	2	*user, movie*	MF, FM	RMSE MAE
context-aware recommendation	regression	Food dataset	3	*user, item, context*	MF, LR, TF, FM, CARS2, COT	RMSE, MAE
lantent collaborative retreval	ranking	Delicious dataset	3	*user, url, tag*	MF, LR, TF, FM, LCR	recall@5, recall@10, recall@20, MAP
click-through rate prediction	classification	Avazu dataset	4/5	*device, application, website, advertisment, (position)*	LR, FM	LogLoss

where the tag appears in the ranked list. We report recall@k, precision@k and F1-score@k with $k = 5$, 10 and 20 in our experiments. The larger the value, the better the performance.

- **Mean Average Precision (MAP)** is another commonly used metric for evaluation in ranking tasks. MAP is a standard metric for evaluating the quality of ranked lists, and its top-bias property is particularly important for ranking tasks such as top-N recommendation and information retrieval. We use it as a global evaluation for latent collaborative retrieval. The larger the value, the better the performance.

- **LogLoss** is commonly used for evaluation in click-through rate prediction. The smaller the value, the better the performance.

5.2 Compared Methods

We compare HIR with both general and task-specific methods:

- **MF** [13] is used as a baseline for modeling interaction between two entities, i.e., general recommendation, ignoring *context* in context-aware recommendation and ignoring *user* in latent collaborative retrieval.

- **LR** is a widely used classifier and used as a method for click-through rate prediction [12, 29]. It can be implemented based on one-hot representation for context-aware recommendation and latent collaborative retrieval.

- **TF** [28] is a state-of-the-art method for context-aware recommendation [4] and tag recommendation [25, 17]. We use it as a baseline for both context-aware recommendation and latent collaborative retrieval.

- **FM** [16] is a compared and used as a baseline method in all the four experiments, as it is a state-of-the-art method used for different applications [20, 19, 14]. We use LibFM[5] to implement the method.

- **CARS2** [21] and **COT** [10] are two state-of-the-art methods for learning contextual representation and used as compared methods for the context-aware recommendation

- **LCR** [27, 2] is a state-of-the-art method for latent collaborative retrieval and implemented on the Delicious dataset in our experiments.

[5]http://www.libfm.org/

5.3 Performance Comparison

5.3.1 General Recommendation

The top part of Table 2 illustrates the results measured by RMSE and MAE on Movielens-10M, which show that HIR achieves the best results in general recommendation compared with MF and FM. HIR, HIR+ and HIR++ improve the performance of FM by 0.6%, 1.1% and 1.5% respectively. The results show that the high-order tensor multiplication in HIR can better represent the joint characteristics of *user-item* pair and thus improve the performance of collaborative prediction.

Table 2: Performance of general recommendation and context-aware recommendation evaluated by RMSE and MAE.

dataset	method	HIRSE	MAE
Movielens-10M	MF	0.8946	0.7159
	FM	0.8912	0.7128
	HIR	0.8863	0.7092
	HIR+	0.8814	0.7054
	HIR++	**0.8772**	**0.7025**
Food dataset	MF	1.1552	0.9484
	LR	1.1263	0.9136
	TF	1.0635	0.8415
	FM	1.0554	0.8453
	CARS2	1.0201	0.8162
	COT	1.0019	0.7921
	HIR	0.9757	0.7816
	HIR+	0.9643	0.7723
	HIR++	**0.9586**	**0.7684**

5.3.2 Context-aware Recommendation

The bottom part of Table 2 shows the results of context-aware recommendation measured by RMSE and MAE. HIR outperforms the state-of-the-art context-aware methods. And from the results, we can see that, comparing with COT, the performance improvements of HIR, HIR+ and HIR++ are 2.7%, 3.8% and 4.4% respectively. The improvement involved by the first and second hidden layer are 1.1% and 0.6% respectively, which proves that hidden layers can improve the performance but yield a smaller improvement than that of HIR itself. Moreover, we can observe that the improvement of hidden layers decreases gradually with its number, which means that the effort of hidden layers has its

Table 3: **Performance of latent collaborative retrieval evaluated by recall, precision and F1-score.**

dataset	method	recall @5	recall @10	recall @20	precision @5	precision @10	precision @20	F1-score @5	F1-score @10	F1-score @20	MAP
Delicious dataset	MF	0.1116	0.1552	0.1952	0.0915	0.0636	0.0401	0.1006	0.0902	0.0665	0.0919
	LR	0.1397	0.1963	0.2576	0.1146	0.0804	0.0527	0.1259	0.1141	0.0875	0.1051
	TF	0.1613	0.2246	0.2931	0.1323	0.0918	0.0601	0.1454	0.1303	0.0997	0.1144
	FM	0.1638	0.2268	0.2965	0.1343	0.0927	0.0607	0.1476	0.1316	0.1008	0.1155
	LCR	0.1654	0.2297	0.3013	0.1356	0.0939	0.0617	0.1491	0.1333	0.1024	0.1164
	HIR	0.1792	0.2484	0.3274	0.1469	0.1017	0.0671	0.1615	0.1443	0.1114	0.1222
	HIR+	0.1856	0.2553	0.3282	0.1522	0.1046	0.0672	0.1672	0.1484	0.1116	0.1255
	HIR++	**0.1867**	**0.2565**	**0.3314**	**0.1531**	**0.1049**	**0.0679**	**0.1682**	**0.1489**	**0.1127**	**0.1266**

own limitation and we do not need to set too many hidden layers.

5.3.3 *Latent Collaborative Retrieval*

Table 3 illustrates the results of latent collaborative retrieval measured by recall, precision, F1-score and MAP on the Delicious dataset. Note that, all the methods are implemented under the BPR framework. The results obviously show that HIR greatly outperform the compared methods. On recall@5, HIR, HIR+ and HIR++ improve the performance of LCR by 8.5%, 12.1% and 12.7% respectively. And on recall@10 and recall@20, the corresponding improvements become 8.3%, 11.4%, 11.8% and 8.6%, 8.9%, 10.1%. Measured by precision and F1-score, the same improvements can be observed. Moreover, on global evaluation metric MAP, our proposed HIR, HIR+ and HIR++ improve the performance by 5.0%, 7.8% and 8.8% respectively. We can draw similar conclusion that the performance improvement of hidden layers decreases gradually with the number of hidden layers in most experiments. The table also shows that, compared with the results on @5 and @10, the second hidden layer of HIR++ on @20 brings a greater improvement, which means that when we generate more predicted results, more hidden layers can be used to further improve the performance.

5.3.4 *Click-through Rate Prediction*

The results of click-through rate prediction measured by LogLoss are illustrated in Table 4. Note that, all the methods are implemented with the same objective function under LogLoss. We can observe that, both latent factor based methods, i.e., FM and HIR, outperform LR, which shows that latent factor based methods can better discover underlying relation of different entities. Moreover, in both experiments, without or with the *position* entity in the advertisement impression, HIR achieves the best performance. Compared with FM, HIR, HIR+ and HIR++ improve the performance by 1.4%, 2.2%, 2.5% and 1.5%, 2.3%, 2.5% respectively in these two experiments, which shows the promising performance of HIR for multi-entity interaction prediction with a number of entities.

5.4 Impact of Dimension

Performance of HIR and compared methods on the Food dataset and the Delicious dataset with varying d is shown in Figure 3. For simplicity, we do not illustrate performance of MF and LR in the figure. Instead of that, we illustrate the performance of several state-of-the-art methods and HIR with 0, 1 and 2 hidden layers in our experiments.

Table 4: Performance of click-through rate prediction evaluated by LogLoss.

dataset	method	*position* excluded	*position* included
Avazu dataset	LR	0.4186	0.4145
	FM	0.4053	0.4025
	HIR	0.3994	0.3962
	HIR+	0.3962	0.3934
	HIR++	**0.3953**	**0.3921**

As shown in Figure 3(a), for all the methods, with increasing d, the value of RMSE decreases at first, then increases after $d = 5$, which means that 5 is the best dimension for all methods. We can also observe that HIR outperforms the compared methods consistently with all dimensions. Moreover, as shown in Figure 3(b), $d = 8$ is the best parameter for all ethods on the Delicious dataset. We can observe that the impact of dimensionality for latent collaborative retrieval is smaller than that for context-aware recommendation, and HIR performs the best compared to other methods.

5.5 Impact of Interacting Order

In previous sections, we have illustrated the order *user, query, document* of information retrieval and the order *user, context, item* of context-aware recommendation. However, for some applications, the orders are sometimes difficult to be determined exactly. In such situations, it will cost lots of labor to determine the proper order. Thus, to examine the impact of interacting order of entities in HIR, we conduct experiments with all possible orders for two tasks: context-aware recommendation on the Food dataset and latent collaborative retrieval on the Delicious dataset. We implement HIR with 0, 1 and 2 hidden layers in this experiment.

Table 5: Performance under different interacting order on the Food dataset evaluated by RMSE of HIR.

order	HIR	HIR+	HIR++
(user,context,item)	0.9757	0.9643	0.9586
(item,context,user)	0.9763	0.9652	0.9583
(user,item,context)	0.9744	0.9633	0.9582
(context,user,item)	0.9786	0.9655	0.9596
(item,user,context)	0.9782	0.9663	0.9603
(context,item,user)	0.9798	0.9687	0.9594
variance	4.12E-06	3.45E-06	6.95E-07

The RMSE results of HIR under different interacting orders on the Food dataset is shown in Table 5. The vari-

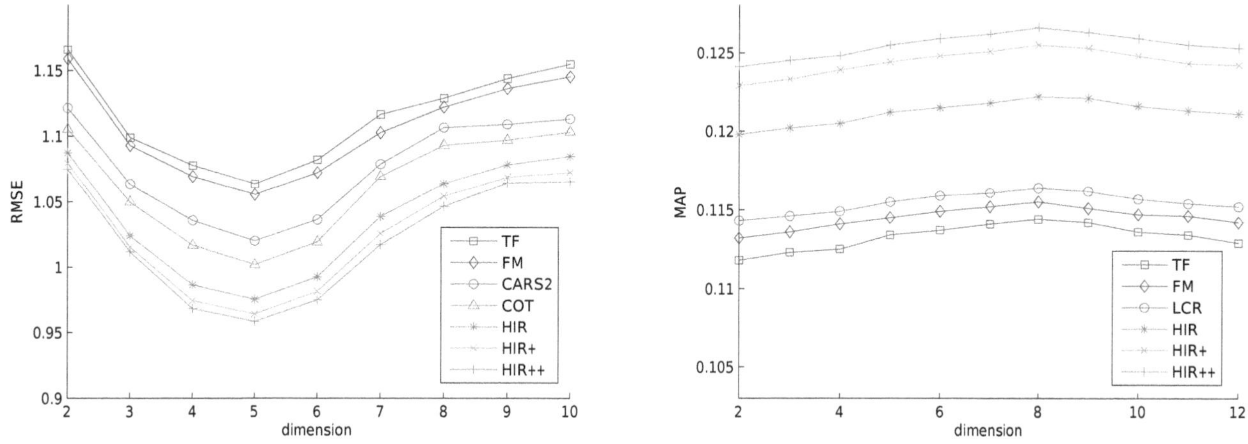

(a) Food dataset (b) Delicious dataset

Figure 3: Performance of HIR and compared methods on the Food dataset and the Delicious dataset with varying d.

Table 6: Performance under different interacting order on the Delicious dataset evaluated by MAP.

order	HIR	HIR+	HIR++
(user,URL,tag)	0.1222	0.1255	0.1266
(tag,URL,user)	0.1243	0.1263	0.1275
(user,tag,URL)	0.1196	0.1234	0.1243
(URL,user,tag)	0.1217	0.1242	0.1262
(tag,user,URL)	0.1232	0.1251	0.1267
(URL,tag,user)	0.1206	0.1228	0.1231
variance	2.91E-06	1.75E-06	2.80E-06

ances of RMSE results are also shown in the table. Note that, these results are all based on the same initialization. With the same number of hidden layers, performances of HIR are approximately the same with different interacting orders. The small variances also show that the impact of the interacting order for context-aware recommendation is not significant. Similar conclusion that the impact of the interacting order for latent collaborative retrieval is not significant can also be drawn from Table 6. In a word, in these applications, different interacting orders often achieve similar performance. The unnecessary of the settled structure can greatly reduce the labor for analyzing the raw data and selecting a suitable order when there is no obvious one.

5.6 Visualization of Representation

Here, using the Delicious dataset as an example, we plan to demonstrate the representations in HIR, and describe some interesting observations. In Figure 4, we use principal component analysis (PCA) to project the representations into a two-dimensional space. The distance in this figure reveals the relation of different representations.

We select three distinguishable users and name them as *Jack*, *Tom* and *Marry*, as shown in Figure 4(a). The representations of *URL* and *tag* are illustrated in Figure 4(b) and Figure 4(c) respectively, in which we can observe that the representations of similar *URLs* or *tags* are close. Figure

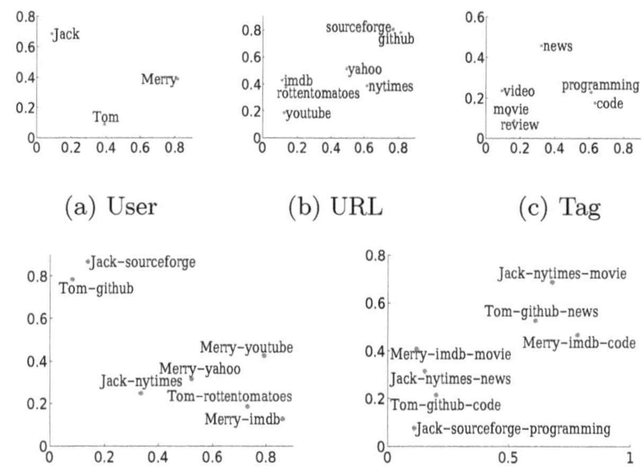

(a) User (b) URL (c) Tag

(d) User-URL (e) User-URL-tag

Figure 4: Visualization of interaction representation in the Delicious dataset.

4(d) shows the joint representations of *user* and *URL*. Although *Jack* and *Tom* have different representations, they have similar interaction representations when visiting programming websites. Similarly, although *Tom* and *Marry* have different representations, they have similar interaction representations when visiting movie websites. Figure 4(e) illustrates the interaction representations of *user*, *URL* and *tag*. We can observe that positive samples and negative samples are clearly divided into two groups in the two-dimensional space according to their interaction representations.

6. CONCLUSIONS AND FUTURE WORK

In this paper, for modeling collaborative multi-entity interaction, a novel method, i.e., HIR, has been proposed. In HIR, we generate the interaction representation of two entities via tensor multiplication and this process is repeated iteratively for the interaction of several entities. This procedure forms a hierarchical structure and can generate the final joint representation. Then the prediction can be calculated based on this representation using various learning methods. The experimental results of four different applications show that HIR outperforms both general methods and state-of-the-art task-specific methods.

In the future, we can further investigate the following directions. First, in HIR, the dimensions of entities can be adjusted for different datasets, which leads lots of hyper-parameters to be determined. So, we need to find a method to determine the dimensions automatically. Second, since there are rich features in real-world applications, we plan to incorporate the entities' feature information in HIR.

7. ACKNOWLEDGMENTS

This work is jointly supported by National Basic Research Program of China(2012CB316300), and National Natural Science Foundation of China (61403390, U1435221, 61175003, 61420106015).

8. REFERENCES

[1] Y. Bengio, A. Courville, and P. Vincent. Representation learning: A review and new perspectives. *TPAMI*, 35(8):1798–1828, 2013.

[2] K.-J. Hsiao, A. Kulesza, and A. Hero. Social collaborative retrieval. In *WSDM*, pages 293–302, 2014.

[3] M. Jamali and L. Lakshmanan. Heteromf: recommendation in heterogeneous information networks using context dependent factor models. In *WWW*, pages 643–654, 2013.

[4] A. Karatzoglou, X. Amatriain, L. Baltrunas, and N. Oliver. Multiverse recommendation: n-dimensional tensor factorization for context-aware collaborative filtering. In *RecSys*, pages 79–86, 2010.

[5] Y. Koren. Factorization meets the neighborhood: a multifaceted collaborative filtering model. In *SIGKDD*, pages 426–434, 2008.

[6] Y. Koren. Collaborative filtering with temporal dynamics. *Communications of the ACM*, 53(4):89–97, 2010.

[7] Y. Koren and R. Bell. Advances in collaborative filtering. In *Recommender Systems Handbook*, pages 145–186. 2011.

[8] Y. Koren, R. Bell, and C. Volinsky. Matrix factorization techniques for recommender systems. *IEEE Computer*, 42(8):30–37, 2009.

[9] K. Li, J. Gao, S. Guo, N. Du, X. Li, and A. Zhang. Lrbm: A restricted boltzmann machine based approach for representation learning on linked data. In *ICDM*, pages 300–309, 2014.

[10] Q. Liu, S. Wu, and L. Wang. Cot: Contextual operating tensor for context-aware recommender systems. In *AAAI*, pages 203–209, 2015.

[11] X. Liu and K. Aberer. Soco: a social network aided context-aware recommender system. In *WWW*, pages 781–802, 2013.

[12] H. B. McMahan, G. Holt, D. Sculley, M. Young, D. Ebner, J. Grady, L. Nie, T. Phillips, E. Davydov, D. Golovin, et al. Ad click prediction: a view from the trenches. In *SIGKDD*, pages 1222–1230, 2013.

[13] A. Mnih and R. Salakhutdinov. Probabilistic matrix factorization. In *NIPS*, pages 1257–1264, 2007.

[14] R. J. Oentaryo, E.-P. Lim, J.-W. Low, D. Lo, and M. Finegold. Predicting response in mobile advertising with hierarchical importance-aware factorization machine. In *WSDM*, pages 123–132, 2014.

[15] C. Ono, Y. Takishima, Y. Motomura, and H. Asoh. Context-aware preference model based on a study of difference between real and supposed situation data. In *UMAP*, pages 102–113. 2009.

[16] S. Rendle. Factorization machines with libfm. *TIST*, 3(3):57–78, 2012.

[17] S. Rendle, L. Balby Marinho, A. Nanopoulos, and L. Schmidt-Thieme. Learning optimal ranking with tensor factorization for tag recommendation. In *SIGKDD*, pages 727–736, 2009.

[18] S. Rendle, C. Freudenthaler, Z. Gantner, and L. Schmidt-Thieme. Bpr: Bayesian personalized ranking from implicit feedback. In *UAI*, pages 452–461, 2009.

[19] S. Rendle, Z. Gantner, C. Freudenthaler, and L. Schmidt-Thieme. Fast context-aware recommendations with factorization machines. In *SIGIR*, pages 635–644, 2011.

[20] S. Rendle and L. Schmidt-Thieme. Pairwise interaction tensor factorization for personalized tag recommendation. In *WSDM*, pages 81–90, 2010.

[21] Y. Shi, A. Karatzoglou, L. Baltrunas, M. Larson, and A. Hanjalic. Cars2: Learning context-aware representations for context-aware recommendations. In *CIKM*, pages 291–300, 2014.

[22] R. Socher, D. Chen, C. D. Manning, and A. Ng. Reasoning with neural tensor networks for knowledge base completion. In *NIPS*, pages 926–934, 2013.

[23] R. Socher, A. Perelygin, J. Y. Wu, J. Chuang, C. D. Manning, A. Y. Ng, and C. Potts. Recursive deep models for semantic compositionality over a sentiment treebank. In *EMNLP*, pages 1631–1642, 2013.

[24] V. Srikumar and C. D. Manning. Learning distributed representations for structured output prediction. In *NIPS*, pages 3266–3274, 2014.

[25] P. Symeonidis, A. Nanopoulos, and Y. Manolopoulos. Tag recommendations based on tensor dimensionality reduction. In *RecSys*, pages 43–50, 2008.

[26] L. R. Tucker. Some mathematical notes on three-mode factor analysis. *Psychometrika*, 31(3):279–311, 1966.

[27] J. Weston, C. Wang, R. Weiss, and A. Berenzweig. Latent collaborative retrieval. In *ICML*, pages 9–16, 2012.

[28] L. Xiong, X. Chen, T.-K. Huang, J. G. Schneider, and J. G. Carbonell. Temporal collaborative filtering with bayesian probabilistic tensor factorization. In *SDM*, pages 211–222, 2010.

[29] L. Yan, W.-J. Li, G.-R. Xue, and D. Han. Coupled group lasso for web-scale ctr prediction in display advertising. In *ICML*, pages 802–810, 2014.

[30] L. Zhang, D. Agarwal, and B.-C. Chen. Generalizing matrix factorization through flexible regression priors. In *RecSys*, pages 13–20, 2011.

Learning to Represent Knowledge Graphs with Gaussian Embedding

Shizhu He, Kang Liu, Guoliang Ji and Jun Zhao
National Laboratory of Pattern Recognition
Institute of Automation, Chinese Academy of Sciences, Beijing, 100190, China
{shizhu.he, kliu, guoliang.ji, jzhao}@nlpr.ia.ac.cn

ABSTRACT

The representation of a knowledge graph (*KG*) in a latent space recently has attracted more and more attention. To this end, some proposed models (e.g., TransE) embed entities and relations of a KG into a *"point"* vector space by optimizing a global loss function which ensures the scores of positive triplets are higher than negative ones. We notice that these models always regard all entities and relations in a same manner and ignore their (un)certainties. In fact, different entities and relations may contain different certainties, which makes identical certainty insufficient for modeling. Therefore, this paper switches to *density-based* embedding and propose **KG2E** for explicitly modeling the certainty of entities and relations, which learn the representations of KGs in the space of multi-dimensional Gaussian distributions. Each entity/relation is represented by a Gaussian distribution, where the mean denotes its position and the covariance (currently with diagonal covariance) can properly represent its certainty. In addition, compared with the symmetric measures used in *point-based* methods, we employ the KL-divergence for scoring triplets, which is a natural asymmetry function for effectively modeling multiple types of relations. We have conducted extensive experiments on link prediction and triplet classification with multiple benchmark datasets (WordNet and Freebase). Our experimental results demonstrate that our method can effectively model the (un)certainties of entities and relations in a KG, and it significantly outperforms state-of-the-art methods (including TransH and TransR).

Categories and Subject Descriptors

I.2.4 [**Artificial Intelligence**]: Knowledge Representation Formalisms and Methods—*Knowledge Graph Representation*

Keywords

Distributed Representation, Gaussian Embedding, Knowledge Graph

1. INTRODUCTION

Knowledge representation and reasoning (*KR&R*) is a fundamental issue for artificial intelligence (*AI*) and knowledge management (*KM*) [6]. To fulfill this aim, recent researchers devote to knowledge graph (*KG*) which provides an effective represent mechanism for knowledge and has become useful resources to support many intelligent applications, such as expert system [10], web search [24][27] and question answering [31][2][11]. Commonly, a KG, such as Freebase[1][1], NELL[2][7] or WordNet[3][18], describes knowledge as many relational data and represent them as interlinked subject-property-object (*SPO*) triplet facts. Usually, a triplet fact (*head entity, relation, tail entity*) (denoted as (*h, r, t*)) consists of two entities and a relation between them.

With the expansion of domains and the increase of data size, representation of KGs is required to support generalization, robust inference and other desirable functionalities [23]. However, traditional representations of KGs are based on a (*hard*) symbolic logic representation framework, which heavily rely on the learned logic inference rules for knowledge reasoning [15][29]. Thus, they lack certain ability for supporting numerical computation in continuous spaces, and cannot be effectively extended to large-scale KGs, such as Freebase. To address this problem, a new approach based on representation learning was recently proposed by attempting to embed a KG into a low-dimensional continuous vector space that preserves certain properties of the original graph [19][13][5]. The representations in (*soft*) latent space could act as a supplement for the symbolic representations, which are learned by optimizing a global loss function that involves all entities and relations in the entire graph. As a result, each entity and relation encodes global KG information through mutual effects and restrictions with the others. These embedding representations can be used in many applications, for example, verifying the correctness of one triplet fact, predicting the relations between two entities and reasoning about the implications among relations.

The promising methods (introduced in Section "Related Work") usually represent an entity as an n-dimensional vector $\mathbf{h}$ (or $\mathbf{t}$) and regard it as a *"point"* in low-dimensional spaces. A relation in KGs is represented as an operation between two *"points"* (e.g., translation as a vector [4], linear transformation as a matrix [20], and mixed operation [25]). In this way, a relation-dependent scoring function $f_r(h,t)$, such as $-||\mathbf{h}+\mathbf{r}-\mathbf{t}||_{\ell_{1/2}}$, is defined to measure the correctness of the fact (h,r,t) in the embedding space. The embedding of a KG is learned to ensure that the score of a positive triplet (e.g., (h,r,t)) is higher (or lower) than that of a corresponding (mostly corrupted) negative triplet (e.g., (h',r,t)).

Based on this paradigm, multiple models are proposed, such as TransE [4], TransH [30], and TransR [16]. Although these models are proved to be effective in many scenarios, we notice that

[1] www.freebase.com/
[2] www.rtw.ml.cmu.edu/rtw/
[3] www.wordnet.princeton.edu/

CIKM'15, October 19–23, 2015, Melbourne, Australia.
© 2015 ACM. ISBN 978-1-4503-3794-6/15/10 ...$15.00.
DOI: http://dx.doi.org/10.1145/2806416.2806502.

different entities and relations often share the same margin when separating a positive triplet and its corresponding negative triplet, and the (un)certainties of entities and relations in KGs are totally neglected. In fact, different entities and relations may contain different certainties, which makes identical certainty insufficient for modeling. We consider that the (un)certainty of one entity/relation represents the confidence for indicating its semantic when scoring a triplet as context. For example, the certainty of relation *spouse* is obviously larger than *nationality* when inferring a person (e.g., for predicting *Hillary Clinton*, we may have more confidence to know who is she when knowing her husband (*spouse*) is *Bill Clinton* than knowing she was born on (*nationality*) *USA*.). Thus, we argue that if we set a larger margin for separating (*spouse*) related positive and negative triplets in the embedding model, we could obtain better performances.

In this paper, we argue that the (un)certainties in KGs could be influenced by multiple factors, including imbalance between the relation's head and tail, different number of the linked triplets for different relations and entities, and the ambiguous of the relations and so on. For example, we hypothesize that an entity containing fewer triplets has more uncertainty, and a relation linking more triplets with more complex contexts has more uncertainty as well. We especially perform statistics on the entities and relations in Freebase[4], and Figure 1 shows the statistics of the *person* type in the *people* domain. In Figure 1, the upper left indicates the diversity numbers of triplets contained in 6 randomly sampled entities; the upper right expresses the distribution of the ratios of entity numbers in the head and tail parts with some typical relations; and the bottom shows the distribution of triplet numbers with multiple relations. This figure illustrates that popular entities (e.g., the politician *Hillary Clinton*) contain more relations and facts than unpopular ones (e.g., the writer *Murray Silverstein*). Furthermore, different parts of relations can contain very different numbers of entities, (such as the *head* part and *tail* part in *gender* or *nationality*), and, high-frequency relations (e.g., *nationality*) link more entity pairs than low-frequency ones (e.g., *religion*). It indicates that the variations of uncertainty with different entities and relations in a KG is vary enormously, and it is desirable to consider this problem when learning the representations of a KG in a latent space.

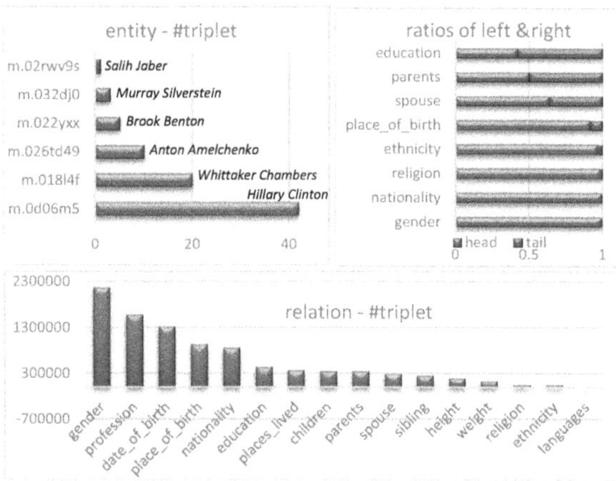

Figure 1: Various densities in a KG.

To address the aforementioned problem, this paper proposes a new *density-based* embedding method, **KG2E**[5], to model KGs and learn the representations in the space of multi-dimensional Gaussian distributions. Inspired by [28], our approach models each entity and relation with a multi-dimensional Gaussian distribution $\mathcal{N}(\boldsymbol{\mu}, \boldsymbol{\Sigma})$ (currently with diagonal covariance for computing efficiency). The mean vector of such multi-dimensional Gaussian distribution indicates its position, and the covariance matrix indicates the corresponding (un)certainty which impacts on others, as shown in Figure 2. Similar to previous methods, we also design a scoring function $f_r(h, t)$ to measure the correctness of the triplet fact (h, r, t) in the embedding space. In our scoring function, the distributions between $\mathcal{H} - \mathcal{T}$ and $\mathcal{R}$ are similar when (h, r, t) holds, where $\mathcal{H}$, $\mathcal{R}$ and $\mathcal{T}$ indicate the Gaussian distributions of h, r and t, respectively. Different from previous methods, which adopts *point-based* scoring functions (dot products, cosine distance, $\ell_{1/2}$ distances, etc.), we employ the KL-divergence between two probability distribution (the entity-pair distribution and the relation distribution) as the scoring function for all triples in KGs, which is a naturally asymmetric and effective way for incorporating covariance (denotes (un)certainties of entities and relations in KGs) into the model. Moreover, we will employ another scoring function based on the expected likelihood [12] to inspect the different performances of asymmetric and symmetric measures.

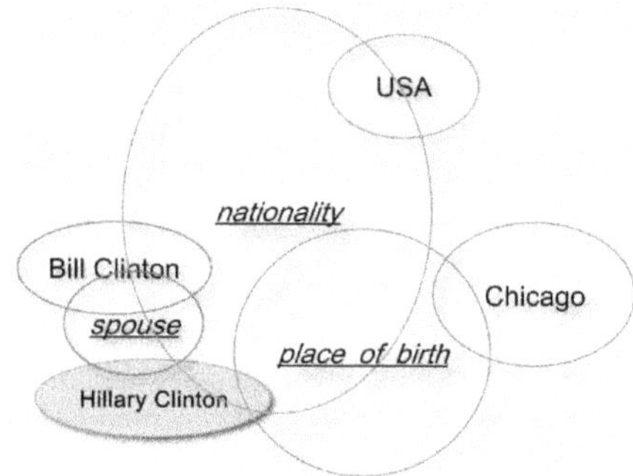

Figure 2: Illustrated of the means and (diagonal) variances of entities and relations in a Gaussian Embedding. The label indicates its position. *Relations* attach with underlined labels. Circles with the same color indicate a fact for *Hillary Clinton*. In the representations, we might infer that *Hillary Clinton* was born in (*place_of_birth*) *Chicago*, and is an (*nationality*) *American*.

We have conducted extensive experiments on link prediction and triplet classification with multiple benchmark datasets such as WordNet and Freebase. The experimental results demonstrate the effectiveness of our method. In particular, the proposed model can effectively address one-to-many, many-to-one and reflexive relations, and significantly outperforms state-of-the-art methods (including TransH [30] and TransR [16]) by as much as ~30% when predicting head (tail) entities in many-to-one (one-to-many) relations.

In summary, our main contributions are as follows:

- We propose a new method for learning the representations of a KG. Different from previous methods, we specially consider the (un)certainties of entities and relations the a KG.
- We model each entity/relation into a Gaussian distribution. In particular, the mean vector denote its position and the covariance matrix (currently diagonal for computing efficiency) are used to describe the (un)certainties of the entities and relations. To our knowledge, the proposed method is the first work which models KGs with *"density-based"* embedding, in contrast to the existing *"point-based"* embedding methods.

[4]We use the dump data released on 2014-06-29.

[5]This name has two meanings. The first indicates mapping **K**nowledge **G**raph *to* **E**mbedding and the second indicates the representation of a **KG** with **G**aussian **E**mbedding.

- We use two methods (symmetric and asymmetric) to compute the scores of triplets and find that the asymmetric method (KL-divergence between two Gaussian distributions) is more suitable for learning the representation of a KG with Gaussian embedding.

- The experimental results demonstrate that our proposed method can effectively model the (un)certainty of entities and relations in a KG, and it significantly outperforms state-of-the-art methods in multiple related tasks.

2. RELATED WORK

Currently, the proposed methods mainly represent KGs in a low-dimensional latent space. We briefly summarize the most relevant work in Table 1[6]. These methods embed entities into a vector space and define a (mainly relation-dependent) scoring function to measure the compatibility of (h, r, t). The differences in these models are the defined scoring functions $f_r(h, t)$.

We first highlight TransE [4] and its variants (TransH [30] and TransR [16]) because they are simple and effective and achieve the state-of-the-art performance in the majority of related tasks, especially in KGs with thousands of relations. Inspired by the word2vec [17], which finds the learning word vectors with a neural network own linear relations, such as, *vec('Paris') - vec('France')* $\approx$ *vec('Rome') - vec('Italy')*, that is, the difference in word vectors is similar when they are attached to the same relation (e.g., *capital_of*, corresponding to the above example), TransE [4] represents a relation as a vector r indicating the semantic translation from the head entity h to the tail entity t, aiming to satisfy the equation $\mathbf{t} - \mathbf{h} \approx \mathbf{r}$ when triplet (h, r, t) holds. TransE effectively handles one-to-one relations but has issues in handling one-to-many, many-to-one and many-to-many relations. For example, consider a one-to-many relation $\mathbf{r}$ with multiple tail entities $\mathbf{t}_i$ satisfying $\mathbf{h} + \mathbf{r} \approx \mathbf{t}_i$ for $\forall i \in \{1, ..., m\}, (h, r, t_i) \in KG$, and it outputs invalid representations ($\mathbf{t}_1 = ... = \mathbf{t}_m$) for distinguishing entities.

To address the aforementioned issues in TransE, TransH [30] and TransR [16] are proposed to enable an entity to have distinct representations when involved in different relations. For a triplet (h, r, t), TransH first projects a head/tail entity vector (**h/t**) into a relation-dependent hyper-plane by the following formulas: $\mathbf{h}_\perp = \mathbf{h}(\mathbf{I} - \mathbf{w}_r^T \mathbf{w}_r)$ and $\mathbf{t}_\perp = \mathbf{t}(\mathbf{I} - \mathbf{w}_r^T \mathbf{w}_r)$, where $\mathbf{w}_r$ is the vector that spans the hyper-plane. It then measures the score using the function $||\mathbf{h}_\perp + \mathbf{r} - \mathbf{t}_\perp||_{\ell_{1/2}}$ in the hyper-plane of the relation r. TransR is slightly different from TransH: it transforms a head/tail entity vector into a relation-dependent sub-space with $\mathbf{h}_r = \mathbf{h}\mathbf{M}_r$ and $\mathbf{t}_r = \mathbf{t}\mathbf{M}_r$, where $\mathbf{M}_r$ represents the transform matrix from entity space to the sub-space of relation r.

However, the TransH and TransR methods only partly address the issues encountered by TransE. For example, consider TransR in a one-to-many relation. It tends to learning $\mathbf{t}_i\mathbf{M}_r = \mathbf{t}_j\mathbf{M}_r$, for $\forall i, j \in \{1, ..., m\}$, (h, r, t_i), and $(h, r, t_j) \in KG$, and as a result, the different part between $\mathbf{t}_i$ and $\mathbf{t}_j$ only depends on the number of eigenvalues equal to zero[7]. In addition, the existing methods have difficulty learning valid representations for reflexive relations because they use the same operation for head and tail entities. For example, when triplets (h, r, t) and (t, r, h) both hold for a reflexive relation r, TransE, TransH and even TransR tend to make ($\mathbf{h} \approx \mathbf{t}$) and ($\mathbf{r} \approx \mathbf{0}$). Whereas $\mathbf{h}$ equals $\mathbf{t}$ may be a good character for a reflexive relation, the same vector ($\mathbf{0}$) for represents all reflexive relations is not helpful for related tasks. Issues often exist in the *"point" based* embedding models, in which "point" vectors are typically compared by dot products, cosine-distance or $\ell_{1/2}$ norm, all of which provide for symmetric comparison between instances. The proposed *"density" based* methods represent entities and relations by Gaussian distributions that explicitly modeling the uncertainty of KGs and the asymmetry function scores (h, r, t) and (t, r, h) using different parameters associated with not only the head and tail entities but also its order.

To our knowledge, Linear Relational Embedding (LRE) [20] is the pioneer work in learning representations of multi-relational data that represent concepts as vectors and binary relations as transform matrices. For concepts and their relations (i, r, j), LRE learns to maximize the generatation probability from concept i and relation r to concept j in proportion to $\exp(-||\mathbf{R_r v_i} - \mathbf{v_j}||^2)$. Subsequently, many approaches have followed this line. The unstructured model (UM) [4] was proposed as the simplified version of TransE by assigning all translation vectors $\mathbf{r} = 0$. However, it cannot distinguish different relations. Structured embedding (SE) [5] adopts two different relation-specific matrices for head and tail entities but cannot capture precious semantics of relations because the two matrices are separated in optimization. The latent factor model (LFM) [13] considers the second-order correlations between entities embedding with a quadratic form. The single layer model (SLM) and neural tensor network (NTN) were proposed by Socher [25]. The SLM is a naive baseline of the NTN and scores triplets using relation-specific weights $\mathbf{u}_r$ with a non-linear operation (tanh) for triplet representation $W_{rh}\mathbf{h} + W_{rt}\mathbf{t} + \mathbf{b}_r$. To date, the NTN is the most expressive model based on multi-layer neural networks. As shown in Table 1, the NTN extends the SLM by considering the second-order correlations between entity embedding (similar to LFM), feeding into a non-linear hidden layer, and then combining with a linear output parameterized by the relation. However, the NTN is not sufficiently simple to handle the large-scale KGs with numerous relations.

In addition to these methods based on the *ranking loss* framework, there is another line of related work that focuses on learning the latent representations for KGs by *tensor (matrix) decomposition and completion*; it was inspired by the wide usage of decomposition in recommended system [14] and relation extraction [32]. The collective matrix factorization model RESCAL [19] was proposed to model KGs, which regarding a KG as a 3-model tensor and learning the latent representations (entity as a vector and relation as a matrix) by reconstructing the original graph. RESCAL can be used to cluster related entities and relations. Clustering concepts have been widely used in modeling multi-relational data, such as tensor factorization based on Bayesian clustering [26] and jointly spectral clustering [8]. We compare our method with RESCAL in our experiments. Vilnis and McCallum firstly proposed the Gaussian Embedding models learning the representations of words [28], which inspired this work. However, they mainly focus on the word representations based on the contexts of text, this work focus on the entity/relation representations in KGs based on the inter-linked relationships between them.

3. REPRESENTING A KG WITH GAUSSIAN EMBEDDING

A Gaussian distribution is capable of representing (un)certainty explicitly. We represent KGs with Gaussian embedding. In this

[6]For convenient comparison, we use a different expression for TransH.

[7]Decompose matrix $\mathbf{M_r}$ with singular value decomposition (SVD): $(\mathbf{t_i} - \mathbf{t_j})\mathbf{M_r} = (\mathbf{t_i} - \mathbf{t_j})\mathbf{S}\begin{pmatrix}\Sigma & 0\\ 0 & 0\end{pmatrix}\mathbf{D} = \mathbf{0}$, ensuring that (most) parts of $\mathbf{t_i}$ and $\mathbf{t_j}$ are equal because the eigenvalues of the upper part of matrix ($\mathbf{S\Sigma D}$) cannot contain zero.

Model	Score function $f_r(h,t)$	# Parameters
LRE (2001) [20]	$\exp(-\|\|\mathbf{W_r h} - \mathbf{t}\|\|^{\mathbf{2}}), W_r \in \mathbb{R}^{k_e \times k_e}$	$k_e n_e + k_r n_r^2$
SE (2011) [5]	$\|\|W_{rh}\mathbf{h} - W_{rt}\mathbf{t}\|\|_{\ell_{1/2}}, W_{rh}, W_{rt} \in \mathbb{R}^{k_r \times k_e}$	$k_e n_e + 2k_r n_r$
LTM (2012) [13]	$\mathbf{h}^T W_r \mathbf{t}, W_R \in \mathbb{R}^{k_e \times k_e}$	$k_e n_e + k_r n_r$
UM (2012) [3]	$\|\|\mathbf{h} - \mathbf{t}\|\|_2^2$	$k_e n_e$
TransE (2013) [4]	$\|\|\mathbf{h} + \mathbf{r} - \mathbf{t}\|\|_{\ell_{1/2}}, \mathbf{r} \in \mathbb{R}_r^k$	$k_e(n_e + n_r)$
SLM (2013) [25]	$\mathbf{u}_r^T g(W_{rh}\mathbf{h} + W_{rt}\mathbf{t} + \mathbf{b}_r), \mathbf{u}_r, \mathbf{b}_r \in \mathbb{R}^s, W_{rh}, W_{rt} \in \mathbb{R}^{s \times k_e}$	$n_e k_e + n_r(2sk_r + s)$
NTN (2013) [25]	$\mathbf{u}_r^T g(\mathbf{h}^T \mathbf{W}_r \mathbf{t} + W_{rh}\mathbf{h} + W_{rt}\mathbf{t} + \mathbf{b}_r), \mathbf{W}_r \in \mathbb{R}^{k_e \times k_e \times s}$	$n_e k_e + n_r(sk_e^2 + 2sk_e + s)$
TransH (2014) [30]	$\|\|\mathbf{h}(\mathbf{I} - \mathbf{w}_r^T\mathbf{w}_r) + \mathbf{r} - \mathbf{t}(\mathbf{I} - \mathbf{w}_r^T\mathbf{w}_r)\|\|_{\ell_{1/2}}, \mathbf{w}_r, \mathbf{r} \in \mathbb{R}_r^k$	$k_e n_e + 2k_r n_r$
TransR (2015) [16]	$\|\|\mathbf{h}\mathbf{M}_r + \mathbf{r} - \mathbf{t}\mathbf{M}_r\|\|_{\ell_{1/2}}, \mathbf{r} \in \mathbb{R}_r^k, \mathbf{M}_r \in \mathbb{R}^{k_r \times k_r}$	$k_e n_e + (k_r + k_r^2)n_r$
KG2E_KL (this paper)	$\frac{1}{2}\{tr(\mathbf{\Sigma}_r^{-1}(\mathbf{\Sigma}_h + \mathbf{\Sigma}_t)) + \boldsymbol{\mu}^T\mathbf{\Sigma}_r^{-1}\boldsymbol{\mu} - \log\frac{det(\mathbf{\Sigma}_h + \mathbf{\Sigma}_t)}{det(\mathbf{\Sigma}_r)}\}, \boldsymbol{\mu} = \boldsymbol{\mu}_h - \boldsymbol{\mu}_t - \boldsymbol{\mu}_r$	$2k_e n_e + 2k_r n_r$
KG2E_EL (this paper)	$\frac{1}{2}\{\boldsymbol{\mu}^T\mathbf{\Sigma}^{-1}\boldsymbol{\mu} + \log\det\mathbf{\Sigma}\}, \mathbf{\Sigma} = \mathbf{\Sigma}_h + \mathbf{\Sigma}_t + \mathbf{\Sigma}_r$	$2k_e n_e + 2k_r n_r$

Table 1: Representative models for representing a KG in a latent space. We mainly compare the models' scoring functions $f_r(\mathbf{h}, \mathbf{t})$ and their complexities (the numbers of parameters). n_e and n_r are the number of unique entities and relations, respectively. k_e and k_r are the dimensions of entity and relation in the latent embedding space, $\mathbf{h}, \mathbf{t} \in \mathbb{R}^{k_e}$. s is the number of slices of a tensor used in NTN. I indicates the identity matrix used in TransH. $g(x)$ is a non-linear function used in neural networks such as $tanh$.

section, we firstly introduce the framework for learning KG embedding. We then present the proposed **KG2E** method and the learning strategy.

First, we describe some common notations: h, r and t denote the head entity, relation and tail entity for a triplet fact (h, r, t). The mathematical symbols $\mathcal{H}$, $\mathcal{R}$ and $\mathcal{T}$ denote the corresponding Gaussian distributions: $\mathcal{H} \sim \mathcal{N}(\boldsymbol{\mu}_h, \mathbf{\Sigma}_h)$ (similarly for $\mathcal{R}$ and $\mathcal{T}$). The mean vector $\boldsymbol{\mu}$ and covariance matrix $\mathbf{\Sigma}$ indicate the corresponding embedding representations for the Gaussian distribution, and $\mathcal{E}$ and $\mathcal{R}$ are the sets of entities and relations in KGs, respectively.

3.1 Background

We follow the *energy-based* framework to learn the representations of a KG, as commonly used in learning word embedding [17] and knowledge graph embedding [4] in a large scale corpus. The core of this framework is an *energy function* $\mathcal{E}_{\boldsymbol{\theta}}(x)$ that scores the input x, parameterized by $\boldsymbol{\theta}$. The goal of *energy-based* learning is to learn the parameters of the energy function to ensure that the score of an observed positive example is higher (or lower, depending on the definition) than those of negative (mainly constructed) examples. This approach is often associated with a loss function $\mathcal{L}$ that provides gradients of the parameters given the predictions of the energy function according to some specific supervision. The framework is also called *ranking loss* learning because the defined loss function is based on the ranks of positive and negative samples.

In *energy-based* KG embedding models, the parameters $\boldsymbol{\theta}$ correspond to our learned representations, and the input x correspond to observed true triplet facts in a KG. That is, the defined *energy function* renders the score of a true fact higher (or lower) than that of a false fact, parameterized with the representations $\boldsymbol{\theta}$.

3.2 Gaussian Embedding for a KG

We will describe the *energy functions* used in our proposed method that measure the score of a triplet (h, r, t). Borrowing concepts from translation-based methods [4][30][16], we consider the transformation result from the head entity to the tail entity to be akin to the relation in the positive triplet. We use the following simple formula to express this transformation: $\mathcal{H} - \mathcal{T}$, which corresponds to the probability distribution $\mathcal{P}_e \sim \mathcal{N}(\boldsymbol{\mu}_h - \boldsymbol{\mu}_t, \mathbf{\Sigma}_h + \mathbf{\Sigma}_t)$ (we hypothesize that the head entity and tail entity are independent with regard to some specific relation). As a result, combined with the probability distribution of relation $\mathcal{P}_r \sim \mathcal{N}(\boldsymbol{\mu}_r, \mathbf{\Sigma}_r)$, the most important step is to measure the similarity between $\mathcal{P}_e$ and $\mathcal{P}_r$.

KL-divergence is a straightforward method of measuring the similarity of two probability distributions and is naturally asymmetric. Moreover, we use another similarity method based on the expected likelihood or probability product kernel [28][12] to inspect the difference in performance between asymmetric and symmetric measures. We illustrate the two similarity measures in detail below.

3.2.1 *Asymmetric similarity: KL-divergence*

We optimize the following energy function based on the KL divergence between the entity-transformed distribution and relation distribution and denote it as KL.

$$\begin{aligned}\mathcal{E}(h,r,t) &= \mathcal{E}(\mathcal{P}_e, \mathcal{P}_r) = \mathcal{D}_{\mathcal{KL}}(\mathcal{P}_e, \mathcal{P}_r) \\ &= \int_{x \in \mathcal{R}^{k_e}} \mathcal{N}(x; \boldsymbol{\mu}_r, \mathbf{\Sigma}_r) \log\frac{\mathcal{N}(x; \boldsymbol{\mu}_e, \mathbf{\Sigma}_e)}{\mathcal{N}(x; \boldsymbol{\mu}_r, \mathbf{\Sigma}_r)} dx \\ &= \frac{1}{2}\Big\{ tr(\mathbf{\Sigma}_r^{-1}\mathbf{\Sigma}_e) + (\boldsymbol{\mu}_r - \boldsymbol{\mu}_e)^T\mathbf{\Sigma}_r^{-1}(\boldsymbol{\mu}_r - \boldsymbol{\mu}_e) \\ &\qquad - \log\frac{det(\mathbf{\Sigma}_e)}{det(\mathbf{\Sigma}_r)} - k_e \Big\}\end{aligned} \tag{1}$$

In the upper formula, $tr(\mathbf{\Sigma})$ and $\mathbf{\Sigma}^{-1}$ indicate the trace and inverse of the covariance matrix, respectively. Considering the simplified diagonal covariance, we can compute the trace and inverse of the matrix simply and effectively.

The gradient of the log determinant is $\frac{\partial \log det A}{\partial A} = A^{-1}$, the gradient $\frac{\partial x^T A^{-1} y}{\partial A} = -A^{-T}xy^TA^{-T}$, and the gradient $\frac{\partial tr(X^TA^{-1}Y)}{\partial A} = -(A^{-1}YX^TA^{-1})^T$ [21]. We can compute the gradients of this energy function with respect to the mean vectors and covariance matrix (currently acting as a vector) as follows:

$$\frac{\partial \mathcal{E}(h,r,t)}{\partial \boldsymbol{\mu}_r} = \frac{\partial \mathcal{E}(h,r,t)}{\partial \boldsymbol{\mu}_t} = -\frac{\partial \mathcal{E}(h,r,t)}{\partial \boldsymbol{\mu}_h} = \Delta'_{hrt} \tag{2}$$

$$\frac{\partial \mathcal{E}(h,r,t)}{\partial \mathbf{\Sigma}_r} = \frac{1}{2}(\mathbf{\Sigma}_r^{-1}\mathbf{\Sigma}_e\mathbf{\Sigma}_r^{-1} + \Delta'_{hrt}\Delta'^T_{hrt} + \mathbf{\Sigma}_r^{-1})) \tag{3}$$

$$\frac{\partial \mathcal{E}(h,r,t)}{\partial \mathbf{\Sigma}_h} = \frac{\partial \mathcal{E}(h,r,t)}{\partial \mathbf{\Sigma}_t} = \frac{1}{2}(\mathbf{\Sigma}_r^{-1} - \mathbf{\Sigma}_e^{-1}) \tag{4}$$

$$where\ \Delta'_{hrt} = \mathbf{\Sigma}_r^{-1}(\boldsymbol{\mu}_r + \boldsymbol{\mu}_t - \boldsymbol{\mu}_h), \mathbf{\Sigma}_e = \mathbf{\Sigma}_h + \mathbf{\Sigma}_t$$

We can define a symmetric similarity measure based on KL divergence as follows:

$$\mathcal{E}(h,r,t) = \frac{1}{2}(\mathcal{D}_{\mathcal{KL}}(\mathcal{P}_e, \mathcal{P}_r) + \mathcal{D}_{\mathcal{KL}}(\mathcal{P}_r, \mathcal{P}_e))$$

However, this measure lacks any gains in performance in terms of link prediction and triplet classification, likely because the discriminative ability of this formula is not distinct from the previous function for positive and negative triplets.

3.2.2 *Symmetric similarity: expected likelihood*

The dot product between the entity mean and relation mean is not a suitable measure of similarity because it does not integrate the covariance and cannot consider the diversity of uncertainty among different entities/relations. Therefore, we take the inner product between two distributions themselves to measure the similarity between $\mathcal{P}_e$ and $\mathcal{P}_r$.

$$\begin{aligned}\mathcal{E}(\mathcal{P}_e, \mathcal{P}_r) &= \int_{x \in \mathcal{R}^{k_e}} \mathcal{N}(x; \boldsymbol{\mu}_e, \boldsymbol{\Sigma}_e)\mathcal{N}(x; \boldsymbol{\mu}_r, \boldsymbol{\Sigma}_r)dx \\ &= \mathcal{N}(0; \boldsymbol{\mu}_e - \boldsymbol{\mu}_r, \boldsymbol{\Sigma}_e + \boldsymbol{\Sigma}_r)\end{aligned} \tag{5}$$

For better computation and comparison, we use the logarithm of the upper formula as the final energy function and denote it as EL.

$$\begin{aligned}\mathcal{E}(h,r,t) &= \log \mathcal{E}(\mathcal{P}_e, \mathcal{P}_r) = \log \mathcal{N}(0; \boldsymbol{\mu}_e - \boldsymbol{\mu}_r, \boldsymbol{\Sigma}_e + \boldsymbol{\Sigma}_r) \\ &= \frac{1}{2}\Big\{(\boldsymbol{\mu}_e - \boldsymbol{\mu}_r)^T(\boldsymbol{\Sigma}_e + \boldsymbol{\Sigma}_r)^{-1}(\boldsymbol{\mu}_e - \boldsymbol{\mu}_r) + \\ &\qquad \log\det(\boldsymbol{\Sigma}_e + \boldsymbol{\Sigma}_r) + k_e \log(2\pi)\Big\}\end{aligned} \tag{6}$$

As in the previous case, we can compute the gradients for this energy function in a closed form.

$$\frac{\partial \mathcal{E}(h,r,t)}{\partial \boldsymbol{\mu}_h} = -\frac{\partial \mathcal{E}(h,r,t)}{\partial \boldsymbol{\mu}_r} = -\frac{\partial \mathcal{E}(h,r,t)}{\partial \boldsymbol{\mu}_t} = \Delta'_{hrt} \tag{7}$$

$$\begin{aligned}\frac{\partial \mathcal{E}(h,r,t)}{\partial \boldsymbol{\Sigma}_h} = \frac{\partial \mathcal{E}(h,r,t)}{\partial \boldsymbol{\Sigma}_r} = \frac{\partial \mathcal{E}(h,r,t)}{\partial \boldsymbol{\Sigma}_t} &= \\ \frac{1}{2}(\Delta'_{hrt}\Delta'^T_{hrt} - \boldsymbol{\Sigma}'^{-1})&\end{aligned} \tag{8}$$

$$where\ \Delta'_{hrt} = \boldsymbol{\Sigma}'^{-1}(\boldsymbol{\mu}_r + \boldsymbol{\mu}_t - \boldsymbol{\mu}_h), \boldsymbol{\Sigma}' = \boldsymbol{\Sigma}_h + \boldsymbol{\Sigma}_t + \boldsymbol{\Sigma}_r$$

3.3 Learning

We define the following margin-based ranking loss for effective discrimination between observed (positive) triplets and incorrect (negative) triplets:

$$\mathcal{L} = \sum_{(h,r,t)\in\Gamma} \sum_{(h',r',t')\in\Gamma'_{(h,r,t)}} [\mathcal{E}(h,r,t) + \gamma - \mathcal{E}(h',r',t')]_+ \tag{9}$$

where $[x]_+ \triangleq \max(0,x)$ aims to obtain the maximums between 0 and x, γ is the margin separating positive and negative triplets, $\mathcal{E}(h,r,t)$ indicates the energy function formula 1 or 6 for scoring triplets, Γ is the set of positive triplets observed in the KG, and $\Gamma'_{(h,r,t)}$ denotes the set of negative triples corresponding to (h,r,t), which will be introduced below.

Under the open world assumption (OWA), existing KGs contain only correct triplets. The routine method for constructing a negative triplet (h',r',t') is to replace the head or tail entity randomly, such as sampling h' for h and obtaining (h',r,t). To obtain practical corrupted triplets, we follow [30] and assign different probabilities for head/tail entity replacement. The main idea is to provide a greater likelihood of replacing the side that will reduce the possibility of generating false-negative instances. For example, with regard to the relation *gender*, replacing *tail* is more likely to generate true-negative triplets. Following the notation in previous methods [30][16], we will denote the traditional sampling method as "unif" and the new method [30] as "bern". We also generate a negative triplet by corrupting the relation and ensure that it is not a false-negative triplet.

To avoid overfitting, we add some regularization while learning the Gaussian embedding. Considering the different geometric characteristics, we use different regularization strategies for the mean and covariance. The following hard constraints are considered when we minimize the loss $\mathcal{L}$:

$$\forall \ell \in \mathcal{E} \cup \mathcal{R}, ||\boldsymbol{\mu}_\ell||_2 \leq 1 \tag{10}$$

$$\forall \ell \in \mathcal{E} \cup \mathcal{R}, c_{min}I \leq \boldsymbol{\Sigma}_\ell \leq c_{max}I, c_{min} > 0 \tag{11}$$

where the constraint 10 ensures that the means remain sufficiently small and the constraint 11 guarantees that the covariance matrices are positive definite and of appropriate size. We can use $\boldsymbol{\Sigma}_{ii} \leftarrow max(c_{min}, min(c_{max}, \boldsymbol{\Sigma}_{ii}))$ to achieve these goals for diagonal covariance.

Algorithm 1: THE LEARNING ALGORITHM OF **KG2E**

Input: An energy function $\mathcal{E}(h,r,t)$, training set $\Gamma = \{(h,r,t)\}$, entity set $\mathcal{E}$ and relation set $\mathcal{R}$, entity and relation sharing embedding dimensions k, margin γ, restriction values c_{min} and c_{max} for covariance, learning rate α and maximum epochs n.

Output: All the Gaussian embeddings (mean vector and covariance matrix) of e and r, where $e \in \mathcal{E}$ and $r \in \mathcal{R}$.

foreach $\ell \in \mathcal{E} \cup \mathcal{R}$ **do**
  ℓ.mean $\leftarrow$ Uniform($\frac{-6}{\sqrt{k}}$, $\frac{6}{\sqrt{k}}$)
  ℓ.cov $\leftarrow$ Uniform(c_{min}, c_{max})
  regularize ℓ.mean and ℓ.cov with constraints 10 and 11
$i \leftarrow 0$
while $i++ \leq n$ **do**
  $\Gamma_{batch} \leftarrow$ sample(Γ, b) //sample a minibatch of size B from Γ
  $T_{batch} \leftarrow \emptyset$ //pairs of triplets for learning
  foreach $(h,r,t) \in \Gamma_{batch}$ **do**
    $(h',r,t') \leftarrow$ negSample((h,r,t)) //sampling negative triplet with "unif" or "bern"
    $T_{batch} \leftarrow T_{batch} \cup ((h,r,t),(h',r,t'))$
    $(h,r',t) \leftarrow$ negSample((h,r,t)) //sampling negative triplet by corrupting relation
    $T_{batch} \leftarrow T_{batch} \cup ((h,r,t),(h,r',t))$
  Update Gaussian embeddings based on Equations 2, 3 and 4 (or 7 and 8, depending on $\mathcal{E}(h,r,t)$) w.r.t. $\mathcal{L} = \sum_{((h,r,t),(h',r',t'))\in T_{batch}} [\mathcal{E}(h,r,t) + \gamma - \mathcal{E}(h',r',t')]_+$
  regularize the means and covariances for each entity and relation in T_{batch} with constraints 10 and 11

We use *Stochastic Gradient Descent* (SGD)[8] in small mini-batches to iteratively update the Gaussian embeddings of entities and relations. In our model, we must first choose an energy function (EL or KL) (hereafter, we denote the corresponding models as KG2E_EL

[8]We also use AdaGrad [9] to optimize the parameters but found no improvement.

and KG2E_KL, respectively.). The detailed learning procedure is described in Algorithm 1. All Gaussian embeddings for entities and relations are first initialized randomly following a uniform distribution. At each main iteration of the algorithm, we first sample a batch of observed triplets, and construct corresponding negative triplets based on the aforementioned sampling methods ("unif" or "bern"). The parameters of Gaussian embedding are then updated by taking a gradient step (using formulas 2, 3 and 4 or 7 and 8, depending on the choice of energy function $\mathcal{E}(h, r, t)$), with a constant learning rate. For each step (including the initial embedding), we ensure that all embeddings satisfy with the constraints 10 and 11.

4. EXPERIMENTS

4.1 Data Sets

In this work, we empirically study and evaluate related methods for two tasks: link prediction [4] and triplet classification [25]. We use datasets commonly used in previous methods, which are built from two typical KGs: WordNet [18] and Freebase [1]. WordNet is a lexical database of the English language. In WordNet, each entity represents a synset consisting of several words, and a word can also belong to different synsets. Relationships between synsets include *hypernym, hyponym, meronym, holonym, troponym* and other lexical relations. We adopt two datasets from WordNet, WN18, used in [4] for link prediction, and WN11, used in [25] for triplet classification. Among them, WN18 contains 18 relations and WN11 contains 11. Freebase is a large collaborative knowledge graph of general world facts. For example, the triplet (*Bill Gates, place_of_birth, Seattle*) indicates that the person with entity *Bill Gates* was born in (*place_of_birth*) the location with entity *Seattle*. We adopt two datasets from Freebase, FB13, used in [25] for triplet classification, and FB15k, used in [4] for link predication and triplet classification. Among them, FB13 contains 13 relations and FB15k contains approximately 15,000 entities. The statistics of these datasets are listed in Table 2.

Dataset	$\#\mathcal{R}$	$\#\mathcal{E}$	#Triplet (Train/Valid/Test)		
WN18	18	40,943	141,442	5,000	5,000
FB15k	1,345	14,951	483,142	50,000	59,071
WN11	11	38,696	112,581	2,609	10,544
FB13	13	75,043	316,232	5,908	23,733

Table 2: Datasets used in the experiments.

4.2 Qualitative Analysis

Before evaluation in each specific task and comparison with other methods, we first examine the effectiveness and ability of our proposed method to represent the uncertainty in a KG with a qualitative analysis. The following surveys and observations are based on the representations of embeddings learned by KG2E and using KL-divergence as a similarity measure in FB15k.

First, we want to know the effect of covariance in modeling the uncertainty in a KG. Based on our ideas, an entity/relation with a higher level of uncertainty has a larger covariance (corresponding with determinant or trace). Considering the uncertainty of an entity, we focus on the relationship between the (log) determinant of covariance matrix and its density. The entity/relation density is indicated by the number of corresponding triplets, and the entity density is measured at different positions: head part, tail part or entire set. As shown in Figure 3, there is a clear tendency for the larger determinant of entity covariance to have fewer corresponding triplets, regardless of position. Considering the uncertainty of a relation, we measure the (log) determinant and trace of covariance for 13 relations with */people/person* as *domain*, as shown in Table 3 (each row includes the following information with a relation: label, number of triplets,number of head entities, number of tail entities, type[9], (log) determinant and trace of covariance matrix). We can draw the following conclusions: 1) the covariance of Gaussian embedding can effectively model the (un)certainty of a relation; 2) relations with complex semantic (e.g., many_to_one (m-1) and many_to_many (m-n) relations) have larger uncertainty, and 3) the more unbalanced the head and tail entities, the larger the uncertainty. For example, the *nationality* relation has the largest uncertainty, and the *parents* relation has the smallest uncertainty among these 13 relations.

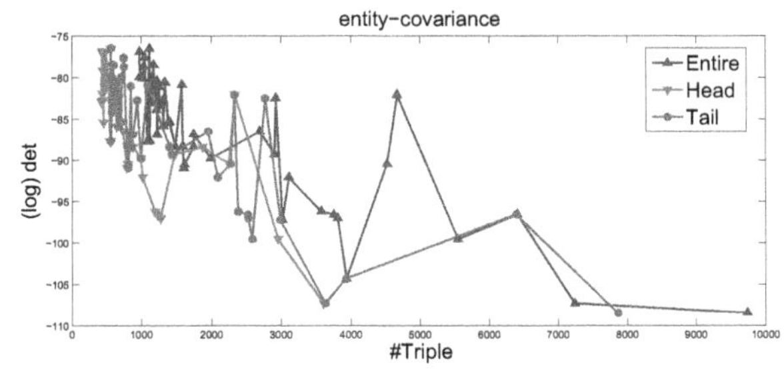

Figure 3: The relationships between the density (linked triplet number) of entity and the determinant of its corresponding covariance.

Relaion	#Triplet	#Head	#Tail	Type	(log) det	trace
nationality	4198	3755	100	m-1	-4.77	67.90
place_lived	3740	2441	784	m-n	-23.02	53.24
profession	11636	4145	152	m-n	-57.45	23.10
gender	3721	3721	2	m-1	-59.53	21.35
place_of_birth	2468	2468	685	m-1	-63.42	19.41
ethnicity	2030	1610	78	m-1	-69.95	15.00
major	260	217	60	m-1	-69.59	14.62
sibling	131	111	113	1-1	-72.98	14.29
religion	1086	963	45	m-1	-75.07	12.98
spouse	427	395	385	1-1	-77.77	12.24
children	77	69	71	1-1	-76.94	12.14
parents	83	74	76	1-1	-77.20	12.03

Table 3: The relationships between some relations and the determinants and traces of their corresponding covariances, sorted by the descending order of trace.

Next, we want to know the ability of Gaussian embedding to learn valid entity/relation representations. Tables 4 and 5 give the top 5 similarity entities/relations with regard to some sampling examples. The tables illustrate that the proposed method can learn a valid representation for modeling KGs.

4.3 Link Prediction

Following the usage in [5][4], link prediction aims to predict the missing h or t for a relation fact triplet(h, r, t). Instead of obtaining one best answer, this task puts more emphasis on ranking a set of candidate entities from the KG. Similar to the setting in [5][4][30][16], we conduct initial experiments using the datasets WN18 and FB15k.

Evaluation protocol. We follow the same protocol as in TransE [4] and its variants [30][16]: In the testing phrase, for each test triplet (h, r, t), we replace the tail entity by all entities e in the

[9]We follow the definition in [4] and measure used in [30].

GNU/Linux	ESPN
Unix	Philips
Solaris Operating System	CNN
Android	AOL
Windows Vista	Parlophone
Project management	64th Primetime Emmy Awards
University of Sydney	**Java (island)**
University of Leeds	Central Java
Seoul National University	East Java
Commonwealth of Nations	West Java
Princeton University	Bandung
Carleton University	Javanese people

Table 4: The top-5 similarity entities with regards to some examples.

people/person/nationality	location/location/contains
location/*division/country	*/country/*divisions
location/hud_county_place/place	location/location/containedby
*/educational/*institution	location/*division/country
base/*/bibs_location/country	biblioness/*location/state
music/artist/origin	*area/capital
film/film/produced_by	***/organization/founders**
film/film/directed_by	*/organizations_founded
film/*/executive_produced_by	people/person/place_of_birth
film/film/written_by	*/location/people_born_here
film/*/performance/actor	*/employer*/person
film/film/story_by	*/award_winner/*/ceremony

Table 5: The top-5 similarity relations with regards to some examples, using a wildcard $*$ to reduce space occupation without ambiguous expression.

KG and rank these entities in descending order of similarity scores, measured by the energy function $\mathcal{E}(h, r, e)$. A similar process is performed for the head entity measure by $\mathcal{E}(e, r, t)$. Based on these entity ranking lists, we use two evaluation metrics by aggregation over all the testing triplets: 1) the average rank of correct entities (denoted as *Mean Rank*) and 2) the proportion of correct entities in the top 10 ranked entities (denoted as *Hits@10*). A good method should obtain lower *Mean Rank* or higher *Hits@10*. Considering the fact that a corrupted triplet for (h, r, t) also exists in a KG, such a prediction should also be deemed correct. However, the above evaluations do not consider the issue and may underestimate the metrics. To eliminate this factor, we remove those corrupted triplets that already appeared in training, valid or testing sets before obtaining the rank entity list of each testing triplet. We term the former evaluation setting as "Raw" and the latter setting as "Filter".

Implementation. Because the testing datasets are the same, we directly compare our models with several baselines reported in [4][30][16]. In learning KG2E, we select the learning rate α for SGD among {0.001, 0.01, 0.05}, the margin γ among {1, 2, 4}, the dimensions of entity and relation sharing embedding k among {20, 50, 100}, the batch size B among {20, 120, 1440, 2480}, and the pair of restriction values c_{min} and c_{max} for covariance among {(0.01, 1), (0.03, 3), (0.05, 5)}. The optimal configuration is determined by the *Hits@10* in the validation set. As the strategy of constructing negative labels can greatly influence the evaluations, we use different parameters for "unif" and "bern". We also use different parameters for KG2E_KL and KG2E_EL. The default configuration for all experiments is as follows: $\alpha = 0.001$, $\gamma = 1$, $k = 50$, $B = 120$, and (c_{min}, c_{max})= (0.05, 5). Below, we list only the non-default parameters. For KG2E_KL, under the "unif" setting, the optimal configuration is as follows: $\alpha = 0.01$, and $\gamma = 4$ on WN18 and $B = 1440$ on FB15k. Under the "bern" setting, the optimal configuration is as follows: $\alpha = 0.01$, $\gamma = 4$, $B = 20$, and (c_{min},c_{max})= (0.03,3) on WN18 and $B = 2480$ on FB15k. For KG2E_EL,under the "unif" setting, the optimal configuration is as follows: $\alpha = 0.01$, $\gamma = 4$, and $B = 20$ on WN18 and $\gamma = 2$ on FB15k. Under the "bern" setting, the optimal configuration is as follows: $\alpha = 0.01$, $\gamma = 4$, $B = 20$, and (c_{min},c_{max})= (0.03,3) on WN18 and $B = 2480$ on FB15k. For both datasets, we traverse all the training triplets for 500 rounds.

Results. The results are reported in Table 6. On WN18, TransE, TransH, TransR, KG2E and even the naive baseline unstructured models outperform other approaches in terms of the *Mean Rank* metric, but the majority of models are poor in terms of the *Hits@10* metric. KG2E with the KL energy function outperforms other baseline models, including TransE, TransH and TransR, in terms of the *Hits@10* metric but achieves a worse *Mean Rank*. One reason may be that WN18 simply contains a small number of relations, and thus, simple methods can judge the correct triplet but cannot rank it in the top position. Another reason is that the *Mean Rank* is easily reduced by an obstinate triplet with a low rank. On FB15k, KG2E_KL consistently outperforms the other baseline models in both *Mean Rank* and *Hits@10*. As the *density* diversity in FB15k is greater than that in WN18, we hypothesize that the improvements are because the *uncertainty* diversities in FB15k are greater than those in WN18, and thus, the *density-based* embedding methods can handle it better. From the observations, we can draw the following conclusions: 1) Gaussian embedding can learn valid representations of KGs for link prediction. 2) KG2E is superior to other baseline methods. 3) KG2E_KL performs better than KG2E_EL, which indicates that the asymmetric energy function is more suitable for learning the representation of KGs with Gaussian embedding. 4) The "bern" sampling strategy works well for most approaches, especially on FB15k, which has many more relation types.

Table 7 shows the evaluation results with separated types of relation properties. Following [4], we divide relations into four types: one-to-one, one-to-many, many-to-one and many-to-many, for which the proportions in FB15k (1345 relations in total) are 24%, 23%, 29% and 24%, respectively, based on the measure used in [30]. KG2E_KL and KG2E_EL significantly outperform TransE, TransH, TransR and other baseline methods in one-to-one, one-to-many, and many-to-one relations. For the difficult tasks of predicting tails in one-to-many relations and predicting heads in many-to-one relations, KG2E_KL obtains 29.3% and 29.9% improvements, respectively. However, the proposed method presents only a slight advantage for many-to-many relations, possibly because there are various fine-grained types within a many-to-many relation that cannot be effectively expressed by one Gaussian embedding. We believe CTransR, proposed by [16], is an effective way to handle this issue by adopting a clustering strategy to divide entity pairs into different sub-types. To better review the modeling improvement of *uncertainty* of KG2E over TransE and its variants, Table 8 shows the *Hits@10* results on some typical one-to-many, many-to-one, many-to-many and reflexive relations. We directly copy the experimental results of TransH from [30] for a fair comparison. We can observe that the asymmetric similarity measure can effectively handle reflexive relations.

4.4 Triplet Classification

This task seeks to judge whether a given triplet (h, r, t) is correct or not. That is, it is a binary classification task for fact triplets, which was first explored in [25] and then widely used to evaluate KGs embedding [30] [16]. In this task, we use three datasets: WN11, FB13 and FB15k.

Evaluation protocol. We follow the same protocol as in NTN [25]. The evaluation of binary classification requires negative triplets.

Data sets	WN18				FB15K			
Metric	Mean Rank		Hits@10		Mean Rank		Hits@10	
	Raw	Filter	Raw	Filter	Raw	Filter	Raw	Filter
Unstructured (Bordes et al. 2012)	315	304	35.3	38.2	1,074	979	4.5	6.3
RESCAL (Nickle, Tresp, and Kriegel 2011)	1,180	1,163	37.2	52.8	828	683	28.4	44.1
SE (Bordes et al. 2011)	1,011	985	68.5	80.5	273	162	28.8	39.8
SME (linear) (Bordes et al.2012)	545	533	65.1	74.1	274	154	30.7	40.8
SME (bilinear) (Bordes et al. 2012)	526	509	54.7	61.3	284	158	31.3	41.3
LFM (Jenatton et al. 2012)	469	456	71.4	81.6	283	164	26.0	33.1
TransE (Bordes et al. 2013)	263	251	75.4	89.2	243	125	34.9	47.1
TransH (unif) (Wang et al. 2014)	318	303	75.4	86.7	211	84	42.5	58.5
TransH (bern) (Wang et al. 2014)	401	388	73.0	82.3	212	87	45.7	64.4
TransR (unif) (Lin et al. 2015)	**232**	**219**	78.3	91.7	226	78	43.8	65.5
TransR (bern) (Lin et al. 2015)	238	225	79.8	92.0	198	77	48.2	68.7
CTransR (unif) (Lin et al. 2015)	243	230	78.9	92.3	233	82	44.0	66.3
CTransR (bern) (Lin et al. 2015)	**231**	**218**	79.4	92.3	199	75	**48.4**	70.2
KG2E_EL (unif)	381	369	74.8	87.8	217	94	38.5	58.6
KG2E_EL (bern)	385	373	74.1	85.0	219	112	39.4	56.7
KG2E_KL (unif)	362	348	**80.5**	**93.2**	**183**	**69**	47.5	**71.5**
KG2E_KL (bern)	342	331	**80.2**	**92.8**	**174**	**59**	**48.9**	**74.0**

Table 6: Experimental results on link prediction.

Tasks	Prediction Head (Hits@10)				Prediction Tail (Hits@10)			
Relation Category	1-to-1	1-to-N	N-to-1	N-to-N	1-to-1	1-to-N	N-to-1	N-to-N
Unstructured (Bordes et al. 2012)	34.5	2.5	6.1	6.6	34.3	4.2	1.9	6.6
SE (Bordes et al. 2011)	35.6	62.6	17.2	37.5	34.9	14.6	68.3	41.3
SME (linear) (Bordes et al.2012)	35.1	53.7	19.0	40.3	32.7	14.9	61.6	43.3
SME (bilinear) (Bordes et al. 2012)	30.9	69.6	19.9	38.6	28.2	13.1	76.0	41.8
TransE (Bordes et al. 2013)	43.7	65.7	18.2	47.2	43.7	19.7	66.7	50.0
TransH (unif) (Wang et al. 2014)	66.7	81.7	30.2	57.4	63.7	30.1	83.2	60.8
TransH (bern) (Wang et al. 2014)	66.8	87.6	28.7	64.5	65.5	39.8	83.3	67.2
TransR (unif) (Lin et al. 2015)	76.9	77.9	38.1	66.9	76.2	38.4	76.2	69.1
TransR (bern) (Lin et al. 2015)	78.8	89.2	34.1	69.2	79.2	37.4	90.4	72.1
CTransR (unif) (Lin et al. 2015)	78.6	77.8	36.4	68.0	77.4	37.8	78.0	70.3
CTransR (bern) (Lin et al. 2015)	81.5	89.0	34.7	**71.2**	80.8	38.6	90.1	**73.8**
KG2E_EL (unif)	49.2	87.9	55.2	53.1	47.8	54.9	88.4	56.2
KG2E_EL (bern)	51.8	89.4	47.9	51.6	52.0	43.6	89.3	55.0
KG2E_KL (unif)	**92.2**	**93.7**	**67.4**	69.1	**91.2**	**69.7**	**93.6**	71.2
KG2E_KL (bern)	**92.3**	**94.6**	**66.0**	**69.6**	**92.6**	**67.9**	**94.4**	**73.4**

Table 7: Experimental results on FB15k by mapping properties of relations. (%)

Relation	Hits@10 (TransH / KG2E_KL)	
	Predict Head	Predict Tail
football_position/players*	100 / 100	22.2 / **100**
production_company/films*	85.6 / **97.3**	16.0 / **29.4**
director/film*	89.6 / **93.4**	80.2 / **85.8**
disease/treatments†	66.6 / 66.6	100 / 100
person/place_of_birth†	**37.5** / 34.1	**87.6** / 84.6
film/production_companies†	21.0 / **44.2**	87.8 / **97.8**
field_of_study/students_majoring‡	66.0 / **86.8**	62.3 / **81.1**
award_winner/awards_won‡	87.5 / **88.4**	86.6 / **89.2**
sports_position/players‡	100 / 100	86.2 / **100**
person/sibling§	63.2 / **89.5**	36.8 / **94.7**
person/spouse§	35.2 / **77.8**	42.6 / **85.2**

Table 8: Hits@10 (Filter) of KG2E_KL and TransH on some examples of one-to-many*, many-to-one†, many-to-many‡, and reflexive relations§.

WN11 and FB13 released by NTN [25] already contain negative triplets, which are built by corrupting the corresponding positive (observed) triplets. As FB15k has not released negative triplets in previous works, we construct negative triplets following the same procedure used in [25] for FB13. The setting for triplet classification is very simple: for each triplet (h, r, t), if the dissimilarity score obtained by the energy function $\mathcal{E}(h, r, t)$ is below a relation-specific threshold δ_r, then the triplet will be classified as positive. Otherwise, it will be classified as negative. The relation-specific threshold δ_r is optimized by maximizing the classification accuracy on the validation set.

Implementation. Considering that the same datasets (negative triplets) are used in WN11 and FB13, we directly compare our models with the baseline methods reported in [16]. For evaluation on FB15k, we use the code released by Lin[10] [16] (running TransE, TransH and TransR) and Socher[11] [25] (running NTN). For TransE, TransH and TransR, we select the learning rate α for SGD among {0.001, 0.01, 0.05}, the margin γ among {0.5, 1, 2}, the dimensions of entity and relation sharing embedding k among {20, 50, 100}, and the batch size B among {20, 120, 1440, 2480}. Other parameters follow the default configuration in the shared codes. For the NTN, we did not change the settings: dimension $k = 100$, and the number of slices equals 3. The optimal configurations are as follows: $\alpha = 0.001$, $\gamma = 1$, and $B = 4800$ for TransE (bern); $\alpha = 0.001$, $\gamma = 2$, and $B = 120$ for TransE (unif); $\alpha = 0.001$, $\gamma = 0.5$, and $B = 4800$ for TransH (bern) $\alpha = 0.01$, $\gamma = 0.5$, and $B = 4800$ for TransH (unif); $\alpha = 0.001$, $\gamma = 1$, and $B = 4800$ for TransR (bern); and $\alpha = 0.001$, $\gamma = 1$, and $B = 120$ for TransR (unif). The dimension $k = 100$ for all the above configurations.

In learning KG2E, we select the learning rate α for SGD among {0.001, 0.01, 0.05}, the margin γ among {1, 1.5, 2}, the dimen-

[10]https://github.com/mrlyk423/relation_extraction
[11]www.socher.org

sions of entity and relation sharing embedding k among {20, 50, 100}, the bach size B among {20, 120, 1440, 2480}, and the pair of restriction values c_{min} and c_{max} for covariance among {(0.01, 1), (0.03, 3), (0.05, 5)}. The optimal configuration is determined by the classification accuracy in the validation set. For all three datasets, we traverse all the training triplets for 1000 rounds. We also use different parameters for KG2E_KL and KG2E_EL. The default configuration for all experiments are as follows: $\alpha = 0.001$, $\gamma = 1$, $k = 50$, $B = 120$, and (c_{min}, c_{max})= (0.05, 5). Below, we list only the non-default parameters. For KG2E_KL, under the "unif" setting, the optimal configuration is as follows: $k = 20$, $\gamma = 2$, and $B = 120$ on WN11; $k = 100$, and $B = 1440$ on FB13. Under the "bern" setting, the optimal configuration is as follows: $k = 20$, and $\gamma = 2$ on WN11 and $k = 100$, and $B = 1440$ on FB13. For KG2E_EL, under the "unif" setting, the optimal configuration is as follows: $k = 20$, $\gamma = 2$, and $B = 120$ on WN11; $k = 100$, and $B = 120$ on FB13 and $\gamma = 1.5$, on FB15k; Under the "bern" setting, the optimal configuration is as follows: $k = 20$, $\gamma = 2$, and $B = 120$ on WN11; $k = 100$ on FB13 and $B = 2480$ on FB15k.

Results. The accuracy of triplet classification on the three datasets is shown in Table 9. On WN11, KG2E_KL and TransR outperform all the other models. The NTN, the powerful model with the most parameters, outperforms the other approaches on FB13, but it performs poorly on FB15k, which contains many more relations. In contrast, on a more practical KG with large-scale relations (such as Freebase), the proposed method KG2E_KL performs much better than the other baseline models, and even the KG2E_EL is also a competitive model. We can draw the following conclusions from the observations: 1) KG2E_KL achieves superior performance compared to other baseline methods for a multi-relational KG, which indicates that Gaussian embedding can effectively model the enormous diversity of uncertainty in a KG. 2) KG2E_KL performs better than KG2E_EL, which is consistent with the results of link prediction. 3) The "bern" sampling strategy outperforms the majority of the approaches (including TransE, TransH, TransR and our proposed models KG2E_EL and KG2E_KG) on all three datasets.

We also compare with CTransR, another model proposed by Lin [16] to handle many-to-many relations with entity-pairs clustering. However, in the NTN [25], another set of results combined with word embedding [17] is reported. There are different ways to improve KG embedding between the aforementioned method and our method, and for fairness, we have not compared their results.

As shown in [30] and [16], the training times of TransE, TransH and TransR are approximately 5 minutes, 30 minutes and 3 hours, respectively. The computational complexities of our proposed methods are lower than that of TransR but higher than those of both TransE and TransH: KG2E_KL and KG2E_EL take approximately 80 and 75 minutes for training, respectively.

Data sets	WN11	FB13	FB15k
SE (Bordes et al. 2011)	53.0	75.2	-
SME (bilinear) (Bordes et al.2012)	70.0	63.7	-
SLM (Socher et al. 2013)	69.9	**85.3**	-
LFM (Jenatton et al. 2012)	73.8	84.3	-
NTN (Socher et al. 2013)	70.4	**87.1**	68.2
TransE (unif) (Bordes et al. 2013)	75.9	70.9	79.2
TransE (bern) (Bordes et al. 2013)	75.9	81.5	81.4
TransH (unif) (Wang et al. 2014)	77.7	76.5	85.4
TransH (bern) (Wang et al. 2014)	78.8	83.3	85.8
TransR (unif) (Lin et al. 2015)	85.5	74.7	83.7
TransR (bern) (Lin et al. 2015)	**85.9**	82.5	86.5
CTransR (bern) (Lin et al. 2015)	**85.7**	-	87.4
KG2E_EL (unif)	73.8	76.3	83.9
KG2E_EL (bern)	75.2	85.2	84.9
KG2E_KL (unif)	83.6	76.4	**88.6**
KG2E_KL (bern)	85.4	**85.3**	**89.3**

Table 9: Experimental results of Triplet Classification (%).

5. CONCLUSIONS

In this paper we propose KG2E, a new method for learning representations of entities and relations in KGs with Gaussian embedding. Each entity and relation is represented by a Gaussian distribution with a mean vector and a covariance matrix (currently with diagonal covariance for computational efficiency), which aims to model the uncertainty of entities and relations in a KG. The (un)certainties vary considerably for different entities and relations: for example, popular entities with fewer uncertainty, which contain more relations and facts than unpopular ones, high-frequency relations with more uncertainty, which link more entity pairs than low frequency ones, and, different parts of relations can contain a very different numbers of entities that sharpen the uncertainties of relations. We use two energy functions (symmetric and asymmetric) to compute the score of a triplet fact. Extensive experiments on link prediction and triplet classification with multiple benchmark datasets (including WordNet and Freebase) demonstrate that the proposed method significantly outperforms state-of-the-art methods.

In the future, we plan to address the following limitations that still exist in the methods:

- Existing methods do not explicitly consider the relationships between relations. For example, triplets with the relations *children* and *parents* (normally, *(X, children, Y)* and *(Y, parents, X)* are mutual implications) affect and restrict with each other. We will explore mixing logical rules into the Gaussian embedding. The same concepts have been successfully used in relation extraction [22].

- Various KGs can supply and verify with each other. For example, NELL contains more *machine learning* related relations (e.g., *mlauthor*) than Freebase but fewer person related relations (e.g., *spouse*), and NELL may extract a false triplet fact (e.g., *(Erma Bombeck, was born in, Dayton)*) with high confidence that can be rectified by Freebase. We will explore the fusion of multiple KGs, learning the representations in a joint model with or without entity linking.

- Compared with other types of relations, KG2E does not significantly outperform previous methods in many-to-many relations, possibly because current entity embedding does not consider the types of entity. For example, even the relation *contains* incorporates many fine-grained relations, such as, *country_contain_university*, *country_contain_city* and *continent_contain_country*. We can ascertain the semantics of relations for the head entity of type *country* and the tail entity of type *city*.

Acknowledgments

The authors are grateful to anonymous reviewers for their constructive comments. This work was supported by the National High Technology Development 863 Program of China (No. 2015AA015405) and the National Natural Science Foundation of China (No. 61272332 and No. 61202329).

6. REFERENCES

[1] K. Bollacker, C. Evans, P. Paritosh, T. Sturge, and J. Taylor. Freebase: a collaboratively created graph database for structuring human knowledge. In *Proceedings of the 2008 ACM SIGMOD international conference on Management of data*, pages 1247–1250. ACM, 2008.

[2] A. Bordes, S. Chopra, and J. Weston. Question answering with subgraph embeddings. In *Proceedings of the Conference on Empirical Methods in Natural Language Processing*, pages 615–620, 2014.

[3] A. Bordes, X. Glorot, J. Weston, and Y. Bengio. A semantic matching energy function for learning with multi-relational data. volume 94, pages 233–259. Springer, 2012.

[4] A. Bordes, N. Usunier, A. Garcia-Duran, J. Weston, and O. Yakhnenko. Translating embeddings for modeling multi-relational data. In *Advances in Neural Information Processing Systems*, pages 2787–2795, 2013.

[5] A. Bordes, J. Weston, R. Collobert, Y. Bengio, et al. Learning structured embeddings of knowledge bases. In *AAAI*, 2011.

[6] R. Brachman and H. Levesque. *Knowledge representation and reasoning*. Elsevier, 2004.

[7] A. Carlson, J. Betteridge, B. Kisiel, B. Settles, E. R. H. Jr., and T. M. Mitchell. Toward an architecture for never-ending language learning. In *Proceedings of the Twenty-Fourth Conference on Artificial Intelligence (AAAI 2010)*, 2010.

[8] X. Dong, P. Frossard, P. Vandergheynst, and N. Nefedov. Clustering with multi-layer graphs: A spectral perspective. *Signal Processing, IEEE Transactions on*, 60(11):5820–5831, 2012.

[9] J. Duchi, E. Hazan, and Y. Singer. Adaptive subgradient methods for online learning and stochastic optimization. *The Journal of Machine Learning Research*, 12:2121–2159, 2011.

[10] F. Hayes-Roth, D. Waterman, and D. Lenat. Building expert systems. 1984.

[11] S. He, K. Liu, Y. Zhang, L. Xu, and J. Zhao. Question answering over linked data using first-order logic. In *Proceedings of the Conference on Empirical Methods in Natural Language Processing*, pages 1092–1103, 2014.

[12] T. Jebara, R. Kondor, and A. Howard. Probability product kernels. *The Journal of Machine Learning Research*, 5:819–844, 2004.

[13] R. Jenatton, N. L. Roux, A. Bordes, and G. R. Obozinski. A latent factor model for highly multi-relational data. In *Advances in Neural Information Processing Systems*, pages 3167–3175, 2012.

[14] Y. Koren, R. Bell, and C. Volinsky. Matrix factorization techniques for recommender systems. *Computer*, (8):30–37, 2009.

[15] N. Lao, T. Mitchell, and W. W. Cohen. Random walk inference and learning in a large scale knowledge base. In *Proceedings of the Conference on Empirical Methods in Natural Language Processing*, pages 529–539. Association for Computational Linguistics, 2011.

[16] Y. Lin, Z. Liu, M. Sun, Y. Liu, and X. Zhu. Learning entity and relation embeddings for knowledge graph completion. In *Proceedings of the Twenty-Eighth AAAI Conference on Artificial Intelligence*, 2015.

[17] T. Mikolov, I. Sutskever, K. Chen, G. S. Corrado, and J. Dean. Distributed representations of words and phrases and their compositionality. In *Advances in Neural Information Processing Systems*, pages 3111–3119, 2013.

[18] G. A. Miller. Wordnet: a lexical database for english. *Communications of the ACM*, 38(11):39–41, 1995.

[19] M. Nickel, V. Tresp, and H.-P. Kriegel. A three-way model for collective learning on multi-relational data. In *Proceedings of the 28th international conference on machine learning (ICML-11)*, pages 809–816, 2011.

[20] A. Paccanaro and G. E. Hinton. Learning distributed representations of concepts using linear relational embedding. volume 13, pages 232–244. IEEE, 2001.

[21] K. B. Petersen, M. S. Pedersen, et al. *The matrix cookbook*, volume 450. 2008.

[22] T. Rocktäschel, S. Singh, and S. Riedel. Injecting logical background knowledge into embeddings for relation extraction. In *Proceedings of the 2015 Human Language Technology Conference of the North American Chapter of the Association of Computational Linguistics*, 2015.

[23] H. Schuetze and C. Scheible. Two svds produce more focal deep learning representations. *arXiv preprint arXiv:1301.3627*, 2013.

[24] W. Shen, J. Wang, P. Luo, and M. Wang. Linking named entities in tweets with knowledge base via user interest modeling. In *Proceedings of the 19th ACM SIGKDD international conference on Knowledge discovery and data mining*, pages 68–76. ACM, 2013.

[25] R. Socher, D. Chen, C. D. Manning, and A. Ng. Reasoning with neural tensor networks for knowledge base completion. In *Advances in Neural Information Processing Systems*, pages 926–934, 2013.

[26] I. Sutskever, J. B. Tenenbaum, and R. R. Salakhutdinov. Modelling relational data using bayesian clustered tensor factorization. In *Advances in neural information processing systems*, pages 1821–1828, 2009.

[27] S. Szumlanski and F. Gomez. Automatically acquiring a semantic network of related concepts. In *Proceedings of the 19th ACM international conference on Information and knowledge management*, pages 19–28. ACM, 2010.

[28] L. Vilnis and A. McCallum. Word representations via gaussian embedding. In *Proceedings of the International Conference on Learning Representations (ICLR 2015)*, 2015.

[29] W. Y. Wang, K. Mazaitis, N. Lao, and W. W. Cohen. Efficient inference and learning in a large knowledge base. *Machine Learning*, pages 1–26, 2015.

[30] Z. Wang, J. Zhang, J. Feng, and Z. Chen. Knowledge graph embedding by translating on hyperplanes. In *Proceedings of the Twenty-Eighth AAAI Conference on Artificial Intelligence*, pages 1112–1119, 2014.

[31] M. Yahya, K. Berberich, S. Elbassuoni, and G. Weikum. Robust question answering over the web of linked data. In *Proceedings of the 22nd ACM international conference on Conference on information & knowledge management*, pages 1107–1116. ACM, 2013.

[32] L. Yao, S. Riedel, and A. McCallum. Probabilistic databases of universal schema. In *Proceedings of the Joint Workshop on Automatic Knowledge Base Construction and Web-scale Knowledge Extraction*, pages 116–121. Association for Computational Linguistics, 2012.

Associative Classification with Statistically Significant Positive and Negative Rules

Jundong Li
Department of Computing Science
University of Alberta
Edmonton, Canada
jundong1@ualberta.ca

Osmar R. Zaïane
Department of Computing Science
University of Alberta
Edmonton, Canada
zaiane@ualberta.ca

ABSTRACT

Rule-based classifier has shown its popularity in building many decision support systems such as medical diagnosis and financial fraud detection. One major advantage is that the models are human understandable and can be edited. Associative classifiers, as an extension of rule-based classifiers, use association rules to associate attributes with class labels. A delicate issue of associative classifiers is the need for subtle thresholds: minimum support and minimum confidence. Without prior knowledge, it could be difficult to choose the proper thresholds, and the discovered rules within the support-confidence framework are not statistically significant, i.e., inclusion of noisy rules and exclusion of valuable rules. Besides, most associative classifiers proposed so far, are built with only positive association rules. Negative rules, however, are also able to provide valuable information to discriminate between classes. To solve the above mentioned problems, we propose a novel associative classifier which is built upon both positive and negative classification association rules that show statistically significant dependencies. Experimental results on real-world datasets show that our method achieves competitive or even better performance than well-known rule-based and associative classifiers in terms of both classification accuracy and computational efficiency.

Categories and Subject Descriptors

D.2.8 [**DATABASE MANAGEMENT**]: Database Applications—*Data Mining*

General Terms

Algorithms

Keywords

Associative Classification; Negative Rules; Statistical Significance

CIKM'15, October 19–23, 2015, Melbourne, Australia.
© 2015 ACM. ISBN 978-1-4503-3794-6/15/10 ...$15.00.
DOI: http://dx.doi.org/10.1145/2806416.2806524.

1. INTRODUCTION

The task of mining association rules over market basket analysis was introduced in [3] which aims to find associations between items or itemsets in a transaction database. The data is typically retail sales in the form of customer transactions, but can be any data if it is transformed to transactions like image data or text data. The problem is formally defined as follows: assume a transaction dataset $\mathcal{D}$ consists of a set of items $\mathcal{I} = \{i_1, i_2, ..., i_m\}$, each transaction T is a set of items such that $T \subseteq \mathcal{I}$ and is associated with a unique identifier. A transaction T is said to contain X, i.e., a set of items in $\mathcal{I}$, if $X \subseteq T$. Then an association rule is an implication of the form "$X \rightarrow Y$", where $X \subseteq \mathcal{I}$, $Y \subseteq \mathcal{I}$, and $X \cap Y = \emptyset$. The rule $X \rightarrow Y$ has a *support* s in the transaction set $\mathcal{D}$ if the percentage of transactions in $\mathcal{D}$ that contain X and Y is s. It is also said that the rule $X \rightarrow Y$ holds in the transaction dataset $\mathcal{D}$ with *confidence* c if the percentage of transactions in $\mathcal{D}$ that contain X also contain Y is c. The problem of discovering all association rules from a set of transactions $\mathcal{D}$ consists of generating association rules that have a *support* and *confidence* greater than given thresholds. These discovered rules are called *strong rules*.

Classification is another common task in data mining and machine learning [15, 19, 26, 27]. A classifier is a system that is able to assign an unlabeled object to one or more predefined classes. Usually, it is created by building a learning model on the training data whose class labels are known in advance, then its ability to discriminate between classes is evaluated on the test data. Associative classification [25] is a classification method that integrates association rule mining and classification together. To build an associative classifier, classification association rules (CARs) with consequent as class labels are first mined by association rule mining techniques. Afterwards, some noisy CARs are pruned to improve the prediction performance, the remaining CARs form the actual associative classifier and these CARs are able to predict classes for unlabeled test data.

Existing associative classification methods mine the training dataset mostly in an Apriori-like way [4] or through a FP-growth approach [22], both of which are based on the support and confidence paradigm. However, appropriate support and confidence thresholds are not easy to determine. Besides, according to Webb [36, 37], traditional association rule mining methods have the risk of false discoveries such that the antecedent part and consequent part of some rules are not strongly correlated. In the worst cases, we may find all spurious rules while miss all rules with strong correlation. On the other hand, most associative classifiers proposed so far use only positive CARs (rules of the form $X \to C$) in the classification process. In addition to positive CARs, negative CARs are also able to provide valuable information to discriminate between classes. A negative CAR is in one of the following form: $X \to \neg C$ or $\neg X \to C$ (where X and $\neg X$ indicate the presence and absence of itemset X, respectively). Let us consider the following example:

Example 1. For a binary classification problem, assume we discover some positive and negative CARs, such as: $X \to c_1$, $Y \to c_2$, $XY \to \neg c_1$. Now we have a new unlabeled instance XY, how to classify it? When only positive CARs $X \to c_1$ and $Y \to c_2$ are considered, both c_1 and c_2 are possible as there is a matching rule for either c_1 or c_2. But the classification task is easier since we have another negative CAR $XY \to \neg c_1$ which reinforces the decision in favor of class c_2.

In this paper, we propose a novel associative classifier to tackle the above mentioned issues. Following traditional associative classification methods, the proposed associative classifier consists of three steps: rule generation, rule pruning and rule classification.

The main contributions of this paper are as follows:

1. A novel associative classifier is proposed, it achieves a competitive or even better performance compared with some well-known rule-based classifiers in terms of both classification accuracy and computational efficiency.

2. By extending the Kingfisher algorithm in [20], we are able to find the complete set of both positive and negative CARs that show statistically significant dependencies efficiently.

3. We develop a novel rule pruning strategy to prune noisy positive and negative CARs simultaneously without jeopardizing the classification accuracy.

4. We present and compare different rule classification methods to investigate how to make a prediction with multiple matching positive and negative CARs.

The reminder of the paper is organized as follows. The overview of related work on associative classifier and negative rule mining is given in Section 2. Section 3 describes the proposed associative classifier in three steps. Section 4 contains the experimental results and the statistical analysis. Section 5 concludes the paper and discusses some possible future work.

2. RELATED WORK

In this section, we review some related work on associative classification and negative rule mining.

2.1 Associative Classification

The first reference to use association rules as CARs is credited to [12], while the first associative classifier, CBA, was introduced by Liu et al. [25]. The main steps in building an associative classifier are as follows:

- Modeling the data into the transaction dataset $\mathcal{D}$ in which the numerical attributes are transformed to discrete attributes.

- Generating the set of CARs from the transaction dataset $\mathcal{D}$. The CARs are in the form of $X \to C$ where X is a conjunction of attributes and C is a class label. The CARs are usually generated by pushing the constraint in the association rule mining process to generate association rules that always have as consequent a class label given minimum support and minimum confidence thresholds.

- Pruning the discovered CARs by some rule pruning strategies. The previous rule generation phase usually generates an overwhelming number of CARs including many noisy CARs and it is very important to prune these rules to make the classifier more effective and efficient. The phase is employed to choose a best subset of CARs and weed out those rules that may introduce errors or are overfitting in the classification stage.

- Classifying a new unlabeled object to a predefined class. At this level a system that can make a prediction for a new object is built. The challenge here is how to rank and make use of the set of rules from the previous phase to give a good prediction.

CBA [25] mines the complete set of CARs through an apriori-like approach, in addition, it ignores rules by "pessimistic error rate" as C4.5 [26]. In the rule pruning phase, CBA adopts a strategy called "database coverage". Database coverage consists of going over all the rules ranked by their confidence values and evaluating them against the training instances. Whenever a rule applies correctly on some instances, the rule is marked and the instances are eliminated until all training instances are covered. Finally, unmarked rules are simply pruned. New instances are classified by a matching rule with the highest ranking.

Motivated by the idea of CBA, many improvements have been proposed to build more accurate associative classifiers. CMAR [24] maintains a CR-tree to compactly store and retrieve rules, the CARs are discovered by a FP-growth approach. In addition to the database coverage method, CMAR also prunes lower ranked and more specific rules. The rule R_1: $P \to C$ with confidence $conf_1$ is a lower ranked and more specific rule w.r.t rule R_2: $P' \to C$ with confidence $conf_2$ if $P' \subsetneq P$ and $conf_1 \leq conf_2$. For a new unlabeled instance, CMAR makes a prediction based on multiple matching rules with a weighted chi-square measure.

In the classification phase, ARC [6] takes all rules that apply within a confidence range, but instead, calculates the average confidence for each set of rules grouped by class labels in the consequent, and selects the class label of the group with the highest confidence average.

There are some other variants of associative classifiers: Harmony [35] is an example which directly mines CARs. It adopts an instance-centric approach to find the highest confidence rule for each training instance and builds the classification model from the union of these rules. It shows to be more effective and scalable than other associative classifiers.

2SARC [9] is a two-stage classification model that is able to automatically learn to select rules for classification. First, an associative classifier is learned by standard techniques. Second, multiple predefined features are computed on the associative classifier, then they act as input to a neural network to achieve a more accurate classification model.

CCCS [10] uses a new measure, "Complement Class Support" (CCS) to mine positively correlated CARs for the imbalanced classification problem. It forces the CCS measure to be monotonic, thus the complete set of CARs are discovered by a row enumeration algorithm. An associative classifier is then built upon these positively correlated CARs.

SPAR-CCC [33] is another associative classifier designed for imbalanced data. It also integrates a new measure, "Class Correlation Ratio" (CCR) into the rule mining phase, the classifier works comparably on balanced datasets and outperforms other associative classifiers on imbalanced datasets.

ARC-PAN [7] is the first associative classifier that uses both positive and negative CARs. It proposes to add Pearson's correlation coefficient on the basis of support and confidence framework to mine positively and negatively correlated CARs. The ability of negative CARs is demonstrated by their usage in the classification phase.

2.2 Negative Rule Mining

A negative association between two positive itemsets X, Y are rules of the following forms: $\neg X \rightarrow Y$ and $X \rightarrow \neg Y$, where $\neg X$ and $\neg Y$ indicate the absence of itemsets X and Y in the transaction dataset $\mathcal{D}$, respectively. Mining association rules from a transaction dataset that contains information about both present and absent itemsets is computationally expensive, traditional association rule mining algorithms cannot be directly applied. This is the reason why new algorithms are needed to efficiently mine association rules with negative itemsets. Here we survey algorithms that efficiently mine some variety of negative association rules from data.

Brin et al. [13] mention for the first time the notion of negative relationships in the literature. They propose to use chi-square test between two itemsets. The statistical test verifies the independence between two itemsets. To determine the nature (positive or negative) of the relationship, a correlation metric is used.

Aggarwal and Yu [1, 2] introduce a new method for finding interesting itemsets in data. Their method is based on mining strongly collective itemsets. The collective strength of an itemset I is defined as $C(I) = \frac{1-v(I)}{1-E[v(I)]} \times \frac{E[v(I)]}{v(I)}$, where $v(I)$ is the violation rate of an itemset I, i.e., the fraction of violations over the entire set of transactions and $E[v(i)]$ is its expected value. An itemset I is in a violation of a transaction if only a subset of its itemsets appears in that transaction. The collective strength ranges from 0 to ∞, where a value of 0 means that the items are perfectly negatively correlated and a value of ∞ means that the items are perfectly positively correlated.

In [29], the authors present a new idea to mine strong negative rules. They combine positive frequent itemsets with domain knowledge in the form of taxonomy to mine negative associations. The idea is to reduce the search space by constraining the search to positive patterns that pass the minimum support threshold. When all the positive itemsets are discovered, candidate negative itemsets are considered based on the used taxonomy.

Wu et al. [38] derive another algorithm for generating both positive and negative association rules. The negative associations discovered are of the following forms: $\neg X \rightarrow Y$, $X \rightarrow \neg Y$ and $\neg X \rightarrow \neg Y$. They add another measure called "mininterest" on top of the support-confidence framework for a better pruning of the frequent itemsets, which is also used to assess the dependency between two itemsets.

The SRM algorithm [30, 31], discovers a subset of negative associations. The authors develop an algorithm to discover negative associations of the type $X \rightarrow \neg Y$. These association rules can be used to discover which items are substitutes for others in market basket analysis.

Antonie and Zaïane [8] propose an algorithm to mine strong positive and negative association rules based on the Pearson's correlation coefficient. In their algorithm, itemset and rule generation are combined and the relevant rules are generated on-the-fly while analyzing the correlations within each candidate itemset.

In [32], the authors extend an existing algorithm for association rule mining, i.e., GRD (generalized rule discovery), to include negative items in the discovered rules. The algorithm discovers top-K positive and negative rules.

Cornelis et al. [16] propose a new Apriori-based algorithm (PNAR) that exploits the upward closure property of negative association rules. With this upward closure property, valid positive and negative association rules can be discovered efficiently. Wang et al. [34] give a more intuitive way to express the validity of both positive and negative association rules, the mining process is very similar to PNAR.

MINR [23] is a method that uses Fisher's exact test to identify itemsets that do not occur together by chance, i.e., with a statistically significant probability. An itemset with a support greater than the positive chance threshold is considered for positive rule generation, while an itemset with a support less than the negative chance threshold is considered for negative rule generation.

Kingfisher [20, 21] is developed to discover both positive and negative dependency rules. The dependency rule can be formulated on the basis of association rule and the statistical dependency of a rule can be calculated by Fisher's exact test. In order to reduce the search space, the author introduces a branch-and-bound search method with three lower bounds for the measure of p_F-value. Another two pruning strategies (pruning by minimality and pruning by principles of Lapis philosophorum) are also included to speed up the search.

A more detailed review of negative rule mining can be referred to [5].

3. PROPOSED ASSOCIATIVE CLASSIFIER

In this section, we introduce details about the proposed associative classifier in three steps: rule generation, rule pruning and rule classification. Before talking about the detailed steps, we introduce some notations and definitions used in this paper.

3.1 Notations and Definitions

Assume $\mathcal{D}$ is a transformed transaction dataset with a set of items $\mathcal{I} = \{i_1, i_2, ..., i_m\}$ and a set of class labels $\mathcal{C} = \{c_1, c_2, ..., c_n\}$. Each transaction T is associated with a set of items X and a class label c_k, where $X \subseteq \mathcal{I}$ and $c_k \in C$. A CAR is in the form of $X \rightarrow c_k$ or $X \rightarrow \neg c_k$, and it is considered dependent if $P(X, c_k) \neq P(X)P(c_k)$ or $P(X, \neg c_k) \neq P(X)P(\neg c_k)$. Since we intend to find statistically significant positive and negative CARs, we take Fisher's exact test [20, 23, 33] as a significance measure. The dependency of the CAR $X \rightarrow c_k$ or $X \rightarrow \neg c_k$ is considered statistically significant at level α, if the probability of observing equal or stronger dependency in the dataset under a null hypothesis model, is not greater than α. X and c_k (or $\neg c_k$) are independent in the null hypothesis. The probability p, i.e., p-value is:

$$p_F(X \to c_k) = \sum_{i=0}^{min\{\sigma(X,\neg c_k)\sigma(\neg X,c_k)\}} \frac{\binom{\sigma(X)}{\sigma(X,c_k)+i}\binom{\sigma(\neg X)}{\sigma(\neg X,\neg c_k)+i}}{\binom{|\mathcal{D}|}{\sigma(c_k)}}$$

$$p_F(X \to \neg c_k) = \sum_{i=0}^{min\{\sigma(X,\neg c_k)\sigma(\neg X,c_k)\}} \frac{\binom{\sigma(X)}{\sigma(X,\neg c_k)+i}\binom{\sigma(\neg X)}{\sigma(\neg X,c_k)+i}}{\binom{|\mathcal{D}|}{\sigma(c_k)}},$$

where the consequent class label c_k can either be present or absent. $\sigma(*)$ denotes the support count of $*$, $*$ can be the conjunction of any itemsets, either being present or absent, for example, it can be X, Xc_k, $\neg Xc_k$, $\neg X\neg c_k$, etc. The significance level α is usually set to be 0.05.

The dependency of the positive CAR $X \to c_k$ or negative CAR $X \to \neg c_k$ is statistically significant, if $p_F(X \to c_k) \leq \alpha$ or $p_F(X \to \neg c_k) \leq \alpha$. In the field of rule mining, an important task is to mine non-redundant rules. Rules are considered redundant when they do not add new information to the remaining rules. Without the non-redundancy property taken into consideration, the number of discovered rules is usually too large for people to read and interpret. In order to reduce the number of rules and to make the classification model more readable, only non-redundant CARs are considered. Following [20], we define non-redundant CARs and minimal CARs as follows:

Definition 1. Non-redundant CARs
The CAR $X \to c_k$ or $X \to \neg c_k$ is considered as non-redundant, if there does not exist any CARs in the form of $Y \to c_k$ or $Y \to \neg c_k$ such that:

$$p_F(Y \to c_k) < p_F(X \to c_k)$$

or

$$p_F(Y \to \neg c_k) < p_F(X \to \neg c_k),$$

where $Y \subsetneq X$.

Definition 2. Minimal CARs
The CAR $X \to c_k$ or $X \to \neg c_k$ is considered as minimal, if and only if $X \to c_k$ or $X \to \neg c_k$ is non-redundant, and, there does not exist any CARs in the form of $Z \to c_k$ or $Z \to \neg c_k$ such that:

$$p_F(Z \to c_k) < p_F(X \to c_k)$$

or

$$p_F(Z \to \neg c_k) < p_F(X \to \neg c_k),$$

where $X \subsetneq Z$.

3.2 Proposed Associative Classifier

3.2.1 Positive and Negative CARs generation

In traditional association rule mining algorithms, the measure of *support* is usually used to prune non-frequent patterns or rules since it has a downward closure property, but it is not the case for the p-value, making it impossible to be used as a monotonic property for some effective pruning. Recently, Kingfisher [20] was proposed to find the complete set of positive and negative rules that show statistically significant dependencies. However, it was designed for the discovery of general rules, not specifically for CARs. Therefore, adaption of the Kingfisher algorithm to enable the discovery of only CARs is necessary as it can reduce the number of discovered rules. To find statistically significant positive and negative CARs, we extend the Kingfisher algorithm by pushing the rule constraint in the rule generation phase.

First, two theorems in [20] are given:

Theorem 1. In a transaction database $\mathcal{D}$, assume $\mathcal{R}$ is the set of all items, for any item $A \in \mathcal{R}$ and $X \subseteq \mathcal{R}\backslash A$, it has $p_F(X \to A) \geq \frac{\sigma(A)!\sigma(\neg A)!}{|\mathcal{D}|!}$ and $p_F(X \to \neg A) \geq \frac{\sigma(A)!\sigma(\neg A)!}{|\mathcal{D}|!}$; if $\sigma(A) \leq \frac{|\mathcal{D}|}{2}$, then for any $B \in \mathcal{R}$, $X \subseteq \mathcal{R}\backslash\{A, B\}$, it has $p_F(XA \to B) \geq \frac{\sigma(A)!\sigma(\neg A)!}{|\mathcal{D}|!}$ and $p_F(XA \to \neg B) \geq \frac{\sigma(A)!\sigma(\neg A)!}{|\mathcal{D}|!}$. Therefore, there exists a threshold $\gamma \leq 0.5$, when $\sigma(A) < \gamma|\mathcal{D}|$, the item A cannot appear in any statistically significant rules.

Theorem 2. In a transaction database $\mathcal{D}$, assume $\mathcal{R}$ is the set of all items, for any item $A \in \mathcal{R}$, $X \subseteq \mathcal{R}\backslash A$ and $Q \subseteq \mathcal{R}\backslash\{X, A\}$, if $\sigma(X) \leq \sigma(A)$ or $\sigma(X) \leq \sigma(\neg A)$ holds, then it has $p_F(XQ \to A) \geq \frac{\sigma(\neg X)!\sigma(A)!}{|\mathcal{D}|!(\sigma(A)-\sigma(X))!}$ or $p_F(XQ \to \neg A) \geq \frac{\sigma(\neg X)!\sigma(\neg A)!}{|\mathcal{D}|!(\sigma(\neg A)-\sigma(X))!}$, respectively.

Given these two theorems, we derive three corollaries to generate positive and negative statistically significant CARs.

COROLLARY 1. *There exists a threshold $\gamma \leq 0.5$ such that the item $I \in \mathcal{I}$ is impossible to be in any statistically significant CARs if its support is smaller than $\gamma|\mathcal{D}|$.*

PROOF. Corollary 1 is a special case of Theorem 1 when $I \in \mathcal{I}$. First we assume that I can be in the consequent part of the rule, then according to Theorem 1, we can find a threshold $\gamma \leq 0.5$ such that when $\sigma(I) < \gamma|\mathcal{D}|$, I cannot appear in any statistically significant rules. Since we only intend to find CARs where item I can only be in the antecedent part, if the condition $\sigma(I) < \gamma|\mathcal{D}|$ holds, item I can cannot appear in any statistically significant CARs. □

Some impossible items are pruned before further analysis by Corollary 1. It is assumed that s items ($s \leq m$) are left. The remaining s items are reordered and renamed in an ascending order by their support count, i.e., $\mathcal{I}_{rest} = \{i_1, i_2, ..., i_s\}$, where $\sigma(i_1) \leq \sigma(i_2) \leq ... \leq \sigma(i_s)$. Then in order to traverse the whole search space, an enumeration tree is built over $\mathcal{I}_{rest}$. For each node in the tree, the antecedent part is a combination of items in the power set of $\mathcal{I}_{rest}$. The consequent part is $2n$ possible class labels (either positive or negative). Therefore, for each node in the enumeration tree, we have to check all $2n$ possible CARs to see if they are statistically significant.

COROLLARY 2. *For any $X \subseteq \mathcal{I}_{rest}$, $Q \subseteq (\mathcal{I}_{rest}\backslash X)$, if $\sigma(X) \leq \sigma(c_k)$ or $\sigma(X) \leq \sigma(\neg c_k)$ holds, we can get $p_F(XQ \to c_k) \geq \frac{\sigma(\neg X)!\sigma(c_k)!}{|\mathcal{D}|!(\sigma(c_k)-\sigma(X))!}$ or $p_F(XQ \to \neg c_k) \geq \frac{\sigma(\neg X)!\sigma(\neg c_k)!}{|\mathcal{D}|!(\sigma(\neg c_k)-\sigma(X))!}$, respectively.*

PROOF. Corollary 2 can be considered as a special case of Theorem 2 when either c_k or $\neg c_k$ is the consequent part of a rule. □

According to Corollary 2, the lowest value of $p_F(XQ \to c_k)$ and $p_F(XQ \to \neg c_k)$ provide the lower bounds for $p_F(X \to c_k)$ and $p_F(X \to \neg c_k)$, respectively. Therefore, if the lower bound exceeds α, the corresponding CAR $X \to c_k$ or $X \to \neg c_k$ is not statistically significant and can be directly pruned. Otherwise, the CAR $X \to c_k$ or $X \to \neg c_k$ is considered as ***PSS***, i.e., "Potentially Statistically Significant".

Definition 3. The CAR $X \to c_k$ or $X \to \neg c_k$ is defined as ***PSS***, i.e., "Potentially Statistically Significant", if it meets either of the following conditions: (1) $\sigma(X) \le \sigma(c_k)$ or $\sigma(X) \le \sigma(\neg c_k)$ holds, and the lower bound $\frac{\sigma(\neg X)!\sigma(c_k)!}{|\mathcal{D}|!(\sigma(c_k)-\sigma(X))!}$ or $\frac{\sigma(\neg X)!\sigma(\neg c_k)!}{|\mathcal{D}|!(\sigma(\neg c_k)-\sigma(X))!}$ is smaller than or equal to α, respectively; (2) $\sigma(X) > \sigma(c_k)$ or $\sigma(X) > \sigma(\neg c_k)$ holds.

If a CAR is ***PSS***, we need to calculate the exact p-value to see if it is indeed statistically significant.

COROLLARY 3. *If CAR $X \to c_k$ or $X \to \neg c_k$ is PSS, then any of its parent rule $Y \to c_k$ or $Y \to \neg c_k$ is also PSS, where $Y \subsetneq X$ and $|Y| = |X| - 1$.*

PROOF. There are two situations making $X \to c_k$ being *PSS*. The first situation is when $\sigma(X) > \sigma(c_k)$, since $Y \subsetneq X$, thus $\sigma(Y) > \sigma(X) > \sigma(c_k)$, and it is easy to see the parent rule $Y \to c_k$ is also *PSS*. The second situation is when $X \to c_k$ but $lowerbound(p_F(XQ \to c_k)) < \alpha$, where $Q \subseteq (\mathcal{I}_{rest} \backslash X)$. Now let $XQ = Y(X\backslash Y)Q = YR$, because $(X\backslash Y) \subseteq (\mathcal{I}_{rest}\backslash Y)$ and $Q \subseteq (\mathcal{I}_{rest}\backslash X) \subseteq (\mathcal{I}_{rest}\backslash Y)$, thus $R = (X\backslash Y)Q \subseteq (\mathcal{I}_{rest}\backslash Y)$ and therefore, there must exists $R \subseteq (\mathcal{I}_{rest}\backslash Y)$ making $lowerbound(p_F(YQ \to c_k)) < \alpha$, i.e., rule $Y \to c_k$ is *PSS*. The proof is similar for the negative CAR $X \to \neg c_k$. □

With these three corollaries, the whole search problem can be summarized as follows: We first use Corollary 1 to prune impossible items, sort and rename the remaining items in an ascending order by their support. Next, all candidate CARs with only one antecedent item are listed. We then use Corollary 2 to check if they are *PSS*, non-*PSS* candidate CARs can be pruned directly without further analysis. *PSS* CARs are further checked to see if they are indeed statistically significant. From *PSS* 1-itemset CARs, we generate candidate *PSS* 2-itemset CARs by Corollary 3. The process repeats until no *PSS* CARs are generated at a certain level. It also needs to be mentioned that in the searching process, the minimality of the CARs is considered, if the CAR is marked as minimal, we stop the expansion from this CAR because all of its children CARs are impossible to get a lower p-value. In fact, checking minimality for a CAR is a hard task, because we have to consider its whole subtree. We use a well-proven result from [20] that if $P(c_k|X) = 1$ or $P(\neg c_k|X) = 1$, the corresponding CAR $X \to c_k$ or $X \to \neg c_k$ is minimal. In other words, the property of minimality can be detected by calculating the conditional probability of c_k or $\neg c_k$ given X. Therefore, for a certain CAR, we do not need to check all its children CARs in its subtree to see if it is minimal anymore. The rule generation process is presented in Algorithm 1.

```
Data: Transaction Dataset D, set of antecedent items
      I, class labels C, significance level α = 0.05.
Result: Statistically significant positive and negative
        CAR sets R_pos and R_neg.
Prune impossible antecedent items I with Corollary 1;
I_rest: the reoredered and renamed antecedent item set;
Create root node and level-1 nodes;
Set l = 1;
while l ≤ |I_rest| do
    for each candidate l-set CAR r do
        if all parent rules of r are PSS and not minimal
        then
            if p_F(r) ≤ α then
                if r is non-redundant then
                    if r is minimal then
                        r.minimal = true;
                    end
                    if r.class is positive then
                        R_pos.add(r);
                    else
                        R_neg.add(r);
                    end
                end
            end
        else
            prune CAR r and all its decedent rules from
            the enumeration tree;
        end
    end
    l = l + 1;
end
```

Algorithm 1: Statistically significant positive and negative CARs generation.

3.2.2 Rule Pruning

In the rule generation phase, redundant (lower ranked and more specific) CARs have been removed, but the number of discovered statistically significant CARs could still be very large. The disadvantages of a large number of CARs are two folds: first, noisy CARs may be included, they may jeopardize the classification performance; second, a classifier with a small number of rules is important since it allows domain experts to tune a classifier by editing rules if necessary.

The most widely used rule pruning strategy is database coverage [25], however, the database coverage heuristic can only be applied to positive CARs and negative CARs in the form of $\neg X \to c_k$. Through our rule generation phase, the discovered CARs are all in the form of $X \to \neg c_k$, to reduce the number of negative CARs in this type, we propose a novel rule pruning strategy to prune noisy positive and negative CARs simultaneously.

We first scan through the set of discovered negative CARs. For each negative CAR $X \to \neg c_k$, if it misclassifies at least one training instance, in other words, if we find an instance t in the training dataset such that $X \subseteq t.antecedent$ and $c_k = t.class$, the negative CAR $X \to \neg c_k$ is pruned, otherwise, it is kept for the following classification phase.

For the positive CARs $X \to c_k$, we first rank them by their confidence values, then use the database coverage method to select a subset of high quality.

Here a problem arises, in some datasets, the number of remaining negative CARs may be much larger than the number of remaining positive CARs. In the extreme case if only negative CARs $X \to \neg c_k$ are left, it is still hard to make a prediction for a new instance, for example, for instance XY, the only information obtained is that class label c_k is not correct. Therefore, we still wish the positive CARs dominate the classification decision phase, while taking negative CARs as a complement to help positive CARs. Considering this, we adjust the number of negative CARs, make it at most as large as the number of positive CARs. To be more specific, let n_{neg} and n_{pos} denote the number of pruned positive and negative CARs, respectively, if $n_{neg} > n_{pos}$, only the first n_{pos} negative CARs and all positive CARs are cho-

Data: Set of positive and negative CARs $\mathcal{R}_{pos}$, $\mathcal{R}_{neg}$ from rule generation phase.
Result: Pruned CARs set $\mathcal{R}_{newpos}$ and $\mathcal{R}_{newneg}$.

```
Ranking R_pos and R_neg according to confidence values;
R_newpos = ∅, R_newneg = ∅;
// 1.  Negative CARs pruning
for each CAR r in R_neg do
    for each training instance t in training dataset D do
        if r.antecedent ⊆ t.antecedent and r.class = t.class then
            R_neg.remove(r);
            break;
        end
    end
end
Assign R_neg to R_newneg;
// 2.  Positive CARs pruning
for each CAR r in R_positive do
    for each training instance t in training dataset D do
        if r.antecedent ⊆ t.antecedent and r.class = t.class then
            R_newpos.add(r);
            remove instances covered by r in D;
        end
    end
end
// 3.  Negative CARs set adjustment
if |R_newneg| > |R_newpos| then
    R_newneg = first |R_newpos| rules in R_newneg;
end
```

Algorithm 2: Positive and negative CARs pruning.

sen as the actual classifier. The whole process is illustrated in Algorithm 2.

3.2.3 *Classification*

The set of statistically significant positive and negative CARs left from the previous rule pruning phase represents the actual associative classifier. Given a new unlabeled object, the classification process searches for the set of CARs that are relevant to this object, and makes the prediction according to the label information of all these relevant rules. Here we discuss how to make predictions for new objects based on the set of rules in the classifier. There are two types of CARs in our classifier: positive CARs in the form of $X \rightarrow c_k$ and negative CARs in the form of $X \rightarrow \neg c_k$. These two types of CARs are both considered in our classification phase. A simple way to classify a new object is to select the matching rule with the highest confidence value and assign its label to the new object. This is the strategy adopted in CBA [25]. But in this way, the negative rule $X \rightarrow \neg c_k$ does not make any sense if it has the highest confidence since it does not allow the labeling. In this way, only positive CARs influence the classification decision. Therefore, we propose to divide all matching rules into groups according to their class labels. The groups are ordered either by average confidence values or sum of confidence values. Then the group with the highest average or sum of confidence values will be assigned to the new object. These three possible classification methods are denoted as BEST, AVE and SUM, representing classifying by the best matching rule, by the average and by the sum of confidence values, respectively.

Data: A new instance o to be classified. Set of positive CARs $\mathcal{R}_{newpos}$ and negative CARs $\mathcal{R}_{newneg}$ from rule pruning phase.
Result: Class label of the new instance o.

```
T_pos = ∅ ;      // set of positive rules matching o
T_neg = ∅ ;      // set of negative rules matching o
for each CAR r in R_newpos do
    if r.antecedent ⊆ o.antecedent then
        T_pos.add(r);
    end
end
for each CAR r in R_newneg do
    if r.antecedent ⊆ o.antecedent then
        r.confidence = −r.confidence;
        T_neg.add(r);
    end
end
Divide T into n subsets by class labels: T_1, T_2, ..., T_n;
// 1.  Classification method BEST
for each subset T_1, T_2, ..., T_n do
    find the CAR with the highest confidence value
end
Assign its class label to o;
// 2.  Classification method AVE
for each subset T_1, T_2, ..., T_n do
    average confidence value of matching CARs in each class
end
Assign the class with the highest average of confidence value to o;
// 3.  Classification method SUM
for each subset T_1, T_2, ..., T_n do
    sum up the confidence values of matching CARs in each class
end
Assign the class with the highest sum of confidence value to o;
```

Algorithm 3: Three methods to classify a new instance.

The detailed descriptions of these classification methods are presented in Algorithm 3.

It is obvious that the confidence values of positive CARs $X \rightarrow c_k$ are added to the class c_i in the classification phase. However, the negative CARs $X \rightarrow \neg c_k$ is treated differently, we choose to subtract its confidence value from the total confidence of the corresponding class c_k.

4. EXPERIMENTAL RESULTS

In this section, we evaluate the proposed associative classifier on 20 datasets from the UCI Machine Learning Repository [11]. In these datasets, the numerical attributes have been discretized by the author of [14], the discretization strategy is different from [24, 25], thus the classification performance may be slightly different from the results reported before. All the experimental results are reported as an average over 10-fold cross validation. To have a fair comparison with some other methods, we also list the classification performance of two rule-based classifier: C4.5 [26] and FOIL [27]; two associative classifier on positive CARs: CBA [25] and CMAR [24]; an associative classifier on both positive and negative CARs: ARC-PAN [7]; a hybrid of rule-based and associative classifier: CPAR [39]; Naïve Bayes [28]

Table 1: **Classification accuracy on 20 UCI datasets by different classifiers.**

Dataset	C4.5	FOIL	CBA	CMAR	CPAR	PAN	NB	SVM	BEST	rules+		rules+-	
										SUM	AVE	SUM	AVE
adult	78.8	84.6	84.2	81.3	77.3	83.1	82.3	75.8	80.8	83.2	76.1	83.2	76.1
anneal	76.7	98.8	94.5	90.7	95.1	86.9	86.3	85.0	94.2	88.0	94.3	91.9	94.5
breast	91.5	89.3	94.1	89.9	93.0	89.4	95.9	95.7	90.0	91.3	90.0	91.3	90.0
cylBands	69.1	74.1	76.1	76.5	70.0	42.2	72.2	76.6	66.1	72.0	65.4	72.2	70.4
flare	82.1	83.8	84.2	84.3	63.9	83.4	71.0	73.8	83.9	83.2	84.0	83.2	84.1
glass	65.9	66.5	68.4	71.1	64.9	48.5	48.6	68.6	70.6	72.0	65.9	72.4	69.2
heart	61.5	55.2	57.8	56.2	53.8	58.8	53.4	55.4	51.5	56.8	51.8	57.4	56.4
hepatitis	84.1	77.8	42.2	79.6	75.5	39.8	84.5	79.3	85.8	83.2	83.2	83.9	82.6
horseColic	70.9	83.4	78.8	82.3	81.2	81.5	77.9	72.5	70.7	76.7	73.6	75.8	71.5
ionosphere	84.6	86.6	32.5	91.5	88.9	83.7	82.6	87.7	80.1	85.0	74.6	82.3	78.6
iris	91.3	94.0	93.3	94.0	94.7	94.6	94.6	94.6	94.7	94.7	95.3	94.7	95.3
led7	73.9	60.5	73.1	73.2	71.3	59.5	73.1	73.6	70.9	73.3	56.6	73.3	56.7
letRecog	50.4	50.0	32.5	28.3	58.2	26.9	64.1	65.2	54.2	61.8	40.6	64.9	54.5
mushroom	92.8	99.5	46.7	100.0	98.5	98.9	95.8	99.8	100.0	100.0	100.0	100.0	100.0
pageBlocks	92.0	92.4	90.9	90.1	92.5	89.9	90.8	91.2	90.7	91.1	90.6	91.2	90.8
penDigits	70.5	84.1	92.3	87.4	80.5	79.5	85.7	86.7	87.4	90.3	75.7	91.3	85.7
pima	71.7	71.9	74.6	74.4	74.0	74.2	75.3	74.0	75.1	67.7	72.9	68.0	72.8
soybean	60.3	88.0	89.2	88.1	83.1	81.8	92.9	88.7	90.3	89.6	90.6	90.5	90.9
wine	75.8	88.2	49.6	92.7	88.2	89.3	96.0	94.9	84.3	88.2	80.9	91.6	89.9
zoo	91.0	93.1	40.7	93.0	94.1	86.1	93.0	92.2	93.1	93.1	93.1	94.1	94.1
Average	76.7	81.1	69.8	81.3	79.9	73.9	80.8	81.6	80.7	82.1	77.8	**82.7**	80.2

and SVM [17]. The parameters of all these classifiers follow the default settings as the original papers.

4.1 Classification Performance

4.1.1 Accuracy

First, we show the classification accuracy by different methods on 20 UCI datasets. The experimental results are shown in Table 1. **Columns 2-9** list the classification accuracies of these compared methods. In **Column 10**, classification accuracy is determined by the best matching rule. **Columns 11-12** show the performance with only positive CARs on two classification methods, SUM and AVE, while **Columns 13-14** list the classification results when negative CARs are also considered.

As can be observed, rules+- with SUM gets the best overall classification performance (82.7%) and wins 4 out of 20 datasets, followed by rules+ with SUM (82.1%). Both of their average classification accuracy outperform the others.

4.1.2 Different rule classification strategies

Then we compare three different classification strategies, SUM, BEST as well as AVE. The classification method SUM is better than the other two classification methods BEST and AVE by winning around 2%-4% average classification accuracy, no matter with only positive CARs or with both positive and negative CARs. When the other two classification methods BEST and AVE are used, the associative classifier still performs comparably to other well-known rule-based and associative classifiers on average of 20 datasets.

4.1.3 Effect of negative CARs

To validate the effect of negative CARs in the associative classifier, we compare rules+- with SUM and AVE to their corresponding alternatives: rules+ with SUM and AVE. The average classification accuracy is higher when negative CARs are included. We also compare the count of wins and losses of rules+- when it is measured against rules+ on SUM and AVE classification methods, when the negative CARs are integrated, both of them win their positive alternatives by 12 times and only loses 2 and 3 times, respectively. It demonstrates the power of negative CARs. They indeed help us get more reliable and more accurate classification results on most datasets.

4.1.4 Effect of rule pruning

In the rule pruning phase, due to the absence of negative rule pruning strategies in the literature, we propose a novel rule pruning method to prune positive and negative CARs simultaneously. We compare the classification performance of three different scenarios: prune both positive and negative CARs, prune only positive CARs and without rule pruning. The comparison is performed on SUM classification methods. In Table 2, **Columns 2-4** show the classification results of these three scenarios on SUM classification method. The average accuracy of **Column 2** (prune both positive and negative CARs) is the highest and it wins 18 out of 20 datasets. Therefore, the proposed rule pruning method not only reduces the number of CARs in the classifier, but also improves the classification performance compared to the associative classifier pruning only positive CARs and the associative classifier without rule pruning phase.

4.2 Statistical Analysis

From Table 1, we can conclude that the associative classifier built with positive and negative CARs is an as good or even better associative classifier compared with other well-known classifiers and the associative classifier with only positive CARs; the SUM classification method is better than BEST and AVE. In Table 2, we show the proposed rule

Table 2: Comparison of rule pruning strategies.

Dataset	rules+- with SUM		
	prune +-	prune +	w/o prune
adult	83.2	82.3	81.9
anneal	91.9	65.7	86.7
breast	91.3	87.0	81.0
cylBands	72.2	63.7	63.7
flare	83.2	78.0	76.6
glass	72.4	60.7	69.6
heart	57.4	60.1	59.7
hepatitis	83.9	82.6	81.3
horseColic	75.8	73.1	72.0
ionosphere	82.3	75.7	75.5
iris	94.7	94.0	94.7
led7	73.3	74.2	73.9
letRecog	64.9	55.1	52.6
mushroom	100.0	97.9	97.7
pageBlocks	91.2	90.4	89.8
penDigits	91.3	83.8	86.8
pima	68.0	65.6	65.1
soybean	90.5	78.2	61.6
wine	91.6	91.6	91.6
zoo	94.1	77.2	94.1
Average	**82.7**	76.9	77.8

pruning strategy is effective. These conclusions are obtained mainly by measuring average classification accuracies and winning times. Although they give us some intuition about the lead of a certain classifier, a certain rule pruning or a classification strategy, the conclusion is not forceful since the dominance is unsurpassed over all 20 datasets.

To better validate the conclusions we get, we use Demsar's [18] method, conducting a set of non-parametric statistical tests to compare different classifiers over multiple datasets. In the first step, Friedman test is applied to measure if there is a significant difference between different classification models on Table 1. We first rank different classifiers on each dataset separately, r_i^j denotes the rank of the j-th of k classifiers on i-th of N datasets. Then the average rank of j-th classifier is computed as:

$$R_j = \frac{1}{N}\sum_i r_i^j$$

In the null hypothesis, the average ranks of different classifiers are equivalent, and the Friedman statistic is:

$$\chi_F^2 = \frac{12N}{k(k+1)}\left(\sum_j R_j^2 - \frac{k(k+1)^2}{4}\right)$$

with $k-1$ degrees of freedom, when $N > 10$ and $k > 5$. If the Friedman statistic exceeds a critical value, the null hypothesis is rejected and we conduct post-hoc tests to make pairwise comparisons between different classifiers, otherwise, there is no statistically significant differences among the k classifiers over these N datasets.

The Friedman statistics of 13 classifiers from Table 1 exceeds the critical value, so we continue to use Wilcoxon signed-ranks test to compare the differences between different classifiers pairwisely. In Wilcoxon signed-ranks test, suppose d_i denotes the classification accuracy difference on the i-th of N datasets. We then rank the difference d_i according to their absolute values, if ties occur, average ranks are assigned. Next, the sum of ranks R^+, R^- are calculated on datasets in which the second classifier outperforms the first classifier and the first classifier outperforms the second classifier, respectively:

$$R^+ = \sum_{d_i>0} rank(d_i) + \frac{1}{2}\sum_{d_i=0} rank(d_i)$$

$$R^- = \sum_{d_i<0} rank(d_i) + \frac{1}{2}\sum_{d_i=0} rank(d_i)$$

Let T be the smaller value of these two sums, when $N \geq 20$, Wilcoxon W statistic tends to form a normal distribution, then we can use z-value to evaluate the null hypothesis that there is no statistical difference between these two classifiers. The z-score is:

$$z = \frac{T - \frac{1}{4}N(N+1)}{\sqrt{\frac{1}{24}N(N+1)(2N+1)}}$$

If $z < -1.96$ then the corresponding p-value is smaller than 0.05, therefore, the null hypothesis is rejected.

A series of Wilcoxon signed-ranks test from Table 1 and Table 2 are listed in Table 3. It shows the count of wins, losses, ties and corresponding p-value for pairwise post-hoc comparisons. **Rows 2-9** show the comparisons of our associative classifier rules+- (SUM) with the other 8 well established classifiers. Our associative classifier always wins more than half of the 20 datasets, but the only strong conclusion we draw is that our method is significantly better than C4.5 and ARC-PAN. ARC-PAN is an associative classifier most similar to our method which also uses the negative CARs, however, it fails to consider the statistical dependency of the discovered CARs. The statistically significant difference between our method and ARC-PAN is very appealing. It shows the power of introducing statistical dependency in the associative classification problem. **Rows 10-11** show SUM method is significantly better than BEST and AVE. Through **Rows 12-13**, we can find that when the negative CARs are included, the associative classifier is significantly better than that with only positive CARs. **Rows 14-16** indicate the effect of the proposed rule pruning strategy, the difference between pruning only positive CARs and without pruning is not statistically significant although pruning only positive rules wins 14 times. But when we also prune negative CARs, the classification performance is greatly improved, the p-value is very small. Therefore, by applying the proposed rule pruning strategy, we get a much better classifier with higher accuracy and fewer rules.

4.3 Running Time Comparison

To test the efficiency of the proposed associative classifier, we compare the running time of rules+- (SUM) with three associative classifiers, CBA, CMAR and ARC-PAN. We only report the results on 6 datasets due to space limit. The results are shown in Table 4. As can be seen from the table, the proposed classifier is faster than the three contender associative classifiers in many cases.

5. CONCLUSION AND FUTURE WORK

In this paper, we introduce a novel associative classifier which is built on statistically significant positive and neg-

Table 3: **Statistical analysis of Table 1 and Table 2; (*) indicates a statistically significant difference.**

row ID	comparisons	wins	losses	ties	p-value
2	rules+-(SUM) vs. C4.5 *	13	7	0	0.011
3	rules+-(SUM) vs. FOIL	12	8	0	0.33
4	rules+-(SUM) vs. CBA	11	9	0	0.24
5	rules+-(SUM) vs. CMAR	12	7	1	0.42
6	rules+-(SUM) vs. CPAR	12	6	2	0.058
7	rules+-(SUM) vs. PAN *	15	5	0	0.014
8	rules+-(SUM) vs. NB	12	7	1	0.32
9	rules+-(SUM) vs. SVM	12	7	1	0.31
10	rules+-(SUM vs. BEST) *	14	4	2	0.028
11	rules+-(SUM vs. AVE) *	13	5	2	0.021
12	SUM(rules+- vs. rules+) *	12	2	6	0.033
13	AVE(rules+- vs. rules+) *	13	4	3	0.011
14	SUM(prune+- vs. prune+) *	17	2	1	0.001
15	SUM(prune+- vs. w/o) *	15	2	3	0.001
16	SUM(prune+ vs. w/o)	14	4	2	0.528

Table 4: Comparison of running time.

Dataset	CBA	CMAR	ARC-PAN	rule+-(SUM)
adult	583.7s	221.6s	561.2s	**177.0**s
cylBands	19.7s	5.9s	74.1s	**3.8**s
ionosphere	57s	95.6s	243.9s	**36.2**s
letRecog	5.9s	**5.2**s	129.2s	10.7s
penDigits	88.6s	257.2s	301.5s	**49.8**s
wine	25.4s	23.2s	98.0s	**11.2**s

ative CARs. The proposed associative classifier consists of three steps: rule generation, rule pruning and rule classification. In the first phase, we extend the Kingfisher algorithm by pushing the rule constraint in the rule generation phase to enable the discovery of statistically significant positive and negative CARs. After the rule generation step, there are still many noisy CARs which may jeopardize the classification phase or overfit the model, therefore we propose a novel rule pruning strategy to prune both positive and negative CARs simultaneously. At the last step, we present and compare different rule classification methods to ensure the correct prediction of unlabeled data.

The experimental results are very encouraging. Our associative classifier achieves a comparably good or even better classification result when measured against other classifiers. Meanwhile, it is also computational efficient. By integrating negative CARs in the classifier, the classification performance indeed improves compared to the classifiers built with only positive CARs. We also propose a novel rule pruning strategy to prune positive and negative CARs simultaneously. The pruning not only reduces the number of CARs, but also greatly improves the performance of the classification. Three different rule classification methods are presented and compared, the SUM method works best, it indicates that to classify a new instance, we should sum up the confidence values of all matching rules and make a class label prediction based on the summations from different classes. A two step statistical test are used to validate all these conclusions.

In the future, we aim to further improve the Kingfisher algorithm to enable the discovery of positive and negative CARs more efficiently. Another challenging task is to find more effective rule pruning strategies post rule generation to further improve the classification performance.

6. REFERENCES

[1] C. C. Aggarwal and P. S. Yu. A new framework for itemset generation. In *Proc. of the 7th ACM SIGACT-SIGMOD-SIGART Symposium on Principles of Database Systems*, pages 18–24, 1998.

[2] C. C. Aggarwal and P. S. Yu. Mining associations with the collective strength approach. *IEEE Transactions on Knowledge and Data Engineering*, 13(6):863–873, 2001.

[3] R. Agrawal, T. Imieliński, and A. Swami. Mining association rules between sets of items in large databases. In *Proc. of the 1993 ACM SIGMOD Intl. Conf. on Management of Data*, pages 207–216, 1993.

[4] R. Agrawal and R. Srikant. Fast algorithms for mining association rules. In *Proc. of the 20th Intl. Conf. on Very Large Data Bases*, pages 487–499, 1994.

[5] L. Antonie, J. Li, and O. Zaiane. Negative association rules. In *Frequent Pattern Mining*, pages 135–145. Springer, 2014.

[6] M.-L. Antonie and O. R. Zaïane. Text document categorization by term association. In *Proc. of the 2002 IEEE Intl. Conf. on Data Mining*, pages 19–26, 2002.

[7] M.-L. Antonie and O. R. Zaïane. An associative classifier based on positive and negative rules. In *Proc. of the 9th ACM SIGMOD Workshop on Research Issues in Data Mining and Knowledge Discovery*, pages 64–69, 2004.

[8] M.-L. Antonie and O. R. Zaïane. Mining positive and negative association rules: an approach for confined rules. In *Proc. of the 8th European Conf. on Principles and Practice of Knowledge Discovery in Databases*, pages 27–38, 2004.

[9] M.-L. Antonie, O. R. Zaïane, and R. C. Holte. Learning to use a learned model: A two-stage approach to classification. In *Proc. of the 6th IEEE Intl. Conf. on Data Mining*, pages 33–42, 2006.

[10] B. Arunasalam and S. Chawla. Cccs: a top-down associative classifier for imbalanced class distribution. In *Proc. of the 12th ACM SIGKDD Intl. Conf. on Knowledge Discovery and Data Mining*, pages 517–522, 2006.

[11] K. Bache and M. Lichman. UCI machine learning repository. `http://archive.ics.uci.edu/ml`, 2013.

[12] R. J. Bayardo Jr. Brute-force mining of high-confidence classification rules. In *Proc. of the 3rd Intl. Conf. on Knowledge Discovery and Data Mining*, pages 123–126, 1997.

[13] S. Brin, R. Motwani, and C. Silverstein. Beyond market baskets: Generalizing association rules to correlations. In *Proc. of the 1997 ACM SIGMOD Intl. Conf. on Management of Data*, pages 265–276, 1997.

[14] F. Coenen. The LUCS-KDD software library. `http://cgi.csc.liv.ac.uk/~frans/KDD/Software/`, 2004.

[15] W. W. Cohen. Fast effective rule induction. In *Proc. of the 12th Intl. Conf. on Machine Learning*, pages 115–123, 1995.

[16] C. Cornelis, P. Yan, X. Zhang, and G. Chen. Mining positive and negative association rules from large databases. In *Proc. of the 2006 IEEE Conf. on Cybernetics and Intelligent Systems*, pages 1–6, 2006.

[17] C. Cortes and V. Vapnik. Support-vector networks. *Machine learning*, 20(3):273–297, 1995.

[18] J. Demšar. Statistical comparisons of classifiers over multiple data sets. *The Journal of Machine Learning Research*, 7:1–30, 2006.

[19] R. O. Duda, P. E. Hart, et al. *Pattern classification and scene analysis*, volume 3. Wiley New York, 1973.

[20] W. Hämäläinen. Efficient discovery of the top-k optimal dependency rules with fisher's exact test of significance. In *Proc. of the 10th IEEE Intl. Conf. on Data Mining*, pages 196–205, 2010.

[21] W. Hämäläinen. Kingfisher: an efficient algorithm for searching for both positive and negative dependency rules with statistical significance measures. *Knowledge and Information Systems*, 32(2):383–414, 2012.

[22] J. Han, J. Pei, and Y. Yin. Mining frequent patterns without candidate generation. In *Proc. of the 2000 ACM SIGMOD Intl. Conf. on Management of Data*, pages 1–12, 2000.

[23] Y. S. Koh and R. Pears. Efficiently finding negative association rules without support threshold. In *Proc. of the 20th Australian Joint Conf. on Artificial Intelligence*, pages 710–714, 2007.

[24] W. Li, J. Han, and J. Pei. Cmar: Accurate and efficient classification based on multiple class-association rules. In *Proc. of the 2001 IEEE Intl. Conf. on Data Mining*, pages 369–376, 2001.

[25] B. Liu, W. Hsu, and Y. Ma. Integrating classification and association rule mining. In *Proc. of the 4th Intl. Conf. on Knowledge Discovery and Data Mining*, pages 80–86, 1998.

[26] J. R. Quinlan. *C4. 5: programs for machine learning*, volume 1. Morgan kaufmann, 1993.

[27] J. R. Quinlan and R. M. Cameron-Jones. Foil: A midterm report. In *Proc. of the 1993 European Conf. on Machine Learning*, pages 3–20, 1993.

[28] S. Russell and P. Norvig. Artificial intelligence: a modern approach. 1995.

[29] A. Savasere, E. Omiecinski, and S. Navathe. Mining for strong negative associations in a large database of customer transactions. In *Proc. of the 14th Intl. Conf. on Data Engineering*, pages 494–502, 1998.

[30] W.-G. Teng, M.-J. Hsieh, and M.-S. Chen. On the mining of substitution rules for statistically dependent items. In *Proc. of the 2002 IEEE Intl. Conf. on Data Mining*, pages 442–449, 2002.

[31] W.-G. Teng, M.-J. Hsieh, and M.-S. Chen. A statistical framework for mining substitution rules. *Knowledge and Information Systems*, 7(2):158–178, 2005.

[32] D. R. Thiruvady and G. I. Webb. Mining negative rules using grd. In *Proc. of the 8th Pacific-Asia Conf. on Knowledge Discovery and Data Mining*, pages 161–165, 2004.

[33] F. Verhein and S. Chawla. Using significant, positively associated and relatively class correlated rules for associative classification of imbalanced datasets. In *Proc. of the 7th IEEE Intl. Conf. on Data Mining*, pages 679–684, 2007.

[34] H. Wang, X. Zhang, and G. Chen. Mining a complete set of both positive and negative association rules from large databases. In *Proc. of the 12th Pacific-Asia Conf. on Advances in Knowledge Discovery and Data Mining*, pages 777–784, 2008.

[35] J. Wang and G. Karypis. Harmony: Efficiently mining the best rules for classification. In *Proc. of the 2005 SIAM Intl. Conf. on Data Mining*, pages 205–216, 2005.

[36] G. I. Webb. Discovering significant rules. In *Proc. of the 12th ACM SIGKDD Intl. Conf. on Knowledge Discovery and Data mining*, pages 434–443, 2006.

[37] G. I. Webb. Discovering significant patterns. *Machine Learning*, 68(1):1–33, 2007.

[38] X. Wu, C. Zhang, and S. Zhang. Efficient mining of both positive and negative association rules. *ACM Transactions on Information System*, 22(3):381–405, 2004.

[39] X. Yin and J. Han. Cpar: Classification based on predictive association rules. In *Proc. of the 3rd SIAM Intl. Conf. on Data Mining*, pages 331–335, 2003.

A Min-Max Optimization Framework For Online Graph Classification

Peng Yang
Institute for Infocomm Research
A*STAR, Singapore 138632
yangp@i2r.a-star.edu.sg

Peilin Zhao
Institute for Infocomm Research
A*STAR, Singapore 138632
zhaop@i2r.a-star.edu.sg

ABSTRACT

Traditional online learning for graph node classification adapts graph regularization into ridge regression, which may not be suitable when data is adversarially generated. To solve this issue, we propose a more general min-max optimization framework for online graph node classification. The derived online algorithm can achieve a min-max regret compared with the optimal linear model found offline. However, this algorithm assumes that the label is provided for every node, while label is scare and labeling is usually either too time-consuming or expensive in real-world applications. To save labeling effort, we propose a novel confidence-based query approach to prioritize the informative labels. Our theoretical result shows that an online algorithm learning on these selected labels can achieve comparable mistake bound with the fully-supervised online counterpart. To take full advantage of these labels, we propose an aggressive algorithm, which can update the model even if no error occurs. Theoretical analysis shows that the mistake bound of the proposed method, thanks to the aggressive update trials, is better than conservative competitor in expectation. We finally empirically evaluate it on several real-world graph databases. Encouraging experimental results further demonstrate the effectiveness of our method.

Categories and Subject Descriptors

H.2.8 [**Database Management**]: Database applications—*Data mining*; I.2.6 [**Artificial Intelligence**]: Learning

General Terms

Learning Theory; Algorithm

Keywords

Min-Max Optimization; Online Learning; Sampling; Graph Node Classification

CIKM'15, October 19–23, 2015, Melbourne, VIC, Australia.

ACM 978-1-4503-3794-6/15/10 ...$15.00.
DOI: http://dx.doi.org/10.1145/2806416.2806548 .

1. INTRODUCTION

Graphs, such as *Facebook*[1], Amazon network, and citation network, play an important role in many real-world applications. In particular, graph node classification has drawn significant attention, for example, to identify the labels of comments on Twitter or to prioritize the potential customers in social networks [23, 27, 11]. To solve this problem, a classification model can be trained on a set of node-label pairs from the graph, in terms of both offline [8] and online settings [21]. Offline learning can query label whenever the nodes are stored, thus demanding a high memory space. In contract, online algorithm learns the nodes in a streaming order. In specific, online learning can only access the label of the current node. After processing the node, the current input is discarded and cannot be stored for further query. As a result, online algorithm is efficient and scalable, especially for the high dimensional and large-scale graph dataset [21].

In fact, most of the online learning algorithms [5, 26, 9] are designed for vector-based data. Unlike the vector data setting, to build an algorithm on graph node, we have to consider the impact of graph structure on these nodes, for example, Gu et al. adapt the graph Laplacian regularization into online setting [18]. Although online learning is quite efficient, it assumes that all labels of nodes are provided. It clearly limits its application to many real-world scenarios, in which labels are scare and labeling all nodes is very expensive. To address this issue, selective sampling is introduced [14, 7, 6, 25, 18], that is an active online learning approach that accesses a fraction of labels to build a model. Its objective is to achieve a good trade-off between classification error and the number of queried labels. A pioneering work of selective sampling on graphs was proposed in [18]. However, it assumes an underline rule to generate a label (i.e. $Pr(y_t = 1|\mathbf{x}_t) = \frac{1+\mathbf{u}^\top \mathbf{x}_t}{2}$), which may not guarantee the performance in an adversarial setting where the actual labels (i.e. $y_t, t \geq 1$) are unknown and they may be chosen adversarially by "nature" for the unlabeled nodes (i.e. $\mathbf{x}_t, t \geq 1$) [32, 21]. This called adversarial classification problem is closely related to intrusion detection in computer networks, weather forecast and biometric authentication, in which malicious instances may weaken the effectiveness of the classifier [16, 28].

To design a robust online classification model in adversarial environments, we propose a new framework for graph node classification, by exploiting a min-max optimization strategy [31]. In this framework, the derived online algorith-

[1]http://www.facebook.com

m, Min-max Optimization for Online Learning on Graph (MOOLG), can bound the choices of an adversary under a stochastic setting of data generation [32, 1]. However, this algorithm will query every node during the learning process, making it inefficient for many real-world applications. To make it scalable on large graphs, we develop a novel confidence-based query method to query only a fraction of labels. This query method not only depends on the margin, but also the prediction confidence on the current nodes, which will query a fraction of labels, on which the MOOLG can achieve a comparable mistake bound with the one of MOOLG that learns on all the labels. Moreover, MOOLG updates the hypothesis only on error trials, thus wasting the correctly predicted labels that are useful to improve the model. To make full use of these labels, we propose another algorithm, Confidence-based randomized Query for Selective Sampling on Graph (CQSSG), hybrids the conservative update with aggressive one, which can conduct updates aggressively even if no error occurs. Theoretical analysis shows that the mistake bound of CQSSG is better than the online model [5] and selective sampling algorithm [7], which can be considered as a theoretical guarantee for our aggressive learning method. Finally, extensive experiments on graph data show the proposed algorithms outperform the existing state-of-the-art online learning methods.

The remainder of this paper is organized as follows. Section 2 provides related work. Section 3 introduces the preliminaries and the setting of graph node classification. Section 4 develops an online learning algorithm on graph. The proposed selective sampling algorithm and its theoretical analysis are present in section 5. Section 6 empirically evaluates the algorithm. Section 7 concludes this paper.

2. RELATED WORK

In this section, we briefly introduce the online learning algorithm and selective sampling algorithm in the setting of vector-based data and graph-based data.

2.1 Online Learning

Online learning has been extensively studied in the machine learning community. Due to the sequential nature of online learning, it is very efficient and scalable to be applied to the large-scale datasets [36, 37, 38, 22]. Online learning algorithm can be categorized into *conservative* algorithms [5, 9, 36] and *aggressive* algorithms [15, 26]. An algorithm is called conservative if it updates the hypothesis on only mistake trials, while an algorithm called aggressive conducts an update even if its prediction is correct.

A pioneering work of online learning on graph data is Graph Percenptron Algorithm (GPA), which is a conservative algorithm [20, 19]. Inspired by this work, Gu et al. proposed an online algorithm, namely OLLGC, which derived the online version of Laplacian regularization [18]. However, all these graph-based online algorithms mentioned above belong to conservative algorithms. In this work, we propose an aggressive online algorithm, which is proved better than the conservative algorithm in both theoretical and empirical results.

2.2 Selective Sampling

Standard selective sampling, designed for vector-based data, combines the setting of online learning and active learning [29, 17, 35]. These algorithms are generally categorized into first-order algorithms [9, 4, 7] and second-order algorithms [25, 6]. A first-order algorithm queries the labels based on a concept of "margin". More specifically, the algorithm is likely to query of a sample that lies close to the decision boundary. However, this kind of model is unable to optimize the direction and scale of the update. To address this issue, a second-order algorithm is proposed recently, which issues a query based on a notion of "uncertainty". It usually chooses an update trial in the direction with little observed instances for current model. However, few methods combine two quantities (margin and uncertainty) to make a query decision, while we will propose a strategy based on both them.

Different from vector-based setting assuming i.i.d. on data, few algorithms are designed for graphs. SSLGC [18] are the most relevant to our work, which is a second-order algorithm that decides to query based on the "uncertainty". Several recent works focus on the active-transductive learning [24, 34]. However, these methods are off-line setting where the observed instances are stored in a pool for further query, which consumes more memory than the online setting.

While extensive works are studied in both fields of selective sampling algorithm under vector-based and graph-based setting, we are the first effort to combine min-max optimization and graph regularization to derive an online algorithm on graph. Moreover, we propose a novel selective sampling algorithm on graph that hybrids the conservative update with aggressive one, which can take full advantage of the queried labels to improve the model.

3. GRAPH CLASSIFICATION

In this section, we first introduce our notations. Then we review a graph regularization framework for classification.

3.1 Notation

In this paper, lower case letter is used as scalar (e.g. x), lower case bold letter as vector (e.g. $\mathbf{v}$), upper case letter as element of a matrix (e.g. D_{ii}) and bold-face upper letter as matrice (e.g. $\mathbf{A}$). An identity matrix is denoted as $\mathbf{I}$ and zero vector as $\mathbf{0}$ with an appropriate size. We denote the transpose of a vector $\mathbf{m}$ as $\mathbf{m}^\top$, the inverse of a matrix $\mathbf{A}$ as $\mathbf{A}^{-1}$, and the pseudo inverse of $\mathbf{L}$ as $\mathbf{L}^\dagger$. Finally, a diagonal matrix is denoted as $\text{diag}(\lambda_1, \ldots, \lambda_n)$ with diagonal elements $\lambda_i, i \in [1, n]$, and the ℓ_2-norm of vector $\mathbf{w} \in \mathbb{R}^d$ as $\|\mathbf{w}\| = \sqrt{\sum_{i=1}^d w_i^2}$.

3.2 Graph Regularization

We define a graph as $G = (V,E)$ with an vertex set $V = \{v_i | i \in [1, n]\}$, and an edge set $E = \{e_{ij} = (v_i, v_j) | v_i, v_j \in V\}$. An adjacency matrix for the graph is denoted as $\mathbf{S} \in \mathbb{R}^{n\times n}$, where the element value $S_{ij} \in \mathbb{R}$ is computed by the edge affinity of a pair $\{v_i, v_j\}$. Graph Laplacian is defined as $\mathbf{L} = \mathbf{D} - \mathbf{S}$, where $\mathbf{D}$ is the diagonal matrix with $D_{ii} = \sum_k S_{ik}$ while the remain elements are 0. Given graph Laplacian $\mathbf{L}$, we denote its eigenvectors as $\mathbf{V} = [\mathbf{v}_1, \ldots, \mathbf{v}_n]$, and its eigenvalues as $\mathbf{\Lambda} = \text{diag}(\lambda_1, \ldots, \lambda_n)$ ($0 = \lambda_1 \leq \ldots \leq \lambda_n$). We assume graph G is connected and undirected in this paper.

Graph regularization [30] is built based on the concept of label smoothness over graph, formatted as $\frac{1}{2}\sum_{i,j=1}^n S_{ij}(f_i - f_j)^2 = \mathbf{f}^\top\mathbf{L}\mathbf{f}$, where $\mathbf{f} = [f_1, \ldots, f_n]^\top \in \mathbb{R}^n$ is the function assigned labels for graph nodes (i.e. $f_i : v_i \to \mathbb{R}$). In this paper,we solve the following problem in the setting of binary classification,

$$\min_{\mathbf{f}} \frac{1}{2}\|\mathbf{f}-\mathbf{y}\|^2 + \frac{b}{2}\mathbf{f}^\top \mathbf{L}\mathbf{f} + \frac{1}{2}\|\mathbf{f}\|^2 \qquad (1)$$

where $\mathbf{y} = [y_1, y_2, \ldots, y_n]^\top$ includes actual labels of graph nodes, and $b > 0$ is a parameter to control the balance of the squared loss and Laplacian regularization. In the classification setting with labeled and unlabeled nodes on graph, this optimization is to learn the function $\mathbf{f}$ with following requirements: (1) the function values for labeled nodes should be close to the given labels for that nodes; (2) nodes should satisfy label smoothness on the whole graph, namely, the points nearby in the graph should have similar labels by $\mathbf{f}$; (3) function values should be regularized without overfitting (i.e. ill-posed problem).

To solve the problem in Eq. (1) with a linear model, we consider its dual form. According to the definition of graph kernel [30, 3], the function $\mathbf{f}$ is defined as,

$$\mathbf{f} = \mathbf{L}^\dagger \beta = \sum_{i=2}^{n} \beta_i (\frac{1}{\lambda_i}\mathbf{v}_i \mathbf{v}_i^{\mathrm{T}}), \qquad (2)$$

where $\mathbf{L}^\dagger$ is the pseudo inverse of $\mathbf{L}$ and β is a parameter vector. Motivated by the work [18], we assume $\mathbf{L}^\dagger \approx \mathbf{M}^\top \mathbf{M}$, where $\mathbf{M} = \sum_{i=2}^{d} \mathrm{diag}(\frac{1}{\sqrt{\lambda_2}}, \ldots, \frac{1}{\sqrt{\lambda_d}})[\mathbf{v}_2, \ldots, \mathbf{v}_d]^\top$ is a low-rank matrix where $d \ll n$. According to Eckart-Young-Mirsky theorem [12], we claim that $\mathbf{M}^\top\mathbf{M}$ is the best rank-d approximation of $\mathbf{L}^\dagger$. Thus the kernel function $\mathbf{f}$ can be rewritten in a linear model form,

$$\mathbf{f}(\mathbf{M}) = \mathbf{M}^{\mathrm{T}}\mathbf{M}\beta = \mathbf{M}^{\mathrm{T}}\mathbf{u}, \qquad (3)$$

where $\mathbf{u} = \mathbf{M}\beta \in \mathbb{R}^d$. Substituting Eq. (3) back into Eq. (1), we get

$$\min_{\mathbf{u}} \frac{1}{2}\|\mathbf{M}^\top\mathbf{u} - \mathbf{y}\|^2 + +\frac{1}{2}\|\mathbf{M}^\top\mathbf{u}\|^2 + \frac{b}{2}\|\mathbf{u}\|^2. \qquad (4)$$

In this way, we derive a formulation similar to ridge-regression, except it contains additional regularization, which makes it shrink the prediction. And Eq. (4) can be used to derive graph-based online learning with new data representation for graph node.

4. ONLINE LEARNING ON GRAPH

Now we are ready to derive the online learning algorithm on graph. We first introduce the problem setting of online learning. Then we exploit a min-max optimization problem [31] to derive the online model on graph.

4.1 Problem Setting

The objective of online learning is to achieve a low regret compared with best linear model in hindsight. Let $\mathbf{m}_1, \ldots, \mathbf{m}_t$ $\mathbf{m}_t \in \mathbb{R}^d$ $(t \le n)$ be a sequence of nodes from columns of $\mathbf{M}$, and $y_i \in \{\pm 1\}$ with $i < t$, the graph regularization in Eq. (4) can be represented as an online version:

$$\min_{\mathbf{u}} \frac{1}{2}\sum_{i=1}^{t}(\mathbf{m}_i^\top\mathbf{u} - y_i)^2 + \frac{1}{2}\sum_{i=1}^{t}(\mathbf{m}_i^\top\mathbf{u})^2 + \frac{b}{2}\|\mathbf{u}\|^2. \qquad (5)$$

At round t, online learning algorithm receives an incoming node $\mathbf{m}_t$, and predicts its binary label $\hat{y}_t = \mathbf{m}_t^\top\mathbf{u} \in \{\pm 1\}$. After prediction, its actual label $y_t \in \mathbb{R}$ is revealed, and the algorithm uses it to update model and then proceeds to the next round. At each iteration, the performance of the online model is evaluated by the squared loss, $\ell_t(alg) = \ell(y_t, \hat{y}_t) = (y_t - \hat{y}_t)^2$. The cumulative loss suffered by the algorithm over T iterations is $L_T(alg) = \sum_{t=1}^{T} \ell_t(alg)$. Given a linear function $\mathbf{u}$, we denote $\ell_t(\mathbf{u}) = (\mathbf{m}_t^\top\mathbf{u} - y_t)^2$ as its instantaneous loss and by $L_T(\mathbf{u}) = \sum_t^T \ell_t(\mathbf{u})$ be its cumulative loss. The goal is to achieve low regret compared with the best linear function. Formally, we define the regret of an algorithm to be

$$R_T(\mathbf{u}) = \sum_{t=1}^{T}(y_t - \hat{y}_t)^2 - \inf_{\mathbf{u}} L_T(\mathbf{u}) \qquad (6)$$

The objective is to let the loss of the online algorithm convergent to the loss of the best linear function $\mathbf{u}$, that is, we have $R_T(\mathbf{u}) = o(T)$. We will solve the problem in Eq. (6) as follows.

4.2 Min-Max Optimization for Online Learning on Graph

To minimize the regret above, we introduce a last-step minmax prediction, proposed by [13] and [31]. Following this optimization approach, the derived online learning outputs a minmax prediction assuming the current iteration is the last one, and $\hat{y}_t$ and y_t serve as min and max quantifiers over the optimization problem, that is, the goal of the learner is to minimize the regret while the goal of the adversary is to maximize it. Note that our objective function is different from [31], since the best model $\mathbf{u}$ is learned from graph regularization. Our motivation is also different from [13], because the derived output is for graph classification. Adapting online graph regularization Eq. (5) into the minmax algorithm, the graph-based online learning predicts,

$$\hat{y}_T = \arg\min_{\hat{y}_T}\max_{y_T} - \inf_{\mathbf{u}}(L_T(\mathbf{u}) + \sum_{t=1}^{T}(\mathbf{m}_t^\top\mathbf{u})^2 + b\|\mathbf{u}\|^2) + \sum_{t=1}^{T}(y_t - \hat{y}_t)^2 \qquad (7)$$

We next compute the actual prediction via solving the minmax optimization in Eq. (7). We start with additional notation,

$$\mathbf{A}_t = b\mathbf{I} + 2\sum_{i=1}^{t}\mathbf{m}_i\mathbf{m}_i^\top \in \mathbb{R}^{d\times d}, \quad \mathbf{b}_t = \sum_{i=1}^{t} y_i\mathbf{m}_i \in \mathbb{R}^d. \ (8)$$

Then we define the internal infimum function,

$$R(\mathbf{u}) = \sum_{t=1}^{T}(\mathbf{m}_t^\top\mathbf{u} - y_t)^2 + \sum_{t=1}^{T}(\mathbf{m}_t^\top\mathbf{u})^2 + b\|\mathbf{u}\|^2,$$

and solve the internal infimum over $\mathbf{u}$ in the following lemma.

Lemma 1. *For all $T \ge 1$, the function $R(\mathbf{u}) = \sum_{t=1}^{T}(\mathbf{m}_t^\top\mathbf{u} - y_t)^2 + \sum_{t=1}^{T}(\mathbf{m}_t^\top\mathbf{u})^2 + b\|\mathbf{u}\|^2$ is minimal at a unique point $\mathbf{u}_T$ given by,*

$$\mathbf{u}_T = \mathbf{A}_T^{-1}\mathbf{b}_T, \quad R(\mathbf{u}_T) = \sum_{t=1}^{T} y_t^2 - \mathbf{b}_T^\top\mathbf{A}_T^{-1}\mathbf{b}_T. \qquad (9)$$

We leave the proof in the Appendix.

Algorithm 1 MOOLG: A Min-max Optimization for Online Learning on Graph

Input: Adjacency matrix $\mathbf{S}$, rank d, and regularization parameter b.
Output: $\mathbf{w}_T$
Compute $\mathbf{L}^{\dagger}$ and $\mathbf{M} \in \mathbb{R}^d$
Initialize: $\mathbf{A}_0 = b\mathbf{I}$, $\mathbf{b}_0 = \mathbf{0}$, $\mathbf{w}_0 = \mathbf{0}$
for $t = 1, \ldots, T$ **do**
  Receive $\mathbf{m}_t \in R^d$
  Compute $\mathbf{A}_t^{-1} = (\mathbf{A}_{t-1} + 2\mathbf{m}_t\mathbf{m}_t^{\top})^{-1}$
  Predict $\hat{y}_t = \text{sign}\ (\mathbf{b}_{t-1}^{\top}\mathbf{A}_t^{-1}\mathbf{m}_t)$
  Query the actual label y_t
  if $\hat{y}_t \neq y_t$ **then**
    Update $\mathbf{A}_t = \mathbf{A}_{t-1} + 2\mathbf{m}_t\mathbf{m}_t^{\top}$
    Update $\mathbf{b}_t = \mathbf{b}_{t-1} + y_t\mathbf{m}_t$.
  else
    $\mathbf{A}_t = \mathbf{A}_{t-1}, \mathbf{b}_t = \mathbf{b}_{t-1}$
  end if
end for

By using lemma 1, we obtain the solution for internal infimum $R(\mathbf{u}_T)$. Substituting (9) back in (7), we obtain the following form of the minmax problem,

$$\min_{\hat{y}_T} \max_{y_T} \ G(\hat{y}_t, y_t), \tag{10}$$

$$\textit{where } G(\hat{y}_t, y_t) = \sum_{t=1}^{T}(y_t - \hat{y}_t)^2 - (\sum_{t=1}^{T} y_t^2 - \mathbf{b}_T^{\top}\mathbf{A}_T^{-1}\mathbf{b}_T).$$

The min-max optimization problem is defined that function $G(\hat{y}_t, y_t)$ should be minimal in $\hat{y}_T$ and maximal in y_T. Equipped with lemma 1, we derive the optimal solution for the min-max problem in Eq. (10) in the following theorem.

THEOREM 1. *For all $T \geq 1$ and $y_t \in \{\pm 1\}$, the optimal prediction for the function $\hat{y}_T = \min_{\hat{y}_T} \max_{y_T} G(\hat{y}_t, y_t)$ is*

$$\hat{y}_T = sign(\mathbf{b}_{T-1}^{\top}\mathbf{A}_T^{-1}\mathbf{m}_T) \tag{11}$$

We leave the proof in the Appendix.

Note that the predicted solution p_T can turn to be a linear predictor by $p_T = \mathbf{w}_{T-1}^{\top}\mathbf{m}_T$ for $\mathbf{w}_{T-1} = \mathbf{A}_T^{-1}\mathbf{b}_{T-1}$. In this case, the form of the derived algorithm can be comparable to the best linear function $\mathbf{u}$. We call the algorithm (defined using (11) and (8)) MOOLG, a Minmax Optimization for Online Learning on Graph. However, it is not efficient for MOOLG to perform update in each iteration. To make it scalable on large graphs, we adopt a mistake-driven update rule, motivated by [5], to let update issued only when an error ($\hat{y}_t \neq y_t$) occurs. Note that our update format is different from [5], because it adds additional input-covariance $\mathbf{m}_t\mathbf{m}_t^{\top}$ to matrix $\mathbf{A}_t$ to avoid overfitting in classification. Moreover, MOOLG is different from OLLGC [18], since it adds the current node into the weight vector $\mathbf{w}_t$ for label prediction. We summarize our proposed online algorithm on graph MOOLG in Algorithm 1.

5. SELECTIVE SAMPLING ON GRAPH

In this section, we first introduce the setting of selective sampling. Then we propose a confidence-based query method and theoretically evaluate the effectiveness of the queried labels.

5.1 Problem Statement

Unlike the traditional online algorithm that queries all labels, selective sampling has to decide whether to query label or not for each coming node $\mathbf{m}_t$ ($t < T$). If label is queried of, the algorithm can update learner with $\mathbf{m}_t$ and y_t; otherwise, no action is performed and learner continues to proceed next one. Query and update decisions are denoted as binary variables Q_t and Z_t at time t. When $Q_t = 1$ iif label y_t is queried of; $Q_t = 0$, no query conducted. The update decision Z_t is similar setting. Note that selective sampling is an online version of active learning. Thus, its best predictor can be derived in a form of online learning with query/update choice on each node, $\mathbf{w}_{t-1} = \mathbf{A}_t^{-1}\mathbf{b}_{t-1}$, where $\mathbf{A}_t = b\mathbf{I} + \sum_{i=1}^{t} Q_i Z_i 2\mathbf{m}_i\mathbf{m}_i^{\top}$ and $\mathbf{b}_t = \sum_{i=1}^{t} Q_i Z_i y_i \mathbf{m}_i$.

The derived model can turn to be a recursive form in terms of $\mathbf{A}_t^{-1}$ and $\mathbf{b}_t$. The recursive form for $\mathbf{b}_t$ is:

$$\mathbf{b}_t = \mathbf{b}_{t-1} + Q_t Z_t y_t \mathbf{m}_t. \tag{12}$$

Using Sherman-Morrisan Identity [2], a non-inverted recursive form for $\mathbf{A}_t^{-1}$ is derived:

$$\begin{aligned} \mathbf{A}_t^{-1} &= (\mathbf{A}_{t-1} + Q_t Z_t 2\mathbf{m}_t\mathbf{m}_t^{\top})^{-1} \\ &= \mathbf{A}_{t-1}^{-1} - \frac{Q_t Z_t \mathbf{A}_{t-1}^{-1}\mathbf{m}_t\mathbf{m}_t^{\top}\mathbf{A}_{t-1}^{-1}}{\frac{1}{2} + \mathbf{m}_t^{\top}\mathbf{A}_{t-1}^{-1}\mathbf{m}_t}. \end{aligned}$$

As a result, matrix $\mathbf{A}_t^{-1}$ can be calculated incrementally with time complexity of $O(d^2)$ whenever the update is invoked (i.e. $Q_t Z_t = 1$).

5.2 Confidence-based Query

The purpose of selective sampling algorithm is to make few mistakes with small amount of queries. To achieve this goal, we propose a randomized query tuning by a confidence score Θ_t: a coin with bias $2h/(2h + \max(0, \Theta_t))$ is flipped; if the coin turns up heads, then actual label y_t is queried; otherwise $Q_t = 0$ and no query performed. The randomized query has been considered in several works [7, 25]. Unlike these methods, we introduce a new confidence Θ_t in a randomized query. We start with the notations below,

$$r_t = \mathbf{m}_t^{\top}\mathbf{A}_{t-1}^{-1}\mathbf{m}_t. \tag{13}$$

Then an additional notation can be derived,

$$\begin{aligned} &\mathbf{m}_t^{\top}\mathbf{A}_t^{-1}\mathbf{m}_t = \mathbf{m}_t^{\top}(\mathbf{A}_{t-1} + 2\mathbf{m}_t\mathbf{m}_t^{\top})^{-1}\mathbf{m}_t \\ &= \mathbf{m}_t^{\top}(\mathbf{A}_{t-1}^{-1} - \frac{\mathbf{A}_{t-1}^{-1}\mathbf{m}_t\mathbf{m}_t^{\top}\mathbf{A}_{t-1}^{-1}}{\frac{1}{2} + \mathbf{m}_t^{\top}\mathbf{A}_{t-1}^{-1}\mathbf{m}_t})\mathbf{m}_t \overset{(13)}{=} \frac{r_t}{1 + 2r_t}. \end{aligned} \tag{14}$$

DEFINITION 1. *(Confidence-based Query) Given any input node $\mathbf{m}_t, t \in [1, T]$, an algorithm predicts label with $p_t = \mathbf{b}_{t-1}^{\top}\mathbf{A}_t^{-1}\mathbf{m}_t$. Given $h > 0$, a probability of query can be computed by a randomized method tuning by Θ_t,*

$$\frac{2h}{2h + \max(0, \Theta_t)}, \tag{15}$$

where $\Theta_t = \Theta(p_t, r_t) = p_t^2 + 2|p_t| - \frac{r_t}{1+2r_t}$.

The Θ_t is a function parameterized by the variables p_t and r_t, which have been used for label query in several works. The quantity p_t, defined as "margin", is a distance of an input to the model boundary [5, 7], while the r_t as "uncertainty" is a projection of current input into the spectrum of observed instances [6, 18, 10]. We observe that Θ_t is positively related to p_t while negatively related to r_t, that is, the query will be not issued only when a node is far from boundary with a large margin (i.e. $|p_t|$) as well as the model has less uncertain (i.e. r_t) towards its prediction. In this condition, the algorithm has a high confidence Θ_t toward its prediction, thus a label can be omitted safely with a low probability of query based on $\frac{2h}{2h+\max(0,\Theta_t)}$. Note that while extensive works mentioned above were studied in both two variables, we proposed a new method to combine p_t and r_t to make a query decision. We will further study the effectiveness of our confidence query in the following theorem.

Intuitively, a query decision is effective iff it can control the probability of making a mistake when the algorithm does not query this label. To analyze the effectiveness of the query decision, we derive a mistake bound for an online algorithm that trains on only queried labels $\{t : Q_t = 1\}$. We start with the following lemma.

LEMMA 2. *For all $t \geq 1$, $R_t(\mathbf{u})$ is an online graph regularization over $\mathbf{u}$. An online algorithm predicts with $p_t = \mathbf{b}_{t-1}^\top \mathbf{A}_t^{-1}\mathbf{m}_t$, then the following equality folds,*

$$(y_t - p_t)^2 + \inf_{\mathbf{u}} R_{t-1}(\mathbf{u}) - \inf_{\mathbf{u}} R_t(\mathbf{u}) = \frac{r_t}{1+2r_t} - r_t p_t^2.$$

PROOF. We omit the proof due to the limited space. But similar proof can be found at [13] Theorem 3. □

In our randomized query, the mistake trials can be partitioned into two disjoint sets, set $\mathcal{S} = \{t : \frac{2h}{2h+\max(0,\Theta_t)} < 1\}$ includes indices on which a stochastic query is conduct, while set $\mathcal{D} = \{t : \frac{2h}{2h+\max(0,\Theta_t)} = 1\}$ includes indices when there is a deterministic query. We denote $\mathcal{M} = \{t : y_t p_t \leq 0\}$ as the set of mistake trials and let $M = |\mathcal{M}|$. We let $\mathcal{U}_t = \{i \leq t : Z_i Q_i = 1\}$ be the set of updates. Finally, we denote $\ell(x)$ is a hinge loss over x.

THEOREM 2. *Let an arbitrary node-label sequence $(\mathbf{m}_t, y_t)$, where $t > 1$, an online learning (i.e. MOOLG) learns on only queried trials $\{t : Q_t = 1, s.t. Q_t \sim \frac{2h}{2h+\max(0,\Theta_t)}\}$ $(h > 0)$, then the following inequality holds for any $\mathbf{u} \in \mathbb{R}^d$,*

$$\mathbb{E}[M] \leq \frac{h}{2}\mathbf{u}^\top \mathbb{E}[A_{\mathcal{U}_T}]\mathbf{u} + \mathbb{E}[\sum_{t\in\mathcal{U}_T} \ell(y_t \mathbf{u}^\top \mathbf{m}_t)] + \frac{1}{2h}\mathbb{E}[\sum_{t\in\mathcal{D}} \frac{r_t}{1+2r_t}].$$

The expectation of queried label is upper bound by $\mathbb{E}[|\mathcal{D}| + \sum_{t\in\mathcal{S}} \frac{2h}{2h+\max(0,\Theta_t)}]$.

PROOF. In lemma 2, if the trial is such that $Z_t Q_t = 0$, then $\mathcal{U}_t = \mathcal{U}_{t-1}$ with no update, which yields $\inf_{\mathbf{u}} R_t(\mathbf{u}) = \inf_{\mathbf{u}} R_{t-1}(\mathbf{u})$. Hence the equality,

$$Z_t Q_t (y_t - p_t)^2 \overset{(13)(14)}{=} \inf_{\mathbf{u}} R_t(\mathbf{u}) - \inf_{\mathbf{u}} R_{t-1}(\mathbf{u}) + Z_t Q_t \frac{r_t}{1+2r_t} - Z_t Q_t r_t p_t^2,$$

holds for all trials t. We drop the term $-Z_t Q_t r_t p_t^2$, which is negative ($r_t \geq 0$ and $p_t^2 \geq 0$), and sum over $t = 1, \ldots, T$. Note that $\inf_{\mathbf{u}} R_1(\mathbf{u}) = 0$, Expanding the squares in both sides and performing manipulation, we obtain

$$\sum_t Z_t Q_t (y_t^2 - 2y_t p_t + p_t^2 - \frac{r_t}{1+2r_t}) = \inf_{\mathbf{u}} R_T(\mathbf{u}) - \inf_{\mathbf{u}} R_1(\mathbf{u}) \leq \sum_t Z_t Q_t (y_t^2 - 2y_t \mathbf{u}^\top \mathbf{m}_t) + \mathbf{u}^\top (b\mathbf{I} + 2\sum_{t=1}^{T} Z_t Q_t \mathbf{m}_t \mathbf{m}_t^\top)\mathbf{u},$$

holding for any $\mathbf{u} \in \mathbb{R}^d$. Since $\mathbf{u}$ is a random variable, we use $h\mathbf{u}$ to replace $\mathbf{u}$ where $h > 0$. Using inequality $1 - x \leq \max\{1 - x, 0\}$ yields $hZ_tQ_t - hZ_tQ_ty_t\mathbf{u}^\top\mathbf{m}_t \leq hZ_tQ_t\ell(y_t\mathbf{u}^\top\mathbf{m}_t)$. Observing $-y_t p_t = |p_t|$ whenever an error $Z_t Q_t = 1$, we simplify with the notations $\mathbf{A}_t$ and Θ_t,

$$\sum_{t=1}^{T} \mathbb{E}[Z_t Q_t (\Theta_t + 2h)] \leq h^2 \mathbf{u}^\top \mathbb{E}[\mathbf{A}_{\mathcal{U}_T}]\mathbf{u} + 2h\mathbb{E}[\sum_{t\in\mathcal{U}_T} \ell(y_t \mathbf{u}^\top \mathbf{m}_t)]. \tag{16}$$

When an error incurs at trial $t \in \mathcal{M}$, the function Θ_t can be positive ($t \in \mathcal{M} \cap \mathcal{S}$) or negative ($t \in \mathcal{M} \cap \mathcal{D}$): In the former subcase, Q_t is random variable with expectation $\mathbb{E}[Q_t] = \frac{2h}{2h+\Theta_t}$ and thus

$$\mathbb{E}[Z_t Q_t (\Theta_t + 2h)] = \mathbb{E}[Z_t]\mathbb{E}[Q_t(\Theta_t + 2h)] = 2h\mathbb{E}[Z_t];$$

In the later subcase, $\mathbb{E}[Q_t] = 1$. We bound

$$\mathbb{E}[Z_t Q_t (p_t^2 + 2|p_t| - \frac{r_t}{1+2r_t} + 2h)] \geq \mathbb{E}[Z_t(-\frac{r_t}{1+2r_t} + 2h)] \geq 2h\mathbb{E}[Z_t] - \mathbb{E}[\frac{r_t}{1+2r_t}].$$

To summarize,

$$\sum_{t=1}^{T} \mathbb{E}[Z_t Q_t (\Theta_t + 2h)] \geq \sum_{t\in\mathcal{M}\cap\mathcal{D}} (2h\mathbb{E}[Z_t] - \mathbb{E}[\frac{r_t}{1+2r_t}]) + \sum_{t\in\mathcal{M}\cap\mathcal{S}} 2h\mathbb{E}[Z_t] \geq 2h\mathbb{E}[M] - \mathbb{E}[\sum_{t\in\mathcal{D}} \frac{r_t}{1+2r_t}].$$

Equipped with Eq. (16), we complete our proof. Note that labels are selected randomly. Thus, all expectations occurring are w.r.t this randomization. □

REMARK 1. *Online algorithm, i.e. MOOLG, run on these queried labels achieves a comparable mistake bound with the fully-supervised algorithm OLLGC ([18], Corollary 5), due to two reasons. First, $\sum_{t\in\mathcal{D}} \frac{r_t}{1+2r_t} \leq \sum_{t\in\mathcal{D}} \mathbf{m}_t A_t^{-1}\mathbf{m}_t \leq \sum_{i=1}^{d} \log(1 + \frac{\lambda_i}{b}) \leq \log T$, where $\lambda_i, i \in [1, d]$ are eigenvalues of matrix A_t. Second, $\mathbf{u}^\top A_{\mathcal{U}_T}\mathbf{u} = \sum_{t\in\mathcal{U}_T} (\mathbf{u}^\top \mathbf{m}_t)^2 \leq \mu\|\mathbf{u}\|^2 = \mu\mathbf{f}^\top\mathbf{L}\mathbf{f}$, assuming $\|\mathbf{m}_t\|^2 \leq B$ and $\mu = MB$. In addition, this mistake bound on the queried labels is comparable with the bound of MOOLG learning on all labels. Similar with loss bound of min-max online algorithm learning on all labels in [13] Theorem 3, MOOLG run on all labels is bound by the cumulative loss of optimal linear predictor and $\log|A_T| \leq \log T$, which is comparable with mistake bound run on queried labels. In general, the MOOLG learning on these queried labels performs not worse than OLLGC and MOOLG that queries all labels in expectation. In other word, our query method is effective to control the probability of making a mistake when it decides not to query this label.*

5.3 The Proposed Algorithm and Theoretical Analysis

Inspired by the confidence-based query, we propose a new selective sampling on graph. We call our algorithm CQSS-G, the Confidence-based Query for Selective Sampling on Graph, as present in Algorithm 2. It maintains two quantities: $\mathbf{A}_t^{-1}$ and $\mathbf{b}_t$ with initial values $\mathbf{A}_0 = b\mathbf{I}$ and $\mathbf{b}_0 = \mathbf{0}$. At each round t, the algorithm observes a node $\mathbf{m}_t$ and predicts its binary label with the learner $\mathbf{w}_t = \mathbf{A}_t^{-1}\mathbf{b}_{t-1}$. Then its actual label y_t is revealed with a probability of $\frac{2h}{2h+\max(0,\Theta_t)}$, which yields to a stochastic query and deterministic query.

Algorithm 2 CQSSG: Confidence-based randomized Query for Selective Sampling on Graph

Input: Adjacency matrix $\mathbf{S}$, rank d, regularization parameter b, query ratio parameter h.
Output: $\mathbf{w}_T$
Compute $\mathbf{L}^{\dagger}$ and $\mathbf{M} \in \mathbb{R}^d$
Initialize: $\mathbf{A}_0 = b\mathbf{I}$, $\mathbf{b}_0 = \mathbf{0}$
for $t = 1, \ldots, T$ **do**
  Receive $\mathbf{m}_t \in R^d$
  Compute $p_t = \mathbf{b}_{t-1}^{\top}\mathbf{A}_t^{-1}\mathbf{m}_t$ and $r_t = \mathbf{m}_t^{\top}\mathbf{A}_{t-1}^{-1}\mathbf{m}_t$
  Compute $\Theta_t = p_t^2 + 2|p_t| - \frac{r_t}{1+2r_t}$
  if $\frac{2h}{2h+\max(0,\Theta_t)} = 1(i.e. \Theta_t \leq 0)$ **then**
    Set $Q_t = 1$ and $Z_t = 1$
    Query label $y_t \in \{\pm 1\}$
  else
    Generate $Q_t \sim \frac{2h}{2h+\max(0,\Theta_t)}$
    if $Q_t = 1$ **then**
      Query label $y_t \in \{\pm 1\}$
      Set $Z_t = 1$ if $y_t \neq \hat{y}_t$ ($Z_t = 0$ otherwise)
    end if
  end if
  Update $\mathbf{b}_t = \mathbf{b}_{t-1} + Q_t Z_t y_t \mathbf{m}_t$
  Update $\mathbf{A}_t^{-1} = \mathbf{A}_{t-1}^{-1} - \frac{Q_t Z_t \mathbf{A}_{t-1}^{-1}\mathbf{m}_t\mathbf{m}_t^{\top}\mathbf{A}_{t-1}^{-1}}{\frac{1}{2}+\mathbf{m}_t^{\top}\mathbf{A}_{t-1}^{-1}\mathbf{m}_t}$
end for

In stochastic query (i.e. $\frac{2h}{2h+\max(0,\Theta_t)} < 1$), update is driven by mistake. If an error occurs ($\hat{y}_t \neq y_t$), the algorithm updates model in terms of $\mathbf{A}_t^{-1}$ and $\mathbf{b}_t$ in a recursive way; otherwise, no action takes place and we proceed the next one with $\mathbf{A}_t = \mathbf{A}_{t-1}$ and $\mathbf{b}_t = \mathbf{b}_{t-1}$. We observe that a deterministic query is issued whenever $\frac{2h}{2h+\max(0,\Theta_t)} = 1$. In this case, an aggressive update is performed, that is, we update model even if no error occurs.

To further understand the aggressive method, we compute under what condition a deterministic query will be issued. A query is issued with probability 1 when $\Theta_t = |p_t|^2 + 2|p_t| - \frac{r_t}{1+2r_t} \leq 0$. By solving for $|p_t|$, we have

$$\Theta_t \leq 0 \Leftrightarrow |p_t| \leq \theta(r_t) = -1 + \sqrt{1 + \frac{r_t}{1+2r_t}}, \tag{17}$$

If $|p_t|$ is less than $\theta(r_t)$, a deterministic query/update is conducted, while $|p_t|$ is above $\theta(r_t)$ (i.e. $\Theta_t > 0$), a query will be issued with a probability strictly less than 1. And the upper bound of $\theta(r_t)$ increases with r_t. If $r_t = 0$ with a minimal uncertainty, a deterministic query is issued only when an input lies on the boundary (i.e. $|p_t| \leq \theta(0) = 0$). However, if $r_t = 1$ with the largest value of uncertainty, this implies that an aggressive query is issued whenever margin $|p_t|$ is no more than $\theta(1) \approx 0.16$.

In the following theoretical analysis, we show the superiority of our aggressive learning algorithm. Besides stochastic query trials $\mathcal{S}$ and deterministic query trials $\mathcal{D}$, we denote $\mathcal{C} = \{t : y_t p_t > 0, \Theta_t \leq 0\}$ as the set of trials where there is an aggressive update without predicted mistake, and let $C = |\mathcal{C}|$. We omit other trials since they do not affect the model. $\mathcal{U}_t = \{i \leq t : Z_i Q_i = 1\}$ is the update trials in Alg. 2.

THEOREM 3. *Let an arbitrary node-label pair sequence be* $(\mathbf{m}_1, y_1), \ldots, (\mathbf{m}_T, y_T)$*, our algorithm (Alg.2) runs on the sequence with* $h > 0$ *and* ℓ *is hinge loss, then for all* $\mathbf{u} \in \mathbb{R}^d$,

$$\begin{aligned}\mathbb{E}[M] \leq \frac{1}{2}h\mathbf{u}^{\top}\mathbb{E}[\mathbf{A}_{\mathcal{U}_T}]\mathbf{u} + \mathbb{E}[\sum_{t\in\mathcal{U}_T} \ell(y_t\mathbf{u}^{\top}\mathbf{m}_t)] \\ + \frac{1}{h}\mathbb{E}[\sum_{t\in\mathcal{D}} \frac{r_t}{1+2r_t}] - \mathbb{E}[C].\end{aligned} \tag{18}$$

The expected number of queries is upper bounded by $\mathbb{E}[|\mathcal{D}| + \sum_{t\in\mathcal{S}} \frac{2h}{2h+\Theta_t}]$.

PROOF. Due to limited space, we omit the theory proof. □

REMARK 2. *It is obvious that this upper mistake bound is strictly lower than the one of MOOLG in Theorem 2, due to the deduction of expectation trials* $\mathbb{E}[C]$*. In addition, The terms of the bound* $\frac{1}{h}\mathbb{E}[\sum_{t\in\mathcal{D}} \frac{r_t}{1+2r_t}] - \mathbb{E}[C]$ *is lower than the corresponding terms of [7] Thm. 3. The reason is that* $\sum_t \frac{r_t}{1+2r_t} = \sum_t \mathbf{m}_t^{\top}\mathbf{A}_t^{-1}\mathbf{m}_t \leqslant \sum_i \log(1 + \frac{\lambda_i}{b})$*. Additionally, our bound is subtracted by the update trials* $\mathbb{E}[C]$*. Hence, we summarize that our mistake bound, thanks to the additional deduction of aggressive update trials* $\mathbb{E}[C]$*, is better than the expectation version of mistake bound of MOOLG in Theorem 2 and one of conservative selective sampling algorithm ([7] Thm. 3), which is considered as a theoretical support for our aggressive learning algorithm.*

REMARK 3. $h > 0$ *is a parameter of the algorithm acting as a scaling actor in the randomized method. The parameter* h *is affected by structure of graph. If we would know in advance, by setting a proper choice*

$$h = \sqrt{\mathbb{E}[\sum_{t\in\mathcal{D}} \frac{r_t}{1+2r_t}]/(\mathbf{u}^{\top}\mathbb{E}[A_{\mathcal{U}_T}]\mathbf{u})},$$

we would minimize the bound and get

$$\begin{aligned}\mathbb{E}[M] \leq & \frac{3}{2}\sqrt{\mathbb{E}[\sum_{t\in\mathcal{D}} \frac{r_t}{1+2r_t}]\mathbf{u}^{\top}\mathbb{E}[A_{\mathcal{U}_T}]\mathbf{u}} + \mathbb{E}[\sum_{t\in\mathcal{U}_T} \ell(y_t\mathbf{u}^{\top}\mathbf{m}_t)] \\ & - \mathbb{E}[C].\end{aligned} \tag{19}$$

The first two terms of this optimized bound is same as an expectation version of the mistake bound for the standard second-order Perceptron (SOP) algorithm, proven in [5]. As it turns out, our bound in Eq. (19) would be sharper than the online algorithm SOP, since the set of updates U_T *is formed by a randomized sampling method, which is typically smaller than the mistake trials in the fully-supervised algorithm (as SOP queries all the labels, it has higher chance to update model). This tends to shrink the three terms* $\frac{1}{2}h\mathbf{u}^{\top}\mathbb{E}[A_{\mathcal{U}_T}]\mathbf{u}$, $\mathbb{E}[\sum_{t\in\mathcal{U}_T} \ell(y_t\mathbf{u}^{\top}\mathbf{m}_t)]$*, and* $\mathbb{E}[\sum_{t\in\mathcal{D}} \frac{r_t}{1+2r_t}]$*, the main components of our proposed bound. Nonetheless, their bounds are not comparable since they depend on the exact update trials in* $\mathcal{U}_T$.

REMARK 4. *As the term* $\sum_{t\in\mathcal{U}_T} \ell(y_t\mathbf{u}^{\top}\mathbf{m}_t)$ *is a cumulative hinge loss over the trials in* $\mathcal{U}_T$ *for all* $\mathbf{u} \in \mathbb{R}^d$*, the mistake bound in (18) can be re-written as one by which the total number of mistakes exceeds a cumulative loss of the best linear model* $\mathbf{u}$ *over the update trials,*

$$\begin{aligned}& \mathbb{E}[M] - \inf_{\mathbf{u}}(\mathbb{E}[\sum_{t\in\mathcal{U}_T} \ell(y_t\mathbf{u}^{\top}\mathbf{m}_t)]) \\ & \leq \frac{1}{2}h\mathbf{u}^{\top}\mathbb{E}[A_{\mathcal{U}_T}]\mathbf{u} + \frac{1}{h}\mathbb{E}[\sum_{t\in\mathcal{D}} \frac{r_t}{1+2r_t}] - \mathbb{E}[C].\end{aligned} \tag{20}$$

The $\mathbf{u}^\top A_{\mathcal{U}_T}\mathbf{u}$ always lies between $\min_k \lambda_k$ and $\max_k \lambda_k$. In particular, $\mathbf{u}^\top A_{\mathcal{U}_T}\mathbf{u} = \lambda_k$ when $\mathbf{u}$ is the eigenvector associated with λ_k. In addition, $\sum_t \frac{r_t}{1+2r_t} \leq \sum_i \log(1+\lambda_i) \leq d\log(1+T)$ is substantially smaller than $d\log T$ whenever the spectrum of matrix $\mathbf{A}_T$ is decreased rapidly. Thus, we conclude that the bound in Eq. (20) can achieve a regret of $O(\log T)$ w.r.t. the best linear model, where T is the number of trials.

6. EXPERIMENTAL RESULTS

In this section, we first introduce data sets and experimental evaluation metrics. Then we present the empirical results to evaluate the proposed algorithms.

6.1 Data Sets and Evaluation Metrics

Data Sets: We use four real-world graph data sets to evaluate the proposed algorithms.

Coauthor[2] is an undirected coauthor graph from *DBLP* dataset in four areas, *data ming, machine learning, information retrieval* and *database*. There are a total number of 1711 authors denoted as nodes, and the numbers of their coauthored papers as the weights of edges.

Cora[2] contains 2485 scientific publications with their citation links. Each publication is categorized into one of seven classes, they are *Case based, Genetic Algorithms, Neural Networks, Probabilistic Methods, Reinforcement Learning, Rule Learning* and *Theory*.

IMDB[3] is a graph that contains up-to-date movie information. The graph is modeled by co-actor association from 17046 movies of four genres: *Romance, Action, Animation* and *Thriller*.

PubMed[4] contains 19717 scientific publications pertaining to diabetes categorized by one of three types. Citation network in PubMed consists of 44338 links.

We assume that graphs are undirected and connected. If some edges are directed, they are transformed into undirected graphs.If they are disconnected, the biggest connected subgraph is selected to study. Table 1 summarizes the statistic results of data sets above.

Table 1: Description of the data sets

	Coauthor	*Cora*	*IMDB*	*PubMed*
#nodes	1,711	2,485	17,046	19,717
#links	7,507	10,138	993,528	88,651
#classes	4	7	4	3

Evaluation Matrics and Parameter Setting: We evaluate the performance of selective sampling with two measures: (i) cumulative error rate, (ii) number of queried labels. Circulative error rate evaluates the prediction accuracy of online learning algorithm while queried label number shows the label efficiency of an algorithm. It indicates that the smaller both two measures, the better the performance of an algorithm. We compare the proposed algorithms with three baselines that are discussed in Section 2. We next introduce the algorithms we study and their parameter settings as follows:

GPA [20] is the state-of-the-art first order nonparametric online learning algorithm on graph. Note that the Perceptron algorithm is not affected by the step-size.

OLLGC and **SSLGC** [18] are two second-order active online learning algorithms on graph. All parameters are tuned with grid search on a held-out random shuffle.

MOOLG and **CQSSG**: are the proposed second-order online learning and selective sampling on graph. For both two methods, the parameter d is set to 100 since these algorithms achieve low error rate with small queried number. We tune b with the grid $\{10^{-3}, 10^{-2}, \ldots, 10\}$ on a held-out random shuffle. In CQSSG, we set $h = 0.01$ for Cora and Coauthor, $h = 0.001$ for IMDB and PubMed due to graph structure variable.

In order to compare these algorithms fairly, we randomly shuffle the sample ordering for each dataset. We run algorithms 20 times for each dataset and compute the average result. Finally, the above algorithms are designed for binary classification. In order to apply the algorithms to those data sets with multiple classes, we use one-vs-other scheme to adapt binary classifiers to the multi-class scenarios.

6.2 Results of Selective Sampling Algorithm

The experimental results are presented in Table 2. We found that CQSSG outperforms all baselines consistently across all four data sets. We also show the results with respect to the round of online learning in Fig.1. In all subfigures, the horizontal-axis represents the rounds of online learning, while the vertical-axis is the cumulative error rate and queried nodes, averaging over 20 times of shuffling order.

We can see the our improvement over GPA are always significant on every data set. This is consistent with previous observations in online learning: second-order algorithms are generally better than first-order algorithm [33]. The reason is due to the matrix $\mathbf{A}_t$ which has a spectral structure to correlate with a best estimator $\mathbf{u}$ for observed instances [5].

MOOLG achieves comparable results with other two algorithms OLLGC or SSLGC. It is because the MOOLG outputs a minmax prediction with a low regret with optimal linear model. However, when graph nodes are adversarially generated, MOOLG can bound the choice of adversary and achieves a more robust performance than the ridge regression model [32].

CQSSG always enjoys smaller error rates than SSLGC with much fewer queried nodes (P-value < 0.001), which shows our algorithm can save the labeling while maintains the high quality of prediction result. Generally speaking, the good performance is due to two reasons. First, the confidence-based query improves the label-efficiency of algorithm. Second, thanks to the aggressive learning, CQSSG can achieve a convergence stage quickly, thus the query rate is reduced further when the model has learned sufficient knowledge of data.

6.3 Sensitivity Study on the Impact of Query Ratio

We study the impact of parameter $h > 0$ in the query method. The selective sampling algorithm with a small h would perform few number of queries. In specific, we set h to $\{10^{-4}, 10^{-3}, \ldots, 1\}$ and calculate the average ratio of query for each value of h over the 20 times of experiments. The comparison results is shown in Fig.2.

We observe that CQSSG achieves the best performance consistently under different ratios of queried nodes, which validates the label-efficiency of our method. SSLGC updates the model only when an error occurs, thus it wastes some

[2]http://www.cs.umd.edu/ sen/lbc-proj/data/
[3]http://www.imdb.com/
[4]http://www.cs.umd.edu/projects/linqs/projects/lbc/

Table 2: Comparison of the online algorithms for graph classification on several datasets.

Algorithm	*Coauthor* Error rate	*Coauthor* # Queried nodes	*Cora* Error rate	*Cora* # Queried nodes
GPA	0.2326±0.0048	1711	0.1169±0.0022	2485
OLLGC	0.1838±0.0032	1711	0.0758±0.0013	2485
SSLGC	0.1854±0.0031	1275.30±21.91	0.0832±0.0019	1525.48±19.32
MOOLG	0.1810±0.0029	1711	0.0760±0.0014	2485
CQSSG	**0.1444±0.0031**	**305.02±46.412**	**0.0566±0.0022**	**299.23±29.34**

Algorithm	*IMDB* Error rate	*IMDB* # Queried nodes	*PubMed* Error rate	*PubMed* # Queried nodes
GPA	0.3362±0.0025	17046	0.2256±0.0025	19717
OLLGC	0.2735±0.0038	17046	0.1804±0.0014	19717
SSLGC	0.2709±0.0064	3453.55±91.32	0.1720±0.0050	5298.55±186.91
MOOLG	0.2710±0.0054	17046	0.1795±0.0010	19717
CQSSG	**0.2259±0.0085**	**1528.5±52.290**	**0.1476±0.0022**	**671.30±38.347**

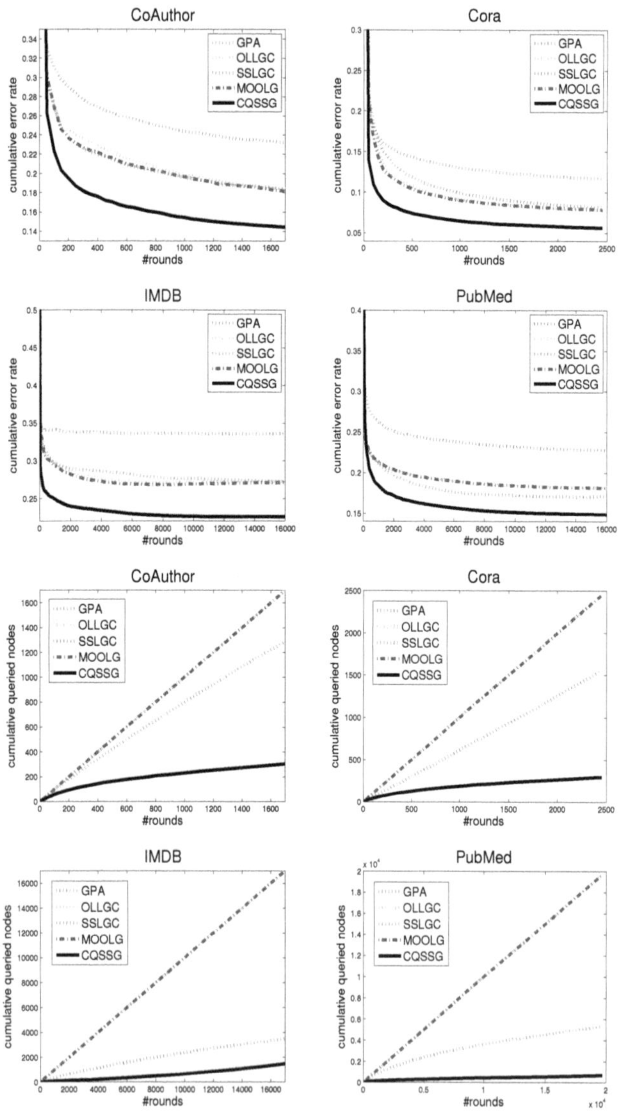

Figure 1: Cumulative error rate and number of label query with respective to online learning rounds on four datasets.

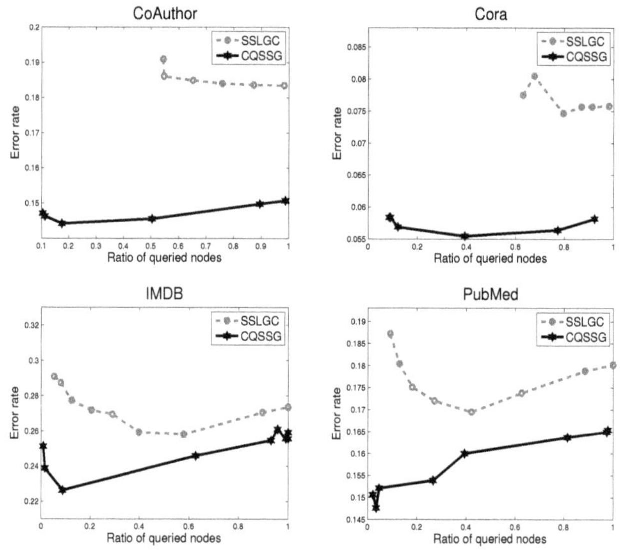

Figure 2: A comparison between CQSSG and SSLGC with respect to different ratios of queried nodes.

correctly predicted labels which are useful to improve the accuracy. Moreover, SSLGC is unable to turn into a small ratio of query in Coauthor and Cora datasets, that cannot guarantee the running process efficiently.

6.4 Sensitivity Study on Low-rank Approximation

The efficiency of the algorithm is also affected by the rank of nodes. To study the impact of low-rank graph nodes on algorithms, we set the parameter d with the grid $\{10, 100, 250, 500, 750\}$. Cora and Coauthor are used as case study since similar conclusions are obtained on IMDB and PubMed. The results in Fig.3 show that CQSSG achieves better performance than SSLGC consistently under different rank approximation.

It is observed that with a high rank, both algorithms need a high number of queries to achieve a low error rate. However, a high queried number yields to a high chance of update. It causes an additional computational cost for the algorithms which update a model with time complexity of $O(d^2)$. To achieve a balance, we choose $d = 100$ in the rest of exper-

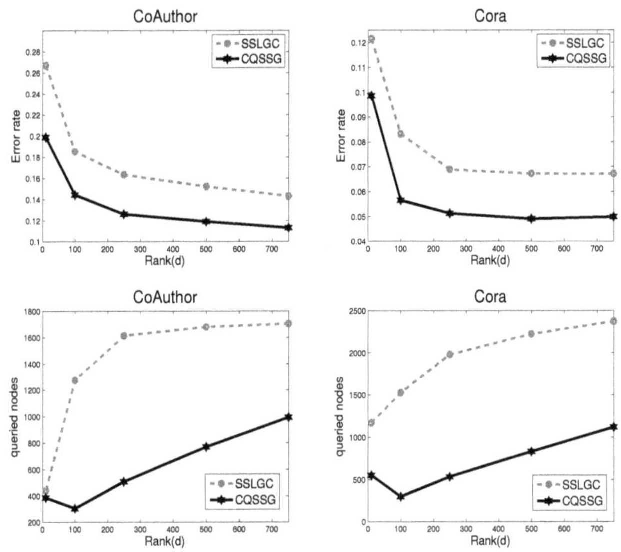

Figure 3: A case study of low rank impact on performance.

iments since the algorithm achieves a good accuracy while the queried number is quite small.

7. CONCLUSION

In this paper, we present a novel online learning and a selective sampling algorithms for graph classification based on min-max optimization. To the best of our knowledge, this is the first effort to combine the graph regularization and min-max optimization for graph classification. The derived online learning algorithm can address online graph classification problem where the labels are adversarially generated, which is realized via the min-max optimization strategy. The selective sampling algorithm can effectively reduce labeling efforts, by only querying a fraction of informative labels. Theoretical result shows that our bounds are better than other second-order online learning and selective sampling algorithms. Finally, we empirically evaluate the proposed algorithms on several real-world datasets. Promising experimental results further validate the effectiveness of the proposed algorithms compared with other baselines in terms of the cumulative error rate and the number of queried labels.

Acknowledgments

We would like to thank the anonymous reviewers for their helpful comments, and Quanquan Gu for his suggestions.

Appendix

Proof of Lemma 1

PROOF. From

$$R(\mathbf{u}) = \sum_{t=1}^{T}(\mathbf{m}_t^\top \mathbf{u} - y_t)^2 + \sum_{t=1}^{T}(\mathbf{m}_t^\top \mathbf{u})^2 + b\|\mathbf{u}\|^2$$
$$= \sum_{t=1}^{T} y_t^2 - 2\sum_{t=1}^{T} \mathbf{u}^\top (y_t \mathbf{m}_t) + \mathbf{u}^\top (b\mathbf{I} + 2\sum_{t=1}^{T} \mathbf{m}_t \mathbf{m}_t^\top)\mathbf{u}$$
$$\overset{(8)}{=} \sum_{t=1}^{T} y_t^2 - 2\mathbf{u}^\top \mathbf{b}_T + \mathbf{u}^\top \mathbf{A}_T \mathbf{u},$$

we have $\nabla R(\mathbf{u}) = 2\mathbf{A}_T\mathbf{u} - 2\mathbf{b}_T = 0$ and $\triangle R(\mathbf{u}) = 2\mathbf{A}_T \geq 0$. Thus $R(\mathbf{u})$ is convex and it achieves a minimal point if $\nabla R(\mathbf{u}) = 0$, i.e. for $\mathbf{u}_T = \mathbf{A}_T^{-1}\mathbf{b}_T$. Substituting the solution $\mathbf{u}_T = \mathbf{A}_T^{-1}\mathbf{b}_T$ back into $R(\mathbf{u}_T)$, and we have

$$R(\mathbf{u}_T) = R(\mathbf{A}_T^{-1}\mathbf{b}_T) = \sum_{t=1}^{T} y_t^2 - \mathbf{b}_T^\top \mathbf{A}_T^{-1}\mathbf{b}_T.$$

□

Proof of Theory 1

PROOF. The adversary can choose any y_T, thus the algorithm predicts $\hat{y}_T$ via minimizing the following maximization problem over y_T,

$$\max_{y_T}(\sum_{t=1}^{T}(y_t - \hat{y}_t)^2 - \sum_{t=1}^{T} y_t^2 + \mathbf{b}_T^\top \mathbf{A}_T^{-1}\mathbf{b}_T).$$

We use the equation below to re-write the optimization problem,

$$\mathbf{b}_T^\top \mathbf{A}_T^{-1}\mathbf{b}_T$$
$$= \mathbf{b}_{T-1}^\top \mathbf{A}_T^{-1}\mathbf{b}_{T-1} + 2y_T\mathbf{b}_{T-1}^\top \mathbf{A}_T^{-1}\mathbf{m}_T + y_T^2 \mathbf{m}_T^\top \mathbf{A}_T^{-1}\mathbf{m}_T.$$

Omitting all terms that are not depending on $\hat{y}_T$ and y_T,

$$\max_{y_T}((y_T - \hat{y}_T)^2 - y_T^2 + 2y_T\mathbf{b}_{T-1}^\top \mathbf{A}_T^{-1}\mathbf{m}_T + y_T^2\mathbf{m}_T^\top \mathbf{A}_T^{-1}\mathbf{m}_T)$$

We manipulate the equation to be the maximization of a polynomial form over y_T, given that $y_T \in \{\pm 1\}$,

$$\max_{y_T \in \{\pm 1\}}((\mathbf{m}_T^\top \mathbf{A}_T^{-1}\mathbf{m}_T)y_T^2 + 2(\mathbf{b}_{T-1}^\top \mathbf{A}_T^{-1}\mathbf{m}_T - \hat{y}_T)y_T + \hat{y}_T^2).$$

This is a convex function, since $\mathbf{m}_T^\top \mathbf{A}_T^{-1}\mathbf{m}_T \geq 0$ given that $\mathbf{A}_T^{-1}$ is positive definite. Thus, we only have to consider $y_T = 1$ or $y_T = -1$, the convex function reaches maximal, as follows,

$$G^{max}(\hat{y}_T) = 2|\mathbf{b}_{T-1}^\top \mathbf{A}_T^{-1}\mathbf{m}_T - \hat{y}_T| + \hat{y}_T^2 + \mathbf{m}_T^\top \mathbf{A}_T^{-1}\mathbf{m}_T.$$

Omitting the term unrelated to y_T and $\hat{y}_T$, we thus have to find a $\hat{y}_T$ in the following minimization form,

$$\hat{y}_T = \arg\min_{\hat{y}_T} 2|\mathbf{b}_{T-1}^\top \mathbf{A}_T^{-1}\mathbf{m}_T - \hat{y}_T| + \hat{y}_T^2. \qquad (21)$$

We consider two cases: 1. $\mathbf{b}_{T-1}^\top \mathbf{A}_T^{-1}\mathbf{m}_T - \hat{y}_T \geq 0$, and 2. $\mathbf{b}_{T-1}^\top \mathbf{A}_T^{-1}\mathbf{m}_T - \hat{y}_T \leq 0$:

1. For $\mathbf{b}_{T-1}^\top \mathbf{A}_T^{-1}\mathbf{m}_T \geq \hat{y}_T$, that is $\hat{y}_T \in [-\infty, \mathbf{b}_{T-1}^\top \mathbf{A}_T^{-1}\mathbf{m}_T]$, the relevant terms in Eq. (21) equals to $2(\mathbf{b}_{T-1}^\top \mathbf{A}_T^{-1}\mathbf{m}_T - \hat{y}_T) + \hat{y}_T^2$, and it achieves minimal at $\min(1, \mathbf{b}_{T-1}^\top \mathbf{A}_T^{-1}\mathbf{m}_T)$.

2. when $\mathbf{b}_{T-1}^\top \mathbf{A}_T^{-1}\mathbf{m}_T \leq \hat{y}_T$, i.e. $\hat{y}_T \in [\mathbf{b}_{T-1}^\top \mathbf{A}_T^{-1}\mathbf{m}_T, +\infty]$, Eq. (21) equals to $2(\hat{y}_T - \mathbf{b}_{T-1}^\top \mathbf{A}_T^{-1}\mathbf{m}_T) + \hat{y}_T^2$, and it reaches minimal at $\max(-1, \mathbf{b}_{T-1}^\top \mathbf{A}_T^{-1}\mathbf{m}_T)$.

Thus if $\mathbf{b}_{T-1}^\top \mathbf{A}_T^{-1}\mathbf{m}_T \in [-1, 1]$, $\hat{y}_T = \mathbf{b}_{T-1}^\top \mathbf{A}_T^{-1}\mathbf{m}_T$ achieves an optimal solution. If $\mathbf{b}_{T-1}^\top \mathbf{A}_T^{-1}\mathbf{m}_T \geq 1$, it achieves optimal at 1. The case $\mathbf{b}_{T-1}^\top \mathbf{A}_T^{-1}\mathbf{m}_T \leq -1$ is similar. In the binary classification setting where $\hat{y}_T \in \pm 1$, we set $\hat{y}_T = \text{sign}(p_T)$ where we define $p_T = \mathbf{b}_{T-1}^\top \mathbf{A}_T^{-1}\mathbf{m}_T$. □

8. REFERENCES

[1] J. Abernethy, A. Agarwal, and P. L. Bartlett. A stochastic view of optimal regret through minimax duality. In *Proceedings of the 22nd Annual Conference on Learning Theory*, 2009.

[2] M. S. Bartlett. An inverse matrix adjustment arising in discriminant analysis. *The Annals of Mathematical Statistics*, pages 107–111, 1951.

[3] M. Belkin, P. Niyogi, and V. Sindhwani. Manifold regularization: A geometric framework for learning from labeled and unlabeled examples. *The Journal of Machine Learning Research*, 7:2399–2434, 2006.

[4] G. Cavallanti, N. Cesa-Bianchi, and C. Gentile. Learning noisy linear classifiers via adaptive and selective sampling. *Machine learning*, 83(1):71–102, 2011.

[5] N. Cesa-Bianchi, A. Conconi, and C. Gentile. A second-order perceptron algorithm. *SIAM Journal on Computing*, 34(3):640–668, 2005.

[6] N. Cesa-Bianchi, C. Gentile, and F. Orabona. Robust bounds for classification via selective sampling. In *ICML-09*, pages 121–128, 2009.

[7] N. Cesa-Bianchi, C. Gentile, and L. Zaniboni. Worst-case analysis of selective sampling for linear classification. *The Journal of Machine Learning Research*, 7:1205–1230, 2006.

[8] O. Chapelle, B. Schölkopf, A. Zien, et al. *Semi-supervised learning*, volume 2. MIT press Cambridge, 2006.

[9] K. Crammer, O. Dekel, J. Keshet, S. Shalev-Shwartz, and Y. Singer. Online passive-aggressive algorithms. *JMLR*, 7:551–585, 2006.

[10] K. Crammer, M. Dredze, and F. Pereira. Confidence-weighted linear classification for text categorization. *JMLR*, 13(1):1891–1926, 2012.

[11] C. Desrosiers and G. Karypis. Within-network classification using local structure similarity. In *Machine Learning and Knowledge Discovery in Databases*, pages 260–275. 2009.

[12] C. Eckart and G. Young. The approximation of one matrix by another of lower rank. *Psychometrika*, 1(3):211–218, 1936.

[13] J. Forster. On relative loss bounds in generalized linear regression. In *Fundamentals of Computation Theory*, pages 269–280, 1999.

[14] Y. Freund, H. S. Seung, E. Shamir, and N. Tishby. Selective sampling using the query by committee algorithm. *Machine learning*, 28(2-3):133–168, 1997.

[15] C. Gentile. The robustness of the p-norm algorithms. *Machine Learning*, 53(3):265–299, 2003.

[16] G. Giacinto, F. Roli, and L. Didaci. Fusion of multiple classifiers for intrusion detection in computer networks. *Pattern recognition letters*, 24(12):1795–1803, 2003.

[17] A. B. Goldberg, X. Zhu, A. Furger, and J.-M. Xu. Oasis: Online active semi-supervised learning. In *AAAI*, 2011.

[18] Q. Gu, C. Aggarwal, J. Liu, and J. Han. Selective sampling on graphs for classification. In *Proceedings of the 19th ACM SIGKDD*, pages 131–139, 2013.

[19] M. Herbster, G. Lever, and M. Pontil. Online prediction on large diameter graphs. In *NIPS-09*, pages 649–656, 2009.

[20] M. Herbster and M. Pontil. Prediction on a graph with a perceptron. In *NIPS-06*, pages 577–584, 2006.

[21] M. Herbster, M. Pontil, and L. Wainer. Online learning over graphs. In *ICML-05*, pages 305–312, 2005.

[22] S. C. Hoi, J. Wang, and P. Zhao. Libol: A library for online learning algorithms. *The Journal of Machine Learning Research*, 15(1):495–499, 2014.

[23] M. Ji, J. Han, and M. Danilevsky. Ranking-based classification of heterogeneous information networks. In *Proceedings of the 17th ACM SIGKDD*, pages 1298–1306, 2011.

[24] D. Kushnir. Active-transductive learning with label-adapted kernels. In *Proceedings of the 20th ACM SIGKDD*, pages 462–471, 2014.

[25] F. Orabona and N. Cesa-Bianchi. Better algorithms for selective sampling. In *ICML-11*, pages 433–440, 2011.

[26] F. Orabona and K. Crammer. New adaptive algorithms for online classification. In *NIPS-10*, pages 1840–1848, 2010.

[27] M. Pennacchiotti and A.-M. Popescu. A machine learning approach to twitter user classification. *ICWSM*, 11:281–288, 2011.

[28] A. A. Ross, K. Nandakumar, and A. K. Jain. *Handbook of multibiometrics*, volume 6. Springer Science & Business Media, 2006.

[29] N. Slonim, E. Yom-Tov, and K. Crammer. Active online classification via information maximization. In *IJCAI*, volume 22, page 1498, 2011.

[30] A. J. Smola and R. Kondor. Kernels and regularization on graphs. In *Learning theory and kernel machines*, pages 144–158. Springer, 2003.

[31] E. Takimoto and M. K. Warmuth. The last-step minimax algorithm. In *Algorithmic Learning Theory*, pages 279–290, 2000.

[32] V. Vovk. Competitive on-line linear regression. *NIPS-98*, pages 364–370, 1998.

[33] J. Wang, P. Zhao, and S. C. Hoi. Exact soft confidence-weighted learning. In *ICML-12*, pages 121–128, 2012.

[34] Z. Yang, J. Tang, and Y. Zhang. Active learning for streaming networked data. In *CIKM-14*, pages 1129–1138, 2014.

[35] P. Zhao and S. C. Hoi. Cost-sensitive online active learning with application to malicious url detection. In *Proceedings of the 19th ACM SIGKDD*, pages 919–927. ACM, 2013.

[36] P. Zhao, S. C. Hoi, and R. Jin. Double updating online learning. *The Journal of Machine Learning Research*, 12:1587–1615, 2011.

[37] P. Zhao, S. C. H. Hoi, R. Jin, and T. Yang. Online AUC maximization. In *Proceedings of the 28th International Conference on Machine Learning, ICML 2011, Bellevue, Washington, USA, June 28 - July 2, 2011*, pages 233–240, 2011.

[38] P. Zhao, S. C. H. Hoi, J. Wang, and B. Li. Online transfer learning. *Artificial Intelligence*, 216:76–102, 2014.

An Inference Approach to Basic Level of Categorization

Zhongyuan Wang [♮,†,1] Haixun Wang [‡,2] Ji-Rong Wen [♮,3] Yanghua Xiao [#,4]

[♮]Renmin University of China, Beijing, China [†]Microsoft Research, Beijing, China [‡]Facebook, Menlo Park, CA, USA [#]Fudan University, Shanghai, China

[1]wzhy@outlook.com [2]haixun@gmail.com [3]jirong.wen@gmail.com [4]shawyh@fudan.edu.cn

ABSTRACT

Humans understand the world by classifying objects into an appropriate level of categories. This process is often automatic and subconscious. Psychologists and linguists call it as *Basic-level Categorization (BLC)*. BLC can benefit lots of applications such as knowledge panel, advertising and recommendation. However, how to quantify basic-level concepts is still an open problem. Recently, much work focuses on constructing knowledge bases or semantic networks from web scale text corpora, which makes it possible for the first time to analyze computational approaches for deriving BLC. In this paper, we introduce a method based on *typicality* and *PMI* for BLC. We compare it with a few existing measures such as *NPMI* and *commute time* to understand its essence, and conduct extensive experiments to show the effectiveness of our approach. We also give a real application example to show how BLC can help sponsored search.

Categories and Subject Descriptors

I.2.4 [**Artificial Intelligence**]: Knowledge Representation Formalisms and Methods—*Representations (procedural and rule-based), Semantic networks*

General Terms

Theory

Keywords

Semantic Network; Conceptualization; Basic Level of Categorization

1. INTRODUCTION

Humans understand the world by classifying objects into concepts. The concepts an object belongs to form a set of hierarchically organized categories, ranging from extremely general to extremely specific [23]. Furthermore, different levels of categorization reflect different levels of abstraction, which associate with different properties.

CIKM'15, October 19–23, 2015, Melbourne, Australia.

ACM 978-1-4503-3794-6/15/10 ...$15.00.
DOI: http://dx.doi.org/10.1145/2806416.2806533 .

1.1 Basic-level category

A human being usually maps an object to an appropriate level of category, and regard the object as equivalent to other objects in the category. For example, one would say `I have a house, a car, and a dog` instead of `I have asset, vehicle, and mammal`. Similarly, when someone sees an `iPhone 6`, he most likely thinks of *high end smartphone* or *Apple's product*, instead of *item* or *popular cellular wireless network phone*. For humans, this process of categorization is often automatic and subconscious, and psychologists call the process *Basic-level Categorization (a.k.a. Basic-level Conceptualization, or **BLC** for short)*.

BLC is important because it provides rich information with little cognitive efforts [23]. When a person obtains the basic-level category of an unfamiliar object, he will associate the object with the known properties of the basic category, and he suddenly understands almost everything about the object. The fact that he can do this with *little cognitive efforts*[1] has intrigued and pushed researchers to better understand BLC. One of the most important properties of BLC was obtained by Rosch et al. [24]. We summarize their findings in Table 1, which shows that, at the basic level, *perceived similarity among category members is maximized and perceived similarities across contrasting categories is minimized.* As a result, the basic-level category of an object is usually in the middle of the object's taxonomic hierarchies.

Category Level	Informative?	Distinctive?
Superordinate	No	Yes
Basic-level	Yes	Yes
Subordinate	Yes	No

Table 1: Differences among category levels

As an example, consider the term `Microsoft`, which can be categorized into a large number of concepts, for example, *company, large company, Redmond IT giant*, etc. Let us take a closer look at the following three concepts:

1. *company*
2. *software company*
3. *largest OS vendor*

Both 1 and 3 are highly related to `Microsoft` in the sense that when we think of `Microsoft`, we think of it as a

[1]It is shown that three-year-olds already master basic-level categorization perfectly [16].

company, and when we think of *largest OS vendor*, we think of `Microsoft`. However, neither of them is an appropriate basic-level concept for `Microsoft`. To see this, assume we want to find objects that are similar to `Microsoft`. If we go through *company*, we may find objects such as `McDonald's` and `ExxonMobil`, which have not much similarity to `Microsoft`. If we go through *largest OS vendor*, we may not be able to find any reasonable object other than `Microsoft`. On the other hand, if we go through *software company*, we may find `Oracle`, `Adobe`, `IBM`, which are a lot more similar to `Microsoft`. Thus, *software company* is a more appropriate basic-level concept for `Microsoft`, or in other words, properties associated with *software company* are more readily applied to `Microsoft`, which is also the reason why through *software company* we can find many objects that are similar to `Microsoft`.

Unfortunately, although much work has been done on this topic, we still do not have a clean formula to infer the basic-level category for any given object. In other words, we do not know how to pick *software company* from thousands of concepts that `Microsoft` belongs to. Psychologists have used word association tests on human subjects to infer concepts that may correspond to the basic-level categories [24]. But such approaches do not scale. On the other hand, an increasing number of applications in the field of information retrieval, natural language understanding, and artificial intelligence require a computational approach for BLC. Short text conceptualization [25, 15, 14, 30] in one of the fundamental techniques. It maps a short text to the concept space, and can benefit web table understanding [28], query intent detection [29], query recommendation [27], etc. BLC is the basic unit of conceptualization, and is crucial for short text conceptualization.

1.2 Applications

For many applications, including query understanding and ads matching, finding an object's basic-level category is important. Here, we give two real life applications that may serve to demonstrate the need of BLC.

- **Knowledge panel**: Search engines display a *knowledge panel* for queries that contain well-known entities. Fig. 1(a) shows the content of Google's knowledge panel when people search for `Albert Einstein`. Similarly, Bing also provides knowledge panel (As Fig. 1(b) shows). It is worth noting that `Albert Einstein` is labeled as a *theoretical physicist*, which, compared to *world famous German-born American physicist* or just *physicist*, is arguably the "just-right" concept to describe `Albert Einstein`. Unfortunately, there is no good inferencing mechanism to derive such "just-right" concepts, and as a result such labels are currently hand-created by human editors.

- **Advertising and recommendation**: Recommending entities similar to a given entity is important in many applications. As an example, for users who show interest in `Samsung Galaxy S5`, we may want to recommend `HTC One M8` or `iPhone 6`, rather than `Samsung LED TV`. As we know, an entity's basic-level category usually contains many entities that are similar to the entity. In the above example, entities in the category of *popular smartphone* or *high end smartphone* may be good candidates. Thus, knowing the basic-level category enables us to provide good recommendations. Currently, good recommendations are usually based on signals from click logs, but click logs are not always available, especially for new entities.

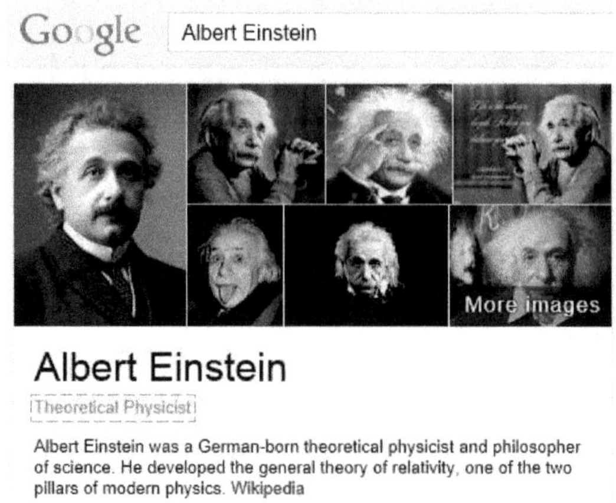

(a) Google's knowledge panel

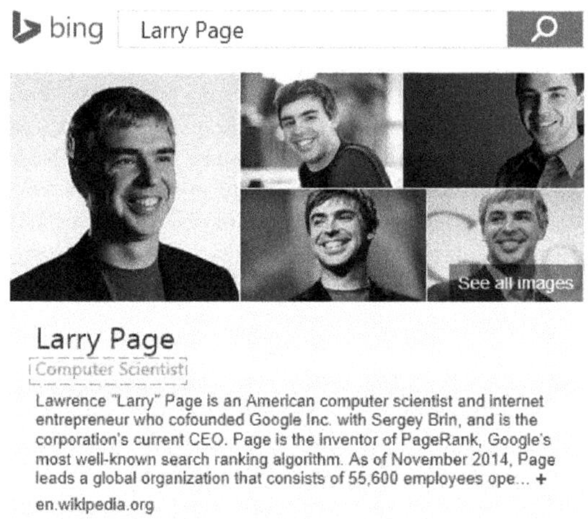

(b) Bing's knowledge panel

Figure 1: Examples of the Application for BLC

1.3 Computational approaches for BLC

The rise of applications such as those mentioned above is pushing for computational approaches for BLC. It has become clear that a better understanding of the human cognitive process helps us build machines that understand the human world. In recent years, a large variety of knowledge bases [3, 26, 9, 32, 5] have been constructed for text understanding and a variety of other tasks. Some of these knowledge bases define a rich concept space, and provides a mapping from a term to the concept space. However, there is no mechanism to determine the basic-level concept for the term, which makes it difficult for machines to "understand" the term, which in turn hampers the impact of such knowledge bases in natural language understanding and other applications.

In this paper, we focus on computational approaches for deriving BLC. Based on previous studies [24], an object's basic-level concept is considered to be in the middle of the taxonomic hierarchies. In other words, basic-level concepts are a trade-off between general concepts and specific concepts. It is also a trade-off between the accuracy of classification and the power of prediction. Based on this observation, we introduce a method based on *typicality* and *PMI* for BLC. We compare our approach with a few existing measures including graph commute time to understand its essence. We also conduct extensive experiments to show the effectiveness of our approach.

1.4 Paper Organization

The rest of the paper is organized as follows. Section 2 introduces background knowledge. Section 3 focuses on computational approaches of BLC. We discuss typicality, PMI, and introduce our own approach. Section 4 compares our approach with existing approaches. We conclude in Section 5.

2. KNOWLEDGE BASES

A large variety of knowledge bases, including lexcial knowledge bases and encyclopedic knowledge bases, have been constructed for various applications. Some of them, such as WordNet [10], Wikipedia [31], Cyc [18], and Freebase [3], are created by human experts or community efforts. Others, such as KnowItAll [9], NELL [5], and Probase [32], are created by data-driven approaches. Because information in data-driven knowledge bases is usage based, it is particularly useful for natural language understanding. More specifically, data-driven-based knowledge bases are special in the following aspects:

1. Data-driven knowledge bases contain more fine-grained concepts than human-crafted ones. For example, Freebase has thousands of human crafted concepts, while Probase has millions of concepts (shown in Fig. 2).

2. Information in data-driven knowledge bases is not black or white, but is associated with various weights and probabilities such as typicality (i.e., how typical is an instance for a concept), etc.

In this paper, we are concerned with basic-level categorization. Many basic-level concepts, such as *high-end smartphone*, *software company*, and *theoretical physicist*, are fine-grained concepts that are not present in manual-crafted knowledge bases. Furthermore, inferring basic-level concepts requires the statistical information associated with the knowledge. Therefore, we choose data-driven knowledge bases for inferring basic-level concepts.

We use Probase[2] [32] to provide us fine-grained concepts and their statistics, but our techniques can be applied to other knowledge bases which meet above requirements, such as KnowItAll and NELL. Probase is acquired from 1.68 billion web pages. It extracts *isa* relations from sentences matching Hearst patterns [12]. For example, from the sentence ... `presidents such as Obama` ..., it extracts evidence for the claim that `Obama` is an instance of the concept *president*. The core version of Probase contains 3,024,814 unique concepts, 6,768,623 unique instances, and 29,625,920 isA relations.

[2]Probase data is publicly available at http://probase.msra.cn/dataset.aspx

Term	Concept
apple	fruit
apple	company
apple	food
apple	movie
apple	guitarist
apple	music track
apple	book

Table 2: The Term `Apple` and Its Concepts

3. BASIC LEVEL OF CATEGORIZATION

In this section, we describe computational approaches for BLC. We start with two popular measures, namely typicality and PMI, and we show why they are insufficient to derive the basic-level category. Based on the insights from these measures, we introduce our approach, and also the intuition why our approach is a better mechanism for BLC.

3.1 Preliminary

Scoring is very useful for machines when they leverage knowledge bases. It can make machines do reasoning like human beings. Without scores, knowledge facts in the knowledge base or semantic network are not easy to use. E.g. for the term `apple`, it may belongs to lots of categories, such as *fruit, company, book, movie,* and *music track.* For human beings, probably they will think of *fruit* or *company* when they see `apple`. For machines, if they do not have scores, they will treat *music track* as important as *fruit* or *company.* This makes machines cannot reason over the knowledge base as human beings. What is worse, according to our observations, all kinds of terms or phrases may be names of *book, movie,* or *music track,* etc. Without scores, machines will think all texts are related, because they all belong to these concepts. This leads to many errors when machines understand texts.

3.2 Typicality

Typicality is an important measure for understanding the relationship between an object and its concept. Each category (concept) may contain one or more typical items, which are ideal or average examples that people extract from seeing real examples [23]. For example, given a concept *bird,* people are more likely to think of `robin` than `penguin`, although `penguin` is also a *bird.* Similarly, when someone mentions `Barack Obama` without a context, we are more likely to think of the concept of *president* than *author,* although `Barack Obama` is actually a best-selling *author* of several books.

More specifically, we use $P(e|c)$ to denote the typical grade of an instance e in concept c, and we use $P(c|e)$ to denote the typical grade of a concept c for instance e. We call $P(e|c)$ and $P(c|e)$ typicality. For our previous examples, we have $P(\texttt{robin}|\textit{bird}) > P(\texttt{penguin}|\textit{bird})$ and $P(\textit{president}|\texttt{Obama}) > P(\textit{author}|\texttt{Obama})$.

How to compute typicality is an interesting and challenging problem. Mervis et al. [21] found that frequency on its own does not predict typicality. For example, `chicken` is a *bird,* and it appears frequently in day-to-day conversations or in texts. But it is much less typical than some much less frequently encountered or discussed birds, such as `robin`. On the other hand, how often an item is thought of as being a member of a category can be used to measure its typi-

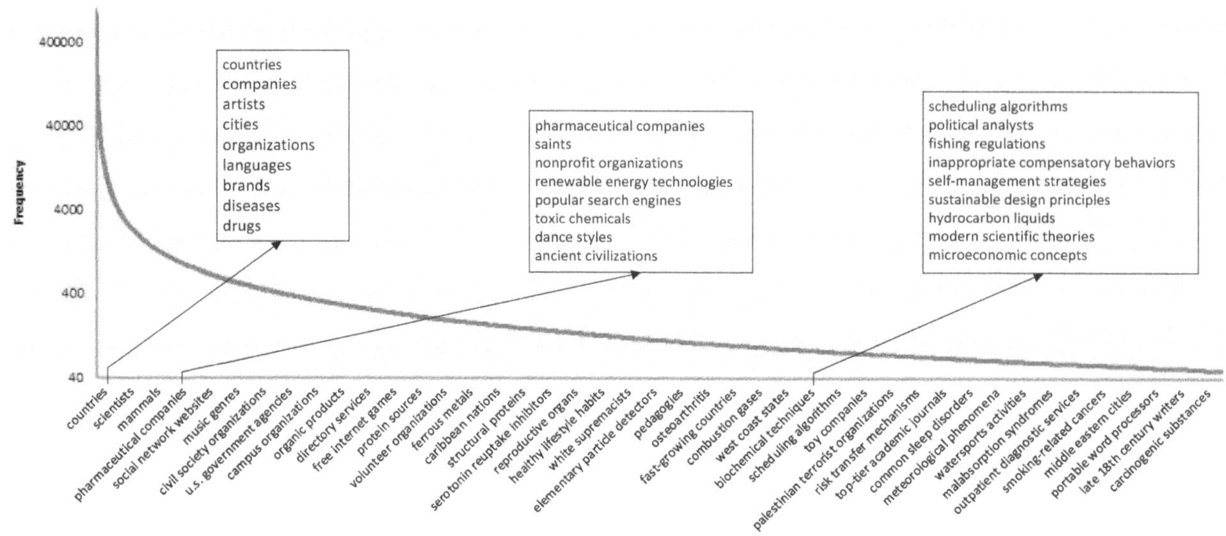

Figure 2: Frequency distribution of the 3 million concepts

cality [1]. For example, by leveraging Hearst patterns [12], we find `chicken` is used as an example of *bird* 130 times in a corpus, while `robin` is used 279 times. This result is consistent with the fact that `robin` is more typical than `chicken` as a *bird*. Based on the above observation, in our work, we derive typicality from co-occurrences of concept and instance pairs:

$$P(e|c) = \frac{n(c,e)}{\sum_{e_i \in c} n(c,e_i)}$$
$$P(c|e) = \frac{n(c,e)}{\sum_{e \in c_i} n(c_i,e)} \tag{1}$$

where $n(c,e)$ is the co-occurrence of concept c and instance e in Hearst patterns' sentences from Web documents.

3.3 Using Typicality for BLC

On the first look, typicality can be used directly for BLC: For a given instance e, how likely is the concept c that maximizes $P(c|e)$ be the basic-level concept for e? Or, how likely is the concept c that maximizes $P(e|c)$?

In this section, we argue that neither is a good candidate for the basic-level concept. Let us go back to the `Microsoft` example we mentioned in Section 1. It is easy to see that *company* is a very typical concept for `Microsoft`, that is, when we think of `Microsoft`, we think of it as a *company*. On the other hand, `Microsoft` is a very typical instance of the concept *largest OS vendor*, that is, when we talk about *largest OS vendor*, we are likely talking about `Microsoft`. In other words, c_1 = *company* has very large typicality $P(c_1|e)$ and c_3 = *largest OS vendor* has very large typicality $P(e|c_3)$, where e = `Microsoft`. But neither is an appropriate basic-level concept for `Microsoft`, for the reasons we described in Section 1. In fact, the two concepts represent two extremes: *company* is a very general concept for *Microsoft*, while *largest OS vendor* is a very specific concept. These two extremes have the following characteristics:

- For the purpose of classifying an instance into the right category, general concepts tend to maximize the accuracy. For example, if we classify instances to general concepts such as *item* or *object*, it may always be correct.
- For the purpose of making prediction, specific concepts tend to have greater power. For example, *largest OS vendor* is able to predict more about *Microsoft* (its properties) with a higher confidence than *company*.

In other words, general concepts may be correct answers to a given instance, but they cannot distinguish different kinds of instances. On the other hand, specific concepts preserve more useful information about instances, but their coverage is limited. What we look for is a compromise of the two.

3.4 Using Typicality with Smoothing for BLC

The typicality score we discussed above tends to give higher score to "extreme" concepts, that is, concepts either very general or very specific. The reason is obvious: (1) when e is given, $P(c|e)$ is proportional to the co-occurrence of c and e, so it tends to map e to some general concepts; (2) when e is given, $P(e|c)$ tends to return those specific concepts that only contain e.

Usually, to address the problem of "extreme" values, we can use the technique of smoothing. We define *smoothed typicality* as follows:

$$P(e|c) = \frac{n(c,e) + \varepsilon}{\sum_{e_i \in c} n(c,e_i) + \varepsilon N_{instance}} \tag{2}$$

where $N_{instance}$ is the total number of instances, and ε is a small constant which assumes every (concept, instance) pair has a very small co-occurrence probability in the real world, no matter whether we observe it or not.

Smoothed typicality reduces extreme values. For example, assume originally we have $P($`Microsoft`$|$*largest OS vendor*$)$ $= 1$. In other words, `Microsoft` is the only instance in the category of *largest OS vendor*. Assume $\varepsilon = 0.001$ and $N_{instance} = 1M$, we derive smoothed typicality according to Eq 2 as $P(e|c) = (1 + 0.001)/(1 + 0.001 * 10^6) = 0.001$, which is much smaller than the original value. This translates to boosting the typicality of other concepts such as *software company*, which makes it possible for us to choose a more appropriate basic-level category.

However, the smoothing approach has two problems. First, the results are very sensitive to ε, which is difficult to tune. Second and more importantly, smoothing helps avoid extreme values using a rationale totally inconsistent with ours. For example, it assumes that there are many *largest OS vendors* for which we do not observe, and as a result it discounts $P(\texttt{Microsoft}|\textit{largest OS vendor})$ to 0.001. But the fact is, `Microsoft` is indeed one of the very few *largest OS vendor*, and reducing its typicality to 0.001 does not make sense. Thus, smoothing does not address the fundamental challenges in finding the basic-level category.

3.5 Using PMI for BLC

Pointwise Mutual Information (PMI) [20] is a common measure of the strength of association between two terms. We may consider using the PMI between concept c and instance e to find the basic-level concepts, that is, we consider $c = \arg\max_c PMI(e, c)$ as e's basic-level concept, where $PMI(e, c)$ is defined as

$$PMI(e,c) = \log \frac{P(e,c)}{P(e)P(c)} \tag{3}$$

This leads to

$$PMI(e,c) = \log \frac{P(e|c)P(c)}{P(e)P(c)} = \log P(e|c) - \log P(e) \tag{4}$$

For a given e, $\log P(e)$ is a constant. Then, ranking concepts by PMI is equivalent to ranking by typicality $P(e|c)$. In other words, PMI is equivalent to typicality. But as we have already shown in Section 3.3, using typicality to find basic-level concept does not work.

In order to make PMI less sensitive to occurrence frequency and at the same time more easily interpretable, Bouma et al [4] proposes a normalized pointwise mutual information ($NPMI$). The $NPMI$ between concept c and instance e is defined as:

$$\begin{aligned} NPMI(e,c) &= \frac{PMI(e,c)}{-\log P(e,c)} \\ &= \frac{\log P(e|c) - \log P(e)}{-\log P(e,c)} \end{aligned} \tag{5}$$

As we can see from Eq 5, similar to PMI and typicality, $NPMI$ also tends to produce concepts either too general or too specific. More specifically,

- when $P(e, c)$ is large (close to 1), $P(e, c)$ dominates $NPMI$ because $-logP(e, c)$ tends to go to 0. This leads to top basic-level concepts too general.
- when $P(e, c)$ is small, $\frac{1}{-\log P(e,c)}$ does not change much when $P(e, c)$ changes, thus, PMI dominates $NPMI$ in this case. As mentioned above, this leads to top basic-level concepts too specific.

3.6 Using $Rep(e, c)$ for BLC

Neither typicality nor PMI produces basic-level concepts. Based on previous studies [24], we know basic-level concepts are concepts neither too general nor too specific. To this end, we make an intuitive compromise and define a scoring function *Rep* as follows:

$$Rep(e,c) = P(c|e) \cdot P(e|c) \tag{6}$$

For an instance e, we use the above score to find its basic-level concept:

$$blc(e) = \arg\max_c Rep(e,c) \tag{7}$$

Intuitively, our measure tries to boost such a concept c for a given instance e: i) concept c is e's typical concept, and ii) instance e is also c's typical instance.

Moreover, if we take the logarithm of our scoring function in Eq 6, we get

$$\begin{aligned} \log Rep(e,c) &= \log \frac{P(e,c)^2}{P(e)P(c)} \\ &= PMI(e,c) + \log P(e,c) \end{aligned} \tag{8}$$

This in fact corresponds to PMI^2, which is a normalized form of PMI in the PMI^k family [7]. PMI^2 is proposed in an attempt to investigate how to improve upon PMI by introducing the $P(e, c)$ inside the logarithm. It normalizes the upper bound of PMI [4]. Therefore, PMI^2 can reduce the extreme values, and help to boost concepts in the middle of the taxonomy.

One important property of an instance's basic-level category is that the category is more likely to contain its similar instances. In our `Microsoft` example in Section 1, we mentioned that going through too general concepts (such as *company*) or too specific concepts (such as *largest OS vendor*) we cannot find instances similar to `Microsoft`. If instead we go through a likely basic-level category (such as *software company*) we find many similar instances. This inspires a graph traversal approach to finding basic-level categories. In the rest of this section, we show that a graph traversal approach is equivalent to our approach of maximizing the scoring function *Rep* in Eq 7.

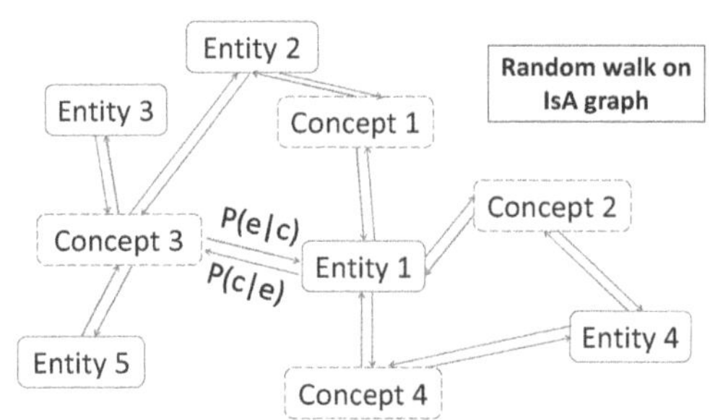

Figure 3: Random Walk on the IsA Network

As we mentioned above, given the instance e, the basic-level concept c should be one of e's typical concepts, in other words, c should have "shortest distance" with e. Similarly, given this basic-level concept c, e should have "shortest distance" with c. Therefore, for an instance e, we consider the process of finding its basic-level concepts as *a process of finding concepts that have shortest expected distance to e*. Intuitively, traversing from node e, it is very likely we arrive at the concept, and traversing from the concept, it is very likely we come back to e. This corresponds to a random walk problem of finding nearest nodes reached by a given node, as shown in Fig. 3. We use commute time [19] as a measure of the distance between two nodes in a graph. Commute time is defined as the expected number of steps that a random walk starting at node i, going through node j once, and returning to i again. The commute time between an instance e and a concept c is:

$$\begin{aligned} Time(e,c) &= \sum_{k=1}^{\infty}(2k) * P_k(e,c) \\ &= \sum_{k=1}^{T}(2k) * P_k(e,c) + \sum_{k=T+1}^{\infty}(2k) * P_k(e,c) \\ &\geq \sum_{k=1}^{T}(2k) * P_k(e,c) \\ &\quad +2(T+1) * (1 - \sum_{k=1}^{T} P_k(e,c)) \end{aligned} \quad (9)$$

where $P_k(e,c)$ is the probability of starting from e to c and back to e in $2k$ steps.

As we are only interested in concepts within a short commute, we may just ignore concepts with commute time larger a threshold of T steps. Let us constrain the random walk within 4 steps, then we have:

$$\begin{aligned} Time'(e,c) &= 2 * P(c|e)P(e|c) + 4 * (1 - P(c|e)P(e|c)) \\ &= 4 - 2 * P(c|e)P(e|c) \\ &= 4 - 2 * Rep(e,c) \end{aligned} \quad (10)$$

This shows that the commute time $Time'(e,c)$ has an inverse relationship with the scoring function *Rep* we defined in Eq 6. Thus, our simple, easy-to-compute scoring method is equivalent to a graph traversal approach of finding the basic-level category under this random walk assumption. But for the complete commute time, our experiments show that the representativeness score is better than it.

4. EXPERIMENTS

To evaluate the effectiveness of scores proposed in this paper, we conduct our experiments on the Probase [32] semantic network. The dataset we use is called "core" version. It contains 3,024,814 unique concepts, 6,768,623 unique instances, and 29,625,920 edges among them.

4.1 Experiment Setting

Conceptualization is one of the essential processes for text understanding. It maps instances in the text to the concept space. In this evaluation, we select top queries from Bing search logs between January 1st, 2015 and January 31st, 2015, then we use the typicality $P(c|e)$, $P(e|c)$, and our approach $Rep(e,c)$ to rank concepts corresponding to these instances. Finally, we generate 1,683 *(instance, concept)* pairs as labeling candidates.

We also compare our approaches with several baselines: MI, $NPMI$, PMI^3. Since PMI is reduced to typicality $P(e|c)$ in our scenario, we do not treat it as another baseline separately. The formulas of these baselines are as follows:

Mutual Information (MI):
$MI(e,c) = \sum P(e,c) \log \frac{P(e,c)}{P(e)P(c)}$

Normalized Pointwise Mutual Information (NPMI): please refer to Equation 5.

PMI^3 [4]: $PMI^3(e,c) = \log \frac{P(e,c)^3}{P(e)P(c)}$

4.2 Metrics

We now discuss how we evaluate the results of different approaches. As there is not ground-truth ranking for conceptualization results. We submitted a labeling task to UHRS (Universal Human Rating System), which is a crowdsourcing and human annotation platform. Each *(instance, concept)* pair is labeled by three workers. Therefore we got 5,049 labeled records. We took the majority of the labels as the final label. If all three annotators did not agree with each other, this pair was sent to the fourth annotator to label, and so on. In this labeling task, the workers did not our labeling goal. They just strictly follow the guideline shown in Table 3.

Label	Meaning	Examples
Excellent	Good matched concepts at the basic level	(bluetooth, wireless communication protocol)
Good	A little general or specific	(bluetooth, accessory)
Fair	Too general or specific	(bluetooth, feature)
Bad	Non-sense concepts	(bluetooth, issue)

Table 3: Labeling Guideline for Conceptualization

Then we employ *precision@K* and $nDCG$ to evaluate the results of different approaches. The *precision@K* is used for evaluating the **correctness** of concepts, and $nDCG$ is used to measure the **ranking** of concepts.

For *precision@K*, we treat *Good/Excellent* as score 1, and *Bad/Fair* as 0. We calculate the precision of top-K concepts as follows:

$$Precision@K = \frac{\sum_{i=1}^{K} rel_i}{K} \quad (11)$$

where rel_i is the score we define above.

For $nDCG$, we treat *Bad* as 0, *Fair* as 1, *Good* as 2, and *Excellent* as 3. Then we calculate $nDCG$ as follows:

$$nDCG_K = \frac{rel_1 + \sum_{i=2}^{K} \frac{rel_i}{\log i}}{ideal\_rel_1 + \sum_{i=2}^{K} \frac{ideal\_rel_i}{\log i}} \quad (12)$$

where rel_i is the relevance score of the result at rank i, and $ideal\_rel_i$ is the relevance score at rank i of an ideal list, obtained by sorting all relevant concepts in decreasing order of the relevance score.

4.3 NDCG & Precision

We show the comparison from two aspects: without smoothing, and with smoothing. Fig. 4 shows the top-20 results for different scoring approaches.

Without smoothing, as Fig. 4(a) shows, the score $Rep(e,c)$ is much better in precision than others. $Rep(e,c)$ is the best for top-2, top-5, and top-10. PMI^3 is also good for top-1, but it is worse for other cases. So it is not stable. For the ranking of top concepts, as Fig. 4(c) shows, $Rep(e,c)$ outperforms all other methods in all cases.

With smoothing, we try different values of ε, from *1e-3* to *1e-7*. We observe that the smoothing technique has a significant effect on the typicality $P(e|c)$, as shown in Fig. 5. For $P(e|c)$, its optimized ε is *1e-4*. With this smoothing setting, as shown in Fig. 4(b) and Fig. 4(d), the typicality $P(e|c)$ outperforms all other methods in both *precision* and $nDCG$

when K is 2, 3, 5, 10, and 15. However, as we mentioned in Section 3.4, the rationale of smoothed typicality is totally inconsistent with our problem. Its top concepts may be good, but not for the rest of concepts. Besides, it is quite sensitive to ε, which is hard to tune. On the other hand, $Rep(e, c)$ is still quite good, and it wins the *precision*@1 when its smoothing ε=*1e-4*.

Based on this evaluation, we have the following conclusions:

- The score $Rep(e, c)$ performs best for conceptualization task overall, and more importantly, it is robust.
- The smoothed typicality $P(e|c)$ is very sensitive to ε. It may have a good performance for top results after a sophisticated tuning on the smoothing value ε.

4.4 Examples

Some examples are shown in Table 4. We find top concepts ranked by $P(c|e)$ tend to be general. E.g. the top 1 concept of `battery` is *item*. Obviously, *item* is not a good concept to predict the instance's features. On the other hand, concepts ranked by $P(e|c)$ (without smoothing) tends to be specific. Though these concepts have greater power on prediction, they have limited coverage. This makes them useless in the computation. E.g. when we compare two related instances with extremely specific concepts, they may have little overlapping information. In Table 4, concepts ranked by $Rep(e, c)$ and $P(e|c)$ with smoothing(ε = *1e-4*) are the best. They are the trade-off between general concepts and specific concepts.

However, as we mentioned in Section 3.4, ε is difficult to tune, and the rationale of smoothed typicality is inconsistent with the problem we want to resolve in this paper. For example, *largest OS vendor* should not be assumed to contain many other instances for which we do not observe. Therefore, smoothed typicality may only be good for top concepts, instead of all concepts.

4.5 Application

With the scores proposed in this paper, the knowledge base becomes usable for machines. In this subsection, we showcase one application leveraging the basic-level concepts. Definitely, more applications can be easily developed for different scenarios.

Sponsored search is one of the most successful business models for search engine companies. It matches user queries to relevant ads. In reality, each ad is associated with a list of keywords. Advertisers bid for keywords, and also specify matching options for these keywords. One option is *exact match* where an ad is displayed only when a user query is identical to one of the bid keywords associated with the ad. Another option is *smart match* which is based on semantic relevance. Exact match targets exact traffic, but it is limited since queries are various. Currently, smart match is the default option provided by mainstream search engines.

In smart match, search engines map the query to bid ad keywords. Since both are short texts, traditional bag-of-words approaches do not work well in this scenario. Therefore, we can leverage the knowledge base for this task in smart match.

For each short text, we first identify instances from the short text (query, or bid keyword), and map it to basic-level concepts with the score $Rep(e, c)$. Then we simply merge the concept vectors of different instances in the short text, and get a single concept vector as the representation of this short text. Finally, we can calculate the semantic similarity between queries and bid keywords by comparing their concept vectors (E.g. using cosine similarity function).

We conduct our experiments on real ads click log of Bing (from January 1st, 2015 to January 31st, 2015). The experiment process is as follows: first, we calculate the semantic similarity score of (query, bid keyword) pairs for each record in the log; Second, we divide all scores into 10 buckets; Third, we aggregate the click number and impression number in the same bucket.

The overall results are illustrated in Fig. 6(a). X-axis represents the bucket number (E.g. *bucket 1* means the similarity score is between 0 and 0.1, and so on). Y-axis is the general click-through rate (CTR) of this bucket, where $CTR = \frac{\#\ of\ clicks}{\#\ of\ impressions}$. From the figure, we observe that: (1) once our semantic similarity score is low, the CTR is low; (2) once our score is high, the CTR is high; (3) the highest CTR is about 3 times of the lowest CTR. This means our semantic similarity score can be a strong feature for the query and ads matching.

We further analyze our results by query frequencies. We separate all queries to 10 deciles in the order of frequency, and each decile has the same total volume of traffic. Generally speaking, decile 1 to 3 are head queries, decile 4 to 6 are torso queries, and decile 7 to 10 are tail queries. Usually, head queries can be covered by exact match. Therefore we mostly focus on torso queries and tail queries. Results are shown in Fig. 6(b) and Fig. 6(c). For both torso and tail queries, the correlation between our semantic similarity score and CTR is preserved. This is quite good because long queries usually are lack of click signals, and the semantics can fill this gap.

5. RELATED WORK

The goal of BLC is for text understanding. Currently, there are two major efforts on semantic analysis and text representation. One is implicit knowledge mining, the other is explicit knowledge mining.

In terms of implicit knowledge mining, some efforts focus on implicit semantic analysis and topic modeling, such as traditional latent semantic analysis (LSA) [8], probabilistic latent semantic indexing (PLSI) [13], and latent Dirichlet allocation (LDA) [2]. They can be also used for basic-level concept reasoning. However, the semantics mined by these approaches cannot be interpreted by human being. Besides, their computation is quite heavy, which makes them cannot be easily applied for large scale data. Other efforts try to get the term embedding by using deep learning techniques [6, 22]. This embedding can be treated as the representation for a given term in high-dimensional semantic space, and benefit lots of applications. But ususally the embedding is not good for those low frequency terms, and it is not easy to tune once its overall quality is bad.

In terms of explicit knowledge mining, explicit semantic analysis (ESA) [11] and conceptualization [25, 15] are the representative work. The former represents the meaning of texts by Wikipedia's article titles. But it is still not the natural way of human thinking, and the "concepts" of a given instance are related articles instead of its categories. The latter is the scope of this paper. But previous work [25, 15] pays attention to short-text level conceptualization, while

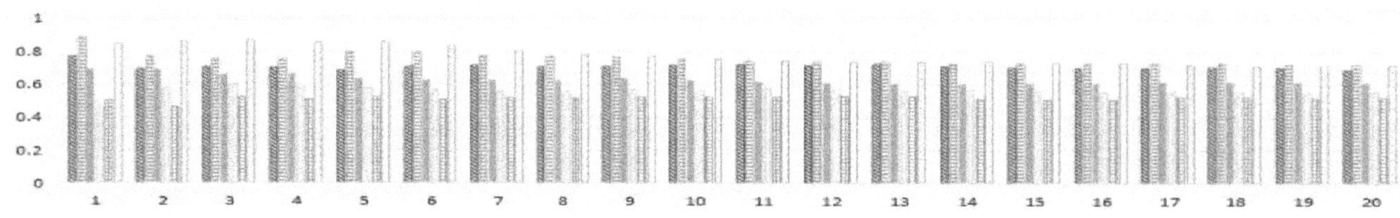

(a) Precision Without Smoothing

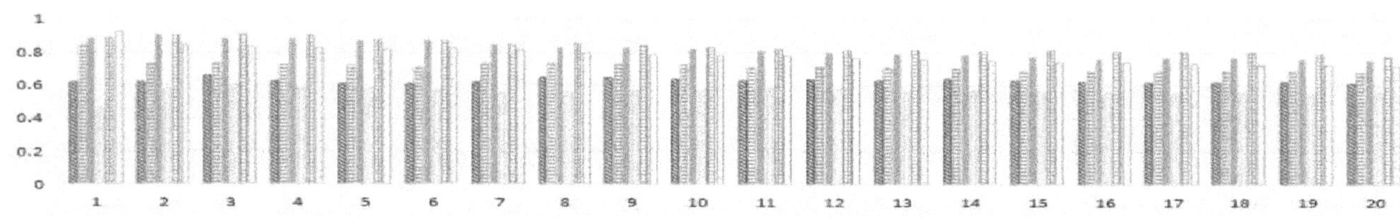

(b) Precision With Smoothing (ε = *1e-4*)

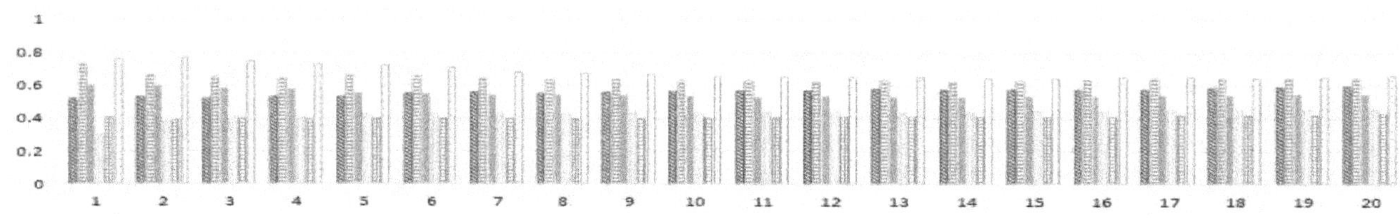

(c) nDCG Without Smoothing

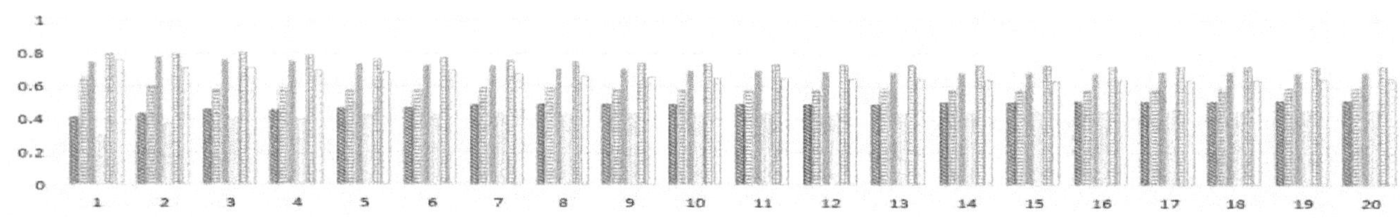

(d) nDCG With Smoothing (ε = *1e-4*)

Figure 4: Precision and nDCG Comparison

our paper focuses on a more fundamental part: instance-level conceptualization. A good instance-level conceptualization mechanism can further improve short-text level conceptualization.

For scores discussed in this paper, typicality and basic-level conceptualization are actively studied in cognitive science and psychology at first. E.g. psychologist Gregory Murphy's highly acclaimed book [23] discusses the typicality and the basic level of concepts from the perspective of psychologists, which is the basis of these two scores proposed in this paper. Other work [17, 32] proposes typicality scores for some special scenarios. Their scoring functions cannot be easily extended to semantic networks. E.g. Lee et al. [17] leverage instances as intermedia for calculating typicality $P(a|c)$ between an attribute a and a concept c. Instead, our typicality is more generic and easy to be adopted by more applications. Besides, we also discuss a smoothing approach and *Rep* score, which have been proved that they are much better than the standard typicality in instance-level conceptualization. Furthermore, we compare our BLC score function with PMI and commute time theoretically, which reveals the essence of BLC score.

6. CONCLUSION

In this paper, we discuss computational approaches for *Basic-level conceptualization (BLC)*. We propose our method based on *typicality* and *PMI*. We make deep analysis and compare it with some popular measures to understand its essence. We conduct extensive experiments and show the effectiveness of our approach. We also use a real example to demonstrate how our score helps current ads system.

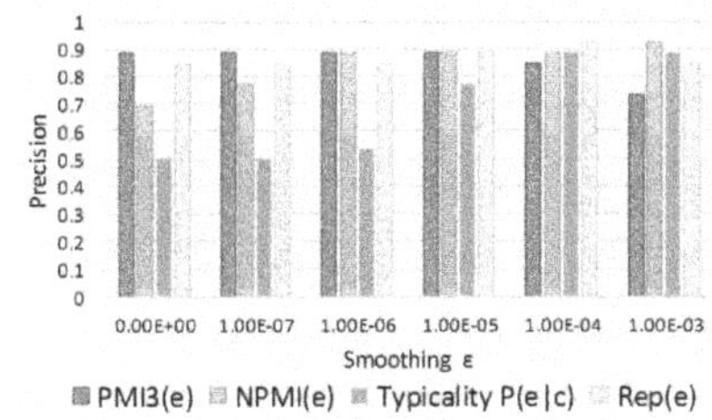

(a) Precision@1

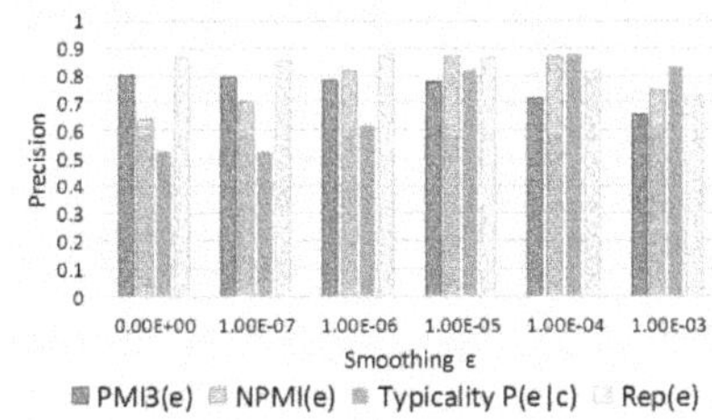

(b) Precision@5

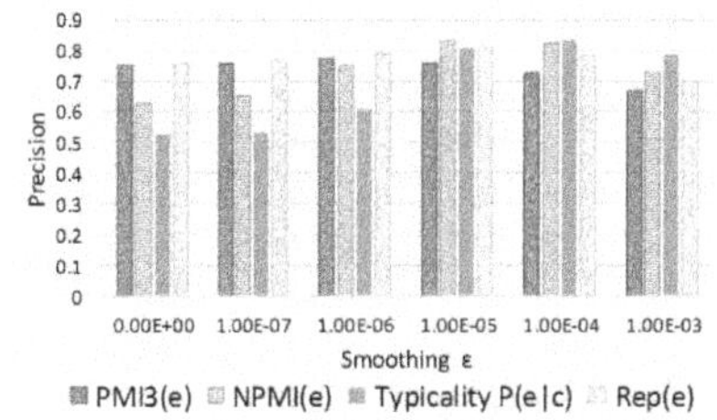

(c) Precision@10

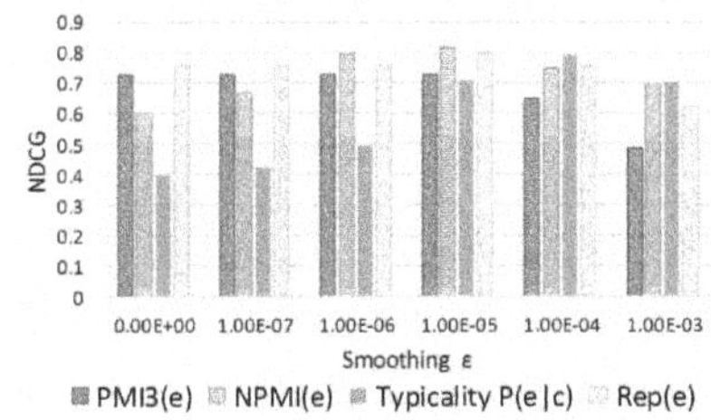

(d) nDCG@1

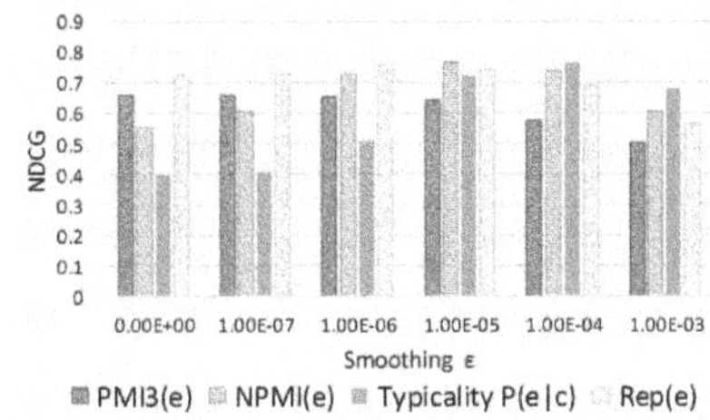

(e) nDCG@5

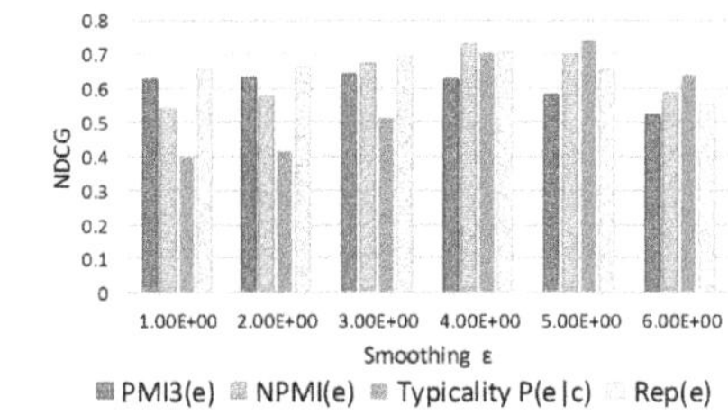

(f) nDCG@10

Figure 5: Precision and nDCG Comparison with Different Smoothing Values

Table 4: Examples of Basic-level Concepts by Different Scoring Approaches

Instance	**Rank by** $P(c\|e)$	**Rank by** $P(e\|c)$ (same as PMI in our scenario)	**Rank by** $Rep(e,c)$ (our approach)	**Rank by** $P(e\|c)$ **with smoothing** (ε = *1e-4*)
Microsoft	1. company 2. vendor 3. corporation	1. standardized technology industry 2. global and leading organization 3. large software maker	1. software company 2. technology company 3. software vendor	1. software company 2. software vendor 3. technology company
Nokia	1. company 2. brand 3. manufacturer	1. leading global MNC handset brand 2. established technology vendor 3. brand-name cell phone product	1. original mobile phone 2. mobile phone manufacturer 3. handset maker	1. mobile phone manufacturer 2. handset maker 3. handset manufacturer
Java	1. language 2. programming language 3. technology	1. built-in language environment 2. controllable language 3. managed language	1. object-oriented language 2. programming language 3. object-oriented programming language	1. object-oriented language 2. programming language 3. object oriented programming system
Bluetooth	1. feature 2. technology 3. wireless technology	1. connectivity facility 2. disable networking capability 3. hands-free communication device	1. wireless technology 2. wireless protocol 3. connectivity option	1. wireless technology 2. connectivity option 3. wireless protocol
battery	1. item 2. accessory 3. power source	1. mobile power source 2. electrical energy storage system 3. auto supply	1. power source 2. power supply 3. energy storage device	1. power source 2. power supply 3. consumable part

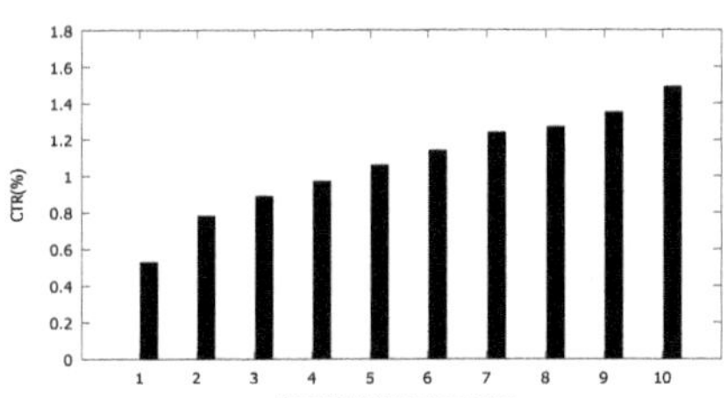

(a) Different SMS Range

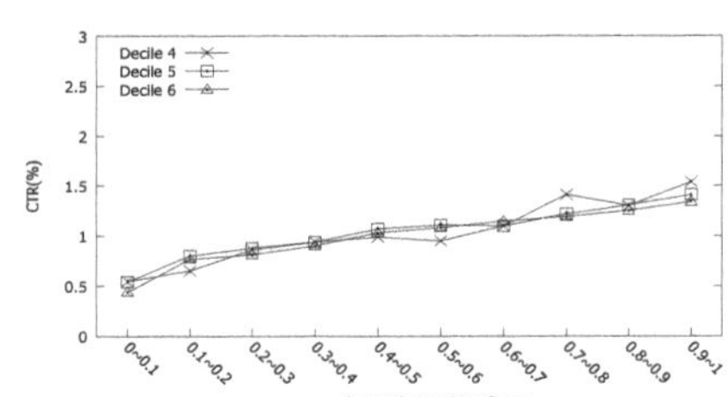

(b) Torso Queries

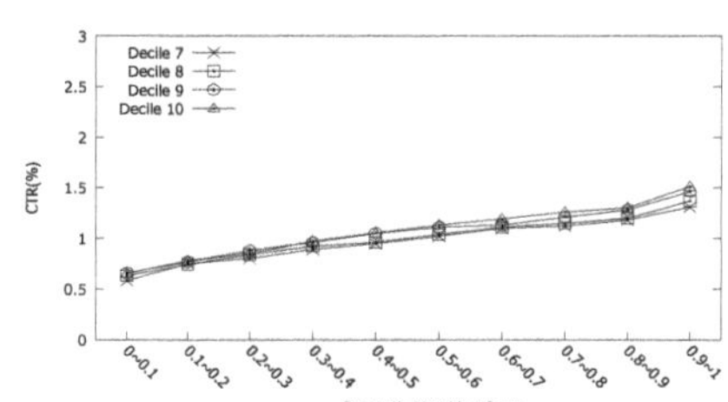

(c) Tail Queries

Figure 6: Correlation between Semantic Matching Score and CTR

7. ACKNOWLEDGMENTS

This work was partially supported by the National Key Basic Research Program (973 Program) of China under grant No. 2014CB340403 & No.2015CB358800, the Natural Science Foundation of China(No.61472085), and the Fundamental Research Funds for the Central Universities & the Research Funds of Renmin University of China.

8. REFERENCES

[1] L. W. Barsalou. Ideals, central tendency, and frequency of instantiation as determinants of graded structure in categories. *JEP:LMC*, 11(4):629–654, 1985.

[2] D. M. Blei, A. Y. Ng, and M. I. Jordan. Latent dirichlet allocation. *the Journal of machine Learning research*, 3:993–1022, 2003.

[3] K. Bollacker, C. Evans, P. Paritosh, T. Sturge, and J. Taylor. Freebase: a collaboratively created graph database for structuring human knowledge. In *SIGMOD*, pages 1247–1250. ACM, 2008.

[4] G. Bouma. Normalized (pointwise) mutual information in collocation extraction. *Proceedings of GSCL*, pages 31–40, 2009.

[5] A. Carlson, J. Betteridge, B. Kisiel, B. Settles, E. R. H. Jr., and T. M. Mitchell. Toward an architecture for never-ending language learning. In *AAAI*, pages 1306–1313, 2010.

[6] R. Collobert, J. Weston, L. Bottou, M. Karlen, K. Kavukcuoglu, and P. Kuksa. Natural language processing (almost) from scratch. *JMLR*, 12:2493–2537, 2011.

[7] B. Daille. *Approche mixte pour l'extraction de terminologie: statistique lexicale et filtres linguistiques.* PhD thesis, 1994.

[8] S. C. Deerwester, S. T. Dumais, T. K. Landauer, G. W. Furnas, and R. A. Harshman. Indexing by latent semantic analysis. *JASIS*, 41(6):391–407, 1990.

[9] O. Etzioni, M. Cafarella, and D. Downey. Webscale information extraction in knowitall (preliminary results). In *International World Wide Web Conference (WWW)*, 2004.

[10] C. Fellbaum, editor. *WordNet: an electronic lexical database.* MIT Press, 1998.

[11] E. Gabrilovich and S. Markovitch. Computing semantic relatedness using wikipedia-based explicit semantic analysis. In *IJCAI*, volume 7, pages 1606–1611, 2007.

[12] M. A. Hearst. Automatic acquisition of hyponyms from large text corpora. In *COLING*, pages 539–545, 1992.

[13] T. Hofmann. Probabilistic latent semantic indexing. In *Proceedings of the 22nd annual international ACM SIGIR conference on Research and development in information retrieval*, pages 50–57. ACM, 1999.

[14] W. Hua, Z. Wang, H. Wang, K. Zheng, and X. Zhou. Short text understanding through lexical-semantic analysis. In *International Conference on Data Engineering (ICDE)*, 2015.

[15] D. Kim, H. Wang, and A. Oh. Context-dependent conceptualization. In *Proceedings of the Twenty-Third international joint conference on Artificial Intelligence (IJCAI)*, pages 2654–2661. AAAI Press, 2013.

[16] G. Lakoff. *Women, fire, and dangerous things: What categories reveal about the mind.* Cambridge Univ Press, 1990.

[17] T. Lee, Z. Wang, H. Wang, and S.-w. Hwang. Attribute extraction and scoring: A probabilistic approach. In *International Conference on Data Engineering (ICDE)*, 2013.

[18] D. B. Lenat and R. V. Guha. *Building Large Knowledge-Based Systems: Representation and Inference in the Cyc Project.* Addison-Wesley, 1989.

[19] L. Lovász. Random walks on graphs: A survey. *Combinatorics, Paul erdos is eighty*, 2(1):1–46, 1993.

[20] C. D. Manning and H. Schütze. *Foundations of statistical natural language processing*, volume 999. MIT Press, 1999.

[21] C. B. Mervis, J. Catlin, and E. Rosch. Relationships among goodness-of-example, category norms, and word frequency. *Bulletin of the Psychonomic Society*, pages 283–284, 1976.

[22] T. Mikolov, K. Chen, G. Corrado, and J. Dean. Efficient estimation of word representations in vector space. In *Proceedings of Workshop at ICLR*, 2013.

[23] G. L. Murphy. *The big book of concepts.* MIT Press, 2004.

[24] E. Rosch, C. B. Mervis, W. D. Gray, D. M. Johnson, and P. Boyes-Braem. Basic objects in natural categories. *Cognitive psychology*, 8(3):382–439, 1976.

[25] Y. Song, H. Wang, Z. Wang, H. Li, and W. Chen. Short text conceptualization using a probabilistic knowledgebase. In *Proceedings of the Twenty-Second international joint conference on Artificial Intelligence (IJCAI)*, pages 2330–2336. AAAI Press, 2011.

[26] F. M. Suchanek, G. Kasneci, and G. Weikum. Yago: a core of semantic knowledge. In *International World Wide Web Conference (WWW)*, pages 697–706, 2007.

[27] F. Wang, Z. Wang, Z. Li, and J.-R. Wen. Concept-based short text classification and ranking. In *ACM International Conference on Information and Knowledge Management (CIKM)*, October 2014.

[28] J. Wang, H. Wang, Z. Wang, and K. Zhu. Understanding tables on the web. In *International Conference on Conceptual Modeling*, October 2012.

[29] Z. Wang, H. Wang, and Z. Hu. Head, modifier, and constraint detection in short texts. In *IEEE 30th International Conference on Data Engineering (ICDE)*, pages 280–291. IEEE, 2014.

[30] Z. Wang, K. Zhao, H. Wang, X. Meng, and J.-R. Wen. Query understanding through knowledge-based conceptualization. In *Proceedings of the Twenty-Fourth International Joint Conference on Artificial Intelligence (IJCAI)*, 2015.

[31] Wikipedia. Plagiarism — Wikipedia, the free encyclopedia, 2004. `http://en.wikipedia.org/w/index.php?title=Plagiarism&oldid=5139350`, [Online; accessed 22-July-2004].

[32] W. Wu, H. Li, H. Wang, and K. Q. Zhu. Probase: A probabilistic taxonomy for text understanding. In *Proceedings of the 2012 ACM SIGMOD International Conference on Management of Data*, pages 481–492. ACM, 2012.

Author Index

www.ingramcontent.com/pod-product-compliance
Ingram Content Group UK Ltd.
Pitfield, Milton Keynes, MK11 3LW, UK
UKHW051419290926
15471UKWH00009B/1685

9 781450 341158